Building a Dream

Building a

Dream

The Art of Disney Architecture

Beth Dunlop

Foreword by Vincent Scully

Harry N. Abrams, Inc.,
Publishers

For Adam

Editor: Eric Himmel

Designer: Judith Hudson

Library of Congress Cataloging-in-Publication Data
Dunlop, Beth, 1947–
    Building a dream : the art of Disney architecture / Beth Dunlop.
    p.   cm.
    Includes bibliographical references and index.
    ISBN 0-8109-3142-7 (hc)
    1. Amusement parks—Design. 2. Walt Disney Company—
    Buildings. 3. Architecture, Modern—20th century. I. Title.
    GV1851.D85 1996
    725'.76—dc20   95–34174

Printed and bound in Hong Kong

contents

| *Disney: Theme and Reality*

The very name "Disney" is so packed with opprobrium for old-line architectural modernists that it took a certain amount of courage for Beth Dunlop to agree to write this book. The decision was surely made easier for her by the fact that Disney was not looking for puffs or apologies and left her strictly alone to write what she pleased, and I for one find it hard to fault the approach she has taken. She writes like an anthropologist, with both eyes open, trying her level best to describe a strange cultural structure unique to our time. There is plenty of special material for her to work with, from the early extravagances of Walt Disney's own "Imagineers" to those of the present stable of famous architects whom Michael Eisner has so assiduously sought out and employed. The unfolding of that story is fascinating enough in itself. The Imagineers and the other company architects come off rather well in it. (I am grateful to John Hench, one of the original Imagineers, for guiding me safely through Disneyland.)

Dunlop does not avoid critical issues. Right at the start, for example, she takes on the issue of "theme." It was the idea of theme, of the Theme Park, that canonical modernists hated most about Disney's architecture. But Dunlop makes it clear that architecture has always been themed. Indeed, it might be argued that abstract modern architecture had an engrossing theme itself, that of its own modernity. For a time that obsessive reduc-tionism was enough to carry it, but after a while it could no longer do so because architecture's traditional themes had always been richer and far more complex than those, say, of the International Style: temples as living divinities, cathedrals as cities of heaven, town halls embodying the communal act, palaces and gardens as earthly images of a cosmic order, towns exploring every conceivable setting for symbolism and ritual. Suburbs and cities expressly themed to tell a story or to shape a special myth were common enough in early twentieth-century America: George Merrick's Coral Gables citing Washington Irving's *Alhambra* in its Mediterranean Revival architecture and the names of its streets, Glenn Curtiss' Opa-Locka illustrating specific tales from the *Thousand and One Nights*, most of Southern California acting out *Ramona* everywhere.

Abstract modernism rejected such symbolic and narrative resources in architecture just as its pictorial models had rejected representation. It was in fact Robert Venturi who reminded us of them in *Complexity and Contradiction in Architecture*, of 1966, and *Learning from Las Vegas*, of 1972. At just about the same time Charles Moore, another leader in this renewed recognition of symbolic content, perceived the significance and effectiveness of storytelling in the architecture and planning of Disneyland, in Anaheim, opened to the public in 1955. There Disney indeed revived architecture as a storytelling device, and he exploited it afresh to explore and embody a number of perhaps simple but artfully interwoven themes. In order to do that he had to create a whole environment all at once, to make a special place, a "land," complete in itself. His architectural model was surely that of the Garden and the result was a condensation of Classic and Romantic garden types into a new unity, one never quite seen before. It was a special kind of American Amusement Park, one with a palace, a castle, at the center of it all.

Disney formed it into a new architectural program, one of the few in American history where many buildings could be arranged in relation to each other to shape a whole place. The American college campus, as Paul Turner has pointed out, is another such program, so far the most conspicuous and important one of all. Nor need the campus necessarily be seen as very different from Disneyland in its objectives and methods: Yale's Gothic and Georgian colleges of the 1930s are certainly theme parks, intended to create secret gardens of mythic character, weaving a special transcendent spell, suggesting the rituals of magic. Indeed their Gothic prototype, Harkness Quadrangle, built in the 'teens, was financed in part by Yale's secret senior societies, and it and its successors are loaded with references, very thinly concealed, to various initiatory rites.

Disneyland is all this. Hence, the "Magic Kingdom" seems to build the very structure of myth, with themes from the depths of the American consciousness sinuously intertwined. Here are tree houses, steamboats, rafts, barren mountains, haunted mansions – and endless disguises involving the eternal

playing of bogus roles. It is no wonder that the river is the major image in Disneyland, and the raft which floats on it is Huck's and Jim's, turning in the eddies under the jungly shores. For this generation it can belong to Herzog's Aguirre on the Amazon, as well. Moreover, the Magic Kingdom is always crowded with humanity; it never leaves us alone for one moment to catch our breaths. We are swept along in the American myth. So, in 1928, Stephen Vincent Benét had written: "Thames and all the rivers of the kings / Ran into Mississippi and were drowned."

But this was not enough for Walt Disney. He clearly hankered after the Campus itself, and Epcot took shape in his mind as a place for teaching, especially of science (how American, who could object to that?), but teaching, of course, accomplished through entertainment. Here, perhaps, we may run into some critical difficulties, involving the character and value of Disney's themes. Epcot is not a Campus. Disney's lands and worlds are invariably noisy (God, those rides are loud), bumptious, and sentimental. That is their style, and it is based on an unacceptably optimistic view of life (if we are speaking seriously), one that is appropriate enough for the American mythology of the Magic Kingdom but not so good if one is professing to deal, as Greek myth, for example, does, with objective reality – as Epcot also professes to do. "When you wish upon a star your dream comes true" makes a lovely fiction for a while, especially when it is sung in front of Cinderella Castle with the magic animals capering about, but it is, after all, pure bullshit in the long run. When you wish upon a star you die like everybody else.

This is a fundamental problem for Disney, dealing with American wish fulfillment – always, like it or not, the very stuff of dreams – as he invariably does. So in the theme parks Disney's focus must be unerringly optimistic, whether dealing with science or not, and it employs a basic American strategy, satirized by Evelyn Waugh in *The Loved One*, where the cemetery is itself a theme park, conceived to deny the reality of death. The skeletons in the haunted houses are jolly fellows after all.

But Disney also conceived of Epcot as a city, where the major issue has to be the shaping of an environment that can realistically endure. And long before Epcot, the central feature of Disneyland and Walt Disney World alike was Main Street, the very soul of every traditional American town, including, we are always told, Walt Disney's own. Here the positive results of Disney's vision have been enormous in the architecture and town planning of the real world, if we can so name it. In the period of the 1950s and 1960s when Disney came up with Main Street, it and indeed all traditional urbanism was despised by modern architects and planners alike. Disney, with whatever hokum, revived it, and in so doing brought into being a public awareness of architecture's fundamental dimension, which has to be that of the town, the city, the human settlement entire. So the visitors to Main Street, pedestrians all, and looking for all the world like actors in a play – how affecting that was, because the city is, after all, a theater for human acts – took back home with them the unshakable conviction that their own Main Streets might be saved from the automobiles and the shopping malls and all the horrors of Redevelopment

that were destroying them everywhere. Ironically enough, they were rarely to give Disney credit for that perception, and the name itself was constantly used by many of them as an image of utter inauthenticity. Nevertheless, for whatever complicated reasons, Historic Preservation grew stronger every year from the opening of Disneyland onward, and the incomparably popular mass movement it represents is beginning to bring to fruition everywhere those revivals of the vernacular and classical traditions of architecture, and of traditional urbanism, which Disneyland, as perceived by Charles Moore long ago, so effectively suggested. This has been the great architectural achievement of the past generation, and Disneyland plays an honorable part in it. It has indeed entered deeply into our consciousness, so that when we come upon a place of absolute vernacular integrity, where people are also buying things, such as New Shoreham on Block Island, we are reminded of Disneyland, where, in return, only Tomorrowland looks dated at all.

There are many paradoxes and ambiguities. For example: the pedestrian experience was essential to Disney's Main Street and, despite monorails and so on, to all of Disneyland from the beginning. But, whether in Anaheim or Orlando, the fundamentally suburban areas in which the theme parks were situated were soon destroyed by the automobile culture engendered by all those millions of people who had to drive to the theme parks in order to walk in them. The orange groves of Anaheim soon gave way to degraded automobile strips, and total physical disorientation set in from Orlando to Kissimmee, most hideously in the miles of roadside mini-theme parks imitating Disney. "Parasites," Disney people call them, but Disney's spectacular success inevitably called them up. There are trolleys, horse-drawn, on Main Street, but none at all, even electrified, nor any other public transportation worthy of the name, in all the miles of sprawl that Disney has occasioned in Florida.

That is why Disney was widely perceived as posing such a threat to northern Virginia, and why Michael Eisner deserves solid credit for having the courage to pull back in time. Eisner's may in fact have been the pivotal decision shaping the future of all Disney worlds to come, because it naturally suggests a reorientation in Disney's thinking about where its theme parks ought to be built. It is now clear that they will inevitably destroy open landscape anywhere, but if set, for example, near the centers of the burned-out cities of the Northeast, anywhere in all those devastated miles alongside the railroad lines, they might become urban saviors, employing, even restoring, various systems of public transportation, in which Disney has always professed its interest, and creating jobs where they are most needed and, perhaps most of all, helping to recreate an environment of delight were hell exists right now.

Disney has clearly thought about these and other urban problems for many years, but the paradoxes have always been present. The company has always refused to build housing for its employees. As a result they are forced to commute, so adding to the automobile congestion and the urban sprawl. Now, however, Disney is building a town for twenty thousand people just south of Walt Disney World in Florida, where, in fact, housing is most desperately needed for those who work in the Orlando-Kissimmee area. It has been called Celebration, a name open to ironic comment and one very much in the theme park vein. But it will not be a company town. Only a certain number of employees, chosen by lot, will be allowed to live there. Better yet, it will not belong to Disney but will enjoy a normal relation to the political structures of the county and the state and will have plenty of citizens to cast votes in it and to decide its future. Probably best of all, it has been designed – by Robert A. M. Stern, Jaquelin Robertson, and other architects – according to the principles of the traditional urbanism which Disney itself helped revive and which have since been developed most fully by Andres Duany and Elizabeth Plater-Zyberk in Miami, Elizabeth Moule and Stefanos Polyzoides in Los Angeles, and Peter Calthorpe in San Francisco. It will be a pedestrian town with a coherent structure of streets and squares eliminating sprawl. House types, defined by code, will be traditional, but there will be some tough and challenging urban structures like the heroically scaled plaza of office blocks designed by Aldo Rossi. There will be no gates; it is not a "gated community" of the kind that is dangerously distorting the objectives of the present urban revival. There will be no company police. It will be traditional Florida cops, wearing mirrored sunglasses, who pull us over. Efforts have been made, perhaps not enough, to enable them, along with other city employees and moderately paid workers in general, to afford to live in the town. There will be a percentage of affordable housing, if none yet subsidized, including a number of those apartments over shops which were so essential to the health of Main Street as it used to be.

Some ambiguities remain, as they do in what has come to be called The New Urbanism as a whole. If towns need the presence of indigent poor as well as of physically and mentally unfortunate citizens in order to sustain instincts of decent humanity in everyone else, how can such factors be designed in? Clearly, they can't quite be. In all likelihood, they will develop out of the normal vagaries of human life as it goes on in the town. In the meantime, it is hoped by its architects that Celebration will be enough like a city to remind its inhabitants of what urban values are – as the gated communities emphatically do not do – so to keep alive somewhere in their minds an awareness of the desperate fate of those human beings who are still forced to live in cities half destroyed. Certainly Celebration, though still irredeemably optimistic in name and objectives, will create a much better environment for life than a similar development would have done only a few years ago, or perhaps, if Disney's Main Street had never come into being, and it may suggest a reasonable shape of reality at last.

Vincent Scully

chapter one | *Architecture with a Plot*

Seven dwarfs, expressing varying degrees of enthusiasm for their task, hold up the roof of Disney's corporate headquarters, the Team Disney Building in Burbank, California, designed by Michael Graves.

Of all the arts, it seems somehow most unlikely that architecture could have a plot. Architecture is proportions and aesthetics, abstraction and allusion, craft and construction. It is not, usually, a medium for storytelling; heroes and villains seldom lurk behind pilaster or parapet. Yet, many of the buildings erected by The Walt Disney Company – first, and still most disarmingly, at Disneyland in Anaheim, California, and later in Orlando, Florida; Tokyo; and Marne-la-Vallée, France – in the past half century seem to have materialized from the pages of picture books or the scenes of animated movies.

At Disney, every architect must turn storyteller, and the results range from the wryly whimsical to the almost abstrusely intellectual. Disney's architecture can be silly, sentimental, profound, enchanting, or challenging – sometimes all in one building. And whichever, it is always somehow cinematic, architecture with the pace and cadence of a film – Scene One, Scene Two – and lots of thematic underpinnings. It is story time.

Architecture had come from the pages of storybooks long before Walt Disney built Disneyland. One could point, for example, to the many themed towns built in America in the early twentieth century – Bavarian villages, Spanish enclaves, Cotswold cottage colonies. They were picturesque, to be sure, artful adaptations of other places, but it wasn't until Disney that the cinematic possibilities of architecture – of letting people step right into the story – started to be explored.

Walt Disney was, of course, the supreme storyteller, the master of a new art. He took the fables and fairy tales of the past and brought them to life in the movies, and so powerful was his imagery that his animated films have become, for many people, the authoritative versions. The characters he animated – from Mickey Mouse and Donald Duck to Snow White and Sleeping Beauty – were made for the screen but soon stepped out of their two-dimensional existence and into the imaginations and toy chests of children around the world. Disney's greatest achievement was in animation, but he also dreamed in three dimensions, creating fantasy worlds for paying visitors, which, in many less easily charted ways, have also had a profound impact on twentieth-century popular culture.

The architecture invariably emanated from actual stories – *Sleeping Beauty* or *The Adventures of Tom Sawyer* – and from fictionalized ideas of what real places might have looked like. Disneyland's Main Street, for example, was said to replicate Disney's hometown of Marceline, Missouri (even though it's really an imaginary turn-of-the-century Main Street, minus the pocks and flaws): in this case, the "tale" being told was Disney's own. "After all," says Marty Sklar, president of Walt Disney Imagineering, "storytelling was one of humankind's basic – and earliest – methods of effective communication – and one of the first ways we learned about the world as children."

In Walt Disney's worlds, architecture was a mesmerist's task of spinning gold from paint and turning stucco into stone. Walt watchers – those who worked with him or studied him closely – will assert that he never intended Disneyland or Walt Disney World to be "real," but, at the same time, they will talk about his preoccupation with making it all completely believable, a pretend world with no jarring intrusions: the oxymoron of totally authentic inauthenticity. "Imagination is the model from which reality is created," Disney once said, showing that he knew exactly what he was doing when he turned fiction into fact, making myth and legend part of everyday life.

"Walt was asked why he worked so hard to make it all look realistic," says Tony Baxter, who as a child rode his bicycle to Disneyland and went on to become one of the chief park and attractions designers as a senior vice president at Walt Disney Imagineering. "He said what we're selling is a belief in fantasy and storytelling, and if the background wasn't believable, people wouldn't buy it." (That urge for ersatz-authenticity has lived on into the 1990s, when bellhops and barmen are dressed to evoke the era or impulse of the various Disney hotels, to blend in with the architecture, as it were.) Marty Sklar recalls walking through Disneyland with Walt Disney when a publicist drove up to them near the Mike Fink Keel Boats. Disney was horrified: "What," he asked, "are you doing with a car here in 1860?"

Walt Disney, in many ways, did see his parks as an extension of the movies he made. Michael Eisner, who became The Walt Disney Company's chairman in 1984, almost two decades after Walt's death in 1966, saw, in architecture, even more potential, the oppor- tunity to create indelible memories by mak- ing hotels, restaurants, even office buildings tell a story. He saw that architecture could have the same enduring magic as an animated film, that architecture, too, could weave a spell. To prove his point, Eisner talks about the beautiful and quite emotional ballroom scene in the 1993 animated feature *Beauty and the Beast* when the two main characters start to dance with one another. "I don't think that anybody watching that can help but be affected," he says. "And that, too, is true of our architecture as well as our art."

Time and space take on new dimensions in the hands of Disney's architects and designers. There is, for example, the Matter- horn at Disneyland, at 147 feet a mere fig- urine of the real mountain, yet somehow larger-than-life in its context; and Big Thun- der Mountain, the attraction – there's one at every Disney theme park – that evokes the splendor and expanse of the West in the course of a roller-coaster ride on a runaway mining train. The castles are not castle-sized, but they are so designed and so placed that they seem to loom over the landscape as they would if they actually were homes to kings and queens, princes and princesses.

When fantasy is the springboard for architec- ture, almost anything is possible, from fairy- tale castles come to life to miniature English villages that reiterate storybook architectural styles as if it were utterly normal for the world of Peter Pan or Toad of Toad Hall to spring to life.

The first "Disney architecture" came in the form of art, sketches for buildings to be used as backgrounds in animated films. Today, The

Walt Disney Company is a global entertainment giant, and yet its buildings remain works of art – inventive, lighthearted, provocative, ingenuous, and always, in one way or another, cinematic. It is telling that top Disney executives preside over a corporate empire that includes four theme parks on three continents, a multifaceted movie studio, a professional sports team, a Broadway theater, new resorts and towns, and even a television network – but do so in a building whose pediment is upheld by Sleepy, Dopey, Grumpy, Sneezy, Happy, Bashful, and Doc, seven very famous and fanciful dwarfs originally drawn at an animator's table for the 1937 animated feature *Snow White and the Seven Dwarfs.*

Today, Disney's animators work in a building in Burbank that has the profile of the Mad Hatter's hat from the 1951 animated film *Alice in Wonderland* and a turret that alludes to the image of Mickey Mouse as the Sorcerer's Apprentice in *Fantasia* of 1940. Every job seeker at Walt Disney World in Orlando must turn door handles that were taken quite literally from the animated version of *Alice in Wonderland,* though these – unlike those in the film – don't talk.

Much of the work done under the auspices of Disney takes images from architectural history – from a humble medieval cottage to a Classical temple – and turns them into popular culture, a kind of designer's wave of the wand: call it alchemy. But the reverse is true, too. Robert Venturi's and Denise Scott-Brown's tiny fire station at Walt Disney World takes popular culture and turns it into high architecture: it is clad in jumbo red "bricks" (actually porcelain panels) and dappled with Dalmatian spots.

Also in Walt Disney World is Arata Isozaki's vast corporate Team Disney Building. Like Venturi, Isozaki is an architect regarded as among the finest anywhere, and this is a memorable work, with its powerful, looming forms and its tumble of geometric forms in bright, unexpected colors. Its entrance – a sequence of freestanding gates leading to the front door – is in the shape of Mickey Mouse's ears.

The Walt Disney Company became a major patron of architecture almost from the moment in 1984 when Michael Eisner took over as chairman. "Architecture, like any great art, is a little threatening. Great architecture and great art have to be intellectually challenging," says Eisner. He immediately saw the potential of architecture as an important way to communicate both myth and metaphor,

Snow White's friends, the Seven Dwarfs, lived in this fanciful cottage in Disney's 1937 animated feature. From the start, it was the animator's imagination that fueled Disney's architecture. Vernacular European country architecture inspired many of the buildings in the theme parks' Fantasylands.

and he didn't necessarily want the stories to be sweet, simple, or easy.

"He was a movie guy – ABC, Paramount," says Peter Rummell, president of the Disney Design and Development Company, which oversees the design and construction of all Disney development projects worldwide, including theme parks, hotels, retail stores, restaurants, entertainment complexes, offices, and community development. "For months, every time he saw PUD on a plan, I'm convinced he thought it meant 'producers using drugs.' [PUD stands for "planned unit development."] But what he did bring was a total understanding of what Disney is; what its strength is; what it represents to the world. You all know the horribly over-used real estate maxim of 'location, location, location' as the key to success. Michael's chant very quickly became 'entertainment, entertainment, entertainment.' He was consistent and unrelenting."

The first architect Eisner hired, Michael Graves, has long generated controversy for his use of powerful and rather intellectual classical images – a vocabulary he expanded, rather than abandoned, for Disney. From there, Eisner has gone on to employ – or try to employ – a legion of the best-known architects of the last decades of the twentieth century. As a kind of testimony to the company's commitment to architecture, the New York architect Robert A. M. Stern – designer of a half-dozen Disney buildings – was made a member of the company's board of directors.

Initially, Disney's – and Eisner's – new architectural venture was a well-kept secret: after Eisner decided he couldn't live with two new hotels that had been designed but not yet built for Walt Disney World before he

assumed his post at Disney, he sought alternative proposals from Robert Venturi and Michael Graves and selected the latter. Graves designed the Swan and Dolphin hotels, and soon other architects, among them Stern, were commissioned for other buildings without any public announcement.

And, indeed, the revelation of it all didn't come with typical Disney hoopla. It came inadvertently after Diane Sawyer and a film crew came to Orlando and followed Eisner around for days. Most of what was filmed for this segment of "60 Minutes" was already under construction, primarily the Disney-MGM Studios and the Grand Floridian Beach Resort, but Eisner was briefly shown standing in front of a scale model of a building.

The night the show aired, Karen Stein, senior editor of *Architectural Record,* was at home in her New York apartment. She had flipped on the TV almost absentmindedly when an image riveted her attention: it was not Eisner; it was the model behind Eisner. She recognized the distinctive architectural style. The next morning, she got on the phone to Michael Graves's office in Princeton, New Jersey. Was he doing a building for Disney? Graves sent her to Burbank: his instructions had been to keep silent about the two hotels and the office building he was designing, but the secret was out.

Soon buildings designed for Disney by Graves, Stern, and Isozaki were appearing on covers of architectural magazines. By then, architecture had become Eisner's passion. He was being regarded, rightly or wrongly, as a "modern Medici," a major patron of architecture. For his part, he had determined that there was little point in commissioning build-

Mickey Mouse as the Sorcerer's Apprentice in the animated movie of *Fantasia* (left) provided Robert A. M. Stern with a motif for two buildings: the Preview Center for Disneyland Paris when it was under construction (above), which has since been demolished, and his monumental Feature Animation Building in Burbank, which is discussed in chapter 10.

The streamlined geometry of Art Deco architecture appealed to both animators and architects in the late 1930s. Pluto (the cartoon dog) lived in a Streamline Moderne doghouse in the 1940 animated short film *Pluto's Dream House*. Architect Kem Weber used much the same approach when he designed the Disney studios in Burbank in 1939.

ings that were dull or ugly, instead setting a goal that his legacy would be architecture that would "have the beauty and the strength" to endure over time.

The new buildings went beyond the expected, at Eisner's behest. (According to Stern, "Disney is very tough, very rigorous and they push people to do something original.") And they weren't always well-received: once, an *Orlando Sentinel* columnist referred to the new buildings Eisner had commissioned as "architorture." There was plenty of debate and discussion, but whether the buildings were liked or disliked, there was no question that Disney had created another world unto itself, a world of architecture.

There was a time, of course, when the name "Disney" was considered little more than a pejorative term in the realm of architecture, a synonym for fake or cute. "Nobody accuses anybody of Paramounting or MGMing something," points out Rummell. "And yet, I don't think we need to apologize for it. I think it's a huge hit and it will endure, long after the Las Vegases have come and gone."

Critics labeled the architecture of the Disney theme parks – the idealized city streets, miniaturized world monuments, houses with toylike proportions painted in gooey colors, and castles recreated in ersatz materials – as purely sentimental. "Disney's worlds often seem to resemble the collective imagination of the middle class, and critics in schools of architecture still use 'Disneyland' as a term of extreme disapprobation to describe projects exhibiting gratuitous sentimentality and straying from serious architectural issues," wrote the architectural historian Bruce Webb.

Yet if Walt Disney chose to make his theme park in Anaheim palpably sweet and nostalgic, it was also notable for being auto-free – a pedestrian environment in an era, the 1950s, when the automobile was king. It offered a vision of buildings and spaces in intricate relationship, at a time when planners were simply cutting vast swathes through cities for urban renewal and for freeways. When Disneyland opened in 1955, the facades of Main Street hid vast storage areas and little more; and, yet, this underscaled, highly sentimentalized rendition of an American small town had the potential to change the way Americans regarded their own towns. It became the inspiration for the restoration of small-town Main Streets from all over America – enough so that real Main Streets tart themselves up to look like the fake

One of Kem Weber's proposals for the gate to the Disney studios (above) had an allosauruslike light fixture looming over the gateway. Not quite fifty years later, in 1987, as part of his commission to design a corporate headquarters building for the Burbank studio lot, Michael Graves proposed an even more whimsical entrance for the studios (left). Neither of these designs was executed, but a faint echo of Weber's pylon can be seen in the design of the gateway to the Disney-MGM Studios in Orlando.

Disney's first substantial studio was built on a lot on Hyperion Avenue in Hollywood that Walt and his brother Roy purchased in 1925. The original one-story white stucco building was enlarged a number of times in the ensuing years, and the two-story animation building, designed in the Spanish Revival style popular in Los Angeles in the 1920s and 1930s, was added in 1931.

Kem Weber designed an entire "campus" for the Burbank studios (right), including sound-stages and offices, for which he designed all the furniture (below) as well.

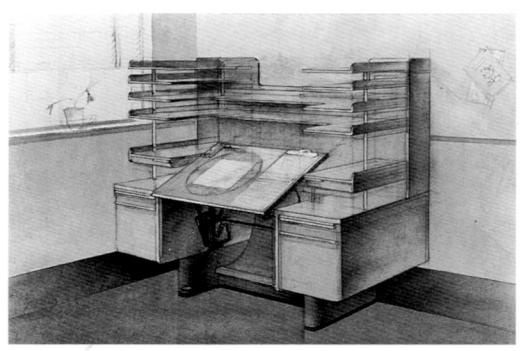

Walt Disney (left, center) oversaw the construction of the Burbank studios, which, when completed, were a fine example of the forward-thinking architecture of the times. These buildings (below) are still in use.

ones – and the source of design ideas for hundreds of shopping malls.

If Disneyland has had its critics, it has also had its admirers – among them the late architect Charles Moore and the urban planner Denise Scott-Brown – who subjected themselves to ridicule when they wrote or talked about the powerful impact of its public spaces. Such commentators may have grasped a contradiction in Walt's ethos. If Disney was the ultimate traditionalist, or what we might call today a neotraditionalist, paying homage to ideals that never really existed, he also had a less well understood fascination with cutting-edge art. Certainly the 1940 film *Fantasia* stands in testimony to this, as did his friendships with writer Ray Bradbury, conductor Leopold Stokowski, and artist Salvador Dalí, who in the 1950s spent months puttering around in Disney's backyard.

As John Hench, senior vice president of Walt Disney Imagineering, points out, despite Disney's enduring grandfatherly image, virtually everything he did was experimental. The first buildings he actually commissioned for his new studio complex in Burbank were designed in the Streamline Moderne Style by the fine – and for the time (1939) progressive – California architect Kem Weber. (In a characteristically sentimental gesture, Walt moved the bungalow on Hyperion Avenue in Hollywood and two other buildings that had first housed his studio to his new Burbank lot, where they still stand.) Weber even designed the animators' desks and other furniture still in use today. An echo of Streamline Moderne Style can be found in such Disney short films as *Modern Inventions* (1937) and *Pluto's Dream House* (1940).

Walt Disney's influence on contemporary architecture was undeniable. Significantly, his enthusiasm for architecture that tells a story got translated into jargon – people spoke of "themed architecture" and "entertainment architecture," the latter a coinage of Michael Eisner's that he came to hate. The widespread use of these terms, however, attests to the level of their acceptance by the architectural establishment. "We've set out to prove that contemporary architects can be part of storytelling just as the derivative architects are," says Rummell. "We've always approached it with the idea that a point of view, a story, goes beyond the architecture. Without the conceit, without the story, there's nothing to test against, there's no frame of reference. A story is the only thing I know that puts everything in context, that gives it a primary reason for being." Speaking on behalf of achitects, Venturi alludes to the "underacknowledged scenographic aspect of architecture," its symbolic dimension.

Eisner has approached architects he admired whether their work promised an easy fit with Disney's mission or not. The list of Disney architects covers a wide range of styles.

There are the historicists or those who will work in regional American styles, such as Peter Dominick of Denver, who designed the masterful and evocative Wilderness Lodge in Walt Disney World, or Robert A. M. Stern, who has designed both hotels and office buildings for Disney. "I was very insistent that my work not be a jokey version of the past, but it could be a hyper-version of the past, more real than reality, in which the architecture intensifies the experience. It's theater. It's hyper-reality. In theater, by buying a ticket you make a pact with the producer that you enter their world," says Stern.

Michael Graves and Robert Venturi tend to be more referential than direct in their borrowings from the vocabulary of styles available to architects, as do the Miami firm of Arquitectonica and the Albuquerque-based architect Antoine Predock, though each in very different ways. Graves, who, like Stern, has designed a number of major buildings for Disney, is known for his occasionally arcane references to classical architecture and art: his work is at once soft and sensual and deep and difficult. In his firehouse for Walt Disney World, Venturi borrows from the traditional language of architecture and from pop culture to make a building that is at once cerebral and very accessible. Arquitectonica's first work for Disney – the comic-strip kitschy All-Star Resorts in Walt Disney World – uses popular images drawn from sports and music. Predock, who designed the Hotel Santa Fe in Disneyland Paris, transforms the vernacular in both literal and oblique ways: for him, the theme is an abstraction but the execution is rather figurative.

Even architects whose work is generally highly abstract – like Arata Isozaki and Charles Gwathmey – will discuss the artistic arguments implicit in the idea of architecture that revolves around a theme or even an invented story line to be entertaining. Isozaki will talk at length about how themes in architecture go back to ancient Greece, as if designing temples to gods could be fairly considered a "theme" (among Disney buildings, Isozaki's Team Disney Building in Walt Disney World probably offers the most exhalted interpretation of themed architec-

ture). "For me, you could say awareness equals entertainment," says Gwathmey, whose New York firm of Gwathmey Siegel & Associates designed the Bonnet Creek Golf Club and the Contemporary Hotel Convention Center in Walt Disney World. "When somebody's stimulated and provoked by a building, there is a certain amount of intensity and revelation that occurs. When you're inspired, that's entertainment." Only Frank Gehry, who designed Festival Disney, a shopping street in Disneyland Paris, and two buildings in Anaheim, finds the idea of themed architecture troubling.

Graves states the case for and against architecture with a theme quite eloquently: "Modern architecture has a theme, if you will, in the machine. Bernini and Michelangelo did themes. I'm not willing to give up the idea that architecture is capable of doing this. Yet the more literal, the closer to likeness a building is, the more difficult it is to say multiple things. As we developed our buildings, we really discovered theming to be very interesting – and very suspect."

From the first, when Graves's Swan Hotel opened in 1989 to plenty of discussion, it was clear that architecture had turned a corner late in the twentieth century: the hotel, and the other buildings by Graves, Stern, and Isozaki that soon followed, contributed to the widespread feeling that high art and popular culture could somehow mesh. "Popular architecture is valid and actually has a long tradition," says Venturi. "Architecture should not be esoteric . . . but it should have opportunity to have many interpretations and work for all kinds of people. And besides, we like to do architecture that children like."

The Sleeping Beauty Castle at Disneyland is seventy-five feet tall. Because the bricks in the upper courses of the base are slightly narrower than those below, the perspective is "forced," making the castle appear taller than it is.

chapter two | *Disneyland*

From the front gates, it unfolds, at once utterly familiar and yet otherworldly, a storybook come to life. In many ways, Disneyland Park is Walt Disney: it is conventional and experimental all at once, its architecture expressing both nostalgia for the past and fervor for the future. To understand Disneyland, it's necessary to understand Disney himself, for he conceived of it and gave it form. If the details of the design came from the hands of others, the ideas behind it were his. He understood the need for a clear, strong visual message: he would tell the Imagineers charged with creating the park that if people didn't understand what they were saying, it was only because of poor design. "It's all very obvious: careful communication, watching what you say, and being explicit and having something to say in the first place," says John Hench.

Disney wanted Disneyland to be "a world of people past and present seen through the eyes of my imagination, a place of warmth and nostalgia, of illusion and color and delight." In the opening paragraph of his 1953 proposal for Disneyland, he wrote, "Like Alice stepping through the Looking Glass, to step through the portals of Disneyland will be like entering another world." It was a prescient allusion, for Alice stepped into a world where experience was heightened by the manipulation of size and shape and color and sound.

The manipulation of scale was a key element of Disney's genius: he loved miniatures, from railroads to tabletop dioramas, and this fascination pervaded many aspects of his life. For example, he sat at a child's table, not a giant desk. Hench recalls that his official office, with all the top-executive trappings, was for show. Disney really worked at a small table in a back room: "He sat on a little stool against the wall, put one script on the table, and everything else would be piled on the floor." Disney once confided that it was a highly successful psychological ploy: when people were angry, they felt like they were towering over him, and when they were asking for something, they felt more comfortable.

This second key element, his instinctive ability to put himself in the shoes of other people, also propelled his imagination. Hench recalls that in the course of screenings, Walt would lean back and muse, "I wonder what they will think." The "they" in question weren't critics or financial backers but people in general, Disney's idealized notion of his audience. It was this sense of identification with the public that enabled Disney to go on television, earnest and grandfatherly, and sell his ideas for what he called "the happiest place on earth."

Disney spent lots of time visiting and studying world fairs, amusement parks, and urban parks, and he wanted Disneyland to look good and feel good to those who went there. If that seems somehow naive and ingenuous, it worked: people flocked to the park.

For several decades designers, planners, historians, and theorists have reckoned with Disneyland, trying to figure out what all its cheerfully optimistic architecture actually means. *New York Times* architecture critic Paul Goldberger called it the town square of Los Angeles. To Charles Moore, it was the "most important single piece of construction in the West in the past several decades," but he bemoaned the fact that the best of Los Angeles's "public" places wasn't actually public, nor was it free. The shopping center developer James Rouse gave a speech at Harvard in 1963 and stepped off the intellectual limb into a more common realm: "I hold a view that may be somewhat shocking to an audience as sophisticated as this," said Rouse, "that the greatest piece of urban design in the United States today is Disneyland. If you think about Disneyland – and think of its performance in relation to its purpose; its meaning to people – more than that its meaning in the process of development – you will find it the outstanding piece of urban design in the United States!"

The cultural historian Karal Ann Marling looks at Disneyland as the "most complex, baffling and beloved work of art produced in postwar America." For Walt, she says, Disneyland was satisfying in a way that making films was not: "It was always perfectible – and that was the real challenge. That was the real fun. The intellectuals who hated Disneyland did not reckon with all that fun."

Speaking for those intellectuals, poet John Ciardi called Disneyland "the heartland of the depthless," adding: "It has to be seen to be disbelieved. The imagination cannot doubt it sufficiently. As Dante almost but not quite did say: I never saw so bright/So blank, so prettified a nothingness/Its very memory marzipans my sight/Mr. Disney's overfrosted cake."

Disneyland didn't have a groundbreaking of record, but on a summer day in July 1954, Walt Disney stuck a shovel in the ground and changed the course of architecture – and of leisure – in America. The start of construction was a quiet affair, without bands or the press or live television.

It opened a year and a day later, on July 17, 1955. The first day was a disaster, with an unexpected crowd of 33,000. Main Street melted, rides broke down, and there was not enough food. Almost forty years later, at the dedication of Mickey's Toontown in 1993, Disney's chairman Michael Eisner called Disneyland "the temple of the entire Walt Disney Company." By then, 350 million visitors had gone through its gates.

Disney's earliest dreams of an amusement park took various forms. In the early 1950s, he put architect-turned-animator Ken Anderson and magazine illustrator Harper Goff to work on a project called "Disneylandia." They were asked to design paintings with themes taken from American life and folklore that Walt himself would model as miniature tableaux. These would be toured around the country: people would pay a quarter a turn to set them into motion. Disney gave the studio the task of creating nine-inch-tall mechanical figures to populate the dioramas, but engineering such tiny figures to move proved impracticable. Eventually, the experiment led by a circuitous route to the creation of life-size *Audio-Animatronics* figures, but that was to come later, after Disneyland had been invented and built. Disneylandia died, but bequeathed its name to a grander scheme.

The first plan was to develop the six-acre tract of land just across Riverside Drive from the Disney Burbank studios: surviving drawings show this was conceived in a much more classical and parklike style than the eventual Anaheim version, but it did include a railroad and – as a hint of the inventions yet to come – a singing waterfall. Disney's colleagues remember watching him walk the open plot, stepping off the measurements, standing silently amid the weeds, trying to envision his park. His ideas soon outgrew the site, however. Today, Disney's new Feature Animation Building occupies the northeast corner of the land, which is now bordered by the Ventura Freeway.

Walt Disney's first idea was to build his theme park in Burbank across the street from his studios. The new Feature Animation Building (see chapter 10) now sits on part of the site.

DISNEYLAND

SCHEMATIC AERIAL VIEW
APPROX. 45 ACRES
WITHIN RAILROAD TRACKS
· DESIGNED BY WED ENTERPRISES ·

The animator Herb Ryman was enlisted by Walt Disney to create an image of Disneyland; he had to do it over a weekend so that Walt and his brother Roy could take the illustration to the financiers who would underwrite the project.

In the summer of 1953, Disney hired the Stanford Research Institute to help him select a site for his new amusement park. Thus he came to buy 160 acres of orange groves in Anaheim, near one of Los Angeles's early amusement parks, Knott's Berry Farm, which at that time included a rather famous restaurant serving chicken and pie and a cyclorama housed in a reconstructed ghost town. The ghost town had begun with an old hotel that had been moved piece by piece from Prescott, Arizona. The Santa Ana Expressway, the road that would link greater Los Angeles to Burbank and Anaheim, was already on the planning boards, which gave the choice of site a certain logic.

Disney had hired Richard Irvine, who had been an art director at 20th Century–Fox, to work with the Los Angeles architecture firm of Pereira & Luckman to do a master plan. He had already talked at length with his architect friend Welton Becket, who had told him that there was no architect at work in America who could produce what Disney dreamed of. "You are going to have to do it yourself," he said. Irvine confirmed

that opinion. As close as Disney was with several important Los Angeles architects and as much as he was pulled by the modernist urge himself, he knew he had to go a different route with Disneyland, and, ultimately, all of the designers and architects of Disneyland came from within Walt Disney Productions or were recruited especially for the project, forming the nucleus of the Imagineering Division. "He had that park all built in his head years and years before he had a place to put it," said Bill Evans, chief landscape architect at Disney, who, with his brother Morgan, also a well-known horticulturist, created – or rather invented – Disneyland's landscape, and stayed on through the landscaping of Walt Disney World and Disneyland Paris, introducing to the theme parks both new plant and tree specimens and new ideas about making landscape tell a story.

Thus, one Saturday morning in September 1953, the artist and animator Herb Ryman got a call as he sat at home, painting. Disney summoned him to the studio and told him of the plans for a $17 million amusement park.

"So I got excited. 'Well gee, I'd like to see it too,' I said.

"He said, 'You're going to do it.'"

The drawings for Disneyland had to be completed right away because Walt's brother Roy was heading for New York to try to drum up the financing. Ryman worked with Disney all weekend translating words into pictures. Ryman, who had been the art director for such MGM classics of the 1930s as *Anna Karenina, The Good Earth,* and *A Tale of Two Cities* before coming to work at Disney, was well-equipped to summon up images of faraway places.

Disney wanted a castle as a centerpiece – it was no coincidence that the studio was at work on *Sleeping Beauty* at the time – in his "magic place." He also wanted a hub in front of the castle that would be a central gathering place, like an Italian piazza. The various "lands" – odes to the future and the past and to the imaginary worlds of Disney's films – would radiate out from this, the hub, which would be a meeting place and orientation point for visitors to the park. "Disneyland," said Walt, "is going to be a place where you can't get lost or tired unless you want to."

Ryman's weekend drawing is in fact a beautiful piece of work, rendered in a rather elegant Beaux-Arts manner and startlingly true to the Disneyland that was to open its doors less than two years later. In ways large and small, it anticipates the theme park as it was built, with its rivers and mountains. A single entrance led down Main Street and into the hub in the shadow of the castle, much as it does today.

Once the financing was clinched, the designers of Disneyland went to work. Virtu-ally all of them were animators, some with backgrounds in architecture and others in art. "All of us came from motion pictures," says Hench. "That's the reason the park is what it is, like stage design. You design the environment for activity, for actions. Walt used a lot of techniques we'd used in motion pictures." (Disney called the theme-park designers "Imagineers." The Imagineering Division now includes among its 1,200 members planners, designers, architects, engineers, computer scientists, and construction managers.)

Indeed, there are long shots and close-ups and carefully laid out sequences unfolding as if they were scenes in a movie. Images materialize and fade, like cinematic dissolves. Hench likened the pieces of the park to scenes in animation, each of which was like a "bead or a charm in a necklace. The same thing was applied as you walk around the park. Continuity was the same. Whether you're slow or fast, what you look at is the same," he said.

In a movie, the images are fleeting and a missed detail might go unnoticed. Disneyland was to be there for the long run, and it was designed to a certain obsessive level of detail. "Walt wanted all the details to be correct," says Hench. "What it amounted to was a kind of visual literacy." He hated finding employees in the wrong costumes for the time or place, just as he hated spoiling illusions with automobiles or other up-to-date paraphernalia.

Of course, for all the attention to detail, there is also an enormous liberty taken with scale, and even with style. On Main Street, the first stories are full scale but the floors above are much smaller: it is not really the 7/8ths scale or 5/8ths scale that is often attributed to Disney, but a play of dimensions far more

Disney's designers put their animation skills to good use in designing Disneyland. Some of the drawings that they prepared, such as the low-level aerial views of Adventureland (above) and Frontierland (opposite), were as much designed to promote the theme park as to aid in the planning process. Walt Disney used such drawings to promote his dream (top). Even the more schematic designs, such as the plan for Fantasyland (right), had a playful feeling.

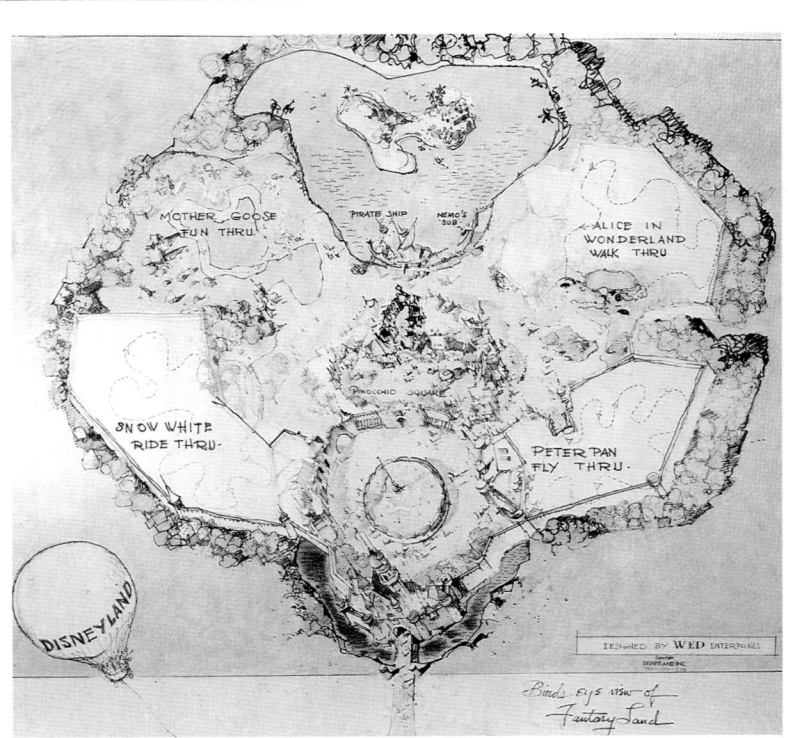

This is a sequence of aerial photographs showing stages of the construction of Disneyland. The first photograph (top left), taken July 16, 1954, shows the site, planted with orange trees, marked by solid white lines. In the second photograph (bottom left), taken on October 20, 1954, the trees are gone and the outline of the park itself is beginning to show. By the time the third photograph (top right) was taken on December 17, 1954, the steel framework for Main Street had been erected, the plantings for Adventureland and Tom Sawyer Island had begun to be installed, and an embankment had been built up to carry the right-of-way for the Disneyland Railroad. By the time the fourth photograph (bottom right) was taken on March 16, 1955, the buildings on Main Street were almost finished and the Sleeping Beauty Castle had begun to rise in its scaffolding. The final photograph (opposite) shows the completed park, which opened to the public on July 17, 1955.

Disneyland took the form of the small towns that were vanishing all across America, with a full complement of sentimentalized nineteenth-century architecture. The first place visitors arrived at was an idealized Town Square, where the tidy buildings – a railroad station, a city hall, an opera house, a bank, a firehouse – symbolized the controlling hand of benevolent authority. Here are the Railroad Station (top) and City Hall (right).

An aerial view of Sleeping Beauty Castle (opposite). Many of the buildings in the Disney theme parks are designed to be seen from street level only. The castles, however, are meant to be convincing from all perspectives.

Adventureland acquired its architecture straight from Hollywood adventure movies. It evolved into a mix of various building styles (African, Polynesian) and what might be called "Castaway Style," summed up by Adventureland's sign (opposite). Almost from the beginning, the Jungle Cruise had its Cambodian Temple, a staple of the adventure genre that inspired George Lucas's Indiana Jones movies. The new Indiana Jones Adventure at Disneyland (above) offers a very sophisticated adaptation of Far Eastern temple architecture.

Frontierland relies on what might be called "ghost-town vernacular," an architecture familiar from hundreds of cowboy movies. State-of-the-art examples can be found on the Big Thunder Mountain Railroad (right).

capricious and cinematic than that. Everything was scaled so that it "looked right," bigger or smaller than it might actually be.

Disney's particular obsession, too, was that everything look freshly painted and clean, even areas alluding to times or places where that was not authentic – Frontierland, say, or New Orleans Square, both of which were representations of places that were tattered and frayed in real life. He said he didn't want his "guests" to see any of the real world while they were in his park. "I want them to feel they are in another world."

Perspective, forced and otherwise, is key to the design of Disneyland. The view down Main Street frames the castle, making it seem grander and more imposing than it actually is. This was one of Disney's cinematic architectural manipulations: in fact, it is a time-tested mechanism for underscoring the prominence of important buildings. Hench, of course, relates it to the movies: "In motion pictures you start out with an establishing shot, a long shot, a wow. The long shot should say something to you. Most cities have the long shot."

As animation historian Donald Britton says, Disneyland betrays a "cartoon sensibility – a liberating sense of the limitless malleability of pictorial space, a freedom to render anything and everything that can be imagined as if it actually existed." Marling, the cultural historian, sees in Disneyland more of a short attention-span television sensibility: "In the movies, the experience is continuous and unbroken, but in Disneyland, it is discontinuous and episodic, like watching television in the privacy of one's own home, each ride a four- or five-minute

segment, slotted in among snacks, trips to the rest room, and 'commercials' in the form of souvenir emporia. And it is always possible to change the channel."

Indeed, it was the ABC television show "Disneyland" that Disney relied on to drum up interest in the project. One consequence of this deal was that America watched Disneyland become a real place – the dredging of the rivers, the fabrication of Main Street, the construction of Sleeping Beauty Castle. It was as if one man's castle was becoming everyman's home. (The ABC network was the original partner in Disneyland, underwriting part of its cost in exchange for one-third ownership of the park – later purchased back by Disney – and the weekly television show. Ironically enough, in 1995 the Disney company acquired ABC.)

From the Town Square at the entrance, Main Street leads to the central plaza, or hub, in front of Sleeping Beauty Castle. From there, the several "lands" unfold. The past – in the form of Frontierland and Adventureland – is to the left; the future, Tomorrowland, is off to the right. Fantasyland is straight ahead.

The transitions between "lands" are planned carefully, with an eye primarily to

After a 1983 renovation, Fantasyland took its predominant architectural styles from the villages of Northern Europe – from the Bavarian Black Forest to the Old English market towns – that gave birth to so many of the fairy tales and folktales that had helped to shape Walt Disney's imagination (above). Almost the only example of traditional American amusement park architecture in Disneyland is the King Arthur Carrousel (opposite), a turn-of-the-century antique rescued from Coney Island, New York. It's a Small World (left), which came to Fantasyland from the 1964-65 New York World's Fair, introduced an unexpected design element to the architecture of Disneyland. The almost flat facade with its bold, abstract forms is an expression of mainstream trends in early 1960s graphic design.

Visitors flocked to Disneyland, in some cases just to stroll through pleasant streets and plazas, among them the Town Square. The visionary architect Charles Moore called Disneyland "the most important" new place in the Western world.

the approach. The Plaza Pavilion restaurant, for example, is two themes in one. The front, in Frontierland, is Victorian, but the back is cued to Adventureland.

Disney and his designers always kept everything – down to banning shirtless or shoeless visitors – under control to provide a kind of visual harmony and psychological order. The amusement park historian Judith Adams notes that it was this control "not only of the design but in the experiencing of the design" that set Disneyland apart from its predecessors. "Everything about the park, including the behavior of the 'guests,' is engineered to promote a spirit of optimism, a belief in progressive improvement toward perfection."

Seldom are there more than two choices at any juncture. The long waits in line are punctuated by music and by what Dick Nunis, chairman of Walt Disney Attractions, calls "random visual detail," which, of course, isn't random at all but consists of carefully placed diversions. The wait at the Haunted Mansion, for example, includes a cemetery with puns or funny poems on all the gravestones.

The science fiction writer Ray Bradbury – Walt Disney's friend and admirer – was an instant proponent of Disneyland. Thirty years ago, he wrote, "In Disneyland, he [Disney] has proven again that the first function of architecture is to make men over, make them wish to go on living, feed fresh oxygen, grow them tall, delight their eyes, make them kind.

"Disneyland liberates men to their better selves. Here the wild brute is gently corralled, not used and squashed, not put upon and harassed, not tromped on by real-estate operators, nor exhausted by smog and traffic."

Hench, the company's long-standing resident intellectual, at eighty-seven is still actively designing for Disney and thinking about it. He calls attention to the gestalt of the place: "It's one of the special charms of Disneyland that not only is the architecture related, but the ideas are related. You get the impression of ambience."

In the 1950s, America was emerging from decades of depression and war, but life wasn't returning to its former predictability. People were newly mobile, moving from cities they'd lived in for generations and starting afresh in California or Florida or New York. Cities were growing rapidly, up and out, and so was government. "Disneyland," says Los Angeles architectural historian Katherine W. Rinne, "was a means of shutting out the realities of life and entering a city perfectly balanced between the safety of the past and the hope of the future." It offered that old dependability, down to the tiniest detail, and yet it held out a promise, of sorts. The dedication plaque at Disneyland, dated July 17, 1955, includes the words, "Here you leave today and enter the world of yesterday, tomorrow and fantasy."

chapter three | *Walt Disney World*

Anthropologists use Mecca as a metaphor for Walt Disney World. Historians find there the expression of arcadian and utopian ideals. Sociologists look at it as a "landscape of power." And in Florida, Walt Disney World looms large enough that economists and journalists often refer to it simply as "The Mouse." *Time* magazine once called it "The Mouse That Roared."

Before Disney, as time is tracked in Orlando, central Florida was a tourist backwater, offering a few old-time attractions. The Works Progress Administration-produced guide to Florida reported in 1939 that Orlando had seventeen hotels, total. By 1995, fifty-six years later, Orlando logged in with more than 80,000 hotel rooms, vying year-by-year with Las Vegas to have the most in the world.

And indeed the allure of Walt Disney World is such that it draws more than 30 million visitors every year by itself. Disneyland, by contrast, is a day trip for Southern Californians or a two-day stop, and draws a comparatively lighter annual crowd of 12 million. Walt Disney World – that is to say, the Magic Kingdom, Epcot, Disney-MGM Studios, Pleasure Island, three water parks, two shopping centers, and dozens of hotels (with about 16,000 rooms) and office buildings, among them Disney's own signature structures, the Casting Center and the Team Disney Building, which are, in their own ways, architectural tourist attractions – is big enough to absorb a tourist's week, and often does.

The anthropologist Alexander Moore has termed Walt Disney World "the cultural climax of its genre," and argues that its form – a "bounded space with entry checkpoints, fully separated from daily life, with specific rituals attending it" – was borrowed "quite unconsciously" from the ancient pilgrimage center of Mecca. It is a shrine for tourists around the world. Another anthropologist, Stephen Fjellman, has studied every facet of Walt Disney World to produce *Vinyl Leaves,* a book-length analysis of what he calls a "pseudoutopia." The Associate Collegiate Schools of Architecture held its 1992 conference in Orlando, during which a number of scholars offered appraisals – analytical, appreciative, and scathing – of Walt Disney World. When the American Institute of Architects held its fiftieth anniversary convention in Orlando in 1987, one full morning session was devoted to the study of the Magic Kingdom's success; the assembled architects sat and listened as Peter Rummell discussed his concept for "entertainment architecture," a term not then in regular use. Marty Sklar, who started with Disney as a college student just before Disneyland opened and went on to become president of the Imagineering Division, issued "Mickey's 10 Commandments," an outline, in plain terms, for making architecture more amenable to the people who experience buildings and places:

"Know your audience; wear your guests' shoes, that is, don't forget the human factor;

The Disney theme parks are built to showcase spectacular visual effects at night. The Cinderella Castle at the Walt Disney World Magic Kingdom is a particularly noteworthy example of design with this use in mind. The distinctive roofs and turrets of Main Street become pleasing, simple geometric shapes when picked out with strings of lights.

organize the flow of people and ideas; create a 'wienie' (that was Walt Disney's somewhat inelegant term for what you might call a visual magnet); communicate with visual literacy; avoid overload – create turn-ons; tell one story at a time; avoid contradictions – maintain identity; for every ounce of treatment provide a ton full of treat; keep it up."

Those 10 Commandments of Mickey's are telling: in Walt Disney World, it is not so much the quality of the architecture, which ranges from bad to brilliant, that draws attention so much as the self-conscious comportment of it all – this is, above all, architecture with good manners. Indeed, there are any number of buildings within the resort's 30,000 acres – among them the cookie-cutter chain hotels at Lake Buena Vista – that are utterly banal works of architecture, but all are maintained with the same obsessive care: "In the Disney theme parks, a dirty floor or an out-of-order facility may individually be of minor significance, but in the long run, they will diminish visitors' expectations of everything we do," says Sklar.

If Disneyland offered a respite from a postwar world in which the automobile was a potent symbol and the group seemed suddenly a more powerful ideal than the individual, Walt Disney World came into being in the midst of the increasingly chaotic 1960s. It was planned as a total, controlled environment and a retreat from the world at large, where order would reign. It would be clean and carefree and predictable, the way the suburbs were supposed to be.

In fact, Walt Disney World is, in many ways, a sealed and often silly environment (imagine parking at Goofy and then passing Chip, Dale, and Pluto). In the long run and in the kindest light, however, its hermetic quality is an inevitable result of design in accordance with Sklar's 10 Commandments, which in themselves are open to wide interpretation: are they motivated by savvy marketing, conscientious design, common sense, or a little bit of each? Alexander Moore's image of the pilgrimage center is the most original and penetrating of all Walt Disney World critiques. He points out that such centers draw people from near and far, to "sacred precincts" away from the routine of their daily lives, to feast on readily comprehensible symbolism and enduring mythology. However, he stops short of attributing a religious meaning to the resort: at Walt Disney World, "magic and fantasy, not religion, reign."

After Disneyland opened in 1955, Walt Disney paid less attention to the everyday business of moviemaking. He'd become preoccupied with solving bigger problems – relating to urban planning, transportation, the quality of life – rather than just offering people a diversion from their daily lives. "The idea preceded the land," says Sklar.

Sklar recalls that Disney was babysitting his grandchildren at his daughter Diane's house and a garbage truck came into the alley at 5:00 A.M., disrupting his sleep. It stimulated a stream of thought about how cities operated. "He began to focus on things that were wrong around the world. It was as broad and as encompassing as that."

Such general concerns were much on Disney's mind when he began looking for a place to build a new park a few years after Disneyland opened. He surveyed the country and chose a site midway between Orlando and Kissimmee, Florida. In choosing the place, he was conceivably making a symbolic gesture: his parents had been married in Kissimmee. Demographically, it made sense. After California, Florida was America's other great tourist destination, and Orlando offered much of what Anaheim did – an empty canvas to paint on plus highway access and little competition from other attractions. The beach is an hour away.

Moreover, the land for the future Walt Disney World – or the "so-called Disney World," as Disney himself wryly referred to it – was partly in Orange County, Florida, and Disneyland was in Orange County, California. Both had orange groves, though the Florida site was more dominantly ranchland and what was then considered swamp, or in today's parlance, wetlands.

Both Florida and California, particularly Southern California, had a certain mythic allure and had been rediscovered and reinvented by successive waves of settlers and tourists. Both had become quintessentially twentieth-century places, where whole towns – and rather lavish and preposterous developments of one sort or another – materialized almost instantly.

In both cases, there were precedents. Knott's Berry Farm, with its restored Arizona ghost town, was in Buena Park, the next town over from Anaheim. And in Florida, there were already some smaller themed attractions – from the waterskiing spectaculars at Cypress Gardens to jungle rides and alligator farms.

By 1964, when Walt Disney decided to build in Florida, these old-style attractions were starting to lose their tourist appeal. The new lure of Florida was living there. People poured into the state every day by the hundreds, buying up the tiny concrete-block houses perched on concrete slabs that developers couldn't build fast enough. Farms and other large plots were rapidly subdivided and sold off. Some even bought lots by mail. Fraud was rampant, and the same piece of unbuildable swamp was often sold dozens of times over.

Thus, it hardly seemed strange when a tough-talking guy named Bob Price Foster, who was Disney's in-house lawyer, showed up in Kissimmee wearing tattered jeans and ragged T-shirts and, using his middle name as his last name, began buying up land through five dummy corporations. He looked like a hick and sounded like a sucker. In eighteen months, he'd bought 27,400 acres of swampland, ranchland, hammock, and citrus groves for just about $200 an acre.

All of this took place in the utmost secrecy; virtually no one in Orlando suspected what was going on. Then, in October 1965, *Orlando Sentinel* reporter Emily Bavar snagged an interview with Walt Disney during a Disneyland press event. The more she probed, the more diligently he denied having any plans for Florida, explaining in much-too-great detail what was wrong with it as a theme park destination. Trusting her instinct, she wrote a speculative story that the *Sentinel* ran on its front page. She was right, of course.

Walt Disney World sprawls over an area the size of San Francisco (Manhattan would fit into it twice over). Disney always regretted he hadn't been able to buy more land in Anaheim, especially when the inevitable ticky-tacky motels and fast-food joints enveloped

Disneyland, so he bought up everything he could in Orlando (the company now owns 30,000 acres).

Because Disney bought land in two counties, Orange and Osceola, he asked the Florida legislature to create a special drainage district called the Reedy Creek Improvement District, which made Walt Disney World literally its own kingdom: here, the district had complete control – over roads, building codes, and land-use planning – as well as responsibility for safety, drainage, waste removal, fire protection, and water and power delivery. The legislation was not especially controversial at the time (a decision to turn a meandering country road into a main access route, thereby forcing its upgrading, caused more hue and cry). Later, however, as the two counties realized what they'd lost and began to assess the impact of uncontrolled growth around Walt Disney World, the Reedy Creek Improvement District came under greater fire, much too late for any governmental bodies to do anything about it.

For Walt himself, the district was a means to an end; he had begun to see himself as an urban planner. By then, late in his life – plans for Walt Disney World were announced just months before his death from cancer in 1966 – he was known to get bored fairly easily, to want to move on to the next challenge. Always driven by forces that were at once Victorian and progressive, Disney wanted everything to be clean and precise, as an antidote to the degradation he saw in the urban environment. He also loved technology of all kinds – from steam locomotives to monorails – and his faith in American corporate know-how was boundless.

Thus, when he drew up plans for Walt Disney World, he pulled all these strains of thought together. He envisioned a theme park, industrial park, residential community, and airport, all connected by a high-speed rail system, with the Magic Kingdom itself at the end of the line. "For somebody who never went to planning school or architecture school, he was amazing," says Wing Chao, Disney's chief architect, who joined the company six years after its founder's death.

John Hench feels that "Disneyland was very courageous on Walt's part, and Florida shows the most guts of anything . . . to take a kind of civilization, make it ideal, and then to make it practical." Indeed, there is a pervasive theme underlying Walt Disney World that seems much less obvious at Disneyland, that of the idealized landscape, which is why so many scholars analyze it in utopian terms. The architectural historian James A. Moore sees it as a meshing of myths: "relentless belief in the perfectibility of the future combined with nostalgic reminiscences of a past long gone."

Walt Disney World is more than 180 times larger than Disneyland. The vistas stretch out, prolonging the drama. To anthropologist Alexander Moore, the Magic Kingdom is reminiscent of the royal hunting parks of Europe, the first grand playgrounds, where space was lavishly squandered on sport and pleasure: "The baroque sundial of avenues is a symbol of the universe as a solar system, whose center, the palace, was once the hub of sovereign power."

The City Hall and Railroad Station in the Walt Disney World Magic Kingdom are bolder and grander, presiding over the

Like that of Disneyland, the Magic Kingdom's plan is a radial one, with the various "lands" connecting to a central Hub in front of Cinderella Castle. Walt Disney always rued the fact that he didn't buy enough land for Disneyland, so in Orlando there's plenty of space for the Magic Kingdom to sprawl.

In general, the Imagineers were more extreme in exaggerating or departing from canons of historical architecture at Walt Disney World's Magic Kingdom than at Disneyland. The Fire House in the Town Square, with its exuberant ornament (opposite), is an excellent example. The

Crystal Palace (above), adjacent to Main Street and Adventureland, and facing the Hub, recalls the conservatories of Victorian England. Victorian architectural idioms are used throughout Disney's theme parks and resorts, both by Imagineers and architects commissioned by the company.

entrance more imposingly than they do at Disneyland. On Main Street (which, at an average width of sixty feet, is just slightly wider than its West Coast counterpart) the elaborate Victorian buildings with their fanciful, ornate detailing would not be out of place in a newly flourishing gold rush town. The castle is a tour de force, a full 170 feet taller than Disneyland's. It is Cinderella's castle, as opposed to Sleeping Beauty's, and it's easy to conclude that Cinderella got herself a much richer prince.

The cacophony of architectural styles reaches a high pitch in Orlando. Adventureland is an ode to a South Seas adventure, a Polynesian show restaurant turned inside out. Liberty Square is a smorgasbord of Colonial and frontier styles. Fantasyland trips lightly across countries and centuries to evoke a Europe found in fairy tales. All this prompted James A. Moore to call it "Banister Fletcher in 3-D," an apt reference to the author of *History of Architecture,* the book architects and students rely on to delineate virtually every style of building ever invented since the start of civilization.

For all that, there is also a certain subtlety and sophistication in Orlando's version of the Magic Kingdom; from the train that circles the theme park, for example, the changing lands (themed to America's Midwest, to the frontier, to fantasy, to the future, and to exotic far-off adventures) are acknowledged by a changing landscape, with vegetation that fits each theme. In Disneyland, by contrast, the ride is fairly hokey.

Even the first two Magic Kingdom hotels were themed to the "lands," though somewhat obliquely, much in the way that the

landscape is themed. Thus came the Contemporary and the Polynesian, the hotels for Tomorrowland and Adventureland. From the start, they looked like opposites – the towering and formidable Contemporary, with the monorail running through it, and the kitschy-exotic and rather relaxed Polynesian, with its flickering torchlight. In fact, they are almost identical in terms of structure; both were designed by the firm of Welton Becket & Associates and built using an innovative modular construction system developed for Disney by the U.S. Steel Corporation.

Myth is layered on myth at Walt Disney World, where the familiar – a shopping center, a water slide – is given a fictional twist and every structure is designed to evoke broad associations with the visitor's mental library of scenes from the world's cultures. Images abound, some of them mere glimpses of another time or place and others protracted illusions, as in the Disney-MGM Studios, a theme park that opened in 1989, where a 1930s Hollywood theme is carried throughout.

In the half century since Disneyland was built, Disney designers – both the in-house

Imagineers and outside architects – have become far more sophisticated about using architecture to arouse emotional responses. At Splash Mountain, for example, the log flume attraction in Walt Disney World's Magic Kingdom and Disneyland based on the 1946 feature film *Song of the South*, the experience is as much visceral as visual. Splash Mountain, designed chiefly by Tony Baxter, is the equivalent of an eight-story building never intended to look like a building at all, and the ride through this structure is loud, soft, musical, talky, hot, cold, wet, dry, tame, scary – all within the space of a few minutes. The experiences come fast, like in a good movie trailer. The whole thing is as hokey as can be. It's full of caricatures of creatures and nature. Real morning glories entwine a garden fence next to oversized and obviously fake kale and carrots. There are luridly bright colors, improbable tableaux, and funny little voices that chirp, croak, sing, gasp.

For this, riders wait in line for as long as an hour because, ultimately, for them Splash Mountain is not just another ride. And that provides a critical insight into the essence of Disney's architecture, to the way it speaks directly to the subconscious mind, the collection of images and sensations that constitutes part of memory. For whether it's Arata Isozaki's highly cerebral Team Disney Building in Orlando, discussed in chapter five, or Baxter's corny Splash Mountain, Disney's architecture works on emotions first and intellect later.

It affects us at first subliminally and then, much later, we begin to perceive its more obvious attributes. Generally speaking, most conventional architecture affects us the other

Three of the most popular rides in the Disney theme parks are called mountains: Space Mountain, Splash Mountain, and Big Thunder Mountain Railroad. The last two, in Frontierland, are literally constructions disguised as mountains while the first is a more conventional building. These attractions work in the landscape of the theme park in much the same way that real mountains shape our experience of a landscape – as goals for the traveler seeking adventure. The Frontierland mountains have their own architecture, which, in the case of Splash Mountain (below), consists of the rustic abodes of the creatures that inhabit it (left and opposite). This is domestic architecture inspired by American country folkways.

The Hollywood Tower Hotel, home of the Tower of Terror, seen here in both a rendering and as completed (left), at Disney-MGM Studios, was loosely based on a number of old Los Angeles hotels built in the 1920s and possesses its own aura of faded glamour.

way around: we take it first at face value, observing and enjoying it, and only afterward understand its subtle persuasive powers. At Disney, however, it is the experience of the architecture that takes hold of us – the fiction of it, not the fact. "Splash Mountain is the closest to literal storytelling that we have," says Tony Baxter. "It is a visceral story of large spaces and small. There's a theatrical magic in that, when it's done, it looks as though you just pulled down the landscape and revealed what's been there all along. Even when it's purposely treated as bad architecture . . . in fact it's good theater."

The Imagineers are always looking for new ways to use architecture as theater. Scary rides, for example, are a staple of amusement parks everywhere, but they almost always rely on simple tricks – abrupt falls, darkness – to achieve their effects. At the Disney theme parks, far more refined stimuli are added, including the associations evoked by architectural style itself. The original 1969 Haunted Mansion at Disneyland was installed in an antebellum plantation house in Frontierland that had been built years previously. For Walt Disney World's Magic Kingdom, John Hench came up with a more satisfying stone and brick Gothic Manse, straight out of Gothic

horror stories. The Twilight Zone Tower of Terror, a 1994 addition to the Disney-MGM Studios in Walt Disney World, uses architecture to evoke a plethora of associations from pop culture, such as 1930s pulp fiction and movies. The Tower – a "ride" that includes a thirteen-story free-fall drop in an elevator – is based on a number of old Los Angeles hotels (among them Arnold Weitzman's Château Marmont, 1928, and Schultze & Weaver's Biltmore Hotel, 1922–23). The hotel itself is simply called the Hollywood Tower Hotel, in keeping with its somewhat spoofy story line about a family checking in and then disappearing into the fifth dimension.

As in many Disney offerings, the metaphors are cavalierly mixed to create the effect of another place in another not quite definable time. For example, Spanish moss (found more often in the swampy South than in Hollywood) is draped from trees in the front garden to give the winding approach a spookier, cobwebby look.

Certainly, the Tower of Terror is a parody, spoofing the whole era of Hollywood glamour, but it is also wonderful entertainment, participatory theater. And, unlike Splash Mountain, it is indeed architecture – and pretty good architecture at that: stripped of

Walt Disney conceived of the Haunted Mansion as a retirement home for ghosts, and the original one in Disneyland is a New Orleans-style plantation house, with a columned portico and filigree railings. For Walt Disney World, Imagineering's John Hench designed a Gothic manse in brick and stone (opposite).

A detailed rendering of Epcot (top) was prepared by Disney's Imagineering division before construction commenced. The theme park, seen in an aerial view taken in 1982 from the same perspective as the rendering (above), is remarkably true to the original conception.

The focal point at Epcot, similar in function to the castles in the Magic Kingdoms, is an immense geodesic dome, actually more a "geosphere," called Spaceship Earth. The Living Seas, visible near the center of the rendering, was finally built in the mid-1980s.

its mottled hot pink "stucco" it would be a creditable offering as a 1990s revival building in any number of cities with a Spanish-Mediterranean tradition.

When Walt Disney envisioned his "land" in Orlando, his interest focused not so much on the Magic Kingdom, which he'd already done once, but on Epcot, which was an acronym for Experimental Prototype Community of Tomorrow. In a press conference in the fall of 1966, only weeks before his death, he described a visionary Epcot that was very different from what was built – an idealized utopian city, its core contained under a vast bubble of glass to guarantee climatic perfection. It was to be a radial city, influenced by the planning ideas of the French modern architect Le Corbusier, with commerce at the center, high-rise apartment living encircling that, then a green belt, and then low-density suburban-styled neighborhoods at the outer edge: "It will be a planned, controlled community; a showcase for American industry and research, schools, cultural and educational opportunities. In Epcot there will be no slum areas because we won't let them develop. There will be no landowners and therefore no voting control. People will rent houses instead of buying them, and at modest rentals. There will be no retirees, because everyone will be employed according to their ability. One of our requirements is that the people who live in Epcot must help keep it alive."

Despite Walt Disney's love for transportation, this was to be a pedestrian city, with cars and trucks relegated to underground roadways. Even residents in the outermost ring, the suburbs, if you will, would be required to leave their cars in garages and take the monorail or electric-powered people movers to travel to work. Under glass there was to be no worry about rain or wind or hot sun.

The Epcot that got built – it opened in 1982 – came in the interim period of the company, between Walt Disney and Michael Eisner. After the Magic Kingdom finally opened in 1971, Walt's more progressive plans were put on hold while the company regrouped. The result was a different Epcot, not experimental and not a community. It was, as Irwin Ross wrote in *Fortune,* "a permanent world's fair that combines popular history with titillating exposure to the marvels of advanced technology and snippets of culture from several foreign countries."

A few of the old ideas remained. Walt's Epcot had country-themed shopping; as built, Epcot has World Showcase, which is a hybrid – part World's Fair pavilions done up authentically to show typical architecture or even famous landmarks of a country, and part shopping promenade.

The utopian Epcot would have included a number of opportunities for corporations to strut their stuff (homes equipped with the newest – and always improving – appliances and electronics were, of course, envisioned). At the actual Epcot, Future World is given over to giant corporate-sponsored pavilions dedicated to "motion" (General Motors), "progress" (General Electric), "energy" (Exxon), and "imagination" (Kodak). Its most notable structure is a huge geodesic dome that long housed a rather conventional Disney-style ride that uses *Audio-Animatronics* figures to tell the story of communication.

Although the two parts of Epcot are

The buildings in Epcot's Future World tend to be most effective at night, when they can be lit in interesting ways. The facade of The Living Seas (overleaf) has a marquee with stylized waves.

In the course of planning the theme parks, the Imagineers create detailed models that help to establish sight lines and determine the exact placement of buildings in relation to one another. Here, the Canada Pavilion in the foreground, with its massive "Hotel du Canada" based on the Chateau Laurier in Ottawa, is set off, in an almost surreal way, by the giant ball that is Spaceship Earth.

physically linked, they are really quite different in terms of their architectural intent. The Future World pavilions are stylized warehouses, basically huge sheds, without much attention to felicity or detail. They share a heritage with the handful of Disney office buildings erected around the same time (among them, the heavy-handed gray concrete Roy O. Disney Building on the studio lot in Burbank and the banal, glass-box Sun Bank Building, which Disney built but then partly leased out, in Orlando).

At the World Showcase, the buildings – France, Italy, Morocco, Mexico, Germany, England, Canada, China, Japan, Norway, and the American Adventure – all sit next to each other like millionaires' mansions arranged around a lake. In size and scale, they may have little relation to buildings in their home-

lands, but they are symbols designed to evoke a sense of place. Perhaps less cinematic than anything else in any Disney Kingdom except Future World, the World Showcase is intended for either the very long view or an extreme close-up.

Some buildings are only effective as icons seen from a distance. For example, there's a diminutive Eiffel Tower on top of France that barely shows up at all except at night when it's lighted, and then, viewed from across the lagoon, it seems a perfect duplicate of the one in Paris. On the other hand, an almost obsessional level of authentic ornamentation can be found here and there throughout the World Showcase. To decorate Morocco, for example, Disney designers went to Morocco to seek out craftsmen and then brought nineteen of them back to Florida.

For those who hoped to find the future at Epcot, or even to see a futuristic world's fair there, it disappointed. "It's not an experimental community or a prototype community or an experimental prototype of a community. It's not a community at all. It may be a prototype adult amusement park for the world of tomorrow, but if it is, I'll wait for the next spaceship, which might be less crowded," wrote the scholar Alfred Heller in *World's Fair Quarterly.*

Writing in *Rolling Stone,* Miami author John Rothchild – now a *Time* magazine writer – said, "Some people describe EPCOT as a permanent world's fair, but it differs in one basic respect. Countries can display their own scientific advancements at world's fairs, but the EPCOT countries are only good for decoration and retail sales, while the future has been handed over to Exxon, General Motors,

Kraft and the Bell System. Perhaps EPCOT is more realistic than a world's fair."

Even those who dismiss Epcot out-of-hand find a certain fascination with it. Heller notes that the "crumpled-silver ball" that is the Spaceship Earth "dominates the dismal Florida swamp no less effectively than the Gothic spires of Chartres Cathedral command reverence and respect across a vast plain." The distinguished historian Elting E. Morison, who worried extensively and quite eloquently about Epcot's iteration of history in an article for *American Heritage* magazine, said of its design: "All elements are brought together in a limited space by a masterly manipulation of scale and proportion that produces a sense of magnificent sizes and distances. It is quite an emplacement."

"It's easy to poke fun at WDW, because WDW in fact welcomes it. It is true, also, that WDW is not a real city – it has no conventional housing yet, no schools yet, no shopping centers yet, no social, economic or political problems, yet," argued architect and editor Peter Blake in his 1972 *Architectural Forum* essay on Walt Disney World. Blake was wowed by Walt Disney World's technology, but he also praised it for being so "unabashedly corny," and pointed out that there was much to be learned from its "urban psychology."

More than two decades later, we admire the latter two qualities much more than the technology; we all can handle technology these days – witness two-year-olds on the computer – but hardly anyone or any city seems to have mastered the psychology part, much less the fun.

China offers temple architecture, in this case a tower inspired by the Temple of Heaven in Peking.

The buildings in Epcot's World Showcase look best from a distance, at dawn or twilight, or in misty weather, when their pictorial qualities emerge, as in the view of the Germany Pavilion at sunset (below). These battlements were modeled after the medieval Eltz Castle on the Moselle River in Germany. The Mexico Pavilion (right) in Epcot's World Showcase is a Mayan pyramid. It looks disconcertingly new and not at all like the romantic ruins that might be found in the Magic Kingdom Adventureland.

The almost obsessive architectural details in the decorative styles of different cultures to be found in the pavilions of World Showcase are interesting in their own right. If there is something incongruous about each pavilion close up, it is perhaps a problem of scale and organization: no matter how large the World Showcase pavilions are, they come nowhere near the size of the real ensembles of buildings on which they are based. Here, clockwise from top left, are aspects of Norway, Japan, Morocco, and Italy.

chapter four | *Enter Eisner*

Michael Eisner couldn't sleep. It was September 23, 1984, only his second day at Disney, and he'd just been shown the drawings for two outsized but utterly ordinary hotels for Walt Disney World that were to be owned and built by the Tishman Company. "I said to myself, this is really horrendous."

Later, long after his – and Disney's – career as a major patron of architecture was well launched, he would articulate the intensity of this feeling more fully. "Buildings, architecture, are something that stay with you in a way nothing else does. It's subliminal. You don't even know what you know about architecture. Yet you get angry or you feel good and you don't understand why you feel good."

Seven days – and seven sleepless nights – after seeing the plans for the two new hotels, Eisner was possessed by a new determination. "We're not doing it," he said to himself, aloud. That week set a new course for Disney.

It was instinct. Eisner had grown up on New York's Upper East Side, without a tutored interest in architecture but with a sense of awe as the city he knew as a child grew in scale and modernity. He remembers a particular fascination with Mies van der Rohe's Seagram Building (1958) – with its proportions and its placement on the street – and with Eero Saarinen's CBS Building (1965). And there were other buildings that amazed or awed him as well, Philip Johnson's Asia House (1960) among them.

In his career-shaping years at ABC and Paramount, he'd never had to deal with architects or architecture; it was out of his realm of experience. Yet, the impulse – to stretch Disney's architectural image, to be daring and even a bit controversial – was there from the start. During that first week at Disney, he was having dinner with a handful of Disney's development executives and suggested building a hotel in the Burbank studio lot in the shape of Mickey Mouse, a hotel that would straddle Riverside Drive and be a tourist attraction in its own right. "It made no economic sense; it made no creative sense, but it was a lark," Eisner later recalled. "I did know that there was more than form and function involved. I knew that architecture could create a business market, that kids in Kansas City were going to tell their parents they wanted to go stay in the hotel shaped like Mickey Mouse." Others who were at that dinner – an informal gathering in the studio commissary – remember it as pivotal, the moment they first knew that Eisner would be different.

The Mickey Mouse project, nonetheless, died stillborn.

But Eisner had launched the kind of architectural exploration he and Disney were to become famous for, buildings that pushed the limits of convention. Eisner started by getting to know the work of the country's top designers and figuring out which ones would be right to vie for particular commissions. It

Workers spray-paint one of the monumental swans atop the Swan Hotel.

was a gamble: would the country's foremost architects, generally known to be captivated by their own seriousness, consent to design in a far giddier realm?

Eisner found his architecture gurus in several places. Within the company there was Wing Chao, now senior vice president of Disney Design and Development, who oversees master planning and design for all Disney building projects world wide. He was born in China and educated in architecture and urban planning at Berkeley and Harvard. The relatively reserved Chao had been at Disney since 1972, working first on the planning of Epcot and later on several of the company's more conservative projects at Lake Buena Vista. He had done his Harvard thesis on what he called a "free-time city" and had already evolved many of the theoretical ideas that were to take hold as Eisner propelled the company on its architectural adventure.

Chao remembers well the dinner at which Eisner proposed the Mickey Mouse Hotel: "All of us were looking at each other, and we don't know if he's kidding or serious, so there's silence. But that gave me the signal right away that he wanted to fire the longest shot possible. Right away I knew he wanted to push us to the edge."

Eisner also turned to an old family friend, the late Victor Ganz, to ask him for advice. Ganz, a noted art collector, had been on the board of the Whitney Museum of American Art in New York. It was Ganz who had helped hone Eisner's aesthetic sense during museum visits in New York and summer trips to Europe; Eisner recalls wandering through Rome with him discussing the buildings.

Thus, it was to Ganz that Eisner came to discuss the question of the proposed hotels. Ganz gave Eisner two names, Philip Johnson and Michael Graves. Johnson, long America's leading modernist, had rekindled his career rather flamboyantly with such commissions as the Chippendale-topped AT&T Building (1979–84) in New York, the Flemish Renaissance–inspired Republic Bank (1981–84) in Houston, and the mirror-glass-Gothic PPG Building (1979–84) in Pittsburgh. Already in his late seventies, he was among the few American architects (I. M. Pei being another) whose name was a household word; certainly he was the most celebrated architect of the early 1980s. He was also eccentric, finicky, and nearing retirement.

Graves, just over fifty, was a Princeton University professor (and, in some ways, a protégé of Johnson's) who had been among the first to break from a group of young architectural abstractionists to develop a distinctive and often controversial style of his own, with classically derived buildings that were lush and deep-hued. His first two prominent works were the Public Services Building (1982) in Portland, Oregon, and a corporate headquarters in Louisville, Kentucky, for the Humana Corporation (1982–85). The Portland building was a mixed success, but the Humana headquarters had immediately garnered widespread admiration. Graves had just been hired to design an addition to the Whitney Museum of American Art in New York, which – after great public debate – was never executed.

Eisner will say now that he was always inclined toward Graves, the up-and-comer. Graves likes to tell a different story, one laced with serendipity: it was intermission time at the New York City Ballet, and Graves and Johnson were standing in the lobby, as was Eisner. Graves's date that night was Kitty Hawks, daughter of the director Howard Hawks and a longtime friend of Eisner's. The two groups converged.

"I can't believe my good fortune," said Eisner.

Johnson did not know Eisner and additionally was having trouble hearing over the din of the intermission, so he excused himself to go get a Perrier, leaving Eisner alone with Graves and Hawks. Graves recalls saying, "Well, I guess you're stuck with me. I can hear."

Some time passed before Graves heard from Eisner. And even then, it was with a complex proposition, one that involved three architects – Graves; Robert Venturi; and Alan Lapidus, who had been the designer of the original hotels. Eisner, wanting to make the competition lively and even intellectually stimulating, had sought out Venturi, who was, in the early 1980s, widely known for his enormously influential writings on architectural theory and a small number of buildings that he had designed with his Philadelphia firm. "He called me," Graves recalled, "and asked if I could work with Bob Venturi. I asked him if that wasn't a little bit like putting Steven Spielberg and George Lucas together, and he replied, 'Remember, I did that.'" Eisner had been at Paramount in 1981 when he teamed Spielberg and Lucas to do *Raiders of the Lost Ark.*

"I knew a lot about literature, a lot about film, a lot about art, and virtually nothing about architecture," says Eisner. That meant he went about hiring architects his own way, with a certain amount of creative tension

and enormous expectations built into the process, more like making a movie, except with higher stakes. Said Eisner, "If you make a movie, even if it's great, it's somewhat transitory. . . . In architecture, the stakes are much higher, the risks greater, but it's much more fun."

Eisner's contemplated collaboration was doomed one day when Venturi and Graves met over breakfast in New York. "After we'd ordered our pancakes," recalls Graves, "Bob said, 'The bomb I'm going to drop on this meeting is that I'm not willing to collaborate. I want a competition.' I said, 'You got it.'"

That set the stage for this competition and many that were to follow.

To be sure, tension abounded. John Tishman, who had thought he was moving right along on his previously planned hotels, was infuriated over Eisner's decision. Before the competition was devised, Tishman had sued Disney under racketeering statutes, asking $375 million and $1 billion in punitive damages. "All I wanted was not to do those buildings," Eisner says, "and instead I got sued for racketeering."

Peter Rummell recalls it this way: "It was Michael at his best and Michael at his worst. He didn't know anything about drawings or design or engineering or the hotel business. He was a movie guy. But he knew we had these hotels, two thousand rooms' worth, going up in a place where we didn't want a hotel."

Eventually, the suit was dropped. Tishman agreed to do the buildings Eisner wanted. A new location near Epcot (as opposed to the original site near the other chain hotels at Lake Buena Vista) was carefully selected. Arthur Levitt, Jr., who worked as Eisner's assistant during those early years and later was to become president of Hard Rock Cafe International in Orlando, was involved in that process. A marine biologist by education who'd recently returned from collecting rare goldfish specimens in Bali, Levitt had been working as a salesman in the furniture design firm of Knoll International when he and Eisner met. He remembers taking both Michael and Jane Eisner out in a four-wheel-drive vehicle into the muck that typifies central Florida's undeveloped lowlands. They drove until they were literally stopped by two huge, slow-moving armadillos at what was to become the hotel site. ("We named one Graves and the other Venturi," Levitt recalls.)

The competition proceeded. Graves knew he was pitted against Venturi's literate simplicity and Lapidus's second-generation hotel savvy. Alan Lapidus's father, Morris, was the Miami Beach architect who created the Fontainebleu and the Eden Roc, and the younger Lapidus had just completed a number of commercially successful Atlantic City hotels.

One rule of the competition was that no building could be higher than eight stories, so that it couldn't be seen from other points in Epcot or at the planned Disney-MGM Studios. Graves had been working with several different ideas, which Chao previewed during a visit to Princeton. Graves was vacillating. He really wanted to use the strong pyramid that ultimately was to become the Dolphin. Chao was impartial and just told him, "Go with your gut feelings, Michael." So Graves did.

"I knew I couldn't have a capital-B building," Graves recalled. "I had to do something that was an illusion there in the muck, in the swamp that was there in central Florida. So I designed a mock mountain, but it went on from there." The second building became a vault, its curved roof gently echoing the curve of the adjacent lagoon. By the time of the presentation in Burbank in July of 1986, the forms of the Dolphin and Swan were pretty well set, but the buildings were without the fish and fowl symbols – water-borne mythic creatures – for which they would be named.

On the day of the competition, Graves's four-by-six-foot scale model – the key visual element in any architectural presentation – went astray in severe thunderstorms. Eventually it was located in Memphis, but Disney was offered only compensation for the mistake, not immediate delivery to California. Levitt, in dire panic, hired a small plane to retrieve the missing model. It arrived ten hours later and covered with frost from the altitude. Graves was to make his presentation just before midnight.

Venturi had come in with a plan that was at once graceful and fanciful. Lapidus presented a "Crystal Palace." But it was Graves's rather formidable scheme that intrigued Eisner the most: it was big and visually intrusive and it broke a major Disney rule, which was never to distract a guest's attention unintentionally: the Dolphin would be visible from many points in Epcot. Still, Eisner liked the strong image of the pyramid with all its mythological, and even archaeological, associations, but he thought the execution of the design was a bit stodgy.

"Lighten up," he told Graves. Graves began to cast about for symbolism that would impart the Disney idea without involving actual Disney characters: he did not want a

Michael Graves's original conception of what was to become the Dolphin Hotel called for an enormous fountain on top of the pyramid (top left). As the design developed and the fountain proved too costly, he dropped it and added the oversized dolphins (above and top right).

predictable cartoon character or a motif from a movie. "I wanted to do something that . . . a child could identify with it but wasn't sappy," he says.

Thus he chose fairy-tale creatures found in gardens and fountains throughout history: dolphins and swans. For indirect inspiration, Graves turned to the seventeenth-century architect Gian Lorenzo Bernini, the great genius of baroque Rome.

Certainly, the mammoth scale of the $225 million, 1,514-room Dolphin and the $120 million, 758-room Swan would have suited the architect of St. Peter's. The Dolphin is twenty-seven-stories tall at the peak of the pyramid, and the Swan rises twelve stories. Both rise startlingly above the treeline, to a height previously broken by only the Disney-MGM Studio's water tower.

The two hotels connect across the lagoon by a walkway topped by gaily striped awnings. Together, they create a memorable composition. Every axis is a studied one, every view is framed. And yet they unfold piece by piece. The hotels are so big that they can only be perceived in fragments rather than as a whole.

The curiously engaging, surprisingly graceful dolphins and swans on top of their respective hotels are sixty-three and forty-seven feet tall, roughly the equivalents of six-story and five-story buildings. Water cascades nine stories down the side of the Dolphin, passing through five shell basins to a fountain where four dolphins hold up a fifty-four-foot clamshell.

Graves originally designed those fountain dolphins to be in three dimensions, just like the ones up top, but they didn't pass muster with either Eisner or Tishman. He flattened them into sophisticated caricatures, which were less naturalistic. With wry wit, he called them the "filets."

Working with Alan Lapidus, who became the production architect, and the interior design firm of Wilson Associates, Graves kept his hand in to an intimate level of detail: he designed the plates in the restaurants, as well as carpets, wallpapers, curtains, and light fixtures. Two dozen set painters were put to work finishing the Dolphin and the Swan, inside and out, and, for the occasion, Graves modified his preferred Tuscan palette of deep teal-green and dark terra-cotta in favor of a more festive and Floridian turquoise and coral. The buildings' facades are flat and painted, the way stucco buildings in Florida often are. On the Dolphin, a pattern of banana leaves grows out of a trellis; at the Swan, waves rhythmically wash across the building.

The exercise in abstraction and the flattening of forms grew to fascinate Graves. He cut out paper dolphins, swans, toucans, and other creatures to use on the backs of chairs, and applied them to "the run-of-the-mill light off the shelf, transformed with a lot more humor and for a lot less money. That two-dimensionality lets you think more broadly. It was a discovery along the way."

Painted ceilings echo carpet patterns. Painted parrots and macaws perch on chandeliers, and cartoony banana leaves grow from huge planters. The lobby of the Swan is a takeoff on a Victorian conservatory; the lobby of the Dolphin is a giant, celebratory tent. Elsewhere in the Dolphin the tent motif recurs, but in paint rather than fabric.

Outside the Swan's ballroom, walls are painted floor to ceiling with a beach scene;

the walls inside the windowless ballroom are the beach viewed through shutters. Similar beach scenes – complete with towels, books, pails, and shovels – also adorn the Dolphin's hallways. In both hotels, doors are painted with stripes, as if they were the entries to cabanas.

In the Swan, the Garden Grove restaurant, contained within a rotunda, has an orange grove motif, and palms grow in the center. Its equivalent at the Dolphin is the Coral Café, which has an underwater theme. Oversized fish dangle from the ceiling, and each one is a pun – there's a "nurse" shark and a "school" of fish and a "cat" fish. In the Dolphin's Copa-banana Lounge, furniture and drink stands represent coconut trees, bananas, pineapples, and pears, as well as an array of melons – watermelon, cantaloupe, honeydew. "To use humor in architecture is a very serious affair," says Graves.

Some people got the jokes. Others didn't.

Both the Swan and the Dolphin, which opened in 1989 and 1990, respectively, received plenty of critical attention, both positive and negative, which plunked them firmly into the polemical realm of modern art by provoking lots of discourse. In the annals of Disney, the Dolphin and Swan were much more fantastic – and much less literal – than anything that had come before. And Graves, always one to engender debate, took as much of the flak and praise as Disney.

Progressive Architecture magazine's Mark Alden Branch termed the Swan a "Busby Berkeley musical, lavish and entertaining but in a genre all its own." Countered Arlene Hirst in *Metropolitan Home* magazine: "Its facade teeters on the edge of self-parody with

The Dolphin and Swan under construction (above). The hotels (overleaf) were the first fruits of a new era of Disney architecture. Painted in Floridian turquoise and coral, they brought a new sophistication (and controversy) to Walt Disney World.

Graves's hotels are identified with a fish and a water bird, and they are watery indeed, without and within. A cheerful but somewhat formal causeway (opposite) links the two buildings. Fountains play throughout both (above), and large interior spaces of the Dolphin Hotel are dressed up with tenting to resemble cabanas (left).

Graves paid attention to the accoutrements of his hotels, creating humorous interior environments such as the Copabanana Lounge.

its five-story painted waves and 45 [actually 47] foot stucco swans. As whimsical ornaments, birds these big just don't fly."

"Thrilling examples of Graves' ability to take the symbols of our culture and turn them into something totally his own," said Kitty Morgan of the *Orange County* (California) *Register*. "It's as if they took an architect, gave him a hallucinogen and asked him to design the kind of hotel he would have liked to stay in when he was 12 years old."

"They are extravagant, flamboyant works of decoration, willfully eccentric and dazzlingly entertaining," said Paul Goldberger, then the architecture critic of the *New York Times*.

"Graves disease strikes the hotel industry," opined the editor of *Building Design and Engineering* magazine.

Eisner knew he'd taken a calculated gamble. At the opening of the Swan he said that though many might dismiss these buildings as being frivolous, he was certain they'd stand up, in the long run, as major works of architecture.

"You don't go in to make it controversial," Eisner said, "but I don't think you can do anything really important without also making it challenging." By then, he had a portfolio – and a legacy – in the making. Robert A. M. Stern's Casting Center had been completed and Arata Isozaki's Team Disney office building was under way. And Graves himself was hard at work on his Team Disney Building in Burbank.

Gwathmey Siegel & Associates' Bonnet Creek Golf Club (1992) at Walt Disney World was a collaboration between Disney and a team of designers that was more modernist in sensibility than any others that the company has commissioned. From the lake, the glass wall of their clubhouse (above) becomes a transparent strip at night. From the road, the building is a cluster of pastel-colored geometric forms. The sculpture out front (top) establishes the theme of the building on two levels: it can be read as an array of monumental golf tees or as an abstract design in keeping with the architure's aesthetic.

chapter five | *Off to Work We Go*

The jumble of forms, patterns, and colors where the two placid, flanking wings of Arata Isozaki's Team Disney Building in Orlando come together is a tour de force of architectural design.

The giant gold letters that spell out CASTING loom large along the highway that connects Orlando and Tampa. One would have to look carefully to see the scuppers set at the cornice line: they are in the shape of Mickey Mouse ears, and on the face of this particular building, they are virtually the only overt reference to Disney.

Yet in many ways the Casting Center, which opened in 1989, says more about Disney architecture than any other building. It is other-worldly and fanciful, as if it were dropped from the pages of a picture book; a stop-frame in an animated film. It seems strangely unreal, this palazzo on the expressway.

Disney had never had much presence along I-4, the east-west highway that bisects Florida. The cluster of hotels and office buildings at Lake Buena Vista were developer offerings, big and plain – and in no way memorable. Disney needed that visibility, not so much for the tourists arriving at Walt Disney World but for the thousands who apply for jobs there each year. By the mid-1980s, "casting" – as Disney likes to call its hiring, even for bus drivers and dishwashers – was contained in a series of tucked-away trailers, and the employment base was rising from 20,000 to 30,000, which meant that the company had to be prepared to do as many as 100,000 employment inter-views every year. "It was a necessity, really," Peter Rummell says. "We needed something out front."

An earlier plan had been to clone the rather nondescript glass-box Sun Bank Build-ing, which Disney owns, and be done with it. But Eisner saw that as an opportunity lost. By then, two years into his job at Disney, he had developed a full-fledged passion for architecture and a personal philosophy to go along with it. Of the Casting Center, he had few preconceptions except that "we didn't want to be too serious."

Enter Robert A. M. Stern. Early in his career, in 1972, the then thirty-three-year-old Stern had designed an apartment for Lester and Maggie Eisner, Michael's parents. Michael was grown and gone by then, already a young married man; he and Stern had only fleeting encounters at the time. Then Stern went on to build a prodigious career, teaching at Columbia University, writing books, and designing buildings, becoming known for his evocative shingle-style beach houses. The slight, silver-tongued, and always-dapper Stern also hosted a six-part public-television series on Ameri-can architecture called "Pride of Place," which was as much an expression of his personal and philosophical take on American architec-ture as it was a documentary history.

Stern's first contact with Disney in 1987 was relatively routine – a phone call followed by an office visit from Wing Chao and his colleague Todd Mansfield, now executive vice president of the Disney Development Com-pany. They wanted him to try his hand at this employment office on I-4, a building with a "small-budget back-office function with a back-office budget and a numero uno front-office location," says Stern. And they wanted it to be lively, diverting, charming, conspicuous, subtle, and memorable. In Orlando, this was to be Disney's billboard. "We really located it the way we would a McDonald's," says Rummell – which is to say out front.

"This was and will be the only building identifying Disney in the public realm," says Stern. "That's quite a burden for such a little building to bear."

Indeed. The building needed to express the idea of Disney without being overly literal and it needed to do so for people traveling at speeds of fifty-five miles per hour on a busy freeway. "In other words," says Rummell, "we needed to define Disney through a rearview mirror."

Stern set to work. Wing Chao gave him the slimmest and firmest of advice: "The building has to be fun. It should be a landmark that makes motorists turn their heads." Rummell puts it this way: "We wanted to give them a sense of Disney and a little pixie dust."

Two days before Stern was to present his concept to the Disney corporate hierarchy, Eisner ran into Chao.

"How is [Stern's] plan?" asked Eisner.

"Interesting," replied Chao rather enigmatically.

"What does that mean?" Eisner persisted. "Does that mean great, good, or terrible?"

Chao replied enthusiastically.

"Great."

Eisner had not monitored the early progress of the design. His first view of it came during a week late in 1987 in Orlando. That was a critical visit. It was the week that the

final build-or-don't-build decision was being made on the Dolphin; the Disney-MGM Studios were under construction, and top Disney executives were walking every street, blueprints and photographic simulations in hand. The almost-finished Grand Floridian Hotel was subjected to a different kind of scrutiny. Eisner, the late Frank Wells (then president of Disney), Rummell, Chao, and others checked out the model rooms, examining wallpaper, sitting in chairs, opening balcony doors.

A film crew for CBS's "60 Minutes" was on hand that week, too, so that when Stern made his presentation on the Casting Center, the cameras caught it and the meeting is preserved in outtakes.

That encounter shows Stern at his intellectual games-playing best and Eisner rising right to the challenge. It is an intriguing bit of video because it records the instant chemistry between the two, Stern leading Eisner down a somewhat circuitous path to his design (which was contained in a precise and comparatively small-scale model kept literally under wraps), Eisner taking the verbal bait.

It helped, of course, that everyone loved the building and understood it immediately. Wells admired the way it explained the company to prospective employees, as "a place where you show off your wares." Stern explained at that first session that even for those who got hired by Disney, the Casting Center "may be the only time you experience the total identity of the corporation. It's very important symbolically."

In spite of its intended identification with the company, the building has little that overtly says "Disney." Stern knew that the imagery couldn't be too subtle, but that if it was too specific, it wouldn't tell the whole story either. "This was about the totality of Disney. You are really trying to say this is this amazing place. I cooked up the iconography, and nobody said put Mickey Mouse on the building. Nobody said try to represent different aspects of Disney on the building."

Furthermore, Stern believed that his Casting Center needed to express its locale, to say something about Florida. As a good scholar of the historicist styles that prevailed in Florida in the early twentieth century, he knew that the style called "Mediterranean Revival" drew extensively on Venetian imagery (in both places, the land is flat and the conjunction of land and water is intimate and abrupt).

He designed his building with this tradition in mind: it is at once serious and capricious, a light-hearted twentieth-century rendition of the sixteenth-century Bridge of Sighs in Venice. He originally intended that it rise out of a small lake as if it were truly a transplanted Venetian building; instead, it got grass and paved parking, somewhat less of an illusion for the allusion. The facade of the Casting Center has a harlequin pattern, also a Venetian reference and one that Stern likes to call the "argyle socks."

From the outside, the references to Disney are in the details. There are those pale blue Mickey Mouse scuppers along the parapet. The entrance is covered by a sleek airplane-wing canopy drawn from futuristic designs for Tomorrowland, with amusing echoes of a medieval drawbridge that are vaguely reminiscent of Disney's castles. The bronze doorknobs come straight from the talking doors in *Alice in Wonderland.*

Disney's architecture has always played with scale in much the same way that Lewis Carroll did when he made Alice grow big or small – and very much the way the animators did in Disney's 1951 version of Carroll's classic. The Casting Center is no exception. The doors – with their Alice-allusion doorknobs – open into a startlingly small rotunda surmounted by a glazed obelisk-shaped cupola. Everyone who goes through those doors feels somewhat bigger, at least for a moment, and yet is still a bit awed by the architecture. The columns that encircle this space are topped with gilded characters – Goofy, Chip, Dale, Donald Duck, Pluto, Minnie Mouse, Dumbo, Pinocchio, Daisy Duck, Roger Rabbit, Thumper, and, of course, Mickey Mouse.

A long ramp, which crosses from one end of the building to the other, leads to the reception desk. Stern says he took the idea of this central corridor – used by visitors, applicants, and employees alike – from Frank Lloyd Wright's Marin County Courthouse in California: "the idea of splitting the building open to have a void in the middle and let the public walk through." The walls alongside this ramp are painted with frescoes of cartoon characters, highway scenes on the side that faces I-4 and images of Walt Disney World on the other. Everything has a humorous patina of age and wear (the brickwork exposed by peeling paint under the bridge that spans the corridor is trompe l'oeil). Up above, on the ceiling, fly Peter Pan, Wendy, John, Michael, and Tinker Bell.

At the top of the ramp is a reception desk, and behind it, the waiting room where prospective employees sit in free-form chairs. Here, centered under another cupola, there is a model of the Cinderella Castle from Disney's archives, offering another play on scale. In the Magic Kingdom, the castle looms large;

here, it is nonetheless a visual focal point, even in miniature. (Amusingly, the ramp invokes Main Street in the Magic Kingdom, with its forced perspective of the castle.)

Disney project director Tim Johnson remembers that Stern fought Disney to keep the reception desk out of the entrance rotunda and won. Johnson looks back on that as a pivotal moment and says that he regards the sequence of rotunda, ramp, rotunda as an epigram for all of Disney's architecture. "Bob was adamant that you enter on the ground floor, and the first time you can ask for a job is at the other end of a hall on the second floor. He said, 'Let them wander. Let them get a taste for Disney before they get there.'" It was a clever stroke, setting the scene as if it were the establishing shot in a movie.

In Stern's work, Disney found an ideal blend of seriousness and whimsy, of history and novelty. Eisner has been known to term him a "superImagineer," and the two have developed a strong friendship. Stern designed

Eisner's vacation house in Aspen; he now sits on the Disney board. He hosted master-planning sessions for Disneyland Paris and coordinated the urban design work for the new Disney town of Celebration. He has designed five hotel complexes (the Yacht and Beach Clubs and the Boardwalk in Walt Disney World and the Newport Bay and Cheyenne in Disneyland Paris), as well as the Feature Animation Building in Burbank.

By the time Stern had been hired to do the Casting Center, Michael Graves had begun work on the Team Disney Building – essentially the company's headquarters, housing many of the senior executives' offices – in Burbank, which opened in 1990. Eisner hired him to do this building in the midst of the Dolphin and the Swan negotiations, giving him a prominent site on the northwest corner of the Studio lot. It was a corporate commission, but more than that it was a personal decision of Eisner's. Thus, Eisner had given

Graves fairly simple marching orders:

"I have only one requirement. I know I'm going to drive to work and park my car every day. I want you to make me smile, because I know I'm going to have an extraordinarily difficult day."

From Eisner, this was actually a pretty straightforward request. Once, he told the architects Charles Gwathmey and Robert Siegel – who were known for buildings of powerful and elegant simplicity – that for the Bonnet Creek Golf Club in Walt Disney World he wanted "the smell of sweat socks more than the look of art. Those were my instructions to the architect: 'We want the look of smelly sweat socks.'"

For the Burbank Disney headquarters, Graves initially designed a lush but somewhat solemn building, without any special ornament on it: no Disney characters, no mythological allusions. "I tried originally to keep that kind of literal decoration off the building. Instead I made a pool, a terrific pool,

with two-dimensional figures in it and water games, fountains that would spray in the eyes of Pluto or Donald Duck."

Eisner rejected that idea, saying he thought it would be too much of an attraction, drawing passersby onto the Disney lot in too great numbers. At the same time, he thought Graves's building facade looked too much like a bank. "I asked Michael for characters," says Eisner. "He first did typical characters. That really looked stupid. But the dwarfs, that was different, and of course, there were enough of them to hold up the roof."

It is the front of this building – made of red Indian sandstone and stucco – that elicits the most attention. It is a classical facade, with, in place of the traditional caryatids, statues of Sleepy, Happy, Grumpy, Doc, Sneezy, and Bashful, in that order, supporting the entablature, and Dopey on the pediment above them, holding up the roof. The statues were modeled at Imagineering and fabricated by an outside contractor.

Robert A. M. Stern designed the Walt Disney World Casting Center as if it were a cartoon version of a sixteenth-century Venetian building. It sits right next to Orlando's I-4 expressway, positioned, says Peter Rummell, the way a fast-food restaurant would be.

A cross-section drawing (below) shows how the long ramp bisects the Casting Center. Right, doorknobs taken from *Alice in Wonderland*.

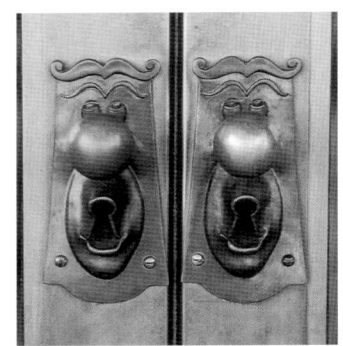

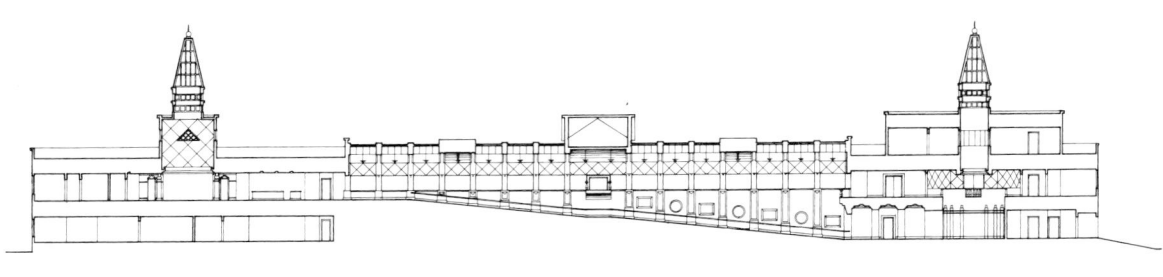

LONGITUDINAL SECTION

The visitor enters the Casting Center under a stainless-steel airplane-wing canopy taken from drawings done for Tomorrowland (above). The main door opens into a small rotunda where there are gilded Disney cartoon characters atop columns (right).

A long ramp leading to the waiting room features painted walls and ceiling with scenes and characters from Disney's animated features (below). Placed centrally in the waiting room of the Casting Center is a scale model of the Magic Kingdom's Cinderella Castle, the grail of the job seeker's journey through the building (right).

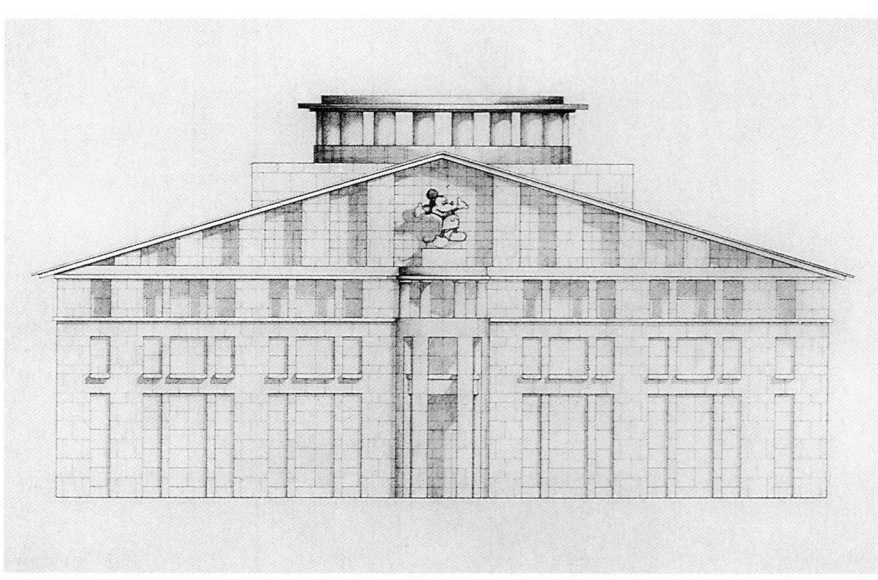

Michael Eisner found the facade of the Team Disney Building too banklike and told the architect to "lighten up." As this early drawing shows, Michael Graves considered adding a statue of Mickey Mouse to the pediment before settling on the Seven Dwarfs.

On a perpendicular axis to the front of the building is an elegant reflecting pool – minus the playful fountains that Graves had originally intended to put in it – surrounded by a pergola that resembles a Roman peristyle.

Inside, immediately adjoining the entry pavilion, is a rotunda, which functions as a pivot, turning the axis of the building to conform to the site. The bulk of the building unfolds from there as a sequence of three courtyards that diminish in size. The first and largest one is open to the sky but has pillared arcades to protect people from the elements; it connects the rotunda and the main section of the building, a massive square block with a quadripartite vault covering each of the four corner bays.

The offices of the top Disney executives are on the upper floors. Eisner had asked Graves to come to him with portfolios of interior designers; he rejected each one out of hand and instead let Graves do the interiors. At the top of the rotunda is the corporate dining room. The circular room is light and airy, with walls painted in pastel motifs typical of Graves's work, at once classical and felicitous, even lighthearted. Here, the Mouse silhouette is unobtrusively designed into every pattern.

Eisner was originally interested in using only American architects, Graves and Stern among them. But by the mid-1980s, architecture was becoming increasingly international, and – as Eisner later said – even the Americans were pointing him to their most interesting counterparts in Europe and Asia.

For the Team Disney Building in Orlando, the Japanese architect Arata Isozaki was

There are six dwarfs on the entablature of Graves's Team Disney Building in Burbank (above): left to right, Sleepy, Happy, Grumpy, Doc, Sneezy, and Bashful; Dopey is on the pediment, holding up the roof. All overlook a long reflecting pool. Right, the dwarfs are singing their way to work in a famous scene from *Snow White and the Seven Dwarfs*.

The various sections of Graves's building are connected by arcaded walkways. The columns have unadorned capitals in a Neo-Classical manner.

The top-floor corporate dining room is decorated with light-hearted painted murals incorporating many Mickey motifs (right). The airy boardroom (below) is the antithesis of a traditional New York corporate boardroom.

The entrance rotunda of the Team Disney Building in Burbank (opposite) features a life-size photo of Walt Disney.

Michael Eisner and Arata Isozaki at the construction site of the Team Disney Building in Orlando, 1990 (right). An early plan for the interior of the central hall (below) envisioned the placement of twelve statues of Disney characters at regular intervals along the walls. This was later abandoned.

selected. Isozaki's first full-fledged American commission – the Museum of Contemporary Art – opened in Los Angeles in 1986 to widespread critical admiration; he was fifty-five years old. A one-time student of Japan's modern master, Kenzo Tange, Isozaki had not by then achieved the stature he now enjoys as Japan's architectural ambassador to the world; he was relatively unknown outside of his native country and, perhaps, Los Angeles. "We wanted him," says Eisner, "because he was just so . . . just so interesting." An early hint of just how interesting Isozaki and his work were to Eisner was that the same stone that was used by Arata Isozaki on the Museum of Contemporary Art in downtown Los Angeles was selected to clad the lower floors of Graves's Team Disney Building in Burbank.

Chao, who had been a student of Tange's at Harvard, recalls, "I got Arata's number in Tokyo and called him cold. I described the project to him and asked him if he was interested in doing it for us." Chao invited Isozaki and his wife, the sculptress Aiko Miyawaki, to Walt Disney World for five days.

Then Isozaki went to work. Some time later he came back with three schemes. There were finished drawings and a model of a mid-rise complex made up of a group of buildings arranged in a fan shape, as well as two very rough cardboard study models: one was a high-rise tower, the other a long low horizontal structure. Isozaki was surprised when Eisner focused his attention on the low-rise approach. (The tower was out of the question since, as Chao says, "Florida is so flat that when you build a single tower you have no relationship or context to other buildings. You're not forming any urban spaces.")

Encouraged by Eisner and Chao, the architect went off to develop the alternative design further. When the group reconvened later, Eisner asked Isozaki which building he wanted to build. Isozaki answered, "The low-rise."

"He came back with this yin-yang theory of positive and negative space, with a central tower that was very powerful, sculptural, looking toward the sky," says Chao. Isozaki's idea was to dramatize the relationship between the covered, air-conditioned work spaces in the building's low, flanking wing – the yin – and the enormous hollowed out vertical cylinder – the yang – that was a sundial open to the sky.

At Disney, even an avant-garde architect like Isozaki has to tell a story, or at least a fragment of one. The idea of a building about "time" – especially a corporate building full of time-conscious workers, and especially for Disney, the company that had grown prosperous by making movies and amusement parks that were always about another time or place – had a great appeal both to Isozaki and Eisner.

Isozaki designed the building originally for a lakeside site near the Caribbean Beach Hotel. Then Disney officials decided to move it to a more prominent – and commercial, as opposed to resort – location by I-4. "I had to call Iso to tell him we were moving his building," remembered Chao. "At the beginning, he was not very receptive. It took some persuasion." Chao recalls that Disney had to ensure that the site was large enough to provide a true north/south orientation for the building.

And Isozaki wanted a lake. "We said we can create a lake," said Chao. "The more he got into it, the more he loved the new site. I pointed out to him: 'This building is going to

The Team Disney Building at Walt Disney World (overleaf). Stand the building on one end and it would be the tallest structure in Florida.

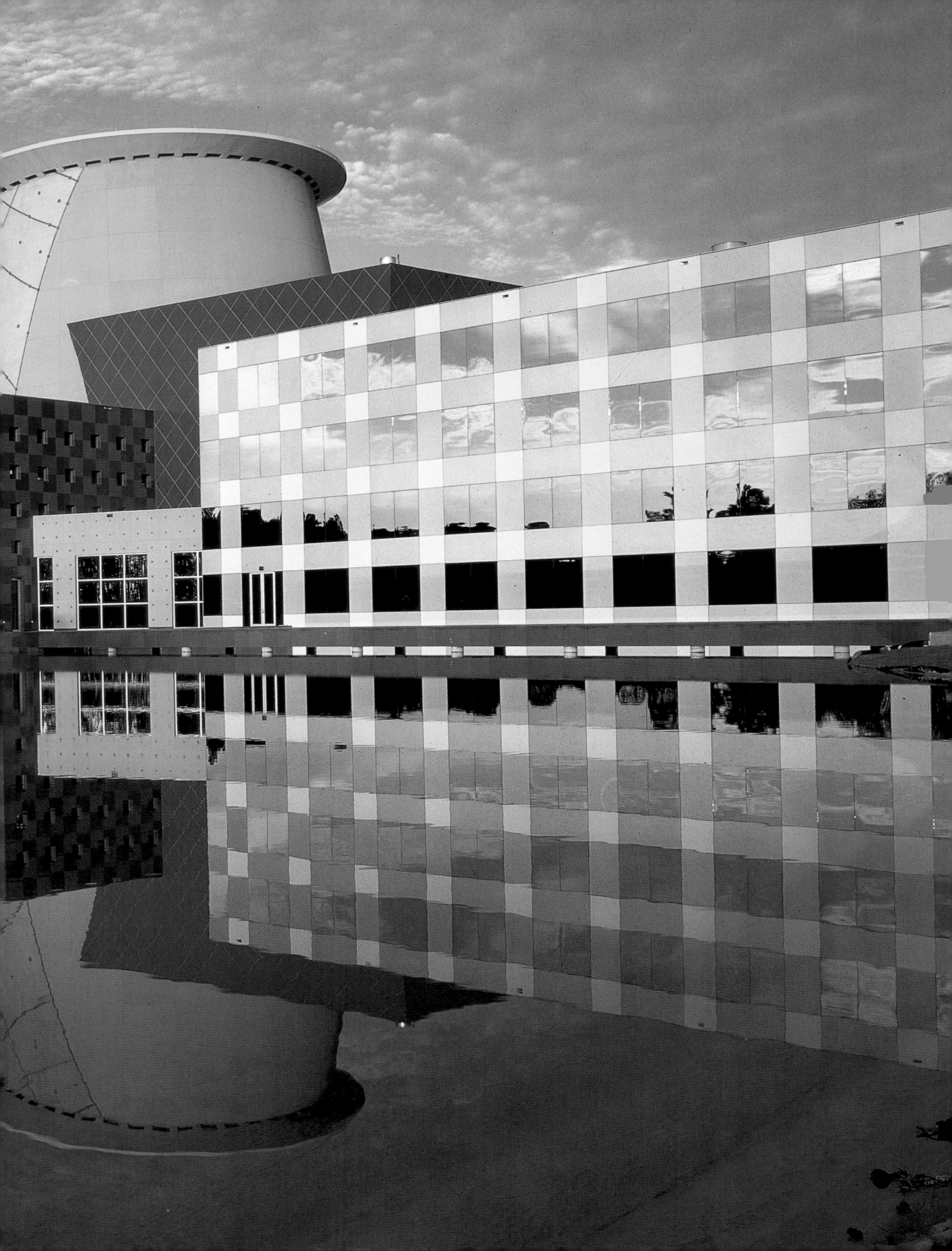

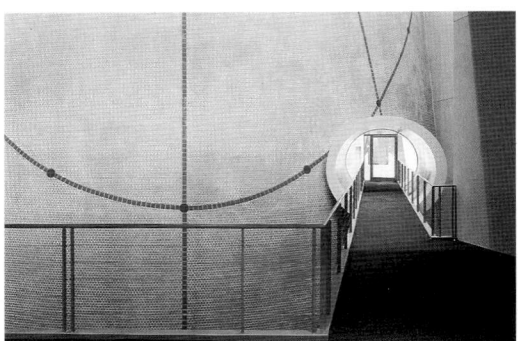

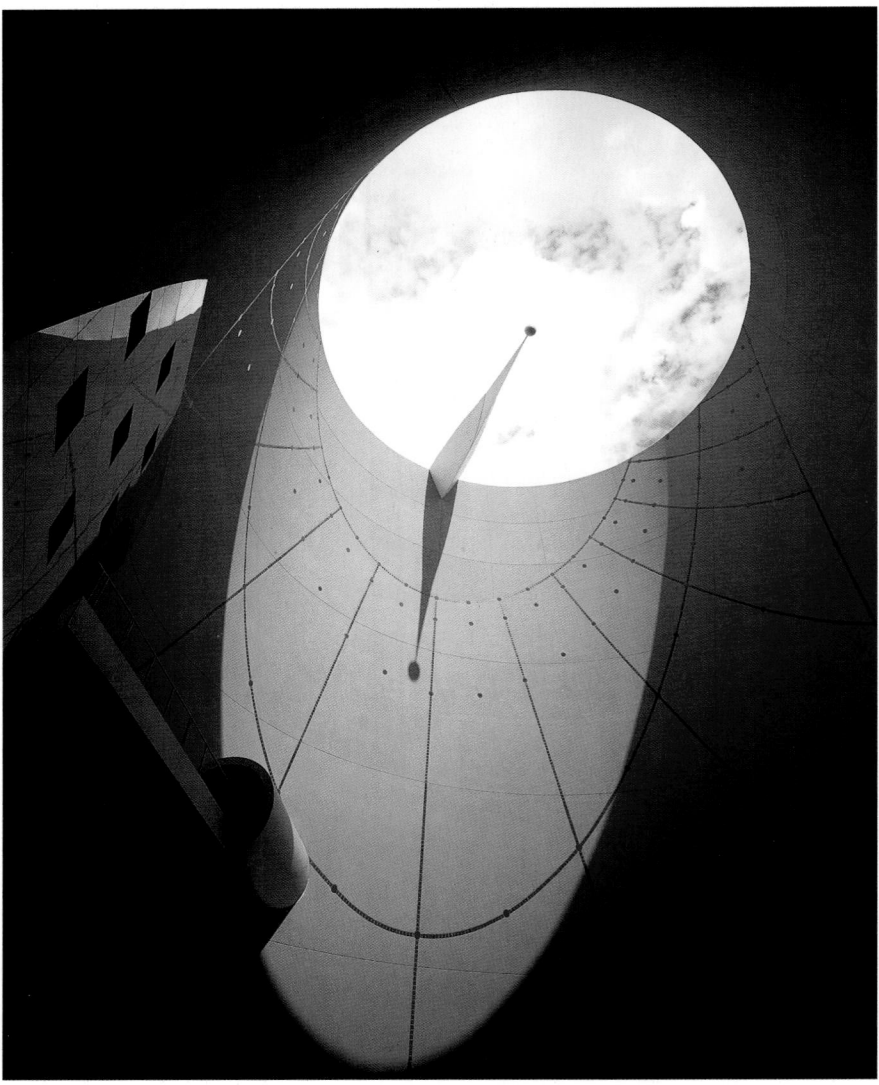

Projecting into the oculus of the central hall is the gnomon of the world's largest sundial (above). In this building, geometry itself is a theme (top).

get lots of exposure every day. Everyone using the Epcot Center Drive will see it.'" Watching Isozaki cope with the changes fascinated Tim Johnson: "He is the one guy I have been able to see design something just sitting there. I've seen him stare at the paper for ten minutes that seemed like an eternity. Then he'd start drawing. What he came up with is better than anything I've ever seen."

The building, which opened in 1991, is an astounding and colorful concoction, long and low like a vast ocean liner, its sleek lines unexpectedly interrupted by a tumble of tile-clad cubes and an open drum that rises above it like a smokestack. It is powerful and playful at once, its strong forms expressed in a profusion of color – pink, gray, red, green, blue, and yellow.

The 120-foot-tall funnel is a sundial, the world's largest. Inside is a Japanese garden of river-washed stones into which is set a circular pattern of granite tiles. On the day of the summer solstice, the shadow cast by the gnomon that is set into the opening above creeps along the granite path throughout the day. Carved into some of the pavers are quotations; Eisner took that job on for himself, sitting up night after night surrounded by books of quotations, poetry, and proverbs seeking the best quotes about time.

"The sundial is no ornamental nicety," said Thomas Fisher, writing in *Progressive Architecture*. It "reminds us, for example, that throughout human history, it has been common to think of time as cyclical and its measurement as relative to particular events, such as the rising and setting of the sun or the change of seasons."

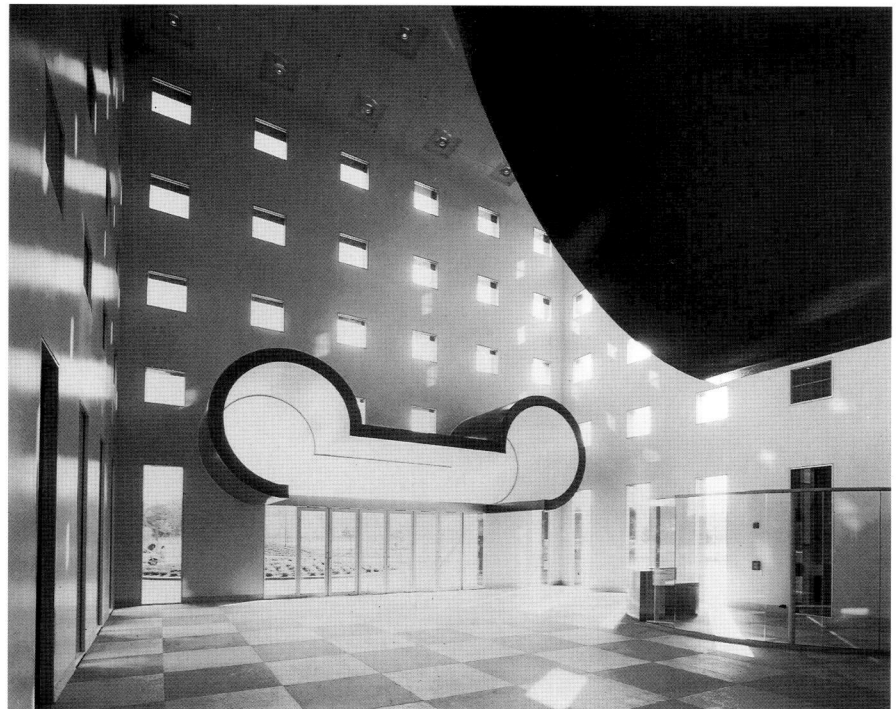

At the base of the sundial (above) is a Japanese garden of river-washed stones. Quotations on the subject of time are carved in the pavers. Mouse ears (left), Isozaki's abstracted nod to the most famous of Disney's cartoon characters, form the arcade of the main entrance to the building.

A three-story-high wall drawing by Sol LeWitt in one of the building's interior atriums.

That the building appears to float is quite an accomplishment, given its massive structure. At 840 feet, it is essentially the length of two city blocks (turned upright, it would be the tallest building in Florida). It houses offices for 1,200 employees. Inside, the four-story wings are painted in pale hues to provide a backdrop for twenty-six Sol LeWitt "wall drawings."

Disney's art consultant, Nancy Rosen, had recommended several artists for the building, among them James Rosenquist and Sol LeWitt. LeWitt was selected. "It was an absolute marriage made in heaven between Sol, Michael, and Isozaki," recalls Rosen. LeWitt first showed a cubic design then, after seeing the building, came back with a starburst motif. "Everybody loved it."

The building – which went on to win Disney its first major architectural award, a national Honor Award from the American Institute of Architects in 1992 – got its public preview during a tour Eisner led for architectural historians and critics. He took them through the new hotels and on to the construction site for Team Disney. The critics were dubious as they approached Isozaki's building, muttering, "I don't know about this one," as they piled out of the bus; doubt turned to amusement when the critics passed through a series of Mickey Mouse-eared metal gates and from amusement to awe as the group continued into the sundial courtyard, an experience Eisner finds to be "almost religious."

"Despite its bright colors and abstracted Mickey Mouse ears in the gates and entry canopy, this is a serious work, as intellectually challenging as it is functionally adept," wrote Fisher.

"Disney has now made its contribution to the history of architecture," proclaimed Paul Goldberger, then the *New York Times* architecture critic, who termed it "an extraordinary composition of geometric forms: intensely colored, fragmented boxes set at clashing angles." Goldberger called the sundial the building's "climactic element."

Isozaki himself has never seen the building finished. Many of the designers from his office came to an opening celebration, but Isozaki, by then at work on the 1992 Olympic stadium in Barcelona, couldn't make it. Disney officials implored him to come see it, but Isozaki demurred. "But you haven't seen it finished," Chao said. "Yes I have," replied Isozaki. "I've seen it. I saw it when I designed it. I saw it in my mind."

chapter six | *Castles (European and American)*

Cinderella Castle at night. Lighting effects are crucial to Disney's design philosophy. This may be the legacy of a company that came to architecture from the perspective of making movies.

The castles of Disney's several kingdoms don't strive for authenticity; they were born in a world of fairy tales and fantasy, and that is where they've stayed. These castles "belong" to Sleeping Beauty or Cinderella, not a long-forgotten baron or princess. They are candy-coated castles, gilded confections, and they have become the enduring architectural symbols of Disney's theme parks. It is to the castle that the tourists turn when they want that last memorable photograph, and it is the image of the castle – a simple, yet memorable, silhouette – that, more than anything else, is used by the company as a symbol in advertisements and commercials.

Before there were castles in the Disney theme parks, there were the memorable castles of the animated features. The castles in *Snow White and the Seven Dwarfs* (1937), *Cinderella* (1950), *Sleeping Beauty* (1959), and the much more recent *Beauty and the Beast* (1991) all share a storybook look. They are slender, turreted, crenellated structures. The buildings in Disney's animated features are always rendered in a painterly style, and the castles gave the animation background artists great opportunity to indulge their most romantic architectural impulses. In *Sleeping Beauty,* for example, a movie whose highly detailed backgrounds were inspired by Early Renaissance paintings, the castle is literally plucked from storybook pages as the film unfolds. The castle, though, was based on

real "storybook" castles, among them the Château of Ussé in France's Loire valley, the compact and beautiful castle that originally moved Charles Perrault to write his *Sleeping Beauty*, and the Bavarian Black Forest castles, which were said to have offered similar inspiration to the Brothers Grimm.

The first three-dimensional castle was almost an impulse. Walt asked for it in the original Disneyland design, and Herb Ryman dutifully put it in the plan he executed so hurriedly over a single weekend. "The first one we sort of invented by going back to some of the stories where the castles were in the backgrounds," says John Hench. The castle was a montage of French and Bavarian castles, drawn from such Loire valley châteaus as Chenonceaux, Chambord, and Chaumont, from the "pleasure courts" of Fontainebleau and Versailles, and from the Bavarian hunting palaces of the Black Forest. The Imagineers also looked at Medieval illuminations, like the famous fifteenth-century illuminated French manuscript called the *Très Riches Heures du Duc de Berry*.

It was, at Walt Disney's request, supposed to be a sweet castle, truly a storybook castle, one proportioned more to the imagination than to history. Ken Anderson recalled that Walt would say, "You know, tyrants in the past built these huge buildings – look how big and powerful I am. And they towered over people to impress people."

Sleeping Beauty Castle, shown
as a rendering (above) and under
construction (right), was the
storybook castle Walt Disney
wanted.

Sleeping Beauty Castle viewed from the west, with the Santa Ana Mountains in the distance.

Later, as a group of designers struggled unhappily to make the castle a three-dimensional reality, Ryman – thinking it looked too much like the flamboyant nineteenth-century castle that King Ludwig II of Bavaria built at Neuschwanstein – impulsively turned the castle top so it sat crosswise on its base, in an utterly unauthentic fashion. Somehow it worked. (Shortly before his death, though, Ryman confided that he nonetheless would have liked to have seen the castle bigger; in the rush to build Disneyland so fast, the castle fell victim to limited funds. It was only when the Magic Kingdom opened in Walt Disney World in 1971 that Ryman got to see the castle as he'd originally envisioned it, in all its excessive glory.) The Disneyland castle started out as Snow White's, but *Sleeping Beauty* was in production in 1954, so a different princess got a house in Anaheim.

Cinderella got her animators' castle in 1950, but it wasn't until almost two decades later, as Walt Disney World's Magic Kingdom was being designed, that it gained its three-dimensional identity. Of the two, the more delicate Disneyland home of Sleeping Beauty and its much grander cousin in the Magic Kingdom, it is the former that became Disney's hallmark. However, it is the Magic Kingdom castle that has been imported to Disneyland Tokyo.

The Disneyland Paris castle presented a special problem, because the designers were acutely aware that the authentic castle that started it all, the Château of Ussé, would be less than an hour away. Tony Baxter put it this way: "Disneyland used Neuschwanstein, and Florida was an amalgam of many French castles. We needed to go to the realm of fairy tales and not tread on anybody's sense of

Cinderella Castle (opposite) in the Walt Disney World Magic Kingdom, from the west. Walt Disney wanted both castles to face south so that visitors would have the best possible light conditions when taking photographs in front of them.

Cinderella Castle is larger and more lavish than Sleeping Beauty Castle. The back of the castle (above) is particularly elaborate, with intricate tracery in the Gothic windows. Left, one of five mosaics in the castle's vault that tells the story of Cinderella.

Le Château de la Belle au Bois Dormant in Disneyland Paris (above and opposite) is even more of a storybook castle than the others. Even the landscaping around the castle seems to have been inspired by children's book illustrations.

integrity. I didn't want to do Gothic columns. I didn't want to do in Fiberglas what you could go into the city [Paris] and see. And right nearby were the finest castle examples in the world. So we created twisted tree forms that kind of grow out of rock as our columns. There's no way you're going to confuse that with the real thing. Likewise, having a fire-breathing dragon in the basement is not the sort of thing you're going to encounter at Chenonceaux." Hence, Le Château de la Belle au Bois Dormant is the most fanciful Disney castle of all.

A cartoon castle brought to three dimensions seems peculiarly American, a somehow appropriate centerpiece for a theme park. Americans, after all, never had real castles, although the grand houses built in the late nineteenth and early twentieth centuries by the Rockefellers and Vanderbilts and others were palatial in scale and intent.

America had hotels, and it was to the grand hotels – opulent and exclusive – that the rich repaired for the social season. The grand hotels became America's castles. Castle imagery abounds, whether the architecture refers more to picturesque French and German castles, as it does, say, at the Mohonk Mountain House (1879) at the edge of the Catskills, or to the romantic Spanish versions, as at the Broadmoor Hotel (1918) in Colorado Springs. The earliest of America's "palace hotels" was the Tremont House in Boston, built in 1829 on an entire city block. The Tremont spawned Holt's Hotel and the Astor House in New York, the St. Charles Hotel in New Orleans, the Parker House in Chicago, and others.

The themed resort hotel was the true American castle and, in some ways, the precursor of the theme park, a destination of fantasy and illusion. The grand hotel, as we grew to call it, was invented almost simultaneously by a number of entrepreneurs across America, capitalists dreaming lavish dreams. If an inventor had to be pinpointed, the distinction might go to Henry Flagler, who arrived – along with his railroad – in St. Augustine, Florida, in 1887. There he found a somnolent and rather frayed town that had been the site of a Spanish fortification; he set out to make it much more than that.

From New York, he quickly brought architects from the prominent firm of Carrère & Hastings to design the Ponce de Leon and Alcazar Hotels. Flagler sent his young architects on a tour of Spain before they got down to work, and, in turn, they gave him hotels in a flamboyant style more Spanish than Spain itself.

The Grand Floridian Hotel was
designed in the style of America's
nineteenth-century "palace
hotels." Its antecedents include
the Hotel del Coronado near
San Diego, California, and the
Ormond Beach Hotel, which was
near Daytona Beach in Florida.

Across the country in San Diego, California, the Hotel del Coronado, designed by architects James and Merritt Reid, was also being built in 1887; a sprawling wood-frame extravaganza, its turrets are said to have inspired L. Frank Baum's description of the Emerald City in *The Wizard of Oz*, a story just as formidable in its impact – at least on the American imagination – as *Sleeping Beauty*. The parallel is worth noting.

It was to these nineteenth-century hotel/palaces that Disney's architects turned for inspiration when planning some of their resort hotels, just as the Imagineers had turned to the castles of Europe to draw and design castles for Sleeping Beauty and Cinderella.

"Walt planted the seed for the idea of themed hotels around the lake," recalled Wing Chao. "He wanted Polynesia, contemporary, Persia, Asia, or Venice." In the original Magic Kingdom plan, a hotel would relate to each of the five different themed areas: the Contemporary was for Tomorrowland, most obviously, and the Polynesian was the extension of Adventureland. The Grand Floridian Beach Resort (1988), the first new hotel to be built at Walt Disney World since the park's opening in 1971, was intended to tie into Main Street, with all its effusive late-nineteenth-century imagery.

Architect Charles Henning – then with the Newport Beach, California, firm of Wimberly, Allison, Tong & Goo, which executed the design originally conceived by Disney's in-house architects – terms the Grand Floridian "the first real Disney hotel," which might seem a bold assertion. "Disney is present everywhere," he says. Indeed, the Grand Floridian is fully themed, from its

The Grand Floridian Hotel evokes a bygone splendor both in its architecture and interior design. Its lobby (below), a five-story space dominated by two huge chandeliers, was inspired by the Brown Palace Hotel in Denver, Colorado.

The Yacht and Beach Clubs are
connected but separately run and
different in design. They share
many common facilities, including
pool, beach, and health club. The
Yacht Club (above) has a "button-
down, navy-blue-blazer look"
while the Beach Club is a more
casual hotel in the shingle style.

five-story lobby with its glass domes and filigreed chandeliers to the posh Victorian decor.

Wimberly, Allison, Tong & Goo had long experience in hotel design, particularly with the posh Ritz-Carlton chain. Partner Gerald Allison describes the style of the Grand Floridian as "American Victorian, basically the Queen Anne Style." "Basically" is the key word there. Like its predecessors among turn-of-the-century hotels, the Grand Floridian wasn't true to only one style or precedent. It drew from the Hotel del Coronado and from several nearby Florida hotels, among them the Belleview Biltmore (1897) and the Ormond Beach (1887). Its lobby, a vast atrium lined with balconies, is taken almost directly from Frank Edbrook's Brown Palace Hotel (1892) in Denver.

Like many Disney offerings, the Grand Floridian is its own exercise in illusion. Real wood is used where people can touch it; out-of-reach, synthetic materials take over. The public spaces at the Grand Floridian carry out the theme effectively. Shops are tucked discreetly to the side and – except for the tea-room that sits at one end of the lobby – so are the restaurants.

Outdoors, it is more ordinary. The pool area is rather more of the 1980s than the 1880s, and bathers in bikinis and flip-flops further destroy the illusion. Disney officials later realized they could turn swimming pools and gardens into flamboyant or glamorous or fully kitschy works of design unto themselves. "The pool is the miss at the Grand Floridian," says Peter Rummell.

That was not to happen again. At the Caribbean Beach Hotel, the pool seems to

One of the most memorable features of the Yacht and Beach Clubs is a small lighthouse at the end of a narrow causeway (top). The Beach Club (above) has elaborate wood trim.

The lakefront facade of the Yacht
Club at night.

emerge from the ruins of a pirate kingdom, with battlements and cannons. Indeed, the shipwreck, a staple of early Disney live-action films, has come to provide a dramatic motif. By anyone's accounting, it is the pool at the Yacht and Beach Clubs that most effectively transforms the experience of swimming into yet another of Disney's worlds, a small water kingdom that becomes an experience in its own right. The pool at the Yacht and Beach Clubs even has its own name, Storma-long Bay, where the wreck of a clipper ship slowly rots on the shore of a romantic New England cove.

Robert A. M. Stern was working on his design for the Casting Center when he first saw the schemes for old-fashioned hotels near Epcot. A group of Disney architects were huddled over plans, photographs, doodles. He noticed, in passing, that one of these was of his much-photographed Lawson House (1979–81) in Quogue, which, though it is not really mod-est, Stern calls a "cottage."

The hotels were a problem. The designers had struggled with Epcot-like themes – ideas for a Bavarian hotel and a French hotel were considered and rejected – but, as Rummell says, "We couldn't compete with Imagineer-ing. We couldn't compete with that really authentic detailed theme look. We realized we really had to get into a different vernacular, something that was smaller and quieter."

The original architects on the job couldn't quite clinch the look Disney was seeking, classy and yet affable, nostalgic and still somehow trendy; thus, Stern came along to be the image-maker. The hotels – they are actually one continuous structure with two

The public spaces in the Yacht Club are formal and elegant (top). The more informal restaurants in the hotels (above) share the ambience of Main Street, but the design is looser and less fussy about period details.

intimately related themes – became the Yacht Club, to conjure up a turn-of-the-century New England club, and the Beach Club, to evoke a mid-Atlantic shore hotel. Compared to the World Showcase at Epcot or Main Street in the Magic Kingdom, or even the Grand Floridian, the Yacht and Beach Clubs (1991) seem restrained. The architectural gestures are more subtle, if amply sentimental, with an abundance of dormers and cupolas, porch railings and wood trim. Each hotel expresses a different regional vernacular. Yacht is gray and slightly more sedate looking, Beach is blue and intended to be somewhat less formidable – as Stern says, "The Yacht Club is shingle style, kind of a button-down, navy-blue-blazer look, while the Beach Club is more stick style." But the idea and the era are similar for both.

And they are a sprawl. End to end, the corridors and breezeways run a mile. At one end, the last door opens right by the Dolphin Hotel; at the other, the next stop is Epcot itself.

Like the Grand Floridian, the Yacht and Beach Clubs impart an idea of civility, and that – more than architecture – is the key to their success. Stern's hotels are more original, today's takes on yesterday's designs, than the Grand Floridian, which is not even apologetic about borrowing from its historical sources and then lightening the overall look by using materials without much heft to them and colors lacking the depth and darkness the Victorians often preferred. However, it is worth noting that even the Yacht and Beach Clubs use a high-compression fiberboard called Werzalit to simulate the traditional beaded clapboard siding of shore hotels in the East.

Americans, of course, didn't limit their hotel/castles to the seaside. As the national parks developed, they engendered their own architectural heritage of hotels and lodges. Many of these arose in the wilderness, as works of rugged splendor, as romantic as their counterparts along the Altantic and Pacific shores.

Thus, when Disney sought a theme for a new hotel on the lake, the idea of creating an ode to one of the great wilderness lodges seemed fitting. This Wilderness Lodge (1994), however, was not to be a re-creation so much as an evocation. Its design, by Peter Dominick of the Urban Design Group of Denver, draws upon a variety of rustic landmarks, including Old Faithful Inn at Yellowstone National Park, Ahwahnee Hotel at Yosemite, Lake McDonald Lodge at Glacier National Park, and Timberline Lodge at Mount Hood, Oregon.

Wilderness Lodge takes some of Disney's successful hotel motifs – the soaring lobby of the Grand Floridian, the themed pool area of the Yacht and Beach Clubs – even further. The six-story lobby is dominated by a giant fireplace with stonework depicting the strata of the Grand Canyon. Columns are carved with birds of prey, starting at eye level with those found in fields and meadows and ascending through lower alpine species to the lords of the upper air. On the grounds, a geyser, a fly-fishing creek, and a waterfall transform Florida scrub and muck into a Western landscape.

Dominick is a successful Western architect and son of a pioneering environmentalist and longtime U.S. senator, and he brought to the design an innate understanding of the West that was integral to the conception of

Bay Lake Approach

WILDERNESS
LODGE

Urban Design Group Inc.

Wilderness Lodge (below) seems set in a Rocky Mountain pine forest, not the swelter of central Florida. An early rendering (left) gives a perspective from the deck of a Western lake steamer.

Wilderness Lodge has its own waterfall (right), a geyser, and a meandering stream (below). This is another watery landscape, of a different sort entirely from the nearby Swan and Dolphin Hotels and the Yacht and Beach Clubs.

the hotel. Despite the spatial and technological demands of building a 728-room hotel, Dominick was able to be faithful to the way in which a log hotel is put together. He describes the experience of designing it as "magical."

Beyond using typical rustic architectural motifs and western materials, Dominick sought to use his commission to express spiritual ideas about the West. He was able to do so, in part, by incorporating as much Native American legend as possible – on columns and totem poles and in patterns in the rugs – and perhaps even more in what was both the philosophical and the structural approach to Wilderness Lodge, by trying to ensure "a roughness and a trueness of how things were put together." At Wilderness Lodge, authenticity is the fantasy.

A totem pole and a giant fireplace dominate the cavernous Wilderness Lodge lobby, a setting worthy of Teddy Roosevelt.

Main Street, U.S.A. (Disney edition), is not an official address, but it is nonetheless one of the most influential streets in America. Dissect it and it is simply this: stage-crafted facades in front of continuously connected shops. But there is much more at work here.

Walt Disney himself might have predicted that the most important architectural symbol of Disneyland would be Sleeping Beauty Castle, but it wasn't. Instead, it was Main Street. No other single element of Disneyland or of the Magic Kingdoms to follow had as much impact.

Main Street was a brilliant gesture. Starting in the 1920s, Main Street, in many small towns, meant the movies. America's images of itself were becoming more universal: Sunset Boulevard was as much America's Main Street as Oak or Elm or Chestnut. But when you went to the movies on Maple Street, you knew everyone in the theater, and afterward you still walked around the town square, stopping for a malt at the soda fountain or to hear a concert at the band shell. Indeed, the small towns of America weren't necessarily the product of a singular vision; they expressed commonly held, everyday aspirations in their architecture, uplifting the mundane to loftier levels, and they continued to cast their spell even as they began to fade in importance.

In the decade after World War II, as Americans were rapidly fleeing their hometowns for cities and suburbs, they also left behind small-town amenities, from the town

A parade on the Magic Kingdom's Main Street celebrates the nation's bicentennial in 1976. Among other things, Main Street in the Disney theme parks is designed for parades, and there is one almost every day in each park.

hall to the village green. In one swoop, Disney's designers encapsulated all the happy associations of small-town America in Disneyland, and his Main Street made Americans yearn once again for the towns and town squares they'd abandoned.

Main Street recalls an era of insouciance and hope for the future that may never have existed; it was created by a master at conjuring fictional memories. Walt Disney had spent his earliest childhood in Marceline, Missouri, a charmless rural small town. More of his boyhood was spent in Kansas City and Chicago, in a family that was seldom either affluent or happy (his father was tyrannical, arbitrary, and hot-tempered). But it was Marceline that Disney was later to romanticize with Main Street.

In the mid-1970s, the historian Richard V. Francaviglia went to see Marceline, Missouri. He found old photographs that showed that the town's unpaved Main Street of Walt's childhood "was rutted and rilled and horse manure helped turn it into a soupy quagmire in wet weather." He pointed out that there really wasn't much of a public square, and telephone poles, "rather than trees," lined the sidewalks. It had little in common with the carefree, colorful, sentimental, ornamental Main Street of Disneyland.

The Main Street that Walt Disney built is a fantasy version of a turn-of-the-century small-town Main Street, the buildings recast pictorially to evoke memories. As is often the

A panoramic view of Main Street in the Walt Disney World Magic Kingdom, looking toward the Railroad Station.

Walt Disney wanted his Main Street to evoke the memory of his childhood home of Marceline, Missouri, but the reality was less romantic than he remembered.

MAIN ST., MARCELINE, MO.
TAYLER'S PHARMACY, MARCELINE, MO.

case in a stage set, the feeling of truth was enhanced by authentic props. Old lamps from Baltimore, Boston, Chicago, and Philadelphia were installed – bought in bulk for as little as 33 cents a pound. Store windows boasted artifacts as well.

"Main Street expressed a general truth about main streets in general – and about how people felt about main street," says John Hench, who helped design the Disney version in the 1950s. "The real period that produced Main Street was an optimistic time. It is so reassuring it is irresistible. It is a communal dream, not some individual saying that life can be good."

The buildings on Main Street are recognizable as archetypes but they aren't authentic. They were drawn the way a town in a picture book or an animated film might be and then transformed into three-dimensional

entities. Francaviglia emphasized "the lushness and harmony of the Main Street, U.S.A., that Disney created." Comparing it to turn-of-the-century Marceline, he noted, "In architectural composition it is far more stereotyped and Victorian, and the colors of its buildings are more coordinated and colorful." This was, of course, a conscious decision: as Hench points out, "Walt had an appreciation for the essence of things. For example, the Main Streets across America have many contradictions in architecture. Walt eliminated the contradictions."

As in storybook illustrations, there is ample play with scale on Disney's Main Street; for example, the first stories are full-sized but those above them are not. The facades are scaled down for a number of reasons – for one, to frame the view of the castle at the end of the street more effectively – but the primary purpose is to make Main Street a palpable experience for those who walk it.

Francaviglia believes that Disney's Main Street is one of the most successful pedestrian environments in the world, calling it "a remarkably effective design for reinforcing experiences, heightening anticipations, and moving traffic." Of course, it serves few of the practical purposes of most small-town main streets. It doesn't have to accommodate cars or parking or parking meters (the only form of transportation is the occasional horse-drawn trolley, fire truck, or omnibus). The street can be narrow and the sidewalks wide, so that even when they are crowded, people are comfortable walking, window-shopping, or even lingering.

"The first Main Street in Disneyland had somewhat more concern with symbolism than with theater," says Hench. It was a powerful statement. "We still get letters from Nebraska or Iowa wanting to redo their Main Street just like ours. But there wasn't ever any Main Street like that."

Indeed, towns that had allowed their main streets to fall into steep decline began to see themselves differently after the opening of Disneyland. Preservationists had been arguing on behalf of restoring rather than demolishing America's small-town "Main Streets," and Disney's versions – first in Anaheim and later in Orlando – influenced millions of Americans to be sympathetic to their goals. In 1980, the National Trust for Historic Preservation began a major program to restore small-city main streets. Now, in cities all over America, blocks of nineteenth- and twentieth-century buildings sit on the National Register of Historic Places; vintage

light fixtures have been restored or re-created, and sentimental signs hang in front of newly renovated storefronts.

In the early 1950s, America's love affair with the automobile was in full tilt, and amenities for pedestrians were not a priority in the planning community. Disney's Main Street anticipated by almost a decade the advent of shopping streets free of cars, such as Morris Lapidus's 1961 transformation of Lincoln Road in Miami Beach to an auto-free outdoor mall and Lawrence Halpern's Nicollet Mall (1963) in Minneapolis. It was only logical that the next step was the enclosed shopping mall.

The earliest enclosed malls, in fact, owed quite a debt to Disney. Linear and traffic-free, they were anchored on each end by department stores that had much the same function as the train station and castle at Disneyland.

An early concept drawing for the Disneyland Main Street suggests that the designers were thinking of the needs of pedestrians from the very beginning.

When Disneyland opened in 1955, its Main Street was little more than facades, scaled slightly smaller than "real" architecture. Eventually, those facades became storefronts. The movie house on Disneyland's Main Street (right) is playing a hit movie from 1928; an antique fire engine frames the view farther down the same side of the street (below). At Disneyland, the ornamentation on the Main Street buildings is less elaborate than at the other Disney theme parks.

Architectural details on Main Street: two buildings at the Magic Kingdom in Orlando (left); Liberty Court in Disneyland Paris (below).

As time went on, the enclosed mall became even more Disney-like. Today, the West Edmonton Mall in the Canadian province of Alberta boasts a Victorian streetscape inside its massive enclosure; at Sawgrass Mills in Sunrise, Florida, the architectural firm of Arquitectonica produced a series of stage-set main streets, each with a different architectural theme. In town centers and malls – and in the "festival marketplaces" that appeared along a number of waterfronts during the 1980s – new cities and older ones alike have sought to evoke or create the old-fashioned feeling of order and freedom that Main Street evokes.

The writer William Zinsser, who set out to visit America's most beloved tourist destinations, calls Main Street Disneyland's "central metaphor." Walking down Main Street, serenaded by waltz music, Zinsser asked himself, "Hadn't I seen it somewhere else? I had. I had seen it replicated in upscale shopping malls in upscale towns across America – towns like Aspen, Colorado, and Naples, Florida. I remembered from a visit to Naples that the two ideas of 'postmodern' (reinventing the past) and 'retro' (re-creating the past) have merged there to form the collective taste." Zinsser cites Georgetown Park, a "Victorian/Federal" styled mall inside an old wharf building on the Potomac River, as "a pure appropriation" of Disneyland.

"We've all been there before, even if we've never lived in – or have been to – a small town," wrote Francaviglia of Main Street. If there's an irony here, it's that we have adopted as a symbol of our common past, a place that never quite existed in the form that Walt's imagination gave it.

Like Main Street, Disney-MGM Studios in Orlando pays homage to another time and another place. In this case, it is an ode to a Hollywood that never really was, much in the way that Main Street is the expression of an architectural idea more than any authentic architectural actuality.

To begin with, there was the mere notion of creating a "studio tour" where there had never been a studio. Movie studio tours were once the stuff of legend, open to a privileged few. Then, in 1974, Universal Studios in Hollywood transformed its back lot into a new kind of theme park with attractions based on Universal movies, where Jaws jumped out of a fake ocean and earthquakes shook passing trams on cue.

Down the street, Disney couldn't do that; its soundstages were in the middle of its Burbank complex, and its small – and dwindling – back lot sat right on Riverside Drive. Furthermore, there were plenty of movie studios in California. The more unexpected move was to create a studio tour at Walt Disney World, where Disney had an enormous amount of land – even though few movies had ever been made in central Florida.

As such, it always seems a bit spoofy, as if you'd dropped in on the back lot on a down day in a studio that is between pictures. Disney-MGM Studios takes a cue from Disneyland, in that it is compactly designed, with the kind of intimate spatial relationships that exist in Anaheim more than in Orlando. Like Main Street, in Disney-MGM Studios a real place has been re-created in idealized form, imparting a sense that all is much better in Hollywood than it actually is or ever really was.

Each building on the studio lot has a specific antecedent: Disney's Imagineers took buildings they liked or admired from all over the real Los Angeles and reassembled them in neat rows. Some of the Disney versions retained more or less the role of the California original: Mayer and Holler's Grauman's Chinese Theater (1927, Hollywood) became The Great Movie Ride; Carl Jules Weyl's Brown Derby (1927, Hollywood) remained a restaurant; and Marcus Miller's Darkroom Camera Shop (1938, Park La Brea) was re-created as a film and camera store. Others were relegated to new uses, sometimes with incongruous results: Fire Station No. 1 (1940, Koreatown), built by the Works Progress Administration, became a newsstand, while S. Charles Lee's Municipal Light, Water, and Power Office Building (c. 1937, Lincoln Heights) became a clothing store called Tailors to the Stars. (Walt Disney World has its own fire stations and power plants, but they are not inside the theme parks, where all buildings tend to be either attractions, stores, or restaurants.)

Interestingly, Disney's Imagineers saw parallels between the roles that Main Street and Hollywood have played in the national mythology. Indeed, Hollywood – or the idea of Hollywood – eventually became a kind of symbolic national Main Street for Americans. The world of movies and moviemaking was a focus of America's optimistic hopes, especially in the dreary years of the Great Depression when the best antidote to the blues was a trip downtown to a picture palace to see a Hollywood extravaganza. It is no coincidence that the predominant architectural style used for Disney-MGM Studios – Art Deco –

Disney-MGM Studios has some of the ambience of Los Angeles, as in this view of Sunset Boulevard (left), taken from the top of the Tower of Terror. The Earffel Tower (above) is one of Walt Disney World's iconographic landmarks – Disney-MGM Studio's answer to the Cinderella Castle and Space-ship Earth.

Real Hollywood Buildings – such as Grauman's Chinese Theater (opposite below), Crossroads of the World (right), and the Darkroom Camera Shop (above) – show up in idealized forms at Disney-MGM Studios. They're out of context, and the scale is different, but they haven't lost their insouciant appeal.

From Disneyland's inception, period automobiles have been used to heighten the atmosphere of streetscapes. Not surprisingly, 1930s cars are scattered throughout Disney-MGM Studios (left). Cars of every era pop up around the Disney theme parks and even at some of the resort hotels, such as the Hotel Santa Fe in Disneyland Paris and All-Star Music in Walt Disney World.

Stage 1 (above), is a handsome, if
heavy, variation on a 1930s Hollywood soundstage. A billboard with
a 1930s feeling (right) heightens
the period ambience established by
the Art Deco ornamentation on a
building at Disney-MGM Studios.

flourished in precisely those years in Los Angeles. Art Deco used dynamic forms – sweeping curves, towers, finials, and exuberant ornamentation – that seemed to express an optimistic faith in machine civilization at a time when the nation's economy seemed fragile at best. It is worth noting that Kem Weber's Streamline Moderne 1939 Burbank studios for Disney were an important contribution to Los Angeles's array of Art Deco buildings.

By extrapolating familiar approaches to design, like the generic late-Victorian style of Main Street and the Art Deco of Disney-MGM Studios, Disney created memorable architectural symbols that are much greater than any of their original parts. Hench refers to these as "archetypal truths," saying, "Painters do this. You can't paint sunflowers without referring to Van Gogh. He expressed a whole truth. Or take Henry the Eighth. There are many versions of Henry the Eighth. We don't even know what he looked like, but we accept Holbein. He owns Henry the Eighth. In much the same way, we own Main Street, because we expressed the archetypal truth about Main Streets everywhere."

The funky Googie architecture of postwar Los Angeles' coffee shops, with its eccentric geometry, provides Disney-MGM Studios with another design theme, especially for signs.

chapter eight | *Designs of the Future*

In 1995, when Tomorrowland at the Walt Disney World Magic Kingdom opened after a complete refurbishment, the Astro-Orbiter (opposite) had been redone to look as if it had come from the pages of a science-fiction fantasy. The new "land" (overleaf) could be home to a family of giant robots.

The new Tomorrowland in Walt Disney World's Magic Kingdom, dedicated in June 1995, appears to have sprung from a giant erector set. Its palette is rich and bold – not the stark black and white of 1960s modernism but vibrant blues, purples, and yellows. The effect is spirited and entirely in tune with the kitsch and nostalgia of the rest of the Magic Kingdom. The future, Magic Kingdom style, is now the future of the past, and therein hangs a tale.

Walt Disney loved the past – be it history or fantasy or fairy tale – but he was always fascinated by the future, too. He mastered the past in the fictional worlds he created for Disneyland and, later, Walt Disney World's Magic Kingdom. The future turned out to be far more difficult to predict.

In the 1950s and 1960s, those years when Disneyland and Walt Disney World were being designed and built, Americans embraced progress and all its manifestations – better toasters, faster cars, rockets to the moon – with naive idealism. "Walt thought the future would be bearable and would turn out to be good if people would get correct information about everything. He thought he could build it," says John Hench. And, indeed, the early drawings for Tomorrowland reflected that buoyant optimism about the future.

Disney's designers – the animators Walt plucked to create Disneyland – produced dozens of sleek, imaginative drawings of Tomorrowland's futuristic facades, many of

them unbuilt reveries about space and time, including an entrance with an "around-the-world" clock that would tell time anywhere on the globe.

Yet when Disneyland opened in 1955, it was clear that the more difficult task was to take the imagined future and give it a palpable reality; even Walt Disney himself was known to refer to Disneyland's Tomorrowland as "Todayland." The original Tomorrowland consisted only of Autopia, which was never especially futuristic, though even today it draws crowds of grown-ups eager to drive little sports cars in circles, and Space Station X-1, offering a satellite view of America, and Rocket to the Moon. The Astro-jets, soon renamed Rocket Jets, were introduced in 1956. But even in the 1950s, Tomorrowland's offerings seemed quaintly out-of-date almost as soon as they were introduced.

Of course, few thought that the future would come so fast. If the future wasn't a fearsome concept in 1955, it also seemed fairly far off, a future that was as fictional and improbable as the one Jules Verne had predicted in the 1880s. If Walt Disney sometimes referred to Tomorrowland as "Todayland," his successors found themselves calling it "Yesterdayland."

Today, a click of a digital watch will tell the time around the world. Rockets – we now call them space shuttles, which shows how compressed the universe has become – routinely head out to explore the cosmos. The

fast-moving changes of the late twentieth century have posed confounding problems for Disney's designers: as John Hench says, "Obviously, it's impossible to design the future . . . this minute it's now and tomorrow it will be yesterday."

Consider the Monsanto House of the Future, which from 1957 to 1967 offered visitors to Disneyland a glimpse of a new domestic future. A modular, plastic structure that looked a bit like a pod dropped from another planet, it had a microwave oven, a hands-free speaker phone with push-button dialing, and a central "climate-control center" – all givens in new houses today.

Three decades ago, computers were cumbersome items, burdensomely expensive and big; there were no fax machines, food processors, videotape recorders, telephone

answering machines, video games, or compact disc players. Devices that seem unimaginable today are tomorrow's clichés. "The future," the architect and theorist Joseph Rykwert wrote, "has always reserved its surprises, which is why, in hindsight, forecasts always seem quaint, even when they are meant to be spine-chilling."

Paradoxically enough, it was the nostalgia of Disneyland that was most prophetic. The architectural historian Chester Leibs once commented on the irony that it was Main Street, the Victorian throwback, that became the progressive expression at the Magic Kingdom, while Tomorrowland looked almost instantly dated. Only the monorail, with its streamlined shape and near-silent glide, continued to seem visionary. The first one, intro-

duced in Disneyland in 1959, gave definition to the idea of the future in three dimensions. Even today, visitors to both Disneyland and Walt Disney World experience the monorails not merely as transportation but as themed attractions, which – considering how rare they are in practical use – seems appropriate.

Part of the chronic problem of Tomorrowland can simply be attributed to the changing nature of architecture. As Tomorrowland gained its full form at Disneyland and was taking shape on the Imagineers' drawing boards for Walt Disney World, the prevailing modernist aesthetic was one of bold, stripped-down forms. The architecture of Tomorrowland inevitably evolved into one of gleaming white buildings with fins and pylons. That this style meshed easily with the architecture of America's corporate realm was no coinci-

Though early drawings for Tomorrowland showed it to be both fantastic and futuristic, the finished product, unveiled in Disneyland in 1967 and shown in a rendering and a photograph (opposite and above), was far more a product of its times, with gleaming glass curtain walls, soaring fins, and a PeopleMover, a tamer and less useful variation on the monorail.

Space Mountain (opposite) was designed in the mid-1970s and is the third "mountain" in the Disney theme parks – the other two being Big Thunder Mountain and Splash Mountain in Frontierland. Unlike the others, it is not naturalistic in the least, and represents the Imagineers' best efforts to envision futuristic architecture in the years between the mid-1960s design of Tomorrowland and the complete rethinking of its look in the late 1980s. The attraction was completely redesigned in the new Tomorrowland style for Discoveryland at Disneyland Paris (above).

The Rocket to the Moon attraction as it looked when Disneyland opened in 1955.

dence. In those decades, Americans fully believed that the future could be entrusted to corporations, and Walt Disney was no exception: much of Tomorrowland was eventually given over to corporate-sponsored pavilions. American Motors, maker of the Nash Rambler (how quickly we forget!), sponsored the original Circarama, an auto tour of the American West projected on a 360-degree screen. Starting in the early 1960s, Disney began his extensive collaboration with such firms as Ford, General Electric, and Pepsi Cola for the New York World's Fair of 1964–65. Later, many of the World's Fair exhibits were moved to Anaheim, and Tomorrowland was redesigned to accommodate them. By 1967, Disneyland's Tomorrowland had gained the form it would then keep for almost thirty years.

By then, Disney had died and the designers were already at work on the next version, at the Magic Kingdom. Disney himself always said he hated sequels, so he had left the theme park future in the hands of others. Instead he had become obsessed in the last year of his life with new ideas that he hoped to express at Epcot, his version of a utopian community. Disney's personal vision of Epcot lives on primarily in a short film presentation and a handful of drawings. By the time Walt Disney World got built, architecture had reached one of its most humdrum moments in history – the late 1960s and 1970s. At Walt Disney World's lands of tomorrow, the Magic Kingdom Tomorrowland, and then Epcot, the future was expressed in comparatively bleak architectural language.

Writing in the *New Republic* in 1982, Hendrik Hertzberg put it this way: "Tomorrowland was the only bit I had really wanted to see as a kid, because it was supposed to show what the future would be like. But this is 1981 and if Tomorrowland is any guide, the future has seen better days."

The Contemporary Hotel, which opened in Walt Disney World in 1971 along with the Magic Kingdom, bears powerful witness to this. It was intended to be Disney's most forward-looking building, a giant structure with a monorail running through it. Instead, it became quickly dated, a cultural and architectural white elephant, bulky and cumbersome. Designed by the Los Angeles firm of Welton Becket and Associates (the same Welton Becket who had so portentously told Walt that he would have to invent the architecture – and the architects – for Disneyland) in collaboration with the Imagineers, it is a cavernous concrete-and-steel A-frame with the top sheared off, a feat of technology in its construction and of derring-do, as far as the monorail was concerned. But it was very much a product of its times, a modernist monolith without many architectural felicities at all. D. Kenneth Mane, writing in *Playboy* in 1973, had this withering assessment: "An A-Frame, it looks like your old pop-up toaster. The monorail passes through it. In fact, the Contemporary seems to exist just so the monorail can pass through it. Inside, baby, it's the Big House: tier after tier of prison walls reaching up. Emptiness architecture. The place is massive and unattractive and superbly inefficient."

In the mid-1980s, the task of transforming the Contemporary Hotel into a warmer, more inviting place fell to Disney chief architect Wing Chao. The first step was to add convention facilities to lure in larger groups.

The monorail has been Disney's real contribution to futuristic thinking about architecture and planning. Especially at Walt Disney World, where it connects distant points, it offers both the excitement of a visionary idea and real practical advantages over automobile travel. It introduces an element of drama to one of Disney's flatter architectural conceptions: the Contemporary Hotel (left), whose lobby has been called "The Grand Canyon" (below).

For this, Disney chose the New York firm of Gwathmey Siegel & Associates, certainly among the country's reigning modernists. "Since the Contemporary Hotel was of a certain ilk, it had a kind of icon perception and needed only a minimal amount of theming," Charles Gwathmey recalls. "Disney does two kinds of architecture, corporate architecture and entertainment architecture, and this was the former. That doesn't mean the corporate kind of building can't be significant."

Gwathmey had known Chao at Harvard, and the two of them set out to transform the rather foreboding approach to the hotel into a landscaped plaza framed by the new wing housing the convention hall. For its part, the new convention hall, with its barrel-vaulted roof, resembled a movie production studio. Gwathmey wanted it all to seem like an assembled collage, using variations in scale, form, and pattern to give new shape not just to his addition but to the ensemble, which would be seen "from the water, from the road, and from the monorail."

At the same time, Tomorrowland, with its heavy-handed concrete buildings and uninterrupted facades, came under scrutiny. Tony Baxter began to confront the challenge of Tomorrowland when he was charged with creating the attractions at Disneyland Paris.

"We were faced with Tomorrowland being pretentious to begin with, but also out of date," Baxter says. The more he looked, the less he liked. When the future took concrete expression, it seemed to lose its poetry and instead become commonplace, yielding structures little differentiated from the thousands of anonymous office buildings and warehouses that line America's cities and suburbs.

"We'd gotten locked into the idea that the future was white stucco and gleaming glass."

In many respects, Baxter went back to the original essence of Tomorrowland. John Hench recalls that Disney's designers had looked first, as they were accustomed to do, to fantasy: "We were using something that would identify the idea of tomorrow, of the future, something that already had been established by cartoons, by Flash Gordon, mainly. That kind of language was understandable, and it was friendly because the future has its own threats. We feel an anxiety about the unknown. This was something we knew was safe and we could survive that kind of tomorrow."

Thus Baxter turned back the clock, looking to historic interpretations of the future. "We conjured Discoveryland [as Disneyland Paris's version of Tomorrowland is called] as homage to the moment in time when the dream of exploring space flourished, homage to all those who envisioned space travel from Leonardo to Jules Verne to George Lucas. We're not trying to say this is the future but that this is the dream."

For Tomorrowland at the Magic Kingdom, designer Eric Jacobson – an Imagineering senior vice president – took his cues more from science fiction. Of the two Tomorrowlands, it was the one at Walt Disney World that seemed the most out of sync with the times, a condition exacerbated by the comparison with Epcot's Future World (though many of those offerings also have suffered from the same affliction). But the presence of Future World was also an asset; it allowed the designers of Tomorrowland more artistic leeway. "We could really push the fantasy of

The New York architecture firm of Gwathmey Siegel & Associates was selected to adapt and add to the Contemporary Hotel. Their convention center addition (above and left) relies on pattern and abstraction inside and out.

Even the signs in Discoveryland (right) have a canny design that mixes old-fashioned and forward-looking elements. A poster (above) offers oxymorons of design syntax symbolic of Discoveryland as a whole: a futuristic side-wheel steamboat and zeppelin in a twenty-first century New Orleans.

science fiction, of the future that never was," says Jacobson.

At first, Eisner needed to be convinced. Jacobson walked him through the existing Tomorrowland and persuaded him that the future needed to be depicted differently. Said Eisner, "How do you show the future when it so quickly becomes the past?" At the Magic Kingdom, the stipulation was that the existing structures had to remain. Thus, the changes are cosmetic, technological and psychological; the by now old-fashioned Mission to Mars, done first for the New York World's Fair and then at Disneyland, was gutted to become Alien Encounter, a fully visceral attraction using a range of special effects, visual and sensory. The rocket ride was given a galaxy of rotating spheres to become the Astro-Orbiter and to make it seem like a new experience.

Movies, books, drawings, comic strips – mostly from the 1930s and 1940s – all provided source material for the new Tomorrowland, among them *Buck Rogers,* drawn by Dick Calkins, and the first science fiction comic strip when it debuted in 1929, and Alex Raymond's *Flash Gordon,* which dates to 1934. In a *Buck Rogers* strip, an alien spaceship might resemble a huge 1930s-style vacuum cleaner with portholes. Thus, in Tomorrowland, there are plenty of visual puns. Everything seems to be bolted down or hinged in place with gigantic pieces of hardware. There's lots of stainless steel.

And as for the technological future, that is now on view in Innoventions at Epcot, a kind of merchandiser's world's fair of technology and invention; it comes closer to the kind of Epcot that Walt Disney imagined just before his death, at least in some ways – an ever-changing showcase for new products with an eye to the ways in which they might change our daily lives. It is the best prognostication available to us, in a time when change seems to have its own constantly accelerating pace.

The new Tomorrowland and Discoveryland are really expressions of yesterday's tomorrow, maybe less a metaphysical concept than a metaphorical one, architecture done as a past vision of the future. "A weird tense," says the Miami landscape architect Douglas Duany, "like the past pluperfect." Walt Disney might not have believed that the future would descend on us so furiously or that it would become the past so rapidly, but that has become the case. Ironically enough, the predictable future – the one that we looked to for many decades – is now a source of nostalgia.

Panoramic view of the Disneyland Paris Discoveryland.

chapter nine | *On to Europe*

Robert A. M. Stern, who was instrumental in the planning of Disneyland Paris, designed a Preview Center for the resort (page 15), which was demolished when the theme park opened to the public. This was the center's small rotunda.

In late 1987, Disney officials began buying up sugar beet fields just south of Paris to fulfill a long-held ambition of building a Disney theme park in Europe. Disney had examined and rejected numerous sites before settling on Marne-la-Vallée, a short rail trip from Paris.

Disney's Imagineers had the difficult task of creating a theme park that would be similar to those in California and Florida but not identical. That was just half the challenge of Disneyland Paris, or EuroDisneyland, as it was then called. The grand plan also included hotels, a golf course, a convention center, and even a water theme park, all designed by an array of internationally renowned architects.

The first designs for the Disneyland Paris resort hotel site plan were sketched in-house. Robert A. M. Stern noticed them one day while he was in Burbank to review his projects in progress: he said the plans looked like a subdivision in Orange County, California. Wing Chao, Disney's chief architect, took the criticism to heart. "I told him, 'Bob, this is not the final site plan,'" Chao says. It was the needed impetus.

That night Stern was intending to host a dinner at Rebecca's Restaurant across Los Angeles in Venice, and the guest list included a number of architectural luminaries, among them Frank Gehry (who had designed the restaurant and who lives in the area), Chicago architect Stanley Tigerman, and Michael Rotondi of the Los Angeles design firm Morphosis.

Chao and Arthur Levitt, Jr., who was then Eisner's special assistant, wanted to harness all that talent to evaluate the master plan. Stern's instant and negative critique had made them realize they needed to start shaping real plans. They called each of Stern's intended guests and told them that the plans had changed, that they were having dinner at Disney's Imagineering design headquarters, a vast warehouse in Glendale. They called Fung Lum's Chinese Restaurant at Studio City and ordered up a feast. They tried, but failed, to locate Stern.

Stern, for his part, got to Rebecca's to find that his dinner had been diverted, and his guests actually hijacked, to Disney. He was furious, but went to Glendale to join the party. The group began to sketch out ideas. Then, as the session heated up, they thought they ought to clue in Eisner. He was in a screening with Jeffrey Katzenberg, then chief of Disney's film operations. The red light was on, which meant, in no uncertain terms, do not enter on peril of your job. Levitt decided to go in anyway; he told Eisner what they were doing and got his approval. "We got," says Chao, "the green light, even though there was a red light."

Out of this first session came the idea of having an ad hoc committee of architects hash out Disneyland Paris. The architects on tap were five of America's most famous – Michael Rotondi dropped out but Michael

to move ahead fast. "We were under the gun," says Chao. He quickly came up with a long list of architects from Europe and Japan as well as the United States for a design competition. The list included Bernard Tschumi, the Swiss-French architect who is dean of Columbia University's School of Architecture; Hans Hollein from Austria; Rem Koolhaas from Holland; Jean Nouvel and Jean-Paul Vigier, both from France; Aldo Rossi of Italy; Arata Isozaki of Japan; and the Americans – Peter Eisenman, Frank Gehry, Michael Graves, Antoine Predock, Robert Stern, Stanley Tigerman, and Robert Venturi. Each was contacted and given three weeks to come up with a concept for a hotel.

The presentations were at Eisner's house in Bel Air over the course of four days, one after another. Isozaki had to explain his proposal by overseas telephone. All the others made it in person. Predock showed up with a drawing so long that it had to be stretched across the lawn.

Eventually, the more abstract European ideas were scotched in favor of a series of hotels intended to express American architecture, American experiences, American icons – all arrayed around a lake that would have to be dug out of a beet field in the French countryside. The whole idea was altogether ambitious. "We were making a destination resort out of whole cloth," says Eisner. "And we went right into the jaws of the lion."

When the dust settled, five architects had been selected – Stern, Graves, Predock, Gehry, and a Frenchman not in the original competition, Antoine Grumbach. Known to oppose the high-tech architecture so popular among many European architects, he was to be the

Graves and Robert Venturi were added – and the only day they had free in common was Easter Sunday, 1988. They ensconced themselves at Stern's offices in an old industrial building on the far West Side of Manhattan. Before the weekend was over, and after many ideas were tried and discarded, Stern, Venturi, Graves, Tigerman, and Gehry would produce a plan for a sequence of five hotels around a lake and along a river. Said Stern, "The basic concept is of a lake of the American architectural experience. Of course, we recognized that a lot of American architecture has its roots in Europe, so we sought the best and clearest examples of what we were all about, what it was to be American." Ideas for hotels themed around lost worlds or new worlds, future worlds or movie worlds were tried and abandoned, left, essentially, on the cutting room floor.

The Easter Sunday resort plan was presented to Eisner, who endorsed it but wanted only European to design a building for the project. Grumbach drew the most romantic assignment, a hotel in the spirit of the great national park lodges of the American West, the same inspiration for Orlando's Wilderness Lodge. Aldo Rossi, whose brooding, beautiful classical buildings have made him one of the most admired architects in the world, had been included in the original group, but ran into difficulties getting along with Disney officials. Pushed in a way he found unaccountable, Rossi, in a letter to Eisner, invoked the travails of an earlier Italian architect in France: in the 1660s, Gian Lorenzo Bernini had been invited to Paris to submit designs for the Louvre and soon found himself at odds with Louis xiv. "I realize I am not Bernini," Rossi wrote Eisner. "But you are not the king of France. I quit." Later, he would reconcile with Disney and design the headquarters of the Disney Development Company in Orlando.

Grumbach's Sequoia Lodge is a heavy, dark, handsome hotel that the architect terms "an ecology building." It is surrounded by trees and, unlike most Disney buildings, is executed largely in natural materials: wood, stone, and copper. In form and execution, it pays homage to Frank Lloyd Wright and Greene & Greene, as well as to the Arts and Crafts Movement in general. It is more serious-minded than any other of the Disneyland Paris hotels, more earnest and open, and perhaps fittingly so. Grumbach, who has taught architecture at both Harvard and Princeton, has a passion for the American national parks and their huge lodges.

Stern drew two assignments, the elegant Newport Bay Club and the kitschy Cheyenne

Sequoia Lodge (left and above), like Wilderness Lodge, is rooted in the early twentieth-century architecture of the American West

For his Newport Bay Club, architect Robert A. M. Stern designed an American "grand hotel" with formal grounds and a rather grand entrance.

Hotel. The Newport Bay Club is the largest hotel in the complex and was basically drawn from his designs for the Yacht and Beach Clubs in Orlando. A series of connected pavilions, with the highest at seven stories, it looks across the Lake of America to Graves's Hotel New York. It is more delicately colored than the two Orlando offerings, "in keeping with the northern light of France," says Stern.

Stern's Cheyenne Hotel, regarded by many critics as one of his best designs ever and as the most successful of all the Disneyland Paris hotels, is laid out as if it were a town in the Old West. It draws entirely on pop-culture imagery from Hollywood westerns, which in turn comes from what might now be called "ghost town vernacular," the flimsy wood-frame architecture left behind after gold rushes went bust and mines petered out.

The counterpart of the theatrical Cheyenne is the cerebral Hotel Santa Fe, designed by Antoine Predock. Predock later spoke of the encounter with Disney as "a moment of truth" for him, because, he says, "I think architecture is about other than theming." He chose to look at his hotel as a "site of imagination." His first thought was "happy trails . . . having trails run through to the sky at different trajectories." Then other ideas

about the West came to mind, among them "legend, monuments, infinite space, water, artifacts." He wanted his design to bear more resemblance to the West depicted by the German filmmaker Wim Wenders in the 1984 movie *Paris, Texas* than to the touristy rendition that is Santa Fe today.

Thus, Predock began with what he terms, somewhat elliptically, as "the extraction of the landscape," looking at the subtle earth colors found in the Southwest and the different manifestations of water – from melting snow trickling down mountainsides to torrential rapids. He found his first high-desert icon, a rotting '57 Ford Fairlane, in Albuquerque at the Coronado U-Pull-It, "a supermarket of junked cars." He later added a '34 Ford Phantom and a '46 Chevy truck, all of which he half-buried on the grounds of the hotel to give the impression that they had been abandoned in the desert.

The Hotel Santa Fe is an ode to the West of Route 66, the old east-west highway – immortalized in a famous rock song and a television series of the early 1960s – that runs through New Mexico just south of Santa Fe and the route most tourists bypass these days as they fly into Las Vegas and then take their rental car to the Grand Canyon. In addition

The Newport Bay Club evokes
the natty and aristocratic world of
New England yacht clubs.

For Disneyland Paris, Stern designed the least expensive and most casual of the hotels, the Cheyenne, themed as a backlot for a cowboy movie (above and opposite). This style of architecture is familiar from Frontierland.

In Stern's hands, more emphasis is placed on the relation of the buildings' forms and proportions of the facades and less on the clutter of detail that visitors expect to find in theme parks.

GUEST HOUSE

HOTEL

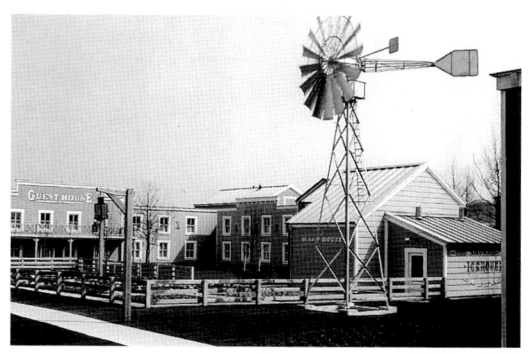

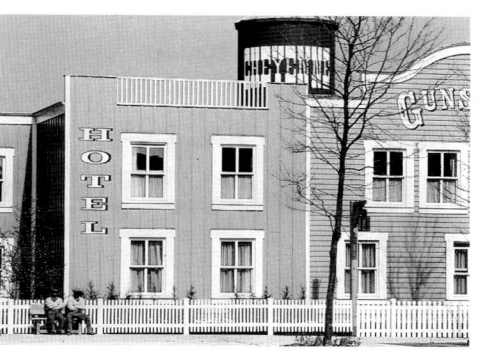

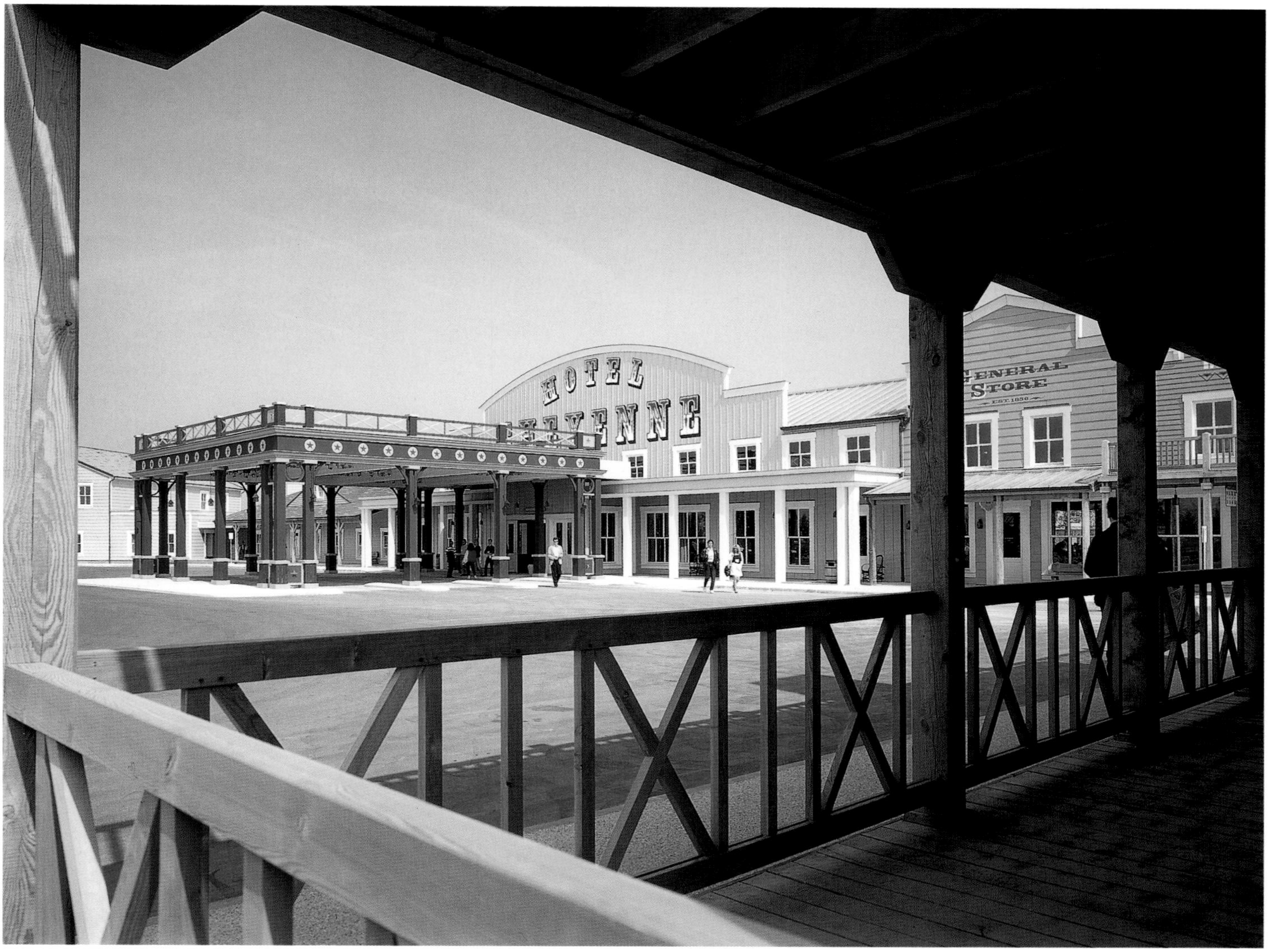
HOTEL
GENERAL STORE

The architect Antoine Predock of New Mexico designed the most cerebral of the Disneyland Paris hotels. The Hotel Santa Fe is abstract and full of metaphors about the endless highways and arid open spaces of the American West.

The Hotel Santa Fe is one of the few architectural projects commissioned by Disney where the facades are almost completely unadorned. They are not, however, exercises in pure form; rather, their "adobe" look is intended to evoke the vernacular architecture of the Pueblo cultures of the Southwest.

Overleaf, the main facade of the Hotel Santa Fe.

Michael Graves was given the task of designing a hotel that evoked New York. To this end, his hotel suggests an urban cityscape as if it were rows of buildings abutting one another. In the courtyard of the hotel is an enormous reflecting pool called the Central Park Fountain (below), with a schematic map of Manhattan on the bottom (right). This becomes an ice-skating rink in the winter.

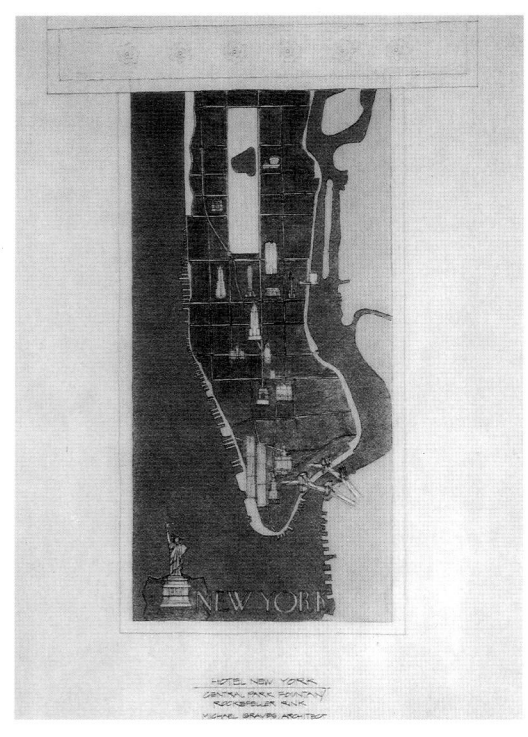

The lobby of the Hotel New York (below) is filled with Big Apple motifs. The pool (bottom) has a more generic "urban cool" feeling.

to the old cars, there are allusions to the great Pueblo Indian ruins of the Southwest, to desert flora, and to Zuni patterns for jewelry. Predock also sought to evoke the feeling of infinite space one experiences while crossing the desert.

To achieve this last effect, Predock wanted one particular icon, a blank drive-in movie screen silhouetted against the sky, "an empty slate and tabula rasa onto which you can inscribe your dreams." Disney wanted an image on the screen. Predock ultimately relented. The drive-in screen bears a huge movie-poster likeness of Clint Eastwood. Says Predock, "If it had to be anybody, Clint's the one."

Graves was given an equally broad assignment, to design a hotel that depicted the iconic American urban experience. Thus came the Hotel New York, with its nods to Manhattan's grand landmarks and numerous design motifs based on familiar New York symbols, especially "big apples," which are ubiquitous. "Bob's [Newport Beach Club] was to be like a hotel," says Graves. "Ours was to be like a city."

The Disneyland Hotel was designed by Disney Imagineers and executed by the firm of Wimberly, Allison, Tong & Goo. Right at the gate of the theme park, it had begun as a ticket-booth design and grown into a full-

The Disneyland Hotel (right and opposite) was conceived by designers from Disney Imagineering to function both as a "castle hotel" and as a gateway to Disneyland Paris (it is the only hotel in the Disney empire that places guests virtually in a theme park). It is a storybook concoction, romantic and pink, that blends in well with Main Street, just on the other side of the building. The renderings of the hotel (below) have a Beaux-Arts flavor.

Frank Gehry designed the shopping and dining concourse for Disneyland Paris. Reluctant to "theme" his architecture, Gehry instead designed an abstract but ebullient Festival Disney. The Be-Bop Diner (opposite below) is a characteristic Gehry building – a podlike shell – inside of which is a restaurant with Googie decor reminiscent of Los Angeles in the 1950s (opposite above).

With its aluminum-clad pylons, vivid neon, and grid of overhead lights, Festival Disney comes alive at night. It connects the Disneyland Hotel and the theme park itself with the other five hotels.

fledged hostelry. "It was conceived as a way to be warm and inviting," says Tony Baxter, who was the park's – and the hotel's – chief designer. "In France," says John Hench, "the light is so diffused that we painted the Disneyland Hotel pink with a red roof, not appliance white like the Grand Floridian, which looks good at nine in the morning when the sun is still a little red. Everyone, even the greatest of the architects, is afraid of pink."

The final piece of high-profile architecture at Disneyland Paris, Festival Disney, fell to Frank Gehry, the celebrated Los Angeles architect, who had never designed for Disney before and who was as dubious about the idea of themed architecture as Predock was. His job was to design the "entertainment center," the shopping "street" that was to link the hotels to the theme park. He chose to do this with an abstracted colonnade with lots of stainless steel to give it glitter: Gehry calls it a "light grid . . . a strip shopping center, in a way." The arcade, says Gehry, "became the same width as the Rue de Rivoli, but it was coincidental."

While the architects were designing their hotels, Baxter was starting to design the theme park. He'd heard about plans for Disneyland Paris early on, and he'd immediately asked for the opportunity to design the park. Baxter had been the creative force behind both Big Thunder Mountain and Splash Mountain, two of Disney's most popular rides. He had gained a reputation for being both thoughtful and completely instinctive about theme park design. This time he wanted "the opportunity to shape some of the things we'd done before in a new way."

At Festival Disney, Gehry makes especially effective use of signage to create a sense of excitement. Here, the vapor trail of a small spaceship becomes a pylon.

Two views toward Main Street
from the Hub in Disneyland
Paris: in the snow (top); and with
the Disneyland Hotel in the background (bottom).

In some ways, the architecture at
Disneyland Paris acknowledges
French culture. The hedge
labyrinth is a traditional feature
of aristocratic estate gardens
in France. For Fantasyland, the
Imagineers designed Alice's
Curious Labyrinth (opposite),
with a confectionary castle for the
Queen of Hearts.

Baxter told his superiors: "We are going
into one of the most culturally developed and
sophisticated cities in the world. I'd like the
challenge of shaping a place against all this art
and architecture, instead of the arid asphalt of
Anaheim or the swampland of Orlando. I'd
like the challenge of amazing people, the challenge of playing against the norm." Later, he'd
say that he also wanted to buck the tendency,
the temptation, to say "We've got a formula.
It's a winner. Let's run with it." The struggle to
design a castle appropriate to a land that had
its own historical castles has already been told
in an earlier chapter.

There were plenty of issues to deal with,
starting with the weather, which proffered,
on the average, 156 gray days a year. ("We just
added coat rooms and built more enclosed
restaurants and arcades.") More daunting
were the countless cultural questions of how
to communicate with many different groups
of Europeans.

To span the culture gap, the attractions
needed to be much more visual. The Haunted
Mansion became a decayed gold rush ghost
house. Pirates of the Caribbean was designed
as a Spanish fort, with pirates and skull and
crossbones out front. And, says Baxter, "we
had the sense of wanting more depth to family experiences. Clearly there needed to be
more integrity and more of a sense of purpose . . . in the objects and the architecture."

For Main Street, the first concept was to
pull it forward into the 1920s, the era in which
the United States and its culture first began
to interest Europeans, with jazz and movies
and even – to a certain extent – gangsters and
speakeasies. Eventually, Main Street remained
Victorian, but the activities it houses are
more modern. "I think we could have been a
bit more bold," says Baxter. "Victorian was
really a European phenomenon that was interpreted in America with lesser materials. Our
challenge was to put an edge on it in terms of
storytelling."

Discoveryland – the Disneyland Paris
version of Tomorrowland – was a major shift,
an ode to the tomorrow of the people who
really invented the future, from Leonardo da
Vinci to Jules Verne, a tomorrow that crosses
cultures and decades far more easily.

By contrast, Frontierland was the simplest
to design. "The first thing you see when you
land in Paris is the Marlboro Man galloping
across Monument Valley," says Baxter. His
Frontierland celebrated the West of the movies,
of the Marlboro Man, of the Mustang commercial. Here is the "rip-roaring and ener-
getic West," where "everything . . . immediately
draws a cliché image. With all the cactus, it's

Miniature architecture has a long pedigree at Disney. When Disneyland opened in 1955, one of the attractions was the Casey Jr. Circus Train, which traveled through the miniature landscape of Storybook Land. At Disneyland Paris, Storybook Land contains a replica of the Beast's castle from the 1991 animated movie *Beauty and the Beast*.

a very effective illusion," says Baxter. "I've stood there and been amazed and said, 'I can't believe I'm twenty minutes from downtown Paris.'"

The opening of Disneyland Paris in the spring of 1992 was at once typically Disney and typically French: Disney stocked the place with stars. All the architects were on hand, posing for photos, joshing with one another. Striking French farmers blocked the entrance to Disneyland Paris just after it opened. In the press, praise for the operation was sparse.

French President François Mitterrand said it wasn't his "cup of tea." Stephen Bayley wrote about it this way in the *International Herald Tribune*: "Twenty miles east of Paris may seem an odd place to start brooding on American national characteristics, but it is here that EuroDisney has landed and the Old World is presented with all the confident, big ticket flimflam of painstaking fakery that this bizarre campaign of reverse-engineered cultural imperialism represents. I like to think that by the turn of the century EuroDisney will have become a deserted city, similar to Angkor Wat or Arc-et-Senans: a haunting reminder of a knowing, but innocent, past age."

Disneyland Paris cost $4 billion to build. It was not an immediate financial success — or even particularly popular. But despite a slow start and much maligning on the part of the French, the Disney formula had its appeal. Even Mitterrand finally and grudgingly admitted to liking it a bit. It is now the most-visited tourist attraction in Europe.

Adventureland at Disneyland Paris has an Arabian motif, reminiscent of the animated film *Aladdin* (1992), which was in production while the park was being built, but also in deference to European conceptions of the exotic.

chapter ten | *The Dream Goes On*

Any building, no matter how minor or mundane, has the potential to transport us to another realm. Architecture can inspire, uplift, entertain, educate, enlighten. Walt Disney instinctively understood that, first in his animated films and then in the buildings at Disneyland, which were little more than what Robert Venturi and Denise Scott-Brown later called "decorated sheds." That isn't to minimize architecture's role as a creator and shaper of space. The world, despite Shakespeare's assertion to the contrary, is not merely a stage. But if there's a lesson from the last half-century of Disney architecture, it is this: Buildings don't have to be boring.

The architecture produced by The Walt Disney Company has progressed far since the opening of Disneyland in July 1955. Now, the buildings of Disney's ever-growing domain are often subtle and highly complex, communicating on many levels, from the overt to the subliminal. The essence of Disney's architecture is that it speaks to a range of emotions and stored images, culling images from memory and appropriating them, even abstracting them.

The Reedy Creek Improvement District Emergency Services Center (1994) by Robert Venturi and Denise Scott-Brown in Walt Disney World looks exactly like what it is, a firehouse, one a child might have drawn. It is clad in porcelain panels that appear to be over-sized red bricks. A large and leaky fire hydrant sits out front; it's actually a fountain. One

wall is dappled with dark brown spots, enough to cover far more than 101 Dalmatians. But there is much more here than meets the eye.

Venturi has always been known for his intelligent and adroit transformations of the classical and the vernacular. He has also long been interested in the idea of the decorated shed and in buildings that are billboards. His firehouse is a true signpost on the road. Its equipment shed is just that, a shed, with a batten-seam aluminum roof and huge glass overhead doors, punctuated by yellow bollards with pink trim. The building's entrance is an arcade marked by blue and pink painted steel columns.

This is the first of Venturi's designs for Disney to be built, and his approach differs from that used in the theme parks. It takes traditional images and exaggerates them, quite wittily, but in a fashion that is clearly architectural, not theatrical. Venturi wanted the design to impart the idea of a turn-of-the-century firehouse in a small town; to appeal to a child's idea of architecture, not a child's mental universe of imaginary characters. In Walt Disney World, where architectural scale is almost always manipulated and perspective forced, this building is no exception. Some of the Dalmatian spots are actually as big as a real dog. There's no real symmetry, though it might seem so on casual inspection: actually, everything is slightly off-kilter, so that the left and right sides of the shed don't match.

A view up into one of the vaults of Robert A. M. Stern's Feature Animation Building. The night sky effect, produced by metal studs in the black-painted vault, was a serendipitous outcome of the construction process.

Robert Venturi and Denise Scott-Brown designed the Reedy Creek Improvement District Emergency Services Center to look like a child's idea of a fire station, complete with a Dalmatian-spotted wall. Although much of it looks as if it were made of oversized bricks, the "bricks" are actually porcelain panels.

For Venturi, the firehouse was an opportunity to express a number of ideas in a small building. Eisner puts it into a literary context, saying: "The firehouse is like a poem. It's far more difficult to write a poem than to write an epic novel."

Here, as elsewhere in Disney's realm, the architecture embraces both order and illusion, which is an unlikely pairing. The firehouse is appropriately whimsical, but as Venturi points out, it had to be a place that worked well because it deals with life and death emergencies; the firehouse also had to be an intelligent, urbane civic landmark. And, he adds, "we weren't afraid to employ convention and symbolism" to achieve those goals.

For a complex of office buildings in Walt Disney World, Disney turned to the Italian architect Aldo Rossi – considered by many to be among the very finest architects of the late twentieth century. Eventually, Disney's planned new town of Celebration will grow up around the Rossi buildings, providing them with a more substantial context.

The first two buildings, completed in the spring of 1995, sit by U.S. Route 192, the franchise-ridden road that approaches Walt Disney World from the south. The buildings are made of inexpensive materials, and yet they are detailed, especially on the front facade of the taller one, which is the headquarters of the Disney Development Company, as if they were designed for a street as affluent as the Via Tornabuoni in Florence.

Aldo Rossi's office complex (above) for Celebration Place is the first of a group of office and commercial buildings planned for the site. In addition to two office buildings, Rossi's complex includes an obelisk, which is a simple marker, and a small folly, left, with provides views of the ensemble through its openings (top).

The main structure is typical of a suburban office building, with work spaces flanking a central corridor, but it is nonetheless Disneyesque, with many of the attributes of buildings on, say, the Magic Kingdom Main Street. Forced perspective makes it seem taller and the public spaces are elegant while the workplaces are plain and unadorned.

There's a reason for this. Eisner, who in his youth in New York had worked as a theater usher on Broadway, recalls his initial shock at the dreariness of backstage spaces, but seeing such works as *Carousel* and *Oklahoma* emerge from the wings was a formative experience: "I have the theory that the beauty grows out of the cesspool of backstage."

When Eisner learned that the Animation Division – long housed just minutes from Burbank in warehouses in Glendale – was going to be moved to leased space in a high-rise, he resisted. "I don't think anybody in the creative world should be in a high-rise," he said. "Waiting for an elevator just saps all that creativity." Instead, he commissioned Robert A. M. Stern to design a building for the animators. During a visit to Stern's New York offices, Eisner looked around and said, "I want it just like this, a cluttered mess."

Later, Eisner elaborated. He told Stern: "I want Ping-Pong tables. I want people playing Frisbee in the halls. I don't want a showplace. I want a workplace."

That imperative propelled Stern in the design of his Feature Animation Building, finished in early 1995. It's a sophisticated work of architecture, and yet in many ways it resembles a converted warehouse, which was really Eisner's goal for his animators. Eisner

wanted "cheap crazy space," says Stern, "like loft space." Stern, of course, had a tough act to follow: the superb animators' building designed by Kem Weber in 1939 for Disney's Burbank studio complex.

Stern chose to be deferential to it, using the same streamlined architectural vocabulary (and a bit of brick detailing), but Weber's building was just a starting point to expound a bit on architecture in Los Angeles. Stern wanted what he calls the building's "rotunda," actually its lobby, a tall oval space with one curved tilted glass wall, to evoke the silly geometry of Googie architecture – the funky fast-food joints and doughnut shops of the 1940s, 1950s, and 1960s that can still be found throughout Los Angeles. The main facade recalls Walter Wurdeman's and Welton Becket's now-demolished Streamline Moderne Pan Pacific Auditorium, built for the 1935 National Housing Exposition on Los Angeles's Miracle Mile, and, more imaginatively, the streamlined buildings occasionally found in animated shorts of the 1930s, a kind of "maushaus" (as opposed to Bauhaus) moderne. "It's not literal," says Stern. "It's my take on it."

The building has an unusual profile – its entrance is tucked under a conical spire, a reference to the hat worn by Mickey Mouse in "The Sorcerer's Apprentice" section of *Fantasia*, an image Stern first turned into architecture at the temporary information kiosk he designed for Disneyland Paris. Running along the south side of the building is a narrow gallery with a high roof that slopes upward toward the main facade, ending in a form like the prow of a ship that Stern calls "the Mohawk," because it does

Its designers termed this top hat a "Mohawk" in reference to the punk hairstyle, but it also alludes to the Mad Hatter in Disney's animated version of *Alice in Wonderland.*

indeed look like the punk haircut. The main
work space is housed in three vast connected
barrel vaults, looking not unlike warehouses,
that form the main bulk of the building.

In much the same way he used the word
"CASTING" on his first Disney building, the
Casting Center in Walt Disney World in
Orlando, Stern uses the word "ANIMATION"
in giant stainless steel letters to identify this
one from the Ventura Freeway that passes
by it to the south.

Inside, it is not really a "cluttered mess"
but well-ordered creative chaos. Under the
vaults, which are painted black with stainless
steel studs that twinkle like stars, and the
girders and air shafts, which have been left
exposed and painted white so that their industrial forms stand out against the dark ceiling,
is generous work space that has been designed
to cater to the special needs of animators.
The funky gallery that runs the length of the
Mohawk does, indeed, permit Frisbee-play-
ing and Ping-Pong.

The entrance rotunda of the
Feature Animation Building
(above) and an example of
the building's interior signage
(left), based on Kem Weber's
designs for the original Disney
Animation Building.

Opposite, Roy Disney's desk in
the top of the building's cone: an
office for a sorcerer.

In Mickey's Toontown, Disney-land's ode to cartoon architecture done up mostly in the Craftsman or Bungalow Style, there are few straight lines. Buildings bulge, tilt, squat, slant, and slop.

In 1988, for the movie *Who Framed Roger Rabbit,* Disney's animators invented "Toon-town," a real place that its cartoon characters called home. Mickey's Toontown, Disney-land's amusement area for younger children, which opened in 1993, layers parody upon parody, joke upon joke. Mickey's Toontown is where Mickey and Minnie are supposed to live (chastely side by side in his-and-her bungalows) along with Goofy, Donald, and, of course, Roger Rabbit. Like Toontown in the movie, Mickey's Toontown as built in Disneyland is painted with a broad brush, with exaggerated details and hardly a straight line to be found. Everything tilts. The build-ings bulge, squeak, slope, and rattle.

Even the "frame" is adapted from car-toons: a cardboard-flat backdrop – like the painted backgrounds Disney pioneered in animation – placed behind and above the houses depicts a landscape of hills straddled by the word "TOONTOWN." The sign play-fully mimicks the famous "HOLLYWOOD" sign in the Hollywood hills – originally erected in 1923 as advertising for a residential development called, ironically, Hollywood-land – that has become an icon for star-struck dreamers.

Meanwhile, in Walt Disney World, Arquitec-tonica offers up its own array of visual puns at All-Star Resorts (1994), a comic book in three dimensions that is to architecture what Pop Art is to art.

Essentially, All-Star is a gigantic sprawling motel with a total of 3,840 rooms, covering 173 acres (that's bigger than Disneyland in Anaheim, including all the parking lots), but

In Toontown, the Imagineers seized every opportunity to crack a good joke. Thus, the Planning Commission didn't leave quite enough room for its sign (upper left). Some of the sight gags in Mickey's Toontown are purely for design cognoscenti, like the parody of a copper Arts and Crafts Style lamp with traces of oxidation (above) in the front hall of Mickey's bungalow (left). The panorama (overleaf) shows part of the wacky town.

the motel units are transformed by American icons of a host of popular preoccupations – from football to rock and roll.

For this project, the given was the use of prefabricated structures for the units. Chief Disney architect Wing Chao asked Laurinda Spear and Bernardo Fort-Brescia, the husband-and-wife partners in the Miami firm, to come up with a theme. Disney had been toying with the idea of using A1A, the old national highway that runs along the Atlantic coast from Maine to Key West, as a theme, incorporating such typically Floridian architectural styles as Mediterranean and Art Deco. Fort-Brescia said in response, "If I want to see that, I'll just drive down the road."

The brainstorming began. Arquitectonica proposed a different approach. "What if we remove ourselves from architectural themes and go more into the theme as an idea, not as a place or a time? Look at popular entertainment, at sports, music, and movies. What if we make those the themes and turn them into popular architecture? After all, it's a very American phenomenon. So we presented it as Pop Art, and it worked," says Fort-Brescia.

At All-Star Sports, there's a Surf's Up section where gigantic surfboards appear to hold up balconies and shark fins pop out of the roof. Another section, called Hoops, offers a bright yellow basketball hoop too high even for Shaquille O'Neal to jam; the staircases are giant megaphones.

At All-Star Music, the visual puns are even more elaborate. There's a swimming pool shaped like a guitar and a second pool that looks like a piano, complete with black-and-white tile steps styled to look like a key-

board. The Broadway section is paved to look like a city street, complete with a yellow Checker cab sitting at the curb. The Rock 'n' Roll section has giant jukeboxes and guitars; Country Music's icons are banjos and boots.

The architecture is all embellishment. The motel units that sprawl for so many acres are identical, literally cast from the same molds; Arquitectonica had to "make" the architecture with the railings, the parapets, the stairwells, and the vertical supports for balconies. Thus surfboards or guitars turn into columns, megaphones or jukeboxes house stairwells. "It comes from the same American culture as roadside architecture," says Fort-Brescia. "You drive down roads in the West and there's a big jack rabbit, a big hat, a big cup of coffee."

All-Star was originally designed for Disneyland Paris as a take on America's kitschy motel architecture. Arquitectonica had begun that project as a coast-to-coast trip from Florida, represented by – say – alligators and palm trees, to the Far West of tepees and cowboy boots. "In that case," says Fort-Brescia, "it was related to the 1950s, but it was there that we started evolving the notion, asking the question of why a theme would have to refer to an actual place. We began to explore the idea of themed architecture without place references but idea references instead."

John Hench points out that "cartoons were so effective because they were so bare bones, just forms, managed images." In many ways, All-Star is similar: it too projects managed images in the same pared down way; the unexpected simplicity of these ideas and images make All-Star so artful – and so much fun.

All-Star Sports: Surf's Up (above),
Hoops (right), and Touchdown
(overleaf).

The later generation of Disney buildings (the buildings from an array of internationally renowned designers all with distinct and memorable buildings to their credit – among them, Isozaki, Rossi, Venturi, and Arquitectonica) do reach a new level of complexity, matched by higher ambitions within the company. In the early 1970s, Wing Chao wrote his graduate thesis at Harvard about the idea of a "free-time city." Now he's overseeing the design of the kind of resort town he started thinking about then, which led him to come to work for Disney in the first place. Now his early thinking has come full circle.

There was a time when skeptical observers would dismiss Disney's architecture as being "Mickey Mouse" because they found it silly or sentimental, but it would be difficult to do so today. And on the books – and even coming out of the ground – are varied projects from a wide range of architects.

The Disney Institute in Walt Disney World was designed by the Chicago-based classicist Thomas Beeby, a former dean of the Yale School of Architecture, to look like a collection of "straw hat" summer theater buildings, as if it were an aggregation of barns and farmhouses. Beeby took that peculiarly American rural imagery and recast it in a sequence of strikingly simple pastel buildings that will house classrooms, studios, workshops, and fitness and spa facilities.

The Boardwalk, Stern's new entertainment center and hotel at Walt Disney World, is an ode to the exuberant architecture of the New Jersey shore. Appropriately enough, it sits across the lake from the Yacht and Beach Clubs, which evoke other East Coast seaside resorts. Graham Gund, a Cambridge, Massachusetts,

All-Star Music: Broadway (opposite), Rock (left), and Country Fair (below).

Frank Gehry's Team Disney Building for Disneyland is as large as
Isozaki's Team Disney Building at
Walt Disney World. The long
stucco structure has awnings of
galvanized sheet-metal and corrugated steel (right). The atrium
inside the main entrance (above)
echoes the dramatic curved forms
of the main facade.

Disney ICE, Frank Gehry's downtown Anaheim skating rink (above), is a recreational center for the community as well as a practice rink for Disney's professional hockey team, the Mighty Ducks. The building has an aluminum skin and the roof is supported by laminated wood beams (left).

Before deciding to build two cruise ships, Disney's naval architecture was limited to the various steamboats and submarines designed by the Imagineers for the theme parks. The new ships will be themed to the great transatlantic liners of the 1930s and 1940s. The Disney cruise ships (above) were designed by Njal R. Eide, Robert Tillberg, Petter Yran, and Bjorn Storbraaten, with consultation by Frogdesign. Right, a concept drawing of one of the ships' interior spaces.

architect, has designed the Disney's Coronado Springs Resort at Walt Disney World as a tribute to the storybook-romantic Spanish Colonial designs of turn-of-the-century California.

Gund also designed Disney's Vero Beach Resort in Florida, and Jaquelin Robertson of New York is designing Disney's Hilton Head Island Resort in South Carolina. These resort complexes are outposts of a new, much more sprawling architectural kingdom for Disney, one that reaches well beyond the precincts of Burbank, Orlando, Paris, and Tokyo. Frank Gehry has completed both Disney ICE, a skating rink, and a Team Disney office building – the third for the company – in Anaheim. These engagingly abstract buildings display his trademark mastery of both form and materials. In Los Angeles, Disney has also renovated two grand old "picture palaces." One of them, the El Capitan on Hollywood Boulevard, has garnered a number of accolades, including an honor award from the National Trust for Historic Preservation. Disney is also currently renovating a Broadway theater in New York. The Miami firm of Arquitectonica has designed a cruise ship terminal for Port Canaveral to house specially commissioned cruise ships to be launched by Disney Cruise Line.

The most ambitious project, however, is one that takes Disney out of the realm of entertainment and leisure and into everyday life. Celebration, located at Walt Disney World, is to be Disney's dream town, and for this company, it breaks new ground. Celebration is to be a town that provides its residents with the opportunity to integrate work, learning, living, and play. A model school designed by William Rawn of Boston with a curriculum and program being developed at Stetson University is to test a progressive curriculum and teaching methods for Osceola County, the political jurisdiction in which Celebration falls. Without getting in a car, Celebration residents will be able to shop at the Town Center and go to work at Rossi's office complex at Celebration Place or at Celebration Health, a health care campus being designed by Stern and developed by Florida Hospital.

"I don't believe there's a challenge anywhere in the world that's more important to people everywhere than finding solutions to the problems of our communities," Walt Disney once said. In the 1960s, the kind of utopian community Disney envisioned – the inspiration came when he was awakened early one morning by the rumbling and clatter of a garbage truck – was a hermetic town under a bubble of glass and removed from real-world problems.

Three decades later, The Walt Disney Company is rising to the challenge. The town that came to be is much different from what the founder envisioned. Cars speed by Celebration; it is within sight of the cacaphonic and cluttered U.S. Route 192 and bounded on one side by the new Orlando "greenway," which is, in fact, a high-speed expressway.

Celebration has been planned as a collaborative venture of Stern and Robertson. For prototypes, they drew on towns they admired, including East Hampton, New York, and Charleston, South Carolina, to create a plan that relies on well-shaped vistas and a sequence of public squares.

Celebration's Town Center will include buildings by some of the twentieth century's most important architects, among them Philip Johnson (more than a decade after he left Michael Eisner and Michael Graves alone together at the ballet), who is designing the Town Hall, a red brick building enveloped by white columns. The "Preview Center" – an information kiosk – was designed by the late Charles Moore, which is fitting, since it was Moore who first understood and expounded on the importance of the public space at Disneyland in his famous essay "You Have to Pay for the Public Life." Venturi, Scott-Brown & Associates designed the bank, Graves the post office, Cesar Pelli the cinema, and Gund the inn. Most of the other "downtown" buildings are being designed by Stern or Robertson.

The houses of Celebration draw on the varied traditions of Southern small-town architecture. The residential neighborhoods will be unlike other suburban subdivisions in that only the elements of the architecture are prescribed in a "Pattern Book," created by Ray Gindroz of the Pittsburgh firm of Urban Design Associates. This Pattern Book, typical of architectural handbooks common in the early twentieth century, lays out the essence of Celebration's housing, which – in turn – will be designed by other architects.

Disney Design and Development president Peter Rummell has high hopes: "I think Celebration is going to change the perception of Walt Disney World. It's going to be a place that deals with real-world issues and real-world problems but deals with them in a relevant way. I think if Celebration just becomes known as a place where a lot of great architects did buildings, we've failed."

Disney has joined the movement (spearheaded by such thinkers as Andres Duany and Elizabeth Plater-Zyberk of Miami, who worked on early versions of Celebration's master plan) that is trying to bring common sense and humanity back to the design of towns and cities. And though Disneyland did just what the new town planners hope to achieve – getting families out of their cars and onto safe sidewalks where they can rediscover such old-fashioned virtues as neighborliness and sociability – it did so in an amusement park – a destination, not a way of life. Back in 1955, those old-fashioned virtues were scoffed at as an exercise in nostalgia. Today, we know that a primary goal of architecture is to provide a common ground for people to gather. And though our world is much too complex to allow us to step back into the fairy-tale that Disneyland has offered for almost a half century, Celebration takes a step toward letting us live happily ever after. It is a bold venture for the 1990s and the next millennium, as powerful a statement as Main Street, Disneyland-style, was in 1955.

And the dream goes on. On the Disney drawing boards or under construction are projects both huge and tiny. At Walt Disney World, Animal Kingdom – a vast and ecologically respectful zoological theme park – is under way; in Tokyo, work has begun on a second theme park "gate," the eclectic and exotic Tokyo Disney Sea. (Even the new gas stations in Walt Disney World will bear the fanciful imprint of such architects as Venturi and Scott-Brown and Hardy Holzman Pfeiffer, looking almost as if they'd sprung into being from an animator's drawing board.) No pro-

ject is too large or too small to get a Disney-styled sprinkling of pixie dust. When imagination reigns, architecture can be magical. Walt Disney knew this from the start; he once said that his work would never be finished as long as there was imagination, and still today, in the company he founded, creativity and fantasy and adventure abound.

"We're not doing this for ego's sake," says Michael Eisner. "We're not just building monuments. We want our buildings to be pleasing to the public, and yet I have no qualms about being completely out there trying something new."

acknowledgments

Many, many people contributed to this project, and I am grateful to them all. With apologies to those I have unintentionally overlooked, I'd especially like to thank Pam Brandon, Bob Mervine, Robbie Pallard, Greg Albrecht, Chris Crary, Charlie Ridgeway, Susan Mitchell Deets, Linda Cummings, Tim Johnson, Eric Jacobson, and Steve Brandon in Orlando; Charlotte Kirk Reynolds, Patty Dorsey, Barbara Lindstrom Rasulo, Michael Eisner, Peter Rummell, Betsy Richman, John Dreyer, John Hench, Bill Evans, Marty Sklar, Tony Baxter, Dave Smith, Andre Tirman, Linda Morganlander, John McClintock, Lou-Anne Capiello, Frank Gehry, Hunter Heller, Heidi Miller, Virginia King, Jonathan Reynolds, and Greg Redlitz in Los Angeles; Bill Farkas, Jean Perwin, Susan and John Rothchild, Cathy Leff, Margot Ammidown, Catharine Lynn, Vincent Scully, Bernardo Fort-Brescia, Laurinda Spear, Jorge Hernandez, Joanna Lombard, Elizabeth Plater-Zyberk, Andres Duany, Beverly Powell, Dan Paul, and Steven Brooke in Miami; Karen Stein, Suzanne Stephens, Danielle Weil Padwa, Eden Ross Lipson and family, Ellen Chesler and family, Robert A. M. Stern, Georgeann Mavrovitis, David Gauld, David Morton, Charles Gwathmey, Robert Siegel, Michael Lynton, Peter Aaron, and Erica Stoller; Michael Graves in Princeton; Robert Venturi in Philadelphia; Peter Dominick in Denver; Antoine Predock in Albuquerque; Aldo Rossi in Milan; Antoine Grumbach in Paris; Arata Isozaki in Tokyo.

Wing Chao, everywhere.

And my tireless assistants and fearless attraction evaluators: Adam Farkas, Eddie Reynolds, Zach and Sam Redlitz, Katie Brandon, Robin-John Gibb, and Omar Wahab.

selected bibliography

In addition to the following sources, three magazines – *Architectural Record, Architecture* (and its predecessor *The AIA Journal*), and *Progressive Architecture* – are notable for their detailed coverage and analysis of the Walt Disney Company's architecture over the years.

Adams, Judith A. *The American Amusement Park Industry*. Boston: Twayne Publishers, 1991.

Allen, Gerald. *Charles Moore*. New York: Whitney Library of Design, 1980.

Association of Collegiate Schools of Architecture. *Architectural Education: Where We Are*. Washington, D.C.: ASCA Press, 1991.

Bright, Randy. *Disneyland Inside Story*. New York: Harry N. Abrams, 1987.

Brown, Patricia Leigh. "Disney Deco." *New York Times Magazine*, 8 April 1990.

Capitman, Barbara, with Michael D. Kinerk and Dennis W. Wilhelm. *Rediscovering Art Deco USA*. New York: Viking, 1994.

Dunlop, Beth. *Arquitectonica*. Washington, D.C.: AIA Press, 1991.

Feifer, Maxine. *Tourism in History: From Imperial Rome to the Present*. New York: Stein & Day, 1985.

Finch, Christopher. *The Art of Walt Disney*. Rev. ed. New York: Harry N. Abrams, 1995.

Findlay, John M. *Magic Lands: Western Cityscapes and American Culture after 1940*. Berkeley: University of California Press, 1992.

Fjellman, Stephen M. *Vinyl Leaves: Walt Disney World and America*. Boulder: Westview Press, 1992.

Francaviglia, Richard V. "Main Street U.S.A.: A Comparison/Contrast of Streetscapes in Walt Disney World." *Journal of Popular Culture* 15 (Summer 1981): 141–56.

——. "Main Street USA: The Creation of a Popular Image." *Landscape*, Spring-Summer 1977, 18–22.

Gebhard, David, and Harriette von Breton. *Kem Weber: The Moderne in Southern California 1920–1941*. Santa Barbara: University of California Press, 1969.

Gehry, Frank. *The Architecture of Frank Gehry*. New York: Rizzoli, 1986.

——. *Frank Gehry: Buildings and Projects*. New York: Rizzoli, 1985.

Goldberger, Paul. "Mickey Mouse Teaches the Architects." *New York Times Magazine*, 22 October 1972.

Graves, Michael. *Michael Graves.* New York: St. Martin's Press, 1994.

———. *Michael Graves: Buildings and Projects 1966–1981.* New York: Rizzoli, 1982.

———. *Michael Graves: Buildings and Projects 1982–1989.* New York: Rizzoli, 1990.

Grover, Ron. *The Disney Touch.* Homewood, Ill.: Business One Irwin, 1991.

Gwathmey, Charles, and Robert Siegel. *Charles Gwathmey and Robert Siegel: Buildings and Projects, 1964–1984.* New York: Harper & Row, 1984.

———. *Gwathmey Siegel: Buildings and Projects, 1982–1992.* New York: Rizzoli, 1993.

Haas, Charlie. "Disneyland Is Good for You." *New West III,* 4 December 1978, 13–19.

Haden-Guest, Anthony. "The Paradise Program: Travels through Muzak, Hilton, Coca-Cola, Texaco, Walt Disney and Other World Empires." New York: William Morrow, 1973.

———. "The Pixie Dust Papers." In *Down the Programmed Rabbit Hole.* London: Hart-Davis MacGibbon, 1972.

Harrington, Michael. "To the Disney Station." *Harper's,* January 1969.

Heimann, Jim, and Rip Georges. *California Crazy: Roadside Vernacular Architecture.* San Francisco: Chronicle Books, 1980.

Heller, Alfred. "Stalled in Epcot's World of Motion." *World's Fair* 3 (Winter 1983): 13–16.

Kammen, Michael. *Mystic Chords of Memory.* New York: Random House, 1993.

Leibs, Chester H. *Main Street to Miracle Mile.* Boston: Little, Brown & Co., 1985.

Marling, Karal Ann. "Disneyland 1955." *American Art,* Winter/Spring 1991, 167–207.

McGinty, Brian. *The Palace Inns: A Connoisseur's Guide to American Hotels.* Harrisburg, Pa.: Stackpole/Cameron House, 1978.

Mechling, Elizabeth Walker, and Jay Mechling. "The Sale of Two Cities: A Semiotic Comparison of Disneyland with Marriott's Great America." *Journal of Popular Culture* 15 (Summer 1987): 166–79.

Moore, Alexander. "Walt Disney World: Bonded Ritual Space and the Playful Pilgrimage Center." *Anthropological Quarterly* 35 (October 1980): 207–18.

Moore, Charles. *Charles Moore: Buildings and Projects 1949–1986.* New York: Rizzoli, 1986.

Moore, Charles, and Gerald Allen. *Dimensions: Space, Shape & Scale in Architecture.* New York: Architectural Record Books, 1976.

Moos, Stanislaus von. *Venturi, Rauch & Scott-Brown: Buildings and Projects.* New York: Rizzoli, 1987.

Morrison, Elting E. "What Went Wrong with Disney's World's Fair?" *American Heritage* 35 (December 1983): 71–78.

Mosley, Leonard. *Disney's World.* Latham, Md.: Scarborough House, 1985.

Ojeda, Oscar Riera. *Moore, Ruble, Yudell, Architects and Planners.* Washington, D.C.: AIA Press, 1994.

Postman, Neil. *Amusing Ourselves to Death: Public Discourse in the Age of Show Business.* New York: Viking Penguin, 1985.

Predock, Antoine. *Antoine Predock, Architect.* New York: Rizzoli, 1994.

Rinne, Katharine W. "You Have to Pay for the Public Life." *LA Architect,* November 1988.

Rossi, Aldo. *Aldo Rossi: Buildings and Projects.* New York: Rizzoli, 1985.

——. *A Scientific Autobiography.* Cambridge: MIT Press, 1981.

Schickel, Richard. *The Disney Version: The Life, Times, Art and Commerce of Walt Disney.* New York: Simon & Schuster, 1968.

Scully, Vincent J. *American Architecture and Urbanism.* New York: Henry Holt, 1988.

——. *Architecture: The Natural and the Man-Made.* New York: St. Martin's Press, 1991.

——. *The Shingle Style and the Stick Style: Architectural Theory and Design from*

Richardson to the Origins of Wright. New Haven: Yale University Press, 1971.

——. *The Shingle Style Today: Or, The Historian's Revenge.* New York: George Braziller, 1974.

Sorkin, Michael, ed. *Variations on a Theme Park.* New York: Hill & Wang, 1992.

Stein, Karen, and Morris Adjmi. *Aldo Rossi: Architecture, 1981–1991.* New York: Princeton Architectural Press, 1991.

Stephens, Suzanne. "The Architectural Mouseketeers." *Avenue,* December 1989, 106–15.

Stern, Robert A. M. *The American Houses of Robert A. M. Stern.* New York: Rizzoli, 1991.

——. *Buildings and Projects, 1981–1985.* Edited by Luis F. Rueda. New York: Rizzoli, 1986.

——. *Buildings and Projects, 1987–1992.* Edited by Elizabeth Kraft. New York: Rizzoli, 1992.

——. *New Directions in American Architecture.* New York: George Braziller, 1977.

——. *Robert A. M. Stern, 1965–1980: Toward a Modern Architecture after Modernism.* Edited by Peter Arnell and Ted Bickford. New York: Rizzoli, 1981.

Stewart, David B. *Arata Isozaki: Architecture, 1960–1990.* New York: Rizzoli, 1991.

Taylor, John. *Storming the Magic Kingdom.* New York: Ballantine Books, 1987.

Thomas, Bob. *Walt Disney: An American Original.* New York: Simon & Schuster, 1976.

Thompson, William Irwin. *Imaginary Landscapes: Making Worlds of Myth and Science.* New York: St. Martin's Press, 1989.

Trillin, Calvin. "U.S. Journal: Disney World, Fla." *New Yorker,* 6 November 1971.

Venturi, Robert. *Complexity and Contradiction in Architecture.* New York: Museum of Modern Art, 1968.

Venturi, Robert, with Denise Scott-Brown and Steve Izenour. *Learning from Las Vegas: The Forgotten Symbolism of Architectural Form.* Cambridge: MIT Press, 1977.

Walker, Derek, ed. *Animated Architecture.* New York: St. Martin's Press, 1982.

Zinsser, William. *American Places.* New York: HarperCollins, 1992.

Zukin, Sharon. *Landscapes of Power: Detroit to Disney World.* Berkeley: University of California Press, 1991.

index

Photograph credits

All of the photographs in this book were provided by the Disney Company with the exception of the following:

©Peter Aaron/ESTO: pp. 76, 80–81, 82 (bottom left and right), 83 (all), 92–93, 94 (both), 95 (both), 96, 109 (both), 110, 111 (both), 141 (both), 146, 149 (both), 150, 151 (all), 152, 153 (bottom), 154 (both), 155 (all), 156–157, 159 (all), 161, 162 (both), 163 (both), 164 (both), 165, 170, 172 (both), 173 (both), 174–175, 177, 178, 179 (both).
©Steven Brooke: pp. 68–69, 72, 73 (all).
Dan Forer, Courtesy Disney Development Company: pp. 113, 114 (both), 115, 185 (both), 186–187, 188, 189 (both).
©Scott Frances/ESTO: p. 153 (top left and right).
©Jeff Goldberg/ESTO: pp. 85, 86 (both), 87, 88 (both), 89.
©Lori and Fred Stocker: pp. 190 (both), 191 (both).
©Tim Street-Porter: p. 181 (top left and right).

contents

fundamentals of I
technical measurement

the process of measurement: 1
an overview — 3

the analog measurand: 2
its time-dependent
characteristics — 23

signal **5**
conditioning   **123**

application of **6**
digital techniques
to mechanical
measurements   **173**

applied mechanical **II** measurements

determination of **10** count, events per unit time, and time interval   **295**

displacement and **11** dimensional measurement   **313**

strain and **12**
stress: measurement
and analysis   **353**

measurement **13**
of force and torque   **413**

measurement **14**
of pressure   **445**

measurement **15**
of fluid flow   **483**

fundamentals
of mechanical
measurements

the process
of measurement:
an overview

1.1 INTRODUCTION

It has been said, "Whatever exists, exists in some amount." The determination of the amount is what measurement is all about. If those things that exist are related to the practice of mechanical engineering, then the determination of their amounts constitutes the subject of *mechanical measurements.**

The process or the act of measurement consists of obtaining a quantitative comparison between a predefined *standard* and a *measurand*. The word *measurand* is used to designate the particular physical parameter being observed and quantified, that is, the input quantity to the measuring process. The act of measurement produces a *result* (see Fig. 1.1).

The standard of comparison must be of the same character as the measurand and usually, but not always, is prescribed and defined by a legal or recognized agency or organization—e.g., the National Bureau of Standards (NBS), the International Organization for Standardization (ISO), or the American National Standards Institute (ANSI). (See Chapter 7.)

Such quantities as temperature, strain, the parameters associated with fluid flow, acoustics, and motion, in addition to the fundamental quantities, mass, length, time, and so on, are typical of those within the scope of mechanical measurements. Unavoidably the measurement of mechanical quantities often also involves consideration of things electrical since it is often convenient or necessary (for reasons we will discuss later) to *transduce* or change a mechanical measurand into a corresponding electrical quantity.

---

* In the context intended, the measurements are not necessarily accomplished by mechanical means: Rather, it is to the quantity itself that the term *mechanical* is directed. The phrase *measurement of mechanical quantities* or parameters would perhaps express more completely the meaning intended. In the interest of brevity, however, the subject is simply called *mechanical measurements.*

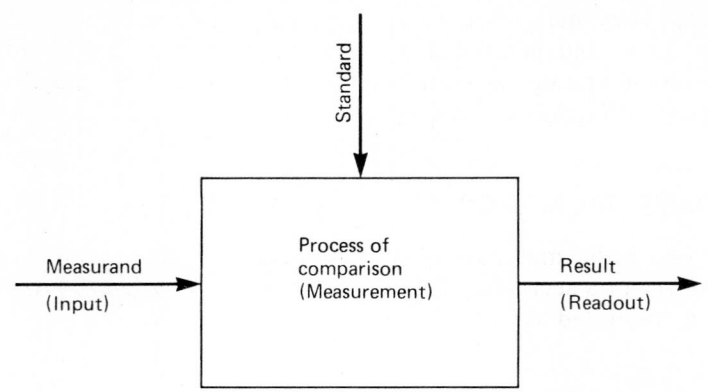

FIGURE 1.1   Fundamental measuring process.

1.2 THE SIGNIFICANCE OF MECHANICAL MEASUREMENT

Measurement provides the fundamental basis for research and development. Development is the final stage of the design procedure. All mechanical design of any complexity involves three elements: the empirical, the rational, and the experimental. The empirical element is based on experience and engineering common sense. The rational element relies on engineering principles, the laws of physics, and so forth. The experimental element is based on measurement, that is, measurement of the various quantities pertaining to the operation and performance of the device or process being developed.

Measurement is also a fundamental element of any control process. The concept of control *requires* the measured discrepancy between the actual and the desired performances. The controlling portion of the system must know the magnitude and direction of the difference in order to react intelligently.

In addition, many daily operations require measurement for proper performance. An example is in the modern central power station. Temperatures, flows, pressures, and vibrational amplitudes must be constantly monitored by measurement to ensure proper performance of the system. Of course, measurement is also the basis for commerce. Costs are established on the basis of *amounts* of materials, power, expenditure of time and labor, and other constraints.

To be useful, measurement must be reliable. Having incorrect information is potentially more damaging than having no information. This, of course, raises the question of degree of certainty or uncertainty. Arnold O. Beckman, founder of Beckman Instruments, has stated, "One thing you learn in science is that there is no *perfect* answer, no *perfect* measure" (emphasis added by authors). It is quite important that engineers interpreting the results of measurement have some basis for evaluating the degree of certainty or uncertainty. Engineers ought *never* simply to read a scale or printout and blindly accept the numbers. They must carefully place realistic tolerances on each of the measured values, and not only should have a doubting mind but equally important, should attempt to quantify their doubts. (We will discuss this topic in more detail in Section 1.8 and as the subject of Chapter 9.)

1.3 FUNDAMENTAL METHODS OF MEASUREMENT

There are two basic methods of measurement: (a) *direct comparison* with either a primary or a secondary standard, and (b) *indirect comparison* through the use of a calibrated system.

1.3.1 Direct Comparison

How would you measure the length of a bar of steel? If you would be satisfied with a measurement to, let us say, one-eighth of an inch (approximately 3 mm), you would probably use a steel tape measure. You compare the length of the bar with a *standard*, and find that the bar is so many inches long because that many inch-units on your standard has the same length as the bar. Thus you have determined the length by *direct comparison*. The standard that you have used is called a secondary standard. No doubt you could trace its ancestry back through no more than four generations to the primary length standard, which is the specific wavelength from krypton 86 (Section 8.4).

Although to measure by direct comparison is to strip the measurement process to its barest essentials, the method is not always adequate. The human senses are not equipped to make direct comparisons of all quantities with equal facility. In many cases they are not sensitive enough. We can make direct comparisons of small distances using a steel rule, with a preciseness of about 1 mm (approximately 0.04 in.). Often we wish for greater accuracy. Then we must call for additional assistance from some more complex form of measuring system. Measurement by direct comparison is less common than is measurement by *indirect comparison*.

1.3.2 Using a Calibrated System

Indirect comparison makes use of some form of transducing device coupled to a chain of connecting apparatus, which we shall call, in toto, the *measuring system*. This chain of devices converts the basic form of input into an analogous form, which it then processes and presents at the output as a known function of the input. Such a conversion is often necessary in order to make the desired information intelligible. The human senses are simply not equipped to detect the strain in a machine member, for instance. Assistance is required from a system that senses, converts, and finally presents an analogous output in the form of a displacement on a scale or chart or in digital form.

Processing of the analogous signal may take many forms. Often it is necessary to increase an amplitude or a power through some form of amplification. Or in another case it may be necessary to extract the desired information from a mass of extraneous input requiring filtering. Then again, a remote reading or recording may be needed, such as ground recording of a temperature or pressure in a missile in flight. This would most certainly require that the pressure or temperature be combined with a radio-frequency signal for transmission to the ground.

In each of the various cases requiring amplification, or filtering, or remote recording, etc., electrical methods suggest themselves. In fact, the majority of transducers in use, *particularly for dynamic mechanical measurements,* convert the mechanical input into an analogous electrical form for processing.

1.4   THE GENERALIZED MEASURING SYSTEM

Most measuring systems fall within the framework of a general arrangement consisting of three phases or stages:

> Stage I   A detector-transducing or *sensor* stage;
>
> Stage II   An intermediate stage, which we shall call the *signal-conditioning* stage;
>
> Stage III A terminating or *read-out* stage.

Each stage consists of a distinct component or group of components that perform required and definite steps in the measurement. These are called *basic elements,* whose scope is determined by their function rather than by their construction. Figure 1.2 and Table 1.1 outline the significance of each of these stages.

1.4.1   First, or Sensor-Transducer, Stage

The prime function of the first stage is to detect or to sense the measurand. At the same time, ideally, it should be insensitive to every other possible input. For instance, if it is a pressure pickup, it should be insensitive to, say,

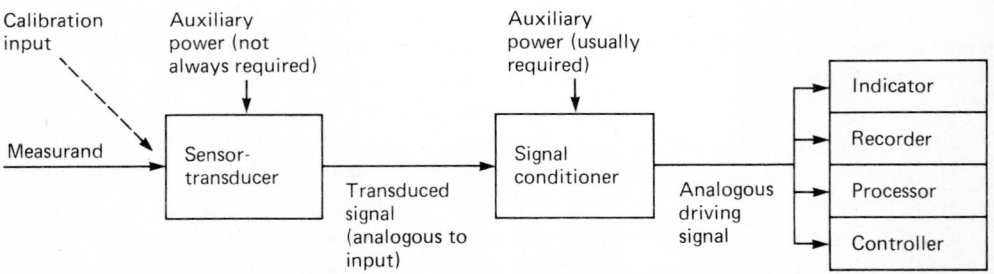

FIGURE 1.2   Block diagram of the generalized measuring system.

TABLE 1.1 Stages of the General Measurement System

Stage One: Sensor-Transducer	Stage Two: Signal Conditioning	Stage Three: Terminating Read-out
Senses desired input to exclusion of all others and provides analogous output.	Modifies transduced signal into form usable by final stage. Usually increases amplitude and/or power, depending on requirement. May also selectively filter unwanted components and convert signal into pulsed form.	Provides an indication or recording in form that can be evaluated by un unaided human sense or by a computer or controller.
Types and Examples	*Types and Examples*	*Types and Examples*
Mechanical: Contacting spindle, spring-mass, elastic devices (e.g., Bourdon tube for pressure, proving ring for force, etc.), gyro.	*Mechanical:* Gearing, cranks, slides, connecting links, cams, etc.	*Indicators* *Displacement types:* Moving pointer and scale, moving scale and index, light beam and scale, electron beam and scale (CRO), liquid column.
Hydraulic–pneumatic: Buoyant float, orifice, venturi, vane, propeller.	*Hydraulic–pneumatic:* Piping, valving, dash-pots, plenum chambers.	*Digital types:* Direct alphanumeric read-out.
Optical: Photographic film, photoelectric cell.	*Optical:* Mirrors, lenses, optical filters, light levers, optical fibers.	*Recorders:* Digital printing, inked pen and chart, light beam and photographic film, direct photography, magnetic recording.
Electrical: Contactor, resistance, capacitance, piezoelectric crystal, thermocouple, etc.	*Electrical:* Amplifying or attenuating systems, matching devices, filters, telemetering systems, various special-purpose integrated-circuit devices.	*Processors:* Various types of computing systems, either special-purpose or general, used to feed read-out/recording devices and/or controlling systems.
		Controllers: All types.

7

acceleration; if it is a strain gage, it should be insensitive to temperature; if a linear accelerometer, it should be insensitive to angular acceleration; and so on. Unfortunately, it is rare indeed to find a detecting device that is completely selective.

Frequently one finds more than a single transduction (change in signal character) in the first stage. This is particularly true if the first-stage output is electrical. (For further discussion see Section 4.3.)

1.4.2 Second, or Signal-Conditioning, Stage

The purpose of the second stage of the general system is to modify the transduced information so that it is acceptable to the third, or terminating, stage. In addition, it may perform one or more basic operations, such as selective filtering, integration, differentiating, or telemetering, as may be required.

Probably the most common function of the second stage is to increase either amplitude or power of the signal, or both, to the level required to drive the final terminating device. In addition it must be designed for proper matching characteristics between first and second and between second and third stages.

1.4.3 Third, or Terminating Read-Out, Stage

The third stage provides the information sought in a form comprehensible to one of the human senses or to a controller. If the output is intended for immediate human recognition, it is, with rare exception, presented in one of the following forms:

1. As a *relative displacement,* such as movement of an indicating hand, displacement of oscilloscope trace or oscillograph light beam, etc., or,

2. In *digital* form, as presented by a counter such as an automobile odometer or one of the modern digital voltmeters, etc.

To illustrate a very simple measuring system, let us consider the familiar tire gage used for checking automobile tire pressure. Such a device is shown in Fig. 1.3(a). It consists of a cylinder and piston, a spring resisting the piston movement, and a stem with scale divisions. As the air pressure bears against the piston, the resulting force compresses the spring until the spring and air forces balance. The calibrated stem, which remains in place after the spring returns the piston, indicates the applied pressure.

The piston–cylinder combination constitutes a force-summing apparatus, sensing and transducing pressure to force. As a secondary transducer (see Section 4.3), the spring converts the force to a displacement. Finally, the transduced input is transferred *without* signal conditioning to the scale and index for read-out (see Fig. 1.3b).

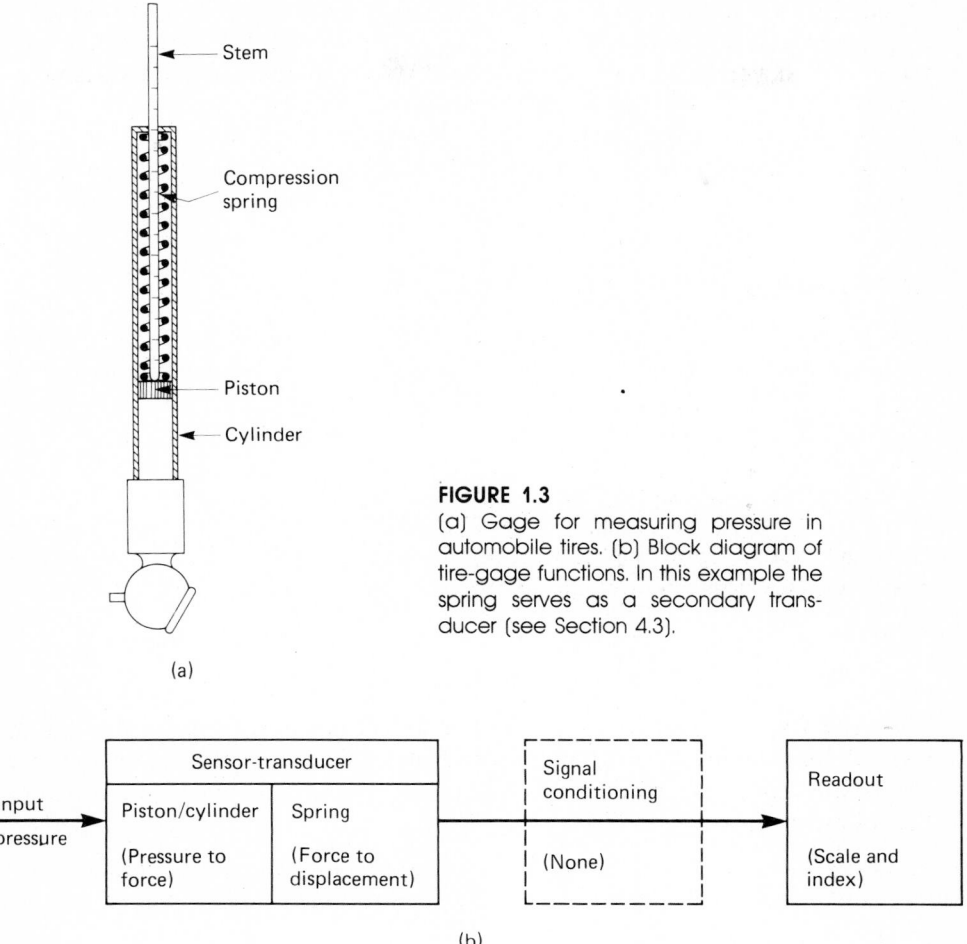

FIGURE 1.3
(a) Gage for measuring pressure in automobile tires. (b) Block diagram of tire-gage functions. In this example the spring serves as a secondary transducer (see Section 4.3).

As an example of a more complex system, let us say that a velocity is to be measured as shown in Fig. 1.4. The first-stage device, the accelerometer, provides an analogous voltage.* In addition to a voltage amplifier, the *second* stage may also include a filter that selectively attenuates unwanted high-frequency components. It may also integrate the analog signal with respect to time, thereby providing a velocity–time relation rather than an acceleration–time signal. Finally, the signal power will probably have to be increased to the level necessary to drive the *third,* or *read-out stage,* which may consist of

---

* Although the accelerometer may be susceptible to an analysis of "stages" within itself, we shall forego such an analysis in this example.

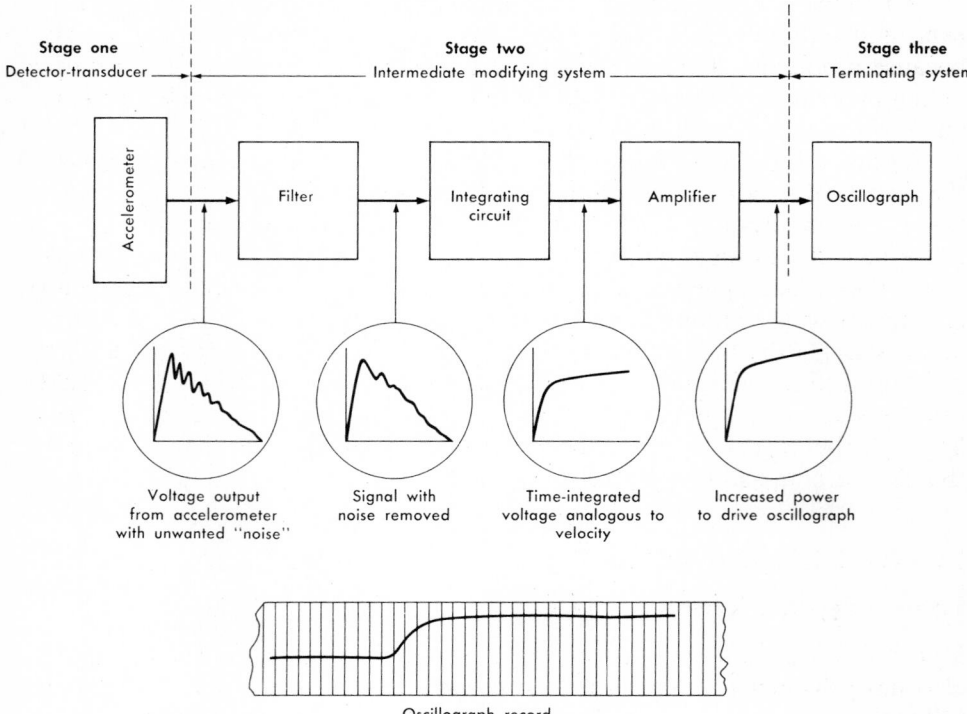

FIGURE 1.4   Block diagram of a relatively complex measuring system.

a galvanometer-type oscillograph (Section 7.9). The final record would then be in the form of a trace (a displacement–time plot) on photographic paper, and with proper calibration an intelligible velocity–time measurement should be the result.

1.5 CALIBRATION

Every measuring system must be *provable,* that is, it must prove its ability to measure reliably. The procedure for this is called *calibration.* It consists of determining the system's scale. At some point during the preparation of the system for measurement, *known* magnitudes of the basic input quantity must be fed into the detector-transducer, and the system's behavior must be observed.

If the system has been proved linear, perhaps *single-point* calibration will suffice, wherein the effect of only a single value of the input is used. If the system is not linear, or if it has not been so proved, a number of values must be used and their results observed.

The input may be static or dynamic, depending on the application; however, quite often dynamic response must be based on static calibration, simply because a practical dynamic source cannot be had. Naturally this is not optimum procedure; the more nearly the calibration standard corresponds to the unknown in all of its characteristics, the better the situation.

Occasionally the nature of the system or one of its components makes the introduction of a sample of the basic input quantity difficult or impossible. One of the important characteristics of the bonded resistance-type strain gage is the fact that through quality control at the time of manufacture, *spot* calibration may be applied to a complete lot of gages. As a result, an indirect calibration of a strain-measuring system may be provided through the gage factor supplied by the manufacturer. Instead of attempting to apply a known unit strain to the gage installed on the test structure, which if possible would often result in an ambiguous situation, a resistance change is substituted. Through the predetermined gage factor, the system's strain response may thereby be obtained (see Sections 12.5 and 12.12).

1.6 TYPES OF INPUT QUANTITIES

1.6.1 Time Relationship

Mechanical quantities, in addition to their inherent defining characteristics, also have distinctive time–amplitude properties, which may be classified as follows:

  I. Static

 II. Dynamic

    A. Steady-state periodic

    B. Nonrepetitive or transient

      1. Single pulse or aperiodic

      2. Continuing or random

Of course, the static, nonchanging measurand is the most easily measured. If the system is terminated by some form of meter-type indicator, the meter pointer has no difficulty in eventually reaching a definite indication. It is the rapidly changing measurand that presents the real measurement challenge.

There are two general forms of dynamic input: steady-state periodic and transient. The steady-state periodic quantity is one whose magnitude has a definite repeating time cycle, whereas the time variation of a transient magnitude does not repeat. "Sixty-cycle" line voltage is an example of a steady-state periodic signal. So also are many mechanical vibrations, after a balance has been reached between a constant input exciting energy and energy dissipated by damping.

An example of a pulsed transient quantity is the acceleration–time relationship accompanying an isolated mechanical impact. Occasionally, the magnitude is temporary, being completed in a matter of milliseconds, with the portions of interest existing perhaps for only a few microseconds. Extremely high rates of change, or wavefronts, exist, placing severe demands on the measuring system. The nature of these inputs is discussed in detail in Chapter 2, and the response of the measuring system is covered in Chapter 3.

1.6.2   Analog or Digital?

Most measurands of interest vary with time in an analog fashion. That is, they vary in a continuous manner over a range of magnitudes. For instance, the speed of an automobile, as it starts from rest, has some magnitude at every instant during its motion, no matter how finely the time intervals between measurements are taken. The speed varies in an analog manner as a function of time. The voltage in utility power lines varies sinusoidally with time. This is an analog quantity also.

Certain quantities, however, may vary digitally, changing in a stepwise manner between two distinct magnitudes: a high and a low voltage, for instance. The revolutions of a shaft could be counted with a cam-actuated electrical switch that is closed or open, depending on the position of the cam. If the switch controls current from a battery, current either flows with a given magnitude or does not flow. The current flow would behave digitally.

Analog-originating mechanical quantities, such as temperatures, fluid flow, stress and strain, and pressure, normally all behave timewise in an analog manner. There may be distinct advantages, however, in converting an analog-type input to an equivalent digital signal for the purposes of signal conditioning and/or read-out. Noise problems are reduced or sometimes eliminated altogether, and data transmission is simpler. Most computers are designed to process digital information and direct numerical display or recording is more easily accomplished by manipulating digital quantities. (Digital techniques are discussed where appropriate throughout this book, but especially in Chapter 6.)

1.7   STANDARDS, DIMENSIONS, AND UNITS OF MEASUREMENT

The term *dimension* connotes the defining characteristics of an entity, and a *unit* is a basis for quantification of the entity. For example, length is a dimension whereas centimeter is a unit of length; time is a dimension and the second is a unit of time. A dimension is unique; however, a particular dimension, say length, may be measured in feet, meters, inches, miles, etc.

Newton's second law may be expressed in various ways, one of which is

A particle acted upon by an external force will be accelerated in proportion to the force magnitude and in inverse proportion to the mass of the particle; the direction of the acceleration will coincide with the line-of-action of the force.

Algebraically,

$$F = ma, \tag{1.1}$$

where

$F =$ the magnitude of the applied force,

$m =$ the mass of particle*, and

$a =$ the resulting acceleration.

From experiment [1] we know that near the earth's surface a particle (body) acted on solely by gravitational attraction accelerates at the rate of about 32.2 ft/s² (9.81 m/s²).† In this situation the acting force is *weight,* which may be expressed in pounds-force (lbf), dynes, etc., depending on the particular system of units that is used, and magnitude of mass may be expressed variously as slugs, pounds-mass (lbm), kilograms, etc. In any case, whichever system is used, a consistent, compatible balance of units must be maintained. The inertial law (Newton's) is of particular interest in this regard because it demands a careful distinction between the units of force and mass. In the United States it has long been the habit to use the abbreviation "lb" as the unit for both mass and force except when a distinction is absolutely required. Then the abbreviations "lbm" and "lbf" are used. The movement toward use of the metric system in the United States with promotion of the SI system of units should help correct this confusion.

Table 1.2 lists the basic units for five different systems. For example, the SI system (Système International d'Unites, or International System of Units) assigns the units of kilograms, meters (or metres), and seconds to the dimensions mass, length, and time, respectively. The unit of force, the newton, is a derived unit. Correspondingly, the English Engineering System uses pounds-force, pounds-mass, feet, and seconds for force, mass, length, and

---

*   *Caution:* Particular note should be made of the use throughout this text of the symbols "m" and "w." The symbol m is used to represent the magnitude of the dimension, *mass,* and carries the units of *kilogram* (kg) or *pound-mass* (lbm). Weight, w, which is a force, carries the units *pounds-force* (lbf) or newtons (N). Note should also be made of the use of the symbol "m," to denote the unit, meter. Context should always make clear the intent.

†   Standard acceleration due to gravity is taken as 32.174 ft/s², or 9.80665 m/s². Of course, the actual value depends on the specific locality.

TABLE 1.2 Systems of Units

Quantity	SI (MKS) (mass, length, time)	Absolute Metric (CGS) (mass, length, time)	English Engineering (force, mass, length, time)	Absolute English (mass, length, time)	Technical English (force, length, time)
			System		
Length	meter (m)	centimeter (cm)	foot (ft)	foot (ft)	foot (ft)
Time	second (s)	second (s)	second (s)	second (s)	second (s)
Mass	kilogram (kg)	gram (g)	pound-mass (lbm)	pound-mass (lbm)	slug
Force	newton (N)	dyne	pound-force (lbf)	poundal	pound-force (lbf)
Energy	joule (J)	erg	foot-(pound-force)	foot-poundal	foot-(pound-force)
Power			= energy/second		
Dimensional constant, g_c	$1\ \dfrac{\text{kg-m}}{\text{N-s}^2}$	$1\ \dfrac{\text{g-cm}}{\text{dyne-s}^2}$	$32.17\ \dfrac{\text{lbm-ft}}{\text{lbf-s}^2}$	$1\ \dfrac{\text{lbm-ft}}{\text{poundal-s}^2}$	$1\ \dfrac{\text{slug-ft}}{\text{lbf-s}^2}$

Note: Four dimensions are involved in each system. For the English Engineering system all four dimensions are assigned. This requires that the dimensional constant carry a value of 32.17. For the other systems that are listed the numerical value of the constant is unity. In each case the constant carries the units necessary to balance the inertial equation.

Note: In the table above, the derived units are underscored.

14

time, respectively. In each case, when the assigned units are applied to Eq. (1.1), a question of compatibility arises. To provide a balance of units it becomes necessary to introduce a factor called the *dimensional constant* g_c, modifying Eq. (1.1) as follows:

$$F/a = W/g = m/g_c \quad \text{or} \quad g_c = ma/F. \tag{1.2}$$

If we select the English system as an example and assume that 1 lbf acts on 1 lbm, which we know results in an acceleration of 32.2 ft/s², then we find that

$$g_c = (1 \text{ lbm})(32.2 \text{ ft/s}^2)/(1 \text{ lbf})$$

$$= (32.2)(\text{lbm-ft/lbf-s}^2).$$

In like manner, we may determine values and units for g_c for the other systems listed in Table 1.2.

To help reinforce the concept of the factor g_c, consider the following.

EXAMPLE   Water of density ρ and absolute viscosity μ flows with velocity V through a pipe of diameter D. Calculate the Reynolds number, R, using the data supplied below, using (a) the English Engineering system of units and (b) the SI system. Before making the numerical calculations, check for balance of units.

Referring to Section 15.2, we see that $R = D\rho V/\mu$ and, as discussed in that section, its value is unitless, hence independent of the system of units used; thus we should obtain the same numerical answers for both parts (a) and (b).

Data   See Appendix A for conversion factors.

$D = 8$ in. $= \frac{2}{3}$ ft $= 0.2032$ m

$\rho = 62.3$ lbm/ft³ $= 997.95$ kg/m³   (see Appendix D)

$V = 4$ ft/s $= 1.219$ m/s

$\mu = 2.02 \times 10^{-5}$ lbf-s/ft² $= 9.6718 \times 10^{-4}$ N-s/m²   (see Appendix D)

Solution   (a) If we enter the units for each of the separate quantities appearing in the equation for R, we have

$$(\text{ft})(\text{lbm/ft}^3)(\text{ft/s})(\text{ft}^2/\text{lbf-s})(1/g_c)$$

or, entering the units for g_c,

$$(\text{ft})(\text{lbm/ft}^3)(\text{ft/s})(\text{ft}^2/\text{lbf-s})(\text{lbf-s/lbm-ft}).$$

We see that the various units cancel, confirming the statement that Reynold's number is unitless.

For magnitude,

$$R = (\tfrac{2}{3})(62.3)(4)/(2.02 \times 10^{-5})(32.2) = 255\ 417.$$

(b) In terms of SI units, we have,

$$(m)(kg/m^3)(m/s)(m^2/N\text{-}s)(1/g_c)$$

or, when the units for g_c are entered,

$$(m)(kg/m^3)(m/s)(m^2/N\text{-}s^2)(N\text{-}s^2/kg\text{-}m).$$

Again we see that the units cancel, once more confirming that Reynold's number is unitless.

For magnitude using SI units,

$$R = (0.2032)(997.95)(1.219)/(9.6718) \times 10^{-4})(1)$$

$$= 255\ 581.$$

Note: The lack of exact numerical agreement in the final numbers is due to inexact conversions.

In the past, physicists have been partial to the Absolute Metric or CGS system, whereas engineers have used either the English Engineering system or the Technical English system. Throughout this book we shall use both the SI and the English Engineering systems.

Standards of measurement are discussed in more detail in Chapter 8.

1.8   CERTAINTY/UNCERTAINTY: VALIDITY OF RESULTS

Error may be defined as the difference between the *measured* result and the *true* value (see Section 9.2). We do not know the true value, hence we do not know the error. We can discuss an error and can estimate (guess) an error, but we can never know its actual magnitude. If we wish to assign a value to our estimate of error, then we commonly refer to that number as *uncertainty*. Uncertainty, then, is our best estimate of error. There are two basic types of error (remember we can discuss it without ever knowing its magnitude): *systematic error* and *random error*.

Should an unscrupulous butcher place a ball of putty under the scale pan, the scale read-outs would be consistently in error. The scale would indicate a weight of product too great by the weight of the putty. This represents one type of systematic error, *zero offset*.

Shrink rules are used to make patterns for the casting of metals. Cast steel shrinks in cooling by about two percent, hence the patterns used for preparing the molds are oversized by the proper percentage amounts. The pattern maker uses a shrink rule on which the dimensional units are increased by that amount. Should a pattern maker's shrink rule for cast steel be inadvertently used for ordinary length measurements, the read-outs would be consistently undersized by 1/50th in one. This is an example of *scale error*.

In each of the foregoing examples the errors are constant and of a systematic nature. Such errors are *not* susceptible to statistical analysis; however, they may be estimated by methods that we discuss in Chapter 9.

An inexpensive frequency counter may use the 60-Hz power-line frequency as a comparison standard. Power-line frequency is held very close to the 60-Hz standard. Although it does slowly wander above and below the average value, over a period of time, say a day, the *average* is very close to 60 Hz. The wandering is random and the moment-to-moment error in the frequency meter read-out (from this source) is called *random error*.

Randomness may also be introduced by lack of *definition* of the measurand. If a number of hardness readings are made on a given sample of steel, a range of readings will be obtained. An average hardness may be calculated and presented as the actual hardness. Single readings will deviate from the average, some higher and some lower. Of course, a primary reason for the variations in this case is the nonhomogeneity of the crystalline structure of the test specimen. The deviations will be random and are due to a lack of definition in the measurand. Random uncertainty (error) is susceptible to statistical treatment and is considered in more detail in Chapter 9.

1.9 RECORDING RESULTS

When experimental setups are made and time and effort are expended to obtain results, it normally follows that some form of written record or report is to be made. The purpose of such a record will determine its form. In fact, in some cases several versions will be prepared. Reports may be categorized as

1. The laboratory note,

2. The progress report,

3. The full or complete report,

4. The technical paper.

Very briefly, the lab note is written to be read by someone thoroughly familiar with the project, such as the immediate supervisor or the experimenter. The full report tells the complete story to someone who is interested in the subject but has not been in direct touch with the specific work—perhaps top officials of a large company or a review committee of a sponsoring agency, etc. A progress report is just that, one of possibly several interim reports describing the current status of an ongoing project, which will eventually be incorporated in a full report. Ordinarily the technical paper is a brief summary of a project, but whose extent must be tailored to fit either a time allotment at a meeting or space in a publication.

There are several factors common to all the various forms. With each type, the first priority is *to make sure* that the *problem or project* that has been tackled *is clearly stated*. There is nothing quite so frustrating as to read details in a technical report, while never being certain of the raison d'être. It is extremely important to make certain that the reader is quickly clued in on the *why,* before one attempts to explain the *how* and the results. A clearly stated objective can be considered the most important part of the report. The entire report should be written in simple language. A rule stated by Samuel Clemens is not inappropriate: "Omit unnecessary adverbs and adjectives."

1.9.1   The Laboratory Note

The lab note is written for a very limited audience, possibly even only as a memory jogger for the experimenter, or perhaps more often, for the information of an immediate supervisor, one who is thoroughly familiar with the work. In some cases a single page may be sufficient, including a sentence or two stating the problem, a block diagram of the experimental setup, and some data presented either in tabular form or as a plotted diagram. Any pertinent observations not directly evident from the data should also be included. Sufficient information should be included so that the experimenter can mentally reconstruct the situation and results a year or even five years hence. A date and signature should always be included and, if there is a possibility of important developments stemming from the work, a second witnessing signature should be included and dated.

1.9.2   The Full Report

The full report must relate all the facts pertinent to the project. It is even more important in this case to make the purpose of the project completely clear, for the report will be read by persons not closely associated with the work.

One format that has much merit is to make the report proper, the main body, short and to the point, relegating the supporting materials, data, detailed descriptions of equipment, review of literature, sample calculations, and so on, to appendixes. Frequent reference to these materials can be made throughout the report proper, but the option to peruse the details is left to the reader. This scheme also provides a good basis for the technical paper, should it be planned.

1.9.3   The Technical Paper

A primary purpose of the technical paper is to make known (advertise) the work of the writer. For this reason two particularly important portions of the writing are the *problem statement* and the *results*. Adequately done, these two items will attract the attention of other workers interested in the particular field who can then make direct contact with the writer(s) for additional details and discussion.

Space, number of words, limits on illustrations, and perhaps time are all factors making the preparation of a technical paper particularly challenging. Once the problem statement and the primary results have been adequately established, the remaining available space may be used to summarize procedures, test setups, and the like.

1.10 FINAL REMARKS

An attempt has been made in this chapter to provide an overall preview of the problems of mechanical measurement. In conformance with the preceding section (1.9), an attempt has been made to "state the problem" as fully as possible in only a few pages. The remainder of the book is used to expand on the topics referred to throughout this chapter.

SUGGESTED READINGS

ASME, *Orientation and Guide for Use of SI Units,* 8th ed., 1978.

Chiswell, B., and E. C. M. Grigg, *S. I. Units: An Introduction.* New York: John Wiley, 1971.

Doeblin, E. A., *Measurement Systems,* rev. ed. New York: McGraw-Hill, 1975.

Greene, M. H., *International and Metric Units of Measurement.* New York: Chemical, 1961.

Hewitt, H. C., Jr., *Scope of Experimental Analysis.* Englewood Cliffs, N.J.: Prentice-Hall, 1973.

Holman, J. P., *Experimental Methods for Engineers,* 3d, ed. New York: McGraw-Hill, 1978.

International Standard ISO 1000, SI Units and Recommendations for Their Use, 1973–02–01, New York: ANSI.

Kapp, R. O., *The Presentation of Technical Information.* New York: Macmillan, 1948.

Klein, H. A., *The World of Measurements.* New York: Simon & Schuster, 1974.

Mechtly, E. A., *The International System of Units, Physical Constants and Conversion Factors. (NASA).* Washington, D.C.: U.S. Government Printing Office, 1964.

Metric Conversion Act of 1975, Public Law 94–168, 94th Congress. H.R.8674, December 23, 1975.

Metric Practice Guide, E 380–72, Philadelphia: ASTM, 1972.

Metric Style Guide, Dimensions/NBS, February, 1977.

Zebrowsky, E., Jr., *Fundamentals of Physical Measurement.* North Scituate, Mass.: Duxbury Press, 1979.

PROBLEMS

1.1 Prepare a list of journals that are pertinent to the subject of this book and that are available in your local or school library. Review several issues of each and prepare short statements covering apparent editorial policies including what, in your opinion, is the clientele toward which each is directed.

1.2 As a semester assignment, write a short synopsis of one article selected from each of the periodicals listed in Problem 1.1.

1.3 A list of general "Suggested Readings" follows each of Chapters 2–18. Select two books from each of these lists and write a short book review for each.

1.4 Scan the headings of each of the following chapters. Select one and as a semester or term assignment summarize articles, papers, advertising, etc., that apply to the selected topic.

1.5 Set up and conduct tests to evaluate your ability to estimate, with the aid of only your judgment and experience, magnitudes of the common quantities listed below. You may wish to determine some measure of improvement with practice.

   a) Linear distances

   b) Weight of small objects of different densities

   c) Time intervals

   d) Frequency of pure sound

   e) Velocity

   f) Temperature of water

   What limits of accuracy in each category do you think you could develop?

1.6 Each of the following devices includes the three basic stages of the generalized measuring system. Analyze each, breaking it into its fundamental stages.

   a) Bourdon-type pressure gage (Fig. 4.1)

   b) Mercury-column–type barometer

   c) Automobile speedometer

   d) Pendulum-type clock

   e) Pendulum-type scale (Fig. 13.6)

   f) Dimensional comparator (Fig. 11.5)

   g) Pressure-type thermometer (Fig. 16.2)

1.7 Assign units and check for unit balance in each of the following relationships. Use each of the five systems given in Table 1.2.

   a) Eqs. (12.4), (13.1b), and (13.9)

   b) Eqs. (14.5) (see Fig. 14.7), (14.6), and (14.20)

   c) Eqs. (15.1), (15.2), (15.5), and (15.9)

   d) Eqs. (16.7), (16.13), and (17.5)

1.8 Absolute viscosity carries the units $N\text{-}s/m^2$ in the SI system and $lbf\text{-}s/ft^2$ in the English system. If the viscosity is known in English units, what multiplication factor should be used to convert it to SI units? Derive the factor.

1.9 What will 1 kg of water weigh (a) in Ft. Egbert, Alaska; (b) in Key West, Florida; (c) on the moon? (See Appendix D for data.)

1.10 What will 1 lbm of water weigh in each of the locations listed in Problem 1.9?

1.11 Very often spring scales of the type shown in Fig. 4.18 carry divisions marked in kilograms. Is this practice fundamentally correct? Basically, what does such a device measure when a mass is suspended from it? What is the relationship between weight and mass?

1.12 Assume that a spring scale of the type referred to in Problem 1.11 is properly calibrated to measure force in newtons. If, on the surface of the moon (gravitational acceleration = 1.67 m/s), a reading of 50 N is obtained when an item is suspended from the scale, what weight would be indicated if the measurement were made under standard conditions on the surface of the earth? What would be the mass of the item in kilograms?

the analog measurand: its time-dependent characteristics

2

2.1 INTRODUCTION

A parameter common to all of measurement is *time:* All measurands have time-related characteristics. As real time progresses, the magnitude of the measurand either changes or does not change. The nature of any change is often fully as important as is that of any discrete amplitude.

In this chapter we will discuss those quantities necessary to define and describe the various time-related factors. In Chapter 1, we classified time-related measurands as

  I. Static
 II. Dynamic
    A. Steady-state periodic
    B. Nonrepetitive or transient
       1. Single pulse or aperiodic
       2. Continuing or random

2.2 SIMPLE HARMONIC RELATIONS

A function is said to be simple harmonic in terms of a variable when its second derivative is proportional to the function but of opposite sign. More often than not, the independent variable is time t, although any two variables may be related harmonically.

One of the most common harmonic functions in mechanical engineering is one relating displacement and time. In electrical engineering many of the variable quantities in a.c. circuitry are harmonic functions of time. The relation is quite basic to dynamic functions, and most quantities that are time functions may be expressed harmonically.

In its most elementary form, *simple harmonic motion* is defined by the relation

$$s = s_0 \sin \omega t, \qquad (2.1)$$

in which

s = instantaneous displacement from equilibrium,

s_0 = amplitude, or maximum displacement from equilibrium,

ω = circular frequency, rad/s, and

t = any time interval measured from the instant when $t = 0$ s.

Pendulum motions of small amplitude, a mass on a beam, a weight suspended by a rubber gum band—all vibrate with simple harmonic motion, or very nearly so.

By differentiation, the following relations may be derived from Eq. (2.1):

$$v = \frac{ds}{dt} = s_0 \omega \cos \omega t \qquad (2.2)$$

and

$$v_0 = s_0 \omega. \qquad (2.2a)$$

Also,

$$a = \frac{dv}{dt} = -s_0 \omega^2 \sin \omega t \qquad (2.3)$$

$$= -s\omega^2. \qquad (2.3a)$$

In addition,

$$a_0 = -s_0 \omega^2. \qquad (2.3b)$$

In the equations above

v = velocity,

v_0 = maximum velocity or velocity amplitude,

a = acceleration,

a_0 = maximum acceleration or acceleration amplitude.

Equation (2.3a) satisfies our word description of simple harmonic motion expressed in the first paragraph of this section: The acceleration a is proportional to the displacement s, but is of opposite sign. The proportionality factor is ω^2.

2.3   THE SIGNIFICANCE OF CIRCULAR FREQUENCY

The idea of *circular frequency* ω, as used above, is very useful in studying cyclic relations. Even if students are completely familiar with its use, the mechanical analogy in the form of the well-known *Scotch-yoke* mechanism may be a helpful adjunct to their thinking.

Figure 2.1(a) shows the elements of the Scotch yoke, consisting of a crank, *OA*, with a slider-block driving the yoke–piston combination. If we measure the piston displacement from its midstroke position, the displacement amplitude will be $\pm OA$. If the crank turns at ω radians per second, then the crank angle θ may be written as ωt. This, of course, is convenient because it introduces time t into the relationship, which is not directly apparent in the term θ. Piston displacement may now be written as

$$s = s_0 \sin \omega t.$$

[This is the same as Eq. (2.1).] One cycle takes place when the crank turns through 2π radians, and if f is the frequency in hertz, then

$$\omega = 2\pi f. \tag{2.4}$$

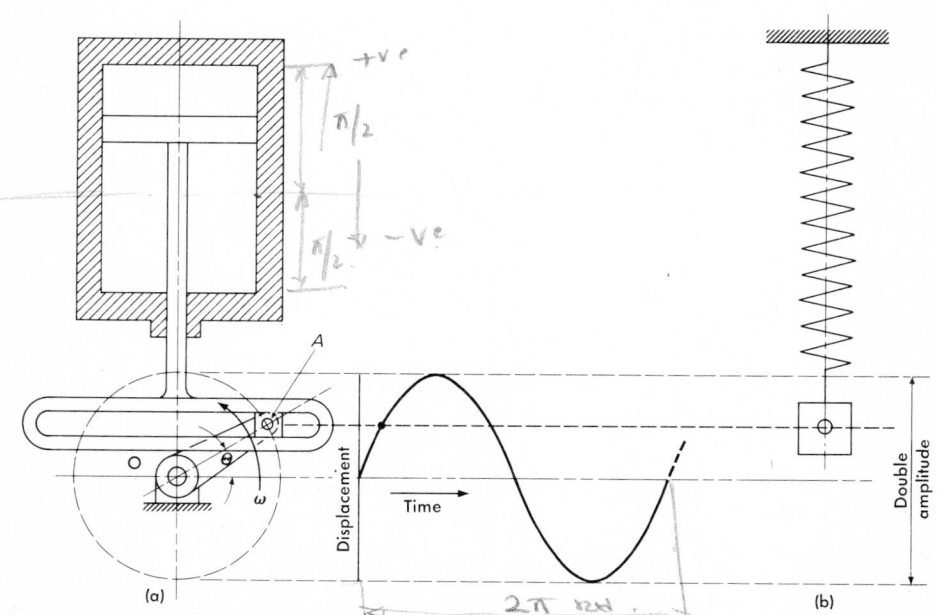

FIGURE 2.1   (a) The Scotch-yoke mechanism that provides a simple harmonic motion to the piston. (b) A spring-mass system that moves with simple harmonic motion.

The displacement equation shows that the yoke–piston combination moves with simple harmonic motion. As mentioned before, there are many other simple harmonic relationships in mechanical and electrical fields. A spring-mass system, as shown in Fig. 2.1(b), is an example. If its amplitude and natural frequency just happen to match the amplitude and frequency of the Scotch-yoke mechanism, then the mass and the piston may be made to move up and down in perfect synchronization.

Or to put it another way, *for every simple harmonic relationship, an analogous Scotch-yoke mechanism may be devised or imagined.* The crank length *OA* will represent the vector amplitude, and the angular velocity of the crank, ω in radians per second, will correspond to the circular frequency of the harmonic relation. If the mass and piston have the same frequencies and simultaneously reach corresponding extremes of displacement, their motions are said to be *in phase*. When they both have the same frequency, but do not oscillate together, the time relation (lag or advance) between their motions may be expressed by an angle referred to as the *phase angle,* φ.

2.4 COMPLEX RELATIONS

Most complex dynamic-mechanical signals, steady-state or transient, whether they are time functions of pressure, displacement, strain, or something else, may be expressed as a combination of simple harmonic components. Each component will have its own amplitude and frequency and will be combined in various phase relations with the other components. A general mathematical statement of this may be written as follows [1]:

$$f(t) = \frac{A}{2} + \sum_{n=1}^{\infty} (A_n \cos n\omega t + B_n \sin n\omega t), \qquad (2.5)$$

in which

$$A, A_n, \text{ and } B_n = \text{amplitude-determining constants called}$$
harmonic coefficients, and

$$n = \text{integers from 1 to } \infty, \text{ called } harmonic$$
orders.

When *n* is unity, the corresponding sine and cosine terms are said to be *fundamental.* For *n* = 2, 3, 4, etc., the corresponding terms are referred to as 2nd, 3rd, 4th *harmonics,* and so on.

Equation (2.5) may be written in the two equivalent forms:

$$f(t) = \frac{A}{2} + \sum_{n=1}^{\infty} C_n \cos (n\omega t - \phi_n) \qquad (2.5a)$$

or

$$f(t) = \frac{A}{2} + \sum_{n=1}^{\infty} C_n \sin (n\omega t + \phi'_n) \tag{2.5b}$$

where the harmonic coefficients, C_n, are determined by the relation

$$C_n = \sqrt{A_n^2 + B_n^2}$$

and the phase relations ϕ_n and ϕ'_n are determined as follows:

$$\tan \phi_n = \left(\frac{B_n}{A_n}\right) \quad \text{and} \quad \tan \phi'_n = \left(\frac{A_n}{B_n}\right).$$

The *phase angles* ϕ_n and ϕ'_n provide necessary timewise relationships among the various harmonic components.

Although Eq. (2.5) indicates that all harmonics may be present in defining the signal–time relation, actually such relations often include only a limited number of harmonics. In fact, all measuring systems have some upper- and some lower-frequency limit beyond which further harmonics will be attenuated. In other words, no measuring system can handle an infinite frequency range.

Although it would be utterly impossible to catalog all the many possible harmonic combinations, nevertheless it may be useful to consider the effects of some of the variables such as relative amplitudes, harmonic orders n, and phase relations ϕ. Therefore Figs. 2.2 through 2.6 are presented for two component relations, in each case showing the effect of one variable only on the overall waveform. Figure 2.2 shows the effect of relative amplitudes; Fig. 2.3 shows the effect of relative frequencies; Fig. 2.4 shows the effect of various phase relations; Fig. 2.5 shows the appearance of the waveform for two components having considerably different frequencies; and Fig. 2.6 shows the effect of two frequencies that are very nearly the same.

EXAMPLE As an example of a relation made up of harmonics, let us consider a relatively simple pressure–time function consisting of two harmonic terms:

$$P = 100 \sin (80t) + 50 \cos \left(160t - \frac{\pi}{4}\right). \tag{2.6}$$

Inspection of the equation shows that the circular frequency of the fundamental has a value of 80 radians per second, or $80/2\pi = 12.7$ Hz. The period for the pressure variation is therefore $1/12.7 = 0.0788$ s. The second term has a frequency twice that of the fundamental, as indicated by its circular frequency of 160 radians per second. It also lags the fundamental by one-eighth cycle, or $\pi/4$ radians. In addition, the equation indicates that the amplitude of the fundamental, which is 100, is twice that of the second harmonic which is 50. A plot of the relation is shown in Fig. 2.7.

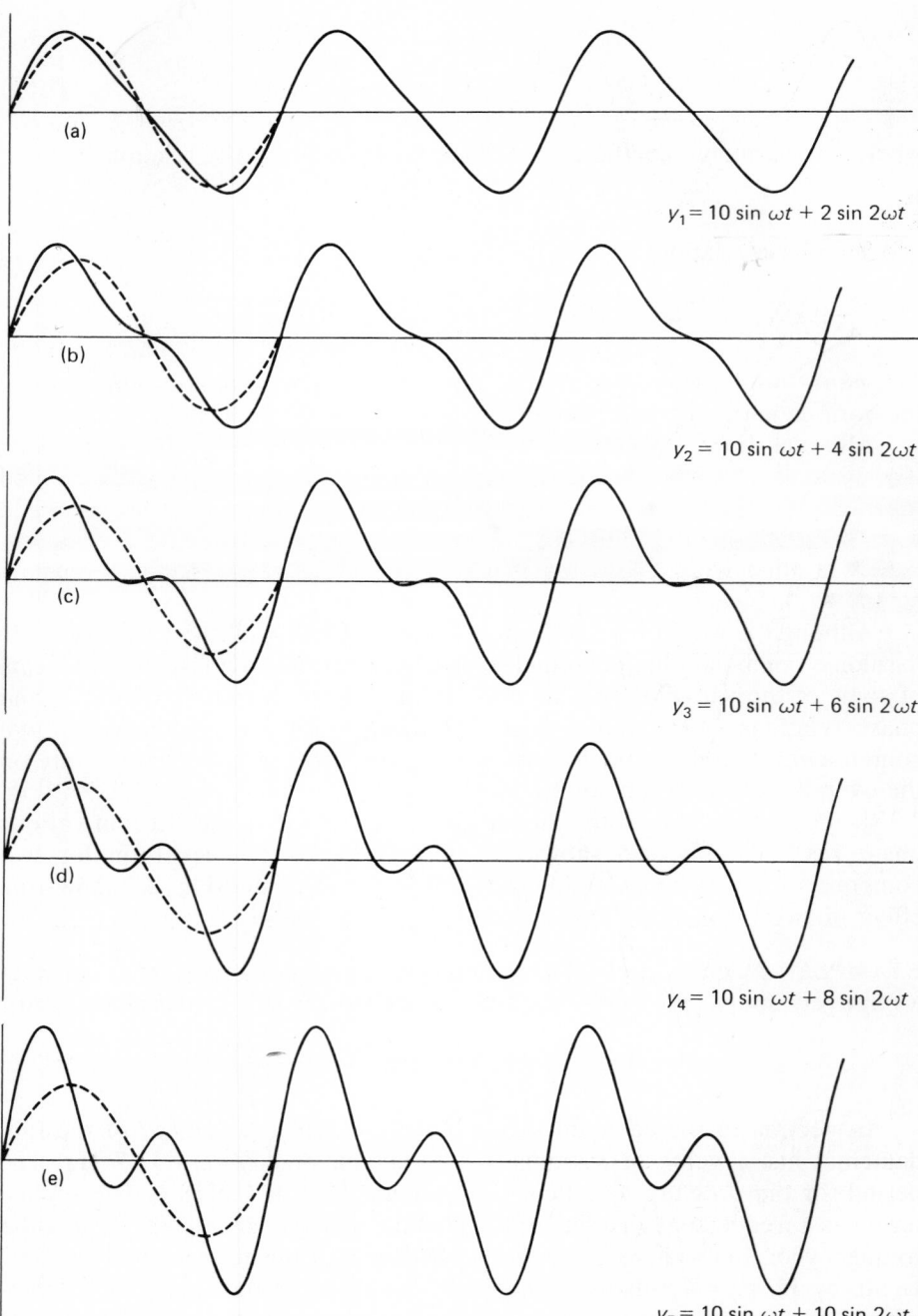

(a)

$y_1 = 10 \sin \omega t + 2 \sin 2\omega t$

(b)

$y_2 = 10 \sin \omega t + 4 \sin 2\omega t$

(c)

$y_3 = 10 \sin \omega t + 6 \sin 2\omega t$

(d)

$y_4 = 10 \sin \omega t + 8 \sin 2\omega t$

(e)

$y_5 = 10 \sin \omega t + 10 \sin 2\omega t$

FIGURE 2.2   Examples of two component waveforms with second harmonic component of various relative amplitudes.

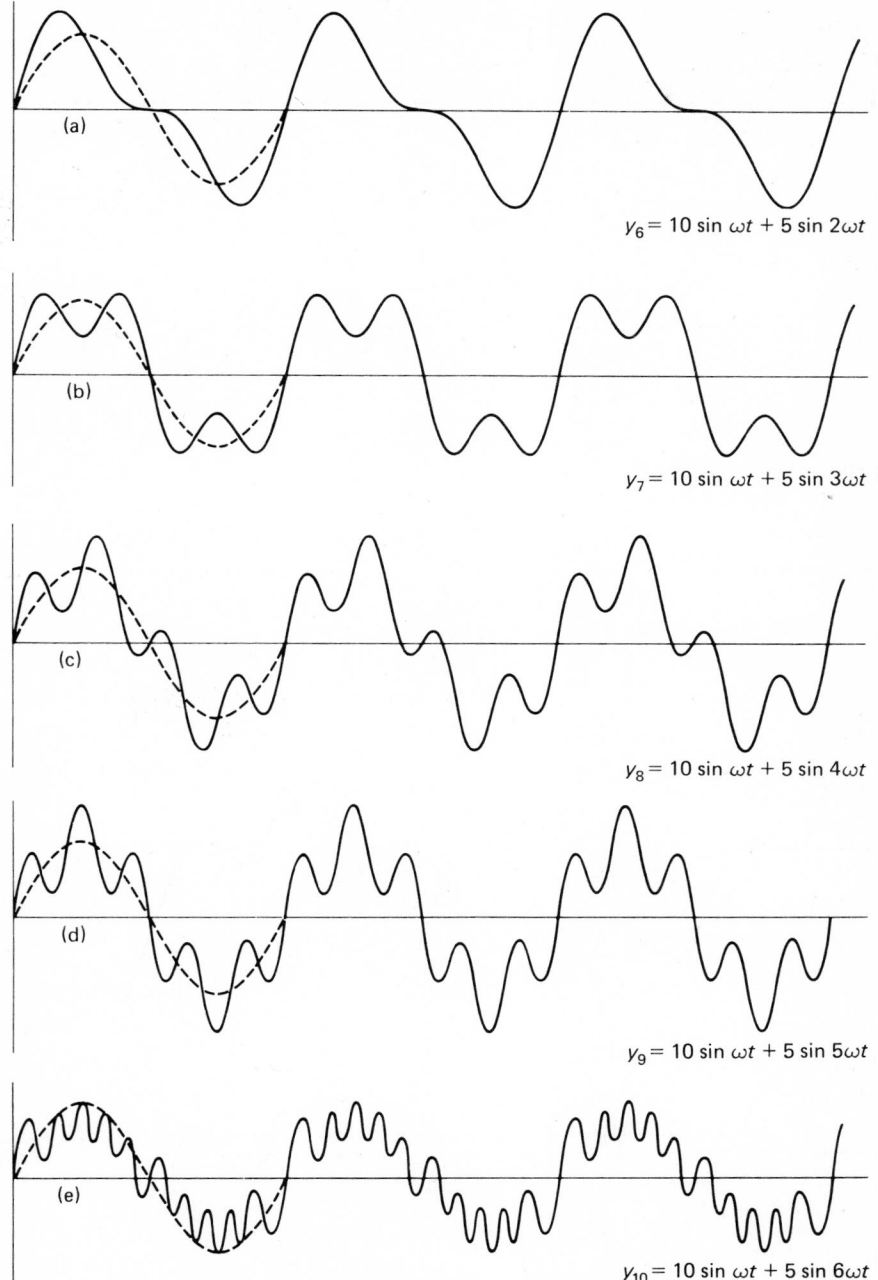

$y_6 = 10 \sin \omega t + 5 \sin 2\omega t$

$y_7 = 10 \sin \omega t + 5 \sin 3\omega t$

$y_8 = 10 \sin \omega t + 5 \sin 4\omega t$

$y_9 = 10 \sin \omega t + 5 \sin 5\omega t$

$y_{10} = 10 \sin \omega t + 5 \sin 6\omega t$

FIGURE 2.3   Examples of two component waveforms with second term of various relative frequencies.

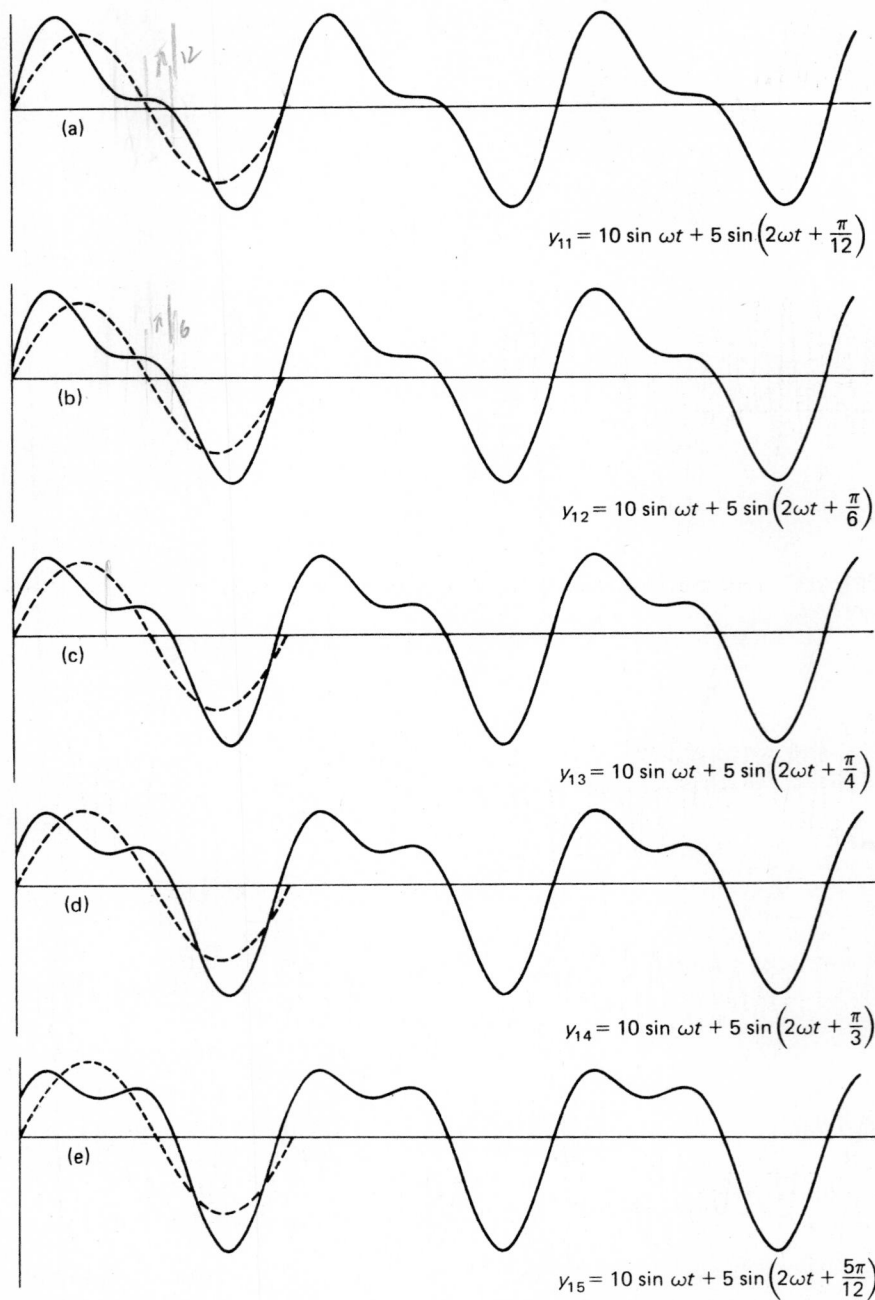

$$y_{11} = 10 \sin \omega t + 5 \sin \left(2\omega t + \frac{\pi}{12}\right)$$

$$y_{12} = 10 \sin \omega t + 5 \sin \left(2\omega t + \frac{\pi}{6}\right)$$

$$y_{13} = 10 \sin \omega t + 5 \sin \left(2\omega t + \frac{\pi}{4}\right)$$

$$y_{14} = 10 \sin \omega t + 5 \sin \left(2\omega t + \frac{\pi}{3}\right)$$

$$y_{15} = 10 \sin \omega t + 5 \sin \left(2\omega t + \frac{5\pi}{12}\right)$$

FIGURE 2.4   Examples of two component waveforms with the second harmonic having various degrees of pfhase shift.

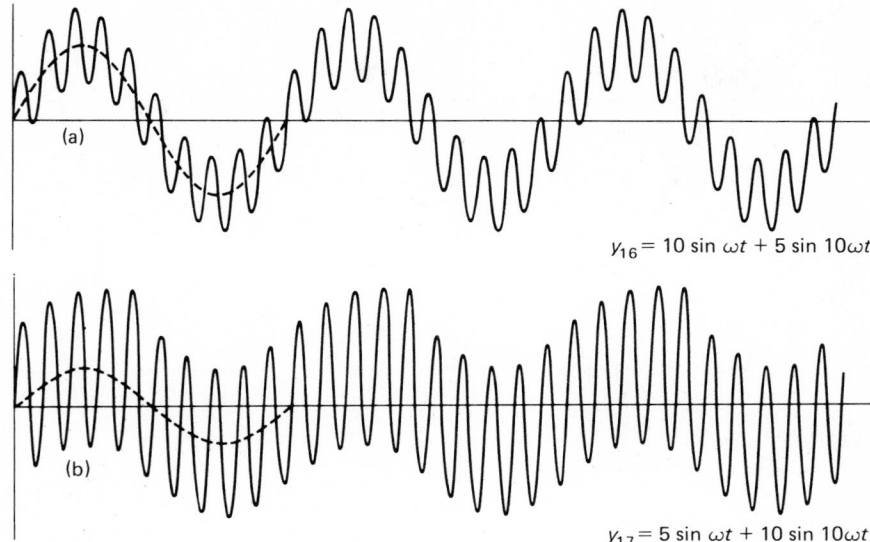

$y_{16} = 10 \sin \omega t + 5 \sin 10\omega t$

$y_{17} = 5 \sin \omega t + 10 \sin 10\omega t$

FIGURE 2.5   Examples of waveforms with the two components having considerably different frequencies.

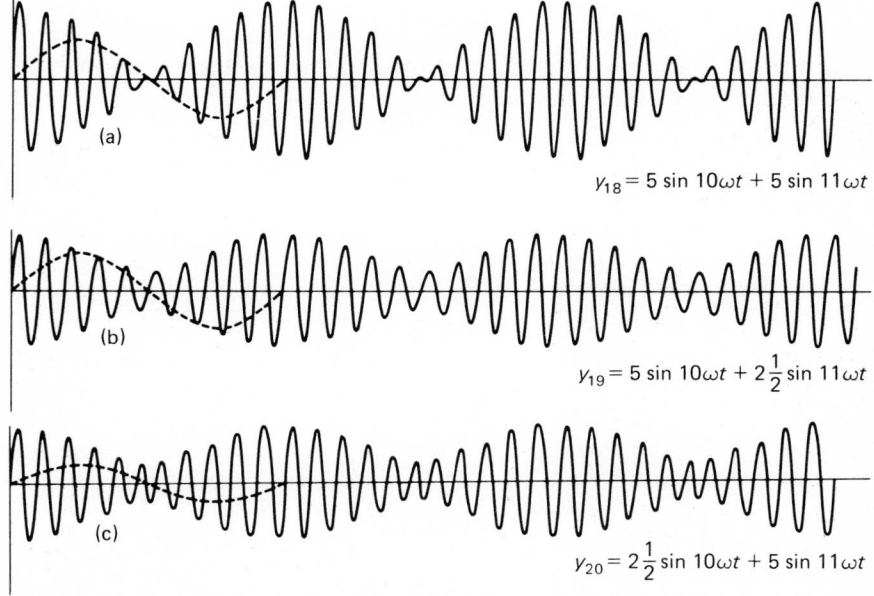

$y_{18} = 5 \sin 10\omega t + 5 \sin 11\omega t$

$y_{19} = 5 \sin 10\omega t + 2\frac{1}{2} \sin 11\omega t$

$y_{20} = 2\frac{1}{2} \sin 10\omega t + 5 \sin 11\omega t$

FIGURE 2.6   Examples of waveforms with two components having frequencies that are very nearly the same.

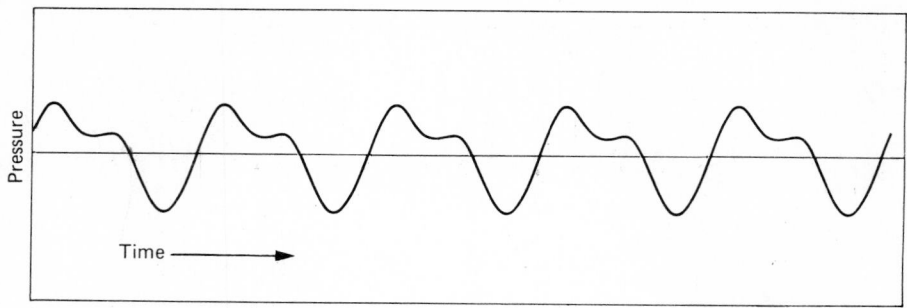

FIGURE 2.7   Pressure–time relation, $P = 100 \sin (80t) + 50 \cos (160t - \pi/4)$.

EXAMPLE As another example, suppose that an acceleration–time relation is expressed by the following equation:

$$a = 3800 \sin (2450t) + 1750 \cos \left(7350t - \frac{\pi}{3} \right) + 800 \sin (36{,}750t), \quad (2.7)$$

where

$$a = \text{acceleration, and}$$

$$t = \text{time, s.}$$

The relation consists of three harmonic components having circular frequencies in the ratio 1 to 3 to 15. Hence the components may be referred to as the fundamental, the third harmonic, and the fifteenth harmonic. Corresponding frequencies in hertz are 390, 1170, and 5850 Hz.

2.5 SPECIAL WAVEFORMS

There are a number of special waveforms whose equations may be written as infinite trigonometric series. Several of these are shown in Fig. 2.8. Table 2.1 lists the corresponding equations.

Both the square wave and the sawtooth are useful in checking the response of dynamic measuring systems. In addition, the skewed sawtooth form, Fig. 2.8(c), is of the form required for the voltage–time relation necessary for driving the horizontal sweep of a cathode-ray oscilloscope. All these forms may be obtained as voltage–time relations from electronic signal generators (Section 8.6.2).

In each case shown in Fig. 2.8 all the terms in the infinite series are necessary if the precise waveform indicated is to be obtained. Of course, with increasing harmonic order their effect on the whole becomes less and less.

As an example of this, consider the square wave shown in Fig. 2.8(a).

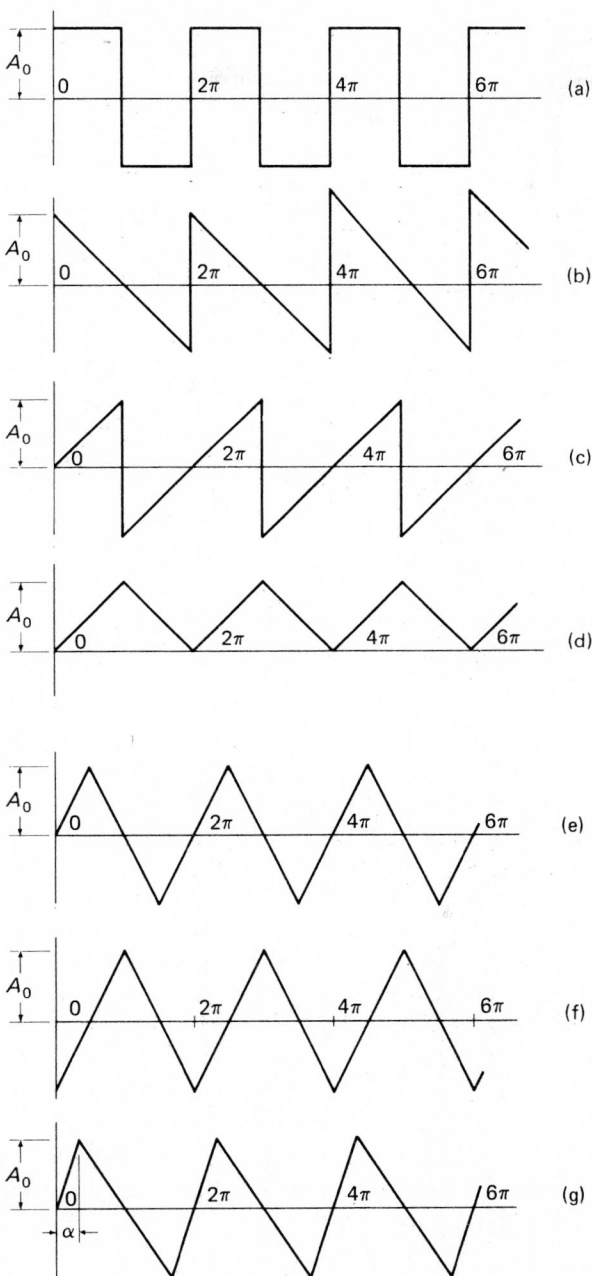

FIGURE 2.8   Various special waveforms of harmonic nature.

TABLE 2.1 Equations for Special Periodic Waveforms Shown in Fig. 2.8

Figure	Equation*
(2.8(a))	$y = \dfrac{4A_0}{\pi}\left(\sin \omega t + \tfrac{1}{3}\sin 3\omega t + \tfrac{1}{5}\sin 5\omega t + \cdots\right) = \dfrac{4A_0}{\pi}\sum_{n=1}^{\infty}\left[\dfrac{1}{2n-1}\sin(2n-1)\omega t\right]$
2.8(b)	$y = \dfrac{2A_0}{\pi}\left(\sin \omega t + \tfrac{1}{2}\sin 2\omega t + \tfrac{1}{3}\sin 3\omega t + \cdots\right) = \dfrac{2A_0}{\pi}\sum_{n=1}^{\infty}\left[\dfrac{1}{n}\sin(n\omega t)\right]$
2.8(c)	$y = \dfrac{2A_0}{\pi}\left(\sin \omega t - \tfrac{1}{2}\sin 2\omega t + \tfrac{1}{3}\sin 3\omega t - \tfrac{1}{4}\sin 4\omega t + \cdots\right) = \dfrac{2A_0}{\pi}\sum_{n=1}^{\infty}\left[\dfrac{(-1)^{n+1}}{n}\sin(n\omega t)\right]$
2.8(d)	$y = \dfrac{A_0}{2} - \dfrac{4A_0}{(\pi)^2}\left(\cos \omega t + \dfrac{1}{(3)^2}\cos 3\omega t + \dfrac{1}{(5)^2}\cos 5\omega t + \cdots\right) = \dfrac{A_0}{2} - \dfrac{4A_0}{\pi^2}\sum_{n=1}^{\infty}\left[\dfrac{1}{(2n-1)^2}\cos(2n-1)\omega t\right]$
2.8(e)	$y = \dfrac{8A_0}{(\pi)^2}\left(\sin \omega t - \dfrac{1}{(3)^2}\sin 3\omega t + \dfrac{1}{(5)^2}\sin 5\omega t - \cdots\right) = \dfrac{8A_0}{(\pi)^2}\sum_{n=1}^{\infty}\left[\dfrac{(-1)^{n+1}}{(2n-1)^2}\sin(2n-1)\omega t\right]$
2.8(f)	$y = -\dfrac{8A_0}{(\pi)^2}\left(\cos \omega t + \dfrac{1}{(3)^2}\cos 3\omega t + \dfrac{1}{(5)^2}\cos 5\omega t + \cdots\right) = \dfrac{8A_0}{(\pi)^2}\sum_{n=1}^{\infty}\left[\dfrac{1}{(2n-1)^2}\cos(n\omega t)\right]$
2.8(g)	$y = \dfrac{2A_0}{\alpha(\pi-\alpha)}\left(\sin \alpha \sin \omega t + \dfrac{1}{(2)^2}\sin 2\alpha \sin 2\omega t + \dfrac{1}{(3)^2}\sin 3\alpha \sin 3\omega t + \cdots\right) = \dfrac{2A_0}{\alpha(\pi-\alpha)}\sum_{n=1}^{\infty}\left[\dfrac{1}{n^2}\sin(n\alpha)\sin(n\omega t)\right]$

* n as used in these equations does not necessarily represent the harmonic order.

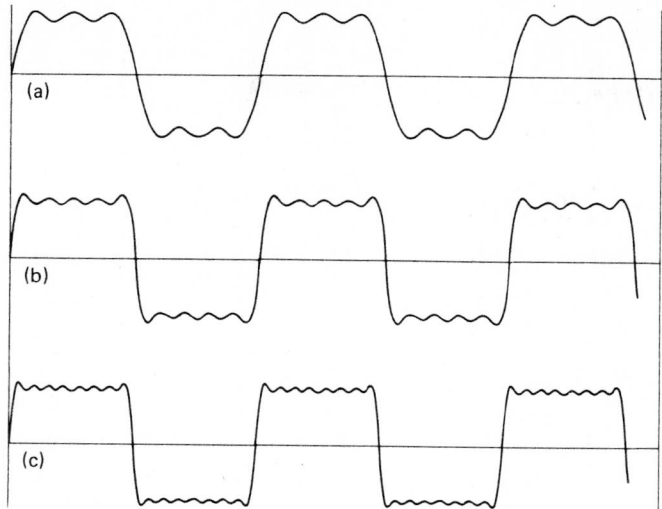

FIGURE 2.9 Plot of square-wave function. (a) Plot of first three terms only (includes the fifth harmonic). (b) Plot of the first five terms (includes the ninth harmonic). (c) Plot of the first eight terms (includes the fifteenth harmonic).

The complete series includes all the terms indicated in the relation

$$y = \frac{4A_0}{\pi} (\sin \omega t + \tfrac{1}{3} \sin 3\omega t + \tfrac{1}{5} \sin 5\omega t + \cdots).$$

By plotting the first three terms only, which includes the fifth harmonic, the waveform shown in Fig. 2.9(a) is obtained. Figure 2.9(b) shows the result of plotting terms through and including the ninth harmonic, and Fig. 2.9(c) shows the form for the terms including the fifteenth harmonic. As more and more terms are added, the waveform gradually approaches the square wave, which results from the infinite series.

Frequency spectrum

Figures 2.2 through 2.6 are plotted using *time* as the independent variable. This is the most common and familiar form. The waveform is displayed as it would appear on the face of the ordinary cathode-ray oscilloscope or in the manner plotted by a stripchart recorder. A second type of plot is the *frequency spectrum,* in which frequency is the independent variable and the amplitude of each frequency component is displayed as the ordinate. For example, the frequency spectrums for the plots shown in Figs. 2.2(a) and 2.2(d) appear as shown in Fig. 2.10. Spectrums corresponding to Figs. 2.3(a) and 2.3(c) are shown in Fig. 2.11, and the frequency spectrum for the square wave is shown in Fig. 2.12.

Interest in frequency spectrum plots has increased since the development of the *spectrum analyzer,* a device that uses a cathode-ray tube to display the

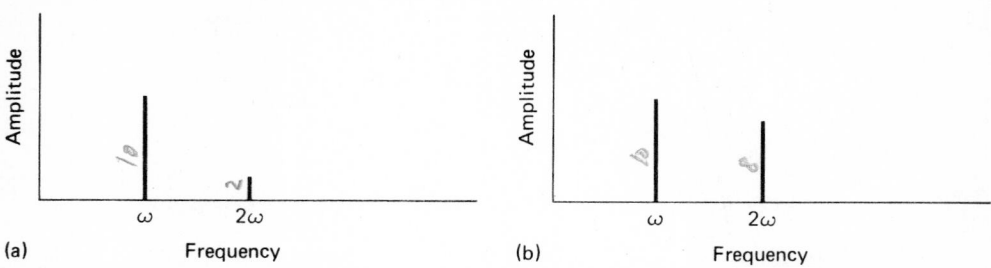

FIGURE 2.10   (a) Frequency spectrum corresponding to Fig. 2.2(a). (b) Frequency spectrum corresponding to Fig. 2.2(d).

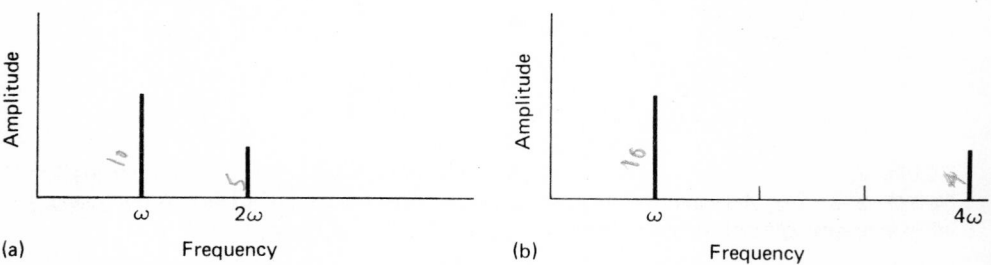

FIGURE 2.11   (a) Frequency spectrum corresponding to Fig. 2.3(a). (b) Frequency spectrum corresponding to Fig. 2.3(c).

frequency spectrum of the input signal. For a further discussion of spectrum analyzers, see Sections 7.13 and 18.5.4.

In the foregoing examples of special waveforms, various combinations of harmonic components were used. In each case the result was a periodic relation repeating indefinitely in every detail. Many mechanical inputs are not repetitive, as for example the acceleration–time relation (Fig. 2.13a) resulting

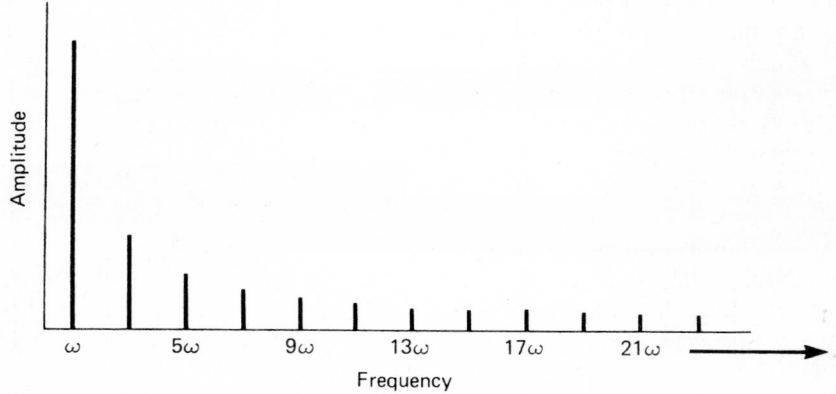

FIGURE 2.12   Frequency spectrum for a square wave, Fig. 2.8(a).

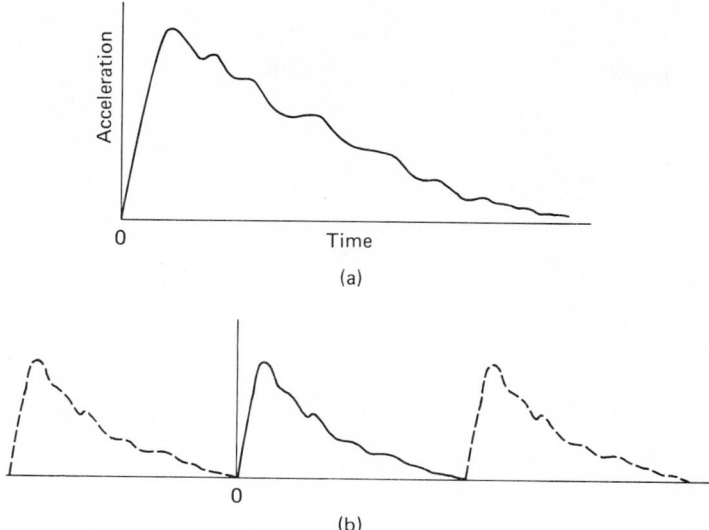

FIGURE 2.13 (a) Acceleration–time relationship resulting from shock-test. (b) Considering the nonrepeating function as one real cycle of a periodic relationship.

from an impact test. Although such a relation is transient, it may be thought of as one cycle of a periodic relation in which all other cycles are fictitious (Fig. 2.13b). On this basis nonperiodic functions may be analyzed in exactly the same manner as are periodic functions.

2.6 HARMONIC OR FOURIER ANALYSIS*

In the previous section, we have shown various forms plotted from given equations. In actual practice, however, our problem would be to obtain the important information from the recorded waveform. We would have the plot, from which we would like to obtain the harmonic components with their relative amplitudes, frequencies, and phase relations, rather than vice versa.

Harmonic analysis, which is the term applied to this process, is a subject of considerable extent, which most certainly cannot receive a thorough discussion here. However, it is possible to present a practical approach to the problem that will serve in most cases. (For detailed information on the subject, the reader is referred to the Suggested Readings for this chapter.)

In essence, the process consists of starting with an analog time-dependent signal, which is then digitized by selecting discrete values at predetermined time intervals. These values are then processed by harmonic analysis through

---

* See Appendix B for the theoretical basis.

TABLE 2.2

	A	B	C	D
I. ½ Period	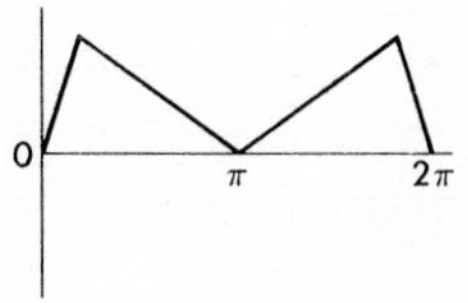 (Cosine terms only)	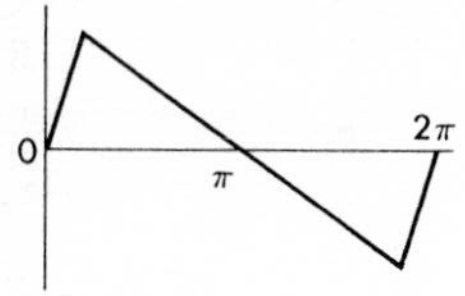 (Sine terms only)	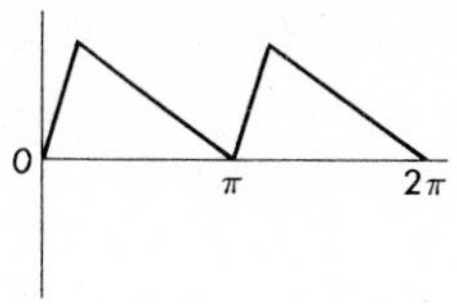 (Even harmonics only)	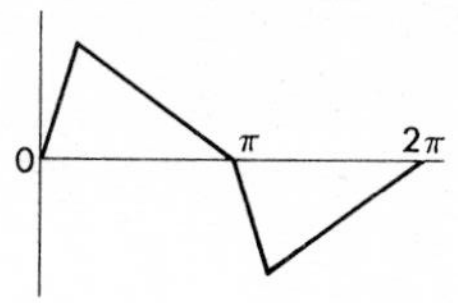 (Odd harmonics only)
II. ¼ Period	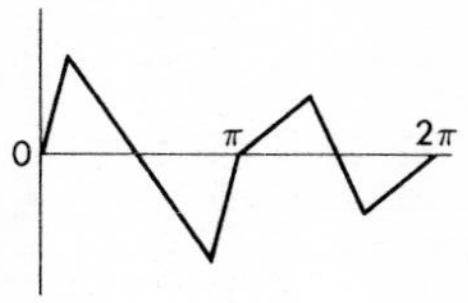 (Odd cosine and even sine terms)	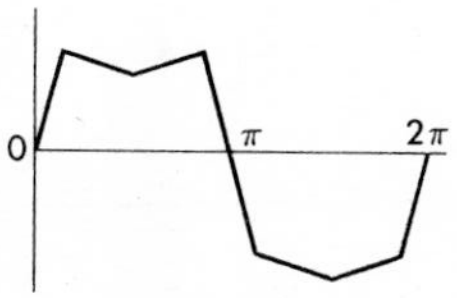 (Even cosine and odd sine terms)	(Odd sine terms only)	(Even sine terms only)
III. Double	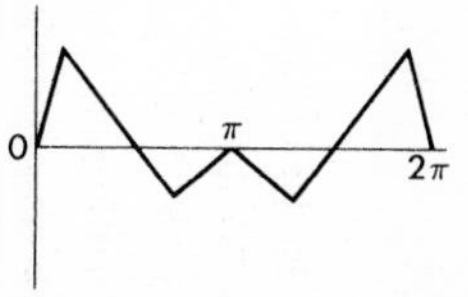 (Odd cosine terms only)	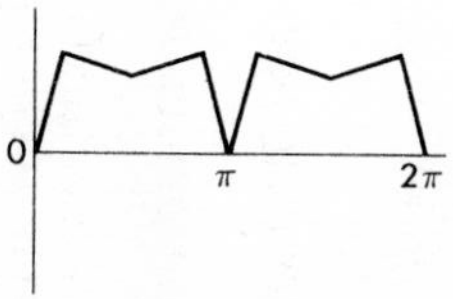 (Even cosine terms only)	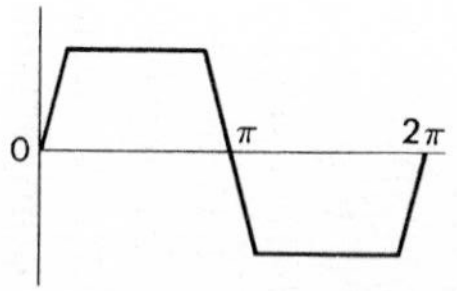	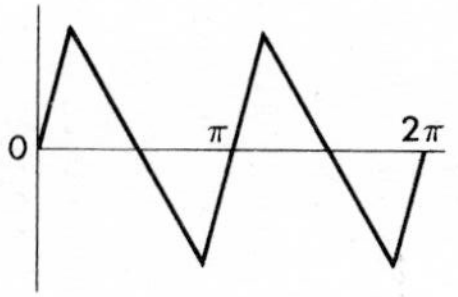

which frequency contribution and relative amplitudes are determined, finally providing a composite functional relationship that defines the original signal.

If we assume that our experimental data can be made to fit relations as expressed in Eqs. (2.5), (2.5a), or (2.5b), our problem becomes that of determining appropriate values for the harmonic orders, coefficients, and phase angles. This may be done by what amounts to a graphical integration, most easily accomplished by numerical methods. It should be noted, however, that the procedure requires considerable time and patience, and previous experience is most helpful in recognizing short cuts reducing the work required. Although digital computer solutions may be used, each student should, at least once, carry out a "longhand" analysis for experience.

Often before beginning actual numerical analysis, we may determine certain facts by inspection. For instance, it may be observed that the positive values for the first half-cycle are repeated as negative values in the second half-cycle. In this situation, it may be shown that only the odd harmonics are present and that the even harmonics may be ignored in the analysis [2, 3]. As will soon be apparent, such an observation considerably reduces the numerical work to be done. Other useful relationships are shown in Table 2.2. In addition, comparison of the unknown relation with typical plots such as those shown in Figs. 2.2 through 2.6 will often indicate the general nature of the function. The presence of higher harmonics in significant amplitudes may often be determined by observation.

2.7 ANALYTICAL PROCEDURE

The analytical procedure may be outlined as follows:

1. Establish the fundamental cycle and assign the values 0 and 2π to its limits. The general form of the desired equation is then

$$f(\theta) = \frac{A}{2} + (A_1 \cos \theta + A_2 \cos 2\theta + A_3 \cos 3\theta + \cdots)$$

$$+ (B_1 \sin \theta + B_2 \sin 2\theta + B_3 \sin 3\theta + \cdots). \tag{2.8}$$

2. Divide the fundamental cycle into m equal intervals, each of width $\Delta\theta$, and determine the corresponding ordinates. (*Note:* Do not include the ordinates for both ends of the interval being analyzed, because this would be a duplication.)

   We should also note that although the computer may make determination of high-order harmonic coefficients feasible, we should not expect to be able to find meaningful coefficients without correspondingly well-defined data. For example, we should not expect to find useful coefficients for the tenth harmonic with only twelve data intervals per cycle. As a

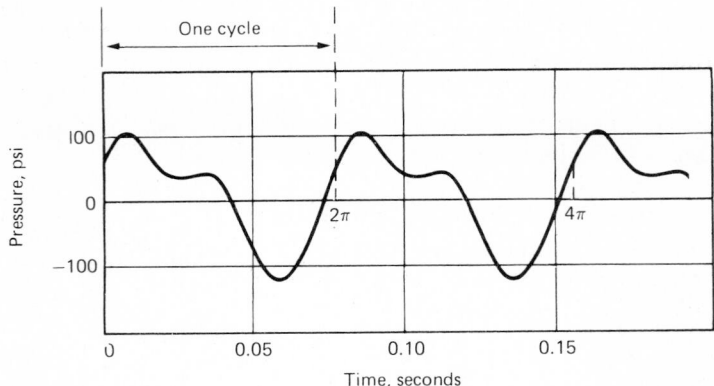

FIGURE 2.14   Enlargement of pressure–time plot shown in Fig. 2.7.

rough rule of thumb we may put down, as a limit, $m \geq 4n$, where m is the number of intervals per cycle and n is the order of coefficient desired.

3. To determine a given coefficient, multiply each of the m ordinates determined in (2) by the corresponding numerical values of the desired trigonometric function. The average value of the resulting column of products will be one-half the coefficient being sought. For example: To determine A_2, multiply each of the values of $f(\theta)$ as determined in step (2) by the corresponding values of cos 2θ. Add all the products together and divide by $m/2$. This will give the numerical value of A_2. Repeat this process for each of the values of A and B that are required.

4. Determine A, which is equal to twice the average of the values of $f(\theta)$.

EXAMPLE   As an exercise, let us assume that we have just obtained the pressure–time trace of Fig. 2.7 by means of an appropriate pressure pickup and recording system. Let us also assume that we now wish to analyze the plot to determine the amplitudes, frequencies, and phase relations that are involved. Since in this example the equation is known, we will be able to easily check our result. As a first step we must determine the unit cycle as shown in Fig. 2.14. The zero pressure and time coordinates will result from our measurements; however, in general, zero time would not be a critical quantity. The pressure scale would be predetermined by system calibration, and the time scale would be established by recorder chart speed. In determining the period, the total time for a number of cycles (say 10 or 20) should be used, provided the frequency did not change with time. A check shows that for our example the period T is equal to 0.079 s, hence $f = 12.75$ Hz and $\omega = 80$ rad/s.

Let us say that the information shown in Fig. 2.14 is the result of our preliminary inspection of the trace. We will now attempt to predict the important components in the function. Comparison of our plot with Figs. 2.2 through 2.6 indicates that we are probably working with a function in which higher harmonics are negligible. We will, therefore, begin our analysis with the assumption that second harmonics only occur in addition to the fundamental. If we are in error on this point, a comparison of our resulting equation with the data will so indicate.

Our next step will be to lift the data from the curve and put it into tabular form. This is done in columns (1) and (2) of Table 2.3. The remainder of the table consists of the numerical determination of the coefficients according to the rules set down in the preceding pages. The columns are calculated as indicated and their sums obtained.

The values of $A/2$ and A_1 indicate that perhaps they should actually be equal to zero, and for the time being at least, we will assume that this is the case. Our equation then may be written as

$$P = 100.03 \sin \theta + 35.4 \cos 2\theta + 35.4 \sin 2\theta. \qquad (2.9)$$

If we convert the 2θ terms into the form of Eq. (3.5b) and substitute $\theta = \omega t = 80t$, we obtain

$$P = 100.03 \sin (80t) + 50 \cos \left(160t - \frac{\pi}{4} \right). \qquad (2.10)$$

Having used, for this example, a trace whose equation was known, we have no problem in checking our analysis. Direct comparison of the relation above with Eq. (2.6) indicates that we have obtained the correct answer. In the usual case, however, we would now use our resulting function to calculate values of pressure for various values of time t. These calculated values would then be compared with the corresponding values on the curve. Reasonable agreement or lack thereof would indicate the measure of our success.

Note also that in the usual case it would probably be more logical to select our time origin ($t = 0$) corresponding to zero pressure. In this case the final equation would contain phase angles other than zero for the fundamental and $\pi/4$ for the second harmonic. However, the same waveform would be defined.

2.8 HARMONIC OR FOURIER ANALYSIS BY MACHINE

2.8.1 Using a Computer

Figure 2.15 illustrates a simple experiment. Each of three sine-wave signal generators is connected to a loudspeaker. Combination A was set to 500 Hz, B to 1000 Hz, and C to 1500 Hz. The three individual sound levels are set separately to peak-to-peak magnitudes of 100 mV as measured by the cathode-ray oscilloscope. Finally the three sources are mixed and the resulting waveform displayed by the CRO from which the data listed in Table 2.4 is taken.

TABLE 2.3

(1)	(2)	(3)	(4)	(5)	(6)	(7)	(8)	(9)	(10)
θ	P = f(θ)	sin θ	f(θ) sin θ	cos θ	f(θ) cos θ	sin 2θ	f(θ) sin 2θ	cos 2θ	f(θ) cos 2θ
0	35	0.000	0.00	1.000	35.00	0.000	0.00	1.000	35.00
10	63	0.174	10.96	0.985	62.06	0.342	21.55	0.940	59.22
20	84	0.342	28.73	0.940	78.96	0.643	54.01	0.766	64.34
30	98	0.500	49.0	0.866	84.87	0.866	84.87	0.500	49.0
40	105	0.643	67.51	0.766	80.43	0.985	103.42	0.174	18.27
50	105	0.766	80.43	0.643	67.51	0.985	103.42	-0.174	-18.27
60	99	0.866	85.73	0.500	49.50	0.866	85.73	-0.500	-49.50
70	90	0.940	84.60	0.342	30.78	0.643	57.87	-0.766	-68.94
80	77	0.985	75.84	0.174	13.40	0.342	26.33	-0.940	-72.38
90	65	1.000	65.00	0.0	0.0	0.0	0.0	-1.000	-65.00
100	53	0.985	52.20	-0.174	-9.22	-0.342	-18.13	-0.940	-49.82
110	44	0.940	41.36	-0.342	-15.05	-0.643	-28.29	-0.766	-33.70
120	38	0.866	32.91	-0.500	-19.00	-0.866	-32.91	-0.500	-19.00
130	36	0.766	27.58	-0.643	-23.15	-0.985	-35.46	-0.174	-6.26
140	36	0.643	23.15	-0.766	-27.58	-0.985	-35.46	0.174	6.26
150	37	0.500	18.50	-0.866	-32.04	-0.866	-32.04	0.500	18.50
160	39	0.342	13.34	-0.940	-36.66	-0.643	-25.08	0.766	29.87
170	39	0.174	6.79	-0.985	-38.41	-0.342	-13.34	0.940	36.66

180	35	0.0	0.0	−1.000	−35.00	0.0	0.0	1.000	35.00
190	28	−0.174	−4.87	−0.985	−27.58	0.342	9.58	0.940	26.32
200	16	−0.342	−5.47	−0.940	−15.04	0.643	10.29	0.766	12.26
210	−2	−0.500	1.00	−0.866	1.73	0.866	−1.73	0.500	−1.00
220	−23	−0.643	14.79	−0.766	17.62	0.985	−22.66	0.174	−4.00
230	−48	−0.766	36.77	−0.643	30.86	0.985	−47.28	−0.174	8.35
240	−74	−0.866	64.08	−0.500	37.00	0.866	−64.08	−0.500	37.00
250	−98	−0.940	92.12	−0.342	33.52	0.643	−63.01	−0.766	75.07
260	−120	−0.985	118.20	−0.174	20.88	0.342	−41.04	−0.940	112.80
270	−135	−1.000	135.00	0.0	0.00	0.0	0.0	−1.000	135.00
280	−144	−0.985	141.84	0.174	−25.06	−0.342	49.25	−0.940	135.36
290	−144	−0.940	135.36	0.342	−49.25	−0.643	92.59	−0.766	110.30
300	−135	−0.866	116.91	0.500	−67.50	−0.866	116.91	−0.500	67.50
310	−118	−0.766	90.39	0.643	−75.87	−0.985	116.23	−0.174	20.53
320	−93	−0.643	59.80	0.766	−71.24	−0.985	91.60	0.174	−16.18
330	−63	−0.500	31.50	0.866	−54.56	−0.866	54.56	0.500	−31.50
340	−30	−0.342	10.26	0.940	−28.20	−0.643	19.29	0.766	−22.98
350	4	−0.174	−0.70	0.985	−3.94	−0.342	−1.37	0.940	3.76
	$\sum = -11$		$\sum = 1800.61$		$\sum = -10.23$		$\sum = 635.62$		$\sum = 637.84$

Note: $A = \dfrac{-11}{18} = -0.6$, $A_1 = \dfrac{-10.23}{18} = -0.56$, $A_2 = \dfrac{637.84}{18} = 35.4$, $B_1 = \dfrac{1800.61}{18} = 100.03$, $B_2 = \dfrac{635.62}{18} = 35.4$.

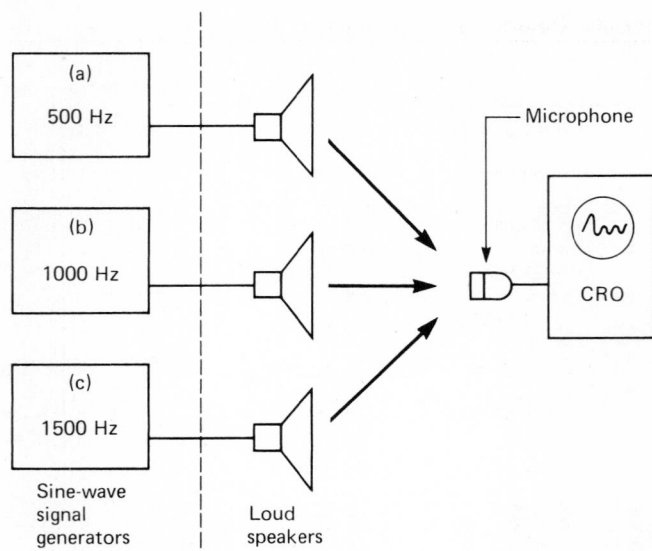

FIGURE 2.15   Experimental setup whereby the combination of pure tones from three sound sources are mixed and displayed on a cathode-ray oscilloscope screen.

TABLE 2.4   Experimental Data

Harmonic angle, degree*	Amplitude, mV
0	0
20	10
40	30
60	70
80	65
100	15
120	− 40
140	− 50
160	15
180	100
220	90
240	− 40
260	− 130
280	− 140
300	− 110
320	− 50
340	− 10
360	0

*   *Position of zero degrees selected arbitrarily.*

TABLE 2.5   Computer-Determined Coefficients

Harmonic order, n	A_n	B_n	Relative magnitudes*
0	-1.04167		
1	-29.11393	46.82849	100%
2	49.08969	52.70029	130.61
3	-21.95833	-47.41489	94.76
4	2.78222	2.22612	6.46
5	1.96661	-0.46995	3.67
6	-0.95833	-0.50519	1.96
7	0.14732	2.93104	5.32
8	-0.37192	-1.11073	2.12
9	-1.08333	-0.00000	1.96

* Relative magnitude $= (A_n^2 + B_n^2)^{1/2}/(29.11393^2 + 46.82849^2)^{1/2}$.

This data is then analyzed using a Fourier computer program and the generated results are shown in Table 2.5 and Fig. 2.16. In the figure the curve is computer-plotted and the original data points are shown. Visually, the fit of curve to data appears perfect.

Eighteen data points are used to define the waveform. If we adhere to the rule given in Section 2.7 that $m \geq 4n$, then we should discount any values

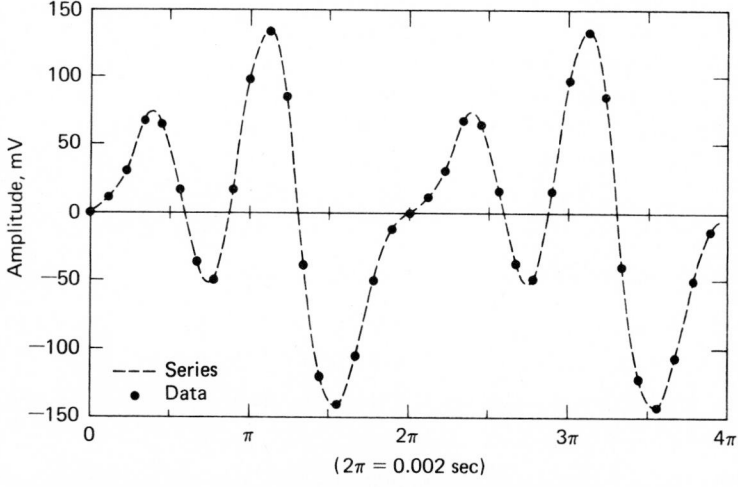

FIGURE 2.16   Comparison of Fourier series with actual test data.

beyond the fourth harmonic order. First, second, and third harmonic inputs were each set to 100%; however, we see that the calculated value for the second is 30% greater than that of the fundamental. In addition to lack of preciseness of the data, a disadvantage is that the test was run in a conventional laboratory environment. Sound reflections from the walls and ceiling were unavoidably added, complicating the input. In spite of this, however, we see that the basic inputs have been adequately extracted from the data. Ideally the exercise should have been run in an anechoic chamber (Section 18.2).

A detailed discussion of a more advanced procedure, the fast Fourier transform analysis technique and its specific application to the analysis of mechanical vibration and acoustic signals, is presented in Sections 18.5.1 and 18.6.

2.8.2 Using the Spectrum Analyzer

Filtering consists of selectively passing desired signal components and rejecting others (Section 5.21). The basis for selection or rejection may be relative amplitude or frequencies. To be used for harmonic analysis, frequency would, of course, be the independent criterion. Through use of very narrow band-pass filtering, complex signal inputs can be broken down and the existence and amplitudes of particular frequency components (or actually very narrow ranges of frequencies) can be isolated. The apparatus for accomplishing this is called the *spectrum analyzer*. See Section 7.12 for a more detailed discussion and examples of its use.

2.9 FINAL REMARKS

In this chapter we have inspected the form of analog signals. We have found that a complex input may be broken down and analyzed as a mixture of harmonic components. When reading the following chapters, keep in mind that in essence all dynamic inputs, those whose magnitudes vary with time, are in reality only combinations of simple sinusoidal building blocks.

In Chapter 6 we will consider some of the properties of digital input signals.

SUGGESTED READINGS

Eagle, A., *Fourier's Theorem and Harmonic Analysis*. London: Green & Co., 1925.

Manley, R. G., *Waveform Analysis*. New York: John Wiley, 1945.

Von Sanden, H., *Practical Mathematical Analysis*. New York: E. P. Dutton, 1924.

Willers, F. A., *Practical Analysis*. New York: Dover, 1948.

Worthing, A. G., and J. Geffner, *Treatment of Experimental Data*. New York: John Wiley, 1943.

PROBLEMS

2.1 Each of the following expressions is written in the form of either Eq. (2.5a), Eq. (2.5b), or both. For each case, determine the period of the function and rewrite the function in the form of Eq. (2.5).

a) $y = 18 \cos (4t - 0.4)$

b) $y = 18 \sin (4t - 0.4)$

c) $y = 2 \sin (0.1t - 0.35) + 4 \cos (0.1t + 0.8)$

d) $y = \cos (18t - 0.8) + \sin (36t + 0.4)$

e) $y = 7 \sin (10t - 0.4) + 4 \cos (20t + 0.7) - 2 \sin (40t - 0.8)$

2.2 The following expressions are written in the form of Eq. (2.5). Assuming that t is measured in seconds, determine the period of each and convert each into the forms of Eqs. (2.5a) and (2.5b).

a) $y = 2.78 \sin (12t) - 1.45 \cos (12t)$

b) $y = 389 \cos (418t) + 217 \sin (418t)$

c) $y = -0.085 \sin (4782t) + 0.111 \cos (4782t)$

d) $y = \sin (0.0046t) - \cos (0.0046t)$

e) $y = 0.82 \cos (5t) + 0.51 \sin (5t) - 0.45 \cos (10t) + 0.38 \sin (10t)$

f) $y = 18 \cos (0.6t) - 9 \sin (0.6t) + 4 \sin (1.2t)$

g) $y = 114 \sin (0.2t) + 21 \cos (0.4t) - 35 \sin (0.4t)$

2.3 The following equation represents the time variation of a mechanical strain:

$\epsilon = 120 + 95 \sin (15t) + 40 \sin (30t) + 18 \sin (45t) - 55 \cos (15t) - 24 \cos (45t)$.

a) What is the fundamental frequency in hertz?

b) Rewrite the equation in terms of cosine components only by combining proper sine and cosine terms.

c) What is the amplitude of the third harmonic component?

2.4 Construct a frequency spectrum diagram for each of the expressions in

a) Fig. 2.5;

b) Fig. 2.6;

c) Fig. 2.8.

2.5 As an exercise, write a relationship involving harmonic terms, such as:

$$f(t) = 4 + 3.6 \sin (\omega t) + 5 \cos (2\omega t) - 2 \sin (2\omega t), \quad \text{etc.}$$

Calculate enough data points to enable the plotting of a complete cycle. Treat the plot as though it were formed experimentally on a CRO screen or on a stripchart from an oscillograph. "Read" data from the plot and perform a Fourier analysis. Prove to yourself that you can make a satisfactory harmonic analysis. Use a computer, if one is available, for each of the steps.

2.6 Table 2.6 lists sets of data, each set derived from a different harmonic series and susceptible to Fourier analysis. The first column, designated t, can be considered the independent variable, tabulated in equal steps. Ordinarily, it would be a measure

TABLE 2.6

t	$f_1(t)$	$f_2(t)$	$f_3(t)$	$f_4(t)$	$f_5(t)$	$f_6(t)$
0	0.00	17.90	3.10	0.00	0.00	1.27
1	8.24	16.63	3.97	0.53	0.22	1.20
2	13.81	11.70	4.49	1.24	0.91	0.99
3	15.15	4.6	3.77	1.65	1.85	1.34
4	12.41	− 2.58	2.39	2.36	2.73	2.03
5	7.28	− 7.91	1.70	2.89	3.35	2.12
6	2.16	− 10.22	2.16	2.57	3.66	1.93
7	− 0.96	− 9.50	2.83	2.22	3.78	2.14
8	− 1.41	− 6.83	2.63	2.29	3.87	2.25
9	− 0.01	− 3.85	1.69	2.04	4.06	1.73
10	1.40	− 2.10	1.10	1.69	4.33	1.18
11	0.95	− 2.40	1.43	1.83	4.54	0.92
12	− 2.17	− 4.48	2.11	1.73	4.53	0.72
13	− 7.29	− 7.15	2.35	1.16	4.24	0.79
14	− 12.42	− 8.76	2.25	1.06	3.73	1.00
15	− 15.16	− 7.91	2.49	1.20	3.20	0.65
16	− 13.82	− 4.04	3.24	0.85	2.82	− 0.04
17	− 8.25	2.26	3.76	0.60	2.68	− 0.13
18	− 0.01	9.35	3.49	0.67	2.70	0.06
19	8.24	15.17	2.95	0.32	2.67	− 0.15
20	13.81	17.90	3.09	0.0	2.39	− 0.26
21	15.15	16.63	3.97	0.53	1.80	0.26
22	12.41	11.7	4.49	1.24	1.02	0.81
23	7.28	4.60	3.77	1.65	0.32	1.07
24	2.16	− 2.58	2.39	2.36	0.0	1.27
25	− 0.96	− 7.91	1.7	2.89	0.22	1.20

of time (ms, hours, days, etc.). Each of the additional columns represents a different function of t. Select a set of data, and perform a Fourier analysis determining the harmonic terms and the coefficients necessary to express the data in an equation. Finally, spot-check several points to assure yourself that the function you have found does indeed agree, within reasonable limits, with the data. (There is undoubtedly some educational merit to performing at least one longhand Fourier analysis during one's lifetime. However, thereafter, the only sensible approach is to use a computer.)

2.7 Duplicate the experiment described in Section 2.8 and compare your results with those given in the text.

measuring 3
system response

3.1 INTRODUCTION

Quite simply, *response* is a measure of a system's fidelity to purpose. It may be defined as an evaluation of the system's ability to faithfully sense, transmit, and present all the pertinent information included in the measurand and to exclude all else.

We would like to know if the output information truly represents the input. If the input information is in the form of a sine wave, a square wave, or a sawtoothed wave, does the output appear as a sine wave, a square wave, or a sawtoothed wave, as the case may be? Is each of the harmonic components in a complex wave treated equally, or are some attenuated, completely ignored, or perhaps shifted timewise relative to the others? These questions are answered by the response characteristics of the particular system, that is, (a) amplitude response, (b) frequency response, (c) phase response, and (d) slew rate.

3.2 AMPLITUDE RESPONSE

Amplitude response is governed by the system's ability to treat all input amplitudes uniformly. If an input of 5 units is fed into a system and an output of 25 indicator divisions is obtained, we can generally expect that an input of 10 units will result in an output of 50 divisions. Although this is the most common case, there are other special nonlinear responses that are occasionally required. Whatever the arrangement, whether it be linear, exponential, or some other amplitude function, discrepancy between design expectations in this respect and actual performance results in poor amplitude response.

Of course no system exists that is capable of faithfully responding over an unlimited range of amplitudes. All systems can be overdriven. Figure 3.1 shows the amplitude response of a voltage amplifier suitable for connecting a strain-gage bridge to an oscilloscope. The usable range of the amplifier is

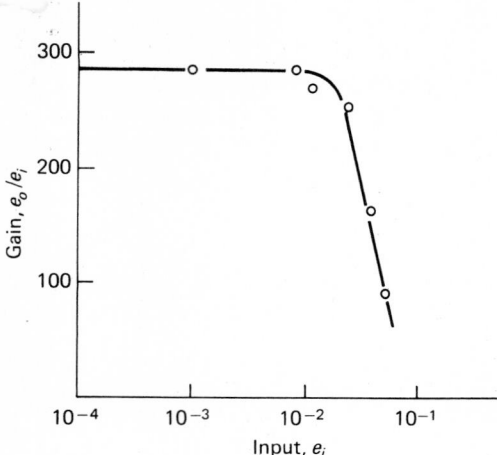

FIGURE 3.1 Gain vs. input voltage for amplifier section of a commercially available strain measuring system. (For frequency = 1 kHz.)

restricted to the horizontal portion of the curve. The plot shows that for inputs above about 0.01 volts the amplifier becomes overloaded and the amplification ceases to be linear.

3.3 FREQUENCY RESPONSE

Good frequency response is obtained when a system treats all *frequency components* with equal faithfulness. If a 100-Hz sine wave with an input amplitude of 5 units is fed into a system, and a peak-to-peak output of $2\frac{1}{2}$ in. results on an oscilloscope screen, we can expect that a 500-Hz sine-wave input of the *same* amplitude would also result in a $2\frac{1}{2}$-in. peak-to-peak output. Changing the frequency of the input signal should not alter the system's output magnitude so long as the input amplitude remains unchanged.

Yet here again there must be a limit to the range over which good frequency response may be expected. This is true for any dynamic system, regardless of its quality. Figure 3.2 illustrates the frequency–response relations for the same voltage amplifier used in Fig. 3.1. Frequencies above about 10 kHz are attenuated and an input below this limit only is amplified in the correct relative proportion.

3.4 PHASE RESPONSE

Amplitude and frequency responses are important for all types of input waveforms, simple or complex. *Phase response,* however, is of importance primarily for the complex wave only.

Time is required for the transmission of a signal through any measuring system. Often when a simple sine-wave voltage is amplified by a single stage of amplification, the output trails the input by approximately 180 degrees, or

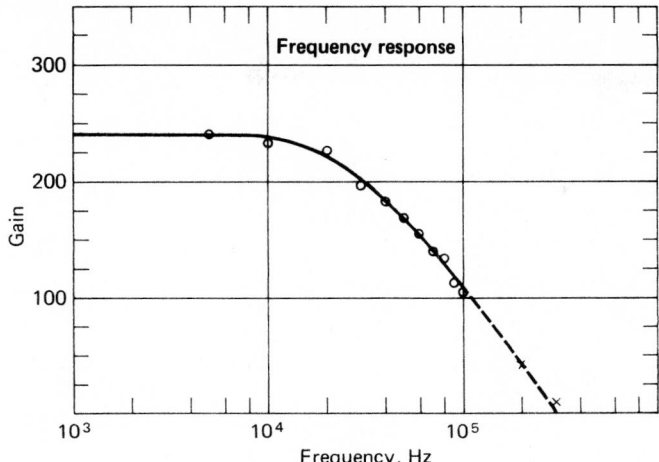

FIGURE 3.2   Frequency response curve for amplifier section of a commercially available strain measuring system. $e_i = 10$mv.

one-half cycle (see Fig. 5.17). For two stages, the shift may be about 360 degrees, and so on. Actually the shift will not be exact multiples of half wavelengths but will depend on the equipment and also on the frequency. It is the frequency-dependent aspect that is important in determining phase response.

For the single sine-wave input, any shift would normally be unimportant. The output produced on the oscilloscope screen could show true waveform, and the proper parameters could be determined. The fact that the shape being shown was actually formed a few microseconds or a few milliseconds after being generated is of no consequence.

Let us consider, however, the complex wave made up of numerous harmonics. Suppose that each component is delayed by a different amount. The harmonic components would then emerge from the system in phase relations different from when they entered. The whole waveform and its amplitudes would be changed, a result of poor phase response.

Figure 3.3 illustrates typical phase–response characteristics for a voltage amplifier.

3.5   PREDICTING PERFORMANCE FOR COMPLEX WAVEFORMS

Response characteristics of an existing system or a component of a system may be determined experimentally by injecting as input a signal of known form, then determining the output, and finally comparing the results (see Section 10.5). Of course, the most basic waveform is the sine wave.

If we know the sine-wave response of a device, can we use this information to predict how it will respond to a complex input, such as a square wave or

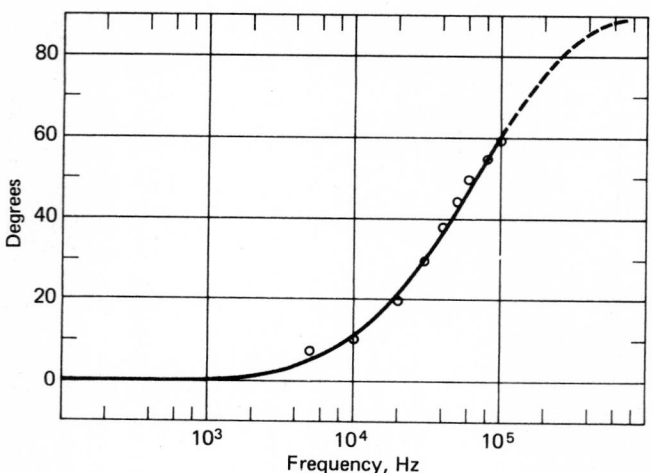

FIGURE 3.3   Phase lag vs. frequency for the same amplifier used for Figs. 3.1 and 3.2.

one of the various sawtooth waveforms? The answer is yes, as we demonstrate in the following example.

EXAMPLE   Using a computer program and information given in Figs. 3.2 and 3.3, predict the form of amplifier output to be expected if a perfect square wave is the input. Do this for fundamental input frequencies of 1000 and 2000 Hz.

Solution   Recall that in Table 2.1 a square wave is defined by the infinite series

$$y = \frac{4A_0}{\pi} \sum_{n=1}^{\infty} \frac{1}{(2n-1)} \sin (2n-1) \, \omega t. \tag{3.1}$$

We may modify Eq. (3.1) by introducing frequency and phase distortion factors:

$$y = \frac{4A_0}{\pi} \sum_{n=1}^{\infty} \frac{K_n}{(2n-1)} \sin [(2n-1) \, \omega t - \phi_n], \tag{3.1a}$$

where

K_n = an amplitude factor based on frequency, and

ϕ_n = a phase distortion factor.

Magnitudes for K_n and ϕ_n for each of the existing harmonic orders can be extracted from the response curves, as shown in Figs. 3.2 and 3.3. Various computer programs can be written. For example, we may write a program including tables of frequency– and phase–response factors taken directly from

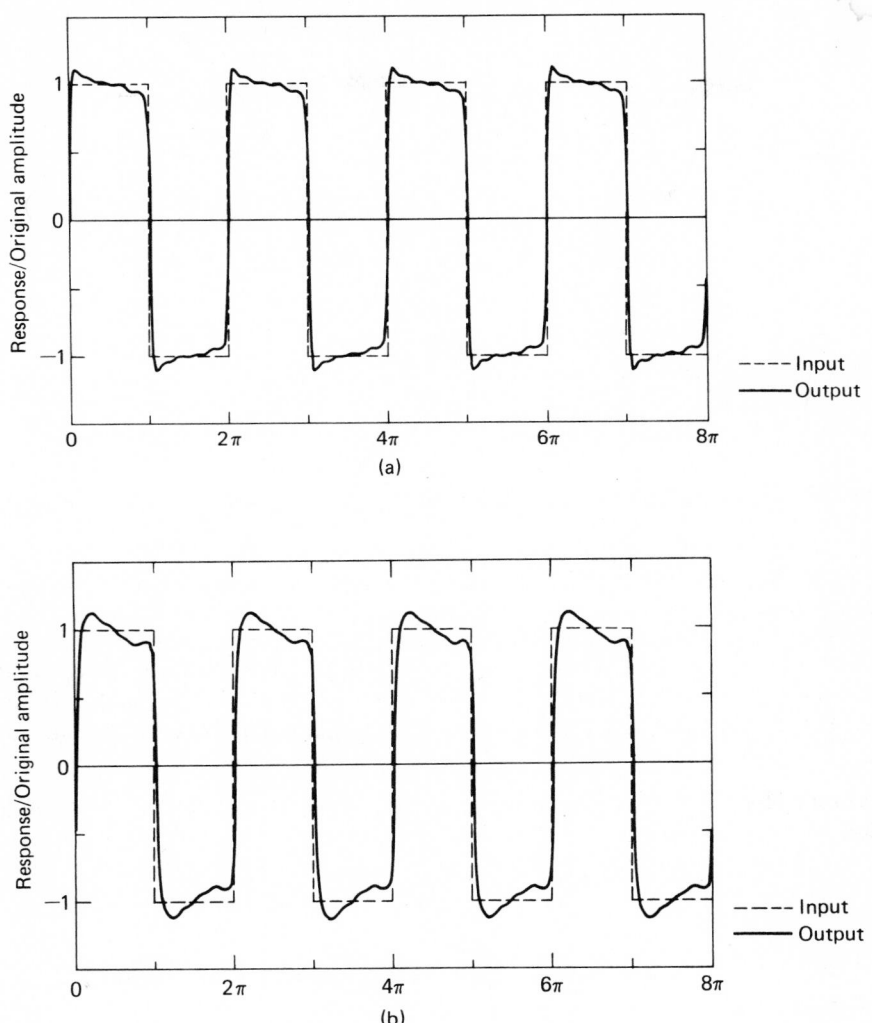

FIGURE 3.4   (a) Computer-determined treatment of a 1000-Hz square wave by the amplifier whose characteristics are shown in Figs. 3.1 through 3.3. (b) Computer-determined treatment of a 2000-Hz square wave by the amplifier whose characteristics are shown in Figs. 3.1 through 3.3.

the curves. The results displayed in Figs. 3.4(a) and 3.4(b) are computer-plotted, based on amplitude and phase distortion factors taken directly from Figs. 3.2 and 3.3.

It should be clear that we can make similar calculations for any waveform for which a harmonic series can be written. For example, we can apply a Fourier analysis to almost any random waveform and use the result to investigate the effects of various response characteristics.

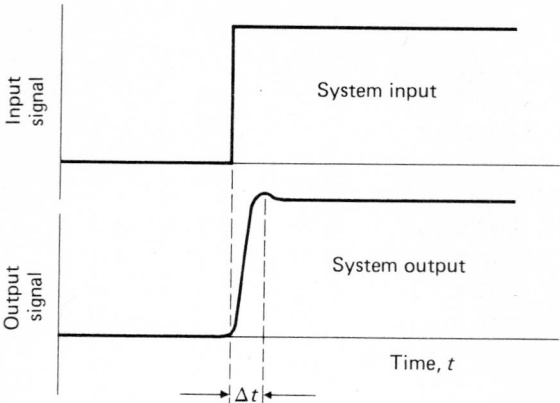

FIGURE 3.5   Response of a typical system to a pulse-type input; Δt is the rise-time.

3.6 DELAY, RISE TIME, AND SLEW RATE

Finally, a fourth type of response, which is actually another form of frequency response, is *delay,* or *rise time.* When a stepped or relatively instantaneous input is applied to a system, the output may lag as shown in Fig. 3.5. The time delay, Δt, after the step is applied but before proper output magnitude is reached is known as delay, or rise time. It is a measure of the system's ability to handle transients.

Slew rate is the *maximum* rate of change that the system can handle. In electrical terms, it is *de/dt,* or volts per unit of time (e.g., 25 volts/microsecond). The term slew rate or slew speed is also used in other ways; for example, the slew speed of the stylus of an *x-y* plotter would be expressed in terms of cm/s, a reference to the maximum speed with which the stylus can traverse its range of motion.

3.7 SIMPLIFIED PHYSICAL SYSTEMS

What basic physical factors govern response? In terms of practical system formation we are confronted with two fundamental segments of construction: mechanical and electrical. The basic mechanical elements are mass, some form of equilibrium-restoring element, and damping. Corresponding electrical elements are resistance, inductance, and capacitance. Although it is true that many, if not most, devices and systems involve both, for our immediate purposes it is advantageous to consider the two separately. In the next several sections we will discuss some of the mechanical aspects; and beginning with Section 3.16 we will consider the electrical.

3.8 MECHANICAL ELEMENTS

A discussion of the dynamic characteristics of an elementary mechanical system necessitates a short description of the elements composing such a system.

3.8.1 Mass

It is obvious that in all cases mass will be a factor. Under certain conditions, however, the masses making up the device or system will not affect its performance. We will consider such cases in Sections 3.13 and 3.14.

By its very nature, mass must be distributed throughout some volume. In many cases, however, it is not only convenient but also correct, or nearly so, to assume that the mass of a member is concentrated at a point. Depending on the geometry of the member and its application, the point of concentration may or may not be the center of gravity. In certain cases, the center of percussion may be the location of effective concentration.

3.8.2 Spring Force

Many mechanical members deflect in direct proportion to the force exerted on them, that is, $\Delta F/\Delta \delta = k = $ a constant, where ΔF is an applied force increment and $\Delta \delta$ is the resulting deflection increment. Most coil springs, beams, and tension/compression members abide by this relationship. It may be noted that the force is opposed to the deflection, that is, the resulting force always attempts to restore equilibrium.

Torsional members commonly adhere to the relationship $\Delta T/\Delta \theta = k_t = $ a constant, where ΔT is an applied torque increment and $\Delta \theta$ is the resulting torsional deflection increment. The constants k and k_t are called *spring constants* or *deflection constants*.

Elasticity is not always the source of the restoring force, however. In certain cases, such as for a beam balance (see Section 3.9), the restoring force may be supplied by gravity.

When the motion of a concentrated mass is constrained by an equilibrium-seeking member (Fig. 3.6a), simple vibration theory shows that the combination will have a natural frequency

$$\omega_n = \sqrt{k \cdot g_c/m}, \tag{3.2}$$

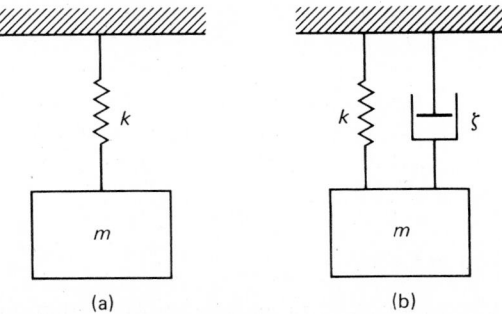

(a) (b)

FIGURE 3.6 Elementary spring-mass systems. (a) Without damping. (b) With viscous damping.

where

ω_n = circular frequency in radians per second (see Section 2.3)

= $2\pi f$, and

f = frequency of vibration in hertz.

A system of this sort is said to have a *single degree of freedom*, that is, it is assumed to be constrained in some way to oscillate in a single mode or manner, needing only one coordinate to fully describe its motion.

3.8.3 Damping

Another factor important to the usefulness of any general system of this type is damping (Fig. 3.6b). Damping in this connection is usually thought of as viscous rather than Coulomb or frictional, and may be obtained by fluids (including gaseous) or electrical means.

Viscous damping is a velocity function, and the force opposing the motion may be expressed as

$$F = -\zeta \frac{ds}{dt},\tag{3.3}$$

where ζ = the damping coefficient and ds/dt = the velocity. We can see that the damping coefficient is an evaluation of force per unit velocity. The negative sign indicates that the resulting force opposes the velocity. The effect of viscous damping on a freely vibrating single-degree-of-freedom system is to reduce the vibrational amplitudes with respect to time according to a logarithmic relation.

Damping magnitude is conveniently thought of in terms of *critical damping*, which is the maximum damping that can be used to just prevent overshoot when a spring-mass–damped system is deflected from equilibrium and then released (see Section 3.10 for further discussion). This limiting condition is shown in Fig. 3.7. The value of the critical damping coefficient, ζ_c, for a simple spring-supported mass m is expressed by the relation

$$\zeta_c = 2\sqrt{m \cdot k/g_c}.\tag{3.4}$$

Damping is often specified in terms of the unitless damping ratio,

$$\xi = \frac{\zeta}{\zeta_c}.$$

Many measuring devices or system components involve elements constrained by gravity or spring force, whose deflection is analogous to the signal input. The ordinary balance scale is an example, as are the D'Arsonval meter movement and the mirror-type galvanometer (Section 7.9). The same is true of

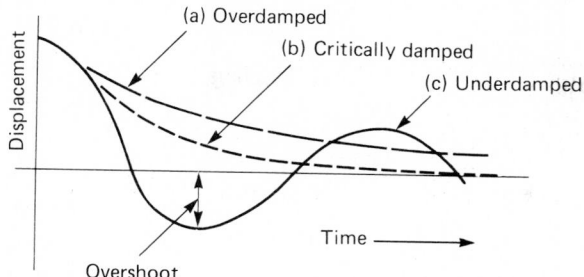

FIGURE 3.7 Time-displacement relations for damped motion. (a) For damping greater than critical. (b) For critical damping. (c) For damping less than critical.

most pressure transducers, elastic-force transducers, and many other measuring devices.

If the system is a translational one, a spring-constrained mass may be involved. Our tire gage illustrates the case in which the piston and stem and a portion of the spring constitute the mass whose motion is controlled by the interaction of the applied pressure and the spring force. Other examples are the seismic-type instruments discussed in Chapter 17.

These devices depend on equilibrium for correct indication. When equilibrium is disturbed by a change of input, the system requires time to readjust to the new equilibrium, and a number of oscillations may take place before the new output is correctly indicated. The rate at which the amplitude of such oscillations decreases is a function of the system's damping. In addition, the frequency of oscillation is a function of both damping and sensitivity.

3.9 AN EXAMPLE OF A SIMPLE MECHANICAL SYSTEM

Let us consider a symmetrical scale beam *without* damping (Fig. 3.8). For simplification, we will assume that the masses of the scale pans and the weights being compared are concentrated at points A and B, and that they are also included in the moment of inertia I, which is referred to the main pivot point O. Further, we will assume that a small difference, ΔW, exists between the two weights being compared, and that points A, B, and O lie along a straight line. We define sensitivity, η, as the ratio of the displacement of the end of the pointer to the length of the pointer, h, divided by ΔW, or

$$\eta = \frac{1}{\Delta W}\frac{d}{h} = \frac{1}{\Delta W}\tan\theta. \tag{3.5}$$

The system behaves as a compound pendulum, and it can be shown that the period of oscillation will be

$$\mathcal{T} = 2\pi\sqrt{I/\bar{r}w_b g_c} \tag{3.6}$$

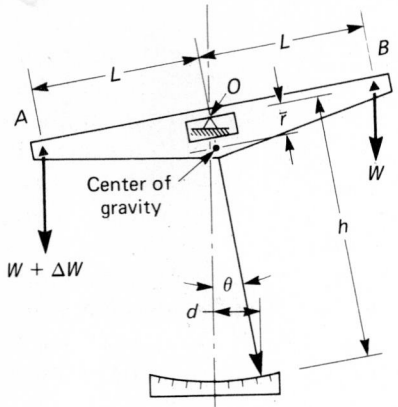

FIGURE 3.8   Schematic of a beam balance.

where

$$I = \text{the moment of inertia,}$$

$$\bar{r} = \text{the distance between the center of gravity}$$
of the beam alone and about pivot
point O, and

$$w_b = \text{the weight of the beam.}$$

With the weights applied,

$$w_b \, \bar{r} \sin \theta = \overline{\Delta W L} \cos \theta \quad \text{or} \quad \tan \theta = \frac{L \overline{\Delta W}}{w_b \, \bar{r}}.$$

Hence using Eq. (3.5), we find that

$$\eta = \frac{L}{w_b \, \bar{r}}. \tag{3.7}$$

Combining Eqs. (3.6) and (3.7), we have

$$\eta = \frac{L}{I} \left(\frac{\mathcal{T}}{2\pi} \right)^2 \cdot g_c = \frac{L}{I} \left(\frac{1}{2\pi f} \right)^2 \cdot g_c, \tag{3.7a}$$

where f = natural frequency.

Equation (3.7a) indicates that the sensitivity is a function of $\mathcal{T}$, the *period of oscillation* of the balance scale, with increased sensitivity corresponding to a long beam and low moment of inertia. In other words, the more sensitive instrument oscillates more slowly than the less sensitive instrument. This is an important observation having significant bearing on the dynamic response of most single-degree-of-freedom instruments.

3.10 THE IMPORTANCE OF DAMPING

The importance of proper damping to dynamic measurement may be understood by assuming that our scale beam in the previous example is part of an instrument that is required to come to *different* equilibriums as rapidly as possible. A situation of this sort exists in the application of light-beam galvanometers to recording oscillographs. The galvanometer suspension is driven by varying frequency inputs, and its ability to follow is governed by its natural period and by damping.

Suppose that our scale beam has very low damping. When a disturbing force is applied, the scale will be caused to oscillate, and the oscillation will continue for a long period of time. A final balance will be obtained only by prolonged waiting, which limits the frequency with which the weighing process may be repeated.

On the other hand, suppose considerable damping is provided—well above critical. An extreme example of this would be to submerge the entire scale in a container of molasses. Balance would be approached at a very slow rate again, but in this case there would be no oscillation. Here, again, excessive time would be required before the next weighing operation could commence. Theoretically, viscous damping does not change the inherent sensitivity of the device; however, sensitivity and natural period are related, as we discussed in Section 3.9.

It appears, therefore, that if we were to design a beam-type scale for quickly determining magnitudes of different masses, the final form would necessarily be a result of compromise. We would like equilibrium to be reached as quickly as possible in order to *get on with the job,* but in addition we would require a certain maximum sensitivity from our instrument, which is one of the factors determining accuracy.

It would seem that there might be an optimum value that should be used. Although this is not exactly the case, because of other factors involved, damping on the order of 60 to 75% of critical is provided in many instruments of this type (see Section 3.15.2 for further clarification of this point). In addition, it would appear that when frequency response is a problem, sensitivities greater than those required by the application should be avoided because sensitivity is gained at the expense of frequency response.

3.11 DYNAMIC CHARACTERISTICS OF SIMPLIFIED MECHANICAL SYSTEMS

By making certain simplifying assumptions, we may place the dynamic characteristics of *most* measuring systems in one of several categories. The basic assumptions are that any restoring element (spring, etc.) is linear, that damping

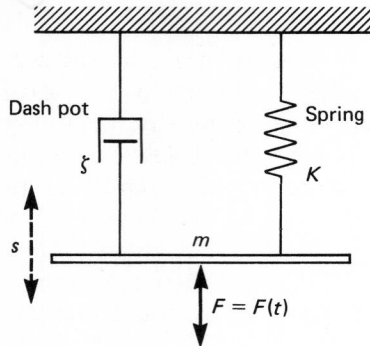

FIGURE 3.9   Mechanical model of a force-excited second-order system.

is viscous, and that the system may be approximated as a single-degree-of-freedom system.

3.12 SINGLE-DEGREE, SPRING–MASS–DAMPER SYSTEMS

Figure 3.9 shows a simple single-degree-of-freedom mechanical system. It is single-degree because only one coordinate of motion is assumed. We will also assume a general form of excitation, $F(t)$, which may or may not be periodic. Forces acting on the mass will result from the spring, damping, and the external force, $F(t)$. Using Newton's second law we can write

$$F(t) - ks - \zeta \frac{ds}{dt} = \frac{m}{g_c}(d^2s/dt^2). \tag{3.8}$$

Note that the spring force will always oppose the displacement and that the damping is a velocity function opposing the velocity direction. This relationship can be rearranged to read

$$\frac{1}{g_c}\left[m\left(\frac{d^2s}{dt^2}\right)\right] + \zeta \left(\frac{ds}{dt}\right) + ks = F(t). \tag{3.8a}$$

If we assume $F(t)$ to be periodic with time we can substitute the appropriate Fourier series for $F(t)$ or, in general (see Section 2.4),

$$F(t) = A/2 + \sum_{n=1}^{\infty} C_n \cos (n\Omega t - \phi_n), \tag{3.9}$$

where

$$C_n = \sqrt{A_n^2 + B_n^2} \quad \text{and} \quad \tan \phi = \frac{B_n}{A_n}. \tag{3.9a}$$

We will consider the general case in Section 3.15.3. First, however, we will consider several special cases.

3.13 THE ZERO-ORDER SYSTEM

A near-trivial case occurs if we remove the spring and damper. The voltage-dividing potentiometer (see Section 4.6) is an example. In its simplest form this device is a single slide-wire. Aside from the mass of the slider and any member attached to it, there is no appreciable resistance to movement. In particular, an equilibrium-seeking force is not present and the output is independent of time, that is,

$$\text{Output} = \text{Constant} \times \text{Input}.$$

Dynamically, the zero-order system requires no further consideration.

3.14 CHARACTERISTICS OF FIRST-ORDER SYSTEMS

If we assume mass, m, in Fig. 3.9 and Eq. (3.8) to be zero, we obtain a *first-order system*. Certain temperature-measuring systems tend to behave according to first-order rules. Of course, we quickly agree that Fig. 3.9 bears no resemblance to a thermocouple (Section 16.6), for instance; however, we will find that the performance relationships that we will develop do correspond quite well with the dynamic response of not only thermocouples, but also other temperature-sensing devices.

For the first-order system we can write

$$\zeta \frac{ds}{dt} + ks = F(t). \tag{3.10}$$

3.14.1 The Step-Forced First-Order System

Let

$$F(t) = 0, \quad \text{for } t < 0$$

and

$$F(t) = F_0, \quad \text{for } t \geq 0.$$

For force equilibrium on the connecting element (which is assumed to be massless),

$$\zeta \frac{ds}{dt} + ks = F_0, \tag{3.11}$$

where

$$t = \text{time,}$$

$$s = \text{displacement,}$$

ζ = the damping coefficient,

k = the deflection constant, and

F_0 = the amplitude of the constant input force,

Then

$$\int_0^t dt = \zeta \int_{s_A}^s \frac{ds}{(F_0 - ks)} ,$$

from which we obtain

$$\frac{F_0 - ks}{F_0 - ks_A} = e^{-kt/\zeta} = e^{-t/r}. \tag{3.12}$$

The units of $\tau = \zeta/k$ are seconds, and this quantity is known as the *time constant*.

Equation (3.12) can be written

$$s = s_\infty[1 - e^{-t/\tau}] + s_A e^{-t/r} = s_\infty + [s_A - s_\infty]e^{-t/r}, \tag{3.13}$$

where

$s_\infty = F_0/k$ = the limiting displacement of the system as $t \to \infty$ and

s_A = any initial displacement at $t = 0$.

We have assumed that the first-order system represents any dynamic condition wherein the elements are essentially massless, the displacement constraint is linear, and a significant viscous rate constraint is present. Generally, Eq. (3.13) can be written

$$P = P_\infty[1 - e^{-t/\tau}] + P_A e^{-t/r}$$

or

$$P = P_\infty + [P_A - P_\infty]e^{-t/r}, \tag{3.14}$$

where

P = the magnitude of any first-order process at $t = t$,

P_∞ = the limiting magnitude of the process as $t \to \infty$, and

P_A = the initial magnitude of the process at $t = 0$.

Although the basic relationship was derived in terms of a spring–dashpot arrangement, other processes that behave in an analogous manner include (a) a heated (or cooled) bulk or mass, such as a temperature sensor subjected to a step-temperature change, (b) simple capacitive-resistive or inductive-resistive circuits, and (c) the decay of a radioactive source with time.

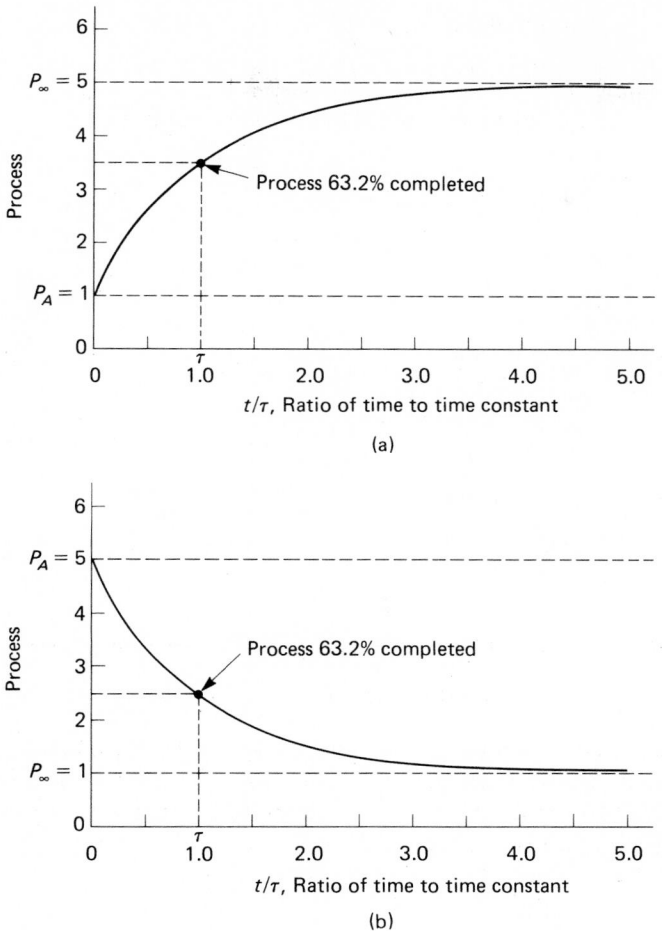

FIGURE 3.10 Characteristics of a first-order system subjected to a step function. (a) For a progressive process. (b) For a decaying process.

Figure 3.10 represents two different process–time conditions for the step-excited first-order system: (a) for a progressive process, wherein the action is an increasing function of time, and (b) for the *decaying* process, wherein the magnitude decreases with time.

Significance of the time constant, τ

If we substitute the magnitude of one time constant for t in Eq. (3.14),

$$ P = P_\infty + (P_A - P_\infty)(0.368), $$

from which we see that $(1 - 0.368)$, or 63.2%, of the dynamic portion of the process will have been completed. Two time constants yield 86.5%; three yield 95.0%; four yield 98.2%; and so on. These percentages of completed processes are important because they will always be the same regardless of the process, provided that the process is governed by the conditions of the step-excited first-order system.

   It is often assumed that a process is completed during a period of five time constants.

EXAMPLE   Assume that the application of a temperature probe approximates first-order conditions,* that the probe has a time constant of 6 s, and that it is suddenly subjected to a temperature step of 75–300°F. What temperature will be indicated 10 s after the process has been initiated?

Solution   Applying Eq. (3.14), we find that

$$P_\infty = 300°F, \qquad P_A = 75°F, \qquad t = 10 \text{ s},$$

$$P = 300 + (75 - 300)e^{-10/6} = 257°F.$$

EXAMPLE   Assume the same conditions as those for the example above, except that the step is 300–75°F. Find the indicated temperature after 10 s.

Solution

$$P_\infty = 75°F, \qquad P_A = 300°F, \qquad t = 10 \text{ s},$$

$$P = 75 + (300 - 75)e^{-10/6} = 117°F.$$

3.14.2   The Harmonically Excited First-Order System

Again referring to Eq. (3.10), let us now consider the case for

$$F(t) = F_0 \cos \Omega t,$$

or

$$\zeta \frac{ds}{dt} + ks = F_0 \cos \Omega t, \tag{3.15}$$

where

$$F_0 = \text{the amplitude of the forcing function, and}$$

$$\Omega = \text{the circular frequency of the forcing function in rad/s.}$$

The solution of Eq. (3.15) yields

$$s = A_1 e^{-t/r} + \frac{F_0/k}{\sqrt{1 + (\tau\Omega)^2}} \cos(\Omega t - \phi), \tag{3.16}$$

---

*   This represents a first approximation for many practical temperature sensors in a given environment. For further discussion see Section 16.10.3.

where

A_1 = the constant whose value depends on the initial conditions,

τ = the time constant = $\dfrac{\zeta}{k}$,

ϕ = the phase lag = $\tan^{-1} \dfrac{\Omega\zeta}{k} = \tan^{-1} \dfrac{2\pi}{\mathcal{T}} \tau$, and $\qquad$ (3.17)

$\mathcal{T} = \dfrac{2\pi}{\Omega}$ = the period of excitation cycle in s.

We see that the first term on the right side of Eq. (3.16), the complementary function, is *transient* and that after a period of several time constants becomes very small. The second term is the *steady-state* relationship and, except for the short initial period, we can write

$$s = \frac{F_0/k}{\sqrt{1 + (\tau\Omega)^2}} \cos{(\Omega t - \phi)} \qquad (3.18)$$

or

$$\frac{s}{s_s} = \frac{\cos{(\Omega t - \phi)}}{\sqrt{1 + (\tau\Omega)^2}},$$

and

$$\frac{s_d}{s_s} = \frac{1}{\sqrt{1 + (\tau\Omega)^2}}$$

$$= \frac{1}{\sqrt{1 + (2\pi\tau/\mathcal{T})^2}}, \qquad (3.19)$$

where

s_d = the maximum amplitude of the periodic dynamic displacement

and

$$s_s = \frac{F_0}{k}.$$

The quantity s_s is the static deflection that would occur, should the force amplitude F_0 be applied as a *static* force. The ratio s_d/s_s is often called the *amplification ratio*. For analogous situations, Eq. (3.19) may be written

$$\frac{P_d}{P_s} = \frac{1}{\sqrt{1 + (2\pi\tau/\mathcal{T})^2}}, \qquad (3.19a)$$

where P represents the magnitude of the applicable process.

Figures 3.11 and 3.12 illustrate the relationships of the phase angle and the magnification ratio described by Eqs. (3.17) and (3.19a), respectively.

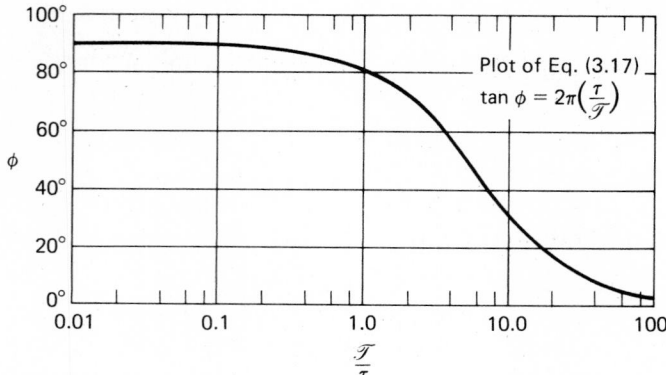

FIGURE 3.11   Phase lag vs. ratio of excitation period to time constant for the harmonically excited first-order sytem.

To a great extent the harmonically excited first-order system is of academic interest only. In most situations involving motion of bodies, a moving mass exists and cannot be ignored. When this is the case, the problem becomes one of second order and will be discussed in subsequent paragraphs.

Although harmonically excited processes that do not involve moving mass are rare, for the purpose of an example we may assume a condition wherein a temperature probe is subjected to a harmonically varying input. Let the time constant of the probe be 10 s. Assume that the probe is inserted into an environment for which the temperature varies harmonically between 75°F and 300°F, with a period of 20 s. Describe the temperature read-out in terms of input.

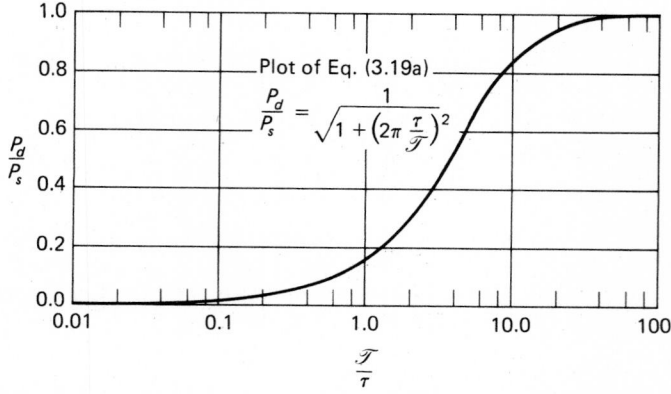

FIGURE 3.12   Amplitude ratio vs. ratio of excitation period to time constant for the harmonically excited first-order system.

In this case the temperature input can be expressed as

$$T(t) = \left(\frac{300 + 75}{2}\right) + \left(\frac{300 - 75}{2}\right) \cos\left(\frac{2\pi}{20}\right)t$$

$$= 187.5 + 112.5 \cos\left(\frac{2\pi}{20}\right)t.$$

From Eq. (3.19a), we find that

$$\frac{T_d}{T_s} = \frac{1}{\sqrt{1 + \left(\frac{2\pi}{20} \times 10\right)^2}}$$

$$T_d = \frac{112.5}{3.3} = 34°F.$$

From Eq. (3.17), we find that the phase lag is

$$\phi = \tan^{-1} 2\pi(\tau/\mathcal{T}) = \tan^{-1}\left(\frac{2\pi \times 10}{20}\right) = \tan^{-1} \pi = 72\tfrac{1}{2}° \quad \text{(angle)}$$

or

$$\text{Time lag} = \frac{72\tfrac{1}{2}}{360} \times 20 = 4 \text{ s.}$$

A graphical representation of the situation is shown in Fig. 3.13. For further discussion of the response of temperature-measuring probes, see Section 16.10.3.

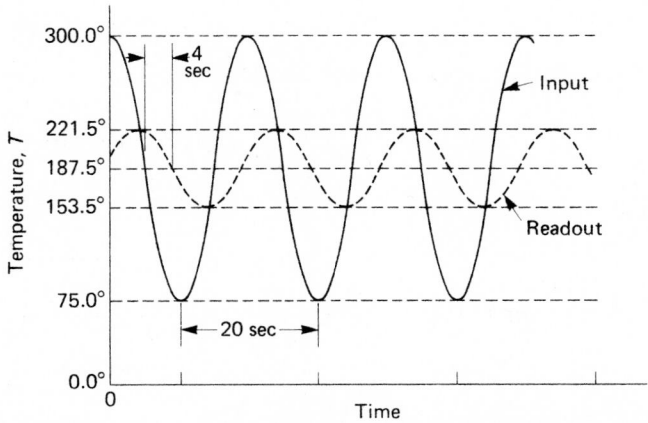

FIGURE 3.13 Response of temperature probe for conditions described in text.

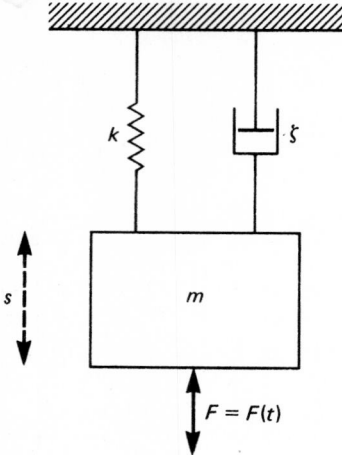

FIGURE 3.14   Schematic of a second-order system.

3.15   CHARACTERISTICS OF SECOND-ORDER SYSTEMS

Figure 3.14 illustrates the essentials of a second-order system. This arrangement approximates many actual mechanical arrangements including simple weighing systems, such as elastic-type load cells supporting mass, D'Arsonval meter movements, including the ordinary galvanometers, and many force-excited mechanical-vibration systems.

As with the first-order system, many excitation modes are possible, ranging from the simple step-function, the simple harmonic, and complex periodic forms. These approximate many actual situations, and since all periodic inputs can be reduced to combinations of simple harmonic components (Section 2.4), the latter can give us insight into system performance when subject to most forms of dynamic input.

3.15.1   Step-Excited Second-Order System

Referring to Fig. 3.14, we let

$$F = 0, \quad \text{when } t < 0$$

and

$$F = F_0, \quad \text{when } t \geq 0.$$

Application of Newton's second law yields

$$d^2s/dt^2 + \left(\frac{\zeta \cdot g_c}{m}\right)\left(\frac{ds}{dt}\right) + \left(\frac{kg_c}{m}\right)s = F_0\left(\frac{g_c}{m}\right). \tag{3.20}$$

If we assume *underdamping*, that is, $(kg_c/m) > (\zeta g_c/2m)^2$ (see Eq. 3.21a), the general solution for Eq. (3.20) can be written as

$$s = e^{-(\zeta \cdot g_c/2m)t} [A \cos \omega_{nd}t + B \sin \omega_{nd}t] + \frac{F_0}{k}, \quad (3.21)$$

where A and B are constants governed by initial conditions and

$$\omega_{nd} = \text{Damped natural frequency}$$

$$= \sqrt{k \cdot g_c/m - (\zeta \cdot g_c/2m)^2}. \quad (3.21a)$$

Note that the exponential multiplier may be written as $e^{-t/\tau}$, where the time constant $\tau = 2m/\zeta \cdot g_c$. If we let $s = 0$ and $ds/dt = 0$ at $t = 0$, and evaluate A and B, then by rearrangement and substitution of terms, we can write Eq. (3.21) as

$$\frac{s_d}{s_s} = 1 - e^{\xi \omega_n t} \left[\frac{\xi}{\sqrt{1 - \xi^2}} \sin \sqrt{1 - \xi^2} \, \omega_n t + \cos \sqrt{1 - \xi^2} \, \omega_n t \right]. \quad (3.22)$$

An alternative form is

$$\frac{s_d}{s_s} = 1 - e^{-\xi \omega_n t} \sqrt{\frac{1}{1 - \xi^2}} \cos (\omega_{nd}t - \beta), \quad (3.22a)$$

$$\beta = \tan^{-1} \left[\frac{\xi}{\sqrt{1 - \xi^2}} \right], \quad (3.22b)$$

where

$\omega_n = \sqrt{k \cdot g_c/m} = $ the undamped natural frequency in rad/s,

$\zeta_c = $ the critical damping coefficient,

$\xi = $ the critical damping ratio, ζ/ζ_c,

$s_s = F_0/k = $ the "static" amplitude, or the amplitude that would result if t approaches infinity, and

$s_d = $ the amplitude of the periodic displacement.

Here again we may introduce the general idea of any applicable process, P, or

$$\frac{P_d}{P_s} = \frac{s_d}{s_s}.$$

For the overdamped condition, $\zeta/\zeta_c > 1$, the solution of Eq. (3.20) can be written as

$$\frac{P_d}{P_s} = \frac{-\xi - \sqrt{\xi^2 - 1}}{2\sqrt{\xi^2 - 1}} e^{(-\xi + \sqrt{\xi^2 - 1})\omega_n t} + \frac{\xi - \sqrt{\xi^2 - 1}}{2\sqrt{\xi^2 - 1}} e^{(-\xi - \sqrt{\xi^2 - 1})\omega_n t} + 1. \quad (3.23)$$

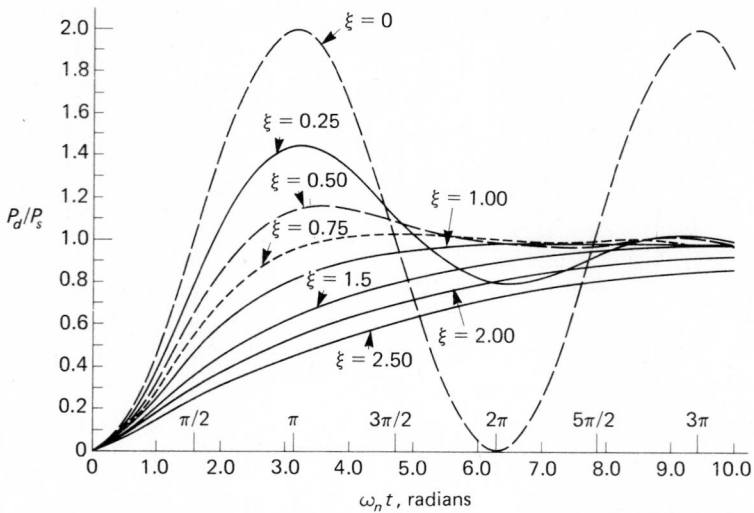

FIGURE 3.15   Response of step-excited second-order system.

Figure 3.15 shows the plots for Eqs. (3.22) and (3.23) for various damping ratios.*

3.15.2 Harmonically Excited Second-Order System

Referring to Fig. 3.9, when

$$F(t) = F_0 \cos \Omega t$$

we can write

$$\frac{m}{g_c} \frac{d^2s}{dt^2} + \zeta \frac{ds}{dt} + ks = F_0 \cos \Omega t. \tag{3.24}$$

For underdamped systems the solution becomes

$$s = e^{-(\zeta g_c /2m)t} \left[A \cos \omega_n t + B \sin \omega_n t \right] + \frac{(F_0/k) \cos (\Omega t - \phi)}{\sqrt{\left[1 - \dfrac{m\Omega^2}{kg_c} \right]^2 + \left(\dfrac{\zeta \Omega}{k} \right)^2}} \tag{3.25}$$

$$= e^{-t/\tau}[A \cos \sqrt{1 - \xi^2}\, \omega_n t + B \sin \sqrt{1 - \xi^2}\, \omega_n t]$$

$$+ \frac{s_s \cos (\Omega t - \phi)}{\sqrt{[1 - (\Omega/\omega_n)^2]^2 + [2\, \xi(\Omega/\omega_n)]^2}} , \tag{3.25a}$$

---

*   Note that the cases of zero damping and critical damping require special treatment.

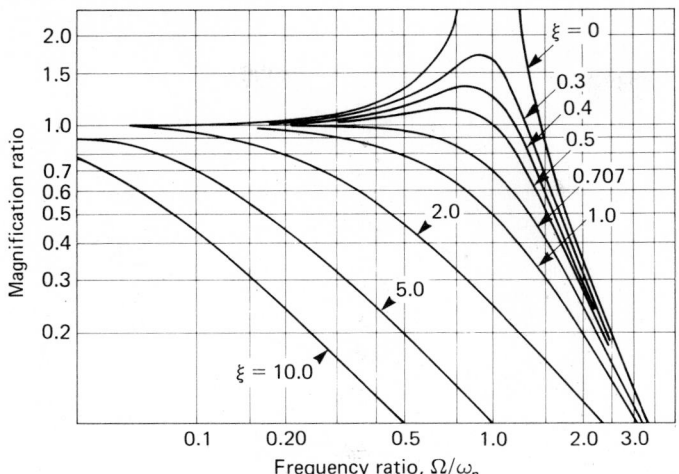

FIGURE 3.16   Plot of Eq. (3.25c) illustrating the frequency response to harmonic excitation of the system shown in Fig. 3.14.

where A and B are constants that depend on particular initial conditions, and

Ω = the frequency of excitation in rad/s, and

$$\phi = \tan^{-1}\left[\frac{2\xi\Omega/\omega_n}{1 - (\Omega/\omega_n)^2}\right] = \text{the phase angle.} \qquad (3.25b)$$

We see that the first term on the right side of Eq. (3.25a) is transient and after several time constants will disappear. The second term is the steady-state relationship, for which we may write*

$$\frac{s_d}{s_s} = \frac{P_d}{P_s} = \frac{1}{\sqrt{[1 - (\Omega/\omega_n)^2]^2 + [2\xi\Omega/\omega_n]^2}} \qquad (3.25c)$$
$$= \text{the magnification ratio.}$$

Figures 3.16 and 3.17 are plots of Eqs. (3.25c) and (3.25b), respectively, for various values of the damping ratio ξ. The ratio s_d/s_s is a measure of the system response to the frequency input. Normally, we hope that this relationship is constant with frequency; that is, we would like the system to be insensitive to changes in the frequency of input $F(t)$. Inspection of Fig. 3.16 shows that the amplitude ratio is reasonably constant for only a limited frequency range and then only for certain damping ratios. We see that for a given damping ratio, ideal conditions ($s_d/s_s = 1$) may occur at only one or

---

* Note that inasmuch as the complementary or homogeneous solution is not involved, this relationship is valid for under-, over-, and critically damped conditions.

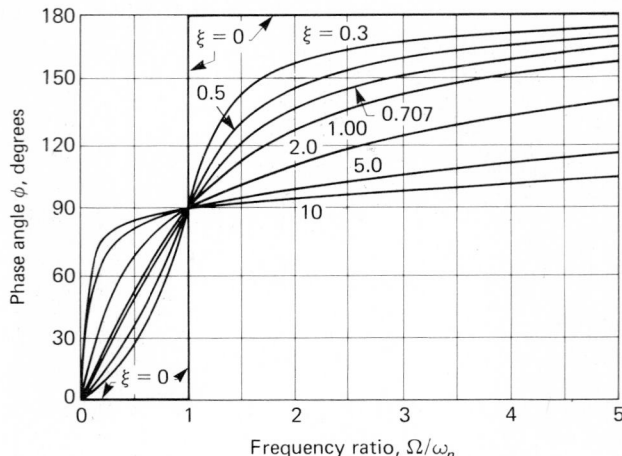

FIGURE 3.17   Plot of Eq. (3.25b) illustrating the phase response of the system shown in Fig. 3.9.

two frequencies. If the system is to be used for general dynamic measurement applications, rather definite damping must be used and an upper frequency limit must be established. Practically, if a damping ratio in the neighborhood of 65–75% is used, then the amplitude ratio will approximate unity over a range of frequency ratios of about 0–40%. Even for these conditions, inherent error ($s_d/s_s - 1$) exists, and a usable system can be had only through compromise.

It should be made clear that the basic reason for optimizing the damping ratio is to extend the usable range of exciting frequency Ω. Certain devices, notably piezoelectric sensors (see Section 4.14), commonly possess such high undamped natural frequencies, ω_n, that the range of normal operating *frequency ratios*, Ω/ω_n, may extend from zero to only 10% or even less. In such cases damping ratio magnitudes are of lesser interest.

Inspection of Fig. 3.17 indicates that damping ratios on the order of 65–75% of critical provide an approximately linear phase shift for the frequency-ratio range of 0–40%. This is desirable if a proper time relationship is to be maintained between the harmonic components of a complex input. (See Sections 17.6.2 and 17.7.1 for further discussion of phase relationships.)

3.15.3   General Periodic Forcing

We now return to the general case of periodic forcing as suggested in Section 3.12. For convenience we will rewrite Eqs. 3.8 and 3.9 as

$$\frac{m}{g_c}\left(\frac{d^2s}{dt^2}\right) + \zeta\left(\frac{ds}{dt}\right) + ks = F(t), \qquad (3.26)$$

where

$$F(t) = \left(\frac{A}{2}\right) + \sum_{n=1}^{\infty} C_n \cos(n\Omega t - \phi_n) \tag{3.26a}$$

and

$$C_n = \sqrt{A_n^2 + B_n^2} \quad \text{and} \quad \tan\phi_n = \frac{B_n}{A_n}. \tag{3.26b}$$

By substituting Eq. (3.26a) into Eq. (3.26) we obtain

$$\frac{m}{g_c}\left(\frac{d^2 s}{dt^2}\right) + \zeta\left(\frac{ds}{dt}\right) + ks = \left(\frac{A}{2}\right) + \sum_{n=1}^{\infty} C_n \cos(n\Omega t - \phi_n). \tag{3.27}$$

Although this appears quite formidable, we can easily recognize that it yields a combination of the solutions given by Eqs. (3.21) and (3.25a). Using the reasoning that the cosine terms on the right side of Eq. (3.27) will give results similar to those of a harmonically forced system, we can write a solution for $\xi < 1$ in the form

$$s = e^{(-\zeta g_c/2m)t}[A \cos\omega_{nd}t + B \sin\omega_{nd}t] \tag{3.28}$$

$$+ r_0 + \sum_{n=1}^{\infty} r_n \cos(n\Omega t - \phi_n - \psi_n)$$

where

$$r_0 = A/2k,$$

$$r_n = \frac{C_n}{k}\left[\frac{1}{\sqrt{\left[1 - \left(\frac{n\Omega}{\omega_n}\right)^2\right]^2 + \left[2\xi n\frac{\Omega}{\omega_n}\right]^2}}\right],$$

$$\tan\psi_n = \frac{2\xi\left(\frac{n\Omega}{\omega_n}\right)}{1 - \left(\frac{n\Omega}{\omega_n}\right)^2}.$$

It helps to recall that

$$\omega_{nd} = \text{the damped natural frequency} = \sqrt{\frac{kg_c}{m} - \left(\frac{\zeta g_c}{2m}\right)^2},$$

$$\omega_n = \text{the undamped natural frequency} = \sqrt{\frac{kg_c}{m}}.$$

As we discussed previously, the first term on the right side of Eq. (3.28) is transient and dies out after several time constants. The remaining terms, then, represent the steady-state response.

EXAMPLE

a) Write an expression for the steady-state response for the single-degree system shown in Fig. 3.14 when subjected to the sawtooth forcing function described in Table 2.1 and shown in Fig. 2.8(b).

b) Let
$m = 1$ kg, or 2.2 lbm,
$k = 1000$ N/m, or 5.71 lbf/in.,
$\zeta = 0.50$, N $\cdot$ s/m or 2.855×10^{-3} lbf $\cdot$ s/in.,
$F_0 = 10$ N, or 2.248 lbf.

Using the data above (use the SI values), determine computer-plotted waveforms for input frequencies of 10, 30, and 50 rad/s.

Solution
a)

$$ s = \frac{A}{2k} + \sum_{n=1}^{\infty} \frac{C_n}{k} \left[\frac{\cos(n\Omega t - \phi_n - \psi_n)}{\sqrt{\left[1 - \left(\frac{n\Omega}{\omega_n} \right)^2 \right]^2 + \left[2\xi n \frac{\Omega}{\omega_n} \right]^2}} \right], $$

$$ \phi_n = \tan^{-1}\left(\frac{B_n}{A_n} \right), $$

$$ C_n = \sqrt{A_n^2 + B_n^2}, $$

$$ \psi_n = \tan^{-1}\left[\frac{2\xi\left(\frac{n\Omega}{\omega_n} \right)}{1 - \left(n\frac{\Omega}{\omega_n} \right)^2} \right]. $$

b) The forcing function varies equally about the x-axis, hence $A = 0$.

$$ \omega_n = \sqrt{\frac{kg_c}{m}} = \sqrt{1000} \approx 31.6 \text{ rad/s} $$

The forcing function contains sine terms only, hence $A_n = 0$.

$$ \phi_n = \tan^{-1}\infty = \frac{\pi}{2}, $$

$$ C_n = \frac{F_0}{k} = \frac{10}{1000} = 1 \text{ cm}, $$

$$\psi_n = \tan \left[\frac{2 \times 0.5 \left(\dfrac{n\Omega}{31.6} \right)}{\sqrt{1 - \left(\dfrac{n\Omega}{31.6} \right)^2}} \right],$$

$$s = \sum_{n=1}^{\infty} \frac{\cos \left(n\Omega t - \dfrac{\pi}{2} - \psi_n \right)}{\sqrt{\left[1 - \left(\dfrac{n\Omega}{31.6} \right)^2 \right]^2 + \left[\dfrac{n\Omega}{31.6} \right]^2}}$$

$$= \sum_{n=1}^{\infty} \frac{\cos \left(n\Omega t - \dfrac{\pi}{2} - \psi_n \right)}{\sqrt{\left[1 - \left(\dfrac{n\Omega}{31.6} \right)^2 \right]^2 + \left(\dfrac{n\Omega}{31.6} \right)^2}}.$$

Note that s is in centimeters.

The only practical approach to obtaining numerical results for this part of the example is through the use of a computer. Computer-plotted results are shown in Figs. 3.18(a) through 3.18(c).

From the foregoing discussions it is apparent that if simple measurements are to be made as rapidly as possible or, more important, if the input signal is continuous and complex, rather definite limitations are imposed by the measuring system. Additional discussion of such limitations can be found in Chapters 7 and 17.

3.16 ELECTRICAL ELEMENTS

As we discussed in Section 3.7, most measurement systems are composed of a combination of mechanical and electrical elements. Very often the basic detecting element of the sensor is mechanical and its output is immediately transduced by a secondary element to an electrical signal. The signal conditioning that follows is largely by electrical means; however, termination often requires conversion to something basically mechanical, such as a galvanometer-type recorder or plotter, controller, etc. It is clear, then, that overall performance results from a combination of mechanical and electrical responses. In previous sections we have discussed the response of simple, purely mechanical systems. In succeeding sections we will look at corresponding electrical elements.

In preparation for the discussion that follows, Table 3.1 lists some fundamental electrical defining quantities and relationships. Table 3.2 lists certain mechanical–electrical analogous equivalents. For verification of these the

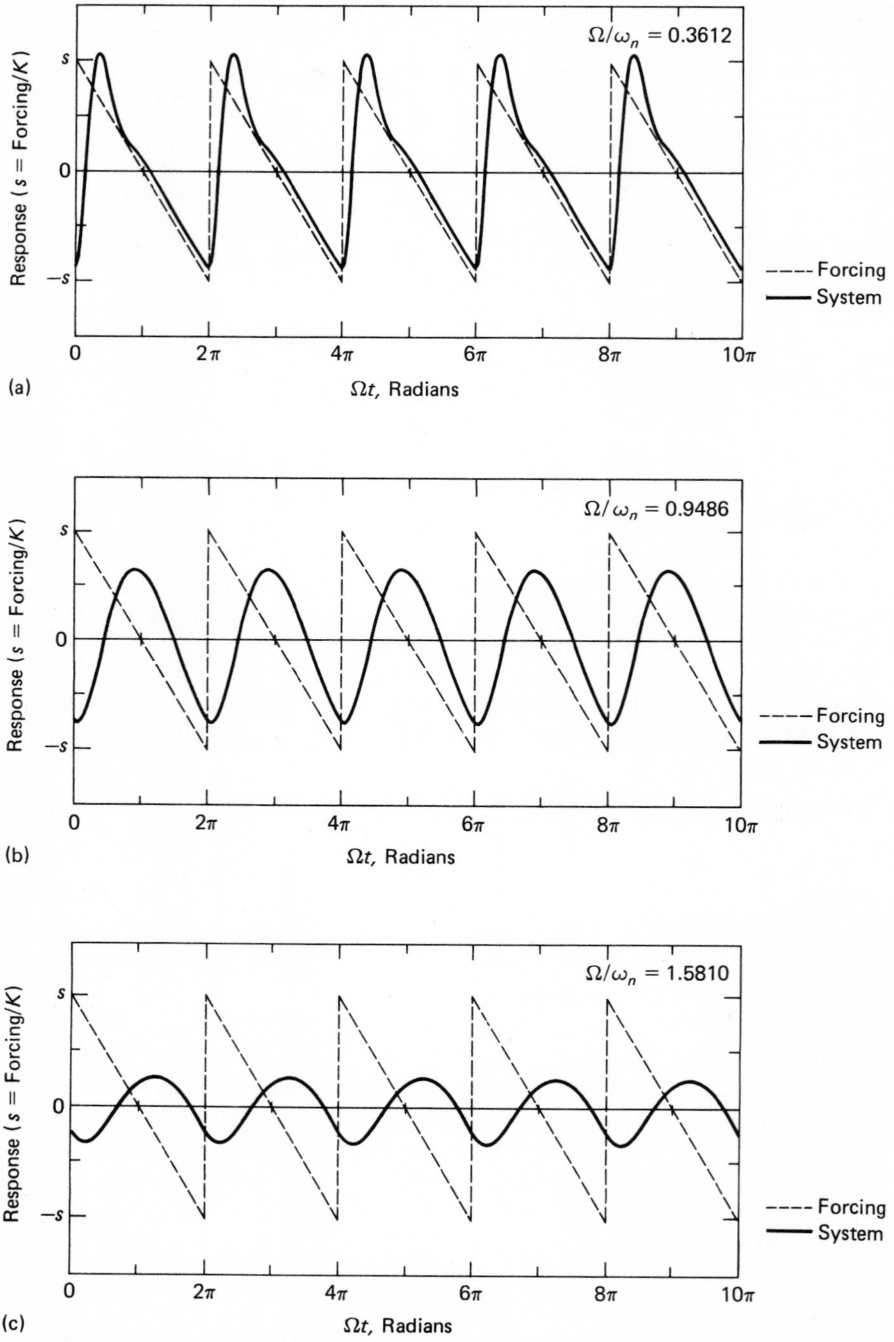

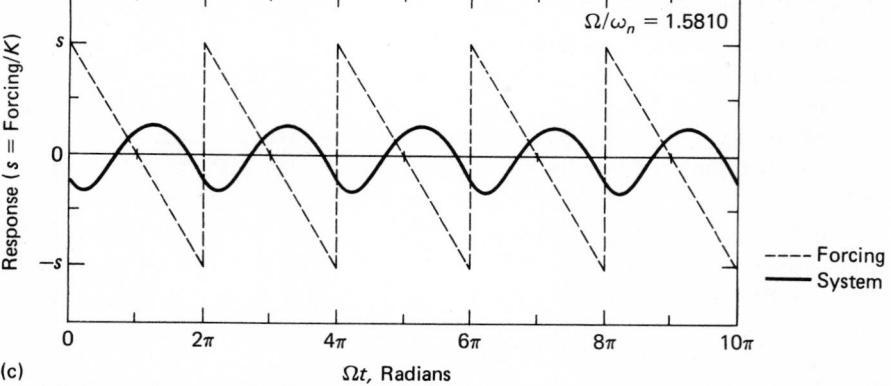

FIGURE 3.18 Computer-plotted saw-tooth wave response for the second-order system specified in the text. (a) For $\Omega = 10$ rad/s. (b) For $\Omega = 30$ rad/s. (c) For $\Omega = 50$ rad/s.

TABLE 3.1 Some Basic Electrical Definitions and Relationships

Symbol	Definition	Unit
E	Electrical potential	Volt (V)
I	Electrical current	Ampere (A)
Q	Electrical charge	Coulomb (C)
R	Electrical resistance	Ohm (Ω)
L	Electrical inductance	Henry (H)
C	Electrical capacitance	Farad (F)

Some defining relationships:

For a capacitance: $I = dQ/dt = C(dE/dt), E = Q/C;$
For a resistance: $E = IR$ *(Ohm's law);*
For an inductance: $E = L(dI/dt) = L(d^2Q/dt^2).$

reader is referred to any basic electrical circuits textbook [1] or physics text [2].

In addition, at this point it is useful to recall Kirchhoff's two laws for electrical circuits, namely,

1. The algebraic sum of all currents entering a junction point is zero, and

2. The algebraic sum of all voltage drops taken in a given direction around a closed circuit is zero.

3.17 FIRST-ORDER ELECTRICAL SYSTEM

Consider the circuit shown in Fig. 3.19. Assume the capacitor carries no initial charge; then let the SPDT (single-pole, double-throw) switch be moved to contact A, thereby inserting the battery into the circuit. By employing Kirchhoff's law of potentials, we may write

$$IR + Q/C - E = 0, \tag{3.30}$$

but

$$I = dQ/dt;$$

hence,

$$dQ/dt + Q/RC - E/R = 0. \tag{3.30a}$$

Solving, we have

$$Q = CE(1 - e^{-t/RC}).$$

Across the capacitor, $E_t = Q/C$, where the time constant $\tau = RC$; hence,

$$E_t = E(1 - e^{(-t/\tau)}). \tag{3.30b}$$

TABLE 3.2 Dynamically Analogous Mechanical and Electrical System Elements

Symbol	Mechanical Quantity	Symbol	Electrical Quantity
m I	Mass, kg (lbm) Moment of inertia, kg · m² (lbm · in²)	L	Inductance, H
k k_t	Deflection constant, N/m (lbf/in.) Torsional deflection constant, N · m/rad (lbf · in./rad)	$1/C$	Reciprocal of capacitance, F⁻¹
ζ ζ_t	Damping coefficient, N · s/m (lbf · s/in.) Torsional damping coefficient, N · m · s/m (lbf · in. · s/in.)	R	Resistance, Ω
f T	Force, N (lbf) Torque, N · m (lbf · in.)	E	Voltage, V
x θ	Translational displacement, m (in.) Angular displacement, rad	Q	Charge, C
dx/dt $d\theta/dt$	Translational velocity, m/s (in./s) Angular velocity, rad/s (rad/s)	dQ/dt	Current, A
Ω	Forcing frequency, rad/s (rad/s)	Ω	Forcing frequency, rad/s
d^2x/dt^2 $d^2\theta/dt^2$	Translational acceleration, m/s² (in./s²) Angular acceleration, rad/s² (rad/s²)	d^2Q/dt^2	Rate of change of current, A/s

Note: The uppercase C has long been used as the symbol for capacitance. It has also been assigned as the symbol for the SI unit for electrical charge, the coulomb. Likewise, Ω is the SI symbol for resistance, ohms. It is also widely used to represent an exciting frequency in radians/second. In this text we will let the symbols retain each meaning. Should the contexts not make clear the meanings intended, we will include clarifying statements.

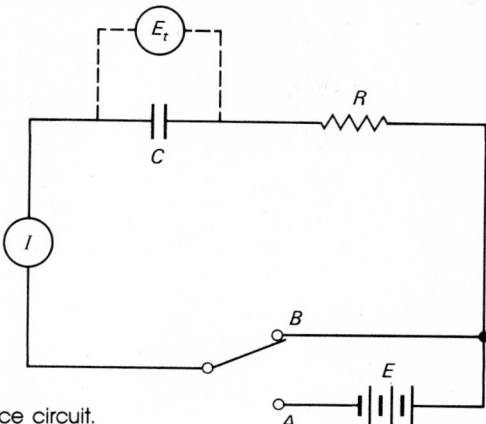

FIGURE 3.19   Series resistance-capacitance circuit.

In a similar manner, after the capacitor is charged, if the switch contact is moved from A to B, we may write the relationship

$$IR + Q/C = 0 \tag{3.31}$$

for which

$$E_t = Ee^{(-t/\tau)}. \tag{3.31a}$$

Furthermore, if an inductance is substituted for the capacitor in Fig. 3.19, similar relationships may be obtained wherein

$$\tau = L/R.$$

It is apparent, then, that Eqs. (3.14) and (3.10), which apply to a mechanical system, hold equally well to the electrical circuit discussed above.

Should the battery in Fig. 3.19 be replaced with a sinusoidal source of voltage, analysis would show that Eqs. (3.17) and (3.19a) would also apply to our electrical systems. In each case it would be necessary only to substitute the appropriate time constant and to properly interpret the response variable.

EXAMPLE   Figure 3.20(a) shows a simple circuit consisting of an inductance, a resistor, and a 5-kHz a.c. voltage source connected in series. Determine the amplitude and phase shift of the voltage appearing across the inductor. Assume that the impedance of the voltage source is relatively small.

Solution

$$\mathcal{T} = 1/f = 2 \times 10^{-4} \text{ seconds} = \text{the period of exciting voltage.}$$

$$\tau = L/R = 0.05/1200$$

$$= 4.167 \times 10^{-5} \text{ s} = \text{the time constant for the circuit.}$$

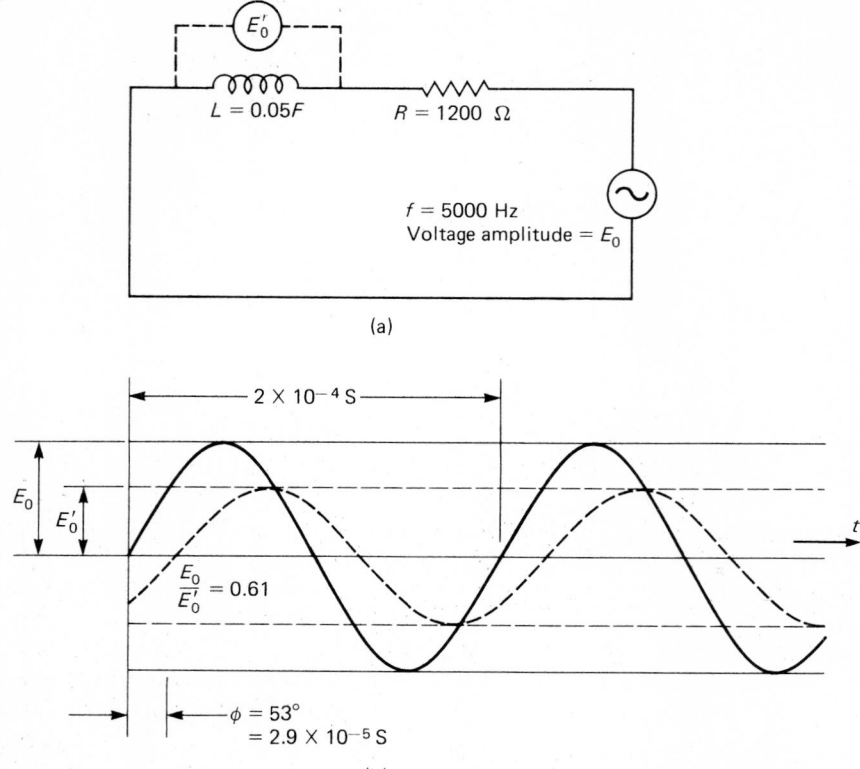

(a)

(b)

FIGURE 3.20   Resistance and inductance in series. (a) Excited by 5000-Hz voltage source. (b) Voltage across the inductance for the circuit shown in (a).

Using Eqs. (3.17) and (3.19a), we have

$$P_d/P_s = E_0'/E_0 = 1/\sqrt{1 + (2\pi\tau/\mathcal{T})} = 0.61,$$

where E_0 is the forcing amplitude and E_0' is the amplitude of the resulting waveform. In addition,

$$\phi = \tan^{-1} (2\pi\tau/\mathcal{T}) = 53 \text{ degrees.}$$

Figure 3.20(b) illustrates the resulting relationship.

3.18   SIMPLE SECOND-ORDER ELECTRICAL SYSTEM

Figure 3.21 illustrates a circuit consisting of R, L, and C elements in series with a voltage source. Referring to Table 3.1 for the voltage drop across each element, then applying Kirchhoff's law for potentials, we can write

$$L(d^2Q/dt^2) + R(dQ/dt) + Q/C = E_0 \cos \Omega t. \tag{3.32}$$

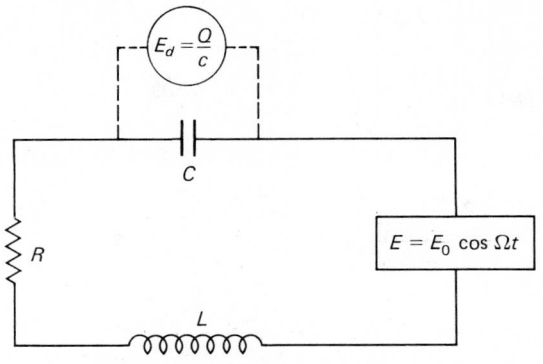

FIGURE 3.21   An *R-L-C* circuit.

We recognize this as having the same form as Eq. (3.24), which permits us to quickly write a solution:

$$Q = e^{-t/\tau}[A \cos \omega_{nd}t + B \sin \omega_{nd}t] + \frac{E_0 \cos (\Omega t - \phi)}{\sqrt{[1/C - L\Omega^2]^2 + (R\Omega)^2}} . \quad (3.32a)$$

If, for example, we consider the steady-state voltage amplitude across the capacitor we may write (see Table 3.1)

$$E_d = \frac{Q}{C} = \frac{E_0}{C\sqrt{[1/C - L\Omega^2]^2 + (R\Omega)^2}} . \quad (3.32b)$$

Using Table 3.2 (see also Section 5.11) we may write

$$\omega_n = \sqrt{1/LC} \quad (3.32c)$$

and

$$R_c = 2\sqrt{L/C}, \quad (3.32d)$$

where

ω_n = a resonant frequency corresponding to the undamped natural frequency of the mechanical system, and

R_c = a critical resistance analogous to critical damping.

By algebraic manipulation, Eqs. (3.32a) and (3.32b) may now be written in the unitless forms, where E_d is the dynamic amplitude of the voltage across C;

$$\frac{E_d}{E_0} = \frac{1}{\sqrt{[1 - (\Omega/\omega_n)^2]^2 + [2(R/R_c)(\Omega/\omega_n)]^2}} \quad (3.32e)$$

and

$$\tan \phi = \frac{2(R/R_c)(\Omega/\omega_n)}{1 - (\Omega/\omega_n)^2} . \quad (3.32f)$$

Except for the symbols we see that Eqs. (3.32e) and (3.32f) are identical to Eqs. (3.25c) and (3.25b), respectively. It follows, then, that Figs. 3.16 and 3.17 apply equally well to the electrical circuit that we have investigated.

3.19 EXPERIMENTAL DETERMINATION OF SYSTEM RESPONSE

The final and positive *proof* of a measuring system's performance is a comparison between the system's read-out in response to a *completely defined and known input*. We again refer to the term *calibration* (Section 1.5). In the present context the word means more than a simple comparison of a static, unchanging input with the system's output. In addition to the basic parameter of the measurand, we must add the time variable. Can we experimentally evaluate the behavior of the system when it is confronted with a measurand that is rapidly changing with time? This becomes a considerable challenge. It is not difficult to produce rapid, or relatively rapid, changes in most measurands, but to do so *and* to assure ourselves that we *really* know the driving function is the crux of the problem.

Calibration sources having simple harmonic (sinusoidal) time variation are undoubtedly the easiest to produce and the most used. Throughout this chapter much of our discussion has implied this. Step inputs are sometimes conveniently used, also. Various classical complex waveforms, such as square waves or sawtooth waveforms, may be useful. For example, the response characteristics of many electrical-type components often may be judged through use of square-wave inputs. A skilled technician frequently can pinpoint reasons for distortions by observing the treatment of a square-wave input to the tested apparatus. Perhaps even more important, such observations can be used to determine limits of usefulness beyond which performances should be questioned.

Measurements of various mechanical measurands, as well as various calibration practices, are considered in Part II of this book. See Sections 14.13, 15.10, 16.12, 17.10, and 18.9.

3.20 FINAL REMARKS REGARDING THEORETICAL STUDIES OF RESPONSE

In the preceding sections we have devoted considerable time to developing the dynamic characteristics of extremely simple—in some sense almost trivial—systems, both mechanical and electrical. Why have we felt this to be so desirable? There are several reasons:

1. By considering the simple systems, we present a basis for establishing fundamental definitions and relationships.

2. The more sophisticated systems are, for the most part, simply combinations of the basic building blocks that we have studied.

3. A study of the analytical complexities experienced in the development of

theoretical bases, even for the simple systems, quickly establishes an appreciation for the difficulties to be met with the more complex combinations.

4. There are indeed certain practical systems that are very close approximations of the simple systems. These include the common D'Arsonval meter movement, especially in the form of either the light-beam or the stylus-type of galvanometers (see Section 7.10). Seismic-type sensors are, in fact, identical to the second-order spring-mass–damped system.

5. The close analogy between the responses of mechanical and electrical elements has been established.

Additional response considerations are found in Chapters 7 and 17.

SUGGESTED READINGS

Cannon, R. H., Jr., *Dynamics of Physical Systems*. New York: McGraw-Hill, 1967.

Vierck, R. K., *Vibration Analysis*. New York: Harper & Row, 1979.

PROBLEMS

3.1 Listed below are the half-lives of various isotopes. Calculate the *time constant* for each.

Calcium 45	152 days
Carbon 14	5500 years
Cobalt 60	5.2 years
Helium 6	0.85 second
Yttrium 90	61 hours

3.2 The motion of a sphere falling due to gravity through a viscous fluid abides by the following relation:

$$V = (F/c) [1 - e^{-(cg/W)t}]$$

where

V = the velocity,

$F = W - B$,

W = the weight of the sphere,

B = the buoyant force,

c = the drag coefficient,

g = gravity acceleration, and

t = time.

a) Write an expression for the time constant.

b) Write an expression for the terminal (maximum) velocity.

c) What are the units of the drag coefficient?

d) How should the relation be modified if the buoyant force exceeds the weight?

3.3 What is the time constant for a single-degree-of-freedom, spring-damper system for which $W = 20$ N and $\zeta = 5$ N-s/m?

3.4 With reference to Problem 3.2, if the sphere weighs 6 N and if, starting from rest, it reaches 80% of its terminal velocity in 8 s, what is the value of the viscous drag coefficient c? Neglect buoyancy.

3.5 Air is pumped into a vessel such that the mass flow may be expressed as

$$dm/dt = k(P_a - P),$$

where

$$m = \text{mass},$$

$$k = \text{a constant},$$

$$P_a = \text{atmospheric pressure, and}$$

$$P = \text{the pressure in the vessel.}$$

If we assume that $PV = mRT$, what is the differential equation relating P and t? (Temperature T, volume V, and R are constants.)

3.6 An experimental arrangement is assembled to determine the time constant of a measuring system A (see Fig. 3.22). The "process" can be controlled to produce a sinusoidal output with respect to time. Measuring system B is used to monitor the process. At the frequencies used in the test, the response of system B may be assumed as perfect. The following data is obtained:

Process amplitude measured by system A = 1.2 units,

Process amplitude measured by system B = 1.4 units,

Process frequency indicated by both systems = 1.25 Hz; however, the output from system A lags behind that from system B by 0.07 s.

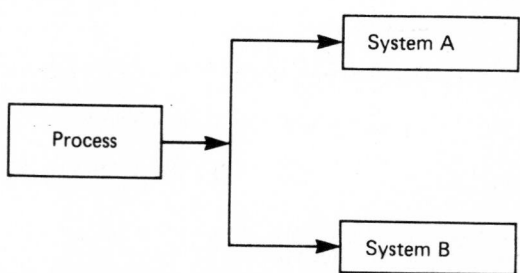

FIGURE 3.22   An experimental arrangement for determining the time constant for a measuring system.

The data provide for two different time-constant calculations for system A. Determine the two values. In which would you place greater confidence? Why?

3.7 A square wave whose amplitude is 1 unit is impressed on a first-order system. Calculate and sketch the responses if

$$\tau = (\tfrac{1}{4})\mathcal{T},$$

$$\tau = (\tfrac{1}{2})\mathcal{T},$$

$$\tau = \mathcal{T},$$

where τ is the system's time constant and $\mathcal{T}$ is the period of excitation.

3.8 A temperature probe is transferred from air at 15°C to air at 30°C, to water at 60°C, and back to air at 30°C. Assume that in each case the transfer is "instantaneous." The effective time constants and the timing sequence are as follows:

In air, probe dry	$\tau = 24$ s;
In water	$\tau = 4$ s;
In air, probe wet	$\tau = 17$ s;

for

$t < 0,$	$T = 15°C$	(T = actual temperature),
$0 < t < 5,$	$T = 30°C$	(dry probe in air),
$5 < t < 10,$	$T = 60°C$	(probe in water),
$10 < t < 20,$	$T = 30°C$	(wet probe in air).

Calculate the indicated temperature at the end of each time interval and sketch the approximate indicated temperature–time relationship between $t = 0$ and $t = 20$ s.

3.9 Assemble a simple RC circuit and voltage source (see Fig. 3.19) and by using an oscilloscope or oscillograph, obtain a voltage-time trace for

a) the "charging" process,

b) the "discharging" process.

Measure the voltage across the capacitor. Do the traces adhere to simple first-order theory?

3.10 Duplicate Problem 3.9 using RL circuit elements.

3.11 Determine the response of a first-order system to the forcing function shown in Fig. 3.23.

3.12 Show that for a harmonically excited first-order system a phase lag greater than 90 degrees is impossible.

3.13 A thermocouple with a time constant of 0.05 second is considered to behave as a first-order system. Over what frequency range(s) can the thermocouple measure

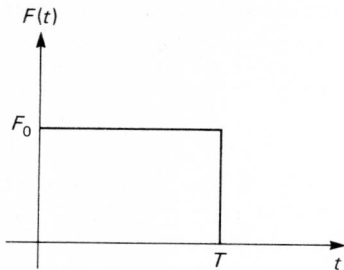

FIGURE 3.23   Forcing function for Problem 3.11.

dynamic temperature fluctuations (assume harmonic) with an error no greater than 5%?

3.14 A thermocouple is subjected to a steady harmonic temperature fluctuation given by

$$T = 300 + 200 \cos \pi t,$$

where T is the temperature in degrees Celsius and t is in seconds. If the thermocouple time constant is 0.10 second, what is the maximum error in degrees Celsius for the indicated temperature?

3.15 A temperature-measuring system is excited by a 0.1-Hz harmonically varying input. From previously run tests the time constant of the system has been measured and found to be 3.5 s. If measured, or indicated, dynamic amplitude is 8°F, what is the true temperature amplitude? What is the phase lag in seconds?

3.16 A slotted motor-driven disk is placed between a light source and a photocell much in the fashion of Fig. 10.3. The disk contains equally spaced "windows" separated by a like number of intervening disk segments. The angle subtended by each window and each segment is 18 degrees. An optical system is used with focus adjusted to provide "instantaneous" transition between light levels. Write an expression $e_0 = f(t)$ for various speeds of disk rotation, where e_0 is the output from the photocell and t is time. Assume first-order behavior and determine the steady-state response waveform.

3.17 Assume that the slotted disk described in Problem 3.16 is replaced with two polarizing disks of Polaroid (TM) sheets. One disk (A) is motor-driven and the other (B) is stationary. In this case the light reaching the photocell varies as the absolute value of sin (Ωt). Write an expression for $e_0 = f(t)$.

3.18 Second-order systems are often torsional rather than translational, based on $T = I\alpha$ rather than $F = Ma$, where T is torque and I the mass moment of inertia. Dimensions for the damping coefficient, ζ_t, are torque divided by angular velocity. Write the basic equations and solutions for the torsional case, specifying proper (common) units for each term.

3.19 Obtain a balance scale used for weighing laboratory chemicals and determine its free unloaded period of oscillation. Displace the rider or apply a small known weight to one of the pans and determine its sensitivity. Apply weights to the pans, balance, and determine the period. What conclusions do you draw from the latter experiment?

3.20 a) The natural frequency of a simple spring-mass system as shown in Fig. 3.6(a) is expressed by,

$$f = (1/2\pi)\sqrt{kg_c/m} \qquad \text{(from Eq. 3.2)}$$
$$= (1/2\pi)\sqrt{kg/w}.$$

If the system has a frequency of 25 Hz on the earth's surface (standard gravity), what will be its frequency of vibration on the surface of the moon? (See Appendix D for data). In gravity-free space?

b) The period of a simple pendulum is expressed by the relationship

$$f = (1/2\pi)\sqrt{g/L},$$

where L is the length of the pendulum. If the length is adjusted to provide a period of 1 Hz on the earth's surface, what would be its period on the moon's surface? In gravity-free space?

3.21 A pressure transducer uses a diaphragm as a pressure-summing device. In application the diaphragm and fluid behave as a second-order, single-degree system. The static displacement is proportional to the applied force (pressure). If the natural undamped frequency of the system is 3600 Hz and the total viscous damping is 75% of critical, determine the frequency range(s) over which the ratio of dynamic amplitude to static amplitude (inherent error) deviates from unity by an amount no greater than 6%. [*Note:* Close inspection of Fig. 3.16 should be helpful.]

3.22 What will be the frequency range(s) for Problem 3.21 if the damping ratio is changed to 0.5?

3.23 Consider the pressure transducer of Problem 3.21 to be damaged such that its viscous damping ratio becomes changed to some unknown value. If the transducer is subjected to a harmonic input of 2400 Hz, the phase angle between output and input is measured as 45 degrees. With this in mind, determine the inherent error of the transducer when used to measure a harmonic pressure signal of 1800 Hz. What will be the phase angle between the output and input at this frequency?

3.24 Consider a second-order system with a critical damping ratio of 0.70 and an undamped natural frequency of 50 Hz. Determine the steady-state response for the forcing function as shown in Fig. 3.24.

FIGURE 3.24   Forcing function for Problem 3.24.

3.25 A force transducer behaves as a simple second-order system. If the undamped natural frequency of the transducer is 1800 Hz and its damping is 30% of critical, what will be the inherent error in amplitude for a harmonic input of 950 Hz? Calculate the phase angle.

3.26 An oscillograph uses a heated stylus-type galvanometer (pen motor), which behaves as a second-order system having a damping ratio of 0.3 and an undamped natural frequency of 120 Hz. If a harmonic input having an amplitude of 12 units at 80 Hz is applied, what dynamic output will be indicated? What is the inherent error under these conditions?

3.27 Figures 3.1, 3.2, and 3.3 present response characteristics for a voltage amplifier. Assuming the following expressions $e_i = f(t)$, write corresponding expressions $e_o = g(t)$, where e_i = the voltage input and e_o = the amplifier output.

$e_i = f(t)$ (waveform from Table 2.1)	A_0, in volts	Frequency, in Hz
Fig. 2.8(a)	4×10^{-4}	5×10^4
Fig. 2.8(b)	1.7×10^{-3}	1×10^4
Fig. 2.8(c)	1×10^{-3}	2×10^4
Fig. 2.8(d)	4×10^{-3}	4×10^4

3.28 Obtain comparative computer plots for each of the input–output pairs listed in Problem 3.27.

3.29 A square wave or stepped pulse is often used to obtain qualitative information regarding performance characteristics of a system. Such an input is used not only for electrical systems, but also for pneumatic, hydraulic, and thermodynamic systems for which inputs may be in the form of such quantities as pressure, temperature, etc. Briefly discuss the reasons for such testing and what information may be obtained. The sawtooth waveform, referred to as "white noise," is often

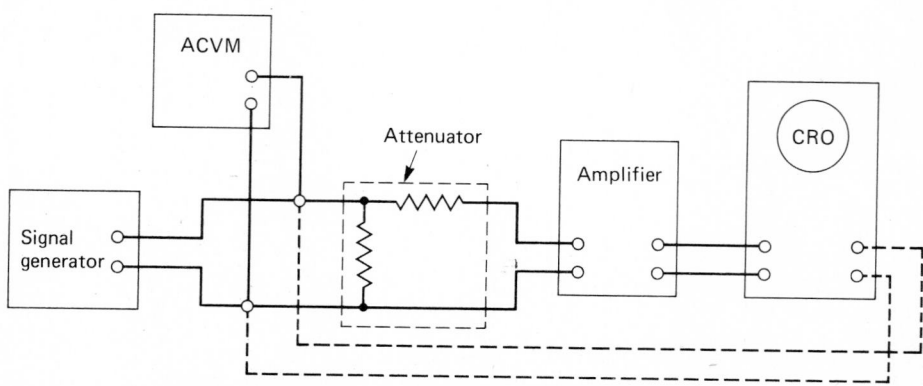

FIGURE 3.25   Experimental set-up described in Problem 3.30.

substituted for the square wave as a test input. What advantage may be claimed for its use?

3.30 Arrange a voltage amplifier, a signal generator, an ACVM, and a CRO as shown in Fig. 3.25.

   a) For a given generator frequency, increase the signal input until distortion is detected in the output waveform displayed on the CRO screen. (Note that distortion is often more readily detected when a Lissajous pattern is displayed. See Section 10.5.) Determine the limiting input voltages for a range of frequencies.

   b) While keeping the input amplitude at a constant value well below the distortion level, determine output voltages vs. frequency, as read from the CRO and the generator. Plot the voltage gain vs. frequency, thereby obtaining a frequency-response curve for the amplifier.

   c) By sampling the generator output and applying it to the horizontal sweep of the CRO (connections shown as dotted lines), determine phase lag through the use of Lissajous diagrams. [*Note:* Beware of any phase shift through an attenuator, if it is used. Check for this separately.]

sensors 4

4.1 INTRODUCTION

In Section 1.4 we divided the general measuring system into three distinct sections: the sensor-detector stage, the signal conditioning stage, and the terminating read-out stage. In this chapter and in Chapters 5 and 7 we will discuss in more detail what goes on in each of these stages.

The first contact that a measuring system has with the quantity to be measured is through the input sample accepted by the detecting element of the first stage (see Section 1.4). This act is usually accompanied by the immediate transduction of the input into an analogous form.

The medium handled is information. The detector senses the information input, I_{in}, and then transduces or converts it to a more convenient form, I_{out}. The relationship may be expressed as

$$I_{out} = f(I_{in}); \tag{4.1}$$

further,

$$\text{Transfer efficiency} = I_{out}/I_{in}. \tag{4.1a}$$

This may not be more than unity, because the pickup cannot generate information, but can only receive and process it. Obviously, as high a transfer efficiency as possible is desirable.

Sensitivity may be expressed as

$$\eta = dI_{out}/dI_{in}. \tag{4.1b}$$

Very often sensitivity approximates a constant, that is, the output is the linear function of the input.

4.2 LOADING OF THE SIGNAL SOURCE

Energy will always be taken from the signal source by the measuring system, which means that the information source will always be changed by the act of measurement. This is a measurement axiom. This effect is referred to as

91

loading. The smaller the load placed on the signal source by the measuring system, the better.

Of course, the problem of loading occurs not only in the first stage, but throughout the entire chain of elements. While the first-stage detector-transducer loads the input source, the second stage loads the first stage, and finally the third stage loads the second stage. In fact, the loading problem may be carried right down to the basic elements themselves.

In measuring systems made up primarily of electrical elements, the loading of the signal source is almost exclusively a function of the detector. Intermediate modifying devices and output indicators or recorders receive most of the energy necessary for their functioning from sources *other* than the signal source. A measure of the quality of the first stage, therefore, is its ability to provide a usable output without draining an undue amount of energy from the signal.

4.3   THE SECONDARY TRANSDUCER

As an example of a system of mechanical elements only, consider the Bourdon tube pressure gage, shown in Fig. 4.1. The primary detecting–transducing element consists of a circular tube of approximately elliptical cross section. When pressure is introduced the section of the flattened tube tends toward a more circular form. This in turn causes the free end A to move outward and the resulting motion is transmitted by link B to sector gear C and hence to pinion D, thereby causing the indicator hand to move over the scale.

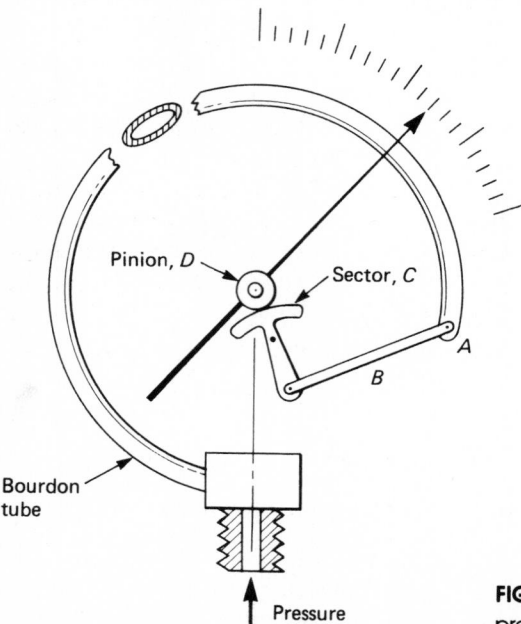

Pinion, *D*

Sector, *C*

A

B

Bourdon tube

Pressure

FIGURE 4.1   Essentials of a Bourdon-tube pressure gage.

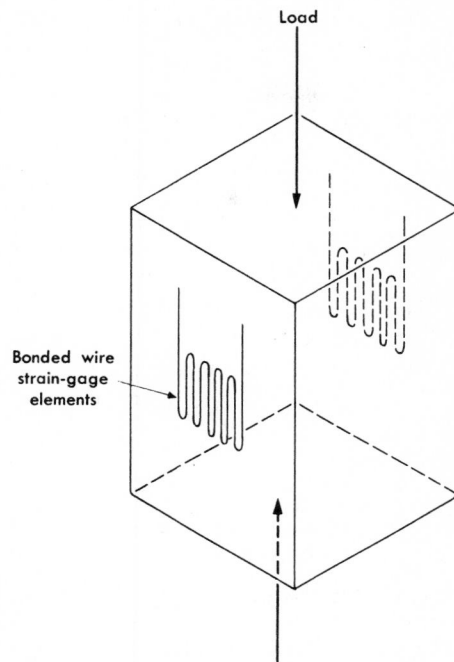

FIGURE 4.2   Schematic of a strain-gage load cell. The block forms the primary detector–transducer and the gages are secondary transducers.

In this example, the tube serves as the primary detector-transducer, changing pressure into near linear displacement. The linkage-gear arrangement acts as a secondary transducer (linear to rotary motion) and as an amplifier, yielding a magnified output.

A modification of this basic arrangement is to replace the linkage-gear arrangement with either a differential transformer (Section 4.11) or a voltage-dividing potentiometer (Section 4.6). In either case the electrical device serves as a secondary transducer, transforming displacement to voltage.

As another example, let us analyze a simplified compression-type force-measuring *load cell* consisting of a short column or strut, with electrical resistance-type strain gages (see Section 4.7) attached (Fig. 4.2). When an applied force deflects or strains the block, the force effect is transduced to deflection (we are interested in the unit deflection in this case). The load is transduced to strain. In turn, the strain is transformed into an electrical resistance change, with the strain gages serving as secondary transducers.

4.4 CLASSIFICATION OF FIRST-STAGE DEVICES

It appears, therefore, that the stage-one instrumentation may be of varying basic complexity, depending on the number of operations performed. This leads to a classification of first-stage devices as follows:

CLASS   I. First-stage element used as detector only.

TABLE 4.1 Some Primary Detector-Transducer Elements and Operations They Perform

Element	Operation
I. Mechanical	
A. Contracting spindle, pin, or finger	Displacement to displacement
B. Elastic member	
1. Load cells (Chapter 13)	
a) Tension/compression	Force to linear displacement
b) Bending	Force to linear displacement
c) Torsion	Torque to angular displacement
2. Proving ring (Chapter 13)	Force to linear displacement
3. Bourdon tube (Chapter 14)	Pressure to displacement
4. Bellows	Pressure to displacement
5. Diaphragm	Pressure to displacement
6. Helical spring	Force to linear displacement
7. Liquid column (also C.4 below)	Pressure to displacement
C. Mass	
1. Seismic mass (Chapter 17)	Forcing function to relative displacement
2. Pendulum	Gravitational acceleration to frequency or period
3. Pendulum (Chapter 13)	Force to displacement
4. Liquid column	Pressure to displacement
D. Thermal (Chapter 16)	
1. Thermocouple	Temperature to electric current
2. Bimaterial (includes mercury in glass)	Temperature to displacement
3. Thermistor	Temperature to resistance change
4. Chemical composition (special)	Temperature to chemical phase
E. Hydropneumatic	
1. Static	
a) Float	Fluid level to displacement
b) Hydrometer	Specific gravity to relative displacement
2. Dynamic (Chapter 15)	
a) Orifice	Fluid velocity to pressure change
b) Venturi	Fluid velocity to pressure change
c) Pitot	Fluid velocity to pressure change
d) Vanes	Velocity to force
e) Turbines	Linear to angular velocity

CLASS II. First-stage elements used as detector and single transducer.

CLASS III. First-stage elements used as detector with two transducer stages.

A generalized first stage may therefore be shown schematically as in Fig. 4.3.

Stage-one instrumentation may be very simple, consisting of no more than a mechanical spindle or contacting member used to transmit the quantity to be measured to a secondary transducer. Or, it may consist of a much more complex assembly of elements. In any event the primary detector-transducer is an *integral* assembly whose function is (1) to selectively sense the quantity of interest, and (2) to process the sensed information into a form acceptable to stage-two operations. It does not present an output in immediately usable form.

TABLE 4.1   *(Continued)*

Element	Operation
II. Electrical	
A. Resistive (Section 4.5)	
1. Contacting	Displacement to resistance change
2. Variable-length conductor	Displacement to resistance change
3. Variable-area conductor	Displacement to resistance change
4. Variable dimensions of conductor	Strain to resistance change
5. Variable resistivity of conductor	Temperature to resistance change
B. Inductive (Section 4.10)	
1. Variable coil dimensions	Displacement to change in inductance
2. Variable air gap	Displacement to change in inductance
3. Changing core material	Displacement to change in inductance
4. Changing core positions	Displacement to change in inductance
5. Changing coil positions	Displacement to change in inductance
6. Moving coil	Velocity to change in inductance
7. Moving permanent magnet	Velocity to change in inductance
8. Moving core	Velocity to change in inductance
C. Capacitive (Section 4.13)	
1. Changing air gap	Displacement to change in capacitance
2. Changing plate areas	Displacement to change in capacitance
3. Changing dielectric	Displacement to change in capacitance
D. Piezoelectric (Section 4.14)	Displacement to voltage and/or voltage to displacement
E. Photoelectric (Section 4.15)	
1. Photovoltaic	Light intensity to voltage*
2. Photoresistive	Light intensity to resistance change*
3. Photoemissive	Light intensity to current*

*   *Also somewhat sensitive to wavelength of light.*

More often than not the initial operation performed by the first-stage device is to transduce the input quantity into an analogous displacement. Without attempting to formulate a completely comprehensive list, let us consider Table 4.1 as representing the general area of the primary detector-transducer in mechanical measurements.

We make no attempt now to discuss all the many combinations of elements listed in Table 4.1. In most cases we have referred in the table to sections

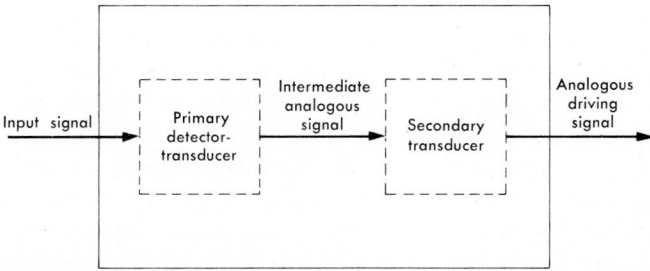

FIGURE 4.3   Block diagram of a first-stage device with primary and secondary transducers.

where thorough discussions can be found. The general nature of many of the elements is self-evident. A few are of minimal importance, included merely to round out the list. However, we can make several pertinent observations at this point.

Close scrutiny of Table 4.1 reveals that whereas many of the mechanical sensors transduce the input to displacement, many of the electrical sensors change displacement to an electrical-type output. This is quite fortunate, for it yields practical combinations in which the mechanical sensor serves as the primary transducer and the electrical sensor as the secondary. The two most commonly used electrical means are variable resistance and variable inductance, although others, such as photoelectric and piezoelectric, are of considerable importance also.

In addition to the inherent compatibility of the mechano-electric transducer combination, electrical elements have several important relative advantages:

1. Amplification or attenuation can be easily obtained.
2. Mass-inertia effects are minimized.
3. The effects of friction are minimized.
4. An output power of almost any magnitude can be provided.
5. Remote indication of recording is feasible.
6. The transducers are commonly susceptible to miniaturization.

Most of the remainder of this chapter is devoted to a discussion of electrical-type transducers and to modification of their outputs (signal conditioning).

4.5   VARIABLE-RESISTANCE TRANSDUCER ELEMENTS

Resistance of an electrical conductor varies according to the following relation:

$$R = \frac{\rho L}{A},\tag{4.2}$$

where

R = resistance, in ohms,

L = the length of the conductor, in cm,

A = cross-sectional area of the conductor, in cm^2,

ρ = the resistivity of material, in ohms · cm.

Probably the simplest mechanical-to-electrical transducer is the ordinary *switch*. It is a yes–no, conducting–nonconducting device that can be used to operate an indicator. Here a lamp is fully as useful for read-out as a meter, since only two values of quantitative information can be obtained. In its simplest form, the switch may be used as a limiting device operated by direct

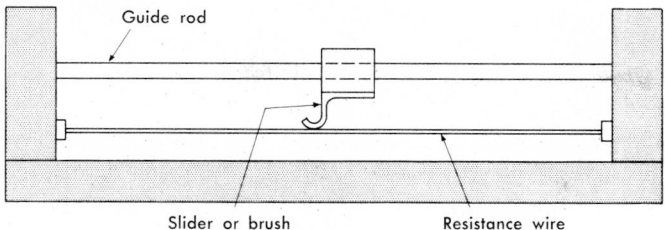

FIGURE 4.4 Variable resistance consisting of a wire and moveable contactor or brush. This is often referred to as a slide wire.

mechanical contact (as for limiting the travel of machine-tool carriages) or it may be used as a position indicator. When actuated by a diaphragm or bellows, it becomes a pressure-limit indicator, or if controlled by a bimetal strip, it is a temperature-limit indicator. It may also be combined with a proving ring to serve as either an overload warning device or a device actually limiting load-carrying, such as a safety device for a crane.

4.6 SLIDING-CONTACT DEVICES

Sliding-contact resistive transducers convert a mechanical displacement input into an electrical output, either voltage or current. This is accomplished by changing the effective length, L, of the conductor in Eq. (4.2). Some form of electrical-resistance element is used, with which a contactor or brush maintains electrical contact as it moves. In its simplest form, the device may consist of a stretched resistance wire and slider, as in Fig. 4.4. The effective resistance existing between either end of the wire and the brush thereby becomes a measure of the mechanical displacement. Devices of this type have been used for sensing relatively large displacements [1].

More commonly, the resistance element is formed by wrapping a resistance wire around a form or *card*. The turns are spaced to prevent shorting, and the brush slides across the turns from one turn to the next. In actual practice, either the arrangement may be wound for a rectilinear movement or the resistance element may be formed into an arc and angular movement used, as shown in Fig. 4.5.

These devices are commonly called *resistance potentiometers,** or simply *pots*. Variations of the basic angular or rotary form are the multiturn, the low-torque, and various nonlinear types [2]. Multiturn potentiometers are available with various numbers of turns, up to 40. See also Section 5.7.

---

* Unfortunately, another entirely different device is also called a potentiometer. It is the voltage-measuring instrument wherein a standard reference voltage is adjusted to counterbalance the unknown voltage (see Section 5.8). The two devices are different and must not be confused.

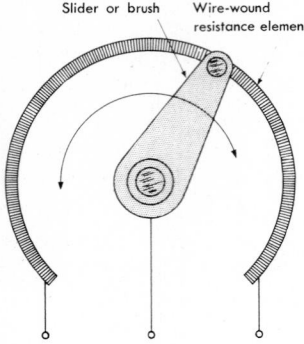
Slider or brush   Wire-wound resistance element

FIGURE 4.5   Angular motion variable resistance, or potentiometer.

4.6.1   Potentiometer Resolution

Resistance variation available from a sliding contact moving over a wire-wound resistance element is not a continuous function of contact movement. The smallest increment into which the whole may be divided determines the *resolution*. In the case of resistance winding, the limiting resolution equals the reciprocal of the number of turns. If 1200 turns of wire are used and the winding is linear, the resolution will be 1/1200, or 0.09083%. The meaning of this quantity is apparent: No matter how refined the remainder of the system may be, it will be impossible to divide, or resolve, the input into parts smaller than 1/1200 of the total potentiometer range.

4.6.2   Potentiometer Linearity

When used as a measurement transducer, a linear potentiometer is normally required. Use of the term *linear* assumes that the resistance measured between one of the ends of the element and the contactor is a direct linear function of the contactor position in relation to that end. Linearity, however, is never completely achieved and deviation limits are usually supplied by the manufacturer.

4.7   THE RESISTANCE STRAIN GAGE

Experiment has shown that each term in Eq. (4.2) is simultaneously affected by the input strain in a resistance strain gage. The resistance element is cemented to the surface of the member to be strained, and as it elongates with application of strain (assuming a tensile strain) its sectional area reduces and a longer length of smaller element results. However, simply accounting for these dimensional changes does not completely explain the behavior of the gage; there is also a change in resistivity with strain.

This device is of sufficient importance in the field of mechanical measurements to warrant a more complete discussion than can be given at this point. Chapter 12 is devoted to the theory and use of strain gages.

4.8 THERMISTORS

Thermistors are thermally sensitive variable resistors made of ceramic-like semiconducting materials. Oxides of manganese, nickel, and cobalt are used in formulations having resistivity values of 100 to 450,000 ohms · cm.

There are two basic applications for these devices: (1) as temperature-detecting elements used to sense temperature changes for the purpose of measurement or control, and (2) as electric-power–sensing devices wherein the thermistor temperature and hence resistance are a function of the power being dissipated by the device. The second application is particularly useful for measuring radio-frequency power.

Further discussion of thermistors will be found in Section 16.5.3.

4.9 THE THERMOCOUPLE

While two dissimilar metals are in contact, an electromotive force exists whose magnitude is a function of several factors, including *temperature*. Junctions of this sort, used to measure temperature, are called *thermocouples*. Often the junction is formed by twisting and welding together two wires.

Because of its small size, its reliability, and its relatively large range of usefulness, the thermocouple is a very important primary element. Further discussion of its application is reserved for Chapter 16 (see especially Section 16.6).

4.10 VARIABLE-INDUCTANCE TRANSDUCER ELEMENTS

A classification of inductive transducers, based on the fundamental principles used, is as follows:

I. Variable self-inductance
    A. Single-coil (simple variable permeance)
    B. Two-coil (or single-coil with center tap) connected for inductance ratio
II. Variable mutual inductance
    A. Simple two-coil
    B. Three-coil (using series opposition)
III. Variable reluctance
    A. Moving iron
    B. Moving coil
    C. Moving magnet

Inductive reactance, which is the evaluation of the inductive effect, may be expressed by the relation

$$X_L = 2\pi f L, \tag{4.3}$$

where

X_L = the inductive reactance, in ohms,

f = the frequency of applied voltage, in Hz,

L = inductance, in henrys.

Inductance, L, is influenced by a number of factors, including the number of turns in the coil, the coil size, and especially the permeability of the flux path. Some coils are wound with only air as the core material. These are usually used at relatively high frequencies; however, they will occasionally be found in transducer circuitry. Often some form of magnetic material will be used in the flux path, commonly in conjunction with one or more air gaps.

An expression that may be used to estimate the inductance of an air-core coil is as follows [3]:

$$L = \frac{a^2 n^2}{22.9a + 25.4b} , \qquad (4.3a)$$

where

L = inductance, in microhenrys,

a = the coil radius, in cm,

b = the coil length, in cm, and

n = the number of turns.

When the flux path includes both a magnetic material (usually iron) and an air gap or gaps, the inductance may be estimated by use of the following relation [4]:

$$L = \frac{1.26 n^2 \times 10^{-8}}{(h_i/\mu a_i) + (h_a/a_a)} , \qquad (4.3b)$$

in which

h_i = the length of the iron circuit, in cm,

h_a = the length of the air gaps, in cm,

a_i = the cross-sectional area of iron, in cm^2,

a_a = the cross-sectional area of the air gap, in cm^2, and

μ = the permeability of the magnetic material at maximum flux density.

In many instances the permeability of the magnetic material is sufficiently high so that only the air gaps need be considered. In such cases, Eq. (4.3b)

reduces to

$$L = 1.26n^2 \frac{a_a}{h_a} \times 10^{-8} \qquad (4.3c)$$

The total impedance of a coil may be expressed by the relation

$$Z = \sqrt{X_L^2 + R^2}, \qquad (4.4)$$

in which R is the d.c. resistance of the coil. The higher the inductance of a coil relative to its d.c. resistance, the higher is said to be its quality, which is designated by the symbol Q. In most cases high Q is desired.

Inductive transducers may be based on any of the variables indicated in the equations above, and most have been tried at one time or another. The following are representative.

4.10.1 Simple Inductance Types

When a simple single coil is used as a transducer element, the mechanical input usually changes the permeance of the flux path generated by the coil, thereby changing its inductance. The change in inductance is then measured by suitable circuitry, indicating the value of the input. The flux path may be changed by a change in air gap (Fig. 4.6); however, a change in either the amount or type of core material may also be used.

Figure 4.7 illustrates a form of *two-coil* self-inductance. (This may also be thought of as a single coil with center tap.) Movement of the core or armature alters the relative inductance of the two coils. Devices of this type

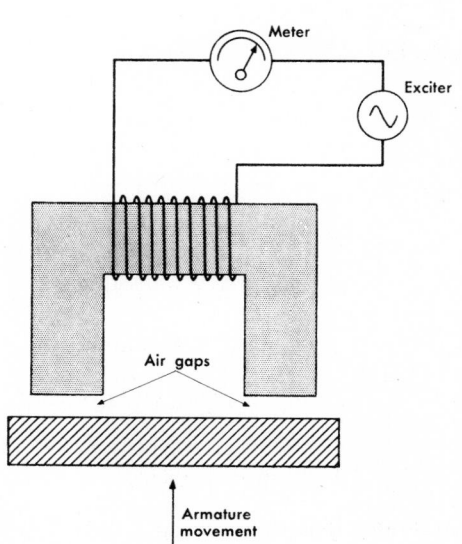

FIGURE 4.6   A simple self-inductance arrangement wherein a change in the air gap changes the pickup output.

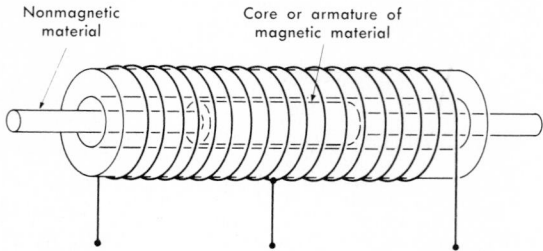

FIGURE 4.7   Two-coil (or center-tapped single coil) inductance–ratio transducer.

are usually incorporated in some form of inductive bridge circuit (see Section 5.10) in which variation in the inductance ratio between the two coils provides the output. An application of a two-coil self-inductance used as a secondary transducer for pressure measurement is described in Section 14.8.2.

4.10.2 Two-Coil Mutual-Inductance Arrangements

Mutual-inductance arrangements using two coils are shown in Figs. 4.8 and 4.9. Figure 4.8 illustrates the manner in which these devices function. The flux from a power coil is coupled to a pickup coil, which supplies the output. Input information, in the form of armature displacement, changes the coupling between the coils. In the arrangement shown, the air gaps between the core and the armature govern the degree of coupling. In other arrangements the coupling may be varied by changing the relative positions of either the coils or armature, linearly or angularly.

Figure 4.9 shows the detector portion of an *electronic micrometer* [5]. Inductive coupling between the coils, which depends on the permeance of the

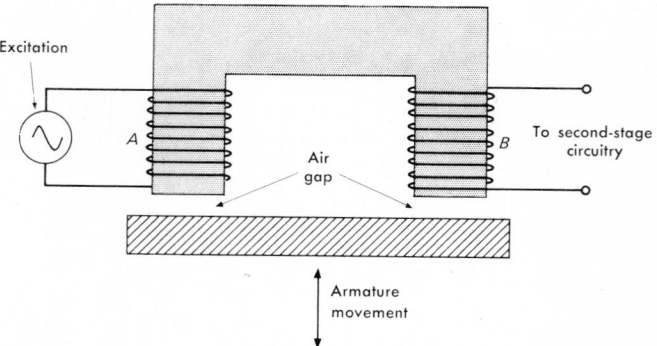

FIGURE 4.8   A mutual-inductance transducer. Coil A is the energizing coil, and B is the pickup coil. As the armature is moved, thereby altering the air-gap, the output from coil B is changed, and this may be used as a measure of armature movement.

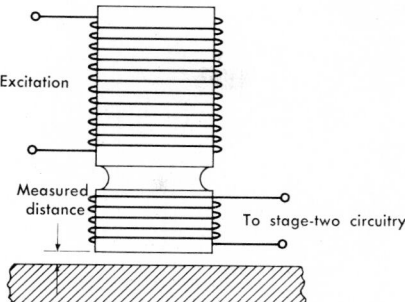

FIGURE 4.9   Two-coil inductive pickup for "an electronic micrometer."

magnetic-flux path, is changed by the relative proximity of a permeable material. A variation of this has been used in a transducer for measuring small inside diameters [6]. In this case the coupling is varied by relative movement between the two coils.

4.11   THE DIFFERENTIAL TRANSFORMER

Undoubtedly the most generally used of the variable-inductance transducers is the differential transformer (Fig. 4.10), which provides an a.c. voltage output proportional to the displacement of the core passing through the windings. It is a mutual-inductance device making use of three coils arranged generally as shown.

The center coil is energized from an a.c. power source, and the two end coils, connected in phase opposition, are used as pickup coils. This device is discussed in detail in Section 11.19.

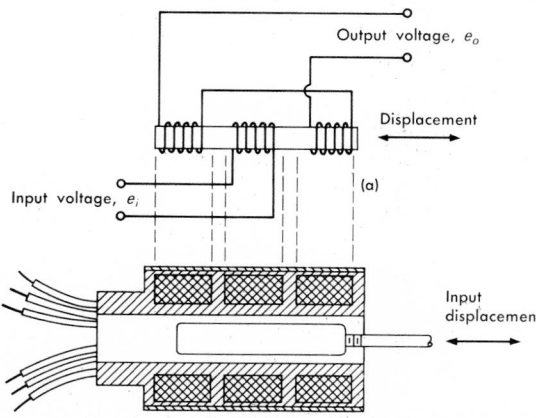

FIGURE 4.10   The differential transformer. (a) Schematic arrangement. (b) Section through typical transformer.

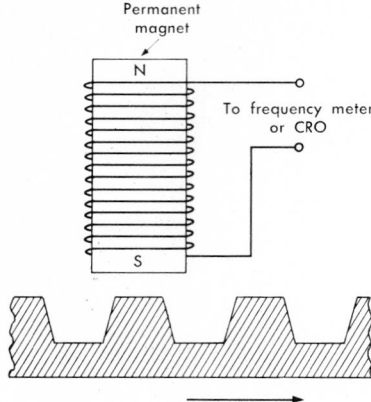

FIGURE 4.11   A simple variable-reluctance pickup.

4.12 VARIABLE-RELUCTANCE TRANSDUCERS

In transducer practice, use of the term *variable reluctance* assumes some form of inductance device incorporating a *permanent magnet*. In most cases these devices are limited to dynamic application, either steady-state or transient, where the flux lines supplied by the magnet are cut by the turns of the coil. Some means of providing relative motion is incorporated into the device.

In its simplest form, the variable-reluctance device consists of a coil wound on a permanent magnet core (Fig. 4.11). Any variation of the permeance of the magnetic circuit causes a change in the flux. As the flux field expands or collapses, a voltage is developed in the coil. Practical applications of this arrangement are discussed in Sections 10.8 and 15.8.1.

Whereas the arrangement above depends on changing permeance, other devices based on variable reluctance depend on relative movement between the flux field and the coil (Section 17.5).

4.13 CAPACITIVE TRANSDUCERS

An equation for calculating capacitance is [7]

$$C = \frac{0.088KA(N-1)}{d},$$

where

C = the capacitance, in picofarads,

K = the dielectric constant ($= 1$ for air),

A = the area of one side of one plate, in cm^2,

N = the number of plates, and

d = the separation of plate surfaces, in cm.

All the terms represented in this equation, except possibly the number of

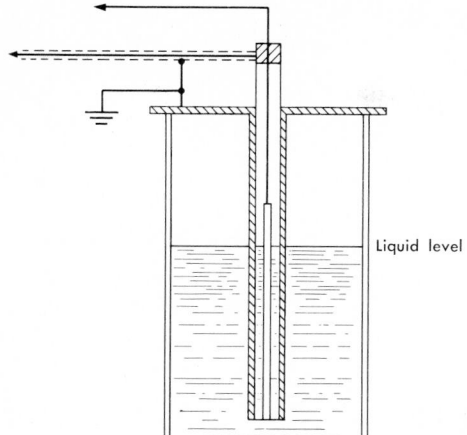

FIGURE 4.12 Capacitance pickup for determining level of liquid hydrogen.

plates, have been used in transducer applications. The following are examples of each.

Changing dielectric constant

Figure 4.12 shows a device developed for the measurement of level in a container of liquid hydrogen [8]. The capacitance between the central rod and the surrounding tube varies with changing dielectric constant brought about by changing liquid level. The device readily detects liquid level even though the difference in dielectric constant between the liquid and vapor states may be as low as 0.05.

Changing area

Capacitance change depending on changing effective area has been used for the secondary transducing element of a torque meter [9]. The device uses a sleeve with teeth or serrations cut axially, and a matching internal member or shaft with similar axially cut teeth. Figure 4.13 illustrates the arrangement.

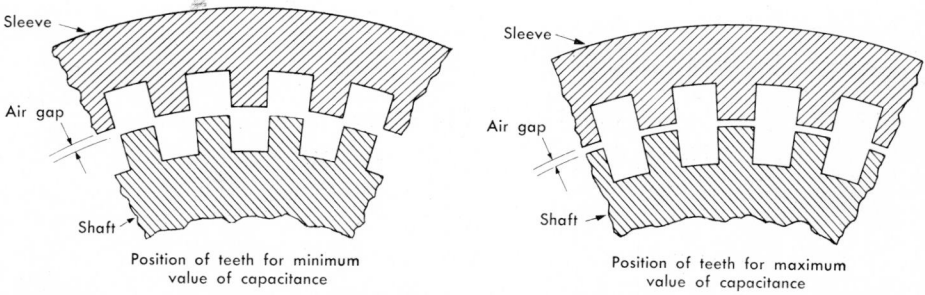

FIGURE 4.13 Section showing relative arrangement of teeth in capacitance-type torque-meter.

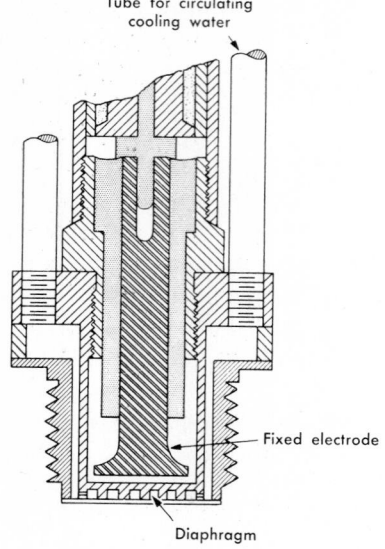

Tube for circulating
cooling water

Fixed electrode

Diaphragm

FIGURE 4.14   Section through capacitance-type pressure pickup.

A clearance is provided between the tips of the teeth, as shown. Torque carried by an elastic member causes a shift in the relative positions of the teeth, thereby changing the effective area. The resulting capacitance change is calibrated in terms of torque.

Changing distance

Changing distance between plates of a capacitor is undoubtedly the more commonly used method for using capacitance in a pickup.

Figure 4.14 illustrates a capacitor-type pressure transducer wherein the capacitance between the diaphragm to which the pressure is applied and the electrode foot is used as a measure of the diaphragm's relative position [10, 11, 12]. Flexing of the diaphragm under pressure changes the distance between itself and the electrode.

4.14 PIEZO-TYPE SENSORS

4.14.1 The Piezoelectric Effect

Certain materials can generate an electrical potential when subjected to mechanical strain or, conversely, can change dimensions when subjected to voltage (Fig. 4.15a). This is known as the *piezoelectric* effect. Pierre and Jacques Curie are credited with its discovery in 1880. Notable among these materials are quartz, Rochelle salt (potassium sodium tartarate), properly polarized

---

*   The prefix "piezo" is derived from the Greek *piezein,* meaning "to press" or "to squeeze."

barium titanate, ammonium dihydrogen phosphate, and even ordinary sugar.

Of all the materials that exhibit the effect, none possesses all the desirable properties, such as stability, high output, insensitivity to temperature extremes and humidity, and the ability to be formed into any desired shape. Rochelle salt provides the highest output, but requires protection from moisture in the air and cannot be used above about 45°C (115°F). Quartz is undoubtedly the most stable, yet its output is low. Because of its stability, quartz is quite commonly used for stabilizing electronic oscillators (Section 8.6.2). Often the quartz is shaped into a thin disk with each face silvered for the attachment of electrodes. The thickness of the plate is ground to the dimension that provides a mechanically resonant frequency corresponding to the desired electrical frequency. This crystal may then be incorporated in an appropriate electronic circuit whose frequency it controls.

Rather than existing as a single crystal, as are many piezoelectric materials, barium titanate is polycrystalline; thus it may be formed into a variety of sizes and shapes. The piezoelectric effect is not present until the element is subjected to polarizing treatment. Although exact polarizing procedure varies with the manufacturer, the following procedure has been used [13]. The element is heated to a temperature above the Curie point of 120°C, and a high d.c. potential is applied across the faces of the element. The magnitude of this voltage depends on the thickness of the element and is on the order of 10,000 V/cm. The element is then cooled with the voltage applied, which results in an element that exhibits the piezoelectric effect.

Figure 4.15(b) shows an equivalent circuit for a piezoelement, consisting of a charge generator and a shunting capacitance, C_T. Charge Q is a fundamental measure of electrical quantity: protons, if positive, and electrons, if negative. The reader should refer to Tables 3.1 and 3.2 for the relationships between charge Q and other electrical units.

When mechanically strained the piezoelement generates a charge $Q(t)$, which is temporarily stored in the element's inherent capacitance, C_T. As with all capacitors, however, the charge dissipates with time due to leakage, a fact that makes piezodevices most valuable when used for dynamic measurements.

Piezoelectric transducers are used to measure surface roughness (Section 11.20), strain (Section 12.13), force and torque (Section 13.6), pressure (Section 14.8.3), motion (Section 17.9), and sound and noise (Section 18.5.1).

Ultrasonic generator elements also use barium titanate. Such elements are used in industrial cleaning apparatus and in underwater detection systems known as *sonar*.

4.14.2 Piezoresistive-Type Sensors

When a conductor of electricity is mechanically strained, its electrical resistance is altered. This is the functional basis for the resistance-type strain gage (see Chapter 12). The resistance change is caused by two factors: (1) R_d due

TABLE 4.2 Photocells

Type	Symbol and Typical Circuit	Form of Output	Relative Frequency Response	Comments
A. *Photoemissive*		Current		Cathode–anode in evacuated glass or quartz envelope. Bulky; requires high voltage; and has given way to solid-state devices.
B. *Photoconductive (or photoresistive)*		Resistance change	Slow	Light-sensitive resistor. Increased light intensity causes reduced resistance.
C. *Photovoltaic (solar cell)*		Voltage	Fast	Typical open-circuit voltage, 0.45. In bright sunlight, 0.4 to 0.5 ma.
D1. *Photodiode (PN junction)* D2. *PIN photodiode*		Current	Fastest acting of all	Primary disadvantage is low output current. "Dark current" very low (nanoampere range), but not zero. PIN diode has "intrinsic" layer between P and N layers that provides response over wider range of light wavelengths. PIN is faster than PN type.
E1. *Phototransistor*		Current		Produces much higher current for given input than photodiode does because of its amplifying ability. Slower acting than photodiode. Base lead, if accessible, is seldom used.
E2. *Photodarlington*		Current	Slower than phototransistor	Much more sensitive than phototransistor.

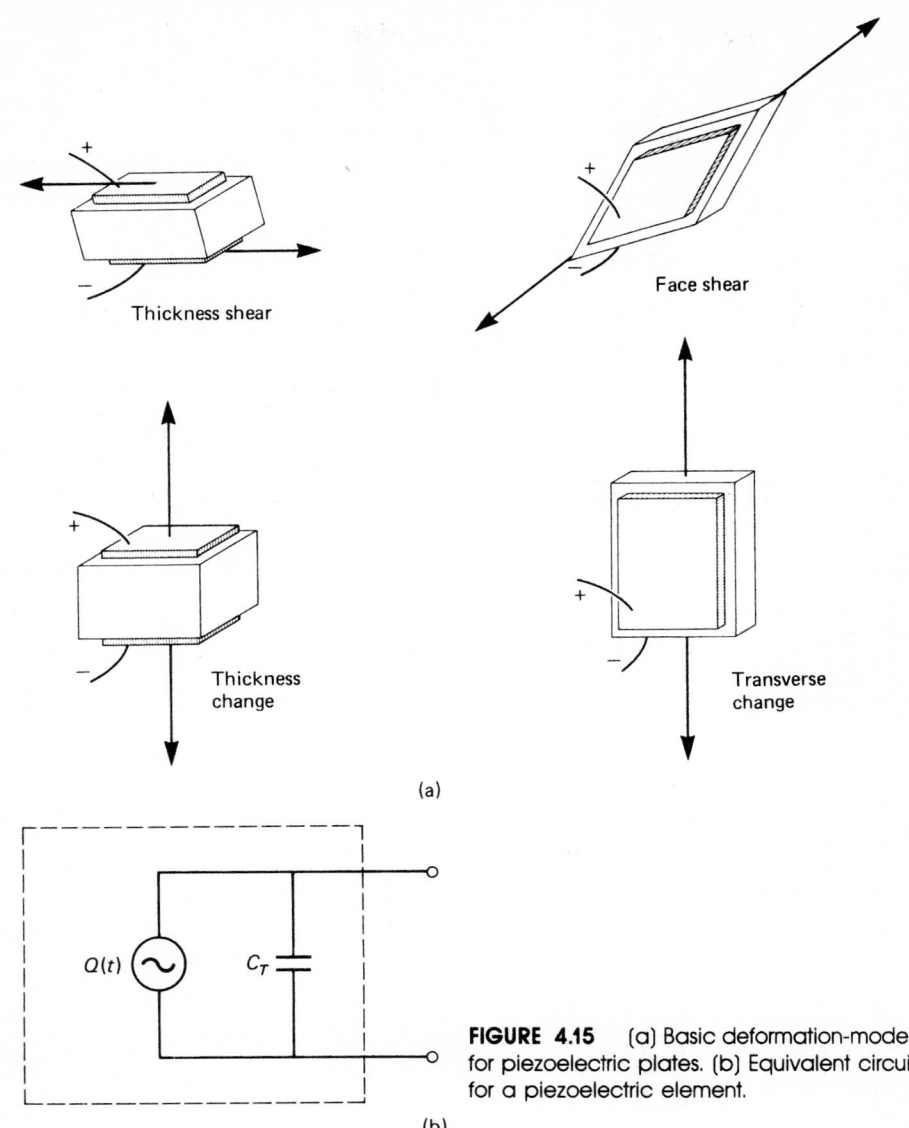

Thickness shear

Face shear

Thickness change

Transverse change

(a)

$Q(t)$ C_T

FIGURE 4.15   (a) Basic deformation-modes for piezoelectric plates. (b) Equivalent circuit for a piezoelectric element.

(b)

to dimensional changes, and (2) R_ρ due to change in resistivity, ρ, of the material. In most cases R_ρ provides the greater contribution to net resistance change. Usually, but not always, this factor is positive. For further discussion of the piezoresistive effect, see Sections 12.5, 12.13, 13.6, 14.8.3, and 17.9.

4.15   PHOTOELECTRIC TRANSDUCERS

Light-sensitive detectors, photosensors, or photocells may be categorized into two types, (a) electronic and (b) solid state, or they may be grouped under the classifications shown in Table 4.2.

Photoemissive types (Type A, Table 4.2) consist of a cathode–anode combination in an evacuated glass or quartz envelope. In the proper circuit (commonly requiring a d.c. source of from 100 to 200 V), light impingement on the cathode frees electrons to flow, thereby providing a small current. With the invention of small solid-state photosensors, this type is seldom used.

Semiconductor photosensors use the electron-hole principle exhibited by certain materials: the flow of electron-hole pairs depends on the intensity of incident light and the surface area exposed.

Photoconductive cells (Type B, Table 4.2) consist of a thin layer of material such as selenium, several of the metallic sulphides, or germanium coated between electrodes on a glass plate. The cell behaves as a light-controlled variable resistor whose resistance is reduced when it is exposed to a light source. In conjunction with resistance-sensitive circuitry (Sections 5.6–5.10) an output may be obtained that is a function of the intensity of the light source.

The *photovoltaic* cell (Type C, Table 4.2) consists of a sandwich of unlike materials, such as an iron base covered with a thin layer of iron selenide. When the cell is exposed to light a voltage is developed across the section. A distinguishing feature of this cell is that it requires no external power other than the light: It is the well-known *solar cell.*

The *photodiode* (Types D1 and D2, Table 4.2) utilizes a PN junction and is similar to the photoconductive cell. Basically it is a light-sensitive variable resistor. The PIN photodiode differs from the common variety in that an additional layer, referred to as the *intrinsic layer,* is inserted between the P and N layers in order to expand the range of sensitivity to light of longer wavelengths.

Both the *phototransistor* and the *photodarlington* cells (Types E1 and E2, Table 4.2) are basically photodiodes followed by one or two stages of amplification incorporated in the same package. This is done to enhance the output.

Photosensors may be made selectively sensitive to light not only in the visible spectrum but also in the infrared and ultraviolet ranges. Heat-seeking

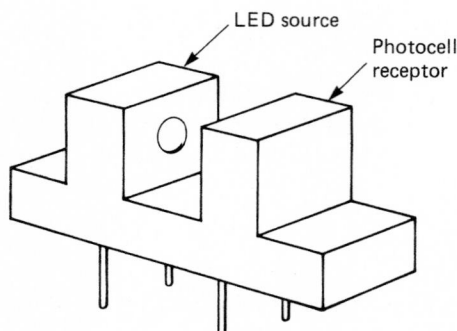

FIGURE 4.16 A photo-interrupter consisting of an LED light source (often infrared) and a photocell sensor. Mechanical interruption of the light path can be used for various purposes, such as counting, triggering, synchronization.

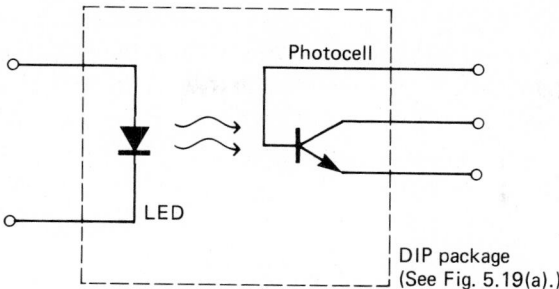

FIGURE 4.17 The essentials of a photo-isolator, used for connecting low-impedance current circuits to high-impedance voltage circuits. The isolator is also useful for providing complete electrical isolation between circuits, sometimes imperative in health-related electronics.

infrared sensors are commonly of the photoconductor type. The response of photosensors to sudden variations in light intensity is not instantaneous. It is determined both by the cell itself and by related circuitry. Rise and fall times, as determined by the cell type, may range from a fraction of a millisecond to several thousand milliseconds [14, 15, 16].

Applications of the photocell in mechanical measurements include simple counting, where the interruption of a beam of light could be used (Fig. 10.1), strain measurement [17], dew-point controls [18], and edge and tension controls [19].

Special packages, optointerrupters and optoisolators, consist of photocells combined with light-emitting diodes (LEDs), arranged so that the light from the LED impinges on the cell (see Figs. 4.16 and 4.17). The interrupter is configured so that some form of mechanical mask may be used to break the light beam between the LED and the cell, thereby providing on–off switching for counting or any of a variety of purposes. The optoisolator is used to match low-impedance current circuits to high-impedance voltage circuits, or vice versa. It also provides a high-impedance isolation between circuits, which is important in some forms of health-related electronics [20].

4.16 SOME DESIGN-RELATED PROBLEMS

Accuracy, sensitivity, dynamic response, repeatability, and the ability to reject unwanted inputs are all qualities highly desired in each component of a measuring system. Many of the parameters that combine to provide these qualities present conflicting problems, and must be compromised in the final design. Response requirements were presented in Chapter 3. At this point we will discuss some additional design problems.

4.16.1 Manufacturing Tolerances

Conception of a component or system on paper is a necessary and important beginning, but to be useful, the apparatus must be produced, and no manufacturing process can reproduce *exact* length or angular dimensions. Dimensions must always be assigned with some specified or implied tolerances. How can one predict the effects of such variations on performance? The following is one approach to the problem.

EXAMPLE   Suppose a spring scale such as that shown in Fig. 4.18 is to be designed. We will assume a force capacity of 50 N and a maximum deflection of 10 cm. This gives us a deflection constant of 5 N/cm.

 Using conventional coil-spring design relations [21], we find that a spring made with a mean coil diameter D_m of 2 cm and a steel wire diameter of 2 mm will meet stress requirements provided we ensure against overload by including appropriate deflection limits or stops. The deflection equation commonly used for coil springs is

$$K = F/y = (E_s D_w^4)/(8 D_m^3 n),$$

where

 K = the deflection constant, in N/m,

 F = the design load, in N,

 y = the corresponding deflection, in m,

 E_s = the torsional elastic modulus, in Pa (about 80×10^9 Pa for steel), and

 n = the number of coils.

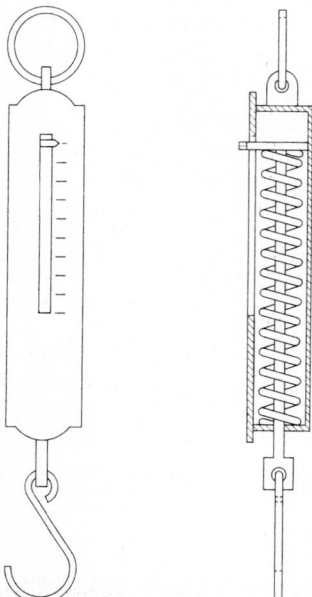

FIGURE 4.18   Common spring-type "fish" scale.

Using this relation and the design values above, we find that 40 coils are needed to provide the required deflection constant. If we apply reasonable tolerances, our specifications become

$$D_w = 2 \pm 0.01 \text{ mm},$$

$$D_m = 2 \pm 0.05 \text{ cm},$$

$$n = 40 \pm \tfrac{1}{3} \text{ coils, and}$$

$$E_s = 80 \times 10^6 \pm 3.5 \times 10^6 \text{ kPa}.$$

Although we realize that it may be confusing to the reader for us to refer to a later chapter, we beg indulgence and mention a relation from Section 9.6, "Treatment of Systematic Uncertainties." (The reader may find it useful to scan that section at this point. We also direct attention to reference [22] for extended coverage.) Equation 9.5 yields an overall evaluation of the interaction of uncertainties. In this case the uncertainties happen to be the ranges of manufacturing tolerances. Inserting the values, including weighting factors, as described in Section 9.6, we have

$$\frac{U_K}{K} = \sqrt{\left(\frac{4 \times 0.01}{2}\right)^2 + \left(\frac{3 \times 0.05}{2}\right)^2 + \left(\frac{0.33}{40}\right)^2 + \left(\frac{3.5}{80}\right)^2}$$

$$= 0.0895 \approx 9\%$$

or

$$K = 500 \pm 45 \text{ N/m}.$$

Note that mm, cm, and m have been used in the above example; hence care must be used in placing decimal points.

We see then that if we lay out the gradations corresponding to nominal values, a force of 50 N may actually be indicated as anything in the range of from 45.5 to 54.5 N, depending on how the manufacturing tolerances may fall. Should this not be satisfactory, our only recourse is (a) to provide better control of the manufacturing tolerances, or (b) to provide some means for adjusting calibration.

Various methods of calibration can be used, depending on the intended "quality" of the device. In this instance, two or three faceplates can be provided, each with gradations scaled to cover a portion of the calibration range. At the time of assembly, a simple calibration would determine the most appropriate plate to use. Section 13.4.1 presents another approach that could be applied to our particular example.

At this point it is appropriate to make an additional observation. *Weight* is basically a *force;* hence we should express the calibration in newtons rather than in kilograms. Should we wish a scale calibrated in kilograms, then, to be completely correct we should include the assumed value of gravity acceleration on the faceplate. The standard due to gravity is 9.80665 m/s^2, and the kilogram-range corresponding to our 50-newton range becomes 0 to 50/9.80665 ≈ 5.1 kg. (Use of the non-SI symbol, kgf, is discouraged.)

It should be clear that the procedures used in the preceding example are applicable to most elastic transducer configurations, as well as to many other tolerance problems.

4.16.2   Some Temperature-Related Problems

An ideal measuring system will react to the design signal only and ignore all else. Of course, this is an ideal that is never completely fulfilled. One of the more insidious extraneous stimuli adversely affecting instrument operation is temperature. It is insidious in that it is almost impossible to maintain a constant temperature environment for the general-purpose measuring system. The usual solution is to accept the temperature variation and to devise methods to compensate for it.

Temperature variations cause dimensional changes and changes in physical properties, both elastic and electrical, resulting in deviations referred to as *zero shift* and *scale error* [23, 24]. Zero shift, as the name implies, results in a change in the no-input reading. Factors other than temperature may cause zero shift; however, temperature is probably the most common cause. In most applications the zero indication on the output scale would be made to correspond to the no-input condition. For example, the indicator or the spring scales referred to earlier should be set at zero pounds when there is no weight in the pan. If the temperature changes after the scale has been set to zero, there may be a differential dimensional change between spring and scale, altering the no-load reading. This change would be referred to as *zero shift*. Zero shift is primarily a function of linear dimensional change caused by expansion or contraction with changing temperature.

Dimensional changes are expressed in terms of the coefficient of expansion by the following familiar relations:

$$\alpha = \frac{1}{\Delta T} \frac{\Delta L}{L_0} \tag{4.5}$$

and

$$L_1 = L_0(1 + \alpha \, \Delta T), \tag{4.6}$$

in which

α = the coefficient of thermal expansion (ppm/deg. temp.) $\times 10^{-6}$,

L/L_0 = the unit change in length,

T = the change in temperature ($T_1 - T_0$),

L_0 = the length dimension at the reference temperature T_0, and

L_1 = the length dimension at any other temperature T_1.

In addition to causing zero shift, temperature changes usually affect scale calibration when resilient load-carrying members are involved. The coil and wire diameters of our spring would be altered with temperature change, and so too would the modulus of elasticity of the spring material. These variations would cause a changed spring constant, hence changed load-deflection calibration, resulting in what is referred to as *scale error*.

The thermoelastic coefficient is defined by the relations

$$c = \frac{1}{\Delta T}\frac{\Delta E}{E_0} \tag{4.7}$$

and

$$E_1 = E_0(1 + c\,\Delta T), \tag{4.8}$$

in which

c = the coefficient for the tensile modulus of elasticity (ppm/deg. temp.) $\times\ 10^{-6}$,

$\Delta E/E_0$ = the unit change in the tensile modulus of elasticity,

E_0 = the tensile modulus of elasticity at temperature T_0, and

E_1 = the tensile modulus of elasticity at temperature T_1.

Similarly, the coefficient for torsional modulus may be written

$$m = \frac{1}{\Delta T}\frac{\Delta E_s}{E_{s0}} \tag{4.9}$$

and

$$E_{s_1} = E_{s0}(1 + m\,\Delta T), \tag{4.10}$$

where

m = the coefficient for the torsional modulus of elasticity (ppm/deg. temp.) $\times\ 10^{-6}$,

$\Delta E_s/E_{s0}$ = the unit change in the torsional modulus of elasticity,

E_{s0} = the torsional modulus of elasticity at temperature T_0, and

E_{s_1} = the torsional modulus of elasticity at temperature T_1.

Representative values of these quantities are given in Table 4.3.

The manner in which temperature changes in elastic properties affect instrument performance can be demonstrated by the following example. Assume that a restoring element in an instrument is essentially a single-leaf

TABLE 4.3 Temperature Characteristics for Some Materials

Material	Tensile modulus of elasticity, E Pa × 10^{-10} (psi × 10^{-6})	Torsional modulus of elasticity, E_s Pa × 10^{-10} (psi × 10^{-6})	Coefficient of linear expansion, d ppm/deg. C (ppm/deg. F)	Coefficient of tensile modulus of elasticity, c^* ppm/deg. C (ppm/deg. F)
High carbon spring steel	20.7 (30)	7.93 (11.5)	11.6 (6.5)	−220 (−122)
Chrome-vanadium steel	20.7 (30)	7.93 (11.5)	12.2 (6.8)	−260 (−145)
Stainless steel Type 302	19.3 (28)	6.9 (10)	16.7 (9.3)	−439 (−244)
Spring brass	10.3 (15)	3.8 (5.5)	20.2 (11.2)	−391 (−217)
Phosphor bronze	10.3 (15)	4.3 (6.3)	17.8 (9.9)	−380 (−211)
Invar†	14.8 (21.4)	5.6 (8.1)	1.1 (0.6)	+48.1 (+27)
Isoelastic†	18.0 (26)	6.3 (9.2)	7.2 (4)	−36 to +13 (−20 to +7.3)
Aluminum	6.9 (10)	2.6 (3.8)	23 (13)	−270 to −400 (−150 to −220)

* c may be used for torsional modulus also.

† Trade names

cantilever spring of rectangular section, for which the deflection equation at reference temperature T_0 is

$$K_0 = \frac{F}{y} = \frac{3E_0 I_0}{L_0^3} = \frac{E_0 w_0 t_0^3}{4L_0^3}, \tag{4.11}$$

in which

K_0 = the deflection constant,

I_0 = the moment of inertia,

w_0 = the width of the section at reference temperature,

t_0 = the thickness of the section at reference temperature, and

L_0 = the length of the beam at the reference temperature.

A second equation may be written for any other temperature, T_1, as follows:

$$K_1 = \frac{[E_0(1 + c\,\Delta T)][w_0(1 + \alpha\,\Delta T)][t_0(1 + \alpha\,\Delta T)]^3}{4[L_0(1 + \alpha\,\Delta T)]^3} \tag{4.12}$$

We also have

$$\begin{array}{l} \text{Percent error in} \\ \text{deflection scale} \end{array} = \left(\frac{K_0 - K_1}{K_0}\right) \times 100$$

$$= [1 - (1 + c\,\Delta T)(1 + \alpha\,\Delta T)] \times 100,$$

which we may simplify, by expanding and discarding the second-order term, to read

$$\text{Percent scale error} = -(c + \alpha)\,\Delta T \times 100. \tag{4.13}$$

If our spring is made of spring brass,

$$\text{Percent scale error/}°\text{F} = -(-217 + 11.2) \times 10^{-6} \times 100 = 0.0206\%.$$

Hence a temperature change of $+50°$F would result in a scale error of about $+1\%$. (This means that the reading is too high; our spring is too flexible, and a given load deflects the spring more than it should.)

It is interesting to note that for our example the scale error is a function of material or materials. It should be clear that we are speaking of the load-deflection relation for resilient members in this connection, and that this would not include members whose duty it is simply to transmit motion, such as the linkage in a Bourdon-tube pressure gage.

Although not a mechanical quantity, another item affected by temperature change is electrical resistance. The basic resistance equation may be written in the form

$$R = \rho\frac{L}{A}, \tag{4.14}$$

TABLE 4.4 Resistivity and Temperature Coefficients of Resistivity for Selected Materials

Material	Composition (for alloys)	Resistivity at 20°C (68°F) ohm·cm × 10^6	Coefficient of resistivity, b, ohm/ohm deg. × 10^6	
			Per deg. C	Per deg. F
Aluminum	—	2.8	3900	2170
Constantan*	60% Cu, 40% Ni	44	11	6
Copper (annealed)	—	1.72	3900	2180
Iron	99.9% pure	10	5000	2800
Isoelastic*	36% Ni, 8% Cr, 4% Mn, Si, and Mo, remainder Fe	48	470	260
Manganin*	9–18% Mn, 1½–4% Ni; remainder Cu	44	11	6
Monel*	33% Cu, 67% Ni	42	2000	1100
Nichrome*	75% Ni, 12% Fe, 11% Cr, 2% Mn	100	400	220
Nickel	—	7	6400	3550
Silver	—	1.6	4000	2250

Note: Values should be considered as quite approximate. Actual values depend on exact composition and, in certain cases, degree of cold work.

* Trade names

where

R = the electrical resistance, in ohms,

ρ = the resistivity, in ohms $\cdot$ cm,

L = the length of the conductor, in cm, and

A = the cross-sectional area of the conductor, in cm^2.

As temperature changes, a change in the resistance of an electrical conductor will be noted. This will be caused by two different factors: dimensional changes due to expansion or contraction, and changes in the current-opposing properties of the material itself. For an unconstrained conductor, the latter is much more significant than the former, causing more than 99% of the total change for copper [25]. Therefore, in most cases it is not very important whether the dimensional effect is accounted for or not. If dimensional changes caused by temperature are ignored, change in resistivity with temperature may be expressed as

$$b = \frac{1}{\Delta T} \frac{\Delta \rho}{\rho_0} \tag{4.15}$$

or

$$\rho_1 = \rho_0 (1 + b\, \Delta T), \tag{4.16}$$

in which

b = the temperature coefficient of resistivity, in ohms $\cdot$ cm/ohms $\cdot$ cm $\cdot$ degree of temperature

ΔT = the temperature change, in degree of temperature

$\Delta \rho / \rho_0$ = the unit change in resistivity,

ρ_0 = the resistivity at the reference temperature T_0, in ohms, and

ρ_1 = the resistivity at any temperature T_1, in ohms.

If we account for temperature-dimensional changes, the equation reads

$$\rho_1 = \frac{R_0 A_0}{L_0} (1 + b\, \Delta T)(1 + \alpha\, \Delta T)$$

$$= \rho_0 (1 + b\, \Delta T)(1 + \alpha\, \Delta T). \tag{4.17}$$

Table 4.4 lists values of the coefficients of resistivity for selected materials.

4.16.3 Methods for Limiting Temperature Errors

Three approaches to a solution of the temperature problem in instrumentation are as follows: (1) *minimization* through careful selection of materials and operating temperature ranges, (2) *compensation* through balancing of inversely reacting elements or effects, and (3) *elimination* through temperature control. Although each situation is a problem unto itself, thereby making specific recommendations difficult, a few general remarks with regard to these possibilities may be made.

Minimization

As we pointed out earlier, temperature errors may be caused by thermal expansion in the case of simple motion-transmitting elements, by thermal expansion and modulus change in the case of calibrated resilient transducer elements, and by thermal expansion and resistivity change in the case of electrical resistance transducers. All these effects may be minimized by selecting materials with low-temperature coefficients in each of the respective categories. Of course, minimum temperature coefficients are not always combined with other desirable features such as high strength, low cost, corrosion resistance, etc.

Compensation

This approach may take a number of different forms, depending on the basic characteristics of the system. If a mechanical system is being used, a form of compensation making use of a composite construction may be employed. If the system is electrical, compensation is generally possible in the electrical circuitry.

An example of composite construction is the balance wheel in a watch or clock. As the temperature rises, the modulus of the spring material reduces and, in addition, the moment of inertia of the wheel (if of simple form) increases because of thermal expansion, both of which cause the watch to *slow down*. If we incorporate a bimetal element of appropriate characteristics in the rim of the wheel, the moment of inertia decreases with temperature enough to compensate for both expansion of the wheel spokes and change in spring modulus. (See also Section 11.6 for a discussion of temperature effect on linear measuring devices.)

Electrical circuitry may use various means for compensating temperature effects. The thermistor, discussed in some detail in Sections 4.8 and 16.5.3, is quite useful for this purpose. Most circuit elements possess the characteristic of increasing d.c. resistance with rising temperature. The thermistor has an opposite temperature-resistance property, along with reasonably good stability, both of which make it ideal for simple temperature-resistance compensation.

Resistance strain gages are particularly susceptible to temperature variations. The actual situation is quite complex, involving thermal-expansion characteristics of both the base material and all the gage materials (support, cement, and grid) and temperature-resistivity properties of the grid material, combined with the fact that heat is dissipated by the grid since it is a resistance device. Temperature compensation is very nicely handled, however, by pitting the temperature-effect output from like gages against one another, while subjecting them differentially to strain. This is accomplished by use of a resistance bridge circuit arrangement, which is used extensively in strain-gage work (see Section 12.11). In addition, through careful selection of grid materials, the so-called "self-compensating" gages have been developed. (See also Section 13.5.)

Elimination

The third method, that is, eliminating the temperature problem by temperature control, really requires no discussion. Many methods are possible, extending from the careful control of large environments to the maintenance of constant temperature in small instrument enclosures. An example of the latter is the "crystal oven" often used to stabilize a frequency-determining quartz crystal.

4.17 CONCLUDING REMARKS

In this short summary we have in no sense exhausted the list of possible devices or principles suitable for sensing mechanical inputs. In certain instances we have discussed others elsewhere in the book, and in Table 4.1 we have attempted to reference these. For further information on basic sensing devices we refer the reader to the suggested readings that follow.

SUGGESTED READINGS

Bube, R. H., *Photoconductivity of Solids*. New York: John Wiley, 1960.

Chappell, A. (ed.), *Optoelectronics, Theory & Practice*. New York: McGraw-Hill, 1978.

Geddes, L. A., *Biomedical Instrumentation*. New York: John Wiley, 1968.

Hix, C. F., Jr., and R. P. Alley, *Physical Laws and Effects*. New York: John Wiley, 1958.

Lion, K. S., *Instrumentation in Scientific Research*. New York: McGraw-Hill, 1959.

Sahm, W. H., *Optoelectronics Manual*. Semiconductor Dept., General Electric Co., 1976.

Wolfe, W. L. (ed.), *Handbook of Military Infrared Technology*. Office of Naval Research. Washington, D.C.: U.S. Government Printing Office, 1965.

PROBLEMS

4.1 A table in an electronics handbook lists the resistance of #32 B & S copper wire as 167.3 ohms per 1000 feet. The diameter of #32 wire is 0.008 inch. Using English units, calculate the resistivity. Compare this with the value listed in Table 4.4. (Note that the resistance of most metals varies considerably with the degree of work-hardening. Unless altered by heat treatment, small-diameter wire will display higher resistivity than large-diameter wire of the same composition.)

4.2 Calculate the maximum capacitance of a torque meter of the type shown in Fig. 4.13 if the device has 50 pairs of teeth and a uniform gap of 0.010 inch, and each tooth face has the dimensions $\frac{1}{2} \times 10$ inches. Calculate the sensitivity in picofarads per degree of rotation.

4.3 Write a general expression for the sensitivity (in henrys per inch) of the device shown in Fig. 4.6. Plot sensitivity vs. h over the range $0.010 \leqslant h \leqslant 0.100$ for gap dimensions of $\frac{3}{8} \times \frac{3}{8}$ inch and $N = 1200$.

4.4 A proving-ring–type force transducer is a very reliable device for checking the calibration of material-testing machines. An equation for estimating the deflection constant of the elemental ring, loaded in compression, is given in Table 13.1. If $D = 10$ in. (25.4 cm) $\pm$ 0.010 in. (0.25 mm), t = the radial thickness of the section = 0.6 in. (15.24 mm) $\pm$ 0.005 in. (0.127 mm), w = the axial width of the section = 2 in. (5.08 cm) $\pm$ 0.015 in. (0.381 mm), and $E = 30 \times 10^6$ lbf/in^2 (20.68 $\times$ 10^{10} N/m^2) $\pm$ 0.5 $\times$ 10^6 lbf/in^2 (0.34 $\times$ 10^{10} N/m^2), calculate the value of K and its uncertainty, using English units.

4.5 Solve Problem 4.4 using SI units.

4.6 A 300-lbf (1334 N) capacity, digital read-out weighing scale uses an aluminum cantilever beam with strain gages (see Fig. 12.30) as the force-sensing element. A lever system is used to attenuate the load by a factor of 18, i.e., a 300-lbf load on the scale exerts 300/18 lbf on the beam. The beam has an effective length $L = 7$ in., and a rectangular section, $w = \frac{1}{2}$ in. (12.7 mm) and $t = \frac{1}{4}$ in. (6.35 mm), oriented as shown in Fig. 12.30. The deflection constant for the beam, loaded in this manner, is $3EI/L^3$ (see Table 13.1). E is Young's modulus (10 $\times$ 10^6 lbf/in^2 or 6.89 $\times$ 10^{10} Pa), and I is the moment of inertia ($I = wt^3/12$). Assign reasonable tolerances to each of the variables and determine the uncertainty in the deflection constant.

signal 5 conditioning

5.1 INTRODUCTION

Once a mechanical quantity has been detected and possibly transduced, it is usually necessary to further modify the stage-one output before it is in satisfactory form for driving an indicator or recorder. We will now consider some of the methods used in this intermediate, signal conditioning step.

Measurement of dynamic mechanical quantities places special requirements on the elements in the signal conditioning stage. Large amplifications, as well as good transient response, are often desired, both of which are difficult to obtain by mechanical, hydraulic, or pneumatic methods. As a result, electrical or electronic elements are usually required.

An input signal is often converted by the detector-transducer to a mechanical displacement (see Table 4.1). It is then commonly fed to a secondary transducer, which converts it into a form, often electrical, that is more easily processed by the intermediate stage. In some cases, however, such a displacement is fed to mechanical intermediate elements, such as linkages, gearing, or cams; these mechanical elements present design problems of considerable magnitude, particularly if dynamic inputs are to be handled.

In the field of dynamic measurements, strictly mechanical systems are much more uncommon than they have been in years past. This is largely due to several inherent disadvantages, which we will discuss only briefly.*

Mechanical amplification by these elements is quite limited. When amplification is required frictional forces are also amplified, resulting in considerable undesirable signal loading. These effects, coupled with backlash and elastic deformations, result in poor response. Inertial loading results in reduced frequency response and in certain cases, depending on the particular configuration of the system, phase response is also a problem.

---

* The first and second editions of this book contain a more thorough discussion of strictly mechanical signal conditioning methods and problems.

5.2   ADVANTAGES OF ELECTRICAL SIGNAL CONDITIONING DEVICES

As we have already seen, many detector–transducer combinations provide an output in electrical form. In these cases, of course, it is convenient to perform further signal conditioning electrically. In addition, in order to minimize friction, inertia, and structural flexibility requirements, we also prefer electrical methods for their ease of *power amplification.* Additional power may be fed into the system to provide a greater output power than input. This is accomplished by the use of power amplifiers, which have no important mechanical counterpart in most instrumentation.* This is of particular value

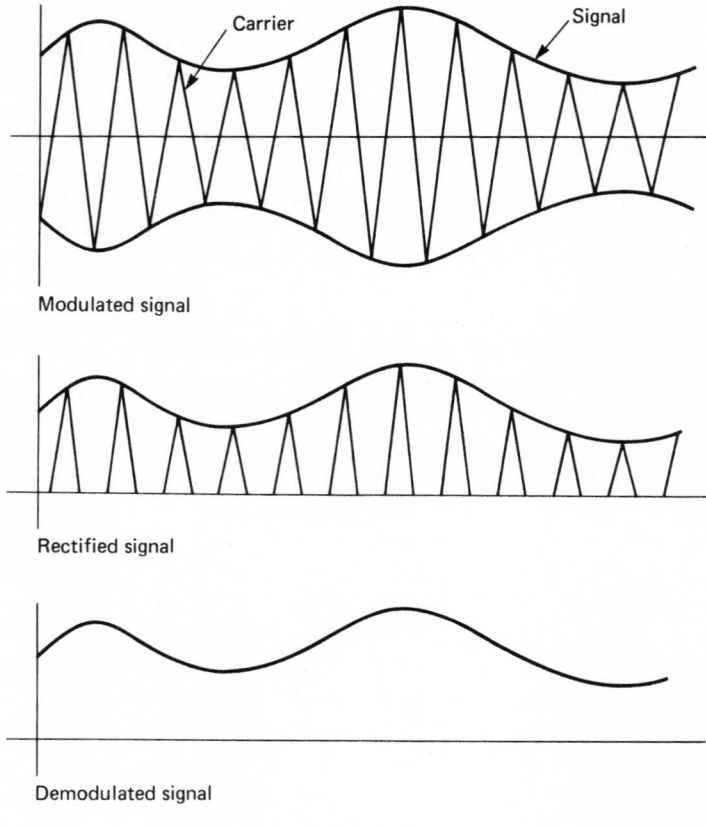

Carrier

Signal

Modulated signal

Rectified signal

Demodulated signal

(a)

FIGURE 5.1   (a) Amplitude modulation whereby the envelope of the carrier contains the signal information.

---

* It is true that hydraulic and pneumatic systems may be set up to increase signal power; however, their use is limited to relatively slow-acting control applications, primarily in the fields of chemical processing and electrical power generation. As in the case of mechanical systems, friction and inertia severely limit transient response of the type required for measurement of dynamic inputs.

when recording procedures employ stylus-type recorders, mirror galvanometers, or magnetic-tape methods.

5.3 MODULATED AND UNMODULATED SIGNALS

Measurands may be "pure" in the sense that the analog electrical signal contains nothing other than the real-time variation of the measurand information itself. On the other hand, the signal may be "mixed" with a *carrier,* which consists of a voltage oscillation at some frequency higher than that of the signal. A common rule of thumb is that the frequency ratio should be at least ten to one. It is said that the signal *modulates* the carrier. The measurand affects the carrier by varying either its amplitude or its frequency. In the former case the carrier frequency is held constant and its amplitude is varied

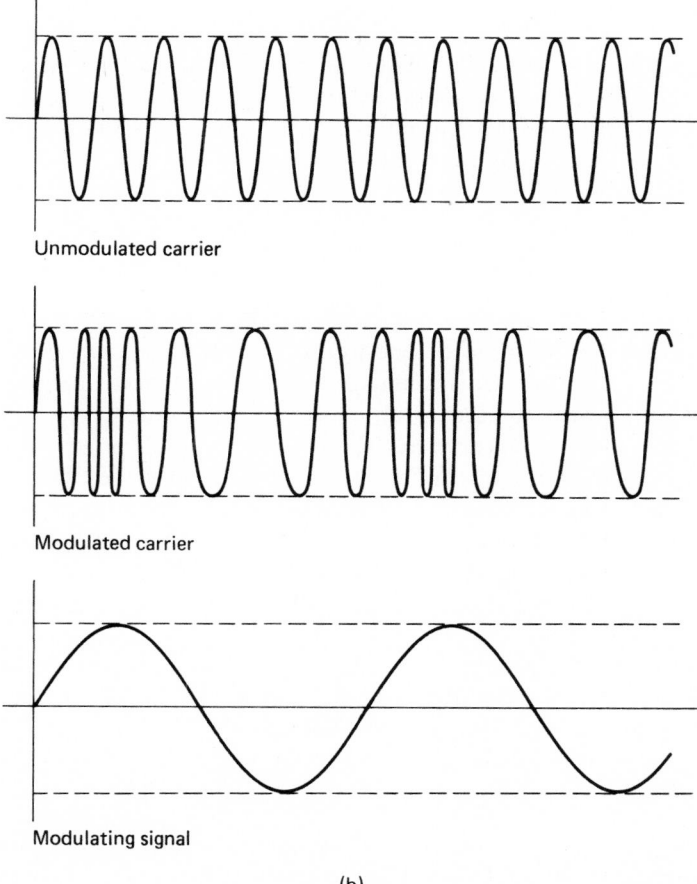

Unmodulated carrier

Modulated carrier

Modulating signal

(b)

FIGURE 5.1(*Continued*)   (b) Frequency modulation whereby the signal information is contained in the frequency variation of the carrier.

by the measurand. This is known as amplitude modulation or AM (Fig. 5.1a). In the latter case the carrier amplitude is held constant and its frequency is varied by the measurand. This is known as frequency modulation or FM (Fig. 5.1b). Of course the most common AM and FM transfer of signals is the familiar AM and FM broadcasts.

When modulation is used in instrumentation, amplitude modulation is the more common form. Nearly any mechanical signal from a passive pickup can be transduced into an analogous AM form. Sensors based on either inductance or capacitance *require* an a.c. excitation. The differential transformer (Section 4.11) is an example of the former, whereas the capacitive pickup for liquid level (Fig. 4.12) is an example of the latter. In addition, however, resistive-type sensors may also use a.c. excitation, as with some strain-gage circuits (e.g., Fig. 12.15).

Extracting the signal information from the modulated carrier is required. When AM is used, this may take several forms. The simplest is merely to display the entire signal using an oscilloscope or oscillograph, and then to "read" the result from the envelope of the carrier. More commonly, the mixed signal and carrier are *demodulated* by rectification and filtering as shown in Fig. 5.1a. FM demodulation is a more complex operation and may be accomplished through the use of frequency discrimination, ratio detection, or IC phase-locked loops. Further discussion is beyond the scope of this text.

5.4 INPUT CIRCUITRY

Electrical detector-transducers are of two general types: (1) *passive,* those requiring an auxiliary source of energy, and (2) *active,* those that are self-powering. The simple bonded strain gage is an example of the former, whereas the piezoelectric accelerometer is an example of the latter.

Although it may be possible to use the active, or self-powering, detector-transducer directly with a minimum of circuitry, the passive type, in general, requires special arrangements to introduce the auxiliary energy. The particular arrangement required will depend on the operating principle involved. For example, resistive-type pickups may be powered by either an a.c. or a d.c. source, whereas capacitive and inductive types, with an exception or two, require an a.c. source.

Although not all-inclusive, the following list classifies the most common forms of input circuits used in transducer work: (1) simple current-sensitive circuits, (2) ballast circuits, (3) voltage-dividing circuits, (4) voltage-balancing potentiometer circuits, (5) bridge circuits, (6) resonant circuits, and (7) amplifier input circuits. These will be discussed in the following sections.

5.5 THE SIMPLE CURRENT-SENSITIVE CIRCUIT

Figure 5.2(a) illustrates a simple current-sensitive circuit in which the transducer may use any one of the various forms of variable-resistance elements.

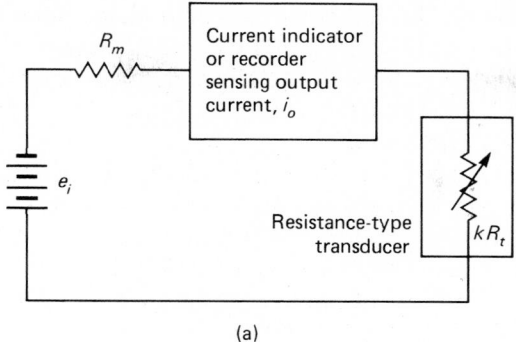

(a)

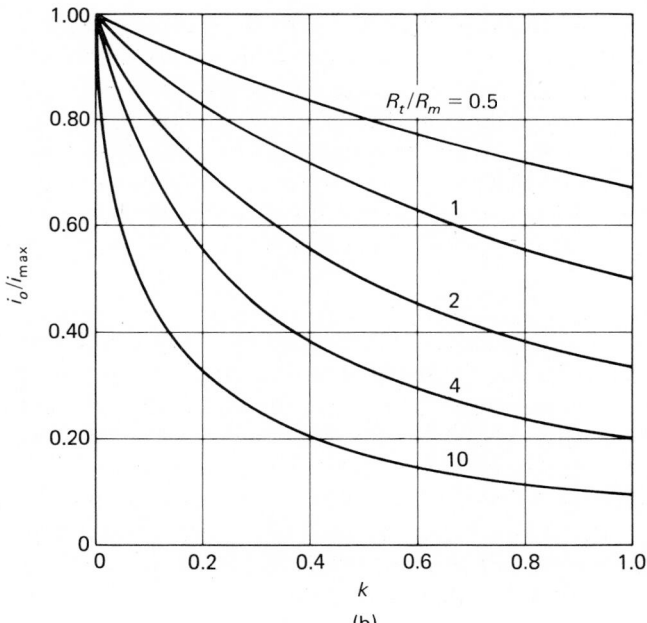

(b)

FIGURE 5.2   (a) Simple current-sensitive circuit. (b) Plot of Eq.(5.2), showing variation of current in terms of input signal k, for a simple current-sensitive circuit.

We will let the transducer resistance be kR_t, where R_t represents the maximum value of transducer resistance and k represents a percentage factor that may vary between 0.0 and 1.0 (0 and 100%), depending on the magnitude of the input signal. Should the transducer element be in the form of a sliding contact resistor, the value of k could vary through the complete range of 0 to 100%. On the other hand, if R_t represents, say, a thermistor, then k would fall within some limiting range not including 0.0%. We will let R_m represent the remaining circuit resistance.

If i_o is the current flowing through the circuit and hence the current indicated by the read-out device, we have, using Ohm's law (Section 3.16)

$$i_o = \frac{e_i}{kR_t + R_m}.$$ (5.1)

This may be rewritten as

$$\frac{i_o}{i_{max}} = \frac{i_o R_m}{e_i} = \frac{1}{1 + \left(\dfrac{R_t}{R_m}\right)k}.$$ (5.2)

Note that maximum current flows when $k = 0$, at which time the current is e_i/R_m.

Figure 5.2(b) shows plots of Eq. (5.2) for various values of resistance ratio. The abscissa is a measure of *signal input* and the ordinate a measure of *output*. First of all, it is observed that the input–output relation is nonlinear, which of course would generally be undesirable. In addition, the higher the relative value of transducer resistance R_t to R_m, the greater will be the output variation or sensitivity. It will also be noted that the output is a function of i_{max}, which in turn is dependent on e_i. This means that careful control of the driving voltage is necessary if calibration is to be maintained.

5.6   THE BALLAST CIRCUIT

Now let us look at a variation of the current-sensitive circuit, often referred to as the *ballast circuit,* shown in Fig. 5.3. Instead of a current-sensitive indicator or recorder through which the total current flows, we shall use a voltage-sensitive device (some form of voltmeter), placed across the transducer. The *ballast resistor, R_b,* is inserted in much the same manner as R_m was used in the previous circuit. It will be observed that in this case, were it not for R_b, the indicator would show no change with variation in R_t; it would always indicate full source voltage. So some value of resistance R_b is necessary for the proper functioning of the circuit.

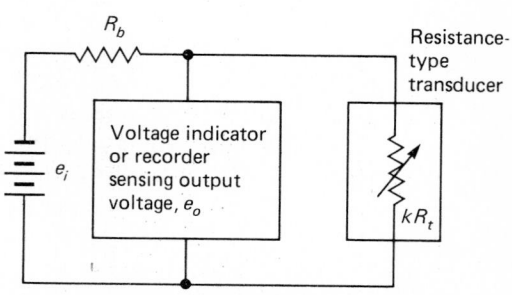

FIGURE 5.3   Schematic of a ballast circuit.

Two different situations may exist, depending on the relative impedance of the meter. First, the meter may be of high impedance, such as would be the case if some form of electronic voltmeter (Section 7.4) were used, in which case any current flow through the meter may be neglected. Second, the meter may be of low impedance, and consideration of such current flow is required.

Assuming a high-impedance meter, we have by Ohm's law

$$i = \frac{e_i}{R_b + kR_t} . \tag{5.3}$$

Then, if e_o = the voltage across kR_t (which is indicated or recorded by the read-out device),

$$e_o = i(kR_t) = \frac{e_i kR_t}{R_b + kR_t} . \tag{5.4}$$

This may be written as

$$\frac{e_o}{e_i} = \frac{kR_t/R_b}{1 + (kR_t/R_b)} \tag{5.5}$$

For a given circuit, e_o/e_i is a measure of the output, and kR_t/R_b is a measure of the input.

Defining η as the sensitivity, or the ratio of change in output to change in input, we have

$$\eta = \frac{de_o}{dk} = \frac{e_i R_b R_t}{(R_b + kR_t)^2} . \tag{5.6}$$

We may change R_b by inserting different values of resistance. If this is done, the sensitivity should be altered, which would mean that there may be some optimum value of R_b so far as sensitivity is concerned. By differentiation with respect to R_b, we should be able to determine this value:

$$\frac{d\eta}{dR_b} = \frac{e_i R_t(kR_t - R_b)}{(R_b + kR_t)^3} . \tag{5.7}$$

The derivative will be zero under two conditions: (1) for $R_b = \infty$, which results in minimum sensitivity, and (2) for $R_b = kR_t$, for which maximum sensitivity is obtained.

The second relation indicates that for full-range usefulness, the value R_b must be based on compromise because R_b, a constant, cannot always have the value of kR_t, a variable. However, R_b may be selected to give maximum sensitivity for a certain point in the range by setting its value to correspond to that of kR_t.

This circuit is occasionally used for dynamic applications of resistance-type strain gages [1, 2]. In this case the change in resistance is quite small compared with the total gage resistance, and the relations above indicate that a ballast resistance equal to gage resistance is optimum.

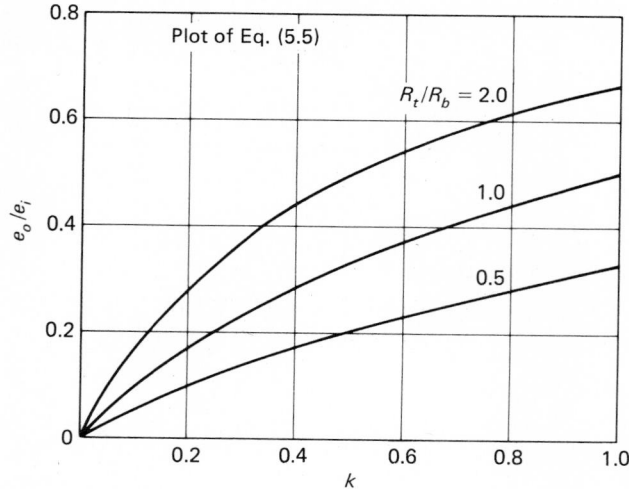

FIGURE 5.4   Curves showing relation between input and output for a ballast circuit.

Figure 5.4 shows the relation between input and output for a circuit of this type as given by Eq. (5.5).

It will be noted that the same disadvantages apply to this circuit as to the current-sensitive circuit discussed previously, namely: (1) a percentage variation in the supply voltage, e_i, results in a greater change in output than does a similar percentage change in k, hence very careful voltage regulation must be used; and (2) the relation between output and input is not linear.

5.7 THE VOLTAGE-DIVIDING POTENTIOMETER CIRCUIT

Figure 5.5 shows a very useful circuit arrangement for sliding-contact resistance transducer elements. This is known as the *voltage-dividing potentiometer circuit*. It will be noted that the voltage source is connected, not to the slider as it would be in the ballast circuit, but across the complete resistance element. The terminating or read-out device is connected to sense the voltage drop across the portion of resistance element R_p as determined by k.

Two different situations may occur with this arrangement, depending on the relative impedance of the resistance element and the indicator–recorder. If the terminating instrument is of sufficiently high relative impedance, no appreciable current will flow through it, and it may be considered a simple "*pressure*-measuring" device. The circuit then becomes a true voltage divider,

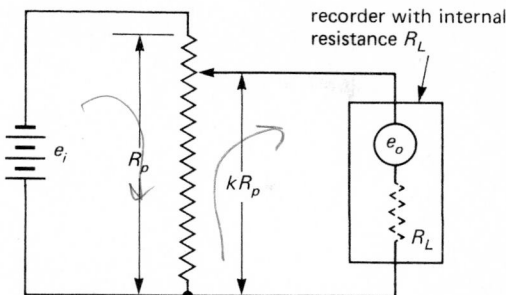

FIGURE 5.5   Simple voltage-dividing potentiometer circuit.

and the indicated output voltage e_o may be determined from the following relation:

$$e_o = ke_i \qquad (5.8)$$

or

$$k = \frac{e_o}{e_i} . \qquad (5.8a)$$

5.7.1 Loading Error

On the other hand, if the read-out device draws appreciable current, a *loading error* (see Section 4.2) will result. This may be analyzed as follows. Referring to Fig. 5.5, we find that the total resistance *seen* by the source of e_i will be

$$R = R_p(1 - k) + \frac{kR_pR_L}{kR_p + R_L}$$

and

$$i = \frac{e_i}{R} = \frac{e_i(kR_p + R_L)}{kR_p^2(1 - k) + R_pR_L} .$$

The output voltage will then be

$$e_o = e_i - iR_p(1 - k)$$

or

$$\frac{e_o}{e_i} = \frac{k}{1 + (R_p/R_L)k - (R_p/R_L)k^2} . \qquad (5.9)$$

If we assume the simpler relation given by Eq. (5.8a) to hold, an error will be introduced according to the following relation:

$$\text{Error} = e_i \left[k - \frac{k}{k(1 - k)(R_p/R_L) + 1} \right]$$

$$= e_i \left[\frac{k^2(1 - k)}{k(1 - k) + (R_L/R_p)} \right]. \tag{5.10}$$

On the basis of *full-scale output* (see Section 9.2), this relation may be written as

$$\text{Percent error} = \left[\frac{k^2(1 - k)}{k(1 - k) + (R_L/R_p)} \right] \times 100. \tag{5.11}$$

Except for the endpoints ($k = 0.0$ or 1.0), where the error is zero, the error will always be on the negative side, i.e., the actual value of voltage will be lower than would be the case if the system performed as a linear voltage divider. Figure 5.6 shows a plot of the variation in error with slider position for various ratios of load to potentiometer resistance. Obviously, the higher the value of load resistance compared with potentiometer resistance, the lower will be the error.

5.7.2 Use of End Resistors

It will be observed that the nonlinearity in the relation between the potentiometer output and the input displacement k may be reduced if only a portion of the available potentiometer range is used. For example, a 1000-ohm potentiometer may be selected, but the input limited to only a 500-ohm portion

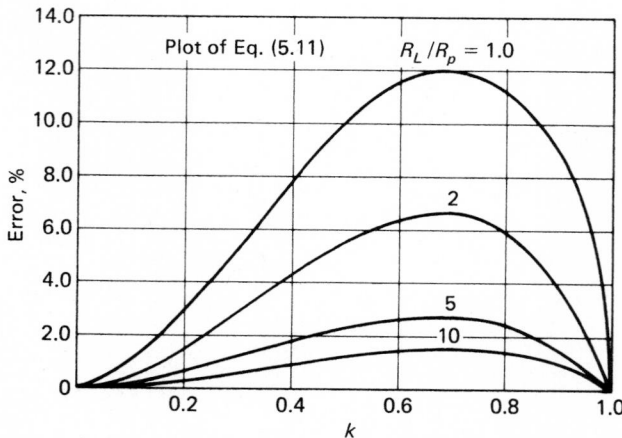

FIGURE 5.6   Curves showing error caused by loading a voltage-dividing potentiometer circuit.

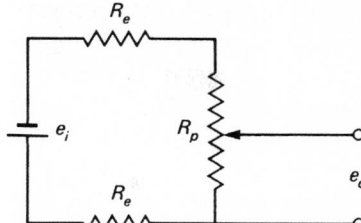

FIGURE 5.7   Methods for improving linearity of potentiometer circuits when low-impedance indicating devices are used. Resistors are termed end resistors.

of the total range. This would reduce the potentiometer resolution and would be generally impractical; however, it would result in a reduction in the deviation from linearity. A similar result may be obtained through use of what are known as *end resistors* (Fig. 5.7). When either an upper- or a lower-end resistor, or both, are used, it is often possible to compensate for reduced potentiometer output caused by the increased resistance by increasing the voltage input e_i by a proportional amount.

5.8   THE VOLTAGE-BALANCING POTENTIOMETER CIRCUIT

Figure 5.8(a) illustrates a simplified form of a circuit that has been used for years, primarily for measuring thermocouple output. Basically the circuit measures small electrical potentials by *comparison*. A known portion of voltage e_m is balanced against the unknown voltage e_i through use of a variable resistor R_s. A galvanometer, G, is used to determine balance. Read-out, or output indication, is obtained from the position of the slider in relation to a calibrated scale. Of course, this simplified circuit would be impractical for

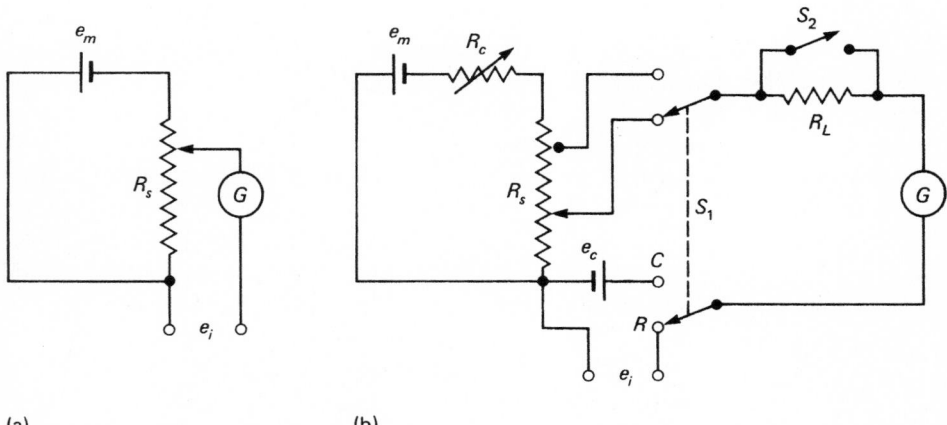

(a)   (b)

FIGURE 5.8   (a) Schematic showing principle of operation of voltage balancing potentiometer circuit. (b) Voltage-balancing potentiometer circuit incorporating means for standardization.

making careful measurement because no provision is made to compensate for variation of battery voltage with use or age.

Figure 5.8(b) illustrates a more useful form of voltage-balancing circuit. Here provision is made for calibrating or standardizing the circuit, thereby providing adjustment for variation in voltage e_m. This is accomplished through the use of a standard cell, e_c. When switch S_1 is thrown to position C, a predetermined voltage is introduced in place of the unknown. Resistance R_c is then adjusted for balance, as indicated by the galvanometer G. After the circuit has been standardized by this means, the precalibrated slide wire becomes usable. Resistance R_L is employed to protect the galvanometer when large unbalance exists. As soon as approximate balance is achieved, switch S_2 is closed for more sensitive adjustment.

A general-purpose instrument of this kind would include additional means for adjusting R_s in the form of shunt and series resistances that could be switched into the circuit, thereby increasing the overall scale of the instrument.

In operation, the instrument is first standardized by the standard cell. The unknown voltage is then measured by balancing it against voltage e_m through use of R_s.

5.9   RESISTANCE BRIDGES

Use of some form of bridge circuit is the most common method for connecting passive transducers to associated equipment in making up a measuring system. Of all the possible configurations, the Wheatstone resistance bridge [3] devised by S. H. Christie in 1833 [4] is undoubtedly used to the greatest extent. Figure 5.9 shows a d.c. Wheatstone bridge consisting of four resistance *arms* with a source of energy (battery) and a detector (meter). Measurement may be accomplished either by *balancing* the bridge by making known adjustments in one or more bridge arms until the voltage across the meter is zero, or by determining the magnitude of *unbalance* from the meter reading. Typical resistance transducers using a circuit of this kind may include resistance thermometers, thermistors, or resistance-type strain gages.

Using Fig. 5.9, we may analyze the requirements for balance as follows: For balance, no current may flow through the meter, hence $i_g = 0$. If this is true, we also know that $i_1 = i_2$ and $i_3 = i_4$. In addition, the potential across the meter must be zero, or $i_1 R_1 = i_3 R_3$ and $i_2 R_2 = i_4 R_4$. By eliminating i_1 and i_3 from the relations above, we obtain the condition for balance, namely,

$$\frac{R_1}{R_2} = \frac{R_3}{R_4} \tag{5.12}$$

or

$$\frac{R_1}{R_3} = \frac{R_2}{R_4} \tag{5.12a}$$

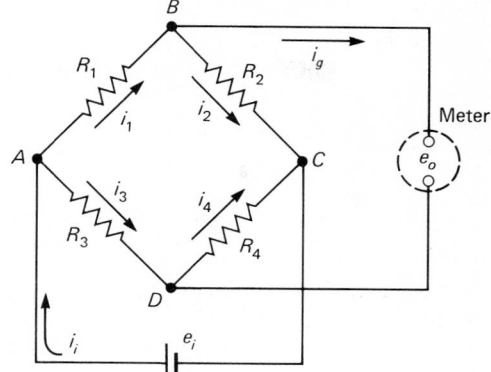

FIGURE 5.9   Simple Wheatstone bridge circuit.

From these two equations we may formulate a statement that should assist us in remembering the necessary balance relation. *In order for the Wheatstone resistance bridge to balance, the ratio of resistances of any two adjacent arms must equal the ratio of resistances of the remaining two arms, taken in the same sense.* (*Note:* "Taken in the same sense" means that if the first resistance ratio is formed from two adjacent resistances reading from left to right, the balancing ratio must also be formed by reading from left to right, etc.)

Basic bridge types are summarized in Table 5.1.

Some of the arrangements that can be used to accomplish bridge balance are shown in Fig. 5.10. An important factor in determining the type to use is bridge sensitivity. If large resistance changes are to be accommodated, large resistance adjustments must be provided; thus one of the series arrangements would be most useful. This could well be the type to use for sliding-contact variable-resistance transducers or thermistors. When small resistance changes are to take place, as in the case of resistance strain gages, then the shunt balance would be used. In order to provide for a range of resistances, a bridge with both series and shunt balances might be utilized.

When the *deflection* bridge is used, bridge unbalance, as indicated by the meter reading, is the measure of input. In this case, provision is generally made for initial zero balance through adjustment of one of the resistance arms. For static inputs, an ordinary meter or galvanometer may be used; for dynamic signals, however, the output may be displayed by a cathode-ray oscilloscope (Section 7.6) or recorded by a stylus-type or light-beam oscillograph (Section 7.9), or the output may be fed to an analog-to-digital converter and a computer for display, recording, or immediate application.

The output from a deflection bridge may be connected to either a high- or a low-impedance device. If the bridge is connected to a simple D'Arsonval meter or most galvanometers, the output circuit will be of low impedance, and appreciable current is required from the bridge. In most cases in which amplification is necessary, the bridge output will be connected to a high-

TABLE 5.1 Types of Electrical Bridge Circuits

Bridge Type	Bridge Features
Voltage-sensitive bridge vs. Current-sensitive bridge	Read-out instrument does not "load" bridge, that is, it requires no current, e.g., electronic voltmeter or CRO.
	Read-out requires current; e.g., a low-impedance indicator such as a simple galvanometer, is used.
Null balance bridge vs. Deflection bridge	Adjustment is required to maintain balance. This becomes source of read-out, e.g., manually adjusted strain indicator.
	Read-out is deviation of bridge output from initial balance, e.g., as required by CRO.
a.c. bridge vs. d.c. bridge	Alternating current/voltage excitation is used.
	Direct current/voltage excitation is used.
Constant voltage vs. Constant current	Voltage input to bridge remains constant; e.g., battery or voltage-regulated power supply is used.
	Current input to bridge remains constant regardless of bridge unbalance; e.g., current-regulated power supply is used.
Resistance bridge vs. Impedance bridge	Bridge arms made up of "pure" resistance elements.
	Bridge arms may include reactance elements.

impedance device and the bridge would supply essentially no current. Such is the case when either an oscilloscope or an electronic voltmeter is used. In the former instance the bridge is *current-sensitive;* in the latter it is *voltage-sensitive.*

5.9.1 The Voltage-Sensitive Wheatstone Bridge

Let us consider the simplest case first, in which the bridge output is connected directly to a high-impedance device, say an oscilloscope. Referring to Fig. 5.9, we find that

$$e_o = i_{ABC}R_1 - i_{ADC}R_3,$$

and making use of relations developed in the derivation for the null-balance condition and Ohm's law, we may write

$$e_o = e_i\left(\frac{R_1}{R_1 + R_2} - \frac{R_3}{R_3 + R_4}\right)$$

$$= e_i\left(\frac{R_1R_4 - R_2R_3}{(R_1 + R_2)(R_3 + R_4)}\right). \tag{5.13}$$

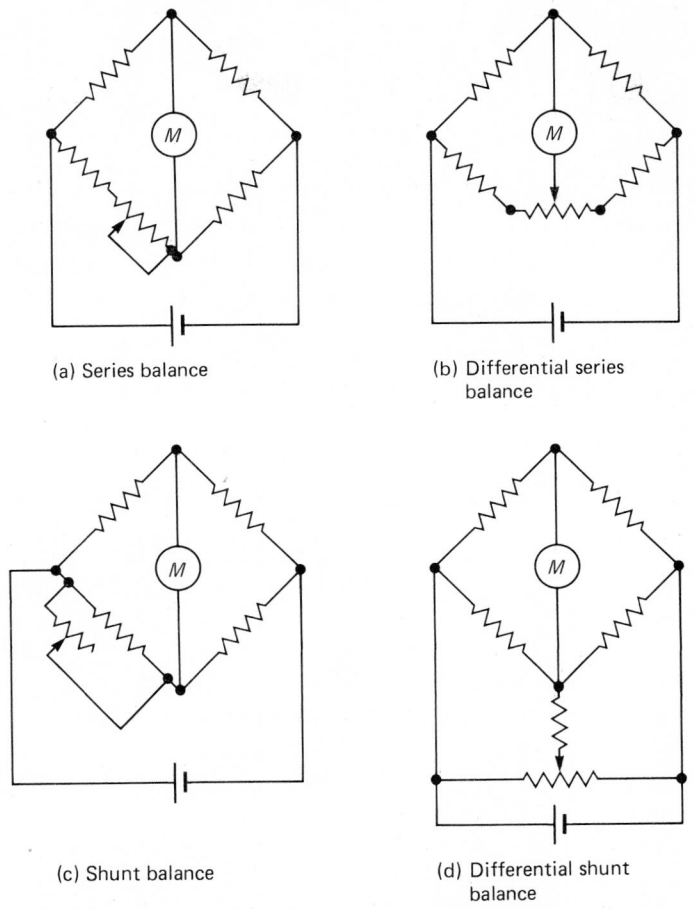

(a) Series balance   (b) Differential series
balance

(c) Shunt balance   (d) Differential shunt
balance

FIGURE 5.10   Methods used to balance d.c. resistance bridges.

We will now assume that resistance R_1 changes by an amount ΔR_1, or

$$\frac{e_o + \Delta e_o}{e_i} = \left[\frac{(R_1 + \Delta R_1)(R_4) - R_2 R_3}{(R_1 + \Delta R_1 + R_2)(R_3 + R_4)} \right]$$

$$= \left\{ \frac{1 + (\Delta R_1/R_1) - (R_2 R_3/R_1 R_4)}{[1 + (\Delta R_1/R_1) + (R_2/R_1)][1 + (R_3/R_4)]} \right\}. \qquad (5.14)$$

The relation may be simplified by assuming all resistances to be initially equal (in which case $e_o = 0$). Then

$$\frac{\Delta e_o}{e_i} = \frac{\Delta R_1/R}{4 + 2(\Delta R_1/R)}. \qquad (5.15)$$

Figure 5.11(a), plotted from Eq. (5.15), shows the relation for the output of a voltage-sensitive deflection bridge whose resistance arms are initially equal. Inspection of the curve indicates that this type of resistance bridge is inherently nonlinear. In many cases, however, the actual resistance change is so small that the arrangement may be assumed linear. This applies to most resistance strain-gage circuits.

5.9.2 The Current-Sensitive Wheatstone Bridge

When the deflection-bridge output is connected to a low-impedance device such as a galvanometer, appreciable current flows and the galvanometer resistance must be considered in the bridge equation. Galvanometer current may be expressed by the following relation [5]:

$$i_g = \frac{i_i(R_2R_3 - R_1R_4)}{R_g(R_1 + R_2 + R_3 + R_4) + (R_2 + R_4)(R_1 + R_3)}, \tag{5.16}$$

in which

$$i_g = \text{the galvanometer current,}$$

$$i_i = \text{the input current, and}$$

$$R_g = \text{the galvanometer resistance, in ohms.}$$

The remaining symbols are as defined in Fig. 5.9.

If we assume that an initial bridge balance is upset by an incremental change in resistance ΔR_1 in arm R_1 and all arms are of equal initial resistance R, we may write

$$\frac{\Delta i_g}{i_i} = \frac{-\Delta R_1/R}{4[1 + (R_g/R)] + [2 + (R_g/R)](\Delta R_1/R)}. \tag{5.17}$$

Figure 5.11(b) shows Eq. (5.17) plotted for various values of R_g/R.

5.9.3 The Constant-Current Bridge

To this point our discussion of bridge circuits has assumed a constant-voltage energizing source (a battery, for example). As the bridge resistance is changed the total current through the bridge will, therefore, also change. In certain instances (see Section 12.10), use of a *constant-current* bridge* may be desirable [6, 7]. Such a circuit is usually obtained through the application of a commercially available *current-regulated* d.c. power supply,† whereby the total current flow through the bridge, i_i (Fig. 5.9), is maintained at a constant

---

*   The term "Wheatstone," as applied to bridge circuits, is commonly limited to the *constant-voltage resistance bridge*. We shall abide by this convention and avoid referring to the constant-current bridge as a Wheatstone bridge.

†   Constant current is obtained by using the voltage drop across a series resistor in the supply-output line to provide a regulating feedback voltage.

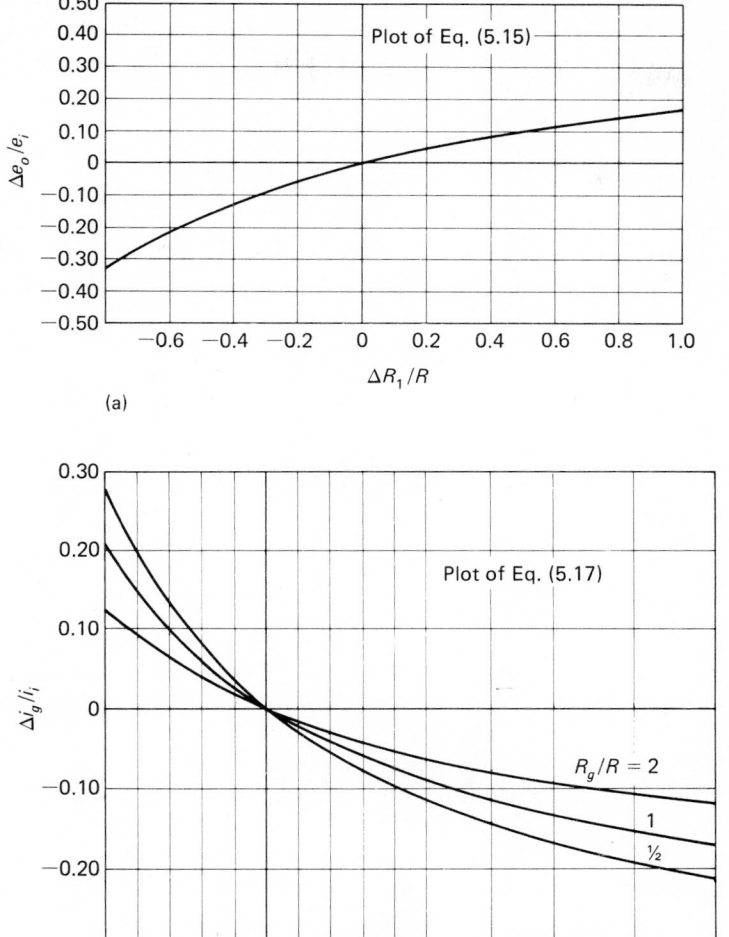

(a)

(b)

FIGURE 5.11 (a) Output from a voltage-sensitive deflection bridge whose resistance arms are initially equal. (b) Output from a current-sensitive deflection bridge whose resistance arms are initially equal, plotted for different relative galvanometer resistances.

value. It should be noted that such a bridge may still be either voltage-sensitive or current-sensitive, depending on the relative impedance of the read-out device.

Relationships for the voltage-sensitive *constant-current* bridge may be developed as follows. Referring to Fig. 5.9, we may write

$$i_i = \frac{e_i}{R_1 + R_2} + \frac{e_i}{R_3 + R_4}, \tag{5.18}$$

or

$$e_i = i_i \left[\frac{(R_1 + R_2)(R_3 + R_4)}{R_1 + R_2 + R_3 + R_4} \right] .$$

Substituting in Eq. (5.13), we have

$$e_o = i_i \left[\frac{R_1 R_4 - R_2 R_3}{R_1 + R_2 + R_3 + R_4} \right] . \tag{5.19}$$

This is the basic equation for the voltage-sensitive constant-current bridge, provided that i_i is maintained at a constant value. If the resistance of one arm, say R_1, is changed by an amount ΔR, then

$$e_o + \Delta e_o = i_i \left[\frac{(R_1 + \Delta R)(R_4) - R_2 R_3}{(R_1 + \Delta R) + R_2 + R_3 + R_4} \right]$$

and

$$\Delta e_o = i_i \left[\frac{(R_1 + \Delta R)R_4 - R_2 R_3}{(R_1 + \Delta R) + R_2 + R_3 + R_4} - \frac{R_1 R_4 - R_2 R_3}{R_1 + R_2 + R_3 + R_4} \right] . \tag{5.20}$$

For equal initial resistances ($R_1 = R_2 = R_3 = R_4 = R$),

$$\Delta e_o = i_i \left[\frac{\Delta R}{4 + \Delta R/R} \right] . \tag{5.21}$$

There is an improved linearity as a result of the constant-current bridge, which is apparent from a comparison of Eqs. (5.15) and (5.21). This coupled with the extreme sensitivity of the semiconductor strain gage is a major reason for the interest in the constant-current bridge. (See Section 12.13.)

5.9.4 The A.C. Resistance Bridge

Resistance bridges powered by a.c. sources may also be used. An additional problem, however, is the necessity for providing reactance balance. In spite of the fact that the Wheatstone bridge, strictly speaking, is a resistance bridge, it is impossible to completely eliminate stray capacitances and inductances resulting from such factors as closely placed lead wires in cables to and from the transducer, and wiring and component placement in associated equipment. In any system of reasonable sensitivity, such unintentional reactive components must be accounted for before satisfactory bridge balance can be accomplished.

Reactive balance can usually be accomplished by introducing an additional balance adjustment in the circuit. Figure 5.12 shows how this may be provided. Balance is accomplished by alternately adjusting the resistance and reactive balance controls, each time reducing bridge output, until proper balance is finally achieved.

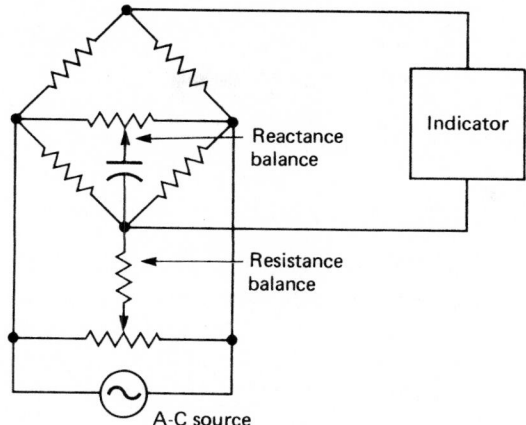

FIGURE 5.12 Circuit arrangement for balancing an a.c. bridge.

5.9.5 Lead-Wire Compensation

Frequently a sensor and a bridge-type instrument must be separated by an appreciable distance. Lead wires are used to connect the two as illustrated in Fig. 5.13(a), which shows the sensor as some type of resistance element such as a resistance thermometer or strain gage. In addition to the extra resistance introduced by the leads (see Sections 12.9.3 and 16.5.2), temperature

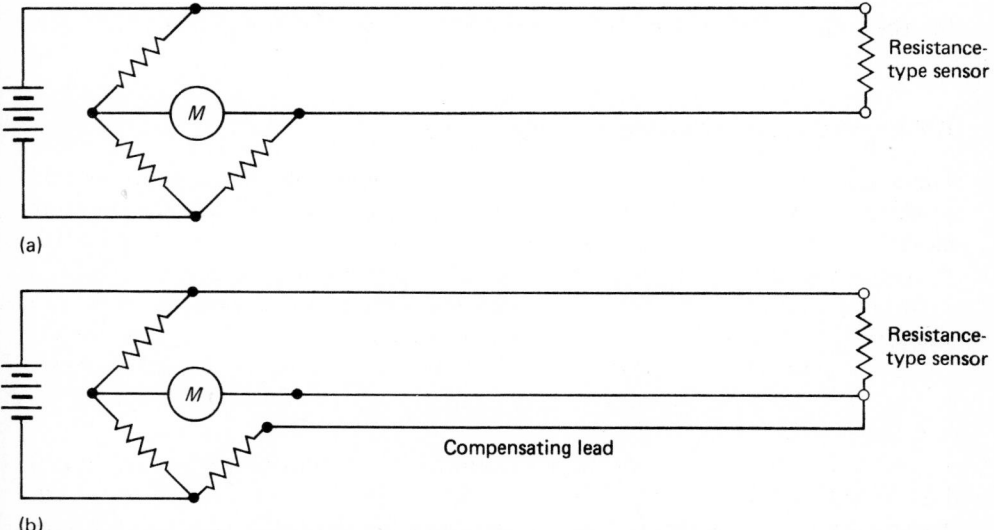

FIGURE 5.13 (a) Simple bridge with remotely located sensor. (b) Circuit similar to that shown in Fig. 5.13(a), but with a compensating leadwire.

gradients along the wires may, in certain cases, cause error. We can compensate for this type of error by using a three-wire circuit as illustrated in Fig. 5.13(b). Inspection shows that the additional lead serves to balance the total lead-wire lengths in the two adjacent arms, thereby eliminating any unbalance from this source.

5.9.6 Adjusting Bridge Sensitivity

There are several reasons for desiring to adjust bridge sensitivity. (1) Such adjustment may be used to attenuate inputs that are larger than desired. (2) It may be used to provide a convenient relation between system calibration and the scale of the read-out instrument. (3) It may be used to provide adjustment for adapting individual transducer characteristics to precalibrated systems. (This method is used to insert the gage factor for resistance strain gages in some commercial circuits.) (4) It provides a means for controlling certain extraneous inputs such as temperature effects (see Section 13.5).

A very simple method of adjusting bridge output is to insert a variable series resistor in one or both of the input leads, as shown in Fig. 5.14. If we assume equal initial resistance R in all bridge arms, the resistance seen by the voltage source will also be R. If a series resistance is inserted, as shown, then thinking in terms of a voltage-dividing circuit, we see that the input to the bridge will be reduced by the factor

$$n = \frac{R}{R + R_s} = \frac{1}{1 + (R_s/R)} . \qquad (5.22)$$

We call n the *bridge factor*. The bridge output will be reduced by a proportional amount, which makes this method very useful for controlling bridge sensitivity.

5.10 REACTANCE OR IMPEDANCE BRIDGES

Reactance or impedance bridge configurations are of the same general form as the Wheatstone bridge, except that reactance elements (capacitors and inductances) are involved in one or more of the arms. Because such elements

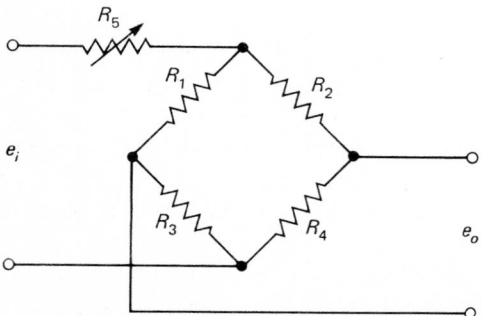

FIGURE 5.14 Method for adjusting bridge sensitivity through use of variable series resistance, R_s.

are inherently frequency-sensitive, impedance bridges are a.c. excited. Obviously the multitude of variations that are possible preclude more than a general discussion in a work of this nature; thus the reader is referred to more specialized works for detailed coverage [8].

Figure 5.15 shows several of the more common a.c. bridges, along with the type of element usually measured and the balance requirements.

5.11 RESONANT CIRCUITS

Capacitance–inductance combinations present varying impedance, depending on their relative values and the frequency of the applied voltage. When connected in parallel, as in Fig. 5.16(a), the inductance offers small opposition to current flow at low frequencies, whereas the capacitive reactance is low at high frequencies. At some intermediate frequency, the opposition to current flow, or impedance, of the combination is a maximum (Fig. 5.16b). A similar but opposite variation in impedance is the series-connected combination.

The frequency corresponding to maximum effect, known as the *resonant frequency,* may be determined by the relation

$$f = \frac{1}{2\pi\sqrt{LC}},\tag{5.23}$$

in which

$$f = \text{the frequency, in hertz,}$$

$$L = \text{the inductance, in henrys, and}$$

$$C = \text{the capacitance, in farads.}$$

It is evident that should, say, a capacitive transducer element be used, it could be in combination with an inductive element to form a resonant combination. Variation in capacitance caused by variation in an input signal (e.g., mechanical pressure) would then alter the resonant frequency, which could then be used as a measure of input.

5.11.1 Undesirable Resonant Conditions

On occasion, resonant conditions occur, introducing spurious outputs. Most circuits are susceptible because they use some combination of inductance and capacitance and most are called on to handle dynamic signal inputs. In certain cases the capacitance and inductance may be not more than the stray values existing between the circuit components, including the wiring. This means that resonant conditions are possible that can result in nonlinearities at certain input or exciting frequencies.

Normally such situations are avoided in the design of commercial equipment insofar as possible. However, the instrument designer is not always in

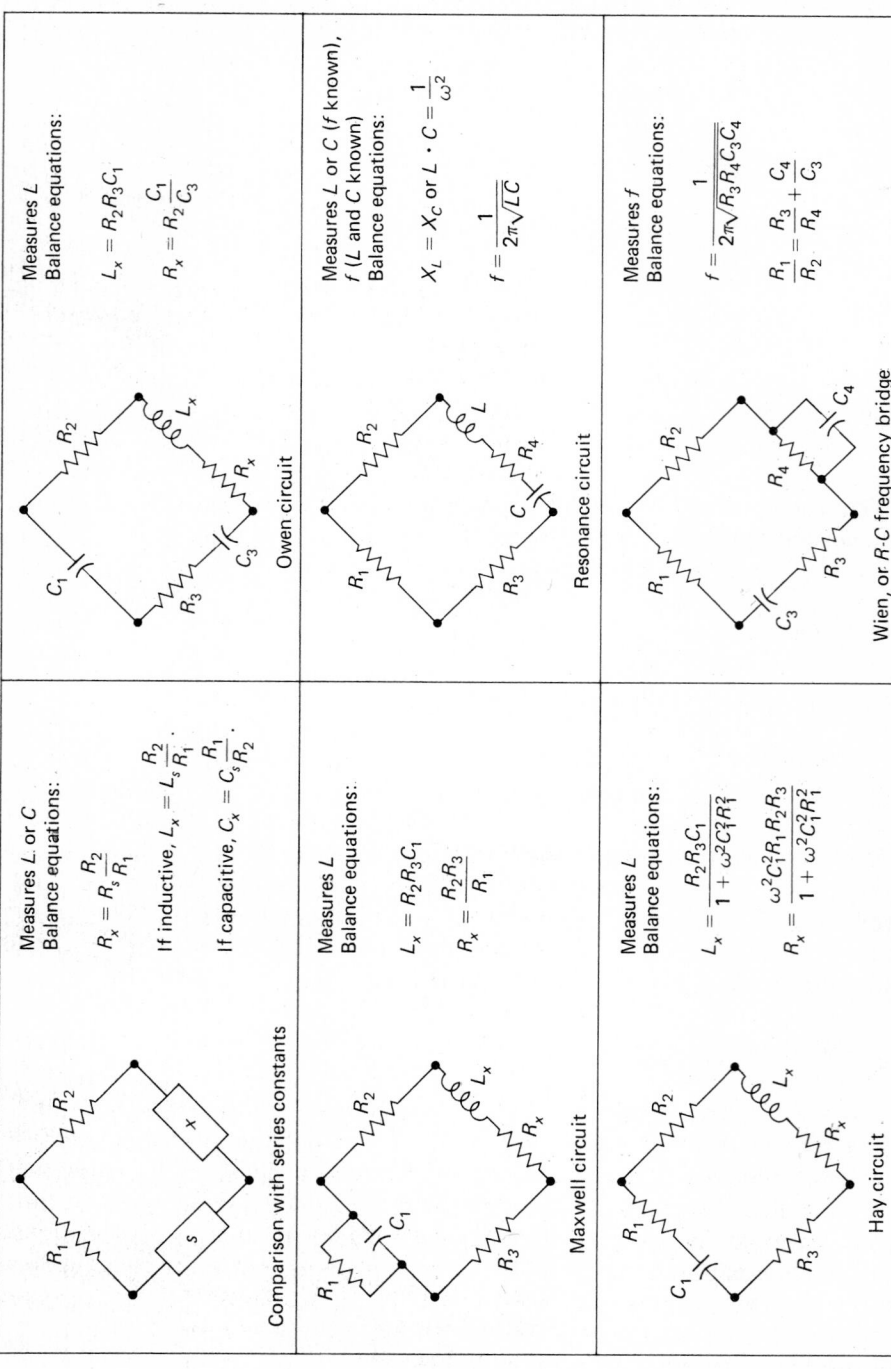

FIGURE 5.15 Impedance bridge arrangements.

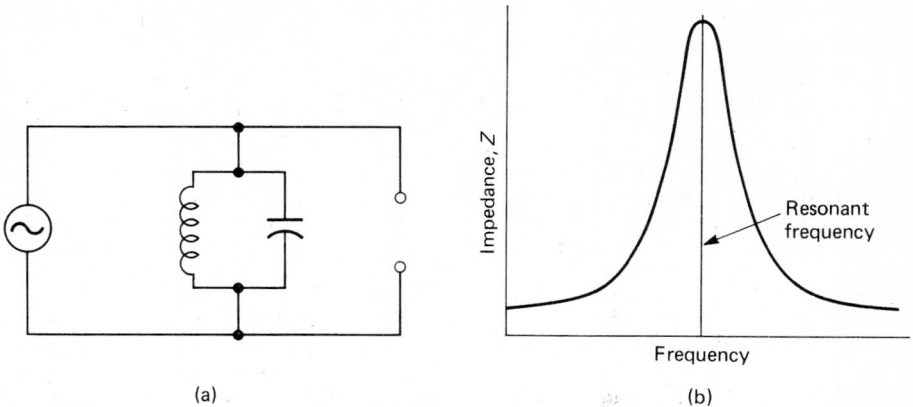

FIGURE 5.16   Parallel *L-C* circuit with curve showing frequency–impedance characteristics.

a position to predict the exact manner in which general-purpose components may be assembled or the exact nature of the input signal fed to the equipment. As a result, it is quite possible to unintentionally set up arrangements of circuit elements combined with frequency conditions that result in undesirable resonant conditions.

5.12 ELECTRONIC AMPLIFICATION OR GAIN

The ratio of output to input for an electronic signal conditioning device is referred to variously as gain, amplification ratio (if greater than unity), or attenuation (if less than unity). It may be defined in terms of voltages, currents, or powers, that is,

Voltage gain = Voltage output/Voltage input,

Current gain = Current output/Current input, and

Power gain = Power output/Power input.

Another way of expressing *power gain* is through use of the *decibel*. A decibel (dB) is one-tenth of a *bel* and is based on a ratio of powers:

$$\text{Decibel (dB)} = 10 \log_{10} (P_2/P_1), \qquad (5.24)$$

where P_2 = the output power and P_1 = the input power, both expressed in the same units.

The average human ear can just detect a loudness change from an audio amplifier when a power ratio change of one decibel is made. It has also been observed that this is nearly true regardless of the power level.

Solving Eq. (5.24) for the ratio P_2/P_1 corresponding to one decibel yields a ratio of 1.26. In other words, for the average human ear to just detect an increase in sound output from an amplifier (feeding some form of earphone or loudspeaker), an increase of approximately 26% in power is required.

For a pure resistance, electrical power may be expressed as

$$\text{Power} = ei = e^2/R = i^2R,$$

where e = the voltage, i = the current, and R is a pure resistance. Substituting either of the last two forms into Eq. (5.24) yields

$$dB = 20 \log (e_1/e_2) + 10 \log (R_1/R_2) \qquad (5.25)$$

or

$$dB = 20 \log (i_2/i_1) + 10 \log (R_2/R_1). \qquad (5.25a)$$

Should $R_1 = R_2$, then the last term in each case reduces to zero.

One must remember that the decibel is fundamentally a *power ratio* and that "forgetting" the R's in the above equations is legitimate only if the two loads are equal.

Amplification calculations based on the decibel offer two important advantages: (1) Reasonably small numbers are involved, and (2) combining the effects of various stages of a system may be accomplished by simple addition.

Voltmeters often carry a decibel scale. When using such a scale one must always be cognizant of three important factors: (1) In reality the measurement is not in decibels, but in voltage; (2) because the decibel is a ratio, the scale must be based on some *reference voltage;* and (3) reference to Eq. (5.25) shows that the scale must assume a *reference load.*

Most voltmeter scales are based on a reference of 1 milliwatt across 600 ohms, or

$$P = e^2/R,$$

hence,

$$e = (PR)^{1/2} = (0.001 \times 600)^{1/2} = 0.7746 \text{ volt}.$$

This means that zero on the decibel scale has been arbitrarily set to correspond to 0.7746 volt. In some instances the references are indicated directly on the meter face. Often the abbreviation dBm is used to indicate the above conventions. Why the 600-ohm load rather than something else? The answer is that this is a long-established industrial standard, predating the field of electronics and originated by telegraph and telephone practices.

Suppose we use a voltmeter to indicate decibels. Suppose also that the signal source impedance is R_s rather than R_r, where the latter is the reference. What correction should be applied? The following provides the proper result [9]:

$$dB_{(corrected)} = dB_{(indicated)} + 10 \log (R_r/R_s). \qquad (5.25b)$$

The derivation is left for the reader (see Problem 5.15 at the end of the chapter).

EXAMPLE   Suppose a reading of 50 dBm is obtained across a 16-ohm load, using a voltmeter with scale referenced to 600 ohms. What is the true dB value?

Solution $dB_{(corrected)} = 50 + 10 \log (600/16) = 65.7$

As we discussed above, corrections must be made to obtain *true* dB values when load and reference conditions differ. Very conveniently, however, if we require only *differences* or changes in decibels, then we may not need corrections in individual readings. This is true if the loads remain unchanged during the actual measurements.

5.13 ELECTRONIC AMPLIFIERS

It is not the purpose of this section, or of the book, to be concerned with electronics or electronic theory beyond the barest minimum required to make intelligent use of such equipment for the purposes of mechanical measurement. The following discussion, therefore, is brief and is directed primarily to applications rather than to specific theory of operation.

Some form of amplification is almost always used in circuitry intended for mechanical measurement. Traditionally, the term "electronic," as opposed to the word "electrical," assumes that in some part of the circuit electrons are caused to flow through space in the absence of a physical conductor, thus assuming the use of vacuum tubes. With the advent of *solid-state* devices (diodes, transistors, and the like) the word electronics has taken on a broader meaning. Throughout the remainder of the book it will be understood that, unless more specific reference is made, the word electronics is being used in its broadest sense.

Electronic amplifiers are used in mechanical measurements to provide one or a combination of the following basic services: (a) voltage gain, (b) current gain (power), and (c) impedance transformation. In most cases in which mechanical or electrical transduction is used, voltage is the electrical output that is the analogous signal. Often the voltage level available from the transducer is very low; thus a voltage amplifier is used to increase the level for subsequent processing. Occasionally, the input signal must finally be used to drive a recording stylus, a galvanometer mirror, or some control apparatus. In this case voltage may not be sufficient in itself, but power must be increased; hence a current or power amplifier is needed. In certain instances a transducer produces sufficient signal level, but is accompanied by an unacceptably high output impedance level. This is true of most piezoelectric-type transducers. A disadvantage of high-impedance lines is their susceptibility to noise. If the signal is to be transmitted any appreciable distance (even a few inches in some cases), the noise pickup from the environment may be unacceptable. Low-impedance lines are much less prone to this problem. Hence it may well be desirable to insert an impedance transformation in the form of an amplifier that will accept a high-impedance input, but produce a low-impedance output.

This type of amplifier is often called a *buffer*.

There are several generalities that can be listed for the ideal (but non-existent) electronic amplifier:

1. Infinite input impedance: no input current, hence no load on the previous stage or device;
2. Infinite gain (lower gain can be obtained by attenuation);
3. Zero output impedance (low noise);
4. Instant response (wide bandwidth);
5. Zero output for zero input;
6. Ability to ignore or reject extraneous inputs.

Although none of these can be completely realized, it is often possible to approach these aims, and their assumption leads to simplified circuit analysis.

5.14   VACUUM-TUBE AMPLIFIERS

Electronic amplification originated with the invention of the triode vacuum tube. Thomas Alva Edison discovered that electrons could flow from a heated cathode to an anode in an evacuated space, hence the term "Edison effect." Lee deForest is credited with showing that the flow could be *controlled* by inserting a third element, the grid, between the cathode and the anode. This resulted in the triode electron tube and, in various configurations, many with additional elements, provided the basis for electronic amplification.

Of course, vacuum tubes are little used today in instrumentation. In certain instances in which high power is required their use may still offer advantages. Most instrumentation-amplification elements are now solid-state, in the form of either discrete circuit elements or integrated circuits.

5.15   SOLID-STATE AMPLIFIERS

Transistorized measurement devices are quite common. The transistor can perform most of the functions of the vacuum tube and can do so without the heated filament, high voltages, and shock-sensitive elements inherent in the construction and operation of the vacuum tube. It is not surprising, then, that transistorized measurement apparatus such as amplifiers and oscillators have gradually taken the place of their vacuum-tube counterparts.

The basic transistor is a three-element device and in this respect is similar to the triode vacuum tube. It is also adaptable to various circuit arrangements, as shown in Fig. 5.17.

Several advantages accrue from the use of transistors in measurement apparatus. The transistor, coupled with module-type integrated circuits, permits considerable weight saving and reduced size. In addition, the inherent characteristics of the transistor permit replacement of relatively high-voltage

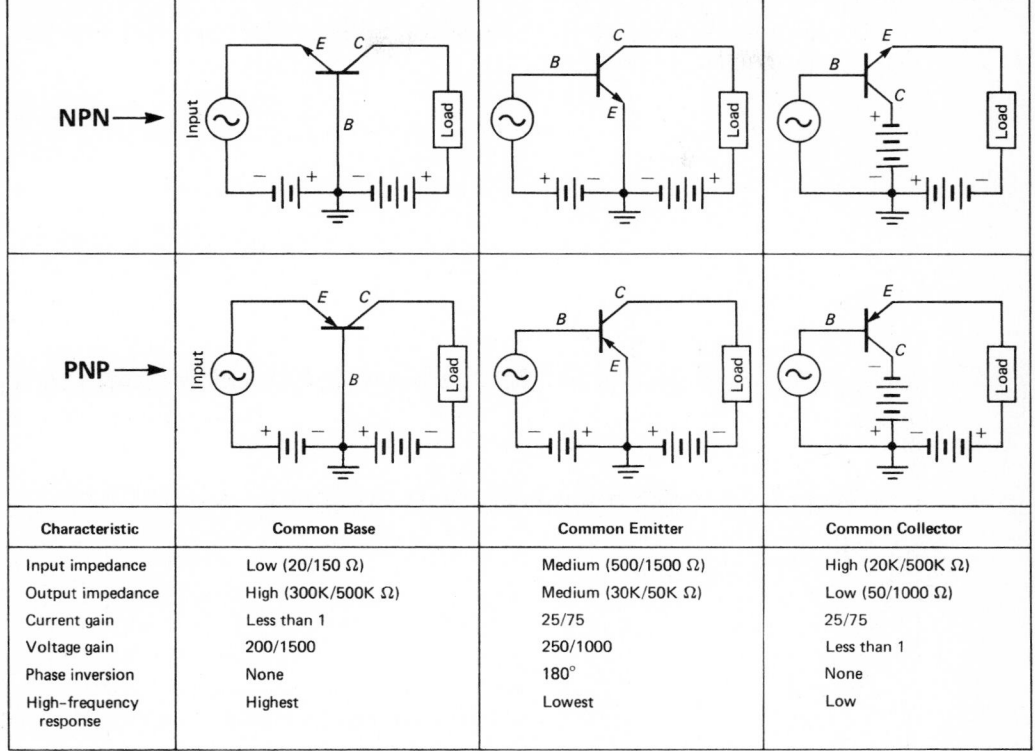

FIGURE 5.17   Basic transistor circuits.

Characteristic	Common Base	Common Emitter	Common Collector
Input impedance	Low (20/150 Ω)	Medium (500/1500 Ω)	High (20K/500K Ω)
Output impedance	High (300K/500K Ω)	Medium (30K/50K Ω)	Low (50/1000 Ω)
Current gain	Less than 1	25/75	25/75
Voltage gain	200/1500	250/1000	Less than 1
Phase inversion	None	180°	None
High–frequency response	Highest	Lowest	Low

plate supplies required by vacuum tubes with much lower voltages, often conveniently supplied by batteries. The latter permits easy field use. Vibration and shock occasionally make vacuum-tube "microphonics" a problem; this is essentially eliminated in transistorized equipment. Among the disadvantages is the fact that transistors are more sensitive to voltage extremes or incorrect polarities. Proper performance is also more temperature-dependent.

Although transistors may be used as discrete, hard-wired circuit elements, they are incorporated more commonly along with other elements into single-package, integrated circuits, or ICs.

5.16 INTEGRATED CIRCUITS*

As the name implies, integrated circuits (ICs) are groups of circuit elements combined to perform specific purposes. For the most part the elements consist

---

* See also Section 6.4.

of transistors, diodes, resistors, and, to a lesser extent, capacitors, all connected and packaged in convenient plug-in units. They form the building blocks used to construct more complex circuits: differential amplifiers, mixers (for combining signals), timers, audio preamps, audio power amplifiers, voltage references, regulators and comparators, and many of the digital devices discussed in Chapter 6. Of particular importance to mechanical measurements is the operational amplifier or op amp. In the following paragraphs we will discuss some of these in more detail.

5.17 OPERATIONAL AMPLIFIERS

The op amp is basically a d.c. differential voltage amplifier. By d.c. we mean that it will process inputs over a frequency range extending down to and *including* a d.c. voltage. As a differential amplifier it has provisions for two inputs and responds to the *difference* in the voltages at the two terminals. One of the inputs, called *noninverting*, is conventionally identified with the (+) symbol (Fig. 5.18). The other, called the *inverting* input, carries the (−) symbol. That portion of the *output* stemming from the (+) source is *in phase* with the input; that portion from the (−) input is 180 degrees out of phase. We can see, then, that the output is a function of the difference between the two input signals, hence the term *differential*. If the (+) and (−) inputs are identical then, ideally, the net output of the op amp will be zero. This leads to a very useful property called *common mode rejection* or CMR. Generally speaking, a useful signal may be applied to one of the inputs while the other is held to zero (grounded). Signal output would then be equal to the input multiplied by the gain. In addition, however, exterior elements, leads, etc., may pick up unwanted noise such as stray 60-cycle line hash. Fortunately such noise is more or less equally applied to both inputs and, therefore, is largely cancelled by the common mode rejection characteristic of the op amp.

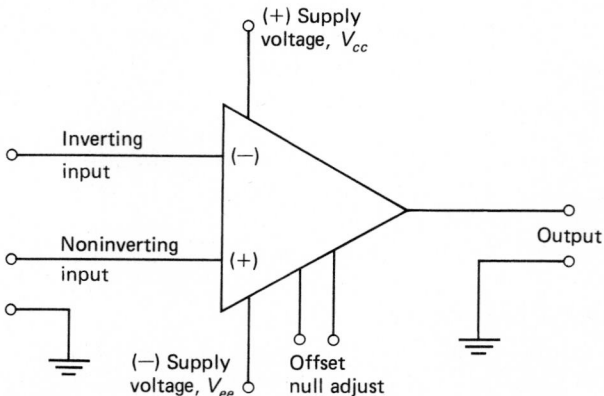

FIGURE 5.18   Diagram showing typical operational–amplifier connections.

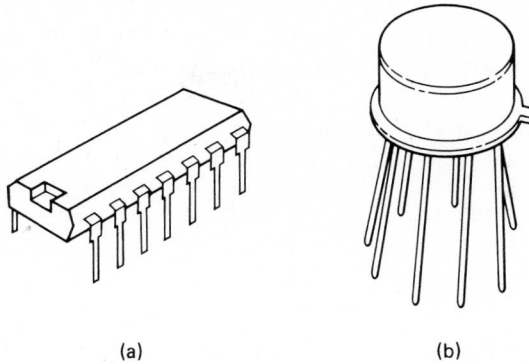

(a)   (b)

FIGURE 5.19   (a) Typical DIP (dual-inline-package) integrated circuit. (b) Typical TO integrated circuit package.

Figure 5.18 shows the configuration of the basic exterior circuitry of the op amp. Two power sources of equal magnitude but opposite polarity ($V_{ee} = -V_{cc}$) are generally required. These values commonly fall somewhere in the range of from 5 to 30 VDC. Quite often common 9-VDC transistor radio batteries may be used. Most op amps are packaged in either the dual-in-line (DIP) form or one of the standard "TO" cans (Figs. 5.19a and b).

Although it is not our purpose or requirement to explore the theory of operation, we point out here that the usual practice in deriving impedance and gain values for the various configurations is to assume that, indeed, the op amp completely satisfies the ideal amplifier requirements given in Section 5.13. No real-life amplifier can actually meet these criteria; yet the op amp comes close to doing so, since:

1. It has very high input impedance (megohms to gigaohms);
2. It has very low output impedance (as low as a fraction of an ohm);
3. It is capable of very high gain [such as 10^6 (120 dB) or greater];
4. It is quite effective in rejecting common mode inputs.

One nonideal characteristic of most op amps is that they do not completely satisfy the differential amplifying property: With both inputs grounded, there is usually a residual output. Internally, the multitude of transistors, diodes, etc., are never perfectly matched. However, it is possible to minimize this shortcoming through use of external trimming components. In addition to power supply and input/output connections, the common op amp is also provided with pins marked "null" or "null offset," which provide the entry for adjusting the unwanted offset voltage. (See Example E6 in Section 5.17.2.)

In addition, it is often necessary to use measures to minimize the thermal drift caused by temperature sensitivities due to both internal and external circuit elements. There is a wide variety of discrete op amps available, and their differences are to a great extent due to attempts to improve drift and frequency deficiencies. Understandably such refinements are reflected in cost.

5.17.1 Typical Op-Amp Specifications

Each op amp is designed to meet certain requirements. Of the types recommended for general application, op-amp 741 is undoubtedly the best known and most widely used. In comparison to more sophisticated op amps, the 741 is quite simple; yet in a package the size of a fingernail, it incorporates 20 transistors, 12 resistors, and one capacitor. Op-amp 741 specifications are as follows:

Open loop gain	to 10^5 (depending on frequency)
Maximum power supply voltages	$\pm$ 18 V
Power dissipation	500 mW
Maximum differential input voltage	$\pm$ 30 V
Maximum single-ended input voltage	$\pm$ 15 V*
Output-short time	Indefinite
Input offset voltage	2 mV
Input offset current	20–200 nA
Input bias current	8 nA
CMRR	90 dB
Output short-circuit current	25 mA
Slew rate	0.5 V/ns

5.17.2 Applications of the Op Amp

Operational amplifiers may be used as the basic components of linear voltage amplifiers, differential amplifiers, integrators and differentiators, voltage comparators, function generators, filters, impedance transformers, and many other devices. They are *not* power amplifiers nor do they have exceptionally wide bandwidth capabilities. Undistorted frequency responses are typically limited to about 1 MHz. In general, their maximum voltage output is limited by the supply voltage.

    Since the number of applications of the op amp to mechanical measurements is almost limitless, we can describe here only a few. Yet this will give the reader some idea of the tremendous versatility of the device and will suggest additional uses. Examples of some basic applications follow (see also the Suggested Readings at the end of the chapter).

---

*   Or supply voltage if supply is below $\pm$ 18 V.

EXAMPLE E1   The open-loop configuration* has the following characteristics:

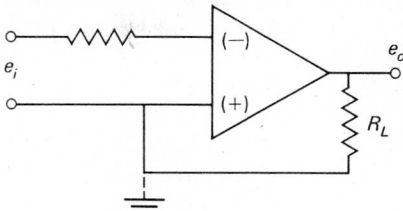

1. No feedback loop (see E2 and E3). R_L is the load resistance. The circuit may be free floating or grounded.
2. Amplifier run wide open. Any input other than zero will drive the amplifier to saturation: A very small input will drive the output to the limit permitted by the power supply.
3. It is seldom used; however, it may be employed as a voltage comparator. With different voltages applied to the (+) and (−), open loop output polarity will be controlled by the larger input. For sinusoidal inputs, a square wave output would result.

EXAMPLE E2   The impedance transformer or voltage follower has:

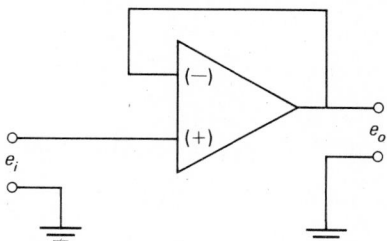

1. Full output fed to (−) input by feedback loop.
2. Gain = 1. Phase of e_o lags e_i by 180 degrees, i.e., $e_o = -e_i$.
3. Input impedance in gigaohms. Output impedance in fractions of an ohm.

EXAMPLE E3   The inverting amplifier

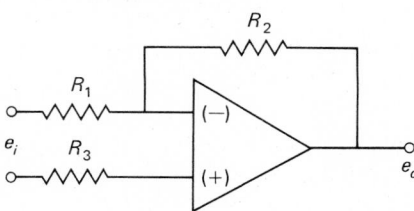

---

* It is conventional in op-amp circuit diagrams to show only those terminals that are used in the particular configuration. Power supply inputs are always required, shown or not. Null adjustment is often not shown, although it may be required for optimum performance (see Example E6).

1. Probably is the most used of all op-amp circuits. Feedback provided by R_2. Differential input across $(-)$ and $(+)$ provides an output equal to the voltage difference multiplied by circuit gain. Output is out of phase with input.

2. Has a circuit gain $= R_2/R_1$.

3. R_3 is commonly made approximately equal to the parallel value of R_1 and R_2, i.e., $R_3 \approx (R_1R_2)/(R_1 + R_2)$. This provides nearly equal input impedances at the $(-)$ and $(+)$ terminals.

EXAMPLE E4   The noninverting amplifier has:

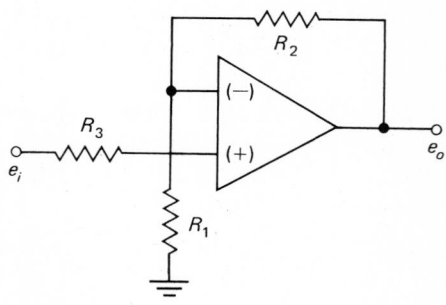

1. An output in phase with input, $e_o = e_i \times$ gain.
2. Gain $= (R_1 + R_2)/R_1$.
3. R_3 serves the same purpose as for inverting amplifier.

EXAMPLE E5   The differential or difference amplifier has:

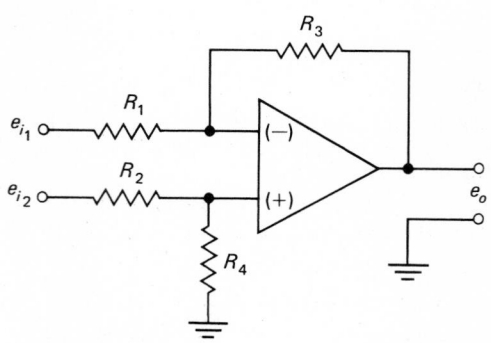

1. $R_1 = R_2$, $R_3 = R_4$, $e_o = (R_3/R_1)(e_{i_1} - e_{i_2})$
2. Minimizes requirement for offset null adjustment (see Example E6), by making input resistances at $(-)$ and $(+)$ equal.

EXAMPLE E6   An amplifier with offset null adjustment

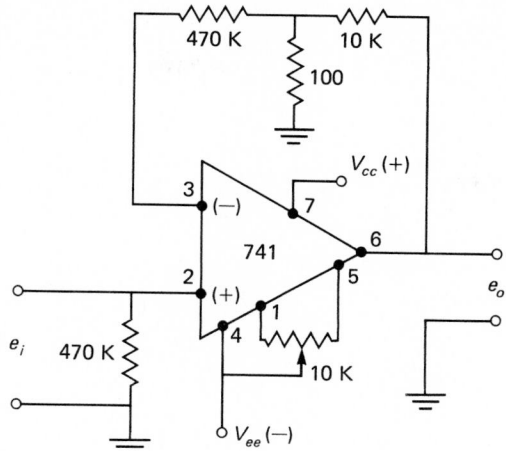

1. Provides trimming for zero output with zero input.
2. Specific example shown to illustrate pin numbering.
3. 470K resistors adjust input impedance and provide nearly equal resistances at pins 2 and 3, thereby reducing demand on null adjustment.

EXAMPLE E7   The voltage comparator has:

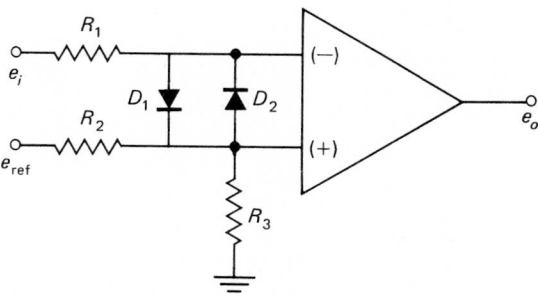

1. A small voltage difference between e_i and e_{ref} swings the output to limit permitted by power supplies. e_{ref} is set to desired reference voltage.
2. When $e_i > e_{ref}$, output is noninverting. When $e_i < e_{ref}$, output is inverted. This provides output indication for relation of e_i to e_{ref}. For example, should e_i be gradually rising, when its value reaches e_{ref} the output polarity would reverse. This could be used to trigger external action. (See Section 6.12.2 for application to analog-to-digital conversion.)
3. $R_1 \approx (R_2 R_3)/(R_2 + R_3)$ to provide near equal impedances at (+) and (−).
4. Diodes serve to limit differential input.

EXAMPLE E8   The summing amplifier has:

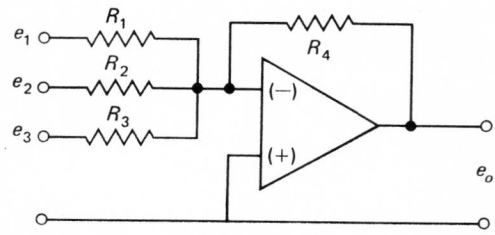

1. $e_o = -[e_1(R_4/R_1) + e_2(R_4/R_2) + e_3(R_4/R_3)]$
2. For $R_1 = R_2 = R_3 = R'$
   $$e_o = -(R_4/R')(e_1 + e_2 + e_3).$$

EXAMPLE E9   The integrator has:

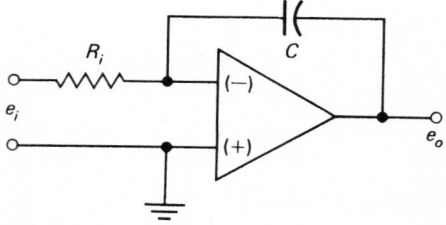

1. $\Delta e_o/\Delta t = -e_i/(R_iC)$
2. $e_o = \int[e_i/(R_iC)]\, dt$

EXAMPLE E10   The differentiator has $e_o = R_fC(de_i/dt)$.

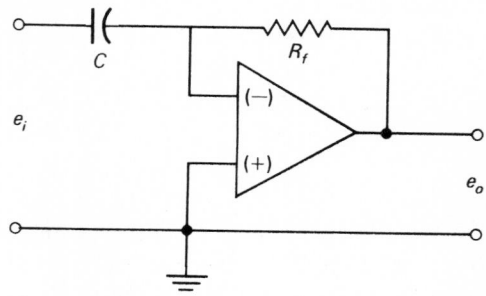

5.18   SPECIAL AMPLIFIERS

5.18.1   Instrument Amplifiers

Figure 5.20(a) shows three op amps arranged in a configuration that is commonly referred to as an *instrument amplifier*. The circuit may be assembled from discrete devices and components or it may be obtained in a single

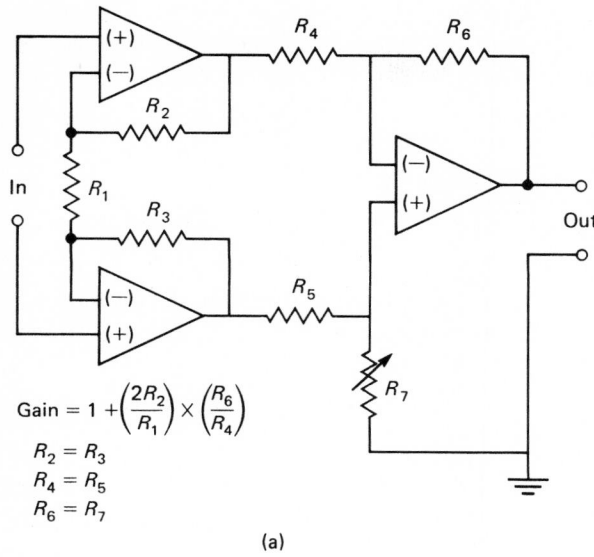

$$\text{Gain} = 1 + \left(\frac{2R_2}{R_1}\right) \times \left(\frac{R_6}{R_4}\right)$$

$R_2 = R_3$
$R_4 = R_5$
$R_6 = R_7$

(a)

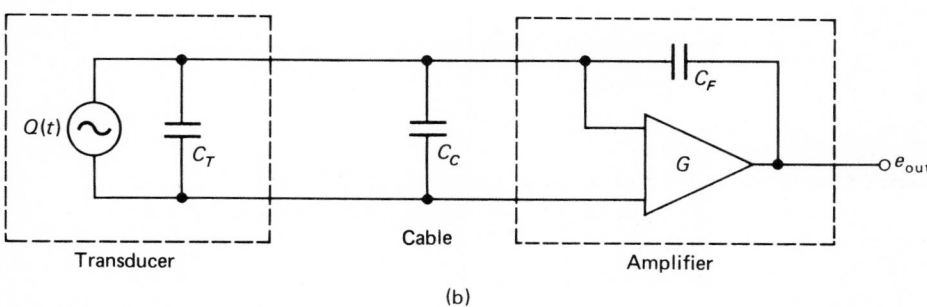

(b)

FIGURE 5.20   (a) An "instrument amplifier" circuit. (b) A charge amplifier circuit.

integrated package. In comparison with single op amps the arrangement provides higher gain and, especially, considerably higher input impedance. The latter is important when signal loading must be minimized.

5.18.2   The Charge Amplifier

A variation of the integrating amplifier (Section 5.17.2, Example E9) is known as a charge amplifier. A primary difference lies in the greater feedback capacitance, C_F. As its name suggests, the device is basically sensitive to charge Q at the input, rather than to voltage. (See Sections 3.16, 3.17, and 3.18 for a short review of charge Q.)

These devices are particularly useful in conjunction with piezoelectric-type transducers (Sections 4.14, 13.6, 14.8.3, 17.8, and 18.5), which possess unusually high source impedances. A typical circuit is shown in Fig. 5.20(b). Transducer, cable, and feedback capacitances are C_T, C_C, and C_F, respectively. The gain for the system can be expressed as [10]

$$\frac{E_{\text{out}}}{Q(t)} = \frac{G}{C_T + C_C - C_F(1 + G)},$$

where G is the amplifier gain.

With C_F quite large when compared to C_T and C_C, the latter two may be ignored. In addition, if G is made much larger than 1, the equation above reduces to

$$E_{\text{out}} \approx - \frac{Q(t)}{C_F}.$$

The output, therefore, is proportional to the charge developed at the transducer and many of the problems associated with high-impedance signal sources are minimized.

5.19   ADDITIONAL IC DEVICES

In the preceding several sections we have discussed at some length only one IC device, the operational amplifier. There is a multitude of additional solid-state devices useful in mechanical measurements, including power amplifiers, solid-state relays, voltage regulators, precision voltage references, voltage comparators, voltage-controlled oscillators (VCO), multiplexers, sample-and-hold circuits, analog-to-digital and digital-to-analog converters, precision timers, frequency-to-voltage converters, temperature transducers, various logic devices, etc. The families of microprocessor ICs form entire systems within themselves.

Discussion of some of these devices will be found in Chapter 6, "Application of digital techniques." For the remainder it is possible only to refer the reader to the Suggested Readings at the end of this chapter.

5.20   FILTERS

As we have seen, measurands that vary with time commonly consist of a combination of many frequency components or harmonics. In addition, very often unwanted inputs (noise) are picked up, resulting in a distortion and masking of the true signal. Often it is possible through the use of appropriate circuitry to selectively filter out some or all of the unwanted noise.

Filtering is the process of attenuating unwanted components of a measurand while permitting the desired components to pass. There are two basic classes of filter: *active* and *passive*. An active filter uses powered components,

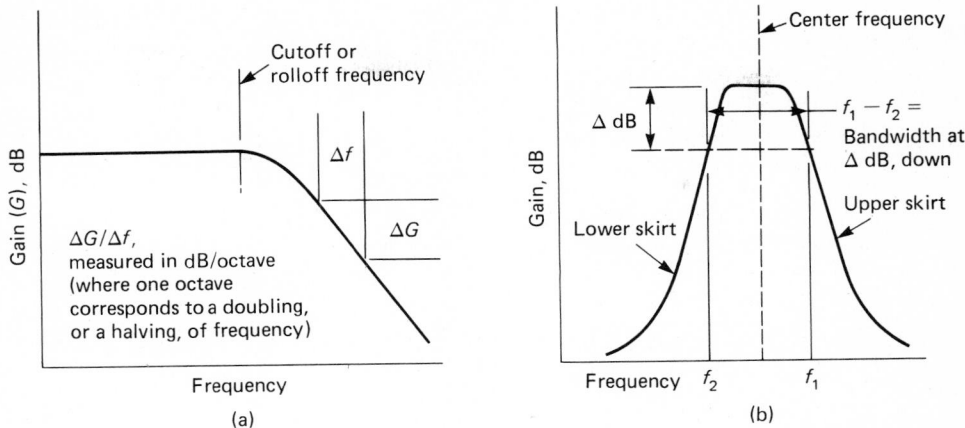

FIGURE 5.21 (a) Some terminology as applied to a low-pass filter. (b) Band-pass filter characteristics.

commonly configurations of op amps, etc., whereas a passive filter is made up of some form of *R-C-L* arrangement. In addition, filters may be classified by the descriptive terms *high-pass, low-pass, band-pass,* and *notch* or *band-reject.* In each case reference is to the signal frequency; for example, the high-pass filter permits components above a certain cutoff frequency to pass through. The notch filter attenuates a selected band of frequency components, whereas the band-pass filter permits only a range of components about its center frequency to pass. Figures 5.21(a) and (b) list certain terms applied to filter design and use. Similar terms are applicable to the high-pass and notch filters, respectively.

5.21 SOME FILTER THEORY

Consider the simple filter (Fig. 5.22a) consisting of an inductor L and a capacitor C. Resistive, capacitive, and inductive reactances may be expressed in complex* form as

$$X_R = R, \tag{5.26}$$

$$X_C = \frac{-j}{\omega C}, \tag{5.26a}$$

and

$$X_L = j\omega L, \tag{5.26b}$$

---

* See any electrical circuits text for reference; e.g., A. E. Fitzgerald, D. E. Higginbotham, and A. Grabel, *Basic Electrical Engineering.* New York: McGraw-Hill, 1967.

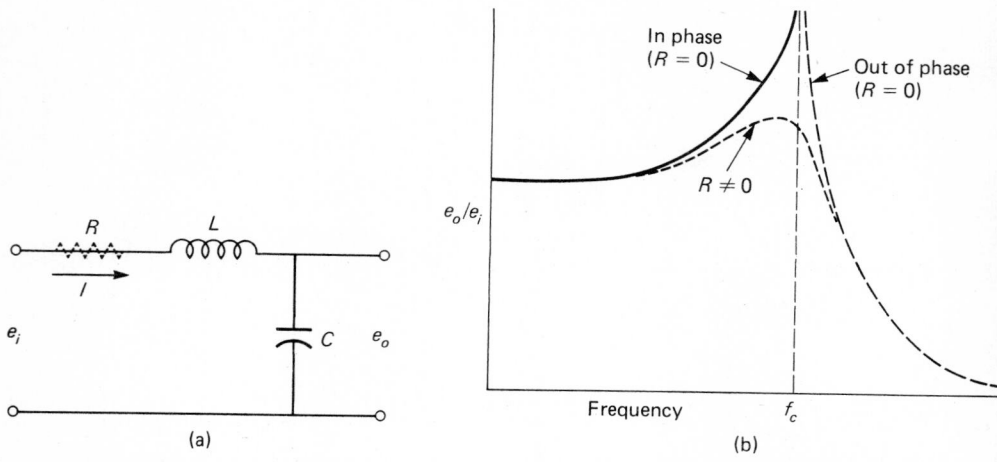

FIGURE 5.22   (a) A simple low-pass filter circuit. (b) Characteristics of circuit shown in Fig. 5.22(a).

where

R = resistance,

ω = circular frequency, $1/s$

C = capacitance, F

L = inductance, H

j = the vector operator (90 degrees ahead of real component).

We may derive the relationship between input and output as

$$e_o = IX_C, \tag{5.27}$$

$$I = e_i/(X_L + X_C), \tag{5.27a}$$

where

I = current,

e_i = input voltage, and

e_o = output voltage.

Solving for I and equating, we get

$$\frac{e_o}{e_i} = \frac{X_C}{(X_C + X_L)} = \frac{(-j/\omega C)}{(-j/\omega C) + j\omega L}, \tag{5.27b}$$

and combining terms yields

$$\frac{e_o}{e_i} = \frac{1}{(1 - \omega^2 LC)}; \tag{5.27c}$$

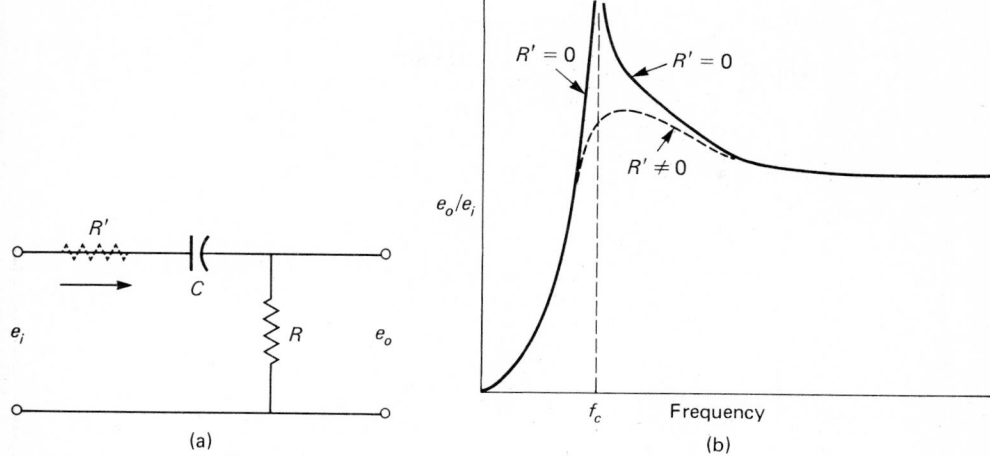

FIGURE 5.23   (a) A simple high-pass filter circuit. (b) Characteristics of circuit shown in Fig. 5.23(b).

for $\omega_c^2 = 1/LC$ (see Section 5.11)

$$\frac{e_o}{e_i} = \frac{1}{[1 - (f/f_c)^2]}$$ (5.27d)

where

$$f_c = \frac{1}{(2\pi\sqrt{LC})} \cdot$$ (5.27e)

The filter gain e_o/e_i may be plotted as shown in Fig. 5.22(b). We see that this simple circuit permits signals below the critical frequency, f_c, to be transmitted while frequencies greater than f_c are blocked. We see also that the critical frequency depends on the product of L and C, Eq. (5.27e); hence if

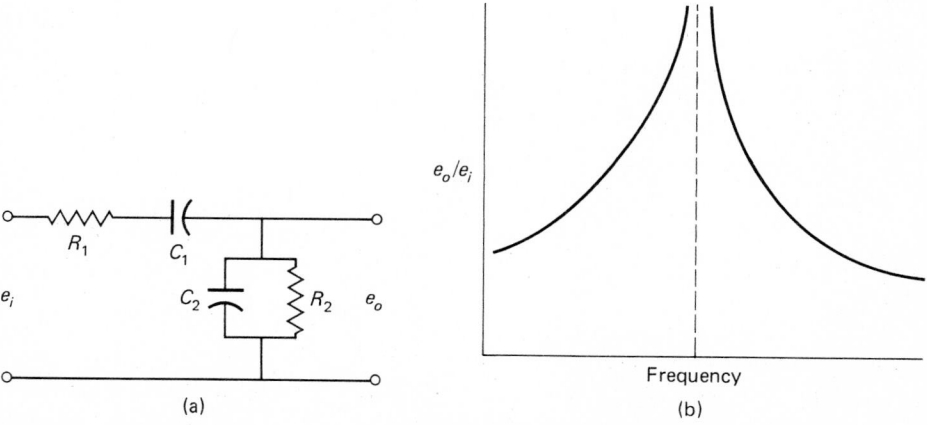

FIGURE 5.24   (a) A circuit for a simple band-pass filter. (b) Performance characteristics of band-pass filter shown in Fig. 5.24(a).

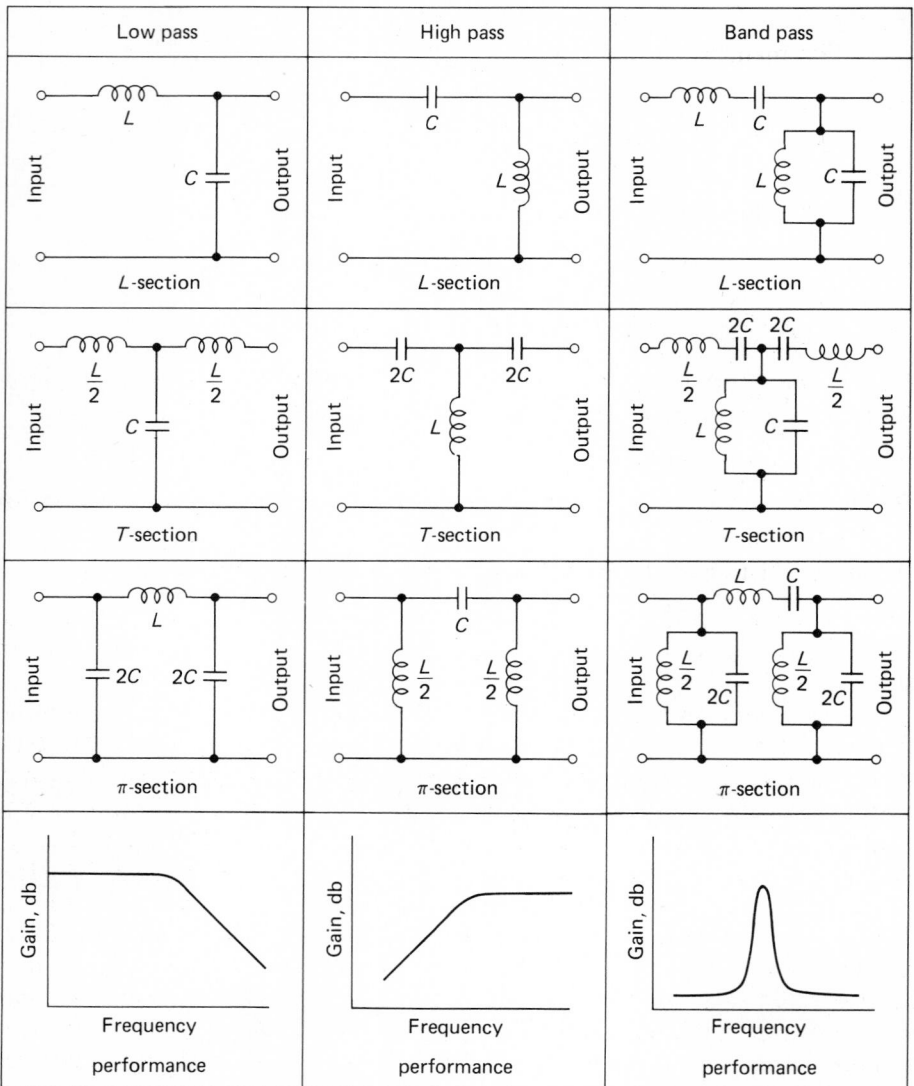

FIGURE 5.25 Examples of *L-C* filter arrangements and their output characteristics.

provision is made for varying LC the circuit may be adjusted or tuned over a range of values.

Using similar procedures, the following relationship may be derived for a simple high-pass filter (Fig. 5.23a):

$$\frac{e_o}{e_i} = \frac{1}{\sqrt{1 + (f_c/f)^2}}. \tag{5.28}$$

The characteristics are shown in Fig. 5.23(b).

In like manner, for a band-pass filter (Figs. 5.24a and b),

$$\frac{e_o}{e_i} = \frac{1}{\sqrt{[1 + (R_1/R_2) + (C_2/C_1)]^2 + [R_1 C_1 \omega - (1/\omega R_1 R_2)]^2}} \ . \tag{5.29}$$

Figure 5.25 illustrates some additional passive-filter configurations.

5.22 MORE COMPLEX FILTERING

Each of the filters discussed in the preceding section is of the very simplest form. As a general rule, the following are desirable filter characteristics:

1. Near flat response over pass or rejection frequency ranges;
2. High values of rolloff for low- and high-pass filters, as measured in dB per octave;
3. Steep skirt characteristics for band-pass and band-rejection types.

Improvements in these characteristics are attained only at the expense of increasingly complex circuits, often incorporating more than one stage of filtering.

Passive-filter circuits are made up of combinations of lumped (discrete) elements of capacitance, inductance, and resistance. In each case the only source of energy is that of the signal itself; thus even the desirable frequency components are attenuated. In addition, the frequencies encountered in mechanical measurements are usually relatively low, extending from d.c. up through the audible range and somewhat beyond; few extend beyond 100 kHz. At these frequencies the required passive components, particularly the inductors, may be quite large and bulky. In addition, optimum inductor values are not always easily attained. Fortunately, filter and amplifier circuits may be integrated into what is commonly called an *active filter,* which (a) can solve any signal attenuation problem; (b) can usually be designed to function without the use of inductors; (c) can be made tunable, i.e., cutoff frequencies and rolloff slopes can be easily adjusted, and (d) are small in size. In most cases they are integrated into a complete instrument package.

Active filters are found in a multitude of forms and have prompted the writing of numerous books devoted entirely to their design. In the very simplest form, they may consist merely of a network of passive elements combined with an op amp whose function is impedance transformation and/or recovery of signal losses (Fig. 5.26). In their more complex forms, multi–op-amp stages are used with the filtering action built into the feedback circuits. For a more detailed discussion of active filters, the reader is referred to the Suggested Readings listed for this chapter.

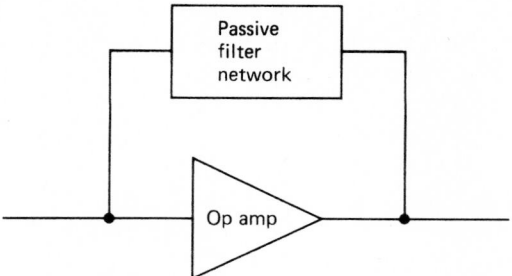

FIGURE 5.26   Circuit for a simple active filter.

5.23 DIFFERENTIATION AND INTEGRATION

Differentiation is obtained when the output is proportional to the time rate of change of the input. Figure 5.27(a) shows a simple R-C differentiation circuit for which we will assume a capacitor reactance that is small compared with the resistance R. Actual resistance and capacitance values, however, must be selected so that the time constant for the circuit is small compared with the period of the input signal. The capacitor reactance depends on frequency, and the output appearing across the resistor will be a function of the rate of change of the input signal, hence its derivative. As a result, a differentiating action is obtained.

By using a somewhat similar circuit, but with component values that provide a time constant that is long compared with the signal frequency, an

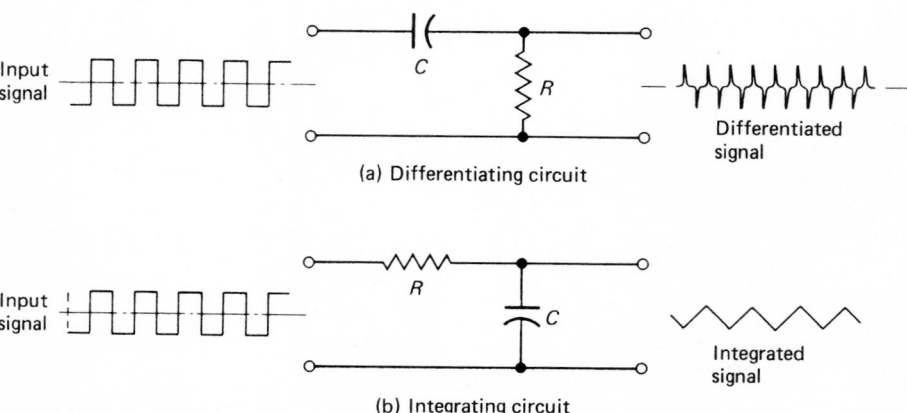

FIGURE 5.27   (a) A differentiating circuit. (b) An integrating circuit.

integrator is obtained. Such a circuit is shown in Fig. 5.27(b). When a long time constant is provided, the capacitor charges slowly and the output becomes a function of the time summation of the input, or its time integral.

Figure 5.27 illustrates typical differentiator and integrator treatments of a square-wave input. Similar actions may be obtained by circuits using inductances.

5.24 COMPONENT COUPLING METHODS

When electrical circuit elements are connected, it is often necessary to give special attention to the coupling methods used. In certain cases, transducer–amplifier, amplifier–recorder, or other component combinations are inherently incompatible, making direct coupling impossible or, at best, causing nonoptimum operation. Coupling problems include obtaining proper impedance match and maintaining proper circuit requirements such as damping. Problems of this nature are usually brought about by desire for maximum energy transfer and optimum fidelity of response.

The importance of exact impedance match, however, varies considerably from application to application. For example, the input impedances of most cathode-ray oscilloscopes and electronic voltmeters are relatively high, yet satisfactory operation may be obtained from directly connected low-impedance transducers. In this case, voltage is the measured quantity and power transfer is incidental. *In most cases, driving a high-impedance circuit component with a low-impedance source presents fewer problems than does the reverse.*

In addition to allowing power transfer, proper coupling may be important in determining dynamic response. An example of this is the amplifier–oscillograph combination. Oscillograph response depends on proper damping, which, in turn, is affected by the electrical circuitry. (Oscillograph damping requirements are discussed in Section 7.10).

There are three special methods of coupling, depending on the circuit elements; they utilize (1) matching transformers, (2) impedance transforming amplifiers, and (3) coupling networks.

An example of transformer coupling is the use of electronic power amplifiers to drive vibration exciters such as those discussed in Section 17.16.1. The problem of connecting the amplifier to the shaker head is similar to that of connecting a speech amplifier to a loudspeaker. In both cases, the output impedance of the driving power source in the amplifier is often higher than the load impedance to which it must be connected. Transformer coupling is generally used as shown in Fig. 5.28(a). Matching requirements may be expressed by the relation

$$\frac{N_S}{N_L} = \frac{Z_S}{Z_L}, \tag{5.30}$$

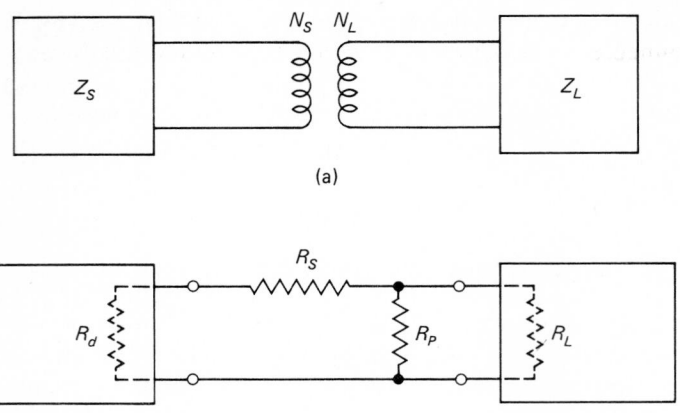

FIGURE 5.28   (a) Impedance matching by means of a coupling transformer. (b) By means of a resistance pad.

in which

$$Z_S = \text{the source impedance,}$$

$$Z_L = \text{the load impedance, and}$$

$$N_S/N_L = \text{the turns ratio of the transformer.}$$

General-purpose devices such as simple voltage amplifiers and oscillators often incorporate a final amplifier stage, called a buffer, to supply a low-impedance output. By reducing the impedance source, one can minimize losses in the connecting lines and the possibility of extraneous signal pickup.

Proper coupling may also be accomplished through use of matching resistance pads. Figure 5.28(b) illustrates one simple form.

If we assume that the driver output and load impedances are resistive, then the requirements for proper matching may be put in simple form as follows: The driving device, which may be a voltage amplifier, *looks* into the resistance network and *sees* the resistance R_s in series with the paralleled combination of R_L and R_p. Hence, for proper matching,

$$R_d = R_s + \frac{R_p R_L}{R_p + R_L}, \tag{5.31}$$

in which

$$R_d = \text{the output impedance of the driver, in ohms,}$$

$$R_L = \text{the load resistance, in ohms,}$$

$$R_p = \text{the paralleling resistance, in ohms, and}$$

$$R_s = \text{the series resistance, in ohms.}$$

The driven device *sees* two parallel resistances, made up of R_p and the series-connected resistances R_s and R_d. Hence, for matching,

$$R_L = \frac{R_p(R_s + R_d)}{R_p + (R_s + R_d)} .$$

(5.31a)

Solving for R_s and R_p, we have

$$R_s = [R_d(R_d - R_L)]^{1/2}$$

(5.32)

and

$$R_p = \left[R_L \left(\frac{R_d R_L}{R_d - R_L} \right) \right]^{1/2} .$$

(5.32a)

Now if R_d and R_L are known, values of R_s and R_p may be determined to satisfy the matching requirements by use of Eqs. (5.32) and (5.32a). It must be realized, however, that in using resistive elements there will be an unavoidable loss in signal energy. Such losses are often referred to as *insertion losses*. In general, however, by providing proper match, the network will provide optimum gain.

5.25 CONCLUDING REMARKS

In this chapter we have discussed system elements under the broad heading "signal conditioning." The devices introduced included those elements required to alter detector-transducer outputs into forms acceptable to the terminating devices, whose duty it is to present the information in intelligible form. Chapter 6 covers the very special subject of digital techniques and their place in mechanical measurement.

SUGGESTED READINGS

Bartholomew, D., *Electrical Measurements and Instrumentation*. Boston: Allyn & Bacon, 1963.

Berlin, H. M., *Operational Amplifiers*. Benton Harbor, Michigan: Heath, 1979.

Booth, S. F., *Precision Measurement and Calibration,* Vol. 1. (Selected NBS technical papers on electricity and electronics). NBS Handbook 77. Washington, D.C.: U.S. Government Printing Office, 1961.

Carr, J., *Op Amp Circuit Design and Applications*. Blue Ridge Summit, Pennsylvania: Tab Books, 1976.

Cowan, J. D., Jr., and H. S. Kirschbaum. *Introduction to Circuit Analysis*. Columbus, Ohio: Charles E. Merrill, 1961.

DeMaw, D. (ed.), *The Radio Amateurs Handbook*. Hartford, Connecticut: American Radio Relay League (annual editions).

Fitzgerald, A. E., D. E. Higginbotham, and A. Grabel, *Basic Electrical Engineering,* 3d ed. New York: McGraw-Hill, 1967.

Knight, A. R., and G. H. Fett, *Introduction to Circuit Analysis*. New York: Harper, 1943.

Linear Data Book. Santa Clara, California: National Semiconductor Corporation.

Morrison, R., *Grounding and Shielding Techniques in Instrumentation*, 2d ed. New York: John Wiley, 1977.

Rhodes, J. D., *Theory of Electrical Filters*. New York: John Wiley, 1976.

Semiconductor Devices. Benton Harbor, Michigan: Heath, 1975.

Shea, R. F. (ed.), *Amplifier Handbook*. New York: McGraw-Hill, 1966.

Stout, D. F., and M. Kaufman, *Handbook of Operational Amplifier Circuit Design*. New York: McGraw-Hill, 1976.

Tobey, G. E., L. P. Huelsman, and G. G. Graeme (eds.), *Operational Amplifiers, Design and Application*. New York: McGraw-Hill, 1971.

PROBLEMS

5.1 A force cell uses a resistance element as a secondary transducer. It is connected to a ballast circuit in which the series resistance R_b has a value one-half the nominal resistance of the transducer. Determine the circuit output e_o in terms of e_i for force inputs of 25, 50, and 75 percent of full range.

5.2 The circuit shown in Fig. 5.29 is used to determine the value of the unknown resistance R_2. If the voltmeter resistance is 10 megohm and the voltmeter reads 4.65 volts, what is the value of R_2?

5.3 Equation (5.11) expresses the loading error for a voltage-dividing potentiometer circuit *based on full scale*. Show that the following equation yields the error *based on reading*:

$$\text{Percent error} = k(1 - k)(R_p/R_1) \times 100.$$

[*Hint:* Note that Eq. (5.9) yields the reading and Eq. (5.10) yields the error.]

5.4 Equations (5.5) and (5.7) are derived on the basis of a high-impedance indicator. Analyze the circuit assuming that the indicator resistance R_m is comparable in magnitude to R_i.

5.5 A 2kΩ voltage-dividing potentiometer is used as the secondary transducer of a vibrometer.

a) What is the limiting value of R_L if the loading error based on full scale is not to exceed 2%?

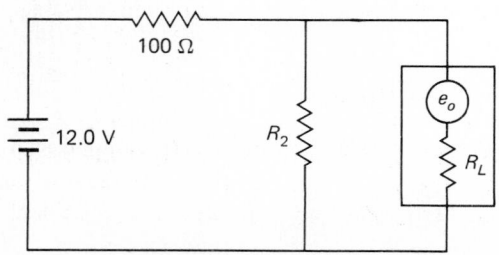

FIGURE 5.29   Circuit for Problem 5.2.

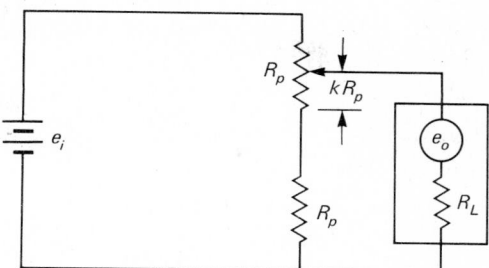

FIGURE 5.30   Voltage-dividing potentiometer circuit for Problem 5.6.

b) What is the limiting value of R_L if the same requirements apply, but the limiting error is based on "reading"?

5.6 The voltage-dividing potentiometer shown in Fig. 5.5 is modified as shown in Fig. 5.30. Determine the relationship for e_o/e_i as a function of k. Compare the results with Eq. (5.9). What advantages or disadvantages does this circuit have over the general voltage-dividing potentiometer?

5.7 A simple Wheatstone bridge as shown in Fig. 5.9 is used to accurately determine the value of an unknown resistance R_1 located in leg 1. If upon initial null balance R_3 is 127.5 Ω, and if when R_2 and R_4 are interchanged null balance is achieved when R_3 is 157.9 Ω, what is the value of the unknown resistance R_1?

5.8 A resistive element of a force cell forms one leg of a Wheatstone bridge. If the no-load resistance is 500 ohms and the sensitivity of the cell is 0.5 ohm per newton, what will be the bridge outputs for applied loads of 100, 200, and 350 newtons, if the bridge excitation is 10 volts and each arm of the bridge is initially 500 ohms?

5.9 Consider the voltage-sensitive bridge shown in Fig. 5.9. If a thermistor whose resistance is governed by Eq. (16.3) is placed in leg 1 of the bridge while $R_2 = R_3 = R_4 = R_0$ determine the bridge output when $T = 400°C$ if $R_0 = 1000$ Ω at $T_0 = 27°C$ and $\beta = 3500$. Plot the bridge output from $T = 27°C$ to $T = 500°C$ and determine the maximum deviation from linearity in this temperature range.

5.10 Figure 5.31 represents a commonly used Wheatstone bridge configuration. R_1 is often a resistance-type transducer (thermistor, resistance thermometer, strain gage, etc.), and R_2, R_3, and R_4 may or may not be fixed resistances; often they, too, are transducer elements (see Section 12.9.1). R_6 is a conventional potentiometer, usually of the multiturn variety. This may be used either for initial nulling of the bridge or as a read-out means. The variable k is a proportional term varying from 0 to 1 (or 0 to 100%) (see Section 5.7). R_s is sometimes called a *scaling resistor*. Its value largely determines the range of effectiveness of R_6. If the nominal resistance of R_1 is 1000 ohms, $R_2 = R_3 = R_4 = 1000$ ohms (fixed), $R_s = 8000$ ohms, and $R_6 = 10,000$ ohms, what null-balance range of ΔR_1 can the bridge accommodate? [*Note:* This is a problem typical of many in that the path to take toward a solution is reasonably clear, although "getting there" may be toilsome. The following problem should suggest a method of attack.]

5.11 Devise a computer program that can be used to solve differential-shunt bridge (see Fig. 5.10d) problems, such as the preceding one. The basic approach is to provide a program for satisfying Eqs. (5.12) and (5.13), including any additional circuit elements.

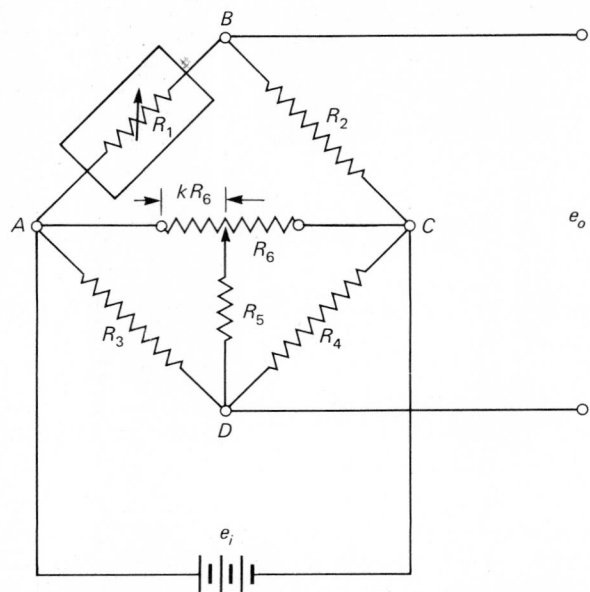

FIGURE 5.31   Resistance bridge circuit for Problem 5.10.

5.12 Using the program developed in Problem 5.11 and the basic resistance values of Problem 5.10, investigate changes in the measurement range of the bridge as affected by

a) changes in R_5

b) changes in R_6

Investigate the linearity of the circuit when used in the null-balance mode, using k as the calibrated read-out.

5.13 Derive the relationships for the Wein bridge circuit shown in Fig. 5.15.

5.14 Derive the relationships for the Maxwell bridge circuit shown in Fig. 5.15.

5.15 Derive Eq. (5.25b).

5.16 Show that an increase of 1 dB corresponds to a power increase of about 26%. Also show that an increase of n dB corresponds to a power increase of approximately $(1.26)^n$.

5.17 Derive the expression for the output e_o in terms of the input e_i for the summing amplifier (Section 5.17.2, Example E8), assuming that the current through the amplifier approximates zero.

5.18 Determine the output–input relationship for the integrator circuit (Section 5.17.2, Example E9) if no appreciable current is drawn by the amplifier.

5.19 Show that $e_o = R_fC(de_i/dt)$ for the differentiator circuit of Example E10, Section 5.17.2.

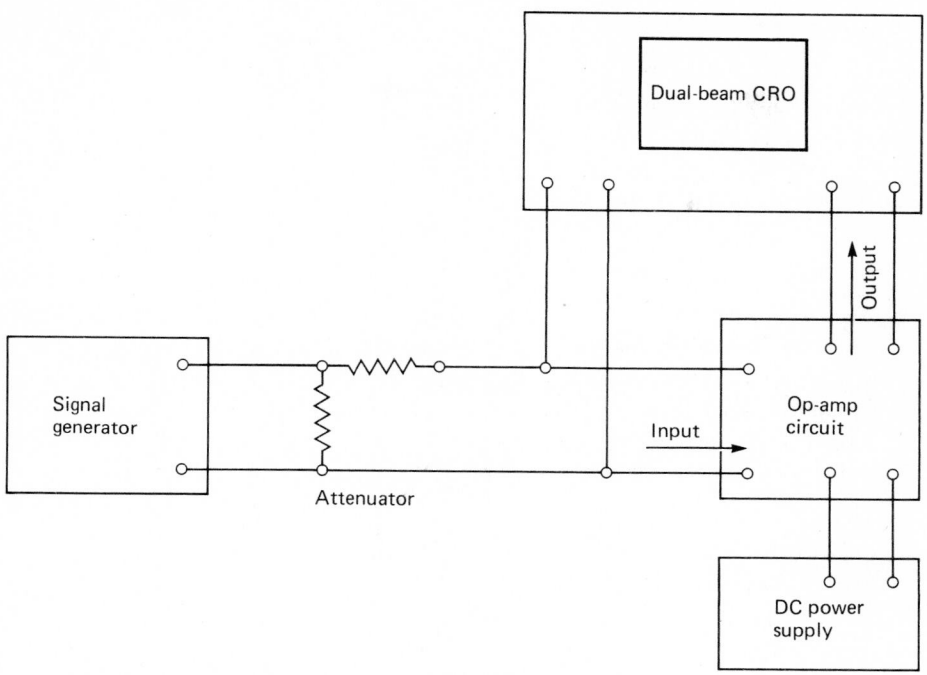

FIGURE 5.32   Circuit for demonstrating op-amp characteristics.

5.20 Figure 5.32 may be used as a guide for demonstrating op-amp performance characteristics. (See also Fig. 3.25.) Circuit values are not given because of the extremely wide choices that are available. Refer to the Suggested Readings at the end of the chapter for specific recommendations.

5.21 For the capacitive-displacement transducer circuit shown in Fig. 5.33, determine an expression for the sensitivity de_o/dd for an excitation frequency f (see Section 4.13).

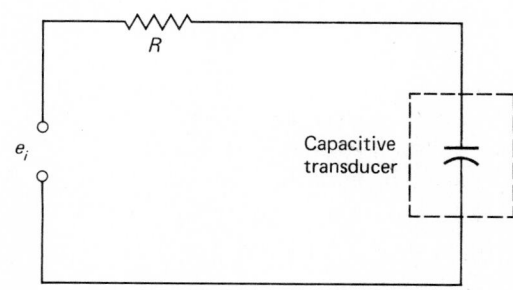

FIGURE 5.33 Capacitive displacement transducer circuit for Problem 5.20.

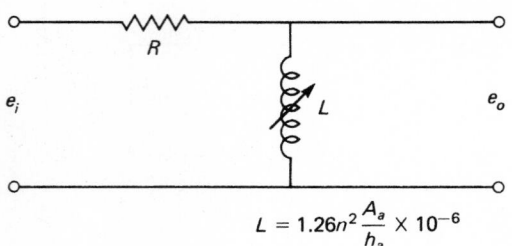

$$L = 1.26n^2 \frac{A_a}{h_a} \times 10^{-6}$$

FIGURE 5.34   Circuit for Problem 5.21.

5.22 For the circuit shown in Fig. 5.34, determine an expression for the circuit-trans-ducer sensitivity $\eta = de_o/dh_a$ for any excitation frequency f.

5.23 Equation (4.3c) governs the performance of an inductive-type transducer. The circuit is shown in Fig. 5.35. Determine the change in output if the air gap changes from 0.15 to 0.25 cm, the excitation frequency is 1000 Hz, the gap cross section is 0.1 cm², and the number of coils is 100.

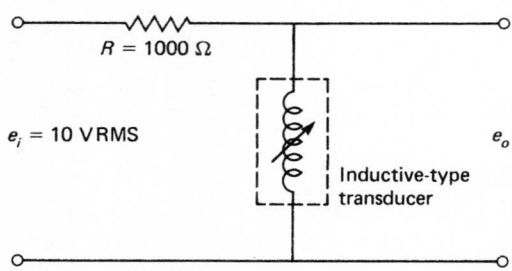

FIGURE 5.35   Inductive   transducer circuit for Problem 5.22.

application of 6 digital techniques to mechanical measurements

6.1 INTRODUCTION

Although in this chapter we will discuss some of the basic uses of digital logic and circuitry as they apply to mechanical measurements, it must be understood at the outset that our purpose is not to attempt an in-depth coverage of digital electronics: The breadth of the subject and space limitations prevent such an aim. Rather, our intent is to sufficiently survey the subject so those in the field of engineering other than electrical will gain some appreciation for the advantages, disadvantages, and general workings of solid-state circuitry, especially of the pulsed logic type.

Most measurands originate in analog form. An analog variable or signal is one that varies with time in a smooth and uniform manner without discontinuity. In many cases the amplitude is the basic variable; in others, the frequency or phase might be. A common example of a quantity in analog form is the ordinary 117-VAC, 60-Hz power-line voltage (Fig. 6.1a). An analog signal, however, need not be simple sinusoidal or periodic in form. The stress–time relationship accompanying a mechanical shock (Fig. 6.1b), is considered analog in form. The pressure variations associated with the transmission of the human voice through the air are also analog. In addition, the readout from the ordinary D'Arsonval meter is considered analog because of the possibility of the uninterrupted movement of the pointer over the scale. An analog scale can be compared to the range of brightness between black and white, including all the variations of gray in between. Digital information, on the other hand, would permit only the time variation of the two brightnesses, black or white.

Digital information is transmitted and processed in the form of *bits* (Fig. 6.1c), each bit being defined by (1) one or the other of two predefined "logic levels," and (2) the time interval assigned to it, called a *bit interval*. The most common basis for the two logic states is predetermined voltage levels, say 0 and 5 VDC. Current or shifts in carrier frequency are also used. The time-

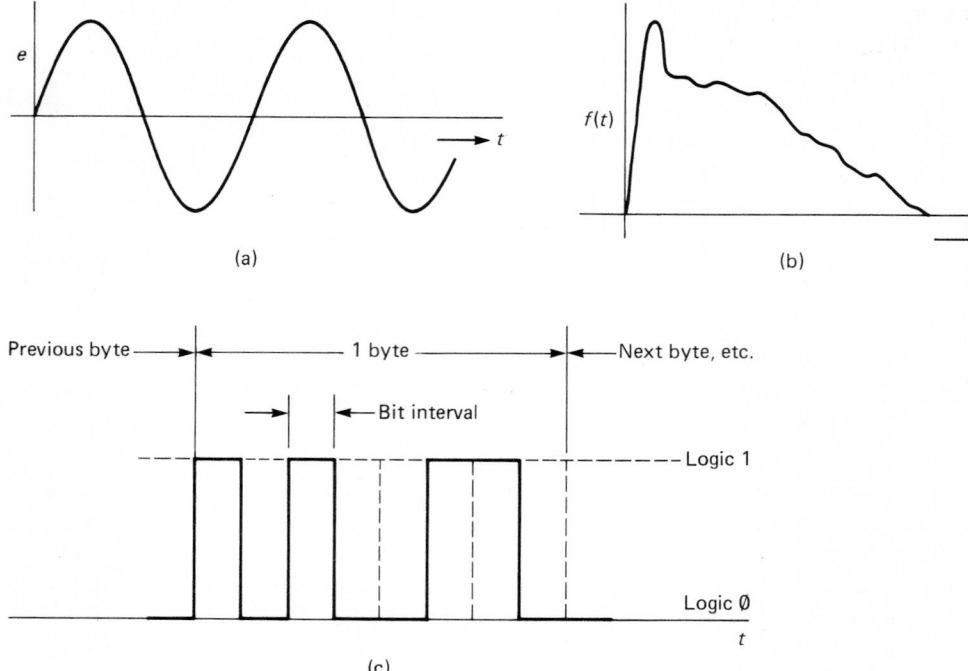

FIGURE 6.1   Examples of voltage–time relationships for analog-type signals (a and b), and a digital signal (c).

rate of the bits is closely controlled, commonly by a crystal-controlled oscillator (or *clock*). The intelligence is then carried by specially coded bit groupings, coded in predetermined sequences; for example, alphanumeric data may be handled by sequences of three, four, or more bits sent in the various possible combinations, each combination or group forming a *word* of information. The term *byte* is applied to an 8-bit word, whereas the term *word* may be applied to *any* unit of digital information. A 16-bit word is two bytes in length. A 4-bit word is sometimes referred to as a *nibble*. (Coding practices are discussed in Section 6.6.)

Figure 6.1(c) shows one possible combination of bits grouped to form one byte. In this case, the sequence of bit values is 10100110. From this we see that a bit need not be a pulse in the sense that it must be a *completed* off/on/off sequence. Indeed a byte of information could well be 00000000 or 11111111, in which case no bit-to-bit changes occur. One bit corresponds to either of two different logic states held constant for one bit interval.

Because most measurement inputs originate in analog form, some type of analog-to-digital (A/D or ADC) converter is usually required (Section 6.12). In certain instances it may also be desirable or necessary to use a digital-to-analog (D/A or DAC) converter somewhere in the measurement chain. A sophisticated example of digital information handling is *pulse-code modulation* (PCM) of the human voice. The spoken word is converted to digital form for transmission over telephone circuits and then converted back to its original analog form at the receiving end. Some of the reasons for this process are discussed in Section 6.2.

6.2 WHY USE DIGITAL METHODS?

One's first contact with digital instrumentation may occur with devices that provide digital rather than analog read-outs. The digital voltmeter (DVM) provides direct numerical display of voltage, whereas the D'Arsonval meter uses the analog pointer and scale. The more advanced DVMs also provide automatic *scaling*, i.e., decimal positioning. Obvious advantages to the use of digital read-outs are that interpolation is not required and that the reading is direct and precise, thereby minimizing errors caused by misinterpretation.

A much greater advantage of the digital technique in instrumentation undoubtedly lies in the fact that digitally based devices may be coupled easily with each other and with either a general-purpose or a dedicated computer. A *dedicated* computer is one that is programmed for a specific application and may be quite simple and inexpensive. The advent of the integrated-circuit central processing unit (CPU) (Section 6.10) has done much to make this possible.

Computer-based instrumentation makes the recording and printout of data easy but of equal importance is that many steps necessary in data reduction can be handled automatically. For example, temperatures, flows, etc., acquired from a process may be combined immediately and reduced to provide on-the-spot overall results. This, of course, does not preclude the automatic recording of the elemental data items for additional study; perhaps to pinpoint the cause of some anomaly. In addition, the outputs may be processed to provide system control. (See Section 6.14.)

There are additional advantages to using digital instrumentation. Digital signals are inherently noise-resistant. The informational content of the digital signal is *not* amplitude-dependent. Rather, it is dependent on the particular sequence of on/off pulses that apply. Therefore, so long as the sequence is identifiable, the *true and complete* form of the input remains unimpaired. Maintenance of accuracy, lack of distortion induced by signal processing and noise pickup, and greater stability are all enhanced in comparison to analog methods. The nature of the digital signal and circuitry permits the signal to be regenerated or reconstituted from point to point throughout the processing chain. The voltage amplitude of the informational pulses is commonly 5 VDC. Unless noise pulses approach this magnitude—a highly unusual condition— they are ignored. This is of particular value in the central control of a large processing system, such as a refinery or power plant, where signals must be relayed over relatively great distances, perhaps a mile or more. This advantage is even more obvious when radio links are used, as in the ground recording of signals originating from a space vehicle.

Digital circuits imply relatively low operational voltages; 5 and 12 VDC are typical. This contrasts with several hundred volts commonly required by many older circuits.

A digital measurement system may hold no particular advantage in cost when a comparison is based on instrumentation alone. However, if savings in a technician's time and the increased reliability and accuracy are considered, digital instrumentation may very well hold a marked cost advantage, particularly as the complexity of the particular problem being solved increases.

6.3   DIGITIZING MECHANICAL INPUTS

To be digitally processed, analog measurands must be

1. Converted to yes/no pulses;
2. Coded in a form meaningful to the remainder of the system; and
3. Synchronized so as to mesh properly with other inputs or control or command signals.

Meeting these three requirements is collectively referred to as *interfacing*.

When some form of computer is a part of the system, not only must the input be converted to digital pulses, but also the pulses must be converted to the language used by the computer, that is, *binary words*. In addition, of course, the computer is unable to give undivided attention to any one signal source: It will also be receiving inputs from other sources, processing the inputted data, and outputting data and control commands. Input from any one source must wait its turn for attention. In other words, all the inputs and outputs must be synchronized through proper interfacing. Before attempting further coverage of interfacing, however (see Sections 6.11, 6.12, and 6.13), we will discuss some of the fundamentals and a few of the simpler types of digital instrumentation.

Single digital-type instruments whose end purpose is to simply *display* the magnitude of an input in digital form (as opposed to an input to be interfaced into a system) often require only that the input be transduced to a frequency. Conventional transducers may be used to sense the magnitude of the measurand and to convert it into an analogous voltage. The voltage can then be amplified and, by a *voltage-controlled oscillator* (VCO), transduced to a proportional frequency. A frequency-measuring circuit (Section 6.7.3) might then be calibrated to display the magnitude of the input. There are many transducers in the field of mechanical measurements that produce voltage outputs, e.g., strain-gage bridges, thermistor bridges, differential transformers, thermocouples, etc. In addition, mechanical motion, both rotational and translational, may often be quickly, easily, and completely converted to digital voltage pulses by proximity transducers (Section 4.12), photocells (Section 4.15), interrupters (Section 4.15), and so on.

6.4 FUNDAMENTAL DIGITAL CIRCUIT ELEMENTS

6.4.1 Basic Logic Elements

An ordinary single-pole single-throw (SPST) switch (Fig. 6.2a) is a digital element in its simplest form. When actuated, it is capable of producing and controlling a *yes–no*, on–off sequence. The ordinary electromechanical relay (Fig. 6.2b) is a slightly more advanced digital device in which an electrical input may be used to change the output condition. More sophisticated switching devices are the triode electronic vacuum tube and the transistor (Fig. 6.2c). When properly biased, a transistor can be made to conduct or not to conduct, depending on the input signal. It is a near-ideal switching device.

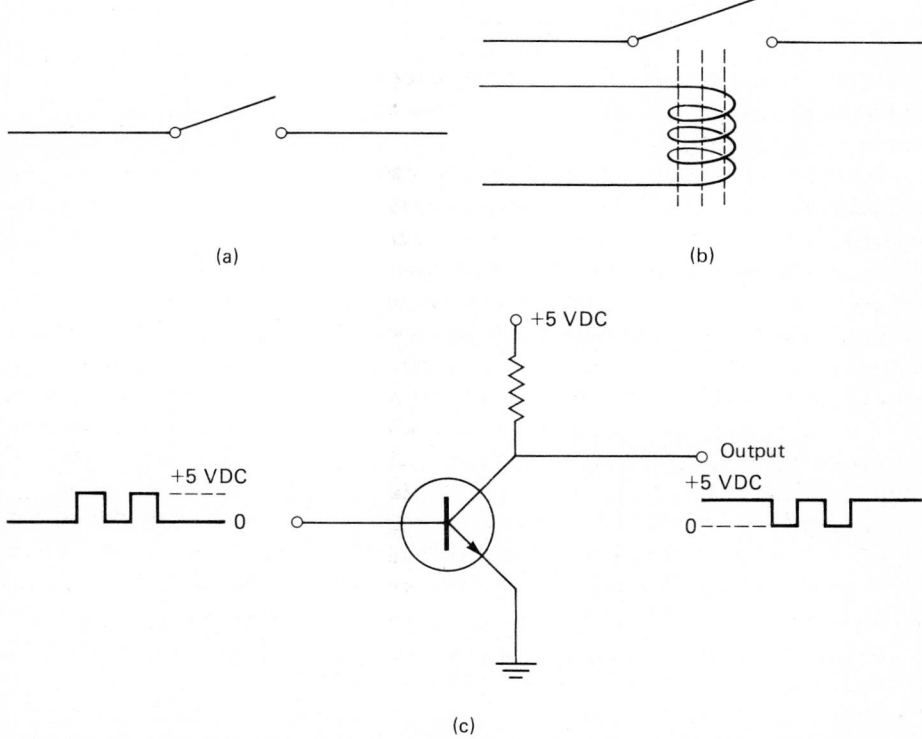

(a) (b) (c)

FIGURE 6.2   Digital switching devices. (a) A simple mechanically operated switch. (b) Electrically controlled relay. (c) A transistor-type switch. For the latter, when the input is "high" the transistor conducts, thereby effectively shorting the output to ground, hence providing near-zero or "low" output. When the input is low the transistor does not conduct, thereby providing near +5 VDC at the output. Additional arrangements are possible if inversion is not desired.

It can function at relatively low control voltages, is capable of switching at rates of hundreds of MHz, can be made extremely small and rugged, is inexpensive, and does not require a heat-producing filament. Initially, discrete transistors were hard-wired into the various circuits. More recently, they have been integrated with other simple elements such as resistors and diodes into special-purpose building blocks—the *integrated circuit chips* or ICs. Figure 6.3 illustrates the outward appearance of a typical chip. The one shown has 14 pins, that is, input/output connections. Others may have as many as 40 or more.

There is a multitude of special-purpose IC chips available to the electronic design engineer. Their variations and complexity are growing at a tremendous rate and much of electronic circuitry is rapidly being converted to their use. Only a few simple elements in various combinations are combined to form most chips. Special shorthand symbols are used to depict their various operations; we discuss several in the following paragraphs. Each symbol represents a combination of solid-state elements, transistors, diodes, resistors, etc., combined to perform the indicated functions. In addition, combinations of logic elements are normally assembled in various configurations in a single chip. The so-called MSI (medium-scale integration) chips may incorporate 50 to 100 individual components per chip. The LSI (large-scale integration) chips contain more than 100.

Figure 6.4 illustrates symbols for common logic elements used in various combinations to form many of the IC chips. Elements 6.4(a) through 6.4(f) are also called *gates*. Figure 6.4(g) represents a simple inverter. Also shown are *logic* or *truth tables*, which list all the possible combinations of inputs and their corresponding outputs. Recall that basic digital operations are based on simple YES/NO, 1/∅, states. For example, the truth table for the AND gate shows that the output is high *only* if the inputs to *both* A and B are high, hence, the *AND rule*:

> For the AND gate, *any* low input will cause a low output; that is, *all* inputs must be high to yield a high output.

In like manner, we can also easily state rules for the other elements. Truth tables are of particular importance to the circuit designer, especially when combinations of circuits increase their complexity.

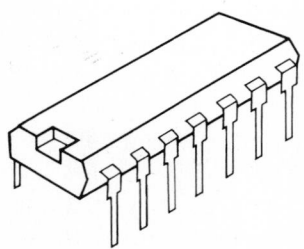

FIGURE 6.3   Outward appearance of a typical 14-pin IC chip. Others may have as few as six pins or as many as 40. This construction is often referred to as a DIP, or "dual-inline-package."

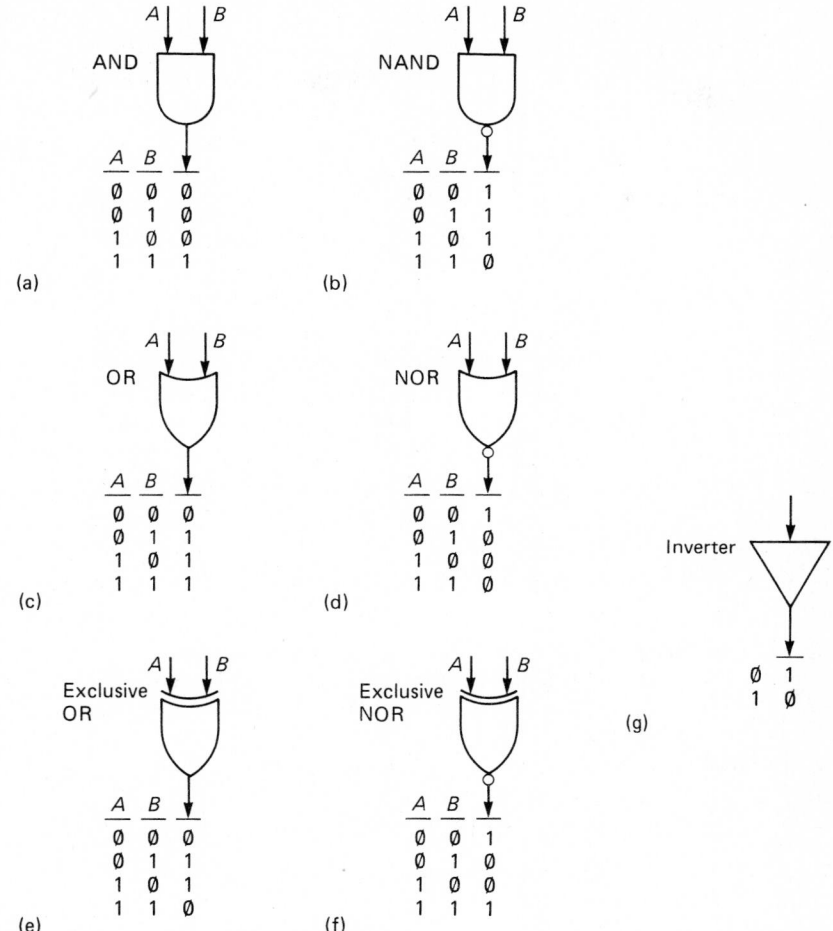

FIGURE 6.4 Symbols for some common digital logic units. Also shown are the respective truth tables for the units.

As a matter of interest, the NAND gate actually contains four transistors, three resistors, and a diode, as shown in Fig. 6.5. Suppose a chain of pulses is applied to input B of the AND gate. We can see that their passage may be controlled by input A. If A is high, the chain will be permitted to pass; if low, the chain will be stopped. From this simple example the origin and significance of the term *gate* is clear.

The various gates may be expanded to provide more than two inputs; see, for example, Fig. 6.6. The IC shown is a three-input NAND gate, for which a zero input level at any one of the input ports permits the passage of pulses from any other port; in other words, all inputs must be high in order for the

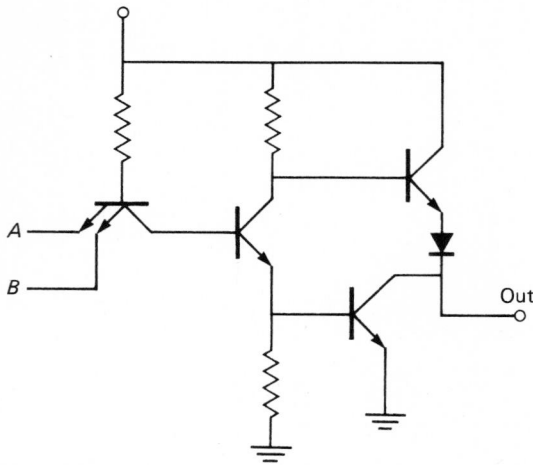

FIGURE 6.5   A schematic showing the internal structure of a NAND gate.

output to be low. With this arrangement, a combination of several control conditions must be met simultaneously to block passage of a signal.

6.4.2 Some Simple Combinations of Logic Elements

The Flip-Flop

Figure 6.7(a) shows two NAND gates connected to form a very useful circuit. As a simple flip-flop, element A is called the SET gate and element B, the RESET gate. Consideration of the individual truth tables, along with their particular interconnections, shows that the following are the only workable conditions:

	S	R	Q	Q′
Condition I	1	1	1	0
Condition II	1	1	0	1
Condition III	0	1	1	0
Condition IV	1	0	0	1

Now suppose that both S and R are initially at logic 1; then either of Conditions I or II may exist, depending on random or programmed preconditions. If either of two outputs can correspond to a given input, the input is referred to as being *bistable*. In some contexts, the circuit is called a *latch*.

Let us momentarily ground input S, i.e., impose logic 0. Condition III, called the SET condition, will result. This is true regardless of whether the

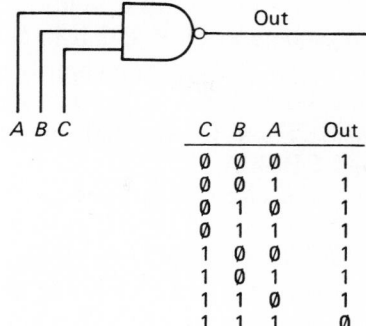

C	B	A	Out
0	0	0	1
0	0	1	1
0	1	0	1
0	1	1	1
1	0	0	1
1	0	1	1
1	1	0	1
1	1	1	0

FIGURE 6.6 NAND gate with three inputs. NAND gates are available with as many as eight inputs permitting 256 input combinations.

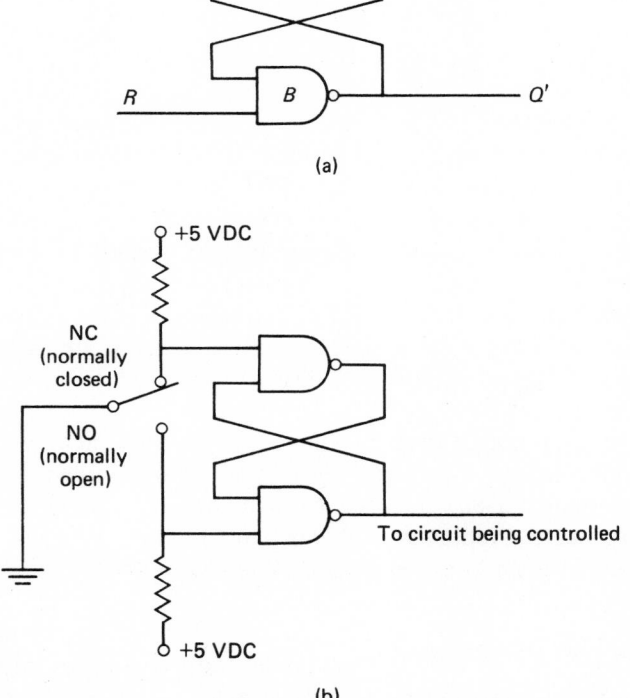

(a)

(b)

FIGURE 6.7 (a) Two NAND gates configured to form a "flip-flop." (b) A switch-debouncer circuit.

circuit is initially in Condition I or II. Return of S to the high state will cause no change in Q or Q': It is *latched*.

Now, if R is momentarily grounded, Condition IV will be instituted, and this state will continue even when R is returned to logic 1. This is called RESET and we see that the outputs are caused to flip and flop between SET and RESET.

The circuit has various important uses. For example, as a latch it may be used to hold (latch) a count in an electronic events counter, then await a RESET input for initiating the next count. The flip-flop is used as a memory cell, capable of holding one bit of information for later use. It also provides the basis for the *switch debouncer*. When an ordinary electrical switch depending on mechanical contacts is closed, numerous contacts are actually made and lost before solid contact is finalized. In a counting circuit, for example, this switch hash cannot be tolerated. By placing a flip-flop or latch in the switch circuit (Fig. 6.7b), we cause the latch to respond to that first momentary contact and then to ignore all that follow, until a RESET signal reinitializes the circuit. These are only several of the uses to which the circuit may be applied; and the particular circuit discussed is only one of a number of different circuits referred to as flip-flops.

6.4.3 IC Families

There are several *families* of integrated chips, each having special characteristics but, in general, all performing essentially the same basic tasks. Common groups are the *resistor–transistor–logic* or RTL group; the *diode–transistor–logic* or DTL group; the *transistor–transistor–logic* or TTL group; and the *complementary–metal–oxide–semiconductor* or CMOS group. In each family the various logic units are combined to perform special functions. For example, the TTL family consists of more than 150 different types of chip. Table 6.1 is a partial list. All have more or less the same outward appearance (see Fig. 6.3), but each is designed to perform a different function. Schematics of several of the TTL family are illustrated in Fig. 6.8. The circuits in Figs. 6.8(a), (b), and (c) are simple enough that the functional performance symbols may be shown. The circuitry of Fig. 6.8(d), however, is so complex (because of the number of elements used) that we have made no attempt to indicate the internal architecture. Application of most of the chips selected for listing in Table 6.1 is covered in later sections of this chapter.

6.4.4 Read-Out Elements

In some situations we may require only simple, single bulbs or lights for an indication or read-out. In other cases we may use combinations of discrete lamps. These may be filament types or, more often, one of the elements discussed below.

TABLE 6.1 A Partial Listing of TTL IC Chips

Type Number	Description
7400	Quad 2-input NAND gate
7404	Hex inverter
7408	Quad 2-input AND gate
7414	Hex Schmidt trigger
7416	Hex driver, inverting
7430	8-input NAND gate
7432	Quad 2-input OR gate
7445	BCD to 1-of-10 decoder driver
7447	BCD to 7-segment decoder driver
7474	Dual D-edge-triggered flip-flop
7475	Quad latch
7483	4-bit full adder
7485	4-bit magnitude comparator
7489	64-bit (16×4) memory
7490	Decade counter
7492	Base-12 counter
74121	Monostable multivibrator
74150	1-of-16 data selector
74154	1-of-16 data distributor
74181	Arithmetic unit (CPU)

Alphanumeric read-out elements normally require one of the following: (a) the cold-cathode nixie-type, (b) the neon type, (c) the liquid-crystal type (LCD), and (d) the light-emitting-diode type (LED). Types (a) and (b) require relatively high voltages not otherwise needed in solid-state circuitry; hence they have been largely superseded. The liquid crystal has a decided advantage in some cases, as, for example, in a digital watch requiring very low power consumption. A disadvantage is the need for proper external illumination. In instrumentation, the LED is undoubtedly the most common of the four. Figure 6.9 shows an arrangement of a typical LED seven-segment digital display. Each segment consists of one or more LED elements and with proper switching supplied by an appropriate IC driver, each of the decimal digits, 0 through 9, can be formed. Quite commonly, the input signal and a 5-V d.c. power source are all that is required for power.

We have presented a smattering of some of the simplest building blocks used to form the more complex IC circuits. Again we state our purpose for this chapter as being to give mechanical engineers a somewhat better understanding of the digital devices that are becoming increasingly important in their measurement systems.

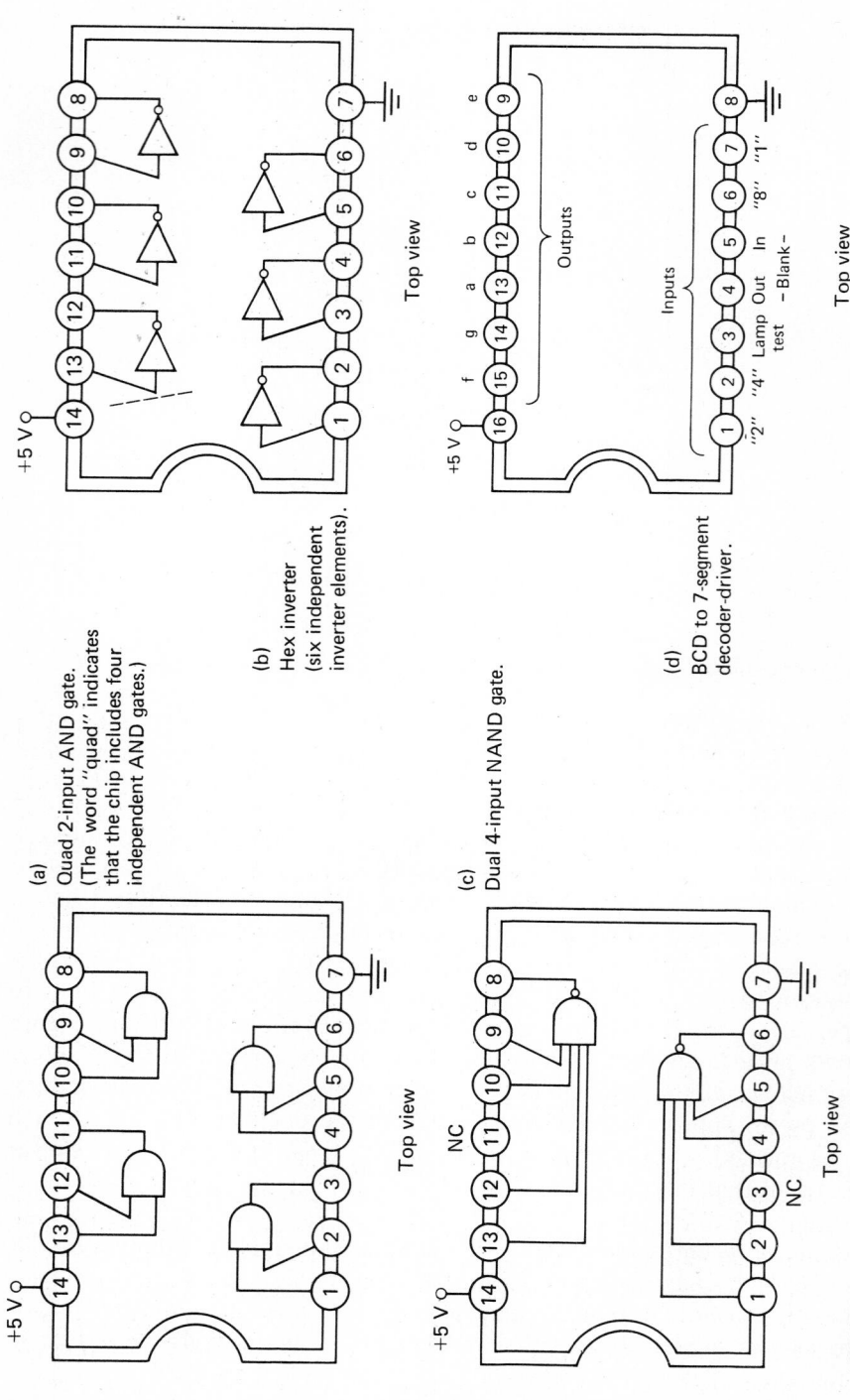

FIGURE 6.8 Diagram showing four typical IC chips. (a) Quad 2-input AND gate. (The word "quad" indicates that the chip contains four independent AND gates). (b) Hex inverter (six independent inverter elements). (c) Dual 4-input NAND gate. (d) BCD (binary coded decimal) to 7-segment decoder-driver.

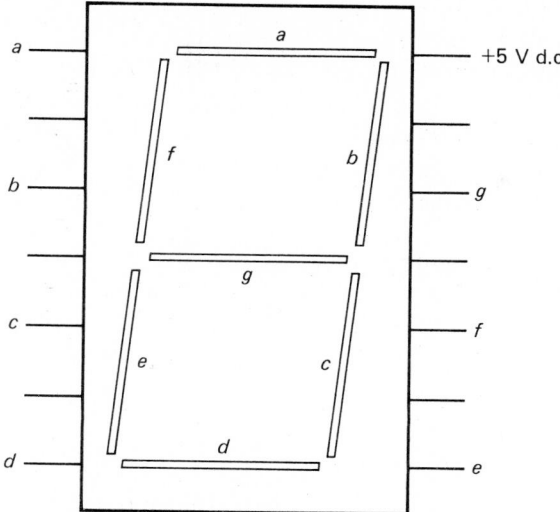

FIGURE 6.9   Typical solid-state numeric display. For example, grounding pin 1(a) through a suitable voltage dropping resistor, lights segment (a).

6.5 NUMBER SYSTEMS

Whether it is in digital or analog form, a measurement signal conveys a magnitude. Magnitudes are expressed in numbers and numbers imply some sort of numbering system or structure. Digital devices with their high–low, yes–no, on–off sequencing suggest the use of a base-2, or binary, system for counting. In this section we will present the essentials of number systems other than decimal that are pertinent to digital operations.

We know that the *position* of each of the digits in a decimal number is important. For example, consider the decimal number 347.25. The "3" is the most significant digit and the "5" is the least significant digit. We know that the number can be expanded to read

$$347.25 = 3 \times 10^2 + 4 \times 10^1 + 7 \times 10^0 + 2 \times 10^{-1} + 5 \times 10^{-2}.$$

It is clear that the various positions of the digits determine the power to which the base ten is raised.

For the binary number, only two different digits are required, a "1" and a "0". The digit "1" may correspond to a "high" condition, say $+5$ V d.c., and the digit "0" to a "low" condition, say 0 V d.c. We have used these designations in an earlier discussion. In the binary system, as in the decimal system, position has meaning. Consider the binary number 11010.01_2. (We add the subscript "2" to make it clear that we are using the binary system.) The first digit "1" is the most significant digit and the last digit "1", the least significant. Each digit is called a *bit* in the sense that it supplies an elemental "bit" of information. Hence, the terms *most significant bit*, or MSB, and *least significant bit*, or LSB, are used. What corresponds to the decimal point in the decimal system is called the *binary point* in the binary system.

As we have observed, in a decimal number each position corresponds to an integral power of 10. By the same token, in a binary number, each position corresponds to an integral power of 2. Whereas the coefficients for the decimal number could be anything between 0 and 9, for the binary system we are limited to $\emptyset$ and 1.

Let's convert the binary number written above to the equivalent decimal number. *Equivalent*, of course, means that the two numbers signify the same true magnitude or quantity (it may be convenient to refer to Table 6.2):

$$11010.01_2$$
$$= 1 \times 2^4 + 1 \times 2^3 + 0 \times 2^2 + 1 \times 2^1 + 0 \times 2^0 + 0 \times 2^{-1} + 1 \times 2^{-2}$$
$$= \quad 16 \quad + \quad 8 \quad + \quad 0 \quad + \quad 2 \quad + \quad 0 \quad + \quad 0 \quad + \quad 1/4$$
$$= 26.25_{10}.$$

We can see that the positional significance of the 0's and 1's lies in the integral powers to which the base (also called the *radix*) is raised. This is true for both the binary and the decimal systems.

Two other systems are commonly used in digital manipulations: the *octal*, or base-8, system; and the *hexidecimal*, or base-16, system. These two systems

TABLE 6.2

n^*	2^n	4^n	8^n	16^n
⋮	⋮	⋮	⋮	⋮
-3	1/8	1/64	1/512	1/4096
-2	1/4	1/16	1/64	1/256
-1	1/2	1/4	1/8	1/16
0	1	1	1	1
1	2	4	8	16
2	4	16	64	256
3	8	64	512	4096
4	16	256	4096	65536
5	32	1024	32768	1048576
6	64	4096	262144	16777216
⋮	⋮	⋮	⋮	⋮

*   *"n" is both the power to which the base is raised and the positional weight.*

have the marked advantage over the decimal system in the ease and convenience of their conversion, by either machine or human, to binary.

For further discussion of number systems, see Appendix C.

6.6 BINARY CODES

In addition to the binary number, which is, of course, limited in magnitude only by the number of positional bits that may be arbitrarily permitted, there are various binary *codes*. At this point we will consider several of them.

Suppose we limit the number of positions to four, i.e., we provide only four on–off switches or their equivalents. We are then limited to the decimal range of 0 to 15 inclusive. The result is what is known as the four-bit *word*, also referred to as a *four-level code*.

A modification of this code is known as *binary-coded decimal* or *BCD*. Although BCD is also a four-bit word, it arbitrarily makes illegal all words greater than 1001_2, or 9_{10}. We see that the BCD code is used because of its convenient relationship to the decimal digits 0 through 9. Table 6.3 lists equivalencies. When the BCD code is used each digit in a decimal number is processed separately as a four-bit sequence (e.g., the decimal number 875_{10} translates to $1000\ 0111\ 0101_2$).

These codes are for the transmission and processing of numeric data. Alphanumeric information must also include provision for the letters of the alphabet and perhaps certain other symbols, such as punctuation marks.

One of the simplest binary codes for transmission of general information (as opposed to numeric data only) is the International Morse Code, which

TABLE 6.3

Decimal Digit	Four-Bit Binary Equivalent	Binary-Coded Decimal Equivalent
0	0000	0000
1	0001	0001
2	0010	0010
3	0011	0011
4	0100	0100
5	0101	0101
6	0110	0110
7	0111	0111
8	1000	1000
9	1001	1001
10	1010	Illegal
11	1011	Illegal
12	1100	Illegal
13	1101	Illegal
14	1110	Illegal
15	1111	Illegal

TABLE 6.4   The American Standard Code for Information Interchange (ASCII)

Binary	Hexadecimal	Character	Binary	Hexadecimal	Character
000 0000	*00*	*NUL*			
			011 1000	38	8
· *Nonprinting control characters*			011 1001	39	9
·			011 1010	3A	:
010 0000	20	Space	011 1011	3B	;
010 0001	21	!			
010 0010	22	"	011 1100	3C	<
010 0011	23	#	011 1101	3D	=
			011 1110	3E	>
010 0100	24	$	011 1111	3F	?
010 0101	25	%			
010 0110	26	&	100 0000	40	@
010 0111	27	'	100 0001	41	A
			100 0010	42	B
010 1000	28	(	100 0011	43	C
010 1001	29	)			
010 1010	2A	*	100 0100	44	D
010 1011	2B	+	100 0101	45	E
			100 0110	46	F
010 1100	2C	,	100 0111	47	G
010 1101	2D	−			
010 1110	2E	.	100 1000	48	H
010 1111	2F	/	100 1001	49	I
			100 1010	4A	J
011 0000	30	0	100 1011	4B	K
011 0001	31	1			
011 0010	32	2	100 1100	4C	L
011 0011	33	3	100 1101	4D	M
			100 1110	4E	N
011 0100	34	4	100 1111	4F	O
011 0101	35	5			
011 0110	36	6			
011 0111	37	7			

uses *pulse-duration modulation* or PDM (also sometimes called pulse-length or pulse-width modulation). The two different pulse widths, the "dot" and the "dash," are used in various combinations to transmit the alphabet, the decimal digits, and certain other special-purpose telegraphic symbols. International Morse Code is an *uneven-length* code in that various time intervals are required for the transmission of the various characters. This code is not important for mechanical measurements.

The *Baudot* or common teletypewriter code is a five-unit, *even-length code*. All characters are formed by a combination of five possible on–off states, each of *uniform* duration. In addition to the five informational intervals, a *start* pulse is required because the idling state is zero logic and the receiving

TABLE 6.4 *(Continued)*

Binary	Hexadecimal	Character	Binary	Hexadecimal	Character
101 0000	50	P	110 1000	68	h
101 0001	51	Q	110 1001	69	i
101 0010	52	R	110 1010	6A	j
101 0011	53	S	110 1011	6B	k
101 0100	54	T	110 1100	6C	l
101 0101	55	U	110 1101	6D	m
101 0110	56	V	110 1110	6E	n
101 0111	57	W	110 1111	6F	o
101 1000	58	X	111 0000	70	p
101 1001	59	Y	111 0001	71	q
101 1010	5A	Z	111 0010	72	r
101 1011	5B	[	111 0011	73	s
101 1100	5C	\	111 0100	74	t
101 1101	5D	]	111 0101	75	u
101 1110	5E	^	111 0110	76	v
101 1111	5F	—	111 0111	77	w
110 0000	60	`	111 1000	78	x
110 0001	61	a	111 1001	79	y
110 0010	62	b	111 1010	7A	z
110 0011	63	c	111 1011	7B	{
110 0100	64	d	111 1100	7C	‖
110 0101	65	e	111 1101	7D	}
110 0110	66	f	111 1110	7E	~
110 0111	67	g	111 1111	7F	Rub Out

machine would otherwise be unable to distinguish between an unimportant idling bit and an information bit for any character that might begin with a zero condition. Also needed is a stop pulse for synchronization. In the traditional teletype machine the pulse sequences are mechanically produced by cam-actuated switch contacts selected by the keys on the keyboard. At the receiving end an ingenious combination of electrical relay and kinematics selects the proper type-bar for actuation.

A popular computer code is known as the *American Standard Code for Information Interchange (ASCII)*. This code is of seven-bit binary form (Table 6.4). Both the upper- and lower-case letters of the English alphabet, plus the decimal digits zero through 9 and certain other control symbols, are included. When writing the binary equivalents of the ASCII code, one generally divides the binary number into two groups of three and four bits each; for example,

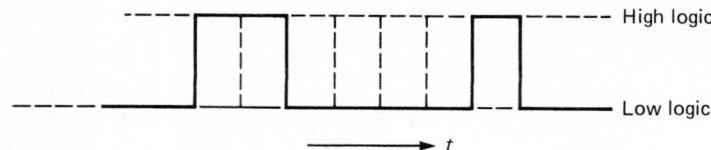

FIGURE 6.10   The ASCII logic sequence for the letter "a."

for the letter "a," the binary equivalent is written 110 0001. The lefthand binary digit is the MSB (most significant bit) and the righthand, the LSB. In processing, the ASCII number for "a" would appear as 1100001. As a function of time it would appear as shown in Fig. 6.10.

The International Morse and the Baudot codes are necessarily of a *serial* type, i.e., the various on/off states occur in sequence, one following another in "bucket-brigade" fashion. If they were transferred by an electrical conductor, only a single transmission circuit would be required. In some cases, an alternative to serial transmission, namely, *parallel* transmission, is used. This means that the bits in a single word are transmitted simultaneously. In its simplest form, this type requires as many transmission circuits as there are code levels, but obviously saves more time. We shall see later that occasionally the one form may be converted into the other. Parallel circuitry is often used within a single instrument or device, whereas serial circuitry is used when distance is important, as, for example, for time-sharing via telephone-interfaced computer circuits.

6.7   SOME SIMPLE DIGITAL CIRCUITRY

6.7.1   Events Counter

Figure 6.11 shows the outward simplicity of one form of digital events counter. Each decade consists of a seven-segment LED display, two IC chips from the TTL family, and a few current-limiting resistors. The 7490 chip is called a *decade counter* (see Table 6.1). It accepts input pulses in serial form through pin 14 and sends as output parallel BCD pulses through pins d, c, b, and a, where d corresponds to the most significant bit and a to the least significant. In addition, this chip provides an output pulse at the *end* of the ninth input pulse. This pulse is available from pin 11 and can be used as the input to the next higher counting decade. We can see that decades may be cascaded easily. As we will note later, this facility obviously also provides a "divide-by-ten" capability.

The BCD outputs from the 7490 chip are fed to a 7447 chip, called a BCD to 7-segment decoder driver (Table 6.1). This chip accepts the parallel BCD input, decodes the input, i.e., converts it to a unit decimal output and switches

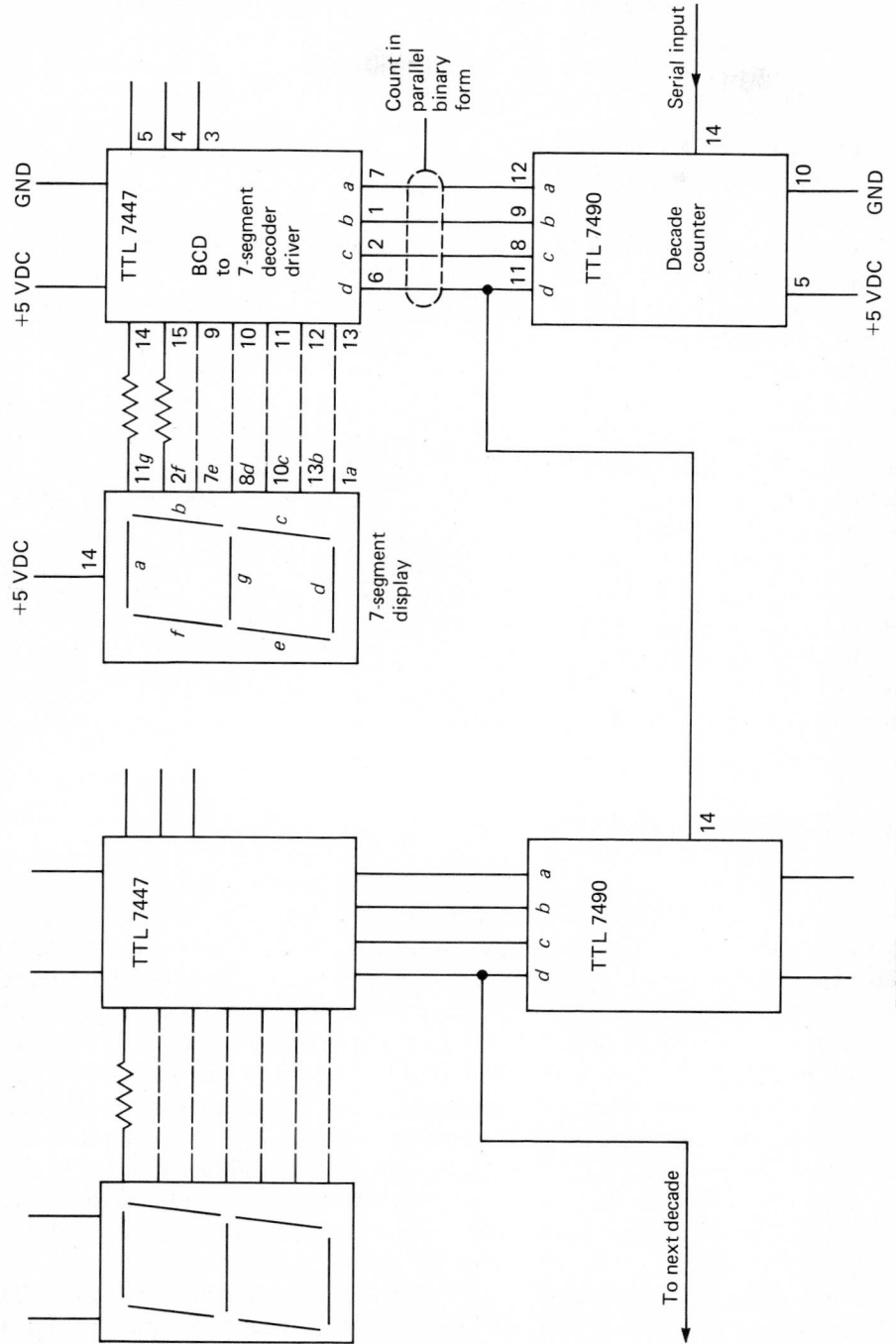

FIGURE 6.11 Circuit schematic for a simple digital events counter.

191

on (grounds) the appropriate segments in the 7-segment read-out, thereby displaying the required decimal digit. This simple circuit is capable of counting at rates of up to about 100 kHz. In addition to this function, IC 7447 also provides control terminals 3, 4, and 5 that may be used for

1. resetting the read-out to zero;
2. blanking unused leading zeros, e.g., making provision so that a five-decade display of the number 25, for instance, would not show as 00025, but simply as 25, with the unnecessary zeros blanked;
3. provisions for displaying appropriate decimal points.

6.7.2 Gating

Suppose the counter circuit shown in Fig. 6.11 is to be used to count a sample of pulses stemming from a continuing sequence of pulses. Can we not use a simple mechanical switch to *gate* the input line? Probably not directly! When the contacts of the mechanical switch (or relay) are closed, there exists a period of indecision. The contacts touch, break, touch again, etc., many times before a final and complete contact is established. This is the source of *switch hash*, which shows on the screen of a cathode-ray oscilloscope. The counter is unable to distinguish between the "good guys" and the "bad guys" and the speed of the counter is sufficient to count them all. Under such circumstances it is necessary to use the *debouncing circuitry* (Section 6.4.2) in the input. This recognizes the first contact, latches, and then ignores the succeeding contacts.

6.7.3 Frequency Meter

Electronic switching or gating would probably be used to switch the counting circuit on and off. Recall the AND gate (see Fig. 6.4). The input pulses may be connected to input A and a control input to B. There will be an ouput only when both are high. This provides an essential part of a digital *frequency meter*. Suppose we introduce an unknown frequency at A and control B with a square-wave oscillator (Fig. 6.12). While both inputs are high, the counter will count. When B is low, counting will stop. Obviously the accuracy of the count will be dependent on the accuracy of the gated time interval. The oscillator will probably be crystal-controlled, and crystals oscillate at relatively high rates. For instance, the fundamental oscillator might have a frequency of 5 megahertz. The period of 1/10 microsecond would certainly be too short for gating most mechanical inputs. Recall, however, that we already have discussed a divide-by-ten IC, the IC 7490 used in the simple counter. By cascading seven divide-by-ten ICs we can reduce the fundamental period to two seconds, one second of which will be high and one second low. By using an AND gate as shown in Fig. 6.12 we can sample one second's worth of the

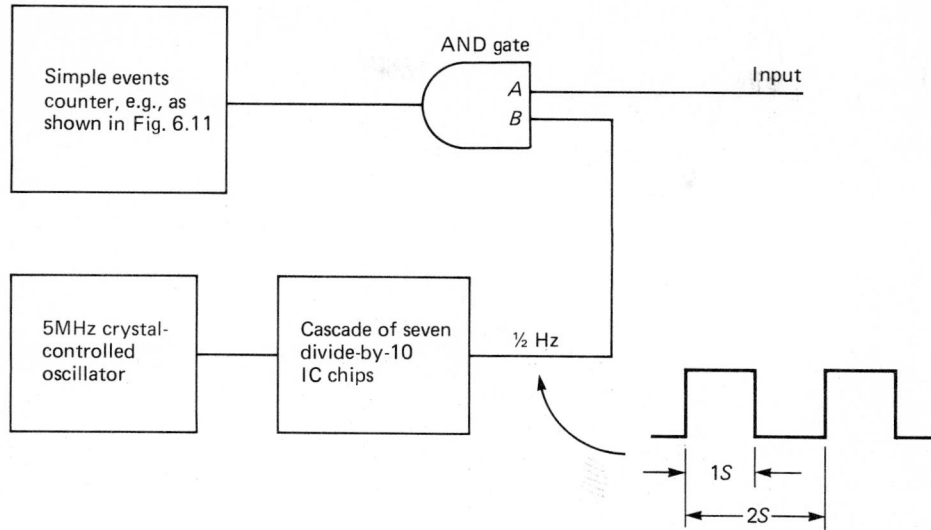

FIGURE 6.12   Circuit schematic for a simple frequency meter.

input, hence its frequency in hertz. Obviously, with the cascade of divide-by-ten chips we can use panel-controlled switches for different gating times by simply tapping the cascade at other points in the chain.

In the example above we have oversimplified to an extent. We have not provided for returning to zero between samplings, and we may perhaps obtain controlled single-pulse gating intervals by better means, e.g., through use of a monostable multivibrator. As we stated earlier in this chapter, our purpose, however, is to give some feel for digital techniques to the mechanical engineer, rather than to cover the multitude of possibilities in depth.

6.7.4 Wave Shaping

Digital logic circuits prefer instant toggling from low to high and back again. Suppose we wish to feed the simple counter we described above with a sine wave, or some other cyclic waveform. If the level is sufficient, our counter may work, but then again it might not. We can convert the sine wave to a pulsed signal by using a *Schmidt trigger* (see TTL 7414 in Table 6.1, for instance). It accepts a gradually rising (or falling) input, but does not become conducting until its "trigger level" is reached. It then becomes fully conducting (or nonconducting on the down side of the cycle). We are therefore able to reshape the input into a series of nearly true square-wave pulses, much preferred by the common IC. If the input is complex, we can use an attenuator to reduce the peaks in relation to the trigger level. In this case the time characteristic of the waveform would have much to do with our success or lack thereof.

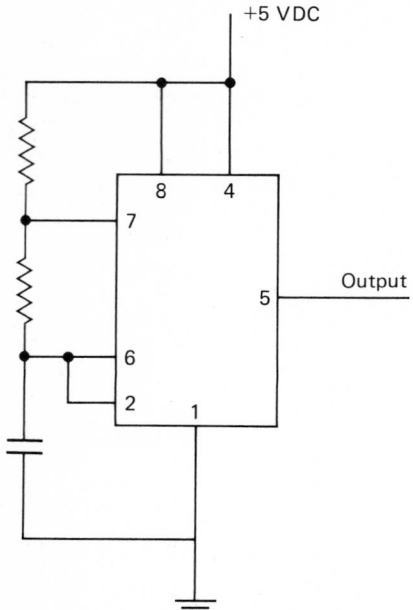

+5 VDC

Output

FIGURE 6.13   Example of "special" IC chips: a 555 astable/monostable multivibrator or oscillator.

6.7.5   An IC Oscillator or Multivibrator

Figure 6.13 illustrates an interesting IC oscillator. The single chip contains 23 transistors, 15 resistors, and 2 diodes. The package is about half the size of a common postage stamp, has eight terminals, and costs less than a package of cigarettes. When configured with two or three external resistors and a capacitor, it becomes capable of either monostable or astable oscillation. When in astable oscillation it is capable of covering a frequency range of from 0.1 Hz to over 100 kHz, with square-wave output. With additional outboard circuit elements it is capable of producing triangular and linear ramp waveforms. The IC oscillator is an example of the wide versatility of a single special-purpose integrated circuit.

6.7.6   Multiplexing and Demultiplexing

Figure 6.14(a) illustrates an IC chip called a *multiplexer*, or a 1-of-16 data selector (see TTL 74150, Table 6.1). In mechanical terms it may be considered a selectable commutator; quite simply, it is similar to a single-pole, 16-position switch (Fig. 6.14b). The particular input (of up to 16) that is permitted to pass is determined by the binary number inserted at the *d, c, b,* and *a* ports, where *d* is the MSB and *a* the LSB.

The demultiplexer, or 1-of-16 data distributor, is similar but with reversed action (see TTL 74154, Table 6.1). It accepts a digital signal through its one

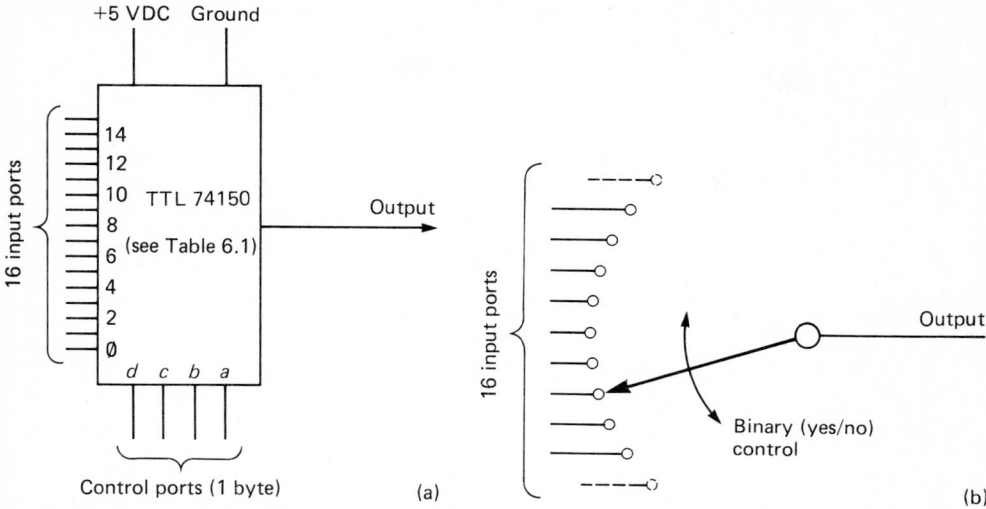

FIGURE 6.14 (a) The TTL 74150 multiplexer or 1 of 16 selector. Each of the 16 possible logic combinations of the *dcba* control port is employed to select a corresponding signal input for connection to the output. (b) Illustration of a nearly equivalent mechanical switching arrangement. A difference, however, lies in the fact that the mechanical device must switch through the sequence in order, whereas this is not true for the multiplexer.

input and then routes it to the particular output selected by the binary value at the control ports.

Why concern ourselves with multiplexers and demultiplexers? In many cases continuous monitoring or recording of a given data source is not necessary: Periodic sampling will suffice. We can see that by sequencing the binary control through 0 to 15, we can consecutively connect 16 different inputs to a given read-out/recording/computing system. This is the economical thing to do in many cases.

Multiplexing may also be used, in certain instances, within the circuitry of a single instrument. Recall the events counter we discussed in Section 6.7.1. Each decade required a 7-segment decoder driver plus 7 current-limiting resistors. More sophisticated counter circuitry uses a multiplexer–demultiplexer combination arranged so that each read-out element is sequentially connected to a single driver–resistor combination. By time-sharing in this manner we can reduce the number of circuit elements and realize quite a saving in cost. The sequencing rate is sufficiently high that the read-out appears to be continuously illuminated.

Data processing may take place at quite some distance from the data source, e.g., in a large industrial complex such as a refinery or power plant. By using multiplexer–demultiplexer combinations, we may also use single, rather than separate, circuits to connect the two positions (Fig. 6.15). We hasten to add that this may not be quite the case because it would also be necessary to synchronize our binary control circuits at the two locations. A

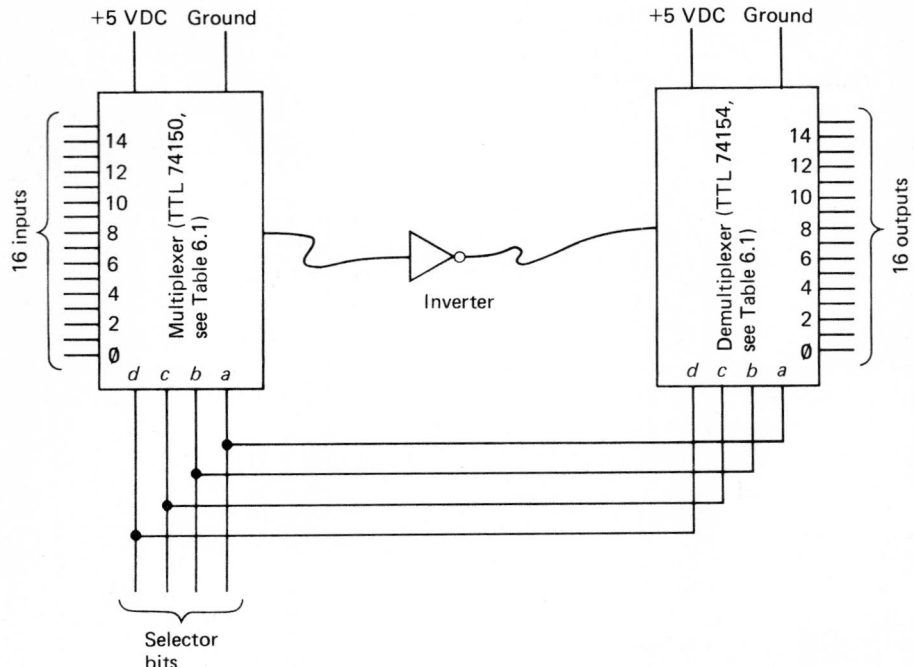

FIGURE 6.15   A multiplexer–demultiplexer circuit.

simple solution is to run four additional wires connecting ports *d, c, b,* and *a.* Thus we would have five circuits instead of sixteen (for the particular combination cited).

There is, however, another possibility through use of more sophisticated ICs. The Universal Asynchronous Receiver/Transmitter (UART) contains what amounts to a multiplexer and a demultiplexer—actually a set of two each—on a single chip. It is capable of converting serial to parallel or parallel to serial data. The word "asynchronous" indicates that the operation need not be synchronized. This is not quite true. What is meant is that the inputs and outputs need not be *perfectly* synchronized: Approximate synchronization, say ±5%, is sufficient. This permits the use of separate control oscillators or "clocks" at the transmitting and receiving ends, whose frequencies are quite close, but not necessarily exactly the same. In this case, directly connected synchronizing circuits between the two locations are not necessary.

6.8 THE DIGITAL COMPUTER AS A MEASUREMENTS SYSTEM TOOL

Small computers, either dedicated or general-purpose, are a natural adjunct to a measurements system. They may be used to simply monitor and record one or more measurands, or they may serve as an interactive part of a more comprehensive measurements–control system.

To connect common measurement circuitry to a computer requires considerably more understanding of the functioning of both systems than it would first appear. Most measurands originate as analog-type signals; however, the computer recognizes only digital quantities. As a result, often the first requirement is to change the language by means of an analog-to-digital converter (ADC). In addition, data from circuitry external to the computer must be fed to the computer in a form and order that the computer is prepared to accept. The computer's connections to the outside (its ports) are generally bidirectional. That is, they may either accept or output data; but this can only be done in a well-defined and orderly manner. The computer must be *told* through software whether a particular port is to handle incoming or outgoing information. Software assignment of port functions is often called *configuring the ports*. Single lines may be all that are required for handling simple limit-switch/warning-light information, but multiple lines may be necessary for processing analog-converted inputs. In addition, input/output may be handled in either serial or parallel form.

In the next few sections we provide an introduction to the use of computers, specifically microcomputers, for mechanical measurements. Since the subject is so broad we limit our discussion to the basic requirements.

6.9 DATA PROCESSORS, COMPUTERS, MICROCOMPUTERS: THE COMPUTER HIERARCHY

To some degree the term "computer" is misused. In its strictest sense, the word restricts the device to arithmetical manipulations. A more appropriate term is *data processor*. However, because of common usage, we will use the two terms interchangeably.

Consider the following:

Microprocessor: A single chip using digital methods to manipulate numerical data. To be practical the unit requires the services of supporting ICs.

Data processor: A microprocessor-based system of memory, input–output devices, some form of resident operating program, power supply, etc., all tied together by buses, thus forming a system for gathering, sorting, rearranging, and analyzing data, including storage and/or printout.

Logic elements represent the most basic type of computer. The elements may be electromechanical or one or more of the various basic integrated circuits. An over-voltage relay is a simple example. It is set to some maximum voltage that, if exceeded, initiates an action—a switch opening accompanied, perhaps, by a latching. An input is thereby permitted to pass only under a certain set of conditions, i.e., provided a voltage is not too great. An op-amp voltage comparator (Section 5.17.2, Example E7) is another simple device whose output is determined on the basis of relative input values. These examples are mentioned simply to describe the least complex data processing.

The *programmable calculator* is intended for number manipulation. It is limited in both the number of steps that may be programmed and the speed with which it operates. In its common form it is constructed to make no more than the most elementary decisions. Ordinarily its programs are volatile (they are lost when power is removed); or it may possess magnetic card storage.

The next step in the hierarchy of data processing is the *microcomputer* or microdata processor. It has the ability to make decisions, to control outputs on the basis of inputs, and to serve, within limits, as a data processor. It is capable of manipulating memories of several thousand words. Its most common form is based on an 8-bit word size, although some use 4-bits and, more recently, some have been introduced with 16-bit capabilities. With proper peripherals, the microcomputer can handle higher languages. The heart of the microcomputer is the LSI (large-scale-integration) IC chip, the *microprocessor*.

The microcomputer may be either *general-purpose* or *dedicated*. The latter is designed and programmed for a specific application such as controlling a solar heating system or an automobile fuel–ignition system. Costs may range from as low as $100 for a simple dedicated type to as much as $15,000 (depending on the array of its peripheral devices).

The *minicomputer* is one step above the microcomputer. It can handle as many as a million 16-bit words and costs from $10,000 up. In large applications such as those required by a chemical processing plant, the minicomputer might very well be served by one or more microcomputers, and, in turn, the minicomputer would feed information to a large-scale computer for processing beyond the minicomputer's capability. The large general-purpose computer, for the most part, has capabilities beyond the direct requirements of mechanical measurement data acquisition and processing and is mentioned here merely to complete our description of the hierarchy. We see, of course, that an initial problem lies in the selection of the proper level of computer required to do a specific job.

We limit the following discussion to the use of microcomputers. Microcomputers are based on microprocessors, which, in turn, must have the support of a family of LSI chips. There are a number of microprocessor families available: the 8080 family of Intel Corporation, the 6800 family of Motorola, the Z80 family of Zilog, the 6502 family of MOS Technology, and others. In general, each system performs similarly; however, in detail, each system uses its own particular set of operational codes. In the following sections, as we refer to specifics, we will use the Motorola 6800 system as our example.

6.10 THE MICROPROCESSOR

As we stated earlier, the heart of the microcomputer is the LSI-IC chip, the *central* processing unit (CPU), or *microprocessor* unit (MPU). Basically, it serves as the control center for directing the flow of digitized information. It is more than a traffic controller for it not only provides the organizational plan for the flow of elemental bits of information, it also assigns the pathways, temporary "parking" spaces, and stop–go gating, and can perform a limited manipulation of the traffic. It accepts inputs in digital form, either data or command instructions, and routes them to predetermined (programmed) destinations over buses (pathways) to displays, memories, controllable devices, etc. Sources of the data or commands may be external memories, keyboards, transducers, and so on.

Figure 6.16 is a highly simplified schematic diagram of the external connections and some of the internal features of one particular CPU, the Motorola 6800. The diagram shows the primary buses into and out of the processor plus some essential internal devices. To be functionally useful, the system requires additional supporting circuitry external to the CPU, including interfacing devices sometimes referred to as buffers, input/output (I/O) facilities, synchronizing clocks, etc. When combined with sufficient peripherals (devices external to the CPU), the combination becomes a microcomputer.

The Motorola 6800 MPU is a single LSI-IC chip housed in a dual in-line package (DIP) similar to, but larger than, the one shown in Fig. 6.3. The dimensions, exclusive of the pins that provide electrical connections, are about $\frac{1}{4} \times \frac{3}{4} \times 2$ inches. The power requirement for the MPU alone is 5 VDC at from 0.6 to 1.2 watts.

The figure shows the following:

1. An *address bus* consisting of sixteen parallel lines for accessing (connecting to) $2^{16} = FFFF_{16} = 65,536_{10}$ different memory locations. The actual number available is, of course, dependent on what may be provided by supporting hardware.

2. A *data bus* consisting of eight bidirectional lines for simultaneously handling eight bits (one byte) of data. This bus is a two-way street, the direction of flow being controlled by gating (Section 6.7.2). Eight bits provide for $2^8 = FF_{16} = 256_{10}$ combinations.

3. Various *control and decode lines*. Bus synchronization, closely akin to multiplexing–demultiplexing (Section 6.7.6), is controlled through use of two external clock signals. Additional lines are shown, their titles in many cases providing a clue to their uses.

Figure 6.16 also shows some of the internal structure of the 6800 CPU. Various *registers* are used. These may be considered as *temporary* storage bins or momentary "parking" locations for data, instructions, or addresses as they are being shunted from one location to another. Essentially, all data and instructions must pass through at least one of the accumulators, *A* or *B*, each having a one byte (eight-bit) handling capability. Primarily for providing manipulation of two-byte (sixteen-bit) addresses, the *index register* (IR), *program counter* (PC), and *stack pointer* (SP) are added.

As illustrated in Fig. 6.16, the *stack* consists of the registers as shown. Their contents are stored in contiguous addresses, the purpose of the stack

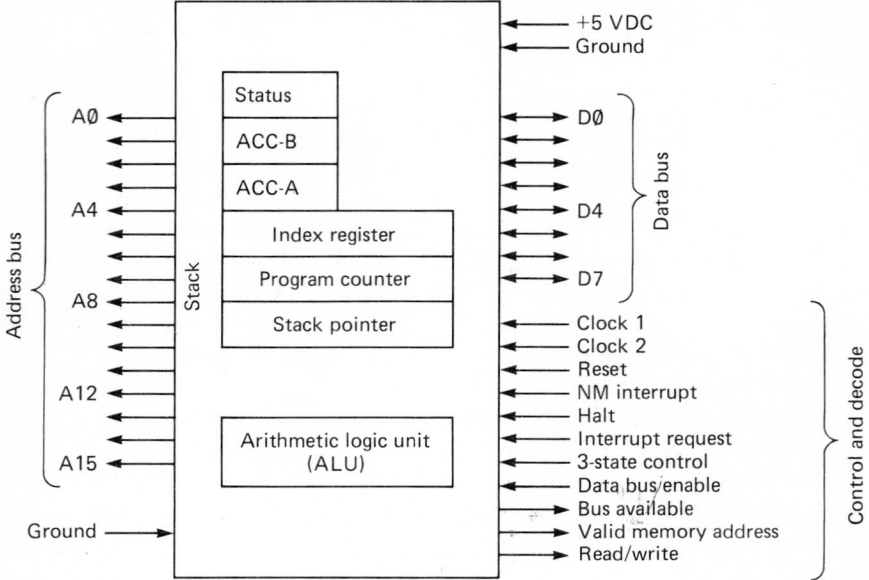

FIGURE 6.16   Simplified schematic of the Motorola 6800 microprocessor.

pointer being to keep track of where the stack information is stored in the external random access memory (RAM). The *program counter* controls the sequencing of any program steps, including the starting point, and the *index register*, in addition to other functions, provides a channel through which two-byte addresses may be handled in a program. The contents of the registers are always available on command.

The arithmetic logic unit (ALU) has a relatively limited capability of manipulating numbers. It can add one byte to another or determine their difference, or it can perform several logic functions, such as AND, OR, and EOR (Section 6.4.1). To handle data in magnitudes requiring several bytes, the add and subtract functions of the ALU may involve carry-overs (for addition) or borrows (for subtraction). It is the responsibility of the status register (SR) (also called the condition code register) to monitor such requirements for possible further program use. *Flags* (primary data bits) in the status register are either set (made equal to 1) or not set (made equal to 0), depending on predetermined conditions. If an addition results in a carry-over from one byte to the next byte, a bit momentarily indicating that fact, stored in the status register, will be added to the byte of the next higher order. Or, if the operation results in a zero, a zero flag in the SR may be used to trigger the decision to branch (or not to branch) to some other point in a program. These are only two of a number of functions of the status register. It is quite powerful and its full importance cannot be covered in a limited summary such as ours.

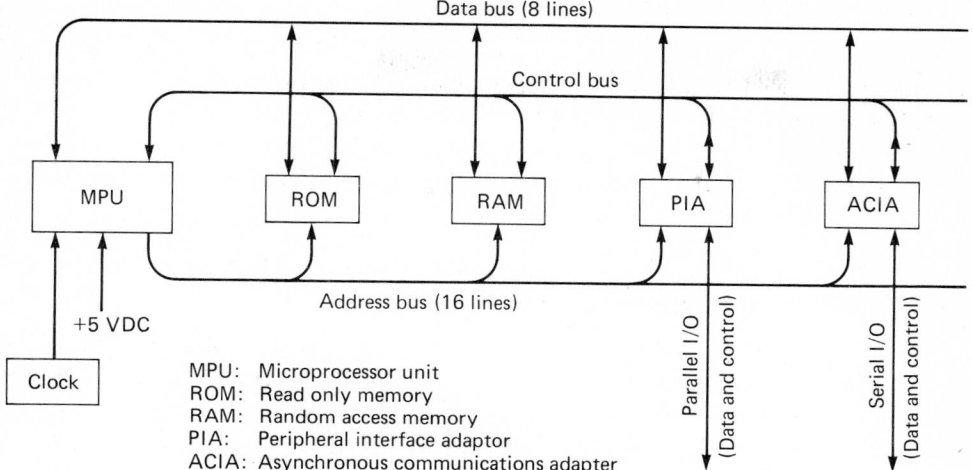

FIGURE 6.17   The essential parts of a microcomputer.

6.11 THE MICROCOMPUTER

As we have stated several times, a microprocessor must be surrounded by a number of servants before it can claim to be a microcomputer. Figure 6.17 is a schematic of the Motorola 6800 system. In addition to the MPU, some combination of the following peripherals is required.

6.11.1 Read Only Memory (ROM)

The schematic shows a single ROM; there might be others. ROM contains what is called the *monitor* or the *executor*. The term executor is particularly apt, because therein are contained the microcomputer's operational orders in the form of various subroutines required for organizing the system and ensuring proper operation. Examples of such subroutines are:

1. Address building;
2. Interrupt sequencing;
3. Memory examine and exchange;
4. Power-up sequence;
5. Code interpretation (e.g., operational instructions, provision for outputting ASCII (Section 6.6) when required);
6. PIA input/output (see Section 6.11.3).

The complete program for a dedicated computer (one assigned a single task only) would also be contained in ROM.

6.11.2 Random Access Memory (RAM)

RAM is the "bank" that is used for temporary deposits and withdrawals of data or information required for the establishment of programs. The program itself may be held in either ROM or RAM. Should the program require modification from time to time, it would require random access, hence RAM. In both RAM and ROM the data or operational instructions are held in the form of single eight-bit bytes.

6.11.3 Peripheral Interface Adapter (PIA)

The PIA provides one form of bridge between the computer and the outside. It handles data in *parallel* fashion in that all eight bits of each byte of information or data are processed simultaneously. It is obvious, then, that eight separate lines into and out of the PIA are required.

Figure 6.18 shows a simplified schematic of the Motorola 6820 PIA. Its operation is actually rather complex. The device provides two separate sections, each serving a *primary* eight-bit port. The in/out buses, designated A and B, with lines PA0 to PA7 and PB0 to PB7, are shown on the right side of the diagram. *Each* separate line in each port can be made to serve as single input or output lines. Any combination of input/output may be had, as required. For example:

1. Lines PA0, PA1, and PA5 could be selected as inputs for receiving information from outside the computer and the remaining lines used (or not) as output lines, or

2. All A-lines could be made outputs and all B-lines inputs, or

3. Any other combination.

Software assignment of the basic line functions is called *configuring*. At appropriate locations in the operating program, the in–out lines must be configured. This leads to two basic and different in–out requirements, as follows:

1. Many situations simply require the handling of limit signals. For example, the input may be simply "yes, a certain event has occurred," or "no, it has not." The two conditions can be signified by a binary 1 for the yes and a binary 0 for the no. In response, through appropriate program manipulation, the output may be simply to trip a relay, light a warning lamp, sound a siren, or shut down the entire plant. In these cases, only *single* input–output lines are required. The ins and outs need not be paired. There can be many inputs, all used to trigger a single output. In an automobile, overheating at any of a number of locations, under-pressure in oil systems, a hood unlatch, etc., could all be used to trigger either a warning lamp, an audible sound, or perhaps an ignition shutoff.

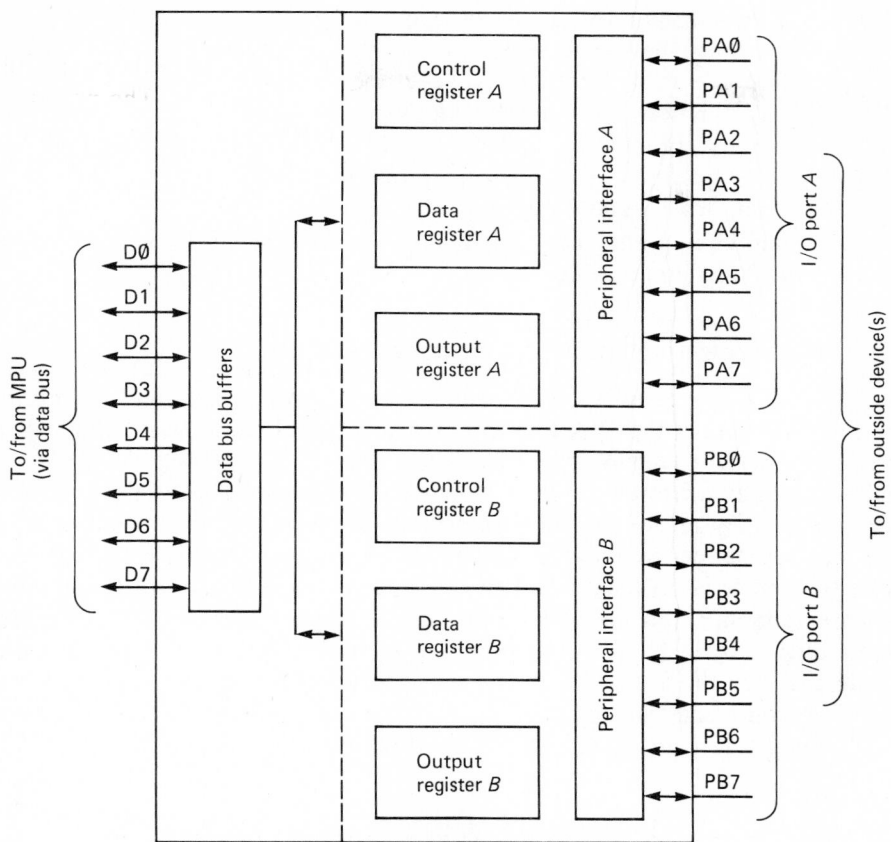

FIGURE 6.18   Schematic diagram of a peripheral interface adapter. Not shown are the input–output control terminals or power connections.

2. On the other hand, the input may stem from an analog quantity from which the application requires the monitoring, sorting, or printout of the input data. In this case a number of lines, the number determined by the desired *resolution*, are required. For example, an analog-to-digital converter (Section 6.12) might provide full eight-bit bytes of information. Then the digital equivalents of the analog input could vary over a range from $00_{16} = 00_{10}$ to a maximum of $FF_{16} = 256_{10}$. This would permit a resolution of 1 in 255_{10} (often rounded to 250_{10}) or 0.4%. We see that in this case the entire primary port, say port *A*, would be absorbed in handling the single data source. Likewise, an eight-bit *output* would require a second full primary port, say port *B*. It should be clear that should a lesser resolution be satisfactory, then fewer data lines may be used. For example, four lines would provide a resolution of 1 in 15, or about 7%.

Programming requirements to configure the lines is beyond the scope of this book and must be left to reference material (see especially, [1]). Suffice it to say that the data direction register and the control register may be addressed through software, and through proper program manipulation, configuring can be accomplished. In fact, should it be desired, a given line, say PA8, could accept *inputs* for *part* of a program reconfigured by software to provide outputs for an additional part of a program.

Most microcomputers can accommodate multiple PIAs; hence a wide range of flexibility is possible.

6.11.4 Asynchronous Interface Adapter (ASCIA)

The ASCIA is a second type of connection, or bridge, into and out of the computer. Whereas the PIA handles data in parallel form, the ASCIA does so serially. Serial transmission of digital information is generally used between such devices as a computer and keyboards, video displays, printers, and the like. Particularly in the case of printers and keyboards, the time required of each mechanical operation is so much greater than that required by the computer that there is no need for speed of transmission. Serial handling is also used for long-line transmission where cost of multiple parallel lines becomes prohibitive. Often a UART (Section 6.7.6) is used to convert from the parallel format used by the computer to the serial format for output.

We recommend that the reader consult the suggested readings at the end of the chapter for details on ASCIA performance and configuring.

6.12 ANALOG-TO-DIGITAL (A/D) AND DIGITAL-TO-ANALOG (D/A) CONVERSION

As we discussed in Section 6.3, certain measurands originate in digital form. Most mechanical inputs, however, exist in analog form. Hence it becomes necessary that before digital processing can be accomplished, there must be an analog-to-digital conversion. In like manner, there are occasions in which the reverse conversion must be performed; that is, the computer's digital output must be converted to analog form for use by other devices.

6.12.1 A Digital-to-Analog Converter

For reasons that will become apparent later, we shall consider D/A conversion first. Referring to Fig. 6.19, we see that four basic factors are involved, as follows:

1. A stable voltage reference (say, 2.55 V d.c.).

2. A ladder arrangement of resistors (note the geometric progression of their values. Note also that their sum is 255R, in ohms).

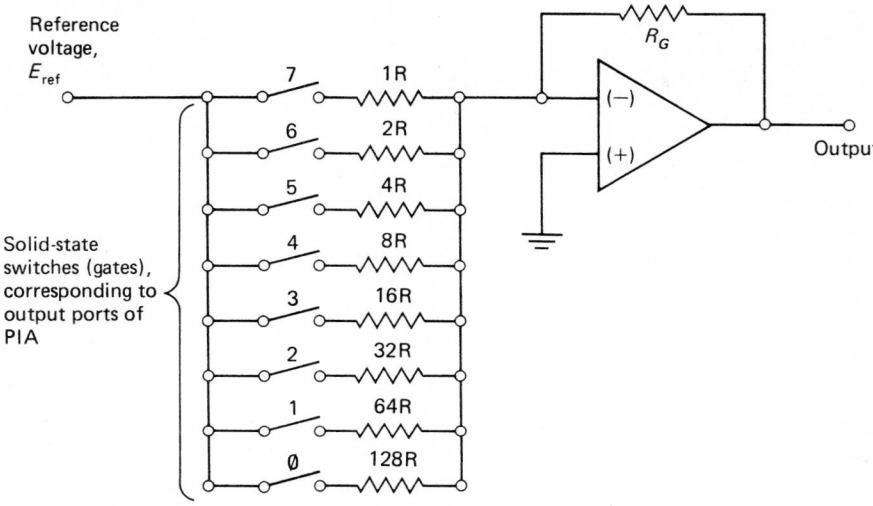

FIGURE 6.19   A simple DAC (digital-to-analog converter).

3. A series of switches. Whereas simple mechanical switches are indicated, in reality these are solid-state gates [e.g., simple AND ICs (Section 6.4.1)]. Since they are eight in number and can be actuated by TTL inputs, their operation may be controlled by the respective bits contained in a single byte of data.

4. Op-amp (Section 5.17) output circuitry, with R_g the gain control resistor selected to *scale* the output, let us say, to a maximum of 2.55 VDC.

When a switch is closed, that particular circuit contributes a current input to the op amp in proportion to its positional number. Switch number 7 corresponds to the most significant bit, b_7, and switch number 0 corresponds to the least significant bit, b_0, etc. In addition, the currents add; thus if switches 1, 6, and 7 are closed, the op-amp input, hence output, becomes proportional to $0110\ 0001_2\ (= 61_{16} = 97_{10})$, etc. The gain of the op amp is scaled to provide the appropriate analog output values.

The above example is only one of several approaches to D/A conversion (see the Suggested Readings).

6.12.2 An Analog-to-Digital Converter

An A/D converter may be created by making a simple addition to the D/A converter and modifying the operating program. As shown in Fig. 6.20, an IC voltage comparator (Section 5.17.2, Example E7) has been added. The resistor ladder is switched by the computer as before, except that this time the switching is in sequentially increasing steps beginning at 00_{16}. This, of

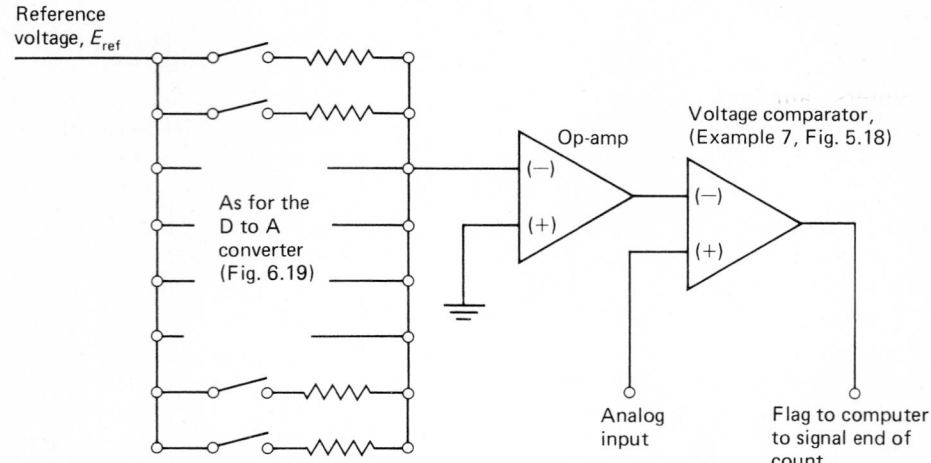

FIGURE 6.20   A simple ADC (analog-to-digital converter).

course, means that increasing values of voltage steps are applied to the $(-)$ input of the op amp. The analog input* is connected to one side of the comparator and the output from the op amp is fed to the other side. As the op-amp output steps sequentially upward from 00_{16} toward FF_{16} $(= 255_{10})$, it eventually reaches the value of the analog input, at which point the state of the comparator changes (either from 0 to 1 or from 1 to 0, depending on the arrangement). This change in state is fed back to the computer, telling it to stop sequencing and to note the number of steps required to reach equality. As with the D/A converter, this number corresponds to the voltage output of the op amp and, with proper scaling, equals the analog voltage input. The computer would then use, store, and/or print out the digital value as required, then reset and repeat the sequence. All of this takes place within microseconds.

As described, the time for sequencing is variable. In one trip the analog input might be low, requiring a small number of steps to reach equality; in the next it could be high, requiring a large number of steps. A somewhat more involved software program begins by comparing the analog input with the midvalue of the reference voltage, then, depending on the comparator output, repeatedly halving the remaining ranges until the value of the analog input is matched. In this case, seven steps are required and the sampling time for each sequence is kept constant.

In practice, the circuit elements shown in Figs. 6.19 and 6.20 are all integrated into single IC chips.

---

* Not shown in Fig. 6.20 is the requirement to properly scale the analog voltage input to match the reference voltage range. In many cases, the analog input signal would be well below the operating voltage of the voltage comparator. The input would, therefore, have to be increased by amplification and the final computer read-out properly scaled to reflect the required change.

6.13 BUSES

If designed to be compatible, black boxes such as power supplies, voltmeters, counters, amplifiers, computers, and the like may be connected to form a *measurements system*. The system may be tailored for specific measurement or control duties and programmed to provide near-automatic functioning. To assemble such a system requires the use of *buses*, the cabling over which the devices communicate. Basically, the buses must provide (a) for data and/or command transfer, plus (b) whatever communication or synchronization for proper functioning is required. The latter requirement is commonly referred to as *handshaking* between the units.

A given device may be a transmitter (talker), a receiver (listener), a controller, or any combination of the three. In the first case, the device is a source of information; in the second, it is a receptor; and in the third, it outputs control signals. Quite often, data lines are bidirectional; that is, information may pass in either direction over the same line. Therefore, a sequencing or synchronization of the line assignments is mandatory, and that is the handshaking function.

Handshaking is a complex matter, to say the least. Certain handshaking actions are dependent on bit level—i.e., either HIGH or LOW—whereas others are determined by the transienting *direction*, either HIGH-to-LOW or vice versa. And all takes place at a rate of microseconds.

Various bus configurations have been "standardized," only two of which, the RS-232C and IEEE 488-1975, will be briefly considered at this point.

The *RS-232C* is used for transfer of *bit-serial* data and specifies a maximum of 25 separate lines, 10 of which are seldom used. It is widely used to transmit digital data over telephone lines, between printers, keyboards, and CRT terminals. In its simplest application, the RS-232C may consist of the following:

1. TRANSMIT DATA (output from A)*;
2. RECEIVE DATA (input to A);
3. SIGNAL GROUND;
4. CARRIER DETECT (synchronous input to A); and
5. DEVICE READY (synchronous output from A).

The IEEE 488-1975 bus is sometimes refered to as an *eight-bit parallel, character-serial* bus. This means that it simultaneously transfers the eight bits of a single character or byte of information, with the bytes (usually ASCII-coded) being transmitted in serial fashion. Obviously, the first requirement is eight separate data lines. In addition, the 488-1975 bus provides eight additional control lines, making a total of sixteen as shown in Fig. 6.21. Some hint of the complexity of the bus application may be inferred from the fact that to state the present standard requires a booklet of eighty pages [2].

---

* In general, at least two devices, say A and B, are assumed.

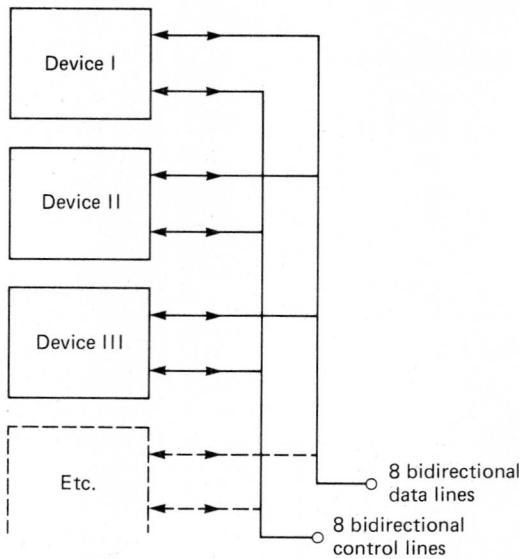

FIGURE 6.21   Simplified schematic of the IEEE-488-1975 bus. Devices I, II, III, and so on may be counters, signal generators, or voltmeters.

More and more commercially available devices are provided with bus connections. Although devices made by the same company are compatible, devices from different sources may not be. That buses are "standardized" does not always mean that such devices will work together. Bits are not always assigned to data lines in a consistent manner, control signals may or may not be similar, some systems may be ASCII-coded and others not, etc. A commercial system with a growing following is the Hewlett Packard HP-IB bus configuration, where IB stands for "interface bus."

It is clear from this brief discussion that system assembly may follow either of two directions: (1) Compatible commercial units may be used and simply plugged together with little or no thought about detailed bus operations, or (2) systems may be "home-brewed" for the particular application. For the former it is necessary only that the user ensure that the devices are truly compatible. For the latter the ground-up design and use of an integrated measurements system of any but the most simple form requires specialized knowledge, in depth, of digital techniques. As a start, the Suggested Readings at the end of the chapter will help.

6.14 GETTING IT ALL TOGETHER

The possibilities for putting together an advanced measurements system for a given project are almost open-ended. The degree of completeness is usually limited by conservation of money and time. A truly integrated system is often

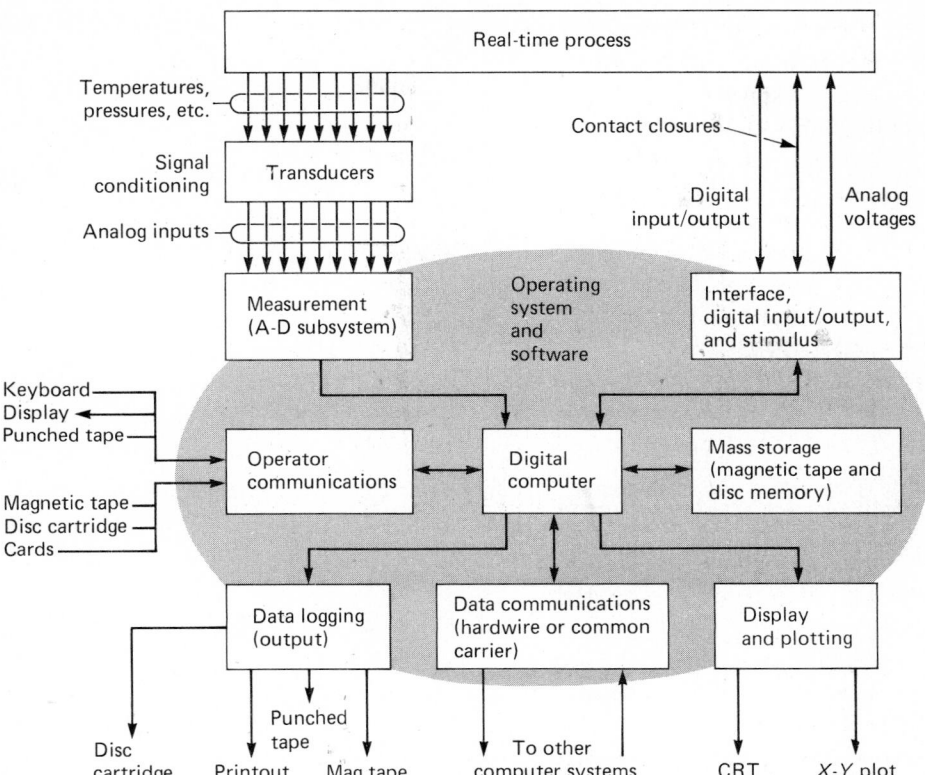

FIGURE 6.22 A block diagram illustrating the potential of an integrated measurements/ control system. Courtesy: Hewlett-Packard Co., Palo Alto, CA.

difficult to justify in terms of budget. In addition, there is always the question of value received. In many situations the design and assembly of a sophisticated system may be more costly in time and money than the project warrants. On the other hand, when great masses of data are to be collected, requiring extensive computational time to digest, funds and time expended in putting together an "automatic" system may very well be cost-conservative.

Figure 6.22 shows the tremendous possibilities for advanced data gathering and processing. Since it is based on materials discussed in this chapter and in Chapter 7, the diagram is self-explanatory.

6.15 FINAL REMARKS

In bringing this chapter to a close, we reiterate that it is presumptuous to attempt to summarize digital techniques in so few pages. We hope, however, that the material that has been presented will serve as an introduction to further study. There is no doubt as to the value of the topic as it relates to mechanical measurements. Further developments will inevitably increase this importance.

SUGGESTED READINGS

Artwick, B. A., *Microcomputer Interfacing*. Englewood Cliffs, N.J.: Prentice-Hall, 1980.

Berlin, H. M., *The 555 Timer Applications Sourcebook, with Experiments*. Derby, Connecticut: E & L Instruments, 1976.

Bibbero, R. J., *Microprocessors in Instruments and Control*. New York: John Wiley, 1977.

Bruck, D. B., *Data Conversion Handbook*. Burlington, Massachusetts: Hybrid Systems Corp., 1974.

CMOS Integrated Circuits. Santa Clara, California: National Semiconductor Co., 1979.

Data Acquisition and Conversion Handbook. Mansfield, Massachusetts: Datel-Intersil, Inc., 1979.

Hilburn, J. L., and P. M. Julich. *Microcomputers/Microprocessors*. New York: Prentice Hall, 1976.

Hoeschele, D. F., *Analog-to-Digital/Digital-to-Analog Conversion Techniques*. New York: John Wiley, 1968.

Introduction to Digital Techniques. Benton Harbor, Michigan: Heath, 1975.

Lesea, A., and R. Zaks, *Microprocessor Interfacing Techniques*. Berkeley, California: Sybex, 1977.

Libes, S., *Digital Logic Circuits*. Rochelle Park, N.J.: Hayden, 1975.

Linear Data Book. Santa Clara, California: National Semiconductor Co., 1979.

Microprocessors. Benton Harbor, Michigan: Heath, 1977.

Motorola Semiconductor Products, Inc., *Microprocessor Applications Manual*. New York: McGraw-Hill, 1975.

Southern, R., *Programming the 6800 Microprocessor*. Ottawa: Southcroft, 1977.

Titus, J. A., *Microcomputer-Analog Converter Software and Hardware Interfacing*. Indianapolis: Howard W. Sam, 1978.

TTL Data Book for Design Engineers. Dallas, Texas: Texas Instruments, Inc., 1979.

PROBLEMS

6.1 Confirm the following:

   a) $16_{10} = 10000_2 = 20_8 = 10_{16}$

   b) $87_{10} = 1010111_2 = 127_8 = 57_{16}$

   c) $419_{10} = 110100011_2 = 643_8 = 1A3_{16}$

   d) $7821_{10} = 1111010001101_2 = 17215_8 = 1E8D_{16}$

   e) $40177_{10} = 1001110011110001_2 = 116361_8 = 9CF1_{16}$

6.2 Prepare tables similar to Tables C1, C2 and C3 in Appendix C for negative powers of the radixes.

6.3 Confirm the following.

a) $0.1_{10} \approx 0.000110011001_2 \approx 0.0631_8 \approx 0.1999_{16}$

b) $0.3_{10} \approx 0.010011001110_2 \approx 0.231_8 \approx 0.4CC_{16}$

c) $0.5_{10} \approx 0.1000_2 \approx 0.4_8 \approx 0.8_{16}$

d) $3.14159264 \approx 11.0010010000111111011_2 \approx 3.110375_8 \approx 3.243F6$

[*Note:* The rules for decimal addition, subtraction, multiplication, and division also apply to the corresponding binary manipulations. Following familiar decimal procedures, confirm the results for the statements listed in Problems 6.4 through 6.7.]

6.4 Using binary arithmetic, confirm the following additions.

a) $(0111_2 + 0111_2) = 1110_2$

b) $(1011_2 + 1101_2 + 1110_2) = 100110_2$

c) $(1111_2 + 1101_2 + 1011_2 + 1001_2) = 110000_2$

6.5 Using binary arithmetic, confirm the following subtractions.

a) $10000_2 - 101_2 = 1101_2$

b) $110110_2 - 10101_2 = 100001_2$

c) $101101110011_2 - 10011110101_2 = 11001111110_2$

6.6 Using binary arithmetic, confirm the following multiplications.

a) $(1011_2) \times (11_2) = 100001_2$

b) $(11001_2) \times (101_2) = 1111101_2$

c) $(10110_2) \times (1101_2) = 100011110_2$

d) $(11111_2) \times (1111_2) = 111010001_2$

6.7 Using binary arithmetic, confirm the following divisions.

a) $(10111_2)/(11_2) = 111_2$ with a remainder of 10_2

b) $(1110110_2)/(101_2) = 10111_2$ with a remainder of 11_2

6.8 Using a truth table, show that the output from the circuit shown in Fig. 6.23 is high, except when the two inputs to either one or both of the AND gates are simultaneously high.

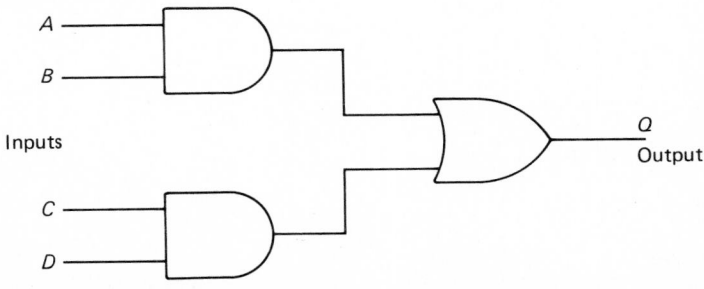

FIGURE 6.23   AND/OR circuit: see Problem 6.8.

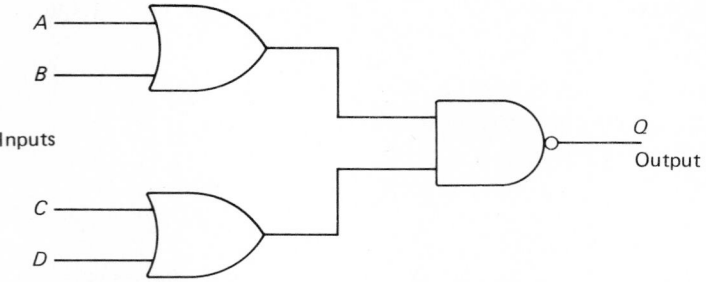

FIGURE 6.24   OR/NAND circuit: see Problem 6.9.

6.9 Using a truth table, show that the output from the circuit shown in Fig. 6.24 will be high only when both inputs of either of the OR gates are simultaneously low.

6.10 Use a truth table to determine under what set(s) of conditions the output from the three-input NAND gate, shown in Fig. 6.25, will be low.

6.11 Table 6.1 lists an eight-input NAND gate (see Fig. 6.6 for the basic concept). Rough-draft a circuit using the TTL 7430 whereby a single LED may be used to monitor eight separate circuits, four of which use NO (normally open) and four NC (normally closed) limit switches. Use additional elements, such as inverters (Fig. 6.4), etc., as needed. The basic transistor switch (Fig. 6.2c) may also be used if required. In practice, the limit switches might be over- or under-pressure, temperature, voltage switches, etc.

6.12 Write a hexidecimal sequence coded in upper- and lower-case ASCII that spells your name. Sketch the high-low sequence to print your initials.

6.13 Write the binary sequence coded in upper-case ASCII that spells your name.

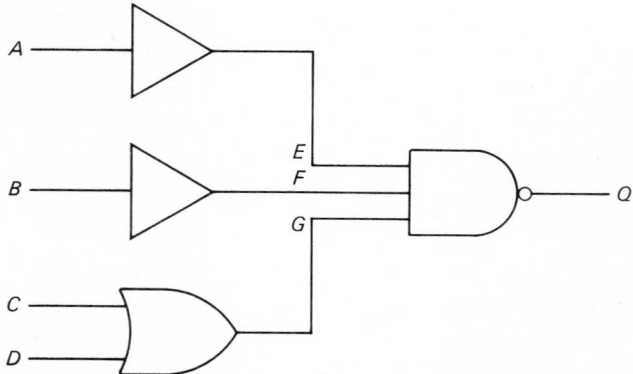

FIGURE 6.25   NAND logic element fed by two inverters and an OR element: see Problem 6.10.

read-out and 7
data processing

7.1 INTRODUCTION

Final usefulness of any measuring system depends on its ability to present the measured output in a form that is comprehensible to the human operator or the controlling device. The primary function of the terminating device is to accept the analogous driving signal presented to it and to either provide the information in a form for immediate reading or record it for later interpretation.

For direct human interpretation, except for simple yes-or-no indication, the terminating device presents the read-out (1) as a relative displacement, or (2) in digital form. Examples of the first are a pointer moving over a scale, a scale moving past an index, a light beam and scale, and a liquid column and scale. Examples of digital output are an odometer in an automobile speedometer, an electric decade counter, and a rotating drum mechanical counter.

Examples of exceptions to the two forms above are any form of yes-or-no limiting-type indicator, such as the red oil-pressure lights in some automobiles, pilot lamps on equipment, and—an unusual kind—litmus paper, which also provides a crude measure of magnitude in addition to a yes-or-no answer. Perhaps the reader can think of other examples.

As we have stated on numerous occasions in previous chapters, measurement of *dynamic* mechanical quantities practically presupposes use of electrical equipment for stages one and two. In many cases the electronic components used consist of rather elaborate systems within themselves. This is true, for example, of the cathode-ray oscilloscope. Sweep circuitry is involved, providing a time basis for the measurement. In addition, the input is carried through further stages of amplification before final presentation. The primary purpose of the complete system, however, is to present the input analogous signal in a form acceptable for interpretation. Such a self-contained system will therefore be classified as an integral part of the terminating device itself.

For the most part, dynamic mechanical measurement requires some form of voltage-sensitive terminating device. Rapidly changing inputs preclude strictly mechanical, hydraulic–pneumatic, and optical systems, either because of their extremely poor response characteristics or because the output cannot be interpreted. Therefore the major portion of this chapter will be concerned with electric indicators and recorders.

The most basic read-out device is undoubtedly the simple counter of items or events. Mechanically constructed counting devices are quite familiar. Most automobile odometers are of this type, simply counting the turns of a drive shaft through a gear reduction, which scales the read-out to miles or kilometers. Modern laboratory-type counters, however, are electronic, such as those discussed in Section 6.7 and in the following paragraphs.

7.2   THE ELECTRONIC COUNTER

Figure 7.1 shows an example of a multipurpose electronic counter, which is much more than a simple counting device. In addition to performing direct counts, this instrument is also capable of measuring events per unit time (EPUT), time interval or period, average period, frequency, or ratio of two different frequencies. Its ranges include count rates of up to 100 MHz and time intervals from 100 ns to 10^5 s. The input impedance is 1 MΩ shunted by 70 pf.

7.2.1   Time-Interval Meter

If a crystal-controlled time base and an electronic switch or *gate* are incorporated into the system, the time interval during which an event occurs may be determined by a counter. All that is necessary is that a pulse be provided

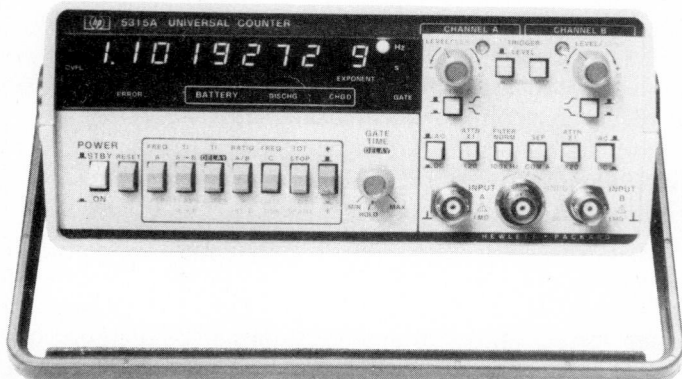

FIGURE 7.1   Hewlett-Packard 5315a Universal Counter. This instrument features frequency measurement by means of period reciprocal, as discussed in the text. Courtesy: Hewlett-Packard Company, Palo Alto, CA.

at the beginning of the event and that a second pulse occur at the end. These pulses are used to start counting and to stop counting the cycles of the time base oscillator.

Figure 7.2(a) illustrates schematically how the system operates. The counter actually counts the cycles from the built-in time base, over a period determined by the external event. The typical counter shown in Fig. 7.1 is provided with a time base of 1 MHz to 10 MHz.

7.2.2 Events-per-Unit-of-Time (EPUT) Meter

By rearranging the basic elements in the universal timer somewhat, an EPUT meter (Fig. 7.2b) may be obtained. In this case the time base is used to control the electronic gate, and the number of pulses from the external source is counted for a preset time interval. This changeover is accomplished by simple switching on the front panel. The counted input pulses may be at a fixed rate, such as from a steady-state vibration, or at an erratic rate, such as would be obtained from a Geiger-counter tube.

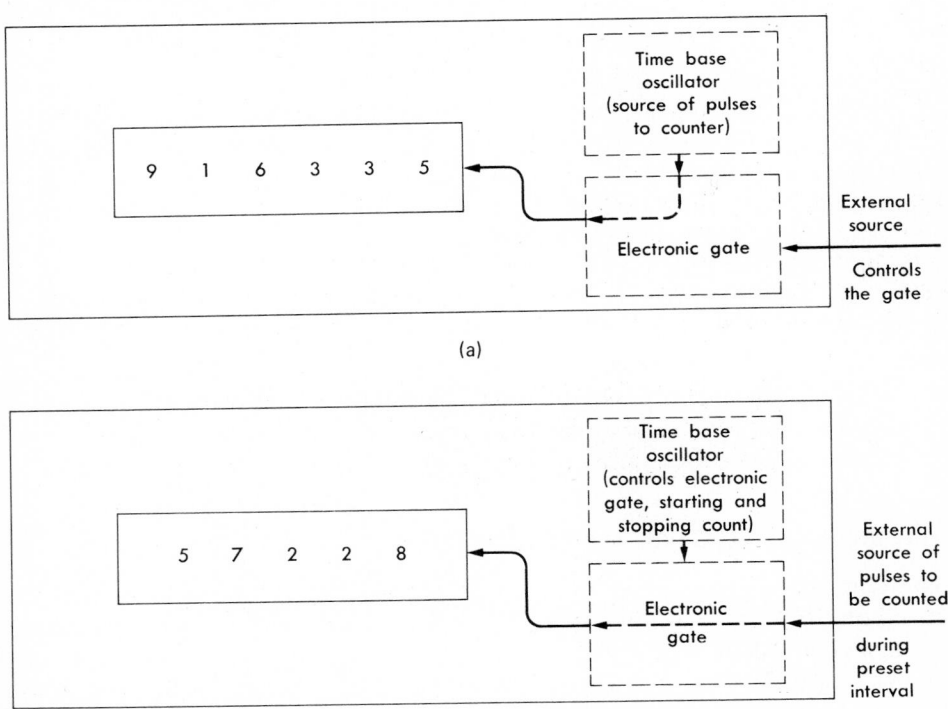

(a)

(b)

FIGURE 7.2   (a) Schematic of a time-interval meter. If the time base were set to 10 kHz, the indicated interval would be 91.6335 s. (b) Schematic of events-per-unit-time (EPUT) meter. If the gate were set to 10 s, the indicated frequency would be 5722.8 Hz.

7.2.3 Variations from the Basic Universal Counter

There are many variations from the basic counter system used for special-purpose applications. For mechanical measurements, a high counting rate may not be required. When such is the case, two or three electronic decades are sometimes used, which feed a simple, solenoid-operated mechancial counter. Other variations use the basic counter as a control unit by providing a control output pulse when a preset total count is reached. A unit of this type may be used for such applications as automatic packaging, coil winding, or sorting. Digital printout recorders are also available, providing automatic count recording. Further application of electronic counters is discussed in Chapter 10.

7.2.4 Count Error

Counting accuracy may involve time base error, trigger error, and a "± 1 count ambiguity." Time base error is concerned with any deviation of the time base oscillator frequency from intended frequency. This may result from a lack of both short- and long-term frequency stability. For most mechanical measurements, this error may be negligible (e.g., after proper warmup a drift or aging rate of less than 3 parts in 10^7 per month may be attained). Trigger error is concerned with the preciseness with which the gating action is known or controlled. The uncertainty of this may be reduced by period averaging.

Finally, a ± 1 count error in electronic counting often exists because of the normal lack of synchronization between the gating and the measured pulses (whether from internal or external sources). It results from the possibility that the gate closing (or opening) may occur so as to barely miss the count of a passing cycle, but still, in fact, include (or exclude) the greater part of that particular cycle's period. For frequency measurement this source of error may be minimized by designing the instrument to measure the *period* of a cycle, then *compute* the reciprocal and display frequency. This feature minimizes the effect of the 1-Hz resolution, particularly at the low frequencies where it might become serious. This method helps to maintain accuracy of frequency measurement over the entire counter range.

7.3 ANALOG ELECTRIC METER INDICATORS

The common electric meter used for measuring either current or voltage is based on the *D'Arsonval movement*. This consists of a coil assembly mounted on a pivoted shaft whose rotation is constrained by spiral hairsprings, as shown in Fig. 7.3. The coil assembly is mounted in a magnetic field, as shown. Electric current, the measurand, passes through the coil and the two interacting magnetic fields result in a torque applied to the pivoted assembly. Rotation occurs until the driving and constraining torques balance. The resulting displacement is calibrated in terms of electric current. The D'Arsonval movement

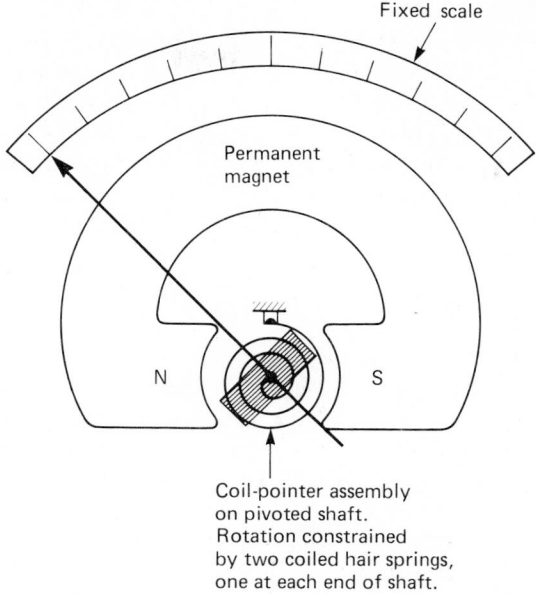

Fixed scale

Permanent
magnet

N   S

Coil-pointer assembly
on pivoted shaft.
Rotation constrained
by two coiled hair springs,
one at each end of shaft.

FIGURE 7.3   The D'Arsonval meter movement.

forms the basis for most electric meters and is also the basis of the stylus and light-beam oscillographs (Section 7.9).

Meter-type indicators may be classified as (1) simple current or voltage meters; (2) ohmmeters and volt-ohm-milliammeters (VOM or multimeters); and (3) meter systems whose read-outs are preceeded by some form of amplification. In the past, the latter type used vacuum tube amplifiers; hence they became known as "vacuum-tube-voltmeters" or VTVMs. The abbreviation is still heard in spite of the fact that solid-state amplifiers are now used.

In the majority of cases, the simple D'Arsonval meter movement is used as the final indicating device. However, moving-iron meters may be used for measuring a.c. current. In the more versatile types, such as the volt-ohm-milliammeter or multimeter, internal shunts or multipliers are provided with switching arrangements for increasing the usefulness of the instrument.

Basically, the D'Arsonval movement is current-sensitive; hence regardless of the application, whether it be as a current meter or as a voltmeter, current must flow. Naturally in most applications, the smaller the current flow, the lower will be the *loading* on the circuit being measured. The meter movement itself possesses internal resistance varying from a few ohms for the less sensitive milliammeter to roughly 2000 ohms for the more sensitive microammeter. Actual meter range, however, is primarily governed by associated range resistors.

Figure 7.4 shows schematically the basic d.c. voltmeter and d.c. current-meter circuits. Either multiplier or shunt resistors are used in conjunction with the same basic meter movement. To minimize circuit loading, it is desirable that total *voltmeter* resistance be much greater than the resistance of the circuit under test. For the same reason, the *current-meter* resistance should be as low as possible. In both cases, meter movements providing large deflections for given current flow through the meter are required for high sensitivity.

7.3.1 Voltmeter Sensitivity

Voltmeter resistance is determined primarily by the series multiplier resistance. High multiplier resistance means that the current available to actuate the meter movement is low and that a sensitive basic movement is required. Because sensitivity may differ from meter to meter even though the meters may be of the same range, it is insufficient to rate voltmeters simply by stating

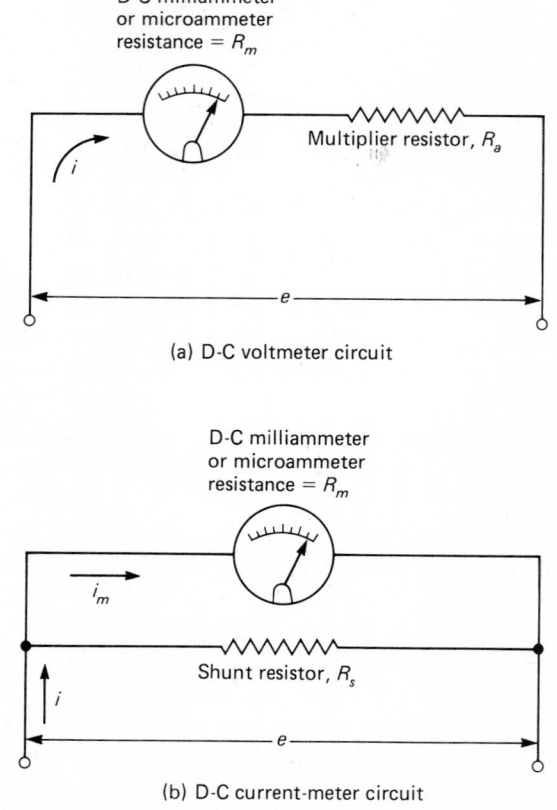

D-C milliammeter
or microammeter
resistance = R_m

Multiplier resistor, R_a

i

e

(a) D-C voltmeter circuit

D-C milliammeter
or microammeter
resistance = R_m

i_m

Shunt resistor, R_s

i

e

(b) D-C current-meter circuit

FIGURE 7.4   (a) D-C voltmeter circuit. (b) D-C current-meter circuit.

total resistance. Rating is commonly stated in terms of *ohms per volt. This value may be thought of as the total voltmeter resistance that a given movement must possess in order for the application of one volt to provide full-scale deflection.* This value combines both resistance and movement sensitivity, and the higher the value, the lower will be the loading effect for a given meter indication.

Simple pocket multimeters generally use a meter of 1 ma and 1000 ohms/volt rating, whereas more expensive multimeters may use movements with a rating of 50 μa and 20,000 ohms/volt.

The value of the series multiplying resistor, R_a, may be determined from the relation (see Fig. 7.4a)

$$R_a = \frac{e}{i} - R_m .$$

7.3.2 The Current Meter

Since current meters are connected in series with the test circuit, the voltage drop across the meter must be kept as low as possible. This means that the combination of meter and shunt must have as low a combined resistance as practical. Referring to Fig. 7.4(b), we may write the relation, based on equal voltage drops across meter and shunt,

$$R_s = \frac{i_m R_m}{i - i_m} .$$

7.3.3 A.C. Meters

Provision for measuring a.c. voltages is made by using a rectifier in conjunction with a d.c. meter movement. Meters of this type are usually calibrated to read in terms of the root-mean-square (rms) value of a sine-wave input. For this reason the careful interpretation of rectifier-type a.c. meter indications is necessary when other than sine-wave inputs are measured.

7.3.4 The Multimeter

A versatile tool around any laboratory is the basic volt-ohm-milliammeter (VOM), which uses switching arrangements for connecting multiplier and shunt resistors and a rectifier into or out of a circuit in order to cover ranges of d.c. and a.c. voltages. In addition, the meter is arranged to measure resistances, using an internal source of current. By switching to the ohmmeter function and connecting the leads to the unknown resistance, one can determine from the meter movement the current flowing through the resistor. The current flow indication is calibrated in terms of resistance, thereby providing a direct means for measurement.

7.4 METERS WITH ELECTRONIC AMPLIFICATION

There are two reasons for amplifying the input to a voltmeter or VOM. The obvious one, of course, is to increase the instrument's sensitivity. Of equal importance, however, is the fact that the input impedance of the meter can be made very much greater, thereby decreasing the effect of the meter load on the tested item.

Although high input resistance is quite desirable in most cases, it is not an unmixed blessing inasmuch as the instrument becomes more susceptible to *noise*, the most troublesome being an extraneous 60-Hz hum radiated from the power lines. Circuitry providing common mode rejection (Section 5.17) is very helpful in this case.

7.5 DIGITAL READ-OUT MULTIMETERS

The advent of the digital counter brought about its application to numerous measurement problems. Basically the counter is simply that—a counter of events. In Section 6.7 we showed how a simple counter circuit can be arranged to display a frequency. A simple way to make use of this capability for measuring a voltage is to combine the meter with a voltage-controlled oscillator (VCO). The frequency output of a VCO (e.g., the National Semiconductor LM566) is determined by the magnitude of the applied voltage. It is easy to visualize that through use of the VCO, a frequency counter, and proper scaling circuitry, a digitally reading voltmeter can be devised. Although this is a simple approach, it possesses certain disadvantages and is not commonly used.

Dual-slope-integration is a much more common method. The essential building blocks for this method are an op-amp integrator (Example E9, Sec. 5.17.2), a clock, and a frequency counter, combined with the necessary scaling and control circuitry. The clock is simply a fixed-frequency oscillator, usually crystal-controlled, that supplies timing pulses.

Through use of IC gating the integrator capacitor is charged for a pre-determined length of time (referenced to the clock frequency). It is then discharged at a constant current rate, and the clock pulses occurring during the discharge period are counted. This becomes the measure of the input voltage. With proper scaling the count is equated to the input magnitude. Other circuitry can be incorporated within the meter, making it a general-purpose multimeter for measuring d.c. or a.c. voltages or currents, or resistance in ohms.

Advantages of the double-slope circuit over others is that aging of either the clock or the integrator causes little or no error. We can see that charge and discharge of the integrator capacitor are each dependent on capacitance value and time interval and that changes in either will be self-compensating. Should the clock slow down with age, the charging time will be reduced, but the discharge time will be increased in like proportion. A similar effect results from small changes in capacitor value.

Other approaches include

1. Single-slope conversion,
2. Charge balance,
3. Linear ramp conversion, and
4. Successive approximation.

These will not be discussed, however, and the reader is referred to the Suggested Readings at the end of the chapter for further information.

Many digital multimeters also include automatic polarity indication and self-ranging ability (automatic placement of the decimal point). Many meters of this type are said to display one-half digits, e.g., a "$3\frac{1}{2}$ digit display." This means the most significant digit can be only a "0" or a "1," excluding all others. A $3\frac{1}{2}$-digit meter, for instance, is not capable of displaying a number greater than 1999.

Figure 7.5 illustrates a compact, digital read-out VOM having the following abbreviated specifications:

d.c. voltmeter ranges to 1200 VDC with accuracies equal to or better than 0.1% of reading + 2 digits;

FIGURE 7.5   Digital readout volt-ohm-milliammeter (VOM). Courtesy: Hewlett-Packard Co., Palo Alto, CA.

a.c. voltmeter ranges to 1200 VAC rms with accuracies equal to or better than 1.5% of reading + 10 digits;

d.c. input resistance = 10 MΩ;

d.c. and a.c. ammeter ranges to 2.0 A;

Ohmmeter ranges to 20 MΩ;

A/D conversion: dual slope.

7.6   THE CATHODE-RAY OSCILLOSCOPE (CRO)

Probably the most versatile read-out device used for mechanical measurements is the cathode-ray oscilloscope (CRO). This is a voltage-sensitive instrument, much the same as the electronic voltmeter, but with an inertialess (at mechanical frequencies) beam of electrons substituted for the meter pointer and a fluorescent screen replacing the meter scale. Figure 7.6 shows a typical general-purpose CRO.

The heart of the instrument is the cathode-ray tube, shown schematically in Fig. 7.7. A stream of electrons emitted from the cathode is focused sharply on the fluorescent screen, which glows at the point of impingement forming a bright spot of light. Deflection plates control the direction of the electron stream and hence the position of the bright spot on the screen. If an electrical potential is applied across the plates, the effect is to bend the pencil of electrons, as shown in Fig. 7.8. With the use of two sets of deflection plates arranged to bend the electron stream both vertically and horizontally, an instantaneous relation between two separate deflection voltages may be obtained.

Figure 7.9 is a block diagram of a typical general-purpose cathode-ray oscilloscope. The nature of the CRO is such that it may appear with many different variations in the form of special controls and input and test terminals.

FIGURE 7.6   Hewlett-Packard Model 1220A cathode-ray oscilloscope. Courtesy: Hewlett-Packard Co., Palo Alto, CA.

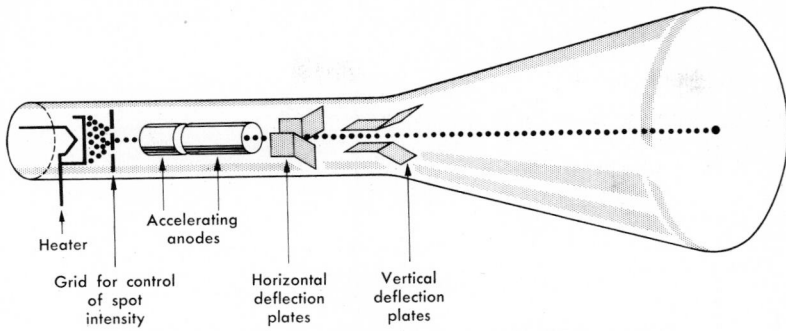

Heater

Grid for control
of spot
intensity

Accelerating
anodes

Horizontal
deflection
plates

Vertical
deflection
plates

FIGURE 7.7   Elements of the basic cathode-ray tube.

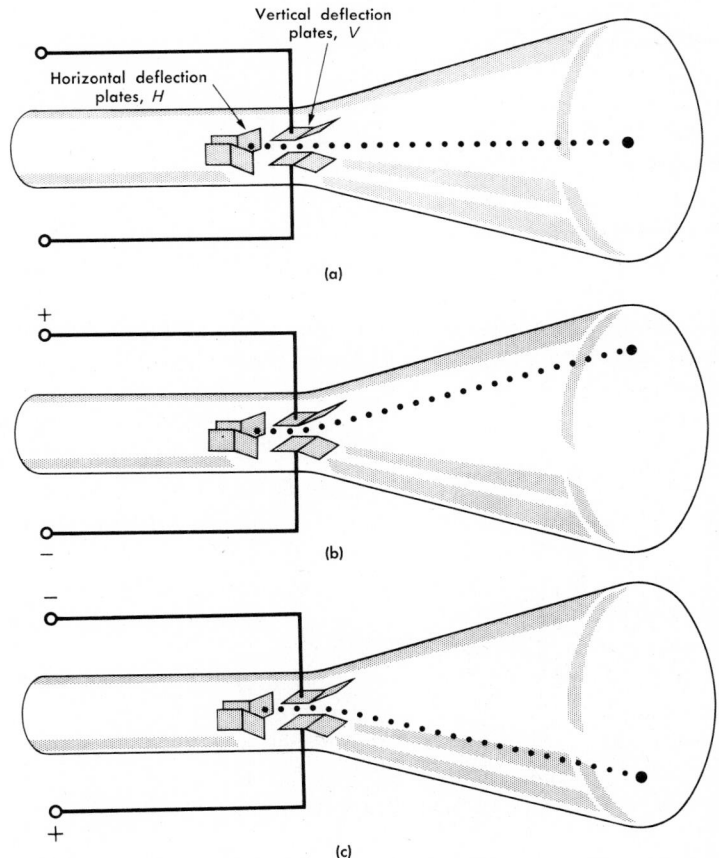

Vertical deflection
plates, V

Horizontal deflection
plates, H

(a)

+

−

(b)

−

+

(c)

FIGURE 7.8   Electrostatic deflection principle. (a) With no voltage applied to the vertical deflection plates, the electron beam is not deflected. (b) When a positive voltage is applied to the upper plate, the electron beam is deflected upward. (c) When the polarity is reversed and positive voltage is applied to the lower plate, the beam is deflected downward.

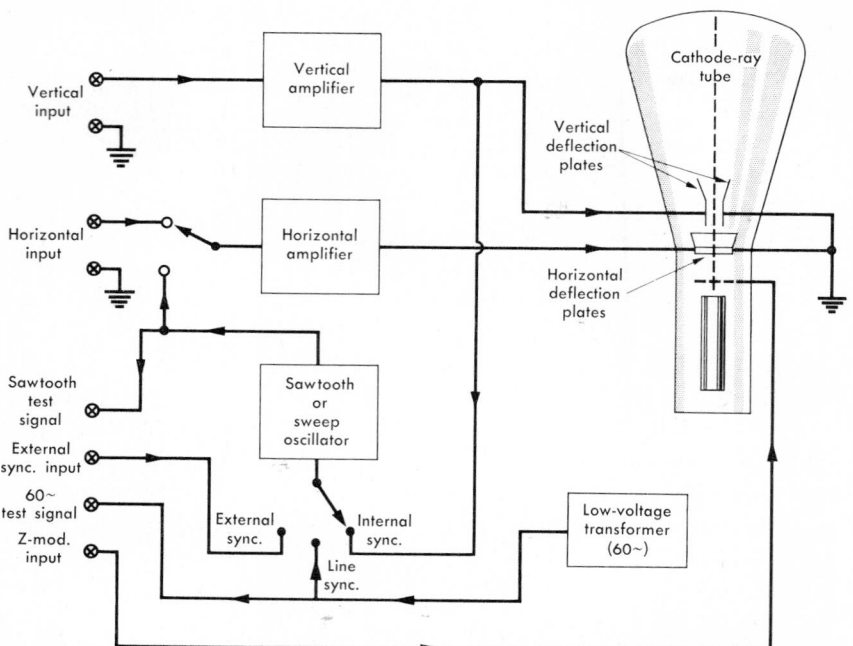

FIGURE 7.9   Block diagram of a typical general-purpose oscilloscope.

The diagram shown is not for any particular commercial instrument. Certain oscilloscopes will have features not shown here, and others may not use certain ones that are shown.

7.6.1 Oscilloscope Amplifiers

The sensitivity of the typical electrostatic cathode-ray *tube* is relatively low, varying from about 0.010 to 0.15 cm deflection per d.c. volt, or from about 6 to 100 V/cm of deflection. This means that in order to be widely useful for measurement work, the CRO should provide means for signal amplification before the signal is applied to the deflection plates. All general-purpose oscilloscopes provide such amplification. Most are equipped for both d.c. and a.c. amplification on both the vertical and horizontal plates.

Some means for varying gain is provided in order to control the amplitude of the trace on the screen. This is often accomplished through use of fixed-gain amplifiers, preceded by variable attenuators.

7.6.2 Sawtooth Oscillator or Time Base Generator

Except for special-purpose applications, the usual cathode-ray oscilloscope is equipped with an integral *sawtooth* or *sweep* oscillator. This is a variable-frequency oscillator that produces an output voltage–time relation in the form shown in Fig. 2.8(c). Ideally, the voltage increases uniformly with time until a maximum is reached, at which point it collapses almost instantaneously.

When the output from the sawtooth oscillator is applied to the horizontal deflection plates of the cathode-ray tube, the bright spot of light will traverse the screen face at a uniform velocity. As the voltage reaches a maximum and collapses to zero, the spot is whipped back across the screen to its starting point, from which it repeats the cycle. The length of the path will then be a measure of the period of the oscillator frequency (called sweep frequency) in seconds, and each point along the path will represent a proportional time interval measured from the beginning of the trace. (By convention, increasing time is measured to the right.) In this manner a very useful *time base* is obtained along the x-axis of the tube face.

As a simple example, let us suppose that ordinary 60-Hz line voltage is applied to the y-deflection plates of the tube and the output from a variable-frequency sweep oscillator is applied to the x-deflection plates. (Usually the sawtooth oscillator is within the case of the CRO and a knob is simply set to "Internal Sweep.") With the two voltages applied, the frequency of the sawtooth oscillator would be adjusted by means of the sweep range and sweep vernier controls on the control panel. If the sawtooth frequency is adjusted *exactly* to 60 Hz, then one complete cycle of the vertical input waveform will appear stationary on the screen, as shown in Fig. 7.10(a). If the sweep frequency is slightly greater or slightly less than 60 Hz, then the waveform will appear to creep backward or forward across the screen. *The reciprocal of the time in seconds required for the waveform to creep exactly one complete wavelength on the screen will be the discrepancy in cycles per second between the sweep frequency and the input frequency.* In certain cases this relationship may be used in making precise measurement of frequency or period.

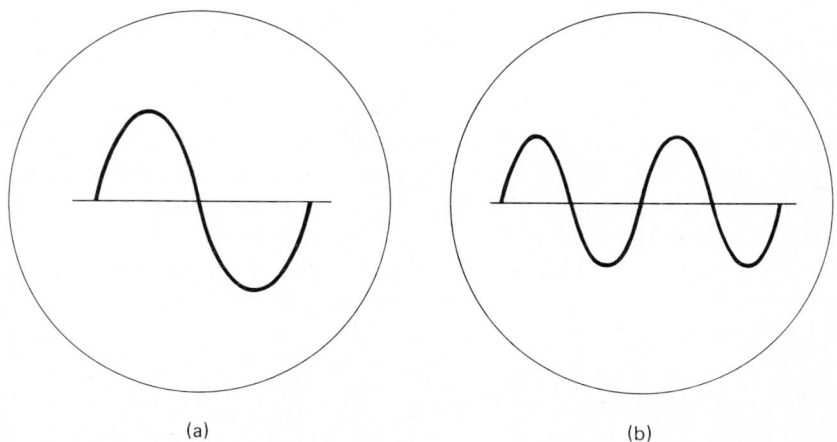

(a)   (b)

FIGURE 7.10   Trace obtained when 60-Hz line voltage is applied to the vertical deflection plates. (a) The horizontal sweep is adjusted to 60 Hz. (b) Trace obtained when a 30-Hz sweep is applied to the horizontal deflection plates.

If the sweep frequency is changed to *exactly* 30 Hz, then two complete cycles of the input signal will appear and remain stationary on the screen, as shown in Fig. 7.10(b).

7.6.3 Synchronization

In the example just referred to, one cycle of the 60-Hz waveform will appear stationary on the screen only if the sweep frequency is exactly 60 Hz. Frequencies from all types of electronic generators tend to shift or drift with time. This is caused by a change in component characteristics brought about by temperature changes due to the warmup of the instrument. Therefore, to hold a pattern on the screen without creep, one must continuously monitor the trace, making adjustments in sweep frequency as required.

When a steady-state signal is applied to the vertical terminals, however, it is possible to lock the sweep oscillator frequency to that of the input frequency, provided the sweep frequency is *first* adjusted to approximately the input frequency or some multiple thereof. This is controlled through use of "Sync. Selector" and "Sync. Amplitude" controls.

In our example, we would wish to use the vertical input as our synchronizing signal source, so we would set the synchronization selector to "Internal" (see Fig. 7.9). Voltage pulses from the input signal would then be applied to the sweep oscillator and would be used to control the oscillator frequency over a small range. If the frequency is initially adjusted to some integral multiple of the input frequency, the sweep oscillator would then lock in step with the input signal and the trace would be held stationary on the screen. Since excessive synchronization voltage tends to distort the trace, only the amount required for synchronization must be applied.

Electrical engineers are often concerned with measurements at 60 Hz; hence oscilloscopes are usually equipped to provide a direct synchronizing signal from the power line. This setting on the synchronization selector is often simply marked "Line."

Finally, it is often desirable to synchronize a CRO trace from an external source closely associated with the input signal. As an example, suppose some form of electrical pressure pickup is being used for measuring the cylinder pressures in a reciprocating-type air compressor. Although the pressure signal from the pickup may be steady state, making internal synchronization a possibility, changing load, erratic valve action, or the like may make this signal an undesirable source for synchronization. An external circuit may be used in a case of this sort. A simple make-and-break contactor could be attached to the compressor shaft, and a voltage pulse could be provided for synchronization through use of a simple dry cell. Such a circuit would be connected between the external synchronization input and the ground, and the Sync. Selector would be set at "External." In this case the horizontal sweep would be set at "Driven" rather than "Recur," and sweeps would take place only when initiated by the external contactor.

This arrangement is also useful when a *single sweep* only is desired. When this is the case, the synchronizing contactor or switch may be simply hand-operated, or it may be incorporated in the test cycle. As an example, a photocell circuit could be arranged so that a beam of light intercepted by a projectile or the like would provide the initiating pulse in synchronization with the test signal of interest.

When the driven sweep is initiated as outlined above, through use of an external source of triggering, the sweep occurs once for each synchronizing pulse. The sweep rate in this case is still controlled by the sweep range and sweep vernier. Of course, the sweep cannot be pulsed at a rate greater than that provided by the sweep-control settings. That is, the electron beam must have returned from the previous excursion before it can be triggered again.

7.6.4 Intensity or Z-Modulation

The fluorescent trace produced by the electron beam may be brightened or darkened by applying a positive or a negative voltage component, respectively, to the grid of the cathode-ray tube. Actually, this is what is done in a television receiver tube to produce the light and dark picture areas. Some oscilloscopes make provision for applying a brightness-modulating voltage from an external source, either through a terminal on the front panel or through a connection on the back of the instrument. This is known as *intensity* or *Z-modulation*. (Z is used in the sense that, along with the x- and y-trace deflections, intensity variation provides the third coordinate.)

If on a normal input trace, say from a pressure pickup, an alternating Z-modulation is superimposed, the trace becomes a dashed line, providing timing calibration as well as the usual y-input information. (See Section 10.4 for further discussion of this application.)

7.6.5 External Horizontal Input

Of course, it is not necessary to use the sweep oscillator for the horizontal input. Input terminals are provided for connecting other sources of voltage. This permits a comparison of voltages, frequencies, and phase relations. (See Section 10.5).

7.7 ADDITIONAL CRO FEATURES

7.7.1 Multiple Trace

In many cases it is desirable to make an accurate time comparison between two continuing inputs, and very often CRO multiple-trace capability is the solution to this problem. Although oscilloscopes are available that permit simultaneous writing of more than two traces, the dual-trace type is the most common.

There are two different basic methods for accomplishing double traces: (1) through use of two separate electron "guns" within a single tube envelope, and (2) by high-speed gating (switching) two inputs to the vertical plates of a conventional one-gun cathode-ray tube. In either case duplicate circuitry (terminals, amplifiers, positioning controls, etc.) is required. The second approach is by far the more common.

When the gating method is used, the oscilloscope-design engineer has a choice of either or both of two different schemes. The first, called the *chopped-trace* method, successively switches from input A to input B and back again many times during a single sweep across the CRT screen. A switching rate of 200 kHz is typical. For many sweep rates the gating is so fast that the two traces appear to be continuous. In addition to being dependent on the relative rates, gating to sweep, the illusion of continuity also depends somewhat on the persistence of the phosphor. However, as the sweep rate is increased, depending on the demands of the measurement, the actual discontinuity of the traces may become a problem.

Alternate gating, the second method, alternately displays the entire traces, first for input A, then B, back to A, and so on. Screen persistence will permit simultaneous viewing of near-simultaneous traces. Many dual-trace scopes provide switch selection of either method.

An oscilloscope accessory called an *electronic switch* may also be used to convert a single-trace CRO to a double-trace one. The same chopped-input method as described above is used, the primary difference being that the circuitry is outboard rather than an integral part of the oscilloscope.

7.7.2 Magnification and Delayed Sweep

Amplification may be used to stretch out or magnify the horizontal sweep to a number of times the size of the CRO screen. This means, coupled with adjustment of the horizontal position control, allows us to magnify a portion of the normal sweep for closer inspection. Oscilloscopes with more advanced circuitry (and higher cost) may use what is called *delayed sweep* to accomplish similar results. That is, the operator may select any small portion of the normal display, which may then be shown at a selected higher sweep rate. The effect of the increased rate over the selected portion of the normal sweep is to expand or magnify the portion that has been pinpointed.

7.7.3 Storage Scopes

In many instances measurands are nonrepeating. Examples are the load or strain resulting from an impulsive load, or the sound wave corresponding to the discharge of a gun. Through proper photographic techniques as described in Section 7.8 and in Chapter 10 a record may be captured on film. These techniques may not be convenient, however, and a series of trials may be required before system adjustments are refined. The answer may be use of a *storage scope*, which is able to "hold" a trace on the CR-tube face for a period of time after it has been written. Eventually the trace fades; however, on some storage scopes the trace may be held for up to an hour.

Digital techniques may also be incorporated in sophisticated oscilloscopes, whereby the contents of the entire screen may be stored and held in memory for repetitive writing, for later recall, or for input into a computer system.

7.8 CRO RECORDING TECHNIQUES

Direct observation of an oscilloscope trace often provides sufficient information. In other cases, however, particularly when transient conditions are being studied, some form of recording is mandatory. This normally dictates the use of photographic methods. Various forms of photographic equipment may be used, but the most satisfactory are special-purpose cameras that can be attached directly to the oscilloscope bezel. Several types are available, including those using ordinary photographic film, the Polaroid Land camera, and moving-film cameras.

Only very simple photographic techniques are required in using the first two types. When the trace is from a steady-state source, the sweep may be synchronized to hold the trace stationary on the screen. It is then only necessary to make an appropriate exposure to capture the record.

When a transient input is to be recorded, single sweep, along with "time" or "bulb" shutter setting on the camera, may be used. The camera shutter is opened, the sweep initiated either internally or externally, and the trace recorded.

7.9 OSCILLOGRAPHS

The oscillograph is basically an adaptation of the D'Arsonval meter movement (Section 7.3), in which either a writing stylus (Fig. 7.11) or a small mirror (Fig. 7.12) replaces the meter pointer or hand. The stylus writes through direct contact on a moving strip of paper. Either an ink pen or a heated stylus on special paper can be used. The mirror-type oscillograph functions by directing a pencil of light onto photographic paper or film. In both cases the meter movement is commonly referred to as the galvanometer. As the stylus (or light beam) is deflected by the input signal, the paper is moved at a known rate, thereby recording the time function of the input. The complete oscillograph incorporates the galvanometer(s), adjustable speed paper drive, and power amplifier(s), plus voltage amplifiers and calibration circuits as needed.

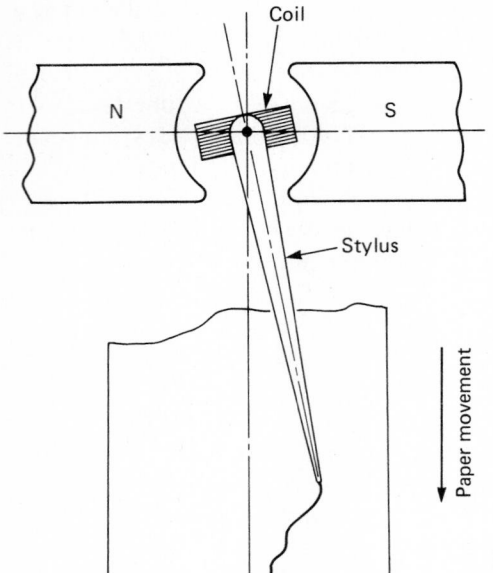

FIGURE 7.11   Essential parts of stylus-type oscillograph.

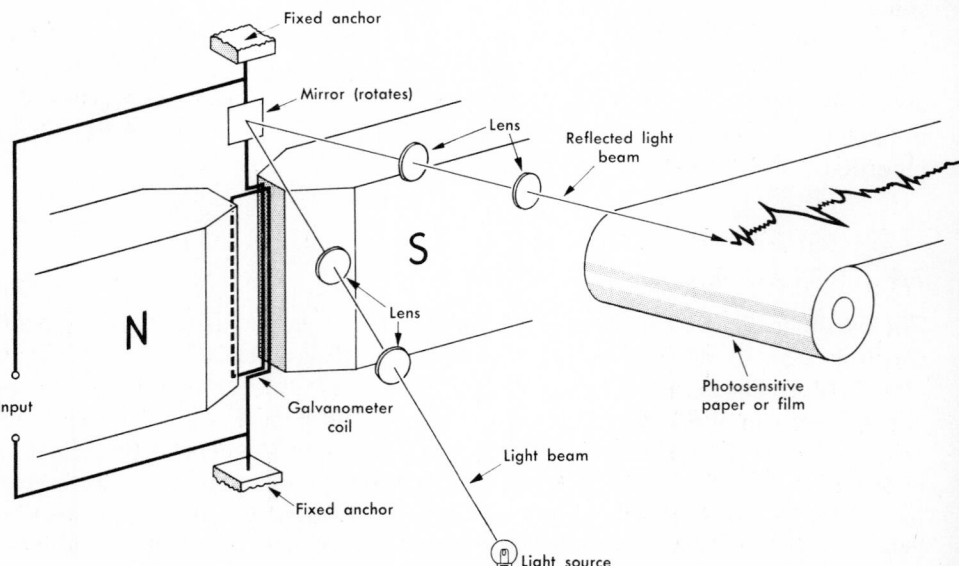

FIGURE 7.12   Essential parts of a light-beam type oscillograph.

TABLE 7.1   Typical Galvanometer Characteristics

Undamped Natural Frequency, Hz	Flat ($\pm 5\%$) Frequency Response, Hz	Sensitivity (with 30-cm Optical Arm)	
		$\mu a/cm$	mV/cm
24	0–15	4	0.5
40	0–40	20	0.6
100	0–60	25	1.3
200	0–120	65	4
400	0–240	200	24
600	0–540	330	105
1000	0–600	5,000	260
5000	0–3,000	50,000	1,600
8000	0–4,800	100,000	3,600

Obviously the frictional drag between paper and pen of the stylus requires considerably more driving torque than does a simple meter or a light-beam galvanometer. In any case an important parameter in the design is the magnitude of the magnetic flux from the permanent magnet. This requires a relatively large and heavy magnet. Commercially available stylus-type oscillographs may have as many as 8 channels and provide flat response from d.c. to about 150 Hz. The light-beam type may have as many as 36 channels with typical responses and sensitivities as listed in Table 7.1.

7.10   GALVANOMETER THEORY

Fundamentally, the galvanometer suspension consists of a mass (the coil and mirror or stylus), whose motion is constrained by a spring, and built-in damping either due to the reversed electromagnetic effect alone or combined with damping from enclosed viscous fluid. The system is driven from an external source, which may be static but which is usually some form of harmonic input. Therefore the motion of the galvanometer suspension must abide by the theory of a damped forced torsional vibration.

Assuming the driving torque to be a simple harmonic function of time, and the damping to be purely viscous, we may write the familiar relation

$$I\frac{d^2\Theta}{dt^2} + \zeta\frac{d\Theta}{dt} + \lambda\Theta = T_0 \cos \Omega t, \qquad (7.1)$$

in which

$$I = \text{the mass moment of inertia,}$$

$$\zeta = \text{the coefficient of viscous damping,}$$

$$\lambda = \text{the torsional spring constant,}$$

$$T_0 = \text{the amplitude of the driving torque,}$$

$$\Theta = \text{the angular displacement of suspension,}$$

$$t = \text{time, and}$$

$$\Omega = \text{the circular frequency of driving torque.}$$

If we assume that the deflections are small, we may write

$$T_0 = ki_0,$$

where

$$i_0 = \text{the amplitude of electrical current driving the galvanometer, and}$$

$$k = \text{the proportionality constant.}$$

When we make this substitution, Eq. (7.1) becomes

$$I\frac{d^2\Theta}{dt^2} + \zeta\frac{d\Theta}{dt} + \lambda\Theta = ki_0 \cos \Omega t. \tag{7.1a}$$

Comparison of this equation with Eq. (3.24) permits us to write relations comparable to Eqs. (3.25c) and (3.25b). For the galvanometer these would be

$$\frac{\theta_0\lambda}{ki_0} = \frac{\theta_0}{\theta_s} = \frac{1}{\sqrt{[1 - (\Omega/\omega_n)^2]^2 + 2[\xi(\Omega/\omega_n)]^2}} \tag{7.2}$$

and

$$\phi = \tan^{-1}\left\{\frac{2[\xi(\Omega/\omega_n)]}{1 - (\Omega/\omega_n)^2}\right\}, \tag{7.3}$$

where ξ is the damping ratio. Figure 7.13 is a plot of Eq. (7.2) for various values of the damping ratio, and ω_n is the undamped natural frequency.

The ratio $\theta_0\lambda/ki_0$ or θ_0/θ_s is a measure of galvanometer dynamic response, which ideally should be a constant over the range of frequencies for which it is used. Inspection of Fig. 7.13 shows that the ratio is reasonably constant only for a limited frequency range and for certain damping ratios. We see that the ratio approximates unity over a frequency span of from d.c. to, let us say, 40% of the undamped natural frequency of the device. In addition, inspection of the figure suggests that damping ratios in the range of about 50 to 100% should be used. Near the lower end of this range one should expect some overtravel when a step change occurs; at the higher ratios a slower slew

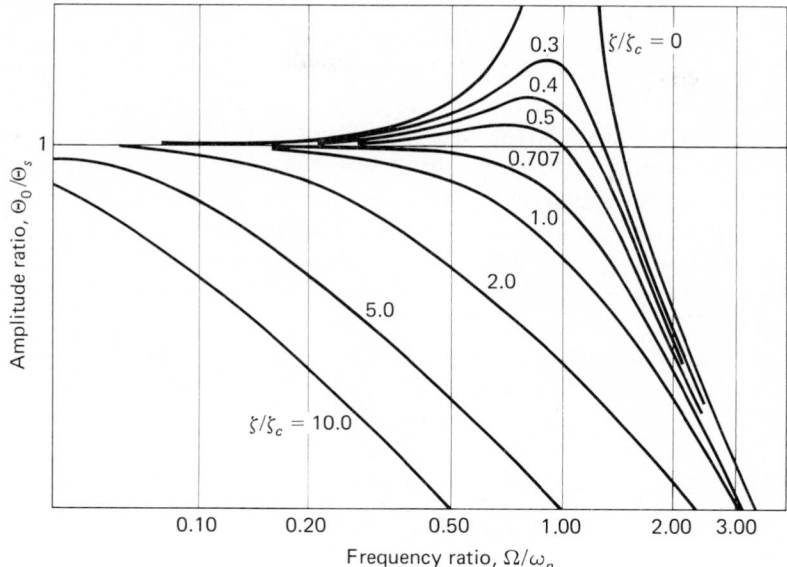

FIGURE 7.13   Amplitude-frequency characteristics of a galvanometer movement.

rate (Section 3.6) would result. There is some evidence that manufacturers opt for the higher damping ratios.

Inspection of Fig. 3.17 (which applies to this case) indicates that damping ratios in the range suggested above provide an approximate linear variation in phase shift with frequency. This is also desirable if the proper time relationship is to be maintained between the harmonic components of a complex input (see Section 17.6.2).

We may say, therefore, that any galvanometer intended for general dynamic measurement should be provided with proper damping. Furthermore, such a galvanometer should not be expected to yield satisfactory information if used at frequencies above about 40 to 50% of its own undamped natural frequency.

Of course, certain assumptions were made in developing the foregoing relations. Those of greatest importance were: (1) that the driving torque was directly proportional to the input current, (2) that the input current was simple harmonic, and (3) that the only damping present was of the viscous type.

In the first place, the driving torque will be constant only so long as the coil turns are working in a constant magnetic field and are moving in a fixed direction relative to it. Although the galvanometer air gaps are arranged to meet this requirement, large excursions result in a certain amount of nonlinearity. In normal use, with a well-designed galvanometer, this is not a serious matter, however.

Dynamic input from a mechanical source is not usually simple harmonic, but is a complex waveform. It would seem, however, that if the complex input were made up of harmonics, all of whose frequencies are below the frequency limit of the instrument, then the waveform would be faithfully reproduced. This is actually the case, and if higher-frequency components are present, it is characteristic of the galvanometer with normal damping to attenuate such components. Usually such higher-frequency harmonics are of small amplitude; this means that although such harmonics will not be faithfully recorded, the instrument's failure will not seriously impair that part of the whole that is recorded. (Discussion of a very similar problem is included in Section 17.6 to which the reader is referred.)

Nonviscous damping, due primarily to ordinary friction and spring hysteresis, is always present to some extent in any oscillatory system. In the case of the stylus-type writing galvanometer, this is obviously so, even though the friction between the stylus and the paper is minimized. Hence the foregoing analysis does not apply quite as completely to this type as it does to the light-beam type. In general, however, both behave very nearly as elementary theory predicts.

7.10.1 Extending the Range of Acceptable Galvanometer Frequency Response

The nature of the stylus-type galvanometer requires that the moving elements, the coil and writing arm, have appreciable mass moments of inertia as compared with the light beam of the mirror type. This in turn results in a relatively low natural frequency if the suspension stiffness is to be made low enough to provide practical sensitivity. However, the usable range is extended beyond the undamped natural frequency of the galvanometer itself through use of an amplifier with compensating characteristics. This is illustrated in Fig. 7.14. The response of the galvanometer alone starts to drop at about 25 Hz. However, when it is combined with a matching amplifier, satisfactory response is extended to 80 or 100 Hz, depending on the acceptable error.

7.10.2 Galvanometer Sensitivity

Galvanometer sensitivity is defined as the ratio of beam or stylus deflection to current, and may be given in centimeters per milliamp or centimeters per microamp. The deflection is measured at the recording end of either the stylus or light beam, the length of which must be considered in making comparisons. Other factors governing sensitivity are density of magnetic flux, number of turns on coil, coil shape, and stiffness of suspension. If all other factors are maintained, the *current sensitivity of a galvanometer is inversely proportional to the square of its natural frequency* [see also Section 3.9 and Eq. (3.7a)]. As a result, the sensitivity drops rapidly as the frequency range is increased.

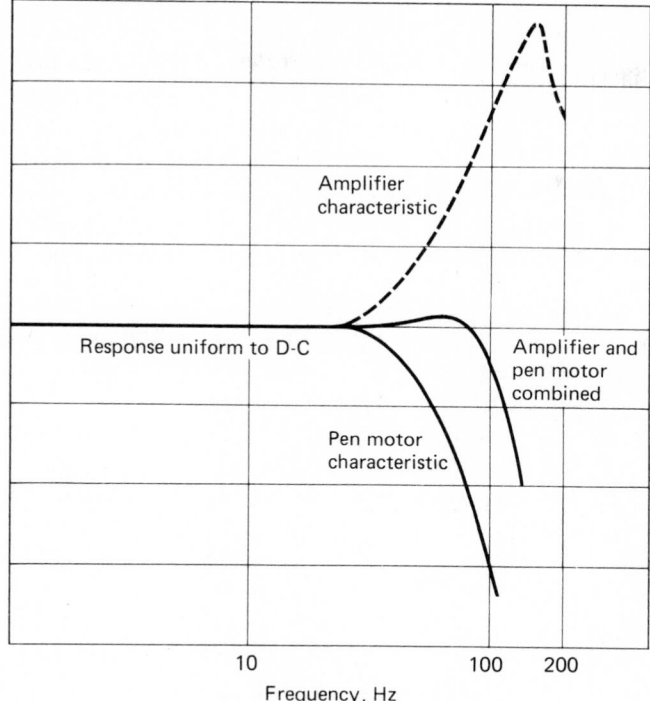

FIGURE 7.14 Compensation of pen motor and amplifier characteristics.

In general, the sensitivity of stylus-type galvanometers is much lower than that of the light-beam variety. Typical stylus-type galvanometer sensitivity is 1 mm/ma and has an upper frequency limit (at reduced amplitude) of about 200 Hz. Representative characteristics of the light-beam types are given in Table 7.1.

7.10.3 Methods of Damping Galvanometers

There are two commonly used methods for damping galvanometers. They are magnetic damping and magnetic damping coupled with fluid damping.

When the galvanometer coil moves in its magnetic field, a back emf is established that produces a current whose effect is to oppose or damp the coil movement. This damping current is superimposed on the original input driving current; however, it may be considered as being independent from the latter. Damping produced in this manner is a velocity function because it depends on the rate at which the lines of flux are cut; hence it satisfies the manner in which we introduced damping in Eq. (7.1).

If the total input circuit resistance, including the source as well as the galvanometer coil, is quite high, little damping current will flow and the system

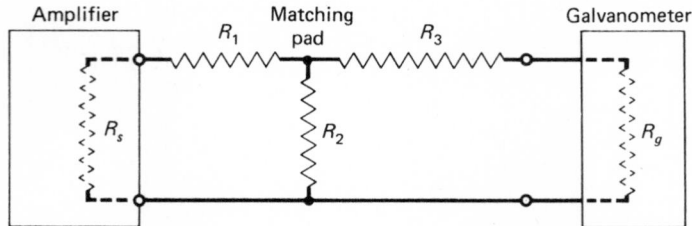

FIGURE 7.15   Matching a galvanometer to an amplifier by means of a resistance pad.

will be underdamped. On the other hand, a low input circuit resistance will cause overdamping. We see, therefore, that proper matching of circuit components is quite important from the standpoint of obtaining the damping that we have already shown to be necessary.

In certain cases, magnetic damping is not sufficient to meet optimum requirements, and fluid damping is also used. This is done by filling the galvanometer case with a fluid of required viscosity. The viscous forces applied to the instrument's parts as they move in the fluid supply added damping. It must be realized, however, that magnetic damping is still present and the requirement for proper external circuit resistance still exists.

Matching resistance pads (see Section 5.24) are normally used for coupling a galvanometer to an amplifier. Figure 7.15 shows an arrangement using a pad. Here R_s and R_g represent the source and galvanometer resistances, respectively, and R_1, R_2, R_3 are the pad resistances. Optimum transfer conditions will occur when the amplifier "sees" the ideal load and the galvanometer "sees" the proper source. Amplifier load is normally equal to, or nearly equal to, the source resistance, R_s. However, the manufacturer may sometimes specify a somewhat different value, R_L. The resistance seen by the galvanometer must be that which provides proper damping as discussed above. This value, R_d, is supplied by the manufacturer of the galvanometer.

Referring to Fig. 7.15, we may write the following relations:

$$R_L = R_1 + \frac{R_2(R_g + R_3)}{R_2 + R_3 + R_g} \tag{7.4}$$

and

$$R_d = R_3 + \frac{R_2(R_1 + R_s)}{R_1 + R_2 + R_s}. \tag{7.5}$$

It is also desired that the galvanometer provide a specified trace for a given input current. (It is up to the amplifier to supply the necessary current, proportional to the transducer output.) Galvanometer sensitivity may be expressed by the relation

$$s = \frac{Ki_0}{D}, \tag{7.6}$$

in which

$$s = \text{sensitivity, in ma/in.,}$$

$$K = \text{a constant,}$$

$$i_0 = \text{current, in ma, and}$$

$$D = \text{trace deflection, in in.}$$

Using elementary circuit analysis, we may also write

$$K = \frac{sD}{i_0} = \frac{R_2}{R_2 + R_3 + R_g}. \tag{7.7}$$

Pad resistances R_1, R_2, and R_3 must be selected to satisfy Eqs. (7.4), (7.5), and (7.7).

7.11   *X–Y* PLOTTERS

The term "*x–y* plotter" is very nearly self-explanatory. It refers to an instrument used to produce a Cartesian graph originated by two d.c. inputs, one plotted along the *x*-axis and the other along the *y*-axis. Of course the great advantage in its use is that the graph is plotted automatically, thereby sidestepping the laborious point-by-point plotting by hand. In addition, families of curves may be plotted easily by varying a third parameter in step fashion from plot to plot. Figure 7.16 shows a typical *x–y* plotter. Basic components

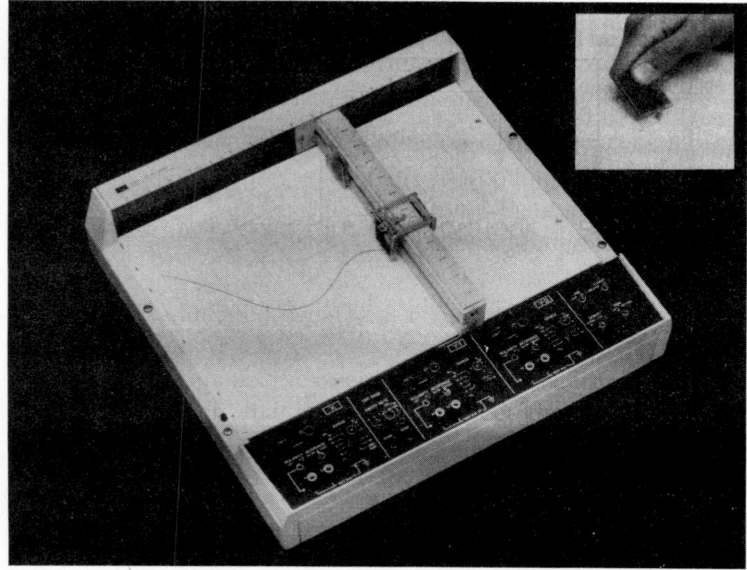

FIGURE 7.16   A two-pen x-y recorder. Courtesy: Hewlett-Packard Co., Palo Alto, CA.

consist of a platen to which the graph paper is either mechanically attached or held by vacuum or by electrostatic means and one or more servo-driven styluses. In addition, amplification of the input signals is normally required.

Performance variables include input ranges (amplitude and frequency), sensitivity, stylus slewing rate and acceleration limit, resolution, resetability and provision for common mode rejection. Slewing rate in cm/s is the maximum velocity with which the stylus can be driven. This becomes a limiting response characteristic, especially when large amplitudes are to be plotted. Limits on the maximum acceleration of the stylus are more often a factor when low-amplitude, high-frequency inputs are plotted.

Common chart sizes are 22 × 28 cm ($8\frac{1}{2}$ × 11 in.) and 28 × 44 cm (11 × 17 in.). Two-stylus (X–Y–Y) models are available for the simultaneous plotting of two curves. These, of course, require three separate drive systems.

7.12   THE SPECTRUM ANALYZER

Figure 7.17 shows a simplified block diagram of the workings of a swept-type spectrum analyzer. Pertinent items are:

1. *A sawtooth waveform generator* running at a fixed frequency, but whose voltage output varies linearly in ramp fashion.
2. *A voltage-controlled oscillator* (VCO), whose output frequency, f_{VCO}, sweeps linearly across a given frequency range. Its voltage amplitude is constant.
3. *A mixer* that combines (mixes) the input signal with the VCO output. This produces sum-and-difference frequency components. For an input frequency, f_{in}, two side frequencies, ($f_{VCO} - f_{in}$) and ($f_{VCO} + f_{in}$), are generated (see Section 10.7).

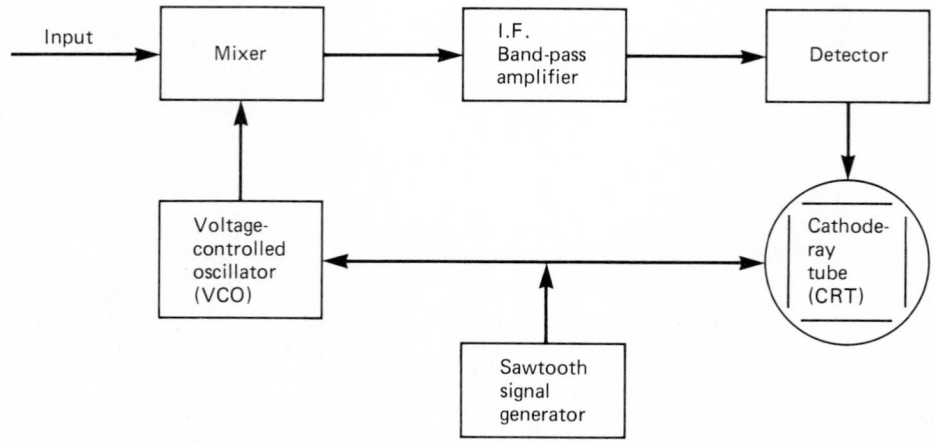

FIGURE 7.17   Block diagram of a spectrum analyzer.

4. An *IF* (intermediate frequency) *band-pass amplifier*, whose pass-band is designed to accommodate a single (ideally) value of $(f_{VCO} - f_{in})$ to the exclusion of other frequencies.

5. A *detector*, which is basically a voltage rectifier, passing a voltage of one polarity (say, positive).

6. A *cathode-ray tube* (CRT), used for display.

In operation, as the output of the sawtooth generator linearly rises from zero, it drives the CRT electron beam along the *x*-axis, across the face of the tube. At the same time, the output frequency from the VCO sweeps linearly upward. When the VCO frequency and the frequency component of the input produce a difference frequency, $(f_{VCO} - f_{in})$, matching the pass-band frequency of the IF amplifier, a signal component passes whose amplitude is proportional to

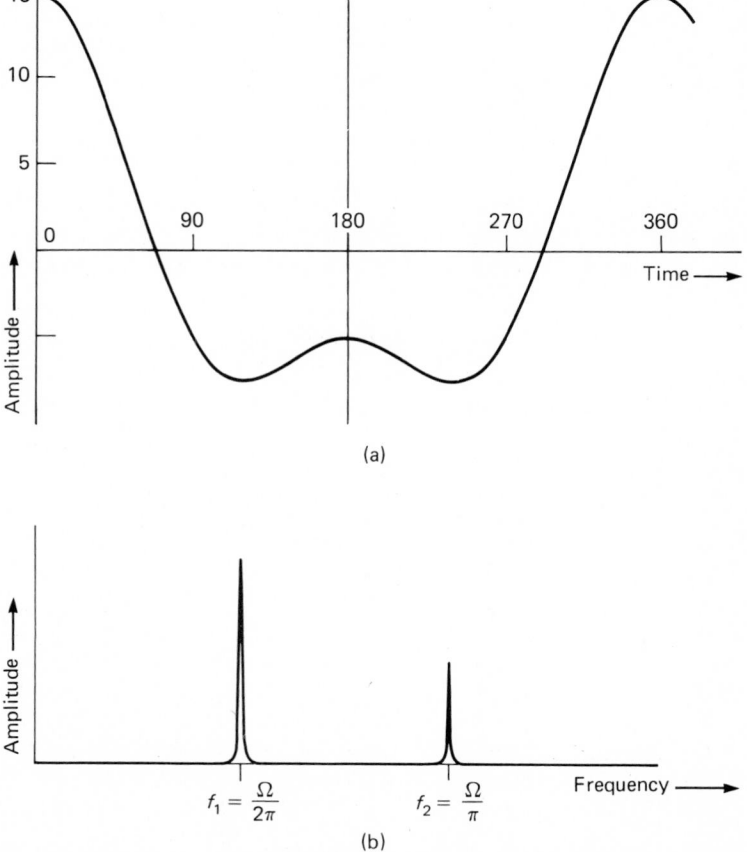

(a)

(b)

FIGURE 7.18   (a) Time domain plot of $A(t) = 10\cos(\Omega t) + 5\cos(2\Omega t)$. (b) Frequency-domain plot of $A(t) = 10\cos(\Omega t) + 5\cos(2\Omega t)$.

that of the input component. This is then rectified and displayed on the CRT screen as a spike located on the horizontal frequency axis at a point corresponding to the difference frequency. Both axes can be calibrated in terms of the input parameters.

To help us visualize the result, let us consider a two-component input:

$$A(t) = 10 \cos \Omega t + 5 \cos (2\Omega t).$$

As an amplitude–time plot, the function would appear as shown in Fig. 7.18(a). Figure 7.18(b) represents the corresponding amplitude–frequency plot as it would be shown by a spectrum analyzer. For an ideal input and an ideal response, the two spikes would be indicated by perfect vertical lines. However, as with all instrumentation, there are limitations and as input frequencies are increased, a broadening of the spikes becomes apparent.

Various adjustments are provided on even the simplest analyzers to accommodate ranges of frequency and amplitude. In addition, the IF band-pass can often be varied to help in isolating frequency components in the input signal. Analyzers are selected on the basis of application: low-frequency analyzers for vibration and sound work, radio-frequency analyzers for RF work, UHF for TV, gigahertz for microwaves, etc.

SUGGESTED READINGS

Analog and Digital Meters. Benton Harbor, Michigan: Heath, 1979.

Sessions, K. W., and W. Fischer, *Understanding Oscilloscopes and Display Waveforms*. New York: John Wiley, 1978.

Van Erk, R., *Oscilloscopes, Functional Operation and Measuring Examples*. New York: McGraw-Hill, 1978.

Oscilloscopes. Benton Harbor, Michigan: Heath, 1979.

PROBLEMS

7.1 Assemble the following equipment: a general-purpose oscilloscope, preferably a single-channel basic CRO, two variable-frequency signal generators (a single oscillator will suffice, if a source of low-level 60-Hz line voltage is available), and an assortment of appropriate leads. Connect one signal source to the vertical input terminals of the CRO and the other to the horizontal terminals. Proceed to "turn the knobs." Experiment until you are familiar with the purpose and action of each of the controls. (Feel free to make any front-panel adjustment that is available, except for possible "screwdriver" balance adjustments. In addition, avoid holding an intense, concentrated, fixed spot on the screen. To do so could cause a local burning of the phosphor.) Refer to Figs. 7.10, 10.10, and 10.13: Can you reproduce these? If the scope has provision for Z-modulation, experiment with this (see Sections 7.6.4 and 10.4.3).

7.2 The cathode-ray oscilloscope is considered a "high-input–impedance" device. The simple D'Arsonval voltmeter is usually considered to be of "low impedance."

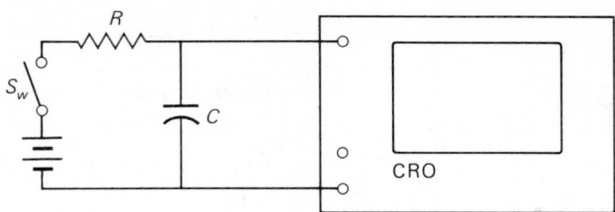

FIGURE 7.19   Circuit used to determine the *RC* time constant for various combinations of *R* and *C*: see Problem 7.3.

What is meant by "high" and "low" impedances in this sense? Discuss the relative merits and disadvantages of each category.

7.3 Use the experimental setup shown in Fig. 7.19 to determine the *RC* time constant for various combinations of *R* and *C*. Compare the results with the theoretical value (see Section 3.17).

Problems 7.4 through 7.9 specify circuits to be inserted as indicated in Fig. 7.20, along with exercises to be performed. Values of circuit elements are not specified since various values as may be available will usually be quite satisfactory. So-called decade boxes of resistances, capacitances, or inductances are particularly useful. These permit selection of a wide range of values. A decade box is simply an assembly of components, in decade steps of value, that may be switch-selected.

7.4 Insert the circuit in Fig. 7.21 into the circuit in Fig. 7.20. Using components of known value, find the *LC* resonant frequency experimentally. Check against Eq. (5.23).

7.5 Duplicate the experiment given in Problem 7.4; however, use the experimentally determined resonant frequency and a known value of capacitance to determine an unknown inductance.

7.6 Using the circuit in Fig. 7.20, experimentally determine the characteristics of the circuit shown in Fig. 5.22(a).

7.7 Using the circuit in Fig. 7.20, experimentally determine the characteristics of the circuit shown in Fig. 5.23(a).

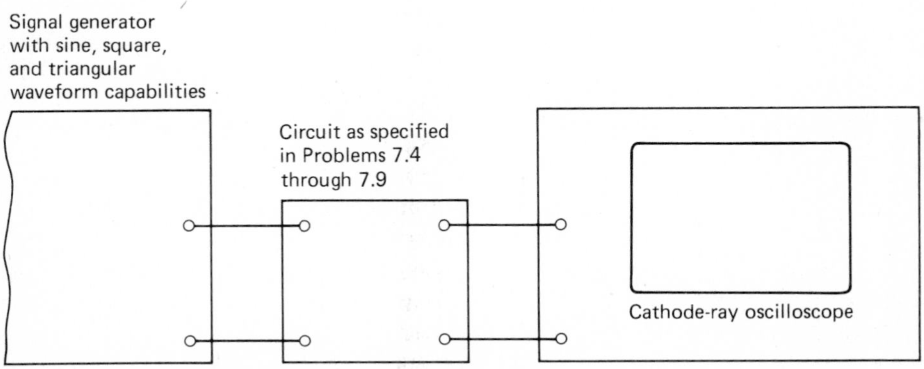

Signal generator
with sine, square,
and triangular
waveform capabilities

Circuit as specified
in Problems 7.4
through 7.9

Cathode-ray oscilloscope

FIGURE 7.20   Block diagram of circuit used in Problems 7.4 through 7.9.

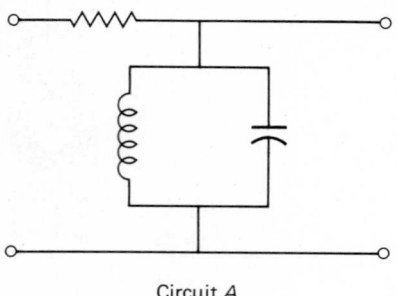

Circuit A

FIGURE 7.21   Parallel *LC* circuit to be used in Problem 7.4.

7.8 Using the circuit in Fig. 7.20, experimentally determine the characteristics of the circuit shown in Fig. 5.24(a).

7.9 Using the circuit in Fig. 7.20, experimentally determine the characteristics of selected circuits from Fig. 5.25.

7.10 Connect the output of a signal generator to the input of an oscillograph and investigate the oscillograph's amplitude and frequency responses. An attenuator may be needed to produce an acceptably low input signal amplitude.

7.11 A pressure pickup is used for measuring the pressure–time relationship in the cylinder of an internal combustion engine. The output is amplified and then applied to the vertical plates of an oscilloscope. Describe arrangements for synchronizing the scope trace with the engine speed (a) using internal sweep and (b) using external sweep. If the pickup is applied to the determination of the pressure–time history resulting from detonations of explosive charges, how should the oscilloscope be configured to obtain satisfactory traces? Assume that the charges are "one-shot," but that they may be repeated as desired.

standards 8
of measurement

8.1 INTRODUCTION

Regardless of the measurement method, some basis for the comparison, a *standard* unit, must be used. There must also be general agreement as to the exact value of such standard units, and for as long as different systems of units may exist, there must be mutual agreement on the basis for conversion from system to system. For example, the relation between the centimeter and the inch must be definitely established, as must the relations among all the basic units. Certain standards fall naturally into place—the average length of the day is one—yet the starting point, or zero, must always be defined.

8.2 LEGAL STATUS OF THE STANDARDS OF MEASUREMENT IN THE UNITED STATES

With regard to the legal status of measurement standards in the United States, the following is of interest. First of all, who or what body shall have authority to control such matters? Quoting from Article 1, Section 8, Paragraph 5, of the United States Constitution: "The congress shall have power to . . . fix the standard of weights and measures." Although Congress was given the power, considerable time elapsed before anything was done about it. In 1866, as found in the Revised Statutes of the United States, Sec. 3569, it was stated "It shall be lawful throughout the United States of America to employ the weights and measures of the metric system. . . ." This simply makes it clear that the metric system *may* be used. In addition, this act established the following relation for conversion:

$$\text{One meter} = 39.37 \text{ in.} \quad \text{(exactly)}.$$

An international convention held in Paris in 1875 resulted in an agreement signed for the United States by the U.S. ambassador to France. The following is quoted therefrom: "The high contracting parties engage to establish and maintain, at their common expense, a scientific and permanent international bureau of weights and measures, the location of which shall be Paris" [1, 2]. Although this established a central bureau of standards, which was set up at Sèvres, a suburb of Paris, it of course did not bind the United States to make use of or adopt such standards.

On April 5, 1893, in the absence of further Congressional action, Superintendent Mendenhall of the Coast and Geodetic Survey issued the following order [1, 3]:

> The Office of Weights and Measures with the approval of the Secretary of the Treasury, will in the future regard the international prototype meter and the kilogram as *fundamental standards,* and the customary units, the yard and pound, will be derived therefrom in accordance with the Act of July 28, 1866.

The Mendenhall Order turned out to be a very important action. First, it recognized the meter and the kilogram as being fundamental units on which all other units of length and mass should be based. Second, it ties the metric and English systems of length and mass together in a definite relationship, thereby making possible international exchange on an exact basis.

In response to requests from scientific and industrial sources, and to a great degree influenced by the establishment of like institutions in Great Britain and Germany,* Congress, on March 3, 1901, passed an act providing that "The office of Standard Weights and Measures shall hereafter be known as 'The National Bureau of Standards' " [4]. Expanded functions of the new bureau were set forth and included development of standards, research basic to standards, and the calibration of standards and devices. The NBS was formally established in July, 1910, and its functions were considerably expanded by an amendment passed in 1950.

Commercial standards are largely regulated by state laws, and to maintain uniformity, regular meetings (National Conferences on Weights and Measures) are held by officials of NBS and officers of state governments. Essentially all state standards of weights and measures are in accordance with the Conference's standards and codes. International uniformity is maintained through regularly scheduled meetings (held at about six-year intervals), called the *General Conference on Weights and Measures* and attended by representatives from most of the industrial countries of the world. In addition, numerous interim meetings are held to consider solutions to more specific problems for later action by the General Conference.

---

* The National Physical Laboratory. Teddington, Middlesex, and Physikalisch-Technische Reichsanstalt, Braunschweig.

8.3 THE METRIC SYSTEM

8.3.1 International Actions

The Eleventh General Conference on Weights and Measures (1960) adopted the International System of Units (SI) and established the rules for the various units. In June 1972, the International Standards Organization (ISO), an assembly of which the United States is a member, approved the International Standard 1000, called *SI Units and Recommendations for the Use of Their Multiples and of Certain Other Units*. The system is often popularly referred to as the *metric system*. Therein are defined three classes of measurement units: (1) base units, (2) supplementary units, and (3) derived units. The seven base units and the two supplementary units are listed in Table 8.1. In addition, various units derived from the base units are listed in the standard. Certain derived units are assigned special names; others are not. For example, area may be expressed simply in terms of meters squared, whereas force (m-kg/s^2) is given the special name, the *newton*. Work and energy, (m^2 · kg/s^2), are called the *joule*. The term *hertz* is used for frequency (s^{-1}) and the term *pascal* (N/m^2) for pressure or stress. Selected derived units are listed in Table 8.2. Note that whereas the assigned words, although often originated from proper names, are not capitalized, many of the corresponding abbreviations are capitalized.

To accommodate the writing of very large or very small values, certain multiplying factors are provided (Table 8.3). For example, 2,500,000 Hz may be written as 2.5 MHz; or 0.000 000 000 005 farad may be expressed as 5 pF.

TABLE 8.1 Base and Supplementary Units

Quantity	Name and Symbol of Unit
Base Units	
Length	meter (m)
Mass	kilogram (kg)
Time	seconds (s)
Electric current	ampere (A)
Thermodynamic temperature	kelvin (K)
Amount of substance	mole (mol)
Luminous intensity	candela (cd)
Supplementary Units	
Plane angle	radian (rad)
Solid angle	steradian (sr)

TABLE 8.2 Derived Units

Quantity	Unit	Symbol	
Area	square meter	m^2	
Volume	cubic meter	m^3	
Frequency	hertz	Hz	(s^{-1})
Density	kilogram per cubic meter	kg/m^3	
Velocity	meter per second	m/s	
Angular velocity	radian per second	rad/s	
Acceleration	meter per second squared	m/s^2	
Angular acceleration	radian per second squared	rad/s^2	
Force	newton	N	(kg·m/s^2)
Pressure	newton per sq meter	N/m^2	
Kinematic viscosity	sq meter per second	m^2/s	
Dynamic viscosity	newton-second per sq meter	N·s/m^2	
Work, energy, quantity of heat	joule	J	(N·m)
Power	watt	W	(J/s)
Electric charge	coulomb	C	(A·s)
Voltage, potential difference, electromotive force	volt	V	(W/A)
Electric field strength	volt per meter	V/m	
Electric resistance	ohm	Ω	(V/A)
Electric capacitance	farad	F	(A·s/V)
Magnetic flux	weber	Wb	(V·s)
Inductance	henry	H	(V·s/A)
Magnetic flux density	tesla	T	(Wb/m^2)
Magnetic field strength	ampere per meter	A/m	
Magnetomotive force	ampere	A	
Luminous flux	lumen	lm	(cd·sr)
Luminance	candela per sq meter	cd/m^2	
Illumination	lux	lx	(lm/m^2)·

8.3.2 Domestic Actions

In May 1965 the United States announced its intention of adopting the metric system. In 1970 passage of Public Law 90-472 authorized the secretary of commerce to make a "U.S. Metric Study," to be reported by August 1971. After prolonged debates, studies, and public pronouncements of ten-year conversion plans, on December 23, 1975, the 94th Congress approved Public Law 94-168, called the Metric Conversion Act of 1975. Its purpose is stated as "To declare a national policy of coordinating the increasing use of the metric system in the United States, and to establish a United States Metric Board to coordinate the voluntary conversion to the metric system." Note especially that the conversion is to be *voluntary* and that no time limit is set. The act makes it clear that in using the term metric, the SI system of units is intended.

The function of the seventeen-member board is to "devise and carry out a broad program of planning, coordination and public education, consistent with other national policy and interests, with the aim of implementing the policy . . ." of the act. Among the various policy statements, which range from publicizing the system to a collection of statistics on its use, is one that is particularly pertinent to our discussion: to "encourage activities of stan-

TABLE 8.3 Multiplying Factors

Multiple and submultiple	Prefix	Symbol	Pronunciation
10^{12}	tera	T	tĕr'à
10^9	giga	G	jĭ' gà
10^6	mega	M	mĕg'à
10^3	kilo	k	kĭl'ô
10^2	hecto	h	hek'tô
10	deka	da	dĕk'à
10^{-1}	deci	d	dĕs'ĭ
10^{-2}	centi	c	sĕn'tĭ
10^{-3}	milli	m	mĭl' ĭ
10^{-6}	micro	μ	mī' krô
10^{-9}	nano	n	năn'ô
10^{-12}	pico	p	pē' cô
10^{-15}	femto	f	fĕm' tô
10^{-18}	atto	a	ăt' tô

dardization organizations to develop, or revise, as rapidly as practicable, engineering standards on a metric measurement basis, and to take advantage of opportunities to promote (a) rationalizations or simplification of relationships, (b) improvements of design, (c) reduction of size variations, (d) increases in economy, and (e) where feasible, the efficient use of energy and conservation of natural resources.''

Although implementation of the system by the public remains voluntary, it seems clear that the metric system will eventually supersede the English system in the United States. As we stated in Section 1.7, we will use both the metric (SI) and English systems throughout this book. In doing so, we hope that some of the difficulties associated with the substitution of a "new" thinking mode for one long established may be minimized.

8.4 THE STANDARD OF LENGTH

Originally, the meter was intended to be one ten-millionth of the earth's quadrant. Until recently it was defined as the length of the International Prototype Meter, the distance between two finely scribed lines on a platinum–iridium bar when subject to certain specified conditions. However, on

October 14, 1960, the Eleventh General Conference on Weights and Measures adopted a new definition of the meter as 1,650,763.73 wavelengths in vacuum of the radiation corresponding to the transition between the levels $2p_{10}$ and $5d_5$ of the krypton atom. The National Bureau of Standards of the United States has adopted this standard, and the inch is now 41,929.39854 wavelengths of the krypton light.

The relation between the meter and the inch as specified by the Mendenhall Order (1 m = 39.37 in.) results in

$$1 \text{ in.} = 2.54000508 \text{ cm} \quad \text{(approximately)}.$$

The convenient relation

$$1 \text{ in.} = 2.54 \text{ cm} \quad \text{(exactly)}$$

has been used in industry and engineering for years and, through adoption of the SI system, now becomes official for all length conversions. The difference between these two standards may be written as

$$2.54000508/2.54 - 1 = 0.000\ 002$$

or 0.0002%. This is about 1/8 inch per mile.

We gain even a better idea of the significance of the difference by considering the following situations. The work of the United States Coast and Geodetic Survey is based on the 39.37 in./m relation and a coordinate system with origin located in Kansas [5]. Changing the metric relation from 39.37 in./m (exactly) to 2.54 cm/in. (exactly) would cause discrepancies of almost 16 ft at a distance of 1500 mi. One can only imagine the confusion over property lines if such a change were made. On the other hand, gage blocks, which are the manufacturing secondary standards, are established on the basis of 2.54 cm/in. If they were measured on the basis of 39.37 in./m, errors of 2 μin./in. would be found. This is in the same order of magnitude as the *tolerance* of the better-quality blocks.

All this would present a very real problem were it not for the fact that geodetic distances and small mechanical displacements need seldom be compared. Hence it is quite probable that the two nearly equal equivalents (sic) will be in use for many years to come.

8.5 THE STANDARD OF MASS

The *kilogram* is defined by the mass of the International Prototype Kilogram, a platinum–iridium mass kept at the International Bureau of Weights and Measures near Paris. Of the basic standards, this remains the only one established by a prototype (*the* original model or pattern, *the* unique example to which all like are referred for comparison). Even this, however, may someday follow the prototype meter bar into the museum and be substituted for by a standard available to any laboratory. Reference [6] alludes to an x-ray interferometry measure of Avogadro's number, enabling the tie of macroscopic mass directly to the atomic-mass unit.

Secondary standards of known relative masses are maintained by each of the primary industrial countries of the world. In the United States, the basic unit of mass is the "United States National Prototype kilogram No. 20," carefully maintained by the National Bureau of Standards.

The Mendenhall Order of 1893 included the following relationship:

$$1 \text{ lb avoirdupois} = 453.592\ 427\ 7 \text{ g.}$$

For 58 years, following the founding of the National Bureau of Standards, the above relation applied. However, on July 1, 1959, the equivalent was altered to

$$1 \text{ lb avoirdupois} = 453.592\ 37 \text{ g.}$$

This change was brought about by the desire to unify the equivalencies used by Australia, Canada, New Zealand, South Africa, the United Kingdom, and the United States.

8.6 TIME AND FREQUENCY STANDARDS

A paradox of scientific measurement is that we measure time without having a very good idea of the nature of the subject with which we are dealing [7]. This has been very ably described by G. M. Clemence [8] of the United States Naval Observatory as follows:

> It is not possible in a scientific journal (or anywhere for that matter) to say much about the nature of time itself. That subject belongs to philosophy rather than to science. It may be permissible, however, to recall a few propositions, not contradicted by experience, which may be thought to be facts.
>
> Time seems to pass more quickly as we grow older. I used to think time was like a suitcase that seemed to grow smaller because there were more and more things to put in it, but later I found that even persons who had nothing to occupy their time experienced the same illusion.
>
> As a rule time passes very quickly in our dreams, and here we have the ability, as we have not when we are awake, to move backward and forward in time, seemingly without effort, and perhaps even against our will.
>
> Time moves, or we move through it, in one direction only. Our senses receive no impression of the future, and we commonly think that we live only in the present. In strictness, however, we know nothing of the present, but only of the past. We are able to speak of the present only because the lag between events in the immediate vicinity and our appreciation of them is so small as to be negligible for most practical purposes. When we regard events outside the earth, the truth is apparent. We observe the moon, not as it is now, but as it was somewhat more than a second ago. Light from the sun requires eight minutes to reach us; from Pluto, five hours. If we could see events on the earth reflected in mirrors placed on

suitable stars at different distances, we could observe the history of the United States, and even of mankind itself, taking place before our very eyes.

What we, as scientists, know about time itself is very little indeed. We can say much more about the measurement of it.

(For an additional philosophical discussion of time, see [9].)

Engineers are not very often interested in the precise *time of day*. Their interest is usually in terms of duration of some event or phenomenon. They require a time base for their observations, but are not particularly interested in knowing the precise instant in history at which an event occurs. This may not always be the case, however, since it is sometimes easier to determine the relative occurrence of events by establishing a time *fix* than by determining the time interval by intraobservation. Even here, of course, the *fix* need only be mutually agreed to and need have no time relation to extraneous events.

Until 1956 the second was defined as 1/86,400 of the average period of revolution of the earth on its axis. Although this seems to be a relatively simple and straightforward definition, problems remained. There is a gradual slowing of the earth's rotation (about 0.001 s/century) [8], and, in addition, the rotation is irregular.

Therefore, in 1956 an improved standard was agreed on; the second was defined as 1/31,556,925.9747 of the time required by the earth to orbit the sun in the year 1900. This is called the *ephemeris second*. Although the unit is defined with a high degree of exactness, implementation of the definition is dependent on astronomical observation, which is incapable of realizing the implied precision.

In the 1950s, atomic research led to the observation that oscillations associated with certain atomic transitions may be measured with great repeatability. One, the hyperfine transition of the cesium atom, was related to the ephemeris second with an estimated accuracy of two parts in 10^9. On October 13, 1967, in Paris, the Thirteenth General Conference on Weights and Measures officially adopted the unit of time of the International System of Units as the second, defined in the following terms: "The second is the duration of 9,192,631,770 periods of the radiation corresponding to the transition between the two hyperfine levels of the fundamental state of the atom of cesium-133" [10].

An atomic beam apparatus [11], commonly called an atomic "clock," is used to produce the frequency of transition. Heated metallic cesium is caused to emit a beam of atoms that is separated into two beams of differing energies depending on the alignment of nuclei and electrons. When an oscillating electromagnetic field is applied having a frequency characteristic of the particular transition, the frequency agreement is detected and appropriately indicated. The frequency of the "master" oscillator may then be used as a standard with which the outputs of other oscillators may be compared.

8.6.1 Frequency Standards

The cesium "clock" is a basic frequency standard. Pendulums, tuning forks, electronic oscillators, etc., may be used as secondary standards. *Frequency* is the number of recurrences of a phenomenon or series of events during a given time interval, and the reciprocal of frequency is *period*. A frequency standard *chops* time into discrete bits that may be used as time standards and, through comparative means, for timing events. The actual source of such a frequency may be mechanical or electrical or, in fact, pneumatic, hydraulic, thermal, etc. In certain cases mechanical frequency sources are used because of their long-time stability. Or the mechanical source, such as a pendulum or tuning fork, may be combined with the electrical, the mechanical being used to control the electrical. Or a strictly electronic source may be used. An electromechanical device that has become very common for providing closely fixed frequencies in the radio frequency range is the piezoelectric crystal. It can be used to maintain very precise frequencies in the range of from 4 kHz to 100 MHz. Such crystals possess the ability to convert mechanical energy into electrical energy, or vice versa. Materials exhibiting this characteristic include quartz, barium titanate, and various crystalline salts. When a small plate or bar of such materials is mechanically strained, a voltage develops across its faces; conversely, when a voltage is applied to the faces, a mechanical strain results. If the voltage is an alternating voltage, the plate or bar may be made to vibrate, and because of its mechanical mass-elastic characteristics, such a member will have a natural frequency of vibration. This fundamental frequency (including overtones) is often used as the basis for very stable control of electronic oscillators.

8.6.2 Electronic Oscillators

Electronic oscillators are sources of periodic voltage variation of either fixed or variable frequency. The rotating a.c. generator is a form of nonelectronic oscillator whose primary purpose is to provide a source of power rather than voltage. However, 60-Hz line voltage is often quite useful as a frequency source. For the purposes of mechanical measurement, it is the voltage output from the oscillator that is of primary value.

In general, electronic oscillators are used for a wide variety of purposes: as energy sources for circuitry measurement, as audio sources for electronic musical instruments, as sweep generators for oscilloscopes and TV receivers, as carriers for radio and TV signal propagation, as "clocks" for synchronizing computer actions, etc. Of course, they can also be used as frequency references that, by suitable comparative means, may be used for timing and phase measurements. See Chapter 10 for additional discussion of this aspect.

Electronic oscillators may be classified as follows:

I. Fixed-frequency oscillators
   A. Simple electronic
   B. Tuning-fork–controlled
   C. Crystal-controlled
II. Variable-frequency oscillators
   A. Sine wave
      1. Audio frequency (0 to 20,000 Hz)
      2. Supersonic (20,000 to 50,000 Hz, roughly)
      3. Radio frequency (50,000 to 10,000,000,000 Hz)
   B. Nonsine wave
      1. Square wave
      2. Sawtooth wave
      3. Random noise

Fixed-frequency oscillators

Fixed-frequency oscillators are of primary value in mechanical measurements for calibrating and recording standard timing signals.

Precise frequency and time standards are available to all through reception of transmissions from the National Bureau of Standards radio stations. Stations WWV, WWVB, and WWVL are located at Fort Collins, Colorado. Station WWVH is in Hawaii. WWV and WWVH are classified as *high frequency* (HF) stations, whereas WWVB transmits at 60 kHz and is classified as *low frequency,* and the frequency of WWVL is 20 kHz, which is called *very low frequency* (VLF). Low and very low frequencies have the advantage of providing more stable reception at a distance because of reduced variations in the transmission paths peculiar to those frequencies. Eventually NBS expects the two lower-frequency stations to have sufficient power to provide a world-wide frequency and time service.*

Variable-frequency oscillators (VFO)

Used for mechanical measurements, these normally produce sine-wave outputs covering a frequency range from about 1 Hz to 100 kHz. Although this exceeds the audible range, oscillators of this type are often referred to as *audio oscillators* to distinguish them from higher-frequency *r.f. oscillators.* A typical audio oscillator has an output of 1 watt at a maximum of 25 volts RMS.

---

* In addition to the United States, many other nations also broadcast timing signals of various types, e.g., CHU in Canada (3.330, 7.335, 14.670 MHz), JJY in Japan (2.5, 5.0, 10.0, 15.0 MHz), MSF in the United Kingdom (2.5, 5.0, 10.0 MHz), and VNG in Australia (4.5, 7.5, 12.0 MHz). (See [12] for an extended listing.)

Complex-wave oscillators

Outputs from sine-wave oscillators may be shaped to provide a variety of waveforms for special applications. Ramp or sawtooth waveforms are used for sweep generators (Section 7.6.2); square waves may be used for evaluating signal conditioner responses (Section 3.19) or for providing synchronization and coding in digital computers. IC chips that provide most or all of these functions are available.

8.7 TEMPERATURE STANDARDS

In 1927 the national laboratories of the United States, Great Britain, and Germany proposed a temperature standard that became known as the International Temperature Scale of 1927 (ITS-27). This standard, adopted by 31 nations, conformed as closely as possible to the thermodynamic scale proposed by Lord Kelvin in 1854. It was based on six fixed-temperature points dependent on physical properties of certain materials, including the ice and steam points of water. Revisions have been made by succeeding conferences, notably in 1948 and 1968. Currently, the International Practical Temperature Scale of 1968 (IPTS-68), adopted by the International Committee on Weights and Measures and authorized by the Thirteenth General Conference, is in effect [13].

The basic unit of temperature, the kelvin (K), is defined as the fraction 1/273.16 of the thermodynamic temperature of the triple point of water; the temperature at which the solid, liquid, and vapor phases of water exist in equilibrium. Degrees Celsius (°C) is defined by the relationship

$$t = T - 273.15,$$

where t and T are *degrees celsius* and *kelvin,* respectively.

In reality, two temperature scales are defined, a *thermodynamic* and a *practical* scale. The latter is the more common basis for measurement. The thermodynamic scale is put in terms of such domains as magnetic, ultrasonic, gas, and optical principles, whereas the practical scale is established in terms of temperature-related physical properties such as thermal expansion and thermoelectrical variations. Both systems are anchored to fixed reference points, with the difference being in the methods of interpolation [14]. Engineering measurement of temperatures is primarily concerned with practical applications, and hence the following discussion is in terms of the International Practical Temperature Scale (IPTS-68).

In addition to defining units, the standard also establishes fixed reference points and provides for interpolation between them. The fixed points are temperatures corresponding to thermal states of materials and are highly reproducible. Zero celsius is the temperature established by equilibrium between pure ice and air-saturated pure water at normal atmospheric pressure. It has been found, however, that a more precise datum, independent of ambient pressure and possible contaminants, uses the so-called *triple point* of water.

This is the temperature at which the solid, liquid, and vapor phases of water exist in equilibrium. The value of 0.0100°C is assigned to this temperature. Simple, easily used apparatus are available for reproducing this fixed temperature point [15].

Primary fixed points listed in Fig. 8.1 and Table 8.4 illustrate the relative positions of certain selected points. The standard also provides numerous *secondary* reference points based on the properties of both elements and compounds such as cadmium, copper, aluminum, and carbon dioxide.

Elaborate interpolation procedures are specified by the IPTS-68 standard for establishment of intermediate reference temperatures. Between the triple

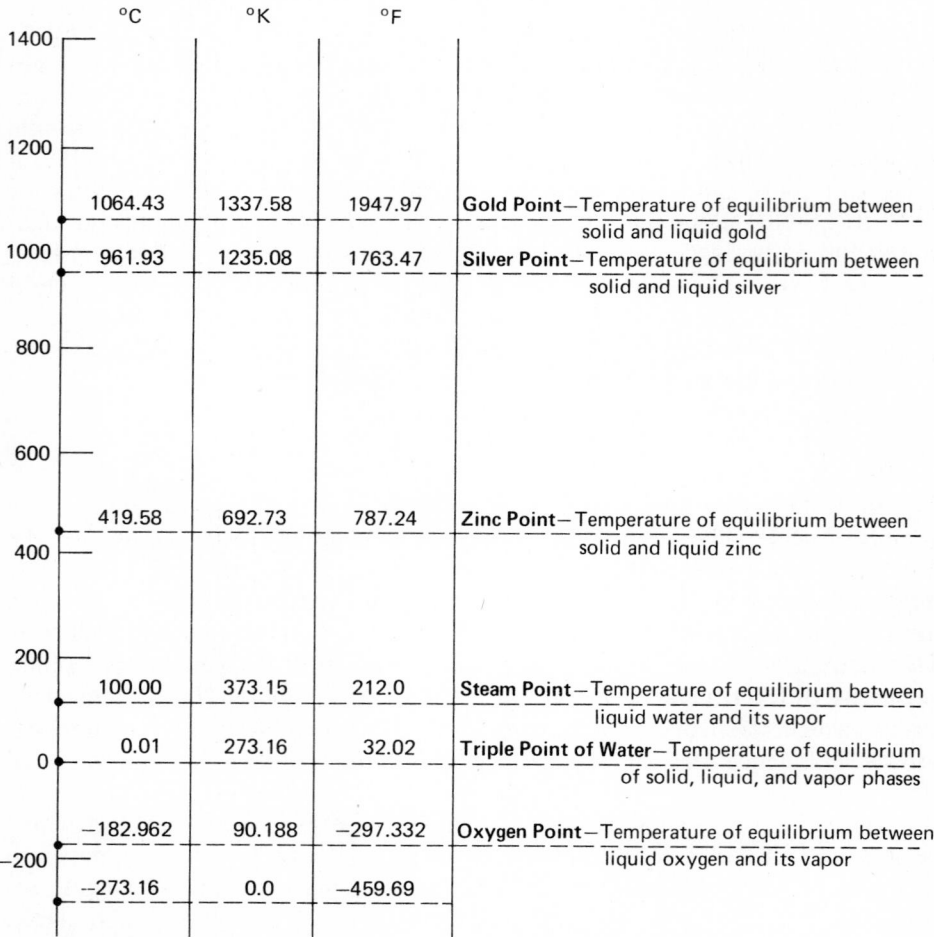

FIGURE 8.1   Some fixed points established by IPTS-68. Others, in kelvins are: triple point of hydrogen, 13.81; boiling point of hydrogen (25/76 atmos.), 17.042; boiling point of hydrogen, 20.28; boiling point of neon, 27.102; triple point of oxygen, 54.361.

TABLE 8.4   Defining Fixed Points of the IPTS-68

Equilibrium State	Assigned Value of International Practical Temperature	
	°K	°C
Triple point* of hydrogen	13.81	−259.34
Boiling point† of hydrogen at 33,330.6 N/m²	17.042	−256.108
Boiling point of hydrogen‡	20.28	−252.87
Boiling point of neon	27.102	−246.048
Triple point of oxygen	54.361	−218.789
Boiling point of oxygen	90.188	−182.962
Triple point of water	273.16	0.01
Boiling point of water	373.15	100
Freezing point of zinc	692.73	419.58
Freezing point of silver	1235.08	961.93
Freezing point of gold	1337.58	1064.43

* Equilibrium between solid, liquid, and vapor phases.

† Equilibrium between liquid and vapor phases.

‡ Except as otherwise noted, equilibrium states correspond to a pressure of standard atmosphere (101,325 N/m²).

point of hydrogen (13.81°K) and the secondary reference point (903.89°K), the freezing point of antimony, use of a platinum resistance thermometer is prescribed (Section 16.4.1). The procedures specified involve subranges and extensive use of tabulated data, too detailed to be presented in this text (see [13] for details). Between 903.89°K and 1337.58°K (the freezing point of gold), a platinum–10%-rhodium/platinum thermocouple is specified as the interpolation device. The following relation is specified for establishing intermediate points:

$$E = a + bt + ct^2,$$

where

E = emf referred to the ice point,

t = the temperature within the specified range °C, and

a, b, and c = constants determined by measuring the value of E with one junction at the ice point and the other successively

at the silver and gold points, plus further determination
at 630.74°C as measured with a platinum resistance
thermometer.

Above the gold point, temperatures are determined by optical means that
evaluate the radiant energy from the unknown temperature source and compare it with that from a source at the gold point. The following relationship
is prescribed:

$$\frac{J_T}{J_{Au}} = \frac{\exp\left[\dfrac{C_2}{\lambda T_{Au}}\right] - 1}{\exp\left[\dfrac{C_2}{\lambda T}\right] - 1} ,$$

where

J_T, J_{Au} = the radiant energy emitted per unit time, per unit area, and
per unit wavelength at wavelength λ, at temperature T, and
at gold-point temperature T_{Au}, respectively.

C_2 = 0.014388 meter-kelvin, and

λ = the wavelength.

Methods for establishing any temperature in the range from 13.81°K
(-259.34°C) to above the gold point are therefore defined. In application to
mechanical development problems, the standardized resistance thermometer,
the standardized thermocouple, or the standardized pyrometer would be used
as secondary devices for calibration of working instruments. (See Chapter
16.)

8.8 ELECTRICAL UNITS

Absolute electrical units are fundamentally derivable from the mechanical
units of length, mass, and time and an assumed value for the permeability of
space, μ_v [16]. Hence with mechanical units standardized, electrical values
are also established. There remains, however, the problem of laboratory usage.
How shall a laboratory provide a basis for calibration? This requires some
form of reproducible source, preferably one having a magnitude as close as
possible to the absolute unit.

Before 1948, electrical standards were based on the "International" Ohm,
Ampere, and Volt, adopted in 1893. The International Ohm was defined as
"the resistance of a column of mercury of uniform cross section, having a
length of 106.300 cm and a mass of 14.4521 gm when the temperature is 0°C."
The International Ampere was defined as "the unvarying current which, when

passed through a solution of silver nitrate in water in accordance with standard specifications, deposits silver at the rate of 0.001118 grams per second.'' The International Volt was defined so that a Clark cell at 15°C had an emf of 1.434 volts.

A primary trouble with this system lay in the fact that as measuring methods inevitably improved, discrepancies between the absolute and the International systems were bound to appear. It soon became apparent that the units as defined above were not consistent with Ohm's law. This was corrected in 1908 by allowing the volt to become a derived unit based on the 1893 definitions of the ampere and the ohm. At that time, however, it was agreed that the *practical* units should be based directly on the derivable absolute units. It was decided that steps should be taken to establish such a standard.

The basis for establishing absolute electrical units lies in theoretically derived relations [17] based on definitions and two experimental procedures. By the first procedure an inductor of accurately determined physical dimensions is constructed and the inductance *calculated*. The reactance of the inductor is then compared with a resistance standard whose resistance is thus determined in dimensional terms. The second procedure consists of accurately determining the force or torque exerted between two coils, in the form of what is known as a *current balance,* when carrying a current [18]. The current is also passed through a resistance, standardized by the first procedure. The potential drop across the resistor is then compared with the output of a *standard-type* cell. On the basis of the data obtained from the current balance, the absolute volt is calculated, thereby standardizing the cell, which in addition to being a standard *type* now becomes a true standard.

From the volt and ohm determined by these experiments, the other electrical units such as the ampere, the henry, and the farad may be derived in absolute terms. Accuracies of a few parts in ten million can be obtained [4].

It was not until 1935, however, that the International Committee on Weights and Measures finally decided that the conversion should be made, setting January 1, 1940, as the date for changeover. The war intervened, and the change to the absolute system was finally made on January 1, 1948. At that time it was found necessary to equate the absolute system to the old International System through use of the following relations:

1 International Ohm $\quad$ = 1.00049 absolute ohms,

1 International Volt $\quad$ = 1.000330 absolute volts,

1 International Ampere = 0.99835 absolute ampere.

Secondary standards in the form of *standard cells* for voltage and *standard resistors* for electrical resistance remain as practical laboratory calibration sources.

SUGGESTED READINGS

ASME, PTC 19.12-1958, *Measurement of Time.*

ASME, PTC 19.16-1965, *Density Determination of Solids and Liquids.*

Blair, B. E., and A. H. Morgan, *Precision Measurement and Calibration.* (Selected NBS papers on frequency and time), NBS Special Publication 300, vol. 5. Washington, D.C.: U.S. Government Printing Office, 1972.

Feather, N., *Mass, Length, and Time.* Baltimore: Penguin Books, 1959.

Hermach, F. L., and R. F. Dziuba, *Precision Measurement and Calibration.* (Selected NBS papers on electricity–low frequency), NBS Special Publication 300, vol. 3. Washington, D.C.: U.S. Government Printing Office, 1968.

"The International Practical Temperature Scale of 1968," (a committee report), *Metrologia,* 5: 2, 35, April 1969.

Kamas, G., and S. L. Howe, *Time and Frequency Users' Manual.* NBS Special Publication 559. Washington, D.C.: U.S. Government Printing Office, 1979.

PROBLEMS

8.1 In 1790, Secretary of State Thomas Jefferson proposed that a standard unit of length be established equal to the length of a seconds pendulum. Write a short report analyzing the merits and problems inherent in such a unit.

8.2 In your own particular position, as an individual, as a student of engineering, as an engineer in industry or at a laboratory, etc., prepare a list of "best" and secondary standards that are directly available to you for any project in which you may be involved. What are your best calibration sources for length, mass, time, temperature, pressure, etc.? Include your best estimates of the calibration uncertainties (see Chapter 9) for each dimension.

8.3 There are various sources of data on local gravity accelerations such as geological surveys, university physics or geology departments, research organizations, and oil, gas, or mining companies. Research values of gravity acceleration for your particular locality.

8.4 Figure 8.2 shows a "constant-moment" beam employed as a secondary strain standard. By use of such an apparatus, the accuracy of strain-measuring systems* may be evaluated simply by comparing strain read-outs with computed strains. Design a standard such as shown in the figure, i.e., after careful consideration, select a material and assign values to dimensions a, b, w, and t; then analyze the design for accuracy. Within what limits do you expect to be able to produce a "standard strain"?

8.5 Answer the following, referring to the apparatus you designed in Problem 8.4.

   a) What range or span of strain should the apparatus have?

   b) List factors that must be considered in selecting the beam material. If metallurgical experts are available, make use of them. Specify a material.

---

*   See Chapter 12 for discussion of strain measurement.

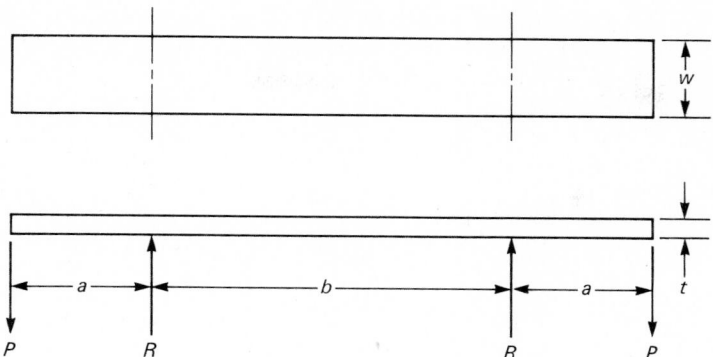

FIGURE 8.2   A "constant moment" beam configuration: see Problem 8.4.

c) How accurately can the beam be made? Assign dimensional tolerances. After it is made, how accurately can the dimensions be checked? Which dimensions are of greatest importance? The value of a on one side may be slightly different than on the other side. What significance would this have?

d) How accurately can the applied loads be determined? If dead weights are to be used, how certain will you be of their magnitudes? In your present circumstance, how would you go about checking the accuracies of any available dead weights? If you were given the job of obtaining "accurate" weights, what would be your procedure? Investigate this matter. The values of P may be slightly different on each side. How nearly equal can they be made? How important is this? Analyze.

e) What value of Young's modulus and Poisson's ratio will you use in your design calculations? (Poisson's ratio may be important if transverse strains are to be considered.) You may wish to determine E and v experimentally. What facilities are available to you to carry out these measurements? With the available facilities, how accurately can you expect to determine E and v? How accurately can the specimens be made, and how accurately can dimensions, loads, and strains be measured? In summary, how accurately do you think you can determine E and v for the material you are using? After careful consideration of all the factors, provide numbers with supporting discussion and findings for the accuracy with which you think values of E and v can be determined.

f) Evaluate the effects of changing ambient temperatures on the strain standard. What problems would be presented if the apparatus were used at extreme temperatures (elevated or cryogenic)?

g) The assumption of "constant moment" between the supports ignores the distributed weight of the beam. Analyze this source of error.

h) There will be certain frictional effects at the support and load points. Analyze them.

i) Bonded-type gages may be applied to the standard for evaluation. They may be used, removed, and others applied. If the surface is mechanically cleaned, how important may the dimensional changes become? Estimate, or better still, experimentally determine such dimensional changes and evaluate the problem. Is it one to worry about? Can local values of E and v be changed by mechanical cleaning?

j) Most of the error sources mentioned above are inherent in the apparatus. Carefully consider any procedural problems that may occur in *using* the apparatus.

k) Can you think of any other factors that may affect the accuracy of the standard? If so, analyze them. What about supporting structure? What about changing barometric pressure? Corrosion? Wear?

8.6 A certain expensive mantel clock uses a torsional pendulum as the means for dividing the passage of time into discrete units. List the variables that control the accuracy of the torsional pendulum. Suggest means for controlling the variables. (See also Problem 9.6).

treatment of 9 uncertainties

9.1 INTRODUCTION

When a number representing the magnitude of a physical quantity is obtained by experimental methods, only through sheer luck will the measured value coincide exactly with the true value—and even then, should this extremely unlikely event occur, it would go unrecognized by the experimenter. The magnitude of the true value can be approached but, in the strictest sense, never evaluated. The difference between the true value (unknown) and the result (best experimentally determined value) is the *error*.

We are clearly confronted with a problem. Since we never know the magnitude of error, should we be so bold as to assign a number to it? We can *attempt* to assign limits within which we are reasonably sure the error will fall, but the fact remains, *we can never be sure*. One option is to coin another term for what we *assume* to be a reasonable numerical value for the error. The word often used in this context is *uncertainty*. Uncertainty is the best estimate (or guess, if you prefer) of the magnitude of the unknown error. None of this, of course, precludes our discussing error or classifying error types or establishing rules for working with error. It is only when we attempt to place a numerical value on the difference between the "measured" and the "true" that we must be careful with our terminology.

The following discussion establishes important nomenclature and outlines some of the procedures applicable to data treatment. It must be understood, however, that only a brief summary can be attempted here; we refer you to the Suggested Readings at the end of the chapter for greater detail.

9.2 NOMENCLATURE

Before proceeding, we must define certain terms applied to the treatment of data.

DATA   Elemental items of information obtained by experimental means herein assumed to be in numerical form.

POPULATION (ALSO CALLED UNIVERSE)   A collection of data, either finite or infinite in number, all supposedly representing the same quantity.

SAMPLE   A portion of a population. A set of values, experimentally obtained, finite in number, representing an actual or a theoretically larger population; that m values are obtained does not normally preclude the possibility of $m + n$ values.

MULTISAMPLE TEST   Repeated measurement of a given quantity using altered test conditions, such as different observers and/or different instrumentation. Merely taking repeated readings with the same procedure and equipment does not provide multisample results. For example, over the years the velocity of light in vacuo has been evaluated by many experimenters, each with different apparatus and techniques and each measuring what is supposedly a unique quantity. Although the results vary, taken together, these findings are multisample results.

SINGLE-SAMPLE TEST   A single reading *or* succession of readings taken under identical conditions except for time. The exactness of a measurement may be estimated only by application of statistics to multiple tests, using as many means and procedures and experimenters as practicable, assuming of course that all methods and equipment are appropriate to the test. When multiple tests, in this sense, are not made, the results are single-sample.

TRUE OR ACTUAL VALUE, V_a Actual magnitude of a measurand. Evaluation of this quantity may be approximated, but in the strictest sense never truly determined.

INDICATED VALUE, V_i The magnitude indication directly supplied by the measuring system. This is the supply of raw or directly recorded data.

CORRECTION   The revision applied to the indicated value, which, it is assumed, improves the worthiness of the result. Such revision may be in the form of either an additive factor or a multiplier or both.

RESULT, V_r Obtained by making all known corrections to the indicated value:

$$V_r = AV_i + B,\tag{9.1}$$

where A and B are multiplying and additive corrections, respectively.

DISCREPANCY   The difference between two indicated values or results determined from a supposedly fixed true value.

ERROR   The *actual* difference between the true value and the result:

$$\text{Error} = V_r - V_a.\tag{9.2}$$

We see that the value of the error is never really known.

ACCURACY   The *maximum* amount by which the result differs from the true value—*measurement with small systematic error:*

$$\text{Accuracy} = \text{Maximum error} = V_{r(\text{max or min})} - V_{a}. \qquad (9.3)$$

In many cases accuracy is expressed as a percentage, based either on the *actual scale reading* or what is called *full-scale reading.* The latter is the maximum value of the particular range being used:

$$\text{Percent accuracy based on reading} = \frac{V_{r(\text{max or min})} - V_{a}}{V_{a}} \times 100, \qquad (9.3a)$$

$$\text{Percent accuracy based on full scale} = \frac{V_{r(\text{max or min})} - V_{a}}{V_{fs}} \times 100, \qquad (9.3b)$$

where V_{fs} is the maximum reading the measuring system is capable of for the particular setting or scale being used. It is most common to find accuracies expressed in terms of full scale.

It should be pointed out that the percent accuracies indicated by Eqs. (9.3a) and (9.3b) are normally used to express equipment accuracies, and when so used do not include procedural and personnel performance. The values do not, therefore, express the true total performance of the measuring system.

PRECISION   The degree of agreement between repeated results—*measurement with small random error.* To cite an extreme example [1]: If all clocks in a jewelry store are set at 8:20 but are not running, the indicated values show precision but are accurate only twice in 24 hours.

Precise data have small dispersion (spread or scatter), but may be far from the true value.

RESOLUTION   The smallest increment of input signal that a measuring system is capable of displaying.

DEFINITION   An evaluation of the consistency of a quantity. For example, the width of a desktop may not be *exactly* defined. The edges are not perfect, nor are the sides *exactly* straight or parallel. Thus even if our measuring system *were* perfect, we could not always expect to obtain consistent results. This variation may be closely associated with uncertainty. However, it is only one component of the latter—the uncertainty of definition.

UNCERTAINTY   Possible error or what one thinks may be the range of error. Although unknown for a given measurement, the error is a definite number. Uncertainty, on the other hand, is the region in which one believes (or guesses) the error to be. This relation may be considered in terms of an analogous idea, a limit dimension. A machined dimension may be specified on a drawing through use of tolerances. When the drawing is made, the dimension of a *particular* part is unknown; however, the range is definitely known. After a part is produced, it then has a definite dimension, deviating a definite amount from nominal. It may be said that this deviation expresses the dimension's *error*, whereas the tolerance span expresses the *uncertainty*.

PROPAGATION OF UNCERTAINTY   The manner in which a combination of uncertainties affect the result. Often a result is derived from a combination of measurements (see Section 9.6), each of which is subject to error. How do they combine to produce an overall uncertainty? Some may simply add; others not. For example, if a micrometer having an inherent error in thread pitch is used to measure two dimensions of a rectangular area, the area calculation will involve errors in both width and thickness and the total error will depend on the interaction of the two errors. On the other hand, if pressure is measured with the simple tire gage shown in Fig. 1.3(a), errors may be introduced by incorrect piston size and incorrect spring constant. In the latter case it is clear that the errors could possibly be compensating, whereas this would be impossible in the first example. The former are called *dependent* errors and the latter *independent* errors. A study of propagation of errors must include consideration of the interrelationships of the various types of error.

In addition, *correlated* errors may be present when a systematic relation exists between two or more quantities. This would occur, for example, when temperature and pressure measurements are both required and a poorly temperature-compensated pressure gage is used.

MEAN (OR AVERAGE)   The summation of results divided by the number of results. This is considered the "best" approximation of the true value of a given measurement.

MEDIAN   The middle value of a series of data representing a given quantity. As many data items fall to one side of the median as to the other side.

MODE   The most frequently occurring result. More than one mode is possible.

RANGE   The difference between the largest and the smallest results.

DISPERSION (OR SCATTER)   The manner in which the results lie about the mean—a measure of reliability.

DEVIATION (ALSO CALLED THE RESIDUAL)   The difference between a single result and the mean of many results, all for the same test quantity.

MEAN DEVIATION (ALSO CALLED PROBABLE ERROR)   The sum of the absolute deviations divided by their number. There is equal probability that a given deviation will be either larger than or smaller than this value.

STANDARD DEVIATION (ALSO CALLED MEAN SQUARE ERROR)   The square root of the mean of the squares of the deviations. This quantity represents a common measure of the preciseness of a sample of data. (*Note:* A "better" value is assumed when the summation of the square is divided by $N - 1$ rather than by N. See Section 9.9.)

PERCENT STANDARD DEVIATION   The ratio of the standard deviation to the mean, expressed as a percentage.

9.3   ERROR CLASSIFICATION

Assigning names to types of error is difficult. Some definitions are overlapping and some may be ambiguous. For our purposes the following are listed.

I. Systematic or fixed errors
   A. Calibration errors
   B. Certain types of consistently recurring human error
   C. Errors of technique
   D. Uncorrected loading errors
   E. Limits of system resolution

II. Random or accidental errors
   A. Errors stemming from environmental variations
   B. Certain types of human error
   C. Errors resulting from variations in definition
   D. Errors derived from insufficient sensitivity of the measuring system

III. Illegitimate errors
   A. Blunders or mistakes
   B. Computational errors
   C. Chaotic errors

Systematic error is of an insidious nature: It is completely unobtrusive, existing unnoticed unless deliberately searched out. As the term indicates, it is repetitive and of a fixed value, recurring consistently every time the measurement is made. It is *not,* therefore, susceptible to statistical analysis.

Error of technique may be due simply to improper usage of measuring apparatus. This type of error could also be listed under (III) above, if it is a blunder. We must note that however sophisticated, no technique is perfect— each is susceptible to improvement. Part II of this book is devoted to applied measurement methods (techniques) and although the state-of-the-art coverage is hoped for, all but the simplest will undoubtedly be improved.

An important source of legitimate systematic error stems from the imprecisenesses of calibration. As we discussed in Section 1.5 and throughout the book, calibration consists of "proving" the measuring system's read-out scales by comparison with a standard. It is obvious, of course, that within all* standards are uncertainties, however small.

Human error may well be systematic, as in the case of an individual's tendency to consistently read high or to "jump the gun" when synchronized readings are to be taken.

The equipment itself may introduce built-in errors resulting from incorrect design, fabrication, or maintenance. Such errors may be caused by *false elements* [2], such as incorrect scale graduations, defective gearing, or linkages of wrong proportions. Certain electronic-amplifier faults also fall under this heading. Errors of this type are consistent with regard to both sign and magnitude, and because of their consistency may sometimes be corrected by calibration. This is not always the case, however, for if the input is of complex form, distortion caused by poor system response would not ordinarily be correctable by calibration.

Loading error is of special significance. It results from the influence exerted by the act of measurement on the physical system being tested. It is basic that *the measurement process inevitably alters the characteristics of both the source of the measured quantity and the measuring system itself, from which it must follow that there will always be some difference between the measured indication and the corresponding to-be-measured quantity.*

This is an important fact that must always be borne in mind. The process must take some energy from the input source; therefore the source will be changed by the process. Placing a probe in an air stream changes the flow pattern. A bonded strain gage mounted on a foil test subject will alter the stiffness. Or the mass of a vibrometer placed on a small beam will alter the characteristics of the quantity being measured. These are obvious examples, but similar conditions exist in all measuring systems, including even optical methods [3].

Random errors are distinguishable by their lack of consistency. An observer may not be consistent when estimating readings, or the process involved may include certain uncontrolled, or poorly controlled, variables causing changing conditions. In the instrumentation itself, such errors may result from *disturbed elements* [2], usually coming from some outside influence such as vibration or temperature variations (vibration- and temperature-measuring systems excepted). Errors of this type are normally of limited time duration or are inherent to specific environment.

Variation of conditions would also include the effects of unconstrained elements caused by such things as backlash and friction. These are design problems involving materials and dimensional tolerances. One means of de-

---

* It might be argued that the uniqueness of certain primary standards (e.g., the mass standard) makes them exceptions to this statement. It is doubtful, however, that the statement can be challenged: certainly not in the practical sense of application. To be practicable, the primary standards require the use of ancillary apparatus, which dilutes the "pureness" of the source.

tecting and often correcting this type of error is to determine results while the measured quantity is first increased and then decreased in magnitude. This is sometimes called the *method of symmetry*.

As their name implies, *illegitimate errors* should not exist. They include outright mistakes that can be eliminated through exercise of care and repetition of the measurement.

Chaotic errors include random disturbances introducing errors of sufficient magnitude to hide the test information. Extreme vibration, mechanical shock of the equipment, or pickup of extraneous noise may be of sufficient magnitude to make testing meaningless. In such cases the test should be stopped until the disturbing elements can be eliminated.

On occasion, the randomness of noise may work against itself. As examples, sophisticated computer systems can extract desired information from an unavoidable overburden of noise, and can enhance photographs being returned from space probes. In such cases the systematic nature of the desired information in comparison to the complete randomness of the noise is used to separate the two. Such techniques are entirely beyond the scope of this book.

9.4 DATA CHARACTERISTICS DICTATED BY THE NATURE OF THE TEST

The numbers obtained by various measurement procedures yield many possible treatments. Consider the following.

9.4.1 Single-Test Data

The nature of the test may preclude check runs. Examples include the launching of a space vehicle or the underground test of a nuclear weapon. In such cases testing redundancy is necessary to ensure adequate data acquisition. In some respects this situation is similar to the example concerning the speed of light that we mentioned in Section 9.2 *Multisample test*. Various comparable data are obtained from a single source, using different test apparatus. On the other hand, certain testing may be included in this category less from the standpoint of possibilities than from factors of convenience, time, and cost. For example, the weighing of a sample of fuel, the measurement of the length of a piece of steel-bar stock, or the measurement of an ambient temperature would probably be done only once, with any checking done simply to preclude gross error, rather than to reduce uncertainty. Although measurements can be repeated, practicality often makes them unnecessary, or even undesirable. This may be true of more complicated measurements also. An example is a test on a turbine generator with a series of runs made under *different* conditions, but with no one set of test conditions repeated in all details.

Data obtained from these tests are referred to as single-test data and can be analyzed by methods developed in Section 9.5.

9.4.2 Variable-Sample Data

In this case testing may be repeated in an attempt to reduce uncertainty; yet the primary source of variableness stems less from the test methods than from the test subject itself. For example, the lack of homogeneity of most materials makes it impossible to test the *same* subject repeatedly. Repeated hardness read-outs obtained from a series of measurements on a given sample of steel will invariably show scatter, which is not derived from the methods used so much as it is from the subject material. This type of randomness is caused more by the measurand and less by the test techniques. Variableness of this sort is susceptible to analysis by statistical methods.

9.4.3 Replicated Test Data

Setups may be made and supposedly identical tests run and rerun to accumulate a mass of data that hopefully represent a single value. This is called *replicated testing*. In truth, of course, the test is never quite duplicated. Small differences in conditions or manipulations, changes in line voltages, and the like may result in randomly dispersed data. Or in some cases the changes may be one-directioned, probably caused by some overlooked effect, such as drift in the gain of an amplifier. Of course, the latter, if observed, should be corrected. If replicated test data are of the random sort, however, about the only value of merit is the arithmetical average of the results. Standard deviations, deviations of the mean, and so on, as discussed in later sections of this chapter, would add little or nothing to interpretation of the result.

9.5 TREATMENT OF SYSTEMATIC AND SINGLE-SAMPLE UNCERTAINTIES

Uncertainties of technique, calibration uncertainties, human uncertainties, and any uncertainties possessing a consistency of magnitude and sign can only be ferretted out and evaluated through diligence and careful and persistent observation, criticism, and evaluation of procedures.

The uncertainty of calibration is perhaps the easiest to consider. Calibration requires a reference (standard) against which the system may be compared. The reference may be *fixed* or *one-valued,* such as the boiling point of water, or, on the other hand, a source capable of supplying a range of inputs comparable to the range of the system. An example of the latter is any one of the commercially available voltage references. Naturally, the uncertainty of the standard should be considerably less than that of the system to be calibrated. Figure 9.1 shows a block diagram of an arrangement that would be used.

Analysis of random uncertainties (considered beginning with Section (9.8) requires a volume of data not always available. In other words, although randomness exists in single-sample testing, a random data analysis is obviously

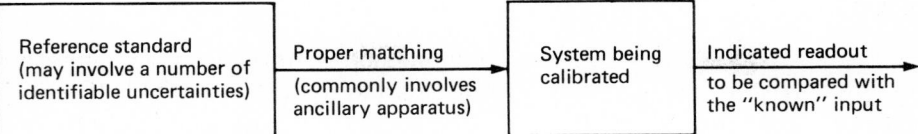

| Reference standard (may involve a number of identifiable uncertainties) | Proper matching (commonly involves ancillary apparatus) | System being calibrated | Indicated readout to be compared with the "known" input |

FIGURE 9.1   Block diagram showing calibration procedure.

precluded by lack of information. In the next several sections we will discuss methods that can be used not only to analyze systematic and single-sample uncertainties, but also to assist in *predicting* uncertainties in as yet unrun tests.

9.6   PROPAGATION OF UNCERTAINTY

Taylor's theorem is a special application of Taylor's series (see most any engineering mathematics text). The theorem can be expressed as

$$f[(x_1 + \Delta x_1), (x_2 + \Delta x_2), \cdots, (x_n + \Delta x_n)] = f(x_1, x_2, \cdots, x_n) + \Delta x_1 \frac{\partial f}{\partial x_1}$$

$$+ \Delta x_2 \frac{\partial f}{\partial x_2} + \cdots + \Delta x_n \frac{\partial f}{\partial x_n}$$

$$+ \text{higher-order terms}, \qquad (9.4)$$

where the x_n's are variables and the Δx_n's are determined *or assumed* incremental variations (uncertainties) in the respective x_n's. The higher-order terms are neglected.

This equation can be rewritten, changing the Δx_n's to u_n's merely to represent uncertainties better:

$$f(|x_1| + |u_{x_1}|), (|x_2| + |u_{x_2}|), \cdots, (|x_n| + |u_{x_n}|) - f(|x_1|, |x_2|, \cdots, |x_n|)$$

$$= u_f = \left| u_{x_1} \frac{\partial f}{\partial x_1} \right| + \left| u_{x_2} \frac{\partial f}{\partial x_2} \right| + \cdots + \left| u_n \frac{\partial f}{\partial x_n} \right|. \qquad (9.4a)$$

Absolute values are indicated because it is assumed that the uncertainties are expressed as equally probable plus and minus values.

Equation (9.4a) evaluates the overall *maximum* uncertainty of the function. It is not likely, however, that we should expect the maximum value to be attained. A more reasonable value corresponds to the Pythagorean summation of the discrete uncertainties, or

$$u_f = \sqrt{\left(u_{x_1} \frac{\partial f}{\partial x_1} \right)^2 + \left(u_{x_2} \frac{\partial f}{\partial x_2} \right)^2 + \cdots + \left(u_{x_n} \frac{\partial f}{\partial x_n} \right)^2} \qquad (9.5)$$

where

$$x_i = \text{nominal values of variables,}$$

$$u_{x_i} = \text{discrete uncertainties, and}$$

$$u_f = \text{overall uncertainty.}$$

As an exercise, let

$$X = AB^m/C^n, \tag{9.6}$$

where A, B, and C are variables. Then

$$\frac{\partial X}{\partial A} = B^m/C^n,$$

$$\frac{\partial X}{\partial B} = \frac{mAB^{(m-1)}}{C^n} \text{ , and}$$

$$\frac{\partial X}{\partial C} = -nAB^m/C^{n+1}.$$

Using Eq. (9.4a), we have

$$u_X = \left| \frac{B^m}{C^n} u_A \right| + \left| \frac{mAB^{(m-1)}}{C^n} u_B \right| + \left| \frac{nAB^m}{C^{(n+1)}} u_C \right|$$

and

$$\frac{u_X}{X} = \left| \frac{u_A}{A} \right| + \left| \frac{mu_B}{B} \right| + \left| \frac{nu_C}{C} \right|;$$

or, using Eq. (9.5),

$$\frac{u_X}{X} = \sqrt{\left(\frac{u_A}{A} \right)^2 + \left(\frac{mu_B}{B} \right)^2 + \left(\frac{nu_C}{C} \right)^2}. \tag{9.6a}$$

Note especially the *weighting factors*, m and n, along with their sources in Eq. (9.6).

9.7 AN EXAMPLE OF SYSTEMATIC ERROR ANALYSIS

Let us consider the following example: Obstruction meters such as venturis and orifices are commonly used to measure steady-state fluid flow. Tables of coefficients are available, which when inserted in theoretical relationships such as Eq. (15.7) yield

$$Q = KA_2\sqrt{2g_c/\rho}\ \sqrt{P_1 - P_2}. \tag{9.7}$$

This provides a means for measuring flow rates in terms of pressure drops across the obstruction. Although published coefficients yield approximate flow rates, accurate measurements require careful experimental determination of the coefficients for a particular installation.

Figure 9.2 shows an arrangement for steady-state calibration of a thin-plate orifice. In this case calibration consists of experimentally determining the coefficient K in the above equation. This is done by collecting the flowing fluid (assume water) in a weigh tank for some convenient time interval. During the calibration period the flow is held as constant as possible and the pressure differential, $(P_1 - P_2) = \Delta P$, is recorded.

Substituting $A_2 = \pi D^2/4$ and $Q = W/\rho t$ in Eq. (9.7) yields

$$K = \frac{4W}{\pi D^2 t} \sqrt{\frac{1}{2g_c \rho \, \Delta P}} . \tag{9.7a}$$

Insertion of the observed values of W, P, and t into the equation, along with appropriate values of D, g_c, and ρ, yields a value for the experimentally determined flow coefficient.

We will now attempt a critical evaluation of the overall systematic uncertainty associated with this experiment. Weight W is measured with a platform scale. What uncertainty exists in the scale measurement? Has the scale's calibration been checked? How recently and against what standard? (See

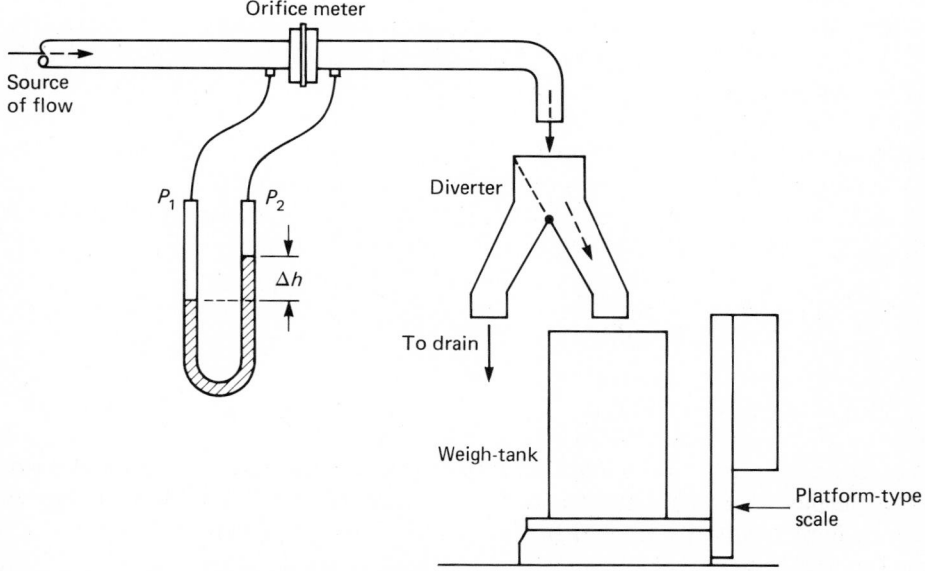

FIGURE 9.2   Setup for calibrating an orifice.

Section 13.1 for further discussion of this point.) Hopefully we have made some sort of check on the scale, at least several point calibrations using reliable proof weights. Let us say that in our judgment we can justify a certainty of 99%, i.e., an uncertainty of 1%. In fact, the uncertainty is undoubtedly dependent to some degree on the relative read-out magnitude and scale range. If warranted, this may be considered.

The diameter of the orifice must be determined. Assume it is a sharp-edged orifice and that we have checked it with an inside micrometer. Did we check the micrometer against gage blocks, or are we accepting its scale verbatim? How experienced are we in using a micrometer? What deviation do we find in repeated readings? How good is the definition of the dimension? Is there out-of-roundness? Let us say that our judgment assigns an uncertainty of $\pm$ 0.008 cm and that the nominal size is 4 cm; $u = \pm 0.2\%$.

How accurate is the determination of the time period t? If a hand-operated diverter is used, precisely when did the flow start and stop; that is, how well is the time period *defined*? If a stopwatch is used, how good is the synchronization between diverter and watch actions? If the nominal time is 5 minutes, let us assume a total uncertainty for this measurement of ± 3 s, or $\pm 1\%$.

We should remark at this point on the real nature of the time determination above. Is this uncertainty really of a systematic nature? To a considerable degree it is more truly of a random nature. If we were to carefully make a series of repeated runs of this particular procedure we would accumulate enough data to permit a random data analysis, should the required precision justify doing so. More often, however, we would probably simply make a judgment analysis and arrive at some reasonable uncertainty estimate, as we did in the preceding paragraph. In this case we would treat the estimate only as a form of systematic uncertainty.

Between 0°C and 38°C, the density of water decreases about 0.7%. For our example, let us assume an uncertainty of $\pm$ 0.2% for this variable. The dimensional constant, g_c, by its nature contains no uncertainty. The value ΔP is measured with a manometer and we will use an uncertainty of $\pm 1\%$ for this quantity. We may observe that in actuality this uncertainty is probably relatively constant and independent of magnitude. To assign a percentage value, therefore, may not be completely realistic without also accounting for the magnitude of ΔP. We will simply use the above value rather than to complicate our example unnecessarily.

What about fluctuations in flow rate over the five-minute test period? Presumably we would monitor this and attempt to fine-tune the flow during the test; however, we should remind ourselves that at this point we are considering *systematic,* not random, error and that any lack of constancy in flow will be primarily random.

On the basis of the above estimates, what is a reasonable value to assign to the uncertainty of the experimentally determined value of K? Summarizing our estimated individual uncertainties, we have:

Scale, u_w	1%
Orifice diameter, u_d	0.2%
Effective time period, u_t	1%
Density of water, u_ρ	0.2%
Δ Pressure, u_p	1%

Taking advantage of the weighting factor, which we demonstrated in Eq. (9.6a), we may write

$$u_K = \left| u_W \frac{\partial K}{\partial W} \right| + \left| u_D \frac{\partial K}{\partial D} \right| + \left| u_t \frac{\partial K}{\partial t} \right| + \left| u_\rho \frac{\partial K}{\partial \rho} \right| + \left| u_{\Delta P} \frac{\partial K}{\partial \Delta P} \right|$$

or

$$\frac{u_K}{K} = \left[\left(\frac{u_W}{W} \right)^2 + \left(2\frac{u_D}{D} \right)^2 + \left(\frac{u_t}{t} \right)^2 + \left(\frac{1}{2}\frac{u_\rho}{\rho} \right)^2 + \left(\frac{1}{2}\frac{u_{\Delta P}}{\Delta P} \right)^2 \right]^{\frac{1}{2}}$$

$$= \left[(1)^2 + (2 \times 0.2)^2 + (1)^2 + \left(\frac{1}{2} \times 0.2 \right)^2 + \left(\frac{1}{2} \times 1 \right)^2 \right]^{\frac{1}{2}}$$

$$= 1.56\%.$$

Inspection of the final evaluation quickly identifies the parameters having little or no influence on the result. Reducing the uncertainties of the weighing and the timing procedures would be most productive. Conservatively, we can say that adhering to the care implied in the discussion we can be assured that the *systematic uncertainty* will be no greater than, say, 2%.

What are the bases for the various individual uncertainties that were used in the analysis? Were the values simple guesses? To a degree, they were, but only to a small degree. Some of the specific factors involved in each of the estimates were discussed, with the final values assigned on the basis of practical engineering judgment; i.e., application of simple common sense. But why not, with common sense, guess at the overall uncertainty and be done with it? In answer, the detailed analysis provides a means for evaluating the weight (effect) of each of the identifiable systematic uncertainties, thereby separating the more important ones from the less important. Furthermore, one is able to evaluate the uncertainties of each of the individual variables with considerably more assurance than one could judge the total.

9.7.1 Designing (Planning) an Experiment

It is obvious from the above discussion that it is unnecessary to wait until after an experiment has been run and data have been collected to make this type of analysis. It should be clear that there is much to recommend making such a study during the planning stage. By so doing, one can readily determine which of the various parameters must be controlled with care and which are of less importance.

9.8 TREATMENT OF RANDOM ERROR

When multisample observations are experimentally obtained, discrepancies displayed by the dispersion or scatter of the data about some average result occur. As an example, Table 9.1 represents the results of a fictitious test in which a pressure is measured 100 times. It is assumed that multisample requirements have been met and that although an attempt is made to hold the test conditions constant, variations in parameters have resulted in a scatter of readings. Any systematic error that may be present simply offsets the entire set of data one way or the other and does *not* affect what we are considering at this point, the dispersion about the average.

In analyzing the dispersion a possible first step is to prepare a *histogram:* a bar diagram displaying the *frequency of occurrence* of the experimental readings versus pressure (Fig. 9.3). In preparing the histogram one must first consider the number of *class intervals* or bars to be used. The number selected may have considerable influence on the final shape of the histogram. A reasonable number can be determined by using an *empirical* relationship known as the Sturgis Rule [4], which is expressed as

$$N = 1 + (3.3) \log (n), \tag{9.8}$$

where n is the total number of data items and N is the suggested number of class intervals. This is merely a guide and in no way dictates a number that

TABLE 9.1

Pressure, P, in MPa	Number of results, n
3.97	1
3.98	3
3.99	12
4.00	25
4.01	33
4.02	17
4.03	6
4.04	2
4.05	1

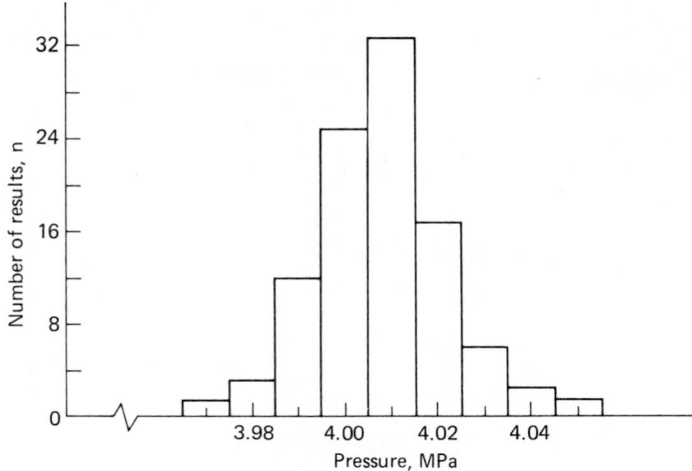

FIGURE 9.3   One of several possible histograms for the data listed in Table 9.1.

must be used. One factor in making the selection may be how neatly the data may be divided. For our example $n = 100$ and $N = 7.6 \approx 8$. In Fig. 9.3 we see that nine class intervals have been used. The reader will follow the reason for this and appreciate the value and limitations of a histogram by using the data given in Table 9.1 to prepare three histograms, one with seven, one with eight, and another with ten class intervals. We also direct the reader's attention to Appendix F for further discussion of class intervals.

9.9 THEORETICAL RELATIONSHIPS*

Experimental data are often dispersed in the familiar bell-shaped curve (Fig. 9.4). On the basis of an *infinite population* the mathematical expression for this curve is

$$f(x) = \frac{1}{\sigma\sqrt{2\pi}} e^{-(x - m)^2/2\sigma^2}, \tag{9.9}$$

where

$x =$ the magnitude of the measured quantity,

$m =$ the mean value of the entire population, and

$\sigma =$ the standard deviation.

Distributions of this sort are said to be Gaussian or *normal*, and the relationship

---

*   The reader is referred to Section 9.2 for definitions of certain terms used in the following discussion.

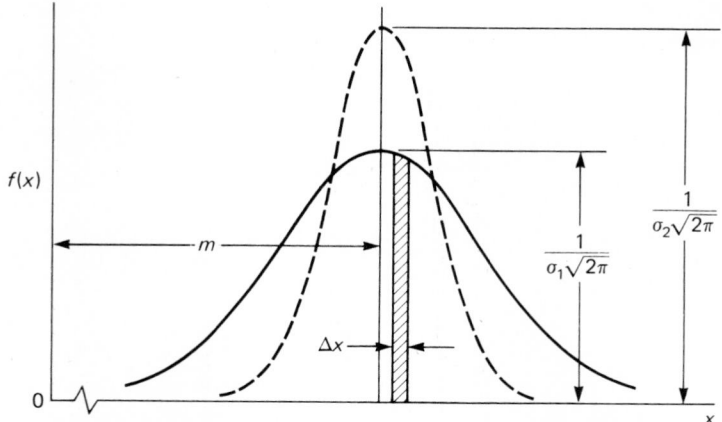

FIGURE 9.4   Normal distribution curve. More precise data are represented by the dashed curve than by the solid curve.

is called the *probability density function*. Another form of the relationship, often more convenient to use, is

$$f(t) = \frac{1}{\sigma\sqrt{2\pi}}\, e^{-(t^2/2)}, \qquad (9.9a)$$

where

$$t = (x - m)/\sigma.$$

Note that whereas the histogram deals with the finite number of data items (100 in our example), Eq. (9.9) and Fig. 9.4 assume an infinite population. The ordinate of the smooth curve must therefore be carefully interpreted. The total *area* under the entire curve corresponds to a probability of unity (100%). A given ordinate does not represent the probability of occurrence of the corresponding value of x, but the area corresponding to an increment, Δx, *does* represent the probability of the occurrence of values falling within the range, Δx.

When data abide by Gaussian or normal distribution rules, plus and minus discrepancies are equally likely, and small discrepancies are more probable than large discrepancies, but there is no real limit to the magnitude of large discrepancies.

In the analysis of multisample data that are assumed to be normally distributed, several important parameters must be defined. It can be shown [5] that if a large number of measurements are all taken with equal care, the most probable value of the measurement is the arithmetic mean, or

$$\bar{x} = \frac{x_1 + x_2 + \cdots + x_n}{n} = \frac{\sum x_i}{n}. \qquad (9.10)$$

By definition the deviation d is the difference $x - \bar{x}$. It can be shown that the arithmetic mean $\bar{x}$ is such that the sum of the squares of the deviations is a minimum. Conversely, if the sum of the squares of the deviations is a minimum, the most probable value of the measured quantity is $\bar{x}$.

9.9.1 Mean and Standard Deviations

The following equation defines the *mean deviation:*

$$\text{Mean deviation} = d_m = \frac{|d_1| + |d_2| + \cdots + |d_n|}{n}. \tag{9.11}$$

Note that the numerical values of the deviations are added without regard to algebraic sign.

Standard or mean-square deviation is defined by the relation*

$$\sigma = \sqrt{\frac{(d_1)^2 + (d_2)^2 + \cdots + (d_n)^2}{n - 1}} \tag{9.12}$$

$$= \sqrt{\frac{\sum (x_i - \bar{x})^2}{n - 1}} \tag{9.12a}$$

$$= \sqrt{\frac{\sum x_i^2 - n\bar{x}^2}{n - 1}}. \tag{9.12b}$$

As we stated previously, the actual value by which a result is in error is never known. There are, however, various ways of estimating random uncertainty. Mean deviation (also known as *probable error*) and standard deviation are two. From the definition of mean deviation, we see that for a given population, there is an equal probability that a randomly selected value will differ from the mean by an amount greater than (or less than) the average deviation. In this connection the term "probable error" is applied to the mean deviation. This quantity is not, however, the most popularly used error estimate.

Standard deviation, σ, has an analogous mechanical counterpart in the radius of gyration, as applied to the moment of inertia. If the area under the normal distribution curve is considered a two-dimensional body rotating about the mean, then the value of σ corresponds to its radius of gyration. Standard deviation is particularly useful in further statistical treatment of data, and is therefore a very commonly used quantity for expressing error estimate.

---

* Note that $(n - 1)$ is used as the divisor in Eq. (9.12). This is the usual practice, the argument being that inasmuch as the entire set of data has already been used to determine the mean, the number of independent deviations is $(n - 1)$. It may also be observed that deviation has meaning only *after* the first result has been obtained.

TABLE 9.2   Summary of Error Estimates Based on Normal Distribution

Name of Error	Symbol	Value in Terms of σ	Percent Certainty	Probability that a Single Value will be Greater
Probable error (also mean deviation)	E_p	0.6745σ	50	1 in 2
Standard deviation	σ	σ	68.3	1 in 3 (approx.)
90% error	E_{90}	1.6449σ	90	1 in 10
Two sigma error	2σ	2σ	95	1 in 20
Three sigma error	3σ	3σ	99.7	1 in 370
Maximum* error	E_{max}	3.29σ	99.9+	1 in 1000

*   *Some regard the 95% error as "maximum." In any case, of course, a practical maximum is being considered. The actual maximum is theoretically infinite.*

For normal distribution, the probability of obtaining a deviation greater than σ is about 31.7%; greater than 2σ is about 5%; greater than 3σ, about $\frac{1}{3}$%; and greater than 4σ, approximately 0.006%. One criterion for discarding suspected data is the 3σ value; any data having a deviation greater than 3σ are arbitrarily thrown out. Table 9.2 compares several of these error estimates.

EXAMPLE   In Section 9.8 and Fig. 9.3 we considered an example involving 100 pressure readings. In Table 9.3 the data are relisted and certain calculations are made. We will assume that all the pertinent corrections have been made and that the first column lists the results. It will be noted that the range is 0.08 MPa as determined from the greatest difference in results. Column 2 lists the frequency of each value, and Fig. 9.5 shows the distribution. Columns 3 and 4 are the deviations and squares thereof, respectively.

The average of the readings is calculated as 4.008 MPa, the mean deviation is 1.046×10^{-2}, and the standard deviation is 13.7×10^{-3}. The latter figure means that should we arbitrarily select any single result, there is a 68.3% chance (see Table 9.2) that it will fall within the region $(4.008 + 13.7 \times 10^{-3}) = 4.0217$ and $(4.008 - 13.7 \times 10^{-3}) = 3.9943$ MPa, provided (*and this is an important proviso*) that the data are truly distributed in accordance with Eq. (9.9). In this connection, it should be clear that the various numerical values relating such quantities as mean deviation and standard deviation (Table 9.2) require a true normal distribution. Although experimental data may approximate normal distribution, they seldom, if ever, fit the bell-shaped curve exactly. *Goodness of fit*, therefore, becomes a legitimate question, and various methods have been devised to evaluate this factor. See the following section and Appendix F.

The question may be asked, "Is it not possible to obtain more than one sample of a given population? If this is so, should we not expect that each

TABLE 9.3

Pressure, P, in MPa	Number of Results, n	Deviation, d	d^2
3.97	1	−0.038	144.4×10^{-5}
3.98	3	−0.028	78.4
3.99	12	−0.018	32.4
4.00	25	−0.008	6.4
4.01	33	0.002	0.4
4.02	17	0.012	14.4
4.03	6	0.022	48.4
4.04	2	0.032	102.4
4.05	1	0.042	176.4
$\sum P = 400.77$	$\sum n = 100$	$\sum d = 1.046$	$\sum d^2 = 1858 \times 10^{-5}$

$P_m = 400.77/100 \approx 4.008$ MPa
$d_m = 1.046/100 = 1.046 \times 10^{-2}$ MPa
$\sigma = \sqrt{1858 \times 10^{-5}/99} \approx 13.7 \times 10^{-3}$ MPa

sample would yield a slightly different average or mean? Hence should it not be possible to treat the resulting means in a statistical manner?'' This is indeed possible, and we can show that the standard deviation of the resulting means may be expressed by the relationship

$$\sigma_m = \sigma/\sqrt{n}, \qquad (9.13)$$

where σ_m is called the *standard deviation of the mean* and is a measure of the probable distribution of the means that would be obtained by taking many samples of a given population.

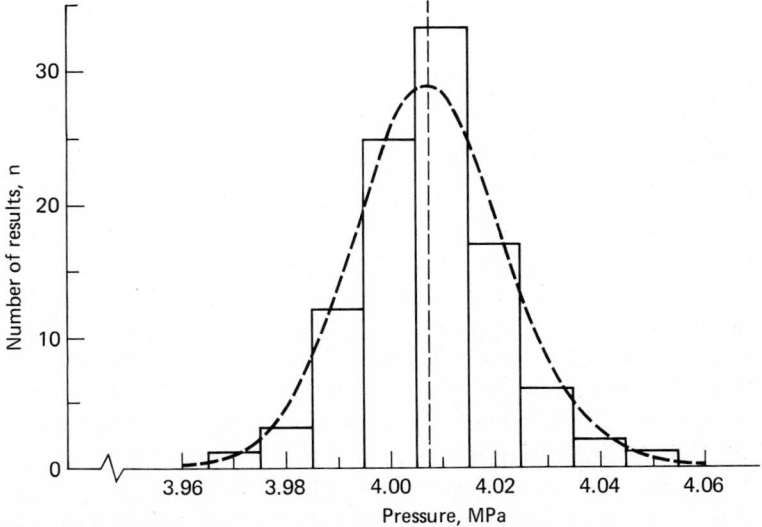

FIGURE 9.5   Histogram of data listed in Table 9.3.

For our example above,

$$\sigma_m = 13.7 \times 10^{-3}/\sqrt{100} = 1.4 \times 10^{-3} \text{ MPa.}$$

If, as a result of our example, we should write

$$\sigma_m = 4.008 \pm 1.4 \times 10^{-3} \text{ MPa,}$$

this should be interpreted as meaning that the arithmetic average of any sample of 100 readings has a 68% chance of falling within the interval $(4.008 + 1.4 \times 10^{-3})$ and $(4.008 - 1.4 \times 10^{-3})$. Perhaps we wish to increase the probability range by using a 2σ tolerance. In this case we would assume a 95% chance that the mean of any sample of 100 readings would fall within the interval $4.008 \pm 2.8 \times 10^{-3}$ MPa.

If multiple samples of a given population are taken, then the resulting standard deviation should be susceptible to similar treatment, and a standard deviation of the standard deviation, σ_σ, should have meaning. It can be shown that

$$\sigma_\sigma = \sigma/\sqrt{2n} = \sigma_m/\sqrt{2}. \tag{9.14}$$

Returning to our example, we have

$$\sigma_\sigma = 13.7 \times 10^{-3}/\sqrt{2 \times 100} \approx 0.97 \times 10^{-3}.$$

This result means that there is a 68% chance that σ will fall within the interval $(13.7 \pm 0.97) \times 10^{-3}$ MPa, giving us a measure of the dispersion of the calculated standard deviation value.

Inspection of Eqs. (9.12), (9.13), and (9.14) shows that in each case, n, the number of experimental data points, enters the relationships *under the radical*. We see, therefore, that results are improved rather slowly as additional data are accumulated.

9.9.2   Uncertainty Distribution

We can always indicate what we *think* uncertainty magnitudes and distribution may be. We can make an educated guess as to their values. The more experienced we are in the nature of the test, the better should be our predictions. By applying the methods of probability and statistics, Kline and McClintock [6] have proposed an analysis procedure using *uncertainty distributions* rather than frequency distributions. They define uncertainty distribution as the error distribution the experimenter *believes* would exist should the data be collected. They also make a case for treating single-sample systematic errors in the same manner as single-sample random errors.

Kline and McClintock suggest that a single-sample result may be expressed in terms of a mean value and an uncertainty interval, based on stated odds.

This may be written as

$$V_a = V_m \pm w \quad (b \text{ to } 1),$$

where

V_m = the value if only one reading is available, or the arithmetic mean of several readings,

w = the uncertainty interval, and

b = the odds, or the chance that the true value lies within the stated range, based on the *opinion* of the experimenter.

For example, an experimentally determined strain may be indicated as

$$V_a = 1248 \pm 35 \text{ ppm} \quad (20 \text{ to } 1).$$

In effect, this states that the experimenter is willing to wager 20 to 1 that the true value of strain lies between 1213 and 1283 ppm.

9.10   GOODNESS OF FIT*

As stated previously, distribution of experimental data often approximately abides by normal or Gaussian rules as expressed by Eq. (9.9). One must continually keep in mind, however, that this is not always the case. For example, fatigue data for some metals commonly approximate the so-called Weibull distribution; there are other distributions as well (see the Suggested Readings at the end of the chapter). Since a given set of data may or may not abide by an assumed distribution and since, at best, the degree of adherence can be only approximate, it is clear that some estimate of *goodness of fit* should be made before reliance is placed on error calculations. In the following paragraphs we will discuss methods that may be applied to the most common: the normal distribution as defined by Eq. (9.9).

At the outset we advise the reader that there is no absolute check in the sense of producing some perfect indisputable figure of merit. At best a qualifying "degree of probability" must be applied, with the final acceptance or rejection left to the judgment of the experimenter.

Of course, the simplest, but rather inadequate, method is simply to plot a histogram and to "eyeball" the result: yes, the distribution appears to approximate a bell-shaped curve; or no, it does not. This can easily result in misleading conclusions. The appearance of the histogram can sometimes be altered quite radically simply by readjusting the number of class intervals. (See Appendix F for clarification of this point.)

---

*   See also Appendix F.

TABLE 9.4 Data on Pressure Listed in Table 9.3 Arranged for Making a Probability Plot (Fig. 9.6)

A	B	C	D
3.967			
	1	1	1.01
3.977			
	3	4	4.04
3.987			
	12	16	16.16
3.998			
	25	41	41.41
4.008 (mean)			
	33	74	74.75
4.018			
	17	91	91.92
4.029			
	6	97	97.98
4.039			
	2	99	99.00
4.049			
	1*	100	100.00

A Limits on class intervals, arbitrarily taken as
    $0.75 \times \sigma = 0.01027$
B Number of data items falling within respective class intervals
C Cumulative number of data items
D Cumulative number of data items in percent

* A rule of thumb often used is to discard arbitrarily any data falling outside a $\pm 3\sigma$ limit. Theoretically, discarding out-of-tolerance items could make a readjustment of the mean and the standard deviation necessary. In this case the changes would be so slight as to make the additional work unprofitable.

A second relatively easy and much more effective method is to make a graphical check, using a *normal probability plot*. This requires a special graph paper* available from most bookstores that deal in technical supplies. One axis of the graph represents the degrees of probability of the summed data frequencies in percent. The other must be scaled to accommodate the range of data values in the sample. The more nearly the data plots as a straight line and the more nearly the line passes through the 50% point, the better the fit to normal distribution. The final determination is subjective; it depends on the judgment of the experimenter. Considerable deviation from a straight line should raise serious doubts as to the value of any Gaussian-based calculations, particularly the value or significance of the calculated standard deviation. The following example demonstrates the procedure.

---

* See [7], p. 25, for directions for preparing one's own normal probability paper.

EXAMPLE We will illustrate the graphical method by using the data on pressure given in Table 9.3. In treating this data we will arbitrarily center our class intervals on the mean and will assume eight intervals, each 0.75σ in width (see Appendix F for further discussion of this step). Using these ground rules we prepare Table 9.4.

The ordinate of the graph is in terms of the *upper limits* of each interval. This quantity correlates with the cumulative values, which are plotted as the abscissa. Data from Column A is simply plotted versus the percentages in Column D, yielding Fig. 9.6. One notes that to plot either 0 or 100% is impossible. For this reason and also because either absence or presence of even one extra data point in the extreme intervals distorts the plot unduly, the two end points are generally given little consideration in making the final judgment. On the basis of Fig. 9.6 we can say that the pressure data has a reasonably good Gaussian distribution.

Figure 9.7 illustrates the general discrepancies that may be discerned from a nonstraight line and normal probability plot, and their causes.

The *Chi² test* is an old and well-known analytical goodness-of-fit procedure. Unfortunately, implementation of the method requires considerable data manipulation and finally, as with the other methods, a judgment on the part of the experimenter is required. In addition, the method does not lend itself well to small samples of data. In application, the procedure is to divide the data sample into a reasonable number of class intervals, determine the number

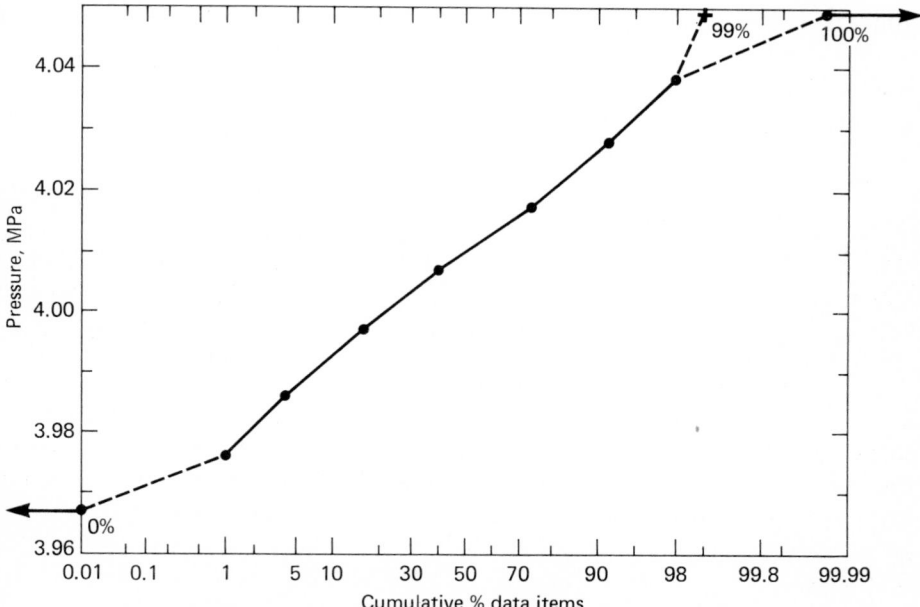

FIGURE 9.6   Normal probability plot of data listed in Table 9.3.

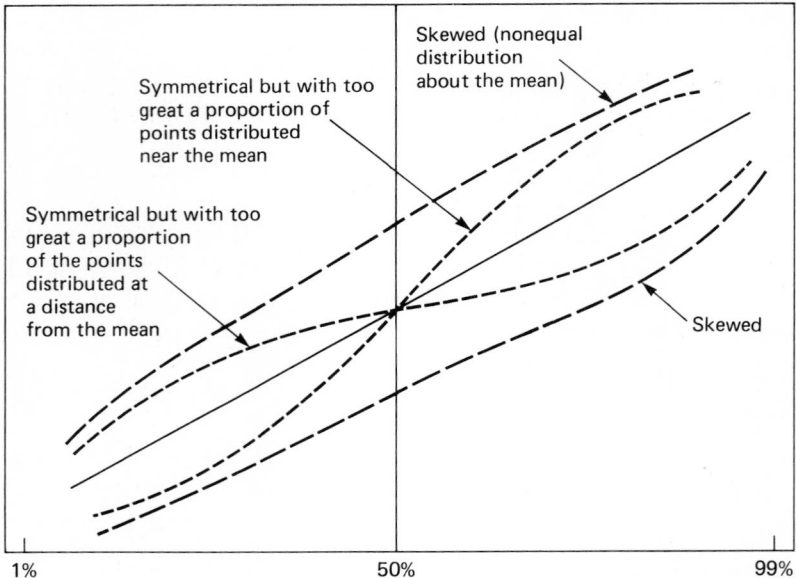

FIGURE 9.7   Graphical effects of data skew and offset as displayed on a normal probability plot.

of observations, O_i, contained in each interval, and then to compare these numbers with an "expected" number of data items E_i, as predicted by normal distribution theory. The comparison is made using the relationship

$$\text{Chi}^2 = \sum_{i=1}^{N} \frac{(O_i - E_i)^2}{E_i} .$$

The value of E_i is usually taken from tables of data.* Chi^2 is calculated for the particular sample and the resulting value, along with an applicable number of *degrees of freedom,* is used to obtain a probability of fit. The probability data may be in tabulated or in plotted form.

Degrees of freedom, DF, depend on the number of class intervals used and on the extent to which the sample has already been used. Quite commonly,

$$\text{DF} = \text{Number of class intervals} - 3.$$

The value 3 stems from the three previous uses to which the sample has been put, i.e., calculation of the mean, the standard deviation, and Chi^2.

---

*   See Appendix F for details of a Chi^2 procedure suggested by the authors.

9.11 CURVE FITTING

In most engineering experiments the measured data (dependent variable) are a function of some independent variable, e.g., the strain in a structural member depends on the applied load. An orthographic plot of the data set invariably improves an understanding of the results. The play of uncertainties commonly causes some scatter of the plotted points; however, it is generally assumed that a continuous relationship between x and y exists. What, therefore, is the "best" function, $y = f(x)$, representing the range of data?

Often the simplest of all plots, the straight line,

$$y = mx + b, \tag{9.15}$$

provides a good approximation. It then becomes a matter of determining a reasonable intercept b and slope m. We will consider three approaches:

1. the "eyeball" method,
2. the zero deviation method, and
3. the least-squares method.

The eyeball approach consists simply of sighting what appears to be a good straight line representing the data. Consciously or unconsciously, the probable tendency is to attempt a zero deviation, i.e., to make

$$\sum_{n=1}^{N} (y - y_n) \approx 0,$$

where, for the various data values of x_n, the value y_n is the experimentally determined ordinate and y is the value from the eyeballed curve. This method might be called the *approximate* zero deviation method.

9.11.1 The Zero Deviation Method

Arithmetically, we can actually sum the deviations between the actual data values and a straight line, make the total equal to zero, and from the manipulation determine the parameters for the line. To do this we divide the data into two subsets and for each subset make the sum of the deviations zero. The procedure is as follows:

1. Divide the total data set into any two subsets.
2. For each subset determine the relationship

$$\sum y_n = Nm + b\sum x_n, \tag{9.16}$$

thereby establishing two equations in m and b that can be solved simultaneously for slope and intercept, where N is equal to the number of data points in the particular subset of data.

By using this scheme, a variety of lines may be determined depending on how the total data set is subdivided.

9.11.2   The Method of Least Squares

A third and undoubtedly the best method for finding a good straight-line representation of $y = f(x)$ from experimental data is the least-squares method, also called the method of linear regression. In this case it may be shown that the most probable straight line is located such that the sum of the squares of the deviations add to a minimum. On the basis of this requirement, two equations may be obtained [8]:

$$b = \frac{\sum y_i \sum x_i^2 - \sum x_i \sum x_i y_i}{N \sum x_i^2 - \sum (x_i)^2} \, , \tag{9.17}$$

$$m = \frac{N \sum x_i y_i - \sum y_i \sum x_i}{N \sum x_i^2 - \sum (x_i)^2} \, . \tag{9.17a}$$

In this case, N is the *total* number of data pairs.

Each of the above equations contains all the original data and when they are solved simultaneously the constants m and b in Eq. (9.15) are found. Although the least-squares method is considered the best of the three methods discussed, one must judge whether or not the amount of work required justifies the gain in precision that is provided by the more complicated method. Many modern scientific calculators contain programs for solving problems with ease using the least-squares method.

Figure 9.8 lists fictitious data for x and y and contains plots and calculations for both a zero deviation and a least-squares solution.

9.11.3   A Variation

Often the problem of fitting curves other than straight lines or polynomials of higher order to a set of data may be treated in similar ways. For example, if we suspect a set of data may fit the function

$$y = ax^m \tag{9.18}$$

we may write

$$\log (y) = \log (a) + m \log (x).$$

Defining

$$Y = \log (y),$$

$$X = \log (x), \text{ and}$$

$$A = \log (a),$$

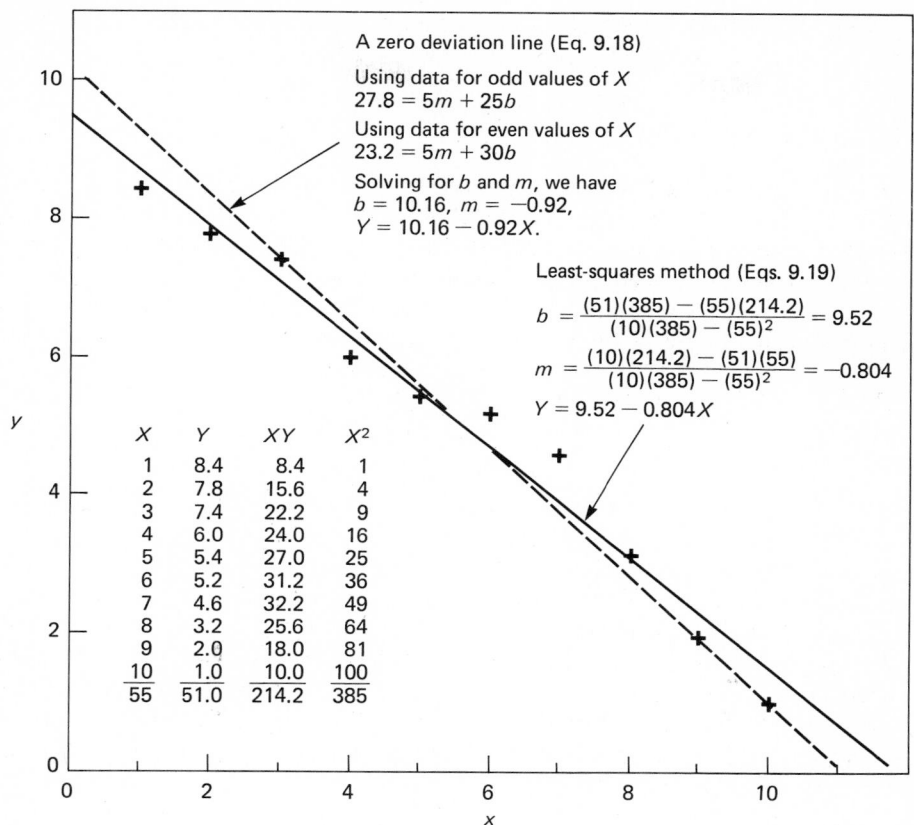

FIGURE 9.8   Examples of straight-line curve-fit.

we can write

$$Y = A + mX. \tag{9.19}$$

The eyeball method and the zero deviation method can then be applied to the modified data and values for A and m determined. (Or, of course, in this case we may simply use log-log graph paper as a shortcut to the same result.)

9.11.4 Application of Least Squares to Second-Order Curve Fitting

The least-squares method may be applied to higher order polynomials; however, the amount of data manipulation increases quite considerably and computer-programmed calculations become quite convenient. For the second-order polynomial

$$y = a + bx + cx^2, \tag{9.20}$$

the equations for fit are [8]

$$\sum y_i = Na + b\sum x_i + c\sum x_i^2, \tag{9.21}$$

$$\sum x_i y_i = a\sum x_i + b\sum x_i^2 + c\sum x_i^3, \tag{9.21a}$$

$$\sum x_i^2 y_i = a\sum x_i^2 + b\sum x_i^3 + c\sum x_i^4, \tag{9.21b}$$

where N is the number of data pairs.

By calculating the summations, the equations may be written and simultaneous solution will provide the coefficients for Eq. (9.20).

SUGGESTED READINGS

Bartee, E. M., *Engineering Experimental Design Fundamentals*. Englewood Cliffs, N. J.: Prentice-Hall, 1968.

Beers, Y., *Theory of Error*. Reading, Mass.: Addison-Wesley, 1957.

Haugen, E. B., *Probabilistic Approaches to Design*. New York: John Wiley, 1968.

Ku, H. H., *Precision Measurement and Calibration*. (Selected papers on statistical concepts), NBS Special Publication 300, vol. 1. Washington, D.C.: U.S. Government Printing Office, 1969.

Lipson, C., and N. J. Seth, *Statistical Design and Analysis of Engineering Experiments*. New York: McGraw-Hill, 1973.

Natrella, M. G., *Experimental Statistics*, NBS Handbook 91. Washington, D.C.: U.S. Government Printing Office, 1963.

Neville, A. M., and J. B. Kennedy, *Basic Statistical Methods for Engineers and Scientists*. Scranton, Pa.: International, 1964.

Schenck, H., Jr., *Theories of Engineering Experimentation,* 2nd ed. New York: McGraw-Hill, 1968.

Whitehead, T. N., *Instruments and Accurate Mechanism*. New York: Dover, 1954.

Willers, A., *Practical Analysis*. New York: Dover, 1948.

Worthing, A. G., and J. Geffner, *Treatment of Experimental Data*. New York: John Wiley, 1943.

Young, H. D., *Statistical Treatment of Experimental Data*. New York: McGraw-Hill, 1962.

PROBLEMS

9.1 A right circular cylinder of nominal height 10 cm and diameter 3 cm is measured with a micrometer. The uncertainty in each dimension is ± 0.005 cm. Determine the uncertainty in the calculated value of the volume.

9.2 A rod of nominal length 3 m and diameter 4 cm is loaded as a cantilever beam with a nominal force of 1000 N. If the uncertainty in length is ± 0.0001 m, in diameter, ± 0.005 cm, and in force, ± 1 N, what is the uncertainty in the calculated value of the maximum bending stress?

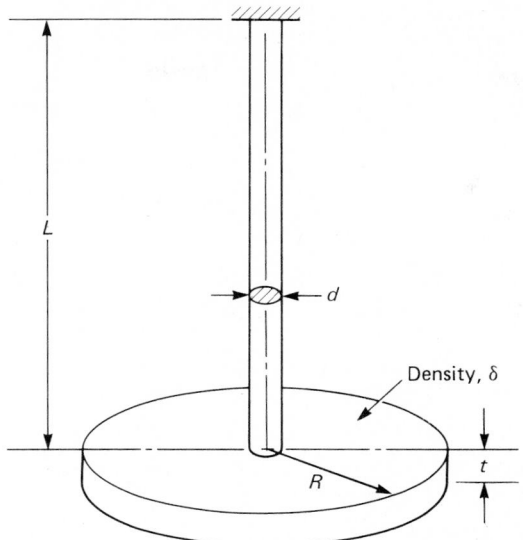

FIGURE 9.9   A torsional pendulum: see Problem 9.6.

9.3 If it is determined that the overall uncertainty in the maximum bending stress for Problem 9.2 may be as great as ± 5%, what maximum uncertainty may be tolerated in the force measurement, if length and diameter uncertainties remain unchanged?

9.4 Basic electronic elements (resistors, capacitors, and inductances) are available in selected standard values and precisions. Often, when a nonstandard value is required, series and/or parallel combinations of elements will be used to "pad" to the desired value.

a) Suppose a 47-kΩ resistor is paralleled with a 6800-ohm resistor, each resistor having a ±5% tolerance. What will be the nominal resistance and uncertainty of the combination?

b) If the values remain the same, except that the tolerance on the 47-kΩ resistor is raised to ±10%, what will be the uncertainty of the combination?

9.5 A capacitor of 0.01 µf ±10% is paralleled with a capacitor of 0.1 µf ±10%.

a) What are the resulting capacitance and uncertainty?

b) What would be the capacitance and uncertainty if the two elements were connected in series?

9.6 A torsional pendulum (Fig. 9.9) is being considered as a frequency standard. The governing relationship for the period $\mathcal{T}$ is

$$\mathcal{T} = 2\pi\sqrt{\frac{I}{K_t g_c}} \, ,$$

where

I = the mass moment of inertia of the disk

$\quad = \frac{1}{2}MR^2 = \frac{1}{2}\pi R^4 t\delta,$

K_t = the torsional deflection constant for the shaft

$\quad = E_s J/L,$

E_s = the shear modulus of elasticity for the torsional member (see Table 4.3),

J = the torsional moment of inertia of the shaft section

$\quad = \pi d^4/32,$ and

g_c = the dimensional constant.

a) "Design" a pendulum to provide a period of 0.1 s. Assign tolerances to each variable and calculate the expected uncertainty.

b) From a practical standpoint, the pendulum may be "fine-tuned" by removal of mass from the disk. If this is to be done by removal of mass (by drilling, perhaps) at a point one-half of the radius from the center, determine the overdesign (additional mass) that must be provided to adjust for maximum probable uncertainty.

9.7 The equation given in Problem 9.6 does not include the effect of the mass of the torsional member. This may be approximated by adding one-third of its mass to the mass of the disk. Rewrite the relationships including this effect and determine its influence on the uncertainty of the period.

9.8 From a sample of 100 marbles having a mean diameter of 1.2 cm and a standard deviation of ±0.34 cm, how many marbles would you expect to find in the range from 1.0 to 1.5 cm? [Note: Refer to a table of integrals of the normal distribution function (Gauss function), found in most elementary statistics texts. See the Suggested Readings listed on page 288 (e.g., Young's *Statistical Treatment of Experimental Data*).]

9.9 Included in Appendix F are sets of pseudo-normally distributed numbers, grouped in sets of twenty-five. For convenience, sums and sums of squares are also included. Select one or several columns and using the data,* determine the following:

a) The mean,

b) The standard deviation,

c) The standard deviation of the mean, and

d) The standard deviation of the standard deviation.

e) Following the suggestions in Appendix F for selection of class intervals, plot a histogram.

f) Using normal probability paper, obtain a graphical measure of goodness of fit.

g) Calculate Chi^2 and determine goodness of fit from Fig. F.2.

---

*   Note that the data may be modified by constant multipliers or additive terms.

9.10 Consider the following expression:

$$Q = \sum_{i=0}^{n} N_i,$$

where

N = values of *uniformly* distributed random numbers, and

i = some number of items, e.g., 12, defining a set of numbers N and a summation Q.

If a number of values Q are generated, their distribution will approximate a *normal distribution*. Write a program to generate sets of numbers by this method and use the results in Problem 9.9.

9.11 The following data describe the temperature condition along a length of heated pipe. Determine the best straight-line fit to the data.

Temperature, in °C	Distance from a Datum, in cm
100	11.0
200	19.0
300	29.0
400	39.0
500	50.5

9.12 The force-deflection data for a spring are tabulated below.

a) Determine a zero deviation fit for the data.

b) Determine the least-squares fit.

Deflection, in in.	Force, in lbf
0.10	9
0.20	19
0.30	22
0.40	40
0.50	52
0.60	59

9.13 Solve Problem 9.12 adding one more set of data, namely, zero deflection under zero load.

9.14 A thermistor was calibrated using a mercury-in-glass thermometer as the standard. The following data were obtained. Using the second-order least-squares relationship, determine (a) $T = f(R)$ and (b) $R = g(T)$.

Temperature T, in °F	Resistance R, in kΩ
78	3.16
76	3.23
72.5	3.89
68	4.24
65	4.47
61	4.76
58	5.31
54	5.77
50.5	6.37
47.5	6.80

See also Problem 16.7.

9.15 Use a hardness tester (Rockwell, Brinell, etc.) to obtain a set of hardness data for a given metallic sample. Using the data, determine

a) the mean,

b) the standard deviation,

c) the standard deviation of the mean, and

d) the standard deviation of the standard deviation.

Plot a histogram and using the Chi^2 procedure, determine the goodness of fit.

applied **II**
mechanical
measurements

determination of **10** count, events per unit time, and time interval

10.1 INTRODUCTION

To be able to count items or events is basic to engineering. Items or events to be counted may be pounds of steam, cycles of displacement, number of lightning flashes, or anything divisible into discrete units. Also, time is often introduced, and the number of items or events per unit of time (EPUT) must be measured. The expressions "EPUT" and "frequency" usually have slightly different connotations. Frequency is thought of as being the events per unit of time for phenomena under steady-state conditions, such as mechanical vibrations, a.c. voltage, or current. EPUT, however, is not dependent on a steady rate, and the term includes the counting of events that take place intermittently or sporadically. An example of this is the counting of any of the various particles radiated from a radioactive source.

Time interval is often desired, and this becomes *period* if it is the duration of a cycle of a periodic event. Or the time interval desired may be that which occurs between events in an erratic phenomenon, or perhaps the duration of a "one-shot" event such as an impulsive pressure or force.

Of course, the problem of counting or timing emerges primarily when the events are too rapid to determine by direct observation, or the time intervals are of very short duration, or unusual accuracy is desired. In general, counting and timing-measurement problems may be classified as follows:

1. *Basic counting,* either to determine a total or to indicate the attainment of a predetermined count.

2. *Number of events or items per unit of time (EPUT)* independent of rate of occurrence.

3. *Frequency,* or the number of cycles of uniformly recurring events per unit of time.

4. *Time interval* between two predetermined conditions or events.

5. *Phase relation,* or percentage of period between predetermined recurring conditions or events.

10.2   USE OF COUNTERS

General-purpose counting equipment, including the various forms of mechanical, electrical, and electronic counters, were discussed in Chapter 7. In addition, general laboratory equipment such as oscilloscopes and oscillographs, used in conjunction with frequency standards, may also be used in various EPUT and time-interval measuring systems, limited only by the ingenuity of the user.

The use of simple mechanical counters or electrically energized mechanical counters requires no particular technique, and further discussion at this point should be unnecessary.

10.2.1   Electronic Counters

Electronic counters used as either basic counting devices or EPUT meters require that the counted input be converted to simple voltage pulses, a count being recorded for each pulse. It should be clear that input functions used to trigger the counter need not be analogous to any quantity other than the count; hence even a simple switch may be used, actuated by the function to be counted. In addition, photocells, variable resistance, inductance, or capacitance devices, Geiger tubes, and the like may be employed. Simple amplifiers may be used, if necessary, to raise the voltage level to that required by the counter, and because most electronic counters have a high-impedance input, no particular power requirement is imposed. Signal inputs may include almost any mechanical quantity, such as displacement, velocity, acceleration, strain, pressure, load, etc., so long as distinct cycles or pulses of the input are provided. The starting or stopping of the counting cycle may be controlled by direct manual-switch operation on the panel or by remote switching. One must not overlook, however, the ±1 count ambiguity referred to in Section 7.2.

A variation of the simple electronic counter is the *count-control* instrument. Provision is made for setting a predetermined count, and when the count is reached, the instrument supplies an electrical output that may be used as a control signal. Figure 10.1 shows how such a device could be used to prepare predetermined batches or lots for packaging.

10.2.2   EPUT Meters

EPUT meters combine the simple electronic counter and an internal time base with a means for limiting the counting process to preset time intervals. This permits direct measurement of frequency and is quite useful for accurate

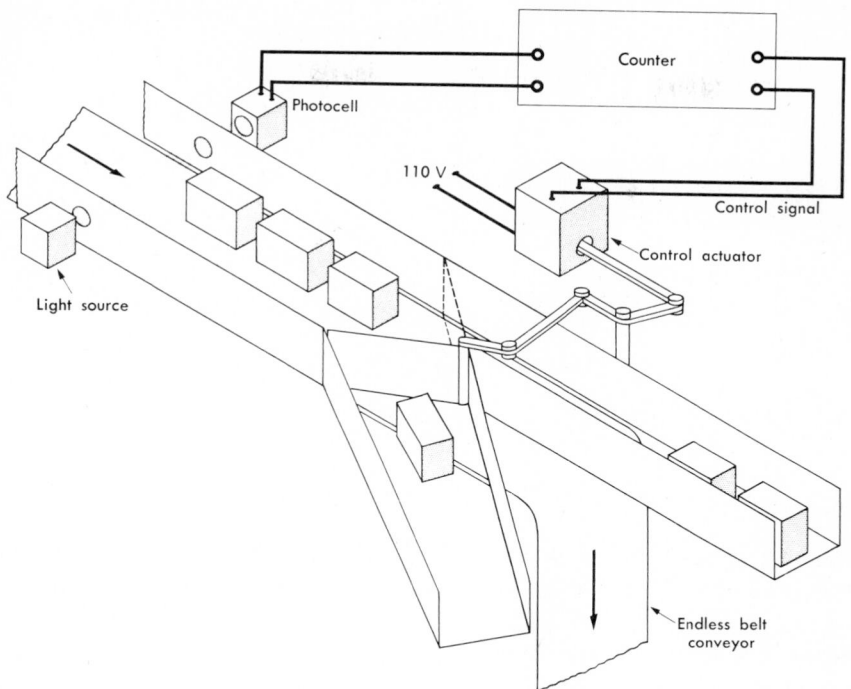

Light source

Photocell

110 V

Counter

Control signal

Control actuator

Endless belt
conveyor

FIGURE 10.1   Counter arrangement to provide a control of a predetermined count.

determinations of rotational speeds (see Section 10.8). The instrument is not limited, however, to an input varying at a regular rate; intermittent or sporadic events per unit of time may also be counted. Other applications include its use as a read-out device for frequency-sensitive pickups such as resonant wire pressure pickups and turbine-type flow meters (see Sections 14.8.4 and 15.8.1).

10.2.3   Time-Interval Meter

By modifying the arrangement of circuitry of an electronic counter, one can obtain a *time-interval meter*. In this case input pulses start and stop the counting process, and the pulses from an internal oscillator make up the counted information. In this manner the time interval taking place between starting and stopping may be determined, provided the frequency of the internal oscillator is known.

Figure 10.2 illustrates a simple application of the time-interval meter. Photocells are arranged so that the interruption of the beams of light provide pulses, first to start the counting process and, second, to stop it. The counter records the number of cycles from the oscillator, which has an accurately known stable output. In the example shown, the count would represent the

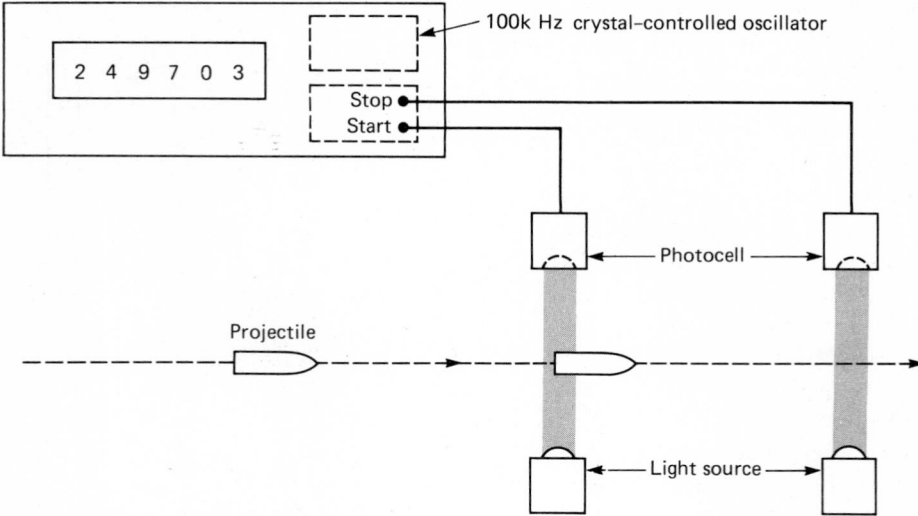

FIGURE 10.2   Time-interval meter arranged to count the number of hundred-thousandths of a second required for the projectile to traverse a known distance between photocells.

number of one-hundred thousandths of a second required for the projectile to traverse the distance between the light beams.

10.3 THE STROBOSCOPE

The term *stroboscope* is derived from two Greek words meaning "whirling" and "to watch." Early stroboscopes used some form of whirling disk arranged somewhat as shown in Fig. 10.3. During the interval when openings in the disk and in the stationary mask coincided, the operator could catch a fleeting glimpse of anything behind the disk. A moving object behind the window of

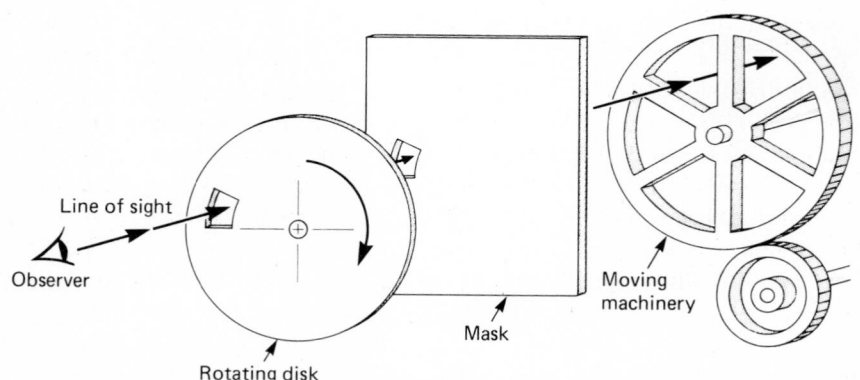

FIGURE 10.3   Essential parts of early disk-type stroboscope.

the stroboscope could actually be made to appear stationary if the movement of the object during the interval of a single observation were small. If the object moved with a repeating or cyclic motion, the speed of the disk could be adjusted so that the object would be occupying the same position each time the windows came into coincidence. By this means, rotating or cyclically moving objects, such as rotating pulleys, gears, or reciprocating valve springs, could be made to appear motionless.

If the disk were made to rotate with a period slightly less than that of the cyclically moving object, the object would have progressed somewhat farther in its cycle for each successive window alignment. In this manner the object could be studied at *slow motion* through every phase of its cycle.

Modern stroboscopes operate on a slightly different principle. Instead of a whirling disk arranged to give intermittent viewing of a moving object, a controllable flashing-light source is used. One such device is called a Strobotac.* Repeated short-duration (10 to 40 μs) light flashes of adjustable frequency are supplied by the lamp. The frequency of flashing is controlled by an internal oscillator; to "stop" a rotating, reciprocating, or oscillating object, the frequency of flashing is varied by means of the knob on the side of the instrument until the flashes are synchronized with the frequency of motion. The range of frequencies for these instruments is about 1 to 2400 Hz. One of the disadvantages of this device is that it cannot be used where the ambient lighting is above a certain value; for it to be most effective, the surrounding lighting must be subdued.

In certain instances it may be difficult to determine proper setting of the instrument for synchronization with the fundamental frequency rather than with some sub- or multifrequency. For example, if the light is directed onto a rotating pulley (Fig. 10.4) having six spokes, it is possible to obtain *apparent* synchronization at frequencies $N/6$ times the fundamental, where N represents any positive integral number. To explain this further, let us suppose a light flash occurs when spoke number one is in the vertical position, then again when spoke number two is vertical, and so on. Each spoke would be "stopped" in turn, in the vertical position, meaning that the stroboscope setting would be six times the correct value. The difficulty lies in determining that the setting is incorrect, for observation of the pulley indicates that it is stationary. Other possibilities would be to stop every other spoke, every third spoke, to catch spoke number one on every other revolution, and so on.

If the spokes are numbered or lettered as shown in Fig. 10.4, false indications can be avoided by comparing any assumed correct setting with submultiples.

Stroboscopic lighting can also be used to study nonrepeating action (see Fig. 10.5).

---

* A registered trademark of GenRad, Inc., Concord, Mass.

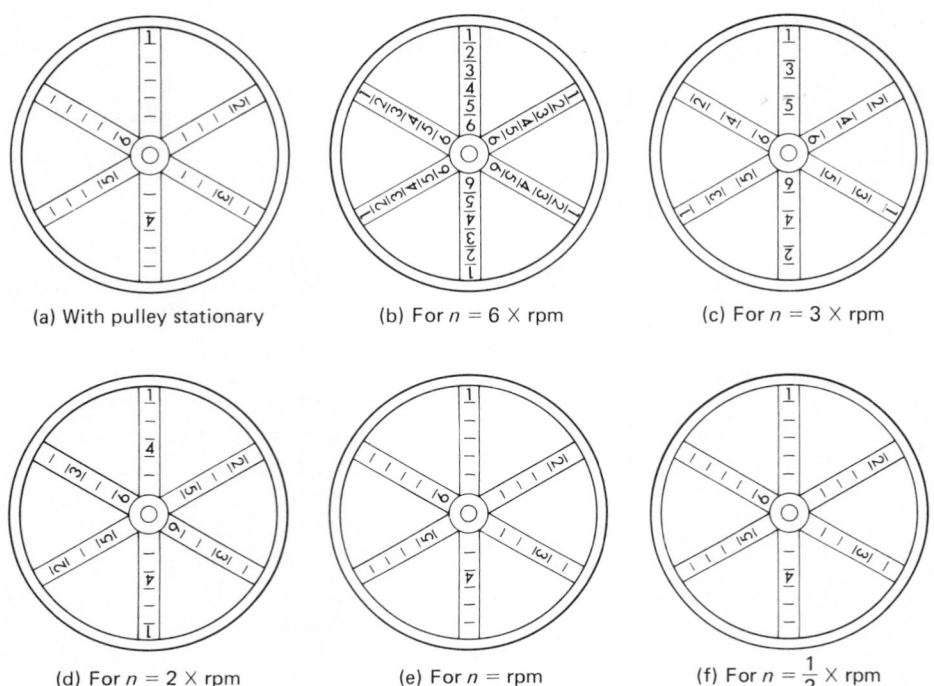

(a) With pulley stationary   (b) For $n = 6 \times$ rpm   (c) For $n = 3 \times$ rpm

(d) For $n = 2 \times$ rpm   (e) For $n =$ rpm   (f) For $n = \frac{1}{2} \times$ rpm

FIGURE 10.4   Example of various phase possibilities that may occur when a spoked wheel is observed with the intermittent light from a stroboscope. The symbol n represents the number of stroboscope flashes per minute.

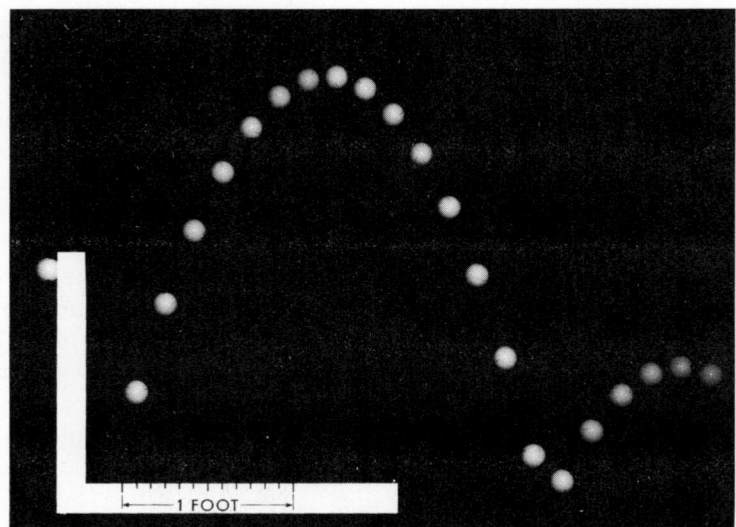

1 FOOT

FIGURE 10.5   Photo obtained by "open-shutter" camera technique and using a Strobotac (TM) set at a flash rate of 20 Hz. Courtesy: GenRad, Inc., Concord, MA.

10.4 DIRECT APPLICATION OF FREQUENCY STANDARDS BY COMPARATIVE METHODS

Probably the simplest and most basic method for measuring frequencies and short time intervals is to make a direct comparison of the unknown with a frequency standard. The problem lies in selecting a usable method for making the comparison.

When multichannel recording equipment is available, the solution is easily obtained. The input or inputs to be measured are simply recorded in terms of time in separate channels. In many cases the speed of the paper is known accurately enough to be used as the time reference, and the necessary time information is obtained automatically. In other cases it may be desirable to simultaneously record the output from a stable oscillator whose frequency is known, and to use this record as the measure of time. Some oscillographs provide a time base as a built-in part of the instrument.

Figure 10.6 shows an arrangement, simple but important because of its fundamental nature. Various inputs are fed to separate channels on a stripchart recorder, one of which is derived from a single generator that supplies a timing reference.

A greater challenge is presented to the engineer equipped only with the simple test equipment found in many laboratories, including the basic item, the general-purpose oscilloscope. The following several examples are presented to illustrate methods for accurately determining frequencies, short time

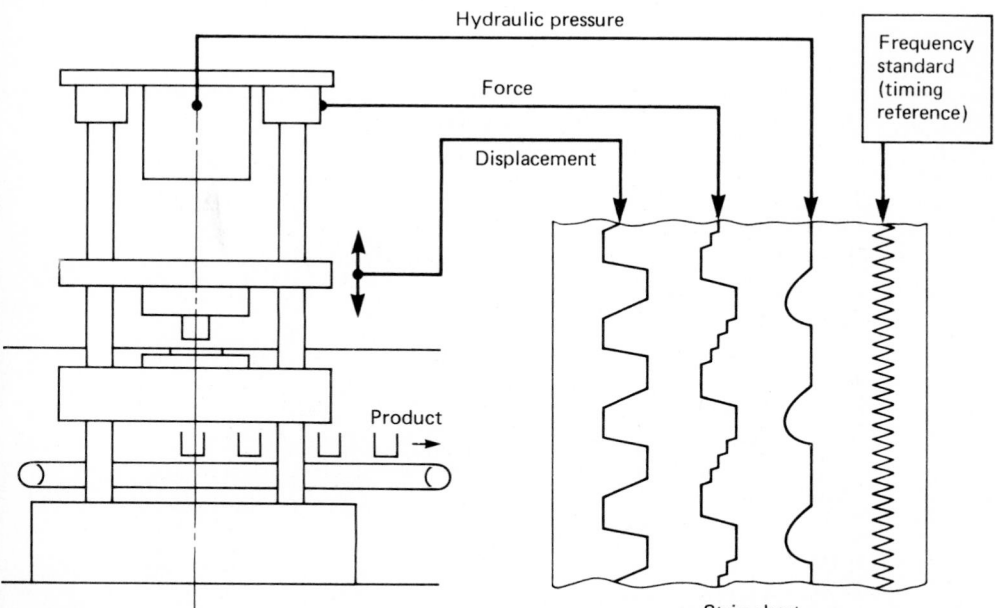

FIGURE 10.6 Stamping press instrumented to produce sychronized outputs on a strip chart. The signal generator supplies a timing reference.

intervals, and phase relations. These by no means exhaust the many possibilities, and the examples given will undoubtedly suggest other equally good arrangements or modifications.

10.4.1 Time Calibration by Substitution And Comparison

EQUIPMENT   (1) Single-trace cathode-ray oscilloscope, with provision for single-sweep triggering; (2) calibrated frequency standard capable of producing a frequency several times that expected from the unknown; (3) a means of recording the oscilloscope trace.

METHOD   Known and unknown signals may be introduced in succession to an oscilloscope, and calibration may be made through delayed comparison. Figure 10.7 shows a possible arrangement for this purpose.

With the camera in place, a record is made, first for the unknown signal and then for the known. If the camera position can be shifted slightly, the timing trace can be displaced on the film so that the two traces are not superimposed. Single sweeps should be used, either through an external synchronization circuit as shown, or perhaps by internal synchronization for the unknown signal and external synchronization for the calibrating signal. In many cases the synchronization may be obtained through a switch, S_2, actuated

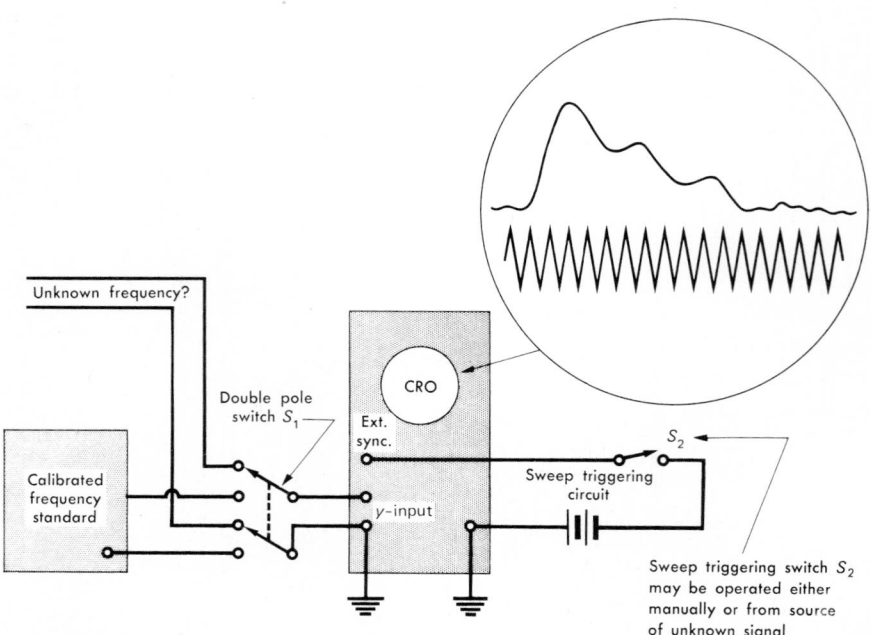

FIGURE 10.7   Arrangement of equipment for frequency or time-interval determination through use of successive sweeps.

by some movement occurring in the system originating the signal source. For example, a lug attached to the side of a rotating gear could be used to close a spring-loaded microswitch. Exact synchronization could be provided by arranging the switch mounting so that the switch could be moved forward or backward, thereby controlling the relation between sweep and cycle. If sound is involved, use of a microphone for sweep triggering may prove feasible.

If we assume that the CRO sweep settings have remained unchanged between the two exposures, it is a simple matter to determine either an unknown frequency or a time interval by direct comparison.

We remind the reader at this point that we are assuming minimum equipment and budget. It is clear that application of a dual-trace scope or a storage scope (Section 7.7) would make the task much easier.

10.4.2 Time Calibration by an Electronic Switch

EQUIPMENT   The same as that used in the preceding example, and including an electronic switch (Section 7.7.1). (This assumes a dual-beam scope is not available.)

METHOD   The equipment is assembled as shown in Fig. 10.8. By proper adjustment of the oscilloscope, the electronic switch, and the frequency stan-

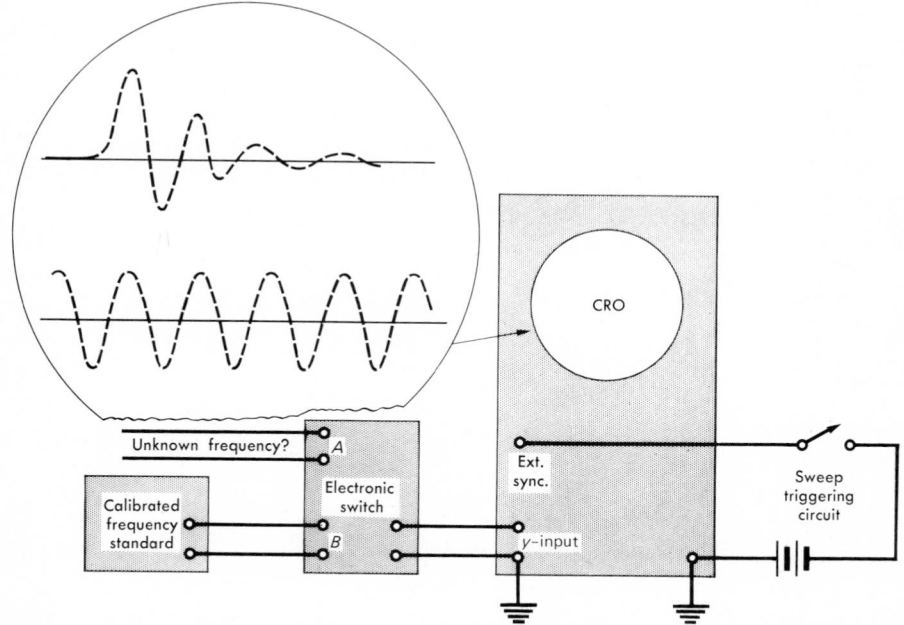

FIGURE 10.8   Application of electronic switch for obtaining comparative frequency or time-interval information.

dard a pattern may be obtained as shown. This may be recorded by approximately the same procedure outlined in the preceding example. In this case, however, only a single photographic exposure will be required. In addition, only external synchronization can be considered. If internal synchronization is attempted, the transients introduced by the electronic switch will cause recurring sweep, resulting in a confused record.

Another limitation in the use of the method lies in the maximum switching rate of the electronic switch. This should be at least *ten times* that of either of the input frequencies. The maximum rate for typical switches is about 500 Hz, which would therefore limit the input frequency to about 50 Hz.

When this method is used, the possibility of changing sweep-rate settings between recording of signal and calibration traces is eliminated.

The unknown frequency or time interval may be determined easily by direct comparison of traces.

10.4.3 Frequency Determination by Z-Modulation (Primarily for Transient Inputs)

EQUIPMENT   (1) Cathode-ray oscilloscope, with provision for Z-modulated input (see Section 7.6.4); (2) calibrated frequency standard, preferably with square-wave output; (3) an oscilloscope camera for recording.

METHOD   Oscilloscope trace intensity may be increased or decreased by applying a voltage to the grid of the cathode-ray tube. This provides a very

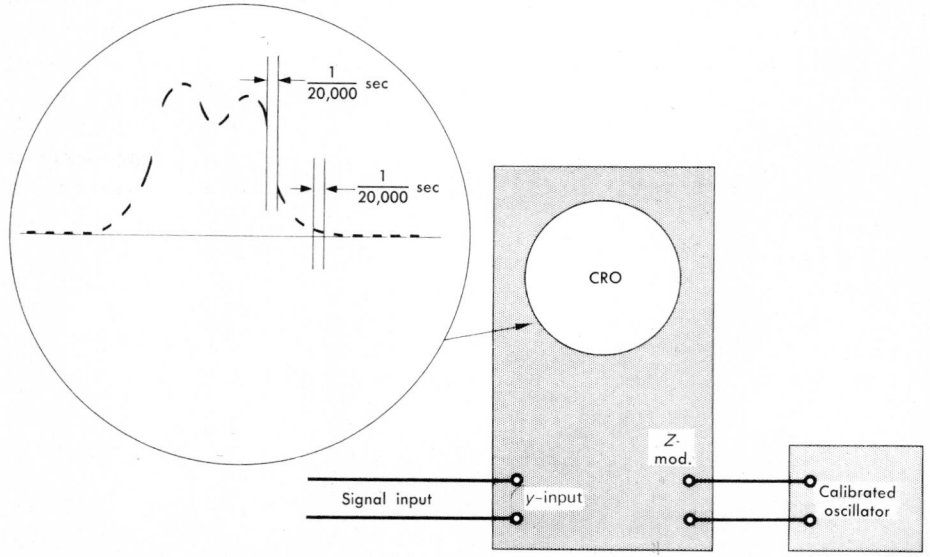

FIGURE 10.9   Arrangement for use of 7-modulation for time-interval or frequency determination.

convenient method for supplying a timing calibration. For example, voltage from a calibrated oscillator may be applied to the Z-modulation terminals, as shown in Fig. 10.9. If the oscillator is set, say, at 10,000 Hz, the CRO intensity and the oscillator voltage output may be adjusted so that blanking occurs at intervals of one every 1/10,000 s. Hence the time required for the trace, or any portion of it, may be determined by counting the markers.

   Square-wave oscillators are preferred for this purpose because the sharp voltage changes provide corresponding intensity changes, thus supplying good definition to the blanking. Sweep triggering may be accomplished by any of the previously described methods, using either internal or external synchronization.

10.5   USE OF LISSAJOUS DIAGRAMS FOR DETERMINATION OF FREQUENCY AND PHASE RELATIONS

EQUIPMENT   (1) Cathode-ray oscilloscope; (2) calibrated variable-frequency standard.

PROCEDURE   Lissajous (Liss-a-ju) diagrams, first studied by Nathanial Bowditch [1], and their interpretation form a basic approach to determining relative characteristics of two different frequency sources, primarily their frequency and phase relations.

   Suppose two 60-Hz sinusoidal voltages from different sources are connected to a cathode-ray oscilloscope, one to the vertical and the other to the horizontal plates. Any of the following several patterns may result.

In-phase relations
If the two voltages are in phase, then as the x-voltage increases, so also does the y-voltage. The x-voltage will deflect the beam along the horizontal axis, and the y-voltage will deflect it in the vertical direction. The resulting trace, then, will be a line diagonally placed across the face of the tube, as shown in Fig. 10.10(a). The angle that the line makes with the horizontal will depend on the relative voltage magnitudes and the oscilloscope gain settings.

90° phase relations
Suppose the two 60-Hz sinusoidal voltages are 90° out of phase. Then as one voltage passes through zero, the other will be at a maximum, and vice versa. The resulting trace will be that shown in Fig. 10.10(b). In general, it will be an ellipse with axes placed horizontal and vertical.

180° phase relations
Figure 10.10(c) shows the pattern that results when the two voltages are 180° out of phase.

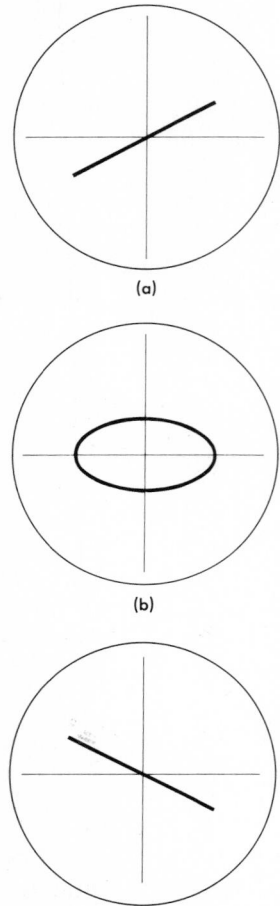

(a)

(b)

(c)

FIGURE 10.10   (a) In-phase Lissajous diagram.
(b) Lissajous diagram for sinusoidal inputs (+/
−)90 degrees out of phase. (c) Lissajous diagram
for inputs 180 degrees out of phase.

Other forms of Lissajous diagrams

Intermediate forms are ellipses with axes inclined to the horizontal. A study
of Fig. 10.11 shows that when the horizontal input is at midsweep, the vertical
precedes it by θ degrees, corresponding to a vertical input of y_1.

From the sine-wave plot of the curve we see that

$$\sin \theta = \frac{y_1}{y_2} = \frac{y\text{-intercept}}{y\text{-amplitude}}.$$

Therefore, by determining the values of y_1 and y_2 from the ellipse, we may
determine the phase relation between the two inputs.

An example of the application of this method is the determination of phase
shift through an amplifier. A sampling of the amplifier input signal would be

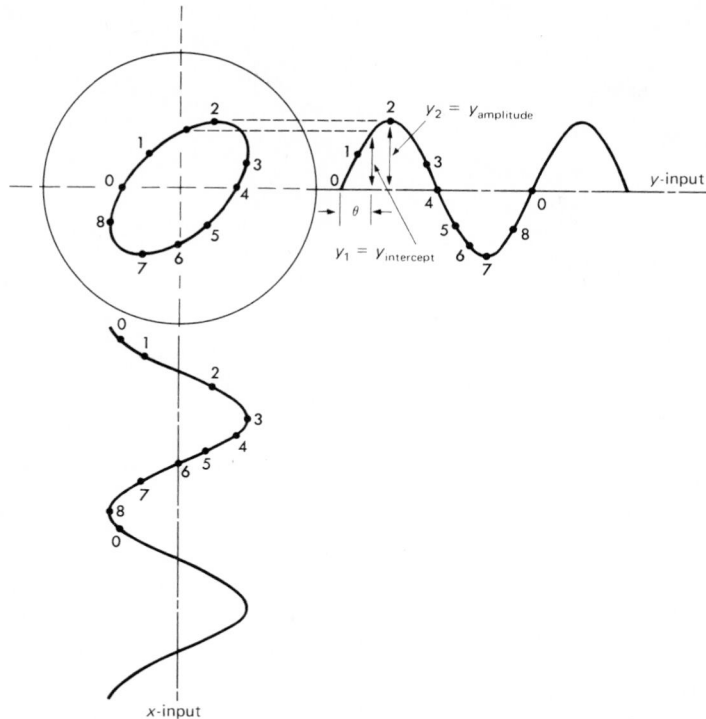

FIGURE 10.11 Lissajous diagram for sinusoidal inputs of the same frequency, but with a phase relation of Θ degrees.

applied to the x-input terminals of a CRO, and the amplifier output would be connected to the y-input terminals as shown in Fig. 10.12. By scanning the frequency range for which the amplifier is intended, one could detect any shift in phase relation. Of course, it would be necessary to know that no shift occurs with frequency in the oscilloscope circuitry or in any of the circuitry external to the amplifier.

It should be obvious by this time how Lissajous diagrams may be used to determine frequencies. Suppose an unknown frequency source with voltage output is connected to the y-input terminals of an oscilloscope, and that the output of a variable-frequency oscillator is connected to the x-input terminals. In general, the two frequencies would be different. However, by adjusting the oscillator frequency, we may obtain equal frequency diagrams such as those shown in Figs. 10.10 and 10.11. When some form of ellipse results, proof would be had that the oscillator and unknown frequencies are equal. With one known, so too would be the other.

Fortunately the method is not limited to equal frequencies. Figure 10.13 shows Lissajous diagrams for several other frequency ratios. By studying

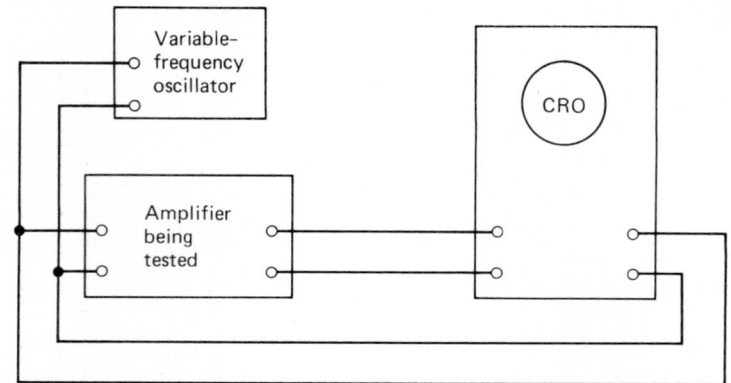

FIGURE 10.12   Arrangement for measuring the phase shift in an amplifier.

these figures, we see that a basic relation may be written as follows:

$$\frac{\text{Vertical input frequency}}{\text{Horizontal input frequency}}$$

$$= \frac{\text{Number of vertical maxima on Lissajous diagram}}{\text{Number of horizontal maxima on Lissajous diagram}} \;.$$

We also see that for the diagram to remain fixed on the screen, either the two input frequencies must each be fixed or they must be changing at proportional rates. In addition, the symmetry of the diagram will depend on the phase relation between the two inputs.

If the frequencies are reasonably fixed, ratios as high as ten to one may be determined without undue difficulty.

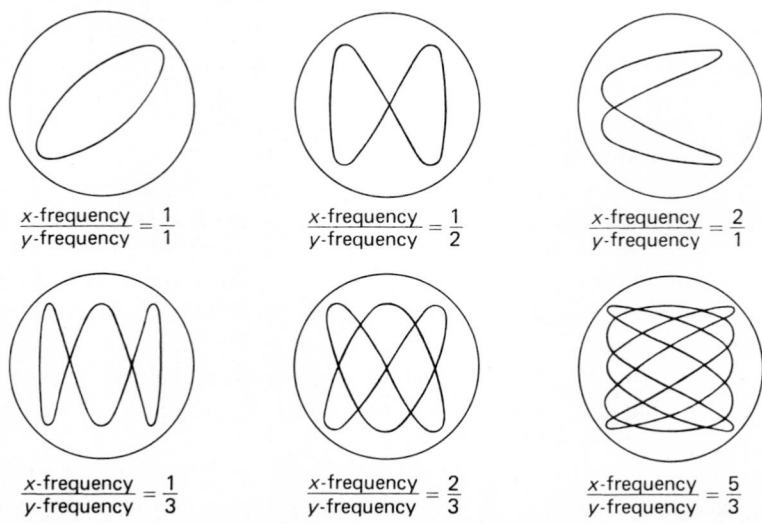

$$\frac{x\text{-frequency}}{y\text{-frequency}} = \frac{1}{1} \qquad \frac{x\text{-frequency}}{y\text{-frequency}} = \frac{1}{2} \qquad \frac{x\text{-frequency}}{y\text{-frequency}} = \frac{2}{1}$$

$$\frac{x\text{-frequency}}{y\text{-frequency}} = \frac{1}{3} \qquad \frac{x\text{-frequency}}{y\text{-frequency}} = \frac{2}{3} \qquad \frac{x\text{-frequency}}{y\text{-frequency}} = \frac{5}{3}$$

FIGURE 10.13   Lissajous displays for sinusoidal inputs at various frequency ratios.

10.6 CALIBRATION OF FREQUENCY SOURCES

These methods suggest means whereby a variable-frequency source, such as an oscillator or signal generator, may be calibrated. By use of a fixed-frequency source, such as the 60-Hz line voltage (through a small step-down transformer), any variable-frequency source may be calibrated for a number of points. Using the ten-to-one relation mentioned above, 60-Hz line voltage may be used to spot-calibrate from 6 to 600 Hz.

In Section 8.6 we discussed various sources of "standard" frequencies. IC divide-by-X solid-state chips, as discussed in Section 6.7.3, are useful for providing a range of frequencies from a single source. National Bureau of Standards radio stations are also available, with proper receiving equipment. Of course, they provide the basic standard for the nation. The stations alternately broadcast signals at 440 and 600 Hz, which provide calibration points between 44 and 6000 Hz. If two or more variable-frequency sources are available, they may be used to extrapolate calibration points to higher frequencies.

It should also be pointed out that pure sine-wave inputs are not always necessary. Figure 10.14 shows a simple arrangement for determining the speed of a fan. In this case the resulting "one-to-one" Lissajous diagram approximates a distorted parallelogram rather than an ellipse.

Various other standardizing sources suggest themselves. In Section 6.7.3 we discussed a crystal-controlled oscillator followed by IC dividers for the purpose of gating a counter. Such a system may be used to form a frequency standard whose accuracy would correspond to that of the crystal.

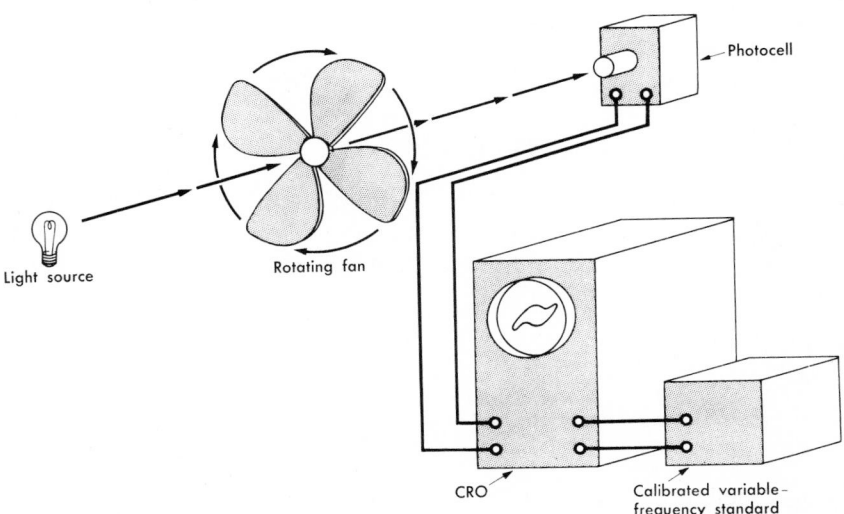

FIGURE 10.14   A method for determining fan speed employing a photoelectric sensor and a frequency standard.

10.7   THE HETERODYNE METHOD OF FREQUENCY MEASUREMENT

Suppose we have two sources of pure audio tones, the two tones having nearly the same frequency. When mixed, a third or beat note (see Fig. 2.6) is produced. The frequency of the beat is a function of the *difference* in the two original notes. If the frequency of one of the sources is known and is adjusted to produce *zero beat,* then the frequency of the other source is also known by comparison. This procedure for determining frequency is called the *heterodyne* method: The two signals are *heterodyned.* Piano tuners make use of this method when adjusting a piano string to zero beat with a tuning fork.

The method is particularly useful for determining frequencies well above the audio range. Radio frequencies are often measured by this method. In this case the standardizing signal originates from a carefully calibrated, variable-frequency oscillator. For radiated signals an ordinary radio receiver covering the desired frequency range may serve as a mixer. The generator frequency is adjusted until the difference between the known and unknown frequencies falls within the audio range, thereby producing the well-known amplitude-modulated squeal so familiar when two radio stations interfere. The generator is then fine-tuned to produce zero beat. True zero beat may be determined by ear within 20 or 30 Hz. The uncertainty, of course, would also include the uncertainty inherent in the standard. By using an oscilloscope or an analog-type electronic voltmeter, the resolution may be reduced to near zero. Provision is made in most signal generators of this type for spot calibration with one or more of the National Bureau of Standards radio signals (Section 8.6.2). One caution should be noted: The signal generator may very well produce many harmonics, any one of which would be suitable as a calibrating source, *provided* one knows which harmonic is being used. This is generally resolved by the fact that the experimenter usually has a fairly good idea of the approximate value of the unknown frequency.

10.8   MEASUREMENT OF ANGULAR MOTION

Probably the most common example of direct counting and EPUT determination is the measurement of angular motion. Many different devices have been used for this purpose, most of which fall under one of the headings in the following classification:

   I. Mechanical
      A. Direct counters
      B. Centrifugal speed indicators
  II. Electrical
      A. Generators (a.c. and d.c.)
      B. Reluctance-type proximity pickups

III. Optical

    A. Stroboscope

    B. Photocells

Mechanical counters may be of the *direct-counting* digital type or may be counters with a gear reducer. In the latter case, angular motion available at a shaft end is reduced by a worm and gear, and the output is indicated by rotating scales. In both examples, rpm is measured by simply counting the revolutions for a length of time as measured with a stopwatch, and calculating the turns per minute from the resulting data.

Modifications incorporate the timing mechanism in the counter. The timer is used to actuate an internal clutch that controls the time interval during which the count is made.

Centrifugal rpm indicators use the familiar *flyball*-governor principles, which balance centrifugal force against a mechanical spring. An appropriate mechanism transmits the resulting displacement to a pointer, which indicates the speed on a calibrated scale. The term *tachometer* is often applied to an instrument of this sort, or to any *direct-indicating,* angular-speed measuring device.

Electrical tachometers generally make use of a small permanent magnet-type d.c. or a.c. generator connected to a simple voltmeter. The d.c. generator requires some form of commutation, which presents the problem of brush maintenance. On the other hand, the a.c. generator requires an instrument rectifier if a simple d.c. meter is to be used for indication. Of course, the advantage of the electrical kind over the mechanical is that the former provides continuous indication that may be displayed or recorded remotely.

A variable-reluctance pickup (discussed in Section 4.12) may be used for angular-speed indication. If the pickup is placed near the teeth of a rotating gear, for example, extremely accurate speed measurements may be made by either an electronic counter, a frequency-sensitive indicator (frequency meter), or, if the speeds are constant, Lissajous techniques (Section 10.5). Photocells may also be used to provide voltage pulses originated by the interruption of a light beam from rotation or movement of a machine member. These pulses may be treated in the same manner.

Finally, any of the various stroboscopic methods discussed in Section 10.3 may also be used for speed measurements.

SUGGESTED READINGS

ASME, PTC 19.13–1961, *Measurement of Rotary Speed.* New York, 1961.

Techniques for Digitizing Rotary and Linear Motion. Wilmington, Mass.: Dynamics Research Corp., 1976.

PROBLEMS

10.1 Using an electronic counter, monitor the local power-line frequency. Use a step-down transformer to avoid the danger of the line voltage. What variations are noted over the period of the test. Compare results using (a) the setting for frequency read-out and (b) the setting for period read-out.

10.2 Using a radio receiver and a CRO, compare the local power-line frequency with the 600-Hz audio tone transmitted by the National Bureau of Standards radio station, WWV.

10.3 Use the power-line frequency to calibrate a signal generator over the range from 10 to 600 Hz. Be sure to use a step-down transformer both to obtain a reasonably low voltage (say, no more than 6 VAC) and to provide isolation from the line.

10.4 Suggest a means of using an oscilloscope for measuring the actuating time of a simple, double-throw electric relay. [Hint: Use the relay actuation voltage to trigger the sweep and a circuit using the relay contacts for the timing-limit switches. Would it be practical to use a debouncing element in the circuit? (See Section 6.4.2.)]

10.5 Make a test arrangement similar to that shown in Fig. 10.14 (or with modifications as may be desired), and determine the time–speed relationship for a common office fan as it accelerates from rest to full speed. The following simple method may be used: Set the signal generator to a predetermined frequency, then simultaneously start the fan and a timer (e.g., a stopwatch). Observe the CRO screen, determining the time for the Lissajous diagram to transit the one-to-one ratio. Repeat for other signal-generator settings, until a sufficient number of data points are obtained to plot a speed–time curve. Check to see if, by chance, the relationship approximates first-order characteristics. Run a similar set of tests to determine the speed–time curve for deceleration.

10.6 Use a flashing-light–type stroboscope and a technique similar to that described in Problem 10.5, and determine the speed–time relationship for a shop-bench–type grinder as it *decelerates*.

10.7 Devise an experimental method for determining the *acceleration* speed–time characteristics of a shop-bench–type grinder.

10.8 Reference [2] describes a simple method for determining the fundamental resonant frequency of a turbine blade. In essence, the method consists of striking the blade with a soft mallet and using a microphone to pick up the sound. The microphone output is fed to a CRO and its frequency is compared with that of a signal generator using the Lissajous technique. Any harmonics of significance would also be displayed. Locate a complex elastic member and use the method to study its characteristics of frequency of vibration.

displacement and dimensional measurement **11**

11.1 INTRODUCTION

The determination of linear displacement is one of the most fundamental of all measurements. The displacement may determine the extent of a physical part, or it may establish the extent of a movement. It is characterized by the determination of a component of space. In *unit* form it may be a measure of either strain (Chapter 12) or angular displacement.

Probably to a greater extent than any other quantity, displacement lends itself to the simplest process of measurement: *direct comparison*. Certainly the most common form of displacement measurement is by direct comparison with a secondary standard. Measurements to least counts on the order of one-half millimeter (about 0.02 in.) may be accomplished without undue difficulty with use of nothing more than a steel rule for a standard. For greater resolutions or sensitivities, measuring systems of varying degrees of complexity are required.

For purposes of discussion, we classify various measuring devices in Table 11.1. With a few exceptions, these systems are used for measuring fixed physical dimensions. Before we discuss any of them in detail, let us consider the following measurement problem.

11.2 A PROBLEM IN DIMENSIONAL MEASUREMENT

Suppose a hole is to be bored to the dimensions shown in Fig. 11.1, and that the part is to be produced in quantity. Such a dimension would probably be checked with some form of plug gage, illustrated in Fig. 11.2. One end of the plug gage is the *Go* end, and the other the *Not go* end. If the *Go* end of the gage fits the hole, we know that the hole has been bored large enough; if the *Not go* end cannot be inserted, the hole has not been bored too large.

Now, the plug gage itself would have to be manufactured, and no doubt drawings of it would be made. A rule of thumb is to dimension the plug gage

TABLE 11.1   Classification of Displacement Measuring Devices

Low-Resolution Devices (to 1/100 in.) (0.25 mm)

1. Steel rule used directly or with assistance of
   a) Calipers
   b) Dividers
   c) Surface gage
2. Thickness gages

Medium-Resolution Devices (to 1/10,000 in.) (2.5×10^{-3} mm)

1. Micrometers (in various forms, such as ordinary, inside, depth, screw thread, etc.) used directly or with assistance of accessories such as,
   a) Telescoping gages
   b) Expandable ball gages
2. Vernier instruments (various forms, such as outside, inside, depth, height, etc.)
3. Specific-purpose gages (variously named, such as plug, ring, snap, taper, etc.)
4. Dial indicators
5. Measuring microscopes

High-Resolution Devices (to a Few Microinches) (2.5×10^{-5} mm)

Gage blocks used directly or with assistance of some form of comparator, such as
a) Mechanical comparators
b) Electronic comparators
c) Pneumatic comparators
d) Optical flats and monochromatic light sources

Super-Resolution Devices

Various forms of interferometers used with special light sources.

with tolerances on the order of 10% of the tolerance of the part to be measured. If this rule is followed, the ends of the plug gage may be dimensioned as shown in Fig. 11.2.

It will be noted that the gage tolerance of 0.0004 in. (10% of the part tolerance, 0.004 in.) is applied symmetrically to the *Not go* end, corresponding to the upper limiting dimension of 1.504 in. On the other hand, the gage tolerance as applied to the *Go* end penalizes the machinist somewhat because, in effect, an extra ten-thousandth of an inch is taken away from what is the machinist's. This is often done to increase the life of the gage by letting the gage wear toward the specified limit. Ideally, the *Go* end will be inserted every time the gage is used and hence will wear, whereas the *Not go* end will never be inserted and will therefore experience no wear.

Provision has now been made for satisfactorily gaging the bored hole, provided the gages themselves are accurately made. How will we know if the gages are within tolerance? We can find out only by measuring them. This leads directly to the *gage block* listed under "High-resolution devices" in Table 11.1. A gage-block set is the basic "company" standard for any small (0.01 to 10 in.) dimension.

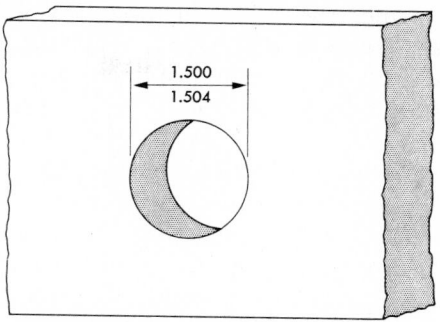

FIGURE 11.1 Typical dimensioning specifications for an internal diameter (English units).

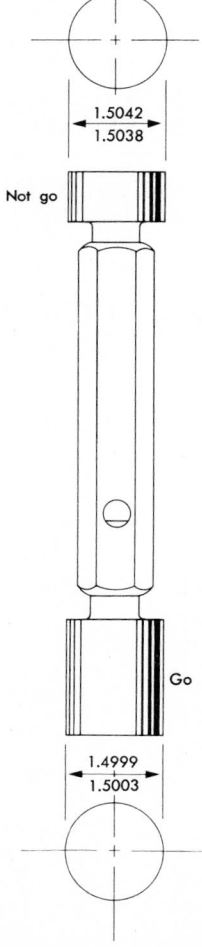

FIGURE 11.2   A Go/Not go plug-type gage.

By use of one of the comparison methods (to be described in a later section), the plug gage would be checked dimensionally. But, of course, we must not overlook the fact that to be useful, the gage blocks themselves must be measured, and so on ad infinitum, at least back to the basic length standard (Section 8.4).

An example may be used to illustrate the extreme importance of measurement standards. Suppose that the 1.500-in. hole described above is in a part to be used by an automobile manufacturer. Very probably the gage would be made by some other company, one that specializes in making gages. Both the gage maker and the automobile manufacturer would undoubtedly "standardize" their measurements by using gage blocks. It is clear that unless the different gage-block sets are accurately derived from the same basic standard, the dimension specified by the automobile manufacturer will not be reproduced by the gage maker.

11.3 GAGE BLOCKS

Gage-block sets are industry's dimensional standards. They are the *known* quantities used for calibration of dimensional measuring devices, for setting special-purpose gages, and for direct use with accessories as gaging devices. They are simply small blocks of steel having parallel faces and dimensions accurate within the tolerances specified by their class. Blocks are normally available in the following classes.

FOR THE ENGLISH SYSTEM OF UNITS:

Tolerance, μin. (microinch)

Class B	"Working" blocks	±8*
Class A	"Reference" blocks	±4
Class AA	"Master" blocks	±2 for all blocks up to 1 in. and ±2 μin./in. for larger blocks

FOR THE SI SYSTEM:

Grade of block	Tolerance, μm (micron)†		
0	±0.10	to	±0.25
1	±0.15	to	±0.40
2	±0.25	to	±0.70
3	±0.50	to	±1.30

---

* For very small displacement or tolerances, the mechanical engineer will commonly use the μm (the micron) or the microinch (1×10^{-6} in.). Physicists commonly use the angstrom (1×10^{-7} mm). Equivalents are 1 μm = 39.37 μin., and 1 angstrom = 0.003937 in. Unit *displacement* (e.g., strain and certain coefficients) is unitless. In this case parts per million or "ppm" is conveniently employed.

† A range of tolerances is listed. Precise values depend on the size of the block.

FIGURE 11.3   A set of 81 gage blocks. Courtesy: The DoAll Co., Des Plaines, IL.

Gage blocks are supplied in sets, with those sets having the largest number of blocks being the most versatile. Figure 11.3 shows a set made up of 81 blocks (plus two wear blocks) having dimensions as follows:

9 blocks with 0.0001-in. increments from 0.1001 to 0.1009 inclusive,

49 blocks with 0.001-in. increments from 0.101 to 0.149 inclusive,

19 blocks with 0.050-in. increments from 0.050 to 0.950 inclusive,

4 blocks with 1-in. increments from 1 to 4 inclusive,

2 tungsten-steel wear blocks, each 0.050 in. thick.

Blocks are made of steel that has been given a stabilizing heat treatment to minimize dimensional change with age. This consists of alternate heating and cooling until the metal is substantially without "built-in" strain. They are hardened to about 65 Rockwell C.

Distribution of sizes within a set is carefully worked out beforehand, and for the set in Fig. 11.3 accurate combinations are possible in steps of one ten-thousandth in over 120,000 dimensional variations.

11.4   ASSEMBLING GAGE-BLOCK STACKS

Blocks may be assembled by *wringing* two or more together to make up a given dimension. Suppose that a dimensional standard of 3.7183 inches is desired. The procedure for arriving at a suitable combination might be determined by successive subtraction as indicated immediately below:

			Blocks used
Desired dimension	=	3.7183	
Ten-thousandths place	=	0.1003	0.1003
Remainder	=	3.618	
Thousandths place	=	0.108	0.108
Remainder	=	3.51	
Hundredths place	=	0.11	0.11
Remainder	=	3.4	
Two wear blocks	=	0.1 (0.05 each)	0.1
Remainder	=	3.3	
Tenths place	=	0.3	0.3
Remainder	=	3.0	
Units place	=	3.0	3.0
Remainder	=	0.0 Check $\cdots$	3.7183

Blocks are not stacked by simply resting them one on top of another. They must be wrung together in such a way as to eliminate all but the thinnest oil film between them. This oil film, incidentally, is an integral part of the block itself; it cannot be completely eliminated, since it was present even at manufacture. The thickness of the oil film is always on the order of 0.2 microinch [1].

A recommended procedure for assembling gage blocks is as follows [1]. Clean the surfaces with alcohol and absorbent cotton; then apply a thin film of petroleum jelly with an otherwise clean cloth. Rub the surface with clean

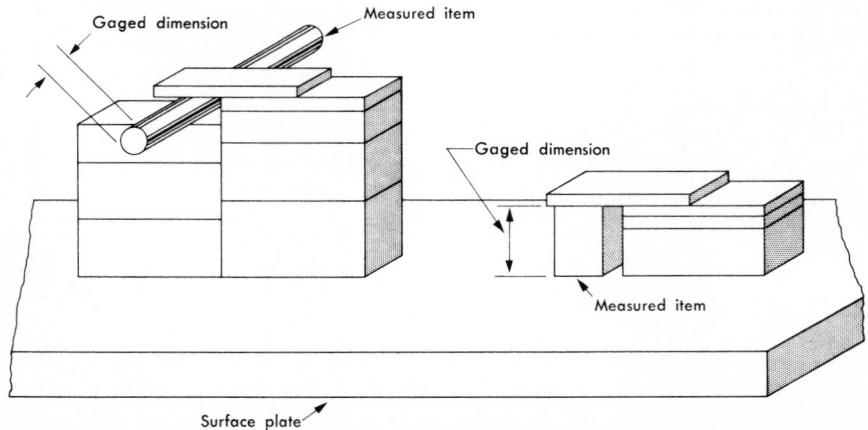

FIGURE 11.4   Two methods for using gage blocks for direct comparison of length-dimension.

surgical cotton until no trace of film can be observed. Bring opposite corners of the two blocks lightly together; then, applying moderate pressure, wipe the two blocks together, sweeping ahead any foreign particles that may be still remaining.

Properly wrung blocks markedly resist separation because the adhesion between the surfaces is about 30 times that due to atmospheric pressure. Unless the assembled blocks exhibit this characteristic, they have not been properly combined. The resulting assembly of blocks may be used for *direct* comparison in various ways. Two simple ways are shown in Fig. 11.4.

11.5 SURFACE PLATES

When blocks are used as shown in Fig. 11.4, some accurate reference plane is required. Such a flat surface is known as a *surface plate,* and must be made with an accuracy comparable to that of the blocks themselves. In years past, carefully aged cast-iron plates with adequate ribbing on the reverse side were used. Such plates were prepared in sets of three, carefully ground and lapped together. When combinations of two are successively worked together, the three surfaces gradually approach the only possible surface common to all three—the true flat.

Machine-lapped and polished granite surface plates have largely replaced the hand-produced cast-iron type. Granite has several advantages. First, it is probably more nearly free from built-in residual stresses than any other material because it has had the advantage of a long period of time for relaxing. Hence, there is less tendency for it to warp when the plates are prepared. Second, should a tool or work piece be accidentally dropped on its surface, residual stresses are not induced, as they are in metals, causing warpage; the granite simply powders somewhat at the point of impact. Third, granite does not corrode.

Optical flats, the uses of which are discussed in Section 11.11, are very similar to surface plates except that they are usually made of fused quartz and are generally much smaller in size.

11.6 TEMPERATURE PROBLEMS

Temperature differences or changes are major problems in accurate dimensional gaging. The coefficient of expansion of gage-block steels is about 11.2 ppm/°C (6.4 ppm/°F). Hence even a shift of one degree in temperature would cause dimensional changes of the same order of magnitude as the gage tolerances. The standard gaging temperature has been established as 20°C (68°F).

Several solutions to the temperature problem are possible. First, the most obvious solution is to use air-conditioned gaging rooms, with temperature maintained at 68°F. This is generally done when the volume of work warrants it. This is not the complete solution, however, for mere handling of the blocks causes thermal changes requiring up to 20 min to correct. For this reason, use of insulating gloves and tweezers is recommended. In addition, care must be exercised to minimize radiated heat from light bulbs, etc. [2].

A constant-temperature bath of kerosene or some other noncorrosive liquid may be used to bring the blocks and work to the same temperature. They may be removed from the bath for comparison, or in extreme cases, measurement may be made with the items submerged.

On the other hand, if temperature control is not feasible, corrections may be used, based on existing conditions. A moment's thought will indicate that *if the gage blocks and work piece are of like materials, there will be no temperature error so long as the two parts are at the same temperature.* In by far the greatest number of applications, steel parts are gaged with steel gage blocks, and although there will probably be a slight difference in coefficients of expansion, and the gage and parts may be at slightly different temperatures, appreciable compensation exists and the problem is not always as great as suggested in the preceding several paragraphs.

If both the part being gaged and the blocks are at temperature T_r (room temperature), corrections may be made by application of the following:

$$L = L_b[1 - (\Delta\alpha)(\Delta T)(10^{-6})], \tag{11.1}$$

where

$$\Delta\alpha = (\alpha_p - \alpha_b),$$

$$\Delta T = (T_r - \text{Standard reference temperature}),$$

and

    L = the true length of the dimension being gaged (at reference temperature),

    L_b = the nominal length of gage blocks determined by summation of dimensions etched thereon,

    α_p = the temperature coefficient of expansion of the part being gaged (ppm/°),

    α_b = the temperature coefficient of expansion of the gage-block material (ppm/°), and

    T_r = the ambient temperature.

In using the above relations, it is very necessary that proper signs be applied to $\Delta\alpha$ and ΔT.

EXAMPLE 1   Let

$$L_b = 10 \text{ cm},$$

$$\alpha_p = 13 \text{ ppm/}° \text{ C},$$

$$\alpha_b = 11.2 \text{ ppm/}° \text{ C, and}$$

$$T_r = 24° \text{ C}.$$

Substituting, we have

$$L = 10\,[1 - (1.8 \times 10^{-6})(4)]$$
$$= 9.999928 \text{ cm.}$$

EXAMPLE 2   Let

$$L_b = 9.7153 \text{ in.,}$$
$$\alpha_p = 5.9 \text{ ppm/}^\circ \text{ F,}$$
$$\alpha_b = 6.4 \text{ ppm/}^\circ \text{ F, and}$$
$$T_r = 62^\circ \text{ F.}$$

Substituting, we have

$$L = 9.7153\,[1 - (-0.5 \times 10^{-6})(-6)]$$
$$= 9.715271 \text{ in.}$$

11.7   USE OF GAGE BLOCKS WITH SPECIAL ACCESSORIES

Gage blocks are sometimes used with special accessories, including clamping devices for holding the blocks. When so used, height gages, snap gages, dividers, pin gages, and the like may be assembled, using the basic gage blocks for establishing the essential dimensions. Use of devices of this type eliminates the necessity for transferring the dimension from the gage-block stack to the measuring device.

11.8   USE OF COMPARATORS

One of the primary applications of gage blocks is that of calibrating a device called a *comparator*. As the name suggests, a comparator is used to compare known and unknown dimensions. One form of mechanical comparator is shown in Fig. 11.5. Some form of displacement sensor is used (the figure shows an ordinary dial indicator) to indicate any dimensional differences as described in the next paragraph. A variety of different sensing devices are found on commercial comparators, including strain-gage types, purely mechanical devices, variable inductance, etc. The resolution and accuracy of the sensing device would add to the gage tolerance in establishing the minimum uncertainty. We see that to use a sensor with the ability to sense discrepancies less than block tolerances would be quite unnecessary.

As an example of a comparator's use, suppose that the diameter of a plug gage is required. The nominal dimension may first be determined by use of an ordinary micrometer. Gage blocks would be stacked to the indicated rough dimension and placed on the comparator anvil, and the indicator would be adjusted on its support post until a zero reading is obtained. The gage blocks

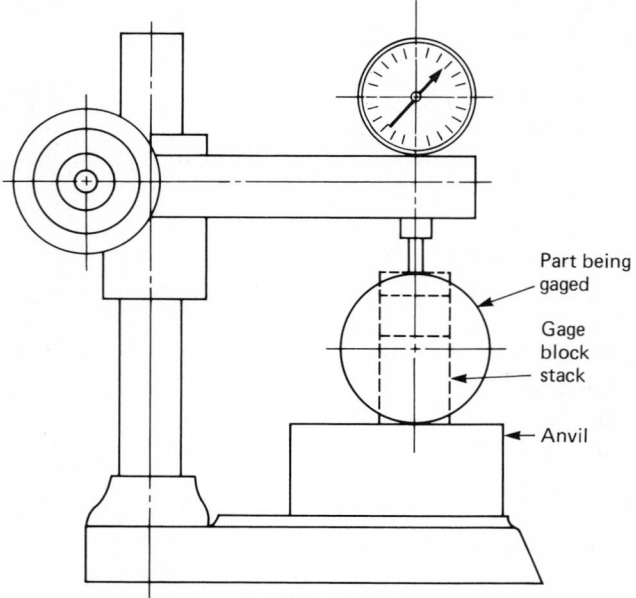

FIGURE 11.5   Comparator employed to measure the difference between a known and an unknown linear dimension.

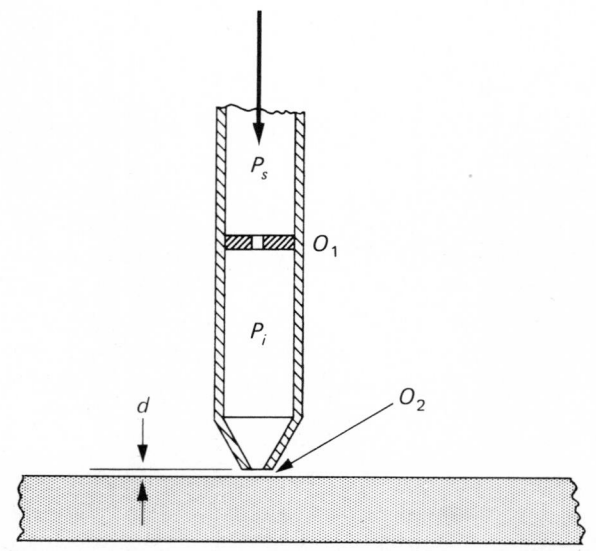

FIGURE 11.6   Schematic showing the principle of operation of the pneumatic comparator.

would then be removed and the part to be measured substituted. A change in the indicator reading would show the difference between the unknown dimension and the height of the stack of blocks. This, of course, would establish the value of the dimension in question. Inasmuch as most gage-block sets contain series having very small changes in base dimensions (e.g., in ten-thousandths of an inch steps for the English system), the gage set may be used quite conveniently for calibrating the comparator.

Pneumatic comparators

Pneumatic gaging is based on a double-orifice arrangement such as that illustrated in Fig. 11.6. Intermediate pressure, P_i, is dependent on the source pressure, P_s, and the pressure drops across the orifices O_1 and O_2. The effective size of orifice O_2 may be varied by a change in distance, d. As d is changed, pressure P_i will change, and this change can be used as a measure of dimension, d. Figure 11.7 shows schematically how this arrangement may be used as a comparator.

Using a double orifice as shown in Fig. 11.7, Graneek [3] determined the following empirical equation for $P_s = 15$ psia and an orifice diameter $O_1 = 0.033$ in.:

$$\left(\frac{A_2}{A_1}\right)^2 = \frac{P_s}{P_i} - \frac{P_i}{P_s}, \tag{11.2}$$

in which A_1 and A_2 are the areas of orifices O_1 and O_2, respectively. For values of P_i/P_s between 0.4 and 0.9, the relation corresponds very nearly to the straight line

$$\frac{P_i}{P_s} = 1.10 - 0.50 \frac{A_2}{A_1}.$$

This indicates that for fixed values of P_s and A_1, P_i may be expected to vary linearly with the value of A_2. In addition, the device may be made quite sensitive, capable of measuring displacements of a few microinches.

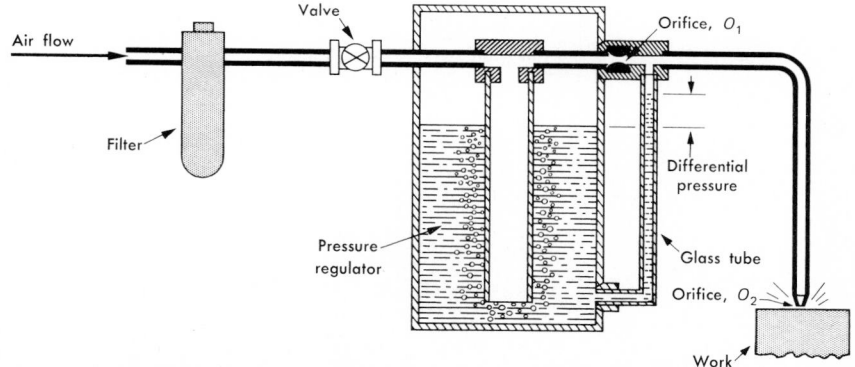

FIGURE 11.7   Circuit diagram for a pneumatic comparator.

Pneumatic gaging is widely used for production work, where reliability and ruggedness are a requirement. Gage blocks are used as standards for calibration. (References [4] and [5] contain additional material on pneumatic gaging methods.)

11.9 OPTICAL METHODS

Optical methods applied to linear measurement may be divided into two general areas as follows: (1) very accurate measurement of small dimension or displacement by methods using light-wave interference or image magnification, and (2) measurement of large dimensions by use of alignment telescopes with accessories and projection systems. Although such a classification can only be quite general, a dimension of about three feet or one meter may be suggested as a rough dividing line, with the realization that there will be overlapping in many cases.

11.10 MONOCHROMATIC LIGHT

The method of interferometry, used for accurate measurement of small linear dimension, is described in subsequent sections. A required tool is a source of monochromatic (one color or wavelength) light.

There are various sources of monochromatic light. Optical filters may be used singly or in combination to isolate narrow bands of approximately single-wavelength light. Or a prism may be employed to "break down" white light into its components and, in conjunction with a slit, to isolate a desired wave-

TABLE 11.2 Approximate Wavelengths of Light of the Various Primary Colors

Color	Range of Wavelengths	
	μm (microns)	μin.
Violet	0.399 to 0.424	15.7 to 16.7
Blue	0.424 to 0.490	16.7 to 19.3
Green	0.490 to 0.574	19.3 to 22.6
Yellow	0.574 to 0.599	22.6 to 23.6
Orange	0.599 to 0.645	23.6 to 25.4
Red	0.645 to 0.699	25.4 to 27.5

TABLE 11.3 Wavelengths from Specific Sources

Source	Wavelengths		Fringe Interval	
	$\mu in.$	μm	$\mu in./fringe$	$\mu m/fringe$
Mercury isotope, Hg^{198}	21.5	0.546	10.75	0.273
Helium	23.2	0.589	11.6	0.295
Sodium	23.56	0.598	11.78	0.299
Krypton 86	23.85	0.606	11.92	0.303
Cadmium red	25.38	0.644	12.69	0.322

length; however, both these methods are quite inefficient. Most practical sources rely on the electrical excitation of atoms of certain elements that radiate light at discrete wavelengths.

Possible sources include mercury, mercury 198, cadmium, krypton, krypton 86, thallium, sodium, helium, and neon [4]. Means are provided for vaporizing the element, if not already gaseous, and to produce a visible light through the application of electrical potential, often at a high voltage and/or frequency. As we have seen, this method is used with krypton 198 for producing the official length standard (Section 8.4).

A common industrial standard is the helium lamp. This standard is obtained by means not unlike those used in the familiar neon signs. A tube is charged with helium and connected to a high-voltage source, which causes it to glow. The resulting light has a narrow range of wavelengths and is intense enough for practical use. The wavelength of this source is 0.589 μm (23.2 μin.). Table 11.2 lists the approximate wavelengths for the various primary colors, and the wavelengths of several specific sources are given in Table 11.3.

11.11 OPTICAL FLATS

An important accessory in the application of monochromatic light to measurement problems is the optical flat (see Fig. 11.8), which is made of a material such as strain-free glass or fused quartz. As the name indicates, at least one of the surfaces is lapped and polished to a close flatness tolerance. Either square or circular flats are available in sizes ranging from 1 to 16 inches (or larger on special order) across a side or diameter. Thicknesses range from $\frac{1}{4}$ inch (6.35 mm) for the small flats to $2\frac{3}{4}$ inches (70 mm) for the large flats. Manufacturing tolerances are as follows: commercial, 8 μin. (0.203 μm); working, 4 μin. (0.101 μm); master, 2 μin. (0.051 μm); reference, 1 μin. (0.025 μm).

FIGURE 11.8   A set of optical flats. Courtesy: The Van Keuren Co., Watertown, MA.

11.12   APPLICATIONS OF MONOCHROMATIC LIGHT AND OPTICAL FLATS

An optical flat and a monochromatic light source may be used to compare gage-block dimensions with unknown dimensions, i.e., they may be used together as a form of dimensional comparator. They may also be used to measure variation from flatness or to determine the contour of an almost flat surface. For these applications the principles involved are as follows.

When light waves are applied to measurement problems, principles of interferometry are used. In general, light waves from a single source may be caused to add or subtract, increasing or decreasing the light intensity, depending on the phase relation. The arrangement shown in Fig. 11.9, making use of an optical flat and a reflective surface, illustrates the basic principles.

Two requirements must be met: (1) *an air gap (a wedge) of varying thickness must exist between the two surfaces,* and (2) *the work surface must be reflective.*

As shown in Fig. 11.9, the light is reflected from both the working face of the flat and the work surface of the part being inspected. At the particular points where multiples of half wavelengths occur, we can see dark interference bands or fringes. Figure 11.10 shows a typical pattern. We see that a fringe represents a locus of separation between work and flat of a definite integral number of half wavelengths of the light used. *Adjacent fringes may be interpreted, therefore, as representing contours of elevation differing by one-half wavelength.* We shall call this distance the *fringe interval.*

Point, or line, of contact

Another item of information that is generally desirable is the point of contact between the flat and the work surface. There will always be one, or possibly

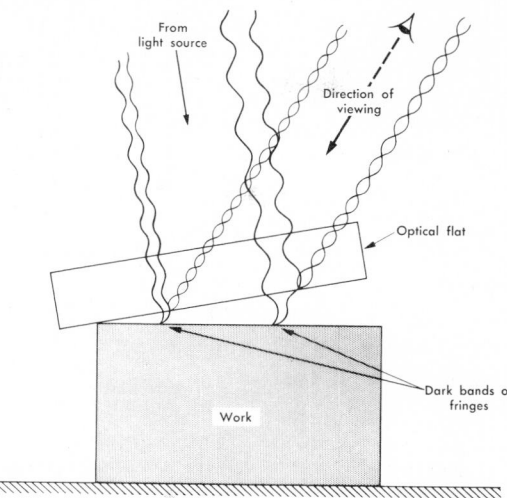

FIGURE 11.9   Sketch illustrating the basic light-interference principle.

more, primary support points for the flat. Sometimes, instead of making contact at a point, the flat will make contact with the work along a line. This can be determined by gently rocking the flat on the surface. Actually, of course, this motion must be very slight in order to maintain an observable pattern, and only a very light pressure need be applied. The general rule is that as the flat is rocked, the point of contact is determined as that spot or line in the pattern that does not shift. Actually in some situations the point will move slightly, but in general it does not stray far from its starting point.

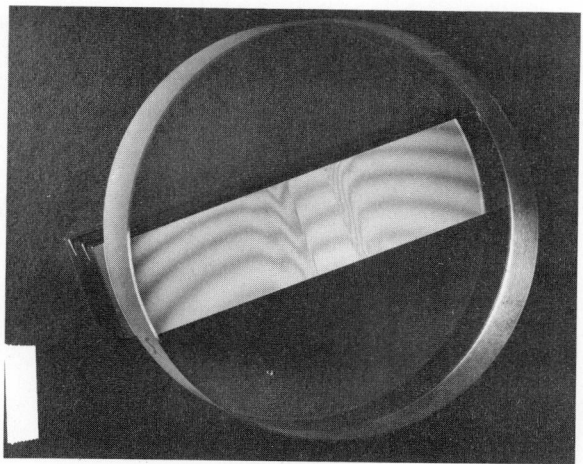

FIGURE 11.10   Photograph showing the interference pattern for a badly worn comparator anvil. Courtesy: The Van Keuren Co., Watertown, MA.

Figure 11.11(a) illustrates the pattern that would be observed if the work surface were spherically convex. The flat rests on the central high spot, and a fringe pattern of concentric circles results. It will be remembered that each adjacent fringe represents a change in elevation, or *fringe interval,* of one-half wavelength of the light that is used. For a helium source, this value would be 0.295 μm (11.6 μin.).

If one edge of the optical flat is pressed gently, it will rock on the high spot and the fringe pattern will shift into a form like that shown in Fig. 11.11(b). The high spot, indicated by the center of the concentric circles, will shift slightly. However, it remains as the primary center of the pattern. In addition, it should be noted *that many of the outer fringes run out at the edge of the work.*

On the other hand, suppose that the surface were spherically concave and that the flat rested on a line extending all the way around the edge, or at least on several points around the edge. If the edge of the optical flat is gently pressed down, it will be observed that although the central point may shift slightly, the edge points (or line) remain stationary and do not move as pressure is varied. From this simple test it can only be concluded that the surface is concave. Having determined the points of contact, we may now map the general contour.

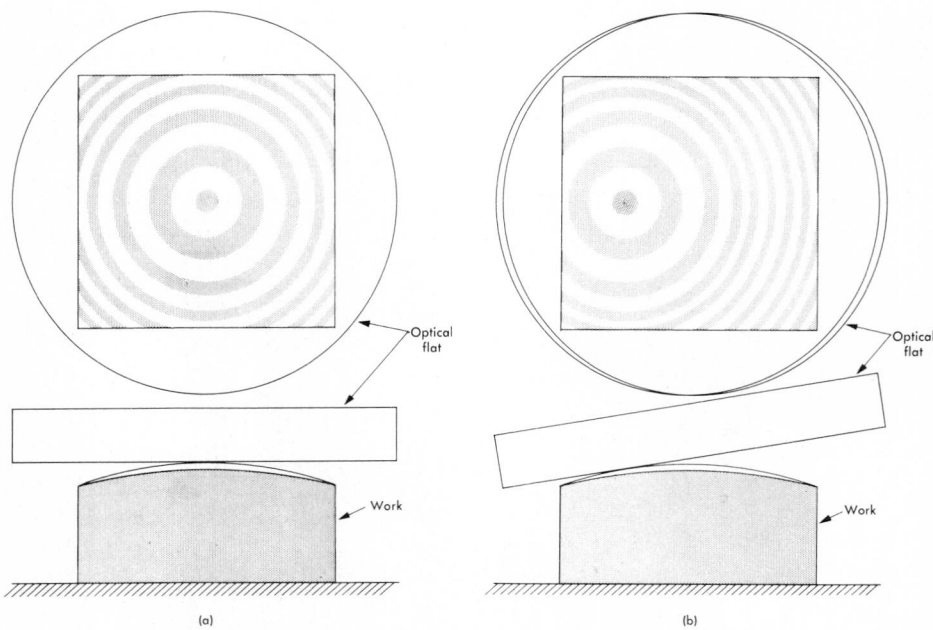

(a)   (b)

FIGURE 11.11   (a) Appearance of interference fringes that occur when an optical flat is placed on a convex spherical surface. (b) Shift of fringe pattern caused by rocking an optical flat.

We may put this on a more formal basis as follows. Let us define the term *fringe order* as the number we would assign a given fringe if we counted them in sequence, starting with a contact point as zero order. We may write the relation

$$\Delta d = (\text{fringe interval}) \times N$$

$$= \frac{\lambda}{2} N, \tag{11.3}$$

in which

Δd = the difference in elevation between contact and the point in question (the contact point will always be the highest point; hence this difference in elevation will always be negative, or away from the face of the optical flat),

N = the fringe order at the point in question, and

λ = the wavelength of the light source used.

11.13 USE OF OPTICAL FLATS AND MONOCHROMATIC LIGHT FOR DIMENSIONAL COMPARISON

Suppose that the diameter of a plug gage (Section 11.2) is to be determined to an uncertainty of several microinches or so. Gage blocks and some form of comparator could be used or, in place of the comparator, an optical flat and a monochromatic light source would serve. If the latter method were used, the procedure would be as follows:

1. The gage diameter is first approximated by use of a micrometer. An estimate to the nearest half-thousandth of an inch (about 0.01 mm) could be expected.

2. Gage blocks are then stacked to the "miked" dimension. At this point it would also be a good idea to check the micrometer against the blocks. If a significant discrepancy is found, the stack of blocks can be reformed.

3. The stack of blocks, along with the plug gage, is then arranged as shown in Fig. 11.12, with the flat resting on top of the combination.

4. If the dimensions of the stack and the plug are nearly the same, an observable fringe pattern will appear over the surface of the gage block. Sometimes considerable patience is required to obtain a good pattern, and experience is certainly helpful. Probably the most important single factor in obtaining good results is cleanliness, because a small bit of lint or a foreign particle will be very large in comparison with the sensitivity of the interference fringes. Ideally, a pattern such as that shown in the figure should finally be obtained.

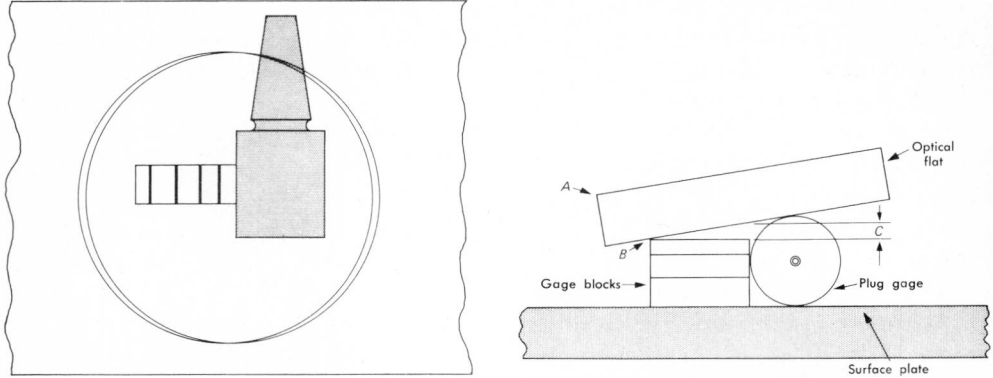

FIGURE 11.12   Arrangement for measurement using gage blocks, optical flat, and mono-chromatic light source.

5. Although Fig. 11.12 indicates that the plug dimension is greater than the stack dimension, this fact must be proved by determining the point of contact between flat and gage block. If the flat were gently pressed downward at point *A*, the fringes would either crowd more closely together (if the plug dimension is the larger) or spread apart (if the stack dimension is the larger). A moment's thought will confirm this if it is remembered that the difference in elevation between adjacent fringes is a fixed quantity. If the situation illustrated exists, then the fringes will crowd more closely together, and contact at *B* between block and flat will be indicated.

6. Now that the point of contact between flat and gage blocks has been determined, the difference in elevation between flat and blocks, *C*, may be determined. This is done by counting the number of fringes, say to the nearest $\frac{1}{5}$ fringe. This number, multiplied by the half wavelength of the light used, gives the height of the flat above the block at *C*.

7. Simple application of similar triangles can now be used to determine the difference between the height of the stack of gage blocks and the plug-gage diameter.

11.14   THE INTERFEROMETER

Measurement of length to, say, 0.5 μin. or about 10^{-5} mm is not commonly required in mechanical development work, but by this time the reader is undoubtedly aware that some accurate and reliable means must be available to establish the absolute length of gage blocks. In other words, how are gage blocks calibrated? We have already discussed methods whereby they may be compared with other gage blocks, but somehow a comparison must be made with the fundamental standard, the wavelength of a specific light source, as discussed in Section 8.4. Interferometers make possible this very basic measurement.

An optical interferometer of great historical significance was devised and used by Albert A. Michelson (1852–1931). It is described in most physics textbooks. Until 1960 the length standard was the meter defined by two finely scribed lines on the platinum–iridium prototype meter bar. Gages of this sort are called *line standards*, whereas the ordinary gage block is an *end standard*. Michelson's primary objective was to determine the wavelengths of light derived from certain sources. Of course the tables are now turned. A specific light source is the standard and the problem is to use it to measure lengths, such as gage-block dimensions.

Gage-block interferometers are available from manufacturers of optical apparatus. Although differing in design details, all make use of essentially the same fundamental methods of operations. The apparatus splits a beam of light into two components, directs each over a different path, and finally reunites the two rays. Recall that two rays from the same initial source will interfere, reinforcing or canceling, depending on the phase relationship. This results in the formation of interference fringes of the type previously described in this chapter. If the source is a white light, the fringes are rather poorly defined sequences of the spectral order. This is generally true; however, if the distances traveled by each of the reunited rays are *identical,* then the resulting interference produces an achromatic fringe, that is, one lacking color, black. White light is used to establish the datum. Monochromatic light is then used to count fringes (half wavelengths of the specific source), corresponding to movement of the reference between two locations. Originally it was necessary to actually count fringes by direct observation. Michelson reduced the problem by devising stepped gages, which he termed *etalons*. His procedure was analogous to using a yard- or meterstick to step off longer distances. For more details on the construction and use of gage-block interferometers, the reader is directed to references [4], [6], and [7].

11.15 MEASURING MICROSCOPES

Figure 11.13 shows a section through a general-purpose low-power microscope. Basically the instrument consists of an objective cell containing the objective lens, an ocular cell containing the eye and field lenses, and a reticle mounting arrangement, all assembled in optical and body tubes. The ocular cell is adjustable in the optical tube, thereby allowing the eyepiece to be focused sharply on the reticle. The complete optical tube is adjustable in the body tube by means of a rack and pinion, for focusing the microscope on the work.

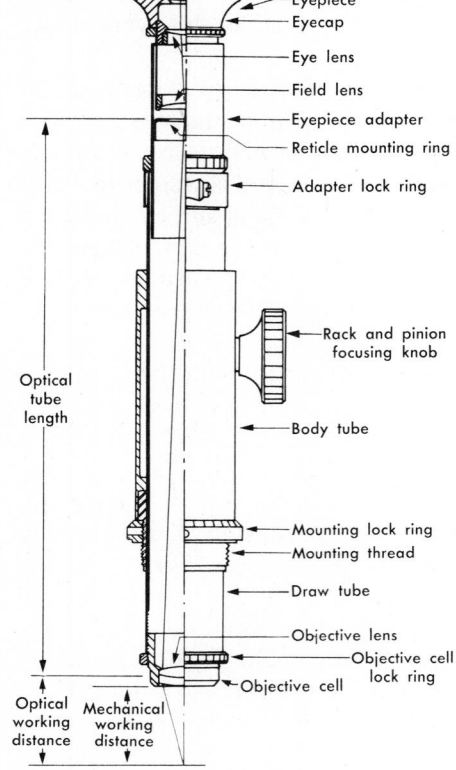

- Eyepiece
- Eyecap
- Eye lens
- Field lens
- Eyepiece adapter
- Reticle mounting ring
- Adapter lock ring
- Rack and pinion focusing knob
- Body tube
- Mounting lock ring
- Mounting thread
- Draw tube
- Objective lens
- Objective cell lock ring
- Objective cell

Optical tube length

Optical working distance   Mechanical working distance

FIGURE 11.13   Section through a simple low-power microscope. Courtesy: The Gaertner Scientific Corp., Chicago, IL.

Aside from the necessary optical excellence required in the lens system, the heart of the measuring microscope lies in the reticle arrangement. The reticle itself may involve almost any type of plane outline, including scales, grids, and lines. Figure 11.14 illustrates several common forms. In use, the images of the reticle and the work are superimposed, making direct comparison

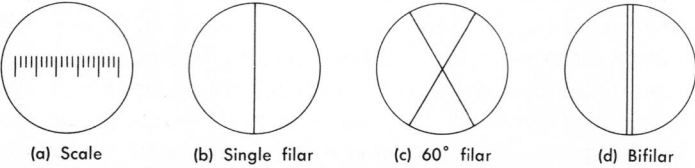

(a) Scale   (b) Single filar   (c) 60° filar   (d) Bifilar

FIGURE 11.14   Examples of measuring microscope reticles. Courtesy: The Gaertner Scientific Corp., Chicago, IL.

possible. If a scale such as Fig. 11.14(a) is used and if the relation between scale and work is known, the dimension may be determined by direct comparison.

Microscopes used for mechanical measurement are of relatively low power, usually less than $100\times$ and often about $40\times$. They may be classified as follows: (1) fixed-scale, (2) filar, (3) traveling, (4) traveling-stage, and (5) draw-tube. The first two, fixed-scale and filar, are intended for measurement of relatively small dimensional magnitudes, from 0.050 to 0.200 in. (1 to 5 mm) in most cases.

11.15.1 Fixed-Scale Microscopes

The fixed-scale measuring microscope uses reticles of the type shown in Fig. 11.14(a). After proper focusing has been accomplished, the scale is simply compared with the work dimension, and the number of scale units is thereby determined. The scale units, of course, must be translated into full-scale dimensions, i.e., the instrument must be calibrated. This is accomplished by focusing on a calibration scale, which is generally made of glass with an etched scale. Typical calibration scales are: 100 divisions with each division 0.1 mm long, and 100 divisions with each division 0.004 in. long. Comparison of the calibration and reticle scales provides a positive calibration. Some microscopes are precalibrated and expected to maintain their calibration indefinitely. However, if the objective is changed or tampered with, recalibration will be necessary.

11.15.2 Filar Microscopes

Filar microscopes make use of moving reticles. Actually in most cases a single or double hairline is moved by a fine-pitch screw thread, with the micrometer drum normally divided into 100 parts for subdividing the turns, as shown in Fig. 11.15. A total range of about 0.25 in. (6 mm) is common. The kind using the double hairline, called a bifilar type, is more common. In use, the double hairline is aligned with one extreme of the dimension, then moved to the other extreme, with the movement indicated by the micrometer drum. It is felt that the bifilar type is more easily used than the single-hairline type. A comparison of the views obtained by both the filar and the bifilar microscopes is shown in Fig. 11.14.

One of the problems in using a filar-measuring microscope is to keep track of the number of turns of the micrometer screw. Two methods for accomplishing this are used. In the first case, a simple counter is attached to the microscope barrel, thus providing direct indication of the number of turns. The more common method is to use a built-in notched bar or *comb* in the field of view. This is shown in Fig. 11.16. Each notch on the comb corresponds

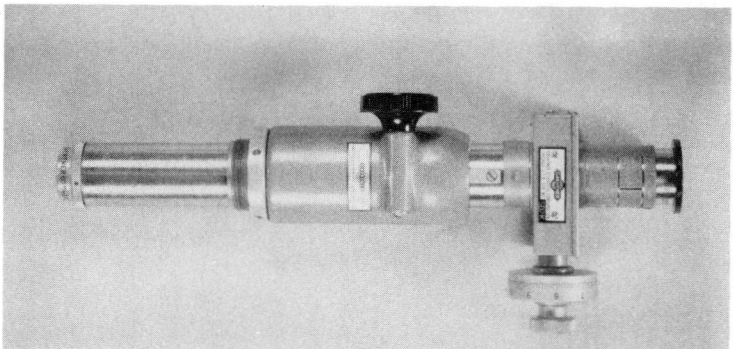

FIGURE 11.15   Filar-type measuring microscope. Courtesy: The Gaertner Scientific Corp., Chicago, IL.

to one complete turn of the micrometer wheel. Further minor and major divisions corresponding to 5 and 10 turns of the wheel are also provided. When the comb is used, a mental scale is applied. As an example, referring to Fig. 11.16, assume that for the initial position the micrometer wheel reads 85. The user might mentally designate the major divisions, reading to the right, as 0, 1000, 2000, 3000, etc. The initial reading would therefore be 085. The hairlines are then moved to the other extreme of the dimension being meas-

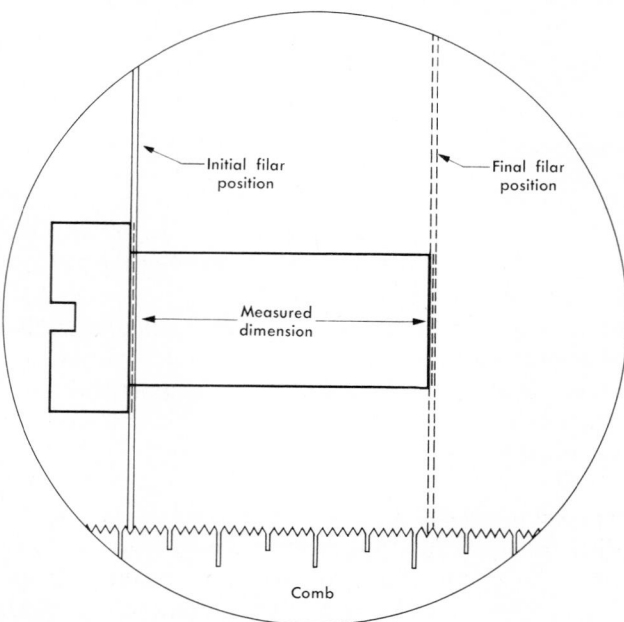

FIGURE 11.16   View through eyepiece of a filar-type microscope showing reference "comb" for indicating turns of the microscope drum. Courtesy: The Gaertner Scientific Corp., Chicago, IL.

ured. Suppose now that the micrometer scale reads 27. Reference to the mental scale applied to the comb supplies the hundreds and thousands places, and the reading should therefore be 3127. The dimension then is 3127 less 85, or 3042 micrometer divisions. From previous calibration, each micrometer division has been determined to be, say, 0.000032 in. Therefore the actual dimension is 3042 × 0.000032, or 0.09734 in.

An example of a special application of the filar microscope is described in Section 17.11.

11.15.3 Traveling and Traveling-Stage Microscopes

A traveling microscope is moved relative to the work by means of a fine-pitch lead screw, and the movement is measured in a manner similar to that used for the ordinary micrometer. In this case the microscope is used merely to provide a magnified index. The traveling-stage type is similar, except that the work is moved relative to the microscope. In both cases the microscope simply serves as an index, and the micrometer arrangement is the measuring means. About 4 or 5 in. is the usual limit of movement, with a least count of 0.0001 in.

An instrument called a *toolmaker's* microscope is an elaborate version of the moving-stage microscope. Special illuminators are used, along with a protractor-type eyepiece.

11.15.4 The Draw-Tube Microscope

This type uses a scale on the side of the optical tube to give a measure of the focusing position. The microscope is used to determine displacements in a direction along the optical axis. For example, the height of a step could be measured. The instrument would be focused on the first level, or elevation, and a reading made; then it would be moved to the second elevation and a second reading made. The difference in readings would be the height of the step.

Vernier scales are normally used, along with microscopes having very shallow depth of focus. A typical range of measurement is $1\frac{1}{2}$ in., with a least count of 0.005 in.

11.15.5 Focusing

Proper focusing of any measuring microscope is essential. First, the eyepiece is carefully adjusted on the reticle without regard to the work image. This is accomplished by sliding the ocular relative to the optical tube, up or down, until maximum sharpness is achieved. Next, the complete optical system is adjusted by means of the rack and pinion until the work is in sharp focus.

Positive check on proper focus may be had by checking for parallax. *When the eye is moved slightly from side to side, the relative positions of the reticle and work images should remain unchanged.* If the reticle image appears to move with respect to the work when this check is made, the focusing has not been properly done.

11.16   OPTICAL TOOLING AND LONG-PATH INTERFEROMETRY

Precision alignment of parts of relatively large dimension is often of great importance. Manufacturers of large aircraft are confronted with problems concerning the assembly of such components as the wings, fuselage, engine mounts, tail surfaces, etc., each made by different companies. Space-vehicle assembly presents similar problems, as does the assembly of large machine tools, turbogenerators, and the like. Tolerances of a few thousandths of an inch or less in a number of feet are often specified. In order to produce dimensions of this precision, special gaging procedures are required, resulting for the most part in the use of optical methods.

Special equipment available for optical tooling includes the following: (1) alignment telescopes, (2) collimators, (3) autocollimators, and (4) accessories. A simple alignment telescope is basically very similar to the familiar surveyor's transit; in fact, surveyors' transits are often used. Basically, the instrument consists of a medium- to high-power telescope with a cross-hair reticle (other special reticles may be used) at the focal point of the eyepiece. The telescopes may be used in the same manner as the surveyor's transit for establishing datum lines and levels. They are particularly useful, however, when used in conjunction with a *collimator.*

A collimator is simply a source of a bundle of *parallel* light rays. Essential parts of the device are a lens tube, a light source, and a lens system for projecting the bundle of rays. Also included are reticles whose images are projected by the collimator. Figure 11.17 shows a schematic with the relative positions of collimator and telescope indicated. Reticle R_2 is at the focal point of the collimator lens system, whereas reticle R_3 is in the collimated light beam. One important feature of the setup is that when reticle R_2 is in place, the observed image at the telescope is a function of *angular alignment only,* independent of lateral or transverse positioning. Another important feature is that when reticle R_3 is observed, its image is dependent only on *lateral position* and is independent of angular alignment. It is therefore possible to first establish correct angular relation between the collimator and the telescope,

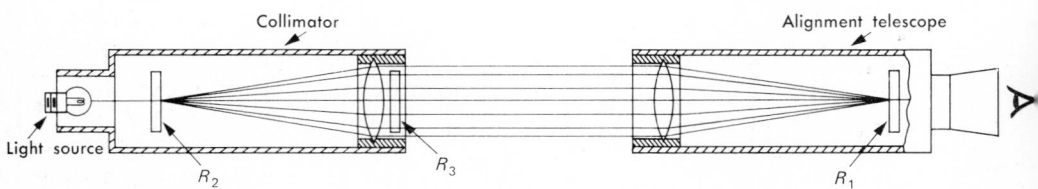

Collimator   Alignment telescope

Light source

R_2 R_3 R_1

FIGURE 11.17   Sketch showing arrangement of alignment telescope and collimator.

and then to determine the magnitude of any lateral misalignment. Magnitudes are independent of distance of separation and are read from scales inscribed on the reticles (Fig. 11.18). Through the use of this type of optical means, widely separated reference points may be established whose relative locations are accurately known. Such points may then be used for establishing shorter local dimensions by means of the more conventional methods.

Another form of instrument is the *autocollimator*. Basically, this device is a combined telescope and collimator that (a) projects a bundle of parallel light rays and (b) uses the same lens system for viewing a reflected image. An important accessory is some form of mirror, which is used as a target for reflecting the light beam. Figure 11.19 shows schematically how it may be used. The autocollimator–target combination provides an optical reference line to which important dimensions may be referred. Intermediate targets may be set up to provide reference points from which dimensional measurements may be made. Instruments of this type also provide for making direct horizontal and vertical measurements of about $\pm \frac{1}{8}$ in. with an accuracy of 0.001 in.

Many accessories are available for these instruments, including special mounts, reticles, optical squares, tooling bars and carriages, targets, etc. A device of great usefulness is the *cube-corner*, a trihedral prism that may be substituted for a mirror to reflect light back toward its origin. The reflected beam emerges parallel to the direction of the incident beam, regardless of alignment.

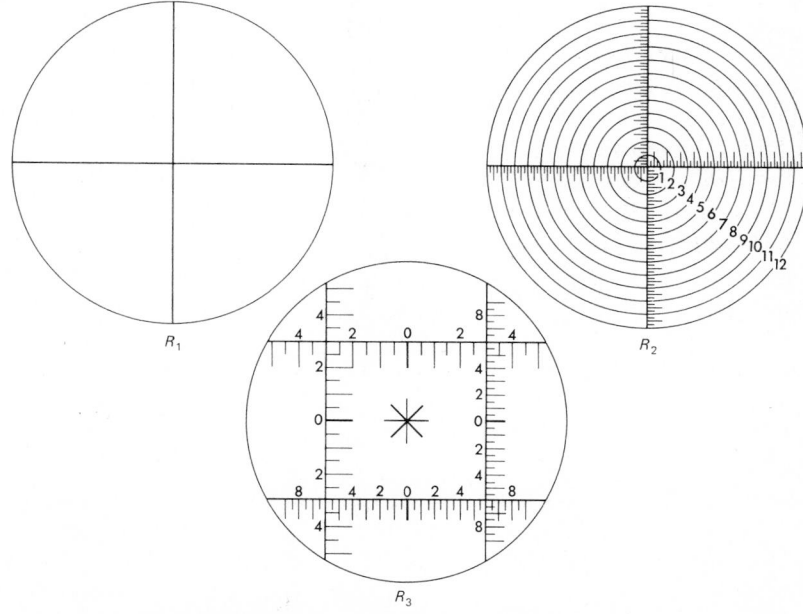

FIGURE 11.18   Examples of reticle designs.

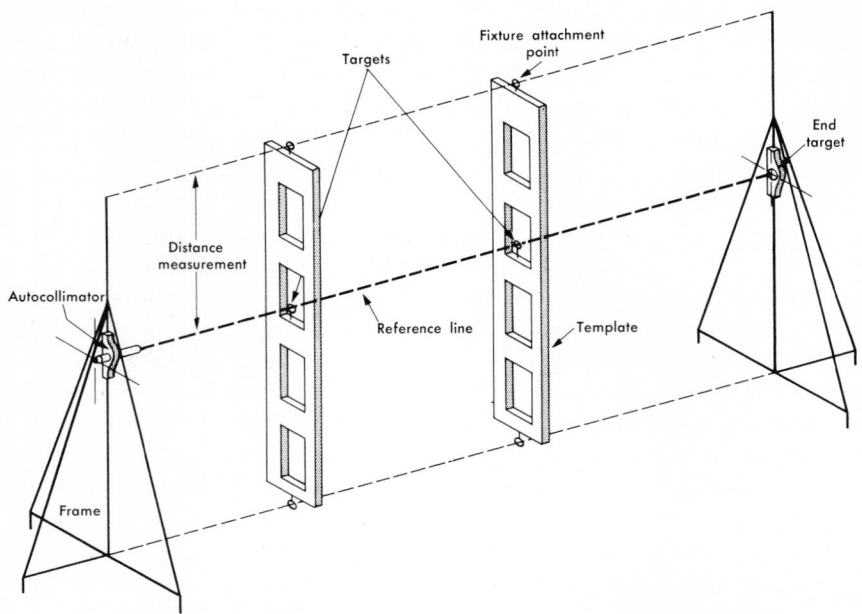

FIGURE 11.19   Sketch illustrating the use of the autocollimator.

An important advance in optical tooling is represented by the laser in-terferometer. In its basic aspects it operates on the same principle as the interferometer using ordinary or simple monochromatic light. Its important feature, however, lies in the use of a gas laser as the light source. This extends the useful range to distances as great as 200 in. as compared to roughly 10 in. for the common methods.

In the strictest sense, no light source has a single frequency or wavelength. For example, the Hg 198 source has a wavelength spread of approximately 0.005 Å (19.685 pico-in.) about a center wavelength of 5461 Å (21.5 μin.). Because of this lack of preciseness, fringes become more poorly defined as the fringe order increases, with reference to the achromatic. For this reason, in practical applications the usefulness of the common metrological light sources is limited to somewhere between 10 inches and one meter; the actual upper limit depends on methods used to minimize the spread. For example, the use of krypton sources may be extended by application of cryogenic temperatures.

Use of the laser as a source provides light that is not only of a very precise wavelength, but also of a coherent nature (as opposed to randomly vibrating light). This maintains the preciseness of fringes over greater dis-tances, greatly extending the range of usefulness.

A commercially available laser interferometer system* makes use of the heterodyning (Section 10.7) of two laser beams, originating from a single source, but of slightly different frequencies. The specifications list a range of up to 200 ft (60 m) with an uncertainty of 5 parts in 10^7. Electronic counting is used and to minimize the problem of air turbulence, a smoothing or averaging mode is provided.

11.17   WHOLE-FIELD DISPLACEMENT MEASUREMENT

Most often mechanical displacements are measured as relative movements between discrete points: Point *A* is displaced by some amount in relation to some reference or datum point. On occasion the relative movements of an array of points may be desired, including a whole-field map, which provides the movements of all points within its bounds. Very commonly the end purpose is related to some form of experimental stress analysis. The reader is directed to Section 12.20 for a discussion of photoelasticity and moiré, which are whole-field techniques.

11.18   DISPLACEMENT TRANSDUCERS

In Chapter 4, we listed a number of devices that are basically displacement-sensitive. These include:

1. Resistance potentiometers (Section 4.6);
2. Resistance strain gages (Section 4.7 and the subject of Chapter 12);
3. Variable-inductance devices (Section 4.10);
4. Differential transformers (Section 4.11 and the subject of further discussion in this section);
5. Capacitive transducers (Section 4.13); and
6. Piezoelectric transducers (Section 4.14).

Most of the other transducers listed in Chapter 4 can be configured to sense displacement. For example, the variable-reluctance transducer is basically velocity-sensitive. Combined with an integrating circuit, the output can be made displacement-related, etc.

Usually variable-inductance, capacitance, piezoelectric, and strain-sensitive transducers are suitable only for small displacements (a few microinches to perhaps $\frac{1}{4}$ in.). The differential transformer may be used over intermediate ranges, say a few microinches to several inches. Although resistance potentiometers are not as sensitive to small displacements as most of the others,

---

*   Hewlett Packard 5526A Laser Measurement System.

there is practically no limit on the maximum displacement for which they may be used [8]. With the exception of the piezoelectric type, all may be used for both static and dynamic displacements.

11.19   THE DIFFERENTIAL TRANSFORMER

Because of its singular importance and because it is fundamentally a mechanical displacement transducer, detailed discussion of the differential transformer was reserved for this chapter.

The device, often referred to as a linear-variable differential transformer, or LVDT, provides an a.c. voltage output proportional to the relative displacement of the transformer core to the windings. Figure 11.20 illustrates the simplicity of its construction. It is a mutual-inductance device using three coils and a core, as shown.

The center coil is energized from an external a.c. power source, and the two end coils, connected together in phase opposition, are used as pickup coils. Output amplitude and phase depend on the relative coupling between the two pickup coils and the power coil. Relative coupling is, in turn, dependent on the position of the core. Theoretically, there should be a core position for which the voltage induced in each of the pickup coils will be of the same magnitude, and the resulting output should be zero. As we will see later, this condition is difficult to attain perfectly.

Typical differential transformer characteristics are illustrated in Fig. 11.21, which shows output vs. core movement. Within limits, on either side of the null position, core displacement results in proportional output. In general, the linear range is primarily dependent on the length of the secondary coils. Although the output voltage magnitudes are ideally the same for equal core

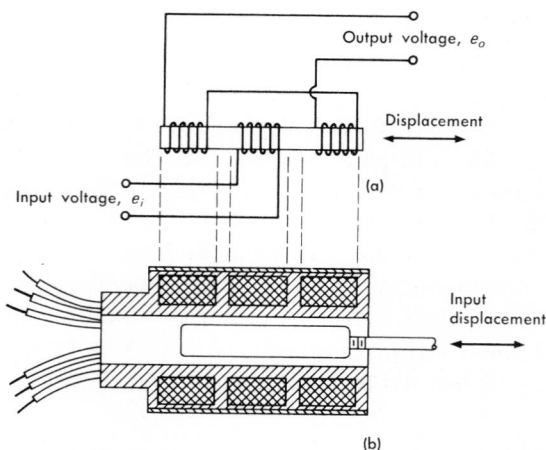

FIGURE 11.20   The differential transformer. (a) Schematic arrangement. (b) Section through a typical transformer

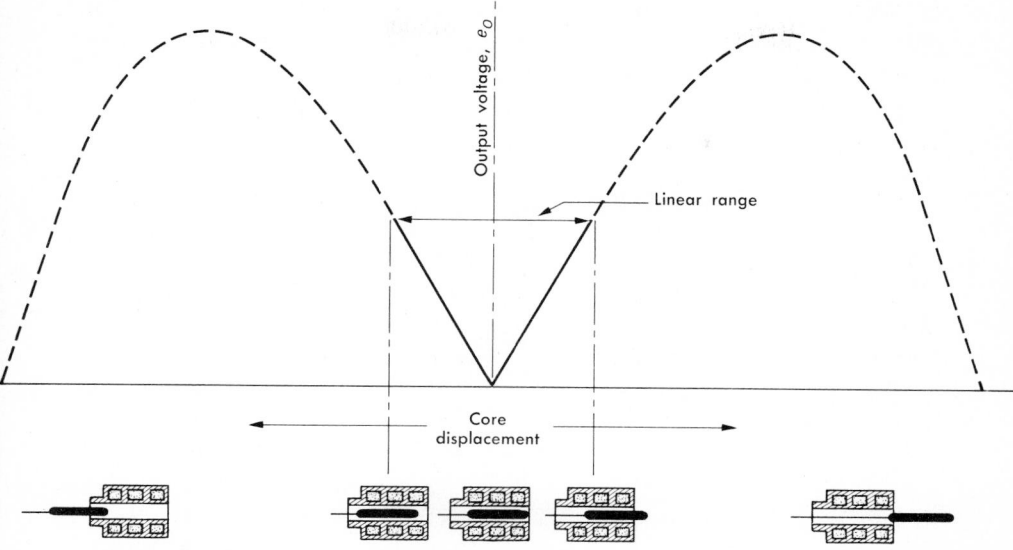

FIGURE 11.21   Typical differential transformer performance characteristics.

displacements on either side of null balance, the phase relation existing between power source and output changes 180 degrees through null. It is therefore possible, through phase determination or the use of phase-sensitive circuitry (discussed later), to distinguish between outputs resulting from displacements on either side of null.

Table 11.4 lists typical differential transformer specifications.

11.19.1 Input Power

Input voltage is limited by the current-carrying ability of the primary coil. In most applications, LVDT sensitivities are great enough so that very conservative ratings can be applied. Many commonly used commercial transformers are made to operate on 60 Hz at 6.3 V. Most of the 60-Hz differential transformers draw less than one watt of excitation power. Generally higher frequencies provide increased sensitivities. However, in order to maintain linearity, design differences, primarily core length, may be required for different frequencies; and, in general, a given LVDT is designed for a specific input frequency.

Exciting frequency, sometimes referred to as *carrier* frequency, limits the dynamic response of a transformer. The desired information is superimposed on the exciting frequency, and a minimum ratio of 10 to 1 between carrier and signal frequencies is usually considered to be the limit. For ratios less than 10 to 1, signal definition tends to become lost. This, therefore, has an important bearing on the selection of an operating frequency.

TABLE 11.4 Typical Variable Differential Transformer Specifications

Linear range, inches	Transformer Size (OD × length), inches	Core Size (diameter × length), inches	Sensitivity mV/0.001 in./V input into high-impedance load Excitation Frequency, Hz				
			60	400	2000	5000	10,000
±0.005	$\frac{3}{8} \times \frac{9}{16}$	0.10 × 0.20	0.40		1.9		
±0.050	$\frac{7}{8} \times 1\frac{1}{8}$	0.25 × $\frac{7}{8}$	0.70	3.00	3.7	3.7	3.75
±0.020	$\frac{1}{2} \times \frac{5}{8}$	0.10 × $\frac{1}{4}$	0.85		3.5		
±0.200	$\frac{7}{8} \times 2\frac{1}{2}$	0.25 × $1\frac{7}{8}$	1.4	2.5	2.5	2.3	2.3
±0.400	$\frac{7}{8} \times 4\frac{3}{8}$	0.25 × $3\frac{3}{8}$	0.8	1.0	1.0	0.5	0.5
±1.0	$\frac{7}{8} \times 6\frac{5}{8}$	0.25 × $4\frac{1}{4}$	0.1	0.3	0.4	0.4	0.3
±5.0	$\frac{7}{8} \times 18$	0.25 × 6	0.05	0.15	0.15	0.15	0.15

Transformer sensitivity is usually stated in terms of *millivolts output per volt input per 0.001-inch core displacement*. It is directly proportional to exciting voltage and, as indicated above, also increases with frequency. Of course, the output also depends on LVDT design, and in general, the sensitivity will increase with increased number of turns on the coils. There is a limit, however, determined by the solenoid effect on the core. In many applications this effect must be minimized; hence design of the general-purpose LVDT is the result of compromise [9].

Solenoid or axial force exerted by the core is zero when the core is centered and increases linearly with displacement. Increasing the excitation frequency reduces this force. Typically, an LVDT having a linear range of ± 0.03 in. exerts an axial force of about 1.80×10^{-4} lbf at 60 Hz and about 1.80×10^{-5} lbf at 1000 Hz, for a driving voltage of 7 V rms.

When utmost sensitivity is required, attainment of a sharp null balance may be difficult without the addition of external components. First of all, in addition to a reactive balance, resistive balance may also be required. This can be accomplished through use of a paralleled potentiometer, inserted as shown in Fig. 11.22(a), whose total resistance is high enough to minimize output loading: 20,000 ohms or higher may be used. In addition to resistive balance, small reactive unbalances may remain at null. These may be caused by unavoidable differences in physical characteristics of the two pickup coils or from external sources present in a particular installation. These unbalances can usually be nulled through use of small capacitances whose values and locations are determined by trial. One or more of the capacitors shown dotted in Fig. 11.22(a) may be required. The figure also shows diodes, D_1 and D_2. These may or may not be added, as desired, to effectively demodulate the output signal, providing plus and minus voltages on either side of null, as shown in Fig. 11.22(b).

The LVDT offers several distinct advantages over many competitive transducers. First, serving as a primary detector-transducer, it converts mechanical displacement into a proportional electrical voltage. As we have found, this is a fundamental conversion. In contrast, the electrical strain gage requires the assistance of some form of elastic member. In addition, the LVDT cannot be overloaded mechanically, since the core is completely separable from the remainder of the device. It is also relatively insensitive to high or low temperatures or to temperature changes, and it provides comparatively high output, often usable without intermediate amplification. It is reusable and of reasonable cost.

Probably its greatest disadvantages lie in the area of dynamic measurement. Its core is of appreciable mass, particularly compared with the mass of the bonded strain gage. And the exciting frequency of the carrier may also be a limiting factor, particularly if the readily available 60-Hz source is used. In addition, the advantage of simple circuitry is lost if the direction from null must be indicated.

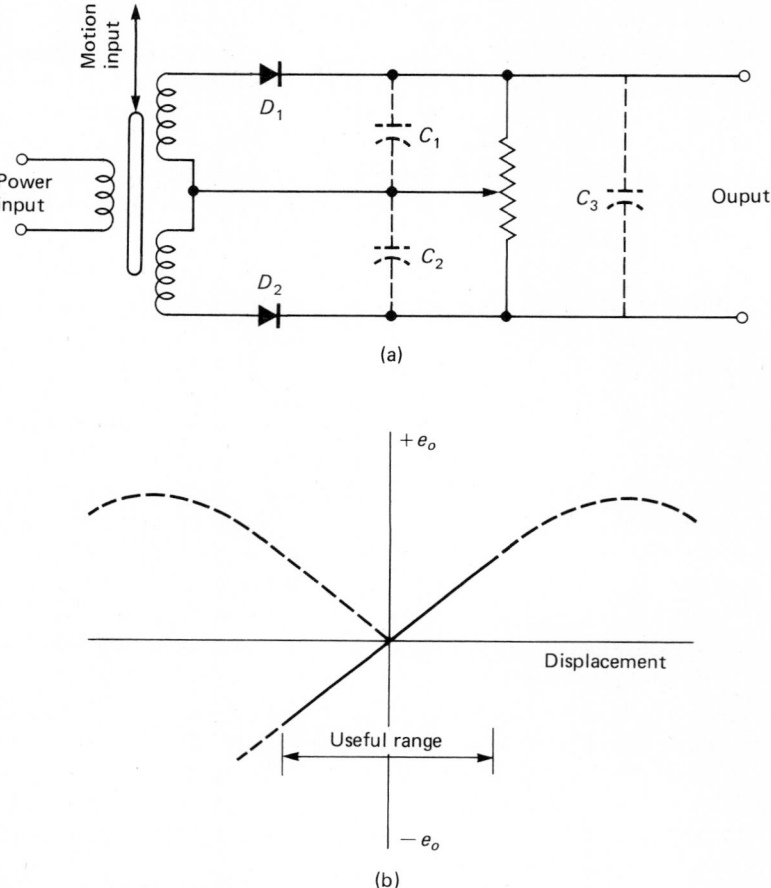

FIGURE 11.22 (a) Arrangement for improving the sharpness of null balance. (b) Demodulated output.

11.20 SURFACE ROUGHNESS [4]

Surface finish may be measured by many different methods, using several different units of measurement. Following is a list of some of the basic methods that have been used or suggested.

1. *Visual comparison* with a *standard* surface. This method is based on appearance, which involves more than the surface roughness.

2. The *tracer method,* which uses a stylus that is dragged across the surface. This is the most common method for obtaining quantitative results.

3. The *plastic-replica method,* wherein a soft, transparent, plastic film is pressed onto the surface, then stripped off. Light is then passed through

the replica and measured. Refraction caused by the roughened surface reduces the transparency, and the intensity of transmitted light is used as the measure.

4. *Reflection of light* from the surface measured by a photocell.

5. *Magnified inspection,* using a binocular microscope or an electron microscope.

6. *Adsorption* of gas or liquid, wherein the magnitude of adsorption is used as the surface-roughness criterion. Radioactive materials have been used for providing a method of quantitative measurement.

7. *Parallel-plane clearance.* Leakage of low-viscosity liquid or gas between the subject surface and a reference flat is used as the measure of roughness.

8. *Electron diffraction* has been proposed, but there are major drawbacks to its use.

9. The *electrolytic method,* which assumes that the electrical capacitance is a function of the actual surface area, the rough surface providing a greater capacitance than a smooth surface.

Suppose Fig. 11.23 represents a sample contour of a machined surface. The values listed thereon may be thought of as actual deviations of the surface from the reference plane x–x, which is located such that the sectional areas above and below the line are equal. These values are also listed in Table 11.5 as absolute values, and their average is calculated to be 12.89 μin. In addition, the root-mean-square (rms) average is calculated as 14.58 μin. We also see that the peak-to-peak height is 27 + 22, or 49 μin. Each of the values—the peak-to-peak height, the arithmetical average deviation, or the root-mean-square average—may be used as measures of roughness.

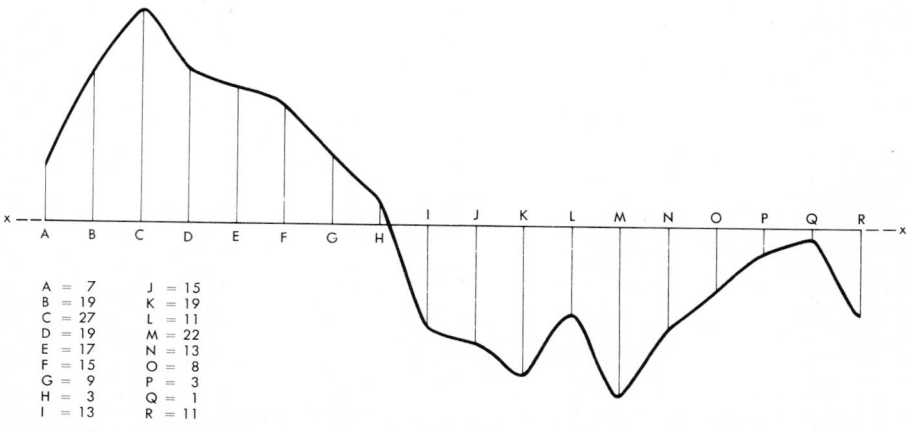

A = 7	J = 15
B = 19	K = 19
C = 27	L = 11
D = 19	M = 22
E = 17	N = 13
F = 15	O = 8
G = 9	P = 3
H = 3	Q = 1
I = 13	R = 11

FIGURE 11.23   Assumed contour of a finished metal surface.

Displacement and Dimensional Measurement

TABLE 11.5 Calculation of Mean Absolute Height and Root-Mean-Square Average

Position	Absolute Elevation from $x-x$, μin.	Square of Elevation
A	7	49
B	19	361
C	27	729
D	19	361
E	17	289
F	15	225
G	9	81
H	3	9
I	13	169
J	15	225
K	19	361
L	11	121
M	22	484
N	13	169
O	8	64
P	3	9
Q	1	1
R	11	121
	Total = 232	Total = 3828

Average absolute height = 232/18 = 12.89

Root-mean-square average = $\sqrt{3828/18}$ = 14.58

The American Standards Association specifies the arithmetical average deviation, defined by the equation

$$Y = \frac{1}{l} \int_0^l |y| \, dx \qquad (11.4)$$

as the standard unit for surface roughness [10]. In this equation,

Y = the arithmetical average deviation,

y = the ordinate of the curve profile from the center line, and

l = the length over which the average is taken.

The term "center line," as used in defining the distance y, corresponds to x–x in Fig. 11.23. We see therefore that the value 12.89 μin. in our example is a practical evaluation of Eq. (11.4).

Many roughness measuring systems using the tracer method yield the rms average. On a given surface, this value will be approximately 11% greater than the arithmetical average deviation [10]. The difference between the two values, however, is less than the normal variations from one piece to another and is commonly ignored.

An idea of the relative values for practical surface finishes may be obtained from Table 11.6.

Although the tracer method for measuring surface roughness is used more than any of the others, it does present several important problems. First, in order for the scriber to follow the contour of the surface, it should have as sharp a point as possible. Some form of conical point with a spherical end is most common. A point radius of 0.0005 in. is often used. Therefore the stylus will not always follow the true contour. If the surface irregularities are primarily what might be referred to as *wavy* or *rolling* hills and valleys of appreciable vertical radius, the stylus may indeed follow the actual contour. If the surface is rugged, on the other hand, the stylus will not extend fully into the valleys.

TABLE 11.6   Relative Values of Surface Finish

Common Name for Finish	rms Roughness, μin.	Average Peak-to-Peak Height, μin.	Usual Tolerance Specified for Finished Part, in.
Mirror	4	15	0.0002
Polished	8	28	0.0005
Ground	16	56	0.001
Smooth	32	118	0.002
Fine	63	220	0.003
Semifine	125	455	0.004
Medium	250	875	0.007
Semirough	500	1750	0.013
Rough	1000	3500	0.025

Second, the stylus will probably actually round off the peaks as it is dragged over the surface. This problem increases as the radius of the tip is decreased. It would seem, therefore, that there are two conflicting requirements with regard to stylus-tip radius. The marring of the surface will in part be a function of the material constants, which of course should have no bearing on the measure of surface roughness.

A third problem lies in the fact that the stylus can never inspect more than a very small percentage of the overall surface.

In spite of these problems, the tracer method is undoubtedly the most commonly used. Various forms of secondary transducers have been employed, including piezoelectric elements (Section 4.14), variable-inductance (Section 4.10), and variable-reluctance (Section 4.12). In each case the stylus motion is transferred to the transducer element, which converts it to an analogous electrical signal.

Read-out devices may be any of the ordinary voltage indicators or recorders, such as the simple meter, an oscillograph, or CRO. The basic indicated value depends on the particular combination of transducing element and indicator used. Piezoelectric variable-inductance and electronic transducers are basically displacement-sensitive, whereas the variable-reluctance type provides an output proportional to velocity. Outputs from the latter, however, may be integrated (Section 5.23), thereby providing displacement information.

An ordinary electronic voltmeter provides a convenient and inexpensive indicator. Outputs from both the piezoelectric and electronic pickups are of sufficient level to provide adequate drive without additional amplification. In addition, if the meter has reasonable frequency–response characteristics, the speed with which the displacement-type pickups are moved over the work need not be carefully controlled.

Of course, the meter, because of its inherent characteristics, indicates rms amplitudes. When some form of oscillograph or oscilloscope is used, peak-to-peak values may be indicated or also recorded. Because of the lower cost, increased portability, and simple operating technique, combinations of displacement-type transducers and meter indicators are the most popular.

SUGGESTED READINGS

ASME, PTC 19.14-1958 Linear Measurements.

American Society of Tool Engineers, *Handbook of Industrial Metrology.* Englewood Cliffs, N.J.: Prentice-Hall, 1967.

Booth, S. F., *Precision Measurement and Calibration,* vol 3 (Selected NBS technical papers on optics, metrology and radiation), NBS Handbook 77. Washington, D.C.: U.S. Government Printing Office, 1961.

Busch, T., *Fundamentals of Dimensional Metrology. Laboratory Experiments.* Albany, N.Y.: Delmar, 1965.

Fullmer, I. H., *Dimensional Metrology* (subject classified with abstracts). NBS Misc. Publ. 265. Washington, D.C.: U.S. Government Printing Office, 1966.

Scarr, A. J. T., *Metrology and Precision Engineering*. London: McGraw-Hill, 1967.

Smith, W. J., *Modern Optical Engineering*. New York: McGraw-Hill, 1966.

PROBLEMS

11.1 Suppose the following data are applied to Fig. 11.12: (a) height of gage-block stack (the sum of the stamped values) = 1.187 in., (b) $4\frac{1}{2}$ fringes from a helium light source are read, (c) nominal width and thickness of the blocks are 1.25 and 1/2 inches, respectively, and (d) the entire assembly is at 68°F. Applying the procedure described in the text, calculate the diameter of the cylindrical plug gage.

11.2 Refer to Fig. 11.12. It is the usual practice to simplify the true geometry of the situation by assuming that the optical flat contacts the plug gage on the vertical center line of the circular section. This, of course, is not precisely true. Using the data given in Problem 11.1, make sufficient calculations to convince yourself of the practicality of the assumption.

11.3 Referring to Problem 11.1, calculate the dimension at standard temperature, 20°C (68°F), if all parts are measured at 35°C (95°F), $4\frac{1}{2}$ fringes are read, and

a) the measured part is of type 302 stainless steel;

b) the measured part is of Invar.

(See Table 4.3 for values of α.)

11.4 Equation (11.1) is written assuming both the blocks and the gaged dimension are at the same nonstandard temperature. Modify the relation to care for a situation in which the blocks and the gaged part are at different temperatures, neither of which is the standard temperature.

11.5 Referring to Problem 11.1, determine how many fringes would appear if the entire assembly were raised to a temperature of 30°C (86°F) and

a) the blocks and the gaged part have identical coefficients of expansion;

b) the gaged part is of aluminum;

c) the gaged part is of type 302 stainless steel.

11.6 The smallest steps in the usual gage-block sets are 0.0001 in. If two blocks A and B are selected such that $h_B - h_A = 0.0001$ in. and the arrangement shown in Fig. 11.24 is used, how many fringes would be produced over block A? Over block B? How does the block width w affect the fringe pattern?

TABLE 11.7 Data for Problems 11.8–11.15

Problem Number	Geometry of Measured Item and Material	a	b	c	d	e	Is $a > (d + e)$?	Light Source	Fringes	Temp., °F
				Inches						
11.8	Rectangular: Carbon steel	1.7839	0.875	1.250	?	0.0	No	Helium	$6\frac{1}{2}$	68
11.9	Cylindrical: Carbon steel	1.7619	1.250	d/2	?	1.4387	Yes	Helium	8	68
11.10	Cylindrical: Aluminum	2.7814	1.000	d/2	2.7805	0	...	Krypton 86	?	68
11.11	Cylindrical: Aluminum	3.7892	1.250	d/2	?	0	No	Hg 198	$15\frac{1}{2}$	90
11.12	Spherical: Brass	1.3470	0.875	d/2	?	1.2750	Yes	Cad. Red	12	75
11.13	Rectangular: Stainless steel	6.3400	1.125	1.500	6.3400*	0	?	Helium	?	98
11.14	Rectangular: Carbon steel	1.7839	0.875	1.250	?	0.0	Yes	Helium	$6\frac{1}{2}$	68
11.15	Cylindrical: Carbon steel	1.7619	1.250	0.400	?	1.4387	Yes	Helium	8	68

Note: Use the following values for thermal coefficients of linear expansion. α, μ in./in.–°F: gage block steel, 6.4; carbon steel, 6.7; stainless steel, 9.4; aluminum, 13.0; brass, 10.0.

* At 68 °F

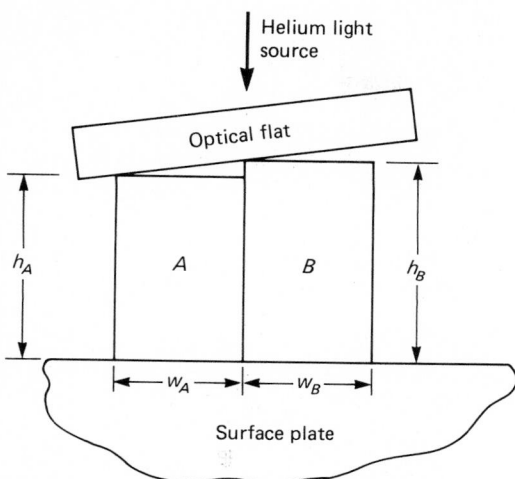

FIGURE 11.24   Arrangement for measuring the difference in lengths between two gage blocks: see Problem 11.6.

11.7 Figure 11.25 illustrates an arrangement of gage blocks, optical flat, and surface plate for measuring the dimension of a hex bar across flats. If the true dimensions are shown, what number of interference fringes would be seen if a helium light source were used?

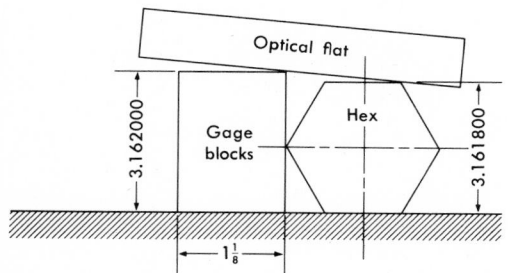

FIGURE 11.25   Arrangement for measuring the "across-flats" dimension of a hexagonal section: see Problem 11.7.

11.8–11.15 Various combinations of values for the parameters defined in Fig. 11.26 are given in Table 11.7. Determine the missing numbers.

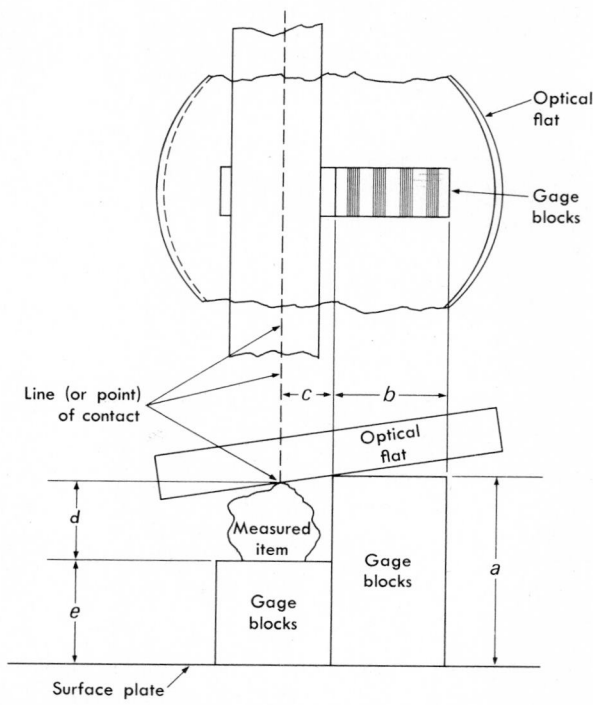

FIGURE 11.26   Gage block and optical flat arrangement to be used for Problems 11.8–11.15; see Problems 11.8–11.15.

strain and 12
stress: measurement and analysis

12.1 INTRODUCTION

All machine or structural members deform to some extent when subjected to external loads or forces. The deformations result in relative displacements that may be normalized as percentage displacement, or strain. For simple axial loading (Fig. 12.1),

$$\varepsilon_a = (L_2 - L_1)/L_1 = \Delta L/L_1, \qquad (12.1)$$

in which

ε_a = axial strain,

L_1 = linear dimension or gage length, and

L_2 = final strained linear dimension.

More correctly, the term *unit strain* should be used for the quantity above, and is generally intended when the word "strain" is used alone. Throughout the following discussion, when the word "strain" is used, we mean the quantity defined by Eq. (12.1). If the net change in a dimension is required, the term *total strain* will be used.

Because the quantity "strain," as applied to most engineering materials, is a very small number, it is commonly multiplied by one million; the resulting number is then called *microstrain*,* or parts per million (ppm).

The stress–strain relation for a uniaxial condition, such as exists in a simple tension-test specimen or at the outer fiber of a beam in bending, is expressed by

$$E = \frac{\sigma_a}{\varepsilon_a}, \qquad (12.2)$$

---

* Considerable use of the term *microstrain* will be made throughout this chapter and elsewhere in the book. For convenience, the abbreviation μs will often be used.

353

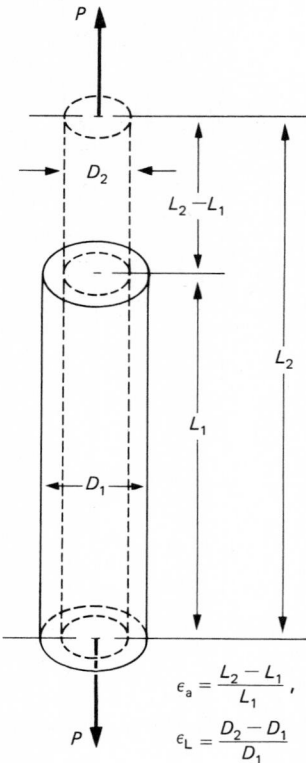

$$\epsilon_a = \frac{L_2 - L_1}{L_1},$$

$$\epsilon_L = \frac{D_2 - D_1}{D_1}$$

FIGURE 12.1   Defining relations for axial and lateral strain.

where

$$E = \text{Young's modulus,}$$

$$\sigma_a = \text{uniaxial stress, and}$$

$$\epsilon_a = \text{the strain in the direction of the stress.}$$

This relation is linear, i.e., E is a constant for most materials so long as the stress is kept below the proportional limit.

When a member is subjected to simple uniaxial stress in the elastic range (Fig. 12.1), lateral strain results in accordance with the following relation:

$$\nu = -\epsilon_L/\epsilon_a \tag{12.2a}$$

where

$$\nu = \text{Poisson's ratio, and}$$

$$\epsilon_L = \text{lateral strain.}$$

A more general condition commonly exists on the free surface of a stressed member. Let us consider an element subject to orthogonal stresses σ_x and σ_y, as shown in Fig. 12.2. Suppose that the stresses σ_x and σ_y are applied one at a time. If σ_x is applied first, there will be a strain in the x-direction equal

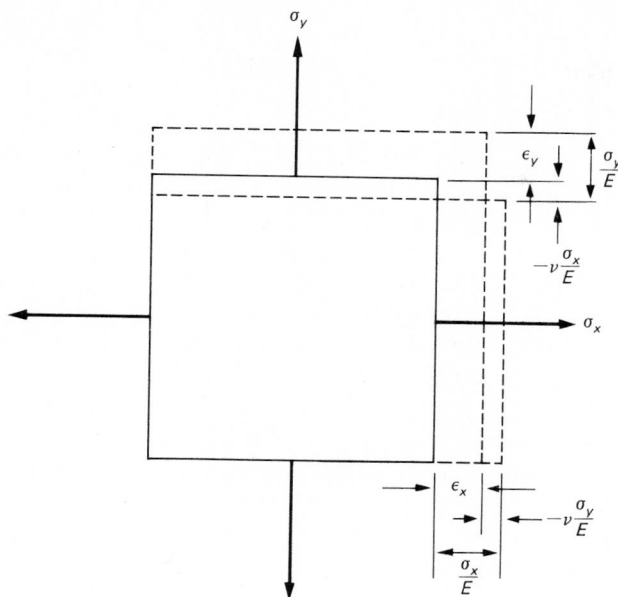

FIGURE 12.2   An element taken from a biaxially stressed condition with normal stresses known.

to σ_x/E. At the same time, because of Poisson's ratio there will be a strain in the y-direction equal to $-\nu\sigma_x/E$.

Now suppose that the stress in the y-direction, σ_y, is applied. This stress will result in a y-strain of σ_y/E and an x-strain equal to $-\nu\sigma_y/E$. The net strains are then expressed by the relations

$$\varepsilon_x = (\sigma_x - \nu\sigma_y)/E \quad \text{and} \quad \varepsilon_y = (\sigma_y - \nu\sigma_x)/E. \quad (12.3)$$

If these relations are solved simultaneously for σ_x and σ_y, we obtain the equations

$$\sigma_x = \frac{E(\varepsilon_x + \nu\varepsilon_y)}{1 - \nu^2} \quad \text{and} \quad \sigma_y = \frac{E(\varepsilon_y + \nu\varepsilon_x)}{1 - \nu^2}. \quad (12.4)$$

When a stress σ_z exists, acting in the third orthogonal direction, the more general three-dimensional relations are

$$\varepsilon_x = \frac{1}{E}\left[\sigma_x - \nu(\sigma_y + \sigma_z)\right],$$

$$\varepsilon_y = \frac{1}{E}\left[\sigma_y - \nu(\sigma_z + \sigma_x)\right], \quad (12.5)$$

$$\varepsilon_z = \frac{1}{E}\left[\sigma_z - \nu(\sigma_x + \sigma_y)\right].$$

Other stress–strain relationships are discussed in Section 12.17 and Appendix E.

12.2 STRAIN MEASUREMENT

Strain may be sensed either directly or indirectly. Electrical resistance strain gages (Section 12.4) are inherently sensitive to strain; that is, their unit resistance change is directly proportional to their unit dimensional change (strain). However, until about 1930 the common experimental procedure consisted of measuring the strain displacement ΔL over some initial gage length L, and then calculating the resulting average strain using Eq. (12.1). An apparatus called an *extensometer* was used. This device generally incorporated either a mechanical or optical lever system and sensed displacements over gage lengths ranging from about 50 mm to as great as 25 cm (about 10 in.). The Huggenberger and the Tuckerman extensometers are representative of the more advanced mechanical and optical types, respectively. Reference [1] provides a good summary of extensometer practices.

12.3 ELECTRICAL-TYPE STRAIN GAGES

As we have already seen, electrical methods yield advantages for dynamic measurements that no other systems provide. These observations also hold for strain measurement; hence most of the discussion that follows in this chapter refers to strain measurement by electrical methods.

Electrical-type strain gages have been devices that use simple resistive, piezoresistive [2, 3], capacitive [4, 5], inductive [6], piezoelectric [7, 8] and photoelectric principles. The resistive types are by far the most popular and will be discussed in considerable detail in sections 12.4 through 12.13. They have advantages, primarily of size and mass, over the other types of electrical gages. On the other hand, strain-sensitive gaging elements used in calibrated devices for measuring other mechanical quantities are often of the inductive type, whereas the capacitive kind is used more for special-purpose applications. Inductive and capacitive gages are generally more rugged than resistive ones and better able to maintain calibration over a long period of time. Inductive gages are sometimes used for permanent installations, such as on rolling-mill frames, etc., for monitoring roll loads. Torque meters often use strain gages in one form or another, both inductive [9] and capacitive [4]. Semiconductor or piezoresistive types (Section 12.13) are extremely sensitive to strain; however, they have the disadvantages of nonlinearity and relatively high temperature sensitivity.

12.4 THE ELECTRICAL RESISTANCE STRAIN GAGE

In 1856 Lord Kelvin described to the Royal Philosophical Society the results of experiments in which he demonstrated that the resistances of copper wire and iron wire change when subject to strain. He made use of a Wheatstone

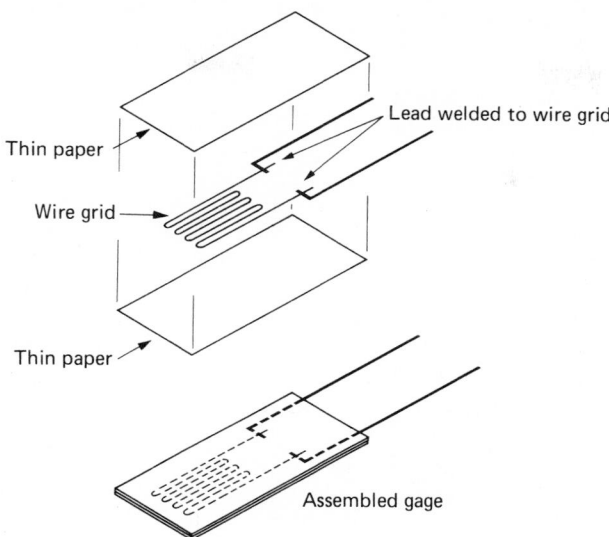

FIGURE 12.3   Construction of bonded-wire type strain gage.

bridge with a galvanometer as indicator [10]. Although the principle had been proved, no practical use was made of the discovery for many years.

Probably the first wire resistance strain gage was that made by Carlson in 1931 [11]. It was of the unbonded type. A force of one pound was required to deflect the gage 0.0005 inch; however, the gage was sensitive to 10 pounds per square inch of stress in concrete. What was probably the first bonded gage was used by Bloach [12]. This consisted of a carbon film applied to the surface of the member in which the strain was to be measured.

In 1938 Edward Simmons made use of a bonded wire gage in a study of stress–strain relations under tension impact [13]. His application consisted of 14 feet of No. 40 constantan wire cemented to the four faces of a steel bar. Glyptal was used as a binder, and the wire was protected by tape. The basic idea (U.S. Patent No. 2,292,549) was to make the cement bond stronger than the wire. At about the same time, Ruge of M.I.T. conceived the idea of making a preassembly of the gage by mounting the wire between thin pieces of paper. Simmons and Ruge were later jointly credited with inventing the gage, and the "SR" in the SR-4 trademark* honors the co-inventors. The basic gage is constructed according to the general arrangement shown in Fig. 12.3.

The unbonded resistance-type gage

Unbonded resistance elements are sometimes used as secondary transducers in pressure sensors, accelerometers, etc. Generally four separate filaments are connected electrically to form a Wheatstone bridge and arranged mechanically

---

*   Baldwin-Lima-Hamilton Corporation, Waltham, Massachusetts.

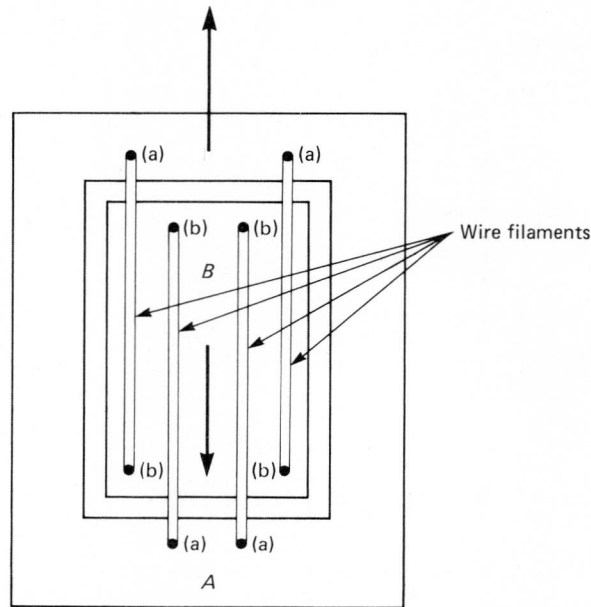

FIGURE 12.4   Schematic of an unbonded resistance-type strain gage. Resistance filaments, under tension, are wrapped around posts (a) and (b), as shown. When block A is moved relative to block B, filament tensions are either increased or decreased and the corresponding resistance changes can be calibrated in terms of strain.

so that filaments in adjacent bridge arms are subjected to strains of opposite sign. Figure 12.4 shows, in schematic form, how such an arrangement works. Assembly must provide a built-in prestrain in the grids greater than the maximum compressive strain to be sensed. (See Fig. 17.8 for an application of an unbonded strain gage.)

The foil strain gage

During the 1950s considerable attention was given to the foil-type gage, which has now essentially replaced the wire gage. The common form consists of a metal foil grid element on a thin epoxy support. Epoxy filled with fiber glass is used for high temperatures and a removable temporary support is sometimes provided for still higher temperatures. The gages are manufactured using printed circuit techniques, hence the configurations are not limited to constant cross sections as is required for the wire elements. This permits the production of many complicated configurations (Fig. 12.5).

The semiconductor gage

Important advances in strain-gage technology have been made through studies of the piezoresistive properties of silicon and germanium. This work has

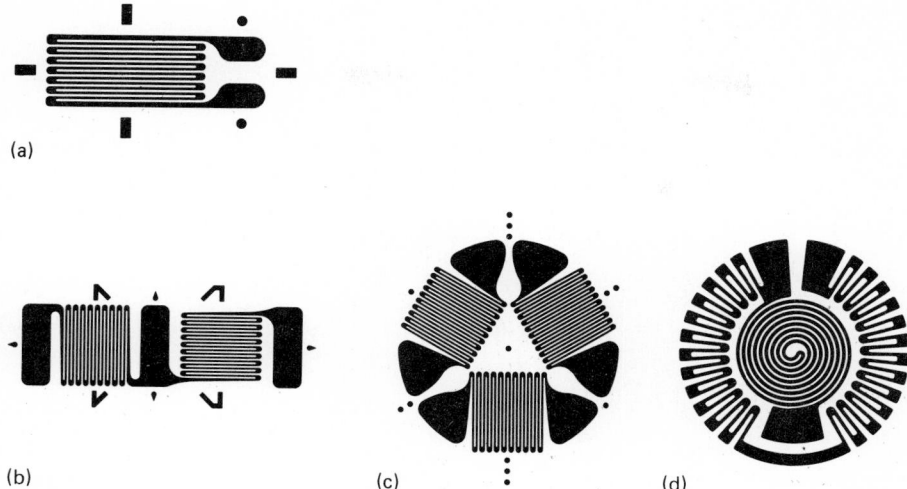

FIGURE 12.5   Typical foil-type gages illustrating the following types: (a) single element, (b) two-element rosette, (c) three-element rosette. (d) One example of many different special-purpose gages. The one shown is for use on pressurized diaphragms.

produced the so-called semiconductor gage,* which is approximately 100 times more sensitive to strain than is the metallic gage. This gain in sensitivity, however, is not without certain important disadvantages, which will be discussed in Section 12.13.

12.5   THE METALLIC RESISTANCE STRAIN GAGE

The theory of operation of the metallic resistance strain gage is relatively simple. When a length of wire (or foil) is mechanically stretched, a *longer* length of *smaller* sectioned conductor results and hence the electrical resistance changes [14]. If the length of resistance element is intimately attached to a strained member in such a way that the element will also be strained, then the measured change in resistance can be calibrated in terms of strain.

A general relation between the electrical and mechanical properties may be derived as follows: Assume an initial conductor length L, having a cross-sectional area CD^2. (In general the section need not be circular; hence, D will be a sectional dimension and C will be a proportionality constant. If the section is square, $C = 1$; if it is circular, $C = \pi/4$, etc.) If the conductor is strained axially in tension thereby causing an increase in length, the lateral dimension should reduce as a function of Poisson's ratio.

---

*   Throughout the remainder of this book the term "semiconductor" or the abbreviation "SC" will be used to designate the germanium- or silicon-type piezoresistive strain gage. The common wire or foil gage will be referred to as the "metallic" or simply the "resistive" gage.

We will start with the relation (Eq. 4.2)

$$R = \frac{\rho L}{A} = \frac{\rho L}{CD^2}. \tag{12.6}$$

If the conductor is strained we may assume that each of the quantities in Eq. (12.6) except for C may change. Differentiating, we have

$$dR = \frac{CD^2(L \, d\rho + \rho \, dL) - 2C\rho \, DL \, dD}{(CD^2)^2}$$

$$= \frac{1}{CD^2}\left((L \, d\rho + \rho \, dL) - 2\rho L\frac{dD}{D}\right). \tag{12.7}$$

Dividing Eq. (12.7) by Eq. (12.6) yields

$$\frac{dR}{R} = \frac{dL}{L} - 2\frac{dD}{D} + \frac{d\rho}{\rho}, \tag{12.8}$$

which may be written

$$\frac{dR/R}{dL/L} = 1 - 2\frac{dD/D}{dL/L} + \frac{d\rho/\rho}{dL/L}. \tag{12.8a}$$

Now

$$\frac{dL}{L} = \varepsilon_a = \text{axial strain,}$$

$$\frac{dD}{D} = \varepsilon_L = \text{lateral strain,}$$

and

$$\nu = \text{Poisson's ratio} = -\frac{dD/D}{dL/L}.$$

Making these substitutions gives us the basic relation for what is known as the *gage factor,* for which we shall use the symbol F:

$$F = \frac{dR/R}{dL/L} = \frac{dR/R}{\varepsilon_a} = 1 + 2\nu + \frac{d\rho/\rho}{dL/L}. \tag{12.9}$$

This is basic for the resistance-type strain gage.

Assuming for the moment that resistivity should remain constant with strain, then according to Eq. (12.9) the gage factor should be a function of Poisson's ratio alone, and in the elastic range should not vary much from $1 + (2)(0.3) = 1.6$. Table 12.1 lists typical values for various materials. Obviously, more than Poisson's ratio must be involved, and if resistivity is the only other variable, apparently its effect is not consistent for all materials. Note the value of the gage factor for nickel. The negative value indicates that a stretched element with increased length and decreased diameter (assuming elastic conditions) actually exhibits a reduced resistance.

TABLE 12.1 Representative Properties of Various Grid Materials

Grid Material	Composition	Approx. Gage Factor, F	Approximate Resistivity Microhm-cm	Approximate Resistivity Ohms per mil-foot	Approximate Temperature Coefficient of Resistance, ppm/°C	Maximum Operating Temp., °C (approx.)
Nichrome V*	80% Ni; 20% Cr	2.0	108	650	400	1100
Constantan*; Copel*; Advance*	45% Ni; 55% Cu	2.0	49	290	11	480
Isoelastic*	36% Ni; 8% Cr; 0.5% Mo; Fe remainder	3.5	112	680	470	. . .
Karma*	74% Ni; 20% Cr 3% Al; 3% Fe	2.4	130	800	18	815
Manganin*	4% Ni; 12% Mn; 84% Cu	0.47	48	260	11	. . .
Platinum-Iridium	95% Pt; 5% Ir	5.1	24	137	1250	1100
Monel*	67% Ni; 33% Cu	1.9	42	240	2000	. . .
Nickel		−12†	7.8	45	6000	. . .
Platinum		4.8	10	60	3000	. . .

* Trade names.

† Varies widely with cold work.

In spite of our incomplete knowledge of the physical mechanism involved, the factor F for metallic gages is essentially a *constant* in the usual range of required strains, and its value, determined experimentally, is reasonably consistent for a given material.

By rewriting Eq. (12.9) and replacing the differential by an incremental resistance change, we obtain the following equation:

$$\varepsilon = \frac{1}{F} \frac{\Delta R}{R} \qquad (12.10)$$

In practical application, values of F and R are supplied by the gage manufacturer, and the user determines ΔR corresponding to the input situation being measured. This is the fundamental procedure for using resistance strain gages.

12.6 SELECTION AND INSTALLATION FACTORS FOR BONDED METALLIC STRAIN GAGES

Five important factors influence metallic-gage characteristics and application:

1. Grid material and construction,
2. Backing material,
3. Bonding material and method,
4. Gage protection,
5. Gage configuration.

About the only opportunity the average strain gage user has to control gage design is through selection of such gages as are made available by commercial sources. The variations are many, however, differing most significantly in types of configurations, but also in grid and backing materials and lead arrangements. In the following paragraphs, we shall discuss some of these factors.

12.6.1 The Grid

Selection of grid materials is based on a compromise of the following desirable factors:

1. High gage factor, F;
2. High resistivity, ρ;
3. Low temperature sensitivity;
4. High electrical stability;
5. High yield point;
6. High endurance limit;

7. Good workability;
8. Good solderability or weldability;
9. Low hysteresis;
10. Low thermal emf when joined with other materials;
11. Good corrosion resistance.

Temperature sensitivity is one of the most worrisome factors in the use of resistance strain gages. In many applications, compensation is provided in the electrical circuitry; however, this does not always eliminate the problem. Two factors are involved: (1) the differential expansion existing between the grid support and the grid proper, resulting in a strain which the gage is unable to distinguish from load strain, and (2) the change in resistivity ρ, with temperature change. The importance of these factors is made apparent by inspection of columns 6 and 7 of Table 12.1, which list the strain increments that may be caused by temperature change in the uncompensated gage. This is commonly called *apparent strain*.

Thermal emf superimposed on gage output obviously must be avoided if d.c. circuitry is used. For a.c. circuitry this factor would be of little importance. Corrosion at a junction between grid and lead could conceivably result in a miniature rectifier, which would be more serious in an a.c. than in a d.c. circuit.

Table 12.1 lists several possible grid materials and some of the properties influencing their use for strain gages. Commercial gages are usually of constantan or isoelastic. The former provides a relatively low temperature coefficient along with reasonable gage factors. Isoelastic gages are some 40 times more sensitive to temperature than are constantan gages. However, they have appreciably higher output, along with generally good characteristics otherwise. They are therefore made available primarily for dynamic application where the short time of strain variation minimizes the temperature problem.

The gage factor listed for nickel is of particular interest, not only because of its relatively high value, but also because of its negative sign. It should be noted, however, that the value of F for nickel varies over a relatively wide range, depending on how it is processed. Cold working has a rather marked effect on the strain- and temperature-related characteristics of nickel and its alloys, and this is taken advantage of to produce special temperature self-compensating gages (see Section 12.11.2).

12.6.2 Backing Materials

The strain-gage grid is normally supported on some form of *backing* material. This provides not only the necessary electrical insulation between grid and tested material, but also a convenient carriage for handling the unmounted gage. Certain types of gages intended for high-temperature applications use

TABLE 12.2   General Recommendations for Strain-Gage Backing Materials and Adhesives

Grid and Backing Materials	Recommended Adhesive	Permissible Temperature Range, °C
Wire or foil on paper	Nitrocellulose (e.g., Duco)	−180 to 90
Foil on epoxy	Cyanoacrylate (e.g., Eastman 910)	−75 to 95
Wire or foil on impregnated paper	Phenolic (e.g., Bakelite)	−240 to 175
Foil on phenol impregnated fiber-glass	Phenolic	−240 to 200
Strippable foil or wire	Ceramic	−240 to 400 (to 1000 for short-time dynamic tests)
Free filament wire	Ceramic	−240 to 650 (to 1100 for short-time dynamic tests)

a *temporary* backing that is removed when the grid is mounted. In this case, at the time of installation the grid is embedded in a special ceramic material that provides the necessary electrical insulation and high-temperature adhesion (see Section 12.19.5).

Desirable characteristics for backing materials include:

1. Minimum thickness consistent with other factors,
2. High mechanical strength,
3. High dielectric strength,
4. Minimum temperature restrictions,
5. Good adherence to cements used,
6. Nonhygroscopic characteristic.

Common backing materials include thin paper, phenolic-impregnated paper, epoxy-type plastic films, and epoxy-impregnated fiber glass. Most foil gages intended for a moderate range of temperatures (−75 to 100°C) use an epoxy film backing. Table 12.2 lists commonly recommended temperature ranges.

12.6.3   Bonding Materials and Methods

Strain gages normally are attached to the test item by some form of cement or adhesive. A multitude of bonding materials are available, which require various detailed techniques for their use. The wide range makes it necessary to give these bonding materials only a general coverage here. The user is referred to the suppliers for more detailed instructions. We can, however, consider general types and ranges of application.

Strain-gage adhesives normally fall into one of the following categories: cellulose, phenolic, epoxy, cyanoacrylate, or ceramic. Table 12.2 summarizes common applications.

In general terms, the following are desirable characteristics of strain-gage adhesives:

1. High mechanical strength,
2. High creep resistance,
3. High dielectric strength,
4. Minimum temperature restrictions,
5. Good adherence,
6. Minimum moisture attraction,
7. Ease of application,
8. The capacity to set up fast.

The mechanical strength of both the backing and the cement is important, since they must transmit the force required to strain the grid. The dielectric strength is also important because this along with moisture absorption determines the electrical leakage resistance to the ground. The recommended minimum resistance between grid and test structure is 50 megohms, with higher values desired. For high stability, resistances to ground should be 1000 megohms or more.

No particular difficulty should be experienced in mounting strain gages if the manufacturer's recommended techniques are carefully followed. However, we may make one observation that is universally applicable. *Cleanliness* is an absolute requirement if consistently satisfactory results are to be expected. The mounting area must be cleaned of all corrosion, paint, etc., and bare base material must be exposed. All traces of greasy film must be removed. Several of the gage suppliers offer kits of cleaning materials along with instructions for their use. These are very satisfactory.

Most of the epoxy cements will set up at room temperature; however, accelerated bonding can be achieved through the application of heat (to a temperature as high as 120 to 175°C). Ceramic cements require curing at temperatures at least as high as the maximum temperature of use.

For simple strain-gage use over a modest temperature range (-75 to 95°C) a most useful cement is the cyanoacrylate type (Eastman 910). Mounting methods are simple and convenient (requiring no temperature cure and a clamping pressure of approximately 10×10^4 Pa (15 psi) for a minute or two). The installation is ready for use almost as quickly as leads can be attached.

12.6.4 Gage Protection

Most gage installations are not complete until provision is made to protect the gage from ambient conditions. The latter may include mechanical abuse, moisture, oil, dust and dirt, and the like.

Once again, gage suppliers provide recommended materials for this purpose, including petroleum waxes, silicone resins, epoxy preparations, and rubberized brushing compounds. A variety of materials is necessary because of the many types of protection required—from such things as hot oil, immersion in water, liquified gases, etc. An extreme requirement for gage protection is found in the case of gages mounted on the exterior of a ship or submarine hull for the purpose of sea trials [15]. Special methods of protection are used, including rubber boots vulcanized over the gages.

12.6.5 Gage Configurations and Sizes

Gages may have one or more elements (see Fig. 12.5). When used for stress analysis, the single-element gage is applied to the uniaxial stress condition; the two-element rosette is applied to the biaxial condition when either the principal axes or the axes of interest are known, and the three-element rosette is applied when a biaxial stress condition is completely unknown (see Section 12.17.2 for a more complete discussion).

Selection of a gage size must be a compromise based on consideration of several factors: axial and transverse strain gradients, and power dissipation. It is desirable to minimize a gage dimension in the direction of greatest strain gradient, either axial or transverse. High strain gradients occur not only near points of stress concentration but also in cases of dynamic loading where propagation of stress waves is being studied. On the other hand, it is sometimes desirable to "average out" the local stress variations that may be caused by nonhomogeneity of material or local, uncontrollable dimensional deviations. An example of the latter would be handling defects or instances of out-of-roundness* in a thin-walled tube which introduce local bending strains. In this case a long gage length may be desirable.

Of course, resistance strain gages are passive transducers requiring external power. The energizing current causes ohmic heating that must be dissipated, largely to the structure upon which the gage is mounted. Foil gages bonded to metal can safely handle about 5 watts per square inch. An approximate maximum current for wire gages is 35 ma. Because sensitivity is, among other things, a function of energizing voltage (hence, power for a given resistance), it is obvious that the larger gage is inherently capable of the

---

* In one instance measurable, but not obvious, out-of-roundness of a pressure vessel with a 30-inch diameter and $\frac{1}{4}$-inch wall caused a strain difference of some 35% at points 90° apart around a free meridian.

**TABLE 12.3 Typical Single Element Strain Gages*

Item	Nominal Resistance, Ohms	Nominal Gage Factor	Length of Grid, inches	Width of Grid, inches	Grid Material and Form	Backing	Remarks
1.	120	2	$\frac{13}{16}$	$\frac{9}{64}$	Constantan wire	Paper	Original commercial gage
2.	300	2	6	$\frac{1}{32}$	Constantan wire	Paper	Extra-long gage
3.	60	1.7	$\frac{1}{16}$	$\frac{1}{16}$	Constantan wire	Paper	Short gage length
4.	500	3.5	1	$\frac{3}{16}$	Isoelastic wire	Paper	
5.	240	2	$\frac{1}{4}$	$\frac{3}{32}$	Constantan wire	Phenolic	
6.	120	2.1	1	0.31	Constantan foil	Epoxy	
7.	120	2.0	0.015	0.020	Constantan foil	Epoxy	Very short gage length
8.	750	2.1	6	0.74	Constantan foil	Epoxy	Long gage length, high resis.
9.	350	2.1	0.12	0.21	Constantan foil	Phenolic	
10.	350	2.2	0.5	0.5	Karma foil	Fiberglass epoxy	
11.	120	2.1	0.50	0.29	Nichrome V foil	Strippable	For elevated temp. use.
12.	120	2.2	$\frac{1}{2}$	$\frac{1}{16}$	Nichrome V foil	Weldable	For elevated temp. use.

* Although the gages listed above are not identified with specific manufacturers, the list does approximate the range of single-element, metallic types presently available. There is a multitude of variations, however, and new gages are being developed at a rapid rate, hence, manufacturers' lists must be consulted for specific applications.

367

greater sensitivity. It may be said, therefore, that it is advantageous to use the largest gage compatible with the strain conditions being measured. An additional dividend gained by using the larger gage is considerably greater ease of installation.

Table 12.3 lists a small but representative sampling of available gages.

12.7 CIRCUITRY FOR THE METALLIC STRAIN GAGE

When the sensitivity of a metallic resistance gage is considered, its versatility and reliability are truly amazing. The basic relation as expressed by Eq. (12.10) is

$$\varepsilon = \frac{1}{F} \frac{\Delta R_g}{R_g}. \tag{12.11}$$

Typical gage constants are

$$F = 2.0, \qquad R_g = 120 \text{ ohms.}$$

Strains of one μs (1 ppm) are detectable with commercial equipment; hence, the corresponding resistance change that must be measured in the gage will be

$$\Delta R_g = FR_g\varepsilon = (2)(120)(0.000001) = 0.00024 \text{ ohm.}$$

This amounts to a resistance change of 0.0002%. Obviously, to measure changes as small as this, instrumentation more sensitive than the ordinary ohmmeter will be required.

Three circuit arrangements are used for this purpose: the simple voltage-dividing potentiometer or ballast circuit (Section 5.6), the Wheatstone bridge (Section 5.9), and the constant-current circuit. Some form of bridge arrangement is by far the more generally useful.

12.8 THE STRAIN-GAGE BALLAST CIRCUIT

Figure 12.6 illustrates a simple strain-gage ballast arrangement. Using Eq. (5.4) and substituting R_g for kR_t, we may write

$$e_o = e_i \frac{R_g}{R_b + R_g}$$

and

$$de_o = \frac{e_i R_b \, dR_g}{(R_b + R_g)^2} = \frac{e_i R_b R_g}{(R_b + R_g)^2} \frac{dR_g}{R_g}.$$

From Eq. (12.11),

$$de_o = \frac{e_i R_b R_g}{(R_b + R_g)^2} F\varepsilon, \tag{12.12}$$

where

$$e_i = \text{the exciting voltage,}$$

$$e_o = \text{the voltage output,}$$

$$R_b = \text{the ballast resistance, in ohms,}$$

$$R_g = \text{the strain-gage resistance, in ohms,}$$

$$F = \text{the gage factor, and}$$

$$\varepsilon = \text{strain.}$$

Some of the limitations inherent in this circuit may be demonstrated by the following example. Let

$$R_b = R_g = 120 \text{ ohms.}$$

A resistance of 120 ohms is common in a strain gage, and it will be recalled that in Section 5.6 we showed that equal ballast and transducer resistances provide maximum sensitivity. Also, let

$$e_i = 8 \text{ volts.}$$

Let

$$F = 2.0,$$

which is a common value. Then

$$e_o = 8\left(\frac{120}{120 + 120}\right) = 4 \text{ volts,}$$

$$de_o = \frac{8 \times 120 \times 120 \times 2 \times \varepsilon}{(120 + 120)^2} = 4\varepsilon.$$

If our indicator is to provide an indication for strain of, say, one microstrain, it must sense a 4-microvolt variation in 4 V, or 0.00010%. This severe requirement practically eliminates the ballast circuit for *static* strain work. We may use it, however, in certain cases for dynamic strain measurement when any static strain component may be ignored. If a capacitor is inserted in an output lead, the d.c. exciting voltage is blocked and only the variable component is allowed to pass (Fig. 12.6). Temperature compensation

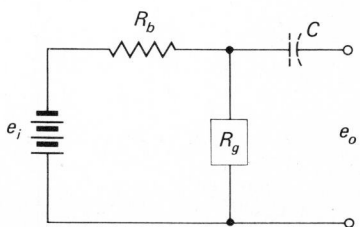

FIGURE 12.6   Ballast circuit for use with strain gages.

is not provided; however, when only transient strains are of interest, this is often of no importance.

12.9   THE STRAIN-GAGE BRIDGE CIRCUIT

A resistance-bridge arrangement is particularly convenient for use with strain gages because it may be easily adjusted to a null for zero strain, and it provides means for effectively reducing or eliminating the temperature effects previously discussed (Section 12.6.1). Figure 12.7 shows a minimum bridge arrangement, where arm 1 consists of the strain-sensitive gage mounted on the test item. Arm 2 is formed by a similar gage mounted on a piece of unstrained material as nearly like the test material as possible and placed near the test location so that the temperature will be the same. Arms 3 and 4 may simply be fixed resistors selected for good stability, plus portions of slide-wire resistance, D, required for balancing the bridge.

If we assume a voltage-sensitive deflection bridge with all initial resistances nominally equal, using Eq. (5.15) we have

$$\frac{\Delta e_o}{e_i} = \frac{\Delta R_1/R}{4 + 2(\Delta R_1/R)} .$$

In addition,

$$\varepsilon = \frac{1}{F}\frac{\Delta R_1}{R} \quad \text{or} \quad \Delta R = FR\varepsilon.$$

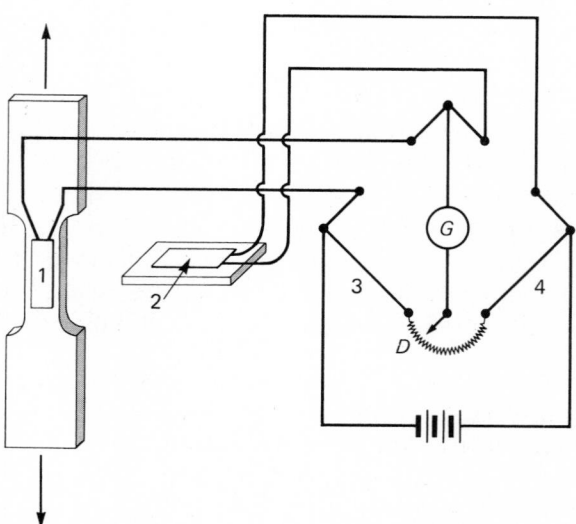

FIGURE 12.7   Simple resistance bridge arrangement for strain measurement.

Then

$$\Delta e_o = \frac{e_i F \varepsilon}{4 + 2F\varepsilon} \ .$$

For $e_i = 8$ volts and $F = 2$,

$$\Delta e_o = \frac{8 \times 2 \times \varepsilon}{4 + (2)(2)\varepsilon} \ .$$

If we neglect the second term in the denominator, which is normally negligible, then

$$\Delta e_o = e_o = 4\varepsilon \text{ volts}$$

or for $\varepsilon = 1$ microstrain, $e_o = 4$ microvolts.

We see that under similar conditions the output increment for the bridge and ballast arrangements is the same. The tremendous advantage that the bridge possesses, however, is that the incremental output is not superimposed on a large fixed-voltage component. Another important advantage, which is discussed in Section 12.11, is that temperature compensation is easily attained through the use of a bridge circuit incorporating a "dummy" or compensating gage.

12.9.1 Bridges with Two and Four Arms Sensitive to Strain

In many cases bridge configuration permits the use of more than one arm for measurement. This is particularly true if a known relation exists between two strains, notably the case of bending. For a beam section symmetrical about the neutral axis, we know that the tensile and compressive strains are equal except for sign. In this case, both gages 1 and 2 may be used for strain measurement. This is done by mounting gage 1 on the tensile side of the beam and mounting gage 2 on the compressive side, as shown in Fig. 12.8 (see also case F in Table 12.5). The resistance changes will be alike but of opposite sign, and a doubled bridge output will be realized.

This may be carried further, and all four arms of the bridge made strain-sensitive, thereby *quadrupling* the output that would be obtained if only a single gage were used. In this case gages 1 and 4 would be mounted to record like strain (say tension) and 2 and 3 to record the opposite type (case G in Table 12.5).

Bridge circuits of these kinds may be used either as null-balance bridges or as deflection bridges (Section 5.9). In the former the slide-wire movement becomes the indicated measure of strain. This is most useful for strain-indicating devices used for static measurement. Most dynamic strain-measuring systems, however, use a voltage- or current-sensitive deflection bridge. After initial balance is accomplished, the output, amplified as necessary, is used to deflect an indicator, such as a cathode-ray oscilloscope beam or a recorder

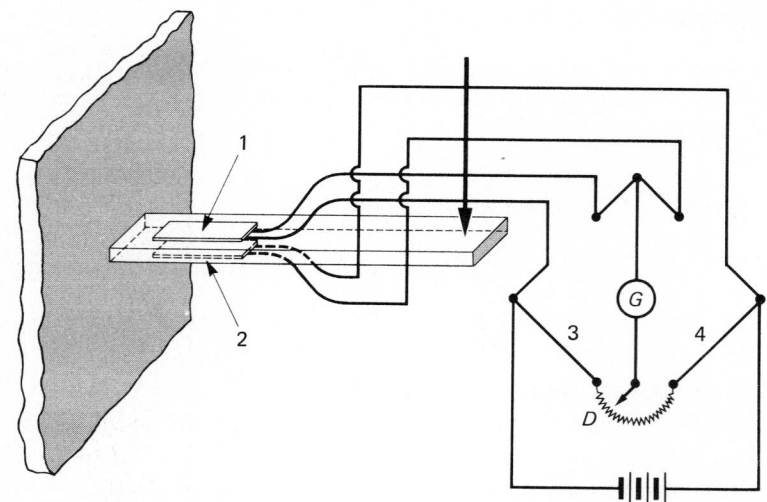

FIGURE 12.8   Bridge arrangement with two gages sensitive to strain.

of the stylus or light-beam types. In addition, the constant-current bridge may offer certain advantages (Section 5.9.3).

12.9.2 The Bridge Constant

At this point we introduce the term *bridge constant,* which we shall define by the following equation:

$$k = A/B, \tag{12.13}$$

where

> k = the bridge constant,
>
> A = the actual bridge output,
>
> B = the output from the bridge if only a single gage,
>   sensing maximum strain, were effective.

In the example illustrated in Fig. 12.8, the bridge constant would be 2. This is true because the bridge provides an output double that which would be had if only gage 1 were strain-sensitive. If all four gages were used, quadrupling the output, the bridge constant would be 4. In certain other cases (Section 12.18), gages may be mounted sensitive to lateral strains that are functions of Poisson's ratio. In such cases bridge constants of 1.3 and 2.6 (for Poisson's ratio = 0.3) are common.

12.9.3 Lead-Wire Error

When it is necessary to use unusually long lead wires between gage and other instrumentation, so-called lead-wire error may be introduced. The reader is referred to Section 5.9.5, where a solution to this problem is discussed.

12.10 THE SIMPLE CONSTANT-CURRENT STRAIN-GAGE CIRCUIT

Measurement of dynamic strains may be accomplished by the simple circuit shown in Fig. 12.9. It is assumed that the power source is a true constant-current supply and that the indicator (CRO is shown) possesses near-infinite input impedance compared to the gage resistance. As the gage resistance changes as a result of strain, the voltage across the gage, hence the input to the CRO, will be

$$e_i = i_i R \qquad (12.14)$$

and

$$\Delta e_i = i_i \, \Delta R. \qquad (12.14a)$$

Dividing Eq. (12.14a) by Eq. (12.14), we have

$$\Delta e_i / e_i = \Delta R / R.$$

Inserting $\Delta R/R$ in Eq. (12.10) gives us

$$\varepsilon = \frac{1}{F} \frac{\Delta e_i}{e_i}. \qquad (12.14b)$$

The CRO should be set in the a.c. mode to cancel the direct d.c. component, and, of course, the CRO amplification capability must be sufficient to provide an adequate read-out.

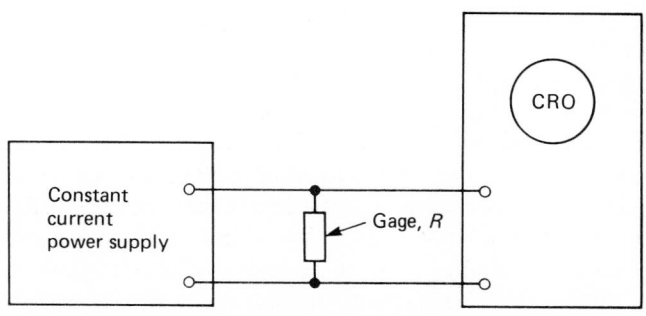

FIGURE 12.9   Single gage, constant-current circuit.

12.11 TEMPERATURE COMPENSATION

As already implied, resistive-type strain gages are normally quite sensitive to temperature. Both the differential expansion between the grid and the tested material and the temperature coefficient of the resistivity of the grid material contribute to the problem. It has been shown (Table 12.1) that the temperature effect may be large enough to require careful consideration. Temperature effects may be handled by (1) cancellation or compensation or (2) evaluation as a part of the data-reduction problem.

Compensation may be provided (1) through use of adjacent-arm balancing or compensating gage or gages or (2) by means of self-compensation.

12.11.1 The Adjacent-Arm Compensating Gage

Consider bridge configurations such as those shown in Figs. 12.7 and 12.8. Initial electrical balance is had when

$$R_1/R_2 = R_3/R_4.$$

If the gages in arms 1 and 2 are *alike* and *mounted on similar materials,* and if both gages experience the same resistance shift, ΔR_t, caused by temperature change, then

$$\frac{R_1 + \Delta R_t}{R_2 + \Delta R_t} = \frac{R_3}{R_4}.$$

We see that the bridge remains in balance and the output unaffected by the change in temperature. When the compensating gage is used merely to complete the bridge and to balance out the temperature component, it is often referred to as the "dummy" gage.

12.11.2 Self-Temperature Compensation

In certain cases it may be difficult or impossible to obtain temperature compensation by means of an adjacent-arm compensating or dummy gage. For example, temperature gradients in the test part may be sufficiently great to make it impossible to hold any two gages at similar temperatures. Or, in certain instances, it may be desirable to use the ballast rather than the bridge circuit, thereby eliminating the possibility of adjacent-arm compensation. Situations of this sort make *self-compensation* highly desirable.

The two general types of self-compensated gages available are the *selected-melt* gage and the *dual-element* gage. The former is based on the discovery that through proper manipulation of alloy and processing, particularly through cold working, some control over the temperature sensitivity of the grid material may be exercised. Through this approach grid materials (both wire and foil) may be prepared that show very low apparent strain versus temperature change

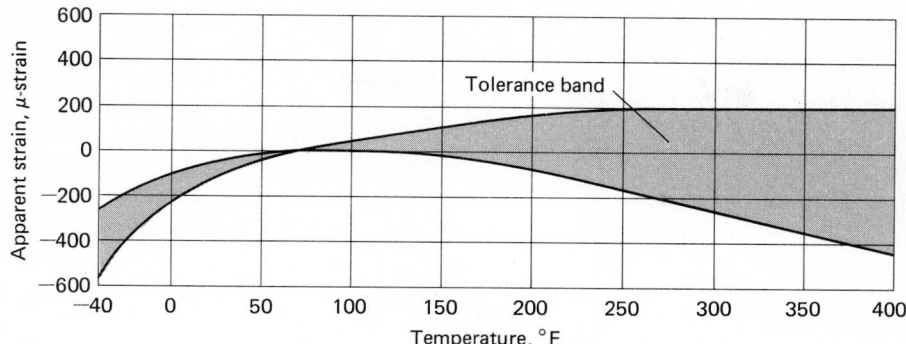

FIGURE 12.10 Approximate range of apparent strain vs. temperature for a typical "selected melt" gage mounted on the appropriate material (e.g., steel at about 11 ppm/deg.C).

over certain temperature ranges when the gage is mounted on a particular test material. Figure 12.10 shows typical characteristics of selected-melt gages compensated for use with a material having a coefficient of expansion 6 ppm/°F, which corresponds to the coefficient of expansion of most carbon steels. In this case, practical compensation is accomplished over a temperature range of approximately 50–250°F. Other gages may be compensated for different thermal expansions and temperature ranges. These curves give some idea of the degree of control that may be had through manipulation of the grid material.

The second approach to self-compensation makes use of two wire elements connected in series in one gage assembly. The two elements have different temperature characteristics and are selected so that the net temperature-induced strain is minimized when the gage is mounted on the specified test material. In general, the performance of this type of gage is similar to that of the selected-melt gage shown in Fig. 12.10.

Neither the selected-melt nor the dual-element gage has a distinctive outward appearance. One company uses color-coded backings to assist in identifying gages of different specifications.

12.12 CALIBRATION

Ideally, calibration of any measuring system consists of introducing an accurately known sample of the variable that is to be measured and then observing the system's response. This ideal cannot often be realized in bonded resistance strain-gage work because of the nature of the transducer. Normally, the gage is bonded to a test item for the simple reason that the strains (or stresses) are unknown. Once bonded, the gage can hardly be transferred to a *known* strain situation for calibration. Of course, this is not necessarily the case if the gage or gages are used as secondary transducers applied to an appropriate elastic member for the purpose of measuring force, pressure,

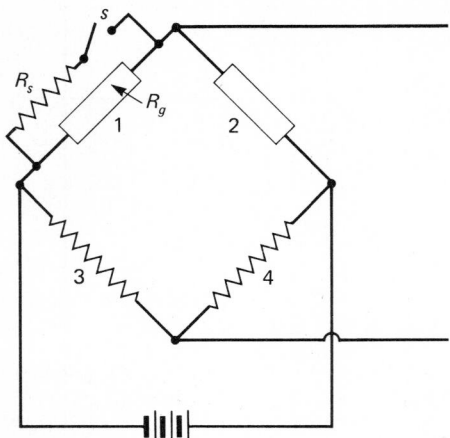

FIGURE 12.11   Bridge employing a shunt resistance for calibration.

torque, etc. In cases of this sort, it may be perfectly feasible to introduce known inputs and carry out satisfactory calibrations. When the gage is used for the purpose of experimentally determining strains, however, some other approach to the calibration problem is required.

Resistance strain gages are manufactured under carefully controlled conditions, and the gage factor for each lot of gages is provided by the manufacturer within an indicated tolerance of about $\pm 0.2\%$. Knowing the gage factor and gage resistance makes possible a simple method for calibrating any resistance strain gage system. The method consists of determining the system's response to the introduction of a known small resistance change at the gage and of calculating an equivalent strain therefrom. The resistance change is introduced by shunting a relatively high-value precision resistance across the gage as shown in Fig. 12.11. When switch S is closed, the resistance of bridge arm 1 is changed by a small amount, as determined by the following calculations.

Let

$$R_g = \text{the gage resistance, in ohms, and}$$

$$R_s = \text{the shunt resistance, in ohms.}$$

Then the resistance of arm 1 before the switch is closed equals R_g, and the resistance of arm 1 after the switch is closed equals $(R_g R_s)/(R_g + R_s)$, as determined for parallel resistances. Therefore the change in resistance is

$$\Delta R = \frac{R_g R_s}{(R_g - R_s)} - R_g = -\frac{R_g^2}{R_g + R_s} .$$

Now to determine the equivalent strain, we may use the relation given by Eq. 12.11.

$$\varepsilon = +\frac{1}{F}\frac{\Delta R_g}{R_g} .$$

By substituting ΔR for ΔR_g, the equivalent strain is found to be

$$\varepsilon_e = -\frac{1}{F}\left(\frac{R_g}{R_g + R_s}\right).$$ (12.15)

EXAMPLE   Suppose that

$$R_g = 120 \text{ ohms,}$$

$$F = 2.1, \quad \text{and}$$

$$R_s = 100 \text{ k}\Omega \quad \text{(i.e., 100,000 ohms).}$$

What equivalent strain will be indicated when the shunt resistance is connected across the gage?

Solution   From Eq. (12.15),

$$\varepsilon_e = -\frac{1}{2.1}\left[\frac{120}{100,000 + 120}\right] = -0.00057$$

$$= 570 \ \mu s.$$

Dynamic calibration is sometimes provided by replacing the manual cal-ibration switch with an electrically driven switch, often referred to as a *chop-per,* which makes and breaks the contact 60 or 100 times per second. When displayed on a CRO screen or recorded, the trace obtained is found to be a square wave. The *step* in the trace represents the equivalent strain calculated from Eq. (12.15).

There are other methods of electrical calibration. One system replaces the strain-gage bridge with a substitute load, initially adjusted to equal the bridge load [16]. A series resistance is then used for calibration. Another method injects an accurately known voltage into the bridge network.

12.13   THE SEMICONDUCTOR, OR PIEZORESISTIVE-TYPE, STRAIN GAGE

A thin sliver of silicon, typically 0.125 by 0.0125 mm in cross-section, is the common transducer element of the semiconductor, or SC, strain gage. Effec-tive lengths may range from roughly 1.25 to 12 mm and the sensitive elements may be either backed or unbacked. Ultrasonic techniques are used to cut the SC gage elements from single crystals of heavily doped silicon. Figure 12.12 illustrates the general construction. Essentially the same types of backing, bonding materials, and mounting techniques as those used for metallic gages are suitable for SC gages.

The major advantage of the silicon SC gage is its high gage factor, currently approximating 130, but which may be increased through further development. This represents a decided improvement in sensitivity compared to the 2–3$\frac{1}{2}$ exhibited by the ordinary metallic element.

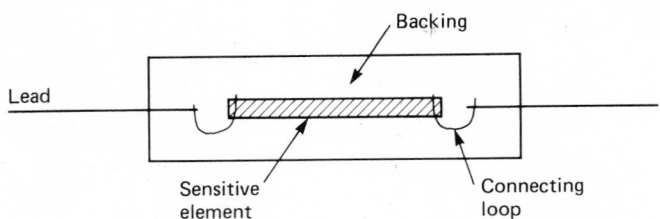

FIGURE 12.12   Typical SC gage construction.

The increased sensitivity, however, is also accompanied by comparative disadvantages, namely:

a) The output of the SC element is inherently nonlinear with strain.

b) Strain sensitivity is markedly temperature dependent.

c) It is somewhat more fragile than the corresponding wire or foil element, though it can be bent to a radius as small as 3 mm.

d) The strain range of the SC gage is roughly limited to 3000 to 10,000 μs (dependent on the specific gage type), as compared to an upper limit of 100,000 μs for some metallic resistance gages.

e) The semiconductor gage is considerably more expensive than the ordinary metallic gage.

f) Because of the high sensitivity of the SC element, the nonlinearity of the simple Wheatstone bridge (see Figs. 5.11a and b) cannot always be ignored, as is normally done when conventional metallic-element gages are used. This may or may not necessitate special instrumentation.

12.13.1 Theoretical Relationships

Semiconductor-gage behavior may be described by the following relation [17]:

$$\frac{\Delta R}{R_0} = \left(\frac{T_0}{T}\right)(F_0)\varepsilon + \left(\frac{T_0}{T}\right)^2 (C_0)\varepsilon^2, \qquad (12.16)$$

where

ΔR = the change in gage resistance, in ohms,

R_0 = the resistance of the unstrained gage element at temperature T_0,

T_0 = the reference temperature, degrees kelvin commonly taken as 298° (or 25°C or 77°F),

T = the temperature, in °K,

F_0 = the gage factor = $(\Delta R/R_0)/\varepsilon$ = the slope of the $\Delta R/R_0$ versus ε curve at *zero strain,* and

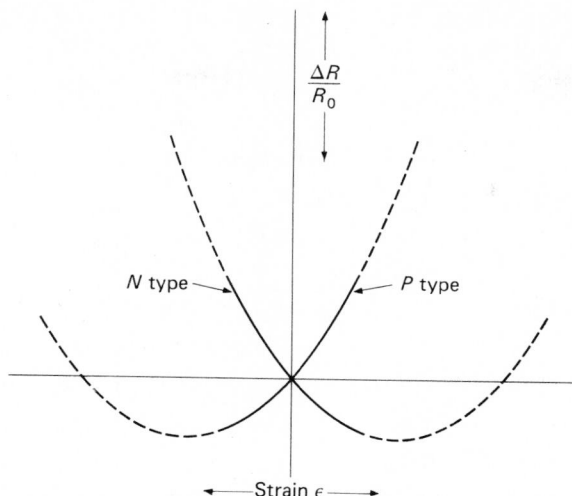

FIGURE 12.13   Characteristic strain-resistance sensitivity of silicon semiconductor strain gage material. (Solid portion of curves indicate practical ranges).

C_0 = a constant for a particular gage,

= a multiplying factor which, along with the temperature, describes the nonlinearity of the gage.

Both F_0 and C_0 are supplied by the manufacturer, but note that F_0 is the value for the original unbacked gage element and that the value may be altered both by the manufacturing process of mounting the element on its backing and by the application process of bonding the gage.

We see that, in terms of strain, the variation of gage sensitivity is parabolic and that increased temperature T reduces both sensitivity and nonlinearity. By control of the impurities (doping) it is possible to obtain gages with a wide variation of characteristics. Figure 12.13 illustrates the characteristics of two basic types, the P or *positive* type and the N or *negative* type. The term "positive" or "negative" refers to the general slope of the curves over the practical strain ranges, i.e., in the vicinity of zero strain.

12.14 COMMERCIALLY AVAILABLE STRAIN MEASURING SYSTEMS

Commercially available systems intended for use with metallic-type gages fall within four general categories:

1. The basic strain indicator, useful for static, single-channel readings.

2. The single-channel system either external to or an integral part of a cathode-ray oscilloscope.

3. Oscillographic systems incorporating either a stylus-and-paper or light-beam and photographic paper read-out.

4. Data acquisition systems (e.g., see Fig. 6.22) whereby the strain data may be:

   a) displayed (digitally and/or by a video terminal),

   b) recorded (magnetic tape or hard-copy printout),

   c) fed back into the system for control purposes.

The wide range of availability and divergence of such systems makes it impractical to attempt any but a superficial coverage in this text. The better source of state-of-the-art details is brochures and technical "aids" provided by many of the commercial suppliers.

12.14.1 The Basic Indicator

Typically, this type consists of a manually balanced Wheatstone bridge with meter-type null-balance indicator, an amplifier, and adjustments to accommodate a range of gage factors. Provision is also common for handling bridges with a single active gage, two-gage, and four-gage configurations. For fewer than four gages, the bridge loop is completed within the instrument. The measurement process consists of zeroing the bridge under initial conditions, then, after applying test conditions, to rebalance the bridge manually. The difference between initial and final readings provides the strain increment. Such instruments are generally precalibrated to provide direct strain read-out, often in digital form.

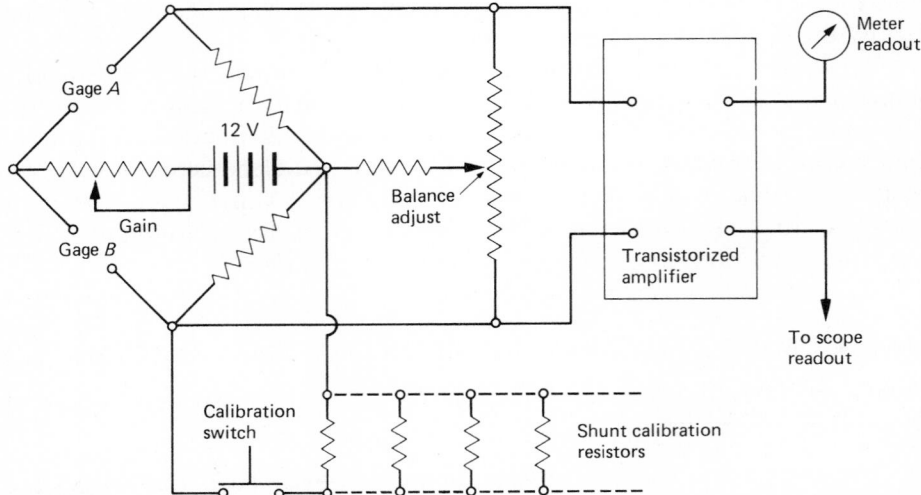

FIGURE 12.14   Schematic circuit diagram for a basic strain-measuring system. Provision is made for meter and/or CRO readouts.

12.14.2   Bridge and Amplifier for Use with Cathode-Ray Oscilloscope

Figure 12.14 shows a simplified circuit diagram for providing single-channel strain input to a CRO. Basically the circuit consists of a d.c. bridge with provision for resistance balance and shunt calibration. Output from the amplifier provides both a meter read-out and an input for driving an oscilloscope. The meter may be used for initial balancing and also for static strain read-out, whereas dynamic inputs may be displayed on the oscilloscope screen.

12.14.3   Multichannel Oscillographic Systems

Either stylus-type or light-beam oscillographs are often used for strain measurement systems. These are commonly general-purpose systems adaptable to various measurement problems through use of plug-in preamplifiers—the preamplifiers configured for the particular purpose, e.g., strain measurement.

Figure 12.15(a) is a block diagram of such a system. As shown the bridge is a.c. excited and, after voltage amplification, the signal is demodulated and fed to a power amplifier needed to drive the galvanometer. Systems such as this are often multichannel, requiring separate bridge–amplifier–galvanometer circuits for each channel, all channels sharing a common power supply, chart drive, and enclosure. Figure 12.15(b) illustrates a typical read-out.

Galvanometers used in these systems may be had with frequency response flat within ±5% to 4800 Hz (Table 7.1). Their use extends the frequency range of measurable strains far above that of the stylus recorder. Many frequencies from mechanical sources fall within the useful range of the light-beam oscillographic recording systems. It will be recalled, however, that wide frequency range can only be obtained at the expense of sensitivity (see Section 7.10).

12.15   STRAIN-GAGE SWITCHING

Mechanical development problems often require the use of many gages mounted throughout the test item, and simultaneous or nearly simultaneous readings are often necessary. Of course, if the data must be recorded at precisely the same instant, it will be necessary to provide separate channels for each gage involved. However, many times steady-state conditions may be maintained or the test cycle repeated, and readings may be made in succession until all the data have been recorded. In other cases, the budget may prohibit duplication of the required instrumentation for simultaneous multiple readings or recordings, and it becomes desirable to switch from gage to gage, taking data in sequence.

Two basic switching arrangements are possible when resistance bridges are used. They are *intrabridge* switching and *interbridge* switching. Figure 12.16 illustrates the first arrangement, in which various gages are switched

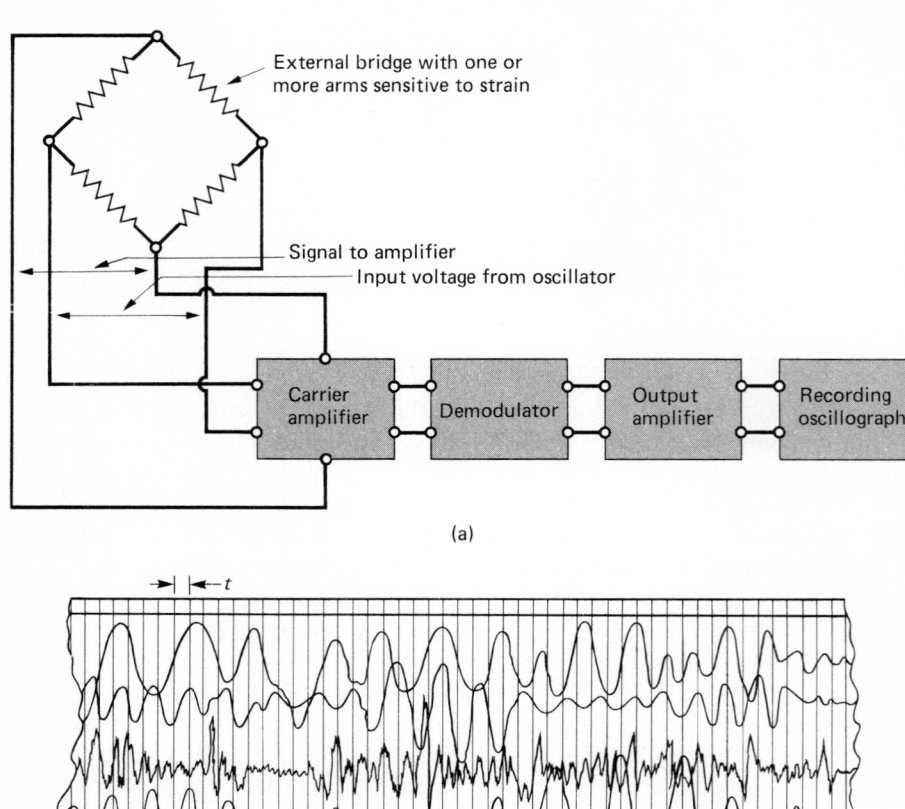

(a)

(b)

FIGURE 12.15   (a) Block diagram of a single-channel oscillographic recording system with carrier amplifier. Multi-channel recording requires duplication of all of the elements shown above, except the oscillograph. (b) Typical record obtained from a multichannel light-beam system.

into and out of a single bridge circuit. Figure 12.17 illustrates the second, in which switch connections are entirely outside the bridges.

When metallic gages and intrabridge switching are simultaneously used, variations in switch resistance can be a very annoying problem. As was shown in Section 12.9, the resistance change due to strain of the metallic gage is very small. It is quite possible that the change in switch resistance from one "switching" to the next may be of the same order of magnitude as the quantity

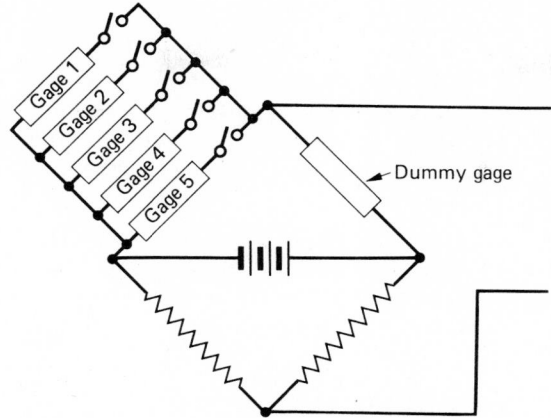

FIGURE 12.16   Intrabridge switching, where gages are switched into and out of a bridge.

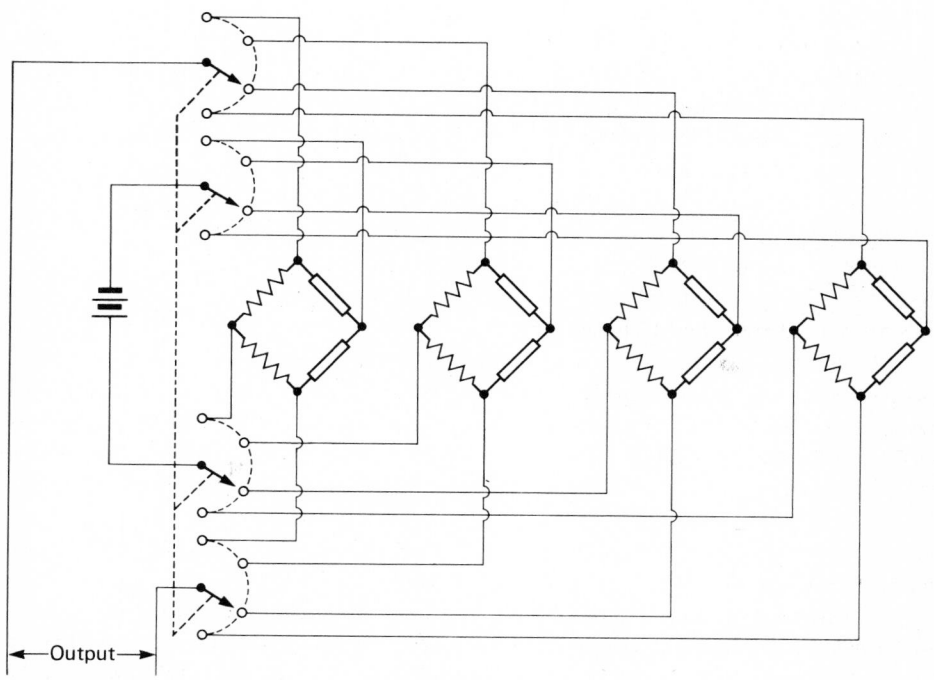

FIGURE 12.17   Interbridge switching where complete bridges are switched into or out of a circuit.

of interest. Unless extreme care and the highest quality of switch components are used, this method of switching may prove entirely impractical.

For really trouble-free strain-gage switching, the method illustrated in Fig. 12.17 is recommended. Here all switch contacts are placed completely outside the bridge ring, and complete bridges are switched into and out of the measuring system. Of course, the same variations in switch resistance occur as do in intrabridge switching, but in this case they do not alter bridge balance. Their effect is to alter bridge sensitivity slightly, although this is not normally measurable. The disadvantage in the latter method lies in the more complicated installation. This disadvantage must be weighed against the possibly questionable data yielded by the simpler setup.

12.16   USE OF STRAIN GAGES ON ROTATING SHAFTS

Strain-gage information may be conducted from rotating shafts in at least three different ways: (1) by direct connection, (2) by telemetering, and (3) by use of slip rings. When a shaft rotates slowly enough and when only a sampling of data is required, direct connections may be made between the gages and the remainder of the measuring system. Sufficient lead length is provided, and the cable is permitted to wrap itself onto the shaft. In fact, the available time may be doubled with a given length of cable if it is first wrapped on the shaft so that the shaft rotation causes it to unwrap and then to wrap up again in the opposite direction. If the machine cannot be stopped quickly enough as the end of the cable is approached, a fast or automatic disconnecting arrangement may be provided. This actually need be no more than soldered connections that can be quickly peeled off. Shielded cable should be used to minimize reactive effects resulting from the coil of cable on the shaft. This technique is somewhat limited, of course, but should not be overlooked, because it is quite workable at slow speeds and avoids many of the problems inherent in the other methods.

A second method is that of actually transmitting the strain-gage information through the use of a radio-frequency transmitter mounted on the shaft and picking up the signal by means of a receiver placed nearby. This method has been used successfully [18], and the procedure and equipment will undoubtedly be perfected for more general use. There is commercially available transistorized FM equipment of relatively small size in which the frequency change of the transmitter RF is a function of the strain. Such a system is quite practical when the added cost can be justified.

Undoubtedly the most common method for obtaining strain-gage information from rotating shafts is through the use of slip rings. Slip-ring problems are similar to switching problems, as discussed in the preceding section, except that additional variables make the problem more difficult. Such factors as ring and brush wear and changing contact temperatures make it imperative that

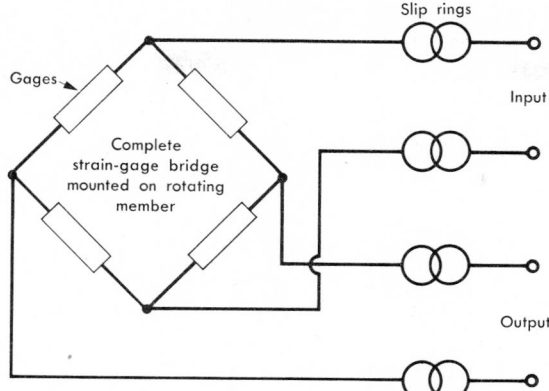

FIGURE 12.18 Slip rings used external to the bridge.

the full bridge be used at the test point and that the slip rings be introduced external to the bridge, as shown in Fig. 12.18.

Commercial slip-ring assemblies are available whose performances are quite satisfactory. Their use, however, presents a problem that is often difficult to solve. The assembly is normally self-contained, consisting of brush supports and a shaft with rings mounted between two bearings. The construction requires that the rings be used at a free end of a shaft, which more often than not is separated from the test point by some form of bearing. This presents the problem of getting the leads from the gage located on one side of a bearing to the slip rings located on the opposite side. It is necessary to feed the leads through the shaft in some manner, which is not always convenient. Where this presents no particular problem, the commercially available slip-ring assemblies are practical and also probably the most inexpensive solution to the problem.

12.17 STRESS–STRAIN RELATIONSHIPS

As previously stated, strain gages are generally used for one of two reasons: to determine stress conditions through strain measurements, or to act as secondary transducers calibrated in terms of such quantities as force, pressure, displacement, and the like. In either case, intelligent use of strain gages demands a good concept of stress–strain relationships. Knowledge of the *plane*, rather than of the general three-dimensional case, is usually sufficient for strain-gage work because it is only in the very unusual situation that a strain gage is mounted anywhere except on the *unloaded surface* of a stressed member. For a review of the plane stress problem, the reader is directed to Appendix E.

12.17.1 The Simple Uniaxial Stress Situation

In bending, or in a tension or compression member, the unloaded outer fiber is subject to a uniaxial stress. However, this condition results in a triaxial strain condition, because we know that there will be lateral strain in addition to the strain in the direction of stress. Because of the simplicity of the ordinary tensile (or compressive) situation and its prevalence (see Fig. 12.1), the fundamental *stress–strain relationship* is based on it. Young's modulus is defined by the relation expressed by Eq. (12.2), and Poisson's ratio is defined by Eq. (12.2a). It is important to realize that both these definitions are made on the basis of the simple, one-direction stress system.

For situations of this sort, calculation of stress from strain measurements is quite simple. The stress is determined merely by multiplying the strain, measured in the axial direction in microstrains, by the modulus of elasticity for the test material.

EXAMPLE 1   Suppose the tensile member in Fig. 12.7 is of aluminum having a modulus of elasticity equal to 6.9×10^{10} Pa (10×10^6 psi) and the strain measured by the gage is 326 μs. What axial stress exists at the gage?

Solution

$$\sigma_a = E\varepsilon_a = (6.9 \times 10^{10}) \times (325 \times 10^{-6}) = 22.4 \times 10^6 \text{ Pa (3250 psi)}$$

EXAMPLE 2   Strain gages are mounted on a beam as shown in Fig. 12.8. The beam is of steel having an estimated modulus of elasticity of 20.3×10^{10} Pa (29.5×10^6 psi). If the total read-out from the two gages is 390 μs, what stress exists at the longitudinal center of the gage? Note that the bridge constant is 2.

Solution

$$\sigma_b = E\varepsilon_b = (20.3 \times 10^{10}) \times (390 \times 10^{-6}/2) = 3958 \times 10^4 \text{ Pa (5700 psi)}$$

12.17.2 The Biaxial Stress Situation

Often gages are used at locations subject to stresses in more than one direction. If the test point is on a free surface, as is usually the case, the condition is termed *biaxial*. A good example of this condition exists on the outer surface, or shell, of a cylindrical pressure vessel. In this case, we know there are *hoop* stresses, acting circumferentially, tending to open up a longitudinal seam. There are also longitudinal stresses tending to blow the heads off. The situation may be represented as shown in Fig. 12.19.

The stress–strain condition on the outer surface corresponds to that shown in Fig. 12.2. The two stresses σ_L and σ_H are principal stresses (no shear in the longitudinal and hoop directions) and the corresponding stresses may be calculated using Eqs. (12.4), if we know (or can estimate) Young's modulus and Poisson's ratio.

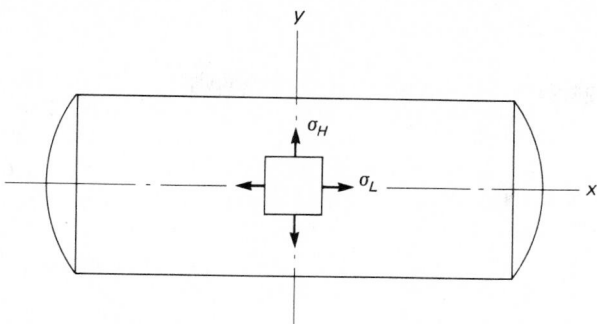

FIGURE 12.19   Element located on the shell of a cylindrical pressure vessel.

EXAMPLE 3 Suppose we wish to determine, by strain measurement, the stress in the circumferential or hoop direction on the outer surface of a cylindrical pressure vessel. The modulus of elasticity of the material is 10.3×10^{10} Pa, and Poisson's ratio is 0.28. By strain measurement the hoop and longitudinal strains are determined to be

$$\varepsilon_H = 425 \ \mu s \quad \text{and} \quad \varepsilon_L = 115 \ \mu s.$$

Solution Using Eqs. (12.4), we have

$$\sigma_H = \frac{E(\varepsilon_H + v\varepsilon_L)}{1 - v^2} = \frac{10.3 \times 10^{10}(425 + 0.28 \times 115) \times 10^{-6}}{1 - 0.28^2}$$
$$= 5110 \times 10^4 \text{ Pa} \quad (7411 \text{ psi}).$$

Although we may not be directly interested, we have the necessary information to determine the longitudinal stress also, as follows:

$$\sigma_L = \frac{E(\varepsilon_L + v\varepsilon_H)}{1 - v^2} = \frac{10.3 \times 10^{10}(115 + 0.28 \times 425) \times 10^{-6}}{1 - 0.28^2}$$
$$= 2615 \times 10^4 \text{ Pa} \quad (3800 \text{ psi}).$$

It may be noted that the 2-to-1 stress ratio traditionally expected for the thin-wall cylindrical pressure vessel does not yield a like ratio of strains. The strain ratio is more nearly 4 to 1.

Use of Eqs. (12.4) permits us to determine the stresses in two orthogonal directions. However, this information gives the *complete* stress–strain picture only when the two right-angled directions coincide with the *principal directions* (see Appendix E). If we do not know the principal directions, our readings would only by chance yield the maximum stress. In general, if a plane stress condition is completely unknown, at least three strain measurements must be made, and it becomes necessary to use some form of three-element *rosette*. (See Fig. 12.5). From the strain data secured in the three directions, we obtain the complete stress–strain picture. Stress–strain relations for rosette gages are given in Table 12.4.

TABLE 12.4 Stress–Strain Relations for Rosette Gages*†

Type of rosette	Rectangular	Equiangular (delta)	T-delta
Principal strains, $\varepsilon_1,\ \varepsilon_2$	$\dfrac{1}{2}\left[\varepsilon_a + \varepsilon_c \pm \sqrt{2(\varepsilon_a - \varepsilon_b)^2 + 2(\varepsilon_b - \varepsilon_c)^2}\,\right]$	$\dfrac{1}{3}\left[\varepsilon_a + \varepsilon_b + \varepsilon_c \pm \sqrt{2(\varepsilon_a - \varepsilon_b)^2 + 2(\varepsilon_b - \varepsilon_c)^2 + 2(\varepsilon_c - \varepsilon_a)^2}\,\right]$	$\dfrac{1}{2}\left[\varepsilon_a + \varepsilon_d \pm \sqrt{(\varepsilon_a - \varepsilon_d)^2 + \tfrac{4}{3}(\varepsilon_b - \varepsilon_c)^2}\,\right]$
Principal stresses, $\sigma_1,\ \sigma_2$	$\dfrac{E}{2}\left[\dfrac{\varepsilon_a + \varepsilon_c}{1-\nu} \pm \dfrac{1}{1+\nu}\sqrt{2(\varepsilon_a - \varepsilon_b)^2 + 2(\varepsilon_b - \varepsilon_c)^2}\,\right]$	$\dfrac{E}{3}\left[\dfrac{\varepsilon_a + \varepsilon_b + \varepsilon_c}{1-\nu} \pm \dfrac{1}{1+\nu}\sqrt{2(\varepsilon_a - \varepsilon_b)^2 + 2(\varepsilon_b - \varepsilon_c)^2 + 2(\varepsilon_c - \varepsilon_a)^2}\,\right]$	$\dfrac{E}{2}\left[\dfrac{\varepsilon_a + \varepsilon_d}{1-\nu} \pm \dfrac{1}{1+\nu}\sqrt{(\varepsilon_a - \varepsilon_d)^2 + \tfrac{4}{3}(\varepsilon_b - \varepsilon_c)^2}\,\right]$
Maximum shear, $\tau_{\max}$	$\dfrac{E}{2(1+\nu)}\sqrt{2(\varepsilon_a - \varepsilon_b)^2 + 2(\varepsilon_b - \varepsilon_c)^2}$	$\dfrac{E}{3(1+\nu)}\sqrt{2(\varepsilon_a - \varepsilon_b)^2 + 2(\varepsilon_b - \varepsilon_c)^2 + 2(\varepsilon_c - \varepsilon_a)^2}$	$\dfrac{E}{2(1+\nu)}\sqrt{(\varepsilon_a - \varepsilon_d)^2 + \tfrac{4}{3}(\varepsilon_b - \varepsilon_c)^2}$
$\tan 2\theta$	$\dfrac{2\varepsilon_b - \varepsilon_a - \varepsilon_c}{\varepsilon_a - \varepsilon_c}$	$\dfrac{\sqrt{3}(\varepsilon_c - \varepsilon_b)}{(2\varepsilon_a - \varepsilon_b - \varepsilon_c)}$	$\dfrac{2}{\sqrt{3}}\dfrac{(\varepsilon_c - \varepsilon_b)}{(\varepsilon_a - \varepsilon_d)}$
$0 < \theta < +90°$	$\varepsilon_b > \dfrac{\varepsilon_a + \varepsilon_c}{2}$	$\varepsilon_c > \varepsilon_b$	$\varepsilon_c > \varepsilon_b$

* References: [1, 19, 20].

† Note: θ = the angle of reference, measured positive in the counterclockwise direction from the a-axis of the rosette to the axis of the algebraically larger stress.

Although only three strain measurements are necessary to completely define a stress situation, the T-delta rosette, which includes a fourth gage element, is sometimes used to advantage for the following reasons.

1. The fourth gage may be used as a check on the results obtained from the other three elements.

2. If the principal directions are approximately known, gage d may be aligned with the estimated direction. Then, if the readings from gages b and c are of about the same magnitude, it is known that the estimate is reasonably correct, and the principal stresses may be calculated directly from Eqs. (12.4), greatly simplifying the arithmetic. If the estimate of direction turns out to be incorrect, complete data are still available for use in the equations from Table 12.4.

3. If the four readings are used in the T-delta equations in Table 12.4, an averaging effect results in better accuracy than if only three readings are used.

In spite of the advantages of the T-delta rosette, the rectangular one is probably the most popular, with the equiangular (delta) kind receiving second greatest use.

EXAMPLE 4   Figure 12.20 illustrates a rectangular rosette used to determine the stress situation near a pressure-vessel nozzle. For thin-walled vessels, the assumption that principal directions correspond to the hoop and longitudinal directions is valid for the shell areas removed from discontinuities. Near an opening, however, the stress condition is completely unknown, and a rosette with at least three elements must be used.

Let us assume that the rosette provides the following data:

$$\varepsilon_a = 72 \ \mu\text{s}, \qquad \varepsilon_b = 120 \ \mu\text{s}, \qquad \varepsilon_c = 248 \ \mu\text{s}.$$

In addition, we shall say that

$$\nu = 0.3, \qquad E = 20.7 \times 10^{10} \ \text{Pa}.$$

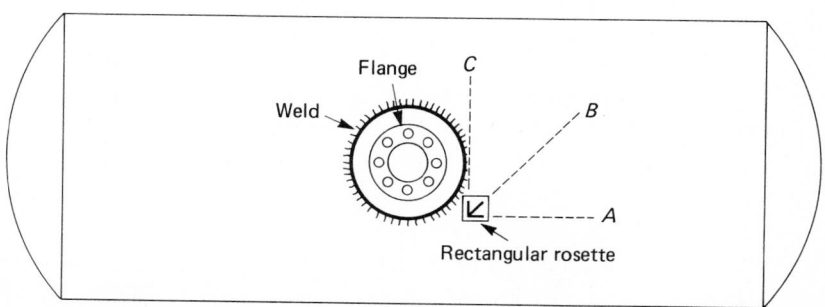

FIGURE 12.20   Rosette installation near a pressure vessel nozzle.

Note: A study of the equation forms in Table 12.4 shows that for each case, the principal strain, the principal stress, and maximum shear relations involve similar radical terms. Therefore, in evaluating rosette data, it is convenient to calculate the value of the radical as the first step. It will also be noted that the second term in the principal stress relations is equal to the shear stress; thus arithmetical manipulations may be kept to a minimum if the shear stress is calculated before the principal stresses are determined. Hence,

$$\sqrt{2(\varepsilon_a - \varepsilon_b)^2 + 2(\varepsilon_b - \varepsilon_c)^2} = \sqrt{2(72 - 120)^2 + 2(120 - 248)^2}$$

$$= 193 \ \mu s$$

and

$$\varepsilon_1 = \tfrac{1}{2}[72 + 248 + 193] = 256.5 \ \mu s,$$

$$\varepsilon_2 = \tfrac{1}{2}[72 + 248 + 193] = 63.5 \ \mu s,$$

$$\tau_{max} = \frac{20.7 \times 10^{10}}{2(1 + 0.3)} (193) \times 10^{-6} = 1537 \times 10^4 \ Pa \quad (2230 \ psi),$$

$$\sigma_1 = \frac{20.7 \times 10^{10}}{2} \times \frac{72 + 248}{0.7} \times 10^{-6} + 1537 \times 10^4$$

$$= (4731 + 1537) \times 10^4 = 6268 \times 10^4 \ Pa \quad (9091 \ psi),$$

$$\sigma_2 = (4731 - 1537) \times 10^4 = 3194 \times 10^4 \ Pa \quad (4632 \ psi).$$

To determine the principal planes, we have

$$\tan 2\theta = \frac{(2\varepsilon_b - \varepsilon_a - \varepsilon_c)}{(\varepsilon_a - \varepsilon_c)}$$

$$= \frac{(2 \times 120) - 72 - 250}{(72 - 150)} = 0.46,$$

$$2\theta = 24.7° \quad \text{or} \quad 204.7°,$$

or

$$\theta = 12.3° \quad \text{or} \quad 102.3°,$$

measured counterclockwise from the axis of element *A*. We must test for the proper quadrant as follows (see the last line in Table 12.4):

$$\frac{\varepsilon_a + \varepsilon_c}{2} = \frac{72 + 248}{2} = 160,$$

which is greater than ε_b. Therefore the axis of maximum principal stress does *not* fall between 0° and 90°. Hence, $\theta = 102.3°$. Figure 12.21 illustrates this condition.

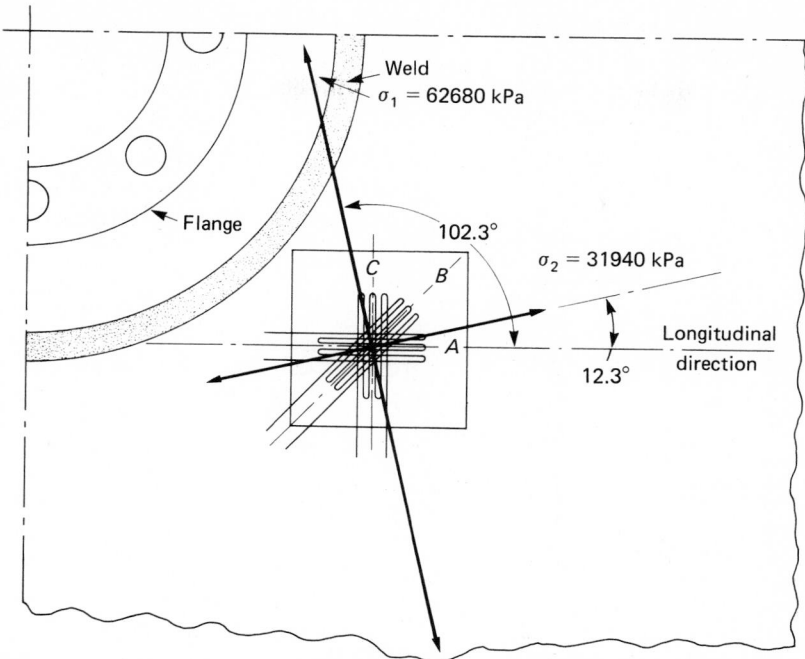

FIGURE 12.21   Stress conditions determined from data obtained by the rosette shown in Fig. 12.20.

12.18   GAGE ORIENTATION AND INTERPRETATION OF RESULTS

In a given situation it is often possible to place gages in several different arrangements to obtain the desired data. Often there is a best way, however, and in certain instances unwanted strain components may be canceled by proper gage orientation. For example, it is often desirable to eliminate unintentional bending when only direct axial loading is of primary interest. Or, perhaps only the bending component in a shaft is desired, to the exclusion of torsional strains.

The following discussion should be helpful in determining the proper positioning of gages and interpretation of the results. We will assume a *standard* bridge arrangement as shown in Table 12.5 and the gages will be numbered in the following examples according to this standard. When fewer than four gages are used it is assumed that the bridge configuration is completed with fixed resistors insensitive to strain.

Recall the relationship given in Eq. (5.13), Section 5.9.1, which evaluates bridge output e_o for a given input e_i, namely,

$$e_o = e_i \frac{R_1 R_4 - R_2 R_3}{(R_1 + R_2)(R_3 + R_4)}. \qquad (12.17)$$

TABLE 12.5 Strain-Gage Orientation

Standard Bridge Configuration

Requirement for null: $R_1/R_2 = R_3/R_4$

$$K = \text{Bridge Constant} = \frac{\text{Output of bridge}}{\text{Output of primary gage}}$$

A	$K = 1$	Compensates for temperature if "dummy" gage is used in arm 2 or arm 3. Does not compensate for bending.
B	$K = 2$	Compensates for bending. Two-arm bridge does not provide temperature compensation. Four-arm bridge ("dummy" gages in arms 2 and 3) provides temperature compensation.
C	$K = 1 + \nu$	Two-arm bridge compensates for temperature and bending.
D	$K = 2(1 + \nu)$	Four-arm bridge compensates for temperature and bending.
E	$K = 1$	Temperature compensation accomplished when "dummy" gage is used in arm 2 or arm 3. Bridge is also sensitive to axial and torsional components of loading.
F	$K = 2$	Temperature effects and axial and torsional components are compensated.
G	$K = 4$	Four-arm bridge. Temperature effects and axial and torsional components are compensated.

392

TABLE 12.5   Strain-Gage Orientation (*Continued*)

Standard Bridge Configuration

Requirement for null: $R_1/R_2 = R_3/R_4$

K = Bridge Constant = $\dfrac{\text{Output of bridge}}{\text{Output of primary gage}}$

H

$K = (a + b)/a$

Temperature effects and axial and torsional components are compensated.

I

$K = 1 + (b/a)\nu$

Temperature effects are compensated.

Axial and torsional load components are not compensated.

Torsion

J

$K = 2$

Two-arm bridge.

Temperature and axial load components are compensated.

Bending components are accentuated.

K

$K = 2$

Two-arm bridge.

Temperature effects and axial load components are compensated.

Relatively insensitive to bending.

L

$K = 4$

Four-arm bridge.

Sensitive to torsion only.

(Gages 1 and 3 are on opposite sides of the shaft from gages 2 and 4.)

If we assume the resistance of each bridge arm to be variable, then

$$de_o = \frac{\partial e_o}{\partial R_1}dR_1 + \frac{\partial e_o}{\partial R_2}dR_2 + \frac{\partial e_o}{\partial R_3}dR_3 + \frac{\partial e_o}{\partial R_4}dR_4. \tag{12.18}$$

By using Eq. (12.17) we can evaluate the various partial derivatives and write

$$\frac{de_o}{e_i} = \frac{R_2 dR_1}{(R_1 + R_2)^2} - \frac{R_1 dR_2}{(R_1 + R_2)^2} - \frac{R_4 dR_3}{(R_3 + R_4)^2} + \frac{R_3 dR_4}{(R_3 + R_4)}, \tag{12.18a}$$

where dR_1, dR_2, dR_3, and dR_4 are the various resistance changes in each of the bridge arms.

Ordinarily the gages used to make up a bridge will be from the same lot and

$$R_1 = R_2 = R_3 = R_4 = R.$$

Each gage may experience a different resistance change, hence we must retain the subscripts on the dR's; however, we can drop them from the R's. Doing so yields

$$\frac{de_o}{e_i} = \frac{dR_1 - dR_2 - dR_3 + dR_4}{4R}. \tag{12.18b}$$

From Eq. (12.10), we have

$$\frac{dR_n}{R_n} = F\varepsilon_n, \tag{12.19}$$

where

$$F = \text{the gage factor, and}$$

$$\varepsilon_n = \text{the strain sensed by gage } n.$$

Combining Eqs. (12.19) and (12.18b) gives us

$$\frac{de_o}{e_i} = \frac{F}{4}\left[\varepsilon_1 - \varepsilon_2 - \varepsilon_3 + \varepsilon_4\right], \tag{12.20}$$

where the ε's are the strains sensed by the respective gages.

Equation (12.20) aids in the proper interpretation of the strain results obtained from the standard four-arm bridge in addition to assisting the stress analyst in the proper placement and orientation of gages for experimental measurements.

For example, when only one active gage is used, Eq. (12.20) reduces to

$$\frac{de_o}{e_i} = \frac{F\varepsilon}{4}.$$

In further discussions we will assume that the term *bridge constant* abides by the definition given in Section 12.9.2.

EXAMPLE 1   The simplest application uses a single measuring gage with an external compensating gage as shown in Fig. 12.7 (also Case A, Table 12.5).

This arrangement is primarily sensitive to axial strain; however, it will also sense any unintentional bending strain. The compensating gage, mounted on a sample of unstrained material identical to the test material, is located so that its temperature and that of the specimen will be the same. In this case,

$$\varepsilon_1 = \varepsilon_a + \varepsilon_b + \varepsilon_T,$$

$$\varepsilon_2 = \varepsilon_T,$$

$$\varepsilon_3 = 0 \quad \text{(a fixed resistor)},$$

$$\varepsilon_4 = 0 \quad \text{(a fixed resistor)},$$

where

ε_a = the strain caused by axial loading,

ε_b = the strain caused by any bending component, and

ε_T = the strain caused by temperature changes.

Substituting in Eq. (12.20) gives us

$$\frac{de_o}{e_i} = \frac{F}{4}\left[\varepsilon_a + \varepsilon_b\right].$$

If the bending strain is negligible,

$$\frac{de_o}{e_i} = \frac{F\varepsilon_a}{4}$$

and the bridge constant is unity. Note that any strains caused by temperature effects cancel.

EXAMPLE 2 The arrangement shown in Case G, Table 12.5 uses gages in each of the four bridge arms. Gages 1 and 4 experience positive-bending strain components and gages 2 and 3 sense negative-bending components. All gages would sense the same strains derived from axial load and/or temperature should these be present. In addition, should the member be subjected to an axial torque, gages 1 and 2 would sense like strains from this source as would gages 3 and 4. All gages would sense strain components of like magnitude from any torque acting about the longitudinal axis of the member; however, strains sensed by gages 1 and 2 would be of opposite sign to those sensed by 3 and 4.

Substitution of all these effects into Eq. (12.20) yields

$$\frac{de_o}{e_i} = (F/4)(4\varepsilon_b) = F\varepsilon_b.$$

We see that only bending strains will be sensed and that the bridge constant is 4.

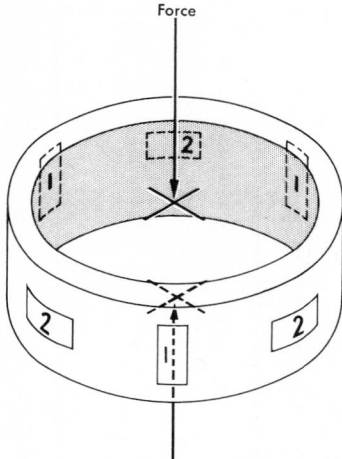

Force

FIGURE 12.22   Load cell employing three series-connected axial gages and three series-connected Poisson-ratio gages.

12.18.1   Gages Connected in Series

Figure 12.22 shows a load-cell element using six gages, three connected in series in each of the bridge arms 1 and 2. At first glance it might be thought that the three gages in series would provide an output three times as great as that from a single gage under like conditions. Such is not the case, for it will be recalled that it is the percentage change in resistance, or dR/R, that counts, not dR alone. It is true that the resistance change for one arm, in this case, is three times what it would be for a single gage, but so also is the total resistance three times as great. Therefore the only advantage gained is that of *averaging* to eliminate incorrect readings resulting from eccentric loading. The remaining two arms (not shown in the figure) may be made up of either inactive strain gages or fixed resistors. The bridge constant = $(1 + v)$.

12.19   SPECIAL PROBLEMS

12.19.1   Cross-Sensitivity

Strain gages are arranged with most of the strain-sensitive filament aligned with the sensitive axis of the gage. However, unavoidably, a part of the grid is aligned transversely. The transverse portion of the grid senses the strain in that direction and its effect is superimposed on the longitudinal output. This is known as *cross-sensitivity*. The error is small, seldom exceeding 2 or 3% and the overall accuracy of many applications does not warrant accounting for it. For more detailed consideration the reader is referred to [21], [22], and [23].

12.19.2 Plastic Strains and the Post-Yield Gage

The average commercial strain gage will behave elastically to strain magnitudes as high as 2 to 3%. This represents a surprising performance when it is realized that the corresponding uniaxial elastic stress in steel would be almost 1,000,000 psi (if elastic conditions in the steel were maintained). It is not very great, however, when viewed by the engineer seeking strain information beyond the yield point. When mild steel is the strained material, strains as great as 10 to 15% may occur immediately following attainment of the elastic limit, before the stress again begins to climb above the yield stress. Hence, the usable strain range of the common resistance gage is quickly exceeded.

Gages known as *post-yield* gages have been developed, extending the usable range to approximately 10 to 20%. Grid material in very ductile condition is used, which is literally caused to flow with the strain in the test material. The primary problem, of course, in developing an "elastic–plastic" grid is to obtain a gage factor that is the same under both conditions. Data reduction presents special problems and for coverage of this aspect, the reader is referred to [24] and [25].

12.19.3 Fatigue Applications of Resistance Strain Gages

Strain gages are subject to fatigue failure in the same manner as are other engineering structures. The same factors are involved in determining their fatigue endurance. In general, the vulnerable point is the discontinuity formed at the juncture of the grid proper and the lead wire to which the user makes connection. Of course, as with any fatigue problem, strain level is the most important factor in determining life.

We have shown that isoelastic grid material performs better under fatigue conditions than does constantan and also that the carrier material is an important factor.

Figure 12.23 illustrates the effects of most of the factors discussed above.

12.19.4 Cryogenic Temperature Applications

Extreme cryogenic temperatures often cause relatively unpredictable performances of resistance strain gages. Adhesives and backings become glass-hard and quite brittle. While the mechanical properties of certain grid materials are drastically curtailed, those of others remain only slightly affected. Large changes in resistivities may be encountered with the effective values dependent to a great degree on trace elements and previous mechanical working of the materials. Much work is being conducted in this area and the state-of-the-art is rapidly changing. Even if all the temperature-related properties were known, however, there would still remain the difficult problem of either controlling the temperature or measuring it.

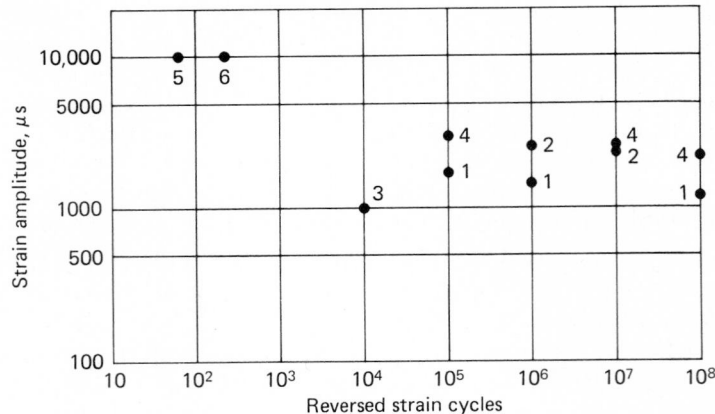

FIGURE 12.23   Relationship of endurance limit to strain level for gages of various materials and constructions. (Data from various sources including manufacturer's literature.)

Telinde reports on a comprehensive evaluation of strain-gage use at temperatures as low as $-452°F$ [26]. His work favors Karma as a grid material, supported on fiberglass-reinforced epoxy.

12.19.5   High-Temperature Applications

Maximum temperatures for short-period use of paper, epoxy, and glass-filled phenolic-base gages with appropriate cements are about 180°, 250°, and 600°F, respectively. Primary limiting factors are decomposition of cement and carrier materials. At these temperatures grid materials present no particular problems. For applications at higher temperatures (to 1800°F) some form of ceramic-base insulation must be used. The grid may be of the strippable support, free-element type with the bonding as described below, or the gage may be of the "weldable" type.

Use of the free-element-type gage involves "constructing" the gage on the spot. Either brushable or flame-sprayed ceramic bonding materials are used. Application of the former consists of laying down an insulating coating upon which the free-element grid is secured with more cement. The process demands considerable skill and carefully controlled baking or curing-temperature cycling.

Flame spraying involves the use of a plasma-type, oxyacetylene gun [27]. Molten particles of ceramic are propelled onto the test surface and used as both the cementing and insulating material for bonding the grid element to the test item. In both cases, leads must be attached by spot-welding to provide the necessary high-temperature properties to the connections. Lead-wire temperature-resistance variations may also present problems.

It is obvious that considerable technique must be developed to satisfactorily use either of these types.

A weldable strain gage consists of a resistance element surrounded by a ceramic-type insulation and encapsulated within a metal sheath. The gage is applied by spot-welding the edges of the assembly to the test member [28].

A novel laser-based extensometer usable at 3500°F or higher and having an overall accuracy of ±0.0002 in. over a 0.3-gage length is described in [29].

12.19.6 Creep

Creep in the bond between gage and test surface is a factor sometimes ignored in strain-gage work. This problem is approximately diametrically opposite to the fatigue problem in that it is of importance only in static strain testing, primarily of the long-duration variety. For example, residual stresses are occasionally determined by measuring the dimensional relaxation as stressed material is removed. In this case, the strain is applied to the gage once and once only. The loading cycle cannot be repeated. Under these circumstances, gage creep will result in direct errors equal to the magnitude of the creep. If the load can be slowly cycled, the creep will appear as a hysteresis loop in the results. This effect is a function of several things, but is primarily determined by the strain level and the cement used for bonding.

12.20 WHOLE-FIELD METHODS

12.20.1 Photoelasticity

Photoelasticity is an experimental technique based on the fact that when certain materials transparent to light are strained, they become optically doubly-refracting (polarizing*) and:

1. The two orthogonal polarizing planes at a given point coincide with the principal stress planes, and

2. The two rays of polarized light corresponding to the two planes emerge from the material out of phase in proportion to the maximum shear stress at the point. Since the maximum shear stress in a two-dimensional stress case is equal to the difference in principal stresses, this difference is also known.

Through use of a polariscope (Fig. 12.24), the two emerging rays are combined, resulting in two sets of interference fringes: one called the *isochromatics* and the other the *isoclinics*. Figure 12.25 illustrates a typical pattern of isochromatics. Basically, the technique is two-dimensional; however,

---

* Distinction must be made between a *polarizer* and a *polarizing filter*. An optical polarizer breaks a random ray of light into two orthogonal components and permits *both* to pass. A polarizing filter breaks the ray into two orthogonal components, suppresses one, but permits the other to pass. The familiar Polaroid® sunglasses use polarizing filters. On the other hand, many materials, particularly when stressed, are polarizers: Glass is one.

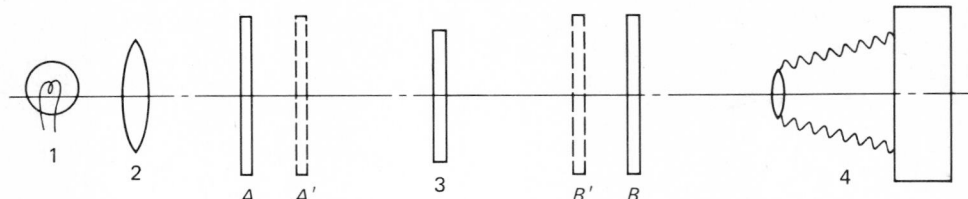

FIGURE 12.24   Photoelastic polariscope.

various methods have been developed whereby three-dimensional conditions may be investigated.

The experimental procedure is as follows:

1. A two-dimensional model of the prototype is prepared from a suitable material, usually an epoxy, and is loaded in a manner simulating the prototype's loading. Note that the stress distribution is not material-dependent so long as elastic conditions prevail.

2. The loaded model is placed between polarizing filters, A and B in Fig. 12.24. Near-monochromatic light (commonly a greenish color) is passed through the model and the resulting fringes are photographed.

When a simple plane-polariscope is used, two superimposed sets of fringes are formed:

1. *Isochromatics,* which are loci of constant principal stress difference, and

2. *Isoclinics,* which are loci of points where the principal stress directions

FIGURE 12.25   Isochromatic pattern for diametrically loaded ring.

are aligned with the optical polarizing axes. We see that by simply rotating the filters A and B, isoclinics for various directions may be obtained.

When what are called quarter-wave plates, A' and B' in Fig. 12.24, are inserted, a circularly polarized polariscope is formed. Under these conditions the isoclinics are suppressed and only the isochromatics remain. In this manner the two sets of fringes may be separated. Figure 12.25 was obtained using a circular polariscope.

To determine stress magnitudes it is necessary to calibrate the stress sensitivity of the material used for the model. This is done by using a circular polariscope and applying the above procedure to a specimen such as a simple tension model, a specimen for which the applied stress may be easily and reliably calculated. The corresponding fringe orders, beginning with fringe #0 (zero stress), are then compared with the calculated stresses, as the load is slowly applied. Actually the principal stress difference is the criterion; however, for a simple tension member the transverse stress is zero.

The photoelastic method may be used quite simply to determine free-boundary stresses for two-dimensional models of any shape, as follows:

1. Stress differences along isochromatics are easily determined from the calibration constant and the fringe order. (Fringe order is easily determined by simply noting the order of their appearances: Fringe #N remains fringe #N regardless of where it may migrate to as the load is changed. There are also other means for confirming the order of a given fringe.

2. On any *free boundary* the two principal planes (two-dimensional case) are normal to and tangent to the boundary, and the stress on the tangent plane is zero. Hence, knowing the difference (from the fringe orders) and the fact that the one stress is zero reveals the magnitude of the remaining stress.

Various methods may be used to separate the principal stresses at interior locations; however, the details are beyond the space limitations of this book. The reader is referred to the Suggested Readings at the end of the chapter for additional information on the subject.

12.20.2 The Moiré Technique

We have all noted the wavy fringe patterns that are produced by the overlapping of two layers of something like window screening. The term *moiré* (a French word for watery) is commonly applied to such a pattern. There is a fabric called silk moiré that is formed by permanently pressing lines nearly, but not exactly, aligned with the threads of the fabric. A "modern" version of moiré occurs when the television image of a newscaster's suit involves a pattern of lines roughly approximating the alignment and pitch of the television receiver's raster. In each case a pattern of fringes is produced and relative movement causes them to shimmer like the reflections from the surface of water.

Moiré patterns properly produced and analyzed may be used for evaluating whole-field *displacements*. The displacements may then be converted to strains and stresses. To accomplish this, a *master* or *reference* pattern, called a *grating,* is required, usually in the form of a photographic film or glass plate. Various patterns may be used; however, gratings consisting of closely packed straight, parallel lines are most common. The line widths and the widths of the intervening spaces are made equal.

Moiré analysis is a two-dimensional technique in much the same sense that the photoelastic method is two-dimensional. The idea on which the method is based is quite simple, but its implementation requires skill and practice. To obtain required sensitivity, one must most often use a low-modulus material, commonly a polyurethane. In addition, sensitivity is a function of the fineness of the grating, i.e., the number of lines per unit length. As would be expected, the greater the number of lines per unit length, the greater the sensitivity of the method and the greater the skill required to produce satisfactory results.

The procedure is as follows:

1. A two-dimensional model of the prototype is prepared using a low-modulus material. If the material is not transparent to light, a reflective surface is required.

2. A working grating is photographically deposited on the surface of the model using the reference grating as the "negative."

3. The master or reference grating is then placed in intimate contact with the model, thereby forming a reference for determining relative displacements. The model is strained by loading, resulting in a pattern of moiré fringes. This may then be photographed and the print used for further analysis. Although it is not entirely necessary, we will assume perfect initial alignment between reference and working gratings. Should we take a right section through the two gratings under zero load conditions we might see something like what is shown in Fig. 12.26(a). With lines in perfect alignment we see no fringes.

4. After straining, we find the condition shown in Fig. 12.26(b). At some point where a *line* on the working grating exactly coincides with a *space* on the reference grating, passage of light is effectively blocked. At other points there will be partial or no blockage. In this manner a pattern of dark and light fringes is formed. As in the case of the photoelastic method, fringe orders, F, may be assigned in integral numerical order, beginning with an arbitrarily chosen zero fringe, F_o.

5. From Fig. 12.26(b) we see that *relative displacements of adjacent fringe sites, in the direction normal to the grating lines, are equal to the pitch*

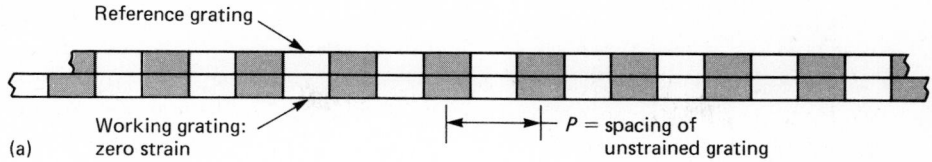

(a)

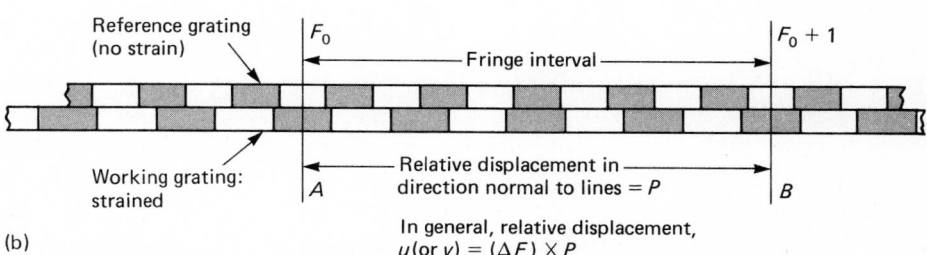

(b)

FIGURE 12.26   Diagram showing how a moiré pattern is generated.

of the reference grating. In other words, if the reference grating lines run in the *y–y*-direction, the relative *x*-displacements along fringe sites equal $(F_m - F_n) \times P$, where F_m and F_n are fringe orders and P is the pitch of the reference grating. For total displacements, both *x*- and *y*-components must be measured and their vector sums determined. This requires two separate test runs. If whole-field *displacements* are the objective, the testing would be completed at this point.

6. Should whole-field strains be desired, further analysis would be required as follows. Figure 12.27(a) shows a random section of fringe pattern obtained with *y–y*-oriented gratings. An origin *O* may be arbitrarily selected. Fringe intersections along the *x*- and *y*-axes are identified. The u_x and u_y displacements corresponding to these points are plotted in Figs. 12.27(b) and (c) versus their respective *x*- and *y*-coordinate positions. The slopes yield the information shown in the diagrams. In like manner, similar *y*-displacements are obtained using *x–x* oriented gratings. This is shown in Figs. 12.28(a), (b), and (c).

7. As shown in Figs. 12.27(b) and (c) and 12.28(b) and (c) the following strains may be determined:

$$\varepsilon_x = \frac{\Delta u}{\Delta x},$$

$$\varepsilon_y = \frac{\Delta v}{\Delta y},$$

$$\gamma_{xy} = \frac{\Delta u}{\Delta y} + \frac{\Delta v}{\Delta x}.$$

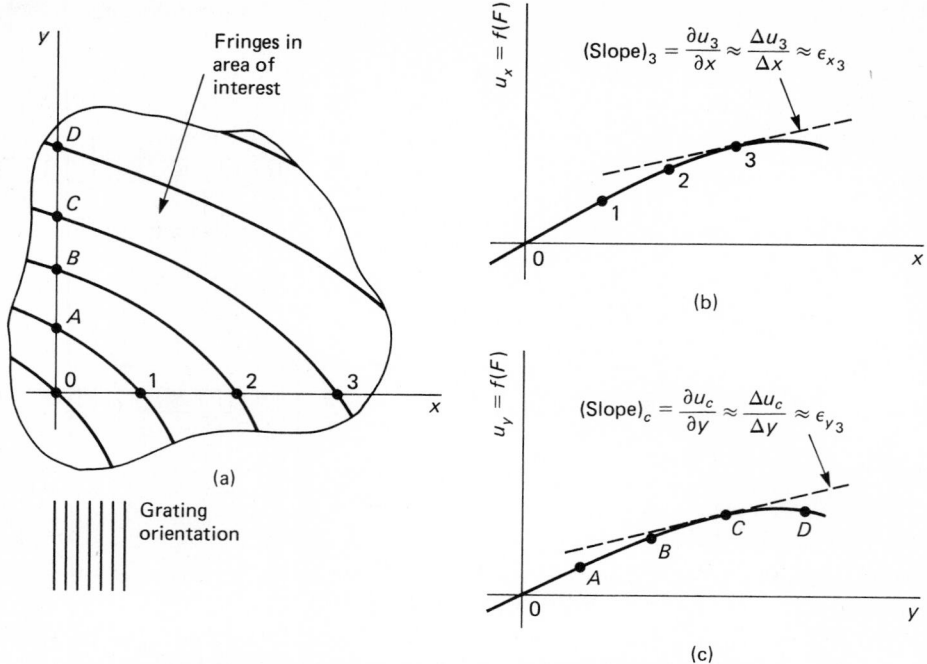

FIGURE 12.27 Graphical procedure for determining X-strains.

In figure (a):
- y axis, x axis
- Fringes in area of interest
- Points D, C, B, A along y axis; points 0, 1, 2, 3 along x axis
- Grating orientation (vertical lines)

In figure (b):
$u_x = f(F)$

$$(\text{Slope})_3 = \frac{\partial u_3}{\partial x} \approx \frac{\Delta u_3}{\Delta x} \approx \epsilon_{x3}$$

Points 1, 2, 3

In figure (c):
$u_y = f(F)$

$$(\text{Slope})_c = \frac{\partial u_c}{\partial y} \approx \frac{\Delta u_c}{\Delta y} \approx \epsilon_{y3}$$

Points A, B, C, D

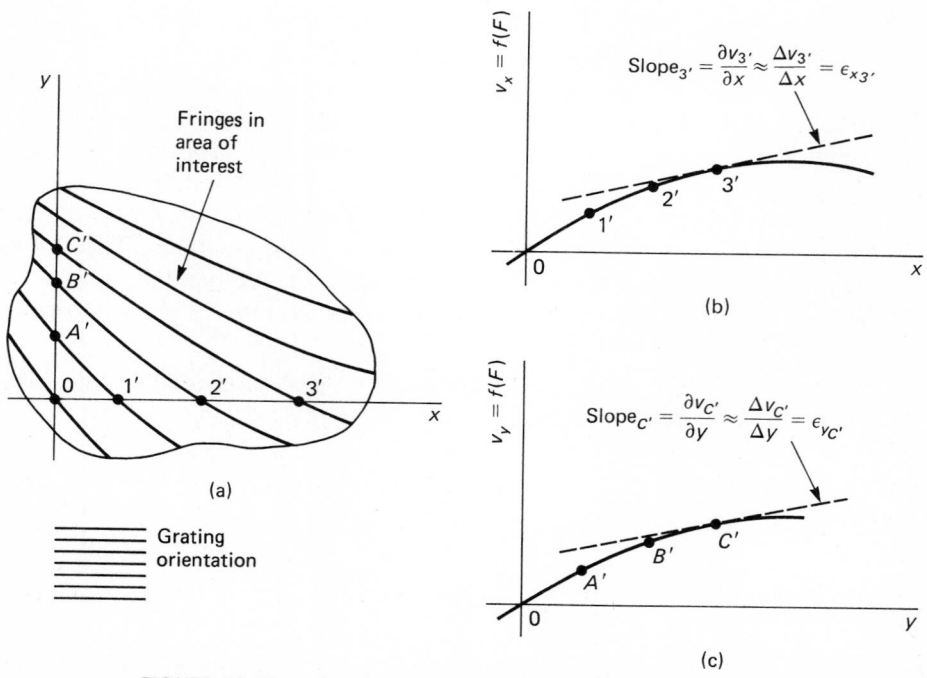

FIGURE 12.28 Graphical procedure for determining Y-strains.

In figure (a):
- y axis, x axis
- Fringes in area of interest
- Points C', B', A' along y axis; points 0, $1'$, $2'$, $3'$ along x axis
- Grating orientation (horizontal lines)

In figure (b):
$v_x = f(F)$

$$\text{Slope}_{3'} = \frac{\partial v_{3'}}{\partial x} \approx \frac{\Delta v_{3'}}{\Delta x} = \epsilon_{x3'}$$

Points $1'$, $2'$, $3'$

In figure (c):
$v_y = f(F)$

$$\text{Slope}_{C'} = \frac{\partial v_{C'}}{\partial y} \approx \frac{\Delta v_{C'}}{\Delta y} = \epsilon_{yC'}$$

Points A', B', C'

From these values, stresses may be determined using the following relations:

$$\sigma_{1,2} = \frac{E}{2}\left[\frac{\varepsilon_x + \varepsilon_y}{1 - \nu} \pm \frac{\sqrt{(\varepsilon_x - \varepsilon_y)^2 + (y_{xy})^2}}{1 + \nu}\right],$$

$$\tan 2\phi = \frac{y_{xy}}{\varepsilon_x - \varepsilon_y}.$$

12.21 CONCLUDING REMARKS

In addition to being the key to experimental stress analysis, strain can be made an analog for essentially any of the various mechanical-type inputs of interest to the engineer: force, torque, displacement, pressure, temperature, motion, etc. For this reason both metallic and SC strain gages are very widely and successfully used as secondary transducers in measuring systems of all types. Their response characteristics are excellent, and they are reliable, relatively linear, and inexpensive. It is important, therefore, that the engineer concerned with experimental work be well versed in the techniques of their use and applications.

SUGGESTED READINGS

Characteristics and Applications of Resistance Strain Gages, NBS Circular 528. Washington, D.C.: U.S. Government Printing Office, 1954.

Dally, J. W., and W. F. Riley, *Experimental Stress Analysis*. New York: McGraw-Hill, 1965.

Dove, R. C., and P. H. Adams, *Experimental Stress Analysis and Motion Measurement*. Columbus, Ohio: Charles E. Merrill, 1964.

Durelli, A. J., *Applied Stress Analysis*. Englewood Cliffs, N. J.: Prentice-Hall, 1967.

Durelli, A. J., and V. J. Parks, *Moiré Analysis of Strain*. Englewood Cliffs, N. J.: Prentice-Hall, 1970.

Frocht, M. M., *Photoelasticity*, vols. 1 and 2. New York: John Wiley, 1941, 1948.

Hendry, A. W., *Elements of Experimental Stress Analysis*. London: The Macmillan Co., 1964.

Hetenyi, M. (ed.), *Handbook of Experimental Stress Analysis*. New York: John Wiley, 1950.

Holister, G. S., *Experimental Stress Analysis*. Cambridge, England: Cambridge University Press, 1967.

Lee, G. H., *An Introduction to Experimental Stress Analysis*. New York: John Wiley, 1950.

Principles of Stresscoat, Chicago, IL: Magnaflux Corp., 1967.

Perry, C. C., and H. R. Lissner, *The Strain Gage Primer,* 2nd. ed. New York: McGraw-Hill, 1962.

PROBLEMS

12.1 A single strain gage is mounted on a tensile member, as shown in Fig. 12.7. If the read-out is 320 μs, what is the axial stress (a) if the member is of steel, and (b) if the member is of aluminum? (See Appendix A for values of E.)

12.2 Two strain gages are mounted on a cantilever beam, as shown in Fig. 12.8. If the *total* strain read-out is 480 μs, what are the outer fiber stresses (a) if the member is of steel, and (b) if the member is of aluminum?

12.3 A simple tension member, 1.25 cm (0.492 in.) in diameter, is subjected to an axial force of 22,500 N (5058 lbf). Strains of 1520 μs and 430 μs are measured in the axial and transverse directions, respectively. Assuming elastic conditions, determine the values of Young's modulus and Poisson's ratio for the material.

12.4 A plastic specimen is subjected to a biaxial stress condition, for which

$$\sigma_x = 710 \text{ psi}, \quad \text{and} \quad \sigma_y = 320 \text{ psi}.$$

Measured strains are

$$\varepsilon_x = 980 \text{ μs} \quad \text{and} \quad \varepsilon_y = 68 \text{ μs}.$$

Calculate Poisson's ratio and Young's modulus.

12.5 Two identical strain gages are mounted on a constant moment beam as shown in Fig. 12.29 (see also Problem 8.5). They are connected into a Wheatstone bridge as shown in Fig. 12.29(b). With no load on the beam the bridge is nulled with all arms having equal resistances. When the loads are applied, a bridge output of 760×10^{-6} volts is measured. Determine the gage factor for the gages, on the basis of the following additional data: $E = 29.4 \times 10^6$ psi, Poisson's ratio = 0.295, and the gage nominal resistance = 121.4 ohms.

12.6 The sensing element of a weighing scale is described in Problem 4.6. Four strain gages are located as shown in Fig. 12.30. The gages are connected in a full bridge (see Case G, Table 12.5). Their nominal resistance is 300 ohms and their gage factors are 3.5. If the bridge is powered with a regulated 5.6-VDC source, what will be the voltage output corresponding to the maximum design load of 300/18 lbf? (See also Problems 13.3 and 13.4.)

12.7 A strain gage is centered along the length of a simply supported beam carrying a centrally positioned, concentrated load. The beam is three gage lengths long. What correction factor should be applied to care for the strain gradients over the gage length?

12.8 A two-element strain rosette is mounted on a simple tensile specimen of steel. One gage is aligned in an axial direction and the other in a transverse direction.

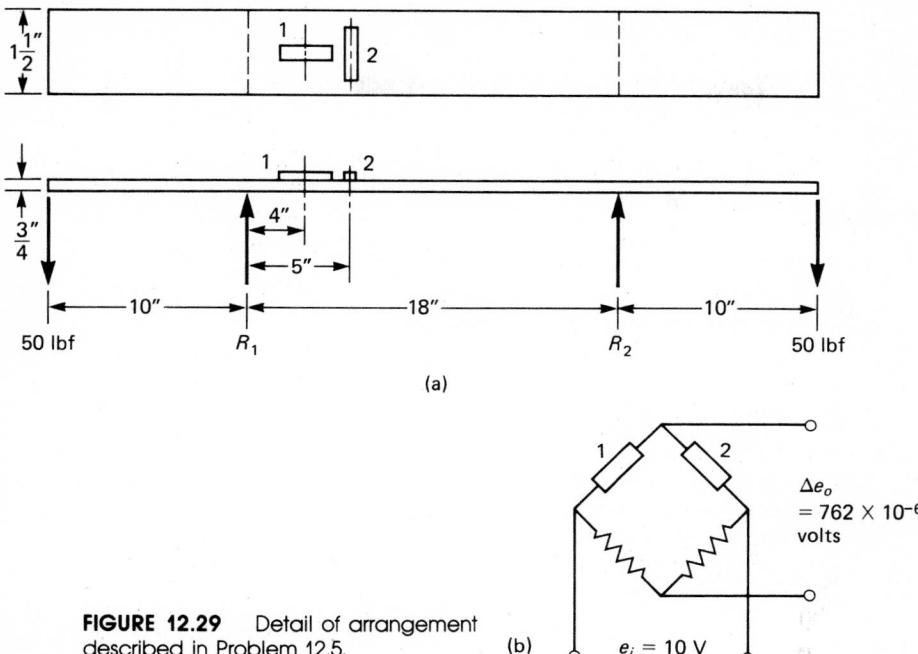

FIGURE 12.29   Detail of arrangement described in Problem 12.5.

(b) $e_i = 10$ V

Δe_o = 762 × 10⁻⁶ volts

The gages are connected in adjacent arms of a bridge. If the total bridge read-out (based on single-gage calibration) is 826 μs, what is the axial stress in pascals? $E = 20 \times 10^{10}$ Pa (29 × 10⁶ psi) and $\nu = 0.3$.

12.9 Show how strain gages may be mounted on a simple beam to sense temperature change while being insensitive to bending strain.

12.10 Assume a system configured as shown in Fig. 12.14, using the conventional oscilloscope for read-out.

  a) Make a list of variables that you feel will have a measurable effect on the overall uncertainty of the system. Indicate those that you would expect to

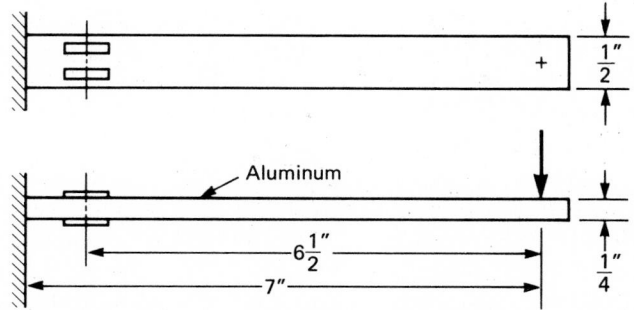

FIGURE 12.30   Strain gage/beam configuration described in Problem 12.6.

TABLE 12.6

	ε_a	ε_b	ε_c	E	ν
(a)	480	200	−710	29×10^6 psi	0.28
(b)	1200	580	0	30×10^6 psi	0.30
(c)	−917	1400	−120	20×10^{10} Pa	0.30
(d)	0	800	−920	7×10^{10} Pa	0.30
(e)	218	−300	1400	15×10^{10} Pa	0.29
(f)	−730	2100	−890	6.9×10^{10} Pa	0.30
(g)	−196	−471	−313	10×10^{10} Pa	0.29
(h)	ε	ε	ε	E	ν
(i)	$-\varepsilon$	ε	ε	E	ν
(j)	$-\varepsilon$	$-\varepsilon$	ε	E	ν

change with input magnitude and those that will be relatively constant. See Eq. (12.11). Include the uncertainty due to limits of resolution of the read-out method and note that some form of system calibration must be used, with its attendant uncertainty.

b) Assign what you believe to be reasonable uncertainties to each factor in your list and determine the overall uncertainty in the final read-out. Finally, divide the uncertainties into two categories: those having a major effect on the overall uncertainty, and those of minor importance.

12.11 A resistance-type strain gage having a factor of 2.00 ± 0.05 and a resistance of 121 ± 2 ohms is used in conjunction with an indicator having an uncertainty of ±2%. What maximum uncertainty may be introduced by these tolerances? What probable uncertainty?

12.12 Each line in Table 12.6 represents a set of data corresponding to a given plane stress condition. The first three items are strains in μs obtained using a three-element *rectangular* rosette. The final two items are material properties. For a selected set of data, determine:

1. the principal strains,

2. the principal stresses,

3. maximum shear stress,

4. principal directions referred to the axis of gage a,

and

5. sketch Mohr's circles for stress, and

6. sketch an element similar to that shown in Fig. 12.21.

Use units corresponding to those given for E.

12.13 Repeat Problem 12.12, (a) through (j), assuming an equiangular rosette.

12.14 If a rectangular-type rosette happens to be aligned such that elements a and c coincide with the principal directions, then measured values of ε_a and ε_c will

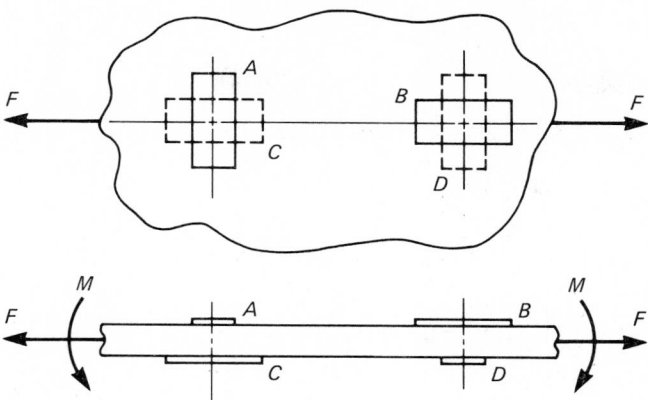

FIGURE 12.31   Arrangement of strain gages described in Problem 12.16.

be ε_1 and ε_2 (or vice versa). Show that under these circumstances the strain magnitude sensed by b will be

$$\frac{1}{2}\left(\varepsilon_1 + \varepsilon_2\right) .$$

12.15 Two strain gages are mounted on a steel shaft ($E = 20 \times 10^{10}$ Pa and Poisson's ratio $= 0.29$), as shown in Case J, Table 12.5. The gage resistance is 119 ohms and $F = 1.23$. When a 250,000-ohm resistor is shunted across gage 1, a 3.4-cm upward shift is recorded on the face of the CRO. When the shaft is torqued, a 5.7-cm shift is measured. For these conditions and assuming bending and axial loading may be neglected:

a) Calculate the maximum torsional stress.

b) What are the three principal stresses on the shaft surface?

c) Plot Mohr's circles for stress.

d) Should a bending moment and/or axial load be present, how would the results be affected?

12.16 Strain gages A, B, C, and D are mounted on a plate subjected to a simple bending moment M and an axial load F, as shown in Fig. 12.31. How should the gages be inserted into a standard bridge (see Table 12.5) in order to accomplish the following:

a) To sense bending only and, under this requirement, provide maximum bridge output?

b) To sense axial stress only (eliminating bending stress)?

In each case, what will be the bridge constant, and will adjacent-arm temperature compensation be accomplished?

12.17 To determine the power transmitted by a 10-cm (3.94-in.) shaft, four strain gages are mounted as shown in Case L, Table 12.5. They are connected as a four-arm bridge and the output is fed to a recording oscillograph. Gage resistances are 118 ohms with a gage factor of 2.1. A 210,000-ohm calibration resistor may be

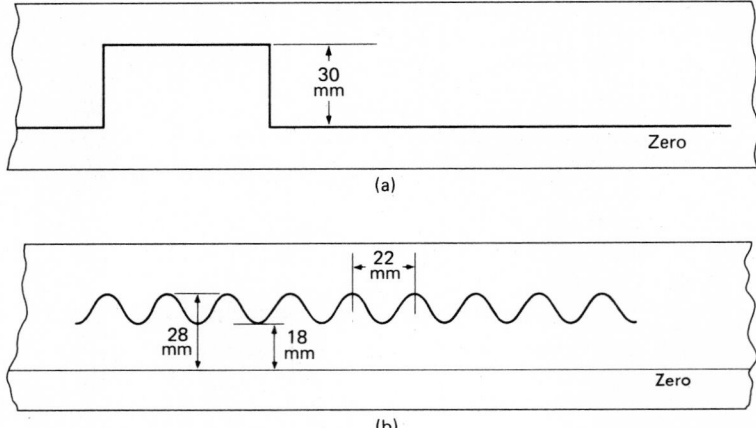

(a)

(b)

FIGURE 12.32   Oscillographic readout for conditions of Problem 12.17.

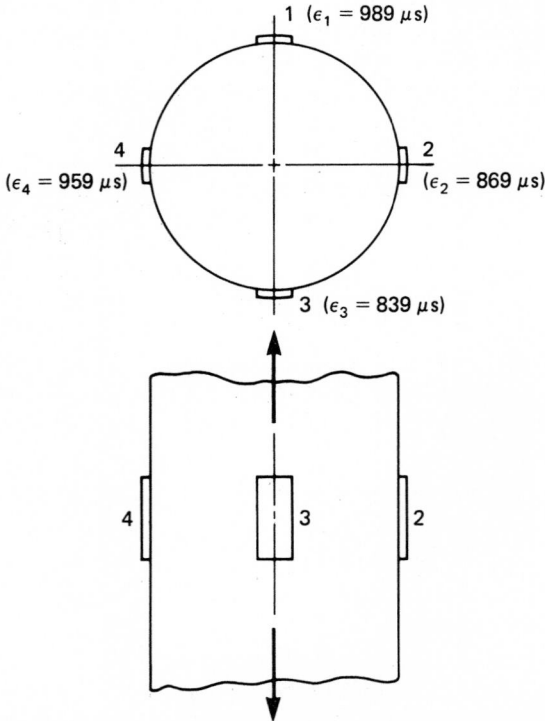

FIGURE 12.33   Configuration of strain gages described in Problem 12.18.

shunted across one of the gages. Figures 12.32(a) and (b) show the calibration and strain records, respectively. The chart speed is 100 mm/s. The shaft is of steel with $E = 20 \times 10^{10}$ Pa and Poisson's ratio = 0.3. Determine the extreme and mean values of transmitted power in watts.

12.18 Four axially aligned, identical strain gages are equally spaced around a $1\frac{1}{4}$-in. (31.75-mm) diameter bar, as shown in Fig. 12.33. The basic load on the bar is tensile; however, because of a small load eccentricity a bending moment also exists. If the strain readings shown on the sketch are determined for the individual gages, what axial load and bending moment must exist? Also determine the position of the neutral axis of bending.

12.19 Four gages are mounted on a thin-wall cylindrical pressure vessel. Two of the gages are aligned circumferentially (these are gages 1 and 4 in the standard bridge, Table 12.5), and the remaining gages 2 and 3 are aligned in the axial direction. (Note that this is not necessarily an optimum configuration.) If the bridge output is 27.8 units when a 300,000-ohm resistor is shunted across gage 1, and an output from the bridge of 47 units is recorded when the vessel is pressurized, what is the circumferential stress? Use $F = 3.5$, $R_g = 180$ ohms, $E = 7 \times 10^{10}$ Pa, and Poisson's ratio = 0.3. Assume that the conventional 2-to-1, circumferential-to-longitudinal stress ratio applies. (See Example 2, Appendix E.)

12.20 Strain read-outs from a rectangular strain rosette are $\varepsilon_a = 620$, $\varepsilon_b = -200$, and $\varepsilon_c = 410$ μs. Assume that under the same conditions an equiangular rosette is mounted and that its a element is aligned with the direction of the a element of the original rectangular rosette. What read-outs should be expected from the delta gage? Assume the same gage factor and resistances for both rosettes. [*Hint:* See Appendix E for Mohr's circles for strain.]

measurement 13
of force and torque

13.1 INTRODUCTION

At this point it may be wise for the reader to reread Section 1.7, "Standards, Dimensions, and Units of Measurement." Mass, time, and displacement are fundamental measurement dimensions. *Mass is the measure of quantity of matter. Force* is a derived unit and *weight* is a force having distinctive characteristics.

Mass is one of the fundamental parameters determining the gravitational attraction (force) exerted between two bodies. Newton's law of universal gravitation is expressed by the relation

$$F = Cm_1m_2/r^2 \tag{13.1}$$

or

$$C = Fr^2/m_1m_2. \tag{13.1a}$$

The units of C are $\text{N·m}^2/(\text{kg})^2$ or $\text{lbf·ft}^2/(\text{lbm})^2$, where

m_1 and $m_2 =$ the masses of bodies 1 and 2, respectively,

$r =$ the distance separating them,

$F =$ the mutual gravitational force exerted, one on the other, and

$C =$ the gravitational constant.

Henry Cavendish (1731–1810), an English scientist, used a sensitive torsional balance (see Fig. 13.1) to determine the value of C. In SI units $C = 6.67 \times 10^{-11} \text{ N·m}^2/(\text{kg})^2$.

When one of the attracting masses is the earth and the second is that of some object on the surface of the earth, the resulting force of mutual attraction is called *weight*. Mass and weight are related through Newton's laws of motion. The gist of his first law is contained in the statement: *If the resultant of all*

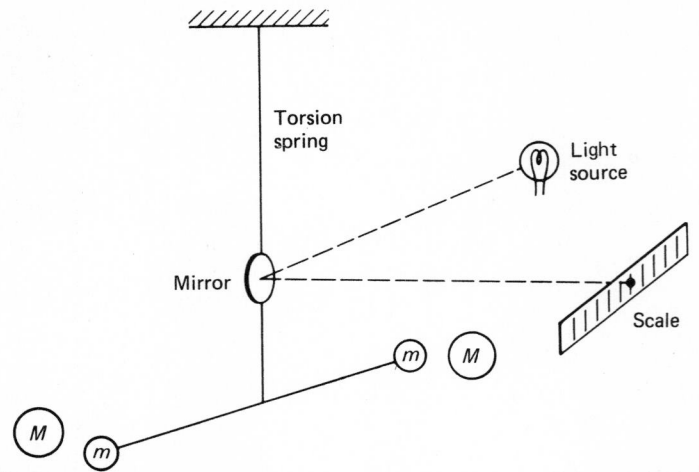

FIGURE 13.1   Balance used by Cavendish to measure gravitational constant.

forces applied to a particle is other than zero, the motion of the particle will be changed.

His second law may be stated as follows: *The acceleration of a particle is directly proportional to and in the same direction as the resultant applied force.* This may be expressed as

$$F_1/a_1 = F_2/a_2 = m/g_c = w/g. \qquad (13.2)$$

To help establish the correctness of Eq. (13.2) let us look at the units (refer to Table 1.2). For the SI system of units we have

$$\frac{F}{a}, \left(\frac{\mathrm{N} \cdot \mathrm{s}^2}{\mathrm{m}} \right) = \frac{m}{g_c}, \left(\frac{\mathrm{kg} \cdot \mathrm{N} \cdot \mathrm{s}^2}{1 \ \mathrm{kg} \cdot \mathrm{m}} \right).$$

Using the English engineering system we have

$$\frac{F}{a}, \left(\frac{\mathrm{lbf} \cdot \mathrm{s}^2}{\mathrm{ft}} \right) = \frac{m}{g_c}, \left(\frac{\mathrm{lbm} \cdot \mathrm{lbf} \cdot \mathrm{s}^2}{32.2 \ \mathrm{lbm} \cdot \mathrm{ft}} \right).$$

A most convenient force to apply is the earth's gravitational attraction for the body or particle, which is the weight. If this is the *only* force, then the resulting acceleration is that of the falling body *in vacuo* at the particular location. Both the weight and the gravitational attraction will vary from location to location. Their ratio, however, remains constant and is proportional to the mass, m, as expressed in Eq. (13.2).

As we can see from Eq. (13.2), neither the ratio m/g_c nor w/g is required for application of Newton's second law. Any ratio F/a, where F is an applied force and a is the resulting acceleration, is just as valid for establishing the necessary value. The ratio w/g is particularly convenient, however, because

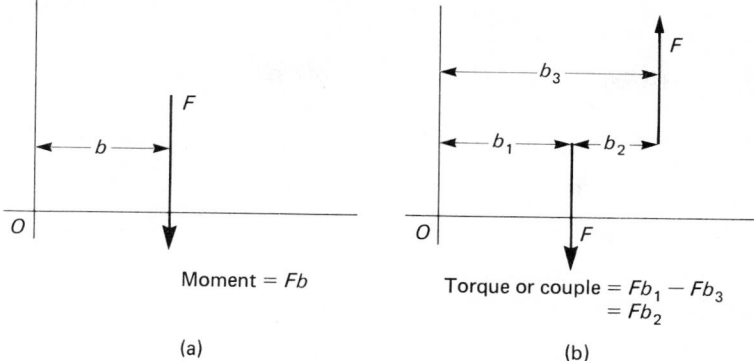

FIGURE 13.2   (a) Definition of moment. (b) Definition of torque or couple.

over the surface of the earth, g is reasonably constant and indeed is often considered a constant in many engineering calculations. As a result, measurement of weight suffices for determining the ratio w/g. The "standard" value of g is 32.1739 ft/s^2, or 9.80665 m/s^2. Rounded values of 32.2 ft/s^2 or 9.81 m/s^2 are commonly used.

Force, in addition to its effect along its line of action, may exert a turning effort relative to any axis other than those intersecting the line of action. Such a turning effect is variously called *torque, moment,* or *couple,* depending on the manner in which it is produced. The term *moment* is applied to conditions such as those illustrated in Fig. 13.2(a), whereas the terms *torque* and *couple* are applied to conditions involving counterbalancing forces, such as those shown in Fig. 13.2(b).

Mass standards

As stated previously (Section 8.5), the fundamental unit of mass is the kilogram, equal to the mass of the International Prototype Kilogram located at Sèvres, France. A gram is defined as a mass equal to one-thousandth of the mass of the International Prototype Kilogram. The commonly used avoirdupois* pound is 0.453,592,37 kilogram, as agreed to in 1959 (Section 8.5). Various classifications and tolerances for laboratory standards are recommended by the National Bureau of Standards [1, 2].

13.2 MEASURING METHODS

As in other areas of measurement, there are two basic approaches to the problem of force and weight measurement: (1) direct comparison, and (2) indirect comparison through use of calibrated transducers. Directly comparative methods use some form of beam balance with a null-balance technique.

---

*   From the French, meaning "goods of weight."

If the beam neither amplifies nor attenuates, the comparison is *direct*. The simple analytical balance is of this type. Often, however, as in the case of a platform scale, the force is attenuated through a system of levers so that a smaller weight may be used to *balance* the unknown, with the variable in this case being the magnitude of attenuation. This method requires calibration of the system.

Question: When an equal-arm balance scale is used, are forces or are masses being compared? (Problem 13.5 expands on this query.)

13.3 MECHANICAL WEIGHING SYSTEMS

Mechanical weighing systems originated in Egypt, and were probably used as early as 5000 B.C. [3]. The earliest devices were of the cord and *equal-arm* type, traditionally used to symbolize justice. *Unequal-arm* balances were apparently first used in the form shown in Fig. 13.3(a). This device, called a Danish steelyard, was described by Aristotle (384–322 B.C.) in his *Mechanics*. Balance is accomplished by moving the beam through the loop of cord, which

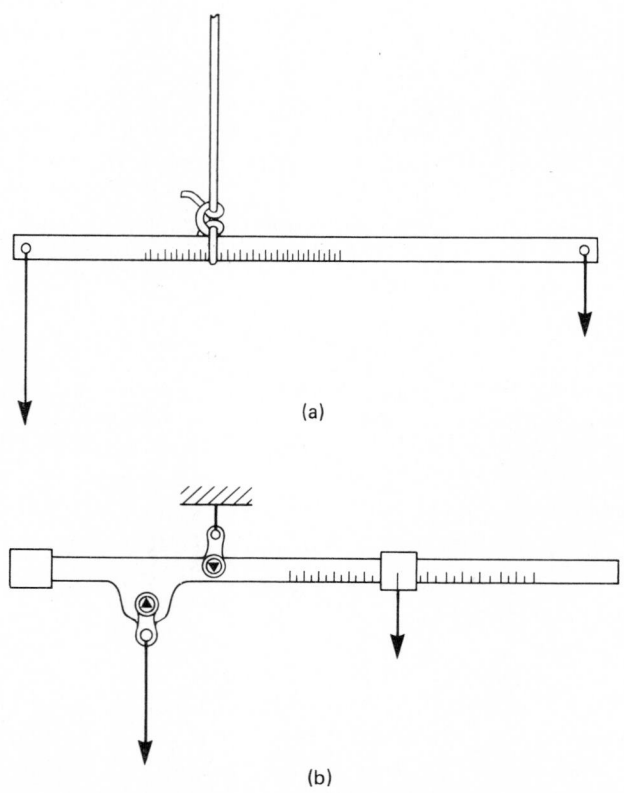

(a)

(b)

FIGURE 13.3   (a) Danish steelyard. (b) Roman steelyard.

acts as the fulcrum point, until balance is obtained. A later unequal-arm balance, the Roman steelyard, which employed fixed pivot points and movable balance weights, is still in use today (Fig. 13.3b).

13.3.1 The Analytical Balance

Probably the simplest weight- or force-measuring system is the ordinary equal-arm beam balance (Fig. 13.4). Basically this device operates on the principle of *moment comparison*. The moment produced by the unknown weight or force is compared with that produced by a known value. When null balance is obtained, the two weights are equal, provided the two arm lengths are identical. A check on arm equivalence may easily be made by simply inter-changing the two weights. If balance was initially achieved and if it is main-tained after exchanging the weights, it can only be concluded that the weights are equal, as are the arm lengths. This method for checking the true null of a system is known as the method of *symmetry*.

A common example of the equal-arm balance is the analytical scale used principally in chemistry and physics. Devices of this type have been con-structed with capacities as high as 400 lb, having sensitivities of 0.0002 lb [4]. In smaller sizes the analytical balance may be constructed to have sen-sitivities of 0.001 mg. Some of the factors governing operation of this type of balance were discussed in Section 3.9.

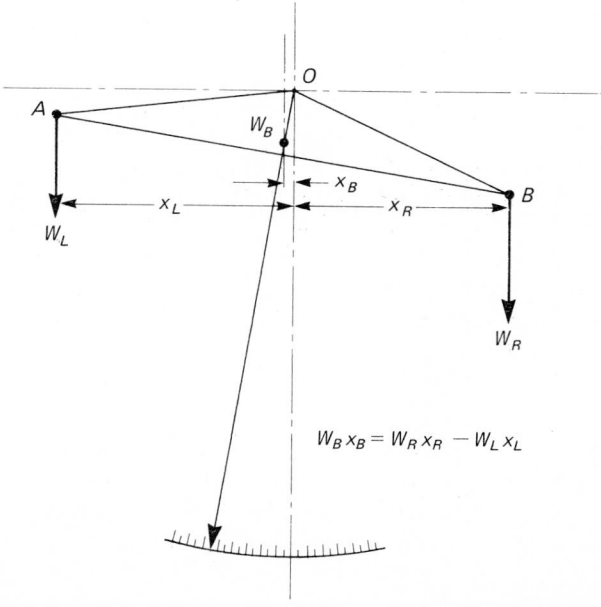

$$W_B x_B = W_R x_R - W_L x_L$$

FIGURE 13.4   Requirement for equilibrium of an analytical balance.

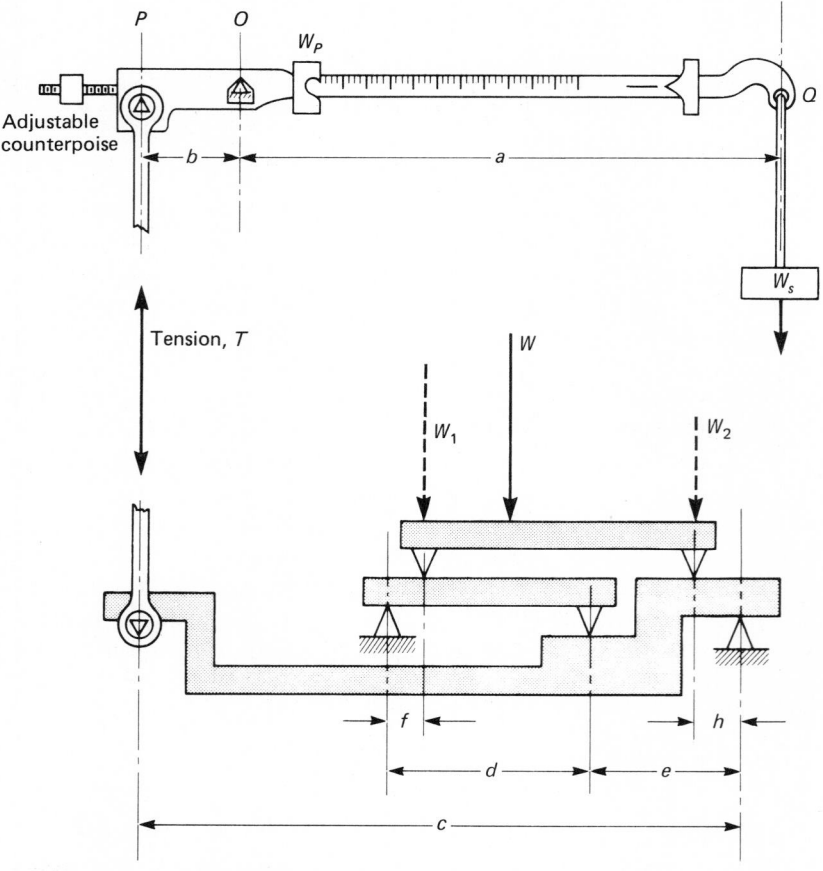

FIGURE 13.5   Multiple-lever system for weighing.

13.3.2 Multiple-Lever Systems

When large weights are to be measured, neither the equal-arm nor the simple unequal-arm balance is adequate. In such cases, multiple-lever systems, shown schematically in Fig. 13.5, are often used. With such systems, large weights W may be measured in terms of much smaller weights W_p and W_s. Weight W_p is called the *poise weight* and W_s the *pan weight*. An adjustable counterpoise is used to obtain an initial zero balance.

We will assume for the moment that W_p is at the zero beam graduation, that the counterpoise is adjusted for initial balance, and that W_1 and W_2 may be substituted for W. With W on the scale platform and balanced by a pan weight W_s, we may write the relations

$$T \times b = W_s \times a \tag{13.3}$$

and

$$T \times c = W_1 \frac{f}{d} e + W_2 h. \tag{13.4}$$

Now if we proportion the linkage such that

$$\frac{h}{e} = \frac{f}{d},$$

then

$$T \times c = h(W_1 + W_2) = hW. \tag{13.4a}$$

From this we see that W may be placed anywhere on the platform and that its position relative to the platform knife-edges is immaterial.

Solving for T in Eqs. (13.3) and (13.4a) and equating yields

$$\frac{W_s a}{b} = \frac{Wh}{c}$$

or

$$W = \frac{a}{b} \frac{c}{h} W_s = R W_s. \tag{13.5}$$

The constant

$$R = \frac{a}{b} \frac{c}{h}$$

is the scale *multiplication ratio.*

Now if the beam is divided with a scale of u lb/in., then a poise movement of v inches should produce the same result as a weight W_p placed on the pan at the end of the beam. Hence,

$$W_p v = uva \qquad \text{or} \qquad u = \frac{a}{W_p}.$$

This relation determines the required scale divisions on the beam for any poise weight W_p.

Dynamic response of a scale of this sort is a function of the natural frequency and damping. The natural frequency will be a function of the moving masses, multiplication ratio, and restoring forces. The latter are determined by the relative vertical placement of the pivot points, primarily those of the balance beam O, P, and Q. If O is below a line drawn from P to Q, then the beam will be unstable, and balance will be unattainable. Pivot O is normally above line PQ, and as the distance above the line is increased, the natural frequency and sensitivity are both reduced.

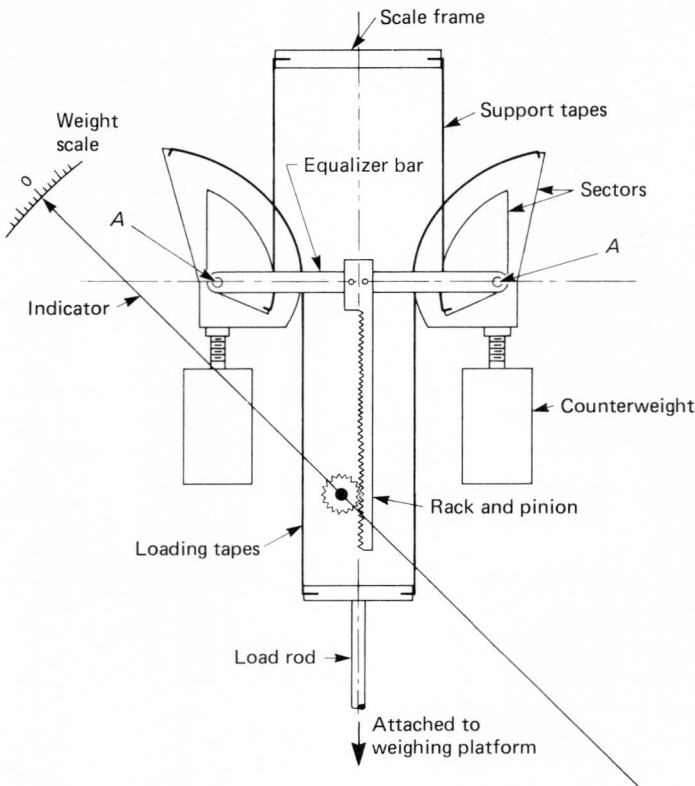

FIGURE 13.6   Essentials of a pendulum scale.

13.3.3 The Pendulum Force-Measuring Mechanism

Another type of moment-comparison device used for measurement of force and weight is shown in Fig. 13.6. This is often referred to as a *pendulum scale*. Basically, the pendulum mechanism is a force-measuring device of the multiple-lever type, with the fixed-length levers replaced by ribbon- or tape-connected sectors. The input, either a direct force or a force proportional to weight and transmitted from a suitable platform, is applied to the load rod. As the load is applied, the sectors rotate about points *A*, as shown, moving the counterweights outward. This movement increases the counterweight effective moment until the load and balance moments are equalized. Motion of the equalizer bar is converted to indicator movement by a rack and pinion, the sector outlines being proportioned to provide a linear dial scale. This device may be applied to many different force-measuring systems, including dynamometers (Section 13.9).

13.4 ELASTIC TRANSDUCERS

Many force-transducing systems make use of some mechanical elastic member or combination of members. Application of load to the member results in an analogous deflection, usually linear. The deflection is then observed directly and used as a measure of force or load, or a secondary transducer is used to convert the displacement into another form of output, often electrical.

Most force-resisting elastic members adhere to the relation

$$K = \frac{F}{y},$$ (13.6)

in which

F = the applied load,

y = the resulting deflection, and

K = the deflection constant.

To determine the value of the deflection constant of an element, it is necessary to write only the deflection equation, and if the deflection is a linear function of the load, K may be found. Table 13.1 lists representative relations indicating the general form.

Design detail of the detector–transducer element is largely a function of capacity, required sensitivity, and the nature of any secondary transducer, and depends on whether the input is static or dynamic. Although it is impossible to discuss all situations, there are several general factors we may consider.

It is normally desirable that the detector–transducer be as sensitive as possible; i.e., maximum output per unit input should be obtained. This would require an elastic member that deflects considerably under load, indicating as low a value of K as possible. There are usually conflicting factors, however, with the final design being a compromise. For example, if we were to measure rolling-mill loads by placing cells between the screwdown and bearing blocks, our application could scarcely tolerate a *springy* load cell, i.e., one that deflected considerably under load. It would be necessary to construct a stiff cell at the expense of elastic sensitivity and then attempt to make up for the loss by using as sensitive a secondary transducer as possible.

Another factor involving sensitivity is response time, or time required to come to equilibrium. This is a function of both damping and natural frequency (see Section 3.10). Fast response corresponds to high natural frequency, requiring a stiff elastic member.

Stress, also, may be a limiting factor in any loaded member. It is especially important that the stresses remain below the elastic limit, not only in gross section, but also at every isolated point. In this respect residual stresses are

TABLE 13.1

	Elastic Element	Deflection Equation	Deflection Constant K_1
A	 F = Load L = Length A = Cross-sectional area y = Deflection at load E = Young's modulus	$y = \dfrac{FL}{AE}$	$K = \dfrac{AE}{L}$
B	 F = Load L = Length E = Young's modulus I = Moment of inertia	$y = \dfrac{1}{48}\dfrac{FL^3}{EI}$	$K = \dfrac{48EI}{L^3}$
C	 F = Load L = Length E = Young's modulus I = Moment of inertia	$y = \dfrac{1}{3}\dfrac{FL^3}{EI}$	$K = \dfrac{3EI}{L^3}$
D	 F = Load D_m = Mean coil diameter N = Number of coils E_s = Shear modulus D_w = Wire diameter	$y = \dfrac{8FD_m^3 N}{E_s D_w^4}$	$K = \dfrac{E_s D_w^4}{8 D_m^3 N}$

E		F = Load D = Diameter of ring E = Young's modulus I = Moment of inertia of section about centroidal axis of bending section	$y = \dfrac{1}{16}\left(\dfrac{\pi}{2} - \dfrac{4}{\pi}\right)\dfrac{FD^3}{EI}$	$K = \dfrac{16}{(\pi/2) - (4/\pi)}\left(\dfrac{EI}{D^3}\right)$
F		K_1 = Deflection constant of member 1 K_2 = Deflection constant of member 2 F = Load	$y = \dfrac{F}{K_1 + K_2}$	$K = K_1 + K_2$
G		K_1 = Deflection constant of member 1 K_2 = Deflection constant of member 2 F = Load	$y = F\left(\dfrac{1}{K_1} + \dfrac{1}{K_2}\right)$	$K = \dfrac{1}{(1/K_1) + (1/K_2)}$

often of significance. While load stresses may be well below the elastic limit for the material, it is possible that when they are added to *locked-in* stresses, the total may be too great. Even though such a situation occurs only at a single isolated point, hysteresis and nonlinearity will result.

Manufacturing tolerances are yet another factor of importance in the design and application of elastic load elements. These were discussed in some detail in Section 4.16.

13.4.1 Calibration Adjustment

Various calibration adjustments may be made to account for variation in characteristics of elastic load members. Sometimes a simple check at the time of assembly and the selection of one of several standard scale graduations may suffice. For the coil spring tolerance example (Section 4.16.1) we determined the deflection constant uncertainty from dimensional tolerances to be 9%. At the time of assembly a quick single calibration check and a choice of two faceplates could cut the uncertainty from this source in half. Four plates would reduce it to $\pm2.5\%$. This scheme is often used not only for load-measuring devices, but for all varieties of inexpensive instruments employing a scale. It does not provide for calibration adjustment in use, however.

When coil springs are used, means are sometimes provided to adjust the number of effective coils through use of an end connection that may be screwed into or out of the spring, thereby changing the number of *active* coils and hence the stiffness of the spring. In other cases, the springs may be purposely overdesigned with regard to stress, and the number of coils specified so that in no case may the tolerances add up to give a spring that is too flexible. Then at the time of assembly the springs are buffed on a wheel to obtain the required deflection constant.

If a secondary transducer is used, we may be able to provide for calibration by making adjustments in its characteristics. As an example, we could use a voltage-dividing potentiometer to sense the load deflection of the spring just discussed. We might do this to provide remote indication or recording. A circuit arrangement could be used in which an adjustable series resistor would be employed to provide calibration for the complete system.

Figure 13.7 illustrates a calibration adjustment scheme that minimizes the need for holding unduly close tolerances. Here the total load is shared between a primary member (a coil spring in this case) and one or more *vernier* members (the small springs in the figure). The design may call on the vernier members to carry 10% or less of the total load. At the time of assembly the verniers are selected from a range of stiffnesses so as to make the uncertainty of the assembly less than some specified value, say $\pm0.2\%$. Schemes of this sort are adaptable to a wide range of elastic devices.

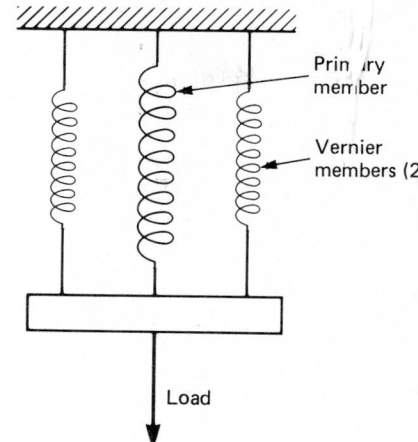

FIGURE 13.7   Approximate calibration method employing paralleling vernier members.

13.4.2   The Proving Ring

This device has long been the *standard* for calibrating tensile-testing machines and is, in general, the means whereby accurate measurement of large static loads may be obtained. Figure 13.8 shows the construction of a compression-type ring. Capacities generally fall in the range of from 300 to 300,000 lbf (1334 N to 1.334 MN) [5].

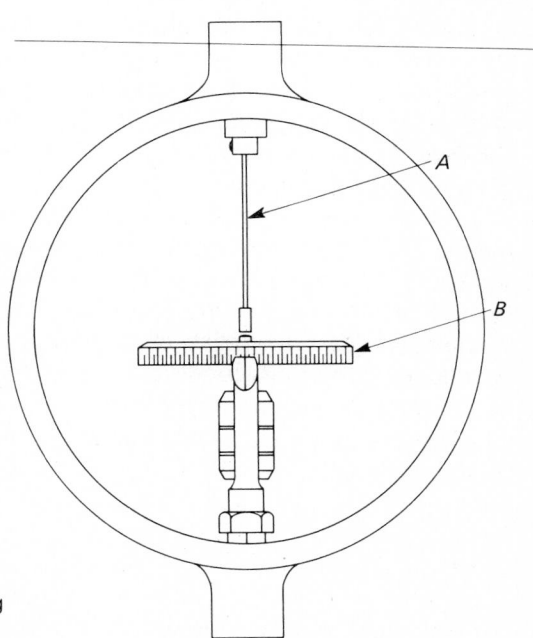

FIGURE 13.8   Compression-type proving ring with vibrating reed.

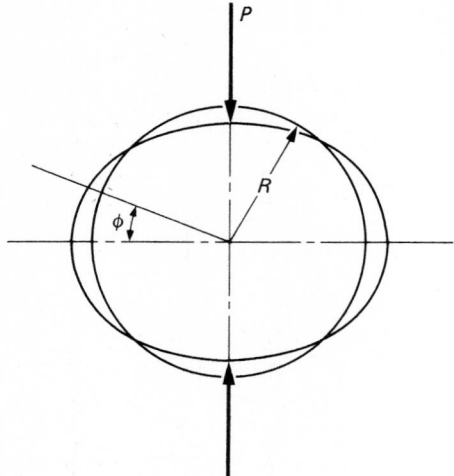

FIGURE 13.9   Ring loaded diametrically in compression.

Here, again, deflection is used as the measure of applied load, with the deflection measured by means of a precision micrometer. Repeatable micrometer settings are obtained with the aid of a vibrating reed. In use, the reed *A* is plucked (electrically driven reeds are also available), and the micrometer spindle *B* is advanced until contact is indicated by the marked damping of the vibration. Although different operators may obtain somewhat different individual readings, consistent differences in readings still will be obtained provided both zero and loaded readings are made by the same person. With 40 to 64 micrometer threads per inch, readings may be made to one- or two-hundred thousandths of an inch [5].

The equation given in Table 13.1 for circular rings is derived with the assumption that the radial thickness of the ring is small compared with the radius. Most proving rings are made with a section of appreciable radial thickness. However, Timoshenko [6] shows that use of the thin-ring rather than the thick-ring relations introduces errors of only about 4% for a ratio of section thickness to radius of $\frac{1}{2}$. Increased stiffness on the order of 25% is introduced by the effects of integral bosses [5]. It is, therefore, apparent that use of the simpler thin-ring equation is normally justified.

Stresses may be calculated from the bending moments *M* determined by the relation [6]

$$M = \frac{PR}{2}\left(\cos\phi - \frac{2}{\pi}\right). \tag{13.7}$$

Symbols correspond to those shown in Fig. 13.9.

13.5 STRAIN-GAGE LOAD CELLS

Instead of using total deflection as a measure of load, the strain-gage load cell measures load in terms of unit strain. Resistance gages are very suitable for this purpose (see Chapter 12). One of the many possible forms of elastic member is selected, and the gages are mounted to provide maximum output. If the loads to be measured are large, the direct tensile-compressive member may be used. If the loads are small, strain amplification provided by bending may be used to advantage.

Figure 13.10 illustrates the arrangement for a tensile-compressive cell using all four gages sensitive to strain and providing temperature compensation for the gages. The bridge constant (Section 12.9.2) in this case will be $2(1 + \nu)$, where ν is Poisson's ratio for the material. Compression cells of this sort have been used with a capacity of three million pounds [7]. Simple beam arrangements may also be used, as illustrated in Table 12.5.

Figure 13.11 illustrates proving-ring strain-gage load cells. In Fig. 13.11(a) the bridge output is a function of the bending strains only, the axial components being canceled in the bridge arrangement. By mounting the gages as shown in Fig. 13.11(b), somewhat greater sensitivity may be obtained because the output includes both the bending and axial components sensed by gages 1 and 4.

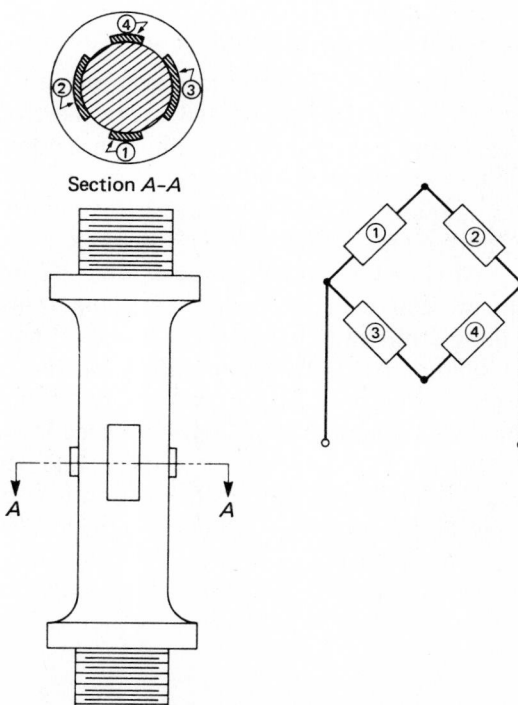

Section A–A

FIGURE 13.10 Tension-compression resistance strain-gage load cell.

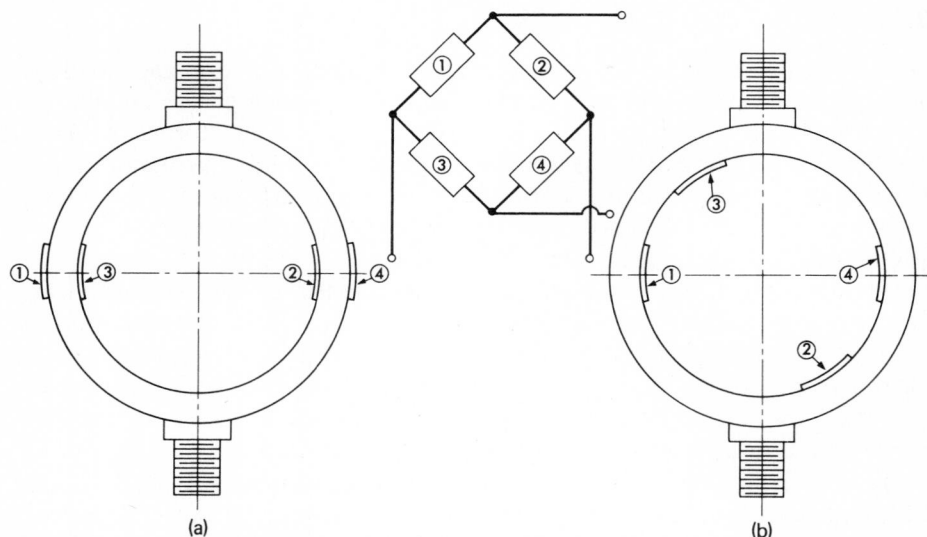

FIGURE 13.11   Two arrangements of circular-shaped load cells employing resistance strain gages as secondary transducers.

Temperature sensitivity

The sensitivity of elastic load-cell elements is affected by temperature variation. This change is caused by two factors: variation in Young's modulus and altered dimensions. Variation in Young's modulus is the more important of the two effects, amounting to roughly $2\frac{1}{2}\%$ per 100°F. On the other hand, the increase in cross-sectional area of a tension member of steel will amount to only about 0.15% per 100°F change.

Obviously, when accuracies of $\pm\frac{1}{2}\%$ are desired, as provided by certain commercial cells, a means of compensation, particularly for variation in Young's modulus, must be supplied. When resistance strain gages are used as secondary transducers, this is accomplished electrically by causing the bridge's electrical sensitivity to change in the opposite direction to the modulus effect. As temperature increases, the deflection constant for the elastic element decreases; it becomes more *springy*, and deflects a greater amount for a given load. This increased sensitivity is offset by reducing the sensitivity of the strain-gage bridge through use of a thermally sensitive compensating resistance element, R_s, as shown in Fig. 13.12.

As discussed in Section 5.9.6, the introduction of a resistance in an input-lead reduces the electrical sensitivity of an equal-arm bridge by the factor expressed as

$$ n = \frac{1}{1 + (R_s/R)} . $$

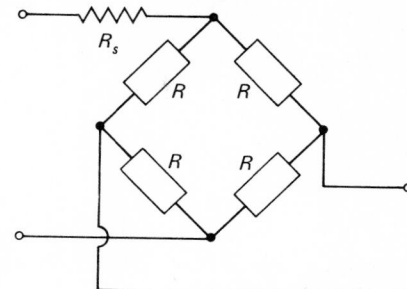

FIGURE 13.12   Schematic diagram of a strain-gage bridge with a compensating resistor.

Requirements for compensation may be analyzed through use of the relation for the initially balanced equal-arm bridge, Eq. (5.15). If we assume

$$2\frac{\Delta R}{R} \ll 4,$$

Eq. (5.15) may be modified to read

$$\frac{\Delta e_o}{e_i} = \frac{k}{4}\frac{\Delta R}{R}.$$

This is true, particularly for a *strain-gage bridge* for which $\Delta R/R$ is always small. A bridge constant, k, is included to account for use of more than one active gage. If all four gages are equally active, $k = 4$. For the arrangement shown in Fig. 13.10, $k = 2(1 + v)$, where v is Poisson's ratio. If we account for the compensating resistor, the equation will then read

$$\frac{\Delta e_o}{e_i} = \frac{k}{4}\frac{\Delta R}{R}\left[\frac{1}{1 + (R_s/R)}\right]. \tag{13.8}$$

Rewriting Eq. (12.10), we have

$$\varepsilon = \left(\frac{1}{F}\right)\left(\frac{\Delta R}{R}\right),$$

and from the definition of Young's modulus, E, Eq. (12.2),

$$P = EA\varepsilon,$$

we may solve for sensitivity:

$$\frac{\Delta e_o}{P} = \left(\frac{e_i}{4}\right)\left(\frac{FRk}{A}\right)\left[\frac{1}{E(R + R_s)}\right]. \tag{13.9}$$

If it is assumed that the gages are arranged for compensation of resistance variation with temperature and that the gage factors F remain unchanged with temperature, and, further, that any change in the cross-sectional area of the elastic member may be neglected, then complete compensation will be accomplished if the quantity $E(R + R_s)$ remains constant with temperature.

Using Eqs. (4.8) and (4.16), we may write

$$E(R + R_s) = E(1 + c \, \Delta T)[R + R_s(1 + b \, \Delta T)], \qquad (13.10)$$

from which we find

$$\frac{R_s}{R} = -\frac{c}{b + c}. \qquad (13.11)$$

This indicates that temperature compensation may possibly be accomplished through proper balancing of the temperature coefficients of Young's modulus, c, and electrical resistivity, b. Because c is usually negative (see Table 4.3), and because the resistances cannot be negative, it follows that

$$b > -c.$$

In addition, we may write (see Eq. 4.2)

$$R_s = \rho \frac{L}{A} = -R\left(\frac{c}{b + c}\right), \qquad (13.12)$$

from which

$$L = -\frac{RA}{\rho}\left(\frac{c}{b + c}\right). \qquad (13.12a)$$

From these relations, specific requirements for compensation may be derived. After a resistance material, generally in the form of wire, is selected, the required length may be determined through use of Eq. (13.12a).

Although a single resistor would serve, commercial cells normally use two modulus resistors, as shown in Fig. 13.13. This ensures proper connections regardless of instrumentation and also permits electrical calibration of the gages by shunt resistances as described in Section 12.12. It is necessary, however, to use two calibration resistors as shown in Fig. 13.14. If each resistor is considered as one-half the total calibration resistance, then the relation given, Eq. (12.15), will remain legitimate.

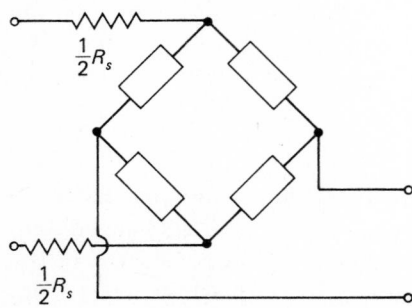

FIGURE 13.13   Strain-gage bridge with two compensating resistors.

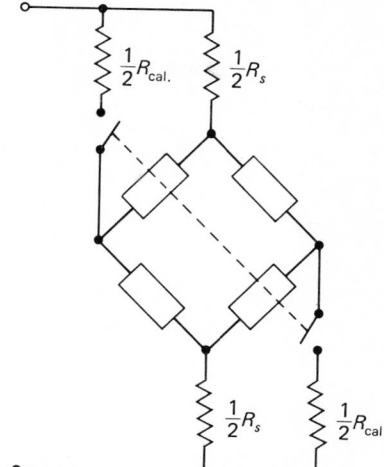

FIGURE 13.14   Schematic diagram of a strain-gage bridge showing how calibration may be accomplished.

13.6 PIEZO-TYPE LOAD CELLS

Piezo load cells may be based on either of two principles: piezoresistivity or the charge-producing piezoelectric basis. The former uses the semiconductor strain gage whose applications have been discussed in Section 12.13.

The piezoelectric transducer produces an electrostatic charge (Section 4.14), which is generally conditioned through use of a charge amplifier (Section 5.18.2). Transducer outputs are in terms of coulombs per unit input, with 10 to 20 pC/lbf being typical. Desirable qualities permit wide ranges of working load in a given unit, excellent frequency response, great stiffness, high resolution, and relatively small size. An important limitation is that piezoelectric devices are inherently of a dynamic, rather than a static, nature. Long-term static output stability is not generally practical.

Multiaxis cells are available. When a quartz master crystal is sliced to produce transducer elements, the selection of slicing planes yields elements with different properties. Slices may be taken to produce elements selectively sensitive to tension–compression, shear, or bending (see Section 4.14). By taking advantage of these characteristics, load cells may be designed that provide various combinations of orthogonal load and/or torque outputs.

13.7 BALLISTIC WEIGHING

Theoretically, if a mass is suddenly applied to a resisting member having a linear load-deflection characteristic, the dynamic deflection will be exactly twice the final static deflection. This is true so long as damping is absent. This fact may be used as the basis for a weighing system. The basic equation for a system of this type is

$$(m/g_c)(d^2y/dt^2) + ky = mg/g_c,$$ (13.13)

in which

m = mass,

k = the deflection constant,

g_c = the dimensional constant,

g = local acceleration due to gravity,

y = deflection, and

t = time.

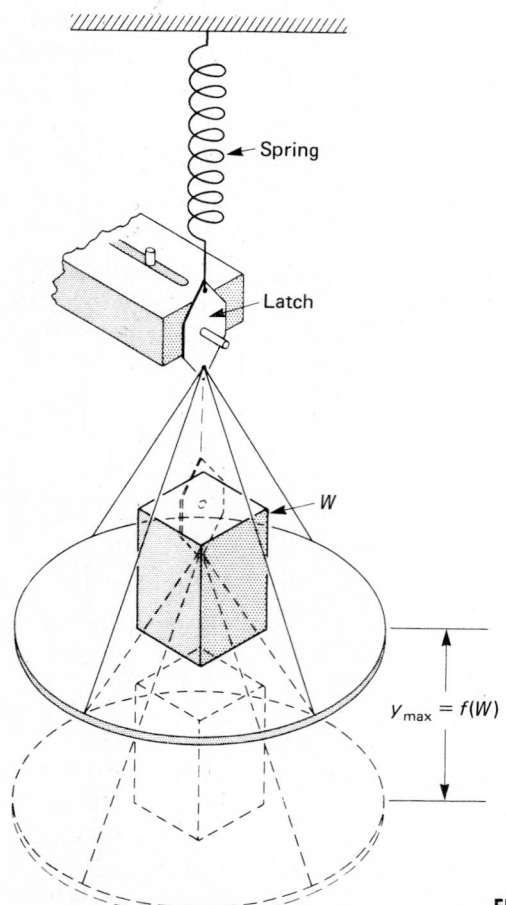

FIGURE 13.15   A ballistic weighing system.

A solution is

$$y = (mg/g_c k)(1 - \cos \omega_n t) \tag{13.13a}$$

for which the maximum value is

$$y_o = (2mg/g_c k) = 2y_{\text{static}} \tag{13.14}$$

when

$$t = \pi/\omega_n \quad \text{and} \quad \omega_n = \text{the undamped natural frequency.} \tag{13.14a}$$

The period of oscillation will be

$$\mathcal{T} = 2\pi \sqrt{m/g_c k}. \tag{13.15}$$

In operation, the platform is locked (Fig. 13.15), then the weight to be measured is put in place, the system is unlocked, and the maximum excursion is measured. If damping is minimized, the maximum displacement will be linearly proportional to the weight and can be used to measure the weight. Of course, the system is useful only for mass measurement and cannot be used to measure force.

13.8 HYDRAULIC AND PNEUMATIC SYSTEMS

If a force is applied to one side of a piston or diaphragm, and a pressure, either hydraulic or pneumatic, is applied to the other side, some particular value of pressure will be necessary to exactly balance the force. This is the principle on which hydraulic and pneumatic load cells are based.

For hydraulic systems, conventional piston and cylinder arrangements may be used. However, the friction between piston and cylinder wall and required packings and seals is unpredictable, making good accuracy difficult to obtain. Use of a *floating* piston with a diaphragm-type seal practically eliminates this variable.

Figure 13.16 shows a hydraulic cell in section. This is similar to the type used in some materials-testing machines. The piston does not actually contact

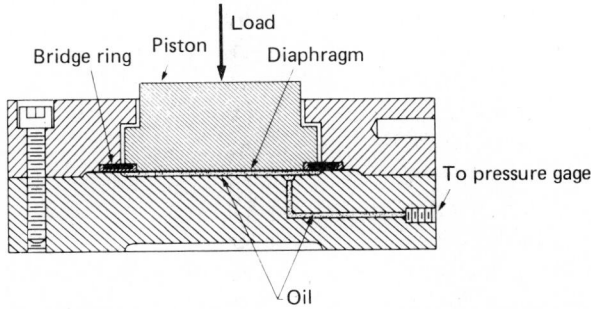

FIGURE 13.16   Section through a hydraulic load cell.

a cylinder wall in the normal sense, but a thin elastic diaphragm, or bridge ring, of steel is used as the positive seal, which allows small piston movement. Mechanical stops prevent the seal from being overstrained.

When force acts on the piston, the resulting oil pressure is transmitted to some form of pressure-sensing system such as the simple Bourdon gage. If the system is completely filled with fluid, very small transfer or flow will be required. Piston movement may be less than 0.002 in. at full capacity. In this respect, at least, the system will have good dynamic response; however, overall response will be determined very largely by the response of the pressure-sensing element.

Very high capacities and accuracies are possible with cells of this type. Capacities to 5,000,000 lbf (22.2 MN) and accuracies on the order of $\pm\frac{1}{2}\%$ of reading or $\pm\frac{1}{10}\%$ of capacity, whichever is greater, have been attained. Since hydraulic cells are somewhat sensitive to temperature change, provision should be made for adjusting the zero setting. Temperature changes during the measuring process cause errors of about $\frac{1}{4}\%$ per 10°F change.

Pneumatic load cells are quite similar to hydraulic cells in that the applied load is balanced by a pressure acting over a resisting area, with the pressure becoming a measure of the applied load. However, in addition to using air rather than liquid as the pressurized medium, these cells differ from the hydraulic ones in several other important respects.

Pneumatic load cells commonly use diaphragms of a flexible material rather than pistons, and they are designed to automatically regulate the balancing pressure. A typical arrangement is shown in Fig. 13.17. Air pressure is supplied to one side of the diaphragm and allowed to escape through a position-controlling *bleed* valve. The pressure under the diaphragm, therefore, is controlled both by source pressure and bleed-valve position. The diaphragm seeks the position that will result in just the proper air pressure to support the load. This, of course, assumes that the supply pressure is great enough so that its value multiplied by the effective area will at least support the load.

We see that as the load changes magnitude, the measuring diaphragm must change its position slightly. Unless care is used in the design, a nonlin-

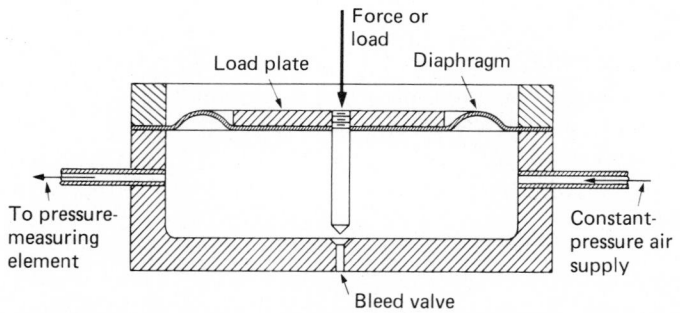

FIGURE 13.17   Section through a pneumatic load cell.

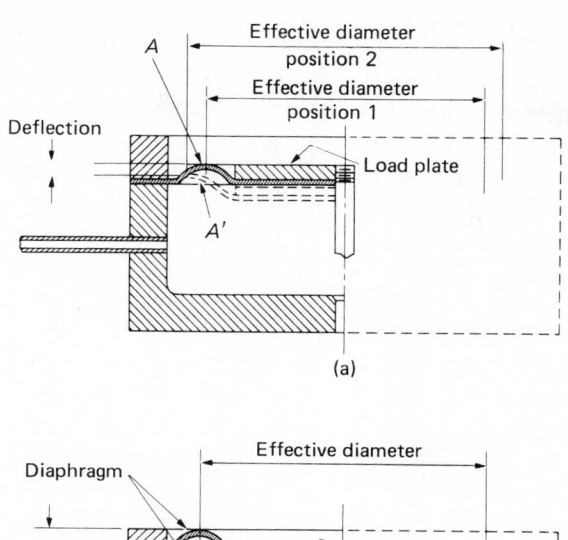

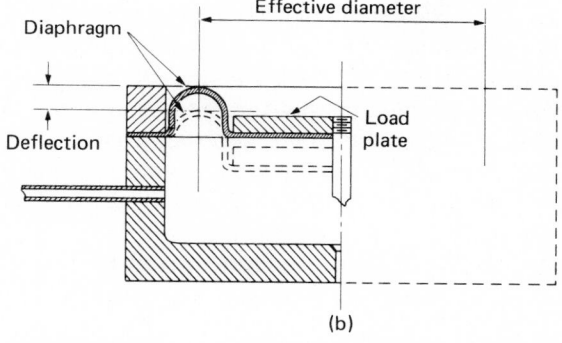

FIGURE 13.18   (a) A section through a diaphragm showing how a change in effective area may take place. (b) When sufficient "roll" is provided, the effective area remains constant.

earity may result, the cause of which may be made clear by referring to Fig. 13.18(a). As the diaphragm moves, the portion between the load plate and the fixed housing will alter position as shown. If it is assumed that the diaphragm is of a perfectly flexible material, incapable of transmitting any but tensile forces, then the division of vertical load components transferred to housing and load plate will occur at points A or A', depending on diaphragm position. We see then that the effective area will change, depending on the geometry of this portion of the diaphragm. If a complete semicircular roll is provided, as shown in Fig. 13.18(b), this effect will be minimized.

Since simple pneumatic cells may tend to be dynamically unstable, most commercial types provide some form of viscous damper to minimize this tendency. Also, additional chambers and diaphragms may be added to provide for *tare* adjustment.

Single-unit capacities to 80,000 lbf (356 kN) may be had, and by use of parallel units practically any total load or force may be measured. Errors as small as 0.1% of full scale may be expected.

13.9   TORQUE MEASUREMENT

Torque measurement is often associated with determination of mechanical power, either power required to operate a machine or power developed by the machine. In this connection, torque-measuring devices are commonly referred to as *dynamometers*. When so applied, both torque and angular speed must be determined. Another important reason for measuring torque is to obtain load information necessary for stress or deflection analysis.

There are three basic types of torque-measuring apparatus, namely, absorption, driving, and transmission dynamometers. *Absorption dynamometers* dissipate mechanical energy as torque is measured; hence they are particularly useful for measuring power or torque developed by power sources such as engines or electric motors. *Driving dynamometers*, as their name indicates, both measure torque or power and also supply energy to operate the tested devices. They are, therefore, useful in determining performance characteristics of such things as pumps and compressors. *Transmission dynamometers* may be thought of as passive devices placed at an appropriate location within a machine or between machines, simply for the purpose of sensing the torque at that location. They neither add to nor subtract from the transmitted energy or power, and are sometimes referred to as *torque meters*.

13.9.1   Mechanical and Hydraulic Dynamometers

Probably the simplest type of absorption dynamometer is the familiar *prony brake*, which is strictly a mechanical device depending on dry friction for converting the mechanical energy into heat. There are many different forms, two of which are shown in Fig. 13.19.

Another form of dynamometer operating on similar principles is the *water brake*, which uses fluid friction rather than dry friction for dissipating the input energy. Figure 13.20 shows this type of dynamometer in its simplest form. Capacity is a function of two factors, speed and water level. Power absorption is approximately a function of the *cube* of the speed, and the absorption at a given speed may be controlled by adjustment of the water level in the housing. This type of dynamometer may be made in considerably larger capacities than the simple prony brake because the heat generated may be easily removed by circulating the water into and out of the casing. Trunnion bearings support the dynamometer housing, allowing it freedom to rotate except for restraint imposed by a reaction arm.

In each of the above devices the power-absorbing element tends to rotate with the input shaft of the driving machine. In the case of the prony brake, the absorbing element is the complete brake assembly, whereas for the water brake it is the housing. In each case such rotation is constrained by a force-measuring device, such as some form of scales or load cell, placed at the end of a reaction arm of radius *r*. By measuring the force at the known radius,

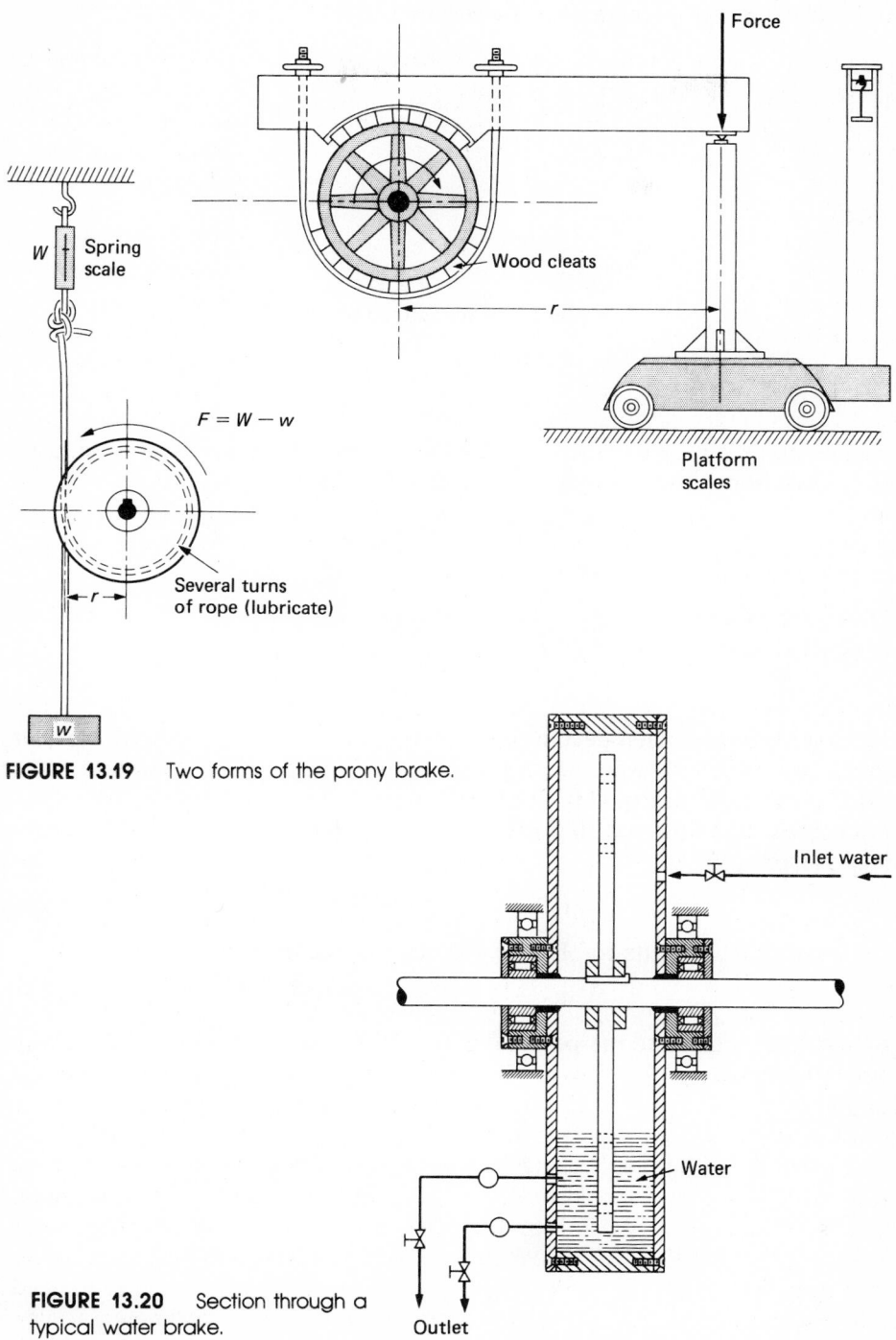

FIGURE 13.19   Two forms of the prony brake.

FIGURE 13.20   Section through a typical water brake.

the torque T may be computed by the simple relation

$$T = Fr. \tag{13.16}$$

If the angular speed of the driver is known, power may be determined from the relation

$$P = 2\pi(T) \text{ (rps)}, \tag{13.17}$$

where

T = torque,

F = the force measured at radius r,

P = power, and

rps = revolutions per second.

At this point it may be wise to carefully consider the units to be used in the above relationships. We may rewrite Eq. (13.17) as follows:

$$P = F(2\pi r \cdot \text{rev})/s = \text{Force} \times \text{Distance/Time}$$

$$= \text{Work/Unit time.}$$

Using the SI system of units, work is measured in joules (J), where one joule is equal to one newton multiplied by one meter, or

$$J = N \cdot m.$$

Mechanical power then becomes $N \cdot m/s = J/s = $ watts. Checking the units in Eq. (13.17) yields watts. Using the English system of units we find power as determined from Eq. (13.17) to yield units of lbf $\cdot$ ft/s. The English system often goes an additional step by assigning the term *horsepower* (HP) to 550 lbf $\cdot$ ft/s or

$$HP = 2\pi(T) \text{ (rps)}/550. \tag{13.18}$$

Conversion from watts to HP may be made using the relation

$$\text{Watts} = 7.457 \times 10^2 \times HP. \tag{13.19}$$

EXAMPLE   Calculate the power if $F = 120$ N (or 26.98 lbf), $r = 75$ cm (or 2.46 ft), and rps = 20.

Solution   Using SI units we have

$$P = 2\pi \cdot 120 \cdot 0.75 \cdot 20 = 11,310 \text{ W.}$$

Using English units we have

$$P = 2\pi \cdot 26.98 \cdot 2.46 \cdot 20 = 8340 \text{ lbf} \cdot \text{ft/s}$$

$$= 15.16 \text{ HP.}$$

A check on equivalence yields

$$11{,}310/15.16 = 746.04 \text{ watts per HP.}$$

13.9.2   Electric Dynamometers

Almost any form of rotating electric machine can be used as a driving dynamometer, or as an absorption dynamometer, or as both. Of course, those designed especially for the purpose are most convenient to use. Four possibilities are: (1) eddy-current dynamometers, (2) d.c. dynamometers or generators, (3) d.c. motors and generators, (4) a.c. motors and generators.

Eddy-current dynamometers are strictly of the absorption type. They are incapable of driving a test machine such as a pump or compressor; hence they are only useful for measuring the power from a source such as an internal combustion engine or electric motor.

The eddy-current dynamometer is based on the following principles. When a conducting material moves through a magnetic flux field, voltage is generated, which causes current to flow. If the conductor is a wire forming a part of a complete circuit, current will be caused to flow through that circuit, and with some form of commutating device a form of a.c. or d.c. generator may be the result. If the conductor is simply an isolated piece of material, such as a short bar of metal, and not a part of a complete circuit as generally recognized, voltages will still be induced. However, only local currents may flow in practically short-circuit paths within the bar itself. These currents, called eddy currents, become dissipated in the form of heat.

An eddy-current dynamometer consists of a metal disk or wheel that is rotated in the flux of a magnetic field. The field is produced by field elements or coils excited by an external source and attached to the dynamometer-housing, which is mounted in trunnion bearings. As the disk turns, eddy currents are generated, and the reaction with the magnetic field tends to rotate the complete housing in the trunnion bearings. Torque is measured in the same manner as for the water brake, and Eqs. (13.16), (13.17), and (13.18) are applicable. Load is controlled by adjusting the field current. As with the water brake, the mechanical energy is converted to heat energy, presenting the problem of satisfactory dissipation. Most eddy-current dynamometers must use water cooling. Particular advantages of this type are the comparatively *small size* for a given capacity and characteristics permitting *good control at low rotating speeds.*

Undoubtedly the most versatile of all types is the *cradled d.c. dynamometer,* shown in Fig. 13.21. This type of machine is usable both as an absorption and as a driving dynamometer in capacities to 5000 hp (238,000 kW). Basically the device is a d.c. motor generator with suitable controls to permit operation in either mode. When used as an absorption dynamometer, it performs as a d.c. generator and the input mechanical energy is converted to electrical

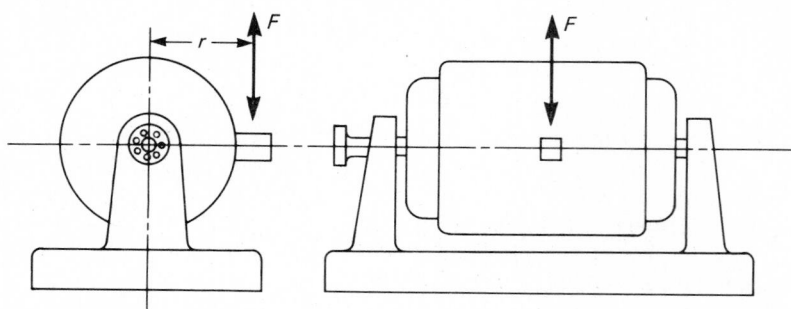

FIGURE 13.21   The general-purpose electric dynamometer.

energy, which is dissipated in resistance racks. This latter feature is important, for unlike the eddy-current dynamometer, the heat is dissipated external to the machine. Cradling in trunnion bearings permits the determination of reaction torque and the direct application of Eqs. (13.16), (13.17), and (13.18). Provision is made for measuring torque in either direction, depending on the direction of rotation and mode of operation. As a driving dynamometer, the device is used as a d.c. motor, which presents a problem in certain instances of obtaining an adequate source of d.c. power for this purpose. Use of either an a.c. motor-driven d.c. generator set or a rectified source is required. *Ease of control* and *good performance at low speeds* are features of this type of machine.

Ordinary *electric motors* or *generators* may be adapted for use in dynamometry. This is more feasible when d.c. rather than a.c. machinery is used. Cradling the motor or generator may be used for either driving or absorbing applications, respectively. By measuring torque reaction and speed, power may be computed. This, of course, requires special effort in designing and fabricating a minimum-friction arrangement. Adjustment of driving speed or absorption load could be provided through control of field current. Load-cell mounting may be used.

Knowledge of motor or generator characteristics versus speed presents another approach. If a d.c. generator is used as an *absorption dynamometer*, then

$$\text{Power (absorbed)} = (e)(i)/\text{Efficiency}, \qquad (13.20)$$

where

$$e = \text{the output voltage, in volts,}$$

$$i = \text{the output current, in amperes, and}$$

$$\text{Efficiency} = \text{the efficiency of the generator.}$$

In like manner, Eq. (13.20) holds if a d.c. motor is used as a *driving* dynamometer, except that e and i are *input* voltage and current, respectively. Both *e* and *i* may be measured separately, or a wattmeter may be used and the electrical power measured directly.

In many applications, only approximate results may be required, in which case *typical* motor or generator efficiencies supplied by the manufacturer should suffice. For more accurate results, some form of dynamometer would be required to determine the efficiencies for the particular machine to be used. The use of a.c. motors or generators, while feasible, is considerably more difficult and will not be discussed here. In any case, application of *general-purpose* electrical rotating machinery to dynamometry must be considered special and will not yield as satisfactory results as equipment particularly designed for the purpose.

13.10 TRANSMISSION DYNAMOMETERS

As mentioned earlier, transmission dynamometers may be thought of as passive devices neither appreciably adding to nor subtracting from the energy involved in the test system. Various devices have been used for this purpose, including gear-train arrangements and belt or chain devices.

Any gear box producing a speed change is subjected to a reaction torque equal to the difference between the input and output torques. When the reaction torque of a cradled gear box is measured, a function of either input or output torque may be obtained.

Belt or chain arrangements, in which reaction is a function of the difference between the tight and loose tensions, may also be used. Torque at either main pulley is also a function of the difference between the tight and loose tensions; hence the measured reaction may be calibrated in terms of torque, from which, with speed information, power may be determined. Mechanical losses introduced by arrangements of these types, combined with general awkwardness and cost, make them rather unsatisfactory except for an occasional special application.

More common forms of transmission dynamometers are based on calibrated measurement of unit or total strains in elastic load-carrying members. A popular dynamometer of the elastic type uses bonded strain gages applied to a section of torque-transmitting shaft [8, 9], as shown in Table 12.5. Such a dynamometer, often referred to as a *torque meter,* is used as a coupling between driving and driven machines, or between any two portions of a machine. A complete four-arm bridge is used, incorporating modulus gages to minimize temperature sensitivity (Section 13.5). Electrical connections are made through slip rings, with means provided to lift the brushes when they are not in use, thereby minimizing wear. Any of the common strain-gage indicators or recorders are usable to interpret the output. Dynamometers of this type are commercially available in capacities of 100 to 30,000 in. · lbf (12 to 3500 N · m). Accuracies to $\frac{1}{4}\%$ are claimed.

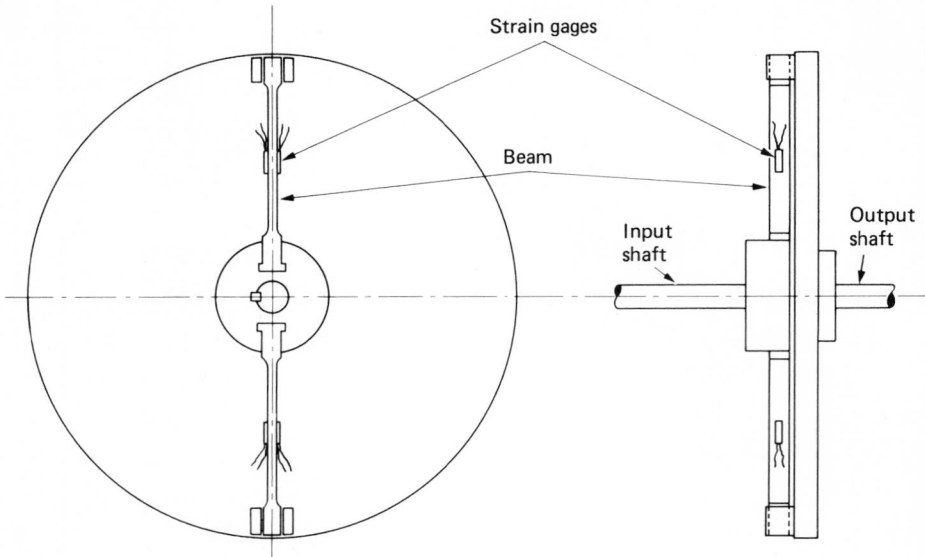

FIGURE 13.22   Transmission dynamometer that employs beams and strain gages for sensing torque.

In most cases resistance strain-gage transducers are most sensitive when bending strains can be used. Figure 13.22 suggests methods whereby torsion may be converted to bending for measurement.

Slip rings are subject to wear and may present annoying maintenance problems when permanent installations are required. For this reason many attempts have been made to devise electrical torque meters that do not require direct electrical connection to the moving shaft. Inductive [10, 11] and capacitive [12] transducers (see Fig. 4.13) have been used to accomplish this.

In addition to temperature sensitivity resulting from variation in elastic constants, further variation may be caused in the inductive type by change in magnetic constants with temperature. This may be compensated for by resistors in a manner similar to that used for strain-gage load cells (Section 13.5).

These types are relatively expensive, and cannot be considered general-purpose instruments. However, in permanent installations they provide the advantage of long service without maintenance problems.

13.11 COMBINED FORCE AND MOMENT MEASUREMENT

Certain special situations require combined force and moment measurement. One example is the measurement of forces and moments on a wind-tunnel model. Another is related to the determination of forces and moments caused by pressure and thermal expansions in a power-piping system. In situations such as these, determination of three force and three moment components

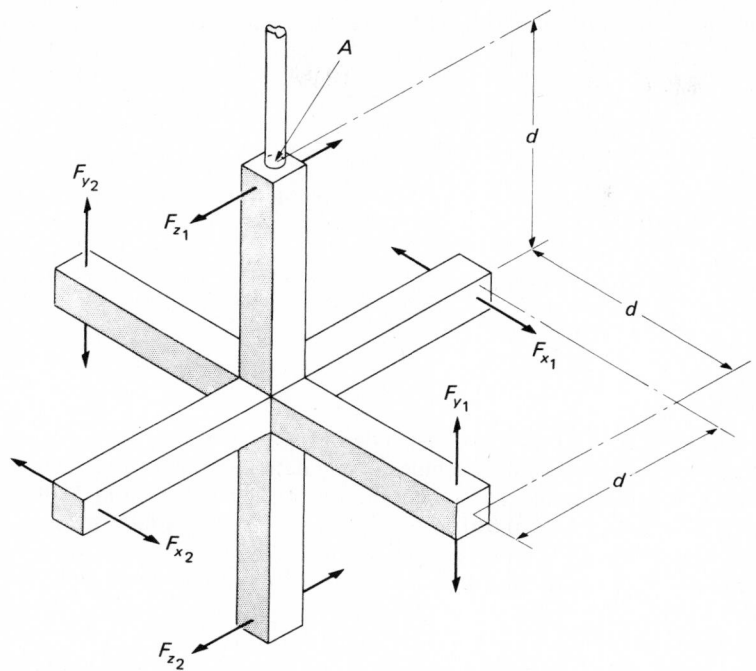

FIGURE 13.23 Cross-type resolver for combined force and moment measurement.

will completely define the condition. Usually the force and moment components are referred to a set of orthogonal axes, x, y, and z.

One of many possible systems will be described briefly. It is applicable to determination of forces and moments in models of power-pipe systems. The method uses a cross-shaped resolver arranged as shown in Fig. 13.23. A model piping-system terminal point is attached to the resolver at point A. Forces required to maintain equilibrium are then applied at the cross extremities. These forces may be designated F_{x_1}, F_{x_2}, F_{y_1}, F_{y_2}, F_{z_1}, and F_{z_2}. Inspection shows that

$$R_x = F_{x_1} + F_{x_2},$$

$$R_y = F_{y_1} + F_{y_2},$$

$$R_z = F_{z_1} + F_{z_2},$$

and also that

$$M_x = d(F_{z_1} - F_{z_2}),$$

$$M_y = d(F_{x_1} - F_{x_2}),$$

$$M_z = d(F_{y_1} - F_{y_2}).$$

Actual measurement of the forces may be made by use of any of the various force transducers that have been discussed.

SUGGESTED READINGS

ASME PTC 19.7-1961, *Measurement of Shaft Horsepower.*

ASME PTC 19.5.1-1964, *Weighing Scales.*

Specifications, Tolerances and Other Technical Requirements for Weighing and Measuring Devices. Washington, D.C.: U.S. Government Printing Office, 1955.

PROBLEMS

13.1 A proving-ring–type force transducer is a very reliable device for checking the calibration of material-testing machines. An equation for estimating the deflection constant of the elemental ring, loaded in compression, is given in Table 13.1. If $D = 10$ in. (25.4 cm) $\pm$ 0.010 in. (0.25 mm), $t =$ the radial thickness of the section $= 0.6$ in. (15.24 mm) $\pm$ 0.005 in. (0.127 mm), $w =$ the axial width of the section $= 2$ in. (5.08 cm) $\pm$ 0.015 in. (0.381 mm), and $E = 30 \times 10^6$ lbf/in^2 (20.68 $\times$ 10^{10} N/m^2) $\pm$ 0.5 $\times$ 10^6 lbf/in^2 (0.34 $\times$ 10^{10}N/m^2), calculate the value of K and its uncertainty, using English units.

13.2 Solve Problem 13.1 using SI units.

13.3 Review Problems 4.6 and 12.6. Using data from these two problems and from Tables 4.3 and 4.4, select a resistance material and determine dimensions for a series resistor to provide compensation for temperature-derived variations in Young's modulus for the beam.

13.4 Assign tolerances to the values given (or determined) in Problems 4.6, 12.6, and 13.3, and calculate an overall uncertainty to apply to the read-out from the beam. [*Note:* Any "electronics" used to evaluate the strain-gage output will also contain uncertainties. Make an estimate for this and include it in the final calculation.]

13.5 Consider a simple balance-beam–type scale (Fig. 13.4). Does the scale compare "weights" or does it compare "masses"? Is the scale sensitive to local gravity? Is it as functional on a mountain top as it is at sea level? Would the scale perform its function in gravity-free space?

measurement **14**
of pressure

14.1 INTRODUCTION

Pressure is the average force exerted by a medium, usually a fluid, on a unit area. It differs from normal stress only in the mode of application. In engineering it is most commonly expressed in terms of pascal (Pa) or pounds-force per square inch. (Pascal is equal to newtons per square meter.) Measuring devices commonly register pressure as a differential quantity, i.e., the difference between two pressures, with atmospheric pressure being the most common reference. The result is called *gage pressure*. When in reference to lack of all pressure, it is said to be *absolute*. For the English system of units these are abbreviated psig and psia, respectively. Figure 14.1 illustrates the relationships.

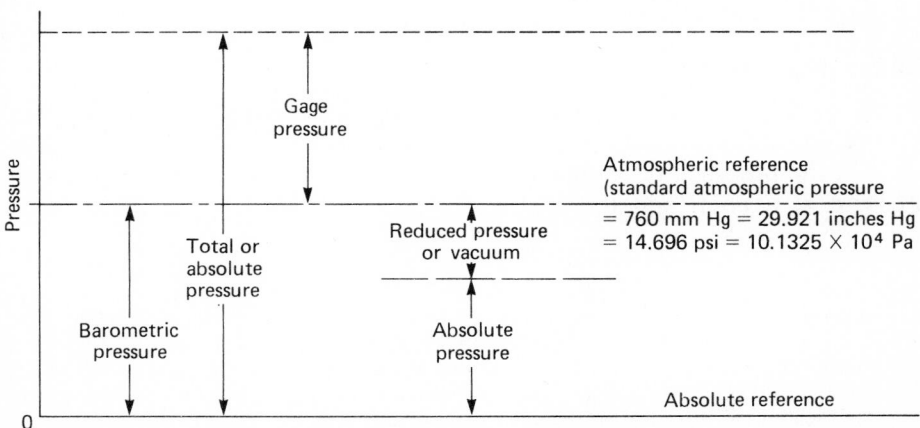

FIGURE 14.1   Relations between absolute, gage, and barometric pressures.

Pressure is often equated to the unit force at the base of a unit column of fluid, such as mercury or water. For example, the atmospheric standard (1.01325×10^5 Pa or 14.696 psia) is approximately* equivalent to the pressure exerted at the bottom of a column of mercury 760 mm (29.921 in.) in height.† Therefore, it is common to find standard atmospheric pressure specified as 760 mm or about 29.9 in. of Hg. It is obvious that fundamentally the unit of pressure is neither millimeters nor inches and that these units have meaning only when used in the proper context.

An absolute pressure less than atmospheric, i.e., a negative gage pressure, is often referred to as a *vacuum*.

In addition to the units mentioned above, the following are commonly used for evaluating low pressure:

1 millibar $= 10^2$ Pa $= 14.5 \times 10^{-3}$ psi,

1 micron $= 10^{-6}$ m Hg $= 19.34 \times 10^{-6}$ psi $= 1.333 \times 10^{-1}$ Pa,

1 torr $= 1$ mm Hg $= 1000$ μ $= 19.34 \times 10^{-3}$ psi $= 1.333 \times 10^2$ Pa.

Extremely high pressure is often designated in terms of atmospheres (atm):

1 atm $= 14.696$ psi $= 101.325 \times 10^3$ Pa   (Note that 1 atm $\approx$ 1 bar.)

14.2 STATIC AND DYNAMIC PRESSURES

When a fluid is in equilibrium, the pressure at a point is identical in all directions and independent of orientation. This pressure is referred to as *static pressure*. When pressure gradients occur within a continuum of pressure, the attempt to restore equilibrium results in fluid flow from regions of higher pressure to regions of lower pressure. In this case, the total pressures are no longer independent of direction.

Sound pressure

Sound propagates in an elastic medium as longitudinal (along the path of propagation) pressure variations, fluctuating above and below the static pressure. In the presence of a sound wave, the instantaneous difference between pressure at a point and the average pressure is called *sound pressure*. A

---

*   Depends on local gravity acceleration and temperature.

†   *Standard atmosphere* may have various meanings. Generally it refers to "standard" conditions at sea level. Traditionally, American engineering practice has been to use 14.696 psia as the standard. SI practice sets two values: *normal* atmosphere as 760 torr (mm of Hg), which converts to $1.01325E + 05$ Pa, and *technical* atmosphere (1 kgf/cm²), which becomes $9.8065E + 04$ Pa. [*Note:* Use of the unit kgf should be avoided.] Aerodynamicists standardize atmosphere over a range of altitudes (from -5000 to $+59,500$ m). This requires a table of several pages in length [1].

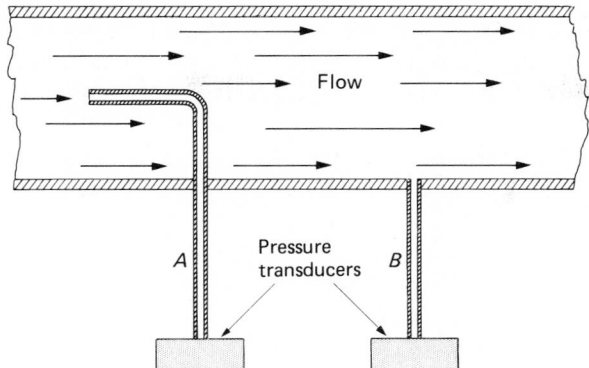

FIGURE 14.2 Impact-pressure and static-pressure tubes.

common unit is the microbar (10^{-1} Pa). Measurement of sound pressure is accomplished through use of a microphone attached to specialized apparatus, as discussed in Chapter 18.

Velocity and impact pressures

Various pressure components exist in a flowing fluid. If we attempt to use a small tube or probe for sampling the pressure in an air duct, we find that the results depend on how the tube is oriented. If the tube or probe is aligned so that the flow impacts against the tube opening as shown at *A* in Fig. 14.2, we obtain one result; if it is positioned as shown at *B,* we obtain another result.

Probe *A* senses a *total* or *stagnation pressure,* whereas tap *B* senses only the *static* component of pressure. Static pressure may be thought of as the pressure one would sense if moving along with the stream, and total pressure may be defined as the pressure that would be obtained if the stream were brought to rest isentropically. If we take the difference between the two pressures, we obtain the pressure due to the fluid motion, referred to as the *velocity pressure,* or

Velocity pressure = Total pressure − Static pressure.

We see, therefore, that to properly obtain and interpret pressure information it is necessary to account for flow conditions. Conversely, to properly interpret flow measurements, consideration must be given to the pressure situation. With the above factors in mind, we shall proceed to consider some of the methods used to measure pressure.

14.3 PRESSURE-MEASURING SYSTEMS

Pressure-measuring systems probably vary over a greater range of complexity than any other type of measuring system. On the one hand, the ordinary

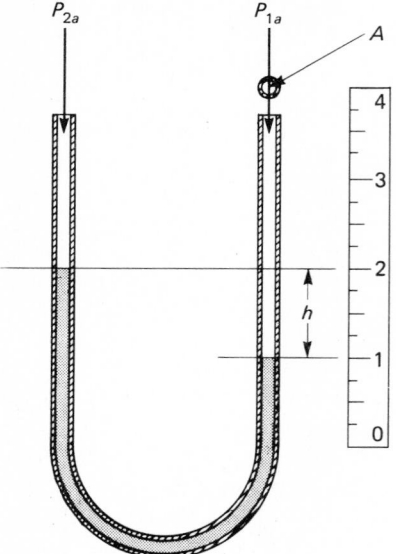

FIGURE 14.3   Simple U-tube manometer.

manometer (Fig. 14.3) is one of the most elementary measuring devices imaginable. It is simple, inexpensive, and relatively free from error, yet it may be arranged to almost any degree of sensitivity. Its major disadvantages lie in certain of its pressure ranges and in its poor dynamic response. It is not very practical for measuring pressures greater than, say, 100 psig, and it is incapable of following any but slowly changing pressures. Another familiar pressure-measuring device, the common Bourdon-tube gage (Fig. 4.1), is quite useful over a wide pressure range, but only for static or slowly changing pressures.

In general, it can be said that when the pressure is *dynamic,* some form of pressure-measuring *system* utilizing electromechanical transducer methods is required. A major portion of this chapter is devoted to discussing applications of devices of this kind.

In accounting for the dynamic response of a pressure-measuring system, the instrumentation and the application must be considered as a whole. The response is not determined by the isolated physical properties of the instrument components alone, but must include the mass-elastic–damping effects of the pressurized media and conducting passageways.

As an example, a diaphragm-type pickup may be used for measuring the pressure at a specific point on an aircraft skin. In such an application, it may be undesirable to place the diaphragm flush with the aircraft surface. Possibly the size of the diaphragm is too great in comparison with the pressure gradients existing; or perhaps flush mounting would disturb the surface to too great a degree; or it may be necessary to mount the pickup internally to protect it from large temperature variations. In such cases, the pressure would be conducted to the sensing element of the pickup through a passageway, and a small space or cavity would exist over the diaphragm. The passageway and cavity become, in essence, an integral part of the transducer, and the mass-elastic–damping properties contribute to the determination of the overall response of the system. It is obvious that it would be insufficient to know only the transducer characteristics.

Ideally, a pressure pickup should be insensitive to temperature change and acceleration; friction should be minimized, and any that is unavoidable should be predictable. Damping should remain constant for all operating conditions. These items will be discussed in more detail later in the chapter.

14.4 PRESSURE-MEASURING TRANSDUCERS

Often pressure is measured by transducing its effect to a deflection through use of a pressurized area and either a gravitational or elastic restraining element. A comprehensive classification of basic pressure-measuring methods is difficult to make. However, the following should suffice for our purposes.

I. Gravitational types
  A. Liquid columns
  B. Pistons or loose diaphragms, and weights
II. Direct-acting elastic types
  A. Unsymmetrically loaded tubes
  B. Symmetrically loaded tubes
  C. Elastic diaphragms
  D. Bellows
  E. Bulk compression
III. Indirect-acting elastic type
  Piston with elastic restraining member

14.5 GRAVITATIONAL-TYPE TRANSDUCERS

The simple well-type manometer (Fig. 14.4) is one of the most elementary forms of pressure-measuring device. A force–equilibrium expression for the net liquid column is

$$(P_{1a}A - P_{2a}A) = Ah\rho(g/g_c) \tag{14.1}$$

or

$$(P_{1a} - P_{2a}) = P_d = h\rho(g/g_c), \tag{14.1a}$$

where

P_{1a} and P_{2a} = the applied absolute pressures,

P_d = the difference or differential pressure,

ρ = the unit density of the fluid, mass/volume, and

h = the net column height, or "head."

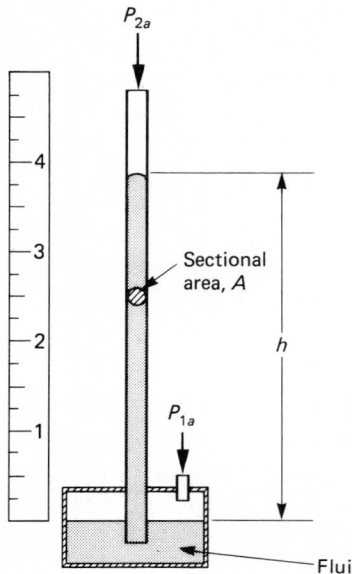

Fluid   **FIGURE 14.4**   Well-type manometer.

In practice, pressure P_{2a} is commonly atmospheric and

$$(P_{1a} - P_{atm}) = P_{1g} = h\rho(g/g_c),\tag{14.2}$$

where

$$P_{1g} = \text{the gage pressure at point 1.}$$

Perhaps it would be wise at this point to make sure we understand the units to be used. In simplified form the above equations may be written as

$$P_d = h\rho(g/g_c)\tag{14.2a}$$

Substituting units in the right-hand side of the equation, we have, for the SI system,

$$(m)(kg/m^3)(m/s^2)(N \cdot s^2/kg \cdot m) = N/m^2 = Pa.$$

Using the English system of units, we have

$$(ft)(lbm/ft^3)(ft/s^2)(lbf \cdot s^2/lbm \cdot ft) = lbf/ft^2.$$

EXAMPLE   Calculate the pressure at the base of a column of water one meter (3.281 ft) in height if the local gravity acceleration is 9.75 m/s² (31.99 ft/s²) and the temperature is 20°C (68°F).

Solution   From Table D.1 (see Appendix D), we find that the density of water at 20°C = 998.2 kg/m³ (62.316 lbm/ft³). Using SI units, we have

$$P_{SI} = (1)(998.2)(9.75/1) = 9732 \text{ Pa}\quad(\text{or N/m}^2);$$

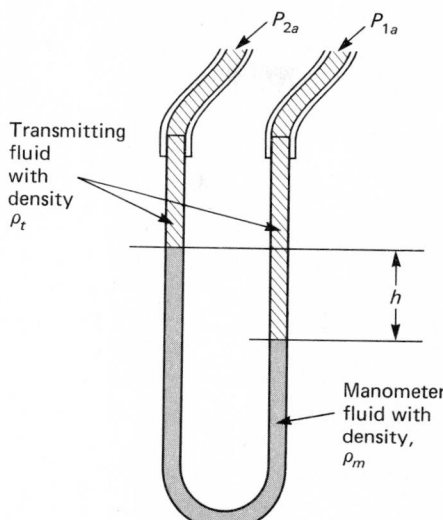

FIGURE 14.5   Dual-fluid U-tube manometer.

using English units, we have

$$P_{\text{Eng}} = (3.281)(62.316)(31.99/32.17) = 203.3 \text{ lbf/ft}^2 = 1.412 \text{ psi}.$$

We see that because the fluid density is involved, accurate work will require consideration of temperature variation; the manometer will possess a certain amount of temperature sensitivity.

When the applied absolute pressure P_{2a} is made to be zero, and P_{1a} is atmospheric, we obtain the ordinary barometer. In this case the fluid is generally mercury.

Figure 14.5 illustrates the function of the simple U-tube manometer. Pressures are applied to both legs of the U, and the manometer fluid is displaced until force equilibrium is attained. Pressures P_{1a} and P_{2a} are transmitted to the manometer legs through some fluid of density ρ_t, while the manometer fluid has some greater density ρ_m. In general we see that

$$P_{1a} - P_{2a} = h(\rho_m - \rho_t)(g/g_c). \tag{14.3}$$

In certain cases the relative densities of the two fluids are great enough that the lesser density may be ignored: when air is the transmitting fluid and water the measuring fluid, for instance. When this is so, Eq. (14.3) reverts to Eq. (14.1a).

EXAMPLE   Suppose the manometer fluids in Fig. 14.5 are water and mercury. This situation might occur when a manometer is used to measure the differential pressure across a venturi meter (see Section 15.3) through which water is flowing. We will consider both systems of units used in this book along with the following pertinent data:

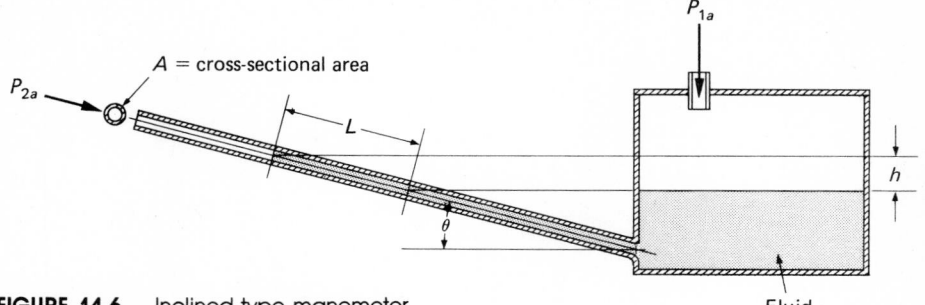

FIGURE 14.6   Inclined-type manometer.   Fluid

$h = 10$ in. or $\frac{5}{6}$ ft (0.254 m),

Density of water $= 62.38$ lbm/ft³ (999.2 kg/m³),

Specific gravities of H_2O and Hg $= 1$ and 13.6, respectively,

Standard gravity acceleration will be used (32.174 ft/s² and 9.80665 m/s²).

Using the English system, determine the differential pressure.

Solution

$$P_{1a} - P_{2a} = (\tfrac{5}{6})(13.6 - 1)(62.38)(32.17/32.17) = 655 \text{ lbf/ft}^2 = 4.55 \text{ psi}$$

For the SI system of units, we have

$$P_{1a} - P_{2a} = (0.254)(12.6)(999.2)(9.80665/1) = 31,360 \text{ Pa}.$$

It is left for the reader to show that the two answers represent the same physical quantity and that the unit balance is proper in each case.

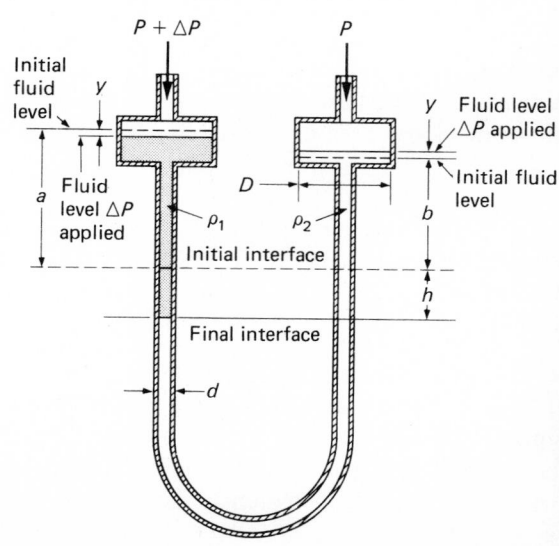

FIGURE 14.7
Two-fluid manometer
with reservoirs.

To obtain displacement amplification one may apply various schemes, two of which are shown in Figs. 14.6 and 14.7. For the single inclined leg (Fig. 14.6),

$$P_{1a} = \rho(L \sin \theta)g/g_c + P_{2a} \qquad (14.4)$$

In the case of the two-fluid type manometer, Fig. 14.7,

$$\text{Sensitivity} = \Delta P/h = [(d/D)^2(\rho_2 + \rho_1) + (\rho_2 - \rho_1)](g/g_c) \qquad (14.5)$$

When compared with the simple U-tube manometer, the deflection amplification equals

$$M = \left[\frac{\rho}{(d/D)^2(\rho_2 + \rho_1) + (\rho_2 - \rho_1)} \right] \qquad (14.5a)$$

where ρ = the density of the fluid in the simple manometer, and $\rho_1 < \rho_2$.

Figure 14.8 illustrates the familiar dead-weight tester that is commonly used as a source of static pressure for calibration purposes but is basically a pressure-producing and pressure-measuring device. When the applied weights and piston area are known, the resulting pressure may be readily calculated.

Figure 14.9 illustrates the principle of operation of the inverted-bell pressure-measuring system. In this case, the force exerted by the pressure against the inner top of the bell is balanced against the net weight of the bell. The net weight depends on the depth of immersion, and as the pressure varies, the bell rises or falls according to pressure magnitude. The primary application of this device is for actuating industrial pressure recorders and controllers.

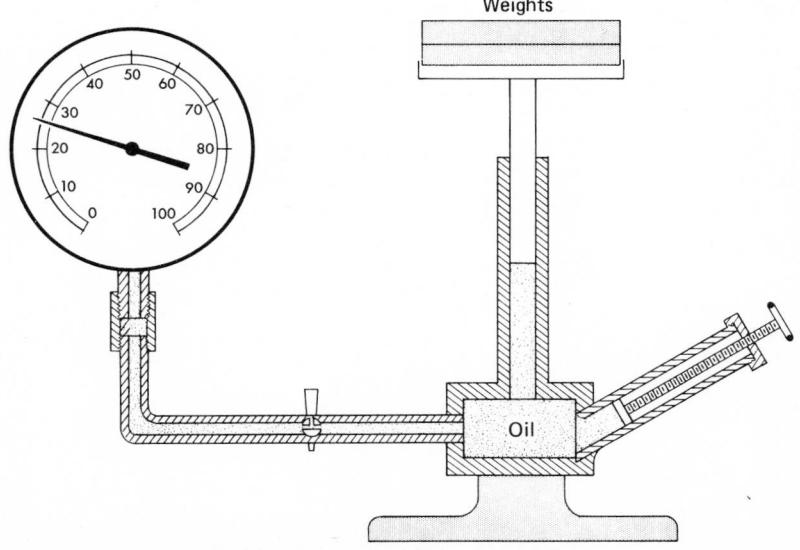

FIGURE 14.8   Dead-weight type tester.

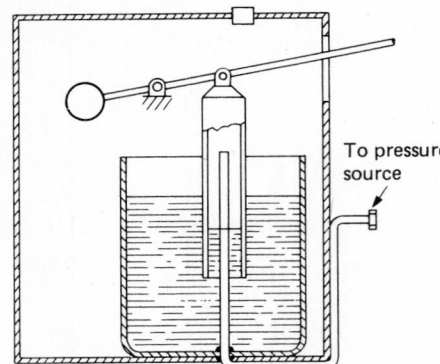

FIGURE 14.9 Inverted bell pressure-measuring device.

Of course, all gravitational-type pressure transducers are sensitive to the local value of gravity acceleration.

14.6 ELASTIC-TYPE TRANSDUCERS

Elastic elements operate on the principle that the deflection or deformation accompanying a balance of pressure and elastic forces may be used as a measure of pressure. A familiar example is the ordinary Bourdon tube (see

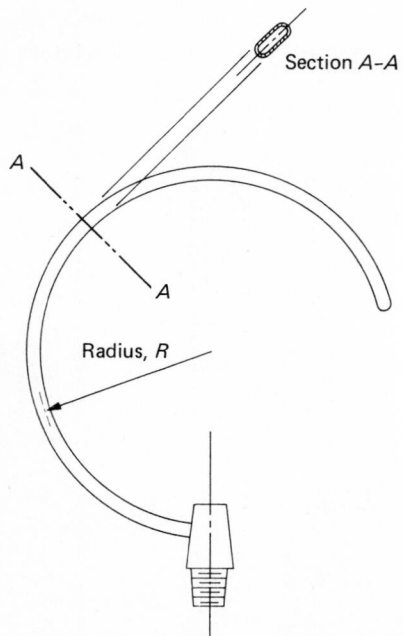

FIGURE 14.10 Basic Bourdon tube.

Fig. 4.1). A tube, normally of oval section, is initially coiled into a circular arc of radius R, as shown in Fig. 14.10. The included angle of the arc is usually less than 360°; however, in some cases, when increased sensitivity is desired, the tube may be formed into a helix of several turns.

As a pressure is applied to the tube, the oval section tends to round out, becoming more circular in section. The inner and outer arc lengths will remain approximately equal to their original lengths, and hence the only recourse is for the tube to uncoil. In the simple pressure gage, the movement of the end of the tube is communicated through linkage and gearing to a pointer whose movement over a scale becomes a measure of pressure. Rigorous treatment of the mechanics of Bourdon-tube action is complex, and only approximate analyses have been made [2].

14.7 ELASTIC DIAPHRAGMS

Many dynamic pressure-measuring apparatus use an elastic diaphragm as the primary pressure transducer. Such diaphragms may be either flat or corrugated; the flat type (Fig. 14.11a) is often used in conjunction with electrical secondary transducers whose sensitivity permits quite small diaphragm deflections, whereas the corrugated type (Fig. 14.11b) is particularly useful when larger deflections are required.

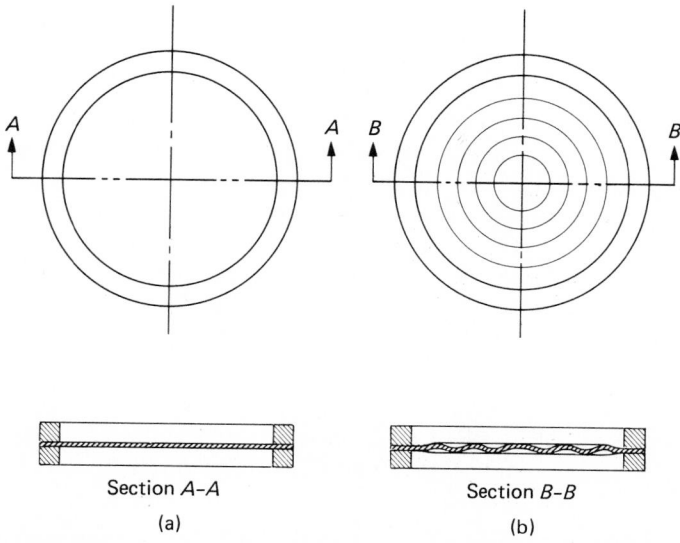

Section *A–A*   Section *B–B*

(a)   (b)

FIGURE 14.11   (a) Flat diaphragm. (b) Corrugated diaphragm.

Diaphragm displacement may be transmitted by mechanical means to some form of indicator, perhaps a pointer and scale as is used in the familiar aneroid barometer. For engineering measurements, particularly when dynamic results are required, diaphragm motion is more often sensed by some form of electrical secondary transducer, whose principle of operation may be resistive, capacitive, inductive, or piezo, as discussed in the following section. The output from the secondary transducer is then processed by appropriate intermediate devices and fed to an indicator, recorder, or controller.

Diaphragm design for pressure transducers generally involves all the following requirements to some degree:

1. Dimensions and total load must be compatible with physical properties of the material used.
2. Flexibility must be such as to provide the sensitivity required by the secondary transducer.
3. Volume of displacement should be minimized to provide reasonable dynamic response.
4. Natural frequency of the diaphragm should be sufficiently high to provide satisfactory frequency response.
5. Output should be linear.

14.7.1 Flat Metal Diaphragms

Deflection of flat metal diaphragms is limited either by stress requirements or by deviation from linearity. It has been found that as a general rule the maximum deflection that can be tolerated maintaining a linear pressure–displacement relation is about 30% of the diaphragm thickness [3].

In certain cases secondary transducers require physical connection with the diaphragm at its center. This is generally true when mechanical linkages are used and is also necessary for certain types of electrical secondary transducers. In addition, auxiliary spring force is sometimes introduced to increase the diaphragm deflection constant. These requirements make necessary some form of boss or reinforcement at the center of the diaphragm face, which reduces diaphragm flexibility and complicates theoretical design analysis.

When a central connection is made, a concentrated force F will normally be applied. In general, therefore, the diaphragm may be simultaneously subjected to two deflection forces, the distributed pressure load and a central concentrated force. Design relationships for the fixed-edge, pressurized diaphragm may be found in [4]; for diaphragms with central bosses, in [5].

Calculations for diaphragm dimensions should not be relied on as representing more than a rough guide for design purposes. There are several factors that cannot be accurately predicted. Among these are: (1) the rigidity of the outer supporting ring and inner boss, which is never as complete as assumed, and (2) the material physical properties, which are seldom accurately known. In addition, an undesirable characteristic of simple flat diaphragms that is often encountered is a nonlinearity referred to as *oil canning*. The term is derived from the action of the bottom of a simple oil can when it is pressed. A slight unintentional dimpling in the assembly of a flat-diaphragm pressure pickup is difficult to eliminate unless special precautions are taken. In addition, oil canning may be aggravated by differential expansions due to changing ambient conditions. It is desirable, therefore, to construct a pressure cell from materials having the same coefficient of expansion. Even this, however, may not always solve the problem because temperature gradients within the instrument itself may result in a different expansion. One solution to this problem is obtained by using a stretched or *radially* preloaded diaphragm [6]. Theoretical solutions for the radially preloaded diaphragm are considerably more involved than those for the simple flat type. Another solution to the oil-canning problem is to use a small external spring load to *bias* the diaphragm. This, of course, adds mass and thereby sacrifices dynamic response. In all cases, care must be exercised to minimize undesirable temperature effects.

14.7.2 Corrugated Diaphragms

Corrugated diaphragms are normally used in larger diameters than the flat types. Corrugations permit increased linear deflections and reduced stresses. Since the larger size and deflection reduce the dynamic response of the corrugated diaphragms as compared with the flat type, they are more commonly used in static applications.

Adding convolutions to a diaphragm increases the complexity of the theoretical design approach. Grover and Bell [7] have used brittle coatings as a means for evaluating approximate theoretical solutions for stresses.

Two corrugated diaphragms are often joined at their edges to provide what is referred to as a *pressure capsule*. This is the type commonly used in aneroid barometers.

Metal bellows are sometimes used as pressure-sensing elements. Bellows are generally useful for pressure ranges from about $\frac{1}{2}$ psi to 150 psi full scale. Hysteresis and zero shift are somewhat greater problems with this type of element than with most of the others.

14.8 SECONDARY TRANSDUCERS USED WITH DIAPHRAGMS

Most electromechanical transducer principles have been applied to diaphragm pressure pickups. The following examples are only representative of many possible variations.

14.8.1 Use of Resistance Strain Gages with Flat Diaphragms

An obvious approach is to simply apply strain gages directly to a diaphragm surface and calibrate the measured strain in terms of pressure. One drawback of this method that is often encountered is the small physical area available for mounting the gages; for this reason, gages with short gage lengths must be used.

Special spiral grids have been used [3, 8]. Grids are mounted in the central area of the diaphragm, with the elements in tension (see Fig. 12.5).

Wenk [3] has found that a satisfactory method for mounting strain gages is the one illustrated in Fig. 14.12. When pressure is applied to the side opposite the gages, the central gage is subject to tension while the outer gage senses compression. The two gages may be used in adjacent bridge arms, thereby adding their individual outputs and simultaneously providing temperature compensation.

14.8.2 Inductive Types

Variable inductance has also been successfully used as a form of secondary transducer used with a diaphragm [6]. Figure 14.13 illustrates one arrangement of this sort. Flexing of the diaphragm due to applied pressure causes it to move toward one pole piece and away from the other, thereby altering the relative inductances. An inductive bridge circuit may be used, as shown.

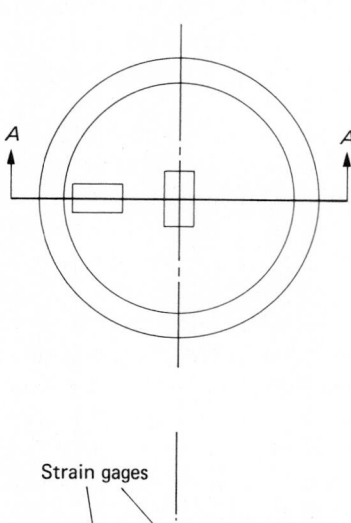

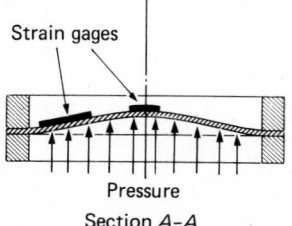

Strain gages

Pressure

Section *A-A*

FIGURE 14.12   Location of strain gages on flat diaphragm.

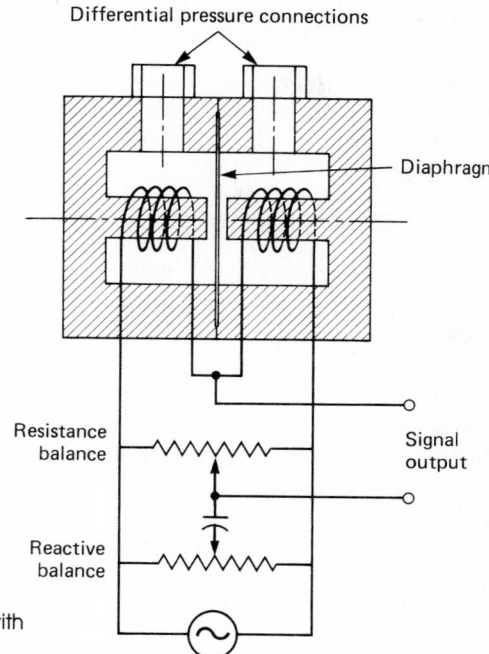

FIGURE 14.13 Differential pressure cell with inductance-type secondary transducer.

Standard laboratory equipment, such as an oscilloscope or electronic voltmeter, as well as recorders, may be used to display the gage output. Available ranges are from 0–1.0 to 0–100 psi.

14.8.3 Piezo-Type Pressure Cells

Literature for commercial piezo-type cells may refer to either of two considerably different types of secondary transducer: (1) piezoresistive elements, or (2) piezoelectric elements. The former are of the passive, semiconductor (SC) strain element type (Section 12.13), whereas the latter use the active, charge-generating "crystal-type" elements (Section 4.14).

When the piezoresistive elements are used, most of the discussion in Section 14.8.1 applies. The primary advantage in using the SC gages rather than the more common simple resistive types lies in the increased sensitivity of the secondary transducer. This permits use of a less sensitive primary transducer (diaphragm, pressure tube, etc.), which in turn allows much stiffer construction, directly resulting in higher dynamic response, greater sturdiness, and/or reduced sizes, without sacrificing overall sensitivity.

Pressure cells using piezoelectric-type secondary transducers have the advantage of very high sensitivities coupled with high natural frequencies. These desirable qualities permit wide ranges of working pressures and excellent frequency response. Typical maximum pressures range to as high as

100,000 psi with resolutions of less than 1 psi. Outputs are in terms of coulombs per unit input and may be on the order of 0.2 pC/psi. A typical resonant frequency is 150,000 Hz. Inasmuch as the output impedance is inherently very high, some form of impedance transformation is required in close proximity to the transducer (Section 5.18.2).

14.8.4 Other Types of Secondary Transducers

Flexing diaphragms have been used to alter capacitance as a means of producing an electrical output (see Fig. 4.14). This method is not so common as those previously discussed, primarily because of low sensitivity and the problems accompanying the requirement for relatively high carrier frequencies.

Another successful method uses an electromechanical resonant system consisting of a fine wire under tensile load vibrating at its natural frequency. One end of the wire is connected to the center of a pressure-sensing diaphragm, which varies the wire tension, depending on the applied pressure. Small permanent magnets provide a magnetic field in which the wire vibrates, causing an a.c. potential to be developed in the wire. After amplification, a portion of this voltage is fed back to energize driving coils that maintain the vibration. Output *frequency* is the measure of pressure.

14.9 STRAIN-GAGE PRESSURE CELLS

Any form of container will be strained when pressurized. Sensing the resulting strain with an appropriate secondary transducer, such as a resistance strain gage, will provide a measure of the applied pressure. The term *pressure cell* has gradually become applied to this type of pressure-sensing device, and various forms of elastic *containers* or cells have been devised.

For low pressures, a pinched tube may be used (Fig. 14.14). This supplies a bending action as the tube tends to round out. Gages may be placed dia-

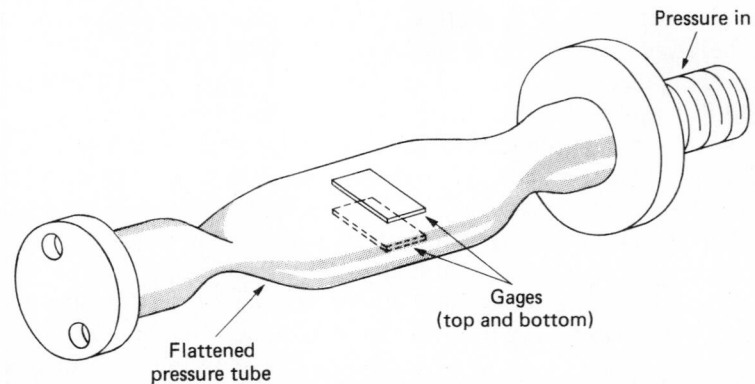

FIGURE 14.14   Flattened-tube pressure cell that employs resistance strain gages as secondary transducers.

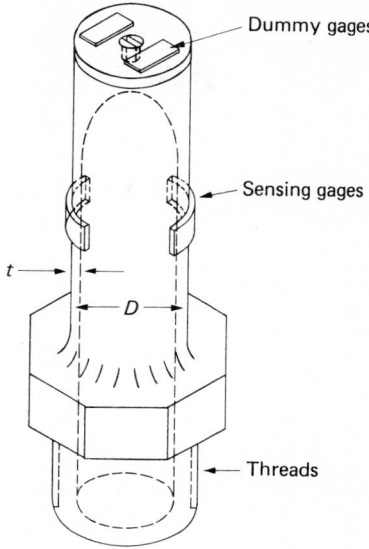

Dummy gages

Sensing gages

t

D

Threads

FIGURE 14.15   Cylindrical type pressure cell.

metrically opposite on the flattened faces, as shown, with two unstressed temperature-compensating gages mounted elsewhere. This arrangement completes the electrical bridge. Cells of this general design are commercially available.

Probably the simplest form of strain-gage pressure transducer is a cylindrical tube such as that shown in Fig. 14.15. In this application two active gages mounted in the hoop direction may be used for pressure sensing, along with two temperature-compensating gages mounted in an unstrained location. Temperature-compensating gages are shown mounted on a separate disk fastened to the end of the cell. Design relationships may be found in most mechanical design texts.

The sensitivity of a pair of circumferentially mounted strain gages (Fig. 14.15) with gage factor F is expressed by the relationship [9]:

$$\frac{\Delta R}{P_i} = \frac{2FRd^2}{E}\left[\frac{2 - v}{D^2 - d^2}\right], \tag{14.6}$$

where

ΔR = the strain-gage resistance change, in ohms,

R = the nominal gage resistance, in ohms,

P_i = the internal pressure,

d = the inside diameter of the cylinder,

D = the outside diameter of the cylinder,

E = Young's modulus, and

v = Poisson's ratio.

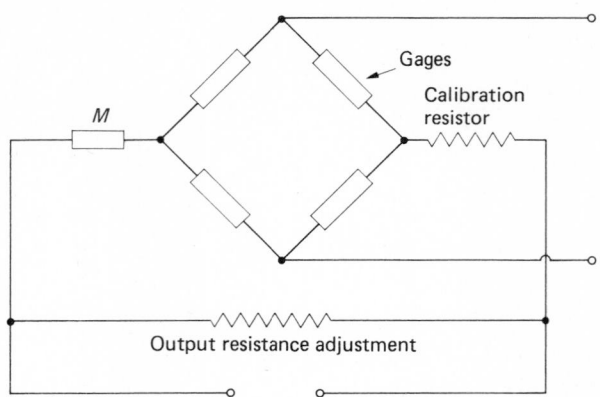

FIGURE 14.16   Strain-gage circuitry for pressure cells employing a modulus gage.

The bridge constant, 2, appears because two circumferential gages are assumed. If a single strain-sensitive gage is to be used, the sensitivity will be one-half that given by Eq. (14.6). Of course, these relations are true only if elastic conditions are maintained and if the gages are located so as to be unaffected by end restraints.

Improved frequency response may be obtained for a cell of this type by minimizing the internal volume. This may be accomplished by use of a solid "filler" such as a plug, which will reduce the flow into and out of the cell with pressure variation.

Figure 14.16 shows the electrical circuitry used for a transducer of this type. Gage M is a modulus gage, discussed in Section 13.5, used to compensate for variation in Young's modulus with temperature. The calibration and output resistors are adjusted to provide predetermined bridge resistance and calibration.

14.10   MEASUREMENT OF HIGH PRESSURES

The high-pressure range has been defined as beginning at about 700 atm and extending upward to the limit of present techniques, which is on the order of 18,000 atm [10]. Conventional pressure-measuring devices, such as strain-gage pressure cells and Bourdon-tube gages, may be used at pressures as high as 3500 to 7000 atm. Bourdon tubes for such pressures are nearly round in section and have a high ratio of wall thickness to diameter. They are, therefore, quite stiff, and the deflection per turn is small. For this reason, high-pressure Bourdon tubes are often made of a number of turns.

Electrical resistance pressure gages

Very high pressures may be measured by electrical resistance gages, which make use of the resistance change brought about by direct application of pressure to the electrical conductor itself. The sensing element consists of a

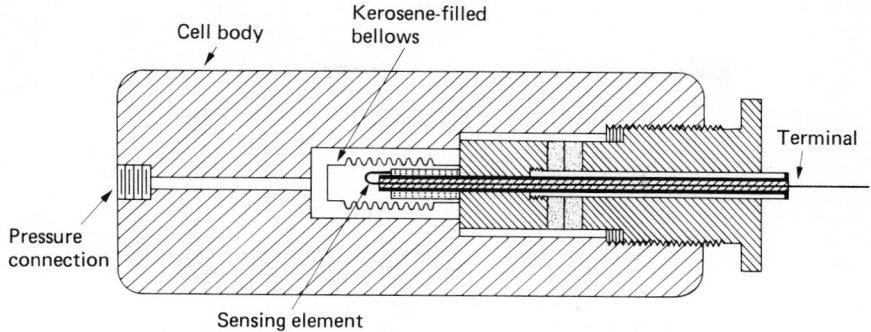

FIGURE 14.17   Section through a bulk-modulus pressure gage.

loosely wound coil of relatively fine wire. When pressure is applied, the bulk-compression effect results in an electrical resistance change that may be calibrated in terhs of the applied pressure.

Figure 14.17 shows a bulk modulus gage in section. The sensing element does not actually contact the process medium, but is separated therefrom by a kerosene-filled bellows. One end of the sensing coil is connected to a central terminal, as shown, while the other end is grounded, thereby completing the necessary electrical circuit.

Although Eq. (12.8) was written with a somewhat different application in mind, it also applies to the situation being discussed. Rewrite this relation,

$$\frac{dR}{R} = \frac{dL}{L} - 2\frac{dD}{D} + \frac{d\rho}{\rho} , \tag{14.7}$$

in which

$$R = \text{the electrical resistance,}$$

$$L = \text{the length of the conductor,}$$

$$D = \text{a sectional dimension, and}$$

$$\rho = \text{resistivity.}$$

The wire will be subject to a biaxial stress condition because the ends, in providing electrical continuity, will generally not be subject to pressure. Using relations of the form expressed by Eqs. (12.3), and assuming that $\sigma_x = \sigma_y = -P$ and $\sigma_z = 0$, we may write

$$\varepsilon_x = \varepsilon_y = \frac{dD}{D} = -\frac{P}{E}(1 - v) \tag{14.8}$$

and

$$\varepsilon_z = \frac{dL}{L} = \frac{2vP}{E} . \tag{14.8a}$$

Combining the above relations gives us

$$\frac{dR}{R} = \frac{2P}{E} + \frac{d\rho}{\rho} \tag{14.9}$$

or

$$\frac{dR/R}{P} = \frac{2}{E} + \frac{d\rho/\rho}{P} . \tag{14.10}$$

Two metals are commonly used for resistance gages, manganin and an alloy of gold and 2.1% chromium. Both metals provide linear outputs with the following sensitivities: 1.692×10^{-7} and 0.673×10^{-7} ohm/ohm · psi for manganin and the gold alloy, respectively. Although the former possesses the greater pressure sensitivity, final selection must also be based on temperature sensitivity. Whereas manganin exhibits a resistance change of about 0.2% for the temperature range of 70–180°F, the corresponding change for the gold alloy is on the order of 0.01% [11]. Because of the difference, the gold alloy is generally preferred. The lower output is compensated for by greater electrical amplification.

14.11 MEASUREMENT OF LOW PRESSURES

Pressures may or may not be referred to the atmospheric datum as depicted in Fig. 14.1. We know, of course, that a *positive* magnitude of absolute pressure exists at all times. It is impossible to reach the absolute zero value. Atmospheric pressure, however, serves as a reference, and in general, pressures below atmospheric may be called low pressures or vacuums.

A common unit of low pressure is the *micron,* which is one-millionth of a meter (0.001 mm) of mercury column. *Very low* pressure may be defined as any below 1 mm of mercury, and an *ultralow* pressure as any less than a millimicron (10^{-3} micron). The torr is also used (Section 14.1).

There are two basic methods for measuring low pressure: (1) *direct* measurement resulting in a displacement caused by the action of force, and (2) *indirect* or *inferential* methods wherein pressure is determined through the measurement of certain other pressure-controlled properties, such as volume, thermal conductivity, etc. Devices included in the first category are spiral Bourdon tubes, flat and corrugated diaphragms, capsules, and various forms of manometers. Since these have been discussed in the preceding pages, they need not be discussed further here except to say that their use is generally limited to a lowest pressure value of about 10 mm of mercury. For measurement of pressures below this value, one of the inferential methods is normally dictated.

14.11.1 The McLeod Gage

Operation of the McLeod gage is based on Boyle's fundamental relation

$$P_1 = \frac{P_2 V_2}{V_1},\tag{14.11}$$

where P_1 and P_2 are pressures at initial and final conditions, respectively, and V_1 and V_2 are volumes at corresponding conditions. By compressing a known volume of the low pressure gas to a higher pressure and measuring the resulting volume and pressure, one can calculate the initial pressure.

Figure 14.18 illustrates the basic construction and operation of the McLeod gage. Measurement is made as follows. The unknown pressure source is connected at point A, and the mercury level is adjusted to fill the volume represented by the darker shading. Under these conditions the unknown pressure fills the bulb B and capillary C. Mercury is then forced out of the reservoir

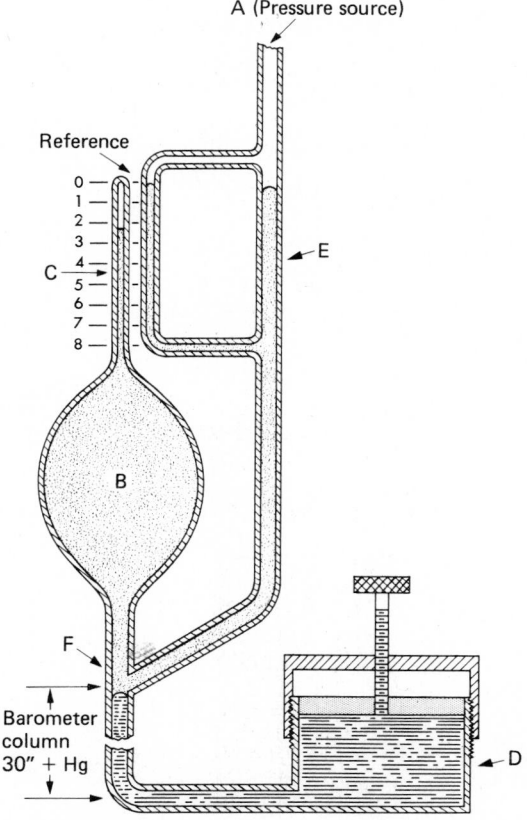

FIGURE 14.18   McLeod vacuum gage.

D, up into the bulb and reference column E. When the mercury level reaches the cutoff point F, a *known* volume of gas is trapped in the bulb and capillary. The mercury level is then further raised until it reaches a zero reference point in E. Under these conditions the volume remaining in the capillary is read directly from the scale, and the difference in heights of the two columns is the measure of the trapped pressure. The initial pressure may then be calculated by use of Boyle's law.

Pressure of gases containing vapors cannot normally be measured with a McLeod gage, for the reason that the compression will cause condensation. By use of instruments of different ranges, a total pressure range of from about 0.01 μ to 50 mm of mercury may be measured with this type of gage.

14.11.2 Thermal Conductivity Gages

The temperature of a given wire through which an electric current is flowing will depend on three factors: the magnitude of the current, the resistivity, and the rate at which the heat is dissipated. The latter will be largely dependent on the conductivity of the surrounding media. As the density of a given medium is reduced, its conductivity will also reduce and the wire will become hotter for a given current flow.

This is the basis for two different forms of gages for measurement of low pressures. Both use a heated filament, but differ in the means for measuring the temperature of the wire. A single platinum filament enclosed in a chamber is used by the *Pirani gage*. As the surrounding pressure changes, the filament temperature, and hence its resistance, also changes. The resistance change is measured by use of a resistance bridge that is calibrated in terms of pressure,

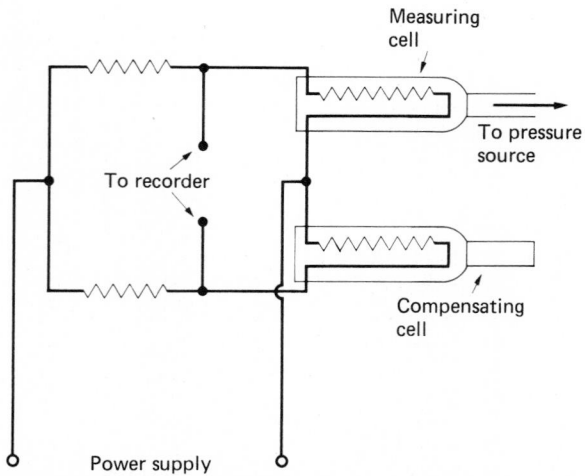

FIGURE 14.19   The Pirani-type thermal conductivity gage.

as shown in Fig. 14.19. A compensating cell is used to minimize variations caused by ambient temperature changes.

A second gage also depending on thermal conductivity is of the thermocouple type. In this case the filament temperatures are measured directly by means of thermocouples welded directly to them. Filaments and thermocouples are arranged in two chambers, as shown schematically in Fig. 14.20. When conditions in both the measuring and reference chambers are the same, no thermocouple current will flow. When the pressure in the measuring chamber is altered, changed conductivity will cause a change in temperature, which will then be indicated by a thermocouple current.

In both cases the gages must be calibrated for a definite pressurized medium, for the conductivity is also dependent on this factor. Gages of these types are useful in the range of 1 to 1000 microns.

14.11.3   Ionization Gages

For measurement of extremely low pressures, an ionization gage, which is usable to pressures down to 0.000001 micron (one-billionth of a millimeter of mercury), is used. The maximum pressure for which an ionization gage may be used is about 1 micron. An ionization cell for pressure measurement is

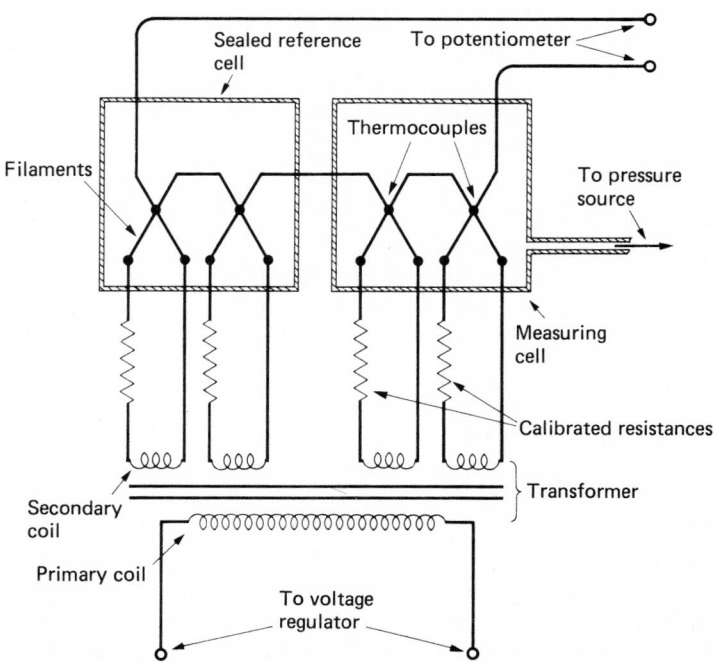

FIGURE 14.20   Thermocouple-type conductivity gage.

very similar to the ordinary triode electronic tube. It possesses a heated filament, a positively biased grid, and a negatively biased plate in an envelope evacuated by the pressure to be measured. The grid draws electrons from the heated filament, and collision between them and gas molecules causes ionization of the molecules. The positively charged molecules are then attracted to the plate of the tube, causing a current flow in the external circuit, which is a function of the gas pressure.

Disadvantages of the heated-filament ionization gage are: (1) Excessive pressure (above 1 or 2 microns) will cause rapid deterioration of the filament and a short life, and (2) the electron bombardment is a function of filament temperature, therefore requiring careful control of filament current. Another form of ionization gage minimizes these disadvantages by substituting a radioactive source of alpha particles for the heated filament.

14.12 DYNAMIC CHARACTERISTICS OF PRESSURE-MEASURING SYSTEMS

Basic pressure-measuring transducers are driven, damped, spring–mass systems whose isolated dynamic characteristics are theoretically similar to the generalized systems discussed in Chapter 3. In application, however, the actual dynamic characteristics of the complete pressure-measuring system are usually controlled more by factors extraneous to the basic pickup than by the pickup characteristics alone. In other words, overall dynamic performance is determined less by the transducer than by the manner in which it is inserted into the complete system.

When the pickup is used to measure a dynamic air or gas pressure, system damping will be determined to a considerable extent by factors external to the pickup. The extraneous pneumatic circuitry will have frequency characteristics of its own, affecting system response. When liquid pressures are measured, the effective sprung mass of the system will necessarily include some portion of the liquid mass. In addition, the elasticity of any conducting tubing will act to change the overall spring constant. Connecting tubing and unavoidable cavities in the pneumatic or hydraulic circuitry introduce losses and phase lags, causing differences between measured and applied pressures. Much theoretical work has been done in an attempt to evaluate these effects [12, 13, 14, 15, 16]. Each application, however, must be weighed on its own individual merits; for this reason only a general summary of some of the factors involved is practical in this discussion.

14.12.1 Gas-Filled Systems

As outlined above, the response of a pressure-measuring system involves more than the pickup characteristics alone. The complete system, including the method of conducting the pressure variation to the pickup, must be accounted for. In many applications it is necessary to transmit the pressure through some form of passageway or connecting tube. Figure 14.21 illustrates typical cases.

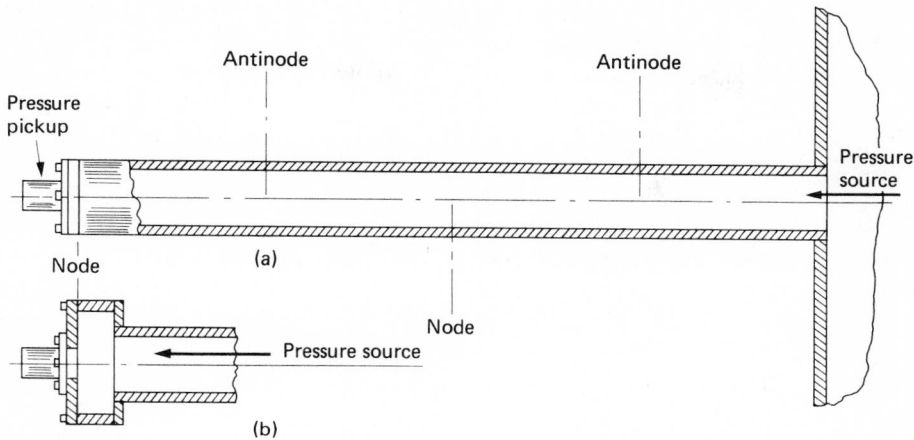

FIGURE 14.21   (a) Gas-filled pressure measuring system. (b) Gas-filled pressure-measuring system with cavity.

If the pressurized medium is a gas, such as air, acoustical resonances may occur in the same manner in which the air in an organ pipe resonates. If sympathetic driving frequencies are present, nodes and antinodes will occur, as shown in the figure. A node, characterized by a point of zero air motion, will occur at the blocked end. (This assumes that the displacement of the pressure-sensing element, such as a diaphragm, is negligible.) Maximum pressure variation takes place at this point. Maximum oscillatory motion will occur at the antinodes, and the distance between adjacent nodes and antinodes equals one-fourth the wavelength of the resonating frequency. Theoretical resonant frequencies may be determined from the relation

$$f = \frac{C}{4L}(2n - 1), \tag{14.12}$$

in which

f = the resonant frequencies (including both fundamental and harmonics), in Hz,

C = the velocity of sound in the pressurized medium,

L = the length of the connecting tube, and

n = any positive integer. (It will be noted from the equation that only odd harmonics occur.)

In many cases a cavity is required at the pickup end to adapt the instrument to the tubing, as shown in Fig. 14.21(b). If we assume that the medium is a gas, and that the elasticity of the containing system, including the pickup device, is relatively stiff compared with that of the gas, we have what is known as a Helmholtz resonator. The column of gas with its mass and elasticity form a spring–mass system having an acoustical resonance whose fundamental frequency may be expressed by the relation [17]

$$f = \frac{C}{2\pi}\sqrt{\frac{a}{V(L + \frac{1}{2}\sqrt{\pi a})}} \, , \tag{14.13}$$

. where

a = the cross-sectional area of the connecting tube, and

V = the net internal volume of the cavity, excluding the volume of the tube.

By proper configuration and proportioning, connecting systems of this type may be used for acoustical filtering [18]. In certain applications, quite sensitive or fragile sensing devices are required to measure small differential pressures. At the same time, high-energy pressure cycles may be present at frequencies above the range of interest and of sufficient intensity to cause pickup failure. This situation is often present in aircraft testing.

14.12.2 Liquid-Filled Systems

When a pressure-measuring system is filled with liquid rather than a gas, a considerably different situation is presented. The liquid becomes a major part of the total sprung mass, thereby becoming a significant factor in determining the natural frequency of the system.

If a single degree of freedom is assumed,

$$f_n = \frac{1}{2\pi}\sqrt{\frac{k_s g_c}{m}} \, , \tag{14.14}$$

in which

f_n = the natural frequency, in Hz,

m = the equivalent moving mass = $m_1 + m_2$,

m_1 = the mass of moving transducer elements,

m_2 = the equivalent mass of the liquid column,

$k_s = \dfrac{k_t k_1}{k_t + k_1}$ = the overall system stiffness,

k_t = the transducer stiffness, and

k_1 = the transmitting medium stiffness.

By simplified analysis, White [19] has determined the following approximate relation for the effective mass of the liquid column:

$$m_2 = \tfrac{4}{3}\,\rho a L (A/a)^2, \tag{14.15}$$

in which

ρ = the fluid density,

a = the sectional area of the tube,

L = the length of the tube, and

A = the effective area of the transducer-sensing element.

It will be noted that A is the *effective* area, which is not necessarily equal to the actual diaphragm or bellows area, but may be defined by the relation

$$A = \Delta V / \Delta y, \tag{14.16}$$

where

Δv = the volume change accompanying sensing-element deflection and

Δy = the significant displacement of the sensing element.

By substitution, we have

$$f_n = \frac{1}{2\pi}\sqrt{\frac{k_s \cdot g_c}{m_1 + \tfrac{4}{3}\rho a L (A/a)^2}}\,. \tag{14.17}$$

In many cases the equivalent mass of the liquid, m_2, is of considerably greater magnitude than m_1, and the latter may be ignored without introducing an appreciable discrepancy. By so doing and substituting, we get

$$a = \pi D^2/4,$$

$$D = \text{tubing I.D.},$$

$$f_n = \frac{D}{8A}\sqrt{\frac{3k_s \cdot g_c}{\pi \rho L}}\,. \tag{14.18}$$

As mentioned before, pressure pickups involve spring-restrained masses in the same manner as do galvanometers and seismic-type accelerometers, and therefore good frequency response is obtainable only in a frequency range well below the natural frequency of the measuring system itself. For this reason it is desirable that the pressure-measuring system have as high a natural frequency as is consistent with required sensitivity and installation requirements. Inspection of Eq. (14.18) indicates that the diameter of the connecting tube should be as large as practical and that its length should be minimized.

In addition, it has been shown that optimum performance for systems of this general type requires damping in rather definite amounts. White [19] gives the following relation for the damping ratio ξ of a system of the sort being discussed:

$$\xi = \frac{4\pi L v (A/a)^2}{\sqrt{k_s m/g_c}} \tag{14.19}$$

$$= \frac{4\pi L v (A/a)^2}{\sqrt{(k_s/g_c)[m_1 + \frac{4}{3}\rho a L (A/a)^2]}}, \tag{14.20}$$

where v = the viscosity of the fluid. If we ignore m_1 and insert $a = \pi D^2/4$, we may write the equation as

$$\xi = \frac{16 v A}{D^2} \sqrt{\frac{3L \cdot g_c}{\pi k_s \rho}}. \tag{14.21}$$

14.13   CALIBRATION METHODS

14.13.1   Methods for Static Pressures

Static calibration of pressure gages presents no particular problems unless the upper pressure limits are unusually high. The familiar dead-weight tester (Fig. 14.8) may be used to accurately supply reference pressures with which transducer outputs may be compared. Testers of this type are useful to pressures as high as 10,000 psi, and by use of special designs, this limit may be extended to 100,000 psi.

Although static calibration is desirable, pickups used for dynamic measurement should also receive some form of dynamic calibration. Dynamic calibration problems consist of (1) obtaining a satisfactory source of pressure, either periodic or pulsed, and (2) reliably determining the true pressure–time relation produced by such a source. These two problems will be discussed in the next few paragraphs.

To be a standard, the precise pressure–time relation must be known. Some sources of dynamic pressure are as follows:

   I. Steady-state periodic sources

      A. Piston and chamber

      B. Cam-controlled jet

      C. Acoustic resonator

      D. Siren disk

  II. Transient sources

      A. Quick-release valve

      B. Burst diaphragm

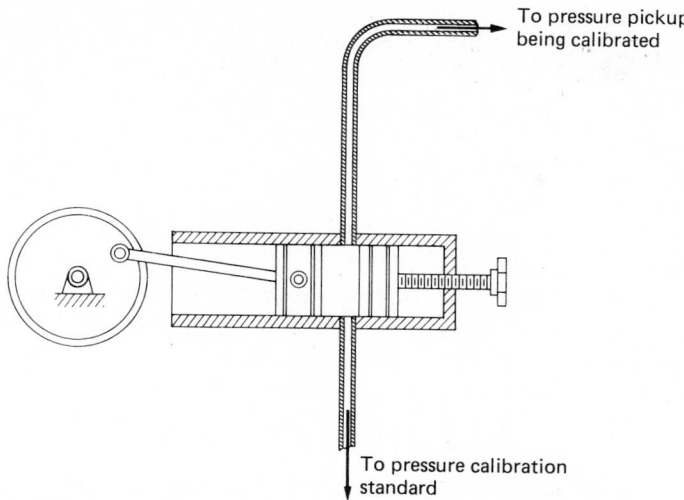

To pressure pickup
being calibrated

To pressure calibration
standard

FIGURE 14.22   Schematic diagram of a piston and cylinder steady-state pressure source.

C. Closed bomb

D. Shock tube

14.13.2 Steady-State Methods

One source of steady-state periodic calibration pressure is simply an ordinary
piston and cylinder arrangement, shown schematically in Fig. 14.22 [20]. If
the piston stroke is fixed, pressure amplitude may be varied by adjusting the
cylinder volume. Although such a system is normally special-purpose, existing
equipment, such as a CFR* engine, may be adapted for this use. Amplitude
and frequency ranges will depend on the mechanical design; however, peak
pressures of 1000 psi and frequencies to 100 Hz may be obtained.

A method very similar to this is used for microphone calibration. In this
case required pressure amplitudes are quite small, and instead of the piston's
being driven with a mechanical linkage, an electromagnetic system is used
[21]. Piston excursion may be determined by the technique described in Section
17.10. This suggests the possibility of using vibration test shakers (Section
17.16) as a source of piston motion for this method of calibration [22].

A variation of the piston source is to drive a diaphragm, bellows, or
Bourdon tube. The latter has been successfully used by flexing it by means
of an eccentric attached to the end of the tube through a link or connecting
rod [23].

---

*   Cooperative Fuels Research.

Figure 14.23 illustrates another method for obtaining a steady-state periodic pressure. A source of this type has been used to 3000 Hz with amplitudes to 1 psi [6]. A variation of this method uses a motor-driven siren-type disk having a series of holes drilled in it so as to alternately vent a pressure source to atmosphere and then shut it off [24].

Another successful system is to use a variable-speed motor to drive a pressure transmitter by means of a circular cam [25]. The transmitter is essentially an adjustable servo valve that controls the output from a constant-pressure source.

Steady-state sinusoidal pressure generators consisting of an acoustically driven resonant system (see Section 14.12.1) have been used. Hylkema and Bowersox [15] obtained pressure fluctuations on the order of 0.5 psi rms, using a 40-inch long pipe energized with a 35-watt loudspeaker type of driving unit. Usable frequencies to about 2000 Hz in integral multiples of the fundamental were obtained.

All the methods suggested above simply supply sources of pressure variation, but in themselves do not provide means for determining magnitudes or time characteristics. They are particularly useful, however, for comparing pickups having unknown characteristics with those of proven performance.

14.13.3 Transient Methods

Steady-state periodic sources used to determine dynamic characteristics of pressure transducers are limited by amplitude and frequency that can be produced. High amplitudes and steady-state frequencies are difficult to obtain simultaneously. For this reason it is necessary to resort to some form of step

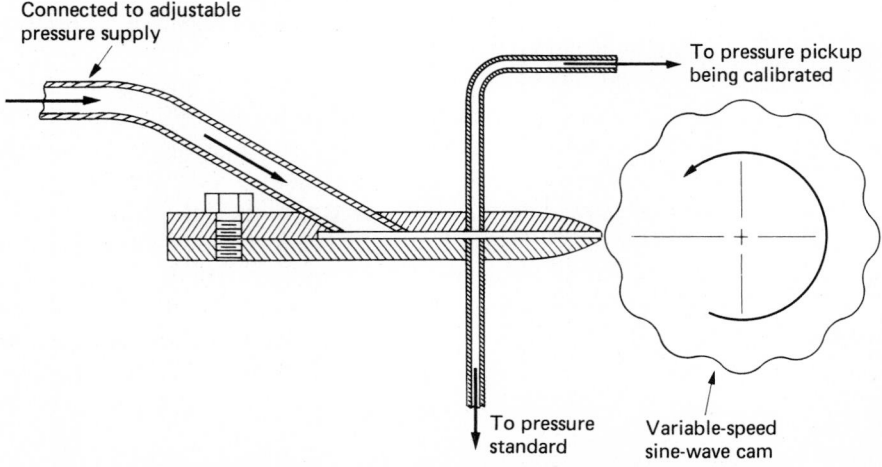

FIGURE 14.23   Jet and cam steady-state pressure source.

function in order to determine high-frequency response of pressure transducers in the higher amplitude ranges.

Various methods are used to produce the necessary pulse. One of the simplest is to use a fast-acting valve between a source of hydraulic pressure and the pickup. Rise times, from 0 to 90% of full pressure, of 10 milliseconds are reported [26].

Pressure steps may also be obtained through use of bursting diaphragms. Two chambers are separated by a thin plastic diaphragm or plate whose failure is mechanically induced by a plunger or knife. It has been found that a pressure drop, rather than a rise, produces a more nearly ideal step function. Drop time on the order of $\frac{1}{4}$ millisecond has been obtained [15].

Still another source of stepped-pressure function is the closed bomb, in which a pressure generator such as a dynamite cap is exploded. Peak pressure is controlled by net internal volume, and pressure steps as high as 700 psi in 0.3 ms have been obtained [15].

Undoubtedly the so-called *shock tube* provides the nearest thing to a transient pressure "standard." Construction of a shock tube is quite simple: it consists of a long tube, closed at both ends, separated into two chambers by a diaphragm, as shown in Fig. 14.24. A pressure differential is built up across the diaphragm, and the diaphragm is burst, either directly by the pressure differential or initiated by means of an externally controlled probe, or *dagger*. Rupturing of the diaphragm causes a pressure discontinuity, or *shock wave,* to travel into the region of the lower pressure and a rarefaction wave to travel through the chamber of initially higher pressure. The reduced pressure wave is reflected from the end of the chamber and follows the stepped pressure down the tube at a velocity that is higher because it is added to the velocity already possessed by the gas particles from the pressure step. Figure 14.25 illustrates the sequence of events immediately following the bursting of the diaphragm.

A relationship between pressures and shock-wave velocity may be expressed as follows [27]:

$$P_1/P_0 = 1 + [2k/(k + 1)][M_0^2 - 1], \qquad (14.22)$$

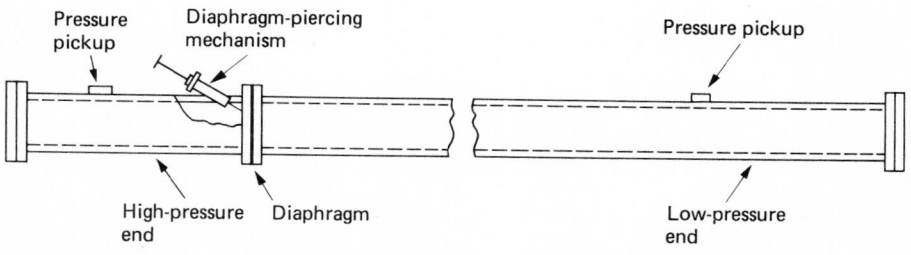

Pressure pickup   Diaphragm-piercing mechanism   Pressure pickup

High-pressure end   Diaphragm   Low-pressure end

FIGURE 14.24 Basic shock tube.

in which

P_1 = the intermediate transient pressure,

P_0 = the lower initial pressure,

k = the ratio of specific heats, and

M_0 = the Mach number corresponding to the lower initial conditions.

We see, then, that if the gas properties are known, measurement of the propagation velocity will be sufficient to determine the magnitude of the pressure pulse. Propagation velocity may be determined from information supplied by accurately positioned pressure pickups in the wall of the tube. By this means, a known transient pressure pulse may be applied to a pressure transducer or to a complete pressure-measuring system simply by mounting the pickup in the wall of the shock tube. The response characteristics, as determined in this manner, may then be used to calculate the general response of the device or system over a spectrum of frequencies [28]. The methods for doing this, however, are beyond the scope of this book, and the large amount of computation required is particularly adaptable to the modern digital computer.

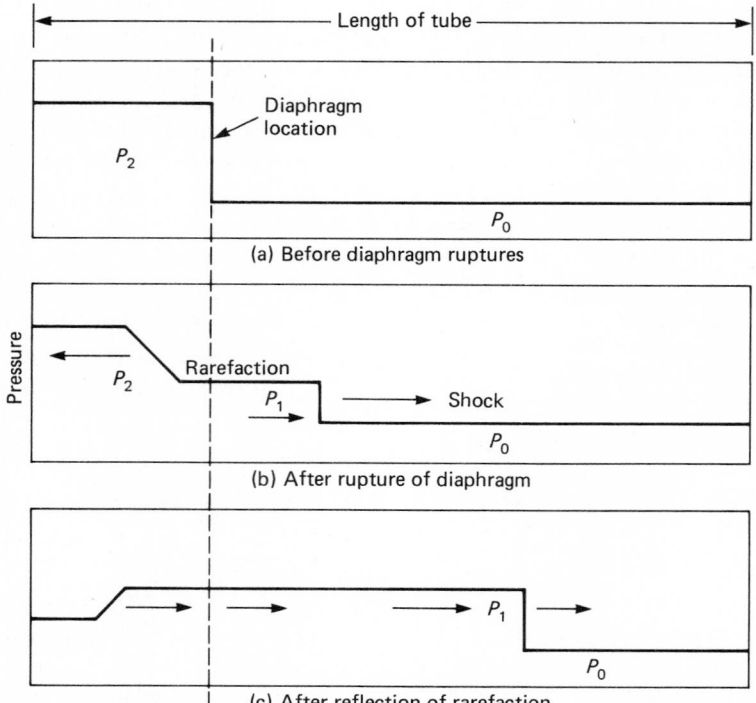

FIGURE 14.25   Pressure sequence in a shock tube before and immediately after diaphragm is ruptured. Abscissa represents longitudinal axis of tube.

14.14 CONCLUDING REMARKS

An attempt has been made in the preceding pages to introduce the reader to some of the problems attending accurate experimental determination of pressure. We realize that many approaches to the problem have been omitted and that in certain respects the coverage has been brief and somewhat superficial. Such is a penalty that must be paid in assembling a book of this nature. For more detailed discussions, the reader is referred to the Suggested Readings for this chapter.

SUGGESTED READINGS

ASME PTC 19.2-1964, *Pressure Measurement.*

Benedict, R. P., *Fundamentals of Temperature, Pressure and Flow Measurements,* 2nd ed. New York: John Wiley, 1977.

Rombacher, W. G., *Survey of Micromanometers.* NBS Monograph 114. Washington, D.C.: U.S. Government Printing Office, 1970.

Schweppe, L. C., et al., *Methods for the Dynamic Calibration of Pressure Transducers.* NBS Monograph 67. Washington, D.C.: U.S. Government Printing Office, 1963.

PROBLEMS

14.1 Standard atmospheric pressure is 1.01325×10^2 kPa. What are the equivalents in (a) newtons per square meter, (b) pounds-force per square foot, (c) meters of water (head), (d) inches of 0.89 specific gravity oil, (e) millibars, (f) microns, and (g) torr?

14.2 Determine the factors for converting pressure in pascals to "head" in (a) meters of water; (b) centimeters of mercury.

14.3 The following are some commonly encountered pressures (approximate). Convert each to the SI units, pascals and kPa: (a) automobile tire pressure of 24 psig; (b) household water pressure of 120 psia; (c) regulation football pressure of 13 psig.

14.4 Rewrite Eq. (14.3) in terms of specific gravities.

14.5 First in SI units and then in English units:

   a) Write expressions relating the height of a fluid column in terms of a reduced gage pressure (a vacuum).

   b) Under standard conditions of atmosphere and gravity, what is the maximum height to which water may be raised by suction alone?

   c) Under similar conditions, to what height may a column of mercury be raised?

   d) On the surface of the moon, what is the height to which water could be raised by suction alone? (See Appendix D for data.)

14.6 The common mercury barometer may be formed by sealing the upper end of a tube (e.g., Fig. 14.4), inverting it and filling it with mercury, then righting the tube into a mercury-filled reservoir. This forms a vacuum over the column and the height of the column is governed primarily by the pressure (air pressure) applied at the base. Under these conditions is a true zero absolute pressure (a complete vacuum) formed over the column? Investigate the vapor pressure of mercury and determine the degree of error introduced if it is ignored.

14.7 The U-tube-type manometer (Fig. 14.5) uses mercury and water as the manometer and transmitting fluids, respectively. What value of h should be expected at 20°C, if the applied differential pressure is 80 kPa (11.6 psig)? (See Appendix D for data.) Use SI units.

14.8 Solve Problem 14.7 using English units.

14.9 Figure 14.26 illustrates a manometer installation. Write an expression for determining the static pressure in the conduit in terms of h_1, h_2, and the other pertinent parameters.

14.10 For the conditions shown in Fig. 14.26, if the manometer fluid is Hg and the conduit fluid is H_2O (both at 20°C), $h_1 = 18.4$ cm (7.24 in.), and $h_2 = 0.7$ m (2.30 ft), what pressure exists in the conduit? Solve using SI units.

14.11 Solve Problem 14.10 using English units.

14.12 Confirm Eq. (14.4).

14.13 Note that Eq. (14.4) is based on a moving datum, namely, the liquid level in the reservoir. Derive an equation for the differential pressure based on the movement of the liquid in the inclined column only. (Note that a practical solution would be to make provision for adjusting the reservoir level to an index or "zero" line.)

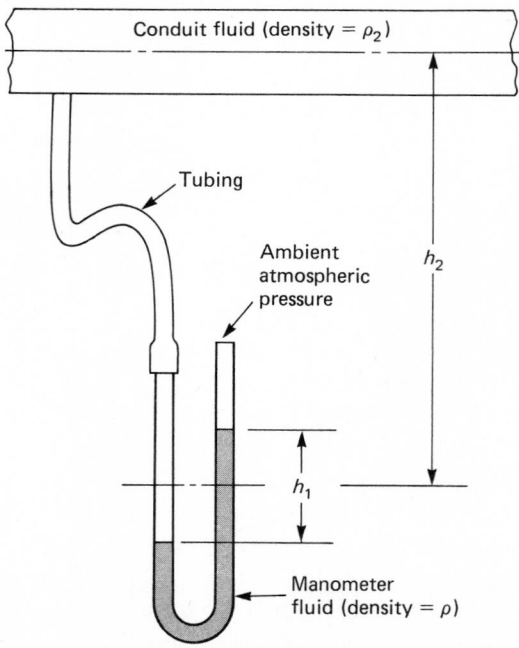

FIGURE 14.26   Manometer arrangement referred to in Problem 14.9.

14.14 Express the ratio of sensitivities of an inclined manometer (Fig. 14.6) to that of a simple manometer in terms of the angle θ. For an inclined manometer six times more sensitive than a simple manometer, what should be the angle of incline?

14.15 Confirm Eqs. (14.5) and (14.5a).

14.16 The manometer shown in Fig. 14.7 uses water and carbon tetrachloride as the two fluids (see Appendix D for data). If the area ratio is 0.01, what magnification will result as compared to the simple manometer using (a) water as the fluid and (b) carbon tetrachloride as the fluid?

14.17 Derive an expression for the two-fluid manometer in Fig. 14.7, substituting reservoirs of diameters D_1 and D_2 for the like-sized reservoirs shown in the figure.

14.18 A two-fluid manometer as shown in Fig. 14.7 uses a combination of kerosene (specific gravity, 0.80) and alcohol-diluted water (specific gravity, 0.83). Also, $d = \frac{1}{4}$ in. (6.35 mm) and $D = 2$ in. (50.8 mm). What amplification ratio is obtained with this arrangement as compared to a simple water manometer? What error would be introduced if the ratio of diameters were ignored?

14.19 For a circular diaphragm of the type and loading shown in Fig. 14.11a, the maximum normal stress occurs in the radial direction at the outer boundary, expressed as follows [29]:

$$\sigma_r = \tfrac{3}{4}(a/t)^2 P.$$

Greatest linear deflection occurs at the center and is equal to

$$Y_{max} = \left(\frac{3}{16}\right)(Pa^4/Et^3)(1 - v^2),$$

where

$$P = \text{pressure,}$$

$$a = \text{radius,}$$

$$E = \text{Young's modulus, and}$$

$$v = \text{Poisson's ratio.}$$

For $a = \frac{1}{4}$ in. (6.35 mm), $E = 30 \times 10^6$ psi (20.68×10^7 kPa), and $v = 0.3$, and for a design stress of 9×10^4 psi (6.2×10^5 kPa), what maximum deflection may be expected if $P = 300$ psi (2.07×10^3 kPa)?

14.20 Solve Problem 14.19 using SI units and reconcile the two answers.

14.21 A thin-wall, cylindrically sectioned tube of nominal diameter D and wall thickness t is subjected to a pressure P. Circumferential (hoop) and longitudinal stresses may be determined from the relations $\sigma_H = PD/2t$ and $\sigma_L = PD/4t$ (see Example E.2, Appendix E). Using Eqs. (12.3) show that the corresponding circumferential and longitudinal strains are

$$\varepsilon_H = (PD/2Et)(1 - \tfrac{1}{2}v) \quad \text{and} \quad \varepsilon_L = (PD/2Et)(\tfrac{1}{2} - v).$$

14.22 A pressure transducer is constructed from a steel tube having a nominal diameter of 15 mm (0.59 in.) and a wall thickness of 2 mm (0.0787 in.).

a) If the design stress is limited to 2.75×10^8 Pa (39,885 psi), what maximum pressure may be applied to the transducer?

b) For the maximum pressure calculated in part (a), determine the circumferential and longitudinal strains that should be expected. Use $E = 20 \times 10^{10}$ Pa (29×10^6 psi) and $\nu = 0.3$.

14.23 Solve Problem 14.22 using English units.

14.24 The simple stress relations given in Problem 14.21 assume a uniform stress distribution through the wall of the cylinder. For "heavy" wall cylinders, this simplifying assumption leads to error and the following more complex relations must be used:

$$\sigma_H = P(D^2 + d^2)/(D^2 - d^2) \text{ on the inner surface,}$$

$$\sigma_H = 2Pd^2/(D^2 - d^2) \text{ on the outer surface,}$$

$$\sigma_L = Pd^2/(D^2 - d^2), \text{ and}$$

$$\sigma_r = -P \text{ on the inner surface.}$$

All are principal stresses (see Appendix E).

a) For a design stress of 2.75×10^8 Pa (39,885 psi), $d = 2$ cm (0.787 in.), and $D = 5$ cm (1.968 in.), what is the maximum pressure that may be applied?

b) If the maximum pressure is applied, what circumferential and longitudinal strains should be expected on the outer surface? Use 0.3 for Poisson's ratio and 20×10^{10} Pa for Young's modulus.

14.25 Solve Problem 14.24 using English units.

14.26 Derive Eq. (14.6).

14.27 The speed of sound in a gas, C, may be expressed by the relation [1]

$$C = [kRTg_c]^{1/2},$$

where

$$k = \text{the ratio of specific heats } (= 1.4 \text{ for air}),$$

$$R = \text{the gas constant} = 288 \text{ J/kg} \cdot \text{K},$$

$$T = \text{absolute temperature, and}$$

$$g_c = \text{the dimensional constant.}$$

Using the above equation and Eq. (14.12), determine the change in frequency in percent, corresponding to a temperature change from 10 to 40°C.

14.28 A pressure-measuring system involves a $\frac{1}{4}$-in. diameter tube, 24 in. long, connecting a pressure source to a transducer. At the transducer end there is a cylindrical cavity $\frac{1}{2}$ in. in diameter and $\frac{1}{2}$ in. long. Proper performance requires that the frequency of applied pressures be such as to avoid resonance. Calculate the resonant frequency of the system.

14.29 Assume that the 24-in. connecting tube used in Problem 14.28 is reduced to zero length. What will be the resonant frequency? (Use Eq. 14.13, letting $L = 0$.)

14.30 A Helmholtz resonator consists of a spherical cavity to which a circularly sectioned tube is attached. It may be considered as approximating the tube and cavity of Problem 14.28. The resonant frequency of a Helmholtz resonator may be estimated by the relation

$$f = \frac{C}{2\pi} \sqrt{\frac{a}{VL}}$$

(see [2] in Chapter 18). (The symbols have the same meaning as in Eq. 14.13.) Use this equation to estimate the resonant frequency of the system described in Problem 14.28.

15.1 INTRODUCTION

Accurate measurement of flow presents many and varied problems. The flowing medium may be liquid, gaseous, a granular solid, or any combination of these. The flow may be laminar or turbulent, steady-state or transient. In addition, there are several very different *basic* approaches to the problem of flow measurement. This section, therefore, will present only an outline of some of the more important aspects of the general topic.

Flow measurement methods may be categorized according to device or method as follows:

I. Primary or quantity methods

  A. Weight or volume tanks, burettes, etc.

  B. Positive-displacement meters

II. Secondary or rate devices

  A. Obstruction meters

   1. The venturi

   2. Flow nozzles

   3. Orifices

   4. Variable-area meters

  B. Velocity probes

   1. Total-pressure probes

   2. Static-pressure probes

   3. Direction-sensing probes

  C. Special methods

   1. Turbine-type meters

   2. Thermal or hot-wire meters

3. Magnetic flowmeters

4. Sonic flowmeters

5. Mass flowmeters

6. Pulse-producing methods

The above outline does not exhaust the list of flow-measuring systems, but does attempt to include those of primary interest to the mechanical engineer. Application of some of the methods listed is so obvious that only passing note will be made of them. This is particularly true of *quantity* methods. Weight tanks are especially useful for steady-state calibration of liquid flow meters, and no particular problems are connected with their use.

There are many forms or variations of displacement meters. Common examples are the water and gas meters used by suppliers to establish charges for services. Basically, displacement meters are hydraulic or pneumatic motors whose cycles of motion are recorded by some form of counter. Only such energy from the stream is absorbed as is necessary to overcome the friction in the device, and this is manifested by a pressure drop between inlet and outlet. Most of the configurations used for motors have been applied to metering. These include reciprocating and oscillating pistons, vane arrangements, including the nutating (or nodding) disk, helical screw devices, etc.

15.2 FLOW CHARACTERISTICS

When fluids move through uniform conduits at very low velocities, the motions of individual particles are generally along lines paralleling the conduit walls. Actual particle velocity is greatest at the center and theoretically zero at the wall, with the velocity distribution as shown in Fig. 15.1(a). Plots of individual loci are called *streamlines,* and the flow is called *laminar* or *viscous.*

As the flow rate is increased, a point is reached when the particle motion becomes more random and complex. Although this change in the nature of flow may appear to occur at a definite velocity, careful observation will show that the change is somewhat gradual over a relatively narrow range of velocities. The *approximate* velocity at which the change occurs is called the *critical velocity,* and the flow at higher rates is referred to as *turbulent.* The corresponding velocity distribution across a circular tube is shown in Fig. 15.1(b).

It has been found that the critical velocity is a function of several factors that may be put in a dimensionless form called the Reynolds number, R_D,* as follows:

$$R_D = D\rho V/\mu, \tag{15.1}$$

---

* The units for absolute viscosity are $N \cdot s/m^2$ (or $lbf \cdot s/ft^2$), depending on the system of units used. We see that although the form of Eq. (15.1) as written is most common, inclusion of g_c is required to obtain a proper unit balance.

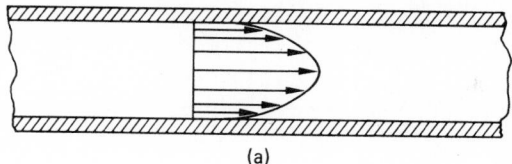

(a)

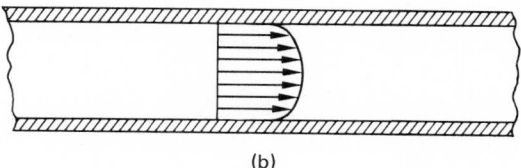

(b)

FIGURE 15.1   Velocity distribution for (a) laminar flow in a pipe or tube, (b) turbulent flow in a pipe or tube.

where

D = a sectional dimension of the fluid stream (normally the diameter if the conduit is a pipe of circular section),[†]

ρ = the density of the fluid,

V = the fluid velocity, and

μ = the absolute viscosity of the fluid.

See Section 1.7 for examples of commonly used units.

It has been shown by many investigators [1] that below the critical-velocity range, friction loss in pipes is a function of R_D only, while for turbulent flow, the Reynolds number combined with surface roughness determines the losses. The critical Reynolds number for pipes is usually between 2000 and 2300.

Bernoulli's equation for the flow of incompressible fluids between points 1 and 2 (Fig. 15.2) may be written

$$(P_1 - P_2)/\rho = (V_2^2 - V_1^2)/2g_c + (Z_2 - Z_1)g/g_c, \qquad (15.2)$$

in which

P = absolute pressure,	lbf/ft²	N/m² (or Pa)
ρ = density,	lbm/ft³	kg/m³

[†]   The subscript D is used to indicate nominal pipe diameter. When Reynolds number is based, for example, on the throat diameter of a venturi or an orifice, the lower-case d is commonly used, e.g., R_d.

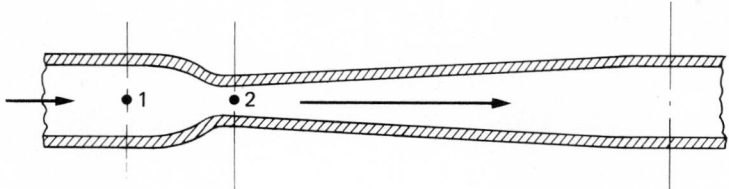

FIGURE 15.2   Section through a restriction in a pipe or tube.

V = linear velocity,	ft/s	m/s
Z = elevation,	ft	m
g = acceleration due to gravity,	32.17 ft/s^2	9.807 m/s^2
g_c = dimensional constant.	32.17 lbm·ft/lbf·s^2	1 kg·m/N·s^2

As written above, the relationship assumes that there is no mechanical work done on or by the fluid and that there is no heat transferred to or from the fluid as it passes between points 1 and 2. This equation provides the basis for evaluating the operation of flow-measuring devices generally classified as *obstruction meters*.

15.3   OBSTRUCTION METERS

Figure 15.3 shows three common forms of obstruction meters: the venturi, the flow nozzle, and the orifice. In each case the basic meter acts as an obstacle placed in the path of the flowing fluid, causing localized changes in velocity. Concurrently with velocity change, there will be pressure change, as illustrated in the figure. At points of maximum restriction, hence maximum velocity, minimum pressures are found. A certain portion of this pressure drop becomes irrecoverable; therefore, the output pressure will always be less than the input pressure. This is indicated in the figure, which shows the venturi, with its guided re-expansion, to be the most efficient. Losses on the order of 30–40% of the differential pressure occur through the orifice meter.

15.3.1   Obstruction Meters for Incompressible Flow

For *incompressible fluids*,

$$\rho_1 = \rho_2 = \rho \quad \text{and} \quad Q = A_1 V_1 = A_2 V_2,$$

where

$$Q = \text{volume/unit time and}$$

$$A = \text{area.}$$

If we let $Z_1 = Z_2$ and substitute $V_1 = (A_2/A_1)V_2$ in Eq. (15.2), we obtain

$$P_1 - P_2 = [V_2^2\rho/2g_c][1 - (A_2/A_1)^2] \tag{15.3}$$

and

$$Q_{\text{ideal}} = A_2 V_2 = \left[\frac{A_2}{\sqrt{1 - (A_2/A_1)^2}}\right]\sqrt{2g_c(P_1 - P_2)/\rho} . \tag{15.4}$$

For a given meter, A_1 and A_2 are established values, and it is often convenient to calculate

$$E = \frac{1}{\sqrt{1 - (A_2/A_1)^2}} . \tag{15.4a}$$

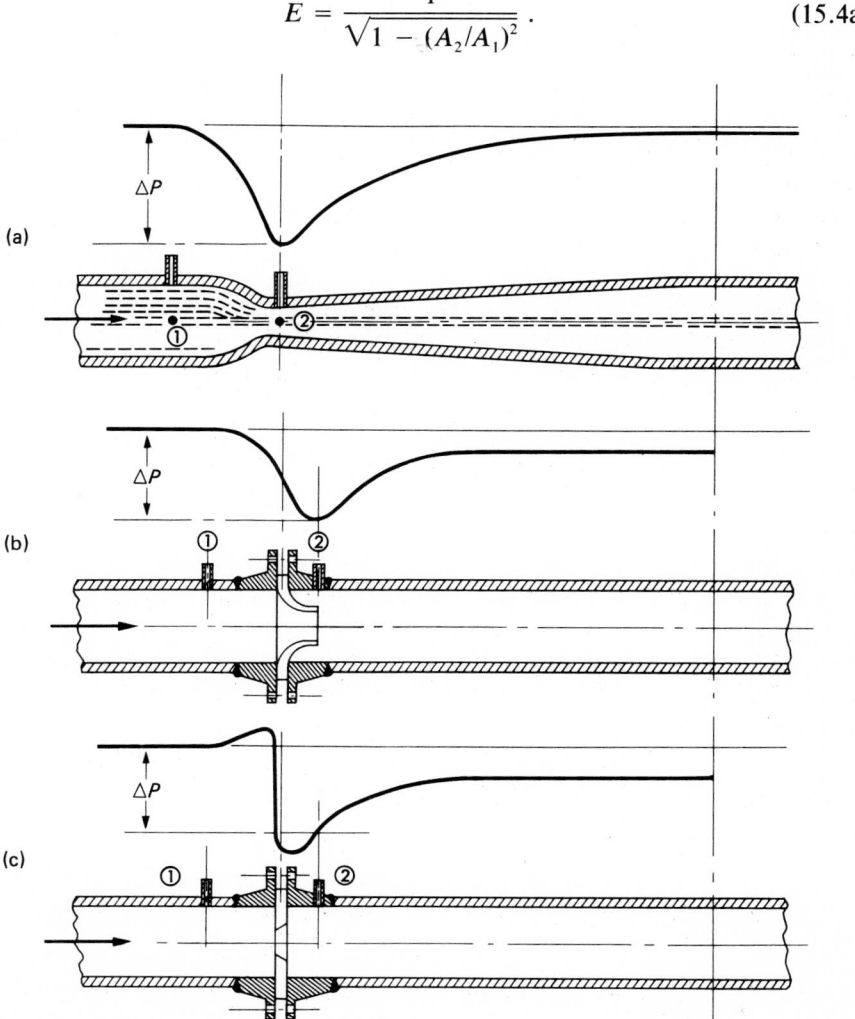

FIGURE 15.3   (a) A venturi. (b) A flow-nozzle. (c) An orifice flowmeter.

For circular sections, the area $= \pi(\text{diameter})^2/4$, hence

$$E = 1/\sqrt{1 - \beta^4} \tag{15.4b}$$

where

$$\beta = d/D$$

and

$$D = \text{the larger diameter and}$$

$$d = \text{the smaller diameter.}$$

We call E the *velocity of approach factor*.

Two additional factors used in obstruction meter calculations are the *discharge coefficient*, C, and the *flow coefficient*, K. These are defined as follows:

$$C = Q_{\text{actual}}/Q_{\text{ideal}} \tag{15.4c}$$

and

$$K = CE = C/\sqrt{1 - \beta^4}. \tag{15.4d}$$

The discharge coefficient C is the factor that accounts for losses through the meter, and the flow coefficient K is used as a matter of convenience, combining the loss factor with the meter constants.

Therefore, we may write

$$Q_{\text{actual}} = KA_2\sqrt{\frac{2g_c}{\rho}}\sqrt{P_1 - P_2}. \tag{15.5}$$

15.3.2   Venturi Characteristics

Venturi proportions are not standardized; however, the dimensional ranges shown in Fig. 15.4 include most cases. They are high-efficiency devices with discharge coefficients falling within a narrow range, depending on the finish of the entrance cone. For the Venturi [2],

$$0.95 < C < 0.98.$$

15.3.3   Flow-Nozzle Characteristics

Figure 15.5 illustrates examples of two "standard" types of flow nozzles. The approach curve must be proportioned to prevent separation between the flow and the wall, and the parallel section is used to ensure that the flow fills the throat. The usual range of discharge coefficients is shown in Fig. 15.6. In addition, the following empirical equation is listed in reference [2] for evaluating the discharge coefficient:

$$C = 0.99622 + 0.00059D - (6.36 + 0.13D - 0.24\beta^2)/R_d. \tag{15.6}$$

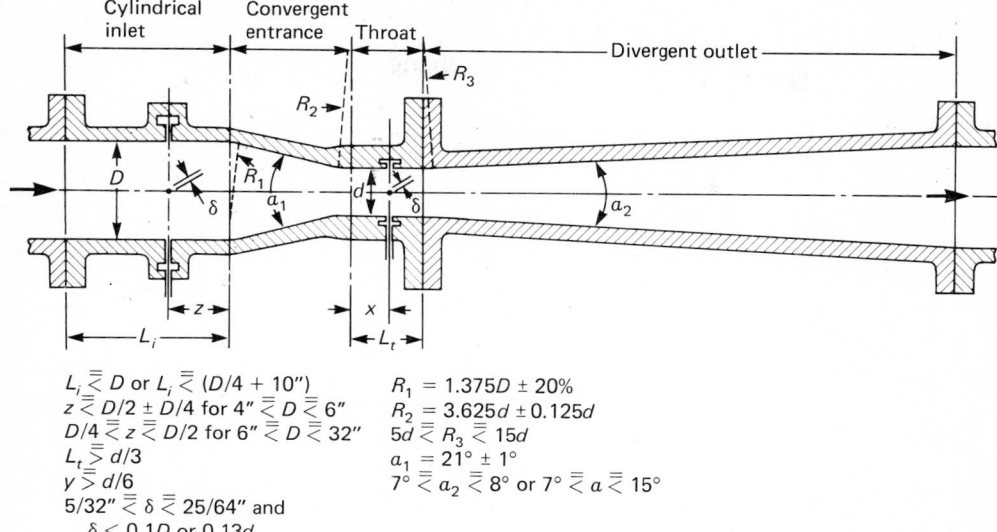

$L_i \gtreqless D$ or $L_i \lesseqgtr (D/4 + 10")$
$z \lesseqgtr D/2 \pm D/4$ for $4" \gtreqless D \lesseqgtr 6"$
$D/4 \gtreqless z \lesseqgtr D/2$ for $6" \gtreqless D \lesseqgtr 32"$
$L_t \gtreqless d/3$
$y \gtrless d/6$
$5/32" \gtreqless \delta \lesseqgtr 25/64"$ and
   $\delta < 0.1D$ or $0.13d$

$R_1 = 1.375D \pm 20\%$
$R_2 = 3.625d \pm 0.125d$
$5d \lesseqgtr R_3 \lesseqgtr 15d$
$a_1 = 21° \pm 1°$
$7° \lesseqgtr a_2 \lesseqgtr 8°$ or $7° \lesseqgtr a \lesseqgtr 15°$

FIGURE 15.4 Recommended proportions of Herschel-type venturi tubes. Source: ASME, *Fluid Meters*, 6th ed., 1971.

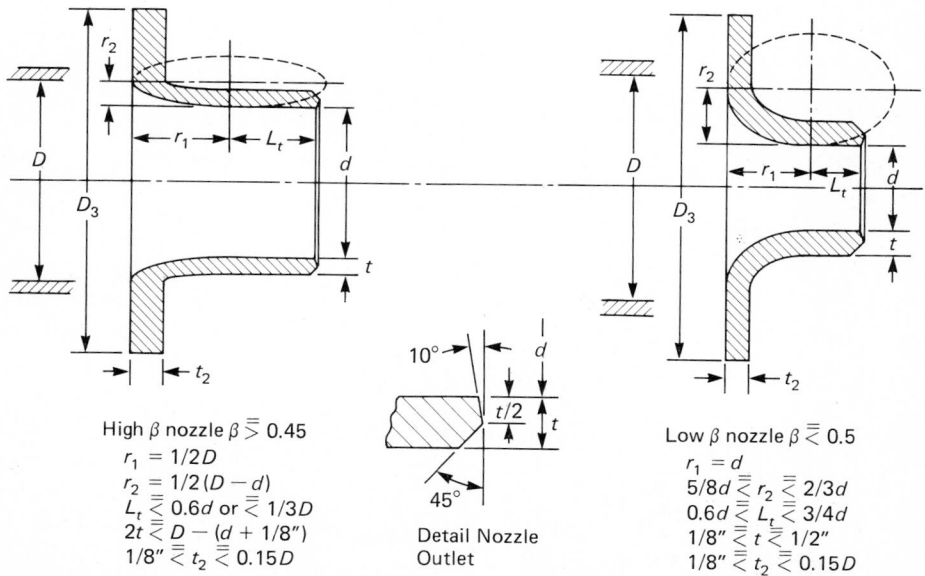

High β nozzle $\beta \gtreqless 0.45$
$r_1 = 1/2D$
$r_2 = 1/2(D - d)$
$L_t \lesseqgtr 0.6d$ or $\lesseqgtr 1/3D$
$2t \lesseqgtr D - (d + 1/8")$
$1/8" \gtreqless t_2 \lesseqgtr 0.15D$

Detail Nozzle
Outlet

Low β nozzle $\beta \lesseqgtr 0.5$
$r_1 = d$
$5/8d \lesseqgtr r_2 \lesseqgtr 2/3d$
$0.6d \lesseqgtr L_t \lesseqgtr 3/4d$
$1/8" \gtreqless t \lesseqgtr 1/2"$
$1/8" \gtreqless t_2 \lesseqgtr 0.15D$

FIGURE 15.5 Dimensional relations for ASME long-radius flow nozzles. Source: ASME, *Fluid Meters*, 6th ed., 1971.

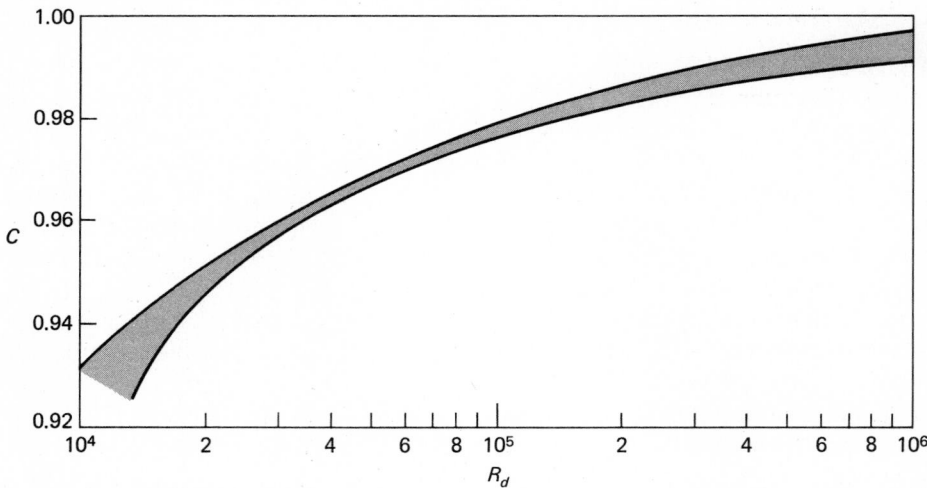

FIGURE 15.6   Range of discharge coefficients for long-radius flow nozzles.

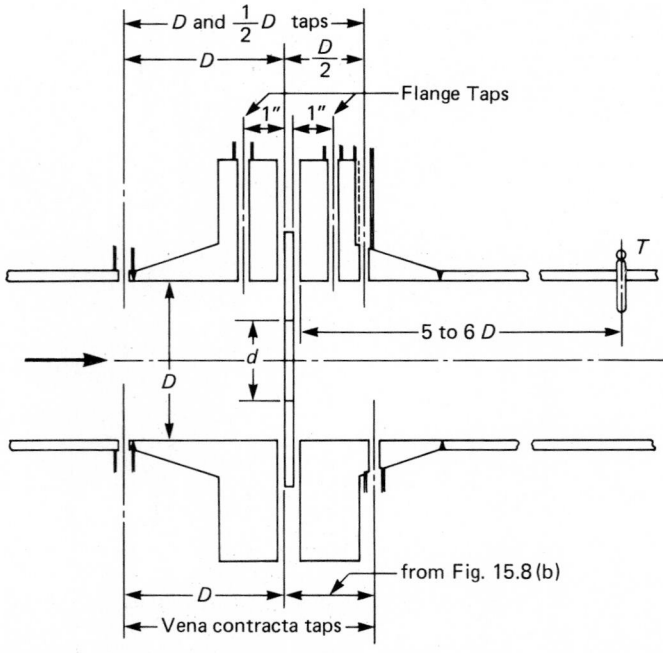

FIGURE 15.7   Locations of pressure-taps for use with concentric, thin-plate, square-edge orifices. Source: ASME, *Fluid Meters*, 6th ed., 1971.

15.3.4 Orifice Characteristics

The primary variables in the use of flat-plate orifices are the ratio of orifice to pipe diameter, tap locations, and characteristics of orifice sections. Various configurations of bevel and rounded edges are used in seeking particular performance characteristics, especially constant coefficients at low Reynolds numbers. Figure 15.7 illustrates typical orifice installations. Three tap locations are indicated: (1) flange taps, (2) "1D" and "$\frac{1}{2}$D" taps, and (3) vena contracta taps. These are all shown in composite fashion in Fig. 15.7; however, only one set would be used for a given installation.

As fluid flows through an orifice, the necessary transverse velocity components imparted to the fluid as it approaches the obstruction carry through to the downstream side. As a result, the minimum stream section occurs not in the plane of the orifice, but somewhat downstream, as shown in Fig. 15.8(a). The term "vena contracta" is applied to the location and conditions of this minimum stream dimension. This is also the location of minimum pressure; hence it explains the interest in the vena contracta tap location. A guide for the location of the vena contracta tap is given in Fig. 15.8(b).

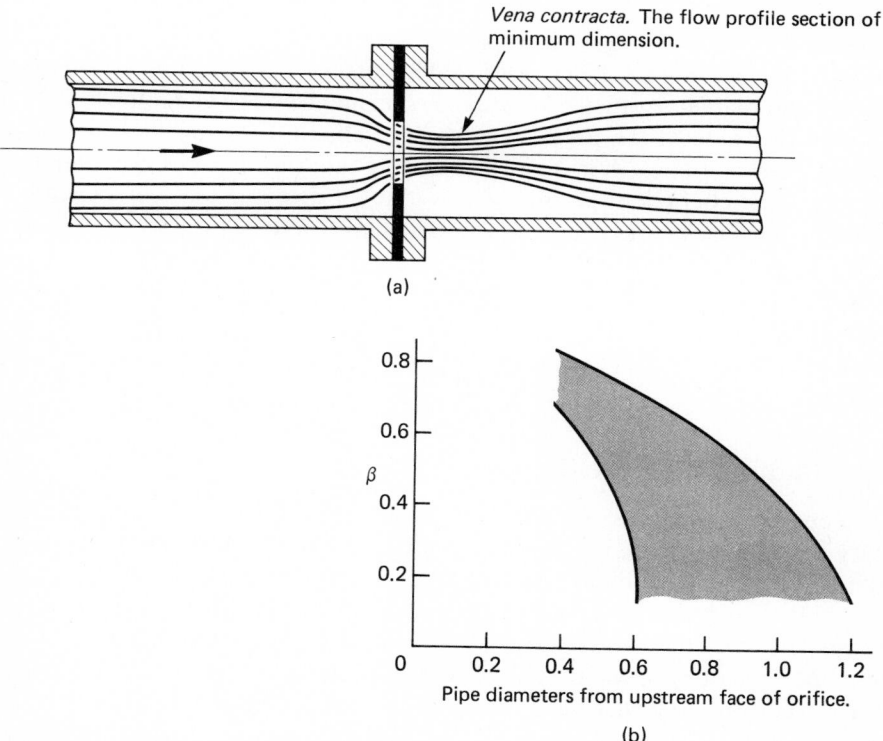

FIGURE 15.8   (a) Diagram illustrating vena contracta location for an orifice. (b) Guide for locating vena contracta as measured from orifice face.

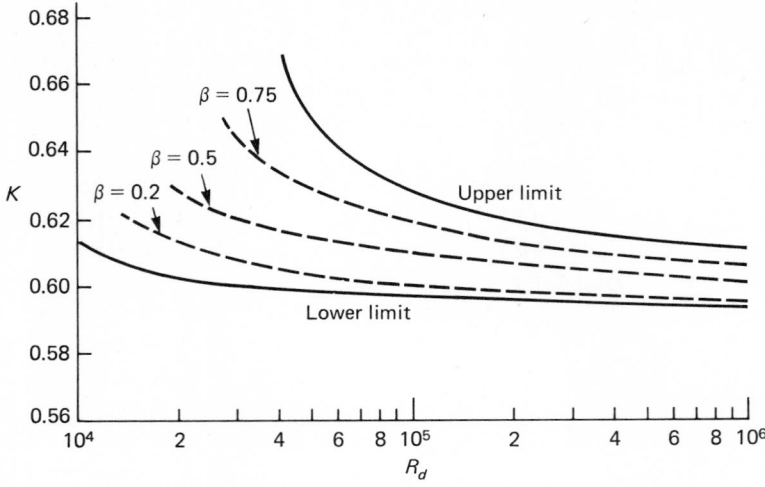

FIGURE 15.9   Range of flow coefficients for flat-plate orifices.

Figure 15.9 shows ranges for typical orifice flow coefficients versus Reynolds number, based on the diameter d. The dashed lines are loci of average values for the diameter ratios indicated. For example, the values for $\beta = 0.5$ range on either side of the $\beta = 0.5$ plot, depending on the tap locations and particular characteristics. It is important to note that this figure is not intended for precise flow coefficient predictions. Rather, it displays the *ranges* within which the values may be expected to fall. The figure may be used for estimates; however, for more precise values the reader is directed to the Suggested Readings at the end of the chapter. In any case, however, the experimenter should be aware that accurate work *requires* careful calibration of each installation. (See also Sections 9.7 and 15.10.)

15.3.5 Relative Merits of the Venturi, Flow Nozzle, and Orifice

High accuracy, good pressure recovery, and resistance to abrasion are the primary advantages of the venturi. These are offset, however, by considerably greater cost and space requirements than with the orifice and nozzle. The orifice is inexpensive, and may often be installed between existing pipe flanges. However, its pressure recovery is poor, and it is especially susceptible to inaccuracies resulting from wear and abrasion. It may also be damaged by pressure transients because of its lower physical strength. The flow nozzle possesses the advantages of the venturi, except that it has lower pressure recovery, plus the added advantage of shorter physical length. It is expensive compared with the orifice and is relatively difficult to install properly.

EXAMPLE   A venturi designed according to the specifications of Fig. 15.4 is placed in an 8-in. diameter (20.32-cm) line passing 500 gallons (1.893 m^3) of water per minute. If the throat diameter is 4 in. (10.16 cm), what differential pressure may be expected across the pressure taps? The water temperature is 70°F (21.1°C).

Solve the problem (a) using the English engineering system of units, (b) using the SI system, and finally, (c) reconcile the two answers. Use the tables in Appendix D for the properties of water.

Solution

a)
$$A_1 = 0.349 \text{ ft}^2,$$

$$A_2 = 0.087 \text{ ft}^2,$$

$$Q = 500 \text{ gpm} = 1.114 \text{ ft}^3/\text{s}.$$

For water at 70°F,

$$\rho = 62.3 \text{ lbm/ft}^3,$$

$$\beta = \frac{4}{8} = 0.5,$$

$$E = 1/\sqrt{1 - \beta^4} = 1.033.$$

From Section 15.3.2, estimate $C = 0.97$:

$$K = CE = 0.97 \times 1.033 = 1.002.$$

Rewriting Eq. (15.5), solving for $P_1 - P_2$, we have

$$P_1 - P_2 = (Q/KA_2)^2(\rho/2g_c)$$

$$= (1.114/1.002 \times 0.087)^2(62.3/2 \times 32.17)$$

$$= 158.13 \text{ lbf/ft}^2 = 1.098 \text{ lbf/in}^2.$$

b)
$$A_1 = 0.0324 \text{ m}^2,$$

$$A_2 = 0.0081 \text{ m}^2,$$

$$Q = 1.893 \text{ m}^3/\text{min} = 0.0316 \text{ m/s}.$$

For water at 21.1°C,

$$\rho = 997.9 \text{ kg/m}^3,$$

$$K = 1.002,$$

as above. Substituting, we have

$$P_1 - P_2 = (0.0316/1.002 \times 0.0081)^2(997.9/2 \times 1)$$

$$= 7563.6 \text{ Pa}.$$

c) From Appendix C, we have that 1 psi = 6894.8 Pa; thus converting the answer for part (b), we obtain

$$P_1 - P_2 = 7563.6/6894.8 = 1.097.$$

(See Problem 15.6.)

15.4 OBSTRUCTION METERS FOR COMPRESSIBLE FLUIDS

When compressible fluids flow through obstruction meters of the types discussed in Section 15.3, the density does not remain constant during the process; that is, $\rho_1 \neq \rho_2$. The usual practice is to base the energy relation, Eq. (15.2), on the density at condition 1 (Fig. 15.2) and to introduce an *expansion factor*, Y, as follows:

$$W = KA_2Y\sqrt{2g_c\rho_1(P_1 - P_2)}, \tag{15.7}$$

where W = the mass flow rate.

The expansion factor, Y, may be determined theoretically for nozzles and venturis and experimentally for orifice meters. For nozzles and venturis values may be calculated from the following relation [2]:

$$Y = \left[\left(\frac{P_2}{P_1}\right)^{2/k}\left(\frac{k}{k-1}\right)\left(\frac{1-(P_2/P_1)^{(k-1)/k}}{1-(P_2/P_1)}\right)\left(\frac{1-\beta^4}{1-\beta^4(P_2/P_1)^{2/k}}\right)\right]^{1/2}, \tag{15.8}$$

in which

$$k = \frac{\text{Specific heat at constant pressure}}{\text{Specific heat at constant volume}}.$$

For square-edged orifices, an empirical relation has been developed that is expressed as follows [2]:

$$Y = 1 - \left[0.41 + 0.35\beta^4\right]\left[\frac{P_1 - P_2}{kP_1}\right]. \tag{15.8a}$$

Expansion factors, Y, for venturis and nozzles and for $k = 1.4$ are shown plotted against pressure ratio in Fig. 15.10(a). Similar values for square-edged orifices are given in Fig. 15.10(b).

EXAMPLE   A sharp-edged orifice is used to measure flow of 30°C air through a 0.25-m diameter circular-sectioned duct. Estimate the flow rate if the differential pressure between vena contracta taps is 20 cm of 0.92 specific gravity oil. The upstream pressure P_1 is 4×10^5 Pa(abs) and $\beta = 0.6$.

FIGURE 15.10   (a) Expansion factors for venturis and nozzles ($k = 1.4$). (b) Expansion factors for square-edged concentric orifices. Source: ASME, *Fluid Meters*, 6th ed., 1971.   ▶

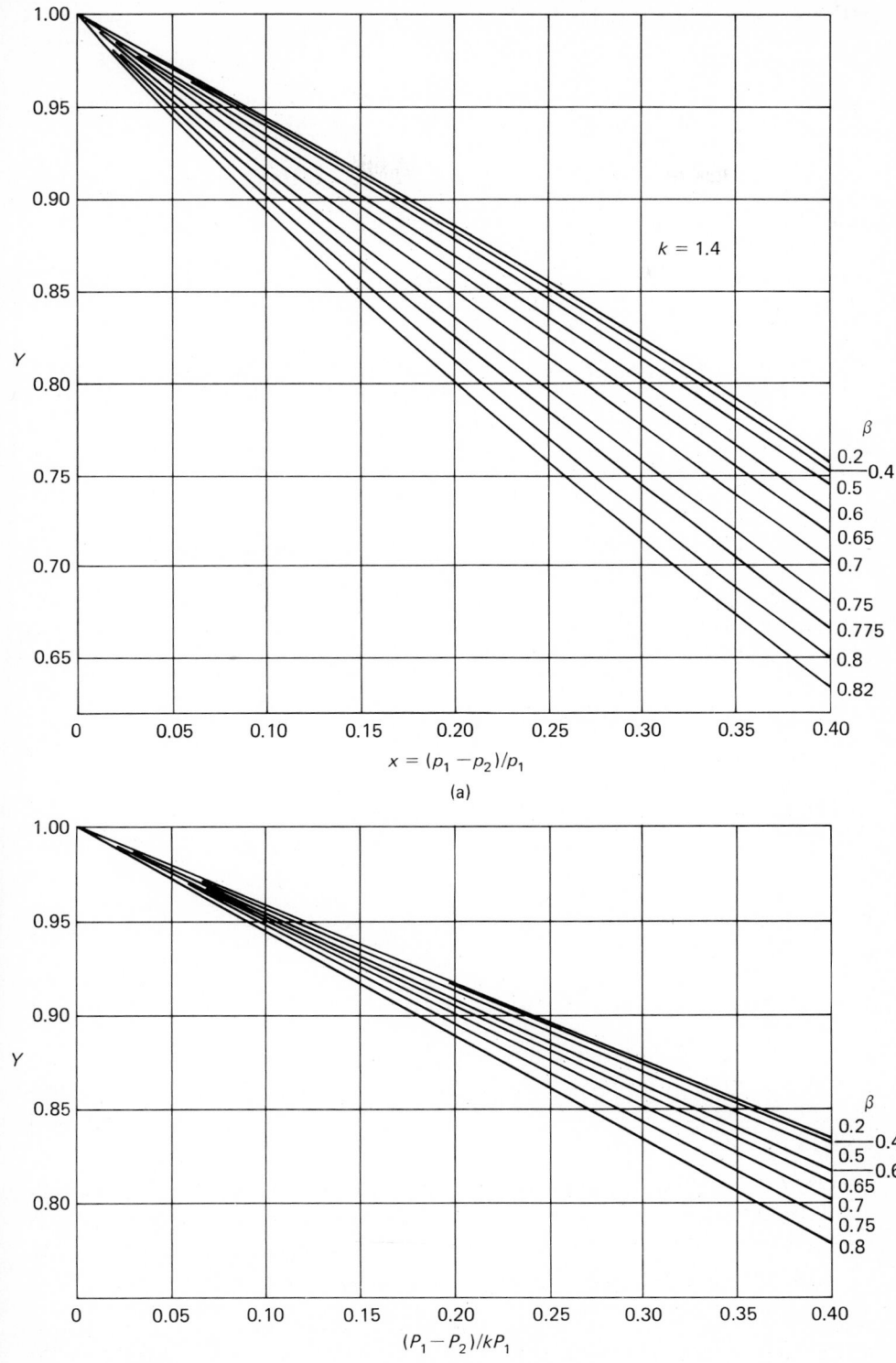

(a)

(b)

Solution

$$A_1 = 0.0491 \text{ m}^2, \qquad A_2 = 0.0177 \text{ m}^2$$

From Fig. 15.9 we may estimate $C \approx 0.6$. (*Note:* At this point we are unable to determine R_d.)

$$E = 1/\sqrt{1 - \beta^4} = 1.0719$$

$$K = CE = 0.643$$

From Table 2 in Appendix D, we have

$$\rho = \rho_{\text{atmos}}(P/P_{\text{atmos}}) = 1.14(4 \times 10^5/1.01325 \times 10^5) \text{ kg/m}^3$$

$$= 4.5 \text{ kg/m}^3,$$

$$g_c = 1 \text{ kg} \cdot \text{m/N} \cdot \text{s}^2.$$

Using Eq. (14.1a), we know that

$$P_1 - P_2 = h\rho_o(g/g_c),$$

where ρ_o is the density of manometer oil. From Table 1 in Appendix D, we find that the density of water at 30°C = 995.7 kg/m³ and

$$P_1 - P_2 = (20/100)(0.92 \times 995.7)(9.807/1) = 1796.7 \text{ Pa.}$$

To determine Y from Fig. 15.10(b) and using $k = 1.4$, we have

$$(P_1 - P_2)/kP_1 = 1796.7/(1.4 \times 4 \times 10^5) = 0.0032.$$

Entering Fig. 15.10(b) gives us $Y \approx 1$, and using Eq. (15.7), we have

$$W = 0.643 \times 0.0177 \times 1\sqrt{2 \times 1 \times 4.5 \times 1796.7}$$

$$= 1.45 \text{ kg/s.}$$

The value of R_d may now be calculated and the reasonableness of our estimate of C determined.

Volume flow rate = W/Density = 1.45/4.5 = 0.32 m³/s,

Velocity = Volume flow rate/Area = 0.32/0.0177 = 18.2 m/s,

Reynolds number = $D\rho V/\mu g_c$

$$= (0.25 \times 0.6)(4.5)(18.2)/1.85 \times 10^{-5}$$

$$= 6.64 \times 10^5.$$

Referring to Fig. 15.9, we have $C \approx 0.61$. This compares reasonably with our assumed value of 0.6, and greater refinement is not warranted.

Choked flow

There is a caution, however, when considering the isentropic flow of compressible fluids. As flow rates are increased, a condition is eventually reached wherein the flow velocity through a constriction reaches the sonic velocity under the existing conditions (Mach number = 1.0). The condition of the Mach number equal to unity at a constriction such as the throat of a nozzle is called a "choked flow" condition [3]. When this occurs, variations in pressure at the constriction or throat, as shown in Fig. 15.3(b) and 15.3(c), no longer influence the mass flow rate. One might interpret this condition by stating that once a Mach number of unity is reached at the throat, the effects of exit pressure variations can no longer be propagated back upstream.

The *critical pressure ratio* for the choked flow condition is expressed in terms of the static upstream and throat pressure as

$$\frac{P_2}{P_1} = \left(\frac{1 + k}{2}\right)^{k/(1 - k)} \tag{15.8b}$$

This can be interpreted as being the limiting ratio for achieving sonic flow in a nozzle; that is, so long as the pressure ratio P_2/P_1 is greater than the value given in Eq. (15.8b), the flow may be predicted by Eq. (15.7). However, when the pressure ratio given by Eq. (15.8b) is reached, the choked flow condition will exist. For air, $k = 1.4$ and this ratio becomes 0.528.

15.5 THE VARIABLE-AREA METER

A major disadvantage of the common forms of obstruction meters (the venturi, the orifice, and the nozzle) is that the pressure drop varies as the square of the flow rate (Eq. 15.5). This means that if these meters are to be used over a wide range of flow rates, pressure-measuring equipment of very wide range will be required. In general, if the range is accommodated, accuracy at low flow rates will be poor. One solution would be to use two (or more) pressure-measuring systems: one for low flow rates and another for high rates.

A device whose indication is essentially linear with flow rate is shown in section in Fig. 15.11. This instrument is a variable-area meter, commonly called a *rotameter*. Two parts are essential, the float and the tapered tube in which the float is free to move. The term "float" is somewhat a misnomer, because it must be heavier than the liquid it displaces. As flow takes place upward through the tube, four forces act on the float: a downward gravity force, an upward buoyant force, pressure, and viscous drag forces.

For a given rate of flow, the float assumes a position in the tube where the forces acting on it are in equilibrium. Through careful design, the effects of changing viscosity or density may be minimized, leaving only the pressure force as a variable. The latter is dependent on flow rate and the annular area between it and the tube. Hence its position will be determined by the flow rate alone. A basic equation for the rotameter has been developed [4] in the following form:

$$Q = A_w C \left[\frac{2gv_f(\rho_f - \rho_w)}{A_f \rho_w}\right]^{1/2}, \tag{15.9}$$

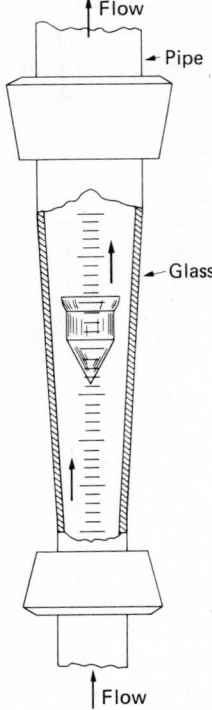

Flow

Pipe

Glass

Flow   **FIGURE 15.11**   Variable-area flow meter.

where

Q = the volumetric rate of flow,

v_f = the volume of the float,

g = acceleration due to gravity,

ρ_f = the float density,

ρ_w = the liquid density,

A_f = the area of the float,

C = the discharge coefficient,

A_w = the area of the annular orifice
     = $\pi/4[(D + by)^2 - d^2]$,

D = the effective diameter of the tube depending on the position of the float,

b = the change in tube diameter per unit change in height,

d = the maximum diameter of the float, and

y = the height of the float above zero position.

Certain disadvantages of the rotameter as compared with the other forms of obstruction meter are: the meter must be installed in a vertical position; the float may not be visible when opaque fluids are used; it cannot be used with liquids carrying large percentages of solids in suspension; for high pressures or temperatures, it is expensive. Advantages include: there is a uniform flow scale over the range of the instrument, with the pressure loss fixed at all flow rates; the capacity may be changed with relative ease by changing float and/or tube; many corrosive fluids may be handled without complication; the condition of flow is readily visible.

15.6 MEASUREMENTS OF FLUID VELOCITIES

Flow is generally proportional to some flow velocity; hence, by measuring the velocity, a measure of flow is obtained. Often velocity *per se* is desired, particularly velocity *relative* to a fluid. An example of the latter is an aircraft moving through the air. The following sections deal with measurement of absolute and relative velocities of fluids.

15.7 PRESSURE PROBES

Point measurement of pressure is accomplished by the use of tubes joining the location in question with some form of pressure transducer. A *probe* or sampling device is intended insofar as possible to obtain a reliable and interpretable indication of the pressure at the signal source. Therein lies a difficulty, however, for the mere presence of the probe will alter, to some extent, the quantity being measured.

A common reason for desiring point-pressure information is to determine flow conditions. Flowing media may be gaseous or liquid in a symmetrical conduit or pipe or in a more complex situation such as a jet engine or compressor.

There are many different types of pressure probes, with the selection depending on the information required, space available, pressure gradients, and constancy of flow magnitude and direction. Basically, pressure probes measure either of two different pressures or some combination thereof (Fig. 15.12). In Section 14.2 we briefly discussed *static* and *total* pressures and indicated that the difference is a result of the flow velocity. This may be expressed as

$$P_t = P_s + P_v. \tag{15.10}$$

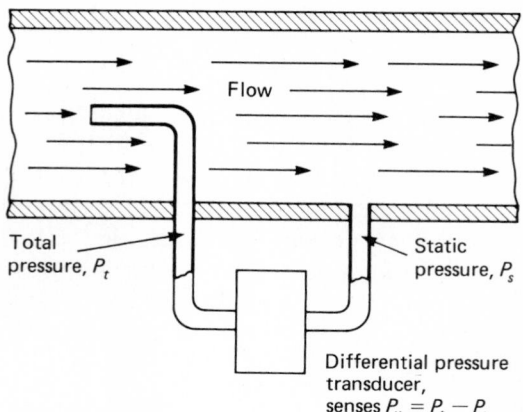

FIGURE 15.12   Total and static pressure probes.

15.7.1 Incompressible Fluids

Referring to Eq. (15.2) for incompressible fluids, we may write

$$P_t = P_s + \rho V^2/2g_c,$$

in which

P_t = the total pressure (often called *stagnation* pressure),

P_s = the static pressure,

P_v = the velocity pressure,

ρ = the fluid density (static),

V = the velocity, and

g_c = the conversion constant.

Solving for velocity, we obtain

$$V = \sqrt{2g_c(P_t - P_s)/\rho_s} = \sqrt{2g_c(\Delta P)/\rho_s} . \qquad (15.11)$$

From this we see that velocity may be determined simply by measuring the difference between the total and static pressures.

15.7.2 Compressible Fluids

For flow of a compressible fluid an isentropic compression occurs at the tip as the pressure changes from P_s to P_t. Under these conditions [2, 5],

$$V = \sqrt{2\left(\frac{k}{k-1}\right)\left(\frac{P_s}{\rho_s}\right)\left[\left(\frac{P_t}{P_s}\right)^{(k-1)/k} - 1\right]g_c}$$

$$= \sqrt{2\left(\frac{k}{k-1}\right)\left(\frac{P_s}{\rho_s}\right)\left[\left(1 + \frac{\Delta P}{P_s}\right)^{(k-1)/k} - 1\right]g_c}, \qquad (15.11a)$$

where k = the ratio of specific heats = c_p/c_v, and $\Delta P = P_t - P_s$.

When velocity is used to measure flow rate, consideration must be given to the velocity distribution across the channel or conduit. A mean may be found by traversing the area to determine the velocity profile, from which the average may be calculated, or a multiplication constant may be determined by calibration (see Problem 15.24).

15.7.3 Total-Pressure Probes

Obtaining a measure of total or impact pressure is usually somewhat easier than getting a good measure of static pressure. This is true except for something such as an open jet, when a barometer reading may be used for the static component. The simple pitot tube (named for Henri Pitot) shown at A in Fig. 14.2 is usually adequate for determining impact pressure. More often, however, the pitot tube is combined with static openings, constructed as shown in Fig. 15.13. This is known as a pitot-static tube, or sometimes as a Prandtl–Pitot tube. For steady-flow conditions, a simple differential manometer, often of the inclined type, suffices for pressure measurement, and $P_t - P_s$ is determined directly. When variable conditions exist, some form of pressure transducer, such as one of the diaphragm types, may be used. Of course, care must be exercised in providing adequate response, particularly in the connecting tubing (see Section 14.12).

A major problem in the use of an ordinary pitot-static tube is to obtain proper alignment of the tube with flow direction. The angle formed between the probe axis and the flow streamline at the pressure opening is called the *yaw angle*. This should be zero, but in many situations the yaw angle may not be constant: The flow may be fixed neither in magnitude nor in direction. In such cases, yaw sensitivity is very important. The pitot-static tube is particularly sensitive to yaw, as shown in Fig. 15.14. Although sensitivity is influenced by orientation of both impact and static openings, the latter probably has the greater effect.

The Kiel tube, designed to measure total or impact pressure only (there are no static openings), is shown in Fig. 15.15. It consists of an impact tube surrounded by what is essentially a venturi. The curve demonstrates the striking insensitivity of this type to variations in yaw. Modifications of the

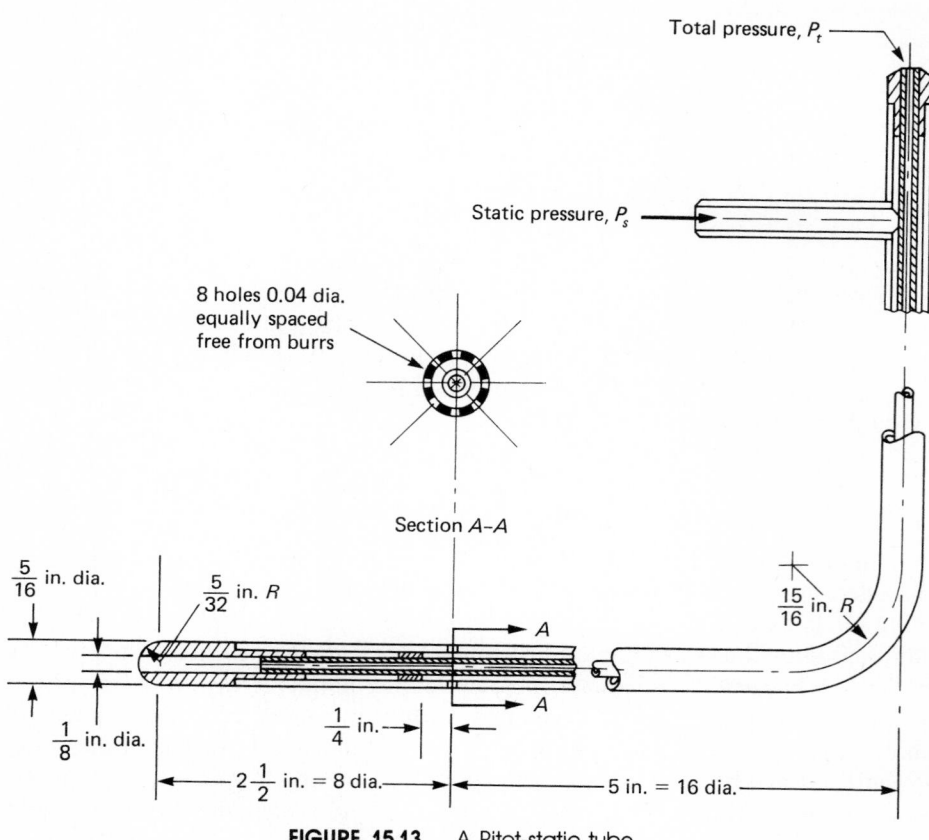

Total pressure, P_t

Static pressure, P_s

8 holes 0.04 dia.
equally spaced
free from burrs

Section *A–A*

$\frac{5}{16}$ in. dia.

$\frac{5}{32}$ in. *R*

$\frac{15}{16}$ in. *R*

A

A

$\frac{1}{8}$ in. dia.

$\frac{1}{4}$ in.

$2\frac{1}{2}$ in. = 8 dia.

5 in. = 16 dia.

FIGURE 15.13   A Pitot-static tube.

Kiel tube make use of a cylindrical duct, beveled at each end, rather than the streamlined venturi. This appears to have little effect on the performance and makes the construction much less expensive.

15.7.4 Static-Pressure Probes

Static-pressure probes have been used in many different forms [7]. Ideally, the simple opening with axis normal to flow direction should be satisfactory. However, slight burrs or yaw introduce appreciable errors. As mentioned previously, in many situations yaw angle may be continually changing. For these reasons, special static-pressure probes may be used. Figure 15.16 shows several probes of this type and corresponding yaw sensitivities.

As mentioned earlier, the mere presence of the probe in a pressure-flow situation alters the parameters to be measured. Probes interact with other probes, with their own supports, and with duct or conduit walls. Such inter-action is primarily a function of geometry and relative dimensional proportions;

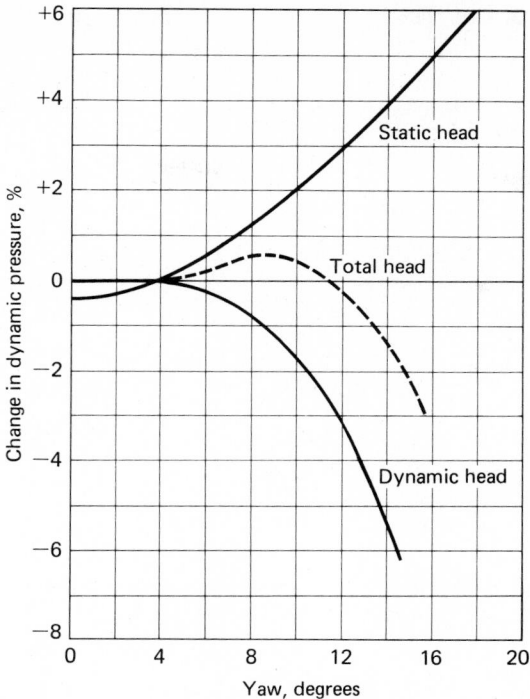

FIGURE 15.14   Yaw sensitivity of a standard Pitot-static tube. Courtesy: The Airflo Instrument Company, Glastonbury, CT.

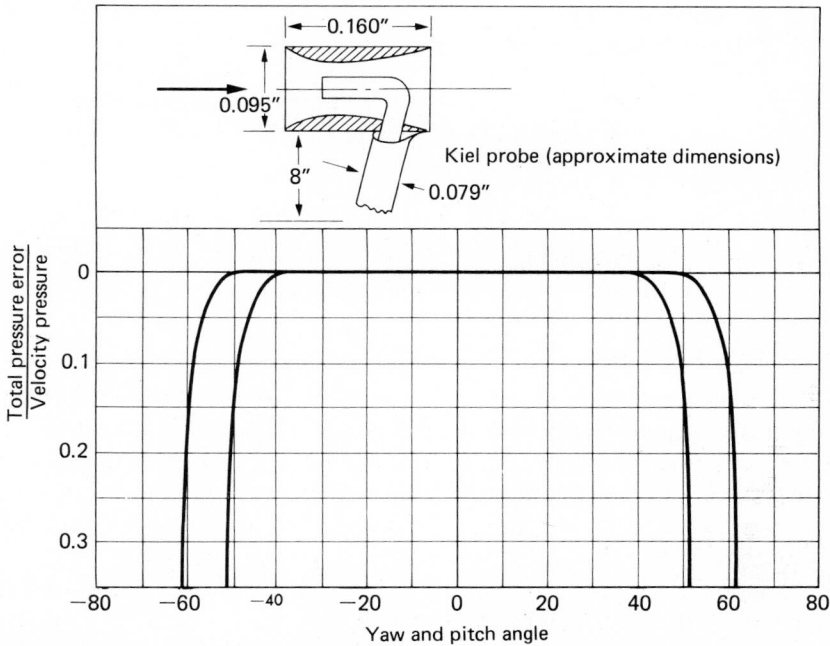

FIGURE 15.15   Kiel-type total-pressure tube and plot of yaw sensitivity. Courtesy: The Airflo Instrument Company, Glastonbury, CT.

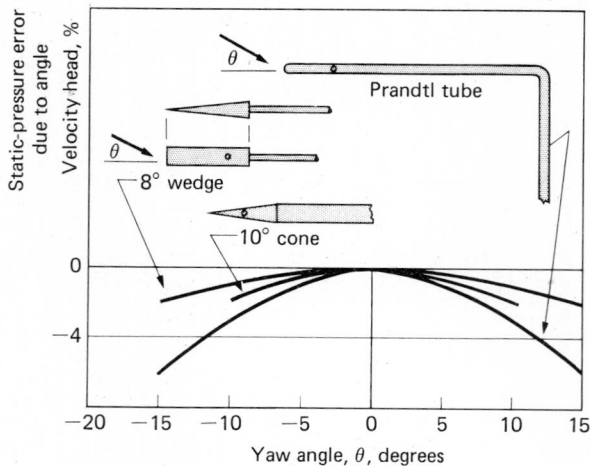

FIGURE 15.16   Angle characteristics of certain static-pressure-sensing elements. Courtesy: Instrument Society of America, Research Triangle Park, NC.

it is also a function of Mach number. Much work has been conducted in this area, and the interested reader is referred to references [8] and [9] for a review of some of these efforts.

15.7.5 Direction-Sensing Probes

Figure 15.17 illustrates two forms of direction-sensing or yaw-angle probes. Each of these probes uses two impact tubes. In each case the probe is placed transverse to flow and is rotatable around its axis. The angular position of the probe is then adjusted until the pressures sensed by the openings are equal. When this is the case, the flow direction will correspond to the bisector of the angle between the openings. Probes are also available with a third opening midway between the other two. The additional hole, when properly aligned, senses maximum impact pressure.

EXAMPLE   A pitot-static tube is used to determine the velocity of air at the center of a pipe. Static pressure is 18 psia (124,106 Pa), the air temperature is 80°F (26.7°C), and a differential pressure of 3.8 in. of water (9.65 cm) is measured. What is the air velocity? Perform the calculations using (a) the English system of units and (b) the SI system.

Solution   a) Using the English engineering system of units, we find from Table D.2 that $\rho_{80} = 0.0735$ lbm/ft^3 at a pressure of 14.7 psia. At 18 psia,

$$\rho_{80} = (0.0735)(18/14.7) = 0.090 \text{ lbm/ft}^3,$$

$$\Delta P = (3.8 \times 144)/(12 \times 2.31) = 19.74 \text{ lbf/ft}^2,$$

$$P_s = 18 \times 144 = 2592 \text{ lbf/ft}^2,$$

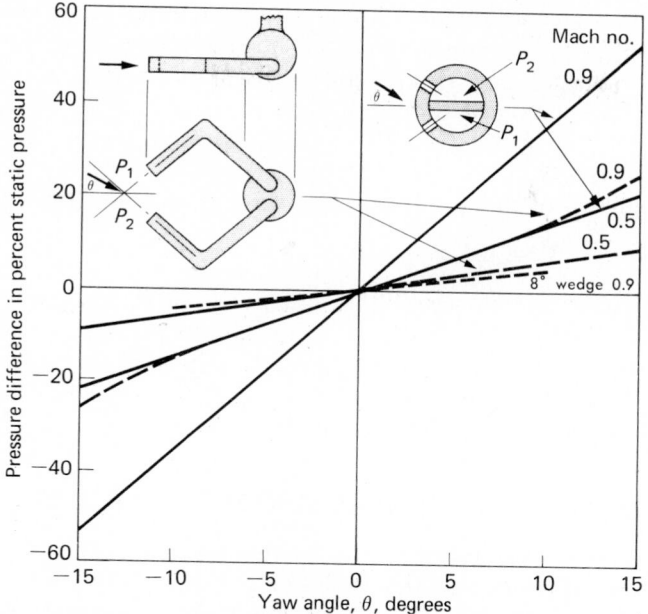

FIGURE 15.17   Special direction-sensing elements and their yaw characteristics. Courtesy: Instrument Society of America, Research Triangle Park, NC.

$$P_t = P_s + \Delta P = 2592 + 19.74 = 2612 \text{ lbf/ft}^2, \text{ and}$$

$$k = 1.4.$$

Substituting in Eq. (15.11a) gives us

$$V = \sqrt{2(1.4/0.4)(2592/0.09)\,[(2612/2592)^{(0.4/1.4)} - 1] \times 32.17}$$

$$= 119 \text{ ft/s (or 36.4 m/s)}.$$

b) Using the SI system of units, we find from Table D.2 that $\rho_{26.7} = 1.153$ kg/m^3 at standard atmospheric pressure. At 124 kPa,

$$\rho_{26.7} = (124/101.35) \times 1.153 = 1.41 \text{ kg/m}^3,$$

1 cm H$_2$O $= 98.06$ Pa,   (*Note:* This is true at 4°C. More accurate calculations would require a correction.)

$$\Delta P = 9.65 \times 98.06 = 946.3 \text{ Pa},$$

$$P_t = P_s + \Delta P = 124{,}106 + 946.3 = 125052 \text{ Pa}.$$

Using Eq. (15.11a), we have

$$V = \sqrt{2(1.4/0.4)(124{,}106/1.41)\,[(125{,}052/124{,}106)^{(0.4/1.4)} - 1] \times 1}$$

$$= 36.58 \text{ m/s}.$$

Close scrutiny of the arithmetical manipulations required in the above example clearly shows that calculation errors of considerable size may easily result from the fact that P_t and P_s are quite commonly of very nearly the same magnitudes: Calculation of the ratio must be quite precise. A much simpler approach would be to use Eq. (15.11) along with an appropriate multiplying coefficient. This commonly falls between 0.96 and 1. If we substitute the values for part (b) of the above example directly into Eq. (15.11) we obtain

$$V = \sqrt{2 \times 1 \times (946.3)/1.41} = 36.6 \text{ m/s}.$$

For our particular example we see that essentially the same answer is obtained. (Problem 15.22 bears on this matter.) Of course, one should always be cautious when using shortcuts of this sort. It has been suggested that the practical use of Eq. (15.11) for compressible fluids and without correction be limited to velocities below 30% of the applicable Mach number [6].

15.8   SPECIAL FLOW-MEASURING METHODS AND DEVICES

Although the preceding discussion covers the common methods of flow measurement, there are many additional methods of relatively specialized nature. In this article we shall consider some of the more important types.

15.8.1   Turbine-Type Meters

The familiar anemometer used by weather stations to measure wind velocity is a simple form of free-stream turbine meter. Somewhat similar rotating-wheel flow meters are used by civil engineers to measure water flow in rivers and streams [10]. Both the cup-type rotors and the propeller types are used for this purpose. In each case the number of turns of the wheel per unit time is counted and used as a measure of the flow rate.

Figure 15.18 illustrates a modern adaptation of these methods to the measure of flow in tubes and pipes. Wheel motion, proportional to flow rate, is sensed by a reluctance-type pickup coil. A permanent magnet is encased in the rotor body, and each time a wheel blade passes the pole of the coil, change in permeability of the magnetic circuit produces a voltage pulse at the output terminal. The pulse rate may then be indicated by a frequency meter, displayed on a CRO screen, or counted by some form of EPUT meter. Frequency converters are also available that convert flow-meter pulses to a proportional d.c. output, permitting use of simple meters for indication. Accuracies within $\pm \frac{1}{2}\%$ are claimed for these devices within specific flow range. Available sizes cover the range from $\frac{1}{8}$ inch to 8 inches. Transient response is good; time constants for stepped pressure pulses are on the order of 2 to 12 milliseconds [11].

In addition to bearing maintenance, a major problem inherent in this type of meter is reduced accuracy at low flow rates. Maximum to minimum ca-

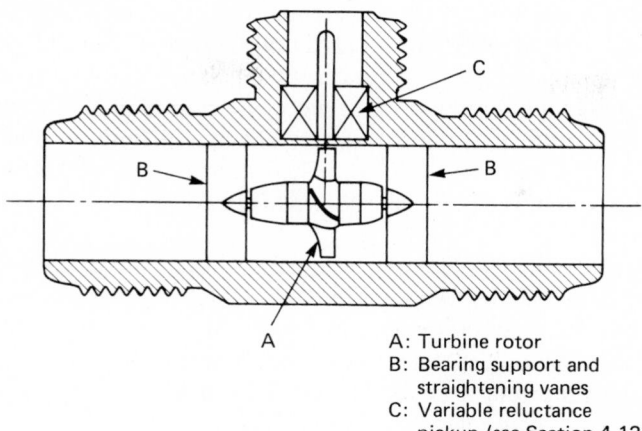

A: Turbine rotor
B: Bearing support and
   straightening vanes
C: Variable reluctance
   pickup (see Section 4.12)

FIGURE 15.18   Turbine-type flowmeter.

pacities vary from about 8 to 1 for small meters to about 40 to 1 for the large
sizes.

15.8.2 Thermal Methods

When an electrically heated wire is placed in a flowing stream (assumed
gaseous), heat will be transferred between the two, depending on a number
of factors, including the flow rate. This type of flow-sensing element is called
the *hot-wire anemometer*. The element consists of a short length of fine wire
stretched between two supports, such as shown in Fig. 15.19. Two methods

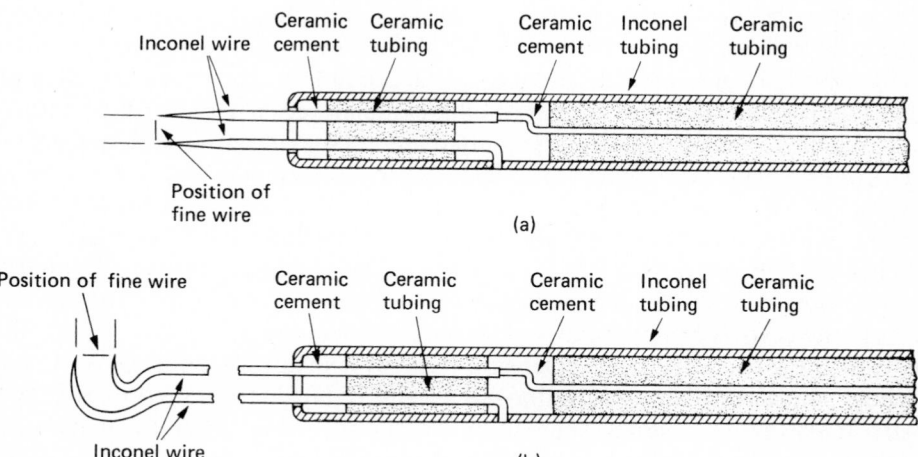

FIGURE 15.19   Two forms of hot-wire anemometer probes. (a) Wire mounted normal to probe
axis. (b) Wire mounted parallel to probe axis.

are used to measure flow. The first technique consists of a constant current passing through the sensing wire. Variation in flow results in changed wire temperature, hence changed resistance, which thereby becomes a measure of flow. The second technique uses a servo system to maintain wire resistance, hence wire temperature. In this case, a change in flow results in a corresponding change in electrical current. The latter is then interpreted as a flow analog. The two methods are called *constant-current* and *constant-temperature,* respectively.

When the hot wire is placed in a flowing stream, heat will be transferred from the wire, primarily by convection. Radiation and conduction are normally negligible. The rate of heat transfer will depend on a number of factors included in the three dimensionless quantities: the Nusselt, Reynolds, and Prandtl numbers. Governing relations have been written as follows [12, 13, 14]:

$$\frac{\text{Power/(Unit length)}}{\text{Temperature difference}} = \frac{i^2 R}{T_w - T_a} = A + B\sqrt{\rho V}, \qquad (15.12)$$

where A and B are constants and

i = the instantaneous current,

R = the resistance of wire per unit length,

T_w = the temperature of the wire,

T_a = the ambient temperature,

ρ = the density of gas, and

V = free-stream velocity.

When the flow past the wire is varying with time, the sensing-element response will lag behind the actual fluctuations because of the heat capacity of the wire. To a considerable extent, it is possible to compensate for lag of this type in the electrical circuitry. This is illustrated in Fig. 15.20.

When a constant-current system is used, compensation is achieved by means of a passive network (Section 5.21) of inductance and resistance, or of capacitance and resistance, or through use of a suitable transformer. However, compensation must be adjusted for the particular flow condition being measured and, in general, is usable only for fluctuations having magnitudes up to about 15% of the mean stream velocity.

In the constant-temperature anemometer, compensation forms an inherent part of the basic system. The sensing element is incorporated in an electrical bridge whose unbalance is used as a measure of current required to maintain wire temperature. Fluctuations of the required current thereby become a measure of the flow variations. An advantage of this system is that a wide range of conditions does not affect the ability of the system to provide flat

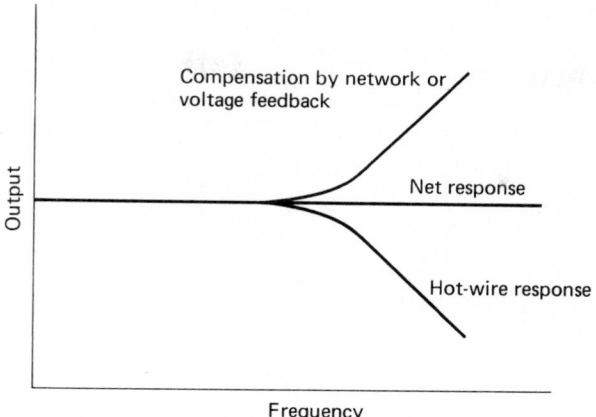

FIGURE 15.20   Effect of compensation on hot-wire anemometer response characteristics.

response. Another very practical advantage is that the system provides inherent protection against wire burnout.

15.8.3 Magnetic Flowmeters

Magnetic flowmeters are based on Faraday's law of induced voltage, expressed by the relation [15]

$$e = Blv \times 10^{-8}, \tag{15.13}$$

where

e = the induced voltage, in volts,

B = the flux density, in gauss,

l = the length of the conductor, in cm, and

v = the velocity of the conductor, in cm/s.

Basic flowmeter arrangement is as shown in Fig. 15.21. The flowing medium is passed through a pipe, a short section of which is subjected to a transverse magnetic flux. Fluid motion relative to the field causes a voltage to be induced proportional to the fluid velocity. This emf is detected by electrodes placed in the conduit walls. Either an alternating or direct magnetic flux may be used. However, if amplification of the output is required, the advantage lies with the alternating field.

Two basic types have been developed. In the first, the fluid need be only slightly electrically conductive, and the conduit must be of glass or some similar nonconducting material. The electrodes are placed flush with the inner conduit surfaces making direct contact with the flowing fluid. Output voltage

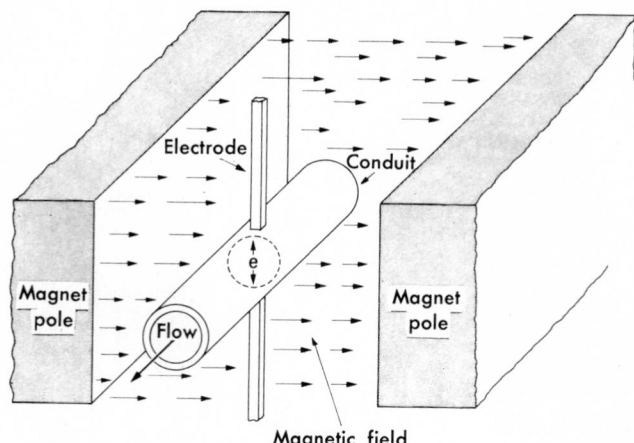

FIGURE 15.21   Schematic showing operation of a magnetic flowmeter.

is quite low, and an alternating magnetic field is used for amplification and to eliminate polarization problems. Special circuitry is required to separate the no-flow output from the signal caused by flow [16].

A second form of magnetic flowmeter is primarily intended for use with highly conductive fluids such as liquid metals. This meter operates on the same basic principle but may use electrically conducting materials for the conduit. Stainless steel is commonly used. A permanent magnet supplies the necessary flux, and the electrodes may be simply attached to diametrically opposite points on the *outside* of the pipe. This provides for easy installation at any time and at any point along the pipe. The output of this type is sufficient to drive ordinary commercial indicators or recorders, and zero output for nonflow conditions is an added advantage [17].

15.8.4   An Ultrasonic Flowmeter [18]

Another type of noncontacting rate meter for measuring flow in pipes uses ultrasonic waves. Similar piezoelectric or magnetostrictive transducers are placed externally on a conduit a few inches apart. One serves as a 100-kHz energy source and the other as the pickup. As the wave travels from source to pickup, its normal velocity in stationary fluid will be either increased or decreased by the Doppler effect resulting from the fluid velocity. In order to minimize errors, the functioning of the two transducers is reversed 10 times per second. In this manner, phase shifts due to both addition and subtraction of the velocities are employed. The relative phase shift is used as the measure of flow rate.

The Doppler effect has been used to construct a combination anemometer and wind direction indicator without moving parts [19]. Ultrasonic genera-

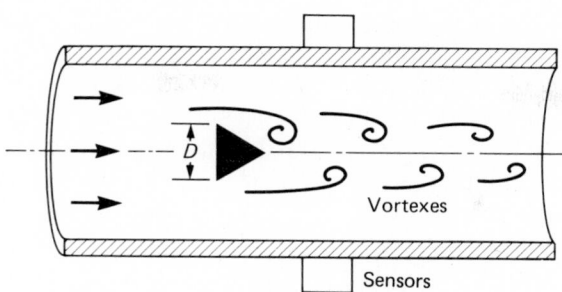

FIGURE 15.22   Vortex stripping caused by bluff-body in flow stream.

tor–receptors are mounted at the four corners of a 3-ft square. Through microcomputer control the generators are sequentially pulsed and the time required for the sound to travel between generators and receptors is input to the computer, programmed to provide both wind velocity and direction readouts. Software temperature compensation is also provided.

15.8.5 Pulse-Producing Methods

The advent of digital electronics has increased the need for flow-measuring devices that provide pulsed outputs. The turbine meter (Fig. 15.18) produces pulses proportional to flow rate; however, its continuously moving rotor subjects it to mechanical maintenance problems. Several meters that circumvent this disadvantage have been developed.

Vortex stripping is based on the fact that when a bluff body is placed in a stream, vortices are alternately formed, first to one side of the obstruction and then to the other (Fig. 15.22). The frequency of formation, f, is a function of flow rate. For incompressible fluids [20],

$$f = kV/d,$$

where

k = a calibration constant,

V = the flow velocity, and

D = the dimension of the obstruction transverse to the flow direction.

For compressible fluids the relation is more complicated, because k is a function of the Reynolds number.

Various schemes are used to sense the frequency of vortex formation. The obstructing body may be mounted on an elastic support and the support oscillation sensed by one of a number of means. Heated thermistors downstream, with one to each side of the obstruction, and the flexing of diaphragms have been used. Fluctuation in resistance is the output parameter. A patented sensing method makes use of an ultrasonic beam that is amplitude modulated by the pulses.*

Yet another approach is the Coanda effect, which is the tendency for a fluid jet to remain in contact with a guiding surface, once contact is established. The effect can be used to produce a hydraulic or pneumatic flip-flop analogous to the electronic counterpart. If designed for self-oscillation, the action indicates a measure of flow rate.

15.9 PREDICTABILITY OF FLOW-METER PERFORMANCE

The foregoing discussion of flow-measuring devices and procedures is based to a great extent on practical information assembled and published by the American Society of Mechanical Engineers (see general references at the end of this chapter). Tables and charts of coefficients for various and precisely prescribed metering methods have evolved through the years from accumulated experiences of many different people and interested commercial and research organizations. This material, stemming from committee actions, probably forms as useful and reliable a guide to flow measurements as is available, and when diligently adhered to, yields satisfactory and practical results. It is recognized, however, that there must be a "limit of accuracy" applied to the values of any generally expressed discharge or flow coefficients or expansion factors and that the charts can only be accurate within a specific tolerance range, and further, that such tolerances can only be approximately determined.

The tolerance ranges in Table 15.1 have been abstracted from reference [2] and apply to coefficient and factor data presented therein. From this tabulation we see that the coefficients may be quite accurately predicted. Of course, it must be remembered that these figures do not include errors of

TABLE 15.1 Tolerance Ranges for Theoretical Flow-Measurement Coefficients and Factors

Type of Element	Tolerances in Percent Coefficient or Factor	
	For Discharge or Flow Coefficients	For Expansion Factors
Venturi tubes	$\pm \frac{3}{4}$ to $1\frac{1}{2}$	± 0.2 to ± 1.2
Flow nozzles, long radius	± 1 to ± 2	± 0.2 to ± 1.2
Square-edge concentric orifices	± 1 to $\pm 5*$	$\pm 1\frac{1}{2}$

* Larger tolerances correspond to smaller sizes and lower values of R_d.

---

* Brooks Instrument Div., Emerson Electric Co., Hatfield, Pa.

observation, errors of subsequent signal conditioning apparatus, etc. For more accurate work, calibration of individual meters along with associated instrumentation is required.

15.10 CALIBRATION OF FLOW-MEASURING DEVICES

Facilities for producing standardized flows are required for flow-meter calibration. Fluid at known rates of flow must be passed through the meter and the rate compared with the meter read-out. When the basic flow input is determined through measurement of time and either linear dimensions (volumetric flow) or weight (mass flow), the procedure may be called *primary calibration*. After receiving a primary calibration, a meter may then be used as a *secondary standard* for standardizing other meters through *comparative calibration*.

Primary calibration is usually carried out at a constant flow rate with the procedure consisting of an integration or summing of the total flow for a predetermined period of time. Volumetric displacement of a liquid may be measured in terms of the liquid level in a carefully measured tank or container. For a gas, at moderate rates, volume may be determined through use of an inverted bell-type *gasometer* or "meter prover." Primary calibration in terms of mass is commonly accomplished by means of the familiar *weigh tank* in which the liquid is collected and weighed. Although the latter method is normally used only for liquids, with proper facilities it may also be used for calibration with gases [21].

Figure 15.23 illustrates a method obviating the requirement for direct weight measurement. A standpipe of known capacity (diameter) is used as a collector. We see that the pressure or head at the base is the analog of the

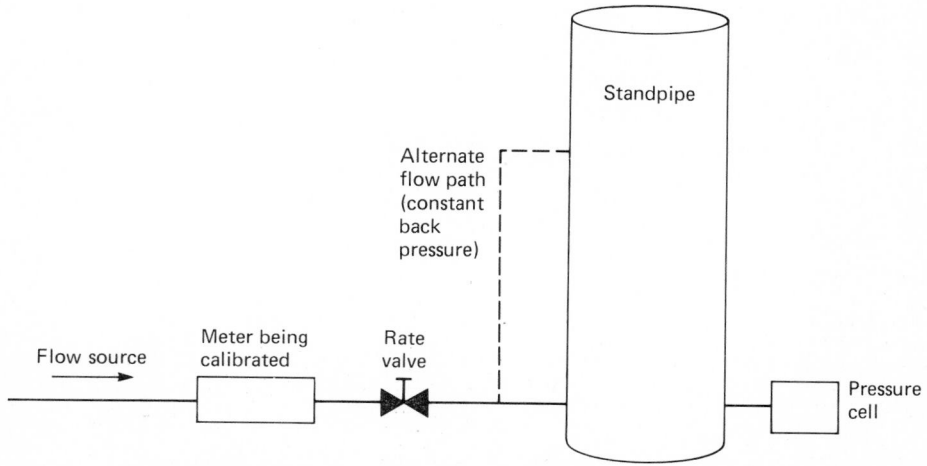

FIGURE 15.23   Standpipe employed for flow-meter calibration.

mass as it is collected. Calibrations within 0.1 percent for meters handling 50 to 600,000 lbm/hr are claimed [22].

Primary calibration is usually considered only at relatively low flow rates; however, on occasion, the cost of large-scale facilities can be justified by the importance of the application. An unusual system adapted to liquid hydrogen flow calibrations, at rates to 7000 gallons per minute, is described in reference [23]. Two 50,000-gallon dewars and an interconnecting flow loop were used and volume rates were determined by means of liquid-level gages. Calibration errors of no more than 4% were claimed for this unusual application.

Secondary calibration may be either *direct* or *indirect*. Direct secondary calibration is accomplished by simply placing a secondary standard in series with the meter to be calibrated and comparing their respective read-outs over the desired range of flow rates. Turbine-type meters are particularly useful as secondary standards for "field" calibration of orifice or venturi meters [24]. It is clear that this procedure requires careful consideration of meter installations, minimizing interactions or other forms of disturbances such as might be caused by nearby line obstructions, e.g., elbows, tees, etc.

Indirect calibration is based on the equivalencies of two different meters. The requirement for similarity is had through maintenance of equal Reynolds numbers, or

$$D_1 \rho_1 V_1 / \mu_1 = D_2 \rho_2 V_2 / \mu_2,$$

where the subscripts 1 and 2 refer to the "standard" and the meter to be calibrated, respectively. The practical significance lies in the fact that, provided that similarity is maintained, discharge coefficients of the two meters will be directly comparable.

We see then that for geometrically similar meters it is possible to predict the performance of one meter on the basis of the experimental performance of another. Meters that are small in physical size may be used to determine the discharge coefficient of large meters. Indeed, coefficients for one fluid may be determined through test runs with another fluid, provided that similarity is maintained through Reynolds numbers. However, when a liquid is used to calibrate a meter intended for a gas, corrections for density and expansion must also be made.

SUGGESTED READINGS

ASME PTC Application, Part II of Fluid Meters, 1972.

ASME Fluid Meters, Their Theory and Applications, 6th ed. ASME, 1971.

Benedict, R. P., *Fundamentals of Temperature, Pressure and Flow Measurements*, 2nd ed. New York: John Wiley, 1977.

Cusick, C. F. (ed.), *Flow Meter Engineering Handbook*, 5th ed. Ft. Washington, Pennsylvania: Honeywell, Inc., Process Control Div., 1977.

Katys, G. P., *Continuous Measurement of Unsteady Flow*. New York: Macmillan, 1964.

Linford, A., *Flow Measurement and Meters*, 2nd ed. London: E & F.N.Spon, Ltd., 1961.

Spink, L. K., *Principles and Practice of Flow Meter Engineering*, 9th ed. Foxboro, Massachusetts: The Foxboro Co., 1978.

PROBLEMS

15.1 Water at 30°C (86°F) flows through a 10-cm (3.94-in.) pipe at an average velocity of 6 m/s (19.68 ft/s). Calculate the value of R_D, using SI units. Check for proper unit balance. Obtain required data from Appendix D.

15.2 Solve Problem 15.1 using English units and check for unit balance. [*Note:* The same numerical result should be obtained in both cases.]

15.3 If Problem 15.1 had specified 4-in., schedule 140 pipe, what would be the resulting R_D? (Check any general engineering handbook for the significance of pipe "schedule" numbers.)

15.4 Check Eq. (15.2) for a balance of units using (a) the SI system of units and (b) the English system.

15.5 Show that Eq. (15.5) may be written as follows

$$Q = KA_2\sqrt{2gh},$$

where h = the differential pressure across the meter, measured in the "head" of the flowing fluid. Check the unit balance.

15.6 When an obstruction meter is placed in a vertical run of pipe (as opposed to a horizontal run), what precautions must be made in measuring the differential pressure?

15.7 A section of vertically oriented conduit is shown in Fig. 15.24. There is a gradual diameter change from 6 in. (15.24 cm) at A to 4 in. (10.16 cm) at B. The velocity

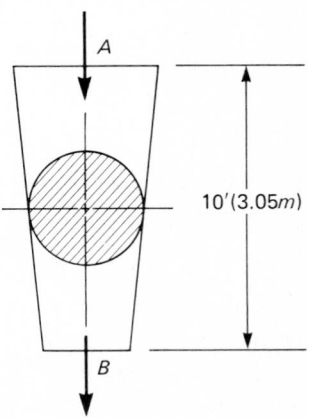

FIGURE 15.24   Vertically oriented conduit described in Problem 15.7.

of 0.87 specific gravity oil is 25 ft/s (7.62 m/s) at A. Assuming no energy loss, what pressure difference should exist between the two points? Check the balance of units.

15.8 Solve Problem 15.7 using SI units. Check the balance of units.

15.9 If the conduit of Problem 15.7 is reoriented into the horizontal position, what differential pressure should be found between points A and B? Solve (a) using SI units and (b) using English units.

15.10 A sharp-edged concentric orifice is used to measure the flow of kerosene in a 6-cm (2.36-in.) diameter line. If $\beta = 0.4$, what differential pressure may be expected for a flow rate of 0.9 m³/min (31.78 ft³/min) when the temperature of the fluid is 10°C (50°F)?

15.11 Solve Problem 15.10 using English units.

15.12 A venturi meter is placed in a horizontal run of $2\frac{1}{2}$-inch IPS (Iron Pipe Size) pipe [ID = 2.47 in. (62.74 mm)] for the purpose of metering heating oil as it is pumped into a storage tank. The throat diameter of the venturi is $1\frac{3}{8}$ in. (34.93 mm). If the differential pressure is held to the equivalent of 22 in. (55.9 cm) of water for one-half hour, how many gallons (liters) of oil should have been pumped? The oil temperature is 60°F (15.6°C) and its specific gravity is 0.86.

15.13 Solve Problem 15.12 using SI units.

15.14 Water at 15°C and 650 kPa flows through a 15 × 10 cm (15-cm pipe and 10-cm throat) venturi. A differential pressure of 25 kPa is measured. Calculate the flow rate (a) in kg/min and (b) in m³/hr.

15.15 A venturi with a 40-cm (15.75-in.) diameter throat is used to meter 15°C (59°F) air in a 60-cm (23.62-in.) duct. If the differential pressure measured across vena contracta taps is 84 mm (3.31 in.) of water and the upstream pressure (absolute) is 125 kPa (18.13 psi), what is the flow rate in kg/s? in m³/s?

15.16 Solve Problem 15.15 using English units.

15.17 Direct secondary calibration is used to determine the flow coefficient for an orifice to meter the flow of nitrogen. For an orifice inlet pressure of 25 psia (172 kPa), the flow rate determined by the primary meter is 9 lbm/min (19.8 kg/m) at 68°F (20°C). If the differential pressure across the orifice being calibrated is 3.1 in. (7.87 cm) of water, the conduit diameter is 4 in. (10.16 cm), and $\beta = 0.5$, what is the value of $(K \times Y)$? (Use $\rho = 0.0726$ lbm/ft³ at 68°F and standard pressure.) Solve using English units.

15.18 Solve Problem 15.17 using SI units.

15.19 Using Eq. (15.8b), plot P_2/P_1 vs. k over a range of $k = 1$ to 1.4.

15.20 A pitot-static tube is used to measure the velocity of 20°C (68°F) water flowing in an open channel. If a differential pressure of 6 cm (2.36 in.) of H_2O is measured, what is the corresponding flow velocity? Check the result by using English units and comparing your answer to the SI result.

15.21 Using the data given in Problem 15.20, what would be the result if the temperature of the flowing water were 50°C, the water in the manometer were at 5°C, and the measurements are made at (a) Key West, Florida, and (b) Ft. Egbert, Alaska? [*Note:* See Appendix D for data and overlook "significant figures," by carrying the results to the degree required to show a difference.]

15.22 A pitot-static tube is used to measure the velocity of an aircraft. If the air temperature and pressure are 5°C (41°F) and 90 kPa (13.2 psia), respectively, what is the aircraft velocity in km/hr if the differential pressure is 450 mm (17.5 in.) of water? (a) Solve using Eq. (15.11), then (b) using Eq. (15.11a).

15.23 Solve Problem 15.22 using English units.

15.24 The velocity profile for turbulent flow in a smooth pipe is sometimes given as [25]

$$V_\tau / V_{center} = [1 - (2r/D)]^{1/n},$$

where

D = the pipe diameter, and

r = the radial coordinate from the center of the pipe,

and n ranges in value from about 6 to 10, depending on Reynolds number. For $n = 8$, determine the value of r at which a pitot tube should be placed to provide the velocity V_{ave}, such that $Q = A V_{ave}$.

15.25 A one-fifth size, geometrically similar model is made of the orifice described in the example in Section 15.4. If water at 70°F is used to experimentally determine the flow coefficient, to what velocity should the flow be adjusted for dynamic similarity?

temperature 16 measurements

16.1 INTRODUCTION

Temperature is a manifestation of the molecular kinetic energy within a body and is readily perceived by the human nervous system. It is a fundamental property in much the same sense as mass, length, and time, and hence is more difficult to define than are derived quantities. Various definitions have been proposed, including "a condition of a body by virtue of which heat is transferred to or from other bodies," and "a quantity whose difference is proportional to the work from a Carnot engine operating between a hot source and a cold receiver." The latter definition assumes some basis for the relation between *hot* and *cold*. For our purposes in this chapter, the concept that temperature is an indication of intensity of molecular activity will suffice.

Temperature cannot be measured by use of basic standards for direct comparison. It can only be determined through some form of standardized calibrated device or system. Its measurement is not based on a tangible entity such as the International Kilogram, but rather on ideas and instructions, as outlined in Section 8.7. When energy in the form of heat is introduced to or extracted from a body, altered molecular activity will be made apparent as a temperature change. Various primary effects may accompany the temperature change, any of which may be used for the purpose of temperature measurement. These include (1) change in physical state, (2) change in chemical state, (3) altered physical dimensions, (4) change in electrical properties, and (5) change in radiating ability.

The first two possibilities are seldom used for direct temperature measurement. However, as we have seen in Chapter 8, actual *establishment* of temperature standards is based on changes in physical state, i.e., freezing or melting and boiling or condensing.

A change in dimensions accompanying a temperature shift is, of course, well known and forms the basis of operation for the common liquid-in-glass, as well as gas and bimetal-type thermometers. Electrical methods include means based on change in electrical conductivity and the well-known thermoelectric effects that produce an electromotive force (emf) at the junction of two dissimilar metals. Another temperature-measuring method, one that makes use of the energy radiated from a hot body, is the basis of operation of optical, radiation, and infrared pyrometers. Table 16.1 outlines approximate ranges and uncertainties of various temperature-measuring methods. It must be understood that the values given in the table are only approximate. There are many untabulated factors, especially applicable to the electrical methods, that may cause deviations from the values listed.

16.2   USE OF BIMATERIALS

16.2.1   Liquid-in-Glass Thermometers

The ordinary thermometer is an example of the liquid-in-glass type. Essential elements consist of a relatively large bulb at the lower end, a capillary tube with scale, and liquid filling both the bulb and a portion of the capillary. In addition, a smaller bulb is generally incorporated at the upper end to serve as a safety reservoir when the intended temperature range is exceeded. As the temperature is raised, the greater expansion of the liquid compared with that of the glass causes it to rise in the capillary or stem of the thermometer, and the height of rise is used as a measure of the temperature. The volume enclosed in the stem above the liquid may either contain a vacuum or be filled with air or another gas. For the higher temperature ranges, an inert gas at a carefully controlled initial pressure is introduced in this volume, thereby raising the boiling point of the liquid and increasing the total useful range. In addition, it is claimed that such pressure minimizes column separation.

There are several desirable properties for a liquid used in a glass thermometer, as follows:

1. The temperature-dimensional relationship should be linear, permitting a linear instrument scale.
2. The liquid should have as large a coefficient of expansion as possible. For this reason, alcohol is better than mercury. Its larger expansion makes possible larger capillary bores, and hence provides easier reading.
3. The liquid should accommodate a reasonable temperature range without change of state. Mercury is limited at the low-temperature end by its freezing point $-37.97°F$ (or $-38.87°C$), and the spirits are limited at their high-temperature ends because of boiling.
4. The liquid should be clearly visible when drawn into a fine thread. Mercury is inherently good in this regard, whereas alcohol is usable only if dye is added.
5. Preferably, the liquid should not adhere to the capillary walls. When rapid temperature drops occur, any film remaining on the wall of the tube will

TABLE 16.1 Survey of Various Temperature-Measuring Elements and Devices (Data From Various Sources)

Type	Useful Range*	Limits of Uncertainty*	Comments
Liquid in Glass			
Mercury filled	−35 to 600°F −37 to 320°C	0.5°F 0.3°C	Low cost. Remote reading not practical.
Pressurized mercury	−35 to 1000°F	"	Lower limit of mercury-filled thermometers determined by freezing point of mercury.
Alcohol	−100 to 200°F −75 to 129°C	1°F 0.6°C	Upper limit determined by boiling point.
Pressure Systems			
Gas (laboratory)	−450 to 212°F −270 to 100°C	0.002 to 0.5°F 0.002 to 0.2°C	Very accurate. Quite fragile. Not easily used.
Gas (industrial)	−450 to 1400°F −270 to 760°C	0.5 to 2% "	Bourdon pressure gage used for read-out. Rugged, with wide range.
Liquid (except mercury)	−125 to 700°F −90 to 370°C	2°F 1°C	Relative elevations of read-out and sensing bulb are critical. Smallest bulb. Up to 10 ft (3 m) capillary.
Liquid (mercury)	−35 to 1200°F −37 to 630°C	$\frac{1}{2}$ to 2% "	"
Vapor pressure	−100 to 650°F	$\frac{1}{2}$ to 2%	Fast response. Nonlinear. Lowest cost.
Bimetal	−80 to 800°F −65 to 430°C	1 to 20°F $\frac{1}{2}$ to 12°C	Rugged. Inexpensive.
Thermocouples			
General	−420 to 4400°F −250 to 2400°C	1°F 0.6°C	Extreme ranges—all types.

TABLE 16.1 Continued

Type	Useful Range*	Limits of Uncertainty*	Comments
Type B (Pt, 30%Rh(+) vs. Pt,6%Rh(−))	1600 to 3100°F	±½%	Not for reducing atmosphere or vacuum. Generates high emf per degree.
Type E (Chromel†(+) vs. Constant†(−))	−300 to 1600°F −184 to 870°C	±½%	Highest output of common thermocouples.
Type J (Fe(+) vs Alumel†(−))	32 to 1400°F	2 to 10°F‡ 1 to 6°C	For reducing or neutral atmosphere. Popular and inexpensive.
Type K (Chromel(+) vs. Alumel†(−))	32 to 2300°F 0 to 1260°C	±¾%‡	For oxidizing or neutral atmosphere. Attacked by sulfur. Most linear of all thermocouples.
Type R(Pt(+) vs. Pt,13%Rh(−))	32 to 2700°F 0 to 1480°C	½‡	Requires protection in all atmospheres. Higher output than Type S. Linearity poor below 1000°F (540°C).
Type S(Pt(+) vs. Pt,10%Rh(−))	32 to 2700°F 0 to 1480°C	½%‡	Requires protection in all atmospheres. Under proper conditions yields highest precision. Used as interpolating device for IPTS-68 (see Section 8.7).
Type T(Cu(+) vs. Constant†(−))	−420 to 650°F −250 to 340°C	1°F 0.6°C	May be used in either oxidizing or reducing atmospheres. Good stability.
W, 5%Rh(+) vs. W,26%Rh(−)	−450 to 4200°F −270 to 2310°C	—	No standards. Reducing or neutral atmospheres. Highest temperature limit of all thermocouples.
Resistance			
Platinum	−450 to 1800°F −180 to 980°C	0.2°F 0.1°C	High repeatability. Linear. Used as an interpolating device for IPTS-68 (see Section 8.7). Sensor can be used as far as 5000 ft (1500 m) from read-out.

	Range	Accuracy	Comments
Nickel	−300 to 500°F	—	High repeatability. Nonlinear. Produces greater resistance change per degree than does Pt. Sensor can be as far as 5000 ft (1500 m) from read-out.
Thermistor	−150 to 600°F / −100 to 315°C	½°F / 1.4°C	Negative temperature coefficient. Highly nonlinear. Less stable than metal types.
Semiconductor	−67 to 300°F / −55 to 150°C	2°F / 1°C	Limited range. Easily adapted to electronic circuitry.
Pyrometers			
Optical	1400 to 6300°F	½ to 2%	Used only for high temperatures. Requires manual manipulation by operator.
Radiation	0 to 7000°F / −15 to 3870°C	"	Can measure "spot" or average temperatures.
Infrared	0 to 6000°F / −15 to 3300°C	"	Portable. Self-contained. Expensive.
Acoustic	−400 to 5600°F / −240 to 3100°C	1%	
Crystal	−420 to 1830°F / −250 to 1000°F	0.4°F / 0.2°C	

* Approximate values. Actual values depend on many factors such as environment, physical size of sensor, purity of materials, etc. Types such as thermocouples and resistance thermometers require additional signal conditioning apparatus. Values given are for sensors only.

† Trade names.

‡ In higher ranges.

524 **Temperature Measurements**

cause a reading that is too low. In this respect, mercury is better than alcohol.

Within its capabilities, mercury is undoubtedly the best liquid for liquid-in-glass thermometers and is generally used in the higher-grade instruments. Alcohol is usually satisfactory. Other liquids are also used, primarily for the purpose of extending the useful ranges to lower temperatures.

16.2.2 Calibration and Stem Correction

High-grade liquid-in-glass thermometers are made with the scale etched directly on the thermometer stem, thereby making it mechanically impossible to shift the scale relative to the stem. The care with which the scale is laid out depends on the intended accuracy of the instrument (and to a large extent governs its cost). The process of establishing *bench marks* from which a scale is determined is known as "pointing," and two or more *marks* or *points* are required. In spite of intentions, a particular thermometer will exhibit some degree of nonlinearity. This may be caused by nonlinear temperature–dimension characteristics of liquid or glass, or by the nonuniformity of the bore of the column. In the simplest case, two points may be established, such as the freezing and boiling points of water, and equal divisions used to interpolate (and extrapolate) the complete scale. For a more accurate scale, additional points—sometimes as many as five—are used. Calibration points for this purpose are obtained through use of fixed temperature points, as discussed in Section 16.12.

Greatest sensitivity to temperature is at the bulb, where the largest volume of liquid is contained; however, all portions of a glass thermometer are temperature-sensitive. With temperature variation, the stem and any upper bulb will also change dimensions, thereby altering the available liquid space and hence the thermometer reading. For this reason, if greatest accuracy is to be attained, it is necessary to prescribe how a glass thermometer is to be subjected to the temperature. Maximum control is obtained when the complete thermometer is entirely immersed in a uniform temperature medium. Often this is not possible, especially when the medium is liquid. A common practice, therefore, is to calibrate the thermometer for a given partial immersion, with the proper depth of immersion indicated by a scribed line around the stem. Thermometer accuracy is then prescribed for this condition only. This, of course, does not ensure absolute uniformity, because the upper portion of the stem is still subject to some variation in ambient conditions.

When the immersion employed is different from that used for calibration, an *estimate* of the correct reading may be obtained from the following relation (for mercury-in-glass thermometers only):

$$T = T_1 + kT'(T_1 - T_2), \tag{16.1}$$

where

    T = the correct temperature, in degrees,

    T_1 = the actual temperature reading, in degrees,

    k = the differential expansion coefficient between liquid and glass (for mercury thermometers, commonly used values are 0.00009 for the Fahrenheit scale and 0.00016 for the Celsius scale),

    T_2 = the ambient temperature surrounding the emergent stem (this may be determined by attaching a second thermometer to the stem of the main thermometer), in degrees,

    T' = degrees of thread emergence to be corrected.

The value T' is determined as follows: For a *total immersion thermometer*, T' should be the actual length of the thread of mercury that is emerging, measured in scale degrees. For the *partial immersion thermometer*, T' should be the number of scale degrees between the scribed calibration immersion line and the actual point of emergence. When the thermometer is too deeply immersed, the value of T' will be *negative*.

Another factor influencing liquid-in-glass thermometer calibration is a variation in the applied pressure, particularly in pressure applied to the bulb. The resulting elastic deformation causes displacement of the column, hence an incorrect reading. Normal variation in atmospheric pressure is not usually of importance, except for the most precise work. However, if the thermometer is subjected to system pressures of higher values, considerable error may be introduced.

16.2.3 Bimetal Temperature-Sensing Elements [1]

When two metal strips having different coefficients of expansion are brazed together, a change in temperature will cause a free deflection of the assembly. Such bimetal strips form the basis for control devices such as the common home heating system thermostat. They are also used to some extent for temperature measurement. In the latter case, the sensing strip is commonly wrapped into a helical form, similar to the simple helical spring. As the temperature changes, the free end of the helix rotates (the diameter of the helix either increasing or decreasing due to the differential action). The rotational motion is directly indicated by the movement of a pointer over a circular scale.

Thermometers with bimetallic temperature-sensitive elements are often used because of their ruggedness, ease of reading, and the convenience of their particular form.

16.3 PRESSURE THERMOMETERS

Figure 16.1 illustrates a simple *constant-volume* gas thermometer. Gas, usually hydrogen or helium, is contained in bulb *A*. A mercury column, *B*, is adjusted so that reference point *C* is maintained. In this manner, a constant volume of gas is held in the bulb and adjoining capillary. Mercury column *h* is a measure of the gas pressure and can be calibrated in terms of temperature.

In this form the apparatus is fragile, difficult to use, and restricted to the laboratory. It does, however, illustrate the working principle of a group of practical instruments called *pressure thermometers*.

Figure 16.2 shows the essentials of the practical *pressure thermometer*. The necessary parts are bulb *A*, tube *B*, pressure-sensing gage *C*, and some sort of filling medium. Pressure thermometers are called *liquid-filled, gas-filled,* or *vapor-filled,* depending on whether the filling medium is completely liquid, completely gaseous, or a combination of a liquid and its vapor. A primary advantage of these thermometers is that they can provide sufficient force output to permit the direct driving of recording and controlling devices. The pressure-type temperature-sensing system is usually less costly than other systems. Tubes as long as 200 ft may be used successfully.

Expansion (or contraction) of bulb *A* and the contained fluid or gas, caused by temperature change, alters the volume and pressure in the system. In the case of the liquid-filled system, the sensing device *C* acts primarily as a differential volume indicator, with the volume increment serving as an analog of temperature. For the gas- or vapor-filled systems, the sensing device serves

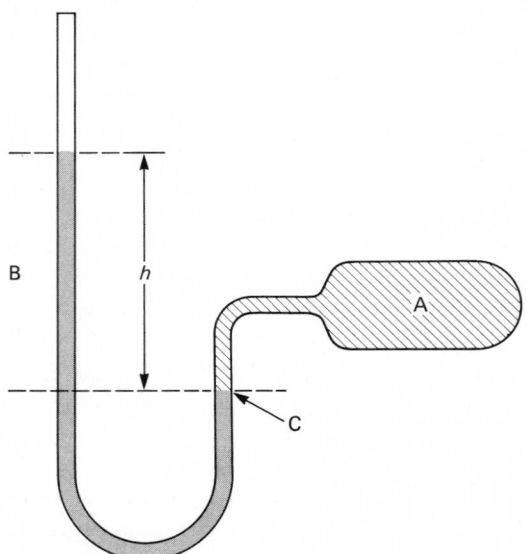

FIGURE 16.1   Sketch illustrating the essentials of a pressure thermometer.

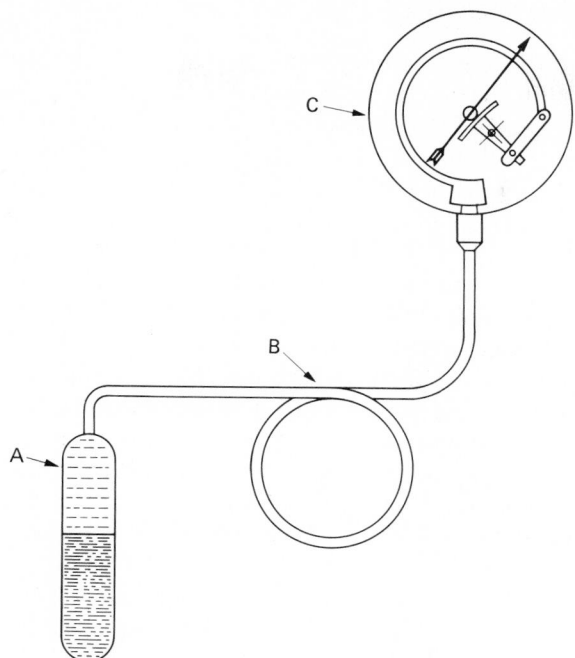

FIGURE 16.2   Schematic diagram showing the operation of a practical pressure thermometer.

primarily as a pressure indicator, with the pressure providing the measure of temperature. In both cases, of course, both pressure and volume change.

Ideally the tube or capillary should serve simply as a connecting link between the bulb and the indicator. When liquid- or gas-filled systems are used, the tube and its filling are also temperature-sensitive, and any difference from calibration conditions along the tube introduces output error. This error is reduced by increasing the ratio of bulb volume to tube volume. Unfortunately, increasing bulb size reduces the time response of a system, which may introduce problems of another nature. On the other hand, reducing tube size, within reason, does not degrade response particularly because, in any case, flow rate is negligible. Another source of error that should not be overlooked is any pressure gradient resulting from difference in elevation of bulb and indicator not accounted for by calibration.

Temperature along the tube is not a factor for vapor-pressure systems, however, so long as a free liquid surface exists in the bulb. In this case, Dalton's law for vapors applies, which states that if both phases (liquid and vapor) are present, only one pressure is possible for a given temperature. This is an important advantage of the vapor-pressure system. In many cases, though, the tube in this type of system will be filled with liquid, and hence the system is susceptible to error caused by elevation difference.

16.4   THERMOELECTRIC THERMOMETRY

Several temperature-sensitive electrical elements are available as measuring means. Of primary importance are thermal emf and both positive and negative variation in resistance with temperature. These are discussed in the following sections.

16.5   THERMORESISTIVE ELEMENTS

We have already seen (Section 4.16.2) that the electrical resistance of most materials varies with temperature. In Sections 12.11 and 13.5 we found this to supply a troublesome extraneous input to the output of strain gages. It can only follow that this relation, which proves so worrisome when unwanted, should be the basis for a good method of temperature measurement.

Traditionally, resistance elements sensitive to temperature are made of metals generally considered to be good conductors of electricity. Examples are nickel, copper, platinum, and silver. A temperature-measuring device using an element of this type is commonly referred to as a *resistance thermometer,* or a *resistance temperature detector,* abbreviated *RTD*. Of more recent origin are elements made from semiconducting materials having large negative resistance coefficients. Such materials are usually some combination of metallic oxides of cobalt, manganese, and nickel. These devices are called *thermistors*.

One important difference between these two kinds of material is that, whereas the resistance change in the thermometer element is small and positive (increasing temperature causes increased resistance), that of the thermistor is relatively large and negative. In addition, the thermometer type provides nearly a linear temperature–resistance relation, whereas that of the thermistor is nonlinear. Still another important difference lies in the temperature ranges over which each may be used. The practical operating range for the thermistor lies between approximately − 100 to 275°C (− 150 to 500°F). The range for the resistance thermometer is much greater, being from about − 250 to 1000°C (− 400 to 1800°F). Finally, the metal resistance elements are more time-stable than the oxides; hence they provide better reproducibility with lower hysteresis.

16.5.1   Resistance Thermometers

Evidence of the importance and reliability of the resistance thermometer may be had by recalling that the International Practical Temperature Scale of 1968 specifies use of a platinum resistance thermometer for interpolation of the scale over the range from − 259.24 to 630.74°C (− 434.63 to 1167.33°F) (see Section 8.7).

Certain properties are desirable in material used for resistance-thermometer elements. The material should have a resistivity permitting fabrication in convenient sizes without excessive bulk, which would degrade time response. In addition, its thermal coefficient of resistivity should be high and as constant as possible, thereby providing an approximately linear output of reasonable magnitude. The material should be corrosion-resistant and should not undergo phase changes in the temperature ranges of interest. Finally, it should be available in conditions providing reproducible and consistent results. In regard to this last requirement, it has been found that to produce precision resistance thermometers, great care must be exercised in minimizing residual strains, requiring careful heat treatment subsequent to forming.

As is generally the case in such matters, there is no universally acceptable material for resistance-thermometer elements. Several materials are commonly used, the choice depending on the compromises that may be accepted. Although the actual resistance-temperature relation must be determined experimentally, for most metals the following empirical equation holds very closely:

$$R_t = R_0(1 + AT + BT^2), \tag{16.2}$$

where

R_t = the resistance at temperature T,

R_0 = the resistance at the reference temperature,

T = the temperature, and

A and B = constants depending on material.

Undoubtedly platinum, nickel, and copper are the materials most commonly used, although others such as tungsten, silver, and iron have also been employed.

Most commonly the elements are of wire wrapped around an insulating support constructed of glass, ceramic, or mica. The latter may have a variety of configurations, ranging from a simple flat strip, as shown in Fig. 16.3, to intricate "bird-cage" arrangements [2]. The mounted element is then provided

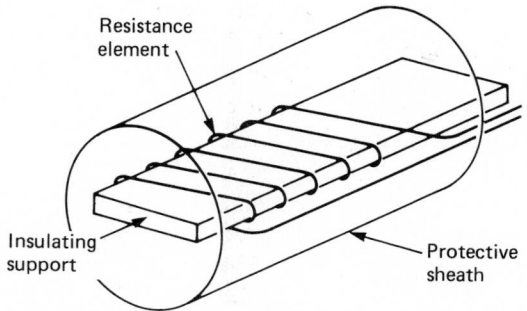

FIGURE 16.3   Section illustrating the construction of a simple RTD (resistance temperature detector).

with a protective enclosure. When permanent installations are made, and when additional protection from corrosion or mechanical abuse is required, a *well* or *socket* may be used, such as shown in Fig. 16.4.

Table 16.2 describes characteristics of several typical, commercially available, resistance-thermometer elements.

Temperature-sensitive resistance elements similar in construction to the resistance-type strain gages are also available; both foil and wire grids are used. They differ from strain gages in that the elements are relatively sensitive to temperature and insensitive to strain. In addition, the circuitry is arranged to enhance the temperature sensitivity. When properly used, common strain gage instrumentation may be used for read-out. Continuous monitoring of temperatures as high as 500°F is possible.

16.5.2 Instrumentation for Resistance Thermometry

Some form of electrical bridge is normally used to measure the resistance change in the RTD. However, particular attention must be given to the manner in which the thermometer is connected into the bridge. Leads of some length

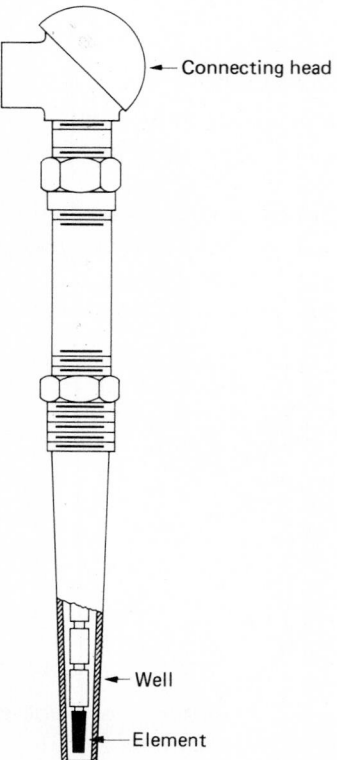

Connecting head

Well

Element

FIGURE 16.4 Installation assembly for an industrial-type resistance thermometer.

TABLE 16.2 Typical Properties of Resistance-Thermometer Elements

Type of Element	Case Material	Temperature Range °C (°F)	Resistance, ohms	Sensitivity, ohms/°C (approx.)	Limits of Error, °C	Response,* s
Platinum (laboratory)	Pyrex glass	−190 to 540 (−310 to 1000)	25 at 0°C	0.09	±0.01	
Platinum (industrial)	Stainless steel	−200 to 125 (−325 to 260)† −18 to 540 (0 to 1000)‡	25 at 0°C 25 at 0°C	—	±1 ±2	10 to 30 10 to 30
Copper	Brass	−75 to 120 (−100 to 250)	10 at 25°C	0.4	±0.5	20 to 60
Nickel	Brass	0 to 120 (32 to 250)	100 at 20°C	—	±0.3	20 to 60

* Time required to detect 90% of any temperature change in water moving at 30 cm/s. The lower value is for the thermometer case only, whereas the higher value is for the thermometer in a protective well.

† Low range.

‡ High range.

appropriate to the situation are required, and any resistance change therein due to any cause, including temperature, may be credited to the thermometer element. It is desirable, therefore, that the lead resistance be kept as low as possible relative to the element resistance. In addition, some modification may be used, providing lead compensation.

Figure 16.5 illustrates three different arrangements used to minimize lead error. Inspection of the diagrams indicates that arms AD and DC each contain the same lead lengths. Therefore, if the leads have identical properties to begin with and are subject to like ambient conditions, the effects they introduce will cancel. In each case the battery and galvanometer may be interchanged without affecting balance. When the Siemen's arrangement is used, however, no current will be carried by the center lead at balance, as shown. This may be considered an advantage. The Callender arrangement is quite useful when thermometers are used in both arms AD and DC to provide an output proportional to temperature differential between the two thermometers. The four-lead arrangement is used in the same way as the one with three leads. Provision is made, however, for using any combination of three, thereby permitting checking for unequal lead resistance. By averaging readings, more accurate results are possible. Some form of this arrangement is used where highest accuracies are desired.

The general practice is to use the bridge in the null-balance form, but the deflection bridge may also be used (see Section 5.9). In general, the null-balance arrangement is limited to measurement of static or slowly changing temperatures, whereas the deflection bridge is used for more rapidly changing

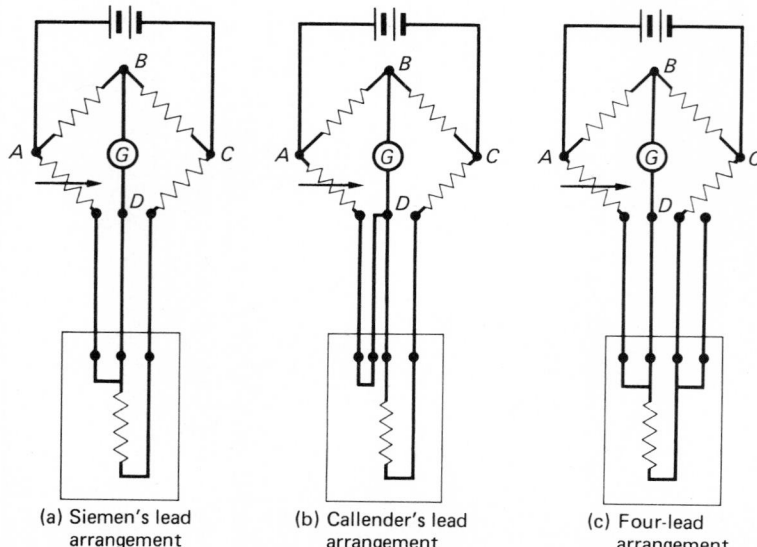

(a) Siemen's lead   (b) Callender's lead   (c) Four-lead
    arrangement   arrangement   arrangement

FIGURE 16.5   Three methods for compensating for lead resistance.

inputs. Dynamic changes are most conveniently recorded rather than simply indicated, and for this purpose either the self-balancing or the deflection types may be used, depending on time rate of temperature change.

When a resistance bridge is used for measurement, current will necessarily flow through each bridge arm. An error may, therefore, be introduced, caused by I^2R heating. For resistance thermometers such an error will be of opposite sign to that caused by conduction and radiation from the element (Section 16.10.1), and in general it will be small because the gross effects in individual arms will be largely balanced by similar effects in the other arms. An estimate of the overall error resulting from ohmic heating may be had by making readings at different current values and extrapolating to zero current.

16.5.3   Thermistors

The thermistor is a thermally sensitive variable resistor made of a ceramiclike semiconducting material. Unlike metals, thermistors respond negatively to temperature. As the temperature rises, the thermistor resistance decreases. Figure 16.6 shows typical temperature–resistance relations.

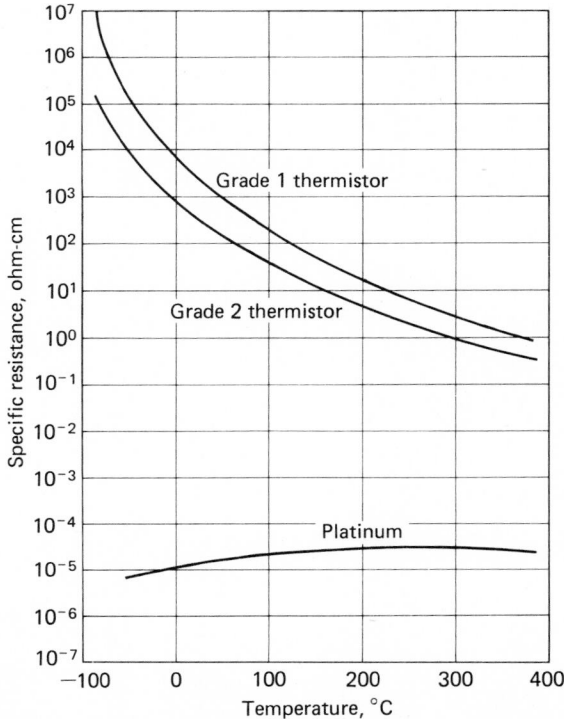

FIGURE 16.6   Typical thermistor temperature–resistance relations.

Thermistors are composed of oxides of manganese, nickel, and cobalt in formulations having resistivities of 100 to 450,000 ohm·cm. They are available in various forms, such as shown in Fig. 16.7. Table 16.3 lists the properties of certain commercially available thermistors.

The temperature–resistance function for a thermistor is given by the relationships

$$R = R_0 e^k \tag{16.3}$$

and

$$k = \beta\left(\frac{1}{T} - \frac{1}{T_0}\right), \tag{16.3a}$$

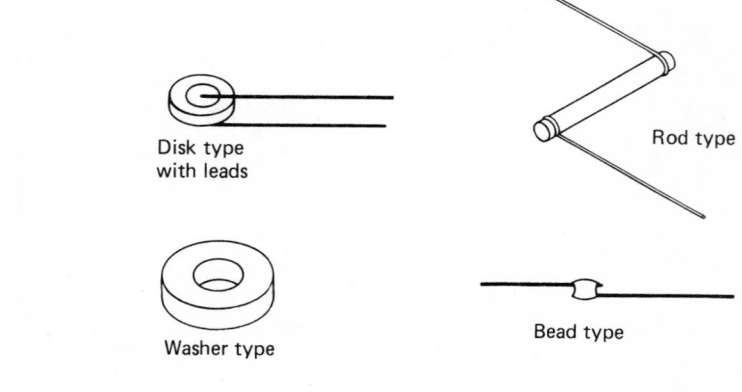

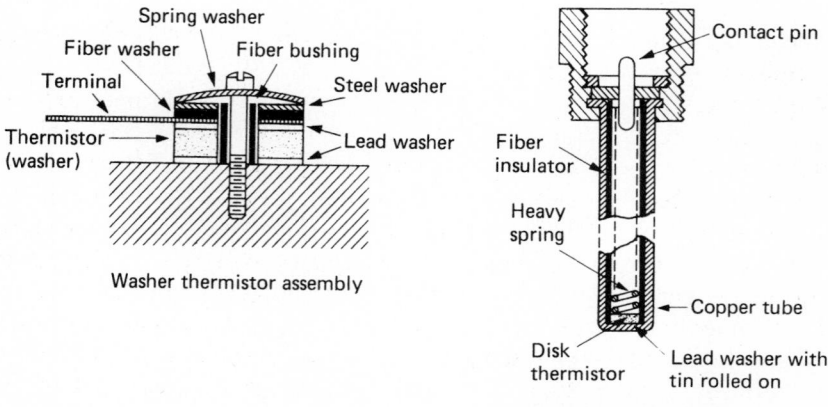

FIGURE 16.7   Various thermistor forms commercially available.

TABLE 16.3   Typical Specifications for Various Commercial Thermistors

Form	Resistance in Ohms at 25°C	Resistance in Ohms at 125°C	Time Characteristics Seconds for ΔT = 50°C	Power Rating, W	Operating Range, °C
Rod A	1K/15K	12½/25	70/160	3½	−10/170
B	2/2M	2.8/52	10/90	0.6/2.4	−40/125
C	1K/150K	7/9	20/125		−60/125
D	1K/100K	20/30	20/100		−80/150
E	90/110K	30	70		−55/150
Disk F	30/10K	20/30	20/100		−80/150
G	½/1M	5/12	2/230		−80/150
H	2½/800K	14/60	10/215	3	−40/125
Bead I	800K/1.2M	52	2	0.18	−55/275
J	30/15M	10/100	0.1/60	0.002/0.15	−55/275
K	60/100M	5/25	½/120		−100/300

in which

R = the resistance at any temperature T, in °K,

R_0 = the resistance at reference temperature T_0, in °K,

e = the base of Naperian logarithms, and

β = a constant.

The constant β generally has a value between 3400 and 3900, depending on the thermistor formulation or grade.

When a thermistor is used in an electrical circuit, current normally flows through it, and ohmic heating is generated by its resistance. This will raise the temperature of the element, the amount depending on the rate with which the heat is dissipated. For given ambient conditions, a temperature equilibrium will occur at which a definite resistance value will exist. Through proper application of thermistor and electrical circuit characteristics, the devices may be used for temperature measurement or control. In addition, they are quite useful for compensating electrical circuitry for changing ambient temperature. This is largely possible because of the *negative* temperature characteristics of the thermistor, in contrast to *positive* characteristics possessed by most electrical components. Also, time-delay actions over large ranges are possible through proper balancing of electrical and heat-transfer conditions. Figure 16.8

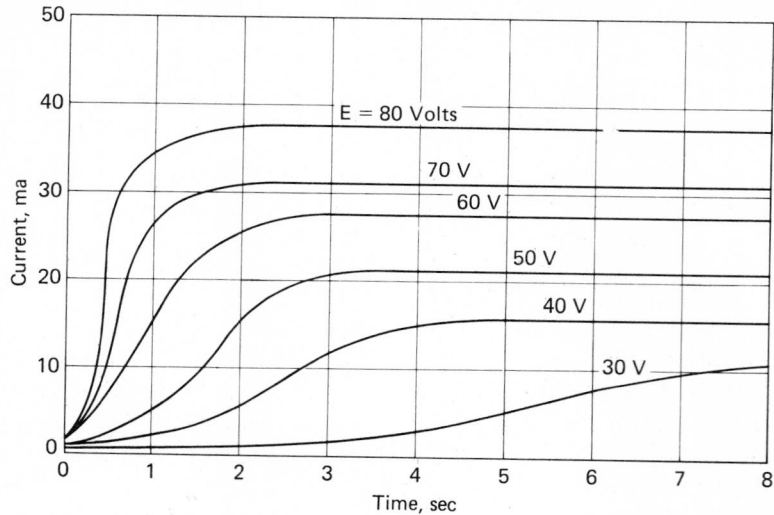

FIGURE 16.8 Typical current–time relations for thermistors.

illustrates typical thermistor self-heating response characteristics. Of course, environment (heat transfer conditions) is a major factor in an actual application.

The inherently high sensitivity possessed by thermistors permits use of very simple electrical circuitry for measurement of temperature. Ordinary ohmmeters may be used within the limits of accuracy of the meter itself. More often one of the various forms of resistance bridge is used (Section 5.9), either in the null-balance form or as a deflection bridge. Simple ballast circuits (Section 5.6) are also usable.

Through use of the thermistor's temperature–resistance characteristics alone, or in conjunction with controlled heat transfer, thermistors have been used for measurement of many quantities, including pressure, liquid level, power, and others. They are also used for temperature control, timing (through use of their delay characteristics in combination with relays), overload protectors, warning devices, etc.

16.6 THERMOCOUPLES

In 1821, T. J. Seebeck discovered that an electromotive force exists across a junction formed of two unlike metals [3]. Later it was shown [4, 5] that the potential actually comes from two different sources: that resulting solely from *contact* of the two dissimilar metals and the *junction temperature,* and that due to *temperature gradients* along the conductors in the circuit. These two effects are named the Peltier and Thomson effects after their respective discoverers. In most cases the Thomson emf is quite small relative to the Peltier emf, and with proper selection of materials may be disregarded. These effects

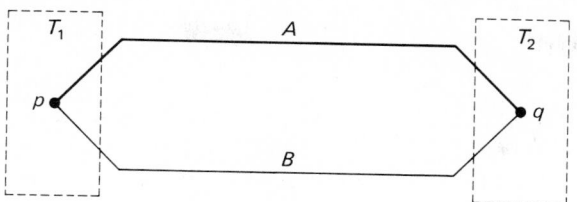

FIGURE 16.9   Elementary thermocouple circuit.

form the basis for a very important temperature-measuring element, the *thermocouple,* often abbreviated TC.

If a circuit is formed including a thermocouple, as shown in Fig. 16.9, a minimum of two conductors will be necessary, unavoidably resulting in two junctions, p and q. If we disregard the Thomson effect, the net emf will be the result of the difference between the two Peltier emf's occurring at the two junctions. If the temperatures T_1 and T_2 are equal, the two emf's will be equal but opposed, and no current will flow. However, if the temperatures are different, the emf's will not balance, and a current *will* flow. The net emf is a function of the two materials used to form the circuit and the *temperatures* of the two junctions. The actual relations, however, are empirical, and the temperature–emf data must be based on experiment. An important fact is that the results are reproducible and therefore provide a reliable method for measuring temperature.

Note particularly that *two* junctions are *always* required. In general, one senses the desired or unknown temperature; this one we shall call the *hot* or *measuring* junction. The second will usually be maintained at a known fixed temperature; this one we shall refer to as the *cold* or *reference* junction.

16.6.1 Application Laws for Thermocouples

In addition to the Seebeck effect, there are certain laws by which thermoelectric circuits abide, as follows:

> *Law of intermediate metals* [6]. *Insertion of an intermediate metal into a thermocouple circuit will not affect the net emf, provided the two junctions introduced by the third metal are at identical temperatures.*

Applications of this law are shown in Fig. 16.10. As shown in part (a) of the figure, if the third metal C is introduced and if the new junctions r and s are both held at temperature T_3, the net potential for the circuit will remain unchanged. This, of course, permits insertion of a measuring device or circuit without upsetting the temperature function of the thermocouple circuit. In Fig. 16.10(b) the third metal may be introduced at either a *measuring* or *reference junction,* so long as couples p_1 and p_2 are maintained at the same temperature T_1. This makes possible the use of joining materials, such as soft

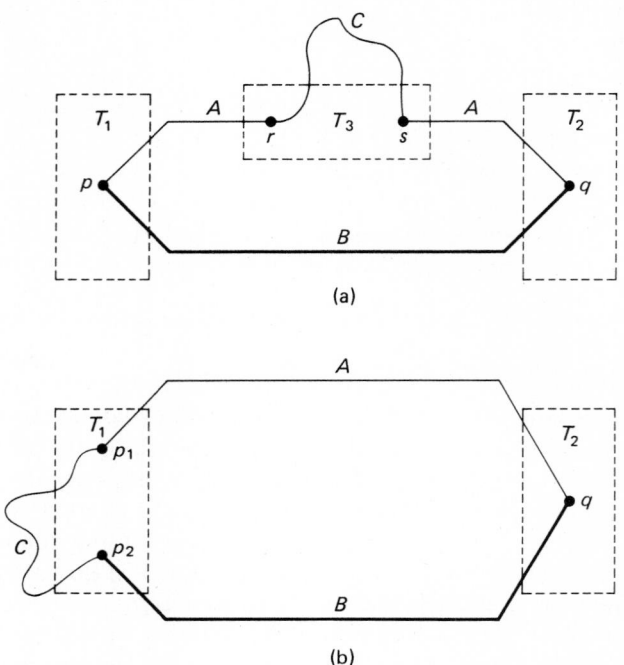

FIGURE 16.10   Diagrams illustrating the law for intermediate metals.

or hard solder, in fabricating the thermocouples. In addition, the thermocouple may be actually embedded directly into the surface or interior of either a conductor or nonconductor without altering the thermocouple's usefulness.

> ***Law of intermediate temperatures*** [6]. *If a simple thermocouple circuit develops an emf, e_1, when its junctions are at temperatures T_1 and T_2, and an emf, e_2, when its junctions are at temperatures T_2 and T_3, it will develop an emf, $e_1 + e_2$, when its junctions are at temperatures T_1 and T_3.*

This makes possible direct correction for secondary junctions whose temperatures may be known but are not directly controllable. It also makes possible the use of thermocouple tables based on a "standard" reference temperature (say 0°C) although neither junction may actually be at the "standard" temperature.

16.6.2 Thermocouple Materials and Installation

Theoretically any two unlike conducting materials could be used to form a thermocouple. Actually, of course, certain materials and combinations are better than others, and some have practically become standard for given temperature ranges. Materials and combinations are listed in Table 16.1. Indicated letter designations are ANSI standards.

Size of wire is of importance. Usually the higher the temperature to be measured, the heavier should be the wire. As the size increases, however, the time response of the couple to temperature change increases. Therefore, some compromise between response and life may be required.

Thermocouples may be prepared by twisting the two wires together and brazing, or preferably welding, as shown in Fig. 16.11. Low-temperature couples are often used bare; however, for higher temperatures, some form of protection is generally required. Figure 16.12 illustrates common methods for separating the wires, and Fig. 16.4 shows a section through a typical protective tube.

16.6.3 Measurement of Thermal emf

The actual magnitude of electrical potential developed by thermocouples is quite small when judged in terms of many standards. Table 16.4 provides some idea of the range of values to be expected. Expanded tables have been developed by the National Bureau of Standards [7]. These are adopted as ANSI and ASTM standards. Table 16.5 is adapted from this source and lists emf values for the type T (copper–constantan) thermocouples. The referenced source contains extended tables for all commonly used thermocouples, typically listing values to six significant places at 1°C increments.

Computer processing of data makes it desirable to incorporate the thermocouple data into computer memory in some manner. To do this the power series given in Tables 16.6 and 16.7 may be used [7]. Values derived from Table 16.6 are referred to as being "exact" and those in Table 16.7 are exact within ± 0.2°C or better. Additional functional relationships are included in reference [7].

Traditionally, thermocouple output has been measured through use of a

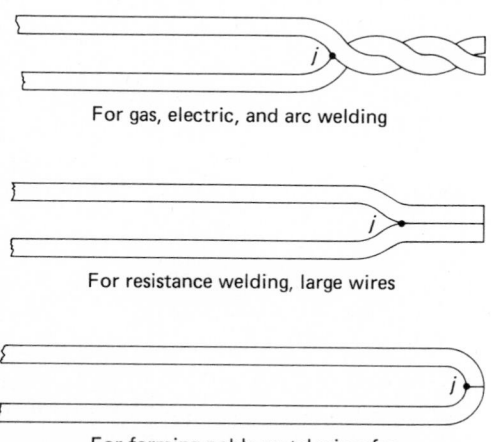

For gas, electric, and arc welding

For resistance welding, large wires

For forming noble-metal wires for electric arc welding

FIGURE 16.11 Common forms of thermocouple construction. (See Section 16.6.5 for significance of point j).

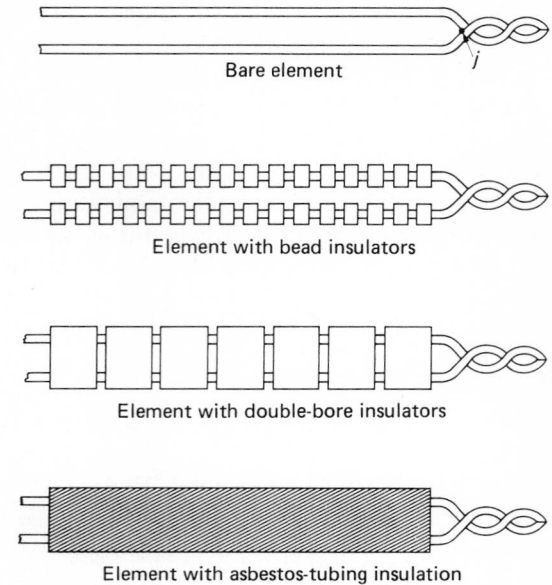

Bare element

Element with bead insulators

Element with double-bore insulators

Element with asbestos-tubing insulation

FIGURE 16.12   Methods for insulating thermocouple leads.

voltage-balancing potentiometer (see Section 5.8), of either the manually or automatically balancing types. In automatic form, the TC output may be chart-recorded, used as a control input, or both. Solid-state innovations are rapidly replacing the older, cumbersome manual methods.

Solid-state temperature-measurement instrumentation includes digital read-out "thermometers" and recorders and controllers. TC thermometers are available for most thermocouple types and provide direct digital read-out. Typical specifications are

Range	− 100 to 1000 (either °F or °C)
Resolution	0.2 to 1 degree
Response time	Less than 2 s
Input impedance	100 M-ohm
Selectable scale (either F or C)	

In the following discussion we will refer to the use of a potentiometer; however, it should be understood that other forms of read-out instrumentation may be substituted.

Figure 16.13 shows a simple temperature-measuring system using a thermocouple as the sensing element and a potentiometer for indication. In this illustration, the thermoelectric circuit consists of a measuring junction, p, and a somewhat less obvious reference junction, q, at the potentiometer. Com-

TABLE 16.4 Values of emf in Absolute Millivolts for Selected Metal Combinations Based on Reference Junction Temperature at 32°F (0 °C)

Temperature °F °C	Thermocouple Type				
	Cu vs. Constantan (T)	Chromel vs. Constantan (E)	Iron vs. Constantan (J)	Chromel vs. Constantan (K)	Platinum vs. Platinum, 10% Rhodium (S)
−300 (−184.4)	−5.341	−8.404	−7.519	−5.632	
−200 (−128.9)	−4.149	−6.471	−5.760	−4.381	
−100 (−73.7)	−2.581	−3.976	−3.492	−2.699	
0 (−17.8)	−0.674	−1.026	−0.885	−0.692	−0.092
100 (37.8)	1.518	2.281	1.942	1.520	0.221
200 (93.3)	3.967	5.869	4.906	3.819	0.597
300 (148.9)	6.647	9.708	7.947	6.092	1.020
400 (204.4)	9.523	13.748	11.023	8.314	1.478
500 (260.0)	12.572	17.942	14.108	10.560	1.962
700 (371.1)	19.095	26.637	20.253	15.178	2.985
1000 (537.8)		40.056	29.515	22.251	4.609
1500 (815.6)		62.240		33.913	7.514
2000 (1093.3)				44.856	10.675
2500 (1371.1)				54.845	14.018
3000 (1648.9)					17.347

parison with Fig. 16.10(b) indicates that the instrument box may be considered an intermediate conductor in the same sense as C in the figure. If we assume the two instrument binding posts to be at identical temperature, the cold junction will then be formed by the ends of the two thermocouple leads as they attach to the posts. If a reference temperature is determined by use of a good liquid-in-glass thermometer placed near the binding posts, application of the law of intermediate metals and use of the tables referred to 0°C permits determination of the hot-junction temperature.

EXAMPLE Let us assume an arrangement as shown in Fig. 16.13, using a type T (copper–constantan) thermocouple, a reference temperature of 20°C, determined as described above, and a potentiometer reading of 2.877 mV. *Object:* Find T_m, the temperature sensed by the measuring couple.

TABLE 16.5 Values of Thermal emf in Millivolts vs. Temperature in Degrees Celsius for Type T Thermocouples [Cu(+) vs. Constantan (−)] and a Reference Temperature of 0°C

°C	0	5	10	15	20
−200	−5.603	−5.522	−5.439	−5.351	−5.261
−175	−5.167	−5.069	−4.969	−4.865	−4.758
−150	−4.648	−4.535	−4.419	−4.299	−4.177
−125	−4.051	−3.923	−3.791	−3.656	−3.519
−100	−3.378	−3.235	−3.089	−2.939	−2.788
−75	−2.633	−2.475	−2.315	−2.152	−1.987
−50	−1.819	−1.648	−1.475	−1.299	−1.121
−25	−.94	−.757	−.571	−.383	−.193
0	0	.195	.391	.589	.789
25	.992	1.196	1.403	1.611	1.822
50	2.035	2.250	2.467	2.687	2.908
75	3.131	3.357	3.584	3.813	4.044
100	4.277	4.512	4.749	4.987	5.227
125	5.469	5.712	5.957	6.204	6.452
150	6.702	6.954	7.207	7.462	7.718
175	7.975	8.235	8.495	8.757	9.021
200	9.286	9.553	9.820	10.090	10.360
225	10.632	10.905	11.180	11.456	11.733
250	12.011	12.291	12.572	12.854	13.137
275	13.421	13.707	13.993	14.261	14.570
300	14.860	15.151	15.443	15.736	16.030
325	16.325	16.621	16.919	17.217	17.516
350	17.816	18.118	18.420	18.723	19.027
375	19.332	19.638	19.945	20.252	20.560

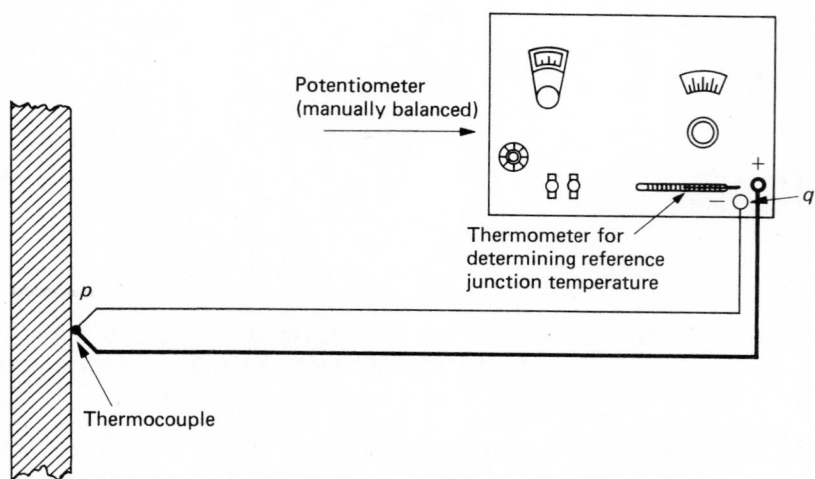

FIGURE 16.13   Schematic diagram illustrating use of potentiometer terminals as a reference junction.

TABLE 16.6 Power Expansion of $E = f(C)$, where $E =$ the Thermocouple emf in mV. Referred to 0°C and $C =$ the temperature in °C

TC Type	Applicable Range	$E = f(C)$
(B), Pt, 30% Rh(+) vs. Pt, 6% Rh(−)	0 to 1820°C	$E = (-2.4674601620 \times 10^{-1} \times C + 5.9102111169 \times 10^{-3} \times C^2 - 1.4307123430 \times 10^{-6} \times C^3 + 2.1509149750 \times 10^{-9} \times C^4 - 3.1757800720 \times 10^{-12} \times C^5 + 2.4010367459 \times 10^{-15} \times C^6 - 9.0928148159 \times 10^{-19} \times C^7 + 1.3299050505137 \times 10^{-22} \times C^8) \times 10^{-3}$
(E), chromel (+) vs. constantan (−)	0 to 1000°C	$E = (+5.8695857799 \times 10 \times C + 4.3110945462 \times 10^{-2} \times C^2 + 5.7220358202 \times 10^{-5} \times C^3 + 5.4020668085 \times 10^{-7} \times C^4 + 1.5425922111 \times 10^{-9} \times C^5 - 2.4850089136 \times 10^{-12} \times C^6 + 2.3389721459 \times 10^{-15} \times C^7 - 1.1946296815 \times 10^{-18} \times C^8 + 2.5561127497 \times 10^{-22} \times C^9) \times 10^{-3}$
(J), Fe(+) vs. constantan (−)	−210 to 760°C	$E = (5.0372753027 \times 10 \times C + 3.0425491284 \times 10^{-2} \times C^2 - 8.5669750464 \times 10^{-5} \times C^3 + 1.3348825735 \times 10^{-7} \times C^4 - 1.7022405966 \times 10^{-10} \times C^5 + 1.9416091001 \times 10^{-13} \times C^6 - 9.6391844859 \times 10^{-17} \times C^7) \times 10^{-3}$
(K), chromel (+) vs. alumel (−)	0 to 1372°C	$E = (-1.8533063273 \times 10 + 3.8918344612 \times 10 \times C + 1.6645154356 \times 10^{-2} \times C^2 - 7.8702374448 \times 10^{-5} \times C^3 + 2.2835785557 \times 10^{-7} \times C^4 - 3.5700231258 \times 10^{-10} \times C^5 + 2.9932909136 \times 10^{-13} \times C^6 - 1.2849848798 \times 10^{-16} \times C^7 + 2.2239974336 \times 10^{-20} \times C^8 - 125\, \exp\left[-\tfrac{1}{2}((C - 127)/65)^2\right]) \times 10^{-3}$
(R), Pt(−) vs. Pt,13% Rh(+)	630 to 1064°C	$E = (-2.6418007025 \times 10^2 + 8.0466800747 \times 10^0 \times C + 2.9892293723 \times 10^{-3} \times C^2 + 2.6876058617 \times 10^{-7} \times C^3) \times 10^{-3}$
	1064 to 1665°C	$E = (+1.4901702702 \times 10^3 + 2.8639867552 \times 10^0 \times C + 8.0823631189 \times 10^{-3} \times C^2 + 1.9338477638 \times 10^{-6} \times C^3) \times 10^{-3}$
(S), Pt,10% (Rh+) vs. Pt(−)	630 to 1064°C	$E = (-2.9824481615 \times 10^2 + 8.2375528221 \times 10^0 \times C + 1.6453909942 \times 10^{-3} \times C^2) \times 10^{-3}$
	1064 to 1665°C	$E = (+1.2766292175 \times 10^3 + 3.4970908041 \times 10^0 \times C + 6.3824648666 \times 10^{-3} \times C^2 - 1.5722424599 \times 10^{-6} \times C^3) \times 10^{-3}$
(T), Cu(+) vs. constantan (−)	0 to 400°C	$E = (+3.8740773840 \times 10 \times C + 3.3190198092 \times 10^{-2} \times C^2 + 2.0714183645 \times 10^{-4} \times C^3 - 2.1945834823 \times 10^{-6} \times C^4 + 1.1031900550 \times 10^{-8} \times C^5 - 3.0927581898 \times 10^{-11} \times C^6 + 4.5653337165 \times 10^{-14} \times C^7 - 2.7616878040 \times 10^{-17} \times C^8) \times 10^{-3}$

TABLE 16.7 Power Expansion of $C = g(E)$, where $C = $ °Celsius and $E = $ the Thermocouple emf in mV. Referred to 0°C

TC Type	Applicable Range	$C = g(E)$
E	0 to 400°C	$C = (+1.7022525 \times 10 \times E - 5.7669892 \times 10^{-3} \times E^4) - 2.2097240 \times 10^{-1} \times E^2 + 5.4809314 \times 10^{-3} \times E^3$
	400 to 1000°C	$C = (+2.9347907 \times 10 + 2.3388779 \times 10^{-4} \times E^3) + 1.3385134 \times 10 \times E - 2.6669218 \times 10^{-2} \times E^2$
J	0 to 400°C	$C = (+1.9750953 \times 10 \times E - 1.3280568 \times 10^{-4} \times E^4) - 1.8542600 \times 10^{-1} \times E^2 + 8.3683958 \times 10^{-3} \times E^3$
	400 to 760°C	$C = (9.2808351 \times 10 + 5.4463817 \times E - 1.3987013 \times 10^{-2} \times E^3 + 9.9364476 \times 10^{-5} \times E^4) + 6.5254537 \times 10^{-1} \times E^2$
K	400 to 1000°C	$C = (-2.4707112 \times 10 + 2.9465633 \times 10 \times E + 6.5075717 \times 10^{-3} \times E^3 - 3.9663834 \times 10^{-5} \times E^4) - 3.1332620 \times 10^{-1} \times E^2$
T	0 to 400°C	$C = (+2.5661297 \times 10 \times E - 3.5500900 \times 10^{-4} \times E^4) - 6.1954869 \times 10^{-1} \times E^2 + 2.2181644 \times 10^{-2} \times E^3$

Solution Because our read-out is referenced to 20°C and the TC tables are referenced to 0°C, we must use the law of intermediate temperatures to correct our emf value, as follows:

$$E_{x_0} = E_{x_{20}} + E_{20_0},$$

where E_{x_0} and $E_{x_{20}}$ are emf's corresponding to the unknown temperature referred to 0 and 20°C, respectively, and E_{20_0} is the emf corresponding to 20°C referred to 0°.

Using Table 16.5 we find $E_{20_0} = 0.789$ mV, hence,

$$E_{x_0} = 2.887 + 0.789 = 3.666 \,\text{mV}.$$

Inspection of the tabulated values yields $T_m = 86 + \,°C$.

Although we would not normally use the relationships in Tables 16.6 and 16.7 for longhand calculations, we will illustrate the use of the polynomials to check a value obtained above. What emf do we obtain from the equation, for 20°C, using a type T thermocouple?

$$E_{20} = 774.8155 + 13.2761 + 1.6571 - 0.3511 + \text{etc.}$$

$$= 0.78943$$

16.6.4 Extension Wires

Thermocouple wire is relatively expensive compared to most common materials, such as ordinary copper. It is therefore often desirable to minimize the use of the more costly materials by employing leads. Arrangements of this are shown in Fig. 16.14. In these cases the measuring junction is shown at p and the reference junction(s) at q. Comparison with Fig. 16.10(a) indicates the similarity. Of course, a requirement for accuracy is that q_1 and q_2 be maintained at the same temperature, and further, that the temperature be accurately known.

An iron–constantan couple is indicated in Fig. 16.14(a), although any of the common materials could be used. Should a copper–constantan couple be used, with copper extension leads, the arrangement would become that shown in Fig. 16.10(b). As before, temperature T_r must be accurately known. This corresponds to the simplified version shown in Fig. 16.10(a).

As indicated above, reference temperature T_r should be known. This may not always be strictly true. In certain commercial equipment, particularly of the recording type, electrical or electromechanical compensation is sometimes built in. When this is done, T_r may not actually be indicated, but its effect is nevertheless recognized and compensated.

Special formulated extension wires are available for each type of TC, minimizing the effects of small temperature variations at intermediate junc-

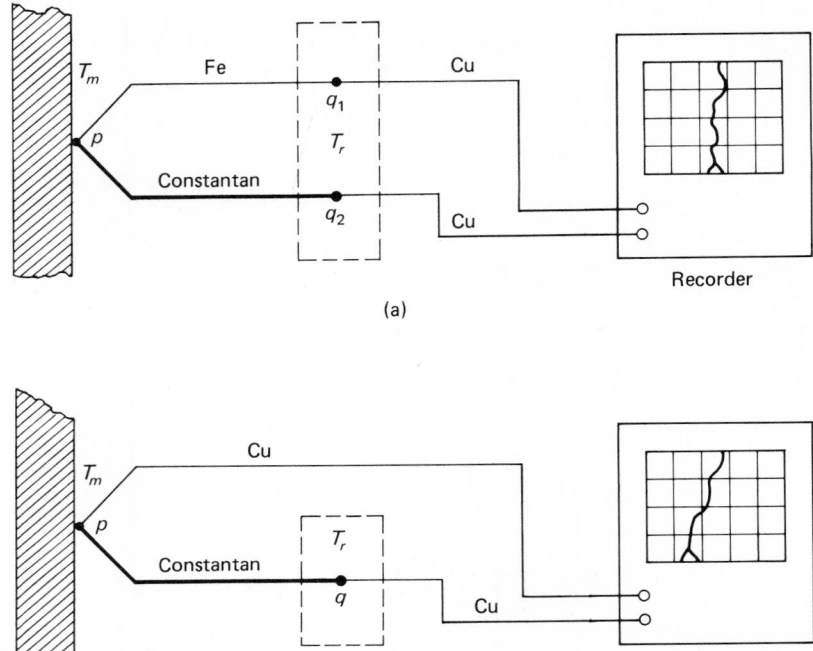

FIGURE 16.14   Diagrams showing use of extension leads.

tions. These are less expensive than primary wire for an entire run, but more expensive than copper wire. Use of the special wires is particularly advisable in critical installations.

Laboratory methods for using thermocouples often employ reference junctions at accurately controlled temperatures. The common arrangements make use of ice baths, such as shown in Fig. 16.15. These systems correspond to simplified circuits shown in Figs. 16.10(a) and (b), respectively. (One circuit uses extension leads, while the other does not.) For the most accurate work, distilled water with ice made therefrom is advisable to eliminate shifts in the freezing point caused by contaminants. Some form of Dewar flask is convenient to use to reduce melting rate. Although the ice bath supplies an easily obtained, accurately controlled reference temperature, any other controlled source could be employed using the same procedures.

16.6.5 Effective Junction

In certain instances it may be highly desirable to know, as precisely as possible, the location of the effective thermocouple junction, i.e., where, within the

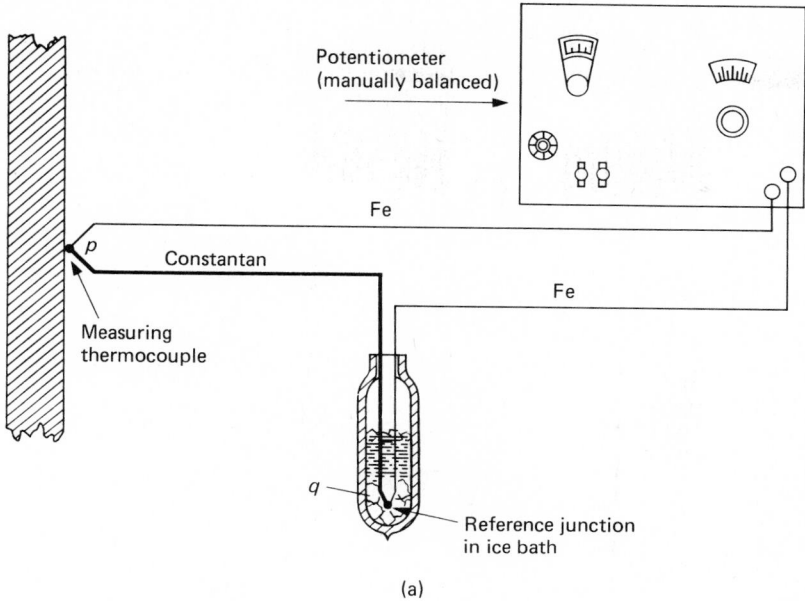

(a)

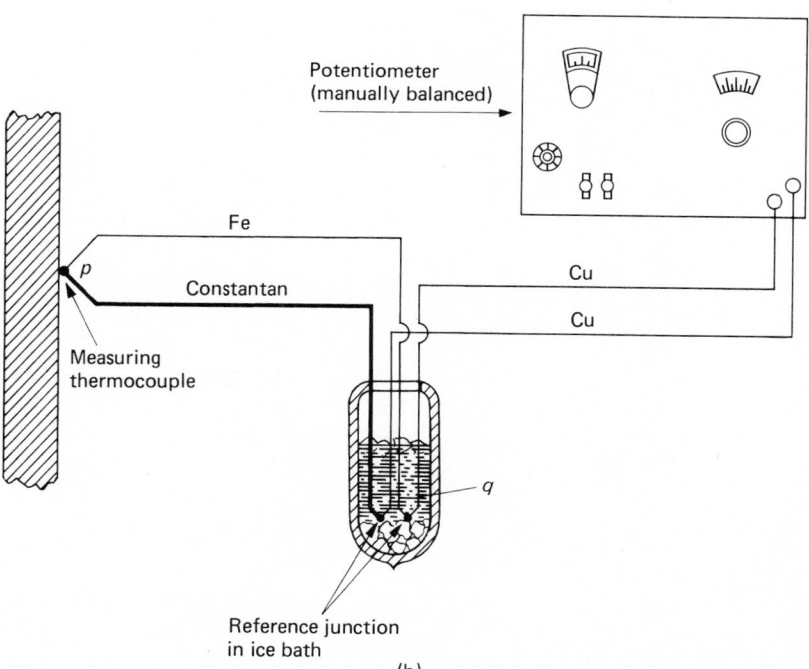

(b)

FIGURE 16.15   Systems with fixed reference temperature (ice bath).

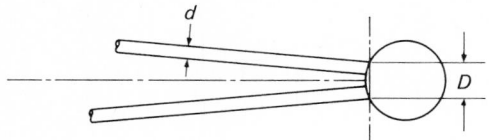

FIGURE 16.16   Region of uncertainty for a bead-type thermocouple.

dimensional extent of the couple, the indicated temperature occurs. This becomes of greater importance as both the temperature gradient and the size of the couple are increased. In general terms, the *effective location* is at the point of junction symmetry nearest the leads (points j in Figs. 16.11 and 16.12). Baker, Ryder, and Baker [8] define the area $D \times d$ (Fig. 16.16) as the region of uncertainty in a "bead-type" couple, when there is a temperature gradient through the junction.

16.6.6   Thermopiles and Thermocouples Connected in Parallel

Thermocouples may be connected electrically in series or parallel, as seen in Fig. 16.17. When connected in series, the combination is generally called a *thermopile*, whereas parallel-connected couples have no particular name.

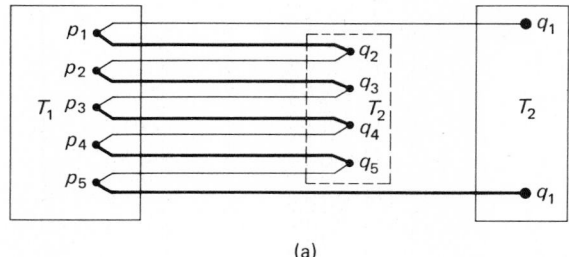

(a)

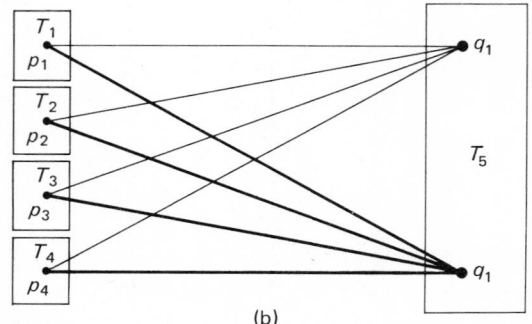

(b)

FIGURE 16.17   (a) Series-connected thermocouples forming a thermopile. (b) Parallel-connected thermocouples.

The total output from n thermocouples connected to form a thermopile (Fig. 16.17a) will be equal to the sums of the individual emf's, and if the thermocouples are identical, the total output will equal n times the output of a single couple. The purpose of using a thermopile rather than a single thermocouple is, of course, to obtain a more sensitive element.

When the couples are combined in the form of a thermopile, it is usually desirable to cluster them together as closely as possible in order to measure the temperature at an approximate point source. It is obvious, however, that when thermocouples are combined in series, the law for intermediate metals, as illustrated in Fig. 16.10(b), cannot be applied to combinations of thermocouples, for the individual thermocouple emf's would be shorted. Care must therefore be used to ensure that the individual couples are electrically insulated one from the other.

Parallel connection of thermocouples provides an averaging, which in certain cases may be advantageous. This form of combination is *not* usually referred to as a thermopile.

16.7 THE LINEAR-QUARTZ THERMOMETER

The interrelationship between temperature and the resonating frequency of a quartz crystal has long been recognized. In general, the relationship is nonlinear, and for many applications very considerable effort has been expended in attempts to minimize the frequency drift caused by temperature variation. Hammond [9] discovered a new orientation called the "LC" or "linear cut," which provides a temperature–frequency relationship of 1000 Hz/°C with a deviation from the best straight line of less than 0.05% over a range of -40 to 230°C (-40 to 446°F). This linearity may be compared with a value of 0.55% for the platinum-resistance thermometer.

Nominal-resonator frequency is 28 MHz and the sensor output is compared to a reference frequency of 28.208 MHz supplied by a reference oscillator. The frequency difference is detected, converted to pulses, and passed to an electronic counter, which provides a digital display of the temperature magnitude. Various probes are available, all with time constants of 1 s. Resolution is dependent on repetitive read-out rate, with a value of 0.0001°C attainable in 10 s. Read-outs as fast as four per second may be obtained. Remote sensing to 3000 m is possible.

16.8 PYROMETRY

The term *pyrometry* is derived from the Greek words *pyros,* meaning "fire" and *metron* meaning "to measure." Literally, the term means general temperature measurement. However, in engineering usage, the word normally (not always) refers to the measurement of temperatures in the range extending upward from about 500°C ($\approx$ 1000°F). Although certain of the thermocouples and resistance-type thermometers can be used above 500°C, pyrometry is generally thought of as consisting primarily of the various forms of thermal-radiation measurement.

Electromagnetic radiation extends over a wide range of wavelengths (frequencies), as illustrated in Fig. 16.18. Pyrometry is based on the sampling and measurement of energies in certain bandwidths of this spectrum. Temperature is then derived from an evaluation of the energy magnitude or wavelength.

There are three distinct instruments referred to as pyrometers: the *total-radiation,* the *optical* (or brightness), and the *infrared* pyrometers. The names are almost self-descriptive. The first accepts a controlled sample of *total* radiation and through determination of the heating effect of the intercepted sample, a measure of temperature is obtained by a thermal sensor such as a thermopile. The optical, or brightness, pyrometer uses the human eye as the detecting means for estimating the change in wavelength of *visual* radiation with temperature. Operation of the infrared pyrometer is similar in principle to that of the total radiation type, except the measurements are restricted to the infrared segment. Also, electronic detectors (photocells) are used as sensors. None of the three is dependent on direct contact with the source and, within reason, none is dependent on distance from the source.

16.8.1 Pyrometry Theory

All bodies above absolute zero temperature radiate energy. Not only do they radiate or emit energy, but they also receive and absorb it from other sources.

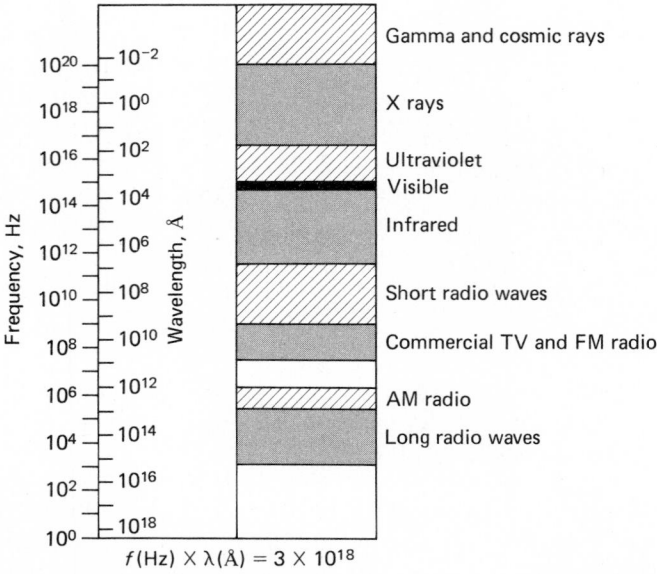

FIGURE 16.18   The electromagnetic radiation spectrum.

We all know that when a piece of steel is heated to about 550°C it begins to glow, i.e., we become conscious of visible light being *radiated* from its surface. As the temperature is raised, the light becomes brighter or more intense. In addition, there is a change in color; it changes from a dull red, through orange to yellow, and finally approaches an almost white light at the melting temperature (1430 to 1540°C).

We know, therefore, that through the range of temperatures from approximately 550 to 1540°C, energy in the form of *light* is radiated from the body. We can also sense that at temperatures below 550°C and almost down to room temperature, the piece of steel is still radiating energy in the form of *heat,* for if the mass is large enough we can feel it even though we may not be touching it. We know, then, that energy is radiated through certain temperature ranges because our senses provide the necessary information. Although our senses are not as good at lower temperatures, on occasion one can actually "feel" the presence of cold walls in a room because heat is being radiated from one's body *to* the walls. Energy transmission of this sort does not require an intervening medium for conveyance; in fact, intervening substances actually interfere with transmission.

The energy of which we are speaking is transmitted as electromagnetic waves traveling at the speed of light. It is known that all substances emit and absorb radiant energy at a rate depending on the absolute temperature and physical properties of the substance. Waves striking the surface of a substance are partially absorbed, partially reflected, and partially transmitted. These portions are measured in terms of *absorptivity,* α, *reflectivity,* ρ, and *transmissivity,* τ, where

$$\alpha + \rho + \tau = 1. \qquad (16.4)$$

For an ideal reflector, a condition approached by a highly polished surface, $\rho \to 1$. Many gases represent substances of high transmissivity, for which $\tau \to 1$, and a *blackbody* approaches the ideal absorber, for which $\alpha \to 1$.

Before a body can emit energy it must have first absorbed it. It follows, therefore, that a good absorber is also a good radiator, and it may be concluded that the *ideal radiator* is one for which the value of α is equal to unity. When we refer to radiation as distinguished from absorption, the term *emissivity,* ε, is used rather than absorptivity, α. However, from Kirchhoff's law

$$\varepsilon = \alpha.$$

Table 16.8 lists values of emissivities for certain materials.

According to the Stefan–Boltzmann law [10], the net rate of exchange of energy between two ideal radiators A and B is

$$q = \sigma(T_A^4 - T_B^4). \qquad (16.5)$$

This may be modified for the nonideal case to read

$$q = \sigma\varepsilon C_A(T_A^4 - T_B^4), \qquad (16.6)$$

TABLE 16.8   Total Emissivity for Certain Surfaces [10]

Surface	Temperature, °C	Emissivity
Polished silver	225–625	0.0198–0.0324
Platinum filament	25–1225	0.036–0.192
Polished nickel	23	0.045
Aluminum foil	100	0.087
Concrete	21	0.63
Roofing paper	20	0.91
Plaster	10–88	0.91
Rough red brick	21	0.93
Asbestos paper	38–371	0.93–0.945
Smooth glass	22	0.937
Water	0–100	0.95–0.963
Blackbody	—	≈1.00

in which

q = radiant heat transfer, in W/m²,

C_A = the configurational factor to allow for relative position and geometry of bodies,

T_A and T_B = the absolute temperatures of bodies A and B, respectively, in K, and

σ = the Stefan–Boltzmann constant

= 5.729×10^{-8} W/m²·K⁴.

The foregoing supplies the theoretical basis for total-radiation pyrometry.

In application, recognition must be made of the fact that the radiators are nonideal. They are of nonoptimum geometry and position; absorption takes place in the intervening media, and the bodies themselves never possess emissivities equal to unity. Account for such things as these *must be made through calibration.*

As we mentioned earlier, the *color* changes. Change in color, of course, corresponds to change in wavelength and the wavelength of *maximum* radiation decreases with increase in temperature. A decrease in wavelength shifts the color from the reds toward the yellows. Steel at 540°C has a deep red color. At 815°C the color is a bright red, and at 1200°C the color appears

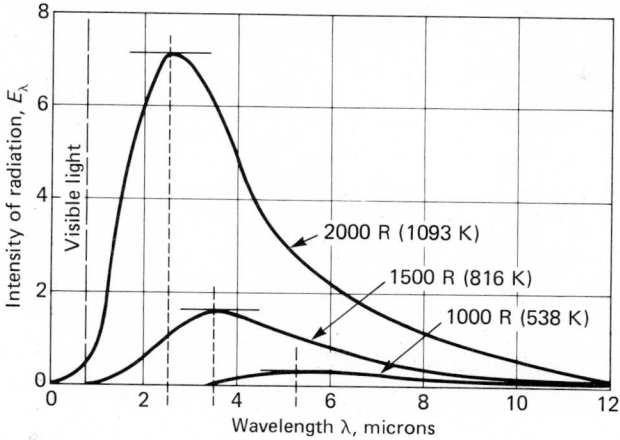

FIGURE 16.19 Graphical representation illustrating basis for Wien's displacement law.

white. The corresponding radiant energy *maximums* occur at wavelengths of 3.5, 2.6, and 1.9 microns, respectively.

If we should heat an ideal radiator and determine the relative intensities at each wavelength, we would obtain the data for a characteristic energy-distribution curve. For different temperatures, curves such as those shown in Fig. 16.19 will be obtained. It will be noted that not only is the radiation intensity of the higher-temperature body increased, but also there is a shift in the wavelength of maximum emission toward the shorter waves (from red toward blue). The rule governing this latter effect, referred to as the *Wien displacement law*, is the primary basis for the optical pyrometer. The intensity relation may be expressed as follows [11]:

$$E_\lambda = C_1 \lambda^{-5}/[e^{(C_2/\lambda T)} - 1], \tag{16.7}$$

in which

$$E_\lambda = \text{the energy emitted by wavelength } \lambda,$$

$$C_1 \text{ and } C_2 = \text{constants},$$

$$e = \text{the base of Naperian logarithms, and}$$

$$T = \text{the absolute temperature of the blackbody.}$$

This forms the basis for temperature measurement by optical means.

16.8.2 Total-Radiation Pyrometry

Figure 16.20 shows, in simplified form, the method of operation of the total-radiation pyrometer. Essential parts of the device consist of some form of

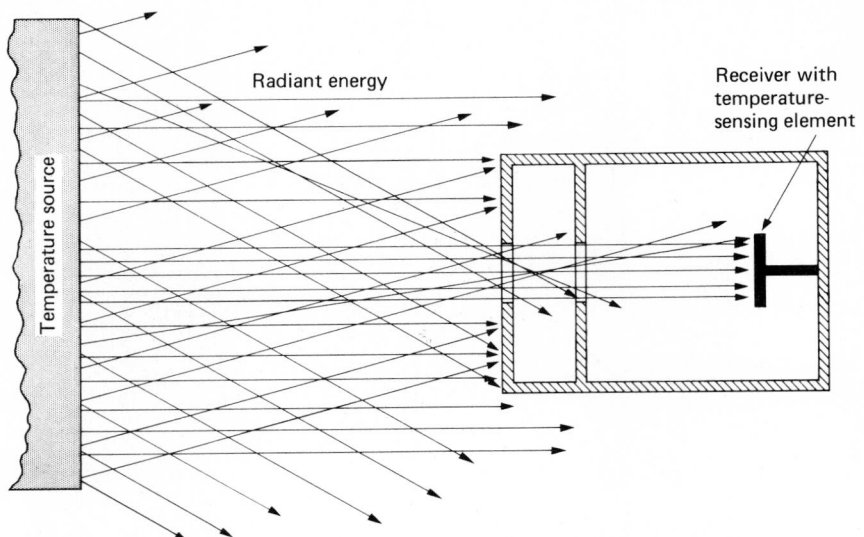

FIGURE 16.20   A simplified form of total-radiation pyrometer.

directing means, shown here as baffles but which is more often a lens, and an approximate blackbody receiver with means for sensing temperature. Although the sensing element may be any of the types discussed earlier in this chapter, it is generally one of the thermoelectric kinds, such as the thermocouple or resistance thermometer. Generally some form of thermopile is used. A balance is quickly established between the energy absorbed by the receiver and that dissipated by conduction through leads and emission to surroundings. The receiver equilibrium temperature then becomes the measure of source temperature, with the scale established by calibration.

Figure 16.21 shows a sectional view of a commercially available pyrometer. Although total-radiation pyrometry is primarily used for temperatures above 550°C, the pyrometer shown is selected to illustrate an instrument sensitive to very low-level radiation (50–375°C). The arrangement, however, is typical of general radiation-pyrometry practice. A lens-and-mirror system is used to focus the radiant energy on a thermopile, whose output is measured by a voltage-balancing potentiometer. Thermocouple reference temperature is supplied by maintaining the assembly at constant temperature through use of a heater controlled by a resistance thermometer. In many cases compensation is obtained through use of temperature-compensating resistors in the electrical circuit.

Particular attention must be given to the optical system of a radiation pyrometer, and appropriate optical glasses must be selected to pass the necessary range of wavelengths. Pyrex glass may be used for the range of from 0.3 to 2.7 microns, fused silica for 0.3 to 3.8 microns, and calcium fluoride

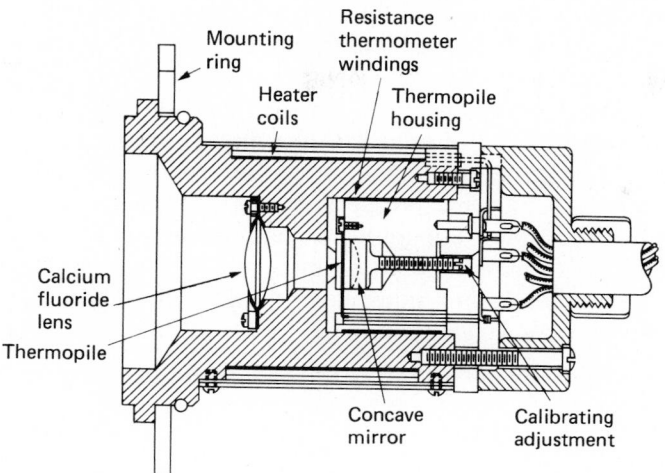

FIGURE 16.21   Section through a commercially available low-temperature, total radiation pyrometer. (Honeywell, Inc., Process Control Division, Ft. Washington, PA 19034.)

for 0.3 to 10 microns. Although Pyrex glass may be used for high-temperature measurement, it is practically opaque to low-temperature radiation, say below 550°C.

Radiation pyrometers are used ideally in applications where the sources approach blackbody conditions, that is, where the source has an emissivity ε approaching unity. In general, however, the radiated energy is a good measure of temperature only if the applicable value of ε is accounted for. This may be made clear by inspection of Eq. (16.6). Although pyrometers calibrated for blackbody conditions are available, in general they must be calibrated for the particular application. They are not normally considered general-purpose instruments. Calibration consists of comparing the pyrometer read-out with that of some standardized device, such as a thermocouple. Often single-point calibration suffices. Devices for adjusting total-radiation pyrometer calibration include the following:

1. Movable aperture in front of the thermopile.
2. Variable thermopile aperture area or pyrometer lens or window area.
3. Movable metal plug screwed into the thermopile housing adjacent to the hot junction.
4. Movable concave mirror reflecting varying amounts of energy back to the thermopile of a lens-type pyrometer (see Fig. 16.21).
5. Variable shunt resistor in the electrical circuit.

Although radiation pyrometers may theoretically be used at any reasonable distance from a temperature source, there are practical limitations that should be mentioned. First, the size of target will largely determine the degree of temperature averaging, and in general, the greater the distance from the source, the greater the averaging. Second, the nature of the intervening atmosphere will have a decided effect on the pyrometer indication. If smoke or dust is present or certain gases, even though they may be optically transparent, or solids are in the path, considerable energy absorption may occur. This will be a particularly troublesome problem if such absorbents are not constant, but are varying with time. For these reasons, minimum practical distance is advisable, along with careful selection of pyrometer sighting methods.

There are three common arrangements used to obtain a sample of radiated energy for the thermopile to sense. They are:

1. A lens system that has the power to concentrate the sampled energy over a smaller area, but is subject to aberrations and must be kept carefully cleaned.
2. An open-end tube (illustrated schematically in Fig. 16.20). In effect, this is a selective "baffle" arranged to transmit energy from a selected area only.
3. A closed-end sighting tube, usually of ceramic, that may be inserted into a furnace or immersed in a liquid bath.

Of course, the primary purpose of these sighting methods and devices is to obtain a true sample from the area or point of interest, uninfluenced by any surrounding conditions.

16.8.3 Optical Pyrometry

Optical pyrometers use a method of matching as the basis for their operation. In general, a reference temperature is provided in the form of an electrically heated lamp filament, and a measure of temperature is obtained by optically comparing the visual radiation from the filament with that from the unknown source. In principle, the radiation from one of the sources, as viewed by the observer, is adjusted to match that from the other source. Two methods are used: (1) The current through the filament may be controlled electrically through a resistance adjustment, or (2) the radiation accepted by the pyrometer from the unknown source may be adjusted optically by means of some absorbing device such as an optical wedge, polarizing filter, or iris diaphragm [12]. In both cases the adjustment required is used as the means for temperature read-out.

Figure 16.22 illustrates schematically an arrangement of a variable-intensity pyrometer. In use, the pyrometer is sighted at the unknown temperature source at a distance such that the objective lens focuses the source in the plane of the lamp filament. The eyepiece is then adjusted so that the filament and the source appear superimposed and in focus to the observer. In general,

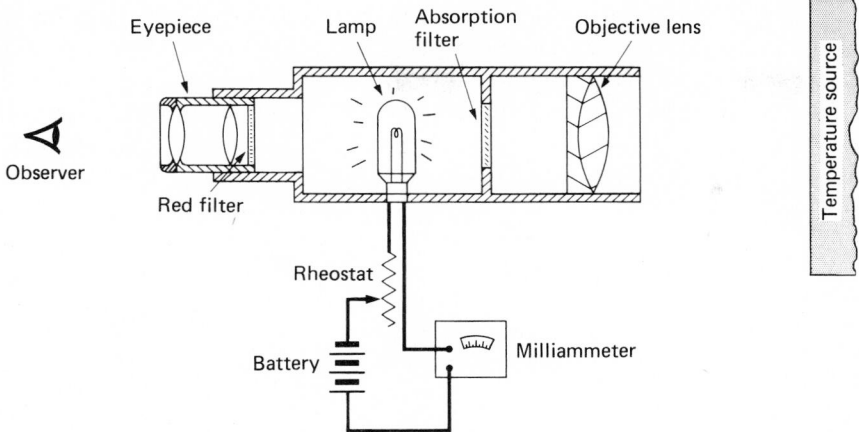

FIGURE 16.22   Schematic diagram of an optical pyrometer.

the filament will appear either hotter than or colder than the unknown source, as shown in Fig. 16.23. By adjusting the battery current, the filament (or any prescribed portion such as the tip) may be made to disappear, as indicated in Fig. 16.23(c). The current indicated by the milliammeter to obtain this condition may then be used as the temperature read-out. Other read-out arrangements use the rheostat setting, in which case battery standardization or some form of potentiometric null-balancing system is required.

A red filter is generally used to obtain approximately monochromatic conditions, and an absorption filter is used so that the filament may be operated at reduced intensity, thereby prolonging its life.

The constant-intensity comparison-lamp method employs the same basic principle of operation as just described for the variable-intensity type, but a different method of adjustment is used. As the name implies, the lamp filament is maintained at constant intensity, whereas the comparative radiation from

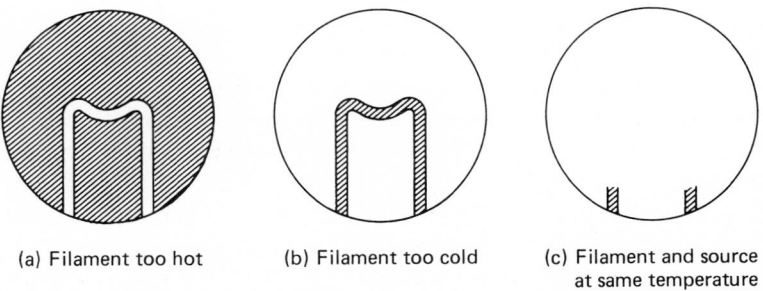

(a) Filament too hot   (b) Filament too cold   (c) Filament and source at same temperature

FIGURE 16.23   Appearance of filament when (a) filament temperature is too high, (b) filament temperature is too low, and (c) filament temperature is correct.

the unknown source is attenuated by methods mentioned earlier. The required adjustment is used for indication of temperature. It is obvious that some means must be employed to standardize filament current. This is accomplished through use of a milliammeter and rheostat in the manner shown in Fig. 16.22.

16.8.4 The Infrared (IR) Pyrometer

As stated earlier, the operating principle of the infrared pyrometer is similar to that of the total-radiation type: A sample of incident radiation is detected and its energy level evaluated. Whereas the total-radiation type makes use of a thermal detector, the IR instrument employs a photocell (photoconductive, photovoltaic, or photoelectromagnetic) to detect proton flux. The d.c. output of the detector is then increased often through use of a chopper-type amplifier, and with calibration the output is displayed as temperature.

Bandwidths are controlled through selection of photocell type (such as cadmium sulphide, lead sulphide, etc.) and by means of optical filters. Because the wavelengths are near the visible spectrum, IR pyrometers may utilize conventional lenses, mirrors, etc. It is therefore possible to control the size of the instrument's target area, thereby reducing averaging. In addition, the response time of the IR pyrometer is faster than those of other types. Finally, the IR pyrometer is not limited to the measuring of "hot" temperatures. Usable temperature ranges may fall within limits of approximately $-40°C$ and $4600°C$.

16.9 OTHER METHODS OF TEMPERATURE INDICATION

Two methods of temperature measurement given in the introduction to this chapter have not been referred to in the intervening pages. They are the application of changes in physical state and of changes in chemical state. Several devices based on these principles should be mentioned.

Seger cones have long been used in the ceramic industry as a means of checking temperatures. These devices are simply small cones made of an oxide and glass. When a predetermined temperature is reached, the tip of the cone softens and curls over, thereby providing the indication that the temperature has been reached. Seger cones are made in a standard series covering a range from 600 to 2000°C.

Somewhat similar temperature-level indicators are available in the forms of crayonlike sticks, lacquer, and pill-like pellets. Each may be calibrated at temperature intervals through a range of about 50 to 1100°C. The crayon or lacquer is stroked or brushed on the part whose temperature is to be indicated. After the lacquer dries, it and the crayon marks appear dull and chalky. When the calibration temperature is reached, the marks become liquid and shiny. The pellets are used in a similar manner, except that they simply melt and assume a shiny liquidlike appearance as the stated temperature is reached.

By using crayons, lacquer, or pellets covering various temperatures within a range, the maximum temperature attained during a test may be rather closely determined.

16.10   SPECIAL PROBLEMS

The number of special problems associated with temperature measurement is unlimited. However, several are significant enough to warrant special note. These will be discussed in the next several pages.

16.10.1   Errors Resulting from Conduction and Radiation

In considering this item, let us think in terms of using a thermocouple to measure the gas temperature in a furnace, bearing in mind, however, that the principles discussed apply to other temperature probes and to many other situations.

Basically, any temperature element senses temperature because heat is transferred between the surroundings and the element until some kind of equilibrium condition is reached. When a bare thermocouple is inserted through the wall of a furnace (assume it to be gas- or coal-fired), heat is transferred to it from the immersing gases by convection. Heat also reaches the element through radiation from the furnace walls and from incandescent solids such as a fuel bed or those carried along by the swirling gases. Finally, heat will flow from the element through any connecting leads by conduction. The temperature indicated by the probe therefore will be a function of all these environmental factors, and consideration must be given to their effects in order to intelligently interpret or control the results.

First of all, in the more common case, the major heat flow will occur directly by forced convection between the gases and the proble. This may be expressed by the relation [13]

$$q_1 = h_c A (T_g - T_t),\tag{16.8}$$

in which

q_1 = the heat transferred,

h_c = the coefficient of heat transfer,

A = the surface area of the probe,

T_g = the gas temperature, and

T_t = the probe temperature.

Although the transfer coefficient, h_c, is a function of a number of things, including viscosity, density, and specific heat of the gas, of particular importance in the application under discussion is the fact that it also is a function of a power of the velocity of gas over the probe.

Radiation effects

Radiation between the probe and any source or sink of different temperature is a function of the difference in the fourth powers of the (absolute) temperatures (see Eq. 16.6). It is generally true, therefore, that radiation becomes an increasingly important source of temperature error as the temperatures and their differences increase. Increased temperature differences generally result from temperature extremes, either high or low, and in either of these cases, particular attention must be given to radiation effects.

As discussed in Section 16.8.1, radiant-heat transfer is also a function of the emissivities of the members involved. For this reason, a bright, shiny probe is less affected by thermal radiation than is one tarnished or covered with soot.

Radiation error may be largely eliminated through proper use of thermal shielding. This consists of placing barriers to thermal radiation around the probe, which prevent the probe from "seeing" the radiant source or sink, as the case may be. For low-temperature work, such shields may simply be made of sheet metal appropriately formed to provide the necessary protection. At higher temperatures, metal or ceramic sleeves or tubes may be used. In applications where gas temperatures are desired, however, care must be exercised in placing radiation shields so as not to cause stagnation of flow around the probe. As pointed out earlier, desirable convection transfer is a function of gas velocity.

Consideration of these factors led quite naturally to the development of an aspirated high-temperature probe known as the *high-velocity thermocouple* (HVT) [14]. Figure 16.24 illustrates an aspirated probe with several types of tips. Gas is induced through the end, over the temperature-sensing element, and either is exhausted to the exterior or, if it will not alter process or measuring functioning, may be returned to the source. A renewable shield provides radiation protection for the element, and through use of aspiration, convective transfer is enhanced. Gas mass-flow over the element should be not less than 15,000 lbm/hr/ft^2 for maximum effectiveness [14].

When a single shield is used, as shown in Fig. 16.24(b), the shield temperature is largely controlled by convective transfer from the aspirated gas through it. Its exterior, however, is subject to thermal-radiation effects, and thus its equilibrium temperature, and hence that of the sensing element, will still be somewhat influenced by radiation. Maximum shielding may be obtained through use of multiple shields, as shown in the lower two sections of Fig. 16.24(b). Thermocouples using multiple shielding are known as *multiple high-velocity thermocouples* (MHVT) [14]. The effectiveness of both the HVT and MHVT relative to a bare thermocouple is graphically illustrated in Fig. 16.25.

Our discussion here of radiation effects has been centered largely on high-

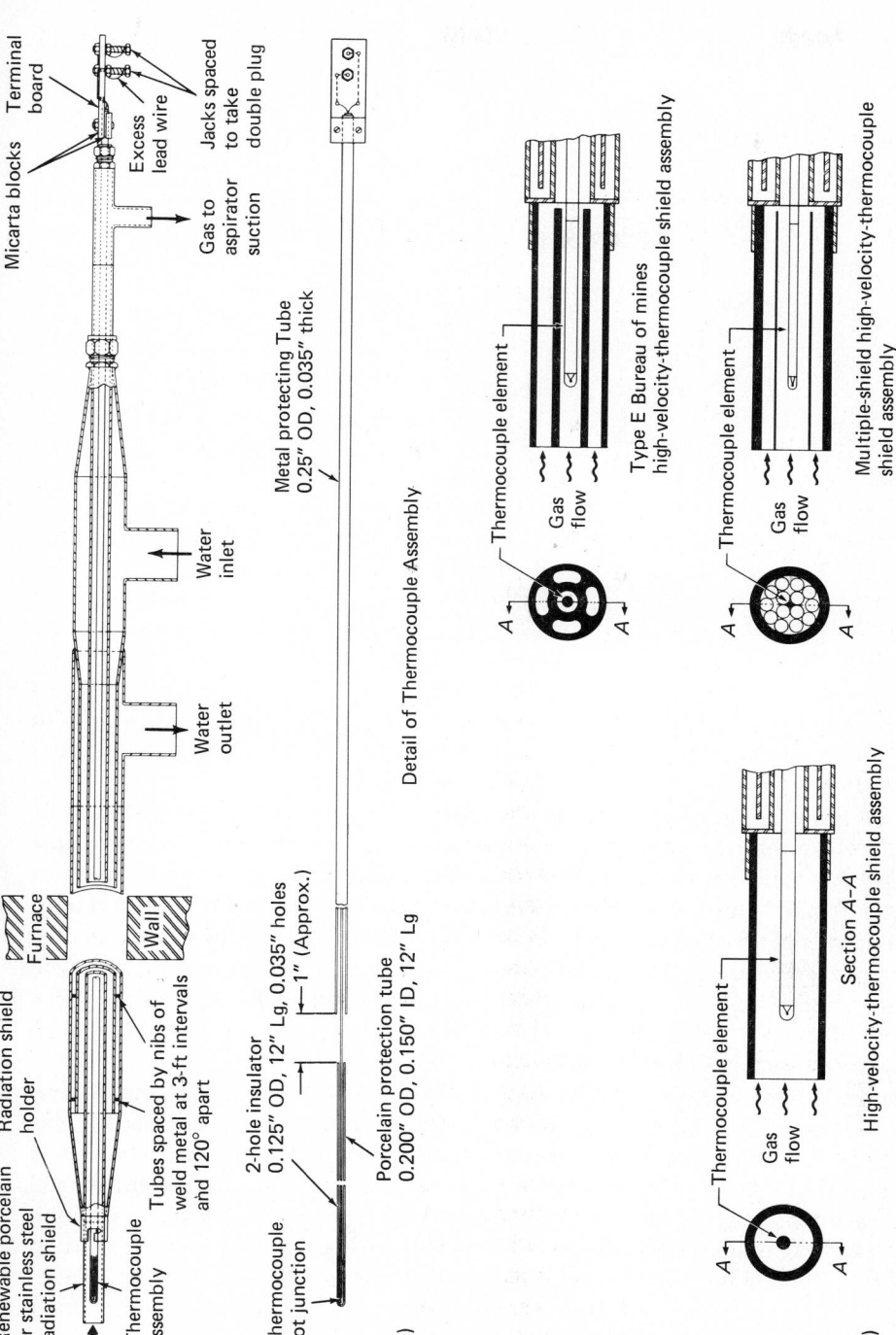

Detail of Thermocouple Assembly

(a)

Section A–A

High-velocity-thermocouple shield assembly

Type E Bureau of mines high-velocity-thermocouple shield assembly

Multiple-shield high-velocity-thermocouple shield assembly

(b)

FIGURE 16.24 (a) Section through an aspirated high-velocity thermocouple, HVT. (b) Various tips used on high-velocity thermocouples. (Courtesy: The Babcock and Wilcox Company, Barberton, OH.)

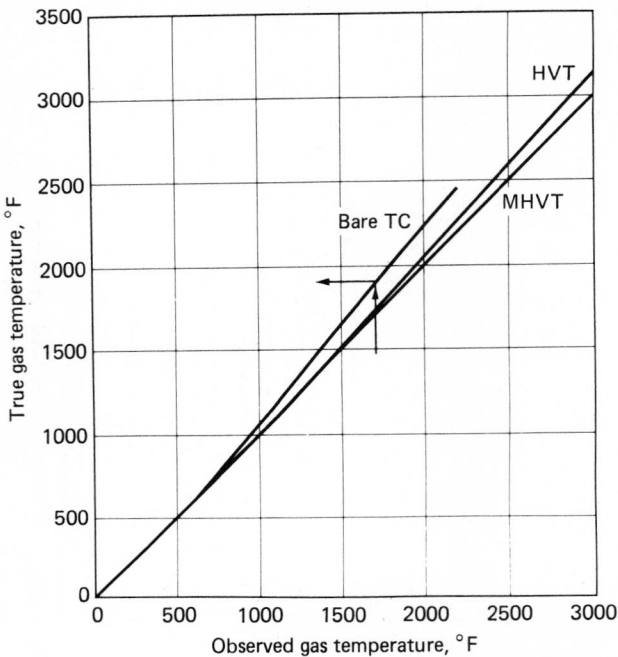

FIGURE 16.25   Graphical representation of the effectiveness of the high-velocity thermo-couple. (Courtesy: The Babcock and Wilcox Company, Barberton, OH.)

temperature application of thermocouples. However, once again it should be made clear that the principles involved apply to *any* temperature-measuring system or situation to one extent or another. Radiation may introduce errors at low temperatures as well as at high ones, and will present similar problems to all types of sensing elements. When the fluids are liquid rather than gaseous, the problem is considerably reduced, however, because most liquids, and even water vapor in air, act as effective thermal-radiation filters.

Errors caused by conduction

All temperature-measuring elements of the probe type must have mechanical support, and, in general, some connection must be made to external indicating apparatus. Such connections provide conduction paths through which heat may be transferred to or away from the sensing element. Such transfer of heat will result in a discrepancy between the indicated temperature and that desired, namely, the temperature that would exist were the instrument not present. Factors influencing such errors may be itemized as follows:

1. Conductivity of lead or support material.
2. Lead and element sizes.

3. Properties of surrounding media.
4. Flow conditions over the probe.
5. Presence of lead insulation or protective well.
6. Configuration of the immersed leads.
7. Temperature magnitudes and the form of temperature gradient along the leads or support.
8. Depth of immersion of the probe.

Johnson, Weinstein, and Osterle [15] have found that except for extreme conditions, variation in the last two factors may generally be ignored. In addition, they show that increasing the ratio of element to lead size reduces the error, or more specifically, a large value of ηL minimizes error. ($\eta^2 = 2h/kd$, where h = the convection coefficient, k = the conductivity of the lead wire, L = a length indicating gradient intensity, and d = the diameter of the lead wire.) It is also shown that the lead error may be reduced to zero by using a reversed lead configuration of proper proportions, as illustrated in Fig. 16.26, wherein the leads are bent back and brought downstream.

16.10.2   Measurement of Temperature in Rapidly Moving Gas

When a temperature probe is placed in a stream of gas, the flow will be partially stopped by the presence of the probe. The lost kinetic energy will be converted to heat, which will have some bearing on the indicated temperature. Two "ideal" states may be defined for such a condition. A *true* state would be that observed by instruments moving with the stream, and a *stagnation* state would be that obtained if the gas were brought to rest and its kinetic energy completely converted to heat, resulting in a temperature rise. A fixed probe inserted into the moving stream will indicate conditions lying between the two states. For exhaust gases from internal combustion

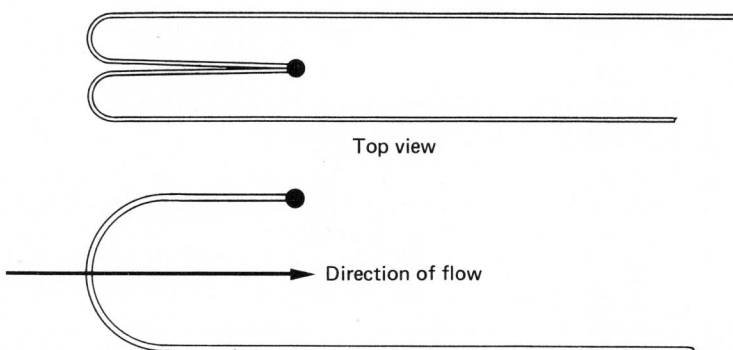

Top view

Direction of flow

FIGURE 16.26   Reversed lead configuration, which may be used to reduce lead error.

engines, we find that temperature differences between the two states may be as great as 200°C [16].

An expression relating stagnation and true temperature for a moving gas, assuming adiabatic conditions, may be written as follows [17]:

$$(T_t - T_s) = V^2/2g_c JC_p. \tag{16.9}$$

This relation may also be written

$$T_s/T_t = 1 + \tfrac{1}{2}(k - 1)M^2, \tag{16.9a}$$

in which

T_s = the stagnation or total temperature, in °K (or Rankine),

T_t = the true or static temperature, in °K (or R),

V = the velocity of flow, in m/s (or ft/s),

g_c = the dimensional constant, 1 kg·m/N·s²(or 32.2 lbm·ft/lbf·s²),

J = the mechanical equivalent of heat, 1 N·m = 1 J (or 778 ft·lbf/BTU),

C_p = the mean specific heat at constant pressure, in joules/kg °K (or BTU/lbm R),

k = the ratio of specific heats, and

M = the Mach number.

A measure of the effectiveness of a probe in bringing about kinetic energy conversion may be expressed by the relation

$$r = \frac{T_i - T_t}{T_s - T_t}, \tag{16.10}$$

where

T_i = the temperature indicated by the probe, and

r = a term called the "recovery factor," which is proportional to the energy conversion.

If $r = 1$, the probe would measure the stagnation temperature, and if $r = 0$, it would measure the true temperature. Experiment has shown that for a given instrument, the recovery factor is essentially a constant and is a function of the probe configuration. It changes little with composition, temperature, pressure, or velocity of the flowing gas [17].

Combining Eqs. (16.9) and (16.10), we obtain

$$T_t = T_i - rV^2/2g_c C_p J \tag{16.11}$$

or

$$T_s = T_i + (1 - r)V^2/2g_c C_p J. \tag{16.11a}$$

The recovery factor, r, for a given probe may be determined experimentally [16]. However, this does not generally provide sufficient information to determine either the true or the stagnation temperature. Inspection of Eqs. (16.11) and (16.11a) indicates that in addition to knowing the indicated temperature T_i and the recovery factor r, we must know the stream velocity and certain properties of the fluid. When these values are known, the relations yield the desired temperatures directly. In many cases, however, it is particularly difficult to determine the flow velocity, and further theoretical consideration of the situation is required.

It has been shown [17] that for sonic velocities ($M = 1$),

$$T_s = \phi T_i, \tag{16.12}$$

in which

$$\phi = \frac{k + 1}{2 + r(k - 1)}. \tag{16.13}$$

One solution to the temperature measurement of high-velocity gases has been to make the measurement at Mach 1, through use of an instrument called a *sonic-flow pyrometer*. Such a device is shown in Fig. 16.27. The basic instrument comprises a temperature-sensing element (thermocouple) located at the throat of a nozzle. Gas whose temperature is to be measured is aspirated (or pressurized by the process) through the nozzle to produce critical or sonic velocity at the nozzle throat. Under these conditions, Eqs. (16.12) and (16.13) apply, and in this manner determination of flow velocity need not be made. It is still necessary to know the ratio of specific heats, but these can usually be determined or estimated with sufficient accuracy. (It may be observed that the dependence of ϕ on k reduces as r is increased.)

16.10.3 Temperature-Element Response

An ideal temperature transducer would faithfully respond to fluctuating inputs regardless of the time rate of temperature change; however, the ideal is not realized in practice. A time lag exists between cause and effect, and the system seldom, if ever, actually indicates true temperature input. Figure 16.28 illus-

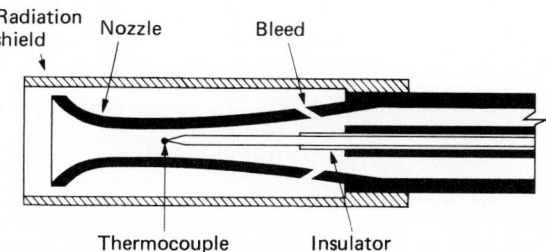

FIGURE 16.27   Schematic of a sonic-flow pyrometer. (Courtesy: National Bureau of Standards.)

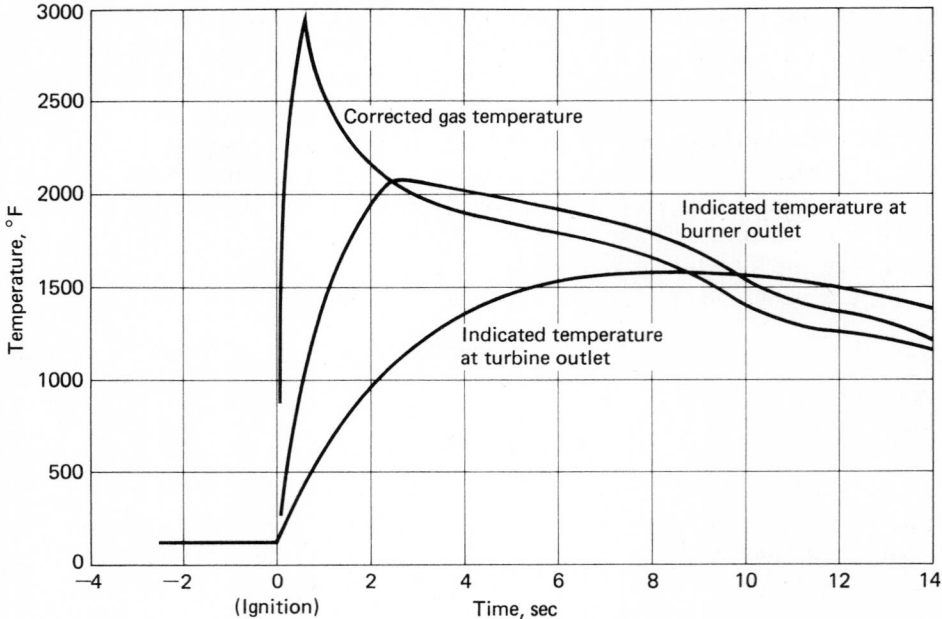

FIGURE 16.28   Temperature–time record made from two thermocouples of different size and location during the starting cycle of a large jet engine. (Courtesy of the Instrument Society of America.)

trates quite graphically the magnitude of errors that may result from poor response.

The time lag that exists is determined by the particular heat-transfer circumstances that apply, and the complexity of the situation depends to a large extent on the relative importance of the convective, conductive, and radiative components. If we assume that radiation and conduction are minimized by design and application, we may equate the heat accepted by the probe per unit time to the rate of heat transferred by convection [18]:

$$Wc(dT_p/dt) = hA(T_g - T_p) \qquad (16.14)$$

or

$$\tau(dT_p/dt) + T_p = T_g, \qquad (16.14a)$$

in which

T_p = the temperature of the probe, in K (or R),

T_g = the temperature of the surrounding gases, in K (or R),

c = the specific heat of the probe, in J/kg·K (or BTU/lbm R),

W = the mass, in kg (or lbm),

t = the time, in s,

h = the convective heat-transfer coefficient, in J/s·m^{2}K (or BTU/ s·ft^2·R),

A = the surface area of the probe exposed to gases, in m^2 (or ft^2), and

$\tau = Wc/hA$ = the time constant, in s.

We may write Eq. (16.14a) as follows:

$$\int_0^t dt = \tau \int_{Tp_0}^T \frac{dT_p}{T_g - T_p}. \tag{16.14b}$$

Solving gives us

$$T_p = T_g - (T_g - T_{p_0})e^{-t/\tau}.$$

If we let

$$\Delta T_p = T_p - T_{p_0},$$

then

$$\Delta T_p = (T_g - T_{p_0})(1 - e^{-t/\tau}). \tag{16.15}$$

This relation corresponds to suddenly exposing the probe at temperature T_{p_0} to a gas temperature T_g. This would be approximated if the probe were quickly inserted through the wall of a furnace or immersed in a liquid bath.

In response to a steady sinusoidal variation in temperature of angular frequency ω, indicated temperature will oscillate with reduced amplitude and will lag in phase and time [18] (see also the example in Section 3.14.2).

The value of τ will be recognized as the *time constant* or *characteristic time* [19] for the probe, or the time in seconds required for 63.2% of the maximum possible change $(T_g - T_p)$ (see Section 3.14.1). Obviously, τ should be as small as possible, and inspection shows, as should be expected, that this corresponds to low mass, low heat capacity, high transfer coefficient, and large area. Probes with low time constant provide fast response, and vice versa.

Even under idealized conditions (convective transfer only), as assumed, the time constant for a given probe is not determined by the probe alone. The convective heat-transfer coefficient is also dependent on the character of the gas flow. For this reason, a given probe may show different time constants when subjected to different conditions.

In general, two parameters, total temperature (Section 16.10.2) and mass velocity, are sufficient to describe the flow. Moffat [19] gives the following empirical equation for evaluating the time constant for bare wire thermocouples:

$$\tau = \frac{3500\rho c d^{1.25}}{T} G^{-15.8/\sqrt{\tau}}, \qquad (16.16)$$

where

d = the wire diameter, in in.,

G = the mass velocity, in lbm/s·ft^2,

T = the total temperature, in °R,

ρ = the *average* density for the two wires, in lbm/ft^3, and

c = the *average* specific heat for the two wires, in Btu/lbm·°F.

A comparison between time constants calculated by Eq. (16.16) and determined from test data is shown in Fig. 16.29.

Although practical probe-response characteristics may, in many cases, be closely approximated by the application of Eq. (16.15), in many other cases more complicated situations exist. Other elements in addition to the actual temperature-sensing element may be involved, resulting in the multiple-time-constant problem.

The case of the common thermometer in a well, or a thermocouple or resistance thermometer in a protective sheath (Fig. 16.4) may be better ap-

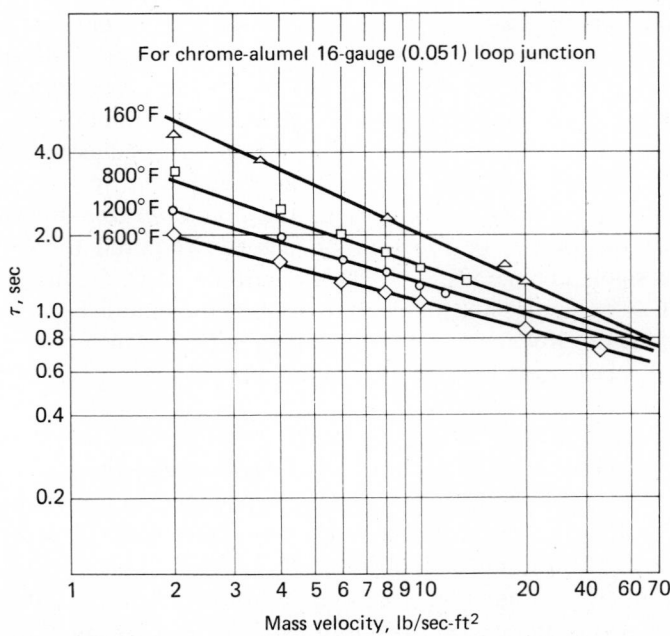

FIGURE 16.29   A comparison of time constants calculated by Eq. (16.16) and determined from test data. (Courtesy of the Instrument Society of America.)

proximated by a two-time-constant model. Both probe and jacket will have characteristic time constants. Let us analyze this situation as follows: We will assume that a probe-jacket assembly (Fig. 16.30) at temperature T_1 is suddenly inserted into a medium at temperature T_2. In the manner of Eq. (16.14), we may write two relationships, as follows:

$$W_j c_j \frac{dT_j}{dt} = h_j A_j (T_2 - T_j) - h_p A_p (T_j - T_p) \tag{16.17}$$

and

$$W_p c_p \frac{dT_p}{dt} = h_p A_p (T_j - T_p), \tag{16.17a}$$

where subscripts j and p refer to the protective jacket and the probe, respectively.

The relationships may be rewritten as

$$\tau_j \frac{dT_j}{dt} = T_2 - T_j - \frac{h_p A_p}{h_j A_j}(T_j - T_p) \tag{16.18}$$

and

$$\tau_p \frac{dT_p}{dt} = T_j - T_p. \tag{16.18a}$$

Simplification may be had if we assume that the last term in Eq. (16.18) may be neglected. This will be legitimate if

$$A_p \ll A_j \quad \text{and/or} \quad T_j - T_p \ll T_2 - T_j.$$

If the above assumption is made, Eqs. (16.18) and (16.18a) may be com-

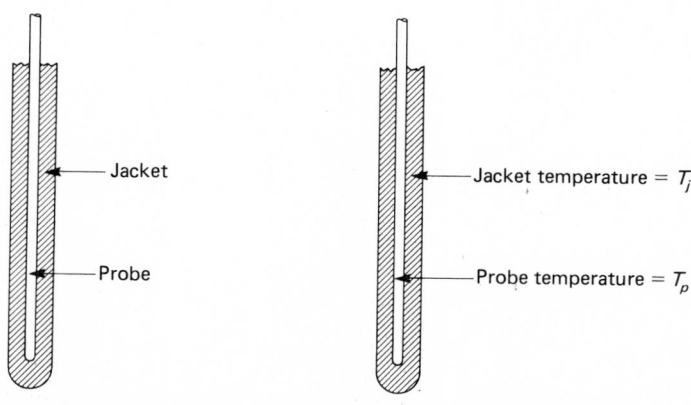

At $t < 0$, all temperatures equal temperatures of the surrounding medium $= T_1$

At $t \geqslant 0$, temperature of surrounding medium $= T_2$

FIGURE 16.30   Temperature probe in jacket subjected to a step-change in temperature.

bined, yielding

$$\tau_j \tau_p \frac{d^2 T_p}{dt^2} + (\tau_j + \tau_p) \frac{dT_p}{dt} + T_p = T_2. \tag{16.19}$$

A solution to this relationship is

$$\frac{T_2 - T_p}{T_2 - T_1} = \frac{\Delta T}{\Delta T_{max}} = \left(\frac{\zeta}{\zeta - 1}\right) e^{-t/\zeta \tau_p} - \left(\frac{1}{\zeta - 1}\right) e^{-t/\tau_p}, \tag{16.20}$$

where

ΔT = the momentary difference between the indicated and actual temperatures,

ΔT_{max} = the difference between the temperature of the medium and the probe temperature at $t = 0$, and

$\zeta = \tau_j / \tau_p$.

Characteristics for various values of ζ are shown in Fig. 16.31. It is seen that for $\zeta = 0$, Eq. (16.20) reverts to Eq. (16.15). In addition, as the time constant for the well is increased, the overall lag is increased, as one would suspect it should be.

Still more refined methods are sometimes applied, using multiple-time-constants and dead times [20, 21]. For example, careful consideration of the simple mercury-in-glass thermometer indicates that the glass envelope, in addition to functioning as a necessary part of the differential-expansion pair, also acts as a thermal shield for the mercury.

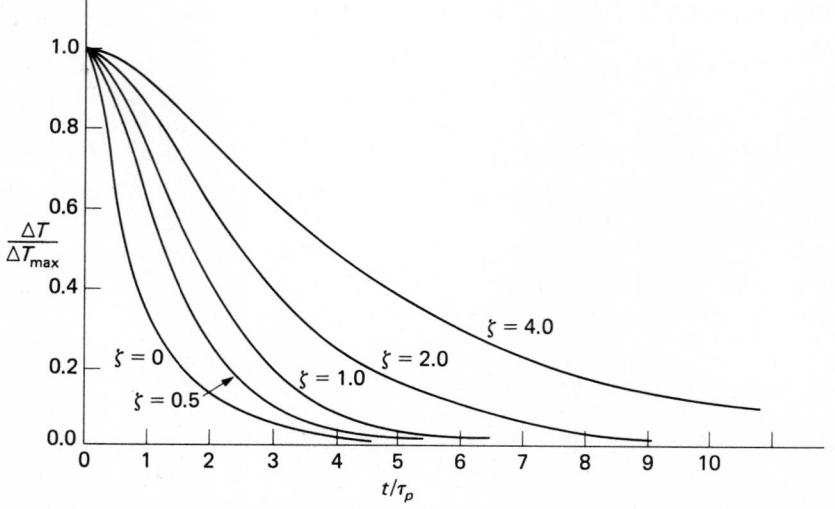

FIGURE 16.31   Two-time constant problem. Plot of $\Delta T/\Delta T_{max}$ versus t/τ_p for various ratios of $\zeta = \tau_j/\tau_p$.

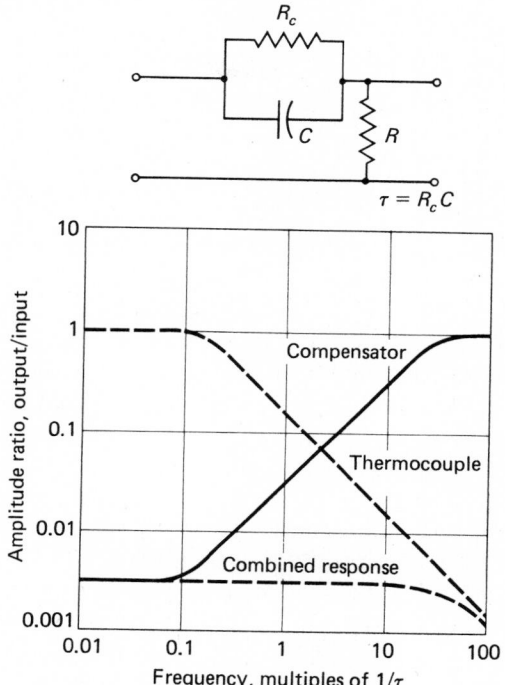

FIGURE 16.32   Curves illustrating compensating action of a simple *R-C* network. (Courtesy of the Instrument Society of America.)

16.10.4 Electrical Compensation

Lag in electrical temperature-sensing elements (thermocouples and resistance thermometers) may be approximately compensated by use of appropriate electrical networks. This is done by selecting a type of filter (Section 5.21) whose electrical-time characteristics complement those of the sensing element [22, 23]. Figure 16.32 illustrates a simple form of such a compensator. In the example illustrated, thermocouple response drops off with increased input frequency. (This is shown in terms of multiples of time-constant reciprocals.) By proper choice of resistors and capacitance, satisfactory combined response may be extended approximately one hundred times.

16.11 MEASUREMENT OF HEAT FLUX

Heat flux may be thought of as the *rate* of heat flow per unit area. The common units are W/m² or BTU/hr·ft². We can write an expression for heat flux as follows:

$$\dot{Q} = -k\partial T/\partial x, \tag{16.21}$$

where

$\dot{Q}$ = heat flux,

k = the thermal conductivity of the material,

T = temperature, and

x = material dimension in direction of flow.

Knowledge of heat flux, rather than temperature, may be of particular importance in locations where *anticipation* of excessive temperatures is desirable. Examples might be at locations on supersonic aircraft, combustion walls of rocket motors, etc.

There are various forms of heat flux meters [24, 25], two of which are of particular importance: the slug type (Fig. 16.33) and the foil or membrane type (Fig. 16.34). The latter is also referred to as the Gardon gage [26].

As shown in Fig. 16.33 the essentials of the slug-type meter include a concentrated mass or slug that is thermally insulated from its surroundings and a temperature sensor, commonly a thermocouple. As heat is applied, the thermal isolation of the slug results in a temperature differential between the slug and its surroundings. The governing relation is

$$\dot{Q} = (Mc/A) \, dT/dt + K \, \Delta T, \tag{16.22}$$

where

M = the mass of the slug,

c = the specific heat of the slug,

A = the area,

t = the time,

K = the coefficient of loss to surroundings, and

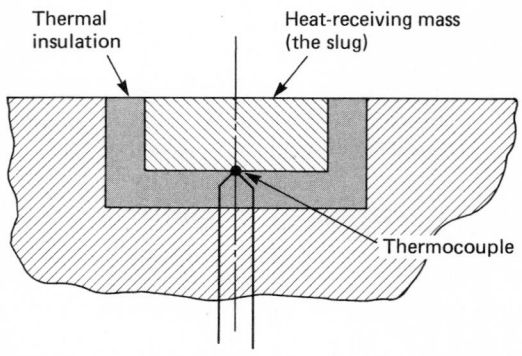

FIGURE 16.33   Section through a plug-type heat flux sensor.

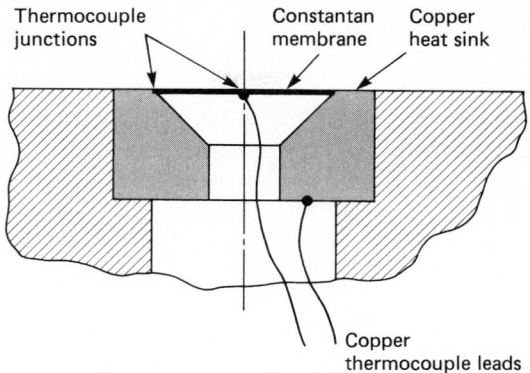

FIGURE 16.34   Section through a foil- or membrane-type heat flux sensor.

ΔT = the temperature difference between the slug and surroundings.

Slug temperature is measured by the sensor and, through calibration, is the analog of flux.

There are two primary disadvantages of this type of flux meter: (1) The assumption is that temperature throughout the slug is uniform at all times, but for high fluxes this will not be true, and (2) the meter is clearly not usable for steady-state conditions.

Construction of the Gardon gage [26] is shown in Fig. 16.34. It consists of an embedded copper heat sink, a thin membrane of constantan, and an integral thermocouple. The nature of the construction provides two copper–constantan thermocouple junctions, one at the center of the membrane and the other at the interface between the membrane and the heat sink. Thermocouple output, therefore, is a function of the differential temperature between the center and the periphery of the membrane. This, in turn, is a function of the heat flow from the membrane to the sink. The governing relationship is

$$\dot{Q} = 2(Sk/R^2)\Delta T \qquad (16.23)$$
$$= Ce,$$

where

S = the membrane thickness,

k = the thermal conductivity of the membrane material,

R = the membrane radius,

ΔT = the temperature difference between the center and the edge of the membrane,

C = a calibration constant, and

e = the millivolt output of the TC.

Calibration of heat flux meters involves radiant, conductive, and convective factors and is not simple [27]. One form of standard is patterned after the slug-type meter and uses a gold or single-crystal copper slug. Emissivities must be carefully controlled and short exposure to a heat source is used to avoid large temperature rise. Water and blackbody standards are also used. Application details are beyond the scope of this book.

16.12 CALIBRATION OF TEMPERATURE-MEASURING DEVICES

As stated in Section 1.5, for the results to be meaningful, measuring procedure and apparatus must be provable. This is true of all areas of measurement, but for some reason the impression seems prevalent that it is less true for temperature-measuring systems than for others. For example, it is generally thought that the only limitation in the use of thermocouple tables is in satisfying the requirement for metal combination indicated in the table heading. Mercury-in-glass scale divisions and resistance-thermometer characteristics are commonly accepted without question. And it is assumed that once proved, the calibrations will hold indefinitely.

Of course, we know that these ideas are incorrect. Thermocouple output is very dependent on purity of elementary metals and consistency and homogeneity of alloys. Alloys of supposedly like characteristics but manufactured by different companies may have temperature–emf relations sufficiently at variance to require different tables. In addition, aging with use will alter thermocouple outputs. Resistance-thermometer stability is very dependent on the degree of freedom from residual strains in the element, and comparative results from like elements require very careful use and control of the metallurgy of the materials.

Methods used to calibrate temperature-measuring systems fall into two general classifications: (1) comparison with the primary standards, the fixed temperature points, or interpolated points as specified by the International Practical Temperature Scale of 1968, and (2) comparison with reliably calibrated secondary standards. (See Section 8.7.)

Basically, the primary temperature standard consists of the fixed physical conditions discussed in Section 8.7. Arbitrary scales are used to relate the following fixed points:

Oxygen point	− 182.97°C	− 297.346°F
Ice point	0	32
Steam point	100.0	212.0
Sulfur point	444.60	832.28

Silver point	960.78	1761.4
Gold point	1063.0	1945.4

Intermediate points are established by specified interpolation procedures. Therefore, for primary calibration, the problems are those of technique attending reproduction of these fundamental points and reproduction of interpolation methods.

Certain secondary references are also specified by the International Temperature Scale (see listings in Table 16.9). For many of these points, commercial "standards" are available. These consist of a sealed container enclosing the reference materials. Glass is used for the container material for the lower temperatures and graphite is used for the higher temperatures. Integral heating coils are employed. To use the standard, the element to be calibrated is placed in a well extending into the center of the container. The heater is then turned on, and the temperature carried above the melting point

TABLE 16.9   Secondary Reference Points [28]

Source	Temperature	
	°C	°F
Sublimation point of carbon dioxide	−78.5	−109.3
Freezing point of mercury	−38.87	−37.97
Triple point of water*	0.0100	32.0180
Triple point of benzoic acid*	122.36	252.25
Boiling point of naphthalene	218.0	424.4
Freezing point of tin	231.9	449.4
Boiling point of benzophenone	305.9	582.6
Freezing point of cadmium	320.9	609.6
Freezing point of lead	327.3	621.1
Freezing point of zinc	419.5	787.1
Freezing point of antimony	630.5	1166.9
Freezing point of aluminum	660.1	1220.2
Freezing point of copper	1083	1981
Freezing point of palladium	1552	2826
Freezing point of platinum	1769	3216

*   Temperature of equilibrium between solid, liquid, and vapor.

of the reference substance and held until melting is completed. It is then permitted to cool, and when the freezing point is reached, the temperature stabilizes and remains constant at the specified value as long as liquid and solid are both present (several minutes). It is claimed that accuracies of approximately 0.1°C may be easily attained and that 0.01°C may be attained if care is exercised.

SUGGESTED READINGS

ASME PTC 19.3-1974, *Temperature Measurement.*

Baker, H. D., E. A. Ryder, and N. H. Baker, *Temperature Measurement in Engineering,* vols. 1 & 2. New York: Wiley, 1953, 1961.

Benedict, R. P., *Fundamentals of Temperature, Pressure and Flow Measurements,* 2d ed. New York: Wiley, 1977.

Booth, S. F. (ed.), *Precision Measurement and Calibration,* vol. 2 (selected NBS technical papers on heat and mechanics), NBS Handbook 77. Washington, D.C.: U.S. Government Printing Office, 1961.

Ginnings, D. C., *Precision Measurement and Calibration* (selected NBS papers on heat), NBS Special Publication 300, vol. 6. Washington, D.C.: U.S. Government Printing Office, 1979.

Kinzie, P. A., *Thermocouple Temperature Measurement.* New York: Wiley, 1973.

Kreith, F., *Principles of Heat Transfer.* New York: Intext Educational Publishers, 1973.

Kutz, M., *Temperature Control.* New York: Wiley, 1968.

Swindells, J. F., *Precision Measurement and Calibration* (selected NBS papers on temperature), NBS Spcl. Publ. 300, vol. 2. Washington, D.C.: U.S. Government Printing Office, 1968.

PROBLEMS

16.1 At what temperature do the Celsius and Fahrenheit scales coincide?

16.2 The temperature indicated by a "total immersion" mercury-in-glass thermometer is 70°C (158°F). Actual immersion is to the 5°C (41°F) mark. What correction should be applied to account for the partial immersion? Assume ambient temperature is 20°C (68°F).

16.3 The following relation [29] may be used to determine the radius of curvature, r, of a bimetal strip that is initially flat at temperature T_0:

$$r = \frac{t\{3(1 + m)^2 + (1 + mn)[m^2 + (1/mn)]\}}{6(\alpha_2 - \alpha_1)(T - T_0)(1 + m)^2},$$

where

t = the combined thickness of the two strips,

m = the ratio of thicknesses of low- to high-expansion components,

n = the ratio of Young's moduluses of low- to high-expansion components,

α_1 and α_2 = the coefficients of linear expansion with $\alpha_1 < \alpha_2$, and

T = the temperature, °C or °F.

If 15-cm long by 1mm thick strips of phos-bronze and Invar are brazed together to form a bimetal temperature sensor, determine the deflection of the free end per degree change in temperature. Recall that for a beam in bending, $1/r = d^2y/dx^2$. See Table 4.3 for material properties. (Let $T_0 = 20°C$ and $T = 100°C$.)

16.4 The element of a resistance thermometer is constructed of a 50-cm (19.7-in.) length of 0.03-mm (0.0012-in.) nickel wire. What will be the nominal resistance of the element? (See Table 12.1 for resistivity.) If we assume that the temperature coefficient of resistivity is constant over the common range of ambient temperatures, what will be the change in resistance of the element per degree C? Per degree F?

16.5 If platinum is substituted for nickel in Problem 16.4, what are the calculated values?

16.6 Search the literature (see the Suggested Readings at the end of the chapter) for the range of values for the constants A and B in Eq. (16.2) for commonly used resistance-thermometer materials.

16.7 Data is presented in Problem 9.14 for the calibration of a thermistor. For each line of data, calculate the value of β, using Eqs. (16.3) and T_0 and R_0 corresponding to the values of 68°F (20°C). Some spread in the results will be found; however, use the average of the calculated values as the magnitude of β. (Use of a programmable calculator or computer is recommended.)

16.8 Write Eqs. (16.3) using the value found in Problem 16.7 for β, plot the result over the range of data, and spot-check several points.

16.9 Investigate the techniques used by the various automobile manufacturers for measuring and indicating engine block temperatures. What accuracies do you think are obtained by the various systems?

16.10 Devise a simple thermistor calibration facility consisting of a variable-temperature environment, an accurate resistance-measuring means that avoids ohmic heating of the element, and a reliable temperature-measuring system to be used as the "standard." Calibrate several thermistors and evaluate their degree of adherence to Eqs. (16.3). (Avoid the problems implied in Problem 16.23.)

16.11 Using the equation for E vs. C for the type T thermocouple, given in Table 16.6, spot-check several points in Table 16.5 to satisfy yourself that the tabulated and calculated values agree.

16.12 Select a thermocouple type (other than type T) and write a computer program to generate an emf vs. temperature table, using the appropriate equation from Table 16.6.

16.13 A computer printout of temperatures derived from thermocouple emf inputs requires an emf-to-temperature conversion. Write and debug a program to accomplish this, using the equation for the type T thermocouple given in Table 16.7.

16.14 An ice-bath reference junction is used with a copper–constantan thermocouple. For four different conditions, millivolt outputs are read as follows: −4.334, 0.00, 8.133, and 11.130. What are the respective junction temperatures (a) in degrees C and (b) in degrees F?

16.15 Copper–constantan thermocouples are used for measuring the temperatures at various points in an air conditioning unit. A reference junction temperature of 22.8°C is recorded. If the following emf outputs are supplied by the various couples, what are the corresponding temperatures? −1.623, −1.088, −0.169, and 3.250

16.16 The temperature difference between two points on a heat exchanger is desired. The measuring and reference junctions of a copper–constantan thermocouple are embedded within the inlet and outlet tubes A and B, respectively, and an emf of 0.381 mV is read. Why does this provide insufficient data to determine the differential temperature accurately? What additional information must be obtained before the answer may be found?

16.17 Use appropriate equations from Table 16.6 and calculate the emfs that are expected for the situations listed below, assuming a circuit such as that shown in Fig. 16.13.

TC Type	Temperature at the Reference Junction, °C	Temperature at the Measuring Junction, °C
B	0	1500
E	20	750
J	0	− 170
K	80	1150
S	700	1580

16.18 Use appropriate equations from Table 16.7 and calculate the temperature at the measuring junction for each of the situations listed below. Assume a circuit such as that shown in Fig. 16.13.

TC Type	Temperature at the Reference Junction, °C	emf, mV
K	400	29.74
K	700	− 8.14
E	56	60.63
E	90	− 4.36
J	15	16.30
J	280	− 11.78

16.19 If you did not work Problems 3.8, 3.13, 3.14, and 3.15 before, you should do them now.

16.20 The following temperature–time data was recorded:

Time, s	Temperature, °C
0	20
4	83
8	123
12	152
20	182
30	194
40	201
50	203

a) Plot the data points.

b) From the plot, determine a time constant for the system.

c) Write an equation assuming first-order process.

d) Calculate sufficient points to plot the theoretical curve.

e) Decide, on the basis of the plot, whether or not the process may be considered a single time-constant first-order type.

16.21 A "two time-constant" temperature transducer has time constants in the ratio $\zeta = 4/1$, where $\tau_p = 1.5$ s. If the transducer, initially at a temperature of 80°C, is suddenly immersed in a 500°C environment, what will be the temperature indicated after 3 seconds?

16.22 If the transducer in Problem 16.21 is initially at 500°C and is suddenly immersed in an 80°C environment, what temperature will be indicated after 3 seconds?

16.23 A small insulated box is constructed for the purpose of obtaining temperature-calibration data for thermistors. Provision is made for mounting a thermistor within the box and bringing suitable leads out for connection to a commercial Wheatstone bridge. The bulb of a standardized mercury-in-glass thermometer is inserted into the box for the purpose of determining reference temperatures. A small heating element (a miniature soldering iron tip) is used as a heat source.

After the heater is turned on, thermistor resistances and thermometer readings are periodically made as the temperature rises from ambient to a maximum. The heater is then turned off and further data are taken as the temperature falls.

It is quickly noted, however, that there is a very considerable discrepancy in the "heating" resistance–temperature relationship compared with the corresponding "cooling" data. Why should this have been expected? Criticize the design of the arrangement described above when used for the stated purpose. How would you make a *simple* laboratory setup for obtaining reasonably accurate calibration data for a thermistor over a temperature range of, say, 80–400°F?

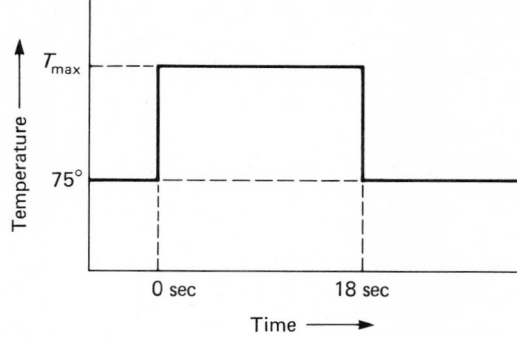

FIGURE 16.35   Temperature–time relationship for Problem 16.24

16.24 The performance of a temperature-measuring system approximates that dictated by two time-constant theory: $\tau_p = 10$ s and $\tau_j = 25$ s. If the system is subjected to the temperature input shown in Fig. 16.35, we see that the probe will not have sufficient time to produce a read-out approximating T_{max}. If, however, at the end of the 18-s pulse, the system indicates 135 degrees, what must be the value of T_{max}?

16.25 The behavior of a temperature-measuring system approximates two time-constant theory with $\tau_p = 6$ s and $\tau_j = 14$ s. If the system experiences a perturbation as shown in Fig. 16.36, what will be the indicated temperature at $t = 15$ s? At $t = 25$ s? At 25 s the temperatures of the probe and the jacket will not be the same; however, on the assumption that both are at probe temperature, estimate the indicated temperature at 60 s. Will the calculated value be too high or too low? State your reasoning in answering the last question.

16.26 Referring to Eq. (16.9a), plot the ratio of static to total temperatures vs. Mach number over the range of $M = 0$ to 3 and for $k = 1.3$, 1.4, and 1.5.

16.27 Referring to Eqs. (16.12) and (16.13), plot the ratio of indicated to static temperatures vs. the recovery factor over the range of $r = 0$ to 1, for $k = 1.3$, 1.4, and 1.5.

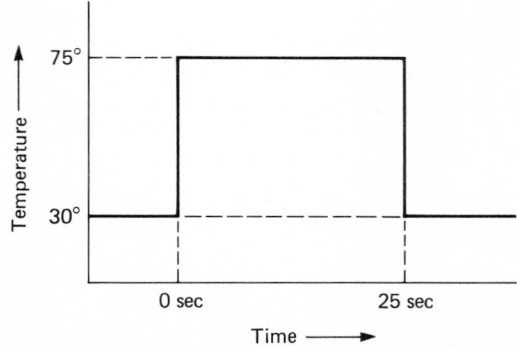

FIGURE 16.36   Temperature–time relationship for Problem 16.25

16.28 We wish to have both a continuous record and an instantaneous read-out of energy flow-rate from heated water passing through a pipe. Temperature, pressure, and rate of flow each vary over a range of values.

a) Analyze the problem and prepare a block diagram of the various measurements and functional problems that must be solved.

b) Insofar as you can, detail the steps to a solution.

[*Note:* Figure 6.22 may help in providing a starting point.]

measurement 17
of motion

17.1 INTRODUCTION

Mechanical motion may be defined in terms of various parameters as listed in Table 17.1. One or more of the values may be constant with time, periodically varying or changing in a complex manner. Measurement of static displacement was discussed in detail in Chapter 11. Very broadly, if the displacement–time variation is of a generally continuous form with some degree of repetitive nature, it is thought of as being a *vibration*. On the other hand, if the action is of a single-event form, a transient, with the motion generally decaying or damping out before further dynamic action takes place, then it may be referred to as *shock*. Obviously, shock action may be repetitive and in any case the displacement–time relationships will normally contain vibratory characteristics. To be so termed, however, shock must in general possess the property of being discontinuous. Additionally, steep wavefronts are often associated with shock action, although this is not a necessary characteristic.

In any event, both mechanical shock and mechanical vibration involve the parameters of frequency, amplitude, and waveform. Basic measurement normally consists of applying the necessary instrumentation to obtain a time-

TABLE 17.1 Motion Parameters

	Defining Relationships	
Motion Parameter	*For Linear Motion*	*For Angular Motion*
Displacement	$s = f(t)$	$\theta = g(t)$
Velocity	$v = ds/dt$	$\Omega = d\theta/dt$
Acceleration	$a = dv/dt = d^2s/dt^2$	$\alpha = d\Omega/dt = d^2\theta/dt^2$
Jerk	da/dt	$d\alpha/dt$

based record of displacement, velocity, or acceleration. Subsequent analysis can then provide such additional information as the frequencies and amplitudes of harmonic components and derivable displacement–time relationships not directly measured.

In many respects, instrumentation used for vibration measurements are directly applicable to shock measurement. On the other hand, testing procedures and methods are quite different.

17.2   VIBROMETERS AND ACCELEROMETERS

Current nomenclature applies the term *vibration pickup* or *vibrometer* to detector-transducers yielding an output, usually a voltage, that is proportional to either displacement or velocity. Whether displacement or velocity is sensed is determined primarily by the secondary transducing element. For example, if a differential transformer (Section 4.11) or a voltage-dividing potentiometer (Sections 4.6 and 5.7) is used, the output will be proportional to a displacement. On the other hand, if a variable-reluctance element (Section 4.12) is used, the output will be a function of velocity.

The term *accelerometer* is applied to those pickups whose outputs are functions of acceleration. There is a basic difference in design and application between vibration pickups and accelerometers.

17.3   ELEMENTARY VIBROMETERS AND VIBRATION DETECTORS

In spite of the tremendous advances made in vibration-measuring instrumentation, one of the most sensitive vibration detectors is the human touch. Tests conducted by a company specializing in balancing machines determined that the average person can detect, by means of his or her fingertips, sinusoidal vibrations having amplitudes as low as 12 microinches [1]. When the vibrating member was tightly gripped, the average minimum detectable amplitude was only slightly greater than *one* microinch. In both cases, by fingertip touch and by gripping, greatest sensitivity occurred at a frequency of about 300 Hz.

When amplitudes of motion are greater than, say, $\frac{1}{32}$ of an inch or about 1 mm, a simple and useful tool is the *vibrating wedge,* shown in Fig. 17.1(a). This is simply a wedge of paper or other thin material of contrasting tone, often black, attached to the surface of the vibrating member. The axis of symmetry of the wedge is placed at right angles to the motion. As the member vibrates, the wedge successively assumes two extreme positions, as shown in Fig. 17.1(b). The resulting double image is quite well defined, with the center portion remaining the color of the wedge and the remainder of the images a compromise between dark and light. By observing the location of the point where the images overlap, marked X, one can obtain a measure of the amplitude. At this point the width of the wedge is equal to the double amplitude of the motion. This device does not yield any information as to the

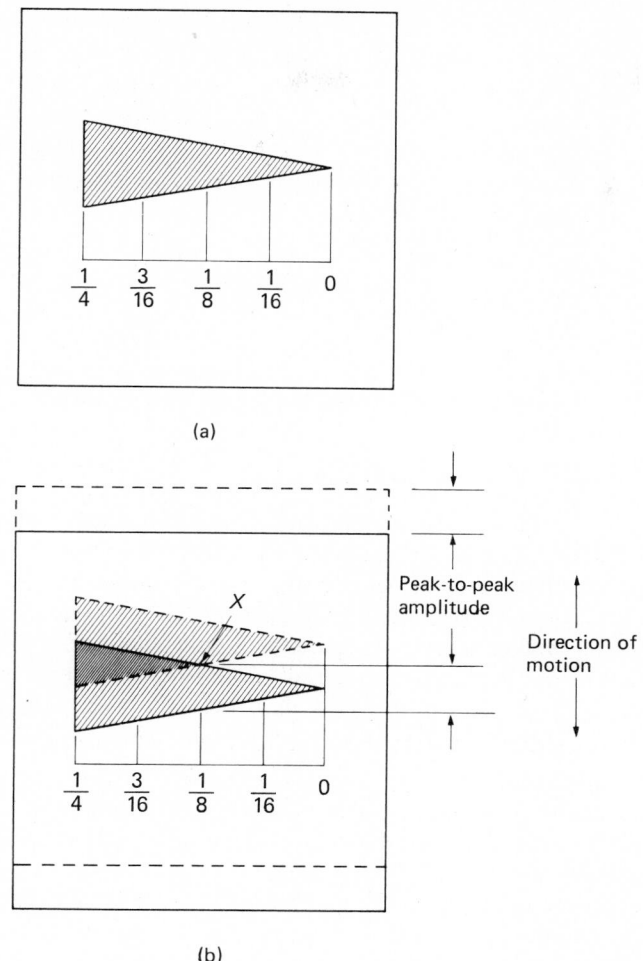

(a)

(b)

FIGURE 17.1   Vibrating-wedge amplitude indicator. (a) Stationary wedge. (b) Extreme positions of wedge.

waveform of the motion. (See Fig. 17.10 for use of a microscope for amplitude measurement.) A simple apparatus for measuring frequency involves a small cantilever beam whose resonant frequency may be varied by changing its effective length. In use, the instrument case is held against the member whose frequency is to be measured, and the beam length is slowly adjusted, searching for the length of beam at which resonance will occur. When this condition is found, the end of the beam whips back and forth with considerable amplitude. The device is quite sensitive, with the accuracy limited only by the resolution of the scale.

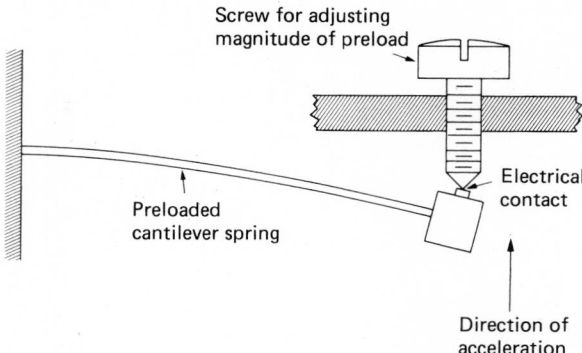

FIGURE 17.2   Preloaded spring-type accelerometer.

17.4   ELEMENTARY ACCELEROMETERS

Probably the most elementary acceleration-*measuring* device is the acceleration-level indicator. There are different forms of this instrument, but they are all of the yes-or-no variety, indicating that a predetermined level of acceleration has or has not been reached. Figure 17.2 is a schematic of one such instrument, which makes use of a preloaded electrical contact [2]. In theory, when the effect of the inertia forces acting on the spring and mass exceed the preload setting, contact will be broken, and this action may then be used to trip some form of indicator. Rather elaborate forms of this arrangement have been devised.

A second acceleration-level indicator is of the *one-shot* type. Acceleration level is determined by whether or not a tension member fractures. Strictly brittle materials should be used for the tension member; otherwise cold working caused by previous acceleration history will change the physical properties and hence the calibration. Since such materials do not exist, this limitation is an important one.

Each of the approaches described above can be considered as providing only rough indications, whose primary value lies in their simplicity.

17.5   THE SEISMIC INSTRUMENT

Vibration pickups and accelerometers are usually of the "seismic mass" form illustrated schematically in Fig. 17.3. A spring-supported mass is mounted in a suitable housing, with a sensing element provided to detect the relative motion between the mass and the housing. As we will see later, damping may also be provided. In the figure this is represented by a dashpot mounted between the mass and the housing.

Basically, the action of the seismic instrument is a function of acceleration through the inertia of the mass. The output, however, is determined by the *relative* motion between the mass and the housing. This results in two varieties

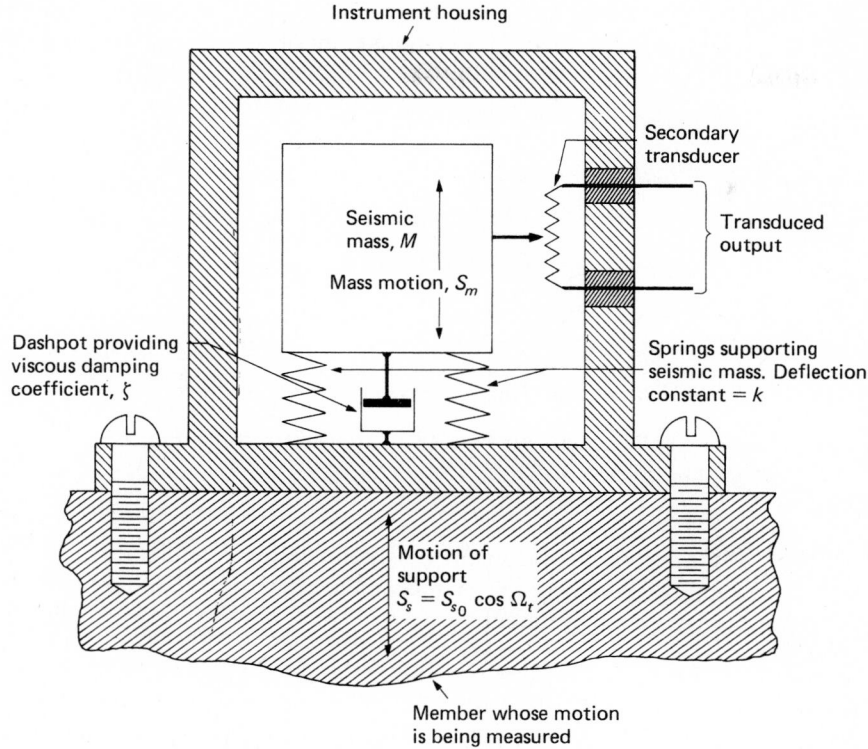

FIGURE 17.3   Seismic type of motion-measuring instrument.

of seismic mass instruments, the *vibrometer* and the *accelerometer*. Several of the more commonly used types of vibration pickups employ a variable-reluctance transducer, in which the relative motion between a coil and the flux field from a permanent magnet is used. In this case, the instrument is velocity-sensitive because the output is proportional to the rate at which the lines of flux are cut.

By proper selection of natural frequency and damping, it is possible to design the seismic instrument so that the relative displacement between mass and housing is a function of acceleration. The output from such an instrument could therefore be calibrated in terms of acceleration, and the instrument would be an accelerometer. The fundamental requirements for the two types of instrument will be developed in the following sections.

17.6   GENERAL THEORY OF THE SEISMIC INSTRUMENT

Figure 17.3 shows a one-degree-of-freedom system with viscous damping, excited by a harmonic motion supplied to the support. Special note should be taken of the fact that *simple harmonic excitation* is assumed, which, strictly speaking, restricts the relations to be developed to a rather limited case. As we will see, however, much can be learned about seismic instruments by studying this special case. Let

M = the mass of the seismic element,

g_c = the dimensional constant,

k = the deflection constant for the spring support,

ζ = the damping coefficient,

S_m = the absolute displacement of mass M, measured from the static equilibrium condition,

S_{m_0} = the displacement amplitude of mass M,

S_{s_0} = the displacement amplitude of the supporting member
     = $S_{s_0} \cos \Omega t$,

$S_r = S_m - S_s$
     = the relative displacement between the mass and the support, which is the displacement that the secondary transducer will detect,

S_{r_0} = the relative displacement amplitude between the mass and the supporting member,

t = any instant of time from $t = 0$,

Ω = the exciting frequency,

ω_n = the undamped natural frequency of the system = $\sqrt{kg_c/M}$,

ϕ = the phase angle, and

k = the deflection constant.

Applying Newton's second law to the free body of mass M, we find that the differential equation for the motion of the mass will be

$$\frac{M}{g_c} \frac{d^2 S_m}{dt^2} + \zeta \frac{dS_r}{dt} + kS_r = 0. \tag{17.1}$$

Each term represents a force: The first is the inertia force, the second is the damping force, and the third is the spring force. Substituting,

$$S_m = S_s + S_r \tag{17.2}$$

we get

$$\frac{M}{g_c} \frac{d^2 S_r}{dt^2} + \zeta \frac{dS_r}{dt} + kS_r = -\frac{M}{g_c} \frac{d^2 S_s}{dt^2}. \tag{17.3}$$

However,

$$S_s = S_{s_0} \cos \Omega t.$$

Then

$$\frac{M}{g_c} \frac{d^2 S_r}{dt^2} + \zeta \frac{dS_r}{dt} + kS_r = \frac{M}{g_c} S_{s_0} \Omega^2 \cos \Omega t. \tag{17.4}$$

This equation is a linear differential equation of the second order, with constant coefficients, and is very similar to Eq. (3.24). Therefore, by comparison, the solution may be written as

$$S_r = e^{-t/\tau} [A \cos \sqrt{1 - (\xi)^2} \omega_n t + B \sin \sqrt{1 - (\xi)^2} \omega_n t]$$

$$+ \frac{(M/kg_c) S_{s_0} \Omega^2 \cos (\Omega t - \phi)}{\sqrt{[1 - (\Omega/\omega_n)^2]^2 + [2\xi(\Omega/\omega_n)]^2}}, \tag{17.5}$$

where ξ = the ratio of the damping coefficient to the critical damping coefficient and

$$\phi = \tan^{-1} \left[\frac{2\xi(\Omega/\omega_n)}{1 - (\Omega/\omega_n)^2} \right]. \tag{17.6}$$

The first term on the right-hand side of Eq. (17.5) provides the transient component and the second term, the steady-state component. If we assume a time interval that is several time constants in length, the transient term may be ignored. We may then write

$$S_{r_0} = \frac{S_{s_0}(\Omega/\omega_n)^2}{\sqrt{[1 - (\Omega/\omega_n)^2]^2 + [2\xi(\Omega/\omega_n)]^2}}. \tag{17.7}$$

17.6.1 The Vibration Pickup

Let us now consider just what we have in Eq. (17.7) by recalling that S_{r_0} is the relative displacement amplitude between the seismic mass M and the support, and that S_{s_0} is the displacement amplitude of the instrument housing and hence of the supporting member to which it is attached. We should also recall that the instrument output will be some function of S_r, the relative displacement, and not a direct function of the quantity we wish to measure, S_s.

An inspection of Eq. (17.7) forces us to the conclusion that if the support amplitude is to be a direct linear function of the relative amplitude, it will be necessary that the total coefficient of S_{s_0} be a constant. For a given instrument, the undamped natural frequency and damping will be *built in*, hence the only variable will be the forcing frequency, Ω. Let us see, then, how the function behaves by plotting the ratio S_{r_0}/S_{s_0} versus Ω/ω_n. This can be done for various damping ratios, thereby obtaining a family of curves. Figure 17.4 is the result. Inspection of the curves shows that for values of Ω/ω_n considerably greater than 1.0, the amplitude ratio is indeed near unity, which is as desired. It may also be observed that the value of the damping ratio is not important for high values of Ω/ω_n. However, in the region near a frequency ratio of 1.0, the amplitude ratio varies considerably and is quite dependent on damping. Below $\Omega/\omega_n = 1.0$, the ratios of amplitude break widely from unity. It may also be observed by inspection of Fig. 17.4 that for certain damping ratios, the amplitude ratio does not stray very far from unity, *even in the vicinity of resonance.*

We may conclude from our inspection that *damping on the order of 65 to 70% of critical is desirable* if the instrument is to be used in the frequency region just above resonance. We also see that, in any case, damping of a general-purpose instrument is a compromise, and inherent errors resulting from the principle of operation will be present. To these would be added errors that may be introduced by the secondary transducer and the second- and third-stage instrumentation.

As an example, let us check the discrepancy for the following conditions:

ξ = the damping ratio = 0.68,

$S_{s0} = 0.015$ in.,

f_n = the natural undamped frequency of the instrument = 4.75 Hz, and

f_e = the exciting frequency = 7 Hz.

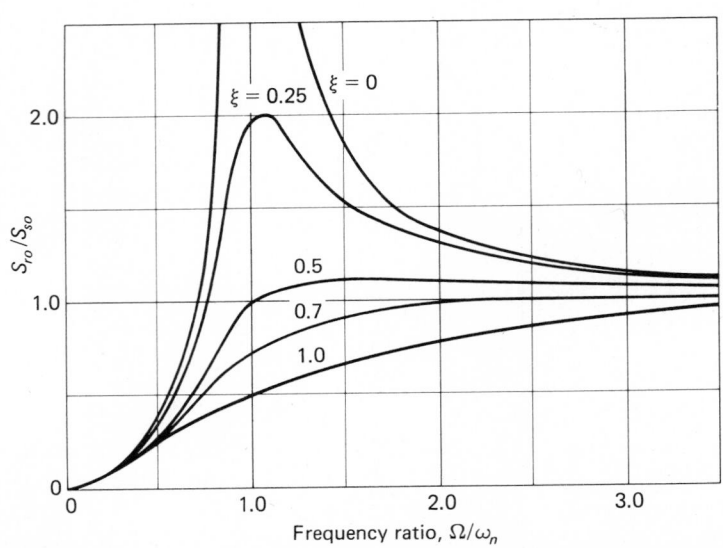

FIGURE 17.4   Response of a seismic instrument to harmonic displacement.

Then

$$\frac{f_e}{f_n} = \frac{7}{4.75} = 1.474, \quad \left(\frac{f_e}{f_n}\right)^2 = 2.17.$$

Using Eq. (17.7), we get

$$S_{r_0} = \frac{2.17 \times 0.015}{\sqrt{[1 - (2.17)]^2 + (2 \times 0.68 \times 1.472)^2}}$$

$$= 0.01404,$$

Inherent error $= \left(\frac{0.01404}{0.015} - 1\right)100 = -6.38\%.$

17.6.2 Phase Shift in the Seismic Vibrometer

Let us now turn our attention to the phase relation between relative amplitude and support amplitude. Naturally it would be very desirable to have a zero phase relation for all frequencies. A plot of Eq. (17.6) is shown in Fig. 17.5. This indicates that for *zero damping* the seismic mass moves exactly in phase with the support (but not with the same amplitude), so long as the forcing frequency is below resonance. Above resonance the mass motion is completely

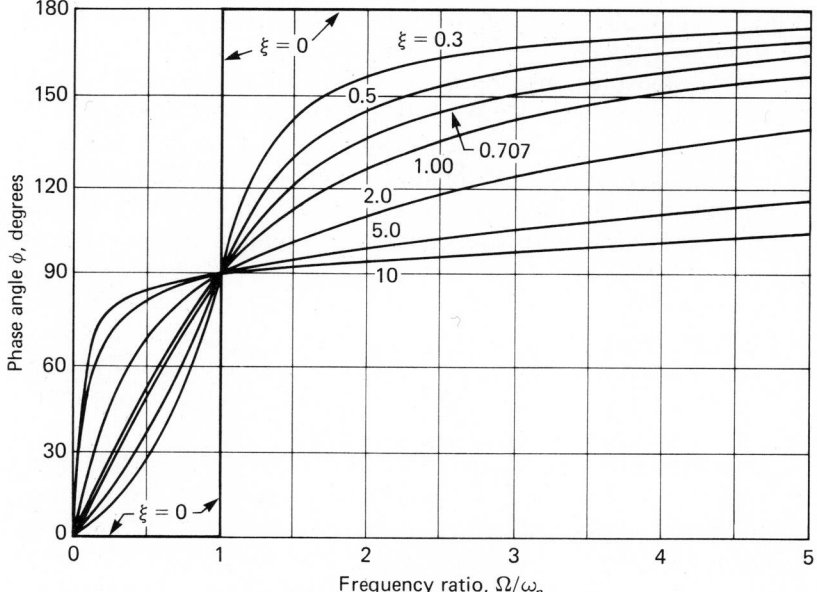

FIGURE 17.5   Relations between phase angle, frequency ratio, and damping for a seismic instrument.

out of phase (180°) with the support motion. At resonance there is a sudden shift in phase. For other damping values, a similar shift takes place, except there is a gradual change with frequency ratio.

A simple experiment verifies this phase-shift relation. A crude support-excited seismic mass can be constructed by tying together five or six rubber bands in series to form a long, soft *spring,* and attaching a mass of, say, one-half pound to one end, while holding the other end in the hand. When the hand is moved up and down, a relative motion is obtained and the natural frequency of the system can easily be found, it being the frequency that provides greatest amplitudes with least effort. Now try moving the hand up and down at a frequency considerably below the natural frequency. It will be observed that the mass moves up and down at very nearly the same time as the hand. The motion of the seismic mass is approximately *in phase* with the motion of the supporting member, the hand. Now move the hand up and down at a frequency considerably above the natural frequency. It will be observed that the mass now moves downward as the hand moves up, and the weight moves up as the hand moves down. The motions are *out of phase.*

Our observations indicate that from the standpoint of phase shift, a "best" solution would be to design an instrument with zero damping (if that were possible). However, the amplitude relation near resonance would then be in serious error.

Perhaps any amplitude and phase-shift effects near resonance, such as we have been discussing, could be accounted for by a calibration! It would seem at first glance that such a possibility would be good, and indeed it would be feasible if *single-frequency* harmonic motions were always encountered. In fact, if simple sinusoidal motion were always to be measured, phase shift would not be of consequence. We would not care particularly whether the peak relative motion coincided exactly with the peak support motion so long as the waveform and measured amplitudes were correct. The difficulty arises when the input is in the complex waveform, made up of the fundamental and many other harmonics, with each harmonic simultaneously experiencing a different phase shift.

As we saw in Section 3.4, if certain harmonic terms in a complex waveform shift relative to the remaining terms, the shape of the resulting wave is distorted, and an incorrect output results. On the other hand, bodily shifts without *relative* changes retain the true shape, and in most applications no problem results.

We find that there are three possible ways in which distortion from phase shift may be minimized. First, if there is no lag for any of the terms, there will be no distortion. Second, if all components lag by 180°, their relative values remain unchanged. And finally, if the shifts are in proportion to the harmonic orders, i.e., there is a linear shift with frequency, correct relative relations will be retained.

Zero shift requires no further comment, other than to suggest that it rarely, if ever, exists. When a 180° shift takes place, all sine and cosine terms will simply have their signs reversed, and their relative magnitudes will remain unaffected.

A phase shift linear with frequency would be of the type in which the first harmonic lagged by, say, ϕ degrees, the second by 2ϕ, the third by 3ϕ, and so on. Let us consider this situation by means of the following relation:

$$f(t) = A_0 + A_1 \cos \omega t + A_2 \cos 2\omega t + A_3 \cos 3\omega t \ldots \quad (17.8)$$

Linear phase shifts would alter this equation to read

$$f(t) = A_0 + A_1 \cos (\omega t - \phi) + A_2 \cos (2\omega t - 2\phi)$$
$$+ A_3 \cos (3\omega t - 3\phi) \ldots$$
$$= A_0 + A_1 \cos \beta + A_2 \cos 2\beta + A_3 \cos 3\beta \ldots , \quad (17.8a)$$

where $\beta = \omega t - \phi$. We see, then, that the whole relation is retarded uniformly, and that each term retains the same relative harmonic relationship with the other terms. Therefore there will be no phase distortion. As we shall see, the vibration pickup approximates the second situation, i.e., 180° phase shift, whereas the accelerometer is of the linear phase-shift type.

Figure 17.5 shows that in the frequency region above resonance, used by a seismic-type displacement or velocity pickup, phase shift approaches 180° as the frequency ratio is increased. The swiftness with which it does so, however, is determined by the damping. For zero damping, the change is immediate as the exciting frequency passes through the instrument's resonant frequency. At higher damping rates, the approach to 180° shift is considerably reduced. We see, therefore, that damping requirements for good amplitude and phase response in this frequency area *are in conflict,* and some degree of compromise is required. In general, however, amplitude response is more of a problem than phase response, and commercial instruments are often designed with 60 to 70% of critical damping, although in some cases the damping is kept to a minimum. In any case, the greater the frequency ratio above unity, the more accurately will the relative motion to which the vibrometer responds represent the desired motion.

17.6.3 General Rule for Vibrometers

We may say, therefore, that in order for a vibration pickup of the seismic mass type to yield satisfactory motion information, use of the instrument must be restricted to input forcing frequencies above its own undamped natural frequency. Hence the lower the instrument's undamped natural frequency, the greater its range. In addition, in the frequency region immediately above resonance, compromised amplitude and phase response must be accepted. Of course, the displacement range that can be accommodated is limited by the design of the particular instrument. In general, the vibrometers of larger physical size permit measurement of larger displacement amplitudes. However, as size is increased, so too is the loading aspect of the signal source.

17.7   THE SEISMIC ACCELEROMETER

We now turn our attention to a similar type of seismic instrument: the accelerometer. Basically, the construction of the accelerometer is the same as that of the vibrometer (Fig. 17.3), except that its design parameters are adjusted so that its output is proportional to the applied acceleration.

Let us rewrite Eq. (17.7) as follows:

$$S_{r_0} = \frac{S_{s_0}\Omega^2}{\omega_n^2\sqrt{[1 - (\Omega/\omega_n)^2]^2 + [2\xi\Omega/\omega_n]^2}} \tag{17.9}$$

or

$$S_{r_0} = \frac{a_{s_0}}{\omega_n^2\sqrt{[1 - (\Omega/\omega_n)^2]^2 + [2\xi\Omega/\omega_n]^2}}, \tag{17.10}$$

in which a_{s_0} is the acceleration amplitude of the supporting member.

Inspection of Eq. (17.10) makes the problem of properly designing and using an accelerometer clear. In order that the relative displacement between the supporting member and the seismic mass may be used as a measure of the support acceleration, the radical in the equation should be a constant. The term ω_n^2 in the denominator is fixed for a given instrument and does not change with application. Hence, if the radical is a constant, the relative displacement will be directly proportional to the acceleration. Let

$$K = \frac{1}{\sqrt{[1 - (\Omega/\omega_n)^2]^2 + [2\xi\Omega/\omega_n]^2}}. \tag{17.11}$$

By plotting K versus Ω/ω_n for various damping ratios, we obtain Fig. 17.6. Inspection of the plot indicates that the only possibility of maintaining a reasonably constant-amplitude ratio as the forcing frequency changes is over a range of frequency ratio between 0.0 and about 0.40 and for a damping ratio of around 0.7. The extent of the usable range will depend on the magnitude of error that may be tolerated.

17.7.1   Phase Lag in the Accelerometer

Referring again to Fig. 17.5 and to the limited accelerometer operating range just indicated—that is, $\Omega/\omega_n = 0$ to about 0.4 and $\xi = 0.70$—we see that the phase changes very nearly linearly with frequency. This is fortunate, for as we have seen, it results in good phase response.

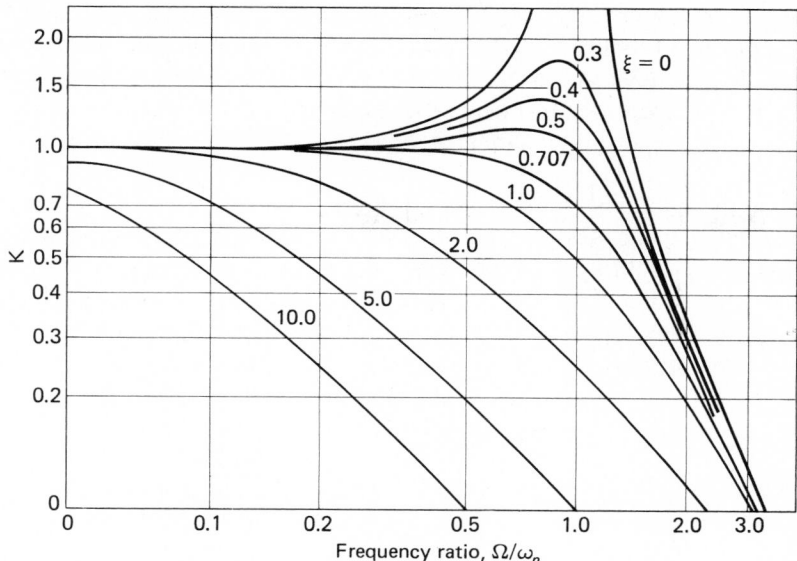

FIGURE 17.6   Response of a seismic instrument to sinusoidal acceleration.

17.7.2   General Rule for Accelerometers

We may now say that in order for a seismic instrument to provide satisfactory acceleration data, it must be used at forcing frequencies *below* approximately 40% of its own undamped natural frequency and the instrument damping should be on the order of 70% of critical damping.

It may be observed that both vibration pickups and accelerometers may use about the same damping; however, the range of usefulness of the two instruments lies on opposite sides of their undamped natural frequencies. The vibration pickup is made to a low undamped natural frequency, which means that it uses a "soft" sprung mass. On the other hand, the accelerometer must be used well below its own undamped natural frequency; therefore it uses a "stiff" sprung mass. This makes the accelerometer an inherently less sensitive but more rugged instrument than the vibration pickup.

Figure 17.3 is a schematic that may be used to represent either a vibrometer or an accelerometer. As developed in Sections 17.6 and 17.7, the basic readout for a seismic instrument is the relative motion between the mass and the supporting structure. To sense this, we require a relative-motion secondary transducer. (The mass–spring combination forms the primary transducer.) Although a voltage-dividing potentiometer is shown in the figure, at one time or another essentially all the appropriate transducing principles discussed in this book have been used for this purpose. A list includes variable-reluctance and variable-inductance devices, both bonded and unbonded strain gages, piezoresistive and piezoelectric sensors, variable-capacitance transducers, and some quite uncommon devices not mentioned in the preceding discussion.

Most of the devices listed above are displacement sensors. Variable reluctance is an exception. In this case the output is a function of velocity: the *rate* at which the magnetic lines of flux are cut. Sensitivity of this type is therefore in volts/unit-velocity, rather than volts/unit-displacement. Variable-reluctance transducers have been quite successfully used as vibrometers. There are two basic designs: (1) A permanent magnet forms a part of the seismic mass, which moves relative to pickup coils anchored to the case, or (2) the magnet is fixed to the housing and the coil forms a part of the seismic mass. Neither has a marked advantage, although it is obvious that for the moving coil, the electrical circuit becomes more critical.

17.8 PRACTICAL ACCELEROMETERS

A popular form of accelerometer, shown in Fig. 17.7, makes use of an *unbonded* strain-gage bridge. The seismic mass, A, is constrained to single-degree motion by small flexure springs (not shown). The unbonded strain-gage element, B, behaves in the same manner as the bonded type discussed in Chapter 12. Damping is accomplished by use of a silicon fluid surrounding the moving mass, and a small diaphragm is used to provide expansion room required by temperature changes.

An advantage enjoyed by this type of accelerometer is the ease with which the secondary transducer, the strain-sensitive elements, may be calibrated in

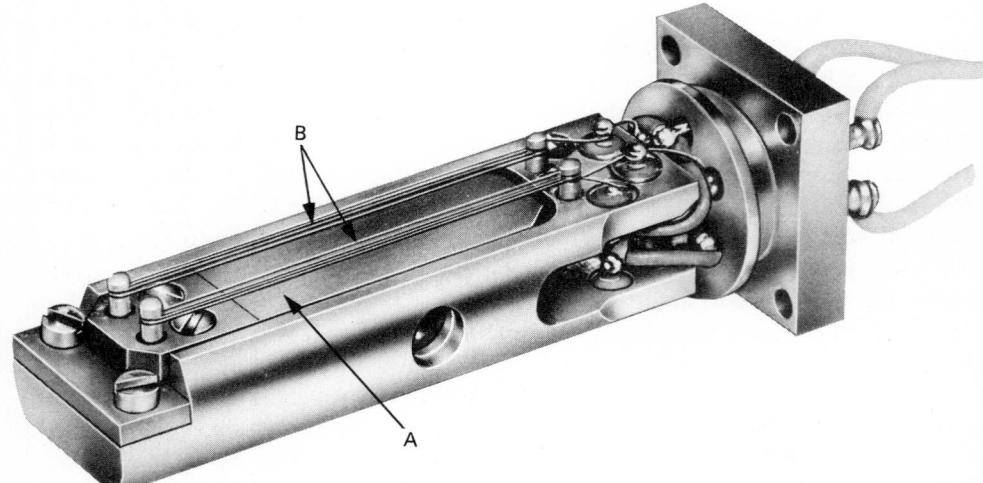

FIGURE 17.7 Internal construction of the Statham Instruments Model A-6 accelerometer. (Courtesy Gould, Inc., Measurement Systems Division, Oxnard, CA, manufacturer of Statham products.)

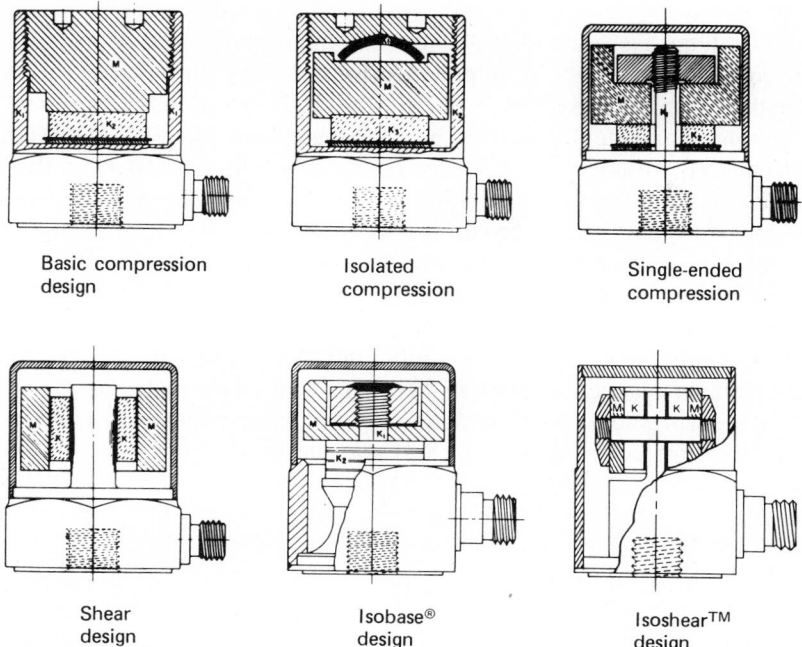

Basic compression design

Isolated compression

Single-ended compression

Shear design

Isobase® design

Isoshear™ design

FIGURE 17.8   Typical piezoelectric-type accelerometer designs. (Courtesy Endevco Corp., San Juan Capistrano, CA)

the field by paralleling calibration resistors (see Section 12.12). Initial calibration of the complete accelerometer is performed by the manufacturer. Instruments of this kind are available covering an acceleration range from 0.5 g to 200 g.

Variable-differential transformers and voltage-dividing potentiometers are also used as secondary transducing elements in accelerometers. When these devices are employed, proper damping is often obtained by means of viscous fluids or through use of eddy-current damping provided by a permanent magnet incorporated into the design.

Undoubtedly the most popular type of accelerometer makes use of a piezoelectric element in some form as shown in Fig. 17.8. Polycrystalline ceramics including barium titanate, lead zirconate, lead titanate, and lead metaniobate are among the piezoelectric materials that have been used [3]. Various design arrangements, as shown in the figure, are also used; the type depends on the characteristics desired, such as frequency range and sensitivity.

Important advantages enjoyed by the piezoelectric type are high sensitivity, extreme compactness, and ruggedness. Although the damping ratio is relatively low (0.002 to 0.25), the useful linear frequency ranges that may be attained are still large because of the high undamped natural frequencies (to 100,000 Hz) inherent in the design.

The output impedance of a piezoelectric device is quite high, and presents certain problems associated with proper matching, noise, and connecting-cable motion and length. Either an impedance-transforming amplifier (Section 5.17) or a charge amplifier (Section 5.18.2) is normally required for proper signal conditioning. Each device has both advantages and disadvantages. Greatest effectiveness is attained when the instrumentation is located near the accelerometer. In fact, modern IC circuitry has made it possible, in some instances, to incorporate the amplifier circuitry within the accelerometer housing. Proper selection of instrumentation will, therefore, depend on application.

The high sensitivity of piezoresistive strain elements (Section 12.13), coupled with small size, makes their use attractive as secondary transducers for accelerometers. They are usually configured in a simple bridge arrangement, mounted on an elastic member in bending. The same instrumentation used for strain measurement (Section 12.13) or for piezoresistive force cells (Section 13.6) or pressure cells (Section 14.8.3) may be used.

17.9 CALIBRATION

To be useful as amplitude-measuring instruments, both vibration pickups and accelerometers must be calibrated. This consists of determining the units of output signal (usually voltage) per unit of input (displacement, velocity, or acceleration). For the accelerometer, volts per g could be determined. Also, the calibration should indicate how such "constants" vary over the useful frequency range.

There are two basic approaches to the calibration of seismic-type transducers: (1) by absolute methods (based directly on the physical concepts of mass, length, and time), and (2) by comparative techniques.

The latter approach uses a "standard" against which the subject transducer is compared. It is clear that the standard must have highly reliable characteristics whose own calibration is not questioned. "Identical" motions are then imposed on subject and standard and the two outputs compared. Although this method would appear to be quite simple and is undoubtedly the one most commonly used, there are many pitfalls to be avoided. Error-free results depend on a number of factors [4, 5].

1. The impressed motions must *indeed* be identical.
2. Read-out apparatus associated with the standard should preferably be and remain a part of the standard, and the *entire* system should have traceable calibration.
3. Associated read-out apparatus in both circuits must have identical responses.
4. The standard must have long-term reliability.

These are all requirements that are not easily achieved.

The motion source used for this purpose is generally some form of exciter system as described in Section 17.16.

The following two sections discuss some of the more fundamental methods applied to calibration of seismic-type transducers.

17.10 CALIBRATION OF VIBROMETERS

Vibration pickups are often calibrated by subjecting them to steady-state harmonic motion of known amplitude and frequency. The output of the pickup is then a sinusoidal voltage that is measured either by a reliable voltmeter or a cathode-ray oscilloscope. The primary problem, of course, is in obtaining a harmonic motion of *known* amplitude and frequency.

Electromechanical exciters are commonly used [6]. Devices of this sort are described in detail in Section 17.16. Exciters of this type are capable of producing usable amplitudes at frequencies to several thousand cycles per second.

The only really positive method for determining actual instrument amplitude in a calibration test of this sort is to measure the excursion directly by means of some form of displacement-measuring device. Measuring microscopes (Section 11.15) are very useful for this purpose [7]. Either the filar type or the graduated reticule type, having a magnification of about 40–100 times, may be used. It is necessary that the microscope be mounted on a rigid support so that the pickup will be credited with no more motion than it is actually experiencing. Figure 17.9 shows schematically the general arrangement that may be used for this method of calibration.

A convenient target to observe is a small patch of #320 grit emery cloth cemented to the exciter table or directly on the pickup. A pinpoint of light is then directed on the emery-cloth patch. The light reflected from the emery cloth appears through the microscope as a myriad of small light sources reflected from the rough sides of the individual crystals, as shown in Fig. 17.10(a). As the exciter table moves, the individual points of light each become bright lines (Fig. 17.10b) having lengths equal to the double amplitude of the motion. The lengths of these lines may easily be measured through the microscope.

One of the requirements of this method is that the center of gravity of the pickup and any mounting fixture must be placed directly on the force axis of the exciter. Otherwise lateral motion may also occur, which must be avoided. Lateral motion will not go unnoticed, however, because if it exists, Lissajous traces (Section 10.5) will be described by the light points and the condition will immediately become obvious.

The following example illustrates the procedure and data for calibrating a velocity pickup. A pickup was shaken sinusoidally by a small electromechanical shaker, and the amplitude was measured through use of a filar mi-

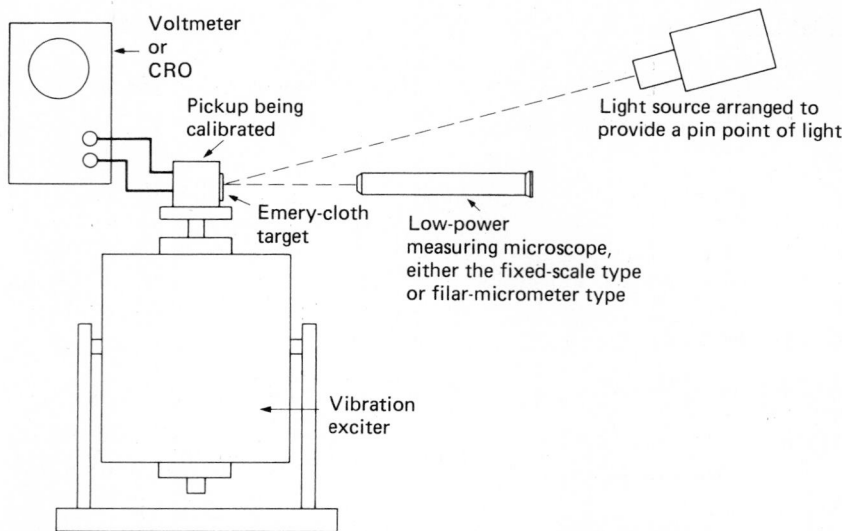

FIGURE 17.9   Schematic diagram of arrangement for calibrating seismic instruments by use of steady-state harmonic motion.

croscope by the procedure outlined immediately above. Data were obtained as follows:

$$f = \text{the frequency} = 120 \text{ Hz},$$

$$A_0 = \text{the amplitude} = 0.0030 \text{ in. } (0.0060 \text{ in. peak to peak), and}$$

$$e = \text{the rms voltage measured by VTVM} = 0.150 \text{ V}.$$

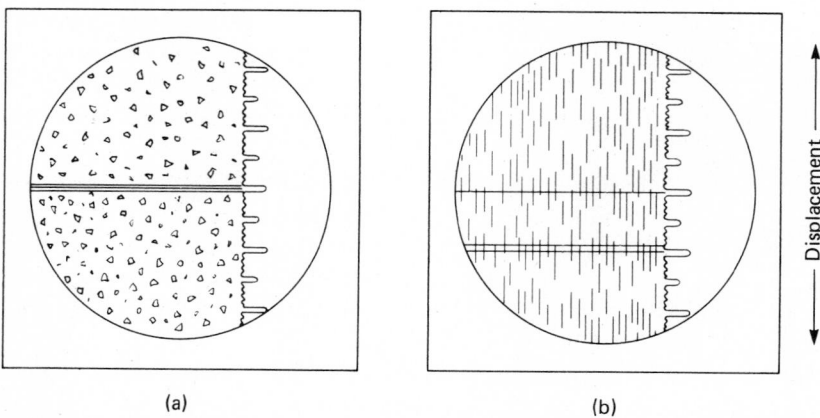

FIGURE 17.10   Views of emery-cloth target observed through a microscope. (a) View when exciter table is stationary, (b) View when table is vibrated.

Calculations:

$$e_0 = \text{the voltage amplitude} = 0.150 \times 1.414 = 0.212 \text{ V},$$
$$V_0 = \text{the velocity amplitude} = 2\pi \times 120 \times 0.0030 = 2.26 \text{ in./s},$$
$$\text{Sensitivity} = e_0/V_0 = 0.212/2.26 = 0.0938 \text{ V/in./s}.$$

(The manufacturer's nominal rating for the sensitivity of this model was 0.0945 V/in./s.)

17.11 CALIBRATION OF ACCELEROMETERS

Accelerometer-calibration methods may be classified as follows:

I. Static
   A. Plus or minus 1-g turnover method
   B. Centrifuge method
II. Steady-state periodic
   A. Rotation in gravitational field
   B. Using a sinusoidal shaker or exciter
III. Pulsed
   A. One-g step, using free fall
   B. Multiple spring–mass device
   C. High-g methods

17.11.1 Static Calibration. Plus and Minus 1-g Turnover Method

Low-range accelerometers may be given a 2-g step calibration by simply rotating the sensitive axis from one vertical position 180° through to the other vertical position, i.e., by simply turning the accelerometer upside down. This method is positive but is, of course, limited in the magnitude of acceleration that may be applied. A simple fixture is described in Reference [8]. Of course, for precise calibration, the value of local gravity acceleration must be used.

Centrifuge method

Practically unlimited values of static acceleration may be determined by a centrifuge or rotating table. The normal component of acceleration toward the center of rotation is expressed by the relation

$$a_n = r(2\pi \text{ rps})^2, \tag{17.12}$$

where

a_n = the acceleration of the seismic mass, and

r = the radius of rotation measured from the center of the table to the center of gravity of the seismic mass.

This assumes the axis of rotaion is vertical. One of the disadvantages of this method, although not serious, is that of making electrical connections to the instrument.

17.11.2   Steady-State Periodic Calibration. Rotation in Gravitational Field

This is simply a variation of the centrifuge method, in which the turntable is rotated about a horizontal axis [9]. To the average static component as determined by Eq. (17.12), a sinusoidal 1-g gravitational component is superimposed.

Using a sinusoidal vibration exciter

A very satisfactory procedure for obtaining a steady-state periodic calibration is that described in Section 17.10 for calibrating a vibration pickup. The primary difference lies in the fact that the input for the accelerometer is the harmonic acceleration,

$$a = -S_{s_0}\Omega^2 \cos \Omega t \qquad (17.13)$$

and

$$a_0 = -S_{s_0}\Omega^2. \qquad (17.14)$$

17.11.3   Pulsed Calibration. The Free-Fall Method

A 1-g stepped acceleration may be obtained by suspending an accelerometer with something like a string. When the support is suddenly cut, the accelerometer is subjected to an acceleration change of 1 g.

High-g methods

Calibration of accelerometers in the high-g range (up to 40,000 g or higher) presents special problems that can be discussed only briefly at this point. Calibration methods are generally based on velocity measurements [10] and use of the following relation:

$$V_2 - V_1 = \int_{t_1}^{t_2} a \, dt. \qquad (17.15)$$

The integration covers the time duration of velocity change.

Various arrangements are used for obtaining the necessary acceleration pulse, including ballistic pendulums, drop testers, air guns, and inclined troughs [3, 10, 11]. The problem consists of obtaining the accelerometer calibration factor,

$$K = e/a, \qquad (17.15a)$$

in which

K = the calibration factor, in volts/unit acceleration,

e = the accelerometer (or accelerometer system) output, in volts, and

a = the acceleration.

To obtain this value the accelerometer is excited by an impact pulse through some means such as a ballistic pendulum (Fig. 17.11; also see Figs. 17.22 and 17.23), and a record is made of the resulting accelerometer output (Fig. 17.12). Substituting the value of a from Eq. (17.15a) into Eq. (17.15) yields

$$K = 1/(V_2 - V_1) \int_{t_1}^{t_2} e \, dt. \qquad (17.16)$$

It will be observed that the integral represents the area under the output curve, which can be obtained graphically. By experimentally determining the velocity change resulting from the impact $(V_2 - V_1)$, we can calculate the value of the calibration factor K. Of course, the method presumes initially that the relation expressed by Eq. (17.15a) is linear. It should also be clear that this method should be used only when high-g calibrations are required, beyond the practical ranges of the simpler methods described previously.

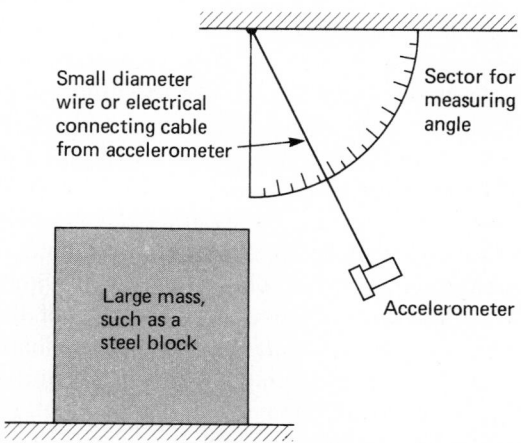

FIGURE 17.11   A simple form of ballistic pendulum for calibrating accelerometers.

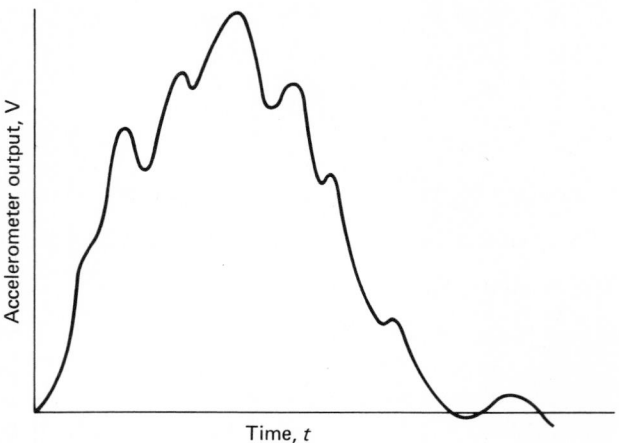

FIGURE 17.12   Typical acceleration–time curve obtained by impact method.

17.12   DETERMINATION OF NATURAL FREQUENCY AND DAMPING RATIO IN A SEISMIC INSTRUMENT

On occasion it may be desirable to determine the dynamic characteristics, including damping ratio, for an *existing* vibration pickup or an accelerometer. This will be necessary, for example, when a special-purpose instrument is constructed by the user, or perhaps to check an instrument before a particularly important testing job, or when instrument damage is suspected.

Two quantities must be determined: the damping ratio and the undamped natural frequency. It should be clear at this point that by undamped *natural frequency*, ω_n, we mean the frequency of oscillation that would occur if damping were zero; we do not mean the *damped natural frequency*, ω_{nd}, that would result if the seismic mass were released from an initially displaced condition. Undamped natural frequency cannot actually be directly measured, because we cannot completely eliminate damping.

Theoretically it is possible to determine the damping ratio and undamped natural frequency of a seismic instrument by subjecting it to a step input and measuring the read-out "overshoot" on the first cycle [12]. Practical limitations associated with this method make its application difficult.

A very workable and accurate solution to the problem may be had by determining the instrument's response over a range of driving frequencies [13]. This may be done by sinusoidally exciting the instrument through a frequency range including the instrument's estimated undamped natural frequency. The output in terms of relative amplitude is obtained (Fig. 17.13).

The frequency–amplitude data thus obtained are then compared with theoretical or "master" curves. If the instrument is a vibration pickup, the master curves would be those shown in Fig. 17.4. If it is an accelerometer, those in Fig. 17.6 would be used. The comparison is most easily done by plotting the

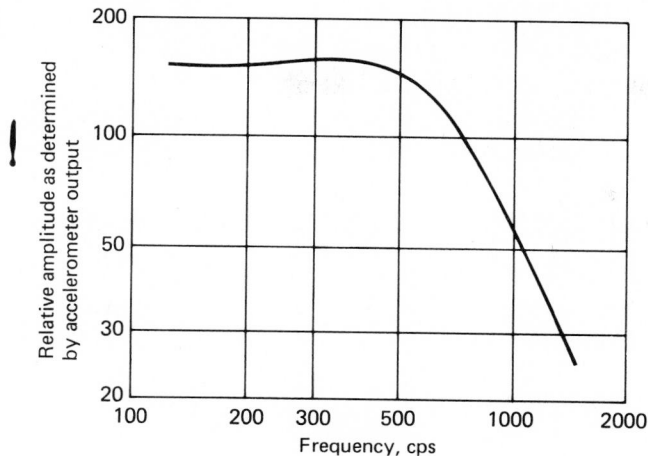

FIGURE 17.13 Experimental response curve obtained from tested instrument.

measured relative amplitudes as ordinates and the corresponding actual frequencies as abscissas on transparent paper having the same logarithmic scales as the master curves. The experimental curve thus plotted is then superimposed on the theoretical curves and adjusted to take its proper place in the family, as determined by its shape. The damping ratio is determined by interpolation, and the experimental frequency corresponding to the dimensionless frequency ratio of 1.0 is the undamped natural frequency. Figure 17.14

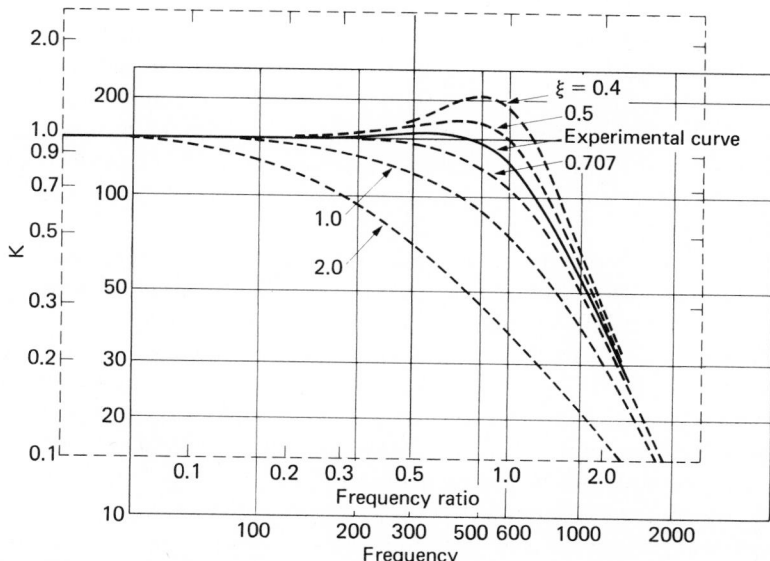

FIGURE 17.14 Experimental response curve (solid) superimposed on family of theoretical curves (dashed). This shows that the experimental instrument has a natural frequency of 60 Hz and a damping ratio of 0.6.

illustrates how this would be done for an accelerometer. The theoretical curves are shown as dashed lines, and the experimental curve, with corresponding scales, is shown as a solid line.

17.13 RESPONSE OF THE SEISMIC INSTRUMENT TO TRANSIENTS

Our discussion of seismic instruments to this point has been largely in terms of simple harmonic motion. How will these instruments respond to complex waveforms and transients? As we saw in Section 2.4 and developed further in Section 3.15, complex waveforms can be analyzed as a series of simple sinusoidal components in appropriate amplitude and phase relationships. It would seem then that a seismic instrument capable of responding faithfully to a range of individual harmonic inputs should also respond faithfully to complex inputs made up of frequency components within that range. Of course if such an assumption is legitimate, the inherent nature of the accelerometer places it initially in a much more restricted area of operation than the vibration pickup. Whereas the accelerometer is limited to a frequency range up to roughly 40% of its own natural frequency, the only frequency restriction on the vibration pickup is that it be operated above its own natural frequency. In comparing the relative merits of the vibrometer and the accelerometer, we must not forget, however, that in terms of phase response the advantage is definitely on the side of the accelerometer (Sections 17.6.2 and 17.7.1). This is an important advantage.

By constructing the vibration pickup with a lightly sprung seismic mass, we can satisfactorily cover almost any frequency range. For the accelerometer, frequency components above the approximate 40% value may be unavoidable. In general, however, higher frequency inputs are attenuated. Figure 17.15 shows the theoretical accelerometer response to square-wave pulses [12, 14, 15]. Results are shown for different damping ratios and undamped natural frequencies.

First of all, these curves confirm our previous conclusion that a damping ratio of about 0.7 is optimum. They also show that insofar as mass response is concerned, use of an instrument with as high an undamped natural frequency as possible is desirable. This is not surprising, because our previous investigation has pointed to this conclusion. A high undamped natural frequency, however, requires a stiff suspension. This means that an extra burden will be placed on the secondary transducer because of the small relative motions between mass and instrument housing. Hence, what is gained in response may be immediately lost in resolution.

The situation emphasizes even more the fact that accelerometer selection must be based on compromise. It means that the accelerometer cannot be

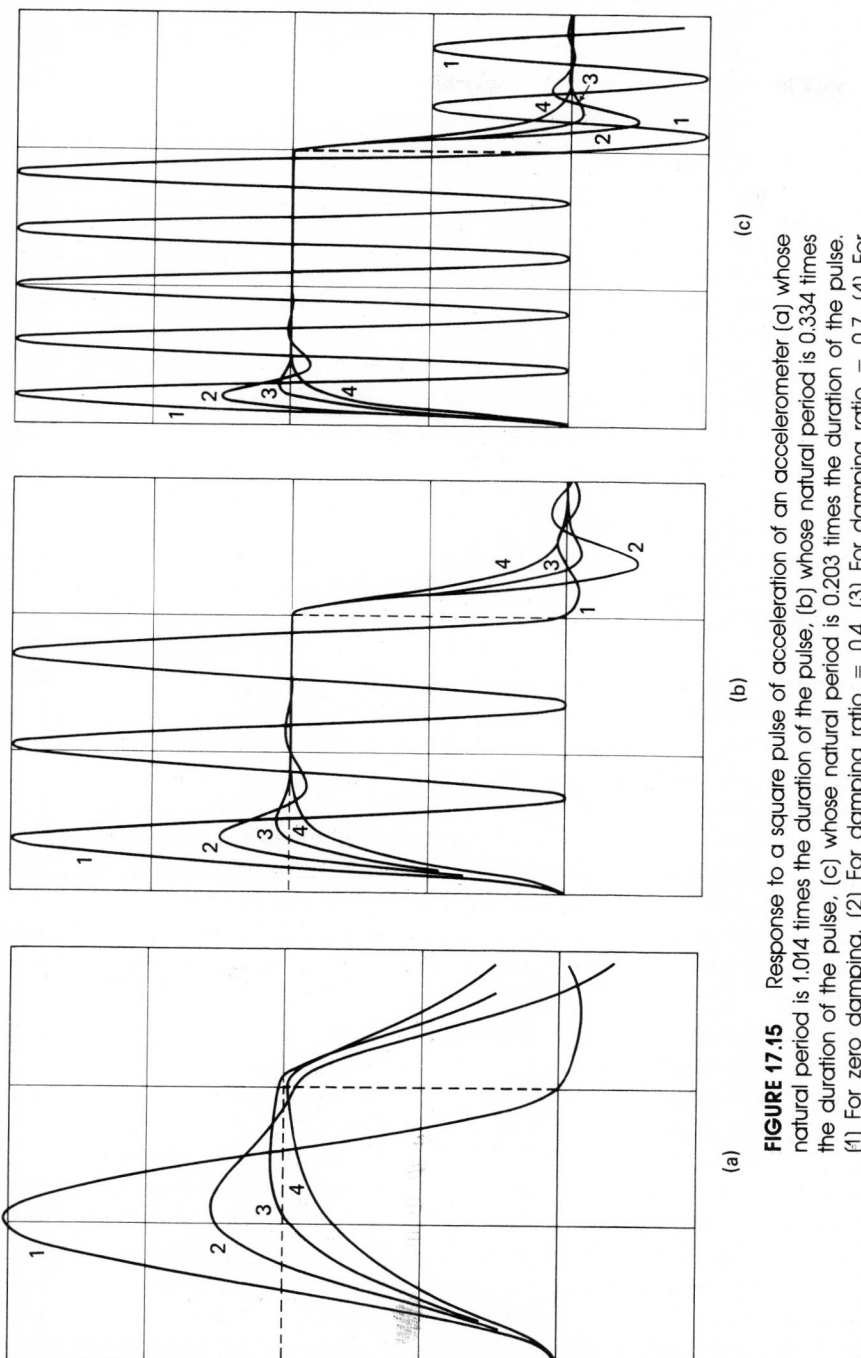

(a)

(b)

(c)

FIGURE 17.15   Response to a square pulse of acceleration of an accelerometer (a) whose natural period is 1.014 times the duration of the pulse, (b) whose natural period is 0.334 times the duration of the pulse, (c) whose natural period is 0.203 times the duration of the pulse. (1) For zero damping, (2) For damping ratio = 0.4. (3) For damping ratio = 0.7. (4) For damping ratio = 1.0. (Courtesy National Bureau of Standards.)

selected entirely on its own merits, but that the whole system must be considered and then the accelerometer selected with the highest undamped natural frequency consistent with satisfactory overall response.

17.14   MEASUREMENT OF VELOCITY WITH SEISMIC INSTRUMENTS

Through proper instrumentation, seismic instruments may be used to measure either periodic or aperiodic velocities. Integration of acceleration–time data will provide the necessary velocity information. Such integration may be performed either by subsequent analytical treatment or by electrical integration at the time of measurement.

To begin with, however, we should understand the real meaning of the term *velocity-sensitive* as applied to seismic instruments. This designation refers to the action of the secondary transducer that may be used, and in general applied to the self-generating types. All seismic-type instruments are *basically* acceleration-sensitive. It is an acceleration or inertia force that produces the relative motion between the seismic mass and the instrument housing. Most so-called velocity-sensitive instruments use some form of variable-reluctance secondary transducer, sensitive to *relative velocity* of mass to housing, which may have only short-term relation to the absolute velocity of the member to which the instrument is attached. Assuming a perfectly responding instrument, we can readily see that if it is subjected to a constant acceleration, only a temporary output will be produced while the initial relative velocity takes place. With constant acceleration, however, the velocity of the supporting member will continue to increase.

Strain-gage, inductive, or capacitive secondary transducers usually provide an output proportional to relative displacement rather than relative velocity of mass to housing. They may be used to determine the characteristics of prolonged motion in a single direction in addition to the characteristics of periodic motions. Absolute velocity may be determined by single integration, whereas displacement requires double integration. The repeated operation required for double integration, however, will unavoidably introduce greater error. Properly designed and used equipment can perform the integration process with errors of less than 1% [16].

17.15   VIBRATION AND SHOCK TESTING

Vibration and shock-test systems are particularly important in relation to numerous R&D contracts. Many specifications require that equipment perform satisfactorily at definite levels of steady-state or transient dynamic conditions. Such testing requires the use of special test facilities, often unique for the test at hand but involving principles basic to all.

Numerous items for civilian consumption require dynamic testing as part of their development. All types of vibration-isolating methods require testing to determine their effectiveness. Certain material-fatigue testing uses vibration test methods. Specific examples of items subjected to dynamic tests include many automobile parts, such as car radios, clocks, head lamps, radiators, ignition components, and larger parts like fenders and body panels. Also, many aircraft components and other items for use by the armed services must meet definite vibration and shock specifications. Missile components are subjected to extremely severe dynamic conditions of both mechanical and acoustic origin.

It might be assumed that dynamic testing should exactly simulate field conditions. However, this is not always necessary or even desirable. First of all, field conditions themselves are often nonrepetitive; situations at one time are not duplicated at another time. Conditions and requirements today differ from those of yesterday. Hence, to define a set of *normal* operating conditions is often difficult if not impossible. Dynamic testing, on the other hand, may be used to pinpoint particular areas of weakness under accurately controlled and measurable conditions. For example, such factors as accurately determined resonant frequencies, destructive amplitude–frequency combinations, and the like may be uncovered in the development stage of a design. With such information the design engineer then may judge whether corrective measures are required, or perhaps determine that such conditions lie outside operating ranges and are therefore unimportant. Another factor making dynamic testing attractive is that the accelerated testing is possible. Field testing, in many cases, would require inordinate lengths of time.

Our discussion of dynamic testing is divided into two parts: vibration testing and shock testing.

17.16   VIBRATIONAL EXCITER SYSTEMS

In order to submit a test item to a specified vibration, a source of motion is required. Devices used for supplying vibrational excitation are usually referred to simply as *shakers* or *exciters*. In most cases, simple harmonic motion is provided, but systems supplying complex waveforms are also available.

There are various forms of shakers, the variation depending on the source of driving force. In general, the primary source of motion may be electromagnetic, mechanical, or hydraulic–pneumatic or, in certain cases, acoustical. Each is subject to inherent limitations, which usually dictate the choice.

17.16.1   Electromagnetic Systems

A section through a small electromagnetic exciter is shown in Fig. 17.16. This consists of a field coil, which supplies a fixed magnetic flux across the air-gap *h,* and a driver coil supplied from a variable-frequency source. Permanent magnets are also sometimes used for the fixed field. Support of the driving coil is by means of flexure springs, which permit the coil to reciprocate when

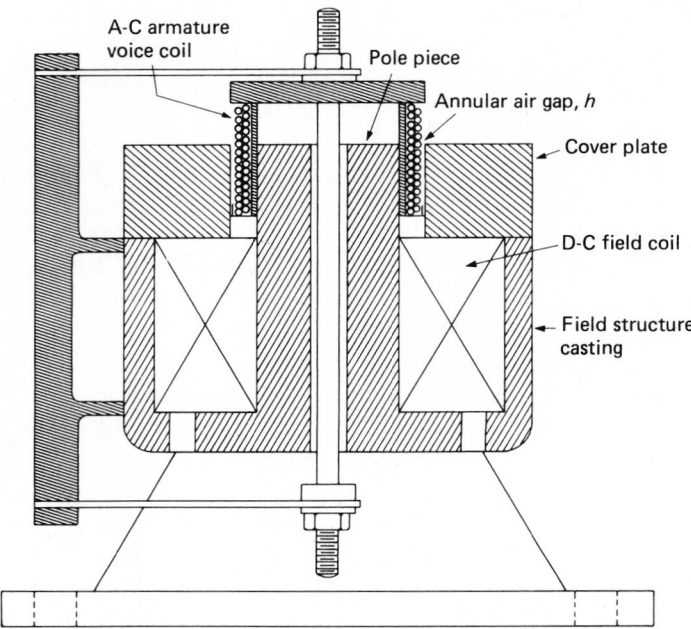

FIGURE 17.16   Sectional view showing internal construction of an electromagnetic shaker head.

driven by the force interaction between the two magnetic fields. We see that the electromagnetic driving head is very similar to the field and voice coil arrangement in the ordinary radio loudspeaker.

An electromagnetic shaker is rated according to its vector-force capacity, which in turn is limited by the current-carrying ability of the voice coil. Temperature limitations of the insulation basically determine the shaker force capacity. The driving force is commonly simple harmonic (complex waveforms are also used) and may be thought of as a rotating vector in the manner of harmonic displacements discussed in Section 2.2. The force used for the rating is the vector force exerted between the voice and field coils.

Rated force, however, is never completely available for driving the test item. It is the force developed within the system, from which must be subtracted the force required by the moving portion of the shaker system proper. This may be expressed as

$$F_n = F_t - F_a, \qquad (17.17)$$

in which

F_n = the net usable force available to shake the test item,

F_t = the manufacturer's rated capacity, or total force provided by the magnetic interaction of the voice and field coils, and

F_a = the force required to accelerate the moving parts of the
shaker system, including the voice coil, table, and
appropriate portions of the voice-coil flexure beams.

In practice, it is often convenient to think in terms of the total vector force, F_t, and to simply add the weight of the shaker's moving parts to that of the test item and any required accessories such as mounting brackets, etc. Table 17.2 lists the specifications for typical commercially available electromagnetic shaker systems.

17.16.2   Mechanical-Type Exciters

There are two basic types of mechanical shakers: the directly driven and the inertia. The directly driven shaker consists simply of a test table that is caused to reciprocate by some form of mechanical linkage. Crank and connecting rod mechanisms, Scotch-yokes, or cams may be used for this purpose.

Another mechanical type uses counter-rotating masses to apply the driving force. Force adjustment is provided by relative offset of the weights and the counter-rotation cancels shaking forces in one, say the X-direction, while supplementing the Y-force. Frequency is controlled by a variable-speed motor.

There are two primary advantages in an inertia system. In the first place, high force capacities are not difficult to obtain, and second, the shaking amplitude of the system remains unchanged by frequency cycling. This means that if a system is set up to provide a 0.05-inch amplitude at 20 Hz, changing the frequency to 50 Hz will not alter the amplitude. The reason for this will be understood if it is remembered that both the *available* exciting force and the *required* accelerating force are harmonic functions of the *square* of the exciting frequency; hence as the requirement changes with frequency, so too does the available force.

17.16.3   Hydraulic and Pneumatic Systems

Important disadvantages of the electromagnetic and mechanical shaker systems are limited load capacity and limited frequency, respectively. As a result, the search for other sources of controllable excitation has led to investigation in the areas of hydraulics and pneumatics.

Figure 17.17 illustrates, in block form, a hydraulic system used for vibration testing [17]. In this arrangement an electrically actuated servo valve operates a main control valve. This in turn regulates flow to each end of a main driving cylinder. Large capacities (to 500,000 lbf) and relatively high frequencies (to 400 Hz), with amplitudes as great as 18 in., have been attained. Of course, the maximum values cannot be attained simultaneously. As would

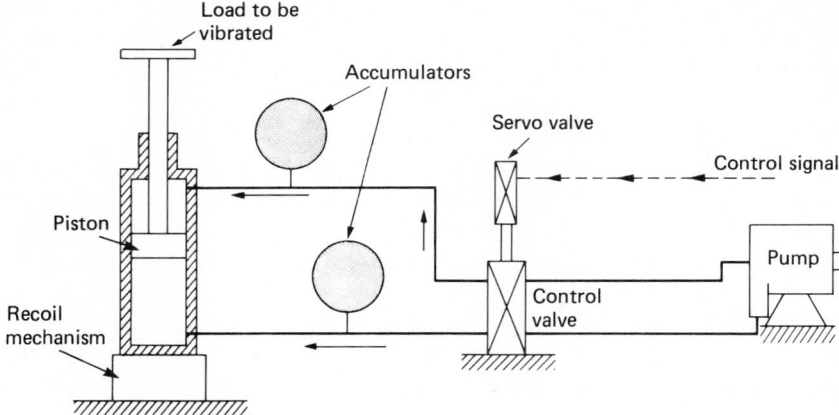

FIGURE 17.17   Block diagram of a hydraulically operated shaker.

be expected, a primary problem in designing a satisfactory system of this sort has been in developing valving with sufficient capacity and response to operate at the required speeds.

17.16.4 Relative Merits and Limitations of Each System. Frequency Range

The upper frequency ranges are available only through use of the electromagnetic shaker. In general, the larger the force capacity of the electromagnetic exciter, the lower its upper frequency will be. However, even the 40,000 lbf shaker listed in Table 17.2 boasts an upper useful frequency of 2000 Hz. To attain this value with a mechanical exciter would require rotative speeds

TABLE 17.2   Specifications for Typical Electromagnetic Exciter Systems

Maximum Rated Force, lbf	Frequency Range, Hz	Maximum Double Amplitude, in.	Weight of Moving Armature, lbm
50	0–5,000	$\frac{1}{2}$	$\frac{3}{4}$
100	0–10,000	1	$1\frac{1}{4}$
300	0–5,000	1	$2\frac{3}{4}$
1,500	0–4,000	$1\frac{1}{4}$	20
3,200	5–3,000	$\frac{1}{2}$	25
20,000	5–3,000	1	95
40,000	2–2,000	1	250

of 120,000 rpm. The maximum frequency available from the smaller mechanical units is limited to approximately 120 Hz (7200 rpm) and for the larger machines to 60 Hz (3600 rpm). Hydraulic units are presently limited to about 2000 Hz.

Force limitations

Electromagnetic shakers have been built with maximum vector-force ratings of 40,000 lbf. Variable-frequency power sources for shakers of this type and size are very expensive. Within the frequency limitations of mechanical and hydraulic systems, corresponding or higher force capacities may be obtained at lower costs by the latter shakers. Careful design of mechanical and hydraulic types is required, however, or maintenance costs become an important factor. Mechanical shakers are particularly susceptible to bearing and gear failures, whereas valve and packing problems are inherent in the hydraulic ones.

Maximum excursion

One inch, or slightly more, may be considered the upper limit of peak-to-peak displacement for the electromagnetic exciter. Mechanical types may provide displacements as great as 5 or 6 in.; however, total excursions as great as 18 in. have been provided by the hydraulic-type exciter.

Magnetic fields

Because the electromagnetic shaker requires a relatively intense fixed magnetic field, special precautions are sometimes required in testing certain items such as solenoids or relays, or any device in which induced voltages may be a problem. Although the flux is rather completely restricted to the magnetic field structure, relatively high stray flux is nevertheless present in the immediate vicinity of the shaker. Operation of items sensitive to magnetic fields may therefore be affected. Degaussing coils are sometimes used around the table to reduce flux level.

Nonsinusoidal excitation

Shaker head motions may be sinusoidal or complex, periodic or completely random. Although sinusoidal motion is by far the most common, other waveforms and random motions are sometimes specified [18]. In this area, the electromagnetic shaker enjoys almost exclusive franchise. Although the hydraulic type may produce nonharmonic motion, precise control of a complex waveform is not easy. Here again, future development of valving may alter the situation.

The voice coil of the ordinary loudspeaker normally produces a complex random motion, depending on the sound to be reproduced. Complex random shaker head motions are obtained in essentially the same manner. Instead of using a fixed-frequency harmonic oscillator as the signal source, either a strictly random or a predetermined random signal source is used. Electronic *noise* sources are available, or a record of the motion of the actual end use of the device may be recorded on magnetic tape and used as the signal source for driving the shaker. As an example, electronic gear may be subjected to combat-vehicle motions by first tape-recording the output of motion trans-ducers, then using the record to drive a shaker. In this manner, controlled repetition of an identical program is possible.

17.17 VIBRATION TEST METHODS [19]

Two basic methods are used in applying a sinusoidal force to the test item: the *brute-force method* and the *resonant method*. In the first case the item is attached or mounted on the shaker table, and the shaker supplies sufficient force to literally drive the item back and forth through its motion. The second method makes use of a mechanical spring–mass fixture having the desired natural frequency. The test item is mounted as a part of the system that is excited by the shaker. The shaker simply supplies the energy dissipated by damping.

17.17.1 The Brute-Force Method

Brute-force testing requires that the exciter supply all the accelerating force to drive the item through the prescribed motion. Such motion is generally sinusoidal, although complex waveforms may be used. The problems inherent in an arrangement of this sort may be shown by the following example.

Suppose a vibration test specification calls for sinusoidally shaking a 10-kg test item at 100 Hz with a displacement amplitude of 2 mm (double amplitude = 4 mm). What force amplitude will be required?

Maximum force will correspond to maximum acceleration, and maximum acceleration may be calculated as follows:

$$\text{Circular frequency} = \Omega = 2\pi \times 100 = 628 \text{ rad/s,}$$

$$\text{Maximum acceleration} = \text{the displacement amplitude} \times (\Omega)^2$$

$$= (2/1000)(628)^2 = 789 \text{ m/s}^2\text{, and}$$

$$\text{Maximum force} = ma/g_c = (10 \times 789)/1 \text{ (kg·m/s}^2)(\text{N·s}^2/\text{kg·m})$$

$$= 7890 \text{ N or about 1770 lbf.}$$

This, of course, is the force amplitude required to shake the test item only. If support fixtures are required, they too must be shaken along with the moving coil of the shaker itself. Suppose these (the fixture and voice-coil assembly) have a mass of 5 kg; then an additional vector force of 3945 N is required. The rated capacity of the shaker must therefore be a minimum of about 12,000 N.

17.17.2 The Resonant Method

The resonant system uses some form of spring-mass fixture to which the test item is attached. Figure 17.18 illustrates a small experimental setup whose characteristics will be described. The test item weighed 7.7 lbm and the test specifications required a sinusoidal vibration at 50 Hz with an amplitude of $\pm\frac{1}{8}$ in. A spring-supported table was designed, as shown in the figure. As initially tested, the resonant frequency was 58 Hz. Addition of a small mass fine-tuned the frequency to 50 Hz. The final weight distribution was as follows:

Test item	7.7
Table with mounting accessories	4.75
Moving weight of exciter	0.35
$\frac{1}{3}$ weight of leaf springs	0.50
Total	13.3 lbm

As a test of the maximum capacity of the system at 50 Hz, it was found that the 5-lbf shaker could actually move the table with test load through an amplitude of ± 0.17 inch at 50 Hz. The force required to accomplish this may be calculated as follows:

Maximum acceleration $= S_0\Omega^2 = (0.17)(2\pi \times 50)^2 = 16,750$ in./s^2,

Necessary accelerating force $= ma/g_c = (16,750/386) \times 13.3 = 577$ lbf.

Obviously the 5-lbf shaker did not supply the force: The necessary accelerating forces were supplied almost in their entirety by the springs.

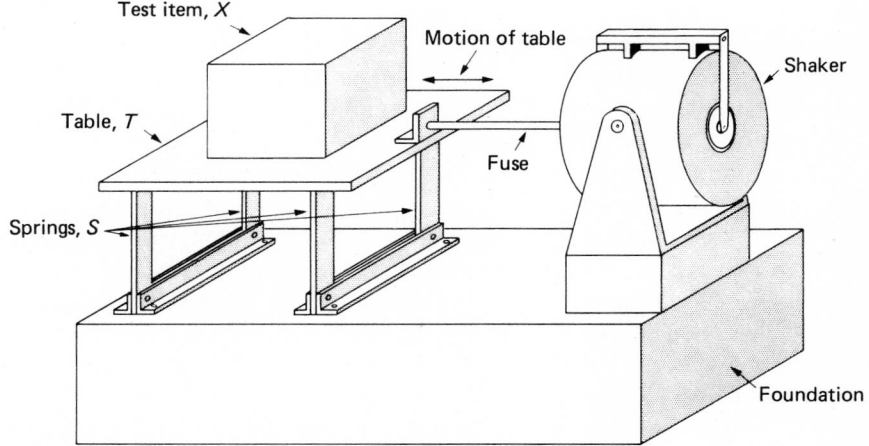

FIGURE 17.18   Exciter-driven table for horizontal motion.

It will be readily realized that a resonant system of this type is limited to *one frequency*. Although a limited range of application might be designed into such a system through use of adjustable springs and masses, in general the system must be designed for the problem at hand and for that only.

Other forms of mechanically resonant systems include vertical spring–mass arrangements, the free-free beam [20, 21], tuning fork systems [20], etc.

17.18   SHOCK TESTING

Mechanical engineers are called on to design machinery to operate at higher and higher speeds. As speed goes up, accelerations increase, for the most part, not in direct proportion, but as the square of the speed. Both the magnitude of acceleration and acceleration gradients are increased. Resulting body loads often become much greater than applied loading, therefore becoming very significant factors in the design. The complexity of many problems has led to an area of investigation generally referred to as *shock testing* [22].

Actually, shock testing is only one of two phases of a broader classification that might better be called *acceleration testing*. Acceleration testing includes any test wherein acceleration loading is of primary significance. This would include tests involving static or relatively slowly changing accelerations of any magnitude. Shock testing, on the other hand, is usually thought of as involving acceleration transients of moderate to high magnitude. In both cases the basic problem is to determine the ability of the test item to continue functioning properly either during or after application of such loading.

The more passive type of acceleration testing involves constant or relatively slowly changing accelerations, which, however, may be of high magnitude. It involves the use of centrifuges, rocket sleds, maneuvering aircraft, etc., for the purpose of testing the capabilities of system components, including the human body, to withstand sustained or slowly changing high-level accelerations. Such tests are usually of quite specialized nature, generally applied to the study of performance in high-speed aircraft and missiles. Therefore, we shall only note this phase in passing and shall devote our primary attention to the first type of acceleration testing—namely, shock testing.

Most military apparatus must satisfactorily pass specified shock tests before acceptance. Equipment aboard ship, for example, is subject to shock from the ship's own armament, noncontact mine explosions, and the like. Aircraft equipment must withstand sharp maneuvering and landing loads, and artillery and communication equipment are subject to severe handling in crossing rough terrain. In addition, many items of industrial and civilian application are also subject to shock, often simply caused by normal handling during distribution, such as railroad-car humping, mail chuting, etc.

As a result, shock testing has become accepted as a necessary step in determining the usefulness of many items. It is becoming generally recognized, however, that to be meaningful, considerably more than magnitude of acceleration must be considered. In addition to magnitude, the rate and duration

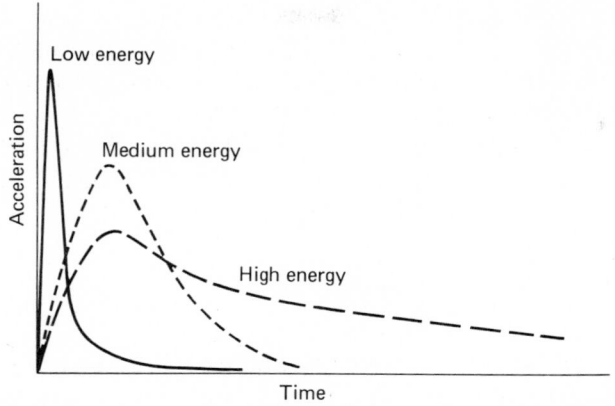

FIGURE 17.19 Typical characteristics of mechanical shock producing machines of low, medium, and high energy.

of application, along with the dynamic characteristics of the test item, must all be studied in setting up a useful shock test.

In general terms, shock testing may be divided into two broad categories: *low-energy* and *high-energy* (Fig. 17.19). Low-energy testing corresponds to the application of high accelerations over short time intervals. The terms "sharp," "intense," "violent," and "abrupt" might be applied. However, the resulting velocities (hence energies) may not be great. On the other hand, high-energy shock is applied for lengths of time permitting the buildup (or deterioration) of relatively high velocities. Acceleration magnitudes accompanying high-energy shock are commonly relatively low. This type of shock might be referred to as "impulsive," "dynamic," etc. Sometimes the latter is referred to as "energy loading" as opposed to "impact loading." The severity of a shock test is very subjective: For certain items, high-energy shock is the more severe; for others, the opposite may be true.

17.19 SHOCK RIGS

Several different methods are used for producing the necessary motion for shock testing. The approach generally taken is to store the required energy in some form of potential energy until needed, then to release it at a rate supplying the desired acceleration–time relation. Methods for doing this include the use of compressed air or hydraulic fluids, loaded springs, and the acceleration of gravity. The latter is the most commonly used.

17.19.1 Air-Gun Shock-Producing Devices

Basically, the air-gun system uses a piston, which moves within a tube or barrel under the action of high-pressure air applied to one face of the piston.

Energy is stored by pressurizing the air in an accumulator. The high pressure is applied to the piston while it is restrained by a mechanical latching mechanism. When released, the piston with test item attached is sharply accelerated. Air trapped in the downstream portion of the cylinder serves to decelerate the piston, finally bringing it to rest. Machines based on this principle of operation have been made with energy capacities of over one million ft-lbf [23].

17.19.2 Spring-Loaded Test Rigs

As the name indicates, these machines use some form of mechanical spring for storing the energy required for acceleration. One machine designed to provide vertical accelerations uses helical tension springs attached at one end to a test carriage and at the other end to anchors that may be moved to put various initial tensions in the springs. With the springs initially tensioned, the test carriage (with test item) is released by a mechanical triggering mechanism and is accelerated suddenly upward. After the carriage has traveled a predetermined distance, the carriage ends of the spring strike stationary hooks. The spring's working stroke is thereby limited; however, the carriage continues upward until stopped by gravity.

17.19.3 A Hydraulic-Pneumatic Rig

The essentials of one hydraulic-pneumatic machine are illustrated in Fig. 17.20. In operation, an initial pneumatic pressure is introduced to chamber B. This

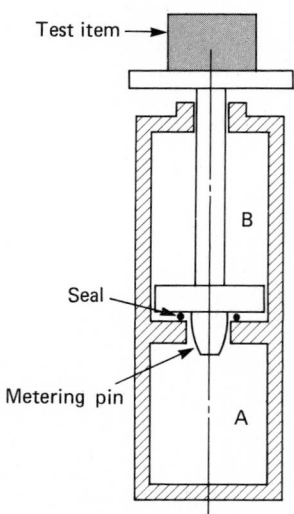

FIGURE 17.20   A form of hydro-pneumatic shock-producing device.

pressure acts over the larger piston area. Hydraulic pressure is then increased in chamber A until the hydraulic pressure over the small area overcomes the pneumatic pressure acting over the larger area. At the instant the piston is lifted, the hydraulic pressure is suddenly applied to the larger area, producing a sharp impulsive-type upward motion. The form of the pulse is controlled by the shape of the metering pin [24, 25].

17.19.4 Gravity Rigs

There are two commonly used gravity-type shock rigs: the drop type and the hammer type. The hammer type is often referred to as a high-g machine and normally provides higher values of acceleration than the drop machine does.

Basically the drop machine consists of a platform to which the test item is attached, an elevating system for raising the platform, a releasing device that allows the platform to drop, and an impact pad or arrester against which the platform strikes. Guides are provided for controlling the fall (Fig. 17.21).

Acceleration–time relations are adjusted by controlling the height of drop and type of arrester pad. Pad selection is of great importance in determining the exact shock characteristics. If the pad is very rigid, for example, an acceleration pulse of very short duration results. On the other hand, a more flexible pad provides a longer time base. *Magnitude* of peak acceleration is controlled by adjusting the height of drop.

Rubber pads shaped to provide the desired acceleration–time pulse may be used. Sand pits have also been used in conjunction with variously shaped

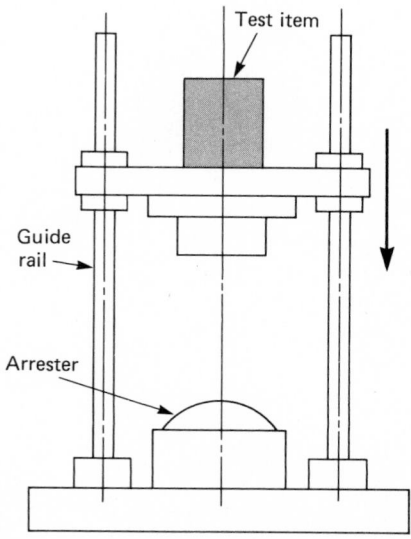

FIGURE 17.21   A drop-type mechanical shock-producing machine.

impacting surfaces. As another example, the test platform may be equipped with shaped pins or punches that strike and penetrate blocks of lead: The shape of the pins is designed to provide the desired pulse form.

Figure 17.22 illustrates the operation of a hammer-type shock-producing device that has been used to study the effects of head injury resulting from an impact. Strain propagation throughout the skull structure resulting from controlled frontal, rear, or side impacts were evaluated. In addition, extensive studies have been conducted on pressure-wave propagation through simulated brain tissue [26].

17.19.5 Relative Merits and Limitations of Each Shock Rig

Each of the shock-testing machines discussed in this section possessed certain distinctive characteristics. The air-gun type produces what may be called a *high-energy* shock. Generally speaking, high energy is synonymous with *high velocity,* and to reach a high velocity, considerable displacement of the test item is required. High velocity can be acquired only by relatively large accelerations, or relatively long time intervals, or a combination of the two. In either case, the test item will be displaced a considerable distance.

On the other hand, the drop and hammer machines are of the low-energy category. High acceleration levels are possible, but only for short time intervals. This results in comparatively low test-item velocities, and hence low energies. The hydraulic–pneumatic machine would be classified as a medium-energy machine.

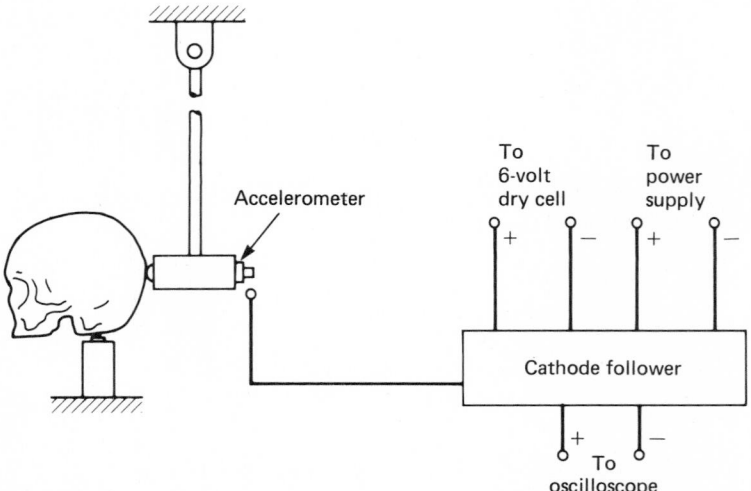

FIGURE 17.22   An application of a pendulum type shock-loading device applied to a research project.

17.20   AN EXAMPLE

Some of the parameters pertinent to shock testing will be illustrated in the following example. Figure 17.23(a) illustrates an arrangement for a laboratory experiment in dynamic-stress analysis. Pendulum OA was caused to swing freely and strike a steel cantilever beam BC on the end of which is mounted a small mass. A small plastic disk was placed at the point of impact to promote inelastic impact. Strain gages on each side of the beam are placed at D. Gage output was appropriately amplified and fed to a CRO for readout. Figure 17.23(b) shows the CRO trace obtained when the pendulum swings from rest through an arc equivalent to $h = 0.18$ in. Calibration-based readout values are shown in the figure.

Applying theoretical relationships, compare analytical and experimental values of (a) maximum strain, (b) time of contact between pendulum tup and beam, and (c) the period of free vibration of the beam. Pertinent dimensions and masses are shown in the sketch. Equivalent mass, m_1, of the pendulum is taken as the mass of the tup plus one-third of the mass of the arm. Equivalent mass, m_2, is taken as the sum of the small mass at B plus one-third of the mass of the beam.

Note that the initial potential energy of the pendulum will be completely converted into kinetic energy at impact (assuming negligible losses). On the basis of the inelastic conditions between masses m_1 and m_2, the law of conservation of momentum will apply, from which the impacting energy loss may be evaluated. The remaining energy must be absorbed by the beam.

Time of contact may be estimated using the assumption that the strain–time relationship is a half-sine wave corresponding to the free vibration of the beam as though both m_1 and m_2 are rigidly attached to it.

Solution

(a) The velocity of initial contact of hammer and beam is

$$V_1 = \sqrt{2gh} = \sqrt{2 \times 386 \times 0.18} = 11.8 \text{ in./s.}$$

The velocity immediately after initial contact may be calculated using conservation of momentum, or,

$$V_2 = (m_1/(m_1 + m_2))V_1 = (1.96/(1.96 + 0.168)) \times 11.8 = 10.9 \text{ in./s.}$$

Therefore, energy to be absorbed by the beam is

$$U_2 = \tfrac{1}{2}(m_1 + m_2)V_2^2/g_c = \tfrac{1}{2}(1.96 + 0.168) \times 10.9^2/386 = 0.327 \text{ in.-lbf.}$$

For the beam,

$$I = bd^3/12 = 0.5 \times 0.188^3/12 = 2.769 \times 10^{-4} \text{ in.}^4$$

Work required to deflect the beam $= U_2 = \displaystyle\int_0^L M_1^2 \, dx/2EI = F^2L^3/6EI,$

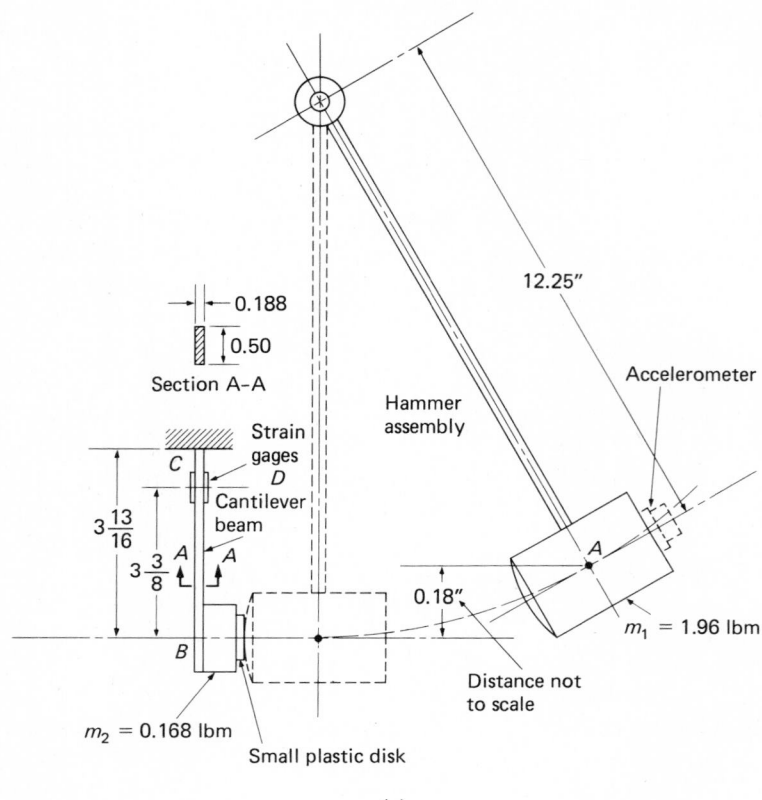

0.188

0.50

Section A-A

12.25″

Accelerometer

Strain
gages

Hammer
assembly

Cantilever
beam

$3\frac{13}{16}$

$3\frac{3}{8}$

C

D

A

A

A

0.18″

$m_1 = 1.96$ lbm

B

Distance not
to scale

$m_2 = 0.168$ lbm

Small plastic disk

(a)

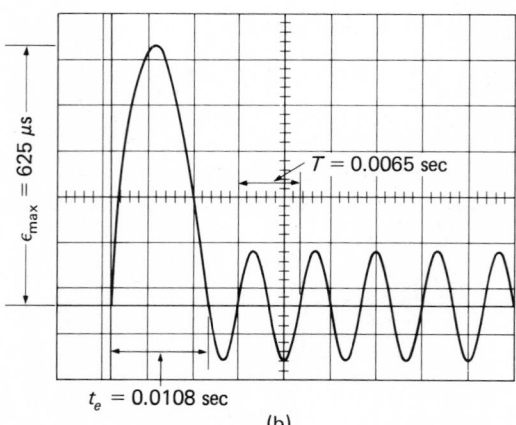

$\epsilon_{max} = 625\ \mu s$

$T = 0.0065$ sec

$t_e = 0.0108$ sec

(b)

FIGURE 17.23   (a) Laboratory setup for demonstrating analysis of mechanical shock. (b) Typical experimental result obtained from apparatus shown at (a).

where

$$M_1 = F_x \quad (0 \leqslant x \leqslant L).$$

Substituting and solving for F_{max},

$$F_{max} = \sqrt{6EIU_2/L^3} = \sqrt{6 \times 30 \times 10^6 \times 2.769 \times 0.327 \times 10^{-4}/3.8125}$$

$$= 17.15 \text{ lbf.}$$

At the strain gages, $M_2 = 3.375 \times F_{max} = 57.88$ in.-lbf.

$$\varepsilon = M_2 c/EI \quad (\text{where } c = 0.188/2)$$

$$= 57.88 \times 0.094/30 \times 10^6 \times 2.769 \times 10^{-4}$$

$$= 655 \text{ micro-strain.}$$

(b) To estimate the time of contact between pendulum tup and beam, assume that for one-half cycle of vibration the tup is rigidly attached to the end of the beam; therefore,

$$\text{Period of vibration} = 2\pi\sqrt{(m_{e_1} + m_{e_2})/kg_c}$$

$$= 2\pi\sqrt{(1.96 + 0.168)/449.7 \times 386}$$

$$= 0.022 \text{ s.}$$

Time for one-half cycle = time of contact = T_1 = 0.022/2 = 0.011 s.

(c) Calculating the period of the free beam (with m_2 at its end),

$$\mathcal{T} = 2\pi\sqrt{m_2/kg_c} = 2\pi\sqrt{0.168/449.7 \times 386} = 0.0062 \text{ s.}$$

17.21 ELEMENTARY SHOCK-TESTING THEORY

An impact or shock test may be simplified as shown in Fig. 17.24. This diagram may be thought of as representing a drop machine of the spring-retarding type. Here M_1 represents the table mass; k_1 is the modulus of the retarding spring; M_2 is the test item, or a portion thereof, supported by a linear spring of modulus, k_2. A viscous damping coefficient, c_2, may be assumed acting between the table and the test mass. If we assume c_2 to be comparatively small, we may write

$$\frac{M_1}{g_c}\frac{d^2S_1}{dt^2} + k_1S_1 - k_2(S_2 - S_1) = 0 \quad (17.18)$$

and

$$\frac{M_2}{g_c}\frac{d^2S_2}{dt^2} + k_2(S_2 - S_1) = 0. \quad (17.18a)$$

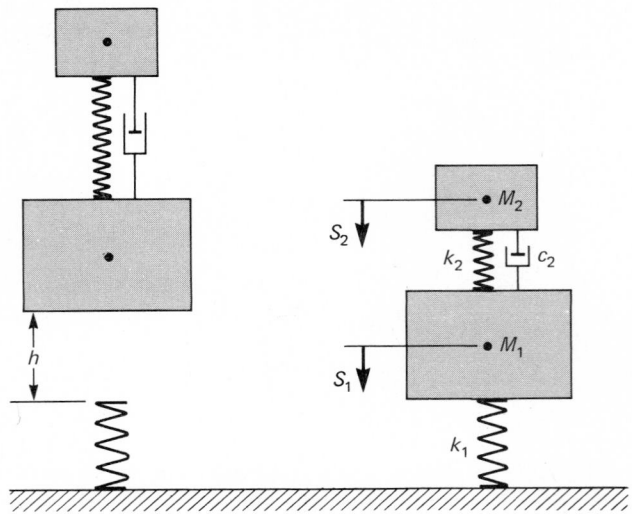

FIGURE 17.24   Idealized shock situation.

Rewriting Eq. (17.18) as

$$\frac{d^2S_1}{dt^2} + g_c\frac{k_1 S_1}{M_1} - g_c\frac{k_2}{M_1}(S_2 - S_1) = 0 \qquad (17.19)$$

and noting that if

$$k_1 \gg k_2 \quad \text{and} \quad M_1 \gg M_2,$$

we have

$$\frac{k_2}{M_1} \ll \frac{k_1}{M_1} \quad \text{and} \quad \frac{k_2}{M_1} \ll \frac{k_2}{M_2}.$$

Thus Eqs. (17.18 and 17.18a) may be written as

$$\frac{d^2S_1}{dt^2} + \omega_1^2 S_1 = 0, \quad \left(0 \leq t \leq \frac{\pi}{\omega_1}\right), \qquad (17.20)$$

$$\frac{d^2S_1}{dt^2} = 0, \quad t \geq \frac{\pi}{\omega_1}, \qquad (17.20a)$$

and

$$\frac{d^2S_2}{dt^2} + \omega_2^2 (S_2 - S_1) = 0, \quad t \geq 0, \qquad (17.20b)$$

where

$$\omega_1^2 = \frac{k_1 g_c}{M_1} \quad \text{and} \quad \omega_2^2 = \frac{k_2 g_c}{M_2}.$$

(Note that although the subscript n is not used, ω_1 and ω_2 represent undamped natural frequencies.) The solution to Eq. (17.20), subject to the initial conditions

$$S_1 = 0 \quad \text{and} \quad \frac{dS_1}{dt} = v_1 = \sqrt{2gh} \quad \text{at } t = 0,$$

can be expressed as

$$S_1(t) = \frac{v_1}{\omega_1} \sin \omega_1 t \qquad \left(0 \leqslant t \leqslant \frac{\pi}{\omega_1}\right). \tag{17.21}$$

Defining the relative displacement between the masses as

$$S = S_2 - S_1,$$

We can write Eq. (17.20b) as

$$\frac{d^2S}{dt^2} + \omega_2^2 S = -\frac{d^2S_1}{dt^2}, \tag{17.22}$$

which gives

$$\frac{d^2S}{dt^2} + \omega_2^2 S = v_1 \omega_1 \sin \omega_1 t \qquad \left(0 \leqslant t \leqslant \frac{\pi}{\omega_1}\right) \tag{17.23}$$

$$\frac{d^2S}{dt^2} + \omega_2^2 S = 0, \quad t > \frac{\pi}{\omega_1}. \tag{17.23a}$$

Considering the initial conditions

$$S = \frac{dS}{dt} = 0 \quad \text{at } t = 0,$$

we can write the solutions to Eqs. (17.23) and (17.23a) as

$$S = \frac{v_1 \omega_1}{\omega_1^2 - \omega_2^2}\left(\frac{\omega_1}{\omega_2} \sin \omega_2 t - \sin \omega_1 t\right), \quad \text{for } 0 \leqslant t \leqslant \frac{\pi}{\omega_1},$$

and

$$S = \frac{2v_1 \omega_1^2 \cos(\pi \omega_2 / 2\omega_1)}{\omega_2(\omega_1^2 - \omega_2^2)} \sin \omega_2\left(t - \frac{\pi}{2\omega_1}\right), \quad \text{for } t \geqslant \frac{\pi}{\omega_1}.$$

Maximum displacements are as follows:

$$S_{\text{max}} = \frac{v_1}{\omega_2[(\omega_2/\omega_1) - 1]} \sin \frac{2n\pi}{(\omega_2/\omega_1) + 1}, \quad \text{for } 0 \leqslant t \leqslant \frac{\pi}{\omega_1},$$

and

$$S_{\text{max}} = \frac{2v_1 \omega_1^2 \cos(\pi \omega_2 / 2\omega_1)}{\omega_2(\omega_1^2 - \omega_2^2)}, \quad \text{for } t \geqslant \frac{\pi}{\omega_1}.$$

Here n is a positive integer, chosen to make the sine term as large as possible, while

$$\frac{2n}{(\omega_2/\omega_1) + 1} < 1.$$

If the gradient of acceleration (d^2S_1/dt^2) is very low so that the peak value $v_1\omega_1$ is reached very slowly, the maximum disturbance experienced by M_2 will be very nearly proportional to (d^2S_1/dt^2). In other words, under such conditions secondary vibrations would not be excited in the supported system. Under these conditions an equivalent static displacement, S_{st}, may be obtained from Eq. (17.23) by dropping the time-dependent terms, or

$$S_{st} = \frac{v_1\omega_1}{\omega_2^2}. \tag{17.24}$$

Mindlin, Stubner, and Cooper [27] call the ratio (S_{max}/S_{st}) the *amplification factor, A.* Solving for A, we obtain

$$A = \frac{\omega_2/\omega_1}{(\omega_2/\omega_1) - 1} \sin\left[\frac{2n\pi}{(\omega_2/\omega_1) + 1}\right], \quad \text{for } 0 \le t \le \frac{\pi}{\omega_1}, \tag{17.25}$$

and

$$A = \frac{2(\omega_2/\omega_1)\cos(\pi\omega_2/2\omega_1)}{1 - (\omega_2/\omega_1)^2}, \quad \text{for } t \ge \frac{\pi}{\omega_1}.$$

It will be observed that the amplification factor is dependent only on the ratio ω_2/ω_1. By plotting Eqs. (17.25), we obtain the upper curve of Fig. 17.25. Damping ratios, $\beta_1 = C_2/2\sqrt{M_2k_2}$, reduce the magnitude of the amplification factor as shown.

The foregoing theoretical consideration of the shock problem is quite elementary from the standpoint that a very simple pulse excitation was assumed and a simple single-degree-of-freedom test situation was considered. In the field, and also when most shock-test machines are used, the exciting pulse or disturbance consists of a complex acceleration–time relation including many frequency components of different amplitude, and the test item will normally possess many degrees of freedom, hence many modes of vibration. The theoretical results are quite useful, however, in providing information on the limiting maxima that may be expected.

Readers interested in pursuing the theoretical aspects of this problem further are directed particularly to reference [28] for this chapter.

SUGGESTED READINGS

Bloss, R. L., and M. J. Orloski (eds.), *Precision Measurement and Calibration* (selected NBS papers on mechanics), NBS Spcl. Publ. 300, vol. 8. Washington, D.C.: U.S. Government Printing Office, 1972.

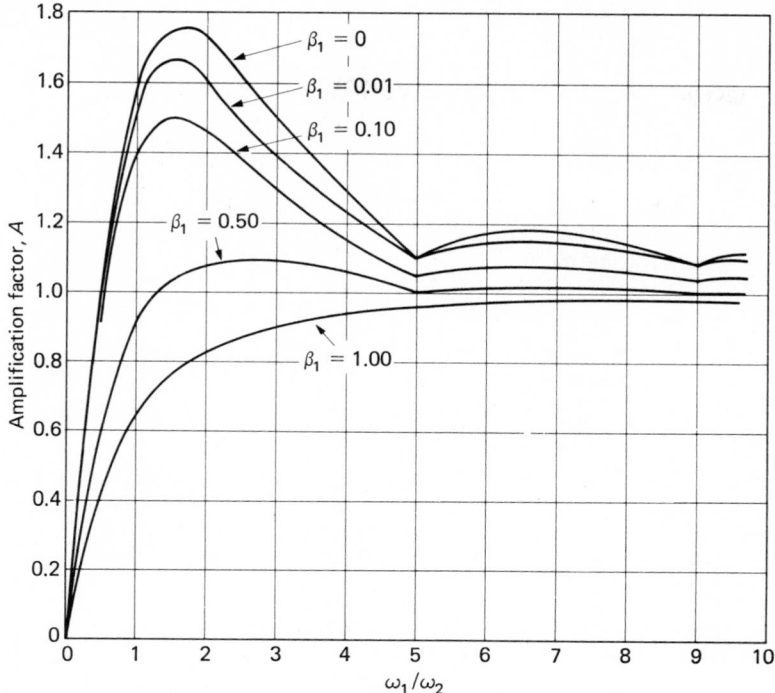

FIGURE 17.25   Amplification factors for linear undamped cushioning with perfect rebound.

Booth, S. F. (ed.), *Precision Measurement and Calibration* (selected papers on heat and mechanics), NBS Hndbk. 77, vol. 2. Washington, D.C.: U.S. Government Printing Office, 1961.

Timoshenko, S., D. H. Young, and W. Weaver, Jr., *Vibration Problems in Engineering*. New York: Wiley, 1974.

PROBLEMS

17.1 A seismic-type vibrometer is characteristically a relatively fragile instrument, whereas an accelerometer is relatively rugged. Explain why this is so.

17.2 The waveform from a mechanical vibration is sensed by a velocity-sensitive vibrometer. The CRO trace indicates that the motion is essentially simple harmonic. A 1-kHz oscillator is used for time calibration and 4 cycles of the vibration are found to correspond to 24 cycles from the oscillator. Calibrated vibrometer output indicates a velocity amplitude ($\frac{1}{2}$ peak-to-peak) of 3.8 mm/s. Determine (a) the displacement amplitude in mm and (b) the acceleration amplitude in standard g's.

17.3 An accelerometer is used for measuring the amplitude of a mechanical vibration. The following data are obtained:

Waveform: simple sinusoidal;

Period of vibration = 0.0023 s;

Output voltage from accelerometer = 0.213 volts rms;

Accelerometer calibration = 0.187 volts/standard g.

What vibrational displacement (amplitude) is sensed by the accelerometer? Express your answer (a) in mm; (b) in in.

17.4 A vibrometer is used to measure the time-dependent displacement of a machine vibrating with the motion

$$y = 0.5 \sin(3\pi t) + 0.8 \sin(10\pi t),$$

where y is in cm, and t in s. If the vibrometer has an undamped natural frequency of 1 Hz and a critical damping ratio of 0.65, determine the vibrometer time-dependent output and explain any discrepancies between the machine vibration and the vibrometer readings.

17.5 An accelerometer is designed to have a maximum practical inherent error of 4% for measurements having frequencies in the range of 0 to 10,000 Hz. If the damping constant is 50 N-s/m, determine the spring constant and suspended mass.

17.6 A simple frequency meter is described in the final paragraph of Section 17.3. The undamped first-mode frequency of a uniformly sectioned cantilever beam may be calculated from the expression [28]

$$f = 3.52\sqrt{EIg_c/mL^4} \quad \text{Hz},$$

where

E = Young's modulus for the material of the beam,

m = the mass of the beam per unit length,

I = the area moment of inertia of the beam section, and

L = the length of the beam.

For a steel wire of $1\frac{1}{2}$-mm (0.0039-in.) diameter, plot the resonant frequencies over a range of L = 10 to 25 cm (3.94 to 9.84 in.). (Use density of steel = 7900 kg/m^3.)

17.7 Referring to Problem 17.6, we may design an instrument of wider range by providing a series of small masses to be attached to the outer end of the beam. In this case,

$$f = \frac{1}{2\pi}\sqrt{3EIg_c/(M_1 + M_B)L^3} \quad \text{Hz},$$

where

M_1 = the mass of the attachment and

M_B = one-third the mass of the beam.

Design a system to cover the range of $50 < f < 2000$ Hz.

17.8 Obtain an inexpensive crystal-type phonograph pickup designed for replaceable phonograph needles. The least expensive will be quite satisfactory. Place a small overhanging mass in the stylus chuck, connect the pickup output to an oscilloscope, and use it to investigate various sources of mechanical vibration. [*Note:* The device should be quite useful as a "frequency" pickup; however, it will not be adequate for meaningful amplitude read-out.]

17.9 Refer to most any introductory vibrations text and review the material on viscous damping including that on the logarithmic decrement. Use such equipment as may be available to obtain a displacement–time record for a decaying damped free vibration, such as that shown in Fig. 17.26(a). The vibrating element may be a simple cantilever beam with concentrated end-mass, as shown in Fig. 17.26(b), etc. The phono-pickup vibration sensor of Problem 17.8 should suffice as a transducer and an oscilloscope or oscillograph as the terminating device. Using data as defined in the figure, determine the damped frequency of vibration and the viscous damping coefficient

$$c = M\omega_{nd}\delta/\pi g_c,$$

where

ω_{nd} = the circular frequency of free vibration and

δ = the logarithmic decrement

$$= \frac{1}{q}\ln\left(S_m/S_{m+q}\right).$$

17.10 An electromagnetic-type sinusoidal vibration exciter having a rated force capacity of 25 N (5.62 lbf) is to be used to excite a test item weighing 3 kg (6.61

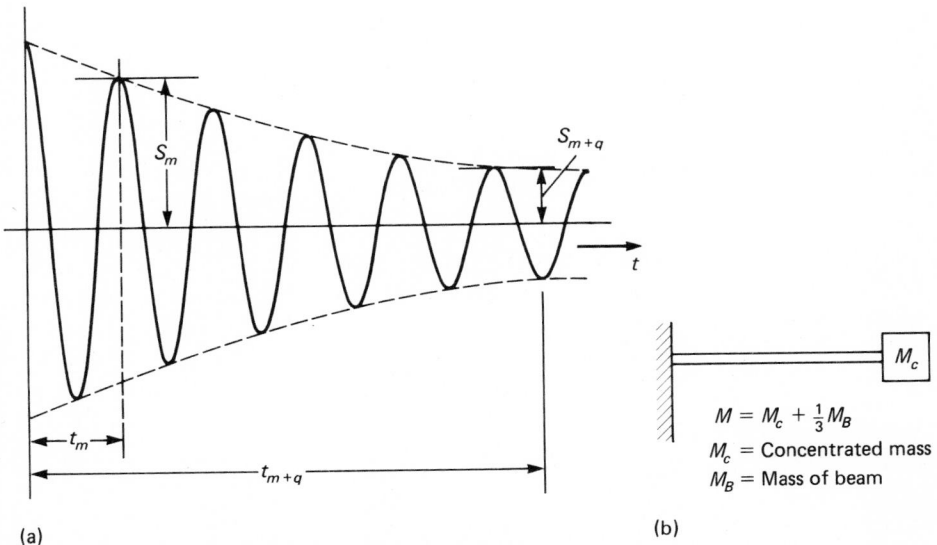

(a)

$M = M_c + \frac{1}{3}M_B$

M_c = Concentrated mass

M_B = Mass of beam

(b)

FIGURE 17.26   See Problem 17.9.

lbm). If the moving parts of the shaker have a mass of 0.75 kg (1.65 lbm) and the amplitude of the vibration is 0.15 mm (0.0059 in.) (double amplitude = 0.30 mm), determine the maximum excitation frequency that can be applied.

17.11 An accelerometer is being calibrated by the procedure illustrated in Fig. 17.9. However, instead of observing straight lines, as shown in Fig. 17.10(b), each of the points of light traces a path similar to that shown in the upper center illustration of Fig. 10.13. This demonstrates an unsatisfactory condition and should be corrected if a good calibration is to be obtained. What is your analysis of the problem?

17.12 An accelerometer is to be calibrated by the high-g method shown in Fig. 17.11. If the effective pendulum length is 1 meter, the initial release angle measured from the vertical is 60°, and the maximum rebound angle is 50°, determine the calibration factor, K, given by Eq. 17.15(a). Assume the acceleration waveform is a half sine wave with an amplitude of 500 mV and a pulse duration of 0.005 s.

acoustical 18
measurements

18.1 INTRODUCTION

Sound may be described on the basis of two considerably different points of view: (a) from the standpoint of the physical phenomenon itself, or (b) in terms of the "psychoacoustical" effect sensed through the human process of hearing. It is very important that these basically different aspects be kept continually in mind. To measure the particular physical parameters associated with a specific sound, either of simple or complex waveform, is a much simpler assignment than to attempt to evaluate the effects of the parameters as sensed by human hearing.

Occasionally, the reasons for measuring a sound may not be associated with hearing. For example, sound pressure variations accompanying high-thrust rocket-motor or jet-engine operation may be of sufficient magnitude to endanger the structural integrity of the missile or aircraft [1]. Structural fatigue failures have been induced by sound excitation. In such cases measurement of the parameters that are involved does not directly include the psycho-acoustical relationship. But in the great majority of cases the effect of the measured sound *is* directly related to human hearing and this added compli-cation is therefore unavoidable.

Noise may be defined as unwanted sound. Noise affects human activities in many ways. Excessive noise may make communication by direct speech difficult or impossible. Noise may be a factor in marketing appliances or other equipment. Prolonged ambient noise levels may eventually cause permanent damage to hearing or, of course, it may simply impair efficiency of workers because of the annoyance factor. All these aspects of sound are unavoidably coupled with human hearing. Seldom are mechanical engineers concerned with the production of *pleasing* sounds. Almost always they are concerned with noise, its abatement, and its control.

Physically airborne sound is, within a certain range of frequencies, a periodic variation in air pressure about the atmospheric mean. The air particles oscillate along the direction of propagation, and for this reason the waveform is said to be longitudinal. For a single tone or frequency (as opposed to a sound of complex form), the oscillation is simple harmonic and may be expressed as [2]:

$$S = S_0 \cos \frac{2\pi}{\lambda} (x \pm ct), \tag{18.1}$$

where

S = the displacement of a particle of the transmitting medium,

S_0 = the displacement amplitude,

λ = the wavelength = c/f,

x = the distance from some origin (e.g., the source), in the direction of propagation,

c = the velocity of propagation,

t = time, and

f = frequency.

For a gaseous medium [2]:

$$p = -B \frac{\partial s}{\partial x} = -B \frac{2\pi}{\lambda} S_0 \sin \frac{2\pi}{\lambda} (ct - x), \tag{18.2}$$

where

p = the pressure variation about an ambient pressure, P, and

B = the adiabatic bulk modulus.

18.2 CHARACTERIZATION OF SOUND (NOISE)

In its simplest form, sound is a *pure tone;* that is, it is of one frequency. Such a source is extremely difficult to produce. In addition to the inherent purity of the signal source and its coupling to the air, it requires the elimination of all reflections from surrounding objects. Such reflections or reverberations produce standing waves that at the point of observation can produce distortions caused by interaction between the directly incident wave and the returning reflections. *Free-field* conditions may be approximated in an *anechoic (no echo) chamber.** The walls of such a chamber are lined with sound-absorbing materials formed in wedges such that small reflections as may result from the

---

*   An imperfect but inexpensive substitute for an anechoic chamber is an open field in as quiet a location as possible. Preferably the site should be on a slight hill or hummock.

initial encounter with the wall are directed again and again into the absorbent materials, until essentially all the energy has been absorbed. In such an environment, sound simply travels outward and away from the source, with no return. Even so, the mere placement of a transducer into the space will cause unwanted distortions.

Random noise, rather than a pure tone, is by far the more common subject of investigation. Random noise is produced from a number of discrete sources whose outputs combine to form the whole. The sounds reaching the transducer (or the ear) are commonly from more than the initiating sources alone. The basic originating sources of sound energy may be called *primary* sources. In mechanical engineering these typically result from interacting machine parts such as gear teeth, bearings, etc.; from vibrating members of a wide variety, such as housing panels, shafts, and supports; or from hydraulic, pneumatic, or combustion sources. Sound waves traveling outward from a primary source are intercepted by surrounding objects such as ceilings, walls, other machinery, etc. A part of such incident waves is absorbed and the remainder is reflected (Fig. 18.1). Each point of reflection then becomes a *secondary source,* "heard" by any pickup device and thereby becoming confused with the initial or primary sounds. Combinations of primary and secondary sounds from *different* reflecting sources produce *standing waves,* resulting in reinforcements and nulls throughout the environment. In the most common situation the primary sounds are not pure tones, but possess certain randomnesses in both amplitudes and frequencies. As a result the standing waves are not necessarily fixed in space, but may be thought of as dancing about throughout the environment: Beats may result (Sections 2.4 and 10.7). It is obvious, then, that evaluation of the parameters associated with a given sound—e.g., from an internal combustion engine or an air compressor—becomes very difficult

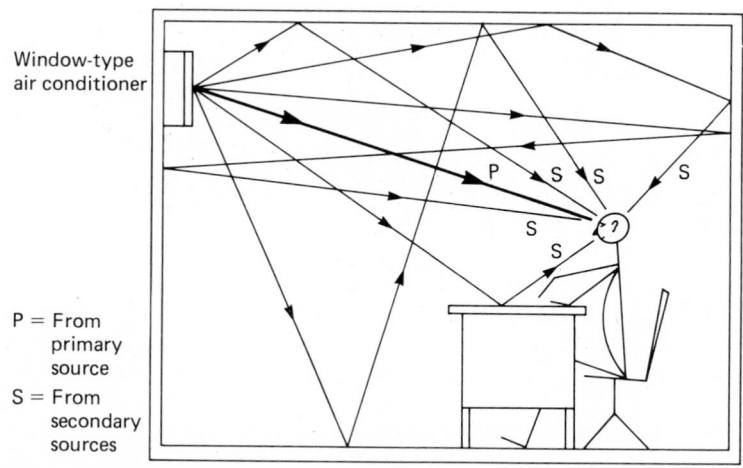

Window-type air conditioner

P = From primary source

S = From secondary sources

FIGURE 18.1   Sketch illustrating primary and secondary sources of sound (noise).

indeed. Under normal circumstances, separation of subject and environment becomes relatively impossible. In fact, one may question the real value of such a separation. Although anechoic-chamber testing may help in understanding or treating certain specific noise sources, to produce meaningful, true-to-life results must necessarily include interaction between both the primary and the secondary sources: The environment is an unavoidable adjunct to any analysis.

18.3 BASIC ACOUSTICAL PARAMETERS

18.3.1 Sound Pressure

In the presence of a sound wave, the instantaneous difference in air pressure and the average air pressure at a point is called *sound pressure*. The unit of measurement is the pascal (Pa), or newtons per square meter, or, more commonly, the micro-newton per square meter ($\mu N/m^2$). The microbar (μbar) is also used. It is equal to one dyne per square centimeter.*

18.3.2 Sound Pressure Level

The ratio between the greatest sound pressure that a person with normal hearing may tolerate without pain and that of the softest discernible sound is roughly 10 million to 1 (Fig. 18.2). This tremendous range suggests the use of some form of logarithmic scale. Recall that the decibel (Section 5.12) provides such a scale and it is on this basis that most sound or noise measurements are made. Basically, the decibel is a measure of *power ratio:*

$$dB = 10 \log_{10} (\text{power}_1/\text{power}_2). \tag{18.3}$$

Because sound power is proportional to the *square* of sound pressure [3], Eq. (18.3) may be written as

$$dB = 20 \log_{10} (p_1/p_0). \tag{18.4}$$

We see that the decibel is not an absolute quantity but a comparative one, which, however, can be used *in the manner of* an absolute quantity if referred to some generally accepted base. This is done and the *rms* value,

$$p_0 = 0.00002 \text{ N/m}^2 = 20 \ \mu N/m^2,$$

is widely accepted as the standard reference for sound pressure level. This value takes on added significance when we note that it corresponds quite closely to the acute threshold of hearing (Fig. 18.2). Therefore,

$$SPL = 20 \log (p/0.00002) \quad re: 20 \ \mu N/m^2, \tag{18.5}$$

---

*   1 $\mu N/m^2$ = 0.00001 μbar.

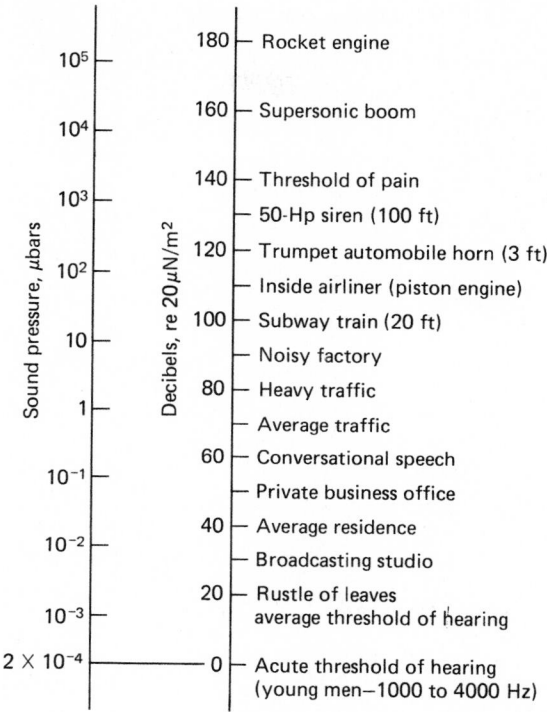

FIGURE 18.2   Typical sound pressures and sound pressure sources.

where

SPL = the sound pressure level, in dB, and

p = the rms pressure from a sound source, in N/m².

Note: Inasmuch as all sound level measurements use base-10 logarithms, the reference will be omitted throughout the remainder of the chapter. In addition, the appended "re: 20 μN/m²" will be omitted with the understanding that this is the standard of reference.

EXAMPLE 1   What is the sound pressure level corresponding to a sound pressure of 1 N/m²?

Solution

$$SPL = 20 \log (1/0.00002) \approx 94 \text{ dB}$$

Special attention should be directed to the use of the word "level." Various terms yet to be discussed use the word: "sound level," "loudness level," "noise level," etc. Use of the word "level" implies a logarithmic scale of measurement expressed in decibels. Remembering this fact should help in keeping the units straight.

18.3.3 Power, Intensity, and Power Level

As suggested by Eq. (18.3), sound involves energy whose magnitude can be expressed in terms of power. The common unit is the watt, W. As the power radiates outward from an ideal point source, it will be continually spread through larger and larger volumes of space. *Sound intensity* at any location is expressed in terms of watts per unit area. For a plane or spherical wave, the intensity I in the direction of propagation is [3]

$$I = (p_{rms})^2/\rho_0 c = W/A, \tag{18.6}$$

where

ρ_0 = the average mass density of the medium, and

c = the speed of sound in the medium,

W = watts,

A = area.

Sound power level (PWL) is expressed in decibels and therefore must be given in terms of a reference level that is usually taken as 10^{-12} W. Power level is therefore defined as

$$PWL = 10 \log (W/10^{-12}), \quad dB \; re \; 10^{-12} \; W. \tag{18.7}$$

There is no instrument for measuring power level directly. However, the quantity can be calculated from sound pressure level measurements [4].

18.3.4 Combination of Sound Pressure Levels

We should note that when two sounds are combined, the resulting sound *pressure level* is *not* the algebraic sum of the two individual sound pressure levels. For example, the SPL from a two-engined aircraft is not twice that of one of the engines alone.

The proper procedure for determining the combined result is to make the addition on the basis of sound power. Let us return to our original definition of the decibel (Section 5.12):

$$dB = 10 \log (pwr/pwr_{ref}) \tag{18.8}$$

or

$$pwr = pwr_{ref}[\log^{-1} (dB/10)] = pwr_{ref}[\log^{-1} (SPL/10)]. \tag{18.8a}$$

Adding two sound powers, each expressed in SPL, yields

$$pwr_1 + pwr_2 = pwr_{ref}[\log^{-1} (SPL_1/10) + \log^{-1} (SPL_2/10)] \tag{18.8b}$$

or, using Eq. (18.8),

$$SPL_{12} = 10 \log [(pwr_1 + pwr_2)/pwr_{ref}]. \tag{18.9}$$

Combining Eqs. (18.8b) and (18.9) yields

$$SPL_{12} = 10 \log[\log^{-1}(SPL_1/10) + \log^{-1}(SPL_2/10)] \qquad (18.10)$$

or, perhaps more simply,

$$\log^{-1}(SPL_{12}/10) = \log^{-1}(SPL_1/10) + \log^{-1}(SPL_2/10). \qquad (18.10a)$$

Generally, we may write

$$\log^{-1}(SPL_t/10) = \sum_{i=1}^{n}\log^{-1}(SPL_n/10), \qquad (18.10b)$$

where SPL_t = the total sound pressure level stemming from the combination of n independent sources of sound pressure level, in dB. It is understood that such a combination has meaning only in reference to a common point in space.

EXAMPLE 2   Two sources of *equal* SPL are combined (e.g., the twin-engined aircraft). What will be the increase in SPL over that of one of the sources alone?

Solution   Let $SPL_1 = SPL_2 = SPL$.

$$SPL_{12} = 10 \log [2 \log^{-1}(SPL/10)]$$

$$= 10 \log 2 + SPL$$

$$= SPL + 3$$

The increase is 3 dB.

EXAMPLE 3   A business machine is added to an office. The original ambient SPL was 68 dB. After the machine was added the sound pressure level rose to 72 dB. What SPL was contributed by the machine?

Solution   Using Eq. (18.10), we have

$$72 = 10 \log [\log^{-1}(68/10) + \log^{-1}(SPL_{mach}/10)]$$

$$\log (SPL_{mach}/10) = 1.59 \times 10^7 - 6.31 \times 10^6$$

$$SPL_{mach}/10 = \log 1.274 \times 10^7 = 6.98$$

$$SPL_{mach} = 69.8 \text{ dB}.$$

The above examples demonstrate that to combine sound pressure levels one must have a calculator or a good source of base-10 logarithms and also must have some facility in manipulating them. Figure 18.3 provides an easy and quick means for sidestepping most of the hard work. Its use is demonstrated by the following examples.

EXAMPLE 4   Use the chart (Fig. 18.3) to check the answer obtained for Example 2.

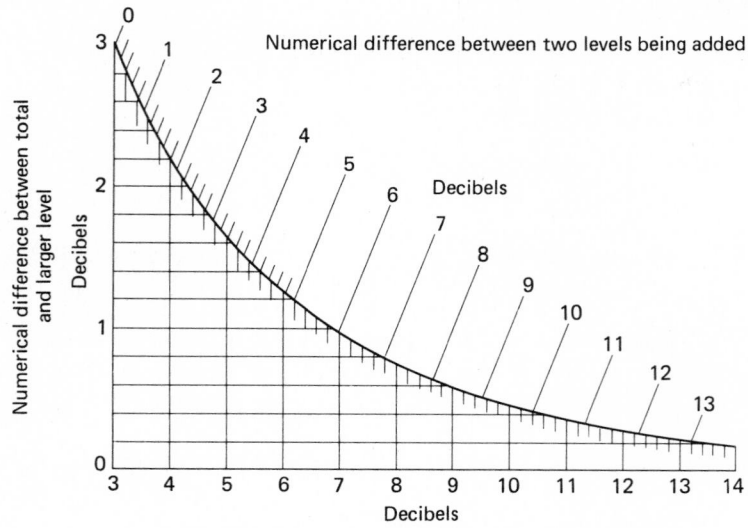

FIGURE 18.3 Diagram for adding or subtracting decibels. Courtesy: GenRad, Inc., Concord, MA.

Solution Because the sound pressure levels are equal, the "numerical difference" is zero. Looking at the zero point on the curved scale one reads 3 dB on both the vertical and horizontal scales. In this case both the "larger" and the "smaller" inputs are the same and either read-out provides confirmation of the answer obtained in Example 2.

EXAMPLE 5 Use the chart to check the result obtained for Example 3.

Solution

$$SPL_1 = 68 \text{ dB} \quad \text{and} \quad SPL_{12} = 72 \text{ dB},$$

$$SPL_{12} - SPL_1 = 4 \text{ dB}.$$

Looking at the horizontal scale at 4 dB, we read

$$SPL_2 - SPL_1 = 1.8 \text{ dB};$$

hence,

$$SPL_2 = 68 + 1.8 = 69.8 \text{ dB},$$

confirming the answer obtained previously. Note that there is no ambiguity in the chart. The horizontal and vertical scales permit only one entry point for a situation such as this.

18.3.5 Attenuation with Distance

In a *lossless, free space* there is a 6-dB decrease in sound pressure level (SPL) for each doubling of distance [5]. This may be shown as follows: From Eq. (18.4), we have

$$SPL_1 = 20 \log (p_1/p_0) \quad \text{and} \quad SPL_2 = 20 \log (p_2/p_0);$$

therefore,

$$SPL_2 - SPL_1 = 20 [\log (p_2) - \log (p_1)] = 20 \log (p_2/p_1). \quad (18.11)$$

From Eq. (18.6), we see that for a spherical wave

$$p^2/\rho c = W/(4\pi r^2);$$

hence

$$p_2/p_1 = r_1/r_2. \quad (18.12)$$

Combining Eqs. (18.11) and (18.12) gives us

$$SPL_2 - SPL_1 = 20 \log (r_1/r_2). \quad (18.13)$$

Question: In a free field, what will be the difference in sound pressure levels between points *A* and *B* if point *B* is twice as far from the source as is *A*?

$$SPL_A - SPL_B = 20 \log r_B/r_A = 20 \log 2 = 6.02$$

Caution: The relation expressed by Eq. (18.13) holds only for free-field conditions. In certain instances the relation may be used to confirm the existence of a free field. (See Section 18.8.)

18.4 PSYCHOACOUSTIC RELATIONSHIPS

As mentioned earlier, in only a relatively few situations is human hearing disassociated from sound measurements. Measuring systems and techniques are therefore unavoidably greatly influenced by the physiological and psychological makeup of the human ear as a transducer and the brain as the final evaluator. In terms of input magnitudes and frequencies, the human hearing system is quite nonlinear. Figure 18.4 shows average thresholds of hearing and tolerances for young persons. It will be noted that the greatest sensitivity occurs at about 4000 Hz and that a considerably greater SPL is required for equal reception at both lower and higher frequencies. Figure 18.5 shows the free-field *equal-loudness* contours for pure *tones* as determined by Robinson and Dadson at the National Physical Laboratories, Teddington, England.

Loudness is a measure of relative sound magnitudes or strengths *as judged by the listener*. It is a subjective quantity depending on both the physical waveform emanating from the source and on the *average* of many human hearing systems (persons) as receptors. The quantity is measured in *loudness*

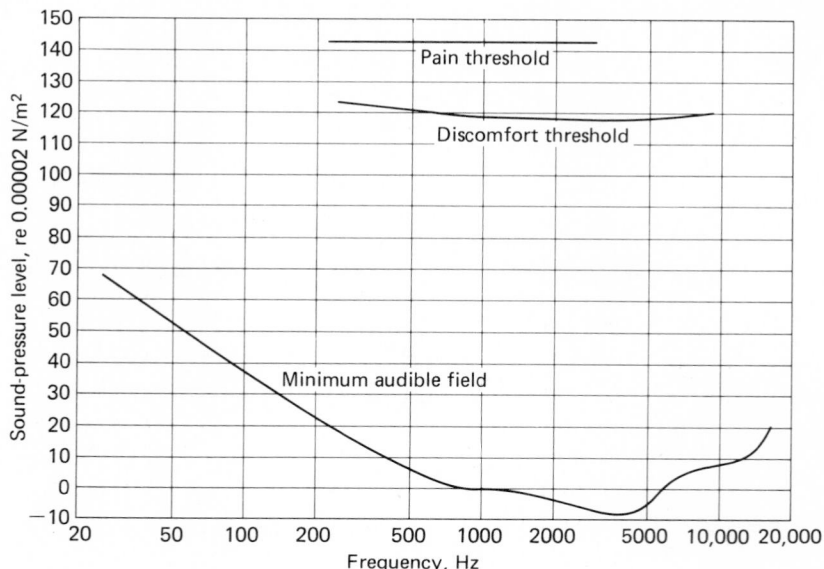

FIGURE 18.4   Thresholds of hearing and tolerance for young people with good hearing. Courtesy: GenRad Inc., Concord, MA.

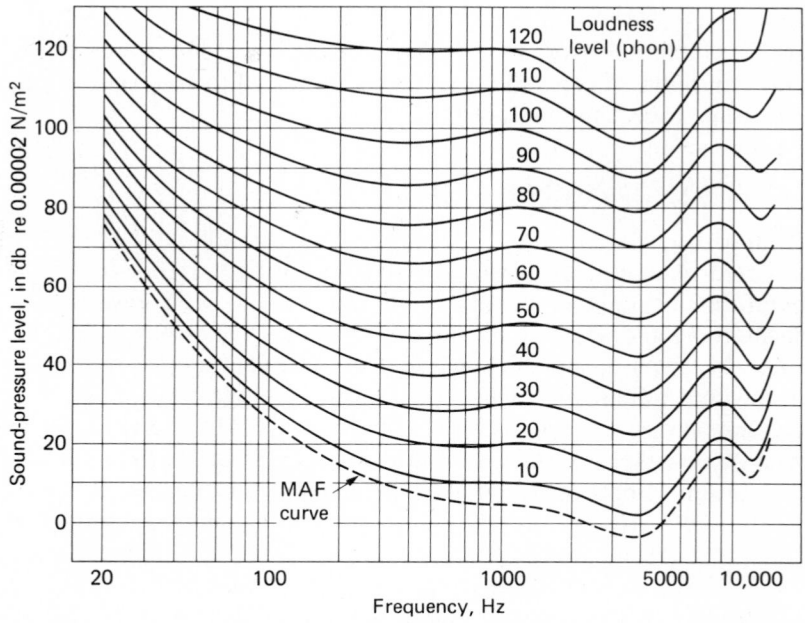

FIGURE 18.5   Free-field equal-loudness contours for pure tones. Courtesy: GenRad, Inc., Concord, MA.

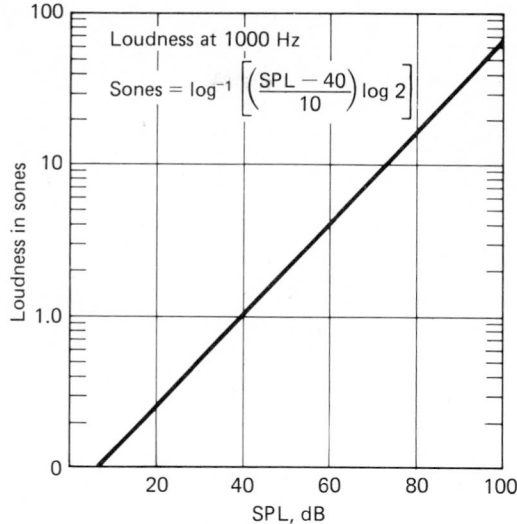

FIGURE 18.6 Relationship between loudness in sones and SPL.

level and the unit is called the *phon* (pronounced "fon" as "up*on*"). The loudness level in phons is numerically equal to the sound pressure level in dB at the frequency of 1000 Hz. Note that for each contour in Fig. 18.5, the loudness level and the sound pressure level are equal at only one point, namely, at 1000 Hz. It is quite important to keep in mind that the equal-loudness contours of Fig. 18.5 are based on *pure tones*. Loudness levels of complex sounds will be considered in Section 18.7.

To further understand the curves in Fig. 18.5, first note that the SPL of 30 dB at 1000 Hz corresponds to 30 phons. On average, for a person to sense a loudness of 30 phons at 100 Hz would require an SPL of 44 dB; at 9000 Hz, 40 dB; and so on.

It is clear that loudness level in terms of the phon is a logarithmic quantity. Although this is quite useful, still another measure of strength is employed. *Loudness* (note the absence of the word "level") is measured with a linear unit, the *sone* (pronounced as in "zone"). One sone is the loudness of a 1000-Hz tone with an SPL of 40 dB (note that this also corresponds to 40 phons). A tone that sounds *n* times as loud has a loudness of *n* sones, etc.

We see that the sone is tied to the SPL at the one common pure tone of 1000 Hz and 40 dB. Figure 18.6 shows values at other sound pressure levels.

18.5 SOUND-MEASURING APPARATUS AND TECHNIQUES

Measurement of the parameters associated with sound use a basic system made up of a detector-transducer (the microphone), intermediate modifying devices (amplifiers and filtering systems), and read-out means (a meter, CRO, or recording apparatus). Most sound-measuring systems are used to obtain psychoacoustically related information. It is therefore necessary to build into the apparatus nonlinearities approximating those of the average human ear. Elaborate filtering networks also provide the basis for analyzers, devices for separating and identifying the various frequency components or ranges of components forming a complex sound.

18.5.1 Microphones

Most microphones incorporate a thin diaphragm as the primary transducer, which is moved by the air acting against it. The mechanical movement of the diaphragm is converted to an electrical output by means of some form of secondary transducer that provides an analogous electrical signal.

Common microphones may be classified on the basis of the secondary transducer, as follows:

1. Capacitor or condenser,
2. Crystal,
3. Electrodynamic (moving coil or ribbon),
4. Carbon.

The *capacitor* or *condenser microphone* is probably the most respected microphone for sound measurement purposes. It is arranged with a diaphragm forming one plate of an air-dielectric capacitor (Fig. 18.7). Movement of the diaphragm caused by impingement of sound pressure results in an output voltage [6]:

$$E \approx Qd, \tag{18.14}$$

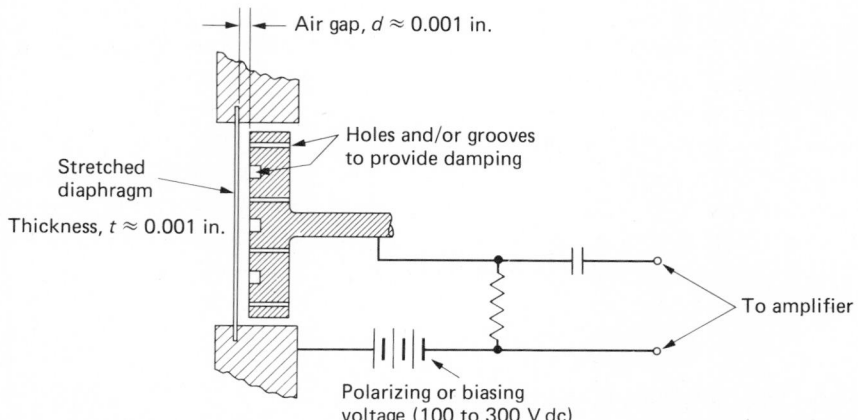

FIGURE 18.7   Schematic of the condenser-type microphone.

where

E = the voltage,

Q = the charge provided by the polarizing voltage (relatively constant), and

d = the separation of the plates.

The capacitive microphone is widely used as the primary transducer for sound measurement purposes.

The *electret microphone* is a special form of the condenser type. Whereas the common condenser type requires an external polarizing voltage, the electret type is self-polarizing. The diaphragm is constructed of a plastic sheet that has a conductive coating on one side. The coating serves as one side of the capacitor.

The Western Electric WE 640AA condenser-type microphone deserves special mention for it was long considered to be the unofficial standard of comparison for all microphones. [7]

The *crystal microphone* uses a piezoelectric-type element (Section 4.14), generally activated by bending. For greatest sensitivity, a cantilevered element is mechanically linked to the diaphragm. Other constructions use direct contact between diaphragm and element, either by cementing (element placed in bending) or by direct bearing (element in compression). Crystal microphones are extensively used for serious sound measurement.

The *electrodynamic microphone* uses the principle of the moving conductor in a magnetic field. The field is commonly provided by a permanent magnet, thereby placing the transducer in the variable-reluctance category (Section 4.12). As the diaphragm is moved, voltage is induced proportional to the *velocity* of the coil relative to the magnetic field, thereby providing an analogous electrical output. Two different constructions are used, the "moving coil" (Fig. 18.8) and the "ribbon" type. The inductive member of the latter type consists of a single element in the form of a ribbon that serves the dual purpose of "coil" and diaphragm.

The secondary transducer of the *carbon microphone* consists of a capsule of carbon granules, the resistance of which varies with change in sound pressure sensed by a diaphragm. Its limited high- and low-frequency response precludes its use for serious sound measurements and it is mentioned here merely to round out the list. The limited-frequency characteristics of the carbon microphone, coupled with its ruggedness, make it ideal for use as the transmitter in the ordinary telephone handset.

Microphone Selection Factors

An ideal microphone used for measurement would have the following characteristics:

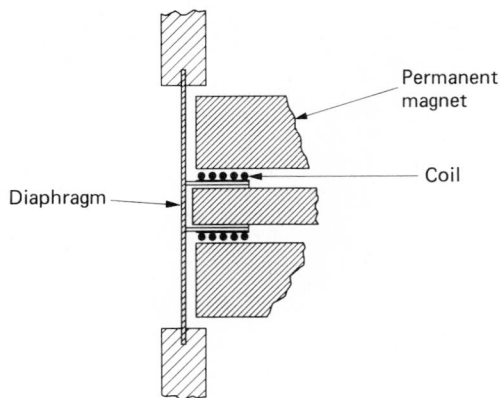

FIGURE 18.8   Schematic of the electrodynamic microphone.

1. Flat frequency response over the audible range;
2. Nondirectivity;
3. Predictable, repeatable sensitivity over the complete dynamic range;
4. At the lowest sound level to be measured, output signal that is several times the system's internal noise level;
5. Minimum dimensions and weight; and
6. Output that is unaffected by all environmental conditions except sound pressure.

The capacitor-type microphone undoubtedly enjoys the top position for sound measurement use, while the crystal type runs a close second. As with all measurement, the presence of the sensor (microphone) unavoidably alters (loads) the signal to be measured. In this application the microphone should be as physically small as possible. It is obvious, however, that size, particularly diaphragm diameter, must have an important influence on both sensitivity and response. Microphones are therefore available in a range of sizes, and final selection must be based on a balance of the requirements for the specific application. Table 18.1 summarizes microphone characteristics.

18.5.2 The Sound-Level Meter

The basic sound-level meter is a measuring system that senses the input sound pressure and provides a meter read-out yielding a measure of the sound magnitude. The sound may be wideband, it may have random frequency distribution, or it may contain discrete tones. Each of these factors will, of course, affect the read-out.

Generally the system includes weighting networks (filters) to roughly match the instrument's response to that of human hearing. The read-out,

TABLE 18.1 Summary of Microphone Characteristics

Type of Microphone	Principle of Operation	Relative Impedance	Linearity	Advantages	Disadvantages
Capacitor	Capacitive	Very high	Excellent	Stable: holds calibration. Low sensitivity to vibration. Wide range.	Sensitive to temperature and pressure variations. Relatively fragile. Requires high polarizing voltage. Requires impedance-coupling device near microphone.
Crystal	Piezoelectric	High	Good to excellent	Self-generating. May be hermetically sealed. Relatively rugged. Relatively inexpensive.	Requires impedance-matching device. Relatively sensitive to vibration.
Electrodynamic	Reluctive	Low	Good	Self-generating.	Physically large.
Carbon	Resistive	Moderate	Poor	Very rugged. Inexpensive.	Severely limited frequency range.

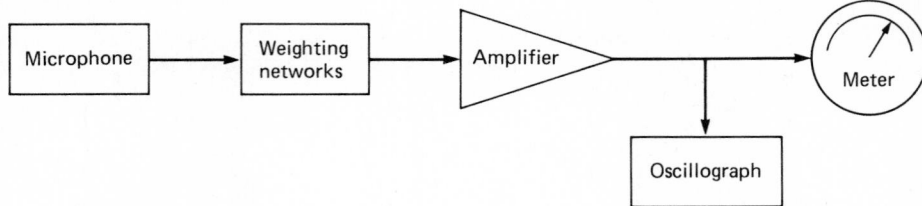

FIGURE 18.9   Block diagram of a typical sound-level meter, or sound-level recorder.

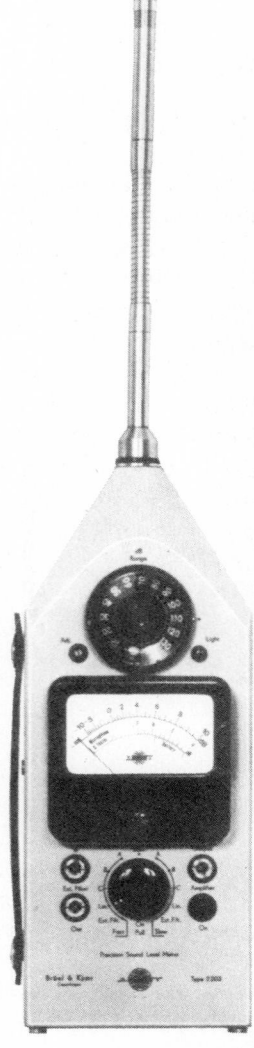

FIGURE 18.10   Sound level meter, Type 2203. Courtesy: Bruel & Kjaer Instruments, Inc., Marlborough, MA.

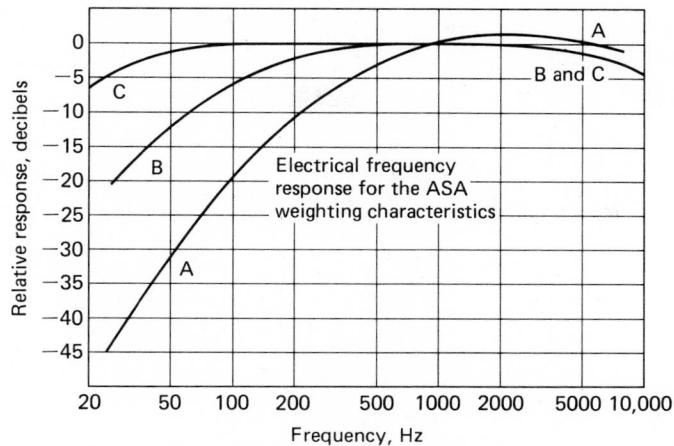

FIGURE 18.11   Standard weighting characteristics for sound-level meters.

therefore, includes a psychoacoustical factor and provides a number ranking the sound magnitude in terms of the ability of the human measuring system.

A block diagram of the basic sound-level meter is shown in Fig. 18.9, and Fig. 18.10 shows a commercially available system. When used in conjunction with an oscillograph, the system is commonly referred to as a *sound-level recorder*.

Figure 18.11 displays the internationally standardized weighting characteristics selectable by panel switch. We can see that the filter responses selectively discriminate against low and high frequencies, much as the human ear does. It is customary to use characteristics *A* for sound levels below 55 dB, *B* for sounds between 55 and 85 dB, and *C* for levels above 85 dB. Certain broad generalities as to the frequency makeup of a sound may be made by taking separate readings with each network.

18.5.3 Frequency Spectrum Analysis

Although determination of a value of sound pressure or sound level provides a measure of sound intensity, it yields no indication of frequency distribution. For noise abatement purposes, for example, it is very desirable to know the predominant frequencies involved. This can often point directly to the prominent noise sources.

Determination of intensities versus frequency is referred to as *spectrum analysis* and is accomplished through the use of pass-band filters (Section 5.21). Various combinations of filters may be used, determined by their relative band-pass widths. Probably the most commonly used are the "full-octave" filters having center frequencies as follows: 31.5, 63, 125, 250, 500, 1000, 2000, 4000, 8000, 16,000 and 31,500 Hz. Figure 18.12 shows such an instrument, and Fig. 18.13 depicts the frequency characteristics of the filters.

FIGURE 18.12   Octave-band sound analyzer. Courtesy: GenRad, Inc., Concord, MA.

In addition to full-octave spectrum division, $\frac{1}{2}$, $\frac{1}{3}$, $\frac{1}{10}$, and other fractional octave divisions are also used. Although the ear may be capable of distinguishing pure tones in the presence of other tones, it does tend to integrate complex sounds over roughly $\frac{1}{3}$-octave intervals [8], thus lending some additional importance to $\frac{1}{3}$-octave analyzers.

Simple analyzers are used by taking a separate reading for each passband. It is seen therefore that an appreciable period of time is required to scan the range. Not only does the bulk of data increase with reduced bandwidth, but the constancy of the sound source becomes of greater importance also as the necessary time for measurement increases. A partial solution to the latter problem is to use a tape recorder for sampling and then analyze the recorded sound at leisure. It is obvious that to be useful for faithfully recording a sound source, the tape recorder must be of highest quality. Commonly available recorders for speech and music are not usable; their frequency response requirements are purposely made nonlinear over the required range of frequencies.

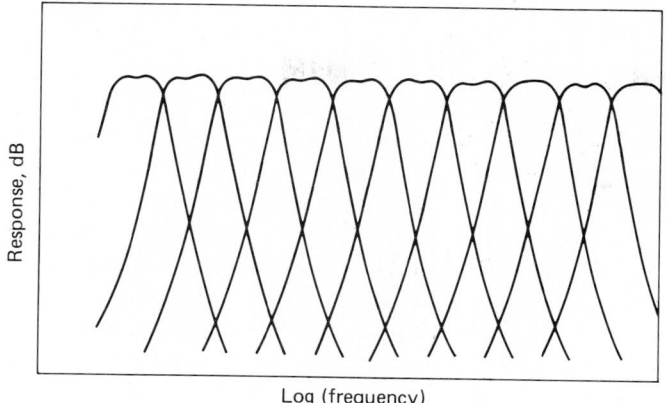

Response, dB

Log (frequency)

FIGURE 18.13   Typical overlapping filter characteristics of band-type sound analyzers.

The spectrum analyzer, along with the fast Fourier transform procedure, provides much greater resolution. These are discussed in the following paragraphs.

18.5.4   The Spectrum Analyzer

Application of the spectrum analyzer is of particular usefulness in acoustical work. It will be recalled (Sections 2.8 and 7.12) that this instrument system produces a CRO amplitude vs. frequency display. It provides a very convenient means for determining the contributions of the various harmonic components making up a complex input. In effect, the spectrum analyzer is a computerized harmonic analyzer. When used in conjunction with the fast Fourier transform technique (discussed in the following section), it is capable of providing ongoing, real-time read-outs.

18.6   APPLIED SPECTRUM ANALYSIS

Harmonic or Fourier analysis of complex waveforms was discussed in Sections 2.6–2.8 and is further mentioned in Appendix B. From the discussions it should be clear that even for relatively simple waveshapes, the number of required numerical manipulations may easily make the procedure prohibitive from a time-benefit standpoint. This limitation becomes especially important when the variety of nonrepetitive conditions needing analysis taxes the capacity of even the larger computers. This has led to a truncated procedure referred to as the *fast Fourier transform,* or *FFT*. If N represents the number of harmonic coefficients to be determined, ordinary harmonic analysis requires roughly N^2 separate computations, whereas FFT requires approximately (N) $\log_2 (N)$. This represents a marked reduction. It has been found that many waveforms encountered in acoustics, mechanical vibrations, and most electrical quantities permit practical application of FFT.

FFT procedures may be hand-calculated in a manner similar to the harmonic analysis problem discussed in Section 2.8. Or, data may be taken from a signal display—from a CRO screen, for instance—and computer-analyzed by using an appropriate program and hand-inputting the data. But, to obtain greatest usefulness from the method, an integrated instrumentation package, the FFT analyzing system, is used. This permits real-time processing with near immediate on-the-scene results.

Figure 18.14 is a schematic of a fast Fourier transform analyzing system. As shown, the signal is sensed by a microphone, vibration pickup, and so on, and is then conditioned by amplification, filtering, etc., as may be required.

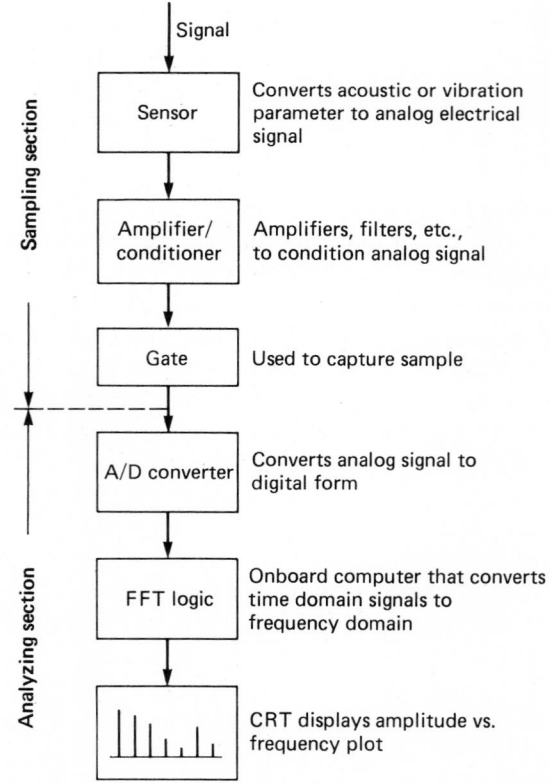

FIGURE 18.14   Block diagram of fast Fourier analyzing system.

A sample of the conditioned input is then taken over a short time interval, Δt. Following this, the time base is divided into an integral number of equal increments: The number is usually a power of 2.* For *each increment* the A/D converter then outputs an amplitude in digital form for analysis by the logic section. The function of the logic section is to transform (convert) the sample from the time domain to the frequency domain for final display or numerical listing.

The output from the FFT calculation usually consists of the amplitude of a sine and cosine pair for each integral multiple of the fundamental frequency.† The number of pairs obtained is just equal to the number of original data points. Each sine and cosine pair can be considered as a vector with real and imaginary parts, which can be combined into a vector with absolute magnitude and a phase angle (see Section 2.4). For many acoustical analyses the phase angle is ignored and the vector magnitude at each integral multiple of the fundamental frequency is used as the result of the analysis.

The squared value of each vector magnitude is sometimes called the *autospectral value* and the set of the squared values the *power spectrum,* even though these values may not represent power at all.

The sampling time interval, Δt, is often referred to as the *data window duration*. The experimenter sets this value by adjustment of the gating time, hence the sampling rate. When obviously repetitive waveforms are encountered, the logical value is clear: the period of the cycle. But when the input is complex and nonrepetitive, the selection of a proper sampling time interval is in doubt. In such a case many primary sources of signal plus secondary sources may be present. In mechanical applications these may consist of gear and bearing noises, elastic resonances, combustion sounds, hydraulic noises, and the like. In the case of acoustical measurements the environment contributes also. In many situations there are identifiable frequency sources such as RPMs, rate of gear tooth meshings, etc. Because of its analyzing speed, the FFT system becomes extremely useful in cases of this sort. A variety of sampling time intervals may be tried and, by comparison of read-outs, a "best" result selected. In certain instances, it may be decided that no significant, constant harmonic relationships are present. Of course, this is pertinent information also.

Some final considerations in the proper use of the FFT analysis include (a) the "shape" of the data window chosen in addition to its time duration and (b) the sampling frequency rate in relation to the highest frequency component desired from the analysis. With regard to (a), the shape of the data

---

* Note that $2^8 = 256_{10}$ is most commonly used. Counting zero as the initial value, this corresponds to 0 to 255_{10} or 0 to FF_{16}, or one byte of information.

† The fundamental frequency here is directly related to the time duration of the waveform being analyzed.

window indicates how the data points will be weighted. For example, a rectangular window indicates that all data points will be treated as equally important, whereas a "raised cosine" or "hanning" window gives greater emphasis to data points in the interior of the interval and lesser importance to those at the ends of the interval. (Reference [9] contains a more detailed discussion of data windows.) For consideration of (b), the simple rule of thumb is that the data sampling rate must be at least twice the highest frequency component desired from the analysis.

18.7 MEASUREMENT AND INTERPRETATION OF RANDOM NOISE MEASUREMENTS

Widely accepted relationships between sound pressure levels and loudness levels are based on the physiological–psychological makeup of the *average* human hearing system and are displayed by the contours shown in Fig. 18.5. It is especially important to realize that these curves are for *pure tones only*. Suppose, however, that we are interested in the loudness level of a random noise source that includes a wide range of frequencies, each of different amplitude. Such a source might be a window-type air conditioner, a regulator valve, any of a variety of production machines, an air compressor, or combinations of many such sources. To obtain a single number adequately expressing the magnitude of loudness, it becomes necessary to adapt the discrete frequency information of Fig. 18.5 to individual segments over the frequency range of the source. Basic data for this purpose are obtained by either full or suboctave band data, which are then modified in accordance with the equal-loudness contours and combined to produce an *effective* loudness number in sones. The procedure makes use of *band loudness indexes* tabulated in Table 18.2. Their use is demonstrated, without comment on theoretical basis, in the following example.

The data in columns 1 and 2 of Table 18.3 correspond to the noise produced by a small portable paint-spray air compressor, as measured at a given indoor location using an octave-band noise analyzer. The data have been corrected for ambient conditions, i.e., ambient noise readings for each pass-band have been subtracted by the methods discussed in Section 18.3.4. The third column lists the appropriate band loudness indexes as extracted from the body of Table 18.2.

The accepted procedure for determining the *computed loudness* in sones is to take 30% of the band loudness index *summation* plus 70% of the maximum band loudness for any one band. For our example, this becomes

Computed loudness = (0.3)(127.8) + (0.7)(30.5) = 59.7 ≈ 60 sones.

From the right-hand two columns in Table 18.2, we see that 60 sones corresponds to approximately 99 phons.

What are the significances of these two numbers? The value of 60 sones is simply another measure of the loudness sensation. It is based on the linear

TABLE 18.2 Band Level Conversion to Loudness Index

Band Level db	Band Loudness Index 31.5	63	125	250	500	1000	2000	4000	8000	Loudness Sones	Loudness Level Phons
20						.18	.30	.45	.61	.25	20
21						.22	.35	.50	.67	.27	21
22					.07	.26	.40	.55	.73	.29	22
23					.12	.30	.45	.61	.80	.31	23
24					.16	.35	.50	.67	.87	.33	24
25				.07	.21	.40	.55	.73	.94	.35	25
26				.12	.26	.45	.61	.80	1.02	.38	26
27					.31	.50	.67	.87	1.10	.41	27
28					.37	.55	.73	.94	1.18	.44	28
29					.43	.61	.80	1.02	1.27	.47	29
30			.07	.16	.49	.67	.87	1.10	1.35	.50	30
31				.21	.55	.73	.94	1.18	1.44	.54	31
32				.26	.61	.80	1.02	1.27	1.54	.57	32
33				.31	.67	.87	1.10	1.35	1.64	.62	33
34				.37	.73	.94	1.18	1.44	1.75	.66	34
35			.12	.43	.80	1.02	1.27	1.54	1.87	.71	35
36			.16	.49	.87	1.10	1.35	1.64	1.99	.76	36
37			.21	.55	.94	1.18	1.44	1.75	2.11	.81	37
38			.26	.62	1.02	1.27	1.54	1.87	2.24	.87	38
39			.31	.69	1.10	1.35	1.64	1.99	2.38	.93	39
40		.07	.37	.77	1.18	1.44	1.75	2.11	2.53	1.00	40
41		.12	.43	.85	1.27	1.54	1.87	2.24	2.68	1.07	41
42		.16	.49	.94	1.35	1.64	1.99	2.38	2.84	1.15	42
43		.21	.55	1.04	1.44	1.75	2.11	2.53	3.0	1.23	43
44		.26	.62	1.13	1.54	1.87	2.24	2.68	3.2	1.32	44

(Continued)

TABLE 18.2   (*continued*)

Band Level	Band Loudness Index									Loudness	Loudness Level
45		.31	.69	1.23	1.64	1.99	2.38	2.84	3.4	1.41	45
46	.07	.37	.77	1.33	1.75	2.11	2.53	3.0	3.6	1.52	46
47	.12	.43	.85	1.44	1.87	2.24	2.68	3.2	3.8	1.62	47
48	.16	.49	.94	1.56	1.99	2.38	2.84	3.4	4.1	1.74	48
49	.21	.55	1.04	1.69	2.11	2.53	3.0	3.6	4.3	1.87	49
50	.26	.62	1.13	1.82	2.24	2.68	3.2	3.8	4.6	2.00	50
51	.31	.69	1.23	1.96	2.38	2.84	3.4	4.1	4.9	2.14	51
52	.37	.77	1.33	2.11	2.53	3.0	3.6	4.3	5.2	2.30	52
53	.43	.85	1.44	2.24	2.68	3.2	3.8	4.6	5.5	2.46	53
54	.49	.94	1.56	2.38	2.84	3.4	4.1	4.9	5.8	2.64	54
55	.55	1.04	1.69	2.53	3.0	3.6	4.3	5.2	6.2	2.83	55
56	.62	1.13	1.82	2.68	3.2	3.8	4.6	5.5	6.6	3.03	56
57	.69	1.23	1.96	2.84	3.4	4.1	4.9	5.8	7.0	3.25	57
58	.77	1.33	2.11	3.0	3.6	4.3	5.2	6.2	7.4	3.48	58
59	.85	1.44	2.27	3.2	3.8	4.6	5.5	6.6	7.8	3.73	59
60	.94	1.56	2.44	3.4	4.1	4.9	5.8	7.0	8.3	4.00	60
61	1.04	1.69	2.62	3.6	4.3	5.2	6.2	7.4	8.8	4.29	61
62	1.13	1.82	2.81	3.8	4.6	5.5	6.6	7.8	9.3	4.59	62
63	1.23	1.96	3.0	4.1	4.9	5.8	7.0	8.3	9.9	4.92	63
64	1.33	2.11	3.2	4.3	5.2	6.2	7.4	8.8	10.5	5.28	64
65	1.44	2.27	3.5	4.6	5.5	6.6	7.8	9.3	11.1	5.66	65
66	1.56	2.44	3.7	4.9	5.8	7.0	8.3	9.9	11.8	6.06	66
67	1.69	2.62	4.0	5.2	6.2	7.4	8.8	10.5	12.6	6.50	67
68	1.82	2.81	4.3	5.5	6.6	7.8	9.3	11.1	13.5	6.96	68
69	1.96	3.0	4.7	5.8	7.0	8.3	9.9	11.8	14.4	7.46	69
70	2.11	3.2	5.0	6.2	7.4	8.8	10.5	12.6	15.3	8.00	70
71	2.27	3.5	5.4	6.6	7.8	9.3	11.1	13.5	16.4	8.6	71
72	2.44	3.7	5.8	7.0	8.3	9.9	11.8	14.4	17.5	9.2	72
73	2.62	4.0	6.2	7.4	8.8	10.5	12.6	15.3	18.7	9.8	73
74	2.81	4.3	6.6	7.8	9.3	11.1	13.5	16.4	20.0	10.6	74

75	11.3	21.4	17.5	14.4	11.8	9.9	8.3	7.0	4.7	3.0	75
76	12.1	23.0	18.7	15.3	12.6	10.5	8.8	7.4	5.0	3.2	76
77	13.0	24.7	20.0	16.4	13.5	11.1	9.3	7.8	5.4	3.5	77
78	13.9	26.5	21.4	17.5	14.4	11.8	9.9	8.3	5.8	3.7	78
79	14.9	28.5	23.0	18.7	15.3	12.6	10.5	8.8	6.2	4.0	79
80	16.0	30.5	24.7	20.0	16.4	13.5	11.1	9.3	6.7	4.3	80
81	17.1	32.9	26.5	21.4	17.5	14.4	11.8	9.9	7.2	4.7	81
82	18.4	35.3	28.5	23.0	18.7	15.3	12.6	10.5	7.7	5.0	82
83	19.7	38	30.5	24.7	20.0	16.4	13.5	11.1	8.2	5.4	83
84	21.1	41	32.9	26.5	21.4	17.5	14.4	11.8	8.8	5.8	84
85	22.6	44	35.3	28.5	23.0	18.7	15.3	12.6	9.4	6.2	85
86	24.3	48	38	30.5	24.7	20.0	16.4	13.5	10.1	6.7	86
87	26.0	52	41	32.9	26.5	21.4	17.5	14.4	10.9	7.2	87
88	27.9	56	44	35.3	28.5	23.0	18.7	15.3	11.7	7.7	88
89	29.9	61	48	38	30.5	24.7	20.0	16.4	12.6	8.2	89
90	32.0	66	52	41	32.9	26.5	21.4	17.5	13.6	8.8	90
91	34.3	71	56	44	35.3	28.5	23.0	18.7	14.8	9.4	91
92	36.8	77	61	48	38	30.5	24.7	20.0	16.0	10.1	92
93	39.4	83	66	52	41	32.9	26.5	21.4	17.3	10.9	93
94	42.2	90	71	56	44	3.53	28.5	23.0	18.7	11.7	94
95	45.3	97	77	61	48	38	30.5	24.7	20.0	12.6	95
96	48.5	105	83	66	52	41	32.9	26.5	21.4	13.6	96
97	52.0	113	90	71	56	44	35.3	28.5	23.0	14.8	97
98	55.7	121	97	77	61	48	38	30.5	24.7	16.0	98
99	59.7	130	105	83	66	52	41	32.9	26.5	17.3	99
100	64.0	139	113	90	71	56	44	35.3	28.5	18.7	100
101	68.6	149	121	97	77	61	48	38	30.5	20.3	101
102	73.5	160	130	105	83	66	52	41	32.9	22.1	102
103	78.8	171	139	113	90	71	56	44	35.3	24.0	103
104	84.4	184	149	121	97	77	61	48	38	26.1	104

(Continued)

TABLE 18.2 *(continued)*

Band Level	Band Loudness Index									Loudness	Loudness Level
105	28.5	41	52	66	83	105	130	160	197	90.5	105
106	31.0	44	56	71	90	113	139	171	211	97	106
107	33.9	48	61	77	97	121	149	184	226	104	107
108	36.9	52	66	83	105	130	160	197	242	111	108
109	40.3	56	71	90	113	139	171	211	260	119	109
110	44	61	77	97	121	149	184	226	278	128	110
111	49	66	83	105	130	160	197	242	298	137	111
112	54	71	90	113	139	171	211	260	320	147	112
113	59	77	97	121	149	184	226	278	343	158	113
114	65	83	105	130	160	197	242	298	367	169	114
115	71	90	113	139	171	211	260	320		181	115
116	77	97	121	149	184	226	278	343		194	116
117	83	105	130	160	197	242	298	367		208	117
118	90	113	139	171	211	260	320			223	118
119	97	121	149	184	226	278	343			239	119
120	105	130	160	197	242	298	367			256	120
121	113	139	171	211	260	320				274	121
122	121	149	184	226	278	343				294	122
123	130	160	197	242	298	367				315	123
124	139	171	211	260	320					338	124
125	149	184	226	278	343					362	125

Source: GenRad, Inc. Handbook of Noise Measurement, 1972.

TABLE 18.3   An Example of Loudness Determination

Octave Bandpass Center Frequency	SPL, in dB*	Band Loudness Index†
31.5	85	6.2
63	80	6.7
125	92	20
250	95	30.5
500	82	15.3
1000	70	8.8
2000	62	6.6
4000	55	5.2
8000	79	28.5
		Total = 127.8

*   Corrected for ambient conditions.

†   From Table 18.2.

scale referred to an SPL of 40 dB at 1000 Hz. Quite simply, the noise from the compressor is approximately 60 times as great as that of a 1000-Hz pure tone having an SPL of 40 dB. In addition to providing a single-number evaluation of loudness level, or simply noisiness, the procedure also provides a basis for making comparisons. In general, the higher the number, the greater the noise, hence annoyance.

The value of 99 phons represents the 1000-Hz equivalent SPL that supposedly produces the *same* sound intensity response (sensation) for the "average" human ear. That is, on average, a 1000-Hz *pure* tone at 99 dB would "seem" to have the same loudness level as the noise from our source, the air compressor, at the given location and in the same environment.

It is extremely important that the numbers be accepted in their proper context: in terms of the degree of preciseness of the entire determination. The values are dependent on the accuracy of the measurement techniques and instrumentation, the oversimplified correspondance to the human hearing system, the somewhat arbitrary equivalence between wideband noise and pure tones, etc.

18.8   NOTES ON SOME PRACTICAL ASPECTS OF SOUND MEASUREMENTS

With all measurements, the act of measuring disrupts the process being evaluated. The sound pressure existing at the microphone diaphragm is *not* the sound pressure that would exist at that location were the microphone not

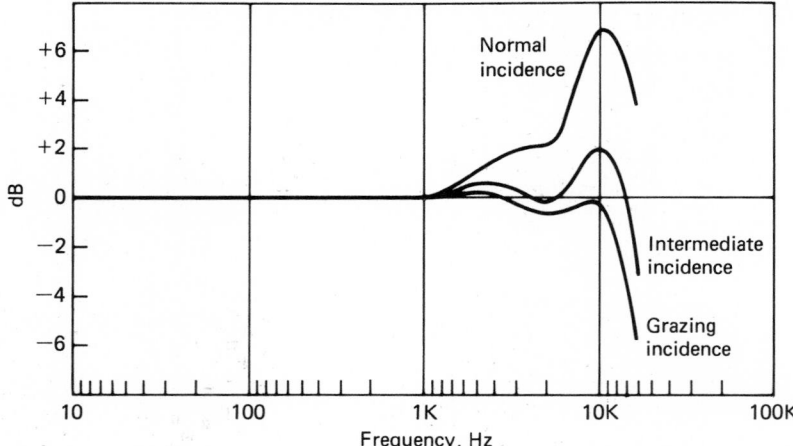

FIGURE 18.15   Variations in microphone response depending on angle of incidence of sound wave.

present. *True* free-field conditions cannot be measured. The diaphragm stiffness characteristics, the housing properties, and so on do not correspond to the properties of the air that they displace. For wavelengths smaller than the diaphragm dimensions (high frequencies), the diaphragm has the characteristics of an infinite wall and for sounds arriving perpendicular to the diaphragm face, the pressures approach twice the value were the diaphragm not present. For wavelengths several times the diaphragm diameter, this effect is negligible. In addition, for other angles on incidence* the effect is reduced. Figure 18.15 illustrates typical response curves for various angles of incidence.

We see therefore that as a general practice, it is advisable to avoid "pointing" the microphone at the sound source. One should use an angle approaching 90 degrees (grazing) incidence. One must remember, however, that in a reverberant field there are multiple sound sources from reflective walls, etc., so one must exercise judgment and carefully consider the individual situation. One reference suggests an angle of incidence of approximately 70 degrees.

An exception to the above occurs when one is attempting to isolate discrete sound inputs, perhaps in conjunction with a spectrum analyzer or band analyzer. In such a case it may be desirable to point the microphone to suspected areas and also to place the microphone much closer to the source than would otherwise be done.

At what distance from the source should the microphone be placed when a general measurement is being made? Figure 18.16 shows a condition typical of many sound fields, produced by such sources as machinery: sources made

---

*   Zero degrees incidence occurs when the microphone axis is parallel to the direction of sound propagation, i.e., the wavefront is parallel to the microphone diaphragm.

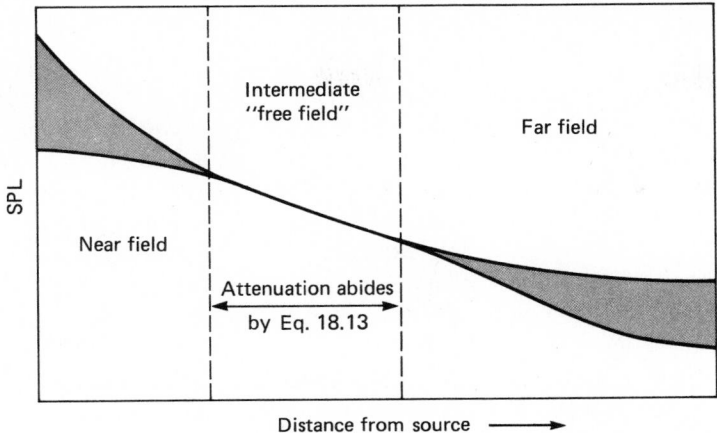

FIGURE 18.16   Typical SPL variations dependent upon microphone placement.

up of many individual noisemakers such as gears, bearings, housings, and so on. The cross-sectional areas in the figure depict distances over which *transverse* movement of the microphone produces variations in SPL readings for a presumably constant input. In the near-distance interval the discrete sources may be identifiable. In the far distances the field is reverberant and reflective sources cause SPL variations.

In the free-field interval, transverse movement of the microphone should make little or no difference in readings. In addition, movement toward or away from the source should provide readings approximating those predicted by Eq. (18.13). This latter fact may be helpful in establishing that free-field conditions do or do not prevail. It is important to note that in many cases the free-field interval is not present: Near- and far-field conditions overlap.

To this point the discussion has assumed sound sources that are of constant or relatively constant amplitude and character. Examples are sound from a blower, an electric motor, or an internal combustion engine running at constant speed and load. Noise from open factory spaces, offices with business machines, or street traffic may also be relatively constant. On the other hand, there may be noise sources of discrete time-wise characteristics. Sources of this type include the impulse of a forging hammer, almost any form of explosion, or the single stroke of a typewriter key.

One form of impact-sound measuring system uses a temporary storage of certain sound parameters for later read-out. Three different sound characteristics may be simultaneously sampled: maximum instantaneous sound level, average sound level, and a continuous indication of sound level. The electrical analogs of the first two quantities are stored in memory for later read-out. The duration of the impact may be estimated through comparison of the average and the instantaneous maximum levels.

18.9 CALIBRATION METHODS

As with most electromechanical measuring systems, sound measurement involves a detector-transducer (the microphone) followed by intermediate electrical/electronic signal conditioning and some sort of read-out stage. Calibration of the complete system involves introducing a known sound-pressure variation and comparing the known with the read-out. In practice such a calibration may be made or, more commonly, the various component stages may be calibrated separately. For example, sound-level meters often provide a simple check of the electrical and read-out stages by substituting a carefully controlled and known voltage for the microphone output and adjusting the read-out to a predetermined value for the particular instrument. This procedure ignores the microphone altogether; however, it does provide a convenient method for checking the remainder of the system.

Comparative methods may also be used whereby a microphone or a complete system is directly compared with a "standard." Of course, as with all comparative methods, it is imperative that great care be exercised to ensure that a true comparison is made. It is necessary that both the standard and the test microphones "hear" the identical sound. Our introductory discussion at the beginning of this chapter should indicate the difficulties in achieving this.

Standard sound sources involve mechanical loudspeaker-type drivers for producing the necessary pressure fluctuations. One system* uses two battery-driven pistons moving in opposition in a cylinder at 250 Hz. A precalibrated pressure level of 124 ± 0.2 dB is produced. A somewhat similar system† uses a small, rugged loudspeaker as the driver. In both cases proper calibration is maintained only if the design coupling cavity is employed between driver and microphone. This restricts this type of calibrator to compatible microphones: those from the same company.

A more basic calibration method is known as *reciprocity* calibration. In addition to the microphone under test, a *reversible,* linear transducer and a sound source with a proper coupling cavity are required. Calibration procedure is divided into two steps. First, both the test microphone and the reversible transducer are subjected to a common sound source and the two outputs; hence their ratio is determined. Second, the reversible transducer is used as a sound source with known input (current), and the output (voltage) of the test microphone is measured. It can be shown [10, 11] that this step provides a relationship that is a function of the product of the two sensitivities: that of the test microphone and that of the reversible transducer. Results of the two steps yield sufficient information to determine the absolute sensitivity of the tested microphone.

---

*   Pistonphone Type 4220, Bruel & Kjaer, Inc., Marlborough, Massachusetts.

†   Type 1562-B Sound-Level Calibrator, GenRad, Inc., Concord, Massachusetts.

18.10 FINAL REMARKS

Sound is a complex physical quantity. Its evaluation through measurement becomes doubly difficult in comparison with evaluation of other engineering quantities because of the necessary involvement of human hearing. It must, therefore, be recognized that the foregoing sections serve merely as an introduction to the subject. The student is directed to the appended list of Suggested Readings for further study.

Little distinction has been made throughout this chapter between sound and noise. The latter has been considered merely as "undesirable" sound. Noise, however, is becoming an increasingly important problem to the engineer due to the controls that are set up by ordinance and statute as well as company–union agreements and court decisions intended to protect the employee. As a result engineers are called on to design "quiet" machinery and processes. They will be increasingly criticized for their part in "silence pollution." It is quite necessary, therefore, that they be knowledgeable not only in the field of noise measurement, but also in the theory and art of noise abatement.

SUGGESTED READINGS

Beranek, L. L. (ed.), *Noise Reduction.* New York: McGraw-Hill, 1960.

Beranek, L. L., *Acoustics.* New York: McGraw-Hill, 1954.

Bloss, R. L., and M. J. Orloski (eds.), *Precision Measurement and Calibration* (selected NBS papers on mechanics), NBS Spcl. Publ. 300, vol. 8. Washington, D.C.: U.S. Government Printing Office, 1972.

Booth, S. F. (ed.), *Precision Measurement and Calibration,* vol. 2 (selected NBS technical papers on heat and mechanics), NBS Handbook 77. Washington, D.C.: U.S. Government Printing Office, 1961.

Fath, J. M., *Standards of Noise, Rating Schemes and Definitions: A Compilation.* NBS Spcl. Publ. 386. Washington, D.C.: U.S. Government Printing Office, 1973.

Hassall, J. R., and K. Zaveri, *Acoustic Noise Measurements,* 4th ed. Marlborough, Mass.: Bruel & Kjaer, 1979.

Lord, H. W., W. S. Gatley, and H. A. Evensen, *Noise Control for Engineers.* New York: McGraw-Hill, 1980.

Peterson, A. P. G., and E. E. Gross, Jr., *Handbook of Noise Measurement,* 8th ed. Concord, Mass.: GenRad, 1980.

Pierce, A. D. *Acoustics: An Introduction to Its Physical Principals and Applications.* New York: McGraw-Hill, 1981.

Rayleigh, J. W. S., *The Theory of Sound,* vols. 1 & 2. New York: Dover, 1945.

PROBLEMS

18.1 It is desired to construct a flow system capable of delivering 1000 gal/min. The available pump styles include a 500 gal/min pump that produces an SPL of 95 dBA or a 250 gal/min pump that produces an SPL of 90 dBA. From a noise-control standpoint, which system is to be preferred? Why?

18.2 The noise level from a factory with 10 identical air compressors running simultaneously is 60 dB, measured at the factory property line. If the maximum SPL permitted at this location is 57 dBA, determine how many compressors may be run simultaneously.

18.3 A sound-pressure level meter used to measure the SPL of an engine without a muffler gave a reading of 120 dBA. After attaching the muffler, the same meter gave a reading of 90 dB. Determine (a) the rms sound pressure before the muffler was attached, and (b) the percentage reduction in rms sound pressure amplitude when the muffler was used.

18.4 The SPL of a single rocket engine on its test stand and at a distance of one-half mile is 108 dBA. What SPL, at the same distance, would result if a cluster of five such engines were tested together? If two of the five were shut down, what drop in SPL would be expected?

18.5 Determine the loudness in sones for the following data as measured by an octave band analyzer. What is the loudness level in phons?

Octave Band Center, Hz	SPL, dB
31.5	79
63	77
125	76
250	81
500	80
1000	82
2000	82
4000	72
8000	67

18.6 If a sawtooth wave having a peak amplitude of 1 unit and a period of 0.0075 s (as shown in Fig. 2.8d) is fed into a spectrum analyzer, determine the frequency spectrum for the first five frequency components, including their relative magnitudes.

18.7 Calculate the SPL and intensity at a distance of 10 m from a uniformly radiating source of 2.0 W.

18.8 In order to determine if free-field conditions are approximated, an engineer finds the SPL at 10 meters from the source to be 89 dBA. What must be the SPL at 7.5 meters in order for free-field conditions to exist?

18.9 Figure 18.17 illustrates a simple experimental setup that may be used to demonstrate a variety of basic principles discussed throughout this book. A small transistor-type loudspeaker (available from most electronic parts dealers) is cemented to a length of plastic pipe (Fig. 18.17a). A signal generator is used to

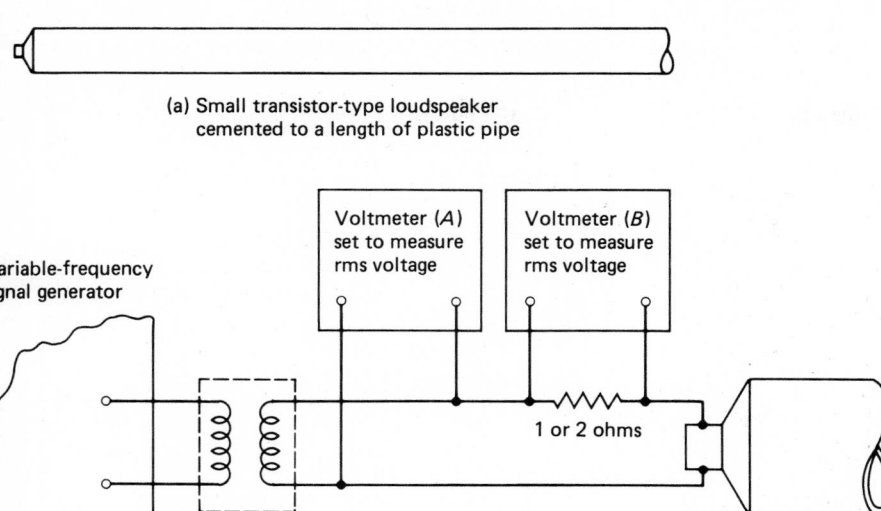

(a) Small transistor-type loudspeaker
cemented to a length of plastic pipe

(b) Electrical circuitry

FIGURE 18.17   See Problem 18.9.

drive the speaker with a sinusoidal waveform (Fig. 18.17b). The tube-speaker
combination possesses two fundamental resonant frequencies, that of the "organ
pipe" (Section 14.12.1) and the acoustical/electrical resonance of the speaker
element. Voltmeter B, along with the 1- or 2-ohm resistor, is used to monitor the
current to the speaker, and voltmeter A monitors the voltage. If voltage measured
by A is held constant as a range of frequencies is swept by the signal generator,
a sharp drop in current will be found at the frequency corresponding to resonance
of the "organ pipe." This is the frequency at which oscillation may be maintained
with minimum *power* expenditure. If the measuring system is sensitive enough,
other resonances may also be determined, that of the speaker itself and the higher
mode frequencies of the pipe. The minimum-power principle is often quite useful
in vibration testing employing shaker-driven systems (Chapter 17). Increased
power transfer may be had by insertion of a matching transformer (Section 5.24).
The turns ratio is not too critical; however, many signal generators have a 600-
ohm output impedance and the input impedance of the speaker may be about 16
ohms. Care must be exercised to prevent overdriving the speaker and destroying
its voice-coil.

standards and A
conversion equations

Standards

Gravity acceleration	9.80665 m/s² (round to 9.81)
	32.174 ft/s² (round to 32.17)
Standard atmospheric pressure	1.01325 E+05 Pa (round to 1.013 E+05)
	14.696 psia (round to 14.7)
Dimensional constants	g_c = 1 kg-m/N-s²
	g_c = 32.174 lbm-ft/lbf-s²

* * *

Conversion Equations

Note: The relationships that follow are in the form of equations, solved for the pertinent SI unit. Consider, for example, the equation for length written in terms of meters and inches:

$$m = 2.540 \text{ E}-02 \times \text{in.}$$

If we wish to find the number of meters corresponding to 36 inches (one English yard), we would make the following substitutions,

$$m = 2.540 \times \frac{36}{100} = 0.9144;$$

that is, 36 inches or one English yard is equal to 0.9144 meters.

On the other hand, if we wish to find the number of inches that are the equivalent of 5 meters, we would solve the equation for inches, thusly,

$$\text{in.} = m \times \frac{100}{2.54} = 5 \times \frac{100}{2.54} = \text{approx. } 196.85.$$

That is, 5 meters and approximately 196.85 inches represent the identical length.

Note also that throughout the listing the computer printout convention for decimal place is used. For example, E+03 = 10^3 = 1000. Also, E−02 = 10^{-2} = 0.01.

Acceleration	$m/s^2 = 3.048 \ E-01 \times ft/s^2$
	$m/s^2 = 2.54 \ E-02 \times in./s^2$
Area	$m^2 = 6.451 \ 6 \ E-04 \times in^2$
	$m^2 = 9.290 \ 304 \ E-02 \times ft^2$
Moment (torque)	$N \times m = 1.129 \ 848 \ E-01 \times lbf \cdot in.$
	$N \times m = 1.355 \ 818 \ E+00 \times lbf \cdot ft$
Energy (work)	$J = 1.055 \ 87 \ E+03 \times BTU(mean)$
	$J = 1.355 \ 818 \ E+00 \times ft \cdot lbf$
	$J = 3.6 \ E+03 \times W \cdot hr$
Force	$N = 2.0 \ E-05 \times dyne$
	$N = 4.448 \ 222 \ E+00 \times lbf$
Length	$m = 1.0 \ E-10 \times angstrom$
	$m = 1.0 \ E-06 \times micron$
	$m = 2.540 \ E-08 \times \mu in.$
	$m = 2.540 \ E-02 \times in.$
	$m = 3.048 \ E-01 \times ft$
	$km = 1.609 \ 344 \times statute \ mile$
Mass	$kg = 4.535 \ 924 \ E-01 \times lbm$
Mass/vol (density)	$kg/m^3 = 1.601 \ 846 \ E+01 \times lbm/ft^3$
	$kg/m^3 = 2.767 \ 990 \ E+04 \times lbm/in^3$
Power	$W = 2.930 \ 711 \ E-01 \times BTU/hr$
	$W = 2.259 \ 697 \ E-02 \times ft \ lbf/min$
	$W = 7.456 \ 999 \ E+02 \times HP(550 \ ft \ lbf/s)$
Pressure (stress)	$Pa = 3.376 \ 850 \ E+03 \times in. \ Hg \ (60°F)$
	$Pa = 2.488 \ 40 \ E+02 \times in. \ H_2O \ (60°F)$
	$Pa = 9.806 \ 38 \ E+01 \times cm \ H_2O \ (4°C)$
	$Pa = 1.333 \ 22 \ E+03 \times cm \ Hg \ (0°C)$
	$Pa = 6.894 \ 757 \ E+03 \times lbf/in^2$
	$Pa = 1.000 \ E+05 \times bar$
Temperature	$K = C + 273.15$
	$K = (F + 459.67)/1.8$
	$C = (F - 32)/1.8$
Velocity	$m/s = 3.048 \ E-01 \times ft/s$
	$m/s = 4.470 \ 4 \ E-01 \times mph$
Viscosity	$Pa \times s = 4.788 \ 026 \ E+01 \times lbf \times s/ft^2$
Volume	$m^3 = 3.785 \ 412 \ E-03 \times U.S. \ liq \ gal$
	$m^3 = 1.638 \ 706 \ E-05 \times in^3$
	$m^3 = 2.831 \ 685 \ E-02 \times ft^3$
Vol/time (flow)	$m^3/s = 2.831 \ 685 \ E-02 \times ft^3/s$
	$m^3/s = 6.309 \ 020 \ E-05 \times U.S. \ liq \ gal/m$

theoretical basis B for Fourier analysis

The theoretical basis for the harmonic-analysis procedure may be described as follows: Any single valued function $f(x)$ that is continuous (except for a finite number of finite discontinuities) in the interval $-\pi$ to π, and which has only a finite number of maxima and minima in that interval, can be represented by a series in the form:

$$f(x) = \frac{A}{2} + A_1 \cos x + A_2 \cos 2x + \cdots + A_n \cos nx$$

$$+ B_1 \sin x + B_2 \sin 2x + \cdots + B_n \sin nx. \quad (B.1)$$

If each term in Eq. (B.1) is multiplied by dx and integrated over any interval of 2π length, all sine and cosine terms will drop out, leaving

$$\int_a^{2\pi+a} f(x)\, dx = \int_a^{2\pi+a} \frac{A}{2} = A\pi$$

or

$$A = \frac{1}{\pi} \int_a^{2\pi+a} f(x)\, dx. \quad (B.2)$$

The factor A_n may be determined if we multiply both sides of Eq. (B.1) by $\cos mx\, dx$ and integrate each term over the interval of 2π.

In general there are the following terms:

$$\int_a^{2\pi+a} \sin nx \cos mx\, dx = 0$$

and

$$\int_a^{2\pi+a} \cos nx \cos mx\, dx = 0, \qquad \text{except for } m = n.$$

667

For the special case $m = n$,

$$\int_a^{2\pi+a} \cos^2 nx \, dx = \frac{1}{2n} [nx + \sin nx \cos nx]_{-\pi}^{\pi}$$

$$= \pi;$$

hence

$$\int_a^{2\pi+a} f(x) \cos nx \, dx = A_n \pi$$

or

$$A_n = \frac{1}{\pi} \int_a^{2\pi+a} f(x) \cos nx \, dx. \tag{B.3}$$

[*Note:* for $n = 0$, Eq. (B.3) reduces to Eq. (B.2).]

In like manner, if we multiply both sides of Eq. (B.1) by $\sin mx \, dx$ and integrate term by term over the interval 2π, we may obtain

$$B_n = \frac{1}{\pi} \int_a^{2\pi+a} f(x) \sin nx \, dx. \tag{B.4}$$

CALCULATION OF FOURIER COEFFICIENTS FOR SPECIAL PERIODIC WAVEFORMS

Square Wave

Considering the square wave shown in Fig. 2.8(a) we have for one full period

$$f(x) = A_o \qquad (0 \leq x \leq \pi)$$
$$f(x) = -A_o \qquad (\pi \leq x \leq 2\pi), \tag{B.5}$$

where $x = \omega t$. Applying Eq. (B.2) to Eq. (B.5) where we choose $a = 0$ for convenience we have

$$A = \frac{1}{\pi} \int_0^{\pi} A_0 \, dx - \frac{1}{\pi} \int_{\pi}^{2\pi} A_0 \, dx,$$

$$A = 0. \tag{B.6}$$

From Eq. (B.3) we have

$$A_n = \frac{1}{\pi} \int_0^{\pi} A_0 \cos nx \, dx - \frac{1}{\pi} \int_{\pi}^{2\pi} A_0 \cos nx \, dx,$$

or

$$A_n = 0. \tag{B.7}$$

Similarly from Eq. (B.4)

$$B_n = \frac{1}{\pi} \int_0^\pi A_0 \sin nx \, dx - \frac{1}{\pi} \int_\pi^{2\pi} A_0 \sin nx \, dx$$

or

$$B_n = \frac{2A_0}{n\pi} [1 - \cos n\pi]$$

and finally

$$B_n = \frac{4A_0}{n\pi} \quad \text{for } n \text{ odd,}$$

$$B_n = 0 \quad \text{for } n \text{ even.}$$

(B.8)

Substituting the results from Eq. (B.6), (B.7), and (B.8) into Eq. (B.1) we obtain

$$f(x) = f(\omega t) = \frac{4A_0}{\pi} \sum_{n=1,2,3}^{\alpha} \frac{\sin(2n-1)\omega t}{(2n-1)}$$

(B.9)

Sawtooth Wave

For the sawtooth wave shown in Fig. 2.8(d) we have

$$f(x) = \frac{A_0}{\pi} x \qquad (0 \le x \le \pi)$$

$$f(x) = 2A_0 - \frac{A_0}{\pi} x \qquad (\pi \le x \le 2\pi).$$

(B.10)

Applying Eqs. (B.2) and (B.3)

$$A = \frac{1}{\pi} \int_0^\pi \frac{A_0 x}{\pi} \, dx + \frac{1}{\pi} \int_\pi^{2\pi} (2A_0 - \frac{A_0}{\pi} x) \, dx = A_0$$

(B.11)

and

$$A_n = \frac{1}{\pi} \int_0^\pi \frac{A_0 x}{\pi} \cos x \, dx + \frac{1}{\pi} \int_\pi^{2\pi} (2A - \frac{A_0}{\pi} x) \cos nx \, dx$$

or

$$A_n = \frac{2A_0}{n^2\pi^2} [\cos n\pi - 1].$$

Considering various integer values for n we obtain

$$A_n = 0 \quad \text{for } n \text{ even, and}$$

$$A_n = \frac{-4A_0}{n^2\pi^2} \quad \text{for } n \text{ odd.}$$

(B.12)

Finally from Eq. (B.4)

$$B_n = \frac{1}{\pi} \int_0^{\pi} \frac{A_0 x}{\pi} \sin nx\, dx + \frac{1}{\pi} \int_{\pi}^{2\pi} \left(2A_0 - \frac{A_0 x}{\pi}\right) \sin nx\, dx,$$

and therefore

$$B_n = 0. \tag{B.13}$$

Using the results of (B.11), (B.12), and (B.13) in Eq. (B.1) the Fourier series for the sawtooth wave becomes

$$f(x) = f(\omega t) = \frac{A_0}{2} - \frac{4A_0}{\pi^2} \sum_{n=1,2,3}^{\alpha} \frac{\cos 1\, (2n - 1)\omega t}{(2n - 1)^2}. \tag{B.14}$$

NUMERICAL INTEGRATION FOR DETERMINATION OF FOURIER COEFFICIENTS

If Eqs. (B.2), (B.3), or (B.4) are plotted separately, but in general as

$$y = \frac{1}{\pi} \int_a^{2\pi + a} \phi(x)\, dx,$$

and the area under the resulting curve is divided into p equal intervals along the x-axis, as shown in Fig. B.1, then

$$A_n (\text{or } B_n) = \frac{1}{\pi}\left(\frac{2\pi}{p}\right)\left[\left(\frac{y_0 + y_1}{2}\right) + \left(\frac{y_1 + y_2}{2}\right) + \cdots + \left(\frac{y_{p-1} + y_p}{2}\right)\right]$$

$$= \frac{1}{(p/2)}\sum_0^p y_n. \tag{B.15}$$

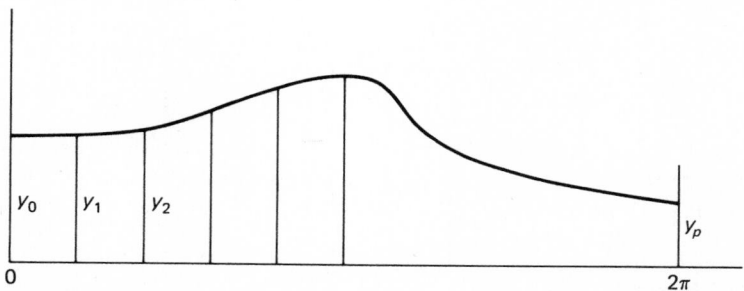

FIGURE B.1   Graphical representation of Eq. (B.15) with ordinates taken at equal intervals.

number C systems

In general:

$$N_b = \sum a_m b^n = \cdots + a_n b^n + a_{(n-1)}b^{(n-1)} + a_{(n-2)}b^{(n-2)} + \cdots$$

where

b = base or radix of the particular system

= the number of distinct character types required to express a quantity or magnitude

N_b = a number in the system

a = coefficient

n = positional value or power.

The Decimal System

The decimal system is based on ten digits, 0 through 9; the base or radix is 10, hence,

$$N_{10} = \sum a_m 10^n$$

For example:

$$524.3_{10} = (5)(10)^2 + (2)(10)^1 + (4)(10)^0 + (3)(10)^{-1}.$$

The digits 5, 2, 4, and 3 are the coefficients corresponding to the respective *positions* or powers 2, 1, 0, and −1. In the decimal system the coefficients may have integral values ranging from 0 through 9, inclusive.

The Binary System

The binary system employs two digits only, namely 1 and 0, and

$$N_2 = \sum a_m 2^n.$$

For example, the representation 1101.1_2 is interpreted as,

$$(1)(2)^3 + (1)(2)^2 + (0)(2)^1 + (1)(2)^0 + (1)(2)^{-1}$$
$$= 8 + 4 + 0 + 1 + \tfrac{1}{2} = 13.5_{10}$$

This example demonstrates the procedure for *converting* a binary number to the equivalent decimal number. The two numbers 1101.1_2 and 13.5_{10} each represent an identical quantity.

The Octal System

This system is based on eight digits, 0 through 7, and,

$$N_8 = \sum a_m 8^n.$$

The coefficients a_m do not include the decimal digits 8 and 9.

EXAMPLE

$$375.3_8 = (3)(8)^2 + (7)(8)^1 + (5)(8)^0 + (3)(8)^{-1}$$
$$= 192_{10} + 56_{10} + 5_{10} + 0.375_{10} = 253.375_{10}$$

The Hexadecimal System

This system employs 16 as the base or radix. Additional digital symbols are required. Those used are $0,1,2,3,4,5,6,7,8,9,A,B,C,D,E,$ and F. These sixteen characters correspond to the base-10 numbers 0 through 15, respectively.

$$N_{16} = \sum a_m (16)^n$$

For example $D8B.2_{16} = (D)(16)^2 + (8)(16)^1 + (B)(16)^0 + (2)(16)^{-1}$

$$= (13)(16)^2{}_{10} + (8)(16)^1{}_{10} + (11)(16)^0{}_{10} + (2)(16)^{-1}{}_{10}$$
$$= 3467.125_{10}$$

Octal and Hexadecimal Formatted Binary

A binary number may be arranged (grouped) in ways that make it easy to convert it to either octal or hexadecimal equivalents.

Consider: 110111001100_2, which we will rewrite as

$$110\ 111\ 001\ 100_2$$

If we consider each subgroup as a single octal digit, we obtain

$$6\ 7\ 1\ 4 \text{ or } 6714_8$$

In like manner we can rearrange the same binary number into subgroups of four, as follows

$$1101\ 1100\ 1100_2$$

This, we see is equal to DCC_{16}.

We can confirm the legitimacy of all of this by converting each number, the binary, the octal, and the hexadecimal to the equivalent decimal number, which we find is equal to 3532_{10}.

Why Need We be Concerned with the Various Number Systems?

1. The decimal system is common in everyday usage but it is not a convenient system around which to build or use a computer. A computer would have to distinguish between ten different states, as opposed to only two when binary is used.

2. Although binary requires a much longer string of symbols to define a given magnitude, the advantage of the simple Yes/No operation more than offsets the use of longer numbers. Machine language employs binary arithmetic.

3. *Why octal or hexadecimal?* The fundamental computer language is binary, but for the human that system would be extremely awkward and error prone. Hexadecimal and/or octal is simply the crutch used by the human to communicate with the computer in the computer's own tongue—machine or assembly language.

CONVERTING A BASE-10 NUMBER TO ONE OF A DIFFERENT RADIX

In the preceding paragraphs we have established procedures for converting numbers of various bases to equivalent magnitudes of base-10. We shall now demonstrate a method* for performing the reverse: converting a base-10 number to equivalent binary, octal, and hexadecimal numbers. We will use Tables C1, C2, and C3.

Decimal to Binary

Let's convert the number 713_{10} to the equivalent binary number. We will do this by successively subtracting the largest values of 2^n that each remainder

---

* There are other methods than the one demonstrated.

will permit. The procedure is demonstrated as follows (refer to Table C.1):

$$
\begin{aligned}
713_{10} & \\
-\underline{512} &= 2^9 \\
201_{10} & \\
-\underline{128} &= 2^7 \\
73_{10} & \\
-\underline{64} &= 2^6 \\
9_{10} & \\
-\underline{8} &= 2^3 \\
1_{10} & \\
-\underline{1} &= 2^0 \\
0 &
\end{aligned}
$$

TABLE C.1   Values of 2^n

n	2^n
Etc. ↑	
-1	0.5
0	1
1	2
2	4
3	8
4	16
5	32
6	64
7	128
8	256
9	512
10	1024
11	2048
12	4096
↓ Etc.	

Recalling that the powers of the radix correspond to the positional orders, we may write:

$$1011001001_2 = 713_{10}.$$

Decimal to Octal

Employ Table C.2 to convert the number 713_{10} to the equivalent octal number. A procedure similar to the one used for the previous example may be used. In this case, however we select the "largest" components in terms of both powers of the radix, 8, and also the required coefficients.

$$
\begin{array}{rl}
713_{10} & \\
-\underline{512} & = 1 \times 8^3 \\
201_{10} & \\
-\underline{192} & = 3 \times 8^2 \\
9_{10} & \\
-\underline{8} & = 1 \times 8^1 \\
1_{10} & \\
-\underline{1} & = 1 \times 8^0 \\
0 &
\end{array}
$$

From this we determine, $713_{10} = 1311_8$.

TABLE C.2   Values of $(a)(8)^n$

Coefficients "a"	Powers "n"						
	6	5	4	3	2	1	0
1	262 144	32 768	4 096	512	64	8	1
2	524 288	65 536	8 192	1 024	128	16	2
3	786 432	98 304	12 288	1 536	192	24	3
4	1 048 576	131 072	16 384	2 048	256	32	4
5	1 310 720	163 840	20 480	2 560	320	40	5
6	1 572 864	196 608	24 576	3 072	384	48	6
7	1 835 008	229 376	28 672	3 584	448	56	7

Decimal to Hexadecimal

In a similar manner convert 713_{10} to the equivalent hexadecimal number using Table C.3.

$$
\begin{array}{rl}
713_{10} & \\
-\,512 & = 2 \times 16^2 \\
\hline
201_{10} & \\
-\,192 & = C \times 16^1 \\
\hline
9_{10} & \\
-\,9 & = 9 \times 16^0 \\
\hline
0 &
\end{array}
$$

From this calculation we may write $713_{10} = 2C9_{16}$.

TABLE C.3   Values of $(a)(16)^n$

Coeffi- cients "a"	Powers, "n"						
	6	5	4	3	2	1	0
1	16 777 216	1 048 576	65 536	4 096	256	16	1
2	33 554 432	2 097 152	131 072	8 192	512	32	2
3	50 331 648	3 145 728	196 608	12 288	768	48	3
4	67 108 864	4 194 304	262 144	16 384	1 024	64	4
5	83 886 080	5 242 880	327 680	20 480	1 280	80	5
6	100 663 296	6 291 456	393 216	24 576	1 536	96	6
7	117 440 512	7 340 032	458 752	28 672	1 792	112	7
8	134 217 728	8 388 608	524 288	32 768	2 048	128	8
9	150 994 944	9 437 184	589 824	36 864	2 304	144	9
A	167 772 160	10 485 760	655 360	40 960	2 560	160	10
B	184 549 376	11 534 336	720 896	45 056	2 816	176	11
C	201 326 592	12 582 912	786 432	49 152	3 072	192	12
D	218 103 808	13 631 488	851 968	53 248	3 328	208	13
E	234 881 024	14 680 064	917 504	57 344	3 584	224	14
F	251 658 240	15 728 640	983 040	61 440	3 840	240	15

some D
useful data

TABLE D.1   Properties of Water: SI System

Temperature	Absolute Viscosity	Density
Degrees C(F)	*Pa-s*	*kg/m³*
5(41)	15.188	1000
10(50)	13.077	999.7
15(59)	11.404	999.1
20(68)	10.050	998.2
25(77)	8.937	997.0
30(86)	8.007	995.7
35(95)	7.225	994.1
40(104)	6.560	992.2
45(113)	5.988	990.3
50(122)	5.494	988.1

TABLE D.2   Properties of Water: English System

Temperature	Absolute Viscosity	Density
Degrees F(C)	(lbf-s/ft² × 10⁵)	(lbm/ft³)
40(4.44)	3.23	62.42
50(10.0)	2.72	62.41
60(15.56)	2.33	62.37
70(21.11)	2.02	62.30
80(26.67)	1.77	62.22
90(32.22)	1.58	62.11
100(37.78)	1.43	61.99
110(43.33)	1.30	61.86
120(48.89)	1.15	61.71

TABLE D.3   Properties of Dry Air at Atmospheric Pressure: SI System

Temperature	Absolute Viscosity*	Density†
Degrees C(F)	(N-sec/m²) × 10⁵	kg/m³
0(32)	1.68	1.26
10(50)	1.73	1.22
20(68)	1.80	1.18
30(86)	1.85	1.14
40(104)	1.91	1.10
50(122)	1.97	1.07
60(140)	2.03	1.04
70(158)	2.09	1.00
80(176)	2.15	0.97
90(194)	2.22	0.94
100(212)	2.28	0.924

*   Over the range from atmospheric pressure to about 7000 kPa (≈1000 psia) the viscosity of dry air increases at a rate of approximately 1% for each 700 kPa (100 psi) increase in pressure.

†   For pressures other than atmospheric, use $\rho/\rho_{atmos} = P/P_{atmos}$.

TABLE D.4   Properties of Dry Air at Atmospheric Pressure: English System

Temperature	Absolute Viscosity*	Density†
Degrees F (C)	*(lbf-s/ft²) × 10⁶*	*lbm/ft³*
40(4.44)	0.362	0.0794
50(10.0)	0.368	0.0779
60(15.6)	0.374	0.0764
70(21.1)	0.379	0.0749
80(26.7)	0.385	0.0735
90(32.2)	0.390	0.0722
100(37.8)	0.396	0.0709
110(43.3)	0.401	0.0697
120(48.9)	0.407	0.0685

*   *Over the range from atmospheric pressure to about 7000 kPa ($\approx$1000 psia) the viscosity of dry air increases at a rate of approximately 1% for each 700 kPa (100 psi) increase in pressure.*

†   *For pressures other than atmospheric, use $\rho/\rho_{atmos} = P/P_{atmos}$.*

TABLE D.5   Some Values of Gravity Acceleration

	m/s²	ft/s²
Standard	9.806 65	32.174
Location		
Ft. Egbert, Alaska	9.821 83	32.224
Key West, Florida	9.789 70	32.118
Batavia, Java	9.781 78	32.092
Karajak Glacier, Greenland	9.825 34	32.235
Pittsburgh, Pennsylvania Latitude 40°, 26′, 40″ Longitude 79°, 57′, 13″ W Elevation 908.35 ft	9.801 05	32.156
Moon	1.67	5.48
Planet Mercury	3.92	12.86
Planet Jupiter	26.46	87.07

TABLE D.6 Specific Gravities* of Selected Materials

Material	Specific Gravity
Mercury	13.596 @ 0 C
	13.546 @ 20 C
	13.690 @ −38.8 C (liquid at freezing point)
	14.193 @ −38.8 C (solid at freezing point)
Gasoline	0.66 to 0.69
Kerosene	0.82
Sea water	1.025
Oil (Meriam Red—a common manometer oil)	0.823
Carbon tetrachloride	1.60
Tetrabromo-ethane	2.96
Ethyl alcohol/water mixture at 20° C—% by weight	
0	1.00
20	0.97
40	0.94
60	0.89
80	0.84
100	0.79

* Specific gravity is the ratio of the mass of a body to that of an equal volume of water at 4° C, or at some other specified temperature.

TABLE D.7 Some Additional Material Properties

Temperature	Medium Heating Oil		Heavy Heating Oil	
°F	Specific gravity	Viscosity: lbf-s/ft²	Specific gravity	Viscosity: lbf-s/ft²
40	0.865	10.82×10^{-5}	0.918	789×10^{-5}
60	0.858	7.85	0.912	390
80	0.851	6.03	0.905	200
100	0.843	4.59	0.899	109

TABLE D.7 (*continued*)

Temperature	Viscosity of kerosene
°C	$n\text{-}s/m^2$
0	28.7×10^{-4}
20	19.2
40	13.4
60	9.6
80	7.7
100	6.7

TABLE D.8 Young's Modulus

For steel	$E \approx 29.5 \times 10^6$ psi $\approx 20.3 \times 10^{10}$ Pa
For aluminum	$E \approx 10 \times 10^6$ psi $\approx 6.9 \times 10^{10}$ Pa

stress and strain relationships E

E.1 THE GENERAL PLANE STRESS SITUATION

Suppose an element dx wide by dy high is selected from a general plane stress situation in equilibrium, as shown in Fig. E.1. Assume that the element is of uniform thickness, t, normal to the paper.

From strength of materials it will be remembered that for equilibrium, τ_{xy} must be equal to τ_{yx}. We will therefore employ the symbol τ_{xy} for both. We will also assume that not only must the complete element be in equilibrium, but so also must be all its parts. Therefore, if the element is bisected by a diagonal ds long, each half of the element must also be in equilibrium.

As shown in Fig. E.2, there must be a normal stress σ_θ and a shear stress τ_θ acting on the diagonal area. If the various stresses shown on the partial element, Fig. E.2, are multiplied by the areas over which they act, forces are obtained as shown in Fig. E.3. Let all the directions be considered positive, as shown. We note that $dy/ds = \cos\theta$ and $dx/ds = \sin\theta$. Summing forces normal to the diagonal plane and solving for σ_θ we obtain,

$$\sigma_\theta = \sigma_x \cos^2\theta + \sigma_y \sin^2\theta + 2\tau_{xy} \sin\theta \cos\theta.$$

A more convenient form of this equation may be had in terms of double angles. By substituting trigonometric equivalents,

$$\sigma_\theta = \tfrac{1}{2}(\sigma_x + \sigma_y) + \tfrac{1}{2}(\sigma_x - \sigma_y) \cos 2\theta + \tau_{xy} \sin 2\theta. \tag{E.1}$$

Using this equation, the stress on any plane may be determined if values of σ_x, σ_y, and τ_{xy} are known.

EXAMPLE   A shaft is subject to a torque, T, which results in a shear stress, $Tc/J = 9500$ psi (Fig. E.4), and at the same time and at the same point a bending moment due to gear loads causes an outer fiber stress, $Mc/I = 4000$ psi. What will be the normal stress on the outer surface in a direction 30° to the shaft center line?

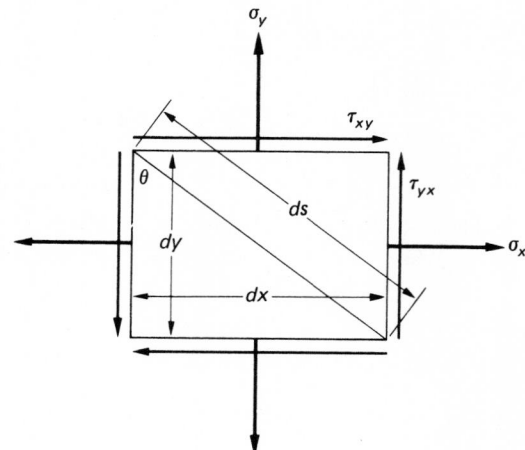

FIGURE E.1   Element subject to plane stresses.

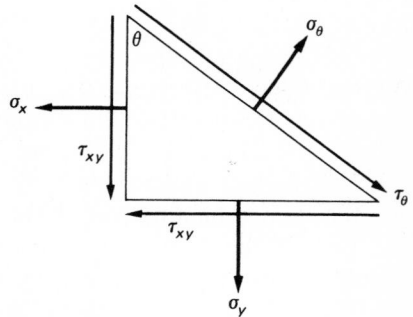

FIGURE E.2   Element used to define positive stress directions.

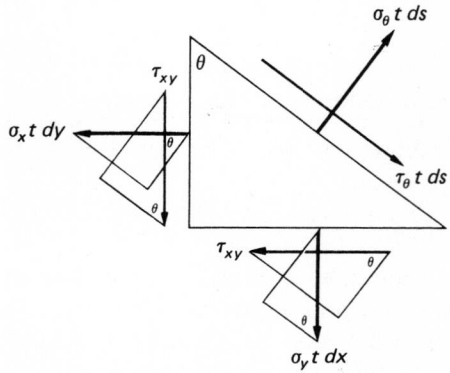

FIGURE E.3   Element illustrating the requirement for force equilibrium.

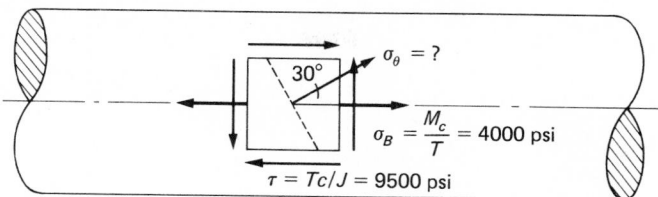

FIGURE E.4 Stresses acting on an element on the outer surface of a shaft subject to torsion and bending.

Solution

$$\sigma_{30°} = \tfrac{1}{2}(\sigma_x + \sigma_y) + \tfrac{1}{2}(\sigma_x - \sigma_y)\cos 2\theta + \tau_{xy}\sin 2\theta$$

$$= \tfrac{1}{2}(4000 + 0) + \tfrac{1}{2}(4000 - 0)\cos 60° + 9500\sin 60°$$

$$= 11,240 \text{ psi.}$$

Of course, the normal stress, 11,240 psi, is not necessarily the maximum normal stress, because the angle 30° was chosen at random; undoubtedly some other angle may result in a larger normal stress.

E.2 DIRECTION AND MAGNITUDES OF PRINCIPAL STRESSES

To calculate the maximum normal stress, the particular angle θ_1 determining the plane over which it will act must be found. This may be done by differentiating Eq. (E.1), with respect to θ, setting the derivative equal to zero, and solving for the angle θ_1. This should also give us the plane over which the normal stress is a minimum.

$$\frac{d\sigma_\theta}{d\theta} = -(\sigma_x - \sigma_y)\sin 2\theta + 2\tau_{xy}\cos 2\theta = 0$$

or

$$\tan 2\theta_{1,2} = \frac{\pm 2\tau_{xy}}{\pm(\sigma_x - \sigma_y)}. \tag{E.2}$$

Two angles, $2\theta_{1,2}$, are determined by Eq. (E.2), and consideration of the trigonometry involved shows that the two angles are 180° apart. This would mean, then, that the two angles $\theta_{1,2}$ are 90° apart, and leads to a very important fact: *The planes of maximum and minimum normal stress are always at right angles to each other.*

The maximum and minimum normal stresses are called the *principal stresses,* and the planes over which they act are called the *principal planes.* We have just found, therefore, that the principal planes are at right angles to each other. If we know the direction of the maximum normal stress, we automatically know the direction of the minimum normal stress.

Now we would like to find an expression for the principal stresses. From Eq. (E.2) we may write

$$\sin 2\theta_{1,2} = \frac{2\tau_{xy}}{\sqrt{(\sigma_x - \sigma_y)^2 + (2\tau_{xy})^2}},$$

$$\cos 2\theta_{1,2} = \frac{(\sigma_x - \sigma_y)}{\sqrt{(\sigma_x - \sigma_y)^2 + (2\tau_{xy})^2}}.$$

(E.3)

Substituting these values in Eq. (E.1) gives us the principal stresses, which we shall designate σ_1 and σ_2, and

$$\sigma_{\theta max} = \sigma_1 = \tfrac{1}{2}(\sigma_x + \sigma_y) + \tfrac{1}{2}\sqrt{(\sigma_x - \sigma_y)^2 + (2\tau_{xy})^2},$$

$$\sigma_{\theta min} = \sigma_2 = \tfrac{1}{2}(\sigma_x + \sigma_y) - \tfrac{1}{2}\sqrt{(\sigma_x - \sigma_y)^2 + (2\tau_{xy})^2}.$$

(E.4)

EXAMPLE Referring to the example in Section E.1, determine the magnitudes of the principal stresses and the positions of the principal planes relative to the shaft center line.

Solution   Using Eq. (E.4),

$$\sigma_1 = \tfrac{1}{2}(4000 + 0) + \tfrac{1}{2}\sqrt{(4000 + 0)^2 + (2 \times 9500)^2}$$

$$= 11,708 \text{ psi}$$

and

$$\sigma_2 = \tfrac{1}{2}(4000 + 0) - \tfrac{1}{2}\sqrt{(4000 + 0)^2 + (2 \times 9500)^2}$$

$$= -7708 \text{ psi}.$$

From Eq. (E.2),

$$\tan 2\theta = \frac{2 \times 9500}{4000 - 0} = \frac{19,000}{4000} = 4.75,$$

$$2\theta = 78.1°,$$

$$\theta = 39.05°.$$

The orientation is as shown in Fig. E.5.

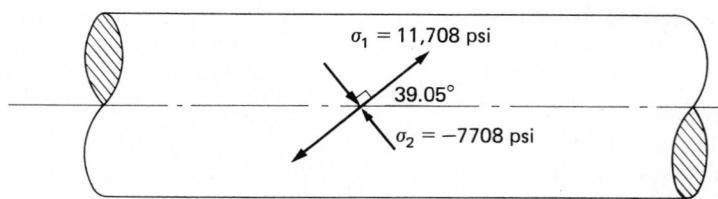

FIGURE E.5   The principal stresses corresponding to the situation shown in Fig. E.4.

E.3   VARIATION IN SHEAR STRESS WITH DIRECTION

Following the same procedure used for normal stresses, and again referring to Fig. E.3, if the forces parallel to the diagonal plane are summed, the following shear relations are obtained. The equation for the shear stress on any plane in terms of σ_x, σ_y, and θ is

$$\tau_\theta = \tfrac{1}{2}(\sigma_x - \sigma_y)\sin 2\theta - \tau_{xy}\cos 2\theta. \tag{E.5}$$

The angle determining the planes over which the shear stresses are maximum and minimum may be determined by the relation

$$\tan 2\theta_s = \frac{\mp(\sigma_x - \sigma_y)}{\pm 2\tau_{xy}}. \tag{E.6}$$

By substituting the angles determined by Eq. (E.6) in Eq. (E.5), relations for maximum and minimum shear stress may be obtained.

$$\text{Maximum shear stress} = \tau_{\theta\text{max}} = \tfrac{1}{2}\sqrt{(\sigma_x - \sigma_y)^2 + (2\tau_{xy})^2},$$

$$\text{Minimum shear stress} = \tau_{\theta\text{min}} = -\tfrac{1}{2}\sqrt{(\sigma_x - \sigma_y)^2 + (2\tau_{xy})^2}. \tag{E.7}$$

We must be careful, however, because the shear stress extremes given by Eq. (E.7) account for only the x- and y-directions. Consideration of the three-dimensional condition often shows the greatest shear stress to occur on yet another plane. See Section E.6.

E.4   SHEAR STRESS ON PRINCIPAL PLANES

Equations (E.7) allow us to determine the shear stress on any plane defined by θ. Therefore, let us substitute the expressions for $\theta_{1,2}$, Eq. (E.2), in Eq. (E.5), and thereby determine the shear stresses acting over the principal planes. Doing this gives

$$\tau_{1,2} = \frac{-\tfrac{1}{2}(\sigma_x - \sigma_y)(2\tau_{xy}) + \tau_{xy}(\sigma_x - \sigma_y)}{\sqrt{(\sigma_x - \sigma_y)^2 + (2\tau_{xy})^2}}$$

$$= 0.$$

This proves a very important fact about any plane stress situation: *The shear stresses on the principal planes are zero.* This in itself often provides the necessary clue to determine the orientation of the principal planes by inspection. In any case where it can be said, "there can be no shear on this plane," then the fact we have just established tells us that the plane we are referring to is a principal plane. Or, often just as important, if it can be said that shear stresses *do* exist on a plane, we know the plane *cannot* be one of the principal planes.

In strain-gage applications, knowing the directions of the principal planes at the point of interest provides a very decided advantage. With this information, gages may be aligned in the principal directions, and usually only two gages are required. More important, however, is the fact that the calculations become much simpler and less time consuming (Section 12.17.2).

E.5 GENERAL STRESS EQUATIONS IN TERMS OF PRINCIPAL STRESSES

Checking back on our original assumptions in Section E.1, we see that we assumed a simple element subject to two orthogonal normal stresses, σ_x and σ_y, and shear stresses, τ_{xy}. Using the information since developed, namely that the principal stresses are at right angles to each other and that the shear stresses are zero on the principal planes, we may now rewrite certain of our equations in terms of principal stresses σ_1 and σ_2.

By selecting just the right element orientation, i.e., aligning it with the principal planes, our basic element could be made to appear as it does in Fig. E.6. σ_1 and σ_2 are orthogonal stresses, and we know also that there will be no shear on the planes over which they act. Therefore, any of our equations written so far may be modified by substituting σ_1 and σ_2 for σ_x and σ_y, respectively, and making the shear stress equal to zero.

Substitution in Eqs. (E.1) and (E.5) yields particularly useful relations. Substitution in most of the others simply confirms our definitions.

Substituting in Eqs. (E.1) and (E.5) gives us

$$\sigma_\theta = \tfrac{1}{2}(\sigma_1 + \sigma_2) + \tfrac{1}{2}(\sigma_1 - \sigma_2) \cos 2\theta, \qquad (E.8)$$

$$\tau_\theta = \tfrac{1}{2}(\sigma_1 - \sigma_2) \sin 2\theta. \qquad (E.8a)$$

These equations are particularly useful in helping us visualize the overall stress condition as shown in the following section.

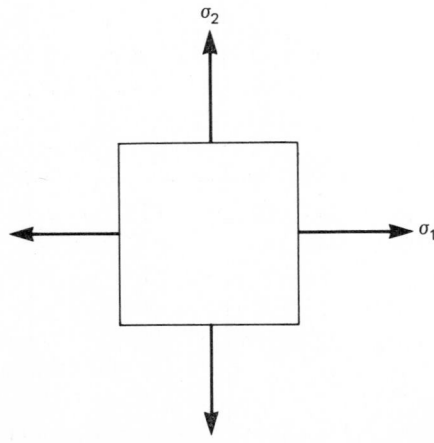

FIGURE E.6   An element subject to principal stresses.

E.6 MOHR'S CIRCLE FOR STRESS

Let us establish a coordinate system with σ_θ plotted as the abscissa and τ_θ as the ordinate (Fig. E.7). The shear stress corresponding to the principal stresses is zero; hence σ_1 and σ_2 will be plotted along the σ_θ-axis.

If a circle is drawn passing through the σ_1 and σ_2 points and having its center on the σ_θ-axis, the construction shown in Fig. E.7 will result. It will be noted that for any point on the circle, the distance along the abscissa represents σ_θ, and the ordinate distance represents τ_θ. This construction, which is very useful in helping to visualize stress situations, is known as Mohr's stress circle.

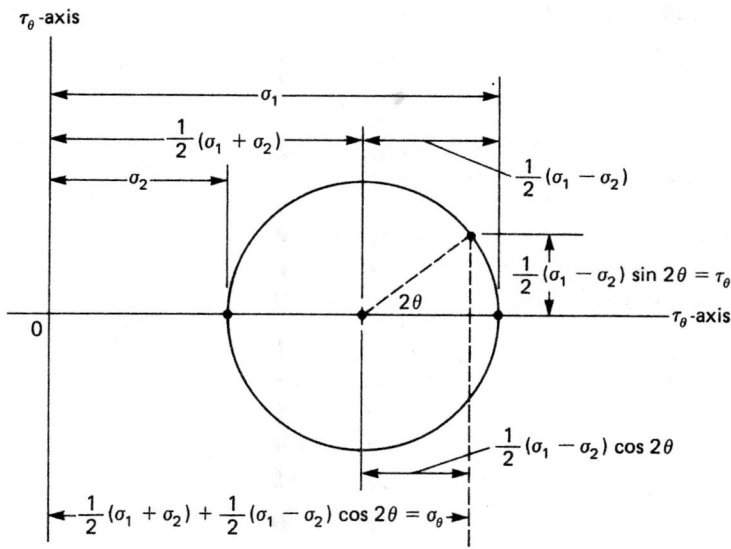

FIGURE E.7 Mohr's circle for plane stresses.

At this point we should consider the third or z-direction. In general three orthogonal stresses σ_x, σ_y, and σ_z, along with corresponding shear stresses τ_{xy}, τ_{yz} and τ_{zx}, will occur on an element, as shown in Fig. E.8a. In this case a third principal plane exists, over which, as for the two-dimensional case, *shear is zero*. Also, it may be shown* that the three principal planes, along with the three principal stresses σ_1, σ_2, and σ_3, are at right angles to one another. By considering the three directions in combinations of two, we may reduce the problem to three related two-dimensional situations. The resulting combined Mohr's diagrams are illustrated in Fig. E.8b.

In the majority of cases, strain gages are applied to free, unloaded surfaces

---

* E.g., in most intermediate solid mechanics books.

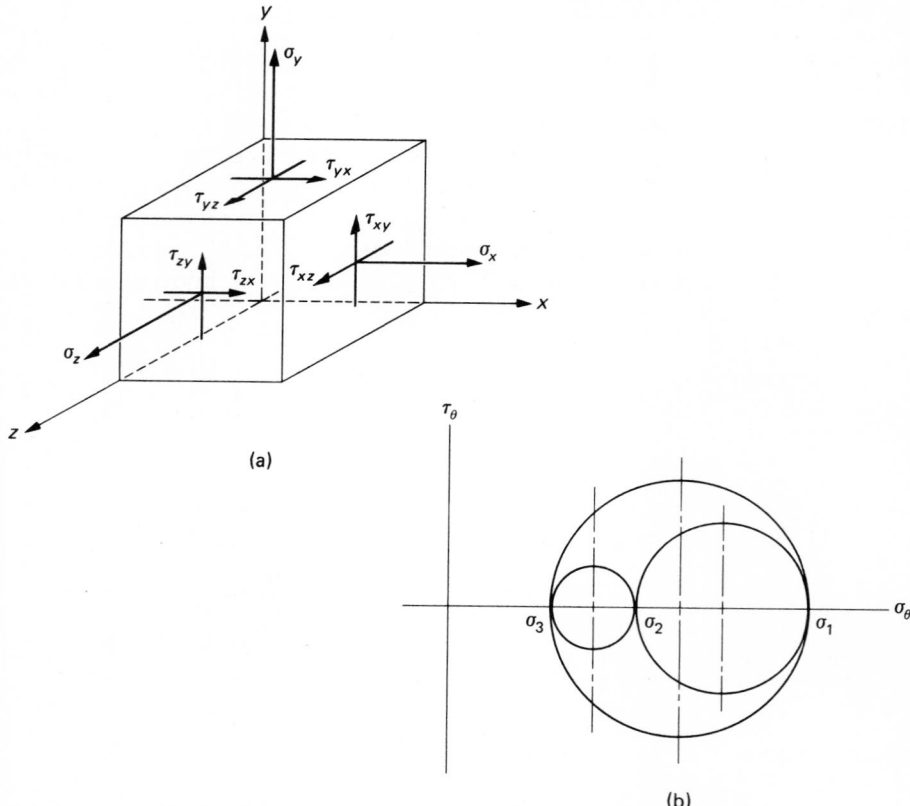

FIGURE E.8   (a) An element subjected to normal and shear stresses on three orthogonal planes. (b) Mohr's circles for stress for the element shown in (a).

and the condition thought of as being two-dimensional. It is well, however, to consider every condition in terms of three dimensions, even though the third stress may be zero, and to plot or merely sketch the three-circle Mohr's diagram. This procedure often reveals a maximum shear which might otherwise be overlooked.

A few examples will demonstrate the power of the Mohr diagram.

EXAMPLE 1   Figure E.9a shows a simple tension member. We know there is no shear stress on a transverse section; hence we know that this must be a principal plane. Since the other principal plane must be normal to the first principal plane and hence be aligned with the axis of the specimen, the normal stress on this plane must be zero. Therefore

$$\sigma_1 = \frac{F}{A} \quad \text{and} \quad \sigma_2 = \sigma_3 = 0.$$

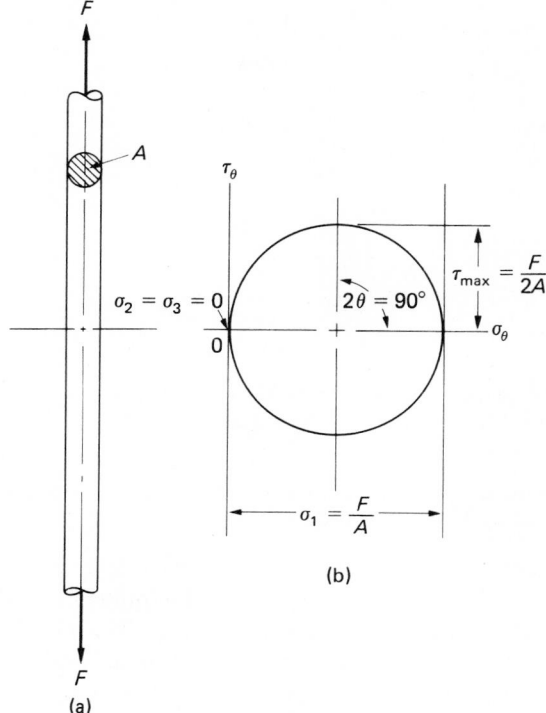

FIGURE E.9   Mohr's circle of stresses for a simple tension member.

Plotting Mohr's circle for this situation gives us Fig. E.9b. One of the Mohr circles degenerates to a point in this case.

By inspection we see that the maximum shear stress is equal to $F/2A$ at an angle $2\theta = 90°$ or $\theta = 45°$ measured relative to the axis of the specimen. This confirms our previous knowledge of the stress condition for this simple situation.

EXAMPLE 2   Figure E.10a shows a thin-walled cylindrical pressure vessel. From elementary theory, the hoop, longitudinal and normal stresses may be calculated by the following relations:

$$\sigma_H = \frac{PD}{2t}, \qquad \sigma_L = \frac{PD}{4t}, \qquad \text{and} \qquad \sigma_N = 0.$$

Consideration of the nature of the stress field makes it difficult to imagine shear stresses on planes parallel to the hoop, longitudinal, or normal directions. Assuming this to be correct, then the circumferential, the longitudinal, and the normal directions must be the principal directions and σ_H, σ_L, and σ_N must be the principal stresses. Mohr's circle for this situation is shown in Fig.

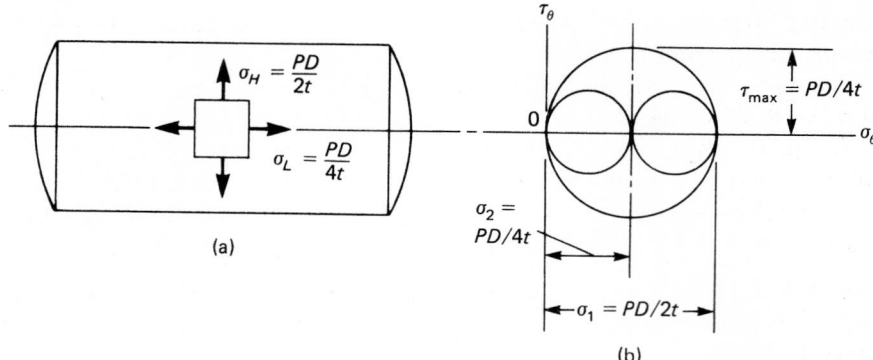

FIGURE E.10   Mohr's circle of stresses for the free surface of a cylindrical pressure vessel. P = pressure; D = shell diameter, and t = shell-wall thickness.

E.10b. The maximum shear is seen to be $PD/4t$, over a plane inclined 45° to the circumferential and normal directions.

EXAMPLE 3   Figure E.11a shows a shaft in simple torsion. From strength of materials we know that the shear stress on the outer fiber acting on a plane normal to the shaft center line is equal to Tc/J. The fact that shear stress exists on this plane eliminates it from consideration as a principal plane. Since principal planes must be normal to each other, we immediately think of the one other symmetrical possibility—the two planes inclined 45° to the shaft center line. Careful consideration of the stresses that may exist on these two planes leads us to conclude that tension would exist on one and compression on the other. The wringing of a wet towel is often used as an example of this situation. In the one 45° direction, the threads of the towel are obviously in tension, while in the other 45° direction, compression is employed to squeeze out the water.

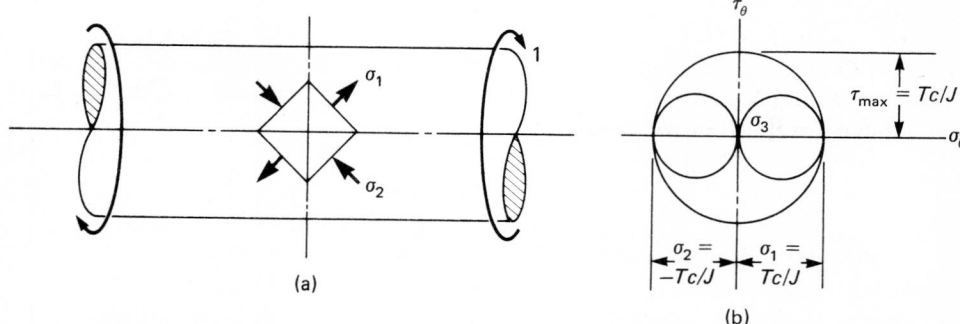

FIGURE E.11   Mohr's circle for a shaft subject to "pure" torsion. T = torque; J = polar moment of inertia of section; C = distance from neutral axis to fiber of interest.

Because of symmetry, we are led to the conclusion that the magnitudes of the two stresses are equal. Plotting equal tensile and compressive principal stresses, using Mohr's circle construction, gives us Fig. E.11b.

The third principal direction is normal to the shaft surface and we see that $\sigma_N = 0$. Although the above discussion can hardly be considered rigorous proof, Fig. E.11b does represent the actual stress situation for a shaft subject to pure torsion. We know that maximum shear stress is equal to Tc/J. Therefore, inspection shows us that the principal stresses σ_1 and σ_2 must also have the same magnitude, Tc/J, tension and compression respectively.

EXAMPLE 4   Figure E.12a shows a thin-wall spherical pressure vessel, for which elementary theory shows that the stress in the wall abides by the following relation:

$$\sigma = \frac{PD}{4t}.$$

In this case it is difficult to see how direction has significance. At any point on the outside of the shell, the normal stresses must be equal in all directions, simply because of symmetry. We must therefore conclude that

$$\sigma_1 = \sigma_2 = \frac{PD}{4t} \qquad \text{and} \qquad \sigma_3 = \sigma_N = 0.$$

Mohr's diagram for this condition is shown in Fig. E.12b, from which it is seen that $\tau_{max} = PD/8t$.

From the preceding discussion and consideration of Mohr's circle construction, we may now make the following general observations:

1. A stress state involving shear without normal stress is impossible.

2. Maximum shear stress always occurs on planes oriented 45° to the principal stresses, and is equal to one-half the algebraic difference of the principal stresses.

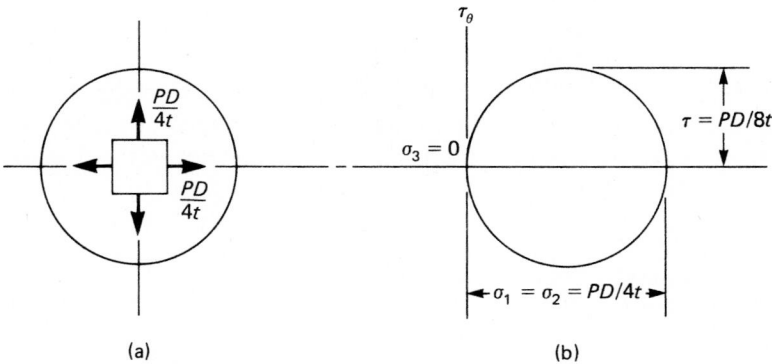

(a)   (b)

FIGURE E.12   Mohr's circle for the free surface of a spherical pressure vessel.

3. The shear stresses on any mutually perpendicular planes are of equal magnitude.

4. The sum of the normal stresses on any mutually perpendicular planes is a constant.

5. The maximum ratio of shear stress to principal stress occurs when the principal stresses are of equal magnitude but opposite sign.

E.7 STRAIN AT A POINT

Through use of Hooke's law and the stress relations developed in the preceding pages, the following relations for strain at a point may be derived:

$$\varepsilon_\theta = \tfrac{1}{2}(\varepsilon_x + \varepsilon_y) + \tfrac{1}{2}(\varepsilon_x - \varepsilon_y)\cos 2\theta + \frac{\gamma_{xy}}{2}\sin 2\theta, \qquad (E.9)$$

$$\frac{\gamma_\theta}{2} = \tfrac{1}{2}(\varepsilon_x - \varepsilon_y)\sin 2\theta - \frac{\gamma_{xy}}{2}\cos 2\theta. \qquad (E.9a)$$

Comparison of the above two equations with Eqs. (E.1) and (E.5), respectively, indicates that with a minor exception [the shear strains γ are divided by 2, whereas their counterparts are not], the stress and the strain relations at a point are functionally alike. It follows, therefore, that we can draw a Mohr's diagram for strain, provided the ordinate is made $\gamma_\theta/2$. This is sometimes useful in treating strain-rosette data.

EXAMPLE 5 Power piping is subject to a combination of loading whose complexity will serve as an interesting example of a combined stress situation. In addition to pressure loading, differential expansion between the hot and cold conditions may superimpose bending, torsional, and axial loading.

Of course, the primary problem involved in piping design is the determination of the loading brought about by pipe expansion, end movements, and movement-limiting stops. In the simple situations good estimates of these loads may be determined analytically, but experimental methods using models are often required (Section 13.11). More recently, the various computer techniques have been applied to the problem.

In this example it will be assumed such preliminary work has been finished and the critically stressed location found. The remaining problem, then, is to combine the stress components and to determine the net stress condition. The problem is as follows:

Pipe data (14 inch, Schedule 100)

Outside diameter = 14 in.,
Wall thickness = 0.937 in.,
Inside diameter = 12.125 in.,
Bending moment of inertia = 825 in⁴,
Bending section modulus = 117.9 in³,
Torsional moment of inertia = 1650 in⁴,

Torsional section modulus = 235.8 in³,
Cross-sectional area = 38.47 in²,
Young's modulus = 23 × 10⁶ psi,
Poisson's ratio = 0.29.

Loading Data

Internal pressure = 620 psi,
Bending moment = 700,000 in·lb,
Torsional moment = 480,000 in·lb,
Axial load = 35,000-lb tension.

Problem. For the outer surface of the pipe, calculate (a) the maximum shear stress, (b) the principal stresses, (c) the direction of the stress σ_1 relative to the axis of the pipe, (d) the axial and circumferential unit strains, and (e) the principal strains. Also, (f) sketch Mohr's diagrams for stress and for strain.

Solution. The stress components are found as follows:

$$\text{The ratio } \frac{\text{I.D.}}{\text{O.D.}} = \frac{12.125}{14} = 0.87,$$

which is the range usually termed "thin wall." Hence,

$$\sigma_H = \text{hoop stress} = \frac{PD}{2t} = \frac{620 \times 12.125}{2 \times 0.937} = 4011 \text{ psi},$$

$$\sigma_L = \text{longitudinal stress} = \frac{PD}{4t} = \frac{1}{2}\sigma_H = 2005 \text{ psi},$$

$$\sigma_B = \text{bending stress} = \frac{Mc}{I} = \frac{700,000}{117.9} = \pm 5937 \text{ psi},$$

$$\tau = \text{torsional stress} = \frac{Tc}{J} = \frac{480,000}{235.8} = 2035 \text{ psi},$$

$$\sigma_A = \text{axial stress} = \frac{F}{A} = \frac{35,000}{38.47} = 910 \text{ psi}.$$

The above conditions are illustrated in Fig. E.13.

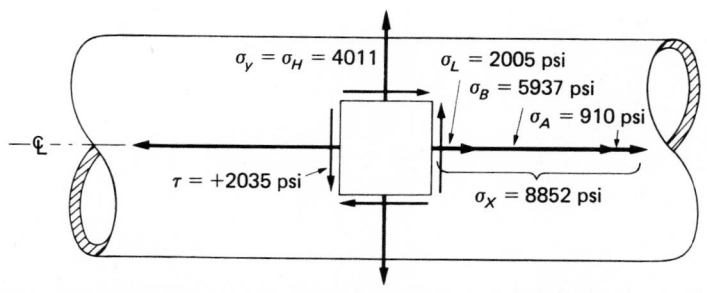

FIGURE E.13   Axial and hoop stresses acting in the pipe of Example 5.

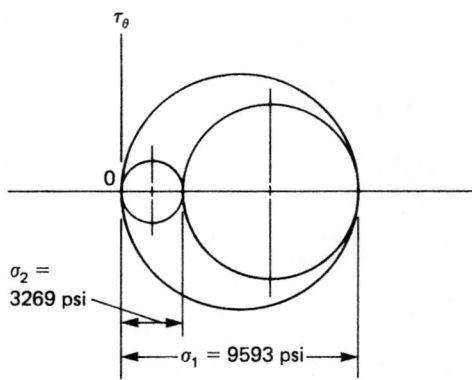

FIGURE E.14   Principal stresses and principal stress directions for the pipe in Example 5.

a) Using Eq. (E.7), we obtain

$$\tau = \tfrac{1}{2}\sqrt{(8852 - 4011)^2 + (2 \times 2035)^2} = 3162 \text{ psi}.$$

From Fig. E.14 we see, however, that the true maximum shear stress is

$$\tau_{\text{max}} = (9593/2) = 4796 \text{ psi}.$$

b) Using Eq. (E.4) (see also Fig. E.15), we get

$$\sigma_1 = \tfrac{1}{2}(8852 + 4011) + 3162 = 9593 \text{ psi},$$

$$\sigma_2 = \tfrac{1}{2}(8852 + 4011) - 3162 = 3269 \text{ psi}.$$

Also,

$$\sigma_3 = \sigma_N = 0.$$

c) Using Eq. (E.2), we obtain

$$\tan 2\theta_{\sigma_1} = \frac{2 \times 2035}{(8852 - 4011)} = \frac{4072}{4841} = 0.8407,$$

$$2\theta_{\sigma_1} = 40°4', \qquad \theta_{\sigma_1} = 20°2'.$$

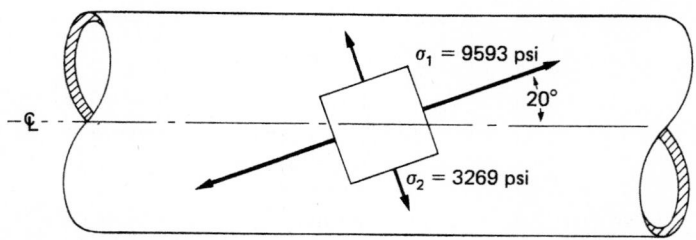

FIGURE E.15   Principal stress element for Example 5.

d) Using Eq. (12.5), we get

$$\varepsilon_x = \frac{1}{23 \times 10^6}[8852 - 0.29(4011 + 0)] = 334 \ \mu s,$$

$$\varepsilon_y = \frac{1}{23 \times 10^6}[4011 - 0.29(0 + 8852)] = 63 \ \mu s,$$

$$\varepsilon_z = \frac{1}{23 \times 10^6}[0 - 0.29(8852 + 4011)] = -162 \ \mu s.$$

e) Again, from Eq. (12.5)

$$\varepsilon_1 = \frac{1}{23 \times 10^6}[9593 - 0.29(3269 + 0)]$$

$$= 376 \ \mu s,$$

$$\varepsilon_2 = \frac{1}{23 \times 10^6}[3269 - 0.29(0 + 9539)]$$

$$= 22 \ \mu s,$$

$$\varepsilon_3 = \frac{1}{23 \times 10^6}[0 - 0.29(9593 + 3269)]$$

$$= -162 \ \mu s.$$

f) Mohr's diagrams for stress and for strain are shown in Figs. E.14 and E.16, respectively.

[*Student assignment:* Modify the above calculations and diagrams for conditions on the inner pipe surface ($\sigma_3 = \sigma_N = -620$ psi).]

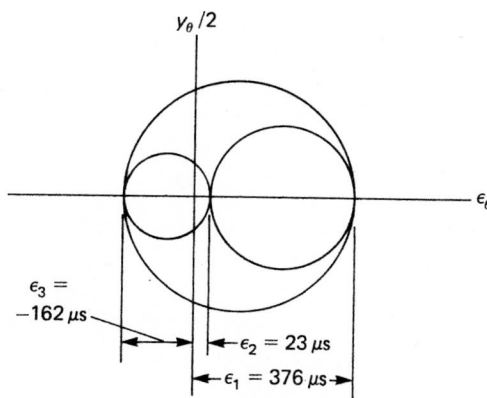

FIGURE E.16   Mohr's strain diagram (outer surface) for Example 5.

further consideration of class intervals and goodness-of-fit

F

There are no basic rules for dividing a data sample into class intervals for the purpose of plotting a histogram or calculating Chi². As discussed in Chapter 9, the particular bounds are normally selected by the experimenter. The authors propose a somewhat more restrictive approach to this step, as follows:

1. Although not a strict requirement, we will center the class interval selection on the mean, $\bar{x}$. That is, the class divisions will be symmetrically disposed about the mean.

2. The class interval increments will be forced to be convenient portions of the standard deviation.

3. Any data beyond about $\bar{x} \pm 3\sigma$ will be assumed improbable and will be rejected. This is often assumed an outer limit for "good" data.* (A minor exception to this may occur when the class interval increment makes an exact 3σ bound inconvenient. See Fig. F.2 as an example.)

Consider Figs. F.1a through F.1g. Each figure shows the normal distribution curve defined by Eq. (9.9). In Fig. F.1a, we have divided the area under the curve into six intervals, each with a width equal to σ. For this division, 34.15% of the data should theoretically fall within each of the intervals adjacent to the mean; 13.57% should fall within each of the next intervals and 2.14% within each of the outer intervals. These values add to 99.72% of the total sample. In accordance with (3) above we assume 0.28% of the sample will fall beyond $\pm 3\sigma$, and are therefore rejected. Figures F.1b through F.1g are prepared in a similar manner but for class interval divisions as shown.

---

* One basis for rejecting data is known as Chauvenet's criterion, which is governed by the number of data items in the sample under consideration. For a sample of 10 items, values beyond about 2σ are rejected; for 1000 items the limits become about $\pm 3.5\sigma$. *Source:* Young, H. D., *Statistical Treatment of Experimental Data.* New York: McGraw-Hill Book Co., 1962, p. 78.

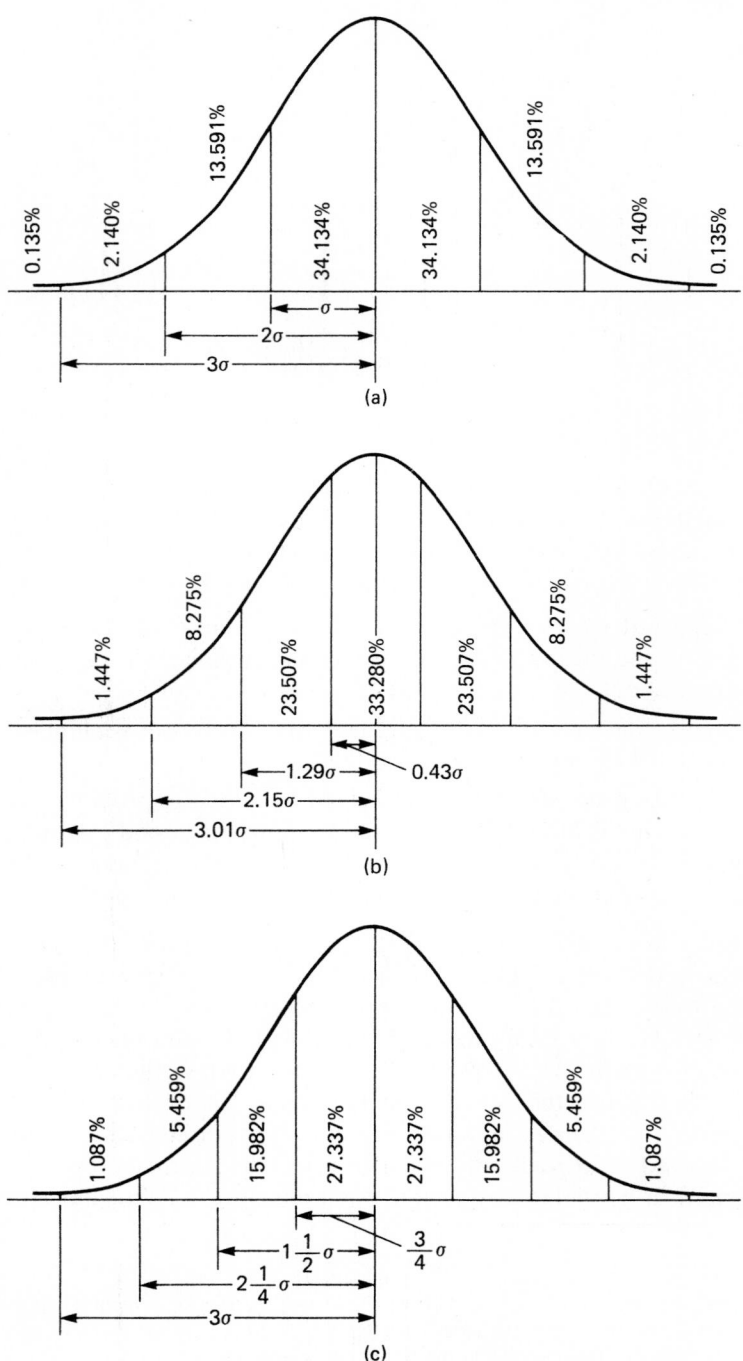

FIGURE F.1 (*See legend on p. 702.*)

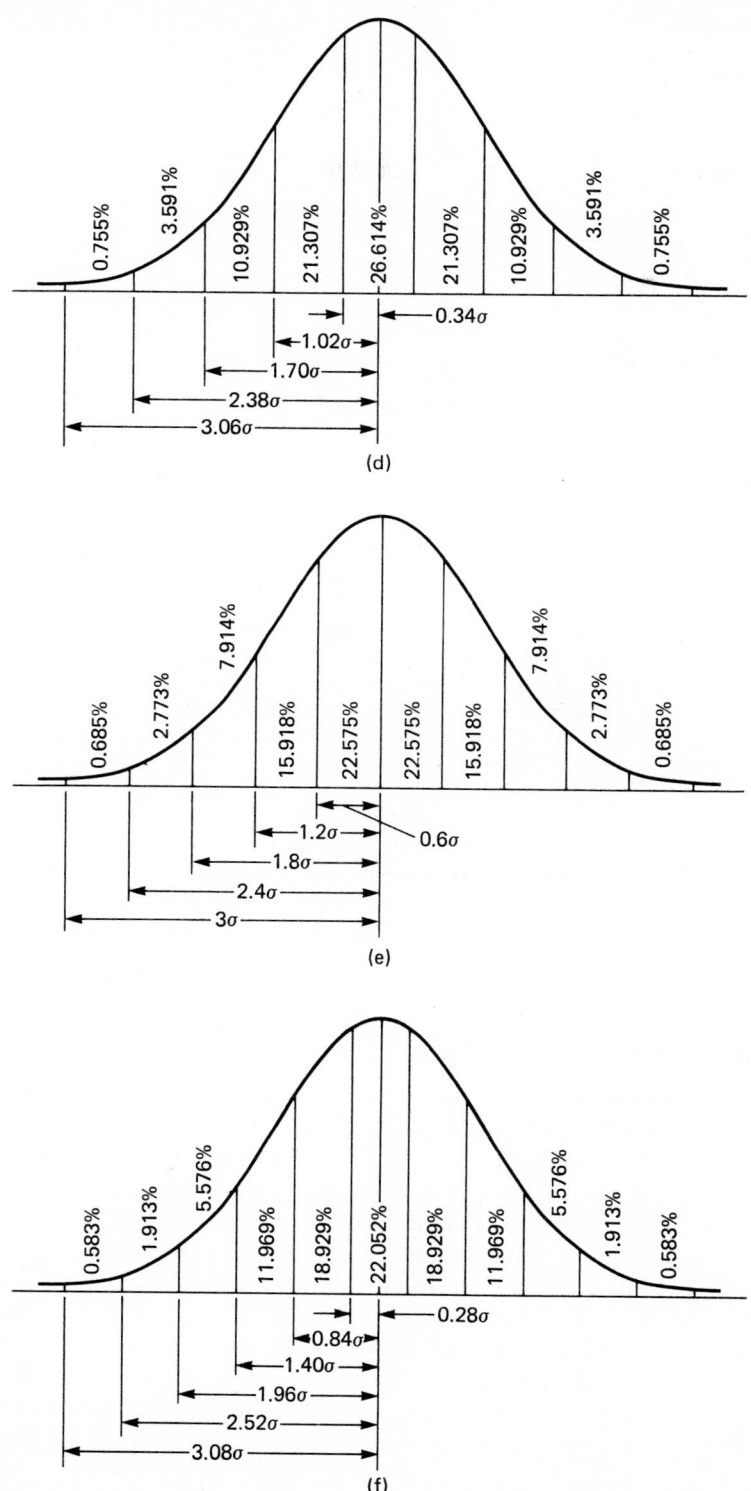

(d)

(e)

(f)

701

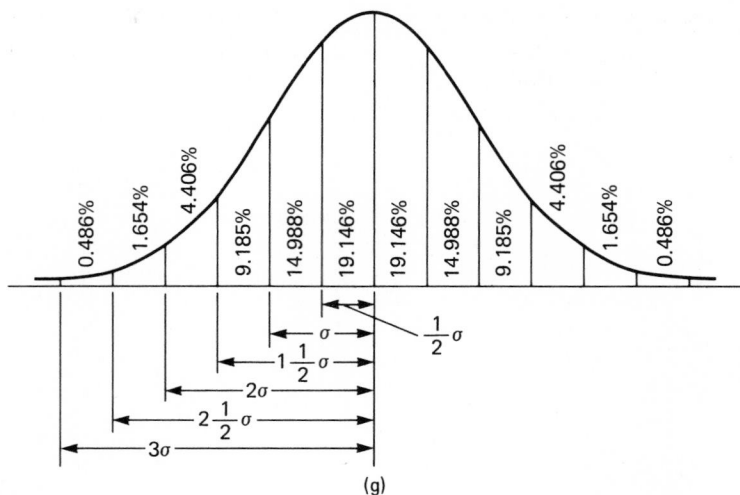

FIGURE F.1   Normal distribution curves. Percentages indicate ideal distribution. (a) Divided into six equal class intervals; interval width = σ. (b) Divided into seven equal class intervals; interval width = 0.86σ. (c) Divided into eight class intervals; interval width = 0.75σ. (d) Divided into nine class intervals; interval width = 0.68σ. (e) Divided into ten class intervals; iinterval width = 0.6σ. (f) Divided into eleven class intervals; interval width = 0.56σ. (g) Divided into twelve class intervals; interval width = 0.5σ.

In the fashion described above we have helped to formalize data division for a given sample. Logically, the larger the sample size the greater should be the number of intervals. In addition to assisting in the plotting of histograms, these "rules" are especially helpful for use with the Chi^2 goodness-of-fit test. Consider the following exercise.

Example of Chi² Calculations

Referring to the data listed in Table 9.3, consisting of 100 items possessing a mean of 4.008 MPa and a standard deviation of 13.7×10^{-3} MPa, we will determine the corresponding Chi^2 using a division of eight intervals.

A preliminary fit of the data show the single maximum value of 4.05 MPa to lie outside the 3σ tolerance limit. We will therefore discard this reading. In doing this we see that to be completely correct (not necessarily too practical, in this case), we must recalculate both the mean and the standard deviation. Doing this, we find, $\bar{x} = 4.007$ MPa and σ = 13.099×10^{-3} MPa. For eight intervals, each interval width will be 0.75σ or 0.09824 MPa. We may now prepare Table F.1 with the first column listing the interval division values; column 2, showing the number of observed data items, "O_i"; column 3 listing the theoretical number of expected items, "E_i"; and the final column listing

TABLE F.1   Calculation of Chi² Using Data from Table 9.1 and Eight Class Intervals

Class Interval Bounds	Number of Data Items within Interval. "O_i"	Number of Data Items Expected. "E_i" (see Fig.F.1c)	ΔChi²
3.968			
	1	1.076	0.005
3.978			
	3	5.404	1.069
3.988			
	12	15.822	0.923
3.997			
	25	27.064	0.157
4.007			
	33	27.064	1.302
4.017			
	17	15.822	0.088
4.027			
	6	5.404	0.066
4.037			
	2	1.076	0.079
4.047			Chi² = 4.39

Note: *The single reading, 4.05 MPa, is rejected because it falls outside the ±3σ tolerance that has been set. Recalculated values for the mean and standard deviation, based on 99 items, yield x̄ = 4.007 MPa and σ = 0.013099 MPa. For eight class intervals each interval width = 0.75σ = 0.00982.*

the calculated Chi² increments determined from

$$\Delta Chi^2 = \frac{(O_i - E_i)^2}{E_i}$$

The sum of the increments is Chi², which is found to be 4.39.

In this case the applicable degrees of freedom, DF, is 8 − 3 = 5. There are eight class intervals (variables), and the data has already been used for determining the mean, the standard deviation and Chi².

Figure F.2 shows the theoretical probability of fit for a range of DF and Chi². Entry into the plot indicates an approximate 50% probability of fit. Is this reasonable? The decision must be made by the experimenter. An extremely high probability is usually viewed with suspicion; suspicion that something must have been forced. A low probability, of course indicates that it is doubtful that the data abides by normal distribution rules. This decision does not invalidate the data, but merely indicates that a different set of rules should be sought, and that although the value of the mean is useful, standard deviation has little meaning.

We should look at another aspect, however. We arbitrarily selected eight class intervals for our calculations. If we recalculate employing intervals rep-

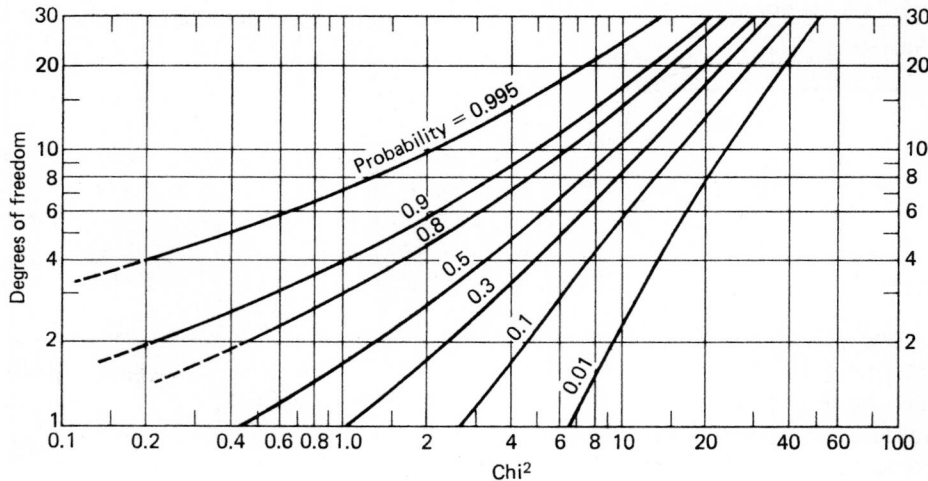

FIGURE F.2   Theoretical probability of fit for ranges of degrees of freedom and Chi^2.

resented by Figs. F.1a through F.1g we obtain the results shown in Table F.2. From these results it is clear that some criterion for establishing an optimum number of intervals is required. The following observations are offered:

1. When data is subdivided into class intervals for the purpose of making a Chi^2 goodness-of-fit calculation and one finds one or more intervals (other than either of the two extreme divisions) containing *no* data items, then either or both of two conditions are automatically indicated:

    a) the data does not fit normal distribution rules, or,

    b) the number of intervals selected is too great in terms of the sample that is being tested.

    In the latter case one should reduce the number of class intervals; however, it is seen that the Chi^2 test easily becomes impractical when a small number of data items are available.

2. When a Chi^2 goodness-of-fit check is made on a sample of data and calculations based on various subdivisions of data are made, the division yielding the greatest probability of fit is the most valid.

The above conclusion is based on the following argument. If for a given sample we write,

$$P = f(N, \text{Chi}^2)$$

where N is the integral number representing the number of class intervals to be considered and P is the corresponding probability of fit based on the Chi^2 test, then we can easily show that P approaches zero for excessively large

TABLE F.2   Effect of Number of Class Intervals on Chi^2 Results. (Data from Table 9.3.)

Number of Class Intervals	Chi^2	Degrees of Freedom	Indicated Probability of Fit
6	15.99	3	Less than 1%
7	8.42	4	About 10%
8	4.39	5	About 50%
9	19.79	6	Less than 1%
10	26.51	7	Nil
11	35.84	8	Nil
12	53.90	9	Nil

or excessively small (in terms of sample size) values of N. At the same time, intermediate values of N may provide greater probabilities of fit (as witness the above example). This, of course, points to the existence of an optimum value of N for each sample of data. It appears logical that the probability corresponding to such an optimum is "best," since neither the data nor the basic Chi^2 concept has been altered in any manner. Determination of the optimum of course remains to be found, and probably the most practical approach is simply to try various data subdivisions until a reasonable value is either found or the conclusion is reached that it does not exist.

Table F.3 consists of pseudo-random, pseudo-normal numbers distributed about a mean of zero. These are presented as a vehicle for statistical exercises. The numbers are presented in columns of 25 along with values of Σx_i and $\Sigma(x_i)^2$. These values may be combined to calculate sample means and standard deviations.

(*Table F.3 is on page 706.*)

TABLE F.3 Pseudo-Random, Pseudo-Normal Numbers Distributed about a Mean of Zero.

-101	19	-26	-67	68	51	56	-136	-9	51	20	-78
-42	-10	119	-181	-104	-139	67	-13	153	-14	150	-100
93	-64	2	21	-28	116	52	-2	-132	124	-60	-17
73	-128	39	-83	60	-32	19	-67	89	-28	51	89
117	-83	67	114	113	9	56	92	255	-60	149	73
-129	23	38	-128	116	163	71	111	-6	21	-61	-111
148	70	-77	-59	148	-61	94	34	73	-88	88	18
22	34	18	147	23	-9	-82	38	-13	-61	-13	20
-3	-105	-16	-213	-82	-131	-29	232	35	11	54	-16
-211	-128	98	-143	-61	22	115	-32	115	-17	-103	-31
116	20	-140	-80	-29	69	157	67	-12	-85	68	2
-15	115	10	97	-33	154	-26	-31	-16	70	-6	51
-215	58	94	-31	53	68	118	-66	-100	39	22	160
154	36	-60	-46	-31	-6	-111	-78	-66	272	-142	0
-201	-63	74	-224	122	-141	-66	-32	-179	-2	55	-107
-14	125	-61	161	-64	-42	112	37	-105	53	164	-99
-47	-86	-18	-66	10	21	-86	-1	4	-1	-131	-77
-144	114	7	88	255	303	22	13	-13	6	227	-9
18	162	50	-6	-65	-5	-180	-3	-1	10	287	68
165	114	-208	-1	-29	-86	-17	94	-7	76	37	-105
50	152	38	23	166	18	-6	-7	99	69	-205	-183
62	-26	19	-191	11	-49	99	167	151	75	-28	69
90	24	5	39	7	18	97	-131	160	165	36	-139
-32	56	71	23	-61	154	-42	-86	-44	-99	-28	-146
-176	19	-104	-100	-13	-1	120	-64	51	-77	50	68
$\sum x_i$											
-222	448	39	-906	552	464	610	136	482	510	681	-600
$\sum (x_i)^2$											
344348	187188	143565	321048	205414	265718	192942	185280	254640	184570	331507	198510

references

CHAPTER 1

1. Cook, A. H. The absolute determination of the acceleration due to gravity. *Metrologia,* 1, 3: 84, 1965.

CHAPTER 2

1. Johnson, W. C. *Mathematical and Physical Principles of Engineering Analysis.* New York: McGraw-Hill Book Co., 1944, p. 241.

2. Doherty, R. E., and E. G. Keller. *Mathematics of Modern Engineering,* Vol. 1. New York: John Wiley & Sons, Inc., 1936, p. 83.

3. Knight, A. R., and G. H. Fett. *Introduction to Circuit Analysis.* New York: Harper and Brothers, 1943, p. 413.

CHAPTER 3

1. Fitzgerald, A. E., D. E. Higginbotham, and A. Grabel. *Basic Electrical Engineering,* 3rd. ed. New York: McGraw-Hill Book Co., 1967.

2. Halliday, D., and R. Resnick. *Fundamentals of Physics* (revised printing). New York: John Wiley & Sons, Inc., 1974.

CHAPTER 4

1. Kneen, W. A review of the electric displacement gages used in railroad car testing. *ISA Proc.* 6: 74, 1951.

2. Gray, H. L., Jr. A guide to applying resistance pots. *Control Engr.* 3, 7: 80, July 1956.

3. *The Radio Amateur's Handbook,* 56th ed. American Radio Relay League, West Hartford, Conn., 1978, pp. 2–11.

4. Hetenyi, M. *Handbook of Experimental Stress Analysis.* New York: John Wiley & Sons, Inc., 1950, p. 239.

5. Electronic micrometer uses dual coils. *Prod. Engr.* 19, 1: 134, Jan. 1948.

6. Brenner, A., and E. Kellogg. An electric gage for measuring the inside diameter of tubes. *NBS J. Res.* 42: 461, May 1949.

7. *The Radio Amateur's Handbook,* 56th ed. American Radio Relay League, West Hartford, Conn., 1978, pp. 2–9.

8. Low temperature liquid level indicator for condensed gases. *NBS Tech. News Bull.* 38: 1, Jan. 1954.

9. Hetenyi, M. *Handbook of Experimental Stress Analysis.* New York: John Wiley & Sons, Inc., 1950, p. 287.

10. Sihvonen, Y. T., G. M. Rassweiler, A. F. Welch, and J. W. Bergstrom. Recent improvements in a capacitor type pressure transducer. *ISA J.* 2: 11, Nov. 1955.

11. Leggat, J. W., G. M. Rassweiler, and Y. T. Sihvonen. Engine pressure indicators, application of a capacitor type. *ISA J.* 2: 9, Aug. 1955.

12. Welch, Weller, Hanysz, and Bergstrom. Auxiliary equipment for the capacitor-type transducer. *ISA J.* 2: 12, Dec. 1955

13. Fleming, L. T. A ceramic accelerometer of wide frequency range. *ISA Proc.* 5: 62, 1950.

14. McDermott, J. R. Control designer's guide to solid state photosensors. *Control Engineering* 71, Oct. 1960.

15. Jamieson, J. A. Detectors for infrared systems. *Electronics* 33, 5: 82, 1960.

16. Bube, R. H. *Photoconductivity of Solids.* New York: John Wiley & Sons, Inc., 1960.

17. Gadd, C. W. and T. C. Van Degrift. A short-gage length extensometer and its application to the study of crankshaft stresses. *J. App. Mech.* 9: A.15, March 1942.

18. *Dew Point Equipment to Measure Moisture in Gases.* General Electric Co., Bulletin GEC-588, Schenectady, NY, 1950.

19. Campbell, J. O. Special electrical applications in the steel industry. *Iron and Steel Engr.* 19: 78–89, Feb. 1942.

20. Carr, J. J. *How to Design and Build Electronic Instrumentation.* Blue Ridge Summit, Penn.: Tab Books, 1978, p. 278.

21. Shigley, J. E. *Mechanical Engineering Design,* 2nd ed. New York: McGraw-Hill Book Co., 1972, Ch. 8.

22. Haugen, E. B. *Probabilistic Approaches to Design.* New York: John Wiley & Sons, Inc., 1968.

23. Gitlin, R. How temperature affects instrument accuracy. *Control Engr.* 2: 5, May 1955.

24. Laws, F. A. *Electrical Measurements,* 2nd ed. New York: McGraw-Hill Book Co., 1938, p. 217.

CHAPTER 5

1. Geldmacher, R. C. Ballast circuit design. *SESA Proc.* 12, 1: 27, 1954.

2. Meier, J. H. Discussion of Ref. 9, in same source, p. 33.

3. Wheatstone, C. An account of several new instruments and processes for determining the constants of a voltaic circuit. *Phil. Trans. Roy. Soc.* (London) 133: 303, 1843.

4. *Encyclopedia Britannica,* Wheatstone's Bridge Encyclopedia Britannica Inc., Chicago, Ill.: William Benton, Publisher, 23, 566, 1957.

5. Laws, F. A. *Electrical Measurements,* 2nd ed. New York: McGraw-Hill Book Co., 1938, p. 217.

6. Bowes, C. A. Variable resistance sensors work better with constant current excitation. *Instrument Technology* March 1967.

7. Sion, N. Bridge networks in transducers. *Inst. Control Systems* August 1968.

8. Hague, B. *Alternating Current Bridge Methods.* London: Pitman Publishing Corporation, 1938.

9. Lenkurt Electric Co. dB and Other Logarithmic Units. *The Lenkurt Demodulator,* 15, 4, 1966.

10. Keast, D. N. *Measurements in Mechanical Dynamics.* New York: McGraw-Hill Book Co., 1967.

CHAPTER 6

1. Southern, R. *Programming the 6800 Microprocessor.* Ottawa, Ont.: Southcroft, 1977.

2. *IEEE Standard Digital Interface for Programmable Instrumentation.* IEEE Std. 488-1975 (also ANSI MC 1.1-1975). The Institute of Electrical and Electronic Engineers, Inc., New York 10017.

CHAPTER 8

1. Units of weight and measure. *NBS Miscel. Pub.* 214: July 1, 1955.

2. Terrien, J. Scientific metrology on the international plane and the bureau international des poids es mesures. *Metrologia* 1, 2: 15, Jan. 1965.

3. U. S. Coast and Geodetic Survey Bulletin 26, April 5, 1893.

4. Cochrane, R. D. *Measures for Progress, A History of the National Bureau of Standards.* U. S. Dept. of Commerce, 1966, p. 47.

5. Silsbee, F. B. Fundamental units and standards. *Instruments* 26: 1520, Oct. 1953.

6. Morrison, P. Book review. *Scientific American* 233, 4: 132, 1975.

7. Cohen, J. Psychological time. *Scientific American* 211, 5: 116, Nov. 1964.

8. Clemence, G. M. Time and its measurement. *Am. Scientist* 40, 2: 260, April 1952.

9. Gardner, M. Can time go backward. *Scientific American* 216, 1: 98, 1967.

10. *NBS Tech. News Bull.* 52, 1: 10, Jan. 1968.

11. Frequency and time standards. *Application Note* 52, Hewlett-Packard Co., Palo Alto, Calif., 1965.

11a. Kamas, G. and S. L. Howe (eds). *Time and Frequency User's Manual.* NBS Spcl. Publ. 559. Washington: U.S. Govt. Printing Office, 1979.

12. The International Practical Temperature Scale of 1968. A Committee Report. English version appearing in *Metrologia* 5: 2, April 1969.

13. Hoge, H. J. and F. G. Brickwedde. Establishment of a temperature scale for the calibration of thermometers between 14 and 83 degrees K. *NBS J. Res.* 22: 351, 1939.

14. Muller, R. H. New precise temperature standard accurate to 5×10^{-4} deg. C. *Anal. Chem.* 32: 103A, Nov. 1950.

15. Silsbee, F. B. Extension and dissemination of the electrical and magnetic units by the National Bureau of Standards. *NBS Circular* 531, 1952.

16. Snow, C. Formulas for computing capacitance and inductance. *NBS Circular* 544, 1954.

17. Driscoll, R. L. and R. D. Cutkosky. Measurement of current with the National Bureau of Standards current balance. *NBS J. Res.* 60: 4, April 1958.

CHAPTER 9

1. Barry, B. A. *Engineering Measurements.* New York: John Wiley & Sons, Inc., 1964.

2. Whitehead, T. N. *Instruments and Accurate Mechanism.* New York: Dover Publications, Inc., 1953.

3. Simpson, H. W. A method of comparing transducers for instrumentation applications. *ISA J.,* 2, 7: 251, July 1955.

4. *RADC Reliability Notebook,* U.S. Dept. of Commerce, PB 161894, Oct. 1959, p. 4-2.

5. Beers, Y. *Introduction to the Theory of Error.* Reading, Mass: Addison-Wesley Publishing Co., 1957.

6. Kline, S. J. and F. A. McClintock. Describing uncertainties in single-sample experiments. *Mech. Engr.* 75: 3, Jan. 1953.

7. Schenck, H., Jr. *Theories of Engineering Experimentation.* New York: McGraw-Hill Book Co., 1968.

8. Lipson, C., and N. J. Sheth. *Statistical Design and Analysis of Engineering Experiments.* New York: McGraw-Hill Book Co., 1973.

CHAPTER 10

1. Curves, Special, *Encyclopedia Britannica,* Encyclopedia Britannica, Inc., Chicago, Ill.: William Benton, Publisher, 6: 892, 1957.

2. Rosard, D. D. Natural frequencies of twisted cantilever beams. *ASME Paper* 52-A-15 (1952).

CHAPTER 11

1. Peters, C. G., and W. B. Emerson. Interference methods for producing and calibrating end standards. *NBS J. Res.,* 44: 427, April 1950.

2. Metrology of gage blocks. *NBS Circular,* U.S. Government Printing Office, Washington, D.C., 581: 67, April 1, 1957.

3. Graneek, M. A pneumatic comparator of high sensitivity. *The Engineer* 172: 414, 1951.

4. American Society of Tool and Manufacturing Engineers. *Handbook of Industrial Metrology.* Englewood Cliffs, N.J.: Prentice-Hall, Inc., 1967.

5. Scarr, A. J. T. *Metrology and Precision Engineering.* New York: McGraw-Hill Publishing Co., 1967.

6. *Metrology of Gage Blocks.* National Bureau of Standards Circular 581, U.S. Government Printing Office, Washington, D.C., 1957.

7. *Precision Measurement and Calibration,* Vol. III. National Bureau of Standards Handbook 77, Washington, D.C.: U.S. Govt. Printing Office, 1966.

8. Kneen, W. A review of electric displacement gages used in railroad car testing. *ISA Proc.* 6: 74, 1951.

9. Boggis, A. G. Design of differential transformer displacement gauges. *SESA Proc.* 9, 2: 171, 1952.

10. American Standard, *Surface Texture* (ASA B46. 1-1962), ASME, New York, 7, NY.

CHAPTER 12

1. Hetenyi, M. *Handbook of Experimental Stress Analysis.* New York: John Wiley & Sons, 1950.

2. Mason, W. P., and R. N. Thurston. Use of piezoresistive materials in the measurement of displacement, force and torque. *J. Acoustical Soc. Am.* 29, 1957.

3. Smith, C. S. Piezoresistive effect in germanium and silicon. *Phys. Rev.* 94, 42: 1954.

4. Brookes-Smith, C. H. W., and J. A. Colls. Measurement of pressure, movement, acceleration and other mechanical quantities by electrostatic systems. *J. Sci. Inst.* (London) 14: 361, 1939.

5. Carter, B. C., J. F. Shannon, and J. R. Forshaw. Measurement of displacement and strain by capacity methods. *Proc. Instn. Mech. Engrs.* 152: 215, 1945.

6. Langer, B. F. Design and application of a magnetic strain gage. *SESA Proc.* 1, 2: 82, 1943.

7. Ripperger, E. A. A piezoelectric strain gage. *SESA Proc.* 12, 1: 117, 1954.

8. Mark, J. W., and W. Goldsmith. Barium titanate strain gages. *SESA Proc.* 13, 1: 139, 1955.

9. Langer, B. F. Measurement of torque transmitted by rotating shafts. *J. App. Mech.* 67, 3: A.39, March 1945.

10. Thompson, K. On the electro-dynamic qualities of metals. *Phil. Trans. Roy. Soc.* (London) 146: 649–751, 1856.

11. Eaton, E. C. Resistance strain gage measures stresses in concrete. *Eng. News Record* 107: 615–616, Oct. 1931.

12. Bloach, A. New methods for measuring mechanical stresses at higher frequencies. *Nature* 136: 223–224, Aug. 19, 1935.

13. Clark, D. S., and G. Datwyler. Stress-strain relations under tension impact loading. *Proc. ASM* 38: 98–111, 1938.

14. Krammer, E. W., and T. E. Pardue. Electric resistance changes of fine wires during elastic and plastic strains. *SESA Proc.* 7, 1: 7, 1949.

15. Mills, D., III. Strain gage waterproofing methods and installation of gages on propeller strut of USS Saratoga. *SESA Proc.* 16, 1: 137, 1958.

16. Frank, E. Series versus shunt bridge calibration. *Instruments and Automation* 31: 648, 1958.

17. Weymouth, L. J., J. E. Starr, and J. Dorsey. Bonded resistance strain gages. *Exp. Mech.* 6, 4: 19A, April 1966.

18. Campbell, W. R., and R. F. Suit, Jr. A transistorized AM-FM radio-link torque telemeter for large rotating shafts. *SESA Proc.* 14, 2: 55, 1957.

19. Baumberger, R., and F. Hines. Practical reduction formulas for use on bonded wire strain gages in two-dimensional stress fields. *SESA Proc.* 2, 1: 133, 1944.

20. Perry, C. C., and H. R. Lissner. *The Strain Gage Primer,* 2nd ed. New York: McGraw-Hill Book Co., 1962, p. 157.

21. Perry, C. C., and H. R. Lissner. *The Strain Gage Primer,* 2nd ed. New York: McGraw-Hill Book Co., 1962, p. 157.

22. Meier, J. H. On the transverse sensitivity of foil gages. *Exp. Mech.* 1: July 1961.

23. Wu, C. T. Transverse sensitivity of bonded strain gages. *Exp. Mech.* 2: 338, Nov. 1962.

24. Pian, T. H. H. Reduction of strain rosettes in the plastic range. *J. Aerospace Sci.* 26, 12: 842, Dec. 1959.

25. Ades, C. S. Reduction of strain rosettes in the plastic range. *Exp. Mech.* 2: 345, Nov. 1962.

26. Telinde, J. C. Investigation of strain gages at cryogenic temperatures. *Douglas Paper No. 3835.* Huntington Beach, CA: Douglas Missile and Space Systems Division, 1966.

27. Leszysnki, S. W. The development of flame sprayed sensors. *ISA Jour.* 9, 7: 35, July 1962.

28. Rastogi, V., K. D. Ives, and W. A. Crawford. High-temperature strain gages for use in sodium environments. *Exp. Mech.* 7, 12: 525, Dec. 1967.

29. Karnie, A. J., and E. E. Day. A laser extensometer for measuring strain at incandescent temperatures. *Exp. Mech.* 7, 11: 485, Nov. 1967.

CHAPTER 13

1. Lashof, T. W., and L. B. Macurdy. Precision laboratory standards of mass and laboratory weights. *NBS Circular 547* (1954).

2. *Precision Measurement and Calibration, Optics, Metrology and Radiation,* Handbook 77, Vol. III. National Bureau of Standards, pp. 588, and 615, 1961.

3. Weighing machines, *Encyclopedia Britannica,* Encyclopedia Britannica, Inc. Chicago, Ill.: William Benton Publisher, 23: 483, 1957.

4. *Instruments,* 25: 1300, Sept. 1952.

5. Wilson, B. L., D. R. Tate, and G. Borkowski. Proving rings for calibrating testing machines. *NBS Circular C454* U.S. Government Printing Office, Washington, D.C. 1946.

6. Timoshenko, S. *Strength of Materials,* Part II, 2nd ed. New York: D. Van Nostrand, Inc., 1941, p. 88.

7. High capacity load calibrating devices. *NBS Tech. News Bull.* 37: 9, Sept. 1953.

8. Ruge, A. C. The bonded wire torquemeter. *SESA Trans.* 1, 2: 68, 1943.

9. Rebeske, J. J., Jr. Investigation of a NACA high-speed strain-gage torquemeter. *NACA Tech. Note 2003,* Jan. 1950.

10. Langer, B. F. Measurement of torque transmitted by rotating shafts. *J. App. Mech.* 67, 3: A.39, March 1945.

11. Langer, B. F., and K. L. Wommack. The magnetic-coupled torquemeter. *SESA Trans.* 2, 2: 11, 1944.

12. Hetenyi, M. *Handbook of Experimental Stress Analysis.* New York: John Wiley & Sons, Inc., 1950, Chapters 6 and 7.

CHAPTER 14

1. Anderson, J. D., Jr. *Introduction to Flight.* New York: McGraw-Hill Book Co., 1978.

2. Wolfe, A. An elementary theory of the bourdon gage. *J. Appl. Mech.* 68, 9: A-207, Sept. 1946.

3. Wenk, E. Jr. A diaphragm-type gage for measuring low pressures in fluids. *SESA Proc.* 8, 2: 90, 1951.

4. Roark, R. J. *Formulas for Stress and Strain,* 4th ed. New York: McGraw-Hill Book Co., 1965.

5. Stedman, C. K. The characteristics of flat annular diaphragms. *Instrument Notes,* No. 31 (Jan. 1957), Statham Laboratories, Los Angeles 64, California.

6. Patterson, J. L. A miniature electrical pressure gage utilizing a stretched flat diaphragm. *NACA Tech. Note 2659* (April 1952).

7. Grover, H. J., and J. C. Bell. Some evaluations of stresses in aneroid capsules. *SESA Proc.* 5, 2: 125, 1958.

8. Werner, F. D. The design of diaphragms for pressure gages which use the bonded wire resistance strain gage. *SESA Proc.* 11, 1: 137, (1935).

9. Beckwith, T. G., and N. L. Buck. *Mechanical Measurements,* 1st ed., Reading, Mass: Addison-Wesley Publishing Company, 1961.

10. Howe, W. H. What's available for high pressure measurement and control. *Control Engr.* 2, 4: 53, April 1955.

11. Howe, W. H. The present status of high pressure measurement. *ISA J.* 2, 3–4: 77, 109, March, April 1955.

12. Wildhack, W. A. Pressure drop in tubing in aircraft instrument installations. *NACA Tech. Note 593* (1937).

13. Iberall, A. S. Attenuation of oscillatory pressures in instrument lines. *NBS J. Res.* 45: 85, July 1950.

14. Moise, J. C. Pneumatic transmission lines. *ISA Proc.* 8: 152, 1953.

15. Hylkema, C. G., and R. B. Bowersox. Experimental and mathematical techniques for determining the dynamic response of pressure gages. *ISA Proc.* 8: 115, 1953, and *ISA J.* 1, 2: 27, Feb. 1954.

16. Stedman, C. K. Alternating flow of fluids in tubes. *Instrument Notes* 30: Jan. 1956, Statham Laboratories, Los Angeles 65, California.

17. Lord Rayleigh, *The Theory of Sound,* Vol. II, 2nd ed. New York: Dover Publications, Inc., 1945, p. 188.

18. Mylius, R. D., and R. J. Reid. Acoustical filters protect pressure transducers. *Control Engr.* 4, 1: 115, Jan. 1957.

19. White, G. Liquid filled pressure gage systems. *Instrument Notes* 7: (Jan.–Feb. 1949), Statham Laboratories, Los Angeles 64, CA.

20. Taback, I. The response of pressure measuring systems to oscillating pressure. *NACA Tech. Note No. 1819* (Feb. 1949).

21. Badmaieff, A. Techniques of microphone calibration. *Audio Engr.* 38: 12, Dec. 1954.

22. Reid, R. Use standard functions to test pneumatic systems. *Control Engr.* 5, 1: 117, Jan. 1958.

23. Baird, R. C., R. L. Solnich, and J. R. Amiss. Calibrator for dynamic pressure transducers. *Inst. Automation* 27: 1074, July 1954.

24. Meyer, R. D. Dynamic pressure transmitter calibrator. *Rev. Sci. Inst.* 17, 5: 199, May 1946.

25. Eckman, D. P., and J. C. Moise. A pneumatic sine-wave generator for process control study. *ISA Proc.* 7: 13, 1952.

26. Davis, W. R. Measuring high pressure transients. *Auto. Control* 4, 1: 24, Jan. 1956.

27. National Bureau of Standards Monograph 67, *Methods for the Dynamic Calibration of Pressure Transducers,* Washington: U.S. Dept. of Commerce, 1963.

28. Bowersox, R. Calibration of high frequency response pressure transducers. *ISA J.* 5: 11, Nov. 1958.

29. Roark, R. J. *Formulas for Stress and Strain.* New York: McGraw-Hill Book Co., 1965, p. 217.

CHAPTER 15

1. Streeter, V. L., and E. B. Wylie. *Fluid Mechanics.* New York: McGraw-Hill Book Co., 1975.

2. ASME, Application—Pt. II of Fluid Meters: Interim Supplement 19.5 on Instruments and Apparatus, 1972, p. 232.

3. Li, W. H., and S. H. Lam. *Principles of Fluid Mechanics.* Reading, Mass: Addison-Wesley Publishing Co., 1964, p. 318.

4. Schoenborn, E. M., and A. P. Colburn. The flow mechanism and performance of the rotameter. *Trans. AI Ch. E.* 35, 3: 359, 1939.

5. Binder, R. C. *Advanced Fluid Dynamics and Fluid Machinery.* New York: Prentice Hall, 1951.

6. Anderson, J. D., Jr. *Introduction to Flight.* New York: McGraw-Hill Book Co., 1978, p. 103.

7. Gracey, W. Measurement of static pressure on aircraft. *NACA Tech. Note 4184,* Nov. 1957.

8. Krause, L. N., and C. C. Gettelman. Effect of interaction among probes, supports, duct walls and jet boundaries on pressure measurements in ducts and jets. *ISA Proc.* 7: 138, 1952.

9. Gettleman, C. C., and L. N. Krause. Considerations entering into the selection of probes for pressure measurement in jet engines. *ISA Proc.* 7: 134, 1952.

10. Nagler, F. A. Use of current meters for precise measurement of flow. *ASME Trans.* 57: 59, 1935.

11. Grey, J. Transient response of the turbine flowmeter. *Jet Propulsion* 26: 2, Feb. 1956.

12. King, L. V. On the convection of heat from small cylinders in a stream of fluid, with applications to hot-wire anemometry. *Phil. Trans. Roy. Soc.* (London) 214, 14, Ser. A: 373–432, 1914.

13. Laurence, J. C., and L. G. Landes. Auxiliary equipment and techniques for adapt-

ing the constant temperature hot-wire anemometer to specific problems in air-flow measurements. *NACA Tech. Note 2843,* Nov. 1952.

14. Laurence, J. C., and L. G. Landes. Application of the constant temperature hot-wire anemometer to the study of transient air-flow phenomena. *ISA J.* 1, 12: 128, Dec. 1953.

15. A. E. Knowlton. *Standard Handbook for Electrical Engineers,* 8th ed. New York: McGraw-Hill Book Co., 1949, pp. 36–40.

16. W. G. James. An A-C induction flow meter, *ISA Proc.* 6: 5, 1951.

17. Gray, W. C., and E. R. Astley. Liquid metal magnetic flowmeters. *ISA J.* 1, 6: 15, June 1954.

18. *NBS Tech. News Bull.* 37, 3, March 1953.

19. N. Dvorak. Sonic anemometry for the hobbyist, *Byte,* 4, 7: 120, 1979.

20. Kiverson, G. Promising newcomers for tough flow measurements. *Machine Design,* Jan. 8, 1976.

21. Collins, W. T., and T. W. Selby. A gravimetric flow standard. *Flow Measurement Symposium.* New York: ASME, p. 290, 1966.

22. Jarret, F. H. Standpipes simplify flowmeter calibration. *Control Engineering* 1, 4: 37, Dec. 1954.

23. Liebenberg, D. H., R. W. Stokes, and F. J. Edeskuty. The calibration of flowmeters with liquid hydrogen in the region between 1000 and 7000 GPM. *Flow Measurement Symposium.* New York: ASME, p. 155, 1966.

24. Bowen, R. P. Designing portability into a flow standard. *ISA J.* 18, 5: 40, May 1961.

25. Hansen, A. G. *Fluid Mechanics.* New York: John Wiley & Sons, Inc., 1967, p. 422.

CHAPTER 16

1. Eskin, S. G., and J. R. Fritze. Thermostatic bimetals. *ASME Trans.,* 62: 7, July 1910.

2. Swindells, J. F., Ed. *Precision Measurement and Calibration, Temperature.* NBS Special Publication 300, Washington, D.C.: U.S. Government Printing Office, 2: 164, 1968.

3. Seebeck, T. J. *Evidence of the Thermal Current of the Combination Bi-Cu by Its Action on Magnetic Needle.* Berlin: Abt. d. Königl, Akad. d. Wiss. 1822–23, p. 265.

4. Peltier, M. Investigation of the heat developed by electric currents in homogeneous materials and at the junction of two different conductors. *Ann. Chim. Phys.* 56: 371, 1834.

5. Thomson, W. Theory of thermoelectricity in crystals. *Trans. Edinb. Soc.* 21: 153, 1847. Also in *Math. Phys. Papers,* 1: 232, 266, (1882).

6. Dike, P. H. *Thermoelectric Thermometry*. Philadelphia: Leeds and Northrup Company, 1954.

7. Powell, R. L., W. J. Hall, C. H. Hyink, Jr., et al. *Thermocouple Reference Tables Based on the IPTS-68*. National Bureau of Standards Monograph 125, Washington, D.C.: U.S. Govt. Printing Office, 1974.

8. Baker, H. D., E. A. Ryder, and N. H. Baker. *Temperature Measurement in Engineering*, Vol. 1. New York: John Wiley & Sons, Inc., 1953, p. 49.

9. Hammond, D. L., and A. Benjaminson. Linear Quartz Thermometer. *Instruments and Control Systems*, 38, 10: 115, 1965.

10. Lee, J. F., and F. W. Sears. *Thermodynamics*. Reading, Mass.: Addison-Wesley Publishing Co., 1955, p. 292.

11. Dike, P. H. *Thermoelectric Thermometry*. Philadelphia: Leeds and Northrup Company, 1954.

12. ASME *Power Test Code* 19.3-1974, Temperature measurement.

13. Lee, J. F., and F. W. Sears. *Thermodynamics*. Reading, Mass.: Addison-Wesley Publishing Co., 1955, p. 281.

14. *Steam, Its Generation and Use*, 38th ed. New York: The Babcock and Wilcox Company, 1975.

15. Johnson, N. R., A. S. Weinstein, and F. Osterle, The influence of gradient temperature fields on thermocouple measurements, *ASME Paper No. 57-HT-18*, Aug. 1957.

16. Hottel, H. C., and A. Kalitinsky, Temperature measurement in high-velocity air streams. *J. App. Mech.*, 67, 3: A25, March 1945.

17. Lalos, G. T., A sonic-flow pyrometer for measuring gas temperatures. *NBS J. Res.* 47, 3: 179, Sept. 1951.

18. Seadron, M. D., and I. Warshawsky. Experimental determination of time constants and nusselt numbers for bare-wire thermocouples in high-velocity air streams and analytic approximation of conduction and radiation errors. *NACA Tech. Note 2599, Jan. 1952.*

19. Moffat, R. J. How to specify thermocouple response. *ISA J.*, 4, 6: 219, June 1957.

20. Lefkowitz, L. Methods of dynamic analysis. *ISA J.* June: 203, 1955.

21. Louis, J. R., and W. E. Hartman. The determination and compensation of temperature sensor transfer functions. *ASME Paper 64-WA/AUT-13.*

22. Shepard, C. E., and I. Warshawsky. Electrical techniques for compensation of thermal time lab of thermocouples and resistance thermometer elements. *NACA Tech. Note 2703,* May 1952.

23. Shepard, C. E., and I. Warshawsky. Electrical techniques for time lag compensation of thermocouples used in jet engine gas temperature measurements. *ISA J.* 119 (Nov. 1953).

24. Harnbaker, D. R., and D. L. Rall. Heat flux measurements: A practical guide. *Instrumentation Technology* 51, Feb. 1968.

25. Baines, D. J. Selecting unsteady heat flux sensors. *Inst. and Control Systems* 80, May 1972.

26. Gardon, R. An instrument for the direct measurement of intense thermal radiation. *Rev. Sci. Instr.,*May 1953.

27. Stempel, F. C. Basic heat flow calibration. *Instr. and Control Systems* 42, 5: 105, 1969.

28. Roeser, W. F., and S. T. Lonberger. Methods of testing thermocouples and thermocouple materials. *NBS Circular 590,* Feb. 1958, 21 pp.

29. Eskin, S. G., and J. R. Fritze. Thermostatic bimetals. *ASME Trans.* 62: 5, 433, 1940.

CHAPTER 17

1. Fibikar, R. J., "Touch and vibration sensitivity," *Prod. Engr.* 27, 11 (Nov. 1956), p. 177.

2. Hudson, D. E., and O. D. Terrell, A preloaded spring accelerometer for shock and impact measurements, *SESA Proc.,* 9, 1 (1951), p. 1.

3. Pennington, D. *Piezoelectric Accelerometer Manual.* Pasadena: Endevco Corporation, 1965.

4. Kistler, W. P., Precision calibration of accelerometers for shock and vibration, *Test Engineering,* May 1966, p. 16.

5. Edelman, S. Additional thoughts on precision calibration of accelerometers, *Test Engineering,* Nov. 1966, p. 17.

6. Lewis, R. C., Electro-dynamic calibration for vibration pickups, *Prod. Engr.,* 22, 9 (Sept. 1951).

7. Unholtz, K., The calibration of vibration pickups to 2000 CPS, *ISA Proc.,* 7 (1952), p. 325.

8. "Easily made device calibrates accelerometer," *N.B.S. Tech. News Bull.,* June 1966, p. 94.

9. Wildhack, W. A., and R. O. Smith, A basic method of determining the dynamic characteristics of accelerometers by rotation, *ISA Paper No. 54–40–3.*

10. Conrad, R. W., and I. Vigness, Calibration of accelerometers by impact techniques, *ISA Proc.,* 8 (1953), p. 166.

11. Perls, T. A., and C. W. Kissinger, "High-g accelerometer calibration by impact methods with ballistic pendulum, air gun, and inclined trough," *ISA Paper No. 54–40–2.*

12. Weiss, D. E., Design and application of accelerometers, *SESA Proc.,* 4, 2 (1947).

13. Burns, J., and G. Rosa, "Calibration and test of accelerometers," *Instrument Notes No. 6* (Dec. 1948), Los Angeles 64, CA: Statham Laboratories.

14. Levy, S., and Wilhelmina D. Kroll, Response of accelerometers to transient accelerations, *NBS J. Res.* 45, 4 (Oct. 1950).

15. Welch, W. P., A proposed new shock-measuring instrument, *SESA Proc.*, 5, 1, p. 39, 1947.

16. Kaufman, A. B., Accelerometer integration, *Radio-Electronic Engr.*, (June 1952).

17. Adler, J. A., Hydraulic shakers, *Test Engineering*, April 1963.

18. Crandall, S. H., *Random Vibration*. New York: John Wiley & Sons, Inc., 1959.

19. Unholtz, K., Factors to consider in setting up vibration test specifications, *Mach. Des.*, 28, 6 (Mar. 22, 1956).

20. Wozney, G. P., Resonant vibration fatigue testing, *Exp. Mech.*, Jan. 1962.

21. "Application and design formulae for free–free resonant beams," *MB Vibration Notebook*, 1, 1, New Haven, Conn.: MB Manufacturing Co., March 1955.

22. Lazarus, M., Shock testing: A design guide, *Machine Design*, Oct. 12, 1967.

23. Armstrong, J. H., Shock-testing technology at the Naval Ordnance Laboratory, *SESA Proc.*, 6, 1 (1948), p. 55.

24. Brown, J., Selection factors for mechanical buffers, *Prod. Engr.*, 21, 11 (Nov. 1950), p. 156.

25. Brown, J., Further principles of buffer design, *Prod. Engr.*, 21, 12 (Dec. 1950), p. 125.

26. Marangoni, R. D., C. A. Saez, D. A. Weyel, and R. A. Polosky, Impact stresses in human head–neck model, *J. Engineering Mechanics Division*, ASCE, Vol. 104, No. EM1, 1978.

27. Mindlin, R. D., F. W. Stuber, and H. L. Cooper, Response of damped elastic systems to transient disturbances," *SESA Proc.*, 5, 2, p. 69.

28. Den Hartog, J. P., *Mechanical Vibrations* (4th ed.). New York: McGraw-Hill Book Co., Inc., 1956, p. 153.

CHAPTER 18

1. Skilling, D. C., Acoustical testing at Northrup Aircraft, *SESA Proceedings*. Vol. 16, No. 2, p. 121, 1959.

2. Randall, R. H., *An Introduction to Acoustics*. Reading, Mass.: Addison-Wesley Publishing Co., 1951.

3. Beranek, L. L., *Acoustics*. New York: McGraw-Hill Book Co., 1954, p. 12.

4. Peterson, A. P. G., *Handbook of Noise Measurement* (9th ed.). Concord, MA: GenRad, Inc, 1980.

5. Beranek, L. L. (Ed.), *Noise Reduction*. New York: McGraw-Hill Book Co., 1960, p. 186.

6. Keast, D. N. *Measurements in Mechanical Dynamics*. New York: McGraw-Hill Book Co., 1967.

7. Beranek, *Op. cit.* (3), p. 158.

8. Ranz, J. R., Noise measurement methods, *Machine Design,* November 10, 1966.

9. Peterson, *Op. cit.,* p. 133.

10. Various papers, Handbook 77, Vol. II, *Precision Measurement and Calibration, Heat and Mechanics,* National Bureau of Standards, 1961.

11. *American Standard Method for Calibration of Microphones,* S1.10–1966, American Standards Association, New York.

answers to
selected problems

CHAPTER 1

1.10 c) $F \approx 0.17$ lbf

1.12 $F_e \approx 293$ N

CHAPTER 2

2.3 $f = 15/2\pi$ Hz, $C_3 = 30$

CHAPTER 3

3.1 $\tau = 219.3$ days (for calcium)

3.3 $\tau = 0.82$ s

3.6 $\tau \approx 0.078$ s (using phase angle)

3.13 $\Omega < 6.57$ rad/s

3.14 $e \approx 9.2$ C

3.15 Lag ≈ 1.8 s

3.22 $0 < f_1 < 1282$ Hz and $3367 < f_2 < 3807$

3.25 $\phi \approx 20.5$ deg.

CHAPTER 4

4.1 $\rho \approx 1.7 \times 10^{-6}$ to 1.8×10^{-6} $\Omega \cdot$ cm

4.2 $\varepsilon \approx 1520$ pf/deg

4.4 $u_k \approx \pm 3\%$, or ± 1800 lbf/in.

4.6 $u_k \approx \pm 3.2$ lbf/in.

CHAPTER 5

5.1 $e_o/e_i = 0.33$ for $k = 0.25$

5.2 $R_2 \approx 63.3$ Ω

5.5 a) $R_L \approx 14,370 \ \Omega$
    b) $R_L \approx 25,000 \ \Omega$

5.7 $R_4 \approx 141.9 \ \Omega$

5.8 $e_o \approx 0.24$V (for $N = 100$)

5.10 For $0 < k < 1$, $938 < R_1 < 1066$

CHAPTER 9

9.1 $u_v/V \approx \pm 0.0034$

9.3 $u_F \approx \pm 49.9$ N

9.4 a) $u_R \approx \pm 262\Omega$

9.5 b) $u_C \approx \pm 0.0008 \ \mu$f

9.8 $N \approx 53$

CHAPTER 11

11.1 $d \approx 1.18708$ in.

11.3 a) $L \approx 1.18698$ in.

11.5 b) $F \approx 9.6$

11.6 $F \approx 8.6$

11.7 $F \approx 7.1$

11.10 $F \approx 54.3$

11.12 $d_{75} \approx 0.07199$ in.

11.15 $d \approx 1.76170$ in.

CHAPTER 12

12.2 a) $\sigma = 7200$ psi
    b) $\sigma = 2400$ psi

12.5 $F = 1.95$

12.6 $e_o = 40.76$ mV d.c.

12.7 Factor $= 1.2$

12.8 $\sigma_a = 6354 \times 10^4$ Pa

12.11 a) 6.2%
    b) 3.6%

12.15 a) 50.23 MPa

12.17 Max pwr. $= 53.8$ kW, Av. pwr. $= 44.2$ kW

CHAPTER 13

13.1 $K = 58,100$ lbf/in., $u_K/K \approx \pm 3.11\%$

CHAPTER 14

14.7 $h = 65.1$ cm

14.10 $P \approx 16.65$ Pa (gage), 117.97 kPa (abs.)

14.16 b) $M = 2.56$

14.18 a) $M \approx 18$

14.22 a) $P \approx 7.3 \times 10^7$ Pa

14.24 a) $P \approx 199$ MPa

14.27 $f_{40}/f_{10} = 1.05$

14.28 $f \approx 306$ Hz

14.29 $f \approx 3408$ Hz

CHAPTER 15

15.1 $R_D \approx 7.46 \times 10^{+5}$

15.7 $\Delta P \approx -228$ lbf/ft^2

15.10 $\Delta P \approx 1.136$ MPa

15.12 $Q \approx 1660$ gal/half hour

15.15 $W \approx 6.65$ kg/s

15.17 $KY = 0.61$

15.20 $V \approx 1.085$ m/s

15.22 a) $V \approx 322$ km/hr

15.24 $r \approx 0.763(D/2)$ for $n = 10$

CHAPTER 16

16.1 $T = -40$

16.4 $R = 55.17\ \Omega$, $\Delta R \approx 0.33\ \Omega/C$

16.14 For -4.334 mV, $T = -213.6$ deg. F

16.15 For $+3.250$ mV, $T = 205$ deg. F

16.20 $\tau \approx 10$ s

16.21 $T \approx 179°C$ after 3 s

16.24 $T_{max} \approx 276$ deg. F or C

CHAPTER 17

17.2   a) $s_0 = 0.0036$ mm   b) $a_0 = 4.06$ g

17.3 $s_0 = 0.0002$ mm

17.5 $M = 0.544$ gr, $k = 13.4$ MN/m

17.6

L, cm	f, Hz
10	676
15	300
20	169
25	108

17.10 $f = 33.6$ Hz

CHAPTER 18

18.2   5 compressors

18.3   a) $P = 20$ N/m^2
       b) 96.8% reduction

18.5   Loudness $= 50$ sones

18.8 $SPL_{7.5} = 91.5$ dB

index

Social Security Tax–2015

Category	Rate	Dollar Limit
OASDI	6.2%	$118,500
Medicare*	1.45%	First $200,000 of wages ($250,000 for joint returns)
	2.35%	Wages greater than $200,000 ($250,000 for joint returns)

*Only the employee is required to pay the additional Medicare tax on wages above $200,000 ($250,000 for joint returns). The employer pays Medicare tax of 1.45% on all wages.

Self-Employment Tax–2015

Category	Rate	Dollar Limit
OASDI	12.4%	$118,500
Medicare	2.90%	First $200,000 of self-employment income ($250,000 combined self-employment income for joint returns)
	3.80%	Self-employment income greater than $200,000 ($250,000 for joint returns)

Alternative Minimum Tax–2015

If AMTI minus the exemption amount is:		The tax is:	
Over—	But Not Over—		Of the Amount Over—
$0	$185,400*	26%	$0
$185,400*		$48,204* + 28%	$185,400

*$92,700 and $24,102 for married taxpayers filing separately.

AMT exemption amounts (before phase-outs and other adjustments):

Unmarried individuals (other than surviving spouses and heads of households)	$53,600
Married individuals filing joint returns and surviving spouses	83,400
Married individuals filing separate returns	41,700

STANDARD DEDUCTION

Filing Status

Married individuals filing joint returns and surviving spouses	$12,600
Heads of households	9,250
Unmarried individuals (other than surviving spouses and heads of households)	6,300
Married individuals filing separate returns	6,300
Additional standard deduction for the aged and the blind	
Individual who is married and surviving spouses	1,250*
Individual who is unmarried and not a surviving spouse	1,550*
Taxpayer claimed as dependent on another taxpayer's return: Greater of (1) earned income plus $350, or (2) $1,050.	

*These amounts are $2,500 and $3,100, respectively, for a taxpayer who is both aged and blind.

PERSONAL AND DEPENDENCY EXEMPTION AND PHASE-OUTS

Personal and dependency exemption	$ 4,000

Phase-outs for high income taxpayers:
Personal and dependency exemptions are reduced by 2% for each $2,500 increment (or part of increment) for AGI above the threshold amount.
Itemized deductions are reduced by 3% for each dollar of AGI above the threshold amounts (taxpayers cannot lose more than 80% of their allowable itemized deductions).
For both provisions, the AGI threshold amounts are:

Married individuals filing joint returns and surviving spouses	$309,900
Heads of households	284,050
Unmarried individuals (other than surviving spouses and heads of households)	258,250
Married individuals filing separate returns	154,950

PRENTICE HALL'S FEDERAL TAXATION

2016

INDIVIDUALS

EDITORS

TIMOTHY J. RUPERT
Northeastern University

THOMAS R. POPE
University of Kentucky

KENNETH E. ANDERSON
University of Tennessee

CONTRIBUTING AUTHORS

D. DALE BANDY
University of Central Florida

N. ALLEN FORD
University of Kansas

ROBERT L. GARDNER
Brigham Young University

LEANN LUNA
University of Tennessee

CHARLENE HENDERSON
Mississippi State University

MICHAEL S. SCHADEWALD
University of Wisconsin—Milwaukee

PEARSON

Boston   Columbus   Indianapolis   New York   San Francisco   Hoboken
Amsterdam   Cape Town   Dubai   London   Madrid   Milan   Munich   Paris   Montreal   Toronto
Delhi   Mexico City   São Paulo   Sydney   Hong Kong   Seoul   Singapore   Taipei   Tokyo

Vice President, Business Publishing: Donna Battista
Senior Acquisitions Editor: Lacey Vitetta
Editorial Assistant: Christine Donovan
Vice President, Product Marketing: Maggie Moylan
Director of Marketing, Digital Services and Products: Jeanette Koskinas
Senior Product Marketing Manager: Alison Haskins
Executive Field Marketing Manager: Lori DeShazo
Senior Strategic Marketing Manager: Erin Gardner
Team Lead, Program Management: Ashley Santora
Program Manager: Mary Kate Murray
Team Lead, Project Management: Jeff Holcomb
Project Managers: Alison Kalil and Melissa Pellerano
Operations Specialist: Carol Melville
Creative Director: Blair Brown
Art Director: Jon Boylan
Vice President, Director of Digital Strategy and Assessment: Paul Gentile
Manager of Learning Applications: Paul DeLuca
Digital Editor: Sarah Peterson
Director, Digital Studio: Sacha Laustsen
Digital Studio Manager: Diane Lombardo
Product Manager: James Bateman
Digital Content Team Lead: Noel Lotz
Digital Content Project Lead: Martha LaChance
Full-Service Project Management, Composition, and Interior Design:
 Integra Software Services
Cover Designer: Jon Boylan
Cover Art: Cristina Ciochina/Shutterstock
Printer/Binder: Courier Kendallville
Cover Printer: Courier Kendallville

Credits: Copyright © 2010. American Institute of Certified Public Accountants, Inc.
All rights reserved. Used or adapted with permission.
Photo credits: chapter openers dgrilla/Fotolia, Rabbit75_fot/Fotolia

PEARSON

10 9 8 7 6 5 4 3 2 1
ISBN-10:   0-13-410590-7
ISBN-13: 978-0-13-410590-1

CONTENTS

ABOUT THE EDITORS

TIMOTHY J. RUPERT

Timothy J. Rupert is a Professor and the Golemme Administrative Chair at the D'Amore-McKim School of Business at Northeastern University. He received his B.S. in Accounting and his Master of Taxation from the University of Akron. He also earned his Ph.D. from Penn State University. Professor Rupert's research has been published in such journals as *The Accounting Review, The Journal of the American Taxation Association, Behavioral Research in Accounting, Advances in Taxation, Applied Cognitive Psychology, Advances in Accounting Education*, and *Journal of Accounting Education*. He currently is the co-editor of *Advances in Accounting Education*. In 2010, he received the Outstanding Educator Award from the Massachusetts Society of CPAs. He also has received the University's Excellence in Teaching Award and the D'Amore-McKim School's Best Teacher of the Year award multiple times. He is active in the American Accounting Association and the American Taxation Association (ATA) and has served as president, vice president, and secretary of the ATA.

THOMAS R. POPE

Thomas R. Pope is the Ernst & Young Professor of Accounting at the University of Kentucky. He received a B.S. from the University of Louisville and an M.S. and D.B.A. in business administration from the University of Kentucky. He teaches international taxation, partnership and S corporation taxation, tax research and policy, and introductory taxation and has won outstanding teaching awards at the University, College, and School of Accountancy levels. He has published articles in *The Accounting Review*, the *Tax Adviser, Taxes, Tax Notes*, and a number of other journals. Professor Pope's extensive professional experience includes eight years with Big Four accounting firms. Five of those years were with Ernst & Whinney (now part of Ernst & Young), including two years with their National Tax Department in Washington, D.C. He subsequently held the position of Senior Manager in charge of the Tax Department in Lexington, Kentucky. Professor Pope also has been a leader and speaker at professional tax conferences all over the United States and is active as a tax consultant.

KENNETH E. ANDERSON

Kenneth E. Anderson is the Pugh CPAs Professor of Accounting at the University of Tennessee. He earned a B.B.A. from the University of Wisconsin–Milwaukee and subsequently attained the level of tax manager with Arthur Young (now part of Ernst & Young). He then earned a Ph.D. from Indiana University. He teaches corporate taxation, partnership taxation, and tax strategy. Professor Anderson also is the Director of the Master of Accountancy Program. He has published articles in *The Accounting Review, The Journal of the American Taxation Association, Advances in Taxation*, the *Journal of Accountancy*, the *Journal of Financial Service Professionals*, and a number of other journals.

ABOUT THE AUTHORS

D. Dale Bandy is the Professor Emeritus in the School of Accounting at the University of Central Florida. He received a B.S. from the University of Tulsa, an M.B.A. from the University of Arkansas, and a Ph.D. from the University of Texas at Austin. He helped to establish the Master of Science in Taxation programs at the University of Central Florida and California State University, Fullerton, where he previously taught. In 1985, he was selected by the California Society of Certified Public Accountants as the Accounting Educator of the year. Professor Bandy has published 8 books and more than 30 articles in accounting and taxation. His articles have appeared in the *Journal of Taxation*, the *Journal of Accountancy, Advances in Taxation*, the *Tax Adviser, The CPA Journal, Management Accounting* and a number of other journals.

N. Allen Ford is the Larry D. Homer/KPMG Peat Marwick Distinguished Teaching Professor of Professional Accounting at the University of Kansas. He received an undergraduate degree from Centenary College in Shreveport, Louisiana, and both the M.B.A. and Ph.D. in Business from the University of Arkansas. He has published over 40 articles related to taxation, financial accounting, and accounting education in journals such as *The Accounting Review, The Journal of the American Taxation Association,* and *The Journal of Taxation.* He served as president of the American Taxation Association in 1979–80. Professor Ford has received numerous teaching awards, at the college and university levels. In 1993, he received the Byron T. Shutz Award for Distinguished Teaching in Economics and Business. In 1996 he received the Ray M. Sommerfeld Outstanding Tax Educator Award, which is jointly sponsored by the American Taxation Association and Ernst & Young and in 1998 he received the Kansas Society of CPAs Outstanding Education Award.

Robert L. Gardner is the Robert J. Smith Professor of Accounting in the School of Accountancy at Brigham Young University (BYU). He received a B.S. and M.B.A. from the University of Utah and a Ph.D. from the University of Texas at Austin. He has authored or coauthored two books and over 25 articles in journals such as *The Tax Advisor, Journal of Corporate Taxation, Journal of Real Estate Taxation, Journal of Accounting Education, Journal of Taxation of S Corporations, and the International Tax Journal.* Professor Gardner has received several teaching awards. In 2001, he received the Outstanding Faculty Award in the Marriott School of Management at BYU. He has served on the Board of Trustees of the American Taxation Association and served as President of the ATA in 1999–2000.

LeAnn Luna is an Associate Professor of Accounting at the University of Tennessee. She is a C.P.A. and holds an undergraduate degree from Southern Methodist University, a M.T. from the University of Denver College of Law, and a Ph.D. from the University of Tennessee. She has taught introductory taxation, corporate and partnership taxation, tax research, and professional standards. Professor Luna also holds a joint appointment with the Center for Business and Economic Research at the University of Tennessee, where she interacts frequently with state policymakers on a variety of policy related issues. She has published articles in the *Journal of Accounting and Economics,* the *National Tax Journal, The Journal of the American Taxation Association, Tax Adviser, State Tax Notes,* and a number of other journals.

Charlene Henderson is a member of the faculty in the Adkerson School of Accountancy at Mississippi State University. She earned her undergraduate and graduate degrees in accounting at Mississippi State University. After working in public and private accounting, she completed the doctoral program at Arizona State University. Her teaching and research interests include both tax and financial accounting. Her research has appeared in several journals, including *Journal of the American Taxation Association, Journal of Accounting Auditing and Finance,* and *Journal of Business Finance and Accounting.*

Michael S. Schadewald, Ph.D., CPA, is on the faculty of the University of Wisconsin-Milwaukee where he teaches graduate and undergraduate courses in business taxation. A graduate of the University of Minnesota, Professor Schadewald is a co-author of several books on multistate and international taxation and has published more than 40 articles in academic and professional journals, including *The Accounting Review, Journal of Accounting Research, Contemporary Accounting Research, The Journal of the American Taxation Association, CPA Journal, Journal of Taxation,* and *The Tax Adviser*. Professor Schadewald also has served on the editorial boards of *The Journal of the American Taxation Association, Journal of State Taxation, International Tax Journal, The International Journal of Accounting, Issues in Accounting Education,* and *Journal of Accounting Education*.

PREFACE

Why is the Rupert/Pope/Anderson series the best choice for you and your students?

The Rupert/Pope/Anderson 2016 Series in Federal Taxation is appropriate for use in any first course in federal taxation, and comes in a choice of three volumes:

Federal Taxation 2016: Individuals
Federal Taxation 2016: Corporations, Partnerships, Estates & Trusts (the companion book to *Individuals*)
Federal Taxation 2016: Comprehensive (14 chapters from *Individuals* and 15 chapters from *Corporations*)

** For a customized edition of any of the chapters for these texts, contact your Pearson representative and they can create a custom text for you.

- The *Individuals* volume covers *all* entities, although the treatment is often briefer than in the *Corporations* and *Comprehensive* volumes. The *Individuals* volume, therefore, is appropriate for colleges and universities that require only one semester of taxation as well as those that require more than one semester of taxation. Further, this volume adapts the suggestions of the Model Tax Curriculum as promulgated by the American Institute of Certified Public Accountants.

- The *Corporations, Partnerships, Estates & Trusts* and *Comprehensive* volumes contain three comprehensive tax return problems whose data change with each edition, thereby keeping the problems fresh. Problem C:3-66 contains the comprehensive corporate tax return, Problem C:9-58 contains the comprehensive partnership tax return, and Problem C:11-64 contains the comprehensive S corporation tax return, which is based on the same facts as Problem C:9-58 so that students can compare the returns for these two entities.

- The *Corporations, Partnerships, Estates & Trusts* and *Comprehensive* volumes contain sections called Financial Statement Implications, which discuss the implications of Accounting Standards Codification (ASC) 740. The main discussion of accounting for income taxes appears in Chapter C:3. The financial statement implications of other transactions appear in Chapters C:5, C:7, C:8, and C:16 (*Corporations* volume only).

What's New to this Edition?

INDIVIDUALS

- Complete updating of significant court cases and IRS rulings and procedures during 2014 and early 2015.
- Complete updating for the Tax Increase Prevention Act of 2014.
- Discussion of the expiration or reduction of some deductions and credits in 2015.
- All tax rate schedules have been updated to reflect the rates and inflation adjustments for 2015.
- Whenever new updates become available, they will be accessible via MyAccountingLab.

CORPORATIONS

- The comprehensive corporate tax return, Problem C:3-66, has all new numbers for the 2014 forms.
- The comprehensive partnership tax return, Problem C:9-58, has all new numbers for the 2014 forms.
- The comprehensive S corporation tax return, Problem C:11-64, has all new numbers for the 2014 forms.
- Changes affecting 2015 tax law have been incorporated into the text where appropriate.
- All tax rate schedules have been updated to reflect the rates and inflation adjustments for 2015.
- Whenever new updates become available, they will be accessible via MyAccountingLab.

MyAccountingLab

MyAccountingLab is an online homework, tutorial, and assessment program designed to work with *Prentice Hall's Federal Taxation 2016* to engage students and improve results. MyAccountingLab's homework and practice questions are correlated to the textbook, they regenerate algorithmically to give students unlimited opportunity for practice and mastery, and they offer helpful feedback when students enter incorrect answers. Combining resources that illuminate content with accessible self-assessment, MyAccountingLab with eText provides students with a complete digital learning experience–all in one place. To register, go to http://www.pearsonmylabandmastering.com.

For Instructors

MyAccountingLab provides instructors with a rich and flexible set of course materials, along with course-management tools that make it easy to deliver all or a portion of your course online.

- **Powerful Homework and Test Manager**   Create, import, and manage online homework and media assignments, quizzes, and tests. Create assignments from online questions directly correlated to this and other textbooks. Homework questions include "Help Me Solve This" guided solutions to help students understand and master concepts. You can choose from a wide range of assignment options, including time limits, proctoring, and maximum number of attempts allowed. In addition, you can create your own questions—or copy and edit ours—to customize your students' learning path.
- **Comprehensive Gradebook Tracking**   MyAccountingLab's online gradebook automatically tracks your students' results on tests, homework, and tutorials and gives you control over managing results and calculating grades. All MyAccountingLab grades can be exported to a spreadsheet program, such as Microsoft® Excel. The MyAccountingLab Gradebook provides a number of student data views and gives you the flexibility to weight assignments, select which attempts to include when calculating scores, and omit or delete results for individual assignments.
- **Department-Wide Solutions**   Get help managing multiple sections and working with Teaching Assistants using MyAccountingLab Coordinator Courses. After your MyAccountingLab course is set up, it can be copied to create sections or "member courses." Changes to the Coordinator Course flow down to all members, so changes only need to be made once.

We will add the most current tax information to MyAccountingLab as it becomes available.

For Students

MyAccountingLab provides students with a personalized interactive learning environment, where they can learn at their own pace and measure their progress.

- **Interactive Tutorial Exercises**   MyAccountingLab's homework and practice questions are correlated to the textbook, and "similar to" versions regenerate algorithmically to give students unlimited opportunity for practice and mastery. Questions offer helpful feedback when students enter incorrect answers, and they include "Help Me Solve This" guided solutions as well as other learning aids for extra help when students need it.
- **Study Plan for Self-Paced Learning**   MyAccountingLab's study plan helps students monitor their own progress, letting them see at a glance exactly which topics they need to practice. MyAccountingLab generates a personalized study plan for each student based on his or her test results, and the study plan links directly to interactive, tutorial exercises for topics the student hasn't yet mastered. Students can regenerate these exercises with new values for unlimited practice, and the exercises include guided solutions and multimedia learning aids to give students the extra help they need.

Strong Pedagogical Aids

- Appropriate blend of technical content of the tax law with a high level of readability for students.
- Focused on enabling students to apply tax principles within the chapter to real-life situations.

Real-World Example

These comments relate the text material to events, cases, and statistics occurring in the tax and business environment. The statistical data presented in some of these comments are taken from the IRS's Statistics of Income at www.irs.gov.

Book-to-Tax Accounting Comparison

These comments compare the tax discussion in the text to the accounting and/or financial statement treatment of this material. Also, the last section of Chapter C:3 discusses the financial statement implications of federal income taxes.

What Would You Do in This Situation?

Unique to the Rupert/Pope/Anderson series, these boxes place students in a decision-making role. The boxes include many *controversies* that are as yet unresolved or are currently being considered by the courts. These boxes make extensive use of **Ethical Material** as they represent choices that may put the practitioner at odds with the client.

Stop & Think

These "speed bumps" encourage students to pause and apply what they have just learned. Solutions for each issue are provided in the box.

Ethical Point

These comments provide the ethical implications of material discussed in the adjoining text. Apply what they have just learned.

Tax Strategy Tip

These comments suggest tax planning ideas related to material in the adjoining text.

Additional Comment

These comments provide supplemental information pertaining to the adjacent text.

Program Components

Materials for the instructor may be accessed at the Instructor's Resource Center (IRC) online, located at **www.pearsonhighered.com/phtax** or within the Instructor Resource section of MyAccountingLab. You may contact your Pearson representative for assistance with the registration process.

- *TaxACT 2014 Software:* Available via online purchase with Individuals, Corporations, and Comprehensive Texts. This user-friendly tax preparation program includes more than 80 tax forms, schedules, and worksheets. TaxACT calculates returns and alerts the user to possible errors or entries. Consists of forms 1040, 1065, 1120, and 1120S.
- *Instructor's Resource Manual:* Contains sample syllabi, instructor outlines, and information regarding problem areas for students. It also contains solutions to the tax form/tax return preparation problems.
- *Solutions Manual:* Contains solutions to discussion questions, problems, and comprehensive and tax strategy problems. It also contains all solutions to the case study problems, research problems, and "What Would You Do in This Situation?" boxes.
- *Test Bank:* Offers a wealth of true/false, multiple-choice, and calculative problems. A computerized program is available to adopters.
- *PowerPoint Slides:* Consists of chapter outlines, featuring images, examples, and problems throughout, to aid in class lectures.
- *Image Library:* Figures, tables, and tax forms featured in the book are provided as individual files for the convenience of instructors and students.
- *Multi-State Tax Chapter:* An entire chapter, complete with problems (and solutions) dedicated to multi-state tax practices.

Acknowledgments

Our policy is to provide annual editions and to prepare timely updated supplements when major tax revisions occur. We are most appreciative of the suggestions made by outside reviewers because these extensive review procedures have been valuable to the authors and editors during the revision process.

We also are grateful to the various graduate assistants, doctoral students, and colleagues who have reviewed the text and supplementary materials and checked solutions to maintain a high level of technical accuracy. In particular, we would like to acknowledge the following colleagues who assisted in the preparation of supplemental materials for this text:

Ann Burstein Cohen	SUNY at Buffalo
Craig J. Langstraat	University of Memphis
Kate Demarest	Carroll Community College
Allison McLeod	University of North Texas
Mitchell Franklin	LeMoyne College
Anthony Masino	East Tennessee State University

In addition, we want to thank Myron S. Scholes, Mark A. Wolfson, Merle M. Erickson, M. L. Hanlon, Edward L. Maydew, and Terry J. Shevlin for allowing us to use the model discussed in their text, *Taxes and Business Strategy: A Planning Approach*, as the basis for material in Chapter I:18.

Please send any comments to Kenneth E. Anderson or Timothy J. Rupert.

CHAPTER

1

AN INTRODUCTION TO TAXATION

LEARNING OBJECTIVES

After studying this chapter, you should be able to

1 ▶ Discuss the history of taxation in the United States

2 ▶ Describe the three types of tax rate structures

3 ▶ Describe the various types of taxes

4 ▶ Discuss the criteria for a "good" tax structure, the objectives of the federal income tax law, and recent tax reform proposals

5 ▶ Describe the tax entities in the federal income tax system

6 ▶ Identify the various tax law sources and understand their implications for tax practice

7 ▶ Describe the legislative process for the enactment of the tax law

8 ▶ Describe the administrative procedures under the tax law

9 ▶ Describe the components of a tax practice

10 ▶ Understand the importance of computer applications in taxation

KEY POINT

In many situations, the use of the tax laws to influence human behavior is deliberate. As will be seen later in this chapter, tax laws are often used to achieve social and economic objectives.

Federal income taxes have a significant effect on business, investor, and personal decisions in the United States. Because tax rates can be as high as 35% on corporations and over 40% on individuals, virtually every transaction is impacted by income taxes. The following examples illustrate the impact of the tax law on various decisions in our society:

▶ Because of the deductibility of home mortgage interest and real estate taxes, an individual may decide to purchase a home rather than to continue to rent an apartment.

▶ An investor may decide to delay selling some stock because of the significant taxes that may result from the sale.

▶ A corporation may get a larger tax deduction if it leases property rather than purchasing the property.

The purpose of this text is to provide an introduction to the study of federal income taxation. However, before discussing the specifics of the U.S. federal income tax law, it is helpful to have a broad conceptual understanding of the taxation process. This chapter provides an overview of the following topics:

▶ Historical developments of the federal tax system

▶ Types of taxes levied and structural considerations

▶ Objectives of the tax law, including a discussion of recent tax reform proposals

▶ Taxpaying entities in the federal income tax system

▶ Tax law sources and the legislative process

▶ Internal Revenue Service (IRS) collection, examination, and appeals processes

▶ The nature of tax practice, including computer applications and tax research

HISTORY OF TAXATION IN THE UNITED STATES

OBJECTIVE 1

Discuss the history of taxation in the United States

HISTORICAL NOTE

The reinstatement of the income tax in 1894 was the subject of heated political controversy. In general, the representatives in Congress from the agricultural South and West favored the income tax in lieu of customs duties. Representatives from the industrial eastern states were against the income tax and favored protective tariff legislation.

EARLY PERIODS

The federal income tax is the dominant form of taxation in the United States. In addition, most states and some cities and counties also impose an income tax. Both corporations and individuals are subject to such taxes.

Prior to 1913 (the date of enactment of the modern-day federal income tax), the federal government relied predominantly on customs duties and excise taxes to finance its operations. The first federal income tax on individuals was enacted in 1861 to finance the Civil War but was repealed after the war. The federal income tax was reinstated in 1894, however, that tax was challenged in the courts because the U.S. Constitution required that an income tax be apportioned among the states in proportion to their populations. This type of tax system, which would be both impractical and difficult to administer, would mean that different tax rates would apply to individual taxpayers depending on their states of residence.

In 1895, the Supreme Court ruled that the tax was in violation of the U.S. Constitution.[1] Therefore, it was necessary to amend the U.S. Constitution to permit the passage of a federal income tax law. This was accomplished by the Sixteenth Amendment, which was ratified in 1913. The Sixteenth Amendment, while being an extraordinarily important amendment, consists of one sentence.

Sixteenth Amendment to the Constitution of the United States

The Congress shall have the power to lay and collect taxes on incomes, from whatever source derived, without apportionment among the several States, and without regard to any census or enumeration.

---

[1] *Pollock v. Farmers' Loan & Trust Co.*, 3 AFTR 2602 (USSC, 1895). Note, however, that a federal income tax on corporations that was enacted in 1909 was held to be constitutional because it was treated as an excise tax. See *Flint v. Stone Tracy Co.*, 3 AFTR 2834 (USSC, 1911).

REVENUE ACTS FROM 1913 TO THE PRESENT

The Revenue Act of 1913 imposed a flat 1% tax (with no exemptions) on a corporation's net income. The rate varied from 1% to 6% for individuals, depending on the individual's income level. However, very few individuals paid federal income taxes because a $3,000 personal exemption ($4,000 for married individuals) was permitted as an offset to taxable income. These amounts were greater than the incomes of most individuals in 1913.

Various amendments to the original law were passed between 1913 and 1939 as separate revenue acts. For example, a deduction for dependency exemptions was provided in 1917. In 1939, the separate revenue acts were codified into the Internal Revenue Code of 1939. A similar codification was accomplished in 1954. The 1954 codification, which was known as the Internal Revenue Code of 1954, included the elimination of many "deadwood" provisions, a rearrangement and clarification of numerous code sections, and the addition of major tax law changes. Whenever changes to the Internal Revenue Code (IRC) are made, the old language is deleted and the new language added. Thus, the statutes are organized as a single document, and a tax advisor does not have to read through the applicable parts of all previous tax bills to find the most current law. In 1986, major changes were made to the tax law, and the basic tax law was redesignated as the Internal Revenue Code of 1986.

The federal income tax became a "mass tax" on individuals during the early 1940s. This change was deemed necessary to finance the revenue needs of the federal government during World War II. In 1939, less than 6% of the U.S. population was subject to the federal income tax; by 1945, 74% of the population was taxed.[2] To accommodate the broadened tax base and to avoid significant tax collection problems, Congress enacted pay-as-you-go withholding in 1943.

A major characteristic of the federal income tax since its inception to today is the manner in which the tax law is changed or modified. The federal income tax is changed on an **incremental** basis rather than a complete revision basis. Under so-called incrementalism, when a change in the tax law is deemed necessary by Congress, the entire law is not changed, but specific provisions of the tax law are added, changed, or deleted on an incremental basis. Thus, the federal income tax has been referred to as a "quiltwork" of tax laws, referring to the patchwork nature of the law. Without question, one of the principal reasons for the complexity of the federal income tax today is the incremental nature of tax legislation.

REVENUE SOURCES

As mentioned earlier, the largest source of federal revenues is individual income taxes. Other major revenue sources include Social Security (FICA) taxes and corporate income taxes (see Table I:1-1). Two notable trends from Table I:1-1 are (1) the gradual increase in social insurance taxes from 1960 to 2014 and (2) the gradual decrease in corporate income taxes for the same period. Individual income taxes have remained fairly stable during the past 50 years.

▼ TABLE I:1-1
Breakdown of Federal Revenues

	1960	1975	1994	2014
Individual income taxes	44%	45%	43%	46%
Social insurance taxes and contribution	16	32	37	34
Corporation income taxes	23	15	11	11
Other	17	8	9	9
Total	100%	100%	100%	100%

Source: Council of Economic Advisers, *Economic Indicators* (Washington, DC: U.S. Government Printing Office, 1967, 1977, 2014).

[2] Richard Goode, *The Individual Income Tax* (Washington, DC: The Brookings Institution, 1964), pp. 2–4.

TYPES OF TAX RATE STRUCTURES

OBJECTIVE 2

Describe the three types of tax rate structures

THE STRUCTURE OF INDIVIDUAL INCOME TAX RATES

Virtually all tax structures are comprised of two basic parts: the **tax base** and the **tax rate**. The tax base is the amount to which the tax rate is applied to determine the tax due. For example, an individual's tax base for the federal income tax is *taxable income,* as defined and determined by the income tax law. Similarly, the tax base for the property tax is generally the fair market value of property subject to the tax. The tax rate is merely the percentage rate applied to the tax base.

Tax rates may be progressive, proportional, or regressive. A **progressive rate** structure is one where the rate of tax increases as the tax base increases. The most notable tax that incorporates a progressive rate structure is the federal income tax. Thus, as a taxpayer's taxable income increases, a progressively higher rate of tax is applied. For 2015, the federal income tax rates for individuals begin at 10% and increase to 15%, 25%, 28%, 33%, 35%, and 39.6% as a taxpayer's taxable income increases.[3] Examples I:1-1 and I:1-2 show how the progressive rate structure of the federal income tax operates.

ADDITIONAL COMMENT

In the 1950s, the top marginal tax rate for individual taxpayers reached 92%. This astonishingly high rate only applied to taxpayers with very high taxable incomes but still is an extremely confiscatory tax rate.

EXAMPLE I:1-1 ▶

LEGISLATIVE BACKGROUND

Beginning with tax year 2013, the top rate for high-income individual taxpayers was increased to 39.6%. The top rate for 2012 was 35%.

Alice, who is single, has $30,000 taxable income in 2015. Her federal income taxes for the year are $4,039, computed as follows: the first $9,225 of taxable income is taxed at 10% and the remaining $20,775 at 15%. (For tax rates, see the inside front cover.)

Allen, who also is single, has taxable income of $60,000. A 10% rate applies to the first $9,225 of taxable income, 15% on the next $28,225, and a 25% rate applies to the taxable income over $37,450. Thus, Allen's total tax is $10,794 [(0.10 × $9,225) + (0.15 × $28,225) + (0.25 × $22,550)].

If Allen's taxable income is $120,000, a 28% rate applies to $29,250 of his taxable income ($120,000 − $90,750) because the 28% rate applies to taxable income above $90,750 for a single individual and his total tax for the year is $26,671. Thus, the tax rates are progressive because the rate of tax increases as a taxpayer's taxable income increases. ◀

Notice in Example I:1-1 that taxable income has doubled in size in the three cases, but the income taxes have more than doubled (i.e., $4,039 to $10,794 to $26,671). This demonstrates how a progressive rate structure operates.

EXAMPLE I:1-2 ▶

Assume the same facts as in Example I:1-1 except that Alice has taxable income of $200,000. Of Alice's taxable income, $10,700 ($200,000 − $189,300) is subject to the 33% rate. Alternatively, if Allen has taxable income of $425,000, $11,800 ($425,000 − $413,200) is subject to the top marginal rate of 39.6%. ◀

A **proportional tax** rate, sometimes called a **flat tax**, is one where the rate of tax is the same for all taxpayers, regardless of the level of their tax base. This type of tax rate is generally used for real estate taxes, state and local sales taxes, personal property taxes, customs duties, and excise taxes. A flat tax has been the subject of considerable discussion over the past twenty years and promises to be a controversial topic as the debate on federal income tax reform continues into the future.

EXAMPLE I:1-3 ▶

Assume the same facts as in Example I:1-1, except that a 17% tax rate applies to all amounts of taxable income. Based on the assumed flat tax rate structure, Alice's federal income tax is $5,100 on $30,000 of taxable income; Allen's tax is $10,200 on $60,000 of taxable income and $20,400 on $120,000 of taxable income. The tax rate is proportional because the 17% rate applies to both taxpayers without regard to their income level. As you can see, a proportional tax rate results in substantially lower taxes for higher income taxpayers.[4] ◀

---

[3] See the inside front cover for the 2015 tax rates and Chapter I:2 for a discussion of the computation procedures. 2014 rate schedules and tax tables are located immediately before Appendix A.

[4] This example assumes the same tax base (taxable income) for the flat tax as with the current federal tax. Most flat tax proposals allow only a few deductions and, therefore, would generate higher taxes than in the example.

A **regressive tax** rate decreases with an increase in the tax base (e.g., income). Regressive taxes, while not consistent with the fairness of the income tax,[5] are found in the United States. The Social Security (FICA) tax is regressive because a fixed rate of tax of 6.20% for OASDI for both the employer and employee is levied up to a ceiling amount of $118,500 for 2015. So, for example, assume Taxpayer A has income subject to Social Security of $80,000 and Taxpayer B income of $400,000. Taxpayer A's OASDI would be $4,960 ($80,000 × 0.062), Taxpayer B's OASDI would be $7,347 ($118,500 × 0.062). Taxpayer A's average rate of OASDI tax is 6.2% while Taxpayer B's average rate of tax is 1.84% ($7,347/$400,000). The sales tax, which is levied by many states, is also regressive when measured against the income base.

THE STRUCTURE OF CORPORATE TAX RATES

Corporations are separate entities and are subject to income tax. The federal corporate income tax reflects a stair-step pattern of progression that tends to benefit small corporations. The corporate rates, which have not changed for several years, are as follows:[6]

Taxable Income[7]	*Tax*
First $50,000	15% of taxable income
Over $50,000 but not over $75,000	$7,500 + 25% of taxable income over $50,000
Over $75,000 but not over $100,000	$13,750 + 34% of taxable income over $75,000
Over $100,000 but not over $335,000	$22,250 + 39% of taxable income over $100,000
Over $335,000	34% of taxable income
Over $10,000,000 but not over $15,000,000	$3,400,000 + 35% of taxable income over $10,000,000
Over $15,000,000 but not over $18,333,333	$5,150,000 + 38% over $15,000,000
Over $18,333,333	35% of taxable income

MARGINAL, AVERAGE, AND EFFECTIVE TAX RATES FOR TAXPAYERS

A taxpayer's **marginal tax rate** is the tax rate applied to an incremental amount of taxable income that is added to the tax base. The marginal tax rate concept is useful for planning because it measures the tax effect of a proposed transaction.

EXAMPLE I:1-4 ▶ Tania, who is single, is considering the purchase of a personal residence that will provide a $20,000 tax deduction for interest expense and real estate taxes in 2015. Tania's taxable income would be reduced from $120,000 to $100,000 if she purchases the residence. Because a 28% tax rate applies to taxable income from $100,000 to $120,000, Tania's marginal tax rate is 28%. Thus, Tania's tax savings from purchasing the personal residence would be $5,600 (0.28 × $20,000). ◀

While the marginal tax rate measures the tax rate applicable to the next $1 of income or deduction for a taxpayer, there are two other tax rates that are used primarily by tax policymakers: average tax rate and effective tax rate. The **average tax rate** is computed by dividing the total tax liability by the amount of taxable income. This represents the average rate of tax for each dollar of taxable income. For example, a single taxpayer with taxable income of $450,000 in 2015 would incur a total tax liability of $134,569. The taxpayer's marginal tax rate is 39.6%, but his average tax rate is 29.9% ($134,569/$450,000).

---

[5] See the discussion of equity and fairness later in this chapter.
[6] For C corporations with taxable income over $100,000, the lower rates of tax on the first $75,000 of income are gradually phased out by applying a 5-percentage-point surtax on taxable income from $100,000 to $335,000 so that benefits of the favorable rates are eliminated once a corporation's taxable income reaches $335,000. Once taxable income exceeds $335,000

the tax equals 34% of taxable income. A 35% tax rate applies to taxable income in excess of $10 million. For corporations with taxable income in excess of $15 million, a 3 percentage-point-surtax applies to taxable income from $15 million to $18,333,333 to eliminate the lower 34% rate that applies to the first $10 million of taxable income.
[7] Also see the inside back cover for the corporation income tax rates.

ADDITIONAL COMMENT

One method of calculating economic income is to start with adjusted gross income (AGI), add back items of excludible income, such as tax-exempt bond interest, proceeds of life insurance policies, etc., and then deduct certain nondeductible business expenses, such as life insurance premiums, penalties and fines, etc.

The **effective tax rate** is the total tax liability divided by total economic income. **Total economic income** includes all types of economic income that a taxpayer has for the year. Thus, economic income is much broader than taxable income and includes most types of excludible income, such as tax-exempt bond interest, and generally permits business deductions but not personal-type deductions. It should be pointed out that economic income is *not* statutorily defined and experts may disagree on a precise calculation. The basic purpose of calculating the effective tax rate is to provide a broad measure of taxpayers' ability to pay taxes. Accordingly, the effective tax rate mainly is used by tax policymakers to determine the fairness of the income tax system.

EXAMPLE I:1-5 ►

Amelia, who is single, has adjusted gross income of $140,000 and economic income of $175,000 in 2015. The difference is attributable to $35,000 of tax-exempt bond interest. If Amelia has deductions of $30,000, then her taxable income is $110,000, and her total tax is $23,871. Her average tax rate is 21.70% ($23,871 ÷ $110,000). Amelia's effective tax rate is 13.64% ($23,871 ÷ $175,000). Amelia's effective tax rate is considerably lower than her average tax rate because of her substantial amount of tax-exempt income. ◄

 STOP & THINK

Question: Gwen, a single taxpayer, has seen her income climb to $200,000 in the current year. She wants a tax planner to help her reduce her tax liability. In planning for tax clients, tax professionals almost exclusively use the marginal tax rate in their analysis rather than the average tax rate. Why is the marginal tax rate much more important in the tax planning process than the average tax rate?

Solution: Because tax planning is done at the margin. A single taxpayer who has taxable income of $200,000 has a marginal tax rate of 33% (at 2015 rates), but an average tax rate of 24.80%, computed as follows:

Taxable income		$200,000
Tax on first $189,300 of taxable income		$46,075.25
Remaining taxable income	$10,700	
Times: Marginal tax rate	× 0.33	3,531.00
Total tax liability		$ 49,606.25

$$\text{Average tax rate} = \frac{\text{Total tax}}{\text{Taxable income}} = \frac{\$\ 49,606.25}{\$200,000} = 24.80\%$$

If a tax planner could reduce Gwen's taxable income by $10,000, Gwen's tax liability would decrease by $3,333 ($10,000 × 0.33). When the taxpayer wants to know how much she can save through tax planning, the appropriate marginal tax rate yields the answer.

Overall, estimated effective federal income tax rates for individuals have increased slightly during the period 2003–2012,[8] amounting to 12.6% in 2012 as compared with 9.1% in 2003. For the highest 20% of households, the effective individual income tax rate increased to 18.0% in 2012 from 14.4% in 2003. The effective tax rate for individuals in the United States is relatively low compared to most other industrialized countries.

ADDITIONAL COMMENT

In the determination of tax rates, one should consider the incidence of taxation that involves the issue of who really bears the burden of the tax. If a city raises the real property tax but landlords simply raise rents to pass on the higher taxes, the tax burden is shifted to their tenants. The concept has important implications in determining any kind of average or effective tax rate.

DETERMINATION OF TAXABLE INCOME AND TAX DUE

As will be discussed in later chapters, the federal income taxes imposed on all taxpayers (individuals, corporations, estates, and trusts) are based on the determination of taxable income. In general, taxable income is computed as follows:

Total income (income from whatever source derived)	$xxx
Minus: Exclusions (specifically defined items, such as tax-exempt bond interest)	(xx)

---

[8] Congressional Budget Office, *Effective Federal Tax Rates Under Current Law, 2001 to 2014* (Washington, DC:U.S. Government Printing Office, August, 2004), p. 10.

Gross income	$xxx
Minus: Deductions (business expenses and itemized deductions)	(xx)
Exemptions (not applicable for corporations)	(xx)
Taxable income	$xxx
Times: Applicable tax rate	× .xx
Income tax before credits	$xxx
Minus: Tax credits	(xx)
Total tax liability	$xxx
Minus: Prepayments	(xx)
Balance due or refund	$xxx

Each different type of taxpayer (individuals, corporations, etc.) computes taxable income in a slightly different manner, but all use the general framework above. An introductory discussion of the various types of taxpayers is provided later in this chapter. More detailed discussions of individual taxpayers (Chapter I:2) and corporation taxpayers (Chapter I:16) are examined in this *Individuals* book. Corporations, estates, and trusts are further examined in *Prentice Hall's Federal Taxation: Corporations, Partnerships, Estates, and Trusts.*

OTHER TYPES OF TAXES

OBJECTIVE 3

Describe the various types of taxes

STATE AND LOCAL INCOME AND FRANCHISE TAXES

In addition to federal income taxes, many states and local jurisdictions impose income taxes on individuals and businesses. These state and local taxes have gradually increased over the years and currently represent a significant source of revenue for state and local governments but also represent a significant tax burden on taxpayers.

State and local income taxes vary greatly in both form and rates.[9] Only seven states do not impose an individual income tax.[10] In most instances, state income tax rates are mildly progressive and are based on an individual's federal adjusted gross income (AGI), with minor adjustments.[11] For example, a typical adjustment to a state income tax return is interest income on federal government bonds, which is subject to tax on the federal return but generally is not subject to state income taxes. Some states also allow a deduction for federal income taxes in the computation of taxable income for state income tax purposes.

ADDITIONAL COMMENT

States that do not impose a state income tax depend on other taxes to support the government mission, principally sales taxes.

States imposing a state income tax generally require the withholding of state income taxes and have established mandatory estimated tax payment procedures. The due date for filing state income tax returns generally coincides with the due date for the federal income tax returns (e.g., the fifteenth day of the fourth month following the close of the tax year for individuals).

ADDITIONAL COMMENT

State income tax rates for individuals have increased significantly in the past twenty years. Twenty-three states now have marginal tax rates of 6% or higher.

Most states impose a corporate income tax, although in some instances the tax is called a **franchise tax**. Franchise taxes usually are based on a weighted-average formula consisting of net worth, income, and sales.

WEALTH TRANSFER TAXES

U.S. citizens are subject to taxation on certain transfers of property to another person. The tax law provides a unified transfer tax system that imposes a single tax on transfers of property taking place during an individual's lifetime (gifts) and at death (estates). (See the inside back cover of the text for the transfer tax rate schedules.) Formerly, the gift and estate tax laws were separate and distinct. The federal estate tax was initially enacted in 1916. The original gift tax law dates back to 1932. The gift tax was originally imposed to prevent widespread avoidance of the estate tax (e.g., taxpayers could make tax-free gifts of property

---

[9] For a thorough discussion of state and local taxes, see the chapter entitled *Multistate Income Taxation* that accompanies this textbook in electronic form on the Prentice Hall Federal Taxation 2016 Web page at www.prenhall.com/phtax.

[10] These states are Alaska, Florida, Nevada, South Dakota, Texas, Washington,

and Wyoming. New Hampshire has an income tax that is levied only on dividend and interest income and Tennessee's income tax applies only to income from stocks and bonds.

[11] See Chapter I:2 for a discussion of the AGI computation.

before their death). Both the gift and estate taxes are wealth transfer taxes levied on the transfer of property and are based on the fair market value (FMV) of the transferred property on the date of the transfer. Following are brief descriptions of the gift tax and estate tax.

The Federal Gift Tax. The **gift tax** is an excise tax that is imposed on the donor (not the donee) for transfers of property that are considered to be a taxable gift. A gift, generally speaking, is a transfer made gratuitously and with donative intent. However, the gift tax law has expanded the definition to include transfers that are not supported by full and adequate consideration.[12] To arrive at the amount of taxable gifts for the current year, a $14,000 (2015) annual exclusion is allowed per donee.[13] In addition, an unlimited marital deduction is allowed for transfers between spouses.[14] The formula for computing the gift tax is as follows:

FMV of all gifts made in the current year			$x,xxx
Minus:	Annual donee exclusions ($14,000 per donee)	$xx	
	Marital deduction for gifts to spouse	xx	
	Charitable contribution deduction	xx	(xxx)
Plus:	Taxable gifts for all prior years		xxx
Cumulative taxable gifts (tax base)			$x,xxx
Times:	Unified transfer tax rates		× .xx
Tentative tax on gift tax base			$ xxx
Minus:	Unified transfer taxes paid in prior years		(xx)
	Unified credit		(xx)
Unified transfer tax (gift tax) due in the current year			$ xx

Note that the gift tax is cumulative over the taxpayer's lifetime (i.e., the tax calculation for the current year includes the taxable gifts made in prior years). The detailed tax rules relating to the gift tax are covered in Chapter C: 12 in both *Prentice Hall's Federal Taxation: Corporations, Partnerships, Estates, and Trusts* and the *Comprehensive* volume. The following general concepts and rules for the federal gift tax are presented as background material for other chapters of this text dealing with individual taxpayers:

▶ Gifts between spouses are exempted from the gift tax due to the operation of an unlimited marital deduction.

▶ The primary liability for payment of the gift tax is imposed on the **donor**. The donee is contingently liable for payment of the gift tax in the event of nonpayment by the donor.

▶ A donor is permitted a $14,000 annual exclusion for gifts of a present interest to each donee.[15]

▶ Charitable contributions are effectively exempted from the gift tax because an unlimited deduction is allowed.

▶ The tax basis of the property to the donee is generally the donor's cost. It is the lesser of the donor's cost and the property's FMV on the date of the gift if the property is sold by the donee at a loss. (See Chapter I:5 for a discussion of the gift tax basis rules.)

▶ A unified tax credit equivalent to a $5,000,000 deduction (adjusted for inflation, the amount is $5,430,000 for 2015) is available to offset any gift tax on taxable gifts that exceed the $14,000 annual exclusion.[16]

EXAMPLE I:1-6 ▶ Antonio makes the following gifts in the year 2015:

▶ $25,000 cash gift to his wife

▶ $15,000 contribution to the United Way

---

[12] Sec. 2512(b).

[13] Sec. 2503(b). The annual exclusion for gift tax purposes had been $10,000 for many years. However, for 2002–2005, the inflation adjustment increased the exclusion to $11,000, for 2006–2008, the exclusion was increased to $12,000, and for 2009–2012 to $13,000. For 2013 and later years, the current exclusion has been increased to $14,000.

[14] Sec. 2523(a).

[15] A gift of a present interest is an interest that is already in existence and the

donee is currently entitled to receive the income from the property. A gift of a future interest comes into being at some future date (e.g., property is transferred by gift to a trust in which the donee is not entitled to the income from the property until the donor dies) and is not eligible for the $14,000 annual exclusion.

[16] The applicable exclusion amount has been $1,000,000 since 2002. However, beginning in 2011, the exclusion was increased to $5,000,000, adjusted for inflation. For further details, see *Prentice Hall's Federal Taxation:Corporations, Partnerships, Estates and Trusts*, 2016 Edition, Chapters C:12 and C:13.

► Gift of a personal automobile valued at $40,000 to his adult son

► Gift of a personal computer valued at $4,000 to a friend

The $25,000 gift to his wife is not taxed because of a $14,000 annual exclusion and a $11,000 marital deduction. The $15,000 contribution to the United Way is also not taxed because of the unlimited deduction for charitable contributions. The $40,000 gift Antonio made to his son is reduced by the $14,000 annual exclusion to each donee, leaving a $26,000 taxable gift.[17] The $4,000 gift to the friend is not taxed because of the annual exclusion of up to $14,000 in gifts to a donee in a tax year. Thus, total taxable gifts for the current year subject to the unified transfer tax are $26,000. ◄

? STOP & THINK

Question: An important but frequently overlooked aspect of gift taxes is the interaction of gift taxes and income taxes. In many cases, gifts are made *primarily* for income tax purposes. Why would a gift be made for income tax purposes?

Solution: Gifts are frequently made to shift income from one family member to another family member who is in a lower marginal tax bracket. For example, assume Fran and Jan are married, have one 25-year-old son, earn $500,000 per year from their business, and generate $100,000 per year in dividends and interest from a substantial portfolio of stocks and bonds. With such a high level of income, Fran and Jan are in the 39.6% marginal tax bracket. If they make a gift of some of the stocks and bonds to their son, the dividends and interest attributable to the gift are taxed to the son at his marginal tax rate (maybe 10% or 15%). If the son's marginal tax rate is lower than 39.6%, the family unit reduces its overall income taxes.

The Federal Estate Tax. The **federal estate tax** is part of the unified transfer tax system that is based on the total property transfers an individual makes both during his or her lifetime and at death. The basic structure of the estate tax is shown in Example I:1-7.

EXAMPLE I:1-7 ►

Amy dies during the current year. The formula for computing the estate tax on Amy's estate is as follows:

Gross estate (FMV of all property owned by the decedent at the date of death)	$xxx,xxx
Minus: Deductions for funeral and administration expenses, debts of the decedent, charitable contributions, and the marital deduction for property transferred to a spouse	(x,xxx)
Taxable estate	$ x,xxx
Plus: Taxable gifts made after 1976	xx
Tax base	$ x,xxx
Times: Unified transfer tax rate(s)	× .xx
Tentative tax on estate tax base	$ xxx
Minus: Tax credits (e.g., the unified tax credit equivalent to a $5,430,000 deduction in 2015)	(xx)
Gift taxes paid after 1976	(xx)
Unified transfer tax (estate tax) due	$ xx ◄

TYPICAL MISCONCEPTION

It is sometimes thought that the federal estate tax raises significant amounts of revenue, but it has not been a significant revenue producer since World War II. Only 9,400 estate tax returns were filed in 2012 generating approximately $8.5 billion in tax revenues. This amount represents about 0.75% of revenues generated by income taxes on individuals.

The federal estate tax has been on a roller coaster ride the last several years, with many changes and uncertainties. For a complete discussion of these developments, see *Prentice Hall's Federal Taxation: Corporations, Partnerships, Estates and Trusts, 2016 Edition, Chapter C:13.* Beginning January 1, 2013, however, more certainty exists to the estate tax law due to recent changes. The computation of the taxable estate and tax base (see Example I:1-7 above) is much the same as in prior years. However, the highest tax rate for tax years after 2012 has been increased to 40% from 35%. More importantly, the unified credit exclusion amount has been made permanent at $5 million per person and is indexed annually for inflation. For 2015, the unified credit exclusion amount is $5,430,000 ($5,340,000 for 2014). In essence, estates of individuals dying in 2015 generally will not be subject to estate taxes if their tax base is equal to or less

---

[17] This example assumes that the automobile is a gift rather than an obligation of support under state law and also assumes that Antonio's wife does not join with Antonio in electing to treat the gift to the son as having been made by both spouses (a gift-splitting election). In such event, donee exclusions of $28,000 (2 × $14,000) would be available, resulting in a taxable gift of only $12,000.

than $5,430,000. With this large exemption amount, most estates will not be subject to estate taxes.

The estate tax rules are discussed in more detail in Chapter C:13 of *Prentice Hall's Federal Taxation: Corporations, Partnerships, Estates, and Trusts* and in the *Comprehensive* volume. The general rules discussed below are provided as background material for subsequent chapters of this text dealing with individual taxpayers:

► The decedent's property is valued at its FMV on the date of death unless the alternative valuation date (six months after the date of death) is elected. The alternative valuation date may be elected only if the aggregate value of the gross estate decreases during the six-month period following the date of death and the election results in a lower estate tax liability.

► The basis of the property received by the estate and by the decedent's heirs is the property's FMV on the date of death (or the alternate valuation date if it is elected).

► Property transferred to the decedent's spouse is exempt from the estate tax because of the estate tax marital deduction provision.

► The unified credit is $2,117,800, based on an exclusion amount of $5,430,000 and is computed as follows: [$345,800 + 0.40 (5,430,000 − 1,000,000)].

EXAMPLE I:1-8 ► Barry died in 2015, leaving a $8,000,000 gross estate. Of the $8,000,000 gross estate, one-half of the estate was transferred to his wife, administrative and funeral expenses are $30,000, Barry had debts of $200,000, and the remainder of the estate was transferred to his children. The estate tax due is computed as follows:

Gross estate	$8,000,000
Minus: Marital deduction	(4,000,000)
Funeral and administrative expenses	(30,000)
Decedent's debts	(200,000)
Taxable estate	$3,770,000
Plus: Taxable gifts made after 1976	0
Tax base	$3,770,000
Tentative tax on estate tax base	$1,453,800[a]
Minus: Tax credits (unified tax credit—see above or inside back cover for table)	(2,117,800)
Unified transfer tax due	$ —0— ◄

[a]$345,800 + [0.40 × ($3,770,000 − $1,000,000)]

Because of the generous credit and deduction provisions (e.g., the unified tax credit and the unlimited marital deduction), few estates are required to pay estate taxes. As can be seen above, the gross estate of the decedent was $8 million but no estate taxes were due primarily because of the large marital deduction and the unified credit. However, estate taxes rise quickly as is demonstrated below in Example I:1-9.

EXAMPLE I:1-9 ► Assume the same facts for Barry as in Example I:1-8 except that Barry's gross estate is $14,000,000 rather than $8,000,000. The estate tax due is computed as follows:

Gross estate	$14,000,000
Minus: Marital deduction	(7,000,000)
Funeral and administrative expenses	(30,000)
Decedent's debts	(200,000)
Taxable estate	$ 6,770,000
Plus: Taxable gifts made after 1976	0
Tax base	$ 6,770,000
Tentative tax on estate tax base	$ 2,653,800[b]
Minus: Tax credits (unified tax credit)	(2,117,800)
Unified transfer tax due	$ 536,000 ◄

[b]$345,800 + [0.40 × ($6,770,000 − $1,000,000)]

OTHER TYPES OF TAXES

Although this text focuses primarily on the federal income tax, some mention should be made of the following other types of taxes levied by federal, state, and local governments.

▶ **Property taxes** are based on the value of a taxpayer's property, which may include both real estate and personal property. Real estate taxes are a major source of revenue for local governments. In addition, some state and local governments levy a personal property tax on intangibles such as securities and tangible personal property (e.g., the value of a personal automobile).

▶ **Federal excise taxes** and **customs duties** on imported goods have declined in relative importance over the years but remain significant sources of revenue. Federal excise taxes are imposed on alcohol, tobacco, gasoline, telephone usage, production of oil and gas, and many other types of goods. Many state and local governments impose similar excise taxes on goods and services.

▶ **Sales taxes** are a major source of revenue for state and local governments. Sales taxes are imposed on retail sales of tangible personal property (e.g., clothing and automobiles). Some states also impose a sales tax on personal services (e.g., accounting and legal fees). Certain items often are exempt from the sales tax levy (e.g., food items or medicines), and the rates vary widely between individual state and local governments. Sales taxes are not deductible for federal income tax purposes unless incurred in a trade or business.

▶ Employment taxes include Social Security (**FICA**) and federal and state unemployment compensation taxes. If an individual is classified as an employee, the FICA tax that is imposed on the employee is comprised of two parts: the old-age survivors, and disability insurance (OASDI) and the Medicare or hospital insurance (HI). The OASDI is 6.2% and is imposed on the first $118,500 (2015) of wages. This tax is imposed on both the employer and the employee at the same rate. Similarly, the HI portion is imposed on both the employer and the employee, but it has no ceiling on wages like the OASDI portion. In fact, the HI portion is generally 1.45% of wages, but beginning in 2013, the employee is required to pay an additional 0.9% on wages above $200,000 ($250,000 for married taxpayers filing a joint return). So while the employer will pay 1.45% on all wages, an employee who is single will pay 1.45% on the first $200,000 of wages and 2.35% on any wages over $200,000.

If an individual is self-employed, a self-employment tax comprised of the OASDI and HI taxes is imposed. The OASDI portion is 12.4% on the individual's self-employment income of up to $118,500 (in 2015). The HI portion is 2.9% on the first $200,000 of self-employment income ($250,000 combined self-employment income for married taxpayers filing a joint return) and 3.8% on any self-employment income over that amount.

▶ Employers are required to pay federal and state unemployment taxes to fund the payment of unemployment benefits to former employees. The federal rate is 6.0% on the first $7,000 of wages for each employee in 2015.[19] However, a credit is granted for up to 5.4% of wages for taxes paid to the state government so that the actual amount paid to the federal government may be as low as 0.6%.[20] The amount of tax paid to the state depends on the employer's prior experience with respect to the frequency and amount of unemployment claims. In California, for example, the highest rate of unemployment tax imposed is 6.2% and this rate is subsequently adjusted down if the employer has a small number of unemployment claims to a minimum of 1.5%.

The types of taxes and structural considerations that were previously discussed are summarized in Topic Review I:1-1.

---

[18] Self-employed individuals receive an income tax deduction equal to 50% of taxes paid on their self-employment income and this deduction is also allowed to compute the amount of self-employment income (see Secs. 164(f) and 1402(a)(12) and Chapter I:14).

[19] Sec. 3301.
[20] Sec. 3302. State unemployment taxes in some states are levied on tax bases above $7,000. For example, the wage base ceiling in North Carolina is $21,700 in 2015.

TOPIC REVIEW I:1-1

Types of Taxes and Tax Structure

TYPE OF TAX	TAX STRUCTURE	TAX BASE
Individuals:		
Federal income tax	Progressive	Gross income from all sources unless specifically excluded by law reduced by deductions and exemptions
State income tax	Progressive	Generally based on AGI for federal income tax purposes with adjustments
Federal gift tax	Progressive	FMV of all taxable gifts made during the tax year
Federal estate tax	Progressive	FMV of property owned at death plus taxable gifts made after 1976
Corporations:		
Federal corporate income tax	Progressive	Gross income from all sources unless specifically excluded by law reduced by deductions
State corporate income tax	Proportional or progressive	Federal corporate taxable income with adjustments
State franchise tax	Proportional	Usually based on a weighted-average formula consisting of net worth, income, and sales
Other Types of Taxes:		
Property taxes	Proportional	FMV of personal or real property
Excise taxes	Proportional	Customs and duties on imported and domestic goods from alcohol to telephone usage
Sales taxes	Proportional	Retail sales of tangible personal property or personal services
FICA and self-employment taxes	Regressive	Based on wages or self-employment income
Unemployment taxes	Regressive	Usually first $7,000 of an employee's wages

CRITERIA FOR A TAX STRUCTURE

Establishing criteria for a "good" tax structure was first attempted in 1776 by economist Adam Smith.[21] Smith's four "canons of taxation"—equity, certainty, convenience, and economy—are still used today when tax policy issues are discussed. Many have added a fifth canon of simplicity. Below is a discussion of these criteria and how they relate to income taxes as well as other taxes.

EQUITY

A rather obvious criteria for a good tax is that the tax be equitable or fair to taxpayers. However, equity or fairness is elusive because of the subjectivity of the concept. What one person may conclude is fair in a particular situation may be considered totally unfair by another person. In other words, fairness is relative in nature and is extremely difficult to measure. For example, the deductibility of mortgage interest on a taxpayer's home certainly seems to be a fair provision for taxpayers. However, for taxpayers who do not own a home but live in a rental apartment, the deductibility of mortgage interest may not be considered as fair because the renter cannot deduct any portion of the rent paid. In other types of situations, the federal tax law includes various measures to ensure that taxpayers are treated fairly. For example, a foreign tax credit is available to minimize the double taxation that would otherwise occur when U.S. taxpayers earn income in a foreign country that is taxed by

[21] Adam Smith, *The Wealth of Nations* (New York: Random House, Modern Library, 1937), pp. 777–779.

both the United States and the country in which it is earned. (See the glossary at the end of this volume for a definition of tax credits and Chapter I:14 for a discussion of the foreign tax credit.) Two aspects of equity are commonly discussed in the tax policy literature, **horizontal equity** and **vertical equity**. Horizontal equity refers to the notion that similarly situated taxpayers should be treated equally. Thus, two taxpayers who each have income of $50,000 should both pay the same amount of tax. Vertical equity, on the other hand, implies that taxpayers who are not similarly situated should be treated differently. Thus, if Taxpayer A has income of $50,000 and Taxpayer B has income of $20,000, Taxpayers A and B should not pay the same amount of income tax. Vertical equity provides that the incidence of taxation should be borne by those who have the **ability to pay** the tax, based on income or wealth. The progressive rate structure is founded on the vertical equity premise.

CERTAINTY

A certain tax (1) ensures a stable source of government operating revenues and (2) provides taxpayers with some degree of certainty concerning the amount of their annual tax liability. A tax that is simple to understand and administer provides certainty for taxpayers. For many years, our income tax laws have been criticized as being overly complex and difficult to administer. Consider the remarks of a noted tax authority at a conference on federal income tax simplification:

> Tax advisers—at least some tax advisers—are saying that the income tax system is not working. They are saying that they don't know what the law provides, that the IRS does not know what the law provides, that taxpayers are not abiding by the law they don't know.[22]

While the above statement is over 30 years old, it is certainly still viable today. This uncertainty in the tax law causes frequent disputes between taxpayers and the IRS and has resulted in extensive litigation.

The federal tax system has made some attempts to provide certainty for taxpayers. For example, the IRS issues advance rulings to taxpayers, which provides some assurance concerning the tax consequences of a proposed transaction for the taxpayer who requests the ruling. The taxpayer may rely on the ruling if the transaction is completed in accordance with the terms of the ruling request. For example, if a merger of two corporations is being considered, the transaction can be structured so that the shareholders and the corporations do not recognize gain or loss. If a favorable ruling is received and the transaction is completed as planned, the IRS cannot later assert that the merger does not qualify for tax-free treatment.

CONVENIENCE

A tax law should be easily assessed, collected, and administered. Taxpayers should not be overly burdened with the maintenance of records and compliance considerations (preparation of their tax returns, payment of their taxes, and so on). One of the reasons that the sales tax is such a popular form of tax for state and local governments is that it is convenient for taxpayers to pay and for the government to collect. The consumer need not complete a tax return or keep detailed records.

ECONOMY

An economical tax structure should require only minimal compliance and administrative costs. The IRS collection costs, amounting to less than 0.5% of revenues, are minimal relative to the total collections of revenues from the federal income tax. Estimates of taxpayer compliance costs are less certain. One indicator of total compliance costs for taxpayers is the demand for tax professionals. Tax practice has been and continues to be one of the fastest growing areas in public accounting firms. Most large corporations also maintain sizable tax departments that engage in tax research, compliance, and planning activities. In addition, many commercial tax return preparer services are available to assist taxpayers who have relatively uncomplicated tax returns.

[22] Sidney L. Roberts, "The Viewpoint of the Tax Adviser: An Overview of Simplification," *Tax Adviser,* January 1979, p. 32.

Complying with the tax laws is enormously expensive for both businesses and individuals in the United States. In 2005, businesses spent an estimated $148 billion to comply with the federal tax laws, while it cost individuals about $111 billion.[23] Compliance with state and local taxes costs another $80 billion. Clearly, the cost of complying with the nation's tax laws is significant, in terms of both money and time.

A more difficult question is whether the tax structure is economical in terms of taxpayer compliance. The issues of tax avoidance and tax evasion are becoming increasingly more important. The General Accounting Office (GAO) reported that sole proprietors underreported their income by 57 percent or $68 billion in 2001.[24]

SIMPLICITY

One of the important measures of any tax system is that of simplicity, or at least, not undue complexity. Taxpayers should be able to understand and comply with any tax system within reasonable boundaries. The sales tax is an example of a tax system that is relatively simple, although the sales tax as it applies to businesses can become fairly complex. The federal income tax system in the United States has become inordinately complex over the years and complexity is one of the major criticisms of the income tax. The following is a quote from the report from the President's Advisory Panel on Federal Tax Reform:[25]

> In short, our current tax code is a complicated mess. Instead of clarity, we have opacity. Instead of simplicity, we have complexity. Instead of fair principles, we have seemingly arbitrary rules. Instead of contributing to economic growth, it detracts from growth. Time and time again, witnesses told the Panel about these failings in the tax code.

While simplicity is an admirable goal of any tax system, achieving this goal in the federal income tax system is difficult and involves the trade-off of other important objectives. For example, simplicity and fairness are almost impossible to achieve together. If the income tax law is extremely simple, like a flat tax rate on all income, the possible result is that many taxpayers will not be treated fairly. Consider this case, two taxpayers, A and B both earn $100,000 per year and we have a flat rate tax of 20% so that each taxpayer will pay $20,000 in income taxes for the year. However, assume that taxpayer B has a severe illness that requires him to pay medical expenses of $60,000 per year. Should both A and B pay the same income tax for the year? There is no absolute correct answer in this case, it depends on your definition of fairness. Thus, making the income tax law simple may not be the top priority in tax reform.

OBJECTIVES OF THE FEDERAL INCOME TAX LAW

The primary objective of the federal income tax law is to raise revenues for government operations. In recent years, the federal government has broadened its use of the tax laws to accomplish various economic and social policy objectives.

ADDITIONAL COMMENT

Among the provisions in the tax law that are designed to enhance the level of health care are the deductibility of medical expenses, deductibility of charitable contributions to hospitals, and exclusion of fringe benefits provided by employers for medical insurance premiums and medical care.

Economic Objectives. The federal income tax law is used as a fiscal policy tool to stimulate private investment, reduce unemployment, and mitigate the effects of inflation on the economy. Consider the following example: Tax credits for businesses operating in distressed urban and rural areas (empowerment zones) are allowed to provide economic revitalization of such areas. This is a clear example of using the federal income tax law to stimulate private investment in specific areas.

---

[23] Scott A. Hodge, J. Scott Moody, and Wendy P. Warcholik, "The Rising Cost of Complying with the Federal Income Tax," Special Report No. 138, *Tax Foundation*, January, 2006, p. 1.
[24] News Report. "Limiting Sole Proprietor Loss Deductions Could Improve Compliance But Would Also Limit Some Legitimate Losses" GAO Report GAO-09-815 Oct. 13, 2009.

[25] Report of the President's Advisory Panel on Federal Tax Reform, *Simple, Fair, & Pro-Growth: Proposals to Fix America's Tax System*, November 2005, p. 2. See the discussion of tax reform in this chapter.

Many items in the tax law are adjusted for inflation by using the consumer price index, including the tax brackets, personal and dependency exemptions, and standard deduction amounts. These inflation adjustments provide relief for individual taxpayers who would otherwise be subject to increased taxes due to the effects of inflation. (See Chapter I:2 for a discussion of the tax computation for individuals.)

Encouragement of Certain Activities and Industries. The federal income tax law also attempts to stimulate and encourage certain activities, specialized industries, and small businesses. One such example is the encouragement of research activities by permitting an immediate write-off of expenses and a special tax credit for increasing research and experimental costs. Special incentives are also provided to the oil and gas industry through percentage depletion allowances and an election to deduct intangible drilling costs.

Certain favorable tax provisions are provided for small businesses, including reduced corporate tax rates of 15% on the first $50,000 of taxable income and 25% for the next $25,000 of taxable income. Favorable ordinary loss (instead of capital loss) deductions are granted to individual investors who sell their small business corporation stock at a loss, provided that certain requirements are met.[26] In addition, noncorporate investors may exclude up to 50% of the gain realized from the disposition of qualified small business stock if the stock is held for more than five years.[27]

Social Objectives. The tax law attempts to encourage or discourage certain socially desirable or undersirable activities. For example:

► Special tax-favored pension and profit-sharing plans have been created for employees and self-employed individuals to supplement the social security retirement system.

► Charitable contributions are deductible to encourage individuals to contribute to charitable organizations.

► The claiming of a deduction for illegal bribes, fines, and penalties has been prohibited to discourage activities that are contrary to public policy.

ADDITIONAL COMMENT

Deductible contributions made by self-employed individuals to their retirement plans (Keogh plans) totaled $20.8 billion in 2012. Charitable deductions totaled over $199 billion that same year.

EXAMPLE I:1-10 ► Able Corporation establishes a qualified pension plan for its employees whereby it makes all of the annual contributions to the plan. Able's contributions to the pension trust are currently deductible and not includible in the employees' gross income until the pension payments are distributed during their retirement years. Earnings on the contributed funds also are nontaxable until such amounts are distributed to the employees. ◄

EXAMPLE I:1-11 ► Anita contributes $10,000 annually to her church, which is a qualified charitable organization. Anita's marginal tax rate is 25%. Her after-tax cost of contributing to the church is only $7,500 [$10,000 − (0.25 × $10,000)]. ◄

EXAMPLE I:1-12 ► Ace Trucking Company incurs $10,000 in fines imposed by local and state governments for overloading its trucks during the current tax year. The fines are not deductible because the activity is contrary to public policy. ◄

The tax law objectives previously discussed are highlighted in Topic Review I:1-2.

Income Tax Reform Proposals. Tax reform has been a much debated topic over the years but has taken center stage recently. There has been a flurry of books, articles, and newspaper editorials that range from installing a completely new tax system to a partial revision of the current income tax. Few people support keeping the income tax

---

[26] Sec. 1244.   [27] Sec. 1202.

TOPIC REVIEW I:1-2

Objectives of the Tax Law

OBJECTIVE	EXAMPLE
Stimulate investment	Provide a tax credit for the purchase of business equipment
Prevent taxpayers from paying a higher percentage of their income in personal income taxes due to inflation (bracket creep)	Index the tax rates, standard deduction, and personal and dependency exemptions for inflation
Encourage research activities that will in turn strengthen the competitiveness of U.S. companies	Allow research expenditures to be written off in the year incurred and offer a tax credit for increasing research and experimental costs
Encourage venture capital for small businesses	Reduce corporate income tax rates on the first $75,000 of taxable income. Allow businesses to immediately expense $500,000 (2014) of certain depreciable business assets acquired each year.
Encourage social objectives	Provide a tax deduction for charitable contributions; provide favorable tax treatment for contributions to qualified pension plans

system as it currently stands. Virtually all reform proposals advocate greater simplicity of the income tax law. Recently, there has been a push to increase income tax rates on high-income individuals. Some proponents of a new tax system advocate substituting a retail sales tax at the federal level for the income tax, others favor a value-added tax system (VAT tax) that is widely used in Europe. A partial revision of what we have now is also a popular option.

At present, it is unclear as to the likelihood of any tax reform proposals. While the recommendations are well thought-out, there are other pressing matters facing Congress that may postpone implementation of tax reform in a comprehensive manner. Piecemeal changes to the tax code certainly may continue and this only ensures continued complexity in the tax law.

ENTITIES IN THE FEDERAL INCOME TAX SYSTEM

OBJECTIVE 5

Describe the tax entities in the federal income tax system

The federal income tax law levies taxes on taxpayers. However, not all entities that file income tax returns pay income taxes. For example, a partnership is required to file a tax return but does not pay any income tax because the income (or loss) of the partnership is allocated to the partners who report the income or loss on their individual tax returns. Therefore, the various entities in the federal income tax system may be classified into two general categories, *taxpaying entities* and *flow-through entities*.[28] Taxpaying entities generally are required to pay income taxes on their taxable income. Flow-through entities, on the other hand, generally do not directly pay income taxes but merely pass the income on to a taxpaying entity. The major entities in each category are as follows:

Taxpaying Entities	*Flow-through Entities*
Individuals	Sole proprietorship
C corporations (regular corporations)	Partnerships
	S corporations
	Limited Liability Company (LLC) or Limited Liability Partnership (LLP)
	Trusts

---

[28] Some entities have characteristics of both categories of entities, including certain types of trusts and S corporations.

Each of these entities is discussed below. The purpose of this section is to provide an overall picture of the various entities in the federal income tax system.

TAXPAYING ENTITIES

Individuals. Individual taxpayers are the principal taxpaying entities in the federal income tax system. In 2014, income taxes paid by individual taxpayers comprised nearly 46% of total federal revenues. If Social Security taxes are included, individual taxpayers paid 80% of total federal revenues (see Table I:1-1 for details). Thus, the study of taxation of individuals is a very important topic and is discussed extensively in this *Individuals* textbook.

Individuals pay income taxes on all gross income minus allowable deductions. Gross income minus allowable deductions is referred to as *taxable income*. Gross income subject to taxation may be broadly classified into three categories:

► Earned income from sources such as salaries and wages, business income, and retirement income.

► Investment income, including interest income, dividends, capital gains, and rents and royalties.

► Flow-through income from partnerships, limited liability companies (LLCs), Subchapter S corporations, estates, and trusts.

Allowable deductions include expenses attributable to the gross income above and certain personal deductions and exemptions specifically allowed under the tax law. Gross income and allowable deductions and exemptions are discussed in detail later in this textbook.

Individual taxpayers use the tax formula below to compute their taxable income:

Total income, from whatever source derived		$xxx
Minus:	Exclusions, as provided in the tax law	(xxx)
Gross income		xxx
Minus:	Deductions for adjusted gross income	(xxx)
Adjusted gross income (AGI)		xxx
Minus:	Deductions from AGI:	
	Greater of itemized deductions or standard deduction	(xxx)
	Personal and dependency exemptions	(xxx)
Taxable income		$xxx

Exclusions are items of income that the tax law specifically exempts from taxation. They include such items as gifts, inheritances, interest income from state and local bonds, loans, and life insurance proceeds. Exclusions are discussed in Chapter I:4.

Once an individual determines that an expenditure is allowed as a deduction for tax purposes, he or she must classify the deduction as *for* AGI or *from* AGI. This classification is very important and is discussed in Chapter I:6. Deductions *for* AGI basically are (1) expenses connected with a taxpayer's business or rental property, or (2) other specified deductions, such as moving expenses, contributions to an Individual Retirement Account (IRA), alimony, and a number of other specific items. Deductions *from* AGI are either itemized deductions or the standard deduction, whichever is greater, and personal and dependency exemptions. Itemized deductions primarily are personal-type deductions of the taxpayer, such as medical expenses, state and local taxes, mortgage interest, and charitable contributions. Itemized deductions are discussed in Chapter I:7. The standard deduction is a set amount that all taxpayers may deduct. For 2015, the standard deduction is $6,300 ($12,600 for married couples filing a joint return) and is indexed annually for inflation. Thus, if a single taxpayer's itemized deductions for 2015 were $5,000, the taxpayer would deduct the standard deduction of $6,300 instead. On the other hand, if the taxpayer's itemized deductions were $7,000, the taxpayer would deduct $7,000 because that amount exceeds the standard deduction.

Personal and dependency exemptions also are specific deductions allowed to individuals. The personal exemption is for the taxpayer and spouse whereas dependency exemptions are for the taxpayer's children or other dependents. The personal and dependency exemption in 2015 is $4,000. So, a husband and wife who have two dependent children would be entitled to a deduction of $16,000 ($4,000 × 4). This exemption amount is phased-out for higher income taxpayers and is indexed annually for inflation. Personal and dependency exemptions are discussed further in Chapter I:2.

Once taxable income is determined, tax rates are applied to this amount to arrive at the income tax liability for the year. Certain credits are allowed that reduce the income tax liability on a dollar-for-dollar basis. Individual income tax rates may be found inside the front cover of this textbook. Because individuals are subject to withholding and estimated tax payment rules, they may pay a balance due or receive a refund upon filing their tax return.

Individual taxpayers are required to file a tax return annually, Form 1040, which is due on or before April 15 of the year following the taxable year. As can be seen from the tax rate schedules located on the inside cover of this textbook, rates range from 10% to 39.6%.

ADDITIONAL COMMENT

Instead of filing Form 1040, some individual taxpayers are eligible to file simplified versions, the form 1040A or Form 1040 EZ.

EXAMPLE I:1-13 ►

Jeff Payne, a single taxpayer, is employed by a large corporation and has the following information for the current year of 2015:

INCOME AND OTHER RECEIPTS

Salary from corporation	$120,000
Interest income from savings account	13,000
Interest on New York City bond	600
Loan from bank	20,000
Share of income from a partnership in which Jeff is a partner	8,600
Gift from Jeff's grandmother	11,000
Total	$173,200

DEDUCTIONS, EXEMPTIONS, AND PAYMENTS

Itemized deductions	17,000
Personal exemption (2015)	4,000
Federal income taxes withheld from salary	30,000

Jeff's taxable income and income tax liability for 2015 would be computed as follows:

Total income		$173,200
Minus: Exclusions:		
Interest on New York City bond	$ 600	
Loan from bank	20,000	
Gift from Jeff's grandmother	$11,000	31,600
Gross income		141,600
Minus: Deductions for AGI		0
Adjusted gross income (AGI)		141,600
Minus: Deductions from AGI:		
Itemized deductions	$17,000	
Personal exemption	4,000	(21,000)
Taxable income		$120,600

The itemized deductions of $17,000 exceed Jeff's allowable standard deduction for 2015 of $6,300 and, therefore, are used to reduce taxable income.

To compute Jeff's income tax liability for the year, the 2015 rate schedules inside the front cover of the textbook are used. Jeff's income tax liability (using single taxpayer rates) would be $26,839.25 [$18,481.25 + 0.28($120,600 − $90,750)]. Since Jeff had $30,000 of federal income taxes withheld from his salary, he would be entitled to a tax refund of $3,160.75 ($30,000.00 − $26,839.25). ◄

Some types of income are taxed at lower rates. For example, dividends from most U.S. corporations are subject to a maximum rate of 20%. This 20% maximum rate also applies to long-term capital gains, such as gains on the sale of stocks and bonds. With these lower rates, a high-income taxpayer in the 39.6% marginal tax bracket would only pay a maximum of 20% on any qualified dividends received or long-term capital gains. The remainder of the taxpayer's income would be subject to the higher rates.

C Corporations. C corporations, many times referred to as regular corporations, also are taxpaying entities. These corporations, both publicly-held corporations traded on stock exchanges and privately-owned corporations, accounted for approximately 11% of total federal revenues in 2014. The percentage of federal revenues provided by C corporations has been steadily declining over the past 40 years, a concern of tax policymakers as more and more taxes are being shifted to individual taxpayers. A major disadvantage of C corporations is they are subject to so-called double taxation. Double taxation results from the corporation paying income tax on its taxable income and shareholders paying income tax on any dividends received from the corporation or on the gain from selling their stock in the corporation. Thus, the same corporate income is subjected to taxation twice—once at the corporate level and again at the shareholder level. For many years, much tax planning has been directed at trying to so arrange the tax affairs of a C corporation to avoid double taxation. This discussion of C corporations is divided into two parts, (1) taxation of C corporations and (2) the operation of double taxation.

Taxation of C corporations. C corporations are taxed on their taxable income in a manner similar to individuals. The major difference between corporations and individuals is that corporations are not allowed personal exemptions and personal deductions. Thus, the concept of AGI does not pertain to corporations. Taxable income for corporations is computed as follows:

Total income, from whatever source derived		$xxx
Minus:	Exclusions, as provided in the tax law	(xxx)
Gross income		xxx
Minus:	Deductions (ordinary and necessary expenses related to the corporation's trade or business)	(xxx)
Taxable income		$xxx

This taxable income is subject to tax rates that range from 15% to 35%. (see rate schedule in the inside rear cover of the textbook). A more detailed discussion of corporation taxation is contained in Chapter I:16 of this *Individuals* textbook and Chapter C:3 of the *Corporations, Partnerships, Estates, and Trusts* volume.

EXAMPLE I:1-14 ▶ During the current taxable year, Crimson Corporation generated gross income of $1,500,000 and had ordinary and necessary deductions of $900,000, resulting in taxable income of $600,000. Based on the corporation rate schedules, Crimson would be subject to taxes of $204,000 [$113,900 + .34($600,000 − 335,000)]. ◀

C corporations are required to file tax returns annually using Form 1120, which is due on or after the 15th day of the third month after the close of the corporation's tax year (e.g., March 15 for calendar year taxpayers).

Double taxation of C corporation earnings. As mentioned previously, C corporations are subject to double taxation. The corporation pays income tax on its taxable income and then shareholders must pay income tax on any dividends paid by the corporation or on the sale of their stock. Tax legislation in 2003 substantially reduced the impact of double taxation by reducing to 15% the maximum tax rate on most corporate dividends received by individuals. Prior to this reduction in tax rates on qualified dividends, dividends were subject to tax at regular tax rates. For tax years 2013 and forward, taxpayers who are in the 10% or 15% regular tax brackets continue to have a 0% tax rate on qualified dividends. Taxpayers who are in a marginal tax bracket above 15% and below 39.6% continue to pay a marginal tax rate of 15% on qualified dividends. However, taxpayers who are in the highest tax bracket of 39.6% now pay a marginal tax rate of 20% on qualified dividends. Thus, under current tax law, a taxpayer in the 35% marginal tax bracket (see tax rate schedules inside the front cover of this textbook) pays only a 15% tax rate on any dividends received. The same reduced tax rates apply to long-term capital gains on the sale of their corporate stock.

EXAMPLE I:1-15 ▶ Using the same facts for Crimson Corporation in Example I:1-14, assume the corporation paid dividends to shareholders during 2015 of $400,000. Further assume that the marginal tax bracket of the shareholders is 39.6%. The shareholders collectively would have to pay individual income taxes of $80,000 ($400,000 × 20%) as the maximum tax rate on qualified dividends is 20%. The total tax on the corporation's taxable income of $600,000, therefore, would be $284,000 ($204,000 paid by Crimson Corporation plus $80,000 paid by the shareholders), or an effective tax rate of 47.3% ($284,000/$600,000). The 47.3% is only federal income taxes and does not include any state or local income taxes that the corporation may have to pay. ◀

While the reduced rate of tax on qualified dividends is certainly favorable to shareholders, the double taxation of C corporation earnings is still an onerous tax. A common method to avoid this double taxation by C corporations with a small number of shareholders is to payout the corporate earnings in the form of salary and bonuses, thereby making the payout deductible by the corporation and eliminating double taxation. The Internal Revenue Service (IRS), however, may attack this plan by asserting that the salary and bonuses are unreasonably large and, in fact, a disguised dividend.

EXAMPLE I:1-16 ▶ Assume in Example I:1-14 that Crimson had only one shareholder, Joe Bank, who also is the president of the corporation. The corporation paid the entire $600,000 to Mr. Bank in the form of a bonus rather than as a dividend. The corporation could deduct the $600,000, thereby reducing its taxable income to zero. Mr. Bank would have to include the $600,000 in his personal income and would pay taxes on this amount. If his average tax rate on the $600,000 was 30%, he would owe $180,000 on the $600,000. The $180,000 would represent the total taxes of both the corporation and shareholder and would save $104,000 ($284,000 − $180,000) from the previous example. The IRS may attack this plan by alleging that Mr. Bank's salary and bonus are unreasonably high and recharacterize part of the $600,000 as a dividend. Because dividends are not deductible by the corporation, the corporation would be subject to additional income taxes. At the same time, if the IRS is successful, the portion of the salary and bonus of Mr. Bank that is recharacterized as a dividend would be subject to the maximum 20% tax rate. ◀

FLOW-THROUGH ENTITIES
The simplest form of a flow-through entity is the sole proprietorship as there are no formal requirements to form such an entity. The net income earned by the proprietor is reported on Schedule C of Form 1040. Thus, the income of the sole proprietorship merely flows to the proprietor's individual tax return. The net income of the sole proprietorship is subject to income tax only once (at the individual level) but is also subject to self-employment tax (Social Security and Medicare taxes).

Flow-through entities, such as partnership, limited liability companies (LLCs), limited liability partnerships (LLPs), and S corporations have the major advantage of being subject to only one level of taxation. All of these entities file tax returns, but, in general, the entities do not pay any income taxes. The income earned by the entity is allocated to the owners based on their proportionate ownership or some other allocation arrangement. Thus, the entity income tax return is really just an information return. The income allocated to the owners is then reported on their own tax returns. The income of the entity, therefore, is subject to a single level of taxation. This single level of tax is a major advantage of the flow-through form over C corporations.

To ensure a single level of taxation for flow-through entities, the tax law employs a unique method of basis adjustments. Every owner of the entity has an *adjusted basis* (basis) in his or her ownership interest. An owner's basis in a flow-through entity is determined as follows:

► Each owner obtains an original basis in his or her ownership interest upon the formation of the entity (investment in the entity) or purchase of the interest.

► The owner's basis increases for any additional capital contributions to the entity in subsequent years.

► The owner's basis increases for the owner's share of income for tax purposes or decreases for losses.

► The owner's basis increases for the owner's share of entity liabilities. Differences exist between partnerships and S corporations as to which liabilities are added to an owner's basis. Details on this topic are covered in later chapters of this textbook.

► The owner's basis decreases for money or property distributed to the owner by the entity.

Without these basis adjustments, the owner could be subject to double taxation upon selling his or her interest or upon dissolution of the entity. Practitioners refer to this basis as "outside basis" as opposed to "inside basis," which is the entity's basis in its assets.

EXAMPLE I:1-17 ► Wildcat Company is a flow-through entity with two owners, Rich and Teresa. Each owner has a $10,000 original basis in the entity. In its first year of operations, Wildcat Company earns $50,000, which is allocated $25,000 to each owner. Thus, each owner reports $25,000 in his individual income tax return even though the entity does not distribute any of the earnings to the owners. At the beginning of the second year, Rich sells his interest to Steve for $35,000. If Rich did not get an increased basis adjustment for his $25,000 of earnings, he would recognize a $25,000 gain ($35,000 selling price − $10,000 basis in the entity) on the sale of his interest, which taxes him twice on the $25,000. However, both Rich and Teresa do increase their bases to $35,000 ($10,000 original basis + $25,000 share of entity earnings) at the end of the first tax year. Therefore, when Rich sells his interest for $35,000, he incurs no additional taxable gain ($35,000 selling price − $35,000 basis in the entity = $0 gain). ◄

Below is a brief description of the four basic types of flow-through business entities.

Partnerships. A partnership is the classic flow-through entity as it has been around the longest. The Internal Revenue Code (IRC) defines a partnership as "a syndicate, group, pool, joint venture, or other incorporated organization" that carries on any business, financial operation, or venture.[29] Thus, if two or more individuals, corporations, trusts, or estates decide to operate a business or financial venture, the business or venture can be classified as a partnership. Unlike a corporation, which must file incorporation documents with the state, partnerships require no legal documentation. However, tax advisors strongly advise partnerships to have written agreements as to the operation of the partnership and how income, deductions, losses, and credits will be allocated to the partners. Most states have laws that govern the rights and restrictions of partnerships and their partners.

Partnerships file an annual income tax return which is just an information return because the partnership entity is not subject to taxation. The return, Form 1065 (U.S. Partnership Return of Income), reports the results of the partnership's operations. An accompanying form, Schedule K-1, reports the separate income, deductions, losses, and credits that flow through to the partners. The partners, in turn, take the information from their Schedule K-1 and report the various items on their individual returns.

EXAMPLE I:1-18 ► Donald and Minnie form a real estate company and decide to operate as a partnership, the DM Partnership. Donald is a 60% partner and Minnie is a 40% partner. Donald invests $60,000 into DM and Minnie contributes real estate with a basis and fair market value of $40,000. In its first year of operation, DM Partnership earns ordinary income of $150,000. The partnership files Form 1065 and reports the $150,000 but is not subject to any income taxation. Included in the

[29] Sec. 761(a).

partnership return are two Schedule K-1s that report $90,000 to Donald ($150,000 × 60%) and $60,000 ($150,000 × 40%) to Minnie. Donald reports $90,000 on his individual income tax return, Form 1040, and Minnie reports $60,000 on her individual return. If the partnership distributed $72,000 to Donald and $48,000 to Minnie during the year, the distributions are considered a return of capital and are not taxable to either partner. Donald's adjusted basis in his partnership interest would be $78,000 ($60,000 + $90,000 − $72,000) and Minnie's adjusted basis would be $52,000 ($40,000 + $60,000 − $48,000). ◀

S Corporations. S corporations are a special form of corporation treated by the tax laws as flow-through entities. They are incorporated under state law just as any other corporation but, if they so elect, are treated as flow-through entities for tax purposes. S corporations are so named because the rules pertaining to this type of entity are located in Subchapter S of the IRC. S corporations have been referred to as "corporations taxed like a partnership." Although this statement is partially true, important differences exist, such as a limitation on the number of shareholders, strict rules on allocation of income or losses, and several other differences. Similar to partnerships, S corporations are not taxed and income, deductions, losses, and credits flow through to its shareholders. Allocations of income, deductions, losses, and credits to shareholders are based on a per share–per day basis. Importantly, S corporation shareholders enjoy limited liability, as do C corporation shareholders.

To achieve S corporation status, the corporation must file an S election and all of its shareholders must consent to that election. S corporations annually file an information return, Form 1120S (U.S. Income Tax Return for an S Corporation), which reports the results of the corporation's operations and, like partnerships, also submits Schedule K-1 to each shareholder which reports the allocable share of income, deduction, loss, and credit that flow through to each shareholder.

Similar to partnerships, S corporations impose only a single level of taxation to its shareholders and the tax law uses basis adjustments to achieve this single level of taxation. The basis adjustments for S corporation shareholders are nearly identical to those for partnerships. The major difference is how liabilities affect the basis of S corporation shareholders. S corporation shareholders obtain basis only for *direct* loans to the corporation and they treat their debt basis separately from stock basis. Partners of a partnership generally increase their basis for all partnership liabilities.

EXAMPLE I:1-19 ▶ Paul and Peter form a corporation in Ohio as equal shareholders. Upon advice from their tax advisor, they decide to elect S corporation status for federal and state tax purposes and file the necessary forms. Both Paul and Peter invest $25,000 in the corporation and each receives 100 shares of common stock of the corporation. During the first year, the corporation reports net ordinary income of $62,000 and a long-term capital gain of $10,000 of Form 1120S. Each shareholder receives a $20,000 distribution from the corporation during the year. In Year 1, the corporation pays no federal or state income taxes, but both Paul and Peter report $31,000 of ordinary income and $5,000 of long-term capital gain on their individual returns. Since the shareholders have sufficient basis, the $20,000 distribution to each shareholder is not subject to taxation. Paul and Peter would each have a basis in their S corporation stock of $41,000 ($25,000 + $31,000 + $5,000 − $20,000) at the end of Year 1. ◀

EXAMPLE I:1-20 ▶ In Year 2, the corporation earns $74,000 of ordinary income and no capital gains. Also, on July 1 of Year 2, Peter sells one-half (50 shares) of his stock to Mary. So, from July 1 to December 31, Paul owns 50% of the corporate stock and Peter and Mary each own 25%. S corporation earnings must be allocated on a per share–per day basis, so the income of $74,000 is allocated to each shareholder as follows:

Paul	$74,000 × 365/365 × 50% = $37,000
Peter	($74,000 × 181/365 × 50%) + ($74,000 × 184/365 × 25%) = $27,674
Mary	$74,000 × 184/365 × 25% = $9,326 ◀

Limited Liability Companies. A limited liability company (LLC) is a legal entity under the laws of all 50 states and the District of Columbia and is a very popular organizational form. LLCs combine the best features of a partnership and a corporation by being treated as a partnership while providing the limited liability protection of a corporation. Thus, LLC owners, called members, are subject to a single level of taxation and are not liable for the liabilties of the LLC.

An LLC is formed under state law similar to a corporation. After formed, the LLC elects whether to be taxed either as a partnership or a corporation.[30] Under Treasury Regulations, an LLC with more than one member is treated as a partnership unless the LLC affirmatively elects to be classified as a corporation. In most cases, LLCs will prefer to be classified as a partnership because of the tax advantages of a single level of taxation. If an LLC elects to be treated as a partnership, it files its tax return on Form 1065 (U.S. Partnership Return of Income). The LLC, however, is not legally a partnership; it is just treated as one for federal income tax purposes. A single member LLC is disregarded for tax purposes and the LLC income, deductions, etc. are reported directly on the member's Schedule C of Form 1040 as a sole proprietor. If an LLC elects to be taxed as a corporation under the Treasury Regulations, it would file Form 1120 (U.S. Corporation Income Tax Return). Further, S corporation status can be achieved by electing to be taxed as a corporation and then make an S election. Thus, the LLC would be considered an LLC for state law purposes but an S corporation for income tax purposes.

EXAMPLE I:1-21 ▶ Karen and David start a wholesale business and decide to operate the business as an LLC. They first must legally form the organization under state law. After the LLC is legally formed, they must decide how the LLC will be treated for income tax purposes. Because they want a single level of taxation, Karen and David elect to be treated as a partnership. Since being treated as a partnership is the default classification under Treasury Regulations, no forms need to be filed with the IRS. At the end of the first year, the LLC will file a Form 1065 and check the box indicating that the entity is an LLC filing as a partnership. All partner allocations, basis adjustments, and all other tax rules for the LLC are identical with partnership rules. ◀

Limited Liability Partnerships. All 50 states and the District of Columbia have statutes that allow a business to operate as a limited liability partnership (LLP). Basically, an LLP is similar to an LLC except that a partner of an LLP *is not* liable for any liability arising from acts of negligence or misconduct or similar acts of another partner of the LLP. Thus, an LLP is much more desirable than a general partnership where partners are liable for all partnership liabilities. Professional service organizations, such as many CPA firms, have adopted the LLP form, primarily to limit legal liability.

EXAMPLE I:1-22 ▶ The accounting firm of Gartman & Kuhn, CPAs, is operating as a general partnership and has 20 partners in the firm. The firm is concerned about the unlimited liability that exists for the partnership, especially in today's litigious environment. The firm decides to convert from a partnership to an LLP. The conversion is simple and tax-free,[31] and protects the partners of the new LLP entity against liabilities of the LLP arising from acts of negligence or misconduct of other partners or employees. ◀

OTHER ENTITIES
Trusts. Trusts are somewhat of a hybrid entity in that they may either be a taxpaying entity or flow-through entity. Also, there are a number of different types of trusts, so the discussion here is very general in nature. Trusts typically are subject to income taxation on all of its net income that is *not* distributed to the beneficiaries. The portion of net income that is distributed to beneficiaries is taxed to the beneficiaries. One drawback to the use of trusts is that the income tax rates are extremely progressive, reaching the 39.6% bracket when the taxable income of the trust reaches $12,300 in 2015. Trusts use Form 1041 to file its tax information.

EXAMPLE I:1-23 ▶ Ben establishes a trust for the benefit of his daughter. The principal amount of the trust is $500,000 and is projected to earn approximately 10% per year. In the current year, the trust earned $50,000 of investment income and had $5,000 of expenses. If the trust did not make any

---

[30] The LLC makes the election pursuant to the "check-the-box" Regulations, Reg. Secs. 301.7701-1 through -4.

[31] Rev. Rul. 95-37, 1995-1 C.B. 130.

distributions during the year to the daughter, the entire $45,000 (less a small exemption) would be subject to income taxation to the trust. Much of the taxable income would be subject to taxation at the 39.6% rate. Alternatively, if the trust distributed the entire $45,000 to the daughter, she would report the $45,000 on her individual tax return. Assuming she does not have significant other income, she would most likely be in the 25% marginal tax bracket. The trust's taxable income would be zero and would have no income tax liability. ◄

TAX LAW SOURCES

The solution to any tax question may only be resolved by reference to tax law sources (also referred to as tax law authority). Tax law sources are generated from all three branches of the federal government, i.e., legislative, executive, and judicial. The principal sources of tax law are as follows:

Branch	*Tax Law Source*
Legislative	Internal Revenue Code
	Congressional Committee Reports
Executive (Administrative)	Income Tax Regulations
	Revenue Rulings
	Revenue Procedures
	Letter Rulings
Judicial	Court Decisions

A thorough knowledge of the various sources above as well as the relative weights attached to each source is vital to tax professionals. Because of the vast volume of tax law sources, the ability to "find an answer" to a tax question is of fundamental importance. In addition, the evaluation of the weight (or importance) of different sources of authority is also crucial in arriving at a proper conclusion. For example, a decision of the U.S. Supreme Court on a tax matter would certainly carry more weight than a Revenue Ruling issued by the Internal Revenue Service.

Clearly, the most authoritative source of tax law is the Internal Revenue Code, which is the tax law passed by Congress. However, Congress is not capable of anticipating every type of transaction that taxpayers might engage in, so most of the statutes in the Code contain very general language. Because of the general language contained in the Code, both administrative and judicial interpretations are necessary to apply the tax law to specific situations and transactions. Thus, the regulations and rulings of the IRS and the decisions of the courts are an integral part of the federal income tax law. For a detailed discussion of tax law sources, see Chapter I:15 (Chapter C:1 of the *Comprehensive* edition). Topic Review I:1-3 provides an overview of the tax law sources.

ENACTMENT OF A TAX LAW

Under the U.S. Constitution, the House of Representatives is responsible for initiating new tax legislation. However, tax bills may also originate in the Senate as riders to nontax legislative proposals. Often, major tax proposals are initiated by the President and accompanied by a Treasury Department study or proposal, and then introduced into Congress by one or more representatives from the President's political party.

STEPS IN THE LEGISLATIVE PROCESS

The specific steps in the legislative process are discussed below and are summarized in Table I:1-2. These steps typically include:

1. A tax bill is introduced in the House of Representatives and is referred to the House Ways and Means Committee.
2. The proposal is considered by the House Ways and Means Committee, and public hearings are held. Testimony may be given by members of professional groups such

TOPIC REVIEW I:1-3

Tax Law Sources

Source	Key Points	Weight of Authority
LEGISLATIVE Internal Revenue Code	Contains provisions governing income, estate and gift, employment, alcohol, tobacco, and excise taxes.	Serves as the highest legislative authority for tax research, planning, and compliance activities.
ADMINISTRATIVE Treasury Regulations	Represents interpretations of the tax code by the Secretary of the Treasury. Regulations may be initially issued in proposed, temporary, and final form and may either be interpretative or legislative in nature.	Legislative regulations have a higher degree of authority than interpretative regulations. Proposed regulations do not have authoritative weight.
IRS Rulings	The IRS issues Revenue Rulings (letter rulings or published rulings), Revenue Procedures, Information Releases, and Technical Advice Memoranda.	These pronouncements reflect the IRS's interpretation of the law and do not have the same level of scope and authority as Treasury Regulations.
JUDICIAL Judicial doctrines	Judicial doctrines are concepts that have evolved from Supreme Court cases that are used by the courts to decide tax issues. Examples include substance over form, tax benefit rule, and constructive receipt.	Judicial doctrines that evolve from Supreme Court cases have substantial weight of authority because they have the force and effect of law.
Judicial interpretations	Tax cases are initially considered by a trial court (i.e., the Tax Court, a Federal district court, or the U.S. Court of Federal Claims). Either the taxpayer or the IRS may appeal to an appeals court. A final appeal is to the U.S. Supreme Court.	A trial court must abide by the precedents set by the court of appeals of the same jurisdiction. An appeals court is not required to follow the decisions of another court of appeals. A Supreme Court decision is the "law of the land."

ADDITIONAL COMMENT

In 2015, the chairman of the House Ways and Means Committee was Rep. Paul Ryan of Wisconsin, and the chairman of the Senate Finance Committee was Sen. Orrin Hatch of Utah.

HISTORICAL NOTE

For many years, only a few members of Congress were CPAs. This trend is changing. As of December, 2014, ten members of the House of Representatives and two members of the Senate are CPAs.

as the American Institute of CPAs and the American Bar Association and from various special-interest groups.

3. The tax bill is voted on by the House Ways and Means Committee and, if approved, is forwarded to the House of Representatives for a vote. Amendments to the bill from individual members of the House of Representatives are generally not allowed.

4. If passed by the House, the bill is forwarded to the Senate for consideration by the Senate Finance Committee, and public hearings are held.

5. The tax bill approved by the Senate Finance Committee may be substantially different from the House of Representatives' version.

6. The Senate Finance Committee reports the Senate bill to the Senate for consideration. The Senate generally permits amendments (e.g., new provisions) to be offered on the Senate floor.

7. If approved by the Senate, both the Senate and House bills are sent to a Joint Conference Committee consisting of an equal number of members from the Senate and the House of Representatives.

8. The Senate and House bills are reconciled in the Joint Conference Committee. This process of reconciliation generally involves substantial compromise if the provisions of both bills are different. A final bill is then resubmitted to the House and Senate for approval.

9. If the Joint Conference Committee bill is approved by the House and Senate, it is sent to the President for approval or veto.

10. A presidential veto may be overturned if a two-thirds majority vote is obtained in both the House and Senate.

▼ **TABLE I:1-2**

Steps in the Legislative Process

1. Treasury studies prepared on needed tax reform
2. President makes proposals to Congress
3. House Ways and Means Committee prepares House bill
4. Approval of House bill by the House of Representatives
5. Senate Finance Committee prepares Senate bill
6. Approval of Senate bill by the Senate
7. Compromise bill approved by a Joint Conference Committee
8. Approval of Joint Conference Committee bill by both the House and Senate
9. Approval or veto of legislation by the President
10. New tax law and amendments incorporated into the Code

11. Committee reports are prepared by the staffs of the House Ways and Means Committee, the Senate Finance Committee, and the Joint Conference Committee as the bill progresses through Congress. These reports help to explain the new law before the Treasury Department drafts regulations on the tax law changes as well as to explain the intent of Congress for passing the new law.

ADMINISTRATION OF THE TAX LAW AND TAX PRACTICE ISSUES

OBJECTIVE 8

Describe the administrative procedures under the tax law

ORGANIZATION OF THE INTERNAL REVENUE SERVICE

The **IRS** is the branch of the Treasury Department that is responsible for administering the federal tax law. It is organized on a type-of-taxpayer basis which allows the IRS to become more specialized. The responsibilities and functions of the various administrative branches include the following:

▶ The Commissioner of Internal Revenue, appointed by the President, is the chief officer of the IRS. This individual is supported by the Chief Counsel's office, which is responsible for preparing the government's case for litigation of tax disputes.

▶ The National Office includes a deputy commissioner, a series of assistants to the commissioner, and a chief counsel. A significant responsibility of the National Office is to process ruling requests and to prepare revenue procedures that assist taxpayers with compliance matters.

▶ Four operating divisions, organized functionally, including (1) Wage and Investment Income, (2) Small Business and Self-Employed, (3) Large Business and International, and (4) Tax Exempt and Government Entities.

ADDITIONAL COMMENT

A survey of members of the American Institute of CPAs found that more than half of the 1,036 members who responded had an unfavorable opinion of the IRS. However, the accountants gave the IRS good marks for courtesy and a willingness to solve problems.

▶ Tax service centers, located around the country, perform tax return processing work, based on the four divisions above. They also select tax returns for audit.

▶ For the 2013 fiscal year, the IRS had approximately 95,000 employees and a budget of $12 billion. In 2013, the IRS collected $2.91 trillion, 91 percent of federal government receipts.

In 1998, Congress enacted legislation with a major objective of reforming the manner in which the IRS administers the tax system. The taxpaying public has been increasingly critical of the IRS, especially with the allegedly insensitive and strong-arm tactics used against taxpayers. Therefore, the legislation placed a greater emphasis on serving the public and meeting taxpayer needs. While substantial organizational and operational changes to the IRS were mandated, only time will tell if this legislation will be successful. Details of the Act are outside the scope of this textbook.

ENFORCEMENT PROCEDURES

All tax returns are initially checked for mathematical accuracy and items that are clearly erroneous. The Form W-2 amounts (e.g., wages, and so on), Form 1099 information return amounts (e.g., relating to dividend and interest payments, and so on) and other forms filed with the IRS by the payer are checked against the amounts reported on the tax return. If differences are noted, the IRS Center merely sends the taxpayer a bill for the corrected amount of tax and a statement of the differences. This type of examination is referred to as a correspondence audit. In some instances, the difference is due to a classification error by the IRS, and the additional assessment can be resolved by written correspondence. A refund check may be sent to the taxpayer if an overpayment of tax has been made.

EXAMPLE I:1-24 ▶

Bart is an author of books and properly reports royalties on Schedule C (Profit or Loss from Business). The IRS computer matching of the Form 1099 information returns from the publishing companies incorrectly assumes that the royalties should be reported on Schedule E (Supplemental Income and Loss). If the IRS sends the taxpayer a statement of the difference and an adjusted tax bill, this matter (including the abatement of added tax, interest, and penalties) should be resolved by correspondence with the IRS. ◀

SELECTION OF RETURNS FOR AUDIT

ADDITIONAL COMMENT

A special task force has recommended that the percentage of returns audited be increased to 2.5%. Many individuals feel that the probability of being audited is so low as to be disregarded.

The U.S. tax system is based on self-assessment and voluntary compliance. However, enforcement by the IRS is essential to maintain the integrity of the tax system. The IRS uses both computers and experienced personnel to select returns for examination. With respect to the use of the computer, a **Discriminant Function System (DIF)** is used to classify returns to be selected for audit. The DIF system generates a "score" for a return based on the potential for the return to generate additional tax revenue. After returns are scored under the DIF system, the returns are manually screened by experienced IRS personnel who decide which returns warrant further examination. In the aggregate, less than 1% of all individual returns are selected for examination each year. Some examples of situations where individuals are more likely to be audited include the following:

ADDITIONAL COMMENT

In 2002, the IRS launched the National Research Program (NRP) to select returns for audit. The NRP will update data compiled in the old TCMP audits and develop new statistical models for identifying returns most likely to contain errors.

▶ Individuals who are sole proprietors and claim expenses in connection with their trade or businesses, especially if significant tax losses are incurred.

▶ Itemized deductions exceeding an average amount for the person's income level

▶ Filing of a refund claim by a taxpayer who has been previously audited, where substantial tax deficiencies have been assessed

▶ Individuals who are self-employed with substantial business income or income from a profession (e.g., a medical doctor)

ETHICAL POINT

A CPA should not recommend a position to a client that exploits the IRS audit selection process.

Audit Procedures. Audits of most individuals are handled through an **office audit procedure** in an office of the IRS. In most cases, an individual is asked to substantiate a particular deduction, credit, or income item (e.g., charitable contributions that appear to be excessive). The office audit procedure does not involve a complete audit of all items on the return.

EXAMPLE I:1-25 ▶

Brad obtains a divorce during the current year and reports a $30,000 deduction for alimony. The IRS may conduct an office audit to ascertain whether the amount is properly deductible as alimony and does not represent a disguised property settlement to Brad's ex-wife. Brad may be asked to submit verification (e.g., a property settlement agreement between the spouses that designates the payments as alimony). ◀

KEY POINT

A taxpayer may appear on his or her own behalf before the IRS during an audit. An attorney or CPA in good standing is authorized to practice before the IRS upon the filing of a written statement that he or she is currently so qualified and is authorized to represent the taxpayer.

A **field audit procedure** often is used for corporations and individuals engaged in a trade or business. A field audit generally is broader in scope than the office audit (e.g., several items on the tax return may be reviewed). A field audit usually is conducted at the taxpayer's place of business or the office of his or her tax advisor.

Most large corporations are subject to annual audits. The year under audit may be several years prior to the current year because the corporation often will waive the statute of limitations pending the resolution of disputed issues.

STATUTE OF LIMITATIONS

Most taxpayers feel a sense of relief after they have prepared their income tax return and have mailed it to the IRS. However, the filing of the tax return is not necessarily the end of the story for that particular taxable year. It is possible, of course, that the IRS may select their tax return for audit after the return has been initially processed or a taxpayer may have filed an amended return to correct an error or omission.

REAL-WORLD EXAMPLE

Based on an IRS audit, the Mustang Ranch, Nevada's most famous legal bordello, was assessed some $13 million in taxes. When the amount owed could not be paid, the IRS sold the property to recoup the taxes.

Both the IRS and taxpayers can make corrections to a return after it has been originally filed. Fortunately, both only have a limited time period in which to make such corrections. This time period is called the **statute of limitations** and prevents either the taxpayer or the IRS from changing a filed tax return after the time period has expired. The general rule for the statute of limitations is three years from the later of the date the tax return was actually filed or its due date.[32] However, a six-year statute of limitations applies if the taxpayer omits items of gross income that in total exceed 25% of the gross income reported on the return.[33] The statute of limitations remains open indefinitely if a fraudulent return is filed or if no return is filed.[34]

EXAMPLE I:1-26 ▶

Betty, a calendar-year taxpayer, is audited by the IRS in February 2015 for the tax year 2013. During the course of the audit, the IRS proposes additional tax for 2013, because Betty failed to substantiate certain travel and entertainment expense deductions. During the course of the audit, the IRS discovers that Betty failed to file a tax return for 2008, and in 2010 an item of gross income amounting to $26,000 was not reported. Gross income reported on the 2010 return was $72,000. Assuming Betty's 2013 return was filed on or before its due date (April 15, 2014), the IRS may assess a deficiency for 2013 because the three-year statute of limitations will not expire until April 15, 2017. A deficiency also may be assessed for the 2010 return because a six-year statute of limitations applies since the omission is more than 25% of the gross income reported on the return. A deficiency also may be assessed for 2008 as there is no statute of limitations for fraud. ◀

ADDITIONAL COMMENT

More than 150 penalties can be imposed on taxpayers. In fact, applying the penalties has become so complicated that the IRS is currently considering ways to consolidate and simplify them.

INTEREST

Interest accrues on both assessments of additional tax due and on refunds that the taxpayer receives from the government.[35] No interest is paid on a tax refund if the amount is refunded by the IRS within 45 days of the day prescribed for filing the return (e.g., April 15) determined without regard to extensions.[36] If a return is filed after the filing date, no interest is paid if the refund is made within 45 days of the date the return was filed.

EXAMPLE I:1-27 ▶

Beverly, a calendar-year taxpayer, files her 2014 tax return on March 1, 2015, and requests a $500 refund. No interest accrues on the refund amount if the IRS sends the refund check to Beverly within 45 days of the April 15, 2015, due date. ◀

ADDITIONAL COMMENT

In addition to the penalties listed on this page, the government also assesses penalties for civil fraud and criminal fraud. Criminal fraud carries a maximum penalty of $100,000, a prison sentence of up to five years, or both.

PENALTIES

Various nondeductible penalties are imposed on the net tax due for failure to comply, including

▶ A penalty of 5% per month (or fraction thereof) subject to a maximum of 25% for failure to file a tax return[37]

---

[32] Secs. 6501(a) and (b)(1). Similar rules apply to claims for a refund filed by the taxpayer. Section 6511(a) requires that a refund claim be filed within three years of the date the return was filed or within two years of the date the tax was paid, whichever is later.

[33] Sec. 6501(e). See also *Stephen G. Colestock*, 102 T.C. 380 (1994), where the Tax Court ruled that the extended six-year limitation period applied to a married couple's entire tax liability for the tax year at issue, not just to items that constituted substantial omissions of gross income. Thus, the IRS was able to assert an increased deficiency and additional penalties attributable to a disallowed depreciation deduction.

[34] Sec. 6501(c).

[35] Sec. 6621(a). The rate is adjusted four times a year by the Treasury Department based on the current interest rate for short-term federal obligations.

The interest rate individual taxpayers must pay to the IRS on underpayments of tax is the federal short-term rate plus three percentage points. The interest rate paid to taxpayers on overpayments of tax is the federal short-term rate plus two percentage points. The annual interest rate on noncorporate underpayments and overpayments for the period January 1, 2015, through March 31, 2015, was 3% (2% in the case of a corporation).

[36] Sec. 6611(e).

[37] Sec. 6651(a)(1). The penalty assessed may be very small in some instances even though the taxpayer owes a large tax bill for the year because penalties are imposed on the net tax due. The percentages are increased to 15% per month (or fraction thereof) up to a maximum of 75% if the penalty is for fraudulent failure to file under Sec. 6651(f).

> ► A penalty of 0.5% per month (or fraction thereof) up to a maximum of 25% for failure to pay the tax that is due[38]

> ► An accuracy-related penalty of 20% of the underpayment for items such as negligence or disregard of rules or regulations, any substantial understatement of income tax, or any substantial misstatement of valuation[39]

> ► A 75% penalty for fraud[40]

> ► A penalty based on the current interest rate for underpayment of estimated taxes[41]

> ► Significant new penalties on tax return preparers have been enacted by Congress for taxable years 2007 and forward. In general, these new penalties are applicable for any position on a tax return where there is a "realistic possibility" (one-in-three chance) that the position would not be upheld in a court of law. The penalty is not assessed if the position is disclosed in the return.

ADMINISTRATIVE APPEAL PROCEDURES

ADDITIONAL COMMENT

Pete Rose, major league baseball's all-time hit leader, was sent to prison in 1990 for income tax evasion.

If an IRS agent issues a deficiency assessment, the taxpayer may make an appeal to the IRS Appeals Division. Some disputes involve a gray area (e.g., a situation where some courts have held for the IRS whereas other courts have held for the taxpayer on facts that are similar to the disputed issue). In such a case, the taxpayer may be able to negotiate a compromise settlement (e.g., a percentage of the disputed tax amount plus interest and penalties) with the Appeals Division based on the "hazards of litigation" (i.e., the probability of winning or losing the case if it is litigated).

COMPONENTS OF A TAX PRACTICE

OBJECTIVE 9

Describe the components of a tax practice

Tax practice is a rapidly growing field that provides substantial opportunities for tax specialists in public accounting, law, and industry. The tasks performed by a tax professional may range from the preparation of a simple Form 1040 for an individual to the conduct of tax research and planning for highly complex business situations. Tax practice consists of the following activities:

► Tax compliance and procedure (i.e., tax return preparation and representation of a client in administrative proceedings before the IRS)

► Tax research

► Tax planning and consulting

► Financial planning

TAX COMPLIANCE AND PROCEDURE

TYPICAL MISCONCEPTION

Many people believe that a tax practitioner should serve in the capacity of a neutral, unbiased expert. They tend to forget that tax practitioners are being paid to represent their clients' interests. A tax practitioner may sometimes recommend a position that is defensible, but where the weight of authority is on the side of the IRS.

Preparation of tax returns is a significant component of tax practice. Tax practitioners often prepare federal, state, and local tax returns for individuals, corporations, estates, trusts, and so on. In larger corporations, the tax return preparation (i.e., compliance) function usually is performed by a company's internal tax department staff. In such a case, a CPA or other tax practitioner may assist the client with the tax research and planning aspects of their tax practice, and may even review their return before it is filed.

An important part of tax practice consists of assisting the client in negotiations with the IRS. If a client is audited, the practitioner acts as the client's representative in discussions with the IRS agent. If a tax deficiency is assessed, the practitioner assists the client if

---

[38] Sec. 6651(a)(2). If the failure to file penalty (5%) and the failure to pay the tax penalty (0.5%) are both applicable, the failure to file penalty is reduced by the failure to pay penalty per Sec. 6651(c)(1). Further, the penalty is increased to 1% per month after the IRS notifies the taxpayer that it will levy on the taxpayer's assets.

[39] Sec. 6662.
[40] Sec. 6663.
[41] Sec. 6654.

an administrative appeal is contemplated with the IRS's Appellate Division. In most instances, an attorney is retained if litigation is being considered.

TAX RESEARCH

Tax research is the search for the best possible defensibly correct solution to a problem involving either a completed transaction (e.g., a sale of property) or a proposed transaction (e.g., a proposed merger of two corporations). Research involves each of the following steps:

▶ Determine the facts.

▶ Identify the issue(s).

▶ Identify and analyze the tax law sources (i.e., code provisions, Treasury Regulations, administrative rulings, and court cases).

▶ Evaluate nontax (e.g., business) implications.

▶ Solve the problem.

▶ Communicate the findings to the client.

Tax research may be conducted in connection with tax return preparation, tax planning, or procedural activities. A more thorough discussion of tax research is presented in Chapter I:15.

TAX PLANNING AND CONSULTING

Tax planning involves the process of structuring one's affairs so as to minimize the amount of taxes *and* maximize the after-tax return. Thus, optimal tax planning is *not* to just pay the least amount of tax but to maximize after-tax cash flows. A text on tax research and planning has delineated the following tax planning principles:[42]

▶ Keep sufficient records.

▶ Forecast the effect of future events.

▶ Support the plan with a sound business purpose.

▶ Base the plan on sound legal authorities.

▶ Do not carry a good plan too far.

▶ Make the plan flexible.

▶ Integrate the tax plan with other factors in decision making.

▶ Conduct research to learn whether a similar plan has previously proved unsuccessful (e.g., a court case involving similar facts may have upheld the IRS's position).

▶ Consider the "maximum" risk exposure of the client (e.g., if the plan is subsequently challenged by the IRS and the tax treatment is disallowed, what is the economic impact upon the taxpayer?).

▶ Consider the effect of timing (e.g., whether it is more beneficial to take a deduction in one year versus another).

▶ Shape the plan to the client's needs and desires.

CPAs and attorneys frequently are engaged by their clients to perform consulting services to optimize the client's tax situation. For example, a major corporation client is considering the acquisition of a major international corporation and wants to make sure that the tax implications of such an acquisition are properly managed. The CPA will be engaged to perform a thorough review of the transaction to ensure that the client is fully aware of the tax results of the acquisition, and possibly may request an advance ruling from the IRS.

Because of the importance of planning in tax practice, subsequent chapters in this text include a separate section on tax planning to discuss issues that are related to the topical coverage. These tax planning principles should be kept in mind when attempting to use the tax planning recommendations. Also, a systematic approach to tax planning

[42] Norton, Fred W., *Federal Taxation: Research, Planning, and Procedures 2Ed*, © 1979. Printed and Electronically reproduced by permission of Pearson Education, Inc., Upper Saddle River, New Jersey.

SELF-STUDY QUESTION

Do large national CPA firms generally stress the importance of tax research in connection with tax-return preparation or tax planning?

ANSWER

The large CPA firms emphasize their skills in tax planning. Sometimes a slight alteration of a proposed transaction can save the client substantial tax dollars. This is high-value-added work and can be billed at premium rates.

ADDITIONAL COMMENT

Several national accounting firms have divided their tax departments into two basic groups, consulting and compliance. The tax consultants work with clients in tax planning and consulting matters and do not prepare tax returns. Tax returns are prepared by the compliance staff.

developed by two noted academicians, Myron Scholes and Mark Wolfson, is discussed in Chapter I:18.

FINANCIAL PLANNING

A relatively new field for tax professionals is that of financial planning for individual clients. Since taxes are an integral part of any financial plan and since a tax specialist regularly meets with his or her clients (filing returns and other tax matters), the area of financial planning has become increasingly a part of tax practice. The typical steps in performing a financial planning engagement include the following steps:

▶ Determine the client's financial goals and objectives.

▶ Review the client's insurance coverage for adequacy and appropriateness.

▶ Recommend an investment strategy, including risk analysis and asset allocation.

▶ Review tax returns to ensure that, through proper tax planning, the client is maximizing his or her after-tax cash flow.

▶ Review the client's retirement plans to assure compliance with the law and possible new alternatives.

▶ Review all documents related to estate and gift planning and work with the client's attorney to minimize all transfer taxes and fulfill the client's objectives.

COMPUTER APPLICATIONS IN TAX PRACTICE

TAX RETURN PREPARATION

To prepare tax returns, most tax practitioners purchase tax preparation software from companies such as Commerce Clearing House or Intuit. This software allows the preparation of accurate and professional-looking tax returns. A word of caution, however, is in order. As with any computer software, the preparation of tax returns using the computer requires as much knowledge and expertise from the preparer as doing the returns by hand. A recent trend in tax return preparation is the **electronic filing** of tax returns, i.e., a "paperless" tax return. Taxpayers send their returns electronically to the IRS for processing, thereby saving enormous amounts of paper and, perhaps, reducing human error.

TAX PLANNING APPLICATIONS

Performing tax planning for clients involves the evaluation of alternative courses of action. This evaluation process can be very time-consuming because of the tax calculations necessary to arrive at an optimal solution. The computer has become an essential tool in this process because of the speed with which the tax calculations can be made. Many tax professionals now use sophisticated software to perform tax planning for their clients. A prime example of the use of the computer in tax planning has been in deciding whether a taxpayer should invest in a Roth Individual Retirement Account (Roth IRA) or a regular IRA (see Chapter I:9 for more details on IRAs). There are many factors to consider, including current and projected tax rates, current and projected level of income, etc. With the computer, a tax professional can vary the assumptions and create a number of alternatives within a relatively short period of time. To perform this task by hand would require an enormous commitment of time. As with most aspects of life, the impact of the computer on tax planning has been highly significant and will only increase in the future.

TAX RESEARCH APPLICATIONS

Computerized information-retrieval systems are used in tax research and are rapidly replacing books as the principal source of tax-related information. Most commercial research services are offered on the internet. The principal Internet services are RIA's *Checkpoint* and CCH's *Tax Research Network*. These commercial Internet services contain a wide range of materials available to tax researchers who subscribe to the service. In addition, the IRS has a home page (www.irs.gov) that taxpayers can access for forms, publications, and other related materials. All of the major accounting firms and many other tax organizations have home pages that allow users to access a myriad of tax information.

PROBLEM MATERIALS

DISCUSSION QUESTIONS

I:1-1 The Supreme Court in 1895 ruled that the income tax was unconstitutional because the tax needed to be apportioned among the states in proportion to their populations. Why would the requirement of proportionality be so difficult to administer?

I:1-2 Why was pay-as-you-go withholding needed in 1943?

I:1-3 Congressman Patrick indicates that he is opposed to tax proposals that call for a flat tax rate because the structure would not tax those individuals who have the ability to pay the tax. Discuss the position of the congressman, giving consideration to tax rate structures (e.g., progressive, proportional, and regressive) and the concept of equity.

I:1-4 The governor of your state stated in a recent political speech that he has never supported any income tax increases as the tax rates have remained at the same level during his entire term of office. Yet, you believe that you are paying more tax this year than in previous years even though your income has not increased. How can both you and the governor be correct? In other words, is it possible for the government to raise taxes without raising tax rates?

I:1-5 Carmen has computed that her average tax rate is 16% and her marginal tax rate is 25% for the current year. She is considering whether to make a charitable contribution to her church before the end of the tax year. Which tax rate is of greater significance in measuring the tax effect for her decision? Explain.

I:1-6 Why are the gift and estate taxes called wealth transfer taxes? What is the tax base for computing each of these taxes?

I:1-7 Cathy, who is single, makes gifts of $50,000 to each of her two adult children.
a. Who is primarily liable for the gift tax on the two gifts, Cathy or the two children?
b. If Cathy has never made a taxable gift in prior years, is a gift tax due on the two gifts?

I:1-8 Carlos inherits 100 shares of Allied Corporation stock from his father. The stock cost his father $8,000 and had a $25,000 FMV on the date of his father's death in 2015. The alternate valuation date was not elected. What is Carlos's tax basis for the Allied stock when it is received from the estate?

I:1-9 Most estates are not subject to the federal estate tax.
a. Why is this the case?
b. Do you believe most estates should be subject to the federal estate tax?

I:1-10 Indicate which of the following taxes are generally progressive, proportional, or regressive:
a. State income taxes
b. Federal estate tax
c. Corporate state franchise tax
d. Property taxes
e. State and local sales taxes

I:1-11 Carolyn operates a consulting business as a sole proprietor (unincorporated). Carolyn has been approached by one of her major clients to become an employee. If she accepts the new job, she would no longer operate her consulting business. From the standpoint of paying Social Security taxes, would Carolyn's Social Security taxes increase or decrease if she becomes an employee? Why? (Assume Carolyn will earn less than $200,000.)

I:1-12 The three different levels of government (federal, state, and local) must impose taxes to carry out their functions. For each of the types of taxes below, discuss which level of government primarily uses that type of tax.
a. Property taxes
b. Excise taxes
c. Sales taxes
d. Income taxes
e. Employment taxes

I:1-13 A "good" tax structure has five characteristics.
a. Briefly discuss the five characteristics.
b. Using the five characteristics, evaluate the following tax structures:
1. Federal income tax
2. State sales tax
3. Local ad valorem property tax

I:1-14 Two commonly-recognized measures of the fairness of an income tax structure are "horizontal equity" and "vertical equity."
a. Discuss what is meant by horizontal equity and vertical equity as it pertains to the income tax.

b. Why is it so difficult to design a "fair" tax structure?

I:1-15 The primary objective of the federal income tax law is to raise revenue. What are its secondary objectives?

I:1-16 If the objectives of the federal tax system are multifaceted and include raising revenues, providing investment incentives, encouraging certain industries, and meeting desired social objectives, is it possible to achieve a simplified tax system? Explain.

I:1-17 Distinguish between *taxpaying entities* and *flow-through entities* from the standpoint of the federal income tax law.

I:1-18 Sally and Tom are married, have three dependent children, and file a joint return in 2015. If they have adjusted gross income (AGI) of $90,000 and itemized deductions of $10,000, what is their taxable income for 2015?

I:1-19 The Bruin Corporation, a C corporation, is owned 100% by John Bean and had taxable income in 2015 of $500,000. John is also an employee of the corporation. In December 2015, the corporation has decided to distribute $400,000 to John and has asked you whether it would be better to distribute the money as a dividend or salary. John is in the 39.6% marginal tax bracket. How would you respond to Bruin Corporation? Consider only income taxes for this problem.

I:1-20 Discuss what is meant by the term "double taxation" of corporations. Develop an example of double taxation using a corporation and shareholder.

I:1-21 Limited liability companies (LLCs) are very popular today as a form of organization. Assume a client asks you to explain what this type of organization is all about. Prepare a brief description of the federal income tax aspects of LLCs.

I:1-22 For flow-through entities, such as partnerships, how does the tax law use partner basis adjustments to prevent double taxation of partnership income?

I:1-23 Partnerships and S corporations are flow-through entities. In connection with filing annual tax returns, these entities must include Form K-1 in the returns. What is Form K-1, what is its purpose, and who receives the form?

I:1-24 The PDQ Partnership earned ordinary income of $150,000 in 2015. The partnership has three equal partners, Pete, Donald, and Quint. Quint, who is single, uses the standard deduction, and has other income of $15,000 (not connected with the partnership) in 2015. He receives a $30,000 distribution from the partnership during the year. What is Quint's taxable income in 2015?

I:1-25 Why is a thorough knowledge of sources of tax law so important for a professional person who works in the tax area?

I:1-26 The Internal Revenue Code is the most authoritative source of income tax law. In trying to resolve an income tax question, however, a tax researcher also consults administrative rulings (Income Tax Regulations, Revenue Rulings, etc.) and court decisions. Why wouldn't the tax researcher just consult the Code since it is the highest authority? Similarly, why is there a need for administrative rulings and court decisions?

I:1-27 Congressional committee reports are an important source of information concerning the legislative enactment of tax law.
a. Name the three Congressional committee reports that are issued in connection with a new tax bill.
b. Of what importance are Congressional committee reports to tax practitioners?

I:1-28 What is the primary service function provided by the National Office of the IRS?

I:1-29 What types of taxpayers are more likely to be audited by the IRS?

I:1-30 Anya is concerned that she will be audited by the IRS.
a. Under what circumstances is it possible that the IRS will review each line item on her tax return?
b. Is it likely that all items on Anya's return will be audited?

I:1-31 **a.** What does the term "hazards of litigation" mean in the context of taxation?
b. Why would the IRS or a taxpayer settle or compromise a case based on the "hazards of litigation"?

I:1-32 If a taxpayer files his or her tax return and receives a tax refund from the IRS, does this mean that the IRS feels that the return is correct and will not be subject to a future audit.

I:1-33 State the statute of limitations for transactions involving:
a. Fraud (e.g., failure to file a tax return)
b. Disallowance of tax deduction items
c. The omission of rental income equal to greater than 25% of the taxpayer's reported gross income

I:1-34 In reference to tax research, what is meant by *the best possible defensibly correct solution*?

I:1-35 The profession of tax practice involves four principal areas of activity. Discuss these four areas.

I:1-36 Many tax professionals have moved into the field of financial planning for their clients.
a. How do taxes impact financial planning for a client?
b. Why do tax professionals have a perfect opportunity to perform financial planning for their clients?

I:1-37 Is the principal goal of tax planning to absolutely minimize the amount of taxes that a taxpayer must pay?

I:1-38 Explain how a computer can assist a tax practitioner in tax planning activities and making complex tax calculations.

PROBLEMS

I:1-39   *Tax Rates.* Latesha, a single taxpayer, had the following income and deductions for the tax year 2015:

INCOME:		
	Salary	$ 80,000
	Business Income	25,000
	Interest income from bonds	10,000
	Tax-exempt bond interest	5,000
	TOTAL INCOME	120,000
DEDUCTIONS:	Business expenses	$ 9,500
	Itemized deductions	20,000
	Personal exemption	4,000
	TOTAL DEDUCTIONS	33,500

    a. Compute Latesha's taxable income and federal tax liability for 2015 (round to dollars).
    b. Compute Latesha's marginal, average, and effective tax rates.
    c. For tax planning purposes, which of the three rates in Part b is the most important?

I:1-40   *Tax Rates.* Based on the amounts of taxable income below, compute the federal income tax payable in 2015 on each amount assuming the taxpayers are married filing a joint return. Also, for each amount of taxable income, compute the average tax rate and the marginal tax rate.
    a. Taxable income of $30,000.
    b. Taxable income of $100,000.
    c. Taxable income of $375,000.
    d. Taxable income of $600,000.

I:1-41   *Marginal Tax Rate.* Jill and George are married and file a joint return. They expect to have $425,000 of taxable income in the next year and are considering whether to purchase a personal residence that would provide additional tax deductions of $80,000 for mortgage interest and real estate taxes.
    a. What is their marginal tax rate for purposes of making this decision?
    b. What is the tax savings if the residence is acquired?

I:1-42   *Gift Tax.* Betty, a married taxpayer, makes the following gifts during the current year (2015): $20,000 to her church, $50,000 to her daughter, and $40,000 to her husband. What is the amount of Betty's taxable gifts for the current year (assuming that she does not elect to split the gifts with her spouse)?

I:1-43   *Estate Tax.* Clay, who was single, died in 2015 and has a gross estate valued at $8,500,000. Six months after his death, the gross assets are valued at $9,000,000. The estate incurs funeral and administration expenses of $125,000. Clay had debts amounting to $150,000 and bequeathed all of his estate to his children. During his life, Clay made no taxable gifts.
    a. What is the amount of Clay's taxable estate?
    b. What is the tax base for computing Clay's estate tax?
    c. What is the amount of estate tax owed if the tentative estate tax (before credits) is $3,235,800?
    d. Alternatively, if, six months after his death, the gross assets in Clay's estate declined in value to $7,500,000, can the administrator of Clay's estate elect the alternate valuation date? What are the important factors that the administrator should consider as to whether the alternate valuation date should be elected?

I:1-44   *Comparison of Tax Entities.*
    a. Keith Thomas and Thomas Brooks began a new consulting business on January 1, 2015. They organized the business as a C corporation, KT, Inc. During 2015, the corporation was successful and generated revenues of $1,300,000. KT had operating expenses of $800,000 before any payments to Keith or Thomas. During 2015, KT paid dividends to Keith and Thomas in the amount of $165,000 each. Assume that Keith had other ordinary taxable income of $130,000, itemized deductions of $40,000, is married (wife has no income), and has no children. Compute the total tax liability of KT and Keith for 2015. Ignore any phaseout of itemized deductions or reduction of personal exemptions.

b. Instead of organizing the consulting business as a C corporation, assume Keith and Thomas organized the business as a limited liability company, KT, LLC. KT made a distribution of $250,000 each to Keith and Thomas during 2015. Compute the total tax liability of KT and Keith for 2015. Ignore any phaseout of itemized deductions, any phase out of personal exemptions, and additional tax on net investment income.

I:1-45 *Partnership Income.* Howard Gartman is a 40% partner in the Horton & Gartman Partnership. During 2015, the partnership reported the total items below (100%) on its Form 1065:

Ordinary income	$180,000
Qualified dividends	10,000
Long-term capital loss	(12,000)
Long-term capital gain	28,000
Charitable contributions	4,000
Cash distributions to partners	150,000

Howard and his wife Dawn, who file a joint return, also had the following income and deductions from sources not connected with the partnership:

Income

Dawn's salary	$40,000
Qualified dividends	3,000

Deductions

Mortgage interest	9,000
Real estate taxes	3,800
Charitable contributions	1,000

Howard and Dawn have two dependent children. During 2015, Dawn had $6,000 in federal income taxes withheld from her salary and Howard made four estimated tax payments of $3,000 each ($12,000 total). Compute Howard and Dawn's Federal income tax liability for 2015 and whether they have a balance due or a tax refund. Ignore the child tax credits and the election to take state sales tax as an itemized deduction.

I:1-46 *Interest and Penalties.* In 2014, Paul, who is single, has a comfortable salary from his job as well as income from his investment portfolio. However, he is habitually late in filing his federal income tax return. He did not file his 2014 income tax return until December 2, 2015 (due date was April 15, 2015) and no extensions of time to file the return were filed. Below are amounts from his 2014 return:

Taxable income	$140,000
Total tax liability on taxable income	32,271
Total federal tax withheld from his salary	26,808

Paul sent a check with his return to the IRS for the balance due of $5,463. He is relieved that he has completed his filing requirement for 2014 *and* has met his financial obligation to the government for 2014.

Has Paul met *all* of his financial obligations to the IRS for 2014? If not, what additional amounts will Paul be liable to pay to the IRS?

I:1-47 *IRS Audits.* Which of the following individuals is most likely to be audited?
a. Connie has a $20,000 net loss from her unincorporated business (a cattle ranch). She also received a $200,000 salary as an executive of a corporation.
b. Craig has AGI of $20,000 from wages and uses the standard deduction.
c. Dale fails to report $120 of dividends from a stock investment. His taxable income is $40,000 and he has no other unusually large itemized deductions or business expenses. A Form 1099 is reported to the IRS.

I:1-48 *Statute of Limitations.* In April 2015, Dan is audited by the IRS for the year 2013. During the course of the audit, the agent discovers that Dan's deductions for business travel and entertainment are unsubstantiated and a $600 deficiency assessment is proposed for the tax year 2013. The agent also examined some prior year returns. The agent discovers that Dan failed to report $40,000 of gross business income on his 2011 return. Gross income of $60,000 was reported in 2011. The agent also discovers that Dan failed to file a tax return in 2006.

Will the statute of limitations prevent the IRS from issuing a deficiency assessment for 2013, 2011, or 2006? Explain.

TAX STRATEGY PROBLEM

I:1-49 Pedro Bourbone is the founder and owner of a highly successful small business and, over the past several years, has accumulated a significant amount of personal wealth. His portfolio of stocks and bonds is worth nearly $5,000,000, owns real estate worth $3,000,000, and generates income from dividends and interest of nearly $250,000 per year. With his salary from the business and his dividends and interest, Pedro has taxable income of approximately $700,000 per year and is clearly in the top individual marginal tax bracket. Pedro is married and has three children, ages 16, 14, and 12. Neither his wife nor his children are employed and have no income. Pedro has come to you as his CPA to discuss ways to reduce his individual tax liability as well as to discuss the potential estate tax upon his death. You mention the possibility of making gifts each year to his children. Explain how annual gifts to his children will reduce both his income during lifetime and his estate tax at death.

CASE STUDY PROBLEM

I:1-50 John Gemstone, a wealthy client, has recently been audited by the IRS. The agent has questioned the following deduction items on Mr. Gemstone's tax return for the year under review:

- A $10,000 loss deduction on the rental of his beach cottage.
- A $20,000 charitable contribution deduction for the donation of a painting to a local art museum. The agent has questioned whether the painting is overvalued.
- A $15,000 loss deduction from the operation of a cattle breeding ranch. The agent is concerned that the ranch is not a legitimate business (i.e., is a hobby).

Your supervisor has requested that you represent Mr. Gemstone in his discussions with the IRS.

a. What additional questions should you ask Mr. Gemstone in an attempt to substantiate the deductibility of the above items?

b. What tax research procedures might be applied to build the best possible case for your client?

TAX RESEARCH PROBLEM

I:1-51 Read the following two cases and explain why the Supreme Court reached different conclusions for cases involving similar facts and issues:

- *CIR v. Court Holding Co.*, 33 AFTR 593, 45-1 USTC ¶9215 (USSC, 1945)
- *U.S. v. Cumberland Public Service Co.*, 38 AFTR 978, 50-1 USTC ¶9129 (USSC, 1950)

2

DETERMINATION OF TAX

LEARNING OBJECTIVES

After studying this chapter, you should be able to

1. Use the tax formula to compute an individual's taxable income

2. Determine the amount of deductions from Adjusted Gross Income

3. Calculate the income tax for individuals

4. Explain the basic income tax rules relating to business entities

5. Explain the basic concepts of capital gains and losses

6. Compute the income tax for high-income individuals

7. Describe tax planning considerations for various tax matters

8. Describe compliance and procedural matters for filing tax returns

Each year, over 140 million individuals and married couples file tax forms on which they compute their federal income tax. The income tax is imposed "on the taxable income of every individual."[1] The amount of tax actually owed by an individual taxpayer is determined by applying a complex set of rules that together make up the income tax law. To understand the income tax, it is necessary to study the basic formula on which the income tax computation is based. Therefore, this chapter introduces the income tax formula and begins the development of its components. Because the income tax formula constitutes the basis of the income tax, most of the remainder of this book is an expansion of the formula. In addition to individual taxpayers, about 6 million corporations and 2 million partnerships file returns each year. These entities are also discussed in this chapter.

FORMULA FOR INDIVIDUAL INCOME TAX

OBJECTIVE 1

Use the tax formula to compute an individual's taxable income

BASIC FORMULA

Most individuals compute their income tax by using the formula illustrated in Table I:2-1. The formula itself appears rather simple. However, the complexity of the income tax results from the intricate rules that must be applied in order to arrive at the amounts that enter into the formula.

The tax formula is incorporated into the income tax form. The tax formula illustrated in Table I:2-1 can be compared with Form 1040, which is reproduced in Figure I:2-1 (see page I:2-8). Some differences exist between the tax formula below and the tax form itself. For example, taxpayers generally are not required to report exclusions (nontaxable income) on their tax returns. One exception does require taxpayers to disclose tax-exempt interest income. A number of separate schedules are used to report various types of income. For example, income from a sole proprietorship is reported on Schedule C, where gross income from the business is reduced by related expenses that are deductions for adjusted gross income (AGI). Only the net income from the business actually appears on Form 1040. Also, Form 1040 is used to collect other taxes such as the self-employment tax. Hence, a line is provided for that tax on Form 1040. The main reason for differences between the formula and the form is administrative convenience. That is, there is no reason to require taxpayers to disclose income if the

ADDITIONAL COMMENT

The IRS estimates that the average taxpayer will spend 3 hours and 59 minutes in preparing just a Form 1040. When the estimated time for recordkeeping, learning about the law, and sending the form is added to the preparation time, the total time estimate jumps to 9 hours and 54 minutes. Each additional form and schedule adds even more time.

ADDITIONAL COMMENT

Comedian Jay Leno's explanation as to why the IRS calls it Form 1040 was, "For every $50 you earn, you get $10 and they get $40."

TYPICAL MISCONCEPTION

As explained in Chapter I:1, the federal income tax includes a progressive tax rate structure, meaning that the tax rate increases as the tax base increases. For example, if a taxpayer is in the 25% marginal tax bracket, some taxpayers incorrectly assume that this means that all of their income is being taxed at 25%. Instead, the actual calculation will include some of the income taxed at 10%, some at 15% and only the last portion of income taxed at 25%.

▼ TABLE I:2-1

Tax Formula for Individuals

Income from whatever source derived	$xxx,xxx
Minus: Exclusions	(xxx)
Gross income	$ xx,xxx
Minus: Deductions for adjusted gross income	(xxx)
Adjusted gross income	$ x,xxx
Minus: Deductions from adjusted gross income:	
Greater of itemized deductions or the standard deduction	(xx)
Personal and dependency exemptions	(xx)
Taxable income	$ x,xxx
Times: Tax rate or rates (from tax table or schedule)	× .xx
Gross tax	$ xx
Minus: Credits and prepayments	(x)
Net tax payable or refund due	$ xx

---

[1] Sec. 1.

income is not subject to tax, it is more simple to report business income on a separate schedule, and it is convenient to collect other taxes on the same tax form.

Examination of the formula reveals terms such as *gross income, exclusions, adjusted gross income, exemptions, gross tax,* and *credits.* These terms and others that make up the formula are defined below.

DEFINITIONS

Income. The term **income** includes both taxable and nontaxable income. Although the term is not specifically defined in the tax law, it does include income from any source.[2] Its meaning is close to that of the term **revenue.** However, it does not include a "return of capital." Thus, in the case of the sale of property, only the gain, not the entire sales proceeds, is viewed as income. This view extends to the sale of inventory, where gross profit is viewed as income, as opposed to the sale price.

Exclusion. Not all income is taxable. An **exclusion** is any item of income that the tax law says is not taxable. Congress, over the years, has specifically excluded certain types of income from taxation for various social, economic, and political reasons. Chapter I:4 discusses specific exclusions and the reasons for their existence. Table I:2-2 contains a sample of the major exclusions from gross income.

Gross Income. **Gross income** is income reduced by exclusions. In other words, it is income from taxable sources and is reported on the return (excluded income need not be disclosed). Section 61(a) contains a partial list of items of gross income. The items listed in Sec. 61(a) are shown in Table I:2-3. Note, however, that Sec. 61(a) states that unless otherwise provided, "gross income means all income from whatever source derived, including (but not limited to)" the listed items of income. Thus, even though an item is omitted from the list does not necessarily mean that the item is excluded. For example, illegal income, although omitted from the list, is taxable.[3]

▼ **TABLE I:2-2**
Major Exclusions

Gifts and inheritances
Life insurance proceeds
Welfare and certain other transfer payments
Certain scholarships and fellowships
Certain payments for injury and sickness
  Personal physical injury settlements
  Worker's compensation
  Medical expense reimbursements
Certain employee fringe benefits
  Health plan premiums
  Group term life insurance premiums (limited)
  Meals and lodging
  Employee discounts
  Dependent care
Certain foreign-earned income
Interest on state and local government bonds
Certain interest of Series EE bonds
Certain improvements by lessee to lessor's property
Child support payments
Property settlements pursuant to a divorce
Gain from the sale of a personal residence (limited)
Distributions from Roth retirement plans

[2] Sec. 61(a).

[3] *U.S. v. Manley S. Sullivan,* 6 AFTR 6753, 1 USTC ¶236 (USSC, 1927).

▼ **TABLE I:2-3**

Gross Income Items Listed in Sec. 61(a)

Compensation for services, including fees, commissions, fringe benefits, and similar items

Gross income derived from business

Gains derived from dealings in property

Interest

Rents

Royalties

Dividends

Alimony and separate maintenance payments

Annuities

Income from life insurance and endowment contracts

Pensions

Income from the discharge of indebtedness

Distributive share of partnership gross income

Income in respect of a decedent

Income from an interest in an estate or trust

Deductions for Adjusted Gross Income. In general, taxpayers may deduct expenses that are specifically allowed by the tax law. Allowable deductions include business and investment expenses generally, along with personal expenses that are specifically provided for in the IRC, such as charitable contributions. Most purely personal expenses are not deductible.

Deductions fall into two categories for individual taxpayers: deductions *for* adjusted gross income and deductions *from* adjusted gross income. In general, **deductions for adjusted gross income** are expenses connected with a trade or business. For the most part, **deductions from adjusted gross income** are personal expenses that Congress has chosen to allow. This classification scheme, however, is not always followed. For example, alimony paid, which is not a business expense, is a deduction *for* adjusted gross income. Table I:2-4 contains a partial list of deductions *for* adjusted gross income that is taken from Sec. 62. Deductions for adjusted gross income are discussed further in Chapter I: 6.

Adjusted Gross Income. Adjusted gross income (AGI) is a measure of income that falls between gross income and taxable income. AGI is important because it is used in numerous other tax computations, especially to impose limitations. For example, AGI is used to establish floors for the medical deduction and casualty loss deduction and to establish a ceiling for the charitable contribution deduction.

Deductions from Adjusted Gross Income. Section 62 lists deductions *for* AGI (see Table I:2-4). Thus, any allowable deduction not listed in Sec. 62 is a deduction *from* AGI. The two categories of deductions *from* adjusted gross income are (1) itemized deductions or the standard deduction and (2) personal and dependency exemptions.[4] Deductions from AGI are discussed further in Chapter I: 7 of this textbook.

Itemized Deductions and The Standard Deduction. As mentioned above, taxpayers generally cannot deduct personal expenses.[5] Congress, however, allows taxpayers to deduct specified personal expenses such as charitable contributions and medical expenses. In addition, taxpayers are allowed to itemize expenses related to the

ADDITIONAL COMMENT

In 2012, there were a total of 145 million individual income tax returns filed. 93.1 million of these returns had AGI under $50,000, and 5.2 million returns filed with AGI over $200,000.

ADDITIONAL COMMENT

Itemized deductions were claimed on 31.5% of all returns filed in 2012.

---

[4] Sec. 63. [5] Sec. 262.

▼ **TABLE I:2-4**
Deductions for Adjusted Gross Income Listed in Sec. 62

Trade and business deductions

Reimbursed employee expenses and certain expenses of performing artists

Losses from the sale or exchange of property

Deductions attributable to rents and royalties

Certain deductions of life tenants and income beneficiaries of property

Contributions to retirement plans (Keoghs and IRAs)

Penalties forfeited because of premature withdrawal of funds from time savings accounts

*One-half of self-employment taxes paid

*Health insurance costs incurred by a self-employed person

Alimony

Moving expenses

Certain required repayments of supplemental unemployment compensation

Jury duty pay remitted to an individual's employer

Certain environmental expenditures (reforestation and clean fuel)

Interest on education loans

Contribution to medical savings account

*Though not actually mentioned in Sec. 62, self-employment taxes and health insurance costs of self-employed persons are defined by Secs. 164(f) and 162(l), respectively, as trade or business deductions thereby indirectly enabling taxpayers to deduct these amounts for AGI.

ADDITIONAL COMMENT

Tax rate schedules, the standard deduction, personal exemptions, and other amounts are adjusted annually for inflation. Because of "rounding conventions," not every amount changes each year.

HISTORICAL NOTE

In 1986, when parents were required merely to list the names of their children to claim them as a dependent, 77 million children were claimed. In 1987, when taxpayers were required to list children's Social Security numbers to prove that the exemptions were valid, the number of children claimed as dependents decreased to 70 million.

HISTORICAL NOTE

As recently as 1986, the highest marginal tax rate was 50%, and as recently as 1980, it was 70%.

production or collection of income, the management of property held for the production of income, and the determination, collection, or refund of any tax.[6]

Taxpayers have the choice of claiming either itemized deductions or the standard deduction. The amount of the standard deduction varies depending on the taxpayer's filing status, age, and vision. As a practical matter, for most taxpayers the standard deduction is greater than the total itemized deductions. Taxpayers with small amounts of deductible expenses do not itemize and, in fact, do not have to keep records of medical expenses and other itemized deductions. The relationship between itemized deductions and the standard deduction is discussed later in this chapter.

Personal and Dependency Exemptions. A **personal exemption** generally is allowed for each taxpayer and his or her spouse and an additional dependency exemption is permitted for each dependent. Both personal and dependency exemptions are equal to $4,000 in 2015 and $3,950 in 2014. The amount of an exemption is adjusted annually for increases in the cost of living.

Taxable Income. **Taxable income** is adjusted gross income reduced by deductions *from* AGI. It is the amount of income that is taxed.

Tax Rates and Gross Tax. Tax rates are the percentage rates, set by Congress, at which income is taxed. There are seven tax rates ranging from 10% to 39.6%.

10%, 15%, 25%, 28%, 33%, 35%, and 39.6%

Taxpayers compute their tax by applying the percentage rates found in the tax rate schedules to taxable income. However, most taxpayers simply look in a tax table to find their gross tax. These two alternatives are discussed in more detail later in this chapter. The gross tax is the amount of tax determined by this process.

[6] Sec. 212.

▼ **TABLE I:2-5**
Partial List of Tax Credits

Refundable

    Withholding from wages and back-up withholding
    Estimated tax payments
    Overpayment of prior year's tax
    Excess Social Security taxes paid
    Earned income credit
    Regulated investment company credit
    Payments made with extension request
    Child credit (in some cases)

Nonrefundable

    Adoption expense credit
    Credit for the elderly and disabled
    Foreign tax credit
    Child and dependent care credit
    Business energy credit
    Research and experimentation credit
    Building rehabilitation credit
    American opportunity and lifetime learning credits

SELF-STUDY QUESTION

If a taxpayer is in the 25% marginal tax bracket, would he or she prefer $100 of tax credits or $300 of tax deductions?

ANSWER

The taxpayer would prefer the $100 of tax credits. The $300 of deductions will result in a tax savings of $75 ($300 × 0.25), whereas the $100 of credits would result in a tax savings of $100.

Credits and Prepayments. **Tax credits,** which include prepayments, are amounts that can be subtracted from the gross tax to arrive at the net tax due or refund due. Credits may be classified as either refundable or nonrefundable tax credits. **Refundable tax credits** are allowed to reduce a taxpayer's tax liability to zero and, if some credit still remains, are refundable (paid) by the government to the taxpayer. Prepayments of tax, which are amounts paid to the government during the year through means such as withholding from wages, and selected other items are classified as **refundable tax credits. Nonrefundable tax credits** are allowances that have been created by Congress for various social, economic, and political reasons such as the child and dependent care credits. Nonrefundable tax credits can be subtracted from the tax and may reduce the tax liability to zero. However, if the nonrefundable credits exceed the tax liability, none of the excess will be paid to the taxpayer. A partial list of refundable and nonrefundable tax credits can be found in Table I:2-5 and are covered in detail in Chapter I:14.

TAX FORMULA ILLUSTRATED

The following example illustrates the tax formula and Form 1040.

EXAMPLE I:2-1 ▶ The following facts relate to Larry S. and Jane V. Lane, who are married and file a joint return in 2014. Betty is their 9-year-old dependent daughter.

Salary	$78,000
Interest Income:	
Taxable	4,000
Exempt	500
Individual Retirement Account (IRA) contribution	5,000
Itemized deductions	15,300
Personal and dependency exemptions (3 × $3,950)	11,850
Federal income taxes withheld from salary	6,000

Their tax is computed as follows:

Income:			
	Salary		$78,000
	Taxable interest		4,000
	Tax-exempt interest		500
	Total		$82,500
Minus:	Exclusion:		
	Tax-exempt interest		(500)
Gross income			$82,000
Minus:	Deductions for AGI:		
	IRA contribution		(5,000)
Adjusted gross income			$77,000
Minus:	Deductions from AGI:		
	Itemized deductions		(15,300)
	Personal and dependency exemptions		(11,850)
Taxable income			$49,850
Gross tax (2014 tax table)			$ 6,574*
Minus:	Credits and prepayments		
	Child credit	(1,000)	
	Federal income tax withheld	(6,000)	(7,000)
Tax refund			$ 426

*The tax rate schedule will yield a tax of $6,570. This small variance results from the ranges in the tax table. ◄

 This tax is also computed on Form 1040 (see Figure I:2-1). Note that certain additional information, such as the taxpayers' address and Social Security numbers, also is included on the return.

DEDUCTIONS FROM ADJUSTED GROSS INCOME

Determine the amount of deductions from Adjusted Gross Income

ADDITIONAL COMMENT

In 2012, the 45.6 million taxpayers who itemized claimed $1.2 trillion in deductions. Taxes paid comprised 39.0% of the total, whereas interest paid made up 28.6%.

ITEMIZED DEDUCTIONS

Itemized deductions are claimed only if the total of such expenses exceeds the standard deduction. Here, consideration is given to which expenses may be itemized and the relationship between itemized deductions and the standard deduction.

Deductible Items. Congress allows taxpayers to itemize specified personal expenses. These specified expenses include medical expenses, taxes, investment and residential interest, charitable contributions, casualty and theft losses, and employee expenses. In addition, taxpayers are allowed to itemize expenses related to the production or collection of nonbusiness income, the management of property held for the production of income, and the determination, collection, or refund of any tax. A partial list of itemized deductions is found in Table I:2-6.

Itemized Deduction Floors. There are four adjusted gross income floors associated with itemized deductions. AGI floors represent amounts subtracted from deductions in arriving at allowable amounts. Three of the floors apply to specific categories of itemized deductions; the remaining floor applies to total itemized deductions. The floors based on AGI are as follows:

► Medical expenses: only medical expenses in excess of 10% of AGI are deductible by taxpayers under age 65. Through 2016, taxpayers aged 65 and older may continue to use the 7.5% of AGI floor applicable to all taxpayers prior to 2013.

► Casualty losses: only casualty losses in excess of 10% of AGI are deductible.

► Miscellaneous itemized deductions: only miscellaneous itemized deductions in excess of 2% of AGI are deductible.

► The overall floor, which reduces total itemized deductions, only applies to high-income taxpayers. It is discussed later in this chapter.

Form **1040**　Department of the Treasury—Internal Revenue Service　(99)
U.S. Individual Income Tax Return
2014　OMB No. 1545-0074　| IRS Use Only—Do not write or staple in this space.

For the year Jan. 1–Dec. 31, 2014, or other tax year beginning	, 2014, ending	, 20	See separate instructions.

Your first name and initial	Last name	Your social security number
Larry S.	Lane	123 45 6789

If a joint return, spouse's first name and initial	Last name	Spouse's social security number
Jane V.	Lane	987 65 4321

Home address (number and street). If you have a P.O. box, see instructions.	Apt. no.
116 E. Edwards	

▲ Make sure the SSN(s) above and on line 6c are correct.

City, town or post office, state, and ZIP code. If you have a foreign address, also complete spaces below (see instructions).
Lubbock, Texas 40401

Presidential Election Campaign
Check here if you, or your spouse if filing jointly, want $3 to go to this fund. Checking a box below will not change your tax or refund.　☐ You　☐ Spouse

Foreign country name	Foreign province/state/county	Foreign postal code

Filing Status
Check only one box.

1　☐ Single
2　[X] Married filing jointly (even if only one had income)
3　☐ Married filing separately. Enter spouse's SSN above and full name here. ▶
4　☐ Head of household (with qualifying person). (See instructions.) If the qualifying person is a child but not your dependent, enter this child's name here. ▶
5　☐ Qualifying widow(er) with dependent child

Exemptions

6a　[X] **Yourself.** If someone can claim you as a dependent, **do not** check box 6a . . . . .
b　[X] **Spouse** . . . .

Boxes checked on 6a and 6b	2

c　**Dependents:**

(1) First name　Last name	(2) Dependent's social security number	(3) Dependent's relationship to you	(4) ✓ if child under age 17 qualifying for child tax credit (see instructions)
Betty　Lane	111 22 3333	Daughter	[X]
			☐
			☐
			☐

If more than four dependents, see instructions and check here ▶ ☐

No. of children on 6c who:
• lived with you　**1**
• did not live with you due to divorce or separation (see instructions)
Dependents on 6c not entered above

d　Total number of exemptions claimed . . . .

Add numbers on lines above ▶	3

Income

Attach Form(s) W-2 here. Also attach Forms W-2G and 1099-R if tax was withheld.

If you did not get a W-2, see instructions.

7	Wages, salaries, tips, etc. Attach Form(s) W-2	7	78,000
8a	**Taxable** interest. Attach Schedule B if required	8a	4,000
b	**Tax-exempt** interest. **Do not** include on line 8a . . .	8b　500		
9a	Ordinary dividends. Attach Schedule B if required	9a	
b	Qualified dividends	9b		
10	Taxable refunds, credits, or offsets of state and local income taxes	10	
11	Alimony received	11	
12	Business income or (loss). Attach Schedule C or C-EZ	12	
13	Capital gain or (loss). Attach Schedule D if required. If not required, check here ▶ ☐	13	
14	Other gains or (losses). Attach Form 4797	14	
15a	IRA distributions .	15a	b Taxable amount . . .	15b	
16a	Pensions and annuities	16a	b Taxable amount . . .	16b	
17	Rental real estate, royalties, partnerships, S corporations, trusts, etc. Attach Schedule E	17	
18	Farm income or (loss). Attach Schedule F	18	
19	Unemployment compensation	19	
20a	Social security benefits	20a	b Taxable amount . . .	20b	
21	Other income. List type and amount _____	21	
22	Combine the amounts in the far right column for lines 7 through 21. This is your **total income** ▶	22	82,000

Adjusted Gross Income

23	Educator expenses	23		
24	Certain business expenses of reservists, performing artists, and fee-basis government officials. Attach Form 2106 or 2106-EZ	24		
25	Health savings account deduction. Attach Form 8889 .	25		
26	Moving expenses. Attach Form 3903	26		
27	Deductible part of self-employment tax. Attach Schedule SE .	27		
28	Self-employed SEP, SIMPLE, and qualified plans . .	28		
29	Self-employed health insurance deduction	29		
30	Penalty on early withdrawal of savings	30		
31a	Alimony paid　b Recipient's SSN ▶ _____	31a		
32	IRA deduction	32	5,000	
33	Student loan interest deduction	33		
34	Tuition and fees. Attach Form 8917	34		
35	Domestic production activities deduction. Attach Form 8903	35		
36	Add lines 23 through 35 . . . . ▶	36	5,000
37	Subtract line 36 from line 22. This is your **adjusted gross income** . . . . . ▶	37	77,000

For Disclosure, Privacy Act, and Paperwork Reduction Act Notice, see separate instructions.　Cat. No. 11320B　Form **1040** (2014)

FIGURE I:2-1 ▶ FORM 1040 (Page 1)

Tax and Credits	38	Amount from line 37 (adjusted gross income)	38	77,000
	39a	Check if: ☐ **You** were born before January 2, 1950, ☐ Blind. ☐ **Spouse** was born before January 2, 1950, ☐ Blind. } Total boxes checked ▶ 39a		
	b	If your spouse itemizes on a separate return or you were a dual-status alien, check here▶ 39b☐		

Standard Deduction for—
- People who check any box on line 39a or 39b **or** who can be claimed as a dependent, see instructions.
- All others:
  Single or Married filing separately, $6,200
  Married filing jointly or Qualifying widow(er), $12,400
  Head of household, $9,100

40	**Itemized deductions** (from Schedule A) **or** your **standard deduction** (see left margin) . .	40	15,300
41	Subtract line 40 from line 38	41	61,700
42	**Exemptions.** If line 38 is $152,525 or less, multiply $3,950 by the number on line 6d. Otherwise, see instructions	42	11,850
43	**Taxable income.** Subtract line 42 from line 41. If line 42 is more than line 41, enter -0- . .	43	49,850
44	**Tax** (see instructions). Check if any from: **a** ☐ Form(s) 8814 **b** ☐ Form 4972 **c** ☐ _____	44	6,574
45	**Alternative minimum tax** (see instructions). Attach Form 6251	45	
46	Excess advance premium tax credit repayment. Attach Form 8962	46	
47	Add lines 44, 45, and 46 . . . . ▶	47	6,574

48	Foreign tax credit. Attach Form 1116 if required	48			
49	Credit for child and dependent care expenses. Attach Form 2441	49			
50	Education credits from Form 8863, line 19	50			
51	Retirement savings contributions credit. Attach Form 8880	51			
52	Child tax credit. Attach Schedule 8812, if required . . .	52	1,000		
53	Residential energy credits. Attach Form 5695	53			
54	Other credits from Form: **a** ☐ 3800 **b** ☐ 8801 **c** ☐	54		54	
55	Add lines 48 through 54. These are your **total credits**			55	1,000
56	Subtract line 55 from line 47. If line 55 is more than line 47, enter -0- . . . . . ▶			56	5,574

Other Taxes	57	Self-employment tax. Attach Schedule SE	57	
	58	Unreported social security and Medicare tax from Form: **a** ☐ 4137 **b** ☐ 8919 . .	58	
	59	Additional tax on IRAs, other qualified retirement plans, etc. Attach Form 5329 if required . .	59	
	60a	Household employment taxes from Schedule H	60a	
	b	First-time homebuyer credit repayment. Attach Form 5405 if required	60b	
	61	Health care: individual responsibility (see instructions) Full-year coverage ☐	61	
	62	Taxes from: **a** ☐ Form 8959 **b** ☐ Form 8960 **c** ☐ Instructions; enter code(s) _____	62	
	63	Add lines 56 through 62. This is your **total tax** . . . . ▶	63	5,574

Payments	64	Federal income tax withheld from Forms W-2 and 1099 . .	64	6,000	
	65	2014 estimated tax payments and amount applied from 2013 return	65		
If you have a qualifying child, attach Schedule EIC.	66a	**Earned income credit (EIC)**	66a		
	b	Nontaxable combat pay election ▎66b			
	67	Additional child tax credit. Attach Schedule 8812	67		
	68	American opportunity credit from Form 8863, line 8 . . .	68		
	69	Net premium tax credit. Attach Form 8962	69		
	70	Amount paid with request for extension to file	70		
	71	Excess social security and tier 1 RRTA tax withheld . . .	71		
	72	Credit for federal tax on fuels. Attach Form 4136 . . .	72		
	73	Credits from Form: **a** ☐ 2439 **b** ▨ Reserved **c** ▨ Reserved **d** ☐	73		
	74	Add lines 64, 65, 66a, and 67 through 73. These are your **total payments** . . . . . ▶	74	6,000

Refund	75	If line 74 is more than line 63, subtract line 63 from line 74. This is the amount you **overpaid**	75	426
	76a	Amount of line 75 you want **refunded to you.** If Form 8888 is attached, check here . . ▶ ☐	76a	426
Direct deposit? ▶ See instructions.	b	Routing number ☐☐☐☐☐☐☐☐☐ ▶ **c** Type: ☐ Checking ☐ Savings		
	d	Account number ☐☐☐☐☐☐☐☐☐☐☐☐☐☐☐☐☐		
	77	Amount of line 75 you want **applied to your 2015 estimated tax** ▶ ▎77		

Amount You Owe	78	**Amount you owe.** Subtract line 74 from line 63. For details on how to pay, see instructions ▶	78	
	79	Estimated tax penalty (see instructions) . . . . ▎79		

Third Party Designee	Do you want to allow another person to discuss this return with the IRS (see instructions)? ☐ **Yes.** Complete below. ☐ **No**

Designee's name ▶	Phone no. ▶	Personal identification number (PIN) ▶

Sign Here
Joint return? See instructions.
Keep a copy for your records.

Under penalties of perjury, I declare that I have examined this return and accompanying schedules and statements, and to the best of my knowledge and belief, they are true, correct, and complete. Declaration of preparer (other than taxpayer) is based on all information of which preparer has any knowledge.

Your signature	Date	Your occupation	Daytime phone number
▶ *Larry S. Lane*	4/15/15	Attorney	555-555-1212
Spouse's signature. If a joint return, **both** must sign.	Date	Spouse's occupation	If the IRS sent you an Identity Protection PIN, enter it here (see inst.)
Jane V. Lane	4/15/15	Student	

Paid Preparer Use Only	Print/Type preparer's name	Preparer's signature	Date	Check ☐ if self-employed	PTIN
	Firm's name ▶			Firm's EIN ▶	
	Firm's address ▶			Phone no.	

FIGURE I:2-1 ▶   FORM 1040 (continued)

▼ TABLE I:2-6
Partial List of Itemized Deductions

Medical expenses (over 10% of adjusted gross income for most taxpayers)
Certain taxes
   State, local, and foreign income and real property taxes
   State and local personal property taxes
Residential interest and investment interest (limited)
Charitable contributions (limited)
Casualty and theft losses (over 10% of adjusted gross income)
Miscellaneous deductions (over 2% of adjusted gross income)
   Employee expenses (e.g., professional and union dues, professional publications, travel, transportation, education, job hunting, office-in-home, special clothing, and 50% of entertainment expenses)
   Expenses for producing investment income (e.g., accounting and legal fees, safe deposit rental, fees paid to an IRA custodian)
   Tax advice and tax return preparation and related costs
Other miscellaneous deductions
   Federal estate tax attributable to income in respect of a decedent
   Gambling losses to the extent of winnings
   Amortization of bond premium
   Amounts restored under claim of right

These floors are discussed in more detail in Chapter I:7.

EXAMPLE I:2-2 ▶ John and Jane, both under age 65, file a joint tax return in 2015 and report AGI of $170,000. Their itemized deductions include $25,000 of medical expenses and home mortgage interest of $10,000. The AGI floor reduces the medical expense deduction to $8,000 [$25,000 − (0.10 × $170,000)]. Thus, the total itemized deductions allowed is $18,000. ◀

STANDARD DEDUCTION

Itemized deductions are claimed only if the total amount of such deductions exceeds the standard deduction. The **standard deduction** is an amount set by Congress. It varies from year to year depending on the taxpayer's filing status, age, and vision.

Filing Status	Standard Deduction 2014	2015
Single individual other than heads of households	$ 6,200	$ 6,300
Married couples filing joint returns and surviving spouses	12,400	12,600
Married people filing separate returns	6,200	6,300
Heads of households	9,100	9,250

KEY POINT

The dollar amount of the standard deduction generally increases each year because it is indexed to the rate of inflation.

The differences between the 2014 and 2015 amounts represent inflation adjustments.

In 2015, a married taxpayer's standard deduction is increased by $1,250 ($1,200 in 2014) if he or she is elderly or blind ($2,500 if the taxpayer is elderly *and* blind) or has a spouse who is elderly or blind (for a maximum possible increase of $5,000 for a married couple). If an unmarried taxpayer is elderly or blind, his or her standard deduction is increased by $1,550 (also $1,550 in 2014) and $3,100 if the taxpayer is elderly *and* blind. Thus, in 2015, a single taxpayer, age 65 and not blind, is entitled to a $7,850 ($6,300 + $1,550) standard deduction. Two special rules relating to age and blindness are noted below.

ADDITIONAL COMMENT
Of all individual returns filed in 2012, 67.1% claimed the standard deduction.

▶ The increase in the standard deduction for elderly taxpayers is available if the taxpayer turns 65 during the tax year. For purposes of this requirement, a taxpayer is considered to be age 65 on the day before his or her sixty-fifth birthday. Thus, a taxpayer who reaches age 65 on January 1 of a year is deemed to have reached age 65 on December 31 of the preceding year. The adjustment is allowed on the final return of a deceased taxpayer only if he or she reached age 65 before death.

▶ The IRC defines blindness as corrected vision in the better eye of no better than 20/200 or a field of no greater than 20 degrees. Vision is determined as of the last day of the tax year or, in the case of a deceased taxpayer, as of the date of death.

The standard deduction simplifies the computation of taxable income. As previously noted, for most taxpayers the standard deduction is greater than total itemized deductions. Those taxpayers do not itemize and, in fact, do not even have to keep records of medical expenses and other itemized deductions.

Who actually itemizes and who does not? High-income taxpayers are more likely to itemize than low-income taxpayers simply because they incur more expenses that can be itemized. This is true even though the AGI floors (previously discussed) affect high-income taxpayers more than low-income taxpayers. Another characteristic of taxpayers who generally itemize their deductions are individuals who own their homes and incur home mortgage expenses and property taxes. These two expenses are deductible and alone often exceed the standard deduction.

EXAMPLE I:2-3 ▶ In 2015, Joan is single and a homeowner who incurs property taxes on her home of $2,000, makes charitable contributions of $500, and pays mortgage interest of $6,000. Joan's adjusted gross income is $32,000. Her taxable income is computed as follows:

Adjusted gross income		$32,000
Minus: Itemized deductions:		
Charitable contributions	$ 500	
Property taxes	2,000	
Mortgage interest	6,000	(8,500)
Minus: Personal exemption		(4,000)
Taxable income		$19,500 ◀

Joan would itemize her deductions because they ($8,500) are greater than her standard deduction ($6,300).

EXAMPLE I:2-4 ▶ Assume the same facts as in Example I:2-3 except that Joan is not a homeowner. Thus, she has no property taxes or mortgage interest but does pay rent of $800 per month for an apartment. Her taxable income is computed as follows:

Adjusted gross income	$32,000
Minus: Standard deduction	(6,300)
Minus: Personal exemption	(4,000)
Taxable income	$21,700 ◀

Joan uses the standard deduction of $6,300 because it is greater than her itemized deductions of $500. Rent paid for a personal apartment is not deductible.

Loss of The Standard Deduction. Congress decided that some taxpayers should not be permitted to use the standard deduction as they possibly would receive an unintended tax benefit.[7] The standard deduction is unavailable to three categories of taxpayers:

► An individual filing a return for a period less than twelve months because of a change in accounting period.

► A married taxpayer filing a separate return in instances where the other spouse itemizes.

► Nonresident aliens.

To illustrate why Congress does not permit certain taxpayers to claim the standard deduction, consider what could happen if a married couple files separate returns but only one spouse itemizes. On a separate return in 2015 when the standard deduction is $6,300, one spouse could claim all itemized deductions while the other uses the standard deduction.

EXAMPLE I:2-5 ► Clay and Joy, a married couple, have incomes of $35,000 and $34,000, respectively. Their itemized deductions total $9,000. They would claim a $12,600 standard deduction on a joint return. If Clay filed a separate return and claimed all of the deductions, his itemized deductions of $9,000 would be greater than the $6,300 standard deduction. If Joy could claim the standard deduction on her return, their total deductions would equal $15,300 ($9,000 + $6,300). The law, however, requires that either they both itemize or they both use the standard deduction. ◄

Limitation on the Standard Deduction. A special rule applies to any individual for whom the dependency exemption is allowable to another taxpayer. The standard deduction of the dependent is limited to the greater of (1) the dependent's earned income plus $350 in 2015 (also $350 in 2014) or (2) $1,050 in 2015 ($1,000 in 2014). The purpose of this limitation is to prevent parents from shifting unearned income, such as interest and dividends, to their children and avoid paying tax on such income. Without this rule, children could use the standard deduction to offset interest and dividends.

EXAMPLE I:2-6 ► Webb and Beth are married, in the 39.6% marginal tax rate bracket, and have one son, Vincent, age 15. Vincent has no income and is claimed as a dependent by his parents. Webb and Beth transfer stocks and bonds that earn $3,000 in dividends and interest to Vincent. Their goal is to shift the $3,000 of income to Vincent to utilize his standard deduction. However, since Vincent is claimed as a dependent by his parents on their return, Vincent's standard deduction is limited to $1,050, i.e., the *greater* of $1,050 or his earned income plus $350 ($0 + $350). ◄

EXAMPLE I:2-7 ► Assume the same facts as in Example I:2-6 except Vincent has a part-time job and earns $2,000 in wages. Vincent's standard deduction would be $2,350 ($2,000 + $350). Alternatively, if Vincent's wages were $7,000, his standard deduction would be $6,300 (the maximum for a single individual). ◄

ADDITIONAL COMMENT

As explained later in the chapter, some high-income taxpayers may have to phase out the personal and dependency exemptions.

PERSONAL EXEMPTIONS

Taxpayers cannot deduct personal expenses except for certain itemized deductions that are specifically authorized under the tax law. Congress has recognized the need to protect a small amount of income from tax in order to allow the taxpayer to meet personal expenses. Thus, almost every individual taxpayer is allowed a personal exemption of $4,000 ($3,950 in 2014). Because there are two taxpayers on a joint return filed by a married couple, they are allowed two personal exemptions. In addition, if a married person files a separate return, the taxpayer can claim a personal exemption for his or her spouse if the spouse has no gross income during the year and the spouse is not the dependent of another taxpayer.[8]

Only one personal exemption is allowed for each person. Therefore, an individual who is claimed as a dependent by another person is not entitled to a personal exemption on his

---

[7] Sec. 63(c)(6).

[8] Sec. 151(b).

or her own return. Despite the loss of the personal exemption, most dependents owe little or no tax because they can usually offset their small income by the standard deduction.

DEPENDENCY EXEMPTIONS

Virtually all taxpayers can claim a *personal exemption* for themselves. In addition, tax-payers may also claim a *dependency exemption* for each dependent.[9] To qualify as a dependent, an individual must meet the definition of either a *qualifying child* or a *qualifying relative*. All dependents must meet several requirements. Four requirements are common to all dependents. All dependents must:

▶ Have a qualifying identification number.

▶ Meet a citizenship test.

▶ Meet a separate return test.

▶ Not themselves claim another person as a dependent.

Additional requirements also must be met depending on whether the dependent is a qualifying child or a qualifying relative.

Requirements for All Dependents. The requirements applicable to all dependents are:

Identification number. Every dependent must have a Social Security number, and that number must be reported on the return.[10]

Citizenship. Dependents must be U.S. citizens[11] or nationals,[12] or residents of the U.S., Canada, or Mexico[13] for some part of the year.

Joint return. Married dependents cannot file joint returns. However, a taxpayer is entitled to the exemption if the dependent files a joint return solely to claim a refund of tax withheld (i.e., there is no tax on the joint return and there would have been no tax on two separate returns).[14] Married dependents should weigh the taxes that would be saved by the family from an exemption against the taxes that would be saved by filing a joint return. Depending on the circumstances, either alternative may be more beneficial.

No dependent. Dependents who file tax returns may not claim personal or dependency exemptions on their returns.

Additional Requirements for Qualifying Children. To claim a dependency exemption for an individual who is considered a *qualifying child*, the following additional requirements must be met:

▶ A relationship test.

▶ An age test.

▶ An abode test.

▶ A support test.

Relationship test. Eligible children include the taxpayer's children (including natural, adopted, foster, and stepchildren) and the taxpayer's siblings (including half-siblings and step-siblings) along with descendants of any of the above. A child is adopted if the child has been legally adopted or has been legally placed in a home for adoption.

---

[9] Sec. 152.

[10] Sec. 151(e). The IRS has the authority to disallow dependency exemptions for otherwise qualified dependents without Social Security numbers and with incorrectly reported Social Security numbers. A missing or incorrectly reported Social Security number may also bar an otherwise eligible individual from claiming head-of-household filing status.

[11] U.S. citizens living in foreign countries can claim dependency exemptions for adopted children even if the children are not U.S. citizens.

[12] A U.S. national is an individual born in an outlying possession such as American Samoa.

[13] A resident is a person who is not a U.S. citizen and who is legally residing in the United States with intent to stay here permanently (see Sec. 7701(b)).

[14] Rev. Rul. 54-567, 1954-2 C.B. 108 and Rev. Rul 65-34, 1965-1 C.B. 86. The theory is that the taxpayer is filing a claim for refund and not actually filing a tax return.

Age test. A qualifying child must be under age 19, a full-time student under age 24, or a permanently and totally disabled child.[15] A child is considered to be a student if he or she is in full-time attendance at a qualified educational institution during at least five months of the year. To be full-time, a student must carry the number of hours or courses the educational institution requires a student to take to be considered full-time.

Abode test. A qualifying child must have the same principal abode as the taxpayer for more than half of the year. A noncustodial parent meets this requirement if the custodial parent agrees in writing.

Support test. A qualifying child may not provide more than one-half of his or her own support during the year. Support is defined below in connection with the discussion of other dependents. Unlike other dependents, there is no requirement that the taxpayer provide more than one-half of the qualifying child's support, only that the dependent cannot provide more than one-half of his or her own support. This can be important in situations such as divorces where one spouse provides support, but the other has custody.

EXAMPLE I:2-8 ▶ Keith and Barbara file a joint return and have one son, Jeff, age 28. Because of a temporary illness, Jeff had to quit his job in June and moved back home to live with his parents. Keith and Barbara provided 70% of Jeff's support. Jeff earned $18,000. Jeff is not a qualifying child for purposes of the dependency exemption. Although Jeff meets the relationship, abode, and support tests, he fails the age test. ◀

Requirements for Other Relatives. A dependency exemption may also be claimed for a *qualifying relative*. To be eligible, dependents must meet the common requirements above and three additional requirements:

▶ Relationship test.

▶ Gross income test.

▶ Support test.

Relationship test. Other relatives must either be related to the taxpayer or reside in the taxpayer's household for the entire year. Although this group is referred to as "other qualifying relatives," that term is misleading because individuals who live with the taxpayer do not actually have to be related to the taxpayer. The relationship between the taxpayer and the dependent cannot violate local law.[16] Relatives who can be claimed as dependents even if they do not live with the taxpayer include the taxpayer's parents and their ancestors and siblings, the taxpayer's stepparents, and specified in-laws (mother, father, brother, sister, son, and daughter) along with qualifying children discussed above. As a result, a qualifying child may be claimed as a dependent if the child meets the tests described here even if the child fails the requirements for qualifying children. Thus, a son who is age 24 can be claimed as a dependent if the son meets the support and gross income tests discussed below even though that son could not be claimed as a dependent under the requirements for a qualifying child.

EXAMPLE I:2-9 ▶ Jesse supports three people, all of whom have gross income of less than $4,000, Tina, an unrelated child who lives with him; his cousin Judy, who lives in another state; and his daughter Vicki, who lives in her own home. Jesse can claim two dependency exemptions: one for Tina, who lives with him (a person who lives with the taxpayer need not be related) and one for his daughter. Jesse cannot claim a dependency exemption for Judy as cousins do not meet the relationship test. ◀

On a joint return the dependent needs to be related to only one spouse.[17] Once established, a relationship is not terminated by death or divorce.

---

[15] As noted, taxpayers attain the age 65, for purposes of the additional standard deduction, on the day before the anniversaries of their births. As a result, an individual whose birthday is January 1 is considered to be age 65 in the year prior to the individual's 65th birthday. A child whose 19th birthday falls on January 1 is considered to be under the age 19 in the previous year. The rule also is followed for purposes of determining whether the child is under age

24, and is used in connection with age 17 threshold associated with the child credit. Rev. Rul. 2003-72, 2003-2 C.B. 353.

[16] Sec. 152(f)(3). The exemption has been disallowed where the relationship constituted "cohabitation" and was illegal in the state (*Cassius L. Peacock*, III, PH T.C. Memo ¶78.030, 37 TCM 177).

[17] Reg. Sec. 1.152-2(d).

EXAMPLE I:2-10 ▶ Ken and Lisa support Lisa's mother and claim her as a dependent on a joint return. Following Lisa's death, Ken continues to support Lisa's mother. Lisa's mother continues to be Ken's mother-in-law and can be claimed as a dependent. ◀

Gross income test. The dependent's gross income must be less than the exemption amount for the year ($4,000 in 2015 and $3,950 in 2014). The statutory definition of gross income is used in applying this limitation. Therefore, nontaxable scholarships, tax-exempt bond interest, and nontaxable Social Security benefits are not considered, but salary, taxable interest, and rent are considered in deciding whether the person meets this test.

EXAMPLE I:2-11 ▶ Jim, age 22, a full-time college student, lives with his cousin who provides more than one-half of Jim's support. Jim earned $8,000 from a summer job. Even though Jim's cousin provided over one-half of his support, Jim cannot be claimed as a dependent as Jim does not meet the gross income test. Alternatively, if Jim lived with and was supported by his brother, he could be claimed as a dependent because, as a brother, Jim is a qualifying child and is exempt from the gross income test. ◀

Support test. The taxpayer must normally provide more than one-half of a dependent's financial support during the year. Support includes amounts spent by the taxpayer, the dependent, and other individuals. Welfare[18] and Social Security benefits[19] spent on support count even if they are excluded from gross income. Scholarships, however, do not count as support if the amounts are tax exempt.

EXAMPLE I:2-12 ▶ Tarer provided $3,000 of support for his mother, Mary. Tarer's sister provided $1,000. Mary spent $4,500 of her savings for her own support. Because Mary provided over one-half of her own support, she cannot be claimed as a dependent. ◀

EXAMPLE I:2-13 ▶

ADDITIONAL COMMENT

A TV set bought by a parent for his 12-year-old child and set up in her bedroom was considered support. A power lawn mower, however, bought by a parent of a 13-year-old child was not considered support. The parent had assigned the child the job of mowing the lawn, and the power mower was intended to make the job more palatable. The lawn mower was considered a family item that benefits all members of the household. (Rev. Rul. 77-282, 1977-2 C.B. 52.)

George's father received Social Security benefits of $6,600, of which $1,800 were deposited into a savings account. He spent the remaining $4,800 on food, clothing, and lodging. George spent $5,600 to support his father. George meets the support test because the amount saved is not counted in the support test. ◀

Support includes amounts spent for food, clothing, shelter, medical and dental care, education, and the like.[20] Support is not limited to these items.[21] Support does not include the value of services rendered by the taxpayer to the dependent.[22] Also, the IRS and the courts have excluded various other expenses from support.[23]

Generally, the amount of support equals the cost of the item, but in the case of support provided in a noncash form, such as lodging, the amount of support equals the fair market value or fair rental value. The cost of an item such as a television or an automobile is included in support if the item actually is support.[24]

EXAMPLE I:2-14 ▶ Vicki's mother lives with her. Vicki purchased clothing for her mother costing $800 and provided her with a room that Vicki estimates she could have rented for $2,800. Vicki spent $2,500 for groceries she shared with her mother and $1,200 for utilities. In addition, Vicki purchased a television for $750 that she placed in the living room. Vicki and her mother both used the television. Vicki's support for her mother, at a minimum, includes:

Clothing	$ 800
Rental value of room	2,800
Food	1,250
Total	$4,850

---

[18] Rev. Rul. 71-468, 1971-2 C.B. 115.
[19] Rev. Ruls. 57-344, 1957-2 C.B. 112, and 58-419, 1958-2 C.B. 57.
[20] Reg. Sec. 1.152-1(a)(2)(i).
[21] Examples of other items that have been held to be support include church contributions (Rev. Rul. 58-67, 1958-1 C.B. 62), telephone (*William K. Price, III*, 1961 PH T.C. Memo ¶61,173, 20 TCM 886), medical insurance premiums (*James Edward Parker*, 1959 PH T.C. Memo ¶52,182, 18 TCM 800), child care (*Marvin D. Tucker*, 1957 PH T.C. Memo ¶57,118, 16 TCM 488), toys (*Loren S. Brumber*, 1952 PH T.C. Memo ¶52,087, 11 TCM 289), and vacations (*George R. Melat*, 1953 PH T.C. Memo ¶53,141, 12 TCM 443).

[22] *Frank Markarian v. CIR.*, 16 AFTR 2d 5785, 65-2 USTC ¶9699 (7th Cir., 1965).
[23] Examples of items that have been excluded are funeral expenses (Rev. Rul. 65-307, 1965-2 C.B. 40), taxes (Rev. Rul. 58-67, 1958-1 C.B. 62), a rifle, lawn mower, boat insurance (*Harriet C. Flower v. U.S.*, 52 AFTR 1383, 57-1 USTC ¶9655 (D.C. Pa., 1957)), and life insurance premiums (*John F. Miller*, 1959 PH T.C. Memo ¶59,155, 18 TCM 673).
[24] Rev. Rul. 77-282, 1977-2 C.B. 52.

Whether a portion of the utilities could be included in support would depend on whether the rental rate for the room included utilities. The fact that the mother used the television set probably would not be sufficient to cause its cost to be viewed as support. On the other hand, if the television set was a gift to the mother, was placed in her room, and was used exclusively by her, the cost probably would qualify as support. ◀

If a taxpayer contributes a lump sum for the support of two or more individuals, the amount is allocated between the individuals on a pro rata basis unless proof exists to the contrary.[25]

EXAMPLE I:2-15 ▶ Jaime pays rent of $9,000 for an apartment occupied by his aunts Alice, Beth, and Cindy. Alice spends $4,000 toward her own support, Beth spends $2,000, and Cindy spends $2,500. Jaime is assumed to have provided $3,000 of support for each aunt. Thus, assuming the other tests are met, Jaime can claim exemptions for Beth and Cindy, but not for Alice. ◀

EXAMPLE I:2-16 ▶ Paul and Mary have three children and are unclear whether they can claim their children as dependents. Information on the children is as follows:

- ▶ Peter, age 25, who served in the military immediately after high school, is a college senior. He worked part-time earning $2,200 and provided 20% of his support.

- ▶ Mark, age 22, graduated from college in May (he was a full-time student for five months of the year), and accepted a job in June. He lived with his parents for the entire year, earned $28,000, and provided 70% of his own support.

- ▶ Ruth, age 18, graduated from high school in May, and moved into an apartment immediately after graduation. She earned $5,500 from a job and provided 30% of her own support for the year.

Assume Paul and Mary provide all the support not provided by the children. The first step is to determine whether any of the children are considered qualifying children. None of the children are qualifying children. Peter is over age 23. Mark provided more than 50% of his own support. Ruth did not live with her parents for more than one-half of the year. The second step is to determine whether any of the children are considered qualifying relatives. Peter is considered as a qualifying relative as he meets the relationship, gross income, and support tests. Mark fails both the gross income and support tests, and Ruth fails the gross income test. Thus, only Peter can be claimed as a dependent. ◀

Tie-Breaker Rules for Dependency Exemptions. More than one person can meet the requirements to claim someone as a dependent. Tie-breakers decide who receives the exemption in such situations, as follows:

- ▶ First, taxpayers who meet the requirements to claim the dependent under the qualifying child rules have priority over individuals who meet the requirements for other relatives.

- ▶ The next priority provides that parents have priority over other individuals.

- ▶ Finally, if neither of the first two tie-breakers apply, the third tie-breaker specifies that the exemption is awarded to the taxpayer with the highest AGI.

Consider a niece who lives with three aunts who contribute equal amounts to her support. Assuming other requirements are met, all three aunts satisfy the requirements to claim the niece as a dependent under the qualifying child rule. Taxpayers who meet the requirements to claim a dependent under the qualifying child rules have priority over individuals who meet the requirements for other relatives. This first tie-breaker would not determine which aunt receives the exemption as each meets the qualifying child requirement.

---

[25] Rev. Rul. 64-222, 1964-2 C.B. 47 and Rev. Rul. 72-591, 1972-2 C.B. 84.

Moving to the second tie-breaker, parents have priority over other individuals. Again, the tie-breaker will not determine which aunt receives the exemption as they are not the child's parent. Thus, in this case, the aunt with the greatest AGI would receive the exemption. In cases involving two parents, the exemption is awarded to the parent with whom the child resided for the longer period of time during the year, and if the child spent equal amounts of time with each parent, the exemption is awarded to the parent with the higher AGI.

Two provisions can override the normal operation of dependency exemption rules:

▶ A Multiple Support Declaration (Form 2120) can enable a taxpayer to claim a dependency exemption in situations where the taxpayer does not provide over one-half of the dependent's support. This can be very important when several individuals contribute to the support of an individual who is not a qualifying child.

▶ A Release of Claim to Exemption for Child of Divorced or Separated Parents (Form 8332) can enable a noncustodial parent to claim an exemption.

Multiple Support Agreements. Often several people contribute to the support of a dependent. When a group provides over one-half of the support of an individual but no one member of the group provides over one-half of the support, eligible members of the group are allowed to designate one group member to claim the exemption. Each eligible member (other than the taxpayer receiving the exemption) must agree in writing. The taxpayer claiming the exemption must complete a Multiple Support Declaration (Form 2120, shown on page I:2-18). An eligible member is one who contributes more than 10% of the dependent's support and meet all requirements for claiming a dependency exemption except the support requirement.[26]

EXAMPLE I:2-17 ▶

John T. Abel lives alone. His support comes from the following sources:

Andy (son)	$ 400
Gabe (son)	2,800
Mable (daughter)	2,000
Betty (friend)	2,800
Total	$8,000

Either Gabe or Mable can claim a dependency exemption if the other agrees in writing. Andy cannot claim the exemption because he did not provide over 10% of John's support. Betty cannot claim a dependency exemption because she is not related and John does not live with her. For this reason, Andy and Betty need not agree in writing. Form 2120 is included in the return of the taxpayer claiming the exemption. A completed Form 2120 is illustrated in Figure I:2-2. ◄

The Multiple Support Declaration can supercede the tie-breaker rules discussed above except that the agreement cannot be used to pass the exemption from a person who is entitled to claim the dependent under the qualifying child rules to a person who is entitled to claim the exemption under the other dependent's rule.[27]

ADDITIONAL COMMENT

Form 8332 may be completed each year by the custodial parent to relinquish the dependency exemption for only that year, or it may be completed once, relinquishing the exemption for all future years.

Parental Release. In the case of divorced or separated parents, the dependency exemption for children generally is awarded to the custodial parent. However, the noncustodial parent may claim the dependency exemption if the custodial spouse signs a completed Form 8332. The signed form is attached to the noncustodial spouse's return for each year the exemption is claimed. In the case of divorces prior to 2008, the noncustodial spouse can substitute a copy of pages from the divorce decree that award the exemption to the noncustodial spouse. In the case of a divorce or separation, the custodial spouse probably would be reluctant to relinquish the dependency exemption for a child. A noncustodial parent, however, might be able to negotiate the exemption in exchange for increased child support payments.

---

[26] Sec. 152(c).

[27] Sec. 152(d)(1)(D).

Form **2120**
(Rev. October 2005)

Department of the Treasury
Internal Revenue Service

Multiple Support Declaration

▶ Attach to Form 1040 or Form 1040A.

OMB No. 1545-0074

Attachment
Sequence No. **114**

Name(s) shown on return

Gabe I. Abel

Your social security number

123 : 45 : 6789

During the calendar year .... 2014 .... , the eligible persons listed below each paid over 10% of the support of:

John T. Abel

Name of your qualifying relative

I have a signed statement from each eligible person waiving his or her right to claim this person as a dependent for any tax year that began in the above calendar year.

Mabel B. Abel

222 : 11 : 0001

Eligible person's name

Social security number

402 N. Lable Lane Lawrence, NJ 08649

Address (number, street, apt. no., city, state, and ZIP code)

Eligible person's name

Social security number

Address (number, street, apt. no., city, state, and ZIP code)

Eligible person's name

Social security number

Address (number, street, apt. no., city, state, and ZIP code)

Eligible person's name

Social security number

Address (number, street, apt. no., city, state, and ZIP code)

FIGURE I:2-2 ▶ FORM 2120

EXAMPLE I:2-18 ▶ Hal and Pam obtain a divorce under the terms of which Pam receives custody of their son. Hal is ordered to pay $600 per month of child support. In absence of a written agreement to the contrary, Pam will receive the dependency exemption for the child. ◀

EXAMPLE I:2-19 ▶ Assume the same facts as in Example I:2-18 except that Pam negotiates child support payments of $800 per month and agrees in writing to allow Hal to claim the dependency exemption for the child. The written agreement will enable Hal to claim the dependency exemption for the child. ◀

EXAMPLE I:2-20 ▶ Andy and Beth obtain a divorce under the terms of which they share custody of their daughter. The divorce decree does not specify who is to receive the dependency exemption. Whoever has custody for the greater part of the year receives the dependency exemption for the daughter unless they agree otherwise in writing. If they share custody equally, the parent with the higher AGI receives the exemption. ◀

SELF-STUDY QUESTION

Beth's mother, who is a U.S. citizen, has moved to France to spend her retirement years. She has retained her U.S. citizenship, but she is now a resident of France. Is it possible for Beth to claim her mother as a dependent?

ANSWER

Yes, the mother need only be a U.S. citizen.

EXAMPLE I:2-21 ▶ In 2015, Lee, a single taxpayer with one dependent, reports AGI of $120,000. Her personal and dependency exemption amount is $8,000 ($4,000 × 2). ◀

The rules for deducting personal and dependency exemptions are summarized in Topic Review I:2-1.

CHILD CREDIT

ADDITIONAL COMMENT

There are now two credits that have similar names: the child tax credit and the child and dependent care credit. They are quite different in how the credit amounts are computed and which dependents qualify.

Under Sec. 24 of the IRC, individual taxpayers may claim a "child credit" of $1,000 for each qualifying child. The credit is reduced by $50 for each $1,000 (or fraction thereof) by which the taxpayer's modified adjusted gross income exceeds a threshold amount ($110,000 on joint returns, $75,000 for single taxpayers, and $55,000 for married persons filing separate returns). Neither the amount of the credit or the phase-out thresholds is indexed for inflation. Modified adjusted gross income is AGI plus any amounts excluded from gross income under Secs. 911, 931, and 933 which relate to certain foreign earned income and possession's income. To qualify for the credit, a child must be under the age of 17 and be a "qualifying child" as defined in the above discussion of dependency exemptions. See Chapter I:14 for more information regarding the child credit.

TOPIC REVIEW I:2-1

Personal and Dependency Exemptions

EXEMPTIONS IN GENERAL

▶ One exemption is available for each taxpayer (except when the taxpayer is the dependent of another) and for each dependent.
▶ The amount of each exemption, which is adjusted annually for inflation, is $4,000 in 2015 and $3,950 in 2014.

DEPENDENCY EXEMPTIONS

▶ One exemption is allowed for each dependent. As explained later in the chapter, the exemptions are phased out for higher income taxpayers.
▶ Each dependent must meet multiple conditions. All dependents (1) must have Social Security numbers reported on the taxpayer's return, (2) must meet a citizenship test, (3) cannot normally file a joint return, and (4) cannot claim others as dependents. Qualifying children must (1) be the taxpayer's child or sibling, (2) be under 19, a full-time student under 24, or disabled, (3) live with the taxpayer, and (4) not be self-supporting. Other qualifying relatives must (1) be related to the taxpayer, (2) have gross income less than the amount of the personal exemption, and (3) receive over one-half of their support from the taxpayer.

EXAMPLE I:2-22 ▶ Jane and Bill have two eligible dependent children and a modified AGI of $120,300. They have excess AGI of $10,300 ($120,300 − $110,000) and are entitled to a credit of $1,450 [(2 × $1,000) − (11 × $50)]. ◀

Through 2017, the child credit is partially refundable. For a taxpayer with one or two qualifying children, the refund is limited to 15% of the taxpayer's earned income in excess of $3,000.

EXAMPLE I:2-23 ▶ Georgia's two dependent children entitle her to a child credit of $2,000. Her salary is $25,000 and her gross income tax is $500. The credit offsets all of Georgia's income tax. In addition, Georgia is entitled to a refund of the balance of the credit ($1,500), as the amount is less than the limitation [$3,300 = 15% × ($25,000 − $3,000)]. ◀

In the case of a taxpayer with three or more qualifying children, the refund is limited to the greater of 15% of the taxpayer's earned income in excess of $3,000 or the excess of the taxpayer's Social Security tax paid over the taxpayer's earned income credit for the year. (See Chapter I: 14 in the Individuals volume for more detail.)

DETERMINING THE AMOUNT OF TAX

OBJECTIVE 3

Calculate the income tax for individuals

After taxable income is computed, the next step is to determine the gross tax. Most individuals determine the amount of gross tax by looking in the tax table. (See page T-2 after Chapter I:8 in *Individuals* volume or after Chapter C:15 in the *Comprehensive* volume.) This method allows the taxpayer to arrive at the gross tax without the need for multiplication and, therefore, simplifies the computation and reduces the number of errors. Individuals are required to use the tax table unless taxable income exceeds the maximum income in the table (currently $100,000), or if the taxpayer files a short period return on account of a change in the annual accounting period.

Taxpayers who cannot use the tax table instead use the tax rate schedule (located after Chapter I:18 and on the inside cover of the text). Taxpayers using the tax rate schedule must actually compute the tax.

EXAMPLE I:2-24 ▶ Liz is single and has taxable income of $48,210. Liz's tax is determined by reference to the tax table for single taxpayers. (At the time of this writing, the 2014 tax table was the most recent available.) The tax from the table is $7,913. ◀

EXAMPLE I:2-25 ▶ Jack and Pam are married, file a joint tax return, and have taxable income of $105,000 in 2015. They use the tax rate schedule to compute their tax. The tax is computed as follows:

Tax on $74,900	$10,313
Tax on remaining $30,100 at 25%	7,525
Gross tax	$17,838	◀

FILING STATUS

There are seven tax brackets applicable to individual taxpayers: 10%, 15%, 25%, 28%, 33%, 35%, and 39.6%. These rates are progressive in that as a taxpayer's income increases, the taxpayer moves into higher tax brackets. The income level at which higher tax brackets begin depends on the taxpayer's filing status. There are five different filing statuses but only four rate schedules and/or tax tables because married couples filing jointly and certain surviving spouses use the same rate schedule or tax table. The five filing statuses are as follows:

▶ Married filing jointly

▶ Surviving spouse

▶ Head of household

▶ Single

▶ Married filing separately

Before 1948, one rate schedule was used by all taxpayers. Married couples often filed separate returns in order to have more income taxed at lower rates. This treatment was deemed to be unfair because various states allocated income between spouses differently. Some states used a community property law system while other states used a common law system. Today, only a few states continue to use the community property law system.[28]

In general, community property law allocates community income equally between a husband and wife, regardless of which spouse actually earns the income. In other states, income belongs to the spouse who produces the income. With a progressive tax system, placing income on one return instead of two can result in a much greater tax. For this reason, couples residing in noncommunity property states often paid more tax than their counterparts who resided in community property states. In 1948, Congress developed the joint-rate schedule to rectify this problem. Unmarried taxpayers who headed families felt they also should receive tax relief because they shared their incomes with their families. So, in 1957, Congress created a rate schedule for heads of households. Below is a discussion of who is covered by each filing status.

JOINT RETURN

Married couples may elect to file joint income tax returns.[29]

▶ To file a **joint return**, a couple must be legally married as of the last day of the tax year. Common law marriages are recognized. An annulled marriage is viewed as never having been valid.

▶ The Supreme Court has recognized same-sex marriages.[30] The IRS has applied the decision to same-sex couples who live in states that do not recognize same-sex marriages as long as the couples were married in states or foreign jurisdictions that permit such marriages. The ruling does not apply to civil unions or domestic partnerships.[31]

▶ Except in the case of death, spouses who file joint tax returns must have the same tax year-end.

▶ Both spouses must be U.S. citizens or residents. An exception allows a joint return if the nonresident alien spouse agrees to report all of his or her income on the return.[32]

 STOP & THINK

Question: Some higher income couples who marry find that their tax liabilities increase even if their combined incomes remain unchanged. Others find that their tax liabilities decrease. Explain why taxes increase for some couples, but decrease for others.

Solution: Couples who marry ordinarily move from two individual returns where incomes are taxed using the rate schedule for single individuals to one return where the combined incomes are taxed using the joint rate schedule. The less progressive joint rate schedule results in a lower tax when one spouse has most of the income because more of that spouse's income is taxed at lower rates. However, when a higher income husband and wife

---

[28] Several states had either adopted or had begun to adopt community property laws in order to reduce the federal taxes paid by their residents. After the joint rate schedule was created, states without a tradition of community property law returned to common law. For a more detailed discussion of community property states, see page I:3-6.

[29] Sec. 6013.

[30] *U.S. v. Edith Windsor*, 111 AFTR2d 2013-2385, 2013-2 USTC ¶50,400. The court declared unconstitutional Sec. 3 of the *Defense of Marriage Act*, which stated that same-sex marriages would not be recognized by the federal government.

[31] Rev. Rul. 2013-17, 2013-38 IRB 201.

[32] Sec. 6013(g). Ordinarily, nonresident aliens are taxed only on U.S.-source income. Permitting a couple to take advantage of the lower tax rates on a joint return while reporting only one spouse's income would result in an unintended tax benefit.

have approximately equal incomes, their combined incomes are taxed at higher rates on one joint return. Even though the joint rate schedule is the least progressive, the combined tax for higher income couples is greater because the 25% and higher brackets in the joint rate schedule are less than twice as wide as the same brackets for single taxpayers. For example, for the tax year 2015, two single individuals with $85,000 of taxable income each are in the 25% tax bracket, while a married couple with $170,000 of taxable income is in the 28% bracket. This is because the 28% bracket begins at $90,750 for single taxpayers, but at $151,200 for married couples. Assuming the taxable income on the joint return is $170,000, the so-called marriage penalty is $564 because $18,800 of income is taxed at 28% instead of 25%. The additional tax is even greater for taxpayers with higher incomes. Nevertheless, because the lower tax brackets were widened in 2003, the additional tax for married couples is considerably less than it has been in the past.

SURVIVING SPOUSE

A widow or widower can file a joint return for the year his or her spouse dies if the widow or widower does not remarry. For the two years after the year of death, the widow or widower can file as a surviving spouse only if he or she meets specific conditions. The **surviving spouse** (sometimes called a qualifying widow or widower) must[33]

▶ Have not remarried as of the year end in which surviving spouse status is claimed.

▶ Be a U.S. citizen or resident.

▶ Have qualified to file a joint return in the year of death.

▶ Have at least one dependent son or daughter[34] living at home during the entire year and the taxpayer must pay over half of the expenses of the home.

In the year of death, a joint return can be filed. On the joint return, the income of the deceased spouse (earned before death) and the survivor are both reported. Personal exemptions are allowed for both spouses. In the two years following death, surviving spouse status can be claimed only if the conditions outlined above are met. Only the surviving spouse's income is reported and, of course, no personal exemption is available for the deceased spouse. What the two situations have in common is that in both instances, the taxpayer can use the more favorable joint rate schedule and standard deduction amount.

EXAMPLE I:2-26 ▶

Connie and Carl are married and have no dependent children. Carl dies in the current year. Connie can file a joint return with Carl even though he did not live the entire year. Alternatively, separate returns can be filed for Connie and Carl applying the rate schedule for married individuals filing separately.

In subsequent years, Connie would file as a single taxpayer. On the other hand, if Connie and Carl had dependent children, Connie could file as a surviving spouse for the two tax years following his death. ◀

 **STOP & THINK**

Question: Most recently-widowed individuals do not qualify for surviving spouse status. Why?

Solution: Most individuals are widowed late in life after their children are grown and have left home. As having a dependent child is a requirement for surviving spouse status, these individuals do not qualify for the special lower tax rate. Such individuals may ordinarily file a joint return in the year of the spouse's death.

HEAD OF HOUSEHOLD

A second rate schedule or tax table is available to a head of household. The head of household rates increase more rapidly than those applicable to married taxpayers filing jointly and surviving spouses, but more slowly than those applicable to other single taxpayers. To claim head-of-household status, a taxpayer must meet all of the following conditions:[35]

---

[33] Sec. 2(a).

[34] Includes an adopted child or a stepchild, but not a foster child.

[35] Sec. 2(b).

▶ Be unmarried as of the last day of the tax year. Exceptions apply to individuals married to nonresident aliens[36] and to abandoned spouses.[37] An individual cannot claim head-of-household status in the year his or her spouse died. Such individuals must file a joint return or a separate return.

▶ Not be a surviving spouse.

▶ Be a U.S. citizen or resident.

▶ Pay over half of the costs of maintaining as his or her home a household in which a dependent lives for more than half of the tax year. An exception permits a taxpayer who maintains a household in which a qualifying child[38] lives for more than half of the tax year to claim head-of-household status when the qualifying child is not the taxpayer's dependent. This comes into play in the case of divorced parents when the dependency exemption goes to the non-custodial parent. A second exception permits a taxpayer to claim head-of-household status if he or she maintains a separate household for a dependent parent. This enables the parent to continue living in his or her own home.

EXAMPLE I:2-27 ▶ Brad and Ellen divorce. Ellen receives custody of their child, and Brad is ordered by the court to pay child support of $6,000 per year. Ellen agrees in writing to allow Brad to claim the dependency exemption for the child. If Ellen maintains the home in which she and her child live, she can claim head-of-household status even though the child is Brad's dependent. ◄

As noted, the taxpayer must pay over half of the costs of maintaining the household. These expenses include property taxes, mortgage interest, rent, utility charges, upkeep and repairs, property insurance, and food consumed on the premises. Such costs do not include clothing, education, medical treatment, vacations, life insurance, transportation, or the value of services provided by the taxpayer.[39]

SINGLE TAXPAYER

An unmarried individual who does not qualify as a surviving spouse or a head of household must file as a single taxpayer. The tax rates progress more rapidly than those that apply to other unmarried taxpayers.

EXAMPLE I:2-28 ▶ Becky, a single taxpayer with no dependents, files her first tax return. She will file as a single taxpayer. ◄

MARRIED FILING A SEPARATE RETURN

Married individuals who choose to file separate returns must use the separate rate schedule. The rates on this schedule increase more rapidly than other individual rate schedules. The implications of joint returns versus separate returns are discussed later in this chapter.

EXAMPLE I:2-29 ▶ On December 31, Rose marries Joe. Because they were married before the year ended, they may elect to file jointly. Alternatively, they may file separate returns with each using the rate schedule applicable to separate returns. ◄

The filing requirements for individuals are summarized in Topic Review I:2-2.

ABANDONED SPOUSE

The particular rate schedule a taxpayer uses can have a great impact on the amount of tax. Without any special rule, an abandoned spouse would be required to file using the rate schedules for a married person filing separately. Congress has provided relief for taxpayers in this situation if they can meet certain conditions. A married individual can claim head-of-household status if[40]

---

[36] Specifically, this refers to an individual married to a nonresident alien if he or she meets the remaining head-of-household requirements.
[37] Abandoned spouse rules are discussed under a separate heading later in this chapter.

[38] Qualifying child has the same meaning as is associated with dependency exemptions except that the child cannot be married and must be a U.S. citizen, resident or national.
[39] Reg. Sec. 1.2-2(d).
[40] Sec. 2(c).

TOPIC REVIEW I:2-2

Filing Status and Requirements

FILING STATUS	MUST MAINTAIN HOUSEHOLD	MUST HAVE DEPENDENT	MARITAL STATUS	MUST BE CITIZEN	TAX RATES
Joint	No requirement	No	Married	Yes	Lowest rates, but two incomes are combined
Surviving spouse	Yes	Yes, son or daughter	Widowed in prior or second prior year	Yes	Uses same schedule as married couple filing joint return
Head of household	Yes	Generally, yes	Generally, single	Yes	Intermediate tax rates
Single	No requirement	No	Single	No	Highest tax rates for unmarried taxpayers
Separate	No requirement	No	Married	No	Highest tax rates

► The taxpayer lived apart from his or her spouse for the last six months of the year.

► The taxpayer pays over half of the cost of maintaining a household in which the taxpayer and a dependent son or daughter live for over half of the year.[41]

► The taxpayer is a U.S. citizen or resident.

The requirement that the taxpayer have a dependent child is met if a taxpayer who is otherwise qualified to claim the child as a dependent signs an agreement that allows the child's noncustodial parent to claim the dependency exemption for the child.[42]

EXAMPLE I:2-30 ► In October, Bob and Gail decide to separate. Gail supports their children after the separation and pays the costs of maintaining their home. Gail cannot claim abandoned spouse status because Bob lived with her for over one-half of the year. If she had obtained a divorce before the end of the year, she could have filed as a head of household. In the absence of a divorce, Gail must file a separate return, unless both Bob and Gail agree to file a joint return. ◄

EXAMPLE I:2-31 ► Assume the same facts as in Example I:2-30 except that Gail continues to support her children and pay household expenses during the next year. She can file as a head of household even if she has not obtained a divorce. ◄

CHILDREN WITH UNEARNED INCOME

In the past, taxpayers in high tax brackets were able to reduce their tax liability by shifting income to children and other dependents. Under prior law, no tax was due if the income was less than the dependent's personal exemption and standard deduction. Even if the shifted income was greater than these amounts, there was a tax savings if the dependent was in a low tax bracket. Under current law, three rules curtail the advantages of shifting income to dependents:

► Dependents do not receive a personal exemption on their own returns.

► A dependent's standard deduction is reduced to the greater of $1,050 in 2015 ($1,000 in 2014) or the dependent's earned income (such as salary) plus $350 (in both 2014 and 2015).

KEY POINT

Children under the age of 18 will not have their net unearned income taxed at their parents' tax rate until the children's unearned income exceeds $2,100.

► The tax on the net unearned income (such as dividends and interest) of a child under age 18 (under age 24 in certain instances described below) is figured by reference to the parents' tax rate if it is higher than the child's rate. This provision is often called the "kiddie tax".

The first two rules have been discussed previously in this chapter. How the "kiddie tax" is computed depends on the child's age.

---

[41] Includes adopted child, stepchild, and foster child.   [42] Sec. 152(e).

Prior to the year a child turns 18, the kiddie tax applies if the unearned income exceeds the $2,100 threshold in 2015 ($2,000 in 2014). For the year the child turns 18 (and only that year), the kiddie tax applies if child's earned income is less than or equal to one-half of his or her support and unearned income exceeds the $2,100 threshold in 2015 ($2,000 in 2014). From the year a child turns 19 up to and including the year the child turns 23, the kiddie tax applies only if the child is a full-time student, the child's earned income is less than or equal to one-half of his or her support, and unearned income exceeds the $2,100 threshold in 2015 ($2,000 in 2014).

EXAMPLE I:2-32 ▶ In 2015, Tim is an 18-year-old who received $2,400 of interest income and $4,500 from a part-time job. His support, which he paid himself, totaled $8,000. As he is self-supporting, his parent's cannot claim him as a dependent. The kiddie tax does not apply as his earned income exceeds one-half of his support. He is entitled to the regular standard deduction and a personal exemption. He owes no tax as these deductions exceed his income. ◀

EXAMPLE I:2-33 ▶ Assume the same facts as in Example I:2-32 except that Tim's parents provided over one-half of his support. Tim saved his earnings for college. Because Tim is a dependent, he is not entitled to a personal exemption. Tim's standard deduction is limited to the greater of $1,050 or his earned income plus $350 (but not more than $6,300). Because his earned income is $4,500, the standard deduction is $4,850 ($4,500 + $350). Therefore, Tim's taxable income is $2,050 ($6,900 AGI − $4,850 standard deduction). The kiddie tax does not apply as his earned income $4,500 exceeds one-half of his support. The application of the kiddie tax is based on whether the child has earned income, not whether the child is self supporting. Tim's regular tax rate of 10% applies resulting in a tax of $205 (10% × $2,050). ◀

When the kiddie tax applies, part of the net unearned income of the child under age 24 is taxed at the child's rate, and part at the parents' marginal tax rate if that rate is higher than the child's rate. This tax can be computed following a three-step process:

1. Compute the child's taxable income in the normal fashion for dependents as discussed earlier in this chapter.
2. Compute the child's net unearned income:

Unearned income (described below)	$xxx
Less: Statutory deduction of $1,000	(xxx)
Less: Greater of	
a. $1,000 of standard deduction, or	
b. Itemized deductions directly connected with the production of the unearned income.	(xxx)
Equals: Net unearned income	$xxx

3. Compute the child's tax:

Net unearned income times parents' marginal tax rate	$xxx
Plus: Difference between taxable income and net unearned income times child's tax rate	xxx
Equals: Child's total tax	$xxx

Unearned income is the child's investment income including dividends, taxable interest, capital gains, rents, royalties and other income that is not earned income (such as salary).[43]

EXAMPLE I:2-34 ▶ Assume the same facts as in Example I:2-32 except that Tim is age 17. His standard deduction is still $4,850 and his taxable income is also $2,050. Since Tim is under age 18, a portion of his unearned income may be subject to tax at his parents' 28% rate. The computation of Tim's tax is as follows:

---

[43] Sec. 1(g)(4).

1. Compute Tim's taxable income:

Wages		$4,500
Interest income		2,400
Adjusted gross income		$6,900
Standard deduction ($4,500 + $350)	$4,850	
Personal exemption	0	4,850
Taxable income		$2,050

2. Compute Tim's net unearned income:

Unearned income: Interest income	$2,400
Statutory deduction	(1,050)
Portion of standard deduction	(1,050)
Net unearned income	$ 300

3. Compute Tim's tax:

Tax on net unearned income: $300 × 28%	$ 84
Tax on taxable income minus net unearned income: ($2,050 − $300) × 10%	175
Total income tax	$ 259 ◀

As discussed in more detail in Chapters I:3 and I:5, dividend income and capital gains are taxed at lower rates than other income. The long-term capital gains and dividend income of individuals in the 25% through 35% brackets are taxed 15%. Individuals in the 10% and 15% tax brackets pay no tax on dividend income or long-term capital gains, while individuals in the 39.6% tax bracket are taxed at 20%. These lower rates also apply to the kiddie tax calculation. In figuring the tax where the parents file separate returns, the tax rate of the parent with the greater taxable income is used. If the parents are divorced, the parent with custody is the relevant parent.

EXAMPLE I:2-35 ▶ 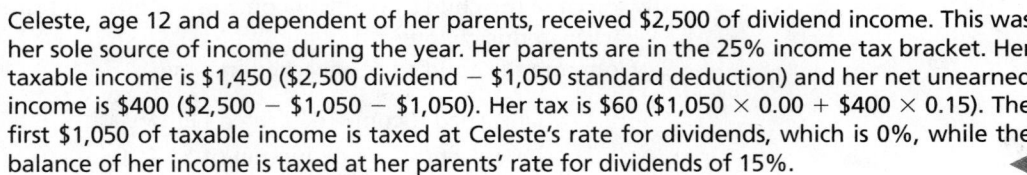 Celeste, age 12 and a dependent of her parents, received $2,500 of dividend income. This was her sole source of income during the year. Her parents are in the 25% income tax bracket. Her taxable income is $1,450 ($2,500 dividend − $1,050 standard deduction) and her net unearned income is $400 ($2,500 − $1,050 − $1,050). Her tax is $60 ($1,050 × 0.00 + $400 × 0.15). The first $1,050 of taxable income is taxed at Celeste's rate for dividends, which is 0%, while the balance of her income is taxed at her parents' rate for dividends of 15%. ◀

Parents of a child subject to the kiddie tax may elect to include the child's dividend and interest income on their own return.[44] This rule eliminates the need to file a tax return for the child. To be eligible for the election, the child's gross income must come solely from dividends and interest, and such income must not exceed $10,500 in 2015 ($10,000 in 2014). Furthermore, there can be no withholding or estimated payment using the child's Social Security number. Parents use Form 8814, Parents' Election to Report Child's Interest and Dividends.

STOP & THINK

Question: Jane and Bill have three dependent teen-age children. Jane operates a retail business and Bill farms. They earn over $200,000 each year. Can they use compensation paid to children as a tax saving device?

Solution: The so called "kiddie tax" does not apply to income earned by children. In many instances, parents can employ their children in family businesses and reduce the family's tax. Individual children may be able to perform a variety of services. They may be assigned chores on the farm such as feeding livestock, milking, gathering eggs, or operating equipment. In the retail business they can be assigned tasks such as filing, answering phones, stocking shelves, making deliveries, and operating cash registers.

Jane and Bill can deduct reasonable compensation paid to the children for the services they provide. The payments are deductible by the parents on their return where it would otherwise be taxed at a high rate. Assuming compensation paid to each child is less than

---

[44] Sec. 1(g)(7).

the amount of the standard deduction, no income tax is owed by them. Assuming the parents continue to provide over one-half of the children's support they remain entitled to dependency exemptions.

BUSINESS INCOME AND BUSINESS ENTITIES

How business income is reported depends on the type of entity. Proprietors report their business income on Schedule C of Form 1040 (Schedule F in the case of farmers). The income is taxed on the proprietor's Form 1040 along with the taxpayer's other income. Approximately 17 million taxpayers report income on Schedule C each year.

Corporations are divided into two groups: C corporations and S corporations. **C corporations**, also called **regular corporations**, are treated as separate entities for tax purposes and pay income taxes on the corporation's taxable income. Shareholders are taxed on dividends they receive from a C corporation but are not taxed on the corporation's undistributed income. Lower tax rates apply temporarily to dividends received by individual taxpayers. See Chapter I:3. Approximately 2 million corporations file the regular corporate return, Form 1120, each year.

The tax formula for C corporations is presented in Table I:2-7. The major difference between the formulas for individual and corporate taxpayers is the fact that there is only one category of deductions for corporations. Personal expenses do not come into consideration. Therefore, there are no itemized deductions, standard deductions, or personal exemptions. The tax rates applicable to C corporations are as follows:[45]

Taxable Income	Tax
First $50,000	15% of taxable income
Over $50,000, but not over $75,000	$7,500 + 25% of taxable income over $50,000
Over $75,000, but not over $100,000	$13,750 + 34% of taxable income over $75,000
Over $100,000, but not over $335,000	$22,250 + 39% of taxable income over $100,000
Over $335,000, but not over $10,000,000	$113,900 + 34% of taxable income over $335,000
Over $10,000,000, but not over $15,000,000	$3,400,000 + 35% of taxable income over $10,000,000
Over $15,000,000, but not over $18,333,333	$5,150,000 + 38% of taxable income over $15,000,000
Over $18,333,333	$6,416,667 + 35% of taxable income over $18,333,333

Note that the corporate tax rates reflect a stair-step pattern of progression, with the two highest rates of 39% and 38% in the middle of the progression. The benefits of the two lowest tax rates of 15% and 25% are completely eliminated by the application of the 39% tax rate to taxable income between $100,000 and $335,000. Likewise, the benefit of the 34% tax rate on taxable income between $335,000 and $10,000,000 is eliminated by the application of a 38% tax rate on taxable income between $15,000,000 and $18,333,333.

The second group of corporations, **S corporations**, generally are not treated as separate entities for tax purposes. They are referred to as flow-through entities. S corporation shareholders are required to report their respective shares of the S corporation's income on their individual tax returns even if the income is not distributed. All shareholders must agree to the S corporation election when it is made. S corporations must also meet a series of conditions, such as having no foreign shareholders. S corporations report ordinary

---

[45] Income of certain personal service corporations is taxed at a flat rate of 35%.

▼ TABLE I:2-7

Tax Formula for C Corporations

Income from whatever source derived	$xxx
Minus: Exclusions	(xxx)
Gross income	$xxx
Minus: Deductions	(xxx)
Taxable income	$xxx
Times: Tax rates	× .xx
Gross tax	$xxx
Minus: Credits and prepayments	(xxx)
Net tax payable or refund due	$xxx

income and special items separately and shareholders in turn report their respective shares of the ordinary income and of each special item. Approximately 4 million corporations file S corporation returns, Form 1120S, each year.

In one sense, there is no formula to compute an S corporation's taxable income because the corporation normally does not pay a tax. S corporations do file returns, but the returns are more informational in nature, much like the returns of a partnership. A residual income total, known as ordinary income, is computed on the return. Special items, such as capital gains and losses and charitable contributions, are kept separate from ordinary income. This is because every item that would receive special treatment on a shareholder's return is passed through to the shareholder with its status intact. Each shareholder reports his or her share of the ordinary income and his or her share of each special item. Losses pass through and generally can be deducted by shareholders up to their respective bases in the corporation's stock. Losses are also subject to other rules, such as the at-risk and passive activity loss rules, which are covered in Chapter I:8.

Partnerships, like S corporations, are flow-through entities for tax purposes. Partners report their respective shares of the partnership's income on their tax returns even if the income is not distributed. Approximately 2 million partnerships file returns, Form 1065, each year. Like S corporations, partnerships report ordinary income and special items separately and the partners report their respective shares of the ordinary income and of each special item. Losses also pass through and generally can be deducted by partners on their returns.

EXAMPLE I:2-36 ► Jane is starting Jane's Computer Services and is considering alternative organizational forms. She anticipates the business will earn $100,000 from operations before compensating her for her services and before charitable contributions. Jane, who is single, has $3,000 of income from other sources and other itemized deductions of $11,000. Her compensation for services will be

WHAT WOULD YOU DO IN THIS SITUATION?

CHOICE OF RATE SCHEDULES

Jane Brown married Jim four years ago. Two years ago Jim lost his job. After looking for work for several months, Jim left town to look for work, and Jane has not heard from him. Jim's brother told Jane that he had heard that Jim lived in Texas, but a friend said he heard that Jim had been killed in an automobile accident.

Jane went back to school and completed a program as a medical technician. She returned to work this year, and she earned $35,000. She has asked you to prepare her tax return this year. She has asked you whether she should file as a single taxpayer, married person filing separately, or as a married person filing jointly. Because she has had a low income until recently, she has taken no legal steps to resolve her status. What should she do?

$50,000. Charitable contributions to be made by the business are expected to be $4,000. Other distributions to her from the business are expected to be $15,000. Compare her income tax for 2015 assuming she operates the business as a proprietorship, an S corporation, and a C corporation. Ignore payroll and other taxes.

	Proprietorship	S Corporation	C Corporation
Business Income			
Operating income	$100,000	$100,000	$100,000
Compensation paid to Jane		(50,000)	(50,000)
Contributions			(4,000)
Net	$100,000	$ 50,000	$ 46,000
Corporate income tax			$ 6,900
Jane's Income			
Business income (above)	$100,000	$ 50,000	
Compensation (above)		50,000	$ 50,000
Dividends			15,000
Other income	3,000	3,000	3,000
Adjusted Gross Income	$103,000	$103,000	$ 68,000
Contributions	($ 4,000)	($ 4,000)	
Other itemized deductions	(11,000)	(11,000)	(11,000)
Personal exemption	(4,000)	(4,000)	(4,000)
Taxable income	$ 84,000	$ 84,000	$ 53,000
Individual income tax	$ 16,794	$ 16,794	$ 7,544
Total tax	$ 16,794	$ 16,794	$ 14,444

In each of the alternatives, Jane reports other income of $3,000 and other itemized deductions of $11,000 on her personal return.

No separate return is filed for the proprietorship. Jane reports the $100,000 income from her business on Schedule C of her Form 1040 and she claims the $4,000 charitable contribution as an itemized deduction on Schedule A along with the other itemized deductions. In this case, whether Jane considers part of the income from the business to be compensation for her services is irrelevant.

With an S election, two returns are filed, a Form 1120S for the corporation and a Form 1040 on Jane's behalf. Because of the S election, the corporation pays no tax. Items reported on the Form 1120S "pass through" the corporation and are reported by Jane on her own return. The $50,000 of compensation paid to Jane by the corporation is deducted by the corporation in computing its income and is taxable to Jane. Jane also reports the remaining $50,000 of the corporation's income on her return and claims the $4,000 charitable contribution as an itemized deduction.

The C corporation is taxed as a separate entity. The corporation files a Form 1120 on which it would deduct the $50,000 of compensation paid to Jane along with the $4,000 charitable contribution and pay a $6,900 (15% × $46,000) tax on the remaining income. Jane reports the $50,000 salary along with the $15,000 dividend distributed by the corporation. Note that the dividend of $15,000 paid by the corporation is not deductible by the corporation. A special provision reduces the "double tax" on the dividends Jane receives from the corporation by subjecting the dividends to a 15% tax rate instead of the 25% rate that would otherwise apply. (See Chapter I:3.) As a result, her tax on the dividends is $2,250 (15% × $15,000) and her tax on her remaining income of $38,000 ($53,000 − $15,000) is $5,294 (from the rate schedule). Her total tax is $7,544. The total tax for the corporation and Jane is $14,444.

As shown, Jane's total current income tax will be lower if she chooses to operate her business as a C corporation even though the $15,000 paid to her as a dividend is taxed twice—once inside the corporation when it is earned and again on Jane's return. The reason the total tax is lower is because the income retained by the corporation is taxed at the corporation's marginal tax rate of 15% instead of being taxed at Jane's marginal rate of 25%. The savings will be lost in the future if the corporation distributes the retained income as a dividend. Clearly, if the plans are to distribute the retained income in the near future, it is desirable to operate as a proprietorship or an S corporation so that the distribution can be made without any future tax.

Self-employment taxes and social security taxes would also be considered when an organizational form is selected for a new business. Although detailed consideration of these taxes is found in Chapter I:14, it is noted here that the self-employment tax, which generally applies to the proprietorship and partnership forms of doing business, would be greater than the social security tax which would apply only to the wages paid to Jane by the S and C corporations. Given the facts in this case, Jane might judge the proprietorship organizational form less favorably when these taxes are taken into consideration. Jane should consider these taxes along with other taxes (e.g., state and local taxes) and other nontax factors such as liability protection before making a final decision. ◀

The detailed rules of C corporations are covered in Chapter I:16 while S corporations and partnerships are covered in Chapter I:17 of the *Individuals* volume. All three are covered more extensively in the *Corporations, Partnerships, Estates, and Trusts* volume and the *Comprehensive* volume.

TREATMENT OF CAPITAL GAINS AND LOSSES

Capital gains and losses have been accorded favored tax treatment since 1922. Favored tax treatment essentially means that capital gains are taxed at a lower rate than is ordinary income. A purpose of the special rules is to distinguish capital appreciation from gains attributable to ordinary business transactions and speculation. This goal is accomplished by defining capital assets to not include certain business property (e.g., inventory and trade receivables) and by requiring taxpayers to hold capital assets for minimum time periods in order to benefit from the lower rates that are available to capital gains.

The discussion below is intended as a brief introduction to capital gains and losses. A detailed discussion of this topic is contained in Chapter I:5.

DEFINITION OF *CAPITAL ASSETS*

A **capital gain** or **loss** is the gain or loss from the sale or exchange of a capital asset. Unfortunately, the tax law merely states what is not a capital asset. In other words, **capital assets** are assets other than those listed in Sec. 1221. A detailed discussion is found in Chapter I:5. Here we simply note the categories of properties included on the list, which are thereby excluded from capital asset status are inventory, trade receivables, certain properties created by the efforts of the taxpayer (such as works of art), depreciable business property and business land, and certain government publications. All other assets are considered capital assets and include investment property (such as stocks and bonds) and personal-use property (such as personal residence or automobile). As noted, a purpose of the rules applicable to capital gains and losses is to distinguish capital appreciation from gains derived from ordinary business operations. The profit from the sale of inventory and trade receivables is viewed as business profit as opposed to capital appreciation. Thus, a gain realized by an artist on the sale of one of his or her own works is ordinary income from personal services. However, gain from the sale of artwork held as an investment or for personal use would be treated as a capital gain.

TAX TREATMENT OF GAINS AND LOSSES

Capital gains and losses are divided into long-term (associated with property held over one year) and short-term (associated with property held one year or less). Individuals in the 10% and 15% tax brackets pay no tax on net long-term capital gains. Individuals in the 25% through 35% brackets are taxed at 15%, and taxpayers in the 39.6% bracket are taxed at 20%. An additional 3.8% tax that applies to investment income, including capital gains and interest, received by higher-income taxpayers is discussed below. A net short-term capital gain is taxed at the same rate as other income.

On the other hand, individuals who suffer net capital losses can deduct only up to $3,000 of the losses from other income. A net capital loss in excess of $3,000 can be carried over and offset against future capital gains or, subject to the $3,000 limitation, deducted from other income.

PROVISIONS APPLICABLE TO HIGHER-INCOME TAXPAYERS

OBJECTIVE 6

Compute the income tax for high-income individuals

In 2013, new rules increased taxes for higher-income taxpayers. Personal and dependency exemptions are now phased out for higher-income taxpayers and itemized deductions are reduced by up to 80%.

Specifically, personal and dependency exemptions are phased out at a rate of 2% for each $2,500 ($1,250 for married persons filing separate returns), or fraction thereof, of AGI above:

	2015	2014
Joint return and surviving spouse	$309,900	$305,050
Head-of-households	284,050	279,650
Single	258,250	254,200
Separate	154,950	152,525

These thresholds are adjusted for inflation.

EXAMPLE I:2-37 ▶ In 2015, Lee, a single taxpayer with one dependent, reports AGI of $200,000. Lee's personal and dependency exemptions of $8,000 ($4,000 × 2) are not subject to the phase-out. ◀

EXAMPLE I:2-38 ▶ In 2015, Jane, a single taxpayer with one dependent, reports AGI of $306,050. Jane's personal and dependency exemptions are reduced as follows:

Gross personal and dependency exemption amount		$8,000
Excess AGI ($306,050 − $258,250)	$47,800	
Phase-out multiples (rounded up) ($47,800/$2,500)	20	
Reduction ($8,000 × 20 × 2%)		(3,200)
Net personal and dependency exemption amount		$4,800 ◀

Itemized deductions are reduced by 3% of AGI in excess of the same thresholds. The reduction cannot exceed 80% of the total itemized deductions (discussed in more detail in Chapter I:7).

EXAMPLE I:2-39 ▶ Jane, from Example I: 2-38, has $10,000 of home mortgage interest and property taxes of $6,000. Her gross itemized deductions of $16,000 are reduced by $1,434 [3% × ($306,050 − $258,250)] to $14,566. ◀

The phase-out of itemized deductions for higher-income taxpayers is discussed in more detail in Chapter I:7.

In addition, taxes enacted in 2010 as part of the Affordable Care Act became effective in 2013. A new payroll tax of 0.9% applies to earned income over $200,000 ($250,000 for married couples). An additional 3.8% tax applies to the lesser of investment income (including interest, capital gains, and dividends) or AGI in excess of $200,000 ($250,000 for married couples). These thresholds are not adjusted for inflation.

TAX PLANNING CONSIDERATIONS

<table>
<tr><td>

OBJECTIVE 7

Describe tax planning considerations for various tax matters

</td></tr>
</table>

SHIFTING INCOME BETWEEN FAMILY MEMBERS

Because of the progressive tax system, families often can reduce their taxes by **shifting income** to family members who are in lower tax brackets.

EXAMPLE I:2-40 ▶ Mary, who is in the 39.6% tax bracket, shifted $5,000 of income to her 25-year-old son, Steve, by making a gift of a 10%, $50,000 corporate bond. Steve had no income as he suffered a business loss. In absence of the shift, 39.6% of the income would have gone for taxes. There is no tax on Steve's return because the income is offset by his loss. ◀

EXAMPLE I:2-41 ▶ Farouk, who is in the 39.6% tax bracket, shifted $2,000 of interest income to his 25-year-old daughter, Dana, who is in the 10% tax bracket. The tax savings from the shift is $592 [(0.396 × $2,000) − (0.10 × $2,000)]. ◀

ADDITIONAL COMMENT

All 50 states have enacted laws that simplify the procedures for making gifts to minors. This type of law, which in most states is called the Uniform Gifts to Minors Act, is especially important when making gifts of securities.

As noted earlier in this chapter, the net unearned income of children under the age of 24 is taxed at their parents' tax rate. Hence, a shifting of income to young children is often an ineffective method of minimizing tax.

Shifting income must be distinguished from assigning income. Earned income is taxed to the person who produces it. Income from property is taxed to the person who owns the property. Ordering income to be paid to another is an assignment of income that does not change who is taxed on the income. Normally, in the case of income from property, ownership of the property must be transferred in order to shift the income.

EXAMPLE I:2-42 ▶ John owns stock in Valley Corporation. John orders the corporation to pay this year's dividends to his daughter. John will be taxed on the income even though he has assigned it to another person. ◀

EXAMPLE I:2-43 ▶ Kay owns stock in Valley Corporation. Kay gives the stock to her 25-year-old son. Future dividends on Valley stock will be taxed to the son instead of to Kay. ◀

Individuals often are unwilling to give property away completely. As a result, personal preference may limit the amount of tax planning that is possible.

SPLITTING INCOME

Splitting income consists of creating additional taxable entities, especially corporations, in order to reduce an individual's effective tax rate.

EXAMPLE I:2-44 ▶ Tom is a taxpayer in the 39.6% tax bracket and is involved in a variety of businesses. One business has been producing $20,000 of income per year for several years. Tom incorporates the business. The first $50,000 of a corporation's income is taxed at a 15% rate. Thus, the tax on the income is reduced by $4,920 [(0.396 × $20,000) − (0.15 × $20,000)]. ◀

The creation of a new corporate entity to split income is not always desirable because the corporation's income will be taxed to the shareholder as a dividend if it is distributed.

In addition, if income is allowed to accumulate in a corporation indefinitely, it may be subject to the accumulated earnings tax.[45]

MAXIMIZING ITEMIZED DEDUCTIONS

Timing expenditures properly often can increase deductions. In general, cash-basis taxpayers deduct expenses in the year paid. If itemized deductions are less than the standard deduction, the taxpayer will receive no tax benefit from the deductions. A taxpayer in that situation could defer some payments or accelerate others to maximize expenses in one year, thereby creating a sufficient amount of deductions in that year.

EXAMPLE I:2-45 ▶ Jean's property taxes are due on January 1 of each year. Jean is a single, cash-basis, calendar-year taxpayer. Itemized deductions other than property taxes total $4,000 in each year. Jean pays the 2015 property taxes of $1,600 on January 1, 2015, and the 2016 property taxes of $1,600 on December 31, 2015. In the absence of doubling up, Jean would not be able to itemize in either year. The itemized deductions of $5,600 ($4,000 + $1,600) would be less than the standard deduction of $6,300. By doubling up, Jean has itemized deductions of $7,200 ($4,000 + $1,600 + $1,600) in 2015. ◀

Medical expenses are deductible only to the extent they exceed 10% of a taxpayer's AGI. In situations where medical expenses are just under the AGI threshold, taxpayers may be able to create a deduction by doubling up.

EXAMPLE I:2-46 ▶ Troy's AGI is $20,000. So far in 2015, Troy's medical expenses have totaled $1,800. Troy has received a bill from his dentist for $500 that is due January 15, 2016. By paying the bill in 2015, Troy will have a deduction for medical expenses of $300 [$1,800 + $500 − (0.10 × $20,000)]. This assumes that Troy's other itemized deductions exceed the standard deduction.[47] ◀

FILING JOINT OR SEPARATE RETURNS

Factors to be Considered. In general, married couples may file either joint or separate returns. As noted earlier, if one spouse has significantly more than half of their combined income, filing separately will increase the couple's total income tax. Because of the potential tax saving from a joint return and because it is simpler to prepare one return than two, most married couples file jointly.

It should be noted that the joint return is not always preferred. Separate returns may result in increased deductions. Because only one spouse's income is reported on a separate return, medical expenses are more likely to exceed the 10% of adjusted gross income floor if one spouse incurs most of the medical expenses. Similarly, casualty losses involving personal-use assets, which are allowable only to the extent that they exceed 10% of AGI, may be deductible on separate returns.

One significant impact of the joint return is the joint income tax liability. Both the husband and wife may be liable for taxes owed on a joint return. This could be a major problem if a couple separates or divorces after filing a return.

EXAMPLE I:2-47 ▶ Jim and Pat file a joint return. They are both informed as to the relevant information pertaining to the return. The next year they separate, and Jim moves out of town without leaving a forwarding address. The IRS audits their joint return and disallows $400 of charitable contributions

---

[46] Amounts accumulated in a corporation in excess of $250,000 may be subject to this tax. However, amounts accumulated for business purposes are exempt. This subject is discussed briefly in Chapter I:16 and extensively in *Prentice Hall's Federal Taxation: Corporations, Partnerships, Estates and Trusts.*

[47] For a discussion of restrictions on the deductibility of prepaid medical expenses, see Chapter I:7.

ETHICAL POINT

Because innocent spouse rules are strict, it may sometimes be safer to file a separate return than run the risk of being held responsible for the acts of another.

deducted on the original return. Pat may be held responsible for the additional taxes owed. The IRS does not have to attempt to locate Jim in order to collect the tax. ◀

Innocent Spouse Provision. When married couples file a joint return, each spouse generally is liable for the entire tax and any penalties imposed.[48] This is the case even if all of the income was earned by one spouse. This rule could prove unfair in some instances, especially where one spouse concealed information from the other. For that reason, the Code contains an **innocent spouse** provision. An innocent spouse is relieved of the liability for tax on unreported income if:

▶ The amount is attributable to erroneous items of the other spouse.

▶ The innocent spouse did not know and had no reason to know that there was such an understatement of tax.

▶ Under the circumstances, it would be inequitable to hold the innocent spouse liable for the understatement.

▶ The innocent spouse elects relief within two years after the IRS begins collection activities.[49]

EXAMPLE I:2-48 ▶ Dan and Joy file a joint return. Dan traveled much of the time and Joy had little information as to his whereabouts or income. Joy worked and her own salary was the sole source of her support. Their return was audited by the IRS. The audit disclosed that Dan had not reported income from a job he had held for several months during the year. In this situation, Joy may be able to use the innocent spouse provision in order to avoid being held liable for the tax on the unreported income. ◀

The election is permitted when the innocent spouse was aware of the understatement, but did not know or have reason to know the extent of the understatement. Relief is limited to the portion of the understatement attributable to the "unknown" amounts.

Separate Liability Election. Couples who file joint returns and are subsequently divorced, widowed, or separated may make a separate liability election. An electing spouse is liable only for the portion of any understatement attributable to him or her.

EXAMPLE I:2-49 ▶ Al and Ann divorce after filing a joint return. An IRS examination of the return reveals $20,000 of unreported income attributable to Al and $10,000 of unallowable deductions attributable to Ann. Together, these amounts result in an understatement of their tax by $9,000. If Ann can establish that she was unaware of Al's unreported income, she can make a separate liability election. She will be liable only for $3,000 of tax as she is responsible for only one third of the understatement. The allocation would not be different because only part of the deductions were disallowed because of an AGI floor. ◀

The election must be made within two years after the IRS begins collections efforts. The election may be made by both spouses. The election is invalid if the spouse responsible for the errors transfers assets to the "innocent" spouse in an effort to avoid payment.

Electing to Change to a Joint Return. In general, a husband and wife who file separate returns for a given year may elect to change to a joint return by filing an amended joint return. This change is permitted after the due date but must occur within three years of the due date including extensions. Taxpayers may not change from a joint return to separate returns after the due date.[50]

---

[48] Sec. 6013(d)(3).
[49] Sec. 6015(b).

[50] Reg. Sec. 1.6013-1(a). However, a couple who filed a joint return whose marriage is later annulled must file amended returns as singles (Rev. Rul. 76-255, 1976-2 C.B. 40).

COMPLIANCE AND PROCEDURAL CONSIDERATIONS

OBJECTIVE 8

Describe compliance and procedural matters for filing tax returns

ADDITIONAL COMMENT

The IRS is encouraging nonfilers (i.e., individuals and businesses who should have filed previous tax returns but did not) to come forward. The IRS estimates that approximately 10 million people fail to file their income tax returns each year.

WHO MUST FILE

Whether an individual must file a tax return is based on the amount of the individual's gross income.[51] The fact that the individual owes no tax does not mean that a return need not be filed. The gross income filing levels for taxpayers under age 65 are as follows:[52]

	2014	2015
Single	$ 10,150	$ 10,300
Married, filing jointly	20,300	20,600
Surviving spouse	16,350	16,600
Married, filing separately	3,950	4,000
Married, living separately from spouse at year-end	3,950	4,000
Head of household	13,050	13,250

There are three situations where taxpayers must file even if the gross income is less than the amounts shown above:

▶ Taxpayers who receive advance payments of the earned income credit (see Chapter I:14) must file regardless of their income levels.

▶ Taxpayers with net self-employment income of $400 or more must file regardless of their total gross income.

▶ Taxpayers who can be claimed as a dependent by another must file if they have either unearned income over $1,050 or total gross income over the standard deduction.

In general, taxpayers must file if their gross income equals or exceeds the sum of the personal exemption and the standard deduction (including the additional standard deduction due to age but not blindness). The blindness allowance and dependency exemptions are not considered. If the disallowance of the standard deduction rules apply, the standard deduction is ignored in determining whether taxpayers must file.

EXAMPLE I:2-50 ▶

In 2015, Carol is a single, self-supporting taxpayer with no dependents. Carol must file if her gross income is $10,300 or greater ($6,300 + $4,000). ◀

KEY POINT

It is possible that a taxpayer may be required to file an income tax return but still have no tax liability.

DUE DATES AND EXTENSIONS

Returns for individuals and partnerships are due on the fifteenth day of the fourth month following the close of the tax year, which for calendar-year taxpayers is April 15.[53] Returns for C corporations and S corporations are due on the fifteenth day of the third month following the close of the tax year, which for calendar-year corporations is March 15.[54] A due date that falls on a Saturday, Sunday, or a holiday is automatically extended to the next day that is not a Saturday, Sunday, or holiday.[55] As noted, individuals are required to file only if their gross income exceeds prescribed thresholds. Partnerships and corporations, however, are required to file even if they have no gross income.

Individuals may obtain an automatic extension of six months by filing Form 4868 (Application for Automatic Extension of Time to File U.S. Individual Income Tax Return). C corporations and S corporations may obtain an automatic extension of six months by filing Form 7004. Partnerships may obtain a 5 month extension by filing Form 7004.

---

[51] *Gross income* has its usual meaning except that the gain excluded from the sale of a personal residence and excluded foreign earned income are included (Sec. 6012(c)).
[52] Sec. 6012(a)(1).

[53] Sec. 6072(a).
[54] Sec. 6072(b).
[55] Sec. 7503.

An extension to file a return is not an extension to pay any tax that is owed. Taxpayers must project their tax liability to the best of their ability and remit with the extension any amount that has not been prepaid through withholding or estimated payments. Interest and penalty may apply to amounts paid after the regular due date. See Chapter C:15 in the *Comprehensive* volume and the *Corporations, Partnerships, Estates, and Trusts* volume for more on payment requirements.

	Individuals	Partnerships	Corporations
Returns	Forms 1040, 1040A, 1040EZ	Form 1065	Forms 1120, 1120S
Return due date	15th day of 4th month	15th day of 4th month	15th day of 3rd month
Automatic extension	Form 4868 (6 months)	Form 7004 (5 months)	Form 7004 (6 months)

ADDITIONAL COMMENT
In 2013, of the 145 million returns filed, nearly 121 million returns were filed electronically, or 83.4%. This compares with 73 million electronic returns in 2006.

USE OF FORMS 1040, 1040EZ, AND 1040A

The primary individual tax return is Form 1040. Complicated returns often involve many additional forms and schedules. Two shorter forms are available to taxpayers with less-complicated tax returns. Form 1040EZ is available to single taxpayers and married individuals who file a joint return. Such taxpayers must have taxable income of less than $50,000 and claim no dependents. To use Form 1040EZ, the taxpayer's income must consist of salary and wages plus no more than $1,500 of taxable interest income. No deductions (other than the standard deduction) or credits (other than withholding from salary and wages) can be taken on the return.

Form 1040A is available to taxpayers who have somewhat more involved returns. Form 1040A can be used by taxpayers claiming any number of exemptions or any filing status. Salary, wages, dividends, interest, pension and annuity income, and unemployment compensation can be reported on Form 1040A. Taxpayers may deduct IRA contributions. Taxpayers may also claim credits for withholding, child care, and earned income.

SELF-STUDY QUESTION
It is sometimes said that the hallmark of the U.S. federal income tax system is voluntary compliance. With so much information being reported to the IRS, how voluntary is the system?

ANSWER
The system is not very voluntary with respect to income subject to reporting. But some sources of income, such as income from self-employment, are not subject to reporting by a third party. Also, the IRS would have to audit a tax return to verify most of the deductions.

SYSTEM FOR REPORTING INCOME

There is a significant and expanding relationship between computers, tax returns, the taxpayer identification system, and information returns. The IRS keeps records based on taxpayer identification numbers. Individual taxpayers report information based on Social Security numbers, whereas employer identification numbers (EIN) are used by corporations, other taxpayers, and tax-exempt entities. Individuals who employ others have both a Social Security number and an employer identification number.

Employers, banks, stockbrokers, savings and loans, and so on report payments they make to others along with the payee's identification number. Today, the IRS computers match much of the reported information with tax returns, using the taxpayer identification number as the cross-reference. The need for accurate information returns is obvious. Some major information returns are listed below:

Basic Form	Type of Payment	Required if Amount Equals or Exceeds
1099-R	Pensions and annuities including lump sum distributions	$600
W-2	Salary, wages, etc.	600
1099-DIV	Dividends	10
1099-INT	Interest	600[56]
1099-B	Sale of a security	All
1099-G	Unemployment compensation, tax refunds, etc.	10
1099-MISC	Rent, royalties, etc.	600

This information-reporting system makes it more difficult for taxpayers to avoid IRS detection if they omit income from their returns.

---

[56] For banks and corporations the amount is $10.

PROBLEM MATERIALS

DISCUSSION QUESTIONS

I:2-1　　a. The tax law refers to gross income, yet the term gross income is not found on Form 1040. Explain.

　　　　　b. Why is it important to understand the concept of gross income even though the term is not found on Form 1040?

I:2-2　　Explain the distinction between income and gross income.

I:2-3　　a. Explain the distinction between a deduction and a credit.

　　　　　b. Which is worth more, a $10 deduction or a $10 credit?

　　　　　c. Explain the difference between refundable and nonrefundable credits.

I:2-4　　List the conditions that must be met in order to claim a dependency exemption for qualifying children and qualifying relatives. Briefly explain each one.

I:2-5　　a. Briefly explain the concept of support.

　　　　　b. If a taxpayer provides 50% or less of another person's support, is it possible for the taxpayer to claim a dependency exemption? Explain.

　　　　　c. Does support include the value of an automobile? Explain.

I:2-6　　Under what circumstances must a taxpayer use a rate schedule instead of a tax table?

I:2-7　　a. What determines who must file a tax return?

　　　　　b. Is an individual required to file a tax return if he or she owes no tax?

I:2-8　　Many homeowners itemize deductions while many renters claim the standard deduction. Explain.

I:2-9　　Tax rules are often very precise. For example, a taxpayer must ordinarily provide "over 50%" of another person's support in order to claim a dependency exemption. Why is the threshold "over 50%" as opposed to "50% or more?"

I:2-10　What is the normal due date for the tax return of calendar-year taxpayers? What happens to the due date if it falls on a Saturday, Sunday, or holiday?

I:2-11　Sometimes taxpayers may not be able to file their tax returns by the normal due date. Are extensions available? How long are the extensions? Do extensions enable taxpayers to delay paying the tax they owe?

I:2-12　Can tax-exempt income qualify as support? Explain.

I:2-13　Can a scholarship qualify as support?

I:2-14　Explain the purpose of the multiple support agreement.

I:2-15　Summarize the rules that explain which parent receives the dependency exemption for children in cases of divorce.

I:2-16　What conditions must be met by a married couple before they can file a joint return?

I:2-17　Explain what is meant by the phrase *maintain a household.*

I:2-18　Under what circumstances, if any, can a married person file as a head of household?

I:2-19　a. Explain the principal difference in the tax treatment of an S corporation and a C corporation.

　　　　　b. Why would a C corporation be used if an S corporation is generally exempt from tax?

I:2-20　Income earned by C corporations is taxed twice, once when the income is earned and again when it is distributed. If so, how is it possible that operating a business as a C corporation can reduce taxes.

I:2-21　a. What assets are excluded from capital asset status?

　　　　　b. Are capital gains given favorable tax treatment?

　　　　　c. What is the significance of an asset being classified as a capital asset?

　　　　　d. Are capital losses deductible?

I:2-22　Is there any tax advantage for an individual who has held an appreciated capital asset for eleven months to delay the sale of the asset? Explain.

I:2-23　a. Explain the difference between income splitting and income shifting.

　　　　　b. Why are taxpayers interested in shifting income from one tax return to another within the same family or economic unit?

　　　　　c. Is there a relationship between the tax on unearned income of a minor and taxpayers who attempt to shift income?

I:2-24　a. Who is liable for additional taxes on a joint return?

　　　　　b. Why is this so important?

I:2-25　Can couples change from joint returns to separate returns? Separate to joint?

ISSUE IDENTIFICATION QUESTIONS

I:2-26 This year, Yung Tseng, a U.S. citizen, supported his nephew who is attending school in the United States. Yung is a U.S. citizen, but his nephew is a citizen of Hong Kong. The nephew has a student visa, but he hopes to become a permanent U. S. resident. Other family members hope to come to the U.S. What issues must be considered by Yung?

I:2-27 Carmen and Carlos, who have filed joint tax returns for several years, separated this year. Carlos works in construction and is often paid in cash. Carlos says he only worked a few weeks this year and made $11,000. In prior years he made approximately $35,000 per year, and Carmen is surprised that his income is so low this year. Carmen received a salary of $38,000 as a medical laboratory technician. They have no dependents and claim the standard deduction. What tax issues should Carmen and Carlos consider?

I:2-28 Jane and Bill have lived in a home Bill inherited from his parents. Their son Jim lives with them. Bill and Jane obtain a divorce during the current year. Under the terms of the divorce, Jane receives possession of the home for a period of five years and custody of Jim. Bill is obligated to furnish over one-half of the cost of the maintenance, taxes, and insurance on the home and pay $6,000 of child support per year. Bill lives in an apartment. What tax issues should Jane and Bill consider?

PROBLEMS

I:2-29 *Computation of Tax.* The following information relates to two married couples:

	Lanes	Waynes
Salary (earned by one spouse)	$32,000	$115,000
Interest income	1,000	10,000
Deductible IRA contribution	5,000	0
Itemized deductions	15,000	15,000
Exemptions	8,000	8,000
Withholding	700	18,700

Compute the 2015 tax due or refund due for each couple. Assume that the itemized deductions have been reduced by the applicable floors. Ignore credits.

I:2-30 *Computation of Taxable Income.* The following information relates to Tom, a single taxpayer, age 18:

Salary	$1,800
Interest income	1,600
Itemized deductions	600

a. Compute Tom's taxable income assuming he is self-supporting.
b. Compute Tom's taxable income assuming he is a dependent of his parents.

I:2-31 *Joint Versus Separate Returns.* Carl and Carol have salaries of $14,000 and $22,000, respectively. Their itemized deductions total $8,500. They are married and both are under age 65.
a. Compute their taxable income assuming they file jointly.
b. Compute their taxable incomes assuming they file separate returns and that Carol claims all of the itemized deductions.

I:2-32 *Joint Versus Separate Returns.* Hal attended school much of 2015, during which time he was supported by his parents. Hal married Ruth in December 2015. Hal graduated and commenced work in 2016. Ruth worked during 2015 and earned $18,000. Hal's only income was $1,100 of interest. Hal's parents are in the 28% tax bracket. Thus, claiming Hal as a dependent would save them $1,120 (0.28 × $4,000) of taxes.
a. Compute Hal and Ruth's gross tax if they file a joint return.
b. Compute Ruth's gross tax if she files a separate return in order to allow Hal's parents to claim him as a dependent.
c. Which alternative would be better for the family? In other words, will filing a joint return save Hal and Ruth more than $1,120?

I:2-33 *Dependency Exemptions.* Wes and Tina are a married couple and provide financial assistance to several persons during the current year. For the situations below, determine whether the individuals qualify as Wes and Tina's dependents. In all of the situations below, assume that any dependency tests not mentioned have been met.

a. Brian is age 24 and Wes and Tina's son. He is a full-time student and lives in an apartment near campus. Wes and Tina provide over 50% of his support. Brian works as a waiter and earned $4,200.

b. Same as Part a except that Brian is a part-time student.

c. Sherry is age 22 and Wes and Tina's daughter. She is a full-time student and lives in the college dormitory. Wes and Tina provide over 50% of her support. Sherry works part-time as a bookkeeper and earned $5,000.

d. Same as Part c except that Sherry is a part-time student.

e. Granny, age 82, is Tina's grandmother and lives with Wes and Tina. During the current year, Granny's only sources of income were her Social Security of $4,800 and interest on U.S. bonds of $4,500. Granny uses her income to pay for 40% of her total support, Wes and Tina provide the remainder of Granny's support.

I:2-34 *Dependency Exemptions.* John and Carole file a joint return and have three children: Jack, age 23; David, age 20; and Kristen, age 15. All three children live at home the entire year. Below is information about each of the children:

- Jack: graduated from college last year and will start medical school next year. This year, Jack worked sparingly as he studied for the medical school entrance exam, but did earn $5,000. John and Carole provided 80% of Jack's support during the year.
- David: a full-time student at State U., earned $6,400 from a part-time job, and provided 40% of his own support.
- Kristen: a full-time student in high school, had no gross income, and provided none of her own support.

a. Based on the above facts, which of the children can be claimed by John and Carole this year?

b. How would your answer to Part a change if Jack began medical school this year?

c. How would your answer to Part a change if Jack earned $3,000 rather than $5,000?

d. How would your answer to Part a change if David was a part-time student rather than a full-time student?

e. How would your answer to Part a change if David provided 60% of his own support rather than 40%?

I:2-35 *Dependency Exemptions and Child Credit.* Robert provides much of the support for his daughter, Jane, and her two children. Jane earned $20,000. Robert, whose AGI is $350,000, paid the rent of $11,000 on Jane's apartment and provided an additional $15,000 support. Jane is age 30, and her children are age 7 and age 4.

a. Can Robert claim a dependency exemption for Jane?

b. Can Jane claim her children as dependents?

c. Who is entitled to the child credit?

I:2-36 *Dependency Exemptions.* Juan helps support his mother Maria, his son Jose, and a niece Norma. How many dependency exemptions can Juan claim given these additional facts?

Maria lives with Juan. She receives $12,000 of Social Security benefits which she uses to pay for food, clothing, medical expenses, and other living expenses. Juan provides Maria's room which has a rental value of $5,000 and pays an additional $4,000 toward her support.

Jose, age 12, lives with his mother, Linda. Juan pays $12,000 per year child support, and Linda provides an additional $4,000 of support.

Norma, age 20, is a part-time college student who lives in an apartment. She earned $6,000 working part-time and received a scholarship of $2,000. Norma's father provided $4,000 toward her support, and Juan provided $7,000.

I:2-37 *Dependency Exemptions.* Anna, age 65, who lives with her unmarried son, Mario, received $7,000, which was used for her support during the year. The sources of support were as follows:

Social Security benefits	$1,500
Mario	2,600
Caroline, an unrelated friend	800
Doug, Anna's son	500
Elaine, Anna's sister	1,600
Total	$7,000

a. Who is eligible to claim Anna as a dependent?

b. What must be done before Mario can claim the exemption?

c. Can anyone claim head-of-household status based on Anna's dependency exemption? Explain.

d. Can Mario claim an old age allowance for his mother? Explain.

I:2-38 *Dependency Exemption and Child Credit: Divorced Parents.* Joe and Joan divorce during the current year. Joan receives custody of their three children. Joe agrees to pay $5,000 of child support for each child.

a. Assuming no written agreement, who will receive the dependency exemption and child credit for the children? Explain.

b. Would it make any difference if Joe could prove that he provided over one-half of the support for each child?

I:2-39 *Filing Status, Dependency Exemptions, and Child Credit.* For the following taxpayers, indicate which tax form should be used, the applicable filing status, and the number of personal and dependency exemptions available, and the number of children who qualify for the child credit.

a. Arnie is a single college student who earned $7,700 working part-time. He had $200 of interest income and received $1,000 of support from his parents.

b. Buddy is a single college student who earned $7,700 working part-time. He had $1,600 of interest income and received $1,000 of support from his parents.

c. Cindy is divorced and received $6,000 of alimony from her former husband and earned $12,000 working as a secretary. She also received $1,800 of child support for her son who lives with her. According to a written agreement, her former husband is entitled to receive the dependency exemption.

d. Debbie is a widow, age 68, who receives a pension of $8,000, nontaxable social security benefits of $8,000, and interest of $4,000. She has no dependents.

e. Edith is married, but her husband left her two years ago and she has not seen him since. Edith supported herself and her daughter, age 6. She paid all household expenses. Her income of $26,000 consisted of a salary of $25,200 and interest of $800.

I:2-40 *Dependency Exemptions and Child Credit.* How many dependency exemptions are the following taxpayers entitled to, assuming the people involved are U.S. citizens? Which dependents qualify for the child credit?

a. Andrew supports his cousin Mary, who does not live with him. Mary has no income and is single.

b. Bob and Ann are filing a joint return. Bob provided over one-half of his father's support. The father received Social Security benefits of $6,000 and taxable interest income of $800. The father is single and does not live with them.

c. Clay provides 60% of his single daughter's support. She earned $3,000 while attending school during the year as a full-time student. She is 22 years old.

d. Dave provided 30% of his mother's support and she provided 55% of her own support. Dave's brother provided the remainder. The brother agreed to sign a multiple support agreement.

I:2-41 *Dependency Exemptions, Child Credits, Tax Rate Schedules, and Divorce.* Juan and Maria, who have two young children, are in the process of obtaining a divorce. Juan expects to have $200,000 of income each year while Maria expects to have $60,000 of income each year. Assume the children will live with Maria after the divorce and that Juan will pay child support.

a. What advice can you provide them regarding the dependency exemptions for the children?

b. What advice can you provide them regarding the child credit?

c. What advice can you provide regarding tax rate schedules?

I:2-42 *Marriage and Taxes.* Bill and Mary plan to marry in December 2015. Bill's salary is $32,000 and he owns his residence. His itemized deductions total $12,000. Mary's salary is $39,000. Her itemized deductions total only $1,600 as she does not own her residence. For purposes of this problem, assume 2016 tax rates, exemptions, and standard deductions are the same as 2015.

a. What will their tax be if they marry before year-end and file a joint return?

b. What will their combined taxes be for the year if they delay the marriage until 2016?

c. What factors contribute to the difference in taxes?

I:2-43 *Filing Requirement.* Which of the following taxpayers must file a 2015 return?

a. Amy, age 19 and single, has $8,050 of wages, $800 of interest, and $350 of self-employment income.

b. Betty, age 67 and single, has a taxable pension of $9,100 and Social Security benefits of $6,200.

c. Chris, age 15 and single, is a dependent of his parents. Chris has earned income of $1,900 and interest of $400.

d. Dawn, age 15 and single, is a dependent of her parents. She has earned income of $400 and interest of $1,600.

e. Doug, age 25, and his wife are separated. He earned $5,000 while attending school during the year.

I:2-44 *Head of Household.* In the following situations, indicate whether the taxpayer qualifies as a head of household.

a. Allen is divorced from his wife. He maintains a household for himself and his dependent mother.

b. Beth is divorced from her husband. She maintains a home for herself and supports an elderly aunt who lives in a retirement home.

c. Cindy was widowed last year. She maintains a household for herself and her dependent daughter, who lived with her during the year.

d. Dick is not divorced, but lived apart from his wife for the entire year. He maintains a household for himself and his dependent daughter. He does not receive any financial support from his wife.

I:2-45 *Filing Status.* For the following independent situations, determine the optimum filing status for the years in question.

a. Wayne and Celia had been married for 24 years before Wayne died in an accident in 2013. Celia and her son, Wally, age 21 in 2013, continued to live at home in 2013, 2014, 2015, and 2016. Wally worked part-time (earning $5,000 in each of the four years) and attended the university on a part-time basis. Celia provided more than 50% of Wally's support for all four years. What is Celia's filing status for 2013, 2014, 2015, and 2016?

b. Juanita is a single parent who maintained a household for her unmarried son Josh, age 19. Josh worked full-time and earned $16,000. Juanita provided approximately 40% of Josh's support but provided all the expenses of maintaining the household. What is Juanita's filing status?

c. Gomer and Gertrude are married and have one dependent son. In April, Gomer left Gertrude a note informing her that he needed his freedom and he was leaving her. As of December, Gertrude had not seen nor heard a word from Gomer since April. Gertrude fully supported her son and completely maintained the household. What is Gertrude's filing status assuming she was still legally married?

I:2-46 *Computation of Taxable Income.* Jim and Pat are married and file jointly. In 2015, Jim earned a salary of $46,000. Pat is self-employed. Her gross business income was $49,000 and her business expenses totaled $24,000. Each contributed $5,000 to a deductible IRA. Their itemized deductions total $13,000. Compute Parts a, b, and c without regard to self-employment tax.

a. Compute their gross income.

b. Compute their adjusted gross income.

c. Compute their taxable income assuming they have a dependent daughter.

I:2-47 *Itemized versus Standard Deduction.* Jan, a single taxpayer, has adjusted gross income of $250,000, medical expenses of $10,000, home mortgage interest of $3,000, property taxes of $2,000. and miscellaneous itemized deductions of $3,500. Should she itemize or claim the standard deduction?

I:2-48 *Kiddie Tax.* Debbie is 23 years old, a full-time student and a dependent of her parents. She earns $4,200 working part-time and receives $2,200 interest on savings. She saves both the salary and interest. What is her taxable income? Would her taxable income or tax be different if Debbie were 16 years old?

I:2-49 *Computation of Taxable Income.* John and Georgia are a married couple with two dependent sons. Their salaries total $130,000. They have a capital loss of $8,000 and tax-exempt interest income of $1,000. They paid home mortgage interest of $10,000, state income taxes of $4,000, and medical expenses of $3,000, and they made charitable contributions of $5,000.

a. Compute their adjusted gross income.

b. Compute their total itemized deductions.

c. What is the amount of their personal exemptions?

d. Compute their taxable income.

I:2-50 **Kiddie Tax.** Mike and Linda have three dependent children who are full-time students in 2015. Mike and Linda's taxable income is $180,000 and they provided $8,000 of support for each child. Information for each child is as follows:

	Karen	Susan	Amelie
Age	21	18	16
Wages	$3,000	$4,500	$5,900
Interest income	2,800	2,400	2,200

Compute each child's tax.

I:2-51 **Computation of Tax.** Georgia, a single taxpayer, operates a business that produces $100,000 of income before any amounts are paid to her. She has no dependents and no other income. She has itemized deductions of $18,000. Compute the *total* income tax that would be paid assuming the following additional facts. Ignore payroll taxes.
a. Georgia operates the business as an S corporation receiving a salary from the corporation of $60,000. The corporation distributes all of its remaining income to the shareholders.
b. She operates the business as a C corporation receiving a salary from the corporation of $60,000. The corporation distributes its after tax income to her as a dividend.
c. How would the total tax change in each of the first two requirements if the corporation made no payments to the owner other than the salary?

I:2-52 **Child Credit.** In 2015, Lana, a single taxpayer with AGI of $85,400, claims exemptions for three dependent children, all under age 17. What is the amount of her child credit?

I:2-53 **Capital Gains and Losses.** Bob and Anna are in the 39.6% tax bracket for ordinary income and the 20% bracket for capital gains (ignore the 3.8% additional tax on investment income for higher-income taxpayers.) They have owned several blocks of stock for many years. They are considering the sale of two blocks of stock. The sale of one block would produce a gain of $10,000. The sale of the other would produce a loss of $15,000. For purposes of this problem, ignore personal exemptions, itemized deductions and other phase-outs. They have no other gains or losses this year.
a. How much tax will they save if they sell the block of stock that produces a loss?
b. How much additional tax will they pay if they sell the block of stock that produces a gain?
c. What will be the impact on their taxes if they sell both blocks of stock?

I:2-54 **Timing of Deductions.** Virginia is a cash-basis, calendar-year taxpayer. Her salary is $20,000, and she is single. She plans to purchase a residence in 2016. She anticipates her property taxes and interest will total $7,200. Each year, Virginia contributes approximately $1,000 to charity. Her other itemized deductions total approximately $800. For purposes of this problem, assume that 2016 tax rates, exemptions, and standard deductions are the same as for 2015.
a. What will her gross tax be in 2015 and 2016 if she contributes $1,000 to charity in each year?
b. What will her gross tax be in 2015 and 2016 if she contributes $2,000 to charity in 2015 but makes no contribution in 2016?
c. What will her gross tax be in 2015 and 2016 if she makes no contribution in 2015 but contributes $2,000 in 2016?
d. Alternative c results in a lower tax than either a or b. Why?

I:2-55 **Tax Forms and Filing Status.** Which tax form is used by the following individuals?
a. Anita is single, age 68, and has a salary of $22,000 and interest of $300.
b. Betty owns an apartment complex that produced rental income of $36,000. Expenses totaled $38,500.
c. Clay's wife died last year. He qualifies as a surviving spouse. His salary is $24,000.
d. Donna is a head of household. Her salary is $27,000 and she has $200 of interest income.

I:2-56 **Computation of Tax.** Maria is a single taxpayer. Her salary is $51,000. Maria realized a short-term capital loss of $5,000. Her itemized deductions total $4,000.
a. Compute Maria's adjusted gross income.
b. Compute her taxable income.
c. Compute her tax liability.

I:2-57 **Kiddie Tax.** Ralph and Tina (husband and wife) transferred taxable bonds worth $30,000 to Pam, their 12-year-old daughter. Pam received $3,500 of interest on the bonds in the current year. Ralph and Tina have a combined taxable income of $83,000.

a. Compute Ralph and Tina's gross tax. Assume they do not include Pam's income on their return.

b. Can Ralph and Tina claim a child credit for Pam?

c. Compute Pam's taxable income and gross tax.

d. What would be Pam's tax if she were age 25?

I:2-58 *Filing Status.* Assume Gail is a wealthy widow whose husband died last year. Her dependent daughter lives with her for the entire year. Gail has interest income totaling $379,900 and she pays property taxes and home mortgage interest totaling $20,000.

a. What filing status applies to Gail?

b. Compute her taxable income and gross tax.

c. Assume that Gail does not have a daughter. What is Gail's filing status?

TAX STRATEGY PROBLEMS

I:2-59 Jack is starting a business that he expects to produce $60,000 of income this year before compensating Jack for his services. He has $1,000 of other income and itemized deductions totaling $10,000. He wants to know whether he should incorporate or operate the business as a proprietorship. If a corporation is formed, he wants to know whether he should make an S election. If he incorporates, the corporation will pay Jack a salary of $40,000. He expects to distribute an additional $5,000 of corporate profits to himself each year. Jack is single.

    Required: Which organizational form, proprietorship, S corporation, or C corporation, will produce the lowest total current income tax liability for Jack and his business? Ignore payroll and other taxes.

I:2-60 Andrea, who is in the 39.6% tax bracket, is interested in reducing her taxes. She is considering several alternatives. For each alternative listed below, indicate how much tax, if any, she would save? (For this problem, ignore additional taxes or phase-outs for high-income taxpayers.)

a. Give $2,000 to a charity. Assume she itemizes.

b. Give $2,000 to a charity. Assume she does not itemize.

c. Make a gift of bonds valued at $8,000 yielding $600 of interest annually to her 15-year-old daughter who has no other income.

d. Sell the bonds from part c for $8,000 and buy tax exempt bonds yielding $300.

TAX FORM/RETURN PREPARATION PROBLEMS

I:2-61 Aida Petosa (SSN 123-45-6789) is the 12-year-old daughter of Alfredo Petosa (SSN 987-65-4321). Her only income is $2,800 of interest on savings. Alfredo qualifies as a head of household, and his taxable income is $52,000. Compute her tax using Form 8615.

I:2-62 James S. (SSN 123-45-6789) and Lulu B. Watson (SSN 987-65-4321) reside at 999 E. North Street, Richmond, Virginia 23174. They have one dependent child, Waldo, age 4 (SSN 111-22-3333) and they are both under 65 years old. They do not wish to take advantage of the presidential election campaign check-off. Other relevant information includes

James's salary as a mechanic	$19,000
Lulu's salary as a teacher	23,000
Interest (First National Bank)	2,100
Withholding	2,000

Complete their Form 1040A.

I:2-63 John R. Lane (SSN 111-44-6666) lives at 1010 Ipsen Street, Yorba Linda, California 90102. John, a single taxpayer, age 66, provided 100% of his cousin's support. The cousin lives in Arizona. He wants to take advantage of the presidential election campaign check-off. John is an accountant. Other relevant information includes

Salary	$20,000
Taxable pension	31,000
Interest income	300
IRA deduction	5,000
Itemized deductions (from Schedule A)	8,000
Withholding	6,000

Assume that Schedule A, if necessary, has already been completed. Complete Form 1040.

CASE STUDY PROBLEMS

I:2-64 Bala and Ann purchased as investments three identical parcels of land over a several-year period. Two years ago they gave one parcel to their daughter, Kim, who is now age 16. They have an offer from an investor who is interested in acquiring all three parcels. The buyer is able to purchase only two of the parcels now, but wants to purchase the third parcel two or three years from now, when he expects to have available funds to acquire the property. Because they paid different prices for the parcels, the sales will result in different amounts of gains and losses. The sale of one parcel owned by Bala and Ann will result in a $20,000 gain and the sale of the other parcel will result in a $28,000 loss. The sale of the parcel owned by Kim will result in a $19,000 gain. Kim has no other income and does not expect any significant income for several years. Bala and Ann, however, are in the 39.6% tax bracket. They do not have any other capital gains this year. Which two properties would you recommend that they sell this year? Why?

I:2-65 Larry and Sue separated at the end of the year. Larry has asked Sue to sign a joint income tax return for the year because he feels that the tax will be lower on a joint return. Larry and Sue both work. Sue received a salary of $25,000 and Larry's salary was $20,000. Larry works as a waiter at a local restaurant and received tips. The restaurant asked Larry to indicate the amount of tips he received so that they could report the information to the IRS. Larry reported to the employer that the tips amounted to $3,000, but Sue believes that the amount was probably $6,000 to $10,000. They do not have enough expenses to itemize. Sue has asked you what are the advantages and risks of filing a joint return.

TAX RESEARCH PROBLEMS

I:2-66 Ed has supported his stepdaughter, her husband, and their child since his wife's death three years ago. Ed promised his late wife that he would support her daughter from a former marriage and her daughter's husband until they both finished college. They live in another state, and meet gross income filing requirements. Is Ed entitled to dependency exemptions for the three individuals?

A partial list of research sources is

- Sec. 152
- Reg. Sec. 1.152-2
- *Desio Barbetti*, 9 T.C. 1097 (1947)

I:2-67 Bob and Sue were expecting a baby in January, but Sue was rushed to the hospital in December. She delivered the baby but it died the first night. Are Bob and Sue entitled to a dependency exemption for the baby?

Research sources include Rev. Rul. 73-156, 1973-1 C.B. 58.

I:2-68 Larry has severe vision problems and, in the past, he has claimed the additional standard deduction available to blind taxpayers. This year Larry's doctor prescribed a new type of contact lens that greatly improved his vision. Naturally, Larry was elated, but unfortunately new problems developed. He suffered severe pain, infection, and ulcers from wearing the new lens. The doctor recommended that he remove the lens and after several weeks his eyes healed. The doctor told him that he could wear the contacts again, but only for brief time periods, or the problems would recur. Can Larry claim the additional standard deduction available to blind taxpayers?

Research sources include *Emanuel Hollman*, 38 T.C. 251 (1963).

CHAPTER

3

GROSS INCOME: INCLUSIONS

LEARNING OBJECTIVES

After studying this chapter, you should be able to

1. Explain the difference between the economic, accounting, and tax concepts of income

2. Explain the principles used to determine who is taxed on a particular item of income

3. Determine when a particular item of income is taxable under both the cash and accrual methods of reporting

4. Apply the rules of Sec. 61(a) to determine whether items such as compensation, dividends, alimony, and pensions are taxable

5. Describe tax planning considerations for inclusions of gross income

6. Describe compliance and procedural considerations for gross income

Computation of an individual's income tax liability begins with the determination of income. Although the meaning of the term *income* has long been debated by economists, accountants, tax specialists, and politicians, no universally operational definition has been accepted.

The Sixteenth Amendment to the Constitution gave Congress the power to tax "income from whatever source derived." To ensure the constitutionality of the income tax, this phrase is incorporated in Sec. 61(a), where **gross income** is defined as follows: "Except as otherwise provided . . . gross income means all income from whatever source derived."

This chapter examines the concept of income for the purpose of determining what items of income are taxable. Chapter I:4 considers items of income that are excluded from gross income. As noted in Chapter I:2, many provisions in the tax law are created by a process of political compromise. Thus, there is no single explanation of why certain items are taxable and others are not. For this reason, determining whether a particular item of income is taxable often proves difficult.

ECONOMIC, ACCOUNTING, AND TAX CONCEPTS OF INCOME

OBJECTIVE 1

Explain the difference between the economic, accounting, and tax concepts of income

ECONOMIC CONCEPT

Economists define *income* as the amount an individual could consume during a period and remain as well off at the end of the period as he or she was at the beginning of the period. To the economist, therefore, income includes both the wealth that flows to the individual and changes in the value of the individual's store of wealth. Or, more simply, income equals consumption plus the change in wealth.

EXAMPLE I:3-1 ▶ Alice earned a salary of $40,000. She consumed $30,000 of food, clothing, housing, medical care, and other goods and services. Assets owned by Alice were worth $100,000 at the beginning of the year. Her assets, including $10,000 of salary that was saved, were worth $115,000 at the end of the year. Her liabilities did not change during the year. Alice's economic income is $45,000 [$30,000 + ($115,000 − $100,000)]. ◀

Under the economist's definition, unrealized gains, as well as gifts and inheritances, are income. Furthermore, the economist adjusts for inflation when measuring income. An individual has no income to the extent that an increase in the measured value of property is caused by a decrease in the value of the measuring unit. In other words, inflation does not increase wealth and, therefore, does not cause an individual to be better off.

ACCOUNTING CONCEPT

Accountants usually measure income when it is *realized* in a transaction. Values measured by transactions are relatively objective as accountants recognize (i.e., report) income, expenses, gains, and losses that have been realized as a result of a completed transaction. Accountants believe that the economic concept of income is too subjective to be used as a basis for financial reporting and, therefore, have traditionally used historical costs in measuring income instead of using unconfirmed estimates of changes in market value. In accounting, the meaning of the term *realization* is critical to the income measurement process. *Realization* generally results upon the occurrence of two events: (1) a change in the form or substance of a taxpayer's property (or phrased another way, a severance of the economic interest in the property) and (2) a transaction with a second party. Realization occurs when a taxpayer sells property. Conversely, the mere increase in value of property owned by a taxpayer will not result in the realization of income because there has been no change in the form of the property and no transaction with a second party.

EXAMPLE I:3-2 ▶ Assume the same facts as in Example I:3-1. The amount consumed by Alice, the increase in the value of the property owned by her, and inflation are all ignored by the accountant in measuring her income. Only when she sells or otherwise disposes of the assets that have increased in value will the accountant recognize the gain. Thus, Alice's accounting income is $40,000. ◄

TAX CONCEPT OF INCOME

The income tax law essentially adopts the accountant's concept of income rather than the economist's. The reasons for this relate to matters of administrative convenience and the wherewithal-to-pay concept. However, as we will see later, there are many differences between income for tax purposes and accounting income.

In general, three conditions must be met for amounts to be taxable.

▶ There must be economic benefit. The economic benefit is not limited to cash payments. Employees who receive a company's stock, rather than cash, are receiving an economic benefit. Taxpayers benefit even if they direct that payments be made to other persons. As a result, employees cannot avoid being taxed on their earnings by ordering that their salaries be paid directly to creditors or family members.

▶ The income must be realized. In general, realization occurs when the earning process is complete and a transaction with another party takes place that permits an objective measure of the income. This objective measurement increases "administrative convenience" which is discussed below. Unlike financial accounting, there are many exceptions that result in income being reported when the taxpayer receives payment even if that is at a time other than when the earning process is complete. These exceptions result in taxes being owed when the taxpayer has the "wherewithal to pay" (see below). Taxpayers who use the "cash method" of reporting, discussed later in the chapter, are normally taxed when payment is received.

▶ The income must be recognized. Some items of income are not taxable because of special provisions in the tax law. For example, certain real estate exchanges and corporate reorganizations are not taxable because of statutory nonrecognition rules. In such cases, the taxpayer receives a lower basis in replacement property, and that often means the income is recognized when the replacement property is sold. The tax law also contains exclusions that exempt specific types of income such as scholarships, inheritances, and municipal bond interest. Within statutory limitations, taxpayers are never taxed on such items of income.

Administrative Convenience. The economic concept of income is considered to be too subjective to be used in determining taxable income. The need for objectivity in taxation is evident. If taxpayers were required to report increases in value as income, some individuals would certainly understate values to reduce their tax liabilities. The IRS and even the most honest taxpayer often would disagree over values and, as a result, the tax system would be extremely difficult to administer. The disputes over valuation issues would be frequent and the courts would be burdened with added litigation. This problem is evidenced by the few situations where valuations are required in the determination of tax. For example, taxpayers who contribute property to charity usually can deduct the value of the property. The courts are continuously having to resolve disputes between taxpayers and the IRS over the value of such contributions. Furthermore, in the case of certain large contributions of property, taxpayers are required to attach to their returns appraisals of the contributed property. Penalties apply to taxpayers who substantially overvalue contributions.

In some instances, objectivity is achieved at the price of equity. For example, a taxpayer who owns land that has substantially declined in value generally cannot recognize the decline in value until it is realized through a disposition of the land. Similarly, an increase in value, no matter how large, is not taxed until a sale or exchange of the property has occurred. A taxpayer with a modest salary may feel that it is unfair that he or she is taxed on the salary while another person is not taxed on unrealized gains amounting to millions of dollars. As noted above, however, it would be practically impossible to fairly and consistantly administer an income tax law that was based on values.

KEY POINT

Section 446(a) states that taxable income shall be computed under the method of accounting on the basis of which the taxpayer regularly computes his or her income in keeping his or her books. This provision would seem to require that tax accounting rules would conform to financial accounting rules. However, as will be seen later in this and other chapters, there are many differences.

Wherewithal to Pay. The wherewithal-to-pay concept holds that a tax should be collected when the taxpayer is in the best position to pay the tax. A taxpayer who sells property and collects the cash is in a better position to pay the tax than a taxpayer who owns property that is merely increasing in value without a sale.

This concept is the rationale for several tax provisions. For example, the tax law allows a taxpayer who sells property on the installment basis to report the gain as the installment payments are collected, rather than at the time of the sale. Losses, on the other hand, cannot be reported on the installment basis, as the wherewithal-to-pay is not an issue. The concept is also used to justify differences between the tax law and financial accounting principles. Prepaid income is not income from an accounting standpoint until it is earned. The tax law, however, takes the position that prepaid income is subject to taxation at the time it is collected, rather than as it is earned. At the time of collection, the taxpayer clearly has the cash available to pay the tax. If the tax were deferred until the income is earned, the taxpayer may no longer have the cash.

KEY POINT

Congress has not adopted any particular concept or theory of income for tax purposes. Except as specifically limited by statute, the definition of income is broad and general.

Gross Income Defined. Section 61(a) provides the following general definition and listing of income items:

> General Definition.—Except as otherwise provided in this subtitle, gross income means all income from whatever source derived, including (but not limited to) the following items:
>
> 1. Compensation for services, including fees, commissions, fringe benefits, and similar items
> 2. Gross income derived from business
> 3. Gains derived from dealings in property
> 4. Interest
> 5. Rents
> 6. Royalties
> 7. Dividends
> 8. Alimony and separate maintenance payments
> 9. Annuities
> 10. Income from life insurance and endowment contracts
> 11. Pensions
> 12. Income from discharge of indebtedness
> 13. Distributive share of partnership gross income
> 14. Income in respect of a decedent
> 15. Income from an interest in an estate or trust

SELF-STUDY QUESTION

Why should taxpayers who are using the cash method of accounting be required to include in gross income the value of property or services received?

ANSWER

If taxpayers were not required to include the value of property or services received in gross income, many taxpayers would arrange their financial affairs so that they would receive property or services instead of cash.

This definition certainly is not all-inclusive. For example, it does not indicate whether specific items of income such as property insurance settlements, gambling winnings, or illegal income are taxable. One point is apparent: The phrase *[e]xcept as otherwise provided* means that all sources of income are presumed to be taxable unless there is a specific exclusion in the income tax law. The IRS does not have to prove that an item of income is taxable. Rather, the taxpayer must prove that the item of income is excluded. Thus, gambling winnings and illegal income are taxable simply because no specific provisions in the tax law exclude such amounts from taxation. As we shall see, life insurance proceeds and certain other insurance proceeds are specifically excluded from gross income.

Form of Receipt. Gross income is not limited to amounts received in the form of cash. According to Reg. Sec. 1.61-1(a), income may be "realized in any form, whether in money, property, or services." The important question is whether the taxpayer receives an economic benefit. This rule covers barter transactions which are direct exchanges of property and services. Each party to the transaction is taxed on the value of the property or services received in the exchange. In general, the cost basis of property given up in a barter transaction can be subtracted from the value of the property received in arriving at the taxable amount.

EXAMPLE I:3-3 ► King Corporation transfers 1,000 shares of its stock to its president. The stock has no restrictions and is part of the president's compensation. The president must include the value of the stock in gross income. ◄

EXAMPLE I:3-4 ► Ali, an attorney, performs legal services for Paul, a painter, in exchange for Paul's promise to paint Ali's residence. Each taxpayer realizes income equal to the value of services received. Thus, Ali must report income in an amount equal to the value of the painting services provided by Paul. Paul must report the value of Ali's legal services. These amounts, assuming an arm's-length transaction, should be the same. ◄

EXAMPLE I:3-5 ► USA Corporation distributes an automobile to Vicki, a shareholder, in lieu of a cash dividend. Vicki must report the value of the automobile as dividend income. ◄

EXAMPLE I:3-6 ► Len has fallen behind on loan payments due to a bank. The bank obtains a court order requiring Len's employer to pay part of Len's wages directly to the bank. Len will be taxed on the full wages even though a portion goes directly to the bank. ◄

EXAMPLE I:3-7 ► Wayne borrowed $3,000 from his employer. The employer awarded year-end bonuses to other employees but told Wayne that the debt was being forgiven in lieu of a bonus. Wayne must include the $3,000 in income. ◄

? STOP & THINK

Question: As noted, income is taxable even if it is paid in a form other than cash. What problems does this produce for the IRS and taxpayers?

Solution: Two major problems are created: valuation and enforcement. First, it is necessary to determine the market value of property and services when income is received in a form other than cash. Determining values can be difficult. Second, enforcement by the IRS is made much more difficult because such income is not documented by canceled checks, credit card receipts, or other records. Thus, as demonstrated in Example I:3-4 above, many of these so-called traded services are not reported as income. This evasion of income represents billions of lost tax revenues to the government.

Indirect Economic Receipt. As indicated earlier, the taxability of income often depends on whether the taxpayer receives an economic benefit. In general, if a taxpayer benefits from an item, it is taxable. Frequently, however, an employer may make an expenditure in which its employees may incidentally or indirectly benefit. For example,

► Security guards patrol an employer's plant, protecting both the employer's property and the employees. The employees receive an indirect benefit for the protection provided by the security guards.

► An employer requires employees to undergo an annual checkup, the cost of which is paid by the employer.

► An employer provides protective clothing worn by employees while on the job.

► A shipping company provides sleeping accommodations to sailors while ships are at sea.

► A company requires certain employees to wear shoes manufactured by the company and provide regular reports on the quality of the shoes.

It is now well-established that taxpayers may exclude such indirect benefits from gross income. This judicially-developed rule holds that a benefit is excludible if it is made in order to serve the business needs of the employer and the benefit to the employee is secondary and incidental.

Congress also has established rules dealing with situations where expenditures are made primarily to benefit employees. While expenditures made by employers that primarily benefit employees are generally taxable, there are instances whereby such expenditures are not taxable. These rules, which are discussed in Chapters I:4 and I:9, permit employees to exclude certain fringe benefits (such as employee discounts) from gross income.

TO WHOM IS INCOME TAXABLE?

OBJECTIVE 2

Explain the principles used to determine who is taxed on a particular item of income

Once it is established that income is taxable, it is necessary to determine to whom it is taxable. Although such determinations are usually easy, there are circumstances where income is not necessarily taxed to the person who receives it. If physical receipt of income was the only test, a family might reduce or eliminate its income tax by having income paid to children and other members who are in low tax brackets or have no tax liability.

ASSIGNMENT OF INCOME

KEY POINT

The law makes a clear distinction between an assignment of income and an assignment of income-producing property. The income is taxable to the assignor in the former case, but where there is a bona fide gift of property the income is taxable to the assignee.

In 1930, the Supreme Court held in a landmark case, *Lucas v. Earl,* that an individual is taxed on the earnings from his or her personal services.[1] Specifically, the Supreme Court held that a husband was taxed on the earnings from his law practice, even though he had signed a legally enforceable agreement with his wife that the earnings would be shared equally. An agreement to assign income does not permit a person to avoid being taxed on the income. The Court used the previously developed analogy that likens income to the fruit and capital to the tree.[2] Accordingly, the fruit (income) could not be attributed to a tree other than the one on which it grew.

In 1940, the Supreme Court, in *Helvering v. Horst,* extended the assignment of income doctrine to income from property.[3] In this case, the taxpayer detached interest coupons from bonds and gave the coupons to his son. The son collected the interest and reported it on his own return. The Supreme Court held that the taxpayer was taxed on the interest income because he owned the bonds. This holding leads to a basic rule that the income from property is taxed to the owner of the property. To transfer the income from property, the taxpayer must transfer ownership of the property itself.[4]

Although married couples may file joint returns today, this privilege did not become available until 1948. Assignment of income is an issue today when other individuals such as parents and children are involved, and it can still be an issue when married couples file separate returns.

ADDITIONAL COMMENT

The community property states are generally located in the western or southwestern United States. Generally these states were settled by immigrants from France and Spain, and their state laws reflect this fact. The common law is derived from English common law.

ALLOCATING INCOME BETWEEN MARRIED PEOPLE

ADDITIONAL COMMENT

Community property laws are sometimes difficult to generalize. Depending on the specific law within a community property state, one-half of estimated taxes paid by one spouse may or may not be used by the other spouse on a separate return.

How income is allocated between a husband and wife depends on the state of residence. Forty-one states follow a common law property system, whereas nine states[5] use a community property system. Under common law, income is generally taxed to the individual who earns the income, either through labor or capital. For example, if a spouse holds stock separately in his or her name, that spouse will be taxed on all of the dividends received from the separately owned stock. Generally, the only **joint income** in a common law state is income from jointly owned property.[6]

In community property states, income may be either separate or community. **Community income** is considered to belong equally to the spouses. In all community property states, the income from the personal efforts of either spouse is considered to belong

---

[1] *Lucas v. Earl,* 8 AFTR 10287, 2 USTC ¶496 (USSC, 1930).
[2] The analogy had been used some ten years earlier in *Eisner v. Myrtle H. Macomber,* 3 AFTR 3020, 1 USTC ¶32 (USSC, 1920). The court originally used the analogy in efforts to distinguish income from capital.
[3] *Helvering v. Horst,* 24 AFTR 1058, 40-2 USTC ¶9787 (USSC, 1940).
[4] A series of rather specific rules allocates income between the former and current owner when income-producing property is transferred. For example, in the case of bonds transferred by gift, the IRS has ruled that interest must be allocated based on the number of days the bonds were held by each owner

during the interest period (Rev. Rul. 72-312, 1972-1 C.B. 22). A similar allocation must be made if bonds are sold (Rev. Rul. 72-224, 1972-1 C.B. 30).
[5] The states are Arizona, California, Idaho, Louisiana, Nevada, New Mexico, Texas, Washington, and Wisconsin. Residents of Alaska may elect to be subject to community property law.
[6] Historically, tenancy by the entirety, a form of joint ownership between spouses, allocated all income to the husband. Today, the laws of many states allocate income from property held in tenancy by the entirety equally between the spouses.

equally to the spouses. Furthermore, income from community property is considered to be community income. Thus, if a wife's salary is used to purchase stock, subsequent dividends are community income.

Couples can have separate property even in community property states. **Separate property** consists of all property owned before marriage and gifts and inheritances acquired after marriage. Whether income from separate property is community or separate depends on the state. In Idaho, Louisiana, Texas, and Wisconsin income from separate property is community income. In Arizona, California, Nevada, New Mexico, and Washington, such income is separate income.

EXAMPLE I:3-8 ▶ A husband and wife file separate returns. The husband's salary is $40,000 and the wife's salary is $48,000. The wife received $1,000 of dividends on stock she had inherited from her parents. Interest of $1,200 was received on bonds that were purchased from the husband's salary. They received $2,600 in rent from farm land that they purchased jointly. The income would be allocated, depending on the state of residence, as follows:

California (Community Property State)	Husband	Wife
Salary	$44,000	$44,000
Dividends		1,000
Interest	600	600
Rent	1,300	1,300
Total	$45,900	$46,900

Texas (Community Property State)		
Salary	$44,000	$44,000
Dividends	500	500
Interest	600	600
Rent	1,300	1,300
Total	$46,400	$46,400

Pennsylvania (Common Law State)		
Salary	$40,000	$48,000
Dividends		1,000
Interest	1,200	
Rent	1,300	1,300
Total	$42,500	$50,300 ◀

These rules are important when couples file separate returns. The community income rules can prove to be a problem if one spouse conceals income from the other. Normally, each spouse is expected to report one-half of all community income. This treatment is inequitable if one spouse is not aware that the community income was earned. Special rules excuse an innocent spouse who fails to report community income on a separate return, provided that the spouse had no knowledge or reason to know of the item and, as a result, the inclusion of the community income would be inequitable.[7] A corresponding provision permits the IRS to include the entire amount in the income of the other spouse.[8]

 **STOP & THINK**

Question: The tax treatment of income earned in a common law state versus a community property state can be very inconsistent. As noted, the Supreme Court, in *Lucas v. Earl,* decided that a husband was taxed on all his income even though he agreed to share that income with his wife. Nevertheless, community income in a community property state is divided equally between husbands and wives even if one spouse earned all of the income. Why the tax distinction?

Solution: Lucas v. Earl dealt with a case in a common law state where the husband was legally entitled to the income, but decided to divide it with his wife. In community property states, couples are legally obligated to share their incomes. The federal income tax law respects the different property law systems of the states and taxes the income of

---

[7] Sec. 66(b).   [8] Sec. 66(c).

persons based on state law.[9] It would be unfairly burdensome to tax individuals on income to which they never had any legal right.

INCOME OF MINOR CHILDREN

As noted earlier, whether a husband or wife is taxed on income is determined by state law. However, earnings of a minor child are taxed to the child regardless of the state's property law system. Therefore, earnings of a child from either personal services (compensation) or from property (dividends, interest, rents, etc.) are taxed to the child, not the child's parents. As noted in Chapter I:2, the unearned income of a child under age 24 may be taxed at the parents' tax rate if it is higher than the child's rate. Alternatively, the parents may elect to include the child's unearned income on their return. In the case of spouses, the spouse who has a legal right to such income determines who is taxed on it. In the case of children, however, the individual who earns the income is the individual who is taxed on it.

WHEN IS INCOME TAXABLE?

OBJECTIVE 3

Determine when a particular item of income is taxable under both the cash and accrual methods of reporting

The year in which income is taxed depends on the taxpayer's accounting method. The three primary overall accounting methods are the **cash receipts and disbursements method**, the **accrual method**, and the **hybrid method**. While taxpayers have the right to choose a method of accounting, the chosen method still must clearly reflect income as determined by the IRS. The IRS has the power to change the accounting method used by a taxpayer if, in the opinion of the IRS, the method being used does not clearly reflect income. Further, the Regulations require taxpayers to use the accrual method for determining purchases and sales when a taxpayer maintains an inventory.[10] However, the IRS has ruled that taxpayers whose annual gross receipts for the three prior years do not exceed $1 million ($10 million if the taxpayer's principal business is not the sale of inventory) are exempt from the requirement and may use the cash method.[11] This exception for small taxpayers is discussed in more detail below.

Section 448 requires C corporations (and partnerships with corporate partners), tax shelters, and certain trusts to use the accrual method of accounting. Qualified personal service corporations, certain types of farms, and entities with average gross receipts under $5 million are exempt from the requirement.

Once an accounting method has been adopted, it cannot be changed without permission of the IRS. See Chapter I:11.

KEY POINT

Neither the IRC nor the Regulations define the terms *accounting* and *accounting method*.

CASH METHOD

ADDITIONAL COMMENT

Taxpayers engaged in more than one trade or business may use a different method of accounting for each separate trade or business.

The **cash receipts and disbursements method** of accounting is used by most individual taxpayers and many small businesses. (See Chapter I:11 for a more complete discussion of who is permitted to use the cash method.) Under this method, income is reported in the year the taxpayer actually or constructively receives the income rather than in the year the income is earned. The income can be received by the taxpayer or the taxpayer's agent and be in the form of cash, other property, or services.[12] In the case of property or services, the amount included in income is the value of the property or services. An accounts receivable or other unsupported promise to pay is considered to have no value under the cash method and, as a result, no income is recognized until the receivable is collected. Topic Review I:3-1 summarizes when various types of income are reported.

ADDITIONAL COMMENT

The use of the cash receipts and disbursements method of accounting gives the taxpayer some control over the timing of the recognition of income and deductions. It also has the advantage of simplicity.

The fact that prepaid income is usually taxed when received, rather than when earned, often results in a mismatching of income and expenses.

EXAMPLE I:3-9 ▶ In December of the current year, Troy, who owns an apartment building, collects the first and last months' rent from a new tenant. Troy must report two months' rent in the current year. The

---

[9] See *Burns Poe v. H. G. Seaborn*, 9 AFTR 576, 2 USTC ¶611 (USSC, 1930). In 2010, the IRS Chief Counsel concluded that the rule also applies to same-sex California couples who enter into domestic partnership agreements based on the fact that California community property law applies to such couples (CCA 201021050).
[10] Reg. Sec. 1.446-1(c)(2)(i).

[11] Rev. Proc. 2002-28, 2002-1 C.B. 815, modified by Rev. Proc. 2012-20, 2012-14 I.R.B. 700.
[12] An agent can be an employee, relative, or other person authorized to receive the income.

TOPIC REVIEW I:3-1

When Income Is Taxable

ITEM	CASH BASIS	ACCRUAL BASIS
Compensation	Year actually or constructively received.	Year earned or year received if prepaid.
Interest	Year actually or constructively received.	Year accrued or year received if prepaid.
Discount on Series E or EE Bonds	Choice of reporting interest as it accrues or at maturity.	Year accrued.
Dividends	Year actually or constructively received.	Year actually or constructively received.
Rent	Year actually or constructively received (does not apply to a deposit).	Year accrued or year received if prepaid (year accrued if services are associated, e.g., in a hotel or motel) (does not apply to a deposit).
Services (maintenance contracts, dance lessons, etc.)	Year actually or constructively received.	Year accrued or year received if prepaid except that a taxpayer may report the income as it accrues if all the services are to be performed by the end of the next tax year.
Sale of goods	Year actually or constructively received.	Year of sale or year cash is received if prepaid except may elect to report in year of sale if goods are not on hand, amount received is less than cost of item, and same accounting method is used for financial accounting.
Subscriptions (newspapers, magazines, etc.)	Year actually or constructively received.	Year earned or year cash is received, if prepaid, except may elect to report income as newspaper, etc., is published.
Memberships (automobile clubs, etc.)	Year actually or constructively received.	Year earned or year received if prepaid (certain nonstock corporations may elect to report prepaid amounts over the membership period, if the period covers three years or less).
Sale of property (other than stock)	Year actually or constructively received.	Year transaction is completed (e.g., the close of escrow in case of sale of real estate).
Sale of stock	Year transaction is executed.	Year transaction is executed.

ADDITIONAL COMMENT
There is no recognized doctrine of constructive payment.

REAL-WORLD EXAMPLE
Paul Hornung, a former football player with the Green Bay Packers, was awarded an automobile in 1961 for being the outstanding player in the NFL championship game, but he did not actually receive it until 1962. He attempted to invoke the constructive receipt doctrine and report the income in 1961. The court held that he could not claim constructive receipt because the car was not set aside in the year of the award. *Paul V. Hornung,* 47 T.C. 428 (1967).

actual expenses associated with the last month's rental are not incurred until the last month. However, Troy must report two months' income this year, but may only deduct one month's expenses. ◄

Reporting prepaid income can have harsh results because it is not offset by related deductions. If the income is taxed before the expenses are incurred, the taxpayer may not have enough cash to pay the expenses when they are incurred.[13] This burden is mitigated, in part, by Treasury Regulations and Revenue Procedures discussed in this chapter (e.g., the treatment of prepaid income, page I:3-11).

Constructive Receipt. As noted, a cash-basis taxpayer must report income in the year in which it is actually or constructively received. Constructive receipt means that the income is made available to the taxpayer so that he may draw upon it at any time. However, income is not constructively received if the taxpayer's control of its receipt is subject to substantial limitations or restrictions. This rule prevents taxpayers from deferring income that is otherwise available by merely "turning their backs" on it. A taxpayer cannot defer income recognition by refusing to accept payment until a later taxable year.

---

[13] This mismatching of income and expenses affects both cash and accrual basis taxpayers.

Examples of constructive receipt where taxpayers are required to report taxable income even though no cash is actually received include:

▶ A check received after banking hours[14]

▶ Interest credited to a bank savings account[15]

▶ Bond interest coupons that have matured but have not been redeemed[16]

▶ Salary available to an employee who does not accept payment[17]

An amount is not considered to be constructively received if:

▶ It is subject to substantial limitations or restrictions.

▶ The payor does not have the funds necessary to make payment.

▶ The amount is unavailable to the taxpayer.

EXAMPLE I:3-10 ▶ Beth owns an ordinary life insurance policy with a cash surrender value. She need not report any income as the cash surrender value increases because the requirement that she cancel the policy in order to collect the cash surrender value constitutes a substantial restriction. If she cancels the policy, she reports as income the difference between the cash surrender value collected and net premiums paid. ◀

EXAMPLE I:3-11 ▶ Cathy has received a paycheck from her employer but has been told to hold the check until the employer has sufficient funds to cover the payroll. Cathy need not report the amount of the check as income until funds are deposited to the employer's account. ◀

EXAMPLE I:3-12 ▶ Dan sold land for $100,000 in December with payment due the following February. During the negotiations, the buyer offered to pay cash. Because the parties did not agree to a cash transaction, there was no constructive receipt in December. Under the terms of the sale, funds were not available at the time of sale. Thus, Dan is permitted to defer the recognition of income until the funds become available the following year. ◀

Exceptions. There are exceptions to the basic rule that cash-basis taxpayers report income when it is actually or constructively received.

▶ The interest on Series E and Series EE U.S. savings bonds need not be reported until the final maturity date, which varies but may be as long as forty years after the date of issue, and can be deferred even longer if the bonds are exchanged within one year of the final maturity date for Series HH U.S. savings bonds.[18] Many taxpayers purchase bonds that mature after retirement when the taxpayers expect to be in a lower tax bracket.

EXAMPLE I:3-13 ▶ Tenisha purchases a Series EE U.S. savings bond for $2,500 that will mature in 10 years. The bond pays no interest until maturity when it will be worth $5,000. Tenisha is not required to report any interest income for tax purposes until the bond matures. At maturity, when Tenisha receives the $5,000, she will report $2,500 of interest income. If she desires to defer the interest further, she could exchange her Series EE bond for a Series HH bond within one year. ◀

▶ Special rules also apply to farmers and ranchers. Farmers may report crop insurance proceeds in the year following receipt if the crop would have ordinarily been sold in the following year. Ranchers who sell livestock on account of a drought, flood, or other weather related condition may delay reporting income until the following year if they can establish that the livestock sale would otherwise have taken place in a later tax year.[19] These rules help taxpayers avoid a bunching of income into one year.

▶ Small taxpayer exception for inventories. As noted above, taxpayers who have average annual gross receipts of $1 million or less for the prior three years ($10 million or less if the taxpayer's principal business is not the sale of inventory) are exempt from maintaining inventories and may use the cash method. The ruling was widely interpreted to

---

[14] *Charles F. Kahler*, 18 T.C. 31 (1952).
[15] Reg. Sec. 1.451-2(b).
[16] Ibid.
[17] *James J. Cooney*, 18 T.C. 883 (1952).
[18] Series E bonds were issued prior to 1980; Series EE bonds were issued after 1979. The interest on the Series HH bonds is taxable as received.

[19] Recognizing the volatile nature of farming and ranching, Congress established a special averaging technique for farmers and ranchers. Electing farmers and ranchers compute their tax on the average income for the current and three preceding years. Sec. 1301.

mean that small taxpayers did not need to account for inventories and could deduct the amount of their purchases in the year of payment. However, the IRS subsequently issued Rev. Proc. 2001-10, whereby it was clarified that the small taxpayer exception will only allow small taxpayers to deduct purchases of inventory in the year of purchase if (1) the inventory purchases are paid for by the end of the year and (2) the inventory is actually sold in such year. The effect of this new ruling basically is to eliminate the small taxpayer exception with respect to inventories.

EXAMPLE I:3-14 ▶

The Cheryl Corporation begins a new retail business in the current year and has sales of $400,000. The corporation has year-end accounts receivable of $15,000 and purchases $240,000 of merchandise during the year. At year-end, the corporation has not paid for $30,000 of the merchandise it had purchased and has $50,000 of inventory on hand. The corporation pays operating expenses of $140,000 during the year. As the average gross receipts are less than $1 million, the corporation can use either the cash or accrual method. The corporation's income computed under both methods is as follows:

	Accrual		Cash	
Sales		$400,000		$385,000
Purchases	$240,000		$210,000	
Ending inventory	50,000		20,000*	
Cost of sales		190,000		190,000
Gross profit		210,000		195,000
Expenses		140,000		140,000
Net income		$ 70,000		$ 55,000

*$50,000 − $30,000 = $20,000

The difference between the accrual and cash methods is that the sales are not reported under the cash method until such sales are actually collected. Thus, the corporation does not include year-end receivables in this year's income. The year-end receivables will be reported when the receivables are collected in later taxable years.

As can be seen above, the cost of sales under both the accrual and cash methods are the same. This is because under Rev. Proc. 2001-10, taxpayers may not deduct inventory unless it is both paid for and sold. Since $30,000 was not paid for by year-end, it is not deductible and the purchases under the cash method are $30,000 less than under the accrual method. The ending inventory under the cash method is the physical inventory of $50,000 reduced by the $30,000 of inventory on hand that has not been paid for by year-end. ◀

ACCRUAL METHOD

Taxpayers using the accrual method of accounting generally report income in the year it is earned. Income is considered to have been earned when all the events have occurred that fix the right to receive the income and when the amount of income can be determined with reasonable accuracy.[20] In the case of a sale of property, income normally accrues when title passes to the buyer.[21] Income from services accrues as the services are performed.

Prepaid Income. A major exception to the normal operation of the accrual method is the rules applicable to the receipt of prepaid income. Prepaid income is generally taxable in the year of receipt. For example, if a lender receives January interest in the preceding December, it is taxable in the year received, whether the lender uses the cash or accrual method. This treatment, of course, differs from financial accounting, where the interest would be reported as it accrues.

Two important exceptions to the general rule are worth noting. Accrual-basis taxpayers may defer recognizing income in the case of certain advance payments for *goods* and in the case of certain advance payments for *services* to be rendered. A taxpayer may defer advance payments for goods (inventory) if the taxpayer's method of accounting for the sale is the same for tax and financial accounting purposes.[22]

---

[20] Reg. Sec. 1.451-1(a).
[21] Regulation Sec. 1.446-1(c)(1)(ii), however, does permit taxpayers the right to accrue income from the sale of inventory when the goods are shipped, when the product is delivered or accepted, or when title passes, as long as the method is consistently used.
[22] Reg. Sec. 1.451-5.

Under Rev. Proc. 2004-34, taxpayers may defer payments for future services to the year following the year in which the payment is received.[23] Revenue relating to services provided in the year payment is received is reported currently. Revenue relating to future years is reported in the year following the year of receipt even if the payments relate to multiple future years. The rule can be applied to a variety of services such as Internet service, dance lessons, maintenance contracts (but not warranties included in the sales price of a product), membership fees, and rent (if services are associated with the rent, such as a hotel or motel). The procedure is available when service and products are provided together. The procedure does not apply to rent (if services are not associated with the rent), insurance premiums, interest, or warranty contracts included in the price of a product.

EXAMPLE I:3-15 ▶

REAL-WORLD EXAMPLE

A dance studio using the accrual method was required to include in taxable income all advance payments for lessons in the form of cash and negotiable notes, plus contract installments due but remaining unpaid at year end. *Mark E. Schlude v. CIR*, 11 AFTR 2d 751, 63-1 USTC ¶9284 (USSC, 1963).

Bear Corporation, a publicly held, accrual-basis taxpayer that uses the calendar year as its tax year, sells computer courses under contracts ranging from three months to two years. When income is reported depends on the length of the contract and the month in which the contract is sold. Assume that Bear sells three contracts on July 1. One is for three months costing $90, a second is for one year costing $300, and the third for two years costing $500. The $90 charged for the three month contract is reported currently as all services are provided currently. One-half of $300 charged for the one year contract is reported currently and one-half is reported next year as one-half of the services are provided currently and one-half will be provided next year. One-fourth of the $500 charged for the two year contract is reported this year and the balance is reported next year. This is because Rev. Proc. 2004-34 does not permit income to be deferred beyond the end of the year following the year in which payment is received.

Length of Contract	Year Includible in Gross Income	
	Current Year	Next Year
3 months	$ 90	
12 months	150	$150
24 months	125	375

HYBRID METHOD

The **hybrid method** of accounting is a combination of the cash and accrual methods. Under the hybrid method, some items of income or expense are reported under the cash basis and others are reported under the accrual method. The method is most often encountered in small businesses that maintain inventories and are required to use the accrual method of accounting for purchases and sales of goods. Such businesses often prefer to use the cash method of reporting for other items because the cash method is simpler and may provide greater flexibility for tax planning. A taxpayer using the hybrid method of accounting would use the accrual method with respect to purchases and sales of goods but would use the cash method in computing all other items of income and expenses.

 STOP & THINK

Question: Taxpayers who are eligible to use the cash method often choose the cash method of reporting income over the accrual method. Why is the cash method generally more favorable for income tax purposes?

Solution: Taxpayers who have the option frequently choose the cash method over the accrual method because it is simpler, offers greater tax planning opportunity, and results in taxes being owed when income is actually received. The cash method is simpler because taxpayers are not required to make the complex accruals associated with the accrual method. Planning opportunities are greater because cash basis taxpayers can deduct expenses when paid, thereby allowing taxpayers to control their tax liability. Under the accrual method, prepaid expenses are not deductible when paid, but must be deducted over the periods benefitted. Finally, cash basis taxpayers do not have to pay taxes until they receive the money. Under the accrual method, income is reported when it is earned even if it has not been received. As a result, accrual basis taxpayers sometimes have to pay the tax before they actually receive the income they have earned.

---

[23] 2004-1 C.B. 991.

ITEMS OF GROSS INCOME: SEC. 61(A)

OBJECTIVE 4

Apply the rules of Sec. 61(a) to determine whether items such as compensation, dividends, alimony, and pensions are taxable

Section 61(a), quoted earlier in this chapter, states that gross income includes, but is not limited to, fifteen specifically listed types of income. Several of these items are discussed below.

COMPENSATION

Compensation is payment for personal services. It includes salaries, wages, fees, commissions, tips, bonuses, and specialized forms of compensation such as director's fees, jury fees, and marriage fees received by clergymen. What the compensation is called, how it is computed, the form and frequency of payment, and whether the compensation is subject to withholding is of little significance. Similarly, the fact that the services are part-time, one-time, seasonal, or temporary is immaterial.

There are exclusions, however, for a variety of employer-provided fringe benefits such as group term life insurance premiums, health and accident insurance premiums, employee discounts, contributions to retirement plans, and education benefits. In addition, there is a limited exclusion applicable to foreign-earned income. Both fringe benefits and the foreign-earned income exclusion are discussed in Chapter I:4.

ADDITIONAL COMMENT

Salaries and wages constituted 68.2% of total AGI reported in 2012.

BUSINESS INCOME

The term *gross income* usually refers to the total amount received from a particular source. In the case of businesses that provide services (e.g., accounting and law), the gross business income is the total amount received. In the case of manufacturing, merchandising, and mining, however, gross income is total sales less the cost of goods sold. Thus, gross income for tax purposes is comparable to gross profit for financial accounting purposes.

The cost of goods sold is, in effect, treated as a return of capital. Chapter I:4 discusses a well-established tax concept that a return of capital is not income and, therefore, cannot be subject to the income tax. Chapter I:11 discusses how inventories are valued.

SELF-STUDY QUESTION

A retail company had sales of $1,000,000 and the following costs: goods sold, $400,000, salaries, $200,000, and rent and other expenses, $100,000. What is the company's gross income?

ANSWER

The gross income is $600,000. The sales figure is reduced by the cost of goods sold.

GAINS FROM DEALINGS IN PROPERTY

Gains realized from property transactions are included in gross income unless a nonrecognition rule applies. As is true with business inventories, taxpayers may deduct the cost of property in order to arrive at the gain from a property transaction.[24] The tax law contains over 30 nonrecognition rules, which allow taxpayers to postpone the recognition of gains and losses from certain types of property transactions. In a few instances, these rules allow taxpayers to permanently exclude gains from gross income.[25]

Losses are not offset against gains in computing gross income. Rather, most losses are deductions *for* adjusted gross income. Furthermore, net capital losses for individuals are subject to provisions that limit the amount that can be deducted from other income to $3,000 per year. Losses from the sale or disposition of an asset held for personal use are not deductible.

TYPICAL MISCONCEPTION

It is sometimes mistakenly assumed that interest paid on federal obligations such as Treasury bonds, notes, and bills will also qualify for tax exemption.

INTEREST

Interest is compensation for the use of money. Taxable interest includes interest on bank deposits, corporate bonds, mortgages, life insurance policies, tax refunds, most U.S. government obligations,[26] and foreign government obligations.[27] Nontaxable interest is discussed below.

Tax-Exempt Interest. Since the inception of the federal income tax in 1913, interest on obligations of states, territories, and U.S. possessions and their political subdivisions has been tax exempt.[28] Bonds issued by school districts, port authorities, toll road commissions, counties, and fire districts have been held to be tax exempt. In addition, Sec. 501(c)(3) organizations may issue up to $225 million of tax-exempt bonds. Such organizations include private universities, hospitals, churches, and similar nonprofit organizations.

---

[24] Note that *business income* and *gains from dealings in property* are overlapping terms. The gross profit from the sale of inventory is actually both business income and a gain from a property transaction. Typically, however, the phrase *gains from dealings in property* may be assumed to mean gains from dealings in property other than inventory, so as to avoid confusion.

[25] For example, Sec. 121 allows taxpayers to exclude a limited amount of gain from a sale of a personal residence.
[26] The interest on many federal obligations issued before March 1, 1942 is tax exempt.
[27] Reg. Sec. 1.61-7.
[28] Sec. 103(a)(1).

As noted above, this exclusion does not extend to interest paid on most U.S. government obligations or foreign government obligations, nor does the exclusion exempt from taxation gains from the sale of state or local government bonds or interest on tax refunds paid by state and municipal governments.

There has always been some uncertainty as to whether the federal government could tax interest on state and local government obligations. The basic question is whether taxing these obligations would violate the doctrine of intergovernmental immunity in that the tax would reduce the ability of state and local governments to finance their operations because taxable bonds usually pay a higher rate of interest than tax-exempt bonds. The belief that taxing state and local government interest is unconstitutional is no longer widely held. While there have been efforts to tax interest on state and local bonds, the only changes have been to limit the use of bonds for private activities,[29] federally insured loans,[30] and arbitrage.[31]

Series EE Savings Bond Exclusion. Taxpayers may purchase and eventually redeem Series EE bonds tax-free if they use the proceeds to pay certain college expenses for themselves, a spouse, or dependents.[32]

To qualify for the exclusion:

▶ The bonds must be purchased after 1989 by an individual who is age 24 or older at the time of the purchase.

▶ The bonds must be purchased by the owner and cannot be a gift to the owner.

▶ The receipts from the bond redemption must be used for tuition and fees, which are first reduced by tax-exempt scholarships, veterans benefits, Hope and Lifetime Learning credits, and other similar amounts.[33]

▶ Married couples living together must file a joint return to obtain the exclusion.

The full amount of interest is excluded only if the combined amount of principal and interest received during the year does not exceed the net qualified educational expenses (tuition and fees reduced by exempt scholarships, etc.), and the taxpayer's 2015 modified adjusted gross income is not over $77,200 ($115,750 for married individuals filing a joint return). The exclusion is fully phased-out for taxpayers whose 2015 modified AGI is more than $92,200 ($145,750 for married individuals filing a joint return).[34]

If the net qualified education expenses are less than the total principal and interest, a portion of the interest is excluded based on the ratio of the qualified educational expenses to the total principal and interest. The tentative exclusion is equal to

$$\text{Series EE interest} \times \frac{\text{Net qualified educational expenses}}{\text{Series EE interest} + \text{Principal}}$$

EXAMPLE I:3-16 ▶ In 2015, Lois redeems Series EE bonds and receives $6,000, consisting of $1,875 of interest and $4,125 of principal. Assume that the net qualifying education expenses total $4,800. Lois's educational expenses equal 80% of the total amount received ($4,800 ÷ $6,000). Thus, her exclusion is limited to $1,500 (0.80 × $1,875). ◀

---

[29] Interest from state and local bonds issued for private activities such as the construction of sports facilities, convention centers, and industrial park sites is taxable. A limited amount of tax-exempt bonds can be issued each year by a state for "qualified" private activities such as airport construction, redevelopment, and student loans. The limit is the greater of $225 million or $75 per resident (Sec. 146(d)). Though exempt from regular income tax, interest from these "qualified" private activity bonds is subject to the alternative minimum tax (see Chapter I:14).

[30] Sec. 149(b).

[31] Sec. 148. Interest from state or local government bonds issued for the purpose of using the proceeds to buy higher-yield investments is taxable. Such bonds are called arbitrage bonds.

[32] Sec. 135(c).

[33] The exclusion is not permitted for amounts paid for sports, games, or hobbies unless they are part of a degree program (Sec. 135(c)(2)(B)).

[34] Each of these amounts is adjusted annually for inflation. In 2014, the phase-out started at $76,000 ($113,950 on joint returns) and ended at $91,000 ($143,950 on joint returns).

ADDITIONAL COMMENT

A child born today will require about $100,000 for a four-year college education. If interest rates are around 6%, one would have to save about $245 a month until the child entered school to be able to pay this amount.

As noted, the amount of the exclusion is further reduced if modified adjusted gross income exceeds a $77,200 threshold ($115,750 for married individuals filing a joint return). Modified adjusted gross income includes the interest from education savings bonds and certain otherwise excludable foreign income.[35] The reduction is computed as follows:

$$\text{Otherwise excludable amount} \times \frac{\text{Excess modified AGI}}{\$15,000\ (\$30,000\ \text{for joint filers})}$$

EXAMPLE I:3-17 ▶ Assume the same facts as in Example I:3-16 and that Lois is single and has other adjusted gross income of $80,325, making her total AGI $82,200 ($80,325 + $1,875). Lois's otherwise available exclusion of $1,500 is reduced by $500 to $1,000. This reduction is computed by dividing the excess modified AGI of $5,000 ($80,325 + $1,875 − $77,200) by $15,000 and multiplying the result by $1,500. ◀

One difficulty with the rules is that the phase-out of the exclusion is based on income in the year the bonds are redeemed, not the year they are purchased. As a result, some taxpayers who purchase bonds anticipating an exclusion find they are ineligible for the exclusion when the bonds are redeemed.

RENTS AND ROYALTIES

Amounts received as rents or royalties are included in gross income. As noted earlier, prepaid rent is taxable when received. Security deposits, which are refundable to tenants upon the expiration of a lease, are not included in gross income. The deposit is included in gross income only if it is not refunded upon the expiration of the lease.

EXAMPLE I:3-18 ▶ In December 2015, Buddy rents an apartment to Gary. Buddy receives the first and last months' rent plus a security deposit of $500. Buddy must include in 2015 gross income both the first and last months' rent. Assume that Gary moves out of the apartment in 2017 and Buddy keeps $300 of the security deposit to cover repairs costing $200 and five days' unpaid rent, which amounts to $100. In 2017, Buddy would include the $300 in gross income and could deduct $200 for repairs. ◀

Royalties from copyrights, patents, and oil, gas, and mineral rights are all taxable as ordinary income. **Royalties** are proceeds paid to an owner by others who do business under some right belonging to the owner. Amounts received by a lessor to cancel, amend, or modify a lease also are taxable.

 **STOP & THINK**

Question: Financial accounting contains extensive rules distinguishing "operating leases" from "capital leases." The IRC has no such rules. While the tax law does require the capitalization of leases that are in substance a purchase of the asset, most authority relating to the distinction comes from court cases. Why doesn't the tax law include specific rules relating to leased property?

Solution: The financial accounting rules that require businesses to capitalize some leases were established because of concern that long-term lease commitments represented unrecorded liabilities. Unrecorded liabilities distort a company's balance sheet, but may not distort reported income. Since the tax law is concerned with the reporting of income rather than the balance sheet, neither Congress nor the Treasury Department has seen the need to adopt leasing rules like those in financial accounting.

Improvements by Lessees. Improvements made by a lessee that increase the value of leased property are included in the lessor's income only if the improvements are made in lieu of paying rent or if rent is reduced because of the improvements. In such situations,

---

[35] Specifically, modified adjusted gross income includes amounts that qualify for the foreign earned income exclusion (Sec. 911), the exclusion for possession's income (Sec. 931), and the exclusion for income from Puerto Rico (Sec. 933). The limitation is determined after taking the partial exclusion for Social Security benefits and railroad retirement (Sec. 86), claiming the allowable deduction for retirement contributions (Sec. 219), and applying the passive loss limitation (Sec. 469).

the lessor must include the fair market value (FMV) of the improvement in gross income when it is made to the property.[36]

EXAMPLE I:3-19 ▶ Rita rents an apartment to Anna. The apartment normally would rent for $1,000 per month, but Rita agrees to accept $400 per month for the first year if Anna builds a block wall around the property. Rita estimates that she would have to pay someone $6,000 to build the wall. Rita is accepting reduced rent and must report gross income of $6,000 when the wall is added to the property. The $6,000 could be added to Rita's basis in the property and should qualify as a depreciable asset. ◀

Improvements not made in lieu of rent are not income to the lessor. No adjustment is made to the lessor's basis in the property and, therefore, no depreciation is allowable. Gain or loss is recognized only when the property is disposed of.[37] Whether the improvements are in lieu of rent depends on the intent of the parties. This determination is based on the facts of the particular situation. The rental rate, the terms of the rental agreement, and whether the improvements have an estimated useful life exceeding the term of the lease may all be indications of intent.

DIVIDENDS

ADDITIONAL COMMENT

Shareholders of closely held corporations generally do not want to receive dividends from their corporations. The reason? They are taxed as ordinary income and the corporation does not receive a tax deduction for the payments.

Dividends are included in shareholder gross income. The result is a so-called double tax because corporations are taxed on income they earn, and shareholders are taxed when the income is distributed as dividends.

As noted in the previous chapter many corporations avoid the problem of "double taxation" by making S elections which result in the corporations and their shareholders being taxed much like partnerships. Two other important provisions reduce the tax burden on dividends:

▶ C Corporation receiving dividends from other C Corporations may claim a "dividends received deduction" that reduces, and in some cases eliminates, the second corporate tax on the income. The amount of the dividend received deduction is generally 70% of dividends received by a corporation owning less than 20% of the distributing corporation, 80% of dividends received by a corporation owning at least 20% but less than 80% of the distributing corporation, and 100% of the dividends received by a corporation owning 80% or more of the distributing corporation. This rule is discussed more in Chapter I:16 and in-depth in *Prentice Hall's Federal Taxation: Corporations, Partnerships, Estates & Trusts* text and the *Comprehensive* volume.

ADDITIONAL COMMENT

Beginning in 2013, higher-income taxpayers (AGI greater than $200,000 for single or $250,000 for married filing jointly) have to pay an additional 3.8% tax on net investment income. Net investment income generally includes interest, dividends, rents, and capital gains.

▶ Lower tax rates apply to qualified dividends received by individuals. There is no tax on qualified dividends received by individuals in the 10% and 15% tax brackets. Dividends received by individuals in the 25% through 35% brackets are taxed at 15%. Dividends received by individuals in the 39.6% bracket are taxed at 20%. These lower rates apply only to stock that meets a special 60-day holding period.

In general, the above provisions apply to domestic corporations because foreign corporations are not automatically subject to the U.S. income tax. Only domestic corporations may make S elections. Dividends received from foreign corporations are generally ineligible for either the dividend received deduction or the lower tax rates discussed above.

EXAMPLE I:3-20 ▶ Georgia is in the 25% tax bracket. She owns 10% of Orange Corporation, an S corporation with $20,000 of income. The corporation distributes $1,000 to Georgia. She receives a $500 dividend from Red Corporation, a U.S. corporation, and $300 from Blue Corporation, a foreign corporation. Georgia will include $2,800 in gross income. This includes her share of Orange Corporation's income or $2,000 (10% × $20,000) along with $500 she received from Red Corporation and $300 she received from Blue Corporation. As Orange Corporation made an S-election, she must include in gross income her share of the corporation's income even though only part of it is distributed. The tax rate that applies to the $2,000 depends on the nature of the income earned by Orange Corporation. For example, part or all of the income could be

---

[36] Reg. Sec. 1.109-1.

[37] Reg. Sec. 1.1019-1.

treated as capital gains or dividend income if Orange earned those types of income while income from operations would be taxed at Georgia's higher tax rate of 25%. The dividend from Red Corporation qualifies for the favorable 15% tax rate as Georgia is in the 25% tax bracket. The dividend from Blue Corporation will be taxed at Georgia's regular tax rate of 25% as it was paid by a foreign corporation. ◄

EXAMPLE I:3-21 ► Celeste is a single taxpayer in 2015 with a salary of $46,750, qualified dividend income of $3,000, and itemized deductions of $8,000. Her taxable income is:

Adjusted gross income	$49,750
Itemized deductions	(8,000)
Personal exemption	(4,000)
Taxable income	$37,750

Her taxable income excluding dividends is $34,750 ($37,750 − $3,000), and is taxed at regular rates. The 15% tax bracket for single taxpayers ends at $37,450. As a result, $2,700 ($37,450 − $34,750) of Celeste's dividends are tax free, and the balance of the dividends or $300 ($3,000 − $2,700) is taxed at 15%.

Tax on ordinary income of $34,750 using rate schedule	$ 4,751
$2,700 of dividend income is tax free	–0–
Tax on $300 of dividend income at 15%	45
Taxable income	$ 4,796

◄

Dividends Defined. Distributions to shareholders are taxable as dividends only to the extent they are made from either the corporation's current earnings and profits (a concept similar, although not identical, to current year's net income for financial accounting purposes) or accumulated earnings and profits (a concept similar, although not identical, to beginning of the year retained earnings).[38] Earnings and profits are discussed in Chapter I:16 and in greater depth in *Prentice Hall's Federal Taxation: Corporations, Partnerships, Estates, and Trusts* text and the *Comprehensive* volume. Distributions in excess of current and accumulated earnings and profits are treated as a nontaxable recovery of capital. Such distributions reduce the shareholder's basis in the stock. Distributions in excess of the basis of the stock are classified as capital gains.

EXAMPLE I:3-22 ► Liz is the sole shareholder in Atlantic Corporation and has owned the stock for five years. The basis of her stock is $50,000. Atlantic distributes $40,000 to Liz. Accumulated earnings and profits at the beginning of the year equal $25,000, and current earnings and profits equal $10,000. Liz will report $35,000 of taxable dividend income and a nontaxable return of capital equal to $5,000. In addition, Liz must reduce her basis in the stock by $5,000. Alternatively, if the distribution to Liz were $100,000, she would report $35,000 of taxable dividend income, $50,000 as a nontaxable return of capital, and a $15,000 long-term capital gain. ◄

Stock Dividends. A **stock dividend** is a distribution by a corporation to its shareholders of the corporation's own stock. In 1920, the Supreme Court held that simple stock dividends could not be taxed because they were not income.[39] More precisely, income had not been realized because there was no real change in the taxpayer's interest or the risks faced by the taxpayer. Over the years, however, the exclusion for stock dividends has been narrowed. If a shareholder has the option of receiving either cash or stock, the shareholder is taxed even if he or she opts to receive stock. The option to receive cash constitutes constructive receipt of the cash. Today, many other features of a stock dividend may cause it to be taxed. For example, a distribution in which preferred stock is distributed to some common shareholders and common stock is distributed to others is taxable.[40] The recipient of a taxable stock dividend includes the value of the stock received in gross income, and that amount becomes the basis of the shares received.

A nontaxable stock dividend has no effect on a shareholder's income in the year received. The basis of the old shares is allocated between the old shares and the new

---

[38] Sec. 316(a). The federal income tax became effective on March 1, 1913. Thus, income accumulated before that date can still be distributed on a tax-exempt basis.

[39] *Eisner v. Myrtle H. Macomber,* 3 AFTR 3020, 1 USTC ¶32 (USSC, 1920).
[40] Reg. Sec. 1.305-4.

shares. Furthermore, the holding period for the new shares starts on the same date as the holding period of the old.

EXAMPLE I:3-23 ► Carol purchases 100 shares of Mesa Corporation stock for $1,100 (or $11 per share). Carol receives 10 shares of Mesa stock as a nontaxable stock dividend. After the dividend, Carol owns 110 shares of stock with a total basis of $1,100 (or $10 per share). All of the stock is assumed to have been acquired at the time of the original purchase. ◄

Capital Gain Dividends. A **capital gain dividend** is a distribution by a regulated investment company (commonly called a *mutual fund*) of capital gains realized from the sale of investments in the fund. Such dividends also include any undistributed capital gains allocated to shareholders by such companies.[41] Capital gain dividends are long-term regardless of how long the shareholder has owned the stock of the regulated investment company.

Constructive Dividends. In many corporations, the same individuals are both shareholders and employees. A corporation may not deduct dividends paid to shareholders but is permitted to deduct reasonable compensation. Questions are often raised as to whether amounts reported as compensation are really disguised dividends. If an amount called compensation is unreasonably high, it will be disallowed and reclassified as a dividend.[42] Often the reasonableness of compensation is determined by comparing the compensation paid to the employee-shareholders with amounts paid to others performing similar services.

EXAMPLE I:3-24 ► Carmen owns 100% of the stock in Florida Corporation and receives a $400,000 salary for serving as president. The corporation reports no taxable income and pays no dividends. Presidents of similar companies received salaries ranging from $75,000 to $160,000. The IRS probably would disallow a portion of Carmen's salary as unreasonable resulting in the corporation owing tax. The disallowed portion would be treated as a dividend. ◄

Constructive dividends are not limited to shareholder-employee compensation payments but may include situations where the shareholder also is a landlord (e.g., property is rented to the corporation at an amount greater than its fair rental value). A shareholder also may receive a constructive dividend because of a creditor or vendor relationship. It is not necessary that a dividend be formally declared or that distributions be in proportion to stock holdings. **Constructive dividends** are often distributions that are intended to result in a deduction to the corporation and taxable income (such as compensation) to the shareholder.[43] Other constructive dividends are intended to produce a nonreportable benefit to the shareholder,[44] or even result in a deduction to the corporation without income to the shareholder.[45]

ALIMONY AND SEPARATE MAINTENANCE PAYMENTS

Any payment pursuant to a divorce or legal separation must be classified as one of the following for tax purposes:

(1) Alimony;

(2) Child support; or

(3) Property settlement.

The treatment of a payment depends on its classification. Alimony is deductible by the payor spouse and taxable to the payee spouse. Neither child support payments nor property settlements have any tax ramifications, that is, they are not subject to tax to the payee spouse nor deductible by the payor spouse.

Example I:3-25 demonstrates the significant difference in taxation that can occur when a payment is classified as either alimony or a property settlement.

---

[41] Sec. 852(b).
[42] Sec. 162(a)(1).
[43] Other examples include excessive royalties (*Peterson & Pegau Baking Co.*, 2 B.T.A. 637 (1925)) and rent (*Limericks, Inc. v. CIR*, 36 AFTR 649, 48-1 USTC ¶9146 (5th Cir., 1948)).
[44] Examples include bargain sales of corporate assets to shareholders (*J. E. Timberlake v. CIR*, 30 AFTR 583, 42-2 USTC ¶9822 (4th Cir., 1942)),

redemptions of a shareholder's stock (Sec. 302), and loans to shareholders that are actually dividends (*George Blood Enterprises, Inc.*, 1976 PH T.C. Memo ¶76,102, 35 TCM 436).
[45] Examples include paying an employee's personal expenses (*The Lang Chevrolet Co.*, 1967 PH T.C. Memo ¶67,212, 26 TCM 1054) and purchasing assets for an employee's use (*Joseph Morgenstern*, 1955 PH T.C. Memo ¶55,086, 14 TCM 282).

EXAMPLE I:3-25 ▶

ADDITIONAL COMMENT

Child-support payments are not treated as alimony and are neither deductible by the payor spouse nor includible in income of the payee spouse.

ADDITIONAL COMMENT

If any amount specified in the divorce instrument will be reduced due to the happening of a contingency relating to a child or reduced at a time that can clearly be associated with such contingency, the amount of the reduction is treated as child support.

ETHICAL POINT

Tax consultants who advise divorcing couples may face an ethical dilemma because advice that benefits one spouse may be detrimental to the other, and because of the need to maintain confidential client relationships.

EXAMPLE I:3-25 ▶

Helen earns $500,000 and, as a result of her divorce, she is required to pay William $250,000. If the payment is a property settlement, Helen cannot deduct any of the $250,000 payment and William is not required to include the payment in his income. However, if the $250,000 is alimony, Helen can deduct the full amount in computing her adjusted gross income. William reports the $250,000 as alimony income. ◀

The tax law has rather specific rules that distinguish alimony, child support, and property settlements. Under current law, in order to be treated as **alimony**, payments must meet all of the following requirements:[46]

▶ Be made in cash (not property)

▶ Be made pursuant to a divorce, separation, or a written agreement between the spouses

▶ Terminate at the death of the payee

▶ Not be designated as being other than alimony (e.g., child support)

▶ Be made between people who are living in separate households

These rules are summarized in Topic Review I:3-2. Certain aspects of these rules will be discussed further.

A **property settlement** is a division of property pursuant to a divorce. In general, each spouse is entitled to the property brought into the marriage and a share of the property accumulated during marriage.[47] A division of property does not result in any income to either spouse, nor does either spouse receive a tax deduction. The basis of property received by either spouse as a result of the divorce or separation remains unchanged.

EXAMPLE I:3-26 ▶

As a result of a divorce, Dawn receives stock that she purchased with her former husband during their marriage for $12,000. At the time of the divorce, the stock was worth $14,000. Neither Dawn nor her former husband reports income from the transfer of the stock because the stock was acquired as a property settlement. If Dawn subsequently sold the stock for $15,000, she would report a $3,000 gain. ◀

TOPIC REVIEW I:3-2

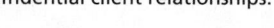

Tax Rules for Alimony

TREATMENT OF RECIPIENT

The recipient of alimony must include the amounts received in gross income. Property settlements and child support payments are not taxable.

TREATMENT OF PAYOR

The payor of alimony may deduct amounts paid *for* adjusted gross income. Property settlements and child support payments are not deductible.

APPLICABLE TO

Payments must be pursuant to a divorce, separation, or a written agreement between spouses.

REQUIREMENTS

Spouses must be living in separate households. Payments must be in the form of cash paid to (or for the benefit of) a spouse or former spouse. Payments must terminate at the death of the payee. Payments may not be designated as being other than alimony (such as child support or a property settlement).

RECAPTURE

If the amount of payments declines in the second or third year, a portion of the early payments may have to be recaptured as income by the payor. The payee may deduct the same recaptured amount.

---

[46] Before 1942, alimony was not deductible (*Gould v. Gould*, 3 AFTR 2958, 1 USTC ¶13 (USSC, 1917)). The original rules were revised in 1984 and again in 1986. Prior rules apply to earlier divorces unless both spouses elect to apply current rules.

[47] How the property accumulated during marriage is divided may be determined by an agreement of the parties, or if they are unable to agree, on a basis of state law.

One unusual rule found in the current law that relates to alimony is the so-called **recapture provision**. This provision was established to prevent a large property settlement that might take place after a divorce from being disguised as alimony so as to produce a deduction for the payor. In essence, the concept of recapture in connection with a divorce means that the payor of the alimony (who has taken a deduction for such amounts in prior years) must report the recapture amount in his or her income. The payee (who has reported the income in prior years) receives a deduction for the recaptured amount. This recapture occurs because the payments that originally were reported as alimony are being reclassified as property settlements.

Recapture occurs if payments decrease sharply in either the second or third year. Specifically, the amount of second-year alimony recaptured is equal to the second-year alimony reduced by the total of $15,000 plus the third-year alimony. The amount of first-year alimony recaptured is equal to the first-year alimony reduced by the total of $15,000 plus the average alimony paid in the second year (reduced by the recapture for that year) and the third year. The calculation of recapture for both the first and second years is shown below.

$$R_2 = A_2 - (\$15,000 + A_3)$$

$$R_1 = A_1 - [\$15,000 + (A_2 + A_3 - R_2)/2]$$

A_i = Alimony paid in first (A_1), second (A_2), and third year (A_3), respectively.

R_i = Recaptured alimony from the first (R_1) and second year (R_2), respectively.

Both first- and second-year amounts are recaptured by requiring the payor to report the excess as income (and allowing the payee to deduct the same amount) in the third year. Recapture is not required if payments cease because of the death of either spouse or remarriage of the recipient.

EXAMPLE I:3-27 ▶ As a result of their divorce, Hal is ordered to pay to Rose $100,000 alimony in 2015 and $20,000 per year thereafter until her death or remarriage. Hal must recapture the amount of the decrease that exceeds $35,000, or $65,000 ($100,000 − $20,000 − $15,000). The $65,000 of alimony in 2015 must be reported by Hal as income during 2017. Also, Rose may deduct the $65,000 *for* AGI in 2017. ◀

EXAMPLE I:3-28 ▶ As a result of their separation, Mary agrees to pay Tom $20,000 per year. The payments are to cease if Tom remarries. In the year after the agreement is reached, Tom remarries and Mary discontinues the payments. No recapture is required because the payments are contingent on the remarriage of the recipient and the payments have been discontinued because of the occurrence of this contingency. ◀

PENSIONS AND ANNUITIES

An **annuity** is a series of regular payments that will continue for a fixed period of time or until the death of the recipient. Taxpayers occasionally purchase annuities from insurance companies to provide a source of funds during retirement years. The insurance company may agree to make payments to the insured for the remainder of the insured's life. The retired individual is assured of a steady flow of funds for life. The price paid for the annuity represents its cost. The insured taxpayer is permitted to recover this cost tax-free.

Individuals receiving an annuity are permitted to exclude their cost, but are taxed on the remaining portion of the annuity. The following steps can be followed to determine the nontaxable portion of the annuity:

▶ Determine the **expected return multiple**. This multiple is the number of years that the annuity is expected to continue and may be a stated term, say ten years, or it may be for the remainder of the taxpayer's life. In the latter situation, the expected return multiple (life expectancy) is determined by referring to a table (see Table I:3-1) developed by the IRS.

▶ Determine the **expected return**. This return is computed by multiplying the amount of the annual payment by the expected return multiple.

▼ TABLE I:3-1
Ordinary Life Annuities (One Life) Expected Return Multiple

Age	Multiple	Age	Multiple	Age	Multiple
5	76.6	42	40.6	79	10.0
6	75.6	43	39.6	80	9.5
7	74.7	44	38.7	81	8.9
8	73.7	45	37.7	82	8.4
9	72.7	46	36.8	83	7.9
10	71.7	47	35.9	84	7.4
11	70.7	48	34.9	85	6.9
12	69.7	49	34.0	86	6.5
13	68.8	50	33.1	87	6.1
14	67.8	51	32.2	88	5.7
15	66.8	52	31.3	89	5.3
16	65.8	53	30.4	90	5.0
17	64.8	54	29.5	91	4.7
18	63.9	55	28.6	92	4.4
19	62.9	56	27.7	93	4.1
20	61.9	57	26.8	94	3.9
21	60.9	58	25.9	95	3.7
22	59.9	59	25.0	96	3.4
23	59.0	60	24.2	97	3.2
24	58.0	61	23.3	98	3.0
25	57.0	62	22.5	99	2.8
26	56.0	63	21.6	100	2.7
27	55.1	64	20.8	101	2.5
28	54.1	65	20.0	102	2.3
29	53.1	66	19.2	103	2.1
30	52.2	67	18.4	104	1.9
31	51.2	68	17.6	105	1.8
32	50.2	69	16.8	106	1.6
33	49.3	70	16.0	107	1.4
34	48.3	71	15.3	108	1.3
35	47.3	72	14.6	109	1.1
36	46.4	73	13.9	110	1.0
37	45.4	74	13.2	111	.9
38	44.4	75	12.5	112	.8
39	43.5	76	11.9	113	.7
40	42.5	77	11.2	114	.6
41	41.5	78	10.6	115	.5

Source: Reg. Sec. 1.72-9, Table V.

Note: This table should be used if any or all investments were made on or after July 1, 1986. If all investments were made before July 1, 1986, use Reg. Sec. 1.72-9, Table I (not shown).

ADDITIONAL COMMENT
If payments are paid other than monthly, the number of anticipated payments is adjusted accordingly. Thus, if payments are made quarterly, the number from the table is divided by three.

▶ Determine the **exclusion ratio.** This ratio is computed by dividing the investment in the contract (its cost) by the expected return (from above).

▶ Determine the **current year's exclusion.** This exclusion is computed by multiplying the exclusion ratio (from above) times the amount received during the year.

EXAMPLE I:3-29 ▶ David, age 65, purchases an annuity for $30,000. Under the terms of the annuity, David is to receive $300 per month ($3,600 per year) for the rest of his life.

▶ The expected return multiple is 20.0. The multiple is obtained from Table I:3-1.

▶ The expected return is $72,000 (20.0 × $3,600).

▶ The exclusion ratio is 0.4167 ($30,000 ÷ $72,000).

▶ The exclusion is $1,500 (0.4167 × $3,600). ◀

After the entire cost of an annuity has been recovered, the full amount of all future payments is taxable. On the other hand, if an individual dies before recovering the entire cost, the remaining unrecovered cost can be deducted as an itemized deduction on that individual's final return. Insurance companies and businesses with retirement plans compute the taxable portion of annuities and report the amounts to recipients on Form 1099.

Qualified Retirement Plan Annuities. Distributions from pensions and other qualified retirement plans are commonly paid in the form of an annuity. Both the employer and the employee often contribute funds to these plans. The employee's cost is limited to after-tax amounts contributed by the employee, usually through withholding. The employee's cost does not include employer contributions or pretax contributions made by the employee to Sec. 401(k) and similar plans.

KEY POINT

The simplified method is used only for annuity distributions from qualified retirement plans. All other annuity distributions are taxed in accordance with the general rules above.

Simplified Method. A simplified method is now used to determine the taxable portion of an annuity paid from a qualified retirement plan. Under the simplified method, the nontaxable portion of each annuity payment is equal to the employee's after-tax investment in the annuity divided by the number of anticipated payments as determined from the following table:

Age of Primary Annuitant on the Start Date	Number of Anticipated Payments
55 and under	360
56–60	310
61–65	260
66–70	210
71 and over	160

EXAMPLE I:3-30 ▶ Jack, age 62, retires, and receives a $1,000 per month annuity from his employer's qualified pension plan. Jack contributed $65,000 to the plan prior to his retirement. Under the simplified method, Jack would exclude $250 per month as a return of capital. This is calculated by dividing $65,000 by 260 anticipated payments. ◀

ADDITIONAL COMMENT

Unlike other retirement plans, all contributions made to Roth plans are from after-tax income. When all Roth requirements are met, distributions are tax-free. See Chapter I:9.

Plan Comparison. Plans that involve a combination of pre- and after-tax contributions are taxed less favorably than plans that have only pretax or only after-tax contributions because income earned on after-tax contributions is taxed when distributed to retired employees. For that reason, many employers today have two separate plans, one with only pretax contributions and a second with only after-tax contributions (like the Roth plan). The result is that all distributions from the pretax plan are taxable, whereas no qualified distributions from the Roth plan are taxable.

KEY POINT

Under current law, a taxpayer must generally pay tax on a portion of each withdrawal made before the normal starting date of the annuity.

Advance Payments. Many pensions contain provisions that allow taxpayers to withdraw amounts before the normal starting date. Under current law, an amount withdrawn from a pension before the starting date is considered to be in part a recovery of the employee's contributions and in part a recovery of the employer's contributions.[48] After all contributions have been withdrawn, additional withdrawals are fully taxable.

EXAMPLE I:3-31 ▶ Dick, age 45 and in good health, withdrew $2,000 from a pension plan during the current year. No exception exempts Dick from the 10% penalty. Dick had made $40,000 of after-tax contributions to the plan, and his employer had contributed $60,000. Dick must include $1,200 (0.60 × $2,000) in income. Because no exception applies, Dick must also pay an additional penalty of $120 (0.10 × $1,200). The penalty is not deductible by Dick. ◀

ADDITIONAL COMMENT

In addition to being subject to the regular income tax, any amount withdrawn may also be subject to a 10% nondeductible penalty. The penalty is not applicable to taxpayers who are age 59 1/2 or older. Other exceptions to the early withdrawal penalty are discussed in Chapter I:9.

INCOME FROM LIFE INSURANCE AND ENDOWMENT CONTRACTS

The face amount of life insurance received because of the death of the insured is not taxable. If the proceeds are left with the insurance company and as a result earn interest, the interest payments are taxable. (See Chapter I:4 for a detailed discussion of life insurance and endowment contracts.)

[48] Sec. 72(e).

INCOME FROM DISCHARGE OF INDEBTEDNESS

In general, the forgiveness of debt is a taxable event. The person who owed the money must report the amount forgiven as income unless one of several exceptions found in the tax law applies. These exceptions are discussed in Chapter I:4.

INCOME PASSED THROUGH TO TAXPAYER

Generally, entities are subject to income tax based on the amount of taxable income. Corporations, as an example, are subject to income taxation. As noted, certain types of entities are not subject to income taxation as their income is taxed directly to their owners rather than to the entities. Such entities are referred to as "flow-through entities." Section 61 specifically lists three such instances: the distributive share of a partnership's income, income in respect of a decedent, and income from an interest in an estate or trust. Though not mentioned in Sec. 61, similar treatment is accorded S corporations, Exchange Traded Funds, Regulated Investment Companies, and Real Estate Investment Trusts. In each case, the income that is produced by the entities merely flows through to the owners or beneficiaries of such entities. The rules can be summarized as follows:

> **KEY POINT**
>
> The pass-through of income by a partnership can create a situation known as phantom income. In this situation, a partner is required to report income on his or her individual tax return, but the partner may not have received a cash distribution from the partnership.

► Each partner reports his or her share of a partnership's income. Each partner deducts his or her share of the partnership's expenses. The income and deductions are reported by the partners whether or not any amount is actually distributed by the partnership during the year. The partnership's income and deductions retain their tax status.

► S corporations are taxed much like partnerships. Each shareholder in the corporation is taxed on his or her proportionate share of the corporation's income whether or not the income is actually distributed.

► Exchange Traded Funds (ETFs), Regulated Investment Companies (RICs), often called mutual funds, and Real Estate Investment Trusts (REITs) are also flow through entities. ETFs and RICs invest in securities and are required to distribute their income to shareholders who are taxed on the distributions. REITs invest in real estate and real estate loans. They too must distribute their income to investors who are taxed on the income. The distributions (dividends, interest, rents, and gains) retain their tax status when reported by ETF, RIC, and REIT investors.

► Income in respect of a decedent is income earned by an individual before death that is paid to another after the death. For example, salary earned by a husband before his death in an automobile accident may be paid to his widow. The recipient, in this case the widow, is taxed on the income if it has not been taxed to the decedent before his death.

► Income earned by estates and trusts is subject to taxation.[49] However, income distributions to beneficiaries are deductible by estates and trusts and are taxable to the beneficiaries. Thus, if a trust with $20,000 of income distributes $15,000 to its beneficiary, the trust is taxed on $5,000, and $15,000 is taxed to the beneficiary. Because of this approach estates and trusts are sometimes referred to as semi-flow-through or hybrid entities. The income taxation of estates and trusts is covered more fully in *Prentice Hall's Federal Taxation: Corporations, Partnerships, Estates, and Trusts.*

OTHER ITEMS OF GROSS INCOME

The preceding discussions considered items of gross income specifically listed in Sec. 61(a). However, the fact that an item of income is listed in Sec. 61(a) does not necessarily cause it to be taxable. Rather, the condition that causes an item of income to be taxable is that it is not specifically excluded. Some items of gross income not mentioned in Sec. 61(a) are discussed below.

---

[49] Note the distinction between income in respect of a decedent and the income of an estate. Income in respect of a decedent is the income earned before death that was never taxed to the decedent. An example would be interest that was accrued but unpaid at death. Income of an estate is income earned after death that is paid to the estate. An example would be interest that accrues after the decedent's death.

PRIZES, AWARDS, GAMBLING WINNINGS, AND TREASURE FINDS

In general, prizes, awards, gambling winnings, and treasure finds are taxable.[50] Winnings in contests, competitions, and quiz shows are taxable.[51] The amount to be included in gross income is the fair market value of the goods or services received. Total gambling winnings must be included in gross income.[52] This includes proceeds from lotteries, raffles, sweepstakes, and the like. Gambling losses (up to the amount of the current year's winnings) are allowable as an itemized deduction.[53] The Regulations state that a treasure find constitutes gross income to the extent of its value in the year in which it is reduced to undisputed possession.[54]

EXAMPLE I:3-32 ▶ Several years ago, Colleen purchased a used piano at an auction for $15. In the current year, she finds $4,500 of currency hidden in the piano. Colleen must report the $4,500 as income in the current year.[55] ◀

ILLEGAL INCOME

Income from illegal activities is taxable.[56] Some people find this part of the tax law surprising, but this fact serves as the basis for many criminal convictions given that few criminals report their illegal income. For example, Al Capone was convicted of income tax evasion, not bootlegging or other crimes. It is not necessary to prove that an individual had illegal income, but merely that the individual had income that was not reported.

Individuals have used varied defenses against this rule. One taxpayer was successful in convincing the Supreme Court that he should not be taxed on embezzlement gains because he had an unconditional obligation to repay the amount embezzled,[57] but the Supreme Court reversed this position in a later case.[58] The court concluded that although an obligation to repay existed, the taxpayer had no "consensual recognition" (intent) to repay. In addition to embezzlement of funds, the courts have held that a kidnapper's ransom was taxable,[59] along with profits from bookmaking,[60] card playing,[61] forgery,[62] stealing,[63] bank robbery,[64] sale of narcotics,[65] illegal sale of liquor,[66] and bribes.[67] (See Chapter I:6 for a discussion of related deductions.)

UNEMPLOYMENT COMPENSATION

For many years, unemployment compensation was excluded from gross income. In 1978, Congress changed the law to fully tax unemployment compensation because these benefits are a substitute for taxable wages.

SOCIAL SECURITY BENEFITS

Social Security benefits were excluded from gross income until 1984. Between 1984 and 1993, up to 50% of Social Security benefits were taxable. Beginning in 1994, up to 85% of Social Security benefits may be taxable. Under Sec. 86, the portion of Social Security benefits that are taxable depends on the taxpayer's provisional income and filing status. *Provisional income* is computed using the following formula:

---

[50] Exclusions for scholarships and fellowships and a limited exclusion for prizes awarded for scientific, charitable, or similar meritorious achievements are discussed in Chapter I:4.
[51] Sec. 74 and Reg. Sec. 1.74-1.
[52] *U.S. v. Manley S. Sullivan,* 6 AFTR 6753, 1 USTC ¶236 (USSC, 1927).
[53] Sec. 165(d).
[54] Reg. Sec. 1.61-14(a).
[55] *Ermenegildo Cesarini v. U.S.,* 26 AFTR 2d 5107, 70-2 USTC ¶9509 (6th Cir., 1970).
[56] Reg. 1.61-14(a).
[57] *CIR v. Laird Wilcox,* 34 AFTR 811, 46-1 USTC ¶9188 (USSC, 1946).
[58] *Eugene C. James v. U.S.,* 7 AFTR 2d 1361, 61-1 USTC ¶9449 (USSC, 1961).

[59] *Murray Humphreys v. CIR,* 28 AFTR 1030, 42-1 USTC ¶9237 (7th Cir., 1942).
[60] *James P. McKenna,* 1 B.T.A. 326 (1925).
[61] *L. Weiner,* 10 B.T.A. 905 (1928).
[62] *Cass Sunstein,* 1966 PH T.C. Memo ¶66,043, 25 TCM 247.
[63] *Mathias Schira v. CIR,* 50 AFTR 1404, 57-1 USTC ¶9413 (6th Cir., 1957).
[64] *Gary Ayers,* 1978 PH T.C. Memo ¶78,341, 37 TCM 1415.
[65] *Antonino Farina v. McMahon,* 2 AFTR 2d 5918, 58-2 USTC ¶9938 (D.C. N.Y., 1958).
[66] *U.S. v. Manley S. Sullivan,* 6 AFTR 6753, 1 USTC ¶236 (USSC, 1927).
[67] *U.S. v. Patrick Commerford,* 12 AFTR 364, 1933 CCH ¶9255 (2nd Cir., 1933).

Adjusted gross income (excluding Social Security benefits)	$xx,xxx
Plus: Tax-exempt interest	x,xxx
Excluded foreign income	x,xxx
50% of Social Security benefits	x,xxx
Provisional income	$xx,xxx

Married Filing Separately. In the case of married couples who live together but file separately, taxable Social Security benefits are equal to the lesser of:

▶ 85% of Social Security benefits, or

▶ 85% of provisional income

Married Filing Jointly. For married couples filing jointly, the computation of the taxable portion of Social Security benefits is as follows:

▶ If provisional income is $32,000 or less, no Social Security benefits are taxable.

▶ If provisional income is over $32,000 (but not over $44,000), taxable Social Security benefits equal the lesser of:
> 50% of the Social Security benefits, or
> 50% of the excess of provisional income over $32,000

▶ If provisional income is over $44,000, taxable Social Security benefits are equal to the lesser of:
> 85% of the Social Security benefits, or
> 85% of provisional income over $44,000, plus the lesser of (1) $6,000 or (2) 50% of Social Security benefits

Single Taxpayers. For single taxpayers (and married persons living separately), the computation of the taxable portion of Social Security benefits is as follows:

▶ If provisional income is $25,000 or less, no Social Security benefits are taxable.

▶ If provisional income is over $25,000 (but not over $34,000), taxable Social Security benefits are equal to the lesser of:
> 50% of the Social Security benefits, or
> 50% of the excess of provisional income over $25,000

▶ If provisional income is over $34,000, taxable Social Security benefits are equal to the lesser of:
> 85% of the Social Security benefits, or
> 85% of provisional income over $34,000, plus the lesser of (1) $4,500 or (2) 50% of Social Security benefits

EXAMPLE I:3-33 ▶ Holly is a single taxpayer with a taxable pension of $22,000, tax-exempt interest of $10,000, and Social Security benefits of $8,000. Her provisional income is $36,000, determined as follows:

Adjusted gross income	$22,000
Plus: Tax-exempt interest	10,000
50% of Social Security benefits	4,000
Provisional income	$36,000

The taxable Social Security benefits are equal to $5,700, which is the lesser of $6,800 (0.85 × $8,000) or $5,700 ($1,700* + the lesser of $4,500 or $4,000**).

*($36,000 provisional income − $34,000 threshold) × 0.85.
**50% of the Social Security benefits.   ◀

The result of the computation excludes from gross income the Social Security benefits received by lower-income individuals but taxes a portion (up to 85%) of the benefits received by taxpayers with higher incomes. As the thresholds are not adjusted for inflation, an increasing number of retirees are finding that a portion of their Social Security benefits is taxable.

The term **Social Security benefits** refers to basic monthly retirement and disability benefits paid under Social Security and also to tier-one railroad retirement benefits. It does not include supplementary Medicare benefits that cover the cost of doctors' services and other medical benefits.

INSURANCE PROCEEDS AND COURT AWARDS

In general, insurance proceeds and court awards are taxable. Two exceptions are accident and health insurance benefits and the face amount of life insurance. (See Chapter I:4 for a discussion of these benefits.)

Insurance proceeds or court awards received because of the destruction of property are included in gross income only to the extent that the proceeds exceed the adjusted basis of the property. Involuntary conversion provisions permit taxpayers to avoid being taxed if they reinvest the proceeds in a qualified replacement property.[68] If the proceeds are less than the property's adjusted basis, they reduce the amount of any deductible loss. Proceeds of insurance guarding against loss of profits because of a casualty are taxable.[69] Similarly, if a taxpayer had to sue a customer to collect income owed to the taxpayer, the amount collected is taxable just as it would have been had the taxpayer collected the income without going to court.

EXAMPLE I:3-34 ▶ Gulf Corporation's factory was destroyed by fire. Gulf Corporation collected insurance of $400,000, which equaled the building's basis, and $250,000 for the profits lost during the time the company was rebuilding its factory. The $400,000 is not taxable because it constitutes a recovery of the basis of the factory. The $250,000 is taxable because it represents lost income. Recall that the income would have been taxable had it been earned by the company from regular operations. ◀

Although few exclusions are designed specifically for insurance proceeds or court awards, such amounts may be covered by other, more general exclusions. For example, Sec. 104(a)(2) excludes "damages (other than punitive damages) received . . . on account of personal physical injuries or sickness." Thus, amounts collected because of physical injury suffered in an automobile accident are excluded (see Chapter I:4).

RECOVERY OF PREVIOUSLY DEDUCTED AMOUNTS

On occasion, a taxpayer may deduct an amount in one year but recover the amount in a subsequent year. In general, the amount recovered must be included in the gross income in the year it is recovered. Cash-basis taxpayers encounter this situation more often than accrual-basis taxpayers because their expenses are generally deductible in the year they are paid. If the amount was overpaid, the taxpayer can anticipate a refund.

EXAMPLE I:3-35 ▶ During 2015, Cindy's employer withheld $1,000 from her wages for state income taxes. She claimed the $1,000 as an itemized deduction on her 2015 federal income tax return. Her itemized deductions totaled $12,000. On her 2015 state income tax return, her state income tax was only $800. As a result, Cindy received a $200 refund from the state in April 2016. Because Cindy deducted the full $1,000 in 2015, she must report the $200 refund as income on her 2016 federal income tax return. ◀

Tax Benefit Rule. As noted above, a taxpayer who recovers an amount deducted in a previous year must report as gross income the amount recovered. The amount recovered need not be included in income, however, if the taxpayer received no tax benefit. A tax benefit occurs only if the deduction reduced the tax for the year.[70] Chapter I:7 provides a more detailed discussion of the tax benefit rule.

---

[68] The involuntary conversion provisions are discussed in Chapter I:12.

[69] *Oppenheim's Inc. v. Kavanagh*, 39 AFTR 468, 50-1 USTC ¶9249 (D.C.-Mich., 1950).

[70] Sec. 111.

EXAMPLE I:3-36 ▶

REAL-WORLD EXAMPLE
An attorney collected fees from clients of his employer. Because the attorney and his employer were engaged in a dispute over ownership of the money, he deposited the disputed amount in a trust account. The attorney was taxable on the amounts in the year received because he had control over the funds under the claim of right doctrine. *Edward J. Costello, Jr.,* 1985 PH T.C. Memo ¶85,571, 50 TCM 1463.

In 2015, Jack's employer withheld $1,200 from his wages for state income tax. Jack claimed the $1,200 as an itemized deduction on his 2015 federal income tax return. Because of a variety of losses incurred by Jack, he reported a negative taxable income of $32,000 during 2015. The state refunded the $1,200 during 2016. Jack will not have to report the $1,200 as gross income on his federal return. He would have owed no federal income tax in 2015 even without the deduction for state income taxes. Therefore, Jack received no tax benefit from the deduction. ◄

CLAIM OF RIGHT

Sometimes taxpayers receive disputed amounts. For example, a contractor may receive payment on a job when the quality of the work is being questioned by the customer, a salesperson may receive commissions when there is a question as to whether the sales are final, or a litigant may receive a court award even though the case is on appeal. Under the claim of right doctrine, the recipient of a disputed amount must include the amount received in gross income as long as the use of the funds is unrestricted.

EXAMPLE I:3-37 ▶

Jane wins a court case against a customer requiring the customer to pay her $10,000. The customer is unhappy with the result of the case and indicates that he plans to appeal, but pays the $10,000 to avoid interest on the amount in the event he loses the appeal. Jane must include the $10,000 in gross income even though she will have to repay the amount if she loses the appeal. ◄

EXAMPLE I:3-38 ▶

Assume the same facts as in Example I:3-37 except that the $10,000 is placed in escrow by the court awaiting the outcome of the appeal. Jane does not have to report the amount as she does not have use of the funds. ◄

Of course, taxpayers may be required to repay the disputed amount in a subsequent year. Such taxpayers may deduct the previously reported amount in the year of repayment. The taxes saved from such a deduction, however, may be considerably less than the original tax. If the repayment is over $3,000, taxpayers have the option of reducing the current tax by the tax paid in the prior year or years on the repaid amount.[71]

EXAMPLE I:3-39 ▶

Assume the same facts as in Example I:3-37, except that after reporting the disputed $10,000 Jane loses the appeal and must repay the $10,000 to her customer. If Jane was in the 25% tax bracket when she reported the disputed amount, she would have paid a $2,500 (0.25 × $10,000) tax on the disputed amount. If she were in the 15% bracket when she made the repayment, she would recover only $1,500 by deducting the $10,000. Because the amount exceeds $3,000, Jane has the option of determining her current year's tax by deducting from the tax she would otherwise pay the $2,500 tax she paid in the earlier year. This credit is allowed in lieu of receiving a $10,000 deduction. ◄

TAX PLANNING CONSIDERATIONS

OBJECTIVE 5

Describe tax planning considerations for inclusions of gross income

SHIFTING INCOME

A family can reduce its taxes by shifting income from family members who are in high tax brackets (e.g., parents) to family members who are in low tax brackets (e.g., children). Assignment of income rules prevent shifting from being done by merely redirecting the payment. Thus, a father cannot avoid a tax on his salary by ordering his employer to pay the salary to his daughter. Nevertheless, income can be shifted by transferring ownership of the property. For example, children may own stock in the family business. Dividends on the stock are taxed to the children. In the case of a child under age 24, however, the

[71] Sec. 1341.

parents' (as opposed to the child's) tax rate often applies to unearned income in excess of $2,100. Series EE bonds may prove useful to avoid the kiddie tax because the interest is deferred until the bond is redeemed or matures. The maturity date, of course, may be after the child reaches age 24. Another shifting technique is for the child to work for the family business and be paid a reasonable salary. Such income is taxed at the child's tax rate, even if the child is under 24 years old, and can be offset by the child's own standard deduction.

Shifting of income is constrained by several factors. As noted, the assignment of income doctrine limits transfers. Reasonableness limitations constrain compensation and other payments. Furthermore, outright gifts of property are subject to gift taxes. Also, individuals are reluctant to transfer wealth to children for a variety of personal reasons. However, the tax saving potential of shifting income is often so great as to prompt many well-to-do families to use available shifting techniques.

ALIMONY

Whether payments made in connection with a divorce or separation are classified as alimony is of major tax significance. Such classification results in a deduction for the payor and income to the payee. Alimony is actually one way to shift income.

EXAMPLE I:3-40 ▶

Tony, who has a 39.6% marginal tax rate, makes payments of $40,000 to his former wife. If it is deductible as alimony, Tony will save $15,840 (0.396 × $40,000) a year in federal income taxes. The amount of tax that the former wife must pay depends on how much other income she has and whether she has deductions that reduce the tax. Her tax might be as high as her former husband's or as little as zero. ◀

ADDITIONAL COMMENT

In 2012, $11.2 billion of alimony paid was reported as a deduction, while only $8.9 billion was reported as taxable income.

Two points are clear. One is that both parties should understand the implication of having amounts treated as alimony. Second, the designation of the payments as alimony may be beneficial to both parties. The payor will, of course, benefit from a tax deduction. The payee may benefit because the payor may agree to make larger alimony payments since the payments are tax deductible.

PREPAID INCOME

As explained earlier in this chapter, prepaid income is generally taxable when received. This accelerated recognition of income may be a significant disadvantage to the taxpayer if the related expenses are incurred in a later tax year. Thus, tax planning for prepaid amounts is essential.

EXAMPLE I:3-41 ▶

Phil owns an apartment complex and requires tenants to pay the first and last months' rent before they move in. Rita, on the other hand, owns an apartment complex and requires tenants to pay the first month's rent and a refundable deposit (which equals one month's rent). Although the full amount received by Phil is taxable when it is received, only one-half of the amount received by Rita is taxable when it is received. Rita is required to refund the deposit, assuming the tenant vacates leaving the property in good condition and having paid all rent. Therefore, the deposit is not taxable. ◀

Taxpayers receiving advance payments in connection with services may be able to meet the requirements of Rev. Proc. 2004-34 (discussed earlier in the chapter); taxpayers receiving advance payments associated with the sale of merchandise may be able to meet the requirements of Reg. Sec. 1.451-5 (also discussed in this chapter). Also, special rules exist for subscription income, membership fees, crop insurance proceeds, and drought sales of livestock, all of which allow taxpayers to defer recognizing income.

TAXABLE, TAX-EXEMPT, OR TAX-DEFERRED BONDS

Which should a taxpayer choose: taxable bonds, tax-exempt bonds, or tax-deferred bonds? The answer depends on the relative interest rates and the taxpayer's current and future tax brackets. **Taxable bonds** yield the highest return, but the interest is taxable. **Tax-exempt bonds** yield a lower return. **Tax-deferred bonds** generally yield a return somewhere close to that of taxable bonds. Interest on U.S. Series EE savings bonds is tax exempt if it is used for educational purposes and if other requirements of Sec. 135 are met (see the discussion earlier in this chapter). If these conditions are not met, the tax is deferred until the bonds are redeemed. The taxpayer may be in a lower bracket when the tax is eventually paid, and in the meantime, the interest that will eventually go to pay taxes is earning additional income.

The decision between taxable and exempt bonds is a rather easy one if the risk of the investments is assumed to be approximately equal. A taxpayer should invest in exempt bonds instead of taxable bonds if the interest on the exempt bonds is greater than the interest on the taxable bonds multiplied by 1 minus the taxpayer's marginal tax bracket (expressed as a decimal). Stated in a formula, this means invest in tax-exempt bonds if

$$\begin{array}{ccc}\text{Return on the} \\ \text{tax-exempt bonds}\end{array} > \begin{array}{ccc}\text{Return on the} \\ \text{taxable bonds}\end{array} \times (1 - \text{Marginal tax bracket})$$

EXAMPLE I:3-42 ▶ Robert's marginal tax bracket is 39.6% and he is trying to decide between tax-exempt bonds, which pay 6% interest, and taxable bonds paying 8% interest. Robert should invest in the exempt bonds because 6% is greater than 4.83% [0.08 × (1 − 0.396)]. ◀

Comparison of taxable bonds or exempt bonds to tax-deferred bonds is more complicated. As noted, the advantages of the tax-deferred bonds are twofold. First, the taxpayer may be in a lower tax bracket when the tax is paid (e.g., taxpayers who plan to redeem the bonds after retirement). Second, the amount that will eventually go to pay the tax earns income until the tax must be paid. Although the computation is not covered here, it is noted that taxpayers who anticipate that they will be in lower tax brackets and who plan to leave funds invested for several years may benefit from choosing Series EE U.S. savings bonds over taxable bonds. See Chapter I:18 in the *Individuals* text for a further discussion of taxable, tax exempt, and tax deferred investments.

REPORTING SAVINGS BOND INTEREST

It may be desirable to purchase Series EE bonds in the child's name despite the fact that such interest is subject to the kiddie tax (see Chapter I:2). This is because there is no income tax as long as the child's annual income is less than $900. However, even if a child is not otherwise required to file a return, it is necessary to report interest on Series EE bonds annually by filing a tax return.[72] Taxpayers who have not been reporting savings bond interest annually may change to annual reporting, but are required to report both current and previously accrued interest in the year of the change.[73]

Taxpayers who report savings bond interest annually are allowed to change to the deferral method without IRS approval.[74] This is particularly useful where the decision to report interest currently was made before the imposition of the kiddie tax. Taxpayers who make this election are bound by it for five years.

---

[72] *Philip Apkin*, 86 T.C. 692 (1986).
[73] Reg. Sec. 1.454-1(a)(4), Ex. (1).

[74] Rev. Proc. 97-37, 1997-2 C.B. 455.

DEFERRED COMPENSATION ARRANGEMENTS

Deferred compensation plans can be used as a means of avoiding the constructive receipt of income. Although income is normally taxable when the funds become available to the taxpayer, an advance contractual agreement can produce different results. Corporate executives, professional athletes, and others often sign agreements providing for compensation to be paid at future dates. Such agreements can produce tax savings because the recipients expect to be in a lower tax bracket. Because the arrangements are advance contractual agreements, the deferral of income does not constitute taxpayers "turning their backs" on the income.

EXAMPLE I:3-43 ▶ Alonzo, a 35-year-old professional basketball player, signs a contract specifying that he will be paid $400,000 per year for ten years even if he does not play. Because of his age, both Alonzo and the team recognize that he will probably play for one or two more years. If the agreement had specified that he was to receive a salary of $1,300,000 per year for two years, most of the income would have been taxed at the highest rates. By spreading the amount over a longer period, Alonzo pays tax at lower rates on much of the income. Alonzo is compensated for the delayed payment by receiving a larger total amount [i.e., $4 million ($400,000 × 10 years) versus $2.6 million ($1.3 million × 2 years)]. ◀

COMPLIANCE AND PROCEDURAL CONSIDERATIONS

Form 1040 lists various types of income. Some items of income (wages, tax refunds, alimony, pensions and annuities, unemployment compensation, Social Security benefits, and other income) are listed directly on Form 1040. Most expenses related to these items of income are deducted as miscellaneous itemized deductions on Schedule A.

Most other types of income (and related deductions) are reported on special schedules.

Topic Review I:3-3 summarizes the procedures for reporting income and related deductions.

EXAMPLE I:3-44 ▶ John J. Alexander has several items of income and related deductions:

ADDITIONAL COMMENT

The dollar amount of tax-exempt interest income is recorded on Form 1040, line 8b, but is not included in the tax base. The IRS requires the reporting of this type of income probably because it may affect the taxability of Social Security benefits.

Salary	$40,000
Deductible alimony payments	6,000
Taxable interest	300
Dividends: Ford Motor Co.	1,150
Omaha Mutual Fund	430
Capital Gain Distribution: Omaha Mutual Fund	50
Rent income (depreciation, interest, repairs, and other related expenses total $9,000)	11,000

KEY POINT

The amount labeled "total income" on line 22 of Form 1040 is not gross income, adjusted gross income, or taxable income.

The reporting of these items of income is illustrated on page 1 of Form 1040 (Figure I:3-1) and on Schedule B of Form 1040 (Figure I:3-2). Salary and interest (because the interest is less than $1,500) are entered directly on Form 1040. Rental income would be entered on Schedule E (not illustrated), and the net income after deducting related expenses is transferred to Form 1040. Alimony received and alimony payments are reported on page 1 of Form 1040. ◀

TOPIC REVIEW I:3-3

Reporting of Income

TYPE OF INCOME	REPORTED ON	RELATED DEDUCTIONS ARE CLAIMED ON
Wages, salaries, tips, etc.	Form 1040	Schedule A and various other forms: moving, Form 3903; travel, transportation, etc., Form 2106
Interest	Form 1040 (if less than $1,500), otherwise Schedule B	Schedule A (miscellaneous deductions, if any, e.g., safe deposit box fees)
Dividends	Form 1040 (if less than $1,500), otherwise Schedule B	Schedule A (miscellaneous deductions, if any, e.g., safe deposit box fees)
Refund of state or local income taxes	Form 1040 (instructions contain a worksheet)	Schedule A (miscellaneous deductions, if any, e.g., fee paid for tax advice)
Alimony	Form 1040	Schedule A (miscellaneous deductions, if any, e.g., legal fee associated with alimony)
Business income	Schedule C or C-EZ (net income or loss is transferred to Form 1040)	Schedule C or C-EZ (e.g., depreciation, advertising, repairs)
Capital gains	Schedule D	Schedule D (capital losses) or Schedule A (investment expenses)
Supplemental gains	Form 4797	Form 4797 (e.g., ordinary losses)
Pensions and annuities	Form 1040 (instructions contain a worksheet)	Schedule A (miscellaneous deductions, if any, e.g., fee paid for tax advice)
Rents, royalties, partnerships, S corporations, estates, trusts, etc.	Schedule E	Schedule E
Farm income	Schedule F	Schedule F
Unemployment compensation	Form 1040	Schedule A (miscellaneous deductions, if any, e.g., fee paid for tax advice)
Social Security benefits	Form 1040 (instructions contain a worksheet)	Schedule A (miscellaneous deductions, if any, e.g., fee paid for tax advice)
Other income	Form 1040	Schedule A (miscellaneous deductions, if any)

PROBLEM MATERIALS

DISCUSSION QUESTIONS

I:3-1 What phrase is found in both the Sixteenth Amendment to the Constitution and Sec. 61(a)? Why does the phrase appear in both locations?

I:3-2 Contrast the accounting and economic concepts of income.

I:3-3 Why does the tax concept of income more closely resemble the accounting concept of income than the economic concept?

I:3-4 Explain the meaning of the term *wherewithal to pay* as it applies to taxation.

I:3-5 If a loan is repaid, the lender does not have to include the repayment in gross income. There is no exclusion in the tax law that permits taxpayers to omit such amounts from gross income. How can this be explained?

I:3-6 A landlord who receives prepaid rent is required to report that amount as gross income when the payment is received. Why would Congress choose to do this? What problem does this create for the taxpayer?

I:3-7 Office space is often rented without carpet, wall covering, or window covering. Furthermore, many rental agreements specify that these improvements cannot be removed by a tenant if removal causes any damage to the property. What issue does this raise?

I:3-8 Does the fact that an item of income is paid in a form other than cash mean it is nontaxable? Explain.

I:3-9 Explain the significance of *Lucas v. Earl* and *Helvering v. Horst.*

I:3-10 Under present-day tax law, community property rules are followed in allocating income between husband and wife. Is this consistent with *Lucas v. Earl*? Explain.

Form 1040

Department of the Treasury—Internal Revenue Service (99)

U.S. Individual Income Tax Return

2014 OMB No. 1545-0074 | IRS Use Only—Do not write or staple in this space.

For the year Jan. 1–Dec. 31, 2014, or other tax year beginning ____ , 2014, ending ____ , 20 ____

Your first name and initial: **John J.**	Last name: **Alexander**
	Your social security number: **123 45 6789**
If a joint return, spouse's first name and initial	Last name
	Spouse's social security number

Home address (number and street). If you have a P.O. box, see instructions.
41 Oak Street Apt. no. ____

City, town or post office, state, and ZIP code. If you have a foreign address, also complete spaces below (see instructions).
Orlando, FL 32816

▲ Make sure the SSN(s) above and on line 6c are correct.

Foreign country name | Foreign province/state/county | Foreign postal code

Presidential Election Campaign
Check here if you, or your spouse if filing jointly, want $3 to go to this fund. Checking a box below will not change your tax or refund. ☐ You ☐ Spouse

Filing Status

Check only one box.

1. ☒ Single
2. ☐ Married filing jointly (even if only one had income)
3. ☐ Married filing separately. Enter spouse's SSN above and full name here. ▶
4. ☐ Head of household (with qualifying person). (See instructions.) If the qualifying person is a child but not your dependent, enter this child's name here. ▶
5. ☐ Qualifying widow(er) with dependent child

Exemptions

6a ☒ **Yourself.** If someone can claim you as a dependent, **do not** check box 6a . . . . .
b ☐ **Spouse**

Boxes checked on 6a and 6b: **1**

c **Dependents:**

(1) First name Last name	(2) Dependent's social security number	(3) Dependent's relationship to you	(4) ✓ if child under age 17 qualifying for child tax credit (see instructions)
			☐
			☐
			☐
			☐

If more than four dependents, see instructions and check here ▶ ☐

No. of children on 6c who:
- lived with you
- did not live with you due to divorce or separation (see instructions)

Dependents on 6c not entered above

d Total number of exemptions claimed . . . .

Add numbers on lines above ▶ **1**

Income

Attach Form(s) W-2 here. Also attach Forms W-2G and 1099-R if tax was withheld.

If you did not get a W-2, see instructions.

7	Wages, salaries, tips, etc. Attach Form(s) W-2	7	40,000
8a	**Taxable** interest. Attach Schedule B if required	8a	300
b	**Tax-exempt** interest. **Do not** include on line 8a . . . 8b		
9a	Ordinary dividends. Attach Schedule B if required	9a	1,580
b	Qualified dividends 9b		
10	Taxable refunds, credits, or offsets of state and local income taxes	10	
11	Alimony received	11	
12	Business income or (loss). Attach Schedule C or C-EZ	12	
13	Capital gain or (loss). Attach Schedule D if required. If not required, check here ▶ ☐	13	50
14	Other gains or (losses). Attach Form 4797	14	
15a	IRA distributions . 15a ___	b Taxable amount . . .	15b	
16a	Pensions and annuities 16a ___	b Taxable amount . . .	16b	
17	Rental real estate, royalties, partnerships, S corporations, trusts, etc. Attach Schedule E	17	2,000
18	Farm income or (loss). Attach Schedule F	18	
19	Unemployment compensation	19	
20a	Social security benefits 20a ___	b Taxable amount . . .	20b	
21	Other income. List type and amount ____	21	
22	Combine the amounts in the far right column for lines 7 through 21. This is your **total income** ▶	22	43,930

Adjusted Gross Income

For AGI

23	Educator expenses . . . 23		
24	Certain business expenses of reservists, performing artists, and fee-basis government officials. Attach Form 2106 or 2106-EZ 24		
25	Health savings account deduction. Attach Form 8889 . 25		
26	Moving expenses. Attach Form 3903 26		
27	Deductible part of self-employment tax. Attach Schedule SE . 27		
28	Self-employed SEP, SIMPLE, and qualified plans . 28		
29	Self-employed health insurance deduction 29		
30	Penalty on early withdrawal of savings 30		
31a	Alimony paid **b** Recipient's SSN ▶ 987 65 4321 31a 6,000		
32	IRA deduction 32		
33	Student loan interest deduction 33		
34	Tuition and fees. Attach Form 8917 34		
35	Domestic production activities deduction. Attach Form 8903 35		
36	Add lines 23 through 35	36	6,000
37	Subtract line 36 from line 22. This is your **adjusted gross income** . . . . . . ▶	37	37,930

For Disclosure, Privacy Act, and Paperwork Reduction Act Notice, see separate instructions. Cat. No. 11320B Form **1040** (2014)

FIGURE I:3-1 ▶ FORM 1040 (PAGE 1)

Interest and Ordinary Dividends

► **Attach to Form 1040A or 1040.**
► **Information about Schedule B and its instructions is at** *www.irs.gov/scheduleb*

OMB No. 1545-0074

20**14**

Attachment
Sequence No. **08**

Name(s) shown on return

John J. Alexander

Your social security number

123-45-6789

			Amount
Part I **Interest** (See instructions on back and the instructions for Form 1040A, or Form 1040, line 8a.) **Note.** If you received a Form 1099-INT, Form 1099-OID, or substitute statement from a brokerage firm, list the firm's name as the payer and enter the total interest shown on that form.	**1**	List name of payer. If any interest is from a seller-financed mortgage and the buyer used the property as a personal residence, see instructions on back and list this interest first. Also, show that buyer's social security number and address ► -- -- -- -- -- -- -- -- -- -- -- -- -- --	**1**
	2	Add the amounts on line 1	**2**
	3	Excludable interest on series EE and I U.S. savings bonds issued after 1989. Attach Form 8815	**3**
	4	Subtract line 3 from line 2. Enter the result here and on Form 1040A, or Form 1040, line 8a . . . . ►	**4**
		Note. If line 4 is over $1,500, you must complete Part III.	**Amount**
Part II **Ordinary Dividends** (See instructions on back and the instructions for Form 1040A, or Form 1040, line 9a.) **Note.** If you received a Form 1099-DIV or substitute statement from a brokerage firm, list the firm's name as the payer and enter the ordinary dividends shown on that form.	**5**	List name of payer ► ----------------------------------- ------------------------ Ford Motor Company ------------------------ ------------------------ Omaha Mutual Fund ----------------------------------- ----------------------------------- ----------------------------------- ----------------------------------- ----------------------------------- ----------------------------------- ----------------------------------- ----------------------------------- ----------------------------------- ----------------------------------- ----------------------------------- -----------------------------------	**5** 1,150 430
	6	Add the amounts on line 5. Enter the total here and on Form 1040A, or Form 1040, line 9a . . . . ►	**6** 1,580
		Note. If line 6 is over $1,500, you must complete Part III.	

		Yes	No
You must complete this part if you **(a)** had over $1,500 of taxable interest or ordinary dividends; **(b)** had a foreign account; or **(c)** received a distribution from, or were a grantor of, or a transferor to, a foreign trust.			
Part III **Foreign Accounts and Trusts** (See instructions on back.)	**7a** At any time during 2014, did you have a financial interest in or signature authority over a financial account (such as a bank account, securities account, or brokerage account) located in a foreign country? See instructions		X
	If "Yes," are you required to file FinCEN Form 114, Report of Foreign Bank and Financial Accounts (FBAR), to report that financial interest or signature authority? See FinCEN Form 114 and its instructions for filing requirements and exceptions to those requirements		X
	b If you are required to file FinCEN Form 114, enter the name of the foreign country where the financial account is located ►		
	8 During 2014, did you receive a distribution from, or were you the grantor of, or transferor to, a foreign trust? If "Yes," you may have to file Form 3520. See instructions on back		X

For Paperwork Reduction Act Notice, see your tax return instructions.   Cat. No. 17146N   Schedule B (Form 1040A or 1040) 2014

FIGURE I:3-2 ► SCHEDULE B

I:3-11 Ricardo owns a small unincorporated business. His 15-year-old daughter Jane works in the business on a part-time basis and was paid wages of $3,000 during the current year. Who is taxed on the child's earnings: Jane or her father? Explain.

I:3-12 Define the term *constructive receipt*. Explain its importance.

I:3-13 Explain three restrictions on the concept of constructive receipt.

I:3-14 When is income considered to be earned by an accrual-basis taxpayer?

I:3-15 a. Explain the difference between the treatment of prepaid income under the tax law and under financial accounting.
b. Why are the two treatments so different?
c. What problem does this treatment create for taxpayers?

I:3-16 Under what conditions is an accrual-basis taxpayer allowed to defer reporting amounts received in the advance of the delivery of goods?

I:3-17 Under what conditions is an accrual-basis taxpayer allowed to defer reporting advance payments received for services?

I:3-18 a. Is the interest received from government obligations taxable? Explain.
b. What impact does the fact that some bond interest is tax exempt have on interest rates?
c. Is an investor always better off buying tax-exempt bonds? Explain.

I:3-19 Corporations are taxed on the income they earn, and shareholders are taxed on the dividends they receive. What provisions in the tax law reduce this "double tax" burden?

I:3-20 Explain the relationship between dividends and earnings and profits.

I:3-21 On what basis did the Supreme Court in *Eisner v. Macomber* decide that stock dividends are nontaxable?

I:3-22 What is the significance of a constructive dividend?

I:3-23 Explain the importance of the distinction between alimony and a property settlement.

I:3-24 a. Are items of income not listed in Sec. 61 taxable? Explain.
b. Because there is no specific exclusion for unrealized income, why is it not taxable?
c. Can income be realized even when a cash-method taxpayer does not receive cash?
d. Does a cash basis taxpayer realize income upon the receipt of a note?

I:3-25 a. Briefly explain the tax benefit rule.
b. Is a taxpayer required to report the reimbursement of a medical expense by insurance as income if the reimbursement is received in the year following the year of the expenditure?

I:3-26 What opportunities are available for a taxpayer to defer the recognition of certain types of prepaid income? That is, what advice could you give someone who wishes to defer the reporting of prepaid income?

I:3-27 Taxpayers who deduct an expense one year but recover it the next year are required to include the recovered amount in gross income. The tax benefit rule provides relief if the original deduction did not result in any tax savings. Does this rule provide relief to taxpayers who are in a higher tax bracket in the year they recover the previously deducted expense?

I:3-28 George, a wealthy investor, is uncertain whether he should invest in taxable or tax-exempt bonds. What tax and nontax factors should he consider?

I:3-29 Do you agree or disagree with the following statement: A taxpayer should not have to report income when debt is forgiven because the taxpayer receives nothing. Explain.

I:3-30 Jack and June are retired and receive $10,000 of social security benefits and taxable pensions totaling $25,000. They have been offered $20,000 for an automobile that they restored after they retired. They did most of the restoration work themselves and the sale will result in a gain of $12,000. What tax issues should Jack and June consider?

ISSUE IDENTIFICATION QUESTIONS

I:3-31 State Construction Company is owned equally by Andy, Bill, and Charlie. Andy works in the corporation full-time, and Bill and Charlie work elsewhere. When Andy left his previous job to work for State, he signed a contract specifying that he would receive a salary of $50,000 per year. This year, Andy felt that the company could expand if it purchased more equipment, and he offered to delay receiving $20,000 of his salary so the funds could be used to purchase the equipment. Bill and Charlie agreed, and the equipment was purchased. It is expected that State will have enough cash to pay Andy by early March of next year. What tax issues should Andy consider?

I:3-32 Lisa and her daughter Jane are equal shareholders in Lisa's Flooring, Inc. Lisa founded the corporation and was the sole owner for over twenty years. The company is very successful and Lisa has accumulated a fairly large estate. When Jane turned age twenty-five last year, Lisa gave her half of the corporation's stock. The gift was properly reported on Lisa's gift tax return. Both Lisa and Jane now work full-time for the corporation. Lisa received a salary of $55,000 per year before Jane started working for the company. After Jane started working, Lisa reduced her salary to $15,000 and started paying Jane a salary of $50,000. Lisa indicates that she still makes most major decisions in the company, but she hopes that Jane will play a more important role as she becomes more familiar with the company. What tax issues should Lisa and the corporation consider?

I:3-33 Larry's Art Gallery sells oil paintings, lithographs, and bronzes to collectors and corporations. Customers often come to Larry looking for special pieces. In order to meet customer needs, Larry often accepts orders and then travels looking for the desired item, which he purchases and delivers to the customer. The pieces are expensive, and Larry requires customers to demonstrate their sincerity by providing deposits. If it turns out that the item costs more than expected, Larry contacts the buyer and asks for additional funds. If the item costs less than expected, Larry refunds the excess amount. Also, Larry sometimes returns amounts he received in advance because he is unable to find what the customer wants. What tax issues should Larry's Art Gallery consider?

PROBLEMS

I:3-34 *Noncash Compensation.* For each of the following items, indicate whether the individual taxpayer must include any amount in gross income.
a. Employees of Eastside Bookstore are given their birthdays off with pay.
b. Westside Hardware, Inc., gave each employee 10 shares of Westside stock worth $100 per share in lieu of a cash bonus.
c. Employees of Northside Manufacturing were allowed to take home the company's old computers when the company purchased new ones.

I:3-35 *Constructive Receipt.* Which of the following constitutes constructive receipt in the current year ended December 31?
a. A salary check received at 6:00 p.m. on December 31, after all the banks have closed.
b. A rent check received on December 30 by the manager of an apartment complex. The manager normally collects the rent for the owner. The owner was out of town.
c. A paycheck received on December 29 that was not honored by the bank because the employer's account did not have sufficient funds.
d. A check received on December 30. The check was postdated January 2 of the following year.
e. A check received on January 2. The check had been mailed on December 30.

I:3-36 *Cash and Accrual Methods.* Carmen opens a retail store. Her sales during the first year are $600,000, of which $30,000 has not been collected at year-end. Her purchases are $400,000. She still owes $20,000 to her suppliers, and at year-end she has $50,000 of inventory on hand. She incurred operating expenses of $160,000. At year-end she has not paid $15,000 of the expenses.
a. Compute her net income from the business assuming she elects the accrual method.
b. Compute her net income from the business assuming she elects the cash method.
c. Would paying the $15,000 she owes for operating expenses before year-end change her net income under accrual method of reporting? under the cash method?

I:3-37 *Series EE Bond Interest.* In 2011, Harry and Mary purchased Series EE bonds, and in 2015 redeemed the bonds, receiving $500 of interest and $1,500 of principal. Their income from other sources totaled $30,000. They paid $2,200 in tuition and fees for their dependent daughter. Their daughter is a qualified student at State University.
a. How much of the Series EE bond interest is excludable?
b. Assuming that the daughter received a $1,000 scholarship, how much of the interest is excludable? Ignore any tax credits that might be available.
c. Assuming the daughter received the $1,000 scholarship and that the parents' income from other sources is $121,250, how much of the interest is excludable?

I:3-38 *Alimony.* As a result of their divorce, Fred agrees to pay alimony to Tammy of $20,000 per year. The payments are to cease in the event of Fred's or Tammy's death or in the event of Tammy's remarriage. In addition, Tammy is to receive their residence, which cost them $100,000 but is worth $140,000.
a. Does the fact that Tammy receives the residence at the time of the divorce mean that there is a reduction in alimony, which will lead to Fred having to recapture an amount in the subsequent year?
b. How will the $20,000 payments be treated by Fred and Tammy?

c. Would recapture of the payments be necessary if payment ceased because of Tammy's remarriage?

d. What is Tammy's basis in the residence?

I:3-39   *Constructive Dividend.* Brad owns a successful corporation that has substantial earnings and profits. During the year, the following payments were made by the corporation:

a. Salary of $250,000 to Brad. Officers in other corporations performing similar services receive between $50,000 and $85,000.

b. Rent of $25,000 to Brad. The rent is paid in connection with an office building owned by Brad and used by the corporation. Similar buildings rent for about the same amount.

c. Salary of $5,000 to Brad's daughter, who worked for the company full-time during the summer and part-time during the rest of the year while she attended high school.

d. Alimony of $40,000 to Brad's former wife. Although Brad was personally obligated to make the payments, he used corporation funds to make the payments.

Discuss the likelihood of these payments being treated as constructive dividends. If a payment is deemed to be a constructive dividend, indicate how such a payment will be treated.

I:3-40   *Constructive Dividend.* Which of the following would likely be a constructive dividend?

a. An unreasonable salary paid to a shareholder.

b. An unreasonable salary paid to the daughter of a shareholder.

c. A sale of a corporation's asset to a shareholder at fair market value.

d. A payment by a corporation of a shareholder's debts.

e. A payment by a corporation of a shareholder's personal expenses.

I:3-41   *Prepaid Rent.* Stan rented an office building to Clay for $3,000 per month. On December 29, 2014, Stan received a deposit of $4,000 in addition to the first and last months' rent. Occupancy began on January 2, 2015. On July 15, 2015, Clay closed his business and filed for bankruptcy. Stan had collected rent for February, March, and April on the first of each month. Stan had received May rent on May 10, but collected no payments afterwards. Stan withheld $800 from the deposit because of damage to the property and $1,500 for unpaid rent. He refunded the balance of the deposit to Clay. What amount would Stan report as gross income for 2014? for 2015?

I:3-42   *Rental Income.* Ed owns Oak Knoll Apartments. During the year, Fred, a tenant, moved to another state. Fred paid Ed $1,000 to cancel the two-year lease he had signed. Ed subsequently rented the unit to Wayne. Wayne paid the first and last months' rents of $800 each and a security deposit of $500. Ed also owns a building that is used as a health club. The club has signed a fifteen-year lease at an annual rental of $17,000. The owner of the club requested that Ed install a swimming pool on the property. Ed declined to do so. The owner of the club finally constructed the pool himself at a cost of $15,000. What amount must Ed include in gross income?

I:3-43   *Gross Income.* Susan's salary is $44,000 and she received dividends of $600. She received a statement from SJ partnership indicating that her share of the partnership's income was $4,000. The partnership distributed $1,000 to her during the year and $600 after year-end. She won $2,000 in the state lottery and spent $50 on lottery tickets. Which amounts are taxable?

I:3-44   *Interest Income.* Holly inherited $10,000 of City of Atlanta bonds in February. In March, she received interest of $500, and in April she sold the bonds at a $200 gain. Holly redeemed Series EE U.S. savings bonds that she had purchased several years ago. The accumulated interest totaled $800. Holly received $300 of interest on bonds issued by the City of Quebec, Canada. What amount, if any, of gross income must Holly report?

I:3-45   *Annuity Income.* Tim retired during the current year at age 58. He purchased an annuity from American National Life Company for $40,000. The annuity pays Tim $500 per month for life.

a. Compute Tim's annual exclusion.

b. How much income will Tim report each year after reaching age 84?

I:3-46   *Pension Income.* Beth retires when she turns 65. She begins receiving a monthly pension of $300 from her employer's qualified retirement plan. While employed, Beth contributed $13,000 to the plan.
  a. Beth uses the simplified method to compute her exclusion. Why?
  b. Compute her monthly exclusion.
  c. How much gross income does she report in the first year if she receives 12 monthly checks?

I:3-47   *Social Security Benefits.* Dan and Diana file a joint return. Dan earned $31,000 during the year before losing his job. Diana received Social Security benefits of $5,000.
  a. Determine the taxable portion of the Social Security benefits.
  b. What is the taxable portion of the Social Security benefits if Dan earned $46,000?

I:3-48   *Social Security Benefits.* Lucia is a 69-year-old single individual who receives a taxable pension of $10,000 per year and Social Security benefits of $7,000. Lucia is considering the possibility of selling stock she has owned for years and using the funds to purchase a summer home. She will realize a gain of $20,000 when she sells the stock, which has been paying $1,000 of dividends each year. Lucia says her brother recommended that she sell half of the stock this year and half next year because selling all of the stock at once would affect the tax treatment of her Social Security benefits.
  a. Compute her AGI under the assumption she sells all of the stock now after receiving $1,000 dividends from the stock.
  b. Repeat the computation under the assumption she sells only half of the stock this year and also receives $1,000 dividends from the stock.

I:3-49   *Social Security Benefits.* Bob is a single individual and received a salary of $27,000 before he retired in October of this year. After he retired, he received Social Security benefits of $3,000 during the year.
  a. What amount, if any, of the Social Security benefits are taxable for the year?
  b. Would the answer be different if Bob also had $1,000 of tax exempt interest?
  c. What if he had had $10,000 of tax exempt interest?

I:3-50   *Adjusted Gross Income.* Amir, who is single, retired from his job this year. He received a salary of $25,000 for the portion of the year that he worked, tax-exempt interest of $3,000, and dividends from domestic corporations of $2,700. On September 1, he began receiving monthly pension payments of $1,000 and Social Security payments of $600. Assume an exclusion ratio of 40% for the pension. Amir owns a duplex that he rents to others. He received rent of $12,000 and incurred $17,000 of expenses related to the duplex. He continued to actively manage the property after he retired from his job. Compute Amir's adjusted gross income.

I:3-51   *Court Awards and Insurance Settlements.* What amount, if any, must be included in gross income by the following taxpayers?
  a. Ann received $2,000 from her insurance company when her automobile which cost $3,000 was stolen.
  b. Barry received $3,000 from his brother. Barry had initiated a lawsuit against his brother in an effort to recover $3,000 he had previously loaned to him. The brother paid Barry back before the case was tried, and Barry dropped the lawsuit.
  c. Carry, an accountant, sued a client in order to collect her fee for doing tax work. Would Carry's accounting method make any difference?
  d. Dave has incurred $6,000 of medical expenses so far this year. He paid $400 of the expenses himself. His insurance company paid $4,000 of the expenses. The hospital is suing Dave and the insurance company for the balance, $1,600.

I:3-52   *Claim of Right.* USA Corporation hired Jesse to install a computer system for the company and paid him $8,000 for the work. USA soon realized that there were problems with the system and asked Jesse to refund the payment. At the end of the year the dispute had not been resolved. Jesse is in the 25% tax bracket in the year he did the original work. During the next year, when he is in the 15% tax bracket, Jesse refunds the $8,000 to USA.
  a. Is the original payment taxable to Jesse when he receives it?
  b. What options are available to Jesse when he repays the $8,000?
  c. What option would have been available to Jesse if he had been asked to repay only $2,000?

I:3-53   *Tax Planning.* Bart and Kesha are in the 39.6% tax bracket. They are interested in reducing the taxes they pay each year. They are currently considering several alternatives. For each of the following alternatives, indicate how much tax, if any, they would save.

    a. Make a gift of bonds valued at $5,000 that yield $400 per year interest to their 24-year-old daughter, who has no other income.

    b. Sell the bonds from Part a rather than give them to their daughter, and buy tax-exempt bonds that pay 6%. Assume the bonds can be sold for an amount equal to their basis of $5,000.

    c. Give $1,000 cash to a charity. Assume they itemize deductions and ignore any phaseout of itemized deductions.

    d. Pay their daughter a salary of $10,000 for services rendered in their unincorporated business.

I:3-54   *Series EE Bond Interest and Kiddie Tax.* In 2015, Ken and Lynn paid $5,000 to purchase Series EE bonds in the name of their 11-year-old son. The son has no other income, and they are in the 28% tax bracket. The taxable interest during the first year will be $400 if an election is made to accrue the interest on an annual basis.

    a. Will the child owe any tax on the bond interest?

    b. Does the son need to file a tax return?

    c. What are the tax consequences in 2015 and subsequent years if annual gifts are made to their son?

COMPREHENSIVE PROBLEMS

I:3-55   Matt and Sandy reside in a community property state. Matt left home in April 2015 because of disputes with his wife, Sandy. Subsequently, Matt earned $15,000. Before leaving home in April, Matt earned $3,000. Sandy was unaware of Matt's whereabouts or his earnings after he left home. The $3,000 earned by Matt before he left home was spent on food, housing, and other items shared by Matt and Sandy. Matt and Sandy have one child, who lived with Sandy after the husband left home.

    a. Is any portion of Matt's earnings after he left home taxable to Sandy?

    b. What filing status is applicable to Sandy if she filed a return?

    c. How much income would Sandy be required to report if she filed?

    d. Is Sandy required to file?

I:3-56   During 2015, Gary earned $57,000 as an executive. Gary, who is single, supported his half sister, who lives in a nursing home. Gary received the following interest: $400 on City of Los Angeles bonds, $200 on a money market account, and $2,100 on a loan made to his brother.

    Gary spent one week serving on a jury and received $50.

    Gary received a refund of federal income taxes withheld during the prior year of $1,200 and a state income tax refund of $140. Gary had itemized deductions last year of $8,000 which included $1,000 of state income taxes.

    Gary received qualified dividends from Ace Corporation of $1,000 and from Tray Corporation of $1,400. Gary's itemized deductions equal $9,000, and withholding for federal income taxes is $8,000. Compute Gary's tax due or refund due for 2015.

TAX STRATEGY PROBLEMS

I:3-57   Kamal is starting a new business in 2015 which will operate as an S corporation. This means that income earned by the corporation will be reported by shareholders even if they do not receive distributions. Kamal has $130,000 of income from other sources, and itemized deductions totaling $15,000. He expects that the new business will produce $30,000 of income each year. He is considering giving his son Rashid 20% of the stock in the corporation. Rashid is age 24, and is Kamal's dependent. Rashid's only other income is $2,000 of interest. Neither Kamal nor Rashid will be employed by the corporation. Which alternative will produce a lower income tax liability—having all stock owned by Kamal or having Kamal own 80% of the stock and Rashid own 20%? Assume Kamal's filing status is head-of-household and Rashid is single. Ignore other taxes. How would the answer be different if Rashid were age 17? Ignore credits.

I:3-58 Assume that it is December 31, and that Jake is considering making a $1,000 charitable contribution. Jake currently is in the 39.6% tax bracket, but expects that his tax bracket will be 28% next year. How much more will the deduction for the contribution be worth if it is made today compared to next year? (Ignore any phase-outs of itemized deductions.)

TAX FORM/RETURN PREPARATION PROBLEM

I:3-59 Sally W. Emanual had the following dividends and interest during the current year:

Acorn Corporation bond interest		$ 700
City of Boston bonds interest		1,000
Camp Bank interest		1,250
Jet Corporation dividend (qualified)		1,300
North Mutual fund		
Capital gain distribution	100	
Ordinary dividend (qualified)	150	
Nontaxable distribution	200	450
Blue Corporation foreign dividend		250

Additional information pertaining to Sally Emanual includes

Salary	$30,000
Rent income	12,000
Expenses related to rent income	14,000
Pension benefits	7,000
Alimony paid to Sally	4,000

The taxable portion of the pension is $7,000. Sally actively participates in the rental activity. Other relevant information includes

Address: 430 Rumsey Place, West Falls, California 92699
Occupation: Credit manager
Social Security number: 123-45-6789
Marital status: Single

Complete Sally's Schedule B and page 1 of her Form 1040. Assume Schedule E has already been prepared.

CASE STUDY PROBLEMS

I:3-60 Jim and Linda are your tax clients. They were divorced two years ago, and the divorce decree stated that Jim was to make monthly payments to Linda. The court designated $300 per month as alimony and $200 per month as child support, or a total of $6,000 per year. Jim has been unemployed for much of the year and paid Linda $2,000 that he said was for child support. In addition, Jim transferred the title to a three-year-old automobile with a $4,000 FMV and basis of $7,000 in exchange for her promise not to pursue any claim she has against him for the unpaid child support and alimony. Does Linda have to report any alimony and is Jim entitled to an alimony deduction? Draft a memo for the file that discusses the tax consequences for both Jim and Linda.

I:3-61 John and Mary (your clients) have two small children and are looking for ways to help fund the children's college education. They have heard that Series EE bonds are a tax-favored way of saving and have requested your opinion on the tax consequences. They have asked your opinion regarding the relative advantages of purchasing Series EE bonds in their names versus the children's names. John and Mary have indicated that they expect to have a high level of income in the future and that their children may receive other income sources from future inheritances. Prepare a client memo making recommendations about the tax consequences of Series EE bond investments for John and Mary.

I:3-62 Lee and Jane have been your firm's clients for most of the twenty years they have been married. Recently Lee came to you and said that he and Jane are obtaining a divorce, and he wants you to help him with some of the tax and financial issues that may come up during the divorce. The next day, Jane called asking you for the same assistance. What ethical issues do you see in this case? What possible conflicts may arise if you represent both Lee and Jane?

TAX RESEARCH PROBLEM

I:3-63   William owns a building that is leased to Lester's Machine Shop. Lester requests that William rewire the building for new equipment Lester plans to purchase. The wiring would cost about $4,000, but would not increase the value of the building because its only use is in connection with the specialized equipment. Rather than lose Lester as a lessee, William agrees to forgo one month's rent of $1,000 if Lester will pay for the wiring. Because Lester does not want to move, he agrees. What amount, if any, must William include in gross income?

A partial list of research sources is

- Sec. 109
- Reg. Sec. 1.109-1
- *CIR v. Grace H. Cunningham*, 2 AFTR 2d 5511, 58-2 USTC ¶9771 (9th Cir., 1958)

CHAPTER

4

GROSS INCOME: EXCLUSIONS

LEARNING OBJECTIVES

After studying this chapter, you should be able to

1. ▶ Determine whether an item is income

2. ▶ Determine which major statutory exclusions are available to a taxpayer

3. ▶ Describe tax planning considerations for exclusions of gross income

4. ▶ Describe compliance and procedural considerations for exclusions of gross income

Chapter I:3 discussed items that must be included in gross income. This chapter considers items that are excluded from gross income. Under Sec. 61(a), all items of income are taxable unless specifically excluded. Taxpayers who wish to avoid being taxed have two basic alternatives. One approach is to establish that the item is not income. If an item is not income (e.g., if it is a return of capital), it is not subject to the income tax. The second approach is to establish that a specific exclusion applies to the item of income.

EXAMPLE I:4-1 ►

KEY POINT

Given the sweeping definition of *income,* it is generally difficult to establish that an item is not income.

Matt borrowed $10,000 from the bank. Although Matt received $10,000, it is not income because he is obligated to repay the amount borrowed. No specific statutory authority states that borrowed funds are excluded from taxation. Presumably, the fact that borrowed funds are not income is considered to be both fundamental and obvious. ◄

EXAMPLE I:4-2 ►

Sheila enrolled in State University. The university awarded her a $1,000 tuition scholarship because of her high admission test scores and grades. Section 117 excludes such scholarships from gross income. As a result, Sheila need not report the scholarship as income. ◄

The major source of exclusions are those specific items contained in the IRC. These exclusions have evolved over the years and were enacted by Congress for a variety of reasons, including social and economic objectives.

Another source of exclusions are referred to as *administrative exclusions.* Exclusions exist because specific provisions in the Internal Revenue Code allow them. While the IRS has no authority to create exclusions, the IRS does have the authority to interpret the meaning of the Code. A liberal interpretation of the statute by the IRS may result in a broad definition of what constitutes an exclusion, and such a broad definition may reasonably be termed an administrative exclusion. For example, Sec. 102 excludes gifts received from gross income. The IRS has followed the practice of excluding certain welfare benefits from gross income, presumably because such benefits may be viewed as gifts.[1] The IRS could take the position that welfare benefits are not gifts. That position would no doubt be challenged in the courts.

REAL-WORLD EXAMPLE

Grants made to Native Americans by the federal government under the Indian Financing Act of 1974 to expand Native American– owned economic enterprises are excludable from gross income. Rev. Rul. 77-77, 1977-1 C.B. 11.

The term *judicial exclusions* should be considered in the same vein. Although the courts cannot create exclusions, they can interpret the statute and decide whether a particular item is covered by a statutory exclusion.

ITEMS THAT ARE NOT INCOME

OBJECTIVE 1

Determine whether an item is income

As noted above, some items are not income and, therefore, are not subject to the income tax. In addition to amounts obtained by a loan (discussed above), four other items are not considered income:

► Unrealized income
► Self-help income
► Rental value of personal-use property
► Gross selling price of property (as opposed to the profit or gain earned on the sale)

TYPICAL MISCONCEPTION

It is sometimes erroneously assumed that severance pay, embezzlement proceeds, gambling winnings, hobby income, prizes, rewards, and tips are not taxable.

UNREALIZED INCOME

Income that is not realized is not subject to income taxation. Thus, owners of appreciated property are not taxed on their unrealized gains.

This issue of the taxability of unrealized income was addressed over 90 years ago in *Eisner v. Macomber,* where the Supreme Court held that a stock dividend cannot be taxed

---

[1] For example, see Rev. Rul. 57-102, 1957-1 C.B. 26, which excludes from gross income public assistance payments to blind persons.

because the taxpayer had "received nothing that answers the definition of income within the meaning of the Sixteenth Amendment."[2] An ordinary stock dividend does not alter the existing proportionate ownership interest of any stockholder, nor does it increase the value of the individual's holdings. In effect, the Court concluded that realization must occur before income is recognized. Although narrowed by subsequent legislation and litigation, ordinary stock dividends continue to be excluded from gross income even today. Perhaps more important, *Eisner v. Macomber* established realization as a criterion for the recognition of income.

SELF-HELP INCOME

Although self-help income is considered as income by economists, it is not recognized as income by the IRS or by the courts. Taxpayers commonly benefit from activities such as painting their own homes or repairing their own automobiles. If a taxpayer hires someone else to do the work, the taxpayer has to earn income, pay tax on the income, and use the after-tax income to pay for the work. In either case, the taxpayer receives the same economic benefit, but the economic benefit derived from self-help is not included in the taxpayer's gross income.

This situation should be contrasted with taxable exchanges of services. A mechanic might agree to repair a painter's automobile in exchange for the painter's promise to paint the mechanic's home. In this instance, when the parties exchange services, each party realizes income equal to the value of the services received.

 STOP & THINK

Question: The discussion of self-help income refers to an exchange of services between two individuals, such as a painter and a mechanic. How can a taxable barter transaction be distinguished from an act of friendship which is repaid?

Solution: When one person helps another without any promise of repayment, the act of kindness does not represent an exchange and is not taxable. Friends help one another from time to time without contractual reciprocity. As a result, such acts are not taxable. The distinction between a taxable barter exchange and acts of friendship is not always easy to make.

RENTAL VALUE OF PERSONAL-USE PROPERTY

Taxpayers are not taxed on the rental value of personally owned property. For example, taxpayers who own their own home receive the economic benefit of occupancy without being taxed on the rental value of the property. It would be very difficult to keep records and value benefits obtained from self-help and the personal use of property. For that reason, no significant effort has ever been made to tax such benefits.[3]

SELLING PRICE OF PROPERTY

If property is sold at a gain, the gain and not the entire sales price is taxable. Because the basic principle is almost universally accepted, the Supreme Court has never had to rule directly on whether the entire sale proceeds could be taxed. The IRS and the courts seemed to accept the basic principle even before the rule became part of the statute.[4] The primary reason for this principle (often referred to as the "recovery of capital" principle) is that a portion of the selling price represents a return of capital to the seller.

---

[2] 3 AFTR 3020, 1 USTC ¶32 (USSC, 1920).

[3] In 1928, the government tried unsuccessfully to tax the value of produce grown and consumed by a farmer (*Homer P. Morris*, 9 B.T.A. 1273 (1928)). The court stated, "To include the value of such products [would be to] in effect include in income something which Congress did not intend should be so regarded." The court did not explain how or why it reached this conclusion. In 1957, the IRS successfully disallowed the deduction of expenses incurred in raising such produce (*Robert L. Nowland v. CIR*, 51 AFTR 423, 57-1 USTC ¶9684 (4th Cir., 1957)).

[4] Section 202(a) of the Revenue Act of 1924 is the predecessor of current Sec. 1001(a), which states that only the gain portion of the sale proceeds is included in gross income. S. Rept. No. 398, 68th Cong., 1st Sess., p. 10 (1924) states that Sec. 202(a) sets forth general rules to be used in the computation of gain or loss. The Senate report further states that the provision "merely embodies in the law the present construction by the Department and the courts of the existing law."

MAJOR STATUTORY EXCLUSIONS

OBJECTIVE 2

Examine the major statutory exclusions that are available to taxpayers

While Congress has created statutory exclusions for a variety of reasons, most exclusions have been enacted for reasons of social policy or reasons of incentive. The concept of social policy, that is, a concept of social generosity or benevolence, has prompted the government to exclude items such as:

▶ Gifts and inheritances (Sec. 102)

▶ Life insurance proceeds (Sec. 101)

▶ Public assistance payments

▶ Qualified adoption expenses (Sec. 137)

▶ Payments for personal physical sickness and injury (Sec. 104)

▶ Discharge of indebtedness during bankruptcy or insolvency (Sec. 108)

▶ Gain on sale of personal residence (Sec. 121)

▶ Partial exclusions for Social Security benefits (Sec. 86)

Other exclusions may be explained in terms of economic incentive, that is, the government's desire to encourage or reward a particular type of behavior.

▶ Awards for meritorious achievement (Sec. 74(b))

▶ Various employee fringe benefits (Secs. 79, 105, 106, 124, 125, 129, 132)

▶ Partial exclusion for scholarships (Sec. 117)

▶ Foreign-earned income (Sec. 911)

▶ Interest on state and local government obligations (Sec. 103)

Other reasons may exist for some of the exclusions listed above. For example, one reason income from the discharge of indebtedness during bankruptcy is excluded from gross income is the fact that such taxpayers would be unlikely to have the resources needed to pay the tax. (See Chapter I:3 for a discussion of tax-exempt interest and Social Security benefits, and Chapter I:12 for the treatment of gain on the sale of a personal residence.)

ADDITIONAL COMMENT

Tax expenditure estimates measure the decreases in individual and corporate income tax liabilities that result from provisions in income tax laws and regulations that provide economic incentives or tax relief to particular kinds of taxpayers.

GIFTS AND INHERITANCES

Congress has excluded the value of gifts and inheritances received from gross income since the inception of the income tax in 1913. Section 102 excludes the value of property received during the life of the donor (*inter vivos* **gifts**) and transfers at death (**testamentary transfers**—bequests, devises, and inheritances).[5] The recipient of such property is taxed on the income produced by the property after the transfer.[6] It should be noted that a donor, under the assignment of income doctrine, cannot avoid the income tax by making a gift of income. To avoid paying tax on income, a donor must make a gift of the underlying property.

TYPICAL MISCONCEPTION

Some people still believe that gifts above the gift exclusion amount of $14,000 are taxable to the donees. They are not since the Code specifically exempts all gifts, regardless of the amount. The donor may, however, depending on the circumstances, pay a gift tax.

EXAMPLE I:4-3 ▶ Stan owns stock in a corporation and orders the corporation to pay dividends on the stock to his daughter. Even though his daughter receives the dividends, Stan must include the dividends in his gross income. Stan could avoid being taxed on future dividends by giving the stock to his daughter. ◀

---

[5] Although excluded from gross income, such transfers may be subject to the gift tax or the estate tax which are imposed on the transferor.
[6] Reg. Sec. 1.102-1(b).

It is often difficult to distinguish gifts, which are not included in the recipient's gross income, from other transfers, which are taxable. Gifts sometimes closely resemble prizes and awards.[7]

EXAMPLE I:4-4 ▶ Tina received a free automobile for being the ten millionth paying guest at an amusement park. The automobile is not considered a gift but a prize and is taxable to Tina. ◀

Also, some payments made to employees by employers may resemble gifts.

EXAMPLE I:4-5 ▶ At Christmas, Red Corporation paid $500 cash to each employee who had been with the company for more than five years. These payments are not considered gifts for tax purposes and are taxable to the employees. ◀

REAL-WORLD EXAMPLE
Amounts received by a dealer from players in the operation of a gambling casino were not excludable as gifts even though impulsive generosity or superstition may be the dominant motive. The amounts were similar to tips, which are taxable. *Louis R. Tomburello,* 86 T.C. 540 (1986).

Whether a transfer is a gift depends on the intent of the donor. Gifts are motivated by love, affection, kindness, sympathy, generosity, admiration, or similar emotions. In the two preceding examples, the transfers were made for business motives and not necessarily for donative reasons. Thus, the automobile is a taxable prize, and the amounts paid to employees represent taxable awards for services rendered, but see the discussion of Sec. 274 later in this chapter.

Transfers of money or property between family members frequently create classification problems. For example, assume a father, who owns a business, hires his 10-year-old son to work in the business. Is the payment to the son a salary (and, therefore, deductible by the business) or is it really just a gift from the father to the son? The answer depends on the fair market value of the services performed by the son. If the son actually performs services that are commensurate with the salary paid, the payment may properly be classified as a salary. On the other hand, if the son is paid an amount that exceeds the value of the services, the excess amount will be treated as a gift.

LIFE INSURANCE PROCEEDS

Life insurance proceeds paid to a beneficiary because of the insured person's death are not taxable.[8] The exclusion applies whether the proceeds are paid in a lump sum or in installments. Amounts received in excess of the face amount of the policy usually are taxable as interest.

EXAMPLE I:4-6 ▶ Buddy is the beneficiary of a $100,000 insurance policy on his mother's life. Upon her death, he elects to receive $13,000 per year for ten years instead of the lump sum. He receives $10,000 per year tax-free ($100,000 ÷ 10), but the remaining $3,000 per year is taxable as interest. ◀

EXAMPLE I:4-7 ▶ Assume the same facts as in Example I:4-6, except that Buddy elects to receive the full $100,000 face amount upon his mother's death. None of the $100,000 is taxable. ◀

The exclusion exists because life insurance benefits closely resemble inheritances, which are not taxable.

There is one exception that may result in a portion of the face amount of a life insurance policy being included in gross income.[9] The life insurance exclusion generally is not available if the insurance policy is obtained by the beneficiary in exchange for valuable consideration from a person other than the insurance company. For example, an individual may purchase an existing life insurance policy for cash from another individual. In this situation, the exclusion for death benefits is limited to the consideration paid plus the premiums or other sums subsequently paid by the buyer.

---

[7] Recall that under Sec. 74 (discussed in Chapter I:3) most prizes and awards are taxable.

[8] Sec. 101(a).
[9] Sec. 101(a)(2).

EXAMPLE I:4-8 ▶

The proceeds of a life insurance policy payable to named beneficiaries can be excluded from the federal estate tax when the decedent does not possess any incidents of ownership. This provision and the exclusion from gross income of life insurance proceeds underscore the favored position of life insurance.

Kwame is the owner and beneficiary of a $100,000 policy on the life of his father. Kwame sells the policy to his brother Anwar for $10,000. Anwar subsequently pays premiums of $12,000. Upon his father's death, Anwar must include $78,000 [$100,000 − ($10,000 + $12,000)] in gross income. However, if Kwame gave the policy to his brother, all of the proceeds would be excluded from gross income because the gift of the policy does not constitute valuable consideration. ◀

The proceeds are excludable under the general exclusion for life insurance proceeds if the beneficiary's basis is found by reference to the transferor's basis (as would be true in the case of a gift), or if the policy is transferred to the insured, the insured's partner, a partnership that includes the insured, or a corporation in which the insured is a shareholder or officer.

Surrender or Sale of Policy. The exclusion for life insurance is available for amounts payable by reason of the death of the insured. In general, if a life policy is sold or surrendered for a lump sum before the death of the insured, the amount received is taxable to the extent that the amount received exceeds the net premiums paid.[10] On the other hand, no loss is recognized if a life insurance policy is surrendered before maturity and premiums paid exceed the cash surrender value.[11]

"Accelerated death benefits" may be excluded from gross income. Accelerated death benefits include payments made to a terminally ill person and periodic payments made to a chronically ill person. A person is terminally ill if a physician certifies that he is reasonably likely to die within 24 months. A person is chronically ill if he has a disability requiring long-term care (e.g., nursing home care). In general, the exclusion for periodic payments made to a chronically ill person is limited to the greater of $330 per day (in 2014 and 2015), or the actual cost of such care. The exclusion covers amounts received from the insurance provider or from a "viatical settlement provider" (i.e., person in the business of providing accelerated death benefits).

EXAMPLE I:4-9 ▶

Harry has been diagnosed with advanced AIDS and is expected to live less than a year. Harry is covered by a life insurance policy with a $100,000 face amount. The insurance company offers terminally ill individuals the option of receiving 75% of the policy face amount. If Harry accepts the settlement, the amount he receives is excludable from gross income because he is terminally ill. ◀

EXAMPLE I:4-10 ▶

Mary suffered a severe stroke and has been admitted to a nursing home where she is expected to remain for the rest of her life. She is certified by a licensed health care practitioner as being a "chronically ill individual." Her nursing home expenses amount to $200 per day. Mary has elected to receive $225 per day from a $1,000,000 face amount life insurance policy as accelerated death benefits. Because she is a chronically ill individual, Mary may exclude the full amount she receives as it is less than the daily limitation of $330 established by law. ◀

Dividends on Life Insurance and Endowment Policies. Dividends on life insurance and endowment policies are normally not taxable because they are considered to be a partial return of premiums paid. The dividends are taxable to the extent that the total dividends received exceed the total premiums paid. Also, if dividends are left with the insurance company and earn interest, the interest is taxable.

---

[10] Sec. 72(e)(2). In some instances where distributions are made before the recipient reaches age 59½, a 10% penalty applies (see Sec. 72(q)).
[11] *London Shoe Co. v. CIR*, 16 AFTR 1398, 35-2 USTC ¶9664 (2nd Cir., 1935).

AWARDS FOR MERITORIOUS ACHIEVEMENT

ADDITIONAL COMMENT

Notice that to exclude awards for meritorious achievement, the award must not come into the possession of the taxpayer.

As noted in Chapter I:3, prizes and awards generally are taxable. An exception is applicable to awards and prizes made for religious, charitable, scientific, educational, artistic, literary, or civic achievement if the recipient:

▶ Was selected without action on his or her part to enter the contest or the proceeding,

▶ Does not have to perform substantial future services as a condition to receiving the prize or award, and

▶ Designates that the payor is to pay the amount of the award to either a government unit or a charitable organization.[12]

The recipient of such an award normally would owe no tax if he or she collected the proceeds and then contributed the proceeds to a charity because the gift would qualify as a deductible charitable contribution. However, the exclusion changes AGI and thereby affects other computations. Also, this rule is beneficial in situations where the taxpayer could not deduct the full amount of the award because of the limitation on the charitable contribution deduction (generally 50% of AGI; see Chapter I:7) or in the case of a small award to a taxpayer who does not itemize.

SCHOLARSHIPS AND FELLOWSHIPS

ADDITIONAL COMMENT

Athletic scholarships for fees, books, and supplies awarded by a university to students who are expected, but not required, to participate in a particular sport can be excludable.

KEY POINT

The exclusion for scholarships does not include amounts received for room, board, and laundry.

Subject to certain limitations, scholarships are excluded from gross income.[13] A scholarship is an amount paid or allowed to a student, whether an undergraduate or graduate, to aid degree-seeking individuals.

The exclusion for scholarships is limited to the amount of the scholarship used for *qualified tuition and related expenses*. Qualified tuition and related expenses typically include tuition and fees, books, supplies, and equipment required for courses of instruction at an educational organization. The value of services and accommodations supplied such as room, board, and laundry are not excluded. The exclusion for scholarships does not extend to salary paid for services even if all candidates for a particular degree are required to perform the services.[14]

EXAMPLE I:4-11 ▶ Becky is awarded a $5,000 per year scholarship by State University. Becky spends $3,000 of the scholarship for tuition, books, and supplies, and $2,000 for room and board. In addition, Becky works part-time on campus and earns $4,000, which covers the rest of her room and board and other expenses. Becky is taxed on the $2,000 of the scholarship spent for room and board and $4,000 of salary earned from her part-time job. ◄

DISTRIBUTIONS FROM QUALIFIED TUITION PROGRAMS

Congress established *qualified tuition plans*, or so-called Section 529 plans, to assist students with higher education costs. Amounts contributed to a qualified tuition plan (QTP) on behalf of a designated beneficiary grow tax-free. Amounts may be withdrawn tax-free by the beneficiary as long as the amounts are used for qualified higher education expenses

---

[12] Sec. 74.
[13] Sec. 117.
[14] Scholarships may need to be reviewed to determine whether the amount constitutes compensation. A "scholarship" awarded to the winner of a televised beauty pageant by a profit-making corporation was ruled to be compensation for performing subsequent services for the corporation (Rev. Rul. 68-20, 1968-1 C.B. 55). An employer-paid "scholarship" was held to be compensation in a situation where the employee was on leave and was required to return to work after finishing the degree (*Richard E. Johnson v. Bingler*, 23 AFTR 2d 69-1212, 69-1 USTC ¶9348 (USSC, 1969)). However, in Ltr. Rul. 9526020 (September 10, 1995) the IRS ruled that grants to law students are not taxable even if they are conditioned upon the students agreeing to practice upon graduation in public, nonprofit, or other low paying sectors.

including tuition, books, fees, supplies, equipment, and room and board.[15] Wealthy individuals may fund QTPs as there is no income limitation. Although parents and grandparents are the most frequent donors, anyone can fund a QTP.

A QTP must be maintained either by a state government or by a private university. Plans may acquire mutual funds and similar investments. State plans (but not private university plans) may provide for the purchase of credit for future tuition in lieu of investments.

Contributions to a QTP may be distributed tax-free. The portion of a distribution that is treated as a contribution is determined under annuity rules discussed in Chapter I:3. The income portion of a QTP distribution may be excluded to the extent it is used for qualified higher education expenses. The amount of the QTP exclusion is reduced by American Opportunity and lifetime learning tax credits claimed by the beneficiary.[16] Any additional distributed income is included to the beneficiary's gross income and is subject to a 10% penalty.

Donors can change the designated beneficiary to another member of the original beneficiary's family without tax consequences. Family members include relatives, as defined for dependency exemption purposes, plus first cousins.

EXAMPLE I:4-12 ▶ For each of his two young children, David contributes $10,000 to a state established Qualified Tuition Program. There is no gift tax as the amounts are less than the $14,000 annual per donee gift tax exclusion. Current and future qualified contributions grow tax-free. Future distributions of income are tax exempt as long as the amounts do not exceed the beneficiary's qualified higher education expenses. Excess distributions are taxable and subject to a 10% penalty. ◀

PAYMENTS FOR INJURY AND SICKNESS

Sec. 104(a) excludes from gross income the "amount of any damages (other than punitive damages) . . . received . . . on account of personal physical injuries or physical sickness." Thus, for example, a taxpayer may exclude an insurance settlement for physical injury that resulted from an automobile accident. Section 104(a) does not cover amounts awarded for nonphysical injuries (such as a damaged reputation or libel) except that taxpayers may exclude reimbursements for medical expenses related to nonphysical injuries.

An attempt to challenge the constitutionality of this provision in the Court of Appeals of the District of Columbia was successful initially, but the court subsequently reversed itself.[17]

EXAMPLE I:4-13 ▶ After she was denied a promotion, Jane sued her employer claiming sex discrimination. She was awarded $5,000 to cover the medical bills she incurred because of the related emotional distress, $20,000 to punish her employer for discrimination, and $10,000 to compensate her for lost wages. The $5,000 awarded to cover medical bills is excluded from gross income, but not the amounts awarded as punitive damages or lost wages. ◀

The exclusion under Sec. 104(a) applies to damages received because of emotional distress in only two situations: (1) when the payments are for medical expenses related to the emotional distress, and (2) when the payments are for emotional distress *attributable* to a physical injury (including physical injury suffered by another person).

---

[15] Room and board is a qualified higher education expense only if the beneficiary is at least a half-time student.

[16] Sec. 529(c)(3)(B)(v). These credits are discussed in Chapter I:14 of this textbook.

[17] *Marrita Murphy v. CIR*, 100 AFTR2d 2007-5075, 2007-2 USTC ¶50,531, (DC Cir., 2007) reversing *Marrita Murphy v. CIR*, 98 AFTR2d 2006-6088, 2006-2 USTC ¶50,476, (DC Cir., 2006).

Sometimes, victims are awarded amounts that are intended to punish the guilty party. These so-called punitive damages are taxable even when they are awarded for physical injuries.

EXAMPLE I:4-14 ▶ Mary was injured in an automobile accident caused by another driver. Mary's daughter, Sarah, was in the automobile, but she was not physically injured. The other driver's insurance company was required by a court to pay Mary $10,000 to cover medical bills relating to her injuries, $5,000 to compensate her for emotional distress caused by the injuries, and $15,000 of punitive damages. Sarah was paid $3,000 to compensate her for distress caused by her witnessing her mother's injuries. Only the $15,000 of punitive damages are taxable to Mary as the other amounts are compensatory damages related to her physical injuries. Sarah's damage award of $3,000 is also excludable. ◄

Sec. 104(a)(3) excludes from gross income amounts collected under an accident and health insurance policy purchased by the taxpayer, even if the benefits are a substitute for lost income. In addition, Sec. 101 specifies that benefits received under a qualified long-term care insurance contract may be excluded from gross income, but limits the exclusion to the greater of $330 per day (in both 2014 and 2015) or the actual cost of such care. Such policies pay for nursing home and other types of long-term care. If the benefits exceed the actual cost of such care but are less than $330 per day, no portion of the benefits is taxable.

EXAMPLE I:4-15 ▶ Chuck purchased a disability income policy from an insurance company. Chuck subsequently suffered a heart attack. Under the terms of the policy, Chuck received $2,500 per month for the five months he was unable to work. The amounts received are not taxable, even though the payments are a substitute for the wages lost due to the illness. ◄

This exclusion is not applicable if the accident and health benefits are provided by the taxpayer's employer.[18]

EXAMPLE I:4-16 ▶ Assume the same facts as in Example I:4-15 except that Chuck's employer paid the premiums on the policy. The amounts received by Chuck are taxable. ◄

EXAMPLE I:4-17 ▶ Ruth suffered a serious stroke and was admitted to a nursing home. During the year, she was in a nursing home for 140 days. Nursing home charges, physician fees, and other related expenses totaled $38,000.

Under her long-term care insurance contract, Ruth received reimbursements of $40,000. The reimbursements are not includible in Ruth's gross income because the amounts are less than the allowed exclusion amount of $46,200 (140 days × $330). This exclusion applies even though she was reimbursed more than her actual costs. Alternatively, if the reimbursements had been $50,200, she would be required to report $4,000 ($50,200 − $46,200) as gross income. ◄

If the cost of the coverage is shared by the employer and the taxpayer, a portion of the benefits is taxable. For example, if the employer paid one-half of the premiums, one-half of the benefits would be taxable. The principal reason for the different tax treatment is that employer-paid coverage represents a tax-free employee fringe benefit, whereas employee-paid premiums are from after-tax dollars.

---

[18] A limited credit is available to taxpayers who receive such benefits. See Chapter I:14 for a discussion of the credit for the elderly and disabled.

In the case of an award intended to reimburse the taxpayer for medical expenses, it follows that the taxpayer cannot deduct the reimbursed medical expenses.[19] If the award exceeds the actual expense, it is not taxable except in the case of employer-financed accident and health insurance and in the case of excess long-term care discussed above.[20]

State worker's compensation laws establish fixed amounts to be paid to employees suffering specific job-related injuries. Section 104(a)(1) specifically excludes worker's compensation from gross income, even though the payments are intended, in part, to reimburse injured workers for loss of future income and even if the injuries are nonphysical.

EMPLOYEE FRINGE BENEFITS

In general, employee compensation is taxable regardless of the form it takes. Nevertheless, the tax law encourages certain types of fringe benefits by allowing an employer to deduct the cost of the benefit, by permitting the employee to exclude the benefit from gross income, or by permitting both the employer deduction and an employee exclusion. Employee fringe benefits subject to special rules include employee insurance, Sec. 132 benefits, meals and lodging, dependent care, and cafeteria plans. These fringe benefits are discussed below.

Employer-Paid Insurance. Employers commonly provide group insurance coverage for employees. In general, employers may deduct the premiums paid for life, health, accident, and disability insurance. Normally an employee does not have to include in gross income premiums paid on his or her behalf for health, accident, and disability insurance. Special rules applicable to life insurance premiums are discussed below.

Benefits received from medical, health, and group term life insurance coverage generally are excluded from an employee's gross income. Benefits received from a disability policy are normally taxable, but may qualify for the credit for the elderly and disabled (see Chapter I:14). The tax treatments of employer-financed and taxpayer-financed insurance coverage are compared in Topic Review I:4-1.

The rules relating to accident and health insurance are more generous than those for some other types of benefits. Under Sec. 106, employers can deduct insurance premiums and employees need not include the premiums in gross income.

STOP & THINK

Question: How does the 2010 *Affordable Care Act* impact employer provided health insurance?

Answer: The law made a number of changes in the tax rules affecting employee health insurance. Collectively, these rules penalize individuals who do not obtain medical insurance coverage and also penalize larger employers who fail to provide adequate employee health benefits. The act creates several new taxes and changes others.

The act mandates that employers report the cost of health insurance benefits provided to employees on employee W-2's. The amount of the benefit is *not* included in employee gross income, but the reporting serves as a basis for imposing a variety of penalties that are part of the law. As noted elsewhere, the law increased the threshold for itemizing medical expense from 7.5% of AGI to 10% and limits the amount that can be contributed to a flexible spending plan for health care ($2,550 in 2015). A credit will help small employers with the cost of providing employees with health insurance coverage.

Industry specific taxes apply to tanning salons, medical device manufacturers, insurance companies, and pharmaceutical companies. Other taxes apply to high income individuals, individuals who do not have health coverage, and large employers who do not provide employee coverage.[21]

These and a number of other taxes will help subsidize health insurance costs for lower and middle income individuals.

[19] See Chapter I:3 for a discussion of the reimbursement of an expense deducted in a preceding year.
[20] Sec. 105(a).
[21] Beginning in 2013, a payroll tax of 0.9% applies to earned income over $200,000 ($250,000 for married couples). These high income taxpayers also face a 3.8% tax on investment income, such as interest, capital gains and dividends. Beginning in 2014, individuals who do not have health insurance coverage will be subject to a tax that will grow to the greater of $695 or 2% of gross income in 2016. Employers with 50 or more employees (100 or more in 2015) who do not provide adequate health insurance coverage must pay a tax of $2,080 (in 2015) for each employee over 30.

TOPIC REVIEW I:4-1

Treatment of Insurance

PREMIUMS PAID BY

	EMPLOYER	*EMPLOYEE*
Medical and health Premiums	Premiums not included in employee's gross income. Premiums deductible by employer.	Premiums deductible as medical expense subject to 10% of AGI limitation (threshold is 7.5% of AGI through 2016 for taxpayers age 65 and older).
Benefits	Excluded from employee's gross income except when benefits exceed actual expenses.	Excluded from gross income.
Disability Premiums	Premiums not included in employee's gross income. Premiums deductible by employer.	Not deductible.
Benefits	Included in employee's gross income. May qualify for credit for elderly and disabled.	Excluded from gross income.
Life insurance Premiums	Included in employee's gross income (except for limited exclusion applicable to group term life insurance). Premiums deductible by employer (assuming employer is not the beneficiary).	Not deductible.
Benefits	Excluded from gross income.	Excluded from gross income.

ADDITIONAL COMMENT

The tax expenditure estimate associated with the exclusion of contributions by employers for medical insurance premiums and medical care for the year 2012 is $117 billion. This is the largest tax expenditure in the U.S. budget.

KEY POINT

The nondiscrimination requirements for self-insured accident and health plans are designed to ensure that such plans do not discriminate against rank-and-file workers.

Some employers provide self-insured accident and health plans to employees. Under such plans the employer pays employee medical expenses directly. Such plans are called Health Reimbursement Arrangements and often supplement health insurance.

Both insured and self-insured plans are subject to nondiscrimination requirements. *Discrimination* is defined in terms of an eligibility test (whether a sufficient number of non-highly compensated employees are covered) and benefits (whether non-highly compensated employees receive benefits comparable to highly compensated employees). Highly compensated employees include the five highest-paid officers, greater-than-10% shareholders, and highest-paid 25% of other employees. If a plan discriminates in favor of highly compensated employees, these employees must include in gross income any medical reimbursements they receive that are not available to other employees.

In general, life insurance premiums paid by an employer on an employee's behalf are deductible by the employer and are includable in the employee's gross income.[22] A limited exception is applicable to group term life insurance coverage. In general, premiums attributable to the first $50,000 of group term life insurance coverage may be excluded from an employee's gross income.[23] To qualify group term life insurance premiums for the exclusion, broad coverage of employees is required. Though somewhat different, the rules may be compared to those associated with self-insurance coverage.[24] The amount of coverage can vary between employees as long as the coverage bears a uniform relationship to each employee's compensation.

---

[22] If the employer is the beneficiary of the policy, the employee receives no economic benefit and, as a result, need not include the premiums in gross income. Such premium payments are not deductible by the employer. Subsequent benefits are not included in the employer's gross income.

[23] Sec. 79(a).

[24] For example, the rules refer to "key employees" as opposed to highly compensated employees. The term *key employee* is somewhat narrower in scope.

▼ TABLE I:4-1

Uniform One-Month Group Term Premiums for $1,000 of Life Insurance Coverage

Employee's age	Premiums
Under 25	$0.05
25 to 29	.06
30 to 34	.08
35 to 39	.09
40 to 44	.10
45 to 49	.15
50 to 54	.23
55 to 59	.43
60 to 64	.66
65 to 69	1.27
70 and above	2.06

EXAMPLE I:4-18 ▶

TYPICAL MISCONCEPTION

Many individuals erroneously believe that all life insurance coverage provided by employers is exempt from income.

Data Corporation provides group term life insurance coverage for each full-time employee. The coverage is equal to one year's compensation. The arrangement constitutes a qualified group term life insurance plan. ◀

In the case of coverage that exceeds $50,000, employees must include in gross income the amount established by the Regulations. (See Table I:4-1.)

EXAMPLE I:4-19 ▶

USA Corporation provides Joy, age 61, with $150,000 of group term life insurance coverage. Joy must include in gross income $792, an amount determined by reference to Table I:4-1 [($100,000/$1,000 × $.66) × 12 = $792]. ◀

The amount that must otherwise be included in an employee's gross income is reduced by any premiums paid by the employee.

If group term life insurance coverage discriminates in favor of key employees, each key employee must include in gross income the greater of the premiums paid on his or her behalf or the amount determined based on Table I:4-1 without any exclusion for the first $50,000 of coverage.

? STOP & THINK

Question: Does the fact that employers can provide health insurance and group term life insurance to employees on a tax-favored basis mean that such benefits should be provided to all employees? Explain.

Solution: No. Providing such benefits to all employees may be inefficient. Some employees have other health coverage (e.g., coverage through a spouse's employer). Employees with no dependents may not want life insurance coverage. As a result, employers who provide all employees with such benefits may be spending money on coverage that some employees neither want nor need. A cafeteria plan, discussed later in this chapter, is often a more efficient option. Such plans permit employees to choose either cash or from a menu of tax-favored benefits. This does have significant social and economic implications. As the cost of health insurance increases, more employees, especially those with lower incomes, choose cash salary over health insurance coverage. This contributes to the growing number of individuals who do not have health insurance. Once the provisions of the Affordable Care Act become effective, larger employers face penalties if employees are not covered by health insurance.

TOPIC REVIEW I:4-2

Summary of Sec. 132 Fringe Benefits

SECTION	BENEFIT	MAY BE MADE AVAILABLE TO	COMMENTS
132(b)	No-additional-cost (e.g., telephone, unused hotel rooms for hotel employees, unused airline seats for airline employees)	Employees, spouses, dependents, and retirees	The services must be of the same types that are sold to customers and in the line of business in which the employee works. Discrimination is prohibited.
132(c)	Qualified employee discounts	Employees, spouses, dependents, and retirees	Discounts on services limited to 20%. Discounts on merchandise are limited to the employer's gross profit percentage. No discount is permitted on real estate, stock, or other investment type property. Discrimination is prohibited.
132(d)	Working condition (e.g., free magazines, out-placement, and memberships)	Employees	Discrimination is permitted. Special rules apply to tuition reductions for employees of educational institutions and to an auto salesperson's demonstrator.
132(e)	De minimis (e.g., free coffee, holiday turkeys, or use of company eating facilities)	Employees	Eating facilities must be made available on a nondiscriminatory basis.
132(f)	Qualified transportation fringes (e.g., transit passes, tokens, and parking)	Employees	Limited exclusion for parking and transportation fringes. Discrimination is permitted.
132(j)(4)	Recreation and athletic facilities (e.g., gyms, pools, saunas, and tennis courts)	Employees, spouses, dependents, and retirees	If discrimination is present, employer loses deduction.
132(j)(8)	Educational assistance	Employees and former employees	Discrimination is prohibited. Now only covers job-related education and training.

ADDITIONAL COMMENT

The nondiscrimination rules do not apply to working condition fringe benefits. For example, if a corporation makes bodyguards available only to key officers, the working condition fringe benefit exclusion would still apply.

Section 132 Fringe Benefits. It has become common for employers to provide employees with such diverse benefits as free parking, membership in professional organizations, and small discounts on products sold by the employer. Section 132 was added to the IRC in 1984 to clarify whether certain types of benefits are taxable. Section 132 lists six types of fringe benefits that may be excluded from an employee's gross income (see Topic Review I:4-2). Any costs incurred by an employer to provide the specified benefits are deductible under Sec. 162 if they meet the "ordinary and necessary" test of that section.[25] Benefits covered by Sec. 132 include:

► No-additional-cost benefits (e.g., a hotel employee's use of a vacant hotel room)
► Qualified employee discounts (e.g., discounts on merchandise sold by the employer)
► Working condition benefits (e.g., membership fees in professional organizations paid by an employer)
► De minimis benefits (e.g., coffee provided by the employer)
► An exclusion of $250 per month (in both 2014 and 2015) is available for employer-financed parking. An exclusion of $130 per month (in both 2014 and 2015) is available for public transportation and commuter highway vehicles.

[25] See Chapter I:6 for a discussion of Sec. 162 and its requirements. Section 274 does provide one exception to the general rule. The costs of maintaining recreational facilities (such as swimming pools) are not deductible if the facilities are made available on a discriminatory basis (e.g., only officers may use the facilities).

► Athletic facilities (e.g., employer-owned tennis courts used by employees)

► Job-related education and training. See Chapter I:9 for a discussion of what constitutes "job-related" education and training. Chapter I:9 also discusses the possible deduction by employees of unreimbursed job-related education costs.

No-additional-cost benefits are limited to services, as opposed to property. Common examples of no-additional-cost benefits include the use of vacant hotel rooms by hotel employees and standby air flights provided to airline employees. The employer may not incur substantial additional costs, including forgone revenue, in providing the services to the employee. Thus, a hotel may allow employees to stay in vacant hotel rooms even though the hotel incurs additional utility and laundry costs as a result of the stay. However, the hotel cannot allow the employees to stay in lieu of paying guests. No-additional-cost benefits are limited to services provided to employees, their spouses, dependent children, and to retired and disabled employees. The term employee includes partners who perform services for a partnership. In addition, the benefits may be extended, on a reciprocal basis, to employees of other companies in the same line of business.

Employers may permit employees to purchase goods and services at a discount from the price charged regular customers. In the case of services, the discount is limited to 20% of the price charged regular customers. In the case of property, the discount is limited to the company's gross profit percent. No discounts are permitted on real property or investment property (e.g., houses or stocks). Further, the discounts must be from the same line of business in which the employee works. The discounts may be provided to the same persons as no-additional-cost benefits except that the discounts may not be provided on a reciprocal basis to employees of companies in the same line of business.

Discrimination is prohibited with respect to certain benefits. The benefits must be made available to employees in general rather than to highly compensated employees only. (See Topic Review I:4-2 for specific rules.)

SELF-STUDY QUESTION

Western Airlines and Central Airlines have a reciprocal agreement that permits employees of the other airline to travel for free on a standby basis. Stan, an employee of Western Airlines, takes a free flight on Central Airlines that would have cost $800. What is Stan's income?

ANSWER

None, reciprocal agreements with regard to no-additional-cost services are permitted.

Employee Awards. As noted earlier, it is often difficult to distinguish between gifts and awards. The de minimis rule mentioned above permits employers to make small gifts such as a holiday turkey or a watch at retirement without the employee having to include the value of the gift in gross income. The employer is entitled to a deduction for the cost of such gifts.

Section 74 provides a similar rule for **employee achievement awards** and **qualified plan awards.**[26] Such awards must be in the form of tangible personal property other than cash and must be based on safety records or length of service. Employee achievement awards are limited to $400 for any one employee during the year. Furthermore, the awards must be presented as part of a meaningful presentation and awarded under circumstances that do not create a significant likelihood of the payment being disguised compensation. Qualified plan awards must be granted under a written plan and may not discriminate in favor of highly compensated employees. The average cost of qualified plan awards is limited to $400, but individual awards can be as large as $1,600.

► An award for length of service cannot qualify under the IRC if it is received during the employee's first five years of employment or if the employee has received a length-of-service award during the year or any of the preceding four years.

► No more than 10% of an employer's eligible employees may receive an excludable safety achievement award during any year. Eligible employees are employees whose positions involve significant safety concerns.

EXAMPLE I:4-20 ► Each year, USA Corporation presents length-of-service awards to employees who have been with the company five, ten, fifteen, or twenty years. The presentations are made at a luncheon sponsored by the company and include gifts such as desk clocks, briefcases, and watches, none of which cost more than $400. The awards, which qualify as employee achievement awards, are deductible by USA Corporation and are not taxable as income to USA's employees. ◄

---

[26] Sec. 74(c). The definitions and requirements for employee achievement awards and qualified plan awards are contained in Sec. 274(j).

Gifts to employees that do not qualify as employee achievement awards or qualified plan awards can be excluded by the employee only if the awards can be excluded as de minimis amounts under Sec. 132(e).

Meals and Lodging. Section 119 provides a limited exclusion for the value of meals and lodging that are provided to employees at either no cost or a reduced cost.

► Meals provided by an employer may be excluded from an employee's gross income if they are furnished on the employer's premises and for the convenience of the employer.

► Lodging provided by an employer may be excluded from an employee's gross income if it is furnished on the employer's premises and for the convenience of the employer, and the employee is required to accept the lodging as a condition of employment.

The requirement that meals and lodging be furnished on the premises of the employer refers to the employee's place of employment.[27] In one case, the Tax Court held that the business premises requirement was met in a situation where a hotel manager lived in a residence across the street from the hotel he managed.[28]

The convenience of the employer test considers whether a substantial noncompensatory business reason exists for providing the meals or lodging. Thus, the test is met if the owner of an apartment complex furnishes a unit to the manager of the complex because it is necessary to have the manager present on the premises even when he or she is off duty.

The value of lodging cannot be excluded from gross income unless the employee is required to accept the lodging as a condition of employment. This requirement is not met if the employee has a choice of accepting the lodging or receiving a cash allowance. Furthermore, meal allowances do not qualify for the exclusion because the employer does not actually provide the meal.[29] Section 132 (discussed earlier in this chapter) provides a de minimis exception. Some employers provide supper money to employees who must work overtime. If such benefits are occasionally provided to employees, the amount is excludable from the employees' gross income.

REAL-WORLD EXAMPLE
Many university presidents are furnished with personal residences, the value of which they can generally exclude from gross income.

REAL-WORLD EXAMPLE
A brewery provided houses on the business premises to officers. The value of the houses was excludable because it was important to have the officers available for around-the-clock operations of the business. *Adolph Coors Co.,* 1968 PH T.C. Memo ¶68, 256, 27 TCM 1351.

EXAMPLE I:4-21 ► A hospital maintains a cafeteria that is used by employees, patients, and visitors. Employees are provided free meals while on duty in order to be available for emergency calls. Since the meals are provided on the employer's premises and for the convenience of the employer, the value of the meals is excluded from the employees' gross income. ◄

EXAMPLE I:4-22 ► A state highway patrol organization provides its officers with a daily meal allowance to compensate them for meals eaten while they are on duty. Officers typically eat their meals at the restaurant of their choice. Because the officers receive cash instead of meals, the amount provided must be included in the officers' gross income. ◄

EXAMPLE I:4-23 ► A large corporation requires five of its employees to work overtime two evenings each year when the company takes inventory. The corporation gives each of the employees a small amount to cover the cost of the dinner for the two evenings. The amounts constitute supper money and are excluded from the employees' gross income. ◄

Section 119 provides that if employees can exclude the value of meals from gross income, the employer can deduct the full cost of the meal. Further, if more than half of the employees who receive meals meet the "convenience of the employer" test, then all employees who receive meals can exclude the value from gross income.

Meals and Entertainment. One obvious question is whether employees who are reimbursed by their employers when they entertain customers must include the reimbursement in gross income. If they must include the reimbursement in gross income, can they deduct the cost of the entertainment and meals? Assuming conditions for deductibility are met, the tax law clearly allows 50% of the cost of entertaining customers to be

[27] Reg. Sec. 1.119-1(c)(1).
[28] *Jack B. Lindeman,* 60 T.C. 609 (1973).
[29] *CIR v. Robert J. Kowalski,* 40 AFTR 2d 77-6128, 77-2 USTC ¶9748 (USSC, 1977).

deducted (discussed in Chapter I:9). Can the employee deduct the meals and entertainment that he personally consumes?

EXAMPLE I:4-24 ▶ Joe is a sales representative for Zero Corporation. As a part of his regular duties, Joe buys lunch for Wayne, a Zero Corporation customer. Fifty percent of the cost of Wayne's meal is deductible either by Joe if he pays for the luncheon without being reimbursed by his employer, or by the Zero Corporation if it reimburses Joe for the cost. Can Joe deduct 50% of the cost of his own meal if he pays for it and is not reimbursed? If Zero pays for the meal, must Joe include in his gross income the cost of his own lunch? ◀

In the above question, Joe apparently can deduct the portion of the luncheon that applies to himself. While this issue is not clear-cut, the IRS has indicated in Rev. Rul. 63-144 that it will not pursue the issue except where taxpayers claim deductions for substantial amounts of personal expenses.[30] In any case, it is an accepted practice today for taxpayers to deduct 50% of the total cost of a meal (taxpayer and customer) unless the practice is considered abusive.[31]

Employee Death Benefits. Occasionally, an employer may make payments to the family or friends of an employee who dies. In some instances, the payments might be viewed as a gift made for reasons such as the financial need of the family, kindness, or charity. Alternatively, the amount might constitute a payment of compensation based on the past services of the deceased employee. Gifts are, of course, excluded from gross income, whereas compensation is taxable. The treatment of payments made to the family or other beneficiaries of the employee's estate is determined by the following rules:

▶ Payments for past services (such as bonuses, accrued wages, and unused vacation pay) are taxable as income to the family and are deductible by the employer. The important issue is whether the employee would have received this amount had he or she lived. If the employer was legally obligated to make the payment at the time of the employee's death, the payments are taxable to the recipient.

▶ Other amounts may be either taxable compensation or excludable gifts depending on the facts and circumstances. If the amount is a gift, it is not deductible by the employer. If the amount is taxable income to the deceased employee's family, it is deductible by the employer.

In determining whether the amount is taxable, the courts have considered such factors as whether the employer derived benefit from the payment, whether the employee had been fully compensated, and whether the payment was made to the family and not to the estate. The Supreme Court stated, "The most critical consideration [in determining whether a transfer is a gift] is the transferor's 'intention'."[32] Although the case did not deal with death benefits, it did establish the importance of motive in determining whether a payment is a gift. Thus, the transfer should be made for reasons such as kindness, sympathy, generosity, affection, or admiration.

It should be noted that it is more difficult to establish that a payment is a gift in situations where the payments are made to persons owning stock in the corporation making the payment. Such payments may be construed as constructive dividends, which are not deductible by the corporation but are taxable income to the recipients.[33]

Dependent Care. **Dependent care assistance programs** are employer-financed programs that provide care for an employee's children or other dependents. An employee may exclude up to $5,000 of assistance each year ($2,500 for a married individual filing a separate return). The care must be of a type that, if paid by the employee, would qualify for the dependent care credit. Furthermore, the credit is scaled down if the employee

ADDITIONAL COMMENT
The $5,000 limit was placed on the exclusion for dependent care assistance programs because it was thought to be inequitable to provide an unlimited dependent care exclusion but a limited child care credit for people who pay their own child care expenses.

---

[30] Rev. Rul. 63-144, 1963-2 C.B. 129.
[31] See, however, *Richard A. Sutter*, 21 T.C. 170 (1953), where the Tax Court ruled that business meals, entertainment, etc. for one's own self are inherently personal and nondeductible. *Sutter* has been cited and upheld some 50 times.

[32] *CIR v. Mose Duberstein*, 5 AFTR 2d 1626, 60-2 USTC ¶9515 (USSC, 1960).
[33] *Ernest L. Poyner v. CIR*, 9 AFTR 2d 1151, 62-1 USTC ¶9387 (4th Cir., 1962).

WHAT WOULD YOU DO IN THIS SITUATION?

FRINGE BENEFIT

National Boats manufactures pleasure boats sold to consumers. The boats range in price from $40,000 to $1,500,000. Jake is the president of National Boats. The company provides Jake with one of its more expensive boats. The company pays for fuel, insurance, and other costs and deducts these expenses along with depreciation on the boat. The company states that Jake is responsible for testing and for demonstrating the boat to possible customers. Jake has had the same boat for two years, and the company plans to provide him with a new boat next month.

You asked Jake how often he uses the boat. He indicated that he uses it once or twice each month on weekends, except during the winter. You asked him who accompanies him, and what types of testing he conducts. He seemed reluctant to answer the question, but acknowledged that his family often accompanies him on the boat, and said that he tests it during ordinary operations to determine how it performs. He added that potential customers who have also accompanied him included neighbors and friends. What tax issues do you see?

KEY POINT

The classification of an employee as highly compensated is made on the basis of the facts and circumstances of each case. Any officers and shareholders owning more than 5% of the stock are classified as highly compensated employees.

ADDITIONAL COMMENT

The Sec. 132 education exclusion discussed earlier is not subject to a dollar limitation, but covers only training related to the employee's work.

ADDITIONAL COMMENT

About half of the large employers in the United States offer flexible spending accounts.

ADDITIONAL COMMENT

While the main benefit of a cafeteria plan is to offer tax-free choices to employees, the plan must also offer at least one taxable benefit.

ADDITIONAL COMMENT

Some plans supplement wages; others are wage reduction plans. In supplemental wage plans, employer funds are used to pay fringe benefits. In the case of wage reduction plans, employees elect to receive reduced wages in exchange for the fringe benefits. In both cases, employees receive benefits without being taxed on them.

receives benefits under the employer's plan. (See Chapter I:14 for a discussion of the child and dependent care rules.) The program cannot discriminate in favor of highly compensated employees or their dependents.[34]

Adoption Expenses. Congress provides tax benefits for qualified adoption expenses in the form of a tax credit (see Chapter I:14) or an exclusion for amounts paid pursuant to the employer's written adoption assistance plan. In 2015, an employee may exclude from gross income up to $13,400 ($13,190 in 2014) of qualified expenses paid by an employer in connection with the adoption of a child under age 18.[35] The exclusion is phased out for employees with modified adjusted gross income between $201,010 and $241,010 (between $197,880 and $237,880 in 2014).

Educational Assistance. Under Sec. 127 educational assistance plans, employers pay employee education expenses. Employees may exclude from gross income annual payments of up to $5,250. The exclusion applies to payments for tuition, fees, books, supplies, and equipment for undergraduate courses or graduate courses as well as other training.

Cafeteria Plans. **Cafeteria plans** are plans that offer employees the option of choosing cash or statutory nontaxable fringe benefits (such as group term life insurance, medical insurance, adoption expenses, child care, etc.). If the employee chooses cash, the cash is taxable. However, if the employee chooses a statutory nontaxable fringe benefit, the value of the benefit is excluded from gross income.[36] In other words, the fact that the employee could have chosen cash does not cause the fringe benefit to be taxed. The plan cannot discriminate in favor of highly compensated employees or their dependents or spouses.[37] Employer plans may specify what benefits are offered and may limit the amount of benefits individual employees may receive.

Cafeteria plans that allow employees to use funds to pay medical expenses are called Flexible Spending Accounts. Typically, the plans supplement medical insurance, and funds are used to pay dental bills and other medical expenses not covered by regular insurance. In general, employees annually elect to set aside funds to pay medical expenses, and the employer pays the expenses using the set-aside funds. One problem with the agreements is that they are binding for one year. As a result, the employee loses the funds if the actual medical expenses are less than the amount set aside. Rules permit employees to carry over up to $500 from one year to the next. Employers, on the other hand, are obligated to pay expenses up to the agreed

---

[34] Sec. 129.
[35] Sec. 137.
[36] Long-term care insurance (sometimes called nursing home insurance) can be offered to employees on a tax-favored basis, but that benefit cannot be offered as part of a flexible spending account.

[37] Sec. 125.

amount even if the full amount has not yet been withheld from the employee's wages. Thus, the employer may lose money if an employee terminates employment after incurring the designated amount of medical expenses but before the full amount is withheld.

Advantage of Fringe Benefits. The major advantage of taking fringe benefits (such as those described above) in lieu of a cash payment is the fact that employees do not have to use after-tax income to obtain the product or service.

EXAMPLE I:4-25 ▶ Dan, an employee of Central Corporation, has a $40,000 life insurance policy and pays the premiums out of his salary. Since his salary is taxable, the premiums are paid on an after-tax basis. Kay, an employee for Western Corporation, is covered by a $40,000 group term life insurance policy financed by Western Corporation. Western Corporation pays the premiums on the policy. Because the premiums are excludable, Kay does not have to report the premiums as income. ◀

EXAMPLE I:4-26 ▶ John's employer establishes a cafeteria plan which allows each employee to set aside up to $5,000 for health insurance premiums and medical reimbursements. John, whose salary has been $30,000, agrees to a salary reduction of $4,000, of which $2,600 is to cover his health insurance premiums and $1,400 is available to reimburse his medical expenses. Under the arrangement, John's salary is reduced to $26,000 for tax purposes. Neither the health insurance coverage nor the medical expense reimbursement is taxable. During the year, John incurs $1,300 of medical expenses not covered by insurance. He receives a reimbursement for all of the expenses. His employer retains the remaining $100. Alternatively, if the medical expenses were $1,800, John would receive a reimbursement of $1,400 and he must pay the remaining $400 of expenses out of after-tax salary dollars. ◀

In 2015, the maximum amount that employees can elect to contribute tax-free to a flexible spending account for health care benefits is $2,550 ($2,500 in 2014). The limitation does not apply to an elective wage reduction for an employee's share of medical insurance premiums, but does apply to reimbursements for dental bills, co-pays, and other medical expenses paid directly by an employee.

STOP & THINK

Question: Employers and employees both pay FICA taxes on salaries. Fringe benefits such as health insurance are exempt from both income taxes and FICA taxes. What is the tax effect of an employee's decision to elect health insurance coverage in exchange for a reduced salary?

Solution: The employee's income and FICA taxes are both lowered. The employer is permitted an income tax deduction for either the salary payment or the payment of the health insurance premium. The employer's FICA tax is reduced because the health insurance benefit also is exempt from that tax.

Availability of Tax-Favored Fringe Benefits to Business Owners. The exclusion for many fringe benefits is only available to employees (and in some cases spouses, dependents, and retirees). Many tax-favored fringe benefits are unavailable to proprietors and partners. As a result, a partnership can provide $50,000 of group-term life insurance to employees on a tax-favored basis, but cannot provide the benefit on a tax-favored basis to its partners. Other fringe benefits that cannot be offered to proprietors or partners on a tax-favored basis include cafeteria plans, disability insurance, medical reimbursements, achievement awards, adoptions assistance, on-premises lodging, moving expense, and commuting and parking benefits (other than de minimis).[38]

Special rules apply to health insurance premiums and retirement plan contributions for proprietors and partners. The owners deduct these payments for AGI. This results in a self-employment tax on the amounts, but no income tax.

---

[38] Benefits that can be offered to proprietors and partners on a tax-favored basis include athletic facilities, de minimis benefits, no additional cost fringe benefits, dependent care assistance, educational assistance, discounts, on-premises meals, and working condition fringes.

Shareholders, as such, are ineligible for tax-favored fringe benefits. In most cases employees of C corporations are eligible for tax-favored fringe benefits based on their wages even if they own stock. This is not true, however, for S corporation employees who own more than 2% of the corporation's stock. They are treated much like partners and proprietors with respect to fringe benefits. Health insurance premiums and retirement plan contributions made for these S corporation employee-shareholders are wages for income tax purposes. Like partners and proprietors, these S corporation employees-shareholders can deduct the amounts for AGI. Unlike partners and proprietors, the amounts are not subject to FICA or self-employment taxes.

The fact that fringe benefits provided to employee-shareholders of C corporations are treated more favorably than benefits provided to the owners of other businesses is an incentive for businesses to operate as C corporations.

FOREIGN-EARNED INCOME EXCLUSION

In general, the income of U.S. citizens is subject to the U.S. income tax even if the income is derived from sources outside the United States. The foreign income of U.S. citizens also may be taxed by the host country possibly leading to a substantial double tax on the same income. The double tax is mitigated by a **foreign tax credit**. Subject to limitations, U.S. citizens may subtract from their U.S. income tax liability the income taxes they pay to foreign countries. (See Chapter I:14 for a discussion of foreign tax credit.)

In the case of foreign-earned income, individuals have available the alternative option of excluding the first $100,800 in 2015 ($99,200 in 2014) of foreign-earned income from gross income.[39] The *exclusion* is available in lieu of the foreign tax credit. If both a husband and wife have foreign-earned income, each may claim an exclusion. Community property rules are ignored in determining the amount of the exclusion. Thus, if only one spouse has foreign-earned income, only one exclusion is available. The principal reasons for the exclusion are to encourage U.S. businesses to operate in foreign countries and to hire U.S. citizens and resident aliens to manage the businesses. The hope is that such operations will improve the balance of payments. Taxpayers who elect the exclusion in one year may switch to the foreign tax credit in any subsequent year. Taxpayers who change from the exclusion to the credit may not reelect the exclusion before the sixth tax year after the tax year in which the change was made.[40] The IRS can waive the six-year limitation in special situations (such as an individual employee changing the location of his or her foreign employment).

Foreign-earned income includes an individual's earnings from personal services rendered in a foreign country. The place where the services are performed determines whether earned income is foreign or U.S. source income. If an individual is engaged in a trade or business in which both personal services and capital are material income-producing factors, no more than 30% of the net profits from the business may be excluded.[41] Furthermore, pensions, annuities, salary paid by the U.S. government, and deferred compensation do not qualify for the exclusion.[42]

To qualify for the foreign-earned income exclusion, the taxpayer must either be a bona fide resident of one or more foreign countries for an entire taxable year, or be present in one or more foreign countries for 330 days during a period of 12 consecutive months.[43] The exclusion limitation for a year must be prorated if the taxpayer is not present in, or a resident of, a foreign country or countries for the entire year.

EXAMPLE I:4-27 ▶

Sondra is given a temporary assignment to work in foreign country T. She arrives in T on October 19, 2015, and leaves on October 1, 2016. Although Sondra does not establish a permanent residence in T, she is present in T for at least 330 days out of a twelve-month period beginning on October 20, 2015. Thus, 73 days fall in 2015 and the rest in 2016. Sondra's exclusion for 2015 is limited to $20,160 [(73 ÷ 365) × $100,800]. She may exclude $20,160 or the income she earns in foreign country T during 2015, whichever is less. Sondra also may claim the foreign earned income exclusion in 2016 for the number of qualified days during the year. ◀

---

[39] Sec. 911(b)(2).
[40] Sec. 911(e)(2).
[41] Sec. 911(d)(2)(B).

[42] Sec. 911(b)(1)(B).
[43] Sec. 911(d).

Deductions directly attributable to the excluded foreign-earned income are disallowed. Expenses attributable to foreign-earned income must be allocated if foreign-earned income exceeds the exclusion. The disallowed portion is determined by multiplying the total amount of such expenses by the ratio of excluded earned income over total foreign-earned income.

EXAMPLE I:4-28 ▶ Connie earned $151,200 while employed in a foreign country for the entire year. She is entitled to an exclusion of $100,800. Connie incurred $12,000 of travel, transportation, and other deductible expenses attributable to the foreign-earned income. She may deduct only $4,000 of such expenses because $8,000 [($100,800 ÷ $151,200) × $12,000] is allocated to the excluded income and, therefore, not deductible. The $4,000 is classified as a miscellaneous itemized deduction and subject to the 2% of AGI floor associated with such deductions. ◀

Housing costs in foreign countries are often higher than in the United States. In such situations, employees may be able to increase their exclusion while self-employed individuals may be able to deduct a portion of their housing costs. Specifically, the exclusion (deduction) is available for housing costs that exceed 16% of the foreign earned income exclusion limitation or $16,128 (0.16 × $100,800) in 2015 ($15,872 in 2014). Because the maximum housing cost exclusion is 30%, the amount that can be excluded for housing costs under this rule generally is limited to $14,112 (0.14 × $100,800) in 2015 ($13,888 in 2014). The IRS provides higher amounts for cities with high cost-of-living. Further, the housing exclusion must be reduced if the taxpayer does not incur cost for the entire year.

EXAMPLE I:4-29 ▶ Wayne is employed in Quebec City, Canada, and earns a salary of $120,000. His housing costs are $38,000 for the year. Wayne can exclude $114,912 ($100,800 + $14,112) from gross income. If the housing costs had been $24,000, Wayne's foreign earned income exclusion would have totaled $108,672 [$100,800 + ($24,000 − $16,128)]. ◀

Taxpayers who exclude a portion, but not all foreign earned income, are subject to a special tax computation. The result of the computation is to apply higher tax rates to the taxable portion of the foreign earned income. (See *Prentice Hall's Federal Taxation: Corporations, Partnererships, Estates, and Trusts*, Chapter 16.) Americans employed abroad are often subject to income and payroll taxes imposed by the host country. Americans employed abroad by foreign companies are generally exempt from FICA taxes while Americans employed abroad by American companies remain subject to FICA taxes except in instances where a tax treaty between the U.S. and the host country subjects Americans to comparable host country taxes.

INCOME FROM THE DISCHARGE OF A DEBT

If debt of a taxpayer is cancelled or forgiven, the taxpayer may have to include the cancelled amount in gross income. It is important to distinguish a debt cancellation from a gift, a bequest, or a renegotiation of the purchase price.

EXAMPLE I:4-30 ▶ Farouk loaned his daughter $4,000 to help her purchase an automobile. Several months after she purchased the automobile, but before she repaid the $4,000, Farouk's daughter married. Farouk told his daughter that he was "tearing up" the $4,000 note as a wedding present. In this instance, the amount forgiven would constitute an excludable gift and would not be taxable as income to the daughter. ◀

EXAMPLE I:4-31 ▶ Clay purchased a used automobile from a dealer for $6,000. He paid $2,000 down and agreed to pay the balance of $4,000 over three years. After Clay purchased the automobile, he determined that it was defective. Clay tried to return the automobile, but the automobile dealer refused. Clay threatened to sue the dealer. To resolve the problem, the dealer offered to reduce the balance due on the purchase-money debt from $4,000 to $2,500. Clay agreed. The transaction constitutes a reduction in the purchase price of the automobile. Clay will not recognize any income, but must reduce the basis in his automobile from $6,000 to $4,500. ◀

EXAMPLE I:4-32 ▶ Blue Corporation issued bonds for $1,000 when interest rates were low. After a few years, interest rates increased and the bond value declined to $850. Blue Corporation purchased the bonds on the open market. Blue will recognize $150 of income from the discharge of indebtedness. ◀

EXAMPLE I:4-33 ► Indy Coal Company has seen its business decline during the past two years. The Company has a significant amount of bank debt that was incurred over the years to fund its coal operations. In order to maintain its operations, Indy entered into an agreement with the bank whereby the bank agreed to cancel 50% of Indy's debt. Assuming Indy was solvent at the time of the cancellation, Indy must report the discharge of indebtedness as gross income. ◄

? STOP & THINK

Question: In Example I:4-33, the bank agreed to cancel 50% of Indy Coal Company's debt. Why would a lender agree to unilaterally cancel a borrower's debt?

Solution: A bank might cancel a portion of a borrower's debt in order to protect the remaining portion of the debt. If the debt forced the company into bankruptcy, the bank may be able to collect none or only a small percentage of the debt. If the cancellation would help stabilize Indy, the bank may be able to collect at least 50% of the debt. Further, if Indy becomes a viable company in the years ahead, the bank will have a good customer to earn profits in the future.

REAL-WORLD EXAMPLE

A taxpayer purchased and retired its own bonds. The purchase resulted in a gain because the bonds were payable in British pounds, which had been devalued. The gain was excludable. *Kentucky & Indiana Terminal Railroad Co. v. U.S.,* 13 AFTR 2d 1148, 64-1 USTC ¶9374 (6th Cir., 1964).

The enforceability of a debt under state law may also determine whether the forgiveness results in income. For example, one case held that the forgiveness of a gambling debt was not included in gross income where the debt was unenforceable under state law.[44]

Discharge in Bankruptcy and Insolvency. Section 61(a)(12) indicates that gross income includes income from the discharge of an indebtedness. Section 108, on the other hand, provides for the following exceptions where the discharge of an indebtedness is not taxable:

► The discharge occurs in bankruptcy.

► The discharge occurs when the taxpayer is insolvent.

These exceptions are intended to allow a "fresh start" for bankrupt and other financially troubled taxpayers. Since a taxpayer is not required to include the discharge in gross income, he is required to reduce certain tax attributes. For example, if the taxpayer has a net operating loss carryover, the NOL carryover must be reduced by the excluded discharge.

If a debt is reduced during bankruptcy proceedings, the taxpayer recognizes no income even if the reduction in debt exceeds the available tax attributes. In the case of an insolvent taxpayer, no income is recognized as long as the taxpayer is insolvent after the reduction in debt takes place. A taxpayer is insolvent if the debts owed by the taxpayer exceed the FMV of assets owned. Thus, an insolvent taxpayer reduces the tax attributes to the point of solvency. From that point on, any reduction in debt results in the recognition of income even if all tax attributes have not been offset.

ADDITIONAL COMMENT

Also excludable is the income from the cancellation of a student loan pursuant to a provision under which part of the debt is discharged due to working for a period of time in certain professions for a broad class of employers.

Student Loan Forgiveness. Under Sec. 108(f)(2), the discharge of certain student loans is excluded from gross income if the discharge is contingent on the individual's performing certain public services. The loans must have been made by governmental, educational, or charitable organizations, and the loan proceeds must have been used to pay the cost of attending an educational institution or used to refinance outstanding student loans. Further, the loan forgiveness must be contingent upon the individual's working for a specified time period in certain professions, and the services must normally be performed for someone other than the lender.

EXAMPLE I:4-34 ► Lee borrowed $60,000 from the federal government to attend medical school. Under the terms of the loan, $20,000 of debt is forgiven for each year she practices medicine in designated low-income neighborhoods. Lee does not have to include the debt forgiveness in gross income. ◄

Home Mortgage Forgiveness. Through 2014, homeowners could exclude debt forgiveness on their principal residence of up to $2 million under Sec. 108(a)(1)(E). This provision applied only to mortgages acquired in connection with the acquisition or improvement of a taxpayer's principal residence. Taxpayers were required to reduce the basis of their residence by the amount of the exclusion.

---

[44] *David Zarin v. CIR,* 66 AFTR 2d 90-5679, 90-2 USTC ¶50,530 (3rd Cir., 1990).

EXCLUSION FOR GAIN FROM SMALL BUSINESS STOCK

Investing in small businesses is risky. To encourage investment, Congress enacted an exclusion for gains realized by noncorporate taxpayers on the sale or exchange of small business stock held over five years.[45] The exclusion for small business stock acquired after August 10, 1993 is 50% (except the exclusion is 75% for stock acquired from February 18, 2009 through September 27, 2010 and is 100% for stock acquired from September 28, 2010 through December 31, 2014).

Any gain remaining after the 50% and 75% exclusion is taxed at a rate of tax not greater than 28%. For each issuer of qualified small business stock, there is a limit on the amount of gain a taxpayer may exclude. The amount of gain eligible for the exclusion may not exceed the greater of $10 million, reduced by amounts previously excluded for gains on the company's stock, or ten times the taxpayer's aggregate adjusted basis of the stock disposed of during the year.[46] When measuring the taxpayer's aggregate basis for the stock to determine the maximum amount of gain to exclude, the fair market value of the assets contributed to the corporation is used.

EXAMPLE I:4-35 ▶ In February 2005, Dennis contributed property with a basis of $1,000,000 and a value of $4,000,000 to a qualified small business corporation for common stock. After holding the stock over five years, Dennis sells it for $14,000,000. He can exclude 50% of the $13,000,000 ($14,000,000 − $1,000,000) realized gain, or $6,500,000, as that amount is less than the maximum gain eligible for the exclusion $40,000,000 [the greater of $10,000,000 or $40,000,000 (10 times $4,000,000)]. If the stock had been acquired in February 2010 and held for over five years, Dennis' exclusion is 75% of the gain, or $9,750,000. If the stock had been acquired in February 2011 and held it over five years, the exclusion is 100% of the gain, or $13,000,000. ◀

Moreover, taxpayers do not have to recognize any gain if they reinvest the proceeds from the sale of small business stock in other small business stock within 60 days of the sale. Gain is recognized only to the extent that the amount realized from the sale exceeds the cost of the replacement stock. The basis of the replacement stock is reduced by the amount of gain not recognized. To qualify for the replacement provision the original stock must have been held for over 6 months.

EXAMPLE I:4-36 ▶ Assume the original facts in Example I:4-35, except that Dennis purchases $13,500,000 of small business investment stock within 60 days. Dennis is taxed only on $500,000 ($14,000,000 − $13,500,000) of his $13,000,000 realized gain. Dennis' basis for the new stock, however, is $1,000,000 ($13,500,000 cost of the new stock − $12,500,000 portion of the gain that is not taxed). ◀

A corporation may issue qualified small business stock only if the corporation is a C corporation that is not an excluded corporation with an aggregate adjusted basis of not more than $50 million of gross assets, and at least 80% of the value of its assets must be used in the active conduct of one or more qualified trades or businesses.[47]

OTHER EXCLUSIONS

The tax law contains other exclusions that are either covered elsewhere in the text or are of limited application. Table I:4-2 lists several such exclusions.

---

[45] §1202(a). The exclusion is 60% in the case of empowerment zone stock (except the exclusion is 75% for empowerment zone stock acquired from February 18, 2009 through September 27, 2010 and is 100% for stock acquired from September 28, 2010 through December 31, 2014).
[46] Sec. 1202(b)(1).

[47] Secs. 1202(d) and (e). Excluded corporations are those engaged in providing professional services (e.g., law and health), financial services (e.g., banking and insurance), hospitality (e.g., hotels and restaurants), farming, and mining and oil and gas production.

▼ **TABLE I:4-2**
Other Exclusions

Section	Applies to	Comments
121	Gain from sale of personal residence	Taxpayers may exclude up to $250,000 ($500,000 in the case of a married couple filing a joint return) of gain from the sale of a personal residence. (See Chapter I:12 for a detailed discussion of this provision.)
101(h)	Annuities paid to survivors of public safety officers	Annuities paid to survivors of public safety officers, such as firefighters and police officers, killed in the line of duty are excluded.
104(a)	Military disability pay	Military personnel may exclude disability pay, combat pay (noncommissioned personnel only), and housing allowances.
112	Combat pay	
134	Military housing allowance	
107	Housing allowance for ministers	Ministers may exclude either the rental value of their homes or a rental allowance if provided in connection with their religious duties.
119	Campus housing	A limited exclusion is provided to employees of educational institutions when they are provided with on-campus housing.
131	Foster care payments	Certain allowances received by foster care providers are excluded from gross income.
162(o)	Rural letter carrier's allowance	Rural letter carriers may exclude the "equipment maintenance allowance" they receive for the use of their personal automobiles in delivering the mail. They receive no deduction for the use of their automobiles.
408A(d)	Roth IRA distributions	Qualified distributions from Roth IRAs are excluded from gross income (see Chapter I:9 for a detailed discussion of the provisions).
530(d)	Education IRA distributions	Qualified distributions from Coverdell Education Savings Account IRAs are excluded from gross income (see Chapter I:9 for a detailed discussion of this provision).
988(e)	Personal foreign currency gains	Individuals are excused from recognizing gain on the disposition of foreign currency in any personal transaction, provided that the gain does not exceed $200.

Tax planning considerations

EMPLOYEE FRINGE BENEFITS

The tax law encourages certain forms of fringe benefits by allowing an employer to deduct the cost of the benefit while permitting the employee to exclude the benefit from gross income. This deduction does not represent an income tax advantage to the employer because compensation, whether in the form of cash or nontaxable fringe benefits, is deductible if reasonable in amount. While employees receive the greatest income tax benefit from the exclusion of fringe benefits from gross income, employers receive a small benefit from the fact that fringe benefits are not subject to Social Security and Medicare taxes.

EXAMPLE I:4-37 ▶

ADDITIONAL COMMENT

A case can be made for the desirability of encouraging employers to provide health insurance and other fringe benefits. However, these provisions may contribute to increases in the cost of insurance and medical care.

USA Company has decided to offer $20,000 of group term life insurance coverage for each of its employees at an average annual premium cost of $100 per employee. Tim, an employee of USA Corporation, is in the 15% tax bracket. Because USA is offering a nontaxable fringe benefit, Tim will owe no additional income tax. If Tim had received a salary increase of $100, he would have had to pay an additional income tax of $15 (0.15 × $100). The remaining $85 of after-tax income would probably not have been sufficient to obtain the same amount of life insurance coverage. ◀

Excluding fringe benefits from gross income favors employees who are subject to higher tax rates.

EXAMPLE I:4-38 ▶ Assume the same facts as in Example I:4-37 except that Tim is in the 39.6% tax rate. Tim would save $39.60 (0.396 × $100) of taxes by receiving the group term life insurance coverage instead of the $100 salary increase. ◀

ADDITIONAL COMMENT
Fringe benefits offered by potential employers are important consideration factors when weighing total compensation packages.

It is not always desirable for employers to offer nontaxable fringe benefits. Some employees are not interested in certain benefits. For example, in the case of married couples where both spouses are employed, it is not necessary for both employers to provide medical insurance coverage for both spouses. Alternatively, single employees may not feel the need for group term life insurance and employees with no children are uninterested in employer-provided child care.

To avoid providing fringe benefits that are unneeded or unwanted, many employers have turned to cafeteria plans. Under cafeteria plans, employees may select from a list of nontaxable fringe benefits. On the other hand, employees who so choose may receive cash in lieu of some or all of the nontaxable benefits. Thus, each employee selects what he or she wants most. One common result is that high-tax-rate employees select the nontaxable fringe benefits, whereas other employees choose to receive cash.

SELF-HELP INCOME AND USE OF PERSONALLY OWNED PROPERTY

As noted earlier in this chapter, self-help income and income derived from the use of personal property are not taxable. Thus, self-help income and personal ownership of property are favored by the tax system. Taxpayers who rent their personal residences cannot deduct rental payments, but taxpayers who own their residences do not pay rent and may deduct interest and real estate taxes as itemized deductions. Thus, the tax law encourages ownership of personal residences.

Effective tax planning necessitates weighing the tax incentives with other nontax factors. Taxpayers with little accumulated funds may find it difficult to purchase a residence despite the availability of tax incentives. Taxpayers who move frequently may find that transaction costs such as real estate commissions and other closing costs are greater than the tax benefits obtained from home ownership. Other factors such as the personal preference of the taxpayer and anticipated inflation rates must also be considered.

Self-help income must be viewed in the same way. Taxpayers who are deciding whether to paint their own residences or hire someone else to do it must consider factors such as personal preference and the amount of income that could be produced if the time were spent working at an activity that produces taxable income.

COMPLIANCE AND PROCEDURAL CONSIDERATIONS

OBJECTIVE 4

Describe compliance and procedural considerations for exclusions of gross income

Taxpayers are usually not required to disclose excluded income on their tax returns. For example, a taxpayer who receives a tax-exempt scholarship need not disclose that income on his or her tax return. An exception is provided for tax-exempt interest and Social Security benefits, which must be disclosed on the tax return. If a taxpayer's only income is from tax-exempt sources, the taxpayer need not file a tax return. Whether an individual must file a return is based on the amount of the individual's gross income for the year (see Chapter I:2).

This chapter considers the taxability of various fringe benefits. The rules regarding the need for an employer to withhold federal income taxes or to report a payment on an employee's Form W-2 (Statement of Income Tax Withheld on Wages) closely parallel the gross income rules. (See Chapter I:14 for a discussion of these reporting requirements.) In general, if a fringe benefit is nontaxable, employers do not withhold from the benefit, nor do they report the benefit on the employee's W-2 at year-end. On the other hand, if the

ADDITIONAL COMMENT
Taxpayers filing Form 1040 are asked to report any tax-exempt interest income on line 8b.

benefit is taxable, it is subject to withholding and is reported on the employee's W-2 at year-end. Thus, employers do not withhold for nontaxable meals and lodging provided to employees[48] or a moving expense reimbursement if the expenses are deductible.[49] Similarly, no withholding is required for the following fringe benefits if they are nontaxable: scholarships and fellowships covered by Sec. 117, dependent care covered by Sec. 129, and miscellaneous fringes covered by Sec. 132.

PROBLEM MATERIALS

DISCUSSION QUESTIONS

I:4-1 What is meant by the terms *administrative exclusion* and *judicial exclusion*?

I:4-2 There is no specific statutory exclusion for welfare benefits. Nevertheless, the IRS has ruled that such benefits are not taxable. Is this within the authority of the IRS?

I:4-3 What was the issue in the tax case *Eisner v. Macomber*? Why is the case important?

I:4-4 Most exclusions exist for one of two reasons. What are those reasons? Give examples of exclusions that exist for each.

I:4-5 a. If a gift of property is made, who is taxed on income produced by the property?
b. How can interfamily gifts reduce a family's total tax liability?

I:4-6 a. What role does intent play in determining whether a transfer is a gift and therefore not subject to the income tax?
b. Are tips received by employees from customers excludable from gross income as gifts? Explain.

I:4-7 What is the tax significance of the face amount of a life insurance policy?

I:4-8 What conditions must be met for an award to qualify for an exclusion under Sec. 74?

I:4-9 Which of the requirements for the Sec. 74 awards exclusion most severely limits its use? Does the exclusion benefit taxpayers more if they itemize their deductions or use the standard deduction?

I:4-10 a. Define the term *scholarship* as it is used in Sec. 117.
b. If a scholarship covers room and board, is it excludable?
c. If an employer provides a scholarship to an employee who is on leave of absence, is that scholarship taxable?
d. Is the amount paid by a university to students for services excludable from the students' gross income?

I:4-11 What special rules are applicable to non-degree candidates who receive scholarships?

I:4-12 Is the personal injury exclusion found in Sec. 104 limited to physical injury? Explain.

I:4-13 Answer the following questions relative to employer-financed medical and health, disability, and life insurance plans.
a. May employers deduct premiums paid on employee insurance?
b. Do employees have to include such premiums in gross income?
c. Are benefits paid to the employee included in the employee's gross income?

I:4-14 Special rules are applicable in situations where group term life insurance coverage exceeds $50,000. How are key employees treated?

I:4-15 a. What are the seven major types of fringe benefits covered by Sec. 132?
b. What tax advantage is offered relative to such benefits?
c. Are such benefits available to employees only or may the benefits also be offered to spouses, dependents, and retirees?
d. Is discrimination prohibited relative to Sec. 132 benefits?
e. What is the tax impact on the employer and employees if an employer's plan is discriminatory?

I:4-16 What conditions must be met if an employee is to exclude meals and lodging furnished by an employer?

I:4-17 The president and vice president of USA Corporation receive benefits that are unavailable to other employees. These benefits include free parking, payment of monthly expenses in a local club, discounts on products sold by the corporation, and payment of premiums on a whole life insurance policy. Which of the benefits must be

---

[48] Reg. Sec. 31.3401(a)-1(b)(9).

[49] See Sec. 3401 for withholding requirements for numerous special situations.

included in the gross income of the president and vice president?

I:4-18 Are the same fringe benefits that are available to employees also available to self-employed individuals?

I:4-19 If an employee takes a customer to lunch and discusses business, can the employee deduct 50% of the meal for both the customer and himself? Explain.

I:4-20 Are income distributions from a qualified state tuition program taxable?

I:4-21 What types of income qualify for the foreign-earned income exclusion?

I:4-22 Are taxpayers who claim the foreign-earned income exclusion entitled to deduct expenses incurred in producing that income? Explain.

I:4-23 a. Why is it important to distinguish debt cancellation from a gift, bequest, or renegotiation of a purchase price?
b. What happens to the basis of an asset if the taxpayer renegotiates its purchase price?

I:4-24 a. Under what conditions is the discharge of indebtedness not taxable?

b. If a father forgives a daughter's debt to him, is she required to include such amount in her gross income?

I:4-25 Bankrupt and insolvent taxpayers do not recognize income if debt is discharged. They must, however, reduce specified tax attributes. What is involved?

I:4-26 Are partners and proprietors at a disadvantage with respect to fringe benefits? Explain.

I:4-27 Why are cafeteria plans helpful in the design of an employee benefit plan that provides nontaxable fringe benefits?

I:4-28 Both high-income and low-income employees are covered by cafeteria plans. Under such plans, all employees may select from a list of nontaxable fringe benefits or they may elect to receive cash in lieu of these benefits.
a. Which group of employees is more likely to choose nontaxable fringe benefits in lieu of cash? Explain.
b. Is this result desirable from a social or economic point of view? Explain.

ISSUE IDENTIFICATION QUESTIONS

I:4-29 Luke, who retired this year, lives in a four-plex owned by Julie. Luke's income decreased when he retired, and he now has difficulty paying his rent. Julie offered to reduce Luke's rent if he would agree to mow the lawn, wash windows, and provide other maintenance services. Luke accepted, and Julie reduced the monthly rental from $650 to $300. What are the tax issues that should be considered by Luke and Julie?

I:4-30 Mildred worked as a maid for 27 years in the home of Larry and Kay. When she retired, they presented her with a check for $25,000, indicating that it was a way of showing their appreciation for her years of loyal service. What tax issues should Mildred and her employer consider?

I:4-31 Troy Department Stores offers employees discounts on merchandise carried in the store. Newly hired employees receive a 10% discount. The discount rate increases 1% each year until employees have 20 years of service when the discount rate is capped at 30%. What tax issues should Troy and the employees consider?

I:4-32 Jerry works in the human resources department of Ajax Corporation. One of his responsibilities is to interview prospective employees. Two or three days each week, Jerry takes a prospective employee to lunch, and Ajax reimburses him for the cost of the meals. What tax issues should Jerry and Ajax Corporation consider?

PROBLEMS

I:4-33 *Self-Help Income.* In which of the following situations would the taxpayer realize taxable income?
a. A mechanic performs work on his own automobile. The mechanic would have charged a customer $400 for doing the same work.
b. A mechanic repairs his neighbor's personal automobile. In exchange, the neighbor, an accountant, agrees to prepare the mechanic's tax return. The services performed are each worth $200.
c. A mechanic repairs his daughter's automobile without any charge.

I:4-34   *Excludable Gifts.* Which of the following would be includable in gross income?

a. Alice appeared on a TV quiz show and received a prize of $5,000.

b. Bart received $500 from his employer because he developed an idea that reduced the employer's production costs.

c. Chuck borrowed $500 from his mother in order to finance his last year in college. Upon his graduation, Chuck's mother told him he did not have to repay the $500. She intended the $500 to be a graduation present.

I:4-35   *Life Insurance Proceeds.* Don is the beneficiary of a $50,000 insurance policy on the life of his mother, Anna. To date, Anna has paid premiums of $16,000. What amount of gross income must be reported in each of the following cases?

a. Anna elects to cancel the policy and receives $20,000, the cash surrender value of the policy.

b. Anna dies and Don receives the face amount of the policy, $50,000.

c. Anna dies and Don elects to receive $15,000 per year for four years.

I:4-36   *Transfer of Life Insurance.* Ed is the beneficiary of a $20,000 insurance policy on the life of his mother. Because Ed needs funds, he sells the policy to his sister, Amy, for $6,000. Amy subsequently pays premiums of $9,000.

a. How much income must Amy report if she collects the face value of the policy upon the death of her mother?

b. Would Amy have to report any income if her brother had given her the policy? Assume the only payment she made was $9,000 for the premiums.

I:4-37   *Settlement of Life Insurance Policy.* Sue is age 73 and has a great deal of difficulty living independently as she suffers from severe rheumatoid arthritis. She is covered by a $400,000 life insurance policy, and her children are named as her beneficiaries. Because of her health, Sue decides to live in a nursing home, but she does not have enough income to pay her nursing home bills which are expected to total $42,000 per year. The insurance company offers disabled individuals the option of either a reduced settlement on their policies or an annuity. Given Sue's age and health she has the option of receiving $3,200 per month or a lump sum payment of $225,000. To date, Sue has paid $80,000 in premiums on the policy.

a. How much income must Sue report if she chooses the lump sum settlement?

b. How much income must Sue report if she elects the annuity?

c. How much income would Sue have to report if her nursing home bills amounted to only $36,000 per year?

I:4-38   *Insurance Policy Dividends.* Hank carries a $100,000 insurance policy on his life. Premiums paid over the years total $8,000. Dividends on the policy have totaled $6,000. Hank has left the dividends on the policy with the insurance company. During the current year, the insurance company credited $600 of interest on the accumulated dividends to Hank's account.

a. How much income is Hank obligated to report in connection with the policy?

b. Would it make any difference if the accumulated dividends equaled $9,000 instead of $6,000?

I:4-39   *Prizes and Awards.* For each of the following, indicate whether the amount is taxable:

a. Peggy won $4,000 in the state lottery.

b. Jane won a $500 prize for her entry in a poetry contest.

c. Linda was awarded $2,000 when she was selected as "Teacher of the Year" by the local school district.

I:4-40   *Scholarships.* For each of the following, indicate the amount that must be included in the taxpayer's gross income:

a. Larry was given a $1,500 tuition scholarship to attend Eastern Law School. In addition, Eastern paid Larry $4,000 per year to work part-time in the campus bookstore.

b. Marty received a $10,000 football scholarship for attending Northern University. The scholarship covered tuition, room and board, laundry, and books. Four thousand dollars of the scholarship was designated for room and board and laundry. It was understood that Marty would participate in the school's intercollegiate football program, but Marty was not required to do so.

c. Western School of Nursing requires all third-year students to work twenty hours per week at an affiliated hospital. Each student is paid $10 per hour. Nancy, a third-year student, earned $10,000 during the year.

I:4-41   *Research Grant.* Otto is a biology professor at State University. The university gave Otto a sabbatical leave to study the surface of the flatworm. During the year he received a salary of $50,000, which is less than his regular salary of $56,000. Otto also received a grant to cover expenses associated with the study. The grant was $2,000, as were his related expenses. Otto also incurred memberships and other employment related expenses totaling $1,000. How much must Otto include in gross income?

I:4-42   *Payments for Personal Injury.* Determine which of the following payments for sickness and injury must be included in the taxpayer's gross income.
a. Pat was injured in an automobile accident. The other driver's insurance company paid him $2,000 to cover medical expenses and a compensatory amount of $4,000 for pain and suffering.
b. A newspaper article stated that Quincy had been convicted of tax evasion. Quincy, in fact, had never been accused of tax evasion. He sued and won a compensatory settlement of $4,000 from the newspaper.
c. Rob, who pays the cost of a commercial disability income policy, fell and injured his back. He was unable to work for six months. The insurance company paid him $1,800 per month during the time he was unable to work.
d. Steve fell and injured his knee. He was unable to work for four months. His employer-financed disability income policy paid Steve $1,600 per month during the time he was unable to work.
e. Ted suffered a stroke. He was unable to work for five months. His employer continued to pay Ted his salary of $1,700 per month during the time he was unable to work.

I:4-43   *Employee Benefits.* Ursula is employed by USA Corporation. USA Corporation provides medical and health, disability, and group term life insurance coverage for its employees. Premiums attributable to Ursula were as follows:

Medical and health	$3,600
Disability	300
Group term life (face amount is $40,000)	200

During the year, Ursula suffered a heart attack and subsequently died. Before her death, Ursula collected $14,000 as a reimbursement for medical expenses and $5,000 of disability income. Upon her death, Ursula's husband collected the $40,000 face value of the life insurance policy.
a. What amount can USA Corporation deduct for premiums attributable to Ursula?
b. How much must Ursula include in income relative to the premiums paid?
c. How much must Ursula include in income relative to the insurance benefits?
d. How much must Ursula's widower include in income?

I:4-44   *Group Term Life Insurance.* Data Corporation has four employees and provides group term life insurance coverage for all four employees. Coverage is nondiscriminatory and is as follows:

Employee	Age	Key Employee	Coverage	Actual Premiums
＊Andy	62	yes	$200,000	$4,000
Bob	52	yes	40,000	700
Cindy	33	no	80,000	600
＊Damitria	33	no	40,000	300

a. How much may Data Corporation deduct for group term life insurance premiums?
b. How much income must be reported by each employee?

I:4-45   *Life Insurance Proceeds.* Joe is the beneficiary of a life insurance policy taken out by his father several years ago. Joe's father dies, and Joe has the option of receiving the $100,000 face value of the policy in cash or receiving annual payments of $1,000 per month for the rest of his life. Joe is now 65. Joe's father paid $32,000 in premiums over the years.
a. How much must Joe include in gross income this year if he accepts the $100,000 face amount?
b. Assume Joe elects to receive the annual payments. What is his life expectancy?
c. What is his annual exclusion?
d. How much must he report as income each year?

I:4-46   *Employee Benefits.* Al flies for AAA Airlines. AAA provides its employees with several fringe benefits. Al and his family are allowed to fly on a space-available basis on AAA Airline. Tickets used by Al and his family during the year are worth $2,000. AAA paid for a subscription to two magazines published for pilots. The subscriptions totaled $80. The

[handwritten note in margin: ＊OVER 50,000, PAY TAXES ON]

airline paid for Al's meals and lodging while he was away from home overnight in connection with his job. Such meals and lodging cost AAA $10,000. Although Al could not eat while flying, he was allowed to drink coffee provided by the airline. The coffee was worth about $50. AAA provided Al with free parking, which is valued at $100 per month. The airline treated Al and his family to a one-week all-expenses-paid vacation at a resort near his home. This benefit was awarded because of Al's outstanding safety record. The value of the vacation was $2,300. Which of these benefits are taxable to Al?

I:4-47 *Employee Benefits.* Jet Corporation is involved in the purchase and rental of several large apartment complexes. Questions have been raised about the treatment of several items pertaining to Jet Corporation and its employees. Jet Corporation employs a manager for each complex. The manager is required to occupy a unit in the complex in order to be available at all hours. The average rental value of the units is $12,000 per year. The corporation's president finds that it is beneficial to the corporation if he entertains bankers and others with whom Jet does business. He does such entertaining about once each month and the corporation pays the cost. Business is discussed at the meals. The cost for the year of such entertaining was $1,500, and about one-third of the cost was attributable to meals consumed by the president.

Each year as the company closes its books, the controller and certain other members of the accounting staff must work overtime. The company pays each employee supper money totaling $25 during this period.

The corporation's vice president is expected to travel on business-related matters to visit various properties owned by the corporation. Because of the distances involved, the vice president must stay away from home several nights. Total meals and lodging incurred on the trips total $3,000, most of which is attributable to the vice president himself.

Which amounts are deductible by the corporation? Which are taxable to the employee?

I:4-48 *Death Benefits.* After a brief illness, Bill died. Bill's employer paid $20,000 to his widow. The corporation sent along a letter with the check indicating that $5,000 represented payment for Bill's accrued vacation days and back wages. The balance was being awarded in recognition of Bill's many years of loyal service. The company was obligated to pay the accrued vacation days and back wages, but the balance was discretionary.
a. Is the employer entitled to deduct the $20,000 paid to Bill's widow?
b. Is Bill's widow required to include the $20,000 in her gross income?

I:4-49 *Foreign-Earned Income Exclusion.* For each of the following cases, indicate the amount of the foreign-earned income exclusion. (Disregard the effect of exemptions for certain allowances under Sec. 912.)
a. Sam, a U.S. citizen, is an assistant to the ambassador to Spain. Sam lives and works in Spain. His salary of $90,000 is paid by the U.S. government.
b. Jim, a U.S. citizen, owns an unincorporated oil drilling company that operates in Argentina, where he resides. The business is heavily dependent on equipment owned by Jim. His profit for the year totaled $100,000.
c. Ken, a U.S. citizen, works for a large Japanese corporation. Ken is employed in the United States, but must travel to Japan several times each year. During the current year he spent sixty days in Japan. This is typical of most years. His salary is $95,000.

I:4-50 *Foreign-Earned Income Exclusion.* On January 5, 2015 Rita left the United States for Germany, where she had accepted an appointment as vice president of foreign operations. Her employer, USA Corporation, told her the assignment would last about two years. Rita decided not to establish a permanent residence in Germany because her assignment was for only two years. Her salary for the year is $301,800. Rita incurred travel, transportation, and other related expenses totaling $6,000, none of which are reimbursed.
a. What is Rita's foreign-earned income exclusion?
b. How much may she deduct for travel and transportation?

I:4-51 *Discharge of Debt.* During bankruptcy, USA Corporation debt was reduced from $780,000 to $400,000. USA Corporation's assets are valued at $500,000. USA's NOL carryover was $400,000.
a. Is USA Corporation required to report any income from the discharge of its debts?
b. Which tax attributes are reduced and by how much? Assume USA does not make any special elections when reducing its attributes.

I:4-52 *Discharge of Debt.* Old Corporation has suffered losses for several years, and its debts total $500,000; Old's assets are valued at only $380,000. Old's creditors agree to reduce

Old's debts by one-half in order to permit the corporation to continue to operate. Old's NOL carryover is $150,000.
a. What impact does the reduction in debt have on Old's NOL?
b. Is Old required to report any income?

I:4-53 *Court and Insurance Awards.* Determine whether the following items represent taxable income.
a. As the result of an age discrimination suit, Pat received a cash settlement of $40,000. One-half of the settlement represented wages lost by Pat as a result of the discrimination and the balance represented an award based on personal injury.
b. Matt sued the local newspaper for a story that reported he was affiliated with organized crime. The court awarded him $50,000 of libel damages.
c. Pam was injured in an automobile accident and received $10,000 from an employer-sponsored disability policy. In addition, her employer-financed medical insurance policy reimbursed her for $15,000 of medical expenses.

I:4-54 *Cafeteria Plan.* Jangyoun is a married taxpayer with a dependent 4-year-old daughter. His employer offers a cafeteria plan under which he can choose to receive cash or, alternatively, choose from certain fringe benefits. These benefits include health insurance that costs $9,000 and child care that costs $2,600. Assume Jangyoun is in the 28% tax bracket.
a. How much income tax will Jangyoun save if he chooses to participate in the employer's health insurance plan? Assume that he does not have sufficient medical expenses to itemize his deductions.
b. Would you recommend that Jangyoun participate in the employer's health insurance plan if his wife's employer already provides comparable health insurance coverage for the family?
c. Would you recommend that Jangyoun participate in the employer-provided child care option if he has the alternative option of claiming a child care credit of $480?

I:4-55 *Exclusion of Gain from Small Business Stock.* In 1996, Jose acquired 100% of Acorn Corporation common stock by transferring property with an adjusted basis of $1,000,000 and fair market value of $4,000,000. Acorn is a qualified small business corporation. On April 1, 2015, Jose sells all of the Acorn Corporation common stock for $16,000,000.
a. What is the amount of gain that may be excluded from Jose's gross income?
b. What would your answer be if the fair market value of the Acorn stock were only $800,000 upon its issue?
c. What would your answer be if the stock were sold after two years?
d. Can Jose avoid recognizing gain by purchasing replacement stock?

COMPREHENSIVE PROBLEM

I:4-56 Pat was divorced from her husband in 2010. During the current year she received alimony of $18,000 and child support of $4,000 for her 11-year-old son, who lives with her. Her former husband had asked her to sign an agreement giving him the dependency exemption for the child but she declined to do so. After the divorce she accepted a position as a teacher in the local school district. During the current year she received a salary of $32,000. The school district paid her medical insurance premiums of $6,900 and provided her with group term life insurance coverage of $40,000. The premiums attributable to her coverage equaled $160. During her marriage, Pat's parents loaned her $8,000 to help with the down payment on her home. Her parents told her this year that they understand her financial problems and that they were cancelling the balance on the loan, which was $5,000. They did so because they wanted to help their only daughter.

Pat received dividends from National Motor Company of $4,600 and interest on State of California bonds of $2,850.

Pat had itemized deductions of $9,100. Compute her taxable income for 2015.

TAX STRATEGY PROBLEMS

I:4-57 Sally owns a small C corporation that has provided health insurance coverage for Sally and the company's three other employees. The insurance coverage for Sally and the three employees is individual coverage, not family coverage. Sally's own family coverage is

uncertain

through a separate private policy. She pays the premiums out of after-tax dollars. Sally's salary is $40,000 and the salary for the other three employees averages $30,000. The premiums on the health insurance policy average $2,000 per employee per year. The provider recently informed Sally that the premiums will increase to $2,500 per employee. The spouses of her two married employees have coverage through their employers. The third employee has announced that he will marry soon and would very much like to have family health insurance coverage. The insurance provider says that family coverage will approximately double the premiums. Sally is finding the cost of providing medical insurance coverage particularly burdensome for her small business. What planning suggestions can you offer?

I:4-58 Maria was planning to paint the interior of her apartment over a three-day weekend. Her employer asked her to work all three days and will pay her $600 overtime. She called a professional painter who offered to do the job for $500. He is willing to use the paint she has already purchased. Maria is in the 28% tax bracket. Will she be better off financially to work the overtime and pay the painter or to turn down the overtime and do the work herself? What other factors should she consider?

TAX FORM/RETURN PREPARATION PROBLEMS

I:4-59 A. J. Paige, Social Security number 111-22-3333, is the vice president of marketing (Australia) for International Industries, Inc. (III). III is headquartered at 123 Main Street, Los Angeles, California 92601. A. J., who is single, accepted the position and became a resident of Australia on July 8 of last year. Her business address is 242 Main, Westview, Australia. Westview is not designated as a high housing cost city. A. J.'s visa permits her to stay in Australia indefinitely. Her only trips to the United States in the current year were for vacations (August 2 to 16 and December 21 to 28). A. J.'s contract specifies that her appointment is to last indefinitely, but states that III is to pay her $4,000 per year to cover the cost of two vacation trips to the United States. Her salary is $140,000, out of which she pays rent on an apartment of $30,000 per year. A. J. has no family or residence in the United States. She paid an income tax in Australia of $23,500. Complete a Form 2555 for 2014.

I:4-60 Alice Johnson, Social Security number 222-23-3334, is a single taxpayer and is employed as a secretary by State University of Florida. She has the following items pertaining to her income tax return for the current year:

- Received a $20,000 salary from her employer, who withheld $3,000 federal income tax.
- Received a gift of 1,000 shares of Ace Corporation stock with a $100,000 FMV from her mother. She also received $4,000 of cash dividends from the Ace Corporation. The dividends are qualified dividends.
- Received $1,000 of interest income on bonds issued by the City of Tampa.
- Received a regular stock dividend (nontaxable under Sec. 305) of 50 shares of Ace Corporation stock with a $5,000 FMV.
- Alice's employer paid $2,000 of medical and health insurance premiums on her behalf.
- Received $12,000 alimony from her ex-husband.
- State University provided $60,000 of group term life insurance. Alice is 42 years old and is not a key employee. The table in the text is applicable.
- Received a $1,000 cash award from her employer for being designated the Secretary of the Year.
- Total itemized deductions are $8,000.

  Complete Form 1040 and accompanying schedules for Alice Johnson's 2014 return.

CASE STUDY PROBLEMS

I:4-61 Able Corporation is a closely held company engaged in the manufacture and retail sales of automotive parts. Able maintains a qualified pension plan for its employees but has not offered nontaxable fringe benefits.

You are a tax consultant for the company who has been asked to prepare suggestions for the adoption of an employee fringe benefit plan. Your discussions with the client's chief financial officer reveal the following:

- Employees currently pay their own premiums for medical and health insurance.
- No group term life insurance is provided.

- The company owns a vacant building that could easily be converted to a parking garage.
- Many of the employees purchase automobile parts from the company's retail outlets and pay retail price.
- The president of the corporation would like to provide a dependent care assistance program under Sec. 129 for its employees.

  Required: Prepare a client memo that recommends the adoption of an employee fringe benefit program. Your recommendations should discuss the pros and cons of different types of nontaxable fringe benefits.

I:4-62 Jay Corporation owns several automobile dealerships. This year, the corporation initiated a policy of giving the top salesperson at each dealership a free vacation trip to Florida. The president believes that this is an effective sales incentive. The cost of the vacations is deductible by the corporation as compensation paid to employees, and is taxable to the recipients. Nevertheless, the president objects to reporting the value of the vacations as income on the W-2s of the recipients and to withholding taxes from wages for the value of the trips. He feels that this undermines the effectiveness of the incentive. What are the implications of this behavior for the corporation and the president?

TAX RESEARCH PROBLEMS

I:4-63 Ann is a graduate economics student at State University. State University awarded her a $1,000 scholarship. In addition, Ann works as a half-time teaching assistant in the Economics Department at State University. She is paid $7,000 per year and her tuition is waived. The salary is equal to that paid other part-time instructors. Her tuition would be $8,000 were it not for the waiver. Ann paid $500 for her books and supplies and she incurred living expenses of $7,400. Determine how much gross income Ann must report.

A partial list of research sources is

- Sec. 117(d)
- Prop. Reg. 1.117-6(d)(5)

I:4-64 Kim leased an office building to USA Corporation under a ten-year lease specifying that at the end of the lease USA had to return the building to its original condition if any modifications were made. USA changed the interior of the building, and at the end of the lease USA paid Kim $30,000 instead of making the required repairs. Does Kim have to include the payment in gross income?

A partial list of research sources is

- Sec. 109
- *Boston Fish Market Corp.*, 57 T.C. 884 (1972)
- *Sirbo Holdings Inc. v. CIR,* 31 AFTR 2d 73-1005, 73-1 USTC ¶9312 (2nd Cir., 1973)

I:4-65 As a result of a fire damaging their residence, the Taylors must stay in a motel for three weeks while their home is being restored. They pay $2,000 for the room and $500 for meals. Their homeowner's policy pays $2,500 to reimburse them for the cost. They estimate that during the five-week period they would normally spend $300 for meals. Is the reimbursement taxable?

A partial list of research sources is

- Sec. 123
- Reg. Sec. 1.123-1

I:4-66 Bold Corporation paid $25 to each full-time employee at year-end in recognition of the holidays. Bold Corporation is interested in whether the amounts are taxable income to its employees, and whether the company can deduct the amounts.

A partial list of research sources is

- Secs. 74(c), 102, 132(c), and 274(b)
- Reg. Sec. 1.132-6(e)(1)
- *Hallmark Cards, Inc. v. U.S.,* 9 AFTR 2d 391, 62-1 USTC ¶9162 (DC-Mo, 1961).
- Rev. Rul. 59-58, 1959-1 CB 17.

CHAPTER

5

PROPERTY TRANSACTIONS: CAPITAL GAINS AND LOSSES

LEARNING OBJECTIVES

After studying this chapter, you should be able to

1 ▶ Determine the realized gain or loss from the sale or other disposition of property

2 ▶ Determine the basis of property

3 ▶ Distinguish between capital assets and other assets

4 ▶ Understand how capital gains are taxed for noncorporate taxpayers

5 ▶ Understand how capital gains are taxed for corporate taxpayers

6 ▶ Recognize when a sale or exchange has occurred

7 ▶ Determine the holding period for an asset when a sale or disposition occurs

8 ▶ Describe tax planning opportunities for property transactions

9 ▶ Describe compliance and procedural considerations for property transactions

HISTORICAL NOTE

A preferential tax rate on capital gains was included in the tax law from 1921 until 1987. A modest preferential rate was reintroduced in 1991, with capital gains for noncorporate taxpayers being subject to a maximum 28% tax rate and ordinary income being subject to a maximum tax rate of 31%. The rates were reduced in 1997 and reduced again in 2003.

ADDITIONAL COMMENT

For a discussion of the justification of preferential tax rates for LTCGs (see page I:5-30).

ADDITIONAL COMMENT

During 2010, many taxpayers sold capital assets to recognize LTCG taxed at 15% because the rates were expected to increase to 20% or even higher.

Gross income includes "gains derived from dealings in property,"[1] and certain "losses from sale or exchange of property"[2] are allowed as deductions from gross income to determine adjusted gross income. All recognized gains and losses must eventually be classified either as *capital* or *ordinary*. Except for a brief time in the mid-to-late 1980s, long-term capital gains (LTCGs) of individual taxpayers have consistently been taxed at lower rates than ordinary gains or short-term capital gains (STCGs).[3] This preferential treatment of capital gains, more precisely LTCGs, has been a much debated topic for many years. A discussion of the reasoning for imposing lower tax rates on LTCGs is provided near the end of this chapter.

The preferential treatment of capital gains has fluctuated widely over the years. For example, in the early 1980s, taxpayers were allowed to deduct 60% of the gain. In 1991, net capital gains were taxed at a maximum rate of 28%, then reduced to 20% for most taxpayers in 1997. Congress started applying different rates to different types of LTCG in 2001, i.e., a LTCG due to the sale of a collectible has a maximum rate of 28% while a LTCG due to the sale of stock has a maximum rate of 15% or 20%. Thus, depending on the political persuasion of the government, tax rates on net capital gains have yo-yoed up and down. A significant change in the rates for adjusted net capital gains occurred in 2003 when the rates were reduced from 20% to 15% for most taxpayers (5% for lower income taxpayers). For tax years beginning after 2007, the rate is zero instead of 5%.[4] With the maximum ordinary tax rate for individuals being 39.6% today, individuals can benefit by having a gain classified as a LTCG rather than as ordinary gain or STCG. Thus, much planning is performed to attempt to arrange one's affairs to take advantage of the lower capital gain rates.

As explained later, a LTCG may be subject to one of five different rates [0%, 15%, 20%, 25%, or 28%] depending on what type of asset is sold and the taxpayer's regular tax rate.

Capital losses must be offset against capital gains, and net capital losses are subjected to restrictions on their deductibility. Thus, most taxpayers prefer to have losses classified as ordinary instead of capital.

Most property transactions have tax consequences to the taxpayer. For example, when a sale, exchange, or abandonment occurs, the taxpayer must determine the realized gain or loss, the portion of the realized gain or loss that must be recognized (if any), and the character of the gain or loss. This chapter focuses on determining the realized gain or loss and the portion of the recognized gain or loss classified as capital or ordinary. When classifying a recognized gain or loss, (i.e., the gain or loss actually reported on the taxpayer's tax return) three important questions must be considered:

► What type of property has been sold or exchanged?

► When has a sale or exchange occurred?

► What is the holding period for the property?

In this chapter, these three questions are considered as well as difficulties associated with determining the basis of the property sold or exchanged and the amount of realized gains or losses.

---

[1] Sec. 61(a)(3).
[2] Sec. 62(a)(3).
[3] See page I:5-29 and below for a discussion of the holding period for capital assets. A capital gain or loss is long-term or short-term depending on the length of time the asset has been held by the taxpayer.

[4] Sec. 1(h)(1)(B).

DETERMINATION OF GAIN OR LOSS

OBJECTIVE 1

Determine the realized gain or loss from the sale or other disposition of property

REALIZED GAIN OR LOSS

To determine the **realized gain** or loss, the amount realized from the sale or exchange of property is compared with the adjusted basis of that property. A gain is realized when the amount realized is greater than the basis, and a loss is realized when the amount realized is less than the basis of the property.[5]

EXAMPLE I:5-1 ▶ Jack sells an asset with an adjusted basis of $10,000 to Judy for $14,000. Because the amount realized is greater than the basis, Jack has a realized gain of $4,000 ($14,000 − $10,000). ◄

Despite the fact that most transfers of property involve a sale, gains and losses may also be realized on certain other types of dispositions of property, such as exchanges, condemnations, casualties, thefts, bond retirements, and corporate distributions. However, gains and losses are generally not realized when property is disposed of by gift or bequest.

EXAMPLE I:5-2 ▶ Alice owns land held for investment with a basis of $20,000. The land is taken by the city by right of eminent domain, and she receives a payment of $30,000 for the land. This condemnation is treated as a sale or disposition for income tax purposes, and Alice's realized gain is $10,000 ($30,000 − $20,000). ◄

EXAMPLE I:5-3 ▶ Two years ago, Bob purchased stock of a newly formed corporation for $10,000. During the current year, he receives a $12,000 distribution, constituting a return of capital, from the corporation. This distribution is treated as a sale. Therefore, Bob has a realized gain of $2,000 ($12,000 − $10,000). Bob's basis for the stock is now zero because his basis of $10,000 has been recovered. ◄

There must be an identifiable event for a sale or other disposition to occur. Mere changes in the value of property are not normally recognized as a disposition for purposes of determining a realized gain or loss.

STUDY AID

Students should pay close attention to the technical terms used in tax law. For example, the similar sounding terms of "realized gain" and "recognized gain" are often different dollar amounts for the sale of an asset.

Many reasons exist for not taxing unrealized gains and losses that arise due to a mere change in value. The Treasury Regulations state that "A loss is not ordinarily sustained prior to the sale or other disposition of the property, for the reason that until such sale or other disposition occurs there remains the possibility that the taxpayer may recover or recoup the adjusted basis of the property."[6] Because of administrative difficulties associated with determining fair market value (FMV), disputes with the Internal Revenue Service (IRS) would be greatly increased if unrealized gains were taxed and unrealized losses were allowed as deductions. In addition, payment of tax on income is generally required only when a taxpayer has the wherewithal to pay the tax (e.g., the taxpayer has received cash from the sale or other disposition of property and can therefore pay the tax on the gain).

Amount Realized. The **amount realized** from a sale or other disposition of property is the sum of any money received, the FMV of all other property received, and any debt assumed by the buyer.

EXAMPLE I:5-4 ▶ Tony sells land to Rita for $15,000 in cash and a machine having a $3,000 FMV. Tony's amount realized is $18,000 ($15,000 + $3,000). ◄

---

[5] Sec. 1001(a).

[6] Reg. Sec. 1.1001-1(c)(1).

The determination of FMV is a question of fact and often creates considerable controversy between taxpayers and the IRS. **Fair market value (FMV)** is "the price at which property would change hands between a willing buyer and a willing seller, neither being under any compulsion to buy or sell."[7] The FMV of the asset given in the exchange may be easier to determine than the FMV of the property received. In those cases, the FMV of the property given may be used to measure the amount realized. If a buyer assumes the seller's liability or takes the property subject to the debt, the courts have included the amount of the liability when determining the amount realized.[8]

EXAMPLE I:5-5 ► Anna exchanges land subject to a liability of $20,000 for $35,000 of stock owned by Mario. Mario takes the property subject to the liability. The amount realized by Anna is $55,000 ($35,000 + $20,000 liability assumed by Mario). If Anna's adjusted basis for the land exchanged is $42,000, her realized gain is $13,000 ($55,000 − $42,000). ◄

In the above example, Anna receives stock with a $35,000 FMV and is relieved of a $20,000 debt. Mario's taking the property subject to the debt is equivalent to providing Anna with cash of $20,000. Thus, the amount realized by Anna is $55,000.

Generally, selling expenses such as sales commissions and advertising incurred in order to sell or dispose of the property reduce the amount realized.

EXAMPLE I:5-6 ► Doug sells stock of Briggs Corporation, with a basis of $10,000, for $17,000. Doug pays a sales commission of $300. The amount realized by Doug is $16,700 ($17,000 − $300), and his realized gain is $6,700 ($16,700 − $10,000). ◄

Adjusted Basis. The initial basis of property depends on how the property is acquired (e.g., by purchase, gift, or inheritance). Most property is acquired by purchase and therefore its initial basis is the cost of the property. However, if property is acquired from a decedent, its basis to the estate or heir is its FMV either at the date of death or, if the alternate valuation date is elected, six months from the date of death. The rules for determining the adjusted basis are discussed in subsequent sections of this chapter. Once the initial basis is determined, it may be adjusted upward or downward. Capital additions (also called capital expenditures) are expenditures that add to the value or prolong the life of property or adapt the property to a new or different use. Capital additions increase the basis. Capital recoveries, such as the deductions for casualty losses, cost recovery, and depreciation, reduce the basis. A property's adjusted basis can be determined by the following equation:

Initial basis
+ Capital additions (e.g., new porch for a building)
− Capital recoveries (e.g., depreciation deduction)
= Adjusted basis

Capital expenditures are distinguished from expenditures that are deductible as ordinary and necessary business expenses. For example, the cost of repairing a roof may be a deductible expense, whereas the cost of replacing a roof is a capital addition. It is sometimes difficult to determine whether an item is a capital expenditure or a business expense. Because of the preference for an immediate tax deduction, taxpayers normally prefer to classify expenditures as expenses rather than capital expenditures.

EXAMPLE I:5-7 ► Ellen pays $2,500 for a major overhaul of an automobile used in her trade or business. The $2,500 is capitalized as part of the automobile's cost rather than deducted as a repair expense. ◄

Capital recoveries reduce the adjusted basis. The most common form of capital recovery is the deduction for depreciation or cost recovery. As discussed in Chapter I:10, the modi-

[7] *CIR v. Homer H. Marshman*, 5 AFTR 2d 1528, 60-2 USTC ¶9484 (6th Cir., 1960).

[8] *Beulah B. Crane v. CIR*, 35 AFTR 776, 47-1 USTC ¶9217 (USSC, 1947).

fied accelerated cost recovery system (MACRS) is mandatory for most tangible depreciable property placed in service after 1986. The accelerated cost recovery system (ACRS) applies to most property placed in service after December 31, 1980, and before 1987.

EXAMPLE I:5-8 ►

ADDITIONAL COMMENT

In addition to depreciation, other capital recoveries that reduce the adjusted basis of property include depletion, amortization, corporate distributions that are a return of basis, compensation or awards for involuntary conversions, deductible casualty losses, insurance reimbursements, and cash rebates received by a purchaser.

Jeremy paid $100,000 for equipment two years ago and has claimed depreciation deductions of $37,000 for the two years. The cost of repairs during the same period was $6,000. At the end of the two-year period, the property's adjusted basis is $63,000 ($100,000 − $37,000). The amount spent for repairs does not affect the basis. ◄

Recovery of Basis Doctrine. The **recovery of basis doctrine** states that taxpayers are allowed to recover the basis of an asset without being taxed because such amounts are a return of capital that the taxpayer has invested in the property. If a taxpayer receives a $12,000 return of capital distribution from a corporation when the taxpayer's basis for its investment in the corporation's stock is $10,000, the first $10,000 received represents a recovery of basis and the $2,000 excess amount is treated as a gain realized on a sale or exchange of the stock investment. In many cases, basis is recovered in the form of a deduction for depreciation, cost recovery, or a casualty loss.

TYPICAL MISCONCEPTION

It is sometimes incorrectly believed that all realized gains and losses are recognized for tax purposes. Although most realized gains are recognized, some realized losses are not. For example, losses on the sale or exchange of property held for personal use are not recognized.

RECOGNIZED GAIN OR LOSS

Realized gain or loss represents the difference between the amount realized and the adjusted basis when a sale or exchange occurs. The amount of gain or loss actually reported on the tax return is the **recognized gain or loss**. In some instances, gain or loss is not recognized due to special provisions in the tax law (e.g., a gain or loss may be deferred or a loss may be disallowed).

Losses are generally deductible if they are incurred in carrying on a trade or business, incurred in an activity engaged in for profit, and casualty and theft losses. Realized losses on the sale or exchange of assets held for personal use are not recognized for tax purposes. Therefore, a taxpayer who incurs a loss on the sale or exchange of a personal-use asset does not fully recover the basis. As explained in Chapter I:8, realized losses on personal-use assets may be recognized to some extent if the property is disposed of by casualty or theft.

EXAMPLE I:5-9 ►

Ralph purchases a personal residence for $60,000. Deductions for depreciation are not allowed because the asset is not used in a trade or business or held for the production of income. If Ralph sells the house for $55,000, the realized loss of $5,000 is a capital loss but not deductible. He recovers only $55,000 of his original $60,000 basis. ◄

BASIS CONSIDERATIONS

OBJECTIVE 2

Determine the basis of property

COST OF ACQUIRED PROPERTY

In most cases, the basis of property is its cost. **Cost** is the amount paid for the property in cash or the FMV of other property given in the exchange. Any costs of acquiring the property and preparing the property for use are included in the cost of the property.

EXAMPLE I:5-10 ►

Penny purchases equipment for $15,000, pays delivery costs of $300, and installation costs of $250. The cost of the equipment is $15,550. ◄

Funds borrowed and used to pay for an asset are included in the cost. Obligations of the seller that are assumed by the buyer increase the asset's cost.

EXAMPLE I:5-11 ►

Peggy purchases an asset by paying cash of $40,000 and signs a note payable to the seller for $60,000. She also assumes a $2,000 lien against the property. Her basis for the asset is $102,000 and the amount realized by the seller is $102,000. ◄

Uniform Capitalization Rules. For financial accounting purposes, businesses must capitalize certain costs in connection with inventory, such as direct materials, direct labor, and overhead. For many years, businesses had a degree of flexibility with respect to capitalizing or expensing certain costs for tax purposes. However, the tax law now mandates one set of capitalization rules applicable to all taxpayers and all types of activities. These uniform capitalization rules, which apply principally to inventory, are provided in Sec. 263A and discussed in Chapter I:11.

The uniform capitalization rules also affect property other than inventory if the property is used in a taxpayer's trade or business or in an activity engaged in for profit. Taxes paid or accrued in connection with the acquisition of property are included as part of the cost of the acquired property. Taxes paid or accrued in connection with the disposition of property reduce the amount realized on the disposition.[9]

EXAMPLE I:5-12 ► The Compact Corporation owns and operates a funeral home. The corporation purchases a hearse for $30,000 and pays sales taxes of $1,500. The cost basis for the hearse is $31,500. ◄

Capitalization of Interest. Interest on debt paid or incurred during the production period to finance production expenditures incurred to construct, build, install, manufacture, develop, or improve real or tangible personal property must be capitalized.[10] The real or tangible personal property must have "a long useful life, an estimated production period exceeding two years, or an estimated production period exceeding one year and a cost exceeding $1,000,000."[11] Property has a long useful life if it is real property or property with a class life of at least 20 years. The production period starts when "production of the property begins and ends when the property is ready to be placed in service or is ready to be held for sale."[12]

EXAMPLE I:5-13 ► The Indiana Corporation started construction of a $3 million motel on July 1, 2014, and borrowed an amount equal to the motel's construction costs. The motel is completed and ready for service on October 1, 2015. Interest incurred for the construction loan for the period from July 1, 2014, through October 1, 2015, is included in the motel's cost. The capitalized interest cost is depreciated over the motel's thirty-nine year recovery period (see Chapter I:10). ◄

Identification Problems. In most cases, the adjusted basis of property sold is easily identified. However, problems arise when property is homogenous in nature such as when an investor owns several blocks of common stock of the same corporation purchased on different dates at different prices. The Regulations require the taxpayer to adequately identify the particular stock sold or exchanged.[13] Many investors allow brokers to hold their stock in street name (i.e., the brokerage firm holds title to the stock certificates) and thus do not make a physical transfer of securities. Such investors need to provide specific instructions to the broker as to which securities should be sold. If the stock sold or exchanged is not adequately identified, the first-in, first-out (FIFO) method must be used to identify the stock. With the FIFO method, the stock sold or exchanged is presumed to come from the first lot or lots acquired.

EXAMPLE I:5-14 ► Judy purchased 300 shares of the Gustavel Corporation stock last year:

Month Acquired	Size of Block	Basis
January	100 shares	$4,000
May	100	5,000
October	100	6,000

In March of the current year, Judy sells 120 shares of the stock for $5,160. If Judy specifically identifies the stock sold as being all of the stock purchased in October and 20 shares purchased in May, her realized loss is $1,840 [$5,160 − ($6,000 + $1,000)]. ◄

[9] Sec. 164(a).
[10] Sec. 263A(f).
[11] Sec. 263A(f)(1)(B).
[12] Sec. 263A(f)(4)(B).
[13] Reg. Sec. 1.1012-1(c)(1).

If Judy does not specifically identify the stock sold, the FIFO method is used, and her realized gain is $160 [$5,160 − ($4,000 + $1,000)].

Owners of shares of mutual funds have more choices when determining the basis of shares sold. In addition to FIFO and specific identification, they may use an average cost method.[14]

EXAMPLE I:5-15 ▶ Colin purchased 100 shares of Bluejay Mutual Fund on May 10, 2013, for $1,000, and has been reinvesting dividends. On December 20, 2015, he sells 115 shares.

ADDITIONAL COMMENT

Because of the difficulty and complexity of tracking basis of shares in a mutual fund, the average cost method is widely used by taxpayers.

	Amount	No. of Shares
Purchase May 10, 2013	$1,000	100
Reinvested Dividend Nov. 1, 2013	125	10
Reinvested Dividends Nov. 1, 2014	140	7
Reinvested Dividends Nov. 1, 2015	185	8
	1,450	125
		$11.60 Average Cost

His basis for the 115 shares sold is $1,225 with FIFO, $1,334 (115 × $11.60) with average cost and could be as high as $1,350 with specific identification. Note that if he sells the shares obtained with the reinvested dividends in 2015, part of the gain or loss is short-term. ◀

PROPERTY RECEIVED AS A GIFT: GIFTS AFTER 1921

The basis of property received as a gift is generally the same as the donor's basis.[15] If the FMV of the property at time of the gift is less than the donor's basis, the donee may have to use one basis if the property is subsequently disposed of at a gain and another if the property is disposed of at a loss. As discussed later in this chapter, the basis may be increased by a portion or all of the gift tax paid because of the transfer.

Current rules for determining the donee's basis for property received as a gift are a function of the relationship between the FMV of the property at the time the gift is made and the donor's basis. If the FMV is equal to or greater than the donor's basis, the donee's basis is the same as the donor's basis for all purposes. However, if the FMV is less than the donor's basis, the donee has a dual basis for the property, that is, a basis for loss and a basis for gain. If the donee later transfers the property at a loss, the donee's basis is the property's FMV at the time of the gift (basis for loss). However, if the donee transfers the property at a gain, the donee's basis is the same as the donor's basis (basis for gain).

ADDITIONAL COMMENT

Upon receipt of property from a relative, one should inquire as to its basis at that time. It might be years later that the asset is sold and the information about the donor's basis may be lost or forgotten.

EXAMPLE I:5-16 ▶ Kevin makes a gift of property with a basis of $350 to Janet when it has a $425 FMV. If Janet sells the property for $450, she has a realized gain of $100 ($450 − $350). If Janet sells the property for $330, she has a realized loss of $20 ($330 − $350). Because the FMV of the property at the time of the gift is more than the donor's basis, the donee's basis is $350 for determining both gain and loss. ◀

The following example illustrates the scenario when a taxpayer has a dual basis. The property is received as a gift when the FMV is less than the donor's basis, so the basis for determining a gain is different from the basis for determining a loss.

EXAMPLE I:5-17 ▶ Chuck makes a gift of property with a basis of $600 to Maggie when the property has a $500 FMV. Maggie's basis for the property is $600 if the property is sold at a gain (i.e., for more than $600), but the basis is $500 if the property is sold at a loss (i.e., for less than $500). If the property is sold for $500 or more but not more than $600, no gain or loss is recognized. ◀

The dual basis rules were designed to prevent tax-avoidance schemes. Taxpayers are prevented from shifting unrealized losses to another taxpayer by making gifts of such "loss" property. For example, a low-income taxpayer who owns property that has depreciated in value might transfer the property by gift to a high-income taxpayer who would receive greater tax benefit from the deduction of the loss upon the subsequent sale of the

---

[14] For mutual fund investors, the IRS has authorized the use of FIFO, specific identification, or two average cost basis methods if only a portion of the fund shares is redeemed or sold. (See Reg. Sec. 1.1012-1(e) and Chapter I:17.)

[15] Sec. 1015(a).

TAX STRATEGY TIP

Donors generally should not make gifts of property that have declined in value below original cost. Since the donee's basis will be the property's FMV, the loss will never be recognized.

KEY POINT

No gift tax can be added to the basis of the property if the donor's basis is greater than the FMV of the property.

property. The loss basis rules prevent the donee from recognizing a loss on the sale of the property because the basis for loss is the lesser of the donor's basis or FMV on the date of the gift.

Effect of Gift Tax on Basis. If the donor pays a gift tax on the transfer of property, the donee's basis may be increased. This increase occurs only if the FMV of the property exceeds the donor's basis on the date of the gift. For taxable gifts after 1976, the increase in the donee's basis is equal to a pro rata portion of the gift tax attributable to the unrealized appreciation in the property. The amount of the addition to the donee's basis is determined as follows:[16]

$$\text{Gift tax paid} \times \frac{\text{FMV at time of the gift} - \text{Donor's basis}}{\text{Amount of the gift}}$$

The amount of the gift is the FMV of the property less the amount of the annual exclusion which is $14,000 in 2015.[17]

EXAMPLE I:5-18 ▶ During the current year, Cindy makes one gift of property with a $24,000 basis to Jessie when the property has a $64,000 FMV. Cindy pays a gift tax of $18,500. The amount of the gift is $50,000 ($64,000 − $14,000). Thus, 80% [($64,000 − $24,000)/$50,000] of the gift tax is added to Jessie's basis. Jessie's basis for the property for determining both gain and loss is $38,800 [$24,000 + (0.80 × $18,500)]. ◀

EXAMPLE I:5-19 ▶ During the current year, Sally makes a gift of property with a basis of $50,000 to Troy when the property has a $40,000 FMV. Sally pays a gift tax of $1,000. Troy's basis for the property is not affected by the gift tax paid by Sally because the FMV is less than the donor's basis at the time of the gift. Troy's basis for the property is $50,000 to determine gain and $40,000 to determine loss. ◀

? STOP & THINK

Question: Pete wants to make a gift of either ABC common stock (basis of $44,000 and FMV of $50,000) or XYZ common stock (basis of $73,000 and FMV of $50,000) to his nephew. Pete and his nephew have the same tax rate. Which stock should he give to his nephew?

Solution: Pete should give the ABC stock to his nephew because the nephew's basis for determining a gain or loss is $44,000 plus a portion of any gift tax Pete pays. The nephew's basis for XYZ common stock is $50,000 to determine a loss and $73,000 to determine a gain. If the nephew sells XYZ stock for less than $73,000, no loss is recognized and thus some of the basis is not used. Note that Pete would have a $23,000 loss if he sells the XYZ stock for $50,000. Furthermore, the nephew's basis for the XYZ stock is not increased if Pete has to pay a gift tax on the $36,000 taxable gift.

PROPERTY RECEIVED FROM A DECEDENT

The basis of property received from a decedent who died in a year other than 2010 is the FMV of the property at the date of the decedent's death or an alternate valuation date (AVD).[18] This provision can result in either a step up (increase) or step down (decrease) in basis, but it is frequently described as the stepped-up basis rule. For decedents dying in 2010, the estate tax was repealed (see the discussion of Carryover Basis Rules below).

EXAMPLE I:5-20 ▶ Patrick inherited property having an $8 million FMV on the date of his sister's death in 2015. The decedent's basis in the property is $3.6 million. The executor of the estate does not elect the AVD. Patrick's basis for the property is $8 million. ◀

EXAMPLE I:5-21 ▶ Dianna inherited property having a $6 million FMV at the date of the decedent's death in 2015. The decedent's basis in the property is $7.2 million. The AVD is not elected. Dianna's basis for the property is $6 million. ◀

---

[16] Sec. 1015(d)(6).
[17] Sec. 1015(d)(2) and Sec. 2503(b). The annual exclusion for gifts was increased to $14,000 starting in 2013. From 2009–2012, the annual exclusion was $13,000. From 2005–2008, an annual exclusion of $12,000 per year was allowed for each donee, from 2002–2004, the annual exclusion was

$11,000. Prior to 2002, the annual exclusion was $10,000. See Chapter I:1 for a limited discussion of the annual exclusion and Chapter C:12 of the *Corporations, Partnerships, Estates & Trusts* and *Comprehensive* volumes for a more detailed discussion.
[18] Sec. 1014(a).

REAL-WORLD EXAMPLE
The alternate valuation date was used in valuing the estates of many individuals owning large portfolios of common stocks who died shortly before the stock market crash in October 1987.

Instead of using the FMV on the date of death to determine the estate tax, the executor of the estate may elect to use the FMV on the AVD. The AVD is generally six months after the date of death. If the AVD is elected, the basis for all of the assets in the estate is their FMV on that date unless the property is distributed by the estate to the heirs or is sold before the AVD. If the AVD is used, property distributed or sold after the date of the decedent's death and before the AVD has a basis equal to its FMV on the date of distribution or the date of disposal.[19]

If the estate is small enough that an estate tax return is not required, the value of the property on the AVD may not be used.[20] An estate tax return must be filed if an individual dies in 2015 and the gross estate plus any previous taxable gifts exceeds $5.43 million.

EXAMPLE I:5-22 ▶ Marilyn inherited all of the property owned by an individual who died in April 2015, when the property had a $100,000 FMV. The value of the property six months later was $90,000. Because of the size of the estate, no estate tax was due. The AVD may not be used, and Marilyn's basis for the property is $100,000. Note that Marilyn does not want the AVD to be used because her basis would be $90,000 instead of $100,000. ◀

As noted above, the basis of the property to the estate and the heirs can be affected if the AVD is used to value the estate's assets. The AVD may be elected only if the value of the gross estate and the amount of estate tax after credits are reduced as a result of using the AVD.[21] This means that the aggregate value of the assets determined by using the AVD may be used only if the total value of the assets decreased during the six-month period.

EXAMPLE I:5-23 ▶ Helmut inherited all of the property owned by an individual who died in March 2015 when the FMV of the property was $5.8 million. Six months after the date of death, the property had a $5.95 million FMV. The property is distributed to Helmut in December. Use of the AVD is not permitted because the value of the gross estate has increased. Therefore, his basis in the property is $5.8 million, the FMV on the date of death. ◀

An executor may elect to use the AVD to reduce the estate taxes owed by the estate. However, the income tax basis of the property included in the estate is also reduced for heirs who inherit the property.

EXAMPLE I:5-24 ▶ Michelle inherited property with a $6.2 million FMV at the date of the decedent's death in 2015. The FMV of the property on the AVD (six months after the date of the decedent's death) is $5.74 million. The executor of the estate elects to use $5.74 million to value the property for estate tax purposes, and Michelle's basis for the property is thus $5.74 million instead of $6.2 million. ◀

ADDITIONAL COMMENT
At least five billionaires, including George Steinbrenner of the New York Yankees, died in 2010, and their estates were probably not subject to the estate tax.

Carryover Basis Rules-Special Rule for 2010. In 2001, Congress eliminated the estate tax for individuals dying in 2010; however, the estate tax was scheduled to return in 2011 and be higher than the estate tax in 2009. Most tax professionals did not expect the estate tax to actually be repealed for the year 2010, but Congress did not take action to reinstate the estate tax retroactively until December of 2010. Congress reinstated the estate tax for 2010 and future years, but estates of individuals dying in 2010 may elect to use the provisions in effect for 2010 and not have the estate tax apply.

The existence of the estate tax has implications for the basis of property transferred to others when one dies. For 2010, a modified carryover basis rule applies if the estate elects to not have the estate tax apply. A taxpayer who inherits the property will take the lesser of the decedent's basis or FMV at time of death, but the basis may be increased if the asset is appreciated. The basis may not be increased to more than the FMV, and the total amount of increase is limited to $1.3 million plus any unused built-in loss or NOL carryover. A surviving spouse may receive an additional $3 million adjustment.

If Patrick's sister in Example 5-20 died in 2010, an estate tax is due unless the estate elected to have the estate tax not apply. Because the exemption equivalent in 2010 was $5 million or less, the estate would probably have elected to pay no estate tax. If so, Patrick's basis is $4.9 million ($3,600,000 + $1,300,000). Patrick's basis is $7.9 million if the decedent was his spouse ($3,600,000 + $1,300,000 + $3,000,000). If the election is not made and the estate tax applies, Patrick's basis is the $8,000,000 FMV.

---

[19] Sec. 2032(a).
[20] Rev. Rul. 56-60, 1956-1 C.B. 443. For a decedent dying in 2011 and 2012, Sec. 6018(a) requires an estate tax return to be filed if the gross estate exceeds $5 million ($3.5 million in 2009, $2 million in 2006–2008 and $1.5 million for decedents dying in 2004 or 2005).

[21] Credits available include the unified transfer tax credit and possibly credits for gift taxes, foreign death taxes, and the credit for taxes on prior transfers.

Dianna's basis in Example 5-21 is $6 million even if the death occurred in 2010. The estate would elect to have the estate tax not apply and avoid any estate tax liability, but the basis is the same under the stepped-up basis rules and the carryover basis rules because the decedent's basis in the property is greater than its FMV.

Community Property. If the decedent and the decedent's spouse own property under community property laws,[22] one-half of the property is included in the decedent's gross estate and its basis to the surviving spouse is its FMV.[23] The surviving spouse's one-half share of the community property is also adjusted to FMV.[24] In effect, the surviving spouse's share of the community property is considered to have passed from the decedent.

EXAMPLE I:5-25 ► Matt and Jane, a married couple, live in Texas, a community property state, and jointly own land as community property that cost $110,000. The land has an $800,000 FMV when Jane dies, leaving all of her property to Matt. His basis for the entire property is $800,000. ◄

In a common law state, one-half of the jointly owned property is included in the decedent's estate and is adjusted to its FMV. The survivor's share of the jointly held property is not adjusted.

EXAMPLE I:5-26 ► Barry and Maria, a married couple, live in Iowa, a common law state, and jointly own land that cost $200,000. The property has a $700,000 FMV when Barry dies, leaving all of his property to Maria. Her basis for the land is $450,000 [$100,000 + (0.50 × $700,000)]. ◄

PROPERTY CONVERTED FROM PERSONAL USE TO BUSINESS USE

Often, taxpayers who own personal-use assets convert these assets to an income-producing use or for use in a trade or business. When this conversion occurs, the property's basis must be determined. The basis for computing depreciation is the lower of FMV or the adjusted basis of the property when the asset is transferred from personal use to an income-producing use or for use in a trade or business.[25] This rule prevents taxpayers from obtaining the benefits of depreciation to the extent that the property has declined in value during the period that it is held for personal use.

EXAMPLE I:5-27 ►

Olga owns a boat that cost $2,000 and is used for personal enjoyment. At a time when the boat has a $1,400 FMV, Olga transfers the boat to her business of operating a marina. The basis for depreciation is $1,400 because the FMV is less than Olga's adjusted basis at the time of conversion to business use. The $600 decline ($2,000 − $1,400) that occurred while Olga used the boat for personal use may not be deducted as depreciation. ◄

If the boat's FMV in Example I:5-27 is more than $2,000, the basis for depreciation is $2,000 because the FMV is higher than its adjusted basis at the time the asset is transferred to business use.

If a personal-use asset is transferred to business use when its FMV is less than its adjusted basis, the basis for determining a loss on a subsequent sale or disposition of the property is its FMV on the date of the conversion to business use less any depreciation taken after the transfer to business use.[26]

EXAMPLE I:5-28 ► Susanna purchased a personal residence in 1990 for $50,000 and converted the property to rental property in 1993 when its FMV was $46,000. Assume depreciation of $20,700 has been deducted after the conversion in 1993, and the property is sold for $21,000. The basis of the property is $25,300 ($46,000 − $20,700), and her loss on the sale is $4,300 ($21,000 − $25,300). ◄

The rule for determining basis, that is, lower of adjusted basis or FMV, applies only to the sale of converted property at a loss. The basis for determining gain is its adjusted basis when converted less depreciation taken after the transfer to business use.

EXAMPLE I:5-29 ► Assume the same facts as in Example I:5-28, except the property is sold for $31,000 instead of $21,000. The basis of the property is $29,300 ($50,000 − $20,700) and her gain is $1,700 ($31,000 − $29,300). ◄

---

[22] Community property states are Arizona, California, Idaho, Louisiana, New Mexico, Nevada, Texas, and Washington. Wisconsin has a marital property law that is basically the same as community property.
[23] Sec. 1014(a).
[24] Sec. 1014(b)(6).
[25] Reg. Sec. 1.167(g)-1.
[26] Reg. Sec. 1.165-9(b)(2).

Without the rule for determining basis of personal-use property converted to business property, taxpayers would have an incentive to convert nonbusiness assets that have declined in value to business use before selling the asset to convert nondeductible losses into deductible losses.

EXAMPLE I:5-30 ▶ Craig owns a personal-use asset with a basis of $80,000 and a $50,000 FMV. If he sells the asset for its FMV, the $30,000 loss ($50,000 − $80,000) is not deductible because losses on the sale of personal-use assets are not deductible. If Craig converts the asset to business use and then immediately sells the asset for $50,000, no loss is realized because the basis of the asset for purposes of determining loss is $50,000, the FMV when property was converted. ◀

ALLOCATION OF BASIS

REAL-WORLD EXAMPLE

A taxpayer purchased a group of lots and allocated the total cost evenly among the lots. The court, however, held that more cost should be allocated to the water-front lots than to the interior lots. *Biscayne Bay Islands Co.,* 23 B.T.A. 731 (1931).

When property is obtained in one transaction and portions of the property are subsequently disposed of at different times, the basis of the property is allocated to the different portions of the property. Gain or loss is computed at the time of disposal for each portion. If a taxpayer purchases a 20-acre tract of land and later sells the entire tract, an allocation of basis is not needed. However, if the taxpayer divides the property into smaller tracts of land for resale, the cost of the 20-acre tract must be allocated among the smaller tracts of land.

Basket Purchase. If more than one asset is acquired in a single purchase transaction (i.e., a basket purchase), the cost must be apportioned to the various assets acquired. The allocation is based on the relative FMVs of the assets.

EXAMPLE I:5-31 ▶ Kelly purchases a duplex for $80,000 to use as a rental property. The land has a $15,000 FMV, and the building has a $65,000 FMV. Kelly's bases for the land and the building are $15,000 and $65,000, respectively. ◀

SELF-STUDY QUESTION

If Kelly in Example I:5-31 paid $2,000 for the cost of a title search and other costs that must be capitalized, what is the basis of the land and building?

Because no depreciation deduction is allowed for land, taxpayers tend to favor a liberal allocation of the total purchase price to the building. Appraisals or other measures of FMV may be used to make the allocation.

ANSWER

Land $15,375
Building $66,625

Common Costs. As in the case of financial accounting, common costs incurred to obtain or prepare an asset for service must be capitalized and allocated to the basis of the individual assets.

EXAMPLE I:5-32 ▶ Priscilla acquires three machines for $60,000, which have FMVs of $30,000, $20,000, and $10,000, respectively. Costs of delivery amount to $2,000, and costs to install the three machines amount to $1,000. The total installation and delivery costs of $3,000 are allocated to the three machines based on their FMVs.

The allocation of the $3,000 of common costs occurs as follows:

$$\text{Machine No. 1: } \frac{\$30,000 \text{ FMV}}{\$30,000 + \$20,000 + \$10,000} \times \$3,000 = \$1,500$$

$$\text{Machine No. 2: } \frac{\$20,000 \text{ FMV}}{\$30,000 + \$20,000 + \$10,000} \times \$3,000 = \$1,000$$

$$\text{Machine No. 3: } \frac{\$10,000 \text{ FMV}}{\$30,000 + \$20,000 + \$10,000} \times \$3,000 = \$500$$

The bases for each of the three machines are $31,500, $21,000, and $10,500, respectively. ◀

Nontaxable Stock Dividends Received. If a nontaxable stock dividend is received, a portion of the basis of the stock on which the stock dividend is received is allocated to the new shares received from the stock dividend.[27] The cost basis of the previously acquired shares is reduced by the amount of basis allocated to the stock dividend shares. If the stock received as a stock dividend is the same type as the stock owned before the dividend, the total basis of the stock owned before the dividend is allocated equally to all shares now owned.

---

[27] Sec. 307(a).

EXAMPLE I:5-33 ▶ Wayne owns 1,000 shares of Bell Corporation common stock with a $44,000 basis. Wayne receives a nontaxable 10% common stock dividend and now owns 1,100 shares of common stock. The basis for each share of common stock is now $40 ($44,000 ÷ 1,100). ◀

If the stock received as a stock dividend is not the same type as the stock owned before the dividend, the allocation is based on relative FMVs.

EXAMPLE I:5-34 ▶ Stacey owns 500 shares of Montana Corporation common stock with a $60,000 basis. She receives a nontaxable stock dividend payable in 50 shares of preferred stock. At time of the distribution, the common stock has a $40,000 FMV ($80 × 500 shares), and the preferred stock has a $10,000 FMV ($200 × 50 shares). After the distribution, Stacey owns 50 shares of preferred stock with a basis of $12,000 [($10,000 ÷ $50,000) × $60,000]. Thus, $12,000 of the basis of the common stock is allocated to the preferred stock and the basis of the common stock is reduced from $60,000 to $48,000. ◀

KEY POINT

Corporations issue stock rights to shareholders so that the shareholders will be able to maintain their same proportional ownership in the corporation. This is called the preemptive right.

Nontaxable Stock Rights Received. Stock rights represent rights to acquire shares of a specified corporation's stock at a specific exercise price when certain conditions are met. The exercise price is usually less than the market price when the stock rights are issued. Stock rights may be distributed to employees as compensation, and they are often issued to shareholders to encourage them to purchase more stock, thereby providing more capital for the corporation.

If the FMV of nontaxable stock rights received is less than 15% of the FMV of the stock, the basis of the stock rights is zero unless the taxpayer elects to allocate the basis between the stock rights and the stock owned before distribution of the stock rights.[28]

EXAMPLE I:5-35 ▶ Tina owns 100 shares of Bear Corporation common stock with a $27,000 basis and a $50,000 FMV. She receives 100 nontaxable stock rights with a total FMV of $4,000. Because the FMV of the stock rights is less than 15% of the FMV of the stock (0.15 × $50,000 = $7,500), the basis of the stock rights is zero unless Tina elects to make an allocation. ◀

REAL-WORLD EXAMPLE

In 1993, United States Cellular Corporation issued one right for each common share held. Each whole right entitled the holder to buy one common share for $33.

If, Tina, in the example above, elects to allocate the basis of $27,000 between the stock rights and the stock, the basis of the rights is $2,000 ([$4,000 ÷ $54,000] × $27,000) and the basis of the stock is $25,000 ([$50,000 ÷ $54,000] × $27,000).

The decision to allocate the basis affects the gain or loss realized on the sale or disposition of the stock rights because the basis of the rights is zero unless an allocation is made. Furthermore, the basis of any stock acquired by exercising the rights is affected by whether or not a portion of the basis is allocated to the rights. The basis of stock acquired by exercising the stock rights is the amount paid plus the basis of the stock rights exercised.

EXAMPLE I:5-36 ▶ George receives 10 stock rights as a nontaxable distribution, and no basis is allocated to the stock rights. With each stock right, George may acquire one share of stock for $20. If he exercises all 10 stock rights, the new stock acquired has a basis of $200 ($20 × 10 shares). If George sells all 10 stock rights for $135, he has a realized gain of $135 ($135 − $0). ◀

If the FMV of a nontaxable stock right received is equal to or greater than 15% of the FMV of the stock, the basis of the stock owned before the distribution must be allocated between the stock and the stock rights.

EXAMPLE I:5-37 ▶ Helen owns 100 shares of NMO common stock with a $14,000 basis and a $30,000 FMV. She receives 100 stock rights with a total FMV of $5,000. Because the FMV of the stock rights is at least 15% of the FMV of the stock, the $14,000 basis must be allocated between the stock rights and the stock. The basis of the stock rights is $2,000 [($5,000 ÷ $35,000) × $14,000] and the basis of the stock is $12,000 [($30,000 ÷ $35,000) × $14,000]. ◀

A recipient of stock rights generally has three courses of action. The stock rights can be sold or exchanged, in which case the basis allocated to the stock rights, if any, is used to determine gain or loss. The stock rights may be exercised, and any basis allocated to the rights is added to the purchase price of the acquired stock. The stock rights may be allowed to expire, in which case no loss is recognized, and any basis allocated to the rights is reallocated back to the stock. If the stock rights received in the above example expire without being exercised, Helen does not recognize a loss and the basis of her 100 shares of common stock is $14,000.

Property basis rules are highlighted in Topic Review I:5-1.

---

[28] Sec. 307(b)(1).

TOPIC REVIEW I:5-1

Property Basis Rules

METHOD ACQUIRED	BASIS OF THE ACQUIRED PROPERTY
1. Acquired by direct purchase	1. Basis includes the amount paid for the property, costs of preparing the property for use, obligations of the seller assumed by the buyer, and liabilities to which the property is subject.
2. Acquired as a gift. (a) FMV on the date of the gift is equal to or greater than the donor's basis (b) FMV on the date of the gift is less than the donor's basis	2. (a) The donee's basis is the same as the donor's basis plus a pro rata portion of the gift tax attributable to the property's unrealized appreciation at the time of the gift. (b) The donee's gain basis is the donor's basis and the loss basis is FMV. No increase for any gift tax paid.
3. Received from a decedent* (a) AVD is not elected (b) AVD is elected	3. (a) The basis is its FMV on the date of death. (b) The basis of nondistributed property is its FMV on the AVD. If the property is distributed or sold before this date, its basis is FMV on the date of sale or distribution.
4. Converted from personal to business use	4. The basis for a loss (as well as for depreciation) is the lesser of its adjusted basis or FMV at date of conversion. The basis for a gain is its adjusted basis at date of conversion.
5. Nontaxable stock dividend	5. Basis of the stock dividend shares includes a pro rata portion of the adjusted basis of the underlying shares owned.
6. Nontaxable stock right	6. If the FMV of the rights is less than 15% of the stock's FMV, the basis of the rights is zero unless an election is made to allocate basis. Basis of the underlying stock is allocated to the rights based on the respective FMVs of the stock and rights.

* Special rules apply to decedents dying in 2010.

DEFINITION OF A CAPITAL ASSET

OBJECTIVE 3

Distinguish between capital assets and other assets

Instead of defining capital assets, Sec. 1221 provides a list of properties that are **not** capital assets. Thus, a capital asset is any property owned by a taxpayer *other* than the types of property specified in Sec. 1221. Property that is not a capital asset includes the following:

1. Inventory or property held primarily for sale to customers in the ordinary course of a trade or business.
2. Property used in the trade or business and subject to the allowance for depreciation provided in Sec. 167 or real property used in a trade or business. (As explained in Chapter I:13, these properties are referred to as *Sec. 1231 assets* if held by the taxpayer more than one year.)
3. Accounts or notes receivable acquired in the ordinary course of a trade or business for services rendered or from the sale of property described in item 1.
4. Supplies of a type regularly used or consumed in the ordinary course of a trade or business.
5. Other assets including
   a. A letter, memorandum, or similar property held by a taxpayer for whom such property was prepared or produced.
   b. A copyright; a literary, musical, or artistic composition; a letter or memorandum; or similar property held by a taxpayer whose personal efforts created such property or whose basis in the property for determining a gain is determined by reference to the basis of such property in the hands of one who created the property or one for whom such property was prepared or produced.

TYPICAL MISCONCEPTION

It is common in financial accounting classes to include property used in a trade or business in the definition of a capital asset. For example, factory buildings, machinery, trucks, and office buildings would be defined as capital assets. However, such items are not capital assets for tax purposes.

c. A U.S. government publication held by a taxpayer who receives the publication by any means other than a purchase at the price the publication is offered for sale to the public.
d. A U.S. government publication held by a taxpayer whose basis in the property for determining a gain is determined by reference to the basis of such property in the hands of a taxpayer in item 5c (e.g., certain property received by gift).

EXAMPLE I:5-38 ▶

Maxine owns a building used in her business. Other business assets include equipment, inventory, and accounts receivable. None of the assets are classified as capital assets. ◀

Chapter I:13 provides an in-depth discussion of business assets such as buildings, land, and equipment. Although these items are not capital assets, Sec. 1231 provides in many cases that the gain on the sale or exchange of such an asset is eventually taxed as LTCG.

EXAMPLE I:5-39 ▶

Eric owns an automobile held for personal use and also owns a copyright for a book he has written. Because the copyright is held by the taxpayer whose personal efforts created the property, it is not a capital asset. The automobile held for personal use is a capital asset. ◀

SELF-STUDY QUESTION

Doug owns a personal residence, an automobile, 100 shares of Ford Motor Company, and a poem he wrote for his girlfriend. Which of these assets are capital assets?

ANSWER

All of the items are capital assets except the poem, which is a literary composition that Doug created. If Doug gives the poem to his girlfriend, the poem is still not a capital asset.

By analyzing Examples I:5-38 and I:5-39, one can conclude that the classification of an asset is often determined by its use. An automobile used in a trade or business is not a capital asset but is a capital asset when held for personal use. Examples of assets that qualify as capital assets include a personal residence, land held for personal use, and investments in stocks and bonds. In addition, certain types of assets are specifically given capital asset status, such as patents, franchises, etc. These and other special assets are discussed later in this chapter.

Recently, Congress made a major change for self-created musical works. Pursuant to Sec. 1221(b)(3), a taxpayer whose personal efforts created such property may now make an election to treat the sale or exchange of musical compositions or copyrights in self-created musical works as a sale or exchange of a capital asset.

INFLUENCE OF THE COURTS

In *Corn Products Refining Co.*, the Supreme Court rendered a landmark decision when it determined that the sale of futures contracts related to the purchase of raw materials resulted in ordinary rather than capital gains and losses.[29] The Corn Products Company, a manufacturer of products made from grain corn, purchased futures contracts for corn to ensure an adequate supply of raw materials. Delivery of the corn was accepted when needed for manufacturing operations, and unneeded contracts were later sold. Corn Products contended that any gains or losses on the sale of the unneeded contracts should be capital gains and losses because futures contracts are customarily viewed as security investments, which qualify as capital assets. The Supreme Court held that these transactions represented an integral part of the business for the purpose of protecting the company's manufacturing operations and the gains and losses should, therefore, be ordinary in nature.

ADDITIONAL COMMENT

If an asset such as an automobile is used in part in a trade or business and in part for personal use, then the business part of the car is not a capital asset, but the other part is a capital asset.

ETHICAL POINT

A CPA should not prepare or sign a tax return for a client unless the position or issue has (1) a realistic possibility of being sustained on its merits or (2) is not frivolous and is adequately disclosed in the return.

Although the *Corn Products* doctrine has been interpreted as creating a nonstatutory exception to the definition of a capital asset when the asset is purchased for business purposes, the Supreme Court ruled in the 1988 *Arkansas Best Corporation* case that the motivation for acquiring assets is irrelevant to the question of whether assets are capital assets. Arkansas Best, a bank holding company, sold shares of a bank's stock that had been acquired for the purpose of protecting its business reputation. Relying on the *Corn Products* doctrine, the company deducted the loss as ordinary. The Supreme Court ruled that the loss was a capital loss because the stock is within the broad definition of the term *capital asset* in Sec. 1221 and is outside the classes of property that are excluded from capital-asset status.[30] *Arkansas Best* apparently limits the application of *Corn Products* to hedging transactions that are an integral part of a taxpayer's system of acquiring inventory.

---

[29] *Corn Products Refining Co. v. CIR,* 47 AFTR 1789, 55-2 USTC ¶9746 (USSC, 1955).

[30] *Arkansas Best Corporation v. CIR,* 61 AFTR 2d 88-655, 88-1 USTC ¶9210 (USSC, 1988).

OTHER IRC PROVISIONS RELEVANT TO CAPITAL GAINS AND LOSSES

A number of IRC sections provide special treatment for certain types of assets and transactions. For example, loss on the sale or exchange of certain small business stock that qualifies as Sec. 1244 stock is treated as an ordinary loss rather than a capital loss to the extent of $50,000 per year ($100,000 if the taxpayer is married and files a joint return).[31]

ADDITIONAL COMMENT

For purposes of Sec. 1236, a security is defined as any share of stock in any corporation, note, bond, debenture, or evidence of indebtedness, or any evidence of an interest in or right to subscribe to or purchase any of the above.

Dealers in Securities. Normally, a security dealer's gain on the sale or exchange of securities is ordinary income. Section 1236 provides an exception for dealers in securities if the dealer clearly identifies that the property is held for investment. This act of identification must occur before the close of the day on which the security is acquired, and the security must not be held primarily for sale to customers in the ordinary course of the dealer's trade or business at any time after the close of the day of purchase.

EXAMPLE I:5-40 ▶ Allyson, a dealer in securities, purchases Cook Corporation stock on April 8, and identifies the stock as being held for investment on that date. Four months later, Allyson sells the stock. Any gain or loss recognized due to the sale is capital gain or loss. ◀

Once a dealer clearly identifies a security as being held for investment, any loss on the sale or exchange of the security is treated as a capital loss.

EXAMPLE I:5-41 ▶ Kris, a dealer in securities, purchases Boston Corporation stock and clearly identifies the stock as being held for investment on the date of purchase. Eight months later, the security is removed from the investment account and held as inventory. If the security is later sold at a gain, the gain is an ordinary gain. However, if the stock is sold at a loss, the loss is a capital loss. ◀

Securities dealers must use the mark-to-market method for their inventory of securities. This method requires that securities be valued at FMV at the end of each taxable year. Dealers in securities recognize gain or loss each year as if the security is sold on the last day of the tax year. Gains and losses are generally treated as ordinary rather than capital. Gains or losses due to adjustments in subsequent years or resulting from the sale of the security must be adjusted to reflect gains and losses already taken into account when determining taxable income.[32]

EXAMPLE I:5-42 ▶ Jim Spikes, a dealer in securities and calendar-year taxpayer, purchases a security for inventory on October 10, 2015, for $10,000 and sells the security for $18,000 on July 1, 2016. The security's FMV on December 31, 2015, is $15,000. Jim recognizes $5,000 of ordinary income in 2015 and $3,000 of ordinary income in 2016. ◀

Real Property Subdivided for Sale. A taxpayer who engages in regular sales of real estate is considered to be a dealer, and any gain or loss recognized is ordinary gain or loss rather than capital gain or loss. A special relief provision is provided in Sec. 1237 for nondealer, noncorporate taxpayers who subdivide a tract of real property into lots (two or more pieces of real property are considered to be a tract if they are contiguous). Part or all of the gain on the sale of the lots may be treated as a capital gain if the following provisions of Sec. 1237 are satisfied:

ADDITIONAL COMMENT

The conversion of an apartment building into condominiums does not qualify under Sec. 1237, even if the property has been held for five years and no substantial improvements have been made.

▶ During the year of sale, the noncorporate taxpayer must not hold any other real property primarily for sale in the ordinary course of business.

▶ Unless the property is acquired by inheritance or devise, the lots sold must be held by the taxpayer for a period of at least five years.

▶ No substantial improvement may be made by the taxpayer while holding the lots if the improvement substantially enhances the value of the lot.[33]

[31] Secs. 1244(a) and (b). (See Chapter I:8 for additional discussion on small business corporation stock losses.)
[32] Sec. 475. The mark-to-market rule also applies to some securities that are not inventory, but does not apply to any security that is held for investment and certain other transactions (see Sec. 475(b)).
[33] Certain improvements are not treated as substantial under Sec. 1237(b)(3) if the lot is held for at least ten years.

▶ The tract or any lot may not have been previously held primarily for sale to customers in the ordinary course of the taxpayer's trade or business unless such tract at that time was covered by Sec. 1237.

The primary advantage of Sec. 1237 is that potential controversy with the IRS is avoided as to whether a taxpayer who subdivides investment property is a dealer. Section 1237 does not apply to losses. Such losses are capital losses if the property is held for investment purposes, or ordinary losses if the taxpayer is a dealer.

If the Sec. 1237 requirements are satisfied, all gain on the sale of the first five lots may be capital gain. Starting in the tax year during which the sixth lot is sold, 5% of the selling price for all lots sold in that year and succeeding years is ordinary income.

EXAMPLE I:5-43 ▶ Jean subdivides a tract of land held as an investment into seven lots, and all requirements of Sec. 1237 are satisfied. The lots have a FMV of $10,000 each and have a basis of $4,000. Jean incurs no selling expenses and sells four lots in 2014 and three lots in 2015. In 2014, all of the $24,000 [four lots × ($10,000 − $4,000)] gain is capital gain. In 2015, the year in which the sixth lot is sold, $1,500 of the gain is ordinary income [0.05 × ($10,000 × three lots)], and the remaining $16,500 {[three lots × ($10,000 − $4,000)] − $1,500} gain is capital gain. ◀

EXAMPLE I:5-44 ▶ Assume the same facts as in the above example, except that all seven lots are sold in 2015. The amount of ordinary income recognized is $3,500 [0.05 × ($10,000 × seven lots)], and the remaining $38,500 {[seven lots × ($10,000 − $4,000)] − $3,500} gain is capital gain. ◀

ADDITIONAL COMMENT

If a taxpayer sells any lots from a tract and does not sell any others for a period of five years, the remaining property is considered a new tract.

Based on Examples I:5-43 and I:5-44, the advantage of selling no more than five lots in the first year should be apparent. Expenditures incurred to sell or exchange the lots are also treated favorably because they are first applied against the portion of the gain treated as ordinary income. Because selling expenses (e.g., commissions) are often equal to or greater than 5% of the selling price, this offset against ordinary income may result in the elimination of the ordinary income portion of the gain. Selling expenses in excess of the gain taxed as ordinary income reduce the amount realized on the sale or exchange.

Nonbusiness Bad Debt. Bad debt losses from nonbusiness debts are deductible only as short-term capital losses (STCLs),[34] regardless of when the debt occurred. A nonbusiness bad debt is deductible only in the year in which the debt becomes totally worthless.

EXAMPLE I:5-45 ▶ Two years ago, Alice loaned $4,000 to a friend. During the current year, the friend declares bankruptcy and the debt is entirely worthless. Assuming that Alice has no other gains and losses from the sale or exchange of capital assets during the year, she deducts $3,000 in determining adjusted gross income (AGI) and has a STCL carry forward of $1,000. ◀

TAX TREATMENT FOR CAPITAL GAINS AND LOSSES OF NONCORPORATE TAXPAYERS

OBJECTIVE 4

Understand how capital gains are taxed for noncorporate taxpayers

To recognize capital gain or loss, it is necessary to have a sale or exchange of a capital asset. Once it is determined that a capital gain or loss has been realized and is to be recognized, it is necessary to classify the gains and losses as either short-term or long-term. If the asset is held for one year or less, the gain or loss is classified as a short-term capital gain (STCG) or a short-term capital loss (STCL). If the capital asset is held for more than one year, the gain or loss is classified as a long-term capital gain (LTCG) or long-term capital loss (LTCL).[35]

---

[34] Sec. 166(d)(1)(B). Also, see discussion of bad debts in Chapter I:8.

[35] While the Taxpayer Relief Act of 1997 reduced the rates for most LTCGs, it increased the required holding period to more than 18 months to be eligible for the lower rates of 10% and 20%. During the last few months of 1997, gain resulting from the sale of a capital asset might be taxed at many different rates depending on whether or not the holding period is one year or less, more

than one year but not more than 18 months, or more than 18 months. These changes in the law dramatically increased the complexity associated with the taxation of capital gains. The 1998 Restructuring and Reform Act eliminated the more than 18-month holding period requirement for tax years ending after 1997 and returned to the more than one year requirement to be LTCG.

ADDITIONAL COMMENT

The rates for long-term capital gains have been lower than rates for ordinary income for many years. However, preferential rates for qualified dividends were enacted in 2003. Qualified dividends are now taxed at a maximum 15% or 20% rate, the same as for long-term capital gains which are ANCG.

CAPITAL GAINS

The first step in determining the taxability of capital gains is to calculate *net capital gains* (NCG), which is defined as the excess of net long-term capital gain over net short-term capital loss.[36] All capital gains are not taxed at the same rate. So, depending on the type of property, NCG could be taxed at zero, 15%, 20%, 25%, or 28%. Once NCG has been determined, a portion of NCG may be classified as *adjusted net capital gain* (ANCG) which is subject to the lower rates of zero, 15%, or 20%.

To compute NCG, first determine all STCGs, STCLs, LTCGs, LTCLs, and then net gains and losses as described below.

Net Short-Term Capital Gain. If total STCGs for the tax year exceed total STCLs for that year, the excess is defined as net short-term capital gain (NSTCG). As discussed later, NSTCG may be offset by net long-term capital loss (NLTCL).

EXAMPLE I:5-46 ▶ Hal has two transactions involving the sale of capital assets during the year. As a result of those transactions, he has a STCG of $4,000 and a STCL of $3,000. Hal's NSTCG is $1,000 and his AGI increases by $1,000. His gross income increases by $4,000, and he is entitled to a $3,000 deduction for AGI. ◀

Net Long-Term Capital Gain. If the total LTCGs for the tax year exceed the total LTCLs for that year, the excess is defined as net long-term capital gain (NLTCG). As indicated earlier, a NCG exists when NLTCG exceeds net short-term capital loss (NSTCL).

EXAMPLE I:5-47 ▶ Clay has two transactions involving the sale of capital assets during the year. As a result of the transactions, he has a LTCG of $5,000 and a LTCL of $3,000. Clay has a NLTCG and a net capital gain of $2,000. His AGI increases by $2,000. ◀

EXAMPLE I:5-48 ▶ Linda has four transactions involving the sale of capital assets during the year. As a result of the transactions, she has a STCG of $5,000, a STCL of $7,000, a LTCG of $10,000, and a LTCL of $2,000. After the initial netting of short-term and long-term gains and losses, Linda has a NSTCL of $2,000 ($7,000 − $5,000) and a NLTCG of $8,000 ($10,000 − $2,000). Because the NLTCG exceeds the NSTCL by $6,000 ($8,000 − $2,000), her NCG is $6,000. ◀

Lower Rates for Adjusted Net Capital Gain (ANCG). The tax rate that applies to a taxpayer's ANCG depends on the taxpayer's tax bracket, and can be zero, 15%, or 20%. Taxpayers with a 10% or 15% marginal tax rate have a zero percent tax rate on their ANCG. Taxpayers with a marginal tax rate more than 15% and less than 39.6% have a preferential rate of 15%, and the preferential rate is 20% if one's marginal tax rate is 39.6%.[37]

EXAMPLE I:5-49 ▶ Sandy is single with taxable income of $100,000 without considering the sale of Merck stock during 2015 for $15,000. The stock was purchased four years earlier for $3,000. Sandy has $12,000 of NLTCG which is ANCG taxed at 15%. To compute her total tax for 2015, ordinary rates would be applied to the $100,000 and then the tax on ANCG (15% × $12,000) is added. ◀

EXAMPLE I:5-50 ▶ Assume the same facts as in Example I:5-49 except Sandy's taxable income without the capital gain is $11,400. The $12,000 ANCG is taxed at a rate of zero because her taxable income is less than $37,450. Taxable income up to $37,450 is subject to ordinary tax rates of no higher than 15%.

LEGISLATIVE UPDATE

The American Tax Relief Act of 2012 retained tax relief of the zero and 15% rates provided by the Bush administration but increased the preferential tax rate to 20% of ANCG for those taxpayers with the highest marginal tax rate, 39.6%.

This change was a compromise between President Obama and most Democrats in Congress who advocated for higher tax rates on taxpayers with higher incomes and most Republicans who opposed any income tax increases.

Computation of the tax becomes more complicated if the ANCG causes taxable income to exceed the $37,450 for a single taxpayer. If a single taxpayer has taxable income of $40,000 that includes $10,000 of ANCG, the taxpayer's tax is determined as follows:

Tax on $30,000 (taxable income without the ANCG)	$4,039	[$922.50 + ($20,775 × 15%)]
+ Tax on $7,450 ($37,450 − $30,000) of the ANCG at zero	0	($7,450 × 0%)
+ Tax on $2,550 ($10,000 − $7,450) at 15% because the taxable income is greater than $37,450	$ 383	($2,550 × 15%)
Total tax	$4,422	

◀

---

[36] Sec. 1222(11).   [37] Sec. 1(h).

SELF-STUDY QUESTION

Mary sells common stock for a gain of $10,000 on December 29, 2015. The settlement date, or date that Mary will receive the proceeds from the stockbroker, is January 2, 2016. Will Mary report the gain on her 2015 or 2016 tax return?

ANSWER

Mary is required to report the gain in the year of the sale (2015). Losses are also recognized in the year of sale.

KEY POINT

Collectibles gain, as explained below, is the net of LTCG and LTCL from the sale of collectibles. Sec. 1202 stock is qualified business stock designed to encourage investment in small businesses.

The Danecks file a joint return with taxable income of $800,000 which includes ANCG of $100,000 and no other investment income. Their tax is determined by adding the tax on $700,000 where marginal tax rate is 39.6% to $20,000 (20% × $100,000). They are also subject to the 3.8% Medicare tax of $3,800 (3.8% × $100,000) on investment income discussed later in the chapter. ◀

ADJUSTED NET CAPITAL GAINS (ANCG)

When computing ANCG, one has to consider that four different types of LTCGs may exist:

1. Collectibles gain
2. Part of the gain (generally 50%) resulting from the sale or exchange of qualified small business stock as defined in Sec. 1202
3. Unrecaptured Sec. 1250 gain[38]
4. All other LTCGs

It is the fourth group of LTCGs that receives the preferential rates of zero, 15%, or 20%. The other three groups receive preferential treatment but not at the zero, 15%, or 20% rate. The first two gains above are referred to as 28% rate gain because the maximum rate for those gains is 28%; the maximum rate for unrecaptured Sec. 1250 gain is 25%. Unrecaptured Sec. 1250 gain, which is taxed at a maximum 25% rate, generally occurs when a building is sold. For the second and third types of LTCG, the special provisions only apply to gains. Net losses from sale of Sec. 1202 stock are treated as normal LTCLs, and one cannot have a loss connected with an unrecaptured Sec. 1250 gain.

ANCG is defined as NCG less the first three gains listed above. However, the computation of ANCG is tricky because one has to consider the impact of net capital losses, both short-term and long-term. Taxpayers are permitted to offset capital losses against capital gains. But, as discussed above, there are four different types of LTCG. So, if a taxpayer has both LTCG and capital losses, the capital losses are first offset within the category (collectibles, Sec. 1202 stock, etc.), then any excess loss is offset against the highest rate LTCG category first and works down to the lowest rate category (i.e., 28% rate gain first, then 25%, then 20% or 15%). This topic is discussed in more detail on page I:5-19 below.

When a taxpayer has no capital losses and no qualified dividends, ANCG is NCG reduced by the first three types of LTCG listed above. Many taxpayers will not have the first three types of LTCG and therefore, NCG and ANCG will often be the same amount.

EXAMPLE I:5-52 ▶

During 2015, Charles, whose tax rate exceeds 15% and is less than 39.6%, sold two publicly-traded stocks. The first stock resulted in a LTCG of $10,000 while the second stock resulted in a LTCG of $15,000. These were his only transactions involving capital assets during the year. Charles' NCG and ANCG is $25,000 and this gain is subject to a maximum tax rate of 15%. ◀

EXAMPLE I:5-53 ▶

Assume in the example above that Charles also had a gain on the sale of a building that resulted in an unrecaptured Sec. 1250 gain of $50,000. Charles has NCG of $75,000 and ANCG of $25,000. The $50,000 gain is taxed at a maximum rate of 25% while the $25,000 of ANCG is taxed at a maximum rate of 15%. ◀

Collectibles Gain. Gains resulting from the sale of collectibles such as artwork, rugs, antiques, stamps and most coins are taxed at a maximum rate of 28%.

EXAMPLE I:5-54 ▶

SELF-STUDY QUESTION

Eliza, who is single, has taxable income of $60,000 including a $1,200 LTCG due to the sale of her baseball card collection. Does she receive preferential tax treatment?

ANSWER

No. Her marginal tax rate is 25% which is less than the maximum 28% rate that applies to collectibles gain. If her taxable income is $200,000, she saves $60 [(33% − 28%)($1,200)].

Danny, whose tax rate is 33%, purchased Bowling common stock and antique chairs three years ago for investment. He sells the assets during the current year and has a gain of $8,000 on the sale of the stock and $10,000 on the sale of the antique chairs. His NLTCG is $18,000, and his NCG is $18,000. His ANCG is $8,000 since $10,000 of the NCG is a collectibles gain. His tax on the capital gains is $4,000 [(15% × $8,000) + (28% × $10,000)]. ◀

Sec. 1202 Gain. Sec. 1202 provides that noncorporate taxpayers may exclude a portion of the gain resulting from the sale or exchange of qualified small business stock (QSBS) issued after August 10, 1993, if the stock is held for more than five years. The exclusion depends on when the stock was acquired, as follows:

Date QSBS Acquired	Exclusion Percentage
Prior to February 18, 2009	50%
February 18, 2009–September 27, 2010	75%
September 28, 2010–December 31, 2014	100%

---

[38] Sec. 1(h)(4).

Since the QSBS must be held for five years, it will be a few years before the 100% exclusion will take effect. A corporation may have QSBS only if the corporation is a C corporation and at least 80% of the value of its assets must be used in the active conduct of one or more qualified trades or businesses.[39]

If the excluded gain on QSBS is either 50% or 75%, the remaining gain is generally taxed at a maximum rate of 28%. However, the amount of any gain eligible for the exclusion may not exceed the greater of $10,000,000 or ten times the aggregate basis of the qualified stock. Thus, if gain on the sale of QSBS is $11.4 million and $5 million of the gain is excluded, $5 million of the gain is taxed at 28% and the remaining $1.4 million gain is taxed at 15% or 20%.

EXAMPLE I:5-55 ►

Raef purchased $200,000 of newly issued Monona common stock on October 1, 2008. On December 15, 2015, he sells the stock for $4 million, resulting in a $3.8 million gain. He excludes $1.9 million of the gain, and the remaining $1.9 million of gain is Sec. 1202 gain taxed at 28%. Alternatively, if Raef purchased the Monona stock on July 11, 2010 and sold it in 2016, he could exclude $2.85 million ($3.8 × 0.75) of the gain. ◄

EXAMPLE I:5-56 ►

Matthew, whose tax rate is 33%, has the following capital gains in 2015:

STCG	$10,000
LTCG (artwork)	12,000
LTCG (stock of AT&T)	17,000
LTCG (acquired in 2006)	200,000

Matthew may exclude $100,000 of the $200,000 Sec. 1202 gain. His NCG is $129,000 ($12,000 + $17,000 + $100,000). His ANCG is $17,000. The increase in his tax is $37,210 [33%($10,000) + 28%($12,000) + 15%($17,000) + 28%($100,000)]. ◄

CAPITAL LOSSES

To have a capital loss, one must sell or exchange the capital asset for an amount less than its adjusted basis. As in the case of capital gains, the one-year period is used to determine whether the capital loss is short-term or long-term.

Net Short-Term Capital Loss. If total STCLs exceed total STCGs for the tax year, the excess is defined as a net short-term capital loss (NSTCL). As indicated above, the NSTCL is first offset against any NLTCG to determine net capital gain. If NSTCL exceeds NLTCG, the capital loss may be offset, on a dollar-for-dollar basis, against a noncorporate taxpayer's ordinary income for amounts up to $3,000 in any one year.[40]

EXAMPLE I:5-57 ►

Bob has gross income of $60,000 before considering capital gains and losses. If Bob has a NLTCG of $10,000 and a NSTCL of $15,000, he has $5,000 of NSTCL in excess of NLTCG and may deduct $3,000 of the losses from gross income. Assuming no other deductions for AGI, Bob's AGI is $57,000 ($60,000 − $3,000). ◄

In the above example, $10,000 of Bob's NSTCL is used to offset the $10,000 of NLTCG, and $3,000 of the NSTCL is used to reduce ordinary income. However, $2,000 of the loss is not used. This net capital loss is carried forward for an indefinite number of years.[41] The loss retains its original character and will be treated as a STCL occurring in the subsequent year. If a taxpayer dies with an unused capital loss carryover, it expires.

EXAMPLE I:5-58 ►

Last year, Milt had a NSTCL of $8,000 and a NLTCG of $2,600. The netting of short-term and long-term gains and losses resulted in a $5,400 excess of NSTCL over NLTCG, and $3,000 of this amount was offset against ordinary income. Milt's NSTCL carryforward is $2,400. During the current year he sells a capital asset and generates a STCG of $800. His NSTCL is $1,600 ($2,400 − $800), and the loss is offset against $1,600 of ordinary income. ◄

Net Long-Term Capital Loss. If total LTCLs for the tax year exceed total LTCGs for the year, the excess is defined as net long-term capital loss (NLTCL). If there is both a NSTCG and a NLTCL, the NLTCL is initially offset against the NSTCG on a dollar-for-dollar basis. If the NLTCL exceeds the NSTCG, the excess is offset against ordinary income on a dollar-for-dollar basis up to $3,000 per year.

---

[39] Sec. 1202.
[40] Sec. 1211(b). A $1,500 limitation applies to a married individual filing a separate return.
[41] Sec. 1212(b) and Reg. Sec. 1.1212-1(b).

EXAMPLE I:5-59 ▶ In the current year, Gordon has a NLTCL of $9,000 and a NSTCG of $2,000. He must use $2,000 of the NLTCL to offset the $2,000 NSTCG, and then use $3,000 of the $7,000 ($9,000 − $2,000) NLTCL to offset $3,000 of ordinary income. Gordon's carryforward of NLTCL is $4,000 [$9,000 − ($2,000 + $3,000)]. This amount is treated as a LTCL in subsequent years. ◀

If an individual has both NSTCL and NLTCL, the NSTCL is offset against ordinary income first, regardless of when the transactions occur during the year.

EXAMPLE I:5-60 ▶ In the current year, Beth has a NSTCL of $2,800 and a NLTCL of $2,000. The entire NSTCL is offset initially against $2,800 of ordinary income. Because capital losses may offset only $3,000 of ordinary income, $200 of NLTCL is used to offset $200 ($3,000 − $2,800) of ordinary income. The NLTCL carryover to the next year is $1,800 ($2,000 − $200). ◀

TAX STRATEGY TIP

Taxpayers who have realized capital gains during the tax year should consider selling securities with a loss during the same year. The losses can be offset against the gains and tax savings result.

Capital Losses Applied to Capital Gains by Groups. Taxpayers separate their LTCGs and LTCLs into three tax rate groups: (1) 28% group, (2) 25% group, and (3) the 15% or 20% group. The 28% group includes capital gains and losses when the capital asset is a collectible held more than one year and part of the gain from the sale of QSBS held for more than five years. The 25% group consists of unrecaptured Sec. 1250 gain discussed in Chapter I:13, and there are no losses for this group. The 15% or 20% group includes capital gains and losses when the holding period is more than one year and the capital asset is not a collectible or Sec. 1202 small business stock.

When a taxpayer has NSTCL and NLTCG, the NSTCL is first offset against NLTCG from the 28% group, then the 25% group, and finally the 15% or 20% group. This treatment of NSTCL is favorable for taxpayers. Note that a taxpayer could have NLTCLs in one group, except the 25% group, and NLTCGs in another group. A net loss from the 28% group is first offset against gains in the 25% group then net gains in the 15% or 20% group. A net loss from the 15% or 20% group is first offset against net gains in the 28% group and then gains in the 25% group.[42]

EXAMPLE I:5-61 ▶ Leroy, whose tax rate is 33%, has NSTCL of $20,000, a $25,000 LTCG from the sale of a rare stamp held 16 months and an $18,000 LTCG from the sale of stock held for three years. The $20,000 NSTCL is offset against $20,000 of the collectibles gain in the 28% group. Leroy's NCG is $23,000 and his ANCG is $18,000. Leroy's tax liability increases by $4,100 [($5,000 × 28%) + ($18,000 × 15%)]. ◀

EXAMPLE I:5-62 ▶ Elizabeth, whose tax rate is 33%, has a $32,000 LTCL from the sale of stock held for four years and the following capital gains:

ADDITIONAL COMMENT

If Elizabeth in Example I:5-62 also had a $9,000 LTCG from the sale of stock held for two years, she would only be able to offset $23,000 of the LTCG in the 28% group.

NSTCG	$40,000
LTCG from sale of collectible	$30,000
LTCG in the 25% group (unrecaptured Sec. 1250 gain)	$10,000

The $32,000 LTCL is offset first against $30,000 of the LTCG in the 28% group (collectibles) and then $2,000 against the unrecaptured Sec. 1250 gain. Her NLTCG is $8,000 taxed at 25% while her $40,000 NSTCG is taxed at her ordinary income rate of 33%. ◀

? STOP & THINK

Question: Srinija has a salary of $100,000. If she sells a non-personal use asset during the year and has a $40,000 loss, why is it important that the asset not be a capital asset?

Solution: Only $3,000 of a $40,000 capital loss is used as a deduction to reduce her gross income each year. Her AGI is $97,000 if the asset is a capital asset, and she has a $37,000 capital loss carryforward. All of the $40,000 loss is used to reduce her gross income if the asset is not a capital asset and her AGI is $60,000. It is possible that Srinija might not care whether or not the asset is a capital asset if she has capital gains that could be reduced by capital losses. If the asset is a personal-use asset, the loss is not deductible regardless of whether or not it is a capital asset.

---

[42] Notice 97-59, I.R.B. 1997-45.

Tax Treatment for Net Capital Gain and Qualified Dividends. Congress eliminated preferential tax rates on NCG in 1986 by making the maximum ordinary income rate equal to the rate on net capital gains at 28%. However, this equality was short-lived as Congress, in 1991, increased the maximum ordinary income rate to 31% but left the NCG rate at 28%.[43] This newly-created preferential treatment for NCG's only applied to taxpayers whose tax rate exceeded 28%. The change in 1997 to rates as low as 10% benefited all noncorporate taxpayers if they held the capital asset for more than one year.

Legislation in 2003 which reduced the tax rate on qualified dividends to 5% (**zero** after 2007) and 15% as of January 1, 2003 dramatically changed investor preferences.[44] The current rate on qualified dividends is zero for a taxpayer with a regular tax rate of 15% or less, and 15% for a taxpayer with a regular tax rate greater than 15% but less than 39.6%. The rate is 20% when the marginal tax rate is 39.6%. This significant reduction of tax rates for dividend income has resulted in an increased interest in stocks with high dividends.

Taxpayers who own mutual funds must recognize their share of capital gains even if no distributions are received. Many mutual fund shareholders reinvest their distributions instead of withdrawing assets from the mutual fund. Mutual funds must classify the gains as short-term or long-term, and long-term gains will need to be separated by rate groups. When shareholders of a mutual fund recognize their share of capital gains when no distribution is actually received, the basis for their shares is increased.

EXAMPLE I:5-63 ▶

Eunice, whose tax rate is 35%, is a shareholder of Canyon Mutual Fund. The basis for her shares is $23,000. At the end of the current year, she received a statement from Canyon indicating her share of the following: qualified dividend income, $200; STCG, $300; 28-percent rate gain, $1,000; and ANCG of $1,500. The increase in her taxes as a result of her ownership of the mutual shares is $640 [($200 × 15%) + ($300 × 35%) + ($1,000 × 28%) + ($1,500 × 15%)]. The basis for her shares of Canyon Mutual Fund is increased to $26,000. ◀

The 3.8% Net Investment Income Tax (NIIT). The Affordable Care Act, which requires most U.S. citizens and legal residents to have health insurance, added a new medicare tax on certain taxpayers' net investment income. Investment income includes interest, dividends, NSTCG, NLTCG, rental, and royalty income. Starting in 2013, individuals are subject to a 3.8% surtax on the lesser of net investment income (NII) or the excess of modified AGI (MAGI) over a certain threshold amount.

MAGI is the sum of AGI plus the net foreign earned income excluded, and NII is gross investment income less allocable investment expenses. The threshold amount is $200,000 for individuals (single or head of household) or $250,000 for married couples (and surviving spouse). The threshold amounts are not indexed for inflation.

EXAMPLE I:5-64 ▶

The Robinsons file a joint return in 2015 with $325,000 of MAGI which includes $100,000 of net investment income. They must pay the new 3.8% medicare tax on $75,000 (net investment income or $325,000 less $250,000 threshold). ◀

EXAMPLE I:5-65 ▶

Pablo is single and a dentist with MAGI of $600,000 and taxable income of $430,000. MAGI includes LTCG of $220,000 from sale of Google stock and qualified dividend income of $60,000. Pablo's NIIT is $10,640 (3.8% × $280,000). Because his taxable income is more than $413,200 his income tax rate on the LTCG and dividend income is 20%, however, his total tax rate is 23.8% after considering the new medicare tax. ◀

TAX TREATMENT OF CAPITAL GAINS AND LOSSES: CORPORATE TAXPAYERS

Most topics covered in this chapter concerning capital gains and losses, including the classification of an asset as a capital asset, rules for determining holding periods, and the procedure for offsetting capital losses against capital gains, apply to both corporate and noncorporate taxpayers. However, a major difference is that the lower tax rates of zero, 15%,

---

[43] For years prior to 1990, a myriad of rules have applied. Prior to 1987, noncorporate taxpayers received a deduction from gross income equal to 60% of the taxpayer's net capital gain. For years 1987–1990, net capital gains were subject to tax at ordinary income rates.

[44] Sec. 1(h)(11).

20%, 25%, and 28% on net capital gain for noncorporate taxpayers do not apply to corporations. A second significant difference relates to the treatment of capital losses: Unlike the noncorporate taxpayer who may deduct up to $3,000 of capital losses from ordinary income, corporations may offset capital losses only against capital gains. Corporate taxpayers may carry capital losses back to each of the three preceding tax years (the earliest of the three tax years first and then to the next two years) and forward for five years to offset capital gains in such years. When a corporate taxpayer carries a loss back to a preceding year or forward to a following year, the loss is treated as a STCL.[45]

EXAMPLE I:5-66 ▶

The Peach Corporation has income from operations of $200,000, a NSTCG of $40,000, and a NLTCL of $56,000 during the current year. The $40,000 NSTCG is offset by $40,000 NLTCL. The remaining $16,000 of NSTCL may not be offset against the $200,000 of other income but may be carried back three years and then forward five years to offset capital gains arising in these years. If Peach has NLTCG and/or NSTCG in the previous three years, a refund of taxes paid during those years will be received during the current year. ◀

HISTORICAL NOTE

The House of Representatives proposed a reduction in corporate net capital gains in 1997, but the proposal was rejected.

TYPICAL MISCONCEPTION

Because the carryover for net operating losses is 20 years, it is sometimes erroneously assumed that the carryover for corporate capital losses is also 20 years instead of five years.

Maximum Rate on Net Capital Gain for Corporations. Unlike individual taxpayers, corporations do not receive any preferential rate reductions for net capital gains. Corporations apply a maximum rate of 35% to the corporation's net capital gain.[46] However, given the present tax rates for corporations, the existence of the 35% alternative rate for net capital gain has no benefit. A corporation subject to a rate of 39% because taxable income is greater than $100,000 but not more than $335,000 does not use the maximum 35% rate. In essence, therefore, corporations are taxed on capital gains at the same rates for ordinary income.

Topic Review I:5-2 summarizes the principal differences in the tax treatment of capital gains and losses for corporate and noncorporate taxpayers.

TOPIC REVIEW I:5-2

Comparison of Corporate and Noncorporate Taxpayers: Capital Gains and Losses

	NONCORPORATE	CORPORATE
A statutory maximum tax rate applicable to net capital gain	Yes, 0%, 15%, 20%, 25%, and 28%	Yes, but rate is 35%
Offset of net capital losses against ordinary income	Yes, up to $3,000	No
Carryback of capital losses	No	Yes, three years as STCLs
Carryforward of capital losses	Yes, indefinitely	Yes, five years as STCLs

SALE OR EXCHANGE

OBJECTIVE 6

Recognize when a sale or exchange has occurred

As previously indicated, capital gains and losses result from the sale or exchange of capital assets. Although Sec. 1222 does not define a sale or an exchange, a **sale** is generally considered to be a transaction where one receives cash or the equivalent of cash, including the assumption of one's debt. An **exchange** is a transaction where one receives a reciprocal transfer of property, as distinguished from a transaction where one receives only cash or a cash equivalent.[47]

EXAMPLE I:5-67 ▶

Two years ago, Bart acquired 100 shares of Alaska Corporation common stock for $12,000 to hold as an investment. Bart sells 50 shares of the stock to Sandy for $10,000 and transfers the other 50 shares to Gail in exchange for land that has a $10,000 FMV. In each transaction, Bart realizes a $4,000 ($10,000 − $6,000) LTCG due to the sale or exchange of a capital asset. The transfer to Sandy qualifies as a sale, and the transfer to Gail qualifies as an exchange. ◀

To qualify as a sale or exchange, the transaction must be bona fide. Transactions between related parties such as family members are closely scrutinized. For example, a sale of property on credit to a relative may be a disguised gift if there is no intention of collecting the debt. If this is the case, a subsequent bad debt deduction due to the debt's

---

[45] Sec. 1212(a).
[46] Sec. 1201.

[47] Reg. Sec. 1.1002-1(d).

worthlessness is disallowed. In some instances, the Code specifically states that a particular transaction or event either qualifies or does not qualify for sale or exchange treatment. For example, the holder of an option who fails to exercise such an option treats the lapse of the option as a sale or exchange.[48] However, abandonment of property is generally not deemed to be a sale or exchange.[49]

WORTHLESS SECURITIES

ADDITIONAL COMMENT

The worthlessness of a security is treated as a sale or exchange so that the taxpayer is not forced to arrange for someone to buy the security for a token amount.

If a security that is a capital asset becomes worthless during the year, Sec. 165(g)(1) specifies that any loss is treated as a loss from the sale or exchange of a capital asset on the last day of the tax year. The term includes stock, a stock option, and "a bond, debenture, note or certificate, or other evidence of indebtedness, issued by a corporation or by a government or political division thereof, with interest coupons or in registered form."[50] Whether a security has become worthless during the year is a question of fact, and the taxpayer has the burden of proof to show evidence of worthlessness.[51]

EXAMPLE I:5-68 ▶ Charlotte purchased $40,000 of bonds issued by the Jet Corporation in March 2014. In February 2015, Jet is declared bankrupt, and its bonds are worthless. Charlotte has a LTCL of $40,000 because the bonds have become worthless and are deemed to have been sold on the last day of 2015. The more-than-one-year holding period requirement is satisfied by the last day of 2015. ◄

REAL-WORLD EXAMPLE

A corporation owned 76% of the stock of another company. The corporation later acquired the remaining 24% of the stock, allegedly for the purpose of avoiding interference by minority shareholders. Later the corporation claimed an ordinary loss on the worthless stock because it owned at least 80% of the stock. The Court treated the loss as a capital loss because the acquisition of the remaining stock was without a business purpose. *Hunter Mfg. Co.,* 21 T.C. 424 (1953).

Securities in Affiliated Corporations. If the security that becomes worthless is a security in a domestic affiliated corporation owned by a corporate taxpayer, the worthless security is not considered a capital asset. Thus, a corporate taxpayer's loss due to owning worthless securities in an affiliated corporation is treated as an ordinary loss. Because capital losses are of only limited benefit to corporate taxpayers, the classification of the loss as ordinary is preferable.

To qualify as an affiliated corporation, the parent corporation must own at least 80% of the voting power of all classes of stock and at least 80% of each class of nonvoting stock. The subsidiary corporation must be engaged in the active conduct of an operating business as opposed to being a passive investment company (i.e., more than 90% of its aggregate gross receipts must be from sources other than passive types of income such as royalties, dividends, and interest).[52]

EXAMPLE I:5-69 ▶ Ace Corporation owns 80% of all classes of stock issued by the same Jet Corporation described in Example I:5-68. Jet Corporation is actively engaged in an operating business and has no income from passive investments before being declared bankrupt. Ace's loss from its worthless stock investment is an ordinary loss instead of a capital loss because Jet is an affiliated corporation. Ace owns at least 80% of all classes of Jet's stock and more than 90% of Jet's gross receipts are from sources other than passive types of income. ◄

RETIREMENT OF DEBT INSTRUMENTS

Generally, the collection of a debt is not a sale or an exchange. However, if a debt instrument is retired, amounts received by the holder are treated as being received in an exchange.[53] Debt instruments include bonds, debentures, notes, certificates, and other evidences of indebtedness.

EXAMPLE I:5-70 ▶ In 2010 the Rocket Corporation issued $50,000 of five-year, interest-bearing bonds that were purchased by Elaine as an investment for $49,800. Elaine receives $50,000 at maturity in 2015. Retirement of the debt instrument is an exchange, and the $200 gain is a LTCG.[54] ◄

Although Congress has provided that retirements of debt instruments are treated as exchanges, Congress is not willing to allow taxpayers to convert large amounts of potential ordinary interest income into capital gain by purchasing debt instruments at a substantial

---

[48] Sec. 1234(b) and Reg. Sec. 1.1234-1(b).
[49] Reg. Secs. 1.165-2 and 1.167(a)-8.
[50] Sec. 165(g)(2).
[51] *Minnie K. Young v. CIR,* 28 AFTR 365, 41-2 USTC ¶9744 (2nd Cir., 1941).

[52] Sec. 165(g)(3).
[53] Sec. 1271(a).
[54] If Rocket Corporation issued the bonds with the intention of calling the bonds before maturity, Sec. 1271(a)(2) treats the gain as ordinary income.

discount. As illustrated in Example I:5-70, a small amount of bond discount is sometimes converted to capital gain. However, if the discount is large enough to be classified as original issue discount, the discount must be amortized and included in gross income for each day the debt instrument is held for both cash and accrual method taxpayers. Original issue discount (OID) is defined as "the excess (if any) of the stated redemption price at maturity over the issue price."[55]

EXAMPLE I:5-71 ► On January 1, 2015, Connie purchases $100,000 of the City Corporation's newly issued bonds for $85,000. The bonds mature in 20 years. In 2015 and in subsequent years Connie must annually recognize as interest income a portion of the $15,000 of OID. ◄

The OID is considered to be zero if the amount of discount "is less than ¼ of 1% of the stated redemption price at maturity, multiplied by the number of complete years to maturity."[56] In Example I:5-70, the $200 discount is not OID because it is less than $625 (0.0025 × $50,000 × 5 years). If Connie pays more than $95,000 for the bonds in Example I:5-71, the OID is zero.

ADDITIONAL COMMENT

Two different types of bonds are sold at a discount: original issue discount (OID) bonds and market discount bonds. OID bonds are issued at a discount, whereas market discount bonds have market discount resulting from a rise in interest rates after the issuance of the bonds.

Original Issue Discount. Instead of spreading the OID ratably over the life of the bond, amortization of the discount is based on an interest amortization method called the **constant interest rate method.** The total amount of interest income is determined by multiplying the interest yield to maturity by the adjusted issue price. With this method of amortizing discount, the amount of OID amortized increases for each year the bond is held. In the above example, Connie recognizes a larger amount of interest income in 2016 than in 2015 due to amortization of the OID.

The daily portion of the OID for any accrual period is "determined by allocating to each day in any accrual period its ratable portion to the increase during such accrual period in the adjusted issue price of the debt instrument."[57] The increase in the adjusted issue price for any accrual period is shown below.

$$\text{increase in the adjusted issue price} = \left[\begin{array}{c} \text{Adjusted issue price at the begining of the accrual period} \end{array} \times \begin{array}{c} \text{Yield to maturity} \end{array} \right] - \begin{array}{c} \text{Interest payments during the accrual period} \end{array}$$

EXAMPLE I:5-72 ► On June 30, 2015, Fred purchases a 10%, $10,000 corporate bond for $9,264. The bond is issued on June 30, 2015, and matures in five years. Interest is paid semiannually, and the effective yield to maturity is 12% compounded semiannually. In 2015, Fred recognizes interest income of $556, as illustrated in Table I:5-1. The adjusted issue price as of January 1, 2016, is $9,320. This is the sum of the issue price plus any amounts of OID includible in the income of any holder since the date of issue. ◄

KEY POINT

The owner of an OID bond is normally required to accrue interest income each year regardless of the owner's method of accounting.

If a debt instrument is sold or exchanged before maturity, part of the OID is included in the seller's income. The amount to be included depends on the number of days the debt instrument is owned by the seller within the accrual period.

EXAMPLE I:5-73 ► Assume the same facts as in the above example, except that Fred sells the corporate bond to Carolyn on February 24, 2018 (the 55th day in the accrual period). Fred must include $23 [(55 days ÷ 181 days in the accrual period) × $75] of accrued interest for the period of January 1, 2018, to February 24, 2018, in income for 2018. Fred's basis for the bond increases by $23. Thus, his basis for determining a gain or loss is $9,603 ($9,580 + $23). ◄

Market Discount Bonds Purchased After April 30, 1993. The sale or exchange of a market discount bond may result in part or all of the gain being classified as ordinary

---

[55] Sec. 1273(a)(1).
[56] Sec. 1273(a)(3).

[57] Sec. 1272(a)(3).

▼ **TABLE I:5-1**

Computation for Interest Income in Examples I:5-72 and I:5-73

	Interest Received (1)	Amortization of Original Issue Discount (2)	Interest Income (3) = (1) + (2)	Taxpayer's Basis for the Bond
6-30-15				$ 9,264
12-31-15	$ 500	$ 56[a]	$ 556	9,320[b]
6-30-16	500	59	559	9,379
12-31-16	500	63	563	9,442
6-30-17	500	67	567	9,509
12-31-17	500	71	571	9,580
6-30-18	500	75	575	9,655
12-31-18	500	79	579	9,734
6-30-19	500	84	584	9,818
12-31-19	500	89	589	9,907
6-30-20	500	93[c]	593	10,000
	$5,000	$736	$5,736	

[a]6% × $9,264 − $500 = $56.
[b]$9,264 + $56 = $9,320.
[c]This figure is adjusted for rounding.

income.[58] A market discount bond is a bond that is acquired in the bond market at a discount. Market discount is the excess of the stated redemption price of the bond at maturity over the taxpayer's basis for such bond immediately after it is acquired.

EXAMPLE I:5-74 ▶ On January 1, Stephano purchased $100,000 of 8%, 20-year bonds for $82,000. The bonds were issued at par by the Solar Corporation two years ago on January 1. The bonds are market discount bonds. ◀

Similar to OID, there is a de minimis rule for determining market discount. Market discount is zero if the discount is less than ¼ of 1% of the stated redemption price of the bond at maturity multiplied by the number of complete years to maturity.[59] If Stephano paid $95,500 or more for the Solar Corporation bonds in Example I:5-74, the bonds would not be market discount bonds.[60]

Gain realized on disposition of the market discount bond is ordinary income to the extent of the accrued market discount.[61] The ratable accrual method (straight line method computed on a daily basis) is used to determine the amount of the accrued market discount recognized as ordinary income.[62] The market discount is allocated on the basis of the number of days the taxpayer held the bond relative to the number of days between the acquisition date and maturity date.

EXAMPLE I:5-75 ▶ Assume the same facts as in the above example except Stephano sells the bonds to Kimberly three years later for $86,400 on January 1st. $3,000 (³⁄₁₈ × $18,000) of the $4,400 ($86,400 − $82,000) gain is ordinary income and the remaining gain is LTCG. If Stephano sold the bond for more than $82,000 but less than $85,000, all of the gain is ordinary income. The entire $18,000 gain is ordinary income if the bond is held to maturity. ◀

---

[58] Ordinary income treatment for accrued market discount does not apply to owners of taxable market discount bonds issued on or before July 18, 1984, if the bonds were acquired before May 1, 1993. Owners of tax-exempt bonds are not required to accrue market discount if the bonds were acquired before May 1, 1993 (regardless of the issue date).

[59] Sec. 1278(a)(2)(C).
[60] $100,000 × .25% × 18 years = $4,500.
[61] Sec. 1276(a)(1).
[62] Sec. 1276(b)(1). A taxpayer may elect to use the constant interest rate method (see Sec. 1276(b)(2)).

OPTIONS

The owner of an option to buy property may sell the option, exercise the option, or allow the option to expire. If the option is exercised, the amount paid for the option is added to the purchase price of the property acquired.[63]

On August 5, 2015, Len pays $600 for an option to acquire 100 shares of Hill Corporation common stock for $80 per share at any time before December 20, 2015. Len exercises the option on November 15, 2015, and pays $8,000 for the stock. Len's basis for the 100 shares of Hill is $8,600 ($8,000 + $600), and the stock's holding period begins on November 15, 2015. ◄

When an option is sold or allowed to expire, a sale or exchange has occurred and gain or loss is therefore recognized.[64] The character of the underlying property determines whether the gain or loss from the sale or expiration of the option is capital or ordinary in nature. If the optioned property is a capital asset, the option is treated as a capital asset and capital gain or loss is recognized on the sale or exchange.

EXAMPLE I:5-77 ►

On March 2, 2015, Holly pays $270 for an option to acquire 100 shares of Arkansas Corporation stock for $30 per share at any time before December 10, 2015. As a result of an increase in the market value of the Arkansas stock, the market price of the option increases and Holly sells the option for $600 on August 2, 2015. Because the Arkansas stock is a capital asset in the hands of Holly, the option is a capital asset and she must recognize a STCG of $330 ($600 − $270). ◄

EXAMPLE I:5-78 ►

On October 12, 2014, Mary paid $400 for an option to acquire 100 shares of Portland Corporation stock for $50 per share at any time before February 19, 2015. The price never exceeds $50 before February 19, 2015, and Mary does not exercise the option. Because the option expires, Mary recognizes a STCL of $400 in 2015. ◄

Transactions in which taxpayers purchase or write options to buy (calls) are quite common today. An investor who anticipates that the market value of a stock or security (e.g., common stock) will increase during the next few months may purchase a call option instead of actually buying the stock. As indicated above, the tax treatment for the option depends on whether the call is exercised, sold, or expires. Someone, however, must be willing to write a call on the stock. Typically an owner of the same stock will write a call option. The writer of the call receives a payment for granting the right to purchase the stock at a fixed price within a given period of time.

If the call is exercised, the writer of the call adds the amount received for the call to the sales price to determine the amount realized.[65] If the call is not exercised within the given time period and thus expires, the writer retains the amount received for the option and recognizes a STCG in the year the call expires. The gain is short-term even if the option is written and held for more than a year.

EXAMPLE I:5-79 ►

Sam owns 100 shares of Madison Corporation common stock, which he purchased on May 1, 2008, for $4,000. On November 8, 2015, Sam writes a call that gives Joan, an investor, the option to purchase Sam's 100 shares of Madison stock at $60 per share any time before April 19, 2016. The current market price of Madison stock is $56 per share, and Sam receives $520 for writing the call. If the call is exercised, Sam has a LTCG of $2,520 [($6,000 + $520) − $4,000] in the year the call is exercised. If the call is not exercised and expires on April 19, 2016, Sam must recognize a STCG of $520 in 2016. ◄

EXAMPLE I:5-80 ►

Assume the same facts as in Example I:5-79, and consider the tax treatment for Joan, the holder of the call. If Joan exercises the call, the basis of the stock is $6,520 ($6,000 + $520). If she does not exercise the call, a STCL of $520 is recognized. If Joan sells the call, the amount received is compared with her basis in the call ($520) to compute Joan's gain or loss. ◄

---

[63] Rev. Rul. 58-234, 1958-1 C.B. 279.
[64] Sec. 1234(a).

[65] Rev. Rul. 58-234, 1958-1 C.B. 279.

PATENTS

To encourage technological progress and to clarify whether a transfer of rights to a patent is capital gain or ordinary income, Congress created Sec. 1235, which allows the holder of a patent to treat the gain resulting from the transfer of all substantial rights in a patent as LTCG. This tax treatment is more favorable than that accorded to producers of artistic and literary works, who receive ordinary rather than capital gain from the sale of their works.

KEY POINT

A copyright held by a taxpayer whose personal efforts created it is omitted from the definition of a capital asset. However, a patent can be considered a capital asset. In effect, the tax law could be said to favor individuals whose efforts lead to scientific or technological advancement.

Requirements for Capital Gain Treatment. Section 1235 provides that the transfer of all substantial rights to a patent by the holder of the patent is treated as a sale or exchange of a capital asset that has been held long-term. Thus, LTCG is recognized on the transfer of a patent regardless of its holding period or the character of the asset. Favorable long-term capital gain treatment applies even if the transferor of the patent receives periodic payments contingent on the productivity, use, or disposition of the property transferred.[66]

EXAMPLE I:5-81 ▶ Clay invents a small utensil used to peel shrimp. He has a patent on the utensil and transfers all rights to the patent to a manufacturing company. Clay receives $100,000 plus 40 cents per utensil sold. Because Sec. 1235 applies, the total of the lump-sum payment and the royalty payments received less his cost basis for the patent is recognized as a LTCG. ◀

Substantial Rights. The principal requirement in Sec. 1235 is that the holder must transfer all substantial rights to the patent. The Regulations state that the circumstances of the whole transaction should be considered in determining whether all substantial rights to a patent have been transferred.[67] All substantial rights have not been transferred if the patent rights of the purchaser are limited geographically within the country of issuance or the rights are for a period less than a patent's remaining life.

EXAMPLE I:5-82 ▶ Bruce, an inventor, transfers one of his U.S. patents on a manufacturing process to a manufacturer located in Utah. The manufacturer's rights to use the patent are limited to the state of Utah. Because the use of the patent is limited to a geographical area, all substantial rights have not been transferred, and Sec. 1235 does not apply. Payments received for the use of the patent are royalties and taxed as ordinary income. ◀

Definition of a Holder. Long-term capital gain treatment applies only to a holder of the patent rights. For purposes of Sec. 1235, a holder is an individual whose efforts created the property or an individual who acquires the patent rights from the creator for valuable consideration before the property covered by the patent is placed in service or used. Furthermore, the acquiring individual may not be related to the creator or be the creator's employer.

Section 1235 may not be used by corporate taxpayers because corporations are not permitted to be classified as holders. Although a partnership is not permitted to be a holder, individual partners may qualify as holders to the extent of the partner's interest in the patent owned by the partnership.

EXAMPLE I:5-83 ▶ Joy purchases a patent from Martin, whose efforts created the patent. The purchase occurs before the property is placed in service or used. Joy and Martin are unrelated individuals, and Joy is not Martin's employer. For purposes of Sec. 1235, both Joy and Martin qualify as holders. ◀

ADDITIONAL COMMENT

The scope of Sec. 1253 is very broad. A franchise "includes an agreement which gives one of the parties to the agreement the right to distribute, sell, or provide goods, services, or facilities within a specified area."

FRANCHISES, TRADEMARKS, AND TRADE NAMES

Before the enactment of Sec. 1253, significant uncertainty existed as to whether the transfer of a franchise, trademark, or trade name should be treated as a sale or exchange or as a licensing agreement. If the transfer is tantamount to a sale of the property, payments received should be treated by the transferor as a return of capital and capital gain, and the transferee should be required to capitalize and amortize such payments. However, if the

---

[66] Sec. 1235(a).

[67] Reg. Sec. 1.1235-2(b).

transfer represents a licensing agreement, the transferor should recognize ordinary income and the transferee should receive an ordinary deduction for such payments.

Section 1253, which applies to the granting of a franchise, trademark, or trade name, as well as renewals and transfers to third parties, attempts to resolve the uncertainty by stating, "A transfer of a franchise, trademark, or trade name shall not be treated as a sale or exchange of a capital asset if the transferor retains any significant power, right, or continuing interest with respect to the subject matter of the franchise, trademark, or trade name."[68]

Examples of some rights that are to be considered a "significant power, right, or continuing interest"[69] include the right to:

▶ Disapprove of any assignment.

▶ Terminate the agreement at will.

▶ Prescribe standards of quality for products, product services, and facilities.

▶ Require the exclusive selling or advertising of the transferor's products or services.

▶ Require the transferee to purchase substantially all of its supplies and equipment from the transferor.

If the transferor does not retain any significant power, right, or continuing interest in the property, the transferor treats the transfer as a sale of the franchise and has the benefits of capital gain treatment. However, any amounts received that are contingent on the productivity, use, or disposition of such property must be treated as ordinary income by the transferor.

EXAMPLE I:5-84 ▶ Rose, who owns a franchise with a basis of $100,000, transfers the franchise to Ruth and retains no significant power, right, or continuing interest. Rose receives a $250,000 down payment when the agreement is signed and annual payments for five years equal to 10% of all sales in excess of $2,000,000. Rose has a capital gain of $150,000 with respect to the initial payment, but all of the payments received during the next five years will be ordinary income because they are contingent payments. ◀

Under Sec. 1253, the transferee may deduct payments that are contingent on the productivity, use, or disposition of such property as business expenses. Generally, other payments are capitalized and amortized over a period of 15 years.[70] In practice, payments received for the transfer of a franchise are generally treated as ordinary income to the transferor and are deductible by the transferee because in most franchise agreements the transferor desires to maintain significant powers, rights, or continuing interests in the franchise operation. Also, in many instances the payments are, in part, predicated on the success of the franchised business and are, therefore, established as contingent payments.

LEASE CANCELLATION PAYMENTS

A lease arrangement may be terminated before the lease period expires, and a lease cancellation payment may be made as consideration for the other party's agreement to terminate the lease. Either a lessor or a lessee may receive such a payment because the payment is normally made by the person who wants to cancel the lease. The tax treatment may differ significantly depending on which party is the recipient.

Payments Received by Lessor. The Supreme Court has ruled that lease cancellation payments received by a lessor are treated as ordinary income on the basis that the payments represent a substitute for rent.[71] Lease cancellation payments are included in the lessor's income in the year received, even if the lessor uses an accrual method.[72]

Payments Received by Lessee. Payments received by a lessee for canceling a lease are considered amounts received in exchange for the lease.[73] If the lease is a capital asset, any gain or loss is a capital gain or loss.

---

[68] Sec. 1253(a). Section 1253(e) prevents the basic Sec. 1253 rules from applying to the transfer of a professional sports franchise.
[69] Sec. 1253(b)(2).
[70] Sec. 197(a).

[71] *Walter M. Hort v. CIR,* 25 AFTR 1207, 41-1 USTC ¶9354 (USSC, 1941).
[72] *Farrelly-Walsh, Inc.,* 13 B.T.A. 923 (1928).
[73] Sec. 1241.

EXAMPLE I:5-85 ▶ Jim has a three-year lease on a house used as his personal residence. The lessor has an opportunity to sell the house and has agreed to pay $1,000 to Jim to cancel the lease. Assuming that Jim has no basis in the lease, the gain of $1,000 is capital gain because the lease is a capital asset. ◄

HOLDING PERIOD

OBJECTIVE 7

Determine the holding period for an asset when a sale or disposition occurs

The length of time an asset is held before it is disposed of (i.e., the *holding period*) is an important factor in determining whether any gain or loss resulting from the disposition of a capital asset is treated as long-term or short-term. To be classified as a long-term capital gain or loss, the capital asset must be held more than one year.[74] To determine the holding period, the day of acquisition is excluded and the disposal date is included.[75]

If the date of disposition is the same date as the date of acquisition, but a year later, the asset is considered to have been held for only one year. If the property is held for an additional day, the holding period is more than one year.

EXAMPLE I:5-86 ▶ Arnie purchased a capital asset on April 20, 2014, and sells the asset at a gain on April 21, 2015. The gain is classified as a LTCG. If the asset is sold on or before April 20, 2015, the gain is a STCG. ◄

ADDITIONAL COMMENT

When determining the holding period for marketable securities, it is important to use the "trade" dates, not the "settlement" dates.

The fact that all months do not have the same number of days is not a factor in determining the one-year period. Acquisitions made on the last day of any month must be held until the first day of the thirteenth subsequent month in order to have been held for more than one year.

EXAMPLE I:5-87 ▶ Alford sells stock held as an investment and recognizes a gain. If the capital asset was purchased on May 31, 2014, the gain is LTCG if the asset is sold on or after June 1, 2015. If sold on or before May 31, 2015, the gain is STCG and the lower preferential rates do not apply. ◄

ADDITIONAL COMMENT

The Securities and Exchange Commission requires investors who purchase or sell securities to deliver the funds to pay for the securities or deliver the certificates to be sold within three days of when the order is placed.

PROPERTY RECEIVED AS A GIFT

If a person receives property as a gift and uses the donor's basis to determine the gain or loss from a sale or exchange, the donor's holding period is added to the donee's holding period.[76] In other words, the donee's holding period includes the donor's holding period. If, however, the donee's basis is the FMV of the property on the date of the gift, the donee's holding period starts on the day after the date of the gift. This situation occurs when the FMV is less than the donor's basis on the date of the gift and the property is subsequently sold at a loss.

EXAMPLE I:5-88 ▶ Cindy receives a capital asset as a gift from Marc on July 4, 2015, when the asset has a $4,000 FMV. Marc acquired the property on April 12, 2015, for $3,400. If Cindy sells the asset after April 12, 2016, any gain or loss is LTCG or LTCL. Cindy's basis is the donor's cost because the FMV of the property is higher than the donor's basis on the date of the gift. Because Cindy takes Marc's basis, Marc's holding period is included. ◄

EXAMPLE I:5-89 ▶ Roy receives a capital asset as a gift from Diane on September 12, 2015, when the asset has a $6,000 FMV. Diane acquired the asset on July 1, 2014, for $6,500. If the asset is sold at a gain (i.e., for more than $6,500), Roy's holding period starts on July 1, 2014, the date when Diane acquired the property, because the donor's basis of $6,500 is used by Roy to compute the gain. If the asset is sold at a loss (i.e., for less than $6,000), Roy's holding period does not start until the day after the date of the gift, September 13, 2015, because Roy's basis is the $6,000 FMV. The FMV is used to compute the loss because it is less than the donor's basis on the date of the gift. ◄

ADDITIONAL COMMENT

The provision permitting the holding period of property received from a decedent to be deemed to be long-term is a rule of convenience. It is not necessary to try to determine when the decedent actually acquired the property.

PROPERTY RECEIVED FROM A DECEDENT

The holding period of property received from a decedent is always deemed to be long-term. If the person who receives the property from the decedent sells the property within one

[74] Sec. 1222. A six-month holding period was applied to property acquired after June 27, 1984 and before January 1, 1988.

[75] *H. M. Hooper,* 26 B.T.A. 758 (1932), and Rev. Rul. 70-598, 1970-2 C.B. 168.
[76] Sec. 1223(1) and Reg. Sec. 1.1223-1(b).

year after the decedent's death, the property is considered to be held for more than one year regardless of how long the property is actually held.[77]

EXAMPLE I:5-90 ▶ The executor of Paul's estate sells certain securities for $41,000 on September 2, 2015, which were valued in the estate at their FMV of $40,000 on June 5, 2015, the date of Paul's death. The estate has a LTCG of $1,000 because the securities are considered to have been held long-term. ◀

NONTAXABLE EXCHANGES

ADDITIONAL COMMENT
The like-kind exchange rules under Sec. 1031 allow taxpayers to trade certain types of business and investment properties with no tax consequences arising from the exchange. Like-kind exchanges are discussed in Chapter I:12.

In a nontaxable exchange, the basis of the property received is determined by taking into account the basis of the property given in the exchange. If the properties are capital assets or Sec. 1231 assets, the holding period of the property received includes the holding period of the surrendered property.[78] In essence, the holding period of the property given up in a tax-free exchange is tacked on to the holding period of the property received in the exchange.

RECEIPT OF NONTAXABLE STOCK DIVIDENDS AND STOCK RIGHTS

If a shareholder receives nontaxable stock dividends or stock rights, the holding period of the stock received as a dividend or the stock rights received includes the holding period for the stock owned by the shareholder.[79] However, if the stock rights are exercised, the holding period for the stock purchased begins with the date of exercise.

EXAMPLE I:5-91 ▶ As a result of owning Circle Corporation stock acquired three years ago, Paula receives nontaxable stock rights on June 5, 2015. Any gain or loss on the sale of the rights is long-term, regardless of whether any basis is allocated to the rights, because the holding period of the rights includes the holding period of the stock. ◀

EXAMPLE I:5-92 ▶ Assume the same facts as in the example above, except that the stock rights are exercised on August 20, 2015. The holding period for the newly acquired Circle stock begins on the date of exercise. ◀

STOP & THINK

Question: Carter owns 500 shares of Okoboji, Inc. (current market price of $310) with a basis of $101,500 acquired three years ago. In May of the current year, she receives 500 stock rights and exercises those rights that entitle her to purchase 500 shares of Okoboji at $300 per share. The current market price of the stock right is $40 per right. She plans to sell the 500 shares obtained by exercising the stock rights in January when she expects the market price to be $400 per share. Why should she elect to allocate basis to the stock rights?

Solution: If she does not allocate basis, her STCG will be $50,000 ($200,000 − $150,000). If she allocates basis to the stock rights, the basis of the 500 shares obtained when she exercises the rights is $161,600 ($150,000 + $11,600), and her STCG will be $38,400 ($200,000 − $161,600). Note that Carter might benefit by waiting a few months before selling because the gain might then be LTCG. She could sell the original 500 shares and have a LTCG.

JUSTIFICATION FOR PREFERENTIAL TREATMENT OF NET CAPITAL GAINS

Preferential treatment for capital gains was first created by the Revenue Act of 1921, which became effective on January 1, 1922. Despite almost continuous controversy concerning the need for preferential treatment, some form of preferential treatment for capital gains has existed since 1922. The range of controversy concerning the need for preferential tax treatment for capital gains is wide. Some maintain that capital gains do not

[77] Sec. 1223(11).
[78] Sec. 1223(1).
[79] Sec. 1223(5) and Reg. Sec. 1.1223-1(e).

HISTORICAL NOTE

In part the preferential treatment of net capital gains was repealed in the Tax Reform Act of 1986 because Congress believed that the reduction of individual tax rates on such forms of capital income as business profits, interest, dividends, and short-term capital gains eliminated the need for a reduced rate for net capital gains.

represent income and should not be taxed, whereas others maintain that capital gains are no different from any other type of income and should be taxed accordingly.[80] A few of the most common arguments are discussed below.

MOBILITY OF CAPITAL

Without some form of preferential treatment, taxpayers who own appreciated capital assets may be unwilling to sell or exchange the asset if high tax rates exist, despite the presence of more attractive investment opportunities. In essence, the taxpayer may be "locked in" to holding an appreciated capital asset instead of shifting resources to more profitable investments.

EXAMPLE I:5-93 ▶ Carmen owns Missouri Corporation stock with a $4,000 basis and a $20,000 FMV. She anticipates that the future after-tax annual return will be 10% on the Missouri stock and 12% on Kansas Corporation stock that has a similar level of risk. Assume her marginal tax rate is 35% (without consideration of favorable capital gain rates). Without preferential treatment of capital gains, Carmen will have to pay a tax of $5,600 ($16,000 × 0.35) on the sale of the Missouri stock and will have only $14,400 ($20,000 − $5,600) to invest in the Kansas stock. With a 12% return, she will receive an investment return of only $1,728 ($14,400 × 0.12), as compared with $2,000 ($20,000 × 0.10) if she maintains the investment in the Missouri stock. ◀

ADDITIONAL COMMENT

According to *The Wall Street Journal,* twelve industrialized nations impose a zero capital gains rate (10-15-07, p. A22).

While the payment of any tax due to the sale of an asset creates somewhat of a "locked-in" effect, the effect can be reduced by lowering the tax rate. The "locked-in" effect is even stronger for older taxpayers if the basis of inherited property is FMV at time of death. A lower tax rate on net capital gain should reduce the taxpayers unwillingness to sell the asset and allow for more mobility of capital. For a brief period in the 1990s, both the top ordinary income rate and the rate on net capital gain were 28%. Today, the top rate on ordinary income is 39.6% and 20% on adjusted net capital gain.

MITIGATION OF THE EFFECTS OF INFLATION AND THE PROGRESSIVE TAX SYSTEM

Because the tax laws do not generally reflect the effect of changes in purchasing power due to inflation, the sale or exchange of a capital asset may produce inequitable results. In fact, taxes may have to be paid even where a transaction results in an inflation-adjusted loss.

EXAMPLE I:5-94 ▶ Beverly purchased a capital asset nine years ago for $100,000. If the asset is sold today for $180,000 and the general price level has increased by 100% during the nine-year period, Beverly will have a taxable gain of $80,000, despite suffering an inflation-adjusted loss of $20,000 [$180,000 sale price − ($100,000 × 200%)]. ◀

ADDITIONAL COMMENT

The American Assembly at Columbia University, in its final report on *Reforming and Simplifying the Federal Tax System* issued in 1985, recommends that capital gains be taxed as ordinary income if they are adjusted for inflation.

With a progressive tax system, the failure to adjust for inflation creates an even greater distortion. However, it should be noted that this distortion applies to all assets, not just capital assets.

LOWERS THE COST OF CAPITAL

By reducing the tax rate on capital gains, investors are more willing to provide businesses with capital and the cost of capital is reduced. A lower cost of capital encourages capital formation to create more jobs and improve our competitive position in the global economy. Reducing the cost of capital is particularly important for the formation and growth of small business.

---

[80] Walter J. Blum, "A Handy Summary of the Capital Gains Argument," *Taxes—The Tax Magazine,* 35 (April 1957), pp. 247–66.

TAX PLANNING CONSIDERATIONS

<table>
<tr><td>**OBJECTIVE 8**</td></tr>
</table>

Describe tax planning opportunities for property transactions

SELECTION OF PROPERTY TO TRANSFER BY GIFT

Many tax reasons exist for making gifts of property, although the donor may incur a gift tax liability if the gift is a taxable gift. For example, taxpayers may give income-producing property to a taxpayer subject to a lower tax rate, or property expected to appreciate in the future may be given away to reduce estate taxes. Individuals may annually give property of $14,000[81] or less to a donee without making a taxable gift.[82]

EXAMPLE I:5-95 ▶ Maya, who is single, owns marketable securities with a $6,200 basis and $10,400 FMV. She makes gifts of the marketable securities to Phil and cash of $14,000 to Roy. Because of the $14,000 annual exclusion per donee, Maya's gifts are not taxable gifts. ◀

EXAMPLE I:5-96 ▶ Harry, who is single and has never made a taxable gift, makes a gift of land in 2015 with a $1,564,000 basis and a $6,214,000 FMV to Rita. Harry's taxable gift is $6,200,000 ($6,214,000 − $14,000), and he incurs a gift tax liability. Rita's basis is $1,564,000 + 75% of the gift tax paid by Harry [($6,214,000 − $1,564,000)/$6,200,000 = 75%]. ◀

Individuals often reduce future estate taxes by making gifts. By using the annual exclusion, an individual may reduce future estate taxes and avoid the gift tax.

EXAMPLE I:5-97 ▶ Christine owns only one asset in 2015—cash of $7.2 million—and has no liabilities. In December of 2015, she gifted $14,000 to each of her five grandchildren. Because of the $14,000 annual exclusion per donee, Christine's gifts were not taxable gifts. By making the gifts, she reduced her potential gross estate by $70,000 (5 × $14,000). ◀

ADDITIONAL COMMENT

A husband and wife can each make a $14,000 gift to their daughter in 2015, enabling her to receive a total of $28,000 annually without the parents having a taxable gift.

The selection of which property to give is important if one is attempting to reduce future estate taxes. It is generally preferable to make gifts of properties that are expected to significantly increase in value during the postgift period before the donor's death. Any increases in value after the date of the gift are not included in the donor's gross estate.

EXAMPLE I:5-98 ▶ In 1994, Hal owned Sun Corporation stock with a $100,000 FMV and Union Corporation stock with a $100,000 FMV. Hal expected the Sun stock to increase in value at a moderate rate and the Union stock to increase at a substantial rate. In 1994, Hal made a gift of the Union stock to Dana. Hal's taxable gift in 1994 was $90,000 ($100,000 − $10,000 annual exclusion in 1994). Hal dies in the current year when the FMVs of the Sun and Union stocks are $180,000 and $425,000, respectively. The postgift appreciation of $325,000 ($425,000 − $100,000) is not included in Hal's gross estate. By giving the Union stock instead of the Sun stock in 1994, Hal reduces his gross estate by $245,000. ◀

Gifts are often made for income tax purposes to shift income to other family members who are in a lower income tax bracket than the donor.

EXAMPLE I:5-99 ▶ In 2015, Anne has a marginal tax rate of 33% and owns Atlantic Corporation bonds, which have a $5,000 basis and $8,000 FMV. The bonds pay interest of $1,400 per year. If Anne gives the bonds to her dependent child, the interest income is shifted to the child. If the child has no other income, the child's taxable income is $350 ($1,400 − $1,050 standard deduction), and the child's marginal tax rate is 10%. The gift results in an annual income tax savings to the family unit of $427 [(0.33 × $1,400) − (0.10 × $350)]. The rate of tax that is imposed may be the parent's rate (see Chapter I:2) if the child is less than 18 years old (possibly less than 24 years old after 2007) and has net unearned income in excess of $2,100.

In addition to shifting the interest income, Anne has also shifted a potential gain of $3,000. The child's basis for the bonds is $5,000 because the donee takes the donor's basis when the FMV of the property at the time of the gift is greater than the donor's basis. No gain is

---

[81] In 2009–2012, the annual exclusion was $13,000.　　　　[82] Sec. 2503(b).

ADDITIONAL COMMENT

In Example I:5-99, Anne may also reduce the new 3.8% Medicare tax on net investment income.

recognized by Anne when the gift is made, and a future sale of the property by the child may be taxed at a lower income tax rate.   ◄

Although gifts of appreciated property may generate desirable income tax benefits, it is not usually advantageous to make a gift of property that has a basis greater than its FMV because the donee's basis for determining a loss is the FMV. The excess of the donor's basis over the FMV at the time of the gift may never generate any tax benefit for the donor or the donee. Therefore, the donor should sell the asset and make a gift of the proceeds if the loss on the sale is deductible.

EXAMPLE I:5-100 ▶

Bob owns Red Corporation stock with an $8,000 basis and $6,000 FMV, which is held as an investment. Bob wishes to make a graduation gift of the marketable securities to Angela, although he expects her to sell the stock and purchase a car. If Angela sells the stock for $6,000, no gain or loss is recognized because her loss basis for the stock is $6,000. In addition, no loss is recognized by Bob on the gift of the stock to Angela. Instead of giving the stock, Bob should sell it to recognize a $2,000 capital loss and then give the proceeds from the sale to Angela.   ◄

SELF-STUDY QUESTION

Doug owns IBM Corporation shares, which have a $50,000 FMV and basis of $75,000. Doug makes a deathbed telephone call to his stockbroker and sells the IBM shares. Assuming that Doug is in the 35% bracket and had no other capital gains or losses, calculate the tax savings associated with the sale.

ANSWER

Doug saves $1,050 ($3,000 × 0.35) unless he has capital gain income that may be offset with the capital loss. It should be noted that the loss is limited to $3,000; if Doug dies, the unused capital loss of $22,000 is lost.

The effect of gift taxes paid by the donor on the donee's basis for property received is another reason why it may be more advantageous to give appreciated property rather than property with a basis greater than its FMV. A portion of the gift taxes paid as a result of giving appreciated property is added to the property's basis. However, payment of gift taxes due to the gift of property that has a basis greater than its FMV does not result in an increase in the donee's basis.

SELECTION OF PROPERTY TO TRANSFER AT TIME OF DEATH

An integral part of gift and estate planning is the selection of property to be transferred to family members and others both during the taxpayer's lifetime and upon death. Usually, taxpayers find it advantageous to retain highly appreciated property in their estates and transfer such property at death to the taxpayer's heirs because the basis of the inherited property will be increased to its FMV at the date of death (or six months from the date of death if the alternate valuation date is elected). Of course, the impact of gift and estate taxes also play a major role in this planning process.

Investment and business assets that have declined in value (i.e., the FMV is less than the basis) should normally be sold before death to obtain an income tax deduction for the loss. If the property is not sold or otherwise disposed of before death, the basis of the inherited property is reduced to its FMV.

EXAMPLE I:5-101 ▶

Paul owns two farms of similar size and quality. Each farm has a $500,000 FMV. Paul's basis for the first farm is $100,000, and his basis for the second farm is $430,000. Eventually, Paul plans for both farms to be owned by Amy. However, he would like to transfer ownership of one farm now and retain the other farm until his death. Paul should make a gift of the second farm and transfer the first farm to Amy upon his death because the second farm has appreciated less in value. When Paul dies and devises the first farm to Amy, she will have a basis for the property equal to its FMV at the date of death even though Paul's basis is only $100,000.   ◄

COMPLIANCE AND PROCEDURAL CONSIDERATIONS

OBJECTIVE 9

Describe compliance and procedural considerations for property transactions

DOCUMENTATION OF BASIS

The importance of being able to determine and document the basis of assets acquired by a taxpayer cannot be overemphasized. Accurate records of asset acquisitions, dispositions, and adjustments to basis are essential. When more than one asset is acquired at the same time, the amount paid must be allocated among the assets acquired based on their relative FMVs. Subsequent adjustments to basis, such as those due to capital improvements and depreciation deductions, must be documented.

Because the basis of property can be determined by reference to another person's basis for that asset (e.g., gifts), taxpayers should be particularly aware of obtaining documentation for that basis at the time of the transfer. In the case of a gift, the taxpayer's basis may be affected by any gift tax paid by the donor. A copy of the donor's gift tax return is useful in documenting the upward adjustment to the donor's basis in determining the donee's basis.

Taxpayers who inherit property may use the decedent's federal Estate Tax Return (Form 706) to determine the FMV at the time of the decedent's death or FMV as of the alternate valuation date. However, the appraised value used for estate tax purposes is only presumptively correct for basis purposes. Although the FMVs used to determine the estate tax are typically used to determine basis, neither the taxpayer nor the IRS is barred from using an FMV for basis purposes that differs from the values used for the estate tax return.[83]

Brokerage firms must report an investor's cost basis in any shares purchased after January 1, 2011 to the IRS when securities are sold. Brokers have been required for many years to report the amount of sales proceeds but must now also provide the basis. The broker will apply a FIFO rule when selecting the securities sold unless the taxpayer notifies the broker that other securities are being sold. If a taxpayer owns securities purchased at different prices and on different dates, the taxpayer may specifically identify those stocks deemed to be sold and thus may affect the amount of the gain or loss and if the gain or loss in ST or LT.

REPORTING OF CAPITAL GAINS AND LOSSES ON SCHEDULE D

Capital gains and losses are reported by individuals on Schedule D, which is then attached to Form 1040. Part I is used to report short-term capital gains and losses, and Part II is used to report long-term capital gains and losses. Part III is a summary of Parts I and II.

Capital gains due to installment sales are first reported on a separate form before being included on Schedule D. The taxpayer's share of capital gains and losses from partnerships, S corporations, and fiduciaries is reported in Parts I and II on lines 5 and 12. The carryover of capital losses is also included in Parts I and II on lines 6 and 14.

EXAMPLE I:5-102 ▶

Virgil Schmidt, a single taxpayer, uses the following information to prepare his Schedule D for 2014. Virgil received $8,000 of qualified dividends during the year. He sold 200 shares of Tennis Corporation stock for $13,000 on June 20, 2014. The shares were purchased on October 2, 2013, for $8,700. He has an STCL carryforward from 2013 of $8,200. He sold a piano for $4,000 on May 30, 2014. The piano was purchased on April 12, 2004, for $2,500 and used by his two sons. Virgil also sold 500 shares of Golf Corporation stock for $18,000 on November 30, 2014. He had purchased the stock on April 1, 2010, for $10,000.

Virgil has STCG of $4,300 that is offset by $8,200 of STCL carryforward on line 6. His NSTCL of $3,900 ($8,200 − $4,300) is shown on line 7. His $1,500 LTCG as a result of the sale of the piano (not a collectible) and his $8,000 LTCG from the sale of the Golf Corporation stock are on lines 9 and 10. Thus, Virgil has a NLTCG of $9,500. He has ANCG of $5,600 ($9,500 − $3,900).

Because Virgil has ANCG of $5,600 and no 28% rate gains or unrecaptured Sec. 1250 gains, he computes his tax on the Qualified Dividends and Capital Gain Tax Worksheet. The preferential treatment for dividends and capital gains saves Virgil $1,768 of federal income taxes in 2014.

Virgil's taxable income including the above dividends and capital gains is $120,000. ◀

The following pages include the Schedule D, Form 8949, and a worksheet that taxpayers use to compute their tax if they have no 28% rate gains or unrecaptured Section 1250 gains. For Virgil in the above example, both stock transactions were reported on Form 1099-B with basis reported to the IRS.

[83] Rev. Rul. 54-97, 1954-1 C.B. 113 and *Achille F. Ford v. U.S.*, 5 AFTR 2d 1157, 60-1 USTC ¶9375 (Ct. Cls., 1960).

SCHEDULE D
(Form 1040)

Department of the Treasury
Internal Revenue Service (99)

Capital Gains and Losses

▶ Attach to Form 1040 or Form 1040NR.
▶ Information about Schedule D and its separate instructions is at *www.irs.gov/scheduled*.
▶ Use Form 8949 to list your transactions for lines 1b, 2, 3, 8b, 9, and 10.

OMB No. 1545-0074

2014

Attachment
Sequence No. **12**

Name(s) shown on return

Virgil Schmidt

Your social security number

| Part I | Short-Term Capital Gains and Losses—Assets Held One Year or Less |

See instructions for how to figure the amounts to enter on the lines below. This form may be easier to complete if you round off cents to whole dollars.	(d) Proceeds (sales price)	(e) Cost (or other basis)	(g) Adjustments to gain or loss from Form(s) 8949, Part I, line 2, column (g)	(h) Gain or (loss) Subtract column (e) from column (d) and combine the result with column (g)
1a Totals for all short-term transactions reported on Form 1099-B for which basis was reported to the IRS and for which you have no adjustments (see instructions). However, if you choose to report all these transactions on Form 8949, leave this line blank and go to line 1b .				
1b Totals for all transactions reported on Form(s) 8949 with **Box A** checked	13,000	8,700		4,300
2 Totals for all transactions reported on Form(s) 8949 with **Box B** checked				
3 Totals for all transactions reported on Form(s) 8949 with **Box C** checked				

4 Short-term gain from Form 6252 and short-term gain or (loss) from Forms 4684, 6781, and 8824 .	**4**	
5 Net short-term gain or (loss) from partnerships, S corporations, estates, and trusts from Schedule(s) K-1	**5**	
6 Short-term capital loss carryover. Enter the amount, if any, from line 8 of your **Capital Loss Carryover Worksheet** in the instructions	**6** (8,200)
7 **Net short-term capital gain or (loss).** Combine lines 1a through 6 in column (h). If you have any long-term capital gains or losses, go to Part II below. Otherwise, go to Part III on the back	**7** (3,900)

| Part II | Long-Term Capital Gains and Losses—Assets Held More Than One Year |

See instructions for how to figure the amounts to enter on the lines below. This form may be easier to complete if you round off cents to whole dollars.	(d) Proceeds (sales price)	(e) Cost (or other basis)	(g) Adjustments to gain or loss from Form(s) 8949, Part II, line 2, column (g)	(h) Gain or (loss) Subtract column (e) from column (d) and combine the result with column (g)
8a Totals for all long-term transactions reported on Form 1099-B for which basis was reported to the IRS and for which you have no adjustments (see instructions). However, if you choose to report all these transactions on Form 8949, leave this line blank and go to line 8b .				
8b Totals for all transactions reported on Form(s) 8949 with **Box D** checked	18,000	(10,000)		8,000
9 Totals for all transactions reported on Form(s) 8949 with **Box E** checked				
10 Totals for all transactions reported on Form(s) 8949 with **Box F** checked.	4,000	(2,500)		1,500

11 Gain from Form 4797, Part I; long-term gain from Forms 2439 and 6252; and long-term gain or (loss) from Forms 4684, 6781, and 8824	**11**	
12 Net long-term gain or (loss) from partnerships, S corporations, estates, and trusts from Schedule(s) K-1	**12**	
13 Capital gain distributions. See the instructions	**13**	
14 Long-term capital loss carryover. Enter the amount, if any, from line 13 of your **Capital Loss Carryover Worksheet** in the instructions	**14** ( )
15 **Net long-term capital gain or (loss).** Combine lines 8a through 14 in column (h). Then go to Part III on the back	**15** 9,500

For Paperwork Reduction Act Notice, see your tax return instructions.   Cat. No. 11338H   Schedule D (Form 1040) 2014

FIGURE I:5-1 ▶ PART I–II OF SCHEDULE D FOR EXAMPLE I:5-102

| **Part III** | **Summary** | | |

16 Combine lines 7 and 15 and enter the result **16**   5,600

- If line 16 is a **gain**, enter the amount from line 16 on Form 1040, line 13, or Form 1040NR, line 14. Then go to line 17 below.
- If line 16 is a **loss**, skip lines 17 through 20 below. Then go to line 21. Also be sure to complete line 22.
- If line 16 is **zero,** skip lines 17 through 21 below and enter -0- on Form 1040, line 13, or Form 1040NR, line 14. Then go to line 22.

17 Are lines 15 and 16 **both** gains?
☐ **Yes.** Go to line 18.
☐ **No.** Skip lines 18 through 21, and go to line 22.

18 Enter the amount, if any, from line 7 of the **28% Rate Gain Worksheet** in the instructions . . ▶   **18**

19 Enter the amount, if any, from line 18 of the **Unrecaptured Section 1250 Gain Worksheet** in the instructions . . . . ▶   **19**

20 Are lines 18 and 19 **both** zero or blank?
☐ **Yes.** Complete the **Qualified Dividends and Capital Gain Tax Worksheet** in the instructions for Form 1040, line 44 (or in the instructions for Form 1040NR, line 42). **Do not** complete lines 21 and 22 below.

☐ **No.** Complete the **Schedule D Tax Worksheet** in the instructions. **Do not** complete lines 21 and 22 below.

21 If line 16 is a loss, enter here and on Form 1040, line 13, or Form 1040NR, line 14, the **smaller** of:

- The loss on line 16 or
- ($3,000), or if married filing separately, ($1,500) } . . . .   **21** ( )

Note. When figuring which amount is smaller, treat both amounts as positive numbers.

22 Do you have qualified dividends on Form 1040, line 9b, or Form 1040NR, line 10b?

☐ **Yes.** Complete the **Qualified Dividends and Capital Gain Tax Worksheet** in the instructions for Form 1040, line 44 (or in the instructions for Form 1040NR, line 42).

☐ **No.** Complete the rest of Form 1040 or Form 1040NR.

Schedule D (Form 1040) 2014

FIGURE I:5-1 ▶ PART III OF SCHEDULE D FOR EXAMPLE I:5-102

Form **8949** | Department of the Treasury Internal Revenue Service

Sales and Other Dispositions of Capital Assets

► Information about Form 8949 and its separate instructions is at *www.irs.gov/form8949.*

► File with your Schedule D to list your transactions for lines 1b, 2, 3, 8b, 9, and 10 of Schedule D.

OMB No. 1545-0074

2014

Attachment Sequence No. **12A**

Name(s) shown on return: Virgil Schmidt

Social security number or taxpayer identification number

Before you check Box A, B, or C below, see whether you received any Form(s) 1099-B or substitute statement(s) from your broker. A substitute statement will have the same information as Form 1099-B. Either may show your basis (usually your cost) even if your broker did not report it to the IRS. Brokers must report basis to the IRS for most stock you bought in 2011 or later (and for certain debt instruments you bought in 2014 or later).

Part I **Short-Term.** Transactions involving capital assets you held 1 year or less are short term. For long-term transactions, see page 2.

Note. You may aggregate all short-term transactions reported on Form(s) 1099-B showing basis was reported to the IRS and for which no adjustments or codes are required. Enter the total directly on Schedule D, line 1a; you are not required to report these transactions on Form 8949 (see instructions).

You *must* check Box A, B, *or* C below. Check only one box. If more than one box applies for your short-term transactions, complete a separate Form 8949, page 1, for each applicable box. If you have more short-term transactions than will fit on this page for one or more of the boxes, complete as many forms with the same box checked as you need.

- ☑ **(A)** Short-term transactions reported on Form(s) 1099-B showing basis was reported to the IRS (see **Note** above)
- ☐ **(B)** Short-term transactions reported on Form(s) 1099-B showing basis was **not** reported to the IRS
- ☐ **(C)** Short-term transactions not reported to you on Form 1099-B

1 (a) Description of property (Example: 100 sh. XYZ Co.)	(b) Date acquired (Mo., day, yr.)	(c) Date sold or disposed (Mo., day, yr.)	(d) Proceeds (sales price) (see instructions)	(e) Cost or other basis. See the **Note** below and see *Column (e)* in the separate instructions	Adjustment, if any, to gain or loss. If you enter an amount in column (g), enter a code in column (f). **See the separate instructions.** (f) Code(s) from instructions	(g) Amount of adjustment	(h) **Gain or (loss).** Subtract column (e) from column (d) and combine the result with column (g)
200 Sh Tennis Corp.	10-2-13	6-20-14	13,000	8,700			4,300
2 Totals. Add the amounts in columns (d), (e), (g), and (h) (subtract negative amounts). Enter each total here and include on your Schedule D, **line 1b** (if **Box A** above is checked), **line 2** (if **Box B** above is checked), or **line 3** (if **Box C** above is checked) ►			13,000	8,700			4,300

Note. If you checked Box A above but the basis reported to the IRS was incorrect, enter in column (e) the basis as reported to the IRS, and enter an adjustment in column (g) to correct the basis. See *Column (g)* in the separate instructions for how to figure the amount of the adjustment.

For Paperwork Reduction Act Notice, see your tax return instructions. Cat. No. 37768Z Form **8949** (2014)

FIGURE I:5-2

Form 8949 (2014)

Attachment Sequence No. **12A**   Page **2**

Name(s) shown on return. Name and SSN or taxpayer identification no. not required if shown on other side	Social security number or taxpayer identification number

Before you check Box D, E, or F below, see whether you received any Form(s) 1099-B or substitute statement(s) from your broker. A substitute statement will have the same information as Form 1099-B. Either may show your basis (usually your cost) even if your broker did not report it to the IRS. Brokers must report basis to the IRS for most stock you bought in 2011 or later (and for certain debt instruments you bought in 2014 or later).

Part II   **Long-Term.** Transactions involving capital assets you held more than 1 year are long term. For short-term transactions, see page 1.

Note. You may aggregate all long-term transactions reported on Form(s) 1099-B showing basis was reported to the IRS and for which no adjustments or codes are required. Enter the total directly on Schedule D, line 8a; you are not required to report these transactions on Form 8949 (see instructions).

You *must* check Box D, E, *or* F below. Check only one box. If more than one box applies for your long-term transactions, complete a separate Form 8949, page 2, for each applicable box. If you have more long-term transactions than will fit on this page for one or more of the boxes, complete as many forms with the same box checked as you need.

- ☑ **(D)** Long-term transactions reported on Form(s) 1099-B showing basis was reported to the IRS (see **Note** above)
- ☐ **(E)** Long-term transactions reported on Form(s) 1099-B showing basis was **not** reported to the IRS
- ☐ **(F)** Long-term transactions not reported to you on Form 1099-B

1 (a) Description of property (Example: 100 sh. XYZ Co.)	(b) Date acquired (Mo., day, yr.)	(c) Date sold or disposed (Mo., day, yr.)	(d) Proceeds (sales price) (see instructions)	(e) Cost or other basis. See the **Note** below and see *Column (e)* in the separate instructions	Adjustment, if any, to gain or loss. If you enter an amount in column (g), enter a code in column (f). See the separate instructions. (f) Code(s) from instructions	(g) Amount of adjustment	(h) Gain or (loss). Subtract column (e) from column (d) and combine the result with column (g)
500 Sh Golf Corp Stock	4-1-10	11-30-14	18,000	10,000			8,000
2 Totals. Add the amounts in columns (d), (e), (g), and (h) (subtract negative amounts). Enter each total here and include on your Schedule D, **line 8b** (if **Box D** above is checked), **line 9** (if **Box E** above is checked), or **line 10** (if **Box F** above is checked) ▶			18,000	10,000			8,000

Note. If you checked Box D above but the basis reported to the IRS was incorrect, enter in column (e) the basis as reported to the IRS, and enter an adjustment in column (g) to correct the basis. See *Column (g)* in the separate instructions for how to figure the amount of the adjustment.

Form **8949** (2014)

FIGURE I:5-2

Form 8949 (2014)

Attachment Sequence No. **12A**   Page **2**

Name(s) shown on return. Name and SSN or taxpayer identification no. not required if shown on other side	Social security number or taxpayer identification number

Before you check Box D, E, or F below, see whether you received any Form(s) 1099-B or substitute statement(s) from your broker. A substitute statement will have the same information as Form 1099-B. Either may show your basis (usually your cost) even if your broker did not report it to the IRS. Brokers must report basis to the IRS for most stock you bought in 2011 or later (and for certain debt instruments you bought in 2014 or later).

Part II   **Long-Term.** Transactions involving capital assets you held more than 1 year are long term. For short-term transactions, see page 1.

Note. You may aggregate all long-term transactions reported on Form(s) 1099-B showing basis was reported to the IRS and for which no adjustments or codes are required. Enter the total directly on Schedule D, line 8a; you are not required to report these transactions on Form 8949 (see instructions).

You *must* check Box D, E, *or* F below. Check only one box. If more than one box applies for your long-term transactions, complete a separate Form 8949, page 2, for each applicable box. If you have more long-term transactions than will fit on this page for one or more of the boxes, complete as many forms with the same box checked as you need.

- ☐ **(D)** Long-term transactions reported on Form(s) 1099-B showing basis was reported to the IRS (see **Note** above)
- ☐ **(E)** Long-term transactions reported on Form(s) 1099-B showing basis was **not** reported to the IRS
- ☑ **(F)** Long-term transactions not reported to you on Form 1099-B

1 (a) Description of property (Example: 100 sh. XYZ Co.)	(b) Date acquired (Mo., day, yr.)	(c) Date sold or disposed (Mo., day, yr.)	(d) Proceeds (sales price) (see instructions)	(e) Cost or other basis. See the **Note** below and see *Column (e)* in the separate instructions	Adjustment, if any, to gain or loss. If you enter an amount in column (g), enter a code in column (f). See the separate instructions. (f) Code(s) from instructions	(g) Amount of adjustment	(h) Gain or (loss). Subtract column (e) from column (d) and combine the result with column (g)
Piano	4-12-04	5-3-14	4,000	2,500			1,500
2 Totals. Add the amounts in columns (d), (e), (g), and (h) (subtract negative amounts). Enter each total here and include on your Schedule D, **line 8b** (if **Box D** above is checked), **line 9** (if **Box E** above is checked), or **line 10** (if **Box F** above is checked) ▶			4,000	2,500			1,500

Note. If you checked Box D above but the basis reported to the IRS was incorrect, enter in column (e) the basis as reported to the IRS, and enter an adjustment in column (g) to correct the basis. See *Column (g)* in the separate instructions for how to figure the amount of the adjustment.

FIGURE I:5-2

Form **8949** (2014)

Taxpayers such as Virgil in Example I:5-102 use the Qualified Dividends Capital Gain Tax Worksheet below if they either have qualified dividends or ANCG *and* do not have any 28% rate gain property or unrecaptured Section 1250 gain. This worksheet applies the lower preferential tax rates of zero or 15% for qualified dividends and ANCG.

2014 Form 1040—Line 44

Qualified Dividends and Capital Gain Tax Worksheet—Line 44

 Keep for Your Records

Before you begin:	✓ See the earlier instructions for line 44 to see if you can use this worksheet to figure your tax.	
	✓ Before completing this worksheet, complete Form 1040 through line 43.	
	✓ If you do not have to file Schedule D and you received capital gain distributions, be sure you checked the box on line 13 of Form 1040.	

1.	Enter the amount from Form 1040, line 43. However, if you are filing Form 2555 or 2555-EZ (relating to foreign earned income), enter the amount from line 3 of the Foreign Earned Income Tax Worksheet .... **1.**	**120,000**
2.	Enter the amount from Form 1040, line 9b* **2.** 8,000	
3.	Are you filing Schedule D?* ☑ **Yes.** Enter the **smaller** of line 15 or 16 of Schedule D. If either line 15 or line 16 is blank or a loss, enter -0- ☐ **No.** Enter the amount from Form 1040, line 13 } **3.** 5,600	
4.	Add lines 2 and 3 .... **4.** 13,600	
5.	If filing Form 4952 (used to figure investment interest expense deduction), enter any amount from line 4g of that form. Otherwise, enter -0- .... **5.** -0-	
6.	Subtract line 5 from line 4. If zero or less, enter -0- .... **6.**	**13,600**
7.	Subtract line 6 from line 1. If zero or less, enter -0- .... **7.**	**106,400**
8.	Enter: $36,900 if single or married filing separately, $73,800 if married filing jointly or qualifying widow(er), $49,400 if head of household. } .... **8.**	**36,900**
9.	Enter the smaller of line 1 or line 8 .... **9.**	**36,900**
10.	Enter the smaller of line 7 or line 9 .... **10.**	**36,900**
11.	Subtract line 10 from line 9. This amount is taxed at 0% ...... **11.**	**-0-**
12.	Enter the smaller of line 1 or line 6 .... **12.**	**13,600**
13.	Enter the amount from line 11 .... **13.**	**-0-**
14.	Subtract line 13 from line 12 .... **14.**	**13,600**
15.	Enter: $406,750 if single, $228,800 if married filing separately, $457,600 if married filing jointly or qualifying widow(er), $432,200 if head of household. } .... **15.**	**406,750**
16.	Enter the smaller of line 1 or line 15 .... **16.**	**120,000**
17.	Add lines 7 and 11 .... **17.**	**106,400**
18.	Subtract line 17 from line 16. If zero or less, enter -0- .... **18.**	**13,600**
19.	Enter the smaller of line 14 or line 18 .... **19.**	**13,600**
20.	Multiply line 19 by 15% (.15) .... **20.**	**2040**
21.	Add lines 11 and 19 .... **21.**	**13,600**
22.	Subtract line 21 from line 12 .... **22.**	**-0-**
23.	Multiply line 22 by 20% (.20) .... **23.**	**-0-**
24.	Figure the tax on the amount on line 7. If the amount on line 7 is less than $100,000, use the Tax Table to figure the tax. If the amount on line 7 is $100,000 or more, use the Tax Computation Worksheet .... **24.**	**22,968**
25.	Add lines 20, 23, and 24 .... **25.**	**25,008**
26.	Figure the tax on the amount on line 1. If the amount on line 1 is less than $100,000, use the Tax Table to figure the tax. If the amount on line 1 is $100,000 or more, use the Tax Computation Worksheet .... **26.**	**26,776**
27.	**Tax on all taxable income.** Enter the **smaller** of line 25 or line 26. Also include this amount on Form 1040, line 44. If you are filing Form 2555 or 2555-EZ, do not enter this amount on Form 1040, line 44. Instead, enter it on line 4 of the Foreign Earned Income Tax Worksheet .... **27.**	**25,008**

If you are filing Form 2555 or 2555-EZ, see the footnote in the Foreign Earned Income Tax Worksheet before completing this line.

FIGURE I:5-3 ▶ QUALIFIED DIVIDENDS AND CAPITAL GAIN TAX WORKSHEET FOR EXAMPLE I:5-102

PROBLEM MATERIALS

DISCUSSION QUESTIONS

I:5-1 What problem may exist in determining the amount realized for an investor who exchanges common stock of a publicly traded corporation for a used building? How is the problem likely to be resolved?

I:5-2 In 2001, Ellen purchased a house for $60,000 to use as her personal residence. She paid $12,000 and borrowed $48,000 from the local savings and loan company. In 2005 she paid $10,000 to add a room to the house. In 200 7 she paid $625 to have the house painted and $800 for built-in bookshelves. As of January 1 of the current year, she has reduced the $48,000 mortgage to $44,300. What is her basis for the house?

I:5-3 Vincent pays $20,000 for equipment to use in his trade or business. He pays sales tax of $800 as a result of the purchase. Must the $800 sales tax be capitalized as part of the purchase price?

I:5-4 Sergio owns 200 shares of Palm Corporation common stock, purchased during the prior year: 100 shares on July 5, for $9,000; and 100 shares on October 15, for $12,000. When Sergio sells 50 shares for $8,000 on July 18 of the current year, he does not identify the particular shares sold. Determine the amount and character of the gain.

I:5-5 On October 21 of the current year, David receives stock of Western Corporation as a gift from his grandfather, who acquired the stock on January 20, 1995. Under what conditions would David's holding period start on?
a. October 22 of the current year?
b. January 20, 1995?

I:5-6 Jim inherits stock (a capital asset) from his brother, who died in March of 2015, when the property had a $6.9 million FMV. This property is the only property included in his brother's gross estate and there is a taxable estate. The FMV of the property as of the alternate valuation date was $6.7 million.
a. Why might the executor of the brother's estate elect to use the alternate valuation date to value the property?
b. Why might Jim prefer the executor to use FMV at time of the death to value the property?
c. If the marginal estate tax rate is 40% and Jim's marginal income tax rate is 25%, which value should the executor use?

I:5-7 Martha owns 500 shares of Columbus Corporation common stock at the beginning of the year with a basis of $82,500. During the year, Columbus declares and pays a 10% nontaxable stock dividend. What is her basis for each of the 50 shares received?

I:5-8 Mario owns 2,000 shares of Nevada Corporation common stock at the beginning of the year. His basis for the stock is $38,880. During the year, Nevada declares and pays a stock dividend. After the dividend, Mario's basis for each share of stock owned is $18. What is the percentage dividend paid by Nevada?

I:5-9 A corporate taxpayer plans to build a $6 million office building during the next 18 months. How must the corporation treat the interest on debt paid or incurred during the production period?

I:5-10 Andy owns an appliance store where he has merchandise such as refrigerators for sale. Roger, a bachelor, owns a refrigerator, which he uses in his apartment for personal use. For which individual is the refrigerator a capital asset?

I:5-11 Why did the Supreme Court rule in the *Corn Products* case that a gain due to the sale of futures contracts is ordinary income instead of capital gain?

I:5-12 When is the gain on the sale or exchange of securities by a dealer in securities classified as capital gain?

I:5-13 In 2002, Florence purchased 30 acres of land. She has not used the land for business purposes or made any substantial improvements to the property. During the current year, she subdivides the land into 15 lots and advertises the lots for sale. She sells four lots at a gain.
a. What is the character of the gain on the sale of the four lots?
b. Explain how the basis of each lot would be determined.

I:5-14 Amy has LTCGs that are taxed at different tax rates, 15%, 25% and 28%. She also has NSTCLs that amount to less than her NLTCG. The procedure for offsetting the NSTCL against the LTCGs is favorable to her. Explain.

I:5-15 Four years ago, Susan loaned $7,000 to her friend Joe. During the current year, the $7,000 loan is considered worthless. Explain how Susan should treat the worthless debt for tax purposes.

I:5-16 Why did the Supreme Court rule in *Arkansas Best* that the stock of a corporation purchased by the taxpayer to protect the taxpayer's business reputation was a capital asset?

I:5-17 The effective tax rate on gain of $1 million resulting from the sale of qualified small business stock obtained in 2005 in an initial public offering and held more than five years is 14%. Do you agree or disagree? Explain.

I:5-18 Nancy and the Minor Corporation own bonds of the East Corporation. Minor Corporation owns 80% of the stock of East Corporation. East Corporation has declared bankruptcy this year, and bondholders will receive only 26% of the face value of the debt. Explain why the loss is a capital loss for Nancy but an ordinary loss for the Minor Corporation.

I:5-19 On January 1 of the current year, the Orange Corporation issues $500,000 of 11%, 20-year bonds for $480,000. Determine the amount of original issue discount, if any.

I:5-20 Today, Juanita purchases a 15-year, 7% bond of the Sunflower Corporation issued four years ago at par. She purchases the bond as an investment at a discount from the par value. If she sells the bonds two years from now, explain why some or all of the gain may be ordinary income.

I:5-21 Judy just obtained a patent on a new product she has developed. Bell Corporation wishes to market the product and will pay 12% of all future sales of the product to Judy. How can she be sure that the payments received will be treated as a long-term capital gain?

I:5-22 When is the transferor of a franchise unable to treat the transfer as a sale or an exchange of a capital asset?

I:5-23 How does a lessor treat payments received for canceling a lease?

I:5-24 What is the first day that an individual could sell a capital asset purchased on March 31, 2015 and have a holding period of more than one year?

I:5-25 Phil, a cash-basis taxpayer, sells the following marketable securities, which are capital assets during 2015. Determine whether the gains or losses are long-term or short-term. Also determine the net capital gain and adjusted net capital gain for 2015.

Capital Asset	Basis	Date Acquired	Trade Date in 2015	Sales Price
A	$40,000	Feb. 10, 2014	Aug. 12	$52,000
B	20,000	Dec. 5, 2014	May 2	17,000
C	30,000	Apr. 9, 2013	Dec. 10	37,400

I:5-26 How might the current treatment of capital losses discourage an individual investor from purchasing stock of a high-risk, start-up company?

I:5-27 An individual taxpayer has realized a $40,000 loss on the sale of an asset that had a holding period of eight months. Explain why the taxpayer may be indifferent as to whether the asset is a capital asset.

I:5-28 If Pam transfers an asset to Fred and the asset is subject to a liability that is assumed by Fred, how does Fred's assumption of the liability affect the amount realized by Pam? How does Fred's assumption of the liability affect his basis for the property?

ISSUE IDENTIFICATION QUESTIONS

I:5-29 Mr. and Mrs. Pickens purchased a used piano in Y1 for their young son who had started taking piano lessons. In Y8 while cleaning the piano, Mrs. Pickens discovered $4,800 of old currency. They exchanged the old currency for new currency.

I:5-30 Lisa and John are in the business of breeding beavers to produce fur for sale. They recently purchased a pair of breeding beavers for $30,000 from XUN, Inc., and agreed to pay interest at 10% each year for five years. After the five-year period, they could pay the debt by delivering seven beavers to XUN, Inc., provided that each beaver was at least nine months old. Identify the tax issues involved in this situation.

I:5-31 Mike, a real estate broker in California, recently inherited a farm from his deceased uncle and plans to sell the farm to the first available buyer. His uncle purchased the property 12 years ago for $600,000. The FMV of the farm on the date of the uncle's death was $500,000. Mike sells the farm for $520,000 seven months after his uncle's death. What tax issues should Mike consider?

I:5-32 Sylvia, a dentist with excellent skills as a carpenter, started the construction of a house that she planned to give to her son as a surprise when he returned from Afghanistan, where he is serving in the military. She began construction on March 23, 2014, and finished the house on July 10, 2015, at a total cost of $70,000. Her son is expected to be home on September 1, 2015.

On July 30, 2015, Roscoe offered Sylvia $245,000 for the house and Sylvia considered the offer to be so attractive that she accepted it. She decided that she could purchase a suitable home for her son for about $200,000. What tax issues should Sylvia consider?

PROBLEMS

I:5-33 *Amount Realized.* Tracy owns a nondepreciable capital asset held for investment. The asset was purchased for $250,000 six years earlier and is now subject to a $75,000 liability. During the current year, Tracy transfers the asset to Tim in exchange for $94,000 cash and a new automobile with a $50,000 FMV to be used by Tracy for personal use; Tim assumes the $75,000 liability. Determine the amount of Tracy's LTCG or LTCL.

I:5-34 *Basis of Property Received as a Gift.* Doug receives a duplex as a gift from his uncle. The uncle's basis for the duplex and land is $90,000. At the time of the gift, the land and building have FMVs of $40,000 and $80,000, respectively. No gift tax is paid by Doug's uncle at the time of the gift.
a. To determine gain, what is Doug's basis for the land?
b. To determine gain, what is Doug's basis for the building?
c. Will the basis of the land and building be the same as in Parts a and b for purposes of determining a loss?

I:5-35 *Sale of Property Received as a Gift.* During the current year, Stan sells a tract of land for $800,000. The property was received as a gift from Maxine on March 10, 1995, when the property had a $310,000 FMV. The taxable gift was $300,000 because the annual exclusion was $10,000 in 1995. Maxine purchased the property on April 12, 1980, for $110,000. At the time of the gift, Maxine paid a gift tax of $12,000. In order to sell the property, Stan paid a sales commission of $16,000.
a. What is Stan's realized gain on the sale?
b. How would your answer to Part a change, if at all, if the FMV of the gift property was $85,000 as of the date of the gift?

I:5-36 *Sale of Asset Received as a Gift.* Bud received 200 shares of Georgia Corporation stock from his uncle as a gift on July 20, 2014, when the stock had a $45,000 FMV. His uncle paid $30,000 for the stock on April 12, 2000. The taxable gift was $45,000, because his uncle made another gift to Bud for $20,000 in January and used the annual exclusion. The uncle paid a gift tax of $1,500.

Without considering the transactions below, Bud's AGI is $45,000 in 2015. No other transactions involving capital assets occur during the year. Analyze each transaction below, independent of the others, and determine Bud's AGI in each case.
a. He sells the stock on October 12, 2015, for $48,000.
b. He sells the stock on October 12, 2015, for $28,000.
c. He sells the stock on December 16, 2015, for $42,000.

I:5-37 *Basis of Property Converted from Personal Use.* Irene owns a truck costing $15,000 and used for personal activities. The truck has a $9,600 FMV when it is transferred to her business, which is operated as a sole proprietorship.
a. What is the basis of the truck for determining depreciation?
b. What is Irene's realized gain or loss if the truck is sold for $5,000 after claiming depreciation of $4,000?

I:5-38 *Sale of Assets Received as a Gift and Inherited.* Daniel receives 400 shares of A&M Corporation stock from his aunt on May 20, 2015, as a gift when the stock has a $60,000 FMV. His aunt purchased the stock in 2005 for $42,000. The taxable gift is $60,000 because she made earlier gifts to Daniel during 2015 and used the annual exclusion. She paid a gift tax of $9,300 on the gift of A&M stock to Daniel.

Daniel also inherited 300 shares of Longhorn Corporation preferred stock when his uncle died on November 12, 2014, when the stock's FMV was $30,000. His uncle purchased the stock in 1995 for $27,600. Determine the gain or loss on the sale of A&M and Longhorn stock on December 15, 2015, under each alternative situation below.
a. A&M stock was sold for $62,600, and Longhorn stock was sold for $30,750.
b. A&M stock was sold for $58,200, and Longhorn stock was sold for $28,650.
c. Assume the same as in Part a except his aunt purchased A&M stock for $71,000 and his uncle purchased Longhorn stock for $31,200.

I:5-39 *Personal-use Property Converted to Rental Property.* Tally owns a house that she has been living in for eight years. She purchased the house for $245,000 and the FMV today is $200,000. She is moving into her friend's house and has decided to convert her residence to rental property. Assume 20% of the property's value is allocated to land.
a. What is the basis of the house for depreciation?
b. If she claims depreciation of $15,000 and sells the property six years later for $260,000 (20% allocated to land), determine the gain on the sale of the building and gain on the sale of the land.
c. How much of the gain is due to depreciation?
d. If the FMV is $290,000 when she converts the house to rental property instead of $200,000, what is the basis of the house for depreciation?

I:5-40 *Stock Rights.* Kathleen owns 500 shares of Buda Corporation common stock which was purchased on March 20, 1999, for $48,000. On October 10 of the current year, she receives a distribution of 500 stock rights. Each stock right has a $20 FMV and the FMV

of the Buda common stock is $100 per share. With each stock right, she may acquire one share of Buda common stock for $95.
a. How much gross income must Kathleen recognize?
b. What is the basis of each stock right received?
c. If she sells the 500 stock rights for $10,600, what is her gain?
d. If she exercises the 500 stock rights on November 10, what is the basis of the 500 shares she receives and when does the holding period for those shares start?

I:5-41 *Stock Rights.* Martha Lou owns 100 shares of Blain Corporation common stock. She purchased the stock on July 25, 1986, for $4,000. On May 2 of the current year, she receives a nontaxable distribution of 100 stock rights. Each stock right has a $10 FMV, and the FMV of the Blain common stock is $70 per share. With each stock right, Martha Lou may acquire one share of Blain common for $68 per share. Assuming that she elects to allocate basis to the stock rights, answer the following:
a. What is the basis allocated to the stock rights?
b. If she sells the stock rights on June 10 for $1,080, determine the amount and character of the recognized gain?
c. If she exercises the stock rights on May 14, what is the basis of the 100 shares purchased and when does the holding period start?
d. If she does not elect to allocate basis to the stock rights, determine the amount and character of the gain if she sells the stock rights on June 10 for $1,080?

I:5-42 *Real Property Subdivided for Sale.* Beth acquired only one tract of land seven years ago as an investment. In order to sell the land at a higher price, she decides to subdivide it into 20 lots. She pays for improvements such as clearing and leveling, but the improvements are not considered to be substantial. Each lot has a basis of $2,000, and a selling price of $6,000. Selling expenses of $480 were incurred to sell two lots last year. This year, ten lots are sold, and selling expenses amount to $1,900. How much ordinary income and capital gain must be recognized in the prior and current year?

I:5-43 *Marginal Tax Rates.* Mr. and Mrs. Dunbar have taxable income of $260,000 without considering the following sales. Consider the following independent cases where capital gains are recognized and determine the marginal tax rate for the capital gain in each case. Ignore the effect of increasing AGI on deductions.
CASE A: $10,000 gain from sale of Storm Lake common stock held for seven months.
CASE B: $10,000 gain from sale of antique clock held for six years.
CASE C: $10,000 gain from sale of Ames preferred stock held for three years.

I:5-44 *Netting Gains and Losses* Trisha, whose tax rate is 35%, sells the following capital assets in 2015 with gains and losses as shown:

Asset	Gain or (Loss)	Holding Period
A	$15,000	15 months
B	7,000	20 months
C	(3,000)	14 months

a. Determine Trisha's increase in tax liability as a result of the three sales. All assets are stock held for investment. Ignore the effect of increasing AGI on deductions and phase-out amounts.
b. Determine her increase in tax liability if the holding period for asset B is 8 months.
c. Determine her increase in tax liability if the holding periods are the same as in Part a but asset B is an antique clock.
d. Determine her increase in tax liability if her tax rate is 39.6%.

I:5-45 *Computing the Tax.* Donna files as a head of household in 2015 and has taxable income of $90,000, including the sale of a stock held as an investment for two years at a gain of $20,000. Only one asset was sold during the year and Donna does not have any capital loss carryovers.
a. What is the amount of Donna's tax liability?
b. What is the amount of Donna's tax liability if the stock is held for 11 months?

I:5-46 *Computing the Tax.* Wayne is single and has no dependents. Without considering his $11,000 adjusted net capital gain (ANCG), his taxable income, which includes no investment income, in 2015 is as follows:

AGI		$258,250
Home mortgage interest	$22,100	
State and local income taxes	8,000	
Charitable contributions	7,000	
Personal exemption	4,000	41,100

Taxable income	$217,150

a. What is Wayne's tax liability without the ANCG?
b. What is Wayne's tax liability with the ANCG?

I:5-47 *Computing the Sales Price.* An investor in a 28% tax bracket owns land that is a capital asset with a $50,000 basis and a holding period of three years. The investor wishes to sell the asset at a price high enough so that he will have $120,000 in cash after paying the income taxes.
a. What is the minimum price the investor could accept?
b. What is the minimum price the investor could accept if all the gain is subject to the Medicare tax on net investment income?

I:5-48 *Capital Gains and Losses.* Consider the four independent situations below for an unmarried individual, and analyze the effects of the capital gains and losses on the individual's AGI. For each case, determine AGI after considering the capital gains and losses.

	Situation 1	Situation 2	Situation 3	Situation 4
AGI (excluding property transactions)	$40,000	$50,000	$60,000	$70,000
STCG	6,000	2,000	5,000	6,000
STCL	2,000	5,000	4,000	15,000
LTCG	3,500	15,000	10,000	9,000
LTCL	2,500	4,000	12,000	4,000

I:5-49 *Capital Losses.* To better understand the rules for offsetting capital losses and how to treat capital losses carried forward, analyze the following data for an unmarried individual for the period 2012 through 2015. No capital loss carryforwards are included in the figures. For each year, determine AGI and the capital losses to be carried forward to a later tax year.

	2012	2013	2014	2015
AGI (excluding property transactions)	$40,000	$50,000	$60,000	$70,000
STCG	4,000	5,000	7,000	10,000
STCL	9,000	3,000	5,000	12,000
LTCG	6,000	10,000	2,200	6,000
LTCL	5,000	21,000	1,000	9,500
AGI (including property transactions)	_____	_____	_____	_____
STCL to be carried forward	_____	_____	_____	_____
LTCL to be carried forward	_____	_____	_____	_____

I:5-50 *Character of Loss.* The Michigan Corporation owns 20% of the Wolverine Corporation. The Wolverine stock was acquired eight years ago to ensure a steady supply of raw materials. Michigan also owns 30% of Spartan Corporation and 85% of Huron Corporation. Stock in both corporations was acquired more than ten years ago for investment purposes. During the current year, Wolverine, Spartan, and Huron are deemed bankrupt, and the stocks are considered worthless. Describe how Michigan should treat its losses.

I:5-51 *Original Issue Discount.* On December 31, 2014, Phil purchased $20,000 of newly issued bonds of Texas Corporation for $16,568. The bonds are dated December 31, 2014. The bonds are 9%, 10-year bonds paying interest semiannually on June 30 and December 31. The bonds are priced to yield 12% compounded semiannually.
a. What is the amount of the original issue discount?
b. For the first semiannual period, what is the amount of the original issue discount Phil must recognize as ordinary income?
c. What is the total amount of interest income Phil must recognize in 2015?
d. What is Phil's basis for the bonds as of December 31, 2015?

I:5-52 On January 1, 2013, Swen paid $184,000 for $200,000 of the 8%, 20-year bonds of Penn Corporation, issued on January 1, 2009, at par. The bonds are held as an investment. Determine the gain and the character of the gain if the bonds are sold on January 1, 2015, for
a. $191,000
b. $185,750
c. $183,000

I:5-53 *Capital Gains and Losses.* During 2015, Gary receives a $50,000 salary and has no deductions for AGI. In 2014, Gary had a $5,000 STCL and no other capital losses or capital gains. Consider the following sales and determine Gary's AGI for 2015.
- An automobile purchased in 2010 for $10,800 and held for personal use is sold for $7,000.
- On April 10, 2015, stock held for investment is sold for $21,000. The stock was acquired on November 20, 2014, for $9,300.

I:5-54 *Call Options.* On February 10, 2015, Gail purchases 20 calls on Red Corporation for $250 per call. Each call represents an option to buy 100 shares of Red stock at $42 per share any time before November 25, 2015. Compute the gain or loss recognized, and determine whether the gain or loss is long-term or short-term for Gail in the following situations:
a. The 20 calls are sold on May 15, 2015, for $310 per call.
b. The calls are not exercised but allowed to expire.
c. The calls are exercised on July 15, 2015, and the 2,000 shares of Red Corporation stock are sold on July 20, 2016, for $50 per share.

I:5-55 *Call Writing.* Dan owns 500 shares of Rocket Corporation common stock. The stock was acquired two years ago for $30 per share. On October 2, 2015, Dan writes five calls on the stock, which represent options to buy the 500 shares of Rocket at $75 per share. For each call, Dan receives $210. The calls expire on June 22, 2016. Consider the following transactions and describe the tax treatment for Dan:
a. The five calls are exercised on December 4, 2015.
b. The calls are not exercised and allowed to expire.

I:5-56 *Corporate Capital Gains and Losses.* Determine the taxable income for the Columbia Corporation for the following independent cases:

Case	Income from Operations	STCG (NSTCL)	NLTCG (NLTCL)
A	$110,000	$30,000	$44,000
B	100,000	(50,000)	65,000
C	80,000	(37,000)	30,000
D	90,000	(15,000)	(9,000)

I:5-57 *Original Issue Discount.* On January 1, 2014, Sean purchased an 8%, $100,000 corporate bond for $92,277. The bond was issued on January 1, 2014, and matures on January 1, 2019. Interest is paid semiannually, and the effective yield to maturity is 10% compounded semiannually. On July 1, 2015, Sean sells the bond for $95,949. A schedule of interest amortization for the bond is shown in Table I:5-2.
a. How much interest income must Sean recognize in 2014?
b. How much interest income must Sean recognize in 2015?
c. How much gain must Sean recognize in 2015 on the sale of the bond?

▼ TABLE I:5-2
Interest Amortization for Problem I:5-57

	Interest Received (1)	Amortization of Discount (2)	Interest Income (3) = (1) + (2)
6-30-14	$4,000	$614	$4,614
12-31-14	4,000	645	4,645
6-30-15	4,000	677	4,677
12-31-15	4,000	711	4,711
6-30-16	4,000	747	4,747
12-31-16	4,000	783	4,783
6-30-17	4,000	823	4,823
12-31-17	4,000	864	4,864
6-30-18	4,000	907	4,907
12-31-18	4,000	952	4,952

I:5-58 *Capital Gains and Losses.* Martha has $40,000 AGI without considering the following information. During the year, she incurs a LTCL of $10,000 and has a gain of $14,000 due to the sale of a capital asset held for more than a year.
a. If the $14,000 gain is not properly classified as a LTCG (i.e., is improperly treated as an ordinary gain), determine Martha's AGI.
b. If the $14,000 gain is properly classified as a LTCG, determine her AGI.
c. If Martha has a $2,500 STCL carryover from earlier years, how would the answers to Parts a and b be affected?

I:5-59 *Capital Gains and Losses.* Without considering the following capital gains and losses, Charlene, who is single, has taxable income of $460,000 and a marginal tax rate of 39.6%. During the year, she sold stock held for nine months at a gain of $10,000; stock held for three years at a gain of $15,000; and a collectible asset held for six years at a gain of $20,000. Ignore the effect of the gains on any threshold amounts and assume that her marginal tax rate of 39.6% does not change.
a. What is her taxable income and the increase in her tax liability after considering the three gains?
b. In addition to the above three sales, assume that she sells another asset and has a STCL of $14,000. What is her taxable income and the increase in her tax liability after considering the four transactions?
c. In addition to the above three sales in Part a, assume that she sells another collectible asset held seven years as an investment and has a $27,000 capital loss. What is her taxable income and the increase in her tax liability after considering the four transactions?
d. Determine her medicare tax on net investment income in (a) if all of the $460,000 of taxable income is due to salary.

I:5-60 *Corporate Capital Gains and Losses.* In 2010, the Ryan Corporation sold a capital asset and incurred a $40,000 LTCL that was carried forward to subsequent years. That sale was the only sale of a capital asset that Ryan made until 2015, when Ryan sells a capital asset and recognizes a STCG of $53,000. Without considering the STCG from the sale, Ryan's taxable income is $250,000.
a. Determine the corporation's NSTCG for 2015.
b. Determine the corporation's 2015 taxable income.
c. If the sale of the asset in 2010 had occurred in 2009, determine the corporation's 2015 taxable income.

COMPREHENSIVE PROBLEM

I:5-61 Betty incurs the following transactions during the current year. Without considering the transactions, her 2015 AGI is $40,000. Analyze the transactions and answer the following questions:

- On March 10, 2015, she sells a painting for $2,000. Betty is the artist, and she completed the painting in 2010. Her basis for the painting is $50.
- On June 18, 2015, she receives $28,500 from the sale of stock purchased by her uncle in 2000 for $10,000, which she inherited on February 20, 2015, as a result of her uncle's death. The stock's FMV on that date is $30,000.
- On July 30, 2015, she sells land for $25,000 that was received as a gift from her brother on April 8, 2015, when the land's FMV was $30,000. Her brother purchased the land for $43,000 on October 12, 2007. No gift tax was paid.

a. What is her NSTCL or NSTCG?
b. What is her NLTCL or NLTCG?
c. What is the effect of capital gains and losses on her AGI?
d. What is her capital loss carryforward to the next year?

TAX STRATEGY PROBLEMS

I:5-62 Dale purchased Blue Corporation stock four years ago for $1,000 as an investment. He intended to hold the stock until funds were needed to help pay for his daughter's college education. Today the stock has a $6,500 FMV and Dale decides to sell the stock and give the proceeds, less any taxes paid on the sale, to Tammy, his 22-year-old daughter. Dale's marginal tax rate is 33%. Tammy has no other gross income and receives more than half of her support from Dale.

a. What advice would you give to Dale?

b. What is the cash savings if Dale follows your advice?

I:5-63 Calvin, whose tax rate is 35% is considering two alternative investments on January 1, 20Y1. He can purchase $100,000 of 10% bonds due in five years or purchase $100,000 of Hobbes, Inc. common stock. The bonds are issued at par, pay interest annually on December 31, and mature at the end of five years. Interest received can be reinvested at 10%. Assume that he knows with relative certainty that the value of the stock will increase 8% each year (i.e., the value of the Hobbes stock will be $108,000 at the end of 20Y1) and the interest and principal for the bonds will be paid as scheduled. On December 31, 20Y5, he will sell the stock or receive the bond principal plus the last interest payment. Which alternative should Calvin select if he wants to have the greater amount of money as of January 1, 20Y6? Provide supporting information for your answer.

I:5-64 On December 20 of the current year, Winneld has decided to sell all of the stock that she owns and reinvest the proceeds in state of Minnesota bonds. Without considering the sales, her taxable income is expected to exceed $500,000 this year and in future years. Information about the stocks are provided below:

Corporation	FMV	Basis	Holding Period
Viking, Inc.	$190,000	$140,000	7 months
Twins, Inc.	200,000	255,000	4 years
Timberwolves, Inc.	382,000	300,000	3 years

She is willing to sell some of the stock this year and the remaining stock next year if it is more advantageous to spread the sales over two years. Assume that the FMV of the stock will not change during the next 30 days, and ignore the effect of a sale on threshold amounts.

Determine the increase in her income tax for each of the following alternatives (a, b, & c) and advise Winneld.

a. Sell all stock this year.

b. Sell Twins and Timberwolves this year and Viking in March of next year.

c. Sell Viking and Twins this year and Timberwolves in March of next year.

d. Determine her Medicare tax on net investment income in Part a if she has no investment income before selling all the stock.

I:5-65 Dallas, whose tax rate is 35%, has recognized a STCL of $11,000 and a LTCG of $10,200 due to the sale of stock. In late December, he is considering the sale of an antique chair held for investment that would result in a LTCG of $5,000. If he sells the chair this year, what is the increase in his tax liability as a result of the sale? Ignore the phase out rules.

TAX FORM/RETURN PREPARATION PROBLEMS

I:5-66 Given the following information for Jane Cole, complete Schedule D of Form 1040 through Part III.

- Stock options, which she purchases on February 14 of the current year for $850, expire on October 1.
- On July 1, she sells for $1,500 her personal-use automobile acquired on March 31, 1990, for $8,000.
- On August 16, she sells for $3,100 her stock of York Corporation purchased as an investment on February 16, for $1,600.
- On March 15, she sells for $5,600 an antique ring, a gift from her grandmother on January 10, 1988, when its FMV was $1,600. The ring was purchased by her grandmother on April 2, 1979, for $1,800.
- She has a STCL carryover of $250 from last year.

I:5-67 Spencer Duck (SSN 000-22-1111) is single and his eight-year-old son, Mitch, lives with him nine months of the year in a rented condominium at 321 Hickory Drive in Ames, Iowa. Mitch lives with his mother, Spencer's ex-wife, during the summer months. His mother provides more than half of Mitch's support and Spencer has agreed to allow her to claim Mitch as her dependent. Spencer has a salary of $39,000 and itemized deductions of $4,000. Taxes withheld during the year amount to $3,221. On July 14 of the current year, he sold the following assets:

- Spencer received a K-1 from a partnership indicating that his share of the partnership STCL is $200.

- Land was sold for $35,000. The land was received as a property settlement on January 10, 2001, when the land's FMV amounted to $30,000. His ex-wife's basis for the land, purchased on January 10, 1991, was $18,600.
- A personal-use computer acquired on March 2 last year for $4,000 was sold for $2,480.
- A membership card for a prestigious country club was sold for $8,500. The card was acquired on October 10, 1993, for $6,000.
- Marketable securities held as an investment were sold for $20,000. The securities were inherited from his uncle, who died on March 10 of the current year when FMV of the securities was $21,000. The uncle purchased the securities on May 10, 1990, for $10,700.

In addition to the above sales, Spencer received a $100 refund of state income taxes paid last year. Spencer used the standard deduction last year to compute his tax liability. Prepare Form 1040 and Schedule D for the current year.

CASE STUDY PROBLEMS

I:5-68   As a political consultant for an aspiring politician, you have been hired to evaluate the following statements that pertain to capital gains and losses. Evaluate the statement and provide at least a one-paragraph explanation of each statement. As you prepare your answer, consider the fact that the aspiring politician does not have much knowledge about taxation.
a. The tax on capital gains is considered a voluntary tax.
b. High-income taxpayers receive the most benefit from preferential treatment for capital gains.

I:5-69   Your client, Apex Corporation, entered into an agreement with an executive to purchase his personal residence at its current FMV in the event that his employment is terminated by the company during a five-year period. The executive's job was terminated before the end of the five-year period and Apex acquired the house for $500,000. Due to a downturn in the real estate market, a $200,000 loss was incurred by the company upon the resale of the house. The chief financial officer of Apex insists that the loss be characterized as ordinary, based on the *Corn Products* doctrine. Your research into this matter reveals that the weight of authority heavily favors capital loss treatment (i.e., case law based on facts identical to the above issue held that the loss was capital rather than ordinary). You therefore conclude that the client's position does not have a realistic possibility of being sustained administratively or judicially on its merits if challenged by the IRS. What responsibility do you have as a tax practitioner relative to preparing the client's tax return and rendering continuing tax consulting services to the client? (See the Section *Statements on Standards for Tax Services* in Chapter I:1 for a discussion of these issues.)

TAX RESEARCH PROBLEMS

I:5-70   Tom Williams is an equal partner in a partnership with the Kansas Corporation. Williams, an inventor, produced a new process while working for the partnership, which has been patented by the partnership. Before making any use of the patent, the partnership entered into a contract granting all rights to use the process for the life of the patent to the Mason Manufacturing Co.

   The time between receiving the patent and entering into the contract with Mason amounted to eight months. Mason agreed to pay 0.3% of all sales revenue generated by products produced as a result of the process. If Mason fails to make payments on a timely basis, Mason's right to use the process is forfeited and the agreement between the partnership and Mason is canceled. Will any of the proceeds collected qualify as LTCG under Sec. 1235?

   A partial list of research sources is

- Reg. Sec. 1.1235-2
- *George N. Soffron*, 35 T.C. 787 (1961)

I:5-71   Lynette, a famous basketball player, is considering the possibility of transferring the sole right to use her name to promote basketball shoes produced and sold by the NIK Corporation. NIK will pay $2 million to obtain the right to use Lynette's name for the next 40 years. NIK may use the name on the shoes and as a part of any of the company's advertisements for basketball shoes. If Lynette signs the contract and receives the $2 million payment, will she have to recognize capital gain or ordinary income?

A partial list of research sources is

- Sec. 1221
- Rev. Rul. 65-261, 1965-2 C.B. 281

I:5-72 Jack, a tenured university professor, has been a malcontent for many years at Rockport University. The university has recently offered to pay $200,000 to Jack if he will relinquish his tenure position and resign. Jack is of the opinion that tenure is an intangible capital asset and the $200,000 received for release of the tenure should be a long-term capital gain. Explain why you agree or disagree.

A partial list of research sources is

- *Harry M. Flower,* 61 T.C. 140 (1973)
- *Estelle Goldman,* 1975 PH T.C. Memo ¶75,138, 34 TCM 639

I:5-73 Web Baker was hired three years ago by the Berry Corporation to serve as CEO for the company. As part of his employment contract, the corporation had agreed to purchase his residence at FMV in the event the company decided to fire him. Last year, Berry, unsatisfied with Web's performance, fired him and purchased the residence for $350,000. Berry immediately listed the house with a real estate agency. Soon after the purchase, the real estate market in the area experienced a serious decline, especially in higher-priced homes. Berry sold the house this year for $270,000 and paid selling expenses of $12,000. How should the Berry Corporation treat the $92,000 loss?

A partial list of research sources is

- Sec. 1221
- Rev. Rul. 82-204, 1982-2 C.B. 192
- *Azar Nut Co. v. CIR,* 67 AFTR 2d 91-987, 91-1 USTC ¶50,257 (5th Cir., 1991)

CHAPTER

6

DEDUCTIONS AND LOSSES

LEARNING OBJECTIVES

After studying this chapter, you should be able to

1 ▶ Distinguish between deductions *for* and *from* AGI

2 ▶ Discuss the criteria for deducting business and investment expenses

3 ▶ Examine the restrictions for deducting expenses

4 ▶ List the substantiation requirements for deducting travel and entertainment expenses

5 ▶ Explain the timing of deductions under both the cash and accrual methods of accounting

6 ▶ Discuss special disallowance rules for deductions

7 ▶ Describe tax planning considerations for deductions and losses

8 ▶ Describe compliance and procedural considerations for deductions and losses

The next five chapters deal with deductions. As you recall from Chapters I:3 and I:4, the IRC uses the "all-inclusive" approach when dealing with items of income; that is, gross income includes all items of income unless the income item is specifically excluded by statute. In contrast, unless the IRC specifically provides a deduction, a taxpayer may not deduct an expenditure or expense. For example, a taxpayer who makes a donation to a charity during the year may deduct the donation only because the IRC specifically allows the deduction of charitable contributions under Sec. 170.

Chapter I:6 discusses the general requirements for the deductibility of taxpayer expenditures and losses. Some of these requirements apply to all taxpayers while others apply only to individuals. Chapter I:7 deals with itemized deductions for individual taxpayers, such as medical expenses, taxes, charitable contributions, interest expense, and other miscellaneous deductions. Chapter I:8 covers two major areas that apply to all taxpayers: the deductibility of losses and bad debts. Chapter I:9 discusses employee compensation and expenses, and Chapter I:10 discusses tax depreciation, amortization, and depletion.

As mentioned above, a taxpayer can only deduct an expenditure if the IRC specifically allows the deduction. However, the IRC cannot possibly specify *every* deductible expense that a taxpayer might incur. Therefore, the IRC contains a framework for analyzing the nature of an expenditure. If the expenditure meets the criteria developed in the framework, the taxpayer generally can deduct the item unless specific disallowance or limitation provisions apply. This framework provides three general categories of deductions:

(1) Expenses incurred in connection with a **trade or business** (Sec. 162);
(2) Expenses incurred by an individual in connection with the **production of income** (Sec. 212);
(3) Other types of expenses that fall within specific provisions of the IRC, such as certain types of interest expense, taxes, bad debts, and other expenditures by individuals for personal items such as medical expenses, alimony, and moving costs.

The first two categories of deductions (business expenses and production of income expenses) are for expenditures the taxpayer incurs in connection with a profit-motivated activity. Here again, the IRC does not attempt to specify every conceivable type of deductible business or investment expense. Rather, the IRC establishes general guidelines that a taxpayer must meet in order to deduct an expense as either a business or investment deduction. Thus, in general, a taxpayer may deduct any expense incurred in connection with a trade or business or for the production of income if the expense (1) falls within the general guidelines and (2) the IRC does not specifically exclude or limit the expense from deductibility. For example, although the IRC does not specifically state that a taxpayer can deduct expenditures for utilities or salaries that the taxpayer incurs in a profit-motivated business, the taxpayer can deduct these business expenses under Sec. 162 as long as the expenses meet the general guidelines of Sec. 162 and they are not subject to a specifically stated limitation or exclusion from deductibility. These general guidelines are discussed later in this chapter.

Section 212, which applies only to individuals, allows an individual to deduct expenses that the individual incurs for the:

▶ Production or collection of income

▶ Management, conservation, or maintenance of property held for the production of income

▶ Determination, collection, or refund of any tax

As explained later in this chapter, the general guidelines that the taxpayer must meet in order to deduct expenses incurred in both of these types of activities require that the expenses must be ordinary, necessary, and reasonable in the context of the activity in which they are incurred. Furthermore, if the taxpayer incurs a loss in either of these types of activities, the amount of the deduction may be limited.

Section 262 also provides a general rule that prevents individuals from deducting personal, living, or family expenses. However, the tax law does specifically allow individuals to deduct certain personal expenditures or losses. For example, a taxpayer may deduct casualty losses (subject to certain limitations) for personal-use property. Taxpayers may also deduct personal expenditures for certain types of interest, taxes, medical expenses, alimony, and retirement savings if the expenditures meet strict requirements. Chapters I:7, I:8, and I:9 discuss deductions and losses for personal expenditures.

CLASSIFYING DEDUCTIONS AS FOR VERSUS FROM ADJUSTED GROSS INCOME (AGI)

OBJECTIVE 1

Distinguish between deductions for *and* from *AGI*

As mentioned in Chapter I:2, the tax formula for individuals divides allowable business, investment, and personal deductions into the following two categories:

▶ Deductions subtracted from gross income in order to calculate adjusted gross income (*for* AGI deductions); and

▶ Deductions subtracted from AGI to calculate taxable income (*from* AGI deductions).

The concept of AGI applies to individual taxpayers, not to other entities such as corporations or partnerships.

Section 62 specifically identifies deductions *for* AGI. All other deductions for individuals are deductions *from* AGI. The more common *for* AGI deductions include the following, subject to certain limitations:

KEY POINT

Most *for* AGI deductions are either expenses the taxpayer incurs in a trade or business or certain investment activities. Most of the deductible personal expenses are deductible *from* AGI.

▶ All allowable expenses incurred in an individual's trade or business, but not including an employee's unreimbursed business expenses

▶ Reimbursed employee business expenses

▶ Certain business expenses incurred by performing artists as well as employees of a state or a political subdivision thereof

▶ Losses from the sale or exchange of trade, business, or investment property

▶ Expenses attributable to the production of rent or royalty income

▶ Contributions to certain pension, profit-sharing, or retirement plan arrangements

▶ Penalties paid to a bank or other savings institution because of the early withdrawal of funds from a certificate of deposit or time savings account

▶ Alimony

▶ Moving expenses

▶ Cash payments made to a qualified Health Savings Account or Archer Medical Savings Account

▶ Up to $2,500 of interest paid on qualified educational loans (student loan interest). As part of the American Taxpayer Relief Act of 2012, Congress permanently extended this *for* AGI deduction.

▶ One-half of the self-employment tax imposed on self-employed individuals and 100% of health insurance costs paid by such individuals.[1]

For individuals, the distinction between deductions *for* AGI and *from* AGI is critical for two reasons. First, as explained in Chapter I:2, the tax formula allows individuals to deduct the greater of the standard deduction or the total of the *from* AGI (itemized) deductions in arriving at taxable income. Thus, a taxpayer does not benefit from these deductions if the total deductible amount for the year does not exceed the standard deduction. Deductions *for* AGI, on the other hand, reduce AGI (and consequently taxable income) even if the taxpayer uses the standard deduction in computing taxable income.

EXAMPLE I:6-1 ▶ Brad, a single individual with no dependents, incurs $6,000 of deductible expenses and earns $75,000 in gross income during 2015. If the expenses are all deductions *from* AGI, Brad will

---

[1] Sections 62, 162(l) and 164(f). Other deductions *for* AGI include deductions for depreciation and depletion for life tenants and income beneficiaries of property, reforestation expenses, required repayments of supplemental unemployment compensation benefits, certain expenses incurred for clean-fuel vehicles and refueling property, jury duty pay the taxpayer remits to an employer, attorney's fees the taxpayer pays out of awards in certain types of lawsuits, and certain trade or business expenses incurred by members of an Armed Forces unit when the individual is more than 100 miles away from home in connection with performing services as a member of that unit. For tax years beginning before 2015, elementary and high school teachers could also take a limited *for* AGI deduction of up to $250 for out-of-pocket expenses they incur as a teacher, and college students in higher education could deduct qualified tuition and related expenses for their higher education up to a limit of $4,000. Currently Congress is considering extending these deductions either temporarily for a few more years, or permanently.

report taxable income of $64,700 (i.e., Brad receives a $4,000 deduction for his personal exemption and a $6,300 standard deduction). Brad receives no direct tax benefit from the expenses because they do not exceed the standard deduction. However, if the $6,000 of expenses are all deductions *for* AGI, Brad reports taxable income of $58,700 (a $6,000 *for* AGI deduction in addition to the $6,300 standard deduction and the $4,000 personal exemption).

KEY POINT

Many individuals lose the benefit of a *from* AGI deduction because that particular deduction is less than its applicable limit, or the total of the itemized deductions is less than the standard deduction. Furthermore, the IRC phases out certain itemized deductions.

	Deductions from AGI	Deductions for AGI
Gross income	$75,000	$75,000
Minus: *For* AGI deductions	0	(6,000)
AGI	$75,000	$69,000
Minus: Standard deduction	(6,300)	(6,300)
Personal exemption	(4,000)	(4,000)
Taxable income	$64,700	$58,700

The second important reason for the proper classification of deductions is that AGI acts as a limit on the amount of *from* AGI itemized deductions that can be taken. This limitation operates in various ways:

▶ Taxpayers may deduct certain itemized deductions such as medical expenses, casualty losses, and miscellaneous itemized deductions only to the extent the particular expense exceeds a prescribed percentage of AGI. For example, pursuant to Sec. 67 an individual may deduct certain miscellaneous itemized deductions only to the extent the sum of these deductions for the year exceeds 2% of the individual's AGI. These expenses include unreimbursed employee business expenses,[2] expenses incurred to produce investment income,[3] and the cost of tax advice and tax return preparation (see Chapter I:7). A taxpayer may deduct medical expenses only to the extent the medical expenses exceed 10% of the individual's AGI for the year (7.5% for individuals 65 or older through 2016). Individual taxpayers must first reduce casualty losses on personal-use property by $100 per casualty event. After this reduction, an individual may deduct casualty losses only to the extent that the sum exceeds 10% of the individual's AGI.

▶ AGI also acts as a limit on the deductibility of certain itemized deductions by placing a limit on the total amount of the deduction. For example, in general the deduction for charitable contributions may not exceed 50% of the taxpayer's AGI.

▶ Under Sec. 68(a) and (b) in 2015 the amount of certain itemized deductions for high-income taxpayers (taxpayers who are married filing jointly with AGI in excess of $309,900 and single taxpayers with AGI in excess of $258,250) is reduced by three percent of the excess. Additionally, the personal exemptions of these same high-income taxpayers also begin to be phased out when their AGI exceeds these same threshold AGI amounts.

Deductions *for* AGI are generally located in two places on the tax return. First, some deductions *for* AGI appear on the front page of Form 1040. These deductions include such items as moving expenses, alimony paid, one-half of self-employment taxes, and student loan interest. Second, other deductions appear on separate schedules, including Schedule C (Profit or Loss from Business), Schedule E (Supplemental Income or Loss), or Schedule F (Profit or Loss from Farming). The net profit or loss from these schedules carries over to the front page of Form 1040 as part of gross income. Thus, the deductions on these schedules are deductions *for* AGI. Figure I:2-1 in Chapter I:2, contains the front page of Form 1040.

---

[2] These employee business expenses include unreimbursed expenditures for travel and transportation, supplies, special clothing or uniforms, union dues, and subscriptions to trade journals. Reimbursed employee expenses are deductible *for* AGI and thus, are deductible in full. (See Chapter I:9.)
[3] These expenses include rental fees for safe deposit boxes used to hold investment property, subscriptions to investment journals, bank service charges on checking accounts used in an investment or income-producing activity, and fees paid for consulting advice. Expenses incurred in an investment or income-producing activity that generates either rental or royalty income are deductions *for* AGI.

CRITERIA FOR DEDUCTING BUSINESS AND INVESTMENT EXPENSES

A taxpayer may deduct business and investment expenses only if certain requirements are met. Thus, deductible business or investment expenses must be:

▶ Related to a profit-motivated activity of the taxpayer (i.e., a business or investment activity rather than a personal expenditure),

▶ Ordinary,

▶ Necessary,

▶ Reasonable in amount,

▶ Properly documented (discussed later in the chapter under the heading Proper Substantiation Requirement), and

▶ An expense of the taxpayer (not someone else's expense).

Furthermore, as discussed later in this chapter under the heading General Restrictions on the Deductibility of Expenses, even if the expense meets the requirements for deductibility above, taxpayers may not deduct expenditures meeting certain other criteria. Thus, generally, a taxpayer cannot deduct an expenditure if it is:

▶ A capital expenditure,

▶ An expense related to tax-exempt income,

▶ Illegal or in violation of public policy, or

▶ Specifically disallowed by the tax law.

Further discussion of these criteria and related matters follows.

BUSINESS OR INVESTMENT ACTIVITY

Deductible expenditures generally originate from a profit-motivated activity. Section 162 provides all taxpayers with a deduction for their business expenses. Additionally, under Sec. 212, individuals can deduct expenses they incur for the production of income or for the maintenance and conservation of income-producing property (an investment activity). Thus, the requirement of an activity being profit-motivated is really two-pronged: (1) a determination of whether an expenditure originates from an activity engaged in for profit and (2) for individuals, a distinction between a trade or business and an investment activity.

Activity Engaged in for Profit. This first part of the test classifies the expense as resulting from either a profit-motivated activity or a personal activity. For individuals, classifying expenses as either profit-motivated or personal can be quite difficult. For example, is the activity of coin collecting a hobby that is personal in nature, a profit-motivated business, or an investment activity? No single objective test is available. Rather, a tax advisor must examine all the facts and circumstances surrounding the activity in which the taxpayer incurs expenses in order to make this distinction. The section in this chapter entitled Hobby Losses discusses these factors in more detail, as well as other issues dealing with the determination of whether or not a particular activity is profit-motivated.

Trade or Business Versus Investment Classification. The second part of the profit-motive test involves the determination of whether a particular activity is a trade or business of the taxpayer or only an investment. This distinction generally is important only to individuals since corporations are assumed to be engaged in a business. It is important to individuals for several reasons. First, if an individual realizes a loss on the sale of an asset that the individual used in a business, the individual may be able to deduct the loss as an ordinary loss.[4] On the other hand, if the taxpayer realizes a loss on the sale of an investment

---

[4] Under Sec. 1231, the exact treatment depends on the total gains and losses from such property for the year. See Chapter I:13 for a discussion of Sec. 1231.

asset, the IRC classifies the loss as a capital loss which, as explained in Chapter I:5, receives different treatment. Second, this distinction may control whether an expense of the activity is a deduction *for* AGI or a deduction *from* AGI. In general, the IRC classifies expenses incurred in a trade or business as deductions *for* AGI whereas investment expenses, other than those incurred to produce rents and royalties, are classified by the IRC as deductions *from* AGI. Additionally, under Sec. 179, taxpayers may elect to currently deduct a specified amount of tangible personal property placed into service during the year if the property is used in a trade or business. For 2015, the maximum amount that a taxpayer may elect to currently deduct under Sec. 179 is $25,000. This $25,000 deductible amount begins to phase out if the taxpayer places into service more than $200,000 of qualified property during 2015. For 2014 the maximum amount that a taxpayer could elect to currently deduct under Sec. 179 was $500,000 and the phase-out began at $2 million. Currently Congress is considering increasing the Sec. 179 deduction and limitation amounts back to what they were in 2014 either temporarily for a few more years, or permanently. (See Chapter I:10 for a discussion of the Sec. 179 expense election for capital expenditures.)

EXAMPLE I:6-2 ▶ Robin is a self-employed financial consultant. She meets daily with a variety of clients to discuss their investments. Because she must keep abreast of the latest market quotes and strategies, Robin subscribes to several trade publications, newsletters, and quote services. During the year, Robin purchased a $4,000 computer to be used exclusively in her consulting business. Robin may deduct the expenses incurred for the publications and services as deductions for AGI because she incurred them in her consulting business. Furthermore, she can currently deduct the $4,000 paid for the computer under the special rules of Sec. 179 because it is a business asset, rather than an investment asset. ◀

Expenses incurred by an individual in an investment activity, other than those incurred to produce rents and royalties, are miscellaneous itemized deductions *from* AGI and are deductible only to the extent they exceed 2% of the taxpayer's AGI for the year (see Chapter I:7).

EXAMPLE I:6-3 ▶ Steve is a wealthy attorney who invests in the stock market and keeps abreast of the latest market quotes and strategies by subscribing to several trade publications and newsletters. This year he purchased a computer he will use exclusively for tracking his investments. Steve generally spends an hour or two each day studying this information and analyzing his portfolio. The subscription expenses are deductions *from* AGI because Steve incurred the expenses in an investment (rather than a business) activity and the expenses do not relate to the production of rents and royalties. Steve cannot currently deduct the entire cost of the computer but must depreciate the cost over a period of five years. Furthermore, the deductibility of all of the above items depends on whether Steve's total miscellaneous itemized deductions exceed 2% of his AGI and whether Steve itemizes his deductions instead of using the standard deduction. ◀

ADDITIONAL COMMENT

A trade or business is an activity with a profit motive and some type of economic activity. An investment activity requires a profit motive but does not require economic activity.

Despite these important differences in treatment, the distinction between an investment activity and a trade or business is not always clear. The IRC and the Treasury Regulations do not provide a precise definition of what constitutes a trade or business. Judicial law, however, does provide some guidelines. In one of the first cases dealing with the issue, the Supreme Court stated that a trade or business involves "holding one's self out to others as engaged in the selling of goods or services."[5]

Later, another Supreme Court case emphasized that one must examine all the surrounding facts and circumstances to determine the underlying nature of an activity.[6] In that case, the taxpayer owned a large portfolio of stocks, bonds, and real estate. The taxpayer's holdings were so large that he rented offices and hired employees to help him manage the properties. The Court, however, regarded these activities as investment activities despite the size of the holdings and the amount of work and effort involved because the taxpayer merely kept records and collected interest and dividends from his securities. Other cases, however, indicate that a taxpayer who invests in stocks and bonds may be considered to be in a business if he or she frequently buys and sells securities in order to make a short-term profit on the daily swings in the market.

[5] *Deputy v. Pierre S. DuPont*, 23 AFTR 808, 40-1 USTC ¶9161 (USSC, 1940).
[6] *Eugene Higgins v. CIR*, 25 AFTR 1160, 41-1 USTC ¶9233 (USSC, 1941). See also *Chang H. Liang*, 23 T.C. 1040 (1955), and *Ralph E. Purvis v. CIR*, 37 AFTR 2d 76-968, 76-1 USTC ¶9270 (9th Cir., 1976); and *Samuel B. Levin v. U.S.*, 43 AFTR 2d 79-612, 79-1 USTC ¶9331 (Ct. Cls., 1979).

Legal and Accounting Fees. Taxpayers may generally deduct legal and accounting fees incurred in the regular conduct of a trade or business or for the production of income. Taxpayers may also deduct fees incurred for the determination, collection, or refund of any tax. These deductions are *for* AGI if incurred in a trade or business or for the production of rents and royalties. Legal and accounting fees incurred in the determination or collection of taxes are also *for* AGI deductions if paid to prepare a taxpayer's Schedule C (Profit or Loss from Business), Part I of Schedule E (Supplemental Income and Loss, which is used to report rental and royalty income), and Schedule F (Farm Income and Expenses).[7] All other deductible legal and accounting fees incurred by the taxpayer are deductible *from* AGI as miscellaneous itemized deductions, subject to the 2% of AGI limitation. A filled-in Schedule C and copies of Schedule E and Schedule F are provided in Appendix B.

Taxpayers may not deduct legal fees they incur in connection with the purchase of property. Instead, taxpayers must capitalize these expenses by adding them to the cost of the property. Likewise, taxpayers generally may not deduct legal expenses they incur for personal purposes.

EXAMPLE I:6-4 ▶ During the current year, Lia pays legal and accounting fees for the following:

Services rendered with regard to a contract dispute in Lia's business	$ 8,000
Services rendered in resolving a federal tax deficiency relating to Lia's business	2,500
Tax return preparation fees:	
Allocable to preparation of Schedule C	1,600
Allocable to preparation of Schedules A and B and to the remainder of	
Form 1040	400
Legal fees incident to a divorce	1,200
Total	$13,700

Lia may deduct $12,100 ($8,000 + $2,500 + $1,600) *for* AGI because these legal expenses are associated with Lia's business. Lia may deduct the remaining $400 of tax preparation fees as a miscellaneous itemized deduction from AGI subject to the 2% of AGI limitation. The legal fees incident to the divorce are personal expenses and generally are not deductible. However, Lia could take a partial deduction *from* AGI as a miscellaneous itemized deduction to the extent these legal fees relate to giving tax advice incident to the divorce. ◄

ORDINARY EXPENSE

A business or investment expense must also be "ordinary" in order for a taxpayer to be able to deduct the expense. Although the IRC does not provide either a definition or an application of this requirement, the Treasury Regulations under Sec. 212 indicate that for an expense to be ordinary it must be reasonable in amount and it must bear a reasonable and proximate relationship to the income-producing activity or property. This means that more than a remote connection must exist between the expense and the anticipated income. It does not mean that the property must be producing income currently.

EXAMPLE I:6-5 ▶ Ahmed purchases a plot of land, on which there is an old vacant warehouse. Ahmed anticipates making a long-term profit from the investment because the value of the land is expected to appreciate eventually due to commercial development in the area. To help cover the costs of holding the property, Ahmed plans to rent storage space in the warehouse. During the current year, although he is unable to rent the warehouse, Ahmed incurs the following expenses:

ADDITIONAL COMMENT

A General Accounting Office report finds that tax cheating is widespread among self-employed taxpayers. These workers represent only 13% of all taxpayers, but account for approximately 40% of all underreported individual income. The report identified truckers as one of the least compliant groups.

Expenses	*Amount*
Property taxes	$1,000
Interest	4,000
Insurance	800
Utilities	200

All of these expenditures qualify as ordinary deductible investment expenses under Sec. 212 because they bear a reasonable and proximate relationship to the income Ahmed hopes to obtain, even though he generated no income from the property during the year. However, Ahmed might not be able to deduct them all in the current year because of the passive loss limitations explained in Chapter I:8. ◄

---

[7] Rev. Rul. 92-29, 1992-1 C.B. 20.

The Supreme Court has ruled that for an expense to be ordinary it must be customary or usual in the context of a particular industry or business community.[8] Thus, an expenditure may be ordinary in the context of one type of business, but not in the context of another.

EXAMPLE I:6-6 ►

For many years, Hank has been an officer in Green Corporation, which is engaged in the grain business. Green Corporation purchases its grain from various suppliers. Last year, Green Corporation went bankrupt and was relieved from having to pay off its debts to its suppliers. In the current year, Hank enters into a contract to act as a commissioned agent to purchase grain for Green Corporation. To reestablish a relationship with suppliers whom Hank knew previously, Hank decides to pay off as many of Green Corporation's debts as he can. Hank is under no legal obligation to do so. Hank's payments are not ordinary. Rather, they are extraordinary expenditures made for goodwill to establish Hank in a new trade or business, and they must be capitalized. ◄

An expense may be ordinary with respect to a taxpayer even though that taxpayer encounters it only once.

EXAMPLE I:6-7 ►

For several years, Health for You, Inc., has been engaged in the business of making and selling dietary supplements. Health for You, Inc., does most of the advertisements, orders, and deliveries of the supplements through the mail. During the current year, the post office judged that some of the advertisements were false. As a result, a fraud order is issued under which the post office stamps "Fraudulent" on all letters addressed to Health for You, Inc., and then returns them to the senders. In an unsuccessful suit to prevent the post office from continuing this practice, Health for You, Inc. expends $50,000 in lawyer's fees. These fees are ordinary business expenses because Health For You, Inc. incurred them in an action that a taxpayer normally or ordinarily would have taken under these circumstances. ◄

The Supreme Court has also indicated that the term *ordinary* in this context refers to an expenditure that is currently deductible rather than an expenditure that must be capitalized.[9]

NECESSARY EXPENSE

In addition to being ordinary, a deductible investment or business expense must also be **necessary**. The Supreme Court has indicated that an expense is considered necessary if it is "appropriate and helpful" in the taxpayer's business.[10] To meet this appropriate or helpful standard, an expenditure need not be necessary in the sense that it is indispensable. Rather, the test is whether a reasonable or prudent businessperson would incur the same expenditure under similar circumstances.

> **REAL-WORLD EXAMPLE**
>
> A corporation made payments to an individual who was a 50% shareholder in the corporation. The corporation made these payments to the individual to prevent him from interfering in the management of the business and damaging the corporation's reputation. The Tax Court held that these payments were necessary business expenses. *Fairmont Homes, Inc.*, 1983 PH T.C. Memo ¶83,209, 45 TCM 1340.

EXAMPLE I:6-8 ►

The expenditures in Example I:6-6 (the payment of debts from a former business) and Example I:6-7 (the payment of legal fees) are both necessary because they are appropriate and helpful in each case. However, the expenditure in Example I:6-6 is not ordinary and, therefore, is not deductible. The expenditure in Example I:6-7 is deductible because it meets both tests. ◄

REASONABLE EXPENSE

Section 162 and Treasury Regulations under Sec. 212 provide that in order to be deductible the business or investment expense must be reasonable. Problems with meeting this standard can arise when a closely-held C corporation pays a salary to an individual who is both a shareholder and an employee. In this situation, a controlling shareholder of a C corporation may receive a payment, characterized as salary, that the IRS asserts is too large for the services the individual employee rendered.

EXAMPLE I:6-9 ►

Central Corporation pays Brian, the controlling shareholder and an employee of Central Corporation, an annual salary of $650,000. Based on several factors, such as the size of Central Corporation's total operations, Brian's duties as an employee, and a comparison of salary received by officers of comparably sized corporations, the IRS contends that Brian's salary should be no higher than $300,000. If Central successfully defends the $650,000 salary, the corporation is able to deduct the full amount as salary expense. If Central Corporation's defense is not successful, the IRS will treat

---

[8] *Thomas H. Welch v. Helvering*, 12 AFTR 1456, 3 USTC ¶1164 (USSC, 1933) and *Deputy v. Pierre S. DuPont*, 23 AFTR 808, 40-1 USTC ¶9161 (USSC, 1940).

[9] *CIR v. S. B. Heininger*, 31 AFTR 783, 44-1 USTC ¶9109 (USSC, 1943). See also *CIR v. Walter F. Tellier*, 17 AFTR 2d 633, 66-1 USTC ¶9319 (USSC, 1966).

[10] *Thomas H. Welch v. Helvering*, 12 AFTR 1456, 3 USTC ¶1164 (USSC, 1933).

KEY POINT

The IRS also applies the reasonable standard in determining whether a salary paid to the owner of an S corporation is too low. This may occur if the owner is attempting to avoid the payment of self-employment taxes.

KEY POINT

Since the Sec. 162(m) compensation deduction limit applies only to publicly-held corporations, privately-held corporations are faced with the general reasonable standard which looks at the particular facts and circumstances.

the excess $350,000 as a dividend to the extent of Central Corporation's earnings and profits, and Central Corporation may not take a deduction for the dividend. In either event, Brian must take the full $650,000 into income. (See the Tax Planning Considerations section in this chapter for a discussion of the use of a payback agreement in these situations.) ◄

In an attempt to link executive compensation to productivity and business performance and to discourage a common practice of increasing executive compensation despite declines in business performance, Congress enacted Sec. 162(m) which disallows a deduction for compensation paid to certain "covered employees" of publicly-held companies that exceeds a yearly amount of $1 million. The definition of a covered employee is based on the Securities Exchange Act of 1934 and states that a covered employee is the publicly-held company's chief executive officer plus the four highest paid corporate officers whose compensation is required to be reported under that Act. In 2006 the Securities Exchange Act was changed to define a covered employee as (1) the corporation's chief executive officer, (2) the corporation's principal financial officer, and (3) the corporation's three highest paid executives whose compensation is required to be reported to the corporation's shareholders. Because of this change in the Securities Exchange Act and a strict technical interpretation of the language of the law, IRS Notice 2007–49 explicitly states that the Sec. 162(m) deduction limit will now be applicable to compensation paid to (1) the company's chief executive officer and (2) the company's three highest paid executives whose compensation is required to be reported to the corporation's shareholders. The company's principal financial officer is not included in this definition. Thus, the company can deduct the principal financial officer's compensation even if the principal financial officer is among the company's three highest paid executives. This limitation does not apply to compensation based on commissions or other performance goals. Special rules and limitations apply to certain employers that are participating in the Troubled Asset Relief Program (TARP). [See Sec. 162(m)(5)].

The tests for determining whether a business or investment expense is deductible are summarized in Topic Review I:6-1.

EXPENSES AND LOSSES INCURRED DIRECTLY BY THE TAXPAYER

Generally, taxpayers may not take a deduction for a loss or expense of another person. This requirement attempts to prevent taxpayers from engaging in manipulative schemes.

EXAMPLE I:6-10 ► Juanita owns 60% of Hot Clothes, Inc. As CEO of Hot Clothes, Juanita travels extensively. This year Hot Clothes purchases a business jet to facilitate Juanita's travel. In addition to her business travel, Juanita also uses the jet to take several family vacations. In general, Hot Clothes may not take a deduction for

TOPIC REVIEW I:6-1

Tests for Deductibility as a Business or Investment Expense

TEST	APPLICATION
Ordinary	► Based on the facts and circumstances. ► Reasonable and proximate relationship to the activity. ► Customary or usual in context of the industry. ► Need not be encountered by the taxpayer more than once.
Necessary	► Based on the facts and circumstances. ► Appropriate and helpful. ► Need not be indispensable. ► Would a reasonable or prudent businessperson incur the same expense?
Reasonable	► Based on the facts and circumstances. ► Applies to all business and investment expenses. ► Compensation paid to an owner-employee of a small corporation is the most commonly contested area. ► Compensation in excess of $1 million payable by a publicly-held corporation to its key executives may not be deductible.

Juanita's personal expenses. In order for the business to deduct these amounts, Juanita and the corporation must follow one of two procedures: (1) Juanita must report as additional compensation an amount that represents the use of the jet for her vacations, or (2) Juanita must reimburse Hot Clothes for the use of the jet for her vacations. However, even if Juanita does follow one of these procedures, the amount Hot Clothes, Inc. may deduct for Juanita's private use of the jet may be limited. ◀

This general rule requiring the taxpayer to directly incur the expense applies to all types of expenditures, whether incurred in a trade or business, an investment activity, or a personal activity for which deductions are allowed. There is one exception: under Sec. 213 taxpayers may take a deduction for medical expenses paid on behalf of a dependent. Individuals may also deduct medical expenses that they pay for a person who would qualify as a dependent except for failing to meet certain other tests (see Chapter I:2). For example, under Sec. 152, the dependent's gross income must be less than the exemption amount to qualify as a qualifying relative, but for Sec. 213 this requirement is disregarded.

EXAMPLE I:6-11 ▶ During the current year, Dan incurs $5,000 in deductible medical expenses. Dan's father, Tom, pays for all of Dan's support. Dan is 23 and is not a full-time student and therefore does not qualify as a dependent under the qualifying child rules of Sec. 152(c). Dan's gross income for the year is $15,000, which exceeds the exemption amount, and therefore Dan is not a qualifying relative of Tom under Sec. 152(d). If Tom pays Dan's medical expenses, Tom may add these expenses to his own itemized medical expenses (subject to the 10% of AGI limitation) because of the modified test in Sec. 213 even though Tom may not take a dependency exemption for Dan. ◀

GENERAL RESTRICTIONS ON THE DEDUCTIBILITY OF EXPENSES

OBJECTIVE 3

Examine the restrictions for deducting expenses

As mentioned earlier on page I:6-5, certain types of expenditures are not deductible. These types of expenditures fall within various categories discussed below.

CAPITALIZATION VERSUS EXPENSE DEDUCTION

General Capitalization Requirements. Under Sec. 162 a taxpayer may currently deduct ordinary, necessary, and reasonable business expenses that the taxpayer incurs for the operation and maintenance of tangible property the taxpayer uses in a business. However, under Sec. 263, expenditures that (1) provide a permanent improvement or "betterment" that increases the value of any property, or (2) "restore" the property are considered **capital expenditures**, which generally must be capitalized and depreciated over an appropriate number of years. The Treasury recently issued new temporary regulations that became effective in 2014. These regulations are very detailed in establishing when certain expenditures may be currently expensed and when the expenditures must be capitalized. Taxpayers must also capitalize the cost of goodwill purchased in connection with the acquisition of the assets of a going concern.[11] (See Chapter I:10 for a discussion of the amortization of goodwill.)

Although taxpayers may depreciate or amortize certain business assets, such as buildings, machinery, equipment, furniture and fixtures, purchased goodwill, and customer lists, other assets, such as land, stock, and partnership interests, are neither depreciable nor amortizable and taxpayers must wait until they sell these assets to recover the cost of the assets. In some instances, it is difficult to ascertain whether an asset is eligible for depreciation or amortization. For example, the Tax Court has held that antique violin bows and an antique bass violin are depreciable property, overriding the IRS's arguments that they should not be depreciable because they were actually appreciating in value and it was impossible to determine their useful life.[12]

As mentioned above, maintenance and repair expenditures that only keep an asset in a normal operating condition are deductible if they do not provide a permanent improvement

---

[11] Reg. Sec. 1.263(a)-2(h). See also *Indopco, Inc., v. CIR*, 69 AFTR 2d 92-694, 92-1 USTC ¶50,113 (USSC, 1992), where expenses incurred by a corporation that was the target of a "friendly" takeover were held to be nondeductible capital expenditures because they provided long-term benefits to the corporation. In this case, the Supreme Court held that these long-term benefits do not need to be associated with a specific identifiable asset.

[12] *Richard L. Simon*, 103 T.C. 247 (1994) and *Brian P. Liddle*, 76 AFTR 2d 95-6255, 95-2 USTC ¶50,488 (3rd Cir., 1959). The IRS has stated it will not follow these decisions. See AOD 96-9, 7/15/96.

ADDITIONAL COMMENT

Some provisions permit taxpayers to depreciate or amortize capital expenditures over a relatively short period of time. For example, there is a rapid write-off available for pollution control facilities under Sec. 169 and for organization costs of corporations under Sec. 248.

or betterment that increases the value of the property or restore the property to its normal usage. Distinguishing between a currently deductible expenditure and a capital expenditure that must be capitalized and depreciated over time can be very difficult. This difficulty has caused a lot of uncertainty and controversy for taxpayers. For example, in an old Tax Court case, the court held that expenditures incurred in replacing support beams and floor joists to shore up a sagging floor were deductible, whereas the court held that the cost of placing a new floor over an old one was a capital expenditure.[13] Because of this difficulty, the Treasury Department has recently issued new Temporary Regulations that provide more clear guidance for taxpayers. These new regulations contain many examples that can help taxpayers and their advisors distinguish the proper tax treatment of these expenditures. In any event, a tax advisor must examine all of the facts and circumstances in light of the guidance contained in these new regulations in order to determine whether any particular expenditure constitutes a deductible expense or a capitalized expenditure.

BOOK-TAX COMPARISON

Although for tax purposes a taxpayer may elect to deduct these capital expenditures, for book purposes capital expenditures must still be capitalized and depreciated or amortized. This difference in treatment gives rise to a book-tax adjustment on Schedule M-1 or M-3 of a corporation's Form 1120 or a partnership's Form 1065.

Election to Deduct Currently. Taxpayers sometimes may elect a current deduction for certain capital expenditures. Taxpayers often prefer a current deduction over capitalizing and depreciating an asset because of the time value of money. Some expenditures that taxpayers may elect to deduct currently[14] include: cost of fertilizers incurred by farmers, cost of soil and water conservation incurred by farmers, intangible drilling costs incurred in drilling oil and gas wells, costs for tertiary injectants, costs for certain mining development projects, costs incurred to remove architectural and transportation barriers to the handicapped and elderly, and costs for certain qualified research and experimental expenditures.

As mentioned previously, under Sec. 179 a taxpayer may also elect to currently deduct a limited amount of capital expenditures for new tangible property the taxpayer purchases to use in a trade or business. Additionally, for years prior to 2015 a taxpayer could elect to currently take a "50% bonus depreciation deduction" for certain qualified new property the taxpayer purchases during the year instead of depreciating the full cost of the property over its depreciable life. Currently Congress is considering extending the bonus depreciation deduction either temporarily for a few more years, or permanently. See Chapter I:10 for a discussion of the limitations of these deductions and how they apply.

Capitalization of Deduction Items. The exceptions mentioned above provide a current deduction for expenditures that are normally capital in nature. Conversely, Section 266 provides for the capitalization of certain expenses that are normally deductible. Section 266 is elective and applies to the following items:

► Interest and employment taxes incurred in transporting and installing personalty (as opposed to realty) up to the time when the taxpayer first puts the property into use.

► Annual property taxes, interest on a mortgage, and other carrying charges incurred on unimproved and unproductive real estate.

► Annual property taxes, interest, employment taxes, and other necessary expenses incurred for the development, improvement, or construction of real property, prior to the time construction is completed. For these expenses to be capitalized, the real property may be either improved or unimproved, productive or unproductive. After construction is completed, these types of expenses are fully deductible when incurred.

A taxpayer may make a new election to capitalize the expenses on unimproved and unproductive real estate each year.

EXAMPLE I:6-12 ▶ During 2015 and 2016, Nancy pays property taxes of $5,000 on a plot of land. During 2015, the land is vacant and unproductive. In 2016, Nancy uses the land as a parking lot, generating $7,000 in income. Nancy can elect to capitalize the taxes in 2015 because the property is both unimproved and unproductive. In 2016, however, the land is productive, and Nancy cannot elect to capitalize the taxes. Because the expenses relate to the production of rental income, Nancy can deduct them *for* AGI. If the land remains unproductive during 2016, Nancy can elect to capitalize the taxes paid in 2016. However, the election is optional and Nancy doesn't need to make the election for 2016 merely because she made the election for 2015. ◀

---

[13] *Standard Fruit Product Co.*, 1949 PH T.C. Memo ¶49,207, 8 TCM 733.   [14] See Secs. 180, 175, 263(c), 193, 616, 190, and 174 respectively.

For the development or construction of real property, if the taxpayer makes the election to capitalize the other expenses incurred during the development or construction period the election remains in effect for that year and for all subsequent years until the end of the construction period. However, a taxpayer may make the election on each new project separately.

EXAMPLE I:6-13 ▶ During the current year, Development, Inc. begins construction of an office building and a hotel. Development, Inc. incurs $20,000 in property taxes during the construction of the office building and $12,000 for the hotel. The election to capitalize the taxes on the office building does not bind Development, Inc. to make the same election with respect to the taxes on the hotel. ◀

If a taxpayer elects to capitalize this type of expense under Sec. 266, the expense increases the taxpayer's basis in the property to which the election pertains. If the property is depreciable, the taxpayer may deduct the expenses as depreciation deductions over a certain period. Taxpayers would want to make this election if they have large net operating loss (NOL) carryovers, or if they expect to be in a significantly higher tax bracket in future years and thus estimate that the benefit of the deduction will be greater in the future.

Under Sec. 263A, certain taxpayers must capitalize certain costs into inventory instead of taking a current deduction. (See Chapter I:11 for a discussion of inventories.)

EXPENSES RELATED TO EXEMPT INCOME

Under Sec. 265, taxpayers may not deduct any expense allocated or related to tax-exempt income. The purpose of this disallowance is to prevent the taxpayer from receiving a double tax benefit.

The IRC specifically disallows interest expense on debt the taxpayer incurs in order to purchase or hold tax-exempt securities. Thus, the disallowance depends on the taxpayer's intended use of the loan proceeds. Intent is generally determined by an examination of all the facts and circumstances surrounding the transaction rather than a mere statement of intent. Intent to hold tax-exempt securities is shown if the tax-exempt securities are used as collateral in securing a loan.[15] If an individual who holds tax-exempt securities later incurs some debt, no disallowance will occur if the debt is incurred to finance personal items for which an interest deduction may be taken (e.g., a mortgage on a personal residence). However, if a taxpayer incurs the debt to finance an investment, a deduction for a portion of the interest is generally disallowed. Even though the debt is not incurred to hold tax-exempt securities, the deductibility of interest may still be limited. For example, if a taxpayer incurs interest on personal debt, this interest is not deductible unless the loan qualifies as home aquisition or home equity indebtedness. (See Chapter I:7 for a discussion of limitations on the deductibility of personal interest.)

EXAMPLE I:6-14 ▶ Asian, Inc. has invested $80,000 in Gold Corporation stock, $120,000 in real estate, and $50,000 in tax-exempt municipal bonds. During the current year, Asian borrows $70,000 for the purpose of investing in a limited partnership. For the year, the company pays $6,000 interest on the loan. Under these circumstances, the IRS will presume that Asian, Inc. has incurred a portion of the debt in order to hold the tax-exempt securities and will disallow a portion of the deduction. Asian may overcome that presumption if it can show that it could not have sold the tax-exempt securities. Merely showing that the sale of the bonds would result in a loss will not overcome this presumption. ◀

EXPENDITURES CONTRARY TO PUBLIC POLICY

Taxpayers may not deduct certain expenditures, if the payment itself is illegal or if the payment is a penalty or fine resulting from an illegal act. These nondeductible expenses generally fall within one of the following categories: illegal payments to government officials or employees; other illegal payments; kickbacks, rebates, and bribes under Medicare and Medicaid; payments of fines and penalties; and payment of treble damages under the federal antitrust laws.

Bribes and Kickbacks. Under Sec. 162(c)(1), any illegal bribe or kickback made to any official or employee of a government is not deductible. This applies to payments made to: federal officials and employees; state, local, and foreign government officials and employees; and officials and employees of an agency of a government.

SELF-STUDY QUESTION

Alpha, Inc., borrows $100,000 at a 10% rate of interest and invests the $100,000 in exempt bonds yielding 8%. Alpha is in the 35% tax bracket. Calculate what Alpha's cash flow on these transactions would be on an after-tax basis if Alpha could deduct these expenses.

ANSWER

Alpha, Inc., has $8,000 of exempt income and $10,000 of interest expense. Cash flows would be equal to ($2,000) since there is no tax benefit for the interest. If the interest expense were deductible, its after-tax cost would be $6,500 ($10,000 − $3,500). Alpha's cash flow would be $1,500 ($8,000 − $6,500), allowing Alpha to make money on an unsound investment.

BOOK-TAX COMPARISON

For book purposes, tax-exempt income and related expenses are included in the calculation of net income. For tax purposes, they are excluded from gross income resulting in a permanent book-tax difference that must be reported on schedule M-1 or M-3.

REAL-WORLD EXAMPLE

A subcontractor involved with the construction of a new shopping mall made kickbacks to the supervisor of the primary contractor. The kickbacks were deductible because they were not illegal, and the kickbacks were also ordinary and necessary because the subcontractor would not have been able to continue to work if the kickbacks had not been made. *Raymond Bertolini Trucking Co. v. CIR*, 54 AFTR 2d 84-5413, 1984-2 USTC ¶9591 (6th Cir., 1984).

---

[15] Rev. Proc. 72-18, 1972-1 C.B. 740 and Rev. Proc. 87-53, 1987-2 C.B. 669. See also *Wisconsin Cheeseman, Inc. v. U.S.*, 21 AFTR 2d 383, 68-1 USTC ¶9145 (7th Cir., 1968).

EXAMPLE I:6-15 ► During February of the current year, Road Corporation enters into a contract with the State of Iowa to construct a five-mile stretch of a new highway. Under the terms of the contract, Road Corporation must complete the project by October 22 of the current year. If it is not completed and accepted by Iowa on or before that date, Iowa will fine Road Corporation $5,000 per day for every day after October 22 until the project is accepted. By October 20, the project foreman realizes that the company will not make the deadline if it complies with all the requirements imposed by the state inspector assigned to the project. To avoid the fine, the foreman arranges for the inspector to "look the other way" on several of the requirements in exchange for a payment of $8,000. Because this payment constitutes an illegal bribe to a government official, the payment is not deductible. On the other hand, assume Road Corporation does not pay the bribe and that it finishes the project four days after the deadline. In this case Road Corporation must pay $20,000 in fines. These fines are not imposed because of an illegal act. Thus, Road Corporation can deduct the $20,000 as an ordinary and necessary business expense. ◄

Taxpayers may not deduct illegal payments to officials or employees of a foreign government if the payment is unlawful under the Foreign Corrupt Practices Act of 1977, unless such payments constitute a normal way of doing business in that country. In all cases, the burden rests on the government to prove the illegality of the payment.

If a taxpayer makes illegal bribes, kickbacks, and other illegal payments to people other than a government official or employee, the payments are nondeductible if they are illegal under a federal law that subjects the payor to a criminal penalty or loss of the privilege of doing business. In addition, illegal payments under a state law imposing the same penalties are nondeductible, but only if the state generally enforces its law. Here, the definition of a kickback includes a payment for referring a client, patient, or customer.

The courts and the IRS have made a distinction between an illegal nondeductible kickback and a rebate on the purchase of an item. If the seller pays a rebate directly to the purchaser, it is an adjustment to the selling price and, as such, is an *exclusion* (rather than a deduction) from gross income.[16] The distinction between the two payments seems to be that the seller and purchaser negotiate the rebate as part of the selling price.

Section 162(c)(3) specifically disallows a deduction for any kickback, rebate, or bribe under Medicare and Medicaid. Disallowed amounts include payments made by physicians or by suppliers and providers of goods and services who receive payment under the Social Security Act or a federally funded state plan. Unlike payments to foreign government or nongovernment employees and officials, these payments need not be illegal under federal or state law.

ETHICAL POINT

A CPA discovers that a client included fines and penalties in a miscellaneous expense section of a previously filed tax return. The CPA should recommend the filing of an amended return. However, the CPA is not obligated to inform the IRS, and the CPA may not do so without the client's permission, except where required by law.

? STOP & THINK

Question: Queen, Inc., is engaged in the ship and boat repair business. Since competition in this industry is very tough, Queen generally kicks back approximately 10% of any repair bill to any ship captain who brings the ship to Queen for repairs. Queen's customers include individual owners of large ocean-going yachts and fishing boats, as well as government vessels owned by state, federal, and foreign governments. During the current year, Queen paid $80,000 in kickbacks to the captains of privately-owned yachts and boats, $40,000 to the owners of privately-owned vessels, and $100,000 to the captains of state, federal, and foreign government vessels. The crews of these government vessels are government employees. What is the proper tax treatment of these payments?

Solution: The $40,000 in kickbacks paid directly to the owners of the privately-owned vessels are treated as merely a rebate in the price of the services and reduces Queen's gross income, unless the payments could result in the imposition of a criminal penalty or loss of the privilege of doing business. The kickbacks paid to the captains of the state and federal vessels are not deductible because they are paid to employees of state and federal governments. The kickbacks paid to the captains of the privately-owned vessels are not deductible if they are illegal and subject the payor to a criminal penalty or loss of the privilege to do business. Likewise, the payments to the captains of the foreign vessels are not deductible if the payments are unlawful under the Foreign Corrupt Practices Act.

[16] Rev. Rul. 82-149, 1982-2 C.B. 56.

Fines and Penalties. Section 162(f) of the IRC also disallows a deduction for the payment of any fine or penalty paid to a government because of the violation of a law.

Furthermore, the IRC disallows a deduction for two-thirds of any payment the taxpayer makes for damages resulting from a conviction (or a guilty or no-contest plea) in an action regarding a criminal violation of the federal antitrust laws.[17]

EXAMPLE I:6-16 ▶ During the current year, the United States files criminal and civil actions against Allen, the president of Able Corporation, and Betty, the president of Bell Corporation, for conspiring to fix and maintain prices of electrical transformers. Both Allen and Betty enter pleas of no contest, and the appropriate judgments are entered. Subsequent to this action, Circle Corporation sues both Able and Bell Corporations for treble damages of $3,000,000. In settlement, Able and Bell Corporations each pay Circle Corporation $750,000. For these damage settlements, Able and Bell Corporations may each deduct $250,000 ($750,000 ÷ 3). ◀

Expenses Relating to an Illegal Activity. Interestingly, although the payment of an illegal bribe or kickback and the payment of a fine or penalty as the result of an illegal act are both nondeductible, other expenses incurred in an illegal business activity are generally deductible if they are ordinary, necessary, and reasonable and the taxpayer reports the income from the illegal activity.[18]

EXAMPLE I:6-17 ▶ Acme, Inc., owns and operates a small financial services business involved in the sale of securities and the lending of money. Acme often sells securities to customers in other states. However, because Acme has not registered the business with the appropriate state or federal authorities, the operation of the business is illegal. During the current year, Acme incurs the following expenses:

Interest	$ 20,000
Salaries	140,000
Depreciation	7,000
Printing	5,000
Bribe to employee of state securities commission	12,000
Total	$184,000

If Acme reports the income from this activity, the deductible expenses for the year total $172,000. The illegal bribe paid of $12,000 to the government employee is not deductible. ◀

One exception to this general rule exists. Section 280E disallows a deduction for expenses incurred in an illegal business of trafficking or dealing in drugs.

OTHER EXPENDITURES SPECIFICALLY DISALLOWED

The IRC also specifically disallows deductions for certain other expenses, even though they might meet all the requirements mentioned previously. These include political contributions and lobbying expenses and, in certain situations, business start-up expenses.

Political Contributions and Lobbying Expenses. Political contributions and lobbying expenses constitute one general category of disallowed expenses. Taxpayers may not deduct expenditures made in connection with the following:

▶ Influencing legislation

▶ Participating or intervening in any political campaign of any candidate for public office

▶ Attempting to influence the general public with respect to elections, legislative matters, or referendums

▶ Communicating directly with the President, Vice President, and certain other federal employees and officials

---

[17] Sec. 162(g).
[18] *CIR v. Neil Sullivan, et al.*, 1 AFTR 2d 1158, 58-1 USTC ¶9368 (USSC, 1958).

Sec. 162(e) also denies a deduction for contributions to tax-exempt organizations that carry on lobbying activities if a principal purpose of the contribution is to obtain a deduction for what otherwise would have been disallowed. Furthermore, the IRC disallows payments made for advertising in a convention or any other program if any part of the proceeds of the publication will directly or indirectly benefit a specific political party or candidate.[19]

Taxpayers may deduct lobbying expenses incurred to influence legislation on a local level if the legislation is of direct interest to the taxpayer's business. Local legislation includes actions by a legislative body of any political subdivision of a state (e.g., city or county council), but does not include any state or federal action. These deductible expenditures include expenses of communicating with or dues paid to an organization of which the taxpayer is a member. For administrative convenience, the deduction disallowance does not apply to any in-house expenditure attributable to such activities as long as the total of such expenditures for the taxable year does not exceed $2,000. In-house expenditures are expenses incurred directly by the taxpayer other than amounts paid to a professional lobbyist or dues that are allocable to lobbying. Additionally, the deduction disallowance does not apply to taxpayers engaged in the business of lobbying.

EXAMPLE I:6-18 ▶ Kensey & Associates is a large New York law firm. It is not in the lobbying business. During the year, the firm spends $6,000 to send some of its employees to Washington, D.C., to testify before a Congressional subcommittee with regard to proposed changes in the Social Security taxes imposed on employers. Such changes directly affect the firm's business because they affect the amount of taxes it must pay on behalf of its employees. The firm's ordinary and necessary expenses incurred with respect to the trip are not deductible because the expenses were incurred to influence federal rather than local legislation. ◀

If the legislation cannot reasonably be expected to directly affect the taxpayer's trade or business, the expenses are not deductible.

EXAMPLE I:6-19 ▶ Realty, LLC is a residential real estate company located in Chicago. The city of Chicago has proposed legislation to increase the hotel room tax. Realty spends time researching and traveling to speak to the Chicago City Council regarding this legislation. Although Realty, LLC incurs these expenses in an effort to influence legislation on the local level, it may not deduct these expenses because they are not of direct interest to its business. ◀

Business Investigation and Preopening Expenses. At the election of the taxpayer, Section 195 of the IRC allows a current deduction in the year in which the business starts for business start-up expenditures. The current deduction amounts to the lesser of the amount of the start-up expenditures or $5,000, with a dollar for dollar phase-out for amounts incurred over $50,000. Taxpayers must capitalize and amortize the remaining portion of start-up expenditures over a period of 180 months starting with the month in which the new business begins. Start-up expenditures specifically include three types of expenditures:

▶ *Business investigation expenses.* These expenses are costs a taxpayer incurs in reviewing and analyzing a prospective business before deciding whether to acquire or create it. The key here is that the taxpayer incurs the expenses before making a decision. These expenses include such items as analyses and surveys of markets, traffic patterns, products, labor supplies, and distribution facilities.

ADDITIONAL COMMENT
Costs incurred in connection with the issuance of stock or securities do not qualify as start-up costs. These costs are charged to Paid-in Capital.

▶ *Preopening or start-up costs.* Preopening or start-up costs are expenses incurred after a taxpayer decides to acquire or create a business but before the business activity itself has started. These costs include expenditures for training employees; advertising; securing supplies, distributors, and potential customers; and professional services in setting up the business' books and records. These costs must be incurred by a taxpayer not engaged in any existing business or engaged in a business unrelated to the business the taxpayer is acquiring or creating.

---

[19] Sec. 276(a). Nondeductible political contributions also include payments for admission to a dinner or program where the proceeds will benefit a party or candidate, or admission to an inaugural ball, party, or concert if the activity is identified with a political party or candidate.

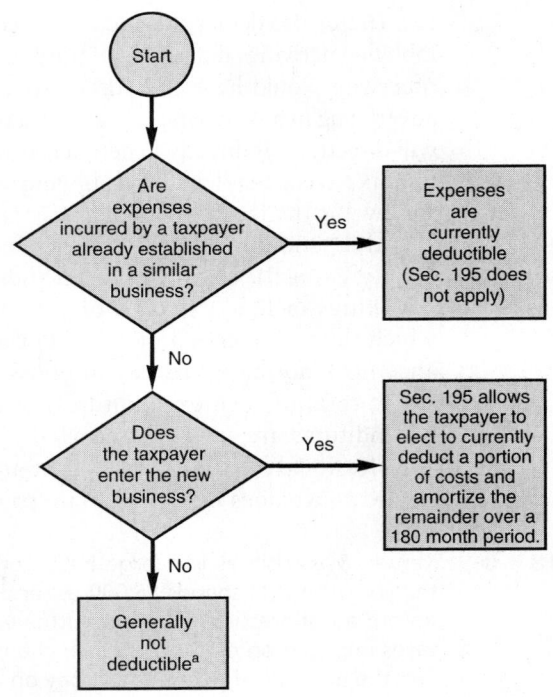

a Rev. Rul. 57-418, 1957-2 C.B. 143 and Rev. Rul. 77-254, 1977-2 C.B. 63; *Morton Frank*, 20 T.C. 511 (1953).

FIGURE I:6-1 ▶ DEDUCTIBILITY OF BUSINESS INVESTIGATION AND START-UP COSTS

▶ *Expenses incurred in connection with an investment activity.* These expenses are costs the taxpayer incurs in connection with an investment activity that the taxpayer anticipates will become an active trade or business.

As defined by Sec. 195, start-up expenditures do not include these same types of expenses when incurred by a taxpayer already engaged in a business similar to the new one being created or acquired. In this case, the taxpayer may deduct these expenditures currently because the expenses originate in the taxpayer's existing business. Figure I:6-1 provides a flowchart to assist in properly classifying these types of expenditures.

STOP & THINK

Question: Shauna works in an automobile manufacturing plant in Detroit, Michigan. In January of the current year, she took a two-week vacation in order to fly to Orlando, Florida. While in Orlando, she spent some time investigating the possibility of opening a store in nearby Coco Beach. In total, she spent $800 on airfare, $1,500 on hotels and food, $300 on equipment rentals, and $300 on a car rental. In addition to spending time on the beach talking to people and checking out the rental equipment, she also spent some time talking to shop owners and real estate agents. After some analysis, however, Shauna decides to keep her job in Detroit. What is the proper tax treatment for these expenditures?

Solution: In general, Sec. 162 of the IRC allows a deduction for expenses incurred in a business. Expenses incurred before the business starts are not incurred in a business and thus are not deductible under Sec. 162. However, under Sec. 195 a portion of certain expenditures such as business investigation expenses and start-up costs can be deducted currently while the remainder is capitalized and amortized over a 180-month period, beginning with the month in which the new business begins. Unfortunately Shauna did not open the new business. Thus, she may not deduct or amortize any of these expenses.

Topic Review I:6-2 summarizes the restrictions on the deductibility of these items.

TOPIC REVIEW I:6-2

Restrictions on the Deductibility of Expense Items

ITEM	RESTRICTIONS IMPOSED
1. Capital expenditures	The general rule is that the expenditure is not currently deductible if its life extends beyond the end of the year. Special elections are available to currently deduct certain capital expenditures (e.g., research and experimental costs under Sec. 174; and limited amounts per year for acquisitions of tangible personal property used in a trade or business under Sec. 179).
2. Carrying charges	An election may be made under Sec. 266 to capitalize certain expenses that are normally deductible such as property and employment taxes, interest, and carrying charges on unimproved unproductive real estate.
3. Expenses related to tax-exempt income	Expenses such as interest incurred on debt used to purchase or carry tax-exempt securities are disallowed under Sec. 265.
4. Expenditures contrary to public policy	Such expenditures are generally not deductible. Examples include bribes and kickbacks, fines and penalties, and expenses of an illegal activity involved with trafficking or dealing in drugs.
5. Legal and accounting fees	Legal and accounting fees can be either *for* AGI deductible business expenses, nondeductible personal use expenditures, or *from* AGI fees incurred in the determination of any tax (e.g., tax return preparation fees).
6. Political contributions and lobby expenses	The general rule is that such items are not deductible (e.g., costs of influencing public opinion), but there are certain exceptions (e.g., costs of appearing before local legislative bodies on topics directly related to the taxpayer's business).
7. Business investigation and preopening expenses	The following rules apply: a. Currently deductible if the taxpayer is already engaged in a similar business. b. Not deductible if the taxpayer is not currently engaged in a similar business and does not enter the new business. c. An amount equal to the lesser of the amount of the expenses or $5,000 reduced by amounts incurred over $50,000 is currently deductible with the remainder to be capitalized and amortized over a 180 month period if the taxpayer enters the new business and makes an election. d. Deductible if expenditures constitute specific items such as legal expenses incurred in drafting purchase documents in an unsuccessful attempt to acquire a specific business. However, general investigation expenditures in search of a new business are not deductible.

PROPER SUBSTANTIATION REQUIREMENT

OBJECTIVE 4

List the substantiation requirements for deducting travel and entertainment expenses

Generally, the burden of proving the existence of a deduction or loss falls on the taxpayer. Thus, a taxpayer must properly substantiate all deductible expenses. Because the IRS may audit a return and request proof, taxpayers should retain items such as receipts, cancelled checks, and paid bills. Occasionally, the courts will allow a deduction that is not properly substantiated by the taxpayer if an expenditure clearly has been made. In these cases, the court estimates the amount of the deduction based on all the facts and circumstances. This procedure is known as the *Cohan* rule and derives its name from a court case in which the judge allowed a deduction for an estimated amount of certain expenses.[20] The most prudent course of action, of course, is to retain proper documentation rather than to rely upon the *Cohan* rule.

EXAMPLE I:6-20 ▶ In April of the current year, Terry took his tax records to a CPA to have his prior year's income tax return prepared. As part of the return, the CPA attached a supplemental schedule listing all of Terry's items of income and expense. After the return was prepared and filed, Terry's records

---

[20] *George M. Cohan v. CIR*, 8 AFTR 10552, 2 USTC ¶489 (2nd Cir., 1930). Interestingly, the *Cohan* case dealt with travel and entertainment expenses. Because of the subsequent enactment of Sec. 274(d), the *Cohan* rule may not

be used to deduct entertainment expenses. It is still effective for other types of expenses.

were stolen. Upon audit two years later, the IRS disallowed Terry's deductions because he had no records to substantiate the expenses. When the case was litigated, the court allowed deductions for an estimated amount of expenses under the *Cohan* rule because of the list that was attached to Terry's return and because the court believed that Terry had testified honestly in his own behalf.[21] ◀

HISTORICAL NOTE

Judge Learned Hand, in permitting a deduction for unsubstantiated amounts in *George M. Cohan v. CIR*, 8 AFTR 10552, 2 USTC ¶489 (2nd Cir, 1930), wrote "absolute certainty in such matters is usually impossible and it is not necessary; the Board should make as close an approximation as it can, bearing heavily if it chooses on the taxpayer whose inexactitude is of his own making."

Additionally, Sections 274 and 280F provide specific and more stringent recordkeeping requirements for travel, entertainment, business gifts, computers, and vehicles used for transportation. In these cases, the taxpayer may not take a deduction unless the taxpayer substantiates the expenditure by either an adequate record or sufficient evidence that corroborates the taxpayer's statement. This substantiation may take the form of account books, diaries, logs, receipts and paid bills, trip sheets, expense reports, and statements of witnesses. The information that requires substantiation includes the following:

▶ Amount of the expense

▶ Time and place of the travel or entertainment

▶ Date and description of the gift

▶ Business purpose of the expenditure

▶ Business relationship to the taxpayer of the person entertained or of the person who received the gift

The *Cohan* rule does not apply to these types of expenses. (See Chapter I:9 for a more complete discussion regarding the deductibility of these types of expenses.)

WHEN AN EXPENSE IS DEDUCTIBLE

OBJECTIVE 5

Explain the timing of deductions under both the cash and accrual methods of accounting

Because the tax law generally requires calculating taxable income annually, the question of when a particular expense is deductible is especially important. The answer to this question largely depends on the taxpayer's method of accounting.[22] The most common methods include the following:

▶ Cash receipts and disbursements method (cash method)

▶ Accrual method

▶ Hybrid method (a combination of the cash and accrual methods where some items are accounted for on the cash method and other items are accounted for on the accrual method)

ADDITIONAL COMMENT

Section 446(b) provides that in cases where no method of accounting has been regularly used or if the method used does not clearly reflect income, then the computation of taxable income is to be made under a method that, in the opinion of the IRS, does clearly reflect income.

Taxpayers normally use the same method for computing taxable income that they use in keeping their financial accounting records. However, except for the use of the last-in, first-out (LIFO) method of accounting for inventory, the tax law does not generally require conformity. For example, many companies use the straight-line depreciation method for financial accounting purposes and the modified accelerated cost recovery system (MACRS) for tax purposes. This difference in depreciation methods, of course, results in a book-tax M-1 or M-3 adjustment.

CASH METHOD

Under the **cash method** of accounting, expenses are generally deductible when actually paid. The cash method considers payment by check a cash payment as long as the bank subsequently honors the check. This is the case even if the payee receives the check so late on the last day of the year that the payee could not have cashed it.[23] If the taxpayer mails the check near the end of the year, the taxpayer must have evidence that the mailing took place in the year

---

[21] *Layard M. White*, 1980 PH T.C. Memo ¶80,582, 41 TCM 671.

[22] Methods of accounting as they relate to the reporting of income are discussed in Chapter I:3. Methods of accounting as they relate to deductibility of expenses and losses are covered in this chapter. For an overall discussion of accounting methods, see Chapter I:11.

[23] *CIR v. Estate of M. A. Bradley*, 10 AFTR 1405, 3 USTC ¶904 (6th Cir., 1932) and *Charles F. Kahler*, 18 T.C. 31 (1952).

for which the taxpayer claims a deduction. Furthermore, the cash method considers payment by credit card a cash payment at the time of the charge rather than at the time the taxpayer pays for the charge.

A mere promise to pay, or the issuance of a note payable, does not constitute a payment under the cash method. Thus, a charge on an open account with a creditor is not deductible until an actual payment of cash satisfies the charge.

EXAMPLE I:6-21 ▶ Fox, Inc., a calendar-year taxpayer, is in the plumbing repair business. The business uses the cash method of accounting. Under an arrangement with one of its suppliers, Fox and its employees can pick up supplies at any time during the month by merely signing for them. At the end of the month, the supplier sends Fox a bill for the charges. Fox always pays the bill in full during the following month. In December of the current year, Fox charges $1,500 for supplies. During the same month Fox purchases a plumbing fixture for $250 from another supplier. Fox uses its charge card at the time of purchase. Fox may deduct the $250 during the current year. However, the $1,500 charged on the open account is deductible when paid in the following year. ◂

Prepaid Expenses. In general, a capital expenditure or the prepayment of expenses by a cash method taxpayer does not result in a current deduction if the expenditure creates an asset having a useful life that extends substantially beyond the close of the tax year. This can occur when a taxpayer makes expenditures for prepaid rent, services, or interest. However, in the case of prepaid rent, a circuit court of appeals decision has held that a taxpayer may take a current deduction for the entire amount of an expenditure if the period covered by the prepayment does not exceed one year and the rent agreement obligates the taxpayer to make the prepayment.[24]

EXAMPLE I:6-22 ▶ On November 1 of the current year, Twyla Corporation enters into a lease arrangement with Rashad to rent Rashad's office space for the following 36 months. By prepaying the rent for the entire 36-month period, Twyla Inc. is able to obtain a favorable monthly lease payment of $1,800. This prepayment creates an asset (a leasehold) with a useful life that extends substantially beyond the end of the taxable year. Thus, only $3,600 ($1,800 × 2 months) of the total payment is deductible in the current year. The rest must be capitalized and amortized over the life of the lease. However, assume that under the terms of the lease, Twyla Inc. is obligated to make three annual payments of $21,600 each November 1 for the subsequent 12 months. On November 1 of the current year, Twyla Inc. pays Rashad $21,600 for the first 12-month period. Because Twyla Inc. is obligated to make the prepayment and the period covered by the prepayment does not exceed one year, the entire $21,600 is deductible in the current year using the reasoning of the previously cited circuit court decision. ◂

Prepaid Interest. The IRC requires taxpayers to deduct prepaid interest expense over the period of the loan to which the interest charge is allocated.[25] Receipt of a discounted loan does not represent prepaid interest expense. Instead, the IRC deems the interest paid when the taxpayer repays the loan.

EXAMPLE I:6-23 ▶ During the current year, Richelle borrows $1,000 from the bank for use in her business. Richelle uses the cash method of accounting in her business. Under the terms of the loan, the bank discounts the loan by $80, issuing Richelle $920. When the loan comes due in the following year, however, Richelle is to repay the full $1,000. Richelle cannot deduct the $80 of interest expense until she repays the loan in the following year. ◂

REAL-WORLD EXAMPLE

A taxpayer made an overpayment of the federal income tax in 1975. In 1979, the IRS offset the overpayment against interest the taxpayer owed to the IRS. The Tax Court held that the interest expense was deductible in 1979 rather than in 1975. *Saverio Eboli*, 93 T.C. 123 (1989).

Taxpayers often prepay interest in the form of points. A point is one percent of the loan amount. Thus, the payment of two points on a $100,000 loan amounts to $2,000. While tax law generally requires the amortization of points over the life of the loan, if a taxpayer pays points in connection with the purchase or improvement of a principal residence, the taxpayer may deduct the points when they are paid. Points that a taxpayer pays in connection with the

---

[24] *Martin J. Zaninovich v. CIR*, 45 AFTR 2d 80-1442, 80-1 USTC ¶9342 (9th Cir., 1980) and *Bonaire Development Co. v. CIR*, 50 AFTR 2d 82-5167, 82-2 USTC ¶9428 (9th Cir., 1982). See also *Stephen A. Keller v. CIR*, 53 AFTR 2d 84-663, 84-1 USTC ¶9194 (8th Cir., 1984).

[25] Sec. 461(g).

purchase (but not the improvement) of a principal residence are automatically deductible in the year paid if they satisfy the following four requirements:

▶ the closing agreement clearly designates the amount as points,

▶ the amount involves a computation as a percentage of the amount borrowed,

▶ the charging of points is an established business practice in the geographic area, and

▶ the points are paid in connection with the purchase of the taxpayer's principal residence which is used to secure the loan.[26]

REAL-WORLD EXAMPLE
The mortgage company will, at the end of the year, mail to the taxpayer a Form 1098 which shows the amount of interest and points paid.

Although points paid on loans incurred to *improve* the taxpayer's principal residence do not fall under this safe harbor rule, they still are currently deductible if the residence is collateral for the loan, the payment of points is an established business practice in the geographic area in which it is incurred, and the amount of the prepayment does not exceed the amount generally charged.

A taxpayer may not currently deduct points paid to refinance a mortgage on a principal residence because the points are not paid in connection with the purchase or improvement of the taxpayer's residence.[27]

EXAMPLE I:6-24 ▶ During the current year, Pam purchases a principal residence for $150,000, paying $50,000 down and financing the remainder with a 30-year mortgage secured by the property. Pam must make monthly payments on the mortgage. At the closing, Pam must pay three points as a loan origination fee. Because these points are paid in connection with the purchase of a principal residence, Pam may deduct $3,000 ($100,000 × 0.03) as interest expense during the current year. In addition, Pam may also deduct the interest portion of each monthly payment made during the year. On the other hand, assume that Pam takes out the $100,000 loan in order to refinance her home at a lower interest rate. The $3,000 prepaid interest is not currently deductible. Instead, Pam must deduct the interest ratably over the term of the loan. Thus, Pam may deduct an additional $8.33 ($3,000 ÷ 360 payments) interest expense for each payment that she makes during the year. ◀

If the taxpayer sells a home and pays off the refinanced mortgage, any unamortized portion of the points is deductible in the year of repayment. The tax law treats points paid by the seller as incurred by the purchaser and, therefore, the points are currently deductible by the purchaser if they meet the other requirements and are subtracted from the purchase price of the residence.[28]

The cash method of accounting provides some degree of flexibility to taxpayers because, under this method, taxpayers can generally deduct expenses when paid rather than when accrued. Thus, subject to the limitations mentioned above with regard to prepaid expenses, taxpayers may to some degree accelerate or defer deductions from one year to another by merely accelerating or deferring payment. However, the IRC imposes limitations on the use of the cash method. For example, taxpayers must account for inventories under the accrual method.[29] Furthermore, under Sec. 448, most C corporations (corporations that have not elected Subchapter S status), partnerships that have a C corporation as a partner, and tax shelters may not use the cash method. The IRC makes exceptions to this general rule for personal service corporations, small businesses with average annual gross receipts of $5 million or less, and businesses involved in the farming and timber businesses. (See Chapter I:11 for a complete discussion of the different accounting methods a taxpayer may use for computing taxable income.)

---

[26] Rev. Proc. 94-27, I.R.B. 94-15, 17. As explained in Chapter I:7, acquisition indebtedness incurred to acquire a personal residence is limited to $1,000,000. Hence, points that are allocated to the loan principal in excess of this limit are not deductible either.

[27] Rev. Rul. 87-22, 1987-1 C.B. 146, and Rev. Proc. 87-15, 1987-1 C.B. 624. However, the Eighth Circuit has allowed a current deduction for points paid upon the refinancing of a mortgage loan because the original loan was merely a "bridge" or temporary loan until permanent financing could be arranged.

See *James R. Huntsman v. CIR*, 66 AFTR 2d 90-5020, 90-2 USTC ¶50,340 (8th Cir., 1990).

[28] Rev. Proc. 94-27, I.R.B. 94-15, 17.

[29] Reg. §1.446-1(c)(2). However, most taxpayers with less than $1,000,000 of average annual gross receipts may use the cash method. See Rev. Proc. 2001-10, 2001-1 CB 272. The cash method may also be used by select taxpayers whose annual gross receipts do not exceed $10,000,000. See Rev. Proc. 2002-28, I.R.B. 2002-18, 815.

ACCRUAL METHOD

An **accrual method** taxpayer deducts expenses in the period in which they accrue. Generally, items accrue when the transaction meets both an **all-events test** and an **economic performance test**.[30]

All-Events Test. The all-events test is met when both of the following occur:

▶ The existence of a liability is established.

▶ The amount of the liability is determined with reasonable accuracy.

EXAMPLE I:6-25 ▶ During the current year, Phil provides services for Granite, Inc. Granite uses the accrual method of accounting. Phil claims that Granite owes $10,000 for the services. Granite admits owing Phil $6,000, but contests the remaining $4,000. Because the amount of the liability can be accurately established only with respect to $6,000, Granite can deduct only that amount. If Granite pays the full $10,000, it may deduct the full amount in the year of payment, even though the contested amount ($4,000) is not resolved until a subsequent taxable year.[31] If Phil loses the lawsuit and repays Granite the $4,000, Granite will include that amount in income in the year of repayment under the tax benefit rule (see Chapter I:11). ◀

Because of the all-events test, taxpayers may not deduct additions to reserves for estimated expenses such as warranty expenses. Instead, the taxpayer deducts the expenses in the year in which such work is actually performed.

EXAMPLE I:6-26 ▶ Best Corporation uses the accrual method of accounting and is engaged in the business of painting and rustproofing automobiles. Best Corporation provides a 5-year warranty for new vehicles and a 2-year warranty for used vehicles. Best Corporation extends the warranty only to the person who owns the car at the time the car is painted. Furthermore, in order to keep the warranty in force, the customer must present the vehicle to Best Corporation for inspection each year. The warranty is void if the vehicle is involved in an accident. Even though for financial accounting purposes Best Corporation may provide a reserve for estimated warranty expenses and deduct a reasonable addition to the reserve on an annual basis, no income tax deduction is allowed until the warranty work is actually done. ◀

ADDITIONAL COMMENT

Because of this difference between the tax treatment and the financial accounting treatment, an M-1 or M-3 adjustment must be made on a corporation's Form 1120.

Economic Performance Test. To be currently deductible under the accrual method, an expense must also meet an economic performance test. Exactly when economic performance occurs depends on the type of transaction. Table I:6-1 contains a listing of various types of transactions that may arise and identifies when economic performance is deemed to have occurred under Sec. 461(h).

EXAMPLE I:6-27 ▶ On December 20 of the current year, Pit Corporation, an accrual method taxpayer, enters into a binding contract with Pat to have Pat do a deep cleaning of its offices. Under the terms of the contract, Pat is to do the work in March of the following year. The total cost of the job is $5,000. Pit pays Pat 10% down at the time the contract is signed. Because the job is not to be done until the following year, economic performance has not occurred in the current year and Pit may not deduct any portion of the expense in the current year. ◀

HISTORICAL NOTE

The economic performance test was added by Congress in the Tax Reform Act of 1984. Congress was concerned that in some situations taxpayers could deduct expenses currently, but the actual cash expenditure might not be made for several years. Taking a current deduction in such situations overstated the real cost because the time value of money was ignored.

An exception to the economic performance test provides that taxpayers may take a current deduction for recurring liabilities if all of the following occur:

▶ The item meets the all-events test during the year.

▶ Economic performance of the item occurs within the shorter of 8½ months after the close of the tax year or a reasonable period after the close of the tax year.

▶ The expense is recurring and the taxpayer consistently treats the item as incurred in the tax year.

▶ Either the item is not material or the accrual of the item in the tax year results in a more proper matching against income than accruing the item in the tax year in which economic performance occurs.

---

[30] Reg. Sec. 1.461-1(a)(2) and Sec. 461(h).

[31] Reg. Sec. 1.461-2(a)(1).

▼ TABLE I:6-1

When Economic Performance Is Deemed to Have Occurred

Event That Gives Rise to Liability	When Economic Performance Is Deemed to Have Occurred (i.e., when the accrual method taxpayer may take the deduction)
Another person provides the taxpayer with property or services	When the person actually provides the services[a]
Taxpayer uses property	As the taxpayer uses the property[a]
Taxpayer must provide property or services to another person	As the taxpayer provides property or services to the other person[b]
Taxpayer must make payments to another, including payments for rebates and refunds, awards or prizes, insurance or service contracts, and taxes	As the taxpayer makes payments to the other person
Taxpayer must make payments to another person because of a tort, breach of contract, violation of law, or injury claim under a worker's compensation act	As the taxpayer makes payments to the other person

[a] Economic performance may be deemed to have occurred at the earlier date of payment if the taxpayer reasonably expects the property or services to be provided within 3½ months after the payment is made. Reg. Sec. 1.461-4(d)(6)(ii).
[b] Economic performance may also occur as the taxpayer incurs costs in connection with the obligation to provide the property or services. Reg. Sec. 1.461-4(d)(4)(i).

The recurring liability exception is available for the first four types of transactions identified in Table I:6-1, but it is not available for the last type of transaction in the table.

EXAMPLE I:6-28 ▶ Beta Inc. is a calendar-year, accrual method taxpayer. Every year at the end of October, Beta enters into a contract with Sam to provide snow removal services for the parking lots at Beta corporate offices. This contract extends for five months through the end of March of the following year. Because the all-events test is met (the liability is fixed), the expense recurs every year, economic performance occurs within the requisite period of time, and the item is not material, Beta may deduct the entire expense in the year in which Beta and Sam enter into the contract. ◀

A special rule under Sec. 461(c) applies to real property taxes. Under this provision, a taxpayer may elect to accrue real property taxes ratably over the period to which the taxes relate. Once made, this election is irrevocable unless the taxpayer obtains permission from the IRS.

EXAMPLE I:6-29 ▶ Under the laws of State X, the lien date for real property taxes for the calendar year 2015 is January 1, 2015. The tax is payable in full on December 15, 2015. Alpha Corporation is an accrual-method taxpayer that has a January 31 fiscal year-end. On January 1, 2015, real property taxes of $100,000 are assessed against a building Alpha owns. Alpha pays the taxes on December 15, 2015. If Alpha does not make the election to use the ratable accrual method, Alpha cannot deduct any of the payment in its fiscal year ending January 31, 2015, because the payment date is more than 8½ months after Alpha's January 31, 2015, year end.

On the other hand, if Alpha makes the election, it may deduct $8,333 ($100,000 × ¹⁄₁₂) in its fiscal year that ends January 31, 2015, and $91,667 ($100,000 × ¹¹⁄₁₂) in its fiscal year that ends January 31, 2016.

If the taxes are paid on September 30, 2015, Alpha would be better off not making the ratable accrual election. In this case, the recurring item exception applies because Alpha makes the payment within 8½ months of its January 31, 2015, fiscal year end. Thus, if Alpha does not make the election, all of the $100,000 is deductible in its fiscal year ending on January 31, 2015. ◀

Topic Review I:6-3 presents the rules for determining when an expense is deductible.

TOPIC REVIEW I:6-3

When an Expense Is Deductible

CASH METHOD: DEDUCTIBLE WHEN PAID

Payment Is Made When
► Cash or other property is transferred.
► A check is delivered or mailed.
► An item is charged on a credit card.
   Note: A mere promise to pay or delivery of a note payable is not deductible under the cash method.

Prepaid Expenses
► Generally are deductible over the period covered.
► Deductible when paid if the period covered does not exceed one year.
► Prepaid interest is generally deductible ratably over the period covered by the loan.
► Points are deductible when paid if:
   —The loan is used to purchase or improve the taxpayer's principal residence.
   —The loan is secured by the residence.
   —Points are established business practice in the geographical area.
   —The points do not exceed the amount generally charged.
   —For points paid to purchase a principal residence, the closing agreement clearly designates the amount as points and the amount must be computed as a percentage of the amount borrowed.

ACCRUAL METHOD: DEDUCTIBLE WHEN ACCRUED

In General
► Taxpayers maintaining inventories must use the accrual method of accounting (except for taxpayers with average annual gross receipts of $10 million or less).
► Accrual occurs when the item satisfies both the all-events test and economic performance.

All-Events Test
► The existence of a liability is established and
► The amount of the liability is determined.

Economic Performance
► When economic performance occurs depends on the transaction involved (see Table I:6-1).
► Occurs in the year the item meets the all-events test and all of the following tests:
   —Actual economic performance occurs within the shorter of:
      8 ½ months after the taxable year or a reasonable period after the taxable year.
   —The expense is recurring and receives consistent treatment from year to year.
   —Either:
      The item is immaterial or
      Deducting the expense in the year it meets the all-events test results in a more proper matching of income and deductions.

SPECIAL DISALLOWANCE RULES

OBJECTIVE 6

Discuss special disallow-ance rules for deductions

In addition to the general rules mentioned above, certain types of transactions are subject to further limitations and disallowances. These include wash sales, transactions between related persons, gambling losses, losses associated with an activity determined to be a hobby, expenses of renting a vacation home, and expenses of an office in the taxpayer's home. Further discussion of these special disallowance rules follows.

WASH SALES
Section 1091 disallows losses incurred on wash sales of stock or securities in the year of sale. For purposes of Sec. 1091, a **wash sale** occurs when:

► A taxpayer realizes a loss on the sale of stock or securities, and

> ▶ The taxpayer acquires "substantially identical" stock or securities within a 61-day period of time that extends from 30 days before the date of sale to 30 days after the date of sale.[32]

The purpose of the wash sale rule is to prevent taxpayers from generating artificial tax losses in situations where taxpayers do not intend to reduce their holdings in the stock or securities sold.

EXAMPLE I:6-30 ▶ Leslie realizes $10,000 in short-term capital gains (STCGs) through dealings in the stock market during the current year. Realizing that STCGs are fully includible in gross income and are taxed at ordinary rates unless they are offset against realized capital losses, Leslie analyzes her portfolio to determine whether she owns any stocks that have declined in value. She finds that the FMV of her Edison Corporation common stock is only $8,000, even though she originally purchased it for $16,000. Despite this paper loss on the stock, Leslie wants to retain the stock because she feels that Edison Corporation is still a good investment. If Leslie attempts to take advantage of the paper loss on the Edison stock by selling the stock she owns and repurchasing a similar number of shares of Edison common stock within the 61-day period, Sec. 1091 disallows the loss. ◀

SELF-STUDY QUESTION

During 2012, you bought 100 shares of X stock on each of three occasions. You paid $158 a share for the first block of 100 shares, $100 a share for the second block, and $95 a share for the third block. On December 21, 2015, you sold 300 shares of X stock for $125 a share. On January 6, 2016, you bought 250 shares of identical X stock. Can you deduct the loss realized on the first block of stock?

ANSWER

You cannot deduct the loss of $33 a share on the first block because within 30 days after the date of sale you bought 250 identical shares of X stock. In addition, you cannot reduce the gain realized on the sale of the second and third blocks of stock by this loss.

At times, taxpayers may attempt to circumvent the wash sale provisions through either a sham transaction or an indirect repurchase of the securities. If this is the case, the wash sale provisions still prevent the recognition of the loss. The Supreme Court has held that losses on sales of stock by a husband were disallowed when the stockbroker was instructed to purchase the same number of shares in his wife's name.[33]

In some instances a taxpayer may attempt to circumvent the wash sale provisions by merely delaying the repurchase of the substantially identical stock. This tactic should work as long as a written agreement to repurchase the stock does not exist at the time of the sale or at any time within the 61-day period mandated by the Sec. 1091 wash sale provisions. If such an agreement exists, the courts will disallow the loss, even though the actual purchase does not occur within the 61-day period.[34]

In certain cases, taxpayers may still recognize losses on transactions that literally fall within the wash sale requirements. For example, a taxpayer may purchase stock and then sell a portion of those shares within 30 days where the intent is merely to reduce the stock holdings. Taken together, these two transactions meet the tests of Sec. 1091. However, because the purpose of the sale is to reduce the taxpayer's holdings rather than to generate an artificial tax loss, Sec. 1091 does not disallow the loss.[35] Section 1091 also does not apply to losses that a dealer in stock or securities realizes in the ordinary course of business.

If the taxpayer acquires fewer shares of stock within the 61-day period than the number of shares disposed of, Sec. 1091 disallows only a proportionate amount of the total loss.

EXAMPLE I:6-31 ▶ Several years ago, Henry purchased 100 shares of New Corporation common stock for $2,000 ($20 per share). On July 2 of the current year, Henry sells all 100 shares for $1,000. On July 30 of the current year, Henry purchases 75 shares (three-fourths of the original shares) of New Corporation common stock. As a result of the reacquisition, three-fourths of the total loss ($750) is disallowed. Henry recognizes the remaining $250 loss. ◀

Substantially Identical Stock or Securities. Only the acquisition of substantially identical stock or securities will cause a loss to be disallowed. The IRC and the Treasury Regulations do not define the term *substantially identical*. Judicial and administrative rulings have held that bonds issued by the same corporation generally are not substantially identical if they differ in terms (e.g., interest rate and term to maturity). However,

---

[32] Here the term *acquire* includes an acquisition of the stock either by purchase or in a taxable exchange. The term *stock or securities* includes contracts or options to acquire or sell stock or securities (see Sec. 1091(a)). The wash sale rules also apply to losses realized on the closing of a short sale of stock or securities if, within the 61-day period, substantially identical stock or securities were sold or another short sale of (or a securities futures contract to sell) substantially identical stock or securities was entered into.

[33] *John P. McWilliams v. CIR*, 35 AFTR 1184, 47-1 USTC ¶9289 (USSC, 1947).

[34] Rev. Rul. 72-225, 1972-1 C.B. 59, and *Frank Stein*, 1977 PH T.C. Memo ¶77,241, 36 TCM 992.

[35] Rev. Rul. 56-602, 1956-2 C.B. 527.

bonds of the same corporation that differ only in their maturity dates (e.g., the bonds do not come due for 16 years and mature within a few months of each other) have been held to be substantially identical. Generally, courts have not considered the preferred stock of a corporation to be substantially identical to the common stock of the same corporation.[36]

Basis of Stock. If the wash sale provisions disallow a loss, then the disallowed loss increases the basis of the recently acquired stock. This increase in basis merely causes the disallowed loss to be deferred. The taxpayer will eventually recognize the loss upon the subsequent sale or disposition of the stock that causes the loss disallowance. If there has been more than one purchase of replacement stock and the amount of stock purchased within the 61-day period exceeds the stock that is sold, the stock that is deemed to have caused the loss to be disallowed is accounted for chronologically. The holding period of the replacement stock includes the period of time the taxpayer held the stock sold.

EXAMPLE I:6-32 ▶ Ingrid enters into the following transactions with regard to Pacific Corporation common stock:

Date	Transaction	Amount
January 4, 2009	Purchases 600 shares	$30,000
October 2, 2015	Purchases 400 shares	10,000
October 12, 2015	Sells original 600 shares	12,000
October 20, 2015	Purchases 200 shares	5,000
October 25, 2015	Purchases 300 shares	8,400

Because Ingrid purchases more than 600 shares within the 61-day period before and after the date of sale (the purchases made on October 2, 20, and 25), the recognition of the entire loss of $18,000 ($30,000–$12,000) is postponed. Four hundred shares (two-thirds of the number of shares sold) are purchased on October 2 and 200 shares (one-third) are purchased on October 20. Thus, the basis of the 400 shares of stock purchased on October 2 is $22,000 [$10,000 purchase price + ($18,000 disallowed loss × 0.667)]. The basis of the 200 shares of stock purchased on October 20 is $11,000 [$5,000 + ($18,000 disallowed loss × 0.333)]. Both of these blocks of stock have a holding period that starts on January 4, 2009.[37] The basis of the 300 shares of stock purchased on October 25 is its purchase price of $8,400. Its holding period begins on October 25, 2015. ◀

? STOP & THINK

Question: With regard to his investments in the stock market, the current year has been like a roller coaster ride for Doug. He now wants to do some year-end tax planning. For the year to date, he has realized a net gain of $12,000 on his stock investments. Although some of his current stock holdings have unrealized losses, he feels that they are excellent investments that will provide excellent returns in the next year or two. His stock broker has suggested that he sell enough of his holdings to realize a $12,000 loss (to offset the $12,000 capital gain) and then simply repurchase some of the stock. What advice would you give Doug as he discusses this strategy with his broker?

Solution: By realizing $12,000 in capital losses this year, Doug may be able to offset the capital gains he has already recognized. In order to recognize these losses, however, he must make sure that the wash sale provisions do not apply. Thus, he must either (1) purchase stock of different corporations or (2) delay the repurchase of the same issue of stock for at least 31 days after the date of sale. Because Doug is happy with his current investments, perhaps the second strategy is the best. Of course, other non-tax issues must also be considered. For example, does Doug think that the prices will go up quickly within the next 30 days? If so, he may lose out on some significant gains while he is waiting to repurchase the stock. Additionally, he must also consider the transaction costs (such as commissions).

---

[36] *Marie Hanlin, Executrix v. CIR,* 39-2 USTC ¶9783 (3d Cir., 1939). However, the IRS held in Rev. Rul. 77-201, 1977-1 C.B. 250, that the convertible preferred stock of a corporation is substantially identical to its common stock if the preferred stock has the same voting rights and is subject to the same dividend restrictions as the common stock, is unrestricted as to its convertibility, and sells at relatively the same price (taking into consideration the conversion ratio).

[37] An asset's holding period is important in determining whether subsequent gain or loss on the asset is long-term or short-term gain or loss. This is explained further in Chapter I:5.

TRANSACTIONS BETWEEN RELATED PARTIES

Section 267 places transactions between certain related parties under special scrutiny because of the potential for tax abuse. For example, a taxpayer could sell a piece of property at a loss to a wholly owned corporation. Without any restrictions on the deductibility of the loss, the individual could recognize the loss while still retaining effective control of the property. Under Sec. 267, related taxpayers may not take current deductions on two specific types of transactions. These transactions are:

▶ Losses on sales of property

▶ Accrued expenses that remain unpaid to the related cash method taxpayer at the end of the tax year

ADDITIONAL COMMENT
Section 267 does not define the word property, but the IRS and the courts have given it a broad meaning.

Related Parties Defined. Section 267 defines the following relationships as related parties:

▶ Individuals and their families. The term family includes an individual's spouse, brothers and sisters (including half-brothers and half-sisters), ancestors, and lineal descendants.

▶ An individual and a corporation in which the individual owns more than 50% of the value of the outstanding stock.

▶ Various relationships between grantors, beneficiaries, and fiduciaries of a trust or trusts, or between the fiduciary of a trust and a corporation if they meet certain ownership requirements.

▶ A corporation and a partnership if the same persons own more than 50% in value of the stock of the corporation and more than 50% of the partnership.

▶ Two corporations if the same persons own more than 50% in value of the outstanding stock of both corporations and at least one of the corporations is an S corporation.

▶ Other complex relationships involving trusts, corporations, and individuals.

TAX STRATEGY TIP
The related party rules many times cause the tax consequences to be different than what was expected. Be sure that your clients provide all details to you ahead of time when related parties are involved in the transaction. You might be able to help structure the transaction in a way that meets your clients' expectations.

Several of these relationships depend on an individual's ownership of a corporation. For example, if a taxpayer does not own more than 50% of a corporation's stock, the individual and the corporation are not related and a loss on the sale of business or investment property between the two is deductible. Occasionally, individuals might attempt to circumvent the related party rules by dispersing the ownership of a corporation (e.g., among close family members) while retaining economic control. To prevent these tactics, Sec. 267 contains constructive ownership rules whereby a taxpayer is deemed to own stock owned by certain other persons. These constructive ownership rules are as follows:

▶ Stock owned by an individual's family is treated as owned by the individual. Here the definition of *family* is the same as that of *related parties* (i.e., spouse, brothers and sisters, ancestors, and lineal descendants).

▶ Stock owned by a corporation, partnership, estate, or trust is treated as owned proportionately by the shareholders, partners, or beneficiaries.

▶ If an individual partner in a partnership owns (or is treated as owning) stock in a corporation, the individual is treated as owning any stock of that corporation owned by any other partner in the partnership. This does not occur, however, if the only stock the individual owns (or is considered to own) is through family attribution.[38]

▶ Stock ownership that is attributed to a shareholder or partner from an entity can be reattributed to another taxpayer under any of the constructive ownership rules. In other words, the same stock can be constructively owned by more than one person. However, stock ownership attributed to a taxpayer under the family or partner rules cannot be reattributed.

---

[38] Reg. Sec. 1.267(c)-1(b), Exs. (2) and (3).

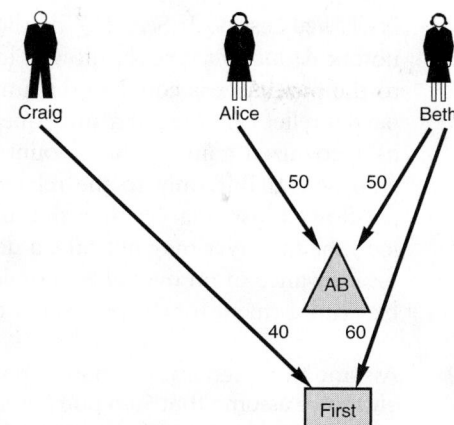

FIGURE I:6-2 ▶ ILLUSTRATION FOR EXAMPLE I:6-33

The following examples illustrate these rules.

EXAMPLE I:6-33 ▶ Alice and Beth are equal partners in the AB Partnership. Beth owns 60% of First Corporation's stock, and Craig, Alice's husband, owns the other 40%. The ownership of the partnership and the corporation is demonstrated in Figure I:6-2. Under the constructive ownership rules, Alice is considered to own Craig's 40% of the First Corporation stock. Alice is not considered to own the First Corporation stock owned by her partner, Beth, because the only First Corporation stock Alice owns (or is considered to own) is the stock owned by her husband. If Alice sells property at a loss to First Corporation, the loss is recognized because Alice does not directly or constructively own more than 50% of the First Corporation stock. ◄

EXAMPLE I:6-34 ▶ Assume the same facts as in Example I:6-33, except that the First Corporation stock is owned 50% by the AB Partnership and 25% each by Beth and Craig. The ownership of the partnership and the corporation is shown in Figure I:6-3. In addition to Craig's 25%, Alice is considered to own 50% of the stock owned by the AB Partnership because of her 50% ownership in AB. The other half of AB's stock ownership is attributed to her partner, Beth. However, Alice is also treated as owning the First Corporation stock Beth owns both actually and constructively (50%). Thus, Alice is treated as owning 100% of the First Corporation stock. In this case, Alice will not be able to recognize a loss on the sale of property to First Corporation. ◄

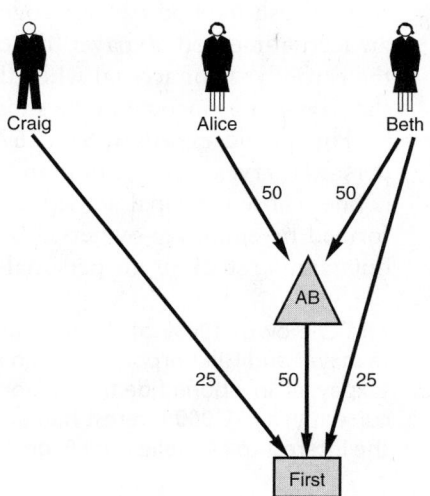

FIGURE I:6-3 ▶ ILLUSTRATION FOR EXAMPLE I:6-34

Disallowed Losses. If Sec. 267 disallows the loss, the original seller of the property receives no tax deduction. The disallowed loss has no effect on the purchaser's basis. The cost basis to the purchaser is equal to the amount paid for the property. However, Sec. 267 provides partial relief because, on a subsequent sale of the property, the related purchaser may reduce its recognized gain by the amount of the disallowed loss. This offsetting of a subsequent gain is available only to the related person who originally purchased the property. If the disallowed loss is larger than the subsequent gain, or if the purchaser sells the property at a loss, the taxpayer may not take a deduction for the unused loss. This may result in a partial disallowance of an overall economic loss for the related parties because there is no upward basis adjustment for the previously disallowed loss (as is the case for a wash sale).

EXAMPLE I:6-35 ▶ Assume three separate scenarios in which Sam sells a tract of land during the current year. In each case assume that Sam purchased the land from his father, Frank, for $10,000. Frank's basis at the time of the original sale was $15,000 in each case. Thus, Frank's $5,000 loss on each land sale was disallowed.

KEY POINT

The loss disallowance rule for related parties is more severe compared to the loss disallowance rule on wash sales. In a related party transaction, it is possible to lose the tax benefit of all or a portion of the economic loss.

	Scenario		
	1	2	3
Selling price	$17,000	$ 12,000	$ 8,000
Minus: Sam's basis	(10,000)	(10,000)	(10,000)
Sam's realized gain (loss)	$ 7,000	$ 2,000	$ (2,000)
Minus: Frank's disallowed loss (up to Sam's gain)	(5,000)	(2,000)	—0—
Sam's recognized gain (loss)	$2,000	—0—	($2,000)

In Scenario 1, Sam and Frank together have incurred an aggregate gain of $2,000 ($17,000 − $15,000). Thus, Frank's full disallowed loss reduces Sam's subsequent gain. In Scenario 2, the aggregate economic loss incurred by Sam and Frank is actually $3,000 ($12,000 − $15,000). However, the actual amount of the tax loss recognized by Sam and Frank is zero. In Scenario 3, the actual tax loss would have been $7,000 ($8,000 − $15,000) instead of $2,000 if Frank had held the land until its eventual sale. ◀

A similar rule found in Sec. 707(b)(1) disallows losses between a partner and a partnership in which the partner owns directly or indirectly over 50% of the partnership and between two partnerships in which the same people own directly or indirectly over 50% in each partnership. The constructive ownership rules of Sec. 267 apply here in determining ownership (see *Prentice Hall's Federal Taxation: Corporations, Partnerships, Estates & Trusts* text or the *Comprehensive* volume).

KEY POINT

The effect of Sec. 267 with respect to unpaid expenses is to place an accrual method taxpayer on the cash method for amounts owed to a related cash method taxpayer.

Unpaid Expenses. Under Sec. 267, a related accrual-method obligor of any accrued but unpaid expenses must defer the deduction for those expenses until the year in which the related cash-method payee recognizes the amount as income. In effect, this rule prevents an accrual-method taxpayer (the payer) from taking a deduction for an unpaid expense in the earlier year of accrual while the related cash-method taxpayer (the payee) recognizes the payment as income in the subsequent year.

For unpaid expenses, Sec. 267 expands the definition of related parties to include a personal-service corporation and any employee-owner.[39] A personal-service corporation is one whose principal activity is the performance of personal services substantially performed by employee-owners. An employee-owner is an employee who owns any of the outstanding stock of the personal-service corporation.[40]

EXAMPLE I:6-36 ▶ Michelle owns 100% of the outstanding stock of Hill Corporation. Michelle is a cash-method taxpayer and Hill Corporation is an accrual-method taxpayer. Both taxpayers are calendar-year taxpayers. In a bona fide transaction, Hill borrows some funds from Michelle. By the end of the current year, $8,000 interest had accrued on the loan. However, Hill Corporation does not pay the interest to Michelle until February of the following year. Because Michelle is a cash-method

---

[39] Sec. 267(a)(2).

[40] Secs. 269A(b) and 441(i)(2). In determining the ownership of an employee-owner, the constructive ownership rules of Sec. 318 as modified by Sec.

441(i)(2) are used. These rules differ substantially from the constructive ownership rules of Sec. 267.

taxpayer, she reports the interest income when she receives it in the following year. Although Hill is an accrual-method taxpayer, it must defer the deduction for the interest expense until it pays the interest in February of the following year. The results are the same if Hill Corporation is a personal service corporation and Michelle is an employee and owns any amount of the Hill stock. ◄

For purposes of these unpaid expenses, the definition of *related parties* also includes various relationships involving partnerships or S corporations and any person who owns (either actually or constructively) any interest in these entities.[41]

HOBBY LOSSES

Certain activities have both profit-motivated and personal attributes. In these cases, a tax advisor must examine all the relevant factors to determine the tax status of the activity since, in general, expenses incurred in a profit-motivated activity such as a business or investment are deductible, whereas most expenses associated with personal activities such as hobbies are not. Reg. Sec. 1.183-2(b) lists the factors the IRS uses to determine whether an activity is profit-motivated. These factors include the following:

► Whether the taxpayer conducts the activity in a businesslike manner.

► The expertise of the taxpayer or the taxpayer's advisors.

► The time and effort expended by the taxpayer in carrying on the activity.

► Whether the assets used in the activity are expected to appreciate in value.

► The taxpayer's success in carrying on other similar activities.

► The taxpayer's history of income or losses with respect to the activity.

► The amount of occasional profits earned, if any.

► The taxpayer's financial status.

► Any elements of personal pleasure or recreation the activity might involve.

ADDITIONAL COMMENT

Many of the court cases dealing with profit motive under Sec. 183 are ranch and farm cases. In fact, Sec. 183, now titled "Activities Not Engaged in for Profit" was originally titled "Farm Losses, etc." in the Tax Reform Act of 1969.

No one of these factors is determinative. In fact, the IRS also may consider other factors not listed. Furthermore, the IRS does not make a determination by merely counting the number of factors that are present. Instead, the decision depends on an examination of all the factors together. The IRS can, therefore, make the decision on a more subjective basis than the taxpayer might like. If the IRS asserts that an activity is a personal one (i.e., a hobby) rather than a business or investment, the burden of proof rests on the taxpayer to prove otherwise.

EXAMPLE I:6-37 ►

Paula, a successful attorney with an annual income of $300,000, also enjoys raising and training quarter horses. She generally spends five to six hours each week training, showing, or racing the horses. Over the last four years her winnings from shows and races have amounted to $16,000. Over that same period, she has generated an additional $8,000 of income from stud fees and the sale of colts. Often Paula uses the horses to take her family or friends riding. In addition, Paula often participates in equestrian clinics and demonstrations for 4-H Clubs and other similar groups. Paula employs a high school student to feed the horses each day and clean the stalls weekly. Paula also hires a professional horse trainer for 4 hours each week to help her train the horses.

In this case, several factors such as the level of earnings, the hiring of professional help, and the amount of time spent in the activity might indicate that Paula is engaged in a business. Other factors, such as the time spent riding with family and friends, the voluntary clinics and demonstrations, and the small amount of revenue generated as compared with Paula's other income, support the position that Paula merely has a hobby of raising horses. ◄

In cases where a clear profit motive cannot be shown under the factors mentioned above, the Code provides a test whereby an activity may be presumed to be engaged in for profit. The activity meets the test if it shows a profit for any three years during a consecutive five-year period. The five-year period consists of the year in question plus the previous four years.[42] This presumption is rebuttable (i.e., if the taxpayer meets the test, the

---

[41] Sec. 267(e). A discussion of these modifications is beyond the scope of this book.
[42] Sec. 183(d). If the major part of the activity involves breeding, training,

showing, or racing horses, the five-year period is extended to a seven-year period, and a profit must be shown in only two, rather than three, of the years covered by that seven-year period.

IRS has the burden of proof to show that the activity *is not* profit motivated). However, if the taxpayer fails to meet this test, the taxpayer must prove that the activity *is* profit motivated.

If the examination of the factors leads to the determination that the activity is a business, the taxpayer generally may deduct all qualified business expenses from the gross income, even if a net loss results.[43] However, if the factors lead to a determination that the activity is a hobby, the taxpayer can generally deduct the expenses as a miscellaneous itemized deduction but only to the extent of the gross income from the activity. A net loss may not be reported from the activity if it is a hobby.

EXAMPLE I:6-38 ▶ Lorenzo, a stockbroker, enjoys raising pedigreed poodles. Although he mainly raises them for recreation and relaxation after work, Lorenzo periodically sells some of his poodles. Lorenzo reports $850 in income and $2,900 in expenses from the activity on his 2015 tax return. Upon auditing Lorenzo's 2015 return, the IRS disallowed the expenses in excess of the income, arguing that the activity is a hobby rather than a business or investment. If Lorenzo can prove that he realized a profit from the poodle-raising operation for any three years from 2011 through 2015 inclusive, the presumption will be made that the poodles are raised for a profit and not for recreation. The IRS then has the burden of proof to show that the activity is really a hobby. If Lorenzo cannot show a profit for three years out of the five-year period, he must rely on the factors mentioned in the Treasury Regulations to convince the IRS and/or the courts that the activity is a business.

If Lorenzo's poodle-raising activity is determined to be a business, Lorenzo will report a net loss of $2,050 ($2,900 expenses − $850 income), assuming the loss is not incurred in a passive activity (see Chapter I:8). If the activity is determined to be a hobby, however, Lorenzo may deduct only $850 of the expenses (up to the amount of the gross income) as an itemized deduction. As explained later, these expenses must be deducted in a certain order. The remaining expenses are not allowed as tax deductions. ◀

Deductible Expenses. Some hobby activities generate gross income, even though profit is not a primary motive for the activity. In such situations, Sec. 183 allows the taxpayer to deduct the expenses related to the hobby, but only to the extent of the gross income from the hobby. Furthermore, a taxpayer may deduct a hobby-related expense only if it would have been deductible if incurred in a trade or business or an investment activity.

In essence, a taxpayer may deduct the hobby-related expenses as long as there is enough gross income from the activity to cover the expenses. However, a taxpayer may not generate a tax loss from a hobby and then use it to offset the taxpayer's other types of income.

Order of the Deductions. If the hobby expenses exceed the amount of gross income generated by the hobby, the expense deductions offset gross income in the following order:

▶ Tier 1: Expenses that are deductible even though not incurred in a trade or business (e.g., itemized deductions such as taxes, certain interest, and casualty losses)

▶ Tier 2: Other expenses of the hobby that could be deductible if incurred in a profit-motivated activity, but which do not reduce the tax basis of any of the assets used in the hobby (e.g., utilities and maintenance expenses)

▶ Tier 3: The expenses of the hobby that could be deductible if incurred in a profit-motivated activity and that reduce the basis of the hobby's assets (e.g., depreciation on fixed assets used in the hobby)[44]

To the extent that the expenses are deductible against the gross income of the activity, they are deductions *from* AGI and are deductible only if the taxpayer has itemized deductions in excess of the standard deduction. Form 1040 reports the tier 1 expenses in their respective sections on Schedule A. The tier 2 and tier 3 expenses allocated to the hobby are miscellaneous itemized deductions; therefore, these expenses are deductible only to the extent

---

[43] If the activity is a passive activity, however, the loss may be deferred or suspended. See Chapter I:8 for a discussion of the passive loss rules.

[44] Reg. Sec. 1.183-1(b).

they exceed 2% of AGI (see Chapter I:7). Form 1040 reports gross income from a hobby as other income. If gross income is not sufficient to cover all of the tier 1 expenses, the taxpayer may also deduct the excess tier 1 expenses as itemized deductions on Schedule A of Form 1040 because the tax law allows deductions for these expenses in any event. The tax law disallows deductions for any remaining expenses in the other two tiers, and the taxpayer may not carry them over to a subsequent year.

If depreciation expense is not deductible, the taxpayer does not need to reduce the cost basis of the asset by the amount of the disallowed depreciation expense.

EXAMPLE I:6-39 ▶

Lynn raises various plants and flowers in a small greenhouse constructed specifically for that purpose. During the current year, Lynn reports gross income from the greenhouse activities of $1,700. Lynn also incurs the following expenses:

Property taxes on the greenhouse	$1,150
Utilities	300
Depreciation (assuming the activity is considered a business)	800

If the greenhouse activity is considered to be a hobby rather than a business, the deductions Lynn may take are computed as follows:

Income from greenhouse		$1,700
Tier 1 Expenses:		
Property taxes	$1,150	
Tier 2 Expenses:		
Utilities	300	
Tier 3 Expenses:		
Depreciation[a]	250	$1,700
Total		$0

[a]Limited to greenhouse income remaining after accounting for the Tier 1 and Tier 2 expenses.

◀

REAL-WORLD EXAMPLE

Good records are very important in establishing the existence of a business rather than a hobby. A taxpayer, who owned and operated an apple orchard, asserted that he maintained sufficient business records, consisting of bank deposit slips, check stubs, and tax forms. A separate bank account was also maintained. But the taxpayer did not present any production records for the apple orchard. In fact, at trial, the taxpayer was not even certain of the exact number of trees in the orchard. Thus, the court found that due to the limited records, the taxpayer's activity was considered to be a hobby rather than a business. *Zdun,* TC Memo 1998-296 (1998).

VACATION HOME

Because owning a second home or dwelling unit may have both personal and profit-motivated attributes, Sec. 280A may disallow or limit deductions for expenses related to the rental of a vacation home that is also used as a residence by the taxpayer.

Residence Defined. For the restrictive rules of Sec. 280A to apply, the property must be a dwelling unit that qualifies as the taxpayer's residence. As used in this context, the term *dwelling unit* is quite expansive. The term dwelling unit may even include property such as boats and mobile homes. The determining factor is whether the property provides shelter and accommodations for eating and sleeping.[45] Thus, a mini-motorhome that contains the appropriate accommodations has been held to be a dwelling unit subject to the rules and limitations of Sec. 280A. The determination disregards the fact that the unit is small and cramped.

A dwelling unit qualifies as a residence if the number of days during which the taxpayer uses the property for personal use throughout the year exceeds the greater of the following:

▶ 14 days, or

▶ 10% of the number of days during the year that the property is rented at a fair rental.[46]

SELF-STUDY QUESTION

What is the maximum number of days during a year that a taxpayer may use a property for personal use and not have it considered to be used as a residence?

EXAMPLE I:6-40 ▶

ANSWER

If a property was rented for 332 days it could be used by the taxpayer for 33 days and not be considered a residence.

Sarah owns a houseboat on Lake Powell that she personally uses for 21 days out of the year. During the year she also rents out the boat for a total of 300 days. Even though Sarah's personal use exceeds 14 days during the year, the houseboat is not considered a residence under Sec. 280A because Sarah's personal use does not exceed 30 days during the year (10% of the 300 rental days for the year).

◀

---

[45] *Ronald L. Haberkorn,* 75 T.C. 259 (1980), and *John O. Loughlin v. U.S.,* 50 AFTR 2d 82-5827, 82-2 USTC ¶9543 (D.C. Minn., 1982).
[46] Sec. 280A(d)(1). In certain cases, this residence test might be met when a taxpayer uses a property as his or her principal residence for part of the year and rents the property for the rest of the year. This could occur, for example, when a taxpayer moves from his or her home and turns the old residence into a rental unit. In such a case, special rules prevent the home from being classified as a residence under Sec. 280A, thus preventing the application of the limitations.

For purposes of the residence test, a day of personal use includes any of the following:

▶ Any day the taxpayer or the taxpayer's family uses the property for personal purposes. Family is defined here as including the taxpayer's spouse, brothers and sisters, ancestors, and lineal descendants.[47]

▶ Any day any individual uses the property under a reciprocal-use arrangement.[48]

▶ Any day any individual uses the property and does not pay a fair rental for its use.[49]

Despite the family-use rule, if a taxpayer rents property at a fair rental to a family member who uses the property as a principal residence, such use does not constitute personal use by the taxpayer.

EXAMPLE I:6-41 ▶ During the current year, Peggy purchases a small house as an investment and rents the property to Stan, her married son, who uses the property as his principal residence. Stan pays his mom a fair rental for the property. Because Stan uses the property as his principal residence and pays Peggy a fair rental for the property, Peggy is not treated as personally using the house for any days during the year. Thus Peggy's personal use does not exceed the greater of 14 days or 10% of the rental days during the year, and the rules of Sec. 280A do not apply to limit the expenses that Peggy may deduct (although the passive loss rules may limit the deduction). ◀

KEY POINT

A second home is classified as either rental property, a residence, or some combination of the two. If it is classified as some combination of rental property and a residence, the expenses of the property must be allocated between the two categories.

Allocation of Expenses. When a taxpayer uses a vacation home personally as well as for rental purposes, the tax law requires the taxpayer to allocate the vacation home expenses between the taxpayer's personal use and rental use. The reason for this required allocation of the vacation home expenses is that the IRC generally allows individuals to deduct expenses attributable to the rental of property (subject to various limitations), whereas individuals generally cannot deduct expenses allocated to personal use property. The taxpayer must allocate the expenses between the two uses whether or not the property qualifies as the taxpayer's residence under the greater of (1) 14 days or (2) 10% of rental days test discussed above. If the property is considered the taxpayer's residence because the taxpayer's personal usage exceeds the greater of 14 days or 10% of the rental days during the year, the taxpayer may deduct the expenses allocated to the rental use as a *for* AGI deduction, but only to the extent of the gross income generated by the property. The property may not generate a loss which could be used to reduce other income of the taxpayer. If the allocated expenses exceed the gross income for the year, the taxpayer may carry over the excess expenses to the following year. However, the deduction in the subsequent year is also limited to the gross income of the property for the subsequent year.[50] The order for deduction of the expenses allocated to the rental use of property is the same as the order for deduction of hobby losses under the rules of Sec. 183. Example I:6-40 illustrates these rules.

Allocation Formula. Sec. 280A uses the following formula to allocate expenses between the personal use and the rental use of the property:[51]

$$\text{Rental use expenses} = \frac{\text{Number of rental days}}{\text{Total number of days used}} \times \text{Total expenses for the year}$$

The denominator of the allocation fraction is the sum of the days the property is rented plus the days the taxpayer uses it for personal purposes. The formula does not include the days that no one uses the property.

---

[47] Sec. 280A(d)(2). A day during which the taxpayer spends substantially full time on repairs and maintenance does not count as a personal-use day.
[48] Sec. 280A(d)(2)(B). A reciprocal-use arrangement is one whereby another person uses the taxpayer's property in exchange for the taxpayer's use of the other person's property.
[49] Sec. 280A(d)(2)(C). Exactly what constitutes a fair rental must be determined by an examination of all the associated facts and circumstances.

[50] Sec. 280A(c)(5)(B). The expenses that are carried over to the subsequent year are deductible to the extent of the property's gross income of that year, even though the property is not used by the taxpayer as a residence during that year.
[51] Sec. 280A(e)(1).

Some courts have modified the allocation formula by using the total number of days in the year as the denominator for qualified residential interest and taxes instead of the number of days the property was used.[52] Use of this ratio allocates less interest and taxes to the rental use, allowing more of the other expenses to be deducted against the rental income. Expenses allocated to the personal use of the vacation home generally are not deductible. However, as explained in Chapter I:7, individuals may take a *from* AGI deduction for real estate taxes paid on personal use property such as a home or vacation home. In addition an individual may also include as a *from* AGI deduction certain interest expenses incurred on a "qualified residence" of the taxpayer. In order for the vacation home to qualify as a "qualified residence" the taxpayer must meet the same residence test discussed above where the taxpayer's personal usage must exceed the greater of (1) 14 days or (2) 10% of the rental days during the year.[53] Example I:6-42 and I:6-43 use the allocation formula for the interest and taxes that is sanctioned by the courts.

EXAMPLE I:6-42 ▶ Joan owns a cabin near the local ski resort. During the year, Joan and Joan's family use the cabin a total of 25 days. Joan also rents the cabin to out-of-state skiers for a total of 50 days during the year, generating rental income of $10,000. Joan incurs the following expenses:

Expense	Amount
Property taxes	$1,500
Interest on mortgage	3,000
Utilities	2,000
Insurance	1,500
Security and snow removal	2,500

Joan would have been entitled to $12,000 depreciation if the property had been entirely rental property held for investment. However, because the property is also used for personal purposes, the amount of deductions (for AGI) Joan may take with respect to the property during the year is as follows:

Item	Calculation	Allocated to Rental	Allocated to Personal	Treatment of Personal Amounts
Rental income		$10,000		
Interest	$ 3,000 × $\frac{50}{365}$	(411)*	($2,589)	Deductible**
Taxes	$ 1,500 × $\frac{50}{365}$	(205)*	(1,295)	Deductible***
Other expenses	$ 6,000 × $\frac{50}{75}$	(4,000)	(2,000)	Not deductible
Depreciation	$12,000 × $\frac{50}{75}$	(5,384)****	(4,000)	Not deductible
Net Rental Income from Property		$0		

The income and expenses allocated to the rental use are reported on Schedule E. Thus, the expenses allocated to the rental use are *for* AGI deductions. The deductible interest and taxes allocated to the personal use are itemized deductions on Schedule A if Joan's total itemized deductions exceed her standard deduction.

* Under the approach favored by the IRS, $2,000 of the interest and $1,000 of the taxes would be allocated to the rental use (50/75 or 2/3 or each expense), leaving only $3,000 of the depreciation to be deducted against the gross income.

** Joan can include the interest allocated to her personal use as an itemized *from* AGI deduction because her personal usage of the cabin (25 days) exceeds 14 days (the greater of 14 days or 10% of the rental days). See Chapter I:7 and Sec. 163(h)(2) and (h)(4)(A).

*** Deductible under Sec. 164(a)(1) as an itemized *from* AGI deduction.

**** Limited to the remaining gross income. If there had been sufficient gross income, Joan could have taken $8,000 depreciation. ◀

---

[52] *Dorance D. Bolton v. CIR*, 51 AFTR 2d 83-305, 82-2 USTC ¶9699 (9th Cir., 1982). See also *Edith G. McKinney v. CIR*, 52 AFTR 2d 83-6281, 83-2 USTC ¶9655 (10th Cir., 1983).

[53] No deduction is allowed for interest incurred with respect to a personal residence if the debt on which the interest is paid is not secured by the property or the taxpayer has not chosen the property as a second residence for purposes of deducting the interest as qualified residential interest (see Chapter I:7). For purposes of the discussion and examples used here, the assumption is made that the interest qualifies as qualified residential interest.

EXAMPLE I:6-43 ▶ Assume all the same facts in Example I:6-42 except that during the year Joan uses the cabin for 16 days and rents the cabin out for 170 days. The allocation and deductibility of the cabin's expenses are as follows:

Item	Calculation	Allocated to Rental	Allocated to Personal	Treatment of Personal Amounts
Rental income		$10,000		
Interest	$\$3,000 \times \dfrac{170}{365}$	(1,397)	($1,603)	Not deductible*
Taxes	$\$1,500 \times \dfrac{170}{365}$	(699)	(801)	Deductible**
Other expenses	$\$6,000 \times \dfrac{170}{186}$	(5,484)	(516)	Not deductible
Depreciation	$\$12,000 \times \dfrac{170}{186}$	(2,420)***	(1,032)	Not deductible

* Joan cannot include the interest allocated to the personal use as an itemized deduction because her personal usage of the cabin doesn't exceed 17 days (the greater of 14 days or 10% of the rental days). See Sec. 163(h)(2) and (h)(4)(A).
**Deductible under Sec. 164(a)(1).
***Limited to the remaining gross income. ◀

Nominal Number of Rental Days. If a property qualifies as a taxpayer's residence under Sec. 280A and the taxpayer rents the property for less than 15 days during the year, the law takes the approach that the property is completely personal in nature. As such, the taxpayer does not have to report the rental income and cannot deduct any of the related expenses. However, expenses such as qualified residential interest and taxes may still be deductible as itemized deductions. (See Chapter I:7 for a discussion of the limitations on interest.)

EXAMPLE I:6-44 ▶ Assume the same facts as in Example I:6-42, except that during the year Joan rents the cabin out for only 12 days and the amount of rental income is $2,400. The cabin qualifies as Joan's residence because her personal use exceeds 14 days. Because the cabin is rented for less than 15 days during the year, Joan may only take itemized deductions of $4,500 for the qualified residential interest and taxes. She may not deduct the other expenses. In addition, she does not include the $2,400 in gross income. ◀

Nominal Number of Personal use Days. If a taxpayer does not have enough personal use days during the year to qualify the property as a residence (i.e., the personal use is not more than the greater of 14 days or 10% of the rental days), the Sec. 280A rules and limitations do not apply. In such a case the taxpayer must still allocate the expenses of the property between the personal use and the rental use days. The taxpayer may deduct the taxes allocated to the personal use as an itemized deduction. However, since the property does not qualify as the taxpayer's residence, the taxpayer may not deduct any of the interest allocated to the personal use because the interest is not "qualified residential interest" (see Chapter I:7 for a discussion of the deductibility of personal interest and qualified residential interest). The taxpayer may not deduct the tier 2 and 3 expenses allocated to the personal use. The income from the property and all of the expenses allocated to the rental use are reported on Schedule E of Form 1040. As such, the expenses are *for* AGI deductions. Any net income or loss from the property is subject to the Sec. 469 passive loss rules, which may limit the deductibility of any losses from the property (see Chapter I:8).

EXAMPLE I:6-45 ▶ Assume the same facts as in Example I:6-42 except that Joan and her family use the cabin only 10 days during the year and rent it out for 65 days of the year. Also assume that Joan chooses to use the IRS's method of allocating the interest and taxes between the personal use and the rental use of the cabin based upon the total number of days used during the year rather than on the total 365 days in the year. Since Joan does not personally use the cabin for at least 14 days, the cabin is not considered her residence and the Sec. 280A rules do not apply. Thus the interest allocated to the personal use is not deductible because it is not "qualified residential interest." Furthermore, the passive loss rules apply to the net income or loss from the property.

KEY POINT

Assume that a taxpayer owns a beachfront condo. The taxpayer personally uses the condo for only 12 days during the year and rents the property for 35 days. Section 280A does not apply because the taxpayer has not used the property for over 14 days. However, if the taxpayer cannot demonstrate a profit motive, it may still be treated as a hobby. Even if a profit motive can be shown, the loss may be limited under the passive loss limitation rules. If so, the deductibility of the expenses allocated to the rental use is limited to the gross income generated by the property. Furthermore, the interest allocated to the personal use of the property is not deductible as qualified residential interest (see Chapter I:7).

	Calculation	*Amount*
Rental income		$10,000
Interest	$ 3,000 \times \dfrac{65}{75}$	(2,600)[a]
Taxes	$ 1,500 \times \dfrac{65}{75}$	(1,300)[a]
Other expenses	$ 6,000 \times \dfrac{65}{75}$	(5,200)
Depreciation	$12,000 \times \dfrac{65}{75}$	(10,400)
	Total	$ (9,500)[b]

[a] Joan would treat the remaining $200 in taxes ($1,500 − $1,300) as an itemized deduction. However, Joan may not deduct the remaining $400 ($3,000 − $2,600) interest because it does not qualify as deductible residential interest.
[b] The deductibility of this $9,500 loss may be limited by the passive loss rules (see Chapter I:8). ◀

The rule of Sec. 280A regarding the rental of residential property is summarized in Figure I:6-4.

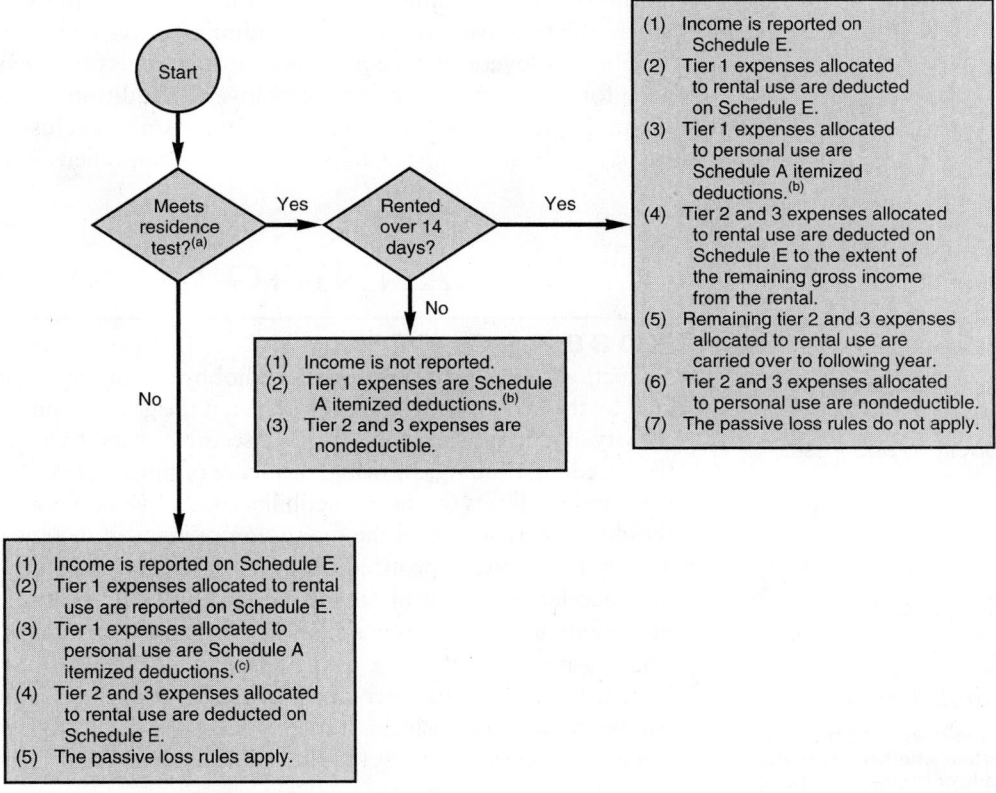

(a) Personal use is more than the larger of (1) 14 days or (2) 10% of rental days.
(b) In order for the interest to be deductible, it must be "qualified residence interest" (see Chapter 7).
(c) In order for the interest to be deductible as qualified residence interest, the property must not have been rented at all during the year. If the property has been rented out, the interest allocated to personal use is not deductible (see Chapter 7).

FIGURE I:6-4 ▶ SECTION 280A: LIMITATION OF DEDUCTIONS ON RENTAL OF RESIDENTIAL PROPERTY

EXPENSES OF AN OFFICE IN THE HOME

Unless the taxpayer meets certain strictly imposed requirements, Sec. 280A disallows any deduction for home office expenses. In general, for a taxpayer to deduct office-in-home expenses, the taxpayer must use the office regularly and exclusively as either of the following:

▶ The principal place of business for a trade or business of the taxpayer, or

▶ A place where the taxpayer meets or deals with clients in the normal course of business.

What would you do in this Situation?

Serious Wine or Hobby Loss?

Mr. Bouteilles Gerbeuses has been your long-time tax client. He has amassed an impressive portfolio of real estate, securities, and joint venture investments. His net worth is substantial.

Despite all his material well-being, Mr. Gerbeuses wants to take on a new challenge—that of producing fine wines. He has not had any formal wine training but he has decided to start his own winery, named *Cuvée de Prestige.* He will pattern it after the great wine houses of Europe.

He already owns several hundred acres of agriculturally zoned land in the wine producing region of the Noir Valley. It happens to adjoin his home in the Wemadeit Country Club and Retirement Resort subdivision. He anticipates a life of semi-retirement by engaging in the art of malolactic fermentation and blending of his *blanc de blancs* and *pinot noir* grapes into his own estate wine. He expects his start-up capital investment to be over $5 million and does not expect the first harvest to take place for at least seven years after the initial planting of grape vines. He expects to offset any losses by his other income.

Assuming Mr. Gerbeuses comes to you for tax advice on his new wine venture, what tax and ethical issues should be considered?

The term "principal place of business" includes a home office used by the taxpayer for administrative or management activities of the business if no other fixed location exists where the taxpayer conducts these administrative or managerial activities.

For employees to take a deduction for home office expenses, the use must also have been for the convenience of the employer. In addition, a separate structure not attached to the taxpayer's house may qualify if regularly and exclusively used in connection with the taxpayer's business. (See Chapter I:9 for a comprehensive discussion of these rules.)

TAX PLANNING CONSIDERATIONS

OBJECTIVE 7

Describe tax planning considerations for deductions and losses

HOBBY LOSSES

Deductions for expenses incurred in a hobby activity may not exceed the gross income generated by the hobby for the year. However, if the gross income exceeds the deductions from the activity in at least three out of five consecutive years (two out of seven for activities involving the breeding, training, showing, or racing of horses), tax law presumes the activity is a business, and the limits on the deductibility of expenses do not apply. Thus, if possible, taxpayers should use care in timing the realization of items of income and expense. For example, if an activity has shown a profit in only two out of the previous four years, a taxpayer may consider accelerating some of the income into the fifth year or deferring some of the expenses of the activity into the following year. Under the cash method of accounting, this can be done by delaying payment for some of the expenses or accelerating income-generating transactions. Note that meeting the three-out-of-five-year test does not automatically ensure the activity will be treated as a business. It merely compels the IRS to prove the activity is *not* a business. Under these circumstances, the IRS is less likely to challenge the deductions.

ETHICAL POINT

In some cases it is difficult to ascertain whether an activity is a trade or business or a hobby. A CPA should not prepare or sign a tax return unless he or she in good faith believes that the return takes a position that has substantial authority.

UNREASONABLE COMPENSATION

If the IRS feels that a salary payment to an officer of a corporation is excessive, it may recharacterize the excess portion as a dividend. If that happens, the corporation cannot deduct the full amount of the salary payment. To prevent a potential future disallowance, the parties may enter into a payback or hedge agreement, which provides that the employee must return to the corporation any payment held to be excessive. Under such an agreement, the employee receives a *for* AGI deduction for any amount he or she repays to the corporation. This deduction is available in the year of repayment. A payback agreement must meet the following requirements to be effective:

▶ The parties must enter into the agreement before actually making the payment.

▶ It must legally obligate the employee to repay the excess amount.[54]

---

[54] *Vincent E. Oswald*, 49 T.C. 645 (1968) and *J. G. Pahl*, 67 T.C. 286 (1976). See also *Ernest H. Berger*, 37 T.C. 1026 (1962).

The IRS may take the position that the existence of the payback agreement itself is evidence that the compensation is excessive. The corporation and employees can avoid this situation if they include the agreement in the general corporate bylaws rather than in a specific contract with a particular employee.[55]

TIMING OF DEDUCTIONS

Because of the time value of money, taxpayers generally prefer to deduct an expenditure as a current expense rather than capitalize it and spread the deductions over the next several years as depreciation or amortization. In addition, some capital expenditures (e.g., land) are not subject to depreciation or amortization. In some situations, however, the taxpayer may prefer to capitalize rather than expense a particular item. For example, if a taxpayer has net operating losses (NOLs) that are about to expire, a current deduction may prevent the use of these losses.[56]

In some cases it is difficult to determine whether an item should be treated as a capital expenditure or a deduction item (e.g., certain repairs may require capitalization). Because of this conflict, the Treasury has recently issued some new regulations that provide very detailed guidance on when an expenditure is to be capitalized and when it may be currently deducted. In addition, the taxpayer may elect to either capitalize or expense certain types of expenditures—such as those for research and experimentation. A tax practitioner should give consideration to the taxpayer's tax situation when making this decision. In making this decision, taxpayers and their advisors should consider NOL carryovers that might be expiring. They should also compare their current marginal tax rate with their anticipated future marginal tax rate.

COMPLIANCE AND PROCEDURAL CONSIDERATIONS

OBJECTIVE 8

Describe compliance and procedural considerations for deductions and losses

PROPER CLASSIFICATION OF DEDUCTIONS

Individuals report trade or business expenses on Schedule C (Profit or Loss from Business or Profession). It is similar to an income statement for business-related income and expenses. Income reported on Form 1040 includes the net income computed on Schedule C, because the process of arriving at the taxable income from the business involves deducting business-related expenses. Thus, these expenses are deductions *for* AGI. Similar treatment is given to expenses attributable to the production of rental and royalty income reported on Schedule E, which is an income statement. The other deductions *for* AGI have specific lines on Form 1040 itself.[57] All of these deductions appear before line 37 (where AGI appears) of Form 1040.

Deductions *from* AGI are reported on Schedule A, where they are totaled and then transferred to Line 40 of Form 1040.

A filled-in Schedule C is provided in Appendix B.

SELF-STUDY QUESTION

A professor in the Department of Accounting also teaches continuing education courses for the state CPA society as a sole proprietor. If she is a member of the state CPA society, are her dues deductible on Schedule C or as an itemized deduction?

ANSWER

Certainly, she would prefer to have the dues deductible on Schedule C so that they will not be subject to the 2% limit on miscellaneous itemized deductions. This question demonstrates the difficulty of classifying some deductions, and the answer probably depends on the primary reason for membership in the organization.

PROPER SUBSTANTIATION

The burden of proving the deductibility of any expense generally rests on the taxpayer. This has always been the case. However, in recent years Congress and the IRS have become increasingly concerned about the propriety of many deductions. In the case of travel and entertainment expenses, the Code states that taxpayers may not take a deduction for an improperly documented expense. This documentation must include the amount of the expense, the time and place of the travel or entertainment activity, the business purpose, and the business relationship of the people entertained.

BUSINESS VERSUS HOBBY

Self-employed individuals who claim a home office deduction on Schedule C must attach a Form 8829, used to allocate direct and indirect expenses to the appropriate use. Form 8829 need not be filed by employees who claim home office expenses on Form 2106.

When an activity has both profit-making and personal attributes, the burden is normally on the taxpayer to prove that the activity is a business. However, if a taxpayer can show that

---

[55] *Charles Schneider and Co. v. CIR,* 34 AFTR 2d 74-5422, 74-2 USTC ¶9563 (8th Cir., 1974). See also *Plastics Universal Corp.,* 1979 PH T.C. Memo ¶79,355, 39 TCM 32. Additionally, some taxpayers have been successful in defending their current level of compensation where they proved that they had been undercompensated in prior years. See *Acme Construction Co., Inc.,* 1995 RIA T.C. Memo ¶95,600, 69 TCM 1596.

[56] A NOL arises when business expenses exceed business income for a year. This excess can be carried to another year (generally back two years and

forward twenty years) and is deducted against the income of that year. If the years to which the NOL is carried do not have enough income, the NOL is lost when the carryover period expires. See Chapter I:8 for a discussion of NOLs.

[57] Some of these expenses, such as employee business expenses (Form 2106) and moving expenses (Form 3903), are summarized on separate forms. These separate forms, however, are not net income statements in the same sense as Schedules C and E.

the activity has generated a profit in at least three out of five consecutive years (two out of seven for activities involving the breeding, training, showing, and racing of horses), the burden of proof shifts to the IRS. Because the statute of limitations generally runs three years after a return is filed for any particular year (i.e., for audit purposes the year closes and the IRS cannot assess any tax deficiency for that year), a potential problem exists for taxpayers who want to rely on this presumption during the first year or two of an activity's life. In these cases, the taxpayer may elect to defer the determination of whether the presumption applies until the fifth (seventh) year of operation. The election keeps the year in question open with respect to that activity until sufficient years have passed to allow for application of the presumptive test. If the taxpayer subsequently does not meet the presumptive test, the IRS can still assess a deficiency for that activity for the prior year, because the year is still open. A taxpayer makes the election by filing Form 5213 (Election to Postpone Determination as to Whether the Presumption That an Activity Is Engaged In for Profit Applies) within three years after the due date for the year in which the taxpayer first engages in the activity.

PROBLEM MATERIALS

DISCUSSION QUESTIONS

I:6-1 Why is the distinction between deductions *for* AGI and deductions *from* AGI important for individuals?

I:6-2 Sam owns a small house that he rents out to students attending the local university. Are the expenses associated with the rental unit deductions *for* or *from* AGI?

I:6-3 During the year, Sara sold a capital asset at a loss of $2,000. She had held the asset as an investment. This is the only capital asset she sold during the year. Is her deduction for this capital loss a deduction *for* or a deduction *from* AGI?

I:6-4 Joe is a single, self-employed individual who owns his own business. During 2015 Joe reported $200,000 gross income and $60,000 expenses from his business. He also paid $30,000 in alimony to his former spouse, $4,000 mortgage interest on his personal home, $6,000 for health insurance premiums, and $2,000 for medicine and doctors. Ignoring any self-employment tax on the business income, what is Joe's AGI for 2015?

I:6-5 For 2015, Mario, a single individual with no dependents, receives income of $55,000 and incurs deductible expenses of $9,000.
a. What is Mario's taxable income assuming that the expenses are deductions *for* AGI?
b. What is Mario's taxable income assuming that the expenses are miscellaneous itemized deductions *from* AGI?

I:6-6 Deductible business or investment expenses must be related to a profit-motivated activity.
a. What are the factors used in determining whether an activity is profit-motivated?
b. Why are these factors so important in making this determination?

I:6-7 If an activity does not generate a profit in three out of five consecutive years, is it automatically deemed to be a hobby? Why or why not?

I:6-8 Because expenses incurred both in a business and for the production of investment income are deductible, why is it important to determine in which category a particular activity falls?

I:6-9 In order for a business expense to be deductible it must be *ordinary, necessary,* and *reasonable.* Explain what these terms mean.

I:6-10 What are the criteria for distinguishing between a deductible expense and a capital expenditure?

I:6-11 Why are expenses related to tax-exempt income disallowed?

I:6-12 Under what circumstances may a taxpayer deduct an illegal bribe or kickback?

I:6-13 Michelle pays a CPA $400 for the preparation of her federal income tax return. Michelle's only sources of income are her salary from employment and interest and dividends from her investments.
a. Is this a deductible expense? If so, is it a deduction *for* or *from* AGI?
b. Assume the same facts as in Part a except that in addition to her salary and investment and dividend income, Michelle also owns a small business. Of the $400 fee paid to the CPA, $250 is for the preparation of her Schedule C (Profit or Loss from Business). How much, if any, of the $400 is a deductible expense? Identify it as either *for* or *from* AGI.

I:6-14 Otter Corporation sends people to the state capital to lobby the legislature to build a proposed highway that is planned to run through the area where its business is located.
a. If Otter Corp. incurs $3,200 of expenses, what part, if any, of its expenses are deductible?
b. Would it make a difference if the proposed road were a city road rather than a state highway, and Otter lobbied its local government?
c. Assume the same facts in Part a except that Otter's total in-house expenses are $1,500. Are these expenses deductible?

I:6-15 During November and December of last year, Tommy's, Inc., incurred the following expenses in investigating the feasibility of opening a new restaurant in town:

Expenses to do a market survey $3,800
Expenses to identify potential
suppliers of goods $2,000
Expenses to identify a proper
location $1,000

Explain the proper treatment of these expenses under the following scenarios:
a. Tommy's, Inc., already owns another restaurant in town and is wanting to expand. Tommy's, Inc. opens the new restaurant in February of the current year.
b. Assume that Tommy's, Inc. is in the book selling business and feels that its bookstore business is not making a high enough return and it wants to move into the restaurant business. It opens the restaurant in February of the current year.
c. Same as Part b except Tommy's decides against opening a restaurant after getting back the results of the investigation.

I:6-16 What documentation is required in order for a travel or entertainment expense to be deductible?

I:6-17 Under what circumstances can prepaid expenses be deducted in the year of payment by a taxpayer using the cash method of accounting?

I:6-18 Under what circumstances would a taxpayer use both the cash method and the accrual method of accounting at the same time?

I:6-19 The timing of when the economic performance test is satisfied depends on the type of transaction and whether the transaction is recurring.
a. When does economic performance occur for a taxpayer who must provide property or services to another person?
b. When does economic performance occur when another person provides the taxpayer with property or services?
c. Explain the exception to the economic performance test for recurring liabilities.

I:6-20 Why did Congress enact the wash sale provisions?

I:6-21 The wash sale rules disallow a loss in the year of sale when substantially identical stock or securities are acquired by the taxpayer within a 61-day period. What types of stock or securities are considered substantially identical?

I:6-22 Under Sec. 267, current deductions may not be taken for certain transactions between related parties.
a. Who is considered a member of a taxpayer's family under the related party transaction rules of Sec. 267?
b. Identify some of the other relationships that are considered related parties for purposes of Sec. 267. Why are these other relationships included in the definition?

I:6-23 Under the related party rules of Sec. 267, why has Congress imposed the concept of constructive ownership?

I:6-24 If property is sold at a loss to a related taxpayer, under what circumstances can at least partial benefit be derived from the disallowed loss?

I:6-25 Assume that Jill is engaged in painting as a hobby. During the year, she earns $1,000 from sales of her paintings and incurs $1,300 expenses for supplies and lessons. Jill's salary from her job is $70,000. What is the tax treatment of the hobby income and expenses?

I:6-26 Under Sec. 280A, what constitutes personal use of a vacation home by the taxpayer?

I:6-27 Under Sec. 280A, how are expenses allocated to the rental use of a vacation home? In what order must the expenses be deducted against the gross income of the property?

I:6-28 Under Sec. 280A, how will a taxpayer report the income and expenses of a vacation home if it is rented out for only 12 days during the year?

ISSUE IDENTIFICATION QUESTIONS

I:6-29 David, a CPA for a large accounting firm, often works 10- to 12-hour days. As a requirement for his position, he must attend social events to recruit new clients. In addition to his job with the accounting firm, he also has private clients in his unincorporated marketing business. David purchased exercise equipment for $3,000. He works out on the equipment to maintain his stamina and good health that enable him to carry such a heavy workload. What tax issues should David consider?

I:6-30 Gus, a football player who was renegotiating his contract with the Denver Broncos, paid his ex-girlfriend $50,000 to drop a sexual assault complaint against him and keep the matter confidential. The Broncos stated that if criminal charges were filed and made public, they would terminate his employment. What tax issues should Gus consider?

I:6-31 Kathleen pays $3,000 mortgage interest on the home that she and her husband live in. Kathleen and her husband live with Molly, Kathleen's mother. The title to the home is in Kathleen's name. However, the mortgage is Molly's obligation. Kathleen claims Molly as her dependent on her current tax return. What tax issues should Kathleen consider?

I:6-32 Katie and Alan are avid boaters and water skiers. They also enjoy parasailing. This year, they started a new parasailing venture to give rides to patrons. Katie and Alan are both employed full-time in other pursuits, but they take patrons out during the summer months, on weekends and holidays. Alan has attended classes on boat operation and parasailing instruction. Katie and Alan have owned a boat for four years, but because of the heavy usage this summer, they replaced their old boat in July. They plan on replacing their boat with a new one every two years now. They use their boat in the parasailing activity and for recreational purposes. This year, Katie and Alan earned $5,400 from chartering activities and incurred $11,600 of expenses associated with their boating and parasailing. What tax issues should Katie and Alan consider?

PROBLEMS

I:6-33 *For or From AGI Deductions.* Roberta is an accountant employed by a local firm. During the year, Roberta incurs the following unreimbursed expenses:

Item	Amount
Travel to client locations	$750
Subscriptions to professional journals	215
Taking potential clients to lunch	400
Photocopying	60
	$1,425

a. Identify which of these expenses are deductible and the amount that is deductible by Roberta. Indicate whether they are deductible *for* or *from* AGI.
b. Would the answers to Part a change if the accounting firm reimburses Roberta for these expenses under an accountable plan?
c. Assume all of the same facts as in Part a, except that Roberta is self-employed. Identify which of the expenses are deductible, and indicate whether they are deductions *for* or *from* AGI.

I:6-34 *For vs. from AGI.* During 2015, Kent, a 40-year-old single taxpayer, reports the following items of income and expense:

Income:	
Salary	$150,000
Dividends from Alta Corporation	800
Interest income from a savings account	1,500
Rental income from a small apartment he owns	8,000
Expenses:	
Medical	6,000
Interest on a principal residence	7,000
Real property taxes on the principal residence	4,300
Charitable contributions	4,000
Casualty loss—personal	6,100
Miscellaneous itemized deductions	1,200
Loss from the sale of Delta Corporation stock (held for two years)	2,000
Expenses incurred on the rental apartment:	
Maintenance	500
Property taxes	1,000
Utilities	2,400
Depreciation	1,700
Insurance	800
Alimony payments to former wife	10,000

Assuming all of these items are deductible and that the amounts are before any limitations, what is Kent's taxable income for the year?

I:6-35 *Capitalization vs. Expense.* Sam owns a small apartment building (this is the only rental building Sam owns). During the year Sam incurs the following expenditures:

Item	Amount
Replace roof and roof underlying structure because of building code requirements	$30,000
Repaint the interior	3,000
Repair door handles and door locks	1,000
Replace broken windows	1,500
Replace crumbling sidewalks and stairs because of building code requirements	25,000

Discuss the proper tax treatment for these expenditures.

I:6-36 *Political Contributions and Lobbying Expenses.* Eljay, LLP owns several apartment complexes and office buildings. The leasing and management of these buildings constitutes Eljay's only business activity. During the current year Eljay incurred the following:

- $900 in airfare and lodging for a trip to Washington, D.C. The purpose of the trip was to protest proposed tax rate increases for individuals and corporations.
- $700 for renting space on billboards along the highway. The billboards express its concern regarding pending legislation that would significantly increase property taxes.
- $500 in airfare and hotel bills incurred on a trip to the state capital. The purpose of the trip was to meet with the legislative subcommittee on property taxation.
- $50 for a subscription to a political newsletter published by a national political party.
- $150 in making a presentation to the county council protesting a proposed increase in the property tax levy.

a. What is the total amount Eljay may deduct because of these expenditures?
b. Assume all the same facts as in Part a except that the expenses for the trip to the state capital are only $300 instead of $500. What amount may Eljay deduct because of these expenditures?

I:6-37 *Legal and Accounting Expenses.* Sam is a sole proprietor who owns, leases, and manages several apartment complexes and office buildings. During the current year, Sam incurs the following expenses. Which of these expenditures are deductible? Are they *for* or *from* AGI deductions?

a. $200 in attorney's fees for title searches on a new property Sam has acquired.
b. $450 in legal fees in an action brought to collect back rents.
c. $500 to his CPA for the preparation of his federal income tax return. $400 is for the preparation of Schedule C (Profit or Loss from Business).
d. $300 in attorney's fees for drafting a will.
e. $250 in attorney's fees in an unsuccessful attempt to prevent the city from rezoning the area of the city where several of his office buildings are located.

I:6-38 *Illegal Payments.* Damian Corporation is engaged in the business of purchasing and importing carpets from Iran. Importing these carpets from Iran is illegal. Following is a list of income and expense items for the year:

Item	Amount
Sales	$750,000
Cost of goods sold	270,000
Salaries	75,000
Freight	22,500
Bribes to customs officials	30,000
Lease payments on warehouses	15,000
Interest expense	12,000

a. What is the taxable income of Damian Corporation from the illegal business activity?
b. Assume the same facts as in Part a except that Damian's business consists of buying and selling marijuana and cocaine. What is Damian's taxable income from this illegal business activity?

I:6-39 *Illegal Payments.* Indicate whether Glenda can deduct the $5,000 payment in each of the following independent situations.

a. Glenda is a supplier of medical supplies. In order to secure a large sales contract to the regional Veterans Affairs Hospital, Glenda makes a gift of $5,000 to the hospital's purchasing agent. The payment is illegal under state law.
b. Assume the same facts as in Part a, except that the payment is made to the purchasing agent of a government-owned hospital in Brazil.
c. Assume the same facts in Part a, except that the payment is made to the purchasing agent of a privately owned hospital in Idaho.

I:6-40 *Business Investigation Expenditures.* During January and February of the current year, Big Bang LLC incurs $3,000 in travel, feasibility studies, and legal expenses to investigate the feasibility of opening a new entertainment gallery in one of the new suburban malls in town. Big Bang already owns two other entertainment galleries in other malls in town.

a. What is the proper tax treatment of these expenses if Big Bang decides not to open the new gallery?
b. What is the proper tax treatment of these expenses if Big Bang decides to open the new gallery?

I:6-41   *Business Investigation Expenditures.* Assume the same facts as in Problem I:6-40, except that Big Bang LLC incurs $41,000 in expenses, it does *not* already own the other entertainment galleries and it does not own anything similar.
   a. What is the proper tax treatment of these expenses if Big Bang does not open the new gallery?
   b. What is the proper tax treatment of these expenses if Big Bang decides to open the new gallery on May 1 of the current year and makes the appropriate election under Sec. 195?

I:6-42   *Timing of Expense Recognition.* Solutions Corporation, a computer vendor and consulting company, uses the accrual method of accounting. Its tax year is the calendar year. The following are three of the corporation's transactions during the current year:
   1. Solutions Corporation hired a contractor to remodel its sales floor. The contractor completed the remodeling on November 30. On December 15, Solutions received a $5,000 bill from the contractor. Solutions immediately contacted the contractor to contest $1,000 of the total charges, arguing that it exceeded the price that was agreed upon. Solutions didn't make any payment on the bill during its current tax year.
   2. Solutions offers a 2-year warranty on all of its computer systems. For sales of computers in the current year, it paid $11,500 to service warranties during the current tax year, and it expects to pay $12,000 to fulfill the remaining warranty obligations next year.
   3. Every year, Solutions offers a series of six trade seminars from November 1 through April 30. It receives all registration fees from participants by October 1, before the seminars begin. As of December 31, two of the six seminars are completed, and the next seminar is scheduled for January 14–15. The expenses incurred in performing the seminars are routine each year. On the first of each month from November through April, Solutions pays the $625 monthly rent for the seminar location. On September 16, Solutions signs a contract with the seminar teacher, a computers expert and excellent public speaker. The contract requires Solutions to pay the teacher $900 after each seminar, a total of $5,400. On October 3, Solutions signs a contract with a local printing company, which will provide text materials for the seminars. Solutions pays the printer $350 after each seminar's materials are delivered the day before the seminar.
   Required:
   a. How should Solutions Corporation treat these transactions? What rules apply?
   b. How would your answers change for each of the transactions if Solutions Corporation were a cash-method taxpayer?

I:6-43   *Prepaid Expenses.* Pamello, Inc., an engineering consulting firm, uses the cash method of accounting and is a calendar year taxpayer. Compute the amount of Pamello's current year deductions for the following transactions:
   a. On November 1 of the current year, it entered into a lease to rent some office space for five years. The lease agreement states that the lease payments are $12,000 per year, payable in advance each November 1 for the following 12-month period. Under the terms of the lease, Pamello is required to pay a $5,000 deposit, refundable upon the termination of the lease.
   b. On December 1 of the current year, Pamello also renewed its malpractice insurance, paying $18,000 for the three-year contract.
   c. On December 31 of the current year, Pamello mailed out a check for $5,000 for drafting services performed for it during the current year by an individual who lives in another city.
   d. On December 31, the firm received a shipment of $700 worth of stationery and other office supplies. Pamello has an open charge account with the office supply company, which bills the firm monthly for charges made during the year.
   e. On December 31, Pamello picked up some work that a local printing company had done for it, which amounted to $1,000. The firm charged the $1,000 with its corporate credit card.

I:6-44   *Prepaid Interest.* During the current year, Richard and Alisha, a married couple who use the cash method of accounting, purchased a principal residence for $320,000. They paid $40,000 down and financed the remaining $280,000 of the purchase price with a 30-year mortgage. At the closing, they also paid $500 for an appraisal, $500 for a title search, and 1.5 points representing additional interest over the term of the loan. At the end of the year, Richard and Alisha received a statement from the mortgage company indicating that $12,000 of their total monthly payments made during the year represents interest and $1,000 is a reduction of the principal balance.
   a. What is the total amount Richard and Alisha may deduct in the current year arising from the purchase and ownership of their home?
   b. What is the treatment of the other items that are not deductible?

I:6-45 *Wash Sales.* Broward Corp. owns 1,500 shares of Silver Fox Corporation common stock. Broward Corp. purchased the 1,500 shares on April 17, 2009, for $20,000. On December 8, 2014, Broward sells 750 shares for $5,000. On January 2, 2015, Broward Corp. buys 250 shares of Silver Fox Corporation common stock for $1,750 and 50 shares of Silver Fox Corporation preferred stock for $1,000. The preferred stock is nonvoting, nonconvertible.
a. What is Broward's realized and recognized loss on the December 8 sale of stock?
b. What is Broward's basis and the holding periods of the stock?

I:6-46 *Wash Sales.* Cougar Corporation owns 1,000 shares of Western Corporation common stock, which it purchased on March 8, 2009, for $12,000. On October 3, 2015, Cougar purchases an additional 300 shares for $3,000. On October 12, 2015, it sells the original 1,000 shares for $8,500. On November 1, 2015, it purchases an additional 500 shares for $4,000.
a. What is Cougar's recognized gain or loss as a result of the sale on October 12, 2015?
b. What are the basis and the holding period of the stock Cougar continues to hold?
c. How would your answers to Parts a and b change if the stock Cougar purchases during 2015 is Western nonvoting, nonconvertible, preferred stock instead of Western common stock?

I:6-47 *Constructive Ownership.* During the current year, Troy sells land to Berry Corporation for $165,000. Troy purchased the land for investment in 2000 for $170,000. Berry Corporation is owned as follows:

Owner	Percentage Ownership
Tom (Troy's son)	20%
Jimmy (Troy's cousin)	15%
Jimmy's father (Troy's uncle)	30%
Angie (Troy's wife)	10%
Nicole (Angie's Sister)	25%

Troy and Jimmy are equal partners in a separate entity, TJ Partnership.
a. What is Troy's constructive ownership in Berry Corporation?
b. What is the amount of loss Troy may recognize?
c. How would your answers to Parts a and b change if TJ Partnership owned 25%, instead of Nicole?

I:6-48 *Constructive Ownership.* PIB Partnership is owned 20% by Sara, 40% by Steve, and 40% by Thann. Burnham, Inc. is owned 70% by PIB Partnership, 10% by Ralph, 10% by Thann, and 10% by Sara. Ralph and Thann are brothers. All other individuals are unrelated. During the current year, Ralph sold a piece of land to Burnham, Inc., for $90,000. Ralph originally purchased the land as an investment a few years ago for $100,000.
a. How much of the loss may Ralph recognize?
b. Now assume all the same facts except that the sale occurred between Thann and Burnham, Inc. How much of the loss may Thann recognize?
c. Now assume the same facts as in b except that Burnham, Inc., is owned 60% by Sara and 40% by Ralph. Thann sells the land to Burnham, Inc. How much of the loss may Thann recognize?

I:6-49 *Related Party Transactions.* Sally is an attorney who computes her taxable income using the cash method of accounting. Sage Corporation, owned 40% by Sally's brother, 40% by her cousin, and 20% by her grandmother, uses the accrual method of accounting. Sally is a calendar-year taxpayer, whereas Sage Corporation's fiscal year ends on January 31. During 2014, Sally does some consulting work for Sage Corporation for a fee of $10,000. The work is completed on December 15 and Sage receives Sally's invoice on that date. For each of the following assumptions, answer the following questions: During which tax year must Sally report the income? During which tax year must Sage Corporation deduct the expense?
a. The payment to Sally is made on December 27, 2014.
b. The payment to Sally is made on January 12, 2015.
c. The payment to Sally is made on February 3, 2015.

I:6-50 *Related Party Transactions.* During the current year, CVI Corporation sells a tract of land for $75,000. The sale is made to Sandi, CVI Corporation's sole shareholder. CVI Corporation originally purchased the land five years earlier for $98,000.
a. What is the amount of gain or loss that CVI Corporation will recognize on the sale during the current year?

    b. Assume that in the following year, Sandi sells the land for $85,000. What is the amount of gain or loss Sandi will recognize? What are the tax consequences to CVI Corporation upon the subsequent sale by Sandi?

    c. Assume that in the following year, Sandi sells the land for $70,000. What is the amount of gain or loss Sandi will recognize?

    d. Assume that in the following year, Sandi sells the land for $105,000. What is the amount of gain or loss Sandi will recognize?

I:6-51 *Hobby Loss Presumptive Rule.* Rachel Schurtz is a high school English teacher. In her spare time, she likes to make her own body lotion, lip-gloss, and bath and shower gel. She uses the bath products herself and gives them to her friends and relatives as gifts. In 2013, Rachel started attending arts and crafts festivals three or four times a year to sell her products. She hands out her business card so her customers can buy directly from her by phone or email. In 2013, Rachel reported a net loss of $375 from the activity. In 2014, she reported a loss of $460. Rachel is audited for the year 2014, and the agent disallows the $460 loss. Rachel is confident she will make a profit on her sales in 2015, and she assumes she will continue to make a profit after 2015. Rachel is not sure that she can prove that her activity is not a hobby right now. What can she do to delay or avoid having to prove to the IRS that her loss is not a hobby loss?

I:6-52 *Hobby Loss Presumptive Rule.* Emily is an interior decorator who does consulting work for several furniture stores. Additionally, she has been designing and creating rubber stamps for the past several years. She sells the stamps to local stationary and novelty shops. Emily has reported the following net income or loss from the rubber stamp activity:

Year	Net Income (Loss)
2010	$ 300
2011	(900)
2012	(400)
2013	600
2014	(550)
2015	(800)

Emily is audited for the year 2015, and the agent disallows the $800 loss. Can Emily make an election for 2015 to keep the year open in anticipation of meeting the presumptive rule for the year? Why or why not?

I:6-53 *Hobby Losses.* Chuck, a dentist, raises prize rabbits for breeding and showing purposes. Assume that the activity is determined to be a hobby. During the year the activity generates the following items of income and expense:

Item	Amount
Sale of rabbits for breeding stock	$800
Prizes and awards	300
Property taxes on rabbit hutches	200
Feed	600
Veterinary fees	500
Depreciation on rabbit hutches	250

    a. What is the total amount of deductions Chuck may take during the year with respect to the rabbit raising activities?

    b. Identify which expenses may be deducted and indicate whether they are deductions *for* or *from* AGI.

    c. By what amount is the cost basis of the rabbit hutches to be reduced for the year?

I:6-54 *Hobby Losses.* Assume the same facts as in Problem I:6-53, except that the income from the sale of rabbits is $1,200.

    a. What is the total amount of deductions Chuck may take during the year with respect to the rabbit raising activities?

    b. Identify which expenses may be deducted and indicate whether they are deductions *for* or *from* AGI.

    c. By what amount is the cost basis of the rabbit hutches to be reduced for the year?

I:6-55
Rental of Vacation Home. During the current year, Kim incurs the following expenses with respect to her beachfront condominium in Hawaii:

Item	Amount
Insurance	$ 500
Repairs and maintenance	700
Interest on mortgage	3,000
Property taxes	1,000
Utilities	800

In addition to the expenses listed above, Kim could have deducted a total of $8,000 depreciation if the property had been acquired only for investment purposes. During the year, Kim uses the condominium 20 days for vacation. She also rents it out for a total of 60 days during the year, generating a total gross income of $9,000.
a. What is the total amount of deductions for and from AGI that Kim may take during the current year with respect to the condominium?
b. What is the effect on the basis of the condominium?

I:6-56
Rental of Vacation Home. Assume all of the same facts as in Problem I:6-55, except that during the year Kim rents the condominium a total of 14 days. How does Kim report the income and deductions from the property?

COMPREHENSIVE PROBLEMS

I:6-57
Bryce, a bank official, is married and files a joint return. During 2015 he engages in the following activities and transactions:
a. Being an avid fisherman, Bryce develops an expertise in tying flies. At times during the year, he is asked to conduct fly-tying demonstrations, for which he is paid a small fee. He also periodically sells flies that he makes. Income generated from these activities during the year is $2,500. The expenses for the year associated with Bryce's fly-tying activity include $125 personal property taxes on a small trailer that he uses exclusively for this purpose, $2,900 in supplies, $270 in repairs on the trailer, and $200 in gasoline for traveling to the demonstrations.
b. Bryce sells a small building lot to his brother for $40,000. Bryce purchased the lot four years ago for $47,000, hoping to make a profit.
c. Bryce enters into the following stock transactions: (None of the stock qualifies as small business stock.)

Date	Transaction
March 22	Purchases 100 shares of Silver Corporation common stock for $2,800.
April 5	Sells 200 shares of Gold Corporation common stock for $8,000. The stock was originally purchased two years ago for $5,000.
April 15	Sells 200 shares of Silver Corporation common stock for $5,400. The stock was originally purchased three years ago for $9,400.
May 20	Sells 100 shares of United Corporation common stock for $12,000. The stock was originally purchased five years ago for $10,000.

d. Bryce's salary for the year is $115,000. In addition to the items above, he also incurs $5,000 in other miscellaneous deductible itemized expenses. Assume that Bryce is not eligible for any other itemized deductions except items listed in the problem (including the election to deduct state and local sales tax instead of state and local income taxes).
Answer the following questions regarding Bryce's activities for the year.
1. Compute Bryce's taxable income for the year.
2. What is Bryce's basis in the Silver stock he continues to own?

I:6-58
Using the following facts, answer the questions below concerning Jaron's 2015 tax liability.
1. Two years ago, in November, 2013, when his wife died, Jaron left the CPA firm he was working for and started his own practice so he could have more time to spend with his four children. Jaron's children are 14, 16, 19, and 24 years old, respectively. The three youngest live at home with their father. Danny, Jaron's 19-year-old son, graduated from high school a year ago and is currently working at a local golf course. Danny earned $17,000 in the current year. Jaron's oldest daughter, Laura, is married and lives in town with her husband, Chad. Laura graduated from college two years ago and now works for a local advertising agency. What are Jaron's filing status and personal and dependency exemptions for 2015?
2. Jaron rents a small office downtown where he meets with clients and conducts business while his children are at school. He keeps all his client files and business records in this

office. In the evening, he uses a converted bedroom in his home as his office. The following expenses are allocated to his home office (by square feet):

- **a.** Depreciation $2,150
- **b.** Taxes $1,500
- **c.** Utilities $75

Can Jaron claim a deduction for his home office?

3. Jaron owns a condominium downtown. He rented it out 270 days during the year. He also allowed Laura and her husband to stay in the home rent-free for 24 days while they were looking for a place to stay. Fortunately, the condominium wasn't rented during the time they needed it. The following items of annual income and expense relate to the condominium:

- **a.** Rental income $18,000
- **b.** Interest $3,150
- **c.** Taxes $1,700
- **d.** Other expenses $6,000
- **e.** Depreciation $7,090

What is the tax treatment of the condominium for Jaron in 2015?

4. On April 6, Jaron sold a parcel of land he had held for investment to a real estate development firm for $75,000. He purchased the land three years earlier from his brother for $70,000. His brother had originally purchased the land for $74,000. What is the amount and character of Jaron's gain or loss on the sale of the land?

5. On May 1, Jaron purchased 1,000 shares in Genomics Ltd. for $10 per share. In December he was forced to sell all 1,000 shares at $8 per share to avoid a conflict of interest. What is the amount and character of Jaron's gain or loss on the sale of the stock?

6. Jaron reported the following items of income and expense from his consulting practice:

- **a.** Consulting fees received $185,000
- **b.** Wages expense $47,400
- **c.** Rent expense $20,000
- **d.** Depreciation $2,100
- **e.** Other expenses $17,000

What is Jaron's net income from his consulting practice?

7. Calculate Jaron's 2015 income tax liability. Ignore any available credits and self employment taxes and assume the standard deduction exceeds any itemized deductions Jaron has.

TAX STRATEGY PROBLEMS

I:6-59   Danielle Anderson, your client and a cash method taxpayer, works full-time at a music store located in a mall. She assists the manager in buying decisions, serves customers on the sales floor, and plays music to draw in customers. On the weekends, she plays in various orchestras, working as an independent contractor. She does not work under a business name, maintain an office, or maintain a separate bank account for her performing activities. She always pays her bills as soon as possible, well before the bill due date. In prior years, she has taken every allowable deduction related to the performing activities. Prior year returns show the following taxable income on her Schedule C:

2011	$(5,000)
2012	2,100
2013	3,000
2014	(1,800)

Danielle has come to you on December 12, 2015. She understands that the IRS can deny losses generated by her performing business if it determines the business is actually a hobby. Because of the uncertainty of the entertainment industry, she will likely continue to generate profits in some years and losses in others. Still, she continues the activities with the intent to earn a profit.

Danielle routinely sends bills to orchestra clients at the end of the month for work she performed during the month. Most of her clients, including the Springville Orchestra, send payment within ten days of when they receive her bill.

The following is a summary of the financial position of the business for 2015 as of 12/12/2015:

Income received to date	$9,000
General expenses paid to date	9,200

Other items:

Bill for refurbishing work on cello, due 1/2/2016	$ 300
Newspaper bill for monthly advertisement, due 1/14/2016	200
Printer bill for business cards, due 1/5/2016	500
Meals eaten while in transit to performance locations	150
Income for 12/3/2015 performance with the Springville Orchestra	1,000

What will you recommend to your client? What issues must you address? What actions will you take to ensure the most favorable tax outcome possible? What advice, if any, will you give your client for the future?

I:6-60   Peter Baumann, your client, wants to sell a printing press to Chamberlain Corporation for $50,000. Pete has used the press in his business for two years and its adjusted basis is $90,000. The Coxmann Partnership; Chloe International, Inc.; Watts, Inc., and Raleigh Corporation own Chamberlain Corporation equally. Pete and Emily Cox each own 50% of the Coxmann Partnership. Emily owns 70% of Chloe International, Inc., and Pete's sister Susan owns the other 30%. Pete's brother, Brian, owns 100% of Watts, Inc. Wade and Catherine Chamberlain, friends of Pete, own Raleigh Corporation equally. Peter wants to know what the tax consequences will be if he sells the printing press to Chamberlain Corporation. In a memo to Pete, explain any tax consequences of the proposed sale and any alternatives that would provide a better result.

TAX FORM/RETURN PREPARATION PROBLEMS

I:6-61   Dave Stevens, age 34, is a self-employed physical therapist. His wife Sarah, age 31, teaches English as a Second Language at a local language school. Dave's Social Security number is 111-11-1111. Sarah's Social Security number is 222-22-2222. Sarah and Dave have three children—Andrew, age 8; Isaac, age 6; and Mira, age 3. The children's Social Security numbers are, respectively, 333-33-3333, 444-44-4444, and 555-55-5555. They live at 12637 Pheasant Run, West Bend, Oregon 74658. They paid $8,900 in qualified residence interest and $2,400 in property taxes on their home. They had cash charitable contributions of $14,000. They also paid $180 to a CPA for preparing their federal and state income tax returns for the prior year, $100 of which was for the preparation of Dave's Schedule C. Sarah and Dave earned interest on CDs of $3,200. Sarah's salary for the year is $32,000, from which $9,600 in federal income tax and $1,400 in state income tax were withheld. Dave's office is located at Suite 402, 942 Woodview Drive, Portland, Oregon 74624, and his employer ID number is 11-1111111. Dave has been practicing for four years, and he uses the cash method of accounting. During the current year, Dave recorded the following items of income:

Revenue from patient visits	$300,000
Interest earned on the office checking balance	225

The following expenses were recorded on the office books:

Property taxes on the office	$ 4,500
Mortgage interest on the office	12,000
Depreciation on the office	4,500
Malpractice insurance	37,500
Utilities	3,750
Office staff salaries	51,000
Rent payments on equipment	15,000
Office magazine subscriptions	150
Office supplies	24,000
Medical journals	330

Dave pays $50 annually for use of a safety deposit box to store certain confidential documents related to his business. In addition to his medical practice, Dave spends 15 hours every week managing his real estate investments. To make sure he is aware of all current investment strategies and best practices, he subscribes to the following journals:

Wall Street Journal	$150
U.S. News & World Report	55
Money Magazine	45

Dave also paid $33,000 in estimated federal income taxes. Prepare Dave and Sarah's tax return (Form 1040, Schedules A, B, C, and SE) for the current year. Disregard any tax credits for which they may be eligible.

I:6-62 Lyle and Kaye James are married, have two minor children, Jessica, age 8 and Jerron, age 4, and are filing a joint tax return in the current year. They are both employed. Lyle and Kaye, ages 38 and 37, respectively, have combined salaries of $240,000, from which $48,000 of federal income tax and $10,000 of state income tax are withheld. Lyle and Kaye own two homes. Their primary residence is located at 11620 N. Mount Ave., New Haven, Connecticut 22222, and their vacation home is on the beach in Fort Lauderdale, Florida. They often rent their vacation home to supplement their income. The following items are related to the James' ownership of the two homes:

Item	New Haven	Fort Lauderdale
Rental income	$ —	$15,000
Qualified residence interest	7,200	5,000
Property taxes	1,400	1,000
Utilities	1,000	1,300
Repairs	200	300
Depreciation	0	3,500
Advertising	0	200
Insurance	1,500	1,500

The James family used their Fort Lauderdale home 20 days during the year. They rented the vacation home 60 days during the year. Lyle and Kaye jointly purchase stock in various corporations and make the following transactions in the current year. (None of the stock qualifies as small business stock.)

Date	Transaction	Price Paid/Sold
2/15	Bought 50 shares of Lake common stock (they own no other Lake stock)	$1,000
5/14	Bought 100 shares of Bass common stock (they own no other Bass stock)	3,000
5/24	Sold 25 shares of Lake common stock	250
5/27	Bought 50 shares of Lake common stock	900
	Sold 50 shares of Bass common stock	1,750
7/12	Bought 100 shares of Bass common stock	2,800

The James' have no other income or expense items. Lyle and Kaye's Social Security numbers are 111-22-3333 and 444-55-6666, respectively. Jessica and Jerron's Social Security numbers are 123-45-6789 and 888-99-1010. The James' use the IRS method of allocating all expenses between personal and rental use.

   File the James' income tax return Form 1040, Schedules A, D, and E using the currently available forms and rates. Disregard the alternative minimum tax and any tax credits for which they may be eligible.

I:6-63 Scarlet Furniture Corporation, an accrual-method taxpayer, retails custom office furniture. On January 1 of the current year, Peter Marlin and John Tanner incorporated Scarlet Furniture Corporation. Peter transferred $350,000 cash for 70% of Scarlet's outstanding stock, and John transferred $150,000 cash for 30% of the outstanding stock. Scarlet generated the following financial statements at the end of its first year of operations:

Scarlet Corporation's Balance Sheet

Assets

Cash	$ 91,400
Inventory	48,000
Other Current Assets	50,000
Office Equipment	170,000
Building	250,000
Accumulated Depreciation	(20,000)
Land	550,000
Total Assets	$1,139,400

Liabilities and Owner's Equity

Accrued Expenses	$ 100,000
Long Term Debt	400,000
Common Stock	500,000
Retained Earnings	139,400
Total Liabilities and Owners' Equity	$1,139,400

Scarlet Corporation's Income Statement

Revenues	$650,000
Costs of Goods Sold	100,000
Gross Income	$550,000
Advertising Expense	40,000
Depreciation Expense	20,000*
Miscellaneous Expense	10,600**
Office Supplies	5,000
Property Tax Expense	60,000
Wages & Salaries Expense	135,000***
Warranty Expense	10,000****
Operating Income	$269,400
Interest Expense	30,000
Federal Income Tax Expense	100,000
Net Income	$139,400

*Depreciation expense for tax purposes was $120,441 because Scarlet made a Sec. 179 election to expense $105,000 of the cost of the equipment purchased this year.
**Miscellaneous expense relates to a $600 penalty fee as a result of a breached customer contract and a $10,000 fine assessed by OSHA for hazardous conditions in its storage facility.
***Wages and salary expense includes Peter's salary of $40,000 and the accrual of $15,000 of bonuses payable to Peter which Scarlet actually paid on February 10 of the following year.
****The actual expenditure paid for warranty repairs during the year is $2,000.

Scarlet does not make any sales or purchases on account. Scarlet's employer identification number is 12-34567. Its address is 789 Presidential Way, Seattle, Washington 54789. Peter Marlin's Social Security number is 555-66-8888. During the current year, the Corporation made federal estimated income tax payments of $50,000.

Prepare a Form 1120 for the initial return for Scarlet.

CASE STUDY PROBLEM

I:6-64 John and Kathy Brown have just been audited and the IRS agent disallowed the business loss they claimed in 2013. The agent asserted that the activity was a hobby, not a business.

John and Kathy live in Rochester, New York, near Lake Ontario. Kathy is a CPA, and John was formerly employed by an insurance firm. John's firm moved in 2008 and John resolved not to move to the firm's new location. Instead of seeking other employment, John felt he could supplement his income by using his fishing expertise. He had been an avid fisherman for 15 years, and he owned a large Chris-Craft fly-bridge that he chartered to paying parties.

In 2009, Kathy and John developed a business plan, established a bank account for the charter activities, developed a bookkeeping system, and acquired insurance to cover the boat and the passengers. John fulfilled all the requirements to receive a U.S. Coast Guard operating license, a New York sport trolling license, and a seller's permit. These licenses and permits were necessary to legally operate a charter boat. The first year of their activity was 2009.

John advertised in local papers and regional sport fishing magazines. He usually had three or four half-day paying parties each week. John spent at least one day per week maintaining and repairing his boat. Kathy usually accompanied John on charters three or four times each year.

John's charter activity was unprofitable the first two years. In 2011, John and Kathy restructured the activity to improve profitability. The restructuring included increasing advertising, participating in outdoor shows, and negotiating small contracts with local businesses. After the restructuring, the activity provided a small profit in 2011 and 2012.

In 2013, John started working with another insurance company in the area on a full-time basis. Even though he returned to the insurance business, John normally took two paying parties and one nonpaying, promotional party each week throughout the fishing season. John's costs unexpectedly increased and he lost $8,000 in the activity during 2013. John and Kathy deducted the entire loss on Schedule C of their 2013 tax return.

Required: Prepare a memo to the Browns recommending what position they should take and why. Show the logic used in arriving at your recommendation.

TAX RESEARCH PROBLEM

I:6-65

Richard Penn lives in Harrisburg, Pennsylvania. Richard is the president of an architectural firm. Richard has become known throughout the community for excellent work and honesty in his business dealings. Richard believes his reputation is an integral part of the success of the firm.

Oil was found recently in the area around Harrisburg and some geologists believed the reserves were large. A few well-respected businesspeople organized Oil Company to develop a few wells. Although some oil was being extracted, the oil corporation lacked capital to develop the oil fields to their expected potential. After reading the geologists' report, Richard felt that Oil Company was a good investment; therefore, he acquired 25% of the company. A short time after Richard's acquisition, the price of foreign oil decreased sharply. The drop in foreign oil prices caused Oil Company to be unprofitable due to its high production costs. Three months later Oil Company filed bankruptcy.

The bankruptcy proceedings were reported in the local newspaper. Many of Oil Company's creditors were real estate developers that engaged Richard's architectural firm to provide designs. After Oil Company declared bankruptcy the architectural firm's business noticeably decreased.

Richard felt the decline in business was related to the bankruptcy of Oil Company. Richard convinced his partner to use the accumulated earnings of the firm to repay all the creditors of Oil Company.

Richard has asked you whether his firm can deduct the expenses of repaying Oil Company's creditors. After completing your research explain to Richard why the expenses are or are not deductible.

A partial list of research sources is as follows:

- Sec. 162
- *Thomas H. Welch v. Helvering*, 12 AFTR 1456, 3 USTC ¶1164 (USSC, 1933)
- *William A. Thompson, Jr.,* 1983 PH T.C. Memo ¶83,487, 46 TCM 1109

TAX RESEARCH CASE

I:6-66

Three years ago, Paul Wilde exercised all his stock options in the start up company he helped establish and walked away with over $100 million. Since that time, he has spent all his energy, time, and effort in managing his portfolio. His investment philosophy is one of steady, careful investment in a well-balanced portfolio. Thus, although each year he engages in several sales and purchases, he generally buys and holds the securities for both the dividends and the growth potential. Consequently, most of the stock sales he makes are of securities he has held for over one year. Because his investment activities have grown so large, this year he rented a suite of offices and hired two investment advisors and five secretaries to help him. He also purchased several new computers and some new office furniture for the office.

Paul has now come to you for some tax help. Specifically, he would like to know if his activities are considered a business or an investment activity. In your explanation, please include whether the expenses incurred in the activity are deductions *for* or *from* AGI.

A partial list of research sources is as follows:

- *Higgins v. CIR*, 25 AFTR 1160, 41-1 USTC §9233 (USSC, 1941)
- *Estate of Louis Yaeger, Deceased, Judith Winters, Ralph Meisels, Abraham J. Weber and the Bank of New York*, 889 F2d 29, 89-2 USTC ¶9633 (CA-2)
- *Frederick Mayer and Jan Perry Mayer*, 67 TCM 2949 (1994)
- *Rudolph W. and Abbie A. Steffler*, 69 TCM 2940 (1995)
- Sec. 179

CHAPTER

7

ITEMIZED DEDUCTIONS

LEARNING OBJECTIVES

After studying this chapter, you should be able to

1 ▶ Identify qualified medical expenses and compute the medical expense deduction

2 ▶ Identify taxes that are deductible as itemized deductions

3 ▶ Identify different types of interest deductions

4 ▶ Compute the amount of a charitable contribution deduction and identify limitations

5 ▶ Discuss casualty and theft losses

6 ▶ Identify certain miscellaneous itemized deductions subject to the 2% of AGI limit

7 ▶ Describe tax planning considerations for itemized deductions

8 ▶ Describe compliance and procedural considerations for itemized deductions

As explained in Chapter I:6, most deductible expenses for individuals fit into three general categories:

► Expenses incurred in a trade or business

► Expenses incurred for the production of income (an investment activity) or for tax advice

► Certain specified personal expenses

If an expense is deductible based on the above categories, the expense must be classified as either *for* AGI or *from* AGI. The distinction between *for* and *from* AGI was discussed in Chapter I:6. This chapter focuses on deductions *from* AGI, also referred to as **itemized deductions**, which include medical expenses, taxes, interest, and charitable contributions. Chapter I:9 discusses other itemized deductions, such as employee business expenses, and Chapter I:8 discusses casualty losses on personal-use property.

In arriving at taxable income, individuals may subtract from AGI the larger of the standard deduction or the sum of all itemized deductions. In calculating the sum of the itemized deductions, certain deductions are subject to reductions and limitations.

MEDICAL EXPENSES

OBJECTIVE 1

Identify qualified medical expenses and compute the medical expense deduction

Medical expenses, which comprise one category of deductible personal expenditures, are deductible because Congress felt that excessive medical expenses might ultimately affect a taxpayer's ability to pay his or her federal income tax. However, under Sec. 213, taxpayers may deduct medical expenses only to the extent the expenses exceed 10% of the taxpayer's AGI. For years before 2016, the AGI limit is 7.5% for taxpayers 65 or older. To qualify as a medical expense deduction, the expenditure must be incurred for the medical care of a qualified individual. Taxpayers may not take a deduction for medical expenses to the extent the expenses are reimbursed (i.e., compensated for by insurance or otherwise).

QUALIFIED INDIVIDUALS

To deduct medical expenses, taxpayers must pay the expenses on behalf of themselves, their spouses, or their dependents.

Taxpayer's Dependent. Deductible medical expenses include those paid on behalf of a taxpayer's dependent as well as on behalf of a person for whom the taxpayer could take a dependency exemption except for the failure to meet the gross income or joint return tests.[1]

EXAMPLE I:7-1 ►

KEY POINT

Medical expenses are deductible for a person who satisfies only the support, relationship, and citizenship dependency tests.

In March of 2015, Jean's son, Steve, is involved in an automobile accident. At the time of the accident Jean is 54 years old and Steve is 25 years old. Steve has worked full-time for part of the year, earning a total of $15,000. Because Steve has no medical insurance and cannot pay the medical bills or support himself as a result of the accident, Jean pays Steve's medical expenses and supports him for the rest of the year. Because Jean provides over one-half of Steve's support for the year and Steve, except for the gross income test, otherwise qualifies as Jean's dependent, (Steve is a qualifying relative rather than a qualifying child because he is over 19 and is not a full-time student) Jean may deduct the medical expenses she pays on his behalf to the extent that these expenses, along with all of Jean's other medical expenses, exceed 10% of her AGI for the year. Jean may not claim a dependency exemption for Steve because the gross income test is not satisfied. ◄

Children of Divorced Parents. As long as one divorced parent qualifies to claim the dependency exemption under Sec. 152(e), the parent who pays medical expenses on behalf of the children may deduct the expenses. The parent taking the medical expense deduction doesn't need to be the parent who may claim the dependency exemption.

[1] Sec. 152. See Chapter I:2 for the tests that must be met to claim a qualifying child or qualifying relative as a dependent.

QUALIFIED MEDICAL EXPENSES

The **medical expense deduction** is available only for expenditures paid for medical care. Section 213 defines *medical care* as amounts paid for

► The diagnosis, cure, mitigation, treatment, or prevention of disease

► The purpose of affecting any structure or function of the body

► Transportation primarily for and essential to the first two items listed above

► Qualified long-term care services

► Insurance covering all of the items listed above

ADDITIONAL COMMENT

In 2012 the deduction for medical expenses totaled $85.3 billion, representing 7.6% of the total dollar amount of the itemized deductions for medical expenses, taxes, interest, and charitable contributions.

Diagnosis, Cure, Mitigation, Treatment, or Prevention of Disease. Although the tax law does not precisely define the term *medical expense,* it is clear that medical expenses are deductible only if paid for procedures or treatments that are legal in the locality in which they are performed. For example, taxpayers may not deduct expenditures for controlled substances.[2] The definition of medical care includes preventive measures such as routine physical and dental examinations. However, other expenses should be "confined strictly to expenses incurred primarily for the prevention or alleviation of a physical or mental defect or illness." Thus, unless they are for routine physical or dental examinations, the expenditures must be for the purpose of curing a specific ailment rather than related to the general health of an individual. This determination is especially critical when the expenditures in question are for items such as vacations, weight loss programs, or stop smoking programs. The taxpayer may or may not incur such expenses for a specific ailment.

EXAMPLE I:7-2 ►

Helmut is nervous and irritable because of pressures at work and begins to suffer angina symptoms. In order to relax and get away from it all, he takes an ocean cruise around the world. Helmut's angina symptoms ease while he is on the cruise. In a case with facts very similar to Helmut's situation, the Tax Court held that a cruise is not a proven medical necessity because the taxpayer's physician did not specifically prescribe it. Although the cruise was beneficial to Helmut's general health, it was not deductible.[3] ◄

EXAMPLE I:7-3 ►

Dave enrolls in a weight reduction program on the advice of two doctors who prescribe the program as a means of relieving his obesity, hypertension, and certain hearing problems. Based on a revenue ruling issued by the IRS, these expenses qualify as deductible medical expenditures because they are incurred for a specific medical condition.[4] ◄

Although a doctor's recommendation appears to lend a great deal of weight to deductibility, it is not always sufficient. For example, a taxpayer could not deduct the cost of dancing lessons for an emotionally disturbed child, even though the lessons proved to be beneficial and were recommended by a physician. Likewise, a taxpayer suffering from arthritis could not deduct the cost of ballroom dance lessons, even though a doctor recommended the lessons. On the other hand, the IRS has ruled that the cost of a clarinet and clarinet lessons was deductible when recommended by an orthodontist to correct a malocclusion of a child's teeth.[5] In short, determining the deductibility of certain expenditures can be difficult.

ADDITIONAL COMMENT

One cannot deduct the cost of nonprescription medicine (except insulin), toothpaste, toiletries, maternity clothes, diaper service, or funeral expenses.

Range of Deductible Medical Services. According to the Treasury Regulations, typical medical expenses include payments for a wide range of medical, dental, and other diagnostic and healing services. Thus, taxpayers may deduct payments to licensed or certified medical professionals such as general practitioners, obstetricians, surgeons, ophthalmologists, opticians, dentists, and orthodontists. Furthermore, deductible medical expenditures

---

[2] Reg. Sec. 1.213-1(e)(1)(ii). See also Rev. Rul. 97-9, 1997-1 C.B. 77 and IRS Publication 502 (2014) which contains the IRS's recommended treatment for a number of medical expenses.

[3] *Daniel E. Mizl,* 1980 PH T.C. Memo ¶80,227, 40 TCM 552. Even if the taxpayer's physician had prescribed the trip, it still may not have been deductible. See Reg. Sec. 1.213-1(e)(1)(ii).

[4] Rev. Rul. 2002-19, 2002-1 C.B. 778. However, taxpayers still may not

deduct the cost of diet foods or weight loss programs directed at general health or appearance. Taxpayers may deduct costs incurred for prescription medications and programs to stop-smoking, but not over-the-counter stop smoking aids. See Rev. Rul. 99-28, 1999-1 C.B. 1269.

[5] *John J. Thoene,* 33 T.C. 62 (1959), *Rose C. France v. CIR,* 50 AFTR 2d 82-5504, 1982-1 USTC ¶9225 (6th Cir., 1982), and Rev. Rul. 62-210, 1962-2 C.B. 89.

include payments for medical services rendered by individuals such as chiropractors, osteopaths, and psychotherapists who may or may not be required to be licensed or certified.[6] Taxpayers may deduct payments to Christian Science practitioners as well as for acupuncture treatment if the taxpayer receives the treatment for a specific medical purpose.[7] Qualified medical expenses also include payment for hospital services, nursing services, laboratory fees, X-rays, artificial teeth or limbs, ambulance hire, eyeglasses, and prescribed medicines and insulin. Nondeductible expenses include expenditures for nonprescription medicines, drugs, vitamins, and other types of health foods that improve the individual's general health.

To deduct costs incurred for schools and camps, the taxpayer must show that the facility has the appropriate medical equipment and regularly engages in providing medical services. For example, a court held that a taxpayer could deduct costs he incurred to send his mentally disabled son to a school with a special curriculum specifically for mentally disabled children. Similarly, another court ruled that a taxpayer could deduct the cost of sending a child with psychiatric problems to a school that specialized in learning disorders. However, taxpayers generally may not deduct the cost of sending children with special medical problems to schools or camps that do not have the proper equipment, facilities, or curriculum for such problems.

TYPICAL MISCONCEPTION

Taxpayers tend to define qualifying medical expenses too narrowly. This may be caused, in part, by comparison with expense reimbursement limitation policies of health insurance companies.

Medical Procedures Affecting any Function or Structure of The Body. Deductible medical expenditures also include payments for services affecting any function or structure of the body, even though no specific illness or disease exists. Thus, qualifying medical expenses include expenditures for such items as physical therapy, obstetrical services, eyeglasses, dental examinations and cleanings, and hearing aids. Under Sec. 213, cosmetic surgery or any other similar procedure does not qualify as a medical expense unless such surgery is necessary to correct a deformity arising from a congenital abnormality, a personal injury resulting from an accident or trauma, or a disfiguring disease. Cosmetic surgery is defined as any procedure undertaken to improve a person's appearance that does not meaningfully promote the proper function of the body or prevent or treat an illness or disease.

Transportation Essential to Medical Care. Taxpayers may deduct transportation expenses that are essential to and incurred primarily for qualified medical care. Thus, taxpayers may deduct actual out-of-pocket automobile expenditures, taxis, airfare, ambulance fees, and other forms of transportation if the travel is for medical reasons. However, the tax law disallows a deduction if the travel is undertaken for recreational purposes or for the general improvement of the taxpayer's health.

ADDITIONAL COMMENT

For 2015, the standard mileage rate for business mileage is 57.5 cents per mile. For medical and moving it is 23 cents, and for charitable purposes it is 14 cents.

In lieu of the actual cost of the use of an automobile, for 2015 the IRS allows a deduction of 23 cents for each mile that the automobile is driven for medical reasons. In addition to this standard mileage rate, taxpayers may also deduct the cost of tolls and parking.

Certain courts have held that the cost of meals and lodging while en route to a medical facility is part of deductible travel costs incurred for medical purposes. However, taxpayers may not deduct the cost of meals eaten on trips that are too short to warrant a stop for meals. Additionally, taxpayers may deduct only 50% of the cost of meals. (See Chapter I:9 for a discussion of the 50% disallowance rule for meals and entertainment.) Sec. 213(d)(2) limits the potential deduction for the cost of lodging to $50 per night. Furthermore, lodging expenses qualify as medical expenditures only if the travel is primarily for and essential to medical care, the medical care is provided in a licensed hospital (or a facility related or equivalent to a licensed hospital), and there is no significant element of personal pleasure or recreation in the travel. The tax law imposes the $50 limitation on lodging on a per-individual basis. Thus, if the patient is unable to travel alone, the taxpayer may deduct an additional $50 per night for the lodging costs of a nurse, parent, or spouse.

---

[6] Reg. Sec. 1.213-1(e)(1) and Rev. Rul. 63-91, 1963-1 C.B. 54. See also Ltr. Rul. 8919009 (February 6, 1989) where a pregnant woman was entitled to a deduction for the cost of childbirth classes to the extent that they prepared her for the childbirth. However, the cost of the classes where she received instructions on the care of the unborn child represented a flat fee that allowed a coach to attend the class with the taxpayer. Thus, one-half of the fee was deemed attributable to the coach and was not allowed as a qualified medical expense.
[7] Rev. Rul. 72-593, 1972-2 C.B. 180 and IRS Special Ruling, February 2, 1943.

Qualified Long-Term Care. Taxpayers may also deduct expenditures for qualified long-term care as medical expenses subject to the 10% of AGI limitation. Long-term care is defined as medical services required by a chronically ill individual which are provided under a prescribed plan of care. Under Sec. 7702B, such items include expenditures for diagnostic, preventive, therapeutic, curing, treating, mitigating, rehabilitative, and personal care services. A chronically ill individual generally is someone who, for a period of at least 90 days, cannot perform at least two daily living tasks such as eating, toileting (including continence), bathing, or dressing. According to Sec. 213(e)(11), if the long-term care service is provided by the individual's spouse or relative, any payment for the long-term care service is not deductible unless the spouse or relative is a licensed professional to be able to provide this care. Furthermore, services provided by a corporation or partnership in which the person owns over 50% are also not deductible.

Expenditures for long-term care insurance premiums qualify as medical deductions, subject to an annual limit based upon the age of an individual.[8]

Capital Expenditures for Medical Care. Generally, taxpayers may not currently deduct capital expenditures for federal income tax purposes. For assets used in a trade or business or held for the production of income, taxpayers must recover such costs through depreciation, cost recovery, or amortization. Capital expenditures incurred for personal medical purposes are not depreciable or amortizable. However, a current deduction is available when the capital expenditure is made to acquire an asset primarily for the medical care of the taxpayer, the taxpayer's spouse, or the taxpayer's dependents. To qualify as a deduction, the taxpayer must incur the expenditure as a medical necessity for primary use by the individual in need of medical treatment, and the expenditure must be reasonable in amount. The following are the three categories of deductible capital expenditures for medical care:[9]

► Expenditures that relate only to the sick or handicapped person, not to the permanent improvement or betterment of the taxpayer's property (e.g., eyeglasses, dogs or other animals that assist the blind or the deaf, artificial teeth and limbs, wheelchairs, crutches, and portable air conditioners purchased for the sole use of a sick or disabled person)

► Expenditures that permanently improve or better the taxpayer's residence for the purpose of providing medical care (e.g., a swimming pool installed in the home of an individual suffering from arthritis)

► Expenditures to remove structural barriers in the home of a physically disabled individual (e.g., costs of constructing entrance ramps, widening doorways and halls, lowering kitchen cabinets, and adding railings)

REAL-WORLD EXAMPLE

The cost of installing an elevator in the home upon the recommendation of a physician to help a patient with a heart condition was deductible to the extent that it did not increase the value of the home. *James E. Berry v. Wiseman*, 2 AFTR 2d 6015, 58-2 USTC ¶9870 (D.C. Okla., 1958).

Capital expenditures that relate only to the sick person (the first category) are fully deductible in the year paid. Expenditures that improve the residence (the second category) are deductible only to the extent that the amount of the expenditure exceeds the increase in the fair market value (FMV) of the residence. Expenditures to remove physical barriers in the home of a physically disabled individual (the third category) are deductible in full (i.e., the increase in the home's value is deemed to be zero). In addition, any costs of operating or maintaining the assets in all three categories are deductible as long as the medical reason for the capital expenditure continues to exist.[10] All of the above expenditures are subject to the 10% of AGI floor.

EXAMPLE I:7-4 ► During the current year, Rita is injured in an industrial accident. As a result, she sustains a chronic disabling leg injury, which requires her to spend much time in a wheelchair. Rita's physician recommends that a swimming pool be installed in her backyard and that she devote several hours each day to physical exercise. During the year, Rita makes the following expenditures:

Wheelchair	$ 2,500
Swimming pool	27,000
Operation and maintenance of the pool	1,800
Entrance ramp and door modification	5,000

---

[8] For 2015, if the individual is 40 years of age or less, the annual deductible limit for the premiums is $380. For individuals over 40 but not over 50, the limit is $710. For those who are 50 but not over 60, the limit is $1,430. For those who are 60 but not over 70, the limit is $3,800. For those who are 70 or older, the limit is $4,750.

[9] Reg. Sec. 1.213-1(e)(1)(iii) and H. Rept. No. 99-841, 99th Cong., 2d Sess., p. II-22 (1986).
[10] Rev. Rul. 87-106, 1987-2 C.B. 67.

REAL-WORLD EXAMPLE
Taxpayers made nonrefundable advance payments required as a condition for an institution's future acceptance of their disabled child for lifetime care in the event that taxpayers could not care for the child. The amounts paid were deductible as expenses for medical care in the year paid. Rev. Rul. 75-303, 1975-2 C.B. 87. This current deduction for prepaid amounts is only available for certain lifetime care expenditures incurred in situations described in this ruling. Rev. Rul. 93-72, I.R.B. 1993-34,7.

A qualified appraiser estimates that the swimming pool increases the value of Rita's home by only $20,000. Rita's medical expenses for the year include $2,500 for the wheelchair, $7,000 for the swimming pool (the excess of the cost of the pool over the increase in the FMV of the home), $1,800 for the operation and maintenance of the pool, and $5,000 for the ramp and door modification. ◀

Costs of Living in Institutions. The entire cost of in-patient hospital care, including meals and lodging, qualifies as a medical expense. However, if an individual is in an institution other than a hospital (e.g., a nursing home or a special school for the disabled), the deductibility of the costs involved depends on the facts of the particular case. If the principal reason for the taxpayer's presence in an institution is the need for and availability of the medical care furnished by that institution, the qualified medical expenditures include the entire costs of meals, lodging, and other services necessary for furnishing the medical care. If medical care is not the principal reason for the taxpayer's presence in the institution, the institutional expenses are not deductible. Only specific medical expenses, such as doctor bills, prescription drugs, etc., are eligible for deduction.

ADDITIONAL COMMENT
A taxpayer cannot deduct the Medicare (hospital insurance benefits) tax that is withheld from wages as part of the Social Security tax.

Medical Insurance Premiums. Qualified medical expenses also include premiums paid for medical insurance, including premiums paid for supplementary medical insurance for the aged under the Social Security Act and premiums paid for qualified long-term care insurance contracts. In many cases, taxpayers pay premiums for insurance coverage that extends beyond mere medical care. For example, in addition to the standard medical care coverage, an insurance policy may provide coverage for loss of income or loss of life, limb, or sight. In such cases, the tax law allows a deduction for the medical care portion of the premium only if the cost of each type of insurance is either separately stated in the contract or furnished to the policyholder by the insurance company in a separate statement.[11]

EXAMPLE I:7-5 ▶ Each month Malazia pays $300 for an insurance policy under which she is reimbursed for any doctor or hospital charges she incurs. In addition, the policy will pay two-thirds of her regular salary each month if she becomes disabled. Finally, the policy will pay her $10,000 for the loss of any limb. At the end of the year, her insurance company issues a statement that allocates two-thirds of the premiums to the medical insurance coverage. Malazia's medical care expenditure is $2,400 ($300 × 12 × 0.667). ◀

If a taxpayer pays the premiums attributable to an individual or group medical insurance plan, the payments are deductible as medical expenses, which are itemized deductions in most cases. Self-employed individuals may deduct 100% of these amounts as deductions *for* AGI. Any amounts paid by the taxpayer's employer are excluded from the employee's gross income and are not includible in the taxpayer's medical expenses.[12]

Chapter I:9 discusses the deduction for certain medical savings accounts established for employees.

AMOUNT AND TIMING OF DEDUCTION

The amount and timing of the allowable medical expense deduction depend on when the taxpayer actually pays the medical expenses, the taxpayer's AGI, and whether the taxpayer receives any reimbursement for the medical expenses.

Timing of The Payment. In general, taxpayers may deduct medical expenses only in the year they actually pay the expenses. This rule applies regardless of the taxpayer's method of accounting or when the event that caused the expenditure occurs.[13] Thus, if taxpayers receive medical care during the year but have not paid for it as of the end of the year, taxpayers must defer the deduction for that care until the year they pay for the medical care. If the obligation is charged on a credit card, payment is deemed to have been

---

[11] Sec. 213(d). See also Rev. Ruls. 66-216, 1966-2 C.B. 100, and 79-175, 1979-1 C.B. 117.
[12] Sections 162 and 106.

[13] Reg. Sec. 1.213-1(a)(1). However, medical expenses paid within one year from the day following the taxpayer's death are treated as paid at the time they are incurred (see Sec. 213(c)).

made on the date of the charge, not on the later date when the taxpayer pays the credit card balance. Conversely, if medical care is prepaid, the deduction is deferred until the year the taxpayer receives the care unless there is a legal obligation to prepay or unless the prepayment is a requirement for the receipt of the medical care.[14]

Limitation on Amount Deductible. As previously noted, other than medical insurance premiums paid by self-employed individuals, the tax law allows a medical expense deduction only for the years in which the taxpayer itemizes his or her deductions and the taxpayer's expenditures for medical care exceed 10% of AGI.

EXAMPLE I:7-6 ► During 2015, Kelly incurs qualified medical expenditures of $6,000. Kelly is 45 and her AGI for the year is $50,000. After subtracting the floor, she has $1,000 ($6,000 − [0.1 × $50,000]) of deductible medical expenses. These medical expenses are added to Kelly's other itemized deductions to determine whether they exceed the standard deduction. ◄

Medical Insurance Reimbursements. Taxpayers may only deduct unreimbursed medical expenditures. It does not matter whether the reimbursement is from an insurance plan purchased from an insurance company, a medical reimbursement plan of an employer, or a payment resulting from litigation.

If the taxpayer receives reimbursement in the same year he or she pays for the medical expenses, the amount of the reimbursement reduces the allowed deduction. If a taxpayer receives a reimbursement in a year subsequent to the year of payment, the taxpayer must include the reimbursement in gross income in the year of receipt to the extent that the taxpayer derived a tax benefit from the deduction in the previous year. If the taxpayer did not take a deduction in the prior year, the taxpayer doesn't need to report the reimbursement as income. This may occur because the taxpayer's total itemized deductions do not exceed the standard deduction or because the taxpayer's total medical expenses do not exceed 10% of AGI. If the taxpayer took a deduction in the prior year, however, the taxpayer must report as income the lesser of the amount of the reimbursement or the amount the medical expenses reduced the taxable income in the prior year.

EXAMPLE I:7-7 ► During 2015, Dan, a single taxpayer under age 65, reports the following items of income and expense:

AGI	$100,000
Total qualified medical expenses	12,500
Itemized deductions other than medical	4,100

Dan's taxable income for 2015 is calculated as follows:

AGI		$100,000
Reduction: Larger of itemized deductions or standard deduction		
Medical expenses	$12,500	
Minus: 10% of AGI	(10,000)	2,500
Other itemized deductions		4,100
Total itemized deductions		$6,600
Greater of itemized deductions or standard deduction ($6,300)		(6,600)
Personal exemption		(4,000)
Taxable income		$89,400

If during 2016 Dan receives a reimbursement of $1,500 for medical expenses he incurred the prior year, he must include $300 (6,600 − 6,300) in gross income for 2016, which is the amount of the tax benefit from the medical expense deduction for the prior year. This amount can be calculated by comparing Dan's actual taxable income for 2015 with what would have been his 2015 taxable income if the reimbursement had been received that year. This calculation is as follows:

[14] Rev. Rul. 78-39, 1978-1 C.B. 73 and *Robert M. Rose v. CIR*, 26 AFTR 2d 70-5653, 70-2 USTC ¶9646 (5th Cir., 1970). See also Rev. Rul. 93-72, Rev. Rul. 1993-2 C.B. 77, Rev. Rul. 75-302, 1975-2 C.B. 86, and Rev. Rul. 75-303, 1975-2 C.B. 87.

AGI		$100,000
Reduction: Larger of itemized deductions or standard deduction		
Medical expenses	$12,500	
Minus: Reimbursement	(1,500)	
Minus: 10% of AGI	(10,000)	1,000
Other itemized deductions		4,100
Total itemized deductions		$5,100
Greater of itemized deductions or standard deduction ($6,300)		(6,300)
Personal exemption		(4,000)
Taxable income (assuming reimbursement was received in 2015)		$89,700
Minus: Actual 2015 taxable income		($89,400)
Tax benefit		$ 300 ◀

Topic Review I:7-1 highlights the principal requirements for the medical expense deduction previously discussed.

 **STOP & THINK**

Question: Vince and Diane are married and file a joint tax return. For the current year they estimate their AGI at $90,000. They also estimate their itemized deductions for taxes, interest, and charitable contributions total $9,000. Up to the current date they have incurred $7,000 in deductible medical expenses. For several months they have been considering laser surgery on Diane's eyes. The total expenditure for the operations will be $5,000 and is not covered by their medical insurance. Since they already have spent so much this year on medical expenses and they do not anticipate such large expenses next year, they are considering delaying the eye operation until next year. They estimate next year's AGI to be approximately $110,000. Does this decision make sense from a tax point of view?

Solution: From a tax point of view, Vince and Diane should consider having and paying for the operation this year. If so, $5,000 is added to the prior $7,000 medical expenditures for a total of $12,000 for the year. After applying the 10% of AGI limitation, $3,000 [$12,000 − ($90,000 × 0.1)] of the medical expenses is deductible. If they wait until next year and if their estimates are correct, none of the medical expenses in either year are deductible because of the 10% of AGI limitation.

TOPIC REVIEW I:7-1

Medical Expense Deductions

ITEMS	DEDUCTION RULES AND LIMITATIONS
Qualifying expenditures	(a) Expenditures for the diagnosis, cure, mitigation, treatment, or prevention of disease and qualified long-term care. (b) Transportation at 23¢ per mile for 2015; lodging limited to $50 per night, per person; and 50% of meals. (c) Medical and qualified long-term care insurance premiums. (d) Capital expenditures (subject to specific limitations).
Qualifying individuals	Taxpayer, spouse, dependents, children of divorced parents even if not dependent, and persons who would qualify as dependent except for the failure to meet gross income or joint return tests.
Amount and timing of the deduction Treatment of insurance reimbursements	Deduct in the year paid unless prepaid, then deductible when medical treatment is received. If prepayment is required or there is a legal obligation to prepay, then deduct in year of prepayment. Medical expenses are subject to a 10% of AGI nondeductible limitation. The deduction is reduced if the reimbursement is received in the year of payment. Reimbursements received in a subsequent year are included in gross income of the year received to the extent that a tax benefit was received in the earlier year.

TAXES

Section 164 provides taxpayers with a deduction for specifically listed taxes paid or accrued during the taxable year. Generally, cash-method taxpayers deduct the taxes when they pay for them, whereas taxpayers using the accrual method deduct taxes in the year the taxes accrue. The tax law specifically lists other taxes as nondeductible. To be deductible as a tax, the assessment in question must be a tax rather than a fee or charge imposed by a government for providing specific goods or services.

DEFINITION OF A TAX

A **tax** is a mandatory assessment levied under the authority of a political entity for the purpose of raising revenue to use for public or governmental purposes. Thus, fees, assessments, or fines imposed for specific privileges or services are not deductible as taxes under Sec. 164. These nontax items include:

► Vehicle registration and inspection fees

► Registration tags for pets

► Toll charges for highways and bridges

► Parking meter charges

► Charges for sewer, water, and other services

► Special assessments against real estate for items such as sidewalks, lighting, and streets

However, if taxpayers incur these nontax fees and charges in a business or income- producing activity, the taxpayers may either capitalize or deduct these items as ordinary and necessary business expenses or ordinary and necessary expenses incurred for the production of income.

DEDUCTIBLE TAXES

The following taxes are specifically deductible under Sec. 164:

► State, local, and foreign real property taxes

► State and local personal property taxes if based on value

► State, local, and foreign income, war profits, and excess profits taxes

► For tax years beginning before January 1, 2015, state and local sales taxes if the taxpayer makes an election to deduct these taxes instead of deducting state and local income taxes.

► The environmental tax imposed by Section 59A. Although the imposition of the Environmental Tax was imposed only for tax years beginning before January 1, 1996, §164(a)(5) still lists the tax as deductible.

► Other state, local, and foreign taxes that are paid or incurred in either a trade or business or an income-producing activity

In general, taxes imposed by the federal government are not deductible in calculating a taxpayer's income tax.[15] However, federal customs and excise taxes incurred in the taxpayer's business or income-producing activity are deductible as ordinary and necessary expenses under Secs. 162 or 212. Furthermore, an employer may deduct the *employer's* portion of Federal Social Security taxes and federal and state unemployment taxes as ordinary and necessary business expenses if the employee works in the employer's business or income-producing activity. A self-employed individual may deduct one-half of the self-employment tax imposed on the individual's self-employment income as a *for* AGI deduction.

---

[15] The generation-skipping transfer tax is imposed by the United States on certain distributions from a trust (see Sec. 2601) and is deductible for federal income tax purposes. Furthermore, under Sec. 691(c) a taxpayer who includes income in respect of a decedent in taxable income may deduct the estate tax attributable to that amount.

STATE AND LOCAL INCOME TAXES

For individuals, state and local income taxes are normally an itemized (*from* AGI) deduction. Thus, a taxpayer does not receive any federal income tax benefit if these taxes, in addition to the taxpayer's other itemized deductions, do not exceed the standard deduction. Cash-method taxpayers deduct all state and local income taxes paid or withheld during the year even if the taxes are attributable to another tax year.

BOOK-TAX DIFFERENCE

For financial accounting purposes, all taxes are expensed in arriving at net income after taxes. However, for tax purposes, only certain taxes are deductible. This gives rise to an M-1 or M-3 adjustment.

EXAMPLE I:7-8 ▶

During 2015, Rita had $1,500 in state income taxes withheld from her salary. On April 15, 2016, Rita pays an additional $400 when she files her 2015 state income tax return. If the sum of her itemized deductions for 2015 exceeds the 2015 standard deduction, for 2015 Rita may deduct as an itemized deduction the $1,500 in state income taxes withheld from her salary during 2015. The $400 that Rita pays on April 15, 2016, is added to her itemized deductions for 2016 even though the liability relates to her 2015 state income tax return. ◀

ADDITIONAL COMMENT

Every state except Alaska, Florida, Nevada, New Hampshire, South Dakota, Tennessee, Texas, Washington, and Wyoming impose a personal income tax. Although New Hampshire and Tennessee do not impose a personal income tax, they do tax interest and dividends at the individual level.

If a taxpayer receives a refund of state income taxes deducted in a prior year, the taxpayer must include the refund as income in the year of the refund to the extent the taxpayer received a tax benefit from the prior deduction. This calculation is similar to the calculation of the tax benefit from a medical expense reimbursement in Example I:7-7.

STATE AND LOCAL SALES TAXES

As mentioned previously, for tax years beginning before January 1, 2015, taxpayers were allowed to deduct state and local sales taxes in lieu of state and local income taxes.[16] Taxpayers electing to deduct state and local sales taxes instead of state and local income taxes had two options for determining the deductible amount. Taxpayers could deduct the actual amount of taxes paid by accumulating receipts showing the actual amount of taxes paid, or they could deduct the appropriate amount from tables provided by the Treasury Department. If a taxpayer used the amount from the tables, sales taxes paid on major purchases could be added to the table amount.

PERSONAL PROPERTY TAXES

Many state and local governments impose personal property taxes. For individuals, the key issue is whether the levy is a deductible tax under Sec. 164 or a nondeductible fee. To qualify as a deductible personal property tax, the levy must meet two basic tests:

▶ The tax must be an ad valorem tax on personal property. In other words, the property's value determines the amount of the tax rather than some other measure such as a vehicle's weight or model year.

▶ The tax must be imposed on an annual basis, even if not collected annually.[17]

If a personal property tax is based partly on value and partly on some other basis, only the ad valorem portion is deductible.

EXAMPLE I:7-9 ▶

Banner County imposes on all passenger automobiles a property tax of 1% of value plus 20 cents per pound. Clay's automobile has a value of $20,000 and weighs 1,500 pounds. Clay may deduct $200 ($20,000 × 0.01) under Sec. 164. Clay may not deduct the remaining $300 (1,500 × 0.20) under Sec. 164; however, he may deduct it as an ordinary business expense if the automobile is used in his business. ◀

ADDITIONAL COMMENT

Several states impose a tax on the value of a taxpayer's investment portfolio. This is an example of a deductible intangible personal property tax.

For individuals, personal property taxes are *from* AGI (itemized) deductions unless the individual incurs the taxes in the individual's trade or business or for the production of rental income.

REAL ESTATE TAXES

Apportionment of Taxes. When real estate is sold during the year, the federal income tax deduction for property taxes imposed on that real estate is allocated between the seller and the purchaser based on the amount of time each taxpayer owns the property during the real property tax year. The real property tax year may or may not coincide with the taxpayer's tax year. The apportionment, based on the number of days each party holds the property during the real property tax year of sale, assumes that the purchaser owns the property on the date of the sale. This apportionment is mandatory for all taxpayers even though one of

---

[16] In years past, Congress has extended this election. At this point in time, Congress has not extended this election beyond 2014, but may do so in the future.

[17] Reg. Sec. 1.164-3(c).

the parties (i.e., the purchaser or seller) may have actually paid the entire property tax bill. The party who actually pays the taxes (either the buyer or the seller) deducts his or her share of the taxes in the year he or she pays the taxes unless the taxpayer makes an election under Sec. 461(c) to accrue the taxes. The tax consequences do not depend on whether the agreement requires proration of the real estate taxes. Both the purchaser and the seller may deduct their apportioned share of the taxes, regardless of who actually pays the taxes. Generally the sales agreement provides for the proper apportionment of property taxes between the buyer and the seller and will state the amount of the taxes apportioned to each party separately from the selling price of the property. If the seller pays all of the taxes prior to the sale, at closing the buyer will reimburse the seller for the payment of these taxes in addition to paying the down payment. On the other hand, if the taxes are to be paid by the buyer after the purchase of the property, the amount collected from the buyer at closing is reduced by the amount of taxes allocated to the seller. This process does not impact the selling price of the property if properly allocated and accounted for at closing.[18]

ADDITIONAL COMMENT

Delinquent taxes of the seller that are paid by the buyer as part of the contract price are not deductible.

EXAMPLE I:7-10 ▶

The real property tax year for Bannock County is the calendar year. Property taxes for a particular real property tax year become a lien against the property as of June 30 of that year, and the owner of the property on that date becomes liable for the tax. However, the taxes are not payable until February 28 of the subsequent year. On May 30 of the current (non-leap) year, Sandy, a cash-method taxpayer, sells a building to Roger, who is also a cash-method taxpayer. The real estate taxes on the property for the current year are $1,095. Although Roger is liable for the payment of the tax, Sandy is treated as having paid $447 ($1,095 × 149/365 [the numerator of 149 is the number of days from January 1 through May 29 and the denominator is the entire real property tax year]) on the date of the sale. Thus, Sandy may deduct $447 in the year of sale. Roger may deduct his share of the taxes, equaling $648 ($1,095 × 216/365), in the subsequent year (i.e., the year during which Roger actually pays the full amount of property tax due of $1,095). On the other hand, if the taxes become a lien against the property on April 1, Sandy is the owner of the building on that date and, since she is liable for the tax, she will be the one who actually pays the tax. Under these circumstances, the result is the same (i.e., Sandy deducts $447 and Roger deducts $648) except that Roger may take the $648 deduction in the year of sale rather than in the year of payment and Sandy takes the $447 deduction in the year of payment rather than the year of sale. ◀

TYPICAL MISCONCEPTION

Taxpayers often fail to differentiate between assessments for new construction and for repairs. For example, an assessment for street repairs is deductible, but an assessment for the construction of a new street is not deductible.

Real Property Assessments for Local Benefits. Local governments often make assessments against real estate for the purpose of funding local improvements. These assessments may be for such items as street improvements, sidewalks, lighting, drainage, and sewer improvements. If the tax assessment is only against the property that benefits from the improvement, it is not deductible, even though the general public may also incidentally benefit.[19] The tax law requires capitalization of such assessments as part of the property's adjusted basis.

Real property taxes incurred on personal-use assets, such as a personal residence, are deductible *from* AGI. Real property taxes incurred on business property or property held for the production of rental income are deductions *for* AGI.

SELF-EMPLOYMENT TAX

Wages paid to an employee are subject to a payroll tax which consists of two components (Social Security, technically called OASDI, and Medicare). Both the employer and the employee pay a share of the taxes imposed. Thus, on wages paid to an employee, the employer and the employee generally each pay a tax of 6.2% for Social Security (a total of 12.4%) and 1.45% (a total of 2.9%) for Medicare. The Social Security tax is imposed on a limited amount of wages. For 2015, this wage limit is $118,500. However, the Medicare tax is imposed on both the employer and the employee without limit on the amount of the wages paid. Self-employed individuals must pay both of these taxes on their self-employment income. Because these taxes are imposed only on the self-employed individual, these taxes are imposed on the individual's self-employment income at the total 2.9% for Medicare and the total 12.4%

---

[18] However, if the agreement does not specifically provide and account for an apportionment of taxes, the apportionment of the taxes is still made and the seller's gain or loss on the sale (and the purchaser's basis in the property) must be adjusted either upward or downward, depending on which party actually pays the taxes.

[19] Reg. Sec. 1.164-4. However, if the assessment against the local benefits is made for maintenance, repair, or interest charges on the benefits, the assessment is deductible. The burden of proof to show how much of the assessment is deductible falls on the taxpayer (see Sec. 164(c)(1)).

(up to self-employment income of $118,500 in 2015) for Social Security. Self-employed individuals may deduct one-half of these self-employment taxes paid as a *for* AGI deduction.[20]

Starting in 2013, an additional surtax is imposed under the Patient Protection and Affordable Care Act passed by Congress in 2012. This new tax is imposed on individuals with over $200,000 in income ($250,000 for married filing jointly) and is imposed at 3.8% on investment income and 0.9% on wages and self-employment income. The reason for this 0.9% (3.8% – 2.9%) difference in these rates is that self-employment income and wages are already subject to the 2.9% Medicare tax whereas investment income is not. This new tax is imposed only on individuals, not on employers. Furthermore, unlike the Social Security tax and the Medicare tax, this new tax is not deductible by individuals.

SELF-STUDY QUESTION

Would a taxpayer normally prefer to deduct foreign taxes or take a foreign tax credit?

ANSWER

Normally the foreign tax credit is better because a credit provides a direct dollar-for-dollar reduction of the tax liability rather than a reduction of taxable income.

NONDEDUCTIBLE TAXES

The following taxes are not deductible under Sec. 164:

► Federal income taxes

► Federal estate, inheritance, legacy, succession, and gift taxes

► Federal import or tariff duties and excise taxes unless incurred in the taxpayer's business or for the production of income

► Employee's portion of Social Security and other payroll taxes

► State and local sales taxes and state inheritance, legacy, succession, and gift taxes (For years prior to 2015 individuals could elect to deduct state and local sales taxes instead of state income taxes)

► Foreign income taxes if the taxpayer elects to take the taxes as a credit against his or her federal income tax liability

► Property taxes on real estate to the extent treated as imposed on another taxpayer

► Tax imposed on wages, self-employment income, and investment income under the Patient Protection and Affordable Care Act

INTEREST

OBJECTIVE 3

Identify different types of interest deductions

In years past, taxpayers could deduct virtually all interest paid or accrued in the taxable year. Gradually, however, Congress has enacted numerous exceptions into the tax law rendering several types of interest nondeductible. For example, individuals may not deduct personal interest expense, such as interest paid on personal credit cards, automobile loans, etc. Interest incurred in connection with a trade or business is deductible. Thus, to determine the amount of interest expense deduction, individuals must properly classify their interest expense for the year. The interest expense categories include the following: active trade or business, passive activity, investment, personal, qualified residence, and student loan.

ADDITIONAL COMMENT

In 2012 the deduction for interest paid totaled $354 billion, representing 31.6% of the total dollar amount of the itemized deductions for medical expenses, taxes, interest, and charitable contributions.

DEFINITION OF INTEREST

Interest is defined as "compensation for the use or forbearance of money."[21] Thus, finance charges, carrying charges, loan discounts, premiums, loan origination fees, and points are all considered interest if they represent a cost for the use of money.

Charge for Services. In addition to interest, borrowers may incur other charges in connection with borrowing money. These service charges include fees for appraisals, title searches, bank service charges, and the annual service charge on credit cards. Unless incurred in a trade or business, these expenses are not deductible because they all represent nondeductible personal expenses. As explained in the section in this chapter entitled Personal Interest, although finance charges on credit cards represent interest rather than service costs (on page 7-16), they likewise are not deductible unless incurred in a trade or business.

Bank Service Charges and Finance Charges. Bank service charges on checking accounts are nondeductible expenses for services rendered rather than interest.

---

[20] Sec. 164(f). In calculating its taxable income subject to the income tax, an employer is able to deduct as a business expense its portion of these Social Security taxes and Medicare taxes. Thus, in order to equate the amount and deductibility of these taxes imposed on self-employed individuals, an adjustment is made to the amount of the self-employed income that is subject to these taxes. (See Chapter I:14 for a discussion of the self-employment tax.)

[21] *Deputy v. Pierre S. DuPont*, 23 AFTR 808, 40-1 USTC ¶9161 (USSC, 1940).

The annual service charge on credit cards is also a charge for services rather than interest. However, finance charges on credit cards are interest. Late payments charged by public utilities are interest expense because they do not relate to any specific service.[22] Of course, if taxpayers incur these expenses in a trade or business, they are deductible.

KEY POINT

In general, the classification of interest expense depends on the use to which the borrowed money is put, not on the nature of the property used to secure the loan.

CLASSIFICATION OF INTEREST EXPENSE

The deductibility of interest generally depends on the purpose for which the taxpayer incurs the indebtedness because interest incurred in certain activities is subject to limitation and disallowance. For example, interest expense incurred in the taxpayer's active business is deductible in full against the business income (a deduction *for* AGI, taken on Schedule C), whereas interest expense allocated to the purchase of the taxpayer's residence is subject to the limitations applicable to that type of interest and is an itemized deduction (a deduction *from* AGI). Except for certain student loan interest and certain interest on a personal residence, taxpayers may not deduct interest allocated to personal-use expenditures.

Pursuant to the Treasury Regulations, taxpayers must allocate interest expense to the different interest expense categories by identifying the use of the borrowed money. Property used as collateral in securing the debt normally has no bearing on the allocation of the interest expense.[23]

EXAMPLE I:7-11 ▶ Cathy pledges some stock and securities as collateral for a $30,000 loan. She then purchases an automobile with the proceeds of the loan. The automobile is used 100% of the time for personal use. Even though the collateral for the loan is investment property, the interest expense is allocated to a personal-use asset and is not deductible. ◄

If the taxpayer deposits borrowed funds in a bank rather than spending them immediately, the deposit is treated as an investment, and the interest on the loan is investment interest until the taxpayer withdraws or expends the funds. Then the taxpayer allocates the interest expense to a category based on the reason for making the expenditure, regardless of when the taxpayer actually pays the interest expense for the debt. This reallocation occurs as of the date the taxpayer writes the check on the account, as long as the delivery or mailing of the check occurs within a reasonable period of time.[24]

EXAMPLE I:7-12 ▶ On March 1 of the current year, José borrows $100,000 and immediately deposits the funds into an account that contains no other funds. José makes no additional deposits or payments. On May 1 of the current year, he withdraws $40,000 from the account and purchases a sailboat to be used for personal purposes. On July 1, José withdraws an additional $50,000 and purchases a passive activity. For the current year, the interest expense on the loan is categorized as follows: from March 1 through April 30, all of the expense is investment interest expense. 40% ($40,000/$100,000) of the interest expense attributable to the period May 1 through June 30 is classified as personal interest and the remainder is investment interest. The interest expense attributable to the period from July 1 to the end of the year is classified as 40% personal interest, 50% passive activity interest, and 10% investment interest. ◄

If both borrowed and personal funds are mingled in the same account, expenditures from that account are treated as coming first from the borrowed funds.[25]

EXAMPLE I:7-13 ▶ On April 1 of the current year, Diane borrows $30,000 and deposits it into a checking account that contains $10,000 of personal funds. On May 1 of the current year, Diane purchases a passive activity for $15,000, and on June 1 she purchases a personal automobile for $20,000. The $15,000 expended for the passive activity on May 1 is treated as coming from the borrowed funds. Thus, as of that date, one-half of the interest expense on the debt is reallocated from

---

[22] Rev. Rul. 73-136, 1973-1 C.B. 68 and Rev. Rul. 74-187, 1974-1 C.B. 48. See also Rev. Rul. 77-417, 1977-2 CB 60, which rules that one-time charges of 2% of each new cash advance and 1% of each new check and overdraft advance on a credit card account is an interest charge if the charges are not for services performed in the maintenance of the account. Of course, interest on a credit card or interest charged by a public utility is not deductible if it is personal interest.

[23] Temp. Reg. Sec. 1.163-8T. The major exception to this rule deals with home equity loans where the funds borrowed may be used for any purpose. Home equity loans are discussed later in this chapter.

[24] Temp. Reg. Sec. 1.163-8T(c). If during any one month several expenditures are made from an account, the taxpayer may elect to treat all the expenditures

as if made on the first day of the month. This election is made on each account separately and is available only for accounts where the borrowed funds are already in the account as of the first day of the month. If the funds are not in the account as of the first day of the month, the expenditures may be treated as made on the date that the borrowed funds are deposited in the account. See Temp. Reg. Sec. 1.163-8T(c)(4)(iv).

[25] Temp. Reg. Sec. 1.163-8T(c)(4)(iii)(B). However, if an expenditure is made out of the mingled funds within 15 days of the deposit of the borrowed funds into the account, the taxpayer may designate the expenditure to which the borrowed funds are allocated.

investment interest to passive activity interest. $15,000 of the funds expended for the personal automobile on June 1 is treated as coming from the borrowed funds, and the remaining $5,000 is treated as coming from the personal funds. Thus, as of June 1, the remaining interest expense on the debt is reallocated to personal interest. ◄

When the taxpayer repays the debt, the allocation of the repayment to the expenditures made with the borrowed funds occurs in the following order: (1) personal expenditures, (2) investment expenditures and passive activity expenditures other than rental real estate, (3) passive activity expenditures in rental real estate, and (4) trade or business expenditures.

Active Trade or Business. Generally, a taxpayer may deduct without limit any interest expense incurred in the taxpayer's active trade or business. As explained in Chapter I:6, the determination of whether a particular activity constitutes a trade or business or an investment depends on an examination of all the relevant facts and circumstances. For individuals, estates, trusts, and certain corporations, however, it is not sufficient that the taxpayer incur the interest in a trade or business. In addition, the taxpayer must *materially participate* in the business. If not, the activity is considered a passive activity, and losses from the activity (including the interest expense) are subject to the passive loss limitation rules (see Chapter I:8 for a discussion of these rules). Interest incurred in an active trade or business is a deduction *for* AGI.

Passive Activity. Individuals, estates, trusts, and certain corporations that incur losses from passive activities are subject to the passive loss limitation rules explained in Chapter I:8. These rules prevent taxpayers from offsetting passive activity losses against other types of income such as salary, interest, dividends, and income from an active business. Taxpayers must include interest expense attributable to the passive activity in computing the net income or loss generated from the activity, and thus may not be able to deduct the interest under these limitation rules (see Chapter I:8 for a discussion of these rules).

Investment Interest. Individuals and other noncorporate taxpayers are limited on the deductibility of interest expense attributable to investments. Without any limitation, high-income taxpayers could realize significant tax savings by borrowing money to invest in assets that are appreciating in value but produce little or no current income. This would enable the taxpayer to offset current highly taxed income with a current interest deduction, while deferring the taxable income from the investment until it is sold at a later date. This technique also would enable taxpayers to increase their future capital gain income and reduce their current ordinary income. This procedure is favorable to individual and noncorporate taxpayers because the tax on capital gains is less than the tax on ordinary income.

Because of these concerns, Sec. 163(d) limits the current deduction for investment interest expense to the noncorporate taxpayer's net investment income for the taxable year. Any investment interest expense disallowed as a current deduction is carried over and treated as investment interest expense incurred in the following year.

EXAMPLE I:7-14 ► In the current year, Rita earns $27,000 in net investment income and incurs $40,000 of investment interest expense. Rita's interest expense deduction for the year is limited to $27,000, the amount of her net investment income.

The remaining investment interest expense of $13,000 ($40,000 − $27,000) may be carried over and deducted in a subsequent year. This carryover amount is treated as paid or accrued in the subsequent year and is subject to the disallowance rules that pertain to the subsequent year. ◄

Investment Interest. **Investment interest** is interest expense on indebtedness properly allocable to property held for investment. This includes property that generates portfolio types of income such as interest, dividends, annuities, and royalties. It does not include business interest, personal interest, qualified residence interest, or interest incurred in connection with any passive activity. Under Sec. 469, all rental activities are passive (see Chapter I:8 for a discussion of the passive loss limitation rules). Thus, interest incurred in owning and renting property is subject to the passive loss limitation rather than the investment interest limitation.

Investment interest also does not include interest expense incurred to purchase or hold tax-exempt securities. This interest is not deductible at all. Without this disallowance, a taxpayer could, in certain circumstances, actually borrow funds at a higher rate of interest than the rate at which they were reinvested, while still generating a positive net cash flow because the government would be subsidizing the transaction through the interest deduction on the borrowings.

Net Investment Income. For purposes of the investment interest limitation, the term **net investment income** means the excess of the taxpayer's investment income over investment expenses. Investment income is gross income from property held for investment, including items such as dividends, interest, annuities, net short-term capital gains, and royalties (if not earned in a trade or business), but excluding qualified dividends and net long-term capital gains taxed at the preferential capital gains tax rates.

Including either of these two items in the definition of investment income would increase the amount of deductible investment interest expense, which might offset other income that is taxed at higher rates. Thus, the definition of investment income generally excludes net capital gain attributable to the disposition of property held for investment and qualified dividends. However, at the election of the taxpayer, net capital gain from the disposition of investment property and qualified dividends can be included in investment income. To the extent the taxpayer elects to include gains from the disposition of investment property and qualified dividends in investment income, these items are taxed at the regular tax rates rather than at the preferential long-term capital gain rates.[26] The calculation of investment income does not include gains on business and personal-use property.

EXAMPLE I:7-15 ►

During the current year, Michael incurs $15,000 investment interest expense, earns $7,000 of qualified dividends and $3,000 interest income. He also reports the following gains and losses from the sale of stocks and bonds during the year:

Short-term capital gains	$4,000
Short-term capital losses	(3,000)
Long-term capital gains	5,000
Long-term capital losses	(2,000)

Considering all of Michael's other income and deductions for the year, assume that he is subject to a 35% marginal tax rate. Michael's net capital gain is $3,000 (net long-term capital gain of $3,000 in excess of net short-term capital losses of $0). He also has a $1,000 ($4,000 – $3,000) net short-term capital gain. Thus, of his total capital gain of $4,000 ($9,000 of total gains – $5,000 of total losses), only $1,000 ($4,000 net gain – $3,000 net capital gain) is included in investment income. In addition, the $7,000 of qualified dividends also are not included in investment income. If Michael does not make an election, his investment income is $4,000 ($3,000 of interest plus $1,000 net short-term capital gain). He may deduct $4,000 of the investment interest expense in the current year. The excess investment interest for the current year of $11,000 ($15,000 – $4,000) is carried over to the next year. The $3,000 net capital gain and the qualified dividends are subject to the 15% tax rate on net capital gain. If Michael makes the election, his investment income is $14,000 (the $3,000 net capital gain and $7,000 of qualified dividends are included), and he may deduct $14,000 of the investment interest expense. Thus, only $1,000 ($15,000 – $14,000) of investment interest expense is not currently deductible and is carried over to the next year. However, his $3,000 net capital gain and $7,000 of qualified dividends are subject to the 35% ordinary income tax rate. ◄

ADDITIONAL COMMENT
Investment expenses are those which are deductible on the tax return, after the 2% limitation.

Investment expenses include all deductions (except interest) that are directly connected with the production of investment income. These expenses include rental fees for safe-deposit boxes, fees for investment counsel,[27] and subscriptions to investment and financial planning journals. As explained later in this chapter (see the section of this chapter titled Miscellaneous Itemized Deductions), these investment expenses are deductible only to the extent they exceed 2% of the taxpayer's AGI for the year. Only the investment

---

[26] Secs. 1(h)(3) and 163(d)(4)(B).
[27] Sec. 163(d)(4)(C). Commissions for the sale or purchase of investment property are not included here. A commission paid on the purchase of property is

added to the purchase price (and the basis) of the property. A commission paid on the sale of property reduces the amount realized.

expenses remaining after application of this limitation are used in computing the net investment income. Furthermore, in computing the amount of the disallowed investment expenses, the 2% of AGI limitation applies to the noninvestment expenses first.[28] Any remaining 2% of AGI limitation then reduces the noninterest investment expenses.

EXAMPLE I:7-16 ▶ Kevin's AGI for the current year is $200,000. Included in his AGI is $175,000 salary and $25,000 of investment income. In earning the investment income, Kevin paid investment interest expense of $33,000. He also incurred the following expenditures subject to the 2% of AGI limitation:

Investment expenses:	
Subscriptions to investment journals	$ 700
Investment counseling	2,000
Safe-deposit box rental	300
Noninvestment expenses:	
Unreimbursed employee business expenses	1,500
Tax return preparation fees (non–business-related)	500

Kevin's investment interest expense deduction for the year is computed by first determining the deductible investment expenses (other than interest) and the net investment income.

Investment expenses:		
Subscriptions	$ 700	
Investment counseling	2,000	
Safe-deposit box rental	300	$3,000
Disallowed by the 2% limitation:		
2% of AGI ($200,000 × 0.02)	$4,000	
Unreimbursed employee expenses	(1,500)	
Tax return preparation fees	(500)	
Investment expenses (remainder of 2% limit allocated to investment expenses)		(2,000)
Deductible investment expenses		$1,000
Net investment income ($25,000 − $1,000)		$24,000

The investment interest expense deduction is limited to $24,000. The remaining investment interest of $9,000 ($33,000 – $24,000) is carried over and deducted in a subsequent year (subject to the disallowance rules that pertain to the subsequent year). ◀

Personal Interest. In general, the tax law does not allow a deduction for interest expense on debt incurred for personal purposes. Thus, taxpayers may not deduct interest on credit cards, car loans, and consumer debt. However, taxpayers generally may deduct interest on debt to acquire a personal residence. Qualified students may also deduct as a *for* AGI deduction interest incurred on certain student loans.

Qualified Residence Interest. Subject to certain limitations discussed below, individuals may deduct **qualified residence interest.** To be qualified residence interest, the interest payment must be either acquisition indebtedness or home equity indebtedness with respect to a qualified residence of the taxpayer. In all cases the residence must secure the debt.[29] A qualified residence (discussed below) may consist of the taxpayer's principal residence and a second residence.

Acquisition Indebtedness. Acquisition indebtedness is any debt secured by the residence and incurred in acquiring, constructing, or substantially improving the qualified residence. Debt may be treated as qualified acquisition indebtedness if the taxpayer acquires the

---

[28] H. Rept. No. 99-841, 99th Cong., 2d Sess., pp. II-153 and 154 (1986). The noninvestment expenses subject to the 2% of AGI limitation include unreimbursed employee business expenses, hobby expenses up to the income from the hobby, and tax return preparation fees.
[29] Sec. 163(h). If the loan is not secured by the residence, it does not qualify. In one instance the taxpayer agreed to purchase her ex-husband's interest in their residence. The terms of the sale were $10,000 down plus an unsecured $25,000 note. In a private ruling, the IRS ruled that because the note was not

secured by the residence, the interest on the note was not qualified residence interest. (See Ltr. Rul. 8752010 September 18, 1987.) However, if under any state or local homestead law the security interest is ineffective or unenforceable, the interest expense still qualifies as qualified residence interest. See Sec. 163(h)(4)(C). In another letter ruling the taxpayer borrowed money to purchase a residence securing the debt by pledging stock and bonds. Here also, the IRS denied the deduction because the loan was not secured by the residence. (See Ltr. Rul. 8906031 November 10, 1988.)

residence within 90 days before or after the date that the debt is incurred. In the case of the construction or substantial improvement of a residence, debt incurred before the completion of the construction or improvement can qualify as acquisition debt to the extent of construction expenditures that are made no more than 24 months before the date the debt is incurred. Furthermore, debt incurred after construction is complete and within 90 days of the completion date may qualify as acquisition indebtedness to the extent of any construction expenditures made within the 24-month period ending on the date the debt is incurred.[30] Making payments of principal on the loan reduces the amount of acquisition debt. The only way to increase the amount of acquisition debt is to make substantial improvements to the property. The taxpayer may refinance acquisition indebtedness (and therefore treat it as acquisition indebtedness) to the extent that the principal amount of the refinancing does not exceed the principal amount of the acquisition debt immediately before the refinancing.

EXAMPLE I:7-17 ▶ Kay acquired a personal residence in 2005 for $220,000 and borrowed $140,000 on a mortgage that was secured by the property. In the current year the principal balance of the mortgage has been reduced to $100,000. Kay's acquisition indebtedness in the current year is only $100,000 and cannot be increased above $100,000 (except by indebtedness incurred to substantially improve the residence). If she refinances the existing mortgage in the current year and the refinanced debt is $110,000, only $100,000 (the principal balance of the existing acquisition indebtedness) qualifies as acquisition indebtedness. ◄

The limitation for qualified acquisition indebtedness is $1,000,000 ($500,000 for a married individual filing a separate return). Qualified acquisition indebtedness incurred before October 13, 1987 (pre-October 13, 1987 indebtedness) is not subject to any limitation. However, the aggregate amount of pre-October 13, 1987 indebtedness reduces the $1,000,000 limitation on the indebtedness incurred after October 13, 1987.

ADDITIONAL COMMENT
Many banks, in attempting to generate new loan business, have heavily advertised the tax advantages of home equity indebtedness.

Home Equity Indebtedness. Taxpayers may also deduct interest incurred on home equity indebtedness (so-called home equity loans). Subject to certain limits, home equity indebtedness is any indebtedness (other than acquisition indebtedness) secured by a qualified residence of the taxpayer. The taxpayer may use the proceeds of the loan for any purpose (including purchasing or improving a qualified residence), as long as the taxpayer's qualified residence secures the loan. However, the tax law limits home equity indebtedness to the lesser of:

▶ The FMV of the qualified residence in excess of the acquisition indebtedness with respect to the residence, or

▶ $100,000 ($50,000 for a married individual filing a separate return)

The $1,000,000 limit on acquisition indebtedness and the $100,000 limit on home equity indebtedness are two separate limits. The maximum amount of indebtedness on which a taxpayer may deduct qualified residence interest is $1,100,000 if an individual has $100,000 or more equity in the property.

EXAMPLE I:7-18 ▶ On April 23 of the current year, Kesha borrows $125,000 to purchase a new sailboat. The loan is secured by her personal residence. On that date, the outstanding balance on the original debt Kesha incurred to purchase the residence is $400,000 and the FMV of the residence is $900,000. The original debt is also secured by Kesha's residence. Kesha may deduct the interest paid on the $400,000 of acquisition indebtedness, plus the interest paid on $100,000 of the home equity loan. The interest on $25,000 ($125,000 − $100,000) is treated as personal interest and is, therefore, not deductible. The home equity loan is limited to the lesser of $100,000 or the FMV of the residence in excess of the outstanding acquisition indebtedness (the lesser of $100,000 or $500,000 ($900,000 − $400,000)). ◄

Points Paid as Qualified Residence Interest. Often taxpayers must pay **points** on real estate debt. A point is equal to 1% of the loan amount. Thus, two points paid on a $120,000 mortgage equal $2,400 (120,000 × .02). Points often represent prepaid interest because the stated

---

[30] Notice 88-74, 1988-2 C.B. 385.

rate of interest for the loan is lower than the current rate of interest. Generally, prepaid interest paid in the form of points must be capitalized and amortized over the life of the loan. However, points paid on a loan incurred to purchase the taxpayer's principal residence (acquisition indebtedness) are automatically deductible when paid if certain requirements are met. The IRS has also indicated that points paid on Veteran Administration (VA) and Federal Home Administration (FHA) loans are also currently deductible as interest if clearly designated as points incurred in connection with the indebtedness.[31]

EXAMPLE I:7-19 ▶

During the current year, Kevin and Donna purchase a new home for $300,000, putting $100,000 down and borrowing $200,000. At the closing, they are required to pay one and one-half points as a loan discount in connection with the loan, which is secured by a mortgage against the home. The practice of charging points is an established business practice where they live.

These points represent prepaid interest on the purchase of a principal residence. Thus, in addition to the interest portion of every payment they make during the year, Kevin and Donna may also deduct $3,000 ($200,000 × 0.015) as interest paid during the year of purchase. ◀

Taxpayers must capitalize points paid on a loan to purchase property other than a principal residence or for refinancing a mortgage on a principal residence. If the property is used in a business, held as an investment, or a qualified residence (the taxpayer's principal residence and one other that the taxpayer chooses) the taxpayer may amortize the points over the life of the loan.[32]

In order for the points to be currently deductible, the purchaser of the principal residence (borrower) must have paid for them with unborrowed funds. However, amounts provided by the borrower as down payments, escrow deposits, earnest money, or other funds are treated as paid for the points. Furthermore, as long as the borrower provides sufficient funds in these other categories, he or she is treated as having paid the points even if the seller has paid for them on behalf of the borrower.[33]

In addition to interest on a qualified residence home acquisition or home equity loan, taxpayers could also deduct mortgage insurance premiums paid or accrued on a qualified residence before 2015. This deduction phased out for taxpayers with AGI in excess of $100,000. The amount of the phase-out was 10% of the amount of the qualified mortgage insurance for each $1,000 (or fraction thereof) that the taxpayer's AGI exceeded $100,000. For taxpayers married filing separately, the amount of the phase-out was 10% of the amount of the qualified mortgage insurance for each $500 (or fraction thereof) that the taxpayer's AGI exceeded $50,000. It is uncertain whether or not Congress will extend this additional deduction for years after 2014.

Qualified Residence. For any tax year, a taxpayer may have two qualified residences:

▶ Taxpayer's principal residence
▶ One other residence selected by the taxpayer, with regard to which the taxpayer meets the residence test of Sec. 280A(d)(1).

In order to meet this residence test, the taxpayer must have personally used the property more than the greater of 14 days or 10% of any rental days during the year.[34]

EXAMPLE I:7-20 ▶

ADDITIONAL COMMENT

Whether property is a residence for tax purposes is based on all the facts and circumstances, including the good faith of the taxpayer. A residence generally includes a house, condominium, mobile home, boat, or house trailer, that contains sleeping space and toilet and cooking facilities. Treas. Reg. § 1.163-10T(p)(3)(ii).

Fred owns a lakeside cabin that he uses for vacations. He also rents the cabin out to others when he is not using it. During the year Fred rents the cabin out at a fair rental for 90 days. Fred personally uses the cabin for a total of 22 days. Because Fred's personal use for the year (22 days) exceeds 14 days [the greater of 14 days or 9 days (10% of the rental days)], the cabin qualifies as his residence for purposes of deducting qualified residence interest for the year. ◀

Despite the residence test, the taxpayer may select a property that has not been rented by the taxpayer at any time during the year as the second residence on which the taxpayer may deduct qualified residence interest.

---

[31] These requirements, are as follows: The points are paid upon the purchase of a principal residence; they are designated as paid in connection with the acquisition debt and are a percentage of the loan; they follow business practices and are secured by the residence. Rev. Proc. 94-27, 1994-1 C.B. 613.

[32] Rev. Rul. 87-22, 1987-1 C.B. 146, and Rev. Proc. 87-15, 1987-1 C.B. 624. The 8th Circuit Court of Appeals has held in one case that points paid on refinancing a "bridge" or temporary loan are currently deductible. *James R.*

Huntsman v. CIR, 66 AFTR 2d 90-5020, 90-2 USTC ¶ 50,340 (8th Cir., 1990), rev'g 91 TC 57 (1988). The IRS will not follow *Huntsman* in other circuits (IRS Action on Decision CC-1991-02, Feb. 11, 1991).

[33] Reg. Sec. 1.6050H-1(f)(3). See also Rev. Proc. 94-27, 1994-1 C.B. 613.

[34] Sec. 280A(d)(1). Use by the taxpayer's family as defined in Sec. 267(c) (4), other individuals under a reciprocal-use arrangement, and anyone when a fair rental is not charged counts as a day of personal use by the taxpayer.

? STOP & THINK

Question: Jana is about to purchase a new sport utility vehicle for $35,000. If she pays $5,000 down, the dealer is prepared to offer her a loan for the remaining $30,000 at 6% interest. In investigating other possible sources of funds, she found out that her brokerage firm would lend her the $30,000 at 7% interest if she pledged her stock as collateral. At her local credit union, she found that she could borrow the $30,000 at 8% interest if she took out a home equity loan by using her home as security. Jana is confused about which loan she should take.

Solution: The best way to analyze this problem is to compare the after-tax interest rates of the loans. Jana may not deduct the interest paid to the car dealer because it is personal interest. Thus, its after-tax interest rate remains at 6%. Furthermore, even though Jana uses her stock holdings as collateral, the interest on the loan from the brokerage firm is non-deductible personal interest because she uses the proceeds of the loan to purchase personal property rather than investment property. Its after-tax interest rate remains at 7%. Only the interest on the home equity loan from the credit union is potentially deductible. This depends, of course, on the amount of Jana's total itemized deductions. Assuming Jana's total itemized deductions exceed the standard deduction and Jana is in the 33% marginal tax bracket, the after-tax interest rate of the home equity loan drops from 8% to 5.33% [8% × (1 − 0.33)].

Student Loan Interest. Individuals may take a *for* AGI deduction for interest paid on qualified education loans. The maximum annual interest deduction for qualified student loans is $2,500. Furthermore, the deduction is phased out if the student reports modified AGI in excess of certain amounts. For 2015 the deduction begins phasing out for a single individual with modified AGI of $65,000 (with a $15,000 phase-out range). For a student who is married filing jointly, the phase-out begins at $130,000 (with a $30,000 phase-out range).[35]

EXAMPLE I:7-21 ▶ During 2015, Ryan pays a total of $2,800 in interest on a loan incurred for qualified education expenses. Ryan is single and reports modified AGI of $74,000 for the year. Because his modified AGI of $74,000 is $9,000 more than $65,000, the maximum deduction of $2,500 is reduced by 60% ($9,000/$15,000). Ryan may take a *for* AGI deduction of $1,000 [2,500 − (60% × 2,500)]. If Ryan pays only $1,800 of interest (rather than $2,800), the potential deduction of $1,800 would be reduced by 60% to $720 [$1,800 − (60% × $1,800)]. ◀

To qualify for this deduction, the interest must be payable on a loan incurred solely to pay for qualified higher education expenses. If a taxpayer takes out a loan to pay for higher education expenses and for other purposes, none of the interest on the loan qualifies. Higher education expenses include tuition, fees, books and equipment, and room and board incurred during a time the taxpayer, the taxpayer's spouse, or the taxpayer's dependent is a student at a qualified higher education institution on at least a half-time basis. However, these qualified expenditures do not include amounts excluded from income under an employer educational assistance program or from United States savings bonds, as well as any scholarship or allowance that is excluded from income. Furthermore, to prevent a double deduction, the tax law allows no deduction to an individual for whom a dependency exemption may be taken on another person's tax return or for any amount that is deductible under any other provision of the Code.

TIMING OF THE INTEREST DEDUCTION

Under Sec. 163, deductible interest becomes deductible in the year the interest is paid or accrued. This generally means that cash method taxpayers deduct interest in the year paid, whereas accrual method taxpayers deduct interest as it accrues. However, the IRC makes exceptions to this general rule.

[35] Modified AGI includes certain excluded income from Guam, American Samoa, or Puerto Rico, as well as any income excluded under the foreign earned income provisions. Furthermore, the deduction for qualified tuition and related expenses is not allowed.

ADDITIONAL COMMENT
Points paid on the refinancing of an existing mortgage must be written off over the life of the new mortgage.

Prepaid Interest. If a cash method taxpayer prepays interest and the prepayment relates to a loan that extends beyond the end of the tax year, generally the taxpayer must capitalize the prepayment and amortize it over the periods to which the interest relates (i.e., the accrual method applies to cash method taxpayers in regards to prepaid interest). As previously discussed, the law makes one exception to this rule involving interest paid in the form of points charged in connection with the purchase or improvement of the taxpayer's principal residence. If these points represent prepaid interest, the taxpayer may deduct them in the year paid.[36]

Interest Paid with Loan Proceeds. Assuming the interest is otherwise deductible, if an individual borrows money from a third party rather than from the original lending institution and uses the funds to make a payment on a previously outstanding loan, the individual generally may deduct the interest portion of the payment. However, if the taxpayer borrows the funds used to pay the interest on the first loan from the same lender to whom the interest is due, and either (1) the purpose of the second loan is to pay the interest on the first or (2) the borrower does not have unrestricted control of the funds, then the borrower may not deduct the interest.[37]

Discounted Notes. Lending institutions often discount notes. In effect, the borrower pays the interest by repaying more money than is received when the note is signed. A cash method taxpayer can deduct this interest at the time of repayment, whereas an accrual method taxpayer must deduct the interest as it accrues over the term of the loan.

EXAMPLE I:7-22 ▶

On December 1, 2015, Stan borrows $1,000 from his credit union to use in his business. Under the terms of the contract, Stan actually receives $970 but is required to repay $1,000 on February 28, 2016 (three months later). Because Stan is a cash-method taxpayer, he may deduct the full $30 interest in 2016 when the note is repaid. If he were an accrual-method taxpayer, he could deduct $10 ($30 × 1/3) in 2015, and $20 ($30 × 2/3) in 2016. ◀

TYPICAL MISCONCEPTION
Taxpayers sometimes mistakenly assume that any business interest paid on loans between related taxpayers is not deductible. However, if the taxpayers are not governed by the Sec. 267 limitation and the interest is paid on a bona fide business loan, it is deductible.

Interest Owed to a Related Party by an Accrual Method Taxpayer. One of the purposes of Sec. 267 is to require related cash method lenders and accrual method borrowers to report the results of their joint transaction in the same year. Thus, an accrual method taxpayer who is related to a cash method creditor must defer the deduction for any accrued expense (including interest) until the year in which the taxpayer actually pays the expense and the creditor reports the income. Section 267 also disallows losses on the sale of property between related parties. Disallowance of losses between related parties is discussed in Chapter I:6.

The relationships covered by this rule are quite extensive. Some of the more common relationships include the following:

▶ Members of a family (defined as an individual's brothers, sisters, spouse, ancestors, and lineal descendants)

▶ An individual and a C corporation in which the individual owns directly or indirectly more than 50% of the outstanding stock

▶ A corporation and a partnership which are both over 50% owned directly or indirectly by the same people

▶ A partnership and any partner of the partnership

▶ An S Corporation and any shareholder of the S Corporation[38]

---

[36] Sec. 461(g). In order for the exception to apply, the home must be used to secure the loan, and the charging of points must be an established business practice in the area where the loan is granted. (See the discussion of the deductibility of points in this chapter under the heading Definition of *Interest* as well as the discussion in Chapter I:6.)

[37] *H. C. Franklin v. CIR*, 50 AFTR 2d 82-5551, 82-2 USTC ¶9532 (5th Cir., 1982) and *Newton A. Burgess*, 8 T.C. 47 (1947). See also *Norman W. Menz*, 80 T.C. 1174 (1983). The IRS has also announced that it will disallow a deduction for interest paid with funds obtained through a second loan from the same lender (see IRS News Release 83-93, July 6, 1983).

[38] Secs. 267(b) and (e). The list of relationships is much more extensive than those mentioned. An S corporation is one that meets certain requirements and has made an election to have its income taxed directly to its shareholders. A C corporation is one that has not made an S election. (See Chapter C:11 of *Prentice Hall's Federal Taxation: Corporations, Partnerships, Estates, and Trusts* text or Chapter C:11 of *Prentice Hall's Federal Taxation: Comprehensive* text.)

EXAMPLE I:7-23 ▶ During the current year, Lisa, a cash method taxpayer, loans some money to her 100%-owned calendar year C corporation, which uses the accrual method of accounting. As of December 31 of the current year, the corporation owes Lisa $3,000 in interest. However, because of a shortage of funds, the corporation does not actually pay the interest until February 15 of the following year. Despite the fact that the corporation uses the accrual method of accounting, the corporation cannot deduct the $3,000 until the corporation actually pays the interest to Lisa in the subsequent year. The result would be the same if the corporation were an S Corporation even if Lisa owned 50% or less of the outstanding stock. ◄

Imputed Interest. Under certain circumstances, if a taxpayer charges less than an adequate rate of interest, the IRS is authorized to impute an interest charge. This may cause the lender to have additional interest income and the borrower to have additional interest expense. The deductibility of this imputed interest expense depends on the classification of the expense (i.e. personal, investment, etc.). (See Chapter I:11 for a discussion of imputed interest.)

Topic Review I:7-2 summarizes the rules for deducting various types of interest.

TOPIC REVIEW I:7-2

Deductibility of Interest Expense

TYPE OF INTEREST	RULES
Business	Deductible in full as a *for* AGI deduction.
Passive	Subject to the passive loss limits (see Chapter I:8).
Investment	Deductible as an itemized deduction to the extent of the taxpayer's net investment income for the year. Any amount not deductible is carried over to subsequent years.
Personal	Not deductible.
Qualified residence	(a) Must be attributable to debt secured by the taxpayer's principal residence and one other qualified residence selected by the taxpayer.
	(b) Interest on up to $1,000,000 of home acquisition indebtedness is deductible as an itemized deduction.
	(c) Interest on home equity debt is deductible as an itemized deduction. Home equity debt is limited to the lesser of $100,000 or the excess of the FMV of the residence over the home acquisition indebtedness.
Student Loan Interest	(a) Payable on loan incurred to pay qualified higher education expenses.
	(b) Taken as a *for* AGI deduction.
	(c) Maximum deductible amount is $2,500. The deduction is phased out ratably for modified AGI between $65,000 and $80,000 ($130,000 and $160,000 for married filing jointly).

CHARITABLE CONTRIBUTIONS

OBJECTIVE 4

Compute the amount of a charitable contribution deduction and identify limitations

Under Sec. 170, individuals who itemize their deductions and corporations can deduct **charitable contributions** to qualified organizations. With the exception of certain contributions made by corporations (explained later in this chapter), a taxpayer takes the deduction in the year the contribution is made, regardless of the taxpayer's method of accounting. The amount of the deduction depends on the type of charity receiving the contribution, the type of property contributed, and the applicable limitations.

QUALIFYING ORGANIZATION

To deduct a contribution for federal income tax purposes, a taxpayer must make the contribution to or for the use of a qualified organization.[39] Contributions made directly to

---

[39] The Supreme Court has ruled that in order for a contribution to be for the use of a qualifying organization, the gift must be held either in a legally enforceable trust or in a similar legal arrangement. (See *U.S. v. Harold Davis*, 65 AFTR 2d 90-1051, 90-1 USTC ¶50,270 (USSC, 1990).)

individuals, even though the individuals may be needy, are generally not deductible.[40] Under Sec. 170, qualified organizations include the following:

▶ The United States, the District of Columbia, a state or possession of the United States, or a political subdivision of a state or possession

▶ A corporation, trust, community chest, fund or foundation created or organized under the laws of the United States, a state, possession, or the District of Columbia[41]

▶ A post or organization of war veterans

▶ A domestic fraternal society, order, or association[42]

▶ Certain cemetery companies

Because of the restrictions and limitations examined later in this chapter, these qualifying non-governmental are further classified into public charities and private nonoperating foundations. Different restrictions and limitations apply to each type of organization.

Public charities include:

▶ Churches or a convention or association of churches

▶ Educational institutions that normally maintain a regular faculty, curriculum, and regularly enrolled students

▶ Organizations such as hospitals and medical schools whose principal function is medical care or medical education and research

▶ Government-supported organizations that exist to receive, hold, invest, and administer property for the benefit of a college or university

▶ Any qualified governmental unit

▶ Organizations that normally receive a substantial part of their support from either a governmental unit or the general public

▶ Certain private operating foundations[43]

TYPE OF PROPERTY CONTRIBUTED

If a taxpayer makes a contribution in cash, the amount of the contribution is easily determinable. However, in order to assure that the contribution has been properly made to a qualified charity, the taxpayer is required to maintain a record of the contribution such as a bank record or a written communication from the donee.[44] If noncash property is donated, the amount of the contribution is not as easy to identify. In the case of noncash property, the amount of the donation depends on two factors: (1) the type of property donated and (2) the type of qualifying organization (public charity or private nonoperating foundation) to whom the property is given. Furthermore, a gift of property that consists of less than the donor's entire interest in the property is not usually considered a contribution of property. Thus, for example, no charitable contribution is allowed when an individual donates the use of a vacation home for a charitable fund-raising auction.[45]

Contribution of Long-Term Capital Gain Property. In general, the amount of a donation of long-term capital gain property is its FMV. Regulation Sec. 1.170A-1(c)(2) defines a property's FMV as the price at which the property would change

[40] Under certain circumstances, a taxpayer may take a deduction (limited to $50 per month) for maintaining a student as a member of his or her household. The student may not be a dependent or relative of the taxpayer and must be placed in the taxpayer's home under an arrangement with a qualifying organization (see Sec. 170(g)).

[41] These organizations must be organized and operated exclusively for religious, charitable, scientific, literary, or educational purposes; to foster national or international amateur sports competition; or for the prevention of cruelty to children or animals.

[42] Furthermore, gifts to these organizations must be made by individuals and must be used exclusively for religious, charitable, scientific, literary, or educational purposes, or for the prevention of cruelty to children or animals.

[43] Sec. 170(b)(1)(F). The distinction between a private operating foundation

and a private nonoperating foundation generally depends on the way the foundation spends or distributes its income and contributions. The details of this distinction are beyond the scope of this text.

[44] Sec. 170(f)(17) and Notice 2008-16. This record must show (1) the name of the donee organization, (2) the date of the contribution, and (3) the amount of the contribution.

[45] Sec. 170(f)(3), Reg. Sec. 1.170A-7(a)(1) and Rev. Rul. 89-51, 1989-1 C.B. 89. Note, however, that certain transfers of partial interests in property do qualify (e.g., the contribution of certain remainder interests to a trust, the transfer of a remainder interest in a personal residence or a farm, or a contribution of an undivided interest in property). These exceptions are beyond the scope of this text.

ADDITIONAL COMMENT

In 2004, new rules were added relating to the contribution of used vehicles and intellectual property. For a used vehicle donated to a charity, in most cases the deduction will be limited to the charity's gross proceeds on the subsequent sale of the vehicle. A taxpayer's deduction for the contribution of a patent or similar intellectual property is the taxpayer's basis in the property.

hands between a willing buyer and a willing seller, neither being under any compulsion to buy or sell and both having reasonable knowledge of relevant facts. For purposes of charitable contributions, **capital gain property** is property held over one year, on which the taxpayer would recognize a long-term capital gain if the taxpayer sold it at its FMV on the date of the contribution. If a capital loss or a short-term capital gain would be recognized on the sale of the capital asset, the property is considered to be ordinary income property for purposes of calculating the amount of the charitable contribution deduction.

Contribution to a Private Nonoperating Foundation. The tax law provides an exception to this general rule for contributions of capital gain property to private nonoperating foundations. In general, a private nonoperating foundation is an organization that does not receive funding from the general public (e.g., the Carnegie Foundation). Private nonoperating foundations distribute funds to various charitable organizations that actually perform the charitable services. The amount of the contribution of long-term capital gain property to a private nonoperating foundation is the property's FMV, reduced by the capital gain that would be recognized if the property were sold at its FMV on the date of the contribution. This means that generally the deductible amount of the contribution is the lesser of the property's adjusted basis or its FMV.[46]

EXAMPLE I:7-24 ▶ Betty purchased some land in 1991 for $10,000. In the current year, she contributes the land to the United Way. At the time of the contribution, the FMV of the property is $25,000. Because the land is long-term capital gain property donated to a public charity, the amount of the contribution is $25,000 (its FMV).

On the other hand, if Betty donates the land to Cherry Foundation, a private nonoperating foundation, the amount of the contribution is $10,000 ($25,000 − $15,000 capital gain that would be recognized if the land were sold). ◀

TYPICAL MISCONCEPTION

Many people do not understand that the unrelated use restriction applies only to tangible personal property. A gift of shares of stock (intangible property) would not be a gift of unrelated use property where the stock is sold by the donee.

Unrelated Use Property. A second exception applies to capital gain property (that is also tangible personal property) contributed to a public charity and used by the organization for purposes unrelated to the charity's function. In such cases, the amount of the contribution deduction is equal to the property's FMV minus the capital gain that would be recognized if the property were sold at its FMV. This amount generally is the property's adjusted basis. Tangible property is all property that is not intangible property (e.g., property other than stock, securities, copyrights, patents, and so on). Personal property is all property other than real estate. The taxpayer is responsible for proving that the property was not put to unrelated use. However, a taxpayer meets this burden of proof if, at the time of the contribution, the taxpayer reasonably anticipates that the property will not be put to unrelated use. The immediate sale of the property by the charitable organization is a use unrelated to its tax-exempt purpose.

EXAMPLE I:7-25 ▶ Laura purchases a painting for $3,000. Several years later she contributes the painting to a local college. The FMV of the painting is $5,000 at the time the property is contributed. The painting is both tangible personal property and capital gain property. The college places the painting in the library for display and study by art students. Because the college uses the painting for purposes related to its function as an educational institution, the amount of Laura's contribution is equal to the painting's FMV ($5,000). On the other hand, if the college had sold the painting immediately after receiving it, the presumption is that the property's use was unrelated to the college's tax-exempt purpose. In this case, Laura's contribution is only $3,000. ◀

Certain Intangibles. Under Sec. 170(e)(1)(B)(iii), a third exception applies to the contribution of certain intangibles to a charitable organization. In this case, the amount of the charitable contribution is the FMV of the property, reduced by the amount of long-term capital gain that would have been recognized if the taxpayer had sold the property. These intangibles include patents, trademarks, a trade name or secret, know-how, a purchased copyright, and certain software.

---

[46] The amount of a contribution of appreciated stock held over one year made to a private nonoperating foundation remains at its FMV.

Contribution of Ordinary Income Property

General Rule. If a taxpayer contributes ordinary income property to a charitable organization, the deduction is equal to the property's FMV minus the amount of gain that would be recognized if the taxpayer had sold the property at its FMV on the date of the contribution. In most cases, this deduction is equal to the property's adjusted basis. This rule applies regardless of the type of charitable organization to which the property is donated.

For this purpose, **ordinary income property** includes any property that would result in the recognition of income taxed at ordinary income rates if the taxpayer sold the property. Thus, ordinary income property includes inventory, works of art or manuscripts created by the taxpayer, capital assets that have been held for one year or less, and Sec. 1231 property to the extent a sale would result in the recognition of ordinary income due to depreciation recapture.[47]

EXAMPLE I:7-26 ▶ During the current year, Beta, Inc. purchases land as an investment for $10,000. Five months later, it contributes the land to the United Way. At the time of the contribution the property's FMV is $15,000. The amount of Beta's contribution is $10,000 ($15,000 − [$15,000 − $10,000]) because it held the land for less than one year. ◀

EXAMPLE I:7-27 ▶ Pork, Inc. purchased a machine a few years ago for $20,000 and used the machine in its business. During the current year, Pork, Inc. donates the machine to a local community college. At the time of the contribution, the machine's adjusted basis is $5,000 and its FMV is $8,000. Because Pork, Inc. would have recognized a $3,000 gain (all ordinary income under Sec. 1245) if the machine were sold at its FMV, the amount of the contribution is $5,000 ($8,000 − $3,000), which is equal to the machine's adjusted basis. ◀

Donation of Inventory by a Corporation. Under certain circumstances, the donation of inventory by a C corporation (not an S corporation) to certain public charities provides a larger charitable contribution deduction than the adjusted basis of the property. One of these enhanced charitable contributions involves the donation of inventory to the charity if the charity uses the inventory solely for the care of the ill, needy, or infants.[48] C corporations may also take an enhanced charitable contribution deduction for donating scientific equipment constructed by the taxpayer and donated to a college, university, or qualified research organization for use in research, experimentation, or research training in the physical or biological sciences.[49] The amount of the enhanced charitable contribution is the property's FMV, reduced by 50% (not 100%) of the ordinary income that the corporation would have recognized if it had sold the property at its FMV. However, the amount of the contribution cannot exceed twice the basis of the property.

EXAMPLE I:7-28 ▶ During 2015, Able Corporation, a manufacturer of medical supplies, donated some of its inventory to the American Red Cross. The Red Cross used the inventory for the care of the needy and ill. At the time of the contribution, the FMV of the inventory was $10,000. Able's basis in the inventory was $3,000. Because this transaction qualifies under the exception, the amount of Able's contribution (before any limitations are applied) is $6,500 [$10,000 − (0.50 × $7,000)] but the actual amount of the contribution is limited to $6,000 (2 × the $3,000 basis in the property). ◀

Contribution of Services. When a taxpayer renders services to a qualified charitable organization, the taxpayer may only deduct the unreimbursed expenses incurred incident to rendering the services. These items include out-of-pocket expenses, transportation expenses, the cost of lodging and 50% of the cost of meals while away from home, and the cost of a uniform that is required to be worn in performing the donated services but is not suitable for general wear. The out-of-pocket expenses are deductible only if the taxpayer who actually renders the services to the charity is the person who incurs these out-of-pocket expenses. Taxpayers cannot take a deduction for expenses while away from home unless they experience no

---

[47] Reg. Secs. 1.170A-4(b)(1) and 1.170A-4(d). Sec. 1231 property includes property used in a trade or business that is subject to depreciation. If it is sold at a gain, part or all of the gain is treated as ordinary income. Any remaining gain is subject to the Sec. 1231 rules. (See Chapter I:13 for an explanation of the depreciation recapture and Sec. 1231 rules.)

[48] Sec. 170(e)(3). These charitable organizations are known as Sec. 501(c)(3) charities. For tax years through 2014, taxpayers other than C corporations

(i.e., individuals) could also take the enhanced charitable deduction if the charitable contribution was food donated for the care of the ill, needy, or infants. [see Sec. 170(e)(3)(c)(iv).]

[49] Sec. 170(e)(4). For tax years before 2012, additional enhanced charitable contribution deductions also included the donation of computer technology and equipment to public libraries and elementary and secondary schools, and the donation of books to a public library.

significant element of personal pleasure, recreation, or vacation in such travel. Instead of the actual costs of operating an automobile while performing the donated services, the law permits a deduction of 14 cents per mile.[50]

EXAMPLE I:7-29 ►

REAL-WORLD EXAMPLE
The cost of newspaper advertising, paper, pencils, and other supplies purchased by volunteers in connection with their involvement in the Volunteer Income Tax Assistance Program (VITA) is deductible. Rev. Rul. 80-45, 1980-1 C.B. 54.

During the current year, Tony spends a total of 100 hours developing an accounting system for the local council of the Boy Scouts of America. As an accountant, Tony earns $200 per hour. During the year, Tony also drives his car a total of 500 miles in performing the services for the Boy Scouts of America. If he uses the automatic mileage method to compute the amount of the charitable contribution, he can deduct $70 (0.14 × 500). No deduction is available for the value of 100 hours of Tony's contributed services.   ◄

DEDUCTION LIMITATIONS

Overall 50% Limitation. The charitable contribution deduction available for any tax year is subject to certain limitations. For individuals, the general overall limitation applicable to public charities is 50% of the taxpayer's AGI for the year. Any contributions in excess of the overall limitation may be carried forward and deducted in the subsequent five tax years. In addition, the tax law imposes further limitations on contributions of capital gain property to either a public charity or a private nonoperating foundation and all types of property contributions to private nonoperating foundations.

KEY POINT
The generosity of Congress in permitting individuals to use FMV is tempered by the 30% of AGI limitation.

30% Limitation. Under certain circumstances, a special 30% of AGI limitation applies. Contributions of capital gain property (capital assets held over one year on which a gain would be realized if sold) to public charities are generally valued at the property's FMV, but the deduction may not exceed an overall limit of 30% of AGI instead of a 50% limit. This special 30% limit does not apply, however, in the following situations:

► Capital gain property (which is tangible personal property) donated to a public charity that does not put the property to its related use. In such cases, the amount of the contribution is reduced by the capital gain that would be recognized if the property were sold.

► The taxpayer elects to reduce the amount of the charitable contribution deduction by the capital gain that the taxpayer would recognize if he or she sold the property.

EXAMPLE I:7-30 ►

Joy donates a painting to the local university during a year in which she has AGI of $50,000. The painting, which cost $10,000 several years before, is valued at $30,000 at the time of the contribution. The university exhibits the painting in its art gallery. Because the painting is put to a use related to the university's purpose, the amount of Joy's contribution is $30,000. If Joy does not make the election, her current year charitable contribution deduction is limited to $15,000 (0.30 × $50,000 AGI). The remaining $15,000 is carried over to the subsequent five years. If she elects to reduce the amount of the contribution by the long-term capital gain, Joy's current year charitable contribution deduction is her basis of $10,000 in the property. She has no charitable contribution carryover. In this case, making the election doesn't make sense.   ◄

The overall deduction limitation of 30% of AGI also applies to the contribution of all types of property other than capital gain property (e.g., cash and ordinary income property) to a private nonoperating foundation. However, further restrictions may apply to the deductibility of certain contributions to this type of charity.

20% Limitation on Capital Gain Property Contributed to Private Nonoperating Foundations. Contributions of capital gain property to private nonoperating foundations may not exceed the lesser of (1) 20% of the taxpayer's AGI or (2) 30% of the taxpayer's AGI, reduced by any contributions of capital gain property donated to a public charity.

Contributions for Athletic Events. If a taxpayer makes a contribution to a college or university and in return receives the right to purchase tickets to athletic events, the taxpayer may deduct only 80% of the payment.

Applying the Deduction Limitations. Contributions subject only to the 50% of AGI limitation are accounted for before the contributions subject to the 30% of AGI limitation.

---

[50] Sec. 170(i).

EXAMPLE I:7-31 ▶ During a year when Ted's AGI is $70,000, he donates $22,000 to his church and $18,000 to a private nonoperating charity. The church contribution is initially subject to the 50% limitation and is fully deductible because the $22,000 contribution is less than the limitation amount of $35,000 (0.50 × $70,000). Ted's deduction for the contribution to the private nonoperating charity (a 30% charity) is limited to $13,000 (the lesser of the following three amounts):

The actual contribution	$18,000
The remaining 50% limitation after the contribution to Ted's church [(0.50 × $70,000) − $22,000]	$13,000
30% of AGI (0.30 × $70,000)	$21,000 ◀

APPLICATION OF CARRYOVERS

As noted earlier, any contributions that exceed the 50% limitation may be carried over and deducted in the subsequent five years. These carryovers are subject to the limitations that apply in subsequent years. Thus, taxpayers may deduct carryovers only to the extent that the limitation of the subsequent year exceeds the contributions made during that year.

These general rules also apply with regard to the special limitations. For example, if the taxpayer donates property subject to the 30% limitation during the current year and the amount of the contribution exceeds the limitation, the excess may carry over to the five subsequent years subject to the 30% limitation in the carryover years. In the carryover year, a deduction may be taken for the excess contribution to the extent that the 30% limitation of the subsequent year exceeds the amount of the property donated during the subsequent year subject to the 30% limitation. Excess contributions of property subject to the 20% limitation may also carry over to the subsequent five years. This carryover is also subject to the special restrictions noted above for the 30% limitation. The carryovers are used in chronological order.

TAX PLANNING

If a taxpayer has contribution carryovers that are about to expire, the taxpayer should consider reducing the current year's contribution so that the carryovers can be deducted.

EXAMPLE I:7-32 ▶ Assume that for the years 2013 through 2015, Joan reports AGI and makes charitable contributions in the following amounts:

	2013	2014	2015
AGI	$40,000	$40,000	$60,000
Cash contributions subject to the 50% of AGI limitation	25,000	23,000	24,000
50% of AGI limitation	20,000	20,000	30,000

The amount of the charitable contribution deduction for each year and the order in which the deduction and carryovers are used are as follows:

	2013	2014	2015
Amount of deduction	$20,000	$20,000	$30,000
Amount of carryover			
From 2013	5,000	5,000	0
From 2014		3,000	2,000 ◀

SPECIAL RULES FOR CHARITABLE CONTRIBUTIONS MADE BY CORPORATIONS

The rules governing charitable contributions made by corporations are generally the same as those pertaining to contributions made by individuals. However, certain differences do exist.

Pledges Made by an Accrual Method Corporation. Generally, taxpayers may only deduct actual contributions (not pledges) made during the tax year. This rule applies to both cash and accrual method taxpayers. A major exception to this general rule exists for accrual method corporations. These accrual method corporations may elect to claim a charitable deduction for the year in which the corporation makes a pledge as long as the actual contribution is made by the fifteenth day of the third month following the close of the year in which the pledge is made.

ETHICAL POINT

A tax practitioner should not be a party to the backdating of a Board of Director's authorization of a charitable contribution pledge so that the corporation may improperly deduct the contribution in the earlier year.

Limitation Applicable to Corporations. Corporate charitable deductions may not exceed 10% of the corporation's taxable income for the year. This amount is computed without regard to the dividends-received deduction, net operating loss or capital loss carrybacks, or any deduction for the charitable contribution itself. Excess contributions may be carried forward for five years and are deductible only if the current-year contributions are less than the current year's 10% limitation. The corporation also uses the carryovers in chronological order.

SUMMARY OF DEDUCTION LIMITATIONS

Topic Review I:7-3 summarizes the rules governing the deduction for charitable contributions.

TOPIC REVIEW I:7-3

Deduction Rules for Charitable Contributions

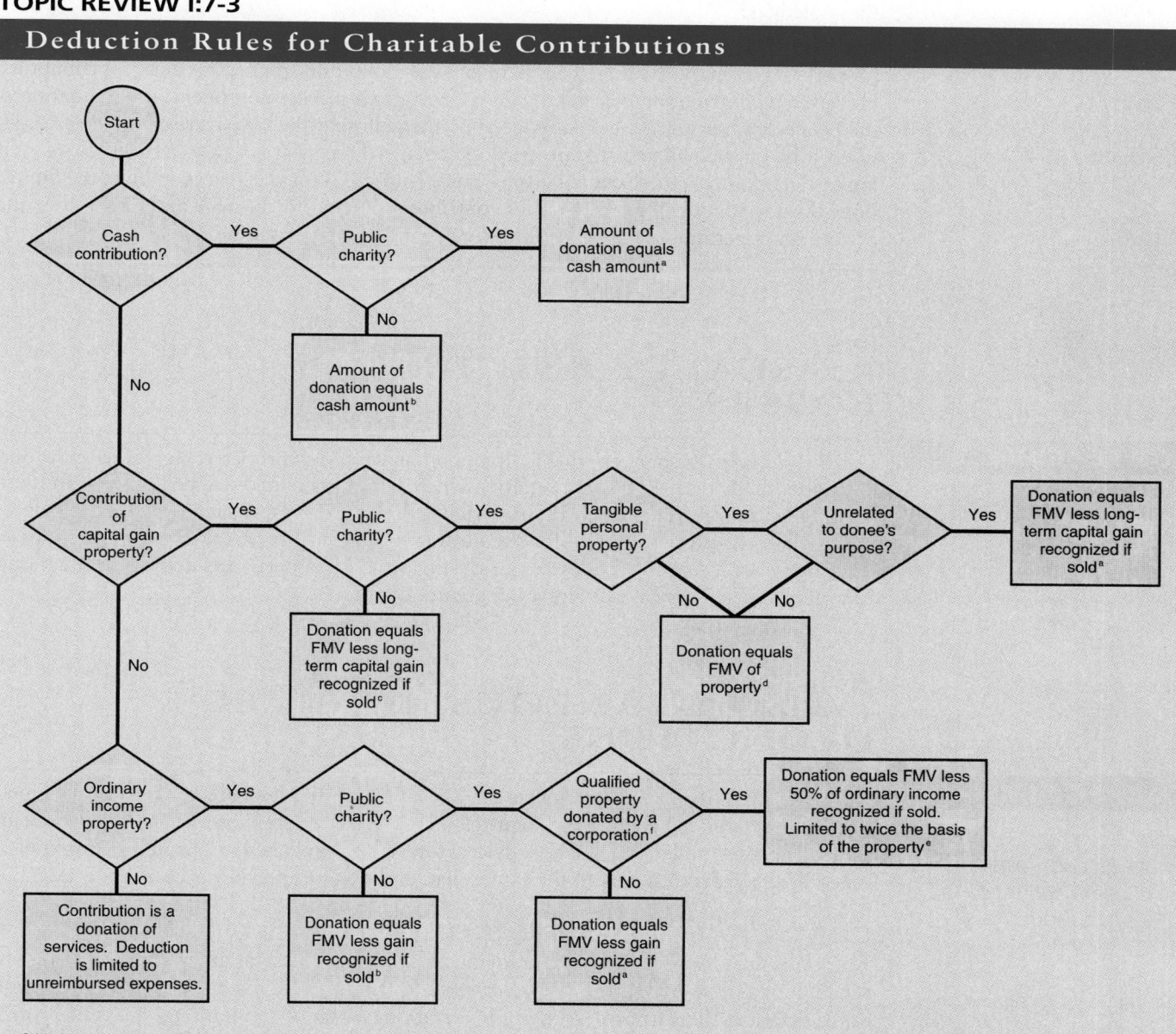

^a Limited to 50% of AGI.
^b Limited to lesser of (1) 30% of AGI or (2) remaining 50% of AGI after accounting for donations to public charities.
^c Limited to lesser of (1) 20% of AGI or (2) 30% of AGI less capital gain contributions to public charities.
^d Taxpayer may elect to scale down the amount of donation by long-term capital gain. If the election is made, limited to 50% of AGI. If no election is made, limited to 30% of AGI.
^e Limited to 10% of the corporation's taxable income without regard to any deduction for charitable contributions, dividends received, a net operating loss carryback or a capital loss carryback.
^f Qualified property consists of either (1) inventory or property used in a trade or business which will be used by a Sec. 501(c)(3) charity for the care of the ill, needy, or infants and (2) inventory constructed by the corporation which will be used by a qualified research institution in the physical or biological sciences.

? STOP & THINK

Question: During the current year, Kim pledges to contribute $10,000 to both the Boy Scouts of America (BSA) and to a private nonoperating foundation. She wants to satisfy those pledges before the end of the year in order to take a deduction this year. She has enough cash to satisfy one of the pledges, but must either sell or donate some land in order to satisfy the other. The land she has in mind has a fair market value of $10,000 and a cost basis of $2,000. She purchased the land four years ago. Kim estimates that she will have AGI of $170,000 and will be in the 28% marginal tax bracket. Assuming that both charities would gladly accept either contribution, how should Kim satisfy these pledges?

Solution: The amount of contribution of capital gain property to a public charity is the property's fair market value. The 30% of AGI limitation applies to such contributions. However, a contribution of capital gain property to a private non-operating foundation is the property's fair market value, reduced by the gain that the taxpayer would have recognized if he or she had sold the property (generally the property's basis). The 50% of AGI limitation applies to these contributions. Since Kim's AGI for the year is so high, the limitations do not apply. Thus, Kim should contribute the land to the BSA and the cash to the private non-operating foundation, for a total charitable contribution of $20,000.

CASUALTY AND THEFT LOSSES

OBJECTIVE 5

Discuss casualty and theft losses

Generally, taxpayers may not deduct losses on personal-use property. However, under Sec. 165 individuals may deduct a casualty or theft loss on personal-use property as an itemized deduction on Schedule A of Form 1040. For individuals, casualty losses on business and investment properties held for the production of rents or royalties are deductions in computing AGI. Other casualty losses on investment property are itemized deductions. Chapter I:8 discusses casualty losses in greater depth.

MISCELLANEOUS ITEMIZED DEDUCTIONS

OBJECTIVE 6

Identify certain miscellaneous itemized deductions subject to the 2% of AGI limit

Taxpayers may deduct various types of expenses as miscellaneous itemized deductions. These deductions include employment-related expenses of employees, certain investment-related expenses, and the cost of tax advice. However, as explained in Chapter I:9, these items generally are deductible only to the extent that, in the aggregate, they exceed 2% of AGI.

CERTAIN EMPLOYEE EXPENSES

Taxpayers may deduct certain employment-related expenses as itemized deductions on Schedule A. These expenses include *unreimbursed* employee expenditures for travel and transportation, dues to professional organizations, costs of job hunting, items of protective clothing or uniforms not suitable for everyday wear, union dues, subscriptions to trade journals, and so on. Chapter I:9 provides a more detailed discussion of this topic.

EXPENSES TO PRODUCE INVESTMENT INCOME

Under Sec. 212, individuals may deduct expenses incurred to produce income. If these expenses arise in an activity that produces either rental or royalty income, they are deductions *for* AGI (see the explanation in Chapter I:6). However, if a taxpayer incurs the expenses in generating other types of investment income, such as interest, dividends, etc., the individual taxpayer may deduct such expenses on Schedule A as itemized deductions. These investment-related expenditures include items such as rental fees for safe-deposit boxes used to hold investment property, subscriptions to investment and trade journals, bank service charges on checking accounts used in an investment activity, and fees paid for consulting advice. These expenses are all subject to the 2% of AGI reduction. Flow-through entities (e.g., partnerships and S corporations) must report these types of investment expenses to their owners as separately stated items so that the 2% of AGI reduction may be applied.

COST OF TAX ADVICE

Section 212 provides individuals with a deduction for expenses incurred in connection with the determination, collection, or refund of any tax, including federal, state, local, and foreign income taxes as well as estate, gift, and inheritance taxes. These items include (1) tax return preparation fees, (2) appraisal fees incurred in determining the amount of a casualty loss, certain capital improvements eligible for a medical deduction, or the FMV of property donated to a qualified charity, (3) fees paid to an accountant for representation in a tax audit, (4) long-distance telephone calls responding to IRS questions, (5) costs of tax return preparation materials and books, and (6) legal fees incurred in planning the tax consequences dealing with estate planning. If an individual incurs these items in connection with the taxpayer's (1) trade or business (reported on Schedule C), (2) farm income (reported on Schedule F), or (3) an activity which produces rents or royalties (reported on Part I of Schedule E), they are *for* AGI deductions.[51] All other expenses incurred for tax advice are miscellaneous itemized deductions subject to the 2% of AGI limitation.

Fees not directly connected with the determination, collection, or refund of a tax or with the taxpayer's trade or business are personal expenses and are not deductible. Thus, legal fees incurred for drafting wills generally are not deductible. However, legal expenses incurred in tax fraud cases in connection with the filing of a fraudulent return generally are deductible.[52] Legal fees relating to a divorce generally are not deductible, unless they deal with tax-related items such as determining who will receive the exemption for dependent children. Chapter I:3 discusses these fees in greater detail.

REDUCTION OF CERTAIN ITEMIZED DEDUCTIONS

Because of concerns with the budget deficit, Congress enacted Sec. 68 several years ago which provides for a reduction in the total amount of certain itemized deductions for high-income taxpayers.[53] This reduction applies only to individuals with AGI in excess of a certain threshold amount. For 2015 this threshold amount is AGI of $309,900 for individuals filing married filing jointly and surviving spouses, $258,250 for single taxpayers, $284,050 for heads of households, and $154,950 for individuals filing married filing separately. This overall reduction applies to all itemized deductions other than medical expenses, investment interest, casualty losses, and wagering losses. The amount of the reduction is the lesser of (1) 3% of the amount the individual's AGI for the year exceeds the threshold level, or (2) 80% of the amount of the taxpayer's itemized deductions other than medical expenses, investment interest, casualty losses, and wagering losses. Furthermore, the reduction is applied after taking into account the other limitations on itemized deductions (e.g., the 2% of AGI limitation on miscellaneous itemized deductions).

[51] Rev. Rul. 92-29, 1992-1 C.B. 20.
[52] Rev. Rul. 68-662, 1968-2 C.B. 69.

[53] In 2001, Congress authorized the elimination of this reduction of itemized deductions for high-income taxpayers. This elimination began in 2006 and by 2010 the reduction was completely eliminated for 2010, 2011, and 2012 but was reinstated for years after 2012.

TAX PLANNING CONSIDERATIONS

OBJECTIVE 7

Describe tax planning considerations for itemized deductions

MEDICAL EXPENSE DEDUCTION

Working With The 10% of Agi Floor. As explained previously, a deduction for medical expenses is available to individuals only to the extent that the taxpayer's medical expenditures exceed 10% of the taxpayer's AGI for the year (7.5% of AGI for taxpayers 65 or older for tax years before 2016). Thus, many individuals find that no deduction is available, even though their medical expenses are relatively high. In these cases, taxpayers may obtain some benefit if they can bunch the medical expenses into one year. Orthodontic work, certain orthopedic treatment, noncosmetic elective surgery, and new eyeglasses are all examples of medical expenditures that may be either accelerated or delayed into a year in which other medical expenses are high or AGI is lower.

Generally, a taxpayer may take a deduction for medical expenses only in the year in which the expense is actually paid. The mere prepayment of future expenses usually does not accelerate the deduction. However, taxpayers may take a deduction in the earlier year of payment if there is a legal obligation to pay or if the prepayment is a requirement for the receipt of the medical care.[54] If the taxpayer has already received the medical treatment, but the taxpayer does not have sufficient cash to pay the bill, the taxpayer may preserve a deduction for the current year by either borrowing the cash to satisfy the bill or by using a credit card.

EXAMPLE I:7-33 ► During the current year, Marty is 40 and he estimates his AGI to be $70,000. Marty has already incurred $5,000 in medical expenses for himself and his family during the year. Because of the 10% of AGI limitation, Marty will not be able to deduct any of the medical expenses. Marty estimates that he will incur $4,000 in medical expenses for orthodontic work for his son next year. He doesn't think he will incur any other major medical expenses next year. Marty also estimates his AGI next year to remain the same as this year. If these estimates are correct, Marty won't be able to deduct any medical expenses in either year because the expenses for each year are less than ($7,000) 10% of his AGI in each of the years. However, if the orthodontic work is started in the current year and Marty pays for the work in the current year, he will incur a total of $9,000 in medical expenses in the current year. Thus, in the current year Marty may deduct $2,000 ($9,000 − $7,000) of the total medical expenses. This, of course, assumes that the total of Marty's itemized deductions exceeds the standard deduction for the year.

Mere prepayment in this case is not sufficient. Marty must have a portion of the orthodontic services performed in the earlier year. If he does not have sufficient cash to pay the bill in the current year, he could borrow the money or use a bank credit card. ◄

KEY POINT

Even if the medical expenses exceed 10% of AGI the taxpayer may not benefit from the deduction if the medical expenses in addition to the other itemized deductions do not exceed the standard deduction.

Multiple Support Agreements. An individual may deduct medical expenses incurred for himself or herself, his or her spouse, dependents, children of divorced parents even if not a dependent, and persons who would qualify as a dependent except for the failure to meet the gross income or joint return test. In cases where a multiple support agreement has been filed, the tax law treats the individual who is the subject of the agreement as the dependent of the taxpayer entitled to the dependency exemption. Thus, to preserve the medical expense deduction, the taxpayer entitled to the dependency exemption should pay all medical expenditures for the dependent individual.

EXAMPLE I:7-34 ► Amy, Bart, Clay, and Donna each provide 25% of the support of their father, Eric. Under the terms of a multiple support agreement, Bart, Clay, and Donna all agree to allow Amy to claim the dependency exemption with respect to Eric. During the year, $3,000 in medical expenses are incurred on Eric's behalf. If Amy pays these expenses, she may deduct them (subject to limitations). However, if Bart, Clay, or Donna pays these expenses, no one may claim the medical expenses as a deduction. ◄

INTEREST EXPENSE DEDUCTION

A taxpayer may deduct qualified residence interest incurred on a principal residence and one other qualified residence that the taxpayer selects. The taxpayer makes this choice annually. The taxpayer may choose any residence that is not a rental property.

---

[54] *Robert M. Rose v. CIR*, 26 AFTR 2d 70-5653, 70-2 USTC ¶9646 (5th Cir., 1970). See also Rev. Ruls. 75-302, 1975-2 C.B. 86, and 75-303, 1975-2 C.B. 87, both clarified by Rev. Rul. 93-72, 1993-2 C.B. 77.

In order for the second residence to qualify, the taxpayer must use it personally for more than the greater of 14 days or 10% of the rental days during the year. If this personal use test is met, however, the Sec. 280A limitations on the rental of vacation homes also apply. As explained in Chapter I:6, under these rules, taxpayers must allocate expenses between the rental use and the personal use of the property. Taxpayers may deduct the expenses allocated to the rental use only to the extent of the rental income. Of the expenses allocated to the personal use, only the taxes and interest (if the residence is selected and if the loan is secured by the residence) are deductible as itemized deductions.

If the personal use by the taxpayer does not meet the test mentioned above, the interest allocated to the personal use cannot qualify as residence interest and it becomes non deductible personal interest. Furthermore, the passive loss rules apply to the rental income and expenses allocated to the rental use of the property (see Chapter I:8). Under these rules, individuals generally can deduct losses generated from a passive activity only to the extent of the individual's passive income. Certain individuals, however, may deduct up to $25,000 of losses from the rental of real estate. Thus, the two alternatives and their consequences are as follows:

▶ Meet the personal use test. No loss from the rental portion of the property is deductible. However, the interest allocated to the personal use portion may be fully deductible as qualified residence interest.

▶ Do not meet the personal use test. The interest allocated to the personal use portion is nondeductible personal interest. However, all of the passive loss from the rental portion is deductible against passive income. Furthermore, certain individuals may deduct up to $25,000 additional passive loss.

The alternative a taxpayer chooses depends on several factors, including the amount of the taxpayer's passive income, the total amount of itemized deductions, and whether the loan is secured by the vacation home.

DEDUCTION FOR CHARITABLE CONTRIBUTIONS

SELF-STUDY QUESTION
What type of property lends itself to the "election to reduce"?

ANSWER
Property on which there is very little appreciation.

Election to Reduce the Amount of a Charitable Contribution. The election to reduce the contribution of capital gain property to public charities by the long-term capital gain that the taxpayer would recognize if he or she sold the property is an annual election that applies to all capital gain property donated to public charities during the year. Because the election increases the ceiling limitation from 30% to 50%, under certain circumstances a taxpayer may actually receive a larger deduction for the year than would normally be available if the taxpayer did not make the election.

EXAMPLE I:7-35 ▶ During the current year, Jane has AGI of $50,000. She donates a painting to the local university during the same year. The painting, valued at $30,000 at the time of contribution, cost her $25,000 several years before. The university displays the painting in its art museum. If Jane does not make the election, the amount of the contribution is equal to its FMV ($30,000). However, Jane's charitable contribution deduction for the year is limited to $15,000 ($50,000 × 0.30). If Jane makes the election to reduce the contribution amount, the deduction is reduced to $25,000 ($30,000 − $5,000 LTCG). The deduction limitation, however, increases to $25,000 for the year because the limitation is now based on 50% of AGI instead of 30%. In this case, Jane will receive a larger deduction for the year by making the election. However, the cost associated with this election is the loss of $5,000 of deduction because the total deduction is reduced from $30,000 to $25,000 if she makes the election. ◄

Many tax practitioners make this election only when preparing the taxpayer's final tax return. The taxpayer makes the election at this time because charitable contribution carryovers to the decedent's estate are not permitted.

ADDITIONAL COMMENT
To help determine the FMV of contributed property, taxpayers can refer to IRS Pub. No. 561, Determining the Value of Donated Property. (2007)

Donation of Appreciated Capital Gain Property. Instead of selling substantially appreciated capital gain property and donating the cash proceeds, the taxpayer should consider donating the property directly to a charity. If property is donated in this way, the donor receives a deduction equal to the FMV of the property and does not recognize any taxable gain on the disposition.

EXAMPLE I:7-36 ▶ Colleen wishes to satisfy a pledge of $100,000 made to a local university. She owns $100,000 worth of marketable securities purchased ten years ago for $30,000. Because the securities are marketable, the university is indifferent as to whether Colleen donates cash or the securities. Although her marginal tax rate is 35%, Colleen would be subject to a tax rate of 15% on the sale of the securities. She has enough AGI to be able to deduct the full contribution in the current year. The following chart summarizes the cash flows to Colleen under two different alternatives:

	Donate Securities	Sell Securities and Donate Cash
Proceeds of sale	0	$100,000
Tax on gain	0	(10,500)[a]
Cash payment to charity		(100,000)
Tax savings from the contribution deduction	$35,000[b]	35,000
Net cash flow	$35,000	$ 24,500

[a]($100,000 − $30,000) × 0.15 = $10,500.
[b]$100,000 × 0.35 = $35,000.

In order to take a tax loss on business or investment property, a taxpayer should not donate property that has decreased in value. Rather, the taxpayer should sell the property, recognize the loss, and donate the cash proceeds.

COMPLIANCE AND PROCEDURAL CONSIDERATIONS

OBJECTIVE 8

Describe compliance and procedural considerations for itemized deductions

MEDICAL EXPENSES

In certain cases, expenditures qualify as both a medical care expense and a dependent care expense (i.e., expenses for household and dependent care services that the taxpayer must pay to be gainfully employed). A taxpayer who incurs an expense that qualifies under both provisions may choose to take either a medical expense deduction or a tax credit under Sec. 21.[55] However, if a taxpayer takes a credit for these expenses, they are not deductible as medical expenses.

EXAMPLE I:7-37 ▶ Joel's daughter, Debbie, has a physical disability. As a result, Joel hires a nurse who provides daily care while he is at work. During the year, Joel pays the nurse a total of $3,000. This amount qualifies for both the dependent care credit and the medical expense deduction. If Joel takes the dependent care credit, he may not deduct the $3,000 as a medical expense. Because of the limitations imposed on each, the determination of which treatment is more advantageous depends on items such as the taxpayer's AGI, other medical expenses, and total itemized deductions. ◀

ADDITIONAL COMMENT

On Form 8283, the charitable organization is required to acknowledge receipt of the gift and to file an information return if the property is sold or disposed of within two years.

CHARITABLE CONTRIBUTIONS

Over the past several years, the IRS has significantly tightened the requirements needed to properly substantiate a charitable contribution in an attempt to prevent abuses in claiming inflated charitable contributions. In order for a taxpayer to take a deduction for a cash contribution of any amount, the taxpayer must be able to substantiate the contribution with either a bank record or a written receipt from the charity. Self-created documents are not sufficient. Previously, this requirement was imposed only on cash contributions of $250 or more. In addition, when a taxpayer donates property other than cash to a qualifying charity, proper determination of the property's FMV is a critical issue. Because of actual and perceived abuses in this area, the IRS often scrutinizes and, if necessary, challenges the valuation of contributed property. This is especially true for contributions of

---

[55] A credit of up to 35% of expenses for child and dependent care services is allowed if the dependent is under age 13 or a spouse or dependent who is mentally or physically incapable of caring for himself or herself. The credit is reduced 1% for every $2,000 (or portion thereof) of AGI over $15,000. However, the credit may not be reduced below 20%. (See the discussion on Personal Tax Credits in Chapter I:14 for a more detailed explanation of the child and dependent care credit.)

property for which no published market quotes exist. Thus, the taxpayer must (1) properly substantiate the fact that the contribution has actually been made, and (2) in the case of the contribution of property, the taxpayer may be required to acquire and retain or provide to the IRS information documenting the property's FMV. As noted below, special detailed substantiation and documentation requirements apply to the contribution of used motor vehicles, boats, and airplanes.

Proper Substantiation. As mentioned above, if the contribution is made in cash, the taxpayer must retain evidence of the donation by keeping a cancelled check or other bank record or a receipt from the charitable organization. If the contribution is in the form of noncash property, the taxpayer must maintain records containing the following:

► Name and address of the charity to which the contribution was made

► Date and location of the contribution

► Description of the property

► FMV of the property

► Method of determining the property's FMV

► Signed copy of the appraisal report if an appraiser was used[56]

For charitable contributions of $250 or more, no deduction is allowed unless the contribution is substantiated by a contemporaneous, written acknowledgment (receipt) by the donee organization. This acknowledgment must contain the following information:

► The amount of cash and a description of any property contributed

► Whether or not the organization provided any goods or services in consideration for the cash or property received, including a description and good faith estimate of the value of any goods or services provided by the organization

The acknowledgment is contemporaneous if obtained by the earlier of the date the taxpayer files a return for the year in question or the extended due date for filing such a return. This substantiation requirement is waived if the donee organization files a return that contains the required information.[57] Additionally, no deduction is allowed for a contribution of clothing or household items unless the items are in "good" condition. Unfortunately, the law does not provide guidance as to what constitutes "good" condition.

Documentation of Property's FMV. In addition to the substantiation requirement, in certain cases the taxpayer must also properly document the property's FMV. The specific documentation requirements depend upon the amount of the claimed deduction for the contributed property. If a claimed deduction for a contribution of property exceeds $500, noncorporate taxpayers (and closely held C corporations and personal service corporations) must include with their tax return a description of the property and any other information the IRS requires, including the type, location, holding period, basis, and FMV of the property. This information is reported on Form 8283 (see Appendix B). If the claimed deduction exceeds $5,000, in addition to the above requirements, all taxpayers must obtain a qualified appraisal of the property and must include with their tax return any additional information that the IRS requires. Finally, if the claimed deduction exceeds $500,000, all taxpayers are additionally required to obtain a qualified appraisal and actually attach the appraisal to their tax return. Because these documentation requirements are based on the amount of a claimed contribution, the donation of similar items of property donated to all charities will be treated as the donation of one property. This requirement prevents taxpayers from avoiding these documentation requirements by spreading out their contributions. If a partnership or an S corporation donates property, these documentation requirements are applied at the entity level. However, if the documentation requirements are not met, the deduction is denied at the partner or shareholder level. In general, these documentation rules do not apply to contributions of cash, certain intangibles, inventory, or publicly traded securities.

---

[56] Reg. Sec. 1.170A-13.

[57] Sec. 170(f)(8) and Reg. Sec. 1.170A-13(f).

Contribution of Used Motor Vehicles, Boats, and Airplanes. Special documentation rules apply to contributions of motor vehicles, boats, and airplanes if the claimed value of the property exceeds $500. However, these rules do not apply if the contributed vehicle, boat, or airplane is inventory in the hands of the donor. If these special rules apply, the substantiation rules for a donation of property exceeding $250 are no longer applicable. Instead, the charity must give the taxpayer and the IRS a contemporaneous written acknowledgment of the contribution. This acknowledgment must be included with the taxpayer's tax return. The information included in the acknowledgment and the date by which the charity must give the acknowledgment to the taxpayer depend upon whether or not the charity sells the vehicle without any significant use or any material improvement of the vehicle. In either case, the acknowledgment must include the name and taxpayer identification number of the taxpayer who donated the vehicle, as well as the vehicle identification number. If the vehicle is sold by the charity before any significant use or material improvement, the acknowledgment must also include (1) a certification that the vehicle was sold in an arm's length transaction to an unrelated party, (2) the gross proceeds from the sale, and (3) a statement that the deductible amount may not exceed the amount of the gross proceeds. This acknowledgment must be given to the taxpayer within 30 days of the contribution of the vehicle to the charity, and, as mentioned earlier, the amount of the deduction for the vehicle is limited to the gross proceeds received from the sale. On the other hand, if the charity uses or improves the vehicle, the acknowledgment must also state: (1) the intended use or improvement and the intended duration of the use and (2) a certification that the vehicle will not be transferred or sold before completion of the intended use or improvement. This acknowledgment must be given to the taxpayer within 30 days of the donation of the vehicle.[58]

EXAMPLE I:7-38 ▶

During the current year, Peter Smith (SSN. 123-45-6789) reports AGI of $250,000. Smith also makes the following charitable contributions during the year:

▶ Smith performs voluntary dental work three days each month in rural areas of the state. Smith drives a total of 4,000 miles on these trips during the year.

▶ Smith makes the following contributions by cash or check: $750 to the city library, $2,000 to the United Way, $500 to a local community college, and $4,000 to his church.

▶ Smith contributes a tract of land to a small rural town. The town plans to erect a public library on the site. Smith purchased the land in 1997 for $5,000. Its appraised value at the time of the contribution is $8,000.

Smith's contributions are reported on the partially completed Schedule A shown in Figure I:7-1. The out-of-pocket expenses of $560 (4,000 miles × $0.14) and the contributions by cash or check of $7,250 (library, United Way, church, and community college) are totaled and reported on line 16. The property contribution of $8,000 is separately stated on line 17. Because Smith contributes property with a value exceeding $500, Form 8283, an appraisal summary, and signed statements by the qualified appraiser and an authorized official of the organization that received the property must be attached to the return. In addition, for the donations that separately exceed $250, Peter must obtain and retain written acknowledgments from the donee organizations in order for the contributions to be deductible. ◀

TAXES

Individuals generally report their deduction for property taxes on Schedule A of Form 1040. However, if the taxpayer incurs the taxes in his or her business, they are reported on Schedule C. Taxes incurred for the production of rents and royalties are reported on Schedule E. Taxes incurred in the taxpayer's farming business are reported on Schedule F. State and local income taxes imposed on individuals are always reported on Schedule A, even if the individual is self-employed.

Real estate brokers must report any real estate tax allocable to the purchaser of a residence. (See the discussion in this chapter regarding the allocation of real estate taxes between the seller and buyer of a residence.)[59] The broker reports this information on Form 1099-S (Proceeds from Real Estate Transactions).

---

[58] Sec. 170(f)(11) and (f)(12).

[59] Sec. 6045(e)(4) and Notice 93-4, 1993-1 C.B. 295.

SCHEDULE A
(Form 1040)

Department of the Treasury
Internal Revenue Service (99)

Itemized Deductions

▶ **Information about Schedule A and its separate instructions is at** *www.irs.gov/schedulea.*
▶ **Attach to Form 1040.**

OMB No. 1545-0074

2014

Attachment
Sequence No. **07**

Name(s) shown on Form 1040

Peter Smith

Your social security number

123 45 6789

Medical and Dental Expenses	**Caution.** Do not include expenses reimbursed or paid by others.			
	1 Medical and dental expenses (see instructions)	**1**		
	2 Enter amount from Form 1040, line 38 **2**			
	3 Multiply line 2 by 10% (.10). But if either you or your spouse was born before January 2, 1950, multiply line 2 by 7.5% (.075) instead	**3**		
	4 Subtract line 3 from line 1. If line 3 is more than line 1, enter -0-		**4**	
Taxes You Paid	5 State and local (**check only one box**):			
	a ☐ Income taxes, **or**	**5**		
	b ☐ General sales taxes			
	6 Real estate taxes (see instructions)	**6**		
	7 Personal property taxes	**7**		
	8 Other taxes. List type and amount ▶ _____	**8**		
	9 Add lines 5 through 8		**9**	
Interest You Paid **Note.** Your mortgage interest deduction may be limited (see instructions).	10 Home mortgage interest and points reported to you on Form 1098	**10**		
	11 Home mortgage interest not reported to you on Form 1098. If paid to the person from whom you bought the home, see instructions and show that person's name, identifying no., and address ▶ _____	**11**		
	12 Points not reported to you on Form 1098. See instructions for special rules	**12**		
	13 Mortgage insurance premiums (see instructions)	**13**		
	14 Investment interest. Attach Form 4952 if required. (See instructions.)	**14**		
	15 Add lines 10 through 14		**15**	
Gifts to Charity If you made a gift and got a benefit for it, see instructions.	16 Gifts by cash or check. If you made any gift of $250 or more, see instructions	**16**	7,810	
	17 Other than by cash or check. If any gift of $250 or more, see instructions. You **must** attach Form 8283 if over $500	**17**	8,000	
	18 Carryover from prior year	**18**		
	19 Add lines 16 through 18		**19**	15,810
Casualty and Theft Losses	20 Casualty or theft loss(es). Attach Form 4684. (See instructions.)		**20**	
Job Expenses and Certain Miscellaneous Deductions	21 Unreimbursed employee expenses—job travel, union dues, job education, etc. Attach Form 2106 or 2106-EZ if required. (See instructions.) ▶ _____	**21**		
	22 Tax preparation fees	**22**		
	23 Other expenses—investment, safe deposit box, etc. List type and amount ▶ _____	**23**		
	24 Add lines 21 through 23	**24**		
	25 Enter amount from Form 1040, line 38 **25**			
	26 Multiply line 25 by 2% (.02)	**26**		
	27 Subtract line 26 from line 24. If line 26 is more than line 24, enter -0-		**27**	
Other Miscellaneous Deductions	28 Other—from list in instructions. List type and amount ▶ _____		**28**	
Total Itemized Deductions	29 Is Form 1040, line 38, over $152,525?			
	☐ **No.** Your deduction is not limited. Add the amounts in the far right column for lines 4 through 28. Also, enter this amount on Form 1040, line 40.		**29**	
	☐ **Yes.** Your deduction may be limited. See the Itemized Deductions Worksheet in the instructions to figure the amount to enter.			
	30 If you elect to itemize deductions even though they are less than your standard deduction, check here ▶ ☐			

FIGURE I:7-1 ▶ PARTIALLY COMPLETED SCHEDULE A

What would you do in this situation?

GIVING TO BOTH: GOODWILL AND THE IRS

Much has been written about abusive practices concerning the valuation of noncash property donated to qualified charities. Under Sec. 170, both corporations and individuals may deduct the FMV of property contributed to charitable organizations. Of course, a number of valuation and percentage limitations and carryover rules are applicable to both individual and corporate taxpayers.

Assume your clients, Mr. and Mrs. Nicholas Nice, come into your office on December 27 for some year-end tax planning. Your review of their tax situation indicates that they have made substantial donations of clothing and household goods to Goodwill Industries. They have obtained proper documentation for donations made during the year but do not know how to qualify for taking a charitable deduction vis-à-vis valuation, forms, and the like. They do know that their original cost basis in the donated goods was $15,000 and that the goods were in good condition at the time of the donation. What tax and ethical issues should be considered?

EXAMPLE I:7-39 ▶ During the year, Andrea incurs $1,500 in property taxes on a two-family duplex. Andrea lives in one unit and rents out the other. She also pays $100 in registration fees and $600 in personal property taxes on her automobile, based on its value. Andrea uses the automobile 80% of the time in an unincorporated business. During the current year, she also pays $2,000 in state income taxes, all of which is attributable to her income of the prior year from the unincorporated business.

Because one-half of the real estate taxes are attributable to property used to produce rental income, $750 (0.50 × $1,500) is reported on Schedule E, and the remaining personal-use portion ($750) is reported on Schedule A. Because 80% of the use of the automobile is in Andrea's business, $80 (0.80 × $100) of the registration fee is deductible as a business expense on Schedule C. The remaining $20 is not deductible because the registration fee is not a tax. However, $480 (0.80 × $600) of the personal property tax on the automobile is deductible as a business expense on Schedule C. The remaining $120 is deductible as a tax on Schedule A. Finally, even though the state income tax is related to Andrea's business income, all $2,000 of the state income tax is reported on Schedule A. Because Andrea pays the state income tax in the current year, it is deductible in the current year. ◀

PROBLEM MATERIALS

DISCUSSION QUESTIONS

I:7-1
a. For which persons may a taxpayer deduct medical expenses?
b. In the case of children of divorced parents, must the parent who is entitled to the dependency exemption pay the medical expenses of the child to ensure that the expenses are deductible? Explain.
c. Who should pay the medical expenses of an individual who is the subject of a multiple support agreement?

I:7-2 What is the definition of medical care for purposes of the medical care deduction?

I:7-3
a. What is the definition of cosmetic surgery under the Internal Revenue Code?
b. Is the cost of cosmetic surgery deductible as a medical expense? Explain.

I:7-4
a. If a taxpayer must travel away from his or her home in order to obtain medical care, which en route costs, if any, are deductible as medical expenses?
b. Are there any limits imposed on the deductibility of these expenses?

I:7-5 What are the rules dealing with the deductibility of the cost of meals and lodging incurred while away from home in order to receive medical treatment as an outpatient?

I:7-6
a. Which types of capital expenditures incurred specifically for medical purposes are deductible?
b. What limitations, if any, are imposed on the deductibility of these expenditures?

I:7-7 Bill, a plant manager, is suffering from a serious ulcer. Bill's doctor recommends that he spend three weeks fishing and hunting in the Colorado Rockies. Can Bill deduct the costs of the trip as a medical expense?

I:7-8 In what cases are medical insurance premiums paid by an individual not deductible as qualified medical expenses?

I:7-9 What is the limit placed on medical expense deductions? When can a deduction be taken for medical care? What if the medical care is prepaid?

I:7-10 a. Which taxes are specifically deductible for federal income tax purposes under Sec. 164?
b. If a tax is not specifically listed in Sec. 164, under what circumstances may it still be deductible?

I:7-11 If Susan overpays her state income tax due to excess withholdings, can she deduct the entire amount in the year withheld? When Susan receives a refund from the state how must she treat that refund for tax purposes?

I:7-12 What is an ad valorem tax? If a tax that is levied on personal property is not an ad valorem tax, under what circumstances may it still be deductible?

I:7-13 When real estate is sold during a year, why is it necessary that the real estate taxes on the property be apportioned between the buyer and seller?

I:7-14 a. Identify the different categories of interest expense an individual may incur. How is the classification of the interest determined?
b. Are these different categories of interest deductible? If so, how?

I:7-15 At times, the term *points* is used to refer to different types of charges. Define the term and describe when points are deductible.

I:7-16 In which year or years are points (representing prepaid interest on a loan) deductible?

I:7-17 Why does Sec. 267 impose a restriction on the deductibility of expenses accrued and payable by an accrual method taxpayer to a related cash method taxpayer?

I:7-18 a. What is the amount of the annual limitation placed on the deductibility of investment interest expense?
b. Explain how net investment income is calculated.
c. Is any disallowed interest expense for the year allowable as a deduction in another year? If so, when?

I:7-19 Explain what acquisition indebtedness and home equity indebtedness are with respect to a qualified residence of a taxpayer. Identify any limitations on the deductibility of interest expense on this indebtedness.

I:7-20 Explain what a qualified residence is for purposes of qualified residence interest.

I:7-21 Why is interest expense disallowed if it is incurred to purchase or hold tax-exempt obligations?

I:7-22 When is interest generally deductible for cash-method taxpayers? Explain if the general rule applies to prepaid interest, interest paid with loan proceeds, discounted notes, and personal interest. If the general rule does not apply, explain when these interest expenses are deductible.

I:7-23 a. For purposes of the charitable contribution deduction, what is capital gain property? Ordinary income property?
b. What is the significance of classifying property as either capital gain property or ordinary income property?

I:7-24 How is the *amount* of a charitable contribution of capital gain property determined if it is donated to a private nonoperating foundation? How does this determination differ if capital gain property is donated to a public charity?

I:7-25 May an individual who is married and files a joint return deduct any charitable contributions if the itemized deductions total $7,000 (of which $3,000 are qualified charitable contributions)?

I:7-26 For individuals, what is the overall deduction limitation on charitable contributions? What is the limitation for corporations?

I:7-27 If a taxpayer's charitable contributions for any tax year exceed the deduction limitations, may the excess contributions be deducted in another year? If so, in which years may they be deducted?

I:7-28 How are charitable contribution deductions reported on the tax return for individuals? What reporting requirements must be met for the contribution of property?

I:7-29 List some of the more common miscellaneous itemized deductions and identify any limitations that are imposed on the deductibility of these items.

I:7-30 Other than the 10% limitation placed on medical expenses, the 10% reduction for casualty losses on personal property, the 2% reduction applied to certain miscellaneous itemized deductions, and the fact that itemized deductions are only deductible if they exceed the standard deduction, are there any other limitations or reductions applied to itemized deductions for individuals?

ISSUE IDENTIFICATION QUESTIONS

I:7-31 Wayne and Maria file a joint tax return on which they itemize their deductions and report AGI of $50,000. During the year they incurred $1,500 of medical expenses when Maria broke her leg. Furthermore, their dentist informed them that their daughter, Alicia, needs $3,000 of orthodontic work to correct her overbite. Wayne also needs a new pair of eyeglasses that will cost $300. What tax issues should Wayne and Maria consider?

I:7-32 This year, Chuck took out a loan to purchase some raw land for investment. He paid $40,000 for the land, and he expects that within 5 years the land will be worth at least $75,000. Chuck is married, and his AGI for the year is $230,000. Chuck paid $4,300 in interest on the loan this year. Chuck has $2,600 in interest income and $1,300 in dividend income for the year. He plans to itemize his deductions so he can use the interest expense to offset his investment income. What tax issues should Chuck consider?

I:7-33 During the current year, George made contributions totaling $40,000 to an organization called the National Endowment for the Preservation of Liberty (NEPL). Later during the year, the NEPL started giving money to a political candidate to help with his campaign expenses. What tax issues should George consider?

I:7-34 During the current year, Bob has AGI of $100,000. He also donated some stock to his church. He purchased the stock two years ago for $55,000. The FMV of the stock at the time of the contribution is $60,000. Bob has $5,000 of unused excess contributions from a prior year. What tax issues should Bob consider?

PROBLEMS

I:7-35 *Medical Expense Deduction.* During 2015, Angela sustains serious injuries from a snow-skiing accident. She incurs the following expenses:

Item	Amount
Doctor bills	$11,700
Hospital bills	9,400
Legal fees in suit against ski resort	3,000

Angela is single and has no dependents. For the year, her salary is $58,000. She pays $600 in medical and dental insurance premiums, which is withheld from her paycheck on an after-tax basis, $2,750 in mortgage interest on her home, and $1,200 in interest on her car loan. Her health insurance provider reimburses her for $10,000 of the medical expenses. What is her 2015 taxable income?

I:7-36 *Reimbursement of Previously Deducted Medical Expenses.* Assume the same facts as in Problem I:7-35. In addition, assume that in 2016, Angela receives an additional $7,000 in a settlement of a lawsuit arising because of the snow-skiing accident. $4,000 of the settlement is to pay Angela's medical bills, and $3,000 is to reimburse her legal expenses. What is the proper tax treatment of this $7,000 settlement?

I:7-37 *Medical Expense Deduction.* Dan lives in Duncan, a small town in Arizona. Because of a rare blood disease, Dan is required to take special medical treatments once a month. The closest place these treatments are available to Dan is in Phoenix, 200 miles away. The treatments are provided on an outpatient basis but require him to stay overnight in Phoenix. During the year, Dan makes 12 trips to Phoenix by automobile to receive the treatments. The motel he always stays in charges $85 per night. For the year, Dan also spends a total of $250 for meals on these trips. $100 of this $250 is spent while en route to Phoenix. What is the amount of Dan's qualified medical expenses for 2015?

I:7-38 *Medical Expense Deduction.* Chad is divorced and has custody of Brett, his 14-year-old son. Chad's ex-wife has custody of their daughter, Sara. During the year, Chad incurs $3,000 for orthodontic work for Sara to correct a severe overbite and $2,000 in unreimbursed medical expenses associated with Brett's broken leg. Chad also pays $900 in health insurance premiums, which is withheld from his paycheck on a pre-tax basis. Both Brett and Sara are covered under Chad's medical insurance plan. In addition, Chad incurs $400 for prescription drugs and $1,000 in doctor bills for himself. Chad's AGI is $40,000. What is Chad's medical expense deduction for the year assuming that his other itemized deductions exceed the standard deduction?

I:7-39 *Medical Expense Deduction.* In 2015, Charla, a single taxpayer with no dependents, was severely hurt in a farm accident. Charla is 38 years old. The accident left Charla's legs 85% paralyzed. After incurring $14,000 of medical expenses at the hospital, the doctor recommended that Charla install a pool at her home for therapy. The pool cost $25,000 to install and increased the value of her home by $22,000. She spent $930 maintaining the pool in 2015 and $1,060 in 2016. Charla also purchased a wheelchair on December 28, 2015, for $2,300, which she charged to her credit card. She paid her credit card bill on January 6, 2016. She also purchased a hospital bed for $3,800 but did not pay for the bed until 2016. Charla paid her physical therapist $4,000 for services performed in 2016. Charla paid $1,200 in medical insurance premiums on an after-tax basis in both 2015 and

2016. In 2016, the insurance company reimbursed Charla $9,000 for her hospital stay in 2015. Her AGI for 2015 and 2016 is $38,000 and $43,000, respectively, not considering any of the above items. Charla has no other itemized deductions in either year.

a. What is Charla's taxable income for 2015?

b. What is Charla's medical expense deduction for 2016? How does she treat the reimbursement?

I:7-40 *Deduction of Taxes.* Joyce is a single, cash-method taxpayer. On April 11, 2014, Joyce paid $120 in state income taxes with her 2013 state income tax return. During 2014, Joyce had $1,600 in state income taxes withheld. On April 13, 2015, Joyce paid $200 with her 2014 state tax return. During 2015, she had $2,100 in state income taxes withheld from her paycheck. Upon filing her 2015 tax return on April 15, 2016, she received a refund of $450 for excess state income taxes withheld. Joyce had total AGI in 2015 and 2016 of $51,000 and $53,500, respectively. In 2015, Joyce also paid $5,500 in qualified residence interest.

a. What is the amount of state income taxes Joyce may include as an itemized deduction for 2014?

b. What is Joyce's allowed itemized deduction for state income taxes for 2015?

c. What is Joyce's taxable income for 2015?

d. What is her AGI for 2016?

I:7-41 Assume the same facts as Problem I:7-40, but change the amount of Joyce's mortgage interest to $3,000.

a. What is her taxable income for 2015?

b. What is her AGI for 2016?

I:7-42 *Deduction of Taxes.* Dawn, a single, cash-method taxpayer, paid the following taxes in 2015: Dawn's employer withheld $5,400 for federal income taxes, $2,000 for state income taxes, and $3,800 for FICA from her 2015 paychecks. Dawn purchased a new car and paid $600 in sales tax and $70 for the license. The car's FMV was $20,000 and it weighed 3,000 pounds. The county also assessed a property tax on the car. The tax was 2% of the car's value and $10 per hundredweight. Dawn uses the car 100% of the time for personal purposes. Dawn sold her house on April 15, 2015. The county's property tax on the home for 2015 is $1,850, payable on February 1, 2015. The county's real property tax year is the calendar year. Dawn's AGI for 2015 is $50,000 and her other itemized deductions exclusive of taxes are $4,000 (disregard any leap year).

a. What is Dawn's deduction for taxes in 2015?

b. Where on Dawn's tax return should she report her deduction for taxes?

I:7-43 *Apportionment of Real Estate Taxes.* On May 1 of the current year, Tara sells a building to Janet for $500,000. Tara's basis in the building is $300,000. The county in which the building is located has a real property tax year that ends on June 30. The taxes are payable by September 1 of that year. On September 1, Janet pays the annual property taxes of $6,000. Both Tara and Janet are calendar-year, cash method taxpayers. The closing agreement does not separately account for the property taxes. Disregard any leap year.

a. What amount of real property taxes may Janet deduct in the current year?

b. What amount of real property taxes may Tara deduct in the current year?

c. If no apportionment on the real property taxes is made in the sales agreement, what is Tara's total selling price of the building? Janet's basis for the building?

I:7-44 *Classification of Interest Expense.* On January 1 of the current year, Scott borrows $80,000, pledging the assets of his business as collateral. He immediately deposits the money in an interest-bearing checking account. Scott already had $20,000 in this account. On April 1, Scott invests $75,000 in a limited real estate partnership. On July 1, he buys a new ski boat for $12,000. On August 1, he makes a $10,000 capital contribution to his unincorporated business. Scott repays $50,000 of the loan on November 30 of the current year. Classify Scott's interest expense for the year.

I:7-45 *Investment Income and Deductions.* During 2015, Travis takes out a $40,000 loan, using stock he owns as collateral. He uses $10,000 to purchase a car, which he uses 100% for personal use. He uses the remaining funds to purchase stocks and bonds. He pays $3,200 interest on the loan. Travis also reports the following for the year:

AGI without any investment income	$130,000
State income taxes paid	8,400
Dividend income	10,000
Interest income	2,100

Investment expenses (exclusive of interest)	8,000
Net short term capital gains	7,300
Net long term capital gain	8,600

Travis is married and files a joint tax return. What is his net taxable income?

I:7-46   *Qualified Residence Interest.* During the current year, Tina purchases a beachfront condominium for $600,000, paying $150,000 down and taking out a $450,000 mortgage, secured by the property. At the time of the purchase, the outstanding mortgage on her principal residence is $700,000. This debt is secured by the residence. The FMV of the principal residence is $1,400,000. She purchased the principal residence in 1997. What is the amount of qualified indebtedness on which Tina may deduct the interest payments?

I:7-47   *Qualified Residence Interest.* Several years ago, Magdelena purchased a new residence for $300,000. Currently, the outstanding mortgage on the residence is $260,000. The current fair market value of the home is $330,000. Magdelena wants to borrow a sizable sum of money to pay for the college education costs of her two children and believes the interest would be deductible if she takes out a home equity loan. For each of the independent situations below, determine the amount of the home equity loan on which Magdelena may deduct the interest as qualified residence interest.
a. Magdelena borrows $50,000 as a home equity loan.
b. Magdelena borrows $80,000 as a home equity loan.
c. Alternatively, assume the current fair market value of her residence is $410,000 and she borrows $110,000 as a home equity loan.
d. Alternatively, assume the current outstanding balance of the mortgage Magdelena incurred to purchase the home is $1,200,000, the home's fair market value is $1,400,000, and she borrows $80,000 as a home equity loan.

I:7-48   *Interest Between Related Parties.* Crown Corporation is an accrual method taxpayer owned 55% by Brett and 45% by Susie. Brett and Susie are good friends and have been business associates for several years. BJ Partnership is a cash method taxpayer, owned 40% by Brett and 60% by Jeremy, Brett's uncle. Both Crown Corporation and BJ Partnership are calendar year entities. On January 5 of the current year, Crown borrows $50,000 from BJ Partnership and pays 8% interest on the loan. Crown must pay the interest on January first of next year.
a. What amount of interest expense can Crown Corporation deduct in the current year?
b. How would your answer change if Jeremy were Brett's brother, instead of his uncle?

I:7-49   *Timing of Interest Deduction.* On April 1 of the current year, Henry borrows $12,000 from the bank for a year. Because the note is discounted for the interest charge and Henry receives proceeds of $10,200, he is required to repay the face amount of the loan ($12,000) in four equal quarterly payments beginning on July 1 of the current year. Henry is a cash method individual.
a. What is the amount of Henry's interest expense deduction in the current year with respect to this loan?
b. Assume the same facts except that the initial starting date when the repayments begin is April 1 of the following year. What is the amount of Henry's interest expense deduction in the current year?
c. Assume the same facts as in Part b, except that Henry is an accrual method taxpayer and the loan will be outstanding for one year. What is the amount of his interest expense deduction in the current year?

I:7-50   *Itemized Deductions.* During 2015, Doug incurs the following deductible expenses: $2,300 in state income taxes, $3,000 in local property taxes, $800 in medical expenses, and $2,000 in charitable contributions. Doug is 33, single, has no dependents, and has $35,000 AGI for the year. What is the amount of Doug's taxable income?

I:7-51   *Computation of Taxable Income.* During 2015, James, a single, cash method taxpayer incurred the following expenditures:

Qualified medical expenses	$ 8,000
Investment interest expense	16,000
Other investment activity expenses	15,000
Qualified residence interest	12,000
Interest on loan on personal auto	2,000
Charitable contributions	3,000

State income tax paid	7,000
State sales tax paid	4,500
Property taxes	4,000
Tax return preparation and consulting fees	5,000

James' income consisted of the following items:

Salary	$70,000
Interest income	20,000
Long-term capital gains	23,000
Long-term capital losses	(15,000)

a. Compute James' taxable income for the year (assuming that he makes an election to have the net capital gain taxed at the regular tax rates). Also assume that James is 67 years old. Thus, his medical expense deduction is subject to the 7.5% rather than the 10% limit.

b. What is James' investment interest carryover (if any)?

I:7-52 *Computation of Taxable Income.* Assume all the same facts as in Problem I:7-51 except that James' salary income is $130,000 instead of $70,000 and that he does not make the election. Compute James' taxable income for the year.

I:7-53 *Charitable Contributions: Services.* Donna is an attorney who renders volunteer legal services to a Legal Aid Society, which provides legal advice to low-income individuals. The Legal Aid Society is a qualified charitable organization. During the current year she spends a total of 200 hours in this volunteer work. Her regular billing rate is $350 per hour. In addition, she spends a total of $800 in out-of-pocket costs in providing these services. She receives no compensation and is not reimbursed for her out-of-pocket costs. What is Donna's charitable contribution for the year because of these activities?

I:7-54 *Charitable Contribution Limitations.* In each of the following independent cases, determine the amount of the charitable contribution and the limitation that would apply. In each case, assume that the donee is a qualified public charity.

a. Sharon donates a tract of land to a charitable organization. She has held the land for seven years. Her basis in the land is $10,000 and its FMV is $40,000.

b. Assume the same facts in Part a, except that Sharon has held the land for only 11 months and that its FMV is $23,000.

c. Jack purchases a historical document for $50,000. He donates the historical document to a charitable organization two years later. The organization plans to use it for research and study. Its FMV at the time of the donation is $100,000.

d. Assume the same facts in Part c, except that the organization plans to sell the document and put the money into an endowment fund.

e. Valerie donates some inventory to a charitable organization. The inventory is not food or clothing. The inventory is purchased for $500 and its FMV is $1,200 at the time of the donation. She held the inventory for seven months.

I:7-55 *Charitable Contributions to Private Nonoperating Foundations.* Assume the same facts as Problem I:7-54, except that the qualified organization is a private nonoperating foundation. Determine the amount of the charitable contribution for Parts a through e.

I:7-56 *Charitable Contribution Limitations.* During the current year, Helen donates stock worth $50,000 to her local community college. Two years ago the stock cost Helen $40,000. Her AGI for the current year is $100,000. Beginning next year, the bulk of her income will be from tax-exempt municipal securities. Thus, she is not interested in any carryover of excess charitable contribution. What is the maximum charitable contribution deduction Helen may take this year?

I:7-57 *Charitable Contribution Limitations.* During the current year, Melissa reports AGI of $200,000. As part of some estate planning, she donates $30,000 to her alma mater, Middle State University, and $65,000 to a private nonoperating foundation.

a. What is the amount of Melissa's charitable deduction for the current year?

b. Assume the same facts in Part a except that she donates $45,000 to Middle State University.

I:7-58 *Corporate Charitable Contributions.* Circle Corporation, an accrual method taxpayer, manufactures and sells mainframe computers. In January of the current year, Circle Corporation donates a mainframe that was part of its inventory to City College. City College will use the computer for physical science research. Circle's basis in the mainframe is $300,000. The computer's FMV is $650,000. On December 15 of the current year, Circle also pledged stock to the Red Cross and promised delivery of the stock by

March 1 of the following year. The stock's FMV is $100,000 and Circle's adjusted basis in the stock is $50,000. Circle has held the stock for over one year. Circle's taxable income (before deducting any charitable contributions) for the current year is $4,000,000.

a. What is the amount of Circle's charitable contribution for the current year?

b. How much of the contribution can Circle deduct in the current year and how much may be carried over, if any?

I:7-59 *Charitable Contribution Carryovers.* Bonnie's charitable contributions and AGI for the past four years were as follows:

	2012	2013	2014	2015
AGI	$50,000	$55,000	$58,000	$60,000
Contributions subject to the 50% limitation	40,000	29,000	25,000	10,000

What is the amount of the charitable deduction for each year and the order in which the deduction and carryovers are used?

COMPREHENSIVE PROBLEM

I:7-60 Tim and Monica Nelson are married, file a joint return, and are your newest tax clients. They provide you with the following information relating to their 2015 tax return:

1. Tim works as a pediatrician for the county hospital. The W-2 form he received from the hospital shows wages of $150,000 and state income tax withheld of $8,500.
2. Monica spends much of her time volunteering, but also works as a substitute teacher for the local schools. During the year, she spent 900 hours volunteering. When she doesn't volunteer, she earns $8.00 per hour working as a substitute. The W-2 form she received from the school district shows total wages of $3,888 and state income tax withheld of $85.
3. On April 13, the couple paid $250 in state taxes with their 2014 state income tax return. The Nelson's state and local sales taxes in 2015 were $5,500.
4. On December 18, the Nelsons donated a small building to the Boy Scouts of America. They purchased the building three years ago for $80,000. A professional appraiser determined the fair market value of the home was $96,000 on December 12.
5. Tim and Monica both received corrective eye surgery, at a total cost of $3,000. They also paid $1,900 in health insurance premiums.
6. On June 1, the couple bought a car for $30,000, paying $18,000 down and borrowing $12,000. They paid $750 total interest on the loan in 2015.
7. On June 10, the Nelsons took out a home equity loan of $20,000 to expand their home. They paid a total of $850 interest with their monthly payments on the loan.
8. The Nelsons paid a total of $2,300 interest on their original home loan.
9. They sold stock in Cabinets, Inc. for $5,200, which they purchased for $7,900 in March of the current year. They also sold stock in The Outdoor Corporation for $12,500, which they purchased several years ago for $8,600.
10. Tim incurred the following expenses related to his profession, none of which were reimbursed by his employer:

Item	Amount
Subscriptions to medical journals	$400
American Medical Association (AMA) annual membership fee	250

11. During the year, the couple paid their former tax advisor $700 to prepare their prior year tax return.
12. The Nelsons do not have children, and they do not provide significant financial support to any family members.

Required: Compute the Nelson's taxable income for 2015.

TAX STRATEGY PROBLEMS

I:7-61 Dean makes a pledge of $30,000 to a local college. The college is willing to accept either cash or marketable securities in fulfillment of the pledge. Dean owns stock in Ajax Corporation worth $30,000. The stock was purchased five years ago for $10,000. Dean's marginal tax rate is 35% and he is subject to the long-term capital gains rate of 15%. Should Dean sell the stock and then donate the cash, or should he donate the stock directly? Compute the net tax benefit from each alternative and explain the difference. (Ignore the 3.8% tax on the net investment income of high-income taxpayers for this comparison.)

I:7-62 On December 1, 2015, Rebecca Ward, a single taxpayer, comes to you for tax advice. At the end of every year, she donates $5,000 to charity. She has no other itemized deductions. This year, she plans to make her charitable donation with stock. She presents you with the following information relating to her stock investments:

Corporation	FMV on Dec. 1	Adjusted Basis	Date Purchased
Sycamore	9,600	7,800	5/22/10
Oak	2,900	3,800	9/10/11
Redwood	5,400	4,900	6/15/15

Which stock should Rebecca donate to charity? What other tax advice would you give her?

TAX FORM/RETURN PREPARATION PROBLEMS

I:7-63 Following is a list of information for Peter and Amy Jones for the current tax year. Peter and Amy are married and have three children, Aubrynne, Bryson, and Caden. They live at 100 Main Street, Anytown, USA 00000. Peter is a lawyer working for a Native American law firm. Amy works part-time in a genetic research lab. The Jones' Social Security numbers and ages are as follows:

Name	S.S. No.	Age
Peter	111-11-1111	32
Amy	222-22-2222	28
Aubrynne	333-33-3333	5
Bryson	444-44-4444	3
Caden	555-55-5555	1

Receipts

Peter's salary	$70,000
Amy's salary	32,000
Interest income on municipal bonds	2,400
Interest income on certificate of deposit (Universal Savings)	3,100
Dividends on GM stock	1,600

Disbursements

Eyeglasses and exam for Aubrynne	$ 600
Orthodontic work for Bryson to correct a congenital defect	2,500
Medical insurance premiums, after-tax basis	1,800
Withholding for state income taxes	7,200
Withholding for federal income taxes	16,000
State income taxes paid with last year's tax return (paid when the return was filed in the current year)	500
Property taxes on home	1,100
Property taxes on automobile	300
Interest on home	9,700
Interest on credit cards	200
Cash contribution to church	3,900

In addition to the above, on September 17, Peter and Amy donate some Beta Trader, Inc. stock to Lakeville Community College. Beta Trader, Inc. is publicly traded. The FMV of the stock on the date of the contribution is $700. Peter and Amy had purchased the stock on November 7, 2003 for $300.

Compute Peter and Amy's income tax liability for the current year using Form 1040, Schedules A and B, and Form 8283, if necessary.

I:7-64 Kelly and Chanelle Chambers, ages 47 and 45, are married and live at 584 Thoreau Drive, Boston, MA 59483. Kelly's Social Security number is 111-11-1111 and Chanelle's is 222-22-2222. The Chambers have two children: Emma, age 23, and Chet, age 19. Their Social Security numbers are 333-33-3333 and 444-44-4444, respectively. Emma is a single college student and earned $8,000 during the summer. Kelly and Chanelle help Emma through school by paying for her room, board, and tuition. Emma lives at home during the summer. Chet has a physical handicap and lives at home. He attends a local university and earned $4,000 working for a marketing firm. In sum, Kelly and Chanelle provide more than 50% of both Emma's and Chet's total support for the year.

Kelly is a commercial pilot for a small airline. His salary is $95,000, from which $19,000 of federal income tax and $8,000 of state income tax were withheld. Kelly also pays premiums for health, disability, and life insurance. $2,000 of the premium was for health insurance, $250 for disability, and $400 for life insurance.

Chanelle owns Alliance Networks, a proprietorship that does network consulting. During the year, Chanelle's gross revenues were $23,000. She incurred the following expenses in her business:

Liability insurance	$ 700
Software rental	5,400
Journals and magazines	150
Training seminars	1,200
Supplies	1,300
Donations to a political campaign fund	800

Kelly enjoys playing guitar and plays in a band. Kelly's band has developed a local following. This year, his gross revenues were $1,200 for playing shows and $700 on CD sales. He incurred the following expenses:

Studio rent expense	$1,300
Sound system repairs	200
CD production	500
New guitar and amplifier	800

Kelly's father passed away during the year. Kelly and Chanelle received $100,000 from the life insurance policy. Neither Kelly nor Chanelle paid any of the premiums.

Chanelle purchased 100 shares of Thurston Co. stock on May 1, 1991, for $1,000. Thurston Co. was declared bankrupt during the current year.

Chet's physician recommended that he see a physical therapist to help with his disability. Kelly paid the therapist $7,000 during the year because his insurance would not cover the bills.

Kelly and Chanelle went to Las Vegas and won $5,000 at the blackjack table. The next night, they lost $6,000.

Kelly and Chanelle gave $900 to their church and, during the year, they had the following other income and expenses:

Real estate taxes	$1,400
Property taxes on car (determined by value)	500
Home mortgage interest	9,000
Credit card finance charges	2,600
Tax return preparation fees ($600 is allocable to Chanelle's business)	1,000
Sales tax on purchases during the year	6,200
Interest from a savings account	800
Interest from City of Boston Bonds	700
Dividend from 3M stock	400

Prepare Kelly and Chanelle's tax return Form 1040 and Schedules A, B, C, D, and SE for the current year.

CASE STUDY PROBLEMS

I:7-65 Brian Brown, an executive at a manufacturing enterprise, comes to you on December 1 of the current year for tax advice. He has agreed to donate a small tract of land to the Rosepark Community College. The value of the land has been appraised at $58,000. Mr. Brown purchased the land 14 months ago for $50,000. Mr. Brown's estimated AGI for the current year is $100,000. He plans to retire next year and anticipates that his AGI will fall to $35,000 for all subsequent years. He does not anticipate making any additional large charitable contributions. He understands that there are special rules dealing with charitable contributions and wants your advice in order to get the maximum overall tax benefit from his contribution. Because the college plans to use the property, selling the land is not an alternative. You are to prepare a letter to Mr. Brown explaining the tax consequences of the different alternatives. His address is 100 East Rosebrook, Mesa, Arizona 85203. For purposes of your analysis, assume that Mr. Brown is married and files a joint return. Also assume that Mr. Brown feels that an appropriate discount rate is 10%. In your analysis, use the tax rate schedules for the current year.

I:7-66 For several years, you have prepared the tax return for Alpha Corporation, a closely held corporation engaged in manufacturing garden tools. On February 20 of the current year, Bill Johnson, the president of Alpha Corporation, delivered to your office the files and information necessary for you to prepare Alpha's tax return for the immediately preceding tax year. Included in this information were the minutes of all meetings held by Alpha's Board of Directors during the year in question.

Then on February 27, Bill stops by your office and hands you an "addendum" to the minutes of the director's meeting held December 15 of the tax year for which you are preparing the tax return. The addendum is dated the same day as the director's meeting, and authorizes a charitable contribution pledge of $20,000 to the local community college. With a wink and a big smile, Bill explains that the addendum had been misplaced. In reviewing the original minutes, you find no mention of a charitable contribution pledge.

What should you do? [See Appendix E and the *Statements on Standards for Tax Services* section in Chapter I:15 (or C:1 of the *Comprehensive* volume) for a discussion of these issues.]

TAX RESEARCH PROBLEMS

I:7-67 Mark Hancock is a self-employed attorney who operates his law practice as an unincorporated sole proprietorship. In 2014, the IRS disallowed several business deductions he took in 2012 and 2013. In addition to paying the deficiency and assessed penalties, he also pays $18,000 in interest on the tax owed. Can he deduct that interest in the current year?

- Sec. 162, Sec. 163
- Reg. Sec. 1.163-9T
- *Kikalos v. Comm.*, 84 AFTR 2d 99-5933

I:7-68 Last year, Mr. Smith was involved in an automobile accident, severely injuring his legs. As part of a long-term rehabilitation process, his physician prescribes a daily routine of swimming. Because there is no readily available public facility nearby, Smith investigates the possibility of either building a pool in his own back yard or purchasing another home with a pool. In the current year he finds a new home with a pool and purchases it for $175,000. He then obtains some estimates and finds that it would cost approximately $20,000 to replace the pool in the home he has just purchased. He also obtains some real estate appraisals, which indicate that the existing pool increases the value of the home by only $8,000. During the current year, Smith also expends $500 in maintaining the pool and $1,800 in other medical expenses. What is the total amount of medical expenses he may claim in the current year? Smith's AGI for the year is $60,000.

- Sec. 213
- Reg. Sec. 1.213-1(e)(1)(iii)
- *Richard A. Polacsek*, 1981 PH T.C. Memo ¶81,569, 42 TCM 1289
- *Paul A. Lerew*, 1982 PH T.C. Memo ¶82,483, 44 TCM 918
- *Jacob H. Robbins*, 1982 PH T.C. Memo ¶82,565, 44 TCM 1254

CHAPTER

8

LOSSES AND BAD DEBTS

LEARNING OBJECTIVES

After studying this chapter, you should be able to

1. ▶ Identify transactions that may result in losses

2. ▶ Determine the proper classification for losses

3. ▶ Examine the tax treatment of passive losses

4. ▶ Identify and calculate the deduction for a casualty or theft loss

5. ▶ Compute the deduction for a bad debt

6. ▶ Compute a net operating loss deduction

7. ▶ Identify tax planning considerations for losses and bad debts

8. ▶ Identify compliance and procedural considerations for losses and bad debts

Taxpayers often sustain losses on property they sell, exchange, or dispose of. If the taxpayer uses the property in a trade or business or holds the property for investment, the tax law generally provides a deduction for these losses. Noncorporate taxpayers may also take a limited deduction for losses on personal-use property that is either stolen or damaged in a casualty. However, in general, taxpayers may not deduct other types of losses on personal-use property (e.g., a loss they realize on the sale of a personal residence or an automobile that they use exclusively for personal purposes). Special rules allow taxpayers to take a deduction for losses they incur because of uncollectible business or nonbusiness debts. This chapter discusses the rules concerning the deductibility of these types of losses.

TRANSACTIONS THAT MAY RESULT IN LOSSES

For taxpayers to deduct a loss on property, the loss must be both *realized* and *recognized* for tax purposes. Generally, *realization* occurs in a completed (closed) transaction evidenced by an identifiable event such as a sale or exchange. This is referred to as the closed transaction doctrine. As a general rule, taxpayers who have realized losses on business or investment property may recognize such losses for tax purposes unless a specific provision holds otherwise (see pages I:8-6 and I:8-7).

EXAMPLE I:8-1 ▶ Capital Corporation purchased 500 shares of Data Corporation stock for $10,000 on February 22 of the current year. By October 31 of the same year, the price of the stock declines to $8,000. Even though Capital has suffered an economic loss on the stock, no realization event has occurred, and the corporation may not deduct the $2,000 loss. However, if Capital sells the stock for $8,000 on October 31, it realizes the loss for tax purposes in the current year. ◀

Losses on property may arise in a variety of transactions, including:

▶ Sale or exchange of the property

▶ Expropriation, seizure, confiscation, or condemnation of the property by a government

▶ Abandonment of the property

▶ Worthlessness of stock or securities

▶ Planned demolition of the property in order to construct other property in its place

▶ Destruction of the property by fire, storm, or other casualty

▶ Theft

▶ Deductible business expenses exceeding business income, giving rise to a net operating loss (NOL)

ADDITIONAL COMMENT

If property is used partly for business and partly for personal use, the loss attributable to the business portion is deductible but the loss on the personal-use portion is not unless the loss was sustained in a casualty.

KEY POINT

Anticipated losses, including those for which reserves have been established, are not deductible.

SALE OR EXCHANGE OF PROPERTY

The amount of the loss a taxpayer incurs in a sale or exchange of property equals the excess of the property's adjusted basis over the amount realized for the property.[1] The amount realized for the property equals the sum of the money received plus the fair market value (FMV) of any other property the taxpayer receives in the transaction. If the property sold or exchanged is subject to a mortgage or other liability, the amount realized by the taxpayer also includes the amount of the liability transferred to the buyer.[2] The treatment of any selling costs depends on the type of property sold or exchanged. If the property is inventory (i.e., property normally held for sale in the taxpayer's business), the selling costs are generally deductible expenses in the year in which the taxpayer incurs the expenses. However, if the sale involves property not normally held for sale by the taxpayer, the selling costs reduce the amount realized from the sale or exchange.

---

[1] Sec. 1001.

[2] *Beulah B. Crane v. CIR*, 35 AFTR 776, 47-1 USTC ¶9217 (USSC, 1947); and Reg. Sec. 1.1001-2.

EXAMPLE I:8-2 ▶ Four years ago, Boyer Corporation purchased a plot of land as an investment for $50,000. Unfortunately, local economic conditions worsened after Boyer, Inc. purchased the land and the land's value declined to $35,000. Boyer sells the property in the current year. At the time of the sale, the land is subject to a $10,000 mortgage. The terms of the sale are $25,000 paid in cash with the purchaser assuming the mortgage. Boyer also incurs $2,000 in sales commissions. The amount realized is $33,000 ($25,000 cash + $10,000 mortgage assumed by the buyer − $2,000 commissions). The loss on the sale is $17,000 ($50,000 basis − $33,000 amount realized). ◄

In general, taxpayers can only deduct losses they incur in the sale or exchange of property used in a trade or business or held for investment. Taxpayers cannot deduct losses they incur in the sale or exchange of personal-use property. Furthermore, the type of deduction a taxpayer may take for a loss realized on the sale or exchange of business or investment property depends on the type of property sold. For example, if inventory is sold, the loss is an ordinary loss. If the asset is a capital asset, the loss is a capital loss (see Chapter I:5). If the sale is of property used in a trade or business (a Sec. 1231 asset), the type of loss depends on the total net gain or loss realized on all the taxpayer's Sec. 1231 transactions during the year (see Chapter I:13).

EXPROPRIATED, SEIZED, CONFISCATED, OR CONDEMNED PROPERTY

A taxpayer may own property that the government expropriates, seizes, confiscates, or condemns. In these cases, the taxpayer incurs a deductible loss if the taxpayer used the property in a trade or business or held it for investment. The Tax Court has held that the confiscation, seizure, condemnation, or expropriation of property does not constitute a theft or a casualty. Rather, it is treated as a sale or exchange. Thus, no deductible loss arises if the seized property is personal-use property.[3] If the seized or condemned property is business or investment property, the classification of the loss depends on the type of property. (See the section in this chapter titled Classifying the Loss on the Taxpayer's Return.) A taxpayer may take the deduction only in the year in which the property is actually seized. Whether formal expropriation or nationalization occurs in a later year is irrelevant.[4] A taxpayer realizes gain if he or she receives compensation for the property in excess of its basis. Under certain circumstances, the taxpayer may defer this gain. (See Chapter I:12 for a discussion of the nonrecognition of gain in an involuntary conversion.)

ABANDONED PROPERTY

If a taxpayer's property becomes worthless or is not worth repairing in order to return the property to a serviceable condition, the taxpayer may simply abandon the property. If the property still has basis, the taxpayer realizes a loss. The taxpayer may not deduct such losses if the property is personal-use property. However, the taxpayer may deduct losses on business or investment property. Furthermore, because the abandonment of property is not a sale or exchange, the loss is an ordinary loss. The amount of the loss is the property's adjusted basis on the date of abandonment. The taxpayer bears the burden of proof to verify that the property was actually abandoned. If the property is depreciable (e.g., machinery and buildings), the taxpayer must actually physically abandon it to take the full amount of the loss.[5]

WORTHLESS SECURITIES

A taxpayer may take a deduction for securities that become completely worthless during the tax year.[6] Because the deduction is only available in the year the security actually becomes worthless, both the taxpayer and the IRS may have problems determining the year in which the security becomes worthless. A mere decline in value is not sufficient to create a deductible loss if the stock has any recognizable value. Furthermore, the sale of the stock for a nominal amount such as $1 does not necessarily establish that the stock became

---

[3] *William J. Powers,* 36 T.C. 1191 (1961) (See also *Gouhari v. U.S.,* 83 AFTR 2d 99-2726 (4th Cir., 1999).).
[4] Rev. Rul. 62-197, 1962-2 C.B. 66 as modified by Rev. Rul. 69-498, 1969-2 C.B. 31. (See also *Estate of Frank Fuchs v. CIR,* 24 AFTR 2d 69-5077, 69-2 USTC ¶9505 (2nd Cir., 1969)).
[5] Reg. Sec. 1.167(a)-8(a)(4).

[6] For this purpose, a *security* is defined in Sec. 165(g)(2) as stock in a corporation, the right to subscribe for or receive a share of stock in a corporation, or a bond, debenture, note, or certificate of indebtedness issued by a corporation or a government either in registered form or with interest coupons. Promissory notes issued by a corporation are generally not securities.

worthless in the year of the sale. The taxpayer must show that the security is completely worthless and that the security became worthless during the year.

Under Sec. 165, once the taxpayer determines the year of worthlessness, the taxpayer treats the loss as a loss from the sale of a capital asset on the last day of the tax year. Although this provision does not help in determining the year of worthlessness, it does establish a definite date for purposes of measuring whether the loss is short- or long-term. In some cases, this provision causes the loss to be long-term because it extends the date of worthlessness to the end of the year.

EXAMPLE I:8-3 ▶ On February 20 of the current year, Control Corporation enters into bankruptcy with no possibility for the shareholders to receive anything of value. Because the amount of Control Corporation's outstanding liabilities exceeds the FMV of its assets on that date, the stock of the corporation becomes worthless. Janet, a calendar-year taxpayer, owns 500 shares of Control's common stock, which she had purchased for $10,000 through her broker on June 17 of the prior year. Under Sec. 165(g), she treats the loss as having arisen from the sale of a capital asset on the last day of the current year. Thus, Janet incurs a $10,000 long-term capital loss because the holding period for the stock is more than one year. On the other hand, if Janet had received the stock directly from Control Corporation in exchange for either money or other property, and if certain other requirements are met, the stock may qualify as Sec. 1244 stock. Individuals who sustain losses on Sec. 1244 stock receive a limited amount of ordinary loss treatment rather than capital loss treatment. (See the discussion in this chapter under the heading "Losses on Sec. 1244 Stock.") ◀

Under certain circumstances, if a domestic corporation owns worthless securities of an affiliated corporation, the domestic corporation treats the loss as having arisen from the sale of a noncapital asset. This allows the corporation to treat the loss as an ordinary loss rather than as a capital loss.[7] For this exception to apply, the corporation must meet the following requirements:

▶ The domestic corporation that is deducting the loss must own at least 80% of the voting power of all classes of the affiliated corporation's stock and 80% of the total value of the affiliated corporation stock.

▶ More than 90% of the affiliated corporation's gross receipts for all its taxable years must be from nonpassive income.[8]

DEMOLITION OF PROPERTY

At times, taxpayers, intent on building their own facilities, purchase land with an existing structure that must first be removed. Taxpayers may also demolish a structure they currently use to construct new facilities. In both cases, taxpayers may not deduct any demolition costs or any loss sustained on account of the demolition. Instead, under Sec. 280B, taxpayers must add these amounts to the basis of the land on which the demolished structure previously stood.

CLASSIFYING THE LOSS ON THE TAXPAYER'S TAX RETURN

If a loss is deductible, the taxpayer must determine whether the loss is an ordinary loss or a capital loss. In addition, individual taxpayers must also identify the deductible amount as either a deduction *for* or *from* AGI.

---

[7] As explained in Chapter I:5, the deductibility of capital losses is limited. For corporate taxpayers, capital losses must initially be offset against capital gains of the current year, and any excess loss is not deductible but may be carried back three years and forward for five years. Individuals may offset capital losses against capital gains and any excess loss is deductible up to $3,000 per year as an offset to ordinary income. Capital losses in excess of this amount

for an individual are carried forward for an indefinite period. Thus, taxpayers generally prefer ordinary losses rather than capital losses.
[8] Sec. 165(g)(3). *Nonpassive income* includes all income other than royalties, rents, dividends, interest, annuities, and gains from the sale or exchange of stocks and securities.

ORDINARY VERSUS CAPITAL LOSS

Whether a deductible loss is ordinary or capital depends on the type of property involved and the transaction in which the taxpayer sustains the loss. To incur a capital loss, a sale or exchange of a capital asset must occur. If both elements (i.e., a sale or exchange and a capital asset) are not present, the deduction generally is an ordinary loss. In general, all assets *except* inventory, notes and accounts receivable, and depreciable property and land used in a trade or business (i.e., property, plant, and machinery) are classified as **capital assets.**[9]

Because a casualty is not a sale or exchange, the destruction of a capital asset in a casualty creates an ordinary rather than a capital loss. Likewise, a deductible loss realized on the abandonment of property is an ordinary loss because an abandonment is not a sale or exchange.

EXAMPLE I:8-4 ▶

BOOK-TAX DIFFERENCE

For book purposes, it makes no difference if a gain or loss is ordinary or capital. The full amount of the loss is deductible. However, because corporations may not deduct a capital loss in excess of its capital gains for the year, a book-tax timing (temporary) difference may arise, making an M-1 or M-3 adjustment necessary.

On July 24 of the current year, Jermaine & Associates, LLP sells some investment property for $75,000. The property's adjusted basis is $85,000. The investment property is a capital asset. Jermaine realizes a $10,000 ($75,000 − $85,000) capital loss. If, instead, the property had been destroyed by fire and the partnership had received $75,000 in insurance proceeds, the $10,000 loss would have been an ordinary loss because a casualty is not a sale or exchange. ◄

Certain transactions, though not actually constituting a sale or exchange, receive sale or exchange treatment. For example, as mentioned previously, if a security owned by an individual investor becomes worthless during the year, the individual treats the loss as a loss from the sale of a capital asset on the last day of the tax year, even though no sale actually occurs. Thus, the loss is a capital loss. Likewise, the taxpayer will treat a seizure or condemnation of property as a sale or exchange.

Section 1231 Property. Whether a loss on a particular transaction is treated as a capital loss may also depend on the gains and losses the taxpayer reports from other property transactions for the tax year. For instance, under Sec. 1231, taxpayers must net certain gains and losses together. If the Sec. 1231 gains exceed the Sec. 1231 losses for the year, the taxpayer treats the net gain as a long-term capital gain. However, if the losses equal or exceed the gains, both the gains and the losses are treated as ordinary. **Section 1231 property** includes real or depreciable property used in a trade or business and held for more than one year. (See Chapter I:13 for a discussion of the netting procedure under Sec. 1231.)

Losses on Sec. 1244 Stock. Taxpayers generally recognize capital gain or loss on the sale of stock or securities. For individuals, the tax law provides an exception for losses from the sale or worthlessness of small business corporation (Sec. 1244) stock. Individuals may deduct these losses as ordinary losses up to a maximum of $50,000 per tax year ($100,000 for married taxpayers filing a joint return). Any remaining loss for the year is a capital loss.

To qualify the loss as ordinary under Sec. 1244, the following requirements must be met:

▶ The stock must be owned by an individual or a partnership.

▶ The stock must have been originally issued by the corporation to the individual or to a partnership in which an individual is a partner.[10]

▶ The stock must be stock in a domestic (U.S.) corporation.

▶ The taxpayer must have received the stock in exchange for cash or property (other than stock or securities) that the taxpayer contributed to the corporation. Stock issued to the taxpayer for services rendered is not eligible for Sec. 1244 treatment.

---

[9] Sec. 1221. Certain other exceptions also exist. The definition of a capital asset is more fully examined in Chapter I:5.

[10] Stock received in certain reorganizations of corporations in exchange for Sec. 1244 stock is also considered Sec. 1244 stock. Section 1244 does not apply to stock that the individual has received through other means such as purchase in a secondary market, exchange, gift, or inheritance.

► The corporation must not have derived over 50% of its gross receipts from passive income sources during the five tax years immediately preceding the year of sale or worthlessness.[11]

► The amount of money and property contributed to both capital and paid-in surplus may not exceed $1 million at the time the corporation issues the stock.

Note that the last test listed above occurs when the corporation *actually issues the stock*. As long as the corporation's capital and paid-in surplus does not exceed $1 million at the time the stock was issued, the individual taxpayer may still report an ordinary loss on the stock even if the corporation has capital and paid-in surplus in excess of the $1 million limit at the time the loss is realized.

? STOP & THINK

Question: Tony, a single taxpayer, incorporated Waffle, Inc. three years ago by contributing $70,000 in exchange for the stock. Waffle owns and operates a small restaurant. Unfortunately, Waffle's business never really became profitable. Tony has been trying to sell the Waffle stock since July of last year, but because the corporation had become insolvent, he couldn't find any buyers. In February of the current year, Waffle was judged to be bankrupt. Tony didn't receive anything for his stock. What issues should Tony's tax advisor address with regard to the Waffle, Inc. stock?

Solution: Tony's tax advisor must determine (1) the amount of any realized loss, (2) the year in which the loss is recognized, and (3) the character of the realized loss. The Waffle, Inc. stock is considered a security under Sec. 165. Whenever a security becomes completely worthless and it is determined that the owner will receive nothing for it, the owner realizes a loss to the extent of the security's basis ($70,000). The loss is deemed to be realized in the year in which the security becomes worthless. While the bankruptcy court ruled the stock to be worthless in February of the current year, the fact that Tony could not find any buyers last year because the corporation was insolvent may indicate that the stock really became worthless last year. This determination is important because Tony must recognize the loss in the year in which the stock becomes worthless. Furthermore, the stock is deemed to become worthless on the last day of that year. Since Tony received the stock directly from the corporation in exchange for contributed cash, Waffle, Inc.'s gross receipts are from business operations, and the capitalization at the time the stock was issued is less than $1 million, the stock qualifies as Sec. 1244 stock. Thus, $50,000 of the loss is characterized as ordinary loss. The remaining $20,000 is a long-term capital loss.

DISALLOWANCE POSSIBILITIES

The tax law may disallow or defer losses incurred in certain transactions and activities. Some of these transactions include:

► Transfers of property to a controlled corporation in exchange for stock of the corporation (see the discussion in Chapter C:2 of *Prentice Hall's Federal Taxation: Corporations, Partnerships, Estates & Trusts* text and Chapter C:2 of the *Comprehensive* volume)

► Exchanges of property for other property considered to be like-kind to the property given up (see the discussion in Chapter I:12)

► Property sold to certain related parties (see the discussion in Chapter I:6)

► Wash sale transactions (see the discussion in Chapter I:6)

► Losses limited because the losses exceed the amount for which the taxpayer is at risk (see the discussion in Chapter C:9 of *Prentice Hall's Federal Taxation: Corporations, Partnerships, Estates & Trusts* text and Chapter C:9 of the *Comprehensive* volume)

In addition, the passive loss rules discussed below may limit the amount of losses that individuals and certain corporations may deduct.

Topic Review I:8-1 contains a summary of loss transactions.

---

[11] For this purpose, passive income sources include royalties, rents, dividends, interest, annuities, and sales or exchanges of stocks and securities. If the corporation has not been in existence for a full five years, the gross receipts test is applied to the shorter period. If the corporation has not been in existence for an entire taxable year, the test is applied to the time period up to the date of the loss (see Sec. 1244(c)(2)).

TOPIC REVIEW I:8-1

Transactions That May Result in Losses

TYPE OF TRANSACTION	RESULT
Sale or exchange	Taxpayers may not deduct a loss on personal-use property. The tax treatment of a loss on business or investment property depends on the type of property. Losses on capital assets result in capital losses. Losses on Sec. 1231 assets are subject to the Sec. 1231 netting rules discussed in Chapter I:13.
Seizure, expropriation, confiscation, or condemnation	Treated as a sale or exchange.
Abandonment	Not treated as a sale or exchange. No deduction is allowed for a loss on personal-use property. Business or investment property is given ordinary loss treatment.
Worthless securities	Treated as a loss from the sale of the securities on the last day of the year in which the securities become worthless. This generally will result in a capital loss. However, if the requirements of Sec. 1244 are met, an individual taxpayer may treat at least part of the loss as an ordinary loss. (See Sec. 1244 stock below.) A loss realized by a corporation on worthless securities of an affiliated corporation results in an ordinary loss.
Demolition	No deductible loss is allowed. Instead, losses and costs of demolition are added to the basis of the land where the demolished structure was located.
Sec. 1244 stock	Individual taxpayers may take an ordinary loss of up to $50,000 per year ($100,000 for married filing jointly) for losses realized on qualified Sec. 1244 stock. The remaining loss is capital. The stock must have been originally issued to the individual for property or cash, and the corporation must meet the requirements to be a small business corporation.

PASSIVE LOSSES

OBJECTIVE 3

Examine the tax treatment of passive losses

Before 1987, taxpayers were able to reduce their income tax liability on their salary or on income from business or investment activities with deductions, losses, and credits arising in other activities. Thus, taxpayers often invested in activities, called **tax shelters**, that would spin off tax deductions and credits. Many of these tax shelters were simply *passive investments* because they did not require the taxpayer's involvement or participation. In some situations, tax shelters had real economic substance, i.e., a taxpayer's economic return in this type of shelter was not based solely on the tax benefits that the activity generated. In many cases, however, tax shelters had no real economic substance other than the creation of deductions and credits that enabled taxpayers to reduce, and sometimes eliminate, the income tax liability from their other business activities. To prevent these perceived and real abuses, Congress enacted Sec. 469, which restricts the current use of losses and credits that arise in rental activities and in other activities in which the taxpayer does not materially participate. These activities constitute passive activities. (See the "Definition of a Passive Activity" section in this chapter for an extended discussion of what constitutes a passive activity.)

HISTORICAL NOTE

Before the passive activity loss limits became effective in 1987, most tax shelters were concentrated in the areas of real estate, oil and gas, equipment leasing, farming, motion pictures, timber, and research and development. Many tax shelters took advantage of liberal depreciation rules during the early 1980s such as the rapid depreciation of real estate over a 15-year period.

COMPUTATION OF PASSIVE LOSSES AND CREDITS

In enacting the passive loss rules, Congress did not want to prevent taxpayers from currently deducting or using losses and credits generated in active business endeavors of the taxpayer. At the same time, Congress realized that certain investments (such as investments that generate interest or dividend income) normally give rise to taxable income, which could itself be sheltered by losses and credits that arise in other passive activities. Thus, Sec. 469 requires certain taxpayers to classify their income into three categories: *active income* (such as wages, salaries, and active business income), *portfolio (or investment) income*, and *passive income*. **Portfolio income** includes dividends, interest, annuities, and royalties (and allocable expenses and interest expense) not derived in the ordinary course of a trade or business. Portfolio income also includes gains and losses on property that produces these types of income if the disposition of the property does not occur in the ordinary course of business.[12] Portfolio income becomes part of net investment income, which is used in computing the deduction limit for investment interest expense. (See Chapter I:7 for a discussion of the investment interest expense limitation.)

Passive Income and Losses. Taxpayers compute income and loss in the passive category separately for each passive activity in which they have invested. In general, for any tax year, a taxpayer may use losses generated in one passive activity to offset income from other passive activities, but may not use them to offset either active or portfolio income.

EXAMPLE I:8-5 ▶ During the year, Kasi, a CPA, reports $100,000 of active business income from his CPA practice. He also owns two passive activities. From activity A, he earns $10,000 of income, and from activity B, he incurs a $15,000 loss. Kasi may use $10,000 of the loss from activity B to offset the $10,000 of income from activity A. However, Kasi may not deduct the $5,000 excess loss from activity B in the current year, even though he has $100,000 of active business income. ◀

CARRYOVERS

A taxpayer carries over disallowed passive activity losses indefinitely and treats them as losses allocable to that specific passive activity in the following tax years. The taxpayer may use these losses, known as **suspended losses,** to offset passive activity income of the subsequent year, but generally may not offset other types of income. If a taxpayer has invested in several passive activities, and for the year some of the activities generate income while others generate losses, the loss carried over for each loss activity is a pro rata portion of the total passive loss for the year.

EXAMPLE I:8-6 ▶ Tammy reports the following income and loss for the year:

Salary	$200,000
Loss from activity X	(40,000)
Loss from activity Y	(10,000)
Income from activity Z	30,000

X, Y, and Z are all passive activities. The losses generated in activities X and Y offset the income from activity Z, but none of the salary income is offset. Thus, Tammy has a net passive loss for the year of $20,000 ($40,000 + $10,000 − $30,000), which must be carried over to subsequent years. The amount of the carryover attributable to each activity is as follows:

$$\text{Activity X:} \qquad \$20,000 \times \frac{\$40,000}{\$50,000} = \$16,000$$

$$\text{Activity Y:} \qquad \$20,000 \times \frac{\$10,000}{\$50,000} = \$\ 4,000 \blacktriangleleft$$

Taxable Disposition of Interest in a Passive Activity. When a taxpayer disposes of a passive activity in a taxable transaction, the taxpayer can compute the economic gain or loss generated by the activity and can deduct the suspended losses of the activity against other income. However, the amount of the total net economic loss from the asset disposed of must first offset any passive income for the year from other passive activities.[13]

EXAMPLE I:8-7 ▶ During the current year, Pam realizes $6,000 of taxable income from activity A, $1,000 of loss from activity B, and $8,000 of taxable income from activity C. All three activities are passive activities with regard to Pam. In addition, $30,000 of passive losses from activity C are carried over from prior years. During the current year, Pam sells activity C for a $15,000 taxable gain. Pam reports salary income of $90,000 for the year. Because Pam sells activity C in a fully taxable transaction, Pam may deduct $2,000 of loss against the salary income:

---

[12] Sec. 469(e)(1). Gain or loss on property dispositions occurring in the ordinary course of business is either passive or active business income, depending on the taxpayer's level of involvement (i.e., material participation) in the activity.

[13] Sec. 469(g). Income from the activity for prior years may also be taken into account in arriving at the net income from all passive activities for the year if it is necessary to prevent avoidance of the passive loss rules.

Income for the year from C	$ 8,000	
Gain from the sale of C	15,000	
Suspended losses from C	(30,000)	
Total loss from C		($7,000)
Income for the year from A	$ 6,000	
Loss for the year from B	(1,000)	5,000
Pam's deduction against salary income		($2,000) ◄

BOOK-TAX DIFFERENCE

Since passive losses are not limited under financial accounting rules, the limitation and carryover of passive losses for tax purposes will create a timing (temporary) difference between book and tax. However, many taxpayers subject to the passive loss rules are individuals who do not use financial accounting rules.

If the taxpayer sells the passive activity to a related party, he or she may not deduct the suspended loss until the related party sells the activity to a nonrelated person. The definition of *related persons* includes spouse, brothers and sisters, ancestors, lineal descendants, and corporations or partnerships in which the individual has a greater than 50% ownership.[14]

Although the death of a taxpayer is not a taxable disposition of the asset, some of the suspended losses may be deductible when a taxpayer dies. The amount of the deduction allowed is the amount by which the suspended losses exceed the increase in basis of the property. The decedent's final income tax return generally includes the deduction for these losses. Any suspended losses up to the amount of the increase in basis will never be deductible.[15]

EXAMPLE I:8-8 ►

At the time that John died, he owned passive activity property with an adjusted basis of $20,000 and a FMV of $35,000. Suspended losses attributable to the property totaled $25,000. Because the increase in the basis of the property is $15,000 ($35,000 − $20,000), $15,000 of the suspended losses are lost. However, $10,000 ($25,000 suspended losses − $15,000 increase in basis) of the suspended losses are deductible on John's final income tax return. ◄

In general, the suspended losses of a passive activity become deductible only when the taxpayer completely disposes of his or her interest in the activity. However, in Treasury Reg. 1.469-4(g) the government has stated that taxpayers may treat the disposition of a substantial part of an activity as the disposition of a separate activity. This treatment is only available, however, if the taxpayer can establish with reasonable certainty the amount of income, deductions, credits, and suspended losses and credits that are allocable to that part of the activity.

Carryovers from a Former Passive Activity. The determination of whether an activity is passive with respect to a taxpayer must be made annually. Thus, an activity that was previously passive may not be passive with respect to the taxpayer for the current year. This is called a **former passive activity.** A taxpayer may deduct any loss carryover from a former passive activity against the current year's income of that activity even though the activity is not a passive activity in the current year. However, any suspended loss in excess of the activity's income for the year is still subject to the carryover limitations. Because the activity is no longer passive for the year, the current year's loss is deductible against active business income.

EXAMPLE I:8-9 ►

Kris owns activity A, which, for the immediately preceding tax year, was considered a passive activity with regard to Kris. $10,000 in losses from activity A were disallowed and carried over to the current year. Because of Kris' increased involvement in activity A in the current year, it is not considered passive with regard to Kris for the current year. During the current year, activity A generates a $5,000 loss. During the current year, Kris also has an investment in activity B, a passive activity. Her share of activity B's income is $7,000. Kris reports $60,000 in salary. Because for the current year activity A is not a passive activity, the $5,000 current year loss is fully deductible against her salary. However, the $10,000 loss carryover from the prior year is deductible only against the $7,000 of income from passive activity B. The $3,000 ($10,000 − $7,000) excess is carried over to the subsequent year. ◄

---

[14] Other relationships described in Secs. 267(b) and 707(b) are also considered related parties for this purpose.

[15] Sec. 469(g)(2). For 2011 and later the basis of inherited property is its FMV on the date of death (see Chapter I:5).

Credits. A taxpayer may only use tax credits generated in a passive activity against the portion of the taxpayer's tax liability that is attributable to passive income. The taxpayer determines this amount by comparing the tax liability on all income for the year with the tax liability on all income excluding the passive income.

EXAMPLE I:8-10 ▶ Dale invests in a passive activity. For the year, he must report $10,000 of taxable income from the passive activity. Dale's share of tax credits generated by the passive activity is $5,000. Assume Dale's precredit tax liability on all income (including the $10,000 from the passive activity) is $25,000, and his precredit tax liability on all income excluding the passive activity income is $22,000. He may use only $3,000 ($25,000 − $22,000) of the tax credits generated by the passive activity. Dale must carry forward the remaining $2,000 of tax credits and can use them in a subsequent year against the portion of his tax liability attributable to his passive activity income in that year. However, these credits may never offset any portion of the tax liability attributable to nonpassive activities. (See Chapter I:14 for a discussion of credits and their carryovers.) ◀

DEFINITION OF A PASSIVE ACTIVITY

The term *passive activity* includes any trade or business in which the taxpayer does not materially participate as well as any rental activity. An important exception applies to a rental activity that is considered to be a *real property trade or business.* This exception is discussed below on page 8–14.[16] The definition of a passive activity is based on two critical elements: an identification of exactly what constitutes an activity and a determination of whether the taxpayer has materially participated in that activity.

Identification of an Activity. Identification of the activity becomes critical for several reasons. (1) The determination of whether a taxpayer materially participates in an activity is determined separately for each activity. (2) A taxpayer may deduct suspended losses of a passive activity when the taxpayer completely terminates his or her ownership of the activity. (3) As explained in a subsequent section of this chapter, taxpayers may deduct currently up to $25,000 of passive losses from rental real estate activities. Thus, taxpayers must not combine losses from passive business and rental real estate activities into one activity.

The way taxpayers combine or separate operations into activities can significantly impact the deductibility of losses generated by the activities. Taxpayers may treat one or more activities as a single activity only if they constitute an "appropriate economic unit."[17] Although the taxpayer makes this determination by examining all the relevant facts and circumstances, the following factors receive the greatest weight:

▶ Similarities and differences in the types of business,

▶ The extent of common control,

▶ The extent of common ownership,

▶ The geographical location, and

▶ Any interdependencies between the operations (i.e., the extent to which the operations purchase or sell goods between each other, have the same customers, are accounted for with a single set of books, etc.).

A taxpayer may treat more than one operation as a single activity, even if all of these factors do not apply. Furthermore, a taxpayer may use any reasonable method of applying the relevant facts and circumstances in grouping the activities.

EXAMPLE I:8-11 ▶ Carla owns a bakery and a movie theater in each of two different shopping malls, one located in Baltimore and the other in Philadelphia. Depending on other relevant facts and circumstances, a reasonable grouping of the operations may result in any of the following:

---

[16] Secs. 469(c)(1) and (c)(2). Sec. 469(c)(6) also includes investment (production of income) activities under Sec. 212 as a passive activity. Section 469(j)(8) defines the term *rental activity* as any activity where payments are principally for the use of tangible property. Pursuant to the Regulations, there are six exceptions to this general rule. These exceptions include (1) providing the use of tangible property where the average period of customer use is seven days or less, (2) the average period of customer use is 30 days or less and significant personal services are provided by the owner in conjunction with the use of the property, (3) extraordinary personal services are provided by the owner in

conjunction with the use of the property, (4) the rental of the property is incidental to a nonrental activity of the taxpayer, (5) the property is customarily made available during defined business hours for nonexclusive use by various customers, or (6) the property is provided for use in a nonrental activity conducted by a partnership, S corporation, or joint venture in which the taxpayer owns an interest. The details of these exceptions are beyond the scope of this text. (See Reg. Sec. 1.469-1(e)(3)(iii).)

[17] Reg. Sec. 1.469-4.

▶ One activity involving all four operations
▶ Two activities: a bakery activity and a theater activity
▶ Two activities: a Baltimore activity and a Philadelphia activity
▶ Four activities

◀

Under the Treasury Regulations, taxpayers apparently have some degree of flexibility in determining the grouping into activities of different business operations. However, once taxpayers establish the activities, they must be consistent in grouping these activities in subsequent years unless material changes in the facts and circumstances clearly make the groupings inappropriate.

In identifying separate activities, taxpayers generally may not group rental operations with trade or business operations. However, a combination is allowed if either the rental operation is insubstantial in relation to the business operation or vice versa. Unfortunately, the Treasury Regulations do not give any guidance with regard to what is insubstantial. Furthermore, because of the special rules dealing with real estate rental activities (explained later in this chapter), the taxpayer may not combine rental activities involving real estate with rental activities involving personal property.

EXAMPLE I:8-12 ▶ Sandy owns a building in which she (1) operates a restaurant and (2) leases out apartments to tenants. Generally the tenants sign apartment leases of one year or longer. Of the total gross income derived from the building, 15% comes from the apartment rentals and 85% comes from the restaurant operation. If the apartment rental operation is insubstantial in relation to the restaurant operation, the taxpayer may combine the two into one activity. If it is not insubstantial, the two operations are considered two separate activities: a business activity and a rental real estate activity. ◀

Partnerships and S corporations (pass-through entities) must identify their business and rental activities by applying these rules at the partnership or S corporation level and then must report the results of their operations by activity to the partners or shareholders. Each partner or shareholder must then take the results from these activities and, using these same rules, combine them where appropriate with operations conducted either directly or through other pass-through entities. In fact, in practice taxpayers often hold real estate passive activities as either partnerships or S corporations.

Material Participation. Once each activity is identified, taxpayers must determine whether the activity is passive or active. If the taxpayer does not **materially participate** in the activity, it is deemed to be a passive activity with respect to that taxpayer. Pursuant to the Treasury Regulations,[18] taxpayers materially participate in an activity if they meet at least one of the following tests:

▶ The individual participates in the activity for more than 500 hours during the year.

▶ The individual's participation in the activity for the year constitutes substantially all of the participation in the activity by all individuals, including individuals who do not own any interest in the activity.

▶ The individual participates in the activity for more than 100 hours during the year, and that participation is more than any other individual's participation for the year (including participation by individuals who do not own any interest in the activity).

▶ The individual participates in "significant participation activities" for an aggregate of more than 500 hours during the year.[19] Thus, an individual who spends over 100 hours each in several separate significant participation activities may aggregate the time spent in these activities in order to meet the 500-hour test.

▶ The individual materially participated in the activity in any five years during the immediately preceding ten taxable years. These five years need not be consecutive.

---

[18] Temp. Reg. Sec. 1.469-5T(a).
[19] A significant participation activity is a trade or business in which the individual participates for more than 100 hours during the year but for which

the individual does not meet the material participation test alone (i.e., with respect to that activity, the individual does not meet one of the other material participation tests). (See Temp. Reg. Sec. 1.469-5T(c).)

▶ The individual materially participated in the activity for any three years preceding the year in question, and the activity is a personal service activity.[20]

▶ The individual participates in the activity on a regular, continuous, and substantial basis during the year, taking into account all the relevant facts and circumstances.

Note that the first four tests are based on the number of hours the taxpayer spent in the activity during the current year. The fifth and sixth tests are based on the material participation of the taxpayer in prior years and are designed to prevent taxpayers from asserting that retirement income is passive and offsetting it with passive losses from tax shelters. To determine whether a taxpayer materially participates in an activity, the participation of the taxpayer's spouse is also taken into account.

Limited Partnerships. A limited partner has limited liability for his or her investment in the partnership and normally is not actively involved in the business of the partnership. As a consequence, a limited partner generally does not meet the material participation test and the limited partner's investment is treated as passive. Thus, most income and deductions passed through to a limited partner from a limited partnership are passive. However, a limited partner can meet the material participation test if the individual meets either the 500 hour test or the fifth or sixth tests above (prior year tests).

Working Interest in an Oil and Gas Property. A working interest is an interest that is responsible for the cost of development or operation of the oil and gas property. This type of interest in an oil and gas property is not a passive activity as long as the taxpayer's liability in the interest is not a limited interest. Thus, even though a taxpayer may not materially participate in the activity, the passive loss rules do not apply. This is so even if the taxpayer holds the interest through an entity such as a partnership.

TAXPAYERS SUBJECT TO PASSIVE LOSS RULES

The passive loss limitation rules apply to:

▶ Individuals, estates, trusts

▶ Any closely held C corporation

▶ Any personal service corporation

▶ Certain publicly traded partnerships

Because the income and losses of partnerships and S corporations are taxed directly to the partners and shareholders, the passive loss rules do not apply to these entities.[21] Rather, the passive loss limitations apply directly at the partner or shareholder level. Thus, the situation may arise where one partner or shareholder is subject to the passive loss rules with regard to an activity conducted by the partnership or S corporation while other partners or shareholders are not.

Generally, regular corporations (i.e., C corporations) are not subject to the passive loss limitation rules. However, to prevent certain individuals from avoiding the passive loss rules through the use of a regular corporation, the passive loss rules do apply to closely held C corporations and personal service corporations.

Closely Held C Corporations. The passive loss rules apply to closely held C corporations but only on a limited basis. A **closely held C corporation** is a C corporation where more than 50% of the stock is owned by five or fewer individuals at any time during the last half of the corporation's taxable year.[22] Without this special rule involving

---

[20] A personal service activity involves rendering personal services in the fields of health, law, engineering, architecture, accounting, actuarial science, performing arts, or consulting. It also includes any other trade or business in which capital is not a material income-producing factor. (See Temp. Reg. Sec. 1.469-5T(d).)

[21] An S corporation is a corporation that has elected for federal income tax purposes to be treated as a flow-through entity. Thus, the income or losses and separately stated items of an S corporation flow through to the shareholders and are reported on their individual tax returns.

[22] Secs. 469(j)(1), 465(a)(1)(B), and 542(a)(2).

closely held C corporations, taxpayers would be motivated to transfer their investments (both portfolio investments and passive activities) to a C corporation where the portfolio income could be offset by the corporation's passive losses. Thus, as applied to a closely held C corporation, the passive loss rules prevent passive activity losses from offsetting portfolio income. However, a closely held C corporation's passive losses may offset its income from active business operations.

EXAMPLE I:8-13 ▶ All of the outstanding stock of Delta Corporation is owned equally by individuals Allen and Beth. During the current year, Delta generates $15,000 taxable income from its active business operations. It also earns $10,000 of interest and dividends from investments and reports a $30,000 loss from a passive activity. Because Delta is a closely held C corporation, the $15,000 of taxable income from the active business is offset by $15,000 of the passive loss. However, the $10,000 of portfolio income may not be offset. Thus, for the current year, Delta reports $10,000 of taxable income from its portfolio income and has a $15,000 passive loss carryover. ◄

Personal Service Corporation. A **personal service corporation** (PSC) is a regular C corporation whose principal activity is the performance of personal services that are substantially performed by owner-employees.[23] However, a corporation is not a PSC unless owner-employees own more than 10% of the value of the stock. In contrast with a closely held C corporation, the passive loss limitation rules apply in their entirety to a PSC. If a corporation is both a PSC and a closely held C corporation, the more restrictive rules for PSCs apply. Thus, a PSC cannot offset its active business income or portfolio income with losses from its passive activities.

Material participation by PSCs and closely held C corporations. Special rules apply for determining whether closely held C corporations or PSCs materially participate in an activity. These corporations materially participate in an activity only if one or more shareholders who own more than 50% in value of the outstanding stock materially participate in the activity. In addition, a closely held C corporation (other than a PSC) materially participates in an activity if it meets *all* of the following tests with regard to an activity:

1. A substantial portion of the services of at least one full-time employee is in the active management of the activity.
2. A substantial portion of the services of at least three full-time nonowner employees is directly related to the activity.
3. The Sec. 162 business deductions of the activity exceed 15% of the activity's gross income for the period.[24]

Publicly Traded Partnerships. In many cases, the tax law provisions for corporations apply to publicly traded partnerships (PTP). For purposes of the passive loss rules, a PTP is defined as any partnership if interests in the partnership are either traded on an established securities market or readily tradable on a secondary market.[25] If the corporate tax provisions apply to a PTP, the passive loss rules generally do not apply. However, if a PTP meets certain gross income requirements, the partnership tax provisions may still apply, causing its items of income, loss, and credit to flow through to the partners.[26] If this is the case, the passive loss rules apply at the partner level separately to the flow through items from each PTP. Thus, partners treat losses from a PTP as separate from any other type of income (passive, active business, or portfolio) and separate from any income from

---

[23] Secs. 469(j)(2) and 269A(b)(1). For this purpose any employee who owns any stock of the corporation is an owner-employee. This stock ownership is determined by using the Sec. 318 constructive ownership rules as modified by Sec. 469(j)(2).

[24] Secs. 469(h)(4) and 465(c)(7). Tests 1 and 2 must be met for the 12-month period ending on the last day of the tax year. Test 3 must be met for the tax year. Furthermore, the Sec. 404 deductions are also included in the 15% of gross income test.

[25] Sec. 469(k)(2). (See Chapter C:10 of *Prentice Hall's Federal Taxation: Corporations, Partnerships, Estates & Trusts* and Chapter C:10 of the *Comprehensive* volume for a definition and discussion of publicly traded partnerships.)

[26] Sec. 7704(c). For the taxable year and all preceding years beginning after Dec. 31, 1987, at least 90% of the PTP's gross income consists of dividends, interest, real property rents, income from certain gas, oil, mineral or timber activities, and gains from the sale of real estate or certain capital assets. Furthermore, certain other PTPs may also elect to continue to be treated as a partnership rather than as a corporation.

other PTPs. Partners can only carry these losses forward and offset them against income generated by that particular PTP in a subsequent year. Furthermore, a PTP loss may not offset any portfolio income that the PTP might generate. Any net income from PTPs is portfolio income.

EXAMPLE I:8-14 ► Mark owns interests in partnerships A and B, both of which are PTPs that are treated as partnerships. During the current year, Mark's share of the income from A is $2,000. Mark's share of B's loss is $1,200. B also generates some portfolio income. Mark's share of B's portfolio income is $800. The $1,200 loss from B may not offset any of B's $800 portfolio income. Furthermore, it may not offset any of the $2,000 income from A. The $2,000 income from A is treated as portfolio income. Thus, Mark reports $2,800 portfolio income and has a $1,200 suspended loss from B. In a subsequent year, Mark's share of any income from B can be offset by the $1,200 of suspended loss that is carried forward. ◄

A partner may deduct suspended losses from a PTP in the year the partner disposes of his or her interest in the PTP. Partners do not recognize a loss in the year that the PTP itself sells a passive activity.

REAL ESTATE BUSINESSES

In general, rental activities are considered passive activities. However, the passive activity loss rules do not apply to certain taxpayers who are involved in real property trades or businesses. Instead, these activities are treated as active businesses. A *real property trade or business* involves the development, redevelopment, construction, reconstruction, acquisition, conversion, rental, operation, management, leasing, or brokering of real property.

This exception only applies to a taxpayer if he or she meets both of the following requirements:

► More than one-half of the personal services the taxpayer performs in all trades or businesses during the year are in real property trades or businesses in which the taxpayer materially participates.

► The taxpayer performs more than 750 hours of work during the taxable year in real property trades or businesses in which the taxpayer materially participates.

In meeting these tests, personal services a taxpayer renders in his or her capacity as an employee are not treated as performed in real property trades or businesses unless the employee owns at least 5% of the employer. Furthermore, for married taxpayers filing a joint return, the exception applies only if one of the spouses separately meets both requirements. The time spent in the activity by both spouses counts toward the determination of whether or not the taxpayer meets the material participation test.

EXAMPLE I:8-15 ► Anwar and Anya are married and file a joint return. They own four large apartment complexes which they manage themselves. Neither is employed elsewhere. During the current year, Anya spent 500 hours keeping records and corresponding with tenants. Anwar spent 700 hours during the year maintaining and repairing the apartments. Even though all of Anya and Anwar's personal services are connected with a real property trade or business in which they materially participate, this rental activity is considered passive because neither Anwar nor Anya alone spends more than 750 hours doing services related to the rental activity. ◄

For a closely held C corporation to meet this rental real estate business exception, the corporation must derive more than one-half of its gross receipts from real property businesses in which it materially participates.

Any deduction allowed under the previously discussed exception for taxpayers involved in real property trades or businesses is not considered in determining the taxpayer's AGI for purposes of the phase-out of the $25,000 deduction available for taxpayers who actively participate in a rental real estate activity. (See the following section in this chapter for a discussion of the $25,000 active participation exception.)

OTHER RENTAL REAL ESTATE ACTIVITIES

Many rental real estate activities are not considered rental real estate businesses and are, therefore, subject to the passive loss rules. However, if an individual taxpayer meets certain requirements, the taxpayer still may deduct against other income up to $25,000 of annual losses from these passive rental real estate activities. To meet this exception, an individual must do both of the following:

► *Actively* participate in the activity

► Own at least 10% of the value of the activity for the entire tax year

Additionally, in order to take a deduction in the current year for a loss sustained in a prior year, Section 469(i) requires the taxpayer to actively participate in the activity during both years.

Active Participation. A taxpayer can achieve *active participation*, as opposed to material participation, without regular, continuous, and material involvement in the activity and without meeting any of the material participation tests. However, the taxpayer still must participate in making management decisions or arranging for others to provide services in a significant and bona fide sense. This includes approving new tenants, deciding on rental terms, approving expenditures, and other similar decisions. Taxpayers may achieve active participation even if they hire a rental agent and others to provide the services. However, a lessor under a net lease arrangement generally does not achieve active participation. Additionally, a limited partner generally cannot actively participate in any activity of a limited partnership.

Limitation on Deduction of Rental Real Estate Loss. Taxpayers must first apply rental real estate losses against other net passive income for the year. Taxpayers may then reduce their portfolio or active business income by up to $25,000. However, the tax law requires reduction of the $25,000 amount by 50% of the taxpayer's AGI in excess of $100,000.[27] For this purpose, AGI does not include any passive activity loss or any loss allowable to taxpayers who materially participate in real property trades or businesses (e.g., a real estate developer). Thus, if a taxpayer has AGI of $150,000 or more, the rental real estate losses are not eligible for the $25,000 deduction and are aggregated with the taxpayer's other passive losses.

EXAMPLE I:8-16 ► During the current year, Penny, a married individual who files a joint return, reports the following items of income and loss:

Salary income	$120,000
Activity A (passive)	15,000
Activity B (nonbusiness rental real estate)	(50,000)

Penny owns over 10% and actively participates in activity B. Her AGI for the year is as follows:

Salary		$120,000
Passive income from activity A	$15,000	
Minus: Passive loss from activity B ($50,000, but limited to $15,000)	(15,000)	–0–
Minus: Maximum rental real estate loss (from activity B)	$25,000	
Reduced by phase-out: [($120,000 − $100,000) × 0.50]	(10,000)	
Deductible amount (but not to exceed actual loss)		(15,000)
AGI		$105,000

Penny may deduct $30,000 of the loss from activity B during the year ($15,000 as an offset to the passive income from activity A + $15,000 deductible against portfolio or active business income). Penny has $20,000 ($50,000 – $30,000) of suspended passive losses from activity B that are carried over to the following year. ◄

---

[27] This provision which allowed taxpayers to either (1) take a current deduction equal to 50% of certain qualified commercial revitalization expenditures on certain buildings, or (2) amortize the qualified expenditures over a 10 year period only applied to property placed into service before January 1, 2010. Even though this provision has been repealed, if a taxpayer elected to amortize the qualified expenditures over a 10 year period, the amount amortized and deducted in years after 2009 is not subject to the $25,000 passive loss limit. Further analysis of this provision is beyond the scope of this discussion. Additionally, AGI is modified by certain items that are beyond this discussion.

The $25,000 limit applies to the sum of both deductions and credits. Thus, in order to properly apply the limit, taxpayers must convert the credits into deduction equivalents. A *deduction equivalent* is an amount that, if taken as a deduction, would reduce the tax liability by an amount equal to the credits. The amount of deduction equivalents can be computed by dividing the amount of the credit by the taxpayer's marginal tax rate. If the sum of the deductions and the deduction equivalents exceeds the $25,000 limit, the taxpayer must first use the deductions.

EXAMPLE I:8-17 ▶ Hal owns over 10% of activity A, in which he actively participates. Activity A is a passive real estate rental activity. Hal's marginal tax rate is 25% and he has AGI of less than $100,000. For the year, activity A generates a $20,000 net loss and $10,000 in tax credits, which amounts to $40,000 in deduction equivalent {$10,000/25%}. After deducting the $20,000 net loss against his active business and portfolio income, Hal has a remaining real estate deduction under the limit of $5,000 ($25,000 − $20,000). Thus, Hal may use $1,250 ($5,000 × 0.25) of the credits. The remaining $8,750 ($10,000 − $1,250) of tax credits must be carried over to subsequent years. ◀

If deductions and credits exceeding the $25,000 limit arise from more than one passive activity, the taxpayer must allocate the deductions and credits between the activities.[28]

EXAMPLE I:8-18 ▶ Mary has AGI of less than $100,000 and a 25% marginal tax rate. During the year she reports a $30,000 loss from activity A and a $10,000 loss from activity B. Additionally, activity A generates $5,000 of tax credits. Both activities A and B are passive real estate rental activities in which Mary actively participates and owns over 10% of each activity. The $25,000 deduction is first allocated to the losses. Because the sum of the losses ($40,000) exceeds the limit, the deductible loss must be allocated ratably between the activities as follows:

$$\text{Activity A:} \quad \$25,000 \times \$30,000 \div \$40,000 = \$18,750$$
$$\text{Activity B:} \quad \$25,000 \times \$10,000 \div \$40,000 = \$6,250$$

Activity A has an $11,250 ($30,000 − $18,750) suspended loss, and activity B has a $3,750 ($10,000 − $6,250) suspended loss. In addition, activity A has $5,000 of suspended tax credits. ◀

Topic Review I:8-2 summarizes the passive activity loss rules.

? STOP & THINK

Question: Jana is a businesswoman who has successfully invested in various stock and bond funds. Now she is considering diversifying her holdings by investing in real estate. One of the alternatives she is considering is purchasing an interest in a limited partnership that invests in real estate. A friend is also urging Jana to go into a partnership with him in order to purchase a small office building they would rent out. Assume that the size of Jana's investment in the two alternatives would be exactly the same and that Jana estimates the economic results to be equivalent (e.g., she expects both to spin off equivalent losses for the first few years and then begin turning a profit). What tax issues should Jana consider when making her investment decision?

Solution: In comparing alternatives such as these, of course, the most important considerations should be the non-tax factors such as cash flow from the investment, the capital appreciation of the assets, the marketability of the investment, and the risk. For example, as a limited partner, Jana will not personally be liable for debts of the partnership or lawsuits filed against the partnership. Purchase of the office building as a general partner with her friend will cause her to be personally liable unless it is done through an LLC or LLP. Additionally, in comparing these two alternatives, certain tax issues may come into play. Both alternatives are investments in rental real estate. However, Jana is not eligible to deduct up to $25,000 of the passive losses from the limited partnership because she will

---

[28] A taxpayer may earn different types of credits, based upon the different types of investments. Furthermore, the phase-out of the $25,000 limit is treated differently for different types of credits. For example, the phase-out for the rehabilitation credit only begins when the taxpayer's AGI exceeds $200,000. Additionally, there is no phase-out applied to the credit for low income housing. (See Sec. 469(e)(3) and Chapter I:14 for a discussion of these credits.) Thus, taxpayers are required to allocate the deductions and credits among the activities and account for them in a specific order. A complete analysis of these rules is beyond the scope of this discussion. Example I:8-18 assumes both activities earn the same type of credit and are subject to the $25,000 limit.

TOPIC REVIEW I:8-2

Passive Losses

Topic	Summary
Taxpayers covered	Individuals, estates, trusts, closely held C corporations, personal service corporations, certain publicly traded partnerships.
Passive activity	Any trade or business activity in which the taxpayer does not materially participate. Includes all rental activities except for certain rental real estate activities and exceptions contained in regulations. Does not include working interests in oil and gas property.
Limitation	Passive losses are deductible against passive income, but not against active or portfolio income. Disallowed losses are carried over to subsequent years (suspended losses). Losses must be accounted for separately by activity. Activities are identified by examining the taxpayer's undertakings.
Suspended losses	Must be allocated and attributed among the passive activities that generated the losses.
Disposition of interest	Suspended losses may be deducted in the year of a taxable disposition. For inherited property, suspended losses in excess of the increase in basis may be deducted on the final return of a decedent. Losses up to the amount of the basis increase are lost.
Material participation	Must be regular, continuous, and substantial. The regulations contain seven separate tests; four based on current-year participation; two based on participation in prior years; and one based on facts and circumstances.
Real property trades or businesses	Passive activity loss rules do not apply to taxpayers who materially participate in real property trade or business activities for more than 750 hours during the year. Additionally, more than one-half of the taxpayer's personal services must be performed in real property trades or businesses in which the taxpayer materially participates.
Rental of real estate	Individuals may deduct losses up to $25,000 against active and portfolio income if they actively participate in the activity and own at least 10% of the value of the activity. Additionally, they may take certain credits generated in passive rental activities in which they actively participate. Active participation is a lesser standard than material participation, but the taxpayer must still participate in management decisions or arranging for others to provide services. The deduction and credits phase out at a 50% rate for AGI in excess of $100,000.

not actively participate in the partnership. On the other hand, if she is involved in management decisions regarding the office building held by the partnership, she will be actively participating and will be eligible for the $25,000 passive loss deduction exception. Of course, the benefit of this exception begins phasing out if her AGI exceeds $100,000.

CASUALTY AND THEFT LOSSES

OBJECTIVE 4

Identify and calculate the deduction for a casualty or theft loss

Taxpayers may deduct losses incurred in connection with business or investment property, but individuals generally are not allowed a deduction for losses on personal-use property. However, under Sec. 165, individuals may take a limited deduction if the loss on personal-use property arises from a fire, storm, shipwreck, other casualty, or theft. In other words, losses on personal-use property are deductible only if the loss results from a casualty. In order for an event to qualify as a casualty, the event must meet certain requirements.

CASUALTY DEFINED

According to the IRS, a deductible **casualty loss** is one that occurs in an identifiable event that is sudden, unexpected, or unusual.[29]

---

[29] Rev. Rul. 79-174, 1979-1 C.B. 99. See also IRS *Publication No. 547, Casualties, Disasters, and Thefts*, 2014, p.2.

Identifiable Event. Because the event that causes the loss must be *identifiable*, the act of losing or misplacing property is generally not considered a casualty.

However, in some cases, taxpayers have proven that the loss of property was the result of an identifiable event.

EXAMPLE I:8-19 ▶ One evening Troy and his wife, Lynn, go to the theater. Troy accidentally slams the car door on Lynn's hand. The impact breaks the flanges holding the diamond in her ring. As a result, the diamond falls from the ring and is lost. In this case, a deductible casualty loss has occurred.[30] ◀

Sudden, Unexpected, or Unusual Events. According to the IRS, a *sudden event* is one that is swift, not gradual or progressive. An *unexpected event* is one that is ordinarily unanticipated and not intended. An *unusual event* is one that is not a day-to-day occurrence and that is not typical of the activity.

Thus, the IRS has ruled that a deductible casualty loss occurred when a taxpayer went ice fishing and his automobile fell through the ice.[31] A taxpayer whose automobile was damaged as the result of an accident also sustained a deductible casualty loss. However, a taxpayer may not deduct losses incurred in an accident caused by the taxpayer's willful negligence or willful act.[32] Damage sustained as the result of an accident in an automobile race was held to be nondeductible because accidents occur often and are not unusual events in automobile races.[33]

The following are a few examples of events that the courts have held to constitute a deductible casualty loss:

▶ Rust and water damage to furniture and carpets caused by the bursting of a water heater

▶ Damage to the exterior paint of a residence caused by a severe, sudden, and unexpected concentration of chemical fumes in the air

▶ Loss caused by fire (unless the taxpayer sets the fire, in which case no deduction is available)

▶ Damage to a building caused by an unusually large blast at a nearby quarry or a jet sonic boom[34]

▶ Death of trees just a few days after a sudden infestation of pine beetles[35]

The following are examples of events that the courts have held *not* to be a casualty:

▶ Water damage to the walls and ceiling of a taxpayer's personal residence as the result of the gradual deterioration of the roof[36]

▶ Trees dying because of gradual suffocation of the root systems

▶ The loss of trees and shrubs because of disease[37]

▶ Damage to carpet and clothing caused by moths and carpet beetles[38]

▶ Damage to a road due to freezing, thawing, and gradual deterioration[39]

▶ Damage to a residence caused by the gradual sinking of the land underneath the home[40]

▶ Damage caused by drought because it occurs through progressive deterioration

▶ The steady weakening of a building caused by normal wind and weather conditions

▶ The rusting and deterioration of a water heater[41]

---

[30] *John P. White*, 48 T.C. 430 (1967), *acq.* 1969-2 C.B. xxv. In another case, the taxpayer convinced the Tax Court to allow a deduction for a lost diamond, even though the taxpayer could not remember a specific blow to the ring. In this instance, the taxpayer obtained an expert witness to testify that the flanges of the ring were strong enough and in good enough repair that the loss of the diamond had to have been caused by a sudden, unexpected blow rather than by progressive deterioration.

[31] Rev. Rul. 69-88, 1969-1 C.B. 58.

[32] *Willie C. Robinson*, 1984 PH T.C. Memo ¶84,188, 47 TCM 1510 and Reg. Sec. 1.165-7(a)(3).

[33] Ltr. Rul. 8227010 (March 30, 1982) contains the above examples.

[34] *Ray Durden*, 3 T.C. 1 (1944), *acq.* 1944 C.B. 8 and Rev. Rul. 60-329, 1960-2 C.B. 67.

[35] Rev. Rul. 79-174, 1979-1 C.B. 99. See also *Charles A. Smithgall v. U.S.*, 47 AFTR 2d 81-695, 81-1 USTC ¶9121 (D.C.-Ga., 1980). However, the IRS has ruled in Ltr. Rul. 8544001 (July 12, 1985) that no casualty loss results when the time interval between the infestation and the death of the trees was too long.

[36] *Lauren Whiting*, 1975 PH T.C. Memo ¶75,038, 34 TCM 241.

[37] *William R. Miller*, 1970 PH T.C. Memo ¶70,167, 29 TCM 741 and Rev. Rul. 57-599, 1957-2 C.B. 142. Modified by Rev. Rul. 79–174, 1979-1 C.B. 99. (See also *Howard F. Burns v. U.S.*, 6 AFTR 2d 6036, 61-1 USTC ¶9127 (6th Cir., 1960).)

[38] Rev. Rul. 55-327, 1955-1 C.B. 25. (See also *J. P. Meersman v. U.S.*, 18 AFTR 2d 6152, 67-1 USTC ¶9125 (6th Cir., 1966).)

[39] *Howard Stacy*, 1970 PH T.C. Memo ¶70,127, 29 TCM 542. However, the breaking up of a road over a 4-month period because of extreme weather conditions was held to be a casualty. See *Emmett J. O'Connell v. U.S.*, 29 AFTR 2d 72-596, 72-1 USTC ¶9312, (D.C. Cal., 1972). (See also *Stephen L. Shaffer*, 1983 PH T.C. Memo ¶83,677, 47 TCM 285.)

[40] *Henry W. Berry*, 1969 PH T.C. Memo ¶69,162, 28 TCM 802. (See also *David McDaniel*, 1980 PH T.C. Memo ¶80,557, 41 TCM 563.)

[41] Rev. Rul. 70-91, 1970-1 C.B. 37 and IRS *Publication No. 547* (Casualties, Disasters, and Thefts), 2014 contain the above examples.

At times it is very difficult to determine under the particular facts whether the necessary requirements of suddenness, unexpectedness, or unusualness exist. For example, as mentioned above, damage caused by the sudden infestation of pine beetles in some instances has been held to be a casualty, but in other instances it has not.[42]

THEFT DEFINED

Under Sec. 165, a taxpayer may also deduct a loss sustained as the result of a theft. This includes theft of business, investment, or personal-use property. The Treasury Regulations state that "the term theft shall be deemed to include, but shall not necessarily be limited to, larceny, embezzlement, and robbery."[43] A determination whether other actions also constitute theft often depends on whether the action involves criminal intent and is illegal under the state law where the action has occurred. Thus, the IRS has stated that blackmail, extortion, and kidnapping for ransom may also constitute theft.[44]

DEDUCTIBLE AMOUNT OF CASUALTY LOSS

The amount of a casualty loss deduction depends on the amount of the loss sustained, any insurance or other reimbursement the taxpayer received, and, in the case of personal-use property, the limitations imposed under the tax law.

Measuring the Loss. As explained below, one measurement of the amount of the loss sustained in a casualty is the amount by which the casualty reduces the property's FMV. This is measured by comparing the property's FMV immediately before and immediately after the casualty.[45] The amount of the loss may not include any reduction in the FMV of the taxpayer's surrounding but undamaged property.

EXAMPLE I:8-20 ►

ADDITIONAL COMMENT

Taxpayers cannot deduct a loss unless they own the damaged property. Therefore, a taxpayer cannot deduct amounts he or she paid to another individual for damage he or she caused to the other individual's property.

Gail purchased a vacation home for $310,000. Shortly after she purchased the property, a mudslide completely destroyed several neighboring cabins. Gail's cabin sustained no damage. After the slide, an appraisal reveals that the FMV of the cabin has declined to $250,000 because of fears that other mudslides might occur. The $60,000 reduction in the FMV of the cabin does not constitute a deductible casualty loss. ◄

The taxpayer must use actual market value, not sentimental value, to compute the reduction in the FMV. Additionally, the cost of protecting property to prevent damage from a casualty is not a deductible loss.

If the property involved in the casualty is only partially destroyed, the amount of the loss is the lesser of the reduction in the property's FMV or the taxpayer's adjusted basis in the property.

EXAMPLE I:8-21 ►

TYPICAL MISCONCEPTION

Taxpayers sometimes think their loss should be based on the total economic loss rather than just the property's basis. Taxpayers should remember that they have not paid a tax on the appreciation in value and, therefore, should not be entitled to a deduction for a loss on the unrealized gain.

Troy purchased a home for $225,000 several years ago. Through the years, the value of the home appreciated until it was appraised at $325,000 in the current year. Shortly after the appraisal, a flood swept through the area and severely damaged Troy's home. After the flood, the value of the home declined to $90,000. Troy does not have any flood insurance. His loss is limited to the $225,000 basis in the home even though the economic loss is $235,000 ($325,000 − $90,000). ◄

If business or investment property is totally destroyed in a casualty, the amount of the loss is the taxpayer's adjusted basis in the property, even if it is greater than the property's FMV. However, if personal-use property is totally destroyed, the amount of the loss is limited to the lesser of the reduction in the property's FMV or the property's adjusted basis.

---

[42] Rev. Rul. 79-174, 1979-1 C.B. 99 and *George K. Notter,* 1985 PH T.C. Memo ¶85,391, 50 TCM 614. A graphic illustration of the controversy that may arise when determining whether an event is a casualty can be made by comparing the following two cases. In one case the taxpayer was washing dishes. Seeing a glass of water on the windowsill, he quickly dumped the contents down the drain and turned on the garbage disposal, not realizing that his wife's rings were in the glass. Damage to the rings in this case was deemed to be a casualty (*William H. Carpenter,* 1966 PH T.C. Memo ¶66,228, 25 TCM 1186). In the second case, the taxpayer gathered up some tissues

from the night stand and flushed them down the toilet, not knowing that his wife's rings were wrapped in one of them. This event was held not to be a casualty (*W.J. Keenan, Jr. v. Bowers,* 39 AFTR 849, 50-2 USTC ¶9444 (D.C.-S.C., 1950)).
[43] Reg. Sec. 1.165-8(d).
[44] Rev. Rul. 72-112, 1972-1 C.B. 60 and IRS *Publication No. 547* (Casualties, Disasters, and Thefts), 2014.
[45] Reg. Sec. 1.165-7(a)(2).

EXAMPLE I:8-22 ▶ A machine Beth uses in her business is completely destroyed by fire. At the time of the fire, the adjusted basis of the machine is $5,000 and its FMV is $3,000. Because the machine is business property, Beth's loss is $5,000. If the machine were a personal-use asset, the amount of the loss would be $3,000, the amount of the reduction in the property's FMV rather than Beth's basis of $5,000. ◀

Generally, taxpayers must establish the reduction in the FMV of the property by an appraisal. If an appraisal is difficult or impossible to obtain, the taxpayer may use the cost of the repairs instead. The repairs must meet all of the following requirements before the taxpayer may use this alternative:

KEY POINT

The reason for this difference is that taxpayers may not deduct a loss on the sale of personal-use property. Thus, taxpayers should not be able to deduct the decline in the personal property's value that occurs before the casualty.

▶ The repairs will bring the property back to its condition immediately before the casualty.

▶ The cost of the repairs is not excessive.

▶ The repairs do no more than repair the damage incurred in the casualty.

▶ The repairs do not increase the value of the property over its value immediately before the casualty.

If the same casualty destroys more than one property, the taxpayer calculates the loss on each property separately.[46] Thus, the taxpayer compares each property's basis with the reduction in the FMV of that property, rather than aggregating the basis and FMV amounts for all the properties destroyed in the casualty.

If the taxpayer receives insurance or any other type of recovery, the taxpayer must reduce the amount of the loss by these amounts. In some cases these payments may actually exceed the taxpayer's basis in the property, causing the realization of a gain. If certain requirements are met, taxpayers may defer or exclude the recognition of these gains. (See the detailed discussion of involuntary conversions in Chapter I:12.)

LIMITATIONS ON PERSONAL-USE PROPERTY

The amount an individual may deduct for a casualty loss on personal-use property is subject to two limitations: (1) losses sustained in each separate casualty must be reduced by $100, and (2) the total amount of all net casualty losses for personal-use property is reduced by 10% of the taxpayer's AGI for the year. For property destroyed in the same casualty, only $100 is deducted from all the properties (i.e., the taxpayer does not reduce the loss from each separate property by $100).

EXAMPLE I:8-23 ▶ During the year a windstorm blows over a large tree in front of Cathy's house, damaging the house and totally destroying her automobile. After the insurance reimbursement, the loss on the house amounts to $3,000, and the loss on the automobile is $2,500. Because the losses occur in the same casualty, the total amount of the loss is reduced to $5,400 ($3,000 + $2,500 − $100). If the damage to the car was sustained in a separate event such as an automobile accident, the total amount of the casualty losses incurred by Cathy during the year would have been $5,300 [($3,000 − $100) + ($2,500 − $100)]. This $5,300 or $5,400 loss is then further reduced by 10% of Cathy's AGI for the year. ◀

EXAMPLE I:8-24 ▶ As the result of a storm, Liz incurs a $4,100 casualty loss on personal-use property during the year. She also sustains a $600 theft loss. Liz's AGI for the year is $50,000. She receives no tax deduction for the casualty and theft losses because they do not exceed the following limitations:

KEY POINT

Many taxpayers cannot deduct their casualty losses because of the $100 floor and 10% of AGI limitation.

	Storm	Theft	Total
Loss before limitations	$4,100	$600	$4,700
Minus: $100 floor	(100)	(100)	(200)
	$4,000	$500	$4,500
Minus: 10% of AGI (0.10 × $50,000)			(5,000)
Deductible loss			0

◀

---

[46] Reg. Sec. 1.165-7(b)(2). For personal-use property, losses on real property and improvements to the property are computed in the aggregate. Thus, no separate basis need be apportioned to the improvements. (See Reg. Secs. 1.165-7(b)(2)(ii) and 1.165-7(b)(3) Example (3).)

Because of these limitations, many taxpayers who sustain casualty and theft losses on personal-use property do not receive a tax deduction. Furthermore, if the taxpayer's insurance covers the property, the taxpayer cannot take a casualty loss deduction unless he or she timely files an insurance claim for the loss. This disallowance relates only to the portion of the loss covered by the insurance.

Below is a summary of the rules concerning deductibility of casualty losses:

Result of Casualty		Business	Investment	Personal Use
Total Destruction	Amount of Casualty[a]	Basis	Basis	Lesser of: basis or decline in FMV, reduced by $100 and 10% of AGI
	Type	For AGI	From AGI (For AGI if Rental)	From AGI
Partial Destruction	Amount of Casualty[a]	Lesser of: basis or decline in FMV	Lesser of: basis or decline in FMV	Lesser of: basis or decline in FMV, reduced by $100 and 10% of AGI
	Type	For AGI	From AGI (For AGI if Rental)	From AGI

[a] All amounts are first reduced by any insurance reimbursement.

NETTING CASUALTY GAINS AND LOSSES ON PERSONAL-USE PROPERTY

Taxpayers must net casualty gains and losses incurred during the year on personal-use assets. These gains and losses are not combined with casualty gains and losses on business and investment property. For purposes of the netting process, the losses should be reduced by any insurance reimbursements and the $100 limitation, but not the 10% of AGI floor. If the gains exceed the losses for the year, all the gains and losses are treated as capital gains and losses.

EXAMPLE I:8-25 ►

During the year, Pat incurs the following casualty gains and losses on personal-use assets. Assets W and X are destroyed in one casualty, and asset Y is destroyed in another. Pat acquired assets X and Y in the current year, whereas she acquired asset W several years ago.

Asset	Reduction in FMV	Adjusted Basis	Insurance	Holding Period
W	$10,000	$3,000	$10,000	More than 12 months
X	3,600	5,000	2,000	Less than one year
Y	1,600	3,000	0	Less than one year

Pat realizes a $7,000 ($10,000 − $3,000) gain on asset W because the insurance proceeds received for the asset exceed its basis. She realizes a $1,600 ($3,600 reduction in FMV − $2,000 insurance) loss on asset X. This loss is reduced to $1,500 because of the $100 reduction for personal casualty losses. She realizes a $1,600 loss on asset Y. Because this loss is realized as a result of the second casualty, the $100 limitation is deducted, resulting in a $1,500 loss from that casualty. Pat realizes a $4,000 [$7,000 − ($1,500 + $1,500)] net casualty gain for the year. Thus, the gain or loss on each asset is treated as a capital gain or loss. Pat must report a $7,000 long-term capital gain on asset W, a $1,500 short-term capital loss on asset X, and a $1,500 short-term capital loss on asset Y. ◄

If the casualty losses on personal-use property exceed the casualty gains for the year, the taxpayer must further reduce the net loss by 10% of AGI. The taxpayer performs all of these calculations (the netting process and reductions) on Form 4684. If any loss remains after the netting and reductions, the taxpayer reports the loss as an itemized deduction on Schedule A of Form 1040.

CASUALTY GAINS AND LOSSES ATTRIBUTABLE TO BUSINESS AND INVESTMENT PROPERTY

Taxpayers must net casualty gains and losses on business and investment property held over one year. (See Chapter I:13 for a discussion of the netting procedure under Sec. 1231.) If the losses exceed the gains, the business losses and losses on investment property that generate rents or royalties are *for* AGI deductions. Losses on other investment property (e.g., the theft of a security) are itemized deductions but are not subject to the 2% of AGI floor or the overall reduction of itemized deductions.[47] The $100 or 10% of AGI limitations do not apply to losses on business and investment property. Casualty gains and losses on business and investment property held one year or less are all treated as ordinary.

TIMING OF CASUALTY LOSS DEDUCTION

In general, taxpayers must deduct casualty losses in the tax year in which the taxpayer sustains the loss. In the following instances, however, taxpayers may deduct the loss in another year:

▶ Theft losses

▶ Insurance or other reimbursements that the taxpayer can reasonably expect to receive in a subsequent year

▶ Certain disaster losses

Theft. Taxpayers must deduct a theft loss in the tax year in which the taxpayer discovers the theft. This rule is equitable and practical because a taxpayer may not discover a theft until a subsequent year.

EXAMPLE I:8-26 ▶

Dale owns a hunting lodge in upstate New York. Sometime after his last trip to the lodge in November 2014, someone breaks into the lodge and steals several guns and paintings. Dale discovers the theft when he returns to the lodge on May 19, 2015. Dale's insurance does not cover the entire cost of the items. The loss is deductible in 2015, even though the theft may have occurred in 2014. ◀

REAL-WORLD EXAMPLE

A taxpayer had property confiscated by the Cuban government in 1960. The taxpayer left the country and could have filed for indemnity but did not because she expected to return. Later, the government took away the right of indemnity in 1961. Since she did not file for indemnity from the Cuban government when she had the chance, she was not allowed a casualty or theft loss. *Vila v. U.S.,* 23 AFTR 2d 69-1311 (1969).

Insurance and Other Reimbursements. Taxpayers must subtract any reimbursement received as compensation for a loss in arriving at the amount of the loss. This is necessary even when the taxpayer has not yet received the reimbursement, as long as there is a reasonable prospect that the taxpayer will receive it in the future. Thus, the taxpayer may not take a deduction in the year of loss if in that year a reasonable expectation of full recovery exists.[48] If no anticipation of full recovery exists, the taxpayer may deduct a loss in the year the casualty occurs for the estimated unrecovered amount. As previously mentioned, the taxpayer may not take a deduction to the extent the taxpayer has insured the personal-use property and the taxpayer does not file a timely insurance claim.

EXAMPLE I:8-27 ▶

In December of the current year, Andrea suffers a $10,000 casualty loss when her personal automobile is struck by a city bus. Although she does not receive any reimbursement from the insurance company by December 31, she reasonably expects to recover the full amount. Andrea may not deduct a casualty loss in the current year. ◀

EXAMPLE I:8-28 ▶

Assume the same facts as in Example I:8-27, except that Andrea reasonably anticipates her reimbursement from the insurance company will be only $7,000. In this case, her casualty loss in the current year is $3,000 (before reduction by the limitations). ◀

If the taxpayer does not receive the full amount of the anticipated recovery in the subsequent year, he or she may deduct the unrecovered portion. However, rather than filing an amended return for the year of loss, the taxpayer deducts the loss in the subsequent year. Thus in some cases, the taxpayer may spread the income tax consequences for a single casualty loss over two years.

---

[47] As explained in Chapter I:6, this overall reduction of itemized deductions applies to taxpayers with AGI in excess of certain threshold amounts. For surviving spouses or taxpayers filing as married filing jointly the threshold is $309,900 for 2015. For heads of households the 2015 threshold is $284,050, and for single taxpayers the 2015 threshold is $258,250. For married taxpayers filing separately the 2015 threshold is $154,950. See Sec. 68(a) and (b).
[48] Reg. Sec. 1.165-1(d)(2)(i).

EXAMPLE I:8-29 ► During the current year, Javier's home is damaged by an exceptionally severe blast at a nearby stone quarry owned by Acme Corporation. Although the amount of the damage is properly appraised at $20,000, Javier can reasonably anticipate a recovery of only $15,000 from Acme Corporation at the end of the current year. He does not receive any recovery from Acme during the current year. Unfortunately, in the subsequent year Acme Corporation is declared bankrupt, and Javier does not receive any reimbursement. Javier's AGI is $40,000 in the current year and $45,000 in the subsequent year. During the current year, Javier may deduct $900 {$5,000 loss reasonably anticipated in the current year − [$100 limitation + (0.10 × $40,000)]}. In the subsequent year, Javier may deduct an additional casualty loss of $10,500 [$15,000 additional loss − (0.10 × $45,000)]. ◄

If a taxpayer receives a subsequent recovery for a previously deducted loss, the taxpayer includes the reimbursement in income in the year of recovery. The taxpayer does not file an amended return. However, the amount that the taxpayer must include in income is limited to the amount of tax benefit the taxpayer received for the previous deduction.

EXAMPLE I:8-30 ► During the current year, Becky's automobile sustains $5,000 in damages when it is struck by another automobile. The driver of the other automobile is at fault and is uninsured, and Becky does not reasonably expect to recover any of the loss. Becky's AGI for the current year is $35,000. Becky deducts $1,400 ($5,000 loss − [$100 + $3,500]). During the subsequent year, the other driver reimburses Becky for the full amount of the damage. Because Becky received a tax benefit of only $1,400 for the loss in the year of the accident, she must only include $1,400 in gross income in the subsequent year, even though she receives a $5,000 reimbursement. Becky does not file an amended return for the year of the accident. ◄

Disaster Losses. Under certain circumstances, a taxpayer may elect to deduct a casualty loss in the year preceding the year in which the loss actually occurs. This election is available to taxpayers who suffer losses attributable to a disaster that occurs in an area subsequently declared by the President of the United States as a disaster area.[49] Thus, an individual can elect to deduct a disaster loss occurring in 2016 on his or her 2015 tax return or report it in the regular way on his or her 2016 return. The taxpayer must file an amended return (Form 1040X) unless he or she has not filed the prior year's return when the disaster is declared. This election allows taxpayers the possibility of receiving financial help sooner from potential tax refunds by filing an amendment to the prior year's return.

Topic Review I:8-3 summarizes the casualty loss deduction rules.

STOP & THINK

Question: Due to a series of hurricanes that hit Florida during the current year, many homes, roads, and other property are destroyed. Because of the tremendous destruction, the President of the United States declares the area a disaster area. One of the properties totally destroyed is Jack's vacation home in Miami. Jack uses the home exclusively for vacationing. The value of the home is $390,000. Unfortunately, Jack had not insured the home against a hurricane. What issues must Jack consider in determining the year in which to take the casualty loss?

Solution: Since the property was destroyed in a disaster and is located in an area which the President subsequently declared as a disaster area, Jack may take the casualty deduction either in the year of the casualty or in the previous year. The year which is most beneficial is based on several factors. The destroyed property was personal use property, so the deduction is an itemized deduction that would normally be subject to the 10% of AGI limitation. Thus, Jack should compare his estimated AGI for the current year with his AGI in the last year. He also should consider his other itemized deductions, including any other casualty losses that might be subject to the $100 or 10% of AGI limitation. In addition, he should compare his marginal tax rates in the two years. Jack should also consider the time value of money, since by taking the deduction on his prior year return, he will receive the tax benefit earlier than if he takes the deduction on the current year return.

[49] Sec. 165(i). Additionally, the same treatment may apply under Sec. 165 to taxpayers who live in a disaster area and who are ordered by a state or local government to move from or relocate their residence because the disaster caused the residence to be unsafe. In order to qualify for this treatment, the order to move must come from the state or local government within 120 days of the date that the President determines the area to be a disaster area. If the property destroyed in a presidentially declared disaster area is the taxpayer's principal residence and the casualty results in a gain, the taxpayer may exclude a portion of the gain if certain conditions are met (see Chapter I:12).

TOPIC REVIEW I:8-3

Casualty Losses

TYPE OF PROPERTY	LIMITATION AND TREATMENT
Personal use	The amount of the loss is the lesser of the property's adjusted basis or the reduction of the asset's FMV. This amount is reduced by any insurance reimbursement. If the insurance reimbursement exceeds the property's basis, a gain is realized. To the extent the property is insured, the taxpayer must file a claim or the loss is disallowed.
	The amount of loss incurred in each separate casualty event during the year is reduced by $100.
	All casualty gains and losses for the year are netted. If the gains exceed the losses, all gains and losses are treated as capital gains and losses. If the losses exceed the gains, the net loss is reduced by 10% of AGI. Any remaining loss is an itemized deduction.
Business or investment	If the property is totally destroyed, the amount of the loss is the adjusted basis of the property. If only partially destroyed, the amount of the loss is the lesser of the property's adjusted basis or the reduction of the asset's FMV. This amount is reduced by any insurance reimbursement. A gain is realized if the insurance reimbursement exceeds the property's basis.
	For property held one year or less, the losses and gains are ordinary losses and gains. For property held over one year, the casualty gains and losses for the year are netted. The treatment depends on the total of the taxpayer's other Sec. 1231 transactions (see Chapter I:13). Business casualty losses and losses on investment property that generate rents or royalties are not subject to the $100 or 10% of AGI limitations.

BAD DEBTS

OBJECTIVE 5

Compute the deduction for a bad debt

In addition to losses on property, taxpayers may also sustain losses generated by uncollectible debts. In dealing with a deduction for **bad debts**, taxpayers must address the following requirements and issues:

▶ A bona fide debtor-creditor relationship must exist between the taxpayer and some other person or entity.

▶ The taxpayer must have basis in the debt.

▶ The debt must actually have become worthless during the year.

▶ The type and timing of a bad debt deduction depend on whether the debt is a business or nonbusiness bad debt.

Generally, taxpayers may use only the specific write-off method of accounting when deducting the bad debt. A partial or complete recovery of a debt that was previously deducted may occur. In many cases a recovery of this type causes income recognition in the year of the recovery.

ADDITIONAL COMMENT

The tax provisions that deal with deductions for losses and the tax provisions that deal with the deductions for bad debts are mutually exclusive, and an amount properly deductible as a loss cannot be deducted as a bad debt or vice versa.

BONA FIDE DEBTOR-CREDITOR RELATIONSHIP

Only items constituting bona fide debt are eligible to be deducted as a bad debt. A **bona fide debt** is one that arises from a valid and enforceable obligation to pay a fixed or determinable sum of money and results in a debtor-creditor relationship.[50]

Related-Party Transactions. Determining whether a bona fide loan transaction has actually taken place is especially critical when the transaction is between the taxpayer and a family member or other related party (e.g., a controlled corporation). The tax advisor must carefully examine all the facts and circumstances surrounding the transaction because a gift does not constitute a debt. The taxpayer's intent is critical. For example, if the taxpayer's intent is to provide property, cash, or services to someone else without receiving

KEY POINT

The fact that the debtor is a related party does not preclude deduction of a bad debt, but the taxpayer must be able to document the debt as being bona fide.

[50] Reg. Sec. 1.166-1(c).

any consideration in return, a gift—not a loan—has been made. Some tests used to determine the taxpayer's intent include the following:

► Does a note or other written instrument exist which evidences an obligation to repay?[51]
► Have the parties established a definite schedule of repayment?
► Have the parties documented a stated reasonable rate of interest?
► Would a person unrelated to the debtor make the loan?[52]

EXAMPLE I:8-31 ►

REAL-WORLD EXAMPLE

A taxpayer advanced $8,500 to his son-in-law who operated a live-stock auction barn. The taxpayer was entitled to a bad debt deduction upon default because notations on the checks indicated that they were loans and undisputed testimony indicated that repayment was to be made within 90 days. *Giffin A. Andrew*, 54 T.C. 239 (1970).

During the current year Maria loaned $20,000 to her son Sam, who used the money in his business. Although they signed no written note or contract, Sam orally promised to repay Maria as soon as his business became profitable. No rate of interest was stated. Unfortunately, the business failed and Sam went out of business in the subsequent year. He never repaid the loan principal or interest.

In this case, no valid debt exists because the taxpayer did not establish an interest rate or a repayment schedule. An unrelated person would not have made a loan to Sam under these conditions. In addition, Maria does not receive any consideration in return for the "loan." Since the facts indicate that the transaction is actually a gift, Maria may not claim a bad debt deduction because of Sam's failure to repay. ◄

Tax advisors should also closely examine other related party transactions. For example, a loan from a shareholder to a controlled corporation may actually be an additional contribution to capital disguised as a loan. Thus, a transfer of cash by a shareholder who owns a controlling (i.e., more than 50%) interest in the stock of a corporation may indicate a capital contribution rather than a loan. Likewise, a "loan" from a corporation to a controlling shareholder may actually be a disguised dividend or a salary payment.

Third Party Debt. In some cases a taxpayer will guarantee or endorse someone else's obligation. If under the terms of the guarantee, the guarantor is required to pay the debtor's remaining outstanding principal as well as any accrued interest on the debt, the relationship between the debtor and the guarantor as well as the terms of the guarantee must be carefully analyzed. The guarantor's intent determines whether the guarantee and subsequent payment of the outstanding principal and accrued interest constitutes a gift to the debtor. If the guarantor's intent was a gift, the guarantor may not deduct the payment of the outstanding principal and accrued interest. On the other hand, if it can be proved that the guarantee was not a gift, the guarantor may deduct the principal and accrued interest as a bad debt issued to the debtor at the time of the payment.

EXAMPLE I:8-32 ►

Ron is the sole shareholder and a full-time employee of Zip Corporation. For Zip Corporation to obtain a bank loan, Ron personally signs a guarantee that the loan will be repaid. Unfortunately, Zip Corporation defaults on the loan and Ron must repay the loan. Assume proof exists that Ron signed the guarantee to preserve his job and enhance his investment in Zip Corporation. Although Ron receives no direct consideration for having signed the note, he does receive indirect consideration in the form of continued job security and protection of his investment. Because a business or investment purpose motivated Ron to sign the loan guarantee, Ron may deduct the bad debt. On the other hand, without proof, this guarantee and subsequent payment of Zip Corporation's debt by Ron may be seen as merely an additional capital contribution by Ron to Zip Corporation. ◄

TAXPAYER'S BASIS IN THE DEBT

For a bad debt to be deductible, the creditor must have basis in the debt. The taxpayer may acquire this basis in different ways. If a taxpayer loans money, the taxpayer's basis in the debt is the amount loaned. If the debt arises because the taxpayer provides property or

---

[51] A written note or other instrument is an evidence of a bona fide debtor-creditor relationship. However, if the note or other instrument is registered or has interest coupons and is issued by a corporation or a government, the bad debt provisions of Sec. 166 do not apply. Instead, the worthless security provisions of Sec. 165 (previously discussed) apply.

[52] *Jean C. Tyler v. Tomlinson*, 24 AFTR 2d 69-5426, 69-2 USTC ¶9559 (5th Cir., 1969). (See also, *C. L. Hunt*, 1989 PH T.C. Memo ¶89,335, 57 TCM 919), where certain loans that the taxpayer made to his children were treated as bona fide loans, whereas others were treated as gifts. In that case, the

children had been trading in silver futures and were required to make margin calls. Because they could not make the calls, the children's positions were involuntarily liquidated. Up to the date of the liquidation, the taxpayer had made loans to the children that were payable on demand and were subject to the prime rate of interest. These loans were evidenced by promissory notes. After the liquidation, the taxpayer continued to make loans to the children. However, these loans were not evidenced by notes. The loans up to the time of the liquidation were treated as bona fide loans and the subsequent loans were treated as gifts.

services for the other party, basis is established only if the taxpayer has previously included the FMV of the property or services in income. This often depends on the taxpayer's method of accounting. An accrual method taxpayer generally reports income in the year the services are performed or the property is provided. (See the discussion in Chapter I:11.) Thus, an accrual method taxpayer has a basis in either a note receivable or an open account receivable equal to the amount included in gross income (i.e., the FMV of the services). A cash method taxpayer, however, reports income only in the year in which the taxpayer receives payment in the form of cash or property. Because a note constitutes the receipt of property, a cash method taxpayer reports income (and establishes basis) in the year the note is received. However, if the cash method taxpayer does not receive a note and the receivable is an open account item, the taxpayer reports no income until the receivable is collected. Thus, the taxpayer has no basis in the receivable and does not receive a bad debt deduction if the receivable is not collected.

EXAMPLE I:8-33 ▶ In October of the current year, Jim performs some legal services for Joy. Jim bills Joy for $10,000. Joy does not sign a note for the debt. As a cash method taxpayer, Jim does not include the $10,000 in his current year's income. After repeated efforts to collect the fee, Jim discovers in June of the subsequent year that Joy has left the city and cannot be found. Jim may not deduct a bad debt for the uncollected amount in the subsequent year because he has not taken the amount into income and he has no basis in the debt. If Joy had signed a note for the debt, Jim would have reported income in the current year in an amount equal to the note's FMV. Thus, Jim can deduct the loss when the note becomes uncollectible in the subsequent year. ◀

DEBT MUST BE WORTHLESS

To deduct a bad debt, the taxpayer must show that the debt is worthless. This determination is made by reference to all the pertinent evidence, including the general financial condition of the debtor and whether the debt is secured by collateral.

In proving the worthlessness of a debt, a taxpayer does not need to take legal action if the surrounding circumstances indicate that legal action probably would not result in the collection of the debt. By simply showing that legal action is not warranted, the taxpayer provides sufficient proof that the debt is worthless.[53] Indications that an unsecured debt is worthless include bankruptcy of the debtor, disappearance or death of a debtor, and repeated unsuccessful attempts at collection. Furthermore, if the surrounding circumstances warrant it, a taxpayer may deduct a worthless debt even before the debt comes due. As will be explained later in this chapter, a nonbusiness debt must be totally worthless before a deduction is allowed. However, a current deduction is allowed for a partially worthless business bad debt.

NONBUSINESS BAD DEBTS

The distinction between a business bad debt and a nonbusiness bad debt is important because the classification of the debt determines its tax treatment. A business bad debt gives rise to an ordinary deduction, whereas a taxpayer must treat a nonbusiness bad debt as a short-term capital loss. All loans made by a corporation are assumed to be associated with the corporation's business; therefore, the provisions for nonbusiness bad debts do not apply to corporations.

Definition of a Nonbusiness Bad Debt. A *nonbusiness debt* is defined as any debt other than (1) a debt created or acquired in connection with a trade or business of the taxpayer or (2) a debt the loss from the worthlessness of which is incurred in the taxpayer's trade or business. This determination depends on an examination of the facts and circumstances surrounding the debt in question.

A debt incurred in a taxpayer's business continues to be a business debt for that taxpayer even if, at the time the debt goes bad, the taxpayer has ceased conducting that particular business (situation (1) above). If another taxpayer acquires a business, any outstanding debt at the time the business is acquired continues to be business debt as long as the purchaser

---

[53] Reg. Sec. 1.166-2.

continues the business (situation (2) above). The debt is a nonbusiness debt if the person who owns the debt when it becomes worthless is not engaged in the business in which the debt is incurred either at the time the debt arose or when it becomes worthless.

EXAMPLE I:8-34 ▶ Matt, an individual who uses the accrual method of accounting, is engaged in the grocery business. During 2015, he extends credit to Jeff on an open account. In 2016, Matt sells his business to Joan, but retains Jeff's account. Jeff's account becomes worthless in 2016. Even though Matt is no longer engaged in the grocery business at the time the debt becomes worthless, he may deduct the loss as a business bad debt in 2016. If Joan purchases Jeff's account upon acquiring the grocery business, Joan is entitled to a business bad debt deduction in 2016 because the debt was incurred in the trade or business in which Joan is currently engaged. ◄

In addition, classification as a business debt requires a proximate relationship between the loan and the taxpayer's business.[54] According to the Supreme Court, this relationship exists if a business motive is the taxpayer's dominant motivation in making the loan. This determination must be made on a case-by-case basis. For example, when an individual stockholder who is also an employee of the corporation loans money to the corporation, is the loan a business or nonbusiness debt? Because an employee is considered to be engaged in the business of working for a corporation, a loan made to the corporation in an attempt to protect the employment relationship may be held to be a business debt. However, if the individual's dominant motive is to protect his or her stock investment, the loan is a nonbusiness debt.[55]

EXAMPLE I:8-35 ▶ Lisa is an individual engaged in the advertising business. If clients occasionally need additional funds to meet their cash-flow obligations, Lisa sometimes lends them money. Lisa's dominant motive for making the loans is to retain the clients. She has no ownership interests in these clients. Under these facts, if any of these loans becomes worthless, it would likely be considered a business bad debt.[56] ◄

Tax Treatment. Individuals deduct nonbusiness debts that become wholly worthless during the year as short-term capital losses. The length of time the debt is outstanding has no bearing on this treatment.

Individuals generally prefer an ordinary deduction rather than a short-term capital loss because capital losses are first used to offset capital gains. If the capital losses exceed the capital gains, the individual taxpayer is limited to an additional $3,000 tax deduction each year. Any loss in excess of this limit is carried over to subsequent years to be included in the capital gain and loss netting process in those years (see Chapter I:5).

EXAMPLE I:8-36 ▶ During 2015, Kim loaned her friend $10,000. The friend used the funds to invest in commodity futures. The transaction had all the characteristics of a bona fide debt rather than a mere gift to a friend. Unfortunately, the commodities market prices declined, and Kim's friend incurred substantial losses. In 2016, Kim's friend declared personal bankruptcy and Kim was unable to collect any of the loan. Kim did not recognize any other capital gains or losses during 2016. The $10,000 bad debt loss recognized in 2016 is treated as a short-term capital loss. Thus, Kim may deduct only $3,000 in 2016. The remaining $7,000 is carried forward indefinitely to 2017 and subsequent years. ◄

TYPICAL MISCONCEPTION

Partial worthlessness means that a debt is still partially recoverable. The term is sometimes erroneously applied to debt where there has been a partial recovery even though there is no prospect for further recovery.

Partial Worthlessness. As previously noted, taxpayers may not deduct a partially worthless nonbusiness debt. Thus, a taxpayer cannot deduct a loss for a nonbusiness debt that is still partially recoverable during the year.

EXAMPLE I:8-37 ▶ Gordon, an individual, made a $5,000, five-year interest-bearing loan to a small company in 2013. Gordon was not in the trade or business of making commercial loans. In 2015, Gordon received word from the attorney who was appointed trustee of the company that bankruptcy proceedings had been filed. The trustee indicated that, although final disposition of the case will not occur until 2016, Gordon can reasonably expect to receive only 20 cents for every $1

[54] Reg. Sec. 1.166-5(b)(2).

[55] *John M. Trent v. CIR*, 7 AFTR 2d 1599, 61-2 USTC ¶9506 (2nd Cir., 1961). See also *Charles L. Hutchinson*, 1982 PH T.C. Memo ¶82,045, 43

TCM 440 and *U.S. v. Edna Generes*, 29 AFTR 2d 72-609, 72-1 USTC ¶9259 (USSC, 1972).

[56] *Stuart Bart*, 21 T.C. 880 (1954), *acq.* 1954-1 C.B. 3.

invested. Because this is a nonbusiness bad debt that is still partly recoverable in 2015, Gordon may not deduct the partial loss as a short-term capital loss in 2015 and must wait until 2016 when the case is finally settled to deduct the nonbusiness bad debt. ◄

BUSINESS BAD DEBTS

The tax treatment of losses from business bad debts differs substantially from the treatment of nonbusiness bad debts. As previously discussed, a business bad debt provides an ordinary loss deduction. Furthermore, taxpayers may also deduct a business debt that has become only partially worthless during the year.

EXAMPLE I:8-38 ► Assume the same facts as in Example I:8-37 except that Gordon's loan is made for business reasons (e.g., to provide assistance to a customer in financial difficulty). Because 80% of the loan is reasonably expected to be unrecoverable during 2015, Gordon may deduct $4,000 (0.80 × $5,000) as an ordinary loss in 2015. If Gordon receives only $600 in 2016 as a settlement, he may deduct an additional $400 of ordinary loss for the year. ◄

BOOK-TAX DIFFERENCES

In general, for tax purposes, taxpayers can use only the specific write-off method of accounting for bad debts. However, a corporation or other taxpayer would probably be required to use the reserve method for financial reporting purposes. This book-tax difference is one of the most common M-1 or M-3 adjustments in filing a Form 1120 for corporate taxpayers.

Accounting for the Business Bad Debt. In general, two basic methods are available to account for business bad debts: the specific write-off method and the reserve method. Except for certain specialized industries, however, taxpayers can use only the specific write-off method for tax purposes. Under the **specific write-off method,** the taxpayer deducts each bad debt individually as it becomes worthless and the taxpayer writes it off as an expense. Taxpayers use this method for (1) business bad debts that are either totally or partially worthless and (2) nonbusiness bad debts that are totally worthless. However, as previously noted, taxpayers take no deduction for partially worthless nonbusiness bad debts.

In the case of a partially worthless business bad debt, taxpayers may only deduct the worthless part of the debt. The taxpayer must prove to the satisfaction of the IRS the amount of the debt that has become worthless.

Recovery of Bad Debts. A taxpayer may collect a debt that was previously written off for tax purposes. Since the taxpayer previously deducted the uncollectible debt, the taxpayer must report the recovery as income in the year it is collected. The amount of the income that must be reported depends on the tax benefit rule discussed in Chapter I:4.

DEPOSITS IN INSOLVENT FINANCIAL INSTITUTIONS

At their election, qualified individuals may treat a loss on deposits in qualified bankrupt or insolvent financial institutions as a personal casualty loss in the year in which the individual can reasonably estimate the loss. The recognized loss is the difference between the taxpayer's basis in the deposit and a reasonable estimate of the amount that the taxpayer will receive. This treatment allows the individual an ordinary loss deduction, but subjects the loss to the personal casualty loss limitations. In lieu of this election, qualified individuals may elect to treat these losses as if they were incurred in a transaction entered into for profit (but not connected with a trade or business). This election is available only with respect to deposits that are not insured under federal law, and is limited to $20,000 ($10,000 if married and filing separately) per institution per year. This limitation is reduced by any insurance proceeds expected to be received under state law. This election also allows the individual an ordinary loss deduction but subjects the loss to the $20,000 limitation as well as the 2% of AGI floor on miscellaneous itemized deductions. If the taxpayer makes neither of these elections, the taxpayer may claim the loss as a nonbusiness bad debt (a short-term capital loss) in the year of worthlessness or partial recovery, whichever comes last.

KEY POINT

If a taxpayer incurs a casualty loss on personal use property, the amount of the deductible loss is first reduced by $100 per casualty, and then the total net casualty losses for the year are further reduced by 10% of the taxpayer's AGI for the year.

A qualified individual is any individual *except* one who:

► Owns at least 1% of the outstanding stock of the financial institution

► Is an officer of the financial institution

► Is a relative of an officer or a 1% owner of the financial institution[57]

---

[57] Sec. 165(l). A *relative* is defined as a sibling, spouse, aunt, uncle, nephew, niece, ancestor, or lineal descendant.

Qualified financial institutions include banks, federal or state chartered savings and loans and thrift institutions, and federal or state insured credit unions.

This election applies to all losses sustained by the individual in the same institution and cannot be revoked unless the taxpayer receives IRS permission.[58]

The treatment of business and nonbusiness bad debts for non-corporate taxpayers is summarized in Topic Review I:8-4.

TOPIC REVIEW I:8-4

Bad Debts

TYPE OF DEBT	RESULTS
Nonbusiness	Deductible as a short-term capital loss.
	Deductible only when the debt is totally worthless.
	The taxpayer must have basis in the debt.
Business	Deductible as an ordinary loss.
	Except for certain specialized exceptions, the specific write-off method must be used. The reserve method is not available.
	May deduct partial worthlessness.
	Must have basis in the debt.

NET OPERATING LOSSES

OBJECTIVE 6

Compute a net operating loss deduction

A **net operating loss (NOL)** under Sec. 172 generally involves only business income and expenses. An NOL occurs when taxable income for any year is negative because business expenses exceed business income. A deduction for the NOL arises when a taxpayer carries the NOL to a year in which the taxpayer has taxable income. Thus, an NOL for one year becomes a deduction against taxable income of another year. This is accomplished in one of two ways:

► The year's NOL is carried back and deducted from the income of a previous year. This procedure provides for a refund of some of the taxes previously paid for the prior year.

► The year's NOL is carried forward and deducted from the income of a subsequent year. This procedure provides a reduction in the taxable income of the subsequent year, thus reducing the tax liability associated with that year.

KEY POINT

If taxpayers were not entitled to a deduction for net operating losses, taxpayers would actually pay a tax on an amount that exceeded their economic income over a period of time. The NOL deduction permits taxpayers to offset taxable income with losses incurred in other years.

The NOL deduction is intended to mitigate the inequity caused by the interaction of the progressive rate structure and the requirement to report income on an annual basis. This inequity arises between taxpayers whose business income fluctuates widely from year to year and those whose business income remains relatively constant.

EXAMPLE I:8-39 ►

John and Julie Jones and Ken and Karen Smith are both married couples and file joint returns. Over a two-year period they both report a total of $140,000 in taxable income. However, John and Julie report $70,000 of taxable income each year; Ken and Karen report $200,000 of taxable income in the first year and a $60,000 loss in the second year. Without the NOL provisions and using the 2015 tax rates for both years, John and Julie will report a $19,156 ($9,578 + $9,578) total tax liability for the two years, whereas Ken and Karen will report a total tax liability of $43,052 on their taxable income of $200,000 in the first year.[59] Under the NOL rules, Ken and Karen can carry back the $60,000 loss in the second year to offset their taxable income in the first year. This allows them to recover a portion of the taxes paid in the first year. Based on 2015 tax rates, they would recover $16,464 of the $43,052 paid, resulting in a net tax liability for both years of $26,588 ($43,052 − $16,464). Although the total tax liability over the two years for the two couples is still unequal ($19,156 for the Joneses, and $26,588 for the Smiths), the ability to carry over NOLs substantially reduces the difference and helps provide some degree of fairness. ◄

---

[58] The rules dealing with this special election are found in Notice 89-28, (1989-1 C.B. 667).

[59] Using the 2015 tax rate schedules for both years.

COMPUTING THE NET OPERATING LOSS FOR INDIVIDUALS

ADDITIONAL COMMENT

In computing the NOL for corporations, only minor adjustments are necessary.

The starting point in calculating an individual's NOL is generally taxable income. As mentioned earlier in this chapter, individuals may deduct three basic types of expenses to arrive at the amount of taxable income: business-related expenses, investment-related expenses, and certain personal expenses. The NOL, however, generally attempts to measure only the economic loss that occurs when business expenses exceed business income. Thus, individual taxpayers must make several adjustments to taxable income to arrive at the amount of the NOL for any particular year. These include adjustments for an NOL deduction, a capital loss deduction, the deduction for personal exemptions, and the excess of nonbusiness deductions over nonbusiness income.

ADDITIONAL COMMENT

If taxpayers were permitted to calculate the NOL for the current year by including NOL carryovers from earlier years, they could possibly extend the carryover period beyond the statutorily established 20-year carryforward period.

Add Back any Nol Deduction. Under certain circumstances, a taxpayer might have taken a deduction for an NOL arising from another tax year in computing the taxable loss for the current loss year. Allowing this deduction to create or increase the NOL of the current loss year would provide an unwarranted benefit. Thus, taxable income for the current loss year must be increased for this deduction.

Add Back any Capital Loss Deduction. To compute taxable income, individuals may deduct up to a maximum of $3,000 capital losses in excess of capital gains in any year. Any capital loss in excess of this limit can be carried over and deducted in a subsequent tax year, subject to the same limitation. Because capital losses have their separate carryover provisions, taxpayers must add back any deduction associated with these losses to taxable income to arrive at the NOL for the current loss year. To make this adjustment, the taxpayer must follow several steps:

Step 1. A taxpayer must separate nonbusiness capital gains and losses from business capital gains and losses. The nonbusiness gains and losses are then netted, while the business gains and losses are netted separately.

Step 2. If the nonbusiness capital gains exceed the nonbusiness capital losses, the excess, along with other types of nonbusiness income, is first used to offset any nonbusiness ordinary deductions. Any nonbusiness capital gain remaining is then used to offset any business capital loss in excess of the business capital gain for the year.[60]

Step 3. If both groups of transactions result in net losses, the capital loss deduction provided by these transactions must be added back. For purposes of the NOL, no deduction is allowed for either business or nonbusiness net capital losses.

Step 4. If the taxpayer's nonbusiness capital losses exceed the nonbusiness capital gains, the losses may not be offset against the taxpayer's excess business capital gains. Allowing this offset would provide an indirect deduction for a nonbusiness economic loss.[61]

EXAMPLE I:8-40 ►

During the current year, Nils recognizes a short-term capital loss of $10,000 on the sale of an investment capital asset. He also recognizes a $5,000 long-term capital gain on the sale of a business capital asset. For taxable income purposes, the loss is netted against the gain, leaving a $5,000 net short-term capital loss. This loss provides a $3,000 deduction from taxable income, with the remaining $2,000 being carried forward to the following year. To compute the NOL, however, none of the $10,000 nonbusiness capital loss is deductible. Thus, the $3,000 deduction as well as the $5,000 loss that offset the business capital gain must be added back because in computing taxable income the taxpayer, in essence, has received a total $8,000 reduction from the nonbusiness capital loss. ◄

Add Back the Deduction for Personal Exemptions. Because the deduction for personal and dependency exemptions is strictly a personal deduction, it must be added back to arrive at the year's NOL.

---

[60] Reg. Sec. 1.172-3. If the nonbusiness deductions exceed the nonbusiness income, the excess is added back. This adjustment is discussed later in the chapter.
[61] Sec. 172(d)(2). Note that all deductible nonbusiness capital losses involve investment property because capital losses on personal-use assets are not deductible in arriving at taxable income. To make the adjustment for any capital loss, the exclusion under Sec. 1202 for gains from small business stock is not allowed (see Chapter I:5).

ADDITIONAL COMMENT

An excess of nonbusiness deductions over nonbusiness income cannot increase the NOL. However, an excess of nonbusiness income over nonbusiness expenses can reduce the NOL.

Add Back Excess of Nonbusiness Deductions over Nonbusiness Income. Because nonbusiness deductions do not reflect an economic loss from business, they are not deductible in arriving at the NOL. However, these deductions do offset any nonbusiness income reported during the year. Nonbusiness income includes sources of income such as dividends and interest, as well as nonbusiness capital gains in excess of nonbusiness capital losses. Wages and salary, even if they are earned in part-time employment, are considered business income. Nonbusiness deductions include itemized deductions such as charitable contributions, medical expenses, and nonbusiness interest and taxes. Casualty losses on personal-use assets, however, are treated as business losses and are excluded from this adjustment.[62] If a taxpayer does not have itemized deductions in excess of the standard deduction, the standard deduction is used as the amount of the nonbusiness deductions.

Following are several independent examples demonstrating these required adjustments. In each case, assume that Nancy is a single taxpayer.

EXAMPLE I:8-41 ▶ During 2015, Nancy, who is single, reports the following taxable income:

Gross income from business		$123,000	
Minus:	Business expenses	(147,000)	($24,000)
Plus:	Interest income		700
	Dividend income		400
AGI			($22,900)
Minus:	Greater of itemized deductions or standard deduction:		
	Interest expense	$ 6,000	
	Taxes	4,000	
	Casualty loss (reduced by the $100 floor)	1,000	
	Total itemized deductions	$ 11,000	
	or		
	Standard deduction	6,300	(11,000)
Minus:	Personal exemption		(4,000)
Taxable income			($37,900)

Nancy's NOL for the year is computed as follows:

Taxable income				($37,900)
Nonbusiness deductions:				
Itemized deductions		$11,000		
Minus:	Casualty loss	(1,000)	$ 10,000	
Minus:	Nonbusiness income:			
	Interest	$700		
	Dividends	400	(1,100)	
Plus:	Excess of nonbusiness deductions over nonbusiness income			8,900
Plus:	Personal exemption			4,000
Net operating loss				($25,000)[a] ◀

[a]Note that the NOL equals the total of the $24,000 net business loss and the $1,000 casualty loss.

EXAMPLE I:8-42 ▶ During 2015, Betsy, who is single, reports the following taxable income:

Gross income from business		$123,000	
Minus:	Business expenses	(147,000)	($24,000)
Plus:	Interest income		700
	Dividend income		400
AGI			($22,900)
Minus	Greater of itemized deductions or standard deduction:		
Interest expense		$ 2,000	
	or		
Standard deduction		6,300	(6,300)
Minus:	Personal exemption		(4,000)
Taxable income			($33,200)

Betsy's NOL for the year is computed as follows:

Taxable income			($33,200)
Nonbusiness deductions:			
Standard deduction		$ 6,300	
Minus: Nonbusiness income:			
Interest	$700		
Dividends	400	(1,100)	
Plus Excess of nonbusiness deductions over nonbusiness income			5,200
Plus: Personal exemption			4,000
Net operating loss			($24,000)[a] ◄

[a]Note that the NOL equals the net business loss for the year.

EXAMPLE I:8-43 ► During 2015, Rachael, who is single, reports the following taxable income:

Gross income from business		$123,000	
Minus Business expenses		(147,000)	($24,000)
Plus: Interest income			700
Dividend income			400
Salary			6,000
Nonbusiness LTCG			10,000
AGI			($6,900)
Minus: Greater of itemized deductions or standard deduction:			
Interest expense		$ 6,000	
Taxes		4,000	
Casualty (reduced by the $100 floor)		1,000	
Total itemized deductions		$ 11,000	
		or	
Standard deduction		6,300	(11,000)
Minus: Personal exemption			(4,000)
Taxable income			($21,900)

Rachael's NOL for the year is computed as follows:

Taxable income			($21,900)
Plus: Nonbusiness deductions:			
Itemized deductions	$11,000		
Minus: Casualty loss	(1,000)	$ 10,000	
Minus: Nonbusiness income:			
Interest	$700		
Dividends	400		
LTCG	10,000	(11,100)	
Excess of nonbusiness deductions over nonbusiness income			0
Plus: Personal exemption			4,000
Net operating loss			($17,900)[a] ◄

[a]Note that the NOL can also be calculated as follows:

Loss from business	($24,000)
Salary	6,000
Casualty loss	(1,000)
Excess of nonbusiness income ($11,100) over nonbusiness deductions ($10,000)	1,100
NOL	($17,900)

CARRYBACK AND CARRYOVER PERIODS

Under Sec. 172, an NOL is initially carried back for two years and is deductible as an offset to the taxable income of the carryback years. Except as noted below, taxpayers must carry the loss back first. If any loss remains, taxpayers may then carry it forward for a period of 20 years.[63] Furthermore, in both the carryback and carryforward periods, the loss must be deducted from the years in chronological order. Thus, if an NOL is sustained

---

[63] For NOLs arising in a farming business, in a qualified small business attributable to a Presidentially declared disaster, or in a casualty or theft sustained by an individual, the carryback period is extended to three years. These NOLs are taken after the regular NOL. Certain "specified liability losses" are entitled to a 10-year carryback. Sec. 172(b)(1)(C) and (f). Likewise, for certain losses occurring in tax years that either begin or end in 2009 or 2010, taxpayers could make a special election to carry the NOLs back for five years.

in 2015, it first must be carried back to 2013, then to 2014, followed by 2016, 2017, and so on until the loss is completely used. Any NOL that is not used during the carryover period expires and is of no further tax benefit.

If the NOL is carried back to a prior year, the taxpayer must file for a refund of taxes previously paid. If the NOL deduction is carried forward, it reduces the taxable income and the tax liability for the carryover year.

Election to Forgo Carryback Period. A taxpayer may elect not to carry back the NOL, but to carry the loss forward. This election, which is made with respect to the entire carryback period, does not extend the carryforward period beyond 20 years. This allows a taxpayer some degree of flexibility in using the NOL deduction to the greatest advantage. (See the Tax Planning Considerations section in this chapter for a discussion of this topic.)

Loss Carryovers from Two or more Years. At times, a taxpayer might have NOL carryovers that are incurred in two or more taxable years. Often these losses are carried to the same years in the carryover period. If such is the case, the loss of the earliest year is always completely used first before deducting any of the loss incurred in a subsequent year. Because of the limited carryover period, this rule is beneficial to the taxpayer.

ADDITIONAL COMMENT

An election to forgo the carry-back period for the NOL of any year is irrevocable.

RECOMPUTATION OF TAXABLE INCOME IN THE CARRYOVER YEAR

When the taxpayer carries back the NOL deduction to a prior year, the taxpayer must recompute that year's taxable income. Because the NOL is attributable to a taxpayer's trade or business, it is deductible *for* AGI. As a result, the recomputation of taxable income for the carryback year may affect the deductible amount of certain itemized deductions because some of the deductions (e.g., the deductions for medical expenses, charitable contributions, and casualty losses) are limited or measured by reference to the taxpayer's AGI. All of these deductions except the deduction for charitable contributions must be recomputed using the reduced AGI amount.[64]

Once the taxpayer determines the tax refund for the carryback year, the taxpayer must calculate the amount of the NOL available to be deducted in subsequent carryover years. This is done by adjusting the recomputed income of the prior carryover year. Although certain differences exist, these adjustments are similar to those mentioned above.

The rules for computing and deducting NOLs are presented in Topic Review I:8-5.

TOPIC REVIEW I:8-5

Net Operating Losses

ITEM	RULES
Computation of NOL (adjustments to taxable income)	Add back any NOL deduction carried to the current year.
	Add back any capital loss deduction.
	Add back the deduction for personal and dependency exemptions.
	Add back the excess of nonbusiness deductions over nonbusiness income. For this purpose, casualty losses on personal-use property are treated as business losses.
Carryover period	May be carried back two years and forward twenty years (certain exceptions apply). Must be carried to the carryover years in chronological order: first carried back to the second prior year, then to the first prior year, then to the first succeeding year, etc. An election may be made to forgo the carryback. This does not extend the carryforward period. If losses from two or more years are carried to the same year, the losses from the earliest year are completely used first.

---

[64] Reg. Sec. 1.172-5(a)(2)(ii).

TAX PLANNING CONSIDERATIONS

BAD DEBTS

To deduct a bad debt, a taxpayer must show that the debt is worthless. At times the IRS might assert that the debt being written off is either not yet worthless or that it became worthless in a previous year. If the taxpayer is unable to overcome the IRS's assertion concerning the year of worthlessness, the taxpayer might be barred from filing an amended return for the prior year because of the statute of limitations.[65] Thus, taxpayers should carefully document all efforts at collection and other facts that show the debt is worthless.

As previously mentioned, a third-party guarantor of a loan who is required to repay the debt may, under certain circumstances, be entitled to a bad debt deduction. The guarantor must demonstrate that he or she received reasonable consideration in the form of cash or property in exchange for guaranteeing the debt. If the taxpayer does not receive proper consideration, the guarantee and subsequent payment of the loan by the guarantor is considered to be a gift rather than a loan. Reasonable consideration is also deemed to be received if the taxpayer enters into the agreement for a good faith business purpose or in accordance with normal business practice. However, if the taxpayer guarantees the debt of a spouse or a relative, the taxpayer must receive the consideration in the form of cash or property.

In the case of an outright loan between related taxpayers, the lender should always make sure to retain proper documentation to substantiate the fact that the transaction is a loan. If the taxpayer does not keep such documentation, the IRS may assert that the transaction is a gift.

KEY POINT

If uncertainty exists as to the year in which a debt became worthless, the issue may not be settled within the normal three-year statute of limitations. For this reason, a taxpayer may claim a deduction for a worthless debt at any time within seven years.

CASUALTIES

A deduction is allowed for stolen property, but no deduction is allowed for lost property. Thus, taxpayers should always carefully document losses of property through theft (e.g., the filing of police reports or claims with the taxpayer's insurance company). In addition, pictures and written appraisals may be helpful to prove the amount of the loss.

NET OPERATING LOSSES

If a taxpayer incurs a net operating loss, the taxpayer should carefully analyze whether to elect to forgo the carryback period. Situations under which a taxpayer might elect to only carry the loss deduction forward include the following:

ADDITIONAL COMMENT

Normally, a taxpayer would want to carry back the NOL because of the possibility of receiving a refund in a short time period by filing the amended return. The carryover of the NOL involves waiting for a year or more to receive a tax benefit.

► A taxpayer might anticipate being in a higher marginal tax rate in future years than in the carryback years. If such is the case, the value of the deduction is higher in the carryforward years than in the carryback years. Taxpayers should consider, however, cash flows and the time value of money (e.g., the tax benefits from a refund of taxes are realized sooner if the NOL is carried back).

► General business and other tax credits that are nonrefundable (i.e., the credits are limited to the tax liability or some percentage thereof) may be reduced or eliminated for the carryback years because these credits must be recomputed based on the adjusted tax liability after applying the NOL carryback. (See Chapter I:14 for a discussion of tax credits.)

COMPLIANCE AND PROCEDURAL CONSIDERATIONS

CASUALTY LOSSES

If a taxpayer sustains a casualty loss in a location that the President of the United States declares a disaster area, he or she may make an election to deduct the loss in the year preceding the year in which the loss occurred. A taxpayer makes this election by either filing

---

[65] However, the statute of limitations for claims for a refund or credit because of a bad debt is extended from three years to seven years under Sec. 6511(d)(1), thus giving the taxpayer additional time if this is the case.

ADDITIONAL COMMENT
Instant access for downloading federal income tax forms, instructions, publications, etc. is available on the Internet (http://www.irs.gov).

the return for the previous year and including the loss in that year (if the return has not already been filed) or filing an amended return or claim for refund for that year.[66] The return should clearly include all the following information:

► That the election is being made

► The date of the disaster giving rise to the loss

► The city, county, and state in which the damaged property is located

The taxpayer must make the election before the due date of the return for the year in which the disaster actually occurs. Although the Regulations state that the election may not be revoked more than 90 days after it is made, the Tax Court has held that this part of the Regulation is invalid.[67]

NET OPERATING LOSSES

When an individual taxpayer carries an NOL deduction back to a prior year, the taxpayer claims a refund of taxes by either filing an amended return on Form 1040X or filing for a quick refund on Form 1045. Corporations use Form 1139. If the taxpayer uses Form 1045, the IRS must act on the application for refund within 90 days of the later of the date of the application or the last day of the month in which the return of the loss year must be filed.[68] A taxpayer must file Form 1045 within one year after the end of the year in which the NOL arose. The taxpayer must attach additional information such as pages 1 and 2 of Form 1040 for the year of loss, a copy of the application for an extension of time to file the return for the year of loss, and copies of forms or schedules for items refigured in the carryback years.

WORTHLESS SECURITIES

As explained earlier in this chapter, securities that become worthless during the taxable year are deemed to have become worthless on the last day of the year. In many cases, this treatment causes the loss to be treated as a long-term capital loss. If the loss from the worthless security is long term, the taxpayer reports it in Part II of Schedule D (Form 1040) along with the other long-term gains and losses for the year. The taxpayer reports short-term capital losses in Part I of Schedule D.

WHAT WOULD YOU DO IN THIS SITUATION?

A client comes to you with an idea to treat a loan that he made to one of his children two years ago as a bad debt. The loan is evidenced by a properly executed note with stated interest and payment dates. However, the client has not collected any loan payments or interest during the two-year period. The child is insolvent and has declared bankruptcy. Before leaving your office, the client also mentions in passing that the child is in London on vacation with other members of the family and will stay in Europe for six weeks. What would you do about classifying this loan as a bad debt?

PROBLEM MATERIALS

DISCUSSION QUESTIONS

I:8-1 What is the closed transaction doctrine, and why does it exist for purposes of recognizing a loss realized on holding property?

I:8-2 When property is disposed of, what factors influence the amount of the deductible loss?

I:8-3 Describe the usual tax consequences that apply to a worthless security.

I:8-4 Under what circumstances will a loss that is realized on a worthless security not be treated as a capital loss?

---

[66] Reg. Sec. 1.165-11(e).
[67] *Chester Matheson*, 74 T.C. 836 (1980), *acq.* 1981-2 C.B. 2.

[68] IRS, 2013 *Instructions for Filing Form 1045.*

I:8-5 What two general requirements must be met for a transaction to result in a capital loss?

I:8-6 What requirements must be met for stock to be considered Sec. 1244 stock?

I:8-7 What tax treatment applies to gains and losses on Sec. 1244 stock?

I:8-8 Describe a situation where a loss on the sale of business or investment property is not currently deductible, and explain why.

I:8-9 a. What is a passive activity?
b. Who is subject to the passive loss limitation rules?

I:8-10 a. For purposes of the passive loss rules, what is a closely held C corporation?
b. In what way do the passive loss rules differ from the regular passive loss rules when applied to closely held C corporations?

I:8-11 Why is it important to identify exactly what constitutes an activity for purposes of the passive activity rules?

I:8-12 a. If a taxpayer is involved in several different business operations during the year, how is the determination made as to how many activities these operations constitute for purposes of the passive activity loss rules?
b. Can a business operation and a rental operation ever be combined into one activity? Explain.

I:8-13 Which of the following activities are considered passive for the year? Explain. Consider each situation independently.
a. Laura owns a rental unit that she rents out to students. The rental unit is Laura's only business and she spends approximately 875 hours per year managing, collecting the rent, advertising, and performing minor repairs. At times she must hire professionals such as plumbers to do the maintenance. Is the rental unit a passive activity with respect to Laura?
b. Kami is a medical doctor who works four days a week in a medical practice that she and five other doctors formed. Last year she and her partners formed another partnership that owns and operates a medical lab. The lab employs ten technicians, one of whom also acts as manager. During the year Kami spent 120 hours in meetings, reviewing records, etc., for the lab. Is the lab a passive activity with respect to Kami?
c. Assume the same facts in part b. In addition, assume that the same group of doctors have formed two other partnerships. One is a medical supply partnership. Kami spent 150 hours working for this partnership. The medical supply partnership has five full-time employees. Kami also spent 250 hours during the year working for the other partnership. This partnership specializes in providing medical services to individuals from out of town who are staying at local hotels and motels. This partnership

hires two full-time and six part-time nurses. Are the lab and the two other partnerships passive activities with respect to Kami?

I:8-14 Explain the difference between materially participating and actively participating in an activity. When is the active participation test used?

I:8-15 a. What requirements must be met in order for a taxpayer to deduct up to $25,000 of passive losses from rental real estate activities against active and portfolio income?
b. What requirements must be met in order for a real estate rental activity to be considered a real estate business that is not subject to the passive loss rules?

I:8-16 Are the losses suspended under the passive loss rules lost forever? Explain.

I:8-17 What tests must be met to qualify a loss as deductible under the casualty loss provisions? Discuss the application of each of these tests.

I:8-18 Explain how a taxable gain on property can be realized because of a casualty event such as a fire or theft. How are these gains treated?

I:8-19 During the current year, Rulon's toilet overflowed because of a mechanical problem. Rulon was outside playing croquet, and by the time he returned, the water had flooded the basement, causing damage to the carpet, walls, and ceiling. The cost of repairing the damage was $9,000. Rulon has homeowners insurance that will cover half of the damage. However, because he has already had claims this year, Rulon does not want to report the incident to his insurance company for fear of a large increase in insurance rates. Instead, Rulon wants to deduct the loss as a casualty loss on his tax return. His AGI for this year is $50,000, and he has other itemized deductions of $6,000. Rulon is single. What amount of the casualty loss may he deduct?

I:8-20 Compare and contrast the computational rules for deducting casualty losses on personal-use property with casualty losses incurred on business or investment property.

I:8-21 Under what circumstances may a loss arising from a casualty or theft be deducted in a year other than the year in which the loss occurs?

I:8-22 For individuals, how are casualty losses on personal-use property reported on the tax return? How are casualty losses on business property reported?

I:8-23 Is the $100 floor on personal-use casualty losses imposed on each individual loss item if more than one item of property is destroyed in a single casualty? Is the floor imposed before or after the casualty gains are netted against the casualty losses?

I:8-24 Sarah loans $50,000 to her best friend, John. John uses the money to open a pizza parlor next to the local high school. Three years later, when John still owed Sarah $15,000, John closed the pizza parlor and declared bankruptcy. Discuss the appropriate tax treatment for Sarah.

I:8-25 Dana is an attorney who specializes in family law. She uses the cash method of accounting and is a calendar-year taxpayer. Last year, she represented a client in a lawsuit and billed the client $5,000 for her services. Although she made repeated attempts, Dana was unable to collect the outstanding receivable. Finally, in November of the current year, she finds out that the individual has moved without leaving any forwarding address. Dana's attempts to locate the individual are futile. What is the amount of deduction that Dana may take with respect to this bad debt?

I:8-26 Under what circumstances may a taxpayer deduct a bad debt even though another party to the transaction is the creditor?

I:8-27 What is the definition of a nonbusiness debt? What is the character of the deduction for a nonbusiness bad debt?

I:8-28 a. What alternatives do individuals have in deducting a loss on a deposit in a qualified financial institution?
b. Explain when it might be better to elect one over the other.

I:8-29 A taxpayer collects a debt that was previously written off as a bad debt. What tax consequences arise if the recovery is received in a subsequent tax year?

I:8-30 What is an NOL deduction, and why is it allowed?

I:8-31 List the adjustments to an individual taxpayer's negative taxable income amount that must be made in computing an NOL for the year. What is the underlying rationale for requiring these adjustments for individuals?

I:8-32 a. What is the NOL carryback and carryover period?
b. Does a taxpayer have any choice in deciding the years to which the NOL should be carried?
c. Explain the circumstances under which a taxpayer might elect not to use the regular carryback or carryover period.

I:8-33 Can a casualty loss on a personal-use asset create or increase an NOL? Explain.

I:8-34 If an NOL is carried back to a prior year, what adjustments must be made to the prior year's taxable income? What are the possible results of the adjustments?

ISSUE IDENTIFICATION QUESTIONS

I:8-35 On January 12 of the current year, Barney Corporation, a publicly-held corporation, files for bankruptcy. During the bankruptcy proceedings it is determined that creditors will only receive 10% of what they are owed and that the shareholders will receive nothing. Sheryl, a calendar-year taxpayer, purchased 1,000 shares of Barney Corporation common stock for $7,000 on February 22 of the prior year. What tax issues should Sheryl consider?

I:8-36 Five years ago, Cora incorporated Gold, Inc., by contributing $80,000 and receiving 100% of the Gold common stock. Gold, Inc. is engaged in a retail business. Cora is single. Gold experienced financial difficulties. On December 22 of the current year, Cora sold all of her Gold stock for $5,000. What tax issues should Cora consider?

I:8-37 In a rage because of personal difficulties, Evan drove recklessly and crashed his automobile, doing $8,000 worth of damage. Fortunately, no one was injured. Since Evan received two speeding tickets during the past year, he is concerned about losing his insurance if he files an insurance claim. What tax issues should Evan consider?

I:8-38 Dan, a full-time employee of Beta, Inc., also owns 10% of its outstanding stock. The other 90% is owned by his three brothers. During the year, the president of Beta came to Dan, expressing grave concern about whether the company had the financial resources to remain in business. He mentioned specifically that a bank was threatening to force Beta to file bankruptcy if it didn't repay its $100,000 loan in full. After some negotiation, Dan agreed to loan Beta the $100,000 for one year until permanent financing could be obtained. A reasonable interest rate was set and a payment schedule was documented. Unfortunately, business did not improve, and Beta discontinued its business and did not repay the loan. What tax issues should Dan consider?

PROBLEMS

I:8-39 *Section 1244 Losses.* During the current year, Karen sells her entire interest in Central Corporation common stock for $22,000. She is the sole shareholder, and originally organized the corporation several years ago by contributing $89,000 in exchange for her stock, which qualifies as Sec. 1244 stock. Since its incorporation, Central has been involved in the manufacture of items that protect personal computers from static electricity. Unfortunately, this market is extremely competitive, and Central Corporation incurs substantial losses throughout its existence.
a. Assuming Karen is single, what are the amount and the character of the loss recognized on the sale of the Central Corporation stock?

b. Assuming Karen is married and files a joint return, what are the amount and the character of the loss recognized on the sale of the Central Corporation stock?

c. How would your answer to Part a change if Karen had originally purchased the stock from another shareholder rather than organizing the corporation?

d. How might Karen have structured the transaction in Part a to receive a greater tax advantage?

I:8-40 *Amount and Character of Loss Transactions.* On September 30 of the current year, Fox Corporation files for bankruptcy. At the time, it estimates that the total FMV of its assets is $725,000, whereas the total amount of its outstanding debt amounts to $950,000. Fox Corporation has been engaged in the resale of tax preparation and tax research-related books and software for several years.

a. At the time of the bankruptcy, Fox is owned by Randall, who purchased the stock from an investor for $250,000 several years ago. Randall is single. What are the amount and character of the loss sustained by Randall upon Fox's bankruptcy?

b. How would your answer to part a change if Randall originally organized Fox Corporation, capitalizing it with $250,000 of cash and assuming Fox qualifies as a small business corporation?

c. How would your answer to Part a change if Randall were a corporation instead of an individual?

d. How would your answer to Part b change if Randall were a corporation instead of an individual?

I:8-41 *Amount and Character of Loss Transactions.* Five years ago, Brian and his brother Boyd formed Stewart Corp., a golf apparel manufacturing corporation. At that time, Brian contributed $300,000 to the corporation in exchange for 50% of its stock. During the current year, Brian needed some cash to purchase a golf course so he sold a third of his interest in Stewart Corp. for $85,000. He also sold stock in the following companies for the amounts indicated:

Corporation	Sales Proceeds	Adjusted Basis	When Acquired
IBM	$15,000	$10,000	52 months ago
Microsoft	25,000	45,000	18 months ago
Tidal Radio	32,000	12,000	7 months ago
Wavetable	20,000	26,000	4 months ago

During the year Brian hired a collection agency to collect a $14,000 loan he made to an old friend, which was due in full on January 1 of the current year. The agency found no trace of his friend. Also during the year, BTR Corporation, in which he owns stock, went bankrupt. His investment was worth $94,000 on January 1, he purchased it six years ago for $100,000, and he expects to receive only $8,000 in redemption of his stock. Finally, Brian's salary for the year was $114,000 for his work as an associate professor.

a. What are the net gains and losses from the above items and their character?

b. What is Brian's AGI for the year assuming he has no other items of income or deduction?

I:8-42 *Passive Losses.* In the current year Alice reports $150,000 of salary income, $20,000 of income from activity X, and $35,000 and $15,000 losses from activities Y and Z, respectively. All three activities are passive with respect to Alice and are purchased during the current year. What is the amount of loss that may be deducted with respect to each of these activities? Also compute the amount of loss that must be carried over for each activity.

I:8-43 *Passive Losses.* In the current year Clay reports income and losses from the following activities:

Activity X	$ 28,000
Activity Y	(10,000)
Activity Z	(20,000)
Salary	100,000

Activities X, Y, and Z are all passive with respect to Clay. Activity Z has $40,000 in passive losses which are carried over from the prior year. In the current year Clay sells activity Z for a taxable gain of $30,000.

a. What is the amount of loss that Clay may deduct and what is the amount that must be carried over in the current year?

b. Based solely on the amounts above, compute Clay's AGI for the current year.

I:8-44 *Passive Losses: Rental Real Estate.* During the current year, Irene, a married individual who files a joint return, reports the following items of income and loss:

Salary	$130,000
Activity X (passive)	10,000
Activity Y (rental real estate, nontrade or business)	(30,000)
Activity Z (rental real estate, nontrade or business)	(20,000)

Irene actively participates in activities Y and Z and owns 100% of both Y and Z.

a. What is Irene's AGI for the year?

b. What is the amount of suspended losses (if any) that may be carried over with respect to each activity?

I:8-45 *Passive Losses.* In 2014, Mark purchased two separate activities. Information regarding these activities for 2014 and 2015 is as follows:

	2014			2015	
Activity	Status	Income (Loss)	Activity	Status	Income (Loss)
A	Passive	($24,000)	A	Active	$10,000
B	Passive	(8,000)	B	Passive	20,000

The 2014 losses were suspended losses for that year. During 2015, Mark also reports salary income of $120,000 and interest and dividend income of $20,000. Compute the amount (if any) of losses attributable to Activities A and B that are deductible in 2015 and any suspended losses carried to 2016.

I:8-46 *Passive Losses.* During the current year, Juan, a single individual, has AGI of $124,000 before taking into account any passive activity losses. He also actively participates and owns 100% of activity A, which is a real estate rental activity. For the year, activity A generates a net loss of $6,000 and $3,000 in tax credits. Juan is in the 28% tax bracket. What is the amount of suspended loss and credit from activity A that must be carried to subsequent years?

I:8-47 *Passive Losses.* In 2015, Julie, a single individual, reported the following items of income and deduction:

Salary	$166,000
Interest income	14,000
Long-term capital gain from sales of stock	22,000
Short-term capital losses from sales of stock	(17,000)
Loss from a passive rental real estate activity	(20,000)
Interest expense on loan to purchase stock	(21,000)
Qualified residence interest on residence	(12,000)
Charitable contributions	(8,000)
Property taxes on residence	(5,000)
Tax return preparation fees	(2,500)
Unreimbursed employee business expenses	(2,000)

Julie owns 100% and is an active participant in the rental real estate activity. What is her taxable income for 2015?

I:8-48 *Casualty Losses.* Tony is a carpenter who owns his own furniture manufacturing business. During the current year, vandals broke into the workshop, damaged several pieces of equipment, stole his delivery truck, and also stole his personal automobile, which he often kept in the workshop garage. The asset descriptions and related values are as follows:

Asset	FMV Before Casualty	FMV After Casualty	Cost to Repair/Replace	Adjusted Basis	Insurance Proceeds
Equipment A	$12,300	$4,000	$ 8,700	$ 9,000	$ 3,700
Equipment B	8,100	0	9,000	3,000	7,800
Equipment C	Not Available	Not Available	13,800	15,300	11,400
Delivery Truck	18,000	0	32,000	17,500	16,000
Automobile	15,000	0	12,000	28,000	12,000

Although he could not obtain its fair market value after the casualties, Troy decided to repair rather than replace Equipment C.

Before considering any deductions because of these casualties, Troy's AGI is $80,000. What deductions may Tony take relating to the vandalism?

I:8-49 *Theft Losses.* On December 17 of the current year, Kelly's business office safe is burglarized. The theft is discovered a few days after the burglary. $3,000 cash from the cash registers is stolen. A diamond necklace and a ring that Kelly frequently wore are also stolen. The necklace cost Kelly $2,300 many years ago and is insured for its $6,000 FMV. Kelly purchased the ring for $3,000 just two weeks before the burglary. Unfortunately, the ring and the cash are not insured. Kelly's AGI for the year, not including the items noted above, is $70,000.
a. What is Kelly's deductible theft loss in the current year?
b. What is Kelly's deductible theft loss in the current year if the theft is not discovered until January of the following year?

I:8-50 *Casualty Losses: Year of Deduction.* Jerry sprayed all of the landscaping around his house with a pesticide in June 2015. Shortly thereafter, all of the trees and shrubs unaccountably died. The FMV and the adjusted basis of the plants were $15,000. Later that year, the pesticide manufacturer announced a recall of the particular batch of pesticide that Jerry used. It also announced a program whereby consumers would be repaid for any damage caused by the improper mixture. Jerry is single and reports $38,000 AGI in 2015 and $42,000 in 2016.
a. Assume that in 2015 Jerry files a claim for his losses and receives notification that payment of $15,000 will be received in 2016. Jerry receives full payment for the damage in 2016. How should the loss and the reimbursement be reported?
b. How will your answer to Part a change if in 2016 the manufacturer files for bankruptcy and Jerry receives $1,500 in total and final payment for his claim?
c. How will your answer to Part a change if the announcement and the reimbursement do not occur until late in 2016, after Jerry has already filed his tax return for 2015?

I:8-51 *Personal-Use Casualty Losses.* In the current year Ned completely destroys his personal automobile (purchased two years earlier for $28,000) in a traffic accident. Fortunately none of the occupants are injured. The FMV of the car before the accident is $18,000; after the accident it is worthless. Ned receives a $14,000 settlement from the insurance company. Later in the same year his house is burglarized and several antiques are stolen. The antiques were purchased a number of years earlier for $8,000. Their value at the time of the theft is estimated at $12,000. They are not insured. Ned's AGI for the current year is $60,000. What is the amount of Ned's deductible casualty loss in the current year, assuming the thefts are discovered in the same year?

I:8-52 *Casualty Losses.* During 2015, Pam incurred the following casualty losses:

Asset	FMV Before	FMV After	Basis	Insurance
Business 1	$18,000	$ 0	$15,000	$ 4,000
Business 2	25,000	10,000	8,000	3,000
Business 3	20,000	0	18,000	19,000
Personal 1	12,000	0	20,000	2,000
Personal 2	8,000	5,000	10,000	0
Personal 3	9,000	0	6,000	8,000

All of the items were destroyed in the same casualty. Before considering the casualty items, Pam reports business income of $80,000, qualified residential interest of $6,000 property taxes on her personal residence of $2,000, and charitable contributions of $4,000. Compute Pam's taxable income for 2015. Pam is single.

I:8-53 *Business Bad Debt.* Elaine is a physician who uses the cash method of accounting for tax purposes. During the current year, Elaine bills Ralph $1,200 for office visits and outpatient surgery. Unfortunately, unknown to Elaine, Ralph moves away leaving no payment and no forwarding address. What is the amount of Elaine's bad debt deduction with respect to Ralph's debt?

I:8-54 *Nonbusiness Bad Debt.* During 2014, Becky loans her brother Ken $5,000, which he intends to use to establish a small business. Because Ken has no other assets and needs cash to establish the business, the agreement provides that Ken will repay the debt if (and when) sufficient funds are generated from the business. Becky and Ken do not establish an interest rate. The business is unsuccessful, and Ken is forced to file for bankruptcy in 2015. By the end of 2015, it is estimated that the creditors will receive only 20% of the amount owed. In 2016 the bankruptcy proceedings are closed, and the creditors receive 10% of the amount due on the debt. What is Becky's bad debt deduction for 2015? For 2016?

I:8-55 *Bad Debt Deduction.* Assume the same facts as in Problem I:8-54, except that Becky and Ken are not related and that under the terms of the loan Ken agrees to repay Becky the $5,000 plus interest (at a reasonable stated rate) over a five-year period. What is Becky's bad debt deduction for 2015? For 2016?

I:8-56 *Net Operating Loss Deduction.* Michelle and Mark are married and file a joint return. Michelle owns an unincorporated dental practice. Mark works part-time as a high school math teacher, and spends the remainder of his time caring for their daughter. During 2015, they report the following items:

Mark's salary	$18,000
Interest earned on savings account	1,200
Interest paid on personal residence	7,100
Itemized deductions for state and local taxes	3,400
Items relating to Michelle's dental practice	
Revenues	65,000
Payroll and salary expense	49,000
Supplies	17,000
Rent	16,400
Advertising	4,600
Depreciation	8,100

a. What is Michelle and Mark's taxable income or loss for the year?
b. What is Michelle and Mark's NOL for the year?

I:8-57 *Net Operating Loss Deduction.* Assume the same facts as in Problem I:8-56, except in addition to the other itemized deductions Michelle and Mark suffer a $4,500 deductible personal casualty loss (after limitations).
a. What is Michelle and Mark's taxable income or loss for the year?
b. What is Michelle and Mark's NOL for the year?

I:8-58 *Net Operating Loss Deduction.* Assume the same facts as in Problem I:8-56, except instead of a $3,400 itemized deduction for state and local taxes, Michelle and Mark have a $3,400 deductible casualty loss (after limitations).
a. What is Michelle and Mark's taxable income or loss for the year?
b. What is Michelle and Mark's NOL for the year?

I:8-59 *Net Operating Loss.* During 2015, Karen, a single taxpayer, reports the following income and expense items relating to her interior design business:

Revenues	$52,000
Cost of goods sold	41,000
Advertising	3,300
Office supplies	1,700
Rent	13,800
Contract labor	28,000

Karen also worked part-time during the year, earning $13,500. She reports a long-term capital gain of $4,200, and a short-term capital loss of $3,800. Her itemized deductions total $5,200.
a. What is Karen's taxable income or loss for the year?
b. What is Karen's NOL for the year?

TAX STRATEGY PROBLEMS

I:8-60 In 2012, Annie Cook and several family members formed Treehouse Rentals, Inc., in Denver, Colorado. Treehouse is a closely held C corporation engaged in the rental real estate business. Treehouse properly classifies its activities as passive. In 2012, 2013, and 2014, the corporation generated net passive losses of ($380,000), ($145,000), and ($194,000), respectively, all of which were properly suspended.

Effective January 2015, Treehouse elected to be taxed as an S corporation. Also during 2015, Treehouse sold two pieces of rental real estate property. The suspended losses related to these properties were ($63,000) and ($112,000).

Write a memo to Treehouse Rentals explaining the tax treatment of the disposition of the rental properties in 2015.

• Sec. 469, Sec. 1371

• TAM 9628002

• *St. Charles Investment Co. v. Comm.*, 86 AFTR 2d 2000-6882 (CA 10, 11/14/2000)

I:8-61 Jace Seaton is a single taxpayer living in Eugene, Oregon. From 2011 to 2014, he worked as the CEO of Wengren & Jeffers, a local architectural firm. In 2015, he left the firm to start his own company as well as spend more time golfing and travelling. On October 25, 2015, he formed Seaton & Associates, a Limited Liability Company (LLC) under Oregon law.

Upon forming the LLC, Jace received an 80% interest in the company. Two other architects, Maria Juarez and Jaman Turhoon, each received a 10% interest in the company. Jace provided all necessary capital, whereas Maria and Jamal provided experience and a commitment to work for the company. Seaton & Associates chose to be taxed as a partnership for federal income tax purposes.

During 2015, Jace worked approximately 300 hours for Seaton & Associates, and received a guaranteed payment of $100,000. Maria and Jamal each worked approximately 600 hours, and each received a guaranteed payment of $150,000. In 2015 the company generated a net loss of $530,000.

Write a memo to Jace explaining how the LLC members, particularly Jace, should treat the loss generated in 2015.

- Reg. 1.469-5T

- *Gregg v. U.S.*, 87 AFTR 2d 2001-337

I:8-62 On November 15, Alex and Deanna Kent come to you for tax advice. The Kents, a married couple that files a joint tax return, own a rental home in Southern California. From January to November 1 of the current year, they rented out the home for 210 days. Since they live in Minnesota, they are considering staying in their rental home from December 10 to 31. If they do not stay in the home during that period, it will sit vacant. They ask you if this decision would have any tax consequences. They also provide you with the following information for the year:

Rental home income and expenses:

Rental income	$16,000
Mortgage interest	12,400
Property taxes	4,300
Homeowners Assoc. Fees	3,500
Depreciation	18,000

Other income and expenses:

Deanna's salary	75,000
Alex's salary	65,000
Passive income (from an investment in a limited partnership)	1,000
Mortgage interest on their Minnesota home	7,800
Charitable contributions	14,200
Medical expenses	8,100
Property taxes on their Minnesota home	2,900
State income taxes	9,700

What do you recommend to the Kents?

I:8-63 Jim had $100,000 in deposits in a savings account at a bank in Page, Arizona. The bank collapsed and Jim did not receive anything for his deposits. The bank was chartered by the state of Arizona and was not insured by federal law. Jim is not sure what his options are in deducting this loss on his tax return. What can Jim do to take advantage of this loss on his tax return? He has an AGI of $110,000 and no capital gains for the current year.

TAX FORM/RETURN PREPARATION PROBLEMS

I:8-64 Heather and Nikolay Laubert are married and file a joint income tax return. Their address is 3847 Jackdaw Path, Madison, WI 58493. Nikolay's Social Security number is 000-00-1111, and Heather's is 000-00-2222. Nikolay is a mechanical engineer, and Heather is a highly renowned speech therapist. She is self-employed. They report all their income and expenses on the cash method. For 2014, they report the following items of income and expense:

Gross receipts from Heather's business	$110,000
Rent on Heather's office	12,000
Receivables written off during the year (received in Heather's business)	1,300
Subscriptions to linguistic journals for Heather	250
Salary for Heather's secretary-receptionist	22,000
Nikolay's salary	78,000
Qualified medical expenses	12,000

Property taxes on their personal residence	4,200
State income tax refund received this year (the tax benefit was received in the prior year from the state income tax deduction)	400
State income taxes withheld on Nikolay's salary	4,600
Federal income taxes withheld on Nikolay's salary	12,000
Heather's estimated tax payments	20,000
Interest paid on residence	11,000
Income tax preparation fee for the prior year's return paid this year ($500 is allocated to preparation of Schedule C)	$940

Heather and Nikolay sold the following assets:

Asset	Acquired	Sold	Sales Price	Cost
KNA stock	2/12/13	3/13/14	$14,000	$ 8,000
AEN stock	3/2/14	7/7/14	20,000	22,000
KLN stock	6/8/09	4/10/14	13,000	17,000
Motorcycle	5/3/06	9/12/14	2,500	6,000

Heather owned the KLN stock and sold it to her brother, Jacob. Heather and Nikolay used the motorcycle for personal recreation.

In addition to the items above, they donate Miner Corporation stock to their community church. The FMV of the stock on the date it is donated (8/18/14) is $6,200. It cost $2,700 when purchased on 3/12/96. Heather and Nikolay's home is burglarized during the year. The burglar stole an entertainment system (FMV $3,500; cost $5,000), an antique diamond ring and pendant (FMV $12,000; cost $10,000), and a painting (FMV $1,500; cost $1,300). The insurance company pays $1,500 for the entertainment system, $4,000 for the jewelry, and $500 for the painting. Complete Heather and Nikolay's Form 1040, Schedules A, C, D, and SE, Form 4684, and Form 8283. For purposes of this problem, disregard the alternative minimum tax and any credits.

I:8-65 Kara and Brandon Arnold are married and file a joint return. Their Social Security numbers are 000-00-1111 and 000-00-2222, respectively. Kara and Brandon have one son, Henry, age 3. His Social Security number is 000-00-3333. They live at 356 Welcome Lane, Woodbury, WA 84653. They report their income on the cash method. During 2014, they report the following items:

Salary	$103,000
Interest income from money market accounts	600
Dividend income from Davis Corp. stock	700
Cash contributions to church	6,000
Rental of a condominium in Lutsen:	
Rental income (30 days)	12,000
Interest expense	7,000
Property taxes	3,200
Maintenance	1,700
Depreciation (entire year)	7,500
Insurance	2,000
Days of personal use	16

The address of the Condo is 1127 Skyline Drive, Lutsen, WA 84666.

During the year the following events also occur:

a. In 2012, Brandon had loaned a friend $3,000 to help pay medical bills. During 2014, he discovers that his "friend" has skipped town.

b. On June 20, 2014, Brandon sells Kim Corporation stock for $16,000. He purchased the stock on December 12, 2009 for $22,000.

c. On September 19, 2014, Kara discovers that the penny stock of Roberts, Inc. she purchased on January 2 of the prior year is completely worthless. She paid $5,000 for the stock.

d. Instead of accepting $60 the utility store offers for their old dishwasher, they donate it to Goodwill on November 21, 2014. They purchased the dishwasher for $750 on March 30, 2006. The new dishwasher cost $900.

e. Kara and Brandon purchased a new residence for $250,000. As part of the closing costs, they pay two points, or $3,800, on the mortgage, which is interest rather than loan processing fees. This payment enables them to obtain a more favorable interest rate for the term of the loan. They also paid $8,400 in interest on their mortgage on their personal residence.

f. They pay $4,100 in property taxes on their residence and $7,500 in state income taxes.

g. On July 20, 2014, Kara and Brandon donate 1,000 shares of Anton, Inc. stock to the local community college. The value of the stock on that date is $10,200. Anton, Inc. is a listed stock. They had purchased the stock on November 10, 2008 for $1,000.

h. $7,000 in federal income tax was withheld during the year.

Complete Kara and Brandon's Form 1040, Schedules A, B, D, and E, Form 8283 and Form 8949. For purposes of this problem, disregard the alternative minimum tax and any credits.

CASE STUDY PROBLEMS

I:8-66

Dr. John Brown is a physician who expects to make $150,000 this year from his medical practice. In addition, Dr. Brown expects to receive $10,000 dividends and interest income.

Last year, on the advice of a friend, Dr. Brown invested $100,000 in Limited, a limited partnership. He spends no time working for Limited. Limited's operations did not turn out exactly as planned, and Dr. Brown's share of Limited's losses last year amounted to $15,000. Dr. Brown has already been informed that his share of Limited's losses this year will be $10,000.

In January of the current year, Dr. Brown set up his own laboratory. Originally he intended to have the lab only do the work for his own practice, but other physicians in the area were impressed with the quick turnaround and convenience that the lab provided and began sending their work. This year, Dr. Brown estimates that the lab will generate $30,000 of taxable income. The work in the lab is done by two full-time qualified laboratory technicians. A part-time bookkeeper is hired to keep the books. Dr. Brown has spent 320 hours to date establishing and managing the lab. He plans to hire another technician who will also manage the lab so that it can operate on its own.

In November, Dr. Brown calls you requesting some tax advice. Specifically, he would like to know what actions he should take before the end of the year in order to reduce his tax liability for the current year.

Write a memo to Dr. Brown, detailing your suggestions. His address is: Dr. John Brown, 444 Physicians Drive, Suite 100, Anytown, USA 88888.

I:8-67

In preparing the tax return for one of your clients, Jack Johnson, you notice that he has listed a deduction for a large business bad debt. Jack explains that the loan was made to his corporate employer when the corporation was experiencing extreme cash flow difficulties. In fact, Jack was very concerned at the time he made the loan that the corporation would go bankrupt. This would have been extremely bad, because not only would he have lost his job, but he also would have lost the $80,000 he had invested in the common stock of the corporation.

You know that if the loan is a business loan Jack will receive an ordinary deduction. However, if the loan is a nonbusiness debt, it becomes a short-term capital loss (and Jack can only currently deduct $3,000).

After thoroughly reviewing all of the facts, you do a complete search of the relevant judicial and administrative authority. There you find that the courts are split as to whether under these circumstances the loan should be treated as a business or nonbusiness bad debt.

What position should you take on Jack's federal income tax return? (See the *Statements on Standards for Tax Services* section in Chapter I:15 and Appendix E for a discussion of this issue.)

TAX RESEARCH PROBLEM

I:8-68

Early in 2015, Keith meets Dan through a business associate. Dan tells Keith that he is directing a business venture that purchases poorly managed restaurants in order to turn them around and make them profitable. Dan mentions that he is currently involved in acquiring a real "gold mine" but needs to raise additional cash in order to purchase it. On the strength of Dan's representations, Keith loans Dan $30,000 for the venture. An agreement is written up between Keith and Dan, wherein Dan agrees to repay Keith the entire amount over a 5-year period plus 14% interest per annum on the unpaid balance. Later in the year, however, Keith discovers that Dan had never intended to purchase the restaurant and, in fact, had used most of the money for his own benefit. Upon making this discovery, Keith sues Dan for recovery of the money, alleging that Dan falsely, fraudulently, and deceitfully represented that the money would be invested and repaid, in order to cheat and defraud Keith out of his money. Unfortunately for Keith, he is never able to recover any amount of the loan. Discuss the tax treatment that Keith may claim with regard to the loss.

A partial list of research sources is:

• *Robert S. Gerstell,* 46 T.C. 161 (1966)

• *Michele Monteleone,* 34 T.C. 688 (1960)

CHAPTER

9

EMPLOYEE EXPENSES AND DEFERRED COMPENSATION

LEARNING OBJECTIVES

After studying this chapter, you should be able to

1 ▶ Determine the classification and limitations of employee expenses

2 ▶ Determine the proper deductible amount for travel expenses

3 ▶ Understand the deductibility of transportation expenses

4 ▶ Determine the proper deductible amount for entertainment expenses under the 50% disallowance rule

5 ▶ Discuss the tax methods concerning reimbursed employee business expenses

6 ▶ Identify deductible moving expenses and determine the amount and year of deductibility

7 ▶ Describe the requirements for deducting education expenses

8 ▶ Determine whether the expenses of an office in home meet the requirements for deductibility and apply the gross income limitations

9 ▶ Discuss the tax treatment and requirements for various deferred compensation arrangements

10 ▶ Describe tax planning considerations for employee expenses

11 ▶ Describe compliance and procedural considerations for employee expenses

This chapter discusses the tax consequences from two types of employee expenses:

▶ Expenditures incurred by an employee in connection with his or her job

▶ Deferred compensation payments made to employees

Employees routinely incur expenses in connection with their jobs, such as travel, entertainment, professional journals, etc. The tax law considers **employee expenses** to be incurred in connection with a trade or business and, therefore are deductible under Sec. 162. However, employee expenses are subject to a myriad of special rules and limitations. Because of the large number of taxpayers who are employees and the importance of the topic, this chapter discusses the rules as well as tax planning opportunities.

Deferred compensation refers to methods of compensating employees that are based on their current service, but the actual payments are deferred until future periods. Deferred compensation arrangements are very popular and widely used in business. The two principal types of deferred compensation arrangements are qualified plans and nonqualified plans. Qualified plans, such as pension and profit-sharing plans, have very favorable tax benefits but also impose strict eligibility and coverage requirements. Nonqualified plans, while not as tax advantageous as qualified plans, are very useful for highly compensated employees. Both of these types of deferred compensation arrangements are discussed later in this chapter.

CLASSIFICATION AND LIMITATIONS OF EMPLOYEE EXPENSES

OBJECTIVE 1

Determine the classification and limitations of employee expenses

Employee expenses, for purposes of the tax law, are divided into two classifications: *reimbursed* employee expenses and *unreimbursed* employee expenses. Reimbursed employee expenses are expenses incurred by the employee that are reimbursed by the employer. IRC Section 62(a)(2) provides that an employee may deduct reimbursed employee expenses *for* AGI. This presumes, of course, that the employee has included the reimbursement in his gross income. Unreimbursed employee expenses are generally deductible by employees, but are deductible *from* AGI. A more detailed discussion of the proper treatment of employee expenses under accountable and nonaccountable plans is presented later in this chapter.

Some of the more frequently encountered employee expenses discussed in this chapter include:

▶ Travel

▶ Transportation

▶ Moving

▶ Entertainment

▶ Education

▶ Office in home

Each of these types of employee expenses are discussed in this chapter.

ADDITIONAL COMMENT

"The income tax has made more liars out of the American people than golf has. Even when you make a tax form on the level, you don't know when its through if you are a crook or a martyr."
—Will Rogers

NATURE OF THE EMPLOYMENT RELATIONSHIP

An individual who provides services for another person or entity may be classified either as an employee or as a self-employed individual (also referred to as an independent contractor). If the individual is classified as self-employed, expenses are deductible *for* AGI under Sec. 162, and are reported on Schedule C of Form 1040. Conversely, expenses of employees are deductible either *for* or *from* AGI depending on whether such expenses are reimbursed or unreimbursed. In addition to the deductibility of expenses, the proper classification is also important due to employment taxes, such as Social Security and Medicare taxes. As is discussed below, self-employed taxpayers must pay both the employee and employer shares of Social Security and Medicare taxes.

KEY POINT

The business expenses of a self-employed individual and the reimbursed business expenses of an employee are deductible *for* AGI. The unreimbursed business expenses of an employee are deductible *from* AGI.

Employer-Employee Relationship Defined. The Treasury Regulations provide that an employer-employee relationship generally exists where the employer has the right to control and direct the individual who provides services with regard to the end result and the means by which the result is accomplished.[1]

EXAMPLE I:9-1 ▶ Carmen is a nurse who assists a group of doctors in a clinic. Carmen is under the direct supervision of the doctors and is told what procedures to perform and when to perform them. Therefore, Carmen is classified as an employee. ◀

EXAMPLE I:9-2 ▶ Carol is a registered nurse who provides in-home services to several elderly patients. She receives instructions from the patients' doctors regarding such items as medications and diet, but Carol is directly responsible for the delivery of nursing care and is in control of the end result. Thus, Carol is self-employed. ◀

ADDITIONAL COMMENT

Anyone in a trade or business making payments of $600 or more to an independent contractor during a year must file Form 1099-MISC.

Importance of Proper Classification. As mentioned above, proper classification is important both to employers and employees. If an individual is classified as an employee, the employer must match the Social Security and Medicare taxes that are paid by the employee. In addition, employers are generally liable for unemployment taxes for their employees. Thus, an employer must pay these employment taxes to the federal and/or state governments in addition to the wages, which means that the cost of an employee generally is higher than for a non-employee. If an individual is *not* considered to be an employee, the individual is classified as self-employed (also called an independent contractor). Amounts paid to a self-employed individual are not considered to be wages and the payor is not responsible for any employment taxes. However, the self-employed individual must pay both the employee and employer portions of Social Security and Medicare taxes. This tax is referred to as the *self-employment tax*. As can be seen from the above discussion, employment taxes are shifted from the employer to the self-employed individual if the individual is not considered to be an employee.

Individuals may prefer to be classified as employees because the employee portion of the Social Security and Medicare taxes (7.65%) is only one-half of the self-employment tax rate (15.3%). Of the 7.65%, 6.2% (12.4% for self-employed individuals) is for the old age, survivors and disability insurance (OASDI) portion of the FICA tax and is assessed on a maximum income amount of $118,500 for 2015 ($117,000 in 2014). The remaining 1.45% (2.9% for self-employed individuals) portion of the FICA tax is for hospital insurance and has no ceiling limitation.[2]

NEW LEGISLATION

As discussed in Chapter I:7, total itemized deductions are subject to a 3% reduction for upper-income taxpayers beginning in 2013.

Litigation Issues and Administrative Enforcement. The determination as to whether an individual who performs services is either an employee or an independent contractor has been a major ongoing area of contention between the IRS and taxpayers. In determining whether a worker is an employee or independent contractor, the facts of the situation must be analyzed and divided into three main categories: behavioral control, financial control, and relationship of the parties. No one factor is necessarily determinative, the totality of the situation must be considered. The first category, behavioral control, entails whether the payor has the right to control how the individual does the work. *Behavioral control* is characterized by the amount of instruction as to how the work is to be done as well as the level of training that is provided to the individual. As to *financial control*, an independent contractor has a significant investment in his or her work, is not reimbursed for expenses, and has the opportunity for profit or loss. An employee generally would not have these characteristics in their role as an employee. The third category is that the *relationship of the parties* and looks at employee benefits and explicit written contracts that show the type of relationship intended. These three categories of tests are an outgrowth of the so-called "20 factor test" that was used for many years to determine whether an individual was considered an employee or independent contractor. Under either system, the determination is still a very difficult and uncertain process.

Substantial litigation has occurred in the interpretation of these factors. For example, truck drivers who were owner-operators and were engaged under contract by an interstate trucking company were considered independent contractors because they selected their

---

[1] Reg. Sec. 31.3401(c)-1(b).

[2] Congress granted taxpayers a 2% reduction in Social Security taxes for employees for 2011 and 2012. Thus, the total rate for Social Security (OASDI) for the two years was 5.65% (4.2% for OASDI and 1.45% for Medicare). No reduction was allowed for the employer share. This 2% payroll reduction in social security was not extended for 2013 or later years. For a more detailed discussion of the self-employment tax, see Chapter I:14.

own routes and were paid a percentage of the company's receipts for shipment.[3] However, drivers for a moving van company were considered employees because the company exercised control over their assignments.[4] The Tax Court held that cosmetologists, nail technicians, and massage therapists who performed services at a spa were not employees but rather independent contractors.[5] The individuals paid weekly rent, set their own hours and fees, and generally provided their own supplies.

LIMITATIONS ON UNREIMBURSED EMPLOYEE EXPENSES

2% Nondeductible Floor. Section 67 imposes a nondeductible floor of 2% of AGI to the following types of itemized deductions:

1) Unreimbursed employee business expenses,
2) Investment expenses,
3) Fees paid for tax advice and/or tax return preparation, and
4) Expenses allowed in connection with a hobby activity (see Chapter I:6 for details on hobby loss activities).

All of these types of expenses are referred to as **miscellaneous itemized deductions** in Sec. 67.[6] Unreimbursed employee expenses that are classified as miscellaneous itemized deductions include:

▶ Professional journals, professional dues, union dues, small tools and supplies
▶ Job-hunting expenses for seeking employment in the same trade or business (e.g., employment agency fees)
▶ The cost and maintenance of special clothing (e.g., uniforms for an airline pilot)

Investment expenses include expenses connected with the earning of investment income, such as publications and safe deposit box rentals. Other miscellaneous itemized deductions include items such as fees for tax return preparation and appraisal fees for charitable contributions.

EXAMPLE I:9-3 ▶ In 2015, Charles incurs and pays $3,000 of unreimbursed employee expenses, $1,000 of investment counseling fees, and $500 for the preparation of his 2014 income tax return. Charles's AGI is $100,000. The total miscellaneous itemized deductions are $4,500 ($3,000 + $1,000 + $500). Charles is limited to a $2,500 deduction ($4,500 − $2,000) because of the application of the 2% nondeductible floor (0.02 × $100,000 AGI = $2,000). ◀

Exceptions to the 2% Floor. The 2% floor applies to most miscellaneous itemized deductions. However, some miscellaneous itemized deductions, such as gambling losses (see footnote 6 below), are not subject to the 2% floor. Further, itemized deductions, such as charitable contributions, mortgage interest and real estate taxes on a principal residence, are not considered miscellaneous itemized deductions and therefore not subject to the 2% nondeductible floor.

EXAMPLE I:9-4 ▶ In the current year Carmelia, who is single, incurs $1,500 of unreimbursed employee expenses, $3,000 of charitable contributions, and $7,000 of mortgage interest and real estate taxes on her principal residence. She has no other miscellaneous itemized deductions or investment expenses, and her AGI is $100,000. The $1,500 of employee expenses are not deductible because the 2% nondeductible floor ($2,000 in this case) is higher than the $1,500 of expenses. The $3,000 of charitable contributions and $7,000 of mortgage interest and real estate taxes are fully deductible as itemized deductions because Carmelia's total itemized deductions of $10,000 exceed the standard deduction amount ($6,300 for a single taxpayer in 2015). The charitable contributions, mortgage interest, and real estate taxes are not subject to the 2% nondeductible floor. ◀

[3] Rev. Rul. 76-226, 1976-1 CB 332
[4] *Richard N. Smith v. U.S.*, 78-1 USTC ¶9263 (CA-5, 1978).
[5] *Cheryl A. Mayfield Therapy Center*, TC Memo 2010-239.

[6] The 2% floor does not apply to certain other miscellaneous itemized deductions, including impairment-related work expenses for handicapped employees, amortizable bond premiums, certain short sale expenses, terminated annuity payments, and gambling losses to the extent of winnings.

TRAVEL EXPENSES

OBJECTIVE 2

Determine the proper deductible amount for travel expenses

DEDUCTIBILITY OF TRAVEL EXPENSES

The deductibility of travel expenses depends on the nature of the expenditure and whether the employee receives a reimbursement from the employer. The following rules apply to the deductibility of travel expenses.

▶ If the taxpayer is engaged in a trade or business as a self-employed individual or is engaged in an activity for the production of rental and royalty income, the travel-related expenditures are deductible *for* AGI and the 2% nondeductible floor is not applicable.

▶ If the taxpayer is an employee and incurs travel expenses in connection with his job, the expenses are deductible either *for* AGI or *from* AGI depending on whether the expenses are reimbursed by the employer.

▶ Personal travel expenses are not deductible.

HISTORICAL NOTE

The partial disallowance of business meals and entertainment of 50% was enacted because Congress believed that prior law had not focused sufficiently on the personal consumption element of deductible business meal and entertainment expenses. Congress felt that taxpayers who could arrange business settings for personal consumption were unfairly receiving a federal tax subsidy for such consumption.

Reimbursed Expenses. If business travel expenses are reimbursed and the reimbursement is included in the employee's gross income, the expenses are deductible *for* AGI.

Unreimbursed Expenses. Generally, if business travel expenses are not reimbursed by the taxpayer's employer, the expenses are a deduction *from* AGI subject to the 2% floor.

The tax rules for reporting reimbursed and unreimbursed employee business expenses are discussed in more detail later in this chapter. Table I:9-1 illustrates how travel expenses are reported.

DEFINITION OF TRAVEL EXPENSES

Travel expenses include transportation, meals, lodging, and other reasonable and necessary expenses incurred by a taxpayer while "away from home" in the pursuit of a trade or business or an employment-related activity. The term *travel expense* is more broadly defined in the IRC than is the term **transportation expense**. If an individual is not away from home, expenses related to local transportation are classified as transportation expenses rather than travel expenses. Transportation expenses for employees are deductible under certain conditions and are discussed later in this chapter.

▼ **TABLE I:9-1**
Classification of Travel Expenses

	TAX TREATMENT		
Situation Facts	**Deductible *for* AGI**	**Deductible *from* AGI**	**Not Deductible**
1. Cindy is a self-employed attorney who incurs travel expenses related to her business.	X[a]		
2. Jose, who lives in Dallas, is the owner of several apartment buildings in Denver. Periodically he travels to Denver to inspect and manage the properties.	X[a]		
3. Clay is an employee who is required to travel to company facilities throughout the U.S. in the conduct of his management responsibilities. Clay is not reimbursed by his employer.		X[b]	
4. Same as Situation 3, except that Clay is fully reimbursed by his employer and includes the reimbursement in his gross income.	X[a]		
5. Colleen works in New York City and travels to her parents' home in Dallas during the holidays.			X

[a] The 2% nondeductible floor is not applicable.
[b] The 2% nondeductible floor is applicable and the expenses are only deductible if in excess of the floor.

EXAMPLE I:9-5 ► Ahmed is away from home overnight on a job-related business trip and incurs airfare, hotel, and taxi fares amounting to $800. Because Ahmed is away from home, the $800 is treated as travel expenses. ◄

EXAMPLE I:9-6 ► Charlotte uses her personal automobile to make deliveries of company products to customers in the same local area of her employer's place of business. Charlotte's automobile expenses are classified as transportation expenses (rather than travel expenses) because she was not away from home when they were incurred. As is discussed later in this chapter, transportation expenses are deductible but are subject to strict recordkeeping rules. If Charlotte stopped to eat lunch alone during her delivery activities, the meals are not deductible as they are neither travel nor transportation expenses. ◄

GENERAL QUALIFICATION REQUIREMENTS

To qualify as a travel expense deduction, the following requirements must be met:

► The purpose of the trip must be connected with a trade or business or be employment-related (e.g., personal vacation trips or commuting to and from a job location are nondeductible personal expenses).[7]

► The taxpayer must be away from his tax home overnight or for a sufficient duration to require sleep or rest before returning home.

Away-from-Tax-Home Requirement. Travel expenses are deductible if the taxpayer is temporarily away from his tax home overnight. While this seems simple enough, there has been considerable controversy as to what the words actually mean. There are three important aspects of this requirement: (1) where is the taxpayer's home, (2) how is *temporarily* distinguished from *indefinite* or *permanent,* and (3) how is the term *overnight* interpreted.

Taxpayer's home: The IRS's position is that a person's tax home is the location of his principal place of employment regardless of where the family residence is maintained. Thus, a taxpayer who works permanently or for an indefinite period of time away from his or her family residence is *not* considered to be away from home and, therefore, travel expenses are not deductible. In this situation, the taxpayer's *tax home* is considered to be his work location.

Temporary vs. Indefinite: To meet the away from home requirement, a taxpayer must be away from home on a temporary basis. Thus, an employee who travels out of town on a three-day business trip clearly meets this requirement. However, an employee whose primary residence is in one location but works on a permanent basis during the week at another location, and possibly has an apartment at the work location, is not considered away from home at the *work location.* In this case, the work location is considered his tax home for income tax purposes, and he is not considered to be away from home.

The determination of whether a taxpayer is away from home temporarily or indefinitely is based upon the length of time the taxpayer is at such location. Work assignments of more than one year are treated as indefinite.[8] Work assignments for one year or less are classified as either temporary or indefinite depending on the facts and circumstances of each case. If an employee is reassigned only for a temporary period, then his tax home does not change and the travel expenses are deductible. However, if the assignment is for an indefinite period, the individual's tax home shifts to the new location. The following bulleted items and examples are taken from Rev. Rul. 93-86[9] and are used to illustrate the IRS's position concerning whether a taxpayer is away from home temporarily for purposes of deducting travel expenses:

► A taxpayer accepts away from home employment where it is realistically expected that the work will be completed in six months. The actual employment period lasts ten months. Because the employment period is realistically expected to last (and does in fact last) for one year or less, the IRS's position is that the employment is temporary and the taxpayer's travel expenses are deductible.

TYPICAL MISCONCEPTION
There is a tendency to erroneously assume that a taxpayer's tax home is the location of his or her primary personal residence.

REAL-WORLD EXAMPLE
A taxpayer was employed by a traveling circus with headquarters in Chicago. The Tax Court held that the taxpayer's home was wherever he happened to be with the circus. Therefore, the cost of his meals and lodging was not deductible. *Nat Lewis,* 1954 PH T.C. Memo ¶54,233, 13 TCM 1167.

---

[7] Travel expenses incurred in the production or collection of income are also deductible from AGI under Sec. 212(1), even though the travel is not connected with employment or with the conduct of a trade or business. See Rev. Rul. 84-113, 1984-2 C.B. 60.

[8] Sec. 162(a). See also Rev. Rul. 99-7, 1999-1 C.B. 361.
[9] Rev. Rul. 93-86, 1993-2 C.B. 71.

► A taxpayer accepts away from home employment where it is realistically expected that the work will be completed in 18 months but the work is actually completed in ten months. In such case the IRS's position is that the employment is treated as indefinite, regardless of whether it actually exceeds one year or not.

► A taxpayer accepts away from home employment where it is realistically expected that the work will be completed in nine months. After eight months the taxpayer is asked to remain for seven more months or a total period of more than one year. Based on these facts, the IRS's position is that the employment is temporary for eight months and the travel expenses are deductible for the eight-month period. The job is considered indefinite for the remaining seven months and no travel expense deduction is allowed for the travel expenses during this period.

Overnight test: To satisfy the overnight test, a taxpayer must show that it was reasonable for him to need to obtain sleep or rest during release time on such trips in order to meet the demands of his job.[10] Generally, costs of meals on one-day business trips are not deductible since the taxpayer was not away from home overnight. The Supreme Court held that a taxpayer who took short rest stops on long one-day business trips was not allowed to deduct his meals.[11] However, whether it is reasonable to need sleep or rest depends on the specific circumstances. A railroad conductor was allowed to deduct lodging, meals, and tips incurred during a six-hour layover on a total trip of 16 hours.[12]

EXAMPLE I:9-7 ► Roberto lives and works in Baltimore. He occasionally travels to New York City on business and stays overnight for two or three days at a time. Roberto clearly meets the away from home test and all of his travel expenses, including airfare, lodging, tips, taxi, and food (subject to the 50% disallowance) are deductible as travel expenses. ◀

EXAMPLE I:9-8 ► Tom lives with his family in Baltimore. In 2015, Tom loses his job in Baltimore and accepts a new full-time position in New York City. However, he decides not to move his family to New York but to rent an apartment and stay there during the week and return home on weekends. Tom's work assignment would be considered indefinite and the cost of his apartment, food, and other incidental expenses would not be deductible travel expenses because his tax home is New York and he is not considered to be away from home. ◀

EXAMPLE I:9-9 ► Gunther lives and works in Baltimore. Gunther's employer asks him to accept a temporary assignment in New York City for approximately seven months to work on a special project. Gunther rents an apartment in New York for the seven months, then returns to his regular office in Baltimore. Gunther's work assignment in New York is considered temporary because it is less than one year, and therefore, all of his apartment rent, food, laundry, and other incidental costs are deductible as travel expenses. Because apartments and food are expensive in New York, his travel expense deduction will be substantial. Good records to substantiate the work assignment and the expenses are very important in this case. ◀

SELF-STUDY QUESTION

A student accepts employment in another state during his summer vacation. Would the cost of his meals and lodging at the job location be deductible?

ANSWER

No, the student did not travel to the job because of the employer's business needs. *Peter F. Janss v. CIR*, 2 AFTR 2d 5927, 58-2 USTC ¶9873 (8th Cir., 1958).

BUSINESS VERSUS PLEASURE

Travel expenses are deductible only if they are incurred in the pursuit of a trade or business activity or are related to the taxpayer's employment. Thus, if a taxpayer takes a trip that is primarily personal in nature but some business is transacted, the only deductions allowed are those that are directly related to the business activity.[13] In such event, all of the traveling expenses to and from the destination are treated as nondeductible personal expenditures. However, if the trip is *primarily related* to business or employment, all of the traveling expenses to and from the destination are deductible, and meals and lodging, local transportation, and incidental expenses are allocated to the business and personal activities, respectively. In effect, an all-or-nothing approach is applied to the deductibility of traveling expenses to and from the destination depending upon the primary purpose for making the trip.

---

[10] Rev. Rul. 75-168, 1975-1 C.B. 58.
[11] *Correll v. U.S.*, 389 U.S. 299 (1968).
[12] *Williams v. Patterson*, 286 F2d 333 (5th Cir. 1961) and Rev. Rul. 75-170, 1975-1 C.B. 60. See also *Marc G. Bissonnette*, 127 T.C. 124 (October 23,

2006), where a six-hour layover on 15-17 hour days for a ferry boat captain was held to be "away from home."
[13] Reg. Sec. 1.162-2(b)(1).

In determining the primary purpose for a trip, the amount of time spent on personal activities compared to the time spent on business activities is an important factor. However, the fact that a taxpayer may spend slightly more time on personal activities than business activities will not automatically prohibit the deductibility of the transportation expenses to and from the destination. The taxpayer must clearly show that the purpose of the trip was *primarily business*.

EXAMPLE I:9-10 ▶ Dana travels to New York on a business trip for her employer and spends $500 for a roundtrip airline ticket and $200 per day for hotel, meals, and incidental expenses. She is not reimbursed for the travel expenses. Dana spends three days in business meetings and vacations for two days. Because the trip is primarily business, the traveling expenses to and from the destination (e.g., airfare) of $500 are fully deductible by Dana. Dana's meals, lodging, and incidental expenses amount to $1,000 (5 days × $200), but only $600 ($200 × 3 business days) of such travel expenses is deductible. The deductible business meal expenses are reduced by 50%, and the total amount of deductible travel expenses are subject to the nondeductible 2% floor on miscellaneous itemized deductions. A proration of the meals, lodging, and incidental expenses based on the number of days may not be appropriate if the expenses are uneven or are directly related to either business or personal activities. ◀

EXAMPLE I:9-11 ▶ Assume that the facts in Example I:9-10 are reversed (i.e., that two days are employment-related and three days are personal). Because more time was spent on personal activities, the general rule would hold that the trip is primarily personal and the traveling expenses to and from the destination of $500 are not deductible. Thus, only $400 ($200 × two business days) of travel expenses related to meals, lodging, and incidental expenses are deductible (subject to the limitations previously discussed). ◀

EXAMPLE I:9-12 ▶ Carroll, who lives and works in St. Louis, is required by his employer to attend a sales meeting in San Francisco. The meeting lasts two days. Carroll decides to take three days of vacation and sightsee in the San Francisco area. Even though Carroll spent more days on personal activities than business activities, Carroll's airfare would be deductible if he can clearly show that the primary purpose of the trip was business. ◀

REAL-WORLD EXAMPLE
It is very difficult to deduct expenses of a spouse who accompanies his or her spouse to a business meeting or convention. The accompanying spouse not only must be an employee of the corporation but the reason for accompanying his or her spouse must be for bona fide business purpose.

The IRS has ruled that the incremental expenses of an additional night's lodging and an additional day's meals that are incurred to obtain "excursion" airfare rates with respect to employees whose business travel extends over Saturday night are deductible business expenses.[14] The reimbursement for these expenses is deductible by the employer (subject to the 50% disallowance for meals). The employer is not required to report the reimbursement on the employee's Form W-2 as gross income or withhold employment taxes.

Stringent rules are applied if the taxpayer is accompanied by family members because of the likelihood that the trip is primarily for personal reasons. No deduction is permitted for travel expenses of a spouse or dependent (or other person accompanying the taxpayer) unless the person is an employee, the travel is for a bona fide business purpose, and the expenses would be otherwise deductible.[15]

FOREIGN TRAVEL
Due to the potential for abuse, special rules apply to foreign travel and foreign convention expenses.[16] Travel expenses related to foreign conventions, seminars, or similar types of meetings are disallowed unless it can be shown that the meeting is directly related to the taxpayer's trade or business (including employment) activity and that it is reasonable for the meeting to be held outside North America. In addition, complex expense allocation rules are applied to business trips made outside the United States.[17]

---

[14] PLR 9237014 (June 10, 1992).
[15] Sec. 274(m)(3).
[16] Secs. 274(c) and (h).
[17] Reg. Sec. 1.274-4. No allocation of total expenses is made to the personal-use (nondeductible) element if an individual is away from home for seven days or less or if less than 25% of the time is devoted to personal purposes. In all other cases, all of the foreign travel expenses (including transportation costs) must be apportioned between business and personal activities based on the relative percentage of time devoted to each activity.

SELF-STUDY QUESTION

Would the cost of going on a safari in Africa be deductible if the taxpayer were in the business of selling guns?

ANSWER

In an actual case, the Court held that the safari expenses were not sufficiently connected to the taxpayer's gun-selling business. Therefore, the safari costs were not deductible. *Vincent W. Eckel,* T.C. Memo 1974-33.

ADDITIONAL LIMITATIONS ON TRAVEL EXPENSES

IRC Section 274 also provides several limitations on the deductibility of certain types of travel expenses, including the following:

▶ Travel deductions are disallowed if the expenses are deductible only as a form of education. For example, a French language professor cannot deduct travel expenses to France if the purpose of the trip is to maintain a general familiarity with the French language and customs.

▶ Deductions allowed for luxury water travel (i.e., ocean liners, cruise ships, or other forms of water transportation) are limited to twice the highest per diem amount allowable for a day of domestic travel by employees in the executive branch of the federal government.

▶ Travel deductions to attend a convention, seminar, or meeting are not allowed if they are related to income-producing activities coming under Sec. 212. Expenses to attend a convention, seminar, or meeting are deductible if directly connected with a taxpayer's trade or business. However, expenses to attend such meetings on a U.S. cruise ship are deductible but only to a maximum amount of $2,000.

EXAMPLE I:9-13 ▶ Dawn travels from Miami on a cruise ship to attend a business meeting in Bermuda. The round-trip cost of the cruise is $6,000, and the travel is for a period of four days. If the highest daily per diem amount is $400 for a government employee, the travel expenses related to the cruise ship are limited to $3,200 ($800 per day × 4 days travel). ◀

EXAMPLE I:9-14 ▶ Assume that Dawn in Example 9-13 went on the cruise to attend a business seminar held on the cruise ship. In this case, Dawn's deductible expenses are limited to a maximum of $2,000. ◀

EXAMPLE I:9-15 ▶ Danielle is an investor in the stock market who attends investment counseling seminars. During the current year, she incurs $4,000 in travel expenses and $1,000 in registration fees to attend the seminars. None of the travel expenses are deductible because the expenses are related to income-producing activities coming under Sec. 212. The registration fees are deductible as an investment expense. If Danielle was employed as a stockbroker (rather than an investor) and attended investment seminars, her travel expenses would be deductible as well as the registration fee. ◀

TRANSPORTATION EXPENSES

OBJECTIVE 3

Understand the deductibility of transportation expenses

The deductibility and classification of transportation expenses also depends on the nature of the expenditure, as follows:

▶ Trade or business-related transportation expenses are deductible *for* AGI and are not subject to specific limitations.

▶ Transportation expenses related to the production of rental and royalty income (e.g., an owner-investor in rental properties) are deductible *for* AGI and are not subject to specific limitations.

▶ Reimbursed employee transportation expenses are deductible *for* AGI (assuming that an adequate accounting is made to the employer; see discussion of reimbursed employee business expenses on page I:9-17).

▶ Unreimbursed employee transportation expenses are deductible *from* AGI as itemized deductions subject to the 2% nondeductible floor for miscellaneous itemized deductions.

▶ Commuting expenses are nondeductible personal expenses.

DEFINITION AND CLASSIFICATION

KEY POINT

The primary difference between travel expenses and transportation expenses for tax purposes is that travel expenses are broad in nature and include transportation, lodging, meals, and other necessary expenses, whereas transportation expenses include only the cost of transportation.

Transportation expenses include such items as taxi fares, automobile expenses, airfares, tolls, and parking fees incurred in a trade or business or employment-related activity. Generally speaking, transportation expenses are those incurred for "local transportation" and are not treated as travel expenses because the away from home requirements have not been met. The cost of commuting to and from an employee's job location are nondeductible personal expenditures regardless of the length of the trip. Both unreimbursed employment-related travel and transportation expenses for employees are subject to the 2% floor on miscellaneous itemized deductions. If a reimbursement is received, such expenses would be deductible *for* AGI.

EXAMPLE I:9-16 ▶ Eurie's employer requires her to call on several customers at different locations in the metropolitan area during the course of the workday. Her transportation expenses (e.g., auto expenses, tolls, and parking) are deductible as transportation expenses because they are related to providing services as an employee. If Eurie is required to travel away from home overnight, the transportation costs are included with meals and lodging and deducted as a travel expense. In either situation, the unreimbursed employment-related expenses are treated as miscellaneous itemized deductions and are subject to the 2% nondeductible floor limitation. If the expenses were reimbursed by Eurie's employer and an adequate accounting is made to the employer, the expenses would be deductible *for* AGI. ◀

EXAMPLE I:9-17 ▶ David accepts a permanent job with a company located 80 miles from his principal residence. He decides not to move to the new location and drives the 160-mile roundtrip each day. None of David's transportation expenses are deductible because they are personal commuting expenses. (Note: Because the job is a permanent assignment, it is for an indefinite period rather than a temporary period and the transportation expenses are not deductible as travel expenses.) ◀

The following exceptions or unusual circumstances should be noted:

▶ Transportation expenses incurred to go from one job to another are deductible if an employee has more than one job. If the employee goes home between jobs, the deduction is only the amount it would have cost him to go directly from the first location to the second.[18]

▶ Certain transportation expenses related to income-producing activities are deductible under Sec. 212. Expenses are deductible *for* AGI if they are related to the production of rental or royalty income whereas expenses connected with other investment-related activities are deductible as miscellaneous itemized deductions subject to the 2% floor.

▶ Transportation expenses related to medical treatment may be deductible from AGI as a medical expense (subject to the limitations on the deductibility of medical expenses discussed in Chapter I:7).

▶ Transportation expenses related to charitable activities may be deductible as a charitable contribution (subject to the limitations on the deductibility of charitable contributions discussed in Chapter I:7).

▶ Transportation expenses incurred in going between the taxpayer's residence and a temporary work location outside the metropolitan area are deductible.[19] Further, assuming a taxpayer has at least one regular work location (such as his primary office location), transportation expenses are deductible in going between the taxpayer's residence and a temporary work location, regardless of the distance.[20] Thus, a CPA who is employed by a CPA firm and who maintains a regular work location (e.g., an office is provided at the CPA firm's work location) may deduct transportation expenses for trips from home to clients in the metropolitan area. Unreimbursed transportation costs for an employee are deductible *from* AGI as unreimbursed employee expenses that are subject to the 2% nondeductible floor. Transportation expenses for a self-employed individual are deductible *for* AGI.

EXAMPLE I:9-18 ▶ As shown in Figure I:9-1, Dick has two jobs that are 10 miles apart. Dick lives 5 miles from the first job site and 8 miles from the second job site. If Dick drives directly from Job 1 to Job 2, he may deduct the automobile costs associated with the 10-mile trip. If he goes home from the first job before driving to the second job, the deduction is still limited to 10 miles, even though he actually travels 13 miles. ◀

EXAMPLE I:9-19 ▶ Diana owns a duplex, which she rents to tenants. She periodically drives from her place of business to this income-producing property to collect the rents and to inspect the property. The

---

[18] IRS, *Publication No. 463* (Travel, Entertainment, Gift, and Car Expenses), 2014.

[19] Rev. Rul. 99-7, 1999-1 C.B. 361.
[20] Ibid.

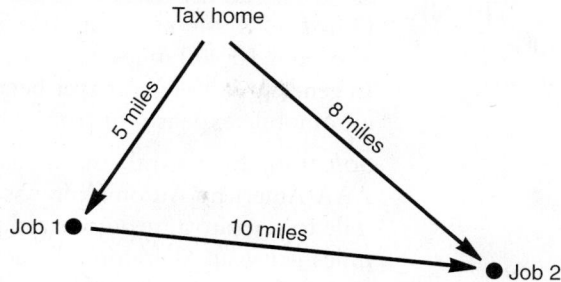

FIGURE I:9-1 ▶   ILLUSTRATION FOR EXAMPLE I:9-17

transportation expenses are deductible *for* AGI as an expense related to the production of rental income under Sec. 212.   ◀

EXAMPLE I:9-20 ▶   Donna, an accountant who is employed by a CPA firm, travels from her home to an audit client located in the local metropolitan area. The firm maintains an office for Donna at their business location. She is not reimbursed for her transportation costs. The transportation costs are deductible *from* AGI as unreimbursed employee expenses that are subject to the 2% nondeductible floor. If Donna were instead a self-employed CPA operating a business from her home, her transportation expenses would be deductible *for* AGI.   ◀

TREATMENT OF AUTOMOBILE EXPENSES

An employee or self-employed person may use either of two methods to deduct allowable automobile expenses. First, actual automobile expenses, including gas, oil, repairs, depreciation, interest, property taxes, license fees, and insurance are deductible based on the percentage of business miles to total miles. Detailed records to support the expenses are necessary in order to properly claim the deduction. To help reduce the burden of detailed recordkeeping, a second method, the standard mileage rate method, is available to taxpayers.

The standard mileage rate method permits a deduction based on a mileage rate of 57.5 cents per mile for the year 2015.[21] Parking and tolls for business purposes are allowed as an addition to this deduction as well as interest expense on an automobile loan and personal property taxes on the automobile. The following restrictions apply when the standard mileage rate is used:

▶ The standard mileage rate method cannot be used for automobiles used for hire, such as taxicabs, or for five or more automobiles used simultaneously by a taxpayer.

> **ADDITIONAL COMMENT**
> It should be remembered that in many cases the taxpayer can choose between the automatic mileage method and calculating the actual costs of operating the car. Although the automatic mileage method has the advantage of convenience, a calculation of the actual costs might produce a larger deduction.

▶ If a taxpayer changes from the standard mileage rate method in one year to the actual expense method in a later year, the basis of the used automobile must be reduced by 24 cents for 2015, 22 cents for 2014, and 23 cents per mile for 2012 and 2013.[22] The modified accelerated cost-recovery system (MACRS) rules (discussed in Chapter I:10) cannot be used for computing depreciation in the year of the change and for the remaining useful life of the automobile. In such case, only the straight-line method under the alternative depreciation system (ADS) may be used (see Chapter I:10).

▶ A change to the standard mileage rate method is not allowed for an automobile that was previously depreciated under the MACRS rules or where an election was made under Sec. 179 to expense part or all of the automobile's cost in the year of acquisition. (See Chapter I:10 for a discussion of the Sec. 179 election.)

▶ The actual expense method is based on the ratio of business or employment-related miles to total miles. (See Chapter I:10 for a discussion of specific restrictions on the computation of depreciation where mixed business- and personal-use automobiles are acquired.)

---

[21] Notice 2014-79, 2014-52 IRB, 12/10/2014. For the taxable year 2014, the standard mileage rate was 56 cents per mile.

[22] The depreciation component of the mileage rate for earlier years was 22 cents per mile for 2011, 23 cents per mile for 2010, 21 cents per mile for 2009 and 2008, 19 cents per mile for 2007, 17 cents per mile for 2006 and 2005, and 16 cents per mile for 2004 and 2003.

STOP & THINK

Question: Assume a taxpayer uses his car (original cost, $20,000) in his business, drives a total of 10,000 miles per year, and can substantiate 80% of the mileage as business use. In general, will the taxpayer benefit more from the standard mileage method of deducting automobile expenses or from the actual expenses method?

Solution: In general, the actual expenses method will yield a higher deduction. The AAA(American Automobile Association) estimates that it costs approximately $0.78 per mile to operate a medium-sized car in the United States in 2014 based on driving 10,000 miles per year. Therefore, the actual cost of operating the automobile would be approximately $7,800 (10,000 miles × $0.78). The deductible amount for tax purposes would be 80% of $7,800, or $6,240 for the actual expense method. Compare this amount with the standard mileage amount of $4,600 (10,000 miles × 80% business usage × .575/mile) and the actual expenses method yields a higher deduction. Of course, each individual situation is different and the actual results can vary based on circumstances, such as the amount of repairs, depreciation, and so on.

EXAMPLE I:9-21 ▶ Danny owns and operates a taxicab in New York City and drives 90,000 miles per year. In deducting his automobile expenses, Danny must use the actual cost method. He is not permitted to use the standard mileage method as the taxicab is an automobile for hire. ◀

EXAMPLE I:9-22 ▶ Doug acquired an automobile for use in his unincorporated business in 2012 and used the standard mileage rate method in 2012–2014. If Doug switches to the actual expense method for 2015 and later years, the automobile's adjusted basis (for depreciation purposes) must be reduced by 23 cents for 2012 and 2013 and 22 cents for 2014. Thus, if the automobile originally cost $20,000 in 2012 and was used 10,000 miles for business purposes during the initial year and 15,000 miles each in 2013 and 2014, the adjusted basis for computing depreciation in 2015 is reduced to $10,950 {$20,000 − [(0.23 × 10,000) + (0.23 × 15,000) + (0.22 × 15,000)]}. The remaining $10,950 basis must be depreciated using straight-line depreciation over the automobile's estimated useful life if the actual expense method is used. ◀

EXAMPLE I:9-23 ▶

HISTORICAL NOTE

Congress enacted a "contemporaneous" records test for substantiating expenses for automobiles and certain other activities. Public outcry caused Congress to repeal this requirement. Currently, the business use of an automobile can be substantiated either by keeping adequate records or by sufficient corroborating evidence, oral or written.

Edith uses her automobile 50% of the time for business and employment-related use and 50% for personal use. These percentages are substantiated by records that document the total usage for the automobile. During 2015, Edith drives 3,000 miles per month or a total of 36,000 miles for the year. If the standard mileage rate method is used, she can deduct $10,350 [(0.575 × 36,000 miles) × 50%] for the business and employment-related use. Additionally, Edith may deduct any business-related parking fees and tolls. ◀

REIMBURSEMENT OF AUTOMOBILE EXPENSES

An employee is entitled to deduct actual automobile expenses (or amounts derived under the standard mileage rate method if applicable) in excess of reimbursed amounts received from the employer. The computation is made on Form 2106 (Employee Business Expenses) and is reported on Schedule A of Form 1040.

EXAMPLE I:9-24 ▶

ADDITIONAL COMMENT

The kind of written record that could corroborate the business use of an automobile would include account books, diaries, logs, trip sheets, expense reports, or written statements from witnesses.

Elizabeth, who makes an adequate accounting to her employer, receives a $8,000 (20,000 miles at 40 cents per mile) reimbursement in 2015 for employment-related business miles. She also drives her car an additional 12,000 miles for personal use, or a total of 32,000 miles. She incurs the following expenses related to both business and personal use:

Gas and oil	$ 6,200
Repairs and maintenance	2,700
Depreciation	3,000
Insurance	1,900
Total	$13,800

Elizabeth also spent $100 on parking fees and tolls that were all related to business. Thus, she uses her car 62.5% (20,000 miles ÷ 32,000 miles) for business use. After subtracting the employer's $8,000 reimbursement and adding the parking fees and tolls, Elizabeth may deduct $725 [($13,800 × 0.625) + $100 − $8,000] as a miscellaneous itemized deduction (subject to the 2% nondeductible floor) in 2015. Alternatively, if 2015 is the first year she used the car in her business, she could have claimed a deduction using the standard mileage rate method. Under the standard mileage rate method her deduction would be $3,600 [(32,000 miles × 62.5% × $0.575) + $100 business-related fees and tolls − $8,000 reimbursement]. ◄

ENTERTAINMENT EXPENSES

OBJECTIVE 4

Determine the proper deductible amount for entertainment expenses under the 50% disallowance rule

Entertainment of business customers and clients is a routine and, in many cases, an essential practice in business. Because entertainment expenses are considered ordinary and necessary practices of a business, they are deductible under either Sec. 162 or Sec. 212. However, the nature of entertainment expenses lend themselves to abuse by taxpayers. There certainly is an element of personal pleasure in taking a client or customer to a hockey game or a Philharmonic orchestra performance and allowing taxpayers to deduct such expenses creates serious enforcement problems for the IRS.

For the reasons above, Congress enacted Sec. 274, which is strictly a disallowance section and contains classification rules, restrictive tests, and specific recordkeeping requirements. To deduct entertainment expenses, taxpayers must first show that the expenditure qualifies for a deduction under Sec. 162 (trade or business expense) or Sec. 212 (investment-type expense). Then the various requirements of Sec. 274 must be adhered to in order for an entertainment expense to be deductible. Over the years, Congress has continued to tighten the rules for the deductibility of entertainment expenses.

50% DISALLOWANCE FOR MEAL AND ENTERTAINMENT EXPENSES

Section 274(n) provides that any expense incurred for either business meals or entertainment must be reduced by 50%. Business meals may be deductible either as travel expenses or as entertainment, depending on the nature of the expenditure. In either case, the 50% limit applies to the cost of food and beverages including tips and taxes but is not applicable to transportation expenses incurred going to and from a business meal. Further, any portion of a business meal that is considered lavish or extravagant is disallowed.[23] In such a situation, the 50% reduction rule is applied to the allowable portion of the business meal.

EXAMPLE I:9-25 ▶ Krishna, a self-employed individual, pays $300 for a business meal plus $18 sales tax and a $60 tip. The total cost of the meal is $378. If $150 of the meal is considered lavish or extravagant, Krishna could deduct $114 [($378 − $150) × 50%]. ◄

If an employee incurs entertainment or business meal expenses that are fully reimbursed by the employer, it is the employer rather than the employee who is limited to a deduction for 50% of the expenses. Assuming the reimbursement is made pursuant to an accountable plan (see discussion later in this chapter), the employee would not include the reimbursement in income and would not be allowed a deduction.

EXAMPLE I:9-26 ▶ Gordon incurs employment-related entertainment expenses of $1,000 and is fully reimbursed by his employer pursuant to an accountable plan. The employer may deduct $500 [$1,000 − ($1,000 × 0.50)] of entertainment expenses. Gordon would not include the $1,000 reimbursement in gross income and would not be allowed to deduct the $1,000 as a deduction. Thus, there is no overall tax effect to Gordon. ◄

Certain meals are not subject to the 50% disallowance, including meals that are treated as compensation to employees, employee picnics or other social gatherings primarily for the benefit of employees, or infrequent meals that would qualify as a de minimus fringe benefit.

CLASSIFICATION OF EXPENSES

If an individual is engaged in a trade or business (but not as an employee), allowable entertainment expenses are deductible *for* AGI. Employees, however, may deduct entertainment expenses only as a miscellaneous itemized deduction (subject to the 2% nondeductible

---

[23] Sec. 274(k).

floor) unless the expenses are reimbursed. The tax rules for reimbursements of employee business expenses are discussed more fully later in this chapter.

EXAMPLE I:9-27 ▶

ADDITIONAL COMMENT

Entertainment expenses are not considered "directly related" if there are substantial distractions. Therefore, if a meeting takes place at a sporting event, theater, or night club, the entertainment cannot be "directly related." This type of entertainment could qualify as an "associated with" expense. An example of a "directly related" expense would be the costs related to a hospitality room at a convention.

ADDITIONAL COMMENT

With respect to the "associated with" type of expense, there is *no* requirement that the business discussion last for any specified period, or that more time be devoted to business than to entertainment.

EXAMPLE I:9-28 ▶

REAL-WORLD EXAMPLE

One common way business people document a business meal is to write on the back of the credit card receipt the other person(s) at the meal and the topic discussed. Then all of the necessary substantiation requirements are present on the one piece of paper: date, time, place, amount, people present, and business discussed.

EXAMPLE I:9-29 ▶

Helen is a self-employed attorney who entertains clients and prospective clients. To the extent that these expenditures meet the Sec. 274 requirements, they are deductible by Helen as a *for* AGI expense on Schedule C of Form 1040 because Helen is engaged in a trade or business activity. The entertainment expenses are subject to the 50% limit but are not subject to the 2% nondeductible floor because the entertainment is deductible when determining AGI as a trade or business expense. ◀

Criteria for Deduction. To be deductible as an entertainment expense, an expenditure must be either **directly related** to the active conduct of a trade or business or **associated with** the active conduct of a trade or business. Different restrictions apply to each of these categories. The Regulations under Sec. 274 provide the substantive rules for the two types of entertainment expenses.

"Directly Related" Expenses. To meet the requirements for a "directly related" **entertainment expense,** some business benefit must be expected from the business conducted other than goodwill and the expense must be incurred in a clear business setting (i.e., where there are no substantial distractions). In other words, business in anticipation of a business benefit must actually be conducted during the entertainment period.

"Associated With" Expenses. To qualify an expense as an "associated with" entertainment expenditure, the taxpayer must show a clear business purpose, such as obtaining new business or encouraging the continuation of an existing business relationship. An added restriction is placed on "associated with" entertainment in that the entertainment must directly precede or follow a bona fide business discussion. This means that the entertainment generally must occur on the same day that business is discussed.

Holly is a lawyer who hosts a birthday party in her home. Most of the guests are law partners or clients. No formal business discussions are conducted either before or immediately following the party. The expenditures for the birthday party are not deductible because they do not meet either the "directly related" or "associated with" tests. ◀

Substantiation Requirements. In addition to both the directly related and associated with requirements, Sec. 274 imposes stringent substantiation requirements for entertainment expenses. In order to deduct entertainment expenses, taxpayers are required to substantiate each expenditure for which a deduction is claimed. Lack of documentation alone will cause the disallowance of a deduction.

BUSINESS MEALS

Business meals related to travel or entertainment activities are subject to the same business-connection requirements as other types of entertainment expenses. Thus, an entertainment deduction is allowed only if the meal meets the "directly related" or "associated with" tests previously discussed. In addition, the expense must not be lavish or extravagant under the circumstances, and the taxpayer (or an employee of the taxpayer) must generally be present when the food or beverages are furnished. These requirements do not apply to a business meal associated with travel where the taxpayer claims a deduction only for his or her own expenses.

Hank is a salesman for a manufacturing supply company. Hank meets Harold, a purchasing agent who is an important customer, for lunch during a normal business day. Business is actually conducted during the lunch, and the lunch expenses are not lavish or extravagant under the circumstances. Hank is fully reimbursed by his employer for the $30 lunch expenses after an adequate accounting of the expenses is submitted. The business meal qualifies as "directly related" entertainment because the entertainment involved the actual conduct of business where some business benefit is reasonably expected and a business discussion was conducted during the meal. Hank's employer may deduct $15 ($30 × 0.50) of entertainment expenses. ◀

WHAT WOULD YOU DO IN THIS SITUATION?

You have recently acquired a new individual tax client, Joe Windsack, who is a manufacturer's representative for a local tool and die company. You have been engaged by Windsack to prepare his individual income tax return for the current year. Before the current tax year is over, you are at a party where Windsack is also a guest. You overhear Windsack bragging to a group of people that he substantially reduces his income tax liability by overstating meal and entertainment expenses. He indicated that he overstates the deductions in several ways: (1) when he goes out to lunch or dinner that is personal in nature, such as with his family, he always uses a credit card and fictitiously writes the name of a client or prospective client on the charge card receipt, (2) when he goes out to lunch with several colleagues from his office (not business related), he charges the entire amount on his credit card (for everyone at the table), collects the cash from his colleagues for the cost of their meals, and then writes the entire amount off as a business-related meal, and (3) whenever he goes to any entertainment event, such as a ballgame, he always says that he took a client to the game with him and deducts the cost of the ticket as a business expense. When Windsack brings his tax information to you a couple of months later and you see a substantial amount of meal and entertainment expenses, what should you do?

EXAMPLE I:9-30 ► Assume the same facts as in Example I:9-29, except that the purchasing agent is a prospective customer and no business is actually discussed either during, directly preceding, or immediately following the meal. Thus, no deduction is allowed because no business is discussed either before, during, or after the meal. ◄

The Regulations provide that the surroundings in which food or beverages are furnished must be in an atmosphere where there are no substantial distractions to the discussion (e.g., a floor show).[24]

EXAMPLE I:9-31 ► Harry is a salesman who takes a customer to a local nightclub to watch a floor show and to have a few drinks. No business is discussed either before, during, or after the entertainment. The expenses for the beverages and floor show are not deductible because neither of the business meal requirements are met (i.e., the floor show produced substantial distractions, and no business was discussed). Even if business was actually discussed, no deduction would be allowed because there were substantial distractions. ◄

ENTERTAINMENT FACILITIES AND CLUB DUES

KEY POINT

Subject to very few exceptions, no deduction is permitted for costs related to yachts, swimming pools, fishing camps, tennis courts, bowling alleys, vacation resorts, etc. This highly visible type of entertainment contributed to the public perception that the tax system was unfair.

No deduction is permitted for costs (e.g., depreciation, maintenance, repairs, and so on) related to the maintenance of facilities that are used for entertainment, amusement, or recreation. Facilities include yachts, hunting lodges, beach cottages, and so on.

No deduction is permitted for any type of club dues (including business, social, athletic, luncheon, and sporting clubs, as well as airline and hotel clubs).[25] Professional, civic and public service organizations (e.g., business leagues, trade associations, chambers of commerce, boards of trade, and real estate boards) are generally not subject to the dues disallowance rules. Initiation fees that are paid only upon joining a club are treated as nondeductible capital expenditures. While club dues are not deductible, other business expenses (e.g., business meals) are deductible if the general requirements for entertainment deductions are met.

EXAMPLE I:9-32 ► Heidi is a self-employed CPA who entertains clients at her country club. Her club expenses include the following:

Annual dues	$ 4,000
Meal and entertainment charges related to business use	3,000
Personal-use meal charges	2,500
Initiation fee	10,000
Total expenses	$19,500

---

[24] Reg. Sec. 1.274-2(f)(2)(i)(b).　　　　[25] Sec. 274(a)(3).

The only expense that is deductible is 50% of the specific business charges relating to the meals and entertainment. Thus, Heidi may deduct $1,500 ($3,000 × 0.50) *for* AGI as a business expense because she is a self-employed CPA. ◀

BUSINESS GIFTS

Business gifts are deductible but are subject to an annual ceiling amount of $25 per donee.[26] Amounts in excess of the $25 limit per donee are disallowed. The following rules and exceptions apply to determine the business gift deduction:

▶ Multiple gifts to each donee are aggregated for purposes of applying the $25 per donee annual limitation. Husbands and wives and other family members are treated as a single donee.

▶ Employee achievement awards made for length of service or safety that are under $400 per individual are excluded.[27]

▶ A gift from an employee to his or her supervisor does not qualify as a business gift because such gifts are personal rather than business related and are, therefore, not deductible.

▶ Business gifts are not subject to the 50% reduction for meals and entertainment.

EXAMPLE I:9-33 ▶

REAL-WORLD EXAMPLE
A taxpayer who had deducted the full cost of two wedding gifts, both of which were in excess of $25 apiece, was able to deduct only $25 for each gift. *Jack R. Howard,* 1981 PH T.C. Memo ¶81,250, 41 TCM 1554.

Jack, an employee, makes the following gifts during the year, none of which are reimbursed by his employer:

Jack's immediate supervisor	$20
Jack's secretary	15
Jeff (a customer of Jack's)	24
Jeff's wife (a noncustomer)	26
Total	$85

Jack's total deduction for business gifts is $40 ($15 + $25) and is classified as a miscellaneous itemized deduction subject to the 2% nondeductible floor as an employee business expense. The $20 gift to Jack's immediate supervisor is not deductible. The gifts of $24 and $26 to Jeff and Jeff's wife must be aggregated and are limited to $25. ◀

LIMITATIONS ON ENTERTAINMENT TICKETS

In addition to the general 50% meals and entertainment limitation, the cost of a ticket for any entertainment activity or facility is limited to the ticket's face value. Thus, the 50% limit applies to the face value of the ticket. Further restrictions are placed on the rental of skyboxes that are leased for more than one event.[28]

EXAMPLE I:9-34 ▶

Able Corporation acquires four tickets to a football game for $2,000 that are used for entertaining customers. The face amount of the four tickets is only $200 in total. Able's deduction for entertainment is initially limited to the $200 face value of the tickets. The deductible amount is $100 ($200 × 0.50) after applying the 50% limit on entertainment expenses. ◀

---

[26] Sec. 274(b)(1).
[27] Sec. 274(j). The total limit including both qualified and nonqualified plan awards is $1,600 per individual (see Chapter I:4).
[28] Sec. 274(l)(2). The cost of a skybox is disallowed to the extent that it exceeds the cost of the highest-priced nonluxury box seat tickets multiplied

by the number of seats in the skybox (e.g., if a skybox contains 30 seats and the cost of the highest-priced nonluxury box seat for a particular event is $200, the deduction for the skybox is limited to $6,000 ($200 × 30) reduced by the 50% limitation applicable to entertainment expenses, or a total of $3,000.

REIMBURSED EMPLOYEE BUSINESS EXPENSES

OBJECTIVE 5

Discuss the tax methods concerning reimbursed employee business expenses

ADDITIONAL COMMENT

While reimbursed business expenses under an accountable plan are technically deductions for AGI, they do not actually appear on the employee's tax return as a deduction. This is because the reimbursement itself is not included on the Form W-2.

The tax treatment of reimbursements received by an employee from his employer for employment-related expenses depends upon whether the reimbursement is made pursuant to an **accountable** or **nonaccountable** plan. An accountable plan is a reimbursement arrangement that meets both of the following two tests.[29]

1. Substantiation—the employee must make an adequate accounting of expenses to his employer, which means that each business expense must be substantiated (an expense report, for example); and
2. Return of excess reimbursement—within a reasonable period of time, the employee is required to return to the employer any portion of the reimbursement in excess of the substantiated expenses.

If both of these tests are not met, amounts paid to an employee generally are treated as paid under a nonaccountable plan. However, a special rule in Reg. Sec. 1.62-2(c) provides that if an employee does not return the excess reimbursement within a reasonable time period, only the portion of the reimbursement in excess of substantiated expenses is considered as being paid under a nonaccountable plan. The portion of the reimbursement for substantiated expenses is considered as being paid under an accountable plan.

Accountable Plan. Under an accountable plan, reimbursements are included in gross income and expenses are deductible *for* AGI. Therefore, a taxpayer's AGI will not increase if employee business expenses are reimbursed under an accountable plan. Because reimbursements and expenses offset each other, when expenses are reimbursed under an accountable plan, taxpayers do not report the reimbursement or the expenses on their tax return. However, if an excess reimbursement is not returned to the employer, the excess reimbursement is included in the employee's gross income.[30]

EXAMPLE I:9-35 ►

Anthony is an employee of the Bluechip Corporation, which maintains an accountable plan for purposes of reimbursing employee expenses. During the current year, Anthony went on a business trip and incurred $1,500 of expenses as follows: airfare, $800; lodging, $450; meals, $200; and tips, $50. Bluechip reimbursed him $1,500. Technically speaking, Anthony has gross income of $1,500 and a deduction for AGI of $1,500. But, because the reimbursement is pursuant to an accountable plan, Anthony will not report the $1,500 reimbursement in his gross income and will not deduct any of the business expenses on his tax return. ◄

EXAMPLE I:9-36 ►

Assume the same facts as in Example I:9-35 except that Bluechip advanced Anthony $1,800, rather than $1,500, for his business trip and his expenses were the same as above. If Anthony returned the excess $300 to Bluechip within a reasonable period of time, the result would be the same as in Example I:9-35. However, if Anthony did not return the excess reimbursement (even though he is required to under the terms of the plan), Anthony must include the $300 in his gross income. The portion of the $1,800 reimbursement that pertains to the substantiated expenses, $1,500, is treated as being paid under an accountable plan. Thus, $1,500 of the reimbursement and the $1,500 of substantiated expenses are netted together and not reported. However, the excess $300 reimbursement is treated as being paid under a non accountable plan and, therefore, includible in Anthony's gross income. ◄

If an employee receives a reimbursement that is not as much as his expenses, a proration is required.

---

[29] Reg. Sec. 1.62-2(c).

[30] In Rev. Rul. 2006-56, 2006-2 C.B. 874, the IRS warned taxpayers that reimbursements from accountable plans must be properly substantiated and excess amounts must be returned to the employer. An accountable plan that reaches the level of a "pattern of abuse" will be reclassified as a nonaccountable plan.

EXAMPLE I:9-37 ► Fred, an employee, incurs employment-related expenses of $4,500 consisting of $1,200 business meals, $1,800 local transportation, and $1,500 entertainment of customers. He is only reimbursed $3,000 from his employer. Since the reimbursement is less than the amount of expenses, Fred must prorate the expenses as follows:

Expense	Total Amount	Reimbursed Expense[a]	Unreimbursed Expense
Business meals	$1,200	$ 800	$ 400
Local transportation	1,800	1,200	600
Entertainment	1,500	1,000	500
Total	$4,500	$3,000	$1,500

The reimbursed expenses of $3,000 are not reported by Fred and the $3,000 reimbursement is not reportable as income. The $1,500 of unreimbursed expenses are deductible *from* AGI (subject to 2% of AGI) as follows:

Business meals ($400 × 50%)	$ 200
Local transportation	600
Entertainment ($500 × 50%)	250
	$1,050

[a]Reimbursements are allocated to each expense category on a prorata basis. For example, the $800 for business meals is computed, $\frac{\$1,200}{\$4,500} \times \$3,000$. ◄

KEY POINT

Why does the government require reimbursements from nonaccountable plans to be included in the employee's gross income? Because these types of plans are often referred to as "expense accounts paid to employees as additional compensation."

Nonaccountable Plan. Under a nonaccountable plan, reimbursements are included in the employee's gross income and the expenses are deductible by the employee as miscellaneous itemized deductions, subject to the 2% of AGI floor and the 50% disallowance for meals and entertainment expenses.

EXAMPLE I:9-38 ► Use the same facts as in Example I:9-35 except that Bluechip does not require its employees to submit an accounting of expenses incurred. Bluechip's plan is a nonaccountable plan. Antoine must include the $1,500 in his gross income and may deduct the expenses as miscellaneous itemized deductions, subject to the 2% of AGI floor, in the amount of $1,400 [$800 + 450 + (200 × 50%) + 50]. ◄

Per Diem Allowances for Meals and Lodging. The IRS permits employers and employees to use optional "per diem allowances" for meals and lodging expenses in lieu of actual expenses. The use of per diem allowances is intended to simplify the burden of keeping detailed records for taxpayers who incur significant travel expenses. Special tables have been issued by the IRS that provide fixed per diem amounts for lodging as well as meals and incidental expenses (M&IE). The per diem allowances vary in amount depending on the city in which the travel took place. The tables list many cities in the United States as well as many cities in foreign countries. Thus, a taxpayer must only substantiate the time, place, and business purpose of the trip and then is permitted to use the per diem allowances. The per diem system is permitted only for payments under an accountable plan, the expenses must be reasonably expected to be incurred, and the amount of expenses should be in reasonable proximity to the expected actual expense amount.[31] A full discussion of this topic is outside the scope of this textbook.

EXAMPLE I:9-39 ► Peyton Boying is an employee of UT, Inc. UT maintains an accountable plan for reimbursing employees for their business expenses. Peyton travels extensively in the United States for business purposes. Instead of requiring Peyton to keep actual records of his travel expenses, UT reimburses Peyton the per diem amounts as allowed by the IRS. Assuming Peyton traveled exclusively in low-cost localities (see footnote below) and was away from home for 100 days, UT could reimburse Peyton in the amount of $17,200 (100 days × $172) without the necessity

---

[31] The IRS tables for per diem allowances paid on or after October 1, 2014, may be found in Notice 2014-57, 2014-41 IRB, or IRS Publication 1542, which is periodically updated. The rate for travel on or after October 1, 2014 for high-cost localities (specifically identified by the IRS) is $259 per day (including $65 for M&IE); low-cost localities are $172 per day (including $52 for M&IE). Further, self-employed individuals who are not reimbursed for their travel expenses may use the M&IE rate, but must substantiate lodging with actual receipts.

of Peyton keeping detailed records of his actual travel expenses. The amount that Peyton actually spent is irrelevant as the IRS will accept the per diem amounts. ◄

Table I:9-2 summarizes the concepts relating to employee business expenses and reimbursements.

▼ **TABLE I:9-2**
Treatment of Employee Reimbursements

TYPE OF PLAN	TAX EFFECT
ACCOUNTABLE PLAN	
Reimbursement = Expense	No effect, amounts are netted and not reported on employee's return.
Reimbursement > Expense	Not permissible under plan, but should it occur, excess reimbursement is included in employee's gross income.
Reimbursement < Expense	Expenses are prorated to amount of reimbursement. Reimbursed expenses—no effect; unreimbursed expenses are deductible as miscellaneous itemized deductions subject to 2% of AGI "floor" or nondeductible amount.
NONACCOUNTABLE PLAN	
Reimbursements	Always included in employee's gross income.
Expenses	Deductible as miscellaneous itemized deductions subject to 2% of AGI "floor" or nondeductible amount.

MOVING EXPENSES

OBJECTIVE 6

Identify deductible moving expenses and determine the amount and year of deductibility

Moving expenses are generally nondeductible personal expenditures. However, Sec. 217 allows a limited deduction for moving expenses for employees and self-employed people. The underlying rationale for this deduction is that such moves are similar to business expenditures because they are either employment-related or connected with a trade or business.

EXAMPLE I:9-40 ►

Ken retires from his job and moves from Tennessee to Arizona. His moving expenses are nondeductible personal expenditures because the move is not employment-related and he is not moving to look for a new job. ◄

ADDITIONAL COMMENT

In 2012, 1.1 million taxpayers deducted moving expenses totaling $3.1 billion.

Two conditions must be met for a moving expense to be deductible:[32]

▶ *Distance requirement.* The new job location must be at least 50 miles farther from the taxpayer's old residence than the old residence was from the former place of employment. If an individual has no former place of employment, the new job must be at least 50 miles from the old residence.

▶ *Time requirement.* A new or transferred employee must be employed on a full-time basis at the new location for at least 39 weeks during the 12-month period immediately following the move. More stringent requirements must be met by self-employed people who either work as an employee at the new location or continue to be self-employed. Such individuals are subject to a 78-week minimum work period during the first two years following the move. At least 39 of the 78 weeks must be in the first 12-month period. A waiver of the time requirements is permitted for both employees and self-employed individuals if the taxpayer becomes disabled, dies, or is

ADDITIONAL COMMENT

The time requirement test ensures that taxpayers cannot use temporary jobs as a pretext for deducting the cost of moving for personal reasons.

---

[32] The requirements for deducting moving expenses are contained in Sec. 217 and the Treasury Regulations thereunder.

involuntarily terminated (other than for willful misconduct). Unemployed or retired individuals are generally not able to deduct moving expenses because they do not meet the 39- or 78-week test.

EXAMPLE I:9-41 ► Ellen is employed by the Able Company in Dallas, Texas. She lives 30 miles from her place of employment in Dallas. If Ellen accepts a new job in Houston, the new job location is 270 miles from her former residence in Dallas. The 50-mile distance requirement is satisfied because the distance from her old residence to her new job in Houston exceeds the distance from her old residence to her old job by 240 miles (270 − 30). In addition, to meet the time requirement, Ellen must be employed on a full-time basis in Houston for at least 39 weeks during the 12-month period immediately following the move. ◄

EXAMPLE I:9-42 ► Assume the same facts as in Example I:9-41, except that Ellen accepts a new job and moves to a new residence in a small town outside of Dallas. Her new job location is 55 miles from her former residence. The 50-mile distance requirement is not met because the distance from her old residence to her new job is 55 miles and the distance from her old residence to her old job is 30 miles; thus, the excess distance is only 25 miles. ◄

ADDITIONAL COMMENT

The individual need not be employed at the location that he or she is leaving. For example, a graduating college student who has not been employed for the most recent four years could deduct moving costs if the distance requirement is satisfied and if he or she has been employed at the *new* location for the minimum time period.

EXPENSE CLASSIFICATION

Moving expenses of an employee or a self-employed individual are deductible *for* AGI.[33] Thus, a taxpayer may receive a tax benefit from the deduction of moving expenses even if the standard deduction is used in lieu of itemizing deductions.

DEFINITION OF MOVING EXPENSES

Direct Moving Expenses. Only direct moving expenses are deductible. These expenses are deductible without limit as long as they are reasonable in amount and include:

KEY POINT

The standard mileage rate for purposes of the moving expense deduction is only 23 cents per mile, compared to the 2015 standard business mileage rate of 57.5 cents per mile.

► The cost of moving household goods and personal effects from the former residence to the new residence (e.g., moving van).
► The cost of traveling (including lodging but excluding meals) from the former residence to the new residence. If the trip is by personal automobile, a deduction of 23 cents per mile (or actual expenses) is allowed for each automobile that is driven in 2015.

The expenses of moving household goods and personal effects do not include storage charges in excess of 30 days, penalties for breaking leases, mortgage penalties, expenses of refitting drapes, or losses on deposits and club memberships.[34]

EXAMPLE I:9-43 ► Gail, a resident of California and a college student in that state, graduates from college and accepts a new position with an accounting firm in Atlanta. Thus, Gail is an employee of the Atlanta firm. Because the move meets the distance requirement (i.e., more than 50 miles), Gail qualifies for the deduction if she also meets the 39-week time requirement. Gail incurs the following expenses pursuant to the move: moving van, $1,200; lodging en route, $400; automobile expenses, $598 (2,600 miles × $0.23 cents per mile); and tolls and parking, $25. Assuming these expenses are reasonable, they qualify as direct moving expenses and are deductible without limitation. The cost of any meals incurred by Gail en route is not deductible. ◄

Otherwise allowable expenses of any individual other than the taxpayer are taken into account only if the individual has both the former residence and the new residence as his principal place of abode and is a member of the taxpayer's household.

EXAMPLE I:9-44 ► Assume the same facts as in Example I:9-43 except that Gail's son Paul is a member of her household. Additional automobile expenses (including tolls and parking) of $275 are incurred during the move because Paul owns an automobile which is driven to the new location. The $275 of additional automobile expenses are deductible as moving expenses because Paul is a member of Gail's household and his principal place of abode includes both the former and the new residences. ◄

---

[33] Sec. 62(a)(15). For years before 1994 moving expenses were deductible *from* AGI as an itemized deduction (not subject to the 2% nondeductible floor).

[34] Reg. Sec. 1.217-2(b)(3). In-transit storage charges for up to 30 consecutive days are allowable moving expenses.

Nondeductible Indirect Moving Expenses. In addition to the disallowed moving expenses previously discussed (e.g., meals en route, storage charges, etc.), the following indirect or moving-related expense items are not deductible:

► Househunting trips including meals, lodging, and transportation

► Temporary living expenses at the new job location

► Qualified expenses related to a sale, purchase, or lease of a residence (e.g., attorney's fees, points, or payments to a lessor to cancel a lease)

TREATMENT OF EMPLOYER REIMBURSEMENTS

Moving expense reimbursements made by an employer, either paid directly or through reimbursement, are excluded from the employee's gross income as a qualified fringe benefit under Sec. 132 to the extent that the expenses meet the requirements for deductibility (i.e., the reimbursement is for moving expenses that are otherwise deductible under Sec. 217). Moving expense reimbursements must be included in gross income if the employee actually deducted the expenses in a prior tax year or if the expenses are otherwise not deductible under Sec. 217.[35]

EXAMPLE I:9-45 ► In 2015, Ralph incurs $2,400 of moving expenses related to moving household effects and traveling to his new residence. He also incurs $2,600 of nondeductible moving-related expenses (e.g., househunting trips and temporary living expenses). Ralph receives a $5,000 reimbursement from his employer. Of the total reimbursement, $2,400 is excluded from gross income as a Sec. 132 fringe benefit. However, the $2,600 reimbursement for nondeductible moving-related expenses is included in Ralph's gross income under Sec. 82. None of the $2,400 of moving expenses may be deducted by Ralph because they were reimbursed by his employer and were not included in Ralph's gross income. ◄

EDUCATION EXPENSES

OBJECTIVE 7

Describe the requirements for deducting education expenses

Generally, education expenses are considered personal expenses and, therefore, are not deductible despite the obvious benefits that accrue to society from the pursuit of such activities. However, education expenses that are necessary in the pursuit of an employment-related or trade or business activity are deductible. It would be inequitable if such educational expenditures were not deductible because they are incurred to produce income from employment or business activities. The education expenses discussed in this chapter pertain to expenses that are related to an individual's trade or business, such as a job in the case of an employee or the business of a self-employed individual. However, there are a number of other provisions in the tax law that provide favorable tax advantages for education expenses. Most of these rules are covered elsewhere in this textbook; however, the major tax provisions dealing with education are summarized below.

► Tax credits—two important provisions benefiting education are the American Opportunity Tax Credit and the Lifetime Learning Credit. Both of these items are credits and are available for the taxpayer and his dependents and are discussed in Chapter I:14.

ADDITIONAL COMMENT

Attendance at a convention or professional meeting is one of the most common deductible education expenses. Almost every profession or occupation has its own society or association. Often these organizations sponsor local, regional, or national meetings. Training sessions or other types of educational activities are normally included on the program.

► Exclusion for scholarships—scholarships received by students are generally excludable from gross income under Sec. 117. See the discussion of scholarships in Chapter I:4.

► Educational assistance for employees—if an employer maintains an educational assistance plan, amounts received by the employee for tuition and other expenses are excludable from the employee's gross income under Sec. 127. This exclusion is also discussed in Chapter I:4.

► Student loan interest—a *for* AGI deduction is permitted for certain student loan interest under Sec. 221. (See Chapter I:6 for a further discussion of this topic.)

[35] Sec. 82 and Sec. 132(g).

▶ Deduction for higher education expenses—taxpayers may deduct up to $4,000 *for* AGI for tuition and related expenses under Sec. 222.[36] This deduction, as is the case for the tax credits and the student loan interest, is subject to a phase-out based on AGI. If a taxpayer's AGI does not exceed $65,000 ($130,000 on a joint return), the taxpayer may deduct up to $4,000. However, taxpayer's with AGI exceeding $65,000 but not exceeding $80,000 may deduct up to $2,000 in qualified expenses. No deduction is permitted for taxpayers with AGI in excess of $80,000 ($160,000 on a joint return). Further, taxpayers are not permitted to claim this deduction and also claim one of the tax credits above using the same expenses.

▶ Qualified state tuition programs—a very popular program for higher income taxpayers is the use of so-called Section 529 plans. These plans allow taxpayers to invest funds to be used for education and the income earned on such funds is not subject to tax. When amounts are withdrawn from the plan, the amounts are also not taxable if used for qualified education expenses. These plans are discussed in Chapter I:4.

▶ Coverdell Education IRA—these special IRAs are discussed later in this chapter and enable a taxpayer to invest up to $2,000 per year in a tax-deferred IRA.

CLASSIFICATION OF EDUCATION EXPENSES

Depending on the nature of the education-related activity, educational expenses may be either personal and nondeductible, deductible *for* AGI, deductible *from* AGI (as a miscellaneous itemized deduction), or reimbursed by an employer and excluded from gross income. Table I:9-3 illustrates the tax consequences that are accorded to various types of education expenses depending on the facts and circumstances and the type of expenditure for each case.

The discussion below focuses on the deductibility of education expenses that are related to a taxpayer's trade or business.

▼ TABLE I:9-3
Classification and Tax Treatment of Educational Expenses

Situation Facts	Classification and Tax Treatment
▶ Jeremy is a college student who is not classified as an employee and is pursuing a general course of study.	▶ The expenses are nondeductible personal expenditures regardless of whether Jeremy or his parents pay them.
▶ Irene is an employee who incurs certain employment-related educational expenses including travel, transportation, tuition, and books. Her expenses are not reimbursed by her employer.	▶ If the expenses meet the two general deduction requirements, the education expenses are deductible *from* AGI as a miscellaneous itemized deduction (subject to the 2% nondeductible floor).
▶ Jesse is an employee who receives educational assistance payments from his employer to reimburse him for certain educational expenses incurred in attending college at the undergraduate level.	▶ Educational assistance payments up to $5,250 per excluded from Jesse's gross income and are deductible by the employer as trade or business expenses if the requirements of Sec. 127 are met.[37]
▶ Jackie is a self-employed CPA who incurs education expenses including travel, transportation, books, registration fees, and so on to attend a continuing education conference.	▶ All of the education expenses are deductible *for* AGI as trade or business expenses.
▶ Jim is an employee who incurs education expenses for a continuing education course related to his employment, and the expenses are reimbursed by the employer.	▶ The reimbursement is deductible by the employer as a trade or business expense. There is no tax effect to the employee because the education expenses are offset by the reimbursement.

---

[36] This deduction was scheduled to expire after December 31, 2013 but has been extended for one year through 2014.
[37] The Sec. 127 exclusion is applicable for expenses paid by an employer for courses taken by employees. Qualified expenses include tuition, fees, and related expenses. Both undergraduate and graduate-level courses qualify for the exclusion.

GENERAL REQUIREMENTS FOR A DEDUCTION

An employee generally may deduct education expenses if either of the following two requirements are met:[38]

▶ The expenditure is incurred to maintain or improve skills required by the individual in his or her employment, trade, or business; or

▶ The expenditure is incurred to meet requirements imposed by law or by the employer for retention of employment, rank, or compensation rate.

Even if one of the two requirements above are met, education expenses are not deductible if:

▶ The education is required to meet minimum educational requirements for qualification in the taxpayer's employment; or

▶ The education qualifies the taxpayer for a new trade or business (or employment activity).

The deductibility of education expenses has been a frequent source of controversy and litigation because of the uncertainty in interpreting the above Regulations. The principal area of disagreement has been the interpretation of the term "qualifies the taxpayer for a new trade or business." If a taxpayer undertakes education and that education will *qualify* her for a new trade or business, then her expenses will not be deductible. For example, several courts have disallowed deductions to IRS agents and accountants for educational expenses incurred in obtaining a law degree, even though such training would be helpful in the taxpayer's employment.[39] The courts reasoned that the taxpayers were qualifying for a new profession (i.e., the practice of law). However, the IRS has ruled that a practicing dentist may deduct educational expenses in becoming an orthodontist under the theory that a dentist becoming an orthodontist is not entering a new trade or business.[40]

? STOP & THINK

Question: The Regulations clearly provide that if the education "qualifies" a taxpayer for a new trade or business, the cost of such education is not deductible. If taken to the extreme, could the IRS argue that *any* course would qualify an individual for a new trade or business? For example, if a person took a basket weaving course, could not the IRS argue that the person is now qualified for the new trade or business of basket weaving? How can a taxpayer support his position that the education does not qualify him for a new trade or business in order to meet the deductibility requirements?

Solution: This is a difficult question and many commentators have written that the Regulations are unfairly harsh toward taxpayers. The courts have required that the IRS be "reasonable" in its interpretations of qualification of a new trade or business. The best way for a taxpayer to support his position is to find a case where the facts are approximately the same as the taxpayer's and where the court has upheld the taxpayer's position in that case.

Generally, a taxpayer must be employed or self-employed to be eligible for an education expense deduction. However, some courts have permitted individuals to qualify if they are unemployed for a temporary period.[41] School teachers have generally qualified for an education expense deduction in situations where the public school system requires advanced education courses as a condition for retention of employment or renewal of a teaching certificate or where state law imposes similar requirements. However, college instructors who are working on a doctorate in a college where the Ph.D. is the minimum degree for holding a permanent position generally have not been permitted to deduct the expenditures made to obtain the degree.[42] The Tax Court allowed a taxpayer to deduct the cost of earning an MBA because the education merely enhanced and maintained the skills he already had and did not qualify him for a new trade or business.[43]

---

[38] Reg. Sec. 1.162-5.
[39] *Jeffry L. Weiler,* 54 T.C. 398 (1970).
[40] Rev. Rul. 74-78, 1974-1 C.B. 44.
[41] *Robert J. Picknally,* 1977 PH T.C. Memo ¶77,321, 36 TCM 1292. The IRS has conceded that a deduction may be warranted in periods where the

cessation of business activity was for periods of a year or less (Rev. Rul. 68-591, 1968-2 C.B. 73).
[42] *Kenneth C. Davis,* 65 T.C. 1014 (1976).
[43] *Daniel R. Allemeier, Jr.,* TC Memo 2005-207.

EXAMPLE I:9-46 ▶ Jane is a self-employed dentist who incurs education expenses attending a continuing education conference on new techniques in her field. Such expenditures are incurred to maintain or improve her skills as a practicing dentist (a trade or business activity). All of her educational expenses are deductible *for* AGI because Jane is currently engaged in a trade or business activity. ◀

EXAMPLE I:9-47 ▶ Juan is a business executive who incurs education expenses in the pursuit of an MBA degree in management. None of the expenses are reimbursed by Juan's employer. The expenses are deductible because they are incurred to maintain or improve Juan's skills as a manager and do not qualify Juan for a new trade or business. All of Juan's education expenses (e.g., travel, transportation, tuition, books, and word processing) are deductible *from* AGI as a miscellaneous itemized deduction (subject to the 2% nondeductible floor). ◀

EXAMPLE I:9-48 ▶ Janet is a high school teacher who is required by state law to complete a specified number of additional graduate courses to renew her provisional teaching certificate. None of the expenses are reimbursed by Janet's employer. The educational expenses are deductible *from* AGI as a miscellaneous itemized deduction (subject to the 2% nondeductible floor) because the expenditures are incurred to meet the requirements imposed by law to retain her job and do not qualify her for a new trade or business. ◀

EXAMPLE I:9-49 ▶ Jean is an accountant with a public accounting firm who incurs expenses in connection with taking the CPA examination (e.g., CPA review course fees, travel, and transportation). None of the expenses are reimbursed by Jean's employer. Even though the expenditures may improve her employment-related skills, they are not deductible because they are incurred to meet the minimum educational standards for qualification in Jean's accounting position.[44] ◀

EXAMPLE I:9-50 ▶ Joy is a tax accountant who incurs expenses to obtain a law degree. Despite the fact that the law school courses may be helpful to Joy to maintain or improve her skills as a tax practitioner, such expenses are not deductible because the taxpayer is qualifying for a new trade or business. If Joy were not a degree candidate at the law school and merely took a few tax law courses for continuing education, the educational expenses would be deductible because they are incurred to maintain or improve Joy's skills as a tax specialist and do not qualify her for a new trade or business. In such a case, the expenses are deductible *for* AGI if Joy is self-employed and *from* AGI as a miscellaneous itemized deduction (subject to the 2% nondeductible floor) if Joy is an employee. ◀

KEY POINT

The deduction for travel expenses is not permitted if the travel itself is the educational activity. Therefore, a high school teacher who teaches Spanish cannot deduct expenses incurred in living in Madrid during the summer.

OFFICE IN HOME EXPENSES

OBJECTIVE 8

Determine whether the expenses of an office in home meet the requirements for deductibility and apply the gross income limitations

Employees or self-employed individuals who use a portion of their home for trade or business or employment-related activities should be entitled to a deduction because the property is used for trade or business or employment-related activities. However, it is often difficult to determine whether a taxpayer is using a portion of the home for business or personal use.

For many years, there has been an ongoing controversy in the tax law as to the deductibility of office in home expenses. Because of the possibility of abuse by taxpayers, the IRC, Treasury Regulations, and the courts[45] have been extremely strict as to who qualifies to deduct office in home expenses. In order to promote fairness and consistency in the tax law, the definition of an office in home that qualifies for a tax deduction was expanded in 1998.

ADDITIONAL COMMENT

Approximately 28 million individuals, or 19% of the work force, work at least part-time at home.

GENERAL REQUIREMENTS FOR A DEDUCTION

Employees and self-employed individuals are permitted to deduct office in home expenses only if the office is exclusively used on a regular basis under any of the following conditions:

▶ The office is used as the principal place of business for *any* trade or business of the taxpayer;

---

[44] Rev. Rul. 69-292, 1969-1 C.B. 84.

[45] See, for example, *CIR v. Nader E. Soliman*, 71 AFTR 2d 93-463, 93-1 USTC 50,014 (USSC, 1993).

▶ The office is used as a place for meeting or dealing with patients, clients, or customers in the normal course of business; or

▶ If the office in home is located in a separate structure which is not attached to the dwelling unit, the office is used exclusively and regularly in connection with the taxpayer's trade or business.[46]

In addition to meeting any of these tests, an employee further must prove that the exclusive use is for the convenience of the *employer*. It is not enough that it is merely appropriate or helpful to the employee.

The first condition above has caused the major controversy in this area. Taxpayers are required to prove that the office is used exclusively as the "principal place of business." Under prior law, the principal place of business was interpreted to mean the "most important or significant place for the business," or more precisely, where the primary services were performed.

EXAMPLE I:9-51 ▶ In the *Soliman* case, Dr. Soliman was a self-employed anesthesiologist who performed medical services at three hospitals, none of which provided him with an office. He spent approximately two hours per day in his office in home where he maintained patient records and correspondence and he performed billing procedures. The office was not used as a place for meeting with or dealing with patients, clients, or customers in the normal course of his business. The U.S. Supreme Court denied a deduction for Dr. Soliman's office in home because it concluded that the essence of professional service rendered by the doctor was the actual medical treatment in the hospitals. A second factor considered by the court was the amount of time spent at the office relative to the total work effort. The effect of this case was to deny a deduction for an office in home for any type of taxpayer in a trade or business where the primary services were performed outside of the office (such as plumbers, electricians). This case was highly criticized. ◄

To combat the perceived unfairness of the *Soliman* case, Congress expanded the definition of "principal place of business" for tax years beginning after December 31, 1998. An office in home now qualifies as a taxpayer's principal place of business if:

1. the office is used by the taxpayer for *administrative or management* activities of the taxpayer's trade or business, and
2. there is no other fixed location of the trade or business where the taxpayer conducts substantial administrative or management activities of the trade or business.[47]

Thus, the law essentially allows a deduction for an office in home even though the taxpayer provides his primary service away from the office. The above tests are clearly intended for self-employed taxpayers. However, they also apply to employees except that the additional "convenience of the employer" test will still apply.

EXAMPLE I:9-52 ▶ David is a self-employed electrician who performs his electrical services at the location of his customers. He also maintains an office where he does his administrative and management duties. David is permitted a deduction for an office in home even though his primary duties of providing electrical services are performed away from his office. ◄

EXAMPLE I:9-53 ▶ Barbara is an employee of DRK, Inc., and is provided with an office on DRK's premises. However, Barbara's job requires significant administrative work after normal working hours and she prefers to perform these duties in her office at home. Barbara may not deduct the costs of her office in home because she uses her office at home for *her* convenience, not her employer's convenience. ◄

As can be seen from the discussion above, the deduction for an office in home is generally restricted to self-employed taxpayers and employees who are not provided with an office by their employer. If a self-employed taxpayer maintains an office in home, the expenses are deductible *for* AGI. Employees must deduct the office in home expenses as miscellaneous itemized deductions, subject to the 2% nondeductible floor.

DEDUCTIONS AND LIMITATIONS

The deduction for home office expenses is computed using the following two categories of expenses: (1) Expenses directly related to the office, and (2) Expenses indirectly related to the office.

---

[46] Sec. 280A(c)(1).
[47] Ibid. For years before 1999, this new definition of principal place of business does not apply. Thus, the restrictive rules promulgated by *Soliman* apply to these years.

Direct expenses include expenses that relate solely to the office, such as painting and decorating just the office. Indirect expenses are the pro rata share of expenses that benefit the entire house or apartment, such as mortgage interest (or rent), real estate taxes, insurance, utilities, and maintenance. The office in the home expense is the sum of the direct expenses plus the pro rata share (generally based on square footage) of indirect expenses.

To compute the office in home deduction, taxpayers first subtract all expenses not connected with the office from the income generated by the business. Then, 100% of the direct expenses of the office and the percentage of indirect expenses based on the pro rata share of the house are deducted. The total of the office in home expenses cannot create a loss.

EXAMPLE I:9-54 ▶

TAX STRATEGY TIP

When a taxpayer depreciates his office in the home, the office becomes business property. Upon the sale of the residence, the portion of the sale price attributable to the office will not be eligible for the sale of principal residence exclusion. Therefore, taxpayers might consider only deducting direct expenses of an in-home office to preserve the exclusion.

Julie works as a full-time employee for a local company. She also operates a mail order business out of her home and maintains an office in her home that is used exclusively for business. The size of her home in total is 2,400 square feet and her office is 300 square feet. During the current year, she generated gross income of $18,000 and had $6,000 of business expenses, supplies, and shipping charges. She also had the following expenses in connection with the office in her home:

Painting of office	$ 600
Decorations in office	900
Mortgage interest (total)	3,200
Real estate taxes (total)	1,800
Insurance (total)	600
Utilities (total)	2,400
Depreciation (total)	800

Julie's home office expense for the current year would be computed as follows:

Direct expenses:		
Painting	$ 600	
Decorations	900	$1,500
Indirect expenses:		
Mortgage interest	3,200	
Real estate taxes	1,800	
Insurance	600	
Utilities	2,400	
Depreciation	800	
	8,800	
Business percentage (300/2,400)	×12.5%	1,100
Total expense for office in home		$2,600

Julie would be allowed to deduct the $2,600 of office in home expenses as they do not exceed the $12,000 ($18,000 − $6,000) of income from the business. If Julie only had $8,000 of gross income and $6,000 of business expenses, her office in home expenses of $2,600 would be limited to $2,000. ◀

As mentioned above, the total allowable office in home expenses may not exceed the taxpayer's net income from the business (or rental) activity.[48] This ceiling limitation on office in home deductions is intended to prevent taxpayers from recognizing tax losses if the business (or rental) activity does not produce sufficient amounts of gross income. Expenses disallowed because of the gross income limitation can be carried forward but are subject to the gross income limitation in the later year and are subject to specific ordering rules.[49]

In early 2013, the IRS issued Rev. Proc. 2013-13, 2013-6 IRB (01/15/2013), which provides for an optional safe harbor that individuals can use to determine the amount of their deductible home office expenses. This safe harbor is effective for tax years beginning on or after January 1, 2013, and the same strict rules as to eligibility for a home office deduction, as discussed previously, will continue to apply. The safe harbor allows taxpayers the option of claiming as their home office deduction $5 times the square feet of qualified use (300 square feet maximum), for a maximum total deduction of $1,500.

TYPICAL MISCONCEPTION

Where a taxpayer is not entitled to an office-in-home deduction, the taxpayer can still deduct directly related business expenses (e.g., the cost of office supplies, and a MACRS deduction on filing cabinets and other equipment).

[48] Sec. 280A(c)(5). Technically, the limitation is gross income less deductions not connected with the home office.
[49] See Prop. Reg. Sec. 1.280A-2 for the ordering rules. These rules are similar, but not identical to the ordering rules for hobby losses under Sec. 183,

as follows: (1) mortgage interest and real estate taxes; (2) other deductions related to the office, such as insurance and utilities; and (3) depreciation.

Taxpayers can alternate the use of the actual expenses or the safe harbor amount each year. So, taxpayers will need to analyze each year which method to use and claim the greater amount.

Employee expense classifications and deduction limitations are summarized in Topic Review I:9-1.

TOPIC REVIEW I:9-1

Classification and Deductibility of Employee Expenses

TYPE OF EXPENDITURE	50% DISALLOWANCE	FOR OR FROM AGI	OTHER LIMITATIONS
Miscellaneous itemized deductions	Applies to unreimbursed meals and entertainment	*From* AGI	Subject to 2% of AGI nondeductible floor.
Reimbursed travel expenses (adequate accounting is made)	Applies to the employer for meals portion of the travel only	*For* AGI	2% of AGI nondeductible floor applies only to employee expenses that exceed the reimbursement.
Unreimbursed travel expenses	Applies to meals portion of travel only	*From* AGI	Subject to the 2% of AGI nondeductible floor. Employee must be away from his or her tax home overnight.
Automobile expenses	Not applicable	*From* AGI	Subject to the 2% of AGI nondeductible floor. Actual costs or the standard mileage rate method may be used.
Moving expenses	Not applicable because meals are not deductible	*For* AGI	Indirect moving-related expenses are not deductible.
Entertainment expenses	Applies to all entertainment expenses	*From* AGI	Subject to the 2% of AGI nondeductible floor. Club dues and initiation fees are not deductible.
Education expenses deductible per Reg. Sec. 1.162-5	Applies to meal portion of education expenses	*From* AGI	Qualifying expenses are subject to the 2% of AGI nondeductible floor.
Office-in-home	Not applicable	*From* AGI; If trade- or business-related, the expenses are for AGI	Employment-related expenses (other than real estate taxes and interest) are subject to the 2% of AGI nondeductible floor. Gross income limitations apply to allowable expenses.

DEFERRED COMPENSATION

OBJECTIVE 9

Discuss the tax treatment and requirements for various deferred compensation arrangements

Various types of benefit plans providing favorable tax treatment are available to employees and self-employed individuals. These tax benefits are provided to stimulate savings accumulations necessary for retirement. Private retirement plans should be the primary source of retirement with the Social Security system as a supplement, although in recent years, more and more retirees rely increasingly on Social Security. Favorable tax consequences generally include the following benefits:

▶ Deferral of taxes on amounts contributed to retirement plans until the individual retires or receives a distribution from the plan

▶ An immediate deduction for contributions to qualified retirement plans for the employer or self-employed individual

▶ Deferral of taxation on income earned on retirement plan assets

▶ Tax-free distributions from certain types of plans (Roth-type plans)

This section discusses *deferred compensation arrangements* including qualified pension and profit sharing plans, nonqualified deferred compensation arrangements, and self-employed retirement plans and individual retirement accounts (IRAs).

QUALIFIED PENSION AND PROFIT-SHARING PLANS

ADDITIONAL COMMENT

The Staff of the Joint Committee on Taxation estimates the revenue loss resulting from the deferral of taxes on contributions and earnings for qualified employer plans, individual retirement plans, and Keogh plans for 2012 will approximate $138 billion. This provision represents one of the largest tax expenditures of the federal government and is designed to encourage employers to establish retirement plans for their employees.

The federal tax law provides favorable tax benefits for *qualified* pension and profit-sharing plans. A **qualified plan** is one that must meet strict requirements, such as not discriminating in favor of highly compensated individuals, be formed and operated for the exclusive benefit of employees, and meet specified vesting and funding requirements. In a qualified plan, both the employer and employee receive significant tax benefits, as follows:

Employer: receives an immediate tax deduction for pension and profit-sharing contributions made on behalf of employees.

Employee: is not taxed on either employer or employee contributions or earnings of the plan assets until funds are withdrawn from the plan at retirement.[50] Thus, funds invested in a qualified plan grow tax-free during an employee's working years. Alternatively, in recent years, Roth-type plans do not allow a deduction for the employee, but all distributions at retirement age can be withdrawn completely tax free.

Types of Plans. Qualified plans[51] include:

► Pension plans
► Profit-sharing plans (including Sec. 401(k) plans)
► Stock bonus plans, including employee stock ownership plans (ESOPs)

Pension Plans. The features that distinguish a *qualified pension plan* include the following:

► Systematic and definite payments are made to a pension trust (without regard to profits) based on formulas or actuarial methods.
► A pension plan may provide for incidental benefits such as disability, death, or medical insurance benefits.

A pension plan may be either contributory or noncontributory. Under a **noncontributory pension plan**, the contributions are made solely by the employer. Under a **contributory pension plan**, the employee makes voluntary contributions into the plan that supplement any contributions made by the employer.

Pension plans also may be either defined contribution plans or defined benefit plans. In a **defined contribution pension plan**, a separate account is established for each participant and certain amounts are contributed based on a specific formula (e.g., a specified percentage of compensation). The benefits payable to the participant at retirement are based on the value of the participant's account (including the amount of earnings that accrue to the account) at the time of retirement.

EXAMPLE I:9-55 ►

Alabama Corporation establishes a qualified pension plan for its employees that provides for employer contributions equal to 8% of each participant's salary. Retirement payments to each participant are based on the amount of accumulated benefits in the employee's account at the retirement date. The pension plan is a defined contribution plan, because the contribution rate is based on a specific and fixed percentage of compensation. ◄

KEY POINT

The trend for most companies in the U.S. is away from defined benefit plans and toward defined contribution plans. Defined contribution plans usually are less costly and the employer liability is fixed at the date of contribution rather than at some future date.

Defined benefit plans establish a contribution formula based on actuarial techniques that are sufficient to fund a fixed benefit amount to be paid upon retirement. For example, a defined benefit plan might provide fixed retirement benefits equal to 40% of an employee's average salary for the five years before retirement.

A distinguishing feature of a defined benefit plan is that forfeitures of unvested amounts (e.g., due to employee resignations) must be used to reduce the employer contributions that would otherwise be made under the plan. In a defined contribution plan, however, the forfeitures related to unvested amounts may either be reallocated to the other participants in a nondiscriminatory manner or used to reduce future employer contributions.

---

[50] An employee may not be liable for federal income taxes but may be subject to Social Security taxes and possibly local or city income taxes.

[51] Qualified plans are generally covered in Secs. 401-417 of the IRC.

Profit-Sharing Plans. A qualified **profit-sharing plan** also may be established by an employer in addition to, or in lieu of, a qualified pension plan arrangement. Profit-sharing plans include the following distinguishing features:

► A definite, predetermined formula must be used to allocate employer contributions to individual employees and to establish benefit payments.

► Annual employer contributions are not required, but substantial and recurring contributions must be made to satisfy the requirement that the plan be permanent.

► Employees may be given the option to receive cash that is fully taxable as current compensation or to defer taxation on employer contributions by having such amounts contributed to the profit-sharing trust. Plans of this type are called Sec. 401(k) plans.[52]

► Forfeitures arising under the plan may be reallocated to the remaining participants to increase their profit-sharing benefits, provided that certain nondiscrimination requirements are met.

► Lump-sum payments made to an employee before retirement may be provided following a prescribed period for the vesting of such amounts.

► Incidental benefits such as disability, death, or medical insurance may also be provided in a profit-sharing arrangement.

Roth-type Plans. **Roth-type plans** are a special type of back-loaded plan. Under such a plan, a taxpayer does not receive a current deduction for any current contribution to the plan, but does not include any qualified distribution from the plan in gross income. The best known of this type of plan is a Roth IRA which was first enacted in 1998 and very popular today. A discussion of Roth IRAs is presented later in this chapter. More recently, in 2006, Congress extended the Roth concept to Sec. 401(k) plans where employees can contribute funds to a Roth 401(k) plan.[53] Similar to Roth IRAs, the employee receives no current tax deduction, but all contributions plus all earnings in the plan grow tax-free. Thus, any qualified distributions (generally, distributions after age 59½) are received tax-free by taxpayer. Participants in 401(k), 403(b), or 457 plans are permitted to roll over amounts in the plan to a "qualified Roth contribution program" for tax years after December 31, 2012.

Stock Bonus Plan. A **stock bonus plan** is a special type of defined contribution plan whereby the investments of the plan are in the employer-company's own stock. The employer makes its contribution to the trust either in cash or in stock. If in cash, the amounts are invested in the company's stock. The stock is allocated and subsequently distributed to the participants. Stock bonus plan requirements are similar to profit-sharing plans. An **employee stock ownership plan (ESOP)** is a type of qualified stock bonus plan.[54] An ESOP, funded by a combination of employer and employee contributions and plan loans, invest primarily in employer stock. The stock is held for the benefit of the employees. ESOPs are attractive because the employer is allowed to reduce taxable income by deducting any dividends that are paid to the participants (or their beneficiaries) in the year such amounts are paid and are taxable to the participant. For employer securities acquired by the ESOP, the dividends-paid deduction is limited to dividends paid on employer stock acquired with an ESOP loan.

ADDITIONAL COMMENT
The tax law with respect to qualified pension and profit-sharing plans is extremely complex. A detailed study of these provisions is beyond the scope of this text.

QUALIFICATION REQUIREMENTS FOR A QUALIFIED PLAN

Qualified pension, profit-sharing, and stock bonus plans must meet complex qualification rules and requirements to achieve and maintain their favored qualifying status. A summary of the important requirements are discussed below.

► Section 401(a) requires that the plan must be for the employee's exclusive benefit. For example, the trust must follow prudent investment rules to ensure that the pension benefits will accrue for the employees' benefit.

► The plan may not discriminate in favor of highly compensated employees. Highly compensated employees are employees who meet either of two tests: (1) own more

---

[52] Sec. 401(k).
[53] Sec. 402A. For 2015, the maximum contribution limit to Roth 401(k) plans is $18,000 ($24,000 for taxpayers 50 years and older).

[54] Secs. 409(a) and 4975(e)(7).

than 5% of the corporation's stock in either the current or prior year or (2) receive compensation of greater than $120,000 in the prior year.[55]

▶ Contributions and plan benefits must bear a uniform relationship to the compensation payments made to covered employees. For example, if contributions for the benefit of the participants are based on a fixed percentage of the employee's compensation (e.g., 4%), the plan should not be disqualified despite the fact that the contributions for highly-compensated employees are greater on an actual dollar basis than those for lower paid individuals.

▶ Certain coverage requirements that are expressed in terms of a portion of the employees covered by the plan must be met.

▶ An employee's right to receive benefits from the employer's contributions must vest (i.e., become nonforfeitable) after a certain period or number of years of employment. The vesting requirement is intended to ensure that a significant percentage of employees will eventually receive retirement benefits. Employer-provided benefits must be 100% vested after 5 years of service.[56] In all cases, any employee contributions to the plan must vest immediately.

EXAMPLE I:9-56 ▶ Ken is a participant in a noncontributory qualified pension plan that provides for no vesting until an employee completes three years of service. Ken terminates his employment with the company after two years of service. Because Ken has not met the minimum vesting requirements, he is not entitled to receive any of the employer contributions that are made on his behalf. ◀

ADDITIONAL COMMENT

Most employees choose to contribute amounts to their qualified retirement plans on a pre-tax basis because of the time value of money. A current deduction (and the related tax savings) is more valuable than a deduction at retirement.

TAX TREATMENT TO EMPLOYEES AND EMPLOYERS

Employer contributions to a qualified plan are immediately deductible (subject to specific limitations on contribution amounts), and earnings on pension fund investments are tax-exempt to the plan. Amounts paid into a plan by or for an employee are not taxable until the pension payments are received, normally at retirement. At the election of the employee, amounts may be treated as having been made from either pre-tax or after-tax earnings. If amounts contributed to a qualified plan by an employee are made on a pre-tax basis, the taxable portion of the employee's earnings is reduced by the contribution amount. This has the effect of permitting a deduction for the contribution amount. When amounts are withdrawn at retirement, the entire distribution is subject to taxation.

EXAMPLE I:9-57 ▶ Larry is an employee of Cisco Corporation, which maintains a Sec. 401(k) plan. Larry contributes 5% of his gross salary into the plan on a pre-tax basis. During the current year, Larry's gross salary is $80,000 so his Sec. 401(k) contribution is $4,000. Since Larry's contribution is made on a pre-tax basis, his taxable salary for the current year will be $76,000. In effect, Larry is able to deduct the $4,000 from his salary in the current year. When Larry retires and begins withdrawing amounts from the plan, the entire amount withdrawn will be subject to income taxation. ◀

Conversely, an employee may elect to contribute to a qualified plan on an after-tax basis. If, in Example I:9-57, Larry contributed to the Sec. 401(k) plan on an after-tax basis, his taxable salary would have been $80,000. The $4,000 contributed to the plan is treated as an investment in the plan and is considered a tax-free return of capital when this amount is withdrawn at retirement.[57]

Employee Retirement Payments. An employee's retirement benefits, other than from Roth-type plans, are generally taxed under the Sec. 72 annuity rules (see Chapter I:3). If the plan is noncontributory (i.e., no employee contributions are made to the plan), all of the pension benefits when received by the employee are fully taxable. If the plan is contributory, the taxability depends on whether the employee's contributions were made on a

---

[55] Sec. 414(q). The $120,000 applicable in 2015 is subject to annual indexing for inflation. The amount for 2013 and 2014 was $115,000. Alternatively, an employer may elect to define a highly- compensated group as employees earning more than $120,000 *and* the top 20% group of employees based on compensation.

[56] Sec. 411(a)(2)(A). An alternative vesting schedule may also be used that provides for 20% vesting each year beginning in the third year of service, Sec. 411(a)(2)(B). Thus, after a total of seven years of service, an employee would

be 100% vested. In addition, a faster vesting schedule is provided in Sec. 411(a)(2)(B) whereby the vesting begins after two years of service and increases at a rate of 20% per year to 100% after six years.

[57] Amounts contributed to a qualified plan on an after-tax basis are treated as an investment in the contract under the annuity rules of Sec. 72. Amounts withdrawn during retirement are taxed under the general rules of Sec. 72. (See Chapter I:3 for a discussion of taxation of annuities.)

pre-tax or after-tax basis. If the contributions were made on a pre-tax basis, *all* retirement payments received by the employee are taxable. Alternatively, if the contributions were made on an after-tax basis, each payment is treated, in part, as a tax-free return of the employee's contributions and the remainder is taxable. The excluded portion is based on the ratio of the employee's investment in the contract to the expected return under the contract. However, the total amount that may be excluded is limited to the amount of the employee's contributions to the plan. If the employee dies before the entire investment in the contract is recovered, the unrecovered amount is allowed as an itemized deduction in the year of death.

As mentioned earlier, qualified distributions from a Roth-type plan, such as a Roth 401(k), are not subject to taxation. Qualified distributions are those that have been invested in the plan for at least five years and the employee is at least age 59½.

EXAMPLE I:9-58 ▶ Kevin retires in 2015 at age 64 and will receive monthly annuity payments of $2,000 for life from his employer's qualified pension plan beginning in January, 2016. Kevin's investment in the contract (represented by his contributions made on an after-tax basis) is $100,000. Kevin's life expectancy per Sec. 72 is 260 months from the annuity starting date. So, for the next 260 months, Kevin can exclude $384.62 ($100,000/260 months). In 2016, Kevin would exclude $4,615.44 ($384.62 × 12 months) and $19,384.56 ($24,000.00 − $4,615.44) would be taxable. After Kevin receives payments for 260 months and his $100,000 investment in the contract is recovered, all subsequent payments are fully taxable. (See Chapter I:3 for a discussion of the annuity formula and related rules.) ◀

EXAMPLE I:9-59 ▶ Assume the same facts as in Example I:9-58 except that Kevin made all of his contributions to the plan on a pre-tax basis. In other words, the amount that he contributed to the plan was subtracted from his salary each year. When Kevin starts receiving payments from the plan, all amounts received will be taxable. Therefore, in 2016, Kevin will include $24,000 in his gross income. Most employees elect to "tax defer" their contributions into retirement plans in order to reduce their current year taxable income and take advantage of the time value of money principle. ◀

EXAMPLE I:9-60 ▶ Keith, age 61 and still employed, has maintained a Roth 401(k) plan for 10 years. All of his contributions into the plan, therefore, have been made on a post-tax basis. Keith may contribute $24,000 into his Roth 401(k) for 2015. The maximum contribution is generally $18,000, but Keith is allowed an additional $6,000 catch-up contribution as he is 50 years old or older. ◀

KEY POINT

For purposes of the limitation on employer contributions, all defined contribution plans maintained by one employer are treated as a single defined contribution plan. Furthermore, under some circumstances a group of employers can be treated as a single employer.

ADDITIONAL COMMENT

Many individuals have the option of taking their retirement savings from traditional pensions, profit-sharing plans, and 401(k)s as a lump sum or an annuity. Those who want to take a lump-sum distribution can delay taxes by transferring the money directly into a tax-deferred IRA.

Limitation on Employer Contributions. The Code places limitations on (1) amounts an employer may contribute to qualified pension, profit-sharing, and stock bonus plans and (2) amounts that the employer may deduct:

▶ Defined contribution plan contributions in 2015 are limited to the lesser of $53,000 or 100% of the employee's compensation.[58]

▶ Defined benefit plans are restricted to an annual benefit to an employee equal to the lesser of $210,000 for 2015 or 100% of the participant's average compensation for the highest three years.[59]

▶ An overall maximum annual employer deduction of 25% of compensation paid or accrued to plan participants is placed on defined contribution, profit-sharing, and stock bonus plans.[60] If an employer has more than one type of qualified plan (e.g., a defined benefit pension plan and a profit-sharing plan), a maximum deduction of 25% of compensation is allowed.

The distinguishing features and major requirements for qualified pension and profit-sharing plans are summarized in Topic Review I:9-2.

---

[58] Sec. 415(c). The deduction limit for 2014 was $52,000. In addition, individuals over 50 years of age are now eligible to contribute extra amounts into their plans. The amount of the so-called catch-up contributions depend on the type of plan.
[59] Sec. 415(b)(1). The benefit amount for 2014 was also $210,000. These amounts are subject to indexing each year. For participants who separated

from service before January 1, 2015, the 100% average is computed by multiplying the participant's compensation limitation by 1.0178.
[60] Sec. 404(a)(3)(A).

TOPIC REVIEW I:9-2

Qualified Pension and Profit-Sharing Plans

DISTINGUISHING FEATURES AND MAJOR REQUIREMENTS

▶ Employer contributions and earnings on contributed amounts are not taxed to employees until distributed or made available. The contributions are immediately deductible by the employer.

▶ Pension plans can be established as either defined contribution or defined benefit plans in which systematic and definite payments are made to a pension trust. Incidental benefits (e.g., death and disability payments) can be provided under the plan.

▶ Profit-sharing plans require the use of a predetermined allocation formula and substantial and recurring contributions must be made although annual employer contributions are not required and the contributions need not be based on profits. Section 401(k) plans can be established where employees have the option to receive cash or to have such amounts contributed to the profit-sharing trust. The employer may also establish an ESOP where the plan is funded by a contribution of the employer's stock.

▶ Qualified plans must be created for the employees' exclusive benefit.

▶ The plans may not discriminate in favor of highly compensated employees.

▶ Contributions and plan benefits must bear a uniform relationship to the compensation of covered employees.

▶ Minimum vesting requirements must be met (e.g., 100% vesting after five years).

▶ Employee benefits are taxed under the Sec. 72 annuity rules.

▶ Total employer contributions to the plan are subject to specific ceiling limitations.

KEY POINT

Because nonqualified plans are not subject to the same restrictions as imposed upon qualified plans, they do not receive the same tax benefits that are available under qualified plans. For example, the employer may not be able to deduct amounts that are set aside for employees.

NONQUALIFIED PLANS

Nonqualified deferred compensation plans are often used by employers to provide incentives or supplementary retirement benefits for executives. Common forms of nonqualified plans include the following:

▶ An unfunded, nonforfeitable promise to pay fixed amounts of compensation in future periods.[61]

▶ Restricted property plans involving property transfers (usually in the form of the employer-company stock), where the property transferred is subject to a substantial risk of forfeiture and is nontransferable.[62]

Distinguishing Characteristics of Nonqualified Plans. Nonqualified plans are not subject to the same restrictions imposed on qualified plans (such as the nondiscrimination and vesting rules), although nonqualified plans may have some vesting rules. Thus, such plans are particularly suitable for use in executive compensation planning. In general, nonqualified plans impose certain restrictions on the outright transfer of the plan's benefits to the employee. This avoids immediate taxation under the constructive receipt doctrine, which does not apply if the benefits are not yet credited, set apart, or made available so that the employee may draw on them. The amount is taxed to the employee upon the lapse of such restrictions, and the employer receives a corresponding deduction in the same year.

Unfunded Deferred Compensation Plans. Unfunded deferred compensation plans are often used to compensate highly compensated employees who desire to defer the recognition of income until future periods (e.g., a professional athlete or a business executive who receives a signing bonus may prefer to defer the recognition of income from the bonus). In general, if the promise to make the compensation payment in a future period is nonforfeitable, the agreement must not be funded (e.g., the transfer of assets to a trust for the employee's benefit) or evidenced by a negotiable note. The employer, however, may establish an *escrow account* on behalf of the employee. Such an account is used to accumulate and invest the deferred compensation amounts. If the requirements for deferral are met, the employee is taxed when the amounts are actually paid or made available, and the employer receives a corresponding deduction in the same year.[63]

---

[61] Rev. Rul. 60-31, 1960-1 C.B. 174, modified by Rev. Rul. 64-279, 1964-2 C.B. 121 and Rev. Rul. 70-435, 1970-2 C.B. 100.

[62] Sec. 83.
[63] Reg. Sec. 1.451-2(a).

EXAMPLE I:9-61 ▶ In 2015, Kelly signs an employment contract to play professional football for the Chicago Skyhawks. The contract includes a $2,000,000 signing bonus that is payable in five annual installments beginning in 2019. The bonus agreement is nonforfeitable and is unfunded. The Skyhawks have agreed to place sufficient amounts of money into an escrow account to fund the future payments to Kelly. None of the $2,000,000 bonus is deductible by the employer or taxable to Kelly when the agreement is signed in 2015. The Skyhawks do not receive a deduction for any amounts that are deposited into the escrow account during the 2015–2018 period. In 2019, Kelly receives $400,000 taxable compensation (plus interest, if any, that accrued and was paid to Kelly is also taxable) upon receipt of the initial payment, and the Skyhawks receive a corresponding tax deduction. ◀

Requirements were enacted several years ago for nonqualified deferred compensation plans.[64] While a detailed examination of these new rules is outside the scope of this textbook, some major features of the law are as follows:

▶ The rules apply to any plan by which executive employees are permitted to defer the receipt and taxability of compensation from the current year to a future year. In prior years, the tax laws in this area were a wide range of cases and rulings.

▶ If deferred amounts under a plan fail to satisfy the requirements at any time during the tax year, the recipient must pay the tax on the deferred compensation plus interest and an additional 20% excise tax.

▶ Distributions from the plan to recipients are subject to strict rules. Deferrals may be distributed to participants no earlier than the time of separation of service, pursuant to a fixed schedule in the plan, death, disability, an unforeseeable emergency, or upon a change in control of the company. Thus, early distributions are not generally permitted. In addition, acceleration of payment amounts are severely curtailed.

▶ Funding rules essentially have remained the same except that employers generally may no longer use offshore trusts.

Because of the complexity of the rules in this area, taxpayers are strongly urged to look closely at their nonqualified deferred compensation plans to ensure that they comply with the rules.

Restricted Property Plans. **Restricted property plans** are used to attract and retain key executives. Under such arrangements, the executive generally obtains an ownership interest (i.e., stock) in the corporation. Restricted property plans are governed by the income recognition rules contained in Sec. 83. Under these rules, the receipt of restricted property in exchange for services rendered is not taxable if the property is nontransferable and subject to a substantial risk of forfeiture.

The employee is treated as receiving taxable compensation based on the amount of the property's fair market value (FMV) (less any amount paid for the property) at the earlier of the time the property is no longer subject to a substantial risk of forfeiture or is transferable. The employer receives a corresponding compensation deduction at the same time the income is taxed to the employee.

EXAMPLE I:9-62 ▶ In 2015, Allied Corporation transfers 1,000 shares of its common stock to employee Karen as compensation pursuant to a restricted property plan. The FMV of the Allied stock is $10 per share on the transfer date. The restricted property agreement provides that the stock is nontransferable by Karen until the year 2017 (i.e., Karen cannot sell the stock to outsiders until year 2017). The stock is also subject to the restriction that if Karen voluntarily leaves the company before the year 2017, she must transfer the shares back to the company and will receive no benefit from the stock other than from the receipt of dividends. The FMV of the stock is $100 per share in year 2017 when the forfeiture and nontransferability restrictions lapse. Because the stock is both nontransferable and subject to a substantial risk of forfeiture from the issue date to year 2017, the tax consequences from the stock transfer are deferred for both Karen and Allied Corporation until the lapse of the nontransferability or forfeiture restrictions in year 2017. Thus, no tax consequences result in 2015 or 2016. In year 2017, Karen must report ordinary (compensation) income of $100,000 ($100 × 1,000 shares), and Allied Corporation is entitled to a corresponding compensation deduction of the same amount. Karen is taxed currently on the dividends she receives because they are not subject to any restrictions. ◀

---

[64] Sec. 409A.

Election to Be Taxed Immediately. An exception which permits an employee to elect (within 30 days after the receipt of restricted property) to recognize income immediately upon receipt of the restricted property is provided in Sec. 83(b). If the election is made, the employer is entitled to a corresponding deduction at the time the income is taxed to the employee. This election is frequently made when the fair market value of the restricted property is expected to increase significantly in the future and the future gain would be taxed as long-term capital gain.

EXAMPLE I:9-63 ►

Assume the same facts as Example I:9-62, except that Karen elects to recognize income in 2015 (i.e., the transfer date). Karen must include $10,000 ($10 × 1,000 shares) in gross income as compensation in the current year and Allied Corporation is entitled to a corresponding deduction in the same year. Karen will report no income in 2017 when the restrictions lapse and her basis in the Allied Corporation stock remains at $10,000. If Karen sells the stock for $100,000 in the year 2017, or a later year after the restrictions lapse, Karen reports a $90,000 ($100,000 − $10,000) long-term capital gain on the sale.[65] If Karen voluntarily leaves the company before the forfeiture restrictions lapse, no deduction is allowed when the forfeiture occurs, despite the fact that Karen is previously taxed on the stock's value on the transfer date (i.e., $10,000 of income is recognized by Karen in the current year). In such event, Allied Corporation must include $10,000 in gross income in the year of the forfeiture (i.e., the amount of the deduction that is taken in the year of the transfer to the extent of any previous tax benefit). ◄

Nonqualified plan features and requirements are summarized in Topic Review I:9-3.

EMPLOYEE STOCK OPTIONS

Stock option plans are used by corporate employers to attract and retain key management employees. Both stock option and restricted property arrangements using the employer's stock permit the executive to receive a proprietary interest in the corporation. Thus, an executive may identify more closely with shareholder interests and the firm's long-run profit-maximization goals. The tax law currently includes two types of stock-option arrangements: the incentive stock option and the nonqualified stock option.[66] Each type is treated differently for tax purposes.

As will be seen in the discussions below, both types of plans have their respective advantages and disadvantages. Incentive stock option arrangements generally are preferred when long-term capital gain rates are low as compared to ordinary income rates. Thus, because long-term capital gain rates are 15% or 20% and marginal tax rates for ordinary income are rather high (39.6%), interest should continue in incentive stock option arrangements. However, an employer is more favorably treated under the nonqualified stock-option rules (i.e., the employer receives a tax deduction for the compensation related to a nonqualified stock option but does not receive a corresponding deduction if an incentive stock-option plan is adopted) and may therefore still prefer to continue to use nonqualified stock options.

TOPIC REVIEW I:9-3

Nonqualified Plans

DISTINGUISHING FEATURES AND MAJOR REQUIREMENTS

1. The employee is taxed upon the lapse of restrictions imposed on the availability or withdrawal of funds and the employer receives a corresponding deduction in the same year.
2. Nonqualified plans may discriminate in favor of highly compensated employees and no minimum vesting rules are required.
3. Restricted property (usually employer stock) may be offered to executives where the incidents of taxation are deferred if the property is nontransferable and subject to a substantial risk of forfeiture. An election may be made under Sec. 83(b) to recognize income immediately upon the receipt of the restricted property.
4. Restrictions must be imposed to avoid immediate taxation to the employee under the constructive receipt doctrine.
5. To avoid immediate taxation, restricted property plans must be both nonforfeitable and subject to a substantial risk of forfeiture.

---

[65] Sec. 1223. The holding period originates on the day following the transfer date because Karen made the election to be taxed immediately under Sec. 83(b).

[66] The incentive stock option rules are provided in Sec. 422, whereas the rules governing nonqualified stock options are contained in Reg. Sec. 1.83-7.

Incentive Stock Option Plans.

Employer Requirements. An **incentive stock option (ISO)** must meet the following plan or employer requirements:[67]

▶ The option price must be equal to or greater than the stock's FMV on the option's grant date.

▶ The option must be granted within ten years of the date the plan is adopted, and the employee must exercise the option within ten years of the grant date.

▶ The option must be both exercisable only by the employee and nontransferable except in the event of death.

▶ The employee cannot own more than 10% of the voting power of the employer corporation's stock immediately before the option's grant date.

▶ The total FMV of the stock options that become exercisable to an employee in any given year may not exceed $100,000 (e.g., an employee can be granted ISOs to acquire $200,000 of stock in one year, provided that no more than $100,000 is exercisable in any given year).

▶ Other procedural requirements must be met (e.g., shareholder approval of the plan).

Employee Requirements. In addition to the above plan requirements, the employee must meet the following requirements:

▶ The employee must not dispose of the stock within two years of the option's grant date nor within one year after the option's exercise date.

▶ The employee must be employed by the issuing company on the grant date and continue such employment until within three months before the exercise date.

If an employee meets the requirements listed above, no tax consequences occur on the grant date or the exercise date. However, the excess of the FMV over the option price on the exercise date is an adjustment for purposes of the alternative minimum tax (see Chapter I:14). When the employee sells the optioned stock, a long-term capital gain or loss is recognized. If the employee meets the two requirements, the employer does not receive a corresponding compensation deduction. If the requirements are not met, the option is treated as a nonqualified stock option.

KEY POINT

Incentive stock options have the disadvantage of not providing a compensation deduction for the employer.

KEY POINT

Incentive stock options can be a valuable tax planning tool because the earliest that they are generally taxed is when they are exercised. Also, when an employee realizes profits from stock options, those profits in certain cases may qualify as capital gains.

EXAMPLE I:9-64 ▶

American Corporation grants an incentive stock option to Kay, an employee, on January 1, 2015. The option price is $100, and the FMV of the American stock is also $100 on the grant date. The option permits Kay to purchase 100 shares of American stock. Kay exercises the option on June 30, 2017, when the stock's FMV is $400. Kay sells the 100 shares of American stock on January 1, 2019, for $500 per share. Because Kay holds the stock for the required period (at least two years from the grant date and one year from the exercise date) and because Kay is employed by American Corporation on the grant date and within three months before the exercise date, all of the requirements for an ISO have been met. No income is recognized on the grant date or the exercise date, although $30,000 [($400 − $100) × 100 shares] is a tax preference item for the alternative minimum tax in 2017. Kay recognizes a $40,000 [($500 − $100) × 100 shares] long-term capital gain on the sale date in 2019. American Corporation is not entitled to a compensation deduction in any year. ◀

EXAMPLE I:9-65 ▶

KEY POINT

With ISOs, the employee does not recognize income when the option is exercised; income is recognized only when the stock is sold. With nonqualified stock options, income is recognized when the option is exercised or on the grant date and when the stock is sold at a gain.

Assume the same facts as Example I:9-64, except that Kay disposes of the stock on August 1, 2017, thus violating the one-year minimum holding period requirement after the exercise date. Kay must recognize ordinary income on the sale date equal to the spread between the option price and the exercise price, or $30,000 [($400 − $100) × 100 shares]. The $30,000 spread between the FMV and the option price is no longer a tax preference item because the option ceases to qualify as an ISO. American Corporation can claim a $30,000 compensation deduction in 2017. Kay also recognizes a $10,000 [($500 − $400 adjusted basis) × 100 shares] short-term capital gain on the sale date, which represents the appreciation of the stock from the exercise date to the sale date. The gain is short-term because the holding period from the exercise date to the sale date does not exceed one year. ◀

[67] Sec. 422.

Nonqualified Stock Option Plans. Stock options that do not meet the plan requirements for incentive stock options are referred to as **nonqualified stock options**. The tax treatment of nonqualified stock options depends on whether the option has a **readily ascertainable fair market value** (e.g., whether the option is traded on an established options exchange).

Readily Ascertainable Fair Market Value. If a nonqualified stock option has a readily ascertainable FMV (e.g., the option is traded on an established options exchange), the employee recognizes ordinary income on the grant date equal to the difference between the stock's FMV and the option's exercise price. The employer receives a compensation deduction on the grant date equal to the same amount of income that is recognized by the employee. In such case, no tax consequences occur on the date the option is exercised, and the employee recognizes capital gain or loss upon the sale or disposition of the stock.

No Readily Ascertainable Fair Market Value. If a nonqualified stock option has no readily ascertainable FMV, no tax consequences occur on the grant date. On the exercise date the employee recognizes ordinary income equal to the spread between the FMV of the stock and the option price, and the employer receives a corresponding compensation deduction. When the stock option is exercised, the employee's basis in the stock is equal to the option price plus the amount reported as ordinary income on the exercise date. Capital gain or loss is recognized upon the subsequent sale of the stock by the employee.

The alternative minimum tax does not apply to nonqualified stock options regardless of whether the option has a readily ascertainable FMV. Table I:9-4 illustrates the tax consequences to employees and employers for such options.

As illustrated in Table I:9-4, Kim reports a total gain of $11,000 from the nonqualified stock option transaction under both circumstances. However, the character of her profit (i.e., ordinary income or capital gain) and the timing of the profit recognition (i.e., grant date or exercise date) depends on whether the option's FMV is readily ascertainable.

The distinguishing features and major requirements for employee stock options are summarized in Topic Review I:9-4.

▼ TABLE I:9-4
Taxation of Nonqualified Stock Options

Situation Facts	Readily Ascertainable FMV	No Readily Ascertainable FMV
Grant date: On January 1, 2013, Kim is granted a nonqualified stock option to purchase 100 shares of stock from Apple Corporation (Kim's employer) at $90 per share. The stock's FMV is $100 on the grant date.	Ordinary income of $1,000 is recognized [($100 − $90) × 100 shares] by Kim in 2013. Apple Corporation receives a corresponding $1,000 compensation deduction in 2013.	No tax consequences to Kim or Apple Corporation.
Exercise date: On January 31, 2015, Kim exercises the option and acquires the 100 shares of Apple Corporation stock for the $90 option price when the FMV is $190.	No tax consequences to Kim or Apple Corporation.	Kim recognizes ordinary income in 2015 of $10,000 [($190 − $90) × 100 shares], and Apple Corporation receives a $10,000 compensation deduction.
Sale date: On February 1, 2016, Kim sells the stock for $200 per share and realizes $20,000 ($200 × 100 shares).	Kim recognizes a $10,000 ($20,000 − $10,000 basis) long-term capital gain.[a]	Kim recognizes a $1,000 ($20,000 − $19,000 basis) long-term capital gain on the sale.[b]

[a] Kim's basis includes the amount paid for the optioned stock of $9,000 plus ordinary income of $1,000 recognized on the grant date. Kim's holding period commences on the January 1, 2013, grant date for determining whether the gain is long-term.

[b] Kim's basis includes the $9,000 paid for the option stock plus the $10,000 ordinary income recognized on the exercise date. Kim's holding period commences on the January 31, 2015, exercise date for determining whether the gain is long-term.

TOPIC REVIEW I:9-4

Employee Stock Options

DISTINGUISHING FEATURES AND MAJOR REQUIREMENTS

▶ For an incentive stock option (ISO) plan no tax consequences occur on the grant or the exercise date (except for the recognition of a tax preference item under the AMT provisions on the exercise date). Capital gain or loss is recognized by the employee upon the sale or exchange of the stock. No deduction is allowed to the employer.

▶ ISOs and nonqualified stock options may be issued to highly-compensated employees without regard to nondiscrimination rules.

▶ If a nonqualified stock option has a readily ascertainable FMV, the employee recognizes ordinary income equal to the spread between the FMV of the stock and the option price on the grant date and the employer receives a corresponding deduction. If the option has no readily ascertainable FMV, income is recognized on the exercise date equal to the spread between the FMV of the stock and the option price and a corresponding deduction is available to the employer.

▶ For an ISO, the option price must be equal to or greater than the FMV of the stock on the grant date, employees cannot own more than 10% of the voting power of the employer's stock, and restrictions are placed on the total FMV of stock options that may be issued.

▶ To qualify under the ISO rules, a two-year holding period from the grant date is required (and at least one year after the exercise date) and the employee must continue to be employed by the company until within three months of the exercise date.

ADDITIONAL COMMENT

If you are self-employed and establish a Keogh plan, you must include any full-time employees in the plan.

PLANS FOR SELF-EMPLOYED INDIVIDUALS

Self-employed individuals, such as sole proprietors or partners who practice as a trade or business, are not considered as employees and are not eligible for the retirement plans offered to employees. However, in recent years, self-employed individuals have their own special types of retirement plans. Retirement plans of self-employed people are generally subject to the same contribution and benefit limitations as other qualified corporate plans. An individual who is an employee and also has a self-employed business generally is able to be covered under an employer-sponsored plan and a self-employed plan. There are overall limitations that apply in these circumstances.

The principal types of retirement plans for self-employed individuals include the following:

▶ H.R. 10 plan—this plan, also referred to as a Keogh plan, was the original self-employed plan and, although still a viable and important type of plan, is not used as much now because of the annual paperwork requirements.

▶ SEP IRA—this plan, a Simplified Employee Pension plan, is similar to an H.R. 10 plan but is easier to set up and administer. SEP IRAs are discussed in more detail below.

▶ SIMPLE plan—SIMPLE plans are relatively easy to use and administer but the contribution limits are lower than those for H.R. 10 or SEP IRA plans. SIMPLE plans are discussed in more detail below.

▶ Solo 401(k) plan—this plan is for solo business owners with no other employees. Solo 401(k) plans provide for a $18,000 deferral for the business owner plus a 25% of salary match by the company. The total contribution limit (including both the deferral plus the company match) in 2015 is $53,000.

KEY POINT

Keogh plans can be either defined benefit or defined contribution plans. Many individuals avoid the defined benefit type of Keogh plan due to the extra paperwork and administrative costs.

For a **defined contribution H.R. 10 plan or SEP IRA,** a self-employed individual in 2015 may contribute the smaller of $53,000 or 25% of earned income from the self-employment activity.[68] *Earned income* refers to net earnings from self-employment. However, for purposes of computing the maximum amount that may be contributed to a Keogh or SEP IRA plan by a self-employed individual, earned income must be reduced by two amounts: (1) the 50% deduction for self-employment taxes and (2) the contribution itself. Since the contribution is based on earned income *after* the contribution, the 25% contribution percentage must be reduced to 20%.[69] To compute the limitations for 2015, a maximum of $265,000 of earned income may be taken into account for any one individual.[70]

---

[68] Sec. 415(c)(1). The limitations are indexed annually for inflation.

[69] This reduction in contribution percentage is computed as follows: $0.25/1.00 + 0.25 = 0.20$. If the Keogh or SEP IRA contribution rate is 15% rather than 25%, the deductible percentage would be 13.0435%, computed as above, $0.15/1.00 + 0.15 = 0.130435$. Other percentages can be calculated accordingly.

[70] Secs. 401(a)(17) and 404(l). The ceiling in 2014 was $260,000.

Larry is a self-employed CPA whose 2015 net earnings from his trade or business (before the H.R. 10 or SEP IRA plan contribution but after the deduction for one-half of the self-employment taxes paid under Sec. 164(f) [see Chapter I:14]) is $100,000. Larry may contribute $20,000 to the plan for 2015. Larry must also provide coverage for all of his eligible full-time employees under the general rules provided in the law for qualified plans (e.g., nondiscrimination, vesting, and so on).[71] ◀

Assume the same facts as in Example I:9-66 except that Larry's earnings from his trade or business (before the plan contribution but after the deduction for one-half of the self-employment taxes) is $300,000. The maximum contribution that Larry can make on his behalf in 2015 is $53,000 ($265,000 × 0.20). Even though his earnings were $300,000, the maximum compensation that can be used to calculate the H.R. 10 or SEP IRA plan contribution in 2015 is $265,000. ◀

KEY POINT

A Keogh plan must be created no later than the last day of your tax year. However, an SEP IRA may be created by the due date of the return.

An H.R. 10 plan must be established before the end of the tax year, but contributions may be made up to the due date for the tax return (including extensions). SEP IRA plans can be setup and funded by the due date of the return, including extensions. Thus, for the tax year 2015, a taxpayer is permitted to establish a SEP IRA by April 15, 2016 (or October 15, 2016, if the return is extended). All pension contributions made by a self-employed individual for *employees* are deductible for AGI on Schedule C. The H.R. 10 or SEP IRA contribution for the self-employed individual is deductible *for* AGI on page 1 of Form 1040.

SIMPLIFIED EMPLOYEE PENSIONS (SEP IRAS)

Due to the administrative complexity associated with qualified pension and profit-sharing plans, small businesses often establish simplified employee pension (SEP IRA) plans for their employees. In an SEP, the employer makes contributions to the IRAs of its employees.[72] The following is a summary of the tax rules that apply to a SEP IRAs:

ADDITIONAL COMMENT

A self-employed person (i.e., a partner or sole proprietor) may establish an SEP rather than using an H.R. 10 plan arrangement because of reduced administrative complexity associated with a SEP.

▶ The employer receives an immediate tax deduction for contributions made under the plan. The annual deductible contributions for each participant are limited to the lesser of 25% of the participant's compensation (up to a ceiling of $265,000 for 2015) and the dollar limitations for defined contribution plans.[73] The maximum amount for 2015 is $53,000.

▶ Contributions are treated as being made on the last day of the tax year if they are made by the due date of the tax return (including extensions).

▶ Employer contributions must be nondiscriminatory.

▶ Distributions from an SEP are subject to taxation based on the IRA rules (previously discussed) including the penalty tax for premature distributions.

SIMPLE RETIREMENT PLANS

Another more recent type of retirement savings plan for small businesses is called the savings incentive match plan for employees (SIMPLE).[74] This type of plan can be adopted by employers who have 100 or fewer employees who received at least $5,000 in compensation from the employer in either of the two preceding years. A SIMPLE plan may be set up either as an IRA for each employee or part of a qualified cash or deferred arrangement (401(k) plan). Essentially, employees are allowed to make elective contributions in 2015 of up to $12,500 per year and employers are required to make matching contributions.

HISTORICAL NOTE

The IRA savings provisions were originally enacted in 1974 to provide a tax-favored retirement savings arrangement to individuals who were not covered under a qualified plan. Beginning in 1982, Congress extended IRA availability to all taxpayers. It was hoped that the extended availability would increase the level of savings and provide a discretionary retirement savings plan that was uniformly available. However, Congress in the Tax Reform Act of 1986 restricted the availability of IRAs because there was no discernible impact on aggregate personal savings.

The unique features of the SIMPLE plans are (1) that elective contributions by employees must be matched by the employer or the employer has the option of making nonelective contributions, (2) that all contributions to an employee's SIMPLE account must be fully vested, and (3) the SIMPLE plans are not subject to the special nondiscrimination rules generally applicable to qualified plans. This last feature is important in that there is no requirement that a set number of employees *participate* in the plan, the only requirement is that all employees who had $5,000 in compensation in the previous year and are reasonably expected to have $5,000 in compensation in the current year must be eligible to participate.

INDIVIDUAL RETIREMENT ACCOUNTS (IRAS)

Under current law, there are three types of IRAs that are available to taxpayers: traditional IRA, Roth IRA, and Coverdell Education Savings Account IRA.[75] Each of these three types of IRAs is discussed below.

---

[71] Sec. 401(d).
[72] Sec. 408(k).
[73] Sec. 404(h)(1).

[74] Sec. 408(p).

[75] The Coverdell Education Savings Account was named after the late Senator Paul Coverdell of Georgia.

TRADITIONAL IRA

Traditional IRAs have been in the law for almost 40 years and taxpayers may make either deductible or nondeductible contributions to the IRA. A contribution to a traditional IRA that is deductible has two principal benefits: (1) the amount contributed to the IRA (maximum $5,500 per year for 2015) is deductible on the taxpayer's return[76] and (2) the income earned on the investments in the IRA is not subject to current taxation. However, when amounts are withdrawn from the IRA at retirement, such amounts are fully subject to taxation. Nondeductible contributions to a traditional IRA may not be deducted on the taxpayer's return, but such contributions are not subject to taxation when withdrawn from the IRA. While contributions are not subject to taxation, any earnings are subject to taxation when withdrawn.

Individuals may make deductible contributions equal to the lesser of $5,500 or 100% of compensation only if either of the following conditions exists:

▶ The individual is *not* an active participant in an employer-sponsored retirement plan, including tax-sheltered annuities, government plans, simplified employee pension plans, and H.R. 10 plans; or

▶ Individuals who are active participants in an employer-sponsored retirement plan must have an AGI equal to or below the following applicable dollar limits for 2015:[77] $61,000 ($60,000 for 2014) for an unmarried taxpayer; $98,000 ($96,000 in 2014) for a married couple filing a joint return; zero for a married individual filing separately. If an individual has AGI above these amounts, the deductible IRA contribution amounts are phased out on a pro rata basis as AGI increases from $61,000 to $71,000 for unmarried taxpayers and from $98,000 to $118,000 for married taxpayers filing a joint return.

EXAMPLE I:9-68 ▶ Laura is an unmarried taxpayer who is not an active participant in an employer-sponsored retirement plan or other qualified plan. In 2015, Laura's AGI is $90,000, consisting of earned income from wages. Laura is not subject to the dollar limitation because she is not an active participant in a qualified plan and may, therefore, contribute and deduct up to $5,500 to a traditional IRA. Laura's AGI is reduced to $84,500 ($90,000 − $5,500) because the amount is deductible *for* AGI. ◀

EXAMPLE I:9-69 ▶ Judy is an unmarried taxpayer and an active participant in her employer's qualified retirement plan. In 2015, Judy's AGI is $65,000, consisting of earned income from wages of $62,000 and interest and dividends of $3,000. Since she is an active participant in a qualified plan and her AGI is over $61,000, her deductible contribution to a traditional IRA is subject to the phaseout. Since the ceiling amount is exceeded by $4,000 ($65,000 − $61,000), the maximum IRA contribution is reduced by 40% ($4,000/$10,000), or $2,200. Thus, the maximum that Judy can contribute *and* deduct to her IRA in 2015 is $3,300 ($5,500 − $2,200). ◀

If a taxpayer's AGI exceeds the above limits, the taxpayer may make a nondeductible contribution of up to $5,500 to a traditional IRA. The benefit of making a nondeductible contribution to an IRA is that the earnings of the IRA investments grow tax-free. Thus, even though the *earnings* of the nondeductible IRA will be taxed when distributed, the ability to allow investments to compound before-tax is a major advantage for taxpayers. However, as will be seen in the discussion of Roth IRAs below, if a taxpayer can qualify for a Roth IRA rather than a traditional nondeductible IRA, the choice clearly favors a Roth IRA. The maximum amount of a nondeductible contribution that may be made to a traditional IRA is $5,500 minus the amount that is allowed as a deduction. Also, a taxpayer may elect for all of his contributions to be nondeductible even though the contributions are otherwise eligible to be deducted.

EXAMPLE I:9-70 ▶ Using the same facts as in Example I:9-69, Judy is permitted to make a nondeductible contribution to her IRA of $2,200 ($5,500 − $3,300). She also could elect to designate all $5,500 as a nondeductible contribution even though she is eligible to deduct the $3,300. ◀

---

[76] The deductible amount to an IRA was increased from $2,000 prior to 2002 to $3,000 for 2002–2004, $4,000 for 2005–2007, $5,000 for 2008–2012, and $5,500 for 2013 and 2014. See Sec. 219 (b)(5). The deductible amount is indexed for inflation. Prior to 2002, the deductible amount was $2,000. In addition, individuals over 50 years of age are now eligible to contribute an extra $500 into their IRA in years 2002–2005 (increasing to $1,000 in 2006 and future years). These extra amounts are referred to as "catch-up contributions."

[77] Sec. 219(g).

Two special rules apply to married couples relative to traditional IRAs. First, if only one spouse is employed and this working spouse is otherwise eligible to make IRA contributions, the nonworking spouse may contribute up to $5,500 per year to an IRA (a so-called spousal IRA). Thus, a total of $11,000 may be deductible by a married couple ($5,500 to each spouse's IRA) even though only one spouse has earned income. It should be noted that even though only the working spouse must have earned income, such working spouse must have at least $11,000 of earned income in order to contribute $11,000 to the two IRAs. Second, if one spouse is covered under a qualified retirement plan but the other spouse is not covered, the non-covered spouse may contribute to a traditional deductible IRA. However, for 2015, the contribution to a traditional deductible IRA is phased out at adjusted gross incomes between $183,000 and $193,000.

EXAMPLE I:9-71 ▶ Gary and Babs are a married couple. Gary is covered under a qualified retirement plan at his job and earned $174,000 in 2015. Babs is employed as a secretary and earned $24,000 but is not covered under a qualified retirement plan. They file a joint return, have interest and dividend income of $16,000, and their AGI, therefore, is $214,000. Neither Gary nor Babs is entitled to deduct contributions to a traditional IRA. Gary cannot contribute and deduct any amount to an IRA because he is covered under another qualified plan and their AGI exceeds $118,000. Babs is also not eligible because their AGI exceeds $193,000. However, both Gary and Babs are allowed to make nondeductible contributions of $5,500 each to the IRA. ◀

EXAMPLE I:9-72 ▶ Assume the same facts as in Example I:9-71 but that Gary's income is $100,000 and their AGI is $130,000. Babs may contribute and deduct $5,500 to a traditional IRA because their AGI is less than $183,000. However, Gary may not make a deductible contribution because he is covered under a qualified plan and their AGI exceeds $118,000. Gary is permitted to make a $5,500 contribution to a nondeductible IRA. ◀

ADDITIONAL COMMENT

A contribution to an IRA for the year 2015 can be made as late as the due date for filing the 2015 return, or April 15, 2016.

The following significant tax rules apply to traditional IRAs:

▶ An IRA plan may be established between the end of the tax year and the due date for the tax return (not including any extensions that are permitted). Any deductible contributions made during this time are treated as a deduction for the prior year. Contributions are deductible if made by the due date for the tax return (i.e., contributions for 2015 must be made no later than April 15, 2016). Contributions to nondeductible IRAs also must be made by April 15 of the following year.

▶ Taxpayers who are 50 years of age or older by the end of the taxable year may contribute an additional $1,000 per year (or a total of $6,500 in 2015).

▶ Distributions from a traditional IRA are taxed under the annuity rules in Sec. 72. Normally distributions from an IRA are fully subject to taxation. However, if nondeductible contributions are made to an IRA, these amounts would represent the investment in the contract in calculating the exclusion ratio.

▶ Withdrawals by a participant before age 59½ are both includible in income and subject to a nondeductible 10% penalty tax.[78]

▶ Withdrawals must begin no later than April 1 of the year following the end of the tax year in which the individual reaches age 70½. IRA contributions that were deducted over the years on the taxpayer's returns are fully taxable as ordinary income when the amounts are distributed.

▶ A nondeductible 6% penalty is levied on excess contributions to an IRA.[79]

ADDITIONAL COMMENT

Some financial advisors recommend the following approach when someone can only afford to have limited amounts set aside for retirement. Have pre-tax dollars withheld from salary up to the employer-matching amount in 401(k) plans, then place $5,500 in a Roth IRA. This maximizes employer contributions and places the maximum amount allowable into the much favored Roth IRA.

ROTH IRA

The Roth IRA[80] is a relatively new type of IRA that is a so-called "backloaded IRA" because the tax benefits come at the end, not at the beginning, of the IRA. Contributions to a Roth IRA are nondeductible but all distributions from the IRA, including earnings, are nontaxable.

---

[78] Sec. 72(t). The amount subject to the 10% penalty is the portion of the amount that must be included in gross income. Exceptions to the 10% penalty are provided in the event of death, disability, and certain non-lump-sum distributions. Two additional exceptions also apply: (1) withdrawals used to pay qualified higher education costs for taxpayer, spouse, children or grandchildren and (2) up to $10,000 to buy or build the principal residence for a "first time homebuyer."

[79] Sec. 4973(b).

[80] Sec. 408A.

The maximum amount that may be contributed to a Roth IRA is $5,500. However, taxpayers who are eligible for both a Roth IRA and a traditional IRA may only contribute a total of $5,500 to both types of IRAs. As with traditional IRAs, Roth IRAs are also subject to AGI phaseout limitations, although the limitation amounts are higher than with traditional IRAs.

All taxpayers may contribute up to the lesser of (1) $5,500 or (2) 100% of the taxpayer's compensation, to a Roth IRA; however, for 2015, this amount is phased-out for single taxpayers if their AGI is between $116,000 ($114,000 in 2014) and $131,000 ($183,000 and $193,000 for married couples filing a joint return and $0 for married individuals filing separate returns). The principal advantage of the Roth IRA is the nontaxability of qualified distributions. One requirement of a qualified distribution is that the distribution must meet a five-year holding period. More specifically, the distribution may not be made before the end of the five-tax-year period beginning with the first tax year for which a contribution was made to the Roth IRA. The first tax year begins on the first day of the tax year (i.e., January 1 in most cases) in which a contribution was made even though such contribution may have been made later in such tax year. In addition to satisfying the five-year test, a qualifying distribution must also meet one of the following:

► made on or after the date on which the individual attains age 59½,

► made to a beneficiary (or the individual's estate) on or after the individual's death,

► attributable to the individual being disabled, or

► a distribution for first-time homebuyer expenses (maximum of $10,000).

An important aspect of distributions from a Roth IRA is a special ordering rule for determining the taxability of nonqualifying withdrawals. Under this rule, distributions are treated as being made from contributions first and, thus, are nontaxable. After all contributions have been withdrawn, any remaining amounts are considered taxable and subject to the 10% penalty.

EXAMPLE I:9-73 ► Ray and Sandy are married and Ray is covered under his employer's qualified retirement plan. Their AGI on a joint return is $130,000. Ray can contribute $5,500 to a Roth IRA. Alternatively, however, if their AGI was $189,000, Ray would be limited to a maximum contribution of $2,200. Since their AGI exceeds the threshold of $183,000 by $6,000, the $5,500 contribution is reduced by 60% ($6,000/$10,000), or $3,300. ◄

EXAMPLE I:9-74 ► Bob, age 60 in 2015, contributes $5,500 each year to a Roth IRA in 2015, 2016, and 2017. On November 30, 2020, the value of the Roth IRA is $20,000. Bob has experienced some financial setbacks and needs to withdraw the money from the Roth IRA. If Bob withdraws $16,500 in 2020 and waits until January 2021 to withdraw the remaining $3,500, none of the distributions are taxable. This result occurs because the first $16,500 is treated as coming from contributions. The remaining $3,500 is nontaxable because Bob has met the five-year test and is over age 59½. Conversely, if Bob withdraws the entire $20,000 in 2020, $3,500 must be included in his income because the five-year test was not met. No penalty will be imposed because he is over age 59½. ◄

A final aspect of Roth IRAs is the ability to "rollover" funds from an existing traditional IRA into a Roth IRA. Since the taxpayer received a deduction for the contribution into the traditional IRA, any rollover amount must be included in gross income in the year the rollover occurred, but is not subject to the 10% penalty for early withdrawals. For years prior to 2010, only taxpayers with AGI of $100,000 or less were eligible to rollover amounts from a traditional IRA to a Roth IRA. However, for tax years after 2009, the $100,000 income limit has been repealed and permits all taxpayers to convert traditional IRAs to Roth IRAs. In addition, as mentioned earlier, this rollover option has been extended to existing 401(k), 403(b), or 457 plans for years beginning in 2013. There is considerable interest in this option for taxpayers. The essential question is whether a taxpayer should convert his or her traditional IRA to a Roth IRA and pay the tax currently or keep the traditional IRA and pay the tax on a current basis as the amounts are withdrawn? The key variable in this analysis is the taxpayer's age. Younger taxpayers would definitely benefit with a Roth IRA as the amounts in the Roth IRA have years to accumulate and compound and such amounts will never be subject to taxation. Other important variables include the taxpayer's assessment of his or her future marginal tax rate and the ability to pay the tax on the rollover out of private funds.

EXAMPLE I:9-75 ▶ John has a traditional IRA that has a balance of $250,000 on June 30, 2014. He is single and has AGI of $180,000. John would like to rollover the $250,000 to a Roth IRA. John is permitted to rollover the $250,000 from his traditional IRA to a Roth IRA in 2014. He must include the $250,000 in his gross income in 2014 but no penalty is imposed. This treatment is now also available for 401(k), 403(b), or 457 plans in addition to traditional IRAs. ◀

Below is a discussion of some of the important tax rules for Roth IRAs:

▶ Like traditional IRAs, Roth IRAs must be established by the due date of the tax return (not including extensions). Similarly, contributions to a Roth IRA also must be made by the due date of the return (i.e., April 15, 2016, for 2015 contributions).

▶ Contributions to a Roth IRA are never deductible.

▶ Contributions to a Roth IRA are subject to special modified AGI limitations.

▶ Contributions to a Roth IRA can be made after the owner has reached age 70½. Similarly, no distributions are required at any age from a Roth IRA. (Remember: owners of traditional IRAs must begin taking distributions in the year after the taxpayer has reached age 70½).

▶ Taxpayers who are 50 years or older by the end of the taxable year may contribute an additional $1,000 per year (or a total of $6,500 in 2015).

▶ Withdrawals from a Roth IRA are not taxable if such withdrawals are "qualified distributions." If a withdrawal is not a qualified distribution, the amount is taxed under special ordering rules and subject to the 10% penalty.

? STOP & THINK

Question: Both nondeductible contributions to a traditional IRA and contributions to a Roth IRA are similar in the sense that neither provides a tax deduction at the date of contribution. Which of the two types would be most advantageous to taxpayers?

Solution: Clearly, if a taxpayer qualifies for a Roth IRA, that type of IRA is superior to a nondeductible contribution to a traditional IRA. The reason is that distributions from a Roth IRA are totally excluded from gross income while only the principal portion of nondeductible contributions to a traditional IRA are excludable. In other words, the earnings generated in a Roth IRA are excluded from gross income whereas earnings associated with nondeductible contributions to a traditional IRA are subject to taxation. Generally, a nondeductible contribution to a traditional IRA will not be advantageous unless the taxpayer's AGI exceeds $193,000.

For a discussion of the decision whether to invest in a traditional deductible IRA or a Roth IRA, see the Tax Planning Considerations later in this chapter. Also, for a more detailed analysis including computations, see Chapter I:18 of the *Individuals* textbook.

Topic Review I:9-5 contains a table which summarizes the eligibility rules for traditional and Roth IRAs.

TOPIC REVIEW I:9-5

Traditional and Roth IRAs—Eligibility

| If 2015 AGI Is | ELIGIBLE FOR IRA (JOINT RETURNS) | | | | |
| | TRADITIONAL IRA (DEDUCTIBLE) | | | ROTH IRA | TRADITIONAL IRA (NONDEDUCTIBLE)* |
	A	B	C		
Up to $98,000	Yes	Yes	Yes	Yes	Yes
$98,000–$118,000	Yes	Partially	Yes	Yes	Yes
$118,000–$183,000	Yes	No	Yes	Yes	Yes
$183,000–$193,000	Yes	No	Partially	Partially	Yes
Over $193,000	Yes	No	No	No	Yes

A   If neither spouse is an active participant in an employer-sponsored plan
B   For the IRA of a spouse who is an active participant in an employer-sponsored plan
C   For the IRA of a spouse who is not an active participant in an employer-sponsored plan

* If AGI is not above $193,000, a nondeductible IRA will not be advantageous.

COVERDELL EDUCATION SAVINGS ACCOUNT

A special type of IRA, referred to as an Education IRA, was established to specifically assist low- and middle-income taxpayers with higher education expenses. The Education IRA was renamed the Coverdell Education Savings Account (CESA) in 2001. CESAs have a number of attractive features:

▶ The maximum annual contribution into such plan is $2,000.[81]

▶ CESAs may be used for elementary and secondary education expenses as well as for higher education expenses, and

▶ Taxpayers can claim either the HOPE scholarship credit or Lifetime Learning Credit as well as excluding distributions from a CESA in the same year.

A contributor can make a *nondeductible* contribution of up to $2,000 per year into a CESA for a designated beneficiary until the beneficiary reaches age 18.[82] The contributor need not be related to the beneficiary and there is no limit on the number of CESAs that can be set up by a contributor. Distributions to the beneficiary are excluded from gross income provided the distribution does not exceed the *qualified education expenses* of the designated beneficiary during the taxable year. Qualified education expenses include tuition, fees, books, supplies, equipment, and room and board. In the case of elementary and secondary education expenses, qualified education expenses include academic tutoring and Internet access fees. Distributions in any tax year in excess of qualified education expenses are includible in the gross income of the beneficiary and subject to a 10% penalty.

Similar to other IRA-type accounts, there are phaseout limits based on the contributor's AGI. The $2,000 annual contribution is phased out for married taxpayers filing joint returns with AGI from $190,000 to $220,000 ($95,000 to $110,000 for other taxpayers). In addition, if the taxpayer claims either the HOPE scholarship credit or the Lifetime Learning Credit, the education expenses used for these credits must reduce the qualified expenses for exclusion from a CESA.

EXAMPLE I:9-76 ▶ Lee and Patsy are married and have two young grandchildren. To assist the grandchildren with their future education expenses, they set up a CESA for each child in 2015 and plan to deposit $2,000 in both accounts. Their AGI for 2015 is $202,000. Because their AGI exceeds $190,000, they are limited to putting $1,200 [$2,000 − $2,000(($202,000 − $190,000)/$30,000)] into the accounts in 2015. In the future, the children can withdraw amounts tax-free from their CESA to pay for qualified education expenses for elementary, secondary, or higher education. ◄

EXAMPLE I:9-77 ▶ Craig Shaw is about to enter State University as a freshman and plans to withdraw amounts from his CESA to help pay his expenses. His expenses for the Fall Semester 2015 are as follows:

Tuition and fees	$2,200
Books	500
Supplies	300
Room and board	2,400
Total	$5,400

Craig's parents plan on paying Craig's tuition and fees, and Craig will pay the remaining $3,200 from his CESA. Craig qualifies as a dependent of his parents for the tax year. Craig's parents plan on claiming the American Opportunity Tax Credit. Craig is not required to include the $3,200 in his gross income in 2015 as his qualified education expenses are at least $3,200. Craig's parents will use $2,200 to claim the AOTC credit. ◄

[81] Pursuant to the American Taxpayer Relief Act of 2012 (ATRA 2012), the contribution limit of $2,000 and other enhancements that were enacted in 2001 are made permanent for 2013 and future years. Without ATRA 2012, the maximum limit would have been reduced to the original limit of $500.

[82] Sec. 530. Contributions are allowed to continue past age 18 for a special-needs beneficiary.

ADDITIONAL COMMENT

Any number of people may contribute funds to a Coverdell Education Savings Account for one child, but all of the contributions may not total more than $2,000 for that child.

HEALTH SAVINGS ACCOUNTS

Health Savings Accounts (HSAs) were established by Congress in 2003 to enable individuals to accumulate funds on a tax-free basis to pay qualified medical expenses currently or in the future.[83] In summary, HSAs operate as follows:

► The individual must be covered by a high-deductible health plan and not covered under any other health plan that is not a high-deductible health plan.

► Taxpayer contributes money into an HSA with a qualified trustee or custodian (much like an IRA). The taxpayer must be an eligible individual and the contributions are subject to limitations. These detailed issues are discussed below.

► The taxpayer is allowed a *for* AGI deduction in the year the contributions are made.

► Distributions from the HSA that are used exclusively to pay for qualified medical expenses (medical expenses as defined in Sec. 213(d), but not health insurance premiums) are excludable from gross income. However, any amount of the distribution that is not used to pay for qualified medical expenses is includable in the gross income of the taxpayer and subject to an additional 10% penalty. The 10% penalty is waived if the beneficiary/taxpayer is age 65 or older.

HSAs are only available to eligible individuals. An eligible individual is any individual who (1) is covered under a high-deductible health plan (HDHP), (2) is not also covered by any other health plan that is not an HDHP, (3) is not entitled to benefits under Medicare (i.e., generally, has not reached age 65), and (4) may not be claimed as a dependent on another person's tax return. An HDHP is a plan for an individual with an annual deductible in 2015 of at least $1,300 and annual out-of-pocket expenses (other than premiums) required to be paid not exceeding $6,450. For family coverage, these amounts are $2,600 and $12,900, respectively.

Annual contributions to an HSA are determined separately for each month the plan is in effect and is $\frac{1}{12}$ of the *lesser* of (1) 100% of the annual deductible under the HDHP (minimum of $1,300) or (2) $3,350. For individuals with family coverage under an HDHP, the amounts are (1) 100% of the annual deductible under the HDHP (minimum of $2,600) or (2) $6,650. Catch-up contributions are permitted for individuals age 55 to 64.

EXAMPLE I:9-78 ► Roy, age 45, established an HDHP for his family with a $3,600 annual deductible on May 1, 2015. Roy is eligible to put $2,400 (8 months × $300) into an HSA for the calendar year 2015. The purpose of the fund is to pay for medical expenses for himself and his family. In 2015, Roy is allowed to deduct the $2,400 as a deduction for AGI. Any earnings of the fund investments are not subject to tax if the distribution is used to pay qualified medical expenses. ◄

EXAMPLE I:9-79 ► In 2018, Roy takes a $5,000 distribution from the HSA to make a down payment on a new automobile. Since the distribution was not used to pay qualified medical expenses, Roy must include the $5,000 in his income and pay a $500 ($5,000 × 10%) penalty in 2018. ◄

TAX PLANNING CONSIDERATIONS

OBJECTIVE 10

Describe tax planning considerations for employee expenses

MOVING EXPENSES

To be eligible for the moving expense deduction, the moving expenses must be paid in connection with the commencement of work by the taxpayer as a full-time employee or self-employed individual. Therefore, it is important to secure full-time employment or to carry on a trade or business as a self-employed individual at the new location. Taxpayers who are approaching retirement are eligible for a moving expense deduction only if they continue to work in the new location before their actual retirement (e.g., 39 weeks in the 12-month period following the move).

EXAMPLE I:9-80 ► Louis decides to quit his job and return to school as a full-time graduate student. Louis incurs substantial long-distance moving expenses that would otherwise be deductible to relocate to the university where the education is to be taken. No deduction is allowed unless Louis is employed on a full-time basis or is engaged in a self-employment activity at the new location. ◄

Reimbursed Amounts. Moving expense reimbursements are often greater than the amounts allowable as a deduction. This is caused by the common practice of reimbursing

---

[83] Sec. 223. Archer Medical Savings Accounts are similar to HSAs but cannot be established after 12/31/05. MSAs have a more restrictive definition of HDHP so there is little incentive to use them.

nondeductible items (e.g., an employer may reimburse an employee for the cost of certain indirect moving expenses such as househunting trips, which do not qualify as deductible moving expenses). This results in an increase in the employee's gross income to the extent of the excess reimbursement. From a tax planning standpoint, the employer may provide an additional payment to compensate the employee for the additional tax cost associated with the move (commonly referred to as a "gross-up").

EXAMPLE I:9-81 ▶

Austin Corporation has a policy of reimbursing transferred employees for 30% of their moving reimbursement that exceeds their deductible expenses to cover the federal and state tax costs associated with the excess reimbursement. Kathy, an employee, is transferred by the company to a new job location and incurs $6,000 of deductible moving expenses and receives an $8,000 reimbursement. Austin also will make an additional payment to Kathy of $600 (0.30 × $2,000) to cover the additional federal and state income tax costs. Kathy must include $2,600 ($2,000 + $600) of the reimbursement in gross income. ◂

PROVIDING NONTAXABLE COMPENSATION TO EMPLOYEES

Employers should consider the tax consequences to employees when changes in fringe benefit and deferred compensation arrangements are evaluated. For example, it is preferable for an employer to pay for fringe benefit items such as group term life insurance (up to $50,000 in coverage), health and accident insurance, employee parking, and so on rather than to give cash raises of a comparable amount. Such payments are nontaxable to the employee up to certain limits, whereas a comparable salary increase is fully taxable. Both types of payments are deductible by the employer.

Consideration should also be given to increased deferred compensation benefit programs for employees, particularly highly-compensated individuals. The use of nonqualified deferred compensation plans, restricted property, and stock options result in tax deferrals and may result in the eventual recognition of capital gains that may be used to offset capital losses or that are taxed at preferential tax rates.

All eligible employees should consider establishing an individual retirement account (IRA) because of the available tax deferral benefits. Even if a premature withdrawal (i.e., before age 59 ½ occurs), the time value of the deferred benefits for the plan contributions and the earnings may be greater than the penalty tax imposed.

REAL-WORLD EXAMPLE

Banks and other financial institutions in their ads sometimes compare the accumulated wealth in an IRA to the accumulated wealth in a fully taxable investment. Although the IRA is generally advantageous, the ads sometimes overstate the advantages because they fail to deduct the tax that will be paid when amounts are withdrawn from the IRA.

ROLLOVERS TO ROTH IRA

Taxpayers have the ability to rollover amounts from traditional IRAs as well as 401(k), 403(b), or 457 plan to a Roth IRA.[84] However, if such a rollover is made, the taxpayer must include the rollover amount in gross income in the year of the rollover. The principal benefit of the rollover is that once the amounts are in the Roth IRA, no further taxes are due on these amounts upon distribution (assuming the five-year test is met). The essential question, therefore, is whether it is advantageous to rollover amounts to a Roth IRA and pay the tax now or keep the original plan intact and pay the tax when regular distributions are made.

The decision rests on several factors, including (1) the marginal tax rate at retirement, (2) age of taxpayer, and (3) payment of tax from rollover from post-tax funds. First, if a taxpayer's marginal tax rate at retirement is expected to be lower than the current tax rate, a rollover may not be advantageous. Second, younger taxpayers are more likely to benefit from a rollover because they have more years to accumulate earnings tax-free and may be in a lower tax bracket today than at retirement. Finally, if the taxes that accrue from the rollover must be paid from the rollover funds, a rollover will probably not be in the taxpayer's favor. In other words, taxpayers should have sufficient funds from other sources to pay the tax, then the entire amount of rollover into the Roth IRA will have maximum ability to grow on a tax-free basis.

Each case must be analyzed based on the unique factors of that particular situation. However, for most taxpayers, it is generally advantageous to rollover funds from a traditional type of plan to a Roth IRA. With the higher tax rates in 2013 and the possibility of even higher tax rates in future years, the desirability of Roth conversions is increased.

---

[84] 401(k), 403(b), and 457 plans must have a separate "designated Roth account" for each participant in the plan.

COMPLIANCE AND PROCEDURAL CONSIDERATIONS

Describe compliance and procedural considerations for employee expenses

KEY POINT

It is extremely important to be able to substantiate travel and entertainment expenses. The *Cohan* Rule that permits a reasonable deduction when substantiation is lacking does not apply to travel and entertainment expenses (see Chapter I:6).

ETHICAL POINT

The CPA has a responsibility to make sure that proper documentation has been furnished by the taxpayer to substantiate travel and entertainment expenses according to the provisions in Sec. 274(d). The CPA cannot rely on the use of estimates for these expenses despite the fact that the *AICPA's Statements on Standards for Tax Services No. 4* (see Appendix E) permits the use of estimates if it is impractical to obtain exact data and the estimated amounts appear to be reasonable.

SUBSTANTIATING TRAVEL AND ENTERTAINMENT EXPENSES

Travel and entertainment expenses are disallowed if the taxpayer does not maintain adequate records or documentary proof of the expenditures.[85] Normally, documentation includes expense statements (diary or account book) and proof of the amount, time, place, and business purpose. Strict substantiation rules are enacted in the law to curb widespread abuses in the so-called expense account living practices engaged in by some taxpayers.

To make compliance easier, the IRS formulated the following administrative procedural rules:

▶ If an employee makes an adequate accounting of the expenditures to the employer, it is not necessary to submit a detailed statement on the employee's tax return unless the expenses exceed the reimbursements.

▶ The standard mileage rate may be used to compute automobile expenses in lieu of actual expenses and is reported on Form 2106 (Employee Business Expenses).

▶ Taxpayers may elect an optional method for computing deductions for business travel and meal expenses in lieu of using actual costs. If a per diem allowance is paid by an employer in lieu of reimbursing actual expenses, the reimbursement is deemed to be substantiated if it does not exceed a federal per diem rate for the travel locality. In lieu of using actual expenses an employee or self-employed individual may use the applicable federal per diem rate. The taxpayer must still provide documentation of time, place, and business purpose for the expenditures.

REPORTING EMPLOYEE BUSINESS EXPENSES

Form 2106 (Employee Business Expenses) is used to report employee business expenses (see Appendix B). Part I of Form 2106 is a recap of travel and transportation expenses. Part II includes a computation of automobile expenses using either actual expenses or the standard rate mileage method. Employer reimbursements must be included in the employee's wages on Form W-2 if an adequate accounting of the expenses is not made. Employer withholding of federal income tax is also required for nonaccountable plan reimbursements. Form 2106-EZ may be used by employees who do not receive an employer reimbursement, and where the standard mileage rate is used for the current year and for the year the taxpayer's automobile was first placed in service.

Moving expenses are reported on Form 3903 (Moving Expenses) instead of Form 2106 because they are treated differently from other employee expenses (e.g., unreimbursed moving expenses are deductible *for* AGI). Expenses such as entertainment, union dues, business gifts, and education expenses are reported on Schedule A of Form 1040 as itemized deductions (see Appendix B).

A filled-in copy of Form 2106 is shown in Figure I:9-2. It includes the computations relating to the information in Example I:9-84.

EXAMPLE I:9-82 ▶

ADDITIONAL COMMENT

Many of the provisions related to employee business expenses are very complex. It has been said of the general complexity of the tax law that "If Patrick Henry thought taxation without representation was bad, he should have seen taxation with representation."

Eric Graber, SSN 000-00-0000, is single and employed as a salesman by the Houston Corporation in 2014. Eric is required to use his personal automobile for employment-related business and placed the current automobile in service on July 1, 2010. He uses only one automobile for business purposes and has elected to use the mileage method for deducting expenses. During 2014, Eric drives his automobile 80% of the time for business use and incurs the following total actual expenses:

Gas and oil	$ 7,400
Repairs	600
Depreciation	1,775
Insurance	1,400
Parking and tolls (all business related)	250
Total	$11,425

[85] Sec. 274(d).

Form **2106**

Department of the Treasury
Internal Revenue Service (99)

Employee Business Expenses

▶ Attach to Form 1040 or Form 1040NR.
▶ Information about Form 2106 and its separate instructions is available at *www.irs.gov/form2106*.

OMB No. 1545-0074

20**14**

Attachment
Sequence No. **129**

Your name	Occupation in which you incurred expenses	Social security number
Eric Graber	Sales	000 ¦ 00 ¦ 0000

Part I Employee Business Expenses and Reimbursements

Step 1 Enter Your Expenses

		Column A Other Than Meals and Entertainment			Column B Meals and Entertainment	
1	Vehicle expense from line 22 or line 29. (Rural mail carriers: See instructions.)	**1**	13,440			
2	Parking fees, tolls, and transportation, including train, bus, etc., that **did not** involve overnight travel or commuting to and from work .	**2**	250			
3	Travel expense while away from home overnight, including lodging, airplane, car rental, etc. **Do not** include meals and entertainment .	**3**	4,050			
4	Business expenses not included on lines 1 through 3. **Do not** include meals and entertainment	**4**				
5	Meals and entertainment expenses (see instructions)	**5**				1,350
6	**Total expenses.** In Column A, add lines 1 through 4 and enter the result. In Column B, enter the amount from line 5	**6**	17,740			1,350

Note: *If you were not reimbursed for any expenses in Step 1, skip line 7 and enter the amount from line 6 on line 8.*

Step 2 Enter Reimbursements Received From Your Employer for Expenses Listed in Step 1

7	Enter reimbursements received from your employer that were **not** reported to you in box 1 of Form W-2. Include any reimbursements reported under code "L" in box 12 of your Form W-2 (see instructions).	**7**	9,600			0

Step 3 Figure Expenses To Deduct on Schedule A (Form 1040 or Form 1040NR)

8	Subtract line 7 from line 6. If zero or less, enter -0-. However, if line 7 is greater than line 6 in Column A, report the excess as income on Form 1040, line 7 (or on Form 1040NR, line 8)	**8**	8,140			1,350

Note: *If **both columns** of line 8 are zero, you cannot deduct employee business expenses. Stop here and attach Form 2106 to your return.*

9	In Column A, enter the amount from line 8. In Column B, multiply line 8 by 50% (.50). (Employees subject to Department of Transportation (DOT) hours of service limits: Multiply meal expenses incurred while away from home on business by 80% (.80) instead of 50%. For details, see instructions.)	**9**	8,140			675
10	Add the amounts on line 9 of both columns and enter the total here. **Also, enter the total on Schedule A (Form 1040), line 21** (or on **Schedule A (Form 1040NR), line 7**). (Armed Forces reservists, qualified performing artists, fee-basis state or local government officials, and individuals with disabilities: See the instructions for special rules on where to enter the total.) . . . . . . ▶	**10**				8,815	

For Paperwork Reduction Act Notice, see your tax return instructions.   Cat. No. 11700N   Form **2106** (2014)

FIGURE I:9-2 ▶   PAGE 1 OF FORM 2106 FOR EXAMPLE I:9-82

Form 2106 (2014)   Page **2**

Part II Vehicle Expenses

Section A—General Information (You must complete this section if you are claiming vehicle expenses.)

			(a) Vehicle 1	(b) Vehicle 2
11	Enter the date the vehicle was placed in service	11	07 / 01 / 10	/ /
12	Total miles the vehicle was driven during 2014	12	30,000 miles	miles
13	Business miles included on line 12	13	24,000 miles	miles
14	Percent of business use. Divide line 13 by line 12	14	80.00 %	%
15	Average daily roundtrip commuting distance	15	8 miles	miles
16	Commuting miles included on line 12	16	2,000 miles	miles
17	Other miles. Add lines 13 and 16 and subtract the total from line 12	17	4,000 miles	miles
18	Was your vehicle available for personal use during off-duty hours?		☑ Yes ☐ No	
19	Do you (or your spouse) have another vehicle available for personal use?		☑ Yes ☐ No	
20	Do you have evidence to support your deduction?		☑ Yes ☐ No	
21	If "Yes," is the evidence written?		☑ Yes ☐ No	

Section B—Standard Mileage Rate (See the instructions for Part II to find out whether to complete this section or Section C.)

22	Multiply line 13 by 56¢ (.56). Enter the result here and on line 1	22	13,440

Section C—Actual Expenses

			(a) Vehicle 1	(b) Vehicle 2
23	Gasoline, oil, repairs, vehicle insurance, etc.	23	9,400	
24a	Vehicle rentals	24a		
b	Inclusion amount (see instructions)	24b		
c	Subtract line 24b from line 24a	24c		
25	Value of employer-provided vehicle (applies only if 100% of annual lease value was included on Form W-2—see instructions)	25		
26	Add lines 23, 24c, and 25	26	9,400	
27	Multiply line 26 by the percentage on line 14	27	7,520	
28	Depreciation (see instructions)	28	1,420	
29	Add lines 27 and 28. Enter total here and on line 1	29	8,940	

Section D—Depreciation of Vehicles (Use this section only if you owned the vehicle and are completing Section C for the vehicle.)

			(a) Vehicle 1	(b) Vehicle 2
30	Enter cost or other basis (see instructions)	30		
31	Enter section 179 deduction (see instructions)	31		
32	Multiply line 30 by line 14 (see instructions if you claimed the section 179 deduction)	32		
33	Enter depreciation method and percentage (see instructions)	33		
34	Multiply line 32 by the percentage on line 33 (see instructions)	34		
35	Add lines 31 and 34	35		
36	Enter the applicable limit explained in the line 36 instructions	36	1,775	
37	Multiply line 36 by the percentage on line 14	37	1,420	
38	Enter the smaller of line 35 or line 37. If you skipped lines 36 and 37, enter the amount from line 35. Also enter this amount on line 28 above	38	1,420	

Form **2106** (2014)

FIGURE I:9-2 ▶ PAGE 2 OF FORM 2106 FOR EXAMPLE I:9-82

During the year, Eric drives a total of 30,000 miles, of which 24,000 are business miles. Of the 6,000 personal miles, 2,000 miles are commuting to and from work (8 miles roundtrip each day). Eric receives a reimbursement of 40 cents per business mile from his employer. Eric also incurred $5,400 of unreimbursed employment-related travel and entertainment expenses. These expenses include the following:

Airfare	$ 2,500
Car rental	250
Business meals at which business was discussed	550
Laundry while traveling	100
Lodging	1,200
Entertainment of customers	800
Total	$ 5,400

Step 1, line 1: Vehicle expense (24,000 × .56)	$13,440
Step 2, line 7: (24,000 miles × $0.40)	$9,600
Section C, line 23: Actual expenses:	
Gas and oil	$7,400
Repairs	600
Insurance	1,400
Total	$ 9,400
Section C, line 28: Depreciation ($1,775 × .80)	$ 1,420

As can be seen from the completed Form 2106, Eric receives a larger deduction from the mileage method. This method has been elected by Eric. Sections C and D of Part II of Form 2106 are not necessary in this case because Eric has elected the mileage method. They are shown for illustrative purposes. ◀

REPORTING MOVING EXPENSES

Employer reimbursements for qualifying moving expenses reduce the otherwise deductible amount for the employee. Reimbursements for nondeductible moving expenses are included in gross income and should be included in total wages on the employee's Form W-2 and reported on page 1 (line 7) of Form 1040. Employers should complete Form 4782 (Employee Moving Expense Information) which summarizes the moving expense payments made to the employee and to third parties. The form is provided to an employee to properly report his moving expenses and reimbursements. Form 3903 (Moving Expenses) is used to compute the allowable moving expenses and is attached to the employee's tax return. Moving expenses are deductible *for* AGI on line 26 of page 1 of the 2014 Form 1040. Moving expenses are not subject to federal income tax withholding if it is reasonable to believe that an employee will be entitled to a deduction for such amounts. Reimbursements in excess of the deductible amounts, however, are subject to the withholding of income and social security taxes.

A taxpayer may deduct moving expenses, even though the tests for qualification have not been met (e.g., the 39-week test). If the individual subsequently fails to satisfy the requirements, gross income for the subsequent year must be increased by the previous tax benefit.[86] Another alternative is to wait until the tests have been met and then file an amended return (Form 1040X) for the prior year.

REPORTING OFFICE IN HOME EXPENSES

Form 8829 (Expenses for Business Use of Your Home) must be used to figure the allowable expenses for business use that are reported on Schedule C (Profit or Loss from Business) and the carryover of any nondeductible amounts from prior years. Form 4562 (Depreciation and Amortization) must also be used to compute depreciation on the office portion of the residence.

KEY POINT

If a taxpayer who is an employee moves in early December, the earliest that the 39-week test could be met would be early September of the following year. This is well after the April 15 due date for the individual return. The taxpayer may nevertheless deduct the moving expenses in the earlier year.

---

[86] Secs. 217(d)(2) and (3).

QUALIFICATION OF PENSION AND PROFIT-SHARING PLANS

The reporting requirements to establish and maintain a qualified pension or profit-sharing plan are too complex for this text. However, it should be noted that it is generally advisable for a taxpayer to obtain advance approval of the plan from the district director of the IRS by requesting a determination letter that all requirements for qualification have been met. A new determination letter should generally be requested when any material (e.g., substantial) modification is made to a plan. Material changes are frequently required when major tax legislation is enacted. In addition, several reports must be filed with the IRS and the U.S. Department of Labor.

PROBLEM MATERIALS

DISCUSSION QUESTIONS

I:9-1 Why is it important to distinguish whether an individual is an employee or an independent contractor (self-employed)?

I:9-2 Determine whether the following expenses are either deductible *for* AGI or *from* AGI or nondeductible on an employee's return. Indicate whether the expenses are subject to the 2% nondeductible floor for miscellaneous itemized deductions.
a. Automobile expenses associated with commuting to and from work
b. Legal expenses incurred to prepare the taxpayer's income tax return
c. Unreimbursed travel and transportation expenses
d. Qualified moving expenses of an employee

I:9-3 Which of the following deduction items are subject to the 2% nondeductible floor applicable to miscellaneous itemized deductions?
a. Investment counseling fees
b. Fees for tax return preparation
c. Unreimbursed professional dues for an employee
d. Gambling losses
e. Interest on a personal residence
f. Unreimbursed employee travel expenses
g. Reimbursed employee travel expenses (an adequate accounting is made to the employer and any excess reimbursement must be repaid)
h. Safe deposit box rental expenses for an investor

I:9-4 In each of the following cases involving travel expenses, indicate how each item is reported on the taxpayer's tax return. Include any limitations that might affect its deductibility.
a. Marilyn lives in Houston and owns several rental properties in Denver. To supervise the management of these properties, Marilyn incurs travel expenses including airfare, lodging, and meals while traveling to and from the location of the rental properties.

b. Marc is an employee who incurs travel expenses as a salesperson. The expenses are fully reimbursed by his employer after an adequate accounting has been made.
c. Assume the same facts as in Part b, except that the expenses are not reimbursed.
d. Kay is a self-employed attorney who incurs travel expenses (including meals) to prepare a court case in a nearby city where she spends the night.

I:9-5 Kelly is an employee who incurs $2,000 of business meal expenses in connection with business entertainment and travel, none of which are reimbursed by her employer. $500 of the business meal costs are considered to be lavish or extravagant. How much can Kelly deduct before applying the 2% nondeductible floor on miscellaneous itemized deductions?

I:9-6 Latoya, a college professor, takes a nine-month leave of absence from her employment at a college in Ohio and accepts a visiting professorship (temporary assignment) at a college in Texas. Latoya leaves her husband and children in Ohio and incurs the following expenses in connection with the temporary assignment:

Airfare to and from the temporary assignment	$ 1,000
Living expenses in the new location (including meals of $1,000)	8,000
Personal clothing	1,500
Total	$10,500

a. Which (if any) of these items can Latoya deduct?
b. Would your answer to Part a change if Latoya, after completing the nine month assignment, resigned her position in Ohio and accepted a full-time assignment with the college in Texas?

I:9-7 Louie is a full-time employee for a large corporation and also an investor in the stock market in his spare time. In the current year, Louie incurs $2,500 of travel expenses and $1,000 in registration fees related to attending investment seminars. He deducts the expenses on his income tax return as a miscellaneous itemized deduction as an investment expense. Are the travel expenses and registration fees deductible? Should they be classified as *for* AGI or *from* AGI?

I:9-8 If an employee receives a specific monthly amount from his or her employer as a reimbursement for employment-related entertainment, travel, and transportation expenses, why is it necessary to allocate a portion of the total reimbursement to each expense category?

I:9-9 If an employee receives a reimbursement of 40 cents a mile from her employer for employment-related transportation expenses, is the employee permitted to deduct the difference between the standard mileage rate and the reimbursement rate as an unreimbursed employee expense? What other alternative is available for claiming the transportation deduction?

I:9-10 If an employee (or self-employed individual) uses the standard mileage rate method for the year in which an automobile is acquired, may the actual expense method be used in a subsequent year? If so, what restrictions are imposed (if any) on depreciation methods? What adjustments to basis are required?

I:9-11 If an employee or self-employed individual uses the actual method of deducting automobile expenses and claims depreciation for the first two years of business use, can the individual switch to the standard mileage rate method for the third year and beyond?

I:9-12 Discuss the reporting procedures that should be followed by an employee to report employment-related expenses on his or her tax return under the following conditions:
a. Expenses are less than reimbursements, and no accounting is made to the employer.
b. Expenses equal reimbursements, and an adequate accounting is made to the employer.
c. Expenses exceed reimbursements, and an adequate accounting is made to the employer.
d. Expenses are less than reimbursements. An adequate accounting is made to the employer and the employee is required to repay any excess amount.

I:9-13 What are the two basic requirements that must be met to permit a deduction for moving expenses?

I:9-14 Does it matter whether a moving expense is incurred by an employee, a self-employed individual, or an unemployed person?

I:9-15 Len incurs $5,000 of deductible moving expenses in the current year and is fully reimbursed by his employer in the same year.
a. How are the expense deduction and the reimbursement reported on Len's tax return if he uses the standard deduction?
b. What tax consequences occur if the reimbursement is $5,000 but only $3,000 of the $5,000 of moving expenses are tax deductible?

I:9-16 Why are strict recordkeeping requirements required for the deduction of entertainment expenses?

I:9-17 Louis incurs "directly related" entertainment expenses of $4,000, but he is reimbursed by his employer for only $3,000 after an adequate accounting is made.
a. How are these amounts reported on Louis's tax return?
b. What are the tax consequences if Louis is unable to provide adequate documentation of the expenditures during the course of an IRS audit of his tax return?

I:9-18 Latasha is a self-employed attorney who entertains clients and potential clients in her home.
a. What requirements must be met to qualify the outlays as deductible entertainment expenses?
b. What is the difference between "directly related" and "associated with" entertainment?

I:9-19 Liz is an employee who regularly entertains customers in connection with her job. In the current year, Liz incurs $6,000 in business meal expenses that are connected with entertainment. Liz's expenses are not lavish or extravagant. She itemizes her deductions in the current year.
a. If none of these expenses are reimbursed by Liz's employer, what amounts are deductible and how are they classified?
b. How are these amounts reported by Liz and her employer if all of her expenses are reimbursed and an adequate accounting is made by Liz?

I:9-20 Atlantic Corporation provides a cafeteria for its employees. The meal charges are set at a sufficiently high level that the employees are not taxed on the subsidized eating facilities. Are Atlantic's cafeteria-related costs subject to the 50% disallowance for business meals?

I:9-21 Lynn is a salesperson who entertains clients at business luncheons. A business relationship exists for the entertainment, and there is a reasonable expectation of business benefit. However, no business discussions are generally conducted before, during, or immediately following the meals. Do the business meal expenditures qualify as entertainment expenses?

I:9-22 If an individual belongs to a country club and uses the facility primarily for business entertainment of customers, what portion of the club dues is deductible?

I:9-23 Bass Corporation purchases 10 tickets to the Super Bowl in February 2015 for entertaining its customers. Due to unusually high demand, the tickets have to be purchased from scalpers for $15,000 (10 × $1,500). The face value of the tickets is only $2,000 (10 × $200). What amount is deductible by Bass in 2015?

I:9-24 a. Discuss the two requirements for an employee expense reimbursement plan to be treated as an accountable plan.
b. How are expenses and reimbursements treated under an accountable plan?
c. How are expenses and reimbursements treated under a nonaccountable plan?

I:9-25 Martin is a tax accountant employed by a public accounting firm. He incurs the following expenses:

CPA review course	$ 400
Law school tuition and books	4,000
Accounting continuing education course (travel, fees, and transportation (including meals of $200)	600
Total	$5,000

Martin is also a degree candidate at the law school. Which (if any) of these expenditures qualify as deductible education expenses? How are they reported?

I:9-26 Discuss whether any of the following individuals are entitled to an office-in-home deduction:
a. Maggie is a self-employed management consultant who maintains an office in her home exclusively used for client meetings and other business-related activities. Maggie has no other place of business and her office is the most significant place for her business. She has substantial income from the consulting practice.
b. Marty is a college professor who writes research papers for academic journals in his office at home which is used exclusively for this purpose. Although Marty has an office at his place of employment, he finds it very convenient to maintain an office at home to avoid distractions from students and colleagues. Marty receives no income from the publication of the research articles for the year in question.
c. Bobby operates his own sole proprietorship as an electrician. He maintains an office at home where he keeps his books, takes phone calls from customers, and does the payroll for his five employees. All of his electrical work is done at the location of his customers.

I:9-27 Compare and contrast the tax advantages accruing to employers and employees from the establishment of a qualified pension or profit-sharing plan versus a nonqualified deferred compensation arrangement (e.g., a restricted property plan).

I:9-28 What is the difference between a defined benefit pension plan and a defined contribution pension plan?

I:9-29 Austin Corporation is proposing the establishment of a pension plan that will cover only employees with salaries in excess of $150,000. No other employees are covered under comparable qualified plans. What problems (if any) do you envision regarding the plan's qualification with the IRS?

I:9-30 Babson Corporation is proposing the creation of a qualified profit-sharing plan for its employees. The proposed plan provides for vesting of employer contributions after 20 years because the company wants to discourage employee turnover and does not feel that short-term employees should qualify for benefits. Will this plan qualify? Why or why not?

I:9-31 Explain how distributions from a qualified pension plan, which are made in the form of annuity payments, are reported by an employee under the following circumstances:
a. No employee contributions are made to the plan.
b. The pension plan provides for matching employee contributions.

I:9-32 Discuss the limitations and restrictions that the Internal Revenue Code places on employer contributions to qualified pension and profit-sharing plans.

I:9-33 Why are nonqualified deferred compensation plans particularly well-suited for use in executive compensation arrangements?

I:9-34 A recently-formed corporation is considering going public and anticipates substantial future appreciation in its stock. Would it be advisable for an executive/employee receiving stock (restricted property) to elect to recognize income immediately under Sec. 83(b)? Contrast the tax consequences of a restricted property arrangement for both the employer and employee when this election is made versus when it is not made. Consider the effect of the subsequent lapsing of the restrictions and the employee's sale of the stock.

I:9-35 List and discuss the qualification requirements for an incentive stock option plan (ISO). Describe the advantages and disadvantages of ISOs compared to nonqualified stock option plans.

I:9-36 What difference does it make if a nonqualified stock option has a readily ascertainable FMV on the grant date?

I:9-37 Is a self-employed individual, who is also employed and covered by an employer's qualified pension plan, eligible to establish an H.R. 10 or an SEP plan on his or her self-employment income?

I:9-38 What limitations are placed on self-employed individuals for contributions made to defined contribution H.R. 10 plans? Must self-employed individuals cover their full-time employees if an H.R. 10 plan is established?

I:9-39 Discuss the essential differences between a traditional IRA and a Roth IRA.

I:9-40 Would you be more favorably inclined to advise a 30-year-old individual to establish a traditional deductible IRA or a Roth IRA? Explain. Consider any tax problems involved if the IRA funds are needed before age 59½. Would your answer change for a 55-year-old individual?

I:9-41 Your client, Charley Long, age 40, has requested your advice with respect to his IRA. He has a traditional IRA with a balance of $250,000 and his current AGI is $250,000. He expects his income to increase slightly when he retires at age 65. Charley has been reading about Roth IRAs and wants your advice as to whether he should rollover the $250,000 from his traditional IRA into a Roth IRA. He has sufficient outside money to pay any taxes due on the rollover. What advice would you give Charley?

I:9-42 Sally, who is single and age 40, made deductible IRA contributions in several early years, but has not been eligible to make deductible IRA contributions for the last 5 years because she is covered under her employer's plan. Her AGI is $100,000. She is interested in making IRA contributions in the current year. What advice would you give her?

I:9-43 Discuss the major features of a Coverdell Education Savings Account (CESA).

I:9-44 The owner of an unincorporated small business is considering whether to establish a simplified employee pension (SEP) plan for its employees.
a. What nontax factors might make an SEP attractive as an alternative to establishing a qualified pension or profit-sharing plan?
b. Is the owner of the small business eligible to make contributions on his or her behalf to the SEP?

ISSUE IDENTIFICATION QUESTIONS

I:9-45 Georgia is an executive who recently completed an assignment with her employer at an away-from-home location. It was realistically expected that the assignment would be completed in 15 months but the actual time period was only 11 months. Georgia incurred $15,000 of away-from-home expenses during the 11-month period, none of which were reimbursed by her employer. What tax issues should Georgia consider?

I:9-46 Jeremy is an executive for Columbia Corporation, which is going through a restructuring of its corporate headquarters operations. Columbia has offered to relocate Jeremy from its New York headquarters to its divisional operation in South Carolina and will reimburse him for both direct and indirect moving expenses. What tax issues should Jeremy consider?

I:9-47 Juan, a self-employed medical doctor, maintains an office in his home where he maintains patient records and performs billing procedures. Most of his time is spent visiting patients and performing surgical procedures in the operating room at several local hospitals. Juan intends to deduct his expenses of his office in his home. What tax issues should Juan consider?

I:9-48 David is on the audit staff of a national accounting firm. He has been with the firm for three years and is a CPA. David has applied and been accepted into a prestigious MBA program. The program is two years in duration. David has decided to resign from the accounting firm even though the firm has indicated that it would very much like David to return to work for the firm after he receives his MBA degree. David is somewhat interested in returning to public accounting but will certainly look at all of his options when he completes the program. David wants to deduct his education expenses. What are the relevant tax issues in this case?

PROBLEMS

I:9-49 *Employment-Related Expenses.* Mike incurs the following employment-related expenses in the current year:

Actual automobile expenses	$ 2,500
Moving expenses (deductible under Sec. 217)	4,000
Entertainment expenses	1,500
Travel expenses (including $500 of business meals)	2,500
Professional dues and subscriptions	500
Total	$11,000

Mike's AGI is $120,000 before any of the above expenses are deducted. None of the expenses listed above are reimbursed by Mike's employer. He has no other miscellaneous itemized deductions and does not use the standard deduction.

a. What is the amount of Mike's deduction for employment-related expenses?

b. How are these items reported in Mike's tax return?

I:9-50 *Travel and Entertainment.* Monique is a self-employed manufacturer's representative (i.e., an independent contractor) who solicits business for numerous clients and receives a commission based on sales. She incurs the following expenditures during the current year:

Airfare and lodging while away from home overnight	$ 4,000
Business meals while traveling at which business is discussed	1,000
Local transportation costs for automobile, parking, tolls, etc. (business-related)	2,000
Commuting expenses	1,000
Local entertainment of customers	2,000
Total	$10,000

a. Which of the expenditures listed above (if any) are deductible by Monique?

b. Are each of these items classified as *for* AGI or *from* AGI deductions?

c. How would your answers to Parts a and b change if Monique were an employee rather than self-employed and none of the expenses were reimbursed by her employer?

I:9-51 *Unreimbursed Employee Expenses.* Mary is an employee of ABC corporation and incurs $3,600 of unreimbursed employment-related travel and entertainment expenses during the current year. These business expenses include the following:

Airfare	$1,500
Taxi fare	100
Meals eaten alone while away from home on business	300
Laundry	50
Lodging	650
Business meals with customers at which business is discussed	500
Entertainment of customers	500
Total	$3,600

Mary also pays $1,000 of investment counseling fees and $500 of tax return preparation fees in the current year. Mary's AGI is $70,000.

a. What is the total amount of Mary's deductible expenses?

b. Are the deductible expenses classified as *for* AGI or *from* AGI?

I:9-52 *Travel Expenses.* Marilyn, a business executive who lives and works in Cleveland, accepts a temporary out-of-town assignment in Atlanta for a period of ten months. Marilyn leaves her husband and children in Cleveland and rents an apartment in Atlanta during the ten-month period. Marilyn incurs the following expenses, none of which are reimbursed by her employer:

Airfare to and from Atlanta	$ 800
Airfare for weekend trips to visit her family	8,000
Apartment rent	10,000
Meals in Atlanta	8,500
Entertainment of customers	2,000
Total	$29,300

a. Which of the expenditures listed above (if any) are deductible by Marilyn (before any limitations are applied)?

b. Are each of these expenditures classified as *for* AGI or *from* AGI deductions?

c. If Marilyn's AGI is $120,000, what is the amount of the deduction for the expenditures?

d. Do the tax consequences change if Marilyn's assignment is for a period of more than one year?

e. Do the tax consequences in Parts a through c change if it was realistically expected that the work would be completed in ten months but after the ten-month period Marilyn is asked to continue for seven more months and if an additional $10,000 of travel expenses are incurred during the extended period?

I:9-53 *Business/Personal Travel Expenses.* In the current year, Mike's AGI is $50,000. Mike has no miscellaneous itemized deductions other than the employment-related expenses listed below. Mike attends a professional trade association convention in Los Angeles. He spends three days at the meeting and two days vacationing before the meeting. Mike's total expenses include the following:

Airfare	$ 450
Meals ($50 per day)	250
Hotel ($100 per day)	500
Entertainment of customers (business is discussed)	500
Total	$1,700

Mike's employer reimburses him for the business-related expenses and, accordingly, Mike receives a reimbursement of $1,400 ($450 + 150 + 300 + 500).
a. How much can Mike deduct for employment-related expenses?
b. How is the reimbursement reported on Mike's tax return?
c. How much of the reimbursement may Mike's employer deduct?
d. How would your answers change if Mike spent two days at the meeting and three days vacationing? Assume Mike received no reimbursement from his employer.

I:9-54 *Employment-Related Expenses and Reimbursements.* Maxine incurs the following employment-related business expenses in the current year:

Professional dues and subscriptions	$1,000
Airfare and lodging	2,000
Local transportation for employment-related business activities	1,000
Customer entertainment (business lunches where business is discussed)	1,000
Total	$5,000

After making an adequate accounting of the expenses, Maxine receives a reimbursement of $3,000 from her employer. Assume that Maxine's AGI is $60,000, she has other miscellaneous itemized deductions of $1,000 and she does not use the standard deduction.
a. What amount of the expenses are deductible by Maxine?
b. Are each of these expenditures classified as *for* AGI or *from* AGI deductions?
c. How would your answers to Parts a and b change if Maxine instead received a $6,000 reimbursement?

I:9-55 *Miscellaneous Itemized Deductions.* In the current year, Melissa, a single employee whose AGI is $100,000 before any of the items below, incurs the following expenses:

Safe deposit box rental for investments	$ 100
Tax return preparation fees	500
Moving expenses (deductible under Sec. 217)	2,000
Mortgage interest on Melissa's principal residence	12,000
Real estate taxes on Melissa's principal residence	1,800
Unreimbursed employment-related expenses (other than business meals and entertainment)	6,000
Unreimbursed employment-related expenses for business meals and entertainment (business is discussed)	1,200
Total	$23,600

a. What is the amount of Melissa's total miscellaneous itemized deductions (after deducting the 2% floor)?
b. What is the amount of Melissa's total itemized deductions?
c. What is the amount of Melissa's total itemized deductions if her AGI, after all adjustments above, is $190,000?

I:9-56

Transportation Expenses. Cassady, an employee of a law firm, maintains an office at the principal business location of her firm. She frequently travels directly from her home to client locations within and outside the metropolitan area. Cassady is not reimbursed for her transportation expenses and has incurred the following:

Transportation expenses associated with trips to clients within the metropolitan area	$2,000
Transportation expenses associated with trips to clients located outside the metropolitan area	3,000
Total	$5,000

a. What is the amount of Cassady's deduction for transportation expenses?
b. How is the deduction reported on Cassady's tax return?
c. What is the amount of Cassady's deduction for transportation expenses and its classification if she is self-employed and operates her office from her home? Assume that the requirements of Sec. 280A are satisfied.

I:9-57

Auto Expenses. Michelle is an employee who must use her personal automobile for employment-related business trips. During 2015, Michelle drives her car 60% for business use and incurs the following total expenses (100% use of car):

Gas and oil	$10,000
Repairs	1,400
Depreciation	4,700
Insurance and license fees	2,800
Parking and tolls (business related)	400
Total	$19,300

Michelle drives her car a total of 40,000 miles (24,000 business miles) during 2015 and receives a reimbursement of 40 cents per business mile from her employer. Assume that an adequate accounting is made to Michelle's employer.

a. What amount is deductible (before the 2% nondeductible floor) if Michelle uses the standard mileage method?
b. What amount is deductible (before the 2% nondeductible floor) if Michelle uses the actual cost method?
c. Can taxpayers switch back and forth between the mileage and actual methods each year?

I:9-58

Auto Expenses. Amelie is an employee who uses her personal automobile in connection with her job. During 2015, Amelie drove her car a total of 28,000 miles. Her business log shows that she drove 22,400 miles for business purposes. She is reimbursed $0.30 per mile from her employer for her business miles and she makes an adequate accounting to her employer. During 2015, Amelie incurred the following actual expenses based on 100% business use, that is, 28,000 miles:

Gas and oil	$ 7,800
Repairs and maintenance	2,300
Depreciation	5,800
Insurance	1,440
Licenses and fees	300
	$17,640

a. Compute Amelie's deduction before the 2% of AGI floor if she uses the actual cost method.
b. Compute Amelie's deduction before the 2% of AGI floor if she uses the standard mileage method.
c. Assume Amelie used the standard mileage method in 2015 and received the 30 cents per mile reimbursement. In addition to the automobile expenses, she made several business trips and incurred the following travel expenses:

Airfare	$ 4,600
Hotel	1,860
Meals and entertainment	720
Taxi fees and tips	280
	$7,460

None of the above expenses were personal in nature and she received total reimbursements (including the mileage reimbursement) from her employer of $11,220. If Amelie's AGI was $120,000, what is her deduction in 2015 after all limitations?

I:9-59 *Entertainment Expenses.* Milt, a self-employed attorney, incurs the following expenses in the current year:

Dues paid to the local chamber of commerce	$ 1,000
Business lunches for clients and prospective clients (Milt does not believe in conducting business discussions during lunch)	4,000
Entertainment of professional associates in his home (immediately following business meetings)	2,000
Country club dues (the club is used exclusively for business)	2,500
Entertainment of clients and prospective clients at the country club (meals and drinks)	1,500
Total	$11,000

a. Which of the expenditures listed above (if any) are deductible by Milt?
b. Are each of these items classified as *for* AGI or *from* AGI deductions?
c. How would your answers change if Milt was an employee rather than self-employed?

I:9-60 *Entertainment Expenses.* Beach Corporation purchases tickets to sporting events and uses them to entertain customers. In the current year Beach Corporation purchases the following tickets:

100 tickets to football games (face value of the tickets is $7,000)	$10,000
A skybox rented for six NFL football games (seating capacity of the skybox is 20, and the highest price of a nonluxury box seat is $100)	30,000

What amount of the entertainment expenses is deductible in the current year?

I:9-61 *Reimbursed Employee Expenses.* Latrisha is an employee of the Cooper Company and incurs significant employment-related expenses. During the current year, she incurred the following expenses in connection with her job:

Travel: Airfare	$ 5,850
Lodging	1,800
Meals	1,200
Entertainment of customers	2,400
Total	$11,250

a. Determine the amount of deductible expenses for both Latrisha and the Cooper Company and, for Latrisha, whether they are deductible *for* AGI or *from* AGI assuming Cooper Company maintains an accountable plan for employee expense reimbursements, if the reimbursements are alternatively:

1. $11,250
2. $9,000
3. $14,000

b. What would be the result in Part a for each of the three situations if the plan was a nonaccountable plan?

I:9-62 *Moving Expenses.* Michael graduates from New York University and on February 1, 2015, accepts a position with a public accounting firm in Chicago. Michael is a resident of New York. In March, Michael travels to Chicago to locate a house and starts to work in June. He incurs the following expenses, none of which are reimbursed by the public accounting firm:

Automobile expense enroute (1,000 miles at 23 cents per mile—standard mileage rate)	$ 230
Cost of meals en route	100
Househunting trip travel expenses	1,400
Moving van expenses	3,970
Commission on the sale of Michael's New York condominium	3,500
Points paid to acquire a mortgage on Michael's new residence in Chicago	1,000
Temporary living expenses for one week in Chicago (hotel and $100 in meals)	400
Expenses incurred in decorating the new residence	500
Total expenses	$11,100

   a. What is Michael's moving expense deduction?
   b. How are the deductible expenses classified on Michael's tax return?
   c. How would your answer to Part a change if all of Michael's expenses were reimbursed by his employer and he received a check for $11,100?

I:9-63   *Education Expenses.* For each of the following independent situations, determine whether any of the expenditures qualify as deductible education expenses in connection with a trade or business (Reg. Sec. 1.162-5). Are the expenditures classified as *for AGI* or *from AGI* deductions?
   a. Law school tuition and books for an IRS agent who is pursuing a law degree: $2,000.
   b. Continuing professional accounting education expenses of $1,900 for a self-employed CPA: travel, $1,000 (including $200 meals); registration fees, $800; books, $100.
   c. MBA education expenses totaling $5,000 for a business executive of a major corporation: tuition, $4,000; transportation, $800; and books, $200.
   d. Tuition and books acquired for graduate education courses required under state law for a schoolteacher in order to renew a provisional certificate: $1,000.
   e. Bar review courses for a recent law school graduate: $1,000.

I:9-64   *Education Expenses.* Anne works for a CPA firm as a secretary/receptionist and earns approximately $27,000 per year. About five years earlier, she had completed 70 credit hours at State U. To increase her career potential, she decided to enroll at the local university to continue her college education and get an undergraduate degree in accounting with the ultimate goal of obtaining her CPA certificate. During 2015, she incurred the following education expenses:

Tuition and fees	$3,500
Books and supplies	800

What are Anne's options as to the deductibility of the above expenses?

I:9-65   *Office in Home.* Nancy is a self-employed artist who uses 10% of her residence as a studio. The studio portion is used exclusively for business and is frequented by customers on a regular basis. Nancy also uses her den as an office (10% of the total floor space of her home) to prepare bills and keep records. However, the den is also used by her children as a TV room. Nancy's net income from the sale of the artwork (other than her home office expenses) amounts to $40,000 in the current year. She also incurs $1,400 of expenses directly related to the office (e.g., painting of the office, window blinds). Nancy incurs the following expenses in the current year related to her residence:

Real estate taxes	$ 2,000
Mortgage interest	5,000
Insurance	500
Depreciation	3,500
Repairs and utilities	1,000
Total	$12,000

   a. Which of the expenditures above (if any) are deductible? Are they *for AGI* or *from AGI* deductions?
   b. Would your answer to Part a change if Nancy's net income from painting were only $2,500 for the year? What is the amount of the office-in-home deduction and the amount of the carryover (if any) of the unused deductions? (Assume that Nancy is not subject to the hobby loss restrictions.)

I:9-66   *Office in Home.* Darrell is a self-employed consultant who uses 15% of his home exclusively as an office. Darrell operates completely out of his home office and makes all of his appointments from the office as well as keeping his books and records in the office. Darrell's gross income from his consulting business is $60,000 in 2015. He incurs $6,000 of expenses that are related to his business, such as computer and office supplies. Below are expenses that relate to Darrell's residence for 2015:

Real estate taxes	$ 4,000
Mortgage interest	8,000
Insurance	1,000
Depreciation	4,000
Repairs and utilities	1,000
Total	$18,000

    a. Which of the above expenditures (if any) are deductible? Are they *for* AGI or *from* AGI deductions?

    b. How would your answer change if Darrell was an employee of a consulting company and maintained an office at home in order to take work home with him so he did not have to spend so many hours at his consulting company office?

I:9-67   *Deferred Compensation Plan Requirements.* Identify whether each of the following plan features is associated with a qualified pension plan, a qualified profit-sharing plan, an employee stock ownership plan, a nonqualifed plan, or none of these plans.

    a. Annual employer contributions are not required, but substantial and recurring contributions must be made based on a predetermined formula.

    b. Annual, systematic, and definite employer contributions are required without regard to profits but based on actuarial methods.

    c. Forfeitures must be used to reduce contributions that would otherwise be made under the plan.

    d. The plan may discriminate in favor of highly compensated individuals.

    e. The trust is funded with the contribution of employer stock, which is subsequently distributed to employees.

I:9-68   *Taxability of Pension Payments.* Pat is a participant in a qualified pension plan. She retires on January 1, 2015, at age 63, and receives pension payments beginning in January 2015. Her pension payments, which will be received monthly for life, amount to $1,000 per month. Pat contributed $30,000 to the pension plan on a pre-tax (or tax-deferred) basis, and the number of anticipated payments based on Pat's age of 63 years is 260 months (see IRS table in Chapter I:3) from the date she starts receiving payments.

    a. What gross income will Pat recognize in 2015 and each year thereafter?

    b. How would your answer to Part a change if Pat made contributions to the plan on an after-tax basis?

    c. If, in Part b, Pat dies in December 2016 after receiving pension payments for two full years, what tax consequences occur in the year of death?

I:9-69   *Restricted Property.* In 2015, Bear Corporation transfers 100 shares of its stock to its employee Patrick. The stock is valued at $10 per share on the issue date. The stock is subject to the following restrictions:

    • Patrick cannot transfer the stock by sale or other disposition (except in the event of death) for a five-year period.

    • The stock must be forfeited to Bear Corporation if Patrick voluntarily terminates his employment with the company within a five-year period.

  In the year 2020, the Bear stock is worth $100 per share when the restrictions expire.

    a. Assuming that no Sec. 83(b) election is made, what are the tax consequences to Patrick and Bear Corporation in 2015?

    b. What are the tax consequences to Patrick and Bear Corporation if Patrick makes a valid Sec. 83(b) election in 2015?

    c. What are the tax consequences to Patrick and Bear Corporation if Patrick forfeits the stock back to the company in 2016 when the stock is worth $20 per share if an election was made under Sec. 83(b)? What would happen if no Sec. 83(b) election were made?

    d. What are the tax consequences to Patrick and Bear Corporation upon the lapse of the restrictions in the year 2020 if an election has been made under Sec. 83(b)? What would the results be if no Sec. 83(b) election were made?

    e. What are the tax consequences to Patrick and Bear Corporation if Patrick sells the Bear stock in the year 2021 for $120 per share if a Sec. 83(b) election is made? if no Sec. 83(b) election is made?

I:9-70   *IRAs.* On February 15, 2016, Jamal, who is single and age 30, establishes a traditional IRA and contributes $5,500 to the account. Jamal's adjusted gross income is $67,000 in 2015 and $57,000 in 2016. Jamal is an active participant in an employer-sponsored retirement plan.

    a. What amount of the contribution is deductible? In what year is it deductible?

    b. How is the deduction (if any) reported (i.e., *for* AGI or *from* AGI)?

    c. How would your answer to Part a change, if at all, if Jamal were not an active participant in an employer-sponsored retirement plan?

    d. How would your answer to Part a change if Jamal were married and files a joint return with his spouse, who has no earned income? (Assume their combined AGI is $85,000.)

I:9-71 *IRAs.* Phil, age 30, is married and files a joint return with his spouse. On February 15, 2016, Phil establishes a traditional IRA for himself and a spousal IRA for his spouse with a $11,000 contribution, $5,500 for himself and $5,500 for his wife. Phil's spouse earned $1,000 in 2015 from a part-time job, and their combined AGI is $75,000. Neither Phil nor his spouse is an active participant in an employer-sponsored retirement plan.

a. What amount of the contribution is deductible?

b. To what year does the contribution apply? (Assume that an election is made to treat Phil's spouse as having no compensation.)

c. Is the deduction reported as *for* AGI or *from* AGI?

d. How would your answer to Part a change, if at all, if Phil and his spouse were active participants in an employer-sponsored retirement plan?

e. If a portion of the contribution is nondeductible in Part d, is it possible for Phil to make a deductible and a nondeductible contribution in the same year? Explain.

f. How would your answer to Part a change if Phil and his spouse's combined AGI were $125,000 in 2015 and Phil was an active participant in an employer-sponsored retirement plan?

I:9-72 *Roth IRA.* Chatham Mae is single, age 35, and wants to make a contribution to an IRA for the year ended December 31, 2015. She is an active participant in a qualified retirement plan sponsored by her employer. Her AGI for 2015 is $122,000 before considering any IRA contribution.

a. What type of IRA, if any, is Chatham Mae eligible to make a contribution to for 2015? If she is eligible to contribute to an IRA, what is the maximum amount that she can contribute to the IRA?

b. Assume Chatham Mae contributes a total of $12,000 over six years to a Roth IRA. In 2021, she withdraws $15,000 to pay off her car loan. Her financial advisor suggested she withdraw the money from the IRA for two major reasons: (1) to eliminate her debt and (2) no tax would be due on distributions from a Roth IRA after five years. Chatham Mae wants to verify the accuracy of her advisor's advice. What would be the tax consequences of this withdrawal? Alternatively, what if Chatham Mae withdrew the $15,000 to purchase a house (she is a first-time homebuyer)?

c. Alternatively to Part b above, assume Chatham Mae has a traditional deductible IRA that has a balance of $50,000. She has been able to deduct all of her contributions to the IRA in prior years. Her financial advisor has recommended that she rollover the funds from her traditional IRA to a Roth IRA in 2015. What are the tax consequences of this rollover in 2015?

I:9-73 *Coverdell Education Savings Accounts.* Jack and Katie have five grandchildren, ages 19, 16, 15, 12, and 10. They have established Coverdell Education Savings Accounts (CESA) for each of the grandchildren and would like to contribute the maximum amount allowable to each CESA for the 2015 taxable year. Jack and Katie's AGI for 2015 is $196,000.

a. How much can Jack and Katie contribute to each grandchild's CESA in 2015?

b. Assume that the 19-year-old granddaughter is a freshman in college and makes a withdrawal of $7,000 from her CESA during the year 2015. Her college expenses for 2015 were as follows:

Tuition	$1,500
Room and board	2,500
Books and supplies	500

The extra amount withdrawn was used as a down payment on a car that the granddaughter purchased during the year. She needed the car in order to drive to school rather than having to either ride the bus or ride with a friend. What are the tax consequences of the $7,000 distribution to the granddaughter?

I:9-74 *H.R. 10 Plans.* Paula is a self-employed doctor and is considering whether to establish a defined contribution H.R. 10 plan. Paula's only employee is a full-time nurse who has been employed by Paula for seven years. Paula's net earnings from self-employment (before the H.R. 10 plan contribution but after the deduction for one-half of self-employment taxes paid) is expected to be $100,000 during the current year and in future years.

a. If the H.R. 10 plan is established, what is the maximum amount Paula can contribute for the nurse's benefit?

b. What is the maximum amount Paula can contribute for herself? Is the amount reported as a *for* AGI or *from* AGI deduction?

c. Is Paula's nurse required to be included in the plan?

d. What are the tax consequences if Paula makes a premature withdrawal from the plan before reaching age 59½?

I:9-75 **Stock Options.** Bell Corporation grants an incentive stock option to Peggy, an employee, on January 1, 2015, when the option price and FMV of the Bell stock is $80. The option entitles Peggy to buy 10 shares of Bell stock. Peggy exercises the option and acquires the stock on April 1, 2017, when the stock's FMV is $100. Peggy, while still employed by the Bell Corporation, sells the stock on May 1, 2019, for $120 per share.

a. What are the tax consequences to Peggy and Bell Corporation on the following dates: January 1, 2015; April 1, 2017; and May 1, 2019? (Assume all incentive stock option qualification requirements are met.)

b. How would your answer to Part a change if Peggy instead sold the Bell stock for $130 per share on May 1, 2017?

I:9-76 **Stock Options.** Bender Corporation grants a nonqualified stock option to Penny, an employee, on January 1, 2015, that entitled Penny to acquire 1,000 shares of Bender stock at $80 per share. On this date, the stock has a $100 FMV and the option has a readily ascertainable FMV. Penny exercises the option on January 1, 2016 (when the FMV of the stock is $150), and acquires 1,000 shares of the stock for $80 per share. Penny later sells the Bender stock on January 1, 2018, for $200 per share.

a. What are the tax consequences to Penny and Bender Corporation on the following dates: January 1, 2015; January 1, 2016; and January 1, 2018?

b. How would your answer to Part a change if the Bender stock were instead closely-held and the option had no readily ascertainable FMV?

COMPREHENSIVE PROBLEM

I:9-77 Dan and Cheryl are married, file a joint return, and have no children. Dan, age 45, is a pharmaceutical salesman and Cheryl, age 42, is a nurse at a local hospital. Dan's SSN is 400-20-1000 and Cheryl's SSN is 200-40-8000 and they reside at 2033 Palmetto Drive, Nashville, TN 28034. Dan is paid according to commissions from sales; however, his compensation is subject to withholding of income and payroll taxes. He also maintains an office in his home as the pharmaceutical company does not have an office in Nashville and when he is not traveling, Dan operates his business from his home office. During 2015, Dan earned total compensation from his job of $125,000, on which $20,000 of federal income taxes were withheld, $7,347 of OASDI, and $1,813 of Medicare taxes. State income taxes of $4,000 were withheld. Cheryl earned a salary during 2015 of $45,400, on which federal taxes withheld were $5,000, OASDI of $2,815, and Medicare taxes of $658.

During 2015, Dan and Cheryl had interest income from corporate bonds and bank accounts of $1,450 and qualified dividends from stocks of $5,950. Dan also actively trades stocks and had the following results for 2015:

LTCG	$4,900
LTCL	(3,200)
STCG	0
STCL	(7,800)

He had no capital loss carryovers from previous years.

Dan does a considerable amount of travel in connection with his job. He uses his own car and is reimbursed $0.30 per business mile. During 2015, Dan drove his car a total of 38,000 miles, of which 32,000 were business related. He also had business-related parking fees and tolls during the year of $280. Dan uses the mileage method for deducting auto expenses. Dan also had the following travel expenses while away from home during the year:

Hotel	$4,200
Meals	820
Entertainment of customers	1,080
Tips	100
Laundry and cleaning	150
Total	$6,350

Dan was reimbursed for the travel expenses by his employer, pursuant to an accountable plan, in the amount of $5,080.

Dan's expenses in connection with his office in the home were as follows:

Office supplies	$ 290
Telephone (separate line)	1,100
Utilities (entire house)	3,400
Homeowners insurance	600
Interest and property taxes (see below for totals)	
Repairs and maintenance (entire house)	800

Dan's office is 300 square feet and the total square footage of the house is 3,000 square feet. Dan and Cheryl purchased the house on June 12, 2000, for $280,000, of which $40,000 is attributable to the land.

Cheryl incurred several expenses in connection with her nursing job. She paid $450 in professional dues, $200 in professional journals, and $350 for uniforms.

Dan and Cheryl had the following other expenditures during the year:

Health insurance premiums (after-tax)	$ 4,400
Doctor bills	470
Real estate taxes on home	2,200
Personal property taxes	400
Mortgage interest	15,600
Charitable contributions—cash	9,000
Charitable contributions—GE stock owned for 5 years:	
FMV	$8,000
Adjusted basis	2,000
Tax preparation fees	750

Compute Dan and Cheryl's income tax liability for 2015. Disregard the alternative minimum tax.

TAX STRATEGY PROBLEM

I:9-78 Paul Price is the president and majority stockholder of Lightmore Communications, Inc. Lightmore is a C corporation and has been extremely successful over the past 20 years. Paul travels extensively in connection with the business to meet with existing and prospective clients. Paul's wife, Laura, would be helpful to Paul in his business entertaining if she could accompany him on many of his business trips and, furthermore, she was unable to go on these trips in the past because of their children at home. Their youngest child is now in college, and Laura's duties at home have diminished. During the current year, Laura has made a number of trips with Paul, but after conferring with the company's tax advisor, had been informed that Laura's expenses would not be deductible for tax purposes. The tax advisor suggested the possibility of putting Laura on the Lightmore payroll as an employee.
a. Would Laura's travel expenses be deductible if she was an employee of the corporation?
b. What other benefits would be available to Laura if she was an employee of the corporation?
c. Are there any detriments to putting Laura on the payroll?

TAX FORM/RETURN PREPARATION PROBLEMS

I:9-79 In 2014, Micah Johnson (SSN 000-22-1111) is employed as a manager and incurs the following unreimbursed employee business expenses:

Airplane and taxi fares	$ 4,000
Lodging away from home	5,000
Meals while away from home	1,000
Automobile expenses (related to 100% of the use of his personal automobile):	
Gasoline and oil	8,500
Repairs	1,000
Insurance	900
Depreciation	1,775
Parking and tolls (includes only business use)	100
Total	$22,275

Johnson receives a $7,800 reimbursement for the travel expenses. He did not receive any reimbursement for the auto expenses. He uses his personal automobile 80% for business use and placed his current automobile in service on October 1, 2010. Total business miles driven during the year (evenly throughout the year) amount to 26,400, his commuting miles in 2014 amount to 2,000 (average daily roundtrip of 7 miles), and other personal miles amount to 4,600 miles. Johnson's AGI is $60,000, and he has no other miscellaneous itemized deductions.

a. Calculate Johnson's expense deduction using the 2014 Form 2106 (Employee Business Expenses) based on actual automobile expenses and other employee business expenses.

b. Calculate Johnson's expense deduction for 2014 using the standard mileage rate method and other employee business expenses. (Assume that none of the restrictions on the use of the standard mileage rate method are applicable.)

I:9-80 George Large (SSN 000-11-1111) and his wife Marge Large (SSN 000-22-2222) live at 2000 Lakeview Drive, Cleveland, OH 49001 and want you to prepare their 2014 income tax return based on the information below:

George Large worked as a salesman for Toyboat, Inc. He received a salary of $80,000 ($8,500 of federal income taxes withheld and $1,800 of state income taxes withheld) plus an expense reimbursement from Toyboat of $5,000 to cover his employee business expenses. George must make an adequate accounting to his employer and return any excess reimbursement, none of the reimbursement was related to the meals and entertainment. Additionally, Toyboat provides George with medical insurance worth $7,200 per year. George drove his car a total of 24,000 miles during the year, and he placed the car in service on June 1, 2012. His log indicates that 18,000 miles were for sales calls to customers at the customers' offices and the remainder was personal mileage. George uses the standard mileage rate method. Assume his business miles were driven evenly during the year. George is a college basketball fan. He purchased two season tickets for a total of $4,000. He takes a customer to every game, and they discuss some business before, during, and after the games. George also takes clients to business lunches. His log indicates that he spent $1,500 on these business meals. George also took a five-day trip to the Toyboat headquarters in Musty, Ohio. He was so well-prepared that he finished his business in three days, so he spent the other two days sightseeing. He had the following expenses during each of the five days of his trip:

Airfare	$200
Lodging	$85/day
Meals	$50/day
Taxicabs	$20/day

Marge Large is self-employed. She repairs rubber toy boats in the basement of their home, which is 25% of the house's square footage. The business code is 811490. She had the following income and expenses:

Income from rubber toy boat repairs	$15,000
Cost of supplies	5,000
Contract labor	3,500
Telephone (business)	500

The Large's home cost a total of $150,000, of which the cost of the land was $20,000. The FMV of the house is $225,000. The house is depreciable over a 39-year recovery period. The Larges incurred the following total other expenses:

Utility bills for the house	$2,000
Real estate taxes	2,500
Mortgage interest	4,500
Cash charitable contributions	3,500

Prepare Form 1040, Schedules A, C, and SE for Form 1040, and Forms 2106 and 8829 for the 2014 year. (Assume no depreciation for this problem and that no estimated taxes were paid by the Larges.)

CASE STUDY PROBLEMS

I:9-81   Ajax Corporation is a young high-growth company engaged in the manufacture and distribution of automotive parts. Its common stock has doubled in value since the company was listed on the NASDAQ exchange about two years ago. Ajax currently has a high debt/equity ratio due to the issuance of debt to finance its capital expansion needs. Despite rapid growth in assets and profitability, Ajax has severe cash flow problems and a poor working capital ratio. The company urgently needs to attract new executives to the organization and to provide financial incentives to existing top management because of recent turnover and high growth. Approximately 55% of the common stock is owned by Andrew Ajax, who is the CEO, and his immediate family. None of the other officers own stock in the company.

   You are a tax consultant for the company who has been asked to prepare suggestions after reviewing the compensation system. Your discussions with several top management individuals reveal the following aspects of corporate strategy and philosophy:

- The company needs to expand the equity capital base because of its concern for the high risk caused by large amounts of debt.
- Improvement in cash flow and liquidity would enhance its stock price and enable the company to continue its high growth rate.
- Top management feels that employee loyalty and productivity would be improved if all employees owned some stock in the company. The company currently offers a qualified pension plan to its employees and executives that provides only minimal pension benefits. No other deferred compensation or bonus arrangements are currently being offered.
- Andrew Ajax feels that the top management group should own a substantial amount of Ajax stock to ensure that the interests of management correspond with the shareholder interests (i.e., the maximization of shareholder wealth).

   The following four types of executive compensation arrangements have been discussed:

- Sec. 401(k) and ESOP plans for employees.
- Encourage all employees and executives to independently fund their retirement needs beyond any Social Security benefits by establishing IRA plans.
- Provide restricted property arrangements (using Ajax stock) to attract new top level executives and to retain existing executives.
- Offer nonqualified or incentive stock options to existing and new executives.

   Required: Prepare a client memo that recommends revisions to Ajax Corporation's existing compensation system for both its employee and executive groups. Your recommendations should discuss the pros and cons of different deferred compensation arrangements and should consider both tax and nontax factors.

I:9-82   Steve is part owner and manager of a small manufacturing company that makes keypads for alarm systems. The keypads are sold to several different alarm companies throughout the country. Steve must travel to several cities each year to meet with current customers and to attract new business. When you meet with Steve to obtain information to prepare his current year tax return, he tells you that he has spent about $5,000 during the current year on airfare and taking his customers out to dinner to discuss business. Because he took most of his trips in the summer and fall, and it is now April of the following year, Steve cannot remember the exact time and places of the business dinners and did not retain any receipts for the cash used to pay the bills. However, he remembers the names of the customers he went to see, the business topics that were discussed, and the restaurants where he had his meals. As Steve's tax consultant, what is your responsibility regarding the treatment of the travel and entertainment expenses under the mandates of the AICPA's *Statements on Standards for Tax Services*? Prepare a client letter explaining to Steve the requirements under Sec. 274(d) for sufficient substantiation of travel and entertainment expenses. (See the *Statements on Standards for Tax Services* section in Chapter I:15 for a discussion of these issues and Appendix E.)

TAX RESEARCH PROBLEM

I:9-83   Charley Long is a truck driver, the 18-wheeler variety. He works for Fishy Co., a seafood company in Mobile, Alabama, and drives a company truck. Charley's job entails leaving Mobile at 4:00 PM each day (five days per week) and delivering fresh fish to restaurants and wholesale fish distributors in Mississippi and Louisiana. His last stop, in Lafayette, Louisiana, is generally around 12:00 midnight. It normally takes Charley about five hours to get back to Mobile.

Charley's routine is varied. Sometimes, he drives straight back to Mobile from Lafayette. On other occasions, he will pull off at a truck stop and sleep in his cab before returning to Mobile. His cab is equipped with sleeping facilities, although small and sparse. Finally, on other occasions, Charley will spend the night in a motel along the road. The Fishy Co. has no preference as to what Charley does and has given him permission to either drive back or stay overnight. However, the company does not reimburse him for his food and lodging expenses.

When Charley drives straight back to Mobile, Charley will eat one meal. When he sleeps overnight (either in his cab or in a motel), he will eat two meals, a late dinner and breakfast. He spends an average of $10.00 for dinner and $6.00 for breakfast. The cost of his motel averages $70.00 per night. When Charley sleeps in the cab, he generally sleeps about 4–5 hours and then drives on to Mobile.

During the current year, Charley incurred the following expenses:

Meals incurred on nonstop trips	$1,000
Meals incurred when: slept in cab	800
slept in motel	600
Lodging	2,800
Total	$5,200

The IRS has disallowed all of the above expenses on the grounds that they are not bona fide travel expenses but personal expenses. Would you advise Charley to contest this issue?

A partial list of research sources is:

- Sec. 162(a)(2) and Reg. Sec. 1.162-2(a)
- *U.S. v. Correll,* 389 U.S. 299 (1967)
- *Williams v. Patterson,* 286 F.2d 333 (5th Cir. 1961)
- Rev. Rul. 75-168, 1975-1 C.B. 58 and Rev. Rul. 75-432, 1975-2 C.B. 60

CHAPTER

10

DEPRECIATION, COST RECOVERY, AMORTIZATION, AND DEPLETION

LEARNING OBJECTIVES

After studying this chapter, you should be able to

1 ▶ Explain the general concepts of tax depreciation and cost recovery

2 ▶ Calculate amortization for intangible assets and distinguish between amortizable and non-amortizable assets

3 ▶ Apply cost and percentage depletion methods and summarize the treatment for intangible drilling costs

4 ▶ Identify tax planning considerations for depreciation

5 ▶ Identify compliance and procedural considerations for depreciation

The income tax law allows taxpayers to deduct a reasonable allowance for the exhaustion, wear and tear, and obsolescence of property used in a trade or business or held for the production of income.[1] Such deductions enable taxpayers to recover the cost of an asset under the "return of capital" doctrine. Depreciation, therefore, is the systematic allocation of the cost of an asset over its estimated economic life. The term *depreciation* relates to deductions for most tangible property; *amortization* relates to deductions for intangible property; and *depletion* relates to deductions for natural resources (oil and gas, coal, etc.) While the concepts of depreciation, amortization, and depletion are similar to those in financial accounting, the income tax rules are unique. This chapter discusses the income tax rules relating to depreciation, amortization, and depletion.

DEPRECIATION AND COST RECOVERY

OBJECTIVE 1

Explain the general concepts of tax depreciation and cost recovery

GENERAL CONSIDERATIONS

Taxpayers must use specific depreciation methods depending on *when* an asset is placed in service. Three separate depreciation and cost recovery systems are currently in place. These three distinct systems are the result of tax law changes in 1981 and 1986. The systems that taxpayers must use are as follows:

▶ Property placed in service after December 31, 1986. Taxpayers must use the Modified Accelerated Cost Recovery System (MACRS) as provided in Sec. 168.

▶ Property placed in service after December 31, 1980 and before January 1, 1987. Taxpayers must use the Accelerated Cost Recovery System (ACRS) as provided in Sec. 168.

▶ Property placed in service prior to 1981. Taxpayers must use the rules contained in Sec. 167. These rules basically follow financial accounting principles.

In this chapter, we emphasize the MACRS rules because most assets placed in service before 1987 are now fully depreciated.

The terms *depreciation* and *cost recovery* are used interchangeably in this text. The rules in Sec. 167 (or pre-ACRS) and the MACRS rules under Sec. 168 both refer to depreciation. However, the deduction under ACRS is referred to as cost recovery. In 1981, Congress initiated the original ACRS system to achieve a number of objectives, including a stimulus for private investment, improving business productivity, simplifying taxpayer compliance, and facilitating IRS administration of the tax law. Therefore, less importance was placed on the financial accounting concept of matching costs and revenues, which is the primary theory that governed the Sec. 167 depreciation rules. Congress' primary objective in 1981 was to allow businesses and investors to recover the cost of capitalized expenditures over a period of time that is substantially shorter than the property's economic useful life. Thus, the term *cost recovery* rather than *depreciation* was used under the ACRS system. The post-1986 MACRS rules more closely follow the concept of economic useful life and, therefore, the MACRS rules refer to depreciation rather than cost recovery.

TYPICAL MISCONCEPTION

It is easy to forget that the depreciation or cost-recovery system that applies to any one asset is the system that was in effect when the property was placed in service. Property acquired in 1986 is not affected by the MACRS rules that became effective in 1987.

HISTORICAL NOTE

Before 1954, except for the limited use of a declining-balance method, taxpayers were required to use the straight-line method.

ADDITIONAL COMMENT

Property is considered to be "placed in service" when it is in a condition or state of readiness and is available for a specifically assigned function. This can be important in attempting to determine the first year that a depreciation deduction is available.

Common Rules of All Systems. Regardless of the particular system of depreciation required (i.e., MACRS, ACRS, etc.), certain rules are common to all systems of depreciation. These common rules are discussed below.

▶ Depreciation may be claimed only on property used in a trade or business or for the production of income. Thus, personal-use assets, such as a personal-use automobile or the taxpayer's personal residence, are not depreciable.

▶ No depreciation is permitted for land or other assets that have an indefinite life. Assets such as works of art are generally not depreciable.

---

[1] Sec. 167(a).

ADDITIONAL COMMENT
A case held that a professional musician could depreciate a nineteenth-century violin bow. The IRS had argued the bow had an indeterminate life, but because the taxpayer played the violin, there was "wear and tear" on the bow and depreciation was allowed. *Simon v. Comm.*, 95-2 USTC ¶50,552 (CA-2, 1995).

▶ First-year depreciation is permitted only in the year the asset is placed in service. For example, a taxpayer may purchase a depreciable asset in December 2014 but not place it in service until January 2015. In this case, depreciation is not allowed until 2015.

▶ Regardless of the depreciation system, consistency is required. Taxpayers must consistently use the method selected in the year the asset was placed in service unless a change of accounting method is requested from the IRS.

▶ The basis of property being depreciated must be reduced by the amount of depreciation that is allowable for each taxable year. An important aspect of depreciation is determining the amount of depreciation that is *allowed* and *allowable*. The depreciation allowed is the actual depreciation claimed by the taxpayer for a particular taxable year. Allowable depreciation is the amount of depreciation to be claimed under the tax law by using the slowest possible method (i.e., straight-line using the longest permissible recovery period). If a taxpayer does not take any depreciation during a particular year, the basis of property must be reduced by the amount of depreciation that should have been taken during the year (i.e., the allowable depreciation).

EXAMPLE I:10-1 ▶

REAL-WORLD EXAMPLE
Harrah's Club in Reno, Nevada, restores antique autos and displays them. The restoration costs cannot be depreciated because the autos have an indefinite life as museum pieces. *Harrah's Club v. U.S.*, 43 AFTR 2d 79-745, 81-2 USTC ¶9677 (Ct. Cls., 1981).

Maria acquires and places in service a machine (7-year property) for $50,000 to be used in her business. She elects straight-line depreciation under MACRS. Maria properly takes depreciation in the first two years in the amount of $10,714 ($3,571 in Year 1 and $7,143 in Year 2, assuming the half-year convention). However, because of a net operating loss in Year 3, Maria did not take any depreciation on the tax return. The allowable depreciation in Year 3 was $7,143. Even though Maria did not claim the $7,143 in Year 3, the basis of the machine must still be reduced by that amount. Thus, at the end of Year 3, the basis of the machine would be $32,143 ($50,000 minus the allowable accumulated depreciation of $17,857). Obviously, Maria should amend her tax return for Year 3 and deduct the allowable depreciation. This would increase her net operating loss for Year 3, which either can be carried back two years or forward 20 years. ◀

Types of Property. For both property law and income tax purposes, there are two basic types of property, tangible and intangible. **Tangible property** refers to property that has physical substance, such as land, buildings, natural resources, equipment, etc. **Intangible property** refers to property that does not have physical substance, such as goodwill, patents, and stocks and bonds. The cost of tangible property (other than land, of course) is systematically written off through depreciation or depletion. Natural resources, such as oil and gas reserves, are recovered through depletion. Intangible property is written off through amortization.

Tangible property is further classified as either real property or personal property. **Real property** (often referred to as real estate or realty) is defined as land or any structure permanently attached to the land, such as buildings. **Personal property** is any tangible property that is not real property, and includes items such as equipment, vehicles, furniture, etc. It is important to distinguish between personal property and personal-use property. **Personal-use property** is any property, tangible or intangible, real or personal, that is used by the taxpayer for his own personal use rather than in a trade or business or for the production of income.

Capitalization Versus Expense. A frequent dilemma for taxpayers is whether an expenditure should be capitalized and expensed through depreciation, or expensed entirely in the current year. As discussed in Chapter I:6, if an expenditure either improves the efficiency of an asset or extends the life of an asset beyond the end of the year, the expenditure should generally be capitalized. However, most taxpayers have established materiality limits to justify the expensing of small expenditures that technically should be considered capital expenditures. Since capitalization-expense decisions are frequently subjective in nature, disputes between the IRS and taxpayers are common.

ADDITIONAL COMMENT
The IRS issued a private letter ruling that required an airline to capitalize engine overhauls rather than expensing such amounts in the current year. The IRS position requires capitalization because the overhauls involve replacement or reconditioning of a large portion of the engine's parts. This ruling has been severely criticized by the airlines industry, saying that the decision could negatively impact passenger safety.

Conversion of Personal-Use Property. If personal-use property is either converted to business-use or held for the production of income (e.g., a principal residence converted to a rental house), the property's basis for depreciation purposes is the lesser of its adjusted basis or its fair market value (FMV) determined as of the conversion date.[2]

---

[2] Reg. Sec. 1.168(i)-4(b)(1).

This lower of cost or market rule prevents taxpayers from depreciating the portion of the cost that represents a nondeductible loss on a personal-use asset. Chapter I:5 discusses the disposition of personal-use property.

EXAMPLE I:10-2 ► Marty acquired a principal residence for $115,000 in 2006. In 2015, he converts the property to rental use because he is unable to sell the house due to a depressed local real estate market. The property's FMV is only $100,000 when it is converted to rental status in 2015. The $15,000 ($115,000 − $100,000) decline in value represents a nondeductible personal loss and is not depreciable. The depreciable basis of the rental property is $100,000 (minus the portion of the property's FMV that represents land, which is not depreciable). ◄

DEPRECIATION METHODS

As mentioned previously, the depreciation method required for income tax purposes depends on the date the asset was placed in service. Assets placed in service prior to 1987 must use the old depreciation methods that were in effect during those years.[3] Under current law, for assets placed in service after 1986, the MACRS system of depreciation is required for most assets. MACRS is different from depreciation methods used for financial accounting purposes in several ways, including the following:

► MACRS does not consider salvage value in the computation of the depreciation amount.

► MACRS uses specific asset classes. Both tangible personal property and real property must be placed into specific asset classes, based on the type of property. Asset classes refer to the number of years over which the asset must be depreciated, such as 5-year property, 7-year property, etc.

► MACRS uses fewer depreciation methods, and the methods are built into the MACRS tables. Both accelerated and straight-line methods are used in MACRS, but accelerated methods are not permissible for real property. The MACRS tables are summarized in Appendix C.

► MACRS uses assumptions about when assets are either placed in service or disposed of rather than using actual dates. The applicable assumption is called a *convention*. The **half-year convention** is generally required for all tangible personal property. It assumes that all asset acquisitions or dispositions are made at the midpoint of the tax year. A special convention that may apply to tangible personal property is the **mid-quarter convention**, discussed later in this chapter. For real estate, the **mid-month convention** is used. It assumes that all asset acquisitions or dispositions are made at the midpoint of the month in which the transaction occurs.

EXAMPLE I:10-3 ► Golden Corporation, a calendar year taxpayer, purchases a business-use machine on March 10, 2015. For depreciation purposes, under the half-year convention, the machine is treated as if it were placed in service on July 1, 2015, and one-half year's depreciation is allowable in 2015. The half-year convention assumes all asset acquisitions and dispositions occur at the midpoint of the tax year. ◄

EXAMPLE I:10-4 ► Assume that Golden Corporation, in Example I:10-3 above, uses the machine for several years and decides to sell the machine on October 30, 2017. To compute the depreciation deduction for the year 2017, under the half-year convention, Golden is permitted one-half year's depreciation. This one-half year's depreciation is required even though the actual sale occurred on October 30. ◄

EXAMPLE I:10-5 ► Silver, Inc., a calendar year taxpayer, purchases a business-use building on March 5, 2015. For depreciation purposes, under the mid-month convention, the building is treated as if it were placed in service on March 15, 2015, and 9½ months of depreciation is allowable in 2015 (one-half of a month for March plus nine full months). ◄

---

[3] For assets placed into service between 1981 and 1986, taxpayers were required to use the ACRS method; for assets placed into service before 1981, a pre-ACRS method was required. Pre-ACRS methods more closely resemble depreciation methods used for financial statement purposes.

CALCULATION OF DEPRECIATION

The annual depreciation deduction involves a number of variables. Below is a discussion of these variables in connection with the two principal types of depreciable property: tangible personal property and real property.

Tangible Personal Property: Classification and Recovery Rates. Tangible personal property, such as equipment, furniture, computers, etc., is depreciable under MACRS if used in a trade or business or held for the production of income. Each piece of tangible personal property acquired must be classified into one of six asset classes.[4] Depreciation is computed using the percentages contained in Table 1 in Appendix C.

The MACRS recovery periods that apply to tangible personal property placed in service after December 31, 1986 are as follows:[5]

ADDITIONAL COMMENT

Most depreciable personal property is classified as 7-year property under MACRS.

KEY POINT

Notice that the recovery period for tax purposes is not necessarily dependent upon the asset's actual economic life. A property's class life and its actual economic life may be different.

► 3-Year — Property with a class life of 4 years or less. This category includes property such as tractor units, race horses over 12 years old, and special tools.

► 5-Year — Property with a class life of more than 4 years but less than 10 years. This category includes property such as automobiles, light and heavy-duty general purpose trucks, computers, and research and experimental (R&E) equipment.

► 7-Year — Property with a class life of 10 years or more but less than 16 years. This category includes property such as office furniture and equipment, horses, single-purpose agricultural or horticultural structures, and property with no class life and not classified elsewhere. Most types of machinery are included in this class.

► 10-Year — Property with a class life of more than 16 years, but less than 20 years. This category includes property such as barges, vessels, and petroleum and food processing equipment.

► 15-Year — Property with a class life of more than 20 years, but less than 25 years. This category includes property such as billboards, service station buildings, and land improvements.

► 20-Year — Property with a class life of 25 or more years, including property such as utilities and sewers.

KEY POINT

Remember that salvage value is not taken into consideration under the MACRS system.

Depreciation rates for the 3-year, 5-year, and 7-year recovery classes are provided in Table I:10-1. (See Table 1 in Appendix C for depreciation rates for all classes of property.) The rates are based on the 200% DB method switching to straight-line when it yields a larger amount. A half-year convention is used in the year of acquisition and zero salvage value is assumed. To properly apply the half-year convention when property is disposed of in a year before the final table year, the amount calculated from the table must be multiplied by one-half.

EXAMPLE I:10-6 ►

In March 2015, Mary acquires and places in service a business machine which costs $20,000 and has a 7-year recovery period under MACRS rules. Assuming no Sec. 179 expensing or bonus depreciation (discussed later), the depreciation deduction for 2015 is $2,858 ($20,000 × 0.1429). MACRS depreciation deduction for the year placed in service also can be computed by applying the accelerated depreciation rate (using the half-year convention) to the basis of the assets. Thus the depreciation deduction for 2015 is $2,857 ($20,000 ÷ 7 years × 200% DB × 0.50 year). Minor differences between the two calculations are due to rounding. ◄

Certain types of property are *excluded* from MACRS depreciation, including:[6]

► Property depreciated under a method not expressed in terms of years, such as the units of production method, where the taxpayer elects to not depreciate the property under MACRS;

► Intangible assets, such as goodwill or copyrights;

► Films, videotapes, or sound recordings.

---

[4] To determine the class life of assets, see Rev. Proc. 87-56, modified by Rev. Proc. 88-22, which sets forth the class life of property for depreciation purposes.

[5] Sec. 168(e)(1).
[6] Sec. 168(f).

▼ **TABLE I:10-1 (a Portion of Table 1 in Appendix C)**

MACRS Percentage Rates for Tangible Personal Property (Using Half-Year Convention)

Recovery Year	Recovery Period		
	3-Year	5-Year	7-Year
1	33.33	20.00	14.29
2	44.45	32.00	24.49
3	14.81	19.20	17.49
4	7.41	11.52	12.49
5	—	11.52	8.93
6	—	5.76	8.92
7	—	—	8.93
8	—	—	4.46

Source: Table 1 of Rev. Proc. 87-57, 1987-2 C.B. 674.

Section 179 Expensing Election. In lieu of depreciating the cost of new or used tangible personal business property under the regular MACRS methods discussed above, taxpayers may elect to expense up to $25,000 (in 2015) of the acquisition cost as an ordinary deduction in the year the property is placed in service.[7] The immediate expensing election is not generally applicable to real estate.[8] The election is made on an annual basis, and the taxpayer must select the assets to which the deduction applies. MACRS rules apply to any amount of an asset's cost not expensed under Sec. 179 or claimed as bonus depreciation (for years bonus is in effect).

The maximum Sec. 179 expense amount (ceiling) has been increasing over the past several years, as shown in Table I:10-2. However, unless Congress acts to extend these higher amounts, the Sec. 179 expense amount is $25,000 for 2015.

EXAMPLE I:10-7 ► In July 2015, Tanya acquires and places in service equipment costing $67,000 with a 7-year MACRS recovery period for 100% business use in her sole proprietorship. Tanya elects to

▼ **TABLE I:10-2**

Section 179 Expense Amounts

Tax Year Beginning In	Maximum Sec. 179 Expense (Ceiling)
2015	$ 25,000
2010–2014	500,000
2008–2009	250,000
2007	125,000
2006	108,000
2005	105,000

---

[7] Sec. 179. The Tax Increase Prevention and Reconciliation Act of 2005 extended the $100,000 base amount to 2008 and 2009 (inflation adjusted), and the Small Business and Work Opportunity Tax Act of 2007 extended it through 2010. The Economic Stimulus Act of 2008 increased the normal inflation-adjusted amount to $250,000 for 2008, the American Recovery and Reinvestment Act of 2009 extended the $250,000 into 2009. The Small Business Jobs Act of 2010 increased the amount to $500,000 for 2010 and 2011. The American Taxpayer Relief Act of 2012 extended the $500,000 amount to 2012 and 2013. The Tax Increase Prevention Act of 2014 extended the $500,000 amount to 2014.

[8] The Small Business Jobs Act of 2010 allowed up to $250,000 of qualified real property to be immediately expensed in 2010 or 2011. For this provision, the qualified real property included: (1) qualified leasehold improvement property, (2) qualified restaurant property, and (3) qualified retail improvement property. The American Taxpayer Relief Act of 2012 extended this treatment to 2012 and 2013, and the Tax Increase Prevention Act of 2014 extended the treatment to 2014.

expense $25,000 of the cost under Sec. 179. Tanya's basis for MACRS depreciation is $42,000 ($67,000 − $25,000). Using the half-year convention (Table 1 of Appendix C), MACRS depreciation is $6,002 ($42,000 × 0.1429). Tanya's total 2015 depreciation is $31,002 ($25,000 + $6,002). ◀

LEGISLATIVE UPDATE

As noted, qualified property for Sec. 179 is generally tangible personal property. From 2002 to 2014, off-the-shelf computer software could be expensed under Sec. 179. This was software that was readily available for purchase by the general public, was subject to a nonexclusive license, and had not been substantially modified. Unless Congress acts to extend this treatment, this computer software will no longer be eligible to be expensed under Sec. 179 after 2014.

ADDITIONAL COMMENT

Married taxpayers who file separate tax returns are each entitled to a maximum of half the regular limitation under Sec. 179.

SELF-STUDY QUESTION

Are corporations entitled to the election to expense up to $25,000 under Sec. 179?

ANSWER

Yes, but larger corporations will not receive the benefit from it because the Sec. 179 deduction is reduced when the cost of qualified property exceeds $200,000.

The following limitations and special rules apply to the Sec. 179 election:

▶ The property must be purchased for use in an active trade or business (more than 50% business-use) as distinguished from property that is acquired for the production of income (e.g., personal property used in a rental activity held by an investor does not qualify).

▶ Qualified property is generally tangible personal property.

▶ The property cannot be acquired from a related party under Sec. 267 or by gift or inheritance.

▶ The Sec. 179 tax benefits are recaptured if the property is no longer predominantly used in a trade or business (e.g., the property is converted to personal use) at any time.[9] In the year of recapture, the taxpayer must include in gross income the amount previously expensed reduced by the amount of depreciation that would have been allowed for the period the property was held for business use.[10]

▶ If the total cost of qualified property placed into service during the year is more than $200,000 (in 2015), the $25,000 ceiling is reduced on a dollar-for-dollar basis by the excess amount. Thus, no deduction is permitted for the 2015 tax year if $225,000 or more of Sec. 179 property is placed in service. No carryovers of Sec. 179 depreciation under this provision are permitted. However, the portion of cost not expensed remains in the property's basis subject to MACRS depreciation.

▶ A second limitation on the total Sec. 179 deduction is that it cannot exceed the taxpayer's taxable income (before deducting the Sec. 179 expense) from the trade or business.[11] Any acquisition cost that cannot be deducted because of the limitation based on taxable income is carried forward for an unlimited number of years and is added to the other amounts eligible for the Sec. 179 deduction in the future year. Such carryover amount will be subject to the taxable income limitation in the carryover year.

EXAMPLE I:10-8 ▶

Pam owns an unincorporated manufacturing business. In 2015, she purchases and places in service $205,000 of qualifying equipment for use in her business. Pam's taxable income from the business (before deducting any Sec. 179 expense) is $17,000. The maximum Sec. 179 deduction of $25,000 is initially reduced by $5,000 ($205,000 − $200,000) because the total cost of qualified property placed in service during the year exceeds $200,000. Pam is allowed no carryover of the $5,000 reduced by this limitation. However, the $5,000 remains part of the equipment's basis subject to MACRS depreciation.

The remaining $20,000 ($25,000 − $5,000) Sec. 179 expense is further limited to business taxable income, so Pam's Sec. 179 deduction in 2015 will be $17,000. She may carry over $3,000 ($20,000 − $17,000) to 2016 as Sec. 179 depreciation in that year. Even though only $17,000 is deductible under Sec. 179, Pam must reduce the cost basis of the equipment by $20,000 to prevent double deduction of the Sec. 179 expense caused by the carryover. Thus, she will depreciate $185,000 ($205,000 − $20,000) using MACRS. ◀

Bonus Depreciation. In response to the terrorist attacks on September 11, 2001, Congress enacted special bonus depreciation for new qualified property placed in service after September 10, 2001 and before January 1, 2005. These special depreciation provisions were

---

[9] Sec. 179(d)(10).
[10] Reg. Sec. 1.179-1(e).
[11] Sec. 179(b)(3). Under Reg. Sec. 1.179-2(c)(6)(iv), employees are considered to be engaged in the active conduct of the trade or business from their employment. Thus, a small business person who is also an employee may

include wages and salary derived from employment in determining taxable income for purposes of this limitation. Such amounts are considered derived from the conduct of a trade or business. For an individual, taxable income is also computed without regard to the deduction for one-half of self-employment taxes paid under Sec. 164(f) (see Chapter I:14).

LEGISLATIVE UPDATE

The American Taxpayer Relief Act of 2012 extended the 50% bonus depreciation that was available in 2012 to 2013. The Tax Increase Prevention Act of 2014 extended 50% bonus depreciation to 2014. Congress has not yet extended bonus depreciation for most property to 2015. However, some limited types of property (e.g., certain aircrafts) are still eligible for bonus depreciation in 2015.

effective in encouraging taxpayers to continue to invest in tangible personal property during that trying period of time. The original bonus depreciation provisions expired after December 31, 2004. However, the Economic Stimulus Act of 2008, the American Recovery and Reinvestment Act of 2009, and the Small Business Jobs Act of 2010 all reinstated 50% bonus depreciation placed in service in 2008, 2009, and 2010. Further, the Tax Relief Act of 2010 provided 100% bonus depreciation for qualified property placed in service after September 8, 2010 and before January 1, 2012. The act also extended the 50% bonus depreciation for 2012. The American Taxpayer Relief Act of 2012 provided 50% bonus depreciation for 2013. The Tax Increase Prevention Act of 2014 provided 50% bonus depreciation for 2014. Unless Congress once again acts to extend the provision, bonus depreciation will not be available after 2014.

While the percentage of bonus depreciation has varied across years, the specific rules discussed below are the same for the bonus depreciation property. Bonus depreciation is automatically deductible for both the regular income tax and the alternative minimum tax (AMT). Taxpayers must elect *out* of bonus depreciation if they do not wish to claim the deduction.

Qualified property (generally non-real estate) includes: (1) MACRS property with a recovery period of 20 years or less; (2) computer software (other than computer software that must be amortized under Sec. 197); or (3) qualified leasehold improvement property (see discussion of qualified leasehold improvement property later in this chapter in connection with real property). To qualify, the property must be new property and original use of the property must begin with the taxpayer. Used property does not qualify for bonus depreciation.

When the bonus depreciation rate is less than 100%, the remaining basis of qualified property is depreciated under the usual rules for depreciating such property. If the taxpayer elects to expense property under Sec. 179, the Sec. 179 expense is deducted first, then the additional first-year bonus depreciation and, third, regular MACRS depreciation.[12] In years after the first year, regular MACRS depreciation is allowable under normal rules.

EXAMPLE I:10-9 ►

On February 10, 2014, Polar Corporation, a calendar year taxpayer, purchased and placed in service equipment costing $625,000. The equipment was 7-year MACRS property and the half-year convention applies. Polar was eligible to expense $500,000 of the cost of the equipment under Sec. 179. Polar also claimed bonus depreciation of $62,500 [($625,000 − $500,000) × 0.50]. MACRS depreciation for 2014 was $8,931 [($625,000 − $500,000 − $62,500) × 0.1429]. Thus, Polar's total 2014 depreciation on the equipment was $571,431. Polar's 2015 depreciation is $15,306 ($62,500 × 0.2449). ◄

KEY POINT

Remember, the mid-quarter convention does *not* apply to real property.

Use of the Mid-Quarter Convention. As mentioned previously, the MACRS system generally uses the half-year convention. However, the MACRS system requires the use of the **mid-quarter convention** if the aggregate basis of all *personal property* placed in service during the last three months of the year exceeds 40% of the cost of all personal property placed in service during the tax year.[13] The 40% test is applied after reducing the property's basis by Sec. 179 expensing, if elected, but not by bonus depreciation, if claimed. If the test is met, the mid-quarter convention must be used instead of the half-year convention, and special mid-quarter tables must be used to compute depreciation under this convention. (See Tables 2 through 5 in Appendix C.) Property placed in service and disposed of during the same tax year is not taken into account for purposes of the mid-quarter test,[14] nor is property expensed under Sec. 179.[15]

---

[12] Temp. Reg. 1.168(k)-1T(d)(3) Example 2.
[13] Sec. 168(d)(3).

[14] Sec. 168(d)(3)(B) and Reg. Sec. 1.168(d)-1(b)(3).
[15] PLR 9126014 (March 29, 1991).

The 40% rule prevents taxpayers from using the half-year convention and thereby obtaining one-half year's depreciation in the year of acquisition when a substantial portion of the assets are placed in service during the last quarter of the tax year.

EXAMPLE I:10-10 ▶ Michael, a calendar year taxpayer, acquires 5-year tangible personal property in 2015, does not elect Sec. 179, and places the properties in service as follows:

Date Placed in Service	Acquisition Cost
January 20	$45,000
April 18	50,000
November 5	77,000
Total	$172,000

Because more than 40% of the property acquired during the year is placed in service in the last three months ($77,000 ÷ $172,000 = 44.8%), the mid-quarter convention applies for all property placed in service during the year. Depreciation for 2015 is computed as follows:

Property Placed in Service	Year 1 MACRS Depreciation	Appendix C Table
January 20	$45,000 × 0.35 = $15,750	Table 2
April 18	50,000 × 0.25 = 12,500	Table 3
November 5	77,000 × 0.05 = 3,850	Table 5
Total	$32,100	

EXAMPLE I:10-11 ▶ Assume the same facts as in Example I:10-10 except Michael elects to expense $25,000 under Sec. 179 and selects the property placed in service on November 5. In this case, the mid-quarter convention would not apply because not more than 40% of property (after the Sec. 179 deduction) was placed in service in the last quarter of the year [($77,000 − $25,000) ÷ ($172,000 − $25,000) = 35.4%]. Therefore, Michael uses the half-year convention, and his depreciation for 2014 is computed using Table 1 in Appendix C as follows:

Date Placed in Service	Year 1 MACRS Depreciation	Sec. 179 Depreciation	Total 2015 Depreciation
January 20	$45,000 × 0.20 = $ 9,000	–0–	$ 9,000
April 18	50,000 × 0.20 = 10,000	–0–	10,000
November 5	52,000* × 0.20 = 10,400	$25,000	35,400
Total			$54,400

* After Sec. 179 depreciation ($77,000 − $25,000)

In this case, the half-year convention yields larger depreciation in the first year. In some cases, the mid-quarter convention can yield a larger depreciation deduction. This situation occurs only when a large amount of property is placed in service in the first quarter of the year, yet enough property is placed in service in the fourth quarter to require the mid-quarter convention. ◄

ADDITIONAL POINT
To reflect the applicable convention, the taxpayer must manually adjust the depreciation factor found in the MACRS table for assets disposed of during the year.

Year of Disposition. The MACRS system requires that depreciation be taken in the year of disposition using the same convention that applied on acquisition (e.g., half-year, mid-month, or mid-quarter convention). Therefore, if property is disposed of during any year in which the half-year convention is applicable, the depreciation for the year of disposition will be one-half of the amount computed by using the table percentages.

EXAMPLE I:10-12 ▶ Michelle acquired machinery in March 2011 that qualified as 7-year MACRS property and had a $100,000 basis for depreciation. The half-year convention applied in the year of acquisition, and Michelle claimed no Sec. 179 depreciation on the machinery. In December 2015, Michelle sells the machinery. Michelle's depreciation deduction in 2015 is $4,465 ($100,000 × 0.0893 × 0.50). See Table 1 in Appendix C. ◄

If property is subject to the mid-quarter convention, it is treated as being disposed of at the midpoint of the quarter.

EXAMPLE I:10-13 ▶ In addition to other property acquired in the last quarter of 2011, Jason acquired $200,000 of 5-year property in May 2011 (second quarter). He depreciated all property acquired in 2011 using the mid-quarter convention. He claimed no Sec. 179 expense. If Jason sells the 5-year property on July 14, 2015 (third quarter), the property will be treated as if it were sold on August 15, 2015, which is the midpoint of the third quarter. Thus, using Table 3 in Appendix C, Jason claims $14,213 of depreciation in 2015 [($200,000 × 0.1137) × (2.5 ÷ 4)]. ◀

KEY POINT

Depreciable real property placed in service after 1986 must be depreciated using the straight-line method.

ADDITIONAL COMMENT

For purposes of determining whether at least 80% of the gross rental income is rental income from dwelling units, a taxpayer living in any part of the building includes the fair rental value of his unit in the gross rental income.

Real property falls into two categories: residential rental property and nonresidential real property. **Residential rental property** is defined as property from which at least 80% of the gross rental income is rental income from dwelling units.[16] Dwelling units include houses, apartments, and manufactured homes that are used for residential purposes but not hotels, motels, or other establishments for transient use. **Nonresidential real property** is any real property other than residential rental property.

Real Property: Classification and Recovery Rates. The MACRS recovery periods that apply to real property placed in service in years after 1986 are:

▶ Residential rental property: 27.5 years (Table 7 in Appendix C)

▶ Nonresidential real property: 39 years[17] (Tables 8 and 9 in Appendix C)

Straight-line depreciation must be used and is reflected in the tables. A mid-month convention is used in the year of acquisition and in the year of disposition.

EXAMPLE I:10-14 ▶ On October 4, 2015, Husker, Inc., acquired an office building to relocate its rapidly-growing staff. The property was purchased for $1,500,000, of which $200,000 was allocated to the underlying land. Because the property is nonresidential real property, it is classified as 39-year property. Depreciation is computed using Table 9 in Appendix C (mid-month convention), totaling $6,955 ($1,300,000 × 0.00535). In 2016, depreciation on the building will be $33,332 ($1,300,000 × 0.02564). ◀

HISTORICAL NOTE

The recovery period for nonresidential real property was extended from 31.5 years to 39 years in 1993 to offset the revenue loss from liberalizing the passive activity loss rules affecting real estate.

Taxpayers owning buildings must depreciate subsequent capital improvements. Capital improvements are depreciated over the full MACRS recovery period of the improvement, not over the remaining life or recovery period of the building. Thus, the cost of a new roof on an office building must be depreciated over 39 years, even though the building may have been placed in service several years ago.

LEGISLATIVE UPDATE

In previous years, Congress provided special treatment for qualified leasehold improvement property by allowing it to be eligible for bonus depreciation in some years and classifying it in the 15-year property class. However, without action from Congress, this treatment ends in 2015.

Qualified Leasehold Improvement Property. Qualified leasehold improvement property (QLIP) is defined as any improvement to an interior portion of nonresidential real property made by either a lessee or a lessor pursuant to a lease. The QLIP must have been placed in service more than three years after the date the building was first placed in service. Expenditures that enlarge a building or expenditures such as an elevator, an escalator, or a structural component that benefits either a common area or the internal structural framework of a building are not considered QLIP.

As discussed previously, bonus depreciation (50% or 30%) was allowed for QLIP placed in service after September 10, 2001 and before January 1, 2005 as well as for QLIP placed in service in 2008 through 2013 (50% or 100%). In recent tax legislation, Congress gave special treatment to QLIP by allowing a 15-year recovery period instead of the 39-year recovery period allowed for nonresidential real property. The shorter recovery period is effective for QLIP placed in service after December 31, 2005 and before January 1, 2015, and requires straight-line depreciation with the half-year or midquarter convention, whichever was applicable.[18]

EXAMPLE I:10-15 ▶ Shaheen Corporation leased office space to operate its business in a 20-year-old building. In early 2014, the corporation made some major leasehold improvements, such as changing the size of offices by rearranging the walls, new ductwork, and other similar capital improvements to the office. The overall size of the office did not change. The leasehold improvements were

---

[16] Secs. 168(e)(2)(A).
[17] Sec. 168(c). A 31.5-year recovery period applied to nonresidential real property placed in service on or after January 1, 1987, and before May 13, 1993.
[18] The shorter recovery period was instituted by the 2004 Jobs Act and extended by the Tax Relief and Health Care Act of 2006 and the Tax Extenders Act of 2008 to QLIP placed in service before January 1, 2010. The Tax

Relief Act of 2010 extended the provision to QLIP placed in service before January 1, 2012. The American Taxpayer Relief Act of 2012 further extended the treatment of QLIP placed in service before January 1, 2014, and 2014 Tax Increase Prevention Act extended the treatment of QLIP placed in service before January 1, 2015.

completed and placed in service on July 15, 2014, at a total cost of $120,000 and were considered qualified leasehold improvement property. Normally, leasehold improvements must be depreciated over 39 years. For 2014, however, Shaheen Corporation was permitted to take both 50% bonus depreciation and 15-year straight line MACRS depreciation on the leasehold improvements. Thus, in 2014, the depreciation deduction was:

Cost of qualified leasehold improvements	$120,000
Minus: Bonus depreciation	(60,000)
Depreciable basis	60,000
Times: Depreciation rate ($\frac{1}{15} \times \frac{1}{2}$)	0.03333
Depreciation on balance	$ 2,000
Total depreciation for 2014	$ 62,000

◄

Straight-Line (Method) Election Under MACRS. Instead of using the accelerated methods previously described under the MACRS rules, taxpayers may elect to use the straight-line method for tangible personal property. If the straight-line election is made, the taxpayer must use either the same depreciation period or an extended period based on the alternative depreciation system, as discussed below.[19]

EXAMPLE I:10-16 ►

In early 2015, Delta Corporation places in service equipment costing $100,000. Delta does not elect Sec. 179 expensing and elects the straight line method under MACRS. Using a 7-year recovery period and half-year convention, Delta's depreciation for 2015 is $7,143 [($100,000 ÷ 7 years) × 0.50]. ◄

Alternative Depreciation System. The MACRS system provides an alternative depreciation system (ADS) that is required for certain property and is also available for all other depreciable assets if the taxpayer so elects.[20] The election is made on a year-by-year basis. Once the election is made for specified property, it is irrevocable. For personal property, the ADS election applies to all property within a class (all 5-year property, for example); for real property, the ADS election may be made on an individual property basis. The principal type of property for which the ADS is *required* is tangible property used predominantly outside the United States. ADS recovery periods are generally longer than recovery periods under MACRS, and ADS requires the use of the straight-line method with a half-year, mid-quarter, or mid-month convention, whichever is applicable. Thus, the ADS election is generally made by taxpayers who want to use the straight-line method over a longer recovery period. These taxpayers frequently have net operating losses or are subject to the alternative minimum tax (see Chapter I:14 for a discussion of the alternative minimum tax).

EXAMPLE I:10-17 ►

In May 2015, Bob Roaster purchases an office building for $300,000 ($50,000 allocated to the land) as rental property. Because he has substantial net operating losses from other business ventures, Roaster elects to depreciate the building using ADS. Depreciation expense for 2015, using the mid-month convention and a 40-year life is $3,908 [$250,000 × .01563 (Table 12, Appendix C)]. If Roaster had not elected ADS, his depreciation would have been $4,013 [$250,000 × .01605 (Table 9, Appendix C)]. The difference is small because the recovery period is 39 years under regular MACRS and 40 years under ADS. ◄

If the taxpayer *elected* ADS, he or she also could use the bonus depreciation allowed in 2001-2004, and 2008–2014. For property *required* to be depreciated under ADS, however, bonus depreciation was not permitted.

The alternate depreciation system also is used to compute earnings and profits (E & P) for a corporation (see Chapter C:4), and a variation of the ADS applies to compute depreciation for property placed into service after 1986 but before 1999 for alternative minimum tax purposes for both individuals and corporations (see Chapter I:14).

Topic Review I:10-1 presents a comparison of the MACRS and ADS rules.

---

[19] Sec. 168(g)(7).   [20] Sec. 168(g). (See Tables 10–12 in Appendix C.)

TOPIC REVIEW I:10-1

Comparison of MACRS and ADS

	MACRS	ADS
Recovery Periods:		
Automobiles	5 years	5 years
Computers	5 years	5 years
Office machinery	5 years	6 years
Office furniture and equipment	7 years	10 years
Residential rental property	27.5 years	40 years
Nonresidential real property	39 years[b]	40 years
Personal property with no specified class life	7 years	12 years
Conventions:		
Personal property	Half-year or mid-quarter[a]	Half-year or mid-quarter[a]
Real property	Mid-month	Mid-month
Depreciation in year of sale:		
Personal property	Yes	Yes
Real property	Yes	Yes

[a] If more than 40% of the cost of personal property (after Sec. 179 expensing) is placed in service during the last quarter of year.
[b] For property placed in service prior to May 13, 1993, the recovery period is 31.5 years.

ETHICAL POINT

The personal use of a corporate automobile by a shareholder-employee may be a constructive dividend. Personal use by a non-shareholder-employee results in additional taxable compensation to the employee.

MACRS RESTRICTIONS

Personal-Use Assets. The personal-use portion of an asset's cost is not depreciable. For example, if a taxpayer owns a duplex and uses one unit as a personal residence, only the unit that is rented to tenants qualifies for depreciation.

Listed Property Rules. Because Congress was concerned about taxpayers claiming large depreciation deductions (using accelerated methods) on certain types of assets that are conducive to mixed business/personal use, it placed restrictions on assets that are classified as *listed property*. Listed property includes automobiles, computers and peripheral equipment, and property generally used for purposes of entertainment, recreation, or amusement (for example, a video recorder).[21] If a listed property's business use is greater than 50% of its total use, the taxpayer may elect Sec. 179 expensing for the business portion and may use regular MACRS tables for the remaining business portion of the asset's cost, including bonus depreciation where applicable. However, if the business use is 50% or less, the taxpayer may not elect Sec. 179 expensing, must use ADS (e.g., 5-year straight-line cost recovery for automobiles and computers), and may not use bonus depreciation (because ADS is required).

EXAMPLE I:10-18 ▶ In June 2015, Patrick acquires an automobile at a cost of $10,000. He uses it 60% for business. Assuming no Sec. 179 election, the depreciation deduction on the business-use portion of the automobile's cost is based on the MACRS system and 5-year recovery class because the automobile is predominantly used in business (i.e., more than 50%). The MACRS depreciation allowance in 2015 is $1,200 [($10,000 × 0.20) × 60% business use percentage]. (Table 1 in Appendix C.) ◀

EXAMPLE I:10-19 ▶ In June 2015, Paula acquires an automobile at a cost of $10,000. She uses it only 40% for business. Paula must use ADS to depreciate the business portion of the automobile, and Sec. 179 expensing is not allowed. The business portion is $4,000 ($10,000 × 0.40). Paula's depreciation allowance in 2015 using the straight-line method and the half-year convention is $400 [($4,000 ÷ 5 years) × 0.50]. ◀

ADDITIONAL COMMENT

Congress enacted the restrictions on automobiles in 1984 because of a concern that the tax system was underwriting the acquisition of automobiles whose cost and luxury far exceeded what was required for business needs.

Additional restrictions apply to employees who acquire listed property (e.g., an automobile, personal computer, etc.) for use in employment-related activities. In addition

---

[21] Before January 1, 2010, cellular telephones were listed property. However, as of January 1, 2010, cellular telephones are no longer listed property.

Taxpayers are now permitted to use common-sense usage percentages. See IRS Notice 2009-46.

to the "more than 50% test," such use must be for the convenience of the *employer* and be required as a condition of employment.[22] This rule is strictly interpreted by the IRS. Further, deductions connected with listed property are also subject to substantial record-keeping requirements, similar to the requirements for entertainment expenses.[23]

EXAMPLE I:10-20 ▶ Raul, a college professor, acquired a personal computer for use at home. He used the computer 60% of the time on teaching- and research-related activities associated with his job. The remaining usage was for personal activities. Raul's employer finds that it is helpful for employees to own a personal computer but does not require them to purchase a computer as a condition of employment. Raul meets the first requirement (i.e., the 60% business usage is greater than the 50% threshold). However, the second requirement for employees (that the use must be for the convenience of the employer and required as a condition of employment) is not met. Thus, no depreciation may be taken because the employment-related use is not deemed to be business use. ◄

Recapture of Excess Cost Recovery Deductions. Taxpayers are subject to depreciation recapture on listed property if MACRS rules were used originally and the property's business-use percentage decreases to 50% or less in a subsequent year. Depreciation deductions for all years are recomputed using ADS. The excess depreciation deducted, including any Sec. 179 expense and bonus depreciation, is recaptured as ordinary income by including it in the taxpayer's gross income in the year the business-use percentage first falls to 50% or below.[24] Once the business use falls to 50% or below, ADS must be used for the current year and for all subsequent years, even if the business-use percentage increases to more than 50% in a subsequent year.

EXAMPLE I:10-21 ▶ Paul, a self-employed attorney, acquired an automobile in June 2013 for $12,000. In both 2013 and 2014, Paul's business-use percentage was 60%. Depreciation under MACRS in 2013 and 2014 were as follows:

2013: Regular MACRS depreciation assuming 100% business use ($12,000 × 0.20)	2,400
Times: Business-use percentage	0.60
Depreciation for 60% business use	$1,440
2014: Regular MACRS depreciation assuming 100% business use ($12,000 × 0.32)	$3,840
Times: Business-use percentage	0.60
Depreciation for 60% business use	$2,304

In 2015, Paul's business-use percentage declines to 40%. Therefore, he must use ADS for 2015 and also recapture the excess depreciation taken in 2013 and 2014. The recapture is computed as follows:

MACRS depreciation taken in 2013 and 2014 ($1,440 + $2,304)		$3,744
2013: Recomputed ADS depreciation ($12,000 × 0.60 × 0.10)	$ 720	
2014: Recomputed ADS depreciation ($12,000 × 0.60 × 0.20)	1,440	(2,160)
Recapture of excess depreciation in 2015 (ordinary income)		$1,584

Paul must use ADS to compute depreciation in 2015 and all subsequent years. His 2015 deduction will be $960 ($12,000 × 0.40 × 0.20). ◄

Limitations on Luxury Automobiles. Because Congress believed that the normal MACRS depreciation deduction for automobiles used for business was too generous, it placed ceilings on deductions related to luxury passenger automobiles. A passenger auto mobile is defined as a 4-wheeled vehicle which is manufactured primarily for use on public streets, roads, and highways and which is rated at 6,000 pounds or less unloaded gross vehicle weight rating (GVWR).[25] In essence, taxpayers are still allowed to fully depreciate luxury cars, but must depreciate them over longer than the normal five-year recovery period.

---

[22] Sec. 280F(d)(3). Any other property used for transportation (e.g., a pickup truck) qualifies as listed property if the nature of the property lends itself to personal use. (See Sec. 280F(b)(4).)

[23] Sec. 274(d)(4).
[24] Sec. 280F(b).
[25] Sec. 280F(d)(5)(A).

EXAMPLE I:10-22 ▶ In 2014, Joe purchases a $60,000 automobile that he uses 100% for business purposes. Under normal MACRS rules and without considering Sec. 179, Joe could deduct depreciation of $12,000 in the first year ($60,000 × 0.20) and $19,200 ($60,000 × 0.32) in the second year. Thus, Joe could deduct 52% ($31,200 ÷ $60,000) of the cost of his automobile in the first two years, creating considerable tax savings.

To prevent such perceived abuse, Congress has implemented ceiling limitations for MACRS depreciation on passenger automobiles placed in service (based on 100% business-use). For 2015, the ceiling limits are:

Year 1 (2015)	$3,160
Year 2 (2016)	5,100
Year 3 (2017)	3,050
Year 4 (2018 and subsequent years)	1,875

(For automobiles placed in service in prior years, see Table 6 in Appendix C.) ◀

ADDITIONAL COMMENT

The limitations on luxury automobiles mean that the depreciation deductions are limited during the normal 5-year recovery period on business automobiles costing more than $15,800 for 2015 ($3,160 ÷ 0.20).

To compute the maximum MACRS depreciation deduction for a passenger automobile for any year, taxpayers must first compute depreciation under normal MACRS rules, including Sec. 179, and then compare this amount to the ceiling limitation for that year.[26] The maximum depreciation deduction allowed for any year cannot exceed the ceiling limitation amount. Due to the ceiling limitation, taxpayers usually do not elect Sec. 179 expensing on passenger automobiles.

EXAMPLE I:10-23 ▶ Amy purchases a $60,000 automobile in 2015 that she uses 100% for business purposes. She is limited to $3,160 of depreciation, as this ceiling amount is less than regular MACRS depreciation ($60,000 × 0.20 = $12,000).

After the first year, the procedure is the same as above. The regular MACRS deduction is computed and compared with the appropriate year of the ceiling limitation and the deduction allowed cannot exceed the ceiling amount. As Table I:10-3 shows, after the regular recovery period ends for passenger automobiles placed in service in 2015, the taxpayer would be entitled to a deduction of $1,875 per year until the automobile is fully depreciated. ◀

Depreciating Mixed-Use Automobiles. Taxpayers who use passenger automobiles less than 100% for business must compute the regular MACRS depreciation amount, identify the ceiling amount, and then reduce each one by the percentage of personal use. The actual depreciation deduction for the year will be the lesser of the two reduced amounts. Complicating the matter, the taxpayer's basis in the automobile will decrease by the lesser of the *unreduced* amounts, even though that was not the amount allowed as a deduction.[27] Example 10-25 and Table 10-3 demonstrate this rule.

EXAMPLE I:10-24 ▶ Phil acquires an automobile for $60,000 in April 2015. He uses the automobile 80% for business and 20% for personal activities during 2015 and all succeeding years. Table I:10-3 lists the depreciation amounts, assuming that the 80% business use continues for the life of the automobile, but no amount is expensed under Sec. 179. At the end of the regular MACRS recovery period, the unrecovered cost of the business-use portion of the automobile may be recovered at an annual rate not to exceed $1,500 ($1,875 × 0.80). ◀

TYPICAL MISCONCEPTION

It is sometimes mistakenly believed that the Sec. 179 expensing allowance can be used to boost the first-year depreciation of luxury automobiles.

Trucks, Vans, and SUVs. As mentioned previously, limitations are placed on "passenger automobiles" that have a gross vehicle weight rating (GVWR) of 6,000 pounds or less. SUVs rated at a GVWR exceeding 6,000 pounds were not subject to the ceiling limitations, so taxpayers could expense up to $100,000 (adjusted for inflation) under Sec. 179, thus creating a major tax planning opportunity. Beginning in 2004, this controversial provision has been curtailed. For SUVs placed into service after October 22, 2004, the maximum Sec. 179

---

[26] Bonus depreciation also applied to property placed in service from September 11, 2001 through December 31, 2004, in 2008, in 2009, in 2010, and 2011, and was reflected in the limitations for those years.

[27] Sec. 280F(d)(8).

▼ TABLE I:10-3

Depreciation Amounts for Example I:10-25 (80% Business-Use Automobile)

	(A) MACRS Deduction: 100% Bus. Use (Table 1)	(B) Ceiling Limit: 100% Bus. Use (Table 6)	Deduction Allowed: 80% × Lesser of MACRS or Ceiling	Unrecovered Basis
2015 Regular MACRS calculation ($60,000 × 0.20)	$12,000	$ 3,160	$ 2,528	$56,840[a]
2016 Regular MACRS calculation ($60,000 × 0.32)	$19,200	$ 5,100	$ 4,080	$51,740
2017 Regular MACRS calculation ($60,000 × 0.192)	$11,520	$ 3,050	$ 2,440	$48,690
2018 Regular MACRS calculation ($60,000 × 0.1152)	$ 6,912	$ 1,875	$ 1,500	$46,815
2019 Regular MACRS calculation ($60,000 × 0.1152)	$ 6,912	$ 1,875	$ 1,500	$44,940
2020 Regular MACRS calculation ($60,000 × 0.0576)	$ 3,456	$ 1,875	$ 1,500	$43,440
Total through 2020	$60,000	$16,935	$13,548	
2021 and subsequent years until fully depreciated Ceiling limit		$ 1,875	$ 1,500	

[a] **Unrecovered basis** equals original basis minus the lesser of A or B [($60,000 − $3,160) in 2015] even though the annual deduction is limited to business usage.

Note: Based on the unrecovered basis of $43,440 at December 31, 2020, it would take Phil 24 more years to fully depreciate the automobile ($34,752/$1,500 = 23.2 years) based on 80% business use. The personal-use portion of the automobile's cost, $12,000 ($60,000 × 0.20), never will be depreciated and will be recovered only upon disposition.

expense amount is $25,000,[28] rather than the typically higher Sec. 179 election amounts. However, SUVs with a GVWR of greater than 6,000 pounds will continue to have significant depreciation advantages over other vehicles because the ceiling limitations do not apply.

To qualify for the truck and van depreciation deduction, a vehicle must be a passenger vehicle built on a truck chassis with an unloaded gross weight of over 6,000 pounds. A vehicle built on an automobile chassis is classified as an automobile regardless of weight, even if its manufacturer calls it an SUV.

EXAMPLE I:10-25 ▶

Two taxpayers purchase vehicles used 100% for business in July 2015, at a cost of $60,000 each. Taxpayer A purchases a BMW sedan that is considered a passenger automobile for tax purposes. Taxpayer B purchases a Ford Expedition which is rated at over 6,000 GVWR and, therefore, is not considered a passenger automobile and not subject to the ceiling limitations. Taxpayer B elects Sec. 179 expensing. The first-year depreciation for each vehicle for 2015 is computed below.

ADDITIONAL COMMENT

Many SUVs have a rated GVWR of greater than 6,000 pounds, such as the Chevrolet Suburban, Dodge Durango, Hummer H1 and H2, and Toyota Sequoia. For a more complete list, go to www.carsdirect.com/home.

BMW: Regular MACRS depreciation from Table 1 ($60,000 × 0.20)	$12,000
Ceiling limitation	3,160

In this case, the maximum depreciation deduction on the vehicle for 2015 is $3,160

Ford Expedition: Section 179 depreciation (maximum)	$25,000

---

[28] Sec. 179(b)(5). Vehicles with a GVWR of more than 14,000 pounds are not considered SUVs and are not subject to the $25,000 limitation.

Regular MACRS depreciation from Table 1 [($60,000 − $25,000) × .020]	7,000
Total depreciation for 2015	$32,000

The Table 6 ceiling limitations do not apply because the vehicle has a GVWR of more than 6,000 pounds. ◄

This example shows the significant tax savings from buying a passenger vehicle on a truck chassis that has a GVWR of more than 6,000 pounds. It should be noted that any vehicle that avoids the ceiling limitations must be used more than 50% for business, under the general listed property rules.

Although some taxpayers avoid the ceiling limitations by purchasing heavy vehicles, other taxpayers who use light trucks and vans (6,000 GVWR or less) in their businesses are hurt by the ceiling limitations. In response to small business concerns, two recent exceptions to the ceiling limitations have been issued: (1) exemption from the ceiling limitations for vehicles that clearly are not for personal use and (2) higher ceiling limitation amounts for other light trucks and vans.

► Exemption from ceiling limitations: Certain "nonpersonal use" vehicles are completely exempt from the ceiling limitations.[29] These vehicles must be specifically modified so that they are not likely to be used more than a de minimis amount for personal purposes. This somewhat vague definition is explained further in the regulations as a van that only has a front bench for seating, has permanent shelving that fills most of the cargo area, or has been painted with advertising or the company's logo.

► Higher ceiling limitations: Even if a light truck or van does not meet the nonpersonal use criteria above, higher ceiling limitations have been issued for vehicles on a truck chassis.[30] For trucks and vans on a truck chassis that have a GVWR of 6,000 pounds or less, the ceiling amounts for 2015 (Table 6) are as follows:

	Annual Ceiling Limitations
Year 1 (2015)	$3,460
Year 2 (2016)	5,600
Year 3 (2017)	3,350
Year 4 (2018 and subsequent years)	1,975

ADDITIONAL COMMENT
The amount that can be deducted for leased automobiles is also limited.

Additional Computations for Leased Vehicles. If a taxpayer leases an automobile or light truck or van for business purposes, the deduction for rental payments is reduced to reflect the luxury auto depreciation limits imposed on purchased vehicles. If these restrictions were not applied to leased automobiles, the ceiling limitations could be avoided by leasing instead of purchasing an automobile. The leasing restriction is accomplished by requiring taxpayers to reduce their deduction by an "inclusion amount" obtained from an IRS table.[31] This amount is based on the automobile's FMV and the tax year in which the lease commences, and is prorated for the percentage of business use and number of days used during the year. Partial lease inclusion tables are provided in Tables 13 and 14 in Appendix C.

EXAMPLE I:10-26 ►

On January 1, 2015, Jim leased and placed in service an automobile with a $39,500 FMV and annual lease payments of $7,200. Jim uses the automobile 80% for business purposes. Jim can deduct 80% of the lease payments ($7,200 × 0.80 = $5,760) but must reduce his deduction by 80% of the inclusion amount from Table 13 to reflect the luxury auto depreciation limitation. For 2015, this reduction was $27 ($34 × 0.80). Thus, Jim's auto lease deduction for 2015 was $5,733 ($5,760 − $27). For 2016, the second year, Jim's auto lease deduction is $5,700 [$5,760 − ($75 × 0.80)]. ◄

Topic Review I:10-2 summarizes the special depreciation elections and restrictions.

---

[29] Temp. Reg. Sec. 1.274-5T(k), T.D. 9064 (6-30-2003) amending T.D. 8061.
[30] Rev. Proc. 2003-75, 2003-2 C.B. 1018.

[31] The latest lease inclusion table is contained in Rev. Proc. 2015-19, 2015-8 I.R.B, 2/6/2015.

TOPIC REVIEW I:10-2

Special Depreciation Elections and Restrictions

SECTION 179 EXPENSING ELECTION

Maximum deduction: $25,000 (in 2015) of the total cost of qualified property placed in service during the year.

Qualified property: New or used tangible personal business-use property.

Limitations on deduction:
1. Cost limitation: The maximum Sec. 179 expense is reduced dollar-for-dollar by the excess of total qualified property cost over $200,000 (in 2015). Taxpayers may not carry forward amounts reduced by this limitation. However, the cost not expensed because of this limitation remains as basis subject to MACRS depreciation,
2. Taxable income limitation: The Sec. 179 expense after cost limitation is further limited to taxable income before the deduction. Taxpayers may carry forward amounts lost because of this limitation.

Basis reduction: The basis of qualified property for MACRS depreciation is reduced by the Sec. 179 expense (after the cost limitation reduction).

BONUS DEPRECIATION

Maximum allowed: 50% in 2014 of the cost of qualified property placed in service during the year. At the time of printing, Congress had not yet extended bonus depreciation to 2015.

Qualified Property: New (not used) property that is (1) MACRS property with a recovery period of 20 years or less, (2) computer software, or (3) qualified leasehold improvement property.

BUSINESS USE RESTRICTION

Listed property: If business use of listed property exceeds 50% of total use, taxpayers may elect Sec. 179 expensing for the business portion and may depreciate the remaining business-use portion using MACRS rules. If business use is 50% or less of total use, taxpayers may not elect Sec. 179 expensing and must depreciate listed property using ADS rules.

AUTOMOBILES, TRUCKS, AND VANS

Table 6 in Appendix C provides annual ceiling amounts for depreciation on 100% business-use automobiles and on 100% business-use trucks and vans with a GVWR of 6,000 pounds or less. The taxpayer computes regular depreciation under MACRS, including Sec. 179 expensing, and then compares that figure to the Table 6 ceiling figure. The deduction is the lesser of these two. If business-use is less than 100%, both figures must be reduced by the personal-use percentage. Basis nevertheless is adjusted by the unreduced figure. Business-use trucks and vans with a GVWR of more than 6,000 pounds are not subject to these limitations.

LEASED VEHICLES

Taxpayers who lease vehicles must subtract from their otherwise deductible lease payments as "inclusion amount" (see Tables 13 and 14 in Appendix C) to adjust the lease expense deduction for the luxury auto depreciation limitations imposed on purchased vehicles. This rule prevents individuals from avoiding the luxury auto depreciation limits by leasing vehicles.

AMORTIZATION

OBJECTIVE 2

Calculate amortization for intangible assets and distinguish between amortizable and non-amortizable assets

Amortization deductions are allowed for a variety of intangible assets. Although amortization periods vary greatly depending on the type of asset, all intangible assets are amortized on a *straight-line basis*. The major intangible assets that may be amortized are as follows:

▶ Goodwill and Other Purchased Intangibles, Sec. 197

▶ Research and Experimental Expenditures, Sec. 174

▶ Computer software

▶ Start-up Expenditures, Sec. 195

▶ Organizational Expenditures, Sec. 248

▶ Pollution Control Facilities, Sec. 169

Several of the above intangibles are discussed below.

HISTORICAL NOTE

Prior to the tax change in 1993, no amortization for goodwill was allowed. So, in business acquisitions, the purchaser typically tried to allocate as little of the purchase price as possible to goodwill. These allocations frequently caused disputes with the IRS. Under current law, these disputes have lessened for purchased goodwill.

SEC. 197 INTANGIBLES

Sec. 197 allows a deduction for the amortization of certain acquired intangible assets. The amortization is deducted on a ratable basis (straight-line) over a 15-year period beginning with the month of acquisition.[32] In general, Sec. 197 applies only to intangible assets that are acquired in connection with the conduct of a trade or business or an activity engaged in for the production of income. Sec. 197 does not apply to an intangible asset that is internally created by the taxpayer, such as a patent resulting from the taxpayer's research and development lab. Internally-created patents and copyrights have definite and limited lives and are therefore amortizable over the defined period.[33] Internally created patents are generally amortized over 17 years; internally created copyrights over 28 years.

EXAMPLE I:10-27 ▶ On January 1, 2015, Central Corporation receives patent approval on an internally created process improvement. Legal costs associated with the patent are $100,000 and the patent has a legal life of 17 years. The patent does not qualify as a Sec. 197 intangible. The patent has a definite and limited life and is amortizable ratably over its legal life of 17 years beginning with the month of its creation. ◀

BOOK-TO-TAX ACCOUNTING COMPARISON

For financial statement reporting, a firm reduces goodwill by an impairment amount rather than by amortization.

Definition of a Sec. 197 Intangible Asset. Sec. 197 intangibles (i.e., intangible assets that are subject to 15-year ratable amortization) include the following:

▶ Goodwill and going concern value. Conceptually, goodwill is an intangible asset that is neither separately identified or valued but possesses characteristics that allow a business to earn greater returns than would be possible without such characteristics. These characteristics include valued employees, superior management team, loyal customer base, strategic location, etc. For income tax purposes, however, goodwill is determined in a much more practical manner. **Goodwill** is defined as the value of a trade or business that is attributable to the expectation of continued customer patronage, whether due to the name or reputation of the trade or business or to any other factor.[34] Going concern value is the added value that attaches to acquired property because it is an integral part of a going concern.

▶ Intangible assets relating to the workforce, such as an information base (e.g., a customer list), know-how, customers, suppliers, or similar items (e.g., the portion of the purchase price of an acquired business that is attributable to an existing employment contract for a key employee.) Know-how related intangibles include patents, copyrights, formulas, and processes.

▶ Licenses, permits, or other rights granted by a governmental unit or agency (e.g., the capitalized cost of acquiring a radio broadcasting license).

▶ Covenants not to compete. A covenant not to compete represents an agreement between a buyer and seller of a business that the seller (i.e., the selling corporation and/or its shareholders) will not compete with the buyer for a limited period. The covenant may also be limited to a geographic area. A covenant not to compete must be amortized over 15 years even though the agreement was only for five years.[35]

▶ Franchises, trademarks, and trade names. A franchise includes any agreement that gives one of the parties the right to distribute, sell, or provide goods, services, or facilities, within a specified area.

EXAMPLE I:10-28 ▶ In January of the current year, Chicago Corporation acquires all the net assets of Coastal Corporation for $1 million. The following intangible assets are included in the purchase agreement:

Assets	Acquisition Cost
Goodwill and going concern value	$100,000
Licenses	55,000
Patents	45,000
Covenant not to compete for five years	90,000

All the intangible assets above qualify as Sec. 197 intangible assets and are amortizable on a ratable basis (straight-line) over 15 years beginning with the month of acquisition. This 15-year amortization period applies to the covenant not to compete even though the convenant is only for five years. ◀

---

[32] Sec. 197(a).
[33] Reg. Sec. 1.167(a)-3.
[34] Reg. Sec. 1.197-2(b)(1).

[35] Frontier Chevrolet Co., 2003-1 USTC ¶50,490 (9th Cir., 2003) aff'g 116 T.C. 289 (2001).

 **STOP & THINK**

Question: When one company purchases the assets of another company, the purchasing company may acquire goodwill. Because purchased goodwill is a Sec. 197 intangible asset and may be amortized over 15 years, determining the cost of goodwill is important. How is the "cost" of goodwill determined in an acquisition?

Solution: The IRS requires that taxpayers use the "residual method" as prescribed in Sec. 1060. Under this method, all of the assets except for goodwill are valued. The total value of these assets is then subtracted from the total purchase price, and the residual is the amount of the purchase price allocated to goodwill.

ADDITIONAL COMMENT

Sec. 1231 generally allows gains to be treated as long-term capital gains and losses to be deducted as ordinary losses. Sec. 1245 requires that gains be classified as ordinary income to the extent depreciation, amortization or depletion was claimed as an ordinary deduction in prior periods (see Chapter I:13).

Classification and Disposition of Intangible Assets. A Sec. 197 intangible asset is treated as depreciable property. Thus, a disposition is given Sec. 1231 treatment if the intangible asset is held for more than one year.[36] Gain on disposition of a Sec. 197 intangible is subject to depreciation recapture under Sec. 1245 (see Chapter I:13).[37] Loss on disposition of a Sec. 197 intangible asset, however, is not deductible if other intangibles acquired in the same acquisition of a trade or business are retained. In such case, the bases of the retained Sec. 197 intangibles are increased by the disallowed loss.[38]

EXAMPLE I:10-29 ►

Assume the same facts as in Example I:10-28. After five years, the covenant not to compete expires. Its adjusted basis is $60,000 [$90,000 − ($\frac{5}{15} \times$ $90,000)]. The $60,000 loss is not deductible, and the disallowed loss is allocated to the retained Sec. 197 assets based on their respective FMVs. ◄

EXAMPLE I:10-30 ►

Assume the same facts as in Example I:10-28. After one year the *patent* is sold for $50,000. In the initial year, $3,000 ($45,000 ÷ 15) of amortization was deducted. The recognized gain on the sale is $8,000 ($50,000 − $42,000). Of the gain, $3,000 is recaptured as ordinary income under Sec. 1245, and $5,000 is classified as Sec. 1231 gain. ◄

RESEARCH AND EXPERIMENTAL EXPENDITURES

TYPICAL MISCONCEPTION

It is sometimes mistakenly believed that if a company constructs a new building to be used entirely as a research facility, the entire cost of the building can be expensed. However, the expensing election applies only to the depreciation allowances on the building.

In general, research and experimental (R&E) expenditures include experimental and laboratory costs incidental to the development of a product.[39] Section 174 was enacted to clarify the income tax treatment of R&E expenditures. Treasury Regulations define items that do and do not qualify as R&E expenditures. These items are summarized in Table I:10-4. For income tax purposes, the following alternatives are available for qualified R&E expenditures:

► Expense in the year paid or incurred.

► Defer (capitalize as deferred expenses) and amortize the costs as a ratable deduction over a period of 60 months or more beginning with the month in which benefits are first realized.

► Capitalize and write off the costs only when the research project is abandoned or is worthless.[40]

A taxpayer must make an election to either expense or defer and amortize the costs in the initial year the R&E expenditures are incurred. If no election is made, the costs must be capitalized. The taxpayer must continue to use the same accounting method for the R&E expenditures unless IRS approval to change methods is obtained.

Below are some important points regarding R&E expenditures:

► Most taxpayers elect to expense the R&E expenditures because they prefer the immediate tax benefit.

► The deferral and amortization method is desirable if the taxpayer is currently in a low tax rate situation or expects initial NOLs during a start-up period.

► If the deferral and amortization method is used, the amortization period of 60 or more months commences with the month in which the benefits from the expenditures are first realized.

---

[36] Sec. 197(f)(7).
[37] Sec. 1245(a)(2)(C).
[38] Sec. 197(f)(1).

[39] Reg. Sec. 1.174-2(a)(2). The Regulations define the term *product* to include any pilot model, formula, invention, technique, patent, or similar product.
[40] Sec. 174.

▼ TABLE I:10-4

Research and Experimental Expenditures

Items That Qualify	Items That Do Not Qualify[a]
▶ Costs incident to the development of an experimental or pilot model, a plant process, a product, a formula, an invention ▶ Costs associated with product improvements ▶ Costs of obtaining a patent, such as attorney fees ▶ Research contracted to others ▶ Depreciation or cost-recovery amounts attributable to capitalized R&E items (e.g., research laboratory and equipment)	▶ Expenditures for ordinary testing or inspection of materials or products for quality control purposes ▶ Efficiency surveys and management studies ▶ Marketing research, advertising, etc. ▶ Cost of acquiring another person's patent, model, production, or process ▶ Research incurred in connection with literary, historical, or similar projects

[a] Certain of these expenses may be deductible as trade or business expenses under Sec. 162, subject to amortization under Sec. 197, or treated as start-up expenditures under Sec. 195.

▶ R&E expenses include depreciation allowances related to capitalized expenditures. Thus, if the deferral and amortization method is used, depreciation allowances are deferred as part of the R&E expenditures that are amortized over a period of at least 60 months. Capital expenditures made in connection with R&E activities cannot be expensed when they are incurred merely because an election to expense R&E costs are made.

▶ A tax credit may apply to certain research expenditures. (See Chapter I:14 for a discussion of the research activities credit.) Taxpayers must reduce any R&E expense deduction by the amount of the credit claimed.

EXAMPLE I:10-31 ▶ In 2015, Control Corporation leases a research laboratory to develop new products and to improve existing products. Control Corporation, a calendar year taxpayer that uses the accrual method of accounting, incurs the following expenditures during 2015:

Laboratory supplies and materials	$ 40,000
Laboratory equipment	60,000[a]
Utilities and rent	50,000
Salaries	50,000
Total expenditures	$200,000

[a] The MACRS recovery period is 5 years at a 20% rate for the initial year.

REAL-WORLD EXAMPLE

An airline company made payments to an aircraft manufacturer to help defray the cost of designing, developing, producing, and testing a supersonic transport prototype aircraft. These payments were considered R&E expenditures. Rev. Rul. 69-484, 1969-2 C.B. 38.

Assume the benefits from the R&E expenditures are first realized in January 2016. If Control Corporation elects to expense the R&E expenditures, the deduction in 2015 is $152,000 ($40,000 laboratory supplies and materials + $12,000 depreciation on the equipment + $50,000 utilities and rent + $50,000 salaries). If the deferral and amortization method is elected, none of the expenditures above are deductible in 2015 because the benefits of the R&E activities are not first realized until January 2016. If the 60-month minimum amortization period is elected, the monthly amortization commencing in January 2016 is $2,533 ($152,000 ÷ 60 months). The $48,000 ($60,000 – $12,000) of laboratory equipment cost is depreciated over the remaining MACRS recovery period beginning in 2016. ◀

COMPUTER SOFTWARE

The amortization or depreciation of computer software depends on the nature of the software and how it is acquired. Basically, computer software is either developed by the taxpayer or acquired (purchased or leased) from an outside party.

Developed Computer Software. The cost of developing computer software that is considered R&E may either be expensed in the year the costs are incurred or, if the taxpayer so elects, capitalized and amortized over 60 months beginning with the month in which the taxpayer first realizes benefits from such expenditures, per Sec. 174. If the costs incurred to develop the software are not considered R&E costs (e.g., the software is not in the experimental stage), such costs should be depreciated on a straight line basis over 36 months beginning with the date the software is placed in service.[41]

Purchased Computer Software. Purchased computer software generally may be depreciated in two alternative ways: (1) if the software is included in the cost of the computer hardware, the software does not have to be separately stated as long as the taxpayer consistently follows this treatment. Therefore, the computer and software would be depreciated together under MACRS over five years; or (2) if the software is purchased separately, the software must be depreciated on a straight-line basis over 36 months. An exception to these rules occurs if computer software is purchased in connection with the acquisition of a number of assets of an existing trade or business. In this case, the computer software is considered to be a Sec. 197 intangible and must be amortized over a period of 15 years.[42]

EXAMPLE I:10-32 ▶ Morris Corporation purchased all the assets of an existing business on April 1, 2015 for $1,000,000. Included in the assets was some computer software that the corporation intends to use in its business. The software is specialized for use by Morris Corporation. Based on relative fair market values, the computer software is allocated a cost of $63,000. The software is considered a Sec. 197 intangible and would be amortized over 15 years beginning in the month of acquisition. For the eight-month period in calendar year 2015, Morris Corporation's amortization deduction would be $2,800 [($63,000 ÷ 15 years) × 8/12]. ◄

EXAMPLE I:10-33 ▶ Using the same facts as in Example I:10-32, if Morris Corporation had purchased computer software on April 1, 2015 (not in connection with an asset acquisition) for $63,000, the software would not be considered a Sec. 197 intangible and would be depreciable under Sec. 167(f) on a straight-line basis over a period of 36 months. Therefore, in 2015, Morris Corporation's depreciation deduction would be $14,000 [($63,000 ÷ 36) × 8 months]. ◄

Leased or Licensed Computer Software. Computer software that is leased or licensed for use in the taxpayer's trade or business generally is deductible in full in the year paid.[43]

DEPLETION, INTANGIBLE DRILLING AND DEVELOPMENT COSTS

OBJECTIVE 3

Apply cost and percentage depletion methods and summarize the treatment for intangible drilling costs

The taxation of natural resources, such as oil and gas, coal, iron ore, etc. has many of its own specific rules. This section of the text discusses some of the concepts that apply to the oil and gas industry. Other natural resources have slightly different rules, but the oil and gas industry demonstrates the normal taxation of natural resources.

The exploration, development, and operation of oil and gas properties require an outlay of various types of expenditures. Below are the four major types of oil and gas property expenditures and their income tax treatment.

▶ Payments for the mineral interest. These costs are capitalized and recovered through depletion.

▶ Intangible drilling and development costs (e.g., labor and other operating costs to clear land, erect a derrick, and drill the well). Taxpayers elect to either capitalize or immediately expense these expenditures.

---

[41] Sec. 167(f)(1) and Rev. Proc. 2007-16, 2007-4 I.R.B. 358.
[42] Sec. 197(e)(3)(A). If the computer software acquired in an asset acquisition is software that is readily available for purchase by the general public, such software would not be considered a Sec. 197 intangible. (See Sec. 197(e)(3)(A)(i).)

[43] Reg. Sec. 1.162-11 and Rev. Proc. 2007-4, 2007-14 I.R.B. 358.

▶ Tangible asset costs (e.g., machinery, pipe). These expenditures must be capitalized and depreciated under the MACRS rules.

▶ Operating costs after the well is producing. These expenditures are deductible under Sec. 162 as ordinary and necessary business expenses.

DEPLETION METHODS

KEY POINT

A depletion deduction is available in the case of mines, oil and gas wells, other natural resources, and timber. However, the percentage depletion method is not available in the case of timber.

Depletion, similar to depreciation, is the using up of natural resources by the process of mining (coal, for example) or drilling (oil and gas). It is calculated under the **cost depletion method** or the **percentage depletion method** for each period. The method used in any year is the one that results in the largest deduction. Thus, percentage depletion may be used in one year and cost depletion may be used in the following year.

Depletion is allowed to the taxpayer who has an **economic interest** in the property. The person who typically has an economic interest in the property is the owner of the natural resource (i.e., the oil, gas, coal, etc.). Thus, depletion may be claimed by the persons who either own the natural resource property or retain a royalty interest. A mining company that only mines coal from a property and does not own (or lease) the underlying coal is not considered to hold an economic interest and, therefore, is not allowed a depletion deduction. The landowner who owns the coal would be entitled to the depletion deduction.

ADDITIONAL COMMENT

Note that a taxpayer will deduct the greater of cost depletion or percentage depletion. If percentage depletion is used, the adjusted basis of the property is reduced by the percentage depletion amount.

Cost Depletion Method. The cost depletion method is similar to the units-of-production method of depreciation. The adjusted basis of the asset is divided by the estimated recoverable units to arrive at a per-unit depletion cost. This per-unit cost is then multiplied by the number of units sold to determine the cost depletion deduction.[44] If the original estimate of recoverable units is subsequently determined to be incorrect, the per-unit cost depletion rate must be revised and used on a prospective basis to determine cost depletion in future years.[45] It is not proper to file an amended return for the years in which the incorrect estimated unit cost was used.

EXAMPLE I:10-34 ▶

Ralph acquires an oil and gas property interest for $100,000 in 2015. The estimate of recoverable units is 10,000 barrels of oil. The per-unit cost depletion amount is $10 ($100,000 ÷ 10,000). If 3,000 units are produced and 2,000 units are sold in 2015, the cost depletion amount is $20,000 (2,000 units × $10 per unit). If cost depletion is used because it exceeds the percentage depletion amount, the cost basis of the property is reduced to $80,000 ($100,000 − $20,000) at the beginning of 2016. If the estimate of remaining recoverable units is revised downward from 8,000 units in 2016 (10,000 − 2,000 units sold in 2015) to 5,000 units (including the 1,000 barrels produced but not sold in 2015), the property's $80,000 adjusted basis is divided by 5,000 units to arrive at a new per-unit cost depletion amount of $16 for 2016. This process is continued each year until the cost of the oil and gas property interest is fully depleted. ◀

REAL-WORLD EXAMPLE

Taxpayers are entitled to a depletion deduction if they have an economic interest in the property. This economic interest may be in the form of a royalty interest where a landowner receives a certain amount per unit extracted from her land, such as $10 for each barrel of oil. The landowner would be entitled to a depletion deduction based on the royalty income received.

Percentage Depletion Method. Percentage depletion generally offers substantial tax benefits for taxpayers in the natural resources industry. The purpose of allowing percentage depletion is to encourage persons to invest and/or operate in an industry that is both capital intensive and high risk but is also vital to our national interests. Percentage depletion may be used by taxpayers for a wide variety of natural resources, such as oil and gas, coal, gold, etc. The percentage depletion method has not been available to *large* oil and gas producers since 1974; but it is still available to *small* oil and gas producers and royalty owners under a specific exemption in the law.[46] Percentage depletion is computed by multiplying the percentage depletion rate times the gross income from the property. However, the depletion amount may not exceed 50% of the taxable income from the property before depletion is deducted (100% for oil and gas properties).[47] Percentage depletion may not be calculated on any lease bonus, advance royalty, or other amount payable without regard to production from the property.

---

[44] Sec. 612.
[45] Sec. 611(a).
[46] Sec. 613A(c). To be classified as a small oil and gas producer or royalty

owner, the maximum depletable quantity is based on average daily production of not more than 1,000 barrels of oil or 6 million cubic feet of natural gas.
[47] Sec. 613(a).

Whether the taxpayer uses cost depletion or percentage depletion, the amount of the depletion deduction reduces the basis of the natural resource property. Once the basis of depletable property has been reduced to zero, a taxpayer may no longer claim depletion using the cost depletion method. However, the taxpayer may continue to claim percentage depletion. Subsequent percentage depletion will not reduce the basis of the property below zero. It should be apparent that percentage depletion is a very advantageous method because the total depletion allowed over the life of the property may exceed the property's cost.[48]

Percentage depletion rates vary by the type of mineral. Depletion rates for selected minerals are as follows:

Mineral	Depletion Rate
Oil and gas	15%[49]
Coal, asbestos	10%
Gold, silver, copper, iron ore	15%
Sulphur and uranium	22%
Gravel, stone	5%
All other minerals	14%

EXAMPLE I:10-35 ▶

In the current year, Carmen acquires for $400,000 an oil and gas property interest with 200,000 barrels of estimated recoverable oil. During the year, 10,000 barrels of oil are sold for $250,000. Intangible drilling and development costs (IDCs) amount to $100,000 and are expensed in the current year. Other expenses are $50,000. Cost depletion is $20,000 [10,000 barrels sold × ($400,000/200,000 barrels)] in the current year. The computation of percentage depletion is as follows:

(1) Percentage depletion before taxable income limitation ($250,000 × 0.15)	$ 37,500
(2) Taxable income ceiling:	
Gross income	$250,000
Minus: Intangible drilling costs (IDCs) expensed	(100,000)
Other expenses	(50,000)
Taxable income before depletion	$100,000
(3) Percentage depletion (lesser of (1) or (2))	$ 37,500

HISTORICAL NOTE

An Arab oil embargo to the United States in 1973 created a situation where oil prices increased significantly. Consequently, most domestic U.S. oil producers reported huge profits. This situation contributed to the repeal of the percentage depletion allowance for large oil and gas producers.

KEY POINT

The use of the percentage depletion method permits recovery of more than the cost of the property.

Carmen's depletion deduction is $37,500 because the percentage depletion amount is greater than the $20,000 of cost depletion. The adjusted basis of the property is reduced by $37,500, the amount of depletion actually claimed. ◀

TREATMENT OF INTANGIBLE DRILLING AND DEVELOPMENT COSTS

Intangible drilling and development costs (IDCs) may either be deducted as an expense or capitalized.[50] IDCs apply only to oil, gas, and geothermal wells and basically include all expenditures, other than the acquisition costs of the underlying property, that are incurred for the drilling and preparation of wells. If the IDCs are capitalized, the amounts are added to the property's basis for determining cost depletion, and the costs are expensed through cost depletion. For a well that is nonproductive (i.e., a dry hole), an ordinary loss is allowed for any IDC costs that have been capitalized and not recovered through depletion. The amount of depletion claimed in a tax year equals the greater of the percentage depletion and cost depletion amounts. If IDCs are capitalized and cost depletion is thereby increased, little or no tax benefit may result because the percentage depletion may still produce a greater deduction than cost depletion. Therefore, it is generally preferable to expense the IDCs if the percentage depletion is expected to be more than the cost depletion and is used to compute the depletion allowance.

---

[48] Depletion in excess of the adjusted basis of the property is a tax preference item under Sec. 57(a)(1).

[49] For small producers and royalty owners of oil and gas properties, there is a further limitation: the percentage depletion deduction may not exceed 65%

of taxable income from all sources before the depletion deduction. Sec. 613A(d)(1).

[50] Sec. 263(c).

EXAMPLE I:10-36 ▶

In the current year, Penny acquires certain rights to oil and gas property for $1,000,000, incurring $300,000 of IDCs. If the IDCs are capitalized, the basis for cost depletion purposes is $1,300,000. Assume that the cost depletion amounts are $100,000 in the current year if the IDCs are expensed and $130,000 if IDCs are capitalized. If the percentage depletion amount is $150,000, percentage depletion will be used because it is greater than either of the cost depletion amounts. Thus, expensing the IDCs permits Penny to deduct the entire $300,000 of IDCs in the current year plus $150,000 of percentage depletion. ◀

TAX PLANNING CONSIDERATIONS

OBJECTIVE 4

Identify tax planning considerations for depreciation

ALTERNATIVE DEPRECIATION SYSTEM UNDER MACRS

In some instances, it may be preferable to elect to use the alternative depreciation system (ADS) rather than the regular MACRS rules. For example, a taxpayer who anticipates losses during the next few years or who currently has NOL carryovers may elect to use ADS, which employs the straight-line method of depreciation over a longer recovery period.

EXAMPLE I:10-37 ▶

ADDITIONAL COMMENT

A taxpayer who is attempting to report a profit in three out of five years in an attempt to avoid the hobby loss rules might want to use the alternative depreciation system.

Delta Corporation has substantial NOL carryovers that will expire if not used during the next few years. Delta anticipates it will not have taxable income for each of the next seven years if the regular MACRS rules are used to depreciate its fixed asset additions. In the current year, Delta acquires new machinery and equipment at a cost of $100,000. Assuming no Sec. 179 election and no bonus depreciation, depreciation deductions using the MACRS rules and a 7-year recovery period are $14,290 (0.1429 × $100,000). Depreciation deductions under the straight-line method using ADS with a 12-year recovery period and the half-year convention are only $4,167 [($100,000 ÷ 12 years) × 0.50 year]. The ADS election increases taxable income in the current year by $10,123 and allows Delta to offset additional loss carryovers (which might otherwise expire) against this income amount. ◀

USE OF UNITS OF PRODUCTION DEPRECIATION

Many times, the MACRS depreciation system requires taxpayers to use a recovery period that is much longer than the actual useful life of the asset. For example, assume a taxpayer uses a machine in his or her business that is classified as 7-year property under MACRS. However, the machine is operated 24 hours a day, seven days a week and will completely wear out in two years. The use of the 7-year recovery period substantially understates depreciation for the machine in the two years of actual use. Under Sec. 168(f), taxpayers may exclude property from the MACRS system if the property is depreciated under the unit-of-production method or any other method not expressed in terms of years. Therefore, if the taxpayer can express the useful life of the machine in terms of some base other than years (such as machine hours, units produced, etc.), it may be possible to depreciate the machine over a much shorter period than the seven years required under MACRS.

STRUCTURING A BUSINESS COMBINATION

REAL-WORLD EXAMPLE

A taxpayer purchased a business that owned retail franchises. The IRS determined that amounts paid in excess of the value of the net assets represented a nondepreciable "indivisible asset." However, the taxpayer was able to show that retail franchises have limited useful lives, and was able to amortize the excess costs. *Super Food Services, Inc. v. U.S.*, 24 AFTR 2d 69-5309, 69-2 USTC ¶9558 (7th Cir., 1969).

When a company purchases the assets of another business, the agreement must specify the amounts paid for the tangible depreciable, nondepreciable, and intangible assets. Also, the company must comply with the reporting requirements of Sec. 1060, which states that both the transferor and the transferee are bound by their written agreement as to the allocation of the purchase price to individual assets unless the IRS determines that such allocation is not appropriate. Amounts paid for tangible assets should be documented by appraisals and evidence of negotiations between the buyer and seller. Within reason, the purchaser should attempt to allocate as much of the total price to tangible depreciable assets, such as machinery and equipment. The purchaser also should consider allocating part of the purchase price to amortizable Sec. 197 intangible assets such as goodwill, covenants not to compete, patents, copyrights, licenses, and customer lists because such asset costs are recovered over a 15-year period. This is preferable to allocating the purchase price to depreciable real estate because such property must be depreciated over 39 years.

WHAT WOULD YOU DO IN THIS SITUATION?

Your CPA firm has a long-standing tax client named Widgets R Us, Incorporated (WRU). WRU has been a worldwide leader in widget technology for years and continues to expand its global market share through a substantial program of basic research and development of widget crystallization processes. You have advised WRU as to which of these expenditures qualify as research and experimental (R&E) expenditures. In addition, you have given timely advice as to when to expense rather than capitalize these expenditures.

You are having your monthly tax conference with Ms. Ima Worthmore, president of WRU, and Mr. Stan Cunning, tax counsel of WMU. Ms. Worthmore relates to you a conversation she had with the local manager of a competitor CPA firm, Ms. Ruth Less. Ms. Less told Ms. Worthmore that she had discovered that WRU was one of the top spenders on research and development in the area and that her firm was "certified" to practice before the IRS and had experienced great success in gaining R&E write-offs for comparable firms. Ms. Less went on to say that, "For you, for this one year only, we offer to prepare your tax returns on a contingent basis. We promise to save you at least $1 million from what you are now paying the IRS through our better use of R&E write-offs, and our fee will only be 30% of the tax savings!"

Ms. Worthmore was excited that WRU might be able to pay considerably lower taxes and is somewhat perturbed because you had not brought this tax opportunity to her attention. She wants your firm to provide her with a counteroffer. How do you ethically respond to your client's request to match or better Ms. Ruth Less' proposal?

COMPLIANCE AND PROCEDURAL CONSIDERATIONS

OBJECTIVE 5

Identify compliance and procedural considerations for depreciation

REPORTING COST RECOVERY, DEPRECIATION, DEPLETION, AND AMORTIZATION DEDUCTIONS

Form 4562 is the primary reporting device for depreciation (cost recovery), depletion, and amortization. Individual taxpayers engaged in trade or business complete Form 4562 and carry the total to Schedule C of their Form 1040, using a separate 4562 for each enterprise. Corporate and other non-corporate taxpayers also use Form 4562, carrying the total to their specific returns. Individuals with rental property complete a 4562 and carry the total to Schedule E of their Form 1040.

Two exceptions to the use of Form 4562: (1) Depreciation on property used by an employee for business purposes is computed along with other employee business expenses on Form 2106, with the total carried to Schedule A of the Form 1040; (2) If a taxpayer computes depreciation only on property placed in service before the current year, Form 4562 is not required. Depreciation totals are entered directly on the applicable primary form. Taxpayers must still maintain detailed depreciation records to support the deduction.

EXAMPLE I:10-38 ▶

Form 4562 for 2014: George Jones, SSN 000-00-1111, is a building contractor who owns the following 100% business-use properties:

▶ Specialized utility repair truck (5-year property that is not listed property), costing $40,000, placed in service on February 15, 2014.

▶ Machinery and equipment (7-year property), costing $535,000, placed in service on June 10, 2014.

▶ Patent, costing $17,000, that was developed and placed in service on June 1, 2014, when it had a remaining legal life of 17 years.

▶ MACRS deduction for assets placed in service before 2014 is $66,000.

Jones had 2014 taxable income of $960,000 (before the Sec. 179 deduction and the deduction for one-half of self-employment taxes). George elected Sec. 179 expensing on the machinery and equipment, but elected out of claiming bonus depreciation on all qualifying property. Depreciation and amortization amounts are reported on Form 4562 and are shown in Figures I:10-1 and I:10-2. ◀

Form **4562**	**Depreciation and Amortization** (Including Information on Listed Property) ▶ Attach to your tax return. ▶ Information about Form 4562 and its separate instructions is at www.irs.gov/form4562.	OMB No. 1545-0172 **2014**
Department of the Treasury Internal Revenue Service (99)		Attachment Sequence No. **179**

Name(s) shown on return	Business or activity to which this form relates	Identifying number
George Jones	Building Contractor	000-00-1111

Part I Election To Expense Certain Property Under Section 179

Note: *If you have any listed property, complete Part V before you complete Part I.*

1	Maximum amount (see instructions)	1	$500,000
2	Total cost of section 179 property placed in service (see instructions)	2	$575,000
3	Threshold cost of section 179 property before reduction in limitation (see instructions)	3	$2,000,000
4	Reduction in limitation. Subtract line 3 from line 2. If zero or less, enter -0-	4	-0-
5	Dollar limitation for tax year. Subtract line 4 from line 1. If zero or less, enter -0-. If married filing separately, see instructions	5	$500,000

6	(a) Description of property	(b) Cost (business use only)	(c) Elected cost	
	Truck	40,000	-0-	
	Machinery and Equipment	535,000	500,000	

7	Listed property. Enter the amount from line 29	7	-0-	
8	Total elected cost of section 179 property. Add amounts in column (c), lines 6 and 7	8	500,000
9	Tentative deduction. Enter the **smaller** of line 5 or line 8	9	500,000
10	Carryover of disallowed deduction from line 13 of your 2013 Form 4562	10	
11	Business income limitation. Enter the smaller of business income (not less than zero) or line 5 (see instructions)	11	500,000
12	Section 179 expense deduction. Add lines 9 and 10, but do not enter more than line 11	12	500,000
13	Carryover of disallowed deduction to 2015. Add lines 9 and 10, less line 12 ▶	13	-0-	

Note: *Do not use Part II or Part III below for listed property. Instead, use Part V.*

Part II Special Depreciation Allowance and Other Depreciation (Do not include listed property.) (See instructions.)

14	Special depreciation allowance for qualified property (other than listed property) placed in service during the tax year (see instructions)	14	
15	Property subject to section 168(f)(1) election	15	
16	Other depreciation (including ACRS)	16	

Part III MACRS Depreciation (Do not include listed property.) (See instructions.)

Section A

17	MACRS deductions for assets placed in service in tax years beginning before 2014	17	66,000
18	If you are electing to group any assets placed in service during the tax year into one or more general asset accounts, check here . . . . ▶ ☐		

Section B—Assets Placed in Service During 2014 Tax Year Using the General Depreciation System

(a) Classification of property	(b) Month and year placed in service	(c) Basis for depreciation (business/investment use only—see instructions)	(d) Recovery period	(e) Convention	(f) Method	(g) Depreciation deduction
19a 3-year property						
b 5-year property		40,000	5 yrs	HY	MACRS	8,000
c 7-year property		*35,000	7 yrs	HY	MACRS	5,002
d 10-year property						
e 15-year property						
f 20-year property						
g 25-year property			25 yrs.		S/L	
h Residential rental property			27.5 yrs.	MM	S/L	
			27.5 yrs.	MM	S/L	
i Nonresidential real property			39 yrs.	MM	S/L	
				MM	S/L	

Section C—Assets Placed in Service During 2014 Tax Year Using the Alternative Depreciation System

20a Class life				S/L	
b 12-year			12 yrs.	S/L	
c 40-year			40 yrs.	MM	S/L

Part IV Summary (See instructions.)

21	Listed property. Enter amount from line 28	21	-0-
22	**Total.** Add amounts from line 12, lines 14 through 17, lines 19 and 20 in column (g), and line 21. Enter here and on the appropriate lines of your return. Partnerships and S corporations—see instructions	22	579,002
23	For assets shown above and placed in service during the current year, enter the portion of the basis attributable to section 263A costs	23	

For Paperwork Reduction Act Notice, see separate instructions.　　　Cat. No. 12906N　　　Form **4562** (2014)

*Line 19c: 535,000 − 500,000

FIGURE I:10-1 ▶ FORM 4562

Form 4562 (2014)   Page **2**

Part V | **Listed Property** (Include automobiles, certain other vehicles, certain computers, and property used for entertainment, recreation, or amusement.)

Note: *For any vehicle for which you are using the standard mileage rate or deducting lease expense, complete **only** 24a, 24b, columns (a) through (c) of Section A, all of Section B, and Section C if applicable.*

Section A—Depreciation and Other Information (Caution: *See the instructions for limits for passenger automobiles.***)**

24a Do you have evidence to support the business/investment use claimed? ☐ **Yes** ☐ **No**   **24b** If "Yes," is the evidence written? ☐ **Yes** ☐ **No**

(a) Type of property (list vehicles first)	(b) Date placed in service	(c) Business/ investment use percentage	(d) Cost or other basis	(e) Basis for depreciation (business/investment use only)	(f) Recovery period	(g) Method/ Convention	(h) Depreciation deduction	(i) Elected section 179 cost
25 Special depreciation allowance for qualified listed property placed in service during the tax year and used more than 50% in a qualified business use (see instructions) . **25**								
26 Property used more than 50% in a qualified business use:								
		%						
		%						
		%						
27 Property used 50% or less in a qualified business use:								
		%			S/L –			
		%			S/L –			
		%			S/L –			

28 Add amounts in column (h), lines 25 through 27. Enter here and on line 21, page 1 . **28**

29 Add amounts in column (i), line 26. Enter here and on line 7, page 1 . . . . **29**

Section B—Information on Use of Vehicles

Complete this section for vehicles used by a sole proprietor, partner, or other "more than 5% owner," or related person. If you provided vehicles to your employees, first answer the questions in Section C to see if you meet an exception to completing this section for those vehicles.

	(a) Vehicle 1		(b) Vehicle 2		(c) Vehicle 3		(d) Vehicle 4		(e) Vehicle 5		(f) Vehicle 6	
30 Total business/investment miles driven during the year (**do not** include commuting miles) .												
31 Total commuting miles driven during the year												
32 Total other personal (noncommuting) miles driven												
33 Total miles driven during the year. Add lines 30 through 32												
34 Was the vehicle available for personal use during off-duty hours?	Yes	No	Yes	No	Yes	No	Yes	No	Yes	No	Yes	No
35 Was the vehicle used primarily by a more than 5% owner or related person? . .												
36 Is another vehicle available for personal use?												

Section C—Questions for Employers Who Provide Vehicles for Use by Their Employees

Answer these questions to determine if you meet an exception to completing Section B for vehicles used by employees who **are not** more than 5% owners or related persons (see instructions).

		Yes	No
37	Do you maintain a written policy statement that prohibits all personal use of vehicles, including commuting, by your employees?		
38	Do you maintain a written policy statement that prohibits personal use of vehicles, except commuting, by your employees? See the instructions for vehicles used by corporate officers, directors, or 1% or more owners . .		
39	Do you treat all use of vehicles by employees as personal use?		
40	Do you provide more than five vehicles to your employees, obtain information from your employees about the use of the vehicles, and retain the information received?		
41	Do you meet the requirements concerning qualified automobile demonstration use? (See instructions.) . . .		

Note: *If your answer to 37, 38, 39, 40, or 41 is "Yes," do not complete Section B for the covered vehicles.*

Part VI | **Amortization**

(a) Description of costs	(b) Date amortization begins	(c) Amortizable amount	(d) Code section	(e) Amortization period or percentage	(f) Amortization for this year
42 Amortization of costs that begins during your 2014 tax year (see instructions):					
Patent	6-01-14	17,000	167	17 yrs.	*583
43 Amortization of costs that began before your 2014 tax year **43**					
44 Total. Add amounts in column (f). See the instructions for where to report **44**					583

*($17,000 ÷ 17 yrs.) = $1,000 x 7/12 = $583

Form **4562** (2014)

FIGURE I:10-2 ► FORM 4562 (CONTINUED)

PROBLEM MATERIALS

DISCUSSION QUESTIONS

I:10-1 Which of the following assets are subject to either amortization, depreciation, or cost recovery? Explain.
   a. An automobile held for personal use.
   b. Excess amounts paid in a business combination that are attributable to goodwill.
   c. Excess amounts paid in a business combination that are attributable to customer lists that have a limited useful life.
   d. A patent created internally which has a legal life of 17 years.
   e. Land held for investment purposes.
   f. A covenant not to compete which is entered into by the buyer and seller of a business.

I:10-2 Rick is a sole proprietor who has a small business currently operating at a loss. He would like to discontinue depreciating the fixed assets of the business for the next few years and to carry the deductions over to a future period. What tax consequences would result if Rick implements the plan to discontinue depreciation and then sells some of the depreciable assets several years later?

I:10-3 Rita acquired a personal residence two years ago for $120,000. In the current year, she purchases another residence and attempts to sell her former residence. Due to depressed housing conditions in the town where she used to live, Rita is unable to sell the house. Her former residence is now being offered for sale at $100,000 (its current FMV according to real estate appraisal experts). Rita has decided to rent the house rather than "give it away." She believes that renting the house on a permanent basis will permit her to write off the original $120,000 investment over its useful life and thus recoup her investment. What restrictions in the tax law may prevent her from accomplishing this objective? Explain.

I:10-4 Daytona Corporation, a manufacturing corporation, acquires the following business assets in the current year:
   • Furniture
   • Plumbing fixtures
   • Land
   • Goodwill and a trademark acquired in the acquisition of a business
   • Automobile
   • Heavy truck
   • Machinery
   • Building used in manufacturing activities
   a. Which of the assets above are eligible for depreciation under the MACRS rules or amortization under Sec. 197?

   b. What recovery period should be used for each of the assets listed above that come under the MACRS rules or under Sec. 197?

I:10-5 Robert is a sole proprietor who uses the calendar year as his tax year. On July 20, 2015 he acquired and placed in service a business machine, a 7-year asset, for $50,000. No other property was acquired in 2015.
   a. What is the amount of depreciation allowed in 2015 and 2016 if Sec. 179 depreciation (first-year expense election) was not elected?
   b. What is the amount of depreciation allowed in 2015 and 2016 if Sec. 179 was elected?

I:10-6 Roberta, a sole proprietor who uses the calendar year as her tax year, acquires and places in service two business machines during 2015. Machine C, a 7-year asset, was acquired on January 20, 2015, for $95,000 and Machine D, a 5-year asset, was acquired on August 1, 2015, for $50,000. No other property was acquired in 2015.
   a. What is the amount of depreciation allowed in 2015 if Sec. 179 is not elected?
   b. What is the amount of depreciation allowed in 2015 if Sec. 179 is elected?

I:10-7 Is a deduction allowed under the MACRS rules for depreciable real estate (used in a business or held for investment) in the year the property is sold? If so, explain how it is calculated.

I:10-8 Jose is considering acquiring a new luxury automobile costing $45,000 that will be used 100% in his business. The salesperson at the automobile dealership states that Jose will be entitled to substantial tax benefits in the initial year (2015) including:

If Sec. 179 is elected:
   • A deduction of $25,000 of the acquisition cost under Sec. 179, and a $4,000 ($20,000 × 0.2) depreciation deduction, for total deductions of $29,000.

If Sec. 179 is not elected:
   • A $9,000 ($45,000 × 0.2) depreciation deduction.

   a. Are the salesperson's assertions relative to the tax benefits accurate? Explain.
   b. Would your answer to Part a differ if the automobile were used only 60% for business purposes?
   c. Would your answer to Part a differ if Jose instead were to lease the automobile?

d. Would your answers to Part a differ if the vehicle were a large SUV (gross vehicle weight rating (GVWR) greater than 6,000 pounds) rather than an automobile?

I:10-9 Would the straight-line MACRS method (using the ADS) be preferable to the regular MACRS method in the following cases? Explain.
a. Ray incurs NOLs in his business for a number of years and has NOL carryovers he would like to use.
b. Rhonda's marginal tax rate is 15% but is expected to increase to 39.6% in three years.

I:10-10 Rudy is considering whether to make the election under Sec. 179 to expense the maximum amount of the acquisition cost related to certain fixed asset additions. What advantages are associated with the Sec. 179 election?

I:10-11 Luby Corporation has maintained an office in a leased building for several years. The corporation has decided to make some significant leasehold improvements to enhance the property. How should Luby Corporation depreciate the leasehold improvements?

I:10-12 Your client is a self-employed attorney who is considering the purchase of a $32,000 automobile that will be used 80% of the time for business and a $4,000 personal computer that will be used 100% of the time for business, but is located in his home.
a. What depreciation methods and recovery periods may be used under MACRS for the automobile and the personal computer?
b. How would your answer to Part a change if your client were an employee and the computer and automobile were not required as a condition of employment?
c. What tax consequences occur in Part a if the business use of the personal computer or the automobile decreases to 50% or less in a succeeding year? Explain.

I:10-13 In recent years (through 2014), Congress enacted provisions in the tax law that permitted bonus depreciation for certain assets.
a. What types of assets typically qualified for bonus depreciation?
b. How does bonus depreciation interface with Sec. 179 first-year expensing?

I:10-14 On March 1, 2015, Sarah entered into a three-year lease of an automobile used exclusively in her business. The automobile's FMV was $58,500 at the inception of the lease. Sarah made ten monthly lease payments of $600 each during 2015. Is Sarah able to avoid the luxury automobile restrictions on depreciation by leasing instead of purchasing the automobile? Explain. (The 2015 inclusion amount for Sarah's automobile is found in Table 13 of Appendix C.)

I:10-15 What difference does it make for income tax purposes whether an intangible asset is (1) acquired in connection with a business acquisition, (2) acquired by the purchase of an individual asset (e.g., a patent), or (3) created internally? Explain.

I:10-16 In January of the current year, Park Corporation incurs $34,000 of legal costs associated with a patent that was developed internally and has a legal life of 17 years. Park also acquired for cash the net assets of Central Corporation for $1,000,000. The following assets are specified in the purchase agreement:

Land	$ 200,000
Goodwill and going concern value	100,000
Covenant not to compete	50,000
Licenses	125,000
Customer lists	25,000
Inventory	100,000
Equipment and other tangible depreciable business assets	400,000
Total	$1,000,000

a. What tax treatment should be accorded the intangible assets?
b. Assuming that you were advising Park Corporation during the negotiations before drafting the purchase agreement, what suggestions would you make regarding the allocation of the total purchase price to the individual assets? How could the purchase price of individual assets be substantiated?

I:10-17 Why do most taxpayers prefer to currently expense research and experimental expenditures?

I:10-18 In a business combination, why does the buyer generally prefer to allocate as much of the purchase price to short-lived depreciable assets, ordinary assets such as inventory, and Sec. 197 intangible assets?

I:10-19 Explain the difference between cost depletion and percentage depletion. Which of these two methods generally provides the largest deduction?

I:10-20 Simon acquires an interest in an oil property for $50,000. Intangible drilling costs (IDCs) in the initial year are $10,000. Cost depletion is $5,000 if the IDCs are expensed and $6,000 if the costs are capitalized. Percentage depletion is $15,000 if the IDCs are expensed and $20,000 if the costs are capitalized. The difference in the percentage depletion amounts is due to the 100% taxable income limitation.
a. What method (i.e., expensing or capitalization and amortization) should be elected for the treatment of the IDCs in the initial year if Simon wants to maximize his deductions?
b. Why are intangible drilling costs expensed by most taxpayers?

ISSUE IDENTIFICATION QUESTIONS

I:10-21 Georgia Corporation acquires a business automobile for $30,000 on December 31 of the current year but does not actually place the automobile into service until January 1 of the following year. What tax issues should Georgia Corporation consider?

I:10-22 Paula is planning to either purchase or lease a $50,000 automobile. She anticipates that business use of the auto will be 60% for the first two years but will decline to 40% in years three through five. Currently, Paula's marginal tax rate is 15% but she anticipates that her marginal tax rate will be 39.6% after a few years. What tax issues should Paula consider relative to the decision to purchase or lease the automobile?

I:10-23 In the current year, Coastal Corporation acquires all of the net assets of Acorn Corporation for $2,000,000. The purchase agreement allocated the following amounts to the individual assets and liabilities:

Land and building	$1,400,000
Accounts receivable	200,000
Inventory	300,000
Goodwill	400,000
Patents (remaining legal life of ten years)	100,000
Covenant not to compete	200,000
Liabilities	(600,000)
Total	$2,000,000

What tax issues should Coastal Corporation consider relative to the asset acquisitions?

I:10-24 Weiskopf, a sole proprietor and a calendar-year taxpayer, purchased $60,000 of equipment during 2015, as follows:

	Cost	Recovery Period
March 1	$20,000	7 years
September 18	$25,000	7 years
October 2	$15,000	5 years

Weiskopf's CPA, to maximize the depreciation deduction, elects $25,000 of Sec. 179 depreciation as follows: $20,000 on the March 1 property and $5,000 on the September 18 property. What tax issue should be considered with respect to the total depreciation deduction for the current year?

PROBLEMS

I:10-25 *Allowed Versus Allowable Depreciation.* Sandy acquired business machinery (which qualified as 7-year MACRS property) on July 15, 2012, for $10,000. In 2012, Sandy claimed a $1,429 regular MACRS depreciation deduction and she elected not to claim Sec. 179 depreciation or bonus depreciation. Because of net operating losses in 2013–2015, Sandy did not claim any depreciation deduction on her tax returns in those years. She sells the machine on July 1, 2015, for $6,000.
a. What is the adjusted basis of the machine on the sale date?
b. How much gain or loss is recognized on the sale of the machine?

I:10-26 *Conversion of Personal Asset to Business Use.* Sid purchased an automobile for personal use on January 18, 2011 for $10,000. On January 1, 2015, Sid starts a small business and begins to use the automobile exclusively in the business. The automobile's FMV on this date is $6,000. MACRS depreciation deductions are based on a 5-year recovery period.
a. What is the automobile's basis for depreciation when converted to business use in 2015?
b. Assuming Sid does not elect Sec. 179 expensing, what is Sid's depreciation deduction in 2015?

I:10-27 *MACRS 40% Test and Bonus Depreciation.* Small Corporation purchased and placed in service the following 100% business-use assets (all of the assets were purchased new). Assume that Small purchased these assets in Year 1, when 50% bonus depreciation was available on eligible property (as "eligible property" has been typically defined for years when bonus depreciation was available). Small claimed bonus depreciation but no Sec. 179 election on all eligible property in Year 1.

- Truck (light-duty, modified non-personal use) costing $20,000: Placed in service on February 15, Year 1 with a 5-year MACRS recovery period.
- Machinery costing $50,000: Placed in service on May 1, Year 1 with a 7-year MACRS recovery period.
- Land costing $60,000: Placed in service on July 1, Year 1.
- Building costing $100,000: Placed in service on December 1, Year 1 with a 39-year MACRS recovery period.
- Equipment costing $40,000:Acquired on December 24, Year 1 and placed in service on January 5, Year 2 with a 5-year MACRS recovery period.

What are Small's total depreciation deductions in Year 1 and Year 2?

I:10-28 *MACRS 40% Test and Partial Year Depreciation.* Large Corporation acquired and placed in service the following 100% business-use assets. Large did not elect Sec. 179 expensing on any of these properties.

- Truck (light-duty, modified non-personal use) costing $36,000: Placed in service on March 3, 2015 with a 5-year MACRS recovery period.
- Machinery costing $85,000: Placed in service on November 15, 2015 with a 7-year MACRS recovery period.
- Land costing $90,000: Placed in service on October 12, 2015.
- Building costing $280,000: Placed in service on December 4, 2015 with a 39-year MACRS recovery period.

a. What is Large's total depreciation deduction in 2015?
b. Large Corporation sells the machinery on February 2, 2017 and sells the building on September 18, 2017. What are the adjusted bases of these two assets on the dates of sale (compute accumulated depreciation to date of sale)?

I:10-29 *Sec. 179 Expensing and MACRS Depreciation.* Ted is in the rental real estate business. During 2015, Ted purchased and placed in service the following assets:

- Apartment building costing $300,000 (exclusive of $80,000 land): Placed in service on May 12 with a 27.5-year MACRS recovery period.
- Office furniture costing $23,000: Placed in service on April 10 with a 7-year MACRS recovery period.
- Office equipment costing $15,000: Placed in service on November 1 with a 5-year MACRS recovery period.

a. What are Ted's total depreciation deductions in 2015 assuming he does not elect Sec. 179 expensing?
b. What are Ted's total depreciation deductions in 2015 assuming he elects Sec. 179 expensing in 2015 for $23,000 on the furniture and $2,000 on the equipment? Assume Ted elects out of bonus depreciation on all qualifying properties.
c. What are Ted's total depreciation deductions in 2015 assuming he elects Sec. 179 expensing in 2015 for $10,000 on the furniture and $15,000 on the equipment?

I:10-30 *Sec. 179 Limitations and Carryovers.* In July 2015, Tish acquires and places in service a business machine costing $40,000 with a 7-year MACRS recovery period. Tish elects the maximum allowable Sec. 179 expense on the machine. In August 2015, she also places in service business equipment costing $165,000, with a 5-year MACRS recovery period. Tish's taxable income (before the Sec. 179 expense and the 50% of SE tax deduction) is $16,000.

a. What is Tish's allowable 2015 Sec. 179 expense on the machine? What amount can she carry over to 2016?
b. What is Tish's total 2015 depreciation deduction?
c. What are the limitations on Tish's ability to use the Sec. 179 carryover in 2016?
d. How would your answer to Part a change if Tish's business taxable income (before the Sec. 179 expense and the 50% of SE tax deduction) were $37,000 in 2015 instead of $16,000?

I:10-31   *MACRS Dispositions.* Tampa Corporation sold the following assets in 2015:

	Date Acquired	Date Sold	Original Cost Basis	Depreciation/ Cost-Recovery Method	Recovery Period (Years)	Sales Price
Automobile	1/1/12	12/1/15[a]	$ 9,000	MACRS	5	$ 1,200
Equipment	1/6/12	9/1/15[a]	20,000	MACRS	7	9,500
Building (nonresidental)	4/1/05	12/10/15	100,000	MACRS	39	240,000

[a] The half-year convention was used in the year of acquisition. Tampa did not elect Sec. 179 expense or bonus depreciation during the acquistion years.

a. What is the depreciation deduction for each asset in 2015?
b. Compute the gain or loss on each asset sold.

I:10-32   *Sec. 179 Expensing Election and MACRS Depreciation.* Thad acquires a machine at a cost of $27,000 for use in his business and places it in service on April 1, 2015. The machine is depreciated under MACRS, with a 7-year recovery period. This machine was his only asset acquisition of the year. Thad elects to expense $25,000 of the acquisition cost under Sec. 179.
a. What is Thad's total depreciation deduction for the machine in 2015?
b. Thad then sells the machine on October 5, 2017 for $10,000. Compute Thad's depreciation deductions for 2015 through 2017, the adjusted basis of the machine on October 5, 2017, and the gain or loss on the sale.

I:10-33   *Sec. 179 Expensing and Mid-Quarter Convention.* During 2015, Rita acquired and placed in service two assets for use in her business, as follows:

• Asset A: Placed in service in February at a cost of $65,000 with a 7-year MACRS recovery period.

• Asset B: Placed in service in November at a cost of $30,000 with a 7-year MACRS recovery period.

Rita elects to expense $25,000 under Sec. 179. Compute Rita's total depreciation deduction for 2015 under each of the following assumptions:
a. Rita allocates the entire $25,000 Sec. 179 expense to Asset A.
b. Rita allocates the entire $25,000 Sec. 179 expense to Asset B.

I:10-34   *Straight-Line Depreciation.* Long Corporation has been unprofitable for several years and has substantial NOL carryovers. Therefore, the company has elected to use straight-line MACRS for property acquisitions. Long acquires, holds, or sells the following assets in 2015:

	Date Acquired	Date Sold	Original Cost Basis	Selling Price	Depreciation Method	Recovery Period (Years)
Equipment	6/1/15	—	$40,000	—	SL ADS	7
Light duty truck (Nonpersonal-use)	5/1/11	12/1/15	30,000	$ 8,000	SL ADS	5
Furniture	3/1/11	—	10,000	—	SL ADS	7
Automobile	7/1/12	12/1/15	12,000	10,000	SL ADS	5

Long did not make the Sec. 179 election in any year, and elects out of bonus depreciation.
a. What is the depreciation deduction for each asset in 2015?
b. What amount of gain or loss does Long recognize on the properties sold in 2015?

I:10-35   *Mixed Personal/Business Use.* In 2015, Trish, a self-employed CPA and calendar year taxpayer, acquires and places in service an automobile and a personal computer. Pertinent data include the following:

Asset	Date Acquired	Total Original Cost Basis	Portion of Business Usage	Sec. 179 Election
Automobile	1/2/15	$21,000	60%	No
Personal computer	7/1/15	4,000	40%	No

For each asset, calculate the MACRS current year depreciation deduction assuming Trish does not elect Sec. 179 expensing.

I:10-36 *Employee Listed Property.* Assume the same facts as in Problem I:10-35, except Trish is an employee who uses the automobile and personal computer for employment-related activities. While both assets are helpful to Trish in performing her job duties, her employer does not require employees to purchase a car or a personal computer as a condition of employment. What is the amount of depreciation for each asset?

I:10-37 *Recapture of Depreciation Deductions Due to Personal Use.* Tammy acquired an automobile for $20,000 on July 1, 2012. She used the automobile partially for business purposes during the 2012–2015 period. The percentage of business use is as follows: 2012, 70%; 2013, 70%; 2014, 40%; 2015, 35%. The automobile is 5-year recovery property, and Tammy did not elect Sec. 179 expensing or bonus depreciation.
a. Compute the MACRS depreciation deductions for 2012–2015.
b. What amount of previously claimed depreciation deductions (if any) must Tammy recapture in 2015?

I:10-38 *Luxury Auto Limitations.* Lutz Corporation acquired a 100% business-use automobile (MACRS 5-year recovery) on July 1, 2015 for $32,000. The company did not elect Sec. 179 expensing. What is depreciation for 2015–2017, and any subsequent years?

I:10-39 *Luxury Auto Limitations.* Luby Corporation acquires a 100% business-use automobile (MACRS 5-year recovery) on July 1, 2015 for $36,000. Luby does not elect Sec. 179. What are depreciation deductions for 2015–2017?

I:10-40 *Luxury Auto Limitations.* Tracy acquires an automobile (MACRS 5-year recovery) on March 1, 2015. He uses the automobile 70% of the time in his business and 30% of the time for personal use. The automobile cost $36,000, and no amount is expensed under Sec. 179.
a. What is depreciation for 2015–2020 and any subsequent years?
b. How would your answer to Part a change if the vehicle were a SUV with a gross vehicle weight rated (GVWR) of over 6,000 pounds and Tracy elected to expense the SUV under Sec. 179?

I:10-41 *Luxury Auto Limitations—Leasing.* Troy entered into a three-year lease of a luxury automobile on January 1, 2015, for use 80% in business and 20% for personal use. The FMV of the automobile at the inception of the lease was $40,500, and Troy made 12 monthly lease payments of $600 in 2015 and 2016.
a. Before considering the effects of any lease inclusions amounts, what amount of lease payments are deductible in 2015 and 2016?
b. What portion, if any, of the "inclusion amount" must reduce Troy's lease deduction in 2015 and 2016?
c. How would your answers to Parts a and b change if the FMV of the auto was $15,000 and the monthly lease payments are $200?

I:10-42 *Amortization of Intangibles.* On January 1 of the current year, Palm Corporation purchases the net assets of Vicki's unincorporated business for $600,000. The tangible net assets have a $300,000 book value and a $400,000 FMV. The purchase agreement states that Vicki will not compete with Palm Corporation by starting a new business in the same area for a period of five years. The stated consideration received by Vicki for the covenant not to compete is $50,000. Other intangible assets included in the purchase agreement are as follows:

• Goodwill: $70,000

• Patents (12-year remaining legal life): $30,000

• Customer list: $50,000

a. How would Vicki's assets be recorded for tax purposes by Palm Corporation?
b. What is the amortization amount for each intangible asset in the current year?

I:10-43 *R&E Expenditures.* Park Corporation incurs the following costs in the initial year of doing business:

Materials and supplies for research laboratory	$ 80,000
Utilities and depreciation on research laboratory and equipment	40,000
Costs of acquiring another entity's patent for a new product	20,000
Market research salaries for surveys relative to proposed new products	60,000
Labor and supplies for quality control tests	50,000
Research costs subcontracted to a local university	35,000
Total	$285,000

Park's controller states that all of these costs are qualifying R&E expenditures and that the company policy is to expense such amounts for tax purposes in the year they are incurred. Which of these expenditures are deductible as R&E costs under Sec. 174?

I:10-44 **R&E Expenditures.** In 2015, Phoenix Corporation acquires a new research facility and hires several scientists to develop new products. No new products are developed until 2016, although the following expenditures were incurred:

Laboratory materials	$ 40,000
Research salaries	80,000
Overhead attributable to the research facility	30,000
R&E equipment placed into service (5-year MACRS recovery period)	100,000
Total	$250,000

a. What are Phoenix Corporation's deductions for R&E expenditures in 2015 and 2016 if the expensing method is elected?

b. How would your answer to Part a change if the deferral and amortization method were elected and the amortization period were 60 months?

I:10-45 **Computer Software.** Phillips Corporation, a construction company that specializes in home construction, uses special computer software to schedule jobs and keep track of job costs. It uses generic software for bookkeeping and spreadsheet analysis. During 2015, Phillips Corporation had the following transactions relating to computer software:

- The corporation purchased a new computer system on May 12, 2015, for $15,000. The system included computer hardware and built-in computer software valued at $3,000. The corporation has never separated computer software from the hardware in prior years when a computer system was purchased.

- The corporation separately purchased new bookkeeping software on September 1, 2015, for $5,760.

- On June 1, 2015, Phillips Corporation acquired another home building company to strengthen its position in higher-priced homes. The total purchase price was $700,000 allocated to specific assets as follows:

Equipment	$500,000
Goodwill	150,000
Computer software	50,000

What amount can Phillips Corporation deduct in 2015 with respect to computer software?

I:10-46 **Cost Depletion.** Tina acquires an oil and gas property interest for $200,000 in the current year. The following information about current year operations is supplied for purposes of computing the amount of Tina's depletion and intangible drilling and development cost (IDC) deductions:

Estimated recoverable units	20,000
Units produced	6,000
Units sold	4,000
IDCs	$20,000
Percentage depletion (after limitations)	$25,000

a. What is the cost depletion amount if the IDCs are expensed?

b. What is the cost depletion amount if the IDCs are capitalized?

c. How much depletion is deducted on the tax return?

d. Should the IDCs be capitalized or expensed? Explain.

I:10-47 *Percentage Depletion.* Tony has owned an oil and gas property for a number of years. The following information is provided about the property's operations in the current year:

Gross income	$500,000
Minus: Expenses (including IDCs of $100,000)	(300,000)
Taxable income (before depletion)	$200,000
Cost depletion (if IDCs are expensed)	$ 20,000
Cost depletion (if IDCs are capitalized)	$ 30,000

a. What is the percentage depletion amount if the IDCs are expensed?
b. What is the percentage depletion amount if the IDCs are capitalized?
c. What is the depletion deduction amount assuming that the IDCs are expensed?
d. Based on the information above, which method should be used for the IDCs? Explain.

COMPREHENSIVE PROBLEM

I:10-48 John and Ellen Brite (SSN 000-00-1111 and 000-00-2222, respectively) are married and file a joint return. They have no dependents. John owns an unincorporated specialty electrical lighting retail store, Brite-On. Brite-On had the following assets on January 1, 2014:

Assets	Cost
Old store building purchased April 1, 1999	$100,000
Equipment (7-year recovery) purchased January 10, 2009	30,000
Inventory valued using FIFO method: 4,000 light bulbs	$5/bulb

Brite-On purchased a competitor's store on March 1, 2014, for $107,000. The purchase price included the following:

New store building	$60,000 (FMV)
Land	18,000 (FMV)
Equipment (5-year recovery)	11,000 (FMV)
Inventory: 3,000 light bulbs	$ 6/bulb (cost)

On June 30, 2014, Brite-On sold the 7-year recovery period equipment for $12,000. Brite-On leased a $30,500 car for $500/month beginning on January 1, 2014. The car is used 100% for business and was driven 14,000 miles during the year.

Brite-On sold 8,000 light bulbs at a price of $15/bulb during the year. Also, Brite-On made additional purchases of 4,000 light bulbs in August 2014 at a cost of $7/bulb. Brite-On had the following revenues (in addition to the sales of light bulbs) and additional expenses:

Service revenues	$64,000
Interest expense on business loans	4,000
Auto expenses (gas, oil, etc.)	3,800
Taxes and licenses	3,300
Utilities	2,800
Salaries	24,000

John and Ellen also had some personal expenses:

Medical bills	$4,500
Real property taxes	3,800
State income taxes	4,000
Home mortgage interest	5,000
Charitable contributions (cash)	600

The Brites received interest income on a bank savings account of $275. John and Ellen made four $5,000 quarterly estimated tax payments. For self-employment tax purposes, assume John spent 100% of his time at the store while Ellen spends no time at the store.

Additional Facts:

• Equipment acquired in 2009: The Brites elected out of bonus depreciation and did not elect Sec. 179.

- Equipment acquired in 2014: The Brites elected Sec. 179 to expense the cost of the 5-year equipment but elected out of bonus depreciation.
- Assume that the lease inclusion rules require that Brite-On reduce its deductible lease expense by $8.

Compute the Brite's taxable income and balance due or refund for 2014.

TAX STRATEGY PROBLEM

I:10-49 Stan Bushart works as a customer representative for a large corporation. Stan's job entails traveling to meet with customers, and he uses his personal car 100% for business use. In 2015, Stan must decide whether to buy or lease a new car. After bargaining with several car dealers, Stan has agreed to a price of $30,000. If he buys the car, he will borrow the entire $30,000 at an annual interest rate of 8%, and his payments will be $608.29 per month over 60 months. Annual principal and interest payments are:

	Total	Principal	Interest
2015	$ 7,299	$ 5,083	$2,216
2016	7,299	5,505	1,794
2017	7,299	5,962	1,337
2018	7,299	6,457	843
2019	7,299	6,993	305
Totals:	$36,495	$30,000	$6,495

If he leases the car, his lease payment will be $450 per month for 60 months. At the end of the lease, he has the option of purchasing the car for $10,000. For simplicity, assume an average lease inclusion amount of $230 per year rather than actual amounts. Stan's marginal tax rate is 28% in each of the five years. Using present value analysis with an 8% discount rate, is Stan better off leasing or buying the car?

If Stan purchases the car, he will not elect Sec. 179 expensing or bonus depreciation. He will sell the car for $10,000 at the end of five years. If he leases the car, assume he merely turns the car in at the end of the lease.

TAX FORM/RETURN PREPARATION PROBLEMS

I:10-50 Thom Jones (SSN 000-00-1111) is an unincorporated manufacturer of widgets. He uses the LCM method to value his inventory and reports the following for 2014:

Sales (less returns and allowances)	$1,250,000
Cost of goods sold	500,000
Office expenses	10,000
Depreciation*	?
Legal services	4,000
Salary expenses	36,000
Travel expenses	30,000
Repair expenses	20,000

* Information related to Mr. Jones's depreciation:

Cost of office furniture acquired and placed in service on April 15, 2014 (7-year recovery).	$480,000
Cost of other property acquired and placed in service on August 1, 2014:	
5-year recovery property (computers-not listed property)	6,000
7-year recovery property (equipment)	54,000
Depreciation on assets purchased prior to 2014:	28,000

Complete Thom's 2014 Form 4562 and Schedule C of Form 1040, assuming Thom elects to expense the maximum amount possible under Sec. 179 but elects out of bonus depreciation.

I:10-51 Using the facts in Problem I:10-48 for John and Ellen Brite, complete their 2014 Form 1040, Schedules A, C, and SE, and Forms 4562 and 4797.

CASE STUDY PROBLEMS

I:10-52
Able Corporation is a manufacturer of electrical lighting fixtures. Able is currently negotiating with Ralph Johnson, the owner of an unincorporated business, to acquire his retail electrical lighting sales business. Johnson's assets include the following:

Assets	Adjusted Basis	FMV
Inventory of electrical fixtures	$ 30,000	$ 50,000
Store buildings	80,000	100,000
Land	40,000	100,000
Equipment: 7-year recovery period	30,000	50,000
Equipment: 5-year recovery period	60,000	100,000
Total	$240,000	$400,000

Mr. Johnson thinks that a total purchase price of $1 million in cash is warranted for the business because of its high profitability and strategic locations, and Able has agreed. Despite the fact that both parties agree that the $600,000 excess payment is goodwill, Able would prefer that it be designated as a 5-year covenant not to compete so that he can amortize it over a 5-year period.

You are a tax consultant for Able who has been asked to make recommendations as to the structuring of the purchase agreement and the amounts to be assigned to individual assets. Prepare a client memo to reflect your recommendations.

I:10-53
In 2013, the Margate Corporation acquired an automobile with a cost of $30,000 for use in its business. Shortly thereafter, Margate Corporation experienced a decline in sales. Several employees were laid off, and the automobile was not immediately needed for any of the sales personnel. Instead of letting the new automobile sit in the corporate lot, the president decided to permit a corporate officer to use the automobile for personal use. The officer used the automobile in 2013 and 2014 only. In 2015, Margate Corporation hired you as their new CPA (tax consultant). You learn that the officer's personal use of the corporate automobile took place for the two prior years without proper accounting to the IRS. As Margate Corporation's tax consultant, what actions (if any) should you take regarding the proper treatment of the automobile? What are your responsibilities as a CPA regarding this matter under the rules of the AICPA's *SSTS* No. 6? (See the *Statements on Standards for Tax Services (SSTS)* in Appendix E).

TAX RESEARCH PROBLEM

I:10-54
The Morriss Corporation is a very successful and profitable manufacturing corporation. The corporation just completed construction of new corporate offices, primarily for its top executives. The president and founder of the corporation, Mr. Timothy Couch, is an avid collector of artwork and has instructed that the lobby and selected offices be decorated with rare collections of art. These expensive works of art were purchased by the corporation in accordance with Couch's directives. Couch justified the purchase of these artworks on the premise that (1) they are excellent investments and should increase in value in the future, (2) they provide an appropriate and impressive office atmosphere when current and prospective customers visit the corporation's offices, and (3) the artwork is depreciable property and the corporation will be able to take sizable writeoffs against income. The Financial Vice-President of the corporation has requested your advice as to whether the works of art are, in fact, depreciable property. Prepare a research memorandum for the Financial Vice-President on this issue.

A partial list of research sources is provided below.

- *Rev. Rul. 68-232*, 1968-1 C.B. 70
- *Shauna C. Clinger*, 60 T.C.M. 598 (1990).
- *Simon v. Comr.*, 103 T.C. 247 (1994), *aff'd*, 95-2 USTC ¶50,552 (2d Cir. 1995) *nonacq.* 1996-2 C.B.I.
- *Liddle v. Comr.*, 103 T.C. 285 (1994), *aff'd*, 95-2 USTC ¶50,488 (3rd Cir. 1995)

CHAPTER

11

ACCOUNTING PERIODS AND METHODS

LEARNING OBJECTIVES

After studying this chapter, you should be able to

1 ▶ Explain the rules for adopting and changing an accounting period

2 ▶ Explain the differences between cash, accrual, and hybrid accounting

3 ▶ Determine what costs must be included in inventory

4 ▶ Identify the amount of income to be reported from special accounting methods

5 ▶ Compute the amount of imputed interest in certain transactions

6 ▶ Determine the tax treatment that results from changes in accounting methods

7 ▶ Describe tax planning considerations for accounting periods and methods

8 ▶ Describe compliance and procedural considerations for accounting periods and methods

An **accounting method** is a system of rules and procedures used to determine the year in which income and expenses are reported for tax purposes. The accounting methods used to compute taxable income generally must be the same as those used in keeping the taxpayer's books and records and determine *when* income and expenses are reported, not whether they are reported. Although the accounting methods used by a taxpayer do not necessarily affect the amount of income reported over the life of a business, they do affect the tax burden in two ways. First, selecting the appropriate accounting method can accelerate deductions or defer income recognition in order to postpone tax payments, and second, because of the progressive tax rate structure, taxpayers can save taxes by spreading income over several accounting periods rather than having income bunched into one period.

EXAMPLE I:11-1 ▶

Jane, a taxpayer using the cash method of accounting, has a 28% marginal tax rate for 2015 and expects to have a 15% marginal tax rate in 2016. Jane plans to make a charitable contribution of $1,000 in January 2016. A contribution in 2016 will reduce Jane's tax by $150 (0.15 × $1,000), whereas a contribution in 2015 will reduce Jane's tax by $280 (0.28 × $1,000). Obviously Jane may wish to accelerate the contribution in order to reduce her tax liability. ◀

ACCOUNTING PERIODS

OBJECTIVE 1

Explain the rules for adopting and changing an accounting period

Taxable income is computed on the basis of the taxpayer's annual **accounting period**, which is ordinarily 12 months (either a calendar year or a fiscal year). A **fiscal year** is a 12-month period that ends on the last day of any month other than December. The tax year must coincide with the year used to keep the taxpayer's books and records. Taxpayers who do not have books (e.g., an individual with wage income) must use the calendar year.[1] A taxpayer with a seasonal business may find a fiscal year to be advantageous. During the slow season, inventories may be lower and employees are available to take inventory and perform other accounting duties associated with the year-end. The tax year is elected on the first tax return that is filed by a taxpayer and cannot be changed without consent from the IRS.[2]

A partnership generally must use the same tax year as the partners who own the majority (greater than 50%) of partnership income and capital. If a majority of partners do not have the same year, the partnership must use the tax year of its principal partners (those with more than a 5% interest in the partnership). If the principal partners do not have the same tax year, the partnership must use the taxable year that results in the least aggregate deferral of income to the partners.[3] An exception is made for partnerships that can establish to the satisfaction of the IRS a business purpose for having a different year.

The purpose of the strict rules for selecting accounting periods is to prevent partners from deferring partnership income by choosing a different tax year for the partnership. For example, calendar-year partners might select a partnership year that ends on January 31. Because partnership income is considered to be earned by the partners on the last day of the partnership's tax year, reporting the profits would thus be deferred 11 months because the partnership year ends after the partner's year. (See the section entitled Required Payments and Fiscal Years in this chapter for further discussion of the calendar-year requirement.)

A similar rule generally requires S corporations and personal service corporations to adopt a calendar year unless the corporation has a business purpose for electing a fiscal year.[4] Taxpayers willing to make required payments or distributions may choose a fiscal year. (See the Required Payments and Fiscal Years section in this chapter.)

 STOP & THINK

Question: The tax rules related to accounting periods require most partnerships, S corporations, and personal service corporations to report on the calendar year basis.

---

[1] Sec. 441(g).
[2] Reg. Sec. 1.441-1(b)(4).

[3] Reg. Sec. 1.706-1(a)(3).
[4] Sec. 1378(a).

Of course, almost all individual taxpayers also report on the calendar year basis. What impact does this have on accountants?

Solution: The principal impact is a compression of tax compliance work into the "accounting busy season." A substantial portion of auditing and other accounting work also takes place at year-end. As a result, these services are also compressed into the accounting busy season. The accounting profession has sought to have these rules changed, but has, at least so far, been unsuccessful.

An improper election to use a fiscal year automatically places the taxpayer on the calendar year.[5] Thus, if the first return is filed late because of oversight, the option to choose a fiscal year is lost.

EXAMPLE I:11-2 ► City Corporation receives its charter but does not begin operations for three years. Tax returns are required for all years. Timely returns are not filed because City's officers are unaware that returns must be filed for inactive corporations. Thus, City Corporation must use the calendar year. City Corporation may petition the IRS for approval to use a fiscal year. ◄

ADDITIONAL COMMENT

The use of a 52–53-week year aids in budgetary matters and statistical comparisons because a four-week period, unlike a calendar month, is a uniform, fixed period.

While most tax years end on the last day of a month, the tax law allows taxpayers to use a tax year that always ends on the same day of the week, such as the last Friday in October. This means that the tax years will vary in length between 52 and 53 weeks. Taxpayers who regularly keep their books over a period that varies from 52 to 53 weeks may elect the same period for tax purposes. A 52–53-week taxable year must end either the last time a particular day occurs during a calendar month (e.g., the last Friday in October) or the occurrence of the particular day that is closest to the end of a calendar month (e.g., the Saturday closest to the end of November).[6] Under the first alternative, the year may end as many as six days before the end of the month, but must end within the month. Under the second alternative, the year may end as many as three days before or after the end of the month.

TYPICAL MISCONCEPTION

It is sometimes mistakenly believed that a tax year can end on a day in the middle of the month.

The 52–53-week year is especially useful to businesses with inventories. For example, a manufacturer might choose a 52–53-week year that ends on the last Friday in December to permit inventory to be taken over the weekend without interfering with the company's manufacturing activity. Similarly, wage accruals would be eliminated for a company with a weekly payroll if the payroll period always ends on Friday.

Although the 52–53-week year may actually end on a day other than the last day of the month, it is treated as ending on the last day of the calendar month for "effective date" changes in the tax law that would otherwise coincide with the year-end.

EXAMPLE I:11-3 ► Eagle Corporation has adopted a 52–53-week year. Eagle's tax year begins on December 29, 2015. Assume that a new tax rate schedule applies to tax years beginning after December 31, 2015. The new tax rate schedule is applicable to Eagle because, in the absence of the 52–53-week year, its tax period would have started on January 1, 2016. ◄

REQUIRED PAYMENTS AND FISCAL YEARS

Virtually all C corporations (other than personal service corporations) have flexibility in choosing an accounting period. Other taxpayers, such as partnerships and S corporations, may use a fiscal year if they have an acceptable business purpose. However, most of these businesses are unable to meet the rather rigid business purpose requirements outlined by the IRS. As a result, these businesses report using the calendar year concentrating most tax work during the early months of the year. Concern over this problem led Congress to enact Sec. 444 which allows partnerships, S corporations, and personal service corporations (such as incorporated medical practices) to elect a taxable year that results in a tax deferral of three months or less (e.g., a partnership with calendar-year partners may elect a September 30 year-end). This is called the **Sec. 444 election**. Furthermore, partnerships,

---

[5] Q.A. *Calhoun v. U.S.*, 33 AFTR 2d 74-305, 74-1 USTC ¶9104 (D.C. Va., 1973).　　[6] Sec. 441(f).

S corporations, and personal service corporations may continue using the fiscal year they were using when the current law was passed in 1986 even if that fiscal year results in a deferral beyond three months.

Partnerships and S corporations making the Sec. 444 election, however, must make annual required payments by April 15 of the following year. The purpose of the required payment is to offset the tax deferral advantage obtained when fiscal years are used.

ADDITIONAL COMMENT

The American Institute of Certified Public Accountants and accounting firms lobbied extensively for the provision that permits partnerships, S corporations, and personal service corporations to continue to use a fiscal year if annual required payments are made.

The amount of the required payment is determined by multiplying the maximum tax rate for individuals plus 1% (40.6%) times the previous year's taxable income times a deferral ratio.[7] The deferral ratio is equal to the number of months in the deferral period divided by the number of months in the taxable year. An adjustment is made for deductible amounts distributed to the owners during the year. If the amount due is $500 or less, no payment is required.

EXAMPLE I:11-4 ▶ ABC Partnership begins operations on October 1, 2015, and elects a September 30 year-end under Sec. 444. The partnership's net income for the fiscal year ended September 30, 2016, is $100,000. ABC must make a required payment of $10,150 ($100,000 × 40.6% × ³⁄₁₂) on or before April 15, 2017. ◀

The owners of businesses making such payments do not claim a credit for the amount paid. Instead, the partnership or S Corporation subtracts the previous year's required payment from the current year's required payment. If the result is negative, then the entity is entitled to a refund.

EXAMPLE I:11-5 ▶ Assume the same facts as in Example I:11-4 except that ABC Partnership's required payment for the year ended September 30, 2017 is $6,000. ABC is entitled to a refund of the difference of $4,150 ($10,150 − $6,000). ◀

Personal service corporations also may elect a fiscal year. However, deductions to shareholder/employees may be limited if distributions to such shareholder/employees during the deferral period do not exceed a minimum amount.[8] Personal service corporations are incorporated medical practices and other businesses owned by individuals who provide their services through the corporation. In general, the rules prevent a distribution pattern that creates a tax deferral. This is achieved by requiring that the deductible payments made to owners during the deferral period be at a rate no lower than during the previous fiscal year.

EXAMPLE I:11-6 ▶ Austin, Inc., is a personal service corporation of attorneys with a fiscal year ending September 30. For the year ended September 30, 2015 the company earned a profit of $480,000 before any salary payments to the owners. The entire profit, however, was paid out as wages to the owners, resulting in a taxable income of zero. To avoid any deduction limitation, Austin must pay salaries to its owners of no less than $120,000 ($480,000 × ³⁄₁₂) during the period October 1, 2015, to December 31, 2015. If less than $120,000 is paid during this deferral period, deductions are limited for the year ended September 30, 2016. ◀

An option allows personal service corporations to compute the amount of the minimum distribution by using a three-year average of income and distributions.

CHANGES IN THE ACCOUNTING PERIOD

Once adopted, an accounting period cannot normally be changed without IRS approval.[9] The IRS will usually approve a change only if the taxpayer can establish a substantial business purpose for the change (e.g., changing to a natural business year).[10] A natural business year ends at or soon after the peak income earning period (e.g., the natural business year for a department store that has a seasonal holiday business may be on January 31). A business without a peak income period may not be able to establish a natural business year and may, therefore, be precluded from changing its tax year. In general, at least

KEY POINT

The use of a natural business year helps in the matching of revenue and expense because the business is normally in a maximum state of liquidity and the problems associated with making estimates involving uncompleted transactions are reduced to a minimum.

---

[7] Sec. 7519(b). The high rate discourages elections by businesses with middle and lower income owners. Businesses do not have to make similar required payments for self-employment and other taxes. As a result, there can be some advantage for businesses with higher income owners.

[8] Sec. 280H(a).
[9] Sec. 442.
[10] Rev. Proc. 2002-39, 2002-1 C.B. 1046.

25% of revenues must occur during the last two months of the year in order to qualify as a natural business year.

EXAMPLE I:11-7 ► USA Department Store's sales peak during the holiday season in December. During January the department store further reduces its inventory through storewide clearance sales. USA elects a "natural" business year-end of January 31 because its inventory levels are lowest at the end of January. Also, USA meets the prescribed test because at least 25% of its revenues for the year occur in December and January. ◄

In a few instances IRS approval is not required to change to another accounting period.

REAL-WORLD EXAMPLE
J.C. Penney, Kmart, and Walmart all use an accounting period ending January 31.

► A newly married person may change tax years to conform to that of his or her spouse so that a joint return may be filed. The election must be made in either the first or second year after the marriage date.[11]

► A change to a 52–53-week year that ends with reference to the same calendar month in which the former tax year ended.[12]

► A taxpayer who erroneously files tax returns using an accounting period other than that on which his or her books are kept is not required to obtain permission to file returns for later years based on the way the books are kept.[13]

► A corporation meeting the following specified conditions may change without IRS approval: (1) There has been no change in its accounting period within the past ten calendar years, (2) the resulting year does not have a net operating loss (NOL), (3) the taxable income for the resulting short tax year when annualized is at least 90% of the taxable income for the preceding full tax year, and (4) there is no change in status of the corporation (such as an S corporation election).[14]

► An existing partnership can change its tax year without prior approval if the partners with a majority interest have the same tax year to which the partnership changes or if all principal partners who do not have such a tax year concurrently change to such a tax year.[15]

There is one instance, however, when a change in tax years is required: A subsidiary corporation filing a consolidated return with its parent corporation must change its accounting period to conform with its parent's tax year.

Application for permission to change accounting periods is made on Form 1128, Application for Change in Accounting Period, on or before the due date of the return including extensions. The application must be sent to the Commissioner of the IRS, Washington, D.C.

The IRS may establish certain conditions for the taxpayer to meet before it approves the change to a new tax year. For example, the IRS has ruled that if the short period that results from a change involves a NOL greater than $50,000, the taxpayer may have to forgo a carryback of the loss.[16]

RETURNS FOR PERIODS OF LESS THAN 12 MONTHS

Most income tax returns cover an accounting period of 12 months. On two occasions, however, a taxpayer's accounting period may be less than 12 months: when the taxpayer's first or final return is filed and when the taxpayer changes accounting periods.

Taxpayers filing an initial tax return and executors filing a taxpayer's final return or corporations filing their last return are not required to annualize the year's income, nor are personal exemptions or tax credits prorated. These returns are prepared and filed, and taxes are paid as though they are returns for a 12-month period ending on the last day of

---

[11] Reg. Sec. 1.442-1(e). A statement should be attached to the resulting short period return indicating that the change is being made.
[12] Reg. Sec. 1.441-2(c)(2). A statement should be attached to the first return filed under the election indicating that the change is being made.
[13] Rev. Rul. 58-256, 1959-1 C.B. 215.

[14] Reg. Sec. 1.442-1(c). A statement should be attached to the return indicating that each condition is met.
[15] Reg. Sec. 1.442-1(b)(2).
[16] Rev. Proc. 2002-37, 2002-1 C.B. 1030.

the short period. An exception permits the final return of a decedent to be filed as though the decedent lived throughout the entire tax year.[17]

EXAMPLE I:11-8 ► ABC Partnership, which has filed its returns on a calendar-year basis, terminates on June 30. ABC's final return is due on October 15. ◄

EXAMPLE I:11-9 ► Joy, a single individual who has filed her returns on a calendar-year basis, dies on June 30. Joy's final return is due the following April 15. ◄

Taxpayers who change from one accounting period to another must annualize their income for the resulting short period. This prevents income earned during the resulting short period from being taxed at lower rates. Income is annualized as follows:

1. Determine modified taxable income. Individuals must compute their taxable income for the short period by itemizing their deductions (i.e., the standard deduction is not allowed) and personal and dependency exemptions must be prorated.[18]
2. Multiply modified taxable income by the following fraction:

$$\frac{12}{\text{Number of months in short period}}$$

3. Compute the tax on the resulting taxable income using the appropriate tax rate schedule.
4. Multiply the resulting tax by the following fraction:

$$\frac{\text{Number of months in short period}}{12}$$

EXAMPLE I:11-10 ► Pat, a single taxpayer, obtains permission to change from a calendar year to a fiscal year ending on June 30, 2015. During the six months ending June 30, 2015, Pat earns $25,000 and has $5,000 in itemized deductions.[19]

Gross Income	$25,000
Minus: Itemized deductions	(5,000)
Personal exemption [(6 ÷ 12) × $4,000]	(2,000)
Modified taxable income	$18,000
Annualized income [(12 ÷ 6) × $18,000]	$36,000
Tax on annualized income	$ 4,939
Gross tax [(6 ÷ 12) × $4,939]	$ 2,470 ◄

Topic Review I:11-1 summarizes the available accounting periods and the rules for changing accounting periods.

? STOP & THINK

Question: Why are taxpayers required to annualize when they change tax years? What provision of the tax law creates this need?

Solution: A change of tax years results in a shortened filing period during the period the change takes place. For example, a taxpayer who changes from a calendar year to a June 30 year-end reports income for only a 6-month period on the first return following the change. Less income is reported, and that income would be taxed at lower rates without annualization. Annualization is necessary because of the progressive tax rate structure.

[17] Reg. Sec. 1.443-1(a)(2).
[18] The exemptions are prorated as follows: exemptions × (number of months in the short period ÷ 12).
[19] An alternative method to compute the tax is provided in Sec. 443(b)(2) and

Reg. Sec. 1.443-1(b)(2) whereby the taxpayer can elect to compute the tax for a 12-month period beginning on the first day of the short period and then convert the tax to a short-period tax.

TOPIC REVIEW I:11-1

Accounting Periods and Changes

AVAILABLE YEARS

► Available tax years include the calendar year, a fiscal year (a year that ends on the last day of any month other than December), and a 52–53-week year (a year that always ends on the same day of the week).

► A partnership must use the tax year of its partners unless the partnership can establish a satisfactory business purpose for having a different year or if the partnership makes required payments.

► Similar rules generally require S corporations and personal service corporations to adopt a calendar year unless the corporation has a business purpose for electing a fiscal year. Taxpayers willing to make required payments or distributions may choose a fiscal year ending on September 30, October 31, or November 30.

CHANGE IN ACCOUNTING PERIODS

► Once adopted, an accounting period normally cannot be changed without approval by the IRS. The IRS is more likely to approve a change to a natural business year. In general, at least 25% of revenues must occur during the last two months of the year in order to qualify as a natural business year.

► Taxpayers who change from one accounting period to another must annualize their income for the resulting short period. This prevents income earned during the resulting short period from being taxed at lower rates.

OVERALL ACCOUNTING METHODS

OBJECTIVE 2

Explain the differences between cash, accrual, and hybrid accounting

A taxpayer's method of accounting determines the year in which income is reported and expenses are deducted. Taxable income must be computed using the method of accounting regularly used by the taxpayer in keeping his or her books if that method clearly reflects income.[20] Permissible overall accounting methods are:

► Cash receipts and disbursements method (often called the cash method of accounting)

► Accrual method

► A combination of the first two methods, often called the hybrid method

KEY POINT

The Code provides the IRS with broad powers in ascertaining whether the taxpayer's accounting method clearly reflects income. It entitles the IRS to more than the usual presumption of correctness.

New taxpayers may generally choose any of the accounting methods listed above. However, the accrual method must be used for sales and cost of goods sold if inventories are an income-producing factor to the business. Exceptions permit businesses with inventories to use the cash method if their average annual gross receipts for the three preceding years do not exceed $1 million ($10 million if the taxpayer's principal business is not the sale of inventory).[21] The fact that an overall accounting method is used in one trade or business does not mean that the same method must be used in a second trade or business or for nonbusiness income and deductions.

EXAMPLE I:11-11 ►

Troy, a practicing CPA, also owns an appliance store. The fact that Troy uses the accrual method of reporting income from the appliance store, where inventories are an income-producing factor, does not preclude Troy from using the cash method to report income from his service-based accounting practice. Troy could also use the cash method for reporting nonbusiness income (such as dividends) and nonbusiness expenses (such as itemized deductions). ◄

REAL-WORLD EXAMPLE

It has been held that the cash method of accounting can be used where inventories are inconsequential. *Michael Drazen,* 34 T.C. 1070 (1960).

The term *method of accounting* is used to include not only overall methods of accounting listed above but also the accounting treatment of any item.[22]

CASH RECEIPTS AND DISBURSEMENTS METHOD

Most individuals and service businesses use the cash receipts and disbursements method of accounting. Taxpayers cannot use the cash method in a business for sales and cost of goods

---

[20] Sec. 446.
[21] Rev. Proc. 2002-28, 2002-1 C.B. 815, modified by Rev. Proc. 2012-20, 2012-14 IRB 700.

[22] Reg. Sec. 1.446-1(a)(1). Examples of accounting methods for specific items include Sec. 174, relating to research and experimentation expenses; Sec. 451, relating to reporting income from long-term contracts; and Sec. 453, relating to reporting income from installment sales.

sold if inventories are an income-producing factor.[23] However, as noted above, businesses with inventories are permitted to use the cash method if their average annual gross receipts for the three preceding tax years do not exceed $1 million ($10 million if the taxpayer's principal business is not the sale of inventory). However, C corporations and partnerships with a corporate partner may use the cash method only if their average annual gross receipts for the three preceding tax years do not exceed $5 million or if the business meets the requirements associated with providing personal services (i.e., if it is owned by professionals who are using the business to provide professional services).[24] Thus, a law or accounting firm can use the cash method even if its average receipts exceed $5 million. However, other C corporations with greater than $5 million average gross receipts must use the accrual method even if they have no inventory.

Under the cash receipts and disbursements method of accounting, a taxpayer is required to report income for the tax year in which payments are actually or constructively received. While it might seem that receipts under the cash method of accounting should only be recognized if the taxpayer receives cash, this is not the case. The Regulations clearly provide that gross income under the cash method includes cash, property, or services.[25] Thus, if a CPA accepts a set of golf clubs as payment from a client for services rendered, the CPA must include the fair market value of the golf clubs in his gross income. However, an accounts receivable or other unsupported promise to pay is considered to have no value and, as a result, no income is recognized until the receivable is collected. Expenses are deducted in the year paid. Because the recognition of expense is measured by the flow of cash, a taxpayer can control the year in which an expense is deductible by choosing when to make the payment. Individual taxpayers do not have the same opportunity to determine the year in which income is recognized, because the constructive receipt rule requires taxpayers to recognize income if a payment is available, even if actual payment has not been received. (See Chapter I:3 for a discussion of constructive receipt.)

Capitalization Requirements for Cash-Method Taxpayers. Taxpayers who use the cash receipts and disbursements method are required to capitalize fixed assets and to recover the cost through depreciation or amortization. The Regulations state that prepaid expenses must be capitalized and deducted over the life of the asset if the life of the asset extends substantially beyond the end of the tax year.[26] Typically, capitalization is required only if the life of the asset extends beyond the close of the tax year following the year of payment.[27]

KEY POINT

A taxpayer using the cash method is entitled to certain deductions that do not involve current year cash disbursements, such as depreciation, depletion, and losses.

EXAMPLE I:11-12 ▶ On July 1, 2015, Acme Corporation, a cash basis, calendar-year taxpayer, pays an insurance premium of $3,000 for a policy that is effective July 1, 2015, to June 30, 2016. The full $3,000 is deductible in 2015. ◀

EXAMPLE I:11-13 ▶ Assume the same facts as in Example I:11-12, except that the premium covers a three-year period beginning July 1, 2015, and ending June 30, 2018. Acme Corporation may deduct $500 in 2015, $1,000 in 2016 and 2017, and $500 in 2018. ◀

One notable exception to the one-year rule denies a deduction for prepaid interest. Cash-method taxpayers must capitalize such amounts and allocate interest over the prepayment period. A special rule allows homeowners to deduct points paid on a mortgage used to buy or improve a personal residence. The payment must be an established business practice in the area and not exceed amounts generally charged for such home loans. (See Chapter I:7 for a discussion of the deductibility of points.)

To be deductible, a payment must be more than just a refundable deposit. A taxpayer who has an option of cancelling delivery and receiving a refund of amounts prepaid is not normally entitled to deduct the amount of the deposit.

[23] Reg. Sec. 1.471-1. However, Sec. 448(b) permits farmers to use the cash method even though they have inventories. Sec. 448(a) denies tax shelters the right to use the cash method even if they do not have inventories.
[24] Secs. 448(b) and (c).

[25] Reg. Sec. 1.446-1(c)(1)(i).
[26] Reg. Sec. 1.461-1(a)(1).
[27] *Bonaire Development Co.*, 76 T.C. 789 (1981), and *Martin J. Zaninovich v. CIR*, 45 AFTR 2d 80-1442, 80-1 USTC ¶9342 (9th Cir., 1980).

Payments can be made either by a check that is honored in due course or by the use of a credit card.[28] Payment by credit card is considered to be the equivalent of borrowing funds to pay the expense. However, a taxpayer's note is not the equivalent of cash, so if a cash method taxpayer gives a note in payment, he or she cannot take the deduction until the note is paid, even if the note is secured by collateral.[29]

ACCRUAL METHOD

For an accrual basis taxpayer, there are two tests used to determine when an item of income must be reported or an expense deducted: the **all-events test** and the **economic performance test**.

All-Events Test. An accrual-method taxpayer reports an item of income when "all events" have occurred that fix the taxpayer's right to receive the item of income and the amount can be determined with reasonable accuracy.[30] Similarly, an expense is deductible when all events have occurred that establish the fact of the liability and the amount of the expense can be determined with reasonable accuracy. For deductions, the all-events test is not satisfied until economic performance has taken place.

Economic Performance Test. Economic performance (of services or property to be provided to a taxpayer) occurs when the property or services are actually provided by the other party.

EXAMPLE I:11-14 ▶ The owner of a professional football team provides medical benefits for injured players through insurance coverage. Economic performance occurs over the term of the policy rather than when the team enters into a binding contract with the insurance company or during the season when the player earns the right to medical benefits. Thus, a one-year premium is deductible over the year of the insurance coverage rather than over the term of the player's contract under which the benefit is earned. But see below for a possible waiver. ◀

Similarly, if a taxpayer is obligated to provide property or services, economic performance occurs in the year the taxpayer provides the property or service.

EXAMPLE I:11-15 ▶ Assume the same facts as in Example I:11-14 except that medical benefits are required under the terms of a player's contract. Also, the team decides to pay medical costs directly. Economic performance occurs as the team actually provides the benefits. Thus, the deduction is permitted only as medical care is provided. ◀

The requirement that economic performance take place before a deduction is allowed is waived if all of the following five conditions are met:

▶ The all-events test, without regard to economic performance, is satisfied.

▶ Economic performance occurs within a reasonable period (but in no event more than 8 ½ months) after the close of the tax year.

▶ The item is recurring in nature, and the taxpayer consistently treats items of the same type as incurred in the tax year in which the all-events test is met.

▶ The taxpayer is not a tax shelter.

▶ Either the amount is not material or the earlier accrual of the item results in a better matching of income and expense.[31]

EXAMPLE I:11-16 ▶ Bass Corporation, a calendar year taxpayer, pays its annual insurance premium each year on April 30, the anniversary of the policy. The premium paid this year is $6,000 while last year's premium was $5,400. Accrual accounting indicates that Bass deduct $4,000 ($8/12 × $6,000) of the premium paid this year along with $1,800 ($4/12 × $5,400) of the premium paid last year, or a total of $5,800. As all of the conditions for the exception to the economic performance requirements are met, Bass Corporation can deduct $6,000 this year. This assumes that Bass has been consistently following the practice and deducted $5,400 last year. ◀

ADDITIONAL COMMENT

The phrase *reasonable accuracy* means that approximate amounts are ascertainable. Although the word *accuracy* means exactness or precision, when it is used with the word *reasonable* it implies something less than an exact amount.

REAL-WORLD EXAMPLE

Before the economic performance test was added to the tax law, a company engaged in strip mining coal was able to deduct the future land reclamation costs as the coal was mined because the liability was certain and the cost could be estimated. *Ohio River Collieries*, 77 T.C. 1369 (1981).

---

[28] Rev. Rul. 78-39, 1978-1 C.B. 73.
[29] *Frank D. Quinn Exec. v. CIR*, 24 AFTR 927, 40-1 USTC ¶9403 (5th Cir., 1940).

[30] Reg. Sec. 1.451-1(a). (See Chapter I:3 for a discussion of the all-events test as it applies to gross income.)
[31] Sec. 461(h).

TYPICAL MISCONCEPTION

It is sometimes mistakenly believed that taxpayers can deduct warranty expenses and bad debts using the allowance method instead of the direct write-off method.

Reserves for items such as product warranty expense and uncollectible accounts are commonly encountered in financial accounting. The all-events and economic performance tests prevent the use of such reserves for tax purposes. This is because the amount of such expense is not usually determinable with sufficient accuracy.

HYBRID METHOD

Taxpayers may use a combination of accounting methods as long as income is clearly reflected. Taxpayers with inventories are required to use the accrual method to report sales and purchases if their average gross receipts for the three preceding years exceeds $1 million ($10 million if the taxpayer's principal business is not the sale of inventory). These taxpayers may use the cash method to report other items of income and expense. To ensure that income is clearly reflected, certain restrictions have been placed on combining accounting methods.

KEY POINT

A taxpayer who uses the cash method in computing gross income from his or her business must use the cash method in computing expenses of such business.

Taxpayers who use the cash method of accounting in determining gross income from a trade or business must use the cash method for determining expenses of the same trade or business. Similarly, taxpayers who use the accrual method of accounting for expenses must use the accrual method in computing gross income from the trade or business.

The basic rules relating to accounting methods, the all-events test, and economic performance are summarized in Topic Review I:11-2.

 **STOP & THINK**

Question: If an accountant does tax work for an automobile dealer, in exchange for free use of an automobile, does the accountant have to report any income? Does it make a difference whether the accountant uses the automobile in her business? When is any taxable income reported?

Solution: The rental value of the automobile must be included in gross income. If the automobile is used in the accountant's business, a portion of the rental value is deductible as a business expense. Although it is not entirely clear, it seems that an accrual basis accountant would report income as tax services are provided to the dealer. A cash basis taxpayer would report income over the time the automobile is used.

TOPIC REVIEW I:11-2

Accounting Methods

AVAILABLE METHODS

▶ Permissible overall accounting methods are the cash receipts and disbursements method, the accrual method, and the hybrid method.

▶ The cash method is available to taxpayers without inventories and to taxpayers with inventories whose average gross receipts during the three preceding years was $1 million or less ($10 million if the taxpayer's principal business is not the sale of inventory). C corporations whose average gross receipts fall between $1 and $5 million thresholds may use the cash method if they do not have inventories. C corporations (other than personal service corporations) may not use the cash method if their average gross receipts in the three preceding tax years exceed $5 million.

ALL-EVENTS TEST AND ECONOMIC PERFORMANCE TEST

▶ An accrual-method taxpayer reports an item of income when all events have occurred that fix the taxpayer's right to receive the item of income and when the amount of the item can be determined with reasonable accuracy.

▶ An expense is deductible when all events have occurred that establish that there is a liability and when the amount of the expense can be determined with reasonable accuracy. The all-events test is not satisfied until economic performance has taken place.

▶ Economic performance takes place when property or services are actually provided.

INVENTORIES

OBJECTIVE 3

Determine what costs must be included in inventory

KEY POINT

Taxpayers cannot always use inventory methods for tax purposes that conform with generally accepted accounting principles.

In general, manufacturing and merchandising companies are required to use the accrual method of accounting for purchases and sales of merchandise. The inventory method used by a taxpayer must conform to the best accounting practice in the trade or business, and it must clearly reflect income. However, best accounting practices (synonymous with generally accepted accounting principles) and clear reflection of income (which is determined by the IRS) occasionally conflict. The Supreme Court has held that the standard of clear reflection of income prevails in a case where the two standards conflict. In the *Thor Power Tool Co.* case, the company wrote off the cost of obsolete parts for both tax and financial accounting purposes even though the parts were kept on hand and their selling price was not reduced.[32] Regulation Sec. 1.471-4(b) states that obsolete or other slow-moving inventory cannot be written down unless the selling price is also reduced.

Although the company's practice conformed with generally accepted accounting principles, it did not, according to the Supreme Court, clearly reflect income. Hence, generally accepted accounting principles are used only when the Regulations do not specify the treatment of an item or, alternatively, when the Regulations provide more than one alternative accounting method.

Taxpayers who value inventory at cost may write down goods that are not salable at their normal price (e.g., damaged, obsolete, or shopworn goods) only after the selling price has been reduced. Items may be valued at a bona fide selling price reduced by the direct cost of disposal.[33] The option to write down this type of merchandise is available even if the taxpayers use the LIFO inventory method.

EXAMPLE I:11-17 ▶

KEY POINT

The uniform capitalization rules, included in the Tax Reform Act of 1986, require the capitalization of significant overhead costs that previously were expensed.

Stone Corporation publishes books for small academic audiences in Sanskrit and other ancient languages. There is typically one printing of a few hundred or perhaps a thousand copies of each book. Stone may sell a few copies a year of each book. Only after several years can the Corporation determine whether they will ever sell all copies of a given work. Based upon the *Thor Power Tool Co.* case, Stone Corporation cannot write off unsold copies unless they are destroyed or otherwise disposed of, and they cannot write down unsold copies unless the selling price is reduced below cost. ◀

ETHICAL POINT

The UNICAP rules must be followed by taxpayers. To bring a business into compliance with these rules, the taxpayer may need to make certain estimates. SRTP No. 4 provides that a CPA may use a client's estimates if such use is generally acceptable or if it is impractical to obtain exact data. If a change in the overhead application rate is contemplated, it may be desirable to request IRS approval.

DETERMINATION OF INVENTORY COST

Inventories may be valued at either cost or at the lower of cost or market value. Taxpayers who use the LIFO inventory valuation method (discussed later in this chapter) may not use the lower of cost or market method. In the case of merchandise purchased, cost is the invoice price less trade discounts, plus freight and other handling charges.

Unlike financial accounting, purchasing costs (e.g., salaries of purchasing agents), warehousing costs, packaging, and administrative costs related to these functions must be allocated between cost of goods sold and inventory. The costs that must be included in inventory are found in Sec. 263A and are referred to as the Uniform Capitalization rules (UNICAP). This requirement is applicable only to taxpayers whose average gross receipts for the three preceding years exceed $10 million.[34]

In the case of goods manufactured by the taxpayer, cost is determined by using the UNICAP rules, which may be thought of as an expanded version of the full absorption costing method. Thus, direct costing and prime costing are not acceptable inventory methods. Direct labor and materials along with manufacturing overhead must be included in inventory. Under UNICAP, the following overhead items are included in inventory:

▶ Factory repairs and maintenance, utilities, rent, insurance, small tools, and depreciation (including the excess of tax depreciation over accounting depreciation)

▶ Factory administration and officers' salaries related to production

▶ Taxes (other than the income tax)

---

[32] *Thor Power Tool Co. v. CIR*, 43 AFTR 2d 79-362, 79-1 USTC ¶9139 (USSC, 1979).

[33] Reg. Sec. 1.471-2(c).

[34] Sec. 263A(b)(2)(B).

> ▶ Quality control and inspection
>
> ▶ Rework, scrap, and spoilage
>
> ▶ Current and past service costs of pension and profit-sharing plans
>
> ▶ Service support such as purchasing, payroll, and warehousing costs

Nonmanufacturing costs (e.g., advertising, selling, and research and experimentation costs) are not required to be included in inventory. Interest must be inventoried if the property is real property, long-lived property, or property requiring more than two years (one year in the case of property costing more than $1 million) to produce.

The main difference between full absorption costing traditionally used for financial reporting purposes and UNICAP costing required for tax purposes is that UNICAP expands the list of overhead costs to include certain indirect costs that have not always been included in overhead for financial reporting purposes. For example, for financial reporting purposes, the costs of operating payroll and personnel departments have sometimes been considered sufficiently indirect or remote to justify omitting them from manufacturing overhead. This is true even though much of the effort of the payroll and personnel departments may be directed toward manufacturing operations. For simplicity and other reasons, overhead costs included in inventory for financial purposes are often limited to those incurred in the factory. UNICAP requires that costs associated with these departments be allocated between manufacturing and nonmanufacturing functions (e.g., sales, advertising, research and experimentation).

EXAMPLE I:11-18 ▶ Best Corporation manufactures traditional style rocking chairs in a small factory with 34 employees. The office staff consists of four employees who handle payroll, receivables, hiring, and other office responsibilities. The sales staff includes three employees who travel the region selling to furniture and craft stores. The remaining 27 employees all work in the factory. Under UNICAP, factory costs including the wages of the 27 factory workers are generally all manufacturing costs. The costs associated with the sales staff are not manufacturing costs. This would include their compensation along with related costs such as travel. Office expenses including the wages paid to the four office workers can be allocated between manufacturing overhead and sales. Reasonable allocation methods are acceptable. One possibility might be to allocate office overhead between sales and manufacturing on a basis as simple as the number of employees in sales (3) and the number in manufacturing (27). Thus, 90% of the cost of the office operation could be treated as manufacturing-related and 10% sales-related. In such case, 90% of the office expenses would be allocated to manufacturing and 10% deducted as a period cost (i.e., selling expenses). The office expenses allocated to manufacturing would in turn be allocated between cost of sales and ending inventory. This allocation could be done on a basis as simple as multiplying the allocated office expenses by the number of chairs in ending inventory and dividing by the number of chairs in the ending inventory plus the total number of chairs made during the year. ◀

A manufacturer may use standard costs to value inventory if any significant variance is reallocated pro rata to ending inventory and cost of goods sold.[35] Taxpayers may determine inventory costs by the following methods: specific identification method; first-in, first-out method (FIFO); last-in, first-out method (LIFO); or average cost method. A few taxpayers, such as an automobile or large appliance dealer, may find it practical to determine the specific cost of items in inventory. Most taxpayers, however, must rely on a flow of goods assumption (e.g., FIFO or LIFO). A discussion of the LIFO method is presented below.

LIFO Method. Many taxpayers use the LIFO cost flow assumption because, during inflationary periods, LIFO normally results in the lowest inventory value and hence the lowest taxable income. Once LIFO has been elected for tax purposes, the taxpayer's financial reports must also be prepared using LIFO.[36] This requirement to conform financial reporting often discourages companies from electing LIFO because lower earnings must be reported to shareholders. However, taxpayers may make footnote disclosure of the amount

---

[35] Reg. Sec. 1.471-11(d)(3).

[36] Sec. 472(c).

of net income that would have been reported under FIFO or other inventory methods.[37] Taxpayers may adopt LIFO by attaching a completed Form 970 (or by a statement acceptable to the IRS) to the return for the tax year in which the method is first used.

? STOP & THINK

Question: As noted, many publicly held companies do not use LIFO inventory valuation. This is, in part, attributed to the fact that LIFO ordinarily results in lower reported income for accounting purposes than FIFO, and management prefers to report higher profits. Many small, closely-held companies also use FIFO even though their earnings are not reported to the public. Why wouldn't closely-held companies use LIFO?

Solution: There are a variety of reasons. Some businesses are very interested in how their financial statements look to banks and other lenders and to potential investors. In some industries, such as electronics, FIFO may actually provide lower inventory values. Also, LIFO cannot be used with lower of cost or market. As a result, some businesses may elect FIFO to be eligible to use lower of cost or market.

Perhaps, however, the main reason is that LIFO is more complex, and small businesses prefer to simplify their accounting. The advent of computers, accounting software, and bar codes may be having some impact on inventory valuation choices. Nevertheless, many accounting packages only track units on hand and sales revenue. They do not track inventory value (cost). Thus, the company must assign a value to inventory at year-end, and the complexity of LIFO remains a deterrent.

REAL-WORLD EXAMPLE

An automobile dealer, using the dollar-value LIFO method in maintaining its inventory, was required to use one pool for new automobiles and a separate pool for new trucks. *Fox Chevrolet, Inc.,* 76 T.C. 708 (1981).

Recordkeeping under LIFO can be cumbersome. For this reason, taxpayers are permitted to determine inventories using "dollar-value" pools and government price indexes rather than by maintaining a record of actual costs.[38] Retailers use appropriate categories in the Consumer Price Index; other taxpayers use categories in the Producer Price Index. Taxpayers using the index method must divide their inventories into one or more pools (groups of similar items). Thus, a department store might create separate pools for tools, appliances, clothing, furniture, and other products. Dividing inventory into pools can be critical because of the different inflation rates associated with various goods and because, if a particular pool is depleted, the taxpayer loses the right to use the lower prices associated with past layers. An important exception permits taxpayers with average annual gross receipts of $5 million or less for the current and two preceding tax years to use the **simplified LIFO method.**[39] The simplified LIFO method uses a single LIFO pool, thereby avoiding problems with multiple pools.

EXAMPLE I:11-19 ▶

In 2015, King Department Store changes its inventory method from FIFO to LIFO. Because King's gross receipts have never exceeded $5 million, the simplified LIFO method is available. King's year-end inventories under FIFO are as follows:

2014	$100,000
2015	$130,000

Assume the 2014 price index is 120% and the 2015 index is 125%. King must convert its 2015 inventory to 2014 prices.

$$\frac{120\%}{125\%} \times \$130,000 = \$124,800$$

A base period inventory of $100,000 is established. The increase in inventory (the 2015 layer) is valued at 2015 prices.

Base inventory (2014)	$100,000
Plus: 2015 layer [(125% ÷ 120%) × ($124,800 − $100,000)]	25,833
2015 ending inventory	$125,833

Assume the 2016 inventory valued under FIFO is $136,000 and the 2016 price index is 130%. The 2016 inventory is converted to 2014 prices.

---

[37] Reg. Sec. 1.472-2(e).
[38] Sec. 472(f).

[39] Sec. 474(c).

$$\frac{120\%}{130\%} \times \$136{,}000 = \$125{,}538$$

The 2016 increase in inventory (the 2016 layer) is valued at 2016 prices.

Base inventory (2014)	$100,000
2015 layer	25,833
2016 layer	800[a]
2016 ending inventory	$126,633

[a] [(130% ÷ 120%) × ($125,538 − $124,800)]. ◀

ADDITIONAL COMMENT

For tax purposes the lower of cost or market method must ordinarily be applied to each separate inventory item, but for financial accounting purposes it can be applied using an aggregate approach.

Lower of Cost or Market Method. Inventory may be valued at the **lower of cost or market**. This option is available to all taxpayers other than those who determine cost using the LIFO method.[40] The term *market* refers to replacement cost. On the date an inventory is valued, the replacement cost of each item in the inventory is compared with its cost. The lower figure is used as the inventory value. The lower of cost or market method must ordinarily be applied to each separate item in the inventory.

Recall the *Thor Power Tool* case (discussed earlier in this chapter) in which the Supreme Court distinguished market value from expected selling price. **Market value** is the price at which the taxpayer can replace the goods in question. Replacement cost is used in the lower of cost or market determination. Obsolete or other slow-moving inventory can be written down below replacement cost only if the selling price has been reduced.

Cycle Inventory Valuation. Computer technology, including bar codes and software, enables businesses to maintain real-time perpetual inventory records. Many businesses, especially those with multiple locations, do not attempt to count all inventory items on the last day of the taxable period. Instead they count inventory following a scheduled cycle. At year-end, businesses adjust quantities shown in perpetual records for shrinkage since the most recent physical count utilizing estimates based on past experiences. The IRS challenged this practice unsuccessfully arguing that the adjustments failed the "all events" test which requires that amounts must be determined with reasonable accuracy.[41] In midst of the litigation, Congress specifically permitted the method in instances where "the taxpayer makes proper adjustment to such inventories and its estimation method [for] actual shrinkage."[42]

WHAT WOULD YOU DO IN THIS SITUATION?

INVENTORY VALUATION

Jack is a new tax client. He says he and his previous accountant did not get along very well. Jack owns an automobile dealership with sales of $12 million. He has provided you with most of the information you need to prepare his tax return, but he has not yet given you the year-end inventory value. You have completed much of the work on his return, but cannot complete it without the inventory figure. You have called Jack three times about the inventory. Each time he has interrupted, and asked you what his tax liability will be at alternative inventory levels. What problem do you see?

---

[40] Reg. Secs. 1.471-2(b) and (c).
[41] *Wal-Mart Stores Inc. v. CIR*, 82 AFTR 2d 5601, 98-2 USTC ¶50,645 (8th Cir., 1998), *Dayton Hudson Corp. v. CIR*, 82 AFTR 2d 5610, 98-2 USTC ¶50,644 (8th Cir., 1998), and *Kroger Co.*, 1997 RIA T.C. Memo ¶97,002, 73 TCM 1637.
[42] Sec. 471(b).

SPECIAL ACCOUNTING METHODS

OBJECTIVE 4

Identify the amount of income to be reported from special accounting methods

The term *method of accounting* is used to include not only overall methods of accounting (i.e., cash, accrual, and hybrid) but also the accounting treatment of specific items. Special rules have been established for two types of transactions that cover long periods of time. One rule applies to installment sales (a sale in which final payment is not received until a subsequent tax year) and a separate set of rules applies to long-term contracts (construction and similar contracts that are not completed in the same year they are started). These special rules permit taxpayers to report income from this type of transaction when they have the wherewithal to pay the tax (i.e., the year in which payment is received).

LONG-TERM CONTRACTS

Long-term contracts include building, installation, construction, or manufacturing contracts that are not completed in the same tax year in which they began.[43] A manufacturing contract is long-term only if the contract involves the manufacture of either a unique item not normally carried in finished goods inventory or items that normally require more than 12 calendar months to complete. Contracts for services (architectural, accounting, legal, and so on) do not qualify for long-term contract treatment.[44]

EXAMPLE I:11-20 ▶ Diamond Corporation manufactures two types of airplanes: small, general aviation planes that require approximately six months to complete and large jet aircrafts sold to airlines that require two years to complete. Diamond maintains an inventory of the small planes but manufactures the large planes to contract specification. Diamond can use long-term contract accounting only for the large planes. Assume Diamond also offers aircraft design assistance to the government and others who seek such services. The long-term contract method of accounting is not available for such services. ◄

HISTORICAL NOTE

The use of the completed contract method was severely restricted in the Tax Reform Act of 1986 because Congress found that several large corporations, particularly those with large defense contracts, had significant deferred taxes attributable to this method. Many of these companies had extremely low or negative tax rates for several years.

The accounting method selected by a taxpayer must be used for all long-term contracts in the same trade or business.[45] In general, the income and expenses associated with long-term contracts may be accounted for by using either the **percentage of completion method** or the **modified percentage of completion method**. In limited instances (explained below), taxpayers may use the **completed contract method**. Under the percentage of completion method, income from a project is reported in installments as the work progresses. Under the completed contract method, income from a project is recognized upon completion of the contract. The modified percentage of completion method is a hybrid that combines two methods (discussed below). Alternatively, taxpayers may use any other accounting method (e.g., the accrual method) that clearly reflects income.

ADDITIONAL COMMENT

In general, a construction contract must involve what has historically been thought of as construction which includes erecting buildings, building dams, roads, and power plants.

Costs Subject to Long-Term Contract Rules. Direct contract costs are subject to the long-term contract rules. Labor, materials, and overhead costs must be allocated to the contract and accounted for accordingly. Thus, under the completed contract method, such costs are capitalized and deducted from revenue in the year the contract is completed. Selling, marketing and advertising expenses, expenses for unsuccessful bids and proposals, and research and development costs not associated with a specific contract may be deducted currently.

In general, administrative overhead must be allocated to long-term contracts. (See the earlier list of overhead items that must be included in inventory.) This is not required of taxpayers (other than homebuilders) using the completed contract method, but as noted below, the use of the completed contract method is limited.

As previously mentioned, interest must be capitalized if the property being produced is real property, long-lived property, or property requiring more than two years (one year in

---

[43] Reg. Sec. 1.451-3(b).
[44] Rev. Proc. 2011-18, 2011-5 I.R.B. 443 and Rev. Proc. 2004-34, 2004-1 C.B. 991, modifying and superseding Rev. Proc. 71-21, 1971-2 C.B. 549, does

establish rules for service contracts that extend into the year following the receipt of payment. These rules are discussed in Chapter I:3.
[45] Reg. Sec. 1.451-3(a)(1).

the case of property costing more than $1 million) to produce. Interest costs directly attributable to a contract and those that could have been avoided if contract costs had not been incurred must be allocated to long-term contracts.

Completed Contract Method. Under the completed contract method of accounting, income from a contract is reported in the taxable year in which the contract is completed. This is true without regard to whether the contract price is collected in advance, upon completion of the contract, or in installments. Costs associated with the contract are accumulated in a work-in-progress account and deducted upon completion. Several courts are in conflict with regard to determining when a contract is completed. Some courts have required total completion and acceptance of the contract.[46] Other courts have held the contract to have been completed when the only work remaining consists of correcting minor defects or furnishing incidental parts.[47]

The use of the completed contract method may only be used in two limited circumstances. The method can be used by smaller companies (those whose average gross receipts for the three preceding tax years is $10 million or less) for construction contracts that are expected to take two years or less to complete and for home construction contracts.[48] It cannot be used by larger companies for manufacturing, or for other long-term contracts other than construction or for construction contracts expected to last longer than two years.

KEY POINT

In general, taxpayers with long-term contracts must compute income under the percentage of completion method for contracts entered into after July 10, 1989.

Percentage of Completion Method. Under the percentage of completion method of reporting income, the taxpayer reports a percentage of the gross income from a long-term contract based on the portion of work that has been completed. The portion of the total contract price reported in a given year is determined by multiplying the total contract price by the percentage of work completed in the year. The percentage is determined by dividing current year costs by the expected total costs.

KEY POINT

After a taxpayer has adopted an accounting method for long-term contracts, he or she must continue to use that method unless permission to change methods is granted.

Modified Percentage of Completion Method. At the beginning of a contract, it is difficult to estimate total costs. For this reason, taxpayers may elect to defer reporting any income from a contract until they have incurred at least 10% of the estimated total cost.[49] This is called the modified percentage of completion method. Under this method, if a contract has just been started as of the end of the year, the taxpayer does not have to estimate the profit on the contract during that year. The next year the taxpayer will report profit on all work that has been completed, including work done during the first year. Of course, this assumes that at least 10% of the work has been completed as of the end of the taxable year. If more than 10% of the costs are incurred during the first year, the modified percentage of completion method is identical to the regular percentage of completion method.

The completed contract method, the percentage of completion method, and the modified percentage of completion method are compared in Example I:11-21.

EXAMPLE I:11-21 ▶ In 2015, a contractor enters into a contract to construct a bridge for $1,400,000. At the outset, the contractor estimates that it will cost $1,200,000 to build the bridge. Actual costs in 2015 are $540,000 (45% of the $1,200,000 total estimated costs). Actual costs in 2016 are less than expected and amount to $600,000. The profits reported in both years of the contract are illustrated below.

	2015	2016
Completed contract		
Revenue	0	$1,400,000
Costs incurred	0	(1,140,000)
Gross profit	0	$ 260,000

[46] *E. E. Black Limited v. Alsup*, 45 AFTR 1345, 54-1 USTC ¶9340 (9th Cir., 1954), and *Thompson-King-Tate, Inc. v. U.S.*, 8 AFTR 2d 5920, 62-1 USTC ¶9116 (6th Cir., 1961).
[47] *Ehret-Day Co.*, 2 T.C. 25 (1943), and *Nathan Wohlfeld*, 1958 PH T.C. Memo ¶58,128, 17 TCM 677.
[48] Sec. 460(e).
[49] Sec. 460(a).

Percentage of completion

Revenue	$630,000[a]	$770,000[b]
Costs incurred	(540,000)	(600,000)
Gross profit	$ 90,000	$170,000

[a] $540,000/1,200,000 \times \$1,400,000 = \$630,000$.
[b] $\$1,400,000 - \$630,000 = \$770,000$.

◄

In Example I:11-21, the modified percentage of completion method results in the same income being reported each year as the percentage of completion method because more than 10% of the estimated costs were incurred during the first year. Note that the completed contract method defers reporting income until the contract is completed, causing all income from the project to be reported in a single year. Thus, the tax is deferred but the taxpayer may end up being taxed at higher rates. As noted, the completed contract is available only for home construction contracts and to certain smaller contractors for projects of two years or less.

Look-Back Interest. Certain contracts (or portions of a contract) accounted for under either the regular or modified percentage of completion method are subject to a **look-back interest** adjustment. When a contract is completed, a computation is made to determine whether the tax paid each year during the contract is more or less than the tax that would have been paid if the actual total cost of the contract had been used rather than the estimated cost.[50] Interest is paid on any additional tax that would have been paid. The taxpayer receives interest on any additional tax that was paid.

Look-back interest is applicable only to contracts completed more than two years after the commencement date. Furthermore, look-back interest is applicable only if the contract price equals or exceeds either 1% of the taxpayer's average gross receipts for the three taxable years preceding the taxable year the contract was entered into or $1 million.[51]

Taxpayers may elect a "de minimis" exception to the "look-back" interest computation. If elected, the exception is applicable to all contracts completed within a year, and the election to use the exception can be revoked only with IRS approval. Under the exception, if income reported each year on a contract is within 10% of the recomputed "look-back income," no interest computation is made for the contract. Whether reported income is within 10% of recomputed income is determined separately for each completed contract.

EXAMPLE I:11-22 ►

The contractor in Example I:11-21 is exempt from the look-back rule because the contract is completed within two years after the commencement date. On the other hand, if the contract took more than two years to complete, interest would be owed on the underpaid taxes for the first and subsequent contract years. The underreported income for the first year would be $33,158 [($260,000 profit × $540,000 first year's costs ÷ $1,140,000 total costs) − $90,000 first year reported income]. Assuming a 35% tax bracket, the underpaid tax for the first year is $11,605. Upon completion of the contract, interest would be paid on this amount and underpaid taxes for other years. Even if elected, the "de-minimis" exception would be inapplicable as the reported income in the first year of the contract ($90,000) is not within 10% of the income that would have been reported if actual costs had been used in the computation ($123,158 = $33,158 + $90,000). ◄

INSTALLMENT SALES METHOD

In general, the gain or loss from the sale of property is reported in the year the property is sold. If the sales proceeds are collected in years after the sale, the taxpayer may find it difficult to pay the tax on the entire amount of the gain in the year of sale. To reduce the burden, the tax law permits taxpayers to spread the gain from installment sales over the collection period. The installment method is applicable only to gains and is used to report income from an installment transaction unless the taxpayer elects not to use the

[50] Sec. 460(b)(3).   [51] Sec. 460(b)(3).

installment method. An **installment sale** is any disposition of property where at least one payment is received after the close of the taxable year in which the disposition occurs. The installment method is *not* applicable to sales of:

▶ inventory, or

▶ marketable securities[52]

Computations Under Sec. 453. Income under the installment sales method is computed as follows:

STEP 1: Compute the gross profit from the sale.

Selling price		$xx,xxx
Minus:	Adjusted basis	(x,xxx)
	Selling expenses	(x,xxx)
	Depreciation recapture[53]	(x,xxx)
Gross profit		$ x,xxx

STEP 2: Determine the contract price.

Contract price (greater of the gross profit from above or the selling price reduced by any existing mortgage assumed or acquired by the purchaser) $xx,xxx

STEP 3: Compute the gross profit percentage.

$$\frac{\text{Gross profit}}{\text{percentage}} = \frac{\text{Gross profit}}{\text{Contract price}} = xx\%$$

STEP 4: Compute the gain to be reported in the year of sale.

Collections of principal received during year (exclusive of interest)	$xx,xxx
Plus: Excess mortgage (if any)[a]	x,xxx
Total	$xx,xxx
Times: Gross profit percentage	× xx%
Net gain recognized in year of sale	$ x,xxx
Plus: Depreciation recapture	x,xxx
Gain reported in year of sale	$ x,xxx

STEP 5: Compute the gain to be reported in subsequent years.

Collections of principal received	$ x,xxx
Times: Gross profit percent	× xx%
Gain reported in each of the subsequent years	$ x,xxx

[a] Mortgage − Basis − Selling expense − Depreciation recapture = Excess mortgage

Note that depreciation recapture (see Chapter I:13) must be reported in the year of the sale even if no payment is received.

EXAMPLE I:11-23 ▶ Gina, a cash basis taxpayer, sells equipment for $200,000. The equipment originally cost $70,000, and $10,000 of MACRS depreciation has been deducted before the sale. The $10,000 of depreciation must be recaptured as ordinary income under Sec. 1245. The buyer assumes the existing mortgage of $50,000, pays $10,000 down, and agrees to pay $10,000 per year for 14 years plus interest at a rate acceptable to the IRS. Selling expenses are $13,000. The selling price is $200,000 [($50,000 + $10,000) + (14 × $10,000)]. The gain to be reported is $127,000 [$200,000 − $13,000 − ($70,000 − $10,000)]. Using the steps listed above, calculations are made as follows:

---

[52] Sec. 453(b)(2) and (k).

[53] For a discussion of depreciation recapture, (see Chapter I:13.)

STEP 1: Compute the gross profit from the sale.

Selling price	$200,000
Minus: Adjusted basis	(60,000)
Selling expenses	(13,000)
Depreciation recapture	(10,000)
Gross profit	$117,000

STEP 2: Determine the contract price.

Greater of gross profit of $117,000 or selling price minus mortgage assumed by purchaser ($150,000 = $200,000 − $50,000)	$150,000

STEP 3: Compute the gross profit percentage.

$$\frac{\text{Gross profit}}{\text{percentage}} = \frac{\text{Gross profit (\$117,000)}}{\text{Contract price (\$150,000)}} = 78\%$$

STEP 4: Compute the gain to be reported in the year of sale.

Principal received during year	$ 10,000
Plus: Excess mortgage	0
Total amount realized	$ 10,000
Times: Gross profit percentage	× 0.78
Gross profit	$ 7,800
Plus: Depreciation recapture	10,000
Gain reported in year of sale	$ 17,800

STEP 5: Compute the gain to be reported in subsequent years.

Principal received	$ 10,000
Times: Gross profit percentage	× 78%
Gain reported in each subsequent year	$ 7,800

Thus, the total gain reported is $127,000 [$17,800 + ($7,800 × 14)]. This is equal to the gross profit of $117,000 (which is the amount of Sec. 1231 gain reported on the sale) plus the $10,000 of depreciation recapture. As a cash basis taxpayer Gina will report the interest income as it is collected. (Figure I:11-1 at the end of this chapter illustrates this computation on Form 6252, Installment Sale Income.) ◄

REAL-WORLD EXAMPLE

When an installment obligation is assigned as collateral for a loan, the transaction is treated as a disposition of the obligation. Rev. Rul. 65-185, 1965-2 C.B. 153.

Disposition of Installment Obligations. A taxpayer who sells property on the installment basis may decide not to hold the obligation until maturity. For example, the holder may sell the obligation to a financial institution for the purpose of raising cash. Alternatively, the holder may not be able to collect the full amount of the installments because of the inability of the buyer to make payments. Thus, the holder must determine the adjusted basis of the obligation in order to compute the gain or loss realized on the disposition. The adjusted basis of an installment obligation is equal to the face amount of the obligation reduced by the gross profit that would be realized if the holder collects the face amount of the obligation. In general, this means the adjusted basis of an obligation is equal to

$$\text{Face amount} \times (100\% - \text{Gross profit percentage})$$

EXAMPLE I:11-24 ► Assume the same facts as in Example I:11-23 except that Gina immediately sells a single $10,000 installment to a bank for $9,700. Gina reports a gain of $7,500 computed as follows:

Selling price	$9,700
Minus: Adjusted basis of installment	(2,200)[a]
Recognized gain	$7,500

[a] $10,000 face amount × (100% − 78% gross profit percentage) = $2,200

Gina would have reported a gain of $7,800 had she decided not to sell the installment but to collect the face amount. Because the obligation is discounted by $300 ($10,000 − $9,700), the reported gain is reduced by $300. If the installment had not been sold immediately, the bank would probably also pay to Gina an amount for the accrued interest. In such a situation Gina would report the gain from the sale and the accrued interest as income. ◀

EXAMPLE I:11-25 ▶ Assume that Gina in Example I:11-24 is unable to collect the final $10,000 installment because the individual who purchases the property declares bankruptcy. Gina would be entitled to a bad debt deduction of $2,200, the basis of the installment. Gina does not receive a bad debt deduction for the accrued interest because the interest has not been included in her gross income. ◀

KEY POINT

A donor of property does not normally recognize gain, but a gift of certain installment obligations causes the recognition of gain.

Certain dispositions of installment obligations, such as gifts, are taxable events.[54] The main objective of this rule is to prevent income from being shifted from one taxpayer to another. Thus, if a corporation distributes an installment obligation as a dividend or if a father gives his daughter an installment obligation, gain or loss is recognized. In general, the gain or loss recognized is equal to the difference between the FMV of the obligation and its adjusted basis. In the case of a gift, the gain recognized is equal to the difference between the face of the obligation and its adjusted basis. However, certain exceptions to this rule exist. Transfers to controlled corporations under Sec. 351, certain corporate reorganizations and liquidations, transfers on the taxpayer's death, transfers incident to divorce, distributions by partnerships, and contributions of capital to a partnership are exceptions to this rule. In these cases, the recipients of the obligations report income when the installments are collected.

Repossessions of Property Sold on the Installment Basis. In general, the repossession of property sold on the installment basis is a taxable event. The gain or loss recognized is generally equal to the difference between the value of the repossessed property (reduced by any costs incurred as a result of the repossession) and the adjusted basis of any remaining installment obligations.

EXAMPLE I:11-26 ▶ Yuji sells stock of a non–publicly traded corporation with a $7,000 adjusted basis for $10,000. Yuji receives a $1,000 down payment, and the balance of $9,000 is due the following year. In the year of the sale Yuji reports a capital gain of $300 (0.30 × $1,000) under the installment method of accounting. Yuji is unable to collect the $9,000 note, and after incurring legal fees of $500, he repossesses the stock. When Yuji repossesses the stock it is worth $8,700. The adjusted basis of the note is $6,300 (0.70 × $9,000). Yuji must report a capital gain of $1,900 ($8,700 − $500 − $6,300). The basis of the stock to Yuji is its FMV at the time it is repossessed ($8,700). ◀

The amount of gain recognized from the repossession of real property is limited to the lesser of (1) the gross profit in the remaining installments reduced by the costs incurred as a result of the repossession or (2) the cash and FMV of other property received from the buyer in excess of the gain previously recognized.[55] In the case of the repossession of either real or personal property, the gain or loss retains the same character as the gain or loss on the original sale.

EXAMPLE I:11-27 ▶ Assume the same facts as in Example I:11-26, except that the property sold is land. Yuji reports a capital gain of $700, which is the lesser of $2,200 [(0.30 × $9,000) − $500] or $700 ($1,000 − $300). The basis of the land is $7,500 [$9,000 − (0.30 × $9,000) unrealized profit + $700 gain previously recognized + $500 legal fees]. ◀

Installment Sales for More Than $150,000. Special rules apply to nondealers who sell property for more than $150,000. The special rules do not apply to sales of personal use property, to sales of property used or produced in the trade or business of farming, or to sales of timeshares or residential lots.

First, if the taxpayer borrows funds using the installment obligations as security, the amount borrowed is treated as a payment received on the installment obligation.[56] This

[54] Sec. 453B(a).
[55] Sec. 1038.
[56] Sec. 453A(d).

prevents the taxpayer from using the installment method to defer tax and yet obtain cash by borrowing against the installment obligation. Second, if the installment method is used, interest must be paid to the government on the deferred tax.[57] This rule, however, applies only to deferred principal payments over $5 million.[58]

KEY POINT

Installment sales between related parties cannot be used to defer the recognition of gain by the original owner when the related purchaser receives cash as result of a resale of the property.

Installment Sales Between Related Persons. Installment sales between related persons are subject to the same rules as other installment sales except when the property is resold by the related purchaser. The primary purpose of the resale rule is to prevent the original owner from deferring gain recognition by selling the property to a related person who, in turn, resells the property.

Sec. 453(e) requires the first seller to treat amounts received by the related person (second seller) as having been personally received. Thus, the first seller would be required to report the gain in the year (or years) in which proceeds are received by the second seller. This acceleration provision is applicable only if the resale takes place within two years of the initial sale. For purposes of Sec. 453(e), the term *related person* includes a spouse, children, grandchildren, and parents. Controlled corporations, partnerships, estates, and trusts are also covered.

DEFERRED PAYMENT SALES

The installment sale rules are not applicable to all sales involving future payments. The installment method cannot be used when the sale of property produces a loss. Also, a taxpayer can elect out of the installment method when a sale results in a gain. The manner in which these transactions are reported depends on the taxpayer's accounting method. For accrual method taxpayers, the total *amount receivable* from the buyer (exclusive of interest) is treated as part of the amount realized. Thus, the entire gain or loss is reported in the year of sale. For cash method taxpayers, the FMV of the installment obligation is treated as part of the amount realized in the year of sale. The amount realized, however, cannot be considered to be less than the FMV of the property sold minus any other consideration received (e.g., cash).[59]

EXAMPLE I:11-28 ▶ USA Corporation, an accrual method taxpayer, sells land for $100,000. USA receives $50,000 down and a $50,000 note payable in 12 months plus 14% interest. Assume the basis of the land is $80,000 and that it is a capital asset. Because of the buyer's poor credit, the value of the note is only $45,000. USA affirmatively elects not to report the installment sale on the installment method. USA reports a capital gain of $20,000 ($100,000 − $80,000). If USA collects the face of the note at maturity, no additional gain or loss is recognized. If USA sells the note for $45,000, a $5,000 capital loss is recognized. ◀

EXAMPLE I:11-29 ▶ Assume the same facts as in Example I:11-28, except that USA is a cash method taxpayer. If the FMV of the land is $100,000 (the stated selling price), the treatment of the transaction is exactly the same as it is using the accrual method. If the FMV of the land is assumed to be $95,000 (cash received plus FMV of the note received), USA recognizes a $15,000 ($95,000 − $80,000) capital gain in the year of the sale. If USA collects the face of the note at maturity, $5,000 of ordinary income is recognized. If USA sells the note for $45,000, no gain or loss is recognized. ◀

ADDITIONAL COMMENT

A contingent payment sale is a sale or other disposition of property in which the aggregate selling price cannot be determined by the close of the tax year in which the sale took place.

Indeterminate Market Value. In certain transactions, the value of obligations received cannot be determined (e.g., a mineral interest is sold for an amount equal to 10% of the value of future production). Under the Regulations, the value of obligations with an **indeterminate market value** is assumed to be no lower than the value of the property sold less the value of other property received.[60] Hence, if the value of property sold is determinable, the recognized gain equals the excess of the value of the property sold over its basis. On occasion, however, neither the value of the obligation received nor the value of property sold can be determined.

Temporary regulations specify how these types of transactions are to be treated.[61] The basic rules relating to special accounting methods are summarized in Topic Review I:11-3.

---

[57] The interest computation is described in Sec. 453A(c).
[58] Sec. 453A(b)(2)(B).
[59] Temp. Reg. Sec. 15A.453-1(d)(2)(ii)(A).

[60] Reg. Sec. 1.453-1(d)(3)(iii).
[61] Temp. Reg. Sec. 15A.453-1(c).

TOPIC REVIEW I:11-3

Special Accounting Methods

LONG-TERM CONTRACTS

▶ Long-term contracts include building, installation, construction, and manufacturing contracts that are not completed in the same tax year in which they are entered into. A manufacturing contract is long-term only if the contract involves the manufacture of either a unique item not normally carried in inventory or an item that normally requires more than 12 calendar months to complete.

▶ Long-term contracts may be reported under the regular or the modified percentage of completion method. Under both methods income is reported as work is completed, except that under the modified percentage of completion method no income is reported until at least 10% of the work is completed.

▶ The completed contract method is available only for home construction contracts, for construction contracts expected to take two years or less to complete, and for use by smaller companies (those whose average gross receipts for the three preceding tax years are $10 million or less).

INSTALLMENT METHOD

▶ Under the installment method gain is reported as the sales proceeds are collected. The installment method is generally not available for sales of inventory or publicly traded property. Furthermore, the method is available only for gains.

▶ Gain is reported as sales proceeds are collected. However, both depreciation recapture and any mortgage in excess of basis must be reported in the year of sale. Gain recognition is also accelerated in certain situations if the seller borrows against the installment obligation or if a related buyer resells the property within two years.

IMPUTED INTEREST

OBJECTIVE 5

Compute the amount of imputed interest in certain transactions

KEY POINT

Imputed interest is important because it alters the amount of gain on the sale and causes an interest expense deduction for the buyer and interest income for the seller.

TYPICAL MISCONCEPTION

Some people mistakenly assumed that the imputed interest rules do not apply if the property is sold for a loss.

Before the enactment of Sec. 1274 and the amendment of Sec. 483, property could be sold on an installment basis in a contract providing for little or no interest. Instead of charging interest, the seller charged a higher price for the property. If the property sold was a capital asset, the result of the arrangement was to reduce the interest income reported by the seller and to increase the amount of favorably taxed capital gain. Sections 483 and 1274 now *impute* interest in a deferred payment contract where no interest or a low rate of interest is provided. Another impact of the **imputed interest rules** on sellers is to reallocate payments received between interest (which is fully taxable) and principal (only the gain portion of which is taxable). The result is often an increase in the income reported in early years and a decrease in later years. The rules are generally applicable to both buyers and sellers. In certain instances, the buyer may want interest to be imputed in order to increase his interest deduction in early years.

The following transactions are exempt from the imputed interest rules:

▶ Debt subject to original issue discount provisions (basically bonds issued for less than face where amortization of the discount is required under Sec. 1274; see Chapter I:5)

▶ Sales of property for $3,000 or less

▶ Any sales where all of the payments are due within six months

▶ Sales of patents to the extent the payment is contingent on the use or disposition of the patent

▶ Certain carrying charges for personal property or educational services covered by Sec. 163(b) when the interest charge cannot be ascertained

▶ Charges for the purchase of personal-use property (purchaser only)[62]

---

[62] Sec. 483(d). The rule lowers the basis of a personal-use asset in order to increase any gain on the future sale of the property.

EXAMPLE I:11-30 ▶ Joan is involved in several transactions during the current year. No interest is stated on any of the transactions. The terms of the transactions and the applicability of the imputed interest rules are summarized below:

Transaction	Imputation of Interest
Purchases furniture costing $8,000 for her residence. Full price is payable within four months.	Not applicable because property is for personal use. Also, all payments are due within six months.
Sells a boat for $2,000. Payment is due in a year.	Not applicable because sales price is not more than $3,000.
Sells land for $100,000. Payment is due in five years.	Interest must be imputed because no exception is applicable.
Purchases a newly issued bond for $650 (face of $1,000).	Not applicable because transaction is subject to the original issue discount rules in Sec. 1274. Also, the price is not more than $3,000. ◀

IMPUTED INTEREST COMPUTATION

In order to avoid the imputation of interest, the stated interest rate must be at least equal to 100% of the applicable federal rate (110% of the applicable federal rate in the case of sale–lease back arrangements). Lower rates are specified for two types of transactions: (1) If the stated principal amount for qualified debt obligations that are issued in exchange for property under Sec. 1274A does not exceed $2.8 million, the interest rate is limited to 9% compounded semiannually; and (2) the interest rate is limited to 6% compounded semiannually in the case of sales of land between related individuals (unless the sales price exceeds $500,000).

The **applicable federal rate** is determined monthly and is based on the rate paid by the federal government on borrowed funds. The rate varies with the terms of the loan. Loans are divided into short-term (not over three years), mid-term (over three years but not over nine years), and long-term (over nine years).

EXAMPLE I:11-31 ▶ Kasi sells land for $100,000 to Bill, an unrelated person. The sales price is to be paid to Kasi at the end of five years in a single installment with no stated interest. Kasi paid $60,000 for the land. Assume the current federal rate is 10%. Because the amount of the stated principal is less than $2,800,000, interest is imputed at a rate not to exceed 9% compounded semiannually. As a result, the effective rate is 9.2025% (9% compounded semiannually), and the present value factor is .64393 ($1 \div 1.092025^5$). Thus, the present value of the final payment is $64,393 (0.64393 × $100,000). Kasi reports a $4,393 ($64,393 − $60,000) gain on the sale of the land and $35,607 ($100,000 − $64,393) interest income instead of a $40,000 gain and no interest income. The buyer is treated as incurring $35,607 in interest and has a $64,393 basis in the land. Whether the interest is deductible depends on a variety of other factors (see Chapter I:7). ◀

ACCRUAL OF INTEREST

Is imputed interest reported under the cash or the accrual method? In other words, is imputed interest reported when it accrues or when it is paid? In general, imputed interest is reported as it accrues. However, there are some major exceptions, as follows:

▶ Sales of personal residences

▶ Most sales of farms for $1 million or less

▶ Sales involving aggregate payments of $250,000 or less

▶ Sales of land between related persons unless the sales price exceeds $500,000[63]

In addition, if the borrower and lender jointly elect, and if the stated principal does not exceed $2 million, accrual of interest is not required. This election is not available if the lender is an accrual method taxpayer or a dealer with respect to the property sold or exchanged.[64]

ADDITIONAL COMMENT

The $2 million and $2.8 million limitations are subject to inflation adjustments.

---

[63] Sec. 1274(c)(4).

[64] Sec. 1274A(c).

EXAMPLE I:11-32 ▶ Assume the same facts as in Example I:11-31. Because the aggregate payments do not exceed $250,000, the transaction is exempt from the requirement that interest be accrued. As a result, Kasi reports interest income and Bill reports interest expense in the fifth year when the final payment is made on the transaction. Under the installment method, $4,393 gain on the sale is recognized in the fifth year. ◀

GIFT, SHAREHOLDER, AND OTHER LOANS

Imputed interest rules are not limited to installment transactions. Sec. 7872 applies to transactions involving related parties whose taxes are lowered as a result of low interest or interest-free loans. These situations include

▶ *Gift loans.* For example, parents in higher tax brackets loan money to their adult children without charging interest. If the children invest the borrowed money and are taxed on the income at a lower rate, the family has reduced its total tax liability in the absence of imputed interest rules.

▶ *Corporation shareholder loans.* In the absence of imputed interest rules, taxes may be saved by a corporation that makes an interest-free loan to a shareholder. If the corporation had invested the money and paid out the resulting income as a dividend, it would have first been taxed on the profit. By making the interest-free loan, the corporation could, in the absence of imputed interest rules, reduce its taxes by avoiding the otherwise taxable income.

▶ *Compensation-related loans.* Employers may loan money to employees without charging interest. Without the requirement to impute interest, this could produce tax savings if the employer was unable to deduct additional compensation because of the reasonable compensation limitation or if the employee was unable to deduct the interest, say, because the borrowed funds were used to purchase personal use property.

▶ *Other tax avoidance loans.* Any other low-interest or interest-free loan that produces tax savings may be subject to the imputed interest rules. For example, a club may offer its members a choice of either paying dues or making a large refundable deposit. The club can invest the money and earn interest perhaps equal to the dues. In the absence of imputed interest rules, the member avoids taxes by not having to report the income that would have been earned if the member personally invested the funds. The club is indifferent between the alternatives because both the dues and the interest income are taxable.

In general, interest is imputed on the above loans by applying the applicable federal rates discussed earlier. The resulting interest income is taxable to the lender. Whether the interest expense is deductible by the borrower is determined by applying the usual interest deduction rules (see Chapter I:7).

The imputation process involves a second step. The lender is treated as returning the imputed interest to the borrower. This is necessary because the interest was not actually paid. For example, in the case of a gift loan, the lender is treated as giving the imputed interest back to the borrower. This would not normally have income tax implications, but if the imputed interest were large enough, it could result in a gift tax. In the case of the corporation-shareholder loan, the corporation is treated as paying the imputed interest back to the shareholder as a dividend. Typically, this does not increase the corporation's tax, but it results in the recognition of dividend income to the shareholder. For compensation-related loans, the second step is to impute compensation paid by the employer and received by the employee. The compensation is taxable to the employee and, if reasonable in amount, is deductible by the employer.

There are several important exceptions intended to limit the application of imputed interest in situations where tax avoidance may be immaterial:

▶ Interest is not imputed on gift loans between two individuals totaling $10,000 or less, except when the borrowed funds are used to purchase income-producing property.

▶ If the gift loans between two individuals total $100,000 or less, the imputed interest is limited to the borrower's "net investment income" as defined by Sec. 163(d)(4). (See Chapter I:7 for a discussion of net investment income.) If the net investment income is $1,000 or less, it is not necessary to impute interest.

▶ Interest is not imputed on compensation-related and corporate shareholder loans totaling $10,000 or less.

These exceptions do not apply when tax avoidance is one of the principal purposes of the loans.

EXAMPLE I:11-33 ▶ Linda made interest-free gift loans to each of her four children: Andy, Bob, Cathy, and Donna. Andy borrowed $9,000 to purchase an automobile. Bob borrowed $25,000 to buy stock. Bob's net investment income is $800. Cathy also borrowed $25,000 to buy stock, but her net investment income is $1,100. Donna borrowed $120,000 to purchase a residence, and her net investment income is $500. Tax avoidance is not a motive for any of the loans. Imputation of interest is not required for the loans to Andy or Bob. The loan to Andy is exempt because the amount is less than $10,000, and the loan to Bob is exempt because his net investment income is under $1,000. Imputation of interest is required for the loans to Cathy and Donna. In the case of Cathy, the amount of imputed interest is limited to her net investment income of $1,100. The imputed interest for Donna, however, is not limited to her net investment income because the amount of the loan is over $100,000. ◀

The imputed interest rules are summarized in Topic Review I:11-4.

CHANGE IN ACCOUNTING METHODS

OBJECTIVE 6

Determine the tax treatment that results from changes in accounting methods

In general, a new taxpayer elects an accounting method by simply applying the selected method when computing income for the initial tax return.[65] If a particular item does not occur in the first year, the accounting method is elected the first year in which the item occurs.

EXAMPLE I:11-34 ▶ Gordon opened a beauty shop several years ago. Because he had no inventory, no inventory method was selected. In the current year, Gordon expanded his business to offer beauty supplies to his customers. Gordon can delay electing an inventory method until the year in which he first has an inventory. ◀

TOPIC REVIEW I:11-4

Imputed Interest

PURPOSE

The imputed interest rules are intended to prevent taxpayers from reducing their taxes by charging little or no interest on installment payment transactions and loans.

APPLIES TO

In most cases applies to both parties, the debtor and the creditor. The result is to impute interest income to the lender and interest expense to the borrower. Several exceptions exempt small transactions from imputed interest. For example, sales involving payments of $3,000 or less are generally exempt as are loans of less than $10,000.

RATE

Interest is imputed at the applicable federal rate if the stated interest rate is lower. The applicable federal rate is the rate the federal government pays on borrowed funds and is determined monthly. In general, the current rate at the time of the transaction is used throughout the term of the loan. The rate varies with the term of the loan. Loans are divided into short-term (not over three years), mid-term (over three years but not over nine years), and long-term (over nine years).

[65] Reg. Sec. 1.446-1(e)(1).

In general, once an accounting method is chosen, it cannot be changed without IRS approval. There are a few exceptions. For example, taxpayers may adopt the LIFO inventory method without prior IRS approval.[66] Once such methods are adopted, however, they cannot be changed without IRS approval.

As previously noted, the term *accounting method* indicates not only the overall accounting method used by the taxpayer, but also the treatment of any item of income or deduction.[67] A change of accounting methods should not be confused with the correction of an error. Errors include mathematical mistakes, posting errors, deductions of the wrong amount for an expense, omission of an item of taxable income, or incorrect computation of a credit. An error is normally corrected by filing an amended return for the tax year or years in which the error occurs. In general, there is a three-year statute of limitations on the correction of errors. After three years, the tax year is closed and changes cannot be made.[68]

Taxpayers wishing to change accounting methods must file Form 3115 with the IRS, on or before the due date of the tax return including extensions. A duplicate copy of Form 3115 must be filed with the tax return for the year. A taxpayer who amends the original income tax return within six months of its due date may request a change of accounting methods with the amended return.[69]

In general, taxpayers initiate a change in accounting methods from an incorrect to a correct method are exempt from penalty and from retroactive application of the new reporting method. Although changes in accounting methods require IRS approval, the IRS states that approval will automatically be granted for a wide variety of changes if the taxpayer meets specific requirements that include proper filing of both Form 3115 and the current year's tax return, agreeing to take into account the Sec. 481(a) adjustment (as described below), not being under examination, and not having changed the same method of accounting within the last four years.[70] Although the IRS retains the right to again change any method of accounting adopted under these procedures it states that such changes will not be retroactive except in rare or unusual circumstances. Examples of situations where retroactive application may occur include misstatement or omission of material facts, change in material facts, and changes in applicable authority.

AMOUNT OF CHANGE

A change in accounting methods usually results in duplications or omissions of items of income or expense.

EXAMPLE I:11-35 ▶

Bonnie, a practicing CPA, has been reporting income using the cash method. In the current year, Bonnie obtains permission to change to the accrual method. At the beginning of the current year, Bonnie has $80,000 of receivables that have not been reported in prior years. The receivables were not reported in prior years because they were not collected. Although the receivables are collected in the current year, they are not taxable because, under the accrual method, Bonnie now reports income as it is earned and the income is not earned in the current year. In this case, the income was earned in prior years.

Also, assume Bonnie has accounts payable of $15,000 at the beginning of the current year. The accounts payable were not deducted in prior years because the expenses had not been paid. Furthermore, the accounts payable are not deductible in the current year even if they are paid. This is because the expenses were incurred in prior years. Obviously, the IRS expects to collect the tax on the $80,000 of receivables, and Bonnie is entitled to deduct the $15,000 of payables. In the absence of any special provision, both amounts would be omitted from the computation of taxable income. On the other hand, if the change were from the accrual

---

[66] A taxpayer may adopt LIFO by merely determining year-end inventory by that method and attaching Form 970 to the tax return for the year (Reg. Sec. 1.472-3(a)).
[67] Reg. Sec. 1.446-1(e)(2)(ii)(b).
[68] Exceptions are applicable when the taxpayer omits from the return an amount of income that is over 25% of the gross income stated on the return (6 years) or where fraud occurs (no limitation).
[69] The extension will be granted if the taxpayer follows procedures outlined in Rev. Proc. 2002-9, 2002-1 C.B. 327.
[70] Rev. Proc. 97-37, 1997-2 C.B. 455.

method to the cash method, both amounts would be reported twice (in the year prior to the change because they had accrued and in the year of the change because they are collected or paid). Thus, a special provision is also needed for duplications. ◄

REPORTING THE AMOUNT OF THE CHANGE

The net amount of the change must be taken into account.[71] A positive adjustment is added to income, whereas a negative adjustment is subtracted from income. This adjustment can, of course, be made in the year of the change. If the amount is small, recognizing the full amount of the net adjustment in the year of the change is both simple and equitable. This is the only option available when the amount of the change is $3,000 or less. On the other hand, reporting a large positive adjustment in one year could push the taxpayer into a higher marginal tax bracket and result in a significant tax increase. Because the extra income is due to changing accounting methods, not increasing cash flows, the taxpayer may not have the wherewithal to pay the additional tax.

As a result, there are alternative methods that may be used to report the amount of the change. The methods that are available depend on whether the change is voluntary (a change that is initiated by the taxpayer) or involuntary (a change from an unacceptable to an acceptable method that is required by the IRS).

In the case of an involuntary change, several alternative methods are available to the IRS.[72]

In the case of voluntary changes, taxpayers must agree to report the adjustment over a period not to exceed four years. When the amount of the adjustment is $25,000 or less, taxpayers may elect to include the full amount in the current year.[73] In the case of a change spread over four years, equal portions of the change are reported in each of the four years beginning with the year of the change.

EXAMPLE I:11-36 ▶ Diana obtains permission to change from the accrual to the cash method of reporting income. The change results in a $30,000 negative adjustment to income. The IRS requires Diana to spread the adjustment over four years. As a result, she may deduct $7,500 per year for four years. Note that because the amount of the adjustment is spread over the current and future years, the tax savings associated with the deduction are deferred. ◄

In general, the amount of the adjustment cannot be spread over a period longer than the method being changed has been used.

OBTAINING IRS CONSENT

Most changes in accounting method require IRS approval. Sec. 446(e) states that a taxpayer changing the method of accounting "on the basis of which he regularly computes his income in keeping his books" must obtain consent before computing taxable income under the new method. This implies that a taxpayer who has been computing taxable income on a method other than that used in computing book income does not need approval to conform the computation of taxable income to the method regularly used on the taxpayer's books. This conclusion is supported by Sec. 441(a), which requires that the same method of accounting be used in computing taxable income as is used in keeping the books. The alternative might be to require the taxpayer to conform his or her book accounting method with the tax accounting method. The answer may well be in how one defines "books." The IRS has ruled that a reconciliation of taxable income with accounting income was a part of the taxpayer's auxiliary records.[74] Hence, the taxpayer was using the same accounting method for book and tax reporting. As a result, a taxpayer who changes the method of accounting used for financial reporting may not be required to change the method of accounting used for tax reporting as long as financial income and book income are reconciled.

---

[71] Sec. 481.
[72] Secs. 481(a), (b)(1), (b)(2), and (c).

[73] Rev. Procs. 2012-20, 2012-14 IRB 700.
[74] Rev. Rul. 58-601, 1958-2 C.B. 81.

TAX PLANNING CONSIDERATIONS

ACCOUNTING PERIODS

New corporations often routinely adopt a calendar year. Consideration should be given, however, to adopting a tax year for the initial reporting period that ends before the amount of taxable income exceeds the amount that is taxed at the lowest tax rates (e.g., when taxable income is $50,000 or less). This is less critical for a corporation suffering losses because the NOLs may be carried forward for a 20-year period.

In the past, taxpayers were able to defer income by selecting different tax years for partners and partnerships or S corporations and shareholders. Current law limits this opportunity. Nevertheless, partnerships and S corporations may adopt a tax year that differs from that of their owners if that year qualifies as a natural business year (i.e., at least 25% of revenues occur during the last two months of the year). Furthermore, deferral is possible in the case of estates, because they are not subject to similar restrictions on the choice of tax years.

ACCOUNTING METHODS

New businesses should consider the tax implications of electing an accounting method. For example, taxpayers may benefit from the LIFO inventory method because LIFO typically reduces gross profit and defers the payment of taxes during inflationary periods. Similarly, service companies usually choose the cash method of reporting income because it permits receivables to be reported when collected rather than when the income is earned. Choosing an accounting method requires an understanding not only of the available accounting methods, but also the nature of the taxpayer's business. Will a specific election be to the tax advantage of the taxpayer? LIFO inventory is often recommended because, during inflationary periods, it tends to reduce inventory values and increase the cost of goods sold. In certain industries, such as the computer industry, however, costs are declining, and LIFO actually may result in a higher inventory value.

In other industries, inventories may fluctuate widely from one year to the next because of changing demand, shortages of materials, strikes, or other causes. LIFO layers may have to be depleted simply to continue business operations. This can cause one of two things to happen: (1) incurring extra recordkeeping costs of LIFO for little or no benefit because the inventories are depleted before they produce significant tax deferrals or (2) depleting low-cost layers from years past, resulting in a substantial increase in taxable income in the year of occurrence.

INSTALLMENT SALES

Taxpayers normally choose the installment method of reporting income from casual sales of property. By spreading the gain from a sale over more than one tax year, the taxpayer normally remains in lower tax brackets and defers the tax. A taxpayer with low current taxable income may elect not to use the installment sale method in order to take advantage of the lower current tax rates.

COMPLIANCE AND PROCEDURAL CONSIDERATIONS

REPORTING INSTALLMENT SALES ON FORM 6252

Form 6252 (Installment Sale Income) is used to report income under the installment method from sales of real property and casual sales of personal property other than inventory. Figure I:11-1 illustrates how an installment sale transaction is reported. The illustration is based on Example I:11-23. A separate Form 6252 is normally used for each installment sale. Form 6252 is used in the year of the sale and any year in which the taxpayer receives a payment from the sale. Taxpayers who do not wish to use the installment method may report the transaction on either Schedule D or on Form 4797.

Form **6252**	**Installment Sale Income**	OMB No. 1545-0228

Department of the Treasury
Internal Revenue Service

► Attach to your tax return.
► Use a separate form for each sale or other disposition of property on the installment method.
► Information about Form 6252 and its instructions is at *www.irs.gov/form6252*.

2014
Attachment
Sequence No. **79**

Name(s) shown on return

Gina Green

Identifying number

123-45-6789

1	Description of property ► Equipment			
2a	Date acquired (mm/dd/yyyy) ► 7-01-2011	**b** Date sold (mm/dd/yyyy) ► 8-31-2014		
3	Was the property sold to a related party (see instructions) after May 14, 1980? If "No," skip line 4 . . .		☐ Yes ☒ No	
4	Was the property you sold to a related party a marketable security? If "Yes," complete Part III. If "No," complete Part III for the year of sale and the 2 years after the year of sale		☐ Yes ☒ No	

Part I   **Gross Profit and Contract Price.** Complete this part for the year of sale only.

5	Selling price including mortgages and other debts. **Do not** include interest, whether stated or unstated			**5**	200,000
6	Mortgages, debts, and other liabilities the buyer assumed or took the property subject to (see instructions)	**6**	50,000		
7	Subtract line 6 from line 5	**7**	150,000		
8	Cost or other basis of property sold	**8**	70,000		
9	Depreciation allowed or allowable	**9**	10,000		
10	Adjusted basis. Subtract line 9 from line 8	**10**	60,000		
11	Commissions and other expenses of sale	**11**	13,000		
12	Income recapture from Form 4797, Part III (see instructions) . . .	**12**	10,000		
13	Add lines 10, 11, and 12			**13**	83,000
14	Subtract line 13 from line 5. If zero or less, **do not** complete the rest of this form (see instructions)			**14**	117,000
15	If the property described on line 1 above was your main home, enter the amount of your excluded gain (see instructions). Otherwise, enter -0-			**15**	
16	**Gross profit.** Subtract line 15 from line 14			**16**	117,000
17	Subtract line 13 from line 6. If zero or less, enter -0-			**17**	
18	**Contract price.** Add line 7 and line 17			**18**	150,000

Part II   **Installment Sale Income.** Complete this part for the year of sale **and** any year you receive a payment or have certain debts you must treat as a payment on installment obligations.

19	Gross profit percentage (expressed as a decimal amount). Divide line 16 by line 18. For years after the year of sale, see instructions			**19**	78%
20	If this is the year of sale, enter the amount from line 17. Otherwise, enter -0-			**20**	
21	Payments received during year (see instructions). **Do not** include interest, whether stated or unstated			**21**	10,000
22	Add lines 20 and 21			**22**	10,000
23	Payments received in prior years (see instructions). **Do not** include interest, whether stated or unstated	**23**			
24	**Installment sale income.** Multiply line 22 by line 19			**24**	7,800
25	Enter the part of line 24 that is ordinary income under the recapture rules (see instructions) . . .			**25**	
26	Subtract line 25 from line 24. Enter here and on Schedule D or Form 4797 (see instructions) . . .			**26**	7,800

Part III   **Related Party Installment Sale Income. Do not** complete if you received the final payment this tax year.

27	Name, address, and taxpayer identifying number of related party

28   Did the related party resell or dispose of the property ("second disposition") during this tax year? . . . . . ☐ Yes ☐ No
29   **If the answer to question 28 is "Yes," complete lines 30 through 37 below unless one of the following conditions is met. Check the box that applies.**

a ☐ The second disposition was more than 2 years after the first disposition (other than dispositions of marketable securities). If this box is checked, enter the date of disposition (mm/dd/yyyy) . . . . . ►
b ☐ The first disposition was a sale or exchange of stock to the issuing corporation.
c ☐ The second disposition was an involuntary conversion and the threat of conversion occurred after the first disposition.
d ☐ The second disposition occurred after the death of the original seller or buyer.
e ☐ It can be established to the satisfaction of the IRS that tax avoidance was not a principal purpose for either of the dispositions. If this box is checked, attach an explanation (see instructions).

30	Selling price of property sold by related party (see instructions)	**30**	
31	Enter contract price from line 18 for year of first sale	**31**	
32	Enter the **smaller** of line 30 or line 31	**32**	
33	Total payments received by the end of your 2014 tax year (see instructions)	**33**	
34	Subtract line 33 from line 32. If zero or less, enter -0-	**34**	
35	Multiply line 34 by the gross profit percentage on line 19 for year of first sale	**35**	
36	Enter the part of line 35 that is ordinary income under the recapture rules (see instructions) . . .	**36**	
37	Subtract line 36 from line 35. Enter here and on Schedule D or Form 4797 (see instructions) . . .	**37**	

For Paperwork Reduction Act Notice, see page 4.   Cat. No. 13601R   Form **6252** (2014)

FIGURE I:11-1 ► REPORTING INSTALLMENT SALE INCOME ON FORM 6252 (BASED ON EXAMPLE I:11-23)

PROCEDURES FOR CHANGING TO LIFO

The LIFO method may be adopted in the initial year that inventories are maintained by merely using the method in that year. In addition, advance approval (e.g., within 180 days following the start of the year) from the IRS is not required for an adoption of the LIFO method in the initial year that inventories are maintained on the LIFO method. However, Form 970 should be filed along with the taxpayer's tax return for the year of the change.[75] The application must include an analysis of the beginning and ending inventories. Further, if a taxpayer is changing to the LIFO method from another method (e.g., FIFO), advance approval from the IRS is also not required. Form 970 must be filed with the return and the beginning inventory for LIFO purposes is the same as under the former inventory method.[76]

If the former inventory is valued based on the lower of cost or market (LCM) method, an adjustment is required to restate the beginning inventory to cost because the LCM method cannot be used under LIFO. Generally, the beginning LIFO inventory is the same as the closing inventory for the prior year, except for the required restatement of previous writedowns to market. This adjustment to the beginning inventory can be spread ratably over the year of the change and the next two years.[77]

EXAMPLE I:11-37 ► Delaware Corporation elects to change to the LIFO inventory method. Delaware's inventories are valued using the LCM method based on the FIFO cost-flow assumption. The FIFO cost for the ending inventory is $50,000, and its LCM amount is $35,000. The initial inventory under LIFO must be restated to its cost, or $50,000. The $15,000 ($50,000 cost − $35,000 LCM value) difference can be included in taxable income over the current year and the next two years. $5,000 is added to taxable income in each year. ◄

PROBLEM MATERIALS

DISCUSSION QUESTIONS

I:11-1 Do accounting rules determine the amount of income to be reported by a taxpayer?

I:11-2 How does a taxpayer's tax accounting method affect the amount of tax paid?

I:11-3 Most individuals use the calendar year as their tax year. What requirement, if any, in the tax law causes this?

I:11-4 Why is it desirable for a new taxpayer to select an appropriate tax year?

I:11-5 What restrictions apply to partnerships selecting a tax year?

I:11-6 Does a similar restriction apply to S corporations? Explain.

I:11-7 How could the 52–53-week year prove to be beneficial to taxpayers? Explain.

I:11-8 Under what circumstances can an individual taxpayer change tax years without IRS approval?

I:11-9 Is there any instance in which a change in tax years is required? Explain.

I:11-10 a. In what situations will a tax year cover a period of less than 12 months?
b. Under what conditions is a taxpayer required to annualize income?
c. Does annualizing income increase or decrease the taxpayer's tax liability? Explain.

I:11-11 When is a final tax return due for an individual who uses a calendar year and who dies during the year?

I:11-12 a. Is it correct to say that businesses with inventories must use the accrual method?
b. What other restrictions apply to taxpayers who are choosing an overall tax accounting method?
c. Why is the cash method usually preferred to the accrual method?

I:11-13 a. Does the term *method of accounting* refer only to overall methods of accounting? Explain.

---

[75] An acceptable election is considered to have been made even if Form 970 is not filed as long as all of the information required by Reg. Sec. 1.472-3(a) is provided by the taxpayer.

[76] Reg. Sec. 1.472-2(c).
[77] Sec. 472(d).

b. Does a taxpayer's accounting method affect the total amount of income reported over an extended time period?

c. How can the use of an accounting method affect the total amount of tax paid over time?

I:11-14 a. When are expenses deductible by a cash method taxpayer?

b. Are the rules that determine when interest is deductible by a cash method taxpayer the same as for other expenses?

c. Is a cash method taxpayer subject to the same rules for depreciable assets as accrual method taxpayers?

I:11-15 Who may use the completed contract method of reporting income from long-term contracts?

I:11-16 When is a cash method taxpayer allowed to deduct deposits?

I:11-17 What constitutes a payment in determining when a cash-basis taxpayer is entitled to deduct an expense?

I:11-18 What is meant by economic performance?

I:11-19 What conditions must be met if the economic performance test is to be waived for an accrual-method taxpayer?

I:11-20 Is an accrual method taxpayer permitted to deduct estimated expenses? What about prepaid expenses? Explain.

I:11-21 What is the significance of the *Thor Power Tool Co.* decision?

I:11-22 a. How are overhead costs treated in determining a manufacturing company's inventory?

b. Do retailers have a similar rule?

c. Are these rules the same as for financial accounting? If not, explain.

I:11-23 What transactions are subject to the long-term contract method of reporting?

I:11-24 a. What conditions must be met in order to use the installment method?

b. Why would a taxpayer elect not to use the installment method?

I:11-25 What is the impact of having the entire gain on an installment sale consist of ordinary income from depreciation recapture?

I:11-26 What impact does the gifting of an installment obligation have on the donor?

I:11-27 What treatment is given to an installment sale involving related people?

I:11-28 What is the primary impact of the imputed interest rules on installment sales?

I:11-29 What changes in accounting method can be made without IRS approval?

I:11-30 Can the IRS require a taxpayer to change accounting methods?

I:11-31 Explain the purpose of the four-year method used in computing the tax resulting from a net adjustment due to a change in accounting methods.

I:11-32 If a taxpayer changes the method of accounting used for financial reporting purposes, must the taxpayer also change his or her method of accounting for tax purposes?

ISSUE IDENTIFICATION QUESTIONS

I:11-33 Judy's Cars, Inc., sells collectible automobiles to consumers. She employs the specific identification inventory valuation method. Prices are negotiated by Judy and individual customers. Judy accepts trade-ins when she sells an automobile. Judy negotiates the allowance for trade with the customer. Occasionally, Judy finds that it can take two or three years to sell a given automobile. Judy now has four automobiles that she has held for over two years. She expects to eventually sell those automobiles, but expects that they will sell for less than their original cost. What tax issues should Judy consider?

I:11-34 Lana operates a real estate appraisal service business in a small town serving local lenders. After noting that lenders must pay to bring in a surveyor from out of town, she completes a course and obtains a surveyor's license that enables her to provide this service also. She now provides both services as a proprietor. What tax issues should Lana consider?

I:11-35 John owns a small farm on a lake. A local developer offers John $400,000 cash for his farm. The developer believes John's farm will be very attractive to home buyers because it is on a lake. After John turns down the initial offer, the developer offers to pay John $250,000 plus an amount equal to 10% of the selling price for the homes that are developed and sold. Identify the tax issues John should consider if he accepts the offer.

I:11-36 Lee is starting a small lawn service. On the advice of his accountant, Lee has formed a corporation and made an S corporation election. The accountant has asked Lee to consider electing a fiscal year ending on the last day in February. The accountant pointed out that Lee's business is likely to slow down in the winter. Also, the accountant indicated that the February year end would permit the accountant to do Lee's accounting work after the busy season in accounting is over. What tax issues should Lee consider?

PROBLEMS

I:11-37 *Allowable Taxable Year.* For each of the following cases, indicate whether the taxpayer has selected an allowable tax year in an initial year. If the year selected is not acceptable, indicate what an acceptable year would be.
a. A corporation selects a January 15 year-end.
b. A corporation selects a March 31 year-end.
c. A corporation selects a year that ends on the last Friday in March.
d. A partnership selects a year that ends on December 31 and has three equal partners whose years end on March 31, April 30, and June 30.
e. An S corporation selects a December 31 year-end.

I:11-38 *Change in Accounting Period.* In which of the following instances is a taxpayer permitted to change accounting periods without IRS approval?
a. A calendar-year taxpayer who wishes to change to a year that ends on the last Friday in December.
b. ABC Partnership has filed its tax return using a fiscal-year ending on March 31 for over 40 years. The partnership wishes to change to a calendar year-end that coincides with its partners' year-end.
c. Iowa Corporation, a newly acquired subsidiary, wishes to change its year-end to coincide with its parent.

I:11-39 *Annualization.* Each of the following cases involves a taxable year of less than 12 months. In which situations is annualization required?
a. A new corporation formed in September elects a calendar year.
b. A calendar-year individual dies on June 15.
c. Jean, who has been using a calendar year, marries Hank, a fiscal-year taxpayer. Soon after the marriage, Jean changes her tax year to coincide with her husband's tax year.
d. A calendar-year corporation liquidates on April 20.

I:11-40 *Short Period Return.* Lavanya, a single taxpayer, is a practicing accountant. She obtains permission to change her tax year from the calendar year to a year ending July 31. Her practice income for the seven months ending July 31 is $40,000. In addition, Lavanya has $3,000 of interest income and $6,500 of itemized deductions. She is entitled to one exemption. What is her tax for the short period?

I:11-41 *Cash Basis Expenses.* How much of the following expenses are currently deductible by a cash basis taxpayer?
a. Medical prescriptions costing $20 paid by credit card (medical expenses already exceed the 10% of AGI floor).
b. Prepaid interest (not related to points) of $200 on a residential loan.
c. Taxpayer borrows $300 from the bank to make a charitable contribution. The $300 is paid to the charitable organization before the end of the tax year.
d. Taxpayer gives a note to his church indicating an intent to contribute $300.
e. A calendar-year individual mails a check for $200 to his church on December 31. The check is postmarked December 31 and clears the bank on January 4.

I:11-42 *Economic Performance.* In light of the economic performance requirement, how much is deductible by the following accrual-basis corporate taxpayers this year?
a. Camp Corporation sells products with a one-year warranty. Camp estimates that the warranty costs on products sold during this year will amount to $80,000. Camp performs $38,000 of warranty work on products sold last year and $36,000 of warranty work on products sold this year.
b. Data Corporation agrees to pay $10,000 this year and $10,000 next year to a software developer. The developer completes all work on the software and delivers the product to Data this year.
c. Palm Corporation pays $5,000 to a supplier to guarantee delivery of raw materials. The $5,000 is refundable if Palm decides not to acquire the materials.
d. This year North Corporation pays a $1,000 security deposit on space it rents for a new office. In addition, North pays current year rent of $18,000. The security deposit is refundable if the property is returned in good condition.

I:11-43 *Manufacturing Inventory.* Which of the following costs must be included in inventory by a manufacturing company?

a. Raw materials
b. Advertising
c. Payroll taxes for factory employees
d. Research and experimental costs
e. Factory insurance
f. Repairs to factory equipment
g. Factory utility costs
h. Factory rent

I:11-44 *Single-Pool LIFO.* Prime Corporation begins operations in late 2015. Prime decides to use the single-pool LIFO method. Year-end inventories under FIFO are as follows:

2015	$110,000
2016	134,000
2017	125,000

The price index for 2015 is 130%; for 2016, 134%; and 2017, 140%. What are 2016 and 2017 inventories?

I:11-45 *Installment Sale.* Ace Construction Company sells a used crane to Go Construction for $80,000. The crane, which originally cost $900,000, is fully depreciated. Under Sec. 1245 depreciation recapture rules, the entire gain is taxable as ordinary income. Ace receives a down payment of $20,000 and is to receive $20,000 per year for three additional years plus interest of 8%, which is greater than the applicable federal rate.
a. Compute the gain from the sale.
b. How much gain is taxable in the year of the sale?
c. What income does Ace report in each of the next three years?

I:11-46 *Inventory Method.* Zap Company manufactures computer hard drives. The cost of hard drives has been declining for years. Sales totaled $4,000,000 last year. Zap's ending inventory was valued at $300,000 under FIFO. The company's new president is trying to cut taxes and asks you whether the company should switch to LIFO. What do you recommend?

I:11-47 *Installment Sales.* First Company sold the following assets during the year. Indicate whether First Company can use the installment method to report each transaction. If not, how is the transaction reported? Assume First Company is an accrual basis taxpayer.
a. First Company sold stock in a publicly held company costing $35,000. First Company received a $20,000 down payment and is to receive $20,000 per year for two years plus interest.
b. First Company sold land costing $150,000. First Company received a $20,000 down payment and is to receive $20,000 per year for five years plus interest.
c. First Company initiated credit sales of merchandise. The company previously sold merchandise only to cash customers. Cash sales this year totaled $4,000,000. Credit sales totaled $500,000. At year end, First Company has receivables of $100,000. The company expects to collect only $85,000 of the current receivables.

I:11-48 *Installment Sale.* In December, Dan sells unlisted stock with a cost of $14,000 for $20,000. Dan collects $5,000 down and is scheduled to receive $5,000 per year for three years plus interest at a rate acceptable to the IRS.
a. How much gain must Dan recognize in the year of the sale? Assume Dan uses the installment method to report the gain.
b. The following January, Dan sells the three remaining installments for a total of $13,800. How much gain or loss must Dan recognize from the sale of the remaining installments?

I:11-49 *Repossession.* Lina, an attorney, sold an antique rug for $45,000 that had been in her home. The rug cost Lina $12,000 several years ago. Lina collected $15,000 down and received a one-year interest bearing note for the balance. She is unable to collect the balance, and after incurring court costs of $500, she repossesses the rug. The rug is damaged when she recovers it and is now worth only $30,000.
a. How much gain must Lina report in the year of the sale?
b. How much gain, if any, must Lina report in the year she repossesses the rug?
c. What is the basis of the rug after the repossession?

I:11-50 *Deferred Payment Sale.* Joe sells land with a $60,000 adjusted basis for $42,000. He incurs selling expenses of $2,000. The land is subject to a $10,000 mortgage. The buyer, who assumes the mortgage, pays $8,000 down and agrees to pay Joe $8,000 per year for three years plus interest. The installment obligations are worth $24,000.

a. How much gain or loss does Joe report in the year of the sale?

b. When does Joe report the interest income from the sale?

c. Does Joe report gain or loss when he collects the installment payments?

I:11-51 *Imputed Interest.* On January 30, 2015, Amy sells land to Bob for a stated price of $200,000. The full $200,000 is payable on January 30, 2017. No interest is stated. Amy, a cash-method taxpayer, purchased the land in 2010 for $130,000.

a. How much interest income must be reported by Amy on the sale? Assume a 9% rate compounded semiannually. The present value factor is 0.83856.

b. In what year is the interest reported?

c. How much gain is reported by Amy on the sale?

d. In what year is the gain reported?

e. What is Bob's basis in the land?

I:11-52 *Change of Accounting Method.* Dana manages real estate and is a cash method taxpayer. She changes to the accrual method in 2016. Dana's business income for 2016 is $30,000 computed on the accrual method. Her books show the following:

	December 31, 2015	December 31, 2016
Accounts receivable	$16,000	$25,300
Accounts payable	15,200	11,800

a. What adjustment is necessary to Dana's income?

b. How should Dana report the adjustment?

I:11-53 *Required Payment.* BCD Partnership has, for many years, had a March 31 year-end. The partnership's net income for the fiscal year ended March 31, 2016 is $400,000. Because of its fiscal year, BCD has $100,000 on deposit with the IRS from 2015.

a. How much must BCD add to the deposit?

b. When must BCD make the addition?

c. Will the partners receive any credit for the deposit? That is, are they permitted to treat the amount as estimated payments?

I:11-54 *Change to LIFO.* Lance Corporation's management has asked whether they may change their inventory valuation method to LIFO. They now report their inventory using FIFO. If they can change, how would they go about it? How is the related adjustment handled?

I:11-55 *Imputed Interest.* Jane loans $80,000 to John, her son, to permit him to purchase a principal residence. The loan principal is secured by John's residence, but the agreement does not specify any interest. The applicable federal rate for the year is 8%. John's net investment income is $800.

a. How much interest is imputed on the loan each year?

b. Assume that the amount of the loan is $125,000. How much interest is imputed on the loan?

c. Is John allowed to deduct the imputed interest?

d. What other tax implications are there for the loan?

I:11-56 *Long-Term Contract.* King Construction Company is engaged in a road construction contract to build a highway over a three-year period. King will receive $11,200,000 for building five miles of highway. King estimates that it will incur $10,000,000 of costs before the contract is completed. As of the end of the first year King incurred $3,000,000 of costs allocated to the contract.

a. How much income from the contract must King report during the first year?

b. Assume King incurs an additional $5,000,000 of costs during the second year. How much income is reported during that year?

c. Assume that King incurs an additional $2,500,000 of costs in the third and final year of the contract. How much does King report during the third year?

d. Will King receive or pay look-back interest? Explain.

COMPREHENSIVE PROBLEM

I:11-57 Dan turned age 65 and retired this year. He owned and operated a tugboat in the local harbor before his retirement. The boat cost $100,000 when he purchased it two years ago. A tugboat is 10-year property. Dan deducted $10,000 of depreciation on the boat the year he purchased it and he deducted $18,000 of depreciation last year. He did not elect Section 179 expensing or bonus depreciation. He sold the tugboat in November of this year for $90,000 collecting an $18,000 down payment. The buyer agreed to pay 8% interest annually on the unpaid balance and to pay $18,000 annually for four years toward the principal. The four $18,000 principal payments and related interest payments begin next year. Dan received $72,000 of business income and incurred other business expenses of $30,000 this year before he retired. He received Social Security benefits of $2,000 and withdrew $10,000 from a regular IRA account. He contributed $4,000 to his church, paid real property taxes of $2,000, and home mortgage interest of $6,500. Dan paid $200 of state income taxes when he filed last year's return earlier this year and he made estimated state income tax payments of $800 during this year and $220 after year end. In addition, Dan made federal estimated payments of $8,000. Dan is a single, cash basis taxpayer. Ignore self-employment taxes and the election to use state sales tax as an itemized deduction.

a. Compute the depreciation for the current year on the tugboat.
b. Compute the amount of gain to be reported currently on the sale of the tugboat. Assume that Dan wants to use the installment method if it can be used. The accumulated depreciation on the tugboat is subject to Sec. 1245 depreciation recapture and must be reported currently.
c. How much interest, if any, must Dan report this year?
d. What is the income from the business, excluding the gain on the sale of the tugboat?
e. What is Dan's AGI?
f. What is the amount of Dan's itemized deductions?
g. What is Dan's taxable income?

TAX STRATEGY PROBLEMS

I:11-58 Leon has a substantial portfolio of stocks and bonds as well as cash from some bonds that have recently matured. He has been looking at investing $200,000 in corporate bonds that pay 7% interest. The $14,000 of annual interest would be used to pay his 24-year-old son's tuition at State University. A friend suggested that Leon loan the money "interest free" to his son, a student who has no other income. The son would then invest the $200,000 in the corporate bonds and use the $14,000 interest to pay his tuition. Leon is in the 28% tax bracket. Would such a strategy reduce his family's tax? Assume the applicable federal rate is 6.5%.

I:11-59 Linda is selling land she has owned for many years. The land cost $80,000 and will sell for $200,000. The buyer has offered to pay $100,000 down and pay the balance next year plus interest at 8%. Assume that Linda's after tax rate of return on investments is 10%. Would she be better off receiving the installment payments or receiving cash? Assume her ordinary income is taxed at 28% and that long-term capital gains are taxed at 15%.

TAX FORM/RETURN PREPARATION PROBLEM

I:11-60 Barbara B. Kuhn (SSN 987-65-4321) purchases a fourplex on January 8, 2011, for $175,000. She allocates $25,000 of the cost to the land, and she deducts MACRS depreciation totaling $16,364. Barbara sells the fourplex on January 6, 2014, for $225,000. The buyer assumes the existing mortgage of $180,000, pays $15,000 down, and agrees to pay $15,000 per year for two years plus 12% interest. Barbara incurs selling expenses of $18,000. Complete Form 6252.

CASE STUDY PROBLEMS

I:11-61 Lavonne just completed medical school and residency. She plans to open her medical practice soon. She is not familiar with the intricacies of accounting methods and periods. On advice of her attorney, she plans to form a professional corporation (a form of organization permitted under the laws of most states that does not have the usual limited liability found with business corporations, but is taxed as a corporation). She has asked you whether she should elect a fiscal year and whether she should use the cash or accrual method of reporting income. Discuss whether the options are available to her and the implications of available choices.

I:11-62   Don owns equipment that he purchased several years ago for $400,000. Over the years he properly deducted $110,000 of depreciation. The depreciation will have to be recaptured as ordinary income on the sale. There is a $90,000 mortgage on the property. Don has an offer for the equipment from an individual who says he will pay $100,000 down and $100,000 per year for five years. There is no mention of interest. As the mortgage is nonassumable, Don will pay off the mortgage using most of the down payment. Don is age 61, and proceeds from the sale along with a pension from his employer will provide for his retirement. Don plans to retire next year. He currently has a 25% marginal tax rate. Discuss the tax implications of the sale. Is there anything Don can do to improve his situation?

I:11-63   Troy Tools manufactures over one hundred different hand tools used by mechanics, carpenters, and plumbers. Troy's cost accounting system has always been very simple. The costs allocated to inventory have included only materials, direct labor, and factory overhead. Other overhead costs such as costs of the personnel department, purchasing, payroll, and computer services have never been treated as manufacturing overhead even though many of the activities of the departments relate to the manufacturing operations. You are preparing Troy's tax return for the first time and determine that the company is not following the uniform capitalization rules prescribed in the tax law. You have explained to the company's president that there is a problem, and she is reluctant to change accounting methods. She says allocating these costs to the many products the company makes will be a time-consuming and expensive process. She feels that the cost of determining the additional amounts to include in inventory under the uniform capitalization rules will probably be more than the additional tax that the company will pay. What is the appropriate way to handle this situation? (See the *Statements on Standards for Tax Services* section in Chapter I:15 for a discussion of these issues.)

TAX RESEARCH PROBLEMS

I:11-64   Eagle and Hill Corporations discuss the terms of a land sale, and they agree to a price of $230,000. Eagle wants to use the installment sale method, but is not sure Hill is a reliable borrower. As a result, Eagle requires Hill to place the entire purchase price in escrow to be released in five yearly installments by the escrow agent. Is the installment method available to Eagle?

     A partial list of research sources is:

- Rev. Rul. 77-294, 1977-2 C.B. 173
- Rev. Rul. 79-91, 1979-1 C.B. 179
- *H. O. Williams v. U.S.*, 46 AFTR 1725, 55-1 USTC ¶9220 (5th Cir., 1955)

I:11-65   Texas Corporation disassembles old automobiles for the purpose of reselling their components (i.e., different types of metals, plastics, rubber, and other materials). Texas sells some of the items for scrap, but must pay to dispose of environmentally hazardous plastics and rubber. At year-end, Texas Corporation has a difficult time determining the cost of the individual parts that are stacked in piles. In fact, it would be very expensive to even weigh some of the materials on hand. Texas has followed the practice of having two experienced employees estimate the weight of different stacks and then price them based on quotes found in trade journals. If Texas must pay to dispose of an item, it is assigned a value of zero. In other words, Texas does not value its inventory using standard FIFO or LIFO methods. Is such a practice acceptable?

     A partial list of research sources is:

- Reg. Secs. 1.471-2(a) and 1.471-3(d)
- *Morrie Chaitlen*, 1978 PH T.C. Memo ¶78,006, 37 TCM 17
- *Justus & Parker Co.*, 13 BTA 127 (1928)

I:11-66   Apple Corporation has never been audited before the current year. An audit is now needed from a CPA because the company is expanding rapidly and plans to issue stock to the public in a secondary offering. A CPA firm has been doing preliminary evaluations of the Apple Corporation's accounts and records. One major problem involves the valuation of inventory under GAAP. Apple Corporation has been valuing its inventory under the cost method and no write-downs have been made for obsolescence. A review of the inventory indicates that obsolescence and excess spare parts in the inventory are two major problems. The CPA states that for GAAP the company will be required to write down its inventory by 25% of its stated amount, or $100,000, and charge this amount against net income from operations for the current period. Otherwise, a "clean opinion" will not be rendered. The company controller asks your advice regarding the tax consequences from the obsolescence and spare parts inventory write-downs for the current year and the procedures for changing to the LCM method for tax purposes. Apple Corporation is on a calendar year, and the date of your contact with the company is December 1 of the current year.

A partial list of research sources is:

- Secs. 446 and 471
- Reg. Secs. 1.446-1(e)(3), 1.471-2 and 1.471-4
- *American Liberty Pipe Line Co. v. CIR*, 32 AFTR 1099, 44-2 USTC ¶9408 (5th Cir., 1944)
- *Thor Power Tool Co. v. CIR*, 43 AFTR 2d 79-362, 79-1 USTC ¶9139 (USSC, 1979)

12

PROPERTY TRANSACTIONS: NONTAXABLE EXCHANGES

LEARNING OBJECTIVES

After studying this chapter, you should be able to

1 ▶ Examine the tax consequences arising from a like-kind exchange

2 ▶ Determine whether gain from an involuntary conversion may be deferred

3 ▶ Determine when a gain resulting from the sale of a principal residence is excluded

4 ▶ Describe tax planning considerations for nontaxable exchanges

5 ▶ Describe compliance and procedural considerations for nontaxable exchanges

KEY POINT

The transactions examined in this chapter override the normal rule that provides for the recognition of realized gains and realized losses on property used in a business or held for investment.

Taxpayers who sell or exchange property for an amount greater or less than their basis in that property have a realized gain or loss on the sale or exchange. Almost any transfer of property is treated as a sale or other disposition (see Chapter I:5). The realized gain or loss must be recognized unless a specific Code section provides for nonrecognition treatment. If the realized gain or loss is not recognized at the time of the transaction, the nonrecognized gain or loss may be deferred in some cases and excluded in others.

The general rules related to the computation of realized and recognized gains or losses are covered in Chapter I:5. This chapter discusses three of the most common transactions that may result in *nonrecognition* of a realized gain or loss:

▶ Like-kind exchanges under Sec. 1031 (deferred gain or loss)
▶ Involuntary conversions under Sec. 1033 (deferred gain)
▶ Sales of a personal residence under Sec. 121 (excluded gain)

Nonrecognition of gain treatment for like-kind exchanges, involuntary conversions, and the sale of a residence may be partially justified by the fact that taxpayers may lack the wherewithal to pay the tax despite the existence of a realized gain. For example, a taxpayer who realizes a gain due to an involuntary conversion of property (damage from fire, storm, etc.) may have to use the amount received to replace the converted property.

A typical requirement in a nontaxable exchange is that the taxpayer is required to maintain a continuing investment in comparable property (e.g., a building is exchanged for another building). In essence, a change in form rather than a change in substance occurs.

A transaction generally considered to be nontaxable may be taxable in part. In a like-kind exchange, for example, the taxpayer may also receive money or property that is not like-kind property. If non–like-kind property or money is received, the realized gain is taxable to the extent of the sum of the money and the fair market value (FMV) of the non–like-kind property received.[1]

LIKE-KIND EXCHANGES

OBJECTIVE 1

Examine the tax consequences arising from a like-kind exchange

Section 1031(a) provides that "No gain or loss shall be recognized on the exchange of property held for productive use in a trade or business or for investment if such property is exchanged solely for property of like-kind which is to be held either for productive use in a trade or business or for investment."[2]

In a **like-kind exchange**, both the property transferred and the property received must be held either for productive use in the trade or business or for investment.

EXAMPLE I:12-1 ▶ Tom owns land used in his trade or business. He exchanges the land for other land, which is to be held for investment. No gain or loss is recognized by Tom because he has exchanged property used in a trade or business for like-kind property to be held for investment. ◀

EXAMPLE I:12-2 ▶ Dawn's automobile is held for personal use. She exchanges the automobile, with a $10,000 basis, for stock of AT&T with a $12,000 FMV. The stock is held for investment. A $2,000 gain is recognized because the automobile is not used in Dawn's trade or business or held for investment. The exchange is not a like-kind exchange because neither personal-use assets nor stock qualify as like-kind property. ◀

REAL-WORLD EXAMPLE

An exchange or trade of professional football player contracts qualifies as a like-kind exchange. Rev. Rul. 71-137, 1971-1 C.B. 104.

Section 1031 is not an elective provision. If the exchange qualifies as a like-kind exchange, nonrecognition of gain or loss is mandatory. To qualify for like-kind exchange treatment, a direct exchange must occur and the property exchanged must be like-kind. A taxpayer who prefers to recognize a loss on an exchange must structure the transaction to avoid having the exchange qualify as a like-kind exchange.

ADDITIONAL COMMENT

The mandatory nonrecognition of loss under Sec. 1031 can be avoided by selling the old property in one transaction and buying the new property in a separate, unrelated transaction.

LIKE-KIND PROPERTY DEFINED
Character of the Property. To be a nontaxable exchange under Sec. 1031, the property exchanged must be like-kind. The Treasury Regulations specify that "the words

---

[1] Sec. 1031(b). [2] Sec. 1031(a).

'like-kind' have reference to the nature or character of the property and not to its grade or quality."[3] Thus, exchanges of real property qualify even if the properties are dissimiliar.

EXAMPLE I:12-3 ► Eric owns an apartment building held for investment. Eric exchanges the building for farmland to be used in his trade or business. The exchange is a like-kind exchange because both the building and the farmland are classified as real property and both properties are used either in business or held for investment. ◄

EXAMPLE I:12-4 ► Trail Corporation exchanges improved real estate for unimproved real estate, both of which are held for investment. The exchange is a like-kind exchange.[4] ◄

ADDITIONAL COMMENT
Real property is often referred to as real estate.

Location of the Property. Transfers of real property located in the U.S. and real property located outside the U.S. after July 9, 1989, are not like-kind exchanges. Exchanges of personal property predominantly used in the United States and personal property used outside of the United States that occur after June 8, 1997, are not like-kind exchanges. To determine where the property is predominantly used, the two-year period ending on the date the property is exchanged is analyzed. For property received, the location of predominant use is determined by analyzing the use during the two-year period after the property is received.

Property Must be the Same Class. An exchange is not a like-kind exchange when property of one class is exchanged for property of a different kind or class.[5] For example, if real property is exchanged for personal property (or vice versa), no like-kind exchange occurs.[6]

EXAMPLE I:12-5 ► Gail exchanges an office building with a $400,000 adjusted basis for an airplane with a $580,000 FMV to be used in business. This is not a like-kind exchange because the office building is real property and the airplane is personal property. Gail must recognize a $180,000 ($580,000 − $400,000) gain. ◄

EXAMPLE I:12-6 ► Gary exchanges a business truck for another truck to use in his business. This is an exchange of like-kind property. ◄

ADDITIONAL COMMENT
The rules in the Regulations dealing with exchanges of personal property are not interpreted as liberally as the rules relating to real property.

Property of a Like Class. The Treasury Regulations provide that personal property of a **like class** meets the definition of *like-kind*.[7] Like class property is defined as depreciable tangible personal properties within the same General Asset Class or within the same Product Class.[8] Property within a General Asset Class consists of depreciable tangible personal property described in one of the asset classes provided in Rev. Proc. 87-56 for depreciation.[9] Some of the General Asset Classes are as follows:

► Office furniture, fixtures, and equipment (Asset Class 00.11)

► Information systems such as computers and peripheral equipment (Asset Class 00.12)

► Automobiles and taxis (Asset Class 00.22)

► Buses (Asset Class 00.23)

► Light general purpose trucks (Asset Class 00.241)

► Heavy general purpose trucks (Asset Class 00.242)

► Vessels, barges, tugs, and similar water-transportation equipment except those used in marine construction (Asset Class 00.28)

For purposes of the like-kind exchange provisions, a single property may not be classified in more than one General Asset Class or more than one Product Class. Furthermore, property in any General Asset Class may not be classified in a Product Class. A property's General Asset Class or Product Class is determined as of the exchange date.

---

[3] Reg. Sec. 1.1031(a)-1(b).
[4] *Ibid.*
[5] *Ibid.*
[6] Real property includes land and property attached to land in a relatively permanent manner. Personal property that is affixed to real property in a

relatively permanent manner is a fixture and is considered part of the real property. Personal property is all property that is not real property or a fixture.
[7] Reg. Sec. 1.1031(a)-2.
[8] Reg. Sec. 1.1031(a)-2(b).
[9] 1987-2 C.B. 674.

EXAMPLE I:12-7 ▶   Wint transfers a personal computer used in his trade or business for a printer to be used in his trade or business. The exchange is a like-kind exchange because both properties are in the same General Asset Class (00.12). ◀

EXAMPLE I:12-8 ▶   Renee transfers an airplane (Asset Class 00.21) used in her trade or business for a heavy general purpose truck to use in her trade or business. The properties are not of a like class because they are in different General Asset Classes. The heavy general purpose truck is in Asset Class 00.242. ◀

Example I:12-8 is taken from the Treasury Regulations, which further state: "Because each of the properties is within a General Asset Class, the properties may not be classified within a Product Class. The airplane and heavy general purpose truck are also not of a like kind. Therefore, the exchange does not qualify for nonrecognition of gain or loss under Sec. 1031."[10]

If two properties are not within a General Asset Class, it still may be possible to be considered like-kind if the properties are within the same Product Class. Property in a Product Class consists of depreciable tangible personal property listed in the North American Classification System prepared by the Office of Management and Budget.[11] The Regulations state that an exchange of a grader for a scraper is an exchange of properties of like class because neither property is in a General Asset Class and both properties are listed in the same Product Class.[12]

There are no like classes for intangible personal property, nondepreciable personal property, or personal property held for investment. To have a like-kind exchange of property held for investment, the property must be exchanged for like-kind property. To determine whether an exchange of intangible personal property is a like-kind exchange, one must consider the type of right involved as well as the underlying property to which the intangible property relates. An exchange of a copyright for a novel for a copyright on a different novel is a like-kind exchange, but the exchange of a copyright on a novel for a copyright on a song is not a like-kind exchange.[13]

ADDITIONAL COMMENT

An exchange can be a like-kind exchange for one party to the transaction but not qualify as a like-kind exchange for the other party.

Non–Like-Kind Property Exchanges. An exchange of inventory or securities does not qualify as a like-kind exchange.[14]

EXAMPLE I:12-9 ▶   Antonio, a dealer in farm equipment, exchanges a new combine for other property in the same General Asset Class to be used in Antonio's trade or business. Because Antonio is a dealer, the new combine is inventory and the exchange does not qualify as a like-kind exchange. ◀

EXAMPLE I:12-10 ▶   Nancy owns Able Corporation stock as an investment. Nancy exchanges the stock for antiques to be held as investments. This exchange is taxable because stock does not qualify as like-kind property. ◀

In most cases, to qualify as a like-kind exchange of personal property, the property must be nearly identical. For example, livestock of different sexes are not like-kind property.[15] An exchange of gold bullion held for investment for silver bullion held for investment is not a like-kind exchange. Silver and gold are intrinsically different metals and primarily are used in different ways.[16] Currency exchanges are not like-kind exchanges,[17] and the exchange of a partnership interest for an interest in another partnership is not a like-kind exchange.[18]

---

[10] Reg. Sec. 1.1031(a)-2(b)(7) Ex. 2.
[11] Reg. Sec. 1.1031(a)-2(b)(3).
[12] Reg. Sec. 1.1031(a)-2(b)(7) Ex. 3.
[13] Reg. Sec. 1.1031(a)-2(c)(1).
[14] Sec. 1031(a)(2). An exchange of stock is not a like-kind exchange. However, an exchange of stock is a nontaxable exchange if the exchange is related to a tax-free reorganization.

[15] Sec. 1031(e).
[16] Rev. Rul. 82-166, 1982-2 C.B. 190.
[17] Rev. Rul. 74-7, 1974-1 C.B. 198.
[18] Sec. 1031(a)(2).

Exchange of Securities. The like-kind exchange rules do not apply to stocks, bonds, or notes.[19] However, Sec. 1036 provides that no gain or loss is recognized on the exchange of common stock for common stock or preferred stock for preferred stock in the same corporation. Sec. 1036 applies even if voting common stock is exchanged for nonvoting common stock of the same corporation. The nontaxable exchange of stock of the same corporation may be between two stockholders or a stockholder and the corporation.[20]

Section 1036 does not apply to exchanges of common stock for preferred stock; stock for bonds of same corporation, or any kind of stock in different corporations.

EXAMPLE I:12-11 ▶ Kelly owns common stock of Best Corporation. Best issues class B common stock to Kelly in exchange for her common stock. No gain or loss is recognized because this is an exchange of common stock for common stock in the same corporation. If Best issues its preferred stock for Kelly's common stock, Kelly will have a recognized gain or loss unless the exchange is part of a tax-free reorganization. ◀

EXAMPLE I:12-12 ▶ Shirley owns 100 shares of Top Corporation common stock. The stock has a $40,000 adjusted basis and a $50,000 FMV. Bob owns 100 shares of Star Corporation common stock with a $50,000 FMV. If Shirley and Bob exchange their stock, the exchange is taxable, and Shirley has a $10,000 ($50,000 − $40,000) recognized gain. The exchange is neither a like-kind exchange nor an exchange of stock for stock of the same corporation. ◀

A DIRECT EXCHANGE MUST OCCUR

To qualify as a like-kind exchange, a direct exchange of property must occur.[21] Thus, the sale of property and the subsequent purchase of like-kind property does not qualify as a like-kind exchange unless the two transactions are interdependent.

EXAMPLE I:12-13 ▶ Karen sells a lathe used in her business to Rashad for an amount greater than the lathe's adjusted basis. After the sale, Karen purchases another lathe from David. The gain is recognized because these two transactions do not qualify as an exchange of like-kind property. ◀

A sale and a subsequent purchase may be treated as an exchange if the two transactions are interdependent. The IRS indicates that a nontaxable exchange may exist when the taxpayer sells property to a dealer and then purchases like-kind property from the same dealer.[22]

THREE-PARTY EXCHANGES

The typical two-party exchange is not always practical. If both parties do not own like-kind property that meets each other's needs, a three-party exchange might be necessary. A three-party exchange is also useful when the taxpayer is willing to exchange property for like-kind property but is not willing to sell the property to a prospective buyer. The taxpayer's unwillingness to sell the property may be motivated by the desire to avoid an immediate tax on a gain resulting from the sale of the property. Therefore, the taxpayer may arrange to have the prospective buyer purchase property from a third party that fulfills the taxpayer's needs. The three-party exchange can be an effective way of allowing the taxpayer to consummate a like-kind exchange.

EXAMPLE I:12-14 ▶ Kathy owns a farm in Nebraska, which Dick offers to purchase. Kathy is not willing to sell the farm but is willing to exchange the farm for an apartment complex in Arizona. The complex is available for sale. Dick purchases the apartment complex in Arizona from Allyson and transfers it to Kathy in exchange for Kathy's farm. The farm and the apartment complex each have a $900,000 FMV. For Kathy, the transaction qualifies as a like-kind exchange because it is a direct exchange of business real property (the farm) for investment real estate (the apartment complex). For Dick, the exchange is not a like-kind exchange. ◀

KEY POINT
Transfers of property in a three-party exchange must be part of a single, integrated plan. It is important that the taxpayers can show their intent to enter into a like-kind exchange even though contractual interdependence is not necessary to the finding of an exchange.

In the example above, the exchange is convenient for all the parties. However, it is not always this convenient to execute a three-party exchange. For example, Kathy may want

[19] Reg. Sec. 1.1031(a)-1(a)(1)(ii).
[20] Reg. Sec. 1.1036-1(a).
[21] Sec. 1031(a).
[22] Rev. Rul. 61-119, 1961-1 C.B. 395.

to own an apartment complex in Arizona, but the property she prefers may not be currently available. In this case, a nonsimultaneous exchange may occur.

TAX STRATEGY TIP
Deferred like-kind exchanges are typically used for real estate transactions. A taxpayer who has highly appreciated real estate can use a deferred, three-party, like-kind exchange to exchange the highly appreciated real estate for other real estate that is more desirable to him.

Nonsimultaneous Exchange. A nonsimultaneous exchange is treated as a like-kind exchange if the exchange is completed within a specified time period. The property to be received in the exchange must be identified within 45 days after the date of the transfer of the property relinquished in the exchange. The replacement property must be received within the earlier of 180 days after the date the taxpayer transfers the property relinquished in the exchange or the due date for filing a return (including extensions) for the year in which the transfer of the relinquished property occurs.[23]

EXAMPLE I:12-15 ▶ On May 5, 2015, Joal transfers property to Lauren, who transfers cash to an escrow agent. The escrow agent is to purchase suitable like-kind property for Joal. Joal does not have actual or constructive receipt of the cash during the delayed period. To be a like-kind exchange for Joal, the suitable like-kind property must be identified by June 19, 2015 (45 days after the transfer), and Joal must receive the property by November 1, 2015 (180 days after the transfer). ◀

EXAMPLE I:12-16 ▶ Assume the same facts as in the above example except that the transfer by Joal occurs on November 10, 2015. To be a like-kind exchange for Joal, the suitable like-kind property must be identified by December 25, 2015, and Joal must receive the property by April 15, 2016, unless Joal files an automatic four-month extension for the filing of his return (i.e., the due date is extended until August 15, 2016). In such a case, the property must be received no later than 180 days following the transfer of the property relinquished in the exchange, or by May 9, 2016 (i.e., 180 days after November 10, 2015). ◀

RECEIPT OF BOOT

TYPICAL MISCONCEPTION
In calculating the amount of gain to be recognized when boot is received, a proportionate approach is used sometimes for financial accounting purposes.

Taxpayers who want to exchange property do not always own property of equal value. To complete the exchange, non–like-kind property or money may be given or received. Cash and non–like-kind property constitute **boot**.

Gain is recognized to the extent of the boot received. However, the amount of recognized gain is limited to the amount of the taxpayer's realized gain.[24] In effect, the realized gain serves as a ceiling for the amount of the recognized gain. The receipt of boot as part of a nontaxable exchange does not cause a realized loss to be recognized.[25]

EXAMPLE I:12-17 ▶ Mario exchanges business equipment with a $50,000 adjusted basis for $10,000 cash and business equipment with a $65,000 FMV. The realized gain is $25,000 ($75,000 − $50,000). The recognized gain is $10,000 because the $10,000 of boot received is less than the $25,000 realized gain. ◀

EXAMPLE I:12-18 ▶ Mary exchanges business equipment with a $70,000 adjusted basis for $20,000 cash and business equipment with a $65,000 FMV. Her realized gain is $15,000 ($85,000 − $70,000). The $20,000 of boot received is more than the $15,000 realized gain, so $15,000 of gain is recognized. ◀

TYPICAL MISCONCEPTION
It is possible to erroneously assume that the receipt of boot causes the recognition of loss.

Taxing part or all of the gain when cash is received in like-kind exchanges is consistent with the wherewithal-to-pay concept. However, boot may not always be in the form of a liquid asset. If non–like-kind property other than cash is received as boot, the amount of the boot is the property's FMV.

EXAMPLE I:12-19 ▶ Jane exchanges land held as an investment with a $70,000 basis for other land with a $100,000 FMV and a motorcycle with a $2,000 FMV. The acquired land is to be held for investment, and the motorcycle is for personal use. Personal-use property is non–like-kind property and constitutes boot. The realized gain is $32,000 [($100,000 + $2,000) − $70,000]. The amount of boot received is equal to the FMV of the motorcycle. The recognized gain is $2,000, the lesser of the amount of boot received ($2,000) or the realized gain ($32,000). ◀

---

[23] Secs. 1031(a)(3)(A) and (B).
[24] Sec. 1031(b).

[25] Sec. 1031(c).

EXAMPLE I:12-20 ►
SELF-STUDY QUESTION

Why is the relief of a liability treated as if one has received cash?

ANSWER
If it were not treated as such, a taxpayer could receive cash shortly before the exchange by borrowing from a bank, using the property as collateral. Then, if the taxpayer is relieved of the debt in the like-kind exchange, he or she would still have cash without having paid a tax on the gain.

Assume the same facts in Example I:12-19 except that Jane uses the motorcycle in a business. The motorcycle is boot, and a $2,000 gain is still recognized because the exchange of real property for personal property is not a like-kind exchange. ◄

Property Transfers Involving Liabilities. If a liability is assumed (or the property is taken subject to a liability), the amount of the liability is considered money received by the taxpayer on the exchange.[26] One who assumes the debt or takes the property subject to a liability is treated as having paid cash, while the party that is relieved of the debt is treated as having received cash. If each party assumes a liability of the other party, only the net liability given or received is treated as boot.[27]

EXAMPLE I:12-21 ►

Mary exchanges land with a $550,000 FMV that is used in her business for Doug's building, which has a $450,000 FMV. Mary's basis in the land is $400,000, and the land is subject to a liability of $100,000, which Doug assumes. Mary's realized gain is $150,000 [($450,000 + $100,000) − $400,000]. Because assumption of the $100,000 liability is treated as boot, Mary recognizes a $100,000 gain. ◄

EXAMPLE I:12-22 ►

Matt owns an office building with a $700,000 basis, which is subject to a liability of $200,000. Susan owns an apartment complex with a $900,000 FMV, which is subject to a $150,000 liability. Matt and Susan exchange buildings and assume the related liabilities. Matt's realized gain is $250,000 [($900,000 + $200,000) − ($700,000 + $150,000)]. Matt receives boot of $50,000 ($200,000 − $150,000) and recognizes a $50,000 gain. ◄

BASIS OF PROPERTY RECEIVED

Like-Kind Property Received. The basis of property received in a nontaxable exchange is equal to the adjusted basis of the property exchanged increased by gain recognized and reduced by any boot received or loss recognized on the exchange.[28]

Basis of property received in a nontaxable exchange	=	Basis of property exchanged	−	Boot received	+	Gain recognized	−	Loss recognized[29]

EXAMPLE I:12-23 ►

ADDITIONAL COMMENT

In effect the formula used to calculate the basis of the new property involves nothing more than journalizing the transaction and adjusting the basis of the new property by an amount needed to make the entry balance.

Chuck, who is in the business of racing horses, exchanges a racehorse with a $30,000 basis for $10,000 cash and a trotter with an $80,000 FMV. Chuck's realized gain is $60,000 [($80,000 + $10,000) − $30,000], and $10,000 of the gain is recognized because the boot received is less than the realized gain. Chuck's basis for the replacement property (i.e., the trotter) is $30,000 ($30,000 basis of property exchanged − $10,000 of boot received + $10,000 of gain recognized). ◄

The basis of the like-kind property received can also be computed by subtracting the unrecognized gain from its FMV or by adding the unrecognized loss to its FMV. Chuck's $30,000 basis for the trotter in Example I:12-23 may be computed by subtracting the $50,000 of unrecognized gain from the $80,000 FMV.

EXAMPLE I:12-24 ►

KEY POINT

The basis adjustment is the mechanism that ensures that gain or loss is temporarily postponed rather than permanently excluded.

Pam, who operates a circus, exchanges an elephant with a $15,000 basis for $3,000 cash and a tiger with a $10,000 FMV. The $2,000 realized loss [($10,000 + $3,000) − $15,000] is not recognized. The receipt of boot does not cause a realized loss to be recognized. Pam's basis for the replacement property (i.e., the tiger) is $12,000 ($15,000 basis of property exchanged − $3,000 boot received). ◄

As indicated earlier, realized gains and losses resulting from nontaxable exchanges are deferred. This deferral is reflected in the basis of property received and is illustrated in the

---

[26] Sec. 1031(d). If a liability is assumed, the taxpayer agrees to pay the debt. If property is taken subject to the liability, the taxpayer is responsible for the debt only to the extent that the property could be used to pay the debt.
[27] Reg. Sec. 1.1031(b)-1(c).

[28] Sec. 1031(d).
[29] A loss is recognized only when the taxpayer transfers boot with a basis greater than its FMV. Transfers of non–like-kind property (i.e., boot) are discussed in a separate section of this chapter.

two preceding examples. In Example I:12-23, the $50,000 ($60,000 − $10,000) unrecognized gain may be recognized when the trotter is sold or exchanged in a taxable transaction, because the basis of the replacement property is less than its FMV by the amount of the deferred gain. For example, if the trotter is sold in a taxable transaction for its $80,000 FMV, the $50,000 ($80,000 − $30,000 basis) of previously unrecognized gain would be recognized. In Example I:12-24, the $2,000 unrecognized loss is reflected in the basis of the tiger. If Pam sells the tiger for its $10,000 FMV, a $2,000 loss ($10,000 − $12,000 basis) is recognized.

If more than one item of like-kind property is received, the basis is allocated among the properties in proportion to their relative FMVs on the date of the exchange.

EXAMPLE I:12-25 ▶ Saul, who operates a zoo, exchanges a boa constrictor with a $300 basis for a python with a $400 FMV and an anaconda with a $600 FMV. The $700 realized gain [($400 + $600) − $300] is not recognized. The total bases of the properties received is $300. This amount is allocated to the properties (i.e., the python and the anaconda) based on their relative FMVs. Saul's basis for the python is $120 [($400 ÷ $1,000) × $300], and the basis for the anaconda is $180 [($600 ÷ $1,000) × $300]. ◀

Non–Like-Kind Property Received. The basis of non–like-kind property received is "an amount equivalent to its FMV at the date of the exchange."[30]

EXAMPLE I:12-26 ▶
KEY POINT
Steve had basis of $20,000 before the exchange. Since he recognized gain of $5,000, the total basis of the two assets should be $25,000.

Steve exchanges a punch press with a $20,000 adjusted basis for a press brake with a $50,000 FMV and $5,000 of marketable securities. Steve's realized gain is $35,000 [($50,000 + $5,000) − $20,000], and $5,000 of the realized gain is recognized due to the receipt of boot. Steve's basis for the marketable securities is $5,000, and the basis for the press brake is $20,000 ($20,000 basis of property exchanged − $5,000 boot received + $5,000 gain recognized). ◀

 **STOP & THINK**

Question: Chris Reedy owns 40 houses that he uses as rental property. All houses have a FMV greater than their adjusted basis. Chris wishes to diversify his investments and is considering selling ten of his houses and using the proceeds to purchase other types of investment assets such as stocks, bonds, commercial parking lots and land near town that he expects to increase in value. He asks you for advice.

Solution: If he sells the ten houses, he will have a gain and must pay taxes on the gain. He could defer the gain by exchanging the houses for like-kind property. Stocks and bonds are not like-kind property, but the commercial parking lots and the land should qualify as like-kind property, therefore the tax law encourages him to exchange the houses for the commercial parking lot and/or the land.

ADDITIONAL COMMENT
The running of the two-year holding period is suspended during any period in which the property holder's risk of loss is substantially diminished.

EXCHANGES BETWEEN RELATED PARTIES

Prior to 1990, related taxpayers could often use the like-kind exchange provisions to lower taxes because the tax basis for the property received is determined by the basis of the property exchanged. Related taxpayers could take advantage of the shift in tax basis to transfer a gain on a subsequent sale to a related party.[31] However, exchanges of property between related parties are not like-kind exchanges under current law if either party disposes of the property within two years of the exchange. Any gain resulting from the original exchange is recognized in the year of the subsequent disposition.[32] Dispositions due to death or involuntary conversion, or for non–tax avoidance purposes are disregarded.[33]

EXAMPLE I:12-27 ▶ Melon Corporation, which is 100% owned by Linda, owned land with a basis of $200,000 that was held for investment. Rick wanted to purchase the land for $900,000. Linda owned an office building with a basis of $750,000 and a FMV of $900,000. Instead of selling the land to Rick, Melon Corporation exchanged the land for Linda's office building in December 2014.

---

[30] Reg. Sec. 1.1031(d)-1(c).
[31] The definition of *related parties* is the same as those for Sec. 267(a) which is discussed in Chapter I:6, and includes brothers, sisters, parents, children, and corporations where the taxpayer owns at least 50% in value. (See Sec. 1031(f)(3).)

[32] Sec. 1031(f)(1)(C).
[33] Sec. 1031(f)(2).

Two months later, Linda sells the land to Rick for $900,000. The exchange of the land for the office building is not a like-kind exchange because one of the related parties disposes of the property within two years of the exchange. In 2015, Melon's recognized gain on the exchange of the land is $700,000 ($900,000 − $200,000) and Linda's recognized gain on the exchange of the office building is $150,000 ($900,000 − $750,000). Because Linda's basis for the land is now $900,000, no gain is recognized on the sale of the land to Rick. ◀

If the parties in Example I:12-27 were not related, a like-kind exchange occurred in 2014 and Linda's gain on the sale of the land to Rick is $150,000 ($900,000 − $750,000). Importantly, the exchange is not a like-kind exchange if Linda does not hold the land for investment or for use in her trade or business after receiving it from Melon.

TRANSFER OF NON–LIKE-KIND PROPERTY

In all of the preceding examples that include a transfer of boot, the transferor (i.e., the taxpayer) received boot. If the taxpayer transfers non–like-kind property, gain or loss equal to the difference between the FMV and the adjusted basis of the non–like-kind property surrendered must be recognized. However, if the non–like-kind property is a personal use asset, the loss is not recognized.

EXAMPLE I:12-28 ▶ Shirley exchanges land with a $30,000 basis ($46,000 FMV) and marketable securities with a $10,000 basis ($14,000 FMV) to David for land with a $60,000 FMV in a transaction that otherwise qualifies as a like-kind exchange. Because the non–like-kind property that Shirley transfers has a FMV greater than its basis, she recognizes $4,000 ($14,000 − $10,000) of gain. Shirley's basis for the land received is $44,000 ($30,000 + $10,000 + $4,000), which is the basis of both assets exchanged plus the gain recognized on the exchange. ◀

EXAMPLE I:12-29 ▶ Paul exchanges timberland held as an investment for undeveloped land with a $200,000 FMV to use in his business. Paul's basis for the timberland is $125,000. His tractor with a $6,000 basis and a $4,000 FMV is also transferred. Because the non–like-kind property (i.e., the tractor) that Paul transfers has a FMV less than its basis, he recognizes a $2,000 ($4,000 − $6,000) loss. Paul's basis for the undeveloped land is $129,000 ($125,000 + $6,000 − $2,000). ◀

In Example I:12-29, Paul recognizes a loss on the non–like-kind property he surrenders, despite receiving property in the aggregate with a FMV greater than the total adjusted basis of the transferred assets. Paul is actually making two exchanges. His exchange of timberland with a basis of $125,000 for undeveloped land with a $196,000 FMV is a like-kind exchange, but his exchange of the tractor with a basis of $6,000 for undeveloped land with a $4,000 FMV is a taxable exchange. In Example I:12-30 below, Ed also makes two exchanges. He has a realized and recognized gain as well as a realized but unrecognized loss.

EXAMPLE I:12-30 ▶ Ed owns equipment used in business with a $20,000 adjusted basis and a $15,000 FMV and marketable securities with a $10,000 basis and an $18,000 FMV. Ed exchanges the marketable securities and the equipment for business equipment in the same General Asset Class with a $33,000 FMV. Although the net realized gain is $3,000 [$33,000 − ($20,000 + $10,000)], Ed recognizes an $8,000 gain because he has transferred non–like-kind property with a $10,000 basis and an $18,000 FMV. The $5,000 realized loss on the transfer of equipment is not recognized due to the nonrecognition of gain or loss rules of Sec. 1031. Ed's basis for the equipment received is $38,000 ($20,000 + $10,000 + $8,000). ◀

HOLDING PERIOD FOR PROPERTY RECEIVED

Like-Kind Property. The holding period of like-kind property received in a nontaxable exchange includes the holding period of the property exchanged if the like-kind property surrendered is a capital asset or an asset that is Sec. 1231 property. In essence, the holding period of the property exchanged carries over to the holding period of the like-kind property received.[34] The rule regarding the holding period carryover is consistent with the notion of a continuing investment in the underlying property that has been transferred.

---

[34] Sec. 1223(1) and Reg. Sec. 1.1223-1(a).

Boot. The holding period for the boot property received begins the day after the date of the exchange.[35]

EXAMPLE I:12-31 ▶ Mario owns a Van Gogh painting acquired on May 1, 1997, as an investment. He exchanges the painting on April 10, 2015, for a Picasso sculpture and marketable securities to be held as investments. The holding period for the sculpture begins on May 1, 1997, and the holding period for the marketable securities starts on April 11, 2015. ◀

The like-kind exchange provisions are summarized in Topic Review I:12-1.

TOPIC REVIEW I:12-1

Section 1031—Like-Kind Exchanges

▶ Gains and losses are not recognized for like-kind exchanges.

▶ Nonrecognition of gains and losses is mandatory if the exchange is a like-kind exchange.

▶ Section 1031 applies to exchanges of property used in a trade or business or held for investment.

▶ Property exchanged and received must be like-kind.

▶ Subject to certain time constraints, a nonsimultaneous exchange may qualify as a like-kind exchange.

▶ Some gain may be recognized if the taxpayer receives or gives non–like-kind property (boot) in an otherwise like-kind exchange.

▶ A loss may be recognized if the taxpayer transfers non–like-kind property (boot) in an otherwise like-kind exchange.

▶ The basis of property received in an exchange is the basis of the property exchanged less the boot received plus the gain recognized and less any loss recognized.

▶ The nonrecognized gain or loss is deferred.

▶ The holding period of like-kind property received includes the holding period of the property exchanged.

▶ Like-kind exchange treatment does not apply between related parties if property is disposed of within two years of exchange.

INVOLUNTARY CONVERSIONS

OBJECTIVE 2

Determine whether gain from an involuntary conversion may be deferred

Taxpayers who realize a gain due to the involuntary conversion of property may elect to defer recognition of the entire gain if qualifying replacement property is acquired within a specified time period at a cost equal to or greater than the amount realized from the involuntary conversion. No gain is recognized if the property is converted "into property similar or related in service or use to the property so converted."[36]

The opportunity provided in Sec. 1033 to defer recognition of the gain reflects the fact that the taxpayer maintains a continuing investment and may lack the wherewithal to pay tax on the gain that would otherwise be recognized. Furthermore, the involuntary conversion is beyond the taxpayer's control.

Note that the gain is deferred, not excluded. The basis of the replacement property is the property's cost reduced by the amount of gain deferred. The tax treatment for an involuntary conversion is similar to the tax treatment of a like-kind exchange.

KEY POINT

Unlike the like-kind exchange provisions which are mandatory, the involuntary conversion provisions are elective. Further, the involuntary conversion rules apply only to gains, not losses.

EXAMPLE I:12-32 ▶

ADDITIONAL COMMENT

Property involved in an involuntary conversion need not be used in a trade or business or held for investment to qualify for the deferral of gain.

Lenea's warehouse with a $500,000 basis is destroyed by a hurricane. She collects $650,000 from the insurance company and purchases a new warehouse for $720,000. Lenea may elect to defer recognition of the $150,000 gain ($650,000 − $500,000). If the election is made, the basis of the new warehouse is $570,000 ($720,000 − $150,000). The $150,000 gain is merely deferred rather than excluded, because an immediate sale of the replacement property at its $720,000 FMV results in a recognized gain equal to the deferred gain on the involuntarily converted property. For example, if the new warehouse is sold for $720,000, the recognized gain is $150,000 ($720,000 − $570,000). ◀

---

[35] Sec. 1223 and Reg. Sec. 1.1223-1(a).

[36] Sec. 1033(a)(1).

TYPICAL MISCONCEPTION

Occasionally, taxpayers fail to realize that Sec. 1033 applies only to gains, not losses.

Section 1033 does not apply to losses realized from an involuntary conversion. A taxpayer may not elect to defer recognition of a loss resulting from an involuntary conversion.

EXAMPLE I:12-33 ►

Barry's offshore drilling rig with an $800,000 adjusted basis is destroyed by a tsunami. He collects $700,000 from the insurance company and purchases a new drilling rig for $760,000. The $100,000 loss ($700,000 − $800,000) is recognized as a casualty loss, and the basis of the new drilling rig is its $760,000 purchase price. ◄

INVOLUNTARY CONVERSION DEFINED

ADDITIONAL COMMENT

Typically, an involuntary conversion consists of either a casualty or a condemnation.

For Sec. 1033 to apply, property must be compulsorily or involuntarily converted into money or other property. An **involuntary conversion** may be due to theft, seizure, requisition, condemnation, or destruction of the property. Destruction of the property may be complete or partial.[37] For purposes of Sec. 1033, destruction of property does not have to meet the "suddenness" test if the cause of destruction otherwise falls within the general concept of a casualty.[38]

An involuntary conversion occurs when a governmental unit exercises its power of eminent domain to acquire the taxpayer's property without the taxpayer's consent. Furthermore, the threat or imminence of requisition or condemnation of property may permit a taxpayer to defer recognition of gain from the sale or exchange of property under the involuntary conversion rules. Taxpayers who transfer property due to such a threat must be careful to confirm that a decision to acquire their property for public use has been made.[39] Written confirmation of potential condemnation is particularly helpful.[40]

EXAMPLE I:12-34 ►

Bruce owns an automobile dealership near a state university campus. On a number of occasions, the president of the university expressed an interest in acquiring Bruce's property for additional parking space. The president is not certain about the availability of funds for the purchase, and the university is reluctant to have the property condemned for its use. Based on the university's interest in the property, Bruce sells the property to the Jet Corporation. The threat or imminence of conversion does not exist merely because the property is being considered for acquisition. The sale does not constitute an involuntary conversion.[41] ◄

Threat of Condemnation. If a threat of condemnation exists and the taxpayer has reasonable grounds to believe that the property will be condemned, Sec. 1033 applies even if the taxpayer sells the property to an entity other than the governmental unit that is threatening to condemn the property.[42]

EXAMPLE I:12-35 ►

ADDITIONAL COMMENT

If the property in Example I:12-35 is later condemned, Marty may be able to defer part or all of the gain.

At its regular meeting on Tuesday night, the city commission authorized the city attorney to start the process of condemning two lots owned by Beth for use as a public park. On Wednesday afternoon, Beth sells the two lots to Marty at a gain. The sale of property to Marty is an involuntary conversion, and Beth may elect to defer recognition of the gain if she satisfies the Sec. 1033 requirements. ◄

Conversion Must be Involuntary. The conversion must be involuntary. For example, an involuntary conversion does not occur when a taxpayer pays someone to set fire to his or her building.[43] An involuntary conversion also does not occur when a taxpayer who is developing a subdivision reserves certain property for a school site and later sells the property to the school district under condemnation proceedings. In this situation, the taxpayer was required to reserve property for a school site in order to receive zoning approval for development of the subdivision.[44]

---

[37] Reg. Sec. 1.1033(a)-1.
[38] Rev. Rul. 59-102, 1959-1 C.B. 200.
[39] Rev. Rul. 63-221, 1963-2 C.B. 332, and *Joseph P. Balistrieri,* 1979 PH T.C. Memo ¶79,115, 38 TCM 526.
[40] Rev. Rul. 63-221, 1963-2 C.B. 332.

[41] *Forest City Chevrolet,* 1977 PH T.C. Memo ¶77,187, 36 TCM 768.
[42] Rev. Rul. 81-180, 1981-2 C.B. 161, and *Creative Solutions, Inc. v. U.S.,* 12 AFTR 2d 5229, 1963-2 USTC ¶9615 (5th Cir., 1963).
[43] Rev. Rul. 82-74, 1982-1 C.B. 110.
[44] Rev. Rul. 69-654, 1969-2 C.B. 162.

Although the typical involuntary conversion generally results from a casualty or condemnation, Sec. 1033 provides that certain transactions involving livestock are to be treated as involuntary conversions.[45] For example, the destruction or sale of livestock because of disease is an involuntary conversion.

TAX TREATMENT OF GAIN DUE TO INVOLUNTARY CONVERSION INTO BOOT

Gain may be deferred if the property is involuntarily converted into money or property that is not similar or related in service or use to the converted property.[46] The taxpayer must make a proper replacement of the converted property within a specific time period and elect to defer the gain.

Realized Gain. The taxpayer's realized gain is the excess of the amount received due to the involuntary conversion over the adjusted basis of the property converted. The total award or proceeds received are reduced by expenses incurred to determine the amount realized (e.g., attorney's fees incurred in connection with determining the settlement to be received from a condemnation). If the payment of the award or proceeds is delayed, any amounts paid as interest are not included in determining the amount realized.[47] Amounts received as interest on an award for property condemned are taxed as ordinary income even if the interest is paid by a state or political subdivision.[48]

REAL-WORLD EXAMPLE
Because of mounting losses and declining property values, a taxpayer decided to burn down his building to collect the fire insurance proceeds. Although the building was converted into money (insurance proceeds) as a result of its destruction, this conversion was not involuntary within the meaning of Sec. 1033. Rev. Rul. 82-74, 1982-1 C.B. 110.

EXAMPLE I:12-36 ▶ Richard's property with a $100,000 basis is condemned by the city of Phoenix. Richard receives a $190,000 award and pays $1,000 in legal expenses for representation at the condemnation proceedings and $800 for an appraisal of the property. The amount realized is $188,200 [$190,000 − ($1,000 + $800)], and the realized gain is $88,200 ($188,200 − $100,000). Richard may elect to defer part or all of the realized gain if the requirements of Sec. 1033 are satisfied. ◀

ADDITIONAL COMMENT
Some or all of the realized gain is recognized if the cost of the replacement property is less than the amount realized.

Gain Recognized. To defer the entire gain, one must purchase replacement property with a cost equal to or greater than the amount realized from the involuntary conversion. If the replacement property is purchased for an amount less than the amount realized, that portion of the realized gain equal to the excess of the amount realized from the conversion over the cost of the replacement property must be recognized.[49] Stated differently, the recognized gain is the lesser of the realized gain or the excess of the amount realized over the cost of the replacement property.

EXAMPLE I:12-37 ▶ Bob owns a restaurant with a $200,000 basis. The restaurant is destroyed by fire, and he receives insurance proceeds of $300,000. Bob's realized gain is $100,000 ($300,000 − $200,000). He purchases another restaurant for $275,000. Bob may elect to defer $75,000 of the gain under Sec. 1033, and $25,000 ($300,000 − $275,000) of Bob's gain must be recognized because he failed to reinvest all of the $300,000 insurance proceeds in a suitable replacement property. ◀

EXAMPLE I:12-38 ▶ Stacey owns a racehorse with a $450,000 basis used for breeding purposes. The racehorse is killed by lightning, and she collects $800,000 from the insurance company. Stacey's realized gain is $350,000 ($800,000 − $450,000). She purchases another racehorse for $430,000. The entire $350,000 of gain is recognized, because the amount realized from the involuntary conversion exceeds the cost of the replacement property by $370,000 ($800,000 − $430,000) which is more than the realized gain. ◀

Basis of Replacement Property. If replacement property is purchased, the basis of the replacement property is its cost less any deferred gain. If the taxpayer elects to defer the gain, the holding period of the replacement property includes the holding period of the converted property.[50]

---

[45] Secs. 1033(d) and (e). If a taxpayer sells or exchanges more livestock than normal because of a drought, the sale or exchange of the excess amount is treated as an involuntary conversion. The livestock must be other than poultry and be held by the taxpayer for draft, breeding, or dairy purposes.
[46] Sec. 1033(a)(2).
[47] *Flushingside Realty & Construction Co.*, 1943 PH T.C. Memo ¶43,286, 2 TCM 259.

[48] *Spencer D. Stewart v. CIR*, 52 AFTR 2d 83-5895, 83-2 USTC ¶9573 (9th Cir., 1983).
[49] Sec. 1033(a)(2)(A).
[50] Sec. 1223(1)(A).

EXAMPLE I:12-39 ▶ Tracy owns a yacht that is held for personal use and has a $20,000 basis. The yacht is destroyed by a storm, and Tracy collects $24,000 from the insurance company. She purchases a new $35,000 yacht for personal use and elects to defer the $4,000 ($24,000 − $20,000) gain. The basis of the new yacht is $31,000 ($35,000 − $4,000). The holding period for the new yacht includes the holding period of the destroyed yacht. ◀

Severance Damages. If a portion of the taxpayer's property is condemned, the taxpayer may receive **severance damages** as compensation for a decline in the value of the retained property. For example, if access to the retained property becomes difficult or if the property is exposed to greater damage from flooding or erosion, its value may decline.

The IRS considers severance damages to be "analogous to the proceeds of property insurance; they represent compensation for damages to the property."[51] Amounts received as severance damages reduce the basis of the retained property, and any amount received in excess of the property's basis is treated as gain.[52]

EXAMPLE I:12-40 ▶ Cindy owns a 500-acre farm with a $200 basis per acre ($100,000 basis). The state condemns ten acres across the northwest corner of her farm to build a major highway. Cindy receives a condemnation award of $500 per acre for the ten acres. The highway separates the farm into a 25-acre tract and a 465-acre tract. Because her ability to efficiently use the 25-acre tract for farming is reduced, the state pays additional severance damages of $90 per acre for the 25 acres. Cindy's gain realized from condemnation of the ten acres is $3,000 [$5,000 − ($200 × 10 acres)]. The $2,250 ($90 × 25 acres) of severance damages reduce the basis of the 25-acre tract from $5,000 to $2,750 [($200 × 25 acres) − $2,250]. The reduction in basis is applied solely to the 25 acres because of its decline in value as farmland. ◀

The Sec. 1033 provisions concerning nonrecognition of gain may apply to severance damages. For instance, if severance damages are used to restore the retained property, only that portion of severance damages not spent for restoration reduces the basis of the retained property. A taxpayer who uses severance damages to purchase adjacent farmland to replace the portion of the farm condemned may use Sec. 1033 to defer a gain due to the receipt of the severance damages.[53]

REPLACEMENT PROPERTY

To qualify for nonrecognition of gain due to an involuntary conversion, the taxpayer must acquire qualified replacement property. With some exceptions, the **replacement property** must be "similar or related in service or use to the property so converted."[54] Taxpayers who own and use the property must use the functional-use test although replacement may be made with like-kind property in certain cases. A taxpayer who owns and leases the property that is involuntarily converted may use the taxpayer-use test.

Functional-Use Test. The **functional-use test** is more restrictive than the like-kind test. To be considered similar or related in service or use, the replacement property must be functionally the same as the converted property. For example, the exchange of a business building for land used in business qualifies as a like-kind exchange. Replacing a building with land does not qualify as replacement property under the involuntary conversion rules. The building must be replaced with a building that is functionally the same as the converted building.

EXAMPLE I:12-41 ▶ Julie's movie theater is destroyed by fire, and she uses the insurance proceeds to purchase a skating rink. The converted property has not been replaced with property that is similar or related in service or use under the functional-use test. The election to defer gain under Sec. 1033 is not available. ◀

---

[51] Rev. Rul. 53-271, 1953-2 C.B. 36.
[52] Rev. Rul. 68-37, 1968-1 C.B. 359.
[53] Rev. Ruls. 69-240, 1969-1 C.B. 199, 73-35, 1973-1 C.B. 367, and 83-49, 1983-1 C.B. 191.
[54] Secs. 1033(a)(2)(A) and 1033(f). The replacement of property requirement

is modified when proceeds from the involuntary conversion of livestock may not be reinvested in property similar or related in use to the converted livestock because of soil contamination or other environmental contamination. Sec. 1033(f) permits the livestock to be replaced with other property, including real property, used for farming purposes.

Replacement with Like-Kind Property. If real property held for productive use in a trade or business or for investment is **condemned**, a proper replacement may be made by acquiring like-kind property.[55] This exception to the functional-use test applies only to real property used in a trade or business or held for investment.

EXAMPLE I:12-42 ▶ Ken owns a building used in his business that is condemned by the state to widen a highway. He uses the proceeds to purchase land to be held for investment. The land is a qualified replacement property because the condemned building is real property used in a trade or business, and the like-kind exchange rule may be applied to the condemnation. ◀

EXAMPLE I:12-43 ▶ Assume the same facts as in Example I:12-42 except that the building is destroyed by a violent windstorm. Ken's purchase of the investment land is not qualified replacement property because the more flexible like-kind exchange rules apply only to condemnations. He must purchase property with the same functional use as the business building. ◀

REAL-WORLD EXAMPLE

A nursery with its trees and shrubs was condemned, and the taxpayer replaced the condemned property with land and green-houses. The replacement was considered to have been made with like-kind property. *Evert Asjes, Jr.,* 74 T.C. 1005 (1980).

If business or investment property is involuntarily converted as a result of a Presidentially declared disaster after 1994, the taxpayer may replace the property with any tangible property that is held for productive use in a trade or business.

Taxpayer-Use Test. The **taxpayer-use test** applies to the involuntary conversion of rental property owned by an investor. This test permits greater flexibility than the functional-use test. The principal requirement is that the owner-investor must lease out the replacement property that is acquired. However, the lessee is not required to use the leased property for the same functional use.[56]

EXAMPLE I:12-44 ▶ Sally owns an apartment complex that is rented to college students. The apartment complex is destroyed by fire. She uses the insurance proceeds to purchase a medical building that is leased to physicians. Sally has acquired a qualified replacement property under the taxpayer-use test, and the gain, if any, may be deferred if an election is made under Sec. 1033. ◀

 **STOP & THINK**

REAL-WORLD EXAMPLE

Taxpayer owned land and a warehouse held for rental purposes. Upon condemnation of this property, taxpayer invested the proceeds in a gas station on land already owned by the taxpayer which was also held for rental purposes. The taxpayer-use test applied, and taxpayer was able to defer the gain. Rev. Rul. 71-41, 1971-1 C.B. 223.

Question: Greg Stacey's motel is destroyed by fire on March 10 of the current year. The basis of the property is $400,000 and he receives $2,000,000 from the insurance company. Greg is concerned about the possibility of having to pay income tax on the $1,600,000 gain and is aware of the tax rules relating to involuntary conversions. Greg is considering replacing the destroyed motel by building either a new motel or an ice skating rink on the vacant lot. The cost of a new motel or an ice skating rink is expected to be $2,500,000, and he expects to borrow 60% of the cost. What tax advice would you give him?

Solution: Greg may defer the $1,600,000 gain if the involuntary conversion requirements are met and he makes a proper election. The principal issue is whether the replacement property is considered to be "similar in service or use" to the converted property. Because the functional-use test is applicable in this case, an ice skating rink is not similar property and the gain of $1,600,000 must be recognized. Conversely, the new motel is similar property and, since Greg is reinvesting an amount greater than $2,000,000, none of the gain is recognized. His basis in the new motel is $900,000 ($2,500,000 − deferred gain of $1,600,000). The fact that he borrows money and does not spend the $2,000,000 insurance proceeds does not prevent him from electing to defer the gain. The tax requirement is only that he must reinvest an amount equal to or greater than the $2,000,000 insurance proceeds. In this case, the tax law clearly encourages the taxpayer to build a new motel rather than an ice skating rink.

OBTAINING REPLACEMENT PROPERTY

The general rule is that the taxpayer must purchase the replacement property.[57] Taxpayers may purchase replacement property indirectly by purchasing control (i.e., 80% or more of the stock) of a corporation that owns the replacement property.[58] However,

---

[55] Sec. 1033(g)(1).
[56] Rev. Rul. 64-237, 1964-2 C.B. 319.
[57] To qualify as a purchase of property or stock under Sec. 1033(a)(2)(A)(ii), the unadjusted basis of the property or stock must be its cost within the

meaning of Sec. 1012 without considering the basis adjustment for the deferred gain. Property acquired by inheritance, gift, or a nontaxable exchange does not qualify as replacement property (see Reg. Sec. 1.1033(a)-2(c)(4)).
[58] Sec. 1033(a)(2)(A) and Reg. Sec. 1.1033(a)-2(c).

this exception is not applicable to the purchase of like-kind property to replace condemned real property used in a trade or business or held for investment.[59]

EXAMPLE I:12-45 ▶ Hank's airplane, used in business, is hijacked and taken to a foreign country. He uses the insurance proceeds to purchase 80% of Fast Corporation stock. Fast Corporation owns an airplane which is qualified replacement property. The involuntary conversion requirements are satisfied if Hank elects to defer any gain realized. ◀

EXAMPLE I:12-46 ▶ Lynn's farm is condemned by the state for public use. She uses the proceeds to purchase 80% of Vermont Corporation stock. Vermont Corporation owns eight parking lots. A qualified replacement property has not been obtained through the stock purchase because the parking lots are not functionally the same as the farm. A qualified replacement does occur if she buys the parking lots from the Vermont Corporation. ◀

TIME REQUIREMENTS FOR REPLACEMENT

To qualify for nonrecognition of gain treatment, the converted property must be replaced within a specified time period. The general rule is that the period begins with the date of disposition of the converted property and ends "two years after the close of the first taxable year in which any part of the gain upon the conversion is realized."[60] If the involuntary conversion is due to condemnation or requisition, or the threat of such, the replacement period begins on the date of the threat or imminence of the requisition or condemnation. The replacement period may be extended by obtaining permission from the IRS.[61]

EXAMPLE I:12-47 ▶ On December 8, 2015, Craig's business property was destroyed by fire. Craig receives insurance proceeds in 2016 and elects to defer recognition of the gain. He must replace the property between December 8, 2015, and December 31, 2018. The two-year time period includes 2018 because the gain is realized when the insurance proceeds are received in 2016. ◀

The replacement period is longer if the involuntary conversion is due to the condemnation of real property (excluding inventory) held for productive use in a trade or business or for investment. The replacement period ends three years after the close of the first tax year in which any part of the gain is realized.[62] This provision for a longer replacement period applies to the same type of real property that may be replaced with like-kind property.

EXAMPLE I:12-48 ▶ Beth owns a building used in her dry cleaning business. In 2015, the state condemns the building and awards Beth an amount greater than the adjusted basis of the building. Beth may replace the property with like-kind property, and the replacement period ends on December 31, 2018. ◀

The involuntary conversion rules are summarized in Topic Review I:12-2.

TOPIC REVIEW I:12-2

Section 1033: Involuntary Conversions

1. Section 1033 applies only to gains, not losses.
2. Nonrecognition of gain under Section 1033 is elective. (Nonrecognition of gain is mandatory in a direct conversion, but direct conversions seldom occur.)
3. Section 1033 applies to involuntary conversions of all types of properties.
4. Some gain may be recognized if the taxpayer replaces the involuntarily converted property with property that costs less than the amount realized in the involuntary conversion.
5. The nonrecognized gain is deferred.
6. The basis of property acquired to replace the involuntarily converted property is the cost of the property less the deferred gain.
7. Property acquired to replace the involuntarily converted property generally must be functionally related property.
8. The required replacement period generally begins with the date of disposition of the converted property and ends two years after the close of the first taxable year in which any part of the gain on the conversion is realized. (A three-year period applies to condemnations of real property used in a trade or business or held for the production of income.)

---

[59] Sec. 1033(g)(2).
[60] Sec. 1033(a)(2)(B).

[61] Sec. 1033(a)(2)(B)(ii).
[62] Sec. 1033(g)(4).

SALE OF PRINCIPAL RESIDENCE

OBJECTIVE 3

Determine when a gain resulting from the sale of a principal residence is excluded

Congress uses the tax law to encourage home ownership in many ways: (1) Real estate taxes and interest on a mortgage used to acquire a principal or second residence are deductible (see Chapter I:7), (2) part or all of the interest on home equity debt may be deductible, and (3) taxpayers may elect to exclude up to $250,000 ($500,000 on a joint return) of gain from the sale of a principal residence.

Individuals who sell or exchange their personal residence after May 6, 1997, may exclude up to $250,000 of gain if it was owned and occupied as a principal residence for at least two years of the five-year period before the sale or exchange. A married couple may exclude up to $500,000 when filing jointly if both meet the use test, at least one meets the ownership test and neither spouse is ineligible for the exclusion because he or she sold or exchanged a residence within the last two years.[63]

The Sec. 121 exclusion is available regardless of age, and taxpayers do not have to purchase a replacement residence. Any gain not excluded is capital gain because a personal residence is a capital asset. If long term, these gains are eligible for preferential tax rates. However, any recognized gain on the sale of a personal residence is considered to be investment income, so the gain may be subject to the 3.8% tax on net investment income due to the so-called Medicare tax on higher-income taxpayers (see Chapter I:5 for further discussion of the preferential rates and the additional tax on net investment income). A loss on the sale or exchange of a personal residence is not deductible because the residence is personal-use property.[64]

EXAMPLE I:12-49 ▶ Maki, who is single and 35 years old, sells her principal residence that she purchased four years ago and realizes a $230,000 gain. Maki may exclude the entire gain regardless of her age or whether she purchases a new principal residence. ◀

EXAMPLE I:12-50 ▶ Assume the same facts as in the above example except the realized gain is $320,000. Maki may exclude $250,000 and recognize a $70,000 LTCG. ◀

EXAMPLE I:12-51 ▶ Assume the same facts as in Example I:12-50 except Maki is married to Yixin, and they have owned and occupied the residence for the last four years. They may exclude the entire $320,000 gain. ◀

ADDITIONAL COMMENT

The elimination of taxes on up to $500,000 of gain from the sale of a personal residence has been a great benefit for many taxpayers who had large built-in gains.

Prior to the Taxpayer Relief Act of 1997, taxpayers could defer gain resulting from sale of a personal residence if they purchased another principal residence within two years at a cost greater than the adjusted sales price. Taxpayers who were at least 55 years old could exclude up to $125,000 of gain resulting from the sale of a personal residence. The deferral provision of Sec. 1034 has been repealed; the exclusion has been increased to $250,000 or $500,000; and taxpayers may exclude gain regardless of age and use the exclusion more than once.

Today, the rules for excluding gain resulting from the sale of a personal residence are more favorable for most taxpayers than the old rules because Congress wanted to eliminate the need for homeowners to maintain records for long periods of time. However, taxpayers who expect to sell their homes and have a realized gain of more than $250,000 ($500,000 if a joint return is filed) still need to maintain records. Also, taxpayers who convert their personal residence to business property or rental property will need to know the property's correct adjusted basis to compute depreciation.

Determining the Realized Gain. Gain realized is the excess of the amount realized over the property's adjusted basis.[65] The amount realized on the sale of the property is equal to the selling price less selling expenses.[66] Selling expenses include commissions, advertising, deed preparation costs, and legal expenses incurred in connection with the sale.[67]

EXAMPLE I:12-52 ▶ Kirby sells his personal residence, which has a $100,000 basis, to Maxine. To make the sale, Kirby pays a $7,000 sales commission and incurs $800 of legal costs. Maxine pays $30,000 cash and assumes Kirby's $90,000 mortgage. The amount realized is $112,200 [($30,000 + $90,000) − ($7,000 + $800)]. The realized gain is $12,200 ($112,200 − $100,000). ◀

---

[63] Sec. 121(a) and (b).
[64] Reg. Secs. 1.165-9(a) and 1.262-1b(4).
[65] Reg. Sec. 1.1034-1(b)(5).

[66] Reg. Sec. 1.1034-1(b)(4).
[67] Reg. Sec. 1.1034-1(b)(4)(i).

Adjusted Basis of Residence. The original basis of a principal residence is a function of how the residence is obtained. It could be purchased, received as a gift, or inherited. The cost of a residence includes all amounts attributable to the acquisition including commissions and other purchasing expenses paid to acquire the residence.[68] Capital improvements, but not repairs, increase the adjusted basis of the residence. The costs of adding a room, installing an air conditioning system, finishing a basement, and landscaping are capital improvements. Expenses incurred to protect the taxpayer's title in the residence are also capitalized. Under Sec. 1034, which was repealed in 1997, a taxpayer who deferred gain on the sale of a principal residence was required to reduce the basis of the replacement residence by the amount of the deferred gain.[69]

EXAMPLE I:12-53 ▶ In 1996, Susan paid $200,000 to purchase a new residence. She paid a realtor $4,000 to help locate the house and paid legal fees of $1,200 to make certain that the seller had legal title to the property. As a result of the purchase, she deferred a gain of $50,000 from the sale a former residence in 1995. In 1997, she added a new porch to the house at a cost of $6,000 and installed central air conditioning at a cost of $5,200. Since purchasing the house, she has paid $1,500 for repairs. The adjusted basis of her house is $166,400 [$200,000 + $4,000 + $1,200 − $50,000 + $6,000 + $5,200]. ◀

Multiple Use of the Exclusion. Previously under Sec. 121, a taxpayer was limited to the exclusion once in their lifetime, and a married taxpayer whose spouse had taken the exclusion could not use the exclusion even if the taxpayer filed as married filing separately. The exclusion is now determined on an individual basis. An individual may claim the exclusion even if the individual's spouse used the exclusion within the past two years. Also, for a married couple filing a joint return when each spouse maintains a separate principal residence, the $250,000 exclusion is available for the sale or exchange of each spouse's principal residence.

EXAMPLE I:12-54 ▶ Krista, who has owned and used a house as her principal residence for the last seven years, marries Josh in January 2015. Josh sold his residence in October 2014 and excluded a $145,000 gain. Krista sells her residence in December 2015 and realizes a gain of $378,000. She may exclude $250,000 of the gain.

Assuming that Krista and Josh use her residence in the above example for a two-year period starting in January 2015, they could exclude up to $500,000 if she waits to sell the house until January 2017. ◀

PRINCIPAL RESIDENCE DEFINED

For Sec. 121 to apply, taxpayers must sell property that qualifies as their principal residence. Whether property is used as the taxpayer's principal residence depends upon all the facts and circumstances. If a taxpayer uses more than one property as a residence during the year, the property used a majority of the time will normally be the principal residence.[70]

EXAMPLE I:12-55 ▶ Lanny, a 40-year-old college professor, owns and occupies a house in Oklahoma. During the summer, he lives in a cabin in Idaho. After owning the cabin for eight years, Lanny sells it for $50,000 and realizes a gain. Gain on the sale of the cabin in Idaho must be recognized because Lanny's principal residence is in Oklahoma. ◀

KEY POINT

A taxpayer may own two or more residences, but only one of them qualifies as the principal residence.

Factors other than use of the property that are relevant when determining a taxpayer's principal residence include place of employment, mailing address for bills and correspondence, address for tax returns and voter registration, and location of religious organizations and recreational clubs with which the taxpayer is affiliated. The principal place of abode for the taxpayer's family members is also relevant.[71]

The property does not have to be one's principal residence at time of the sale to qualify for the exclusion. The exclusion applies if the property has been used as a principal residence for at least two of the five years before the sale or exchange and the exclusion has not been used within the past two years.

---

[68] Reg. Sec. 1.1034-1(c)(4).
[69] Sec. 1034(e).

[70] Reg. Sec. 1.121-1(b)(2).
[71] Reg. Sec. 1.121-1(b)(2).

EXAMPLE I:12-56 ▶ Canan owned and used a house in Buffalo as her principal residence from March 10, 2011, until November 21, 2013, when she purchased a new house in Kansas on December 1, 2013. Her brother lives in the house in Buffalo until Canan sells it on July 10, 2015, and realizes a gain of $288,000. She may exclude $250,000 and recognize a $38,000 LTCG. ◀

Condominium apartments, houseboats, and housetrailers may qualify as principal residences.[72] Stock held by a tenant-stockholder in a cooperative housing corporation is a principal residence if the dwelling that the taxpayer is entitled to occupy as a stockholder is used as his or her principal residence.[73]

ADDITIONAL COMMENT

The taxpayer does not have to be occupying the old residence at the date of sale. The taxpayer may have already moved to a new residence and be renting the old residence temporarily before its sale.

SALE OF MORE THAN ONE PRINCIPAL RESIDENCE WITHIN A TWO-YEAR PERIOD

The new exclusion provided by Sec. 121 applies to only one sale or exchange every two years. However, a portion of the gain may be excluded in certain circumstances even if the two-year requirement is not satisfied.

If a principal residence is sold within two years of a previous sale or exchange of a residence, part of the gain may be excluded if the sale or exchange is due to a change in employment, health or unforseen circumstances. The portion of the gain excluded is based on a ratio with a numerator in days or months and a denominator of 730 days or 24 months.[74] The numerator is the shorter of:

(1) the period during which the ownership and use tests were met during the five-year period ending on the date of sale, or
(2) the period of time after the date of the most recent prior sale or exchange for which the exclusion applied until the date of the current sale or exchange.[75]

The amount excluded is $250,000 or $500,000 times the above ratio.

EXAMPLE I:12-57 ▶

ADDITIONAL COMMENT

If Winnie's gain in Example I:12-57 is $100,000, she may exclude $86,986 (254/730 × $250,000).

Winnie, who is single, sold her principal residence in Detroit on November 1, 2015, and excluded the $127,000 gain because she owned and used the residence for two of the last five years. Winnie had purchased another residence in Cleveland on October 1, 2015. She occupies the residence in Cleveland until June 12, 2016, when she moves to Dallas to accept a new job. She sells the residence in Cleveland on November 15, 2016, and realizes a gain of $40,000. Winnie may exclude all of the gain because the sale of her Cleveland residence was due to a change in employment and 254/730 of $250,000 is more than the $40,000 realized gain. She owns and uses the residence in Cleveland for 254 days, and the period between the sale of the residence in Detroit and the sale in Cleveland is 378 days. ◀

Ownership and Use Tests. If a principal residence is sold before satisfying the ownership and use tests, part of the gain may be excluded if the sale is due to a change in employment, health, or unforeseen circumstances. The portion of the gain excluded is determined by multiplying the amount of the exclusion (i.e., $250,000 or $500,000) by a fraction whose numerator is the number of days the use and ownership tests were met and whose denominator is 730 days (or 24 months).

EXAMPLE I:12-58 ▶ Tim, a single taxpayer who purchased his home on January 1, 2015, for $500,000, recently became ill and sells his home in order to move closer to a relative who can care for him. Tim sells his principal residence on June 14, 2015, for $620,000, realizing a gain of $120,000. Because he owned and occupied the residence for 164 days and the sale was due to a change in his health, he may exclude $56,164 ($250,000 × 164/730). ◀

For purposes of the two-year ownership rule, a taxpayer's period of ownership includes the period during which the taxpayer's deceased spouse owned the residence. When a taxpayer receives a residence from a spouse or an ex-spouse incident to a divorce, the taxpayer's period of owning the property includes the time the residence was owned by the spouse or ex-spouse.[76] When attempting to determine if the taxpayer has occupied the residence for two years, short temporary absences such as for vacation or other seasonal absence are counted as use by the taxpayer.[77]

[72] Rev. Rul. 64-31, 1964-1 C.B. 300.
[73] Reg. Sec. 1.1034-1(c)(3).
[74] Reg. Sec. 1.121-3(g).

[75] Sec. 121(c).
[76] Sec. 121(d)(2) and (3).
[77] Reg. Sec. 1.121-1(c)(2)(i).

EXAMPLE I:12-59 ▶ Sachie receives an $800,000 residence owned for six years by Richard, her former spouse, as part of a divorce settlement. Richard's basis for the residence is $430,000. They lived in the house for five years prior to the divorce. Three months after transfer of the residence to Sachie, she sells it for $825,000, and $250,000 of her $395,000 realized gain is excluded. Sachie must recognize a $145,000 LTCG. Sachie's period of ownership includes the six years Richard owned the residence. ◀

ADDITIONAL COMMENT

The five-year period does not include any period up to ten years during which the taxpayer or the taxpayer's spouse is on qualified official extended duty as a member of the uniformed services.

Change Due to Employment, Health, or Unforeseen Circumstances. The Treasury has issued Regulations to provide guidance as to how a homeowner may qualify for partial exclusion if the sale was before the two-year use and ownership test is satisfied or if the sale occurs within two years of a previous sale where the exclusion was used. The exceptions may apply even if a person other than the taxpayer has a change in employment or health.

A taxpayer is viewed as being eligible for partial exclusion if she sells her residence because a qualified individual has a change in employment that satisfies the test under Sec. 217 for the moving expense deduction. A qualified individual includes the taxpayer, the taxpayer's spouse, co-owner of the residence, or a person who uses the residence as a principal place of abode. Taxpayers may qualify for the exclusion and the moving expense deduction if moving to take a new job, continue with present employer or accept a job if the 50-mile distance test is satisfied. The change in employment must occur when the taxpayer is satisfying the ownership and use test for the residence except for the two-year requirement.[78]

EXAMPLE I:12-60 ▶ Mark has lived in his first house for one year in Omaha when he marries Karen. Six months later, Karen receives a job offer and they move to Florida. Mark may exclude a realized gain equal to 18/24 of $250,000, because the move is due to a change in employment of a qualified individual. ◀

When determining if the sale or exchange of the residence is due to a change in health, the definition of a "qualified individual" is expanded to include relatives who satisfy the relationship test used to determine if one is a dependent of the taxpayer. The relative must satisfy the relationship test but does not have to be a dependent to be a qualified individual. A sale or exchange is because of health if the primary reason is "to obtain, provide, or facilitate the diagnosis, cure, mitigation, or treatment of a disease, illness, or injury of a qualified individual."[79]

EXAMPLE I:12-61 ▶ Daniel has lived in his first house in Virginia for eight months when he sells the house and moves to Texas to take care of his 60-year-old father who recently suffered a stroke. Daniel may exclude a realized gain equal to 8/24 of $250,000 because the primary reason for the sale is due to the health of a qualified individual. ◀

REAL-WORLD EXAMPLE

In LTR 200601009, taxpayers who sold their home within two years of the purchase because they became aware of various criminal activities occurring in their neighborhood were allowed to utilize Sec. 121. In addition to their son being assaulted and threatened, one of the taxpayers was assaulted by the neighbors.

A sale or exchange is due to unforeseen circumstances if the primary reason for the sale or exchange is an event that the taxpayer could not reasonably have anticipated before purchasing and occupying the residence. For the unforeseen circumstances exception, a qualified individual is the same as a qualified individual for the change in employment test.

The following are specific events considered to qualify as unforeseen circumstances:

1. Involuntary conversion of residence;
2. Natural or man-made disasters or acts of war or terrorism resulting in a casualty to the residence;
3. Death of a qualified individual;
4. Loss of employment by a qualified individual if the individual is eligible for unemployment compensation;
5. Change of employment that results in the taxpayer's inability to pay housing costs and reasonable basic living expenses;
6. Divorce or legal separation;
7. Multiple births from the same pregnancy.[80]

Note that marriage and adoption are not included in the above safe-harbor list of unforeseen circumstances. One who sells her residence before meeting the two-year test because she has adopted a child will not be assured of qualifying for possible exclusion

---

[78] Reg. Sec. 1.121-3(c).
[79] Reg. Sec. 1.121-3(d).

[80] Reg. Sec. 1.121-3T(e).

under the unforeseen circumstances exception. She will have to argue that the facts and circumstances justify her use of the partial exclusion.

The IRS has issued a number of letter rulings that suggest that it is willing to consider many different reasons for selling due to unforeseen circumstances. In LTR 200601022, a taxpayer purchased a house, but then married someone with a child who attended a school in a different school district. They decided to temporarily use their house as rental property and rent another house for their use located in the child's school district. While living in the rented house, they had a child and decided to sell the first house because it was too small for their expanding family. Despite the fact that the taxpayer did not use the house as a principal residence, they were allowed to utilize Sec. 121.

EXAMPLE I:12-62 ►

Benjamin purchases a house near the airport and sells it four months later because of noise caused by planes. He may not exclude any of the gain, because the airport noise is not an unforeseen circumstance. ◄

STOP & THINK

REAL-WORLD EXAMPLE
Unlike Example I:12-62, a taxpayer in LTR 200702032 was able to utilize Sec. 121 when he sold his principal residence located near an airport because he was mislead about the amount of noise, despite his considerable efforts to determine if noise would be a problem. He sold the house at a loss, but he sued the real estate agents and the seller for their failure to disclose the excessive noise during peak periods in the early morning and evening. The defendants settled and the settlement proceeds were treated as additional proceeds from the sale of the residence resulting in a gain which the taxpayer was able to exclude.

Question: Rebecca's uncle told her that she could purchase his house for $150,000 in five years provided that she could pay at least $30,000 of the purchase price in cash. Rebecca has $15,000 and is considering two alternative methods to obtain the remaining $15,000 in five years. The first alternative is to purchase $15,000 of non-dividend paying stock that she expects to increase in value to $30,000 within five years. The second alternative is to purchase an $80,000 residence by paying $15,000 and borrowing $65,000. Payments on the mortgage will be interest only for five years and amount to $450 per month. Insurance, property taxes, and other home ownership expenses average $90 per month. She expects the house to be worth $95,000 at the end of five years. She will rent an apartment for $540 per month, including utilities, if she buys the stock. Ignoring transaction costs and assuming that she does not itemize deductions, should Rebecca purchase the stock or the house?

Solution: The $15,000 gain resulting from sale of the stock is LTCG and probably taxed at 15%. If the rate is 15%, she must pay taxes of $2,250 and has only $27,750 available to purchase her uncle's house. She will have a gain of $15,000 if she sells the house but the gain is excluded. She has $30,000 of cash and is able to buy her uncle's house. The tax law encourages Rebecca to buy a principal residence.

NONQUALIFIED USE AFTER 2008

A taxpayer who owns a principal residence and a second home (rental property, vacation home, etc.) that has appreciated in value has an incentive to convert the second home to a principal residence if planning to sell the second home. The Housing Assistance Tax Act of 2008 reduced the advantage of converting residences that have not been the principal residence to one's principal residence.

Gain from the sale of a principal residence that is allocable to periods of nonqualified use after 2008 is not excluded from income. Gain allocated to periods of nonqualified use after 2008 is based on the ratio which the aggregate periods of nonqualified use after 2008 bears to the total time the property was owned. A period of nonqualified use is any period that the property is not used as a principal residence after 2008. As under prior law, any depreciation attributable to periods of business use is subject to taxation.

Any portion of the five-year period ending on the date of sale that is after the property ceases to be used as a principal residence is not considered nonqualified use, thus the taxpayer may vacate the residence before selling it without recognizing that time after moving out as nonqualified use. Absences due to change in employment, health condition, or other unforeseen circumstances are not considered nonqualified use. Also, nonqualified use does not include any period in which the taxpayer or taxpayer's spouse is serving on qualified official extended duty.

EXAMPLE I:12-63 ►

The Eberts have owned and lived in a house on Mill Street as their personal residence for 20 years. They also own a house on Elm Street that has been used as rental property for 18 years. On May 1, 2008, they moved into the Elm Street house and used it as their principal residence until the current year when they sell the Elm Street property and realize a $700,000 gain. Any of the gain due to depreciation must be recognized, but they are eligible to exclude up to $500,000 of the remaining gain. The use of the property as rental property is not nonqualified use because it occurred before 2009. ◄

EXAMPLE I:12-64 ▶ Assume the same facts as in Example I:12-63 except the Eberts did not move into the Elm Street property until May 1, 2013, and sell the property on December 22, 2015. In this case, the period from January 1, 2009 through April 30, 2013 is nonqualified use and a prorata share of the gain after considering the gain due to depreciation is not eligible for the $500,000 exclusion. ◀

EXAMPLE I:12-65 ▶ Dale owned a house and used it as rental property for seven years until January 1, 2013, when he moved into the house and used it as a principal residence. Depreciation for the seven years that it was used as rental property is $30,000. If he sells the house on January 1, 2016, and realizes a gain of $210,000, the first $30,000 of gain is recognized because of depreciation. He may exclude 6/10* of the remaining gain of $180,000, and must recognize another $72,000 (4/10* of $180,000) due to the nonqualified use in 2009, 2010, 2011 and 2012. He used the property as a principal residence for three years, and the three years before 2009 are not considered to be nonqualified use. So, six years* of the ten-year period are eligible for the Sec. 121 exclusion. He must recognize $102,000 of the $210,000 gain and may exclude $108,000.

> * To further clarify the calculations in this example, below is an explanation of the relevant time periods:
> 10 years = total ownership period, 1/1/06 – 1/1/16.
> 4 years = nonqualified use period, 1/1/09 – 12/31/12.
> 6 years = qualified use years, 1/1/06 – 12/31/08 and 1/1/13 – 1/1/16. ◀

INVOLUNTARY CONVERSION OF A PRINCIPAL RESIDENCE

Ordinarily, the involuntary conversion of a principal residence is governed by Sec. 1033, discussed earlier in this chapter. A gain due to an involuntary conversion of a personal residence may be deferred if the requirements of Sec. 1033 are satisfied. The functional-use test must be satisfied regardless of the type of involuntary conversion.

For purposes of Sec. 121, the destruction, theft, seizure, requisition, or condemnation of property is treated as a sale.[81] Thus, taxpayers may exclude a gain of up to $250,000 or $500,000 due to the involuntary conversion of a principal residence if the use and ownership tests are satisfied. Taxpayers normally prefer to exclude gain if the use and ownership tests are satisfied rather than defer gain under the involuntary conversion provisions.

If taxpayers make a proper and timely replacement of the residence subject to the involuntary conversion, gain may be excluded up to $250,000, or $500,000, and the remaining gain may be deferred. For purposes of applying the involuntary conversion provisions, the amount realized due to the involuntary conversion is reduced by any gain excluded under Sec. 121.[82]

EXAMPLE I:12-66 ▶ The Kochs' principal residence, with an adjusted basis of $200,000, has been used and owned by them for nine years. The house is destroyed by a hurricane, and the Kochs receive insurance proceeds of $820,000. Four months later, they purchase another residence for $900,000. The Kochs have a realized gain of $620,000 and may exclude $500,000 under Sec. 121. The remaining $120,000 gain may be deferred and the basis of their replacement residence is $780,000 ($900,000 − $120,000). ◀

Because the amount realized is reduced by the gain excluded, the Kochs could have deferred the $120,000 gain in the above example by investing only $320,000 in a replacement residence.

If gain due to the involuntary conversion of a principal residence is deferred under Sec. 1033, the holding period of the replacement residence includes the holding period of the converted property for purposes of satisfying the use and ownership tests of Sec. 121.[83] The Kochs satisfy the use and ownership requirements for Sec. 121 with respect to their new residence in Example I:12-66 because gain is deferred under Sec. 1033.

A loss due to a condemnation of a personal residence is not recognized. If the loss is due to a casualty, the loss is deductible and is treated like other casualty losses of nonbusiness property (see Chapter I:8).

TAX PLANNING CONSIDERATIONS

OBJECTIVE 4

Describe tax planning considerations for nontaxable exchanges

AVOIDING THE LIKE-KIND EXCHANGE PROVISIONS

In some cases, a taxpayer may prefer a taxable exchange to a nontaxable like-kind exchange. For instance, if the gain is taxed as a capital gain and the taxpayer has capital

[81] Sec. 121(d)(5)(A).
[82] Sec. 121(d)(5)(B).

[83] Sec. 121(d)(8).

losses to offset the gain, the taxpayer may prefer to recognize the gain during the current year. If gain on the exchange is recognized instead of deferred, the basis of the property received in the exchange is higher.

EXAMPLE I:12-67 ►
Connie owns land with a $20,000 basis. The land is held as an investment. Connie exchanges the land for a duplex with a $100,000 FMV. Because the exchange qualifies as a like-kind exchange, no gain is recognized and Connie's basis for the duplex is $20,000. If the exchange does not qualify as a like-kind exchange (e.g., the land is a personal-use asset), Connie recognizes an $80,000 capital gain. Connie's basis for the duplex is $100,000. The basis of the duplex, except for the portion allocable to land, is eligible for depreciation. ◄

If an exchange qualifies as a like-kind exchange, no loss on the exchange is recognized. A taxpayer who prefers to recognize a loss should avoid making a like-kind exchange. It may be advantageous to sell the property to recognize the loss and then purchase the replacement asset in two independent transactions. If the sale and purchase transactions are with the same party, the IRS may maintain that the like-kind exchange rules apply because the two transactions are in substance a like-kind exchange (i.e., the judicial doctrine of substance over form might be applied).

SALE OF A PRINCIPAL RESIDENCE

Election Provision. When the requirements of Sec. 121 are satisfied, gain is excluded unless the taxpayer elects not to have Sec. 121 apply.[84]

EXAMPLE I:12-68 ►
Paula has owned a house in Wyoming for eight years and occupied it until 18 months ago when she moved to Idaho and purchased a new house. She sells the house in Wyoming on May 23, 2015, and the realized gain is $25,000. Paula anticipates that she will move next year and have to sell the house in Idaho which has appreciated more than $100,000 since purchased. Paula may want to elect not to have Sec. 121 apply and recognize the $25,000 gain and then use the exclusion when she sells the house in Idaho next year. ◄

Property Used as Residence and for Business. If a house is used for both residential use and business use, the tax treatment depends on whether or not the business portion of the house is conducted in a separate structure. If the business portion of the house is conducted in a separate structure, the sale should be treated as a sale of two assets, the residence and the portion of the property used as a business. The Sec. 121 exclusion only applies to the residence portion of the property.

EXAMPLE I:12-69 ►

ADDITIONAL COMMENT

As explained in Chapter I:13, Mormor's $24,000 gain in Example 69 is a Sec. 1231 gain and $4,000 is taxed at a maximum rate of 25% because it is unrecaptured Sec. 1250 gain.

Mormor owns a one-acre lot with a house she uses as her residence and a barn that she uses to display and sell antiques. She purchased the property in 1990 for $100,000 and $10,000 of the purchase price was allocated to the barn. Depreciation of $4,000 has been allowed for the barn. She sells the property during the current year for $300,000 and estimates that 10% of the price received is for the barn. She may exclude the $180,000 ($270,000 − $90,000) gain on the sale of the residence. Her $24,000 ($30,000 − $6,000) gain on the sale of the barn is recognized. ◄

If the business activity is conducted within the house and not in a separate structure, the sale does not have to be treated as a sale of two different assets. However, gain attributable to depreciation after May 6, 1997, is not eligible for the exclusion. The remaining gain is eligible for the exclusion.

EXAMPLE I:12-70 ►
Kate purchased a house in 2005 for $200,000 and uses 15% of the house as an office. The office is used on a regular and exclusive basis and is her principal place of business. Depreciation of $3,400 has been deducted when she sells the house for $430,000. Her gain is $233,400 ($430,000 − $196,600), and she may exclude $230,000 but must recognize $3,400 of the gain. ◄

The government's decision to allow Kate to treat the property in the above example as one property instead of two is beneficial for her. If the property was viewed as two properties or if the office was in a separate structure, only $195,500 ($365,500 − $170,000) of the gain would qualify for the exclusion.

---

[84] Sec. 121(f).

EXAMPLE I:12-71 ▶ Bobbi purchased a house on March 1, 2004 and used it as her principal residence until March 1, 2006, when she rented the house to the Allens while she lived with her mother. On November 1, 2013, the Allens' lease expired and Bobbi moved back into the house. She sells the house on July 12, 2015, and realizes a gain of $210,000. She may not exclude any of the gain because she has not used the property as her principal residence for two of the last five years. ◀

If Bobbi in the above example did satisfy the two-out-of-five-year requirement, gain equal to depreciation would first be recognized. A portion of the remaining gain could not be excluded because of the nonqualified use after 2008.

EXAMPLE I:12-72 ▶ Assume the same facts as in the above example except that Bobbi sells the house on December 1, 2015. Because she has used the property as her principal residence for two of the last five years, she may exclude part of the excess of the $210,000 gain over depreciation allowed after May 6, 1997. 58 months of the use is nonqualified use because of its use as rental property for 58 months after 2008. Because she owned the property for 141 months and nonqualified use amounted to 58 months, 58/141 of the gain remaining after gain recognized due to depreciation is recognized. ◀

COMPLIANCE AND PROCEDURAL CONSIDERATIONS

OBJECTIVE 5

Describe compliance and procedural considerations for nontaxable exchanges

REPORTING OF INVOLUNTARY CONVERSIONS

The election to defer recognition of the gain from an involuntary conversion is made by not reporting the gain as income for the first year in which gain is realized. All details pertaining to the involuntary conversion (including those relating to the replacement of the converted property) should be reported for the taxable year or years in which any of the gain is realized.[85]

ADDITIONAL COMMENT
The failure to include gain from an involuntary conversion in gross income is deemed to be an election even though the details are not reported.

A taxpayer who elects to defer recognition of the gain but does not make a proper replacement of the property within the required period of time must file an amended return for the year or years for which the election was made. An amended return may be needed if the cost of the replacement property is less than expected at the time of the election. All details pertaining to the replacement of converted property must be reported in the year in which replacement occurs.[86]

EXAMPLE I:12-73 ▶ Bob's property, with a $40,000 adjusted basis, was destroyed by a storm in 2014. Bob received $45,000 insurance proceeds in 2014 and planned to purchase property similar to the converted property in 2015 at a cost of $47,000. Bob elected to defer recognition of the gain in 2014. In 2015 the replacement property is purchased for $44,500. Bob must file an amended return for 2014 and recognize a $500 ($45,000 − $44,500) gain. ◀

ADDITIONAL COMMENT
The replacement period may be extended if special permission is obtained from the IRS.

A taxpayer who either is ineligible or does not want to defer the gain must report the gain in the usual manner. If a taxpayer does not elect to defer the gain in the year the gain is realized and the replacement period has not expired, a subsequent election may be made. In such an event, a refund claim should be filed for the tax year in which the gain was realized and previously recognized.[87]

Taxpayers who do not initially elect to defer the gain from an involuntary conversion may later make the election, but the election may not subsequently be revoked. The Tax Court has ruled that the Treasury Regulations allow the filing of an amended return for a year in which the election is made only if proper replacement is not made within the specified time period or the replacement is made at a cost lower than anticipated at the time of the election.[88] The IRS takes the position that taxpayers who designate qualifying property as replacement property may not later designate other qualifying property as the replacement property.[89]

EXAMPLE I:12-74 ▶ In 2013 Troy collected $200,000 from an insurance company as the result of the destruction of rental property with a $140,000 basis. He made the election to defer the gain realized in 2013 and attached a supporting schedule of details regarding the involuntary conversion including

---

[85] Reg. Sec. 1.1033(a)-2(c)(2).
[86] *Ibid.*
[87] *Ibid.*

[88] *John McShain*, 65 T.C. 686 (1976).
[89] Rev. Rul. 83-39, 1983-1 C.B. 190.

a designation of replacement property to be acquired in 2014. In 2014 Troy purchased the designated replacement rental property for $225,000. In 2015 Troy purchases other rental property for $400,000 and now wants to designate that property as the replacement property for the property destroyed in 2013. Troy may not designate the property acquired in 2015 as the replacement property because the rental property purchased in 2014 was already designated as such. ◀

REPORTING OF SALE OR EXCHANGE OF A PRINCIPAL RESIDENCE

Taxpayers only have to report the sale if any of the gain is not excluded. If the taxpayer does not qualify to exclude all of the gain or elects not to exclude the gain, the entire gain realized is reported on Schedule D either on line 1, if residence is held for one year or less, or on line 8. On the line below where the entire gain is shown, the taxpayer should indicate on the following line the amount of the gain that is being excluded as a loss (i.e., show in parentheses).

Publication 523, Selling Your Home, provides the following worksheet that may be used to determine if any gain is recognized. If the taxpayer has to utilize the exceptions to the two-year ownership and use tests, a different worksheet is provided.

Worksheet 2. **Taxable Gain on Sale of Home**

Part 1. Gain or (Loss) on Sale

1.	Selling price of home	1. _____
2.	Selling expenses (including commissions, advertising and legal fees, and seller-paid loan charges)	2. _____
3.	Subtract line 2 from line 1. This is the amount realized	3. _____
4.	Adjusted basis of home sold (from Worksheet 1, line 13)	4. _____
5.	**Gain or (loss)** on the sale. Subtract line 4 from line 3. If this is a loss, stop here	5. _____

Part 2. Exclusion and Taxable Gain

6.	Enter any depreciation allowed or allowable on the property for periods after May 6, 1997. If none, enter -0-	6. _____
7.	Subtract line 6 from line 5. If the result is less than zero, enter -0-	7. _____
8.	Aggregate number of days of nonqualified use after 2008. If none, enter -0-. If line 8 is equal to zero, skip to line 12 and enter the amount from line 7 on line 12	8. _____
9.	Number of days taxpayer owned the property	9. _____
10.	Divide the amount on line 8 by the amount on line 9. Enter the result as a decimal (rounded to at least 3 places). But do not enter an amount greater than 1.00	10. _____
11.	Gain allocated to nonqualified use. (Line 7 multiplied by line 10)	11. _____
12.	Gain eligible for exclusion. Subtract line 11 from line 7	12. _____
13.	If you qualify to exclude gain on the sale, enter your maximum exclusion (see *Maximum Exclusion*). If you qualify for a reduced maximum exclusion, enter the amount from Worksheet 3, line 7. If you do not qualify to exclude gain, enter -0-	13. _____
14.	**Exclusion.** Enter the smaller of line 12 or line 13	14. _____
15.	**Taxable gain.** Subtract line 14 from line 5. Report your taxable gain as described under *Reporting the Sale.* **If the amount on line 6 is more than zero, complete line 16**	15. _____
16.	Enter the **smaller** of line 6 or line 15. Enter this amount on line 12 of the Unrecaptured Section 1250 Gain Worksheet in the instructions for Schedule D (Form 1040)	16. _____

PROBLEM MATERIALS

DISCUSSION QUESTIONS

I:12-1 Evaluate the following statement: The underlying rationale for the nonrecognition of a gain or loss resulting from a like-kind exchange is that the exchange constitutes a liquidation of the taxpayer's investment.

I:12-2 Why might a taxpayer want to avoid having an exchange qualify as a like-kind exchange?

I:12-3 Debbie owns office equipment with a basis of $300,000 and a holding period starting on May 10, 2004. Debbie exchanges the equipment for other office equipment owned by Doug on July 23, 2015. Doug's equipment has an FMV of $500,000. Both Debbie and Doug use the equipment in their businesses.
a. What is Debbie's basis for the office equipment received in the exchange and when does the holding period start for that equipment?
b. If Debbie and Doug are related taxpayers, explain what action could occur that would cause the exchange not to qualify as a like-kind exchange.

I:12-4 Kay owns equipment used in her business and exchanges the equipment for other like-kind equipment and marketable securities.
a. Will Kay's recognized gain ever exceed the realized gain?
b. Will Kay's recognized gain ever exceed the FMV of the marketable securities?
c. What is the basis of the marketable securities received?
d. When does the holding period of the marketable securities begin?

I:12-5 Demetrius sells word processing equipment used in his business to Edith. He then purchases new word processing equipment from Zip Corporation.
a. Do the sale and purchase qualify as a like-kind exchange?
b. When may a sale and a subsequent purchase be treated as a like-kind exchange?

I:12-6 When determining whether property qualifies as like-kind property, is the quality or grade of the property considered?

I:12-7 What is personal property of a like class that meets the definition of like-kind?

I:12-8 When does a nonsimultaneous exchange qualify as a like-kind exchange?

I:12-9 Burke is anxious to purchase land owned by Kim for use in his trade or business. Kim's basis for the land is $150,000, and Burke has offered to pay $800,000 if she will sell within the next 10 days. Kim is interested in selling but wants to avoid recognizing gain. What advice would you give?

I:12-10 Lanny wants to purchase a farm owned by Jane, but Jane does not want to recognize a gain on the transfer of the appreciated property. Explain how a three-party exchange might be used to allow Lanny to obtain the farm without Jane having to recognize a gain.

I:12-11 Does the receipt of boot in a transaction that otherwise qualifies as a like-kind exchange always cause the exchange to be at least partially taxable?

I:12-12 When must a taxpayer who gives boot recognize a gain or loss?

I:12-13 What is the justification for Sec. 1033, which allows a taxpayer to elect to defer a gain resulting from an involuntary conversion? May a taxpayer elect under Sec. 1033 to defer recognition of a loss resulting from an involuntary conversion?

I:12-14 Must property be actually condemned for the conversion of property to be classified as an involuntary conversion? Explain.

I:12-15 What are severance damages? What is the tax treatment for severance damages received if the taxpayer does not use the severance damages to restore the retained property?

I:12-16 The functional use test is often used to determine whether the replacement property is similar or related in service or use to the property converted. Explain the functional use test.

I:12-17 In what situations may a gain due to an involuntary conversion of real property be deferred if like-kind property is purchased to replace the converted property?

I:12-18 Prior to the Taxpayer Relief Act of 1997, taxpayers could defer a gain on the sale of a principal residence sold before May 7, 1997, if they purchased and occupied a new principal residence within two years before or after the sale and the cost of the new residence was at least equal to the adjusted sales price of the old residence. Some taxpayers who were at least 55 years old had a once-in-a-lifetime exclusion up to $125,000 if they owned and used the property as a principal residence for at least three years of the five-year-period ending on the date of sale. Discuss why current law with respect to the sale of a personal residence is more favorable than the law prior to the Taxpayer Relief Act of 1997.

I:12-19 One reason Congress expanded the exclusion of gain on the sale of a principal residence and eliminated the deferral provision was to eliminate the need for many taxpayers to keep records of capital improvements that increase the basis of their residence. Why might taxpayers still need to maintain such records to substantiate the adjusted basis of their principal residence?

I:12-20 Steve maintains that the cost of wallpapering his three-bedroom house is a capital expenditure while Martha maintains that the cost of wallpapering her three-bedroom house is an expense. Steve uses his house as his personal residence while Martha's house is rental property. Explain why Steve and Martha view the cost of wallpapering differently.

I:12-21 The Nelsons purchased a new residence in 1992 for $300,000 from David who owned and used the residence as rental property. When the Nelsons wanted to purchase the property, it was being rented to tenants who had four months remaining on their lease. The Nelsons paid the tenants $1,000 to relinquish the lease and vacate the property. In 1996, they added a family room to the house at a cost of $79,200. In 1998, they suffered hail damage to the roof and received $7,000 from the insurance company. They did not repair the damaged roof, and no casualty loss deduction was allowed. What is their adjusted basis for the house today?

I:12-22 What requirements must be satisfied by an unmarried taxpayer under Sec. 121 to be eligible for the election to exclude a gain up to $250,000 on the sale or exchange of a principal residence?

ISSUE IDENTIFICATION QUESTIONS

I:12-23 John owns 25% of the ABC Partnership and Jane owns 25% of the XYZ Partnership. The ABC Partnership owns a farm and produces corn and the XYZ Partnership owns a farm and produces soybeans. John and Jane agree to exchange their partnership interests. What tax issues should John and Jane consider?

I:12-24 Chauvin Oil Corporation operates primarily in the United States and owns an offshore drilling rig with an adjusted basis of $400,000 that it uses near Louisiana. Chauvin exchanges the rig for a new rig with a FMV of $1,000,000, and Chauvin also pays $250,000. Chauvin plans to expand its drilling operations to offshore sites near Finland. What tax issues should the Chauvin Oil Corporation consider?

I:12-25 Jaharta, Inc., owns land used for truck farming and cattle raising. The California Division of Highways condemned 36 acres of Jaharta's land to build a new highway. Jaharta owned a 50% interest in property being used for apricot, prune, and walnut orchards. Jaharta used the proceeds received as a result of the condemnation to purchase the remaining interest in the property being used for orchards. What tax issues should Jaharta consider?

PROBLEMS

I:12-26 *Like-Kind Property.* Which of the following exchanges qualify as like-kind exchanges under Sec. 1031?
a. Acme Corporation stock held for investment purposes for Mesa Corporation stock also held for investment purposes
b. A motel used in a trade or business for an apartment complex held for investment
c. A pecan orchard in Texas used in a trade or business for an orange grove in Florida used in a trade or business
d. A one-third interest in a general partnership for a one-fourth interest in a limited partnership
e. Inventory for equipment used in a trade or business
f. Unimproved land held as an investment for a warehouse used in a trade or business
g. An automobile used as a personal-use asset for marketable securities held for investment

I:12-27 *Like-Kind Property.* Which of the following exchanges qualify as like-kind exchanges under Sec. 1031?
a. A motel in Texas for a motel in Italy
b. An office building held for investment for an airplane to be used in the taxpayer's business
c. Land held for investment for marketable securities held for investment
d. Land held for investment for a farm to be used in the taxpayer's business

I:12-28 *Like-Kind Exchange: Boot.* Determine the realized gain or loss, the recognized gain or loss, and the basis of the equipment received for the following like-kind exchanges:

Basis of Equipment Exchanged	FMV of Boot Received	FMV of Equipment Received
$20,000	$ –0–	$85,000
45,000	14,000	70,000
60,000	25,000	65,000
70,000	38,000	60,000
90,000	22,000	55,000

I:12-29 *Like-Kind Exchange: Personal Property.* Beach Corporation owns a computer with a $34,000 adjusted basis. The computer is used in the company's trade or business. What is the realized and recognized gain or loss for each of the following independent transactions where the computer is exchanged for?
a. A used computer with a $70,000 FMV plus $16,000 cash.
b. A used computer with a $18,000 FMV plus $7,000 cash.
c. Marketable securities with a $61,000 FMV.

I:12-30 *Like-Kind Exchange: Personal Property.* Boise Corporation exchanges a machine with a $14,000 basis for a new machine with an $18,000 FMV and $3,000 cash. The machines are used in Boise's business and are in the same General Asset Class.
a. Determine Boise Corporation's recognized gain and the basis for the new machine.
b. How would your answer to Part a change if the corporation's machine is also subject to a $6,000 liability, and the liability is assumed by the other party?

I:12-31 *Exchange of Personal Property.* Lithuania Corporation operates a ferry service and owns four barges. Lithuania exchanges one of the barges with an adjusted basis of $350,000 for a used smaller barge with a FMV of $444,000 and a $26,000 computer. Without considering the exchange, Lithuania Corporation's taxable income is $700,000. Determine Lithuania's
a. realized gain on the exchange.
b. recognized gain.
c. basis of the new barge.
d. basis of the computer.
e. Assume that the recognized gain is $26,000 and the gain is not capital gain. What is the increase in Lithuania's tax liability as a result of the exchange?

I:12-32 *Like-Kind Exchange: Liabilities.* Paul owns a building used in his business with an adjusted basis of $340,000 and a $750,000 FMV. He exchanges the building for a building owned by David. David's building has a $950,000 FMV but is subject to a $200,000 liability. Paul assumes David's liability and uses the building in his business. What is Paul's
a. realized gain?
b. recognized gain?
c. basis for the building received?

I:12-33 *Like-Kind Exchange: Liabilities.* Helmut exchanges his apartment complex for Heidi's farm, and the exchange qualifies as a like-kind exchange. Helmut's adjusted basis for the apartment complex is $600,000 and the complex is subject to a $180,000 liability. The FMV of Heidi's farm is $770,000 and the farm is subject to a $100,000 liability. Each asset is transferred subject to the liability. What is Helmut's recognized gain and the basis of the new farm?

I:12-34 *Like-Kind Exchange: Liabilities.* Carol owns land used in her business with a basis of $70,000 and a fair market value of $90,000. She is planning to exchange the land for a warehouse owned by Jeff and used in his business. Jeff's warehouse has a basis of $50,000 and a fair market value of $110,000. The warehouse is also subject to a liability of $20,000. Carol has agreed to assume the liability for Jeff. What is Jeff's recognized gain and his basis in the new land?

I:12-35 *Like-Kind Exchange: Transfer of Boot.* Wayne exchanges unimproved land with a $50,000 basis and marketable securities with a $10,000 basis for an eight-unit apartment building having a $150,000 FMV. The land and marketable securities are held by Wayne as investments, and the apartment building is held as an investment. The marketable securities have a $25,000 FMV. What is his realized gain, recognized gain, and the basis for the apartment building?

I:12-36 *Like-Kind Exchange: Related Parties.* Bob owns a duplex used as rental property. The duplex has a basis of $86,000 and $300,000 FMV. He transfers the duplex to Cindy, his sister, in exchange for a triplex that she owns. The triplex has a basis of $279,000 and a

$300,000 FMV. Two months after the exchange, Cindy sells the duplex to a business associate for $312,000. Determine:
a. Bob's realized and recognized gain on the exchange.
b. Cindy's realized and recognized gain on the exchange.

I:12-37 *Like-Kind Exchange: Related Parties.* Assume the same facts as in I:12-36 except Cindy sells the duplex to a nonrelated individual more than two years after the exchange with Bob. Ignore any changes in adjusted basis due to depreciation that would have occurred after the exchange. Determine:
a. Bob's realized and recognized gain on the exchange.
b. Cindy's realized and recognized gain on the exchange.
c. Cindy's realized and recognized gain on the sale.

I:12-38 *Involuntary Conversion.* Duke Corporation owns an office building with a $400,000 adjusted basis. The building is destroyed by a tornado. The insurance company paid $750,000 as compensation for the loss. Eight months after the loss, Duke uses the insurance proceeds and other funds to acquire a new office building for $682,000 and machinery for one of the company's plants at a $90,000 cost. Assuming that Duke elects to defer as much of the gain as possible, what is the recognized gain, the basis for the new office building, and the basis for the machinery acquired?

I:12-39 *Involuntary Conversion: Replacement Period.* The Madison Corporation paid $3,000 for several acres of land in 1993 to use in its business. The land is condemned and taken by the state in March 2015. The company receives $25,000 from the state. Whenever possible, the corporation elects to minimize taxable income. For each of the following independent cases, what is the recognized gain or loss in 2015 on the conversion and the tax basis of the replacement property (replacement land will be purchased in July)?
a. 2016 for $22,500.
b. 2017 for $28,500.
c. 2018 for $23,600.

I:12-40 *Involuntary Conversion of Real Property.* On April 27, 2015, an office building owned by Newark Corporation, an offshore drilling company that is a calendar-year taxpayer, is destroyed by a hurricane. The basis of the office building is $600,000, and the corporation receives $840,000 from the insurance company.
a. To defer the entire gain due to the involuntary conversion, what amount must the corporation pay for replacement property?
b. To defer the gain due to the involuntary conversion, by what date must the corporation replace the converted property?
c. If Newark replaces the office building by purchasing a 900,000 gallon storage tank for $810,000, may it defer any of the gain due to the involuntary conversion?
d. Will answers to Parts b and c change if the office building had been condemned by the state? Explain.

I:12-41 *Involuntary Conversion: Different Methods of Replacement.* On September 3, 2015, Federal Corporation's warehouse is totally destroyed by fire. $800,000 of insurance proceeds are received, and the realized gain is $300,000. Whenever possible, Federal elects to defer gains. For each of the following independent situations, what is the amount of gain recognized? Explain why the gain is not deferred, if applicable.
a. On October 23, 2015, Federal purchases a warehouse for $770,000.
b. On February 4, 2016, Federal purchases 100% of the Park Corporation, which owns a warehouse. Federal pays $895,000 for the stock.
c. On November 20, 2017, Federal purchases an apartment complex for $900,000.
d. On March 26, 2018, Federal purchases a warehouse for $888,000.

I:12-42 *Severance Damages.* Twelve years ago, Marilyn purchased two lots in an undeveloped subdivision as an investment. Each lot has a $10,000 basis and a $40,000 FMV when the city condemns one lot for use as a municipal sewage treatment plant. As a result of the condemnation, Marilyn receives $40,000 from the city. Because the value of the other lot is reduced, the city pays $7,500 severance damages. She does not plan to replace the condemned lot. What is her:
a. recognized gain due to the condemnation?
b. recognized gain from the receipt of the severance damages?
c. basis for the lot she continues to own?

I:12-43 *Sale of a Principal Residence.* Marc, age 45, sells his personal residence on May 15, 2015, for $180,000. He pays $8,000 in selling expenses and $900 in repair expenses to help sell the residence. He has lived in the residence since 1980, when he purchased it for $55,000. In 1996, he paid $6,000 to install central air conditioning. If Marc purchases a new principal residence in December of the current year for $162,000, what is the realized gain, recognized gain, and the basis for the new residence?

I:12-44 *Sale of a Principal Residence.* Mr. and Mrs. Rusbarsky purchased a residence on June 12, 2012, for $200,000. On March 12, 2015, they sell the residence for $300,000, and selling expenses amount to $11,000. They purchase another house in a new subdivision for $275,000. Determine the gain realized and recognized.

I:12-45 *Sale of a Principal Residence.* On January 10, 2015, Kirsten married Joe. Joe sold his personal residence on October 25, 2014, and excluded the entire gain of $175,000. Although they had originally planned to live in the house that Kirsten had received as a gift from her parents in 2006, they decided to purchase a larger house, and Kirsten sold her house 60 days after their wedding and realized a $370,000 gain.
a. If they file a joint return, how much of the $370,000 gain may be excluded?
b. If Kirsten files as married filing separately, how much of the $370,000 gain may be excluded?

I:12-46 *Involuntary Conversion of Principal Residence.* Mr. and Mrs. Snell own and live in a house, with an adjusted basis of $300,000, that was purchased in 1994. The house is destroyed by a tornado on March 10 of the current year, and the Snells receive insurance proceeds of $410,000. They purchase another residence for $480,000 four months later.
a. May they exclude the $110,000 gain, and if so, what is the basis of the residence purchased in July?
b. May they defer the $110,000 gain, and if so, what is the basis of the residence purchased in July?

I:12-47 *Sale of a Principal Residence.* Mr. and Mrs. Kitchens purchased their first home in Ohio for $135,000 on October 1, 2014. Because Mr. Kitchens' employer transferred him to Utah, they sold the house for $160,000 on January 10, 2015. How much of the gain is recognized?

I:12-48 *Sale or Other Disposition of a Principal Residence.* In 1970, Mr. and Mrs. Self purchased their first principal residence for $80,000. In 1995, they sold the house for $300,000 and purchased a new residence for $1.5 million. At that time, the Selfs were allowed to defer the $220,000 gain because they purchased a more expensive residence, but the basis of the residence was reduced by the gain deferred. The Taxpayer Relief Act of 1997 eliminated this deferral provision and made it easier for taxpayers who sell a principal residence to exclude the gain resulting from the sale even if they do not purchase a replacement residence.

In 2001, the Selfs spent $200,000 to add a porch to their house that overlooks the small pond behind their house. In 2004, they hired painters to paint the entire house at a cost of $18,000. They estimate that $20,000 has been spent on routine repairs since 1995, but insurance of $11,000 was collected for the repairs resulting from a small tornado in 2008. No casualty loss deduction was allowed. They hold the residence as joint tenants.

1. What is the current adjusted basis of the house?
2. Mrs. Self is an employee of Bulldog Consulting and has a nice office on the business premises; however, she finds it helpful to use one of the bedrooms as an office to do work in the evenings and on weekends. May the Selfs claim a deduction for depreciation?
3. Determine their recognized gain and character if they sell the house today for $2.8 million.
4. If the property is owned by Mrs. Self instead of owned jointly, determine their recognized gain and character if they sell the house today for $2.8 million.
5. If the property is owned by Mrs. Self instead of owned jointly and Mr. Self dies, will the basis of the house be increased?
6. Determine their recognized gain if they exchange the house today for an apartment complex valued at $2.8 million. The Selfs will purchase another house and hire someone to manage the apartment complex.
7. If the house is destroyed by a fire when its FMV is $2.8 million and the Selfs receive $2.6 million, determine their casualty loss deduction and gain recognized, if any. The Selfs do not plan to purchase another residence.
8. If the Selfs want to purchase another principal residence after collecting the insurance in question #7 above, what is the minimum amount they would have to pay for the new residence to avoid recognizing any gain?

I:12-49 *Unqualified Use.* Sherron, who is single, purchased a house to use as rental property on April 1, 2007, for $300,000. He moved into the house on June 1, 2014, and used it as a personal residence until August 1, 2015, when he sells the house for $500,000. Depreciation allowed while property was used as rental property amounts to $25,000. Determine his:
a. realized gain on the sale
b. recognized gain on the sale
c. recognized gain on the sale if the house is not sold until August 1, 2016, for $500,000

I:12-50 *Sale of a Principal Residence: Rental Property.* For the last five years, Mr. and Mrs. Cockrell rented their furnished basement to local college students. When determining their taxable income each year, they deducted a portion of the utilities, property taxes, interest, and depreciation based on the fact that 15% of the house is used for rental purposes. The original basis of the property is $100,000, and depreciation of $4,000 has been allowed on the rental portion of the property. During the current year, Mr. and Mrs. Cockrell sell the house for $300,000. No selling expenses or fixing-up expenses are incurred. Determine:
a. realized gain on the sale.
b. recognized gain on the sale.

I:12-51 *Multiple Sales of a Principal Residence.* Consider the following information for Mr. and Mrs. Di Palma:

- On June 10, 2014, they sold their principal residence for $80,000 and incur $6,000 of selling expenses. The basis of the residence, acquired in 2004, is $50,000.
- On June 25, 2014, they purchased a new principal residence for $90,000 and occupied it immediately.
- On May 10, 2015, they purchase their neighbor's residence for $115,000 and occupy the residence immediately.
- On August 29, 2015, they sell the residence purchased on June 25, 2014, for $148,000. They pay $7,000 of selling expenses. Determine:
a. realized gain on the sale of the residence in 2014.
b. recognized gain on the sale of the residence in 2014.
c. realized gain on the sale of the residence in 2015.
d. recognized gain on the sale of the residence in 2015.

I:12-52 *Multiple Sales of a Principal Residence.* Consider the following information for Mr. and Mrs. Gomez:

- On May 26, 2014, they sold their principal residence, acquired in 1999, for $200,000. They paid $8,000 of selling expenses. Their basis in the residence was $70,000.
- On July 25, 2014, they purchased a new principal residence for $250,000.
- On June 2, 2015, Mr. Gomez, a bank officer, is transferred to another bank in the northern part of the state and they vacate their house.
- On July 1, 2015, they purchase a new principal residence for $420,000.
- On October 6, 2015, they sell the residence that was purchased on July 25, 2013, for $520,000. They pay $30,000 of selling expenses. Determine:
a. realized gain on the sale of the residence in 2014.
b. recognized gain on the sale of the residence in 2014.
c. realized gain on the sale of the residence in 2015.
d. recognized gain on the sale of the residence in 2015.

COMPREHENSIVE PROBLEM

I:12-53 Paden, who is single and has been employed as an accountant for 27 years with Harper, Inc., lost his job due to company downsizing. His last day of employment is July 31, 2015, and Harper provides a $9,000 severance payment. The severance payments are based on an employee's time of employment. During the year, Paden received a salary from Harper of $36,000. Harper also paid $1,500 of Paden's medical insurance premiums.

In May 2015, Paden, who had always wanted to be associated with a football team, applied for the head coaching job at Hawk University in Iowa and, much to his surprise, received the job beginning on August 1. In June and July, Paden paid $4,500 to take courses in sports management at the local university. Hawk University is substantially short of funding and Paden paid $2,000 for entertainment expenses related to his job and $500 for supplies. No reimbursement was received.

His salary from Hawk is $4,000 per month payable at the end of each month. His salary for December was not received until January 6, 2016.

On August 1, he sold his house for $329,000 in Texas and paid a sales commission of $14,000. He inherited the house 20 years ago when his mother died. Her basis for the house was $37,000 and the FMV when she died was $50,000. Property taxes for the 2015 calendar year amount to $3,600, and property taxes were apportioned at the closing. Property taxes are payable on October 1. He paid $12,000 of interest on home equity debt of $150,000.

To move to Iowa, he drove 700 miles and spent $45 for meals during the trip in July. Movers charged $4,150 to move his household items. Use the standard mileage rate for moving expenses for 2015 which is 23 cents per mile. He purchased a new house in Iowa for $150,000 on August 15 and borrowed $110,000. He also agreed to pay all property taxes for 2015. Real property taxes for the home in Iowa will be paid on January 30, 2016, and amount to $1,500. Interest on the $110,000 debt during the current year is $1,475. To obtain the loan, Paden paid points of $1,000.

He contributed common stock (basis of $1,000 and FMV of $6,000) held as an investment for three years to Hawk University. He also paid state income taxes of $1,765 (which was greater than state sales taxes for the year) as well as personal property taxes of $435 for his car.

Paden sold 200 shares of Dell Corporation stock on April 10 for $100 per share. His basis was $145 per share. On May 1, he purchased 300 shares of Dell at $89 per share.

Determine:
1. gross income without considering the sale of his house or the Dell Corporation stock.
2. recognized gain due to the sale of his house.
3. net capital gain.
4. adjusted gross income.
5. total amount of itemized deductions.
6. taxable income.
7. basis of his house in Iowa.
8. if the sales price for his home was $470,000 instead of $370,000, would his taxable income increase by more than $100,000. If yes, explain.

TAX STRATEGY PROBLEM

I:12-54 *Sale of a Principal Residence.* Ray and Ellie have each owned a principal residence used for more than five years. Ray's residence has an adjusted basis of $100,000 and a FMV of $325,000, while Ellie's residence has an adjusted basis of $300,000 and a FMV of $490,000. They plan to marry and will purchase another house.
a. Should they sell their houses before the marriage in order to minimize their taxes?
b. Will your answer to Part a change if the FMV of Ellie's house is $690,000?
c. In Part b, what tax strategy should Ray and Ellie consider?

TAX FORM/RETURN PREPARATION PROBLEMS

I:12-55 On October 29, 2014, Miss Joan Seely (SSN 123-45-6789) sells her principal residence for $150,000 cash. She purchased the residence on May 12, 2005, for $85,000. She spent $12,000 for capital improvements in 2005. To help sell the house, she pays $300 for minor repairs. The realtor's commission amounts to $7,500. Her old residence is never rented out or used for business. Complete the worksheet on page 12-24 for Miss Seely for 2014.

I:12-56 At the beginning of 2014, Donna Harp was employed as a cinematographer by Farah Movie, Inc., a motion picture company in Los Angeles, California. In June, she accepted a new job with Ocala Production in Orlando, Florida. Donna is single and her Social Security number is 000-00-1111. She sold her house in California on August 10 for $500,000. She paid a $14,000 sales commission. The house was acquired on March 23, 1987, for $140,000.

The cost of transporting her household goods and personal effects from California to Orlando amounted to $2,350. To travel from California to Florida, she paid travel and lodging costs of $370 and $100 for meals.

On July 15, she purchased a house for $270,000 on 1225 Minnie Lane in Orlando. To purchase the house, she incurred a 20-year mortgage for $170,000. To obtain the loan, she paid points of $3,400. The $3,600 of property taxes for the house in Orlando were prorated with $1,950 being apportioned to the seller and $1,650 being apportioned to the buyer. In December of the current year she paid $3,600 for property taxes.

Other information related to her return:

Salary from Farah Movie, Inc.	$30,000
Salary from Ocala Production, Inc.	70,000
Federal income taxes withheld by Farah	6,000
Federal income taxes withheld by Ocala	22,000
FICA taxes withheld by Farah	2,295
FICA taxes withheld by Ocala	5,355
Interest income from Sun National Bank	1,800
Dividend income	10,000
Interest paid for mortgage:	
Home in California	6,780
Home in Orlando	3,800
Property taxes paid in California	4,100
Sales taxes paid in California and Florida	3,125
State income taxes paid in California	2,900

Prepare Form 1040 including Schedules A, B, and D. Prepare Form 3903 and Form 8960. Use the worksheet on page 12-24 to determine the amount of recognized gain on the sale of the residence.

I:12-57 Jim Sarowski (SSN 000-00-2222) is 70 years old and single. He received Social Security benefits of $16,000. He works part-time as a greeter at a local discount store and received wages of $7,300. Federal income taxes of $250 were withheld from his salary. Jim lives at Rt. 7 in Daingerfield, Texas.

In March of 2014, he purchased a duplex at 2006 Tennessee Street to use as rental property for $100,000, with 20% of the price allocated to land. During the year, he had the following receipts and expenditures with respect to the duplex:

Rent receipts	$8,800
Interest paid	5,900
Property taxes	1,400
Insurance	800
Maintenance	300

Other expenditures during the year:

Contributions to the church	$2,600
Personal property taxes	225
Sales tax	345

On July 24, he exchanged ten acres of land for a car with a $16,500 FMV to be held for personal use. The land was purchased on November 22, 1991, for $18,000 as an investment. Because of pollution problems in the area, the value of the land declined.

On December 1, he sold his residence, which had been his home for 30 years, for $475,000. Sales commissions of $16,000 were paid, and the adjusted basis for his home is $110,000. He plans to rent an apartment and does not plan to purchase another home. His only other sale of a principal residence occurred 32 years ago.

Prepare Forms 1040 and 4562 and Schedules D and E. Use the worksheet on page 12-24 to determine the amount of recognized gain on the sale of the residence.

CASE STUDY PROBLEM

I:12-58 The Electric Corporation, a publicly held corporation, owns land with a $1,600,000 basis that is being held for investment. The company is considering exchanging the land for two assets owned by the Quail Corporation: land with a FMV of $4,000,000 and marketable securities with a $1,000,000 FMV. Both assets will be held by the Electric Corporation for investment, although the corporation is considering the possibility of developing the land and building residential houses. The president of the corporation has hired you to prepare a report explaining how the exchange will affect the corporation's reported net income and its tax liability. The corporation has a tax rate of 34%.

TAX RESEARCH PROBLEMS

I:12-59 For the last nine years, Mr. and Mrs. Orchard live in a residence located on eight acres. In January of the current year they sell the home and two acres of land. The purchaser of the residence does not wish to own the entire eight acres of land. In December they sell the remaining six acres of land to another individual for $60,000. The house and the land have never been used by the Orchards in a trade or business or held for investment. The realized gains resulting from the two sales are computed as follows:

	House and Two Acres January Sales	Eight Acres December Sale
Selling price	$140,000	$60,000
Minus: Selling expenses	(8,000)	(3,000)
Amount realized	$132,000	$57,000
Minus: Basis	(80,000)	(18,000)
Realized gain	$ 52,000	$39,000

As a result of the sales described above, what is the amount of realized gain that must be recognized during the current year?

A partial list of research sources is:

• Reg. Sec. 1.121-1(b)

I:12-60 George, age 68, decides to retire from farming and is considering selling his farm. The farm has a $100,000 basis and a $400,000 FMV. George's two sons are not interested in farming. Both sons have large families and would like to own houses suitable for their needs. The Iowa Corporation is willing to purchase George's farm. George's tax advisor suggests that Iowa Corporation should buy the two houses the sons want to own for $400,000 and then exchange the houses for George's farm. After the exchange, George could make a gift of the houses to the sons.

a. If the transactions are executed as suggested by the tax advisor, George's recognized gain will be $300,000. Explain why the transaction does not qualify as a like-kind exchange.

b. George wants the exchange to qualify as a like-kind exchange and still help his sons obtain the houses. What advice do you have for him?

A partial list of research sources is:

• *Dollie H. Click*, 78 T.C. 225 (1982)

• *Fred S. Wagensen*, 74 T.C. 653 (1980)

I:12-61 On March 10, 2012, Elizabeth, a college professor, purchased a house for $300,000. She did not move into the house until August 8, 2012. On August 1, 2013, she accepted a position as a visiting professor at Hogwatts University for one year and moved to Liverpool where she rented an apartment. While away at Hogwatts, two of her former students lived in the house but did not pay rent. She returned to the house on August 1, 2014, and lived in the house until July 15, 2015, when she sold the house for $500,000. The realtor's commission was $35,000. Determine her recognized gain.

A partial list of research sources is:

• Reg. Sec. 1.121-1(c)

I:12-62 Mr. and Mrs. Hattan have lived in their residence for 20 years and purchased the house for $100,000 as joint tenants with right of survivorship. Mr. Hattan died in May of the current year when the house's FMV was $800,000. Mrs. Hattan wants to sell the house. What is the tax effect of selling the house this year for $825,000 or next year for $830,000?

A partial list of research sources is:

• Sections 121 and 1014

I:12-63 Joseph Allen, who is single, purchased his first house in Orono, ME one year ago for $200,000. Katahdin wants to purchase the house for $360,000. Refer to the regulations to determine if he may exclude part of the gain in the following independent cases:

a. He has been unemployed for 16 months and has a chance to start work for Penobscot Manufacturing whose plant is located 62 miles from Joseph's home in Orono.

b. His dependent son, Ryan, has chronic asthma, and the son's doctor has advised Joseph that Ryan should live in a warm, dry climate to mitigate the chronic asthma. Joseph and Ryan move to Nevada.

c. Joseph has become increasingly annoyed at the amount of traffic in his neighborhood although the amount of traffic has not increased much compared to the traffic when he purchased the house.

A partial list of research sources is:

- Reg. Sec. 1.121-3(c), (d) and (e)

13

PROPERTY TRANSACTIONS: SECTION 1231 AND RECAPTURE

LEARNING OBJECTIVES

After studying this chapter, you should be able to

1 ▶ Understand the basic tax treatment for Sec. 1231 transactions

2 ▶ Identify Sec. 1231 property

3 ▶ Understand the tax treatment for Sec. 1231 transactions

4 ▶ Apply the recapture provisions of Sec. 1245

5 ▶ Apply the recapture provisions of Sec. 1250

6 ▶ Understand recapture provisions for corporations

7 ▶ Describe other recapture applications

8 ▶ Describe tax planning considerations for Sec. 1231 assets

9 ▶ Describe compliance and procedural considerations for Sec. 1231 assets

KEY POINT

Taxpayers normally prefer to have gains treated as capital gains, and losses treated as ordinary losses. Because Sec. 1231 property receives the preferable treatment for both net gains and losses, it has been said that this property enjoys the best of both worlds.

ADDITIONAL COMMENT

Beginning in 2013, higher-income taxpayers also have to pay an additional 3.8% tax on net investment income, which includes capital gains. Generally, for this provision, higher-income taxpayers are defined as those with modified AGI of greater than $200,000 if single or head of household and $250,000 if married, filing jointly. More information on this additional tax can be found in Chapter I:5.

Chapter I:5 states that all recognized gains and losses must eventually be designated as either capital or ordinary. However, gains or losses on certain types of property are designated as Sec. 1231 gains or losses, which are given preferential treatment under the tax law. Section 1231 property primarily is business property, either real or depreciable property used in a trade or business.[1] A net Sec. 1231 loss, defined as the excess of Sec. 1231 losses over Sec. 1231 gains, is treated as an ordinary loss.[2] Net Sec. 1231 gain, the excess of Sec. 1231 gains over Sec. 1231 losses, is generally treated as long-term capital gain.[3] However, the preferential treatment of Sec. 1231 gains is diminished, principally by the so-called depreciation recapture rules and the five-year lookback rule. This chapter discusses the important rules dealing with Sec. 1231 gains and losses and depreciation recapture.

HISTORY OF SEC. 1231

During the depressed economy of the early and mid-1930s, business property was classified as a capital asset. Many business properties were worth less than their adjusted basis. Instead of selling business properties, taxpayers found it advantageous to retain assets that had declined in value because they could recover the full cost as depreciation. Capital losses had only limited deductibility during this period. To encourage the mobility of capital (i.e., the replacement of business fixed assets), the Revenue Act of 1938 added business property to the list of properties not considered to be capital assets.

From 1938 to 1942, gains and losses on the sale or exchange of business property were treated as ordinary gains and losses. Favorable capital gain treatment was eliminated and taxpayers with appreciated business properties were reluctant to sell the assets because of the high tax cost. This restriction on the mobility of capital was more significant than usual because business assets had to be shifted into industries that were heavily involved in the production of military goods. Furthermore, taxpayers were often forced to recognize ordinary gains because the government used the condemnation process to obtain business property for the war effort. In 1942, Congress created the predecessor of Sec. 1231, which allowed taxpayers to treat net gains from the sale of business property as capital gains and net losses as ordinary losses. Before 1987, only 40% of an individual's net capital gain might be subject to tax because of the 60% long-term capital gain deduction.

The Tax Reform Act of 1986 eliminated the 60% long-term capital gain deduction for net capital gains. Favorable long-term capital gain treatment was reinstated into the tax law in 1991 in the form of a 28% maximum tax rate applying to net capital gains for noncorporate taxpayers. The Taxpayer Relief Act of 1997 significantly increased the preferential tax treatment by reducing the maximum rate to 20% for net capital gain that is adjusted net capital gain. The maximum rate was reduced by the Jobs and Growth Tax Relief Reconciliation Act of 2003 (2003 Tax Act) to 15%, for sales after May 5, 2003. The American Tax Relief Act of 2012 increased the maximum rate to 20% starting in 2013 for unmarried taxpayers with taxable income above $400,000 ($413,200 in 2015) and $450,000 ($464,850 in 2015) for married taxpayers (i.e., those taxpayers with a marginal tax rate of 39.6%).

It may also be advantageous to have gains classified as capital or Sec. 1231 if taxpayers have capital losses or capital loss carryovers because of the limitations imposed on the deductibility of capital losses. Furthermore, there are other situations where it may be important for the property to be Sec. 1231 property (e.g., a contribution of appreciated property to a charitable organization).

---

[1] (See page I:13-5 for a more complete definition of Sec. 1231 property.)
[2] Secs. 1231(c)(4) and (a)(2).

[3] Secs. 1231(c)(3) and (a)(1). There are several exceptions to this rule that are covered later in this chapter.

OVERVIEW OF BASIC TAX TREATMENT FOR SEC. 1231

Understand the basic tax treatment for Sec. 1231 transactions

NET GAINS

At the end of the tax year, Sec. 1231 gains are netted against Sec. 1231 losses. If the overall result is a net Sec. 1231 gain, the gains and losses are treated as long-term capital gains (LTCGs) and long-term capital losses (LTCLs), respectively.[4] For the sake of expediency, it is often stated that a net Sec. 1231 gain is treated as a LTCG. However, a portion or all of the net Sec. 1231 gain may be treated as ordinary income because of a special five-year lookback rule (see discussion below).

EXAMPLE I:13-1 ▶ Dawn owns a business that has $20,000 of Sec. 1231 gains and $12,000 of Sec. 1231 losses during the current year. Because the Sec. 1231 gains exceed the Sec. 1231 losses, the gains and losses are treated as LTCGs and LTCLs. After the gains and losses are offset, there is an $8,000 net long-term capital gain (NLTCG). ◀

EXAMPLE I:13-2 ▶ Assume the same facts as in Example I:13-1 except that Dawn also recognizes a $7,000 LTCG from the sale of a capital asset. After considering the $8,000 net Sec. 1231 gain, which is treated as a LTCG, Dawn has a $15,000 NLTCG ($8,000 + $7,000). ◀

NET LOSSES

If the netting of Sec. 1231 gains and losses at the end of the year results in a net Sec. 1231 loss, the Sec. 1231 gains and losses are treated as ordinary gains and losses.[5] For expediency, it is often stated that the net Sec. 1231 loss is treated as an ordinary loss.

EXAMPLE I:13-3 ▶ David owns an unincorporated business and has $30,000 of Sec. 1231 gains and $40,000 of Sec. 1231 losses in the current year. Because the losses exceed the gains, they are treated as ordinary losses and gains. ◀

EXAMPLE I:13-4 ▶ Assume the same facts as in Example I:13-3 except that David receives a $67,000 salary as a corporate employee. David has no other income, losses, or deductions affecting his adjusted gross income (AGI). The Sec. 1231 gains and losses are treated as ordinary gains and losses, and David's AGI is $57,000 ($67,000 salary − $10,000 of ordinary loss). The $40,000 of ordinary losses offsets the $30,000 of ordinary gains and $10,000 of David's salary. ◀

TYPICAL MISCONCEPTION

It is sometimes erroneously thought that each Sec. 1231 gain should be treated as a LTCG and each Sec. 1231 loss as an ordinary loss. However all Sec. 1231 gains and losses must be combined to determine whether the Sec. 1231 gains and losses are LTCGs and LT-CLs or ordinary gains and losses.

One important advantage of Sec. 1231 is illustrated in Example I:13-4. Because the Sec. 1231 gains and losses are treated as ordinary, the $10,000 net Sec. 1231 loss is fully deductible in the current year. If the gains and losses were classified as long-term capital gains and losses, David would have a $10,000 net long-term capital loss (NLTCL). Only $3,000 of the $10,000 NLTCL would have been deductible against David's other income. As explained in Chapter I:5, only $3,000 of net capital losses may be deducted from noncapital gain income per year for individual taxpayers.

ADDITIONAL COMMENT

A taxpayer's share of a Sec. 1231 loss from a partnership or S Corporation may be subject to the passive activity loss rules.

Five-Year Lookback Rule Beginning in 1985, the benefits of Sec. 1231 were reduced. For tax years beginning after 1984, any net Sec. 1231 gain is ordinary gain to the extent of any nonrecaptured net Sec. 1231 losses from the previous five years.[6] This provision is referred to as the *five-year lookback rule*. In essence, net Sec. 1231 losses previously deducted as ordinary losses are recaptured by changing what would otherwise be a LTCG into ordinary income.

EXAMPLE I:13-5 ▶ In 2015, Craig recognizes $25,000 of Sec. 1231 gains and $15,000 of Sec. 1231 losses. In 2011, Craig reported $14,000 of Sec. 1231 losses and no Sec. 1231 gains. No other Sec. 1231 gains or losses were recognized by Craig during the five-year period, 2010–2014. The $10,000

---

[4] Sec. 1231(a)(1).
[5] Sec. 1231(a)(2).

[6] Sec. 1231(c)(1).

($25,000 − $15,000) of net Sec. 1231 gain in 2015 is treated as ordinary income due to the $14,000 of nonrecaptured net Sec. 1231 losses. ◀

To determine the amount of nonrecaptured net Sec. 1231 losses, compare the aggregate amount of net Sec. 1231 losses for the most recent preceding five tax years with the amount of such losses recaptured as ordinary income for those preceding tax years. The excess of the aggregate amount of net Sec. 1231 losses over the previously recaptured loss is the nonrecaptured net Sec. 1231 loss. In Example I:13-5, the remaining $4,000 of nonrecaptured net Sec. 1231 losses could be recaptured in 2016. In 2016, the preceding five-year period includes 2011 through 2015.

TAX RATE FOR NET SEC. 1231 GAIN

In general, net Sec. 1231 gains are taxed similarly to net long-term capital gains. Thus, a Sec. 1231 gain may be taxed at a rate of 15% (or zero if the taxpayer's regular tax rate is 15% or less) or 20% if taxable income is above $413,200 for unmarried taxpayers and $464,850 for married taxpayers. Section 1231 property must have a holding period of more than one year. Recall from Chapter I:5 that adjusted net capital gain (ANCG) is net capital gain (NCG) determined *without* regard to:

(1) the 28% rate gain, and
(2) unrecaptured Sec. 1250 gain, which is taxed at no more than 25% as explained later.

ANCG might be taxed at 15% or zero. The tax rate on ANCG for taxpayers in the 10% or 15% tax brackets is 0%. If Sec. 1231 property is sold at a gain, the Sec. 1231 gain is LTCG if there are no Sec. 1231 losses or nonrecaptured net Sec. 1231 losses. However, all or part of this gain is unrecaptured Section 1250 gain if the asset is a building. Thus, net Sec. 1231 gain might be taxed today at 15%, 20%, or 25% depending on the taxpayer's tax rate and whether or not the gain is unrecaptured section 1250 gain. Part or all of Sec. 1231 gain due to the sale of real property subject to depreciation that is unrecaptured Sec. 1250 gain is taxed at a maximum of 25%.

EXAMPLE I:13-6 ▶ Savannah, whose tax rate is 28% and AGI is less than $413,200, sells land at a gain of $10,000 and other land at a gain of $15,000. Both tracts of land qualify as Sec. 1231 property. She has no other transactions involving capital assets or 1231 property and no nonrecaptured net Sec. 1231 losses. Savannah has net Sec. 1231 gain of $25,000 that is NLTCG and her NCG is $25,000. Her ANCG is $25,000 taxed at a rate of 15%. ◀

EXAMPLE I:13-7 ▶ Assume the same facts as in Example I:13-6 except Savannah also has a $7,000 loss from the sale of a third tract of land that is Sec. 1231 property. Her net Sec. 1231 gain is $18,000. Her NCG is $18,000 and her ANCG is $18,000 taxed at a rate of 15%. ◀

EXAMPLE I:13-8 ▶ Grace, whose tax rate is 15% or less, sells land that is Sec. 1231 property at a gain of $2,000. She has no other transactions involving capital assets or 1231 property and no nonrecaptured net Sec. 1231 losses. The $2,000 gain is not taxed since her tax rate for ANCG is zero. ◀

Applying the Five-Year Lookback Rule. As explained earlier, net Sec. 1231 gain is ordinary income to the extent of nonrecaptured net Sec. 1231 losses. Net Sec. 1231 gain is recharacterized as ordinary income under the five-year lookback rule in the following order:

(1) Net Sec. 1231 gain in the 25% group (unrecaptured Sec. 1250 gain)
(2) Net Sec. 1231 gain in the 20% or 15% group

EXAMPLE I:13-9 ▶ Chris, whose tax rate is 33%, has nonrecaptured net Sec. 1231 losses of $20,000 at the beginning of the current year when he recognizes gains from the sale of two assets used in his trade or business and held more than one year. Asset #1 is a building and the entire $14,000 Sec. 1231 gain is unrecaptured Sec. 1250 gain. Asset #2 is land and the Sec. 1231 gain is $15,000. All gain resulting from the sale of asset #1 is ordinary income and $6,000 of the gain from the sale of asset #2 is ordinary income because of the five-year lookback rule. The remaining $9,000 gain from the sale of asset #2 (land) is taxed at 15%. ◀

SECTION 1231 PROPERTY

OBJECTIVE 2

Identify Sec. 1231 property

SECTION 1231 PROPERTY DEFINED

Section 1231 property includes the following types of property:

▶ Real property or depreciable property used in a trade or business with a holding period of more than one year

▶ Timber, coal, or domestic iron ore

▶ Livestock

▶ Unharvested crops

Each of these types of Sec. 1231 assets are discussed below.

REAL OR DEPRECIABLE PROPERTY USED IN TRADE OR BUSINESS

KEY POINT

Inventory, free publications of the U.S. government, and copyrights, as well as literary, musical, or artistic compositions are not capital assets.

As noted in Chapter I:5, the IRC does not provide a definition of a capital asset. Instead, Sec. 1221 provides a list of noncapital assets. This list includes both depreciable property and real property used in a trade or business.[7] These properties are treated as Sec. 1231 properties if held for more than one year. Depreciable property and real property used in a trade or business and held for **one year or less** are neither capital assets nor Sec. 1231 property. Any gain or loss resulting from the disposition of such assets is ordinary.

EXAMPLE I:13-10 ▶ The Prime Corporation owns land held as an investment and land used as an employee parking lot. The land held as an investment is a capital asset. The land used as a parking lot is real property used in a trade or business and is not a capital asset. The land used as a parking lot is a Sec. 1231 asset if held for more than one year. ◀

EXAMPLE I:13-11 ▶ Dale, a self-employed plumber, owns an automobile held for personal use and a truck used in his trade. The automobile is a capital asset, but the truck is a Sec. 1231 asset if held for more than one year. As described later, a portion or all of any gain realized on the sale of the truck may be taxed as ordinary income due to the Sec. 1245 depreciation recapture provisions which are explained on page 8. ◀

KEY POINT

Only property used in a trade or business is included in the definition of Sec. 1231 property. Gains and losses on property held for investment may be included only if the result of a condemnation or casualty.

Certain types of property do not qualify as Sec. 1231 property, even if used in a trade or business. For example, inventory is not Sec. 1231 property. Thus, a sale of inventory results in ordinary gain or loss. Publications of the U.S. Government received other than by purchase at its regular sale price; a copyright; literary, musical, or artistic compositions; letters or memorandums; or similar properties held by certain taxpayers, such as their creator, are not classified as Sec. 1231 property.[8]

EXAMPLE I:13-12 ▶ Carl, who owns a recording studio, writes a musical composition and obtains a copyright that is sold to a record company. Because the musical composition is created by the personal efforts of the taxpayer, the musical composition is not Sec. 1231 property, and the sale results in ordinary gain from the sale of an ordinary asset. ◀

KEY POINT

The record company in example I:13-12 may amortize the cost of the copyright. The copyright is Sec. 1231 property if held more than one year.

Timber. Section 631 allows taxpayers to elect to treat the cutting of timber as a sale or exchange of such timber. To be eligible to make this election, the taxpayer must own the timber or hold the contract right on the first day of the year and for more than one year. Furthermore, the timber must be cut for sale or for use in the taxpayer's trade or business.[9]

REAL-WORLD EXAMPLE

Christmas trees can be included in the definition of Sec. 1231 property.

The gain or loss is determined by comparing the timber's adjusted basis for depletion with its fair market value (FMV) on the first day of the tax year in which it is cut. If the timber is eventually sold for more or less than its FMV (determined on the first day of the year the timber is cut), the difference is ordinary gain or loss.

---

[7] Sec. 1221(2).
[8] Sec. 1231(b)(1).

[9] Sec. 631(a) and Reg. Sec. 1.631-1.

EXAMPLE I:13-13 ▶ Vermont Corporation owns timber with a $60,000 basis for depletion. The timber, acquired four years ago, is cut during the current year for use in the corporation's business. The FMV of the timber on the first day of the current year is $200,000. Vermont Corporation may elect to treat the cutting of the timber as a sale or exchange and recognize a $140,000 ($200,000 − $60,000) gain. ◀

SELF-STUDY QUESTION

Is the possible inclusion of timber and coal or domestic iron ore in the definition of Sec. 1231 property favorable to the taxpayers who produce these items?

ANSWER

Yes, it can result in income being taxed at rates applicable for LTCG instead of ordinary income from the sale of inventory.

ADDITIONAL COMMENT

Livestock includes cattle, hogs, horses, mules, donkeys, sheep, goats, fur-bearing animals, and other mammals but excludes poultry, fish, frogs, and reptiles.

ADDITIONAL COMMENT

The treatment of unharvested crops as a Sec. 1231 asset is largely a rule of convenience. If the taxpayer were not permitted to treat the crops in this fashion, it would be necessary to allocate the selling price between the land and crops.

If the election is made to treat the cutting of timber as a sale or exchange, the timber is considered Sec. 1231 property.[10] Thus, the $140,000 gain in Example I:13-13 is Sec. 1231 gain. If the taxpayer does not make the election, the character of any gain or loss depends on whether the timber is held for sale in the ordinary course of the taxpayer's trade or business, held for investment, or held for use in a trade or business.

Coal or Domestic Iron Ore. An owner who disposes of coal (including lignite) or domestic iron ore while retaining an economic interest in it must treat the disposal as a sale.[11] The coal or iron ore is considered Sec. 1231 property.[12] The owner must own and retain an economic interest in the coal or iron ore in place.[13] An economic interest is owned when one acquires by investment any interest in mineral in place and seeks a return of capital from income derived from the extraction of the mineral.

Livestock. Livestock held by the taxpayer for draft, breeding, dairy, or sporting purposes is considered Sec. 1231 property if held for 12 months or more from the date of acquisition. However, cattle and horses must be held for 24 months or more from the date of acquisition to qualify as Sec. 1231 property.[14]

Unharvested Crops and Land. An unharvested crop growing on land used in a trade or business is considered Sec. 1231 property if the crop and the land are both sold at the same time to the same person and the land is held more than one year.[15] Section 1231 does not apply to the sale or exchange of an unharvested crop if the taxpayer retains any right or option to reacquire the land.[16]

If Sec. 1231 applies to the sale or exchange of an unharvested crop sold with the land, no deductions are allowed for expenses attributable to the production of the unharvested crop.[17] Instead, costs of producing the crop must be capitalized.

INVOLUNTARY CONVERSIONS

Gains and losses from involuntary conversions of property used in a trade or business generally are classified as Sec. 1231 gains and losses. Involuntary conversions of capital assets that are held in connection with a trade or business or in a transaction entered into for profit also generally qualify for Sec. 1231 treatment. The property that is involuntarily converted must be held more than one year. Certain involuntary conversions are treated differently for income tax purposes. For example, the tax rules are different for condemnations and casualties, even though both are involuntary conversions of property.

CONDEMNATIONS

Gains and losses resulting from condemnations of Sec. 1231 property and capital assets held more than one year are classified as Sec. 1231 gains and losses. As indicated above, the capital assets must be held in connection with a trade or business or with a transaction entered into for profit.[18]

EXAMPLE I:13-14 ▶ Kathryn owns land with a $20,000 basis and a $30,000 FMV as well as a building with a $40,000 adjusted basis and a $26,000 FMV. Both assets are used in her trade or business and have been held for more than one year. As a result of the state exercising its powers of requisition or

---

[10] Sec. 1231(b)(2) and Reg. Sec. 1.631-1(d)(4).
[11] Sec. 631(c) and Reg. Sec. 1.631-3(a)(1).
[12] Sec. 1231(b)(2) and Reg. Sec. 1.631-3(a)(2).
[13] Reg. Sec. 1.631-3(b)(4).
[14] Sec. 1231(b)(3).

[15] Sec. 1231(b)(4) and Reg. Secs. 1.1231-1(c)(5) and 1(f).
[16] Reg. Sec. 1.1231-1(f).
[17] Sec. 268 and Reg. Sec. 1.268-1.
[18] Secs. 1231(a)(3)(A) and (4)(B).

condemnation, Kathryn is required to transfer both properties to the state for cash equal to their FMVs. No other transfers of assets occur during the current year. The $10,000 gain due to condemnation of the land is a Sec. 1231 gain and the $14,000 loss due to condemnation of the building is a Sec. 1231 loss. ◄

OTHER INVOLUNTARY CONVERSIONS

TYPICAL MISCONCEPTION

The inclusion of gains and losses from condemnations in the netting of the other involuntary conversions is a common error.

Gains or losses resulting from an involuntary conversion arising from fire, storm, shipwreck, other casualty, or theft are not classified as Sec. 1231 gains or losses if the recognized losses from such conversions exceed the recognized gains.[19] In such a case, the involuntary conversions are treated as ordinary gains and losses. However, if the gains from such involuntary conversions exceed the losses, both are classified as Sec. 1231 gains and losses.

EXAMPLE I:13-15 ►

Jose owns equipment having a $50,000 adjusted basis and a $42,000 FMV and a building having a $30,000 adjusted basis and a $35,000 FMV which are used in Jose's trade or business. The straight-line method of depreciation is used for the building. Both assets are held for more than a year. As a result of a fire, both assets are destroyed, and Jose collects insurance proceeds equal to the assets' FMV. No other transfers of assets occur during the current year. Because the $8,000 ($42,000 − $50,000) recognized loss exceeds the $5,000 ($35,000 − $30,000) recognized gain, the recognized loss and gain are both treated as ordinary. ◄

PROCEDURE FOR SEC. 1231 TREATMENT

OBJECTIVE 3

Understand the tax treatment for Sec. 1231 transactions

After determining the recognized gains and losses from transfers of property qualifying for Sec. 1231 treatment, it is necessary to determine whether any gain must be recaptured as ordinary income under Secs. 1245 and 1250. The recaptured gain, discussed later in this chapter, is not eligible for Sec. 1231 treatment. After eliminating the gain recaptured as ordinary income due to the recapture of depreciation, the procedure for analyzing Sec. 1231 transactions is as follows:

STEP 1. Determine all gains and losses resulting from casualties or thefts of Sec. 1231 property and non–personal-use capital assets held for more than one year. Gains and losses are netted and the net gain is treated as Sec. 1231 gain if the gains exceed the losses.

If the losses exceed the gains, both are treated as ordinary losses and gains and do not, therefore, enter into the Sec. 1231 netting procedure. Recall from Chapter I:7 that business casualty losses are deductible *for* AGI and other casualty losses are deductible *from* AGI.

KEY POINT

Gains that are recaptured under Secs. 1245 and 1250 are not eligible for Sec. 1231 treatment.

STEP 2. Combine the following gains and losses to determine whether Sec. 1231 gains exceed Sec. 1231 losses or vice versa:

► Net casualty and theft *gains* resulting from Step 1, if any

► Gains and losses resulting from the sale or exchange of Sec. 1231 property

► Gains and losses resulting from the condemnation of Sec. 1231 property and non–personal-use capital assets held more than one year.

If a net Sec. 1231 loss is the result, the losses and gains are treated as ordinary losses and gains. If a net Sec. 1231 gain is the result, the gains and losses are treated as LTCGs and LTCLs, although a portion or all of the capital gain may be recaptured as ordinary income as outlined in Step 3 (five-year lookback rule) below.

STEP 3. If a net Sec. 1231 gain is the result of Step 2, determine if the taxpayer has any nonrecaptured net Sec. 1231 losses. Nonrecaptured net Sec. 1231 losses are the excess of aggregate net Sec. 1231 losses for the preceding five years over losses previously recaptured as ordinary income due to the recapture provision of Sec. 1231. Net Sec. 1231 gains to the extent of any nonrecaptured net Sec. 1231 losses are treated as ordinary income. Section 1231 gain that is unrecaptured Sec. 1250 gain is first treated as ordinary income to the extent of nonrecaptured net Sec. 1231 losses. Any net Sec. 1231 gain in excess of nonrecaptured net Sec. 1231 loss is treated as a LTCG.

[19] Sec. 1231(a)(4)(C).

EXAMPLE I:13-16 ▶

ADDITIONAL COMMENT

If Danielle has AGI of $80,000 without considering the gains and losses in Example I:13-16, her AGI is $93,000.

The following gains and losses pertain to Danielle's business assets that qualify as Sec. 1231 property. Danielle does not have any nonrecaptured net Sec. 1231 losses from previous years, and the portion of gain recaptured as ordinary income due to the depreciation recapture provisions has been considered.

Gain due to an insurance reimbursement for fire damage	$10,000
Loss due to condemnation	(19,000)
Gain due to the sale of Sec. 1231 property	22,000

The $10,000 casualty gain is classified as a Sec. 1231 gain because gains resulting from casualties or thefts of Sec. 1231 property exceed losses. Danielle has $32,000 ($10,000 + $22,000) of Sec. 1231 gains and a $19,000 Sec. 1231 loss. Danielle's $13,000 net Sec. 1231 gain is treated as a LTCG. No portion of the $13,000 LTCG is recaptured as ordinary income because Danielle does not have any nonrecaptured net Sec. 1231 losses during the preceding five-year period. ◀

EXAMPLE I:13-17 ▶

Assume the same facts as in Example I:13-16 except that Danielle has a $10,000 loss because of the fire instead of a $10,000 gain. The $10,000 casualty loss is an ordinary loss, not a Sec. 1231 loss because losses resulting from casualties or thefts of Sec. 1231 property exceed gains. Because the loss is a business loss, it is deductible *for* AGI. Due to the $19,000 condemnation loss and the $22,000 of Sec. 1231 gain, she has a $3,000 net Sec. 1231 gain that is treated as a LTCG. ◀

EXAMPLE I:13-18 ▶

ADDITIONAL COMMENT

If Danielle has AGI of $80,000 without considering the gains and losses in Example I:13-17, her AGI is $73,000.

The following gains and losses recognized in 2015 pertain to Fred's business assets that were held for more than one year. The assets qualify as Sec. 1231 property.

Gain due to an insurance reimbursement for a casualty	$15,000
Gain due to a condemnation	25,000
Loss due to the sale of Sec. 1231 property	(12,000)

A summary of Fred's net Sec. 1231 gains and losses for the previous five-year period is as follows:

Year	Sec. 1231 Gain	Sec. 1231 Loss	Cumulative Nonrecaptured Net Sec. 1231 Losses (from five prior years)
2010	$ 5,000		–0–
2011		$2,000	$2,000
2012		6,000	8,000
2013	13,000		–0–
2014		9,000	9,000

The $15,000 gain due to the insurance reimbursement for a casualty is treated as a Sec. 1231 gain. The $25,000 gain from the condemnation is also a Sec. 1231 gain. Fred's net Sec. 1231 gain in 2015 is $28,000 [($15,000 + $25,000) − $12,000]. However, $9,000 of the Sec. 1231 gain is recaptured as ordinary income due to the $9,000 of nonrecaptured net Sec. 1231 loss existing at the end of 2014. The remaining $19,000 of net Sec. 1231 gain is a LTCG. ◀

RECAPTURE PROVISIONS OF SEC. 1245

OBJECTIVE 4

Apply the recapture provisions of Sec. 1245

In 1962, Congress enacted Sec. 1245, which substantially reduced the advantages of Sec. 1231. A gain from the disposition of Sec. 1245 property is treated as ordinary income to the extent of the total amount of depreciation (or cost-recovery) deductions allowed since January 1, 1962. The gain recaptured as ordinary income cannot exceed the amount of the realized gain.

EXAMPLE I:13-19 ▶

Adobe Corporation sells equipment used in its trade or business for $95,000. The equipment was acquired several years ago for $110,000 and is Sec. 1245 property.[20] The equipment's adjusted basis is $60,000 because $50,000 of depreciation was deducted. The entire $35,000 ($95,000 − $60,000) gain is treated as ordinary income because the total amount of depreciation taken ($50,000) is greater than the $35,000 realized gain. ◀

---

[20] Throughout this chapter, property is considered to be placed in service when it is purchased or acquired. The term *Sec. 1245 property* is used here to refer to either recovery property under the ACRS or MACRS rules or nonrecovery property that falls outside of the ACRS or MACRS rules.

TYPICAL MISCONCEPTION

It is sometimes thought that only tangible property is subject to Sec. 1245 recapture. In fact, both tangible and intangible personal property are included.

The recapture provisions of Sec. 1245 apply to the total amount of depreciation (or cost recovery) allowed or allowable for Sec. 1245 property. It makes no difference which method of depreciation is used.[21]

Generally, the entire gain from the disposition of Sec. 1245 property is recaptured as ordinary income because the total amount of depreciation (or cost recovery) is greater than the gain realized. A portion of the gain will receive Sec. 1231 treatment if the realized gain exceeds total depreciation or cost recovery.

EXAMPLE I:13-20 ▶

Assume the same facts as in Example I:13-19 except that the asset is sold for $117,000. Because the $57,000 ($117,000 − $60,000) realized gain is greater than the $50,000 of total depreciation, $50,000 of the gain is ordinary income and the remaining $7,000 is a Sec. 1231 gain. ◀

ADDITIONAL COMMENT

Section 1245 does not apply to losses because in these cases the taxpayers have not taken more depreciation than the asset's decline in value.

PURPOSE OF SEC. 1245

The purpose of Sec. 1245 is to eliminate any advantage taxpayers would have if they were able to reduce ordinary income by deducting depreciation and subsequently receive Sec. 1231 treatment when the asset was sold. For individuals, Sec. 1245 recapture prevents net Sec. 1231 gain from being treated as LTCG. The conversion of Sec. 1231 gain to Sec. 1245 ordinary income also prevents taxpayers from possibly using capital losses.

EXAMPLE I:13-21 ▶

KEY POINT

On the sale of Sec. 1245 property, a portion of the gain is treated as Sec. 1231 gain only if the property is sold for more than the original cost. This is very unlikely for factory equipment, trucks, office equipment, and other Sec. 1245 property.

During the current year, Coastal Corporation has capital losses of $50,000 and no capital gains for the current year or the preceding three years. The corporation owns equipment purchased several years ago for $90,000, and depreciation deductions of $48,000 have been allowed. If Coastal sells the equipment for $72,000, the entire $30,000 ($72,000 − $42,000) gain, which is due to the depreciation deductions, is Sec. 1245 ordinary income. Without Sec. 1245, the $30,000 gain is a Sec. 1231 gain that could be offset by $30,000 of the corporation's capital loss if Coastal has net Sec. 1231 gain. ◀

Note that Sec. 1245 does not apply to losses. If Coastal Corporation sells the equipment in Example I:13-21 for $40,000, a $2,000 ($40,000 − $42,000 basis) Sec. 1231 loss is recognized.

KEY POINT

Property must be depreciable or amortizable to be considered Sec. 1245 property.

Section 1245 Property. **Section 1245 property** is certain property subject to depreciation and, in some cases, amortization. The most common example of Sec. 1245 property is depreciable personal property such as equipment. Automobiles, livestock, railroad grading, and single-purpose agricultural or horticultural structures are Sec. 1245 properties as well as intangible assets subject to amortization under Sec. 197 (see Chapter I:10).[22] Except for certain buildings placed in service after 1980 and before 1987, buildings and structural components generally are not Sec. 1245 property.[23]

EXAMPLE I:13-22 ▶

Buckeye Corporation owns the following assets acquired in 2009: equipment, a patent, an office building (including structural components), and land. The equipment and patent are Sec. 1245 property. The office building and the land are not Sec. 1245 property. ◀

REAL-WORLD EXAMPLE

Pipelines, electric transmission towers, blast furnaces, greenhouses, and oil tanks are examples of real property that are included in the definition of Sec. 1245 property.

In many cases, taxpayers are allowed preferential treatment with respect to amortizing certain costs. For example, taxpayers may elect to expense up to $15,000 of the cost of making any business facility more accessible to handicapped and elderly people,[24] or to amortize pollution control facilities over 60 months[25] and reforestation expenditures over 84 months.[26] If taxpayers have amortized the costs of any real property under the special provisions, Sec. 1245 applies to the gain resulting from the disposition of such property.[27]

If taxpayers elect to expense certain depreciable property under Sec. 179, the amount deducted is treated as a depreciation deduction for purposes of the Sec. 1245 recapture provisions.[28]

---

[21] As explained later in this chapter, the method of cost recovery used determines whether certain real property is treated as Sec. 1245 recovery property.
[22] Sec. 1245(a)(3).
[23] Sec. 1245(a)(3)(B)(i). Tangible real property "used as an integral part of the manufacturing, production, extraction, or furnishing of transportation, communication, electrical energy, gas, water, or sewage disposal services" is Sec. 1245 property.
[24] Sec. 190.

[25] Sec. 169(a).
[26] Sec. 194(a).
[27] Sec. 1245(a)(3)(C). The Sec. 1245 rules recapture amortization deductions claimed on real property under Secs. 169, 179, 185, 188, 190, 193, and 194.
[28] Sec. 1245(a)(2)(C). The maximum amount deductible under Sec. 179 is $25,000 in 2015 unless Congress decides to increase the amount, $500,000 in 2010–2014, $250,000 in 2008–2009, $125,000 in 2007, $108,000 in 2006, and $105,000 in 2005.

EXAMPLE I:13-23 ▶ Compact Corporation purchased $90,000 of five-year equipment on March 10, 2014, and elected to expense $20,000 of the cost under Sec. 179. Compact sells the equipment on July 30, 2015, for $95,000. Regular depreciation allowed under MACRS for 2014 and 2015 is $14,000 and $11,200 (1/2 year), respectively. The adjusted basis of the equipment on the date of sale is $44,800 ($90,000 − $20,000 − $25,200 depreciation). The realized gain is $50,200 ($95,000 − $44,800), and $45,200 ($20,000 + $25,200) of the gain is Sec. 1245 ordinary income. The remaining $5,000 is Sec. 1231 gain. ◀

TYPICAL MISCONCEPTION

The categorization of nonresidential real estate acquired between 1981 and 1986 on which an accelerated depreciation method was used as Sec. 1250 property rather than as Sec. 1245 property is a common error.

Application of Sec. 1245 to Nonresidential Real Estate. Most real property is not affected by Sec. 1245. However, Sec. 1245 does apply to nonresidential real estate that qualified as recovery property under the ACRS rules (i.e., placed in service after 1980 and before 1987) unless the taxpayer elected to use the straight-line method of cost recovery.[29] Section 1245 does not apply to depreciable real estate acquired after 1986.

EXAMPLE I:13-24 ▶

HISTORICAL NOTE

Taxpayers acquiring nonresidential real property between 1981 and 1986 were confronted with choosing between straight-line ACRS and ACRS using the statutory rates. In making the decision, these taxpayers should have considered the number of years the property would be held, the estimated selling price, the present value of the tax savings due to deducting depreciation sooner, and any preferential treatment for net capital gains.

Brad sells two warehouses during the current year that are totally depreciated because their recovery period is 19 years.

	Warehouse 1	Warehouse 2
Year of purchase	1985	1985
Cost*	$720,000	$900,000
Cost recovery—straight line ACRS	720,000	
Cost recovery—ACRS statutory rates (accelerated)		900,000
Adjusted basis	0	0
Selling price	700,000	800,000

*does not consider the cost of land

Both warehouses were placed in service after 1980 and before 1987 and qualify as recovery property under ACRS. The $700,000 ($700,000 − $0) gain on the sale of Warehouse 1 is a Sec. 1231 gain. Section 1245 does not apply because Brad elected to use the straight-line method of cost recovery. Section 1245 applies to the sale of Warehouse 2 because ACRS was used and the property is nonresidential real estate placed in service after 1980 and before 1987. Therefore, the $800,000 ($800,000 − $0) gain is Sec. 1245 ordinary income because the $800,000 gain is less than the $900,000 total ACRS cost-recovery allowance. ◀

As illustrated in the example above, nonresidential buildings placed in service after 1980 and before 1987 are Sec. 1245 property if an accelerated method of cost recovery was used.

If the properties in Example I:13-24 were acquired before 1981 or after 1986, they would not be subject to the Sec. 1245 recapture rules regardless of the method of depreciation used.

The Sec. 1245 recapture rules are summarized in Topic Review I:13-1.

RECAPTURE PROVISIONS OF SEC. 1250

OBJECTIVE 5

Apply the recapture provisions of Sec. 1250

In 1964, Sec. 1250 was enacted to extend the recapture concept to include most depreciable real property. Unlike Sec. 1245, where the recapture is based upon the total amount of depreciation (or cost recovery) allowed, Sec. 1250 applies solely to additional depreciation. **Additional depreciation,** also referred to as **excess depreciation,** is the excess of the actual amount of accelerated depreciation (or cost-recovery deductions under ACRS) over

---

[29] Sec. 1245(a)(5).

TOPIC REVIEW I:13-1

Section 1245 Recapture

▶ Section 1245 affects the character of the gain, not the amount of gain. Character refers to gain being classified as either ordinary income or Sec. 1231 gain.

▶ Section 1245 does not apply to assets sold or exchanged at a loss.

▶ Section 1245 ordinary income is never more than the realized gain.

▶ Section 1245 recapture applies to the total depreciation or amortization allowed or allowable but not more than the realized gain.

▶ Section 1245 property includes depreciable personal property and amortizable intangible assets (e.g., a patent).

▶ Section 1245 property includes nonresidential real estate placed in service after 1980 and before 1987 under the ACRS rules *unless* the taxpayer elected to use the straight-line method of cost recovery.

▶ Section 1245 does not apply to any buildings placed in service after 1986.

the amount of depreciation that would be deductible under the straight-line method. Any gain due to excess depreciation is Sec. 1250 ordinary income.

EXAMPLE I:13-25 ▶

ADDITIONAL COMMENT

Since buildings generally must be depreciated on a straight-line basis since 1987, Sec. 1250 depreciation recapture becomes less and less applicable as time passes.

Wyatt sells a building that was placed in service before 1981 and the gain is $50,000. Accelerated depreciation was used and excess depreciation amounts to $74,000. All $50,000 of the gain is Sec. 1250 ordinary income. If the gain is $90,000, $74,000 is Sec. 1250 ordinary income and $16,000 is Sec. 1231 gain. ◀

PURPOSE OF SEC. 1250

Section 1250 has the effect of converting a portion of the Sec. 1231 gain into ordinary income when real property is sold or exchanged. The incremental benefits from using accelerated depreciation or ACRS cost recovery may be recaptured when the property is sold. Noncorporate taxpayers can avoid Sec. 1250 recapture by either using the straight-line method of depreciation or cost recovery or holding the Sec. 1250 property for its entire useful life or recovery period.

The Sec. 1250 recapture rules are applied solely to the additional depreciation amount instead of total depreciation allowable as is the case for Sec. 1245 property. Sec. 1250 provides for less depreciation recapture than Sec. 1245.

SECTION 1250 PROPERTY DEFINED

ADDITIONAL COMMENT

Elevators and escalators are Sec. 1245 property if placed in service before 1987, but Sec. 1250 property if placed in service after 1986.

KEY POINT

An apartment building is the most common type of property classified as residential real estate.

Section 1250 property is any depreciable real property other than Sec. 1245 property.[30] As stated on page 10, nonresidential real estate placed in service after 1980 and before 1987 is Sec. 1245 property unless the straight-line method of cost recovery is elected. The property is Sec. 1250 property if straight-line cost recovery is elected.

Depreciation recapture is not required on real property placed in service after 1986 because such property must be depreciated under the straight-line MACRS rules.[31]

EXAMPLE I:13-26 ▶

ADDITIONAL COMMENT

If the building in Example I:13-26 was placed in service after 1980 and before 1987, the building is Sec. 1245 property if Frances uses accelerated cost recovery and not the straight-line method.

Frances, whose marginal tax rate is less than 39.6%, sells an office building during the current year for $800,000. The office building was purchased before 1981 for $700,000* and depreciation of $500,000 has been allowed using an accelerated method of depreciation. If the straight-line method was used, depreciation would be $420,000. The office building is Sec. 1250 property. Her recognized gain is $600,000 and $80,000 is Sec. 1250 ordinary income due to excess depreciation ($500,000 − $420,000). The remaining $520,000 gain is Sec. 1231 gain.

If Frances purchased the building after 1986, she was required to use the straight-line method. Thus her recognized gain is $520,000 ($800,000 − $280,000) with straight-line depreciation being $420,000. None of the gain is Sec. 1250 ordinary income. The gain is Sec. 1231 gain. ◀

*does not consider the cost of land

[30] Sec. 1250(c).
[31] As explained in the Additional Recapture for Corporations section in this chapter, corporations may have depreciation recapture under Sec. 291(a) despite the use of straight-line depreciation.

As explained below, $420,000 of the Sec. 1231 gain in Example 13-26 is taxed at a maximum rate of 25% and $100,000 is taxed at 20% if there are no Sec. 1231 losses, nonrecaptured net Sec. 1231 losses, and no capital gains and losses from other transactions. Recall from Chapter I:5 that the tax rate on adjusted net capital gain may be 20%, 15%, or zero.

UNRECAPTURED SECTION 1250 GAIN

For sales of real property, some or all of the Sec. 1231 gain may be LTCG that is unrecaptured Sec. 1250 gain taxed at a maximum rate of 25%. Unrecaptured Sec. 1250 gain is the amount of LTCG which would be taxed as ordinary if Sec. 1250 provided for the recapture of all depreciation instead of additional (excess) depreciation. When a taxpayer sells Sec. 1250 property (e.g., an office building) at a gain, any gain due to excess depreciation is ordinary income. Any remaining gain is Sec. 1231 gain and may be LTCG; however, any of the LTCG due to depreciation other than excess depreciation is unrecaptured Sec. 1250 gain taxed at a maximum rate of 25%.

An individual taxpayer who uses straight-line depreciation for Sec. 1250 property does not have any additional depreciation that would be recaptured as ordinary gain under Sec. 1250. Therefore, for buildings placed in service after 1986, all of the Sec. 1231 gain to the extent of the depreciation is unrecaptured Sec. 1250 gain subject to a maximum tax rate of 25% because only straight-line depreciation may be used.

EXAMPLE I:13-27 ▶

Linnie owns a building used in her trade or business that was placed in service in 1995. She has no Sec. 1231 losses, nonrecaptured net Sec. 1231 losses or capital gains and losses. The building cost $400,000* and depreciation-to-date amounts to $172,000. If she sells the building for $350,000, her $122,000 gain ($350,000−$228,000) is Sec. 1231 gain and there is no depreciation recapture under Sec. 1250 because straight-line depreciation was allowed. The $122,000 Sec. 1231 gain is LTCG taxed at a maximum rate of 25% because it is unrecaptured Sec. 1250 gain. ◀

*does not consider the cost of land

 STOP & THINK

Question: What is the difference between *Sec. 1250 depreciation recapture* and *unrecaptured Sec. 1250 gain*?

Solution: Section 1250 depreciation recapture is the recharacterization of some or all of the Sec. 1231 gain on a building to ordinary income. Section 1250 depreciation recapture only applies to a noncorporate taxpayer if accelerated depreciation was used. Because accelerated depreciation is not allowed after 1986, this provision does not apply to noncorporate taxpayers for buildings placed in service after 1986. Unrecaptured Sec. 1250 gain is taxed at a maximum rate of 25% and occurs when there is a sale or an exchange of a building that is not Sec. 1245 property. If straight-line depreciation is used for a building, the gain is Sec. 1231 gain and the portion of the gain due to depreciation is unrecaptured Sec. 1250 gain. Part or all of the Sec. 1231 gain is taxed at a maximum rate of 25% with any excess taxed at 15% (or 20% if regular marginal tax rate is 39.6%).

EXAMPLE I:13-28 ▶

Assume the same facts as in Example I:13-27 except Linnie has a marginal tax rate less than 39.6% and sells the building for $500,000. Her Sec. 1231 gain is $272,000 ($500,000−$228,000), and $172,000 of the gain is taxed at 25% because it is unrecaptured Sec. 1250 gain. The remaining $100,000 of gain is taxed at 15%. ◀

TAXATION OF GAINS ON SALE OR EXCHANGE OF DEPRECIABLE REAL PROPERTY

Noncorporate taxpayers who placed real property in service after 1963 and before 1981 may have to recognize Sec. 1250 ordinary income if they used a depreciation method greater than straight-line. Only noncorporate taxpayers may have gain treated as unrecaptured Sec. 1250 gain and the amount of unrecaptured Sec. 1250 gain is not greater than the amount of depreciation allowed.

There is a difference between Sec. 1250 ordinary income and unrecaptured Sec. 1250 gain. Section 1250 ordinary income could be taxed at 39.6% after 2012 for noncorporate taxpayers while unrecaptured Sec. 1250 gain is taxed at a maximum rate of 25%. To have unrecaptured Sec. 1250 gain, the property must have a holding period greater than one year.

EXAMPLE I:13-29 ▶ Erin, whose tax rate is 35%, owns an office building purchased for $1 million* on April 10 of last year. The building is sold on March 28 of the current year for $990,000 when its adjusted basis is $966,850. The $23,150 gain is not Sec. 1231 gain and none of the gain is unrecaptured Sec. 1250 gain because the holding period is not more than one year. The $23,150 gain is ordinary taxed at 35%. If the holding period was more than one year, the Sec. 1231 gain of $23,150 is LTCG that is unrecaptured Sec. 1250 gain taxed at 25%. ◀

*does not consider the cost of land

The proper tax treatment for depreciable real estate depends on the method of depreciation, when the property was placed in service, and how the property is used. Section 1245 applies to a building placed in service after 1980 and before 1987 if accelerated cost recovery is allowed and the building is not used as residential rental property.

Real property used as residential rental property placed in service before 1987 may be taxed more favorably than other types of real property because the Sec. 1250 recapture of excess depreciation rules apply only to additional depreciation allowed after 1975 for residential rental property. Also, buildings used as residential rental property are never subject to the Sec. 1245 recapture rules.

For a building or structure to qualify as residential rental property, 80% or more of the gross rental income from the building or structure must be rental income from dwelling units. Residential rental property does not include any unit in a hotel, motel, inn, or other establishment if more than one-half of the units are used on a transient basis.[32]

When a building is sold at a gain, different tax rates may apply to portions of the gain:

Rate for ordinary income − Sec. 1250 due to recapture of excess depreciation or 1245 due to recapture of depreciation

25% − unrecaptured Sec. 1250 gain

20%, 15%, or zero − portion of Sec. 1231 gain that becomes adjusted net capital gain

Depreciable Real Property Placed in Service Before 1981. Taxpayers who elected to use accelerated depreciation on real property placed in service before 1981 may have some or all of their gain treated as Sec. 1250 ordinary income. Gain due to excess depreciation allowed after 1963 is Sec. 1250 ordinary income unless the building is used as residential rental property where gain due to excess depreciation after 1975 is ordinary income. The Sec. 1250 recapture rules are the same for residential rental property and other real property placed in service after 1975.

EXAMPLE I:13-30 ▶ Buddy sells an apartment complex used as residential rental property and placed in service on January 1, 1977. The cost of the apartment complex is $900,000,* and the complex is sold on January 1, 2015, for $700,000. Depreciation claimed by Buddy on the property is as follows:

ADDITIONAL COMMENT

If the selling price in Example I:13-30 is $172,000, all of the gain is Sec. 1250 ordinary income.

Selling Price	$172,000
Adjusted Basis	100,000
Realized Gain	$ 72,000
Ordinary Gain	$ 72,000

Time Period	Depreciation Allowed	Straight-Line Depreciation	Excess Depreciation
Jan. 1, 1977–Jan. 1, 2015	$800,000	$710,000	$90,000

On the date of sale, the adjusted basis of the apartment is $100,000 ($900,000 − $800,000) and the realized gain is $600,000 ($700,000 − $100,000). All $90,000 of excess depreciation allowed is recaptured as Sec. 1250 ordinary income because the excess depreciation is less than the realized gain. The remaining $510,000 ($600,000 − $90,000) of gain is a Sec. 1231 gain. The Sec. 1231 gain is LTCG if 1231 gains exceed 1231 losses and is taxed at 25% because it is unrecaptured Sec. 1250 gain. ◀

*does not consider the cost of land

---

[32] Reg. Sec. 1.167(j)-3(b)(1)(i).

EXAMPLE I:13-31 ▶ Assume the same facts as in Example I:13-30 except the building is nonresidential real estate such as a warehouse, manufacturing plant or an office building. The tax treatment is the same for both examples. Buddy has $90,000 of ordinary income and Sec. 1231 gain of $510,000. The Sec. 1231 gain is LTCG if 1231 gains exceed 1231 losses and is taxed at 25% because it is unrecaptured Sec. 1250 gain. ◀

There is no excess depreciation, and thus no Sec. 1250 ordinary income if the building is fully depreciated when sold or exchanged. As each year passes, noncorporate shareholders are increasingly less likely to have Sec. 1250 ordinary income.

EXAMPLE I:13-32 ▶ Assume the same facts as in Examples 30 and 31 except the buildings are fully depreciated and the selling price is $720,000. For both buildings, the realized gain of $720,000 is Sec. 1231 gain and is unrecaptured Sec. 1250 gain taxed at a maximum rate of 25%. ◀

Depreciable Real Property Placed in Service After 1980 and Before 1987. Gain due to excess depreciation for buildings used as residential rental property placed in service after 1980 and before 1987 is Sec. 1250 ordinary income. Because the recovery period for buildings placed in service during this period is 15, 18 or 19 years, all such buildings will be fully depreciated if sold in 2015, thus there is no excess depreciation and no Sec. 1250 ordinary income.

The method of depreciation used for other buildings placed in service during this period is a critical factor in determining the tax treatment when sold. If accelerated cost recovery was used, the nonresidential real estate is Sec. 1245 property where all gain due to depreciation is ordinary income. If the straight-line method is used, the property is Sec. 1250 property and none of the gain is ordinary income for noncorporate taxpayers.

EXAMPLE I:13-33 ▶ Ford purchased three buildings (A, B and C) in 1982 for $500,000 each*. The recovery period for each building is 15 years, so each building is fully depreciated when he sells the buildings during the current year for $400,000 each.

*does not consider the cost of land

Building	Use of Property	Method of Cost Recovery (Depreciation)
A	residential rental property	accelerated or straight-line
B	office building	accelerated
C	warehouse	straight-line

Building B is Sec. 1245 property, and the $400,000 gain is Sec. 1245 ordinary income. For buildings A and C, the $400,000 gain is Sec. 1231 gain and is unrecaptured Sec. 1250 gain because the gain is due to depreciation. ◀

EXAMPLE I:13-34 ▶ Assume the same facts as in Example I:13-33 except the selling price is $570,000. For building B, Ford must recognize $500,000 of Sec. 1245 ordinary income and $70,000 of Sec. 1231 gain taxed at 15% or 20%. For buildings A and C, the $570,000 gain is Sec. 1231 gain with $500,000 taxed at 25% and $70,000 taxed at 15% or 20%. ◀

Depreciable Real Property Placed in Service After 1986. The straight-line method of depreciation is the only method of depreciation allowed for buildings placed in service after 1986, and thus noncorporate taxpayers will not have any Sec. 1250 ordinary income when they sell or exchange buildings placed in service after 1986. Gain due to depreciation is unrecaptured Sec. 1250 gain subject to a maximum tax rate of 25%.

The tax treatment for residential rental property and other real property placed in service after 1986 is the same, but taxpayers may depreciate residential rental property over 27.5 years and other real property placed in service after May 12, 1993, over 39 years.

EXAMPLE I:13-35 ▶ Stella purchased an apartment complex on October 10, 2008, for $275,000 (exclusive of land) while Mack purchased an office building for $275,000 on the same day. Stella and Mack sell the

▼ **TABLE I:13-1**

CHARACTER OF GAIN ON SALE OR EXCHANGE OF DEPRECIABLE REAL PROPERTY FOR NONCORPORATE TAXPAYERS

	Sec. 1245 Ordinary	Sec. 1250 Ordinary	Sec. 1231	Unrecaptured Sec. 1250 (Maximum rate of 25%)
RESIDENTIAL RENTAL				
Placed in Service Before 1981				
Use straight-line depreciation	No	No	Yes	Yes
Use accelerated depreciation	No	Yes*	Yes**	Yes
Placed in Service After 1980 & Before 1987				
Use straight-line depreciation	No	No	Yes	Yes
Use accelerated depreciation	No	Yes*	Yes**	Yes
Placed in Service After 1986				
Use straight-line depreciation	No	No	Yes	Yes
NONRESIDENTIAL				
Placed in Service Before 1981				
Use straight-line depreciation	No	No	Yes	Yes
Use accelerated depreciation	No	Yes*	Yes**	Yes
Placed in Service After 1980 & Before 1987				
Use straight-line depreciation	No	No	Yes	Yes
Use accelerated depreciation	Yes	No	Yes***	No
Placed in Service After 1986				
Use straight-line depreciation	No	No	Yes	Yes

* Portion of gain due to excess depreciation
** To extent gain is greater than excess depreciation
*** To extent gain is greater than total depreciation

buildings on April 22, 2015, for $250,000. At the date of sale, Stella's adjusted basis in the apartment complex is $210,005 based on a 27.5 year recovery period and Mack's adjusted basis in the office building is $229,166 based on a 39 year recovery period. Stella has a Sec. 1231 gain of $39,995 [$250,000 − $210,005 adjusted basis], and all of the gain is unrecaptured Sec. 1250 gain. Mack has a Sec. 1231 gain of $20,834 [$250,000 − $229,166 adjusted basis], and all of the gain is unrecaptured Sec. 1250 gain. ◀

LOW-INCOME HOUSING

Congress has provided incentives for the construction and rehabilitation of low-income housing. For tax years after 1986, a low-income housing credit is available to owners of qualified low-income housing projects.[33]

If the low-income housing unit is held for 16 years and 8 months, none of the additional depreciation is subject to recapture as ordinary income.[34] Thus noncorporate taxpayers will not have any Sec. 1250 ordinary income if the low-income housing is sold after 2002.

The Sec. 1250 recapture rules for noncorporate taxpayers are summarized in Topic Review I:13-2.

---

[33] Sec. 42.

[34] Secs. 1250(a)(1)(B)(i), (ii), (iii), and (iv).

TOPIC REVIEW I:13-2

Section 1250 Recapture for Noncorporate Taxpayers

▶ Section 1250 affects the character of the gain, not the amount of gain.

▶ Section 1250 does not apply to assets sold or exchanged at a loss.

▶ Section 1250 ordinary income is never more than the realized gain.

▶ Section 1250 ordinary income is never more than the *additional* (excess) depreciation allowed. (Note, that this statement is not true for corporate taxpayers.)

▶ Section 1250 property includes depreciable real property unless the real property is nonresidential real estate placed in service in 1980 and before 1987 under the ACRS rules and the straight-line method is not elected.

▶ Section 1250 ordinary income does not exist if the straight-line method of depreciation is used. (This statement is not true for corporate taxpayers because of the additional recapture requirements under Sec. 291.)

ADDITIONAL RECAPTURE FOR CORPORATIONS

OBJECTIVE 6

Understand recapture provisions for corporations

Corporations are subject to additional recapture rules under Sec. 291 if depreciable real estate is sold or otherwise disposed of. This recapture is in addition to the normal recapture rules under Sec. 1250. The additional ordinary income that is recaptured effectively reduces the amount of the Sec. 1231 gain.

The additional recapture amount under Sec. 291 is equal to 20% of the difference between the amount that would be recaptured if the property was Sec. 1245 property and actual recapture amount under Sec. 1250.[35]

KEY POINT

Section 291 has no effect on Sec. 1245 property because gain is already recaptured to the extent of all depreciation.

ADDITIONAL COMMENT

Corporations are subject to an additional 20% depreciation recapture rule under Sec. 291 on sales of Sec. 1250 property.

EXAMPLE I:13-36 ▶

In 1980, Orlando Corporation purchased an office building for $500,000* for use in its business. The building is sold during the current year for $480,000. Pertinent details relating to depreciation of the building and realized gain on the sale are below:

▶ Total depreciation allowed for the building is $420,000.

▶ If straight-line depreciation had been used, depreciation allowed would have been $360,000.

▶ Building's adjusted basis is $80,000 ($500,000 − $420,000).

▶ Realized and recognized gain is $400,000 ($480,000 − $80,000).

To determine the character of the $400,000 gain, the following analysis must be made:

▶ Excess depreciation is $60,000 ($420,000 − $360,000). Gain to the extent of excess depreciation is recaptured as Sec. 1250 ordinary income.

▶ Section 291 depreciation recapture applies because the taxpayer is a corporation. If the property was Sec. 1245 property, $400,000 of the gain would be ordinary income.

▶ Because of Sec. 291, Orlando has more Sec. 1250 ordinary income: $68,000 [0.20 × ($400,000 − $60,000)].

In summary, $128,000 of the total recognized gain of $400,000 is recaptured as ordinary income ($60,000 + $68,000) and the remaining $272,000 ($400,000 − $128,000) is Sec. 1231 gain. ◀

*does not consider the cost of land

SELF-STUDY QUESTION

If the taxpayer in Example I:13-36 is a noncorporate taxpayer, how much of the gain is Sec. 1250 ordinary income?

ANSWER

$60,000

EXAMPLE I:13-37 ▶

Pacific Corporation purchased an office building in 1981 for $800,000* for use in its trade or business. The building is sold during the current year for $850,000. Pacific elected to use the straight-line method of cost recovery and $800,000 cost-recovery deductions have been allowed. The realized gain is $850,000 ($850,000 − 0). None of the gain is ordinary income under Sec. 1250 if Sec. 291 is not considered. If the building were instead Sec. 1245 recovery property, $800,000 of the gain would be treated as ordinary income.

---

[35] Sec. 291(a)(1).

The amount of Sec. 1250 ordinary income under Sec. 291 for a corporate taxpayer is $160,000 [0.20 × ($800,000 − $0)]. The remaining $690,000 ($850,000 − $160,000) gain is Sec. 1231 gain.   ◀

*does not consider the cost of land

For corporations, none of the Sec. 1231 gain is unrecaptured Sec. 1250 gain.

SUMMARY OF SECS. 1231, 1245, AND 1250 GAINS

Section 1231 property is depreciable property and nondepreciable real property used in one's trade or business and held for more than one year. Net Sec. 1231 gain, the excess of Sec. 1231 gain over Sec. 1231 loss, is LTCG unless the five-year lookback rule applies in which case the gain is ordinary to the extent of the nonrecaptured net Sec. 1231 loss. Net Sec. 1231 loss, the excess of Sec. 1231 loss over Sec. 1231 gain, is ordinary.

Section 1245 applies to depreciable personal property and amortizable intangible assets. It also applies to certain nonresidential real property placed in service during ACRS (after 1980 and before 1987) if accelerated cost recovery is used. Gain to the extent of depreciation is ordinary income. All of the gain resulting from the sale of Sec. 1245 property is ordinary income unless the asset is sold for more than its original basis.

Section 1250 property is depreciable real property, and gain is ordinary income to the extent of excess depreciation, the excess of accelerated depreciation over straight-line. After 1986, the straight-line method must be used for real property and thus noncorporate taxpayers will not have any Sec. 1250 ordinary income on the sale of depreciable real property placed in service after 1986. Unfortunately, Congress made the sale and exchange of buildings more complicated in 1997 when it created the concept of unrecaptured Sec. 1250 gain that is taxed at 25%. When a noncorporate taxpayer sells depreciated buildings at a gain, any gain to the extent of straight-line depreciation is Sec. 1231 gain but is taxed at a rate no higher than 25% because it is unrecaptured Sec. 1250 gain.

To further illustrate Sec. 1231, 1245, and 1250, refer to Topic Review I:13-3 where a noncorporate taxpayer with a 35% tax rate sells various assets during the current year. Each asset was purchased in 1997 and the selling price is $450,000 for each of the first three assets. All assets are used in a trade or business. There are no other gains and losses and no nonrecaptured net Sec. 1231 losses.

TOPIC REVIEW I:13-3

Sections 1231, 1245, and 1250—Comparison of Various Assets

The taxpayer is a noncorporate taxpayer with a 35% tax rate who sells each of the first three assets for $450,000. Each asset was purchased in 1997 and is used in a trade or business. The difference between the original basis and the adjusted basis of the equipment and building is attributable to depreciation. There are no other gains and losses and no nonrecaptured net Sec. 1231 losses, thus the Sec. 1231 gain becomes LTCG.

	ORIGINAL BASIS	ADJUSTED BASIS	TAX TREATMENT
1. Land	$400,000	$400,000	$50,000 Sec. 1231 gain taxed at 15%.*
2. Equipment	600,000	400,000	$50,000 Sec. 1245 ordinary income taxed at 35%. All gain is due to depreciation.
3. Building	500,000	400,000	$50,000 Sec. 1231 gain which is unrecaptured Sec. 1250 gain taxed at 25%.

For assets 4, 5, & 6, assume the selling price is $700,000.

	ORIGINAL BASIS	ADJUSTED BASIS	TAX TREATMENT
4. Land	$400,000	$400,000	$300,000 Sec. 1231 gain taxed at 15%.*
5. Equipment	600,000	400,000	$200,000 Sec. 1245 ordinary income taxed at 35% and $100,000 Sec. 1231 gain taxed at 15%.*
6. Building	500,000	400,000	$300,000 Sec. 1231 gain with $100,000 of unrecaptured Sec. 1250 gain taxed at 25% and $200,000 taxed at 15%.*

* 20% if unmarried with taxable income above $413,200 or married with taxable income above $464,850.

RECAPTURE PROVISIONS—OTHER APPLICATIONS

Describe other recapture applications

Sections 1245 and 1250 recapture provisions take precedence over other provisions of the tax law.[36] Unless an exception or limitation is specifically stated in Secs. 1245 or 1250, gain is recognized under Secs. 1245 or 1250 despite the existence of provisions elsewhere in the IRC that allow nonrecognition of gain.[37]

GIFTS OF PROPERTY SUBJECT TO RECAPTURE

A gift of appreciated depreciable property does not result in the recapture of depreciation or cost-recovery deductions under Secs. 1245 or 1250.[38] The donee must consider the recapture potential when disposing of the property. The recapture amount for the donee is computed by including the recaptured amount attributable to the donor.[39]

EXAMPLE I:13-38 ▶

Ashley makes a gift of equipment with an $8,200 FMV to Helmut. Ashley paid $10,000 for the equipment and deducted $4,000 of depreciation before making the gift. Ashley does not have to recapture any depreciation when making the gift. Helmut's basis for the equipment is $6,000 and the potential depreciation recapture carries over to Helmut. ◀

EXAMPLE I:13-39 ▶

ADDITIONAL COMMENT

If the taxpayer in Topic Review I:13-3 is a corporation, the character of the gain is the same for assets 1, 2, 4, and 5. For asset 3, $10,000 of the gain is Sec. 1250 ordinary income because of Sec. 291 and $40,000 is Sec. 1231 gain. For asset 6, $20,000 is Sec. 1250 ordinary income because of Sec. 291 and $280,000 is Sec. 1231 gain.

Assume the same facts as in Example I:13-38 except that Helmut uses the equipment in a trade or business, deducts $1,500 of depreciation, and sells the equipment for $7,100. When determining the amount of depreciation subject to recapture, Helmut must also consider the depreciation allowed to Ashley. The entire $2,600 [$7,100 − ($6,000 − $1,500)] gain is recaptured as ordinary income because it is less than the $5,500 ($4,000 + $1,500) of depreciation claimed. ◀

TRANSFER OF PROPERTY SUBJECT TO RECAPTURE AT DEATH

The transfer of appreciated property at death does not cause a recapture of depreciation deductions to the decedent's estate under Secs. 1245 and 1250.[40] In addition, recapture potential does not carry over to the person who receives the property from the decedent.

EXAMPLE I:13-40 ▶

KEY POINT

Death is one of the few ways to avoid the recapture provisions.

Jackie dies while owning a building with a $900,000 FMV. The building is Sec. 1245 property acquired in 1985 for $800,000* on which cost-recovery deductions of $800,000 have been claimed. Pam inherits the building from Jackie. Pam's basis for the building is $900,000, and the $800,000 of cost-recovery deductions are not recaptured. If Pam immediately sells the building, there is no depreciation recapture attributable to the $800,000 of cost-recovery deductions taken by the decedent. ◀

*does not include cost of land

CHARITABLE CONTRIBUTIONS

As discussed in Chapter I:7, the deduction for a charitable contribution of appreciated ordinary income property is generally limited to its adjusted basis (i.e., the amount of the contribution deduction is equal to the FMV of the property less the amount of gain that would not have been LTCG [or Sec. 1231 gain] if the contributed property had been sold by the taxpayer at its FMV).[41] Thus, the contribution deduction for recapture property is reduced to reflect the ordinary income that would be recognized if the property were sold rather than contributed to the charity.

EXAMPLE I:13-41 ▶

Ralph makes a gift of an organ to a church. The organ is used in Ralph's trade or business and has a $6,300 FMV. Ralph paid $10,000 for the organ, and $8,000 depreciation has been claimed. If the organ were sold for its $6,300 FMV, the realized and recognized gain would be $4,300 ($6,300 − $2,000) and all of the gain would be ordinary income due to the recapture of depreciation under Sec. 1245. The charitable contribution deduction is limited to $2,000 ($6,300 − $4,300), because none of the $4,300 gain would be taxed as a LTCG if the organ were sold. ◀

---

[36] Secs. 1245(d) and 1250(i).
[37] Reg. Secs. 1.1245-6(a) and 1.1250-1(c)(1).
[38] Secs. 1245(b)(1) and 1250(d)(1).

[39] Reg. Secs. 1.1245-2(a)(4) and 1.1250-2(d).
[40] Secs. 1245(b)(2) and 1250(d)(2).
[41] Sec. 170(e)(1)(A).

LIKE-KIND EXCHANGES

A taxpayer who receives boot (i.e., non–like-kind property) in a transaction that otherwise qualifies as a like-kind exchange recognizes gain equal to the lesser of the realized gain or the amount of boot received. If the property is Sec. 1245 or 1250 property, the gain is first considered to be ordinary income up to the maximum amount of the gain that is subject to the recapture provisions.

EXAMPLE I:13-42 ▶

The Krider Corporation owns a purebred bull used in its trade or business that cost $300,000 two years ago. During the current year, the bull is exchanged when its adjusted basis is $115,000 for another bull with an FMV of $187,000 and $200,000 of cash. Gain realized on the exchange is $272,000 [($187,000 + $200,000) − $115,000], and gain recognized is the lesser of the $200,000 boot received or the $272,000 gain realized. Because the $200,000 recognized gain is greater than depreciation allowed of $185,000, $185,000 is Sec. 1245 ordinary income and $15,000 is Sec. 1231 gain. ◀

If gain is not recognized in a like-kind exchange, the recapture potential carries over to the replacement property (i.e., any recapture potential associated with the property exchanged attaches to the property received in the exchange).[42]

EXAMPLE I:13-43 ▶

Melissa owns a Chevrolet pickup truck used in her trade or business that cost $10,000 and has a $6,000 adjusted basis due to $4,000 in depreciation deductions she has claimed. The truck is exchanged for a Ford pickup truck with a $9,000 FMV. The Ford truck is used in Melissa's business. Melissa does not recognize any portion of the $3,000 realized gain because the exchange qualifies as a like-kind exchange and no boot is received. Her basis for the Ford truck is $6,000 (i.e., a substituted basis).

After deducting $2,000 of depreciation, Melissa sells the Ford truck for $7,300. All of the recognized gain of $3,300 ($7,300 − $4,000) is ordinary income. The depreciation recapture amount under Sec. 1245 is equal to the total $6,000 in depreciation (including $4,000 on the Chevrolet pickup truck) but the recognized gain is only $3,300.[43] ◀

INVOLUNTARY CONVERSIONS

If an involuntary conversion of Sec. 1245 property occurs and all or a portion of the gain is not recognized,[44] the amount of gain considered to be Sec. 1245 ordinary income is limited and cannot be more than the recognized gain.[45] A similar provision exists for the involuntary conversion of Sec. 1250 property.[46]

EXAMPLE I:13-44 ▶

The Ryan Corporation's printing equipment with original cost of $600,000 and adjusted basis of $200,000 is destroyed by fire. Ryan, Inc. receives $550,000 of insurance proceeds and purchases $510,000 of printing equipment. If the corporation elects to defer gain, it must recognize a $40,000 gain which is Sec. 1245 ordinary income. The basis of the printing equipment acquired is $200,000. ◀

INSTALLMENT SALES

As discussed in Chapter I:11, gain resulting from an installment sale is generally recognized as payments are received. Thus, the gain may be spread over more than one accounting period. An installment sale of depreciable property may result in all of the recaptured gain being taxed in the year of the sale.[47] Recapture income is "the aggregate amount which would be treated as ordinary income under Sec. 1245 or 1250 for the taxable year of the disposition if all payments to be received were received in the taxable year of disposition."[48] Recapture income must be recognized in the year of sale, even if no payments are received.

---

[42] Reg. Sec. 1.1245-2(c)(4).
[43] Reg. Sec. 1.1245-2(a)(4).
[44] As discussed in Chapter I:12, one may elect to defer recognition of the gain if the Sec. 1033 requirements are satisfied.

[45] Sec. 1245(b)(4) and Reg. Sec. 1.1245-4(d)(1).
[46] Sec. 1250(d)(4) and Reg. Sec. 1.1250-3(d).
[47] Sec. 453(i)(1).
[48] Sec. 453(i)(2).

Pat owns equipment with a $100,000 acquisition cost and a $42,000 adjusted basis. During the current year, Pat sells the property for $30,000 cash and a $60,000 interest-bearing note to be paid over a ten-year period. The realized gain is $48,000 ($90,000 − $42,000), and the recapture income amount is $48,000 (the lesser of total depreciation deductions of $58,000 or the $48,000 realized gain). The $48,000 gain is all recognized as ordinary income in the current year, despite the fact that the transaction qualifies as an installment sale and only $30,000 of cash is received in the year of sale. ◀

If gain realized from the installment sale exceeds the recapture income, the excess gain is reported under the installment method.[49] The amount of recapture income recognized is added to the adjusted basis to determine the gross profit ratio.

Bob owns an office building acquired for $700,000* in 1986 and subject to the Sec. 1245 recapture rules. After claiming $700,000 of cost recovery deductions, Bob sells the building to Janet in 2015 for $1 million. Bob receives $200,000 in cash and an $800,000 interest-bearing note. The note is to be paid with annual principal payments of $100,000 and interest on the unpaid balance beginning in 2016. The total amount of realized gain is $1 million ($1,000,000 − 0). In 2015, Bob recognizes $700,000 of Sec. 1245 ordinary income. The gross profit ratio is determined by adding $700,000 recapture income to the $0 basis. The gross profit ratio is 30% [($1,000,000 − $700,000) ÷ $1,000,000]. In addition to recognizing $700,000 of ordinary income, Bob recognizes $60,000 (0.30 × $200,000) Sec. 1231 gain in 2015 because a $200,000 cash down payment was received in the year of the sale. In 2016 and in each subsequent year, $30,000 (0.30 × $100,000) of Sec. 1231 gain is recognized as the cash payments on the principal are received. ◀

*does not include cost of land

SECTION 179 EXPENSING ELECTION

In lieu of capitalizing the cost of new or used tangible personal business property, taxpayers may elect to expense up to $25,000 of the acquisition cost in 2015.[50] (see Chapter I:10). If the property is subsequently converted to nonbusiness use, previous tax benefits derived from the immediate expensing election must be recaptured and added to the taxpayer's gross income in the year of the conversion.[51] The recaptured amount equals the difference between the amount expensed under Sec. 179 and the total depreciation that would otherwise have been claimed for the period of business use.

Behren purchased business equipment (a five-year recovery period) in 2014 for $18,100 and elected to expense the entire amount under Sec. 179. In 2015, he converts the equipment to nonbusiness use. Depreciation of $3,620 (0.20 × $18,100) under the MACRS rules would have been allowed during the period the equipment was held for business use if Behren had not elected to expense the $18,100 cost. Behren must recognize $14,480 ($18,100 − $3,620) of Sec. 1245 ordinary income in 2015. ◀

CONSERVATION AND LAND CLEARING EXPENDITURES

Taxpayers engaged in the business of farming may deduct expenditures paid or incurred during the taxable year for soil and water conservation or the prevention of erosion. The expenditures must be made with respect to land used in farming and would be capital expenditures except for this provision.[52]

The deductions for conservation expenditures may be partially or fully recaptured as ordinary income if the farmland is disposed of before the land is held for more than nine years.[53] The amount of deductions recaptured as ordinary income under Sec. 1252 is a percentage of the aggregate deductions allowed for conservation expenditures. The amount of ordinary income recognized under Sec. 1252 is limited to the lesser of the taxpayer's realized gain or the applicable recapture percentage times the total conservation expenditures.

---

[49] Sec. 453(i)(1)(B).0.
[50] Secs. 179(a) and (b)(1). In 2015, the maximum Sec. 179 deduction is $25,000 with a dollar for dollar reduction when the cost of qualifying property placed in service exceeds $200,000. In recent years, Congress has changed the law to allow for a larger deduction ($500,000 in 2014).

[51] Sec. 179(d)(10) and Reg. Sec. 1.179-1(e).
[52] Sec. 175(a).
[53] Sec. 1252(a)(1).

WHAT WOULD YOU DO IN THIS SITUATION?

You recently graduated with an advanced degree in taxation and have accepted a job with a CPA firm in the tax department. One of the firm's clients, a wealthy individual, was in need of cash and decided to sell some assets to raise the cash. The client asked the firm to advise him, from a tax standpoint, which assets he should sell. The client is in the 35% tax bracket. You suggested in a written memo that the client sell one of the client's jet airplanes. The plane you recommended to be sold had originally cost $16 million and now had an adjusted basis of $5 million. A buyer had offered to buy the plane for $12 million on the installment basis, paying $4 million per year for three years plus interest at 9%. The principal reason for selling that particular plane is that it would raise $12 million over three years, but the tax could be spread over three years by using the installment sale method. The client took your advice and sold the plane in the current year.

Later, when preparing the client's tax return, you realize that gain due to depreciation of the airplane must be recognized in the year of sale, even if the property is sold under the installment sale method. Thus, *all* of the gain on the sale of the plane must be recognized in the year of sale, not spread over three years. You go to your manager and tell him about your major mistake. Your manager, who reviewed your original memo, indicates that he thinks that the two of you should not tell anyone about the mistake as it will negatively impact both of your careers. The manager thinks that because the client has such a large amount of income, reporting the entire gain on the sale of the plane on the client's return might not be detected by the client. Thus, the manager instructs you to prepare the current year return with the entire $7 million of gain and not tell anyone about the mistake. What should you do in this situation?

KEY POINT
There is no recapture of conservation costs if the farmland is held for at least 10 years.

The recapture percentage is 100% if the farmland is disposed of within five years after the date it is acquired. The percentage declines by 20 percentage points for each additional year the property is held. If the land is disposed of after being held for more than nine years, none of the expenses are recaptured.[54]

EXAMPLE I:13-48 ▶

Paula owns farmland with a $400,000 basis. She has deducted $50,000 for soil and water conservation expenditures. After farming the land for six years and five months, Paula sells the land for $520,000. The realized gain is $120,000 ($520,000 − $400,000) and the recapture percentage is 60%, because the farmland is disposed of within the seventh year after it was acquired. The amount of ordinary income due to recapture under Sec. 1252 is $30,000, the lesser of the $120,000 realized gain or the $30,000 (0.60 × $50,000) recapture amount. ◀

ADDITIONAL COMMENT
Intangible drilling and development costs represent the major cost of operations and can provide investors with working interests in oil and gas properties with a first-year write-off of substantially all of their investment.

INTANGIBLE DRILLING COSTS AND DEPLETION

Taxpayers may elect to either expense or capitalize intangible drilling and development costs (IDC).[55] If the election to expense is not made, the costs are capitalized and recovered through additional depletion deductions. Intangible drilling and development costs include "all expenditures made by an operator for wages, fuel, repairs, hauling, supplies, etc., incident to and necessary for the drilling of wells and the preparation of wells for the production of oil or gas."[56]

Part or all of the gain from the sale of oil and gas properties may be recaptured as ordinary income due to the recapture of the IDC deduction and the deduction for depletion. However, the amount of ordinary income recognized from the recapture of IDC and depletion is limited to the gain realized from disposition of the property.[57]

EXAMPLE I:13-49 ▶

In 2008, Marty purchased undeveloped property to drill for oil and gas. Intangible drilling and development costs of $400,000 were paid in 2008, and Marty elected to expense the IDC. During the current year, Marty sells the property and realizes a $900,000 gain. $300,000 of cost depletion was also allowed. Marty must recognize $700,000 of ordinary income because of the recapture of IDC ($400,000) and the recapture of depletion ($300,000). The remaining $200,000 ($900,000 − $700,000) gain is Sec. 1231 gain. ◀

---

[54] Sec. 1252(a)(3).
[55] Sec. 263(c).
[56] Reg. Sec. 1.612-4(a).
[57] Sec. 1254(a)(1).

In 2007, Tina acquired oil and gas properties for $700,000 and paid $200,000 for intangible drilling costs. During 2007, she elected to expense the $200,000 of IDC. Total depletion allowed was $80,000. During the current year, Tina sells the property for $840,000 and realizes a $220,000 [$840,000 − ($700,000 − $80,000)] gain. The amount of ordinary income due to recapture is $220,000, because both IDC and depletion must be recaptured only to the extent of the gain. ◄

GAIN ON SALE OF DEPRECIABLE PROPERTY BETWEEN RELATED PARTIES

All gain recognized on the sale or exchange of property between related parties is ordinary income if the property is subject to depreciation in the hands of the transferee (i.e., the person who purchases the property). The sale or exchange may be direct or indirect.[58]

Phil owns a building with a $500,000 adjusted basis and $800,000 FMV. The building, which cost $700,000, is used in his business, and the straight-line method of depreciation is used. $200,000 of depreciation deductions were allowed. If the building is sold to Phil's 100%-owned corporation for $800,000, the $300,000 realized gain ($800,000 − $500,000) is treated as ordinary income under Sec. 1239, because the property is subject to depreciation in the hands of the transferee and the corporation and Phil are related parties. ◄

A sale or exchange of property could be subject to depreciation recapture under Sec. 1245 or 1250 as well as the Sec. 1239 related party rules. If so, recapture under Sec. 1245 or 1250 is considered before recapture under Sec. 1239.[59]

Assume the same facts as in Example I:13-51 except that Phil sells equipment to the corporation instead of a building. All of the $300,000 realized gain is treated as ordinary income. The recapture amount under Sec. 1245 is $200,000, and Sec. 1239 applies to the remaining $100,000 gain. ◄

Purpose of Sec. 1239. Without Sec. 1239, a taxpayer could transfer appreciated depreciable property to a related party and recognize a Sec. 1231 gain on the sale. Net Sec. 1231 gain is treated as LTCG. The related purchaser of the property would receive a step up in the depreciable basis of the property to its FMV and be able to claim a larger amount of depreciation. In Example I:13-51, Phil might prefer to recognize a $300,000 Sec. 1231 gain if the 100%-owned corporation was able to obtain a step-up in the property's basis to $800,000. Because Sec. 1239 applies, Phil must recognize $300,000 of ordinary income rather than Sec. 1231 gain. This rule prevents an individual taxpayer from receiving favorable Sec. 1231 gain treatment and prevents all taxpayers having large capital loss carryovers from using a related party to recognize a Sec. 1231 or capital gain which can be offset against their capital losses.

Related Parties. A person is related (1) to any corporation if the individual owns (directly or indirectly) more than 50% of the value of the outstanding stock and (2) to any partnership in which the person has a capital or profits interest of more than 50%.[60] Constructive ownership rules apply when determining whether the person owns more than 50% of the corporation or has more than a 50% interest in the partnership. Thus, an individual is considered to own stock owned by other family members and related entities (e.g., corporations, partnerships, estates, and trusts).

Tony sells a truck used for nonbusiness purposes to the Able Corporation for $15,000 when its original cost basis is $12,000. Tony owns 30% of Able and his spouse owns 40% of Able. Tony and Able are related parties because Tony is deemed to own 70% of Able under the constructive ownership rules and $3,000 of ordinary income must be recognized under Sec. 1239. ◄

A person is related to any trust in which such a person or the person's spouse is a beneficiary.[61] Section 1239 also applies to a sale or exchange of depreciable property between two corporations if the same individual owns more than 50% of each corporation.[62]

---

[58] Sec. 1239(a).
[59] Reg. Sec. 1.1245-6(f).
[60] Sec. 1239(c).

[61] Sec. 1239(b)(2).
[62] Rev. Rul. 79-157, 1979-1 C.B. 281.

TAX PLANNING CONSIDERATIONS

<table>
<tr><td>

OBJECTIVE 8

Describe tax planning considerations for Sec. 1231 assets

</td><td>

For noncorporate taxpayers, net Sec. 1231 gains are generally preferable to ordinary gains because of the possible lower tax rate applicable to net capital gains. The tax rate could be zero, 15%, 20%, or 25%. For corporate taxpayers, however, after 1986 it usually does not make any difference whether a gain is classified as Sec. 1231 or ordinary unless the corporation has capital losses. Corporations do not have preferential tax rates on net capital gains.

</td></tr>
</table>

EXAMPLE I:13-54 ▶ Western Corporation has taxable income of $550,000 without considering the sale of equipment for $400,000 during the current year. The equipment originally cost $500,000 and has a $350,000 adjusted basis after deducting depreciation. The corporation has no other gains and losses during the year or any capital loss carryovers from previous years. For Western Corporation, it does not make any difference whether the gain is Sec. 1245 ordinary income or Sec. 1231 gain. The effect on the corporation's taxable income and tax liability is the same regardless of whether the gain is classified as capital or ordinary. ◀

The avoidance of the recapture provisions is important to both corporate and noncorporate taxpayers if capital loss carryovers exist. For example, if Western Corporation has a capital loss carryforward of $40,000 in Example I:13-54, the corporation's taxable income is increased by $10,000 ($50,000 − $40,000) if the $50,000 gain is Sec. 1231 gain. However, because the gain is Sec. 1245 ordinary income, the corporation's taxable income is increased by $50,000. The $40,000 capital loss carryforward is deductible only if Western has capital gain or net Sec. 1231 gain which becomes capital gain.

AVOIDING THE RECAPTURE PROVISIONS

In view of the pervasiveness of the recapture provisions discussed in this chapter, recapture is difficult to avoid. In some cases, recapture can be avoided by holding the property a specific length of time before disposing of it (e.g., the recapture of conservation and land clearing expenses can be avoided by holding the farmland for more than nine years).[63] Contributing appreciated property to a qualified charitable organization cannot be used to circumvent the recapture provisions because in such case the amount of the charitable contribution is reduced by the amount of the gain that would not be a LTCG if the property were sold by the taxpayer.[64]

Although it is often difficult to avoid the recapture provisions, taxpayers may dispose of the property and defer recapture if the disposition is a nontaxable exchange. In a like-kind exchange where no boot is received, the recapture potential is carried over to the property received in the exchange.

Proper timing of the asset's disposition may be advantageous. Disposition may be delayed until the taxpayer's tax rate is low or the property can be sold in the same year that the taxpayer has an NOL that is about to expire.

Taxpayers can shift the recapture potential to other taxpayers by making a gift of property subject to recapture. The recapture potential remains with the property and must be considered when the donee disposes of the property.

Transfer Property at Death. One way to avoid the recapture provisions is to transfer the property at death. No recapture occurs at the time of the transfer, and the basis of property received from a decedent is generally the FMV of the property at the date of the decedent's death.[65] The property's recapture potential does not carry over to the beneficiary as in the case of a gift made to a donee.

---

[63] Sec. 1252(a)(1).
[64] Sec. 170(e)(1)(A).

[65] Sec. 1014(a). For property inherited in 2010, it is possible that carryover basis rules might be used.

COMPLIANCE AND PROCEDURAL CONSIDERATIONS

Form 4797, Supplemental Schedule of Gains and Losses, is used to report gains and losses from sales or exchanges of assets used in a trade or business (see Figures I:13-1 through I:13-3). The form is also used to report gains or losses resulting from involuntary conversions, other than casualties or thefts, of property used in the trade or business and capital assets held more than a year. If gains or losses due to casualties or thefts of property used in a trade or business or property held to produce income are recognized, they are reported on Form 4684, Casualties and Thefts (see Figure I:13-3). If such casualties or thefts occur, Form 4684 is prepared either before or at the same time as Form 4797.

REPORTING SEC. 1231 GAINS AND LOSSES ON FORM 4797

Part I of Form 4797, which is reproduced in Figure I:13-1, is used to report gains and losses resulting from

▶ The sale or exchange of Sec. 1231 property

▶ An involuntary conversion, other than a casualty or theft, of Sec. 1231 property

▶ An involuntary conversion, other than a casualty or theft, of capital assets held more than one year and used to produce income.

As indicated on lines 3 through 6 in Part I of Form 4797, gains and losses recorded on other forms and in Part III of Form 4797 are reported in Part I. The netting of Sec. 1231 gains and losses occurs in Part I of Form 4797. All gains and losses are recorded in column (g). If line 7(g) has a loss, Sec. 1231 losses exceed Sec. 1231 gains and the net loss is reported on line 11 as ordinary loss. If there is no nonrecaptured net section 1231 losses, all gain reported on line 7(g) is transferred to Schedule D. If the taxpayer does have nonrecaptured net Sec. 1231 losses, that amount is reported on line 8. Gains reported on line 7(g) will be recharacterized as ordinary income to the extent of the nonrecaptured net Sec. 1231 losses and reported as ordinary income on line 12.

Ordinary gains and losses recognized including those recorded on other forms and in Parts I and III of Form 4797 are reported on lines 11 through 17 in Part II of Form 4797.

REPORTING GAINS RECAPTURED AS ORDINARY INCOME ON FORM 4797

Part III of Form 4797 for 2014, reproduced in Figure I:13-2, is completed before Parts I and II to determine and report ordinary income due to the recapture provisions of Secs. 1245, 1250, 1252, 1254, and 1255. To illustrate the use of Part III, assume an individual sells equipment (7-year recovery) used in a trade or business for $60,000 on April 30, 2014. The equipment cost $58,000 on March 10, 2012, and depreciation deductions through the date of sale of $27,565 were allowed. The $29,565 ($60,000 − $30,435) total gain is reported on line 24. On line 30, total gains resulting from the sale of all properties ($29,565 in this illustration) reported in Part III are combined. The total amount of ordinary income due to the recapture provisions ($27,565 in this illustration) is reported on line 31 and then reported as ordinary income on line 13 in Part II. The excess of the gain over the amount of ordinary income is reported on line 32. The portion of this gain not due to casualty or theft ($2,000 in this illustration) is a Sec. 1231 gain and is reported on line 6 of Part I of Form 4797. If any of the gain is due to casualty or theft, that portion of the gain is reported on Section B of Form 4684.

REPORTING CASUALTY OR THEFT GAIN OR LOSS ON FORM 4684

Section A of Form 4684 is used to report gains and losses resulting from a casualty or theft of personal-use property. These gains and losses are not Sec. 1231 transactions, and Sec. A of Form 4684 is not discussed in this chapter.

Section B of Form 4684, reproduced in Figure I:13-3, is used to report gains and losses resulting from a casualty or theft of property used in a trade or business or held for the

Form **4797**	**Sales of Business Property**	OMB No. 1545-0184
	(Also Involuntary Conversions and Recapture Amounts Under Sections 179 and 280F(b)(2))	20**14**
Department of the Treasury Internal Revenue Service	► **Attach to your tax return.** ► **Information about Form 4797 and its separate instructions is at** *www.irs.gov/form4797.*	Attachment Sequence No. **27**

Name(s) shown on return	Identifying number

1 Enter the gross proceeds from sales or exchanges reported to you for 2014 on Form(s) 1099-B or 1099-S (or substitute statement) that you are including on line 2, 10, or 20 (see instructions) **1**

Part I   **Sales or Exchanges of Property Used in a Trade or Business and Involuntary Conversions From Other Than Casualty or Theft—Most Property Held More Than 1 Year** (see instructions)

2	**(a)** Description of property	**(b)** Date acquired (mo., day, yr.)	**(c)** Date sold (mo., day, yr.)	**(d)** Gross sales price	**(e)** Depreciation allowed or allowable since acquisition	**(f)** Cost or other basis, plus improvements and expense of sale	**(g) Gain or (loss)** Subtract (f) from the sum of (d) and (e)

3	Gain, if any, from Form 4684, line 39	**3**	
4	Section 1231 gain from installment sales from Form 6252, line 26 or 37	**4**	
5	Section 1231 gain or (loss) from like-kind exchanges from Form 8824	**5**	
6	Gain, if any, from line 32, from other than casualty or theft	**6**	2,000
7	Combine lines 2 through 6. Enter the gain or (loss) here and on the appropriate line as follows: . . .	**7**	2,000

Partnerships (except electing large partnerships) and S corporations. Report the gain or (loss) following the instructions for Form 1065, Schedule K, line 10, or Form 1120S, Schedule K, line 9. Skip lines 8, 9, 11, and 12 below.

Individuals, partners, S corporation shareholders, and all others. If line 7 is zero or a loss, enter the amount from line 7 on line 11 below and skip lines 8 and 9. If line 7 is a gain and you did not have any prior year section 1231 losses, or they were recaptured in an earlier year, enter the gain from line 7 as a long-term capital gain on the Schedule D filed with your return and skip lines 8, 9, 11, and 12 below.

8	Nonrecaptured net section 1231 losses from prior years (see instructions)	**8**	
9	Subtract line 8 from line 7. If zero or less, enter -0-. If line 9 is zero, enter the gain from line 7 on line 12 below. If line 9 is more than zero, enter the amount from line 8 on line 12 below and enter the gain from line 9 as a long-term capital gain on the Schedule D filed with your return (see instructions)	**9**	

Part II   **Ordinary Gains and Losses** (see instructions)

10 Ordinary gains and losses not included on lines 11 through 16 (include property held 1 year or less):

11	Loss, if any, from line 7	**11**	( )
12	Gain, if any, from line 7 or amount from line 8, if applicable	**12**	
13	Gain, if any, from line 31	**13**	27,565
14	Net gain or (loss) from Form 4684, lines 31 and 38a	**14**	
15	Ordinary gain from installment sales from Form 6252, line 25 or 36	**15**	
16	Ordinary gain or (loss) from like-kind exchanges from Form 8824	**16**	
17	Combine lines 10 through 16	**17**	27,565

18 For all except individual returns, enter the amount from line 17 on the appropriate line of your return and skip lines a and b below. For individual returns, complete lines a and b below:

a If the loss on line 11 includes a loss from Form 4684, line 35, column (b)(ii), enter that part of the loss here. Enter the part of the loss from income-producing property on Schedule A (Form 1040), line 28, and the part of the loss from property used as an employee on Schedule A (Form 1040), line 23. Identify as from "Form 4797, line 18a." See instructions . . **18a**

b Redetermine the gain or (loss) on line 17 excluding the loss, if any, on line 18a. Enter here and on Form 1040, line 14   **18b**   27,565

For Paperwork Reduction Act Notice, see separate instructions.   Cat. No. 13086I   Form **4797** (2014)

FIGURE I:13-1 ►   PART I AND PART II OF FORM 4797

Part III Gain From Disposition of Property Under Sections 1245, 1250, 1252, 1254, and 1255
(see instructions)

19	(a) Description of section 1245, 1250, 1252, 1254, or 1255 property:		(b) Date acquired (mo., day, yr.)	(c) Date sold (mo., day, yr.)
A	Equipment		3-10-12	4-30-14
B				
C				
D				

	These columns relate to the properties on lines 19A through 19D. ▶		Property A	Property B	Property C	Property D
20	Gross sales price (**Note:** See line 1 before completing.) .	20	60,000			
21	Cost or other basis plus expense of sale	21	58,000			
22	Depreciation (or depletion) allowed or allowable. . .	22	27,565			
23	Adjusted basis. Subtract line 22 from line 21	23	30,435			
24	Total gain. Subtract line 23 from line 20	24	29,565			
25	**If section 1245 property:**					
a	Depreciation allowed or allowable from line 22 . . .	25a	27,565			
b	Enter the **smaller** of line 24 or 25a	25b	27,565			
26	**If section 1250 property:** If straight line depreciation was used, enter -0- on line 26g, except for a corporation subject to section 291.					
a	Additional depreciation after 1975 (see instructions) .	26a				
b	Applicable percentage multiplied by the **smaller** of line 24 or line 26a (see instructions)	26b				
c	Subtract line 26a from line 24. If residential rental property **or** line 24 is not more than line 26a, skip lines 26d and 26e	26c				
d	Additional depreciation after 1969 and before 1976. .	26d				
e	Enter the **smaller** of line 26c or 26d	26e				
f	Section 291 amount (corporations only)	26f				
g	Add lines 26b, 26e, and 26f.	26g				
27	**If section 1252 property:** Skip this section if you did not dispose of farmland or if this form is being completed for a partnership (other than an electing large partnership).					
a	Soil, water, and land clearing expenses	27a				
b	Line 27a multiplied by applicable percentage (see instructions)	27b				
c	Enter the **smaller** of line 24 or 27b	27c				
28	**If section 1254 property:**					
a	Intangible drilling and development costs, expenditures for development of mines and other natural deposits, mining exploration costs, and depletion (see instructions)	28a				
b	Enter the **smaller** of line 24 or 28a	28b				
29	**If section 1255 property:**					
a	Applicable percentage of payments excluded from income under section 126 (see instructions) . . .	29a				
b	Enter the **smaller** of line 24 or 29a (see instructions) .	29b				

Summary of Part III Gains. Complete property columns A through D through line 29b before going to line 30.

30	Total gains for all properties. Add property columns A through D, line 24	30	29,565
31	Add property columns A through D, lines 25b, 26g, 27c, 28b, and 29b. Enter here and on line 13	31	27,565
32	Subtract line 31 from line 30. Enter the portion from casualty or theft on Form 4684, line 33. Enter the portion from other than casualty or theft on Form 4797, line 6	32	2,000

Part IV Recapture Amounts Under Sections 179 and 280F(b)(2) When Business Use Drops to 50% or Less
(see instructions)

			(a) Section 179	(b) Section 280F(b)(2)
33	Section 179 expense deduction or depreciation allowable in prior years.	33		
34	Recomputed depreciation (see instructions)	34		
35	Recapture amount. Subtract line 34 from line 33. See the instructions for where to report . .	35		

Form **4797** (2014)

FIGURE I:13-2 ▶ PART III OF FORM 4797

Name(s) shown on tax return. Do not enter name and identifying number if shown on other side. | Identifying number

SECTION B—Business and Income-Producing Property

Part I **Casualty or Theft Gain or Loss** (Use a separate Part I for each casualty or theft.)

19 Description of properties (show type, location, and date acquired for each property). Use a separate line for each property lost or damaged from the same casualty or theft. **See instructions if claiming a loss due to a Ponzi-type investment scheme and Section C is not completed.**

Property **A** _____

Property **B** _____

Property **C** _____

Property **D** _____

		Properties			
		A	**B**	**C**	**D**
20 Cost or adjusted basis of each property	**20**				
21 Insurance or other reimbursement (whether or not you filed a claim). See the instructions for line 3	**21**				
Note: *If line 20 is **more** than line 21, skip line 22.*					
22 Gain from casualty or theft. If line 21 is **more** than line 20, enter the difference here and on line 29 or line 34, column (c), except as provided in the instructions for line 33. Also, skip lines 23 through 27 for that column. See the instructions for line 4 if line 21 includes insurance or other reimbursement you did not claim, or you received payment for your loss in a later tax year	**22**				
23 Fair market value **before** casualty or theft	**23**				
24 Fair market value **after** casualty or theft	**24**				
25 Subtract line 24 from line 23	**25**				
26 Enter the **smaller** of line 20 or line 25	**26**				
Note: *If the property was totally destroyed by casualty or lost from theft, enter on line 26 the amount from line 20.*					
27 Subtract line 21 from line 26. If zero or less, enter -0-	**27**				

28 Casualty or theft loss. Add the amounts on line 27. Enter the total here and on line 29 **or** line 34 (see instructions) | **28**

Part II **Summary of Gains and Losses** (from separate Parts I)

(a) Identify casualty or theft	**(b)** Losses from casualties or thefts		**(c)** Gains from casualties or thefts includible in income
	(i) Trade, business, rental or royalty property	**(ii)** Income-producing and employee property	

Casualty or Theft of Property Held One Year or Less

29 _____	( )	( )	
_____	( )	( )	
30 Totals. Add the amounts on line 29 **30**	( )	( )	

31 Combine line 30, columns (b)(i) and (c). Enter the net gain or (loss) here and on Form 4797, line 14. If Form 4797 is not otherwise required, see instructions | **31**

32 Enter the amount from line 30, column (b)(ii) here. Individuals, enter the amount from income-producing property on Schedule A (Form 1040), line 28, or Form 1040NR, Schedule A, line 14, and enter the amount from property used as an employee on Schedule A (Form 1040), line 23, or Form 1040NR, Schedule A, line 9. Estates and trusts, partnerships, and S corporations, see instructions | **32**

Casualty or Theft of Property Held More Than One Year

33 Casualty or theft gains from Form 4797, line 32 | **33**

34 _____	( )	( )	
_____	( )	( )	

35 Total losses. Add amounts on line 34, columns (b)(i) and (b)(ii) **35** | ( ) | ( ) |

36 Total gains. Add lines 33 and 34, column (c) | **36**

37 Add amounts on line 35, columns (b)(i) and (b)(ii) | **37**

38 If the loss on line 37 is **more** than the gain on line 36:

  a Combine line 35, column (b)(i) and line 36, and enter the net gain or (loss) here. Partnerships (except electing large partnerships) and S corporations, see the note below. All others, enter this amount on Form 4797, line 14. If Form 4797 is not otherwise required, see instructions | **38a**

  b Enter the amount from line 35, column (b)(ii) here. Individuals, enter the amount from income-producing property on Schedule A (Form 1040), line 28, or Form 1040NR, Schedule A, line 14, and enter the amount from property used as an employee on Schedule A (Form 1040), line 23, or Form 1040NR, Schedule A, line 9. Estates and trusts, enter on the "Other deductions" line of your tax return. Partnerships (except electing large partnerships) and S corporations, see the note below. Electing large partnerships, enter on Form 1065-B, Part II, line 11 | **38b**

39 If the loss on line 37 is **less** than or **equal** to the gain on line 36, combine lines 36 and 37 and enter here. Partnerships (except electing large partnerships), see the note below. All others, enter this amount on Form 4797, line 3 | **39**

Note: *Partnerships, enter the amount from line 38a, 38b, or line 39 on Form 1065, Schedule K, line 11. S corporations, enter the amount from line 38a or 38b on Form 1120S, Schedule K, line 10.*

Form **4684** (2014)

FIGURE I:13-3 ▶ SECTION B OF FORM 4684

production of income. Note that a separate Part I is used for each different casualty or theft. Gains are reported on line 26, and losses are reported on line 32. For properties held a year or less, the gains and losses are reported on lines 33 through 36 of Part II. These gains and losses are either recorded as ordinary gains and losses on line 14 of Part II of Form 4797 or as itemized deductions on Schedule A of Form 1040.

For properties held more than a year, the gains and losses are reported on lines 40 and 41. If gains exceed losses, the net gain is reported on line 43 and then on line 3 of Part I of Form 4797 (i.e., the gains and losses are treated as Sec. 1231 gains and losses). If the losses exceed the gains, all or part of the gains and losses are reported as ordinary in Part II of Form 4797 and/or on Schedule A of Form 1040.

PROBLEM MATERIALS

DISCUSSION QUESTIONS

I:13-1 Explain how the gain on the sale or exchange of land could be classified as either ordinary income, a Sec. 1231 gain, or a LTCG, depending on the facts and circumstances.

I:13-2 Why were taxpayers reluctant to sell appreciated business property between 1938 and 1942? What effect did this reluctance have on the tax law?

I:13-3 Alice owns timber, purchased six years ago, with an adjusted basis of $50,000. The timber is cut for use in her furniture business on October 1, when the FMV of the timber is $200,000. The FMV of the timber on January 1 is $190,000. May Alice treat any of the gain as Sec. 1231 gain? If so, how much?

I:13-4 Explain how the gain from an involuntary conversion of business property held more than one year is taxed if the involuntary conversion is the result of a condemnation. Explain the tax treatment if the involuntary conversion is due to a casualty.

I:13-5 When is livestock considered Sec. 1231 property?

I:13-6 When is a net Sec. 1231 gain treated as ordinary income?

I:13-7 Carlie who is single has a Sec. 1231 gain of $10,000 and no Sec. 1231 losses during the current year. Explain why the gain might be taxed at (a) 15%, (b) 39.6%, (c) 25%, (d) 20%, or (e) zero.

I:13-8 Why is it unlikely that gains due to the sale of equipment will be treated as Sec. 1231 gains?

I:13-9 Hank sells equipment used in a trade or business for $25,000. The equipment costs $30,000 and has an adjusted basis of $25,500. Why is it important to know the holding period?

I:13-10 Jackie purchases equipment during the current year for $800,000 that has a seven-year MACRS recovery period. She expects to sell the property after three years. Jackie anticipates that her marginal tax rate in the year of sale will be significantly higher than her current marginal tax rate.

Why might it be advantageous for her to use the straight-line method of depreciation?

I:13-11 Karen purchased a computer three years ago for $15,300 to use exclusively in her business. She expensed the entire cost of the computer under Sec. 179. If she sells the computer during the current year for $3,721, what is the amount and character of her recognized gain?

I:13-12 Sheila owns a motel that is used in a trade or business. If she sells the motel, the gain will be Sec. 1245 ordinary income. During what period of time was the motel placed into service?

I:13-13 Will an individual taxpayer ever have to recognize Sec. 1250 ordinary income on the sale of a building used for business and placed in service after 1986? Explain.

I:13-14 Marty sells his fully depreciated building at a gain to an unrelated party. The building is purchased before 1981. Is any of the gain taxed as ordinary income?

I:13-15 Which of the following assets (assume all assets have a holding period of more than one year) do not qualify as Sec. 1231 property: inventory, a pig held for breeding, land used as a parking lot for customers, and marketable securities?

I:13-16 When is an office building subject to the depreciation recapture rules of Sec. 1245?

I:13-17 Does a building that is 60% rented for residential use and 40% for commercial use qualify as residential rental property?

I:13-18 Roger owns an apartment complex with a FMV of $2 million. If he sells the apartment complex, $700,000 of the gain is Sec. 1231 gain with $600,000 taxed at 25% because it is unrecaptured Sec. 1250 gain. If he dies before selling the apartment complex and his estate sells the property for $2 million, how much ordinary income must the estate recognize?

I:13-19 Rashad owns a duplex used 100% as residential rental property. Under what conditions, if any, will any gain that he recognizes be Sec. 1245 ordinary income?

I:13-20 John and Karen are unrelated individuals. John sold land that is Sec. 1231 property held for three years and recognized a $50,000 gain. Karen sold a building that is Sec. 1231 property held for three years and recognized a $50,000 gain. Straight-line depreciation was used. John and Karen both have a 33% tax rate, no other transactions involving capital assets or 1231 assets, and no nonrecaptured Sec. 1231 losses. Except for the sales of different assets, their tax situation is exactly the same. As a result of selling his Sec. 1231 property, will John pay more, less or the same amount of taxes than Karen as a result of selling her Sec. 1231 property? Explain.

I:13-21 Why may a corporation recognize a greater amount of ordinary income due to the sale of Sec. 1250 property than a noncorporate taxpayer?

I:13-22 Assume a taxpayer sells equipment used in a trade or business for a gain that is less than the depreciation allowed. If the taxpayer is a corporation, will a greater amount of Sec. 1245 income be recognized than if the taxpayer is an individual? Explain.

I:13-23 Dale owns business equipment with a $100,000 FMV and an adjusted basis of $60,000. The property was originally acquired for $150,000. Which one of the following transactions would result in recognition of $40,000 ordinary income by Dale due to the depreciation recapture rules of Sec. 1245?
a. He makes a gift of the property to a daughter.
b. He contributes the property to a qualified charitable organization.
c. He disposes of the equipment in an installment sale and receives $10,000 cash in the year of sale.

I:13-24 Carlos owns equipment with an $800,000 acquisition cost, a $270,000 adjusted basis, and a $500,000 FMV. Carlos makes a gift of the equipment to a charitable organization. The equipment is used by the charity in its exempt function. What is the amount of his charitable contribution deduction?

I:13-25 Ted owns a warehouse that cost $850,000 in 1984 and is subject to depreciation recapture under Sec. 1245. The warehouse, which has an adjusted basis of zero, is destroyed by a tornado and Ted receives $580,000 from the insurance company. Within nine months, he pays $500,000 for a new warehouse and an election is made to defer the gain under Sec. 1033. What is the amount and character of Ted's recognized gain?

I:13-26 When a taxpayer disposes of oil, gas, or geothermal property, part or all of the gain may be recaptured as ordinary income. Explain how the recapture amount is determined for oil and gas and geothermal properties.

I:13-27 William owns two appreciated assets, land and a building, which have been used in his trade or business since purchased in 1990. If he sells the two assets to his 100%-owned corporation, will William have to recognize any ordinary income? Explain.

ISSUE IDENTIFICATION QUESTIONS

I:13-28 Six years ago Joelle started raising chinchillas. She separates her chinchillas into two groups, a breeding group and a market group. During the year, she had the following sales of chinchillas from her market group: 400 to producers of fur products; 100 to pet stores; and 25 to individuals to use as pets. From her breeding stock, she sold six chinchillas to Rebecca, an individual who is starting a chinchilla ranch, and five to Fur Pelts, a producer of fur products. All 11 chinchillas from the breeding group have been held for at least 22 months, and the five sold to Fur Pelts were poor performers.

I:13-29 Green Acres, Inc., owns 1,400 acres adjacent to land owned by the U.S. government. The government, wanting to sell timber from its land, had to assure prospective bidders of access to the timber. The government entered into an agreement with Green Acres for a logging road easement across land owned by Green Acres. The government agreed to pay $2 per thousand board feet of timber removed up to a maximum of $130,000. Bidders for the rights to obtain the government's timber had to agree to pay the fee to Green Acres as part of their bids for the timber. Stanley Lumberyard, Inc. provided the highest bid and paid $80,000 to Green Acres during the first year of cutting and removing the timber and $50,000 during the second year. What tax issues should Green Acres and Stanley Lumberyard consider?

I:13-30 Sarah, who has been in the business of erecting, maintaining, and renting outdoor advertising displays for 18 years, has an offer to purchase her business. Two basic types of advertising displays are used in her business: structure X and structure Y. Structure X consists of a single sign face nailed to a wooden support frame and attached to wooden poles 30 feet long. Its structure is rather easy to dismantle and move from one location to another. In contrast, structure Y is a permanent sign that is designed to withstand winds of up to 100 miles per hour. None of the Structure Y signs have ever been moved. What tax issues should Sarah consider?

I:13-31 Sylvester owns and operates an unincorporated pizza business that delivers pizza to customers. Three years ago, he acquired an automobile for $10,000 to provide delivery service. Recently, Sylvester hired an employee who prefers to use his personal automobile to make the deliveries. Thus, Sylvester decided to permit his 18-year old daughter to use the automobile for her personal use. The automobile's adjusted basis is $3,080 and its FMV is $4,700. What tax issues should Sylvester consider?

PROBLEMS

I:13-32 *Secs. 1231, 1245, and 1250 Transactions.* All assets listed below have been held for more than one year. Which assets might be classified as Sec. 1231, Sec. 1245, or Sec. 1250 property? An asset may be classified as more than one type of property.
a. Land on which a factory is located
b. Equipment used in the factory
c. Raw materials inventory
d. Patent purchased to allow use of a manufacturing process
e. Land held primarily for sale
f. Factory building acquired in 1986 (the straight-line ACRS recovery method is used)

I:13-33 *Sec. 1231 Gains and Losses.* Vivian's AGI is $40,000 without considering the gains and losses below. Determine her revised AGI after the inclusion of any applicable gains or losses for the following independent cases. Assume she has no nonrecaptured net Sec. 1231 losses at the beginning of the year.

	Case A	Case B	Case C	Case D
Sec. 1231 gain	$19,000	$10,000	$30,000	$ 5,000
Sec. 1231 loss	5,000	22,000	39,000	12,000
LTCG	–0–	–0–	6,300	–0–
LTCL	–0–	–0–	–0–	4,200

I:13-34 *Sec. 1231 Gains and Losses.* Edith, who has no other sales or exchanges and no nonrecaptured Sec. 1231 losses, sells three tracts of land that are used in her trade or business. Edith is single, and her regular income tax rate is 33%.
Asset #1—$15,000 gain and holding period of 20 months
Asset #2—$17,000 loss and holding period of 25 months
Asset #3—$ 5,000 gain and holding period of 13 months
a. What is the increase in her taxes as a result of the three sales?
b. If the holding period for Asset #2 is nine months, what is the decrease in her taxes as a result of the three sales?
c. Same as part a except her tax rate is 39.6%.

I:13-35 *Sec. 1231 Transactions.* Which of the following transactions or events is treated as a Sec. 1231 gain or loss? All assets are held for more than one year.
a. Theft of uninsured diamond ring, with an $800 basis and a $1,000 FMV.
b. Gain due to condemnation of land used in business.
c. Loss on the sale of a warehouse.
d. Gain of $4,000 on the sale of equipment. Depreciation deductions allowed amount to $10,000.

I:13-36 *Capital Loss Versus Sec. 1231 Loss.* Vicki has an AGI of $70,000 without considering the sale of a nondepreciable asset for $23,000. The asset was acquired six years ago and has an adjusted basis of $35,000. She has no other sales or exchanges. Determine her AGI for the following independent situations when the asset is:
a. A capital asset.
b. Sec. 1231 property.

I:13-37 *Ordinary Income Versus Sec. 1231 Gain.* At the beginning of 2015, Silver Corporation has a $95,000 capital loss carryforward from 2014. During 2015, the corporation sells land, held for four years, and realizes an $80,000 gain. Silver has no unrecaptured net Sec. 1231 losses, and it made no other sales during the current year. Determine the amount of capital loss carryforward that Silver can use in 2015 if the land is:
a. Sec. 1231 property.
b. Not a capital asset or Sec. 1231 property.

I:13-38   *Sec. 1231 Transactions.* During the current year, Sean's office building is destroyed by fire. After collecting the insurance proceeds, Sean has a $50,000 recognized gain. The building was acquired in 1998, and the straight-line method of depreciation has been used. He does not plan to acquire a replacement building. In addition to the gain on the building, consider the following independent cases and determine his total net capital gain. For each case, include the $50,000 casualty gain described above.

a. Land used in his trade or business and held more than a year is condemned by the state. The recognized gain is $60,000.

b. Assume the same facts as in Part a, except the condemnation results in a $60,000 loss.

c. An apartment building used as residential rental property and held more than one year is destroyed by a sudden, unexpected mudslide. The building is not insured, and the loss amounts to $200,000.

I:13-39   *Nonrecaptured Net Sec. 1231 Losses.* Consider the following summary of Sec. 1231 gains and losses recognized by Janet during the period 2010–2015. Janet had no nonrecaptured Sec. 1231 losses at the beginning of 2010. If Janet has no capital gains and losses during the six-year period, determine her net capital gain for each year.

	Sec. 1231 Gains	Sec. 1231 Losses
2010	$ 9,000	$ 7,000
2011	20,000	24,000
2012	12,000	19,000
2013	9,000	4,000
2014	25,000	13,200
2015	10,000	17,000

I:13-40   *Nonrecaptured Net Sec. 1231 Losses.* Dillion whose taxable income is less than $300,000 has a tax rate of 33% on his ordinary income and $40,000 of net nonrecaptured Sec. 1231 losses at the start of the year. During the year, he recognizes a Sec. 1231 gain of $53,000 from the sale of land. As a result of the sale, how much does Dillion's tax liability increase?

I:13-41   *Sec. 1245.* The Pear Corporation owns equipment with a $300,000 adjusted basis. The equipment was purchased six years ago for $650,000. If Pear sells the equipment for the selling prices given in the three independent cases below, what are the amount and character of Pear's recognized gain or loss?

Case	Selling Price
A	$407,000
B	752,000
C	245,000

I:13-42   *Sec. 1245.* Elizabeth owns equipment that cost $500,000 and has an adjusted basis of $230,000. If the straight-line method of depreciation had been used, the adjusted basis would be $300,000.

a. What is the maximum selling price that she could sell the equipment for without having to recognize Sec. 1245 ordinary income?

b. If she sold the equipment and had to recognize $61,000 of Sec. 1245 ordinary income, what was the selling price?

I:13-43   *Sale of Business and Personal-Use Property.* Arnie, a college student, purchased a truck in 2013 for $6,000. He used the truck 70% of the time as a distributor for the local newspaper and 30% of the time for personal use. The truck has a five-year recovery period, and he claimed depreciation deductions of $840 in 2013 and $1,344 in 2014. Arnie sells the truck on June 20, 2015, for $3,000.

a. What is the amount of allowable depreciation in 2015?

b. Determine Arnie's realized and recognized gain or loss and its character.

I:13-44   *Like-Kind Exchange of Sec. 1245 Property.* General Corporation owns equipment which cost $70,000 and has a $44,000 adjusted basis. General exchanges the equipment for other equipment ($42,000 FMV) and marketable securities ($30,000 FMV). Determine the following:

a. Realized gain

b. Recognized gain

c. Gain treated as ordinary income

d. Gain treated as Sec. 1231 gain

e. Basis of marketable securities received

f. Basis of equipment received

I:13-45 *Like-Kind Exchange of Sec. 1245 Property.* Leroy owns a truck used in his trade or business that cost $50,000 and has an adjusted basis of $34,000. The truck is exchanged for a new truck that is like-kind property with a FMV of $40,000. Prior to selling the new truck two years later, Leroy is allowed depreciation of $13,000 for the new truck. Determine:
  a. Realized gain on the exchange
  b. Recognized gain on the exchange
  c. Basis of truck received
  d. Recognized gain, and the character of the gain, if the sales price of the truck is $41,000
  e. Recognized gain, and the character of the gain, if the sale price of the truck is $52,000

I:13-46 *Purpose of Sec. 1245.* Martin owns equipment used in his trade or business purchased four years ago for $200,000. Martin sells the equipment in the current year for $110,000 when its adjusted basis is $52,000. No other sales or exchanges are made this year or the preceding five years. His tax rate is 35% for all years since the year of purchase.
  a. Determine the increase in Martin's AGI for the current year as a result of the sale if Sec. 1245 did not exist.
  b. Determine the increase in Martin's AGI for the current year as a result of the sale if Sec. 1245 does exist.
  c. Given that Sec. 1245 does exist, how much higher is his tax in (b) than in (a)?

I:13-47 *Secs. 1231 and 1250-Real Property Placed in Service Before 1981.* Charles owns an office building and land that are used in his trade or business. The office building and land were acquired in 1978 for $800,000 and $100,000, respectively. During the current year, the properties are sold for $900,000 with 20% of the selling price being allocated to the land. The assets as shown on the taxpayer's books before their sale are as follows:

Building	$800,000	
Accumulated depreciation	690,000[a]	$110,000
Land		100,000

[a]If the straight-line method of depreciation had been used, the accumulated depreciation would be $560,000.

  a. What is the recognized gain due to the sale of the building?
  b. What is the character of the recognized gain due to the sale of the building?
  c. What is the recognized gain and character of the gain due to the sale of the land?

I:13-48 Assume the same facts as in Problem I:13-47 except the taxpayer is a corporation and answer the same questions.

I:13-49 *Secs. 1231, 1245, and Unrecaptured Sec. 1250.* Brigham is single and is in the 33% marginal income tax bracket. He has the sales or exchanges below. At the beginning of the year, he has nonrecaptured net Sec. 1231 losses of $10,000. Determine the increase or decrease in Brigham's tax liability as a result of the following independent sales or exchanges.
  a. Sells equipment used in his trade or business for $40,000. The equipment was purchased for $100,000 and depreciation allowed amounts to $72,000.
  b. Sells land used in his trade or business for $80,000. The land was purchased four years ago for $61,000.
  c. He sells a building used in his trade or business for $163,000. The building was purchased in 1988 for $250,000 and depreciation allowed amounts to $110,000.
  d. Same as Part c except he sells the building for $127,000.

I:13-50 *Secs. 1245 and 1231.* The LaPoint Corporation placed in service $350,000 of used equipment (7-year recovery property) on June 3, 2014 and elected to expense $250,000 as Sec. 179 depreciation expense. LaPont sold the equipment for $150,000 on November 22, 2015. Determine the following:
  a. Depreciation allowed in 2014
  b. Depreciation allowed during 2015
  c. Amount of gain or loss and character

I:13-51 *Unrecaptured Sec. 1250 Gain and 1231.* Mr. Briggs purchased an apartment complex on January 10, 2013, for $2 million with 10% of the price allocated to land. He sells the complex on October 22, 2015, for $2.5 million. Assume that 10% of the $2.5 million selling price is allocated to land and 90% is allocated to the building.
  a. How much depreciation was allowed for 2013?
  b. How much depreciation is allowed for 2015?
  c. Will any of the gain be ordinary income?
  d. What is the amount of gain and the character of the gain on the sale of the building?

e. What is the amount of gain and the character of the gain on the sale of the land?

f. Will any of the gain be taxed at 25%?

I:13-52 *Sec. 1250 Residential Rental Property-Placed in Service After 1981 and Before 1987.* Jesse owns a duplex used as residential rental property. The duplex cost $100,000 in 1986, and 10% of the cost was allocated to the land. Total cost-recovery deductions allowed amount to $90,000. The statutory percentages were used to compute cost-recovery deductions. If the straight-line method of cost recovery were used instead, $90,000 of cost-recovery deductions would have been allowed.

a. What is the amount of recognized gain and the character of the gain if Jesse sells the duplex for $125,000 with 10% of the price allocated to land?

b. Same as (a) except the building is an office building.

I:13-53 *Sec. 1250-Real Property Placed in Service Before 1981.* Rosemary owns an office building placed in service in 1980 that cost $625,000 and has an adjusted basis of $227,000. If the straight-line method of depreciation were used, the adjusted basis would be $300,000.

a. What is the maximum selling price that she could sell the building for without having to recognize Sec. 1250 ordinary income?

b. If she sold the building and had to recognize $51,000 of Sec. 1250 ordinary income, what was the selling price?

I:13-54 *Nonresidential Real Property-Noncorporate Taxpayer.* Consider three office buildings placed in service as shown below and answer the following true-false questions. Assume all assets are sold by a noncorporate taxpayer at a gain and there are no other sales or exchanges or nonrecaptured Sec. 1231 loss unless told otherwise. None of the buildings are fully depreciated when sold and the taxpayer's tax rate is more than 25%.

	Placed in Service
Building #1	Before 1981
Building #2	After 1980 and before 1987
Building #3	After 1986

1. Some or all of the gain on sale of #1 is ordinary if accelerated depreciation was used.
2. If the straight-line method of depreciation was used for #1, some or all of the gain may be taxed at 25%.
3. Gain on the sale of #2 could be Sec. 1245 ordinary income.
4. Gain on the sale of #2 could be Sec. 1231 gain.
5. Part of the gain on the sale of #2 could be Sec. 1245 ordinary income and part could be Sec. 1231 gain.
6. If the straight-line method of depreciation was used for #2, some or all of the gain may be taxed at 25%.
7. Some or all of the gain on the sale of #3 could be Sec. 1245 ordinary income.
8. Some or all of the gain on the sale of #3 could be taxed at 25%.
9. Some of the gain on the sale of #3 could be Sec. 1250 ordinary income.
10. If the taxpayer has a nonrecaptured Sec. 1231 loss of $30,000 and the gain on the sale of #3 is $40,000, all $40,000 of the gain is taxed as ordinary income.

I:13-55 *Nonresidential Real Property-Corporate Taxpayer.* Assume the same facts as in Problem I:13-54 except the taxpayer is a corporate taxpayer with a 34% tax rate and answer the ten true-false questions.

I:13-56 *Secs. 1231 and 1250-Placed in Service After 1986.* Molly, whose tax rate is 39.6%, sells an apartment complex for $4.5 million with 10% of the price allocated to land. The apartment complex was purchased in 1993. She has no other sales or exchanges during the year and no nonrecaptured net Sec. 1231 losses. Information about the assets at the time of sale is:

	Building	*Land*
Original Cost	$2,700,000	$300,000
Accumulated Depreciation	1,000,000	0

a. What is the recognized gain on the sale of the building and the character of the gain?

b. What is the recognized gain on the sale of the land and the character of the gain?

c. How much of the Sec. 1231 gain is taxed at 25%?

d. If Molly has NSTCL of $50,000, will the capital loss reduce the Sec. 1231 gain taxed at 25% or 20%?

I:13-57 *Secs. 1231 and 1250 for Corporate Taxpayer.* Assume the same facts as in Problem I:13-56 except the taxpayer is a corporation instead of an individual.
a. What is the recognized gain on the sale of the building and the character of the gain?
b. What is the recognized gain on the sale of the land and the character of the gain?
c. How much of the Sec. 1231 gain is taxed at 25%?

I:13-58 *Charitable Contribution of Sec. 1231 Property.* Raquel owns land used in her trade or business for more than one year. The basis is $10,000 and its FMV is $40,000. Her tax rate is 33% and her AGI is $250,000. She makes no other charitable contributions except for the ones considered below.
a. If she gives the land to a university, determine her tax savings.
b. If she sells the land for $40,000, pays the tax and then contributes the remainder of the cash to the charity, determine her tax savings because of the contribution and the amount that the university receives. Assume that she has no other sales or exchanges during the year.

I:13-59 *Secs. 1231, 1245 and 1250.* Glen, whose tax rate is 33%, sells each of the following assets for $200,000. Each case is an independent case.

	Sec. 1231 Gain (Loss)	Ordinary Income	Taxed at 33%	Taxed at 25%	Taxed at 20%	Taxed at 15%
Building purchased in 1999 for $220,000 with adjusted basis of $165,000						
Equipment purchased in 2011 for $300,000 with adjusted basis of $144,000						
Land purchased in 1992 for $30,000 to use as a building site						
Building purchased in 1997 for $150,000 with adjusted basis of $112,000						
Equipment purchased in 2012 for $180,000 with adjusted basis of $140,000						

I:13-60 *Recapture of Soil and Water Conservation Expenditures.* Bob owns farmland with a $600,000 basis, and he elects to expense $100,000 of expenditures incurred for soil and water conservation purposes. Bob sells the farmland after farming for seven years and four months. What is the amount of the recognized gain and the character of the gain if the selling price is
a. $825,000
b. $615,000

I:13-61 *Recapture of Intangible Drilling Costs.* Jeremy purchased undeveloped oil and gas property five years ago. He paid $300,000 for intangible drilling and development costs and elected to expense the $300,000. During the current year, Jeremy sells the property, which has an $800,000 adjusted basis, for $900,000. What is the amount of gain treated as ordinary income under Sec. 1254 because of the election to expense intangible drilling and development costs?

I:13-62 *Recapture of Intangible Drilling Costs and Depletion.* In 2009, Jack purchased undeveloped oil and gas property for $900,000 and paid $170,000 for intangible drilling and development costs. He elected to expense the intangible drilling and development costs. During the current year he sells the property for $950,000 when the property's adjusted basis is $700,000. Depletion of $200,000 was allowed on the property.
a. What is the realized gain and how much of the gain is ordinary income?
b. For Jack to have a Sec. 1231 gain, the selling price must exceed what amount?

I:13-63 *Related Party Transactions.* Ed operates a storage business as a sole proprietorship and owns the following assets acquired in 1996:

Warehouse	$400,000
Minus: Accumulated depreciation	(230,000)

Adjusted basis	$170,000
Land	65,000

The FMV of the warehouse and the land are $500,000 and $200,000, respectively. Ed owns 75% of the stock of the Crane Corporation. If he sells the two assets to Crane at a price equal to the FMV of the assets, determine the recognized gain and its character due to the sale of the:
a. Building
b. Land

COMPREHENSIVE PROBLEM

I:13-64 Betty, whose tax rate is 33%, is in the business of breeding and racing horses. Except for the transactions below, she has no other sales or exchanges and she has no unrecaptured net Sec. 1231 losses. Consider the following transactions that occur during the year:

- A building with an adjusted basis of $300,000 is destroyed by fire. Insurance proceeds of $500,000 are received, but Betty does not plan to replace the building. The building was built 12 years ago at a cost of $430,000 and used to provide lodging for her employees. Straight-line depreciation has been used.

- Four acres of the farm are condemned by the state to widen the highway and Betty receives $50,000. The land was inherited from her mother 15 years ago when its FMV was $15,000. Her mother purchased the land for $10,300. Betty does not plan to purchase additional land.

- A racehorse purchased four years ago for $200,000 was sold for $550,000. Total depreciation allowed using the straight-line method amounts to $160,000.

- Equipment purchased three years ago for $200,000 is exchanged for $100,000 of IBM common stock. The adjusted basis of the equipment is $120,000. If straight-line depreciation had been used, the adjusted basis would be $152,000.

- An uninsured pony, with an adjusted basis of $20,000 and FMV of $35,000, that her daughter uses only for personal use is injured while attempting a jump. Because of the injury, the uninsured pony has to be destroyed by a veterinarian.

a. What amount of Sec. 1245 ordinary income must be recognized?
b. What amount of Sec. 1250 ordinary income must be recognized?
c. Will the loss resulting from the destruction of her daughter's pony be used to determine net Sec. 1231 gains or losses?
d. What is the amount of the net Sec. 1231 gain or loss?
e. After all of the netting of gains or losses is completed, will the gain resulting from the involuntary conversion of the building be treated as LTCG?
f. What is the amount of her Sec. 1231 gain that is unrecaptured Sec. 1250 gain?

TAX STRATEGY PROBLEMS

I:13-65 Russ has never recognized any Sec. 1231 gains or losses. In December 2015, Russ is considering the sale of two Sec. 1231 assets. The sale of one asset will result in a $20,000 Sec. 1231 gain while the sale of the other asset will result in a $20,000 Sec. 1231 loss. Russ has no other capital or Sec. 1231 gains and losses in 2015 and does not expect to have any other capital or Sec. 1231 gains and losses in 2015. He is aware that it might be advantageous to recognize the Sec. 1231 gain and the Sec. 1231 loss in different tax years. However, he does not know whether he should recognize the Sec. 1231 gain in 2015 and the Sec. 1231 loss in 2016 or vice versa. His marginal tax rate for each year is expected to be 33%. Advise the taxpayer with respect to these two alternatives:
a. Recognize the $20,000 Sec. 1231 loss in 2015 and the $20,000 Sec. 1231 gain in 2016.
b. Recognize the $20,000 Sec. 1231 gain in 2015 and the $20,000 Sec. 1231 loss in 2016.

I:13-66 Holly has recognized a $9,000 STCL. She has no other recognized capital gains and losses in 2015. She is considering the sale of a Sec. 1231 asset held for four years at a $5,000 gain in 2015. She had not recognized any Sec. 1231 losses during the previous five years and does not expect to have any other Sec. 1231 transactions in 2015. Her marginal tax rate for 2015 is 33%. What is the amount of increase in her 2015 taxes if Holly recognizes the $5,000 Sec. 1231 gain in 2015?

TAX FORM/RETURN PREPARATION PROBLEMS

I:13-67 George Buckner sells an apartment building on October 10 for $1.75 million. The building was purchased on January 1, 1995, for $2 million. Depreciation of $420,000 has been taken. The figures given above do not include the purchase price or the selling price of the land. Mr. Buckner's adjusted basis for the land is $200,000, and the sales price is $350,000. Mr. Buckner, who owns and operates a taxi business, sells one of the automobiles for $1,800 on November 14th. The automobile's adjusted basis is zero, and the original cost is $15,000. The automobile was purchased on April 25, 2006. Mr. Buckner has no other gains and losses during the year, and nonrecaptured net Sec. 1231 losses amount to $32,000. Prepare Form 4797.

I:13-68 Julie Hernandez is single and has no dependents. She operates a dairy farm and her Social Security number is 000-00-1111. She lives at 1325 Vermont Street in Costa, Florida. Consider the following information for the current year:

- Schedule C was prepared by her accountant and the net profit from the dairy operations is $48,000.
- Itemized deductions amount to $4,185.
- Dividend income (qualified dividend) amounts to $280.
- State income tax refund received during the year is $125. She did not itemize last year.
- In June, a burglar broke into her house and stole the following two assets, which were acquired in 1988:

	Basis	FMV	Insurance Proceeds Received
Painting	$2,000	$10,000	$9,000
Sculpture	1,700	1,500	0

The following assets used in her business were sold during the year:

	Acquisition Date	Original Cost	Depreciation to Date of Sale	Date of Sale	Selling Price
Tractor	June 10, 2004	$25,000	$25,000	Oct. 20	$ 8,300
Barn	May 23, 1994	90,000	61,000	May 13	87,000
Land	May 23, 1994	15,000	–0–	May 13	27,000
Cows	Sept. 7, 2012	20,000	13,000	Nov. 8	21,000

In August, three acres of the farm were taken by the state under the right of eminent domain for the purpose of building a highway. The basis of the three acres is $1,500, and the state paid the FMV, $22,000, on February 10. The farm was purchased on August 12, 1976.

Nonrecaptured net Section 1231 losses from the five most recent tax years preceding the current year amount to $7,000. Estimated taxes paid during the year amount to $32,000.

Prepare Forms 1040, 4684 Section A, 4797, and Schedule D. (Do not consider the alternative minimum tax or self-employment taxes discussed in Chapter I:14.)

CASE STUDY PROBLEMS

I:13-69 Your client, Kent Earl, whose tax rate is 35%, owns a bowling alley and has indicated that he wants to sell the business for $1 million and purchase a minor league baseball franchise. His business consists of the following tangible assets:

	Acquisition Date	Original Cost	Adjusted Basis
Equipment	2003	$600,000	$150,000
Building	2003	900,000	494,000
Land	1988	100,000	100,000
Inventory	Current year	50,000	50,000

Because you have another client, Tom Quick, who is interested in purchasing a business, you informed Tom of Kent's interest in selling. Tom wants to purchase the bowling alley, and the price sounds right to him. The bowling alley business has been very profitable in the last few years because Kent has developed a loyal group of customers by promoting bowling leagues during the week days and a special Saturday afternoon session for children in the elementary school grades. Kent and Tom have come to you and want to know how the transaction should be handled for the best tax results. You know that the $1 million purchase price will have to be allocated among the assets and it will be necessary to estimate the FMV of all assets. Because FMV is often subjective, Kent and Tom recognize that some flexibility might exist in allocating the purchase price. For example, it might be just as easy to justify a FMV of $300,000 or $325,000 for the equipment.

a. What advice do you have for Kent with respect to the allocation (i.e., should he be interested in allocating more to some assets than others)? Explain the reasoning for your advice.

b. Would your advice to Kent be different if he had a large amount of capital losses and no nonrecaptured net Sec. 1231 losses?

c. What advice do you have for Tom with respect to the allocation (i.e., should he be interested in allocating more of the purchase price to some assets than to others)? Explain the reasoning for your advice.

d. What advantages might result from having Kent sign an agreement not to compete (i.e., operate a bowling alley)?

e. Should you have a concern about the ethical implications of advising both Kent and Tom?

I:13-70 Assume the same facts as in Case Study Problem I:13-69 except you have the following market values as a result of an appraisal:

Equipment	$ 250,000
Building	500,000
Land	140,000
Inventory	110,000
Total	$1,000,000

Tom insists that $150,000 of the purchase price should be allocated to inventory and $100,000 should be allocated to land. He refuses to complete the purchase unless the allocation is made as he requests. What action should you take with respect to Tom's request? (See Chapter I:10 for a discussion of valuation issues in the purchase and sale of a business.)

TAX RESEARCH PROBLEM

I:13-71 Berkeley Corporation has a policy of furnishing new automobiles to the athletic department of the local university. The automobiles are used for short periods of time by the extremely popular head basketball coach. When the automobiles are returned to Berkeley Corporation, they are sold to regular customers. The owner of Berkeley Corporation maintains that any such cars held for more than one year should qualify as Sec. 1231 property. Do you agree?

Research sources include:

• Rev. Rul. 75-538, 1975-2 C.B. 34

14

SPECIAL TAX COMPUTATION METHODS, TAX CREDITS, AND PAYMENT OF TAX

LEARNING OBJECTIVES

After studying this chapter, you should be able to

1 ▶ Calculate the alternative minimum tax

2 ▶ Describe self-employment income and compute the self-employment tax

3 ▶ Describe the various business and personal tax credits

4 ▶ Describe and compute the premium tax credit and the shared responsibility payment

5 ▶ Explain the mechanics of the federal withholding tax system and the requirements for making estimated tax payments

6 ▶ Describe tax planning considerations for AMT, tax credits, and payment of taxes

7 ▶ Describe compliance and procedural considerations for AMT, tax credits, and payment of taxes

Chapter I:2 discussed the basic tax computation for individuals using the tax table and tax rate schedules. This chapter completes the discussion of the tax computation by examining three principal topics:

1. Two additional taxes: the alternative minimum tax and self-employment tax;
2. Various tax credits that reduce tax liability; and
3. Methods for prepayment of an individual's tax liability, including wage withholding and estimated tax payments.

ALTERNATIVE MINIMUM TAX

OBJECTIVE 1

Calculate the alternative minimum tax

Over the years, Congress has used the income tax law for a variety of purposes beyond raising revenue to fund government operations, such as enacting provisions to promote economic and social goals. As the number of special tax provisions increased, many taxpayers were able to plan their financial affairs to substantially reduce or eliminate their income tax liability. As a result, in 1969, Congress passed a new set of rules to ensure that all taxpayers would pay at least a minimum amount of income tax. Thus was born what is known today as the **alternative minimum tax (AMT)**.

The present AMT system operates as a separate tax system, parallel to the regular income tax system. Taxpayers first determine their regular income tax liability and then determine their tax liability under the AMT system. They must pay the *greater* of the regular income tax or their tax under the AMT system.

The AMT system applies to individuals, corporations, estates, and trusts.[1] It requires taxpayers to modify the amount of their regular taxable income for a number of adjustments and preferences and to subtract an AMT exemption, with the result being the tax base for the AMT system. AMT tax rates are applied to compute the tax, which is called the Tentative Minimum Tax (TMT).

Few individual taxpayers pay the AMT. Only approximately 1 percent of taxpayers were subject to AMT during the late 1990s, but that number has increased, with almost 3 percent of taxpayers paying AMT in 2012.[2]

EXAMPLE I:14-1 ▶ Ricardo and Sue are married and file a joint return for 2015 with regular taxable income of $50,000 and tax preferences and adjustments of $12,000. Their alternative minimum taxable income (AMTI) is $62,000 ($50,000 + $12,000), but the alternative minimum tax base is zero because of the $83,400 exemption. Thus, their tax liability is based on the regular tax computation, and they owe no AMT liability. ◀

EXAMPLE I:14-2 ▶ Assume the same facts for Ricardo and Sue as in Example I:14-1 except they have tax preferences and adjustments of $61,000. Their alternative minimum taxable income (AMTI) is $111,000. Their tentative minimum tax (TMT) is $7,176 [($111,000 − $83,400) = $27,600 × 0.26 = $7,176.] Regular tax on taxable income of $50,000 is $6,578. Ricardo and Sue must pay the TMT of $7,176 because it exceeds the regular tax of $6,578. ◀

---

[1] The AMT applicable to corporations is discussed in Chapter C:5 of *Prentice Hall's Federal Taxation: Corporations, Partnerships, Estates, and Trusts* text and in the *Comprehensive* volume.
[2] IRS, *Statistics of Income Bulletin*, Fall 2014.

HISTORICAL NOTE

The original add-on minimum tax, enacted in 1969, was 10% of the taxpayer's tax preferences in excess of a $30,000 statutory exemption.

HISTORICAL NOTE

The original add-on minimum tax, enacted in 1969, was 10% of the taxpayer's tax preferences in excess of a $30,000 statutory exemption.

ADDITIONAL COMMENT

Some tax advisors recommend accelerating income into a year in which the taxpayer is subject to the AMT because the income will be taxed at a 26% or a 28% rate rather than a possibly higher rate in a later year.

AMT COMPUTATION

The individual AMT uses the approach outlined below to determine the AMT tax base and the amount of AMT imposed, if any.[3]

> TAXABLE INCOME   (determined under the regular income tax system)
>   Plus: AMT preference items
>   Plus or minus: AMT adjustments
>
> =ALTERNATIVE MINIMUM TAXABLE INCOME (AMTI)
>   Minus: AMT exemption amount (see table below)
>
> =ALTERNATIVE MINIMUM TAX BASE
>   Multiplied by AMT tax rates[4]
>
> =TENTATIVE MINIMUM TAX
>   Minus: Regular income tax
>
> ALTERNATIVE MINIMUM TAX

From 2001 to 2011, three elements in the AMT computation—the AMT exemption amount, the AMT exemption phase-out range, and the AMT tax brackets—were not automatically adjusted for annual inflation. Almost annually, Congress acted to "patch" the amount of the AMT exemption. In the American Taxpayer Relief Act of 2012, Congress provided for future years with a provision for automatic annual inflation adjustments for all three elements (Sec. 55(d)(4)). The inflation adjusted amounts for the 2015's AMT exemption and phase-out range appear in the table below.

AMT TAX RATES AND BRACKETS

The AMT for 2015 (2014) is imposed on the AMT base at 26% of the first $185,400 ($182,500) and at 28% on AMTI over $185,400 ($182,500).

AMT EXEMPTION AMOUNT

The AMT exemption operates as a buffer to reduce the impact of AMT. The buffer is ineffective for high-income taxpayers both because of the limited amount of the basic exemption and because the exemption amount is disallowed (phased-out) as income rises over a threshold amount. The exemption is reduced by 25 cents per dollar of AMTI over the threshold: Exemption allowed = Basic exemption amount − 25% (AMTI − Threshold). The phase-out concludes when the amount of AMTI is sufficient to reduce the exemption allowed to $0.

Filling Status	2015 Basic Exemption	2014 Basic Exemption	2015 Phaseout Threshold	2014 Phaseout Threshold
Married jointly	$83,400	$82,100	$158,900	$156,500
Single	$53,600	$52,800	$119,200	$117,300
Married separately	$41,700	$41,050	$ 79,450	$ 78,250

---

[3] Sec. 55(b)(1).
[4] The AMT rate on net capital gains corresponds with the reduced rates on net capital gains and qualified dividends for regular tax purposes: 20% if the taxpayer's top regular tax rate is 39.6%; 15% if the taxpayer's top regular tax rate is 25%, 28%, 33%, or 35%; and 0% if the taxpayer's top regular tax rate is 15%. (Sec. 1(h)(1)).

EXAMPLE I:14-3 ▶

KEY POINT

For purposes of the alternative minimum tax, no deduction is allowed personal exemptions or the standard deduction.

HISTORICAL NOTE

In the Revenue Reconciliation Act of 1993, Congress created a two-tier alternative minimum tax schedule in order to make the individual income tax system more progressive.

EXAMPLE I:14-3 ▶ Rita, an unmarried taxpayer filing single, has regular taxable income of $185,000 in 2015, a regular tax liability after credits of $43,271 ($44,871 − $1,600), a positive AMT adjustment (due to limitations on itemized deductions) of $25,300, and tax preferences of $10,000. Rita's non-refundable tax cedits were an adoption credit of $1,000 and a dependent care credit of $600. Rita's alternative minimum tax is calculated as follows:

Taxable income		$185,000
Plus:	Tax preferences	10,000
Plus:	AMT Adjustment for itemized deductions	25,300
Plus:	AMT Adjustment for personal exemption	4,000
Alternative minimum taxable income (AMTI)		$224,300
Minus:	Exemption amount ($53,600 − $26,275)[a]	(27,325)
Alternative minimum tax base		$196,975
Tax on first $185,400: ($185,400 × 0.26)		$ 48,204
Tax on excess over $185,400: ($11,575 × 0.28)		3,241
Tentative minimum tax		$ 51,445
Minus:	Nonrefundable tax credits	$ (1,600)
	Regular tax	(43,271)
Alternative minimum tax (AMT)		$ 6,574

[a]Exemption phaseout: [0.25 × ($224,300 − $119,200)] = $26,275   ◀

AMT TAX PREFERENCE ITEMS

ADDITIONAL COMMENT

Most taxpayers will not have tax preference items. Over the years, tax preference items have diminished in importance while adjustments have increased in impacting AMT liabilities.

Certain provisions in the Internal Revenue Code grant favorable treatment to taxpayers. However, because of concern that some taxpayers may overuse these favorable provisions, Congress has classified them as tax preferences (IRC Sec. 57). For example, though the regular tax system allows deductions for depletion in excess of the property's basis, the AMT system limits depletion deductions to the property's basis. So, an AMT preference item (equal to depletion deducted in excess of basis) is a required addition. All AMT tax preference items are additions toward AMTI. However, only certain items receiving preferential regular tax treatment are tax preference items.

ADDITIONAL COMMENT

Under the American Recovery and Reinvestment Act of 2009, interest on private activity bonds issued in 2009 or 2010 is not treated as a tax preference item.

To compute the AMT tax base, the tax preferences designated in Sec. 57 must be added to regular taxable income. Some common tax preference items designated in Sec. 57 include:

▶ The excess of accelerated depreciation expense over a hypothetical straight-line depreciation amount for real property placed in service before 1987 (computed on an item-by-item basis).

▶ Tax-exempt interest on certain private activity bonds. In general, private activity bonds are state or local bonds that are issued to help finance a private business.

▶ The excess of depletion expense over the adjusted basis of the underlying natural resource asset.

EXAMPLE I:14-4 ▶ Richard, a single taxpayer, has the following tax preference items for the current year:

▶ $15,000 ACRS cost-recovery deduction on real property placed in service before 1987 and held for investment. The straight-line ACRS deduction would have been $10,000.

▶ $10,000 of tax-exempt interest on private activity bonds.

ADDITIONAL COMMENT

Some tax advisors recommend that cash basis taxpayers prepay their local property taxes or state income taxes before the end of the year to reduce the current year's tax liability. However, if the taxpayer is subject to the AMT, this may not be effective in reducing the current tax liability.

Richard's total tax preferences are $15,000, consisting of $5,000 excess cost recovery deductions and $10,000 tax-exempt interest on the private activity bonds.   ◀

AMT ADJUSTMENTS

For most individual taxpayers, adjustments fall into three categories: (1) regular tax itemized deductions disallowed in computing AMTI, (2) the AMT system's disallowance of the standard deduction (if taken) and personal exemptions, and (3) timing differences relating to the deferral of income or the acceleration of deductions under the regular tax rules.

Itemized Deductions. Only certain itemized deductions are allowed in computing AMTI. The more significant itemized deductions that *are not deductible* for the AMT include:

▶ Miscellaneous itemized deductions.

▶ State, local and foreign income taxes and real and personal property taxes.

▶ Home mortgage interest expense that is *not* "qualified housing interest." Qualified housing interest includes only interest on debt incurred to acquire/build/improve taxpayers' principal residence or second home, and

▶ Medical and dental expenses that exceed the AGI ceiling for regular tax but do not exceed the AGI ceiling for AMT. For most taxpayers, the AGI ceiling is 10% for both regular tax and the AMT. However, for tax years 2013–2016, taxpayers who are age 65 or over have a 7.5% AGI ceiling for regular tax but a 10% AGI ceiling for AMT.

Standard Deduction and Personal Exemptions. Although allowed for regular tax, a standard deduction is not allowed for AMTI. In addition, personal and dependency exemptions are not allowed as deductions in determining AMTI.

EXAMPLE I:14-5 ▶ Robin, a single taxpayer with no dependents, has AGI of $100,000 and the following itemized deductions for the current tax year:

Charitable contributions	4,000
Medical expenses, net of insurance	10,500
Mortgage interest on Robin's personal residence	18,400
Real estate taxes	4,000
State income taxes	6,000
Personal casualty loss, net of insurance	$15,000

From the information above, Robin's regular taxable income would be:

AGI			$100,000
Itemized deductions:			
Charitable contributions		$ 4,000	
Medical expenses	$10,500		
Less 10.0% of AGI	(10,000)	500	
Mortgage interest			
(100% qualified housing interest)		18,400	
Real estate taxes		4,000	
State income taxes		6,000	
Personal casualty loss	$15,000		
Less $100 floor	(100)		
Less 10% of AGI	(10,000)	4,900	(37,800)
Personal exemption			(4,000)
Taxable income			$58,200

To compute her AMTI, Robin must make adjustments to her regular taxable income. Assume that Robin also has $20,000 of tax preferences. Her AMTI would be computed as follows:

Taxable income	$58,200
Tax preferences	20,000
AMT adjustments:	
Medical expenses: ($500 allowed for regular taxable income and for AMTI)	0
Real estate and state income taxes (not allowed for AMTI)	10,000
Personal exemption (not allowed for AMTI)	4,000
AMTI	$92,200 ◀

Timing Differences. Other adjustments are required when the rules for calculating regular taxable income permit the taxpayer temporarily to defer the recognition of income or to accelerate deductions (timing differences). The most common AMT adjustments for timing differences include:

▶ For personal property placed in service after 1998, the difference between the MACRS depreciation deduction and the hypothetical amount determined by using the 150%

declining balance method over the recovery period used for regular tax purposes. Bonus depreciation, where applicable, is allowed in full for purposes of the AMT.

▶ For real property placed in service after 1986 and before January 1, 1999, the difference between the MACRS depreciation claimed using the property's actual recovery period and a hypothetical straight-line depreciation amount calculated using a 40-year life (see Chapter I:10 for a discussion of the alternative depreciation system).[5]

▶ For incentive stock options, the excess of the option's fair market value over the price paid by the individual for the option. This adjustment is measured on the date the rights to the underlying stock are freely transferable or are not subject to a substantial risk of forfeiture.

▶ For research and experimental (R&E) expenditures, the difference between the regular tax deduction and the deduction that would have been allowed if the expenditures were capitalized and amortized over a ten-year period.[6]

EXAMPLE I:14-6 ▶ Rob has the following AMT adjustments caused by timing differences in 2015:

▶ Depreciation of $3,636 on residential rental property costing $100,000 and placed in service in January 1998 (using the straight-line method and a 27 1/2-year recovery period under MACRS). Depreciation for AMT purposes is $2,500 (using the straight-line method and a 40-year recovery period under the alternative depreciation system). Thus, the positive AMT adjustment is $1,136 ($3,636 − $2,500).

▶ Depreciation is $2,000 on a computer used in business costing $10,000 and placed in service in January 2015 based on MACRS rules. Depreciation for AMT purposes is $1,500 based on the alternative depreciation system (i.e., 150% DB method, half-year convention, and a five-year recovery period). Thus, the positive AMT adjustment is $500 ($2,000 − $1,500).

ADDITIONAL COMMENT

For corporate taxpayers only, there is a 0.12% environmental tax imposed on the excess of the corporation's modified alternative minimum taxable income over $2 million. This additional tax levy is primarily imposed on corporations larger than "mom and pop" entities.

▶ R&E expenditures amounting to $50,000 are expensed in the current year. For AMT purposes, the R&E deduction would be $5,000 ($50,000 ÷ 10 years) since the expenditures are capitalized and amortized over a 10-year period. Thus, the positive AMT adjustment is $45,000 ($50,000 − $5,000).

Rob's total positive AMT adjustment to taxable income to arrive at AMTI is $46,636 ($1,136 + $500 + $45,000). ◀

AMT CREDITS

Credits that Reduce AMT. As discussed later in this chapter, a number of credits are allowed to reduce a taxpayer's regular tax liability. However, only the foreign tax credit and nonrefundable personal credits are allowed to reduce AMT. The foreign tax credit that applies to the AMT is a specially computed credit, called the "alternative minimum tax foreign tax credit" and is beyond the scope of this text. Nonrefundable personal tax credits are allowed against both regular tax and the AMT. They are discussed on pp. I:14-10–19 and are summarized in Topic Review I:14-2.

 STOP & THINK

Question: What are the most common characteristics of taxpayers who are subject to the AMT?

Solution: While each situation is unique, certain taxpayers are more likely to be subject to the AMT. First, taxpayers who have materially invested in real estate before January 1, 1999 are likely candidates for the AMT because they will have a large positive adjustment caused from differences in depreciation. Second, as discussed above, taxpayers who use credits to reduce their regular tax liability may be subject to the AMT because only certain credits reduce the AMT. Third, taxpayers who have very large itemized deductions, primarily from large state and local tax liabilities, may be subject to the AMT because state and

---

[5] For real property being depreciated under the straight-line method and placed in service after 1998, the Taxpayer Relief Act of 1997 eliminates this adjustment.

[6] Sec. 56(b)(2). However, this adjustment does not apply if the taxpayer materially participates in the activity, Sec. 56(b)(2)(D).

local taxes are not deductible for AMT purposes. Fourth, taxpayers who have numerous personal exemptions (large families) may be subject to the AMT.

Minimum Tax Credit (MTC) Under Sec. 53, individual taxpayers are allowed a credit for AMT paid in past years against future years' *regular tax liability*. The logic is as follows: the AMT may be caused by adjustments that will reverse in the future, and the taxpayer will actually pay a higher regular tax in those future years. Thus, the combination of a prior year AMT and current year regular tax essentially constitutes double taxation. A taxpayer who paid AMT in prior years but is not subject to AMT in the current year may be entitled to an MTC against his regular tax liability in the current year.[7]

SUMMARY ILLUSTRATION OF THE AMT COMPUTATION

EXAMPLE I:14-7 ▶

Roger and Kate are married, file a joint return, and have four dependent children. All the children are under age 17. The following items were used to compute regular taxable income for the current year:

Gross income:		
Salary		$ 70,000
Interest income		10,000
Business income		30,000[a]
AGI		$110,000
Itemized deductions:		
State and local taxes	$9,400	
Mortgage interest (100% qualified housing interest)	12,000	
Charitable contributions	3,000	(24,400)
Personal and dependency exemptions ($4,000 × 6)		(24,000)
Taxable income		$ 61,600
Regular tax		$8,318
Child tax credit		(4,000)
Net regular tax		$ 4,318

[a]MACRS depreciation deductions of $75,000 on personal property placed in service after 1986 were claimed in arriving at business income. Only $50,000 of depreciation would be claimed under the alternative depreciation system using the 150% declining balance method.

Their AMT is computed as follows:		
Taxable income		$ 61,600
AMT adjustments:		
Personal and dependency exemptions	$24,000	
Excess depreciation ($75,000 − $50,000)	25,000	
State and local taxes	9,400	58,400
AMTI		$120,000
AMT exemption		(83,400)
Alternative Minimum Tax base		$ 36,600
Tax rate		× 0.26
Tentative minimum tax before credit		$ 9,516
Child tax credit		(4,000)
Tentative minimum tax		$ 5,516
Net regular tax after child tax credit		(4,318)
Alternative minimum tax		$ 1,198[b]

The total tax liability for Roger and Kate is $5,516 ($4,318 + $1,198).

[b]An AMT credit may be available in future years to offset regular tax. However, the AMT credit applies only to the AMT that results from timing differences (e.g., depreciation adjustments) and not from exclusions (e.g., personal exemptions and taxes). ◀

---

[7] The Minimum Tax Credit applies to timing adjustments rather than permanent adjustments. A detailed discussion of the rules for computing this credit for individuals is beyond the scope of this book.

SELF-EMPLOYMENT TAX

OBJECTIVE 2

Describe self-employment income and compute the self-employment tax

An individual may work either as an employee or as an independent contractor. The distinction generally hinges on the degree of influence and control an individual has over his work.[8] The classification is important in determining the responsible party for employment taxes imposed under the Federal Insurance Contribution Act (FICA). FICA includes old-age, survivors, and disability insurance (OASDI, commonly referred to as Social Security) and hospital insurance (Medicare).

Individuals classified as *employees* pay the employee part of FICA on their earnings as they are earned through withholding, and their employers pay the employer part of employment taxes on the same earnings. Because employers report and remit both the withheld employee portion and the employer portion of FICA taxes to the U.S. Treasury, it is not necessary for employees to report employment taxes within their federal income tax returns.

Individuals classified as *self-employed* are responsible for paying both the employee share and employer share of employment taxes. This tax is called the self-employment (SE) tax, and it is imposed on net earnings from self-employment (defined below). It is reported as part of the self-employed individual's federal income tax return.

A combined FICA rate of 15.3% applied for the years 1989 through 2010 and will hold for years after 2012. The rate includes the following:

1) Social Security tax imposed at a rate of 12.4% on wages (6.2% by withholding for the employee portion and 6.2% for the employer portion) and on net earnings from self-employment (SE);[9] and,

2) Medicare tax imposed at a rate of 2.9% on wages (1.45% by withholding for the employee portion and 1.45% for the employer portion) and on net earnings from self-employment. (See next page for separate discussion of the Additional Medicare Tax)

Social Security tax is imposed on wages and net earnings from SE up to a ceiling amount (adjusted for inflation annually). For 2015, the ceiling equals $118,500 ($117,000 for 2014). The regular Medicare tax is imposed on all wages and net earnings from SE—without limit.

Net earnings from SE is defined as 92.35% of self-employment income The SE tax is imposed only if net earnings from SE equals or exceeds $400.

Self employed individuals are entitled to deduct—*for AGI*—50% of the employer portion of their SE tax.[10]

EXAMPLE I:14-8 ▶ Robert, a cabinet maker, works as a sole proprietor. For 2015, his self-employment earnings totaled $75,000. His net earnings from SE equal $69,263 ($75,000 × 0.9235). His SE tax of $10,596 includes Social Security tax and Medicare tax. His deduction for SE tax equals $5,298.

Social Security tax: 0.124 × ($69,263) = $8,589
Medicare tax: 0.029 × ($69,263) = $2,009
SE tax deduction: 0.50 × ($8,589 + $2,009) = $5,299. ◀

EXAMPLE I:14-9 ▶ The facts are identical to I:14-8 except Robert's self-employment earnings totaled $175,000. His net earnings from SE equal $161,613 (0.9235 × 175,000).

His SE tax of $19,381 includes Social Security tax and Medicare tax. His deduction for SE tax equals $9,691.

Social Security tax: 0.124 ($118,500 ceiling) = $14,694
Medicare tax: 0.029 ($161,613) = $4,687
SE tax deduction: 0.50 ($14,694 + $4,687) = $9,691 ◀

Individuals who work as employees but also operate a business are subject to self-employment tax on net earnings from self-employment (SE). For Social Security tax, the tax base

---

[8] Rev. Rul. 87-41 provides a list of twenty factors to be considered in evaluating whether an employer-employee relationship exists.

[9] PL 112-78. During 2011 and 2012, a temporary payroll tax holiday applied, reducing the OASDI rate for employees to 4.2% (OASDI rate of 10.4% and combined FICA rate of 13.3%).

[10] In 2011 and 2012, the deductible portion of Social Security tax was based on the employer portion (6.2%/(4.2% + 6.2%) = 59.6%), and 50% of the Medicare tax was deductible.

equals the lesser of (1) net earnings from self-employment or (2) the Social Security tax ceiling reduced by the individual's earnings as an employee. The Medicare tax is imposed on net earnings from SE (without limit).

EXAMPLE I:14-10 ► In the current year, Sandy earns $75,000 in employee wages. In addition, from her small consulting practice, she earns $10,000 of income from self-employment. The tax base for her Social Security tax equals the smaller of $9,235 (0.9235 × $10,000) or $43,500 ($118,500 − $75,000). Sandy's SE tax equals $1,413, including Social Security tax of $1,145 ($9,235 × 0.124), and Medicare tax of $268 ($9,235 × 0.029). Her deduction for SE tax equals $707 (0.50 × $1,413). ◄

EXAMPLE I:14-11 ► Assume the facts in Example 14-10 apply except that Sandy earns $125,000 in employee wages. The tax base for her Social Security tax equals $0 because her employee earnings exceed the Social Security tax ceiling (more precisely, the tax base equals the smaller of $9,235 [0.9235 × $10,000] or $0 [$118,500 − $125,000]). The Medicare tax (and the SE tax) totals $268 ($9,235 × 0.029). Her deduction for SE tax equals $134 (0.50 × $268). ◄

For tax years after 2012, a new hospital insurance tax (Additional Medicare Tax) of 0.9% applies to self-employment income (Sec. 1401(b)(2)) of individuals whose earned income exceeds threshold amounts (table below). Unlike the regular Medicare Tax of 2.9%, the Additional Medicare Tax is *not* included in the "for AGI" deduction allowed to self-employed taxpayers for the employer portion of SE tax (Sec. 164(f)(1)).

ADDITIONAL COMMENT

For some self-employed taxpayers, the amount of SE tax exceeds the amount of income tax for the year. For example, a married couple with two children and $17,000 of self-employment income would not owe any income tax, but would have a $2,402 (17,000 × .9235 × 15.3%) SE tax liability.

Filing Status	Threshold Amount
Married Jointly	$250,000
Single	$200,000
Married Separately	$125,000

Because the new tax applies to all earned income, in determining the amount of earned income subject to the new tax, the threshold amount is used first against employee compensation, and any remainder used against self-employment income.

EXAMPLE I:14-12 ► Henry, an unmarried taxpayer filing single for 2015, earns a salary of $130,000 plus self-employment income of $145,000 in consulting fees. His net SE income is $133,908 ($145,000 × .9235).

ADDITIONAL COMMENT

If an individual works for more than one employer during the year and earns (in total) more than the Social Security tax ceiling, the employers will have withheld more than the employee's required Social Security tax. The taxpayer is entitled to a credit (or refund) for the overpaid tax against his regular income tax liability.

For regular SE tax, Henry will not pay Social Security tax on his SE income from consulting (his salary subject to this tax exceeds the $118,500 ceiling). He will pay Medicare tax of $3,883 ($133,908 × .029). One-half of the Medicare tax, $1,942, is allowed as a for AGI deduction.

Henry will pay the Additional Medicare Tax because his earned income exceeds $200,000. The $200,000 threshold first will exempt his salary from the additional tax ($200,000 threshold − $130,000 = $70,000 remaining), and the remainder will exempt all but $63,908 of his self-employment income ($133,908 − $70,000 remaining threshold = $63,908).

The Additional Medicare tax imposed will equal $575 ($63,908 × 0.009). A deduction for AGI is not allowed for the Additional Medicare Tax. ◄

WHAT CONSTITUTES SELF-EMPLOYMENT INCOME

Individuals who carry on a trade or business as a proprietor or partnership are subject to the SE tax. If an individual has two separate self-employment activities, the *net* earnings from each activity are aggregated. However, where a husband and wife file a joint return and both have self-employment income, the SE tax must be computed for each individual separately.

EXAMPLE I:14-13 ► Bob and Ruth are married and file a joint return. Bob has $93,000 net earnings from a consulting business and a $4,000 net loss from a retail store that he operates as a sole proprietorship. Ruth has wages of $50,000 from her employer that are subject to FICA taxes. Bob's net earnings from self-employment are $82,192 ($89,000 × 0.9235). No reduction in Bob's SE tax base is allowed for Ruth's wages. The SE tax is computed separately for Bob and Ruth. ◄

KEY POINT

In the case of married taxpayers filing joint returns, it is important on Schedule SE of Form 1040 to fill in the name and Social Security number of the spouse with the self-employment income. This information is used to establish specific benefit eligibility.

Among the items that constitute earnings subject to the SE tax are:

► Net earnings from a sole proprietorship

> ► Director's fees[11]
>
> ► Taxable research grants
>
> ► Distributive share of partnership income plus guaranteed payments from the partnership[12]

The self-employment tax is computed on Schedule SE of Form 1040 (see Appendix B). The rules for computing the SE tax are summarized in Topic Review I:14-1.

TOPIC REVIEW I:14-1

Self-Employment Tax Summary

► The tax base is generally net earnings from SE which equals 92.35% of self-employment income.

► The Social Security tax is imposed at 12.4% of net earnings from SE, and the Medicare tax is imposed at 2.9% of net earnings from SE.

► For years after 2012, an Additional Medicare Tax is imposed on earnings from employment (employee and self-employed). The tax is imposed at a rate of 0.9% on earnings in excess of a threshold amount.

► In 2015, a ceiling of $118,500 applies to the amount of SE earnings subject to Social Security tax. No ceiling applies to the Medicare portion of the tax.

► SE tax is computed separately for each spouse for married individuals filing joint returns.

PERSONAL AND BUSINESS TAX CREDITS

OBJECTIVE 3

Describe the various business and personal tax credits

USE AND IMPORTANCE OF TAX CREDITS

Tax credits often serve as incentives for activities supporting broader policy objectives. For example, tax credits may help to increase employment, encourage energy conservation and research and experimental activities, and provide tax relief for low-income taxpayers. Tax credits are also used to mitigate the effects of double taxation on income from foreign countries. Thus, tax credits are an important part of the income tax law.

Credits are classified into two broad categories, **nonrefundable** and **refundable**. Nonrefundable credits only offset tax liability. Refundable credits, on the other hand, not only offset tax liability but if the credits exceed the tax liability, the excess will be paid (refunded) directly to the taxpayer. At the end of the section, Topic Review I:14-2 provides a summary of selected tax credits and the rationale for their inclusion in the tax law. Taxes withheld from employee wages are prepayments of tax, but are also referred to as refundable credits.

VALUE OF A CREDIT VERSUS A DEDUCTION

As discussed in Chapter I:2, tax credits reduce tax liability on a dollar-for-dollar basis. This is in contrast to tax deductions, which reduce taxable income. The value of a tax deduction increases with the taxpayer's marginal tax rate, so tax deductions are more valuable to high-income taxpayers than to lower-income taxpayers. Tax credits, however, benefit all taxpayers in the same amount regardless of their marginal tax rate.

ADDITIONAL COMMENT

The American Recovery and Reinvestment Act of 2009 has expanded and increased both nonrefundable and refundable credits.

EXAMPLE I:14-14 ►

Tasha and Sean are both single taxpayers. Each has an $800 expenditure that qualifies as either a tax deduction or a 20% credit. Tasha is in the 15% marginal tax bracket while Sean is in the 33% marginal tax bracket. If the $800 is claimed as a deduction, Tasha would receive a tax benefit of $120 ($800 × 15%) whereas Sean would receive a tax benefit of $264 ($800 × 33%). Conversely, if the credit is claimed, Tasha and Sean would benefit equally from a $160 credit ($800 × 20%). In this case, Tasha would prefer the credit while Sean would prefer the tax deduction. ◄

---

[11] Rev. Rul. 57-246, 1957-1 C.B. 338. It is a factual question whether an officer who also serves as a director is performing services as an employee or as an independent contractor. The courts have recognized that an individual can perform services as a director and also perform employment-related services, but the director fees may be recharacterized by the courts if the fees are in reality compensation for services rendered as an employee. (See *Peter H. Jacobs,* 1993 RIA T.C. Memo ¶ 93, 570, 66 TCM 1470.)

[12] A limited partner's share of partnership income is not considered SE income (Sec. 1402(a) (13)) given the inability of limited partners to participate in managing the partnership. LLPs and LLCs developed as business entities long after 1977, when Sec. 1402(a)(13) was added to the law. Individuals are considered members of LLCs, and they participate in management (like general partners). But, they have limited liability. Thus, determination of whether LLC (and LLP) earnings are considered SE income is unsettled.

NONREFUNDABLE PERSONAL TAX CREDITS

As a result of tax legislation in the last few years, the number of personal tax credits for individual taxpayers has increased significantly. For tax years after 2010, nonrefundable personal credits offset an individual's regular tax and AMT.[13] The more important nonrefundable personal tax credits are discussed below.

Child and Dependent Care Credit. The child and dependent care credit provides tax savings for taxpayers who incur child and dependent care expenses because of employment activities. To qualify for the credit, an individual must meet two requirements: (1) expenses for the care of a qualifying individual are incurred to enable the taxpayer to be gainfully employed, and (2) the qualifying individual is either a qualifying child under age 13 or an incapacitated dependent or spouse who lived with the taxpayer for more than one-half of the year. The credit equals 35% of qualified expenditures.

EXAMPLE I:14-15 ▶ Tim and Tina are married and have two children under age 13. They incur child care expenses (e.g., a housekeeper and nurse) to enable both Tim and Tina to work on a full-time basis. These expenditures are eligible for the child and dependent care credit because Tim and Tina incurred them for qualifying individuals and to be gainfully employed. Alternatively, if Tina were not employed, but incurred the child care expenses to volunteer at the city library, the expenditures would not be eligible for the credit. ◀

Qualifying Employment-Related Expenses. Eligible expenses include amounts paid for care inside the home or outside the home for a qualifying individual. If care is provided in the home, amounts paid for care and household maintenance (e.g., housekeeper who cares for the child, and serves as maid and cook) are qualifying expenses. If the care is provided outside the home by a dependent care facility (e.g., a day care facility), the amounts will be eligible expenses only if the dependent care facility operates in compliance with federal, state and local law.[14] Amounts paid for services outside of the taxpayer's household (e.g., adult day care) that are spent for the care of an incapacitated dependent or spouse qualify only if the individual lives in the taxpayer's home for at least eight hours a day.

EXAMPLE I:14-16 ▶ Tony is divorced and has two children under age 13. He is employed and incurs child care expenses at a preschool nursery for one of the children. He also relies on a live-in nanny who cares for both children and provides housekeeping services and a gardener to care for his yard. All of the expenditures for the preschool nursery and the nanny qualify because these services constitute eligible household services, and care of qualifying individuals. However, the payments to the gardener are not eligible because they do not constitute qualifying household services. ◀

The following additional limitations apply:

1) Ceiling on qualifying expenses: The maximum amount of child and dependent care expenses that qualify for the credit equals $3,000 for one qualifying individual and $6,000 for two or more qualifying individuals. No carryover is permitted for expenses in excess of the maximum amounts.

2) Earned income limit: Maximum qualifying expenses cannot exceed the taxpayer's earned income. For married individuals, the limitation is applied to the earned income of the spouse with the smaller earned income. Gratuitous services performed by the taxpayer for charitable organizations are not considered gainful employment.[15] A spouse who is a full-time student or incapacitated is deemed to have an earned income of $250 per month ($500 per month if there are two or more qualifying individuals in the household).[16]

3) Payments to a relative are qualifying expenses unless the relative is a dependent or a child (under age 19) of the taxpayer.[17]

4) The credit will not be allowed unless the qualifying individual's Social Security number and the dependent care provider's social security number (or employer ID number) are reported on the return on which the credit is claimed.

EXAMPLE I:14-17 ▶ Troy and Tracy are married and incur qualifying child care expenses of $4,000 to take care of their two children, ages 1 and 3. Tracy's earned income is $20,000, and Troy's earned income

---

[13] Before 2011, these credits could offset a taxpayer's AMT liability only to the extent of tentative minimum tax over regular tax (the AMT).

[14] Employment-related expenses do not include amounts paid for services outside of the taxpayer's household at an overnight-stay camp.

[15] Rev. Rul. 73-597, 1973-2 CB 69.

[16] Sec. 21(d)(2). To qualify as a full-time student, the individual must enroll in an educational institution on a full-time basis for at least five calendar months of the year (Reg. Sec. 1.44A-2(b)(3)(B)(ii)).

[17] Sec. 21(e)(6).

KEY POINT

The percentage used to calculate the credit varies from 20% to 35% depending on the taxpayer's AGI.

from a part-time job is $3,500. Although their expenses do not exceed the overall qualifying expense limitation of $6,000, the earned income limitation applies because Troy's earned income ($3,500) is less than the child care expenses ($4,000). Therefore, the amount of child care expenses eligible for the credit is limited to $3,500. ◄

Credit Rate and Amount. Though generally, the credit equals 35% of qualifying expenses, the credit rate is reduced by one percentage point for each $2,000 (or

Credit rates for the child care credit across AGI levels

Adjusted Gross Income	Applicable Percentage	Adjusted Gross Income	Applicable Percentage
$ 0 to $15,000	35%	29,001 to 31,000	27%
15,001 to 17,000	34	31,001 to 33,000	26
17,001 to 19,000	33	33,001 to 35,000	25
19,001 to 21,000	32	35,001 to 37,000	24
21,001 to 23,000	31	37,001 to 39,000	23
23,001 to 25,000	30	39,001 to 41,000	22
25,001 to 27,000	29	41,001 to 43,000	21
27,001 to 29,000	28	43,001 and above	20

fraction thereof) of adjusted gross income in excess of $15,000. The rate goes no lower than 20%.

EXAMPLE I:14-18 ► Mark and Vicki are married, file a joint return, and have three children under age 13. Mark and Vicki's employment-related earnings are $25,000 and $10,000, respectively. Including all sources of income, their AGI is $36,000. They incur $8,000 of child care expenses during the year. First, their eligible child care expenses are limited to $6,000 because Mark and Vicki have more than one qualifying child. Second, the credit rate equals 24%, computed as follows:

Adjusted gross income (AGI)	$36,000
Base amount	(15,000)
Excess	21,000
Divided by $2,000	10.5
Rounded up to	11
Applicable credit (35% − 11%)	24%

Mark and Vicki's child and dependent care credit for the year is $1,440 ($6,000 × 0.24). ◄

Other Sources of Tax Benefits for Dependent Care. Employees may be eligible for two types of employer supported dependent care assistance that exclude from employees' gross income payments made by their employer for the provision for dependent care. The assistance is through dependent care assistance programs (IRC Section 129)[18] and employee funding of flexible spending arrangement (IRC Section 125). Qualifying employment-related expenses for purposes of the child and dependent care credit are reduced to the extent dependent care costs are funded through either of these types of plans.

EXAMPLE I:14-19 ► Assume the same facts as in Example I:14-18 except that Mark was reimbursed $4,100 by his employer under a qualified dependent care assistance program and this amount was excluded from his gross income. Thus, expenses eligible for the child and dependent care credit are reduced to $1,900 ($6,000 − $4,100) and the child care credit is $456 ($1,900 × 0.24). ◄

ADDITIONAL COMMENT

The tax credit for the elderly or disabled has been declining in recent years and amounted to only $16.2 million in 2011.

Tax Credit for the Elderly and Disabled. A limited credit is provided for certain low-income individuals who have attained age 65 before the end of the tax year or who retired because of a permanent and total disability.

The maximum credit is 15% of an initial amount of $5,000 ($7,500 for married individuals filing jointly if both spouses qualify).[19] This initial amount is reduced by:

---

[18] Sec. 129. (See Chapter I:4 for a discussion of the requirements for exclusion.)
[19] Sec. 22(c)(2).

1) Nontaxable Social Security, railroad retirement, or Veterans Administration pension or annuity benefits, and

2) One-half of AGI in excess of $7,500 for a single individual ($10,000 (MFJ)).[20]

Most elderly or disabled taxpayers are ineligible for the credit because they either receive Social Security benefits in excess of ceiling limitations or they have AGI amounts in excess of the limitations, which effectively reduces or eliminates the allowable credit.

EXAMPLE I:14-20 ▶ Wayne and Tammy are both 67 years old and file a joint return. They have AGI of $11,000 and receive nontaxable Social Security benefits of $3,000 during the current year. Their tax credit for the elderly is computed as follows:

Initial ceiling amount		$7,500
Minus: Nontaxable social security benefits	$3,000	
One-half of excess AGI (0.50 × [$11,000 − $10,000])	500	(3,500)
Total credit base		$4,000
		× 0.15
Tax credit		$ 600

◀

Adoption Credit. A nonrefundable credit is allowed for qualified adoption expenses in 2015 of up to $13,400 for adoption of an eligible child ($13,190 in 2014).[21] The credit generally is allowable in the year the adoption is finalized. If adoption expenses are paid prior to the year in which the adoption is finalized, such expenses are not eligible for the credit until the year the adoption is finalized. If expenses are paid during or after the year the adoption is finalized, the credit is allowable in the year the expenses are paid or incurred.

The credit is phased out (ratably over a $40,000 range) for high income taxpayers. The 2015 phaseout begins at AGI of $201,010 (2014 at $197,880).[22]

Qualified adoption expenses include reasonable and necessary adoption fees, court costs, attorney fees, and other expenses that are directly related to the legal adoption of an eligible child. Qualified adoption expenses are reduced by any reimbursements from an employer plan. An eligible child is defined as a child who has not reached 18 years old when the adoption takes place, or one who is physically or mentally incapable of self-care.

Taxpayers adopting a special needs child are treated as having incurred qualified adoption expenses of the maximum credit amount even if actual expenses are less.

EXAMPLE I:14-21 ▶ Oscar and Betty began proceedings in June 2014 to adopt a child. They incurred $7,000 of attorney fees and adoption agency fees in 2014. In 2015, they incurred an additional $8,000 of qualified adoption expenses, and the adoption became final. Oscar and Betty's AGI in 2015 equals $215,000. The adoption credit is allowable in 2015, computed as follows:

Total qualified adoption expenses	$15,000
Maximum credit (lesser of $15,000 or $13,400)	13,400
Phase-out percentage [($215,000 − $201,010) / $40,000] = 34.98%	
Amount of credit disallowed ($13,400 × 34.98%)	(4,687)
Amount of credit allowed	$ 8,713

---

[20] The AGI ceiling is $5,000 for married individuals filing a separate return.
[21] The credit as well as the AGI phaseout amounts are adjusted for inflation each year.

[22] For purposes of the phase-out, AGI is modified and determined without regard to the exclusions from gross income for foreign earned income, after the application of the rules relating to the taxation of Social Security, and other items. (See Sec. 36B(2).)

Oscar and Betty can take a credit for $8,713 of expenses and must claim the credit in 2015, the year the adoption becomes final. ◀

Child Tax Credit. Taxpayers are allowed a credit of $1,000 for each qualifying child. The definition of qualifying child for the child tax credit requires that the child is the taxpayer's dependent based on the category "qualifying child" under the conditions for the dependency exemption,[23] and that the child is under age 17.

The credit begins to phase out when modified AGI[24] reaches a threshold amount ($110,000 (MFJ), $75,000 (Single), or $55,000 (MFS)). The credit lost to phaseout is determined by the following.

$$[(\text{Modified AGI} - \text{Threshold})/\$1,000]^* \times \$50$$
*rounded up to the next whole number

Thus, a married couple filing jointly with one qualifying child and modified AGI of $123,500 will have a tentative child tax credit of $1,000. The credit will be subject to a phaseout of $700 [($123,500 − $110,000) ÷ $1,000 = 13.5 and 14 × $50 = $700]. Their allowable credit will be $300.

ADDITIONAL COMMENT

For taxpayers with three or more qualifying children, the refundable child tax credit equals the lesser of (1) the unclaimed portion of the credit or (2) the greater of a) 15% of the taxpayers earned income in excess of $3,000 or b) the taxpayer's social security taxes in excess of the taxpayer's earned income credit.

The child tax credit is generally *nonrefundable*. However, for tax years 2009–2017, if a taxpayer's tentative child tax credit is greater than the total tax liability, part of the credit (the "additional" child tax credit) is *refundable*. The refundable portion is the lesser of (1) the unclaimed portion of the credit or (2) 15% of taxpayer's earned income in excess of $3,000. Form 8812 is used to compute the refundable portion of the child tax credit.

Higher Education Costs Tax Credits. Two credits are available to taxpayers who incur higher education expenses. The two credits are the "American Opportunity Tax Credit (AOTC)" and the "Lifetime Learning Credit (LLC)."[25]

American Opportunity Tax Credit.[26] Under the AOTC, taxpayers are allowed a credit for up to $2,500 for qualified tuition and related expenses paid during the taxable year for each eligible student. The credit allowed equals 100% of the first $2,000 of qualified expenses plus 25% of up to $2,000 of qualified expenses in excess of the first $2,000 ($2,000 + 25%($2,000)) = $2,500, maximum credit amount).

Qualified tuition and related expenses include tuition and fees required for enrollment and course materials, including textbooks. They do not include room and board, student activity fees, and other expenses unrelated to an individual's academic coursework. Qualified expenses are limited to those paid for the first four years of postsecondary education. This requirement is based on whether the educational institution has awarded the student four years of academic credit as of the *beginning* of the tax year. Qualified expenses include those paid during the tax year for an eligible student, including the taxpayer, the taxpayer's spouse, or the taxpayer's dependent. An eligible student must (1) be enrolled in or attending an eligible education institution and (2) be taking courses on at least one-half of a full-time load for at least one academic term at that educational institution. Students are considered ineligible if they have been convicted of a federal or state felony drug offense by the end of tax year.

ADDITIONAL COMMENT

In addition to the AOTC and Lifetime Learning credits, there have been a plethora of new tax laws that encourage education, including:
(1) Sec. 529 plans;
(2) Improved student loan interest deduction rules;
(3) Increased limits for Coverdell Education IRAs.

Other requirements include the following items.

▶ If a taxpayer pays qualified expenses in one year but the expenses relate to an academic period that begins during January, February, or March of the next taxable year, the academic period is treated as beginning during the taxable year in which the payment is made. Thus, a payment of tuition in December 2014 for the Spring Semester, 2015 (which begins in January 2015) would be eligible for the AOTC in 2014.

---

[23] Under IRC Section 152(c) for the dependency exemption, a qualifying child must 1) be a relative of the taxpayer (descendent, sibling, or descendent of a sibling), 2) reside in the taxpayer's household for more than one-half of the year, 3) be supported by the taxpayer, 4) not file a joint return with a spouse, and 5) be younger than the taxpayer and under age 19 (or a student under age 24). For the child tax credit, the age requirement in the dependency exemption is modified to under age 17.

[24] Modified AGI means AGI increased by any amount excluded from gross income under Secs. 911, 931, or 933. Sec. 911, 931, and 933 are special exclusions in the international tax area.
[25] Sec. 25A.
[26] The provisions discussed for the AOTC apply for tax years 2009–2017, and represent those of the "expanded" Hope Scholarship credit.

► Qualified tuition and related expenses eligible for the AOTC must be reduced by amounts received under other sections of the tax law, such as scholarships (Sec. 117), employer-sponsored educational reimbursement plans (Sec. 127), education IRAs (Sec. 530), or other provisions of the tax law.

The allowable credit is phased out for high income taxpayers. The phase-out occurs over a $20,000 range (for married filing joint taxpayers) and begins when modified AGI is $160,000 as follows:

$$\text{Tentative AOTC} \times \frac{\text{Modified AGI} - \$160,000}{\$20,000} = \text{Phaseout for MFJ taxpayers}$$

For taxpayers other than joint filers, phase-out occurs over a $10,000 range, beginning at $80,000 of modified AGI. Modified AGI is AGI before exclusions for foreign earned income and foreign housing costs.

It is important to understand that the AOTC applies to each student. Thus, parents who have two children in their first four years of college may claim up to $2,500 for each child. For tax years 2009 through 2017, up to 40% of the allowable AOTC is refundable.

Lifetime Learning Credit. The LLC allowed equals 20% of up to $10,000 of qualified education expenses paid (per year). Education expenses of students eligible for AOTC must first be considered for AOTC. None of the expenses of a student for whom an AOTC credit is allowed are eligible for the LLC (LLC cannot be combined with AOTC to yield LLC on expenses in excess of those yielding maximum AOTC).

Like AOTC, qualified education expenses include those paid during the tax year for an eligible student, who may be the taxpayer, the taxpayer's spouse, or the taxpayer's dependent. However, for LLC, qualified education expenses include only tuition and academic fees, not course materials.

In some aspects, the LLC is more expansive than the AOTC: qualified expenses for LLC include those paid for any year (not limited to the first four years of postsecondary education), whether taken as part of a postsecondary degree program or to acquire or improve job skills. The expenses of a student with a record of conviction a felony drug offense qualify for LLC.

In other ways, the LLC is more restrictive than AOTC. Importantly, the $10,000 limitation on qualified expenses for LLC applies at the "family" level. For example, assuming a family pays $12,000 of qualified tuition, $6,000 for each of two dependent children who are eligible students. If the expenses qualify only for LLC, the maximum credit allowed equals $2,000. Had the expenses qualified for AOTC, the AOTC credit would equal $5,000 (2 students × $2,500 each). The LLC phases out more quickly for high-income taxpayers because the phase-out range begins at lower income levels and is indexed for inflation. For 2015, the LLC phase-out occurs for married taxpayers over a $20,000 range, beginning at $110,000 (at $108,000 in 2014) and for single taxpayers, phase-out occurs over a $10,000 range, beginning at $55,000 (at $54,000 in 2014).[27] Finally, the LLC is nonrefundable.

ADDITIONAL COMMENT

The education expenses for the AOTC and lifetime learning credits must be incurred at an educational institution that is eligible to participate in Department of Education student aid programs.

EXAMPLE I:14-22 ► Mark and Jane Green are married, file a joint return, and have three dependent children in college, Ron, Susan, and Bill. Ron and Susan attend State University and Bill attends Private University. The Greens' modified AGI in 2015 is $164,000. Details are as follows:

	Spring Semester 2015 (Paid in January 2015)	Fall Semester 2015 (Paid in August 2015)	AOTC Eligible Expenses
Ron:	Senior	5th year Senior	
Tuition and fees	$1,500	$1,550	$3,050
Course materials (books)	300	300	600
Room and board	3,500	3,700	—

---

[27] Note that inflation adjustments apply only to the phase-outs under LLC, not AOTC.

Susan:	Junior	Senior	
Tuition and fees	$1,500	$1,550	$3,050
Course materials (books)	300	300	600
Room and board	3,500	3,700	—
Bill:		Freshman	
Tuition and fees	—	$3,700	$3,700
Course materials (books)	—	300	300
Room and board	—	3,700	—

In 2015, the Greens are allowed to claim the American Opportunity Tax credit (AOTC) and the Lifetime Learning Credit (LLC) as follows:

Ron has not completed four years of postsecondary education at the beginning of 2015, so he qualifies as an eligible student for *all* of 2015. Assuming the AOTC has not been used for Ron in four prior tax years, his 2015 qualifying education expenses include his tuition and fees and course materials, totaling $3,650 ($1,500 + $1,550 + $300 + $300).

Ron's tentative AOTC equals $2,413 ((100% × $2,000) + (25% × $1,650)).

Susan qualifies for the AOTC in both semesters. Her tentative AOTC is $2,413 [(100% × $2,000) + ($1,650 × 25%)]. Bill qualifies for the AOTC only in Fall 2015 because he began postsecondary education in that semester. His tentative credit is $2,500 [(100% × $2,000) + (the next $ 2,000 x 25%)], based on qualifying expenses of $4,000.

The Greens' total tentative AOTC is $7,326 ($2,413 + $2,413 + $2,500). The phaseout is $1,465 ($7,326 × ($164,000 − $160,000)/$20,000). Thus, the Greens' total allowable AOTC is $5,861 ($7,326 − $1,465).

> Note: If the AOTC has been used for Ron in four prior tax years, the Greens' total allowable AOTC is $3,930. Their total tentative AOTC is $4,913 ($0 + $2,413 + $2,500), and their phaseout is $983 ($4,913 × ($164,000 − $160,000)/$20,000).
>
> If the AOTC has already been claimed for Ron for four years, Ron qualifies for the LLC in 2015 because the LLC is not limited to four years of postsecondary education. His qualified education expenses for 2015 total $3,050, so the Greens' tentative LLC is $610 ($3,050 × 20%). The phaseout is $610 ($610 × ($164,000 − $110,000)/$20,000). Thus, the Greens' total allowable LLC is zero. ◀

Residential Energy Credits. Congress has enacted a wide range of incentives for both individuals and businesses to promote domestic energy production and conservation. Most of these incentives are in the form of tax credits. Two major credits for individual taxpayers are (1) the nonbusiness energy property credit, and (2) the residential energy efficient property credit.

Nonbusiness Energy Property Credit. Individuals are allowed a nonrefundable tax credit for nonbusiness residential energy property (qualified windows, exterior doors, insulation, heat pumps, furnaces, central air conditioners, and water heaters). The credit equals 10% of the cost of building components (exterior doors and insulation, for example) plus the cost of energy property (water heaters and furnaces, for example). The credit's lifetime limit is $500 per taxpayer. It applies to property placed into service after December 31, 2008, and before January 1, 2015.[28]

Residential Energy Efficient Property (REEP) Credit. For tax years beginning after December 31, 2005 and before January 1, 2017, a tax credit is allowed for several types of energy efficient property installed on a taxpayer's principal residence:[29] Solar hot water heaters, Qualified solar electric property, Fuel cell property, Residential wind property, and Geothermal heat pumps.

The credit is 30% of the cost of eligible property. Other features of the REEP credit are:

▶ Labor costs to install the property are included in the qualified cost of the property.

▶ Second homes or vacation homes do not qualify for some parts of the credit.

---

[28] Sec. 25C(g), as amended by the Tax Increase Prevention Act of 2014.

[29] Sec. 25D, as amended by the American Recovery and Reinvestment Act of 2009.

▶ If less than 80% of the use of the dwelling is for nonbusiness use, then only the percentage of nonbusiness use can be taken into account.

▶ The taxpayer's basis in the property is reduced by the amount of the credit.

▶ The credit is not available for use with swimming pools or hot tubs.

▶ Credits earned but not used in the current year can be carried forward to the next year.

Alternative Motor Vehicle Credit. Congress has enacted several nonrefundable personal credits to encourage taxpayers to invest in alternative vehicles. The comprehensive alternative motor vehicle credit (AMVC) contains the: Qualified fuel cell credit, Advanced lean-burn technology credit, Qualified hybrid credit, Qualified alternative fuel refueling property credit, Plug-in conversion credit, Plug-in electric vehicle credit. Under current law, only the provision for the credit for a fuel cell motor vehicle is active. It is allowed for qualifying vehicles purchased before January 1, 2015. Details on these credits are beyond the scope of this text.

Qualified Retirement Savings Contributions Credit ("Saver's Credit"). To encourage low and middle income taxpayers to save for retirement, a *permanent,* nonrefundable credit for contributions or deferrals to qualified retirement plans has been established for tax years beginning after December 31, 2001.[30] The saver's credit is allowed *in addition* to otherwise allowable exclusions or deductions from gross income for retirement plan contributions or deferrals.

To be eligible for the credit, a taxpayer must be at least 18 years of age as of the close of the tax year, must not be claimed as a dependent on another taxpayer's tax return, and must not be a full-time student[31] for purposes of the dependency exemption (full-time student for at least 5 calendar months).

The saver's credit is computed by multiplying the amount contributed (maximum $2,000 per eligible individual per year) by an applicable percentage. The percentage for 2015 depends on the taxpayer's adjusted gross income, as shown in the following table:

Applicable Percentage	MFJ AGI Over	Not Over	Head of Household AGI Over	Not Over	All Other Statuses AGI Over	Not Over
50%	$ 0	$36,500	$ 0	$27,375	$ 0	$18,250
20%	36,500	39,500	27,375	29,625	18,250	19,750
10%	39,500	61,000	29,625	45,750	19,750	30,500
0%	61,000		45,750		30,500	

Annual qualified retirement savings contribution equals the sum of contributions or deferrals by the taxpayer to specified retirement plans, including IRAs (Roth and Traditional), 401(k) plans, 403(b) plans, and certain other plans, reduced by any distributions from such plans. The maximum contribution eligible for the credit for each individual is $2,000 per year.

EXAMPLE I:14-23 ▶ Steve is 20 years old, unmarried, filing single and has AGI of $17,000 in 2015. During the year, he contributes $2,000 to his Roth IRA. Steve is eligible for a Qualified Retirement Savings Contributions Credit in the amount of $1,000 ($2,000 × 50%). The credit would be the same if he contributed $2,000 to a traditional IRA, but in addition to the $1,000 credit, Steve would be permitted to deduct the $2,000 contribution to the traditional IRA on his individual return. ◀

Limitation on Nonrefundable Personal Credits. Nonrefundable personal credits may not exceed the regular tax liability minus foreign tax credit. After passage of the 2012 American Taxpayer Relief Act, these credits may offset AMT as well.

[30] Sec. 25B. The Pension Protection Act of 2006 made the credit permanent. [31] Sec. 152(f)(2).

FOREIGN TAX CREDIT

U.S. citizens, resident aliens, and U.S. corporations are subject to U.S. taxation on their worldwide income.[32] The foreign-source portion of worldwide income is also subject to taxation by the foreign country. To reduce possible double taxation, U.S. tax law provides a foreign tax credit (FTC) for income taxes paid or accrued to a foreign country or a U.S. possession.

In lieu of the FTC, taxpayers may elect to take a deduction for foreign taxes paid or accrued.[33] In general, the FTC results in a greater tax benefit because (as previously discussed) a credit is fully offset against the tax liability, while a deduction merely reduces taxable income. Finally, in lieu of the FTC, taxpayers may elect to exclude foreign earned income from U.S. gross income (Sec. 911). (See chapter I:4 for more information).

Computation of Allowable Credit. The FTC equals the lesser of (1) foreign tax paid or accrued, or (2) the portion of U.S. income tax liability attributable to income earned in all foreign countries (FTC limitation).[34] This limitation restricts claiming the benefit from foreign tax credit if the effective foreign tax rate on foreign earnings exceeds the effective U.S. tax rate on these earnings. The FTC limitation is computed using the following formula:

$$\frac{\text{Foreign source taxable income}}{\text{Worldwide taxable income}} \times \text{U.S. income tax before credits} = \text{FTC limitation}$$

EXAMPLE I:14-24 ▶ Robert Albertson has $200,000 of U.S. source taxable income and $100,000 of foreign source taxable income from country A. Robert's worldwide taxable income is $300,000 ($200,000 + $100,000). Country A levies $40,000 in foreign income taxes on the foreign source taxable income (i.e., a 40% effective tax rate). His U.S. tax before credits is $100,250 on the $300,000 of worldwide taxable income. Using the formula given above, the overall FTC limitation is computed as follows:[35]

$$\frac{\$100,000}{\$300,000} \times \$100,250 = \$33,417$$

Because the foreign tax payments ($40,000) exceed the U.S. tax attributable to the foreign source income ($33,417), the limitation applies. Thus, Robert's net U.S. tax equals $66,833 ($100,250 − $33,417) and, $6,583 ($40,000 − $33,417) of FTC cannot be used in the current year. ◀

STOP & THINK

Question: Since a credit is generally more valuable than a deduction, under what circumstances would it be beneficial for a taxpayer to take a deduction for foreign taxes in lieu of the foreign tax credit?

Solution: If a taxpayer has foreign source taxable income from one country and an equal loss from another foreign country, the foreign tax credit limitation is zero because the net foreign-source taxable income is zero. Because none of the taxes paid in the foreign country in which taxable income was produced can be claimed as a credit, the taxpayer may choose to deduct them (unless the unused credits can be carried back or forward.)

---

[32] Certain exceptions are provided by treaty agreements between the United States and foreign countries whereby certain types of foreign-source income may be exempt from taxation or taxed at a reduced tax rate in the foreign country.
[33] Sec. 164(a)(3).
[34] Sec. 904.

[35] Two types of income have a separate foreign tax credit limitation: passive income and all other income. (See Chapter C:16 of *Prentice Hall's Federal Taxation: Corporations, Partnerships, Estates, and Trusts* for a more detailed discussion of these separate limitations.)

Treatment of Unused Credits. Unused foreign tax credits may be carried back one year and then forward for ten years to tax years where the limitation is not exceeded (i.e., the foreign tax payment is lower than the U.S. taxes attributable to the foreign-source income in the carryback or carryover years). Unused credits are lost if they are not used by the end of the ten-year carryover period.

BUSINESS RELATED TAX CREDITS

General Business Credits. The tax credits commonly available to businesses are grouped into a special category called **general business credits**. These credits are combined for the purpose of computing an overall dollar limitation based on the taxpayer's tax liability (discussed in more detail on page I:14-23). If the general business credits earned in the current year exceed the limitation, the excess may be carried back one year and carried forward 20 years. The credits are used in order of time generated with carryforward credits used first, current year credits next, and then carryback credits.[36]

EXAMPLE I:14-25 ►

Eastern Corporation had unused general business tax credits of $10,000 in 2014 that are carried forward to 2015. Eastern earns $5,000 of additional credits in 2015 and computes an overall credit limitation of $12,000 for the year. The allowable $12,000 credit consists of the $10,000 carryover and $2,000 from 2015. The $3,000 of unused 2015 credit ($5,000 − $2,000) is carried forward to 2016. ◄

The more important general business credits are discussed below. All are nonrefundable.

Tax Credit for Rehabilitation Expenditures. Congress provides a credit for investments in the rehabilitation of older industrial and commercial buildings and certified historic structures.[37]

The credit equals 10% of qualified rehabilitation expenditures (QRE) for buildings originally placed in service before 1936 and 20% of QRE for certified historic structures. The credit applies only to depreciable trade or business property and depreciable property held for investment. Residential rental property does not qualify unless the building is a certified historic structure. Rehabilitation includes renovation, restoration, or construction of a building, but not an enlargement or new construction. For buildings other than certified historic structures, a rehabilitation project must meet certain structural tests and must be substantial (QRE exceed the greater of $5,000 or the building's adjusted basis).[38]

The following additional provisions apply.

REAL-WORLD EXAMPLE

Taxpayers incurred substantial rehabilitation expenditures on an old factory building, but the tax credit was not allowed because the taxpayers did not use the straight-line depreciation method. *Frank DeMarco,* 87 T.C. 518 (1986).

► For certified historic structures, the total rehabilitation must be certified by the Department of the Interior as being consistent with the historic character of the building.

► Straight-line depreciation generally must be used with the applicable Sec. 168 recovery periods with respect to rehabilitation expenditures. The regular MACRS depreciation rules apply to the portion of the property's basis that is not eligible for the credit.

► The basis of the property for depreciation is reduced by the full amount of the credit taken.[39]

► The rehabilitation credit is recaptured at a rate of 20% per year if the property is disposed of within five years of the date placed in service.

---

[36] Sec. 38(d).
[37] Secs. 47(a)(1) and (2). A certified historic structure must be certified by the Department of the Interior and must be located in a registered historic district or listed in the *National Register.*

[38] Sec. 47(c)(1)(A).
[39] Sec. 50(c)(1).

EXAMPLE I:14-26 ► During the current year, Ted incurs $40,000 of qualified rehabilitation expenditures (QRE) in connection with a certified historic structure used in his business. The adjusted basis of the certified historic structure was $38,000 at the time the rehabilitation began. The property qualifies for the rehabilitation credit because:

► It is used in Ted's trade or business and is depreciable.

► The property is a certified historic structure.

► The amount of the QRE exceeds the greater of the property's $38,000 adjusted basis or the $5,000 statutory minimum.

Thus, the credit is $8,000 (0.20 × $40,000). The building's depreciable basis attributable to the $40,000 of QRE rehabilitation expenditures is reduced by the full amount of the credit to $32,000 ($40,000 − $8,000). If the property is disposed of after one year, $6,400 of the credit ($8,000 − $1,600) is recaptured. ◄

ADDITIONAL COMMENT

The American Recovery and Reinvestment Act of 2009 expanded or added several new business energy tax credits.

Business Energy Tax Credits. To encourage energy conservation measures, credits are available to businesses that invest in energy-conserving properties (e.g., solar and geothermal property).[40] The credit for geothermal energy property is 10% of the property's basis. The credit for solar energy property and qualified fuel cell property purchased in tax years ending after December 31, 2005 and before January 1, 2016 is 30% of the property's basis. Construction, reconstruction, or erection of the property must be completed by the taxpayer, and its original use must begin with the taxpayer.

Recent tax law changes have set up a complex interaction among the energy credit, renewable energy grants, and an electricity production credit. Details are beyond the scope of this text, but essentially, taxpayers must choose to receive grants or take credits, but not both.

Employer-Provided Child Care Credit. The employer-provided child care credit is an incentive for businesses to provide child care for their employees. The credit is the *sum* of the following two amounts:

► 25% of qualified child care expenses. These expenses are amounts paid to acquire, construct, rehabilitate, expand, and operate a qualified child care facility or paid under contract to a qualified child care facility for services to employees; plus

► 10% of qualified child care resources and referral expenditures. These are expenses paid or incurred by a taxpayer under a contract to provide child care resource and referral services to employees.

These are several special rules with regard to the credit, including:

► The total credit amount allowed for any given year cannot exceed $150,000.

► Employers claiming this credit cannot claim a deduction for child care expenses and also claim the credit. Expenses that would be otherwise deductible must be reduced by the amount of the credit claimed.

► If, within 10 years of the year in which a child care facility is placed in service, an employer terminates its use as a qualified child care facility, the credit must be recaptured. The recapture rate begins at 100% (terminate within the first three years), and declines steadily as the years of facility use increase.

This credit is part of, and is subject to, the limitations of the general business credit.

EXAMPLE I:14-27 ► Gamechicken Partnership began a child care facility for its employees during the current year. The business incurred the following expenses:

Rent on facility	$ 25,000
Leasehold improvements	60,000
Equipment, toys, etc.	18,000
Salaries of child care employees	30,000
Other operating expenses of facility	12,000
Qualified child care referral fees*	8,000
Total expenses	$153,000

*Fees paid to a firm to place children in other facilities.

---

[40] Sec. 48(a)(2).

Gamechicken's credit for the year would be $37,050 [($145,000 × 25%) + ($8,000 × 10%)]. All of the above amounts are also deductible after reduction by the amount of the credit. So, the rent, salaries, and operating expenses of $67,000 ($25,000 + $30,000 + $12,000) must be reduced by a total of $16,750 ($67,000 × 25%), the referral fees must be reduced by $800 ($8,000 × 10%), and the basis of the leasehold improvements and equipment must be reduced by $19,500 ($78,000 × 25%). ◀

Disabled Access Credit. A nonrefundable tax credit is available to eligible small businesses for expenditures incurred to make existing business facilities accessible to disabled individuals. The disabled access credit equals 50% of eligible expenditures that exceed $250 but do not exceed $10,250.[41] Thus, the annual credit limitation is $5,000 [0.50($10,250 − $250)].

Eligible expenditures include payments for removing architectural, communication, physical, or transportation barriers that prevent a business from being accessible. Expenditures made in connection with *new facility* construction are not eligible for the credit. The allowed credit reduces the deduction for eligible expenses. An eligible small business is any business that either (1) had gross receipts of $1 million or less in the preceding year or, (2) in the case of a business failing the first test, had no more than 30 full-time employees in the preceding year and makes a timely election to claim the credit.

EXAMPLE I:14-28 ▶ In the previous year, Crane Corporation (an S Corp) had 14 employees and $2 million of gross receipts. During the current year, Crane installed concrete access ramps at a total cost of $14,000. Crane is an eligible small business because the company had 30 or fewer full-time employees during the preceding year. Only $10,000 of eligible expenditures qualify for the credit, thereby limiting the credit to $5,000 ($10,000 × 0.50). The depreciable basis of the property must be reduced by the credit amount to $9,000 ($14,000 − $5,000). ◀

Credit for Increased Research Activities. To encourage businesses to conduct research and experimentation, a credit is allowed under Sec. 41. The research credit is equal to the sum of the regular research credit, the university basic research credit, and the energy research consortium credit. The last two are beyond the scope of this book.

This credit is allowed for increased research expenses and at a rate of 20% of the excess of qualified research expenses over the base amount. It applies to qualified expenses incurred before January 1, 2015. Qualified research expenses (QRE) are defined as internal and external research expenses that are incident to the development or improvement of a product or component. Only incremental expenditures (the excess over a base amount) are eligible for the credit. Research conducted after the start of commercial production does not qualify for the credit, nor do marketing, advertising, or production expenses.

The base amount equals the greater of (1) the product of the taxpayer's fixed-base percentage and average annual gross receipts over the four years prior to the credit year, and (2) 50% of credit year qualified research expenditures. The fixed-base percentage is the historical ratio of qualified research expenditures to gross receipts and is limited to 16%. The table below specifies the historical period used based on the years in which the taxpayer incurred qualified research expenses, assuming the taxpayer is considered a start-up company.[42]

---

[41] Sec. 44.   [42] Sec. 41(c)(3)(B)

History of Incurred QREs	*Fixed base percentage*
First year through fifth year	3%
Sixth year	1/6*(QRE /gross receipts for years 4 & 5)
Seventh year	1/3*(QRE /gross receipts for years 5 & 6)
Eighth year	1/2*(QRE /gross receipts for years 5, 6 & 7)
Ninth year	2/3*(QRE /gross receipts for years 5, 6, 7 & 8)
Tenth year	5/6*(QRE /gross receipts for years 5, 6, 7, 8 & 9)

After the tenth year in which the taxpayer incurs QREs, the fixed base percentage equals the ratio of QRE accumulated across any five years in the year 5 to year 10 range divided by the gross receipts for the same five year range.

EXAMPLE I:14-29 ▶ Northern Inc. (an S Corp). began operations in 2010 and had the following gross receipts for the previous four-year period.

2010	$4,500,000
2011	7,000,000
2012	8,000,000
2013	8,500,000

Northern's average annual gross receipts for the four-year prior period is $7,000,000. In 2014, Northern incurred $500,000 of qualified research expenditures. Assuming Northern Inc. uses a fixed-base percentage of 3%, the corporation's base amount equals the greater of (1) $210,000 ($7,000,000 × 3%) or (2) $250,000 ($500,000 × 50%). The 2014 regular research credit would be $50,000 [($500,000 − $250,000) × 20%]. ◀

Taxpayers may elect a simplified credit in lieu of the regular credit, effective for tax years ending after December 31, 2006. This simplified credit is not based on historical gross receipts, thus opening the research credit to new businesses. The base and credit percentage is computed as follows:

▶ For tax years after 2008, 14% of the excess of qualified research expenses of the current year over 50 percent of the average qualified research expenses for the three preceding taxable years; or

▶ 6% of qualified research expenses of the current year if the taxpayer has no qualified research expenses in any one of the three preceding taxable years.

EXAMPLE I:14-30 ▶ Howell Company is a calendar year taxpayer. In 2014, it incurs $175,000 of qualified research expenses. In the three preceding tax years, Howell's qualified research expenses averaged $40,000 per year. Howell can elect a simplified research credit of $21,700 [($175,000 − 50% ($40,000) × 0.14)]. If Howell had no qualified research expenses in the three preceding years, its credit would be $10,500 ($175,000 × .06). ◀

A business deduction is allowed for research and experimentation expenditures under Sec. 174. This deduction must be reduced by the amount of the research credit.[43]

General Business Credit Overall Limitation. There is an overall dollar limitation of the general business credit based on tax liability. The general business credit may not exceed the smaller of:[44]

---

[43] Sec. 280(c)(2).

[44] The limitation discussed above must be separated into two parts: (1) all general business credits other than the empowerment zone and New York Liberty Zone employment credits and (2) the empowerment zone and New York Liberty Zone employment credits. Only the first part is covered here. The second part allows these credits to reduce, in whole or part, the AMT. (See Sec. 38(c) for details.)

1. Net income tax – Tentative AMT, and
2. Net income tax – 0.25 (Net regular tax – $25,000)

Net income tax means the sum of the net regular tax liability and the AMT, reduced by the nonrefundable personal credits and the foreign tax credit. *Net regular tax liability* means the regular tax reduced by nonrefundable personal credits and the foreign tax credit. The limitation also prevents a taxpayer from claiming a general business credit in the same tax year that the taxpayer has alternative minimum tax. The overall credit limitation is demonstrated in the example below.

EXAMPLE I:14-31 ▶

Steve's general business tax credit before limitation is $50,000 (a $50,000 research credit). Steve's regular tax liability (before credits) is $45,000, and his tentative minimum tax is $10,000. His nonrefundable tax credits also include a $1,200 child and dependent care credit and an $1,800 foreign tax credit. Steve's general business tax credit is initially limited to the smaller of (A) and (B) below. Thus, the limitation on the $50,000 of general business tax credit is $32,000, and Steve's general business credit is limited to $32,000. This credit reduces his tax liablity to $13,000,

A) Net income tax – Tentative AMT
[($45,000 − $1,200 − $1,800) − ($10,000)] = $32,000
B) Net income tax − $25% (Net regular tax − $25,000)
{($45,000 − $1,200 − $1,800) − 25% [($45,000 − $1,200 − $1,800) − $25,000] = $37,750} ◀

REFUNDABLE PERSONAL CREDITS

As mentioned earlier, refundable credits not only offset a taxpayer's income tax liability but can create a refund. If the refundable credits exceed the tax liability, such excess will be refunded to the taxpayer.

Earned Income Credit. The earned income credit (EIC) is a special type of "negative income tax" designed to encourage individuals to become employed or to continue work despite low earnings.[45] The credit is based on earned income, which includes wages, salaries, tips, and other employee compensation plus net earnings from self-employment. Earned income does not include any form of employee compensation that is not includible in the taxpayer's income for the year.

The EIC is not available to taxpayers whose "disqualified income" exceeds $3,400 in 2015 ($3,350 in 2014). Disqualified income includes taxable interest income and dividends, tax-exempt interest income, net income from nonbusiness rents or royalties, net capital gains, and net passive activity income.

The credit is available to individuals with qualifying children[46] (see Chapter I:2 for the uniform definition of a qualifying child) and to individuals without children.[47] Individuals without children are eligible only if the following requirements are met:

▶ The individual's principal place of abode is in the United States for more than one-half of the tax year.

▶ The individual (or spouse if married) is at least age 25 and not more than age 64 at the end of the tax year.

▶ The individual is not a dependent or qualifying child of another taxpayer for the tax year.[48]

Married taxpayers must file a joint return to be eligible for the credit. Earned income credit percentages and the maximum amount of earned income allowed for the credit in

---

[45] (See Chapter I:2 for a discussion of the relationship between the child tax credit and the earned income credit.)

[46] Any qualifying child's name, age, and taxpayer identification number must be reported on the tax return.

[47] Sec. 32(c).

[48] Sec. 32(c)(1)(A), as amended by the 2008 Adoption Act.

2015 are summarized in Table I:14-1. These vary by the number of qualifying children and the taxpayer's filing status. The allowable credit phases out when the taxpayer's AGI or earned income (whichever is greater) exceeds a specified amount (Table I:14-1).[49]

EXAMPLE I:14-32 ▶ Vivian is not married, has one qualifying child, and is eligible for the earned income credit in 2015. Vivian's AGI is $19,500 ($15,900 of wages and $3,600 of alimony). The wages are considered earned income; the alimony is not earned income. The tentative credit is $3,359 (0.34 × $9,880). The phaseout is $222 [15.98% × ($19,500 AGI − $18,110)]. The allowable credit is therefore $3,137 ($3,359 − 222), and this amount is refundable to Vivian. ◀

▼ TABLE I:14-1
2015 Earned Income Credit Table

Number of Qualifying Children	Credit Rate	Credit Base (Earned Income)	Maximum Credit	Phase-out Rate*	Phase-out Threshold for Taxpayers Married Filing Joint (Not Married Filing Joint)
0	7.65%	$ 6,580	$ 503	7.65%	$13,750 ($8,240)
1	34%	$ 9,880	$3,359	15.98%	$23,630 ($18,110)
2	40%	$13,870	$5,548	21.06%	$23,630 ($18,110)
3 or more	45%	$13,870	$6,242	21.06%	$23,630 ($18,110)

ᵃapplied to Earned Income (or AGI if larger) in excess of phase-out threshold.

PROVISIONS RELATED TO HEALTH INSURANCE

OBJECTIVE 4

Describe and compute the premium tax credit and the shared responsibility payment

HEALTH INSURANCE PREMIUM ASSISTANCE CREDIT (ALSO KNOWN AS PREMIUM TAX CREDIT)

For years after 2013, a credit is allowed for a portion of taxpayers' health insurance premiums (Sec. 36B). The credit allowed equals the excess of qualifying premiums over the premium amount deemed affordable based on the taxpayer's household income. Qualifying premiums are based on the purchase of health insurance through a state American Health Benefit exchange or a federal exchange. The qualifying premiums are calibrated to premiums in the taxpayer's residential area. Plans are categorized by the portion of cost of benefits covered by the plan, and they range from Bronze to Silver to Gold to Platinum. Qualifying premiums for the credit are set at the cost of premiums for the second-lowest-cost Silver plan. Premium amounts are reported by state and family characteristics on the federal website HealthCare.gov (https://www.healthcare.gov/health-plan-information/).

Credit-eligible taxpayers (1) must not have access through employer health insurance or other government sponsored plans to minimum affordable essential coverage (affordable: premiums ≤ 9.56% of household income and essential: plan covers 60% or more of the cost of allowed plan benefits), (2) must file jointly if married, and (3) may not be eligible as a dependent of another taxpayer. Furthermore, to be eligible for the credit, the taxpayer must have household income that falls between 100% and 400% of the federal poverty line (FPL).[50] Household income is a taxpayer's modified AGI plus the AGI of dependent family members required to file a federal income tax return.[51] The 2015 FPL minimums for the 48 contiguous U.S. states are outlined in the following table:

---

[49] The percentages are adjusted annually for inflation.

[50] THE FPL is defined in Sec. 36B(d)(3) based on its definition in the Social Security Act (42 USC 1397jj(c)(5)). The U.S. Department of Health and Human Services publishes these guidelines annually.

[51] Section 36B(d)(2). Modified AGI includes nontaxable Social Security benefits, tax-exempt interest income, and any excluded foreign earned income.

▼ TABLE I:14-2
2015 Federal Poverty Guidelines[52]

People in Household	Poverty Guideline (100%)	People in Household	Poverty Guideline (100%)
1	$11,770	5	$28,410
2	$15,930	6	$32,570
3	$20,090	7	$36,730
4	$24,250	8	$40,890

Beyond 8, add $4,160 for each additional person beyond 8

▼ TABLE I:14-3
Premium Levels Deemed Affordable as a Percent of Household Income–2015

Categories of Household Income Relative to the FPL	Affordable Premium as a Percent of Household Income	
	Initial %	Final %
100% up to 133% FPL	2.01%	2.01%
Over 133% up to150% FPL	3.02%	4.02%
Over 150% up to 200% FPL	4.02%	6.34%
Over 200% up to 250% FPL	6.34%	8.10%
Over 250% up to 300% FPL	8.10%	9.56%
Over 300% up to 400% FPL	9.56%	9.56%

EXAMPLE I:14-33 ► Bryan and Heather Delane (27 and 26 years old, respectively) are eligible taxpayers and have household income of $29,600. Their income and household size put them at 186% ($29,600/$15,930) of the FPL. ◄

Neither has available coverage from their employers. For 2015, the Delanes enroll in the second-lowest-cost Silver plan available through their state's health care exchange, for which total premiums will cost $5,500. Determine the amount of the Delanes' health insurance premium tax credit.

1st: Affordable premium

The Delanes' household income relative to the FPL equals 186% and falls in the 150%–200% range of the FPL. The share of the premium deemed affordable for them must be based on the initial rate (4.02%) plus a prorated portion of the distance to the final rate (6.34%).

FPL range: 200% − 150% = 50   Distance from initial range = 186% − 150% = 36

Range of rates within FPL range: 6.34% − 4.02% = 2.32%
   Delanes' rate = Initial rate + prorated portion of range of rates
      = 4.02% + 36/50 (2.32%) = 5.69%

Delanes' affordable premiums = 5.69% ($29,600 household income) = $1,684

2nd: Credit amount

Premium tax credit = cost of coverage (total premiums) − personal share (affordable premiums) = $5,500 − $1,684 = $3,816

This credit may be available as an advance payment directly from the U.S. Treasury to the issuer of the health insurance plan. This approach reduces the taxpayer's periodic payment required for the personal share of the total premiums. The tax credit reported on the taxpayer's individual income tax return reflects the computed credit reduced by advance

---

[52] http://aspe.hhs.gov/poverty/15poverty.cfm.

payments of the credit (Sec. 36B(f)). Any excess of the credit over advance payments represents an additional credit. Any shortfall is an additional tax liability.

SHARED RESPONSIBILITY PAYMENT

After 2013, individuals without the required minimum essential health insurance coverage (for taxpayer and dependents) must pay an excise tax commonly referred to as the "shared responsibility payment" (Sec. 5000A). The shared responsibility payment equals the lesser of (1) the cost of bronze level insurance coverage in a health plan ($207 per month or $2,484 per individual for 2015) or (2) the calculated penalty. The calculated penalty equals the greater of (1) the applicable dollar amount ($325 for 2015) or (2) 2% of household income in excess of the filing threshold. The filing threshold is the sum of the deduction for exemptions and the standard deduction amount for non-itemizers.

EXAMPLE I:14-34 ▶ In 2015, Robert Dice is single, has no dependents, has no health insurance, and has gross income of $75,000. The annual cost of qualified health insurance for him at the bronze level would have been $2,484. The penalty for Robert will equal the greater of (a) $325, the flat dollar amount for a single person with no dependents, or (b) $1,294, the excess income amount based on 2.0% of Robert's household income in excess of his filing threshold ($75,000 − $4,000 personal exemption − $6,300 standard deduction). Robert's shared responsibility payment will equal $1,294, the lesser of the annual cost of insurance, $2,484 or the penalty amount, $1,294. ◀

TOPIC REVIEW I:14-2

Summary of Selected Tax Credits Discussed in Chapter 14

TAX CREDIT ITEM	RATIONALE FOR INCLUSION IN TAX LAW
NONREFUNDABLE PERSONAL CREDITS:	
Adoption credit (Sec. 23)	Provides relief for taxpayers who incur expenses in the adoption of children
Child tax credit (Sec. 24)	Reduces the tax burden on families with dependent children
Child and Dependent care credit (Sec. 21)	Provides relief for employed parents and other individuals who incur expenses for dependent care
Elderly and Disabled credit (Sec. 22)	Provides relief for elderly taxpayers who are not substantially covered by Social Security
American Opportunity Tax Credit and Lifetime Learning Credit (Sec. 25A)	Assists students and families with the cost of post-secondary education
Qualified retirement savings contributions credit (Sec. 25B)	Encourages low- and middle-income taxpayers to save for retirement
Residential energy credits (Sec. 25C & D)	Encourages energy conservation measures on principal residences
MISCELLANEOUS CREDITS:	
Foreign tax credit (Sec. 27)	Mitigates the effects of double taxation on foreign-source income
GENERAL BUSINESS CREDITS:	
Business energy credits (Sec. 48)	Encourages energy conservation measures
Disabled access credit (Sec. 44)	Encourages small businesses to provide access for disabled persons
Employer-provided child care credit (Sec. 45F)	Provides incentive for businesses to provide child care for employees
Rehabilitation expenditures credit (Sec. 21)	Encourages the rehabilitation of older buildings
Research credit (Sec. 41)	Encourages research and experimental activities
REFUNDABLE PERSONAL CREDITS:	
Earned income credit (Sec. 32)	Provides incentive for low-income individuals to work
Overpayment of social security taxes (Sec. 31)	Provides a credit or refund for social security taxes overpaid when a taxpayer has multiple employers
Taxes withheld from wages and other income (Sec. 31)	Recognizes taxpayer's prepayment of tax
Premium Tax Credit (Sec. 36B)	Reduces the cost of health insurance for households with low and modest incomes.

PAYMENT OF TAXES

Explain the mechanics of the federal withholding tax system and the requirements for making estimated tax payments

The IRS collects federal income taxes during the year ("pay as you go") through withholding on wages and quarterly estimated tax payments. If the total of withholdings and estimated taxes is less than the amount of tax liability, the taxpayer must pay the balance of the tax due when the tax return is filed. If there has been an overpayment of tax, the taxpayer may either request a refund or apply the overpayment to the following year's estimated tax.

Substantial penalties are imposed if an employer fails to withhold federal income tax and pay such amounts to the IRS.[53] In addition, taxpayers may be subject to penalties for underpayment of estimated tax.[54]

WITHHOLDING OF TAXES

Employers must withhold federal income taxes and FICA taxes from an employee's wages. No withholdings are required if an employer-employee relationship does not exist (e.g., an individual who performs services as an independent contractor). Generally, unless a specific exemption is provided, withholding is required on all forms of employee compensation (salaries, fees, bonuses, dismissal payments, commissions, vacation pay, and taxable fringe benefits).[55] Below are some special rules relating to withholding of federal taxes:

REAL-WORLD EXAMPLE

A teacher claimed a credit for Social Security taxes that had been withheld from his salary. He believed that the Social Security tax was illegally withheld because he did not authorize the collection of the tax. The Tax Court held that the Social Security tax is mandatory for designated employees and does not allow a person to elect not to contribute. *Richard L. Feldman,* 1967 PH T.C. Memo ¶67,091, 26 TCM 444.

▶ *More than one employer during the same year.* Each employer must withhold FICA and federal income taxes without regard to the fact that the employee has more than one employer. As mentioned on page I:14-9, this may cause an overwithholding of FICA taxes if the employee's wages exceed the ceiling amount on the OASDI portion of the tax. In the event of overwithholding of FICA taxes, the employee may credit the excess amount as an additional payment of tax. However, the matching employer excess FICA contributions are not refundable or creditable against the tax liabilities of either employer or employee.

HISTORICAL NOTE

The withholding of federal income taxes by employers began during World War II.

▶ *Overall exemption.* Taxpayers are exempt from income tax withholding in the current year if they (1) had no tax liability in the prior year; (2) expect no tax liability in the current year; and (3) can be claimed as dependent by another taxpayer and report no more than $950 total income, no more than $300 of which is unearned. The earnings of such individuals are still fully taxable, and an employer may be liable for FICA tax payments on these earnings.

▶ *Exemption for certain employment activities.* Certain employees, such as agricultural laborers, ministers, household employees, newspaper carriers under age 18, and those earning tips of less than $20 per month from an employer, are exempt from withholding. The earnings of such individuals are still fully taxable, and an employer may be liable for matching FICA tax payments on these earnings.[56]

▶ *Special rules for supplemental wage payments.* Supplemental wages payments include items such as bonuses, commissions, overtime, accumulated sick pay, severance pay, awards, prizes, back pay, and retroactive pay increases. If an employee receives supplemental wage payments, the federal income tax withholding amount is determined under either of two methods:[57]

---

[53] Sec. 3403. Employers are liable for payment of the full amount that must be withheld and paid to the IRS. In addition, responsible individuals (e.g., corporate officers, directors, and consultants) may be held personally liable for payment of the tax. (See *Renate Schiff v. U.S.,* 69 AFTR 2d 92-804, 92-1 USTC ¶50,248 (D.C. NV, 1992), *Ted E. Tsouprake v. U.S.,* 69 AFTR 2d 92-821, 92-1 USTC ¶50,249 (D.C. FL, 1992), and *Ralph M. Guito, Jr. v. U.S.,* 67 AFTR 2d 91-1066, 92-1 USTC ¶ 50,231 (D.C. FL, 1991).)

[54] Sec. 6654.
[55] Reg. Sec. 31.3401(a)-1(a)(2).
[56] Reg. Sec. 31.3401(a)(10)-1(a). An employer is liable for FICA tax payments for domestic servants if $1,400 or more is paid to an individual in any calendar year.
[57] Reg. Sec. 31.3402(g)-1(a).

- Concurrent payments—if the supplemental wages are included in the payment of regular wages, the tax is withheld as if the combined wages were a single wage payment for the payroll period.
- Separate payments—if the supplemental wages are paid separately, the tax withheld is either a flat 25%, or the percentage that applies to the aggregate of the supplemental wage payment with wages paid within the same calendar year for the last preceding payroll period or the current payroll period.

▶ *Backup withholding.* Backup withholding rules were enacted to prevent abusive noncompliance situations, such as not providing the payor of a dividend with the payee's Social Security number. A 28% withholding rate is required on most types of payments that are reported on Form 1099 (e.g., interest, dividends, royalties, etc.) where a proper taxpayer identification number is not provided.

▶ *Other special rules.* There are many other special rules on withholding in certain circumstances, such as for fringe benefits, pension and annuity payments, etc. that are beyond the scope of this text.

REAL-WORLD EXAMPLE

It has been held that the employer's withholding of federal income taxes is not an improper taking of property without due process in violation of the Fifth Amendment. *Michael O. Campbell v. Amax Coal Co.,* 610 F.2d 701, 45 AFTR 2d 80-564, 80-1 USTC ¶9185 (10th Cir., 1980).

Withholding Allowances and Methods. On beginning a new job, each employee must file with his/her employer an employee's withholding allowance certificate (Form W-4), which lists the employee's marital status and number of withholding allowances. The W-4 provides the employer with the information needed to determine the amount of federal income tax to be withheld from the employee's earnings. If an employee's circumstances change (e.g., a married taxpayer is divorced during the year), an amended Form W-4 must be provided to the employer within 10 days.

The number of withholding allowances claimed on Form W-4 is typically the same as the number of personal and dependency exemptions that will be taken on the employee's tax return for the year. An additional withholding allowance (reflecting the standard deduction) may be claimed by a taxpayer who has one job or, if married, has a spouse who is unemployed.[58] Further additional withholding allowances may be claimed if an individual has deductions, losses, or credits from a wide variety of sources, including itemized deductions, alimony payments, moving expenses, and losses from a trade or business, rental property, or a farm. Form W-4 contains tables and a worksheet to help employees compute the number of additional withholding allowances.[59]

EXAMPLE I:14-35 ▶ Sam and Sally are married and have three dependent children. They file a joint tax return. Sally is not employed, and Sam does not claim additional withholding allowances for unusually large deductions or tax credits. Sam may claim six allowances (two personal exemptions [for Sam and Sally] plus three dependency exemptions, plus one special allowance to reflect the standard deduction). The special allowance is available because Sally is not employed and Sam has only one job. ◀

⑧ STOP & THINK

Question: Many taxpayers believe that they must claim the same number of withholding allowances for withholding purposes as the number of personal exemptions on their income tax return. Why is this not correct?

Solution: While the starting point for determining withholding allowances is the taxpayer's marital status and number of personal exemptions, taxpayers are allowed to claim more or fewer withholding allowances based on their individual situation. Taxpayers may claim additional withholding allowances for two principal reasons: (1) a taxpayer has high deductions, losses, or credits; or (2) an unmarried taxpayer qualifies

---

[58] Sec. 3402(f)(1)(E).
[59] Married taxpayers who are both employed may allocate withholding allowances between them as they see fit as long as the same allowance is not claimed more than once.

for head of household filing status. The withholding tables are constructed assuming that the taxpayer will use the standard deduction. Therefore, if a taxpayer has much higher itemized deductions than the standard deduction, the withholding tables may prescribe too much withholding, and the taxpayer would have a large refund at the end of the year. To alleviate this situation, taxpayers are allowed to claim additional withholding allowances. Similarly, the withholding tables only have two categories for marital status, single or married. Thus, if an unmarried taxpayer qualifies for head of household status, the "single" withholding tables may cause over-withholding of tax.

Computation of Federal Income Tax Withheld. Employers use either wage bracket tables or an optional percentage method to compute the actual amount of withholding. The two methods produce approximately the same results. Wage bracket tables are available for daily, weekly, biweekly, and monthly payroll periods. Separate tables are used for single (including heads-of-household) and married individuals. Partial wage bracket tables for married and single persons using a monthly payroll period for wages are located in the Tax Tables and Rate Schedules in the Tables beginning on page T-15.

EXAMPLE I:14-36 ▶

Henry is married and claims four withholding allowances. His monthly salary is $3,000. The federal income tax, Social Security tax and Medicare tax withheld per month for 2015 using the wage bracket table on page T-17 is $328.03. ◀

ESTIMATED TAX PAYMENTS

ADDITIONAL COMMENT

The IRS does not mail reminder statements for the required quarterly estimated payments.

Certain types of income are not subject to withholding (e.g., investment income, rents, income from self-employment, and capital gains). Taxpayers who earn this type of income must make quarterly estimated tax payments.

The purpose of the estimated tax payment system is to ensure that all taxpayers have pre-paid enough tax by the end of the tax year to cover most of their tax liability. Thus, estimated tax payments may also be required if insufficient tax is being withheld from an individual's salary, pension, or other income (although many taxpayers prefer to file an amended Form W-4 to reduce the number of withholding allowances). The amount of estimated tax is the taxpayer's estimated tax liability (including self-employment tax and alternative minimum tax) reduced by withholdings and tax credits.

Required Estimated Tax Payments. For calendar-year individuals, required quarterly payments are due by April 15, June 15, September 15 of the current year, and January 15 of the following year. To avoid an underpayment penalty,[60] total estimated tax payments must equal or exceed any of the following three "safe harbor" amounts:

1) 90% of current year tax liability;

2) 100% of the prior year tax liability shown if the taxpayer's AGI in the prior year was $150,000 or less.

   110% of the prior year tax liability if the taxpayer's AGI in the prior year was more than $150,000.

3) 90% of current year tax liability computed on an annualized basis (helpful for taxpayers who do not earn taxable income evenly through the year).

In addition, no penalty is imposed if (1) the estimated tax for the current year is less than $1,000, or (2) the individual had no tax liability for the prior year.

---

[60] Sec. 6654.

WHAT WOULD YOU DO IN THIS SITUATION?

THE NANNY TAX: DON'T PAY NOW, WORRY LATER

You are a CPA engaged in tax practice, and one of your clients is Mr. Throckmorton D. Princeton, J.D. He is a senior partner in the prestigious employment litigation firm of Huey, Dewey and Fooey. Mr. Princeton is known for his ruthless litigation style.

Things were rosy for Mr. Princeton until last week, when there was some speculation in the press about his being appointed to a cabinet-level position by the President. A TV news magazine show looked into Mr. Princeton's domestic worker situation. It appears that Mr. Princeton has long engaged in the practice of hiring part-time workers in his household to clean his house, tend to his gardens, walk his dogs, cook his meals, service his car, and nurse him when he is ill. All told, he used over twenty-five people at one time or another in the past year. These workers were paid as little as possible, and all were asked to sign a contract with Mr. Princeton stating that they were to be classified as independent contractors. The total amount paid to these workers was $50,000. Mr. Princeton paid no payroll taxes, although he did file Forms 1099 with the IRS. What tax and ethical issues should be considered?

EXAMPLE I:14-37 ▶ Sarah does not make quarterly estimated tax payments for 2015, even though she has a substantial amount of income not subject to withholding. Her taxable income is $140,000. Her actual tax liability (including self-employment taxes and the alternative minimum tax) for the current year is $40,000. Withholdings from her salary are $30,000. She pays the $10,000 balance due to the IRS when she files her return on April 3, 2016. Sarah's tax liability for the prior year was $28,000. No underpayment penalty is imposed because she meets the second exception: the $30,000 of withholdings is more than 100% of her $28,000 prior year tax liability. ◀

EXAMPLE I:14-38 ▶ Assume the same facts in Example I:14-37 except Sarah's AGI in the prior year was $180,000. Since her AGI exceeded $150,000, the second safe harbor amount is 110% (instead of 100%) of the prior year's tax or $30,800 ($28,000 × 1.10). Because the $30,000 of withholding for 2015 is less than 110% of her previous year tax liability, Sarah would not meet either exception and would be subject to the underpayment penalty. ◀

Form 2210 (see Appendix B) should be completed and submitted with the tax return if a possible underpayment of tax is indicated. This form is used to determine whether one of the exceptions applies and, if not, to compute the amount of the underpayment penalty. Topic Review I:14-3 summarizes the withholding tax and estimated payment requirements.

TAX PLANNING CONSIDERATIONS

OBJECTIVE 6

Describe tax planning considerations for AMT, tax credits, and payment of taxes

AVOIDING THE ALTERNATIVE MINIMUM TAX

Taxpayers with substantial amounts of tax preference items and/or positive AMT adjustments and a correspondingly low regular tax liability may be subject to the AMT. These taxpayers need to engage in tax planning to minimize or avoid the AMT.

A liberal AMT exemption is provided for most individuals, so taxpayers can plan for full use of the exemption by timing certain income and deduction items each year. For example, the AMT may be avoided by delaying payment of certain itemized deductions (e.g., state and local taxes) that reduce the regular income tax but do not reduce the AMT. A cash method taxpayer who defers payment of state income taxes into the

TOPIC REVIEW I:14-3

Withholding Taxes and Estimated Payments

EMPLOYER WITHHOLDING OF TAXES:

	FICA	**INCOME TAX**
Subject to withholding:	For Social Security tax, all employee earnings up to $118,500 in 2015 per employer. No ceiling applies to Medicare portion.	All employee compensation including wages, salaries, fees, bonuses, commissions, taxable fringe benefits.[a]
Withholding amounts:	7.65% of FICA wages including 6.2% on Social Security earnings and 1.45% on Medicare earnings.	Determined using withholding tables or the percentage method based on an individual's filing status and number of withholding allowances.

[a]Exceptions are provided for certain nontaxable fringe benefits.

ESTIMATED TAX PAYMENTS:

► To avoid an underpayment penalty, estimated tax payments and withholdings for the year must equal or exceed: 90% of the current year tax liability; or 100% of the prior year tax liability (110% if prior year AGI exceeds $150,000); or 90% of the current year tax liability computed on an annualized basis.

► The underpayment penalty is not deductible for income tax purposes.

► Form 2210 is used to determine the underpayment penalty amount.

KEY POINT

The alternative minimum tax can be avoided or its impact lessened by various tax strategies.

following year, triggers an increase in the regular tax for the current year. This increase can eliminate the AMT liability. However, it is necessary to consider tax effects for both the current and following years, because state income taxes are deductible for purposes of the regular tax calculation when payment is made in the following year. This reduction may affect the AMT calculation in the following year and increase the amount of tax owed then.

Certain tax-exempt investments, such as interest on private activity bonds, generate additional tax preferences for the investor. Before acquiring such investments, an investor should determine the potential AMT impact.

AVOIDING THE UNDERPAYMENT PENALTY FOR ESTIMATED TAX

Many taxpayers find it difficult to estimate their taxes for the purposes of making quarterly estimated payments and are uncertain whether their withholdings and estimated tax will equal or exceed 90% or more of their actual tax liability for the year. A common planning technique to avoid a possible underpayment tax penalty is to make estimated tax payments and withholdings in an amount that is at least 100% (or 110% if AGI was in excess of $150,000 for the prior year) of the actual tax liability for the prior year, thereby meeting one of the exceptions that prevents the underpayment penalty from being imposed.

EXAMPLE I:14-39 ►

Yong expects his 2015 federal income tax withholdings to total $14,000 and estimates that his income tax liability will be $24,000. Yong's actual federal income taxes in the prior year were $20,000. If estimated taxes of at least $6,000 are paid during 2015, Yong's estimated taxes plus withholding will be at least 100% of his prior year's tax liability ($14,000 + $6,000 = $20,000), and no underpayment penalty will be imposed, despite the $4,000 ($24,000 − $20,000) balance due on the 2015 return. If Yong's prior year AGI exceeded $150,000, his estimated taxes plus withholding must be at least 110% of his prior year tax liability or $22,000 (1.10 × $20,000) to avoid the underpayment penalty. Thus, his estimated tax payments must total at least $8,000. ◄

CASH-FLOW CONSIDERATIONS

Assuming that the underpayment penalty can be avoided, it is generally preferable to have a balance due to the government at the time for filing the return rather than to receive a refund of an overpayment of tax. No interest is paid on a refund if the IRS pays the refund within 45 days from the later of the due date of the return or its filing date.[61] In addition, the IRS has, in effect, received an interest-free loan from the taxpayer during the period such overpayment exists. To avoid an overpayment, a taxpayer may file an amended W-4 form and claim additional withholding allowances if the requirements are met (e.g., the taxpayer has unusually large itemized deductions, tax credits, alimony payments, etc.).

If an individual anticipates that her combined estimated tax payments and withholdings will be insufficient to avoid the underpayment penalty, it may be preferable to increase amounts withheld near the end of the tax year rather than increase the estimated tax payments.[62] This technique may be advantageous because the penalty's quarterly calculation treats withholdings as made evenly over the year, even when withholding amounts are increased near the end of the year. Another way to avoid the underpayment penalty is to accelerate certain deductions (e.g., real estate taxes on a personal residence) by paying such amounts before the end of the current tax year. Additionally, otherwise deductible contributions to an IRA made after the end of the tax year but by the due date for the tax return may be treated as a deduction for the prior year, thereby avoiding the underpayment penalty (see Chapter I:9).

USE OF GENERAL BUSINESS TAX CREDITS

Taxpayers must consider the priority and interrelated aspects of credits to ensure that a particular credit is fully used. For example, an individual's nonrefundable personal tax credits reduce tax liability before the foreign tax credit limitation is applied. Then, the nonrefundable personal tax credits and foreign tax credit are deducted from the individual's tax liability before limitations are applied to the general business tax credit.

FOREIGN TAX CREDITS AND THE FOREIGN EARNED INCOME EXCLUSION

Individuals who accept foreign job assignments should consider federal income tax implications, because U.S. citizens are subject to U.S. tax on their worldwide income. Assuming that certain requirements and limitations are met, an individual may elect to take either a foreign tax credit or a foreign-earned income exclusion of $100,800 in 2015 ($99,200 in 2014) with respect to salaries, allowances, and other forms of earned income that are earned while on extended non-U.S. assignments.[63] Any taxes paid or accrued with respect to the excluded income are not available as a foreign tax credit. In general, when the effective foreign tax rate is less than the effective U.S. tax rate, the exclusion is preferable because the foreign tax credit that can be claimed does not equal the gross U.S. tax owed on the income. When the effective foreign tax rate exceeds the effective U.S. tax rate, U.S. taxpayers ordinarily elect not to use the exclusion. Instead, the excess tax credits on earned income are used to offset the U.S. taxes owed on other types of foreign income. Detailed coverage of the interaction between foreign tax credits and the exclusion is contained in Chapter C:16 of the *Prentice Hall's Federal Taxation: Corporations, Partnerships, Estates & Trusts* text.

---

[61] Sec. 6611(e).
[62] To completely avoid the underpayment penalty, the tax law generally requires the estimated payments to be made equally on the four installment dates.

[63] Sec. 911(a). The foreign income exclusion requirements are discussed in Chapter I:4.

COMPLIANCE AND PROCEDURAL CONSIDERATIONS

OBJECTIVE 7

Describe compliance and procedural considerations for AMT, tax credits, and payment of taxes

ALTERNATIVE MINIMUM TAX (AMT) FILING PROCEDURES

Individual taxpayers use Form 6251 to compute the AMT, and corporations use Form 4626 (see Appendix B for both forms). Form 6251 must be completed and attached to an individual's income tax return in any of the following situations:

► An AMT tax liability actually exists.

► The taxpayer has tax credits that are limited by the tentative minimum tax.

► The AMT base exceeds the AMT exemption amounts, and the individual has AMT adjustment or tax preference items.

WITHHOLDINGS AND ESTIMATED TAX PAYMENTS

Taxpayers who have income taxes withheld from wages, pensions, and other income should receive a Form W-2 (or Form 1099-R for pensions) from the employer by January 31. These forms should be attached to the individual's tax return to substantiate the amount of withholdings.

Taxpayers who make quarterly estimated tax payments may not file Form 1040A or Form 1040EZ. Married individuals may make either joint or separate estimated tax payments. If joint estimated tax payments are made and the married individuals subsequently file separate returns (e.g., in the case of a divorce that is pending or a divorce completed before the end of the year), the joint estimated tax payments are divided in proportion to each spouse's individual tax if no agreement is reached concerning an appropriate division.

EXAMPLE I:14-40 ► George and Alice are married and make joint estimated tax payments of $10,000 during 2015. George and Alice are separated in February 2016 and Alice refuses to file a joint return with George. George's tax liability for 2015 on his separate return is $20,000 and Alice's tax liability on her separate return is $5,000. If no agreement is reached concerning the allocation of the joint estimated payments of $10,000, Alice is entitled to claim $2,000 of the estimated tax payments on her return [($5,000/($20,000 + $5,000) × $10,000]. The remaining $8,000 is apportioned to George. ◄

GENERAL BUSINESS TAX CREDITS

The computation of the business energy credit is made on Form 3468. Form 3800 must be filed if any other general business credits are claimed.

NONREFUNDABLE PERSONAL TAX CREDITS

KEY POINT

The earned income credit is available even in cases where the taxpayer has no tax liability. The refund of taxes not paid or incurred is often called a negative income tax.

Nonrefundable personal tax credits are deducted from the taxpayer's tax liability before other credits. The credits section on page 2 of Form 1040 limits the deduction for nonrefundable personal tax credits to the amount of tax due. Form 2441 (see Appendix B) must be filed to claim the child and dependent care credit. Taxpayers who claim the child and dependent care credit must also include the care provider's name, address, and taxpayer identification number on their tax return. If the caregiver will not provide the required information, the taxpayer has the option to supply the name and address of the caregiver on Form 2441 and attach a statement explaining that the caregiver has refused to provide his or her taxpayer identification number (TIN). Schedule R of Form 1040 is filed to claim the credit for the elderly and disabled. An eligible individual may elect to have the IRS compute the tax and the amount of the tax credit.[64]

---

[64] Sec. 6014. (See Form 1040 instructions for more reporting details.)

The earned income tax credit is refundable to an individual even if no income tax is owed. The IRS will automatically compute the credit amount.[65] However, helpful tax tables are included in the IRS instructions to Forms 1040, 1040A and 1040 EZ. Schedule EIC is filed if the taxpayer has a qualifying child for the earned income credit.

The foreign tax credit for individuals is computed on Form 1116.

PROBLEM MATERIALS

DISCUSSION QUESTIONS

I:14-1 Why are most taxpayers not subject to the alternative minimum tax (AMT)?

I:14-2 Does the AMT apply if an individual's tax liability as computed under the AMT rules is less than his or her regular tax amount?

I:14-3 Which of the following are tax preference items for purposes of computing the individual AMT?
a. Net long-term capital gain
b. Excess depreciation for real property placed in service before 1987
c. Straight-line depreciation on residential real estate acquired in 1992
d. Appreciated portion of the value of capital gain real property contributed to charity

I:14-4 Which of the following are individual AMT adjustments?
a. Itemized deductions that are allowed for regular tax purposes but not allowed in computing AMTI.
b. Excess of MACRS depreciation over depreciation computed under the alternative depreciation system for real property placed in service after 1986 and before 1999.
c. Excess of MACRS depreciation over depreciation computed under the alternative depreciation system for personal property placed in service after 1986.
d. Tax-exempt interest earned on State of Michigan bonds.

I:14-5 Which of the following itemized deductions are deductible when computing the alternative minimum tax for individuals?
a. Charitable contributions

b. Mortgage interest on a loan used to acquire a personal residence
c. State and local income taxes
d. Interest related to an investment in undeveloped land where the individual has no investment income
e. Medical expenses amounting to 9% of AGI

I:14-6 Why are most individuals not subject to the self-employment tax?

I:14-7 Tony, who is single and 58 years old, is considering early retirement from his salaried job. He currently has $70,000 salary and also earns $50,000 profit from a consulting business. What advice would you give Tony relative to the need to make Social Security tax payments if he retires and continues to be actively engaged as a consultant during his retirement?

I:14-8 Theresa is a college professor who wants to work for a consulting firm during the summer. She will be working on special projects relating to professional development programs. What advantages might accrue to the consulting firm if the engagement is set up as a consulting arrangement rather than an employment contract?

I:14-9 Brian and Jennifer are a married couple who believe they may be subject to the AMT this year. Currently, they calculate their alternative minimum taxable income (AMTI) to be $160,000.
a. What is their AMT exemption amount?
b. They are considering an opportunity that would allow them to earn additional income this year. As a result of this additional income, they believe that their AMTI will increase by $200,000. What will their AMT exemption be if they recognize the additional income?

---

[65] Sec. 6695(g) requires preparers to meet due diligence requirements with respect to the earned income tax credit (EIC). If the EIC is incorrectly computed or overlooked, the *preparer* could be subject to a $100 penalty.

I:14-10 Discuss the underlying rationale for the following tax credit items:
  a. Foreign tax credit
  b. Research credit
  c. Business energy credit
  d. Premium tax credit
  e. Dependent care credit
  f. Earned income credit
  g. American Opportunity credit
  h. Adoption credit

I:14-11 If Congress is considering a tax credit or deduction as an incentive to encourage certain activities, is a $40 tax credit more valuable than a $200 tax deduction for a taxpayer with a 15% marginal rate? a 25% marginal rate?

I:14-12 What are the more significant tax credit items included in the computation of the general business tax credit?

I:14-13 Discuss the limitations that have been imposed on the general business tax credit, including the following:
  a. Overall ceiling limitation based on the tax liability
  b. Priority of general business and personal credits
  c. Carryback and carryover of unused credits (including the application of the FIFO method)

I:14-14 Sarah, a married taxpayer who files a joint return, is considering a foreign assignment for two years. In 2015, she will earn $120,000 in the foreign country. Sarah has no other income. She will be eligible for either the foreign tax credit or the foreign-earned income exclusion. The average tax rate on Sarah's earnings if fully taxable under U.S. law would be 30%. The average tax rate for the foreign salary is 20% under the foreign country's laws.
  a. Discuss in general terms the computation of the foreign tax credit and its limitation.
  b. Would Sarah be better off electing the foreign tax credit or the foreign earned income exclusion? Explain.

I:14-15 Although it became law in 2010, one of the key features of the Affordable Care Act, the Premium Assistance Credit, became effective in 2014. Describe the tax costs to a taxpayer who does not purchase health insurance coverage for 2015. Assume the taxpayer is single, 40 years old, has no dependents, has household income of $55,000, and does not meet any of the conditions to be exempt from the tax.

I:14-16 Queen Corporation has been in business since 1989. During the preceding year, the company had 25 full-time employees and gross receipts of $8,000,000. During the current year, Queen spent $15,000 to install access ramps for disabled individuals. Is Queen Corporation eligible for the disabled access credit? If so, what is the credit amount and the basis reduction (if any) for the depreciable property?

I:14-17 Discuss the special tax rules that apply to the tax credit for rehabilitation expenditures including the following:
  a. Types of eligible expenditures
  b. Applicable tax credit rates
  c. Calculation of basis for expenditures
  d. Restrictions on depreciation methods
  e. Potential recapture of the credit

I:14-18 What types of business property qualify for the business energy credit?

I:14-19 What are the underlying reason for enactment of many of the personal tax credits?

I:14-20 Discuss the difference between a refundable tax credit and a nonrefundable tax credit. Give at least one example of each type of credit.

I:14-21 If an individual is not employed and has no earned income, is it possible to take a child and dependent care credit for otherwise qualifying child and dependent care expenses? Explain.

I:14-22 Discuss the major differences between the American Opportunity credit and the Lifetime Learning credit. Include in your discussion the type of taxpayers who would likely qualify for each of the credits.

I:14-23 What is the maximum child and dependent care credit available to an employed individual who has $8,000 of qualifying child care expenses and two or more qualifying dependents?

I:14-24 Vivian is a single taxpayer with two children who qualify for the child and dependent care credit. She incurred $7,000 of qualifying child care expenses during the current year. She also received $4,000 in reimbursements from her employer from a qualified employee dependent care assistance program. What is the maximum child and dependent care credit available to Vivian if her AGI is $24,500?

I:14-25 The adoption credit is intended to assist taxpayers with the financial burden of adopting children.
  a. Discuss how the credit is computed.
  b. Why did Congress impose a phase-out of the credit for taxpayers based on AGI?

I:14-26 Alice is a single mother, 37 years old, and has two qualifying children, ages 3 and 6. She receives $3,600 alimony and earns $18,000 in wages resulting in $21,600 of AGI in 2015. Is Alice eligible for the earned income credit? If so, is it possible for her to receive advance payments of the credit rather than receiving a tax refund when her tax return is filed?

I:14-27 Why are most elderly people unable to qualify for the tax credit for the elderly?

I:14-28 If an employer fails to withhold federal income taxes and FICA taxes on wages or fails to make payment to the IRS, what adverse tax consequences may result? May corporate officers or other corporate officials be held responsible for the underpayment?

I:14-29 Taxpayers are permitted to contribute money to qualified retirement plans and receive very favorable tax benefits. Congress has provided further incentives to contribute money to such plans by enacting the Qualified Retirement Savings Contributions Credit.

a. Why did Congress enact this credit when such contributions already receive favorable tax treatment?

b. Briefly describe how the credit is computed.

I:14-30 The credit for employer-provided child care has two major components, a credit for qualified child care expenses and a credit for qualified child care resources and referral expenditures.

a. Discuss each of the two components. What type of expenses are included in each component?

b. The two components are added together to compute the credit for employer-provided child care. Discuss the rates for each component, the limitation for the credit, and the tax result if the employer ceases to offer child care operations within the first three years after claiming the credit.

I:14-31 A credit is allowed to encourage businesses to conduct research and experimentation. One feature of the research credit is that only incremental expenditures are eligible. Explain the concept that the credit is allowed for *increasing* research activities.

I:14-32 Although Virginia is entitled to five personal and dependency exemptions on her income tax return, she claims only one withholding allowance on Form W-4.

a. Is it permissible to claim fewer allowances than an individual is entitled to?

b. Why would an individual claim fewer allowances?

c. Is it possible for Virginia to claim more than five withholding allowances?

I:14-33 Mario is a college student who had no income tax liability in the prior year and expects to have no tax liability for the current year.

a. What steps should Mario take to avoid having amounts withheld from his summer employment wages?

b. What are the cash-flow implications to Mario if the employer withholds federal income taxes?

I:14-34 What is backup withholding? What is its purpose?

I:14-35 In March 2016, Vincent anticipates that his actual tax liability for the tax year 2015 will be $12,000 and that federal income taxes withheld from his salary will be $9,000. Thus, when he files his income tax return in early 2016, he will have a $3,000 balance due. In the previous year, his actual federal income tax liability was $8,000 and his AGI was less than $150,000.

a. Is Vincent required to make estimated tax payments in 2015?

b. If no estimated tax payments are made, will Vincent be subject to an underpayment penalty if the actual tax liability for 2015 is $12,000? Why or why not?

c. Will Vincent be subject to an underpayment penalty if his 2014 AGI was $175,000? Why?

I:14-36 An individual has increasing levels of income each year and is uncertain regarding the amount of his estimated taxable income for any given year. What tax planning strategy can you suggest to avoid the penalty for underpayment of estimated tax?

I:14-37 From a cash-flow perspective, why is it generally preferable to have an underpayment of tax (assuming no underpayment penalty is imposed) rather than an overpayment of tax?

I:14-38 Why do many taxpayers intentionally overpay their tax through withholdings to obtain a tax refund?

ISSUE IDENTIFICATION QUESTIONS

I:14-39 Daryl is an executive who has an annual salary of $120,000. He is considering early retirement so he can pursue a career as a management consultant. Daryl estimates that he could earn approximately $80,000 annually from his consulting business. What tax issues should Daryl consider?

I:14-40 Jennifer recently received a check for $30,000 and securities with an FMV of $200,000 from her former husband pursuant to a divorce. The $30,000 represents alimony and the securities were transferred pursuant to the property settlement. The property settlement is nontaxable to Jennifer. Assuming the alimony is taxable and no income taxes are withheld, what tax issues should Jennifer consider?

I:14-41 Dale Eisen is saving as much as possible to fund a down payment on his first home. He is young (25 years old) and healthy, and has declined health insurance coverage offered by his employer because he would have to pay one-third of the cost (another $100 would be withheld from his monthly paycheck). He earns $65,000 per year. He received a notice from his employer indicating that unless he declined coverage, he would automatically be enrolled in the employer's basic health insurance plan ($5,000 deductible, employee pays one-third of the premium or $100 per month). Dale made an appointment with the human resources (HR) manager, intending to decline coverage. Assume you are the HR manager, and explain the costs to Dale of accepting coverage and declining coverage.

Notes: Remember that the $200 of cost paid by the employer is not treated as taxable income to Dale. For simplicity, assume any health insurance premiums paid by Dale do not exceed the 10% floor to become itemized deductions.

PROBLEMS

I:14-42 **AMT Computation.** William and Maria Smith are a married couple filing jointly. They have no children and report the following items in 2015:

Taxable income	$70,000
Tax preferences	20,000
AMT adjustments related to itemized deductions	15,000
Regular tax liability	9,578

a. What is the Smith's AMT liability?

b. What would be William's AMT liability if he were an unmarried taxpayer filing single with a regular tax liability of $13,294?

I:14-43 **AMT Computation.** Jose, an unmarried taxpayer filing single with no dependents, has AGI of $200,000 and reports the following items in 2015:

Taxable income	$160,000
Tax preferences	10,000
AMT adjustments related to itemized deductions	30,000
Regular tax liability	37,871

What is Jose's AMT liability for 2015?

I:14-44 **AMT Computation.** Harry and Mary Prodigious are married filing jointly and have 12 dependent children. Six of the children are under age 17. With the large number of children, they live in a very austere manner. Harry, in his spare time, works a large garden that provides most of their food. Mary makes all the children's clothes. Harry works for a local engineering firm and earns a salary of $100,000 annually. Mary does not work outside the home. The only other income is taxable interest in the amount of $8,000. For 2015, they claim the standard deduction and have no tax preferences or adjustments for purposes of the AMT.

a. Compute Harry and Mary's regular tax and AMT under the facts above.

b. Comment on the tax policy implications of your answer in Part a above.

I:14-45 **AMT Adjustments and Computation of Tax.** Allen, an unmarried taxpayer filing single, has no dependents and reports the following items on his 2015 federal income tax return:

Adjusted gross income	$82,450
Taxable income	47,950
Regular tax liability	7,781
Tax preferences	20,000
Itemized deductions including:	
Charitable contributions	7,500
Medical expenses (before AGI floor)	10,000
Mortgage interest on personal residence	10,000
State income taxes	5,000
Real estate taxes	8,000

a. What is the amount of Allen's AMT adjustments related to itemized deductions?

b. What is Allen's AMT liability for 2015?

I:14-46 **Self-Employment Tax.** Amelia has wages of $45,000 and net income from a small unincorporated business of $70,000 for 2015.

a. What is the amount of Amelia's self-employment (SE) tax and deduction *for* AGI for her SE tax?

b. How would your answer to Part a change if Amelia's wages were $120,000 rather than $45,000?

I:14-47 **Self-Employment Tax.** Arnie and Angela are married and file a joint return in 2015. Arnie is a partner in a public accounting firm. His share of the partnership's income in the current year is $40,000, and he receives guaranteed payments of $35,000. Angela receives wages of $50,000 from a large corporation. What is each taxpayer's self-employment tax amount? (Hint: Guaranteed payments received from a partnership are considered self-employment income.)

I:14-48 **Self-Employment Tax.** Anita, a single taxpayer, reports the following items for 2015:

Salary (subject to withholding)	$20,000
Income for serving on the Board of Directors for XYZ Corporation	11,000
Consulting gross income	9,000
Expenses related to consulting practice	(15,000)

a. What is the amount of Anita's self-employment tax?
b. How would your answer to Part a change if Anita's salary were $120,000?

I:14-49 *Computation of Tax Credits.* During the current year, Becky has personal credits (P) as well as business credits (B) related to her sole proprietorship. Her tentative tax credits for the current year include the following:

Child tax credit	$ 2,000 P
Disabled access credit	$ 900 B
Child and dependent care credit	1,200 P
Business energy credit	600 B

Becky's regular tax liability before credits is $4,000. Assume that she has no alternative minimum tax liability.
a. What is the amount of allowable personal tax credits?
b. What is the amount of allowable business tax credits?
c. What treatment is accorded to the unused tax credits for the current year?

I:14-50 *Child and Dependent Care Credit.* In each of the following independent situations, determine the amount of the child and dependent care tax credit. (Assume that both taxpayers are employed and the year is 2015).
a. Brad and Bonnie are married and file a joint return, with earned income of $40,000 and $14,000, respectively. Their combined AGI is $52,000. They have two children, ages 10 and 12, and employ a live-in nanny at an annual cost of $9,000.
b. Assume the same facts as in Part a, except that Brad and Bonnie employ Bonnie's mother, who is not their dependent, as the live-in nanny.
c. Bruce is divorced and has two children, ages 10 and 16. He has AGI and earned income of $27,000. Bruce incurs qualifying child care expenses of $8,000 during the year, incurred equally for both children. Bruce's employer maintains an employee dependent care assistance program. $1,000 was paid to Bruce from this program and excluded from Bruce's gross income.
d. Buddy and Candice are married and file a joint return. Their combined AGI is $50,000. Buddy earns $46,000, and Candice's salary from a part-time job is $4,000. They incur $5,000 of qualifying child care expenses for a day-care facility for their two children, ages 2 and 4.
e. Ben and Bunny are married and file a joint return. Their AGI is $75,000, all earned by Bunny. Ben was a full-time student for two semesters (10 months) at State University during the year. They incur $7,000 of qualifying child care expenses for their two children, ages 6 and 4.

I:14-51 *Adoption Credit.* Brad and Valerie decided to adopt a child and contacted an adoption agency in August 2014. After extensive interviews and other requirements (such as financial status, etc.), Brad and Valerie were approved as eligible parents to adopt a child. The agency indicated that it might take up to two years to find a proper match. In March 2015, the adoption became final, and Brad and Valerie adopted an infant daughter (not a special needs child). Below is a list of expenses that they incurred:

2014:	Agency fees (first installment)	$5,000
	Travel expenses for interviews, etc.	1,500
	Publications for prospective adoptive parents	300
	Legal fees connected with the adoption	1,000
	Kennel fees for dog while on adoption trips	250
2015:	Agency fees (final installment)	$4,000
	Travel expenses	400
	Court costs for adoption	1,500
	Kennel fees	100
	Nursery furniture (baby's room) and supplies	2,000

Brad and Valerie's AGI in 2014 was $70,000, and in 2015 was $90,000.
a. Compute Brad and Valerie's qualified adoption expenses for 2014 and 2015
b. Compute Brad and Valerie's adoption credit. In which year(s) may the credit be taken?
c. Would your answer to Part b change if the adopted child was a special needs child and if a grant covered all adoption cost except for legal fees?

I:14-52 *American Opportunity Tax Credit and Lifetime Learning Credit.* Lou and Stella North are married, file a joint return, and have two dependent children in college, Phil and Jaci. Phil attends a State University in a neighboring state, and Jaci attends a State University in their home state. Neither receives any type of financial assistance. The Norths' modified AGI in 2015 is $112,000. The children's classifications and expenses are as follows:

	Spring Semester 2015 (paid in January 2015)	Fall Semester 2015 (paid in July 2015)
Phil:	Senior	Master's candidate
Tuition	$7,500	$8,000
Laboratory fees	500	500
Student activity fees	100	100
Course materials (books)	400	450
Room and board	3,200	3,200
Jaci:	Sophomore	Junior
Tuition	$1,600	$1,750
Student activity fees	100	100
Course materials (books)	250	300
Room and board	3,500	3,700

a. Compute any education credits that the Norths may claim in 2015.
b. How would your answer in Part a change if Phil received an academic scholarship of $3,000 (excluded from gross income) for each semester in 2015?
c. How would your answer in Part a change if Lou and Stella's modified AGI for 2015 was $175,000?
d. How would your answer in Part a change if Phil had been a junior during Spring semester 2015 and a senior during Fall semester 2015?

I:14-53 *Tax Credit for the Elderly.* Caroline, age 66 and filing single as a dependent of another, received the following income items for 2015:

Social Security benefits (nontaxable)	$ 3,000
Pension benefits (taxable)	6,450
Interest income (taxable)	2,050
Total	$11,500

Caroline's tax liability (before credits) is $200.
a. What is Caroline's tentative tax credit for the elderly (before the tax liability limitation is applied)?
b. What is Caroline's allowable tax credit?

I:14-54 *General Business Tax Credit Limitation.* During the current year, Joule Company, a sole proprietorship, earned general business tax credits of $30,000 for energy conservation and rehabilitation expenditures. The owner, Mark Joule, knows that the overall credit will be limited. He provides you with the following information for the current year: regular tax (before credits) = $37,500; tentative minimum tax = $20,200; alternative minimum tax = $0; foreign tax credit = $4,500; other nonrefundable credits = $6,100. Mark also has a $3,000 carryforward of general business credit from the prior year.
a. What is the current year limitation on Mark's general business credit?
b. What is Mark's allowable general business credit in the current year and where does it come from?
c. What is Mark's general business credit carryover?

I:14-55 *Foreign Tax Credit.* Laser Corporation, a U.S. corporation, has a foreign office that conducts business in France. Laser pays foreign taxes of $74,000 on foreign-source taxable income of $185,000. Its U.S.-source taxable income is $320,000, total U.S. taxable income (worldwide) of $505,000, and U.S. tax liability (before reductions for the foreign tax credit) is $171,700. What is Laser's foreign tax credit? What is Laser's foreign tax credit carryback or carryover?

I:14-56 *Premium Tax Credit.* Randall and Dianne Wall live in St. Louis, Missouri. Randall and Dianne are each 30 years old, neither smokes, and they have no children or other dependents.

Randall is attending law school full time and working part time (2015 earnings = $9,000). Dianne works full time (2015 earnings = $38,200). Their 2015 household income is more than 200% of the FPL (but not more than 300% of the FPL).

Dianne's employer does not offer employee health insurance coverage. The Walls choose to purchase insurance through the federal exchange operating in Missouri. They are credit eligible for all 12 months in 2015.

Their premiums for coverage vary by the type of plan.
- Under a Gold plan, monthly premiums are $585 (covers 2) per month, so the annual cost of coverage is $7,020.
- The second-least-expensive Silver plan (the benchmark plan) involves premiums of $468 per month (covers 2), or $5,616 per year.
- Under a Bronze plan, monthly premiums are $390 (covers 2) per month, so the annual cost of coverage is $4,680.

What is the 2015 after-tax-credit cost of health insurance for the Walls under each of the plans described above?

I:14-57 *Rehabilitation Tax Credit.* Bob acquired a certified historic structure and placed it in service August of the current year, as an office for his business. He paid $20,000 for the building (exclusive of the land) and spent $40,000 for renovation costs.
a. What is the rehabilitation tax credit (before limitations)?
b. What is the basis of the building for MACRS depreciation purposes?
c. Compute the depreciation that Bob can take on the building for the current year.

I:14-58 *Research Credit.* Pharm Inc. is a small pharmaceutical company (organized four years ago) that is heavily involved in drug research. During the current year, Pharm Inc. incurred the following expenditures related to the company's research efforts:

Salaries of research scientists and technicians	$180,000
Supplies and materials	162,000
Depreciation on research equipment	30,000

For the previous four years, Pharm Inc. had average gross receipts of $5,000,000. The company's fixed-base percentage is 3%. Compute Pharm Inc.'s current year credit for research activities. Is Pharm Inc. entitled to claim any deduction for research and experimentation expenses for the current year?

I:14-59 *Earned Income Credit.* Carolyn is unmarried and has one dependent child, age 6, who lived with her for the entire year. In 2015, she has income of $16,000 in wages and $6,000 in alimony. Her AGI is $22,000.
a. What is Carolyn's tentative earned income credit (before phaseout)?
b. What is Carolyn's allowable earned income credit?
c. If Carolyn has no income tax liability (before the earned income credit is subtracted), is she entitled to a refund in the current year?
d. How will your answers to Parts a and b change if Carolyn is married filing a joint return?

I:14-60 *Earned Income Credit.* Jose is unmarried with no qualifying children. He has $8,300 of 2015 wages and is otherwise eligible for the earned income credit. Jose has $200 of interest income and no *for* AGI deductions.
a. What is Jose's tentative earned income credit before phaseout?
b. What is Jose's allowable earned income credit?
c. If Jose has no income tax liability (before the earned income credit is subtracted), is he entitled to a refund for the current year?
d. Would your answer to Part b change if Jose had dividend and interest income of $3,700 during the taxable year?

I:14-61 *Refundable Credits.* Latisha is an unmarried taxpayer, filing head of household. She has two dependent children (7 year old twins) who lived with her all year. Her 2015 earned income was $18,600, her AGI was $22,700, and she uses the standard deduction. Determine her:
1. Taxable income and regular tax before credits
2. Earned income credit (EIC).
3. Balance due or refund.

I:14-62 *Penalties for Nonpayment of Withholding and FICA Taxes.* Lake Corporation has some severe cash-flow problems. You are the company's financial and tax consultant. The treasurer of the company has informed you that the company has failed to make FICA and federal income tax withholding payments to the IRS (both the employer and employee contributions) for a period of approximately six months.

a. What advice can you give to the company treasurer regarding the nonpayment of taxes?

b. Can the liability for payment of the taxes extend to parties other than the corporation? Explain.

I:14-63 *Exemptions from Withholding.* Which of the following categories of individuals or income are exempt from the federal income tax withholding requirements?

a. Household employees

b. Independent contractors

c. Newspaper carriers over age 18

d. Bonuses

e. Commissions

f. Vacation pay

g. Tips under $20 per month from a single employer

I:14-64 *Withholding Exemptions.* Barry is a college student who is employed as a waiter during the summer. He earns approximately $1,500 during the summer and estimates that he will not be required to file a tax return and will have no federal income tax liability. Last year, however, he made $6,000 and was required to file a return and pay $400 in taxes. Barry is unmarried and is supported by his parents. He has no dependents and does not have any other sources of income or deductions.

a. Can Barry claim exempt status on Form W-4 for withholding purposes?

b. Can Barry claim more than one exemption on Form W-4 (e.g., additional withholding allowances or the standard deduction allowance) to minimize the amount withheld? Explain.

I:14-65 *Withholding Allowances.* Bart and Jane Lee are married, file a joint return and have two dependent children. Bart begins a new job in 2015 and is asked to fill out a Form W-4. His monthly gross earnings will be $3,200. Jane does not work outside their home. Bart can claim three additional withholding allowances because he will have a large for-AGI deduction for substantial alimony paid to his ex-wife, Sue.

a. What is the correct number of withholding allowances on Form W-4?

b. What is the federal income tax, FICA and Medicare tax to be withheld using the wage bracket tables (see withholding table on page T-15)?

c. What disclosure procedures must Bart's employer follow if Bart claims more than ten allowances?

I:14-66 *Estimated Tax Requirements.* Anna does not make quarterly estimated tax payments even though she has substantial amounts of income that are not subject to withholding. In the previous year, Anna's tax liability was $18,000 and her AGI was $135,000. In the current year, Anna's actual tax liability is $30,000, and $18,200 was withheld from her salary.

a. Is Anna subject to the underpayment penalty? Why?

b. If Anna's withholdings were only $15,000, would she be subject to the underpayment penalty? Why?

c. If Anna is subject to an underpayment penalty, can she deduct this amount as interest? Explain.

I:14-67 *Estimated Tax Underpayment Penalty.* Jane's estimated tax payments for the current year total $14,000, and federal income taxes withheld from her salary amount to $12,000. Jane's actual tax liability for the current year is $30,000. Her income was earned evenly throughout the current year. Jane's AGI for the prior year was $160,000 and her tax liability was $25,000. Is Jane subject to the underpayment penalty? Explain.

COMPREHENSIVE PROBLEM

I:14-68 Mike Webb, married to Nancy Webb, is employed by a large pharmaceutical company and earns a salary. In addition, Mike is an entrepreneur and has two small businesses on the side, both of which operate as sole proprietorships. One is a profitable consulting business where Mike provides financial and retirement advice to pharmacists. The other involves the manufacture of Christmas novelties in China, selling the products in gift shops in the U.S. This business is struggling. However, Mike feels the Christmas novelty business has great potential. Mike reports the following for 2015:

Salary			$150,000
Consulting practice:	Revenues	$65,000	
	Ordinary expenses	12,000	53,000
Sole proprietorship:	Revenues	$22,000	
	Ordinary Expenses	40,000	(18,000)
Interest (none tax-exempt)			3,000
Dividends, qualified			9,000
LTCG		$24,000	
STCL		(4,000)	20,000
Itemized deductions:			
State and local taxes		$14,000	
Real estate taxes		8,000	
Mortgage interest on personal residence		7,000	
Charitable contributions		8,000	37,000

Child care expenses:
The Webb's have two dependent children, ages 13 and 11, and pay child care expenses of $4,000 per year for each child. Nancy is not employed, but is a full-time student (all of 2015) at State University, majoring in Accounting.

Federal income tax withheld from salary	$21,000
Estimated taxes paid for 2015	14,000

For 2014, Mike and Nancy's AGI was $175,000 and their actual federal income tax liability was $29,000.

a. Compute the Webbs regular federal income tax liability for 2015, including self-employment taxes.
b. Are the Webbs subject to AMT in 2015?
c. Are the Webbs due a refund for 2015?
d. Are the Webbs subject to any underpayment penalties for 2015?

TAX STRATEGY PROBLEM

I:14-69 Jeff and Linda Foley are married and file a joint income tax return. Jeff is a lawyer and a partner in the firm of Foley & Looby, Attorneys at Law. Jeff is a 50% partner in the firm along with his partner, John Looby who is the other 50% partner. Foley & Looby (F&L) currently rent office space in a prestigious building and pay rent of $6,000 per month or $72,000 per year for their 4,000 square foot office. Thus, the firm pays $18 per square foot per year. As no equity is being generated by paying rent, Jeff and John are considering buying an office building. They have two buildings under consideration, as follows:

Building #1

Building #1 is a relatively new building and has 10,000 square feet of space. The new building can be purchased for a total price of $1,000,000. F&L would only use 4,000 square feet of the space and have other businesses that would rent the other 6,000 square feet from F&L for $15 per square foot per year, a total of $90,000 per year. Maintenance costs would amount to approximately $10 per square foot per year. The building is in excellent condition and is ready to be moved into immediately and would require very few other outlays by F&L.

Building #2

Building #2 is located in the downtown area in a certified historic district and would qualify as a certified historic structure. This building, nearly 80 years old, also has 10,000 square feet and, like Building #1, the other 6,000 square feet can be rented to other tenants at $15 per square foot per year, a total of $90,000 per year. However, Building #2 is not in as good condition as Building #1. The purchase price of the building would be $400,000, and Jeff and John estimate that approximately $600,000 would have to be invested in capital expenditures to make the building suitable for their business. After the significant capital expenditures, F&L estimates the maintenance costs to be similar to Building #1, or $10 per square foot per year.

Both buildings can be 100% financed at 8% annual interest rate for 15 years. The annual cash payment on the $1,000,000 mortgage would be $117,000. Assume both buildings will appreciate at a rate of 8% per year.

Jeff and John have come to you as their financial and tax advisor to help them make the decision as to which building to purchase. If the buildings are equally desirable from a non-financial and non-tax standpoint, what is the best decision for them? That is, should they stay where they are and rent, or purchase one of the two buildings? Assume both Jeff and John are in the top 35% marginal tax bracket.

TAX FORM/RETURN PREPARATION PROBLEMS

I:14-70 Len and Christy Vole, ages 42 and 39 respectively, are married and file jointly in 2014. Len is a contractor operating as a sole proprietorship (EIN 11-1111111). Christy is employed, earning $24,000 as a part-time paralegal. They have two dependent children, Jill, age 8 and Lee, age 5. In 2014, they received $4,550 from Good Bank in taxable interest income. Their allowable itemized deductions include state income tax $3,700; home mortgage interest $6,000; and charity $5,000. Federal income tax withholding was $7,500 and estimated tax payments were $13,000. The Voles also incurred $7,000 of qualifying child care expenses to enable them to work ($3,500 for each child). It was paid to HiTop Daycare, 327 Fowler St., Indianapolis, IN 46802 (EIN 22-2222222).

Len earns $95,000 in profit in a sole proprietorship. He incurred the following expenses that qualify for the general business credit: $6,000 for disabled access. No adjustments are required to this credit and there are no carrybacks or carryforwards.

Social security numbers are: Len, 111-11-1111; Christy, 222-22-2222; Jill, 333-33-3333; Lee, 444-44-4444.

Complete the Voles' Form 1040 for 2014, along with supporting Schedules A, B, C, and SE, Form 2441 (child and dependent care credit), Form 3800 (general business credit), Form 8826 (disabled access credit), and Form 5884 (work opportunity credit). Show detail of the child tax credit computation (with any phaseout) at the bottom of Form 1040, page 2.

I:14-71 Harold J. Milton (SSN 000-22-1111) is 45 years old and unmarried, filing single with no dependents. He had the following income and deductions for 2014:

Salary	$177,000	State income taxes	$18,000
Interest income from State Bank	12,000	Mortgage interest expense on	
Dividend income (qualified)	18,000	residence (100% acquisition	
Deductible IRA contribution	5,000	debt)	19,000
Tax-exempt interest income		Interest expense on car loan	3,000
from municipal bonds	24,000	Real estate taxes	
Charitable contributions	27,000	on residence	2,000
		Miscellaneous deductions—other	
		(before the 2% AGI floor)	7,000
		Income taxes withheld	20,000
		Estimated tax payments	
		($2,500 per quarter)	10,000

Complete Milton's 2014 Form 1040, Schedule A, B, D, and Form 6251. In 2013, Milton had AGI of $200,000 and his income tax liability was $46,000.

CASE STUDY PROBLEMS

I:14-72 Barbara was divorced in 2012. However, the final property settlement and determination of alimony payments was not made until February 2015 because of extended litigation. Barbara received a $20,000 payment of back alimony in March 2015 and will receive monthly alimony payments of $2,000 for the period April through December 2015.

Last year, Barbara's income consisted of $15,000 salary and $2,000 of taxable interest income, and her tax liability was $1,900. She expects to continue working at an annual salary of $15,000 and will have $2,000 of interest income. Federal income taxes withheld from her salary in 2015 will be $1,500. Her monthly alimony payments of $2,000 are also expected to continue for an indefinite period.

In early April 2015 Barbara requests your advice regarding the payment of quarterly estimated taxes for 2015. Prepare a memo to your client that discusses these requirements, including any possible penalties for not making quarterly payments and nontax issues such as cash-flow and investment income decisions.

I:14-73 Chips-R-Us is a computer technology corporation that designs hardware and software for use in large businesses. The corporation regularly pays individuals to install programs and give advice to companies that buy their software. In the current year, Simone, a computer expert, was sent to a customer of Chips-R-Us to perform computer services. Simone is not a regular employee of the corporation and the corporation did not train Simone for the task. Simone keeps track of the time spent on the job at the customer and reports to the corporation, which pays Simone for her services. The corporation specifies the work to be done for their client. The corporation can also replace Simone with another individual if her work is not satisfactory. Chips-R-Us treats Simone as an independent contractor for employment tax purposes.

In the current year the IRS challenges the corporation that it has failed to remit FICA taxes and income taxes that should have been withheld with respect to Simone's employment. Chips-R-Us refuses to pay the amount, stating that it is not required to do so because Simone is not an employee of the corporation. What will be the likely outcome of the IRS's challenge concerning Simone's status as an employee or independent contractor? Who may be liable for payment of the employment taxes, interest, and penalties to the government? What ethical responsibilities should be followed in the remittance of withheld employee taxes?

TAX RESEARCH PROBLEM

I:14-74 Lean Corporation was incorporated in 1981 by Bruce Smith, who has served as an officer and member of the Board of Directors. Carl Jones has served as the secretary-treasurer of the company as a convenience to his friend Bruce. Carl acted as a part-time bookkeeper but did not run the everyday business affairs and paid only the bills he was instructed to pay. Carl was an authorized signatory for the corporate bank accounts but had no final control over expenditures.

Beginning in the last quarter of 2012, the company failed to pay all of the taxes withheld from employees and the employer's share of FICA taxes to the IRS. Despite this delinquency, the corporation continued to pay other creditors, including its employees, in preference to the IRS.

In January, 2014 Lean Corporation entered into an installment agreement with the IRS to keep current on its withholding taxes and to make payments on the past due balance until paid in full. The company subsequently defaulted on the agreement in April 2014. During this period, Bruce Smith was serving as chief financial officer and was a member of the board of directors. He had the authority to make policy decisions. He was responsible for negotiating the installment agreement with the IRS and the decision to default on the agreement.

Who is liable for the penalty for the nonpayment of the payroll tax withholdings?

A partial list of research sources is:

- Sec. 6672

- *Ernest W. Carlson v. U.S.,* 67 AFTR 2d 91-1104, 91-1 USTC ¶50,262 (D.C. UT, 1991)

CHAPTER

15

TAX RESEARCH

LEARNING OBJECTIVES

After studying this chapter, you should be able to

1 ▶ Distinguish between closed fact and open fact tax situations

2 ▶ Describe the steps in the tax research process

3 ▶ Explain how the facts influence tax consequences

4 ▶ Identify the sources of tax law and assess the authoritative value of each

5 ▶ Consult tax services to research an issue

6 ▶ Apply the basics of Internet-based tax research

7 ▶ Use a citator to assess tax authorities

8 ▶ Describe the professional guidelines that CPAs in tax practice should follow

9 ▶ Prepare work papers and communicate to clients

This chapter introduces the reader to the tax research process. Its major focus is the sources of the tax law (i.e., the Internal Revenue Code and other tax authorities) and the relative weight given to each source. The chapter describes the steps in the tax research process and places particular emphasis on the importance of the facts to the tax consequences. It also describes the features of frequently used tax services and computer-based tax research resources. Finally, it explains how to use a citator.

The end product of the tax research process—the communication of results to the client—also is discussed. This text uses a hypothetical set of facts to provide a comprehensive illustration of the process. Sample work papers demonstrating how to document the results of research are included in Appendix A. The text also discusses two types of professional guidelines for CPAs in tax practice: the American Institute of Certified Public Accountants' (AICPA's) *Statements on Standards for Tax Services* (reproduced in Appendix E) and Treasury Department *Circular 230*.

OVERVIEW OF TAX RESEARCH

OBJECTIVE 1

Distinguish between closed fact and open fact tax situations

Tax research is the process of solving tax-related problems by applying tax law to specific sets of facts. Sometimes it involves researching several issues and often is conducted to formulate tax policy. For example, policy-oriented research would determine how far the level of charitable contributions might decline if such contributions were no longer deductible. Economists usually conduct this type of tax research to assess the effects of government policy.

Tax research also is conducted to determine the tax consequences of transactions to specific taxpayers. For example, client-oriented research would determine whether Smith Corporation could deduct a particular expenditure as a trade or business expense. Accounting and law firms generally engage in this type of research on behalf of their clients.

This chapter deals only with client-oriented tax research, which occurs in two contexts:

1. **Closed fact or tax compliance situations:** The client contacts the tax advisor after completing a transaction or while preparing a tax return. In such situations, the tax consequences are fairly straightforward because the facts cannot be modified to obtain different results. Consequently, tax saving opportunities may be lost.

ADDITIONAL COMMENT

Closed-fact situations afford the tax advisor the least amount of flexibility. Because the facts are already established, the tax advisor must develop the best solution possible within certain predetermined constraints.

EXAMPLE I:15-1 ▶

Tom informs Carol, his tax advisor, that on November 4 of the current year, he sold land held as an investment for $500,000 cash. His basis in the land was $50,000. On November 9, Tom reinvested the sales proceeds in another plot of investment property costing $500,000. This is a closed fact situation. Tom wants to know the amount and the character of the gain (if any) he must recognize. Because Tom solicits the tax advisor's advice after the sale and reinvestment, the opportunity for tax planning is limited. For example, the possibility of deferring taxes by using a like-kind exchange or an installment sale is lost. ◀

ADDITIONAL COMMENT

Open-fact or tax-planning situations give a tax advisor flexibility to structure transactions to accomplish the client's objectives. In this type of situation, a creative tax advisor can save taxpayers dollars through effective tax planning.

2. **Open fact or tax planning situations:** Before structuring or concluding a transaction, the client contacts the tax advisor to discuss tax planning opportunities. Tax-planning situations generally are more difficult and challenging because the tax advisor must consider the client's tax and nontax objectives. Most clients will not engage in a transaction if it is inconsistent with their nontax objectives, even though it produces tax savings.

EXAMPLE I:15-2 ▶

Diane is a widow with three children and five grandchildren and at present owns property valued at $30 million. She seeks advice from Carol, her tax advisor, about how to minimize her estate taxes and convey the greatest value of property to her descendants. This is an open-fact situation. Carol could advise Diane to leave all but $5 million of her property to a charitable organization so that her estate would owe no estate taxes. Although this recommendation would eliminate Diane's estate taxes, Diane is likely to reject it because she wants her children or grandchildren to be her primary beneficiaries. Thus, reducing estate taxes to zero is inconsistent with her objective of allowing her descendants to receive as much after-tax wealth as possible. ◄

When conducting research in a tax planning context, the tax professional should keep a number of points in mind. First, the objective is not to minimize taxes per se but rather to maximize a taxpayer's after-tax return. For example, if the federal income tax rate is a constant 30%, an investor should not buy a tax-exempt bond yielding 5% when he or she could buy a corporate bond of equal risk that yields 9% before tax and 6.3% after tax. This is the case even though his or her explicit taxes (actual tax liability) would be minimized by investing in the tax-exempt bond.[1] Second, taxpayers typically do not engage in unilateral or self-dealing transactions; thus, the tax ramifications for all parties to the transaction should be considered. For example, in the executive compensation context, employees may prefer to receive incentive stock options (because they will not recognize income until they sell the stock), but the employer may prefer to grant a different type of option (because the employer cannot deduct the value of incentive stock options upon issuance). Thus, the employer might grant a different number of options if it uses one type of stock option versus another type as compensation. Third, taxes are but one cost of doing business. In deciding where to locate a manufacturing plant, for example, factors more important to some businesses than the amount of state and local taxes paid might be the proximity to raw materials, good transportation systems, the cost of labor, the quantity of available skilled labor, and the quality of life in the area. Fourth, the time for tax planning is not restricted to the beginning date of an investment, contract, or other arrangement. Instead, the time extends throughout the duration of the activity. As tax rules change or as business and economic environments change, the tax advisor must reevaluate whether the taxpayer should hold onto an investment and must consider the transaction costs of any alternatives.

One final note: the tax advisor should always bear in mind the financial accounting implications of proposed transactions. An answer that may be desirable from a tax perspective may not always be desirable from a financial accounting perspective. Though interrelated, the two fields of accounting have different orientations and different objectives. Tax accounting is oriented primarily to the Internal Revenue Service (IRS). Its objectives include calculating, reporting, and predicting one's tax liability according to legal principles. Financial accounting is oriented primarily to shareholders, creditors, managers, and employees. Its objectives include determining, reporting, and predicting a business's financial position and operating results according to Generally Accepted Accounting Principles. Because tax and financial accounting objectives may differ, planning conflicts could arise. For example, management might be reluctant to engage in tax reduction strategies that also reduce book income and reported earnings per share. Success in any tax practice, especially at the managerial level, requires consideration of both sets of objectives and orientations.

STEPS IN THE TAX RESEARCH PROCESS

In both open- and closed-fact situations, the tax research process involves six basic steps:

1. Determine the facts.
2. Identify the issues (questions).
3. Locate the applicable authorities.
4. Evaluate the authorities and choose those to follow where the authorities conflict.
5. Analyze the facts in terms of the applicable authorities.
6. Communicate conclusions and recommendations to the client.

---

[1] For an excellent discussion of explicit and implicit taxes and tax planning see M. S. Scholes, M. A. Wolfson, M. Erickson, L. Maydew, and T. Shevlin, *Taxes and Business Strategy: A Planning Approach,* fourth edition (Upper Saddle River, NJ: Pearson Prentice Hall, 2008). Also see Chapter I:18 of the *Individuals* volume. An example of an implicit tax is the excess of the before-tax earnings on a taxable bond over the risk-adjusted before-tax earnings on a tax-favored investment (e.g., a municipal bond).

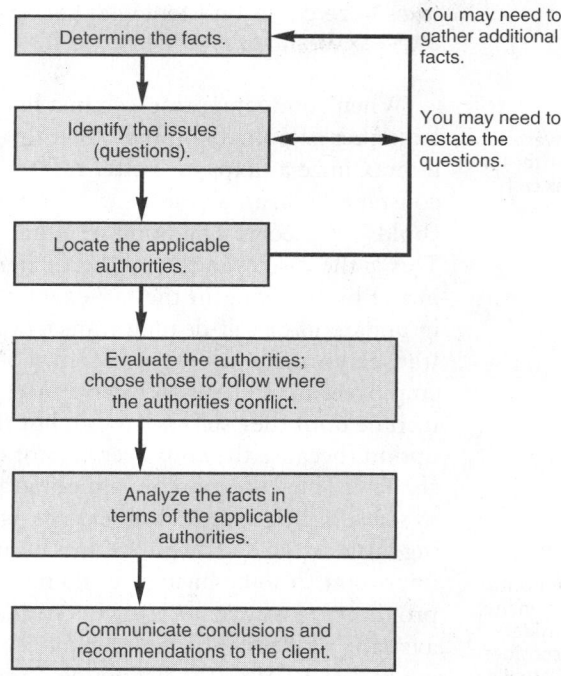

FIGURE I:15-1 ▶ STEPS IN THE TAX RESEARCH PROCESS

Although the above outline suggests a linear approach, the tax research process often is circular. That is, it does not always proceed step-by-step. Figure I:15-1 illustrates a more accurate process, and Appendix A provides a comprehensive example of this process.

In a closed-fact situation, the facts have already occurred, and the tax advisor's task is to analyze them to determine the appropriate tax treatment. In an open-fact situation, by contrast, the facts have not yet occurred, and the tax advisor's task is to plan for them or shape them so as to produce a favorable tax result. The tax advisor performs the latter task by reviewing the relevant legal authorities, particularly court cases and IRS rulings, all the while bearing in mind the facts of those cases or rulings that produced favorable results compared with those that produced unfavorable results. For example, if a client wants to realize an ordinary loss (as opposed to a capital loss) on the sale of several plots of land, the tax advisor might consult cases involving similar land sales. The advisor might attempt to distinguish the facts of those cases in which the taxpayer realized an ordinary loss from the facts of those cases in which the taxpayer realized a capital loss. The advisor then might recommend that the client structure the transaction based on the fact pattern in the ordinary loss cases.

Often, tax research involves a question to which no clearcut, unequivocally correct answer exists. In such situations, probing a related issue might lead to a solution pertinent to the central question. For example, in researching whether the taxpayer may deduct a loss as ordinary instead of capital, the tax advisor might research the related issue of whether the presence of an investment motive precludes classifying a loss as ordinary. The solution to that issue might be relevant to the central question of whether the taxpayer may deduct the loss as ordinary.

Identifying the issue(s) to be researched often is the most difficult step in the tax research process. In some instances, the client defines the issue(s) for the tax advisor, such as where the client asks, "May I deduct the costs of a winter trip to Florida recommended by my physician?" In other instances, the tax advisor, after reviewing the documents submitted to him or her by the client, identifies and defines the issue(s) himself or herself. Doing so presupposes a firm grounding in tax law.[2]

---

[2] Often, in an employment context, supervisors define the questions to be researched and the authorities that might be relevant to the tax consequences.

Once the tax advisor locates the applicable legal authorities, he or she might have to obtain additional information from the client. Example I:15-3 illustrates the point. The example assumes that all relevant tax authorities are in agreement.

EXAMPLE I:15-3 ▶ Mark calls his tax advisor, Al, and states that he (1) incurred a loss on renting his beach cottage during the current year and (2) wonders whether he may deduct the loss. He also states that he, his wife, and their minor child occupied the cottage only eight days during the current year.

This is the first time Al has dealt with the Sec. 280A vacation home rules. On reading Sec. 280A(d), Al learns that a loss is *not* deductible if the taxpayer used the residence for personal purposes for longer than the greater of (1) 14 days or (2) 10% of the number of days the unit was rented at a fair rental value. He also learns that the property is *deemed* to be used by the taxpayer for personal purposes on any days on which it is used by any member of his or her family (as defined in Sec. 267(c)(4)). The Sec. 267(c)(4) definition of family members includes brothers, sisters, spouse, ancestors (e.g., parents and grandparents), or lineal descendants (e.g., children and grandchildren).

Mark's eight-day use is not long enough to make the rental loss nondeductible. However, Al must inquire about the number of days, if any, Mark's brothers, sisters, or parents used the property. (He already knows about use by Mark, his spouse, and his lineal descendants.) In addition, Al must find out how many days the cottage was rented to other persons at a fair rental value. Upon obtaining the additional information, Al proceeds to determine how to calculate the deductible expenses. Al then derives his conclusion concerning the deductible loss, if any, and communicates it to Mark. (This example assumes the passive activity and at-risk rules restricting a taxpayer's ability to deduct losses from real estate activities will not pose a problem for Mark. See Chapter I:8 for a comprehensive discussion of these topics.) ◀

Many firms require that a researcher's conclusions be communicated to the client in writing. Members or employees of such firms may answer questions orally, but their oral conclusions should be followed by a written communication. According to the AICPA's *Statements on Standards for Tax Services* (reproduced in Appendix E),

> Although oral advice may serve a client's needs appropriately in routine matters or in well-defined areas, written communications are recommended in important, unusual, substantial dollar value, or complicated transactions. The member may use professional judgment about whether, subsequently, to document oral advice.[3]

In addition, Treasury Department *Circular 230* covers all written advice communicated to clients. These requirements are more fully discussed at the end of this chapter and in Chapter C:15.

IMPORTANCE OF THE FACTS TO THE TAX CONSEQUENCES

OBJECTIVE 3

Explain how the facts influence tax consequences

Many terms and phrases used in the Internal Revenue Code (IRC) and other tax authorities are vague or ambiguous. Some provisions conflict with others or are difficult to reconcile, creating for the researcher the dilemma of deciding which rules are applicable and which tax results are proper. For example, as a condition to claiming another person as a dependent, the taxpayer must provide a certain level of support for such person.[4] Neither the IRC nor the Treasury Regulations define "support." This lack of definition could be problematic. For example, if the taxpayer purchased a used automobile costing $8,000 for an elderly parent whose only source of income is $7,800 in Social Security benefits, the question of whether the expenditure constitutes support would arise. The tax advisor would have to consult court opinions, revenue rulings, and other IRS pronouncements to ascertain the legal meaning of the term "support." Only after thorough research would the meaning of the term become clear.

---

[3] AICPA, *Statement on Standards for Tax Services*, No. 7, "Form and Content of Advice to Taxpayers," 2010, Para. 6.

[4] Sec. 152(e)(1)(A) and Sec. 152(d)(1)(C).

In other instances, the legal language is quite clear, but a question arises as to whether the taxpayer's transaction conforms to a specific pattern of facts that gives rise to a particular tax result. Ultimately, the peculiar facts of a transaction or event determine its tax consequences. A change in the facts can significantly change the consequences. Consider the following illustrations:

Illustration One

Facts: A holds stock, a capital asset, that he purchased two years ago at a cost of $1,000. He sells the stock to B for $920. What are the tax consequences to A?

Result: Under Sec. 1001, A realizes an $80 capital loss. He recognizes this loss in the current year. A must offset the loss against any capital gains recognized during the year. Any excess loss is deductible from ordinary income up to a $3,000 annual limit.

Change of Facts: A is B's son.

New Result: Under Sec. 267, A and B are related parties. Therefore, A may not recognize the realized loss. However, B may use the loss if she subsequently sells the stock at a gain.

Illustration Two

Facts: C donates to State University ten acres of land that she purchased two years ago for $10,000. The fair market value (FMV) of the land on the date of the donation is $25,000. C's adjusted gross income is $100,000. What is C's charitable contribution deduction?

Result: Under Sec. 170, C is entitled to a $25,000 charitable contribution deduction (i.e., the FMV of the property unreduced by the unrealized long-term gain).

Change of Facts: C purchased the land 11 months ago.

New Result: Under the same IRC section, C is entitled to only a $10,000 charitable contribution deduction (i.e., the FMV of the property reduced by the unrealized short-term gain).

Illustration Three

Facts: Acquiring Corporation pays Target Corporation's shareholders one million shares of Acquiring voting stock. In return, Target's shareholders tender 98% of their Target voting stock. The acquisition is for a bona fide business purpose. Acquiring continues Target's business. What are the tax consequences of the exchange to Target's shareholders?

Result: Because the transaction qualifies as a reorganization under Sec. 368(a)(1)(B), Target's shareholders are not taxed on the exchange, which is solely for Acquiring voting stock.

Change of Facts: In the transaction, Acquiring purchases the remaining 2% of Target's shares with cash.

New Result: Under the same IRC provision, Target's shareholders are now taxed on the exchange, which is not solely for Acquiring voting stock.

CREATING A FACTUAL SITUATION FAVORABLE TO THE TAXPAYER

TYPICAL MISCONCEPTION

Many taxpayers believe tax practitioners spend most of their time preparing tax returns. In reality, providing tax advice that accomplishes the taxpayer's objectives is one of the most important responsibilities of a tax advisor. This latter activity is tax consulting as compared to tax compliance.

Based on his or her research, a tax advisor might recommend to a taxpayer how to structure a transaction or plan an event so as to increase the likelihood that related expenses will be deductible. For example, suppose a taxpayer is assigned a temporary task in a location (City Y) different from the location (City X) of his or her permanent employment. Suppose also that the taxpayer wants to deduct the meal and lodging expenses incurred in City Y as well as the cost of transportation thereto. To do so, the taxpayer must establish that City X is his or her tax home and that he or she temporarily works in City Y. (Section 162 provides that a taxpayer may deduct travel expenses while "away from home" on business. A taxpayer is deemed to be "away from home" if his or her employment at the new location does not exceed one year, i.e., it is "temporary.") Suppose the taxpayer wants to know the tax consequences of his or her working in City Y for ten months and then, within that ten-month period, finding permanent employment in City Y. What is tax research likely to reveal?

Tax research will lead to an IRS ruling stating that, in such circumstances, the employment will be deemed to be temporary until the date on which the realistic expectation about the temporary nature of the assignment changes.[5] After this date, the employment

---

[5] Rev. Rul. 93-86, 1993-2 C.B. 71.

will be deemed to be permanent, and travel expenses relating to it will be nondeductible. Based on this finding, the tax advisor might advise the taxpayer to postpone his or her permanent job search in City Y until the end of the ten-month period and simply treat his or her assignment as temporary. So doing would lengthen the time he or she is deemed to be "away from home" on business and thus increase the amount of meal, lodging, and transportation costs deductible as travel expenses. The taxpayer should compare the tax savings to any additional personal costs of maintaining two residences.

THE SOURCES OF TAX LAW

Identify the sources of tax law and assess the authoritative value of each

The language of the IRC is general; that is, it prescribes the tax treatment of broad categories of transactions and events. The reason for the generality is that Congress can neither foresee nor provide for every conceivable transaction or event. Even if it could, doing so would render the statute narrow in scope and inflexible in application. Accordingly, interpretations of the IRC—both administrative and judicial—are necessary. Administrative interpretations are provided in Treasury Regulations, revenue rulings, revenue procedures, and several other pronouncements discussed later in this chapter. Judicial interpretations are presented in court opinions. The term *tax law* as used by most tax advisors encompasses administrative and judicial interpretations in addition to the IRC. It also includes the meaning conveyed in reports issued by Congressional committees involved in the legislative process.

THE LEGISLATIVE PROCESS

Tax legislation begins in the House of Representatives. Initially, a tax proposal is incorporated in a bill. The bill is referred to the House Ways and Means Committee, which is charged with reviewing all tax legislation. The Ways and Means Committee holds hearings in which interested parties, such as the Treasury Secretary and IRS Commissioner, testify. At the conclusion of the hearings, the Ways and Means Committee votes to approve or reject the measure. If approved, the bill goes to the House floor where it is debated by the full membership. If the House approves the measure, the bill moves to the Senate where it is taken up by the Senate Finance Committee. Like Ways and Means, the Finance Committee holds hearings in which Treasury officials, tax experts, and other interested parties testify. If the committee approves the measure, the bill goes to the Senate floor where it is debated by the full membership. Upon approval by the Senate, it is submitted to the President for his or her signature. If the President signs the measure, the bill becomes public law. If the President vetoes it, Congress can override the veto by at least a two-thirds majority vote in each chamber.

Generally, at each stage of the legislative process, the bill is subject to amendment. If amended, and if the House version differs from the Senate version, the bill is referred to a House-Senate conference committee.[6] This committee attempts to resolve the differences between the House and Senate versions. Ultimately, it submits a compromise version of the measure to each chamber for its approval. Such referrals are common. For example, in 1998 the House and Senate disagreed over what the taxpayer must do to shift the burden of proof to the IRS. The House proposed that the taxpayer assert a "reasonable dispute" regarding a taxable item. The Senate proposed that the taxpayer introduce "credible evidence" regarding the item. A conference committee was appointed to resolve the differences. This committee ultimately adopted the Senate proposal, which was later approved by both chambers.

Committee reports can be helpful in interpreting new legislation because they indicate the intent of Congress. With the proliferation of tax legislation, committee reports have become especially important because the Treasury Department often is unable to draft the needed regulations in a timely manner.

After approving major legislation, the Ways and Means Committee and Senate Finance Committee usually issue official reports. These reports, published by the U.S. Government Printing Office (GPO) as part of the *Cumulative Bulletin* and as separate documents, explain the committees' reasoning for approving (and/or amending) the legislation.[7] In addition, the GPO publishes both records of the committee hearings and transcripts of the floor debates. The records are published as separate House or Senate documents. The transcripts are incorporated in the *Congressional Record* for the day of the

---

[6] The size of a conference committee can vary. It is made up of an equal number of members from the House and the Senate.

[7] The *Cumulative Bulletin* is described in the discussion of revenue rulings on page I:15-12.

debate. In tax research, these records, reports, and transcripts are useful in deciphering the meaning of the statutory language. Where this language is ambiguous or vague, and the courts have not interpreted it, the documents can shed light on **Congressional intent**, i.e., what Congress *intended* by a particular term, phrase, or provision.

EXAMPLE I:15-4 ►

In 1998, Congress passed legislation concerning shifting the burden of proof to the IRS. This legislation was codified in Sec. 7491. The question arises as to what constitutes "credible evidence" because the taxpayer must introduce such evidence to shift the burden of proof to the IRS. Section 7491 does not define the term. Because the provision was relatively new, few courts had an opportunity to interpret what "credible evidence" means. In the absence of relevant statutory or judicial authority, the researcher might have looked to the committee reports to ascertain what Congress intended by the term. Senate Report No. 105-174 states that "credible evidence" means evidence of a quality, which, "after critical analysis, the court would find sufficient upon which to base a decision on the issue if no contrary evidence were submitted."[8] This language suggests that Congress intended the term to mean evidence of a kind sufficient to withstand judicial scrutiny. Such a meaning should be regarded as conclusive in the absence of other authority. ◄

THE INTERNAL REVENUE CODE

The IRC, which comprises Title 26 of the United States Code, is the foundation of all tax law. First codified (i.e., organized into a single compilation of revenue statutes) in 1939, the tax law was recodified in 1954. The IRC was known as the Internal Revenue Code of 1954 until 1986, when its name was changed to the Internal Revenue Code of 1986. Whenever changes to the IRC are approved, the old language is deleted and new language added. Thus, the IRC is organized as an integrated document, and a researcher need not read through the relevant parts of all previous tax bills to find the current version of the law. Nevertheless, a researcher must be sure that he or she is working with the law in effect when a particular transaction occurred.

ADDITIONAL COMMENT

The various tax services, discussed later in this chapter, provide IRC histories for researchers who need to work with prior years' tax law.

The IRC contains provisions dealing with income taxes, estate and gift taxes, employment taxes, alcohol and tobacco taxes, and other excise taxes. Organizationally, the IRC is divided into subtitles, chapters, subchapters, parts, subparts, sections, subsections, paragraphs, subparagraphs, and clauses. Subtitle A contains rules relating to income taxes, and Subtitle B deals with estate and gift taxes. A set of provisions concerned with one general area constitutes a subchapter. For example, the topics of corporate distributions and adjustments appear in Subchapter C, and topics relating to partners and partnerships appear in Subchapter K. Figure I:15-2 presents the organizational scheme of the IRC.

An IRC section contains the operative provisions to which tax advisors most often refer. For example, they speak of "Sec. 351 transactions," "Sec. 306 stock," and "Sec. 1231 gains and losses." Although a tax advisor need not know all the IRC sections, paragraphs, and parts, he or she must be familiar with the IRC's organizational scheme to read and interpret it correctly. The language of the IRC is replete with cross-references to titles, paragraphs, subparagraphs, and so on.

EXAMPLE I:15-5 ►

Section 7701, a definitional section, begins, "When used in this title . . ." and then provides a series of definitions. Because of this broad reference, a Sec. 7701 definition applies for all of Title 26; that is, it applies for purposes of the income tax, estate and gift tax, excise tax, and other taxes governed by Title 26. ◄

EXAMPLE I:15-6 ►

Section 302(b)(3) allows taxpayers whose stock holdings are completely terminated in a redemption (a corporation's purchase of its stock from one or more of its shareholders) to receive capital gain treatment on the excess of the redemption proceeds over the stock's basis instead of ordinary income treatment on the entire proceeds. Section 302(c)(2)(A) states, "In the case of a distribution described in subsection (b)(3), section 318(a)(1) shall not apply if. . . ." Further, Sec. 302(c)(2)(C)(i) indicates "Subparagraph (A) shall not apply to a distribution to any entity unless. . . ." Thus, in determining whether a taxpayer will receive capital gain treatment in a stock redemption, a tax advisor must be able to locate and interpret various cross-referenced IRC sections, subsections, paragraphs, subparagraphs, and clauses. ◄

---

[8] S. Rept. No. 105-174, 105th Cong., 1st Sess. (unpaginated) (1998).

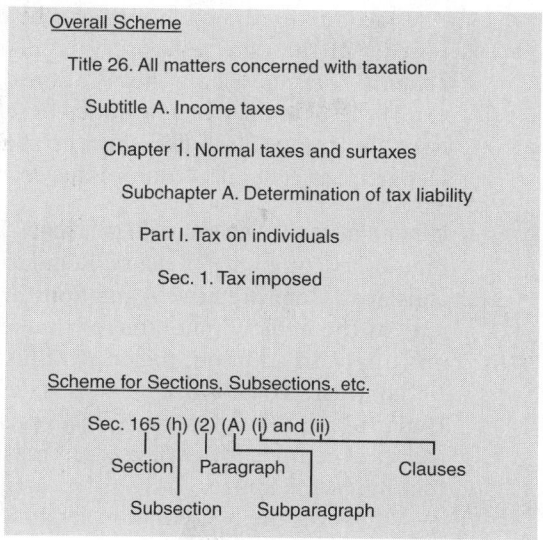

FIGURE I:15-2 ▶ ORGANIZATIONAL SCHEME OF THE INTERNAL REVENUE CODE

TREASURY REGULATIONS

The Treasury Department issues regulations that expound upon the IRC. Treasury Regulations often provide examples with computations that assist the reader in understanding how IRC provisions apply. Treasury Regulations are formulated on the basis of Treasury Decisions (T.D.s). The numbers of the Treasury Decisions that form the basis of a Treasury Regulation usually are found in the notes at the end of the regulation.

Because of frequent IRC changes, the Treasury Department does not always update the regulations in a timely manner. Consequently, when consulting a regulation, a tax advisor should check its introductory or end note to determine when the regulation was adopted. If the regulation was adopted before the most recent revision of the applicable IRC section, the regulation should be treated as authoritative to the extent consistent with the revision. Thus, for example, if a regulation issued before the passage of an IRC amendment specifies a dollar amount, and the amendment changed the dollar amount, the regulation should be regarded as authoritative in all respects except for the dollar amount.

Proposed, Temporary, and Final Regulations. A Treasury Regulation is first issued in proposed form to the public, which is given an opportunity to comment on it. Parties most likely to comment are individual tax practitioners and representatives of organizations such as the American Bar Association, the Tax Division of the AICPA, and the American Taxation Association. The comments may suggest that the proposed rules could affect taxpayers more adversely than Congress had anticipated. In drafting a final regulation, the Treasury Department generally considers the comments and may modify the rules accordingly. If the comments are favorable, the Treasury Department usually finalizes the regulation with minor revisions. If the comments are unfavorable, it usually finalizes the regulation with major revisions or allows the proposed regulation to expire.

Proposed regulations are just that—proposed. Consequently, they carry no more authoritative weight than do the arguments of the IRS in a court brief. Nevertheless, they represent the Treasury Department's official interpretation of the IRC. By contrast, **temporary regulations** are binding on the taxpayer. Effective as of the date of their publication, they often are issued immediately after passage of a major tax act to guide taxpayers and their advisors on procedural or computational matters. Regulations issued as temporary are concurrently issued as proposed. Because their issuance is not preceded by a public comment period, they are regarded as somewhat less authoritative than final regulations.

Once finalized, regulations can be effective the earliest of (1) the date they were proposed; (2) the date temporary regulations preceding them were first published in the *Federal Register*, a daily publication that contains federal government pronouncements; or (3) the date on which a notice describing the expected contents of the regulation was issued to the public.[9] For changes to the IRC enacted after July 29, 1996, the Treasury Department generally cannot issue regulations with retroactive effect.

Interpretative and Legislative Regulations. In addition to being officially classified as proposed, temporary, or final, Treasury Regulations are unofficially classified as interpretative or legislative. **Interpretative regulations** are issued under the general authority of Sec. 7805 and, as the name implies, merely make the IRC's statutory language easier to understand and apply. In addition, they often illustrate various computations. **Legislative regulations**, by contrast, arise where Congress delegates its rule-making authority to the Treasury Department. When Congress believes it lacks the expertise necessary to deal with a highly technical matter, it instructs the Treasury Department to set forth substantive tax rules relating to the matter.

Whenever the IRC contains language such as "The Secretary shall prescribe such regulations as he may deem necessary" or "under regulations prescribed by the Secretary," the regulations interpreting the IRC provision are legislative. The consolidated tax return regulations are an example of legislative regulations. In Sec. 1502, Congress delegated to the Treasury Department authority to issue regulations that determine the tax liability of a group of affiliated corporations filing a consolidated tax return. As a precondition to filing such a return, the corporations must consent to follow the consolidated return regulations.[10] Such consent generally precludes the corporations from later arguing in court that the regulatory provisions are invalid.

Authoritative Weight. Final Treasury Regulations are presumed to be valid and have almost the same authoritative weight as the IRC. Despite this presumption, taxpayers occasionally argue that a regulation is invalid and, consequently, should not be followed.

Prior to 2011, courts held interpretive and legislative regulations to different standards, giving more authority to legislative regulations that Congress specifically delegated to the Treasury Department to draft. The difference in authoritative weight largely disappeared, however, in 2011 with the Supreme Court decision in *Mayo Foundation*.[11] Going forward, both types of regulations will have the same authoritative weight and will be overturned only in very limited cases such as when, in the Court's opinion, the regulations exceed the scope of power delegated to the Treasury Department,[12] are contrary to the IRC,[13] or are unreasonable.[14]

In assessing the validity of long-standing Treasury Regulations, some courts apply the **legislative reenactment doctrine**. Under this doctrine, a regulation is deemed to receive congressional approval whenever the IRC provision under which the regulation was issued is reenacted without amendment.[15] Underlying this doctrine is the rationale that, if Congress believed that the regulation offered an erroneous interpretation of the IRC, it would have amended the IRC to conform to its belief. Congress's failure to amend the IRC signifies approval of the regulation.[16] This doctrine is predicated on Congress's constitutional authority to levy taxes. This authority implies that, if Congress is dissatisfied with the manner in which either the executive or the judiciary has interpreted the IRC, it can invalidate these interpretations through new legislation.

KEY POINT

The older a Treasury Regulation becomes, the less likely a court is to invalidate the regulation. The legislative reenactment doctrine holds that if a regulation did not reflect the intent of Congress, lawmakers would have changed the statute in subsequent legislation to obtain their desired objectives.

 STOP & THINK

Question: You are researching the manner in which a deduction is calculated. You consult Treasury Regulations for guidance because the IRC states that the calculation is to be done "in a manner prescribed by the Secretary." After reviewing these authorities, you

---

[9] Sec. 7805(b).
[10] Sec. 1501.
[11] *Mayo Foundation for Medical Education & Research, et al. v. U.S.,* 107 AFTR 2d 2011-341, 131 S.Ct. 704 (2011).
[12] *McDonald v. CIR,* 56 AFTR 2d 85-5318, 85-2 USTC ¶9494 (5th Cir., 1985).
[13] *Jeanese, Inc. v. U.S.,* 15 AFTR 2d 429, 65-1 USTC ¶9259 (9th Cir., 1965).
[14] *United States v. Vogel Fertilizer Co.,* 49 AFTR 2d 82-491, 82-1 USTC ¶9134 (USSC, 1982).

[15] *United States v. Homer O. Correll,* 20 AFTR 2d 5845, 68-1 USTC ¶9101 (USSC, 1967).
[16] One can rebut the presumption that Congress approved of the regulation by showing that Congress was unaware of the regulation when it reenacted the statute.

conclude that another way of doing the calculation arguably is correct under an intuitive approach. This approach would result in a lower tax liability for the client. Should you follow the Treasury Regulations, or should you use the intuitive approach and argue that the regulations are invalid?

Solution: Because of the language "in a manner prescribed by the Secretary," the Treasury Regulations dealing with the calculation are legislative. Whenever Congress calls for legislative regulations, it explicitly authorizes (directs) the Treasury Department to write the "rules." Thus, a challenge based on the existence of a reasonable alternative method is unlikely to succeed in court. Under the *Mayo Foundation* decision, you should reach the same conclusion even if dealing with an interpretive Treasury Regulation.

Citations. Citations to Treasury Regulations are relatively easy to understand. One or more numbers appear before a decimal place, and several numbers follow the decimal place. The numbers immediately following the decimal place indicate the IRC section being interpreted. The numbers preceding the decimal place indicate the general subject of the regulation. Numbers that often appear before the decimal place and their general subjects are as follows:

Number	General Subject Matter
1	Income tax
20	Estate tax
25	Gift tax
301	Administrative and procedural matters
601	Procedural rules

The number following the IRC section number indicates the numerical sequence of the regulation, such as the fifth regulation. No relationship exists between this number and the subsection of the IRC being interpreted. An example of a citation to a final regulation is as follows:

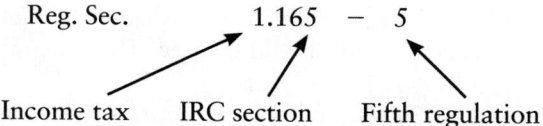

Reg. Sec.   1.165 — 5

Income tax   IRC section   Fifth regulation

Citations to proposed or temporary regulations follow the same format. They are referenced as Prop. Reg. Sec. or Temp. Reg. Sec. For temporary regulations the numbering system following the IRC section number always begins with the number of the regulation and an upper case T (e.g., -1T).

Section 165 addresses the broad topic of losses and is interpreted by several regulations. According to its caption, the topic of Reg. Sec. 1.165-5 is worthless securities, which also is addressed in subsection (g) of IRC Sec. 165. Parenthetical information following the text of the Treasury Regulation indicates that the regulation was last revised on March 11, 2008, by Treasury Decision (T.D.) 9386. Section 165(g) was last amended in 2000. A researcher must always check when the regulations were last amended and be aware that an IRC change may have occurred after the most recent regulation amendment, potentially making the regulation inapplicable.

When referencing a regulation, the researcher should fine-tune the citation to indicate the precise passage that supports his or her conclusion. An example of such a detailed citation is Reg. Sec. 1.165-5(j), Ex. 2(i), which refers to paragraph (i) of Example 2, found in paragraph (j) of the fifth regulation interpreting Sec. 165.

ADMINISTRATIVE PRONOUNCEMENTS

The IRS interprets the IRC through **administrative pronouncements,** the most important of which are discussed below. After consulting the IRC and Treasury Regulations, tax advisors are likely next to consult these pronouncements.

Revenue Rulings. In **revenue rulings**, the IRS indicates the tax consequences of specific transactions encountered in practice. For example, in a revenue ruling, the IRS might indicate whether the exchange of stock for stock derivatives in a corporate acquisition is tax-free.

The IRS issues more than 50 revenue rulings a year. These rulings do not rank as high in the hierarchy of authorities as do Treasury Regulations or federal court cases. They simply represent the IRS's view of the tax law. Taxpayers who do not follow a revenue ruling will not incur a substantial understatement penalty if they have substantial authority for different treatment.[17] Nonetheless, the IRS presumes that the tax treatment specified in a revenue ruling is correct. Consequently, if an examining agent discovers in an audit that a taxpayer did not adopt the position prescribed in a revenue ruling, the agent will contend that the taxpayer's tax liability should be adjusted to reflect that position.

Soon after it is issued, a revenue ruling appears in the weekly *Internal Revenue Bulletin* (cited as I.R.B.), published by the U.S. Government Printing Office (GPO). Revenue rulings later appear in the *Cumulative Bulletin* (cited as C.B.), a bound volume issued semiannually by the GPO. An example of a citation to a revenue ruling appearing in the *Cumulative Bulletin* is as follows:

Rev. Rul. 97-4, 1997-1 C.B. 5.

This is the fourth ruling issued in 1997, and it appears on page 5 of Volume 1 of the 1997 *Cumulative Bulletin*. Before the GPO publishes the pertinent volume of the *Cumulative Bulletin*, researchers should use citations to the *Internal Revenue Bulletin*. An example of such a citation follows:

Rev. Rul. 2013-8, 2013-15 I.R.B. 763.

For revenue rulings (and other IRS pronouncements) issued after 1999, the full four digits of the year of issuance are set forth in the title. For revenue rulings (and other IRS pronouncements) issued before 2000, only the last two digits of the year of issuance are set forth in the title. The above citation represents the eighth ruling for 2013. This ruling is located on page 763 of the *Internal Revenue Bulletin* for the fifteenth week of 2013. Once a revenue ruling is published in the *Cumulative Bulletin*, only the citation to the *Cumulative Bulletin* should be used. Thus, a citation to the I.R.B. is temporary.

Revenue Procedures. As the name suggests, **revenue procedures** are IRS pronouncements that usually deal with the procedural aspects of tax practice. For example, one revenue procedure deals with the manner in which tip income should be reported. Another revenue procedure describes the requirements for reproducing paper substitutes for informational returns such as Form 1099.

As with revenue rulings, revenue procedures are published first in the *Internal Revenue Bulletin*, then in the *Cumulative Bulletin*. An example of a citation to a revenue procedure appearing in the *Cumulative Bulletin* is as follows:

Rev. Proc. 97-19, 1997-1 C.B. 644.

This pronouncement is found in Volume 1 of the 1997 *Cumulative Bulletin* on page 644. It is the nineteenth revenue procedure issued in 1997.

In addition to revenue rulings and revenue procedures, the *Cumulative Bulletin* contains IRS notices, as well as the texts of proposed regulations, tax treaties, committee reports, and U.S. Supreme Court decisions.

Letter Rulings. **Letter rulings** are initiated by taxpayers who ask the IRS to explain the tax consequences of a particular transaction.[18] The IRS provides its explanation in the form of a letter ruling, a response personal to the taxpayer requesting an answer. Only the

---

[17] Chapter C:15 discusses the authoritative support taxpayers and tax advisors should have for positions they adopt on a tax return.

[18] Chapter C:15 further discusses letter rulings.

taxpayer to whom the ruling is addressed may rely on it as authority. Nevertheless, letter rulings are relevant for other taxpayers and tax advisors because they offer insight into the IRS's position on the tax treatment of particular transactions.

Originally the public did not have access to letter rulings issued to other taxpayers. As a result of Sec. 6110, enacted in 1976, letter rulings (with confidential information deleted) are accessible to the general public and have been reproduced by major tax services. An example of a citation to a letter ruling appears below:

Ltr. Rul. 200130006 (July 30, 2001).

The first four digits (two if issued before 2000) indicate the year in which the ruling was made public, in this case, 2001.[19] The next two digits denote the week in which the ruling was made public, here the thirtieth. The last three numbers indicate the numerical sequence of the ruling for the week, here the sixth. The date in parentheses denotes the date of the ruling.

Other Interpretations

Technical Advice Memoranda. When the IRS audits a taxpayer's return, the IRS agent might ask the IRS national office for advice on a complicated, technical matter. The national office will provide its advice in a **technical advice memorandum,** released to the public in the form of a letter ruling.[20] Researchers can identify which letter rulings are technical advice memoranda by introductory language such as, "In response to a request for technical advice. . . ." An example of a citation to a technical advice memorandum is as follows:

T.A.M. 9801001 (January 2, 1998).

This citation refers to the first technical advice memorandum issued in the first week of 1998. The memorandum is dated January 2, 1998.

Information Releases. If the IRS wants to disseminate information to the general public, it will issue an **information release.** Information releases are written in lay terms and are dispatched to thousands of newspapers throughout the country. The IRS, for example, may issue an information release to announce the standard mileage rate for business travel. An example of a citation to an information release is as follows:

I.R. 86-70 (June 12, 1986).

This citation is to the seventieth information release issued in 1986. The release is dated June 12, 1986.

Announcements and Notices. The IRS also disseminates information to tax practitioners in the form of **announcements** and **notices.** These pronouncements generally are more technical than information releases and frequently address current tax developments. After passage of a major tax act, and before the Treasury Department has had an opportunity to issue proposed or temporary regulations, the IRS may issue an announcement or notice to clarify the legislation. The IRS is bound to follow the announcement or notice just as it is bound to follow a revenue procedure or revenue ruling. Examples of citations to announcements and notices are as follows:

Announcement 2007-3, 2007-1 C.B. 376.
Notice 2007-9, 2007-1 C.B. 401.

The first citation is to the third announcement issued in 2007. It can be found on page 376 of the first *Cumulative Bulletin* for 2007. The second citation is to the ninth

---

[19] Sometimes a letter ruling is cited as PLR (private letter ruling) instead of Ltr. Rul.

[20] Technical advice memoranda are discussed further in Chapter C:15.

notice issued in 2007. It can be found on page 401 of the first *Cumulative Bulletin* for 2007. Notices and announcements appear in both the *Internal Revenue Bulletin* and the *Cumulative Bulletin*.

JUDICIAL DECISIONS

Judicial decisions are an important source of tax law. Judges are reputed to be unbiased individuals who decide questions of fact (the existence of a fact or the occurrence of an event) or questions of law (the applicability of a legal principle or the proper interpretation of a legal term or provision). Judges do not always agree on the tax consequences of a particular transaction or event. Therefore, tax advisors often must derive conclusions against a background of conflicting judicial authorities. For example, a U.S. district court might disagree with the Tax Court on the deductibility of an expense. Likewise, one circuit court might disagree with another circuit court on the same issue.

Overview of the Court System. A taxpayer may begin tax litigation in any of three courts: the U.S. Tax Court, the U.S. Court of Federal Claims (formerly the U.S. Claims Court), or U.S. district courts. Court precedents are important in deciding where to begin such litigation (see page I:15-21 for a discussion of precedent). Also important is when the taxpayer must pay the deficiency the IRS contends is due. A taxpayer who wants to litigate either in a U.S. district court or in the U.S. Court of Federal Claims must first pay the deficiency. The taxpayer then files a claim for refund, which the IRS is likely to deny. Following this denial, the taxpayer must petition the court for a refund. If the court grants the taxpayer's petition, he or she receives a refund of the taxes in question plus accrued interest. If the taxpayer begins litigation in the Tax Court, on the other hand, he or she need not pay the deficiency unless and until the court decides the case against him or her. In that event, the taxpayer also must pay interest and penalties.[21] A taxpayer who believes that a jury would be sympathetic to his or her case should litigate in a U.S. district court, the only forum where a jury trial is possible.

If a party loses at the trial court level, it can appeal the decision to a higher court. Appeals of Tax Court and U.S. district court decisions are made to the court of appeals for the taxpayer's circuit. The appeals court system is comprised of 11 geographical circuits designated by numbers, the District of Columbia Circuit, and the Federal Circuit.[22] Table I:15-1 shows the states that lie in the various circuits. California, for example, lies in the Ninth Circuit. When referring to these appellate courts, instead of saying, for example, "the Court of Appeals for the Ninth Circuit," one generally says "the Ninth Circuit." All decisions of the U.S. Court of Federal Claims are appealable to one court—the Court of Appeals for the Federal Circuit—irrespective of where the taxpayer resides or does business.[23] The only cases the Federal Circuit hears are those that originate in the U.S. Court of Federal Claims.

The party losing at the appellate level can petition the U.S. Supreme Court to review the case under a **writ of certiorari.** If the Supreme Court agrees to hear the case, it grants certiorari.[24] If it refuses to hear the case, it denies certiorari. In recent years, the Court has granted certiorari in only about six to ten tax cases per year. Figure I:15-3 and Table I:15-2 provide an overview and summary of the court system with respect to tax matters.

The U.S. Tax Court. The U.S. Tax Court was created in 1942 as a successor to the Board of Tax Appeals. It is a court of national jurisdiction that hears only tax-related cases. All taxpayers, regardless of their state of residence or place of business, may litigate in the Tax Court. It has 19 judges, including one chief judge.[25] The President, with the consent of the Senate, appoints the judges for a 15-year term and may reappoint them for an additional

SELF-STUDY QUESTION

What are some of the factors that a taxpayer should consider when deciding in which court to file a tax-related claim?

ANSWER

(1) Each court's published precedent pertaining to the issue, (2) desirability of a jury trial, (3) tax expertise of each court, and (4) when the deficiency must be paid.

ADDITIONAL COMMENT

Because the Tax Court deals only with tax cases, it presumably has a higher level of tax expertise than do other courts. Tax Court judges are appointed by the President, in part, due to their considerable tax experience. The Tax Court typically maintains a large backlog of tax cases, sometimes numbering in the tens of thousands.

---

[21] Revenue Procedure 2005-18, 2005-1 C.B. 798, provides procedures for taxpayers to make remittances or apply overpayments to stop the accrual of interest on deficiencies.
[22] The Federal Circuit has nationwide jurisdiction to hear appeals in specialized cases, such as those involving patent laws.
[23] The Court of Claims was reconstituted as the United States Court of Claims in 1982. In 1992, this court was renamed the U.S. Court of Federal Claims.

[24] The granting of certiorari signifies that the Supreme Court is granting an appellate review. The denial of certiorari does not necessarily mean that the Supreme Court endorses the lower court's decision. It simply means the court has decided not to hear the case.
[25] The Tax Court also periodically appoints, depending on budgetary constraints, a number of trial judges and senior judges who hear cases and render decisions with the same authority as the regular Tax Court judges.

▼ TABLE I:15-1

Federal Judicial Circuits

Circuit	States Included in Circuit
First	Maine, Massachusetts, New Hampshire, Rhode Island, Puerto Rico
Second	Connecticut, New York, Vermont
Third	Delaware, New Jersey, Pennsylvania, Virgin Islands
Fourth	Maryland, North Carolina, South Carolina, Virginia, West Virginia
Fifth	Louisiana, Mississippi, Texas
Sixth	Kentucky, Michigan, Ohio, Tennessee
Seventh	Illinois, Indiana, Wisconsin
Eighth	Arkansas, Iowa, Minnesota, Missouri, Nebraska, North Dakota, South Dakota
Ninth	Alaska, Arizona, California, Hawaii, Idaho, Montana, Nevada, Oregon, Washington, Guam, Northern Marina Islands
Tenth	Colorado, Kansas, New Mexico, Oklahoma, Utah, Wyoming
Eleventh	Alabama, Florida, Georgia
D.C.	District of Columbia
Federal	All jurisdictions (for taxpayers appealing from the U.S. Court of Federal Claims)

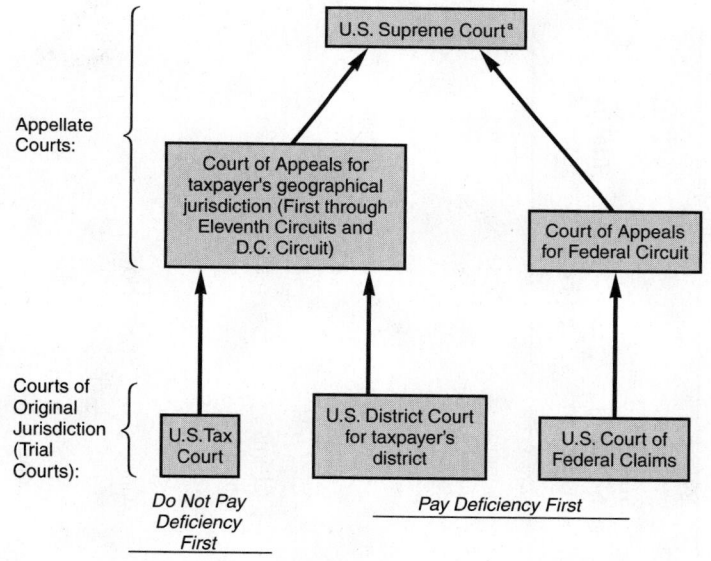

ᵃ Cases are heard only if the Supreme Court grants certiorari.

FIGURE I:15-3 ▶ OVERVIEW OF COURT SYSTEM—TAX MATTERS

term. The judges, specialists in tax-related matters, periodically travel to roughly 100 cities throughout the country to hear cases. In most instances, only one judge hears a case.

The Tax Court issues both regular and memorandum (memo) decisions. Generally, the first time the Tax Court decides a legal issue, its decision appears as a **regular decision.** **Memo decisions,** on the other hand, usually deal with factual variations of previously decided cases. Nevertheless, regular and memo decisions carry the same authoritative weight.

At times, the chief judge determines that a particular case concerns an important issue that the entire Tax Court should consider. In such a situation, the words *reviewed by the court* appear at the end of the majority opinion. Any concurring or dissenting opinions follow the majority opinion. A judge who issues a concurring opinion agrees with the basic outcome of the majority's decision but not with its rationale. A judge who issues a dissenting opinion believes the majority reached an erroneous conclusion.

▶ TABLE I:15-2
Summary of Court System—Tax Matters

Court(s) (Number of)	Number of Judges on Each	Personal Jurisdiction	Subject Matter Jurisdiction	Determines Questions of Fact	Trial by Jury	Precedents Followed	Where Opinions Published
U.S. district courts (over 95)	1–28*	Local	General	Yes	Yes	Same court Court for circuit where situated U.S. Supreme Court	Federal Supplement American Federal Tax Reports United States Tax Cases
U.S. Tax Court (1)	19	National	Tax	Yes	No	Same court Court for taxpayer's circuit U.S. Supreme Court	Tax Court of the U.S. Reports CCH Tax Court Memorandum Decisions RIA Tax Court Memorandum Decisions
U.S. Court of Federal Claims (1)	16	National	Claims against U.S. Government	Yes	No	Same court Federal Circuit Court U.S. Supreme Court	Federal Reporter (pre-1982) U.S. Court of Federal Claims American Federal Tax Reports United States Tax Cases
U.S. Courts of Appeals (13)	About 20	Regional	General	No	No	Same court U.S. Supreme Court	Federal Reporter American Federal Tax Reports United States Tax Cases
U.S. Supreme Court (1)	9	National	General	No	No	Same court	U.S. Supreme Court Reports Supreme Court Reporter United States Reports, Lawyers' Edition American Federal Tax Reports United States Tax Cases

*Although the number of judges assigned to each court varies, only one judge hears a case.

Another phrase sometimes appearing at the end of a Tax Court opinion is *Entered under Rule 155.* This phrase signifies that the court has reached a decision concerning the tax treatment of an item but has left computation of the deficiency to the two litigating parties.

SELF-STUDY QUESTION

What are some of the considerations for litigating under the small cases procedure of the Tax Court?

ANSWER

The small cases procedure gives the taxpayer the advantage of having his or her "day in court" without the expense of an attorney. But if the taxpayer loses, the decision cannot be appealed.

Small Cases Procedure. Taxpayers have the option of having their cases heard under the **small cases procedure** of the Tax Court if the amount in controversy on an annual basis does not exceed $50,000.[26] This procedure is less formal than the regular Tax Court procedure, and taxpayers can represent themselves without an attorney.[27] The cases are heard by special commissioners instead of by one of the 19 Tax Court judges. A disadvantage of the small cases procedure for the losing party is that the decision cannot be appealed. The opinions of the commissioners generally are not published and have no precedential value.

Acquiescence Policy. The IRS has adopted a policy of announcing whether, in future cases involving similar facts and similar issues, it will follow federal court decisions that are adverse to it. This policy is known as the IRS **acquiescence policy.** If the IRS wants taxpayers to know that it will follow an adverse decision in future cases involving similar facts and issues, it will announce its "acquiescence" in the decision. Conversely, if it wants taxpayers to know that it will not follow the decision in such future cases, it will announce its "nonacquiescence." The IRS does not announce its acquiescence or nonacquiescence in every decision it loses.

ADDITIONAL COMMENT

The only cases with respect to which the IRS will acquiesce or nonacquiesce are decisions that the government loses. Because the majority of cases, particularly Tax Court cases, are won by the government, the IRS will potentially acquiesce in only a small number of cases.

The IRS publishes its acquiescences and nonacquiescences as "Actions on Decision" first in the *Internal Revenue Bulletin,* then in the *Cumulative Bulletin.* Before 1991, the IRS acquiesced or nonacquiesced in regular Tax Court decisions only. In 1991, it broadened the scope of its policy to include adverse U.S. Claims Court, U.S. district court, and U.S. circuit court decisions.

In cases involving multiple issues, the IRS may acquiesce in some issues but not others. In decisions supported by extensive reasoning, it may acquiesce in the result but not the rationale (*acq. in result*). Furthermore, it may retroactively revoke an acquiescence or nonacquiescence. The footnotes to the relevant announcement in the *Internal Revenue Bulletin* and *Cumulative Bulletin* indicate the nature and extent of IRS acquiescences and nonacquiescences.

These acquiescences and nonacquiescences have important implications for taxpayers. If a taxpayer bases his or her position on a decision in which the IRS has nonacquiesced, he or she can expect an IRS challenge in the event of an audit. In such circumstances, the taxpayer's only recourse may be litigation. On the other hand, if the taxpayer bases his or her position on a decision in which the IRS has acquiesced, he or she can expect little or no challenge. In either case, the examining agent will be bound by the IRS position.

ADDITIONAL COMMENT

If a particular case is important, the chief judge will instruct the other judges to review the case. If a case is reviewed by the entire court, the phrase *reviewed by the court* is inserted immediately after the text of the majority opinion. A reviewed decision provides an opportunity for Tax Court judges to express their dissenting opinions.

Published Opinions and Citations. Regular Tax Court decisions are published by the U.S. Government Printing Office in a bound volume known as the *Tax Court of the United States Reports.* Soon after a decision is made public, Research Institute of America (RIA) and Commerce Clearing House (CCH) each publish the decision in its respective reporter of Tax Court decisions. An official citation to a Tax Court decision is as follows:[28]

MedChem Products, Inc., 116 T.C. 308 (2001).

The citation indicates that this case appears on page 308 in Volume 116 of *Tax Court of the United States Reports* and that the case was decided in 2001.

---

[26] Sec. 7463. The $50,000 amount includes penalties and additional taxes but excludes interest.

[27] Taxpayers also can represent themselves in regular Tax Court proceedings even though they are not attorneys. Where taxpayers represent themselves, the words *pro se* appear in the opinion after the taxpayer's name. The Tax Court is the only federal court before which non-attorneys, including CPAs, may practice.

[28] In a citation to a case decided by the Tax Court, only the name of the plaintiff (taxpayer) is listed. The defendant is understood to be the Commissioner of Internal Revenue whose name usually is not shown in the citation. In cases decided by other courts, the name of the plaintiff is listed first and the name of the defendant second. For non-Tax Court cases, the Commissioner of Internal Revenue is referred to as *CIR* in our footnotes and text.

From 1924 to 1942, regular decisions of the Board of Tax Appeals (predecessor of the Tax Court) were published by the U.S. Government Printing Office in the *United States Board of Tax Appeals Reports*. An example of a citation to a Board of Tax Appeals case is as follows:

J.W. Wells Lumber Co. Trust A., 44 B.T.A. 551 (1941).

This case is found in Volume 44 of the *United States Board of Tax Appeals Reports* on page 551. It is a 1941 decision.

ADDITIONAL COMMENT

Once the IRS has acquiesced in a federal court decision, other taxpayers generally will not need to litigate the same issue. However, the IRS can change its mind and revoke a previous acquiescence or nonacquiescence. References to acquiescences or nonacquiescences in federal court decisions can be found in the citators.

If the IRS has acquiesced or nonacquiesced in a federal court decision, the IRS's action should be denoted in the citation. At times, the IRS will not announce its acquiescence or nonacquiescence until several years after the date of the decision. An example of a citation to a decision in which the IRS has acquiesced is as follows:

Security State Bank, 111 T.C. 210 (1998), *acq.* 2001-1 C.B. xix.

The case appears on page 210 of Volume 111 of the *Tax Court of the United States Reports* and the acquiescence is reported on page xix of Volume 1 of the 2001 *Cumulative Bulletin*. In 2001, the IRS acquiesced in this 1998 decision. A citation to a decision in which the IRS has nonacquiesced is as follows:

Estate of Algerine Allen Smith, 108 T.C. 412 (1997), *nonacq.* 2000-1 C.B. xvi.

KEY POINT

To access all Tax Court cases, a tax advisor must refer to two different publications. The regular opinions appear in the *Tax Court of the United States Reports,* published by the U.S. Government Printing Office, and the memo decisions are published by both RIA (formerly PH) and CCH in their own court reporters.

The case appears on page 412 of Volume 108 of the *Tax Court of the United States Reports*. The nonacquiescence is reported on page xvi of Volume 1 of the 2000 *Cumulative Bulletin*. In 2000, the IRS nonacquiesced in this 1997 decision.

Tax Court memo decisions are not published by the U.S. Government Printing Office. They are, however, published by RIA in *RIA T.C. Memorandum Decisions* and by CCH in *CCH Tax Court Memorandum Decisions*. In addition, shortly after its issuance, an opinion is made available electronically and in loose-leaf form by RIA and CCH in their respective tax services. The following citation is to a Tax Court memo decision:

Edith G. McKinney, 1981 PH T.C. Memo ¶81,181 (T.C. Memo 1981-181), 41 TCM 1272.

ADDITIONAL COMMENT

In its Internet-based tax service (see Page I:15-26), RIA uses a different format for its Tax Court Memorandum Decisions, which in this textbook appear in parentheses after the "official" RIA citation.

McKinney is found at Paragraph 81,181 of Prentice Hall's (now RIA's)[29] 1981 *PH T.C. Memorandum Decisions* reporter, and in Volume 41, page 1272, of CCH's *Tax Court Memorandum Decisions*. The 181 in the PH citation indicates that the case is the Tax Court's 181st memo decision of the year. A more recent citation is formatted in the same way but refers to RIA memo decisions.

Paul F. Belloff, 1992 RIA T.C. Memo ¶92,346 (T.C. Memo 1992-346), 63 TCM 3150.

U.S. District Courts. Each state has at least one U.S. district court, and more populous states have more than one. Each district court is independent of the others and is thus free to issue its own decisions, subject to the precedential constraints discussed later in this chapter. Different types of cases—not just tax-related—are adjudicated in this forum. A district court is the only forum in which the taxpayer may have a jury decide questions of fact. Depending on the circumstances, a jury trial might be advantageous for the taxpayer.[30]

District court decisions are officially reported in the *Federal Supplement* (cited as F. Supp.) published by West®. Some decisions are not officially reported and are referred

---

[29] Several ownership changes have occurred for publishers of tax service materials. Thomson Reuters added the former Prentice Hall tax materials to the product line of its RIA tax publishing division. RIA and West® are members of Thomson Reuters, Tax and Accounting Division, and CCH is a member of the Wolters Kluwer Tax, Accounting and Legal Division.

[30] Taxpayers might prefer to have a jury trial if they believe a jury will be sympathetic to their case.

to as **unreported decisions.** Decisions by U.S. district courts on the topic of taxation also are published by RIA and CCH in secondary reporters that contain only tax-related opinions. RIA's reporter is *American Federal Tax Reports* (cited as AFTR).[31] CCH's reporter is *U.S. Tax Cases* (cited as USTC). A case not offically reported nevertheless might be published in the AFTR and USTC. An example of a complete citation to a U.S. district court decision is as follows:

Alfred Abdo, Jr. v. IRS, 234 F. Supp. 2d 533, 90 AFTR 2d 2002-7484, 2003-1 USTC ¶50,107 (DC North Carolina, 2002).

ADDITIONAL COMMENT

A citation, at a minimum, should contain the following information: (1) the name of the case, (2) the reporter that publishes the case along with both a volume and page (or paragraph) number, (3) the year the case was decided, and (4) the court that decided the case.

In the example above, the **primary citation** is to the *Federal Supplement.* The case appears on page 533 of Volume 234 of the second series of this reporter. **Secondary citations** are to *American Federal Tax Reports* and *U.S. Tax Cases.* The same case is found in Volume 90 of the second series of the AFTR, page 2002-7484 (meaning page 7484 in the volume containing 2002 cases) and in Volume 1 of the 2003 USTC at Paragraph 50,107. The parenthetical information indicates that the case was decided in 2002 by the U.S. District Court for North Carolina. Because some judicial decisions have greater precedential weight than others (e.g., a Supreme Court decision versus a district court decision), information relating to the identity of the adjudicating court is useful in evaluating the authoritative value of the decision.

ADDITIONAL COMMENT

The U.S. Court of Federal Claims adjudicates claims (including suits to recover federal income taxes) against the U.S. Government. This court usually hears cases in Washington, D.C., but will hold sessions in other locations as the court deems necessary.

U.S. Court of Federal Claims. The U.S. Court of Federal Claims, another court of first instance that addresses tax matters, has nationwide jurisdiction. Originally, this court was called the U.S. Court of Claims (cited as Ct. Cl.), and its decisions were appealable to the U.S. Supreme Court only. In a reorganization, effective October 1, 1982, the reconstituted court was named the U.S. Claims Court (cited as Cl. Ct.), and its decisions became appealable to the Circuit Court of Appeals for the Federal Circuit. In October 1992, the court's name was again changed to the U.S. Court of Federal Claims (cited as Fed. Cl.).

Beginning in 1982, U.S. Claims Court decisions were reported officially in the *Claims Court Reporter,* published by West® from 1982 to 1992.[32] An example of a citation to a U.S. Claims Court decision appears below:

Benjamin Raphan v. U.S., 3 Cl. Ct. 457, 52 AFTR 2d 83-5987, 83-2 USTC ¶9613 (1983).

The *Raphan* case appears on page 457 of Volume 3 of the *Claims Court Reporter.* Secondary citations are to Volume 52, page 83-5987 of the AFTR, Second Series, and to Volume 2 of the 1983 USTC at Paragraph 9613.

Effective with the 1992 reorganization, decisions of the U.S. Court of Federal Claims are now reported in the *Federal Claims Reporter.* An example of a citation to an opinion published in this reporter is presented below:

Jeffrey G. Sharp v. U.S., 27 Fed. Cl. 52, 70 AFTR 2d 92-6040, 92-2 USTC ¶50,561 (1992).

The *Sharp* case appears on page 52 of Volume 27 of the *Federal Claims Reporter,* on page 6040 of the 70th volume of the AFTR, Second Series, and at Paragraph 50,561 of Volume 2 of the 1992 USTC reporter. Note that, even though the name of the reporter published by West® has changed, the volume numbers continue in sequence as if no name change had occurred.

---

[31] The *American Federal Tax Reports* (AFTR) is published in two series. The first series, which includes opinions issued up to 1957, is cited as AFTR. The second series, which includes opinions issued after 1957, is cited as AFTR 2d. The *Alfred Abdo, Jr.* decision cited as an illustration of a U.S. district court decision appears in the second *American Federal Tax Reports* series.

[32] Before the creation in 1982 of the U.S. Claims Court (and the *Claims*

Court Reporter), the opinions of the U.S. Court of Claims were reported in either the *Federal Supplement* (F. Supp.) or the *Federal Reporter, Second Series* (F.2d). The *Federal Supplement* is the primary source of U.S. Court of Claims opinions from 1932 through January 19, 1960. Opinions issued from January 20, 1960, to October 1982 are reported in the *Federal Reporter, Second Series.*

Circuit Courts of Appeals. Lower court decisions are appealable by the losing party to the court of appeals for the circuit in which the litigation originated. Generally, if the case began in the Tax Court or a U.S. district court, the case is appealable to the circuit for the individual's residence as of the appeal date. For a corporation, the case is appealable to the circuit for the corporation's principal place of business. The Federal Circuit hears all appeals of cases originating in the U.S. Court of Federal Claims.

As mentioned earlier, there are 11 geographical circuits designated by numbers, the District of Columbia Circuit, and the Federal Circuit. In October 1981, the Eleventh Circuit was created by moving Alabama, Georgia, and Florida from the Fifth to a new geographical circuit. The Eleventh Circuit has adopted the policy of following as precedent all decisions of the Fifth Circuit during the time the states currently constituting the Eleventh Circuit were part of the Fifth Circuit.[33]

EXAMPLE I:15-7 ▶ In the current year, the Eleventh Circuit first considered an issue in a case involving a Florida taxpayer. In 1980, the Fifth Circuit had ruled on the same issue in a case involving a Louisiana taxpayer. Because Florida was part of the Fifth Circuit in 1980, under the policy adopted by the Eleventh Circuit, it will follow the Fifth Circuit's earlier decision. Had the Fifth Circuit's decision been rendered in 1982—after the creation of the Eleventh Circuit—the Eleventh Circuit would not have been bound by the Fifth Circuit's decision. ◀

As the later discussion of precedent points out, different circuits may reach different conclusions concerning similar facts and issues.

Circuit court decisions—regardless of topic (e.g., civil rights, securities law, and taxation)—are now reported officially in the *Federal Reporter, Third Series* (cited as F.3d), published by West®. The third series was created in October 1993 after the volume number for the second series reached 999. The primary citation to a circuit court opinion should be to the *Federal Reporter*. Tax decisions of the circuit courts also appear in the *American Federal Tax Reports* and *U.S. Tax Cases*. Below is an example of a citation to a 1994 circuit court decision:

> *Leonard Greene v. U.S.,* 13 F.3d 577, 73 AFTR 2d 94-746, 94-1 USTC ¶50,022 (2nd Cir., 1994).

The *Greene* case appears on page 577 of Volume 13 of the *Federal Reporter, Third Series.* It also is published in Volume 73, page 94-746 of the AFTR, Second Series, and in Volume 1, Paragraph 50,022, of the 1994 USTC. The parenthetical information indicates that the Second Circuit decided the case in 1994. (A *Federal Reporter, Second Series* reference is found in footnote 33 of this chapter.)

ADDITIONAL COMMENT

A judge is not required to follow judicial precedent beyond his or her jurisdiction. Thus, the Tax Court, the U.S. district courts, and the U.S. Court of Federal Claims are not required to follow the others' decisions, nor is a circuit court required to follow the decision of a different circuit court.

U.S. Supreme Court. Whichever party loses at the appellate level can request that the U.S. Supreme Court hear the case. The Supreme Court, however, hears very few tax cases. Unless the circuits are divided on the tax treatment of an item, or the issue is deemed to be of great significance, the Supreme Court probably will not hear the case.[34] Supreme Court decisions are the law of the land and take precedence over all other court decisions, including the Supreme Court's earlier decisions. As a practical matter, a Supreme Court interpretation of the IRC is almost as authoritative as an act of Congress. If Congress does not agree with the Court's interpretation, it can amend the IRC to achieve a different result and has in fact done so on a number of occasions. If the Supreme Court declares a tax statute to be unconstitutional, the statute is invalid.

All Supreme Court decisions, regardless of subject, are published in the *United States Supreme Court Reports* (cited as U.S.) by the U.S. Government Printing Office, the *Supreme Court Reporter* (cited as S. Ct.) by West®, and the *United States Reports, Lawyers' Edition* (cited as L. Ed.) by LexisNexis®. In addition, the AFTR and USTC

---

[33] *Bonner v. City of Prichard,* 661 F.2d 1206 (11th Cir., 1981).
[34] *Vogel Fertilizer Co. v. U.S.,* 49 AFTR 2d 82-491, 82-1 USTC ¶9134 (USSC, 1982), is an example of a case the Supreme Court heard to settle a split in

judicial authority. The Fifth Circuit, the Tax Court, and the Court of Claims had reached one conclusion on an issue, while the Second, Fourth, and Eighth Circuits had reached another.

reporters published by RIA and CCH, respectively, contain Supreme Court decisions concerned with taxation. An example of a citation to a Supreme Court opinion appears below:

Boeing Company v. U.S., 537 U.S. 437, 91 AFTR 2d 2003-1088, 2003-1 USTC ¶50,273 (USSC, 2003).

According to the primary citation, this case appears in Volume 537, page 437, of the *United States Supreme Court Reports*. According to the secondary citation, it also appears in Volume 91, page 2003-1088, of the AFTR, Second Series, and in Volume 1, Paragraph 50,273, of the 2003 USTC.

Table I:15-3 provides a summary of how the IRC, court decisions, revenue rulings, revenue procedures, and other administrative pronouncements should be cited. Primary citations are to the reporters published by West® or the U.S. Government Printing Office, and secondary citations are to the AFTR and USTC.

Precedential Value of Various Decisions.

Tax Court. The Tax Court is a court of national jurisdiction. Consequently, it generally rules uniformly for all taxpayers, regardless of their residence or place of business. It follows U.S. Supreme Court decisions and its own earlier decisions. It is not bound by cases decided by the U.S. Court of Federal Claims or a U.S. district court, even if the district court has jurisdiction over the taxpayer.

In 1970, the Tax Court adopted what is known as the *Golsen* Rule.[35] Under this rule, the Tax Court departs from its general policy of adjudicating uniformly for all taxpayers and instead follows the decisions of the court of appeals to which the case in question is appealable. Stated differently, the *Golsen* Rule mandates that the Tax Court rule consistently with decisions of the court for the circuit where the taxpayer resides or does business.

EXAMPLE I:15-8 ▶ In the year in which an issue was first litigated, the Tax Court decided that an expenditure was deductible. The government appealed the decision to the Tenth Circuit Court of Appeals and won a reversal. This is the only appellate decision regarding the issue. If and when the Tax Court addresses this issue again, it will hold, with one exception, that the expenditure is deductible. The exception applies to taxpayers in the Tenth Circuit. Under the *Golsen* Rule, these taxpayers will be denied the deduction. ◀

U.S. District Court. Because each U.S. district court is independent of the other district courts, the decisions of each have precedential value only within its own jurisdiction (i.e., only with respect to subsequent cases brought before that court). District courts must follow decisions of the U.S. Supreme Court, the circuit court to which the case is appealable, and the district court's own earlier decisions regarding similar facts and issues.

EXAMPLE I:15-9 ▶ The U.S. District Court for Rhode Island, the Tax Court, and the Eleventh Circuit have decided cases involving similar facts and issues. Any U.S. district court within the Eleventh Circuit must follow that circuit's decision in future cases involving similar facts and issues. Likewise, the U.S. District Court for Rhode Island must decide such cases consistently with its previous decision. Tax Court decisions are not binding on the district courts. Thus, all district courts other than the one for Rhode Island and those within the Eleventh Circuit are free to decide such cases independently. ◀

U.S. Court of Federal Claims. In adjudicating a case, the U.S. Court of Federal Claims must rule consistently with U.S. Supreme Court decisions, decisions of the Circuit Court of Appeals for the Federal Circuit, and its own earlier decisions, including those rendered when the court had a different name. It need not follow decisions of other circuit courts, the Tax Court, or U.S. district courts.

---

[35] The *Golsen* Rule is based on the decision in *Jack E. Golsen*, 54 T.C. 742 (1970).

▼ TABLE I:15-3
Summary of Tax-related Primary Sources—Statutory and Administrative

Source Name	Publisher	Materials Provided	Citation Example
U.S. Code, Title 26	Government Printing Office	Internal Revenue Code	Sec. 441(b)
Code of Federal Regulations, Title 26	Government Printing Office	Treasury Regulations (final)	Reg. Sec. 1.461-1(c)
		Treasury Regulations (temporary)	Temp. Reg. Sec. 1.62-1T(e)
Internal Revenue Bulletin	Government Printing Office	Treasury Regulations (proposed)	Prop. Reg. Sec. 1.671-1(h)
		Treasury decisions	T.D. 8756 (January 13, 1998)
		Revenue rulings	Rev. Rul. 2009-33, 2009-40 I.R.B. 447
		Revenue procedures	Rev. Proc. 2009-52, 2009-49 I.R.B. 744
		Committee reports	S.Rept. No. 105-33, 105th Cong., 1st Sess., p. 308 (1997)
		Public laws	P.L. 105-34, Sec. 224(a), enacted August 6, 1997
		Announcements	Announcement 2007-3, 2007-4 I.R.B. 376
		Notices	Notice 2009-21, 2009-13 I.R.B. 724
Cumulative Bulletin	Government Printing Office	Treasury Regulations (proposed)	Prop. Reg. Sec. 1.671-1(h)
		Treasury decisions	T.D. 8756 (January 12, 1998)
		Revenue rulings	Rev. Rul. 84-111, 1984-2 C.B. 88
		Revenue procedures	Rev. Proc. 77-28, 1977-2 C.B. 537
		Committee reports	S.Rept. No. 105-33, 105th Cong., 1st Sess., p. 308 (1997)
		Public laws	P.L. 105-34, Sec. 224(a), enacted August 6, 1997
		Announcements	Announcement 2006-8, 2006-1 C.B. 344
		Notices	Notice 88-74, 1988-2 C.B. 385

Summary of Tax-related Primary and Secondary Sources—Judicial

Reporter Name	Publisher	Decisions Published	Citation Example
U.S. Supreme Court Reports	Government Printing Office	U.S. Supreme Court	*Boeing Company v. U.S.*, 537 U.S. 437 (2003)
Supreme Court Reports	Thomson Reuters/West	U.S. Supreme Court	*Boeing Company v. U.S.*, 123 S. Ct. 1099 (2003)
Federal Reporter (1st–3rd Series)	Thomson Reuters/West	U.S. Court of Appeal Pre-1982 Court of Claims	*Leonard Greene v. U.S.*, 13 F.3d 577 (2nd Cir., 1994)
Federal Supplement Series	Thomson Reuters/West	U.S. District Court	*Alfred Abdo, Jr. v. IRS*, 234 F. Supp. 2d 553 (DC North Carolina, 2002)
U.S. Court of Federal Claims	Thomson Reuters/West	Court of Federal Claims	*Jeffery G. Sharp v. U.S.*, 27 Fed. Cl. 52 (1992)
Tax Court of the U.S. Reports	Government Printing Office	U.S. Tax Court regular	*Security State Bank*, 111 T.C. 210 (1998), acq. 2001-1 C.B. xix
Tax Court Memorandum Decisions	Wolters Kluwer/CCH	U.S. Tax Court memo	*Paul F. Belloff*, 63 TCM 3150 (1992)
RIA Tax Court Memorandum Decisions	Thomson Reuters/RIA	U.S. Tax Court memo	*Paul F. Belloff*, 1992 RIA T.C. Memo ¶92,346 (T.C. Memo 1992-346)
American Federal Tax Reports	Thomson Reuters/RIA	Tax: all federal courts except Tax Court	*Boeing Company v. U.S.*, 91 AFTR 2d 2003-1 (USSC, 2003)
U.S. Tax Cases	Wolters Kluwer/CCH	Tax: all federal courts except Tax Court	*Ruddick Corp. v. U.S.*, 81-1 USTC ¶9343 (Ct. Cls., 1981)

EXAMPLE I:15-10 ▷ Assume the same facts as in Example I:15-9. In a later year, a case involving similar facts and issues is heard by the U.S. Court of Federal Claims. This court is not bound by precedents set by any of the other courts. Thus, it may reach a conclusion independently of the other courts. ◄

Circuit Courts of Appeals. A circuit court is bound by U.S. Supreme Court decisions and its own earlier decisions. If neither the Supreme Court nor the circuit in question has already decided an issue, the circuit court has no precedent that it must follow, regardless of whether other circuits have ruled on the issue. In such circumstances, the circuit court is said to be writing on a clean slate. In rendering a decision, the judges of that court may adopt another circuit's view, which they are likely to regard as relevant.

EXAMPLE I:15-11 ▷ Assume the same facts as in Example I:15-9. Any circuit other than the Eleventh would be writing on a clean slate if it adjudicated a case involving similar facts and issues. After reviewing the Eleventh Circuit's decision, another circuit might find it relevant and rule in the same way. ◄

In such a case of "first impression," when the court has had no precedent on which to base a decision, a tax practitioner might look at past opinions of the court to see which other judicial authority the court has found to be "persuasive."

Forum Shopping. Not surprisingly, courts often disagree on the tax treatment of the same item. This disagreement gives rise to differing precedents within the various jurisdictions (what is called a "split in judicial authority"). Because taxpayers have the flexibility of choosing where to file a lawsuit, these circumstances afford them the opportunity to **forum shop.** Forum shopping involves choosing where among the courts to file a lawsuit based on differing precedents.

An example of a split in judicial authority concerned the issue of when it became too late for the IRS to question the tax treatment of items that "flowed through" an S corporation's return to a shareholder's return. The key question was this: if the time for assessing a deficiency (limitations period) with respect to the corporation's, but not the shareholder's, return had expired, was the IRS precluded from collecting additional taxes from the shareholder? In *Kelley,*[36] the Ninth Circuit Court of Appeals ruled that the IRS would be barred from collecting additional taxes from the shareholder if the limitations period for the *S corporation's* return had expired. In *Bufferd,*[37] *Fehlhaber,*[38] and *Green,*[39] three other circuit courts ruled that the IRS would be barred from collecting additional taxes from the shareholder if the limitations period for the *shareholder's* return had expired. The Supreme Court affirmed the *Bufferd* decision,[40] establishing that the statute of limitations for the shareholder's return governed. This action brought about certainty and uniformity within the judicial system.

Dictum. At times, a court may comment on an issue or a set of facts not central to the case under review. A court's remark not essential to the determination of a disputed issue, and therefore not binding authority, is called *dictum.* An example of dictum is found in *Central Illinois Public Service Co.*[41] In this case, the U.S. Supreme Court addressed whether lunch reimbursements received by employees constitute wages subject to withholding. Justice Blackman remarked in passing that earnings in the form of interest, rents, and dividends are not wages. This remark is dictum because it is not essential to the determination of whether lunch reimbursements are wages subject to withholding. Although not authoritative, dictum may be cited by taxpayers to bolster an argument in favor of a particular tax result.

---

[36] *Daniel M. Kelley v. CIR,* 64 AFTR 2d 89-5025, 89-1 USTC ¶9360 (9th Cir., 1989).
[37] *Sheldon B. Bufferd v. CIR,* 69 AFTR 2d 92-465, 92-1 USTC ¶50,031 (2nd Cir., 1992).
[38] *Robert Fehlhaber v. CIR,* 69 AFTR 2d 92-850, 92-1 USTC ¶50,131 (11th Cir., 1992).

[39] *Charles T. Green v. CIR,* 70 AFTR 2d 92-5077, 92-2 USTC ¶50,340 (5th Cir., 1992).
[40] *Sheldon B. Bufferd v. CIR,* 71 AFTR 2d 93-573, 93-1 USTC ¶50,038 (USSC, 1993).
[41] *Central Illinois Public Service Co. v. CIR,* 41 AFTR 2d 78-718, 78-1 USTC ¶9254 (USSC, 1978).

? STOP & THINK

Question: You have been researching whether an amount received by your new client can be excluded from her gross income. The IRS is auditing the client's prior year tax return, which another firm prepared. In a similar case decided a few years ago, the Tax Court allowed an exclusion, but the IRS nonacquiesced in the decision. The case involved a taxpayer in the Fourth Circuit. Your client is a resident of Maine, which is in the First Circuit. Twelve years ago, in a case involving another taxpayer, the federal court for the client's district ruled that this type of receipt is not excludable. No other precedent exists. To sustain an exclusion, must your client litigate? Explain. If your client litigates, in which court of first instance should she begin her litigation?

Solution: Because of its nonacquiescence, the IRS is likely to challenge your client's tax treatment. Thus, she may be compelled to litigate. She would not want to litigate in her U.S. district court because it would be bound by its earlier decision, which is unfavorable to taxpayers generally. A good place to begin would be the Tax Court because it is bound by appellate court, but not district court, decisions and because of its earlier pro-taxpayer position. No one can predict how the U.S. Court of Federal Claims would rule because no precedent that it must follow exists.

ADDITIONAL COMMENT
A tax treaty carries the same authoritative weight as a federal statute (IRC). A tax advisor should be aware of provisions in tax treaties that will affect a taxpayer's worldwide tax liability.

TAX TREATIES

The United States has concluded **tax treaties** with numerous foreign countries. These treaties address the alleviation of double taxation and other matters. A tax advisor exploring the U.S. tax consequences of a U.S. corporation's operations in another country should determine whether a treaty between that country and the United States exists. If one does, the tax advisor should ascertain the applicable provisions of the treaty. (See Chapter C:16 for a more extensive discussion of treaties.)

KEY POINT
Tax articles can be used to help *find* answers to tax questions. Where possible, the underlying statutory, administrative, or judicial sources referenced in the tax article should be cited as authority and not the author of the article. The courts and the IRS will place little, if any, reliance on mere editorial opinion.

TAX PERIODICALS

Tax periodicals assist the researcher in tracing the development of, and analyzing tax law. These periodicals are especially useful when they discuss the legislative history of a recently enacted IRC statute that has little or no administrative or judicial authority on point.

Tax experts write articles on landmark court decisions, proposed regulations, new tax legislation, and other matters. Frequently, those who write articles of a highly technical nature are attorneys, accountants, or professors. Among the periodicals that provide in-depth coverage of tax-related matters are the following:

The Journal of Taxation
The Tax Adviser
Practical Tax Strategies
Taxes—The Tax Magazine
Tax Law Review
Tax Notes
Corporate Taxation
Business Entities
Real Estate Taxation
Estate Planning

The first six journals are generalized; that is, they deal with a variety of topics. As their titles suggest, the next four are specialized; they deal with specific subjects. All these publications (other than *Tax Notes,* which is published weekly) are published either monthly or quarterly. Daily newsletters, such as the *Daily Tax Report,* published by Bloomberg BNA in print and electronic formats, are used by tax professionals when they need updates more timely than can be provided by monthly or quarterly publications.

Tax periodicals and tax services are secondary authorities. The IRC, Treasury Regulations, IRS pronouncements, and court opinions are primary authorities. In presenting research results, the tax advisor should always cite primary authorities.

TAX SERVICES

Various publishers provide multivolume commentaries on the tax law in what are familiarly referred to as **tax services**. Researchers often consult tax services at the beginning of the research process because a tax service helps identify the tax authorities pertaining to a particular tax issue. The actual tax authorities (e.g., IRC, Treasury Regulations, IRS pronouncements, and court cases), and not the tax services, are generally cited as support for a particular tax position. The services are available in print form via the publishers and electronic form via the Internet. (See further discussion at "The Internet as a Research Tool" later in this chapter). Although each major tax service is an outstanding resource, significant differences exist in the content and organizational scheme from one publisher to the next. For example, each service has its own special features and editorial approach to tax issues along with a great deal of proprietary content. The best way to acquaint oneself with the various tax services and the advantages and disadvantages of each is to use them in researching hypothetical or actual problems.

Organizationally, tax services fall into two types: annotated and topical (although this distinction has become somewhat blurred in the Internet version of these services). An **annotated tax service** is organized by IRC section. The IRC-arranged subdivisions of this service are likely to encompass several topics. The annotations accompany editorial commentaries and include digests or summaries of IRS pronouncements and court opinions that interpret a particular IRC section. They are classified by subtopic and cite pertinent primary authorities. A **topical tax service**, on the other hand, is organized by broad topic, including income taxes, estate and gift taxes, and excise taxes. The topically arranged subdivisions of this service are likely to encompass several IRC sections.

Annotated tax services include the *United States Tax Reporter* and the *Standard Federal Income Tax Reporter* services, both of which are organized by IRC section. Many tax advisors find these reporters easy to use because of their extensive indexing system. Topical tax services include RIA's *Federal Tax Coordinator 2d* and Bloomberg BNA's *Tax Management Portfolios*. *Tax Management Portfolios* are popular with many tax advisors because they are very readable yet still provide a comprehensive discussion of a broad range of tax issues. Each portfolio (e.g., Passive Loss Rules, Portfolio 549) covers a particular topic in great detail. However, because the published portfolios do not cover all areas of the tax law, another service may be necessary to supplement the gaps in a portfolio's coverage. Table I:15-4 summarizes the organization and key features of the major tax services.

▼ TABLE I:15-4
Summary of Key Features of Tax Services

Name	Publisher	Organization	Key Features
United States Tax Reporter	Thomson Reuters/RIA	IRC section number	• Editorial commentary • Index and findings list • Annotations
Standard Federal Income Tax Reporter	Wolters Kluwer/CCH	IRC section number	• Editorial commentary • Index and findings list • Annotations
Federal Tax Coordinator 2d	Thomson Reuters/RIA	Tax topic (income tax by topic, estate and gift taxes, excise taxes)	• Commentary organized by topic with references to primary authority and tabbed access to IRC and Treasury Regulations.
Tax Management Portfolios	Bloomberg BNA	U.S. income, foreign income, state tax, estate and gift tax	• Over 400 specialized booklets with extensive commentary by topic, heavily footnoted and referenced to primary authority.

THE INTERNET AS A RESEARCH TOOL

OBJECTIVE 6

Apply the basics of Internet-based tax research

Internet databases are rapidly replacing print-based services as the principal source of tax related information. These databases encompass not only the IRC, Treasury Regulations, court cases, state laws, and other primary authorities, but also citators and secondary sources such as tax service reporters, treatises, journals, and newsletters. The principal advantages of using Internet-based tax services are ease and speed of access. These services eliminate the need for searching through several volumes of text, the need for consulting numerous cumulative supplements, and the time required to regularly update a print-based library. In addition, Internet based research tools put a vast amount of information in the hands of a tax practitioner without the cost and space requirements of a well equipped print-based tax library.

ADDITIONAL COMMENT

To apply the online research tools discussed in this chapter, textbook users must have access to the described Internet-based tax services at their institution.

Because of these advantages, the Internet has become the principal medium for conveying tax related information to professionals. The most widely used Internet-based research services are RIA's Checkpoint™ (hereafter CHECKPOINT), accessible at *checkpoint.riag.com*, and CCH IntelliConnect™ (hereafter INTELLICONNECT), accessible at *intelliconnect.cch.com*. Westlaw®[42] and LexisNexus are online legal research services that are predominately used by legal professionals.[43] This chapter limits its discussion to CHECKPOINT and INTELLICONNECT. Both subscription-based services are updated continuously and store information in databases, called libraries, principal among which are the following:[44]

CHECKPOINT	INTELLICONNECT
Newsstand	Tax News, Journals, and Newsletters
Federal	Federal Tax
State and Local	State Tax
International	International Tax
Estate Planning	Financial and Estate Planning
Pension and Benefits	Pension
Payroll	Payroll

Newsstand on CHECKPOINT and *Tax News, Journals, and Newsletters* on INTELLICONNECT provide daily updates on recent tax developments. The *Federal* library on both series contains the text of the IRC, Treasury Regulations, IRS pronouncements, court opinions, and other primary sources. In addition to primary sources, the *Federal* library on CHECKPOINT contains the RIA citator, *Federal Tax Coordinator 2d*, and *United States Tax Reporter* annotations and explanations. The *Federal* library on INTELLICONNECT contains the *Standard Federal Income Tax Reporter* and the *Standard Federal Income Tax Reporter Explanations*. Tax reporters for all 50 states as well as multistate tax guides are found in the *State and Local* library on CHECKPOINT and the *State Tax* library on INTELLICONNECT. International tax treaties are found in the *International* library of both services. CHECKPOINT's *Estate Planning* offers the text of estate tax treaties, newsletters, journals, and Warren, Gorham & Lamont tax treatises. INTELLICONNECT's *Financial and Estate Planning* library supplies the *Federal Estate and Gift Tax Reporter*, as well as the text of estate and gift tax statutes, cases, and rulings. Finally, *Pension and Benefits* on CHECKPOINT and *Pension* on INTELLICONNECT contain the text of the Employee Retirement Income Security Act (ERISA), related Treasury Regulations, and Congressional committee reports, while *Payroll* provides the text of state and federal employment regulations and current withholding tables.

---

[42] Westlaw® is owned by Thomson Reuters.
[43] The research products discussed in this section (e.g., CHECKPOINT, INTELLICONNECT, Westlaw®, and LexisNexus) generally are available only to paid subscribers.

[44] INTELLICONNECT has numerous other databases, including Accounting and Audit, Banking, Corporate Government, Energy & Natural Resources, Health Care Compliance and Reimbursement. These specialty areas generally fall outside the tax arena and therefore are not described in this chapter.

CHECKPOINT and INTELLICONNECT libraries and databases can be searched in four basic ways:

- ► By keyword
- ► By index
- ► By citation
- ► By content

EXAMPLE I:15-12 ► Rhonda Researcher's client is a real estate developer and wants to exchange an office building for a residential condominium in the same town. The client wants to know if he can structure the transaction in a tax advantaged way. Rhonda immediately recognizes the situation as a potential like-kind exchange of real property. Therefore, she undertakes a keyword search of INTELLICONNECT using the term *like kind exchange* to quickly uncover potentially applicable documents. She also knows that Sec. 1031 is the relevant IRC section and can search the IRC or Treasury Regulations by citation. On the other hand, if she were unfamiliar with the topic, she could employ several other options. For example, INTELLICONNECT's Federal Tax editorial content has a heading for Standard Federal Tax Reporter topical index. The "Exchange of property" term in the topical index directs Rhonda to "See Like-kind Exchanges; Sales and Exchanges; and Tax-free Exchanges." The index entries under these headings direct Rhonda to a number of entries potentially applicable to the transaction. Rhonda also conducts a similar research procedure on CHECKPOINT to see whether this alternative service provides any additional information. In particular, she searches in the *Federal Tax Coordinator 2d,* which is RIA's topical service. ◄

KEY WORD SEARCHES

Searching CHECKPOINT and INTELLICONNECT by keyword is relatively simple, particularly if the researcher is familiar with the Internet. The first step is to activate a database or multiple databases, perform an initial keyword search, and refine the results after the initial query. The researcher can choose to search across any combination of the available databases. The CHECKPOINT Federal databases include primary sources such as the Internal Revenue Code, Treasury Regulations, and Federal Tax Cases along with editorial databases such as RIA's *Federal Tax Coordinator 2d.* Similar choices exist for INTELLICONNECT. Deciding which database to include in the search depends partly on the expected complexity of the research question and on the researcher's familiarity with the topic.

The search engines within the services look for the terms selected and many variations of the terms. For example, the search for *auto* will return documents with auto, car, automobile, motor vehicle, passenger vehicle, sedan, and others.[45] Searches will include both singular and plural variations. Any document with the term or terms is returned and ranked by best match according to the search. If two terms are used, the best matches generally are documents where the terms are close together. Picking key words and search terms is critical to success. The search must be broad enough to include relevant documents but not so broad to include hundreds or thousands of documents unlikely to be on point.

For example, if the researcher selects only the INTELLICONNECT Cases database, the term *property exchange* returns thousands of results that have both the words *property* and *exchange* somewhere in the document. Clearly this outcome is too broad for a researcher just beginning his or her research. Fortunately, several methods of narrowing the search exist. For example, the search for *property exchange* can be limited to all terms, any terms, near phrase, or exact phrase. Specifically, the keyword search "property exchange" that uses quotation marks around the search phrase will return documents only with that exact phrase. Thus, quotation marks should be used sparingly and only when the researcher knows the precise phrase. Using Boolean connectors is helpful as well. These connectors force the search engine to narrow the search based on the parameters set. Table I:15-5 provides a partial list of connectors available in CHECKPOINT and INTELLICONNECT.

Another way to narrow a search is to focus on terms unique to the research question at hand. The goal is to identify tax related terms likely to appear only in relevant tax

---

[45] Both CHECKPOINT and INTELLICONNECT provide a thesaurus tool, which can identify synonyms and suggest alternative terms related to search terms used by the researcher. The search engine automatically searches for synonyms unless the researcher restricts the search to specific terms using Boolean connectors or quotation marks. For example, a search for the specific phrase "automobile depreciation" will not return documents that refer to *auto, car,* or *vehicle.*

▼ TABLE I:15-5
Connectors Used in INTELLICONNECT and CHECKPOINT

INTELLICONNECT	CHECKPOINT	Description	Examples
and	&, and	Retrieves documents with both terms.	INTELLICONNECT: property and exchange CHECKPOINT: property & exchange
or	|, or	Retrieves documents with either term.	INTELLICONNECT: property or exchange CHECKPOINT: property | exchange
not	^, not	Retrieves documents with one term but not the other.	INTELLICONNECT: property not exchange CHECKPOINT: property ^ exchange
w/n	/n	Retrieves documents in which the first term is separated from the second term by no more than n number of words.	INTELLICONNECT: property w/5 exchange CHECKPOINT: property /5 exchange Locates property within 5 words of exchange
w/sen	/s	Retrieves documents that contain the first term within 20 words of the second term (or within the same sentence for RIA).	INTELLICONNECT: property w/sen exchange CHECKPOINT: property /s exchange
w/par	/p	Retrieves documents that contain the first term within 80 words of the second term (or within the same paragraph for RIA).	INTELLICONNECT: property w/par exchange CHECKPOINT: property /p exchange
" "	" "	Exact phrase.	INTELLICONNECT and CHECKPOINT: "property exchange"
*	*	Keyword variation.	Deprecia* returns depreciation, depreciate, depreciated, depreciating
?	?	Keyword variation.	Advis?r returns advisor and adviser

authorities. For example, stamps are a type of collectible, but the term also will appear in documents discussing taxation of distilled spirits, food stamps, and store stamps and coupons. The researcher should begin the search with limiting terms such as *collectible* rather than the broader term *stamps*. Also, researchers with a good working knowledge of the IRC quickly learn that using IRC sections in search terms is a great way to obtain relevant documents.

Searching using key words is a skill that improves with practice. Researchers becoming familiar with using the databases will learn to craft search terms that include the most relevant elements of the question at hand. Once the researcher finds a document on point, the information within that document often can be used to narrow future searches. The search can be repeated by adding terms, or the documents returned originally can be searched using a new set of terms. Also, the "search within results" feature offered by both CHECKPOINT and INTELLICONNECT is helpful when the search returns too many documents. However, if searches by key word search do not return the desired results, other options exist.

SEARCH BY INDEX
Both CHECKPOINT and INTELLICONNECT offer traditional indexes. With INTELLICONNECT, the user can click on most databases to see an index of the contents. For example, clicking on the *Standard Federal Income Tax Reporter* Topical Index listed in the Federal Tax Editorial content database reveals a list from A to Z, and the researcher can easily click on a hyperlink for any letter and scroll through the alphabetized topics list. As an example, one can find the letter C, then scroll through the screens and find the topic "casualty losses" that directs the researcher to a variety of subheadings. CHECKPOINT has an Indexes option under the GO TO area of the Search tab. In CHECKPOINT, the researcher can choose the *Federal Tax Coordinator 2d* Topic Index database. Again, the

researcher will find the letter C and scroll through the topics to find "casualty losses," which leads the researcher to subheadings with hyperlinks to CHECKPOINT's editorial materials.

In addition, both INTELLICONNECT and CHECKPOINT have topical indexes that use hyperlinks to the Internal Revenue Code. In INTELLICONNECT, the researcher begins with the Topical Index option located under Federal Tax Primary Sources, selects the Current Internal Revenue Code Topical Index, and begins his or her research with an A to Z list. In CHECKPOINT, the researcher selects the Current Code Topic Index located in the Indexes link on the Search tab.

SEARCH BY CITATION

Often the desired document is a specific IRC section, Treasury Regulation, court case, IRS pronouncement, or other document. If so, both services offer searches by specific citation. Researchers must be careful to use exact citations using this tool because close matches will not return the desired document.

Both CHECKPOINT and INTELLICONNECT citation search tools provide dedicated boxes in which to type the specific type of document requested. For example, to search for IRC Sec. 267, the researcher simply types 267 in the box labeled Current Code in CHECKPOINT under the "Find by Citation" link, or IRC Code & Hist. Sec. in INTELLICONNECT under the "Citations" link. Specific boxes also exist for various court decisions, revenue rulings, revenue procedures, and other IRS pronouncements.

SEARCH BY CONTENT

Each database also can be searched by content. Clicking on the hyperlink for each database will return a table of contents. Clicking through an entry will take the researcher further into the table of contents. For example, in INTELLICONNECT, several documents discussing adoption credits can be located by clicking on the following series of hyperlinks:

> Federal Tax
> > Federal Tax Editorial Content
> > > Standard Federal Tax Reporter
> > > Credits
> > > > Adoption expenses – Sec. 23

CHECKPOINT also has a Table of Contents tab. Documents discussing adoption credits may be found by clicking on the following series of hyperlinks:

> Federal Library
> > Federal Editorial Materials
> > > Federal Tax Coordinator 2d
> > > > Chapter A Individuals and Self-Employment Tax
> > > > A-4400 Adoption Expense Credit

NONCOMMERCIAL INTERNET SERVICES

Many noncommercial institutions, such as governments and universities, allow access to their tax-related databases via the Internet. In "tax-surfing" the Internet, the researcher might first visit the IRS site located at *www.irs.gov*. Although oriented to the layman, this site contains a wealth of information useful to the tax professional. Such information includes guidelines for electronic filing, IRS forms and instructions, the full text of Treasury Regulations, and recent issues of the *Internal Revenue Bulletin*. Other useful sites include those maintained by the Library of Congress at *www.loc.gov* and the U.S. Government Printing Office Federal Digital System at *www.gpo.gov/fdsys/*. From these sites, the researcher can retrieve the text of recent court opinions, tax legislation, committee reports, state and federal tax laws, and much more.

An excellent gateway for starting tax related research is the Tax, Accounting, and Payroll Sites Directory at *www.taxsites.com*, maintained by AccountantsWorld,

LLC. This site provides hundreds of hyperlinks to federal, state, and international tax law and tax form databases. Instrumental in financial accounting searches is the Electronic Data Gathering, Analysis, and Retrieval (EDGAR) site at *www.sec.gov/edgar.shtml*. EDGAR is a document filing and retrieval service sponsored by the U.S. Securities and Exchange Commission (SEC). It provides access to the full text of documents filed with the SEC by publicly traded companies. These documents include annual financial statements on Form 10-K, quarterly financial statements on Form 10-Q, proxy statements, and prospectuses. The EDGAR database extends from January 1994 to the present and is accessible by company name, central index key, document file number, and keyword.

CITATORS

OBJECTIVE 7

Use a citator to assess tax authorities

Citators serve two functions. First, they trace the judicial history of a particular case (e.g., if the case under analysis is an appeals court decision, the citator indicates the lower court that heard the case and whether the Supreme Court reviewed the case). Second, they list other authorities (e.g., cases and IRS pronouncements) that cite the case or authority in question. These listed authorities are called *citing cases* or *citing rulings*. The judicial history also indicates whether the case is affirmed, reversed or remanded.[46]

Because tax law relies heavily on precedent, the citator provides an index of citing cases and rulings that help the researcher determine the strength of the case or ruling he or she is evaluating. The citator gives full citations for the citing case and lists where the citing cases can be found. It is important to note that the same case may have as many as three decisions (i.e., lower court, court of appeals, and Supreme Court) with each listing having its own list of citing cases. Therefore, if a citing case cites only the Supreme Court decision, the citator will list it only under the Supreme Court cite.

Two principal tax related commercial citators are those in INTELLICONNECT and CHECKPOINT. Both citators allow the researcher to enter case names or case citations. The discussion in this section focuses on the electronic version of the citators, although both CCH and RIA offer print versions as well.

The INTELLICONNECT citator analyzes every decision reported in the *Standard Federal Income Tax Reporter*, the *Excise Tax Reporter*, and the *Federal Estate and Gift Tax Reporter* and selectively lists cases that cite the decision under analysis. INTELLICONNECT lists only the citing cases that its editors believe will influence the precedential weight of the decision under analysis.

The CHECKPOINT citator also provides the history of each authority and lists the cases and pronouncements that have cited the authority. This citator, however, differs from the INTELLICONNECT citator in a couple of important ways. First, CHECKPOINT lists all citing cases, and not just those that the editors believe will serve as relevant precedent. Second, the CHECKPOINT citator provides additional information about the citing case, showing whether the citing authorities comment favorably or unfavorably on the cited case or whether they can be distinguished from the cited case.[47]

In addition to tax cases, the CHECKPOINT and INTELLICONNECT citators evaluate revenue rulings and other IRS pronouncements and lists any status changes. Before relying on a revenue ruling or pronouncement, a researcher must confirm that the pronouncement reflects the current position of the IRS. For example, a revoked ruling is

---

[46] If a case is *affirmed*, the decision of the lower court is upheld. *Reversed* means the higher court invalidated the decision of the lower court because it reached a conclusion different from that derived by the lower court. *Remanded* signifies that the higher court sent the case back to the lower court with instructions to address matters consistent with the higher court's ruling.

[47] When a court distinguishes the facts of one case from those of an earlier case, it suggests that its departure from the earlier decision is justified because the facts of the two cases are different.

▼ TABLE I:15-6

Terms to Describe Status Changes to IRS Rulings

Term	Description of Term
Amplified	No change in the prior published position has occurred, but the prior position is extended to cover a variation of the fact situation previously addressed.
Clarified	Language used in a prior published position is being made clear because the previous language has caused or could cause confusion.
Distinguished	The ruling mentions a prior ruling but points out an essential difference between the two rulings.
Modified	The substance of a previously published ruling is being changed, but the prior ruling remains in effect.
Obsoleted	A previously published ruling is no longer determinative with respect to future transactions, e.g., because laws or regulations have changed, or the substance of the ruling has been adopted into regulations.
Revoked	A previously published ruling has been determined to be incorrect, and the correct position is being stated in the new ruling.
Superseded	The new ruling merely restates the substance of a previously published ruling or series of rulings.
Supplemented	The ruling expands a previous ruling, e.g., by adding items to a list.
Suspended	The previously published ruling will not be applied pending some future action, such as the issuance of new or amended regulations.

Source: www.irs.gov.

one in which the ruling is no longer correct and the correct position is being stated in the new ruling. The IRS does not remove the old ruling from the *Internal Revenue Bulletin* or *Cumulative Bulletin*, but the old ruling does not have authority regarding a transaction occurring after the revocation. Thus, failure to confirm its status could result in an incorrect conclusion. Table I:15-6 provides a list of terms the IRS uses to describe changes in the status of a ruling.

USING THE CITATOR

Internet-based versions of the citators are easier to use than print-based citators. For example, assume the researcher is currently reading *Leonarda C. Diaz v. Commissioner of Internal Revenue*, 70 TC 1067 (1978). Using INTELLICONNECT, the researcher can click on the Citator button in the left column at the top left of the page, and the service opens up a new tab with a summary of activity of the case. The information in bold print with bullets to the left denotes that the *Diaz* case was first decided by the Tax Court (i.e., TC), and then by the Second Circuit Court of Appeals (i.e., CA-2). It shows that the Second Circuit affirmed (upheld) the Tax Court's decision. The four cases underneath the Second Circuit decision cite the *Diaz* decision and might be useful for the researcher to better understand the impact of the case. The seven cases listed beneath the Tax Court decision cite the Tax Court's opinion.

The CHECKPOINT citator is similarly easy to use. Once again, if the researcher is reading the *Diaz* case, he or she simply clicks on the Citator button at the top of the case window. The two main decisions (Tax Court and Second Circuit) appear in a list. Clicking on either case brings up the court decisions that have cited the *Diaz* decision. CHECKPOINT sometimes lists more cases than does INTELLICONNECT. In this example, CHECKPOINT lists 11 cases that have cited the *Diaz* Second Circuit decision and 26 cases that have cited the Tax Court decision. CHECKPOINT also adds a brief description of the type of citation—cited favorably, cited unfavorable, case distinguished, or reasoning followed.

PROFESSIONAL GUIDELINES FOR TAX SERVICES

Describe the professional guidelines that CPAs in tax practice should follow

Professional guidelines for tax services are contained in both government-imposed and professional-imposed tax standards. The following sections briefly describe two types of guidelines—Treasury Department *Circular 230* (Rev. 8-2011) and the American Institute of Certified Public Accountants (AICPA) *Statements on Standards for Tax Services (SSTSs)*. A fuller discussion of these standards appears in Chapter C:15.

TREASURY DEPARTMENT *CIRCULAR 230*

Circular 230 sets forth rules to practice before the Internal Revenue Service and pertains to certified public accountants, attorneys, enrolled agents, and other persons representing taxpayers before the IRS. It presents the duties and restrictions relating to such practice and prescribes sanctions and disciplinary proceedings for violating these regulations.

Circular 230 rules, however, are not ethical standards. Instead, the document focuses on the right to represent clients before the IRS. These standards differ from the AICPA's SSTSs in the following ways:

▶ They apply only to federal tax issues and not state authorities.

▶ They generally apply only to federal income tax practice.

▶ They do not provide the depth of guidance found in the SSTSs.

▶ They give the government the authority to impose monetary penalties for violations of the rules.

Circular 230 provides guidelines for written advice to taxpayers. In June 2014, the IRS substantially revised and simplified the rules and eliminated the distinction between covered opinions and other written advice. Under the new rules, all written advice is held to a "reasonable practitioner standard" that will vary based on the nature and extent of the advice. An email to a client answering a routine tax question will be held to a different standard than will an opinion on the tax effects of a complex transaction. The written advice rules do not apply to training or educational presentations but do apply to marketing and sales presentations.

For all written advice, the practitioner is expected to base the advice on reasonable assumptions, consider relevant facts and circumstances, identify the facts relevant to the advice, be properly skeptical of representations by the taxpayer and others, relate applicable law and authority to the facts, and not base an opinion on the chances that a transaction will or will not be identified by IRS and subject to audit. The revised Section 10.37 of *Circular 230* does note that the IRS representative will consider the "additional risk" associated with opinions related to tax shelters.

AICPA'S STATEMENTS ON TAX STANDARDS

Tax advisors confronted with ethical issues frequently turn to a professional organization for guidance. Although the guidelines set forth by such organizations are not *legally* enforceable, they carry significant moral weight, and may be cited in a negligence lawsuit as the proper "standard of care" for tax practitioners. They also may provide grounds for the termination or suspension of one's professional license. One such set of guidelines is the *Statements on Standards for Tax Services* (SSTSs),[48] issued by the American Institute of Certified Public Accountants (AICPA) and reproduced in Appendix E.

The SSTSs provide an ethical framework to govern the normative relationship between a tax advisor and his or her client, where, unlike an auditor, a tax advisor acts as the client's advocate. Thus, his or her primary duty is to the client, not the IRS. In

---

[48] AICPA, *Statements on Standards for Tax Services*, 2009, effective January 1, 2010.

fulfilling this duty, the advisor is bound by the highest standards of care. The most recent version of the SSTSs includes seven standards that provide guidance for AICPA members in their professional tax practice.

SSTS No. 1—Tax Return Positions. Tax professionals often provide tax advice in situations where the authority is unclear or evolving. Frequently this advice involves recommending positions that could be reversed upon audit. This statement describes the minimum level of confidence a CPA must achieve to recommend a tax return position to a taxpayer. Members first must determine and comply with all standards imposed by the various taxing authorities. Regardless of those standards, a member should not recommend a position unless he or she has a good faith belief that the position has a "realistic possibility" of being sustained administratively or judicially on its merits if challenged. Members are not permitted to take the probability of audit into account.

If the position does not meet the realistic probability standard, a member still may recommend a tax return position if he or she concludes that the position has a "reasonable basis" and the position is properly disclosed. When recommending a tax return position and when preparing or signing a return on which a tax return position is taken, a member should, when relevant, advise the taxpayer regarding potential penalty consequences of such tax return position and the opportunity, if any, to avoid such penalties through disclosure. The member also may consider any GAAP requirements to disclose aggressive tax positions under the portion of Accounting Standards Codification 740 formerly known as FIN 48.

The standard highlights the dual responsibility of the member. The U.S. tax system can function only when taxpayers file "true, correct, and complete" returns, but taxpayers also have no obligation to pay more in tax than they legally owe. The tax professional's duty is to meet his or her responsibilities to both the tax system and the taxpayer client.

SSTS No. 2—Answers to Questions on Returns. Return preparers often must sign a declaration that the return is "true, correct, and complete." A member should make a reasonable effort to obtain from the taxpayer the information necessary to provide appropriate answers to all questions on a tax return before signing as preparer. However, in certain circumstances, questions or information applicable to the taxpayer may be omitted. Reasonable grounds include the following situtations:

▶ The omitted information is not readily available or is immaterial and has little effect on taxable income or loss or the tax liability.

▶ The meaning of the question as it relates to the taxpayer is uncertain.

▶ The requested information is voluminous, in which case the taxpayer can attach a statement indicating that the requested information will be supplied upon request.

SSTS No. 3—Certain Procedural Aspects of Preparing Returns. Tax returns are based on information provided by the client. This statement sets forth the applicable standards for members concerning this information. Specifically, in preparing or signing a return, members are not required to examine or verify a client's supporting data. A member may rely on information supplied by the taxpayer unless the information appears to be incorrect, incomplete, inconsistent, or unreasonable under the circumstances. However, if the applicable law or regulations impose a specific record keeping requirement to claim a deduction, the member should inquire and satisfy himself or herself that the required records do exist.

Members are specifically encouraged to make use of a taxpayer's returns for one or more prior years in preparing the current return, whenever feasible. The practice should help avoid the omission or duplication of items and provide a basis for the treatment of similar or related transactions.

SSTS No. 4—Use of Estimates. For various reasons, precise information about an amount required on a tax return might not be available at the time the tax return is prepared. For example, the taxpayer might not have a record of small transactions or might be missing certain records. In such cases, a member may advise on estimates used in the preparation of the tax return, but the taxpayer has the responsibility to provide the estimated data. Appraisals and valuations are not considered estimates.

If estimates are used, they generally need not be labeled as estimates, but they should not be presented in a manner that provides a misleading impression about the degree of factual accuracy. However, disclosure that estimates were used should be made in some unusual situations, including:

▶ A taxpayer has died or is ill at the time the return is prepared.

▶ A taxpayer has not received a schedule K-1 at the time the tax return is to be filed.

▶ Litigation is pending that affects the return.

▶ Fire, computer failure, or a natural disaster has destroyed the relevant records.

Notwithstanding this statement, the tax practitioner may not use estimates when such use is implicitly prohibited by the IRC. For example, Sec. 274(d) disallows deductions for certain expenses (e.g., meals and entertainment) unless the taxpayer can substantiate the expenses with adequate records or sufficient corroborating information. The documentation requirement effectively precludes the taxpayer from estimating such expenses and the practitioner from using such estimates.

SSTS No. 5—Departure from a Position Previously Concluded in an Administrative Proceeding or Court Decisions. Members can take positions that differ from a position determined in an administrative proceeding with respect to the taxpayer's prior return (such as an IRS audit, IRS appeals conference, or a court decision.) Departure might be warranted because of a change in the law or regulations, or favorable court decisions. In any event, if the member can otherwise meet the standards of SSTS No. 1, departure from previous positions is permissible.

SSTS No. 6—Knowledge of Error: Return Preparation and Administrative Proceedings. For purposes of this standard, the definition of an error has the common meaning, including a mathematical error, but the definition also encompasses any position that does not meet the standards of SSTS No. 1. A position also qualifies as an error if it met the standard when a return was originally filed but no longer does because of a retroactive legislative or legal proceeding. An error for this purpose does not include immaterial items.

A member should inform the taxpayer promptly upon becoming aware of (1) an error in a previously filed return, (2) an error in a return that is the subject of an administrative proceeding (e.g., an IRS audit or appeals conference), or (3) a taxpayer's failure to file a required return. A member should advise the taxpayer of the potential consequences of the error and recommend corrective measures to be taken. This advice can be given orally. The member is not obligated to inform the taxing authority of an error and, in fact, may not do so without the taxpayer's permission except when required by law.

However, if the taxpayer requests that a member prepare the current year's return and the taxpayer has not taken appropriate action to correct an error in a prior year's return, the member should consider whether to withdraw from preparing the return and whether to continue a professional or employment relationship with the taxpayer.

The standard recognizes that conflicts can arise between the member's interests and those of the client. For example, withdrawal from an engagement could have an adverse impact on the taxpayer. In some situations, the member should consult his or her own legal counsel before deciding on recommendations to the taxpayer and whether to continue the engagement. In situations involving potential fraud or criminal charges, the member should advise the client to consult with an attorney before taking any action.

SSTS No. 7—Form and Content of Advice to Taxpayers. A member should use professional judgment to ensure that tax advice provided to a taxpayer reflects competence and appropriately serves the taxpayer's needs. The advice can be communicated in writing or orally. When communicating tax advice to a taxpayer in writing, a member should comply with relevant taxing authorities' standards applicable to written tax advice. A member should use professional judgment about any need to document oral advice.

In deciding on the form of advice provided to a taxpayer, a member should consider factors such as:

► The importance of the transaction and the amounts involved

► The technical complexity involved

► The existence of authorities and precedents

► The tax sophistication of the taxpayer

► The need to seek other professional advice

► The potential penalty consequences of a tax return position and whether any penalties can be avoided through disclosure

This statement implies that practitioner-taxpayer dealings should not be casual, non-consensual, or open ended. Rather, they should be professional, contractual, and definite. Oral advice may be appropriate in routine matters, but written communications are recommended in important, complicated, or significant dollar value transactions.

In addition to these obligations, the tax advisor has a strict duty of confidentiality to the client. Although not encompassed under the SSTSs, this duty is implied in the accountant client privilege. (For a discussion of this privilege, see Chapter C:15.)

? STOP & THINK

Question: As described in the Stop & Think box on pages I:15-10 and I:15-11, you are researching the manner in which a deduction is calculated. The IRC states that the calculation is to be made "in a manner prescribed by the Secretary." After studying the IRC, Treasury Regulations, and committee reports, you conclude that another way of doing the calculation is arguably correct under an intuitive approach. This approach would result in a lower tax liability for the client. According to the *Statements on Standards for Tax Services,* may you take a position contrary to final Treasury Regulations based on the argument that the regulations are not valid?

Solution: You should not take a position contrary to the Treasury Regulations unless you have a "good-faith belief that the position has a realistic possibility of being sustained administratively or judicially on its merits." However, you can take a position that does not meet the above standard, provided you adequately disclose the position, and the position has a reasonable basis. Whether or not you have met the standard depends on all the facts and circumstances. Chapter C:15 discusses tax return preparer positions contrary to Treasury Regulations.

WHAT WOULD YOU DO IN THIS SITUATION?

Regal Enterprises and Macon Industries, unaffiliated corporations, have hired you to prepare their respective income tax returns. In preparing Regal's return, you notice that Regal has claimed a depreciation deduction for equipment purchased from Macon on February 22 at a cost of $2 million. In preparing Macon's return, you notice that Macon has reported sales proceeds of $1.5 million from the sale of equipment to Regal on February 22. One of the two figures must be incorrect. How do you proceed to correct it? Hint: See SSTS No. 3 in Appendix E.

SAMPLE WORK PAPERS AND CLIENT LETTER

<table>
<tr><td>

Prepare work papers and communicate to clients
</td><td>

Appendix A presents a set of sample work papers, including a draft of a client letter and a memo to the file. The work papers indicate the issues to be researched, the authorities addressing the issues, and the researcher's conclusions concerning the appropriate tax treatment, with rationale therefor.

The format and other details of work papers differ from firm to firm. The sample in this text offers general guidance concerning the content of work papers. In practice, work papers may include less detail.
</td></tr>
</table>

PROBLEM MATERIALS

Note: To complete the online research problems for this chapter, textbook users must have access to the Internet-based services described in the chapter.

DISCUSSION QUESTIONS

I:15-1 Explain the difference between closed-fact and open-fact situations.

I:15-2 According to the AICPA's *Statements on Standards for Tax Services*, what duties does the tax practitioner owe the client?

I:15-3 Explain what is encompassed by the term *tax law* as used by tax advisors.

I:15-4 The U.S. Government Printing Office publishes both hearings on proposed legislation and committee reports. Distinguish between the two.

I:15-5 Explain how committee reports can be used in tax research. What do they indicate?

I:15-6 A friend notices that you are reading the Internal Revenue Code of 1986. Your friend inquires why you are consulting a 1986 publication, especially when tax laws change so frequently. What is your response?

I:15-7 Does Title 26 contain statutory provisions dealing only with income taxation? Explain.

I:15-8 Refer to IRC Sec. 301.
   a. Which subsection discusses the general rule for the tax treatment of a property distribution?
   b. Where should one look for exceptions to the general rule?
   c. What type of Treasury Regulations would relate to subsection (e)?

I:15-9 Why should tax researchers note the date on which a Treasury Regulation was adopted?

I:15-10 a. Distinguish between proposed, temporary, and final Treasury Regulations.
   b. Distinguish between interpretative and legislative Treasury Regulations.

I:15-11 Which type of regulation is more difficult for a taxpayer to successfully challenge, and why?

I:15-12 Explain the legislative reenactment doctrine.

I:15-13 a. Discuss the authoritative weight of revenue rulings.

   b. As a practical matter, what consequences are likely to ensue if a taxpayer does not follow a revenue ruling and the IRS audits his or her return?

I:15-14 a. In which courts may litigation dealing with tax matters begin?
   b. Discuss the factors that might be considered in deciding where to litigate.
   c. Describe the appeals process in tax litigation.

I:15-15 May a taxpayer appeal a case litigated under the Small Cases Procedure of the Tax Court?

I:15-16 Explain whether the following decisions are of the same precedential value: (1) Tax Court regular decisions, (2) Tax Court memo decisions, (3) decisions under the Small Cases Procedures of the Tax Court.

I:15-17 Does the IRS acquiesce in decisions of U.S. district courts?

I:15-18 The decisions of which courts are reported in the AFTR? In the USTC?

I:15-19 Why do some revenue ruling citations refer to the *Internal Revenue Bulletin* (I.R.B.) and others to a *Cumulative Bulletin* (C.B.)?

I:15-20 Explain the *Golsen* Rule. Give an example of its application.

I:15-21 Assume that the only precedents relating to a particular issue are as follows:

Tax Court—decided for the taxpayer
Eighth Circuit Court of Appeals—decided for the taxpayer (affirming the Tax Court)
U.S. District Court for Eastern Louisiana—decided for the taxpayer
Fifth Circuit Court of Appeals—decided for the government (reversing the U.S. District Court of Eastern Louisiana)
   a. Discuss the precedential value of the foregoing decisions for your client, who is a California resident.

b. If your client, a Texas resident, litigates in the Tax Court, how will the court rule? Explain.

I:15-22 Which official publication(s) contain(s) the following:
    a. Transcripts of Senate floor debates
    b. IRS announcements
    c. Tax Court regular opinions
    d. Treasury decisions
    e. U.S. district court opinions
    f. Technical advice memoranda

I:15-23 Under what circumstances might a tax advisor find the provisions of a tax treaty useful?

I:15-24 What two functions does a citator serve?

I:15-25 Describe two ways that the information available from the CHECKPOINT citator differs from that available from the INTELLICONNECT citator.

I:15-26 List four methods of searching the CHECKPOINT and INTELLICONNECT databases.

I:15-27 Access INTELLICONNECT at *http://intelliconnect .cch.com* and RIA CHECKPOINT™ at *http:// checkpoint.riag.com.* Then answer the following questions:
    a. What are the principal primary sources found in both Internet tax services?
    b. What are the principal secondary sources found in each Internet tax service?

I:15-28 Compare the features of the computerized tax services with those of Internet sites maintained by noncommercial institutions. What are the relative advantages and disadvantages of each? Could the latter sites serve as a substitute for a commercial tax service?

I:15-29 According to the *Statements on Standards for Tax Services,* what belief should a CPA have before taking a pro-taxpayer position on a tax return?

I:15-30 List an advisor's duties that are excluded under the AICPA's *Statements on Standards for Tax Services.*

I:15-31 List three requirements that apply to written advice under Treasury Department *Circular 230.*

I:15-32 Explain how Treasury Department *Circular 230* differs from the AICPA's *Statements on Standards for Tax Services.*

PROBLEMS

I:15-33 *Interpreting the IRC.* Under a divorce agreement executed in the current year, an ex-wife receives from her former husband cash of $25,000 per year for eight years. The agreement does not explicitly state that the payments are excludable from gross income.
    a. Does the ex-wife have gross income? If so, how much?
    b. Is the former husband entitled to a deduction? If so, is it for or from AGI? Refer only to the IRC in answering this question. Start with Sec. 71.

I:15-34 *Interpreting the IRC.* Refer to Sec. 385 and answer the questions below.
    a. Whenever Treasury Regulations are issued under this section, what type are they likely to be: legislative or interpretative? Explain.
    b. Assume Treasury Regulations under Sec. 385 have been finalized. Will they be relevant to estate tax matters? Explain.

I:15-35 *Using IRS Rulings.* Locate PLR 8733007 and Rev. Rul. 81-219.
    a. Briefly summarize the tax issue and conclusion of each ruling.
    b. Under what circumstances can a researcher rely on the private letter ruling?
    c. Under what circumstances can a researcher rely on the revenue ruling?

I:15-36 *Using Treasury pronouncements.* Which IRC section(s) does Rev. Rul. 2001-29 interpret? (Hint: consult the official pronouncement of the IRS.)

I:15-37 *Using CHECKPOINT for a Keyword Search.* The objective is to locate a general overview of available home office deductions. On the main research tab, select the *United States Tax Reporter—Explanations (RIA)* library. How many results does CHECKPOINT return for each search term if the terms and connectors option is selected?
    a. Search term: home office deduction.
    b. Search term: "home office" deduction.
    c. Search term: "home office" /5 deduction.
    d. Perform the search in Part a above. Select *Sort by Relevance.* How does this sort change the results? Does the sort make it easier to locate relevant documents?
    e. How do your answers change to Parts a–c if you use the intuitive search?

I:15-38 *Using INTELLICONNECT for a Keyword Search.* The search objective is to determine the amount generally excludable on the sale of a married couple's home. Using Browse, locate the *Standard Federal Tax Reporter—Explanations* library. How many results does INTELLICONNECT return for each search term?
    a. Search term: home sale gain exclusion.
    b. Search term: "home sale" gain exclusion and turn off "apply thesaurus" under Advanced Search.

    c. Does limiting the results to only those documents containing the specific term "home sale" improve your results?

    d. How do most tax documents refer to a person's home?

I:15-39 *Determining Acquiescence.*

    a. What official action (acquiescence or nonacquiescence) did the IRS Commissioner take regarding the 1985 Tax Court decision in *John McIntosh*, 85 T.C. 31 (1985)? (Hint: Consult Actions on Decisions.)

    b. Did this action concern *all* issues in the case? If not, explain. (Before answering this question, consult the headnote to the court opinion.)

I:15-40 *Determining Acquiescence.*

    a. What original action (acquiescence or nonacquiescence) did the IRS Commissioner take regarding the 1952 Tax Court decision in *Streckfus Steamers, Inc.*, 19 T.C.1 (1952)? (Hint: Consult Actions on Decisions.)

    b. Was the action complete or partial?

    c. Did the IRS Commissioner subsequently change his mind? If so, when?

I:15-41 *Determining Acquiescence.*

    a. What original action (acquiescence or nonacquiescence) did the IRS Commissioner take regarding the 1982 Tax Court decision in *Doyle, Dane, Bernbach, Inc.*, 79 T.C. 101 (1982)? (Hint: Consult Actions on Decisions.)

    b. Did the IRS Commissioner subsequently change his mind? If so, when?

I:15-42 *Evaluating a Case.* Look up *James E. Threlkeld*, 87 T.C. 1294 (1988) and answer the questions below.

    a. Was the case reviewed by the court? If so, was the decision unanimous? Explain.

    b. Was the decision entered under Rule 155?

    c. Consult a citator. Was the case reviewed by an appellate court? If so, which one?

I:15-43 *Evaluating a Case.* Look up *Bush Brothers & Co.*, 73 T.C. 424 (1979) and answer the questions below.

    a. Was the case reviewed by the court? If so, was the decision unanimous? Explain.

    b. Was the decision entered under Rule 155?

    c. Consult a citator. Was the case reviewed by an appellate court? If so, which one?

I:15-44 *Writing Citations.* Provide the proper citations (including both primary and secondary citations where applicable) for the authorities listed below. (For secondary citations, reference both the AFTR and USTC.)

    a. *National Cash Register Co.*, a 6th Circuit Court decision

    b. *Thomas M. Dragoun v. CIR*, a Tax Court memo decision

    c. *John M. Grabinski v. U.S.*, a U.S. district court decision

    d. *John M. Grabinski v. U.S.*, an Eighth Circuit Court decision

    e. *Rebekah Harkness*, a 1972 Court of Claims decision

    f. *Hillsboro National Bank v. CIR*, a Supreme Court decision

    g. Rev. Rul. 78-129

I:15-45 *Writing Citations.* Provide the proper citations (including both primary and secondary citations where applicable) for the authorities listed below. (For secondary citations, reference both the AFTR and USTC.)

    a. Rev. Rul. 99-7

    b. *Frank H. Sullivan*, a Board of Tax Appeals decision

    c. *Tate & Lyle, Inc.*, a 1994 Tax Court decision

    d. *Ralph L. Rogers v. U.S.*, a U.S. district court decision

    e. *Norman Rodman v. CIR*, a Second Circuit Court decision

I:15-46 *Interpreting Citations.* Indicate which courts decided the cases cited below. Also indicate on which pages and in which publications the authority is reported.

    a. *Lloyd M. Shumaker v. CIR*, 648 F.2d 1198, 48 AFTR 2d 81-5353 (9th Cir., 1981)

    b. *Xerox Corp. v. U.S.*, 14 Cl. Ct. 455, 88-1 USTC ¶9231 (1988)

    c. *Real Estate Land Title & Trust Co. v. U.S.*, 309 U.S. 13, 23 AFTR 816 (USSC, 1940)

    d. *J. B. Morris v. U.S.*, 441 F. Supp. 76, 41 AFTR 2d 78-335 (DC TX, 1977)

    e. Rev. Rul. 83-3, 1983-1 C.B. 72

    f. *Malone & Hyde, Inc. v. U.S.*, 568 F.2d 474, 78-1 USTC ¶9199 (6th Cir., 1978)

I:15-47 *Using a Tax Service.* Use the topical index of the *United States Tax Reporter* to locate authorities dealing with the deductibility of the cost of a facelift.

    a. In which paragraph(s) does the *United States Tax Reporter* summarize and cite these authorities?

    b. List the authorities.

    c. May a taxpayer deduct the cost of a facelift paid in the current year? Explain.

I:15-48 ***Using a Tax Service.*** Locate Reg. Sec. 1.302-1 using either CHECKPOINT or INTELLI-CONNECT. Does this Treasury Regulation reflect recent amendments to the IRC? Explain.

I:15-49 ***Using a Tax Service.*** Using the topical index of the *Standard Federal Income Tax Reporter* in INTELLICONNECT, locate authorities addressing whether termite damage constitutes a casualty loss.
a. In which paragraph(s) does the *Standard Federal Income Tax Reporter* summarize and cite these authorities?
b. List three authorities cited by the Reporter.

I:15-50 ***Using a Tax Service.***
a. Using the *Standard Federal Income Tax Reporter* in INTELLICONNECT, locate where Sec. 303(b)(2)(A) appears. This provision states that Sec. 303(a) applies only if the stock in question meets a certain percentage test. What is the applicable percentage?
b. Locate Reg. Sec. 1.303-2(a) in the same service. Does this Treasury Regulation reflect recent amendments to the IRC with respect to the percentage test addressed in Part a? Explain.

I:15-51 ***Using a Tax Service.*** Using the BNA tax service, identify the number of the BNA portfolio for the following subjects.
a. Innocent spouse relief.
b. Accounting methods.
c. Involuntary conversions.
d. IRAs.
e. Deductibility of legal and accounting fees, bribes, and illegal payments.

I:15-52 ***Using a Tax Service.*** This problem deals with CHECKPOINT's *Federal Tax Coordinator 2d.* Use the topical index CHECKPOINT to locate authorities dealing with the deductibility of the cost of work clothing by ministers (clergymen). List the authorities.

I:15-53 ***Using a Citator.*** Trace *Biltmore Homes, Inc.,* a 1960 Tax Court memo decision, in both the INTELLICONNECT and CHECKPOINT citators.
a. According to the CHECKPOINT citator, how many times has the Tax Court decision been cited by other courts on Headnote Number 5?
b. How many issues did the lower court address in its opinion? (Hint: Refer to the case headnote numbers.)
c. Did an appellate court review the case? If so, which one?
d. According to the INTELLICONNECT citator, how many times has the Tax Court decision been cited by other courts?
e. According to the INTELLICONNECT citator, how many times has the circuit court decision been cited by other courts on Headnote Number 5?

I:15-54 ***Using a Citator.*** Trace *Stephen Bolaris,* 776 F.2d 1428, in both the INTELLICONNECT and CHECKPOINT citators.
a. According to the CHECKPOINT citator, how many times has the Ninth Circuit's decision been cited?
b. Did the decision address more than one issue? Explain.
c. Was the decision ever cited unfavorably? Explain.
d. According to the INTELLICONNECT citator, how many times has the Ninth Circuit's decision been cited?
e. According to the INTELLICONNECT citator, how many times has the Tax Court's decision been cited on Headnote Number 1?

I:15-55 ***Interpreting a Case.*** Using either CHECKPOINT or INTELLICONNECT refer to the *Holden Fuel Oil Company,* RIA T.C. Memo ¶72,045 (T.C. Memo 1972-45), 31 TCM 184.
a. In which year was the case decided?
b. What controversy was litigated?
c. Who won the case?
d. Was the decision reviewed at the lower court level?
e. Was the decision appealed?
f. Has the decision been cited in other cases?

I:15-56 ***Internet Research.*** Access the IRS Internet site at *www.irs.gov* and answer the following questions:
a. How does one file a tax return electronically?
b. How can the taxpayer transmit funds electronically?
c. What are the advantages of electronic filing?

I:15-57 *Internet Research.* Access the IRS Internet site at *www.irs.gov* and indicate the titles of the following IRS forms:
a. Form 4506
b. Form 973
c. Form 8725

I:15-58 *Internet Research.* Access the Federation of Tax Administrators Internet site at *www. taxadmin.org/fta/link/forms.html* and indicate the titles of the following state tax forms and publications:
a. Minnesota Form M-100
b. Illinois Individual Schedule CR
c. New York State Corporate Form CT-3-C

I:15-59 *Internet Research.* Access the Urban Institute and Brookings Institution Tax Policy Center at *taxpolicycenter.org.* On the home page, search for *state individual income tax rates* and locate the Tax Policy Center's latest summary of each state's rates. Researchers also can locate the file by looking under the TAX FACTS tab and then the *State* tab, *Main Features of State Tax Systems.*
a. How many states do not have a state individual income tax?
b. How many states tax only interest and dividends for individuals?
c. What is the top marginal individual income tax rate in Oregon?
d. Of those that do impose an income tax, which state's top marginal rate is lowest?

COMPREHENSIVE PROBLEM

I:15-60 Your client, a physician, recently purchased a yacht on which he flies a pennant with a medical emblem on it. He recently informed you that he purchased the yacht and flies the pennant to advertise his occupation and thus attract new patients. He has asked you if he may deduct as ordinary and necessary business expenses the costs of insuring and maintaining the yacht. In search of an answer, consult either INTELLICONNECT's *Standard Federal Income Tax Reporter* or CHECKPOINT's *United States Tax Reporter.* Explain the steps taken to find your answer.

TAX STRATEGY PROBLEM

I:15-61 Your client, Home Products Universal (HPU), distributes home improvement products to independent retailers throughout the country. Its management wants to explore the possibility of opening its own home improvement centers. Accordingly, it commissions a consulting firm to conduct a feasibility study, which ultimately persuades HPU to expand into retail sales. The consulting firm bills HPU $150,000, which HPU deducts on its current year tax return. The IRS disputes the deduction, contending that, because the cost relates to entering a new business, it should be capitalized. HPU's management, on the other hand, firmly believes that, because the cost relates to expanding HPU's existing business, it should be deducted. In contemplating legal action against the IRS, HPU's management considers the state of judicial precedent: The federal court for HPU's district has ruled that the cost of expanding from distribution into retail sales should be capitalized. The appellate court for HPU's circuit has stated in *dictum* that, although in some circumstances switching from product distribution to product sales entails entering a new trade or business, improving customer access to one's existing products generally does not. The Federal Circuit Court has ruled that wholesale distribution and retail sales, even of the same product, constitute distinct businesses. In a case involving a taxpayer from another circuit, the Tax Court has ruled that such costs invariably should be capitalized. HPU's Chief Financial Officer approaches you with the question, "In which judicial forum should HPU file a lawsuit against the IRS: (1) U.S. district court, (2) the Tax Court, or (3) the U.S. Court of Federal Claims?" What do you tell her?

CASE STUDY PROBLEM

I:15-62 A client, Mal Manley, fills out his client questionnaire for the previous year and on it provides information for the preparation of his individual income tax return. The IRS has never audited Mal's returns. Mal reports that he made over 100 relatively small cash contributions totaling $24,785 to charitable organizations. In the last few years, Mal's charitable contributions have averaged about $15,000 per year. For the previous year, Mal's adjusted gross income was roughly $350,000, about a 10% increase from the year before.

Required: Applying *Statements on Standards for Tax Services* No. 3, determine whether you can accept at face value Mal's information concerning his charitable contributions. Now assume that the IRS recently audited Mal's tax return for two years ago and denied 75% of that year's charitable contribution deduction because the deduction was not substantiated. Assume also that Mal indicates that, in the previous year, he contributed $25,000 (instead of $24,785). How do these changes of fact affect your earlier decision?

TAX RESEARCH PROBLEMS

I:15-63 The purpose of this problem is to enhance your skills in interpreting the authorities that you locate in your research. In answering the questions that follow, refer only to *Thomas A. Curtis, M.D., Inc.,* 1994 RIA TC Memo ¶94,015 (T.C. Memo 1994-15), 67 TCM 1958.
a. What was the principal controversy litigated in this case?
b. Which party—the taxpayer or the IRS—won?
c. Why is the corporation instead of Dr. and/or Ms. Curtis listed as the plaintiff?
d. What is the relationship between Ellen Barnert Curtis and Dr. Thomas A. Curtis?
e. Approximately how many hours a week did Ms. Curtis work, and what were her credentials?
f. For the fiscal year ending in 1989, what salary did the corporation pay Ms. Curtis? What amount did the court decide was reasonable?
g. What dividends did the corporation pay for its fiscal years ending in 1988 and 1989?
h. To which circuit would this decision be appealable?
i. According to *Curtis,* what five factors did the Ninth Circuit mention in *Elliotts, Inc.* as relevant in determining reasonable compensation?

I:15-64 Josh contributes $5,000 toward the support of his widowed mother, aged 69, a U.S. citizen and resident. She earns gross income of $2,000 and spends it all for her own support. In addition, Medicare pays $3,200 of her medical expenses. She does not receive financial support from sources other than those described above. Must the Medicare payments be included in the support that Josh's mother is deemed to provide for herself?
Prepare work papers and a client letter (to Josh) dealing with the issue.

I:15-65 Amy owns a vacation cottage in Maine. She predicts that the time during which the cottage will be used in the current year is as follows:

By Amy, solely for vacation	12 days
By Amy, making repairs ten hours per day and vacationing the rest of the day	2 days
By her sister, who paid fair rental value	8 days
By her cousin, who paid fair rental value	4 days
By her friend, who paid a token amount of rent	2 days
By three families from the Northeast, who paid fair rental value for 40 days each	120 days
Not used	217 days

Calculate the ratio for allocating the following expenses to the rental income expected to be received from the cottage: interest, taxes, repairs, insurance, and depreciation. The ratio will be used to determine the amount of expenses that are deductible and, thus, Amy's taxable income for the year.

For the tax manager to whom you report, prepare work papers in which you discuss the calculation method. Also, draft a memo to the file dealing with the results of your research.

I:15-66 Look up *Summit Publishing Company,* 1990 PH T.C. Memo ¶90,288, 59 (T.C. Memo 1990-288) TCM 833, and *J.B.S. Enterprises,* 1991 PH T.C. Memo ¶91,254, (T.C. Memo 1991-254) 61 TCM 2829, and answer the following questions:
a. What was the principal issue in these cases?
b. What factors did the Tax Court consider in resolving the central issue?
c. How are the facts of these cases similar? How are they dissimilar?

I:15-67 Your supervisor would like to set up a single Sec. 401(k) plan exclusively for the managers of your organization. Concerned that this arrangement might not meet the requirements for a qualified plan, he has asked you to request a determination letter from the IRS. In a brief memorandum, address the following issues:

a. What IRS pronouncements govern requests for determination letters?
b. What IRS forms must be filed with the request?
c. What information must be provided in the request?
d. What actions must accompany the filing?
e. Where must the request be filed?

CHAPTER

16

CORPORATIONS

LEARNING OBJECTIVES

After studying this chapter, you should be able to

1. ▶ Define the types of entities that can be classified as a corporation for federal income tax purposes

2. ▶ Examine specific rules that apply to corporations

3. ▶ Calculate the corporate income tax liability

4. ▶ Apply the nonrecognition of gain or loss rules for corporate capitalizations

5. ▶ Understand the significance of earnings and profits

6. ▶ Determine the tax consequences of noncash distributions and stock redemptions

7. ▶ Understand the tax implications of a corporate liquidation for the liquidating corporation and its shareholders

8. ▶ Describe tax planning considerations for corporations

9. ▶ Describe compliance and procedural considerations for corporations

ADDITIONAL COMMENT

In 2013, total federal tax collections were $2,855 billion. Corporate income taxes accounted for 10.9% of federal tax revenues. Noncorporate (individual, trust, estate, etc.) income taxes accounted for 54.8% of federal tax revenues.

A business may be organized and operated as a **sole proprietorship, C corporation, S corporation, partnership, limited liability company (LLC),** or **limited liability partnership (LLP)**. These business forms fall into two major categories: taxable entities and flow-through entities. The latter category also is referred to as tax conduits or pass-through entities. Sole proprietorships and C corporations fall into the taxable entity category although sole proprietorships are subject to a single level of tax, while C corporations are subject to two levels of tax. A sole proprietorship is not taxed directly because it is not considered to be a separate legal entity. Rather, the individual owner is taxed directly and reports the sole proprietorship's business income and expenses on Schedule C of Form 1040 (U.S. Individual Income Tax Return). The C corporation also is taxed directly and reports its tax results on Form 1120 (U.S. Corporation Income Tax Return). In addition, the corporation's shareholders are taxed if the C corporation pays dividends to them or if the shareholders sell their stock at a gain.[1] In this way, the C corporation organizational form results in two levels of taxation: once at the corporate level when income is earned and again at the shareholder level when income is distributed.

Despite its double taxation and sometimes complicated legal form, the corporation has the dual advantages of facilitating external financing and limiting the shareholders' legal liability. Some tax analysts question whether the burden of corporate taxation is borne directly by the corporate enterprise. These analysts argue that, depending on market conditions and terms of trade, the corporate enterprise might be able to shift the burden to consumers in the form of higher prices, employees in the form of lower salaries and wages, tenants in the form of higher rents, and shareholders in the form of lower dividends and stock values.

Flow-through entities, such as S corporations, partnerships, and limited liability companies, entail only one level of taxation at the ownership level. Accordingly, the entities themselves are not taxed, and the income and losses pass through to the shareholders of the S corporation, the partners of the partnership, or the members of the limited liability company. The owners then report the pass-through items on their separate tax returns and may offset a pro rata share of entity losses against their separate income. Some of these entities, such as S corporations and limited liability companies, offer the advantage of limiting all of their owners' legal liability. Such a feature is advantageous, especially where the business incurs extraordinary liability. Nevertheless, flow-through entities involve certain legal complexities and restrictions, which is one disadvantage of this form of organization. A comparison of the number of tax returns filed and taxable income for the four major business forms through tax year 2013 can be found in Table I:16-1.

This chapter explores the tax consequences of forming, operating, and liquidating a C corporation. Chapter I:17 discusses the basic tax rules pertaining to flow-through entities, and Table I:17-2 at the end of that chapter compares the alternative forms of business organizations. Detailed coverage of these two areas of taxation are reserved for this text's companion volume titled *Prentice Hall's Federal Taxation: Corporations, Partnerships, Estates, and Trusts.*

DEFINITION OF A CORPORATION

OBJECTIVE 1

Define the types of entities that can be classified as a corporation for federal income tax purposes

Under Treasury Regulations,[2] a business entity with two or more owners may be classified as either a corporation or a partnership. An entity having only one owner may be classified as a corporation or a sole proprietorship. A business entity is a corporation if it is organized under a federal or state statute that refers to the entity as incorporated or as a corporation, body corporate, body politic, joint-stock company, or joint-stock association. Corporations also include insurance companies, state-chartered banks, and business entities wholly owned by a state or political subdivision. In general, with rare exceptions if a business entity incorporates, it is taxed as a corporation.

---

[1] A corporate liquidation is treated as a sale in which a shareholder receives cash and/or other assets from the liquidating corporation in exchange for his or her stock. The shareholder's recognized gain or loss upon a liquidating distribution generally is capital in character (IRC Sec. 331(a)). This topic is explored in greater detail in a later section of this chapter.

[2] Reg. Secs. 301.7701-1, -2, and -3.

▼ TABLE I:16-1

Comparison—Types of Returns

Taxpayer Class	Number of Returns Filed (in millions)				
	2013	2012	2011	2010	2009
Individuals	145.996	146.244	143.608	141.167	144.103
Partnerships	3.686	3.626	3.574	3.509	3.565
S corporations	4.566	4.580	4.545	4.508	4.496
C corporations[a, b]	2.248	2.263	2.313	2.356	2.476
Estates and Trusts	3.192	3.061	3.106	3.074	3.143

IRS, *Data Book*, 2013.
[a]The number shown includes returns for various types of domestic and foreign corporations and associations.
[b]Tax-exempt organizations filed 1,132,000 Form 990 series returns in 2009, 1,343,000 in 2010, 1,385,000 in 2012, 1,367,000 in 2012, and 1,463,000 in 2013.

On the other hand, if the business entity has two or more owners and is organized as a partnership, limited liability company, or limited liability partnership, the entity can elect to be *taxed* as either a partnership or corporation. The "check-the-box" regulations replace prior entity classification rules that involved subjective judgment and opened the door to manipulation.

EXAMPLE I:16-1 ► Al and Jane incorporate a business in Delaware. Because it is legally incorporated, the business is taxed as a corporation. Bill and Max form a limited liability company in Florida. For federal income tax purposes, the limited liability company can elect to be taxed as a corporation or a partnership. ◄

SIMILARITIES AND DIFFERENCES BETWEEN THE TAXATION OF CORPORATIONS AND INDIVIDUALS

Similarities. The computation of corporate taxable income is similar to that of sole proprietorship income. For example, under Sec. 162 corporations can deduct ordinary and necessary business expenses. They also may exclude from gross income items such as tax-exempt interest and life insurance proceeds. Corporations also can deduct interest, depreciation, and other business-related expenses in a manner similar to that of unincorporated businesses.

In general, the IRC authorizes all taxpayers to use one of three methods of accounting—the accrual method, the cash method, and the hybrid method.[3] However, with certain exceptions C corporations generally must use the accrual method of accounting unless they meet certain conditions. Sec. 448 permits corporations engaged in a farming business, qualified personal service corporations, and entities having less than $5 million in gross receipts for each of the three prior tax years to use the cash method of accounting.[4] To simplify recordkeeping requirements for small businesses, Rev. Proc. 2002-28 permits qualified small businesses to adopt the cash method of accounting instead of the accrual method.[5]

[3] For a more complete discussion of accounting methods, (see Chapter I:11).
[4] Sec. 448(b).
[5] Rev. Proc. 2002-28, 2002-1 C.B. 815 as modified by Rev. Proc. 2012-20,

2012-14 I.R.B. 700. An eligible business has gross receipts of $10 million or less for all prior three-taxable year periods and not prohibited under Sec. 448 from otherwise using the cash method of accounting.

Corporations are entitled to many of the tax benefits available to sole proprietorships. C corporations can elect to claim the Sec. 179 expensing deduction that is available to sole proprietorships and partnerships. They also are eligible to claim the first-year bonus depreciation when available. In addition, owners of small corporations are eligible for a special exclusion of part or all of their gain on the sale of qualifying stock under Sec. 1202. Since 2003, capital gains rates on individuals have been lowered, thereby reducing the effective cost of selling a stock investment. Most investors will pay a 15% marginal tax rate on a stock gain. Similarly, most dividend income earned by individuals is now taxed at the same low rate.

ADDITIONAL COMMENT

According to a Tax Foundation estimate, Fortune 500 companies spend an average of $2.4 million per year on income-tax compliance. Approximately 70% is attributable to the federal income tax, especially provisions relating to foreign-source income and the alternative minimum tax.

Differences. One principal difference in computing corporate taxable income compared to individual taxable income is that personal, consumption-type expenditure write-offs and exemptions apply solely to individuals. A few differences are worth noting:

▶ Computation of *adjusted gross income* (AGI) applies only to individuals.

▶ Corporations are not entitled to the standard deduction or personal and dependency exemptions.

▶ Corporations are entitled to a dividends-received deduction of 70%, 80%, or 100% for qualifying dividends.

▶ Dividends received by an individual from a domestic corporation are typically taxed at 15%, although the rate for some taxpayers is 0% or 20%. The 0% rate applies only to individuals whose income falls in the 10% or 15% tax bracket. The 20% rate applies only to individuals whose income falls in the 39.6% bracket.

ADDITIONAL COMMENT

Because dividends are subject to the 3.8% surtax on net investment income beginning in 2013, the overall rate on qualified dividends for some taxpayers is 23.8%.

▶ Corporations are not allowed preferential tax treatment for net long-term capital gains nor are they allowed to deduct net capital losses against ordinary income. Individuals are allowed preferential tax treatment for net long-term capital gains and may deduct up to $3,000 per year of net capital losses against ordinary income.

▶ Corporate charitable contribution deductions are limited to 10% of taxable income (with certain adjustments described on page I:16-7 of this chapter), whereas individual charitable contribution deductions generally are limited to 50% of AGI.

SPECIFIC RULES APPLICABLE TO CORPORATIONS

OBJECTIVE 2

Examine specific rules that apply to corporations

CAPITAL GAINS AND LOSSES

The rules for netting long- and short-term capital gains and losses, netting Sec. 1231 (i.e., business fixed assets) gains and losses, and capital gain and loss holding periods are the same for both corporations and individuals. The netting process can be summarized as follows (see Schedule D of Form 1120–Capital Gains and Losses available on the IRS website):

▶ Long-term capital gains (LTCGs) are netted against long-term capital losses (LTCLs).

▶ Short-term capital gains (STCGs) are netted against short-term capital losses (STCLs).

▶ A net long-term capital gain (NLTCG) is then offset against a net short-term capital loss (NSTCL).

▶ A net long-term capital loss (NLTCL) is then offset against a net short-term capital gain (NSTCG).

▶ Following this initial netting process, if a corporation reports both a NLTCG and a NSTCG, both the NSTCG and the NLTCG are taxed at ordinary income rates.

▶ NSTCGs are netted against NLTCLs, and any excess is taxed at ordinary income rates.

▶ NLTCLs and NSTCLs may not be deducted from ordinary income.

EXAMPLE I:16-2 ▶ Gulf Corporation realizes the following capital gains and losses during the current year:

LTCG	$15,000
LTCL	5,000
STCG	3,000
STCL	8,000

Gulf has a $10,000 NLTCG and a $5,000 NSTCL. The NLTCG is offset against the NSTCL, resulting in a $5,000 net capital gain that is taxed at ordinary income rates. ◀

EXAMPLE I:16-3 ▶ High Corporation realizes the following capital gains and losses during the current year:

LTCG	$15,000
LTCL	5,000
STCG	10,000
STCL	8,000

High has a $10,000 NLTCG and a $2,000 NSTCG. Both the $2,000 NSTCG and the $10,000 NLTCG are taxed at ordinary income rates. ◀

EXAMPLE I:16-4 ▶ Huge Corporation realizes the following capital gains and losses during the current year:

LTCG	$ 5,000
LTCL	15,000
STCG	8,000
STCL	10,000

Huge Corporation has a $10,000 NLTCL and a $2,000 NSTCL. In computing its current year taxable income, Huge may not deduct either net loss against its ordinary income. ◀

SELF-STUDY QUESTION

What are the major differences in the taxation of the capital gains and losses of individuals and corporations?

Corporate Capital Loss Limitations. For corporations, neither a NLTCL nor a NSTCL is deductible against ordinary income in the year it is incurred. Instead, it is eligible for a 3-year carryback and 5-year carryforward and may be offset against capital gains in those years.[6] Both the NSTCL and the NLTCL are treated as STCLs for purposes of the carryback and carryforward. The corporate capital loss limitations and carryback-carryforward rules differ from those applicable to noncorporate taxpayers (see the discussion in Chapter I:5).[7]

EXAMPLE I:16-5 ▶ Assume the same facts as in Example I:16-4. The $10,000 NLTCL and the $2,000 NSTCL are nondeductible in the current year. The $12,000 ($10,000 + $2,000) is carried back as a STCL to the third previous year. If the net gains in the carryback years are insufficient to absorb the $12,000 STCL, the excess is carried over up to 5 years. ◀

ANSWER

First, an individual can offset $3,000 of capital losses against ordinary income. Second, an individual has an indefinite carryforward instead of a 3-year carryback and a 5-year carryforward that applies to corporations. Third, all corporate capital loss carrybacks and carryforwards are treated as STCLs. Finally, noncorporate taxpayers receive a preferential tax rate on most net capital gains. A 0% maximum rate applies to taxpayers in tax brackets of 15% or lower, a 15% rate applies for taxpayers in the 25% through 35% tax brackets, and a 20% rate applies to taxpayers in the 39.6% tax bracket. However, taxpayers whose modified AGI exceeds $200,000 ($250,000 for married filing jointly) have to apply an additional 3.8% rate to net investment income.

DIVIDENDS-RECEIVED DEDUCTION

Corporations may deduct 80% of dividends received from a domestic corporation if the recipient corporation owns 20% or more of the voting power and value of the dividend-paying corporation's stock.[8] If a corporation owns less than 20% of the dividend-paying corporation's stock, the deduction is 70% of dividends received. The percentage increases to 100% if the dividend is received from an 80%-or-more-owned corporation for which a consolidated tax return election has not been made. This deduction mitigates the onerous effects of triple taxation, where one corporation (a subsidiary) pays dividends to a corporate shareholder (its parent corporation), which in turn distributes an equal amount to its shareholders.

The following table sets forth the dividends-received deduction percentages.

Percentage of Stock Owned	Dividends-Received Deduction
Less than 20%	70%
20% through 79.99%	80%
80% or more	100%

---

[6] Secs. 1211(a) and 1212(a).
[7] Noncorporate taxpayers (e.g., individuals) can deduct up to $3,000 of net capital losses against ordinary income annually. Unused capital losses of a noncorporate taxpayer are carried over (but not carried back) for an indefinite time period and retain their character as long- or short-term.
[8] The dividends-received deduction rules are set forth in Secs. 243 and 246.

The 80% and 70% **dividends-received deductions** are subject to the following limitations:

▶ The dividends-received deduction is limited to 80% (or 70%) of taxable income computed without regard to the net operating loss (NOL) deduction, the dividends-received deduction, or capital loss carrybacks to the limitation year.

▶ The limitation does not apply if the corporation generates an NOL in the current year after taking the dividends-received deduction determined under the general rules.

▶ The dividends-received deduction is not available if the distributing corporation's stock is held by the distributee for 45 or fewer days within the 90-day period that commences 45 days before the ex-dividend date.

EXAMPLE I:16-6 ▶ King Corporation reports the following income and expense items during the current year:

Net income from operations	$ 50,000
Dividends from two 20%-owned corporations	200,000

The dividends-received deduction determined under the general rule is $160,000 (0.80 × $200,000 dividends). The deduction limitation is $200,000 (0.80 × $250,000 of taxable income before the dividends-received deduction). Because the limitation ($200,000) exceeds the dividends-received deduction determined under the general rule ($160,000), the entire $160,000 dividends-received deduction is allowed. ◀

EXAMPLE I:16-7 ▶ Assume the same facts as in Example I:16-6, except that the corporation incurred a $10,000 net loss from operations. The dividends-received deduction determined under the general rule is $160,000 (0.80 × $200,000 dividends). The limitation under the general rule is based on taxable income before the dividends-received deduction of $190,000 ($200,000 − $10,000). The limitation is $152,000 (0.80 × $190,000). As illustrated below, no NOL results after deducting the entire 80% dividends-received deduction determined under the general rule:

Net loss from operations	$ (10,000)
Plus: Dividends received from 20% (or more) owned corporations	200,000
Minus: Dividends-received deduction (0.80 × $200,000)	(160,000)
Taxable income as determined under the general rule	$ 30,000

Because the dividends-received deduction is limited to $152,000, the recognized taxable income for the year is $38,000 ($190,000 − $152,000). ◀

EXAMPLE I:16-8 ▶ Assume the same facts as in Example I:16-7, except that the loss from operations is $50,000. The dividends-received deduction determined under the general rule is $160,000 (0.80 × $200,000 dividends). The limitation is $120,000 (0.80 × $150,000 of taxable income before the dividends-received deduction). The limitation, however, does not apply because a $10,000 NOL results after taking the entire dividends-received deduction determined under the general rule.

Net loss from operations	$ (50,000)
Plus: Dividends received	200,000
Minus: Dividends-received deduction (0.80 × $200,000)	(160,000)
Taxable income	$ (10,000)

Therefore, the entire $160,000 dividends-received deduction is allowed. ◀

EXAMPLE I:16-9 ▶ On June 1, Lean Corporation acquires 5% of Madison Corporation stock. Madison pays a cash dividend to all shareholders of record on June 15. Lean receives the dividend on June 20. On July 1, Lean sells its Madison stock. A dividends-received deduction is not allowed because Lean does not own the Madison stock for the required 46 days within the 90-day period that commences 45 days before the ex-dividend date (June 15). ◀

NET OPERATING LOSSES

Unlike the computation of individual NOLs, the computation of a corporate **net operating loss (NOL)** does not involve adjusting nonbusiness deductions and capital gains and losses. (See Chapter I:8 for a discussion of these adjustments for individuals.[9]) In the

---

[9] The NOL rules are set forth in Sec. 172.

corporate NOL computation, the full dividends-received deduction is allowed. However, no deduction for an NOL carryover or carryback from a preceding or succeeding year is allowed.

EXAMPLE I:16-10 ▶ The computation of Maine Corporation's NOL for 2015 is based on the following taxable items:

Operating income	$ 400,000
Plus: Dividends received from 20% (or more) owned corporations	300,000
Gross income	$ 700,000
Minus: Business operating expenses	(600,000)
Dividends-received deduction (0.80 × $300,000)	(240,000)
Net operating loss	$(140,000)

In general, NOLs are carried back two years (beginning with the earliest NOL tax year). Any excess amounts are carried forward up to 20 years to offset taxable income in those years. Thus, Maine's NOLs can be carried back to 2013 and 2014. Any remaining NOL is carried forward to years 2016–2035.[10] ◄

A corporation may elect to forgo the NOL carryback and instead carry the loss forward. For example, if the corporation has taxable income less than $75,000 in the carryback year(s) subject to tax rates less than 34%, the tax benefit of an NOL carryback might be limited because the carryback offsets income taxed at relatively low rates. The tax benefit of the NOL might be greater if the carryback is forgone and the NOL is carried over to a year in which the marginal tax rate is 34% or higher. However, the carryover would defer tax savings, whereas a carryback would produce an immediate tax benefit. The election, if made, applies to all carryback years, and the NOL carries forward for up to 20 years.

CHARITABLE CONTRIBUTIONS

Some of the charitable contribution rules applicable to individuals also apply to corporations (e.g., the restriction on contributions of ordinary income property discussed in Chapter I:7).[11] The following rules apply solely to corporations:

▶ Under the general rule, a payment must be made before a contribution deduction is allowed. However, corporations using the accrual method of accounting may accrue a contribution deduction in the year preceding payment if before the end of the tax year the contribution is authorized by the board of directors and is made within 2½ months of the end of the tax year.

▶ Section 170(e) allows an increased charitable deduction for certain corporate property contributions. The increased deduction is available for (1) property used to care for the ill, needy, or infants; (2) scientific research property used by colleges or universities for research and experimentation; and (3) computer technology, software, and peripherals donated to educational institutions for use in grades kindergarten through 12. In each case the amount of the deduction equals the donor's adjusted basis in the property plus one-half of the excess of the property's FMV over its adjusted basis (not to exceed twice the property's adjusted basis).

▶ Corporate charitable contributions are limited to 10% of taxable income (computed without regard to the charitable contribution deduction, NOL and capital loss carry-*backs*, or the dividends-received deduction).

▶ Unused contribution amounts are carried forward 5 years. In the carryover year, the current year's contribution amount first is deducted to the extent of the 10% limitation. Contribution carryovers from the earliest year then are deducted to the extent of any unused limitation amount.

---

[10] NOLs incurred in tax years beginning before August 6, 1997 are carried back three years and forward 15 years. IRC Sec. 172(f) contains special rules that permit three-year or longer carryback periods. Corporate losses eligible for special carrybacks include presidentially declared disaster area losses (one year), product liability losses (10 years), and losses arising in 2001 and 2002 (five years). Losses incurred after 1998 may be carried forward up to 20 years.

[11] Rules pertaining to charitable contributions are set forth in Sec. 170.

EXAMPLE I:16-11 ▶ Mesa Corporation reports the following results for 2015:

Taxable income (before deducting dividends-received and charitable contributions)	$130,000
Dividends-received deduction	10,000
Charitable contributions	20,000

Mesa has never incurred an NOL. The limitation on contributions is $13,000 ($130,000 × 0.10), and taxable income is $107,000 ($130,000 − $13,000 − $10,000). The $7,000 ($20,000 − $13,000) excess contribution amount carries forward 5 years (2016–2020). ◀

EXAMPLE I:16-12 ▶ Assume that the same facts in Example I:16-11 in 2016, except that taxable income (before deducting dividends-received and charitable contributions) is $220,000. The contribution limitation now is $22,000 ($220,000 × 0.10). The $20,000 charitable contribution for 2016 first is deducted to the extent of the $22,000 limitation, leaving a $2,000 unused excess. Thus, $2,000 of the carryforward from 2015 is deductible to the extent of this unused limitation, leaving a $5,000 carryforward from 2015, which may be used in tax years 2017 through 2020. ◀

COMPENSATION DEDUCTION LIMITATION FOR PUBLICLY HELD CORPORATIONS

A publicly held corporation is denied a deduction for compensation paid to its chief executive officer and its four highest-compensated officers if the compensation for that individual exceeds $1 million per year.[12] Includible compensation includes both cash and noncash benefits. The following types of compensation are not taken into account for purposes of calculating the $1 million limitation:

▶ Remuneration payable on a commission basis

▶ Compensation based on individual performance goals (if approved by certain outside directors and shareholders)[13]

▶ Payments to a qualified retirement plan

▶ Tax-free employee benefits (such as employer-provided health care and Sec. 132 fringe benefits)

EXAMPLE I:16-13 ▶ Pine Corporation is a publicly held company whose securities are listed on the New York Stock Exchange. In the current year, Pine compensates its chief executive officer, Rodney, as follows: salary, $1,200,000; commissions based on sales generated by Rodney, $400,000; payments to a qualified pension plan, $25,000; and tax-free fringe benefits, $10,000. The commissions, payments to the qualified pension plan, and tax-free fringe benefits are not subject to the $1 million annual deduction limitation. Thus, $200,000 ($1,200,000 − $1,000,000) of Rodney's salary is not deductible by Pine even though Rodney is taxed on the entire $1,200,000. ◀

U.S. PRODUCTION ACTIVITIES DEDUCTION

Congress created a special deduction to reduce taxes on U.S. manufacturing activities. Effective as of 2005, the deduction is calculated as a percentage of the lesser of qualified production activities income or taxable income (before considering this deduction). The current percentage for the deduction is 9%.

---

[12] Sec. 162(m). A publicly held corporation is any corporation issuing any class of securities required to be registered under Section 12 of the Securities Exchange Act of 1934. This corporation generally has securities listed on a national securities exchange, or has at least $5 million or more of assets and 500 or more shareholders.

[13] (See Reg. Sec. 1.162-27 for the requirements relating to the attainment of performance goals.)

The deduction is available for income derived from qualified production property manufactured, produced, grown, or extracted in whole or in significant part in the U.S. The deduction is broad in scope because the definition of qualified production property is quite expansive. Qualified production property includes any tangible personal property, computer software, sound recording, qualified firm, electricity, natural gas, or potable water, erection or renovation of buildings or infrastructure, and architectural or engineering services related to construction.

EXAMPLE I:16-14 ▶ Cedar Corporation manufactures widgets in its factory in Birmingham, Alabama. In the current year, its taxable income (before the production deduction) is $300,000 and its net income from qualified production activities is $237,000. Cedar has a qualified production activities deduction of $21,330 (9% of the lesser of $237,000 or $300,000). After claiming this deduction, its taxable income for the current year is $278,670 ($300,000 − $21,330). ◀

For a summary of the rules relating to corporate capital gains and losses, dividends-received deduction, net operating losses, charitable contribution deduction, compensation deduction, and U.S. production activities deduction, see Topic Review I:16-1.

TOPIC REVIEW I:16-1

Summary of Rules for Calculating Corporate Taxable Income

CAPITAL GAINS AND LOSSES

▶ If a net loss results from netting long-term and short-term capital gains and losses, none of this loss can be deducted from ordinary income. Instead, the loss may be carried back 3 years and forward up to 5 years and is treated as short-term in character (i.e., STCL).

▶ Corporate net capital gains do not receive favorable tax treatment. The 15% preferential tax rate for net capital gains (or 0% for lower-income taxpayers and 20% for higher-income taxpayers) applies to individuals but not C corporations.

DIVIDENDS-RECEIVED DEDUCTION

▶ The dividends-received deduction is 80% if the corporate shareholder owns 20% or more of stock in the dividend-paying corporation, and 70% if the corporate shareholder owns less than 20%. A 100% deduction is available for dividends received from an 80%-or-more-owned member of an affiliated group that does not file a consolidated tax return.

▶ The dividends-received deduction is limited to 80% (or 70% as the case may be) of taxable income (after adjustments for the NOL deduction, the dividends-received deduction, and capital loss carrybacks) unless the corporate shareholder generates an NOL after deducting the full amount of dividends-received.

CHARITABLE CONTRIBUTIONS

▶ Accrual-basis corporate donors may accrue a current year deduction if the contribution is authorized by the board of directors and paid within 2½ months after the end of the current tax year.

▶ Corporations are allowed increased deductions for contributions of qualifying property used (1) to care for the ill, needy, or infants, (2) to conduct research or experimentation in colleges or universities, or (3) by educational institutions in grades kindergarten through 12.

▶ Contributions are limited to 10% of taxable income (adjusted for certain taxable items).

▶ Unused charitable contributions are carried forward up to 5 years.

NOLs, COMPENSATION, AND PRODUCTION ACTIVITIES

▶ In general, NOLs may be carried back 2 years (beginning with the earlier year), then forward up to 20 years. The corporation may elect to forgo the 2-year carryback.

▶ Publicly held corporations are denied a deduction for compensation exceeding $1 million paid to certain key executives.

▶ Businesses engaged in manufacturing activities may deduct 9% of the lesser of qualified production activities income or taxable income (before this deduction) for tax years 2010 and after.

COMPUTATION OF TAX

OBJECTIVE 3

Calculate the corporate income tax liability

COMPUTATION OF TAXABLE INCOME

Table I:16-2 illustrates the computation of *taxable income* for a C corporation.

COMPUTATION OF REGULAR TAX

The corporate tax rate schedule is graduated, as follows:[14]

If Taxable Income Is:		The Tax Is:	Of the Amount
Over ...	But Not Over ...		Over ...
$0	$50,000	15%	$0
50,000	75,000	$7,500 + 25%	50,000
75,000	100,000	13,750 + 34%	75,000
100,000	335,000	22,250 + 39%	100,000
335,000	10,000,000	113,900 + 34%	335,000
10,000,000	15,000,000	3,400,000 + 35%	10,000,000
15,000,000	18,333,333	5,150,000 + 38%	15,000,000
18,333,333		6,416,667 + 35%	18,333,333

▼ TABLE I:16-2

Computation of Corporate Taxable Income

Sales	$600,000
Minus: Cost of goods sold	(300,000)
Gross profit	$300,000
Plus: Other income	
Dividends from 25%-owned corporation	$100,000
Interest	10,000
Long-term capital gain	90,000
Gross income	$500,000
Minus: Deductions:	
Salaries	$ 80,000
Repairs	20,000
Bad debts	27,000
Taxes	10,000
Contributions (subject to the 10% corporate limitation, as discussed on page I:16-7)	5,000
Depreciation	20,000
Pension and profit-sharing contributions	35,000
Total deductions	$197,000
Taxable income before special deductions	$303,000
Minus: Special deductions:	
Net operating loss deduction	(15,000)[a]
Dividends-received deduction	(80,000)[b]
U.S. production activities deduction	(12,600)[c]
Taxable income	$195,400

ADDITIONAL COMMENT

Most states impose an income tax on C corporations. Some states exempt S corporations from the state corporate income tax.

[a]This amount represents a net operating loss carried over from a prior year.
[b]0.80 × $100,000 = $80,000 dividends-received deduction.
[c]Assume qualified production income is $140,000. Taxable income before the U.S. production activities deduction is $208,000. Therefore, the U.S. production activities deduction (in years 2010 and after) is $12,600 ($140,000 × 0.09).

[14] Sec. 11(b)(1).

EXAMPLE I:16-15 ▶ Able Corporation's taxable income for the current year is $100,000. Its regular tax liability is computed as follows:

0.15 × $50,000	=	$ 7,500
0.25 × $25,000	=	6,250
0.34 × $25,000	=	8,500
Total tax		$22,250

The total tax due on the $100,000 of taxable income is $22,250. This tax can be computed directly through the tax rate schedule shown on the previous page (or on inside back cover of this textbook). ◀

The 15% and 25% tax rates on the first $75,000 of taxable income, as compared to a flat 34% rate, provide an $11,750 benefit (tax reduction) computed as follows:

Tax on $75,000 at 34%	$25,500
Minus: Tax on $75,000 (from tax rate schedule)	(13,750)
Tax benefit of lower rates	$11,750

Congress wanted only small corporations to obtain this benefit, so it imposed a 5% surtax on taxable income between $100,000 and $335,000. This 5% surtax is reflected in the 39% (34% + 5%) marginal rate in the corporate tax schedule. After taxable income reaches $335,000, the entire benefit of the lower rates is recaptured ($235,000 × 0.05 = $11,750). Thus, corporations with taxable income between $335,000 and $10,000,000 pay a flat tax equal to 34% times taxable income.

EXAMPLE I:16-16 ▶ Ajax Corporation's taxable income for the current year is $335,000. Its tax liability is computed as follows:

0.15 × $ 50,000	=	$ 7,500
0.25 × $ 25,000	=	6,250
0.34 × $260,000	=	88,400
0.05 × $235,000	=	11,750
Total tax		$113,900

The $113,900 tax liability also can be calculated by multiplying 34% times $335,000. Thus, the benefit of the lower rates on the first $75,000 of taxable income is completely phased-out when taxable income reaches $335,000. ◀

KEY POINT

The corporate income tax is essentially flat for corporations with substantial taxable income.

A 35% rate applies to taxable income exceeding $10 million. An additional 3% surtax (reflected in the 38% rate) applies to taxable income between $15 million and $18,333,333. This surtax eliminates the benefit of the 34% rate when taxable income equals or exceeds $18,333,333. Thus, a flat 35% rate applies to taxable income exceeding $18,333,333.

EXAMPLE I:16-17 ▶ Ajax Corporation's taxable income for the current year is $18,333,333. Its tax liability is computed as follows:

0.34 × $10,000,000	=	$3,400,000
0.35 × $ 5,000,000	=	1,750,000
0.38 × $ 3,333,333	=	1,266,667
Total tax		$6,416,667

Effectively, at $18,333,333 of taxable income, the average tax rate is 35% (0.35 × $18,333,333 = $6,416,667). ◀

Special Rule for Personal Service Corporations. Certain personal service corporations are not subject to graduated rates.[15] Rather, a flat 35% rate applies. Applicable personal service corporations are those that perform services in the fields of

---

[15] Sec. 11(b)(2).

health, law, engineering, architecture, accounting, actuarial science, performing arts, or consulting, where substantially all of the corporate stock is held by current or retired employees, or by the estates of deceased employees.

COMPUTATION OF THE CORPORATE ALTERNATIVE MINIMUM TAX (AMT)

The alternative minimum tax (AMT) for corporations is similar to that for individuals (see Chapter I:14 for a discussion of the AMT for individuals).[16] The AMT ensures that taxpayers with substantial economic income pay a minimum amount of federal tax.[17] If a corporation's AMT liability is greater than its regular (income) tax liability, the corporation must pay both the excess amount and the regular tax.

The corporate AMT is 20% of alternative minimum taxable income (AMTI) net of an exemption based on the entity's AMTI. The exemption amount for corporations is $40,000 reduced by 25% of the excess of AMTI over $150,000. This exemption is phased-out when AMTI exceeds $310,000 [$150,000 + (1.0/0.25 × $40,000)].

EXAMPLE I:16-18 ► Allied Corporation reports $200,000 of AMTI before the AMT exemption. The $40,000 exemption amount is reduced by $12,500 [0.25 × ($200,000 − $150,000)] to $27,500 ($40,000 − $12,500). Thus, the AMT base is $172,500 ($200,000 − $27,500). ◄

ADDITIONAL COMMENT

For AMTI through $150,000, the exemption amount is $40,000. For AMTI of $310,000 or more, the exemption amount is $0. Thus, the reduction formula need be applied only when AMTI is between $150,000 and $310,000. For all practical purposes, few corporations will benefit from the exemption as their AMTI will exceed $310,000.

Computation of AMTI. AMTI equals regular taxable income modified by certain adjustments and increased by tax preference items. Tax preference items are subject to some type of preferential tax treatment in the regular income tax system. As with the individual AMT, these items are *added* to regular taxable income to compute AMTI. Because corporations are more likely to have AMT adjustments than tax preferences,[18] only AMT adjustments are discussed in this chapter.

AMT Adjustments. AMT adjustments reflect timing differences relating to deferred income or accelerated deductions. These adjustments generally increase the AMT tax base, while the reversal of these differences may result in a reduction of the AMT tax base over time. When an AMT is paid, an AMT tax credit is available to the corporation to reduce the regular tax liability in subsequent years if its regular tax exceeds its tentative minimum tax. (See Chapter I:14 for a detailed discussion of this topic.) The most common AMT adjustments include the following:

► For real property placed in service after 1986 and before 1999, the difference between the MACRS income tax depreciation claimed and a hypothetical straight-line depreciation amount computed under the alternative depreciation system and a 40-year cost recovery period (see Chapter I:10 for a discussion of the alternative depreciation system).

► For personal property placed in service after 1986, the difference between the MACRS income tax depreciation claimed and the amount calculated under the 150% declining balance method and alternative depreciation system.

► 75% of the excess of adjusted current earnings (ACE) over AMTI (as calculated before the ACE adjustment and the alternative tax NOL deduction but after all other adjustments and tax preference items).[19]

► Regular taxable income (the starting point for calculating AMTI) is net of the U.S. production activities deduction. For regular tax purposes, the deduction is 9% (in 2010 and after) times the lesser of qualified production activities income or taxable income before the deduction. For corporate AMTI purposes, the computation is based on the lesser of qualified production activities income or AMTI before the deduction.

---

[16] The AMT rules are set forth in Secs. 55–58.

[17] The Taxpayer Relief Act of 1997 repealed the corporate AMT for *small corporations* (measured by gross receipts) for tax years beginning after December 31, 1997. For details, see the discussion below.

[18] (See Sec. 57 for a list of tax preference items. Also, see Chapter I:14 for a discussion of these items.)

[19] The term *adjusted current earnings* is based on the earnings and profits definition found in Sec. 312. (See Chapter C:5 of *Prentice Hall's Federal Taxation: Corporations, Partnerships, Estates, and Trusts* for a detailed discussion of this AMT adjustment.)

EXAMPLE I:16-19 ▶

In the current year, Camp Corporation earns taxable income of $100,000, and its regular tax liability is $22,250. Camp's AMT adjustments other than ACE are $80,000, and it has $340,000 of adjusted current earnings. Camp's AMT liability is computed as follows:

Regular taxable income	$100,000
Plus: AMT adjustments other than ACE	80,000
AMTI (before ACE adjustment)	$180,000
Plus: ACE adjustment [0.75 × ($340,000 − $180,000)]	120,000
AMTI	$300,000
Minus: Exemption ($40,000 − [($300,000 − $150,000) × 0.25])	(2,500)
AMT base	$297,500
Times: AMT rate	× .20
Tentative minimum tax	$ 59,500
Minus: Regular tax	(22,250)
AMT liability	$ 37,250

ADDITIONAL COMMENT

Because of the AMT credit, the AMT essentially is a prepaid tax on preference items and adjustments; it affects the timing of the corporation's tax payments.

Camp's total current year tax liability is $59,500 ($22,250 regular tax + $37,250 AMT). In effect, the corporation pays the greater of the regular tax or the tentative minimum tax. Camp also carries over the $37,250 AMT to next year as an AMT credit. For example, if next year's regular tax liability is $30,000 and the tentative minimum tax is $20,000, Camp applies a $10,000 credit against next year's regular tax liability and carries over the remaining $27,250 ($37,250 − $10,000) AMT credit to the following year. The AMT credit has an indefinite life. ◀

STOP & THINK

Question: Corporations that are subject to the AMT typically must alter their tax planning to minimize their overall tax liability. How might a corporation plan the timing of income recognition and deductions for AMT purposes?

Solution: Under the regular tax regime, a corporation might accelerate deductions to the current year and defer income recognition until a future year. While this technique reduces the regular tax, it increases the AMT and for some corporations may produce no tax benefit. Under the AMT regime, the corporation might consider reversing this strategy by accelerating income recognition and deferring deductions. The interplay of regular tax and AMT planning converges to a point where the income tax is reduced to the lowest possible amount without triggering the AMT.

Exception to AMT for Small Corporations. For tax years beginning after 1997, the AMT does not apply to small business corporations. A small business corporation is a corporation whose average gross receipts for each of the three years preceding the year in which the exemption is claimed is $7.5 million or less.[20]

STOP & THINK

Question: Why might Alternative Minimum Taxable Income (AMTI) approximate income for financial accounting purposes to a greater extent than would regular taxable income?

Solution: AMTI could approximate financial accounting income to a greater extent than would regular taxable income for three reasons: First, AMTI includes certain items recognized for financial accounting purposes but not regular tax purposes (e.g., interest on private activity bonds). Second, AMTI generally is based on conservative accounting methods (e.g., less accelerated depreciation rates) that often are adopted for financial accounting purposes, but not regular tax purposes. Third, certain deductions allowed in deriving regular taxable income (e.g., U.S. production activities deduction) are not allowed in deriving either AMTI or financial accounting income. As a result, the liability that a company accrues for AMT purposes could approximate the tax expense that it recognizes for financial accounting purposes to a greater extent than would its regular tax liability.

---

[20] The AMT exemption also applies to a noncorporate entity that elects to be taxed as a C corporation under the check-the-box rules. The calculation of gross receipts is based on the entity's tax year. The $7.5 million maximum is reduced to $5 million for the corporation's first three year period that begins after 1993.

PENALTY TAXES

Intended to deter otherwise abusive tax planning practices are two penalty taxes: the accumulated earnings tax and the personal holding company tax. The computation of both taxes is based on complex rules that are discussed in more detail in the companion volume to this text, *Prentice Hall's Federal Taxation: Corporations, Partnerships, Estates, and Trusts*. These rules are summarized below.

Accumulated Earnings Tax. The **accumulated earnings tax** aims at discouraging companies from retaining excessive earnings invested in assets unrelated to business needs.[21] A company might avoid liability for this tax if its earnings are reinvested in operating assets or retained for the reasonable needs of the business. If not for this tax, closely held corporations might not pay dividends to their shareholders (thereby avoiding the double taxation of their earnings). The retained earnings then might be used for passive investment purposes.

Reasonable needs of the business are associated with numerous activities, including the following:

▶ Reasonably anticipated business expansion and plant replacement

▶ Acquiring the assets or stock (other than portfolio investments) of another business

▶ Providing working capital for the business

▶ Establishing a sinking fund to retire corporate debt

▶ Investing or lending to suppliers or customers

The accumulated earnings tax generally is imposed on closely held corporations. However, the tax may be imposed on a publicly held corporation if effective control is in the hands of a few related shareholders.[22]

The accumulated earnings tax base is the corporation's accumulated taxable income for a particular year. The accumulated earnings tax rate is 20%. Shareholders subject to a tax rate less than 20% on dividends can reduce the corporation's accumulated earnings tax exposure by having the corporation distribute dividends, taxed to the shareholders at a 0% or 15% rate. Accumulated taxable income is computed as follows:

Taxable income	
Plus:	Dividends-received deduction
	Net operating loss deduction
Minus:	Net capital losses
	Net long-term capital gains over net short-term capital losses (less federal income tax on such net gains)
	Federal income tax liability
	Charitable contributions exceeding 10% corporate limitation
	Deductions for dividends paid or deemed paid[23]
	Accumulated earnings credit
Accumulated taxable income	

The accumulated earnings credit equals the greater of (1) $250,000 minus accumulated earnings and profits (E&P) at the beginning of the year[24] or (2) the amount of E&P for the tax year that is retained for the reasonable needs of the business. The reasonable needs of the business are determined at year-end and are reduced by accumulated E&P at the beginning of the year. Thus, only the amount of E&P that is retained to meet the increase in reasonable business needs may be claimed as a credit. (E&P is defined later in this chapter.)

ADDITIONAL COMMENT

When the highest marginal tax rate on individuals was considerably higher than the corporate tax rate, corporations commonly were used as tax shelters. During these years, the accumulated earnings tax and the personal holding company tax had greater importance. In recent years, the highest marginal tax rate for individuals and the corporate tax rate were relatively similar. The accumulated earnings tax rate was reduced to 15% for tax years beginning after December 31, 2002, to match the tax rate on dividends that would apply to most shareholders if the accumulated earnings of the corporation were distributed to the shareholders. In 2013, the accumulated earnings tax rate was increased to 20% to match the highest tax rate on dividends for individuals.

ADDITIONAL COMMENT

The accumulated earnings tax can be avoided by the payment of a large enough dividend or by making an S corporation election. The accumulated earnings tax does not apply during the years the S corporation election is in effect.

---

[21] The basic rules for the accumulated earning tax are set forth in Code Secs. 531–537.

[22] Sec. 532(c) and *Golconda Mining Corp. v. CIR*, 35 AFTR 2d 75-336, 74-2 USTC ¶9845 (9th Cir., 1974).

[23] Sec. 561. The deduction for dividends paid includes dividends actually paid during the tax year and consent dividends (e.g., hypothetical dividends) where

the shareholders agree to be taxed on such amounts. Under Sec. 563, dividends paid during the first 2½ months following the end of the tax year are considered paid on the last day of the preceding tax year.

[24] The $250,000 credit amount is reduced to $150,000 for service corporations engaged in the field of health, law, engineering, architecture, accounting, actuarial science, performing arts, or consulting.

EXAMPLE I:16-20 ▶ In the current year, Compact Corporation earns taxable income of $100,000. Compact's federal tax liability is $22,250, and the corporation paid $10,000 in dividends to its shareholders. Compact claims a deduction of $80,000 for $100,000 of dividends received. Accumulated E&P at the beginning of the year for the reasonable needs of the business is $200,000. Compact's reasonable needs of the business at year-end require $220,000 of funding. Accumulated taxable income and the accumulated earnings credit are computed as follows:

Taxable income		$100,000
Plus: Dividends-received deduction		80,000
Minus: Federal income tax liability		(22,250)
Dividends-paid deduction		(10,000)
Accumulated earnings credit—the greater of:		
(1) $250,000 (statutory exemption) − $200,000 (accumulated E&P at the beginning of the year)	$50,000	
	or	
(2) E&P retained for the increased reasonable needs of the business ($220,000 − $200,000)	$20,000	(50,000)
Accumulated taxable income		$ 97,750

Compact's accumulated earnings tax liability is $19,550 (0.20 × $97,750). It pays this tax in addition to its regular income tax. Compact's total federal tax liability is $41,800 ($22,250 + $19,550). ◀

An IRS auditor will likely examine Schedules L and M-2 of Form 1120 (U.S. Corporation Income Tax Return) to determine if accumulated earnings are excessive. The auditor will examine Schedule L (the balance sheet) to identify the assets owned by the business. Substantial marketable securities, loans to shareholders, and nonbusiness assets (for example, a boat or resort condominium) might suggest that the corporation is retaining excessive earnings. The corporation could have distributed these earnings to its shareholders in the form of dividends. Loans to shareholders might suggest the corporation's reluctance to distribute its earnings. The IRS auditor will look at Schedule M-2 to see if the corporation has declared and paid any dividends to the shareholders. To avoid the accumulated earnings tax the corporation might argue that it has consistently paid dividends.

WHAT WOULD YOU DO IN THIS SITUATION?

Scott, Steve, and Sean own 100% of the outstanding stock of Sofa Corporation for all of the current year. In its first twelve years of existence, Sofa Corporation, a manufacturer of custom-made sofas, never paid a dividend to its shareholders. It preferred instead to retain its earnings for working capital, additional machinery, and short-term investments. Scott and Steve would like to borrow money from Sofa because Scott is planning to open a florist shop, and Steve needs a loan to pay off personal debts. For these reasons, Sofa will not pay a dividend in the current year. However, the company intends to pay dividends next year when the two loans have been paid off. Sofa has accumulated E&P (before any distributions) exceeding $250,000. As Sofa's tax consultant, you inform the shareholders of

the possibility that the company will be liable for the accumulated earnings tax. The shareholders ask you if they should inform the IRS of potentially excessive earnings, voluntarily pay the tax, or just wait to be audited by the IRS.

a. What advice would you give the shareholders regarding reporting the potentially excessive earnings and the payment of the tax? (See the *Statements on Responsibilities in Tax Practice* section in Chapter I:15 and Appendix E.)

b. What advice would you give the shareholders if the corporation instead reported low operating profits from its sofa-making business and met both personal holding company requirements in the current year?

Personal Holding Company Tax. A corporation is considered a personal holding company if both of the following tests are met:[25]

▶ More than 50% of the value of its outstanding stock is owned by five or fewer individuals at some time during the last six months of the tax year.

▶ 60% or more of its adjusted ordinary gross income is personal holding company income. Personal holding company income consists of passive income, including dividends, interest, and in some circumstances, rent.

Many closely held corporations pass the 50% stock ownership test because of family ownership attribution rules. For example, 20 family shareholders (e.g., spouses, children, and grandchildren) may count as a single shareholder for purposes of applying the 50% and five or fewer shareholder tests.

The personal holding company tax discourages the conversion of closely held operating companies into nonoperating companies that reinvest substantial earnings in passive investments (e.g., stocks and bonds of other companies). The tax compels a company to distribute its earnings to shareholders if the earnings are not reinvested in operating assets. Liability for the personal holding company tax does not require a tax-avoidance motive. By contrast, liability for the accumulated earnings tax does require an intent to avoid the tax on dividends.

The accumulated earnings tax cannot be imposed in the same year the corporation is deemed to be a personal holding company. Often, a corporation that gradually converts itself into a nonoperating company by reinvesting its earnings in passive investments will incur an accumulated earnings tax liability before incurring a personal holding company tax liability. However, this is not always the case. For example, a newly-formed corporation that temporarily invests surplus funds in nonoperating assets may be deemed to be a personal holding company in its first year of operation, while the $250,000 accumulated earnings credit temporarily shields the same company from the accumulated earnings tax.

Computation of Personal Holding Company Tax. The **personal holding company tax** is the product of the personal holding company tax rate times undistributed personal holding company income. Various adjustments are made to regular taxable income to derive the personal holding company tax base. These adjustments are similar to those made in calculating the accumulated earnings tax, as illustrated in Example I:16-20. The personal holding company tax rate is 20%.

EXAMPLE I:16-21 ▶ Crane Corporation has four shareholders who together own more than 50% of the value of Crane stock at all times during the current year. More than 60% of Crane's adjusted gross income is personal holding company income (dividends, interest, etc.). Crane is a personal holding company for the current year because both the stock ownership and the income tests are met. Crane receives a $25,000 dividend for which it claims a $20,000 dividends-received deduction. It pays $18,750 of dividends to its shareholders. Crane has $200,000 of regular taxable income and a $61,250 regular tax liability.

Crane's personal holding company tax is computed as follows:

Regular taxable income	$200,000
Adjustments:	
Federal income tax liability	(61,250)
Dividends-received deduction	20,000
Dividends-paid deduction[26]	(18,750)
Undistributed personal holding company income	$140,000
Times: Personal holding company tax rate	× 0.20
Personal holding company tax	$ 28,000

---

[25] The basic rules for personal holding companies are set forth in Secs. 541–547.

[26] Secs. 547 and 561. The dividends-paid deduction is available for dividends paid during the tax year, dividends paid within 2½ months following the end of the tax year (subject to certain limitations), consent dividends, and dividends paid within 90 days following an IRS determination that a personal holding company tax is owed (i.e., deficiency dividends). Deficiency dividends are not allowed in computing the accumulated earnings tax.

TOPIC REVIEW I:16-2

Comparison of the Two Corporate Penalty Taxes

ITEM	ACCUMULATED EARNINGS TAX—SEC. 531	PERSONAL HOLDING COMPANY (PHC) TAX—SEC. 541
Reason for imposing the penalty tax	To discourage companies from retaining excessive earnings if such earnings are invested in nonoperating assets. A primary purpose is to compel the distribution of excessive earnings.	To discourage the conversion of closely held operating companies into passive investment companies. A primary purpose is to compel the distribution of passive income.
Elements of the tax formula	The tax base is regular taxable income plus or minus certain adjustments. The tax computation involves subjective judgment because the accumulated earnings credit (which often reduces the tax base to zero) is a function of retaining earnings for the reasonable needs of the business.	The determination of whether a corporation is a personal holding company and the computation of the tax is mechanical. Once the corporation is deemed to be a PHC, its tax base is regular taxable income plus or minus certain adjustments.
Computation of tax	Adjustments are made to taxable income for items such as the dividends-received deduction, the dividends-paid deduction, the federal income tax liability, and the accumulated earnings credit (see Example I:16-20). The tax rate is 20% of accumulated taxable income.	Adjustments are made to regular taxable income for items such as the dividends-received deduction, dividends-paid deduction, and the federal income tax liability to derive undistributed PHC income (see Example I:16-21). The tax rate is 20% of undistributed PHC income.

Crane's total federal tax liability is $89,250 ($61,250 + $28,000). Payment of the $28,000 personal holding company tax may be avoided if Crane distributes all of the personal holding company income to its shareholders. Special rules allow personal holding companies to distribute this income and avoid the personal holding company tax even after the corporation's year-end. Crane shareholders then pay the regular income tax on the dividend distribution. ◀

Topic Review I:16-2 compares the accumulated earnings tax and personal holding company tax rules.

COMPUTATION OF TAX FOR CONTROLLED GROUPS

Shareholders in one corporation could realize substantial tax savings by dividing the business into two or more corporations. These tax savings result from the corporations' benefitting from the lower corporate rates for taxable income less than $100,000. To prevent this type of tax avoidance, a **controlled group** must apportion the lower rates among group members as if only one corporation exists.[27] An equal apportionment to each member is required unless all group members consent to a disproportionate allocation. A controlled group, as discussed below, is a group of corporations that are, in general, owned by the same shareholder or group of shareholders.

EXAMPLE I:16-22 ▶ West and East Corporations are members of a controlled group. In the current year West and East each earn taxable income of $100,000. If each corporation were taxed separately, each's tax liability would be $22,250, or a total of $44,500. However, because West and East are members of a controlled group, the lower marginal tax rates must be apportioned to each corporation. The tax liability for each corporation under an equal apportionment is computed as follows:

---

[27] Sec. 1561.

Tax Calculation	Corporation	
	West	East
Tax on initial $50,000 of taxable income apportioned equally between West and East (0.15 × $25,000)	$ 3,750	$ 3,750
Tax on next $25,000 apportioned equally between West and East (0.25 × $12,500)	3,125	3,125
Tax on next $25,000 apportioned equally between West and East (0.34 × $12,500)	4,250	4,250
Tax on remaining $50,000 of taxable income for each corporation (0.39 × $50,000)	19,500	19,500
Tax on $100,000 of taxable income for each corporation	$30,625	$30,625

ADDITIONAL COMMENT

A controlled group of corporations must apportion not only the lower tax rates but also the $250,000 accumulated earnings credit and the $40,000 alternative minimum tax exemption.

The result of being members of a controlled group is that West and East must pay a total tax of $61,250, which is $16,750 ($61,250 − $44,500) more than the amount that each would pay if it were a separate, unrelated corporation. The total tax liability of $61,250 would have resulted if West and East were, in fact, one corporation. ◀

If taxable income of the controlled group exceeds $10 million, a comparable allocation must be made to reflect the lower 34% rate applicable to taxable income up to $10 million. Controlled groups may be classified into three types: brother-sister, parent-subsidiary, and combined. These three types are discussed below.

Brother-Sister Controlled Group. The IRC sets forth two definitions of a **brother-sister controlled group.** This textbook will refer to them as the 80%-50% definition and the 50%-only definition. Under the 80%-50% definition, a brother-sister controlled group exists if the following conditions are met:

▶ Five or fewer individuals, estates, or trusts own at least 80% of the voting power or value of all classes of stock of each corporation.[28]

▶ The shareholders commonly own more than 50% of the total voting power or value of all classes of stock. For the purpose of this condition, stock is counted only to the extent that each shareholder owns an identical interest in each corporation.[29] The term *identical interest* means the smallest overlapping percentage of stock owned by the shareholder in any corporation included in the brother-sister group.

ADDITIONAL COMMENT

In practice, brother-sister corporations are associated with one or a small number of taxpayers, owning several small, closely-held corporations.

Thus, under the 80%-50% definition, the five or fewer shareholders not only must have more than 50% common ownership in the corporations, but also must own at least 80% of the stock in each brother-sister corporation. This definition is narrow because the shareholders must meet two tests.

The 50%-only definition is broader because the five or fewer shareholders must satisfy only the 50% common ownership test. Consequently, in situations where the 50%-only definition applies, more corporations may be deemed to be members of a controlled group than under the 80%-50% definition.

The 50%-only definition applies for apportioning the lower marginal tax rates as illustrated in Example I:16-22. It also applies for apportioning the accumulated earnings credit and the AMT exemption. The 80%-50% definition applies for other purposes, such as apportioning the Sec. 179 expense limitation.

EXAMPLE I:16-23 ▶ The single classes of stock in First, Second, and Third Corporations are owned by Amir, Beth, Carol, Dawn, and Edith as follows:

---

[28] The 80% test is met if 80% or more of the total combined voting power of all classes of voting stock *or* at least 80% of the total value of all classes of stock of each corporation is held by five or fewer shareholders on December

31. To be counted for the 80% test, a shareholder must own stock in each corporate member of the brother-sister controlled group.
[29] Sec. 1563(a)(2).

Individuals	Corporation			Identical Interest
	First	Second	Third	
Amir	40%	20%	20%	20%
Beth	30	30	60	30
Carol	10	40	10	10
Dawn	10	10	—	—
Edith	10	—	10	—
Total	100%	100%	100%	60%

This group meets both the 80%-50% test and the 50%-only test. The 80%-50% test is met because five or fewer individuals own at least 80% of First, Second, and Third stocks and because Amir, Beth, and Carol own 80% of First stock and 90% of Second and Third stocks. For purposes of the 80% test the stock ownership of Dawn and Edith is not counted because they do not own stock in each of the three corporations. The 50% test also is met because common ownership exceeds 50% (60% of identical interests). For purposes of the 50%-only test, the stock ownership of Dawn and Edith is not counted because they do not own stock in each of the three corporations. In this example, the 50%-only test also is met. ◄

Parent-Subsidiary Controlled Groups. A **parent-subsidiary controlled group** exists if the following conditions are met:

▶ A common parent corporation owns at least 80% of the stock in at least one subsidiary.[30]

▶ At least 80% of the stock in each other member of the controlled group is owned by other members of the controlled group.

EXAMPLE I:16-24 ▶ Federal Corporation owns 100% of Apex Corporation stock and 30% of Giant Corporation stock. Apex also owns 50% of Giant stock. Each corporation has only one class of stock outstanding. Because Federal owns at least 80% of Apex stock, it is the common parent of the Federal-Apex-Giant parent-subsidiary controlled group. Giant also is a member of the controlled group because at least 80% of Giant stock is owned by members of the controlled group (Federal and Apex together own 80% [30% + 50%]). The parent-subsidiary controlled group consists of Federal, Apex, and Giant. ◄

Combined Controlled Groups. A combined controlled group exists if the following two conditions involving three or more corporations are met:

▶ A common parent owns at least 80% of at least one subsidiary (a parent-subsidiary group), and

▶ The common parent is a member of a brother-sister controlled group.[31]

Based on the facts of Example I:16-24, a combined controlled group would have existed if Federal was a member of a brother-sister controlled group that also included National, a situation that would have resulted from Viki's owning 100% of the single classes of stock of Federal and National. Then, Federal, National, Apex, and Giant would have constituted a combined controlled group and would have had to apportion the various tax benefits.

BOOK-TAX ACCOUNTING COMPARISON

Corporations eligible to file a consolidated tax return may differ from those eligible to report on a consolidated financial accounting basis. 80% stock ownership is needed to file a consolidated tax return while only 50% stock ownership is needed to issue a consolidated financial statement.

CONSOLIDATED RETURNS

Corporations that are members of a parent-subsidiary affiliated group are eligible to file a consolidated tax return if they elect to do so under the consolidated return Treasury Regulations. Note, however, that an affiliated group is not the same as a controlled group. (See Chapter C:8 of the *Prentice Hall's Federal Taxation: Corporations, Partnerships, Estates, and Trusts* text for a detailed discussion of the requirements for filing a consolidated tax return.) Brother-sister controlled groups never can file consolidated tax returns. The parent-subsidiary members of a combined controlled group might

---

[30] Sec. 1563(a)(1).   [31] Sec. 1563(a)(3).

constitute an affiliated group and thus could elect to file a consolidated tax return. Although the parent's sister corporation is a member of the same controlled group, the parent's sister may not join in the consolidated tax return election. Once the election is made, IRS permission to discontinue filing on a consolidated basis is required.[32]

The consolidated return regulations treat the affiliated group as a single entity, thereby providing the following advantages: (1) net operating losses of one or more members can be used to offset profits of other members; (2) capital losses of one or more members can be used to offset capital gains of other members; and (3) transactions involving two or more group members are treated as occurring among divisions of a single entity, thus the taxation of profits and gains from such transactions is deferred until a subsequent transaction involving a group member and a party outside the affiliated group.

? STOP & THINK

Question: P Corporation owns 100% of S-1 Corporation stock and P and S-1 Corporations each own 50% of S-2 Corporation stock. P and S-1 have owned stock in S-2 since its incorporation. Both P and S-1 are highly profitable and are subject to a flat 34% corporate tax rate. S-2 has generated a net operating loss (NOL) in each year of its existence. Would filing a consolidated tax return benefit P, S-1, and S-2?

Solution: Filing a consolidated return would benefit the corporations because S-2's current year losses can be used to offset P's and S-1's current year profits. Because S-2 has never earned a profit, it would not be able to use the NOL if it filed a separate return. In addition, S-2's prior year losses might be used to offset profits reported by S-1 in current year and future year consolidated tax returns. Filing a consolidated return allows the NOLs of one or more members of an affiliated group to offset the profits of other members and reduce the group's overall tax liability.

TRANSFERS OF PROPERTY TO CONTROLLED CORPORATIONS

OBJECTIVE 4

Apply the nonrecognition of gain or loss rules for corporate capitalizations

Section 351 permits investors to defer recognition of gain or loss on the transfer of property to a corporation. The property may be transferred when a new corporation is formed or when additional capital is contributed to an existing corporation. Without the Sec. 351 nonrecognition rules, an investor, sole proprietorship, or partnership might be discouraged from incorporating because the transfer of appreciated property to the corporation would constitute a taxable event, thereby resulting in a recognized gain.

SECTION 351 NONRECOGNITION REQUIREMENTS

KEY POINT

The nonrecognition provisions of Sec. 351 are mandatory rather than elective if all its conditions are met.

The deferral of gain or loss under Sec. 351 can be justified because the assets merely have been transferred to a corporation that is controlled by the transferors. In addition, the transferors do not have the wherewithal-to-pay the tax on the gains that otherwise would be recognized because they receive only stock in the transferee (controlled) corporation. Section 351 prevents recognition of losses on transfers of property that have declined in value.

Gain or loss is not recognized if all the following conditions are met:

ADDITIONAL COMMENT

In Sec. 351 transactions, the term "transferor" refers to the shareholder, and the term "transferee" refers to the controlled corporation.

▶ Property (other than services) is transferred to the corporation solely in exchange for stock in the transferee corporation.[33]

▶ Immediately after the exchange, the transferor-shareholders in the aggregate control the transferee corporation through ownership of at least 80% of its stock.[34]

---

[32] Reg. Sec. 1.1502-75(c).

[33] Section 351(d) provides that services do not qualify as "property". Thus, if an individual transfers services in exchange for stock, the individual is not deemed to be a transferor for purposes of meeting the 80% control requirement, unless the individual also transfers sufficient property. The rendering of services results in the service provider's recognizing ordinary income equal to the FMV of the services rendered.

[34] Sec. 368(c). "Control" means the ownership of at least 80% of the total combined voting power of all classes of stock and at least 80% of the total number of shares of all other classes of stock.

▶ If a transferor receives money or property (other than stock in the transferee corporation), the transferor recognizes gain (but not loss) equal to the lesser of the "boot" (i.e., money plus the FMV of nonstock property) received or the realized gain.[35] In addition, a corporation that transfers appreciated property (other than its own stock or debt obligations) to the transferor-shareholders also recognizes gain on the exchange.[36]

▶ The character of any gain recognized by the transferor depends on the type of property transferred as follows: capital gain on capital assets, Sec. 1231 gain on Sec. 1231 property, and ordinary income on other property (e.g., inventory).

▶ Depreciation is not recaptured in a Sec. 351 transfer unless the transferor recognizes gain on the depreciable property transferred.[37]

EXAMPLE I:16-25 ▶ Carlos and Fred merge their sole proprietorships by forming the Miami Corporation. Carlos transfers to Miami land and a building with a $50,000 adjusted basis and a $100,000 FMV in exchange for 40% of Miami stock. Fred transfers to Miami equipment with a $60,000 adjusted basis and a $150,000 FMV in exchange for 60% of Miami stock. Miami is controlled by Carlos and Fred because immediately after the exchange together they own at least 80% of Miami's single class of stock. Carlos and Fred recognize no gain because all of the Sec. 351 requirements are met and they received no property other than Miami stock. The depreciation recapture potential on the building and equipment is inherited by Miami. ◀

EXAMPLE I:16-26 ▶ Gail and Gary form Michigan Corporation. Gail transfers inventory with a $50,000 adjusted basis and a $100,000 FMV to Michigan in exchange for $20,000 cash and 50% of Michigan stock worth $80,000. Michigan generated the cash through bank borrowings. Gary transfers equipment with a $150,000 adjusted basis and a $100,000 FMV in exchange for 50% of stock worth $80,000 and a Michigan 10-year note valued at $20,000. The Section 351 requirements are met because property is transferred by the two transferors who together control more than 80% of the Michigan stock immediately after the exchange. The tax consequences to Gail and Gary are as follows:

	Gail	Gary
FMV of stock received	$ 80,000	$ 80,000
Plus: Cash or note received	20,000	20,000
Amount realized	$100,000	$100,000
Minus: Adjusted basis of property transferred	(50,000)	(150,000)
Gain (loss) realized	$ 50,000	$ (50,000)
Gain (loss) recognized	$ 20,000	$ —0—

Gail's recognized gain is the lesser of the $20,000 boot she received or her $50,000 realized gain. This gain is ordinary in character because Gail transferred inventory. Because Gary realized a loss, he recognizes no gain or loss even though he received $20,000 of boot. ◀

BASIS CONSIDERATIONS

ADDITIONAL COMMENT

When different classes of stock are received in a Sec. 351 exchange, the total substituted basis must be allocated among the different classes in proportion to their relative FMVs.

Stock Received by the Transferor. In Sec. 351 transactions, substituted basis rules apply to stock received by the transferors and carryover basis rules apply to property transferred to the corporation. The transferor's stock basis is computed as follows:

Basis of property transferred to the corporation
Plus: Any gain recognized by the transferor
   on the exchange (e.g., as a result of boot received)
Minus: Amount of money received (including any transferor
   liabilities assumed by the transferee corporation)
   FMV of any noncash boot property received
_____
Basis of stock received[38]

Any boot property received by the tranferor takes a FMV basis.

---

[35] Sec. 351(b). Recognized gain is calculated on an asset-by-asset basis.
[36] Secs. 351(f) and 311(b).
[37] Secs. 1245(b)(3) and 1250(d)(3). The transferee corporation recaptures depreciation if it subsequently sells or disposes of the asset.

[38] Sec. 358(a).

EXAMPLE I:16-27 ▶ George and Gina form New Corporation. George transfers to New land and a building with a $60,000 adjusted basis and a $100,000 FMV in exchange for 50% of New stock. Gina transfers equipment with a $120,000 adjusted basis and a $100,000 FMV for 50% of New stock. George realizes a $40,000 gain, and Gina realizes a $20,000 loss. However, George and Gina recognize no gain or loss because the Sec. 351 requirements have been met. George's basis in his New stock is $60,000, and Gina's basis in her New stock is $120,000. ◀

? STOP & THINK

Question: In Example I:16-27, George and Gina recognized no gain or loss. Why does this treatment represent tax deferral rather than permanent nonrecognition?

Solution: George's $40,000 unrecognized gain is reflected in a $60,000 stock basis that is $40,000 *below* its $100,000 FMV. Thus, if George immediately sells his stock for its FMV, he recognizes the $40,000 deferred gain ($100,000 selling price − $60,000 stock adjusted basis). Similarly, Gina's $20,000 unrecognized loss is reflected in a $120,000 stock basis that is $20,000 *above* its $100,000 FMV. Thus, if Gina immediately sells her stock for its FMV, she recognizes the $20,000 deferred loss ($100,000 selling price − $120,000 stock adjusted basis). In this way, the substituted basis rules ensure that realized gains and losses are deferred.

BOOK-TAX ACCOUNTING COMPARISON

Financial accounting requires that the corporation record the transferred assets at their fair market values.

Property Received by Transferee Corporation. Generally, carryover basis rules apply to property received by the transferee corporation. The basis of this property is computed as follows:

$$\frac{\text{Transferor's adjusted basis in property}}{\text{Basis of property to the transferee corporation}^{39}}$$ Plus: Gain recognized by the transferor

EXAMPLE I:16-28 ▶ In a tax-free exchange under Sec. 351, North Corporation receives property with a $60,000 adjusted basis and a $100,000 FMV. If no gain is recognized on the transfer, the transferor's $60,000 adjusted basis becomes the transferee corporation's asset basis, as well as the shareholder's stock basis. If the transferor instead had recognized a $10,000 gain because she received boot (e.g., cash) North's asset basis would have been $70,000 ($60,000 adjusted basis in the transferor's hands + $10,000 gain recognized by the transferor), and the transferor's stock basis would have been $70,000. ◀

A special IRC provision is intended to discourage investors from attempting to generate double losses by transferring loss property to a corporation in connection with a Sec. 351 exchange.[40] In general, if the FMV of contributed property is less than the shareholder's adjusted basis in such property, the transferee corporation is required to use the FMV of the loss property as its asset basis.

TREATMENT OF LIABILITIES

TYPICAL MISCONCEPTION

When a corporation assumes a shareholder's liabilities and the shareholder recognizes no gain, one might mistakenly assume that the shareholder's stock basis is not reduced by the liabilities assumed.

Nonrecognition of Gain. Section 357(a) provides for the nonrecognition of gain upon the transferee corporation's assumption of liabilities or its taking property subject to liabilities. Accordingly, under the general rule, shareholders recognize no gain when they transfer liabilities to a controlled corporation. The shareholders, however, must reduce their stock basis by the amount of liabilities assumed or acquired. This rule is logical because, if a shareholder transfers net assets of $10,000 (i.e., gross assets of $100,000 and liabilities of $90,000), the net contribution to capital is only $10,000 even though the shareholder has transferred $100,000 in gross assets.

EXAMPLE I:16-29 ▶ In a transaction qualifying as tax-free under Sec. 351, Ira transfers land with an $80,000 adjusted basis and a $100,000 FMV to Mega Corporation in exchange for 100% of Mega stock with a $60,000 FMV. The transferred property is subject to a $40,000 liability that the corporation assumes. The tax consequences to Ira are as follows:

---

[39] Sec. 362(a). [40] Sec. 362(e).

FMV of stock received	$ 60,000
Plus: Liability assumed by Mega	40,000
Amount realized	$100,000
Minus: Adjusted basis of property transferred	(80,000)
Gain realized by Ira	$ 20,000
Gain recognized by Ira	$ –0–
Adjusted basis of property transferred	$ 80,000
Minus: Liability assumed by Mega	(40,000)
Ira's adjusted basis in Mega stock received	$ 40,000

In addition, Mega takes an $80,000 carryover basis in the land. ◀

Exceptions. Two exceptions to the general rule of Sec. 357 require gain recognition upon the transfer of liabilities to a corporation. The first exception relates to the nature of the exchange. If the principal purpose for the assumption of the liabilities is tax avoidance or if the transaction does not have a bona fide business purpose, all of the transferor's liabilities assumed by the transferee corporation are treated as boot, potentially resulting in gain recognition.[41]

EXAMPLE I:16-30 ▶ In a transaction purportedly meeting the requirements of Sec. 351, Helen transfers to Orlando Corporation land and a building with a $70,000 adjusted basis and a $100,000 FMV in exchange for 100% of Orlando stock. Shortly before the transfer, Helen mortgages the property for $60,000 and uses the mortgage loan to pay off personal debts. The corporation then assumes the $60,000 mortgage and issues to Helen stock worth $40,000. The mortgage assumption lacks a bona fide business purpose because it is intended to place cash in Helen's hands without her recognizing gain under the boot rules. Consequently, for the purpose of determining gain recognized, Helen must treat the entire $60,000 liability assumed as boot. The tax consequences to Helen are as follows:

FMV of stock received	$ 40,000
Plus: Liability assumed by Orlando	60,000
Amount realized	$100,000
Minus: Adjusted basis of property transferred	(70,000)
Gain realized	$ 30,000
Gain recognized	$ 30,000
Adjusted basis of property transferred	$ 70,000
Plus: Gain recognized	30,000
Minus: Liability assumed by Orlando	(60,000)
Adjusted basis of stock received	$ 40,000

Although total boot is $60,000 (the liability assumed), Helen's recognized gain does not exceed her $30,000 realized gain. In addition, the stock basis equals its FMV because Helen recognizes the entire realized gain, with no gain to defer. Finally, Orlando's basis in the land and building is $100,000 ($70,000 adjusted basis in the transferor's hands + $30,000 gain recognized by the transferor). ◀

REAL-WORLD EXAMPLE

Customer deposits representing obligations to perform future services were considered liabilities. Because these liabilities exceeded the basis of the assets transferred to the corporation, gain was recognized. *William P. Orr,* 78 T.C. 1059 (1982).

A second exception applies to excess liabilities. If a transferor's total liabilities assumed by the transferee corporation exceeds the total basis of assets (including cash) transferred by that transferor, the transferor must recognize gain to the extent of the excess.[42] Without this rule, the transferor would take a negative basis in the stock received. Gain is recognized because the transferor has derived a net economic benefit to the extent the liabilities assumed exceed the adjusted basis of the transferred assets.

---

[41] Sec. 357(b).

[42] Sec. 357(c). Accounts receivable and accounts payable with a zero basis for a cash basis transferor are disregarded for purposes of Sec. 357(c). (See Sec. 357(c)(3).)

EXAMPLE I:16-31 ▶ In a transaction otherwise qualifying as tax-free under Sec. 351 Jack transfers to Maple Corporation assets with a $60,000 adjusted basis and a $100,000 FMV. Simultaneously, Maple assumes $75,000 of Jack's liabilities. Jack recognizes a $15,000 gain because the liabilities assumed by Maple exceed the basis of the assets transferred ($75,000 − $60,000). The character of Jack's recognized gain depends on the type(s) of property (capital assets, Sec. 1231 property, inventory, etc.) Jack transferred.[43] Jack's net economic benefit from the exchange is $15,000 ($75,000 liabilities assumed by Maple − $60,000 adjusted basis of assets transferred). Jack's basis in the stock received is zero ($60,000 asset adjusted basis + $15,000 gain recognized − $75,000 liabilities assumed). Because Jack's realized gain is $40,000 of which he recognizes $15,000, only $25,000 of the gain is deferred ($25,000 FMV of stock − $0 basis). Maple's basis in the assets is increased from $60,000 to $75,000 because of Jack's $15,000 recognized gain. ◀

Topic Review I:16-3 summarizes the general rules relating to the transfer of property to a controlled corporation.

CORPORATE CAPITAL STRUCTURE

A corporation may be capitalized with both equity (generally common or preferred stock) and debt. The use of debt in the capital structure offers the following advantages:

▶ Interest on debt is deductible by the corporation, while dividends on stock are not deductible.

▶ Stock redemptions may result in dividend or capital gain recognition by the shareholders (see pages I:16-28 through I:16-30), while debt repayment represents a tax-free return of capital.

If the corporation is too thinly capitalized (e.g., excessive debt relative to equity), the IRS may attempt to recharacterize part or all of the debt as equity and deny the corporation an interest deduction.

ADDITIONAL COMMENT
Thin capitalization is primarily a problem for closely-held corporations where the shareholders also hold the debt. It is not normally a problem for large publicly-held corporations.

TOPIC REVIEW I:16-3

Sec. 351 Requirements, Gain Recognition Rules, and Basis Rules

▶ Sec. 351 nonrecognition treatment requires an exchange of property solely for stock. The transferor-shareholders must control (i.e., 80% or more stock ownership) the corporation immediately after the exchange.
▶ Nonqualifying property (e.g., cash, noncash property, or debt obligations of the transferee corporation) received by the transferors is treated as boot.
▶ The transferors recognize gain equal to the lesser of the boot received or the realized gain.
▶ Generally, the transferors recognize no gain if they transfer liabilities to a controlled corporation. Exceptions to the nonrecognition rule apply if (1) the principal purpose of the liability transfer is tax avoidance, (2) no bona fide business purpose for the transfer exists, or (3) total liabilities assumed by the corporation exceed the transferor's adjusted basis in the transferred assets.
▶ Substituted basis rules referencing the basis of the asset(s) transferred apply to the stock received by the transferors. Generally, carryover basis rules apply to property contributed to the transferee corporation. However, if the FMV of the property is less than the carryover basis, the corporation must use a FMV basis.

---

[43] Reg. Sec. 1.357-2(a).

EARNINGS AND PROFITS

OBJECTIVE 5

Understand the significance of earnings and profits

CALCULATION OF EARNINGS AND PROFITS

Earnings and profits (E&P) measures a C corporation's economic ability to pay dividends out of its current and accumulated earnings without impairing its capital. If the corporation has no E&P, a distribution is treated as a tax-free return of capital, and possibly a capital gain, rather than a taxable dividend.

Current E&P is calculated by making various adjustments to the corporation's regular taxable income.[44] This calculation, as well as the determination of accumulated E&P, is set forth in Table I:16-3.

EXAMPLE I:16-32 ►

BOOK-TAX ACCOUNTING COMPARISON

E&P is similar to retained earnings in financial accounting although numerous differences exist between the two accounts. For example, issuance of a stock dividend usually reduces retained earnings but does not affect E&P.

Park Corporation, an accrual method taxpayer, reports $100,000 of taxable income in the current year. Its tax accountant made the following adjustments to derive current E&P and the addition to accumulated E&P:

Taxable income	$100,000
Plus:	
Tax-exempt bond interest	2,000
Key officer life insurance proceeds (nontaxable)	10,000
Dividends-received deduction	20,000
MACRS depreciation in excess of ADS depreciation	15,000
Percentage depletion in excess of cost depletion	10,000
U.S. production activities deduction	3,000
	$160,000
Minus:	
Federal income taxes accrued[a]	(22,250)
Net capital losses	(5,000)
Key officer life insurance premiums (not deductible because the corporation is the beneficiary)	(2,000)
Charitable contributions exceeding the 10% limitation	(3,000)
Fine for overweight trucks on city streets	(5,000)
Current E&P	$122,750
Minus: Money distribution	(5,000)
Addition to accumulated E&P	$117,750

[a]An accrual method of accounting corporation reduces its E&P by its accrued federal income taxes for the tax year. A cash method of accounting corporation reduces its E&P by its actual federal income taxes paid during the tax year.

SELF-STUDY QUESTION

Should Sue, an individual, consider transferring her $100,000 in municipal bonds to her controlled C corporation?

ANSWER

No; although the interest income on the municipal bond is excludable from the corporation's taxable income, the tax-exempt interest creates E&P for a C corporation, which causes a cash distribution to Sue to be taxable as a dividend.

To derive E&P, regular taxable income is increased by nontaxable income—the tax-exempt bond interest and the life insurance proceeds—received by Park. Taxable income also is increased for deductions claimed when calculating regular taxable income but not allowed when calculating E&P. Three of these deductions do not represent economic outlays—the dividends-received deduction, U.S. production activities deduction, and percentage depletion in excess of cost. Another adjustment represents a timing difference that will reverse in later tax years—MACRS depreciation in excess of Alternative Depreciation System (ADS) depreciation. Regular taxable income is reduced by negative adjustments for economic outlays that are not deductible in calculating regular taxable income. These E&P reductions include federal income taxes, capital losses in excess of capital gains, key officer life insurance premiums, excess charitable contributions, and fines. ◄

CURRENT VERSUS ACCUMULATED E&P

Current and accumulated E&P must be distinguished because tracing rules determine whether a distribution is made out of current or accumulated E&P. For example, a distribution to shareholders is deemed to be made first out of current E&P and is therefore taxed as a dividend, even if accumulated E&P is negative. Accumulated E&P represents

---

[44] These adjustments are set forth in Sec. 312 and the related Treasury Regulations.

▼ TABLE I:16-3

Calculation of Earnings and Profits

Regular taxable income

Plus: Exclusions from regular taxable income:
>Tax-exempt interest
>
>Life insurance proceeds where the corporation is the beneficiary
>
>Recoveries of bad debts and other prior-year deductions for which the corporation received no tax benefit
>
>Federal income tax refunds from prior years

Plus: Income deferred to a later year for taxable income purposes:
>Deferred gain on installment sales
>
>Deferred gain on like-kind exchanges

Plus or minus: Adjustments for items that must be recomputed:
>Income on long-term contracts based on percentage of completion method rather than completed contract method
>
>Excess of pre-ACRS accelerated depreciation over straight-line depreciation
>
>Excess of ACRS depreciation over straight-line ACRS depreciation with an extended recovery period
>
>Excess of regular MACRS depreciation over Alternative Depreciation System (ADS) depreciation
>
>Excess of percentage depletion over cost depletion

Plus: Deductions not allowed in computing E&P:
>Dividends-received deduction
>
>NOL carryovers, charitable contribution carryovers, and capital loss carryovers from prior years
>
>U.S. production activitives deduction

Minus: Expenses and losses not deductible in computing regular taxable income:
>Federal income taxes
>
>Life insurance premiums where the corporation is the beneficiary
>
>Excess capital losses not deductible in current year
>
>Excess charitable contributions not deductible in current year
>
>Expenses related to production of tax-exempt income
>
>Nondeductible losses on related party sales
>
>Nondeductible penalties and fines
>
>Nondeductible political contributions

Current E&P (or E&P deficit)

Minus: Distributions to shareholders (but not in excess of current E&P)

Addition to accumulated E&P (if any)

the total of all prior years' undistributed current E&P as of the first day of the tax year. Distributions are deemed to be made out of accumulated E&P only after the current E&P balance (if any) is exhausted.[45]

EXAMPLE I:16-33 ▶ Pacific Corporation, a calendar-year taxpayer, reports a $100,000 accumulated E&P deficit and $30,000 of current E&P as of January 1. Pacific makes a $40,000 distribution to its shareholders. In the distribution, $30,000 is treated as a taxable dividend to the extent of current E&P, and the remaining $10,000 is treated as a tax-free return of capital (to the extent that Pacific's shareholders have stock basis) because of the accumulated E&P deficit, which is not increased as a result of the tax-free distribution. ◀

If a shareholder's stock basis is reduced to zero because of a property distribution treated as a tax-free return of capital, the excess of the distribution amount over this basis is treated as a capital gain.

[45] Reg. Sec. 1.316-2.

EXAMPLE I:16-34 ▶ Peach Corporation, a calendar-year taxpayer, has one shareholder, Georgia, who has owned her Peach stock for several years. At the beginning of the current year, Peach has $30,000 of current E&P and $20,000 of accumulated E&P. Georgia's stock basis is $10,000. At the end of the current year, Peach distributes $65,000 to Georgia. The $65,000 distribution is reported as follows:

Taxable dividend paid out of current E&P	$30,000
Taxable dividend paid out of accumulated E&P	20,000
Total taxable dividend	$50,000
Tax-free return of capital	10,000
Long-term capital gain	5,000
Total distribution	$65,000

In addition, Georgia's stock basis is reduced to zero because of the $10,000 portion treated as a return of capital. ◀

If the distributing corporation has a current E&P deficit and a positive accumulated E&P balance, the current deficit and accumulated E&P balance are netted as of the distribution date.[46] The current E&P deficit for the year is prorated on a daily basis unless a nonratable allocation is more appropriate.

EXAMPLE I:16-35 ▶ On January 1 of the current (nonleap) year, Prime Corporation, a calendar-year taxpayer, has a $100,000 positive accumulated E&P balance and a $35,500 current E&P deficit. Prime makes a $30,000 distribution to its shareholders on July 1 (the 182nd day of the year). Because the current deficit is allocated ratably over the year unless the corporation can show that a nonratable allocation is more appropriate, E&P as of July 1 is $82,201 [$100,000 accumulated E&P − (183/365 × $35,500 current E&P deficit)]. The entire $30,000 distribution is taxable as a dividend. ◀

NONCASH DISTRIBUTIONS

OBJECTIVE 6

Determine the tax consequences of noncash distributions and stock redemptions

TAX CONSEQUENCES TO THE SHAREHOLDERS

Occasionally, a corporation distributes noncash property (i.e., assets other than its stock or stock rights) to its shareholders. If noncash property is distributed, the following tax consequences generally ensue:

▶ The distribution amount equals the FMV of the property (reduced by any associated liabilities).

▶ The distribution amount is treated as a taxable dividend if the corporation has sufficient E&P.

▶ The basis of the distributed property equals its FMV (without reduction for any associated liabilities).

EXAMPLE I:16-36 ▶

REAL-WORLD EXAMPLE

A distribution of $20 Double Eagle gold coins was a noncash distribution rather than a money distribution because the gold coins were withdrawn from circulation and had numismatic value. *Warren C. Cordner v. U.S.,* 49 AFTR 2d 82-1353, 82-1 USTC ¶9275 (9th Cir., 1982).

Red Corporation distributes land and a building having a $50,000 adjusted basis and a $100,000 FMV to its sole shareholder, Irene. Red has current and accumulated E&P exceeding $100,000. The property is subject to a $40,000 mortgage, which Irene assumes. The amount distributed to Irene is $60,000 ($100,000 FMV − $40,000 liability). Irene reports a $60,000 taxable dividend because the corporation has E&P exceeding the distribution amount. Irene's basis in the property is its $100,000 FMV. ◀

TAX CONSEQUENCES TO THE DISTRIBUTING CORPORATION

As a general rule, the corporation recognizes no gain or loss upon distributing noncash property to its shareholders.[47] However, if a corporation distributes appreciated noncash property, the corporation is treated as if it sold the property to the shareholder for its FMV immediately before the distribution and thus recognizes any realized gain.[48] On the

---

[46] Reg. Sec. 1.316-2(b).
[48] Sec. 311(b).

[47] Sec. 311(a).

other hand, a corporation does not recognize loss when it distributes depreciated noncash property, even though the sale of such property might otherwise have resulted in a deductible tax loss.

EXAMPLE I:16-37 ▶ Rocket Corporation distributes to its shareholder Peter $75,000 in cash, along with land having a $50,000 adjusted basis and a $60,000 FMV. Rocket recognizes $10,000 ($60,000 − $50,000) of gain on the land distribution. Alternatively, if the land had a $60,000 adjusted basis and a $50,000 FMV, the corporation would not have recognized the $10,000 ($50,000 − $60,000) realized loss. ◀

If the property distributed is subject to a liability that exceeds the property's basis, for the purpose of calculating gain, the FMV of such property is deemed to be the greater of the actual FMV or the amount of the liability.[49]

EXAMPLE I:16-38 ▶ Assume the same facts as in Example I:16-37 except that the land is subject to a $70,000 mortgage. Rocket recognizes a $20,000 ($70,000 − $50,000) gain on the distribution because the mortgage exceeds the land's FMV. ◀

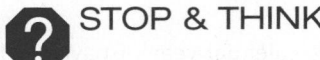 **STOP & THINK**

Question: What are the tax consequences of a pro rata stock dividend, that is, a corporation's issuing additional shares of its own single class of stock to existing shareholders?

Solution: The shareholder's economic position does not change as a result of the stock dividend. Although the shareholders receive additional shares of stock, they still own the same proportion of stock in the corporation. Consequently, they realize no economic gain on the stock dividend. Accordingly, they spread the basis of their old shares over their old and new shares, thereby decreasing the per share basis while leaving the total basis unchanged. In addition, the corporation recognizes no gain or loss and does not reduce its E&P balance. Some stock dividends, such as those involving a shareholder election to receive either stock or cash, are taxable.[50] (See Chapter 4 of *Prentice Hall's Corporations, Partnerships, Estates, and Trusts*).

STOCK REDEMPTIONS

Two possible tax consequences ensue when a corporation repurchases (redeems) some of its outstanding stock:

▶ The redemption is treated as a taxable dividend to the shareholder to the extent of the corporation's E&P

▶ The redemption is treated as a sale of stock, generally resulting in the shareholder recognizing capital gain or loss

The first prescribed treatment is intended to discourage corporations from paying a disguised dividend in the form of a stock redemption taxable as a capital gain. For example, the corporation might redeem 10% of its sole shareholder's stock rather than pay a cash dividend. After the redemption, the shareholder continues to own all of the outstanding stock, retains the same degree of control over the corporation, and holds the distributed money or other property. Taxing the redemption as a sale would reduce the tax burden on the shareholder without reducing his/her ownership interest.

The second prescribed tax treatment is significant because individual shareholders are generally subject to a 15% or 20% maximum rate on their net capital gains. In addition, sale treatment is preferable if the shareholders have unused capital losses or capital loss carryovers that otherwise would be of limited tax benefit. Moreover, sale treatment affords shareholders a tax-free recovery of their stock investment. Such a tax-free recovery does not result if the distribution is treated as a dividend.

ADDITIONAL COMMENT
Because an incremental 3.8% rate applies to net investment income for taxpayers whose modified AGI exceeds $200,000 ($250,000 for married filing jointly), some taxpayers may pay a higher rate than 15% or 20% on their net capital gains.

---

[49] Secs. 311(b)(2) and 336(b).   [50] Sec. 305(b).

EXAMPLE I:16-39 ▶ Ajax Corporation has two equal shareholders, Rita and Harry. Each shareholder has owned 10 shares of Ajax stock for several years. Each share has a $100 basis and a $150 FMV. Ajax, which has sufficient E&P, redeems 5 shares from each shareholder for the $150 FMV. As a result of the redemption, Rita and Harry each recognize $750 ($150 FMV × 5 shares) of dividend income because each still owns 50% of Ajax stock. Rita's total $1,000 basis in her stock is not decreased as a result of the dividend treatment. On the other hand, her per share basis increases from $100 ($1,000 ÷ 10 shares) to $200 ($1,000 ÷ 5) per share.

If instead, Ajax redeems 5 of Rita's shares but none of Harry's, Rita has substantially reduced her proportionate ownership interest in Ajax. Consequently, she is entitled to sale treatment and recognizes a $250 capital gain calculated as follows:

Redemption proceeds ($150 × 5)	$750
Minus: Basis of stock redeemed ($100 × 5)	(500)
Capital gain	$250

The capital gain is generally long-term and is taxed at a preferential rate (for most taxpayers, 15%). Moreover, only $250 is taxed in the case of sale treatment as opposed to $750 in the case of dividend treatment. In the former case, Rita's total $1,000 basis is reduced to $500. The basis of her 5 shares redeemed offsets the $750 redemption amount. Rita's per share basis remains at $100 ($500 ÷ 5 shares) after the redemption. Example I:16-40 on page I:16-30 explains why the first redemption warrants dividend treatment while the second redemption warrants sale treatment. ◄

DETERMINING WHETHER A REDEMPTION IS A DIVIDEND OR CAPITAL GAIN

A redemption is treated as an exchange taxed as a capital gain or loss if any of the following conditions are met:[51]

▶ The redemption is substantially disproportionate with respect to the shareholder's interest [Sec. 302(b)(2)].

▶ The redemption is not essentially equivalent to a dividend [Sec. 302(b)(1)].[52]

▶ The redemption completely terminates the shareholder's interest [Sec. 302(b)(3)].

Substantially Disproportionate. Constructive stock ownership rules apply to determine whether a redemption is substantially disproportionate.[53] **Constructive stock ownership** means that the redeemed shareholder is considered to own the stock of certain related parties. These related parties include family members, partnerships and corporations in which the shareholder owns an interest, and trusts and estates of which the shareholder is a beneficiary.

For a redemption to be substantially disproportionate, all of the following tests must be met immediately after the redemption:

▶ The shareholder must own less than 80% of his or her former percentage of voting stock (including stock held by related parties).

▶ The shareholder must own less than 80% of his or her former percentage of common (voting and nonvoting) stock (including stock held by related parties).

▶ The shareholder must own less than 50% of all the voting stock (including stock held by related parties).

Under Sec. 302(b)(2) a redemption of solely nonvoting stock will not qualify for capital gains treatment.

Not Essentially Equivalent to a Dividend. A redemption that is not essentially equivalent to a dividend results in a meaningful reduction in the shareholder's interest.[54] In determining whether a meaningful reduction has occurred, the IRS looks at the shareholder's interest in the following: (1) voting power, (2) participation in earning

---

[51] Sec. 302.

[52] For example, sale treatment has been allowed where the redeemed shareholder's voting control, right to share in current earnings, and right to receive corporate assets upon liquidation have been significantly reduced. Ordinarily, this occurs when a shareholder's majority interest is converted to a 50% interest, a majority interest is converted to a minority (less than 50%) interest, or a

minority interest is significantly reduced. (See, for example, Rev. Ruls. 75-502 and 76-364 cited in footnotes 55 and 56.)

[53] Sec. 318.

[54] *U.S.* v. *Maclin P. Davis*, 25 AFTR 2d 70-827, 70-1 USTC ¶9289 (USSC, 1970).

and profits, and (3) share of net assets upon liquidation.[55] This approach usually is adopted if the redemption fails the objective tests for a substantially disproportionate redemption. Specifically, if a shareholder's interest falls below 50% after the redemption, but the redemption does not meet the 80% test, the shareholder might argue that the redemption is not essentially equivalent to a dividend. For example, a reduction in ownership from 27% to 22% fails the 80% test for substantially disproportionate redemptions (80% × 27% = 21.6%) but could be regarded as a meaningful reduction in the shareholder's interest.[56]

EXAMPLE I:16-40 ▶

In Example I:16-39, the redemption of both Rita and Harry's stock failed the substantially disproportionate test. For Rita and Harry to pass the test, each shareholder's current ownership percentage must be less than 80% of his or her former ownership percentage, or 40% (80% × 50% prior ownership) and less than 50% on an absolute basis. After the redemption, Rita and Harry each still own exactly 50% of Ajax's single class of stock, thereby failing both the 80% and 50% tests.

On the other hand, the redemption of only Rita's 5 shares qualifies for sale treatment because, after the redemption, Rita owns 33⅓% (5 shares Rita still owns ÷ 15 total shares outstanding) of Ajax's single class of stock. Thus, Rita's post-redemption ownership is less than the 40% and 50% thresholds, thereby making the redemption substantially disproportionate. ◀

EXAMPLE I:16-41 ▶

Jane owns 60 shares of Fast Corporation's single class of stock. Her mother owns 20 additional shares of Fast stock. The remaining 20 Fast shares are owned by Peter, who is unrelated to Jane or her mother. Fast redeems 30 shares of Jane's stock for $100,000. Jane's percentage interest before the redemption is 80% [(60 + 20 shares) ÷ 100 shares]. Immediately after the redemption, her percentage interest is 71.4% [(30 + 20 shares) ÷ 70 shares]. To meet the 80% test, Jane's interest must be less than 64% (80% × 80%). Therefore, Jane does not meet the 80% test. Also, Jane does not meet the 50% test because she does not own less than 50% of Fast stock after the redemption. Both tests must be met for the redemption to qualify as substantially disproportionate. Jane likely will not qualify for Sec. 302(b)(1) "not essentially equivalent to a dividend" treatment because she has not reduced her stock interest to 50% or less. Therefore, the $100,000 is treated as a dividend and is taxable to Jane to the extent of Fast's E&P. ◀

Complete Termination. Under Sec. 302(b)(3), a complete termination of a shareholder's stock interest also qualifies for capital gain or loss treatment. At first glance, this rule appears redundant because the substantially disproportionate rule also applies to a redemption that results in a complete termination of a shareholder's interest. However, the complete termination provision permits a waiver of the family ownership attribution rules. These rules are waived if the former shareholder files an agreement with the IRS that for 10 years he or she will acquire no interest other than that as a creditor of the corporation.[57]

EXAMPLE I:16-42 ▶

REAL-WORLD EXAMPLE

All of a father's stock in a corporation was redeemed, and his children were the remaining shareholders. Then the father entered into a long-term contract with the corporation to perform consulting and advisory services. The contract represented an interest in the corporation and the family attribution rules were not waived. Rev. Rul. 70-104, 1970-1 C.B. 66.

Assume the same facts as in Example I:16-41 except that Fast Corporation redeems all of Jane's 60 shares for $200,000, and Jane's basis in her shares is $90,000. The family ownership attribution rules are waived if Jane agrees not to acquire any interest in Fast for 10 years. Jane's interest is deemed to be completely terminated, and the redemption is treated as a sale of stock, thus eligible for capital gains treatment. Jane recognizes a capital gain of $110,000 ($200,000 − $90,000). If the waiver is not effective because Jane remains an employee of Fast, the substantially disproportionate tests would be applied to determine whether the redemption qualifies as an exchange. Jane would be deemed to own 50% of the stock (20 shares owned ÷ 40 outstanding shares) immediately after the redemption. Thus, the substantially disproportionate test would not be met. Without an effective waiver, the redemption does not qualify as a complete termination because Jane is deemed to own her mother's stock. Consequently, the redemption would be treated as a dividend unless it could qualify for sale treatment under the Sec. 302(b)(1) "not-essentially-equivalent-to-a-dividend" test. ◀

---

[55] Rev. Rul. 75-502, 1975-2 C.B. 111.
[56] Rev. Rul. 76-364, 1976-2 C.B. 91.
[57] Sec. 302(c)(2). The former shareholder cannot serve as an officer, director, or employee for at least 10 years and must notify the IRS if additional stock is acquired (other than by bequest or inheritance). If such stock is subsequently acquired, it usually causes the redemption to be recharacterized as a dividend.

CORPORATE DISTRIBUTIONS IN COMPLETE LIQUIDATION

OBJECTIVE 7

Understand the tax implications of a corporate liquidation for the liquidating corporation and its shareholders

TYPICAL MISCONCEPTION

It is sometimes assumed that corporate liquidation always is associated with the discontinuance of business activities. Sometimes, however, the business is operated as a limited liability company, partnership, or sole proprietorship after the liquidation.

Sometimes shareholders may wish to terminate a corporation's existence. A complete liquidation is similar to a stock redemption except that all (rather than a portion) of the corporation's stock is redeemed. In a complete liquidation, the assets are either distributed in kind to the shareholders in exchange for their stock or sold for cash, which is then distributed to the shareholders in exchange for their stock. The liquidated corporation usually is dissolved under state law.

Surprisingly, the reasons for a complete termination are not always associated with unprofitable operations. For example, a highly-successful closely-held company may have management continuity problems because key officers and shareholders are approaching retirement age. Also, for reasons of organizational management, a parent corporation may wish to liquidate a subsidiary and continue its operations as a separate division of the parent.

TAX CONSEQUENCES TO THE LIQUIDATING CORPORATION

Distribution of Assets. In a liquidation, the liquidating corporation is treated as if it had sold its assets for their FMV to its shareholders and thus recognizes gain or loss.[58] If the distributed property is subject to a liability, the FMV of the property is deemed to be the greater of the property's actual FMV or the amount of the liability.

EXAMPLE I:16-43 ▶

In a complete liquidation, Southern Corporation distributes the following assets to its shareholders:

▶ Inventory: $12,000 basis, $20,000 FMV

▶ Investment land: $5,000 basis, $40,000 FMV, subject to a $30,000 liability

▶ Marketable securities: $20,000 basis, $15,000 FMV

Southern recognizes $8,000 ($20,000 − $12,000) of ordinary income on the distribution of the inventory, $35,000 ($40,000 − $5,000) of capital gain on the distribution of the land, and $5,000 ($15,000 − $20,000) of capital loss on the distribution of the marketable securities. ◀

Sale of Assets. The tax consequences of an asset sale closely parallel those of a liqui-dating distribution. If a corporation sells its assets in a complete liquidation and then distributes the sales proceeds to its shareholders, all gain or loss realized on the sale is recognized by the corporation.

Limitation on Loss Recognition. Under the general rule, upon liquidating, the corporation recognizes both gains and losses. To prevent abuses, three special rules limit the recognition of losses. First, a liquidating subsidiary recognizes neither gain nor loss when it distributes property to its parent. In addition, a liquidating subsidiary recognizes gain (but not loss) when it distributes property to minority shareholders. (The special rules applying to the liquidation of a subsidiary are set forth below.) Second, a liquidating corporation recognizes no loss when it distributes property to a related person, unless the property is distributed ratably to all shareholders and the property was not contributed in a Sec. 351 transaction or otherwise as capital within the preceding five years. Finally, losses are not recognized upon the sale, exchange, or distribution of property where the property was contributed in a Sec. 351 transaction or otherwise as capital, the principal purpose of which was loss recognition. These special loss limitations are explained further in Chapter C:6 of *Prentice Hall's Federal Taxation: Corporations, Partnerships, Estates, and Trusts.*

---

[58] Sec. 336.

Tax Attributes. Tax attributes, such as NOL carryovers, E&P balances, capital loss carryovers, and tax credits, are extinguished in a corporate liquidation.

TAX CONSEQUENCES TO THE SHAREHOLDERS

KEY POINT

An appraisal may be necessary to determine the FMV of the distributed assets.

Under the general rule for complete liquidations, shareholders are deemed to have sold their stock to the corporation in exchange for money or other property.[59] If the stock is a capital asset, the shareholder recognizes capital gain or loss equal to (1) the money plus the FMV of other property distributed to the shareholder less (2) the adjusted basis of the shareholder's stock.[60] The value of property distributed to a shareholder is its FMV on the distribution date.[61]

EXAMPLE I:16-44 ▶

In a complete liquidation, Sun Corporation distributes land with a $70,000 adjusted basis and a $100,000 FMV to shareholder John, in exchange for his Sun stock. John's adjusted basis in the stock is $40,000. Joan, another shareholder, receives $100,000 cash for her shares. Joan's adjusted basis in her stock is $120,000. John recognizes a $60,000 ($100,000 − $40,000) capital gain. Joan recognizes a $20,000 ($100,000 − $120,000) capital loss. The basis of the land received by John is $100,000 (the land's FMV on the distribution date). ◀

SECTION 332: LIQUIDATION OF A SUBSIDIARY CORPORATION

Gain and Loss Considerations. Section 332 carves out an exception to the general rule that gain or loss is recognized in a liquidating distribution. Under this exception, neither a parent nor its 80% or more owned subsidiary recognizes gain or loss when the parent liquidates the subsidiary.[62] In a Sec. 332 liquidation, the subsidiary usually is dissolved, and its assets and liabilities transferred to the parent. The Section 332 nonrecognition rule is mandatory, not elective, if its requirements are met.

KEY POINT

Section 351 permits a parent corporation to incorporate a subsidiary corporation tax-free. Section 332 permits a parent corporation to liquidate a controlled subsidiary corporation without adverse tax results where the subsidiary's property has significantly appreciated in value.

For nonrecognition treatment, the subsidiary must:

▶ Distribute all its assets to the parent in complete liquidation within a single tax year.

▶ Make a series of distributions resulting in a complete liquidation over a three-year period that commences at the close of the tax year in which the first liquidating distribution is made.

If a minority interest also is liquidated, the exception does not apply. The subsidiary recognizes gain (but not loss) on property distributed to a minority shareholder. In addition, the minority shareholder(s), recognize(s) gain or loss.

KEY POINT

A parent corporation whose basis for its subsidiary's stock exceeds the tax basis of its share of the subsidiary's net assets loses the tax benefit of the economic loss if the subsidiary is liquidated under the Sec. 332 rules.

Basis Considerations. The basis of the subsidiary's assets carry over to the parent, and the adjusted basis of the parent's stock in the subsidiary disappears.[63] This rule could create inequities because the parent may have paid an amount for the subsidiary stock that is greater (or less) than the parent's basis in the subsidiary's net assets.

EXAMPLE I:16-45 ▶

Several years ago Tampa Corporation acquired 100% of Top Corporation stock for $100,000. In the current year, Top is liquidated, and assets having a $130,000 FMV and a $50,000 basis are transferred to Tampa. Upon receiving the assets, Tampa recognizes no gain or loss. Tampa's $100,000 basis in the Top stock disappears, and Tampa takes only a $50,000 basis in the Top assets. Tampa would recognize an $80,000 ($130,000 − $50,000) gain should it sell the assets for their $130,000 FMV immediately after the liquidation. The character of the gain would depend on the type of assets received by Tampa. ◀

When these carryover basis rules apply, the parent corporation also inherits the tax attributes of the subsidiary.[64] For example, the liquidated subsidiary's NOL and capital

---

[59] Sec. 331(a)(1).
[60] Certain losses on the sale of small business stock are ordinary in character if the requirements of Sec. 1244 are met (see Chapter I:8).
[61] Sec. 334(a).
[62] Under Sec. 1504(a)(2), the parent corporation must own at least 80% of the

total combined voting power of all classes of stock entitled to vote and at least 80% of the total value of all classes of stock.
[63] Sec. 334(b)(1).
[64] Sec. 381.

loss carryovers and E&P balances carry over to the parent. In addition, the subsidiary recognizes no gain under the depreciation recapture rules. Instead, this recapture potential remains with the subsidiary assets distributed to the parent.

Topic Review I:16-4 summarizes the complete liquidation rules.

TAX PLANNING CONSIDERATIONS

OBJECTIVE 8

Describe tax planning considerations for corporations

CAPITAL STRUCTURE AND SECTION 1244

As mentioned earlier in the chapter, the issuance of long-term debt to capitalize a profitable closely-held C corporation could bolster the corporation's total economic returns and thus increase share values. However, if the corporation is no longer profitable and goes bankrupt, the corporate debt becomes worthless and is treated by noncorporate shareholders as nonbusiness bad debt. As is discussed in Chapter I:8, nonbusiness bad debt is deductible as a short-term capital loss subject to the $3,000 per year limitation.

TOPIC REVIEW I:16-4

Distributions in Complete Liquidation

SEC. 331 GENERAL LIQUIDATION RULES	LIQUIDATING CORPORATION	SHAREHOLDERS
Gain or loss recognition	Gain or loss equal to the FMV of the property distributed less the property's adjusted basis generally is recognized.	Capital gain or loss equal to the amount of money plus the FMV of other property received less the shareholder's basis of stock in the liquidating corporation is recognized.
Exception to the gain or loss rule	Losses are not recognized on distributions of property to related parties, or property acquired in certain tax-free transactions, where the principal purpose for the transaction is tax avoidance.	Sec. 1244 ordinary loss treatment is available only to individual shareholders.
Basis considerations	Not applicable.	The basis of noncash property received is its FMV.
Tax attributes	Tax attributes (e.g., NOL carryovers and E&P) disappear upon liquidation.	Not applicable.

SEC. 332 SUBSIDIARY CORPORATION LIQUIDATION RULES	SUBSIDIARY	PARENT
General requirements	The subsidiary is liquidated, and its assets and liabilities are transferred to its minority shareholders and parent.	Sec. 332 is mandatory. The parent must own at least 80% of subsidiary stock.
Gain or loss recognition	No gain or loss is recognized on the transfer of assets to the parent. Gain but not loss is recognized on distributions to minority shareholders.	The parent recognizes no gain or loss. Minority shareholders recognize gain or loss.
Basis considerations	None.	The basis of subsidiary assets carry over to the parent. Minority shareholders take a FMV basis in the assets they receive.
Tax attributes	Tax attributes are extinguished in the liquidation.	Tax attributes (e.g., NOL carryovers and E&P) are inherited by the parent.

As an alternative to debt, shareholders could capitalize the corporation with stock (equity). If certain conditions are met, this stock would be Sec. 1244 stock (small business corporation stock, see Chapter I:8 for details). If it becomes worthless, the shareholder may deduct up to $50,000 ($100,000 on a joint return) of its value as an ordinary loss. From a tax perspective, ordinary loss treatment is generally preferable to capital loss treatment that applies to nonbusiness bad debts.

The two principal components of capital structure clearly yield different results, depending on whether the corporation is profitable or unprofitable. Thus, deciding how to capitalize a corporation ultimately involves an evaluation of its potential profitability. If the owners of a new corporation believe the venture will be profitable, they should prefer debt because of the deductibility of interest payments. Because few entrepreneurs assume that their business will be unsuccessful, advising them to capitalize it with substantially more equity than debt might be difficult.

DIVIDEND POLICY

ADDITIONAL COMMENT

The reasonableness of a salary payment is a question of fact to be determined in each case. No formula can be used to determine a reasonable amount of compensation.

Dividends paid out of E&P are taxable to shareholders and nondeductible by the corporation. Consequently, in a closely held corporation, where ownership and management are the same, the owner-managers may wish to increase shareholder-employee compensation rather than increase dividends. Likewise, a shareholder may wish to lease property to the corporation instead of contribute it as capital. Even though the increased salary or rental payments are taxable to the shareholders (as are dividends), the corporation may deduct them as long as the amounts are reasonable.

EXAMPLE I:16-46 ▶ Mario and Nancy are equal owners of highly profitable Texas Corporation, which has substantial E&P. Mario and Nancy are the key officers. Each is paid $150,000 compared to $200,000 paid to others in similar positions. To increase earnings distributions to the owners, additional salary of $50,000 might be paid to both Mario and Nancy (rather than increase dividends by the same amount) because the corporation can deduct salary but not dividends. The salary payments result in a single level of taxation, while the dividend payments result in double taxation. The additional $50,000 compensation would subject the employer and the two shareholders to additional payroll taxes (e.g., the 1.45% Medicare portion of the FICA tax. There is no ceiling on the Medicare tax base.) ◀

USE OF LOSSES

A corporation should carefully plan how to use its net operating loss and capital loss carryovers. For example, the sale of appreciated business assets could result in a Sec. 1231 gain that could offset capital loss carryovers. Net Sec. 1231 gains are treated as capital in character. Alternatively, as a result of depreciation recapture, the sale of assets could give rise to ordinary income. Such income could be offset by expiring NOLs.

If a business expects to generate net operating losses or capital losses during its start-up phase, an S corporation election might be desirable because the losses flow thru to the shareholders' separate returns. The S corporation election might be terminated when the corporation becomes profitable so that C corporation treatment is preferred. (See Chapter I:17 for a discussion of S corporations.)

REAL-WORLD EXAMPLE

An accrual basis corporation that attempted to treat a contribution paid within 2½ months following year-end as a charitable contribution in the earlier year was denied a charitable contribution deduction because no written declaration of the resolution of the board of directors authorizing the contribution was attached to the return. *Donald G. Griswold,* 39 T.C. 620 (1962).

CHARITABLE CONTRIBUTIONS

Many owners of closely held corporations prefer to make charitable contributions through their corporations rather than as individuals because the corporations might be able to take a larger deduction. An accrual method corporation may accelerate a charitable contribution deduction if its board of directors approves the contribution before year-end, and the corporation makes the contribution within 2½ months of the corporation's tax year-end. The alternative to a corporate contribution could be a nondeductible dividend payment to the owner(s) who make(s) (an) individual contribution(s).

DIVIDENDS-RECEIVED DEDUCTION

Corporate shareholders may deduct 80% (in some cases, 70%) of dividends received. However, this deduction is limited to 80% (in some cases, 70%) of taxable income unless the deduction creates or increases an NOL. Thus, a substantial scale-down of the dividends-received deduction may result if taxable income (before this deduction) is positive, but negligible. If the limitation is likely to diminish the magnitude of the deduction, the corporation might either accelerate business deductions into the current year or postpone the recognition of income to a later year. Either measure could result in the generation of an NOL that renders the limitation inapplicable. (See Examples I:16-7 and I:16-8.)

REDUCED TAXES ON TAXPAYER STOCK SALES

IRC Section 1202(a)(1) permits noncorporate investors to exclude up to 50% of any gain realized on the sale or exchange of small business stock. This exclusion applies only to stock issued by C corporations that meet certain requirements; i.e., a stock holding period of five years or more, the use of at least 80% of the corporation's assets in the active conduct of a business, and a corporate asset value of $50 million or less at the time of stock issuance.

COMPLIANCE AND PROCEDURAL CONSIDERATIONS

OBJECTIVE 9

Describe compliance and procedural considerations for corporations

KEY POINT

All corporations must file an income tax return. The filing requirements are not based on minimum amounts of gross income, as in the case of individual taxpayers.

FILING REQUIREMENTS

A corporation must file Form 1120 (U.S. Corporation Income Tax Return) even if the corporation exists for only part of the year. Supplementing this form is a separate Schedule D that reports capital gains and losses. In addition, the corporation must file Form 4626 (Alternative Minimum Tax—Corporations) even if no alternative minimum tax is due. Corporations with less than $250,000 of gross receipts and less than $250,000 in assets can avoid reporting on Schedules L, M-1, and M-2 of their Form 1120.

The regular due date for the corporate return is the fifteenth day of the third month following the end of the tax year (e.g., March 15 for calendar-year corporations). The corporation can obtain an automatic 6-month extension by filing Form 7004 (Application for Automatic Extension of Time to File Corporation Income Tax Return). If an extension is granted, the full amount of the estimated tax must be paid on or before the due date (e.g., March 15 for calendar-year corporations).

Quarterly estimated tax payments must be made on the fifteenth day of the fourth, sixth, ninth, and twelfth months of the tax year. In general, the total required estimated tax payments are the lesser of 100% of the corporation's tax liability for the current year or 100% of the tax shown on the preceding year's return.[65] However, a corporation need not base the quarterly payments on the preceding year's tax liability if that liability was zero.[66] The corporation is subject to a nondeductible penalty to the extent the quarterly payments are less than the actual amounts due.

Through its e-file program, the IRS has developed an electronic procedure for filing Forms 1120 and 1120S. For tax years ending on or after December 31, 2005, corporations with at least $10 million in assets that file at least 250 returns annually are required to file electronically. Corporations not required to file electronically may choose to do so voluntarily. Currently, an amended tax return cannot be filed electronically.

---

[65]Exceptions are provided for large corporations and corporations that earn their income unevenly during the tax year. Large corporations—those with taxable income exceeding $1 million in any of the three preceding tax years—must make quarterly estimated tax payments based on 100% of the tax shown on their current year return. Alternatively, they are permitted to make their first-quarter payment based on 100% of the preceding year's tax liability [Sec. 6655(d)]. Section 6655(e) permits corporations to use an annualized income installment method, or seasonally adjusted installment method if the latter installments are less than the normally-required installment [Sec. 6655(e)].

[66] Rev. Rul. 92-54 1992-2 C.B. 320.

BOOK-TAX ACCOUNTING COMPARISON

The Schedule M-1 adjustments highlight the differences between financial accounting and tax accounting.

SCHEDULE M-1 AND M-2 RECONCILIATIONS

Schedule M-1 is used to reconcile financial accounting net income with taxable income before certain deductions (the NOL and dividends-received deductions). Figure I:16-1 shows a completed Schedule M-1 based on the following adjustments:

Net income per books	$100,000
Plus:	
Federal income tax liability	3,000
Net capital losses	2,000
Nondeductible premiums on life insurance covering key officers	4,000
Minus:	
Tax-exempt interest income	(9,000)
Excess of tax depreciation over financial accounting depreciation	(75,000)
Taxable income (before certain deductions)	$ 25,000

KEY POINT

Many small corporations who file Form 1120 are not required to complete Schedules M-1 and M-2. The exception is applicable to companies with gross receipts and assets below $250,000.

Schedule M-2 reconciles retained earnings (for financial accounting purposes) at the beginning of the year with retained earnings at year-end. This reconciliation accounts for changes in the balance sheet reported on Schedule L, or for items of income, gain, or loss components of retained earnings that have not been reported as part of net income. Figure I:16-2 illustrates a completed Schedule M-2 based on the above facts and the following assumptions: a $140,000 retained earnings balance on January 1, $100,000 of net income for financial accounting purposes, and the payment of a $40,000 cash dividend.

Schedule M-1 — **Reconciliation of Income (Loss) per Books With Income per Return**
Note: The corporation may be required to file Schedule M-3 (see instructions).

1	Net income (loss) per books	100,000	7	Income recorded on books this year not included on this return (itemize):	
2	Federal income tax per books	3,000		Tax-exempt interest $ 9,000	
3	Excess of capital losses over capital gains	2,000			
4	Income subject to tax not recorded on books this year (itemize):				9,000
5	Expenses recorded on books this year not deducted on this return (itemize):		8	Deductions on this return not charged against book income this year (itemize):	
a	Depreciation . . . . $		a	Depreciation . . $75,000	
b	Charitable contributions $		b	Charitable contributions $	
c	Travel and entertainment $				
	Premium on Life Insurance 4,000	4,000	9	Add lines 7 and 8	84,000
6	Add lines 1 through 5	109,000	10	Income (page 1, line 28)—line 6 less line 9	25,000

FIGURE I:16-1 ▶ Form 1120, Schedule M-1

Schedule M-2 — **Analysis of Unappropriated Retained Earnings per Books (Line 25, Schedule L)**

1	Balance at beginning of year	140,000	5	Distributions:	a	Cash	40,000
2	Net income (loss) per books	100,000			b	Stock	
3	Other increases (itemize):				c	Property . . .	
			6	Other decreases (itemize):			
			7	Add lines 5 and 6			40,000
4	Add lines 1, 2, and 3	240,000	8	Balance at end of year (line 4 less line 7) .			200,000

FIGURE I:16-2 ▶ Form 1120, Schedule M-2

SCHEDULE M-3 RECONCILIATION

Schedule M-3 (Net Income (Loss) Reconciliation for Corporations with Total Assets of $10 Million or More) reconciles a C corporation's book-tax differences. Reg. Sec. 1.6011-4(b)(6), defines significant book-tax difference in terms of a transaction with respect to which the amount of any item or items of income, gain, expense, or loss for tax purposes differs by more than $10 million in any tax year from the amount of the same item for book purposes. The amount of an item for book purposes is determined under Generally Accepted Accounting Principles.

Each member of an affiliated group must file a separate Schedule M-3. The entire group must file a consolidated Schedule M-3. The IRS is likely to use this schedule as a tool to determine whether or not to audit a corporation. A sample Schedule M-3 is presented on pages I:16-38 to I:16-40.

MAINTENANCE OF E&P RECORDS

Companies are not required to compute E&P on their tax return. They should, however, maintain adequate records of E&P items because the limitations period for contesting these items is indefinite, and the taxpayer has the burden of proof. Thus, if the IRS discovers that a company has current or accumulated E&P and treats a distribution as a taxable dividend rather than a tax-free return of capital, the taxpayer must show that the prescribed IRS treatment is erroneous.

Form 5452 (Corporate Report of Nondividend Distributions) must be filed by any corporation that makes a return-of-capital distribution. This form requires a computation of E&P and a schedule of differences between taxable income and E&P. This form also requires a year-by-year computation of accumulated E&P.

PROBLEM MATERIALS

DISCUSSION QUESTIONS

I:16-1 William Bonney and Pat Garrett incorporate Sales, Inc. on January 1, of the current year, under the laws of the State of Florida.
  a. How should the new corporation be regarded under the check-the-box rules?
  b. Are any entity elections available for Sales, Inc. under the IRC or the check-the-box rules?
  c. How would your answers to Parts a and b change (if at all) should William Bonney be the sole shareholder of Sales, Inc.?

I:16-2 Under the present tax system, C corporation income is taxed twice, once when earned and again when the shareholders receive dividends or sell their stock. Nevertheless, the C corporation form is widely used in the United States, especially for large enterprises. Why would an entrepreneur choose C corporation status instead of one of the flow-through entity forms?

I:16-3 Some tax analysts contend that many corporations can shift the burden of corporate taxation to consumers in the form of higher prices. In what other ways might a corporation attempt to shift the burden (e.g., to employees, tenants, and/or shareholders)?

I:16-4 For most individual investors, net long-term capital gains and dividends are taxed at the same rate. Yet, in some circumstances, an investor's generating long-term capital gains is more advantageous than earning a dividend. What are these circumstances and why?

I:16-5 Acorn Corporation has a $5,000 NSTCG and a $9,000 NLTCL in the current year. Last year, Acorn had a $3,000 NLTCG. No other capital gains or losses were reported in prior tax years.
  a. Do the NSTCG and NLTCL have to be offset against one another in the current year?
  b. Is any portion of the NLTCL deductible in the current year?
  c. What loss carryback or carryover rules should be applied to any unused capital losses incurred in the current year?

I:16-6 C corporations are allowed a dividends received deduction (DRD) for dividends received from domestic corporations.
  a. What is the purpose of the DRD?
  b. Does the taxable income limitation on the DRD serve any purpose?
  c. What additional tax liability is incurred by a C corporation when it receives $10,000 of dividend income from a 10%-owned domestic

| SCHEDULE M-3
(Form 1120)

Department of the Treasury
Internal Revenue Service | **Net Income (Loss) Reconciliation for Corporations
With Total Assets of \$10 Million or More**
▶ Attach to Form 1120 or 1120-C. ▶ Information about Schedule M-3 (Form 1120) and its
separate instructions is available at *www.irs.gov/form1120*. | OMB No. 1545-0123

20**14** |

| Name of corporation (common parent, if consolidated return) | Employer identification number |

Check applicable box(es):   (1) ☐ Non-consolidated return   (2) ☐ Consolidated return (Form 1120 only)

(3) ☐ Mixed 1120/L/PC group   (4) ☐ Dormant subsidiaries schedule attached

Part I   Financial Information and Net Income (Loss) Reconciliation (see instructions)

1a Did the corporation file SEC Form 10-K for its income statement period ending with or within this tax year?
   ☐ **Yes.**   Skip lines 1b and 1c and complete lines 2a through 11 with respect to that SEC Form 10-K.
   ☐ **No.**   Go to line 1b. See instructions if multiple non-tax-basis income statements are prepared.

 b Did the corporation prepare a certified audited non-tax-basis income statement for that period?
   ☐ **Yes.**   Skip line 1c and complete lines 2a through 11 with respect to that income statement.
   ☐ **No.**   Go to line 1c.

 c Did the corporation prepare a non-tax-basis income statement for that period?
   ☐ **Yes.**   Complete lines 2a through 11 with respect to that income statement.
   ☐ **No.**   Skip lines 2a through 3c and enter the corporation's net income (loss) per its books and records on line 4a.

2a Enter the income statement period: Beginning   MM/DD/YYYY   Ending   MM/DD/YYYY

 b Has the corporation's income statement been restated for the income statement period on line 2a?
   ☐ **Yes.**   (If "Yes," attach an explanation and the amount of each item restated.)
   ☐ **No.**

 c Has the corporation's income statement been restated for any of the five income statement periods immediately preceding the period on line 2a?
   ☐ **Yes.**   (If "Yes," attach an explanation and the amount of each item restated.)
   ☐ **No.**

3a Is any of the corporation's voting common stock publicly traded?
   ☐ **Yes.**
   ☐ **No.**   If "No," go to line 4a.

 b Enter the symbol of the corporation's primary U.S. publicly traded voting common stock . . . .

 c Enter the nine-digit CUSIP number of the corporation's primary publicly traded voting common stock . . . .

4a	Worldwide consolidated net income (loss) from income statement source identified in Part I, line 1 .	**4a**
b	Indicate accounting standard used for line 4a (see instructions): (1) ☐ GAAP (2) ☐ IFRS (3) ☐ Statutory (4) ☐ Tax-basis (5) ☐ Other (specify) _____	
5a	Net income from nonincludible foreign entities (attach statement)	**5a** ( )
b	Net loss from nonincludible foreign entities (attach statement and enter as a positive amount) . . .	**5b**
6a	Net income from nonincludible U.S. entities (attach statement)	**6a** ( )
b	Net loss from nonincludible U.S. entities (attach statement and enter as a positive amount)	**6b**
7a	Net income (loss) of other includible foreign disregarded entities (attach statement)	**7a**
b	Net income (loss) of other includible U.S. disregarded entities (attach statement)	**7b**
c	Net income (loss) of other includible entities (attach statement)	**7c**
8	Adjustment to eliminations of transactions between includible entities and nonincludible entities (attach statement)	**8**
9	Adjustment to reconcile income statement period to tax year (attach statement)	**9**
10a	Intercompany dividend adjustments to reconcile to line 11 (attach statement)	**10a**
b	Other statutory accounting adjustments to reconcile to line 11 (attach statement)	**10b**
c	Other adjustments to reconcile to amount on line 11 (attach statement)	**10c**
11	**Net income (loss) per income statement of includible corporations.** Combine lines 4 through 10 .	**11**

Note. Part I, line 11, must equal Part II, line 30, column (a) or Schedule M-1, line 1 (see instructions).

12 Enter the total amount (not just the corporation's share) of the assets and liabilities of all entities included or removed on the following lines.

	Total Assets	Total Liabilities
a Included on Part I, line 4 . . . . ▶		
b Removed on Part I, line 5 . . . . ▶		
c Removed on Part I, line 6 . . . . ▶		
d Included on Part I, line 7 . . . . ▶		

For Paperwork Reduction Act Notice, see the Instructions for Form 1120.   Cat. No. 37961C   **Schedule M-3 (Form 1120) 2014**

FIGURE I:16-3a ▶ Form 1120, Schedule M-3

Schedule M-3 (Form 1120) 2014   Page **2**

Name of corporation (common parent, if consolidated return)	Employer identification number

Check applicable box(es): **(1)** ☐ Consolidated group   **(2)** ☐ Parent corp   **(3)** ☐ Consolidated eliminations   **(4)** ☐ Subsidiary corp   **(5)** ☐ Mixed 1120/L/PC group

Check if a sub-consolidated: **(6)** ☐ 1120 group   **(7)** ☐ 1120 eliminations

Name of subsidiary (if consolidated return)	Employer identification number

Part II **Reconciliation of Net Income (Loss) per Income Statement of Includible Corporations With Taxable Income per Return** (see instructions)

Income (Loss) Items (Attach statements for lines 1 through 12)	(a) Income (Loss) per Income Statement	(b) Temporary Difference	(c) Permanent Difference	(d) Income (Loss) per Tax Return
1 Income (loss) from equity method foreign corporations				
2 Gross foreign dividends not previously taxed				
3 Subpart F, QEF, and similar income inclusions				
4 Section 78 gross-up				
5 Gross foreign distributions previously taxed				
6 Income (loss) from equity method U.S. corporations				
7 U.S. dividends not eliminated in tax consolidation				
8 Minority interest for includible corporations				
9 Income (loss) from U.S. partnerships				
10 Income (loss) from foreign partnerships				
11 Income (loss) from other pass-through entities				
12 Items relating to reportable transactions				
13 Interest income (see instructions)				
14 Total accrual to cash adjustment				
15 Hedging transactions				
16 Mark-to-market income (loss)				
17 Cost of goods sold (see instructions)	( )			( )
18 Sale versus lease (for sellers and/or lessors)				
19 Section 481(a) adjustments				
20 Unearned/deferred revenue				
21 Income recognition from long-term contracts				
22 Original issue discount and other imputed interest				
23a Income statement gain/loss on sale, exchange, abandonment, worthlessness, or other disposition of assets other than inventory and pass-through entities				
b Gross capital gains from Schedule D, excluding amounts from pass-through entities				
c Gross capital losses from Schedule D, excluding amounts from pass-through entities, abandonment losses, and worthless stock losses				
d Net gain/loss reported on Form 4797, line 17, excluding amounts from pass-through entities, abandonment losses, and worthless stock losses				
e Abandonment losses				
f Worthless stock losses (attach statement)				
g Other gain/loss on disposition of assets other than inventory				
24 Capital loss limitation and carryforward used				
25 Other income (loss) items with differences (attach statement)				
26 **Total income (loss) items.** Combine lines 1 through 25				
27 **Total expense/deduction items** (from Part III, line 38)				
28 Other items with no differences				
29a Mixed groups, see instructions. All others, combine lines 26 through 28				
b PC insurance subgroup reconciliation totals				
c Life insurance subgroup reconciliation totals				
30 **Reconciliation totals.** Combine lines 29a through 29c				

Note. Line 30, column (a), must equal Part I, line 11, and column (d) must equal Form 1120, page 1, line 28.

Schedule M-3 (Form 1120) 2014

FIGURE I:16-3b ▶ Form 1120, Schedule M-3

Name of corporation (common parent, if consolidated return)	Employer identification number

Check applicable box(es): **(1)** ☐ Consolidated group   **(2)** ☐ Parent corp   **(3)** ☐ Consolidated eliminations   **(4)** ☐ Subsidiary corp   **(5)** ☐ Mixed 1120/L/PC group

Check if a sub-consolidated: **(6)** ☐ 1120 group   **(7)** ☐ 1120 eliminations

Name of subsidiary (if consolidated return)	Employer identification number

Part III **Reconciliation of Net Income (Loss) per Income Statement of Includible Corporations With Taxable Income per Return—Expense/Deduction Items** (see instructions)

Expense/Deduction Items	(a) Expense per Income Statement	(b) Temporary Difference	(c) Permanent Difference	(d) Deduction per Tax Return
1 U.S. current income tax expense				
2 U.S. deferred income tax expense				
3 State and local current income tax expense . . .				
4 State and local deferred income tax expense . . .				
5 Foreign current income tax expense (other than foreign withholding taxes)				
6 Foreign deferred income tax expense				
7 Foreign withholding taxes				
8 Interest expense (see instructions)				
9 Stock option expense				
10 Other equity-based compensation				
11 Meals and entertainment				
12 Fines and penalties				
13 Judgments, damages, awards, and similar costs .				
14 Parachute payments				
15 Compensation with section 162(m) limitation . . .				
16 Pension and profit-sharing				
17 Other post-retirement benefits				
18 Deferred compensation				
19 Charitable contribution of cash and tangible property				
20 Charitable contribution of intangible property . .				
21 Charitable contribution limitation/carryforward . .				
22 Domestic production activities deduction				
23 Current year acquisition or reorganization investment banking fees				
24 Current year acquisition or reorganization legal and accounting fees				
25 Current year acquisition/reorganization other costs .				
26 Amortization/impairment of goodwill				
27 Amortization of acquisition, reorganization, and start-up costs				
28 Other amortization or impairment write-offs . . .				
29 Reserved				
30 Depletion				
31 Depreciation				
32 Bad debt expense				
33 Corporate owned life insurance premiums . . .				
34 Purchase versus lease (for purchasers and/or lessees)				
35 Research and development costs				
36 Section 118 exclusion (attach statement)				
37 Other expense/deduction items with differences (attach statement)				
38 **Total expense/deduction items.** Combine lines 1 through 37. Enter here and on Part II, line 27, reporting positive amounts as negative and negative amounts as positive				

Schedule M-3 (Form 1120) 2014

FIGURE I:16-3c ▶ Form 1120, Schedule M-3

corporation? From a 25%-owned domestic corporation?From a more-than-80% owned domestic corporation?Assume that the entity's additional taxable income is taxed at a 34% marginal rate.

d. What is the effective tax rate on the dividend income? Hint: the effective tax rate equals the increase in a C corporation's tax liability divided by the additional gross income that it reports.

I:16-7 Under what circumstances might a corporation elect not to carry back an NOL to its prior tax years?

I:16-8 What conditions must be met for an accrual-basis corporation to deduct a charitable contribution in a year before it is made?

I:16-9 Acorn Corporation is publicly traded on the American Stock Exchange. Its chief executive officer, Carl, currently receives an annual salary of $1 million. The board of directors is considering increasing his compensation by $200,000.
  a. What are the income tax consequences to Acorn if Carl's salary is increased to $1,200,000?
  b. What alternatives might be considered to increase Carl's annual compensation that would produce more favorable tax consequences for Acorn?

I:16-10 Current tax law imposes a $1 million limitation on the deductibility of executive compensation. Should such limitation be retained or repealed? Give reasons for your opinion.

I:16-11 The current corporate tax structure contains phase-outs (via surtaxes) at various levels of taxable income that eliminate the benefits of lower tax brackets. Identify the two phase-outs in the corporate tax rate structure. How do these phase-outs affect a corporation's marginal and average tax rates? In your opinion, should phase-outs be retained in the tax law or repealed?

I:16-12 Explain the following statement:For a C corporation earning taxable income in excess of $10,000,000, the corporate income tax is in essence a flat tax imposed at a 34% rate.

I:16-13 The production activities deduction is available based only on income related to U.S. production activities (or taxable income, if a smaller amount). Why did Congress restrict the calculation of the deduction only to income from domestic production?

I:16-14 Spurrier Corporation's taxable income is $50,000, and its tax preference items and positive adjustments for the alternative minimum tax (AMT) are $100,000.
  a. Is Spurrier subject to the AMT (assume the corporation is not excluded from the AMT under the small business exception)?If so, what additional taxes (if any) are owed because of the AMT rules?

b. What AMT reporting requirements must Spurrier satisfy in preparing its tax return?
  c. Can Spurrier avoid paying the corporate AMT by electing to pay more dividends to its shareholder?What is the tax tradeoff between paying the AMT and paying dividends to a shareholder?

I:16-15 Current tax law provides for a dual system, the regular tax and alternative minimum tax. In effect, a corporation pays the greater of the regular tax or the tentative minimum tax. Why did Congress enact such a dual system? How could Congress replace the dual system with a single tax system?

I:16-16 Collins Corporation pays a $30,000 alternative minimum tax in the current year. What AMT benefit (if any) is available to reduce federal income taxes paid in a prior tax year, in the current tax year, or in a future tax year?

I:16-17 The accumulated earnings tax is effectively a penalty on corporations.
  a. What is the purpose of the accumulated earnings tax?
  b. Why does the "reasonable needs of the business" exception either reduce or eliminate the accumulated earnings tax burden for many corporations?

I:16-18 Acme Corporation is a highly profitable closely held corporation that has never paid a dividend. During the past five years, after-tax earnings of $200,000 per year have been retained in the business. All of the earnings ($1 million) have been reinvested in operating assets and to finance an expansion of the business. Is the corporation subject to the accumulated earnings tax because no dividends have been paid?

I:16-19 The personal holding company tax imposes a penalty on corporations.
  a. What is the purpose of the personal holding company tax?
  b. Two tests are used to classify a corporation as a personal holding company. What are these tests, and how do they serve the purpose of the personal holding company tax?

I:16-20 In terms of a corporation's incurring liability for the tax, what is the difference between the personal holding company tax and the accumulated earnings tax? Do both taxes require a tax avoidance motive?

I:16-21 Why are controlled groups of corporations required to apportion among group members the lower rates applicable to taxable income up to $75,000?

I:16-22 Discuss the underlying rationale for the nonrecognition of gain or loss in a Sec. 351 transaction.

I:16-23 Corporate formation transactions are either taxable or tax-free events depending on whether the requirements of Sec. 351 are met. Debate the pros and cons of the following statement: All corporate formations should be treated as taxable events. Teams of two to four persons should conduct the debate. A summary of items for the "pro" and "con" positions should be presented.

I:16-24
a. Brett Nelson transfers a building having a $75,000 FMV and a $30,000 adjusted basis to Gator Corporation. An advantage of the asset transfer under Sec. 351 is that Brett can defer his $45,000 ($75,000 FMV − $30,000 adjusted basis) realized gain. What disadvantages accrue to Gator as a result of the post-transfer aspects of the transaction?
b. Assume the same facts as in Part a except that the building's FMV is instead $30,000 and its adjusted basis is $75,000. What tax disadvantage results from the transfer as presently structured? Are there any suggestions that you can offer to Brett to improve his tax benefits?
c. Explain why the basis of gain property that is contributed to a corporation in a Sec. 351 exchange is not equal to its FMV on the date of the exchange. Is the basis of the property that is contributed to the corporation adjusted when gain is recognized by the transferor?
d. How would your answers to Part a change if Brett Nelson transferred a $25,000 mortgage along with the land and received stock having a value less than the amount of the liability?

I:16-25 Carmen transfers land and a building having a $60,000 adjusted basis and a $100,000 FMV to Bass Corporation in a transaction ostensibly qualifying as tax-free under Sec. 351. Immediately before the exchange, Carmen incurs a $50,000 mortgage on the property. The mortgage is assumed by the corporation, and the mortgage proceeds are used by Carmen to remodel her personal residence.
a. What are the likely tax consequences of the asset transfer?
b. What is the rationale for this result?

I:16-26 Sato, Jose, and Satish form a new corporation. Each individual contributes $100,000 in appreciated property and receives a one-third (equity) ownership interest. Jose and Satish also lend the corporation $250,000 cash in exchange for two 30-year notes (debt) bearing annual interest at a below-market rate of 3.5%.
a. From the corporation's and the shareholders' perspectives, what are the principal advantages of capitalizing with debt as opposed to equity?
b. What are the tax consequences to Sato, Jose, and Satish if the property transfer meets the requirements of Sec. 351?
c. What tax consequences to the corporation and its shareholders would ensue if the IRS recharacterizes the debt as equity?

I:16-27 Chang and George, high income taxpayers, are starting a new business that manufactures and sells explosives. They expect the business to sustain $500,000 in losses in its first two years of operation, then gradually generate profits. Given their high income level, the nature of their business, and its projected operating results, what entity form(s) might Chang and George find advantageous, and why?

I:16-28 Under current tax law, a corporation may deduct interest but not dividends paid to shareholders. What potential problems are created by this disparate treatment? Should the law be changed to either disallow the interest deduction or allow a dividends-paid deduction?

I:16-29 Why is it generally preferable to structure the redemption of a shareholder's stock to meet the substantially disproportionate test or the complete termination test rather than the not-essentially-equivalent-to-a-dividend requirement?

I:16-30 Compare the three types of redemptions (i.e., substantially disproportionate, not essentially equivalent to a dividend, and complete termination of shareholder interest) in terms of the following features:
a. Often permissible, even where percentage stock ownership does not decrease by more than 80%.
b. Constructive ownership rules may be waived under certain conditions.
c. Treated as an exchange taxed as a capital gain or loss.
d. Stock not surrendered in exchange for corporate distribution.

I:16-31 If the requirements for a complete termination of a shareholder's interest are met, should not the substantially disproportionate redemption requirements also be met? What is the major difference between these two requirements?

I:16-32 How does the liquidation of a controlled subsidiary differ from the liquidation of a corporation owned by a single individual? What is the reason for the difference?

I:16-33 A corporate formation can take place tax-free when an individual transfers the assets of a business to a corporation and no boot property is distributed by the corporation to the shareholder. A corporate liquidation, on the other hand, is taxable to both the liquidating corporation and its shareholder(s). Why does the tax law differentiate between the two transactions?

I:16-34 Why is Sec. 1244, which pertains to small business corporation stock, in the tax code? What advantages and disadvantages are afforded to owners of Sec. 1244 stock?

I:16-35 Why is it generally preferable to increase salaries, interest, or rental payments to employee-shareholders in a closely held corporation rather than increase dividends?

I:16-36 What advantages and disadvantages accrue to a corporation and its shareholders of (1) electing C corporation status for the business, or (2) electing S corporation status?

I:16-37 Explain the purpose of Schedule M-3 in corporate income tax reporting. Explain which C corporations must file this form and which C corporations need not file this form.

I:16-38 Besides M-1 and M-2, what other schedules are incorporated in Form 1120, and what do they purport to report? *(Hint: go to www.irs.gov. Retrieve and review the form.)*

ISSUE IDENTIFICATION QUESTIONS

I:16-39 Acorn Corporation is a very profitable closely held corporation that is owned solely by Helen, age 55, who plans to retire in 10 years. Management continuity is a problem because neither the existing employees nor Helen's children are interested in or capable of managing the company. Acorn has never paid a dividend and does not intend to do so in the future because dividends are not deductible by the corporation and would be taxable to the shareholders. Helen does not wish to expand the business and plans to have the corporation reinvest its earnings in securities. What tax issues should Helen consider in the short run? In the long run?

I:16-40 Hugo and Helga each own unincorporated businesses. They plan to form a corporation to which they would transfer all of their business assets and liabilities in exchange for all of the corporation's stock. Hugo's assets have substantially appreciated over time. A transfer of all of his assets and liabilities would result in an excess of liabilities over the adjusted basis of the assets. Helga has substantial unrealized losses on some of her business properties (e.g., land and a building). Her tax accountant has recommended that she sell the properties to a third party or to the corporation to recognize capital losses or Sec. 1231 losses that could be used to offset personal capital or ordinary gains. The sales proceeds then could be invested in the new corporation. What tax issues should Hugo and Helga consider with respect to the asset transfer, the organizational expenditures, the capital structure, and other aspects of the corporate formation?

I:16-41 Eastern Corporation is formed by John and Joy with an initial capitalization of $500,000. Two alternative capitalization plans are being considered: (1) John and Joy, who are unrelated, each would receive $200,000 of 8% 15-year bonds and $50,000 of Eastern stock, or (2) John and Joy each would receive $250,000 of Eastern stock. John's business assets that would be transferred to Eastern have significantly appreciated over time, and John does not want to recognize any gain on the transfer of these assets. Organizational costs of $3,000 are expected to be incurred. What tax issues should John and Joy consider with respect to the asset transfer, the organizational expenditures, the capital structure, and other aspects of the corporate formation?

PROBLEMS

I:16-42 *Capital Gains and Losses.* First Corporation, in its fifth year of operations, realizes the following capital gains and losses in the current year:

LTCG	$20,000
LTCL	(8,000)
STCG	16,000
STCL	(40,000)

Taxable income (exclusive of the capital gains and losses) is $60,000.
a. What is First's net capital gain or loss?
b. What is First's taxable income for the current year?
c. Assuming that the gains and losses reported in the current year are the first capital gains and losses ever reported by the corporation and then that the corporation had reported an excess of capital gains over capital losses in its prior tax years, explain the tax treatment of any unused capital losses

I:16-43 *Capital Loss Carrybacks and Carryovers.* Federal Corporation realizes the following net capital losses in 2015:

STCL	$ 80,000
LTCL	120,000

NLTCGs were incurred in 2012 through 2014 as follows:

2012	$20,000
2013	20,000
2014	60,000

a. What are the amount and character of any capital loss carryback to 2012 through 2014?
b. What treatment should be accorded any unused capital loss amount after the carryback?
c. What is the character of any unused capital loss carryovers?

I:16-44 *Netting of Gains and Losses.* For each of the four independent scenarios below, compute the additional amount of income tax (or tax savings if a loss) that would result from current gains and losses for (a) Able Corporation that is taxed at a 35% marginal tax rate or (b) a sole proprietorship whose ordinary income is taxed at a 39.6% rate and long-term capital gains, at a 20% rate. (Ignore the 3.8% net investment income tax for higher-income taxpayers for this problem.)

Scenario	LTCG or (LTCL)	STCG or (STCL)	Sec. 1231 Gains	Sec. 1231 Losses
1	$10,000	$ 5,000	$10,000	$ 5,000
2	$10,000	$ 15,000	$20,000	$ 5,000
3	$10,000	$(15,000)	$ –0–	$15,000
4	$20,000	$ 5,000	$10,000	$15,000

I:16-45 *Dividends-Received Deduction.* During the current year, Florida Corporation reports the following results:

Net income from operations	$100,000
Dividend from a 20%-owned corporation (qualifying for the dividends-received deduction)	200,000

a. What is the amount of Florida's dividends-received deduction?
b. How would your answer to Part a change if Florida instead reported a $20,000 loss from operations?
c. How would your answer to Parts a and b change if the dividend income were instead from a 10%-owned corporation and the loss from operations in Part b were instead $70,000?

I:16-46 *Dividends-Received Deduction.* Calculate the dividends-received deduction and taxable income for each independent scenario below. Assume there are no other income or deduction items.
a. During the current year, Purple Corporation reports $260,000 of gross income from operations and $170,000 of allowable business deductions. In addition, Purple receives dividends of $200,000 from Blue Corporation. Purple owns 25% of Blue and the dividends qualify for the dividends-received deduction.
b. During the current year, Yellow Corporation reports $160,000 of gross income from operations and $180,000 of allowable business deductions. In addition, Yellow receives dividends of $220,000 from Green Corporation. Yellow owns 15% of Green common stock and the dividends qualify for the dividends-received deduction.

I:16-47 *Net Operating Losses.* Alpha Corporation reports $500,000 of gross income from business operations and $625,000 of allowable business deductions. It also received from a domestic corporation $150,000 in dividends for which it is entitled to an 80% dividends-received deduction. What is Alpha's taxable income reported on Form 1120?

I:16-48 *Charitable Contributions.* On May 15 of the current year, the board of directors of Georgia Corporation authorized a $40,000 donation to a qualified charity. The corporation donated the $40,000 to the charity on December 1 of the current year. It made no other charitable contributions during the year. Georgia reports the following results for the current year:

Taxable income (before the dividends-received deduction and charitable contributions)	$250,000
Dividends-received deduction	10,000

a. What amount of charitable contributions is deductible in the current year?

b. How are any excess contributions treated?

c. How would your answer to Part a change if Georgia incurs a $50,000 NOL in the next year that is carried back to the current year?

I:16-49 *Corporate Tax Rates.* Calculate Ajax Corporation's regular tax liability for the following amounts of taxable income:

a. $90,000

b. $300,000

c. $5 million

d. $12 million

e. $17 million

f. $20 million

g. Alternatively, for Parts a, b, and c above, compute Ajax's regular tax liability if it were a personal service corporation.

I:16-50 *Corporate Tax Rates.* In December of the current year, Colorado Corporation considers a sale of certain corporate assets that would result in the recognition of a $50,000 LTCG. Colorado's controller estimates that taxable income for the current year will be $60,000 (excluding the LTCG). She also estimates that taxable income for next year will be $200,000 (excluding the LTCG).

a. What is Colorado's tax liability for the two years if the assets are sold in the current year?

b. What is Colorado's tax liability for the two years if the assets are sold next year?

c. Should Colorado sell the assets in the current year or next year? Explain.

I:16-51 *Alternative Minimum Tax.* In an audit of Control Corporation, you were assigned to review the company's current-year tax accrual (e.g., provision for federal income taxes and the related liability). Control was incorporated in 2000. The following tax information is available for your review:

• Taxable income for regular tax purposes is $150,000.

• Depreciation for regular tax purposes is $100,000. Depreciation for AMT purposes is $71,000.

• Adjusted current earnings is $370,000.

• No AMT adjustment for the U.S. production activities deduction.

Assume that Control is not eligible for the small corporation AMT exemption.

a. What is the total amount of Control's AMT adjustments for the current year?

b. Calculate the following amounts for Control:
  • Alternative minimum taxable income
  • AMT base
  • Tentative minimum tax
  • Alternative minimum tax
  • Total tax liability

I:16-52 *Accumulated Earnings Tax.* The IRS is auditing Crane Corporation, a manufacturer of widgets, to determine whether the company is liable for the accumulated earnings tax in a prior tax year. Crane is owned by 20 shareholders who are unrelated and was not a personal holding company in the year in question. Crane reported the following results for the current year:

Taxable income	$150,000
Federal income taxes	41,750
Dividends-received deduction	85,000
Dividend paid on June 1	20,000

The accumulated E&P balance on January 1 is $180,000, and the company can justify the retention of the $180,000 of E&P at the beginning of the year plus $80,000 of earnings earned in the current year in terms of meeting its reasonable business needs. In fact, all of the January 1 earnings were retained for the reasonable needs of the business.

a. What is Crane's accumulated taxable income?

b. What is Crane's accumulated earnings tax liability?

c. If Crane potentially owes the accumulated earnings tax, what steps can it take to reduce or eliminate the liability?

I:16-53   *Personal Holding Company Tax.* Delta Corporation is being reorganized as an investment company because its retained earnings have been used for passive investments. The company is owned by three shareholders, and more than 60% of its income is personal holding company income. George, the president of Delta believes that personal holding company status is not detrimental because the company has paid dividends to its shareholders for several years and therefore should not be liable for any penalty tax.

Delta reports the following results for the current year:

Taxable income	$50,000
Federal income tax liability	7,500
Dividends paid	6,000
Dividends-received deduction	80,000

a. Do you agree or disagree with George? Explain.

b. What is Delta's personal holding company tax liability, if any, for the current year?

c. How could Delta avoid liability for the personal holding company tax?

I:16-54   *Controlled Group.* Eagle and East Corporations are members of a brother-sister controlled group. Eagle's taxable income is $75,000, and East's taxable income is $50,000.

a. What is Eagle and East's total federal income tax liability?

b. What is Eagle and East's total federal income tax liability if they are not members of a controlled group?

I:16-55   *Controlled Group.* Alfred, Barbara, and Cathy own stock in First, Second, and Third Corporations as follows:

Individuals	First	Second	Third
Alfred	40%	40%	40%
Barbara	30%	60%	30%
Cathy	30%	–0–	30%

Which corporations are members of a brother-sister controlled group under the 80%-50% test?

I:16-56   *Corporate Formation.* In the current year, Jack, Karen, Latoya, and Marc transfer the following property to Giant Corporation (an existing corporation), which is owned equally by the four transferors.

• Jack transfers land and a building with a $60,000 adjusted basis and a $100,000 FMV for additional Giant stock having an $80,000 FMV and $20,000 of marketable securities having an adjusted basis of $15,000 in Giant's hands. $10,000 of MACRS straight-line depreciation on the building was claimed by Jack prior to the transfer.

• Karen transfers equipment with a $120,000 adjusted basis and a $100,000 FMV for additional Giant stock having an $80,000 FMV and a $20,000 20-year Giant note. $25,000 of MACRS depreciation on the equipment was claimed by Karen prior to the transfer.

• Latoya transfers inventory with a $70,000 adjusted basis and a $100,000 FMV for additional Giant stock having an $80,000 FMV and $20,000 cash.

• Marc transfers land with a $30,000 adjusted basis and a $100,000 FMV, subject to a $40,000 mortgage, which Giant assumes, for additional Giant stock having a $60,000 FMV.

a. What amount and character of gain or loss does Jack recognize? What is Jack's basis in the Giant stock and the marketable securities? What is Giant's basis in the land and building?

b. What amount and character of gain or loss does Karen recognize? What is Karen's basis in the Giant stock and note? What is Giant's basis in the equipment?

c. What amount and character of gain or loss does Latoya recognize? What is Latoya's basis in the Giant stock? What is Giant's basis in the inventory?

d. What amount and character of gain or loss does Marc recognize? What is Marc's basis in the Giant stock? What is Giant's basis in the land?

e. What amount and character of gain or loss does Giant recognize on the distribution of its stock, note, and other property to its shareholders?

I:16-57 *Corporate Formation.* Linda and Cynthia decide to form a corporation in a transaction that meets the requirements of Sec. 351. Linda transfers machinery she has held for several years with a basis of $45,000 and a fair market value of $70,000 for 60% of the new corporation's stock. The machinery was originally purchased for $100,000 and is subject to a liability of $10,000 that the corporation has agreed to assume. Cynthia transfers land held for investment with a basis of $32,000 and a fair market value of $40,000 for the remaining 40% of the corporation's stock.
a. Determine Linda's basis in her shares and any gain or loss recognized.
b. Determine Cynthia's basis in her shares and any gain or loss recognized.

I:16-58 *Corporate Formations: Transfer of Liabilities.* In a transaction that meets the requirements of Sec. 351, Matt transfers to Hill Corporation land with a $600,000 adjusted basis and a $1,000,000 FMV that was used in his business. The land is subject to an $800,000 mortgage, which Hill assumes. Matt receives 100% of Hill stock.
a. What amount and character of gain or loss are recognized by Matt?
b. What is Matt's basis in the Hill stock?
c. What is Hill's basis in the land?

I:16-59 *Earnings and Profits (E&P).* During the current year, Nevada Corporation distributed $100,000 in cash to its sole shareholder. Because the corporation has a $300,000 accumulated E&P deficit at the beginning of the current year and only $30,000 of taxable income in the current year, Nevada's controller believes that the distribution should be treated as a tax-free return of capital to the shareholder. Your investigation reveals the following information that may have an effect on the computation of current E&P:

Federal income tax liability	$ 4,500
Dividends-received deduction	60,000
Excess of MACRS depreciation over	
Alternative Depreciation System depreciation	30,000
Excess charitable contributions	9,000
U.S. production activities deduction	10,000

a. What is Nevada's current E&P?
b. How much (if any) of the $100,000 cash distribution is taxable as a dividend to the sole shareholder?
c. What is the amount of Nevada's accumulated E&P balance (deficit) on the last day of the current year?

I:16-60 *Earnings and Profits (E&P).* North Corporation has $200,000 of accumulated E&P at the beginning of the current year. North distributed $300,000 cash during the current year to its shareholders. The company's operating results for the current year are as follows:

Taxable income	$100,000
Tax-exempt bond interest	10,000
Dividends-received deduction	7,000
Federal income tax liability	22,250
Net capital losses	27,000
U.S. production activities deduction	12,000

a. What is North Corporation's current E&P?
b. How much of the $300,000 cash distribution is taxable as a dividend?
c. What is North's accumulated E&P balance (deficit) at the end of the current year?

I:16-61 *Earnings and Profits (E&P).* At the beginning of the current year Ohio Corporation has a $40,000 accumulated E&P balance and a $73,000 current E&P deficit. The corporation distributes $60,000 cash to its sole shareholder on May 5. The shareholder's tax basis in her Ohio stock at the beginning of the year is $325,000.
a. What amount of the $60,000 distribution is taxable as a dividend (assume a ratable allocation of the deficit)?
b. What are the amount and character of any nondividend distributions to the shareholder?
c. What is the amount of Ohio's accumulated E&P balance (deficit) on the last day of the year?

I:16-62 *Property Distributions.* Old Corporation has liquidity problems but wants to maintain its existing dividend policy. Old distributes investment land to its two shareholders. The land has a $30,000 adjusted basis and a $100,000 FMV. Old has an E&P balance of $300,000 (excluding the effects of the distribution). Nancy receives 50% of the land, and Palm Corporation receives the remaining 50%. Assume no taxable income or loss from current year operations.
a. What distribution amount is taxable to Nancy and Palm?
b. What is the basis of the property to Nancy and Palm?
c. What are the income tax consequences of the distribution to Old?

I:16-63 *Property Distributions.* Without liquidating, Park Corporation distributes equipment with a $70,000 adjusted basis and a $80,000 FMV to Pam. The equipment is subject to a $25,000 mortgage assumed by Pam. Park has $300,000 of E&P (excluding the distribution).
a. How much gain (if any) does Park recognize on the distribution of the equipment?
b. What distribution amount is taxable as a dividend to Pam?
c. What is Pam's basis in the equipment?

I:16-64 *Withdrawing Earnings from a Business.* Galadriel Corporation reports pre-tax earnings of $500,000 during the current year. The corporation wishes to distribute $100,000 to Gabby, its sole owner and CEO, in a manner that will minimize taxes for Galadriel and Gabby. The corporation is subject to the regular corporate tax rates. Gabby's tax rate is a flat 39.6%. Ignoring FICA employment taxes paid by the corporation and Gabby, compare the after-tax income reported if the $100,000 is paid to Gabby as (1) salary and (2) as a qualifying dividend.

I:16-65 *Stock Redemptions.* Private Corporation redeems some of its stock from Jane, a major shareholder. Before the redemption Jane owns 50 of the 100 outstanding shares, and her daughter Jill owns 40 shares. The remaining ten shares are owned by unrelated individuals. Private redeems for $600,000 in cash 40 of Jane's shares, having a $200,000 basis. Private has $900,000 of current and accumulated E&P. Jane's basis in her remaining ten shares is $50,000.
a. What are the tax consequences of the redemption to Jane?
b. What is Jane's basis in her remaining ten shares after her 40 shares are redeemed?
c. How would your answers to Parts a and b change if Jane and Jill were not related?

I:16-66 *Stock Redemption.* Prime Corporation redeems some of its stock from two of its shareholders on the same date. Frank and his son Sam own 50 and 20 shares, respectively, of the 100 shares outstanding before the redemption. The remaining 30 shares are owned by unrelated individuals. Prime redeems for $50,000 10 of Frank's shares having a $15,000 basis. All of Sam's shares, having a $30,000 basis, are redeemed for $100,000. Sam files an agreement with the IRS that he will acquire no interest in the corporation other than as a creditor for 10 years. Prime has current and accumulated E&P of $200,000.
a. What are the tax consequences of the redemption to Frank and Sam?
b. What are the tax consequences of the redemption to Sam if he does not file the agreement or if he violates the agreement during the 10-year period?

I:16-67 *Corporate Liquidation.* Queen Corporation adopts a plan of complete liquidation on January 1 of the current year. The corporation sells the assets listed below to King Corporation during the current year. This sale is followed by the assumption of Queen's liabilities by King Corporation and a single liquidating distribution of $1,200,000 cash to Ahmed (Queen's sole shareholder) on December 12 of the current year. Ahmed has a $400,000 basis in his Queen stock, which he has held for seven years. The following facts are relevant:
• Inventory costing $600,000 is sold to customers for $1,000,000.
• Depreciable fixed assets with a $2,000,000 adjusted basis are sold for $3,000,000. Depreciation recapture under Sec. 1245 is $800,000.
• Land held as a capital asset with a $4,000,000 adjusted basis is sold for $5,000,000.
a. What are the tax consequences of the liquidation to Queen?
b. What are the tax consequences to Ahmed upon his receiving the liquidating distribution?
c. How would your answers to Parts a and b change if the assets were instead distributed to Ahmed in exchange for his Queen stock and Ahmed then proceeded to sell the assets for the prices indicated above?

I:16-68 *Corporate Liquidation.* Several years ago, Tampa Corporation acquired 100% of Union Corporation stock for $1,000,000. In the current year, Tampa liquidates Union and receives all of its assets and liabilities. Tampa continues to operate Union as a division. On the liquidation date, the basis and FMV of Union's assets are $700,000 and $2,500,000, respectively. Union also has $100,000 of liabilities that were owed to third parties and E&P of $125,000 on the liquidation date.

a. How much gain or loss does Union recognize as a result of the liquidation?

b. What is Tampa's basis in the Union assets?

c. What Union tax attributes (if any) carry over to Tampa?

TAX STRATEGY PROBLEMS

I:16-69 Sandra and John, unrelated individuals, own all of Alpha and Beta corporation stock. John owns 60% of Alpha stock and 40% of Beta stock. Sandra owns 40% of Alpha stock and 60% of Beta stock. For five years, Alpha has conducted manufacturing activities and sold machine parts primarily in the eastern United States. Alpha reported $75,000 of operating profits in each of the last two years. Alpha's operating profits are expected to grow to $150,000 during the next five years. Alpha still has $100,000 of NOLs that must be used before it incurs federal income tax liability.

One-fourth of Alpha's output is sold to Beta, which is attempting to establish a market niche for reselling Alpha products in the southwestern United States. In the start-up phase of this effort, Beta incurred $200,000 of NOLs. Under the sales arrangement with Alpha, the best that Beta can hope to do in the short run is break-even.

What suggestions can you offer Sandra and John about the short-term possibility of offsetting Alpha and Beta's NOLs against the profits that Alpha expects to earn and minimizing their overall tax liabilities if both businesses become profitable? Sandra has specifically asked about merging the two companies into a single entity so that the losses of one entity can offset the profits of the other and defer federal income taxes. Sandra indicates that the two companies were created for non-tax reasons. The operating situation has changed, and according to Sandra, now may be the time to consolidate the entities. John is not sure that combining the two businesses is a good idea.

I:16-70 Penny and Rick, equal partners in a partnership, recently attended a business-planning seminar held in their town. While at the seminar they learned about limiting their personal liability by using the corporate form of business association. Penny and Rick's business has incurred product liability because it manufactures replacement parts for motorcycles. The most important information that Penny and Rick acquired from the seminar was the tax and legal advantages of incorporating their partnership business. According to a speaker at the seminar, incorporation would protect Penny and Rick from losing their personal wealth if someone sued them. Following a phone call from the partners to set up an appointment, you have scheduled a meeting with Rick and Penny for this afternoon. In preparation for the meeting you draft a list of points to discuss with the couple. What kinds of tax and non-tax strategies should you include in this list?

I:16-71 Peter Martin owned an equity interest in retail hardware stores for a nationwide chain. The eleven stores operate in a single midwestern state under the name Martin Corporation. Peter has been the chief financial officer of the company for fifteen years. His retirement plans call for him to take his pension from Martin in six months and play golf in sunny Gainesville, Florida. Since Peter's son and daughter will be operating the company, Peter will probably drop by the office to see family and old friends and to provide management advice. Peter will continue to serve on Martin's board of directors. The Martin stock is owned as follows: Peter and his wife Jaclyn, 25%; Peter's son and daughter-in-law, 25%; Peter's daughter and son-in-law, 25%. All six individuals serve on Martin's board of directors, along with six outside directors. The outside directors and Martin employees (other than those listed above) own the remaining 25% of the stock. Peter is thinking about his post-retirement years. He would like to withdraw money from the company, in addition to his pension and board of directors compensation. He would like to redeem some of his stockholdings each year. What advice can you provide Peter about the tax consequences of the redemption(s)?

I:16-72 Gertrude, age 67 and widowed, owns 50 acres of land on the Chattahoochee River that she and her husband purchased for $10,000 when they were newlyweds in 1970. The land is near Atlanta and is now worth at least $1,500,000 if sold undivided. Gertrude is considering selling the land to her wholly owned ABC Corporation for its $1,500,000 market value. Alternatively, Gertrude is considering transferring ownership of the land to ABC in exchange for additional ABC stock.

ABC will subdivide the land and sell it off as 50 one-acre lots with total proceeds of the lot sales expected to be at least $3,000,000. Land development costs will be approximately $300,000 and sales commissions will be 5% of the sales price.

Analyze the tax implications of Gertrude's two choices. Assume that Gertrude's marginal tax rate on ordinary income is 39.6% and that she has never generated capital gains. Assume that ABC would recognize ordinary income on the lot sales taxed at a marginal tax rate of 34%. (Ignore the 3.8% net investment income tax for higher-income taxpayers for this problem.)

TAX FORM/RETURN PREPARATION PROBLEMS

I:16-73 The financial accounting balance sheet for Zane, a retail sales corporation, as of the end of the current year is as follows:

Assets

Cash	$ 50,000
Accounts receivable	20,000
Inventory	10,000
Land	20,000
Buildings (net of $30,000 accumulated depreciation)	100,000
Equipment (net of $50,000 accumulated depreciation)	150,000
Intangibles	60,000
Total assets	$410,000

Liabilities & Owner's Equity

Accounts payable	$ 40,000
Mortgage payable	40,000
Long-term debt	60,000
Capital stock	100,000
Retained earnings	170,000[a]
Total liabilities and stockholders' equity	$410,000

[a]The retained earnings balance at the beginning of the current year was $70,000. Beginning inventory was $15,000. Dividends in the amount of $25,000 were paid.

Using the accrual method Zane reports the following financial accounting operating results for the current year:

Sales	$550,000
Minus: Costs of goods sold	(350,000)
Gross profit	$200,000
Dividend income from a 20%-owned domestic corporation	75,000
Net long-term capital gains	150,000
Total income	$425,000
Expenses:	
Salaries (including officer's salary of $40,000)	$120,000
Repairs	30,000
Bad debts	10,000
State and local taxes	20,000
Amortization	5,000
Contributions	35,000
Depreciation (straight-line)	40,000
Total expenses (before federal income tax expense)	$260,000
Operating profit	$165,000
Minus: Provision for federal income taxes	(40,000)
Net income	$125,000

All dividends qualify for the dividends-received deduction. In addition, the following items should be taken into account:

Current-year estimated tax payments	$15,000
MACRS depreciation for tax purposes	60,000

Prepare a current year Form 1120 (U.S. Corporation Income Tax Return) for Zane. Disregard beginning-of-the-year balance sheet amounts other than retained earnings. Also, leave spaces blank on Form 1120 for information not provided.

I:16-74   Huge Corporation reports the following balance sheet for the current year:

	Beginning of Year	End of Year
Cash	$ 40,000	$ 70,000
Accounts receivable	23,000	21,500
Inventories	26,000	53,000
Marketable securities	30,000	30,000
Investment in 100%-owned subsidiary	100,000	115,000
Depreciable assets	100,000	100,000
Less: Accumulated depreciation	(20,000)	(30,000)
Total assets	$299,000	$359,500
Accounts payable	$ 50,000	$ 80,000
Short-term loans payable	20,000	35,000
Mortgage payable	80,000	79,000
Common stock	1,000	1,000
Additional paid-in capital	49,000	49,000
Retained earnings	99,000	115,500
Total liabilities and stockholders' equity	$299,000	$359,500

Huge reports the following income and expenses for the year:

Sales	$720,000
Purchases	570,000
Dividend from 100%-owned subsidiary	30,000
Dividend from less-than-20%-owned corporation	10,000
Salaries (including officers' salaries of $30,000)	90,000
Repairs	12,000
Contributions	60,000
State and local taxes	7,500
Interest expense	11,000
Financial accounting depreciation	10,000
MACRS depreciation	17,490
Federal income tax expense per books	10,000

In addition, Huge reported an NOL carryover of $12,000 from the preceding year and paid current year estimated taxes of $10,000.

Prepare a current year Form 1120 (U.S. Corporation Income Tax Return) for Huge. Leave spaces blank on Form 1120 for information not provided. Note: You should prepare a schedule of net income per books to complete Line 1 of Schedule M-1.

CASE STUDY PROBLEMS

I:16-75   Frank, Paul, and Sam are considering merging their respective unincorporated businesses into a new C corporation called FPS. Frank would transfer land and a building with a $50,000 adjusted basis and $100,000 FMV to the corporation in exchange for $100,000 of FPS common stock. Paul would transfer inventory with an adjusted basis of $60,000 and $100,000 FMV in exchange for $50,000 of FPS stock and $50,000 of FPS 10-year notes. Sam would contribute equipment with an adjusted basis of $80,000 and $60,000 FMV along with legal services worth $40,000 in exchange for $100,000 of FPS stock.

Prepare a client memo that details the tax consequences of the transactions to FPS, Frank, Paul, and Sam.

I:16-76   Beth, who is married, is the sole shareholder of Pet Store Inc., a C corporation. She also manages the store. She wishes to expand the business, but the corporation needs additional capital for her to do so. Fortunately, she has saved $50,000 cash and plans to contribute it to the corporation. However, she does not know whether to contribute the cash in exchange for additional stock or lend the cash in exchange for a note.

Prepare a client memo that explains the tax consequences and requirements of each alternative so that Beth can make an informed decision.

TAX RESEARCH PROBLEMS

I:16-77 The income tax laws for a particular state depend on the business entity's organizational status. Answer the following four questions using the web site for a particular department of state (for example, Florida's information can be found at http://dos.state.fl.us/).

a. What business entity forms are permitted in the state selected?

b. Must a business that uses one of the basic business forms (for example, corporation, partnership, or LLC) organized and operating in the state register with a state agency? If so, which agency?

c. Must a business that uses one of the basic business forms that is organized outside of the state (for example, Georgia) but which operates in the state (for example, Florida) register with an agency in the state of organization? In the state in which it operates? In both states?

d. Does the state selected impose an income tax on corporations organized in the state? On foreign corporations (corporations formed outside of the state selected) who conduct part or all of their business in their home state and part in the state selected?

I:16-78 Charlie Corporation acquired 100% of Delta Corporation common stock on July 1 of the current tax year. Prior to the acquisition, Delta supplied Charlie with about 50% of the raw materials and other components used in producing its plastic toys. Delta will continue to be Charlie's major supplier as well as a supplier to other toy makers. Both corporations have been profitable for years and expect to be profitable after the acquisition. Charlie's CEO asks you if the two corporations, filing a single consolidated tax return would be less costly (in terms of both taxes paid and filing fees) than their filing two separate tax returns. How do you respond to this inquiry?

I:16-79 Ted is the sole shareholder of Zero Corporation. Before his retirement from the company, he gave 100 shares of Zero stock to his son. A few months later, Ted sold his remaining 1,900 shares to Zero for $2 million. The company has E&P exceeding $2 million. Ted's basis in his 2,000 shares before the two transfers was $80,000. Ted requested a waiver of the Sec. 318 attribution rules and treated the redemption of Zero stock as a long-term capital gain. Ted also agreed to serve as a consultant to the company. The terms of the agreement are that Ted will be paid as an independent contractor $175 per hour plus expenses. The agreement does not specify a minimum number of hours of services to be provided each month. Three years later the IRS audits Ted's return and argues that the redemption should be treated as a dividend under Sec. 301. Have the Sec. 302(c)(2) requirements that permit a waiver of the family attribution rules been met?

A partial list of research sources is:

- Secs. 302(c)(2) and (b)(3)
- Reg. Sec. 1.302-4
- *Estate of Milton S. Lennard v. CIR*, 61 T.C. 554 (1974)
- *William M. Lynch v. CIR*, 58 AFTR 2d 86-5970, 86-2 USTC ¶9731 (9th Cir., 1986)

I:16-80 Beth in Case Study Problem I:16-76 also wants to know whether she can make a $50,000 capital contribution to the corporation without the corporation's issuing additional shares. If so, should she have the corporation issue the shares or not? Assume that Beth's basis in her stock is $40,000 and that she files a joint return with her husband.

A partial list of research sources is:

- Sec. 1244(d)(1)(B)
- Reg. Secs. 1.1244(c)-1(b) and 1.1244(d)-2(a)
- *Sol Lessinger v. CIR*, 63 AFTR 2d 89-1055, 89-1 USTC ¶9254 (2nd Cir., 1989)
- *James D. Pierce*, 1989 PH T.C. Memo ¶89,647, 58 TCM 865 (1989).

I:16-81 In 2012, Peter purchased 150 shares of Able Manufacturing Corporation stock for $75,000. Able is a C corporation that has 40 shareholders. None of the other 39 shareholders own more than 5% of the 5,000 shares outstanding. No events have occurred that have changed either the number of shares of stock that Peter owns, or Peter's total basis in his shares. Peter is unhappy with Able's management. It is now Spring 2015 and Peter would like to sell part or all of his Able stock and reinvest the proceeds in the stock of another small corporation. At present, his total unrealized gain is $300,000. Peter was told by his stockbroker that he may be eligible to exclude part or all of his profit on the sale of the Able shares from current taxable income. What advice on reducing the tax cost of the sale can you give him?

A partial list of research sources is:

- Sec. 1(h)
- Sec. 1202
- Sec. 1044
- Sec. 1045
- Sec. 1244

I:16-82 Erin Brinson founded BCD Corporation in 1991 with a contribution of $50,000 cash. The entity has always been a C corporation and Erin has not made any other capital contributions nor has BCD made any distributions. When she retired in 2015, Erin transferred ownership of BCD to her son, Evan, and two other employees. Evan now owns 60% of BCD stock and the two other employees each own 20%. The transaction was consummated by BCD redeeming 90% of Erin's shares for a $2,000,000 note payable over the next 15 years and Evan and the two other employees' buying the remaining 10% for notes totaling $250,000 payable over the next 15 years. All notes bear market rates with interest and principal payable twice a year on a regular basis. Erin owned the building in which BCD operates. As part of this transaction, Erin agreed to a new 5-year lease to BCD at market rental rates. How should the transfers of stock in BCD be taxed? Must Erin take measures to qualify for the most favorable tax treatment?

A partial list of research sources is:

- Sec. 302(b)
- Reg. Sec. 1.302
- Rev. Rul. 77-467, 1977-2 CB 92
- *Hurst*, 124 TC No. 2 (2005)

CHAPTER

17

PARTNERSHIPS AND S CORPORATIONS

LEARNING OBJECTIVES

After studying this chapter, you should be able to

1. Compare and contrast the various types of pass-through entities

2. Determine the tax implications of forming and operating a partnership, including partnership distributions

3. Explain the requirements for electing and maintaining S corporation status, and apply operating rules for S corporations

4. Identify tax planning opportunities for partnerships and S corporations

5. Comply with procedural and reporting requirements for partnerships and S corporations

KEY POINT

Pass-through entities (also called flow-through entities) entail taxation only at the ownership level. This single level of taxation is achieved by (1) exempting the entity from taxation; (2) passing income, deductions, losses, and credits through to the owners; and (3) adjusting the basis of the owner's interest in the entity.

Pass-through or conduit business entities, such as partnerships, S corporations, limited liability companies, and limited liability partnerships, have the major advantage of entailing only one level of taxation.[1] These legal organizational forms thus represent an interesting blend of what tax theorists call the entity and aggregate theories of taxation. In some ways, they are treated as entities separate from their owners. For example, the entity files a tax return (for information purposes), makes elections pertaining to accounting periods and methods, and computes the results of business operations. In other ways, however, a pass-through entity is treated as a mere aggregation of its owners. For example, the entity is generally not taxed, and the entity's income, deductions, losses, and credits are allocated to the owners based on their proportionate ownership or some other allocation arrangement. These allocated items then pass through to the owners to be reported in their own tax returns.

Aside from exempting pass-through entities from entity level taxation, the tax law preserves the single level of taxation in another important way: basis adjustments made to the owner's interest in the entity. Each owner obtains an original basis in his or her ownership interest upon acquiring the interest via formation of the entity, purchase of the entity interest, gift of the entity interest, etc. Subsequently, the owner's basis increases if the entity earns income or if the owner contributes additional money or property to the entity. Conversely, the owner's basis decreases if the entity incurs a loss or if the entity distributes money or property to the owner. In short, the owner's basis increases as the entity expands, and the owner's basis decreases as the entity contracts. Without these basis adjustments, the owner could be subject to double taxation upon selling his or her interest or upon the liquidation of the entity.

EXAMPLE I:17-1 ▶

Conduit Company is a pass-through entity with two owners, George and Flo. Each owner has a $10,000 original basis in the entity. In its first year of operations, Conduit earns $30,000, which is allocated $15,000 to each owner. Thus, each owner reports $15,000 in his or her individual tax return even though the entity does not distribute the earnings to the owners. At the beginning of the second year, Flo sells her interest to Fred for $25,000. If Flo did not get an increased basis adjustment for her $15,000 of earnings, she would recognize a $15,000 ($25,000 selling price − $10,000 basis in the entity) gain on the sale of her interest, which taxes her twice on the $15,000. However, both George and Flo do increase their bases to $25,000 ($10,000 original basis + $15,000 share of entity earnings) at the end of the first year. Therefore, when Flo sells her interest for $25,000, she incurs no addition taxable gain ($25,000 selling price − $25,000 basis in the entity = $0 gain). ◀

The next section of this chapter briefly describes the four basic types of pass-through business entities. Afterward, the chapter provides more detail on the tax treatment of partnerships and S corporations.

TYPES OF PASS-THROUGH ENTITIES

OBJECTIVE 1

Compare and contrast the various types of pass-through entities

PARTNERSHIPS

Of the pass-through business entities, partnerships have been around the longest. The IRC defines a **partnership** as "a syndicate, group, pool, joint venture, or other unincorporated organization" that carries on any business, financial operation, or venture. The definition of a partnership, however, does not include a trust, estate, or corporation.[2] A partner is a member of such syndicate, group, pool, joint venture, or organization, and the partner can be an individual, corporation, trust, or estate. Unlike a corporation, which must file incorporation documents with the state, partnerships require no legal documentation although most states have laws that govern the rights and restrictions of partnerships. Moreover, most states model their laws on the Uniform Partnership Act (UPA) or the

---

[1] Trusts and estates also are conduit entities to some extent in that they are not taxed on income that is distributed. Trusts and estates are not generally used to conduct business activities. Income taxation of trusts and estates is discussed in Chapter C:14 of the *Prentice Hall Federal Taxation of Corporations, Partnerships, Estates & Trusts* text.

[2] Secs. 761(a) and 7701(a)(2).

Uniform Limited Partnership Act (UPLA). A partnership must have at least two partners but can have an unlimited number beyond two.

A partnership can be either a general partnership or a limited partnership. In a general partnership, each partner has unlimited liability for partnership debts. Thus, these partners are at risk for more than their investment in the partnership. In a limited partnership, at least one partner must be a general partner, and at least one partner must be a limited partner. As in a general partnership, the general partners are liable for all partnership debts, but the limited partners are liable only to the extent of their investment plus any amount they commit to contribute to the partnership if called upon. Moreover, limited partners may not participate in the management of the partnership.

A major document for a partnership is the partnership agreement. In this agreement, the partners set out the terms of how the partnership will operate and how income, deductions, losses, and credits will be allocated to the partners. The partners, therefore, should take great care in drafting this agreement.

A partnership files an annual information return with the IRS. This return, Form 1065 (U.S. Partnership Return of Income), reports the results of the partnership's operations and indicates the separate income, deduction, loss, and credit items that pass through to the partners. A sample Form 1065 appears in Appendix B of the *Comprehensive* and *Corporations, Partnerships, Estates & Trusts* volumes.

ADDITIONAL COMMENT

A number of states allow a variation on the limited partnership, called the limited liability limited partnership (LLLP). The LLLP is a partnership formed under a state's limited partnership laws but that can elect under the state's laws to provide the general partners with limited liability.[3]

S CORPORATIONS

An **S corporation** is so designated because rules pertaining to this entity are located in Subchapter S of the Internal Revenue Code (IRC). S corporations are corporations that have elected to be treated by the tax laws as pass-through entities. Similar to partnerships, therefore, S corporations are not taxed, and income, deduction, loss, and credit items pass through to the shareholders. These entities, however, still are corporations so that corporate tax rules apply to them unless overridden by the Subchapter S provisions.[4] As with C corporations, the shareholders enjoy limited liability, but S corporations offer less flexibility than do partnerships. For example, the number and type of shareholders are limited, and the shareholders cannot agree to allocate income, deduction, loss, and credit items in a way that differs from their proportionate stock ownership.

To achieve S corporation status, the corporation must file an S election, and its shareholders must consent to that election. An electing S corporation files an information return, Form 1120S (U.S. Income Tax Return for an S Corporation), which reports the results of the corporation's operations and indicates the separate income, deduction, loss, and credit items that pass through to the shareholders. A sample Form 1120S appears in Appendix B of the *Comprehensive* and *Corporations, Partnerships, Estates & Trusts* volumes.

REAL-WORLD EXAMPLE

S corporation returns represented about 67% of all corporate tax returns filed in 2013. The total number of S corporations has grown from 736,900 returns filed in 1985 to a 4.6 million in 2013.

LIMITED LIABILITY COMPANIES

A qualifying **limited liability company** (LLC) combines the best features of a partnership and a corporation even though it is neither. Specifically, it provides the limited liability protection of a corporation for all the LLC's owners, called members. An LLC can have an unlimited number of members who can be individuals, corporations, estates, or trusts.

An LLC may elect to be taxed as either a corporation or a partnership under the check-the-box regulations.[5] Under these Treasury Regulations, an LLC with more than one member is treated as a partnership unless the LLC affirmatively elects to be classified as a corporation. In most cases, LLCs will prefer to be classified as a partnership because of the tax advantages of that organizational form. Assuming the LLC opts for its default partnership classification, it annually files Form 1065 (U.S. Partnership Return of Income). Nevertheless, an LLC is not legally a partnership; it just is treated as one for tax purposes. A single member LLC may choose to be taxed as a corporation or

ADDITIONAL COMMENT

The LLC type of entity has been legislatively adopted by all 50 states.

---

[3] For a detailed discussion, see Shop Talk, "Service Firms Practicing as LLLPs: What are the Tax Consequences?," *Journal of Taxation*, August 2005.

[4] Sec. 1371(a)(1).
[5] Reg. Secs. 301.7701-1 through -4.

to be disregarded for tax purposes. If the entity is disregarded, income earned by the single member LLC is generally taxed to its owner under the sole proprietorship rules.

LIMITED LIABILITY PARTNERSHIPS

Many states also have statutes that allow a business to operate as a **limited liability partnership (LLP)**. This partnership form is particularly attractive to professional service partnerships, such as public accounting firms. As a result, many professional firms have adopted the LLP form, primarily to limit legal liability. Under state LLP laws, partners are liable for their own acts and the acts of individuals under their direction. However, LLP partners are not liable for the negligence or misconduct of other partners. Thus, from a liability perspective, an LLP partner is like a limited partner with respect to other partners' acts but like a general partner with respect to his or her own acts.

TAXATION OF PARTNERSHIPS[6]

OBJECTIVE 2

Determine the tax implications of forming and operating a partnership, including partnership distributions

FORMATION OF A PARTNERSHIP

Upon forming a partnership, the partners often contribute property (e.g., money, business equipment, and inventory previously used in a proprietorship) or services to the partnership. In exchange for this property and/or services, the partners receive an interest in the partnership. For each partner, a **partnership interest** represents an equity interest similar to corporate stock and is a capital asset.

KEY POINT

The nonrecognition provisions of Sec. 721 apply not only at the time of the formation of a partnership but also to subsequent capital contributions.

Section 721: Nonrecognition Rules. Section 721 prevents the recognition of gain or loss upon either the transfer of property in exchange for a partnership interest or subsequent transfers of property by the partners in exchange for a pro rata increase in their partnership interests. Without this nonrecognition provision, gain on a transfer of appreciated property would be recognized, and the partners might not have sufficient liquidity (e.g., cash) to pay the tax. In addition, the transfer of property to the partnership represents a mere change in ownership form, which is not a recognition event under the tax laws. Finally, the depreciation recapture rules do not apply if no gain is recognized under Sec. 721.

The following exceptions to the Sec. 721 nonrecognition rules should be noted:

▶ The Sec. 721 nonrecognition of gain or loss rules do not apply if the partner acts in a capacity other than as partner. For example, if a partner sells property to the partnership in an arm's-length transaction, the sale would be taxable.[7]

▶ If a partner contributes services instead of cash or property in exchange for an unrestricted partnership interest, the fair market value (FMV) of the services is taxed as compensation to the contributing partner because services do not qualify as property.[8]

▶ The contributing partner recognizes gain if liabilities transferred to the partnership exceed the partner's basis in the partnership.[9]

▶ The contributing partner recognizes gain if the partnership would be treated as an investment company had it incorporated under Sec. 351.[10]

KEY POINT

The substituted basis of the partnership interest is consistent with the nonrecognition of gain or loss.

Basis of a Partnership Interest. If the Sec. 721 nonrecognition rules apply, Sec. 722 provides a substituted basis rule for determining the basis of a partnership interest. In a simple case where no liabilities exist, the basis of the contributing partner's

---

[6] The rules described in this chapter apply generally to partnerships. However, special rules apply to electing large partnerships (those having at least 100 partners). A brief discussion of these rules is provided on pages I:17-17 and I:17-18.

[7] Reg. Sec. 1.721-1(a).

[8] Reg. Sec. 1.721-1(b)(1). In May 2005, the IRS issued proposed regulations which would bring partnership interests issued in exchange for services under Sec. 83 rules. If and when these regulations become final, they will significantly change the taxation of a partnership interest received for services.

[9] (See Example I:17-4 and the discussion of the partnership basis rules.)

[10] Sec. 721(b). The partnership is considered to be an investment company if 80% or more of the transferred assets (excluding cash and nonconvertible debt obligations) consist of marketable stocks or securities. This restriction prevents investors from diversifying their portfolios by creating a partnership through a nontaxable transfer of securities in exchange for a partnership interest.

partnership interest equals the sum of money contributed plus the adjusted basis of other property transferred to the partnership.

EXAMPLE I:17-2 ▶ Allen contributes business equipment having a $10,000 FMV and a $4,000 adjusted basis to the ABC Partnership in exchange for a 30% interest in the partnership. The basis of Allen's partnership interest is $4,000 because he recognizes no gain or loss on the asset transfer under Sec. 721. ◄

If a contributing partner renders services to the partnership in exchange for a partnership interest, the contributing partner's basis equals the amount of income recognized from rendering the services (i.e., the FMV of the services).[11] The FMV basis is permitted because the partner recognizes ordinary income equal to the FMV of the services.

EXAMPLE I:17-3 ▶ Angela contributes property having a $10,000 FMV and a $4,000 adjusted basis and renders services valued at $10,000 in exchange for a 60% interest in the ABC Partnership. Section 721 protects Angela from gain recognition on the property transfer. However, Angela recognizes $10,000 of ordinary income for the services rendered. Thus, the basis of Angela's partnership interest equals $14,000 ($4,000 adjusted basis of the property plus the $10,000 FMV of the services). ◄

ADDITIONAL COMMENT

A partner's basis in the partnership interest commonly is called "outside basis."

Section 752 Basis Adjustments. A partner's basis for his or her partnership interest includes the partner's ratable share of partnership liabilities as well as the basis attributable to any property and services contributed to the partnership. In addition, the following rules apply if a partnership assumes a partner's liability or if the partner transfers property to the partnership subject to a liability:

▶ An increase in partnership liabilities is treated as a cash contribution by all partners, which increases their bases by their share of the assumed liabilities.

▶ The partnership's assumption of a partner's liability is treated as a cash distribution to the partner whose liability it assumed, which decreases that partner's basis in the partnership.

EXAMPLE I:17-4 ▶ Brad contributes a building to a newly formed partnership, BCD Partnership, in exchange for a one-third interest in the partnership. The building has a $90,000 FMV, an $80,000 adjusted basis, and is subject to a $60,000 mortgage. The partnership assumes the mortgage but has no other liabilities. Carol and Dale each contribute $30,000 of cash for a one-third interest in the partnership. After the contributions, the partners have the following bases in their partnership interests:

	Brad	Carol	Dale
Adjusted basis of property or amount of cash contributed	$80,000	$30,000	$30,000
Plus: Share of mortgage assumed by the partnership ($60,000 × 1/3 to each)	20,000	20,000	20,000
Minus: Decrease in Brad's personal liabilities	(60,000)	–0–	–0–
Basis in partnership interest	$40,000	$50,000	$50,000 ◄

Under the general rules of Sec. 752, a partner's basis in the partnership interest increases by the partner's share of any changes in the partnership's liabilities during the year. For example, if total partnership liabilities (including accounts and notes payable, mortgages, bank loans, etc.) increase during the year from $100,000 to $200,000, the basis of a partner with a 50% interest in the partnership increases by $50,000 ($100,000 increase in liabilities × 0.50).

Negative Basis Rule. The basis of a partnership interest cannot be negative. Therefore, Sec. 731 requires recognition of gain in situations where a negative basis would otherwise occur.

EXAMPLE I:17-5 ▶ Becky transfers property having a $100,000 FMV and a $25,000 adjusted basis, which is subject to a $60,000 mortgage, in exchange for a one-third interest in the BCD Partnership. The

---

[11] Reg. Sec. 1.722-1. Also, see footnote 8.

partnership owes no other liabilities. Becky, Cindy, and Dan each have a one-third interest in the partnership. The $60,000 reduction in Becky's individual liabilities is treated as a distribution of money. Thus, Becky recognizes a $15,000 gain because the distribution exceeds her $45,000 ($25,000 + $20,000) basis in the partnership interest. Becky's basis in the partnership interest is zero after the distribution. The basis is computed as follows:

Adjusted basis of property transferred	$25,000
Plus: Becky's share of the mortgage assumed by the partnership ($60,000 × 1/3)	20,000
Basis before deemed distribution	45,000
Minus: Decrease in Becky's individual liabilities	(60,000)
Becky's basis in the partnership interest (cannot be negative)	$ –0–

The cash deemed distributed in excess of Becky's predistribution basis causes her to recognize a $15,000 ($60,000 – $45,000) gain. Becky reduces her basis to zero by the deemed distribution because her basis in the partnership interest cannot be less than zero. ◀

 **STOP & THINK**

Question: In Example I:17-5, Becky transferred property subject to a liability exceeding the property's adjusted basis. How does the treatment of excess liabilities in a partnership differ from the treatment when such property is transferred to a corporation?

Solution: In a corporate situation, the shareholder recognizes gain to the extent that total liabilities exceed the total basis of property transferred by that shareholder. Thus, had Becky transferred the same property to a corporation in a Sec. 351 transaction, she would have recognized gain for the entire $35,000 ($60,000 mortgage − $25,000 adjusted basis) excess liability. In a partnership, however, the transferor partner recognizes gain only if the deemed money distribution associated with the liability exceeds the partner's basis in the partnership interest. Thus, in Example I:17-5, Becky recognized only a $15,000 gain. If she had substantial basis in an existing partnership, she would have recognized no gain.

Holding Period for a Partnership Interest. If a partner contributes only cash to the partnership in exchange for a partnership interest, the holding period begins the day after the partner acquires the interest. If the partner contributes property, the holding period for the partnership interest generally includes the holding period of the contributed property. However, if the contributed property is other than a capital asset or Sec. 1231 property, the holding period begins on the date the partnership interest is acquired.[12]

EXAMPLE I:17-6 ▶ In the current year, Johanna contributes business machinery to the JK Partnership in exchange for a partnership interest. Johanna originally acquired the machinery in 2012. Because the machinery is Sec. 1231 property, Johanna's holding period for her partnership interest begins in 2012 (the date she acquired the machinery). If Johanna had contributed inventory instead of machinery, the holding period would begin the day after the inventory contribution date. ◀

ADDITIONAL COMMENT

When property that has been held for personal use is contributed to a partnership, the basis equals the lesser of the property's FMV or adjusted basis on the contribution date.

Basis of Partnership Assets. Section 723 provides a carryover basis rule for property contributed to the partnership. Generally the partnership's basis in the property is the same as that of the transferor partner, even if the contributing partner recognizes gain. Without this rule, partners could increase the basis of their property for depreciation and subsequent sale purposes merely by contributing appreciated property to a partnership. When the carryover basis rule applies, the partnership's holding period for the property includes the period the property was held by the contributing partner.[13]

EXAMPLE I:17-7 ▶ In the current year, Carlos contributes equipment with a $6,000 adjusted basis and an $8,000 FMV to the CDE Partnership and receives a one-third interest in the partnership. Carlos acquired the equipment in 2013. CDE's basis for the equipment is $6,000, its adjusted basis in the hands of the contributing partner. Carlos recognizes no gain due to the Sec. 721

---

[12] Reg. Sec. 1.1223-1(a).

[13] Sec. 1223(2) and Reg. Sec. 1.723-1.

nonrecognition rules. CDE's holding period for the equipment begins in 2013 because it includes Carlos' holding period for the property. ◄

ADDITIONAL COMMENT

A partnership's basis in its assets commonly is called "inside basis."

An individual who contributes property encumbered with a liability to a partnership may have to recognize gain on the transfer if the deemed cash distribution from the partnership's assumption of the liability exceeds the partner's basis in the partnership (see Example I:17-5). The adjusted basis of Becky's partnership interest in Example I:17-5 is reduced by this release from the liability (but not below zero). It is not increased by the gain Becky recognizes, however, because the gain recognition is due to a distribution of money on the release from the liability and not from the contribution of the property to the partnership. For a similar reason, the partnership does not increase its basis in contributed property by the partner's recognized gain.[14]

BOOK-TAX ACCOUNTING COMPARISON

For many items, the partnership must maintain separate sets of records for tax purposes, partnership "book" purposes, and financial accounting (GAAP) purposes.

Book Accounting Considerations. Like all publicly traded entities, publicly traded partnerships must produce financial statements prepared in accordance with GAAP. However, one of the most confusing aspects of partnership tax accounting is that Treasury Regulations require the maintenance of another set of accounting "books" based on the requirements of Reg. Sec. 1.704-1(b)(2)(iv). These regulations for properly maintaining partnership capital accounts mandate "book" accounting that is similar (but not identical) to GAAP financial accounting partnership rules. Under these partnership book rules, the carryover basis rules used in taxation do not apply for book accounting. For example, if property is contributed to a partnership, its book value is recorded at the contributed property's FMV while the tax basis is recorded as a carryover. This book accounting treatment in the regulations results in differences between the tax bases and book values of contributed assets. These differences between tax and book values will be important in our study of special allocations (page I:17-8). Just remember that when the text mentions book accounting for partnerships, it is the accounting required by Reg. Sec. 1.704-1(b)(2)(iv) and not financial statements prepared according to GAAP.

EXAMPLE I:17-8 ►

BOOK-TAX ACCOUNTING COMPARISON

The difference between book value and tax basis also causes GAAP, book, and tax depreciation to differ if a partner contributes depreciable property.

Anwar contributes cash of $30,000 and Beth contributes land having a $30,000 FMV and a $20,000 adjusted basis to the AB Partnership. Each partner receives a 50% interest in the partnership. For book accounting purposes, the cash and land are each recorded at $30,000. For tax purposes, the carryover basis of the land to the partnership is $20,000. The partnership realizes no gain or loss for book accounting purposes if it later sells the land for $30,000. However, the partnership recognizes a $10,000 gain under the tax rules because the land's adjusted basis for tax purposes is only $20,000. The $10,000 precontribution gain must be allocated to Beth. (See the section titled Special Allocations on page I:17-8 for a discussion of precontribution gains and losses.) ◄

Topic Review I:17-1 highlights the nonrecognition of gain or loss provisions and basis rules.

ADDITIONAL COMMENT

If a partnership claims the amortization deduction in its first year, the partnership is deemed to have properly made the election. If the partnership chooses to forgo the deemed election, it can elect to capitalize the expenditures (without amortization) on a timely filed tax return for the tax year the partnership begins business. See Reg. Sec. 1.709-1.

Organizational and Syndication Fees. A partnership can deduct up to $5,000 of costs of organizing the partnership in the year the partnership begins business. The deduction is limited to the lesser of (1) the amount of organizational expenditures or (2) $5,000, reduced by the amount by which such organizational expenditures exceed $50,000. Any organizational expenditures exceeding the first year deduction can be deducted ratably over the 180 month period beginning with the month the partnership begins business.[15] Organizational expenditures that qualify for this amortization treatment include items such as the attorney's fees for drafting the partnership agreement, the accountant's fees for setting up the financial record system, and filing fees.

The partnership must capitalize expenses attributable to syndicating the partnership. These expenses, however, are *not* amortizable. **Syndication fees** are expenses incurred to promote and market partnership interests (usually associated with tax-sheltered limited partnership interests). Examples of nondeductible syndication fees include brokerage and registration fees, legal fees of the underwriter and issuer, and printing costs associated with the prospectus and promotional materials.

---

[14] Rev. Rul. 84-15, 1984-1 C.B. 158. [15] These rules are contained in Sec. 709.

TOPIC REVIEW I:17-1

Section 721 Formations: Nonrecognition of Gain or Loss Rules

▶ Neither the partnership nor the partners recognize gain or loss on the transfer of property to a partnership in exchange for a partnership interest or an increase in a partnership interest.

▶ A partner's basis in his or her partnership interest is adjusted upward for the following items:
  Amount of cash contributed to the partnership
  Adjusted basis of noncash property contributed
  FMV of services contributed
  Section 752 adjustment for liabilities

▶ The partnership's basis in transferred property carries over from the transferor partners.

▶ With exceptions pertaining to contributions of cash and ordinary income property, a partner's holding period for his or her partnership interest includes the holding period of the contributed property.

▶ The partnership's holding period in contributed property includes the transferor's holding period.

▶ The nonrecognition rules do not apply to services contributed. The contributing partner recognizes ordinary income equal to the FMV of the services, and the partner's basis in the partnership interest is increased by the amount of income recognized from rendering the services.

▶ The depreciation recapture rules generally do not apply to contributed property. Instead, the depreciation recapture potential carries over to the partnership.

PARTNERSHIP OPERATIONS

The partnership tax return (Form 1065) provides information regarding the measurement and reporting of income, deductions, losses, and credits that pass through to the partners. Certain separately stated items (e.g., capital gains and losses, charitable contributions, and Sec. 1231 gains and losses) pass through to the partners without losing their identity. Such items must be separately stated because their tax effect depends on the partner's particular tax situation. These items are reported on Schedules K and K-1 of the partnership return. Schedule K reports tax information for the entire partnership, and a separate Schedule K-1 summarizes the results for each partner.

Items that do not have special tax effect are netted at the partnership level and are reported on page 1 of Form 1065. The netting of such items results in partnership ordinary income or ordinary loss, which then is allocated to the partners depending on the profit and loss sharing ratios contained in the partnership agreement. Table I:17-1 contains a list of commonly encountered separately stated items and items that make up partnership ordinary income or loss.

ADDITIONAL COMMENT

Many states impose an income tax on each nonresident partner's share of income produced by the partnership in that state, which can cause a partner to file several state income tax returns when a partnership conducts business in those states.

SPECIAL ALLOCATIONS

Section 704 permits partners some latitude in allocating income, deductions, losses, and credits among the individual partners. Special allocations are unique to partnerships and permit flexible arrangements among the partners for sharing specific income and loss items. A partner's distributive share of such items generally is determined by the partnership agreement. However, the special allocation provisions restrict the partners' freedom to shift tax benefits among individual partners. For example, the special allocation must have substantial economic effect (e.g., it cannot be a tax sham). In addition, a special allocation must be made for property contributed by the partners when determining the allocation of depreciation deductions and the amount of gain or loss recognized when the partnership eventually sells the property. Essentially, the allocation of the depreciation deductions and the amount of recognized gain or loss must take into account the difference between the partnership's basis for the contributed property and the property's FMV at the time of the contribution.

ADDITIONAL COMMENT

In general, partnership income or loss is allocated according to the partnership agreement, which can be amended any time up to the due date for filing the partnership return.

EXAMPLE I:17-9 ▶ Clay and Dana formed an equal partnership five years ago. Clay contributed cash of $100,000, and Dana contributed land having a $60,000 adjusted basis and a $100,000 FMV.

▼ TABLE I:17-1

Segregation of Ordinary Income and Separately Stated Items

Items	Separately Stated Items (Schedules K and K-1)	Partnership Ordinary Income (or Loss) (Page 1 of Form 1065)
Sales minus cost of goods sold (gross profit)		X
Salaries and wage expense		X
Guaranteed payments to partners[a]	X	X
Tax, bad debt, and repair expenses		X
Charitable contributions	X	
Investment income (interest, dividends, etc.) and expense	X	
Foreign income taxes paid or accrued	X	
Specially allocated income, deduction, loss, gain, and credit items that differ from the general profit and loss allocation ratios	X	
Tax-exempt interest income	X	
Capital gains and losses	X	
Sec. 1245 and Sec. 1250 depreciation recapture		X
Unrecaptured Sec. 1250 gain	X	
Sec. 1231 gains or losses	X	
Sec. 179 expensing	X	
Tax credits	X	
Tax preference items	X	

[a]Guaranteed payments appear in both columns because the partnership deducts them to arrive at partnership ordinary income (or loss), and they are reported separately and are taxable to the partner who receives the payments.

The partnership's basis for the land is $60,000 (Dana's carryover basis). If the partnership sells the land in the current year for $110,000, it recognizes $50,000 ($110,000 − $60,000) of gain. If a special allocation of the gain were not required, Clay and Dana each would be allocated $25,000 of the gain based on their equal profit and loss sharing ratios. The special allocation rules, however, require $45,000 of the gain to be allocated to Dana ($40,000 appreciation accruing before her transfer of property to the partnership plus $5,000, which is one-half of the $10,000 of post-contribution appreciation). The remaining $5,000 of post-contribution gain is allocated to Clay [($110,000 − $100,000) × 0.50]. ◄

WHAT WOULD YOU DO IN THIS SITUATION?

Alex and Alicia plan to form a partnership in the current year with each partner making an equal capital contribution to the partnership. The partnership agreement will specify that the partners share equally in partnership profits and losses. Among other things, the partnership will invest in taxable and tax-exempt bonds. The partners expect the taxable and tax-exempt bonds each to generate $2,500 of interest per year. For the next several years, Alex expects to be in the 15% tax bracket and Alicia expects to be in the 33% individual tax bracket. Without a special allocation, each partner would be allocated $1,250 of each type interest. Instead, however, they want a special allocation in the partnership agreement that allocates (1) all $2,500 of taxable interest to Alex plus $188 ($1,250 × 0.15) of tax-exempt interest to compensate him for the additional taxes owed on the extra $1,250 of taxable interest and (2) the remaining $2,312 ($2,500 − $188) of tax-exempt interest to Alicia. Alex and Alicia seek your advice on the propriety of this special allocation. Hint: Prepare a schedule of after-tax interest income to the partners with and without the special allocation.

ALLOCATION OF PARTNERSHIP INCOME, DEDUCTIONS, LOSSES, AND CREDITS TO PARTNERS

If a partner's interest in the partnership changes during the year (e.g., due to the sale of a partnership interest or the entry of a new partner who contributes property to the partnership in exchange for an interest), all the partners must determine their distributive share of the partnership income, deductions, losses, and credits according to their varying interests in the partnership during the year.[16] Retroactive allocations (e.g., an allocation of deductions or losses incurred before admission of a new partner to the partnership) may not be made to new partners admitted during the partnership's tax year.

EXAMPLE I:17-10 ▶ Colleen and Dan are equal partners in the CDE Partnership, which uses the calendar year as its tax year. On December 1 of the current year, Ed contributes $50,000 cash for a one-third interest in the partnership. The partnership reports a $9,000 ordinary loss for the current tax year ending on December 31. The partners must report their shares of the partnership loss based on their varying interests as follows:[17]

Partner		Loss Allocation
Colleen	1/2 × $9,000 × 11/12	$4,125
	1/3 × $9,000 × 1/12	250
	Colleen's share of loss	$4,375
Dan	Same as Colleen	4,375
Ed	1/3 × $9,000 × 1/12	250
	Total allocation of loss	$9,000

Ed's loss is limited to his ratable (one-third) share of the loss incurred after his entry into the partnership, or $250. This result occurs even if the partnership agreement provides that Ed would receive one-third of all losses for the entire year. ◀

BASIS ADJUSTMENTS FOR OPERATING ITEMS

Under Sec. 705, the basis of each partnership interest is adjusted to reflect the partner's share of income and deduction items. This basis adjustment is necessary to ensure the single level of taxation of partnerships. Basis adjustments for income and deduction items are made currently regardless of whether the partners receive an actual distribution from the partnership. In addition, each partner's basis in the partnership interest is adjusted for capital contributions, withdrawals, and changes in liabilities that occur during the year. Each partner's basis is increased by the partner's distributive share of partnership ordinary income and separately stated income and gain items. The basis of the partnership interest is increased whether the income is taxable to the partners or is tax-exempt.[18]

A partner's basis is decreased (but not below zero) by partnership distributions and by the partner's distributive share of partnership ordinary loss, separately stated losses and deductions, and expenditures that are nondeductible in computing partnership ordinary income or loss (e.g., charitable contributions made by the partnership).

Partners also increase their basis by their share of partnership liabilities. That share depends on whether the partnership liabilities are recourse or nonrecourse. A recourse liability is one where the lender has recourse to all partnership assets as well as general partners' other assets for satisfaction of the loan. In other words, the lender has recourse to the general partners, so they have what is called the economic risk of loss. Thus, recourse liabilities are allocated to the partners based on their economic risk of loss. A nonrecourse liability is one where the lender has recourse only to specified partnership property, such as real estate, for satisfaction of the loan. In other words, the lender has no recourse to the

---

[16] Sec. 706(d)(1).

[17] Regulation Sec. 1.706-1(c)(2) provides for alternative allocation methods. The partners may elect to use the interim closing method as an alternative to the pro rata allocation method used in Example I:17-10.

[18] If the partnership includes oil and gas properties, an increase in basis is made for the excess of percentage depletion claimed over the basis of the property subject to depletion, and a reduction in basis is made for the depletion deduction claimed under Sec. 611.

partners. Nonrecourse liabilities are allocated based on the partners' profit sharing percentages.

EXAMPLE I:17-11 ▶ David and Edith form a partnership in the current year and share profits and losses equally. However, David is a general partner, and Edith is a limited partner. Thus, David has all the economic risk of loss for recourse liabilities. The partnership agreement provides for no special allocations. The following transactions occur during the year:

▶ David contributes land having a $60,000 basis and a $100,000 FMV in exchange for his initial partnership interest.

▶ At the end of the year, the partnership has $100,000 of nonrecourse liabilities and $30,000 of recourse liabilities.

▶ The partnership earns $50,000 of ordinary income.

▶ The partnership earns $5,000 of tax-exempt interest income.

▶ The partnership incurs $10,000 of capital losses.

▶ The partnership makes a $15,000 charitable contribution.

▶ The partnership distributes $20,000 in cash to David.

David's year-end basis is determined as follows:

Capital contribution of land (adjusted basis)		$ 60,000
Plus:	Share of partnership nonrecourse liabilities ($100,000 × 0.50)	50,000
	Share of partnership recourse liabilities ($30,000 × 1.00)	30,000
	Share of ordinary income ($50,000 × 0.50)	25,000
	Share of tax-exempt interest income ($5,000 × 0.50)	2,500
Minus:	Distribution to David	(20,000)
	Share of charitable contribution ($15,000 × 0.50)	(7,500)
	Share of capital losses ($10,000 × 0.50)	(5,000)
David's basis at the end of the current year		$135,000

◄

? STOP & THINK

Question: Why do partners increase the basis of their partnership interests by their share of tax-exempt income?

Solution: Increasing the basis ensures that the income will retain its tax-exempt character when the partnership income is subsequently distributed in the form of cash or the partner's interest in the partnership is sold or exchanged.

LIMITATIONS ON LOSSES AND RESTORATION OF BASIS

Although a partner's distributive share of the partnership's ordinary loss and any separately stated losses and deductions passes through to the partner, Sec. 704(d) limits deductibility of the losses to the partner's adjusted basis in his or her partnership interest as determined at the end of the partnership's tax year.[19] All positive and negative adjustments referred to in Example I:17-11 (except the loss) are made before the limitation is considered. If the loss limitation rule did not apply, the partner's interest could have a negative basis. Any unused losses and deductions carry over indefinitely and are allowed in subsequent years when the partner again has a positive basis in his or her partnership interest.

EXAMPLE I:17-12 ▶ Ellen, who has a 50% interest in the EF Partnership, has a $10,000 basis in her partnership interest at the end of Year 1 (before deducting her share of losses). The EF Partnership incurs a $50,000 ordinary loss in Year 1. Ellen's share of the loss is $25,000 ($50,000 × 0.50), but Ellen can deduct only $10,000 in Year 1. The remaining $15,000 of loss carries over to Year 2. The deductible loss reduces Ellen's partnership basis to zero at the end of Year 1. ◄

---

[19] Two other rules also restrict the deductibility of losses. The at-risk rules contained in Sec. 465 limit loss deductions to the partner's at-risk basis. In addition, Sec. 469 contains passive activity loss rules that disallow virtually all net passive activity losses. These restrictions are discussed in Chapter I:8 of this text and in Chapter C:9 of *Prentice Hall's Federal Taxation: Corporations, Partnerships, Estates & Trusts.*

EXAMPLE I:17-13 ▶

BOOK-TAX ACCOUNTING COMPARISON

Although a partner's basis in his or her partnership interest may not go below zero, a partner's book capital account (equity) may be negative.

TAX STRATEGY TIP

Taxpayers can control to a limited degree when they use partnership and S corporation losses in their individual tax returns. If loss pass-throughs exceed the partner's end-of-year basis in his or her investment, the loss will not be deductible until the partner again has basis in his or her investment. If a taxpayer incurs a loss in the current year and wants to deduct the loss on next year's personal tax return, he or she must make an additional capital contribution after year-end. Alternatively, a shareholder can loan money to his or her S corporation before year-end to ensure having sufficient basis to use the loss currently. A partner can make similar capital contributions. A partnership (but not an S corporation) can control the timing of the loss deductions for its partners through additional borrowings it makes prior to the end of the tax year.

Assume the same facts as in Example I:17-12 except in Year 2 Ellen's share of partnership liabilities increases by $5,000, Ellen's share of Year 2 ordinary income is $5,000, and Ellen makes a $5,000 additional capital contribution. Ellen's basis increases by a total of $15,000 due to the three items. Therefore, in Year 2, she deducts the $15,000 loss carryover from Year 1. The deduction reduces Ellen's partnership basis to zero at the end of Year 2. A zero tax basis for a partnership interest does not necessarily mean that the interest is worthless. The FMV of the partnership's net assets and accounting book value, nevertheless, may be substantial. ◀

Topic Review I:17-2 summarizes the allocation and basis rules.

Passive Activity Loss Limitations. The passive activity loss limitations discussed in Chapter I:8 apply to partners who do not materially participate in the business of the partnership. The passive activity loss rules apply at the *partner* level, that is, each partner must determine whether he or she materially participates in the partnership. If a loss is determined to be passive, a partner may not deduct the loss against either earned income or portfolio income (e.g., dividends and interest) but may deduct the loss only against other passive income. These rules are highly significant and play a major role in determining the deductibility of partnership losses by partners.

TRANSACTIONS BETWEEN A PARTNER AND THE PARTNERSHIP

Sometimes a partner may independently engage in transactions with the partnership. For example, a partner may sell property to the partnership rather than make a capital contribution of the property. In such transactions, the partner is treated as an outside independent party.[20] Thus, a partner recognizes gain or loss on the sale of property to the partnership, and the partnership receives a cost basis equal to the amount of consideration paid. Because the partner and the partnership are not truly independent parties, abuse of this provision is possible. For example, the partners might want to recognize losses by selling certain assets at a loss to the partnership while still retaining those assets in the partnership. Alternatively, a partner may wish to sell certain depreciable business assets (Sec. 1231 property) at a gain taxable to the partner at favorable capital gains rates while the partnership receives a stepped-up FMV basis in the assets for depreciation purposes. Section 707(b) forestalls such potential abuses by disallowing losses and by providing ordinary income (rather than capital gain) treatment under the following circumstances:

TOPIC REVIEW I:17-2

Allocation Rules and Basis Adjustments

▶ When a partner contributes property to a partnership, any unrecognized precontribution gain or loss must be allocated to the contributing partner when the partnership sells the property.

▶ Partnership income, gains, deductions, losses, and credits are allocated to the partners on a daily basis based on each partner's interest in the partnership.

▶ Special allocations of income, gains, deductions, losses, and credits are permitted as long as they have substantial economic effect.

▶ Basis in the partnership interest is increased by the partner's share of ordinary income, separately stated income items, and tax-exempt income. Basis is reduced by a partner's share of ordinary loss, separately stated deductions and losses, and nondeductible expenditures. Basis also is adjusted for capital contributions, distributions, and changes in partnership liabilities. Basis cannot be decreased below zero.

▶ Ordinary losses and separately stated deduction and loss items that exceed a partner's basis carry over indefinitely until the partner again has a positive basis in his or her partnership interest.

---

[20] Rules for transactions taking place between a partner and the partnership are found in Sec. 707.

ADDITIONAL COMMENT

Defining a partner's interest in a partnership is not always an easy matter. These determinations become difficult if a partner has varying interests in different types of income.

▶ Losses are disallowed on sales or exchanges between a partner and the partnership if the partner owns more than a 50% interest in the partnership. A loss also is disallowed if a sale or exchange of property occurs between two partnerships in which the same persons own more than a 50% interest. The Sec. 267 constructive ownership rules apply to determine whether the 50% test is met. If the purchaser (i.e., the partner or the partnership) of the property later sells the asset to an outsider, the gain recognized is reduced by the previously disallowed loss.

▶ Gains are treated as ordinary income (rather than capital gains) if the partner owns (directly or indirectly) more than a 50% interest in the partnership and if the exchanged asset is not a capital asset in the transferee's hands.[21] Again, the Sec. 267(b) constructive ownership rules apply.

EXAMPLE I:17-14 ▶ Ira has a 60% interest in the HI Partnership. Ira sells land with a $100,000 adjusted basis to the partnership for its $60,000 FMV. Ira does not recognize the $40,000 ($60,000 − $100,000) loss because Ira owns more than a 50% interest in the partnership. The partnership takes a $60,000 cost basis in the land. If the partnership later sells the land to an outsider for $110,000, the partnership recognizes only $10,000 of gain because the $50,000 ($110,000 − $60,000) realized gain is reduced by Ira's $40,000 previously disallowed loss. ◀

EXAMPLE I:17-15 ▶ Helen has a 90% interest in the HI Partnership. Helen sells a building used in her business with a $60,000 adjusted basis to the HI Partnership for its FMV of $100,000. After the purchase, the partnership continues to use the building in its business activities. Before the sale, Helen had taken straight-line depreciation. Had Helen instead sold the building to an outsider, she would have recognized $40,000 of unrecaptured Sec. 1231 gain, which usually receives capital gain treatment. However, Helen's $40,000 gain is treated as ordinary income because she sold the building to a partnership in which she owns a more than 50% interest, and the building is not a capital asset to the partnership. The ordinary income does not qualify for a reduced tax rate, nor can it be used to offset capital losses. HI Partnership takes a $100,000 cost basis in the building. ◀

ADDITIONAL COMMENT

A partner generally has to make estimated tax payments to cover the income and self-employment taxes on a guaranteed payment.

Guaranteed Payments. Even though a partner does not qualify as an employee of the partnership for tax purposes, the partnership agreement may provide for fixed salary payments that are not based on partnership income. Generally, the partnership deducts such payments as guaranteed payments to arrive at partnership ordinary income. They are includible in the partner's gross income in the tax year received. The partnership also can make guaranteed payments in lieu of interest payments on the amount of the partner's capital investment. Such payments are deductible by the partnership to arrive at partnership ordinary income and are includible in the partner's gross income.

EXAMPLE I:17-16 ▶

ADDITIONAL COMMENT

Although José receives a fixed "salary," he is not considered to be an employee of the partnership. The "salary" is treated as self-employment income.

José owns a 40% interest in the JKL Partnership. The partnership agreement provides that José is to receive a fixed salary of $20,000 plus 10% interest on his average capital balance. The partnership makes no guaranteed payments to the other partners. If his average capital balance for the year is $50,000, the partnership would pay $5,000 (0.10 × $50,000) of interest as a guaranteed payment. If partnership ordinary income is $10,000 before deducting the guaranteed payments, the partnership ordinary loss is $15,000 ($10,000 income − $25,000 of guaranteed payments to José). José reports $25,000 of ordinary income for the year, consisting of the $20,000 salary and the $5,000 interest. He also reports a $6,000 ($15,000 × 0.40) ordinary loss. The other partners in total report a $9,000 ($15,000 × 0.60) ordinary loss. ◀

PARTNERSHIP DISTRIBUTIONS

A distribution of cash or property from the partnership to a partner generally is treated as a nontaxable return of capital. This treatment closely parallels the nontaxable consequences resulting from a capital contribution of property made in exchange for a partnership interest under Sec. 721.

A distribution may result in a reduction of a partner's capital interest in the partnership. This type of distribution is called a **nonliquidating distribution**. The partnership may

---

[21] Gains also are converted to ordinary income if the sale is between two partnerships in which the same persons own directly or indirectly more than a 50% interest in the partnership. In determining the 50% ownership rule, the Sec. 267 constructive ownership rules apply.

KEY POINT

The adjusted basis of a property distributed by a partnership generally measures the taxability of the distribution. The difference between the property's FMV and basis can be important, however, in determining the property's basis when the partnership distributes multiple properties.

SELF-STUDY QUESTION

Carl, a partner with a $10,000 basis in the ABC Partnership, receives property having a FMV of $20,000 and a basis of $8,000 in a nonliquidating distribution. How much gain does Carl recognize?

ANSWER

None. A partner recognizes gain only when the amount of cash distributed exceeds the basis of the partnership interest.

wish to liquidate a partner's entire interest due to retirement, death, or other business reasons. These distributions are called **liquidating distributions**. In such cases, the liquidating distribution is treated as a sale or exchange of the partnership interest.

Due to the complex nature of this topic, this chapter includes only an abbreviated coverage of these materials, and the discussion of liquidating distributions is omitted. Chapter C:10 of *Prentice Hall's Federal Taxation: Corporations, Partnerships, Estates & Trusts* includes detailed coverage of these topics.

Nonliquidating Distributions. As a general rule, neither the partner nor the partnership recognize gain or loss if the partnership distributes money or other property to the partner.[22] Such nonliquidating distributions usually are treated as nontaxable returns of capital. If the amount of money received by the partner exceeds the partner's basis for the partnership interest, however, the partner recognizes gain to the extent of the excess.[23] If the partnership distributes property other than money (e.g., land and machinery) to the partner, the basis of the partnership interest is reduced by the adjusted basis of the distributed assets. As previously mentioned, neither the partnership nor the distributee partner recognize gain or loss even if the adjusted basis of the distributed property exceeds the partner's basis in his or her partnership interest. In this case, the basis of the property to the partner is reduced to equal the basis of the partnership interest. If the partnership distributes both money and property, the money distribution reduces the basis of the partnership interest before any adjustment for the property distribution.

EXAMPLE I:17-17 ▶ Jane receives a nonliquidating distribution of $10,000 cash from the JK Partnership. At the distribution date, Jane's basis in her partnership interest is $8,000. Of the $10,000 distribution, $8,000 is a nontaxable free return of capital, which reduces Jane's basis to zero. The remaining $2,000 is a capital gain.[24] ◀

EXAMPLE I:17-18 ▶ Jeff receives a nonliquidating distribution of land having a $6,000 adjusted basis and a $10,000 FMV from the JK Partnership. Jeff's predistribution basis in his partnership interest is $8,000. Neither Jeff nor the partnership recognize gain or loss on the distribution. Jeff's basis in the land is $6,000, and his basis in his partnership interest is reduced by $6,000 (the adjusted basis of the property distributed). Thus, following the distribution, Jeff's basis in his partnership interest is $2,000 ($8,000 − $6,000). ◀

EXAMPLE I:17-19 ▶ Jean receives from the JK Partnership a nonliquidating distribution of $5,000 cash plus land having a $6,000 adjusted basis and a $10,000 FMV. Jean's predistribution basis in her partnership interest is $8,000. Her basis initially is reduced by the $5,000 cash distribution to reflect a nontaxable return of capital treatment. The remaining $3,000 basis in her partnership interest is allocated to the land, and neither Jane nor the partnership recognize gain or loss on the distribution. Jean's basis for her partnership interest is zero after the distribution. ◀

Topic Review I:17-3 summarizes the gain or loss recognition rules relating to nonliquidating distributions.

SALE OF A PARTNERSHIP INTEREST

Recognition of Gain or Loss. A partnership interest is a capital asset similar to a corporate security. It may be sold or exchanged as existing partners retire or withdraw from the business. The remaining partners may acquire the selling partner's interest, or the outgoing partner may sell the interest to an outsider.

Capital gain or loss generally arises from the sale of a partnership interest because the interest is a capital asset in the hands of the selling partner. For noncorporate partners,

ADDITIONAL COMMENT

A sale of a partnership interest is treated as a sale even though the sale results in the termination of the partnership. For example, if one partner in a two-person partnership sells his or her interest to the other partner, the transaction is treated as a sale.

---

[22] Sections 731 through 733 contain the partnership distribution rules. Distribution of marketable securities also can trigger gain recognition.
[23] Exceptions apply if unrealized receivables and inventory items, referred to as Sec. 751 assets, remain in the partnership or are distributed to the partner. In such instances, the partnership and/or the partner may recognize gain on the distribution.

[24] A portion of this gain may be converted to ordinary income if Jane's share of any Sec. 751 assets (i.e., unrealized receivables and substantially appreciated inventory items) held by the partnership changes as a result of the cash distribution.

TOPIC REVIEW I:17-3

Nonliquidating Distributions

▶ Generally, neither the partner nor the partnership recognize gain or loss on a nonliquidating distribution of money or other property. However, if the distributed money exceeds the distributee partner's basis in the partnership interest, the partner recognizes gain on the excess. For this purpose, any release from partnership liabilities is treated as money distributed to the partner.

▶ The partner's basis in the partnership interest is reduced (but not below zero) by the amount of money distributed. If the partnership distributes property other than money, the following two points apply.

• If the adjusted basis of distributed property does not exceed the partner's basis in the partnership interest (after reduction for money distributions), the basis of the distributed property carries over to the partner, and the partner's basis in the partnership interest is reduced by the distributed property's adjusted basis.

• If the adjusted basis of distributed property exceeds the partner's basis in the partnership interest (after reduction for money distributions), the distributed property takes a basis equal to the partner's remaining basis in the partnership interest, and the partner's basis in the partnership interest is reduced to zero.

ADDITIONAL COMMENT

The applicable long-term capital gains tax rate can be 0%, 15%, or 20% depending on the taxpayer's ordinary tax bracket. Specifically, the capital gains rate is 0% for taxpayers in tax brackets of 15% and below, 15% for taxpayers in the 25% through 35% tax brackets, and 20% for taxpayers in the 39.6% tax bracket. In addition, an incremental 3.8% rate applies to net investment income for taxpayers whose modified AGI exceeds $200,000 ($250,000 for married filing jointly).

the long-term capital gain is taxed at the applicable capital gains rate. In this case, a partnership is viewed as an entity separate and distinct from the partners. However, under Sec. 751, a partner is considered to own a proportionate interest in each partnership asset (i.e., the partnership is viewed as a conduit), which results in part capital gain and part ordinary income treatment depending on the character of the underlying assets.

Under the general rules of Sec. 741, gain or loss is measured by the difference between the amount realized and the selling partner's adjusted basis in the partnership interest. The amount realized includes the partner's share of partnership liabilities from which the partner is released as a result of the sale. The basis of the partnership interest also is adjusted by the selling partner's distributive share of partnership income or loss, which must be computed up to the sale date.

EXAMPLE I:17-20 ▶

On October 1, Jesse sells his interest in the JK Partnership to Paula, an outsider, for $150,000 cash plus release from $30,000 of partnership liabilities. Jesse's basis in his partnership interest is $74,000 before taking into account his distributive share of partnership income for the period ending on the sale date and his share of any increase in partnership liabilities during the same period. For the current year, Jesse's share of the partnership income for the period up to the date of sale is $20,000, and his share of increased partnership liabilities is $6,000. Thus, at the sale date, Jesse's basis in his partnership interest is $100,000 ($74,000 basis on January 1 + $20,000 share of partnership income + $6,000 share of increased partnership liabilities). The amount realized on the sale is $180,000 ($150,000 selling price + $30,000 liability release). Thus, Jesse recognizes an $80,000 gain on the sale, which is capital gain unless ordinary income is triggered under Sec. 751. (See Example I:17-21 for an illustration of Sec. 751 treatment.) ◀

Section 751 Ordinary Income Treatment. Ordinary income rather than capital gain treatment may result under Sec. 751 if a partnership has unrealized receivables or inventory items when the partner sells a partnership interest. A sale of Sec. 751 assets by the partnership results in ordinary income, which passes through to the partners. Thus, this rule prevents a partner from converting ordinary income into capital gain by selling or liquidating the partnership interest before the partnership sells or collects on the Sec. 751 assets. Section 751 assets include the following:

▶ Inventory items include the traditional definition of inventory plus any other property except capital assets and Sec. 1231 property

▶ Unrealized receivables for services rendered or goods delivered, such as accounts receivable of a cash method partnership (i.e., receivables having a zero basis)

▶ Unrealized receivables also include Sec. 1245 and 1250 depreciation recapture potential (i.e., amounts that would be recaptured as ordinary income if Sec. 1245 or 1250 property were sold by the partnership) or recapture potential arising under certain other IRC sections

EXAMPLE I:17-21 ▶

Joy's basis in her partnership interest is $100,000, and the amount realized on its sale is $180,000, which results in an $80,000 gain. The cash basis partnership has accounts receivable with a zero basis and a $30,000 FMV. Joy's share of these receivables is $10,000. Thus, $10,000 of the amount realized on the sale of the partnership interest is attributed to Joy's share of the accounts receivable. Because her share of the receivables has a zero basis and a $10,000 FMV, $10,000 ($10,000 − $0) of the gain is ordinary income to Joy as though she had sold her share of the receivables. The remaining $70,000 ($80,000 − $10,000) of gain from the sale of Joy's partnership interest is a capital gain. ◀

ADDITIONAL COMMENT

In addition to the rates described in the adjoining paragraph, an incremental 3.8% rate applies to net investment income for taxpayers whose modified AGI exceeds $200,000 ($250,000 for married filing jointly).

Other Special Treatments. In addition to Sec. 751 ordinary income treatment, Sec. 1(h) applies various other tax rates on the sale of a partnership interest. First, a 28% rate applies to gain the partner would have recognized had the partnership sold its collectibles and small business (Sec. 1202) stock. Second, a 25% rate applies to unrecaptured Sec. 1250 gain the partner would have recognized had the partnership sold its Sec. 1250 property (i.e., depreciable real property). These two special rules are in lieu of the 15% or 20% rate that generally applies to capital gains of a partner selling his or her partnership interest. Thus, any gain on the sale of a partnership interest allocable to these items will be taxed at a 25% or 28% tax rate rather than 15% or 20%.

OPTIONAL AND MANDATORY BASIS ADJUSTMENTS

Section 754 provides an election that permits a basis adjustment to the assets of a continuing partnership when a partner sells or exchanges a partnership interest or when certain distributions occur. This election, made by the partnership, prevents inequities that might arise because the basis of partnership assets are not adjusted under general partnership tax accounting rules. The election is binding for all future years unless the IRS consents to a revocation of the election. In addition, a partnership may have to make mandatory basis adjustments in certain circumstances even if a Sec. 754 election is not in effect.

EXAMPLE I:17-22 ▶

Jim acquires Antonio's one-third partnership interest in the ABC Partnership for $40,000. The partnership's balance sheet on the sale date includes the following:

	Adjusted Basis	FMV
Assets:		
Cash	$20,000	$ 20,000
Accounts receivable	10,000	10,000
Inventory	15,000	20,000
Depreciable assets	15,000	85,000
Total	$60,000	$135,000
Liabilities	$15,000	$ 15,000
Capital accounts:		
Antonio	15,000	40,000
Beth	15,000	40,000
Carmen	15,000	40,000
Total	$60,000	$135,000

If the partnership has a Sec. 754 election in effect, Jim's optional basis adjustment equals the difference between his basis in the partnership interest of $45,000 ($40,000 amount paid + $5,000 of ABC's liabilities) and his $20,000 ($60,000 × 1/3) share of basis in the underlying partnership assets. Thus, Jim steps up the basis of his share of partnership assets from $20,000 to $45,000. The election does not affect the remaining partners' underlying basis in partnership assets.

The election would be favorable only to Jim because his share of the appreciated partnership assets (inventories and depreciable assets) would be stepped up by $25,000, based on the relative amounts of appreciation for each asset. Jim then would be entitled to additional depreciation deductions on the increased basis of the depreciable assets. In addition, Jim would receive an increased basis for calculating gain on the sale of the inventory. If this election were not in effect and the inventory were sold, Jim would report $1,667 (1/3 × $5,000) gain from the sale of his one-third interest in the inventory even though he paid $6,667 (1/3 × $20,000) for such interest. ◀

Once the election is in effect, its application may be detrimental because a downward adjustment is required if the amount paid for a partnership interest is less than the adjusted basis of the assets (i.e., the assets have declined rather than appreciated in value).

In addition, the IRC contains provisions to prevent shifting of losses using the optional basis adjustment mechanism. Under these rules, the partnership must make a mandatory basis adjustment following a transfer of partnership interest, whether or not the partnership has made a Sec. 754 election, if the partnership's basis in its partnership property is more than $250,000 above the FMV for partnership property (i.e., a built-in loss of $250,000 or more). This rule, and a similar rule related to distributions, are an attempt to prevent taxpayers from transferring losses on partnership property or on property contributed to a partnership.

ELECTING LARGE PARTNERSHIPS

ADDITIONAL COMMENT

Congress enacted the electing large partnership provisions for two basic reasons: (1) to ease the reporting burden of partners who own a relatively small interest in a large partnership and (2) to ease the computer matching effort of the IRS.

Partnerships meeting the definition of a large partnership can elect under Sec. 775 to be treated as an electing large partnership. To qualify, a partnership must satisfy the following four requirements:

► Must not be a service partnership

► Must not be engaged in commodity trading

► Must have at least 100 partners

► Must file an election

Section 775(b) defines a service partnership as one in which substantially all the partners perform substantial services in connection with the partnership activities or the partners are retired but in the past performed substantial services in connection with the partnership's activities. For example, a partnership that performs accounting services cannot be an electing large partnership. In addition, the partnership must have 100 or more partners excluding those partners who provide substantial services in connection with the partnership's business activities.

The calculation of an electing large partnership's taxable income includes separately stated income and other income. However, the items separately stated under Sec. 772(a) for an electing large partnership are much different from other partnerships. For example, under Sec. 773(b)(3), miscellaneous itemized deductions for an electing large partnership are combined at the partnership level and subject to a 70% disallowance at the partnership level. After the 70% disallowance, the remaining miscellaneous itemized deductions are combined with other income items and pass through to the partner. Because the miscellaneous itemized deductions are combined with other partnership income, the deductions are not subject to the 2% nondeductible floor at the partner level. Under Sec. 773(b)(2), charitable contributions made by an electing large partnership are subject to a 10% of taxable income limit similar to the limit applying to a C corporation.

Section 773(a)(3) requires an electing large partnership to apply the Sec. 179 expensing deduction limitation at only the entity level instead of at both the partnership and partner levels. Under Sec. 773(a)(4), Sec. 1231 gains and losses are netted at the partnership level. The partnership reports net Sec. 1231 losses with other ordinary taxable income or loss and reports net Sec. 1231 gains with capital gains and losses. The capital gains and losses are netted at the partnership level with only a single, net number reported to the partners. The capital gain or loss is treated as long-term, unless the net is a short-term capital gain, in which case it gets combined with ordinary income. Many of the partnership's tax credits are combined at the partnership level into a single number with the exception of the four credit categories listed below as being separately reported.

The separate items reported to the partners under Sec. 772(a) include:

► Taxable income or loss from passive loss limitation activities

► Taxable income or loss from other partnership activities

► Net capital gain or loss from passive loss limitation activities

► Net capital gain or loss from other partnership activities

► Tax-exempt interest

▶ Net alternative minimum tax adjustments, which are computed separately for passive loss limitation activities and other activities

▶ Separate credit passthroughs for only the general credits, low income housing credit, rehabilitation credit, and foreign income taxes

▶ Any other item the IRS determines should be separately stated

EXAMPLE I:17-23 ▶

The JLK Partnership elects to be treated as an electing large partnership. The partnership reports the following activities for the current year. It has no passive activities.

Ordinary income	$120,000
Sec. 1231 gain	60,000
Tax-exempt income	12,000
Net long-term capital loss	40,000
Charitable contributions	30,000

JLK Partnership reports the following results to its partners:

Ordinary income	$106,000
Net long-term capital gain	20,000
Tax-exempt income	12,000

The partnership's net Sec. 1231 gain ($60,000) is treated as a long-term capital gain and off-sets the net long-term capital loss ($40,000), thereby producing a $20,000 net long-term capital gain. Ordinary income is reduced only by the charitable contribution. However, the 10% contribution deduction limitation restricts the deduction to $14,000 [($120,000 + $20,000) × 0.10]. The remaining $16,000 of contributions carry forward. The partnership's ordinary income is $106,000 ($120,000 − $14,000). ◀

An electing large partnership must provide a Schedule K-1 to its partners on or before March 15 following the close of the partnership tax year without regard to when the partnership tax return is due. Partnerships other than electing large partnerships need only provide the Schedule K-1 by the due date for the partnership's tax return. The March 15 date is different from the April 15 deadline otherwise applied to calendar year partnerships. Unlike other partnerships, an electing large partnership does not terminate for tax purposes when a substantial change in ownership occurs. Instead, an electing large partnership terminates only when the partners cease to conduct any business, financial operation, or venture using the partnership form.

Partners of an electing large partnership must report all items of partnership income, gain, loss, or deduction the same way that the partnership reports the item. Deviations from the required reporting will be "corrected" by the IRS in the same say that a math mistake is corrected. An electing large partnership is subject to special audit rules and will be audited only at the partnership level.

PARTNERSHIP ELECTIONS

Tax Year Restrictions. When a partnership's tax year ends, each partner's distributive share of the partnership income (including guaranteed payments) is reported on each partner's Form 1040 (or Form 1120 for corporate partners). With no restrictions about partnership tax year ends, this rule would allow significant deferral of partnership income. Thus, if a partnership's tax year ends on January 31 and the partners report on a calendar year ending December 31, partnership income earned from February 1 of Year 1 through December 31 of Year 1 (as well as partnership income earned in January of Year 2) is reported in the partners' Year 2 federal income tax returns (filed in Year 3). This situation results in an effective 11-month income deferral.

EXAMPLE I:17-24 ▶

Kim is admitted to the ABC Partnership on April 1 of Year 1. Kim is a calendar-year taxpayer who previously was an employee of the partnership from January 1 of Year 1 until her admission to the partnership. Kim's earnings as an employee for the three-month period are $8,000. She received monthly distributions of $3,000 for the last nine months of the year that represent draws against her share of estimated partnership income for the partnership year ending January 31 of Year 2. Kim's distributive share of the partnership income for the period April 1 of Year 1 through January 31 of Year 2 is $60,000. Because distributions to a partner are treated as made on the last day of the partnership's tax year (January 31 of Year 2) and because the partnership tax year ends after December 31 of Year 1, Kim's income for Year 1 is only $8,000 (her salary as an employee for the first three months of Year 1). Kim reports her $60,000 share of partnership income for the year ending January 31 of Year 2, on her Year 2 tax return, which she files in Year 3. ◄

To prevent or minimize opportunities for deferring partnership income as illustrated in Example I:17-24, Sec. 706 provides the following requirements on the selection of a tax year by the partnership:

► A partnership uses the tax year of the one or more partners who, in aggregate, own a majority interest (more than 50%) in the partnership. This majority interest tax year rule is determined on the first day of the partnership's existing tax year.

► If partners having a majority interest in the partnership do not have the same tax year, the partnership uses the same tax year as *all* of its principal partners (a **principal partner** has a 5% or greater interest in the partnership).

► If the principal partners do not have the same tax year and no majority of its partners have the same tax year, the partnership uses the tax year that allows the "least aggregate deferral." (See Chapter C:9 of *Prentice Hall's Federal Taxation: Corporations, Partnerships, Estates & Trusts* for a detailed discussion of this requirement.)

EXAMPLE I:17-25 ►

ABC Partnership has one corporate partner, Ace Corporation, with a fiscal year-end of March 31. Ace Corporation has a 25% interest in the ABC Partnership. The other partners are individuals with a calendar year for tax purposes, none of whom has a 5% or more interest in the ABC Partnership. ABC Partnership must use a calendar year for tax purposes (the tax year of the individual partners who in aggregate own a 75% majority interest). ◄

The rules given above have three exceptions. First, a partnership with all calendar year partners can adopt or change to a fiscal year if it can convince the IRS that a business purpose exists for the choice. For example, if the partnership owns a ski resort, it probably could make a good case for closing the partnership tax year on May 31, shortly after the ski season ends, rather than on December 31, which is in the middle of the ski season. However, the IRS must agree that a valid business purpose exists for using the fiscal year.

Second, a partnership may adopt or change to a fiscal year-end if the business recognizes 25% or more of its annual gross receipts in the last two months of the fiscal year, with this being the case for three consecutive 12-month periods. Third, a partnership may elect a maximum three-month deferral if it agrees to make a special tax payment each year that approximates the income deferral benefit.[25] The net effect of these rules is to restrict any deferral opportunities for partnerships in choosing their tax year-end.

(See Chapter C:9 of *Prentice Hall's Federal Taxation, Corporations, Partnerships, Estates & Trusts* for a detailed discussion of partnership tax years.)

Cash Method of Accounting Restrictions. A partnership may elect with its first tax return any method of accounting that clearly reflects income. Unlike the tax year election, partnerships may elect an accounting method without regard to the methods used by its partners. The two most commonly used methods are the cash method and the accrual method. Under the cash method, the partnership reports income as received and expenses when actually paid. Under the accrual method, the partnership reports income when earned even if the cash has not yet been received. Similarly, the partnership reports expenses when incurred, not when actually paid.

Congress understands that the cash method does not always reflect the economic realities of a business. However, Congress also concedes that the cash method is much simpler to use than the accrual method. Because of its simplicity, the cash method still is an

---

[25] Secs. 444 and 7519.

option, but Congress has restricted its use. For example, partnerships that have a C corporation for a partner and that have average gross receipts exceeding $5 million during the prior three years are not allowed to use the cash method of accounting.[26] Tax shelters, no matter what their size, may not use the cash method under any circumstances. (See Chapter I:11 for a discussion of permissible accounting methods.)

TAXATION OF S CORPORATIONS

OBJECTIVE 3

Explain the requirements for electing and maintaining S corporation status, and apply operating rules for S corporations

QUALIFICATION REQUIREMENTS

To qualify as an S corporation, a business must meet the definition of a small business corporation.[27] To meet this definition, the entity[28]:

▶ Must be a domestic (U.S.) corporation rather than a foreign corporation
▶ Must not be an ineligible corporation[29]
▶ Must not have more than 100 shareholders[30]
▶ Must have only individuals, estates, certain kinds of trusts, and certain kinds of tax-exempt organizations as shareholders
▶ Must not have a nonresident alien as a shareholder
▶ Must issue only one class of stock

All the above requirements must be met for the initial election to be made. Once the corporation makes an S election, the requirements must be met on every day of each tax year the S election is in effect. Otherwise, the election terminates.

100-Shareholder Limitation. The S corporation rules place no restriction on the amount of an S corporation's assets or income. Nevertheless, most large, publicly-traded corporations have more than 100 shareholders and therefore are not eligible for S corporation status.

Members of a family count as one shareholder for the 100-shareholder limitation. Members of a family include a common ancestor, the lineal descendants of the common ancestor, and the spouses (or former spouses) of the lineal descendants or common ancestor. The common ancestor must not be more than six generations removed from the youngest shareholder at the time the corporation makes the election. This is a surprisingly large group treated as a single shareholder. For example, if the common ancester marries only once and has two children, and each of his descendants does the same, the generation that is six generations removed from the common ancestor includes 64 direct descendants and their 64 spouses. Also, the common ancestor need not be living at the time of the election. The requirement is only that the group of individuals who are to be treated as one family shareholder must have a common ancestor no more than six generations removed.

SELF-STUDY QUESTION

At any one time, how many different individuals could be shareholders in a single S corporation?

ANSWER

The number could be huge because 100 different families could be shareholders.

EXAMPLE I:17-26 ▶ Adobe Corporation, a qualifying S corporation, has 100 shareholders, including both Brad and Vanessa, who are married and are counted as one shareholder. No other shareholders are members of one family. Brad dies and wills his stock to his two best friends, who do not already own Adobe stock. Before the estate distributes the stock, the estate and Vanessa count as one shareholder, and the S corporation remains qualified under the 100-shareholder limitation. Adobe becomes disqualified as an S corporation when the estate distributes the stock to the two friends because the corporation then has 102 shareholders. ◀

---

[26] Sec. 448(a)(2). Section 448(b) provides exceptions for farming businesses and certain qualified personal service corporations.
[27] These qualification rules are in Sec. 1361.
[28] An S corporation does not have to be a corporation. Under the check-the-box regulations, a noncorporate entity can make an S election, in which case the entity is automatically deemed to have elected to be treated as a corporation under the check-the-box regulations. (See Reg. Secs. 301.7701-1, -2, and -3 that describe the tax consequences of a noncorporate entity electing to be

taxed under the check-the-box regulations.) Most LLCs and partnerships will not make an S election because of the additional benefits available with the more liberal partnership tax rules.
[29] Ineligible corporations include insurance companies, certain financial institutions, U.S. possessions corporations, and Domestic International Sales Corporations.
[30] Members of a single family are counted as one shareholder for tax years beginning after December 31, 2004.

TAX STRATEGY TIP

The lower a shareholder's marginal tax rate is in relation to the C corporation tax rate, the more attractive is the S corporation election.

Type of Shareholder Restrictions. A qualifying shareholder must be an individual (other than a nonresident alien), estate, qualifying trust, or qualifying tax-exempt organization.[31] Thus, a C corporation or a partnership may not own stock in an S corporation. If a C corporation or partnership were permitted to own stock, the 100-shareholder limitation easily could be avoided through indirect ownership of the S corporation stock through another corporation or partnership having many shareholders or partners.

Subsidiaries of S Corporations. Although an S corporation may not have a corporate shareholder, it may own stock of a C corporation. If this stock ownership equals or exceeds 80%, however, the S corporation (parent) and the C corporation (subsidiary) are considered an affiliated group under Sec. 1504. Nevertheless, an S corporation may not file a consolidated tax return with its 80%-owned subsidiaries.[32] In addition, an S corporation may have a Qualified Subchapter S Subsidiary (QSub).[33] The subsidiary is a QSub if the parent S corporation owns 100% of the QSub stock and elects to treat the QSub as such. Under this election, the QSub is not treated as a separate corporation for income tax purposes. Instead, all assets, liabilities, income, deductions, and credits of the QSub are treated as those of the parent S corporation.

One Class of Stock Restriction. An S corporation can have only one class of stock outstanding. This requirement simplifies problems that otherwise would result from determining how corporate income and losses should be allocated to the shareholders.

TAX STRATEGY TIP

If a corporation needs to issue preferred stock for estate planning reasons (e.g., freezing the value of the stock), the S corporation is not an available choice because the preferred stock is a second class of stock.

The requirement for one class of stock, however, can be troublesome if an S corporation is thinly capitalized (i.e., significant amounts of debt exist in the capital structure) because the debt may in fact be equity and represent a second class of stock. To reduce the uncertainty regarding the second class of stock issue, a safe-harbor rule provides that straight debt shall not be treated as a second class of stock if it meets certain requirements. To qualify as straight debt, the interest rate cannot be contingent on profits,[34] the debt cannot be convertible into stock, and the creditor must be either a person otherwise eligible to be an S corporation shareholder or a person actively and regularly engaged in the business of lending money.

Aside from the debt issue, Treasury Regulations provide that a corporation is treated as having only one class of stock if all outstanding shares of stock confer identical rights to distribution and liquidation proceeds. This test is based on the corporate charter, articles of incorporation, bylaws, applicable state law, and any binding agreements relating to distribution or liquidation proceeds.[35] Nevertheless, shares of common stock can have different voting rights without violating the one-class-of-stock restriction.

EXAMPLE I:17-27 ▶ Dale is the sole owner of an S corporation. For estate tax planning purposes, Dale wishes to make gifts of certain shares of the corporation's stock to his children while still retaining control of the company. A class of S corporation common stock with limited or no voting rights may be issued to Dale in exchange for a capital contribution. Dale can subsequently make gifts of this new stock to his children without disqualifying the S election. ◀

ELECTION REQUIREMENTS

The corporation files an election for S corporation status, and all shareholders who own stock on the date of the S election must consent to the election.[36] The election and consent are filed with the IRS on Form 2553 (Election by a Small Business Corporation). Shareholders who own stock during any part of the tax year including the election date must consent to the election even if they are not shareholders on the election date. A shareholder who sells his or her stock during the year but before the election will receive an allocation of the S corporation's income or loss for the portion of the election year he or she owned the stock.

---

[31] Qualifying trusts include voting trusts, Sec. 678 grantor trusts, electing small business trusts, and qualified Subchapter S trusts. Qualifying tax-exempt organizations include qualified retirement plan trusts and charitable organizations. (See Chapter C:11 of *Prentice Hall's Federal Taxation: Corporations, Partnerships, Estates & Trusts* for a discussion of these trusts.)

[32] Sec. 1504(a)(8).

[33] Sec. 1361(b)(3).

[34] The interest rate, however, may vary with the prime rate or a similar factor unrelated to the debtor corporation.

[35] Reg. Sec. 1.1361-1(l).

[36] Election and termination rules are in Sec. 1362.

A corporation may make the election in the tax year preceding the election year or on or before the fifteenth day of the third month of the election year. An election after the fifteenth day of the third month of the election year is treated as made for the next tax year. Once made, the election remains in effect until revoked or terminated.

The tax law, however, provides some relief for improper elections. First, if the corporation misses the deadline for making the S election, the IRS can treat the election as timely if the IRS determines that the corporation had reasonable cause for making the late election. Second, if the election was ineffective because the corporation inadvertently failed to qualify as a small business corporation or because it inadvertently failed to obtain shareholder consents, the IRS can nevertheless honor the election if the corporation and shareholders take steps to correct the deficiency within a reasonable time period.

EXAMPLE I:17-28 ▶

Circle Corporation is a calendar year C corporation. To elect S corporation status for Year 2, it must file the election any time in Year 1 (the preceding year) or during the period January 1 through March 15 of Year 2. If Circle makes the election on March 31 of Year 2, the corporation remains a C corporation for all of Year 2 and becomes an S corporation in Year 3. However, if Circle can show reasonable cause for making the late election, the IRS may allow the election to be effective for Year 2. ◀

TAX STRATEGY TIP

S corporations have been around since the 1960s. Limited liability companies (LLC) and limited liability partnerships (LLP) have become quite popular since the mid-1990s. Sometimes, shareholders may want to change their S corporation to an LLC or LLP. Careful planning is essential to avoid unintended results. Changing from an S corporation to an LLC can be costly because the S corporation is liquidated for income tax purposes. Shareholders may recognize substantial gains in addition to legal and accounting costs in making the transition.

TERMINATION CONDITIONS

Revocation of S Corporation Status. A corporation may terminate an S election either voluntarily via a revocation or involuntarily by failing to continue to meet the requirements for a small business corporation (e.g., if on any day in any year the S corporation has more than 100 shareholders or issues a second class of stock). A voluntary revocation requires consents from shareholders owning more than 50% of the corporation's stock.

General Effective Date. Under the general rules, a revocation is effective for the entire tax year if the corporation files a statement on or before the fifteenth day of the third month of the tax year. If the corporation files the revocation after this date (e.g., after March 15 for a calendar year S corporation), the effective date is the first day of the next tax year.

EXAMPLE I:17-29 ▶

Shareholders owning more than 50% of the stock of a qualifying calendar year S corporation consent to a voluntary revocation statement filed by the corporation on March 12 of Year 1. Because the corporation filed the revocation on or before March 15, it is taxed as a C corporation for all of Year 1. If the corporation does not file the revocation until March 16 of Year 1, it continues to be treated as an S corporation during Year 1, and it becomes a C corporation in Year 2. ◀

KEY POINT

An election to be treated as an S corporation becomes effective only as of the beginning of a tax year, but a termination can become effective before the end of the normal tax year.

Specified Revocation Date. The law provides an exception when the corporation and its shareholders specify a prospective revocation date. In this case, the revocation takes effect as of the specified date. If the corporation specifies a prospective date other than the first day of a tax year, the revocation results in a short tax year for the final S corporation tax return and a short tax year for the initial C corporation tax return. In this case, the income or loss is allocated between the two short years on a prorated daily basis.[37]

EXAMPLE I:17-30 ▶

Assume the same facts as in Example I:17-29 except that the corporation specifies a prospective termination date of July 1 of Year 1. The revocation is effective as of this date, and the corporation files an S corporation short-period return for the period January 1 through June 30 of Year 1, and files a C corporation short-period return for the period July 1 through December 31 of Year 1. The income or loss is prorated to each return on a daily basis. Unless extended, the S corporation return is due September 15 of Year 1, and the C corporation return is due March 15 of Year 2. ◀

---

[37] The first day of the C corporation tax year is the day on which the revocation occurs. Under Sec. 1377(a)(2), a special election may be made to use the interim closing method (i.e., the books are closed as of the termination date) if all affected shareholders consent to this method.

Involuntary and Inadvertent Terminations. An S corporation may involuntarily lose its special tax status and revert to a C corporation if it fails to meet the small business corporation requirements or if it has excessive amounts of passive (investment) income for each year in a three-year period (i.e., more than 25% of gross receipts).[38] However, if the IRS deems that the termination was inadvertent and the S corporation or its shareholders take the necessary steps within a reasonable time period to restore its small business corporation status, the S corporation status is considered to have been continuously in effect.

EXAMPLE I:17-31 ► A calendar year S corporation adds an unqualified shareholder on June 4. The S corporation status terminates on June 3. The corporation files a short-period S corporation tax return for the period January 1 through June 3 and files a C corporation tax return for the period from June 4 through December 31. Income or loss is prorated to the two tax returns on a daily basis. ◄

EXAMPLE I:17-32 ► Assume the same facts as in Example I:17-31 except the termination is deemed to be inadvertent, and the violation of shareholder requirements is corrected within a reasonable time period. The S corporation status is considered to have been continuously in effect, and no C corporation tax return is required. A single S corporation tax return will be filed for the year. ◄

Election After Termination. If an S corporation terminates its election either by ceasing to be a small business corporation or by revocation, the corporation may not reelect S corporation status for five years unless the IRS consents to an early reelection.

Topic Review I:17-4 summarizes the S corporation qualification, election, and termination rules.

S CORPORATION OPERATIONS

Income, gains, losses, deductions, and credits pass through to the S corporation's shareholders in a manner similar to the partnership rules. Some common separately stated items include:

► Short-term and long-term capital gains and losses

► Sec. 1231 gains and losses

► Unrecaptured Sec. 1250 gains

► Charitable contributions[39]

► Credits

► Interest on investment indebtedness

► AMT adjustments and tax preference items

► Foreign taxes paid or accrued

► Dividends and other portfolio income

Table I:17-1, appearing earlier in this chapter, provides a list of comparable items for partnerships. These separately stated items are segregated from the computation of ordinary income (or loss) because each item affects the tax returns of the various shareholders differently, depending on their particular tax situation. The residual income or loss amount (i.e., the amount remaining after removing the separately stated items) represents the S corporation's ordinary income (or loss). Separately stated items and S corporation ordinary income (or loss) pass through to the shareholders as of the last day of the S corporation's tax year.[40] The S corporation computes its ordinary income (or loss) on page 1 of Form 1120S (U.S. Income Tax Return for an S Corporation), and it reports all items on

---

[38] The passive income restrictions apply solely to S corporations that were previously taxed as C corporations in pre-election years and have accumulated Subchapter C earnings and profits from those years on the last day of three consecutive S corporation tax years. Thus, a corporation that elects S corporation status in its initial tax year and continually retains such status is not subject to the restrictions. If the restrictions apply and the S corporation has passive income exceeding 25% of its gross receipts for three consecutive tax years, the S election automatically terminates on the first day of the fourth

tax year. In addition, a penalty tax equal to 35% of the corporation's excess net passive income is imposed during each year of the three-year period.

[39] The IRS has ruled in Rev. Rul. 2000-43, 2000-2 C.B. 333, that charitable contributions made by an S corporation cannot be reported using the accrual method permitted for C corporations under Sec. 170(a)(2).

[40] Sec. 1363. Special rules apply if the S election terminates during the tax year. These rules are beyond the scope of this text.

TOPIC REVIEW I:17-4

S Corporation Qualification, Election, and Termination Rules

QUALIFICATION REQUIREMENTS

▶ An S corporation must be a domestic corporation.

▶ A maximum of 100 shareholders are allowed. Members of a family count as one shareholder, and each beneficiary of a qualifying trust is a separate shareholder.

▶ Only individuals (citizens or resident aliens), estates, certain kinds of trusts, and certain kinds of tax-exempt organizations can be shareholders. No corporate or general partnership shareholders are permitted.

▶ Only one class of stock generally may be issued and outstanding. Multiple classes of stock can be used if the only difference between the classes is voting rights.

▶ Certain corporations that maintain special tax statuses are ineligible.

▶ If an S corporation has an 80%-or-more-owned subsidiary, it cannot file a consolidated tax return with that subsidiary. Special rules apply to a Qualified Subchapter S Subsidiary (QSub).

ELECTION REQUIREMENTS

▶ All shareholders on the S election date must consent to the election and the corporation must file Form 2553. To be effective for the election year, the corporation must file the S election and consent form on or before the fifteenth day of the third month of the election year. Otherwise, the election is effective for the next tax year.

▶ The IRS can waive the election deadline if the corporation shows reasonable cause for late filing.

▶ The IRS can grant relief for improper elections if they are inadvertent and subsequently corrected.

TERMINATION RULES

▶ To effect a voluntary revocation, shareholders owning more than 50% of the S corporation's stock must consent. The revocation is effective for the entire year if made on or before the fifteenth day of the third month of the tax year. Otherwise, the revocation is effective the first day of the next tax year unless the corporation specifies a prospective revocation.

▶ An involuntary termination occurs if (1) the S corporation fails to meet any of the small business corporation requirements (e.g., it has more than 100 shareholders) or (2) it has excessive passive investment income in a three-year period (assuming the corporation has prior C corporation accumulated E&P). If the IRS deems the involuntary termination to be inadvertent, the S corporation status is considered to have been continuously in effect provided the corporation and shareholders correct the defect.

▶ Aside from the inadvertent termination exception, a corporation may not reelect S corporation status for five years after a termination or revocation.

ADDITIONAL COMMENT

A shareholder of a corporation also can be an employee of the corporation. Payments with respect to the employment status are considered salary whereas payments with respect to ownership of stock are treated as corporate distributions.

ADDITIONAL COMMENT

A corporation is deemed to make the election to deduct and amortize organizational expenditures unless it chooses to forgo the election.

Schedule K of that return. Then, the corporation prepares a Schedule K-1, which reports to each shareholder his or her share of the S corporation items. The shareholders use the Schedule K-1 information to prepare their individual tax returns (Form 1040).

The tax treatment of some S corporation items is similar to that for C corporations. For example, the S corporation deducts salaries paid to its shareholders in the calculation of ordinary income or loss and not as a separately stated item on Schedule K-1. In addition, S Corporations can deduct up to $5,000 in organizational expenditures in the year in which business begins. The deduction is limited to the lesser of the organizational expenditures or $5,000, reduced by the amount by which such organizational expenditures exceed $50,000. Any excess organizational expenditures may be amortized over 180 months beginning with the month the S Corporation's business begins. S corporations, however, are not entitled to certain other corporate deductions, such as the dividends-received deduction or the net operating loss deduction because dividends and net operating losses pass through to the S corporation's shareholders.

EXAMPLE I:17-33 ▶ Ajax Corporation, an S corporation owned equally by Linda and Hal, reports the following operating results for the current year (a non-leap year):

SELF-STUDY QUESTION

Compare the manner in which income of an S corporation is allocated among the shareholders to the manner in which partnership income is allocated among the partners.

ANSWER

In the case of an S corporation, the income must be allocated based on the percentage of stock owned on a daily basis. Partners have much greater flexibility. The partnership agreement serves as the basis for allocation, with special allocations being permitted. No special allocations are permitted for an S corporation.

Sales	$10,000
Minus: Cost of goods sold	(2,000)
Gross profit	$ 8,000
Plus: Long-term capital gains	3,000
Total income	$11,000
Minus: Administrative expenses	(800)
Repairs	(200)
Sec. 1231 losses	(1,100)
Charitable contributions	(900)
Net income	$ 8,000

The S corporation reports these items on its tax return as follows:

	Schedule K Ordinary Income	Separately Stated Items	Linda's K-1	Hal's K-1
Sales	$10,000			
Cost of goods sold	(2,000)			
Administrative expenses	(800)			
Repairs	(200)			
Total ordinary income	$ 7,000		$3,500	$3,500
Long-term capital gains		$ 3,000	1,500	1,500
Sec. 1231 losses		(1,100)	(550)	(550)
Charitable contributions		(900)	(450)	(450)

Linda and Hal each report $3,500 of ordinary income plus 50% of each separately stated item on their individual tax returns. ◄

Income, gains, losses, deductions, credits, and other separately stated items are allocated to the shareholders based on the number of shares of stock owned on each day of the S corporation's tax year. Thus, if a shareholder sells S corporation stock during the year, ordinary income (or loss) and separately stated items are allocated on a daily basis to the seller and purchaser of the stock.[41]

EXAMPLE I:17-34 ► Assume the same facts as in Example I:17-33 except Linda sells her stock to Mark on the 181st day of the tax year. Income through the date of the transfer is allocated to Linda. Thus, Linda reports $1,736 [0.50 × (181 ÷ 365)× $7,000] of the ordinary income and a similar portion of each separately stated item. Mark reports the ordinary income and separately stated items for the remainder of the year. The sale does not affect the way Hal reports his share of the income. ◄

BASIS ADJUSTMENTS TO S CORPORATION STOCK

Usually, a shareholder's original basis for S corporation stock is either the amount paid for the stock or a substituted basis from a nontaxable transaction (e.g., a Sec. 351 corporate formation).[42] Adjustments subsequently are made for ordinary income (or loss) and separately stated items that pass through to the shareholders, as well as additional capital contributions by shareholders and distributions to shareholders.[43] These basis adjustments apply in the following order: (1) positive adjustments for contributions, S corporation ordinary income, and separately stated income and gain items; (2) negative adjustments for distributions; and (3) negative adjustments for S corporation ordinary loss and separately stated deduction and loss items.

---

[41] If the corporation makes a special election under Sec. 1377(a)(2), the income is allocated according to the accounting methods used by the S corporation (instead of on a daily basis) when a shareholder terminates his or her interest during the tax year.

[42] The death or gift tax basis rules also may be used to determine the initial basis for S corporation stock.

[43] Sec. 1367.

EXAMPLE I:17-35 ► During the current year, Juan pays $40,000 for 100 shares of Allied Corporation stock. Allied is a calendar year S corporation. Juan's share of Allied's current year ordinary income is $10,000. In addition, his share of separately stated items includes $4,000 of long-term capital gains and $2,000 of Sec. 1231 losses. Allied also distributes $5,000 cash to Juan during the year. Juan's basis in the S corporation stock on December 31 is computed as follows:

Original basis (cost)		$40,000
Plus:	Share of ordinary income	10,000
	Share of long-term capital gains	4,000
Minus:	Cash distribution to Juan	(5,000)
	Share of Sec. 1231 losses	(2,000)
Basis of stock on December 31		$47,000 ◄

The logic behind these basis adjustments is the same as for partnerships. They prevent double taxation of income or double deductions for losses.

EXAMPLE I:17-36 ► Kayla is in the 39.6% tax bracket for ordinary income and faces a 23.8% tax rate on long-term capital gains (including the 3.8% tax on net investment income). She plans to form Alpha Corporation by contributing $100,000 in exchange for Alpha stock. Alpha will invest the contributed funds in its business operations. During the next ten years, Kayla expects Alpha to earn $900,000 of ordinary income before taxes. At the end of the ten-year period, Kayla plans to sell her Alpha stock. If Alpha operates as an S corporation, Kayla will recognize $900,000 of pass-through income on which she must pay taxes. So that Kayla will have sufficient cash to pay these taxes, Alpha will distribute $356,400 ($900,000 × 0.396) over the ten-year period. On the other hand, if Alpha operates as a C corporation, it will pay taxes at its 35% tax rate (assumed) and will make no distributions to Kayla. If an S corporation, Alpha's value at the end of ten years will be $643,600 ($100,000 contribution + $900,000 pretax earnings − $356,400 distributed). If a C corporation, its value will be $685,000 ($100,000 contribution + $900,000 pretax earnings − $315,000 corporate taxes paid). Thus, Kayla will sell the stock at one of these amounts, depending on whether Alpha operates as an S corporation or a C corporation. The results of these alternatives are as follows:

	S Corporation with Stock Basis Adjustments	C Corporation with No Stock Basis Adjustments
Selling price of stock	$ 643,600	$685,000
Original contribution	$ 100,000	$100,000
Kayla's pass-through income	900,000	–0–
Distributions to Kayla	(356,400)	–0–
Adjusted basis of Alpha stock	$ 643,600	$100,000
Gain on sale of stock	$ –0–	$585,000
Times: Capital gains tax rate	0.238	0.238
Tax on capital gain	$ –0–	$139,230
After-tax proceeds (selling price − tax)	$ 643,600	$545,770

Thus, the S corporation results in the higher after-tax proceeds primarily because its shareholder is subject to only one level of taxation rather than the double taxation afforded by the C corporation, that is, the corporate-level tax and the tax upon selling the C corporation stock. ◄

S CORPORATION LOSSES AND LIMITATIONS

An ordinary loss and any separately stated loss and deduction items of an S corporation are allocated among the shareholders based on the number of shares of stock owned on each day of the S corporation's tax year.[44] The last day of the S corporation's tax year determines when the shareholders report the loss on their tax return.[45] Most S corporations must use a calendar tax year, although an S corporation can use a fiscal year if that year can be shown to be a natural business year because the corporation's operations are cyclical.

---

[44] Sec. 1366(a)(1).

[45] The same rule applies for reporting ordinary income and separately stated income and gain items.

EXAMPLE I:17-37 ▶ Sigma Corporation is an S corporation whose tax year ends on January 31 of each year because Sigma has a natural business year that ends on that date. All of its shareholders report their taxes using a calendar year. Sigma reports a $100,000 ordinary loss for the 12-month period ending January 31 of Year 2. The shareholders report the entire loss on their calendar Year 2 returns. ◀

KEY POINT

An S corporation shareholder gets debt basis, separate from stock basis, for amounts the shareholder lends directly to the corporation, but the shareholder gets no basis for corporate liabilities owed to third parties. This treatment differs from that of partnership liabilities.

ADDITIONAL COMMENT

The loss carryover period is indefinite but does not transfer to another taxpayer if the shareholder disposes of all his or her stock or if the shareholder dies. Furthermore, if the S election terminates, the loss must be used against any basis of the former S corporation stock by the end of a one-year post-termination transition period.

A shareholder's deduction for ordinary losses and separately stated items cannot exceed his or her basis for the S corporation stock plus the debt basis for any shareholder loans made to the S corporation.[46] A shareholder, however, obtains no debt basis for corporate-level liabilities even if he or she guarantees them. The following rules apply in determining the deductibility of ordinary loss and separately stated loss items:

▶ Positive basis adjustments increase stock basis for ordinary income or separately stated income or gain items incurred during the year before ordinary losses, and separately stated losses and deductions reduce stock basis.

▶ The shareholder's deduction for pass-through losses is limited to the sum of (1) stock basis after the above positive adjustments and after distributions but before negative adjustments for losses and deductions and (2) the shareholder's debt basis.[47]

▶ A shareholder's pass-through loss first reduces the shareholder's stock basis (but not below zero).

▶ If the loss exceeds the shareholder's stock basis, the remaining pass-through loss reduces the shareholder's debt basis (but not below zero).

▶ If the loss exceeds both the stock and debt basis, the shareholder carries over the excess loss and deducts it in a subsequent year when the shareholder again has basis in the stock or debt.

EXAMPLE I:17-38 ▶ Matt owns 20% of the stock of an S corporation. His stock basis is $18,000 at the end of Year 1 after adjustments for separately stated income and gain items. Matt also loans the S corporation $12,000 during Year 1. The S corporation incurs a $200,000 ordinary loss in Year 1. Matt's share of the ordinary loss is $40,000 (0.20 × $200,000). Matt's deduction and carryover of the unused loss are as follows:

Basis in stock	$18,000
Minus: Ordinary loss applied against stock basis	(18,000)
Basis in stock after ordinary loss	$ –0–
Debt basis in loan	$12,000
Minus: Ordinary loss applied against debt basis	(12,000)
Debt basis in loan after ordinary loss	$ –0–
Share of ordinary loss	$40,000
Minus: Loss allowed in Year 1 ($18,000 + $12,000)	(30,000)
Carryover of ordinary loss to Year 2	$10,000 ◀

If a shareholder's basis is insufficient to absorb the entire amount of ordinary loss (and separately stated loss and deduction items), the pass-through of each item is pro rated. For example, if a shareholder's basis is $5,000 and he or she has a $6,000 ordinary loss and a $4,000 capital loss, the total deduction is limited to $5,000. This deduction consists of a $3,000 [($6,000 ÷ $10,000) × $5,000] ordinary loss and a $2,000 [($4,000 ÷ $10,000) × $5,000] capital loss. The shareholder also has a $3,000 ($6,000 − $3,000) ordinary loss carryover and a $2,000 ($4,000 − $2,000) capital loss carryover.

Restoration of Basis. If a shareholder's debt basis is reduced by a loss deduction, subsequent net increases in a future year initially increase the debt basis until that basis

---

[46] Sec. 1366(d)(1). The deductible loss is treated as a deduction for AGI on an individual shareholder's tax return. S corporation shareholders also are subject to special limitations on losses and deductions that pass through from the S corporation (e.g., at-risk limitations under Sec. 465 and passive activity losses under Sec. 469). (See Chapter C:11 of *Prentice Hall's Federal Taxation: Corporations, Partnerships, Estates & Trusts* for a discussion of these additional limitations.)
[47] Secs. 1366(d)(1)(A) and 1367(a)(2).

reduction is fully restored. Any excess positive adjustment then increases the shareholder's stock basis.

EXAMPLE I:17-39 ▶ Assume the same facts as in Example I:17-38, and in Year 2 the S corporation's ordinary income is $140,000. Matt's share of the income is $28,000 (0.20 × $140,000). The $28,000 of income earned in Year 2 permits Matt to deduct the $10,000 ordinary loss carryover from Year 1. Matt's net increase is $18,000 ($28,000 − $10,000 loss carryover). Thus, Matt restores debt basis by $12,000, its original amount. The remaining $16,000 of income increases stock basis. Accordingly, stock and debt basis are adjusted as follows:

ADDITIONAL COMMENT

In a manner similar to partners, S corporation shareholders may be subject to the passive activity loss limitations on their pass-through losses if they do not materially participate in the S corporation's business. See Chapter I:8 for a detailed discussion of the passive activity loss limitations rules.

	Stock Basis	Debt Basis
Basis at beginning of year	$ –0–	$ –0–
Plus: Income for the year ($28,000)	16,000	12,000
Minus: Loss carryover from prior year	(10,000)	–0–
Basis at end of year	$ 6,000	$12,000 ◀

If the debt basis is not fully restored, gain results when the corporation repays the loan. If the loan is in the form of a note, the repayment results in a capital gain because the note constitutes a capital asset.[48] However, ordinary income results if the loan is an unsecured advance.[49]

Topic Review I:17-5 summarizes the basic tax rules for S corporation shareholders.

OTHER S CORPORATION CONSIDERATIONS

Distributions of Cash and Property to Shareholders. A money or property distribution made by an S corporation to its shareholders is treated as a return of capital if the S corporation has no accumulated earnings and profits from pre-S corporation years.[50] As such, the amount of money or FMV of the noncash property distributed to a shareholder reduces the basis of the shareholder's S corporation stock. If distributions exceed the shareholder's stock basis, the excess is treated as a capital gain if the stock is a capital asset.[51]

ADDITIONAL COMMENT

Another important difference between partnerships and S corporations involves the tax consequences of property distributions. An S corporation recognizes gain if it distributes appreciated property to its shareholders, but a partnership would not recognize such gain. Also, the property's FMV is used for S corporation distributions while the property's adjusted basis is used for partnership distributions.

The S corporation recognizes gain (but not loss) if it distributes noncash property to its shareholders.[52] The distribution is treated as if the corporation sold the property to the shareholders at its FMV. The gain passes through to the shareholders who increase their stock basis accordingly. The distributed property's FMV then reduces the shareholders' stock bases.

TOPIC REVIEW I:17-5

Basic Tax Rules for S Corporation Shareholders

▶ Ordinary losses and separately stated loss and deduction items are allocated to shareholders on a per share per day basis.

▶ The last day of the S corporation's tax year determines the year in which the shareholders report their share of income, gain, deductions, losses, credits, and other separately stated items.

▶ Basis cannot be reduced below zero. Positive basis adjustments are made for ordinary income and separately stated income or gain items before basis reductions for distributions, ordinary losses, and separately stated loss and deduction items.

▶ Losses initially reduce the shareholder's stock basis (but not below zero). Any excess losses then reduce a shareholder's basis in debt owed by the S corporation to the shareholder.

▶ Unused losses are suspended and carried over until the shareholder again has basis to absorb the losses.

▶ Net positive basis adjustments in subsequent years initially increase the shareholder's debt basis until fully restored. Any additional positive basis adjustments increase the shareholder's basis in S corporation stock.

---

[48] Rev. Rul. 64-162, 1964-1 C.B. 304.
[49] Rev. Rul. 68-537, 1968-2 C.B. 372.
[50] The tax consequences of property distributions to an S corporation's shareholders are discussed in Chapter C:11 of *Prentice Hall's Federal Taxation: Corporations, Partnerships, Estates & Trusts.*
[51] Sec. 1368(b). The S corporation also can have accumulated E&P from a

tax year in which it was taxed as a C corporation. The tax consequences of a distribution made by an S corporation having accumulated E&P are complex. These rules are beyond the scope of this text but are discussed in Chapter C:11 of *Prentice Hall's Federal Taxation: Corporations, Partnerships, Estates & Trusts.*
[52] Sec. 311(b).

EXAMPLE I:17-40 ▶ Austin Corporation, an S corporation, distributes land (a capital asset) to its sole shareholder Sue. The land has a $10,000 basis and a $90,000 FMV. Prior to the distribution, Sue's stock basis is $200,000. The S corporation recognizes an $80,000 capital gain, which passes through to Sue. Sue increases her Austin stock basis by the $80,000 pass-through gain and decreases it by the $90,000 FMV of the distribution. Thus, after the distribution, her stock basis is $190,000, and her basis in the land is $90,000 (its FMV). ◀

Tax Year Restrictions. S corporations must use a calendar year unless the corporation can establish a business purpose (i.e., a natural business year) for choosing a fiscal year-end.[53] These year-end restrictions prevent shareholders from deferring pass-through income for up to 11 months (e.g., if a January 31 fiscal year-end were permitted). Also, like a partnership, an S corporation may elect a maximum three-month deferral if it agrees to make a special tax payment each year that approximates the deferral benefit.

ADDITIONAL COMMENT

For purposes of calculating which shareholders own more than 2% of the S corporation's outstanding stock, the Sec. 318 attribution rules apply.

Treatment of Fringe Benefits. S corporation shareholders who own more than 2% of the outstanding stock are not eligible for some nontaxable corporate employee fringe benefits, including the following examples:

▶ The group term life insurance exclusion for premiums paid for up to $50,000 coverage (Sec. 79)

▶ The exclusion from income for premiums paid for accident and health insurance and medical reimbursement plans (Secs. 105 and 106)[54]

▶ The exclusion for cafeteria plan benefits (Sec. 125)

▶ Meals and lodging furnished for the convenience of the employer (Sec. 119)

A more-than-2% shareholder includes the fringe benefits listed above in gross income as compensation, which is deductible by the S corporation. Amounts received by a shareholder owning 2% or less of the S corporation's stock are excluded from the shareholder's gross income and deductible by the corporation as they would be for an employee of a C corporation.

EXAMPLE I:17-41 ▶ Bass Corporation, an S corporation, pays health insurance and group term life insurance premiums for its employee-owner group, all of whom own more than 2% of the Bass stock. The owner-employees include the premiums in their gross income, and the S corporation deducts the premiums. Employee-shareholders who own more than 2% of the S corporation's stock can deduct 100% of the amount includible in gross income as being paid for medical insurance for themselves, their spouses, and their dependents.[55] The premiums would not be included in the gross income of employees who did not own any Bass stock, or who owned 2% or less of the Bass stock. ◀

Many S corporation fringe benefits are not subject to special treatment for a more-than-2% shareholder. A partial list of such fringe benefits includes:

▶ Stock options

▶ Nonqualified deferred compensation

▶ Compensation for injuries and sickness (Sec. 104)

▶ Educational assistance programs (Sec. 127)

▶ Dependent care assistance programs (Sec. 129)

▶ Certain fringe benefits (Sec. 132)

The employee reports these fringe benefits under the general gross income inclusion rule applicable to the fringe benefit, and the corporation deducts them as ordinary business expenses under Sec. 162.

---

[53] Sec. 1378(b).
[54] Rev. Rul. 91-26, 1991-1 C.B. 184, clarified by Ann. 92-16, 1992-5 I.R.B. 53. Rules similar to those applying to more than 2% S corporation shareholders will apply to all partners in a partnership. The payment is deductible by the partnership and includible in the partner's gross income. Notice 2008-1, 2008-1 C.B. 251, eases the for-AGI deductibility of health insurance premiums.
[55] Sec. 162(l)(1) and (5).

ADDITIONAL COMMENT

A special rule provides reduced recognition periods for tax years beginning in 2009 through 2014. As an example, for 2011 through 2014, a calendar year S corporation recognizes no built-in gains tax if the fifth year of the recognition period precedes the applicable year.

Corporate Tax on Built-in Gains. A 35% corporate tax on built-in gains applies if a corporation that previously was a C corporation elects S corporation status.[56] The built-in gains tax does not apply to a corporation that always has been an S corporation or that elected S corporation status before 1987. A built-in gain exists if the FMV of an asset exceeds its adjusted basis on the day the S election becomes effective. If the corporation sells an asset with a built-in gain within the ten-year recognition period beginning on the effective date for the election, the S corporation pays tax on the built-in gain. Built-in losses existing on the first day of the S election period can reduce built-in gains. Any appreciation on the asset that occurs after conversion from a C corporation to an S corporation is subject to the regular S corporation pass-through rules but is not taxed under the built-in gains tax. Assets acquired after the first day of the S corporation election period also are exempt from the built-in gains tax.

EXAMPLE I:17-42 ▶

KEY POINT

Congress enacted the built-in gains tax to prevent C corporations from avoiding double taxation in a corporate liquidation or asset sale by electing S corporation status immediately before the liquidation or sale.

Beach Corporation, an accrual basis taxpayer, incorporated six years ago and subsequently elected S corporation status beginning January 1 of last year. On January 1 of last year, Beach owned land with a $50,000 basis and a $200,000 FMV. Beach sold the land this year for $225,000. Thus, Beach reports a total gain of $175,000 ($225,000 − $50,000). The first $150,000 of the gain is subject to the built-in gains tax at the corporate level and passes through to the shareholders. The remaining $25,000 of post-conversion appreciation also is subject to the regular S corporation pass-through rules but is not subject to the built-in gains tax. In addition, the built-in gains tax paid by the corporation passes through as a loss to the shareholders. ◀

Tax on Excess Net Passive Income. A 35% excess net passive income tax applies when an S corporation has passive investment income for the tax year that exceeds 25% of its gross receipts and, at the close of the tax year, the S corporation has E&P that accumulated while it was a C corporation.[57]

EXAMPLE I:17-43 ▶

Acorn Corporation made an S election last year after having been a C corporation for several years. Acorn has accumulated C corporation E&P at the end of the current year. During the current year, Acorn's excess net passive income is $10,000, comprised of dividends and interest. The excess net passive income tax is $3,500 ($10,000 × 0.35). The tax reduces (on a pro rata basis) the passive income items (e.g., dividends and interest) that pass through to Acorn's shareholders. ◀

STOP & THINK

Question: Suppose shareholders of an S corporation wanted to convert the business into a limited liability company (LLC). What tax obstacles might they encounter?

Solution: The shareholders would have to liquidate the corporation and recontribute the assets to the LLC. Because the S corporation must comply with general corporate tax rules, the liquidation will cause gain and loss recognition at the corporate level for property distributed (Sec. 336). This gain (loss) will pass through to the shareholders and be taxable (deductible) to them. In addition, the liquidation might trigger the corporate level tax on built-in gains (Sec. 1374). Thus, conversion from an S corporation to an LLC could have adverse tax consequences. Contrast these major tax obstacles with the conversion of a partnership to an LLC. The IRS has ruled that the conversion of a partnership to an LLC is a nontaxable event.[58]

Sale of S Corporation Stock. If an S corporation shareholder sells his or her stock, he or she recognizes a capital gain. Unlike under the partnership rules discussed earlier, the S corporation shareholder does not have to convert any of the gain to ordinary income as under Sec. 751 or to unrecaptured Sec. 1250 gain under Sec. 1(h). If the S corporation owns collectibles, however, gain attributable to those assets would be subject to the

---

[56] Sec. 1374. This discussion is only a sketch of these complex rules.

[57] Sec. 1375(a). These rules are discussed in greater detail in Chapter C:11 of *Prentice Hall's Federal Taxation: Corporations, Partnerships, Estates & Trusts.*

[58] Rev. Rul. 95-37, 1995-1 C.B. 130.

28% capital gains tax rate.[59] Aside from this exception and other rare exceptions, the shareholder's gain would be taxed at the applicable capital gains rate if he or she has held the stock for more than one year.

TAX PLANNING CONSIDERATIONS

OBJECTIVE 4

Identify tax planning opportunities for partnerships and S corporations

USE OF OPERATING LOSSES

Often, the decision to select a particular form of business organization involves both tax and nontax issues. For example, owners may prefer the corporate form because of nontax attributes such as limited liability, the relative freedom to transfer ownership interests, and the ability to raise outside equity capital.

In many instances, however, the tax attributes dominate, making the partnership or S corporation form preferable to the C corporation. If the owners expect operating losses in the initial years of operation, they may prefer the partnership (or LLC) form to either the C corporation or the S corporation form of organization. In a C corporation, the operating losses do not benefit the shareholders directly and may be of no benefit if the corporation cannot generate sufficient profits in future years to offset the loss carryovers.[60] In a partnership, the losses pass through to the partners, limited by their basis for the partnership interest. The basis of a partner's interest, however, includes his or her share of partnership liabilities. In contrast, an S corporation's ability to pass through losses is limited to the shareholder's basis in the stock and any shareholder loans to the corporation. Other S corporation liabilities are not included in determining the shareholder's loss limitation. Thus, the partnership (or LLC) form of conducting business may provide its owners a greater opportunity to deduct losses than does the S corporation form.

EXAMPLE I:17-44 ►

Mary and Marty are considering whether to operate a new business venture as a C corporation, S corporation, LLC, or a partnership. Regardless of the form chosen, Mary and Marty will materially participate in the business. Mary and Marty plan to invest $50,000 of equity and raise an additional $50,000 from outside creditors (e.g., accounts payable and a mortgage). They expect initial losses of $20,000 per year for five years. Three alternatives are available. If they use a C corporation, the corporate losses are not deductible (i.e., the corporation has net operating loss carryovers of $100,000 after the five-year period). If they elect S corporation status, Mary and Marty can deduct only $50,000 because the general corporate debt is not included in their stock basis. The remaining $50,000 loss carries forward indefinitely at the shareholder level unless the shareholders lend $50,000 of additional funds to the corporation (instead of having the corporation borrow these amounts from outside creditors) or make $50,000 of additional capital contributions. If they form a partnership or LLC, Mary and Marty can deduct the full $100,000 of losses because their basis includes their ratable share of the partnership's liabilities.[61] Assuming Mary and Marty have sufficient other sources of income to absorb the losses, the value of these additional deductions in the first five years favors the partnership or LLC form of organization. A nontax factor that might influence the decision is the limited liability protection offered by the corporate or LLC forms. ◄

? STOP & THINK

Question: Paul, a single taxpayer, owns a business that produces $50,000 of annual profits. If the business were incorporated, it could justify retaining all of its earnings and pay little or no dividends. Paul also has $100,000 of taxable income from other sources. Should Paul organize the business as an S corporation or as a C corporation?

Solution: Although many factors would be involved, one important tax factor is that Paul's $50,000 of income from the business would be taxed at a 28% marginal tax rate (in 2015) if the business is an S corporation because the $50,000 increases his taxable

---

[59] Reg. Sec. 1.1(h)-1. An incremental 3.8% rate also applies to net investment income for taxpayers whose modified AGI exceeds $200,000 ($250,000 for married filing jointly).

[60] In a C corporation, net operating losses carry back two years and forward 20 years. In a newly formed corporation with initial losses, the carryback

rules would not apply because the corporation has no income in the carryback years.

[61] Taxpayers also must satisfy the at risk rules of Sec. 465 and the passive activity loss rules of Sec. 469. These topics are discussed in Chapter I:8.

income to $150,000. In contrast, the C corporation tax rate is 15% on the first $50,000 of taxable income. Thus, the marginal tax rate on the $50,000 is much lower with the C corporation form. Additional taxation would result, however, if Paul withdrew profits as a dividend or recognized a capital gain upon selling his stock or liquidating the corporation.

INCOME SHIFTING AMONG FAMILY MEMBERS

Subject to gift tax rules and restrictions, an attractive tax planning strategy is to shift income from higher tax bracket family members to children or others who are subject to lower tax rates. With an S corporation, parents may gift nonvoting common stock and shift income to their children if the children are not subject to the kiddie tax. Thus, a portion of the S corporation income is taxed to the children even though the parents retain all voting rights for the corporate stock. A partnership interest also may be gifted to other family members. However, the IRS generally does not recognize the family member as a partner where capital (e.g., inventory, plant, and equipment) is a material income-producing factor unless the individual is the real owner of the interest and has dominion and control over it. If property is given to a child subject to the kiddie tax, a 10% or 15% marginal tax rate could apply to the unearned income generated from the property. Should the child's unearned income exceed $2,100 (in 2015), however, it is taxed at the parents' higher tax rate. Therefore, if S corporation stock or a partnership interest is given to a child subject to the kiddie tax, the child's share of S corporation or partnership income will be taxed to the child at the parents' highest marginal tax rate if it exceeds the $2,100 threshold (see Chapter I:2).

With an S corporation or a partnership, family members (e.g., children) can be hired as employees. Thus, income may be shifted to lower tax bracket family members. The kiddie tax rules discussed previously have no effect on earned income even if derived from a parent's business. In a partnership and an S corporation, however, the IRS will reallocate income to reflect the value of the services and capital contributions if the entity pays unreasonable salaries.[62]

EXAMPLE I:17-45 ► Paul, the sole owner of an S corporation, gifts 20% of the corporation's stock equally to his children Kelly, age 25, and Joslyn, age 12. The S corporation's ordinary income is $100,000 after deducting a $10,000 salary paid to Paul. If a reasonable salary for Paul's services is $50,000, the IRS may reduce ordinary income by the additional $40,000 of salary to $60,000 ($100,000 − $40,000) and increase Paul's taxable compensation to $50,000. Thus, the share of ordinary income that passes through to the children is reduced from $20,000 (0.20 × $100,000) to $12,000 (0.20 × $60,000). Kelly's $6,000 ([$60,000 × 0.20] × 0.50) of income is taxed at her regular tax rate because she is not subject to the kiddie tax. On the other hand, $3,900 ($6,000 − $2,100) of Joslyn's income is taxed at her parents' marginal tax rate. ◄

ADDITIONAL COMMENT

The Sec. 754 election may be revoked only with the approval of the IRS. The IRS, however, will not approve a revocation if the primary purpose is to avoid stepping down the basis of partnership assets.

OPTIONAL BASIS ADJUSTMENT ELECTION UNDER SEC. 754

A basis adjustment election under Sec. 754 usually is desirable for an incoming partner whose partnership interest cost more than the tax basis of his or her share of partnership assets. The excess amount increases the new partner's basis for his or her interest in the partnership's assets. If the partnership made a Sec. 754 election in a prior year, the election continues in effect and automatically applies to subsequent years. When made, all partners must agree to the election because the partnership makes the election rather than the individual partner.

Therefore, before consummating a sale, an incoming partner should attempt to obtain assurances from the remaining partners that the partnership will make the election in the current year if the election is not already in effect. The partnership makes the election by attaching a statement to a timely filed tax return for the year the transaction occurs. The partnership cannot make a retroactive election for prior years.[63] A Sec. 754 election,

---

[62] Secs. 1366(e) and 704(e).

[63] Reg. Sec. 1.754-1(b).

however, may have adverse effects in subsequent years if the amount paid for a partnership interest is less than the tax basis of partnership assets because the incoming partner must reduce his or her share of basis in partnership assets. However, if the partnership assets have a built-in loss exceeding $250,000, the downward basis adjustment would be mandatory even without the Sec. 754 election. See Chapter C:10 of *Prentice Hall's Federal Taxation of Corporations, Partnerships, Estates & Trusts* for additional coverage of this topic.

COMPLIANCE AND PROCEDURAL CONSIDERATIONS

OBJECTIVE 5

Comply with procedural and reporting requirements for partnerships and S corporations

PARTNERSHIP FILING REQUIREMENTS AND ELECTIONS

Partnerships must file Form 1065 (U.S. Return of Partnership Income) on or before the fifteenth day of the fourth month following the close of its tax year (by April 15 for a calendar year partnership). The partnership, however, can obtain an automatic five-month extension by filing Form 7004 (Application for Automatic Extension of Time to File Certain Business Income Tax, Information, and Other Returns).[64] The IRS imposes penalties for failure to file a timely or complete partnership return.

Partnership Elections. The partnership makes most elections affecting the computation of partnership income. These elections include:

▶ Selection of a tax year

▶ Selection of an overall accounting method

▶ Inventory valuation method

▶ Depreciation methods

▶ Amortization method for organizational expenditures

▶ Optional basis adjustments under Sec. 754

An election made at the partnership level is binding on all partners.

In addition, each partner also makes certain elections. The common elections falling into this category are the partners' own accounting periods and methods and the election to take a credit or deduction for foreign income taxes.

REAL-WORLD EXAMPLE

A partnership reported its capital gain on a sale in one tax year rather than on the installment basis. The partners could not use the installment method because this is a partnership election. *George Rothenberg*, 48 T.C. 369 (1967).

REPORTING PARTNERSHIP ITEMS ON FORM 1065

A partnership reports ordinary income or loss on page 1 of Form 1065 while Schedule K summarizes all the separately stated items (e.g., capital gains and losses, tax credits, and charitable contributions). Schedule K also includes guaranteed payments made to partners and the partnership's ordinary income or loss, even though reported on page 1. The partnership prepares a separate Schedule K-1 for each partner. The Schedule K-1 reports each partner's share of the Schedule K items, depending on the agreed upon ratio for sharing income, deduction, loss, and credit items. This schedule becomes the primary input for preparing each partner's federal income tax return.

ADDITIONAL COMMENT

Most partnerships having more than ten partners must select a partner to serve as the tax matters partner. This partner will be in charge of administrative matters in the event of a partnership audit.

A partnership also must prepare a balance sheet (Schedule L), a reconciliation of income per books with income per tax (Schedule M-1), and an analysis of capital accounts (Schedule M-2). A partnership must file Schedule M-3 in lieu of Schedule M-1 if any one of the following conditions holds: (1) the amount of total assets reported in Schedule L exceeds $10 million; (2) the amount of adjusted total assets equals or exceeds $10 million, where adjusted total assets equal the Schedule L amount plus the following items that appear in Schedule M-2: (a) capital distributions made during the year, (b) net book loss for the year, and (c) other

---

[64] Form 7004 allows five-month extensions for some entities (e.g., a partnership) and six-month extensions for other entities (e.g., C and S corporations).

adjustments; (3) total receipts equal or exceed $35 million; or (4) a reportable entity partner owns at least a 50% interest in the partnership on any day of the tax year, where a reportable entity partner is one that had to file its own Schedule M-3.

S CORPORATION FILING REQUIREMENTS AND ACCOUNTING METHOD ELECTIONS

ADDITIONAL COMMENT

Because calendar year S corporation returns are due on March 15, a six-month extension runs to September 15, which is one month prior to the extended due date for individuals. This equalizes treatment of S corporations with partnerships as discussed on the previous page.

An S corporation must file its corporate tax return no later than the fifteenth day of the third month following the end of the tax year. The S corporation reports its results on Form 1120S (U.S. Income Tax Return for an S Corporation). An S corporation can obtain an automatic six-month extension of time for filing its tax return by filing Form 7004 (Application for Automatic Extension of Time to File Certain Business Income Tax, Information, and Other Returns).

The S corporation, rather than the shareholders, makes the accounting method elections used to compute ordinary income or loss and the separately stated items. As with a partnership, the corporation makes these elections independently of the accounting method elections made by its shareholders.

REPORTING S CORPORATION ITEMS ON FORM 1120S

Page 1 of Form 1120S summarizes the ordinary income and deduction items for the S corporation. If the corporation owes any tax due to the excess net passive income tax or the ≠built-in gains tax, such amounts also are reported on page 1 of the return. Schedule K lists the separately stated items and ordinary income or losses for the S corporation, S corporation distributions, and selected other items. The corporation prepares a Schedule K-1 for each shareholder reflecting his or her share of the ordinary income (loss) and separately stated items. The Schedule K-1 becomes the basis for preparing each shareholder's federal income tax return. The S corporation also must prepare a balance sheet (Schedule L) and a reconciliation of income per books with income per tax (Schedule M-1). An S corporation must file Schedule M-3 in lieu of Schedule M-1 if the amount of total assets reported in Schedule L equals or exceeds $10 million.

COMPARISON OF ALTERNATIVE FORMS OF BUSINESS ORGANIZATIONS

Table I:17-2 provides a comparison of sole proprietorships, partnerships, S corporations, and C corporations. The partnership comments also apply to entities treated as partnerships for tax purposes such as LLCs or LLPs.

PROBLEM MATERIALS

DISCUSSION QUESTIONS

I:17-1 Distinguish between the partnership, S corporation, and C corporation forms regarding the following:
  a. Incidence of taxation on the organization's business income
  b. Taxation of distributions to owners
  c. Application of the conduit and separate entity concepts of taxation
  d. Limitation on number and type of owners.

I:17-2 Explain how the following types of business entities are treated under the check-the-box regulations. What alternative treatments are available other than the default classification?

  a. Corporation
  b. Partnership (general and limited)
  c. Limited liability company (LLC)
  d. Limited liability partnership (LLP)

I:17-3 Anya is considering whether to become a limited partner in a real estate investment partnership by making a $10,000 investment. The limited partnership will generate substantial operating losses for its first five years. Discuss the advantages and disadvantages of the entity electing to be taxed as a C corporation versus being treated as a partnership or S corporation.

▼ **TABLE I:17-2**

Comparison of Alternative Forms of Business Organizations

Attributes	Sole Proprietorship	Partnership	S Corporation	C Corporation
Application of the separate entity versus the conduit (pass-through) concepts.	Single level of taxation. The proprietor is the same person as the individual taxpayer. The sole proprietor reports proprietorship income, gains, deductions, losses, and credits in his or her individual tax return.	Conduit with a single level of taxation. The partnership is not taxed. Instead, its income, gains, deductions, losses, and credits pass through to the partners to be taxed in their tax returns.	Conduit with a single level of taxation. Similar to a partnership in that its income, gains, deductions, losses, and credits pass through to the shareholders to be taxed in their tax returns. In special cases, the S corporation may pay entity level taxes on built-in gains and excess net passive income.	Entity with double taxation. The corporation is taxed at the entity level, and its shareholders are taxed again when they receive dividends, sell their stock, or liquidate the corporation.
Applicable income tax rates	Individual tax rates apply to the proprietorship's income, which is included in the proprietor's total taxable income.	Individual tax rates apply to individual partners; corporate tax rates apply to corporate partners; and estate and trust tax rates apply to fiduciary partners.	Individual tax rates apply to individual shareholders; estate and trust tax rates apply to fiduciary shareholders.	Corporate tax rates apply to a corporation's taxable income. Individual, corporate, or estate and trust tax rates apply to shareholders receiving dividends from the C corporation. Qualified dividends are taxed at the applicable capital gains rate (see Additional Comment on page I:17-15).
Ownership restrictions	By definition, a sole proprietorship can have only one owner.	A partnership can have an unlimited number of partners, and these partners can be individuals, corporations, estates, or trusts.	An S corporation can have up to 100 shareholders (with members of a family counting as one). Shareholders are limited to individuals, estates, certain trusts, and certain tax-exempt organizations.	A C corporation can have an unlimited number of shareholders of any type.
Personal liability	The sole proprietor is liable for debts of the proprietorship.	General partners have unlimited liability. Limited partners have liability to the extent of their investment.	Shareholders have limited liability.	Shareholders have limited liability.
Other nontax factors	A sole proprietorship has management continuity problems and may have difficulty raising outside capital.	A partnership has management continuity problems and restrictions on the transfer of partnership interests. It may have difficulty raising outside capital although limited partners, who are pure investors, mitigate this problem.	S corporations have the same characteristics as C corporations. An additional cost may arise if the state income tax law does not recognize the conduit form of taxation and taxes the S corporation as a C corporation.	Along with limited liability, C corporations have continuity of life, centralized management, and free transferability of ownership interests. These factors may outweigh the disadvantages of double taxation.

▼ **TABLE I:17-2 (Continued)**

Comparison of Alternative Forms of Business Organizations

Attributes	Sole Proprietorship	Partnership	S Corporation	C Corporation
Basis	A sole proprietor has basis in the business's assets but has no basis in the entity.	A partnership has basis in its assets, and its partners have basis in their partnership interests. A partner's basis includes his or her share of partnership liabilities. A partner's basis is adjusted for his or her share of partnership transactions.	An S corporation has basis in its assets. Shareholders have basis in their stock and a separate debt basis in their loans to the corporation. A shareholder's basis does not include corporate level liabilities. A shareholder's stock basis is adjusted for his or her share of corporate transactions. Debt basis is adjusted downward for pass-through losses and increased for restorations.	A C corporation has basis in its assets, and shareholders have basis in their stock. Stock basis is adjusted upward only for additional contributions to the corporation and downward for distributions that exceed the corporation's E&P.
Treatment of losses	No limitations apply to the proprietor's NOLs assuming the at-risk and passive activity loss limitations do not apply. Unused proprietor NOLs carry back two years and carry over 20 years.	Partners' pass-through losses are limited to the basis of their partnership interests. At-risk and passive activity loss limitations also may apply.	Shareholders' pass-through losses are limited to their stock and debt basis. At-risk and passive activity loss limitations also may apply.	C corporation losses do not pass through to its shareholders. Unused corporate level NOLs carry back two years and carry over 20 years at the corporate level.
Choice of accounting methods	The sole proprietor can elect the cash or accrual method for business items. However, the accrual method for sales and purchases is required if inventory is a material income producing factor.	Partnerships can elect the cash or accrual method unless they are tax shelters or have a C corporation as a partner, in which case they must use the accrual method. Also, the accrual method for sales and purchases is required if inventory is a material income producing factor.	S corporations can elect the cash or accrual method unless they are tax shelters, in which case they must use the accrual method. Also, the accrual method for sales and purchases is required if inventory is a material income producing factor.	C corporations must use the accrual method unless they are personal service corporations or have annual gross receipts less than $5 million, in which case they can elect the cash or accrual method.
Choice of tax year	A sole proprietorship must use the same tax year as the sole proprietor, usually a calendar year.	The tax year is restricted to that of the majority partners, principal partners, or the least aggregate deferral. The partnership can use a fiscal year if it establishes a business purpose (e.g., a natural business cycle). Other special rules allow a tax year resulting in a maximum three-month deferral.	The tax year is restricted to a calendar year unless the corporation establishes a business purpose (e.g., a natural business cycle) for a fiscal year. Other special rules allow a tax year resulting in a maximum three-month deferral.	C corporations can use a calendar year or any fiscal year. Personal service corporations, however, face restrictions similar to those for S corporations.

▼ **TABLE I:17-2 (Continued)**

Comparison of Alternative Forms of Business Organizations

Attributes	Sole Proprietorship	Partnership	S Corporation	C Corporation
Employment related tax considerations	A sole proprietor is not considered an employee of the business and must pay self-employment taxes on business earnings. Special tax treatment for corporate fringe benefits, such as group term life insurance, are not available to the proprietor.	A partner is not considered an employee of the partnership and must pay self-employment taxes on business earnings. Special tax treatment for corporate fringe benefits, such as group term life insurance, are not available to the partners.	Same as partnerships for shareholders owning more than 2% of the S corporation's stock. S corporation shareholders may be treated as employees, however, for Social Security tax purposes if they receive a salary.	A shareholder-employee may be treated as an employee for Social Security tax and fringe benefits purposes.

I:17-4 Paula transfers two assets to a partnership in separate transactions:
   a. Land with a $60,000 adjusted basis and a $100,000 FMV in exchange for a 20% interest in the partnership.
   b. A machine with a $50,000 adjusted basis and a $40,000 FMV. The partnership signs a note for $40,000 as consideration for the exchange.
Explain whether Paula recognizes gain or loss for either or both of these transactions, and discuss the reason for any difference in tax treatment.

I:17-5 In the current year, Penny contributes machinery to a partnership in exchange for a minority partnership interest. She acquired the machinery five years earlier. It now has a $50,000 adjusted basis and a $90,000 FMV. What are Penny's basis and holding period for the partnership interest? What is the partnership's basis and holding period for the machine? Why are the partnership formation rules structured in their current format?

I:17-6 Compare the Sec. 721 partnership formation rules for a new partnership with the Sec. 351 corporate formation rules for a new C corporation.

I:17-7 How is Mario's basis in his accrual method partnership interest affected by each of the following changes in partnership assets and liabilities (assuming he has a 50% interest in the partnership)?
   a. Mario contributes a building with a $100,000 FMV, and a $70,000 adjusted basis. The building is subject to a $50,000 mortgage, which the partnership assumes.
   b. The partnership's accounts payable increase by $50,000 during the tax year.
   c. The partnership pays off a $40,000 bank note that was outstanding for several years.
   d. The partnership distributes $10,000 cash each to Mario and his partner.

I:17-8 Sally contributes farm machinery with a $150,000 FMV, a $125,000 basis, and a $50,000 note owed to the AB Bank to a new partnership in exchange for a 25% partnership interest. Total partnership liabilities after Sally's contribution are $340,000. What gain or loss do Sally and the partnership recognize on the property contribution to the partnership? What is the partnership's basis and holding period in the machinery? What is Sally's basis in her partnership interest? How would your answers to this problem change (if at all) had Sally's asset contribution instead been made to an existing corporation for a 25% stock interest?

I:17-9 Assume the same basic facts as in Problem I:17-8. How would your answer change if the entity is a new corporation with all owners making property contributions? The corporation makes a timely election to be treated as an S corporation beginning with its first year.

I:17-10 What are the tax consequences to a partner who contributes liabilities that exceed the total basis of assets transferred to a new partnership in exchange for a partnership interest? How does your answer change if the same assets and liabilities are instead transferred to form a new C corporation?

I:17-11 What inequities might result if partners were not required to make special allocations for pre-contribution gains and losses on noncash property contributed to a partnership?

I:17-12 Indicate whether a partner's basis in the partnership interest increases, decreases, or is not affected by the partner's share of the following operating items:
   a. Ordinary income
   b. Ordinary loss
   c. Tax-exempt income
   d. Capital loss
   e. Capital gain
   f. Charitable contribution made by the partnership
   g. Distributions of cash to the partners
   h. Distributions of appreciated noncash property to the partners
   i. Guaranteed payments

I:17-13 Phyllis owns a 30% interest in the PQR Partnership and has a $20,000 basis in her partnership interest (before adjustments for Phyllis's share of current year partnership income or loss). During the current year, the PQR Partnership reports a $100,000 ordinary loss and no change in partnership liabilities. Phyllis materially participates in the business in the current year.
   a. What amount of the loss can Phyllis deduct in the current year?
   b. What is Phyllis's basis in her partnership interest at the end of the current year?
   c. What happens to Phyllis's unused ordinary loss (if any)?
   d. What advice can you give Phyllis about reducing the amount of unused loss (if any) that was not deductible in the current year?

I:17-14 Ralph sells an asset to the RST Partnership at a loss. In which of the following situations does he recognize a loss?
   a. Ralph owns a 20% direct interest in the partnership, and his son also owns a 20% interest.
   b. Ralph owns a 35% direct interest in the partnership, and his daughter also owns a 35% interest.
   c. Ralph owns a 35% direct interest in the partnership, and his 100%-owned C corporation also owns a 35% interest.

I:17-15 Jose owns a 60% interest in the JKL Partnership. What are the amount and character of the recognized gain or loss in each of the following situations?
   a. Jose sells common stock held as an investment with a $1,000 adjusted basis and a $3,000 FMV to the partnership. Jose held the stock for more than one year as an investment before the sale. The partnership also held the stock as an investment after the sale.
   b. Jose sells a parcel of land held for investment purposes with a $10,000 adjusted basis and a $25,000 FMV to the partnership. The land is used in the partnership's business.
   c. The partnership sells Jose a building used in its business with a $100,000 adjusted basis and a $60,000 FMV.

I:17-16 Ursula is a 30% partner in the UV Partnership. The partnership agreement states that she shall receive 30% of partnership profits computed before considering guaranteed payments. However, she is not to receive less than $10,000.
   a. What is Ursula's income if the partnership earns $60,000? How much of her income is a guaranteed payment?
   b. What is Ursula's income if the partnership earns $20,000? How much of her income is a guaranteed payment?

I:17-17 The SJ Partnership, in which Sandy and Jack are equal partners, reported the following income and losses in the current year:

Interest from muncipal bonds	$ 30,000
Interest from corporate bonds	25,000
LTCL from stock sale	20,000
Net income from operations	125,000

How do the partners treat these items?

I:17-18 Explain the circumstances that cause a partner to recognize gain or loss if the partnership distributes money or other property in a nonliquidating partnership distribution.

I:17-19 Explain why a partner who sells his or her interest in the partnership for cash must include his or her share of the partnership liabilities in the amount realized from the sale.

I:17-20 What are the tax consequences to a partner who sells his or her partnership interest if the partnership has Sec. 751 assets (i.e., unrealized receivables or inventory items)? What is the reason for this result?

I:17-21 What requirements must a partnership meet to make an election to use the simplified reporting rules available to electing large partnerships?

I:17-22 What are the major differences between the reporting of business profits and losses earned by an electing large partnership having 200 partners and a regular partnership having two partners?

I:17-23 What are the primary advantages of using an S corporation instead of a C corporation?

I:17-24 What are the tax consequences to an S corporation and its shareholders if one of the requirements for a small business corporation is not met at some time in a tax year?

I:17-25 An S corporation issues straight debt obligations to its shareholders. Is it possible for the debt to be treated as a second class of stock, which would terminate the S election? Explain.

I:17-26 Andrew sells his Ajax Corporation stock to Angela on March 1. On March 15, Ajax elects S corporation status for the current year. Ajax is a calendar year taxpayer. Which shareholder(s) must consent to the election? Why? Which shareholder(s) receive an allocation of the S corporation's profits? Losses? For what time period is the allocation received by each shareholder?

I:17-27 An S corporation's shareholder wants the corporation to voluntarily revoke the S election. What percentage of the stock interests must agree to the revocation? When is the revocation effective?

I:17-28 Under what conditions will an S corporation involuntarily lose its special tax status and revert to being a C corporation? What remedies are available if the S corporation termination is deemed to be inadvertent?

I:17-29 Indicate whether the following items are reported on the tax return of an S corporation as part of ordinary income (or loss) or as separately stated items:

a. Repairs
b. Long-term capital gains
c. Short-term capital losses
d. Section 1231 gains
e. Tax-exempt interest income
f. Tax credits
g. Tax preference items
h. Salary paid to an S corporation shareholder

I:17-30 Explain why the basis of S corporation stock is increased by the stockholder's share of ordinary income and separately stated gain and income items and reduced by the stockholder's share of an ordinary loss and separately stated loss and deduction items.

I:17-31 Anne has a $10,000 basis in her S corporation stock on January 1 of the current year. On March 1 of the current year, Anne lends the corporation $8,000. Her share of the S corporation's ordinary loss for the current year (which has not yet ended) is expected to be $28,000. Anne expects her marginal tax rate to be 15% in the current year. She expects that her marginal tax rate will increase to 33% next year, and she anticipates substantial profits for the S corporation next year. Advise Anne regarding the deductibility of her share of the losses and the desirability of making additional capital contributions or loans to the S corporation in either year.

I:17-32 Allied Corporation, an S corporation, is considering making a distribution of land to its sole shareholder. Allied acquired the land three years ago and used it in its business activities. The land now has a $30,000 adjusted basis and a $130,000 FMV. Allied has been an S corporation since its inception 12 years ago. Explain the tax consequences of the land distribution to the corporation and to the shareholder.

I:17-33 Barry and Bart are considering whether to start a new manufacturing business. Alternative forms of business organization being considered include operating as a partnership, a limited liability company, an S corporation, or a C corporation. Barry and Bart are calendar year taxpayers but would like to use a January 31 year-end for the business to obtain an 11-month income deferral. Discuss the implications and restrictions of operating under each alternative form of business organization being considered.

I:17-34 Assume the same facts as in Problem I:17-33 except Barry and Bart instead are considering the treatment of fringe benefits. Barry and Bart want to provide group term life insurance and accident and health insurance for themselves and their employees and plan to make the premium payments from business funds. Explain any restrictions that apply to each form of business organization.

I:17-35 Explain the circumstances in which an S corporation is subject to taxation at the corporate level.

ISSUE IDENTIFICATION QUESTIONS

I:17-36 Bert and José plan to combine their unincorporated businesses by forming a partnership. Bert has substantially appreciated business assets. Moreover, if he transfers all the business' liabilities and assets, the liabilities will exceed the adjusted basis of the assets but not their FMV. José will render services to the entity in addition to transferring his business assets. What tax issues should Bert and José consider?

I:17-37 Helen and Helga are equal partners in the HH Partnership. However, Helen devotes most of her time managing the business and believes that she should be given additional compensation in the form of a guaranteed payment. Currently, the partnership is operating at a break-even point (i.e., zero ordinary income and no separately stated items of income or loss). The basis of each partner's partnership interest also is negligible. Helen has requested a $40,000 guaranteed payment as compensation for her additional efforts. What tax issues should Helen and Helga consider?

I:17-38 Coastal Corporation has been a C corporation for several years and has substantial earnings and profits. Its tangible business assets are highly appreciated, and the corporation has paid no dividends for several years. The board of directors and its key shareholders are now recommending making an S election, selling the appreciated property, and paying a substantial cash distribution in the initial S corporation tax year. What tax issues should Coastal and its shareholders consider?

PROBLEMS

I:17-39 *Formation of Partnership and Treatment of Liabilities.* Andrea, Robert, and Agatha form the ARA Partnership as equal general partners. Andrea contributes land with a

$20,000 basis and a $40,000 FMV along with cash of $60,000. Andrea has held the land for two years as an investment. Robert contributes equipment with a $50,000 adjusted basis and a $100,000 FMV. Robert has used the equipment in his sole proprietorship for three years and has claimed $40,000 of accelerated depreciation. Agatha contributes accounts receivable from her sole proprietorship with a zero basis and a $45,000 FMV along with cash of $35,000. In addition, Agatha set up the accounting system for the business. She normally would charge $20,000 to do the same job for a client. On the first day of business, the partnership borrows $90,000 (recourse debt) from their bank to begin the business. The partners have equal risk of loss for these liabilities.

a. How much gain, loss, or income must each partner recognize on the formation of the partnership? What is the character of any gain, loss, or income recognized?
b. How much gain, loss, income, or deduction will the ARA Partnership recognize on the formation?
c. What is the partnership's basis in its property on the day the business begins?
d. What is each partner's basis in his or her partnership interest?

I:17-40 *Formation of a Partnership and Treatment of Liabilities.* Bonnie, Carlos, and Dale form the BCD Partnership as equal partners. Bonnie contributes land and a building having a $50,000 adjusted basis and a $200,000 FMV that is subject to a $100,000 mortgage assumed by the partnership. The land and the building originally cost $200,000, with $180,000 allocated to the building and $20,000 allocated to the land. Bonnie had claimed $150,000 of straight-line depreciation on the building. Carlos contributes cash of $100,000, and Dale contributes land (a capital asset) having a $200,000 adjusted basis and a $100,000 FMV. All assets have been held for more than one year. Assume the partners have an equal economic risk of loss.

a. What are the amount and character of Bonnie's recognized gain or loss on the transfer?
b. What is Bonnie's basis in her partnership interest?
c. What is Carlos's basis in his partnership interest?
d. What are the amount and character of Dale's recognized gain or loss on the transfer?
e. What is Dale's basis in his partnership interest?
f. What is the partnership's basis for each of the contributed properties?

I:17-41 *Formation of a Partnership and Treatment of Liabilities.* In the current year, Dana transfers to the DE Partnership land and a building having a total $25,000 adjusted basis and an $80,000 FMV. In addition, the property is subject to a $70,000 mortgage. The land and the building cost $105,000 when Dana acquired them in 1987, and Dana has claimed $80,000 of straight-line depreciation on the building. The land and building originally cost $20,000 and $85,000, respectively. Dana, who is active in the management of the partnership, receives a one-half interest in the partnership. Assume the partners' economic risk of loss is equal to their interest in the partnership.

a. What are the amount and character of Dana's recognized gain or loss on the transfer?
b. What is Dana's basis in her partnership interest?
c. When does Dana's holding period for the partnership interest begin?
d. What is the basis of the contributed properties to the DE Partnership?

I:17-42 *Formation of a Partnership and Loss Limitation.* Dan, who is active in the management of the partnership, contributes $10,000 in cash to the newly formed DEF Partnership for a 10% interest in the partnership. The partners transfer no liabilities to the partnership. During the partnership's first year, DEF borrows $75,000 from a bank and is liable for accounts payable amounting to $180,000 at the end of the current year. The DEF Partnership incurs a $400,000 ordinary loss during the current year.

a. How much of the ordinary loss may Dan deduct on his individual tax return?
b. What is Dan's basis in his partnership interest at the end of the current year?
c. How much of the loss (if any) carries over to future years?

I:17-43 *Expenses of Forming a Partnership.* The ABC Partnership, a calendar year entity, is formed and begins business on July 1 of the current year. ABC incurs the following expenditures on the date the partnership is formed:

Legal fees incident to the organization of the partnership	$ 6,000
Printing costs associated with the syndication of the partnership	4,000
Brokerage fees associated with underwriting efforts to sell limited partnership interests	5,000
Legal fees associated with asset transfers by three partners	10,000
Accounting services incurred during the organizational period	3,000

a. What is the appropriate tax treatment (i.e., capitalization, capitalization subject to amortization, or immediate expensing) for each of these items?

b. How much amortization should the partnership deduct for the current year?

I:17-44 *Pass-Through of Income and Separately Stated Items.* Damien and Donna are equal partners in the DD Partnership. The passive activity loss and the at-risk rules are not applicable to the partners. The partnership reports the following items on its Schedule K during the current year:

Ordinary loss	$10,000
Long-term capital gains	40,000
Research and experimentation credit	4,000
AMT tax preference items	6,000
Distribution to the partners	25,000

Damien's basis in his partnership interest is $80,000 at the beginning of the current year. The DD Partnership's liabilities increased by $20,000 during the current year.

a. What amounts should Damien report on his individual tax return as a result of DD Partnership's activities?

b. What is Damien's basis in his partnership interest after taking into account the Schedule K items?

I:17-45 *Special Allocations on Contributed Property.* Ed contributes land (a capital asset) having a $60,000 adjusted basis and a $100,000 FMV, and Gail contributes $100,000 cash to the EG Partnership. Ed and Gail each receive 50% interests in the partnership. Two years later the partnership sells the land (still a capital asset) for $110,000. What are the amount and character of the EG Partnership's gain or loss? How much of EG's gain or loss is allocated to Ed? To Gail? Are the results equitable?

I:17-46 *Loss Allocations.* Alice and Bruce are equal partners in the calendar year AB Partnership. On November 1 of the current year, Carl joined the partnership by making a $100,000 cash contribution in exchange for a one-third interest. Alice and Bruce's partnership interests are each reduced to one-third. The partners want to provide that Carl will receive a retroactive allocation of one-third of all partnership profits and losses incurred for the entire year. The AB Partnership reports a $90,000 ordinary loss for the tax year ending on December 31. How much of the partnership's loss is allocated to Alice, Bruce, and Carl?

I:17-47 *Basis of a Partnership Interest.* Anita has a one-half interest in the AB Partnership. Anita's basis in her interest at the beginning of the current year is $75,000. During the year, the following events occur:

- Partnership liabilities increase by $50,000.
- Partnership earns $60,000 of ordinary income.
- Partnership recognizes $20,000 of capital losses.
- Partnership incurs $3,000 of nondeductible expenses.
- Partnership earns $10,000 of tax-exempt interest.
- Anita withdraws $15,000 in cash.
- Anita contributes land having a $20,000 adjusted basis and a $100,000 FMV as an additional capital contribution without increasing her interest in the partnership.

a. What gain (if any) does Anita recognize on the transfer of the land to the partnership?

b. What is Anita's basis in her partnership interest at the end of the current year?

I:17-48 *Partnership Losses and Basis.* Keith has a one-half interest in the KL Partnership. His basis in the partnership interest at the end of the current year (before deducting his share of partnership losses) is $40,000. His share of the partnership's ordinary loss in the current year is $180,000. Next year, Keith makes a $60,000 additional capital contribution, and the partnership's ordinary income is $100,000. Assume that no change occurs in Keith's partnership interest as a result of the capital contribution and that he materially participates in the business. Partnership liabilities do not change.

a. How much ordinary loss can Keith deduct in the current year?

b. What is Keith's basis in his partnership interest at the end of the current year?

c. How much ordinary income or loss does Keith report next year?

d. What is Keith's basis in his partnership interest at the end of next year?

e. How much loss can Keith use in future years? What has to happen to enable him to use the loss?

I:17-49 *Transactions Between the Partners and the Partnership.* Kevin has a 30% interest in the KLM Partnership. Louis (Kevin's son) also has a 30% interest. An individual unrelated to either Kevin or Louis holds the remaining 40% interest. Kevin sells the following assets to the partnership during the year:

- Common stock (a capital asset held more than one year) having a $10,000 basis and a $25,000 FMV and selling price.
- Land (a Sec. 1231 asset) having a $100,000 adjusted basis and a $60,000 FMV and selling price.
- Machine having a $50,000 adjusted basis and a $70,000 FMV and selling price. The original cost of the machine was $60,000, and Kevin deducted $10,000 in MACRS depreciation before the transfer.

a. What are the amount and character of Kevin's recognized gain or loss on the sale of the common stock? The land? The machine?
b. What gain or loss would the partnership recognize if it sells the land two years later for $90,000?

I:17-50 *Guaranteed Payments.* Laura and Mark are equal partners in the LM Partnership. Laura receives a $35,000 guaranteed payment in the current year and also withdraws $15,000 of her partnership capital in cash. Partnership ordinary income is $100,000 after deducting the guaranteed payments for the current year. What amounts must Laura include in her gross income for the current year?

I:17-51 *Nonliquidating Distributions.* Lynn's basis in her partnership interest is $9,000 when she receives a nonliquidating distribution of $5,000 cash and land having a $6,000 adjusted basis and a $12,000 FMV.
a. What gain or loss does the partnership recognize when making the distribution?
b. What are the amount and character of the income or gain Lynn must recognize on the distribution?
c. What is Lynn's basis in the land?
d. What is Lynn's basis in her partnership interest after the distribution?

I:17-52 *Sale of a Partnership Interest.* The balance sheet of the ABC Partnership at December 31 of the current year is as follows:

	Adjusted Basis	FMV
Assets:		
Cash	$ 10,000	$ 10,000
Accounts receivable	20,000	20,000
Inventory	15,000	21,000
Land, buildings, and machinery	60,000	84,000[a]
Total	$105,000	$135,000
Liabilities and capital:		
Accounts payable	$ 5,000	$ 5,000
Notes payable	10,000	10,000
Allen's capital account (⅓)	30,000	40,000
Beth's capital account (⅓)	30,000	40,000
Candace's capital account (⅓)	30,000	40,000
Total	$105,000	$135,000

[a]Assume that $3,000 would be ordinary income under the depreciation recapture rules and $5,400 would be unrecaptured Sec. 1250 gain if the partnership sold the assets.

All partners have an equal interest in the partnership. Allen sells his partnership interest to an outsider on December 31 of the current year for $40,000. Allen's basis in the partnership interest is $35,000 (which includes Allen's share of partnership liabilities).
a. What amount does Allen realize on the sale?
b. What are the amount and character of Allen's recognized gain or loss on the sale?

I:17-53 *Reporting Partnership Income.* Rita, a calendar year taxpayer, is an employee of the RST Partnership, which has a June 30 year-end. The partnership pays Rita a salary of $2,500 per month for the period January 1 through June 30, 2015. On July 1, she joins the partnership and receives monthly drawings of $2,500 for the 12-month period ending June 30, 2016. The drawings reflect her approximate share of partnership income for the period July 1, 2015, through June 30, 2016. On June 30, 2016, Rita's share of partnership ordinary income is $40,000.

a. What amount of income does Rita report on her 2015 individual tax return?

b. What amount of income does Rita report on her 2016 individual tax return?

c. Which part (if any) of Rita's income is subject to Social Security taxes?

I:17-54 *Electing Large Partnerships.* JLK Partnership is an electing large partnership with 100 partners. The partnership reports the following operating results from the current year:

Ordinary income	$2,000,000
Net Sec. 1231 gain	250,000
Tax-exempt interest income	100,000
Net long-term capital gain	150,000
Charitable contributions	200,000
Miscellaneous itemized deductions	50,000

None of JLK's activities is passive. During the year, JLK distributed $5,000 to each of its partners.

a. What income, gains, losses, and deductions must the JLK Partnership report to each of its partners?

b. How are the items from Part a reported by JLK's partners?

I:17-55 *S Corporation Terminations.* Which of the following events will cause termination or revocation of the S election for a calendar year corporation? When is the termination or revocation effective? (Assume all other requirements for an S election are met and that any termination is not inadvertent.)

a. Best Corporation has 100 qualifying S corporation shareholders. Sam dies on October 13, and the estate holds his stock for the rest of the year.

b. Assume the same facts as in Part a except the estate distributes the stock to Sam's child before the end of the tax year. Sam's child did not previously own any Best stock.

c. Best issues nonvoting common stock to Susan's two children during the current year. Susan's children did not previously own any Best stock.

d. Shareholders Susan, Ted, and Tim, who own 60% of the Best stock, file the necessary form on October 1 to revoke the election as of this date. All three shareholders are calendar year taxpayers.

I:17-56 *S Corporation Ordinary Income and Separately Stated Items.* The income statement for Central Corporation, an S corporation, reports the following:

Sales	$260,000
Cost of goods sold	(60,000)
Repair expense	(5,000)
Depreciation expense	(20,000)
Salary expense	(30,000)
Long-term capital losses	(15,000)
Charitable contributions	(5,000)
Sec. 1231 losses	(8,000)
Net income per tax books	$117,000

a. What is Central's ordinary income (or loss) for the year?

b. Which of the above items appear as separately stated items on Schedule K?

c. Carol owns 50% of Central's stock, which has a $75,000 basis (before taking into account any of the items listed above). What is Carol's stock basis after all adjustments for Carol's share of Central's ordinary income or loss and separately stated items?

I:17-57 *Basis of S Corporation Stock.* Cathy is a 40% shareholder of City Corporation. City is a calendar year S corporation. Cathy acquired her stock on January 1 of the current year for $80,000. In the current year, City reports the following results of operations, cash distributions, and salary payments:

Ordinary income allocable to Cathy	$30,000
Salary payments to Cathy	40,000
Long-term capital loss allocable to Cathy	5,000
Cash distributions to Cathy	17,000

a. What is Cathy's stock basis at the end of the current year?

b. What amounts should Cathy include in her individual tax return for the current year?

I:17-58 **S Corporation and Partnership Losses.** In the current year, Harold and Faye form Entity Company by each contributing $50,000 to the company in exchange for a 50% ownership interest. In addition, the company borrows $40,000 from First Bank. In the current year, the company incurs a $110,000 loss from operations.
  a. How much of the loss can each partner deduct in the current year if Entity is a partnership, and what is each partner's basis in his or her partnership interest at the end of the year?
  b. How much of the loss can each shareholder deduct in the current year if Entity is an S corporation, and what is each shareholder's basis in his or her stock at the end of the year?

I:17-59 **S Corporation Losses and Stock Basis.** Chris owns one-third of Coastal Corporation's stock, and he materially participates in the business. Coastal, an S corporation, uses the calendar year as its tax year. On January 1 of the current year, Chris's stock basis is $25,000, and he has a $10,000 loan outstanding to the corporation. In the current year, Coastal reports a $180,000 ordinary loss.
  a. What amount of loss can Chris deduct on his individual tax return?
  b. What is Chris's basis in his stock and debt at December 31?
  c. How much of the loss (if any) carries over to subsequent years?
  d. If Coastal reports ordinary income of $90,000 during the next year, what is Chris's basis in his stock and debt at the end of next year?

I:17-60 **S Corporation Basis for Stock and Debt.** Because of earlier losses, Cindy has a zero basis in her S corporation stock and a zero basis in her $10,000 loan to the corporation. During the current year, Cindy acquires additional shares of the S corporation stock for $8,000, and her share of the S corporation income is $7,000.
  a. What are Cindy's stock and debt bases on December 31?
  b. What are the tax consequences to Cindy if the corporation fully repays her loan (secured by a note) on January 1 of the following year?

I:17-61 **S Corporation Distributions and Stock Basis.** Control Corporation distributes $11,000 cash to shareholder Craig whose stock basis is $8,000 before this year's income or the distribution. Craig's share of ordinary income for the current year is $1,000, and the corporation has no separately stated items. Control always has been an S corporation.
  a. What are the tax consequences of the distribution (i.e., amount and character of income or gain to Control and Craig)?
  b. What is Craig's stock basis at the end of the tax year?

I:17-62 **S Corporation and Partnership Property Distributions.** Omega Company has two equal owners, William and Mary. Prior to a property distribution, each owner has a $200,000 basis in his or her ownership interest. In the current year, Omega distributes property to William having a $50,000 FMV and a $30,000 basis and distributes property to Mary having a $50,000 FMV and a $60,000 basis. The property is a capital asset. In Parts a and b, determine Omega's gain or loss recognized (if any), the owners' gain or loss recognized (if any), and the owners' basis in his or her ownership interest after the distribution.
  a. Omega is partnership.
  b. Omega is an S corporation.
  c. In the S corporation case, is distributing the loss property to Mary a good idea? Why or why not?

I:17-63 **S Corporation Distributions and Basis of Property.** Compact Corporation, an S corporation, distributes land used in its business to Clay, its sole shareholder. The land has a $75,000 adjusted basis and a $125,000 FMV. Clay assumes a $20,000 mortgage secured by the land distributed to him. Immediately before the distribution, Clay's basis in the Compact stock is $170,000, which includes his share of ordinary income and separately stated items for the current year (other than any gains or losses recognized because of the distribution). Compact always has been an S corporation.
  a. What are the tax consequences of the distribution to Compact and Clay?
  b. What is Clay's basis in the land?
  c. How would your answer to Part a change if the land instead had a $100,000 adjusted basis and a $75,000 FMV?

I:17-64 **S Corporation Fringe Benefits.** Copper Corporation formed two years ago and immediately elected S corporation status. In the current year, the corporation pays the following insurance premiums for its employees:

Group term life insurance for shareholder-employees, all of whom own more than 2% of the stock	$3,000
Accident, health, and medical reimbursement plan insurance premiums for shareholder-employees, all of whom own more than 2% of the stock	5,000
Group term life insurance premiums for employees who are not shareholders	1,000
Accident, health, and medical reimbursement plan insurance premiums for employees who are not shareholders	2,000

a. What tax consequences result from Copper's payment of the insurance premiums?
b. What are the tax consequences to the shareholder-employees and to the employees who are not shareholders?

I:17-65 *S Corporation Built-in Gains Tax.* Delta Corporation made an S election on January 1 of the current year. Delta had been a C corporation since its inception in 1983. The corporation has the following operating results during the current year:

Ordinary income	$200,000
Long-term capital gains	130,000

The adjusted basis and FMV of capital assets held on January 1 and sold during the current year were $200,000 and $320,000, respectively, as of the January 1 beginning of the S election period.
a. Is Delta Corporation subject to the built-in gains tax under Sec. 1374? Explain.
b. What is the corporation's tax liability on the built-in gain (if applicable)?
c. How would your answers to Parts a and b change if Delta Corporation instead had made its S election on January 31, 1986?

COMPREHENSIVE PROBLEM

I:17-66 Charles is a 60% partner in CD Partnership, a calendar year partnership. For 2015, Charles received a Schedule K-1 that reported his share of partnership items as follows:

Partnership ordinary income	$105,000
Tax-exempt income	1,000
Qualified dividend income	3,000
Short-term capital loss	20,000
Sec. 1231 loss	17,000
Charitable contributions	2,000
Cash distribution	60,000
Guaranteed payment	40,000

In addition, Charles and his wife, Charlene, had the following items relating to activities outside the partnership:

Charlene's salary	$80,000
Long-term capital gain	49,000
Interest income from corporate bonds	5,000
Mortgage interest expense	12,000
State income taxes	8,000
Property taxes on home	3,000
Charitable contributions	5,500
Withholding on Charlene's salary	18,000
Estimated tax payments (paid one-fourth on each of the quarterly due dates)	24,000

Charles and Charlene have two dependent children, ages 7 and 9, and file a joint tax return. Calculate the following items for Charles and Charlene:
a. Adjusted gross income (AGI)
b. Taxable income
c. Tax liability
d. Taxes due or refund

TAX STRATEGY PROBLEMS

I:17-67 Joann and Bob, both single taxpayers in their mid-40s, own an employment business. The firm finds temporary employment for students in the college town of Gainesville, Florida. They have operated the business as a two-person equal partnership for five years. Profits have grown in each of the first five years until the partnership earns approximately $320,000 per year. Bob's parents operate a small grocery store in Nebraska and have successfully used the C corporation form for many years. They have become confused with all the new business forms—limited liability companies, limited liability partnerships, S corporations, etc.—that people have recommended to them. Bob mentions that he and Joann each has been taking $60,000 out of his and Joann's business each year as distributions. They have come to you for help in determining whether their partnership form of business is the way to operate the business in the future. What strategies can you develop for improving Joann's and Bob's personal and business tax positions?

I:17-68 Peter, Paul, and Mary plan to create a new business that buys, restores, and sells classic cars. The three individuals have been involved in a number of business deals dating back to the 1990s. Each individual has a net worth of at least $2 million. Peter has located an old auto dealership to be the showroom for the classic cars. Paul has restored many classic cars so he has developed the network for purchasing restorable cars. Mary is a well-established promoter of new businesses and is in charge of determining the business plan, selecting the entity form, obtaining the external financing, and hiring the firm's accountant. She also will handle most of the day-to-day management. Mary has narrowed the business entity choice down to a partnership, C or S corporation, or limited liability company. You have talked with Mary about this project at length in three different meetings. She wants your advice about selecting the appropriate business entity for the business. Prepare a short list of the pros and cons of using each of the four business forms and be prepared to make a final recommendation to Mary at your next meeting with her.

I:17-69 Steve and Erin started a general partnership to do landscaping and sell gardening supplies. Both will work in the business full time and need to withdraw approximately $40,000 a year each to live on. The partnership has purchased substantial capital assets that it will hold until the cash from their sale is needed in the business. For the first five years of operations, the partnership expects to earn approximately $70,000 of ordinary income and $50,000 of long-term capital gain each year before distributions to the two owners. Steve and Erin are single taxpayers and have income from other sources so their partnership earnings will be taxed at a 25% marginal rate. Should the two set up $40,000 guaranteed payments for each, or should they take out the $40,000 as draws from their distributive shares of partnership income? Consider self-employment taxes in your analysis.

TAX FORM/RETURN PREPARATION PROBLEMS

I:17-70 The XYZ Partnership reports the following items during 2014:

Sales	$400,000
Cost of goods sold	120,000
Dividends—all qualified	6,000
Interest income on certificate of deposit held as an investment	2,000
Tax-exempt interest	1,500
Salaries to employees	130,000
Federal employment taxes	9,000
Rental expense	5,000
Guaranteed payments to partners	40,000
Net long-term capital gain	12,000
Net short-term capital loss	5,000
Repairs	3,000
MACRS depreciation	10,000
Section 1231 losses	8,000
Charitable contributions	3,500
Amortization of organizational expenditures	1,000
Research and experimentation credit	2,500
Cash distributions to partners	20,000

Calculate ordinary income (or loss) by completing page 1 of Form 1065, and complete Schedule K (Partners' Shares of Income, Credits, Deductions, etc.). Leave spaces blank on Form 1065 if information is not provided.

I:17-71 Eagle Corporation, an S corporation, reports the following items during 2014:

Sales	$500,000
Cost of goods sold	150,000
Dividends—all qualified	7,000
Interest income on certificate of deposit held as an investment	2,500
Tax-exempt interest income	1,200
Employees' salaries (other than officers)	90,000
Federal employment taxes	6,000
Rental expense	8,000
Officers' salaries (all shareholders)	40,000
Net long-term capital gain	8,000
Net short-term capital loss	10,000
Repairs	2,000
MACRS depreciation	12,000
Section 1231 losses	4,000
Charitable contributions	2,000
Amortization of organizational expenditures	1,000
Research and experimentation credit	3,500
Cash distributions to shareholders	12,000

Calculate ordinary income (or loss) by completing page 1 of Form 1120S, and complete Schedule K (Shareholders' Shares of Income, Credits, Deductions, etc.). Leave spaces blank on Form 1120S if information is not provided.

CASE STUDY PROBLEMS

I:17-72 Peggy, Phil, and Ralph each have unincorporated accounting practices, and they wish to pool their resources and operate as a single business entity. Peggy owns a building that has appreciated in value since she purchased it eight years ago. They intend to use this building for their office. Other than the building, they own office equipment, computer equipment, and furniture, none of which is worth more than book value. They all have substantial outstanding accounts receivable with a zero basis because each individual uses the cash method of accounting. Each individual has substantial amounts of portfolio income (i.e., dividends and interest) earned outside of their business activities. Under the plan, accounts payable with a zero basis from the unincorporated accounting practices would be transferred to the new entity.

Each accountant has two or three employees. They all agree on the importance of providing benefits to their employees, such as group health insurance, group term life insurance, and a retirement plan of some kind. Additionally, they wish to have their staff participate in the profits of the company and have some form of equity interest in the company.

Peggy, Phil, and Ralph use different computerized accounting and billing systems. They also have different documentation requirements for their client files. The computerized accounting records, billing records, and client files will all have to be consolidated from three systems to one system. The conversion will take place over a period of time. For this reason, they anticipate reporting a loss for their first tax year.

Peggy, Phil, and Ralph have agreed that they want to operate as a pass-through entity because they wish to avoid double taxation, and they want to use the losses from the first year immediately. They have come to you for advice. Prepare a client memo comparing the pros and cons of operating the accounting practice as a partnership or an S corporation.

I:17-73 Dan is the partial owner of an S corporation that currently has 100 shareholders. In March of the current year, Dan sold some of his S corporation stock to each of his two adult children. In August, Dan redeemed the stock he sold because he is in the midst of a divorce and was fearful of the consequences associated with giving voting rights for his business to his children. Dan informs you, his tax consultant, of the stock sale and subsequent redemption. You explain to Dan that by selling the stock he created 102 shareholders between the months of March and August and that the S election had been terminated on the day preceding the date on which the corporation first had more than 100 shareholders. Dan tells you that he sees no reason to inform the IRS of the termination because he bought back the stock within the same tax year, and the IRS probably would not discover the event. What are your responsibilities as a CPA under the SSTS rules as mandated by the AICPA concerning the S election termination? (See the *Statements on Standards for Tax Services* in Appendix E for a discussion of these issues.) What advice can you offer Dan concerning reinstatement of the S election under the rules for inadvertent terminations?

TAX RESEARCH PROBLEMS

I:17-74 Sandra is an employee of the Beach Group, an organization active in the Florida real estate industry. Sandra finds real estate property on Miami Beach and subsequently organizes partnerships to acquire and finance the property. Sandra was particularly interested in one building in the Art Deco district that was to be purchased and renovated. She gathered interested investors who formed the Deco Partnership, consisting of two general partners and several limited partners. In exchange for her services in organizing the partnership, Sandra received a 3% limited partnership interest only in the profits of the Deco Partnership. As part of the agreement, the profits interest was transferable only at the discretion of the general partners. Based on the uncertainty in the South Florida real estate industry at the time, the partners could not estimate whether profits or losses would be generated when the renovation was completed in three years. Based on these facts, will Sandra's receipt of the limited partnership interest be a taxable event?

A partial list of research sources is:

- Sec. 721
- Reg. Sec. 1.721-1(a)
- *William G. Campbell v. CIR,* 68 AFTR 2d 91-5425, 91-2 USTC ¶50,420 (8th Cir., 1991)
- *Sol Diamond v. CIR,* 33 AFTR 2d 74-852, 74-1 USTC ¶9306 (7th Cir., 1974)
- Rev. Proc. 93-27, 1993-2 C.B. 343
- Notice 2005-43, 2005-43 C.B. 1221

I:17-75 Chuck, Cindy, and Clay are equal shareholders of Able Corporation common stock. Able was incorporated in the current year. Able elects to be treated as an S corporation starting in its initial year. Chuck, Cindy, and Clay each contributed $10,000 cash to Able in exchange for their common stock. Able borrows $60,000 from a bank, and Chuck, Cindy, and Clay personally guaranteed the corporation's loan. In the current year, Able suffers a $90,000 ordinary loss. How much of the corporation's loss can Chuck, Cindy, and Clay deduct? (Assume the at-risk and passive activity loss limitation rules do not apply.)

A partial list of research sources is:

- Sec. 1366(d)(1)
- *Estate of Daniel Leavitt v. CIR,* 63 AFTR 2d 89-1437, 89-1 USTC ¶9332 (4th Cir., 1989)
- *Edward M. Selfe v. U.S.,* 57 AFTR 2d 86-464, 86-1 USTC ¶9115 (11th Cir., 1986)
- *Dennis E. Bolding v. U.S.,* 80 AFTR 2d 97-5481, 97-2 USTC ¶50,553 (7th Cir., 1997).

I:17-76 In January 2014, Joey contributed investment land he had held two years with a FMV of $6,000 and an adjusted basis of $10,000, and Rachel contributed $6,000 cash to form the Green Partnership as equal general partners. During 2014, the partnership earned ordinary income of $10,000 and made no distributions. On January 1, 2015, while the partnership still held the land, Joey sold his interest in the partnership to Phoebe for $11,000. In April 2015, Green partnership sold for $5,400 the land that Joey contributed. What are the tax consequences of these transactions?

A partial list of research resources includes:

- Sec. 721
- Sec. 704(c)
- Sec. 705
- Sec. 741
- Reg. Sec. 1.704-1(c)

18

TAXES AND INVESTMENT PLANNING

LEARNING OBJECTIVES

After studying this chapter, you should be able to

1 ▶ Apply the investment models to various investment alternatives

2 ▶ Use the investment models to make entity choices and compensation decisions

3 ▶ Recognize the role of implicit taxes in investment decisions

This chapter has been derived from a book originally written by Myron S. Scholes and Mark A. Wolfson and takes what has become known as the Scholes-Wolfson approach to investment strategy.[1] Consequently, the chapter differs significantly from other chapters in this text. First, the chapter does not present details of tax law. Instead, it introduces a conceptual framework for understanding how taxes affect basic investment decisions. Second, the chapter develops and illustrates models for determining the after-tax outcomes of various investment alternatives. Although these models may look strange at first, they become familiar and manageable after some study and practice. Third, the chapter extends the models' application to the flow-through versus C corporation choice and the current salary versus deferred compensation decision. Fourth, the chapter introduces the role of implicit taxes as well as explicit taxes in investment decisions. As demonstrated later, the before-tax rate of return of a tax-favored asset will be reduced by market forces as investors increase their demand for these investments. This reduced rate of return is an implicit tax that investors need to consider when making their decisions.

INVESTMENT MODELS

OBJECTIVE 1

Apply the investment models to various investment alternatives

The investment models described in this chapter fall into four categories depending on how investment earnings are taxed. We refer to these models as follows:

▶ The Current Model—Investment earnings are taxed currently.

▶ The Deferred Model—Investment earnings are taxed at the end of the investment period.

▶ The Exempt Model—Investment earnings are exempt from explicit taxation.

▶ The Pension Model—The initial investment is deductible or excludable from gross income, and the entire accumulation, not just earnings, is taxed at the end of the investment period.

These models in their basic form reflect the following assumptions:

▶ The investment's before-tax rate of return is constant over the investment period.

▶ The investor's marginal tax rate is constant over the investment period.

▶ Investment earnings are reinvested at the same rate of return as earned by the original investment.

▶ The investor knows future rates of returns and tax rates with certainty.

▶ The investor incurs no transaction costs.

KEY POINT

Future values are necessary to compare all amounts at the same point in time. This comparable time frame is critical in evaluating alternative investment opportunities.

The models can be modified, however, to accommodate changes to these assumptions. For example, we later show how to adapt the Current Model for changing tax rates (see Example I:18-5).

For simplicity, this chapter generally uses the following individual marginal tax rates for ordinary income: 40%, 35%, 30%, 25%, and 15%. Although these rates do not conform exactly to current tax rates, they are sufficient to demonstrate the concepts in this chapter. In addition, the chapter assumes a 20%, 15%, or 0% capital gains tax rate for transactions not subject to the Sec. 1202 exclusion. For regular C corporations, the chapter uses the following marginal tax rates: 39%, 35%, 34%, 25%, and 15%.

ADDITIONAL COMMENT

This chapter ignores the additional 3.8% tax rate on net investment income that could apply to taxpayers having modified AGI exceeding $200,000 ($250,000 for married filing jointly).

THE CURRENT MODEL

The Current Model gives the future value of an investment having the following characteristics:

▶ Only after-tax dollars are invested.

▶ The earnings on the investment are taxed annually (currently); thus, the reinvested earnings grow at the after-tax rate of return.

---

[1] M. S. Scholes, M. A. Wolfson, M. M. Erickson, M. L. Hanlon, E. L. Maydew, and T. J. Shevlin, *Taxes and Business Strategy: A Planning Approach*, Fifth Edition (Upper Saddle River, NJ: Pearson Prentice Hall, 2014).

Common examples of investments taxed this way are savings accounts, money market funds, and taxable bonds, if the investor reinvests the after-tax earnings annually.

Investment with no Taxation. Before developing the Current Model, however, we first illustrate how an investment grows when compounded annually in a no-tax situation, and we introduce the notions of before-tax dollars and the before-tax rate of return. We then show the relationship between before-tax dollars and after-tax dollars and between before-tax and after-tax rates of return. Finally, we incorporate these concepts into the Current Model.

EXAMPLE I:18-1 ▶ Carla, an individual investor, lives in a land of no taxation and earns $1,000 of salary. She invests this amount in a bond that pays interest at 10% per year and holds the bond for three years, reinvesting the interest annually at the same 10% return. The following schedule details the investment's cash flow over the three years:

ADDITIONAL COMMENT

The rates of return used in this chapter do not attempt to reflect the actual returns in the current economy.

(1) Year	(2) Cumulative Investment at Beginning of Year	(3) Interest Income[a]	(4) Cumulative Investment at End of Year[b]
1	$1,000	$100	$1,100
2	1,100	110	1,210
3	1,210	121	1,331

[a]Column 2 × 10%
[b]Column 2 + Column 3

ADDITIONAL COMMENT

Definitions of variables:
ATA: After-tax accumulation
BT$: Before-tax dollars
AT$: After-tax dollars
BTROR or R: Before-tax rate of return
ATROR or r: After-tax rate of return
t: Marginal tax rate, generally
t_o: Marginal tax rate at time of investment
t_n: Marginal tax rate at end of investment horizon
n: Investment horizon
Also see Topic Review I:18-1 on page I:18-16.

Thus, at the end of three years, the $1,000 original investment accumulates to $1,331. ◄

The three-year accumulation determined in Example also can be calculated as follows: $1,000 (1.1)^3 = $1,331$, which is $1,000 compounded at 10% for three years. Thus, the general form of the compounding formula is:

$$\text{Accumulation} = \text{BT\$}(1 + R)^n$$

In this formula, BT$ stands for before-tax dollars invested. For instance, in Example I:18-1, Carla invested the entire $1,000 because taxes did not reduce her salary. Also in the formula, R is the before-tax rate of return (BTROR). Again, this return is a before-tax percentage because, as in Example I:18-1, the interest on the investment is not taxed. Consequently, the investor can reinvest all the interest with nothing siphoned away as taxes. Finally, n equals the number of years the investor holds the investment or, in other words, n represents the investment horizon. Thus, the formula gives the future value (accumulation) of before-tax dollars invested for n years while earning a BTROR equal to R.

The Current Model. Now assume our investor is subject to taxation at marginal tax rate t. In this case, any earned income, such as salary, will be subject to taxes, leaving only after-tax dollars available for investment.

EXAMPLE I:18-2 ▶ Assume the same facts as Example I:18-1 except Carla's $1,000 salary is subject to tax, and her marginal tax rate is 40%. That is, t = 40% or 0.4. In this case, Carla has only $600 to invest. This amount is computed as follows:

TAX STRATEGY TIP

Although this chapter focuses on federal income taxes, a taxpayer must consider all applicable taxes when making investment decisions.

Salary before taxes	$1,000
Minus: Taxes ($1,000 × 0.4)	(400)
After-tax dollars available to invest	$ 600

◄

The $600 amount determined in Example I:18-2 also can be calculated as follows:

$$
\begin{aligned}
\text{After-tax dollars} &= \$1,000 - (\$1,000 \times 0.4) \\
&= \$1,000 (1 - 0.4) \quad \text{(Factoring out the \$1,000 salary)} \\
&= \$1,000 \times 0.6 = \$600
\end{aligned}
$$

In general, then, the relationship between before-tax dollars (BT\$) and after-tax dollars (AT\$) can be expressed as follows:

$$AT\$ = BT\$(1 - t)$$

Now assume that the interest our investor earns also is taxed at her marginal tax rate. The following example shows the impact on the investor's after-tax cash flows.

EXAMPLE I:18-3 ▶ Carla (from the two previous examples) again earns $1,000 of salary, but because of taxation at 40%, she has only $600 to invest, as shown in Example I:18-2. She invests the $600 in a bond for three years that yields 10% interest per year before taxes. However, in this case, the interest income also is taxed at 40%. The following schedule details the investment's cash flow over the three years:

(1)	(2)	(3)	(4)	(5)	(6)
		Before-Tax		After-Tax	
Year	Cumulative Investment at Beginning of Year	Interest Income[a]	Tax on Interest[b]	Interest Income[c]	Cumulative Investment at End of Year[d]
1	$600.00	$60.00	$24.00	$36.00	$636.00
2	636.00	63.60	25.44	38.16	674.16
3	674.16	67.42	26.97	40.45	714.61

[a]Column 2 × 10%
[b]Column 3 × 40%
[c]Column 3 − Column 4
[d]Column 2 + Column 5

◀

In Example I:18-3, after-tax interest in Column 5 for Year 1 also can be calculated as follows:

$$
\begin{aligned}
\text{After-tax interest} &= \$600(0.1) - \$600(0.1)(0.4) \\
&= \$600(0.1)(1 - 0.4) \quad \text{(Factoring out the \$600 after-tax salary} \\
&\quad \text{and the 10\% before-tax rate of return)} \\
&= \$600(0.1)(0.6) \\
&= \$600(.06) = \$36
\end{aligned}
$$

ADDITIONAL COMMENT

An easy way to remember that r is the ATROR and R is the BTROR is that taxation shrinks big R down to little r.

Thus, although the BTROR is 10%, the after-tax rate of return (ATROR) is only 6%. In general, the relationship between the BTROR and the ATROR can be expressed as follows:

$$r = R(1 - t)$$

As before, R equals the BTROR, and t equals the investor's marginal tax rate. The new variable, r, equals the ATROR, which is easy to remember because taxes reduce big R to little r.

With knowledge of this ATROR, the three-year accumulation in Example I:18-3 also can be calculated as follows: After-tax accumulation (ATA) = $600 $(1.06)^3$ = $714.61, which is $600 compounded at 6% for three years. Thus, the general form of the after-tax compounding formula is:

> The Current Model:
> $$ATA = AT\$(1 + r)^n \text{ or}$$
> $$ATA = AT\$[1 + R(1 - t)]^n$$

Note that, because of current taxation, investments conforming to the Current Model provide no deferral advantages because all earnings are taxed currently. As demonstrated later in this chapter, the other three models reflect certain tax advantages.

EXAMPLE I:18-4 ▶ At the beginning of Year 1, Harry invests $5,000 (AT$) in a money market fund that pays a 5% annual return before taxes. Harry's marginal tax rate is 30%, and he allows all after-tax earnings to remain in the money market fund. That is, he withdraws only enough cash to pay taxes on the fund's annual earnings. The following table shows Harry's after-tax accumulation for various investment horizons. In this table, note that Harry's ATROR equals 3.5%, which is 5% $(1 - 0.30)$. Thus, the Current Model appears as $5,000 $[1 + 0.05 (1 - 0.30)]^n$ or $5,000 $(1.035)^n$.

Investment Horizon (n)	Computation	After-Tax Accumulation
5 years	$5,000 $(1.035)^5$	$5,938.43
10 years	$5,000 $(1.035)^{10}$	$7,052.99
20 years	$5,000 $(1.035)^{20}$	$9,948.94 ◀

Changes to Assumptions. As stated earlier, the Current Model (as well as other models) assumes that R and t are constant over the investment period. However, the model can be modified to accommodate changes to these assumptions. This modification is accomplished by breaking the model into separate components, as demonstrated in the next example.

EXAMPLE I:18-5 ▶ At the beginning of Year 1, Dan invests $5,000 (AT$) in a money market fund that pays a 5% annual return before taxes. He plans to leave the after-tax earnings in the fund for 15 years. Dan expects his marginal tax rate to be 25% over the next five years but expects his tax rate to be 35% for the subsequent ten years. Thus, his ATROR for the first five years equals 3.75%, which is 5% $(1 - 0.25)$. For the remaining ten years, his ATROR equals 3.25%, which is 5% $(1 - 0.35)$. Dan's after-tax accumulation (ATA) after 15 years is calculated as follows:

$$ATA = \$5,000(1.0375)^5(1.0325)^{10} = \$8,275.82$$

Note that the first part of this calculation, $5,000 $(1.0375)^5$ = $6,010.50, gives the accumulation after the five years during which Dan's tax rate is 25%. This accumulation then continues to grow at the 3.25% ATROR for the remaining ten years as follows: $6,010.50 $(1.0325)^{10}$ = $8,275.82. ◀

THE DEFERRED MODEL

KEY POINT

Deferral is beneficial because the tax dollars not used currently to pay tax can be reinvested to help generate additional earnings.

The Deferred Model gives the future value of an investment having the following characteristics:

▶ Only after-tax dollars are invested (as with the Current Model).

▶ The earnings on the investment are not taxed annually; thus, they grow at the BTROR.

▶ The accumulated earnings are taxed at the end of the investment horizon when the investor cashes out of the investment; thus, taxation of these earnings is deferred.

The traditional nondeductible IRA described in Chapter I:9 is a classic example of the Deferred Model. Recall that, if the taxpayer or the taxpayer's spouse is covered by an employer-sponsored qualified retirement plan and the taxpayer's AGI exceeds a specified amount,[2] the taxpayer may not deduct contributions to a traditional IRA. Moreover, if the taxpayer's AGI exceeds another threshold,[3] the taxpayer may not contribute to a Roth IRA. Nevertheless, a taxpayer precluded from making *deductible* contributions to a traditional IRA or contributions to a Roth IRA still may make *nondeductible* contributions up to $5,500 (in 2015) per year to a traditional IRA. These nondeductible contributions are after-tax dollars.

EXAMPLE I:18-6 ▶ Marsha is in the 35% tax bracket and is ineligible to make deductible or Roth IRA contributions. Nevertheless, she wishes to contribute the maximum $5,500 to a traditional nondeductible IRA. She wants to know how much taxable salary she must earn to have $5,500 left for the contribution. Recall that AT$ = BT$$(1 - t)$. Rearranging these terms gives BT$ = AT$$/(1 - t)$.

---

[2] In 2015 for a taxpayer covered by an employer plan, this AGI amount is $118,000 for married filing jointly and $71,000 for other taxpayers except those married filing separately. If the taxpayer is not covered by an employer plan but his or her spouse is covered, the AGI amount is $193,000.

[3] The AGI amount in 2015 is $193,000 for married filing jointly and $131,000 for other taxpayers except those married filing separately.

In other words, we can "gross up" after-tax dollars by dividing after-tax dollars by one minus the tax rate. Accordingly, the before-tax dollars necessary to yield $5,500 after taxes equals $8,462, which is $5,500/(1 − 0.35). Thus, Marsha must earn $8,462 of salary before taxes. The tax on this amount equals $2,962, which is $8,462 × 0.35, leaving $5,500 available for contribution to the nondeductible IRA. ◀

EXAMPLE I:18-7 ▶ Suppose Marsha makes the $5,500 contribution to a traditional nondeductible IRA in the current year and makes no subsequent contributions. Suppose further that investments in the IRA yield 8% per year before taxes and that Marsha allows her investment to accumulate in the IRA for 15 years. At the end of 15 years, she withdraws all amounts from the IRA, at which time her marginal tax rate still is 35%. The following calculation demonstrates one way to determine Marsha's after-tax accumulation in the IRA:

(1) Before-tax accumulation in the IRA [$5,500(1.08)^{15}$]	$17,447
(2) Minus: Original contribution	(5,500)
(3) Accumulated earnings before taxes	$11,947
(4) Times: Tax rate	0.35
(5) Tax on accumulated earnings	$ 4,181
(6) After-tax accumulation (Line 1 − Line 5)	$13,266 ◀

The calculation in Example I:18-7 also can be formulated as follows:

$$\text{ATA} = \$5{,}500(1.08)^{15} - [\$5{,}500(1.08)^{15} - \$5{,}500] \times 0.35$$

The first term, $\$5{,}500\,(1.08)^{15}$, gives the total before-tax accumulation; the subtraction in brackets gives the accumulated before-tax earnings; and the multiplication by 35% gives the tax on the accumulated earnings. Subtracting these taxes from the first term gives the total after-tax accumulation. Factoring out the $5,500 investment yields the following expression:

$$\text{ATA} = \$5{,}500\{(1.08)^{15} - [(1.08)^{15} - 1] \times 0.35\}$$

Substituting our general symbols into this expression yields the following model, the component parts of which are shown in Figure I:18-1:

$$\text{ATA} = \text{AT\$}\{(1 + R)^n - [(1 + R)^n - 1] \times t_n\}$$

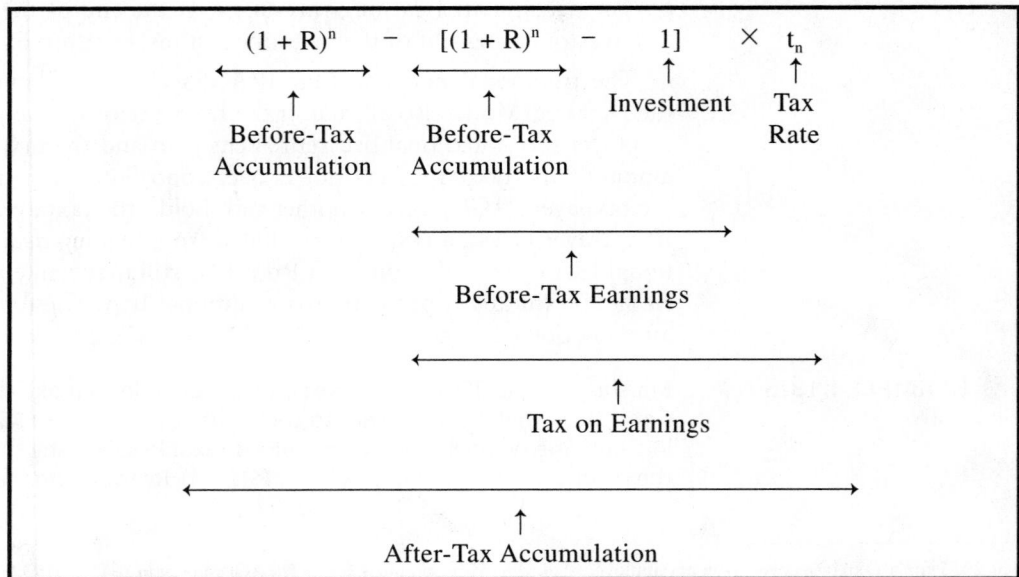

FIGURE I:18-1 ▶ Deferred Model before Algebraic Simplification

The subscript n on the tax rate emphasizes that the rate in Year n applies rather than the rate in the investment year or any intervening year. To make the model easier to use computationally, we can simplify this model algebraically with the following three steps. Multiplying through by t_n yields:

$$ATA = AT\$\{(1 + R)^n - [t_n (1 + R)^n - t_n]\}$$

Carrying the first minus sign through yields:

$$ATA = AT\$[(1 + R)^n - t_n (1 + R)^n + t_n]$$

Factoring out $(1 + R)^n$ yields:

> The Deferred Model:
> $$ATA = AT\$[(1 + R)^n(1 - t_n) + t_n]$$

We call this model the Deferred Model because the tax on investment earnings is deferred until the investor cashes out of the investment. This characteristic causes the Deferred Model investment to outperform the Current Model investment given equal BTRORs and constant tax rates.

EXAMPLE I:18-8 ▶ Phillip can invest $1,000 (AT$) directly in a taxable bond outside an IRA, or he can contribute the $1,000 to a traditional nondeductible IRA and invest in the same bond through the IRA vehicle. In either case, the bond yields an annual 10% BTROR. Phillip's marginal tax rate is 35%, and he expects it to remain so for the entire investment horizon. The two alternatives give the following after-tax accumulations after 20 years:

Bond outside the IRA (Current Model):

$$\$1,000[1 + 0.1(1 - 0.35)]^{20} = \$1,000(1.065)^{20} = \$3,523.65$$

Bond inside the IRA (Deferred Model):

$$\$1,000[(1.1)^{20} \times (1 - 0.35) + 0.35] = \$4,722.87$$

The Deferred Model investment outperforms the Current Model investment because, within the IRA, the interest on the bond grows at the BTROR (10%), with taxation deferred until Year 20. ◄

Annualized Atror. As we explained earlier, the ATROR in the Current Model is $r = R(1 - t)$. That is, an investment that fits the Current Model yields this ATROR annually. The annual ATROR is a useful number for comparison to annual ATRORs of other models. However, the annual ATROR of other models, such as the Deferred Model, is not always obvious. Therefore, to determine this comparable number, we compute a variable called the annualized ATROR. The annualized ATROR is the rate of return that would cause a Current Model investment to yield the same accumulation per after-tax dollar invested as does the model under consideration.

For example, we derive the annualized ATROR for the Deferred Model as follows:

$$(1 + r_{ann})^n = [(1 + R)^n(1 - t_n) + t_n]$$

Here, the left-hand side of the equation is the Current Model investment compounding at the annualized ATROR, which we symbolize as r_{ann}. The right-hand side is the Deferred Model with one after-tax dollar invested. Taking the nth root of each side yields:

$$(1 + r_{ann}) = [(1 + R)^n(1 - t_n) + t_n]^{1/n}$$

Subtracting 1 from each side yields:

$$r_{ann} = [(1 + R)^n(1 - t_n) + t_n]^{1/n} - 1$$

The general form for this relationship, which can be used for any model, is:

> Annualized ATROR:
> $$r_{ann} = [\text{Accumulation per AT\$ invested}]^{1/n} - 1$$

EXAMPLE I:18-9 ▶ Consider the same facts as in Example I:18-8. The annualized ATROR for the investment outside the IRA is 6.5%. No additional computation is necessary because the model already is in the Current Model form. The accumulation per AT\$ invested inside the IRA (the Deferred Model) can be determined two ways. First, divide the total accumulation ($4,722.87) by the $1,000 (AT\$) invested, which yields 4.72287. Alternatively, compute the accumulation per AT\$ as follows: $[(1.1)^{20}(1 - 0.35) + 0.35] = 4.72287$. The annualized ATROR, then, is computed as follows: $r_{ann} = (4.72287)^{1/20} - 1 = 0.0807128$ or 8.07128%. Thus, on an annualized basis, a 20-year investment outside the IRA (the Current Model) yields 6.5% after taxes, while a 20-year investment inside the IRA (the Deferred Model) yields 8.07128% after taxes. To check this result, simply put the 8.07128% annualized ATROR in the Current Model to see that it yields the same result as did the Deferred Model.

$$\text{ATA} = \$1,000(1.0807128)^{20} = \$1,000(4.72287) = \$4,722.87 \quad ◀$$

Capital Assets. The Deferred Model also describes the after-tax growth of a capital asset. For example, suppose a stock grows annually at rate R and does not pay dividends, that is, the stock is strictly a growth stock. In n years, the stock will be worth $(1 + R)^n$. If the investor then sells the stock for its fair market value (FMV), the investor pays tax on the capital gain. Consequently, the tax on the gain is deferred until the investor sells the asset, which reflects the realization principle of taxation. Moreover, the capital gain may be taxed at a preferential capital gains tax rate. Thus, when applied to capital assets, the Deferred Model provides two tax advantages: deferral and a preferential tax rate.

When Figure I:18-1 is applied to this situation, the before-tax accumulation represents the selling price at the FMV, and the before-tax earnings represent the capital gain.

EXAMPLE I:18-10 ▶ Brian purchases stock for $5,000. The stock appreciates (grows) at an 8% rate before taxes. Brian sells the stock ten years later for $10,795, which is $5,000 $(1.08)^{10}$. At the time of sale, his regular tax rate is 40%, but his long-term capital gains tax rate is 20%. One way to calculate Brian's after-tax proceeds is as follows:

(1) Selling price [$5,000(1.08)^{10}$]	$10,795
(2) Minus: Original investment (basis)	(5,000)
(3) Long-term capital gain	$ 5,795
(4) Times: Long-term capital gains tax rate	0.20
(5) Tax on capital gain	$ 1,159
(6) After-tax proceeds (Line 1 − Line 5)	$ 9,636

Alternatively, the after-tax proceeds can be determined quickly with the Deferred Model as follows:

$$\text{ATA} = \$5,000 \times [(1.08)^{10}(1 - 0.20) + 0.20] = \$9,636 \quad ◀$$

Comparing Current and Deferred Models. As mentioned earlier, a Deferred Model investment always outperforms a Current Model investment if BTRORs are constant over time and equal across models and if tax rates also are constant and equal. However, when these conditions are not present, the models must be compared to determine which is preferable. One way to make this comparison is to set up a spreadsheet of the various alternatives.

EXAMPLE I:18-11 ▶ As in Example I:18-8, assume that Phillip can invest $1,000 (AT\$) in a taxable bond either outside or inside a traditional nondeductible IRA. The bond yields 10% per year before taxes, and

Phillip's marginal tax rate is 35%. Assume also that Phillip will be younger than 59½ when he withdraws the funds from the IRA. As described in Chapter I:9, a taxpayer who withdraws amounts from a traditional IRA before reaching age 59½ generally must pay a 10% penalty tax on the taxable portion of the withdrawal. This penalty, in effect, increases the applicable tax rate in the Deferred Model. Thus, the following models apply (the Deferred Model with no penalty is repeated for comparison):

Bond outside the IRA (Current Model):

$$\$1,000[1 + 0.1(1 - 0.35)]^n = \$1,000(1.065)n$$

Bond inside the IRA (Deferred Model)—No penalty:

$$\$1,000[(1.1)^n \times (1 - 0.35) + 0.35]$$

Bond inside the IRA (Deferred Model)—With penalty:

$$\$1,000[(1.1)^n \times (1 - 0.45) + 0.45]$$

Notice that the 10% penalty effectively increases the marginal tax rate to 45%. Given the 10% penalty, which investment is better, the Current Model or the Deferred Model? The answer depends on the length of the investment horizon. Table I:18-1 schedules the after-tax accumulations and related annualized ATRORs for various investment horizons (n) from one to 20 years.

Before considering the penalty situation, observe the no penalty case. For all values of n above one, the Deferred Model investment produces a greater after-tax accumulation than does the Current Model investment (compare Columns 2 and 3). This result also is apparent in

▼ **TABLE I:18-1**

Comparison of Current and Deferred Models

	After-Tax Accumulations			Annualized ATRORs[d]		
(1)	(2)	(3)	(4)	(5)	(6)	(7)
n	Current Model[a]	Deferred Model No Penalty[b]	Deferred Model with Penalty[c]	Current Model	Deferred Model No Penalty	Deferred Model with Penalty
1	$1,065	$1,065	$1,055	6.5%	6.500%	5.500%
2	1,134	1,137	1,116	6.5	6.607	5.617
3	1,208	1,215	1,182	6.5	6.711	5.733
4	1,286	1,302	1,255	6.5	6.813	5.848
5	1,370	1,397	1,336	6.5	6.913	5.961
6	1,459	1,502	1,424	6.5	7.009	6.073
7	1,544	1,617	1,522	6.5	7.103	6.182
8	1,655	1,743	1,629	6.5	7.195	6.289
9	1,763	1,883	1,747	6.5	7.283	6.394
10	1,877	2,036	1,876	6.5	7.368	6.497
11	1,999	2,205	2,019	6.5	7.451	6.597
12	2,129	2,390	2,176	6.5	7.531	6.694
13	2,267	2,594	2,349	6.5	7.608	6.789
14	2,415	2,818	2,539	6.5	7.682	6.881
15	2,572	3,065	2,747	6.5	7.753	6.970
16	2,739	3,337	2,977	6.5	7.822	7.057
17	2,917	3,635	3,230	6.5	7.888	7.140
18	3,107	3,964	3,508	6.5	7.952	7.221
19	3,309	4,325	3,814	6.5	8.013	7.299
20	3,524	4,723	4,150	6.5	8.071	7.375

[a] $1,000(1.065)^n$
[b] $\$1,000[(1.1)^n(1 - 0.35) + 0.35]$
[c] $\$1,000[(1.1)^n(1 - 0.45) + 0.45]$
[d] $[(\text{ATA per AT\$})^{1/n} - 1] \times 100$

the annualized ATRORs. For all values of n above one, the Deferred Model investment produces an annualized ATROR greater than 6.5% (compare Columns 5 and 6). Moreover, the greater the n, the greater the annualized ATROR from the Deferred Model investment. This result occurs because tax deferral increases as the investment horizon lengthens. Thus, the longer the deferral, the better the annualized ATROR produced by the Deferred Model investment.

Now compare the Current Model to the Deferred Model with the 10% penalty. For investment horizons up to ten years, the Current Model investment outperforms the Deferred Model investment, while for horizons greater than ten years, the Deferred Model investment beats the Current Model investment (compare Columns 2 and 4). This result can be seen more easily with the annualized ATRORs, where beginning in Year 11, the annualized ATRORs for the Deferred Model investment exceed 6.5% (compare Columns 5 and 7). The Current Model investment is better for short horizons because the applicable tax rate is 35% rather than 45% (rate + penalty). However, after ten years, the deferral benefit of the Deferred Model investment overcomes the penalty's detrimental effect. Thus, if an investor has a long enough investment horizon, a traditional nondeductible IRA subject to the 10% penalty may be the preferred method of accumulating savings, assuming the investor is ineligible for the Roth IRA. ◀

THE EXEMPT MODEL

The Exempt Model gives the future value of an investment having the following characteristics:

▶ Only after-tax dollars are invested (as with the Current and Deferred Models).

▶ Earnings on the investment are exempt from explicit taxation (unlike the Current and Deferred Models).

In fact, the Exempt Model is a special case of either the Current Model or the Deferred Model with the tax rate equal to zero. Consequently, the investment grows at the BTROR and appears as follows:

The Exempt Model:
$$ATA = AT\$(1 + R)^n$$

State and local government obligations, such as municipal bonds, are classic examples of the Exempt Model. Section 103 excludes interest on these instruments from gross income.

EXAMPLE I:18-12 ▶ Carmen invests $10,000 (AT$) in tax-exempt municipal bonds, which yield 5% per year. She reinvests the interest and holds the bonds for ten years. Thus, the investment accumulates to $16,288.95, which is $10,000 (1.05)^{10}. ◀

Other examples of the Exempt Model are the Roth IRA (see Chapter I:9) and the Roth option for Sec. 401(k) and Sec. 403(b) plans. Like the traditional nondeductible IRA, the Roth IRA does not allow a deduction for contributions. However, upon withdrawals, the accumulated earnings are not taxed. We will say more about the Roth IRA after developing the Pension Model.

STOP & THINK

Question: Does the Exempt Model imply that no taxation occurs in the tax system for investments of this type?

Solution: No. Taxation occurs because the taxpayer invests after-tax dollars, which means the invested amount comes from some taxable source. If no taxation occurred at all, the model would appear as Accumulation = BT\$ $(1 + R)^n$, which is the situation described on page I:18-3 just after Example I:18-1.

THE PENSION MODEL

The Pension Model gives the future value of an investment in a qualified retirement plan having the following characteristics:

▶ Before-tax dollars are invested (unlike the previous three models).

▶ The annual earnings on the investment grow at the BTROR (as with the Deferred and Exempt Models).

▶ The entire accumulation, not just the earnings, is taxed at the end of the investment horizon when the investor cashes out of the plan.

Thus, the Pension Model provides two levels of tax deferral. First, salary or earned income contributed to the plan escapes taxation when contributed but is taxed later upon withdrawal. Second, earnings on the underlying investment are not taxed while in the plan but also are taxed later upon withdrawal. This double deferral contrasts with the Deferral Model, in which only the taxes on investment earnings are deferred.

Deductible IRAs and H.R. 10 plans described in Chapter I:9 are classic examples of the Pension Model. The taxpayer deducts the IRA or H.R. 10 contribution from gross income, the underlying investments grow at before-tax rates of return, and the taxpayer later includes any withdrawals in gross income.

EXAMPLE I:18-13 ▶ Frank, whose marginal tax rate is 35%, earns $1,000 of salary and wishes to contribute this amount to a deductible IRA (Pension Model). He may do so because he can deduct the $1,000 contribution from gross income, leaving the entire $1,000 available for contribution. If, instead, Frank contributes to a traditional nondeductible IRA (Deferred Model) or a Roth IRA (Exempt Model), he can contribute only $650 because he must pay $350 of taxes on the $1,000 salary. Thus, Frank can contribute $1,000 before-tax dollars to a deductible IRA as contrasted with $650 after-tax dollars to a traditional nondeductible IRA or a Roth IRA. ◀

Other examples of the Pension Model include cash or deferred arrangements, commonly known as Sec. 401(k) plans, and tax-deferred annuities, sometimes referred to as Sec. 403(b) plans. Both of these type plans operate through a salary reduction agreement whereby the employee elects to have a specified amount of his or her salary contributed to the plan. The employee excludes the amount of salary contributed to the plan from his or her gross income. However, annual contributions are limited to $18,000 (in 2015).[4] As with IRA and H.R. 10 plans, the underlying investments in Sec. 401(k) and Sec. 403(b) plans grow at before-tax rates of return, and the employee later includes any withdrawals in gross income. Withdrawals before the employee reaches age 59 1/2, however, are subject to a 10% penalty in addition to the tax. Although most employers can offer Sec. 401(k) plans, only educational institutions and certain tax-exempt organizations may provide Sec. 403(b) plans.

Employer-sponsored qualified retirement plans also fit the Pension Model. In this case, the employer makes a deductible contribution on the employee's behalf, and the employee excludes the contribution from gross income. Upon retirement, the employee's retirement payments are fully taxed.

EXAMPLE I:18-14 ▶ Frank in Example I:18-13 makes the $1,000 contribution to a deductible IRA. The investment in the IRA will earn 10% per year before taxes, and Frank will withdraw all accumulated amounts from the IRA after 20 years. He expects his tax rate to be 25% at that time, and he will not be subject to the 10% penalty for early withdrawals. The following calculation demonstrates one way to determine Frank's after-tax accumulation in the IRA:

Before-tax accumulation in the IRA [$1,000(1.1)^{20}]	$6,728
Minus: Tax on withdrawn accumulation ($6,728 × 0.25)	(1,682)
Accumulated earnings after taxes	$5,046 ◀

The calculation in Example I:18-14 also can be formulated as follows:

$$ATA = \$1,000(1.1)^{20} - [\$1,000(1.1)^{20}] \times 0.25$$

---

[4] Section 402(g) imposes this dollar limitation. In addition, Sec. 414(v) increases the limitation for taxpayers age 50 or older. This additional catch-up limitation is $5,500 in 2015. Percentage of compensation limitations also apply to contributions to Sec. 401(k) and Sec. 403(b) plans, but these limitations are complex and beyond the scope of this chapter. (See Chapter I:9 and Secs. 403(b) and 415(c).)

Factoring out the before-tax accumulation of $1,000(1.1)^{20}$ yields the following expression:

$$ATA = \$1,000(1.1)^{20}(1 - 0.25)$$

Substituting our general symbols into this expression yields:

The Pension Model:
$$ATA = BT\$(1 + R)^n(1 - t_n) \text{ or}$$

$$ATA = AT\$\left[\frac{1}{(1 - t_o)}(1 + R)^n(1 - t_n)\right]$$

Recall that $BT\$ = AT\$/(1 - t)$. That is, before-tax dollars equal after-tax dollars grossed up by one minus the tax rate. Thus, the second form of the Pension Model is equivalent to the first form. The second form, however, has the same format as the other three models: AT$ times a future value formula. This format allows the investor to compare all four models without considering a specific level of investment because each model in this format is stated in terms of the after-tax accumulation per AT$ invested. In these models, t_o is the tax rate in Year 0, and t_n is the tax rate in Year n.

EXAMPLE I:18-15 ▶ Given four options listed below, Beth wants to know the after-tax accumulation and annualized ATROR of each.

▶ Current Model: $R = 10\%$, $t = 25\%$, $n = 5$
▶ Deferred Model: $R = 9\%$, $t_n = 35\%$, $n = 5$
▶ Exempt Model: $R = 8\%$, $n = 5$
▶ Pension Model: $R = 10\%$, $t_o = 25\%$, $t_n = 35\%$, $n = 5$

The results of the four options are as follows:

Model	Computation	After-Tax Accumulation	Annualized ATROR
Current	$[1 + 0.1(1 - 0.25)]^5$	1.4356	7.50%
Deferred	$(1.09)^5(1 - 0.35) + 0.35$	1.3501	6.19%
Exempt	$(1.08)^5$	1.4693	8.00%
Pension	$[1/(1 - 0.25)](1.1)^5(1 - 0.35)$	1.3958	6.90%

ADDITIONAL COMMENT

The tax rates (t_o and t_n) in these comparisons are those faced by a particular individual because of changing tax laws and/or because of an individual's changing circumstances, e.g., levels of income at the time of investment versus at the end of the investment horizon.

Comparing Exempt and Pension Models. With equal BTRORs, constant tax rates (i.e., $t_o = t_n$), and no limitation on contributions, the Exempt and Pension Models are equivalent because the $1/(1 - t_o)$ and $(1 - t_n)$ terms cancel out, leaving the Pension Model (second form) to appear as $AT\$(1 + R)^n$. However, if t_o and t_n differ for a particular individual, this equivalency disappears. Thus, the following relationships hold:

▶ If $t_o = t_n$, ATA per Exempt Model = ATA per Pension Model.
▶ If $t_o > t_n$, ATA per Exempt Model < ATA per Pension Model.
▶ If $t_o < t_n$, ATA per Exempt Model > ATA per Pension Model.

EXAMPLE I:18-16 ▶ Consider the following situations:

▶ $R = 10\%$, $t_o = 30\%$, $t_n = 30\%$, $n = 10$
▶ $R = 10\%$, $t_o = 40\%$, $t_n = 30\%$, $n = 10$
▶ $R = 10\%$, $t_o = 30\%$, $t_n = 40\%$, $n = 10$

The after-tax accumulations (ATAs) for the three situations are as follows:

Situation	Exempt Model	Pension Model
$t_o = 30\%$, $t_n = 30\%$	$(1.1)^{10} = 2.5937$	$[1/(1 - 0.30)](1.1)^{10}(1 - 0.30) = 2.5937$
$t_o = 40\%$, $t_n = 30\%$	$(1.1)^{10} = 2.5937$	$[1/(1 - 0.40)](1.1)^{10}(1 - 0.30) = 3.0260$
$t_o = 30\%$, $t_n = 40\%$	$(1.1)^{10} = 2.5937$	$[1/(1 - 0.30)](1.1)^{10}(1 - 0.40) = 2.2232$

Deductible IRA versus Roth IRA. The Exempt and Pension models can be used to compare investment in a traditional deductible IRA versus a Roth IRA. If the amount of before-tax dollars available for investment does not exceed the $5,500 limitation (in 2015),[5] the comparative results are similar to those in Example I:18-16.

EXAMPLE I:18-17 ▶ Marcy has $5,500 of salary before taxes available for contribution to either a traditional deductible IRA or a Roth IRA. The underlying investments will earn a 10% BTROR. After ten years, Marcy plans to withdraw the entire accumulation without penalty. If her marginal tax rate is 30% in the contribution year, she can contribute either $5,500 (BT$) to the deductible IRA or $3,850 (AT$) to the Roth IRA. If her marginal tax rate upon withdrawal is 30%, she will have the following after tax accumulations under each alternative:

Roth IRA: [$3,850(1.1)^{10}$] $9,986

Deductible IRA: [$5,500(1.1)^{10}(1 - 0.30)$] $9,986

TAX STRATEGY TIP

When given a choice between a Roth IRA and a traditional *non*deductible IRA, the taxpayer always should choose the Roth IRA. However, if the taxpayer's AGI exceeds the limitation for contributions to a Roth IRA, the taxpayer can contribute to a traditional nondeductible IRA and then immediately roll over the traditional IRA contribution into a Roth IRA. The Roth rollover (also called a conversion) has no AGI limitation.

Thus, with constant tax rates, the two alternatives yield the same after-tax accumulation.

If Marcy's current tax rate is 40%, and her later tax rate is 30%, the two alternatives yield the following after-tax accumulations:

Roth IRA: [$3,300(1.1)^{10}$] $8,559

Deductible IRA: [$5,500(1.1)^{10}(1 - 0.30)$] $9,986

Thus, with decreasing tax rates, the deductible IRA yields the better result.

Finally, if Marcy's current tax rate is 30%, and her later tax rate is 40%, the two alternatives yield the following after-tax accumulations:

Roth IRA: [$3,850(1.1)^{10}$] $9,986

Deductible IRA: [$5,500(1.1)^{10}(1 - 0.4)$] $8,559

Thus, with increasing tax rates, the Roth IRA yields the better result. ◀

In Example I:18-17, the before-tax dollars available for contribution did not exceed the $5,500 limitation on IRA contributions. However, suppose the taxpayer wishes to compare a $5,500 contribution to a deductible IRA with a $5,500 contribution to a Roth IRA. In this case, the two contributions are not equivalent because the taxpayer makes the contribution to the deductible IRA with before-tax dollars and to the Roth IRA with after-tax dollars. To have $5,500 after-tax dollars available for a Roth IRA contribution, the taxpayer must have $5,500/(1 - t_o)$ before-tax dollars available for investment. If the taxpayer has this amount available and contributes $5,500 to a deductible IRA, the taxpayer will have some available funds left over for investment outside the deductible IRA.[6]

EXAMPLE I:18-18 ▶ Mark wants to contribute $5,500 to either a deductible IRA or a Roth IRA. His current marginal tax rate is 30%. To contribute $5,500 (AT$) to a Roth IRA, his before-tax dollars available for investment must be $7,857, which is computed as BT$ = $5,500/(1 - 0.30). On the other hand, if he contributes $5,500 (BT$) to a deductible IRA, he has $2,357 remaining. This $2,357 is subject to tax so that, after taxes at 30%, Mark will have $1,650 (AT$) remaining for investment outside the IRA.

A convenient short-cut method to determine the amount remaining for outside investment is to multiply the $5,500 deduction by the tax rate to arrive at the tax savings from the traditional IRA deduction. Specifically, the $5,500 deduction will generate $1,650 of tax savings for outside investment, computed as $5,500 × 0.30 = $1,650. This shortcut, however, works only if the taxpayer considers contributing the maximum amount to the deductible or Roth IRA. ◀

Given the previous discussion, the deductible IRA versus Roth IRA decision can be framed as follows:

---

[5] For taxpayers age 50 or older, the limitation is increased by $1,000 in 2015, called a catchup limitation.

[6] Participants in Sec. 401(k) and Sec. 403(b) plans can opt to have their elective deferrals treated as Roth contributions. For a detailed analysis of this decision, (see K. E. Anderson and D. P. Murphy, "The New Roth Option for 401(k) and 403(b) Plans: A Decision Framework," *Journal of Financial Service Professionals*, January 2002, pp. 45–56).

Roth IRA	$5,500(1 + R)^n$
Versus	
Deductible IRA	$5,500(1 + R)^n(1 - t_n)$
Plus	
Outside Investment	$5,500(t_o)[1 + R(1 - t)]^n$

In this framework, $5,500(t_o)$ is the tax savings from the traditional IRA deduction, which the taxpayer invests in an investment conforming to the Current Model. If the taxpayer's outside investment conforms to the Deferred Model or some other model, the alternative model can be substituted for the Current Model in this decision framework.

EXAMPLE I:18-19 ▶ Helen wishes to invest $5,500 in either a deductible IRA or a Roth IRA. The underlying investments will earn a 10% BTROR. After ten years, Helen plans to withdraw the entire accumulation without penalty. Her marginal tax rate is 30% in the contribution year, and she expects her marginal tax rate upon withdrawal to be 30%. If she contributes to the deductible IRA, she will invest the tax savings in an investment yielding a 10% BTROR and which is currently taxable at 30%. The alternative investments yield the following results:

Roth IRA [$5,500(1.1)^{10}$]	$14,266
Deductible IRA [$5,500(1.1)^{10}(1 - 0.30)$]	$ 9,986
Plus: Outside investment [$5,500(0.30)(1.07)^{10}$]	3,246
Total	$13,232

With constant tax rates, the Roth IRA produces the better result because, with the deductible IRA, part of the investment goes to an outside investment taxed less favorably than the IRA. Note also that, because the $5,500 limitation is after-tax dollars for the Roth IRA but before-tax dollars for the deductible IRA, constant tax rates no longer produce equivalent results.

Suppose instead that Helen expects her tax rate to be 15% when she withdraws the IRA accumulation. In this case, the alternative investments yield the following results:

Roth IRA [$5,500(1.1)^{10}$]	$14,266
Deductible IRA [$5,500(1.1)^{10}(1 - 0.15)$]	$ 12,126
Plus: Outside investment [$5,500(0.30)(1.07)^{10}$]	3,246
Total	$15,372

Thus, with a reduced tax rate in the withdrawal year, the deductible IRA (plus the outside investment) yields the better result. ◀

MULTIPERIOD STRATEGIES

All previous examples assumed a single amount invested for a specified time period. However, suppose an investor wants to invest a certain amount each year over several years. In this case, the investor may optimize his or her after-tax accumulation by investing in one type of investment in early years and another type investment in late years.

EXAMPLE I:18-20 ▶ For the next 15 years, Jack wishes to invest $10,000 (AT$) at the beginning of each year into either nondividend paying stock that increases in value at 8% per year before taxes or a taxable bond that yields 10% per year before taxes. Jack's regular tax rate is 30%, but he pays only 15% on long-term capital gains. Jack wants to know which asset to invest in for each of the 15 years. The following models apply to this situation:

Stock (Deferred Model):

$$\$10,000[(1.08)^n(1 - 0.15) + 0.15]$$

Taxable bond (Current Model):

$$\$10,000[1 + 0.1(1 - 0.30)]^n = \$10,000(1.07)^n$$

Table I:18-2 schedules the alternatives for each year. The stock produces the larger after-tax accumulations for investments made in Years 1 through 9. For Years 10 through 15, however, the taxable bonds outperform the stock. Consequently, Jack should invest in stock for each of

▼ TABLE I:18-2
Multiperiod Investments

(1) Year	(2) n	(3) Amount Invested	(4) Stock[a] (Deferred Model)	(5) Taxable Bond[b] (Current Model)	(6) Greater of Column 4 or 5
1	15	$10,000	$ 28,463	$ 27,590	$ 28,463
2	14	10,000	26,466	25,785	26,466
3	13	10,000	24,617	24,098	24,617
4	12	10,000	22,904	22,522	22,904
5	11	10,000	21,319	21,049	21,319
6	10	10,000	19,851	19,672	19,851
7	9	10,000	18,492	18,385	18,492
8	8	10,000	17,233	17,182	17,233
9	7	10,000	16,068	16,058	16,068
10	6	10,000	14,988	15,007	15,007
11	5	10,000	13,989	14,026	14,026
12	4	10,000	13,064	13,108	13,108
13	3	10,000	12,208	12,250	12,250
14	2	10,000	11,414	11,449	11,449
15	1	10,000	10,680	10,700	10,700
Total ATA with no switching			$271,756	$268,881	
Total ATA with switching strategy					$271,953

[a]$10,000 [(1.08)^n(1 - 0.15) + 0.15]$
[b]$10,000 (1.07)^n$

the first nine years and hold the stock for the rest of the 15-year investment horizon. For the remaining six years, he should invest in taxable bonds. This switching strategy maximizes the total after-tax accumulation compared to investing in either stock or bonds for the entire 15-year period (compare Column 4 and 5 totals to Column 6 total).

The stock outperforms the taxable bonds for the first nine years even though the taxable bonds yield a higher BTROR than does the stock. This result occurs because the deferral benefit outweighs the lower BTROR for long investment horizons. ◄

SUMMARY AND COMPARISON OF BASIC INVESTMENT MODELS

Topic Review I:18-1 summarizes the models along with simple examples. In the examples, each model assumes an investment earning 10% before taxes and assumes a constant 30% tax rate. With these assumptions, the Exempt and Pension Models outperform the Current and Deferred Models, and the Deferred Model outperforms the Current Model.

OTHER APPLICATIONS OF INVESTMENT MODELS

OBJECTIVE 2

Use the investment models to make entity choices and compensation decisions

In the previous section of this chapter, we developed four investment models and applied them to currently taxable investments, capital gains assets, tax-exempt bonds, and retirement plans. In this section, we present two additional applications: (1) the flow-through entity versus the C corporation form of business operations and (2) current salary versus deferred compensation.

TOPIC REVIEW I:18-1

Summary of Investment Models

INVESTMENT MODEL	INITIAL INCOME	INVESTMENT EARNINGS OR CAPITAL GAIN	EXAMPLES[a]	ATA	ATA/AT$	r_{ann}
Current: $AT\$[1 + R(1-t)]^n$ — or — $AT\$(1+r)^n$	Taxed currently	Taxed annually	$\$700(1.07)^5$	\$ 981.79	1.4026[b]	7.00%
Deferred: $AT\$[(1+R)^n(1-t_n) + t_n]$	Taxed currently	Tax deferred	$\$700[(1.1)^5(0.7) + 0.30]$	\$ 999.15	1.4274[c]	7.38%
Exempt: $AT\$(1+R)^n$	Taxed currently	Tax exempt	$\$700(1.1)^5$	\$1,127.36	1.6105[d]	10.00%
Pension: $BT\$(1+R)^n(1-t_n)$ — or — $AT\$\left[\dfrac{1}{(1-t_o)}(1+R)^n(1-t_n)\right]$	Tax deferred	Tax deferred	$\$1,000(1.1)^5(0.7)$ — or — $\$700(1/0.7)(1.1)^5(0.7)$	\$1,127.36	1.6105[e]	10.00%

Definitions of Variables:

ATA = After-tax accumulation (future value of an investment)
BT$ = Before-tax dollars
AT$ = After-tax dollars
  R = Before-tax rate of return (BTROR)
  r = After-tax rate of return (ATROR)
r_{ann} = Annualized ATROR
  n = Investment horizon
  t = Marginal tax rate, generally and for Current Model
  t_o = Marginal tax rate in the year of investment (Year 0) for Pension Model
  t_n = Marginal tax rate at the end of the investment horizon (Year n) for Deferred and Pension Models

[a]Initial before-tax income (BT$) = \$1,000; AT$ = \$1,000(0.7) = \$700; R = 10%; t = t_o = t_n = 30%; n = 5
[b]Also: $(1.07)^5 = 1.4026$
[c]Also: $(1.1)^5(0.7) + 0.30 = 1.4274$
[d]Also: $(1.1)^5 = 1.6105$
[e]Note that the \$1,127.36 after-tax accumulation is divided by \$700, not \$1,000, because \$700 is the after-tax dollar equivalent of \$1,000 before taxes.
Also: $(1/0.7)(1.1)^5(0.7) = 1.6105$

FLOW-THROUGH ENTITY VERSUS C CORPORATION

Chapter I:16 described how the government taxes C corporations and their shareholders, and Chapter I:17 introduced the tax consequences of operating as a flow-through entity (also called a pass-through entity). Flow-through entities include partnerships, limited liability companies (LLCs), limited liability partnerships (LLPs), and S corporations. A flow-through entity's primary characteristic is that income escapes taxation at the entity level and flows through to be taxed at the ownership level. Corporate income, on the other hand, is taxed once at the entity level and again at the owner level. Taxation at the owner level occurs when the corporation distributes its earnings, when the shareholder sells his or her stock, or when the corporation liquidates.

In this section, we show that the Current Model describes a flow-through entity and that a variation of the Deferred Model describes a C corporation. These models can be used to decide which form of business is best from a tax perspective. At first, one might think the flow-through entity is the better form because it avoids double taxation. But, in fact, the better alternative depends on a combination of factors, specifically, rates of returns, the corporate tax rate, the owner's tax rate, and the entity's expected life span (investment horizon).

The Flow-Through Model. To keep matters simple, we assume an S corporation with only one shareholder. The one-owner assumption allows us to focus on the entity decision without worrying about distributive shares and differential individual tax rates among owners. The model also applies to an S corporation, a partnership, an LLC, or an LLP with more than one owner. In addition, the model applies to a sole proprietorship because that form of business also entails one level of taxation.

ADDITIONAL COMMENT

As the income and deductions flow through to the owners of partnerships and S corporations, they retain their character. For example, ordinary income at the entity level is ordinary income to the owner, and capital gains at the entity level flow through as capital gains.

EXAMPLE I:18-21 ▶ Assume the following facts. Rebecca forms an S corporation by contributing $10,000 to the corporation in exchange for all the corporation's stock. The S corporation invests in assets that produce a 10% BTROR per year. At the end of each year, the S corporation distributes cash to Rebecca equal to the taxes she must pay on the S corporation's flow-through earnings. The corporation reinvests the remaining earnings in its business. Rebecca's tax rate is 40%. Immediately after the end of the second year, the S corporation liquidates, selling the assets and distributing the cash proceeds to Rebecca. Because the corporation reinvested its retained earnings, the total basis of the corporation's assets increased as well. Assuming the FMV of the assets increased similarly, the sale produces no realized gain at the entity level. The following schedule shows the results of these transactions at the entity and owner levels:

	Year 1	Year 2
Entity level:		
Investment at beginning of year	$10,000	$10,600
Plus: Earnings on investment (10% × investment)	1,000	1,060
Minus: Distribution to shareholder (40% × earnings)	(400)	(424)
Investment at end of year	$10,600	$11,236
Owner level:		
Stock basis at beginning of year	$10,000	$10,600
Plus: Increase due to flow-through income	1,000	1,060
Minus: Decrease due to distribution	(400)	(424)
Stock basis at end of year	$10,600	$11,236

Upon liquidation, the S corporation sells the assets and distributes the $11,236 to Rebecca. Because Rebecca's stock basis equals $11,236, she recognizes no additional gain on the liquidation. Thus, after two years, she ends up with $11,236 on a $10,000 original investment. ◀

In Example I:18-21, the S corporation could reinvest only its earnings after paying the shareholder's tax. Thus, the investment grew at a 6% ATROR, which is 10% $(1 - 0.4)$. Consequently, the shareholder's after-tax accumulation also can be calculated as follows: ATA = $10,000(1.06)^2 = $11,236$. From the owner's viewpoint, then, the flow-through entity resembles the Current Model. In general terms, the owner's after-tax accumulation can be expressed as:

> The Flow-Through Model:
> $$ATA = \text{Contribution}[1 + R_f(1 - t_p)]^n$$

In this model, R_f equals the flow-through entity's BTROR, t_p is the owner's marginal tax rate (p is for personal), and n is the investment horizon. Although Example I:18-21 assumes a liquidating distribution at the end of the investment, the same result would have occurred had the owner sold her ownership interest (stock in this case) to another party.

The C Corporation Model.   Again, to keep matters simple, we assume a C corporation with only one shareholder, and we further assume that the corporation retains all earnings after paying corporate level taxes. That is, the corporation pays no dividends. The model could be modified to reflect annual dividend payments, but such a model becomes extremely complicated and is beyond the scope of this chapter.

EXAMPLE I:18-22 ▶ Assume the same facts as in Example I:18-21 except Rebecca forms a C corporation instead of an S corporation. In this case, the corporation makes no annual distributions to Rebecca. Instead, the corporation pays its own taxes at a 35% rate and reinvests the after-tax retained earnings. Thus, the shareholder has no owner-level taxes until the corporation liquidates. Rebecca's ordinary tax rate remains 40%, but her capital gains tax rate is 20%. As in Example I:18-21, the sale prior to liquidation produces no realized gain at the entity level. The following schedule shows the results of these transactions at the entity and owner levels:

	Year 1	Year 2
Entity level:		
Investment at beginning of year	$10,000	$10,650
Plus: Earnings on investment (10% × investment)	1,000	1,065
Minus: Corporate taxes (35% × earnings)	(350)	(373)
Investment at end of year	$10,650	$11,342
Owner level:		
Stock basis	$10,000	$10,000
(1) Liquidation proceeds		$11,342
(2) Minus: Stock basis		(10,000)
(3) Capital gain on liquidation		$ 1,342
(4) Times: Long-term capital gains tax rate		0.20
(5) Tax on capital gain		$ 268
(6) After-tax proceeds (Line 1 − Line 5)		$11,074

Because the corporation is a C corporation, Rebecca makes no adjustments to her stock basis, which remains at $10,000. Consequently, she recognizes a capital gain upon liquidation, and after two years she ends up with $11,074 on a $10,000 original investment. ◀

In Example I:18-22, the C corporation was able to reinvest only its after-tax earnings. Thus, at the corporate level, the investment grew at a 6.5% ATROR, which is 10% $(1 - 0.35)$. Consequently, the corporate-level accumulation before distribution to the shareholders can be calculated as follows: $\$10,000[1 + 0.1(1 - 0.35)]^2 = \$10,000(1.065)^2 = \$11,342$. In general terms, this expression is: Contribution$[1 + R_c(1 - t_c)]^n$, or Contribution $[1 + r_c]^n$. This formulation is a variation of the Current Model, where R_c is the corporation's BTROR, r_c is the corporation's ATROR, and t_c is the corporation's marginal tax rate.

Upon liquidation, the shareholder receives the corporate-level accumulation and pays tax at rate t_p on the difference between the distribution and her stock basis. Thus, the shareholder's after-tax accumulation in Example I:18-22 can be formulated as follows:

$$ATA = \$10,000(1.065)^2 - [\$10,000(1.065)^2 - \$10,000] \times 0.20$$

The first term, $\$10,000(1.065)^2$, gives the corporate-level after-tax accumulation; the subtraction in brackets gives the shareholder's liquidation gain before shareholder-level taxes; and the multiplication by 20% gives the tax on the liquidation gain. Subtracting this tax from the first term gives the shareholder's total after-tax accumulation on the investment in the C corporation. Factoring out the $10,000 contribution yields the following expression:

$$ATA = \$10,000\{(1.065)^2 - [(1.065)^2 - 1] \times 0.20\}$$

Substituting our general symbols into this expression yields the following model, which is a variation of the Deferred Model shown earlier in Figure I:18-1:

$$ATA = \text{Contribution}\{(1 + r_c)^n - [(1 + r_c)^n - 1] \times t_p\}$$

As done earlier with the Deferred Model, we can simplify this model algebraically to obtain:

> The C Corporation Model:
> $$ATA = \text{Contribution}[(1 + r_c)^n(1 - t_p) + t_p] \text{ or}$$
> $$ATA = \text{Contribution}\{[1 + R_c(1 - t_c)]^n(1 - t_p) + t_p\}$$

In the first form of this model, the corporation's ATROR (r_c) plays the same role as the BTROR plays in the Deferred Model developed earlier in this chapter. More specifically, in terms used in Example I:18-10, r_c is the appreciation (growth) rate of the shareholder's stock investment, assuming the stock value reflects increases in the corporation's after-tax retained earnings. Thus, the corporation's ATROR functions as the shareholder's BTROR on his or her stock investment. The second form of the C Corporation Model emphasizes that the corporate-level accumulation (the Current Model) is embedded in the shareholder's after-tax accumulation model (the Deferred Model). Topic Review I:18-2 summarizes these models.

Comparing the Flow-Through and C Corporation Models. Given these two models, an owner can compare whether operating as a flow-through entity or a C corporation provides the better result.

EXAMPLE I:18-23 ▶

ADDITIONAL COMMENT

For qualified small business stock (Sec. 1202 stock) acquired after February 17, 2009 and before September 28, 2010, the exclusion is 75%. For qualified Sec. 1202 stock acquired after September 27, 2010 and before January 1, 2015, the exclusion percentage is 100%. In both instances, the five-year holding period requirement remains in effect. The text discussion assumes a 50% exclusion.

Assume the following facts. Mark forms Wolfson Corporation by contributing $5 million in exchange for the corporation's stock. The corporation expects to earn 18% per year before taxes on this investment. The corporate tax rate is 34%, and Mark's individual tax rate on ordinary income is 40%. On capital gains other than Sec. 1202 gains, Mark's tax rate is 20%. Because Wolfson stock qualifies as small business stock under Sec. 1202, any gain recognized on disposition of the stock after a five-year holding period qualifies for a 50% exclusion. The maximum capital gain rate on the included gain is 28% rather than 20%. Thus, Mark's effective rate on the *entire* capital gain is 20% if he holds the stock for five years or less and is 14% if he holds the stock for more than five years (that is, 28% of half the gain is equivalent to 14% of the entire gain). Wolfson can operate either as an S corporation or a C corporation. If the corporation elects S corporation status, each year it will distribute exactly enough cash for Mark to pay taxes on any flow-through income, and it will reinvest the remaining earnings in the business. If the corporation operates as a C corporation, it will make no annual distributions, reinvesting all after-tax earnings in the business. In either case, the corporation will liquidate at the end of the investment horizon. Mark wants to know how long he must operate the corporation to make the C corporation form better than the S corporation form. Table I:18-3 gives Mark's after-tax accumulation for each alternative.

According to Table I:18-3 in Columns 1 and 2, if Mark decides to operate the corporation for ten years or less, the corporation should make the S corporation election. However, if he plans to operate for more than ten years, the corporation should remain a C corporation. Alternatively, if Mark formed the corporation in a year when the Sec. 1202 exclusion percentage

▼ **TABLE I:18-3**

S Corporation Versus C Corporation

Years of Operation (n)	(1) S Corporation[a]	(2) C Corporation[b] (50% Exclusion)	(3) C Corporation[c] (100% Exclusion)
1	$ 5,540,000	$ 5,475,200	$ 5,475,200
2	6,138,320	6,006,854	6,006,854
3	6,801,259	6,601,668	6,601,668
4	7,535,794	7,267,146	7,267,146
5	8,349,660	8,011,683	8,011,683
6	9,251,424	9,133,021	9,805,839
7	10,250,577	10,134,864	10,970,772
8	11,357,640	11,255,726	12,274,100
9	12,584,265	12,509,746	13,732,263
10	13,943,365	13,912,744	15,363,656
11	15,449,249	15,482,418	17,188,859
12	17,117,768	17,238,570	19,230,895

[a]For all n, ATA = $5,000,000[1 + 0.18(1 − 0.4)]^n
[b]For n = 1 through 5, ATA = $5,000,000\{[1 + 0.18(1 − 0.34)]^n(1 − 0.20) + 0.20\}$
For n > 5, ATA = $5,000,000\{[1 + 0.18(1 − 0.34)]^n(1 − 0.14) + 0.14\}$
[c]For n = 1 through 5, the same as in Column 2
For n > 5, $5,000,000 [1 + 0.18 (1 − 0.34)]^n

was 100%, the C corporation form would beat the S corporation form for all holding periods exceeding five years (see Column 3). This result occurs because his effective marginal tax rate on any shareholder-level capital gain would be zero after a five-year holding period and because his individual ordinary tax rate exceeds the corporate tax rate. ◀

 **STOP & THINK**

Question: Assume that a flow-through entity and a C corporation earn the same BTROR, that is, $R_f = R_c$. Given the following comparisons of the corporate tax rate (t_c) and the owner's tax rate (t_p), can you tell from just looking at the two models which entity form is better from a tax perspective?

Comparison 1: $t_c = t_p$
Comparison 2: $t_c > t_p$
Comparison 3: $t_c < t_p$

Solution: In Comparisons 1 and 2, the flow-through entity is always better than the C corporation (given $R_f = R_c$). In Comparison 3, however, the answer is not obvious. Consider the two models:

Flow-through: $[1 + R_f(1 - t_p)]^n$
C corporation: $[1 + R_c(1 - t_c)]^n(1 - t_p) + t_p$

Notice that, if $R_f = R_c$ and $t_c = t_p$, the bracketed terms in the two models will be equal, which means the flow-through entity accumulation equals the corporate-level accumulation. The C corporation, however, entails additional taxation at the shareholder level, which is represented by the terms following the bracketed term. This additional tax makes the C corporation worse than the flow-through entity. If $t_c > t_p$, the bracketed term in the C corporation model accumulates to a lesser amount than does the flow-through model, and the shareholder-level tax just makes matters worse. Thus, the flow-through entity again is the preferred form. Finally, if $t_c < t_p$, the bracketed term in the C corporation model accumulates to a greater amount than does the flow-through model, but the shareholder level tax lessens the overall benefit. However, whether the overall effect causes the C corporation to be better than the flow-through entity depends on how much t_p exceeds t_c and on how long the investment horizon (n) is. Thus, the answer is not obvious.

CURRENT SALARY VERSUS DEFERRED COMPENSATION

Chapter I:9 introduced the characteristics of a nonqualified deferred compensation plan. This arrangement differs from current salary in that the employer's deduction and the employee's inclusion in gross income occur later than with current salary. The key question, then, is whether an employee should choose current salary or deferred compensation. The decision model developed in this section helps answer this question. Because both the employer and the employee are affected by the timing of compensation, the decision model must incorporate these dual effects. Specifically, the model includes the current and future tax rates of the employer and employee as well as the employer's and employee's ATRORs.

The Employee's Point of View. The employee can choose between current salary in Year 0 or deferred compensation in Year n. If the employee chooses current salary, the employee immediately pays taxes on the salary and invests the after-tax amount at his or her ATROR.[7] If, instead, the employee receives deferred compensation, the employee pays taxes on this compensation in Year n, leaving an after-tax amount of deferred compensation. These two alternatives are comparable because both are stated in terms of future values.

REAL-WORLD EXAMPLE

To successfully defer income in nonqualified deferral compensation plans, taxpayers must satisfy strict requirements set forth in Sec. 409A. Essentially, the requirements discourage taxpayers from taking early distributions or accelerated benefits from such plans. The rules also dictate when the taxpayer must make the election to defer: generally the year before the deferral or, for compensation based on performance over 12 months, at least six months before year-end. Failure to meet the Sec. 409A requirements results in immediate recognition of previously deferred income plus a 20% penalty.

---

[7] The employee also could spend the current salary. However, this current consumption is equivalent to the future consumption available if the employee invests and spends later. In this case, the investment assumption gives the future value of current consumption. Thus, whether the employee actually spends or invests, the investment assumption provides the future value of that decision.

TOPIC REVIEW I:18-2

Flow-Through and C Corporation Models

Flow-Through Model:
$$ATA = Contribution[1 + R_f(1 - t_p)]^n$$

C Corporation Model:
$$ATA = Contribution[(1 + r_c)^n(1 - t_p) + t_p]$$

or

$$ATA = Contribution\{ [1 + R_c(1 - t_c)]^n(1 - t_p) + t_p\}$$

Definitions of Variables:
R_f = Flow-through entity's BTROR
R_c = C corporation's BTROR
t_p = Owner's marginal tax rate
t_c = C corporation's marginal tax rate
r_c = C corporation's ATROR
n = Investment horizon

EXAMPLE I:18-24 ▶ Bruce works for Xeron Corporation and is considering receiving either $10,000 of current salary or $25,000 of deferred compensation in ten years. His current tax rate is 40%, but he expects his tax rate to be 25% ten years from now. Bruce can invest any after-tax current salary at a 10% ATROR. If Bruce receives current salary and invests the after-tax amount, his investment will accumulate as follows:

$$\$10,000(1 - 0.4)(1.1)^{10} = \$15,562$$

Bruce's after-tax salary is $6,000, which grows to $15,562 in ten years if invested at a 10% ATROR. Thus, this calculation, which is an application of the Current Model, gives the future value of Bruce's after-tax current salary. Alternatively, if Bruce receives deferred compensation, his after-tax deferred compensation is calculated as follows:

$$\$25,000(1 - 0.25) = \$18,750$$

In this case, Bruce prefers the deferred compensation alternative because he will have $18,750 in ten years instead of $15,562 under the current salary alternative. ◄

Using general terms, we can state the employee's current salary and deferred compensation alternatives as follows:

$$CSI = BT\$(1 - t_{po})(1 + r_p)^n$$
$$DCI = BT\$(D_n)(1 - t_{pn})$$

In these formulas, CSI stands for current salary income and is the employee's after-tax future value of current salary; DCI stands for deferred compensation income and is the employee's after-tax future value of deferred compensation; and BT$ stands for before-tax current salary. In the second formula, D_n is the amount of deferred compensation received in lieu of $1 currently. Accordingly, BT$ × D_n gives total deferred compensation before taxes. For example, in Example I:18-24, BT$ = $10,000, and BT$ × D_n = $25,000. Thus, D_n = 2.50. In other words, Bruce could choose between $1 of current salary or $2.50 of deferred compensation, before taxes. The factor, BT$, converts these per dollar amounts to total dollars of current salary or deferred compensation. The other variables in the formulas are defined as follows:

▶ t_{po} = The employee's marginal tax rate in Year 0

▶ t_{pn} = The employee's marginal tax rate in Year n

► r_p = The employee's ATROR

► n = The number of years until the employee receives the deferred compensation

The employee prefers deferred compensation if DCI exceeds CSI. From the previous formulas, this relationship can be expressed as follows:

$$DCI > CSI \text{ or}$$

$$BT\$(D_n)(1 - t_{pn}) > BT\$(1 - t_{po})(1 + r_p)^n$$

Solving the second expression for D_n yields:

$$D_n > \frac{(1 - t_{po})(1 + r_p)^n}{(1 - t_{pn})}$$

The level of D_n that exactly equals the right-hand side of this expression makes the employee indifferent to receiving current salary or deferred compensation. That is, at the indifference level of D_n, the employee's current salary income (CSI) equals the employee's deferred compensation income (DCI). Levels of D_n above the indifference level make deferred compensation more beneficial than current salary to the employee.

EXAMPLE I:18-25 ▶

Assume the same facts as in Example I:18-24. Bruce prefers deferred compensation rather than $1 of current salary if D_n exceeds 2.0750, calculated as follows:

$$D_n > \frac{(1 - 0.4)(1.1)^{10}}{(1 - 0.25)} = 2.0750$$

Therefore, D_n = 2.0750 is Bruce's indifference level, as shown by the following calculation for $1 of current salary:

$$CSI = \$1\,(1 - 0.4)(1.1)^{10} = \$1.5562$$
$$DCI = \$1\,(2.0750)(1 - 0.25) = \$1.5562$$

Given a choice between $10,000 of current salary (BT$) and deferred compensation, Bruce will prefer deferred compensation to current salary if the deferred compensation exceeds $20,750, which is $10,000 × 2.0750. ◀

The Employer's Point of View. The issue from the employer's point of view is whether the employer is willing to pay deferred compensation in lieu of current salary. If the employer pays current salary, the employer takes a business deduction and obtains an immediate tax benefit. The current salary net of the tax benefit is the employer's after-tax salary expense. This after-tax amount must be projected to Year n to be comparable to the alternative deferred compensation expense. We compound the after-tax salary expense at the employer's ATROR because, if the employer does not pay the salary, the employer will have the after-tax amount available for investment in its business. This investment, in turn, grows at the employer's ATROR. Thus, compounding determines the future value of the employer's after-tax salary expense. If instead of paying salary the employer pays deferred compensation, the employer deducts the deferred compensation expense in Year n. The deferred compensation net of the Year n tax benefit is the employer's after-tax deferred compensation expense.

EXAMPLE I:18-26 ▶

Again consider the facts in Example I:18-24, that is, $10,000 of current salary versus $25,000 of deferred compensation in ten years. In addition, the employer's current tax rate is 39%, but the employer expects its tax rate to be 34% ten years from now. The employer's ATROR is 10%. If the employer pays current salary, its after-tax salary expense projected to Year n is calculated as follows:

$$\$10,000(1 - 0.39)(1.1)^{10} = \$15,822$$

Alternatively, the after-tax deferred compensation expense is calculated as follows:

$$\$25{,}000(1 - 0.34) = \$16{,}500$$

In this case, the employer's after-tax deferred compensation expense ($16,500) exceeds its after-tax salary expense ($15,822). Consequently, the employer is unwilling to pay Bruce the $25,000 of deferred compensation even though Bruce prefers that alternative. ◀

Using general terms, we can state the employer's current salary and deferred compensation alternatives as follows:

$$CSE = BT\$(1 - t_{co})(1 + r_c)^n$$
$$DCE = BT\$(D_n)(1 - t_{cn})$$

In these formulas, CSE stands for current salary expense and is the employer's after-tax salary expense projected to Year n; DCE stands for deferred compensation expense and is the employer's after-tax deferred compensation expense in Year n; and BT$ stands for before-tax current salary. As before, D_n equals the amount of deferred compensation paid in lieu of $1 currently. Accordingly, $BT\$ \times D_n$ gives total deferred compensation before taxes. The other variables in the formulas are defined as follows:

▶ t_{co} = The employer's marginal tax rate in Year 0
▶ t_{cn} = The employer's marginal tax rate in Year n
▶ r_c = The employer's ATROR
▶ n = The number of years until the employer pays the deferred compensation

The employer will pay deferred compensation only if DCE does not exceed CSE. From the previous formulas, this relationship can be expressed as follows:

$$DCE \leq CSE \text{ or}$$
$$BT\$(D_n)(1 - t_{cn}) \leq BT\$(1 - t_{co})(1 + r_c)^n$$

Solving the second expression for D_n yields:

$$D_n \leq \frac{(1 - t_{co})(1 + r_c)^n}{(1 - t_{cn})}$$

The level of D_n that exactly equals the right-hand side of this expression makes the employer indifferent to paying current salary or deferred compensation. That is, at the indifference level of D_n, the employer's current salary expense (CSE) equals the employer's deferred compensation expense (DCE). Levels of D_n below the indifference level make deferred compensation more beneficial than current salary to the employer.

EXAMPLE I:18-27 ▶ Assume the same facts as in Example I:18-26. Compared to $1 of current salary, the employer will pay deferred compensation only if D_n does not exceed 2.3972, calculated as follows:

$$D_n \leq \frac{(1 - 0.39)(1.1)^{10}}{(1 - 0.34)} = 2.3972$$

Therefore, $D_n = 2.3972$ is the employer's indifference level, as shown by the following calculation for $1 of current salary:

$$CSE = \$1(1 - 0.39)(1.1)^{10} = \$1.5822$$
$$DCE = \$1(2.3972)(1 - 0.34) = \$1.5822$$

Given a choice between $10,000 of current salary (BT$) and deferred compensation, the employer will pay deferred compensation instead of current salary only if deferred compensation does not exceed $23,972, which is $10,000 × 2.3972. ◀

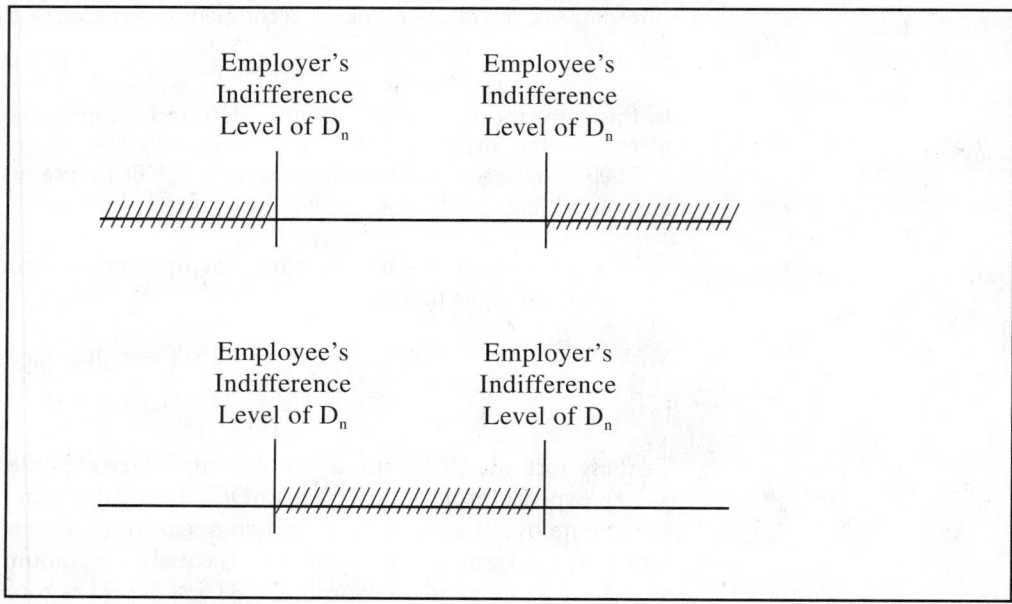

FIGURE I:18-2 ► Comparing the Employee's and Employer's Views

Comparing the Employee's and Employer's Views. Knowledge of the employee's and employer's acceptable levels of D_n gives the two parties the necessary tools to decide whether deferred compensation is preferable to current salary. Specifically, the employee and employer can apply the following decision rules:

► If the employee's indifference level of D_n exceeds the employer's indifference level of D_n, the employee must accept current salary because the employer will not pay the employee's required deferred compensation.

► If the employee's indifference level of D_n is less than the employer's indifference level of D_n, the employer can pay deferred compensation up to its indifference level.

Figure I:18-2 shows these decision rules graphically. In both graphs, the shaded portion of the lines indicates the employee's and employer's acceptable levels of D_n. In the top graph, these areas are separated, leaving the middle part of the line empty. This empty region indicates the employee and employer cannot agree on a mutually acceptable level of D_n. In the bottom graph, however, the employee's and employer's acceptable levels of D_n overlap in the middle part of the line. Thus, both parties can accept any level of D_n in this region. For example, in Examples I:18-25 and I:18-27 the parties could agree on deferred compensation between $20,750 and $23,972.

EXAMPLE I:18-28 ► Marsha and Todd are employed by Omega Corporation. They want to compare deferred compensation two years from now (n = 2) to $10,000 of current salary. Assume the following tax rates and rates of return:

	Year 0	Year n	ATROR
Marsha	$t_{po} = 0.30$	$t_{pn} = 0.15$	$r_p = 0.10$
Todd	$t_{po} = 0.40$	$t_{pn} = 0.15$	$r_p = 0.10$
Omega Corporation	$t_{co} = 0.39$	$t_{cn} = 0.25$	$r_c = 0.10$

The indifference level of D_n for each party is as follows:

Marsha:
$$D_n = \frac{(1 - 0.30)(1.1)^2}{(1 - 0.15)} = 0.9965$$

Todd:
$$D_n = \frac{(1 - 0.4)(1.1)^2}{(1 - 0.15)} = 0.8541$$

Omega Corporation:
$$D_n = \frac{(1 - 0.39)(1.1)^2}{(1 - 0.25)} = 0.9841$$

Compared to $10,000 of current salary, Omega Corporation will pay no more than $9,841 of deferred compensation. Consequently, Marsha must settle for $10,000 of current salary because she requires more than $9,965 of deferred compensation to make that alternative preferable. This amount exceeds what Omega Corporation is willing to pay as deferred compensation.

Todd, on the other hand, can benefit from a deferred compensation arrangement. He requires deferred compensation exceeding $8,541, and Omega Corporation is willing to pay up to $9,841 of deferred compensation. ◀

We can provide additional insight into the salary versus deferred compensation decision by carrying Example I:18-28 a bit further. If Omega Corporation pays Todd $9,841 of deferred compensation, Omega Corporation incurs the same after-tax expense it would have incurred had it paid $10,000 of current salary. Thus, Omega Corporation remains indifferent, and Todd obtains the full benefit of the deferred compensation arrangement. This outcome can be seen with the following income and expense amounts:

Todd:
$$CSI = \$10,000(1 - 0.4)(1.1)^2 = \$7,260$$
$$DCI = \$10,000(0.9841)(1 - 0.15) = \$8,365$$

Omega Corporation:
$$CSE = \$10,000(1 - 0.39)(1.1)^2 = \$7,381$$
$$DCE = \$10,000(0.9841)(1 - 0.25) = \$7,381$$

Because Omega Corporation pays its indifference level of D_n, its current salary and deferred compensation expenses are equal. Under the deferred compensation arrangement, however, Todd ends up with $8,365 rather than $7,260.

Suppose instead that Omega Corporation pays deferred compensation that makes Todd indifferent. In this case, Todd obtains the same amount of after-tax income as under the salary option, and Omega Corporation obtains the full benefit of the deferred compensation arrangement. This outcome can be seen with the following income and expense amounts:

Todd:
$$CSI = \$10,000(1 - 0.4)(1.1)^2 = \$7,260$$
$$DCI = \$10,000(0.8541)(1 - 0.15) = \$7,260$$

Omega Corporation:
$$CSE = \$10,000(1 - 0.39)(1.1)^2 = \$7,381$$
$$DCE = \$10,000(0.8541)(1 - 0.25) = \$6,406$$

Because Omega Corporation pays Todd's indifference level of D_n, Todd's current salary and deferred compensation income are equal. Under the deferred compensation arrangement, however, Omega Corporation's deferred compensation expense ($6,406) is less than the alternative current salary expense ($7,381).

In each case, one party was made indifferent while the other party benefited from the deferred compensation alternative. However, Omega Corporation also could pay deferred compensation somewhere between the two indifference levels of D_n. The shaded middle region in the bottom graph of Figure I:18-2 depicts this range. For example, suppose Omega Corporation chose $D_n = 0.92$. The following outcomes would occur:

Todd:
$$CSI = \$10,000(1 - 0.4)(1.1)^2 = \$7,260$$
$$DCI = \$10,000(0.92)(1 - 0.15) = \$7,820$$

Omega Corporation:
$$CSE = \$10,000(1 - 0.39)(1.1)^2 = \$7,381$$
$$DCE = \$10,000(0.92)(1 - 0.25) = \$6,900$$

In this case, Todd's deferred compensation income is $7,820 rather than $7,260 of current salary income. In addition, Omega Corporation's deferred compensation expense is $6,900 rather than the $7,381 current salary expense. Thus, both parties are better off with the deferred compensation arrangement than with current salary. However, neither party is as well off had the other party remained indifferent. In short, they share the benefit.

The preceding analysis incorporated tax rates and ATRORs in the decision model for current salary versus deferred compensation. The outcomes in the examples, however, depended only on the differential tax rates across taxpayers and over time because the

ATRORs of the employer and employees were the same. In other situations, the employer's ATROR may differ from that of the employees, further influencing the results.

? **STOP & THINK**

Question: What nontax factors might affect the current salary versus deferred compensation decision, possibly overriding the tax factors?

Solution: In addition to tax factors, the parties must consider their cash-flow requirements. If the employee needs cash now, he or she may be unwilling to defer income despite a better result from the decision model. Similarly, an employer short on current cash may prefer deferred compensation even though the decision model suggests current salary as the better alternative. Deferred compensation also carries some risk. Under nonqualified deferred compensation plans, the employee becomes a general creditor of the employer. Consequently, if the employer runs into financial difficulties later, the employer may not be able to pay the deferred compensation. The employee, therefore, may decide for the safe alternative, current salary, regardless of the decision model outcome. Finally, deferred compensation may lock the employee into continued employment unless the deferred compensation contract makes adequate provision for the employee's severance.

Summary. The decision model developed in this section provides an analytic tool for employees and employers to plan current salary versus deferred compensation arrangements. The model takes into account the tax and ATROR attributes of both parties to the transaction. This approach prevents one party benefiting at the disadvantage of the other and therefore leads to the best overall solution. Topic Review I:18-3 summarizes the decision model.

TOPIC REVIEW I:18-3

Current Salary Versus Deferred Compensation

EMPLOYEE'S POINT OF VIEW

$$CSI = BT\$(1 - t_{po})(1 + r_p)^n$$
$$DCI = BT\$(D_n)(1 - t_{pn})$$

$$D_n = \frac{(1 - t_{po})(1 + r_p)^n}{(1 - t_{pn})}$$

EMPLOYER'S POINT OF VIEW

$$CSE = BT\$(1 - t_{co})(1 + r_c)^n$$
$$DCE = BT\$(D_n)(1 - t_{cn})$$

$$OD_n = \frac{(1 - t_{co})(1 + r_c)^n}{(1 - t_{cn})}$$

Decision rules:

▶ If the employee's indifference level of D_n exceeds the employer's indifference level of D_n, the employee must accept current salary because the employer will not pay the employee's required deferred compensation.

▶ If the employee's indifference level of D_n is less than the employer's indifference level of D_n, the employer can pay deferred compensation up to its indifference level.

Definitions of Variables:

CSI = Current salary income; employee's after-tax future value of before-tax current salary
DCI = Deferred compensation income; employee's after-tax future value of deferred compensation
CSE = Current salary expense; employer's after-tax salary expense projected to Year n
DCE = Deferred compensation expense; employer's after-tax deferred compensation expense in Year n
$BT\$$ = Before-tax current salary
D_n = Amount of deferred compensation paid in lieu of $1 of current salary
t_{po} = Employee's marginal tax rate in Year 0
t_{pn} = Employee's marginal tax rate in Year n
r_p = Employee's ATROR
t_{co} = Employer's marginal tax rate in Year 0
t_{cn} = Employer's marginal tax rate in Year n
r_c = Employer's ATROR
n = Number of years until the deferred compensation is paid

IMPLICIT TAXES AND CLIENTELES

OBJECTIVE 3

Recognize the role of implicit taxes in investment decisions

Several of the investment vehicles we modeled earlier have certain tax benefits compared to other investments. For example, interest earned on tax-exempt investments, such as state and local bonds, is excluded from gross income. The Exempt Model reflects this tax benefit. As another example, assets that generate long-term capital gains also are tax favored. The taxation of the capital gain is deferred until realization, and then the realized gain may be subject to the applicable capital gains tax rate. The Deferred Model, when applied to capital gain assets, reflects this preferential taxation. For the sake of simplicity, however, this section focuses on tax-exempt bonds to introduce the concept of implicit taxes and clientele effects.

Implicit Taxes. Consider what happens in the marketplace for tax-favored assets. Given a choice between a fully-taxable investment and a tax-favored investment, investors will prefer the tax-favored investment, assuming the two investments are equally risky. This preference manifests itself as an increased demand for the tax-favored investment, thereby driving up the asset's price. The increased price, in turn, causes the asset's BTROR to decrease. For example, the BTROR on a bond with an unlimited life (a perpetuity) is as follows:

$$BTROR = \frac{\text{Annual cash flow}}{\text{Bond's price}}$$

If the bond's price increases, the BTROR must decrease.

The difference between the BTRORs of the fully-taxable and tax-favored investments is an implicit tax, which can be expressed as follows:

$$IT = R_b - R_e$$

In this formula, IT stands for implicit tax, R_b is the BTROR on a fully-taxable benchmark investment, and R_e is the BTROR on a tax-favored investment having the same risk level as the benchmark. (Later in this chapter, we will show the problem with comparing investments of unequal risk.) Dividing the implicit tax by the benchmark BTROR (R_b) converts the implicit tax (IT) to an implicit tax *rate* (t_I), expressed as follows:

$$t_I = \frac{R_b - R_e}{R_b}$$

EXAMPLE I:18-29 ▶ Maria invests $1,000 in a taxable bond that yields a 10% BTROR and another $1,000 in a tax-exempt bond that yields a 7.5% BTROR (i.e., $R_b = 10\%$, and $R_e = 7.5\%$). Maria's marginal tax rate is 25% (i.e., t = 25%). The two investments yield the following earnings each year:

	Taxable Bond	Tax-Exempt Bond
Before-tax interest	$100	$75
Minus: Explicit tax on interest	(25)	0
After-tax interest	$ 75	$75

Although the tax-exempt bond is free from explicit taxation, it reflects a 2.5% implicit tax, which is $R_b - R_e = 10\% - 7.5\% = 2.5\%$. Here, we express the implicit tax as a 2.5% reduction in the BTROR. Stated in dollars, the implicit tax is $1,000 × 0.025 = $25. Thus, Maria incurs a $25 explicit tax on the taxable bond and a $25 implicit tax on the tax-exempt bond. Maria's implicit tax *rate* on the tax-exempt bond is 25%, calculated as follows:

$$t_I = \frac{R_b - R_e}{R_b} = \frac{10\% - 7.5\%}{10\%} = 0.25 \text{ or } 25\%$$

Thus, Maria incurs a 25% explicit tax *rate* on the taxable bond and a 25% implicit tax *rate* on the tax-exempt bond.

Maria's ATROR on each bond is 7.5%. For the taxable bond, the ATROR is calculated as follows: $r_b = R_b(1 - t) = 10\%(1 - 0.25) = 7.5\%$. For the tax-exempt bond, the ATROR is the same as the BTROR. ◀

Equilibrium Condition and Clienteles. The degree to which R_e falls in relation to R_b depends on the marginal investor's tax rate. By definition, marginal investors are indifferent between fully-taxable and tax-favored investments. As marginal investors compete for a tax-favored investment, supply and demand forces drive up its price (and reduce its BTROR) to the point where the ATRORs of the fully-taxable and tax-favored investments are equal. That is, in equilibrium for marginal investors, the ATRORs for investments meet the following condition: $r_b = r_e$. For example, in Example I:18-29, Maria is a marginal investor because $r_b = r_e = 7.5\%$. Thus, Maria is indifferent between the two investments. (Note that, for tax-exempt bonds, $r_e = R_e$.)

In Example I:18-29, Maria incurred a 25% tax rate on each investment, explicit on the fully-taxable bond and implicit on the tax-exempt bond. Thus, Maria did not realize a tax benefit on the tax-exempt bond. In fact, the term *tax-exempt* is a misnomer when implicit taxes are considered. The issuer of the tax-exempt bond, however, received a tax subsidy in the form of a reduced interest rate. Therefore, the transaction works as though Maria paid a tax while the bond issuer received a subsidy.

This result leads to the following question: Can any investor benefit from tax-exempt bonds? In a flat-rate tax system where only one tax rate prevails, the answer is no because all investors are marginal investors. In a progressive tax rate system, however, the answer is yes for an investor whose marginal tax rate exceeds that of the marginal investor. In this situation, investors form natural clienteles for the alternative investments.

EXAMPLE I:18-30 ▶ Assume the same facts as in Example I:18-29, where Maria is the indifferent marginal investor. Consider two other investors, Silvia and Bob. Silvia's tax rate is 40%, and Bob's tax rate is 15%. If Silvia invested in a fully-taxable bond, her ATROR would be as follows: $r_b = 10\%(1 - 0.4) = 6\%$. Consequently, Silvia will prefer the tax-exempt bond that yields a 7.5% ATROR (which also equals its BTROR). Silvia's high tax rate puts her in the clientele for tax-exempt bonds. By investing in the tax-exempt bond, Silvia converts her 40% explicit tax rate into a 25% implicit tax rate, thereby giving her the higher ATROR.

If Bob invests in the fully-taxable bond, his ATROR will be as follows: $r_b = 10\%(1 - 0.15) = 8.5\%$. Thus, Bob prefers the fully-taxable bond because he obtains an 8.5% ATROR rather than 7.5% from the tax-exempt bond. Bob's low tax rate puts him in the clientele for taxable bonds. If he mistakenly invests in the tax-exempt bond, he will convert a 15% explicit tax rate into a 25% implicit tax rate. Therefore, he should avoid the tax-exempt bond. ◀

Risky Assets. A key requirement for calculating the implicit tax rate on a tax-favored investment is that the risk level be the same as the benchmark investment. The BTROR of a risky asset has two components, the riskless return and a risk premium. This relationship can be formulated as follows:

$$\tilde{R} = R + P$$

In this formula, $\tilde{R}$ is the risky return, R is the riskless return, and P is the risk premium. Investors who invest in risky assets require this premium as an incentive to make the investment. If the benchmark investment is a fully-taxable, riskless bond, the tax-favored investment's BTROR must be adjusted to remove this risk premium to obtain an accurate measure of the implicit tax rate.

EXAMPLE I:18-31 ▶ A tax-exempt bond issued by Troubled City is highly risky and therefore yields a 12% BTROR, which is composed of a 7% riskless return and a 5% risk premium. A riskless benchmark investment yields a 10% BTROR. Computing the implicit tax rate with the 12% return yields the following incorrect (and negative) implicit tax rate:

$$t_I = \frac{R_b - \tilde{R}_e}{R_b} = \frac{10\% - 12\%}{10\%} = -0.2 \text{ or } -20\%$$

The correct implicit tax rate is calculated with the risk-adjusted return as follows:

$$t_I = \frac{R_b - R_e}{R_b} = \frac{10\% - 7\%}{10\%} = 0.30 \text{ or } 30\%$$ ◀

Summary. Market forces drive down the BTRORs of tax-favored assets. This reduced return is an implicit tax. Thus, potential tax benefits to a marginal investor are competed away, thereby providing an implicit subsidy to the asset's issuer or seller. Investors whose tax rate exceeds that of the marginal investor, however, still can reap some benefit through the clientele effect. Topic Review I:18-4 summarizes the implicit tax rate formula.

TOPIC REVIEW I:18-4

Implicit Taxes

Implicit tax:
   $IT = R_b - R_e$

Implicit tax rate:

   $$t_I = \frac{R_b - R_e}{R_b}$$

Equilibrium condition for marginal investor:
   $r_b = r_e$.

Definitions of Variables:
   IT = Implicit tax
   t_I = Implicit tax rate
   R_b = BTROR on a fully-taxable benchmark investment
   R_e = Risk-adjusted BTROR on a tax-favored investment
   r_b = ATROR on a fully-taxable benchmark investment
   r_e = Risk-adjusted ATROR on a tax-favored investment

PROBLEM MATERIALS

DISCUSSION QUESTIONS

I:18-1 What is the primary distinguishing feature that causes the Current Model, Deferred Model, and Pension Model to differ?

I:18-2 What is an annualized ATROR, and why is it useful?

I:18-3 Why might an investment in a capital asset be preferable to an investment that is fully taxed currently even though the capital asset's BTROR is less than that of the fully-taxable investment?

I:18-4 Suppose a taxpayer is trying to decide between saving outside an IRA or saving through a traditional IRA. If the taxpayer needs the savings before reaching age 59½, should he or she necessarily avoid the IRA because of the 10% early withdrawal penalty? Why or why not? If the taxpayer must make a withdrawal before age 59½, which IRA might be better, the traditional IRA or the Roth IRA?

I:18-5 How does the length of the investment horizon affect the annualized ATROR of an investment conforming to the Deferred Model?

I:18-6 Under what conditions are the Exempt Model and Pension Model equivalent? Under what conditions would one model perform better than the other? How does the $5,500 limitation on deductible and Roth IRA contributions (in 2015) affect the comparison of these two vehicles?

I:18-7 What characteristics of a C corporation cause the shareholder's stock investment to conform to the Deferred Model?

I:18-8 How does the tax treatment of deferred compensation differ from the tax treatment of current salary?

I:18-9 What is the variable, D_n, and why is it important to the current salary versus deferred compensation decision?

I:18-10 Why might the employee and/or employer prefer salary over deferred compensation even in cases where deferred compensation provides the better tax results?

I:18-11 Why might an investment conforming to the Exempt Model have a lower BTROR than would an equivalent-risk investment conforming to the Current Model?

I:18-12 What is an implicit tax, and how does it arise?

I:18-13 What forces cause ATRORs of various investments to be equal for marginal investors?

I:18-14 What is a clientele effect, and what conditions are necessary for it to occur?

I:18-15 An article that appeared in a financial publication several years ago made a statement similar to the following:

At the highest federal tax rates, interest from private sector investments are taxed at 40%, capital gains at 20%, while interest from state and local debt instruments isn't taxed at all.

What problem do you see with the author's statement?

I:18-16 Why would a flat-rate tax system eliminate clientele effects?

I:18-17 Why might the BTROR on a tax-favored investment be higher than the BTROR on a fully-taxable investment even though implicit tax theory says that it should be lower?

I:18-18 We have discussed implicit taxes using tax-exempt bonds as an example, and we have mentioned capital gains assets as another case where implicit taxes might occur. Give one or two other specific tax provisions that might cause implicit taxes to arise. In so doing, explain:
- How the implicit tax is manifested (e.g., increased prices, reduced returns, increased costs, etc.).
- Who "pays" the implicit tax.
- Who "receives" the implicit subsidy.

PROBLEMS

I:18-19 *Tax-Exempt Bond.* Laura, who is in the 35% tax bracket, notices that tax-exempt municipal bonds are yielding a 7% return. What before-tax rate of return on a fully-taxable bond must Laura obtain to make her prefer the taxable bond over the tax-exempt bond?

I:18-20 *After-Tax Rates of Return.* Suppose a bond is taxable for both federal and state purposes. Let R_b = the BTROR on the bond, t_{fed} = the federal tax rate, and t_{st} = the state tax rate. Determine the ATROR (i.e., after federal and state taxes) if:
a. The state tax is *not* deductible for either federal or state purposes.
b. The state tax *is* deductible for federal but not for state purposes.
After algebraic simplification, each answer should take the form: $R_b($), with the rest of the answer inside the parentheses.
c. After determining the formulas for Parts a and b, determine the ATRORs assuming that the BTROR (R_b) is 8%, the federal tax rate (t_{fed}) is 40%, and the state tax rate (t_{st}) is 6%.

I:18-21 *Investment Models.* David can make a single investment in one of three alternatives. The first investment conforms to the Current Model, the second investment conforms to the Deferred Model, and the third investment conforms to the Pension Model. The investment horizon is seven years, and the BTROR for each alternative is 10%. David will incur no penalties upon withdrawal.
a. Assuming David's tax rate will be 15% for all seven years, what is the accumulation and annualized ATROR for each investment? Which alternative should David choose?
b. Assuming David's tax rate will be 15% for the first six years but will be 25% in the seventh year, what is the accumulation and annualized ATROR for each investment? Which alternative should David choose?

I:18-22 *Investment Models.* Mark is considering investing in either a tax-exempt municipal bond that yields 7% or a nondeductible IRA that contains investments that yield 10% before taxes. (Mark is ineligible to contribute to a Roth IRA.) Mark's current tax rate is 35%, and he plans to make a single investment now with a 15-year investment horizon.
a. Using after-tax accumulations and annualized ATRORs, show that the nondeductible IRA outperforms the municipal bonds assuming Mark's tax rate remains at 35%. Assume no additional penalty upon withdrawal from the IRA.
b. How high would Mark's tax rate have to rise in Year n to make the municipal bond more attractive than the nondeductible IRA? Assume the 7% and 10% BTRORs remain constant over time.

I:18-23 *Investment Models and IRAs.* Brenda has $5,500 of before-tax dollars available for a one-time investment. She is in the 25% bracket and expects to remain in this bracket indefinitely. She can invest directly in a taxable bond yielding 8% before taxes, or she can open an IRA and invest in the bond within the IRA. She knows that she will need the accumulated funds before she reaches age 59½. Thus, if she invests in an IRA, she will incur a 10% penalty on taxable amounts withdrawn from the IRA. Note: The two parts to this problem are best solved using a spreadsheet.

   a. If she invests in an IRA that allows immediate deduction of contributed amounts (i.e., a traditional deductible IRA), how many years must she wait before the IRA is a better vehicle than direct investment in the bond outside the IRA?

   b. How many years must she wait if she invests in a Roth IRA? Reminder: Withdrawals from a Roth IRA first come from contributions and are a nontaxable return of capital. However, if Brenda withdraws the *entire* accumulation before she attains age 59½, the accumulated earnings will be fully taxable and also subject to the 10% early withdrawal penalty. Hence, in this situation, the Roth IRA operates exactly like a traditional nondeductible IRA (the Deferred Model instead of the Exempt Model).

I:18-24 *Investment Planning.* Martha, who is in the 35% tax bracket, has $40,000 of before-tax income with which she wants to make a one-time investment. She wants to put $20,000 of this income in a deductible H.R. 10 plan, and she wants to invest any remaining after-tax income outside the H.R. 10 plan. Assume that Martha has sufficient self-employment income such that her contribution does not exceed the H.R. 10 contribution limit. Two investments are available: (1) a taxable bond yielding a 10% BTROR and (2) a nondividend paying stock that appreciates at a 10% annual rate before taxes. She is considering two alternatives:

   1. Have the H.R. 10 plan invest in the stock, and Martha will invest in the bond outside the H.R. 10 plan.

   2. Have the H.R. 10 plan invest in the bond, and Martha will invest in the stock outside the H.R. 10 plan.

The investment horizon is ten years with tax rates constant over this period. Capital gains upon sale of stock outside the H.R. 10 plan are taxed at 15%. However, if the stock is placed in the H.R. 10 plan, the H.R. 10 plan will sell the stock after ten years and distribute the proceeds to Martha, triggering ordinary income recognition to Martha. Assume no early withdrawal penalties on H.R. 10 plan distributions. Determine the total after-tax accumulation of Alternative 1 and of Alternative 2. Which of the two alternatives should Martha choose?

I:18-25 *Roth IRA Versus Deductible IRA.* Harry wants to contribute either $5,500 (BT$) to a traditional deductible IRA or $5,500 (AT$) to a Roth IRA. His current tax rate is 30% for ordinary income and 15% for capital gains. He expects his IRA investment to earn a 12% BTROR, and he plans to withdraw the IRA accumulation in 25 years, at which time he will be over age 59½. If he contributes to a deductible IRA, he will invest the tax savings from the deduction in a nondividend paying stock that he expects to grow at a 12% BTROR. Harry will sell the stock at the same time he withdraws the IRA accumulation.

   a. Compare the two alternatives assuming that, at the time of withdrawal, Harry's tax rate will be 30% for ordinary income and 15% for capital gains.

   b. Compare the two alternatives assuming that, at the time of withdrawal, Harry's tax rate will be 15% for ordinary income and 0% for capital gains.

I:18-26 *Roth IRA Versus Deductible IRA.* Beth wants to contribute to either a traditional deductible IRA or a Roth IRA. However, she can afford to contribute only $4,800 after-tax dollars to a Roth IRA even though the maximum contribution is $5,500. Alternatively, she can contribute a comparable amount to a deductible IRA plus an outside investment if necessary. (Remember that deductible IRA contributions are made with before-tax dollars and are limited to $5,500.) Beth's current tax rate is 25%, and she expects her tax rate to remain at 25% throughout the investment period. In addition, she expects her IRA investment to earn a 10% BTROR, and she plans to withdraw the IRA accumulation in 30 years, at which time she will be over age 59 1/2. Any outside investment will conform to the Current Model earning a 10% BTROR. Determine the after-tax accumulation from each IRA alternative. Which of the two IRA types will give Beth the greater after-tax accumulation?

I:18-27   *Multiperiod Investment Strategy.* Given the following facts and assumptions, determine what investment strategy Karen should follow to maximize accumulations and how much she will have accumulated at the *beginning* of Year 10 (including her last paycheck).

- Karen's ordinary tax rate is 25%, and her long-term capital gains tax rate is 15%. These rates will remain constant over her investment horizon.
- Karen earns $40,000 per year, which she receives on the first day of each year.
- Karen saves all her income after paying income taxes on her earnings. Taxes are payable immediately upon receiving her paycheck.
- At the beginning of each year, Karen can invest her savings in any of three vehicles:
  1. A money market fund yielding 6% per year before taxes,
  2. A traditional deductible IRA that yields 6% per year before taxes, and/or
  3. Capital assets that grow at 5.21% per year before taxes.
- IRA contributions are limited to $5,500 per year and are deductible up to that amount. Assume this limit applies to all years under consideration.
- At the beginning of Year 10, Karen saves no more income. Instead, she withdraws any IRA and/or money market accumulations and sells her capital assets for their accumulated FMV before taxes. She also receives a $40,000 paycheck at the beginning of Year 10.
- IRA accumulations are taxable immediately upon withdrawal with no additional penalty.
- Ignore itemized deductions, standard deductions, exemptions, etc.

I:18-28   *Proprietorship Versus C Corporation.* Myron has $10,000 to invest in a business. He can either (1) operate as a sole proprietor or (2) form a regular C corporation by contributing the $10,000 in exchange for corporate stock. In either case, the $10,000 will be invested in business assets and will earn a 10% BTROR for the first five years and an 18% BTROR for years six through 15. All after-tax earnings will be reinvested in the business. If Myron uses the corporate form, the corporation will liquidate at the end of the investment horizon. Myron's personal tax rate is 40%; the corporate tax rate is 25%; and the tax rate on capital gains for individuals is 20% (assume no Sec. 1202 exclusion for gain on the sale of small business stock). Determine whether Myron should operate as a sole proprietor or form a C corporation if the investment horizon is 15 years. Show the after-tax accumulation and annualized after-tax rate of return for each alternative.

I:18-29   *Flow-Through Versus C Corporation.* Twelve years ago, your client formed a C corporation with a $100,000 investment (contribution). The corporation's BTROR (R_c) has been and will continue to be 10%. The corporate tax rate (t_c) has been and will continue to be 35%. The corporation pays no dividends and reinvests all after-tax earnings in its business. Thus, the corporation's value grows at its ATROR. Your client's marginal ordinary tax rate (t_p) has been 33%, and her capital gains rate has been 15%. Your client expects her ordinary tax rate to drop to 25% at the beginning of this year and stay at that level indefinitely. Her capital gains tax rate will remain at 15%. Assume the corporate stock does not qualify for the Sec. 1202 exclusion for gain on the sale of small business stock. Your client wants you to consider three alternatives:

(1) Continue the business in C corporation form for the next 20 years and liquidate at that time (32 years in total).

(2) Liquidate the C corporation at the end of the 12-year period, invest the after-tax proceeds in a sole proprietorship, and operate as a sole proprietorship for the next 20 years.

(3) Make an S corporation election effective at the beginning of this year, operate as an S corporation for the next 20 years, and liquidate the S corporation at that time (32 years in total).

Regarding Alternatives 2 and 3, the sole proprietorship's or S corporation's BTROR (R_p) also will be 10% for the next 20 years. Earnings from the sole proprietorship or S corporation will be taxed currently at your client's ordinary tax rate, and your client will withdraw just enough from the business to pay her taxes. The remaining after-tax earnings will remain in the business until the end of the investment horizon (20 years from now). Show the results of each alternative along with supporting models and calculations. Which alternative should your client adopt? Ignore the accumulated earnings tax for C corporations.

I:18-30 *Flow-Through Versus C Corporation.* Assume the corporation in Problem I:18-29 had been an S corporation for its first 12 years, during which it distributed just enough cash for the shareholder to pay taxes on the flow-through income. Thus, the S corporation reinvested after-tax income. Now the corporation is considering revoking its S election and operating as a C corporation for the remaining 20 years with no dividend distributions. Show the results of remaining an S corporation versus revoking the election. Also show supporting models and calculations. Which alternative should the corporation adopt? Ignore the accumulated earnings tax for C corporations. How does your answer change if the C corporation's tax rate is 15% instead of 35%?

I:18-31 *S Corporation Versus C Corporation.* Consider the following facts:

$$R_f = R_c = 18\%$$
$$t_c = 34\%$$
$$t_p = 40\% \text{ for ordinary income}$$
$$= 20\% \text{ for capital gains}$$
$$n = 5, 25, \text{ or } 50 \text{ years}$$

Other information:
- The corporation is formed with a $10,000 contribution.
- The corporation pays no dividends.
- Assume the Sec. 1202 exclusion for gain on the sale of small business stock does not apply.

a. Using the format below, compare after-tax accumulations for each investment horizon. Should the corporation make the S election for any of these investment horizons?

b. How does your answer change if t_p for ordinary income is 35% instead of 40%?

c. Now assume the 100% Sec. 1202 exclusion applies. How does your answer change in comparison to the S corporation alternative in Part b?

	Years (n)		
	5	25	50
S corporation ($t_p = 40\%$)			
C corporation (no exclusion)			
S corporation ($t_p = 35\%$)			
C corporation (100% exclusion)			

I:18-32 *Current Salary Versus Deferred Compensation.* Consider Marsha and Todd from Example I:18-28 in the text. Suppose these employees worked for Learned University, a tax-exempt organization, instead of a taxable corporation. The university's BTROR equals its ATROR, i.e., $R_c = r_c = 0.10$. Would the university be willing to pay deferred compensation to either employee? If so, how much? That is, what is the university's indifference level of D_n?

I:18-33 *Current Salary Versus Deferred Compensation.* Consider the following facts:

Variables	Case 1	Case 2	Case 3
BT$	$10,000	$10,000	$10,000
t_{po}	.30	.30	.40
t_{pn}	.40	.40	.30
r_p	.10	.10	.10
t_{co}	.35	.35	.35
t_{cn}	.35	.35	.25
r_c	.15	.20	.10
n	3	3	3

a. Complete the following table for each case:

	Case 1	Case 2	Case 3
Employer's D_n			
Employee's D_n			
Decision (CS or DC?)			
CSI			
DCI (employer indiff.)			

CSE
DCE (employer indiff.)
CSI
DCI (employee indiff.)
CSE
DCE (employee indiff.)

b. Suppose in Case 2 from Part a that the employer and employee negotiate a D_n of 1.62. Compute CSI, DCI, CSE, and DCE with this D_n to show that each party to the deferred compensation contract shares in the tax benefit.

I:18-34 *Current Salary Versus Deferred Compensation.* Sandy will earn a $100,000 bonus that can be split between current and deferred compensation in any of the following ways:

Current (BT$)*	Deferred (BT$)*
$100,000	$ –0–
80,000	20,000
60,000	40,000
40,000	60,000
20,000	80,000
–0–	100,000

* The numbers in the above lists are BT$ as in the text formulas. Thus, the numbers in the second column are not BT$ $\times$ D_n.

Assume that Sandy is subject to the following progressive tax rate schedule in the current and future years:

Income Range	Marginal Tax Rate	Computation of Tax
$ 0–20,000	30.0%	$0.30 \times TI$
20,001–40,000	32.5	$ 6,000 + 0.325(TI − $20,000)$
40,001–60,000	35.0	$12,500 + 0.35(TI − $40,000)$
60,001–80,000	37.5	$19,500 + 0.375(TI − $60,000)$
Over 80,000	40.0	$27,000 + 0.4(TI − $80,000)$

- Corporate tax rates are as follows: $t_{co} = .35$, $t_{cn} = .34$.
- Rates of return are as follows: $r_c = .08$; $r_p = .07$.
- The length of deferral is five years, i.e., $n = 5$.

a. What is the best way for Sandy to split the $100,000 bonus given a level of D_n that makes the corporation indifferent?
b. Now assume the bonus allocations are not restricted to $20,000 increments. What is the optimal allocation of the current and deferred bonus given the level of D_n that makes the employer indifferent?

I:18-35 *Implicit Tax Rates and Clientele Effects.* Terry's marginal tax rate is 30%. He can invest in a taxable bond yielding 7.5% before taxes. What is the implicit tax rate on a tax-exempt bond of equivalent risk that yields 6%?
a. Which bond should Terry invest in? Why?
b. How would your answer to Part a change if Terry's statutory marginal tax rate were 15%?

I:18-36 *Implicit Tax Rates and Clientele Effects.* Consider three taxpayers who are in the following tax brackets:

Alice	25%
Brad	35%
Camille	40%

The BTROR on a benchmark investment is 10% (i.e., $R_b = 10\%$). Compute the equilibrium BTROR and the implicit tax rate on a tax-exempt bond under each of the following three alternative assumptions.
a. Alice is the marginal investor.
b. Brad is the marginal investor.
c. Camille is the marginal investor.
d. Which taxpayer (Alice, Brad, or Camille) would Camille like to see be the marginal investor? Why?

2014 TAX TABLES AND RATE SCHEDULES

2015 WITHHOLDING TABLES (PARTIAL)

2014 Tax Table

See the instructions for line 44 to see if you must use the Tax Table below to figure your tax.

Example. Mr. and Mrs. Brown are filing a joint return. Their taxable income on Form 1040, line 43, is $25,300. First, they find the $25,300-25,350 taxable income line. Next, they find the column for married filing jointly and read down the column. The amount shown where the taxable income line and filing status column meet is $2,891. This is the tax amount they should enter on Form 1040, line 44.

Sample Table

At Least	But Less Than	Single	Married filing jointly*	Married filing separately	Head of a household
			Your tax is—		
25,200	25,250	3,330	2,876	3,330	3,136
25,250	25,300	3,338	2,884	3,338	3,144
25,300	25,350	3,345	(2,891)	3,345	3,151
25,350	25,400	3,353	2,899	3,353	3,159

If line 43 (taxable income) is—		And you are—			
At least	But less than	Single	Married filing jointly *	Married filing separately	Head of a household
			Your tax is—		
0	5	0	0	0	0
5	15	1	1	1	1
15	25	2	2	2	2
25	50	4	4	4	4
50	75	6	6	6	6
75	100	9	9	9	9
100	125	11	11	11	11
125	150	14	14	14	14
150	175	16	16	16	16
175	200	19	19	19	19
200	225	21	21	21	21
225	250	24	24	24	24
250	275	26	26	26	26
275	300	29	29	29	29
300	325	31	31	31	31
325	350	34	34	34	34
350	375	36	36	36	36
375	400	39	39	39	39
400	425	41	41	41	41
425	450	44	44	44	44
450	475	46	46	46	46
475	500	49	49	49	49
500	525	51	51	51	51
525	550	54	54	54	54
550	575	56	56	56	56
575	600	59	59	59	59
600	625	61	61	61	61
625	650	64	64	64	64
650	675	66	66	66	66
675	700	69	69	69	69
700	725	71	71	71	71
725	750	74	74	74	74
750	775	76	76	76	76
775	800	79	79	79	79
800	825	81	81	81	81
825	850	84	84	84	84
850	875	86	86	86	86
875	900	89	89	89	89
900	925	91	91	91	91
925	950	94	94	94	94
950	975	96	96	96	96
975	1,000	99	99	99	99

If line 43 (taxable income) is—		And you are—			
At least	But less than	Single	Married filing jointly *	Married filing separately	Head of a household
			Your tax is—		
1,000					
1,000	1,025	101	101	101	101
1,025	1,050	104	104	104	104
1,050	1,075	106	106	106	106
1,075	1,100	109	109	109	109
1,100	1,125	111	111	111	111
1,125	1,150	114	114	114	114
1,150	1,175	116	116	116	116
1,175	1,200	119	119	119	119
1,200	1,225	121	121	121	121
1,225	1,250	124	124	124	124
1,250	1,275	126	126	126	126
1,275	1,300	129	129	129	129
1,300	1,325	131	131	131	131
1,325	1,350	134	134	134	134
1,350	1,375	136	136	136	136
1,375	1,400	139	139	139	139
1,400	1,425	141	141	141	141
1,425	1,450	144	144	144	144
1,450	1,475	146	146	146	146
1,475	1,500	149	149	149	149
1,500	1,525	151	151	151	151
1,525	1,550	154	154	154	154
1,550	1,575	156	156	156	156
1,575	1,600	159	159	159	159
1,600	1,625	161	161	161	161
1,625	1,650	164	164	164	164
1,650	1,675	166	166	166	166
1,675	1,700	169	169	169	169
1,700	1,725	171	171	171	171
1,725	1,750	174	174	174	174
1,750	1,775	176	176	176	176
1,775	1,800	179	179	179	179
1,800	1,825	181	181	181	181
1,825	1,850	184	184	184	184
1,850	1,875	186	186	186	186
1,875	1,900	189	189	189	189
1,900	1,925	191	191	191	191
1,925	1,950	194	194	194	194
1,950	1,975	196	196	196	196
1,975	2,000	199	199	199	199

If line 43 (taxable income) is—		And you are—			
At least	But less than	Single	Married filing jointly *	Married filing separately	Head of a household
			Your tax is—		
2,000					
2,000	2,025	201	201	201	201
2,025	2,050	204	204	204	204
2,050	2,075	206	206	206	206
2,075	2,100	209	209	209	209
2,100	2,125	211	211	211	211
2,125	2,150	214	214	214	214
2,150	2,175	216	216	216	216
2,175	2,200	219	219	219	219
2,200	2,225	221	221	221	221
2,225	2,250	224	224	224	224
2,250	2,275	226	226	226	226
2,275	2,300	229	229	229	229
2,300	2,325	231	231	231	231
2,325	2,350	234	234	234	234
2,350	2,375	236	236	236	236
2,375	2,400	239	239	239	239
2,400	2,425	241	241	241	241
2,425	2,450	244	244	244	244
2,450	2,475	246	246	246	246
2,475	2,500	249	249	249	249
2,500	2,525	251	251	251	251
2,525	2,550	254	254	254	254
2,550	2,575	256	256	256	256
2,575	2,600	259	259	259	259
2,600	2,625	261	261	261	261
2,625	2,650	264	264	264	264
2,650	2,675	266	266	266	266
2,675	2,700	269	269	269	269
2,700	2,725	271	271	271	271
2,725	2,750	274	274	274	274
2,750	2,775	276	276	276	276
2,775	2,800	279	279	279	279
2,800	2,825	281	281	281	281
2,825	2,850	284	284	284	284
2,850	2,875	286	286	286	286
2,875	2,900	289	289	289	289
2,900	2,925	291	291	291	291
2,925	2,950	294	294	294	294
2,950	2,975	296	296	296	296
2,975	3,000	299	299	299	299

(Continued)

* This column must also be used by a qualifying widow(er).

(Continued on page T-3)

2014 Tax Table —*Continued*

3,000

If line 43 (taxable income) is—		And you are—			
At least	But less than	Single	Married filing jointly *	Married filing separately	Head of a household
		Your tax is—			
3,000	3,050	303	303	303	303
3,050	3,100	308	308	308	308
3,100	3,150	313	313	313	313
3,150	3,200	318	318	318	318
3,200	3,250	323	323	323	323
3,250	3,300	328	328	328	328
3,300	3,350	333	333	333	333
3,350	3,400	338	338	338	338
3,400	3,450	343	343	343	343
3,450	3,500	348	348	348	348
3,500	3,550	353	353	353	353
3,550	3,600	358	358	358	358
3,600	3,650	363	363	363	363
3,650	3,700	368	368	368	368
3,700	3,750	373	373	373	373
3,750	3,800	378	378	378	378
3,800	3,850	383	383	383	383
3,850	3,900	388	388	388	388
3,900	3,950	393	393	393	393
3,950	4,000	398	398	398	398

4,000

At least	But less than	Single	Married filing jointly *	Married filing separately	Head of a household
4,000	4,050	403	403	403	403
4,050	4,100	408	408	408	408
4,100	4,150	413	413	413	413
4,150	4,200	418	418	418	418
4,200	4,250	423	423	423	423
4,250	4,300	428	428	428	428
4,300	4,350	433	433	433	433
4,350	4,400	438	438	438	438
4,400	4,450	443	443	443	443
4,450	4,500	448	448	448	448
4,500	4,550	453	453	453	453
4,550	4,600	458	458	458	458
4,600	4,650	463	463	463	463
4,650	4,700	468	468	468	468
4,700	4,750	473	473	473	473
4,750	4,800	478	478	478	478
4,800	4,850	483	483	483	483
4,850	4,900	488	488	488	488
4,900	4,950	493	493	493	493
4,950	5,000	498	498	498	498

5,000

At least	But less than	Single	Married filing jointly *	Married filing separately	Head of a household
5,000	5,050	503	503	503	503
5,050	5,100	508	508	508	508
5,100	5,150	513	513	513	513
5,150	5,200	518	518	518	518
5,200	5,250	523	523	523	523
5,250	5,300	528	528	528	528
5,300	5,350	533	533	533	533
5,350	5,400	538	538	538	538
5,400	5,450	543	543	543	543
5,450	5,500	548	548	548	548
5,500	5,550	553	553	553	553
5,550	5,600	558	558	558	558
5,600	5,650	563	563	563	563
5,650	5,700	568	568	568	568
5,700	5,750	573	573	573	573
5,750	5,800	578	578	578	578
5,800	5,850	583	583	583	583
5,850	5,900	588	588	588	588
5,900	5,950	593	593	593	593
5,950	6,000	598	598	598	598

6,000

If line 43 (taxable income) is—		And you are—			
At least	But less than	Single	Married filing jointly *	Married filing separately	Head of a household
		Your tax is—			
6,000	6,050	603	603	603	603
6,050	6,100	608	608	608	608
6,100	6,150	613	613	613	613
6,150	6,200	618	618	618	618
6,200	6,250	623	623	623	623
6,250	6,300	628	628	628	628
6,300	6,350	633	633	633	633
6,350	6,400	638	638	638	638
6,400	6,450	643	643	643	643
6,450	6,500	648	648	648	648
6,500	6,550	653	653	653	653
6,550	6,600	658	658	658	658
6,600	6,650	663	663	663	663
6,650	6,700	668	668	668	668
6,700	6,750	673	673	673	673
6,750	6,800	678	678	678	678
6,800	6,850	683	683	683	683
6,850	6,900	688	688	688	688
6,900	6,950	693	693	693	693
6,950	7,000	698	698	698	698

7,000

At least	But less than	Single	Married filing jointly *	Married filing separately	Head of a household
7,000	7,050	703	703	703	703
7,050	7,100	708	708	708	708
7,100	7,150	713	713	713	713
7,150	7,200	718	718	718	718
7,200	7,250	723	723	723	723
7,250	7,300	728	728	728	728
7,300	7,350	733	733	733	733
7,350	7,400	738	738	738	738
7,400	7,450	743	743	743	743
7,450	7,500	748	748	748	748
7,500	7,550	753	753	753	753
7,550	7,600	758	758	758	758
7,600	7,650	763	763	763	763
7,650	7,700	768	768	768	768
7,700	7,750	773	773	773	773
7,750	7,800	778	778	778	778
7,800	7,850	783	783	783	783
7,850	7,900	788	788	788	788
7,900	7,950	793	793	793	793
7,950	8,000	798	798	798	798

8,000

At least	But less than	Single	Married filing jointly *	Married filing separately	Head of a household
8,000	8,050	803	803	803	803
8,050	8,100	808	808	808	808
8,100	8,150	813	813	813	813
8,150	8,200	818	818	818	818
8,200	8,250	823	823	823	823
8,250	8,300	828	828	828	828
8,300	8,350	833	833	833	833
8,350	8,400	838	838	838	838
8,400	8,450	843	843	843	843
8,450	8,500	848	848	848	848
8,500	8,550	853	853	853	853
8,550	8,600	858	858	858	858
8,600	8,650	863	863	863	863
8,650	8,700	868	868	868	868
8,700	8,750	873	873	873	873
8,750	8,800	878	878	878	878
8,800	8,850	883	883	883	883
8,850	8,900	888	888	888	888
8,900	8,950	893	893	893	893
8,950	9,000	898	898	898	898

9,000

If line 43 (taxable income) is—		And you are—			
At least	But less than	Single	Married filing jointly *	Married filing separately	Head of a household
		Your tax is—			
9,000	9,050	903	903	903	903
9,050	9,100	908	908	908	908
9,100	9,150	915	913	915	913
9,150	9,200	923	918	923	918
9,200	9,250	930	923	930	923
9,250	9,300	938	928	938	928
9,300	9,350	945	933	945	933
9,350	9,400	953	938	953	938
9,400	9,450	960	943	960	943
9,450	9,500	968	948	968	948
9,500	9,550	975	953	975	953
9,550	9,600	983	958	983	958
9,600	9,650	990	963	990	963
9,650	9,700	998	968	998	968
9,700	9,750	1,005	973	1,005	973
9,750	9,800	1,013	978	1,013	978
9,800	9,850	1,020	983	1,020	983
9,850	9,900	1,028	988	1,028	988
9,900	9,950	1,035	993	1,035	993
9,950	10,000	1,043	998	1,043	998

10,000

At least	But less than	Single	Married filing jointly *	Married filing separately	Head of a household
10,000	10,050	1,050	1,003	1,050	1,003
10,050	10,100	1,058	1,008	1,058	1,008
10,100	10,150	1,065	1,013	1,065	1,013
10,150	10,200	1,073	1,018	1,073	1,018
10,200	10,250	1,080	1,023	1,080	1,023
10,250	10,300	1,088	1,028	1,088	1,028
10,300	10,350	1,095	1,033	1,095	1,033
10,350	10,400	1,103	1,038	1,103	1,038
10,400	10,450	1,110	1,043	1,110	1,043
10,450	10,500	1,118	1,048	1,118	1,048
10,500	10,550	1,125	1,053	1,125	1,053
10,550	10,600	1,133	1,058	1,133	1,058
10,600	10,650	1,140	1,063	1,140	1,063
10,650	10,700	1,148	1,068	1,148	1,068
10,700	10,750	1,155	1,073	1,155	1,073
10,750	10,800	1,163	1,078	1,163	1,078
10,800	10,850	1,170	1,083	1,170	1,083
10,850	10,900	1,178	1,088	1,178	1,088
10,900	10,950	1,185	1,093	1,185	1,093
10,950	11,000	1,193	1,098	1,193	1,098

11,000

At least	But less than	Single	Married filing jointly *	Married filing separately	Head of a household
11,000	11,050	1,200	1,103	1,200	1,103
11,050	11,100	1,208	1,108	1,208	1,108
11,100	11,150	1,215	1,113	1,215	1,113
11,150	11,200	1,223	1,118	1,223	1,118
11,200	11,250	1,230	1,123	1,230	1,123
11,250	11,300	1,238	1,128	1,238	1,128
11,300	11,350	1,245	1,133	1,245	1,133
11,350	11,400	1,253	1,138	1,253	1,138
11,400	11,450	1,260	1,143	1,260	1,143
11,450	11,500	1,268	1,148	1,268	1,148
11,500	11,550	1,275	1,153	1,275	1,153
11,550	11,600	1,283	1,158	1,283	1,158
11,600	11,650	1,290	1,163	1,290	1,163
11,650	11,700	1,298	1,168	1,298	1,168
11,700	11,750	1,305	1,173	1,305	1,173
11,750	11,800	1,313	1,178	1,313	1,178
11,800	11,850	1,320	1,183	1,320	1,183
11,850	11,900	1,328	1,188	1,328	1,188
11,900	11,950	1,335	1,193	1,335	1,193
11,950	12,000	1,343	1,198	1,343	1,198

(Continued)

* This column must also be used by a qualifying widow(er).

(Continued on page T-4)

2014 Tax Table — *Continued*

12,000

If line 43 (taxable income) is—		And you are—			
At least	But less than	Single	Married filing jointly *	Married filing separately	Head of a household
		Your tax is—			
12,000	12,050	1,350	1,203	1,350	1,203
12,050	12,100	1,358	1,208	1,358	1,208
12,100	12,150	1,365	1,213	1,365	1,213
12,150	12,200	1,373	1,218	1,373	1,218
12,200	12,250	1,380	1,223	1,380	1,223
12,250	12,300	1,388	1,228	1,388	1,228
12,300	12,350	1,395	1,233	1,395	1,233
12,350	12,400	1,403	1,238	1,403	1,238
12,400	12,450	1,410	1,243	1,410	1,243
12,450	12,500	1,418	1,248	1,418	1,248
12,500	12,550	1,425	1,253	1,425	1,253
12,550	12,600	1,433	1,258	1,433	1,258
12,600	12,650	1,440	1,263	1,440	1,263
12,650	12,700	1,448	1,268	1,448	1,268
12,700	12,750	1,455	1,273	1,455	1,273
12,750	12,800	1,463	1,278	1,463	1,278
12,800	12,850	1,470	1,283	1,470	1,283
12,850	12,900	1,478	1,288	1,478	1,288
12,900	12,950	1,485	1,293	1,485	1,293
12,950	13,000	1,493	1,298	1,493	1,299

13,000

At least	But less than	Single	Married filing jointly *	Married filing separately	Head of a household
13,000	13,050	1,500	1,303	1,500	1,306
13,050	13,100	1,508	1,308	1,508	1,314
13,100	13,150	1,515	1,313	1,515	1,321
13,150	13,200	1,523	1,318	1,523	1,329
13,200	13,250	1,530	1,323	1,530	1,336
13,250	13,300	1,538	1,328	1,538	1,344
13,300	13,350	1,545	1,333	1,545	1,351
13,350	13,400	1,553	1,338	1,553	1,359
13,400	13,450	1,560	1,343	1,560	1,366
13,450	13,500	1,568	1,348	1,568	1,374
13,500	13,550	1,575	1,353	1,575	1,381
13,550	13,600	1,583	1,358	1,583	1,389
13,600	13,650	1,590	1,363	1,590	1,396
13,650	13,700	1,598	1,368	1,598	1,404
13,700	13,750	1,605	1,373	1,605	1,411
13,750	13,800	1,613	1,378	1,613	1,419
13,800	13,850	1,620	1,383	1,620	1,426
13,850	13,900	1,628	1,388	1,628	1,434
13,900	13,950	1,635	1,393	1,635	1,441
13,950	14,000	1,643	1,398	1,643	1,449

14,000

At least	But less than	Single	Married filing jointly *	Married filing separately	Head of a household
14,000	14,050	1,650	1,403	1,650	1,456
14,050	14,100	1,658	1,408	1,658	1,464
14,100	14,150	1,665	1,413	1,665	1,471
14,150	14,200	1,673	1,418	1,673	1,479
14,200	14,250	1,680	1,423	1,680	1,486
14,250	14,300	1,688	1,428	1,688	1,494
14,300	14,350	1,695	1,433	1,695	1,501
14,350	14,400	1,703	1,438	1,703	1,509
14,400	14,450	1,710	1,443	1,710	1,516
14,450	14,500	1,718	1,448	1,718	1,524
14,500	14,550	1,725	1,453	1,725	1,531
14,550	14,600	1,733	1,458	1,733	1,539
14,600	14,650	1,740	1,463	1,740	1,546
14,650	14,700	1,748	1,468	1,748	1,554
14,700	14,750	1,755	1,473	1,755	1,561
14,750	14,800	1,763	1,478	1,763	1,569
14,800	14,850	1,770	1,483	1,770	1,576
14,850	14,900	1,778	1,488	1,778	1,584
14,900	14,950	1,785	1,493	1,785	1,591
14,950	15,000	1,793	1,498	1,793	1,599

15,000

If line 43 (taxable income) is—		And you are—			
At least	But less than	Single	Married filing jointly *	Married filing separately	Head of a household
		Your tax is—			
15,000	15,050	1,800	1,503	1,800	1,606
15,050	15,100	1,808	1,508	1,808	1,614
15,100	15,150	1,815	1,513	1,815	1,621
15,150	15,200	1,823	1,518	1,823	1,629
15,200	15,250	1,830	1,523	1,830	1,636
15,250	15,300	1,838	1,528	1,838	1,644
15,300	15,350	1,845	1,533	1,845	1,651
15,350	15,400	1,853	1,538	1,853	1,659
15,400	15,450	1,860	1,543	1,860	1,666
15,450	15,500	1,868	1,548	1,868	1,674
15,500	15,550	1,875	1,553	1,875	1,681
15,550	15,600	1,883	1,558	1,883	1,689
15,600	15,650	1,890	1,563	1,890	1,696
15,650	15,700	1,898	1,568	1,898	1,704
15,700	15,750	1,905	1,573	1,905	1,711
15,750	15,800	1,913	1,578	1,913	1,719
15,800	15,850	1,920	1,583	1,920	1,726
15,850	15,900	1,928	1,588	1,928	1,734
15,900	15,950	1,935	1,593	1,935	1,741
15,950	16,000	1,943	1,598	1,943	1,749

16,000

At least	But less than	Single	Married filing jointly *	Married filing separately	Head of a household
16,000	16,050	1,950	1,603	1,950	1,756
16,050	16,100	1,958	1,608	1,958	1,764
16,100	16,150	1,965	1,613	1,965	1,771
16,150	16,200	1,973	1,618	1,973	1,779
16,200	16,250	1,980	1,623	1,980	1,786
16,250	16,300	1,988	1,628	1,988	1,794
16,300	16,350	1,995	1,633	1,995	1,801
16,350	16,400	2,003	1,638	2,003	1,809
16,400	16,450	2,010	1,643	2,010	1,816
16,450	16,500	2,018	1,648	2,018	1,824
16,500	16,550	2,025	1,653	2,025	1,831
16,550	16,600	2,033	1,658	2,033	1,839
16,600	16,650	2,040	1,663	2,040	1,846
16,650	16,700	2,048	1,668	2,048	1,854
16,700	16,750	2,055	1,673	2,055	1,861
16,750	16,800	2,063	1,678	2,063	1,869
16,800	16,850	2,070	1,683	2,070	1,876
16,850	16,900	2,078	1,688	2,078	1,884
16,900	16,950	2,085	1,693	2,085	1,891
16,950	17,000	2,093	1,698	2,093	1,899

17,000

At least	But less than	Single	Married filing jointly *	Married filing separately	Head of a household
17,000	17,050	2,100	1,703	2,100	1,906
17,050	17,100	2,108	1,708	2,108	1,914
17,100	17,150	2,115	1,713	2,115	1,921
17,150	17,200	2,123	1,718	2,123	1,929
17,200	17,250	2,130	1,723	2,130	1,936
17,250	17,300	2,138	1,728	2,138	1,944
17,300	17,350	2,145	1,733	2,145	1,951
17,350	17,400	2,153	1,738	2,153	1,959
17,400	17,450	2,160	1,743	2,160	1,966
17,450	17,500	2,168	1,748	2,168	1,974
17,500	17,550	2,175	1,753	2,175	1,981
17,550	17,600	2,183	1,758	2,183	1,989
17,600	17,650	2,190	1,763	2,190	1,996
17,650	17,700	2,198	1,768	2,198	2,004
17,700	17,750	2,205	1,773	2,205	2,011
17,750	17,800	2,213	1,778	2,213	2,019
17,800	17,850	2,220	1,783	2,220	2,026
17,850	17,900	2,228	1,788	2,228	2,034
17,900	17,950	2,235	1,793	2,235	2,041
17,950	18,000	2,243	1,798	2,243	2,049

18,000

If line 43 (taxable income) is—		And you are—			
At least	But less than	Single	Married filing jointly *	Married filing separately	Head of a household
		Your tax is—			
18,000	18,050	2,250	1,803	2,250	2,056
18,050	18,100	2,258	1,808	2,258	2,064
18,100	18,150	2,265	1,813	2,265	2,071
18,150	18,200	2,273	1,819	2,273	2,079
18,200	18,250	2,280	1,826	2,280	2,086
18,250	18,300	2,288	1,834	2,288	2,094
18,300	18,350	2,295	1,841	2,295	2,101
18,350	18,400	2,303	1,849	2,303	2,109
18,400	18,450	2,310	1,856	2,310	2,116
18,450	18,500	2,318	1,864	2,318	2,124
18,500	18,550	2,325	1,871	2,325	2,131
18,550	18,600	2,333	1,879	2,333	2,139
18,600	18,650	2,340	1,886	2,340	2,146
18,650	18,700	2,348	1,894	2,348	2,154
18,700	18,750	2,355	1,901	2,355	2,161
18,750	18,800	2,363	1,909	2,363	2,169
18,800	18,850	2,370	1,916	2,370	2,176
18,850	18,900	2,378	1,924	2,378	2,184
18,900	18,950	2,385	1,931	2,385	2,191
18,950	19,000	2,393	1,939	2,393	2,199

19,000

At least	But less than	Single	Married filing jointly *	Married filing separately	Head of a household
19,000	19,050	2,400	1,946	2,400	2,206
19,050	19,100	2,408	1,954	2,408	2,214
19,100	19,150	2,415	1,961	2,415	2,221
19,150	19,200	2,423	1,969	2,423	2,229
19,200	19,250	2,430	1,976	2,430	2,236
19,250	19,300	2,438	1,984	2,438	2,244
19,300	19,350	2,445	1,991	2,445	2,251
19,350	19,400	2,453	1,999	2,453	2,259
19,400	19,450	2,460	2,006	2,460	2,266
19,450	19,500	2,468	2,014	2,468	2,274
19,500	19,550	2,475	2,021	2,475	2,281
19,550	19,600	2,483	2,029	2,483	2,289
19,600	19,650	2,490	2,036	2,490	2,296
19,650	19,700	2,498	2,044	2,498	2,304
19,700	19,750	2,505	2,051	2,505	2,311
19,750	19,800	2,513	2,059	2,513	2,319
19,800	19,850	2,520	2,066	2,520	2,326
19,850	19,900	2,528	2,074	2,528	2,334
19,900	19,950	2,535	2,081	2,535	2,341
19,950	20,000	2,543	2,089	2,543	2,349

20,000

At least	But less than	Single	Married filing jointly *	Married filing separately	Head of a household
20,000	20,050	2,550	2,096	2,550	2,356
20,050	20,100	2,558	2,104	2,558	2,364
20,100	20,150	2,565	2,111	2,565	2,371
20,150	20,200	2,573	2,119	2,573	2,379
20,200	20,250	2,580	2,126	2,580	2,386
20,250	20,300	2,588	2,134	2,588	2,394
20,300	20,350	2,595	2,141	2,595	2,401
20,350	20,400	2,603	2,149	2,603	2,409
20,400	20,450	2,610	2,156	2,610	2,416
20,450	20,500	2,618	2,164	2,618	2,424
20,500	20,550	2,625	2,171	2,625	2,431
20,550	20,600	2,633	2,179	2,633	2,439
20,600	20,650	2,640	2,186	2,640	2,446
20,650	20,700	2,648	2,194	2,648	2,454
20,700	20,750	2,655	2,201	2,655	2,461
20,750	20,800	2,663	2,209	2,663	2,469
20,800	20,850	2,670	2,216	2,670	2,476
20,850	20,900	2,678	2,224	2,678	2,484
20,900	20,950	2,685	2,231	2,685	2,491
20,950	21,000	2,693	2,239	2,693	2,499

(Continued)

* This column must also be used by a qualifying widow(er).

(Continued on page T-5)

2014 Tax Table — Continued

21,000

If line 43 (taxable income) is—		And you are—			
At least	But less than	Single	Married filing jointly *	Married filing separately	Head of a household
		Your tax is—			
21,000	21,050	2,700	2,246	2,700	2,506
21,050	21,100	2,708	2,254	2,708	2,514
21,100	21,150	2,715	2,261	2,715	2,521
21,150	21,200	2,723	2,269	2,723	2,529
21,200	21,250	2,730	2,276	2,730	2,536
21,250	21,300	2,738	2,284	2,738	2,544
21,300	21,350	2,745	2,291	2,745	2,551
21,350	21,400	2,753	2,299	2,753	2,559
21,400	21,450	2,760	2,306	2,760	2,566
21,450	21,500	2,768	2,314	2,768	2,574
21,500	21,550	2,775	2,321	2,775	2,581
21,550	21,600	2,783	2,329	2,783	2,589
21,600	21,650	2,790	2,336	2,790	2,596
21,650	21,700	2,798	2,344	2,798	2,604
21,700	21,750	2,805	2,351	2,805	2,611
21,750	21,800	2,813	2,359	2,813	2,619
21,800	21,850	2,820	2,366	2,820	2,626
21,850	21,900	2,828	2,374	2,828	2,634
21,900	21,950	2,835	2,381	2,835	2,641
21,950	22,000	2,843	2,389	2,843	2,649

22,000

At least	But less than	Single	Married filing jointly *	Married filing separately	Head of a household
22,000	22,050	2,850	2,396	2,850	2,656
22,050	22,100	2,858	2,404	2,858	2,664
22,100	22,150	2,865	2,411	2,865	2,671
22,150	22,200	2,873	2,419	2,873	2,679
22,200	22,250	2,880	2,426	2,880	2,686
22,250	22,300	2,888	2,434	2,888	2,694
22,300	22,350	2,895	2,441	2,895	2,701
22,350	22,400	2,903	2,449	2,903	2,709
22,400	22,450	2,910	2,456	2,910	2,716
22,450	22,500	2,918	2,464	2,918	2,724
22,500	22,550	2,925	2,471	2,925	2,731
22,550	22,600	2,933	2,479	2,933	2,739
22,600	22,650	2,940	2,486	2,940	2,746
22,650	22,700	2,948	2,494	2,948	2,754
22,700	22,750	2,955	2,501	2,955	2,761
22,750	22,800	2,963	2,509	2,963	2,769
22,800	22,850	2,970	2,516	2,970	2,776
22,850	22,900	2,978	2,524	2,978	2,784
22,900	22,950	2,985	2,531	2,985	2,791
22,950	23,000	2,993	2,539	2,993	2,799

23,000

At least	But less than	Single	Married filing jointly *	Married filing separately	Head of a household
23,000	23,050	3,000	2,546	3,000	2,806
23,050	23,100	3,008	2,554	3,008	2,814
23,100	23,150	3,015	2,561	3,015	2,821
23,150	23,200	3,023	2,569	3,023	2,829
23,200	23,250	3,030	2,576	3,030	2,836
23,250	23,300	3,038	2,584	3,038	2,844
23,300	23,350	3,045	2,591	3,045	2,851
23,350	23,400	3,053	2,599	3,053	2,859
23,400	23,450	3,060	2,606	3,060	2,866
23,450	23,500	3,068	2,614	3,068	2,874
23,500	23,550	3,075	2,621	3,075	2,881
23,550	23,600	3,083	2,629	3,083	2,889
23,600	23,650	3,090	2,636	3,090	2,896
23,650	23,700	3,098	2,644	3,098	2,904
23,700	23,750	3,105	2,651	3,105	2,911
23,750	23,800	3,113	2,659	3,113	2,919
23,800	23,850	3,120	2,666	3,120	2,926
23,850	23,900	3,128	2,674	3,128	2,934
23,900	23,950	3,135	2,681	3,135	2,941
23,950	24,000	3,143	2,689	3,143	2,949

24,000

At least	But less than	Single	Married filing jointly *	Married filing separately	Head of a household
24,000	24,050	3,150	2,696	3,150	2,956
24,050	24,100	3,158	2,704	3,158	2,964
24,100	24,150	3,165	2,711	3,165	2,971
24,150	24,200	3,173	2,719	3,173	2,979
24,200	24,250	3,180	2,726	3,180	2,986
24,250	24,300	3,188	2,734	3,188	2,994
24,300	24,350	3,195	2,741	3,195	3,001
24,350	24,400	3,203	2,749	3,203	3,009
24,400	24,450	3,210	2,756	3,210	3,016
24,450	24,500	3,218	2,764	3,218	3,024
24,500	24,550	3,225	2,771	3,225	3,031
24,550	24,600	3,233	2,779	3,233	3,039
24,600	24,650	3,240	2,786	3,240	3,046
24,650	24,700	3,248	2,794	3,248	3,054
24,700	24,750	3,255	2,801	3,255	3,061
24,750	24,800	3,263	2,809	3,263	3,069
24,800	24,850	3,270	2,816	3,270	3,076
24,850	24,900	3,278	2,824	3,278	3,084
24,900	24,950	3,285	2,831	3,285	3,091
24,950	25,000	3,293	2,839	3,293	3,099

25,000

At least	But less than	Single	Married filing jointly *	Married filing separately	Head of a household
25,000	25,050	3,300	2,846	3,300	3,106
25,050	25,100	3,308	2,854	3,308	3,114
25,100	25,150	3,315	2,861	3,315	3,121
25,150	25,200	3,323	2,869	3,323	3,129
25,200	25,250	3,330	2,876	3,330	3,136
25,250	25,300	3,338	2,884	3,338	3,144
25,300	25,350	3,345	2,891	3,345	3,151
25,350	25,400	3,353	2,899	3,353	3,159
25,400	25,450	3,360	2,906	3,360	3,166
25,450	25,500	3,368	2,914	3,368	3,174
25,500	25,550	3,375	2,921	3,375	3,181
25,550	25,600	3,383	2,929	3,383	3,189
25,600	25,650	3,390	2,936	3,390	3,196
25,650	25,700	3,398	2,944	3,398	3,204
25,700	25,750	3,405	2,951	3,405	3,211
25,750	25,800	3,413	2,959	3,413	3,219
25,800	25,850	3,420	2,966	3,420	3,226
25,850	25,900	3,428	2,974	3,428	3,234
25,900	25,950	3,435	2,981	3,435	3,241
25,950	26,000	3,443	2,989	3,443	3,249

26,000

At least	But less than	Single	Married filing jointly *	Married filing separately	Head of a household
26,000	26,050	3,450	2,996	3,450	3,256
26,050	26,100	3,458	3,004	3,458	3,264
26,100	26,150	3,465	3,011	3,465	3,271
26,150	26,200	3,473	3,019	3,473	3,279
26,200	26,250	3,480	3,026	3,480	3,286
26,250	26,300	3,488	3,034	3,488	3,294
26,300	26,350	3,495	3,041	3,495	3,301
26,350	26,400	3,503	3,049	3,503	3,309
26,400	26,450	3,510	3,056	3,510	3,316
26,450	26,500	3,518	3,064	3,518	3,324
26,500	26,550	3,525	3,071	3,525	3,331
26,550	26,600	3,533	3,079	3,533	3,339
26,600	26,650	3,540	3,086	3,540	3,346
26,650	26,700	3,548	3,094	3,548	3,354
26,700	26,750	3,555	3,101	3,555	3,361
26,750	26,800	3,563	3,109	3,563	3,369
26,800	26,850	3,570	3,116	3,570	3,376
26,850	26,900	3,578	3,124	3,578	3,384
26,900	26,950	3,585	3,131	3,585	3,391
26,950	27,000	3,593	3,139	3,593	3,399

27,000

At least	But less than	Single	Married filing jointly *	Married filing separately	Head of a household
27,000	27,050	3,600	3,146	3,600	3,406
27,050	27,100	3,608	3,154	3,608	3,414
27,100	27,150	3,615	3,161	3,615	3,421
27,150	27,200	3,623	3,169	3,623	3,429
27,200	27,250	3,630	3,176	3,630	3,436
27,250	27,300	3,638	3,184	3,638	3,444
27,300	27,350	3,645	3,191	3,645	3,451
27,350	27,400	3,653	3,199	3,653	3,459
27,400	27,450	3,660	3,206	3,660	3,466
27,450	27,500	3,668	3,214	3,668	3,474
27,500	27,550	3,675	3,221	3,675	3,481
27,550	27,600	3,683	3,229	3,683	3,489
27,600	27,650	3,690	3,236	3,690	3,496
27,650	27,700	3,698	3,244	3,698	3,504
27,700	27,750	3,705	3,251	3,705	3,511
27,750	27,800	3,713	3,259	3,713	3,519
27,800	27,850	3,720	3,266	3,720	3,526
27,850	27,900	3,728	3,274	3,728	3,534
27,900	27,950	3,735	3,281	3,735	3,541
27,950	28,000	3,743	3,289	3,743	3,549

28,000

At least	But less than	Single	Married filing jointly *	Married filing separately	Head of a household
28,000	28,050	3,750	3,296	3,750	3,556
28,050	28,100	3,758	3,304	3,758	3,564
28,100	28,150	3,765	3,311	3,765	3,571
28,150	28,200	3,773	3,319	3,773	3,579
28,200	28,250	3,780	3,326	3,780	3,586
28,250	28,300	3,788	3,334	3,788	3,594
28,300	28,350	3,795	3,341	3,795	3,601
28,350	28,400	3,803	3,349	3,803	3,609
28,400	28,450	3,810	3,356	3,810	3,616
28,450	28,500	3,818	3,364	3,818	3,624
28,500	28,550	3,825	3,371	3,825	3,631
28,550	28,600	3,833	3,379	3,833	3,639
28,600	28,650	3,840	3,386	3,840	3,646
28,650	28,700	3,848	3,394	3,848	3,654
28,700	28,750	3,855	3,401	3,855	3,661
28,750	28,800	3,863	3,409	3,863	3,669
28,800	28,850	3,870	3,416	3,870	3,676
28,850	28,900	3,878	3,424	3,878	3,684
28,900	28,950	3,885	3,431	3,885	3,691
28,950	29,000	3,893	3,439	3,893	3,699

29,000

At least	But less than	Single	Married filing jointly *	Married filing separately	Head of a household
29,000	29,050	3,900	3,446	3,900	3,706
29,050	29,100	3,908	3,454	3,908	3,714
29,100	29,150	3,915	3,461	3,915	3,721
29,150	29,200	3,923	3,469	3,923	3,729
29,200	29,250	3,930	3,476	3,930	3,736
29,250	29,300	3,938	3,484	3,938	3,744
29,300	29,350	3,945	3,491	3,945	3,751
29,350	29,400	3,953	3,499	3,953	3,759
29,400	29,450	3,960	3,506	3,960	3,766
29,450	29,500	3,968	3,514	3,968	3,774
29,500	29,550	3,975	3,521	3,975	3,781
29,550	29,600	3,983	3,529	3,983	3,789
29,600	29,650	3,990	3,536	3,990	3,796
29,650	29,700	3,998	3,544	3,998	3,804
29,700	29,750	4,005	3,551	4,005	3,811
29,750	29,800	4,013	3,559	4,013	3,819
29,800	29,850	4,020	3,566	4,020	3,826
29,850	29,900	4,028	3,574	4,028	3,834
29,900	29,950	4,035	3,581	4,035	3,841
29,950	30,000	4,043	3,589	4,043	3,849

(Continued)

* This column must also be used by a qualifying widow(er).

(Continued on page T-6)

2014 Tax Table — Continued

30,000

At least	But less than	Single	Married filing jointly *	Married filing separately	Head of a household
30,000	30,050	4,050	3,596	4,050	3,856
30,050	30,100	4,058	3,604	4,058	3,864
30,100	30,150	4,065	3,611	4,065	3,871
30,150	30,200	4,073	3,619	4,073	3,879
30,200	30,250	4,080	3,626	4,080	3,886
30,250	30,300	4,088	3,634	4,088	3,894
30,300	30,350	4,095	3,641	4,095	3,901
30,350	30,400	4,103	3,649	4,103	3,909
30,400	30,450	4,110	3,656	4,110	3,916
30,450	30,500	4,118	3,664	4,118	3,924
30,500	30,550	4,125	3,671	4,125	3,931
30,550	30,600	4,133	3,679	4,133	3,939
30,600	30,650	4,140	3,686	4,140	3,946
30,650	30,700	4,148	3,694	4,148	3,954
30,700	30,750	4,155	3,701	4,155	3,961
30,750	30,800	4,163	3,709	4,163	3,969
30,800	30,850	4,170	3,716	4,170	3,976
30,850	30,900	4,178	3,724	4,178	3,984
30,900	30,950	4,185	3,731	4,185	3,991
30,950	31,000	4,193	3,739	4,193	3,999

31,000

At least	But less than	Single	Married filing jointly *	Married filing separately	Head of a household
31,000	31,050	4,200	3,746	4,200	4,006
31,050	31,100	4,208	3,754	4,208	4,014
31,100	31,150	4,215	3,761	4,215	4,021
31,150	31,200	4,223	3,769	4,223	4,029
31,200	31,250	4,230	3,776	4,230	4,036
31,250	31,300	4,238	3,784	4,238	4,044
31,300	31,350	4,245	3,791	4,245	4,051
31,350	31,400	4,253	3,799	4,253	4,059
31,400	31,450	4,260	3,806	4,260	4,066
31,450	31,500	4,268	3,814	4,268	4,074
31,500	31,550	4,275	3,821	4,275	4,081
31,550	31,600	4,283	3,829	4,283	4,089
31,600	31,650	4,290	3,836	4,290	4,096
31,650	31,700	4,298	3,844	4,298	4,104
31,700	31,750	4,305	3,851	4,305	4,111
31,750	31,800	4,313	3,859	4,313	4,119
31,800	31,850	4,320	3,866	4,320	4,126
31,850	31,900	4,328	3,874	4,328	4,134
31,900	31,950	4,335	3,881	4,335	4,141
31,950	32,000	4,343	3,889	4,343	4,149

32,000

At least	But less than	Single	Married filing jointly *	Married filing separately	Head of a household
32,000	32,050	4,350	3,896	4,350	4,156
32,050	32,100	4,358	3,904	4,358	4,164
32,100	32,150	4,365	3,911	4,365	4,171
32,150	32,200	4,373	3,919	4,373	4,179
32,200	32,250	4,380	3,926	4,380	4,186
32,250	32,300	4,388	3,934	4,388	4,194
32,300	32,350	4,395	3,941	4,395	4,201
32,350	32,400	4,403	3,949	4,403	4,209
32,400	32,450	4,410	3,956	4,410	4,216
32,450	32,500	4,418	3,964	4,418	4,224
32,500	32,550	4,425	3,971	4,425	4,231
32,550	32,600	4,433	3,979	4,433	4,239
32,600	32,650	4,440	3,986	4,440	4,246
32,650	32,700	4,448	3,994	4,448	4,254
32,700	32,750	4,455	4,001	4,455	4,261
32,750	32,800	4,463	4,009	4,463	4,269
32,800	32,850	4,470	4,016	4,470	4,276
32,850	32,900	4,478	4,024	4,478	4,284
32,900	32,950	4,485	4,031	4,485	4,291
32,950	33,000	4,493	4,039	4,493	4,299

33,000

At least	But less than	Single	Married filing jointly *	Married filing separately	Head of a household
33,000	33,050	4,500	4,046	4,500	4,306
33,050	33,100	4,508	4,054	4,508	4,314
33,100	33,150	4,515	4,061	4,515	4,321
33,150	33,200	4,523	4,069	4,523	4,329
33,200	33,250	4,530	4,076	4,530	4,336
33,250	33,300	4,538	4,084	4,538	4,344
33,300	33,350	4,545	4,091	4,545	4,351
33,350	33,400	4,553	4,099	4,553	4,359
33,400	33,450	4,560	4,106	4,560	4,366
33,450	33,500	4,568	4,114	4,568	4,374
33,500	33,550	4,575	4,121	4,575	4,381
33,550	33,600	4,583	4,129	4,583	4,389
33,600	33,650	4,590	4,136	4,590	4,396
33,650	33,700	4,598	4,144	4,598	4,404
33,700	33,750	4,605	4,151	4,605	4,411
33,750	33,800	4,613	4,159	4,613	4,419
33,800	33,850	4,620	4,166	4,620	4,426
33,850	33,900	4,628	4,174	4,628	4,434
33,900	33,950	4,635	4,181	4,635	4,441
33,950	34,000	4,643	4,189	4,643	4,449

34,000

At least	But less than	Single	Married filing jointly *	Married filing separately	Head of a household
34,000	34,050	4,650	4,196	4,650	4,456
34,050	34,100	4,658	4,204	4,658	4,464
34,100	34,150	4,665	4,211	4,665	4,471
34,150	34,200	4,673	4,219	4,673	4,479
34,200	34,250	4,680	4,226	4,680	4,486
34,250	34,300	4,688	4,234	4,688	4,494
34,300	34,350	4,695	4,241	4,695	4,501
34,350	34,400	4,703	4,249	4,703	4,509
34,400	34,450	4,710	4,256	4,710	4,516
34,450	34,500	4,718	4,264	4,718	4,524
34,500	34,550	4,725	4,271	4,725	4,531
34,550	34,600	4,733	4,279	4,733	4,539
34,600	34,650	4,740	4,286	4,740	4,546
34,650	34,700	4,748	4,294	4,748	4,554
34,700	34,750	4,755	4,301	4,755	4,561
34,750	34,800	4,763	4,309	4,763	4,569
34,800	34,850	4,770	4,316	4,770	4,576
34,850	34,900	4,778	4,324	4,778	4,584
34,900	34,950	4,785	4,331	4,785	4,591
34,950	35,000	4,793	4,339	4,793	4,599

35,000

At least	But less than	Single	Married filing jointly *	Married filing separately	Head of a household
35,000	35,050	4,800	4,346	4,800	4,606
35,050	35,100	4,808	4,354	4,808	4,614
35,100	35,150	4,815	4,361	4,815	4,621
35,150	35,200	4,823	4,369	4,823	4,629
35,200	35,250	4,830	4,376	4,830	4,636
35,250	35,300	4,838	4,384	4,838	4,644
35,300	35,350	4,845	4,391	4,845	4,651
35,350	35,400	4,853	4,399	4,853	4,659
35,400	35,450	4,860	4,406	4,860	4,666
35,450	35,500	4,868	4,414	4,868	4,674
35,500	35,550	4,875	4,421	4,875	4,681
35,550	35,600	4,883	4,429	4,883	4,689
35,600	35,650	4,890	4,436	4,890	4,696
35,650	35,700	4,898	4,444	4,898	4,704
35,700	35,750	4,905	4,451	4,905	4,711
35,750	35,800	4,913	4,459	4,913	4,719
35,800	35,850	4,920	4,466	4,920	4,726
35,850	35,900	4,928	4,474	4,928	4,734
35,900	35,950	4,935	4,481	4,935	4,741
35,950	36,000	4,943	4,489	4,943	4,749

36,000

At least	But less than	Single	Married filing jointly *	Married filing separately	Head of a household
36,000	36,050	4,950	4,496	4,950	4,756
36,050	36,100	4,958	4,504	4,958	4,764
36,100	36,150	4,965	4,511	4,965	4,771
36,150	36,200	4,973	4,519	4,973	4,779
36,200	36,250	4,980	4,526	4,980	4,786
36,250	36,300	4,988	4,534	4,988	4,794
36,300	36,350	4,995	4,541	4,995	4,801
36,350	36,400	5,003	4,549	5,003	4,809
36,400	36,450	5,010	4,556	5,010	4,816
36,450	36,500	5,018	4,564	5,018	4,824
36,500	36,550	5,025	4,571	5,025	4,831
36,550	36,600	5,033	4,579	5,033	4,839
36,600	36,650	5,040	4,586	5,040	4,846
36,650	36,700	5,048	4,594	5,048	4,854
36,700	36,750	5,055	4,601	5,055	4,861
36,750	36,800	5,063	4,609	5,063	4,869
36,800	36,850	5,070	4,616	5,070	4,876
36,850	36,900	5,078	4,624	5,078	4,884
36,900	36,950	5,088	4,631	5,088	4,891
36,950	37,000	5,100	4,639	5,100	4,899

37,000

At least	But less than	Single	Married filing jointly *	Married filing separately	Head of a household
37,000	37,050	5,113	4,646	5,113	4,906
37,050	37,100	5,125	4,654	5,125	4,914
37,100	37,150	5,138	4,661	5,138	4,921
37,150	37,200	5,150	4,669	5,150	4,929
37,200	37,250	5,163	4,676	5,163	4,936
37,250	37,300	5,175	4,684	5,175	4,944
37,300	37,350	5,188	4,691	5,188	4,951
37,350	37,400	5,200	4,699	5,200	4,959
37,400	37,450	5,213	4,706	5,213	4,966
37,450	37,500	5,225	4,714	5,225	4,974
37,500	37,550	5,238	4,721	5,238	4,981
37,550	37,600	5,250	4,729	5,250	4,989
37,600	37,650	5,263	4,736	5,263	4,996
37,650	37,700	5,275	4,744	5,275	5,004
37,700	37,750	5,288	4,751	5,288	5,011
37,750	37,800	5,300	4,759	5,300	5,019
37,800	37,850	5,313	4,766	5,313	5,026
37,850	37,900	5,325	4,774	5,325	5,034
37,900	37,950	5,338	4,781	5,338	5,041
37,950	38,000	5,350	4,789	5,350	5,049

38,000

At least	But less than	Single	Married filing jointly *	Married filing separately	Head of a household
38,000	38,050	5,363	4,796	5,363	5,056
38,050	38,100	5,375	4,804	5,375	5,064
38,100	38,150	5,388	4,811	5,388	5,071
38,150	38,200	5,400	4,819	5,400	5,079
38,200	38,250	5,413	4,826	5,413	5,086
38,250	38,300	5,425	4,834	5,425	5,094
38,300	38,350	5,438	4,841	5,438	5,101
38,350	38,400	5,450	4,849	5,450	5,109
38,400	38,450	5,463	4,856	5,463	5,116
38,450	38,500	5,475	4,864	5,475	5,124
38,500	38,550	5,488	4,871	5,488	5,131
38,550	38,600	5,500	4,879	5,500	5,139
38,600	38,650	5,513	4,886	5,513	5,146
38,650	38,700	5,525	4,894	5,525	5,154
38,700	38,750	5,538	4,901	5,538	5,161
38,750	38,800	5,550	4,909	5,550	5,169
38,800	38,850	5,563	4,916	5,563	5,176
38,850	38,900	5,575	4,924	5,575	5,184
38,900	38,950	5,588	4,931	5,588	5,191
38,950	39,000	5,600	4,939	5,600	5,199

(Continued)

* This column must also be used by a qualifying widow(er).

(Continued on page T-7)

2014 Tax Table — *Continued*

39,000

At least	But less than	Single	Married filing jointly *	Married filing separately	Head of a household
39,000	39,050	5,613	4,946	5,613	5,206
39,050	39,100	5,625	4,954	5,625	5,214
39,100	39,150	5,638	4,961	5,638	5,221
39,150	39,200	5,650	4,969	5,650	5,229
39,200	39,250	5,663	4,976	5,663	5,236
39,250	39,300	5,675	4,984	5,675	5,244
39,300	39,350	5,688	4,991	5,688	5,251
39,350	39,400	5,700	4,999	5,700	5,259
39,400	39,450	5,713	5,006	5,713	5,266
39,450	39,500	5,725	5,014	5,725	5,274
39,500	39,550	5,738	5,021	5,738	5,281
39,550	39,600	5,750	5,029	5,750	5,289
39,600	39,650	5,763	5,036	5,763	5,296
39,650	39,700	5,775	5,044	5,775	5,304
39,700	39,750	5,788	5,051	5,788	5,311
39,750	39,800	5,800	5,059	5,800	5,319
39,800	39,850	5,813	5,066	5,813	5,326
39,850	39,900	5,825	5,074	5,825	5,334
39,900	39,950	5,838	5,081	5,838	5,341
39,950	40,000	5,850	5,089	5,850	5,349

40,000

At least	But less than	Single	Married filing jointly *	Married filing separately	Head of a household
40,000	40,050	5,863	5,096	5,863	5,356
40,050	40,100	5,875	5,104	5,875	5,364
40,100	40,150	5,888	5,111	5,888	5,371
40,150	40,200	5,900	5,119	5,900	5,379
40,200	40,250	5,913	5,126	5,913	5,386
40,250	40,300	5,925	5,134	5,925	5,394
40,300	40,350	5,938	5,141	5,938	5,401
40,350	40,400	5,950	5,149	5,950	5,409
40,400	40,450	5,963	5,156	5,963	5,416
40,450	40,500	5,975	5,164	5,975	5,424
40,500	40,550	5,988	5,171	5,988	5,431
40,550	40,600	6,000	5,179	6,000	5,439
40,600	40,650	6,013	5,186	6,013	5,446
40,650	40,700	6,025	5,194	6,025	5,454
40,700	40,750	6,038	5,201	6,038	5,461
40,750	40,800	6,050	5,209	6,050	5,469
40,800	40,850	6,063	5,216	6,063	5,476
40,850	40,900	6,075	5,224	6,075	5,484
40,900	40,950	6,088	5,231	6,088	5,491
40,950	41,000	6,100	5,239	6,100	5,499

41,000

At least	But less than	Single	Married filing jointly *	Married filing separately	Head of a household
41,000	41,050	6,113	5,246	6,113	5,506
41,050	41,100	6,125	5,254	6,125	5,514
41,100	41,150	6,138	5,261	6,138	5,521
41,150	41,200	6,150	5,269	6,150	5,529
41,200	41,250	6,163	5,276	6,163	5,536
41,250	41,300	6,175	5,284	6,175	5,544
41,300	41,350	6,188	5,291	6,188	5,551
41,350	41,400	6,200	5,299	6,200	5,559
41,400	41,450	6,213	5,306	6,213	5,566
41,450	41,500	6,225	5,314	6,225	5,574
41,500	41,550	6,238	5,321	6,238	5,581
41,550	41,600	6,250	5,329	6,250	5,589
41,600	41,650	6,263	5,336	6,263	5,596
41,650	41,700	6,275	5,344	6,275	5,604
41,700	41,750	6,288	5,351	6,288	5,611
41,750	41,800	6,300	5,359	6,300	5,619
41,800	41,850	6,313	5,366	6,313	5,626
41,850	41,900	6,325	5,374	6,325	5,634
41,900	41,950	6,338	5,381	6,338	5,641
41,950	42,000	6,350	5,389	6,350	5,649

42,000

At least	But less than	Single	Married filing jointly *	Married filing separately	Head of a household
42,000	42,050	6,363	5,396	6,363	5,656
42,050	42,100	6,375	5,404	6,375	5,664
42,100	42,150	6,388	5,411	6,388	5,671
42,150	42,200	6,400	5,419	6,400	5,679
42,200	42,250	6,413	5,426	6,413	5,686
42,250	42,300	6,425	5,434	6,425	5,694
42,300	42,350	6,438	5,441	6,438	5,701
42,350	42,400	6,450	5,449	6,450	5,709
42,400	42,450	6,463	5,456	6,463	5,716
42,450	42,500	6,475	5,464	6,475	5,724
42,500	42,550	6,488	5,471	6,488	5,731
42,550	42,600	6,500	5,479	6,500	5,739
42,600	42,650	6,513	5,486	6,513	5,746
42,650	42,700	6,525	5,494	6,525	5,754
42,700	42,750	6,538	5,501	6,538	5,761
42,750	42,800	6,550	5,509	6,550	5,769
42,800	42,850	6,563	5,516	6,563	5,776
42,850	42,900	6,575	5,524	6,575	5,784
42,900	42,950	6,588	5,531	6,588	5,791
42,950	43,000	6,600	5,539	6,600	5,799

43,000

At least	But less than	Single	Married filing jointly *	Married filing separately	Head of a household
43,000	43,050	6,613	5,546	6,613	5,806
43,050	43,100	6,625	5,554	6,625	5,814
43,100	43,150	6,638	5,561	6,638	5,821
43,150	43,200	6,650	5,569	6,650	5,829
43,200	43,250	6,663	5,576	6,663	5,836
43,250	43,300	6,675	5,584	6,675	5,844
43,300	43,350	6,688	5,591	6,688	5,851
43,350	43,400	6,700	5,599	6,700	5,859
43,400	43,450	6,713	5,606	6,713	5,866
43,450	43,500	6,725	5,614	6,725	5,874
43,500	43,550	6,738	5,621	6,738	5,881
43,550	43,600	6,750	5,629	6,750	5,889
43,600	43,650	6,763	5,636	6,763	5,896
43,650	43,700	6,775	5,644	6,775	5,904
43,700	43,750	6,788	5,651	6,788	5,911
43,750	43,800	6,800	5,659	6,800	5,919
43,800	43,850	6,813	5,666	6,813	5,926
43,850	43,900	6,825	5,674	6,825	5,934
43,900	43,950	6,838	5,681	6,838	5,941
43,950	44,000	6,850	5,689	6,850	5,949

44,000

At least	But less than	Single	Married filing jointly *	Married filing separately	Head of a household
44,000	44,050	6,863	5,696	6,863	5,956
44,050	44,100	6,875	5,704	6,875	5,964
44,100	44,150	6,888	5,711	6,888	5,971
44,150	44,200	6,900	5,719	6,900	5,979
44,200	44,250	6,913	5,726	6,913	5,986
44,250	44,300	6,925	5,734	6,925	5,994
44,300	44,350	6,938	5,741	6,938	6,001
44,350	44,400	6,950	5,749	6,950	6,009
44,400	44,450	6,963	5,756	6,963	6,016
44,450	44,500	6,975	5,764	6,975	6,024
44,500	44,550	6,988	5,771	6,988	6,031
44,550	44,600	7,000	5,779	7,000	6,039
44,600	44,650	7,013	5,786	7,013	6,046
44,650	44,700	7,025	5,794	7,025	6,054
44,700	44,750	7,038	5,801	7,038	6,061
44,750	44,800	7,050	5,809	7,050	6,069
44,800	44,850	7,063	5,816	7,063	6,076
44,850	44,900	7,075	5,824	7,075	6,084
44,900	44,950	7,088	5,831	7,088	6,091
44,950	45,000	7,100	5,839	7,100	6,099

45,000

At least	But less than	Single	Married filing jointly *	Married filing separately	Head of a household
45,000	45,050	7,113	5,846	7,113	6,106
45,050	45,100	7,125	5,854	7,125	6,114
45,100	45,150	7,138	5,861	7,138	6,121
45,150	45,200	7,150	5,869	7,150	6,129
45,200	45,250	7,163	5,876	7,163	6,136
45,250	45,300	7,175	5,884	7,175	6,144
45,300	45,350	7,188	5,891	7,188	6,151
45,350	45,400	7,200	5,899	7,200	6,159
45,400	45,450	7,213	5,906	7,213	6,166
45,450	45,500	7,225	5,914	7,225	6,174
45,500	45,550	7,238	5,921	7,238	6,181
45,550	45,600	7,250	5,929	7,250	6,189
45,600	45,650	7,263	5,936	7,263	6,196
45,650	45,700	7,275	5,944	7,275	6,204
45,700	45,750	7,288	5,951	7,288	6,211
45,750	45,800	7,300	5,959	7,300	6,219
45,800	45,850	7,313	5,966	7,313	6,226
45,850	45,900	7,325	5,974	7,325	6,234
45,900	45,950	7,338	5,981	7,338	6,241
45,950	46,000	7,350	5,989	7,350	6,249

46,000

At least	But less than	Single	Married filing jointly *	Married filing separately	Head of a household
46,000	46,050	7,363	5,996	7,363	6,256
46,050	46,100	7,375	6,004	7,375	6,264
46,100	46,150	7,388	6,011	7,388	6,271
46,150	46,200	7,400	6,019	7,400	6,279
46,200	46,250	7,413	6,026	7,413	6,286
46,250	46,300	7,425	6,034	7,425	6,294
46,300	46,350	7,438	6,041	7,438	6,301
46,350	46,400	7,450	6,049	7,450	6,309
46,400	46,450	7,463	6,056	7,463	6,316
46,450	46,500	7,475	6,064	7,475	6,324
46,500	46,550	7,488	6,071	7,488	6,331
46,550	46,600	7,500	6,079	7,500	6,339
46,600	46,650	7,513	6,086	7,513	6,346
46,650	46,700	7,525	6,094	7,525	6,354
46,700	46,750	7,538	6,101	7,538	6,361
46,750	46,800	7,550	6,109	7,550	6,369
46,800	46,850	7,563	6,116	7,563	6,376
46,850	46,900	7,575	6,124	7,575	6,384
46,900	46,950	7,588	6,131	7,588	6,391
46,950	47,000	7,600	6,139	7,600	6,399

47,000

At least	But less than	Single	Married filing jointly *	Married filing separately	Head of a household
47,000	47,050	7,613	6,146	7,613	6,406
47,050	47,100	7,625	6,154	7,625	6,414
47,100	47,150	7,638	6,161	7,638	6,421
47,150	47,200	7,650	6,169	7,650	6,429
47,200	47,250	7,663	6,176	7,663	6,436
47,250	47,300	7,675	6,184	7,675	6,444
47,300	47,350	7,688	6,191	7,688	6,451
47,350	47,400	7,700	6,199	7,700	6,459
47,400	47,450	7,713	6,206	7,713	6,466
47,450	47,500	7,725	6,214	7,725	6,474
47,500	47,550	7,738	6,221	7,738	6,481
47,550	47,600	7,750	6,229	7,750	6,489
47,600	47,650	7,763	6,236	7,763	6,496
47,650	47,700	7,775	6,244	7,775	6,504
47,700	47,750	7,788	6,251	7,788	6,511
47,750	47,800	7,800	6,259	7,800	6,519
47,800	47,850	7,813	6,266	7,813	6,526
47,850	47,900	7,825	6,274	7,825	6,534
47,900	47,950	7,838	6,281	7,838	6,541
47,950	48,000	7,850	6,289	7,850	6,549

(Continued)

* This column must also be used by a qualifying widow(er).

(Continued on page T-8)

2014 Tax Table — Continued

If line 43 (taxable income) is—		And you are—			
At least	But less than	Single	Married filing jointly *	Married filing separately	Head of a household
		Your tax is—			

48,000

At least	But less than	Single	MFJ *	MFS	HoH
48,000	48,050	7,863	6,296	7,863	6,556
48,050	48,100	7,875	6,304	7,875	6,564
48,100	48,150	7,888	6,311	7,888	6,571
48,150	48,200	7,900	6,319	7,900	6,579
48,200	48,250	7,913	6,326	7,913	6,586
48,250	48,300	7,925	6,334	7,925	6,594
48,300	48,350	7,938	6,341	7,938	6,601
48,350	48,400	7,950	6,349	7,950	6,609
48,400	48,450	7,963	6,356	7,963	6,616
48,450	48,500	7,975	6,364	7,975	6,624
48,500	48,550	7,988	6,371	7,988	6,631
48,550	48,600	8,000	6,379	8,000	6,639
48,600	48,650	8,013	6,386	8,013	6,646
48,650	48,700	8,025	6,394	8,025	6,654
48,700	48,750	8,038	6,401	8,038	6,661
48,750	48,800	8,050	6,409	8,050	6,669
48,800	48,850	8,063	6,416	8,063	6,676
48,850	48,900	8,075	6,424	8,075	6,684
48,900	48,950	8,088	6,431	8,088	6,691
48,950	49,000	8,100	6,439	8,100	6,699

49,000

At least	But less than	Single	MFJ *	MFS	HoH
49,000	49,050	8,113	6,446	8,113	6,706
49,050	49,100	8,125	6,454	8,125	6,714
49,100	49,150	8,138	6,461	8,138	6,721
49,150	49,200	8,150	6,469	8,150	6,729
49,200	49,250	8,163	6,476	8,163	6,736
49,250	49,300	8,175	6,484	8,175	6,744
49,300	49,350	8,188	6,491	8,188	6,751
49,350	49,400	8,200	6,499	8,200	6,759
49,400	49,450	8,213	6,506	8,213	6,769
49,450	49,500	8,225	6,514	8,225	6,781
49,500	49,550	8,238	6,521	8,238	6,794
49,550	49,600	8,250	6,529	8,250	6,806
49,600	49,650	8,263	6,536	8,263	6,819
49,650	49,700	8,275	6,544	8,275	6,831
49,700	49,750	8,288	6,551	8,288	6,844
49,750	49,800	8,300	6,559	8,300	6,856
49,800	49,850	8,313	6,566	8,313	6,869
49,850	49,900	8,325	6,574	8,325	6,881
49,900	49,950	8,338	6,581	8,338	6,894
49,950	50,000	8,350	6,589	8,350	6,906

50,000

At least	But less than	Single	MFJ *	MFS	HoH
50,000	50,050	8,363	6,596	8,363	6,919
50,050	50,100	8,375	6,604	8,375	6,931
50,100	50,150	8,388	6,611	8,388	6,944
50,150	50,200	8,400	6,619	8,400	6,956
50,200	50,250	8,413	6,626	8,413	6,969
50,250	50,300	8,425	6,634	8,425	6,981
50,300	50,350	8,438	6,641	8,438	6,994
50,350	50,400	8,450	6,649	8,450	7,006
50,400	50,450	8,463	6,656	8,463	7,019
50,450	50,500	8,475	6,664	8,475	7,031
50,500	50,550	8,488	6,671	8,488	7,044
50,550	50,600	8,500	6,679	8,500	7,056
50,600	50,650	8,513	6,686	8,513	7,069
50,650	50,700	8,525	6,694	8,525	7,081
50,700	50,750	8,538	6,701	8,538	7,094
50,750	50,800	8,550	6,709	8,550	7,106
50,800	50,850	8,563	6,716	8,563	7,119
50,850	50,900	8,575	6,724	8,575	7,131
50,900	50,950	8,588	6,731	8,588	7,144
50,950	51,000	8,600	6,739	8,600	7,156

51,000

At least	But less than	Single	MFJ *	MFS	HoH
51,000	51,050	8,613	6,746	8,613	7,169
51,050	51,100	8,625	6,754	8,625	7,181
51,100	51,150	8,638	6,761	8,638	7,194
51,150	51,200	8,650	6,769	8,650	7,206
51,200	51,250	8,663	6,776	8,663	7,219
51,250	51,300	8,675	6,784	8,675	7,231
51,300	51,350	8,688	6,791	8,688	7,244
51,350	51,400	8,700	6,799	8,700	7,256
51,400	51,450	8,713	6,806	8,713	7,269
51,450	51,500	8,725	6,814	8,725	7,281
51,500	51,550	8,738	6,821	8,738	7,294
51,550	51,600	8,750	6,829	8,750	7,306
51,600	51,650	8,763	6,836	8,763	7,319
51,650	51,700	8,775	6,844	8,775	7,331
51,700	51,750	8,788	6,851	8,788	7,344
51,750	51,800	8,800	6,859	8,800	7,356
51,800	51,850	8,813	6,866	8,813	7,369
51,850	51,900	8,825	6,874	8,825	7,381
51,900	51,950	8,838	6,881	8,838	7,394
51,950	52,000	8,850	6,889	8,850	7,406

52,000

At least	But less than	Single	MFJ *	MFS	HoH
52,000	52,050	8,863	6,896	8,863	7,419
52,050	52,100	8,875	6,904	8,875	7,431
52,100	52,150	8,888	6,911	8,888	7,444
52,150	52,200	8,900	6,919	8,900	7,456
52,200	52,250	8,913	6,926	8,913	7,469
52,250	52,300	8,925	6,934	8,925	7,481
52,300	52,350	8,938	6,941	8,938	7,494
52,350	52,400	8,950	6,949	8,950	7,506
52,400	52,450	8,963	6,956	8,963	7,519
52,450	52,500	8,975	6,964	8,975	7,531
52,500	52,550	8,988	6,971	8,988	7,544
52,550	52,600	9,000	6,979	9,000	7,556
52,600	52,650	9,013	6,986	9,013	7,569
52,650	52,700	9,025	6,994	9,025	7,581
52,700	52,750	9,038	7,001	9,038	7,594
52,750	52,800	9,050	7,009	9,050	7,606
52,800	52,850	9,063	7,016	9,063	7,619
52,850	52,900	9,075	7,024	9,075	7,631
52,900	52,950	9,088	7,031	9,088	7,644
52,950	53,000	9,100	7,039	9,100	7,656

53,000

At least	But less than	Single	MFJ *	MFS	HoH
53,000	53,050	9,113	7,046	9,113	7,669
53,050	53,100	9,125	7,054	9,125	7,681
53,100	53,150	9,138	7,061	9,138	7,694
53,150	53,200	9,150	7,069	9,150	7,706
53,200	53,250	9,163	7,076	9,163	7,719
53,250	53,300	9,175	7,084	9,175	7,731
53,300	53,350	9,188	7,091	9,188	7,744
53,350	53,400	9,200	7,099	9,200	7,756
53,400	53,450	9,213	7,106	9,213	7,769
53,450	53,500	9,225	7,114	9,225	7,781
53,500	53,550	9,238	7,121	9,238	7,794
53,550	53,600	9,250	7,129	9,250	7,806
53,600	53,650	9,263	7,136	9,263	7,819
53,650	53,700	9,275	7,144	9,275	7,831
53,700	53,750	9,288	7,151	9,288	7,844
53,750	53,800	9,300	7,159	9,300	7,856
53,800	53,850	9,313	7,166	9,313	7,869
53,850	53,900	9,325	7,174	9,325	7,881
53,900	53,950	9,338	7,181	9,338	7,894
53,950	54,000	9,350	7,189	9,350	7,906

54,000

At least	But less than	Single	MFJ *	MFS	HoH
54,000	54,050	9,363	7,196	9,363	7,919
54,050	54,100	9,375	7,204	9,375	7,931
54,100	54,150	9,388	7,211	9,388	7,944
54,150	54,200	9,400	7,219	9,400	7,956
54,200	54,250	9,413	7,226	9,413	7,969
54,250	54,300	9,425	7,234	9,425	7,981
54,300	54,350	9,438	7,241	9,438	7,994
54,350	54,400	9,450	7,249	9,450	8,006
54,400	54,450	9,463	7,256	9,463	8,019
54,450	54,500	9,475	7,264	9,475	8,031
54,500	54,550	9,488	7,271	9,488	8,044
54,550	54,600	9,500	7,279	9,500	8,056
54,600	54,650	9,513	7,286	9,513	8,069
54,650	54,700	9,525	7,294	9,525	8,081
54,700	54,750	9,538	7,301	9,538	8,094
54,750	54,800	9,550	7,309	9,550	8,106
54,800	54,850	9,563	7,316	9,563	8,119
54,850	54,900	9,575	7,324	9,575	8,131
54,900	54,950	9,588	7,331	9,588	8,144
54,950	55,000	9,600	7,339	9,600	8,156

55,000

At least	But less than	Single	MFJ *	MFS	HoH
55,000	55,050	9,613	7,346	9,613	8,169
55,050	55,100	9,625	7,354	9,625	8,181
55,100	55,150	9,638	7,361	9,638	8,194
55,150	55,200	9,650	7,369	9,650	8,206
55,200	55,250	9,663	7,376	9,663	8,219
55,250	55,300	9,675	7,384	9,675	8,231
55,300	55,350	9,688	7,391	9,688	8,244
55,350	55,400	9,700	7,399	9,700	8,256
55,400	55,450	9,713	7,406	9,713	8,269
55,450	55,500	9,725	7,414	9,725	8,281
55,500	55,550	9,738	7,421	9,738	8,294
55,550	55,600	9,750	7,429	9,750	8,306
55,600	55,650	9,763	7,436	9,763	8,319
55,650	55,700	9,775	7,444	9,775	8,331
55,700	55,750	9,788	7,451	9,788	8,344
55,750	55,800	9,800	7,459	9,800	8,356
55,800	55,850	9,813	7,466	9,813	8,369
55,850	55,900	9,825	7,474	9,825	8,381
55,900	55,950	9,838	7,481	9,838	8,394
55,950	56,000	9,850	7,489	9,850	8,406

56,000

At least	But less than	Single	MFJ *	MFS	HoH
56,000	56,050	9,863	7,496	9,863	8,419
56,050	56,100	9,875	7,504	9,875	8,431
56,100	56,150	9,888	7,511	9,888	8,444
56,150	56,200	9,900	7,519	9,900	8,456
56,200	56,250	9,913	7,526	9,913	8,469
56,250	56,300	9,925	7,534	9,925	8,481
56,300	56,350	9,938	7,541	9,938	8,494
56,350	56,400	9,950	7,549	9,950	8,506
56,400	56,450	9,963	7,556	9,963	8,519
56,450	56,500	9,975	7,564	9,975	8,531
56,500	56,550	9,988	7,571	9,988	8,544
56,550	56,600	10,000	7,579	10,000	8,556
56,600	56,650	10,013	7,586	10,013	8,569
56,650	56,700	10,025	7,594	10,025	8,581
56,700	56,750	10,038	7,601	10,038	8,594
56,750	56,800	10,050	7,609	10,050	8,606
56,800	56,850	10,063	7,616	10,063	8,619
56,850	56,900	10,075	7,624	10,075	8,631
56,900	56,950	10,088	7,631	10,088	8,644
56,950	57,000	10,100	7,639	10,100	8,656

(Continued)

* This column must also be used by a qualifying widow(er).

(Continued on page T-9)

2014 Tax Table — *Continued*

57,000

At least	But less than	Single	Married filing jointly *	Married filing separately	Head of a household
57,000	57,050	10,113	7,646	10,113	8,669
57,050	57,100	10,125	7,654	10,125	8,681
57,100	57,150	10,138	7,661	10,138	8,694
57,150	57,200	10,150	7,669	10,150	8,706
57,200	57,250	10,163	7,676	10,163	8,719
57,250	57,300	10,175	7,684	10,175	8,731
57,300	57,350	10,188	7,691	10,188	8,744
57,350	57,400	10,200	7,699	10,200	8,756
57,400	57,450	10,213	7,706	10,213	8,769
57,450	57,500	10,225	7,714	10,225	8,781
57,500	57,550	10,238	7,721	10,238	8,794
57,550	57,600	10,250	7,729	10,250	8,806
57,600	57,650	10,263	7,736	10,263	8,819
57,650	57,700	10,275	7,744	10,275	8,831
57,700	57,750	10,288	7,751	10,288	8,844
57,750	57,800	10,300	7,759	10,300	8,856
57,800	57,850	10,313	7,766	10,313	8,869
57,850	57,900	10,325	7,774	10,325	8,881
57,900	57,950	10,338	7,781	10,338	8,894
57,950	58,000	10,350	7,789	10,350	8,906

58,000

At least	But less than	Single	Married filing jointly *	Married filing separately	Head of a household
58,000	58,050	10,363	7,796	10,363	8,919
58,050	58,100	10,375	7,804	10,375	8,931
58,100	58,150	10,388	7,811	10,388	8,944
58,150	58,200	10,400	7,819	10,400	8,956
58,200	58,250	10,413	7,826	10,413	8,969
58,250	58,300	10,425	7,834	10,425	8,981
58,300	58,350	10,438	7,841	10,438	8,994
58,350	58,400	10,450	7,849	10,450	9,006
58,400	58,450	10,463	7,856	10,463	9,019
58,450	58,500	10,475	7,864	10,475	9,031
58,500	58,550	10,488	7,871	10,488	9,044
58,550	58,600	10,500	7,879	10,500	9,056
58,600	58,650	10,513	7,886	10,513	9,069
58,650	58,700	10,525	7,894	10,525	9,081
58,700	58,750	10,538	7,901	10,538	9,094
58,750	58,800	10,550	7,909	10,550	9,106
58,800	58,850	10,563	7,916	10,563	9,119
58,850	58,900	10,575	7,924	10,575	9,131
58,900	58,950	10,588	7,931	10,588	9,144
58,950	59,000	10,600	7,939	10,600	9,156

59,000

At least	But less than	Single	Married filing jointly *	Married filing separately	Head of a household
59,000	59,050	10,613	7,946	10,613	9,169
59,050	59,100	10,625	7,954	10,625	9,181
59,100	59,150	10,638	7,961	10,638	9,194
59,150	59,200	10,650	7,969	10,650	9,206
59,200	59,250	10,663	7,976	10,663	9,219
59,250	59,300	10,675	7,984	10,675	9,231
59,300	59,350	10,688	7,991	10,688	9,244
59,350	59,400	10,700	7,999	10,700	9,256
59,400	59,450	10,713	8,006	10,713	9,269
59,450	59,500	10,725	8,014	10,725	9,281
59,500	59,550	10,738	8,021	10,738	9,294
59,550	59,600	10,750	8,029	10,750	9,306
59,600	59,650	10,763	8,036	10,763	9,319
59,650	59,700	10,775	8,044	10,775	9,331
59,700	59,750	10,788	8,051	10,788	9,344
59,750	59,800	10,800	8,059	10,800	9,356
59,800	59,850	10,813	8,066	10,813	9,369
59,850	59,900	10,825	8,074	10,825	9,381
59,900	59,950	10,838	8,081	10,838	9,394
59,950	60,000	10,850	8,089	10,850	9,406

60,000

At least	But less than	Single	Married filing jointly *	Married filing separately	Head of a household
60,000	60,050	10,863	8,096	10,863	9,419
60,050	60,100	10,875	8,104	10,875	9,431
60,100	60,150	10,888	8,111	10,888	9,444
60,150	60,200	10,900	8,119	10,900	9,456
60,200	60,250	10,913	8,126	10,913	9,469
60,250	60,300	10,925	8,134	10,925	9,481
60,300	60,350	10,938	8,141	10,938	9,494
60,350	60,400	10,950	8,149	10,950	9,506
60,400	60,450	10,963	8,156	10,963	9,519
60,450	60,500	10,975	8,164	10,975	9,531
60,500	60,550	10,988	8,171	10,988	9,544
60,550	60,600	11,000	8,179	11,000	9,556
60,600	60,650	11,013	8,186	11,013	9,569
60,650	60,700	11,025	8,194	11,025	9,581
60,700	60,750	11,038	8,201	11,038	9,594
60,750	60,800	11,050	8,209	11,050	9,606
60,800	60,850	11,063	8,216	11,063	9,619
60,850	60,900	11,075	8,224	11,075	9,631
60,900	60,950	11,088	8,231	11,088	9,644
60,950	61,000	11,100	8,239	11,100	9,656

61,000

At least	But less than	Single	Married filing jointly *	Married filing separately	Head of a household
61,000	61,050	11,113	8,246	11,113	9,669
61,050	61,100	11,125	8,254	11,125	9,681
61,100	61,150	11,138	8,261	11,138	9,694
61,150	61,200	11,150	8,269	11,150	9,706
61,200	61,250	11,163	8,276	11,163	9,719
61,250	61,300	11,175	8,284	11,175	9,731
61,300	61,350	11,188	8,291	11,188	9,744
61,350	61,400	11,200	8,299	11,200	9,756
61,400	61,450	11,213	8,306	11,213	9,769
61,450	61,500	11,225	8,314	11,225	9,781
61,500	61,550	11,238	8,321	11,238	9,794
61,550	61,600	11,250	8,329	11,250	9,806
61,600	61,650	11,263	8,336	11,263	9,819
61,650	61,700	11,275	8,344	11,275	9,831
61,700	61,750	11,288	8,351	11,288	9,844
61,750	61,800	11,300	8,359	11,300	9,856
61,800	61,850	11,313	8,366	11,313	9,869
61,850	61,900	11,325	8,374	11,325	9,881
61,900	61,950	11,338	8,381	11,338	9,894
61,950	62,000	11,350	8,389	11,350	9,906

62,000

At least	But less than	Single	Married filing jointly *	Married filing separately	Head of a household
62,000	62,050	11,363	8,396	11,363	9,919
62,050	62,100	11,375	8,404	11,375	9,931
62,100	62,150	11,388	8,411	11,388	9,944
62,150	62,200	11,400	8,419	11,400	9,956
62,200	62,250	11,413	8,426	11,413	9,969
62,250	62,300	11,425	8,434	11,425	9,981
62,300	62,350	11,438	8,441	11,438	9,994
62,350	62,400	11,450	8,449	11,450	10,006
62,400	62,450	11,463	8,456	11,463	10,019
62,450	62,500	11,475	8,464	11,475	10,031
62,500	62,550	11,488	8,471	11,488	10,044
62,550	62,600	11,500	8,479	11,500	10,056
62,600	62,650	11,513	8,486	11,513	10,069
62,650	62,700	11,525	8,494	11,525	10,081
62,700	62,750	11,538	8,501	11,538	10,094
62,750	62,800	11,550	8,509	11,550	10,106
62,800	62,850	11,563	8,516	11,563	10,119
62,850	62,900	11,575	8,524	11,575	10,131
62,900	62,950	11,588	8,531	11,588	10,144
62,950	63,000	11,600	8,539	11,600	10,156

63,000

At least	But less than	Single	Married filing jointly *	Married filing separately	Head of a household
63,000	63,050	11,613	8,546	11,613	10,169
63,050	63,100	11,625	8,554	11,625	10,181
63,100	63,150	11,638	8,561	11,638	10,194
63,150	63,200	11,650	8,569	11,650	10,206
63,200	63,250	11,663	8,576	11,663	10,219
63,250	63,300	11,675	8,584	11,675	10,231
63,300	63,350	11,688	8,591	11,688	10,244
63,350	63,400	11,700	8,599	11,700	10,256
63,400	63,450	11,713	8,606	11,713	10,269
63,450	63,500	11,725	8,614	11,725	10,281
63,500	63,550	11,738	8,621	11,738	10,294
63,550	63,600	11,750	8,629	11,750	10,306
63,600	63,650	11,763	8,636	11,763	10,319
63,650	63,700	11,775	8,644	11,775	10,331
63,700	63,750	11,788	8,651	11,788	10,344
63,750	63,800	11,800	8,659	11,800	10,356
63,800	63,850	11,813	8,666	11,813	10,369
63,850	63,900	11,825	8,674	11,825	10,381
63,900	63,950	11,838	8,681	11,838	10,394
63,950	64,000	11,850	8,689	11,850	10,406

64,000

At least	But less than	Single	Married filing jointly *	Married filing separately	Head of a household
64,000	64,050	11,863	8,696	11,863	10,419
64,050	64,100	11,875	8,704	11,875	10,431
64,100	64,150	11,888	8,711	11,888	10,444
64,150	64,200	11,900	8,719	11,900	10,456
64,200	64,250	11,913	8,726	11,913	10,469
64,250	64,300	11,925	8,734	11,925	10,481
64,300	64,350	11,938	8,741	11,938	10,494
64,350	64,400	11,950	8,749	11,950	10,506
64,400	64,450	11,963	8,756	11,963	10,519
64,450	64,500	11,975	8,764	11,975	10,531
64,500	64,550	11,988	8,771	11,988	10,544
64,550	64,600	12,000	8,779	12,000	10,556
64,600	64,650	12,013	8,786	12,013	10,569
64,650	64,700	12,025	8,794	12,025	10,581
64,700	64,750	12,038	8,801	12,038	10,594
64,750	64,800	12,050	8,809	12,050	10,606
64,800	64,850	12,063	8,816	12,063	10,619
64,850	64,900	12,075	8,824	12,075	10,631
64,900	64,950	12,088	8,831	12,088	10,644
64,950	65,000	12,100	8,839	12,100	10,656

65,000

At least	But less than	Single	Married filing jointly *	Married filing separately	Head of a household
65,000	65,050	12,113	8,846	12,113	10,669
65,050	65,100	12,125	8,854	12,125	10,681
65,100	65,150	12,138	8,861	12,138	10,694
65,150	65,200	12,150	8,869	12,150	10,706
65,200	65,250	12,163	8,876	12,163	10,719
65,250	65,300	12,175	8,884	12,175	10,731
65,300	65,350	12,188	8,891	12,188	10,744
65,350	65,400	12,200	8,899	12,200	10,756
65,400	65,450	12,213	8,906	12,213	10,769
65,450	65,500	12,225	8,914	12,225	10,781
65,500	65,550	12,238	8,921	12,238	10,794
65,550	65,600	12,250	8,929	12,250	10,806
65,600	65,650	12,263	8,936	12,263	10,819
65,650	65,700	12,275	8,944	12,275	10,831
65,700	65,750	12,288	8,951	12,288	10,844
65,750	65,800	12,300	8,959	12,300	10,856
65,800	65,850	12,313	8,966	12,313	10,869
65,850	65,900	12,325	8,974	12,325	10,881
65,900	65,950	12,338	8,981	12,338	10,894
65,950	66,000	12,350	8,989	12,350	10,906

(Continued)

* This column must also be used by a qualifying widow(er).

(Continued on page T-10)

2014 Tax Table — Continued

66,000

At least	But less than	Single	Married filing jointly *	Married filing separately	Head of a household
66,000	66,050	12,363	8,996	12,363	10,919
66,050	66,100	12,375	9,004	12,375	10,931
66,100	66,150	12,388	9,011	12,388	10,944
66,150	66,200	12,400	9,019	12,400	10,956
66,200	66,250	12,413	9,026	12,413	10,969
66,250	66,300	12,425	9,034	12,425	10,981
66,300	66,350	12,438	9,041	12,438	10,994
66,350	66,400	12,450	9,049	12,450	11,006
66,400	66,450	12,463	9,056	12,463	11,019
66,450	66,500	12,475	9,064	12,475	11,031
66,500	66,550	12,488	9,071	12,488	11,044
66,550	66,600	12,500	9,079	12,500	11,056
66,600	66,650	12,513	9,086	12,513	11,069
66,650	66,700	12,525	9,094	12,525	11,081
66,700	66,750	12,538	9,101	12,538	11,094
66,750	66,800	12,550	9,109	12,550	11,106
66,800	66,850	12,563	9,116	12,563	11,119
66,850	66,900	12,575	9,124	12,575	11,131
66,900	66,950	12,588	9,131	12,588	11,144
66,950	67,000	12,600	9,139	12,600	11,156

67,000

At least	But less than	Single	Married filing jointly *	Married filing separately	Head of a household
67,000	67,050	12,613	9,146	12,613	11,169
67,050	67,100	12,625	9,154	12,625	11,181
67,100	67,150	12,638	9,161	12,638	11,194
67,150	67,200	12,650	9,169	12,650	11,206
67,200	67,250	12,663	9,176	12,663	11,219
67,250	67,300	12,675	9,184	12,675	11,231
67,300	67,350	12,688	9,191	12,688	11,244
67,350	67,400	12,700	9,199	12,700	11,256
67,400	67,450	12,713	9,206	12,713	11,269
67,450	67,500	12,725	9,214	12,725	11,281
67,500	67,550	12,738	9,221	12,738	11,294
67,550	67,600	12,750	9,229	12,750	11,306
67,600	67,650	12,763	9,236	12,763	11,319
67,650	67,700	12,775	9,244	12,775	11,331
67,700	67,750	12,788	9,251	12,788	11,344
67,750	67,800	12,800	9,259	12,800	11,356
67,800	67,850	12,813	9,266	12,813	11,369
67,850	67,900	12,825	9,274	12,825	11,381
67,900	67,950	12,838	9,281	12,838	11,394
67,950	68,000	12,850	9,289	12,850	11,406

68,000

At least	But less than	Single	Married filing jointly *	Married filing separately	Head of a household
68,000	68,050	12,863	9,296	12,863	11,419
68,050	68,100	12,875	9,304	12,875	11,431
68,100	68,150	12,888	9,311	12,888	11,444
68,150	68,200	12,900	9,319	12,900	11,456
68,200	68,250	12,913	9,326	12,913	11,469
68,250	68,300	12,925	9,334	12,925	11,481
68,300	68,350	12,938	9,341	12,938	11,494
68,350	68,400	12,950	9,349	12,950	11,506
68,400	68,450	12,963	9,356	12,963	11,519
68,450	68,500	12,975	9,364	12,975	11,531
68,500	68,550	12,988	9,371	12,988	11,544
68,550	68,600	13,000	9,379	13,000	11,556
68,600	68,650	13,013	9,386	13,013	11,569
68,650	68,700	13,025	9,394	13,025	11,581
68,700	68,750	13,038	9,401	13,038	11,594
68,750	68,800	13,050	9,409	13,050	11,606
68,800	68,850	13,063	9,416	13,063	11,619
68,850	68,900	13,075	9,424	13,075	11,631
68,900	68,950	13,088	9,431	13,088	11,644
68,950	69,000	13,100	9,439	13,100	11,656

69,000

At least	But less than	Single	Married filing jointly *	Married filing separately	Head of a household
69,000	69,050	13,113	9,446	13,113	11,669
69,050	69,100	13,125	9,454	13,125	11,681
69,100	69,150	13,138	9,461	13,138	11,694
69,150	69,200	13,150	9,469	13,150	11,706
69,200	69,250	13,163	9,476	13,163	11,719
69,250	69,300	13,175	9,484	13,175	11,731
69,300	69,350	13,188	9,491	13,188	11,744
69,350	69,400	13,200	9,499	13,200	11,756
69,400	69,450	13,213	9,506	13,213	11,769
69,450	69,500	13,225	9,514	13,225	11,781
69,500	69,550	13,238	9,521	13,238	11,794
69,550	69,600	13,250	9,529	13,250	11,806
69,600	69,650	13,263	9,536	13,263	11,819
69,650	69,700	13,275	9,544	13,275	11,831
69,700	69,750	13,288	9,551	13,288	11,844
69,750	69,800	13,300	9,559	13,300	11,856
69,800	69,850	13,313	9,566	13,313	11,869
69,850	69,900	13,325	9,574	13,325	11,881
69,900	69,950	13,338	9,581	13,338	11,894
69,950	70,000	13,350	9,589	13,350	11,906

70,000

At least	But less than	Single	Married filing jointly *	Married filing separately	Head of a household
70,000	70,050	13,363	9,596	13,363	11,919
70,050	70,100	13,375	9,604	13,375	11,931
70,100	70,150	13,388	9,611	13,388	11,944
70,150	70,200	13,400	9,619	13,400	11,956
70,200	70,250	13,413	9,626	13,413	11,969
70,250	70,300	13,425	9,634	13,425	11,981
70,300	70,350	13,438	9,641	13,438	11,994
70,350	70,400	13,450	9,649	13,450	12,006
70,400	70,450	13,463	9,656	13,463	12,019
70,450	70,500	13,475	9,664	13,475	12,031
70,500	70,550	13,488	9,671	13,488	12,044
70,550	70,600	13,500	9,679	13,500	12,056
70,600	70,650	13,513	9,686	13,513	12,069
70,650	70,700	13,525	9,694	13,525	12,081
70,700	70,750	13,538	9,701	13,538	12,094
70,750	70,800	13,550	9,709	13,550	12,106
70,800	70,850	13,563	9,716	13,563	12,119
70,850	70,900	13,575	9,724	13,575	12,131
70,900	70,950	13,588	9,731	13,588	12,144
70,950	71,000	13,600	9,739	13,600	12,156

71,000

At least	But less than	Single	Married filing jointly *	Married filing separately	Head of a household
71,000	71,050	13,613	9,746	13,613	12,169
71,050	71,100	13,625	9,754	13,625	12,181
71,100	71,150	13,638	9,761	13,638	12,194
71,150	71,200	13,650	9,769	13,650	12,206
71,200	71,250	13,663	9,776	13,663	12,219
71,250	71,300	13,675	9,784	13,675	12,231
71,300	71,350	13,688	9,791	13,688	12,244
71,350	71,400	13,700	9,799	13,700	12,256
71,400	71,450	13,713	9,806	13,713	12,269
71,450	71,500	13,725	9,814	13,725	12,281
71,500	71,550	13,738	9,821	13,738	12,294
71,550	71,600	13,750	9,829	13,750	12,306
71,600	71,650	13,763	9,836	13,763	12,319
71,650	71,700	13,775	9,844	13,775	12,331
71,700	71,750	13,788	9,851	13,788	12,344
71,750	71,800	13,800	9,859	13,800	12,356
71,800	71,850	13,813	9,866	13,813	12,369
71,850	71,900	13,825	9,874	13,825	12,381
71,900	71,950	13,838	9,881	13,838	12,394
71,950	72,000	13,850	9,889	13,850	12,406

72,000

At least	But less than	Single	Married filing jointly *	Married filing separately	Head of a household
72,000	72,050	13,863	9,896	13,863	12,419
72,050	72,100	13,875	9,904	13,875	12,431
72,100	72,150	13,888	9,911	13,888	12,444
72,150	72,200	13,900	9,919	13,900	12,456
72,200	72,250	13,913	9,926	13,913	12,469
72,250	72,300	13,925	9,934	13,925	12,481
72,300	72,350	13,938	9,941	13,938	12,494
72,350	72,400	13,950	9,949	13,950	12,506
72,400	72,450	13,963	9,956	13,963	12,519
72,450	72,500	13,975	9,964	13,975	12,531
72,500	72,550	13,988	9,971	13,988	12,544
72,550	72,600	14,000	9,979	14,000	12,556
72,600	72,650	14,013	9,986	14,013	12,569
72,650	72,700	14,025	9,994	14,025	12,581
72,700	72,750	14,038	10,001	14,038	12,594
72,750	72,800	14,050	10,009	14,050	12,606
72,800	72,850	14,063	10,016	14,063	12,619
72,850	72,900	14,075	10,024	14,075	12,631
72,900	72,950	14,088	10,031	14,088	12,644
72,950	73,000	14,100	10,039	14,100	12,656

73,000

At least	But less than	Single	Married filing jointly *	Married filing separately	Head of a household
73,000	73,050	14,113	10,046	14,113	12,669
73,050	73,100	14,125	10,054	14,125	12,681
73,100	73,150	14,138	10,061	14,138	12,694
73,150	73,200	14,150	10,069	14,150	12,706
73,200	73,250	14,163	10,076	14,163	12,719
73,250	73,300	14,175	10,084	14,175	12,731
73,300	73,350	14,188	10,091	14,188	12,744
73,350	73,400	14,200	10,099	14,200	12,756
73,400	73,450	14,213	10,106	14,213	12,769
73,450	73,500	14,225	10,114	14,225	12,781
73,500	73,550	14,238	10,121	14,238	12,794
73,550	73,600	14,250	10,129	14,250	12,806
73,600	73,650	14,263	10,136	14,263	12,819
73,650	73,700	14,275	10,144	14,275	12,831
73,700	73,750	14,288	10,151	14,288	12,844
73,750	73,800	14,300	10,159	14,300	12,856
73,800	73,850	14,313	10,169	14,313	12,869
73,850	73,900	14,325	10,181	14,325	12,881
73,900	73,950	14,338	10,194	14,338	12,894
73,950	74,000	14,350	10,206	14,350	12,906

74,000

At least	But less than	Single	Married filing jointly *	Married filing separately	Head of a household
74,000	74,050	14,363	10,219	14,363	12,919
74,050	74,100	14,375	10,231	14,375	12,931
74,100	74,150	14,388	10,244	14,388	12,944
74,150	74,200	14,400	10,256	14,400	12,956
74,200	74,250	14,413	10,269	14,413	12,969
74,250	74,300	14,425	10,281	14,425	12,981
74,300	74,350	14,438	10,294	14,438	12,994
74,350	74,400	14,450	10,306	14,450	13,006
74,400	74,450	14,463	10,319	14,463	13,019
74,450	74,500	14,475	10,331	14,477	13,031
74,500	74,550	14,488	10,344	14,491	13,044
74,550	74,600	14,500	10,356	14,505	13,056
74,600	74,650	14,513	10,369	14,519	13,069
74,650	74,700	14,525	10,381	14,533	13,081
74,700	74,750	14,538	10,394	14,547	13,094
74,750	74,800	14,550	10,406	14,561	13,106
74,800	74,850	14,563	10,419	14,575	13,119
74,850	74,900	14,575	10,431	14,589	13,131
74,900	74,950	14,588	10,444	14,603	13,144
74,950	75,000	14,600	10,456	14,617	13,156

(Continued)

* This column must also be used by a qualifying widow(er).

(Continued on page T-11)

2014 Tax Table — *Continued*

75,000

At least	But less than	Single	Married filing jointly *	Married filing separately	Head of a household
75,000	75,050	14,613	10,469	14,631	13,169
75,050	75,100	14,625	10,481	14,645	13,181
75,100	75,150	14,638	10,494	14,659	13,194
75,150	75,200	14,650	10,506	14,673	13,206
75,200	75,250	14,663	10,519	14,687	13,219
75,250	75,300	14,675	10,531	14,701	13,231
75,300	75,350	14,688	10,544	14,715	13,244
75,350	75,400	14,700	10,556	14,729	13,256
75,400	75,450	14,713	10,569	14,743	13,269
75,450	75,500	14,725	10,581	14,757	13,281
75,500	75,550	14,738	10,594	14,771	13,294
75,550	75,600	14,750	10,606	14,785	13,306
75,600	75,650	14,763	10,619	14,799	13,319
75,650	75,700	14,775	10,631	14,813	13,331
75,700	75,750	14,788	10,644	14,827	13,344
75,750	75,800	14,800	10,656	14,841	13,356
75,800	75,850	14,813	10,669	14,855	13,369
75,850	75,900	14,825	10,681	14,869	13,381
75,900	75,950	14,838	10,694	14,883	13,394
75,950	76,000	14,850	10,706	14,897	13,406

76,000

At least	But less than	Single	Married filing jointly *	Married filing separately	Head of a household
76,000	76,050	14,863	10,719	14,911	13,419
76,050	76,100	14,875	10,731	14,925	13,431
76,100	76,150	14,888	10,744	14,939	13,444
76,150	76,200	14,900	10,756	14,953	13,456
76,200	76,250	14,913	10,769	14,967	13,469
76,250	76,300	14,925	10,781	14,981	13,481
76,300	76,350	14,938	10,794	14,995	13,494
76,350	76,400	14,950	10,806	15,009	13,506
76,400	76,450	14,963	10,819	15,023	13,519
76,450	76,500	14,975	10,831	15,037	13,531
76,500	76,550	14,988	10,844	15,051	13,544
76,550	76,600	15,000	10,856	15,065	13,556
76,600	76,650	15,013	10,869	15,079	13,569
76,650	76,700	15,025	10,881	15,093	13,581
76,700	76,750	15,038	10,894	15,107	13,594
76,750	76,800	15,050	10,906	15,121	13,606
76,800	76,850	15,063	10,919	15,135	13,619
76,850	76,900	15,075	10,931	15,149	13,631
76,900	76,950	15,088	10,944	15,163	13,644
76,950	77,000	15,100	10,956	15,177	13,656

77,000

At least	But less than	Single	Married filing jointly *	Married filing separately	Head of a household
77,000	77,050	15,113	10,969	15,191	13,669
77,050	77,100	15,125	10,981	15,205	13,681
77,100	77,150	15,138	10,994	15,219	13,694
77,150	77,200	15,150	11,006	15,233	13,706
77,200	77,250	15,163	11,019	15,247	13,719
77,250	77,300	15,175	11,031	15,261	13,731
77,300	77,350	15,188	11,044	15,275	13,744
77,350	77,400	15,200	11,056	15,289	13,756
77,400	77,450	15,213	11,069	15,303	13,769
77,450	77,500	15,225	11,081	15,317	13,781
77,500	77,550	15,238	11,094	15,331	13,794
77,550	77,600	15,250	11,106	15,345	13,806
77,600	77,650	15,263	11,119	15,359	13,819
77,650	77,700	15,275	11,131	15,373	13,831
77,700	77,750	15,288	11,144	15,387	13,844
77,750	77,800	15,300	11,156	15,401	13,856
77,800	77,850	15,313	11,169	15,415	13,869
77,850	77,900	15,325	11,181	15,429	13,881
77,900	77,950	15,338	11,194	15,443	13,894
77,950	78,000	15,350	11,206	15,457	13,906

78,000

At least	But less than	Single	Married filing jointly *	Married filing separately	Head of a household
78,000	78,050	15,363	11,219	15,471	13,919
78,050	78,100	15,375	11,231	15,485	13,931
78,100	78,150	15,388	11,244	15,499	13,944
78,150	78,200	15,400	11,256	15,513	13,956
78,200	78,250	15,413	11,269	15,527	13,969
78,250	78,300	15,425	11,281	15,541	13,981
78,300	78,350	15,438	11,294	15,555	13,994
78,350	78,400	15,450	11,306	15,569	14,006
78,400	78,450	15,463	11,319	15,583	14,019
78,450	78,500	15,475	11,331	15,597	14,031
78,500	78,550	15,488	11,344	15,611	14,044
78,550	78,600	15,500	11,356	15,625	14,056
78,600	78,650	15,513	11,369	15,639	14,069
78,650	78,700	15,525	11,381	15,653	14,081
78,700	78,750	15,538	11,394	15,667	14,094
78,750	78,800	15,550	11,406	15,681	14,106
78,800	78,850	15,563	11,419	15,695	14,119
78,850	78,900	15,575	11,431	15,709	14,131
78,900	78,950	15,588	11,444	15,723	14,144
78,950	79,000	15,600	11,456	15,737	14,156

79,000

At least	But less than	Single	Married filing jointly *	Married filing separately	Head of a household
79,000	79,050	15,613	11,469	15,751	14,169
79,050	79,100	15,625	11,481	15,765	14,181
79,100	79,150	15,638	11,494	15,779	14,194
79,150	79,200	15,650	11,506	15,793	14,206
79,200	79,250	15,663	11,519	15,807	14,219
79,250	79,300	15,675	11,531	15,821	14,231
79,300	79,350	15,688	11,544	15,835	14,244
79,350	79,400	15,700	11,556	15,849	14,256
79,400	79,450	15,713	11,569	15,863	14,269
79,450	79,500	15,725	11,581	15,877	14,281
79,500	79,550	15,738	11,594	15,891	14,294
79,550	79,600	15,750	11,606	15,905	14,306
79,600	79,650	15,763	11,619	15,919	14,319
79,650	79,700	15,775	11,631	15,933	14,331
79,700	79,750	15,788	11,644	15,947	14,344
79,750	79,800	15,800	11,656	15,961	14,356
79,800	79,850	15,813	11,669	15,975	14,369
79,850	79,900	15,825	11,681	15,989	14,381
79,900	79,950	15,838	11,694	16,003	14,394
79,950	80,000	15,850	11,706	16,017	14,406

80,000

At least	But less than	Single	Married filing jointly *	Married filing separately	Head of a household
80,000	80,050	15,863	11,719	16,031	14,419
80,050	80,100	15,875	11,731	16,045	14,431
80,100	80,150	15,888	11,744	16,059	14,444
80,150	80,200	15,900	11,756	16,073	14,456
80,200	80,250	15,913	11,769	16,087	14,469
80,250	80,300	15,925	11,781	16,101	14,481
80,300	80,350	15,938	11,794	16,115	14,494
80,350	80,400	15,950	11,806	16,129	14,506
80,400	80,450	15,963	11,819	16,143	14,519
80,450	80,500	15,975	11,831	16,157	14,531
80,500	80,550	15,988	11,844	16,171	14,544
80,550	80,600	16,000	11,856	16,185	14,556
80,600	80,650	16,013	11,869	16,199	14,569
80,650	80,700	16,025	11,881	16,213	14,581
80,700	80,750	16,038	11,894	16,227	14,594
80,750	80,800	16,050	11,906	16,241	14,606
80,800	80,850	16,063	11,919	16,255	14,619
80,850	80,900	16,075	11,931	16,269	14,631
80,900	80,950	16,088	11,944	16,283	14,644
80,950	81,000	16,100	11,956	16,297	14,656

81,000

At least	But less than	Single	Married filing jointly *	Married filing separately	Head of a household
81,000	81,050	16,113	11,969	16,311	14,669
81,050	81,100	16,125	11,981	16,325	14,681
81,100	81,150	16,138	11,994	16,339	14,694
81,150	81,200	16,150	12,006	16,353	14,706
81,200	81,250	16,163	12,019	16,367	14,719
81,250	81,300	16,175	12,031	16,381	14,731
81,300	81,350	16,188	12,044	16,395	14,744
81,350	81,400	16,200	12,056	16,409	14,756
81,400	81,450	16,213	12,069	16,423	14,769
81,450	81,500	16,225	12,081	16,437	14,781
81,500	81,550	16,238	12,094	16,451	14,794
81,550	81,600	16,250	12,106	16,465	14,806
81,600	81,650	16,263	12,119	16,479	14,819
81,650	81,700	16,275	12,131	16,493	14,831
81,700	81,750	16,288	12,144	16,507	14,844
81,750	81,800	16,300	12,156	16,521	14,856
81,800	81,850	16,313	12,169	16,535	14,869
81,850	81,900	16,325	12,181	16,549	14,881
81,900	81,950	16,338	12,194	16,563	14,894
81,950	82,000	16,350	12,206	16,577	14,906

82,000

At least	But less than	Single	Married filing jointly *	Married filing separately	Head of a household
82,000	82,050	16,363	12,219	16,591	14,919
82,050	82,100	16,375	12,231	16,605	14,931
82,100	82,150	16,388	12,244	16,619	14,944
82,150	82,200	16,400	12,256	16,633	14,956
82,200	82,250	16,413	12,269	16,647	14,969
82,250	82,300	16,425	12,281	16,661	14,981
82,300	82,350	16,438	12,294	16,675	14,994
82,350	82,400	16,450	12,306	16,689	15,006
82,400	82,450	16,463	12,319	16,703	15,019
82,450	82,500	16,475	12,331	16,717	15,031
82,500	82,550	16,488	12,344	16,731	15,044
82,550	82,600	16,500	12,356	16,745	15,056
82,600	82,650	16,513	12,369	16,759	15,069
82,650	82,700	16,525	12,381	16,773	15,081
82,700	82,750	16,538	12,394	16,787	15,094
82,750	82,800	16,550	12,406	16,801	15,106
82,800	82,850	16,563	12,419	16,815	15,119
82,850	82,900	16,575	12,431	16,829	15,131
82,900	82,950	16,588	12,444	16,843	15,144
82,950	83,000	16,600	12,456	16,857	15,156

83,000

At least	But less than	Single	Married filing jointly *	Married filing separately	Head of a household
83,000	83,050	16,613	12,469	16,871	15,169
83,050	83,100	16,625	12,481	16,885	15,181
83,100	83,150	16,638	12,494	16,899	15,194
83,150	83,200	16,650	12,506	16,913	15,206
83,200	83,250	16,663	12,519	16,927	15,219
83,250	83,300	16,675	12,531	16,941	15,231
83,300	83,350	16,688	12,544	16,955	15,244
83,350	83,400	16,700	12,556	16,969	15,256
83,400	83,450	16,713	12,569	16,983	15,269
83,450	83,500	16,725	12,581	16,997	15,281
83,500	83,550	16,738	12,594	17,011	15,294
83,550	83,600	16,750	12,606	17,025	15,306
83,600	83,650	16,763	12,619	17,039	15,319
83,650	83,700	16,775	12,631	17,053	15,331
83,700	83,750	16,788	12,644	17,067	15,344
83,750	83,800	16,800	12,656	17,081	15,356
83,800	83,850	16,813	12,669	17,095	15,369
83,850	83,900	16,825	12,681	17,109	15,381
83,900	83,950	16,838	12,694	17,123	15,394
83,950	84,000	16,850	12,706	17,137	15,406

(Continued)

* This column must also be used by a qualifying widow(er).

(Continued on page T-12)

2014 Tax Table — Continued

If line 43 (taxable income) is—		And you are—			
At least	But less than	Single	Married filing jointly *	Married filing separately	Head of a house-hold
		Your tax is—			

84,000

At least	But less than	Single	Married filing jointly *	Married filing separately	Head of a household
84,000	84,050	16,863	12,719	17,151	15,419
84,050	84,100	16,875	12,731	17,165	15,431
84,100	84,150	16,888	12,744	17,179	15,444
84,150	84,200	16,900	12,756	17,193	15,456
84,200	84,250	16,913	12,769	17,207	15,469
84,250	84,300	16,925	12,781	17,221	15,481
84,300	84,350	16,938	12,794	17,235	15,494
84,350	84,400	16,950	12,806	17,249	15,506
84,400	84,450	16,963	12,819	17,263	15,519
84,450	84,500	16,975	12,831	17,277	15,531
84,500	84,550	16,988	12,844	17,291	15,544
84,550	84,600	17,000	12,856	17,305	15,556
84,600	84,650	17,013	12,869	17,319	15,569
84,650	84,700	17,025	12,881	17,333	15,581
84,700	84,750	17,038	12,894	17,347	15,594
84,750	84,800	17,050	12,906	17,361	15,606
84,800	84,850	17,063	12,919	17,375	15,619
84,850	84,900	17,075	12,931	17,389	15,631
84,900	84,950	17,088	12,944	17,403	15,644
84,950	85,000	17,100	12,956	17,417	15,656

85,000

At least	But less than	Single	Married filing jointly *	Married filing separately	Head of a household
85,000	85,050	17,113	12,969	17,431	15,669
85,050	85,100	17,125	12,981	17,445	15,681
85,100	85,150	17,138	12,994	17,459	15,694
85,150	85,200	17,150	13,006	17,473	15,706
85,200	85,250	17,163	13,019	17,487	15,719
85,250	85,300	17,175	13,031	17,501	15,731
85,300	85,350	17,188	13,044	17,515	15,744
85,350	85,400	17,200	13,056	17,529	15,756
85,400	85,450	17,213	13,069	17,543	15,769
85,450	85,500	17,225	13,081	17,557	15,781
85,500	85,550	17,238	13,094	17,571	15,794
85,550	85,600	17,250	13,106	17,585	15,806
85,600	85,650	17,263	13,119	17,599	15,819
85,650	85,700	17,275	13,131	17,613	15,831
85,700	85,750	17,288	13,144	17,627	15,844
85,750	85,800	17,300	13,156	17,641	15,856
85,800	85,850	17,313	13,169	17,655	15,869
85,850	85,900	17,325	13,181	17,669	15,881
85,900	85,950	17,338	13,194	17,683	15,894
85,950	86,000	17,350	13,206	17,697	15,906

86,000

At least	But less than	Single	Married filing jointly *	Married filing separately	Head of a household
86,000	86,050	17,363	13,219	17,711	15,919
86,050	86,100	17,375	13,231	17,725	15,931
86,100	86,150	17,388	13,244	17,739	15,944
86,150	86,200	17,400	13,256	17,753	15,956
86,200	86,250	17,413	13,269	17,767	15,969
86,250	86,300	17,425	13,281	17,781	15,981
86,300	86,350	17,438	13,294	17,795	15,994
86,350	86,400	17,450	13,306	17,809	16,006
86,400	86,450	17,463	13,319	17,823	16,019
86,450	86,500	17,475	13,331	17,837	16,031
86,500	86,550	17,488	13,344	17,851	16,044
86,550	86,600	17,500	13,356	17,865	16,056
86,600	86,650	17,513	13,369	17,879	16,069
86,650	86,700	17,525	13,381	17,893	16,081
86,700	86,750	17,538	13,394	17,907	16,094
86,750	86,800	17,550	13,406	17,921	16,106
86,800	86,850	17,563	13,419	17,935	16,119
86,850	86,900	17,575	13,431	17,949	16,131
86,900	86,950	17,588	13,444	17,963	16,144
86,950	87,000	17,600	13,456	17,977	16,156

87,000

At least	But less than	Single	Married filing jointly *	Married filing separately	Head of a household
87,000	87,050	17,613	13,469	17,991	16,169
87,050	87,100	17,625	13,481	18,005	16,181
87,100	87,150	17,638	13,494	18,019	16,194
87,150	87,200	17,650	13,506	18,033	16,206
87,200	87,250	17,663	13,519	18,047	16,219
87,250	87,300	17,675	13,531	18,061	16,231
87,300	87,350	17,688	13,544	18,075	16,244
87,350	87,400	17,700	13,556	18,089	16,256
87,400	87,450	17,713	13,569	18,103	16,269
87,450	87,500	17,725	13,581	18,117	16,281
87,500	87,550	17,738	13,594	18,131	16,294
87,550	87,600	17,750	13,606	18,145	16,306
87,600	87,650	17,763	13,619	18,159	16,319
87,650	87,700	17,775	13,631	18,173	16,331
87,700	87,750	17,788	13,644	18,187	16,344
87,750	87,800	17,800	13,656	18,201	16,356
87,800	87,850	17,813	13,669	18,215	16,369
87,850	87,900	17,825	13,681	18,229	16,381
87,900	87,950	17,838	13,694	18,243	16,394
87,950	88,000	17,850	13,706	18,257	16,406

88,000

At least	But less than	Single	Married filing jointly *	Married filing separately	Head of a household
88,000	88,050	17,863	13,719	18,271	16,419
88,050	88,100	17,875	13,731	18,285	16,431
88,100	88,150	17,888	13,744	18,299	16,444
88,150	88,200	17,900	13,756	18,313	16,456
88,200	88,250	17,913	13,769	18,327	16,469
88,250	88,300	17,925	13,781	18,341	16,481
88,300	88,350	17,938	13,794	18,355	16,494
88,350	88,400	17,950	13,806	18,369	16,506
88,400	88,450	17,963	13,819	18,383	16,519
88,450	88,500	17,975	13,831	18,397	16,531
88,500	88,550	17,988	13,844	18,411	16,544
88,550	88,600	18,000	13,856	18,425	16,556
88,600	88,650	18,013	13,869	18,439	16,569
88,650	88,700	18,025	13,881	18,453	16,581
88,700	88,750	18,038	13,894	18,467	16,594
88,750	88,800	18,050	13,906	18,481	16,606
88,800	88,850	18,063	13,919	18,495	16,619
88,850	88,900	18,075	13,931	18,509	16,631
88,900	88,950	18,088	13,944	18,523	16,644
88,950	89,000	18,100	13,956	18,537	16,656

89,000

At least	But less than	Single	Married filing jointly *	Married filing separately	Head of a household
89,000	89,050	18,113	13,969	18,551	16,669
89,050	89,100	18,125	13,981	18,565	16,681
89,100	89,150	18,138	13,994	18,579	16,694
89,150	89,200	18,150	14,006	18,593	16,706
89,200	89,250	18,163	14,019	18,607	16,719
89,250	89,300	18,175	14,031	18,621	16,731
89,300	89,350	18,188	14,044	18,635	16,744
89,350	89,400	18,201	14,056	18,649	16,756
89,400	89,450	18,215	14,069	18,663	16,769
89,450	89,500	18,229	14,081	18,677	16,781
89,500	89,550	18,243	14,094	18,691	16,794
89,550	89,600	18,257	14,106	18,705	16,806
89,600	89,650	18,271	14,119	18,719	16,819
89,650	89,700	18,285	14,131	18,733	16,831
89,700	89,750	18,299	14,144	18,747	16,844
89,750	89,800	18,313	14,156	18,761	16,856
89,800	89,850	18,327	14,169	18,775	16,869
89,850	89,900	18,341	14,181	18,789	16,881
89,900	89,950	18,355	14,194	18,803	16,894
89,950	90,000	18,369	14,206	18,817	16,906

90,000

At least	But less than	Single	Married filing jointly *	Married filing separately	Head of a household
90,000	90,050	18,383	14,219	18,831	16,919
90,050	90,100	18,397	14,231	18,845	16,931
90,100	90,150	18,411	14,244	18,859	16,944
90,150	90,200	18,425	14,256	18,873	16,956
90,200	90,250	18,439	14,269	18,887	16,969
90,250	90,300	18,453	14,281	18,901	16,981
90,300	90,350	18,467	14,294	18,915	16,994
90,350	90,400	18,481	14,306	18,929	17,006
90,400	90,450	18,495	14,319	18,943	17,019
90,450	90,500	18,509	14,331	18,957	17,031
90,500	90,550	18,523	14,344	18,971	17,044
90,550	90,600	18,537	14,356	18,985	17,056
90,600	90,650	18,551	14,369	18,999	17,069
90,650	90,700	18,565	14,381	19,013	17,081
90,700	90,750	18,579	14,394	19,027	17,094
90,750	90,800	18,593	14,406	19,041	17,106
90,800	90,850	18,607	14,419	19,055	17,119
90,850	90,900	18,621	14,431	19,069	17,131
90,900	90,950	18,635	14,444	19,083	17,144
90,950	91,000	18,649	14,456	19,097	17,156

91,000

At least	But less than	Single	Married filing jointly *	Married filing separately	Head of a household
91,000	91,050	18,663	14,469	19,111	17,169
91,050	91,100	18,677	14,481	19,125	17,181
91,100	91,150	18,691	14,494	19,139	17,194
91,150	91,200	18,705	14,506	19,153	17,206
91,200	91,250	18,719	14,519	19,167	17,219
91,250	91,300	18,733	14,531	19,181	17,231
91,300	91,350	18,747	14,544	19,195	17,244
91,350	91,400	18,761	14,556	19,209	17,256
91,400	91,450	18,775	14,569	19,223	17,269
91,450	91,500	18,789	14,581	19,237	17,281
91,500	91,550	18,803	14,594	19,251	17,294
91,550	91,600	18,817	14,606	19,265	17,306
91,600	91,650	18,831	14,619	19,279	17,319
91,650	91,700	18,845	14,631	19,293	17,331
91,700	91,750	18,859	14,644	19,307	17,344
91,750	91,800	18,873	14,656	19,321	17,356
91,800	91,850	18,887	14,669	19,335	17,369
91,850	91,900	18,901	14,681	19,349	17,381
91,900	91,950	18,915	14,694	19,363	17,394
91,950	92,000	18,929	14,706	19,377	17,406

92,000

At least	But less than	Single	Married filing jointly *	Married filing separately	Head of a household
92,000	92,050	18,943	14,719	19,391	17,419
92,050	92,100	18,957	14,731	19,405	17,431
92,100	92,150	18,971	14,744	19,419	17,444
92,150	92,200	18,985	14,756	19,433	17,456
92,200	92,250	18,999	14,769	19,447	17,469
92,250	92,300	19,013	14,781	19,461	17,481
92,300	92,350	19,027	14,794	19,475	17,494
92,350	92,400	19,041	14,806	19,489	17,506
92,400	92,450	19,055	14,819	19,503	17,519
92,450	92,500	19,069	14,831	19,517	17,531
92,500	92,550	19,083	14,844	19,531	17,544
92,550	92,600	19,097	14,856	19,545	17,556
92,600	92,650	19,111	14,869	19,559	17,569
92,650	92,700	19,125	14,881	19,573	17,581
92,700	92,750	19,139	14,894	19,587	17,594
92,750	92,800	19,153	14,906	19,601	17,606
92,800	92,850	19,167	14,919	19,615	17,619
92,850	92,900	19,181	14,931	19,629	17,631
92,900	92,950	19,195	14,944	19,643	17,644
92,950	93,000	19,209	14,956	19,657	17,656

(Continued)

* This column must also be used by a qualifying widow(er).

(Continued on page T-13)

2014 Tax Table — *Continued*

93,000

If line 43 (taxable income) is— At least	But less than	Single	Married filing jointly *	Married filing separately	Head of a household
			Your tax is—		
93,000	93,050	19,223	14,969	19,671	17,669
93,050	93,100	19,237	14,981	19,685	17,681
93,100	93,150	19,251	14,994	19,699	17,694
93,150	93,200	19,265	15,006	19,713	17,706
93,200	93,250	19,279	15,019	19,727	17,719
93,250	93,300	19,293	15,031	19,741	17,731
93,300	93,350	19,307	15,044	19,755	17,744
93,350	93,400	19,321	15,056	19,769	17,756
93,400	93,450	19,335	15,069	19,783	17,769
93,450	93,500	19,349	15,081	19,797	17,781
93,500	93,550	19,363	15,094	19,811	17,794
93,550	93,600	19,377	15,106	19,825	17,806
93,600	93,650	19,391	15,119	19,839	17,819
93,650	93,700	19,405	15,131	19,853	17,831
93,700	93,750	19,419	15,144	19,867	17,844
93,750	93,800	19,433	15,156	19,881	17,856
93,800	93,850	19,447	15,169	19,895	17,869
93,850	93,900	19,461	15,181	19,909	17,881
93,900	93,950	19,475	15,194	19,923	17,894
93,950	94,000	19,489	15,206	19,937	17,906

94,000

At least	But less than	Single	Married filing jointly *	Married filing separately	Head of a household
94,000	94,050	19,503	15,219	19,951	17,919
94,050	94,100	19,517	15,231	19,965	17,931
94,100	94,150	19,531	15,244	19,979	17,944
94,150	94,200	19,545	15,256	19,993	17,956
94,200	94,250	19,559	15,269	20,007	17,969
94,250	94,300	19,573	15,281	20,021	17,981
94,300	94,350	19,587	15,294	20,035	17,994
94,350	94,400	19,601	15,306	20,049	18,006
94,400	94,450	19,615	15,319	20,063	18,019
94,450	94,500	19,629	15,331	20,077	18,031
94,500	94,550	19,643	15,344	20,091	18,044
94,550	94,600	19,657	15,356	20,105	18,056
94,600	94,650	19,671	15,369	20,119	18,069
94,650	94,700	19,685	15,381	20,133	18,081
94,700	94,750	19,699	15,394	20,147	18,094
94,750	94,800	19,713	15,406	20,161	18,106
94,800	94,850	19,727	15,419	20,175	18,119
94,850	94,900	19,741	15,431	20,189	18,131
94,900	94,950	19,755	15,444	20,203	18,144
94,950	95,000	19,769	15,456	20,217	18,156

95,000

At least	But less than	Single	Married filing jointly *	Married filing separately	Head of a household
95,000	95,050	19,783	15,469	20,231	18,169
95,050	95,100	19,797	15,481	20,245	18,181
95,100	95,150	19,811	15,494	20,259	18,194
95,150	95,200	19,825	15,506	20,273	18,206
95,200	95,250	19,839	15,519	20,287	18,219
95,250	95,300	19,853	15,531	20,301	18,231
95,300	95,350	19,867	15,544	20,315	18,244
95,350	95,400	19,881	15,556	20,329	18,256
95,400	95,450	19,895	15,569	20,343	18,269
95,450	95,500	19,909	15,581	20,357	18,281
95,500	95,550	19,923	15,594	20,371	18,294
95,550	95,600	19,937	15,606	20,385	18,306
95,600	95,650	19,951	15,619	20,399	18,319
95,650	95,700	19,965	15,631	20,413	18,331
95,700	95,750	19,979	15,644	20,427	18,344
95,750	95,800	19,993	15,656	20,441	18,356
95,800	95,850	20,007	15,669	20,455	18,369
95,850	95,900	20,021	15,681	20,469	18,381
95,900	95,950	20,035	15,694	20,483	18,394
95,950	96,000	20,049	15,706	20,497	18,406

96,000

At least	But less than	Single	Married filing jointly *	Married filing separately	Head of a household
96,000	96,050	20,063	15,719	20,511	18,419
96,050	96,100	20,077	15,731	20,525	18,431
96,100	96,150	20,091	15,744	20,539	18,444
96,150	96,200	20,105	15,756	20,553	18,456
96,200	96,250	20,119	15,769	20,567	18,469
96,250	96,300	20,133	15,781	20,581	18,481
96,300	96,350	20,147	15,794	20,595	18,494
96,350	96,400	20,161	15,806	20,609	18,506
96,400	96,450	20,175	15,819	20,623	18,519
96,450	96,500	20,189	15,831	20,637	18,531
96,500	96,550	20,203	15,844	20,651	18,544
96,550	96,600	20,217	15,856	20,665	18,556
96,600	96,650	20,231	15,869	20,679	18,569
96,650	96,700	20,245	15,881	20,693	18,581
96,700	96,750	20,259	15,894	20,707	18,594
96,750	96,800	20,273	15,906	20,721	18,606
96,800	96,850	20,287	15,919	20,735	18,619
96,850	96,900	20,301	15,931	20,749	18,631
96,900	96,950	20,315	15,944	20,763	18,644
96,950	97,000	20,329	15,956	20,777	18,656

97,000

At least	But less than	Single	Married filing jointly *	Married filing separately	Head of a household
97,000	97,050	20,343	15,969	20,791	18,669
97,050	97,100	20,357	15,981	20,805	18,681
97,100	97,150	20,371	15,994	20,819	18,694
97,150	97,200	20,385	16,006	20,833	18,706
97,200	97,250	20,399	16,019	20,847	18,719
97,250	97,300	20,413	16,031	20,861	18,731
97,300	97,350	20,427	16,044	20,875	18,744
97,350	97,400	20,441	16,056	20,889	18,756
97,400	97,450	20,455	16,069	20,903	18,769
97,450	97,500	20,469	16,081	20,917	18,781
97,500	97,550	20,483	16,094	20,931	18,794
97,550	97,600	20,497	16,106	20,945	18,806
97,600	97,650	20,511	16,119	20,959	18,819
97,650	97,700	20,525	16,131	20,973	18,831
97,700	97,750	20,539	16,144	20,987	18,844
97,750	97,800	20,553	16,156	21,001	18,856
97,800	97,850	20,567	16,169	21,015	18,869
97,850	97,900	20,581	16,181	21,029	18,881
97,900	97,950	20,595	16,194	21,043	18,894
97,950	98,000	20,609	16,206	21,057	18,906

98,000

At least	But less than	Single	Married filing jointly *	Married filing separately	Head of a household
98,000	98,050	20,623	16,219	21,071	18,919
98,050	98,100	20,637	16,231	21,085	18,931
98,100	98,150	20,651	16,244	21,099	18,944
98,150	98,200	20,665	16,256	21,113	18,956
98,200	98,250	20,679	16,269	21,127	18,969
98,250	98,300	20,693	16,281	21,141	18,981
98,300	98,350	20,707	16,294	21,155	18,994
98,350	98,400	20,721	16,306	21,169	19,006
98,400	98,450	20,735	16,319	21,183	19,019
98,450	98,500	20,749	16,331	21,197	19,031
98,500	98,550	20,763	16,344	21,211	19,044
98,550	98,600	20,777	16,356	21,225	19,056
98,600	98,650	20,791	16,369	21,239	19,069
98,650	98,700	20,805	16,381	21,253	19,081
98,700	98,750	20,819	16,394	21,267	19,094
98,750	98,800	20,833	16,406	21,281	19,106
98,800	98,850	20,847	16,419	21,295	19,119
98,850	98,900	20,861	16,431	21,309	19,131
98,900	98,950	20,875	16,444	21,323	19,144
98,950	99,000	20,889	16,456	21,337	19,156

99,000

At least	But less than	Single	Married filing jointly *	Married filing separately	Head of a household
99,000	99,050	20,903	16,469	21,351	19,169
99,050	99,100	20,917	16,481	21,365	19,181
99,100	99,150	20,931	16,494	21,379	19,194
99,150	99,200	20,945	16,506	21,393	19,206
99,200	99,250	20,959	16,519	21,407	19,219
99,250	99,300	20,973	16,531	21,421	19,231
99,300	99,350	20,987	16,544	21,435	19,244
99,350	99,400	21,001	16,556	21,449	19,256
99,400	99,450	21,015	16,569	21,463	19,269
99,450	99,500	21,029	16,581	21,477	19,281
99,500	99,550	21,043	16,594	21,491	19,294
99,550	99,600	21,057	16,606	21,505	19,306
99,600	99,650	21,071	16,619	21,519	19,319
99,650	99,700	21,085	16,631	21,533	19,331
99,700	99,750	21,099	16,644	21,547	19,344
99,750	99,800	21,113	16,656	21,561	19,356
99,800	99,850	21,127	16,669	21,575	19,369
99,850	99,900	21,141	16,681	21,589	19,381
99,900	99,950	21,155	16,694	21,603	19,394
99,950	100,000	21,169	16,706	21,617	19,406

$100,000
or over
use the Tax
Computation
Worksheet

* This column must also be used by a qualifying widow(er).

2014 Tax Rate Schedules

The Tax Rate Schedules are shown so you can see the tax rate that applies to all levels of taxable income. Do not use them to figure your tax. Instead, see chapter 30.

Schedule X—If your filing status is **Single**

If your taxable income is: Over—	But not over—	The tax is:	of the amount over—
$0	$9,075	.... 10%	$0
9,075	36,900	$907.50 + 15%	9,075
36,900	89,350	5,081.25 + 25%	36,900
89,350	186,350	18,193.75 + 28%	89,350
186,350	405,100	45,353.75 + 33%	186,350
405,100	406,750	117,541.25 + 35%	405,100
406,750	....	118,118.75 + 39.6%	406,750

Schedule Y-1—If your filing status is **Married filing jointly** or **Qualifying widow(er)**

If your taxable income is: Over—	But not over—	The tax is:	of the amount over—
$0	$18,150	.... 10%	$0
18,150	73,800	$1,815.00 + 15%	18,150
73,800	148,850	10,162.50 + 25%	73,800
148,850	226,850	28,925.00 + 28%	148,850
226,850	405,100	50,765.00 + 33%	226,850
405,100	457,600	109,587.50 + 35%	405,100
457,600	....	127,962.50 + 39.6%	457,600

Schedule Y-2—If your filing status is **Married filing separately**

If your taxable income is: Over—	But not over—	The tax is:	of the amount over—
$0	$9,075	.... 10%	$0
9,075	36,900	$907.50 + 15%	9,075
36,900	74,425	5,081.25 + 25%	36,900
74,425	113,425	14,462.50 + 28%	74,425
113,425	202,550	25,382.50 + 33%	113,425
202,550	228,800	54,793.75 + 35%	202,550
228,800	....	63,981.25 + 39.6%	228,800

Schedule Z—If your filing status is **Head of household**

If your taxable income is: Over—	But not over—	The tax is:	of the amount over—
$0	$12,950	.... 10%	$0
12,950	49,400	$1,295.00 + 15%	12,950
49,400	127,550	6,762.50 + 25%	49,400
127,550	206,600	26,300.00 + 28%	127,550
206,600	405,100	48,434.00 + 33%	206,600
405,100	432,200	113,939.00 + 35%	405,100
432,200	....	123,424.00 + 39.6%	432,200

Combined Federal Income Tax, Employee Social Security Tax, and Employee Medicare Tax Withholding Tables

SINGLE Persons—MONTHLY Payroll Period

(For Wages Paid through December 2015)

And the wages are—		And the number of withholding allowances claimed is—										
At least	But less than	0	1	2	3	4	5	6	7	8	9	10
		The amount of income, social security, and Medicare taxes to be withheld is—										
$ 0	$220	7.65%	7.65%	7.65%	7.65%	7.65%	7.65%	7.65%	7.65%	7.65%	7.65%	7.65%
220	230	$20.21	$17.21	$17.21	$17.21	$17.21	$17.21	$17.21	$17.21	$17.21	$17.21	$17.21
230	240	21.98	17.98	17.98	17.98	17.98	17.98	17.98	17.98	17.98	17.98	17.98
240	250	23.74	18.74	18.74	18.74	18.74	18.74	18.74	18.74	18.74	18.74	18.74
250	260	25.51	19.51	19.51	19.51	19.51	19.51	19.51	19.51	19.51	19.51	19.51
260	270	27.27	20.27	20.27	20.27	20.27	20.27	20.27	20.27	20.27	20.27	20.27
270	280	29.04	21.04	21.04	21.04	21.04	21.04	21.04	21.04	21.04	21.04	21.04
280	290	30.80	21.80	21.80	21.80	21.80	21.80	21.80	21.80	21.80	21.80	21.80
290	300	32.57	22.57	22.57	22.57	22.57	22.57	22.57	22.57	22.57	22.57	22.57
300	320	35.72	23.72	23.72	23.72	23.72	23.72	23.72	23.72	23.72	23.72	23.72
320	340	39.25	25.25	25.25	25.25	25.25	25.25	25.25	25.25	25.25	25.25	25.25
340	360	42.78	26.78	26.78	26.78	26.78	26.78	26.78	26.78	26.78	26.78	26.78
360	380	46.31	28.31	28.31	28.31	28.31	28.31	28.31	28.31	28.31	28.31	28.31
380	400	49.84	29.84	29.84	29.84	29.84	29.84	29.84	29.84	29.84	29.84	29.84
400	420	53.37	31.37	31.37	31.37	31.37	31.37	31.37	31.37	31.37	31.37	31.37
420	440	56.90	32.90	32.90	32.90	32.90	32.90	32.90	32.90	32.90	32.90	32.90
440	460	60.43	34.43	34.43	34.43	34.43	34.43	34.43	34.43	34.43	34.43	34.43
460	480	63.96	35.96	35.96	35.96	35.96	35.96	35.96	35.96	35.96	35.96	35.96
480	500	67.49	37.49	37.49	37.49	37.49	37.49	37.49	37.49	37.49	37.49	37.49
500	520	71.02	39.02	39.02	39.02	39.02	39.02	39.02	39.02	39.02	39.02	39.02
520	540	74.55	41.55	40.55	40.55	40.55	40.55	40.55	40.55	40.55	40.55	40.55
540	560	78.08	45.08	42.08	42.08	42.08	42.08	42.08	42.08	42.08	42.08	42.08
560	580	81.61	48.61	43.61	43.61	43.61	43.61	43.61	43.61	43.61	43.61	43.61
580	600	85.14	52.14	45.14	45.14	45.14	45.14	45.14	45.14	45.14	45.14	45.14
600	640	90.43	57.43	47.43	47.43	47.43	47.43	47.43	47.43	47.43	47.43	47.43
640	680	97.49	64.49	50.49	50.49	50.49	50.49	50.49	50.49	50.49	50.49	50.49
680	720	104.55	71.55	53.55	53.55	53.55	53.55	53.55	53.55	53.55	53.55	53.55
720	760	111.61	78.61	56.61	56.61	56.61	56.61	56.61	56.61	56.61	56.61	56.61
760	800	118.67	85.67	59.67	59.67	59.67	59.67	59.67	59.67	59.67	59.67	59.67
800	840	125.73	92.73	62.73	62.73	62.73	62.73	62.73	62.73	62.73	62.73	62.73
840	880	132.79	99.79	65.79	65.79	65.79	65.79	65.79	65.79	65.79	65.79	65.79
880	920	139.85	106.85	72.85	68.85	68.85	68.85	68.85	68.85	68.85	68.85	68.85
920	960	146.91	113.91	79.91	71.91	71.91	71.91	71.91	71.91	71.91	71.91	71.91
960	1,000	154.97	120.97	86.97	74.97	74.97	74.97	74.97	74.97	74.97	74.97	74.97
1,000	1,040	164.03	128.03	94.03	78.03	78.03	78.03	78.03	78.03	78.03	78.03	78.03
1,040	1,080	173.09	135.09	101.09	81.09	81.09	81.09	81.09	81.09	81.09	81.09	81.09
1,080	1,120	182.15	142.15	108.15	84.15	84.15	84.15	84.15	84.15	84.15	84.15	84.15
1,120	1,160	191.21	149.21	115.21	87.21	87.21	87.21	87.21	87.21	87.21	87.21	87.21
1,160	1,200	200.27	156.27	122.27	90.27	90.27	90.27	90.27	90.27	90.27	90.27	90.27
1,200	1,240	209.33	163.33	129.33	96.33	93.33	93.33	93.33	93.33	93.33	93.33	93.33
1,240	1,280	218.39	170.39	136.39	103.39	96.39	96.39	96.39	96.39	96.39	96.39	96.39
1,280	1,320	227.45	177.45	143.45	110.45	99.45	99.45	99.45	99.45	99.45	99.45	99.45
1,320	1,360	236.51	186.51	150.51	117.51	102.51	102.51	102.51	102.51	102.51	102.51	102.51
1,360	1,400	245.57	195.57	157.57	124.57	105.57	105.57	105.57	105.57	105.57	105.57	105.57
1,400	1,440	254.63	204.63	164.63	131.63	108.63	108.63	108.63	108.63	108.63	108.63	108.63
1,440	1,480	263.69	213.69	171.69	138.69	111.69	111.69	111.69	111.69	111.69	111.69	111.69
1,480	1,520	272.75	222.75	178.75	145.75	114.75	114.75	114.75	114.75	114.75	114.75	114.75
1,520	1,560	281.81	231.81	185.81	152.81	119.81	117.81	117.81	117.81	117.81	117.81	117.81
1,560	1,600	290.87	240.87	192.87	159.87	126.87	120.87	120.87	120.87	120.87	120.87	120.87
1,600	1,640	299.93	249.93	199.93	166.93	133.93	123.93	123.93	123.93	123.93	123.93	123.93
1,640	1,680	308.99	258.99	208.99	173.99	140.99	126.99	126.99	126.99	126.99	126.99	126.99
1,680	1,720	318.05	268.05	218.05	181.05	148.05	130.05	130.05	130.05	130.05	130.05	130.05
1,720	1,760	327.11	277.11	227.11	188.11	155.11	133.11	133.11	133.11	133.11	133.11	133.11
1,760	1,800	336.17	286.17	236.17	195.17	162.17	136.17	136.17	136.17	136.17	136.17	136.17
1,800	1,840	345.23	295.23	245.23	202.23	169.23	139.23	139.23	139.23	139.23	139.23	139.23
1,840	1,880	354.29	304.29	254.29	209.29	176.29	142.29	142.29	142.29	142.29	142.29	142.29
1,880	1,920	363.35	313.35	263.35	216.35	183.35	149.35	145.35	145.35	145.35	145.35	145.35
1,920	1,960	372.41	322.41	272.41	223.41	190.41	156.41	148.41	148.41	148.41	148.41	148.41
1,960	2,000	381.47	331.47	281.47	231.47	197.47	163.47	151.47	151.47	151.47	151.47	151.47
2,000	2,040	390.53	340.53	290.53	240.53	204.53	170.53	154.53	154.53	154.53	154.53	154.53
2,040	2,080	399.59	349.59	299.59	249.59	211.59	177.59	157.59	157.59	157.59	157.59	157.59
2,080	2,120	408.65	358.65	308.65	258.65	218.65	184.65	160.65	160.65	160.65	160.65	160.65
2,120	2,160	417.71	367.71	317.71	267.71	225.71	191.71	163.71	163.71	163.71	163.71	163.71
2,160	2,200	426.77	376.77	326.77	276.77	232.77	198.77	166.77	166.77	166.77	166.77	166.77
2,200	2,240	435.83	385.83	335.83	285.83	239.83	205.83	172.83	169.83	169.83	169.83	169.83
2,240	2,280	444.89	394.89	344.89	294.89	246.89	212.89	179.89	172.89	172.89	172.89	172.89
2,280	2,320	453.95	403.95	353.95	303.95	253.95	219.95	186.95	175.95	175.95	175.95	175.95
2,320	2,360	463.01	413.01	363.01	313.01	263.01	227.01	194.01	179.01	179.01	179.01	179.01
2,360	2,400	472.07	422.07	372.07	322.07	272.07	234.07	201.07	182.07	182.07	182.07	182.07

Combined Federal Income Tax, Employee Social Security Tax, and Employee Medicare Tax Withholding Tables

SINGLE Persons—MONTHLY Payroll Period

(For Wages Paid through December 2015)

And the wages are—		And the number of withholding allowances claimed is—										
At least	But less than	0	1	2	3	4	5	6	7	8	9	10
		The amount of income, social security, and Medicare taxes to be withheld is—										
$2,400	$2,440	$481.13	$431.13	$381.13	$331.13	$281.13	$241.13	$208.13	$185.13	$185.13	$185.13	$185.13
2,440	2,480	490.19	440.19	390.19	340.19	290.19	248.19	215.19	188.19	188.19	188.19	188.19
2,480	2,520	499.25	449.25	399.25	349.25	299.25	255.25	222.25	191.25	191.25	191.25	191.25
2,520	2,560	508.31	458.31	408.31	358.31	308.31	262.31	229.31	196.31	194.31	194.31	194.31
2,560	2,600	517.37	467.37	417.37	367.37	317.37	269.37	236.37	203.37	197.37	197.37	197.37
2,600	2,640	526.43	476.43	426.43	376.43	326.43	276.43	243.43	210.43	200.43	200.43	200.43
2,640	2,680	535.49	485.49	435.49	385.49	335.49	285.49	250.49	217.49	203.49	203.49	203.49
2,680	2,720	544.55	494.55	444.55	394.55	344.55	294.55	257.55	224.55	206.55	206.55	206.55
2,720	2,760	553.61	503.61	453.61	403.61	353.61	303.61	264.61	231.61	209.61	209.61	209.61
2,760	2,800	562.67	512.67	462.67	412.67	362.67	312.67	271.67	238.67	212.67	212.67	212.67
2,800	2,840	571.73	521.73	471.73	421.73	371.73	321.73	278.73	245.73	215.73	215.73	215.73
2,840	2,880	580.79	530.79	480.79	430.79	380.79	330.79	285.79	252.79	218.79	218.79	218.79
2,880	2,920	589.85	539.85	489.85	439.85	389.85	339.85	292.85	259.85	225.85	221.85	221.85
2,920	2,960	598.91	548.91	498.91	448.91	398.91	348.91	299.91	266.91	232.91	224.91	224.91
2,960	3,000	607.97	557.97	507.97	457.97	407.97	357.97	307.97	273.97	239.97	227.97	227.97
3,000	3,040	617.03	567.03	517.03	467.03	417.03	367.03	317.03	281.03	247.03	231.03	231.03
3,040	3,080	626.09	576.09	526.09	476.09	426.09	376.09	326.09	288.09	254.09	234.09	234.09
3,080	3,120	635.15	585.15	535.15	485.15	435.15	385.15	335.15	295.15	261.15	237.15	237.15
3,120	3,160	644.21	594.21	544.21	494.21	444.21	394.21	344.21	302.21	268.21	240.21	240.21
3,160	3,200	653.27	603.27	553.27	503.27	453.27	403.27	353.27	309.27	275.27	243.27	243.27
3,200	3,240	662.33	612.33	562.33	512.33	462.33	412.33	362.33	316.33	282.33	249.33	246.33
3,240	3,280	671.39	621.39	571.39	521.39	471.39	421.39	371.39	323.39	289.39	256.39	249.39
3,280	3,320	680.45	630.45	580.45	530.45	480.45	430.45	380.45	330.45	296.45	263.45	252.45
3,320	3,360	692.51	639.51	589.51	539.51	489.51	439.51	389.51	339.51	303.51	270.51	255.51
3,360	3,400	705.57	648.57	598.57	548.57	498.57	448.57	398.57	348.57	310.57	277.57	258.57
3,400	3,440	718.63	657.63	607.63	557.63	507.63	457.63	407.63	357.63	317.63	284.63	261.63
3,440	3,480	731.69	666.69	616.69	566.69	516.69	466.69	416.69	366.69	324.69	291.69	264.69
3,480	3,520	744.75	675.75	625.75	575.75	525.75	475.75	425.75	375.75	331.75	298.75	267.75
3,520	3,560	757.81	684.81	634.81	584.81	534.81	484.81	434.81	384.81	338.81	305.81	272.81
3,560	3,600	770.87	693.87	643.87	593.87	543.87	493.87	443.87	393.87	345.87	312.87	279.87
3,600	3,640	783.93	702.93	652.93	602.93	552.93	502.93	452.93	402.93	352.93	319.93	286.93
3,640	3,680	796.99	712.99	661.99	611.99	561.99	511.99	461.99	411.99	361.99	326.99	293.99
3,680	3,720	810.05	726.05	671.05	621.05	571.05	521.05	471.05	421.05	371.05	334.05	301.05
3,720	3,760	823.11	739.11	680.11	630.11	580.11	530.11	480.11	430.11	380.11	341.11	308.11
3,760	3,800	836.17	752.17	689.17	639.17	589.17	539.17	489.17	439.17	389.17	348.17	315.17
3,800	3,840	849.23	765.23	698.23	648.23	598.23	548.23	498.23	448.23	398.23	355.23	322.23
3,840	3,880	862.29	778.29	707.29	657.29	607.29	557.29	507.29	457.29	407.29	362.29	329.29
3,880	3,920	875.35	791.35	716.35	666.35	616.35	566.35	516.35	466.35	416.35	369.35	336.35
3,920	3,960	888.41	804.41	725.41	675.41	625.41	575.41	525.41	475.41	425.41	376.41	343.41
3,960	4,000	901.47	817.47	734.47	684.47	634.47	584.47	534.47	484.47	434.47	384.47	350.47
4,000	4,040	914.53	830.53	747.53	693.53	643.53	593.53	543.53	493.53	443.53	393.53	357.53
4,040	4,080	927.59	843.59	760.59	702.59	652.59	602.59	552.59	502.59	452.59	402.59	364.59
4,080	4,120	940.65	856.65	773.65	711.65	661.65	611.65	561.65	511.65	461.65	411.65	371.65
4,120	4,160	953.71	869.71	786.71	720.71	670.71	620.71	570.71	520.71	470.71	420.71	378.71
4,160	4,200	966.77	882.77	799.77	729.77	679.77	629.77	579.77	529.77	479.77	429.77	385.77
4,200	4,240	979.83	895.83	812.83	738.83	688.83	638.83	588.83	538.83	488.83	438.83	392.83
4,240	4,280	992.89	908.89	825.89	747.89	697.89	647.89	597.89	547.89	497.89	447.89	399.89
4,280	4,320	1,005.95	921.95	838.95	756.95	706.95	656.95	606.95	556.95	506.95	456.95	406.95
4,320	4,360	1,019.01	935.01	852.01	769.01	716.01	666.01	616.01	566.01	516.01	466.01	416.01
4,360	4,400	1,032.07	948.07	865.07	782.07	725.07	675.07	625.07	575.07	525.07	475.07	425.07
4,400	4,440	1,045.13	961.13	878.13	795.13	734.13	684.13	634.13	584.13	534.13	484.13	434.13
4,440	4,480	1,058.19	974.19	891.19	808.19	743.19	693.19	643.19	593.19	543.19	493.19	443.19
4,480	4,520	1,071.25	987.25	904.25	821.25	752.25	702.25	652.25	602.25	552.25	502.25	452.25
4,520	4,560	1,084.31	1,000.31	917.31	834.31	761.31	711.31	661.31	611.31	561.31	511.31	461.31
4,560	4,600	1,097.37	1,013.37	930.37	847.37	770.37	720.37	670.37	620.37	570.37	520.37	470.37
4,600	4,640	1,110.43	1,026.43	943.43	860.43	779.43	729.43	679.43	629.43	579.43	529.43	479.43
4,640	4,680	1,123.49	1,039.49	956.49	873.49	789.49	738.49	688.49	638.49	588.49	538.49	488.49
4,680	4,720	1,136.55	1,052.55	969.55	886.55	802.55	747.55	697.55	647.55	597.55	547.55	497.55
4,720	4,760	1,149.61	1,065.61	982.61	899.61	815.61	756.61	706.61	656.61	606.61	556.61	506.61
4,760	4,800	1,162.67	1,078.67	995.67	912.67	828.67	765.67	715.67	665.67	615.67	565.67	515.67
4,800	4,840	1,175.73	1,091.73	1,008.73	925.73	841.73	774.73	724.73	674.73	624.73	574.73	524.73
4,840	4,880	1,188.79	1,104.79	1,021.79	938.79	854.79	783.79	733.79	683.79	633.79	583.79	533.79
4,880	4,920	1,201.85	1,117.85	1,034.85	951.85	867.85	792.85	742.85	692.85	642.85	592.85	542.85
4,920	4,960	1,214.91	1,130.91	1,047.91	964.91	880.91	801.91	751.91	701.91	651.91	601.91	551.91
4,960	5,000	1,227.97	1,143.97	1,060.97	977.97	893.97	810.97	760.97	710.97	660.97	610.97	560.97
5,000	5,040	1,241.03	1,157.03	1,074.03	991.03	907.03	824.03	770.03	720.03	670.03	620.03	570.03

| $5,040 and over | Do not use this table. See page 48 for instructions. |

Combined Federal Income Tax, Employee Social Security Tax, and Employee Medicare Tax Withholding Tables

MARRIED Persons—MONTHLY Payroll Period

(For Wages Paid through December 2015)

And the wages are—		And the number of withholding allowances claimed is—										
At least	But less than	0	1	2	3	4	5	6	7	8	9	10
		The amount of income, social security, and Medicare taxes to be withheld is—										
$ 0	$720	7.65%	7.65%	7.65%	7.65%	7.65%	7.65%	7.65%	7.65%	7.65%	7.65%	7.65%
720	760	$58.61	$56.61	$56.61	$56.61	$56.61	$56.61	$56.61	$56.61	$56.61	$56.61	$56.61
760	800	65.67	59.67	59.67	59.67	59.67	59.67	59.67	59.67	59.67	59.67	59.67
800	840	72.73	62.73	62.73	62.73	62.73	62.73	62.73	62.73	62.73	62.73	62.73
840	880	79.79	65.79	65.79	65.79	65.79	65.79	65.79	65.79	65.79	65.79	65.79
880	920	86.85	68.85	68.85	68.85	68.85	68.85	68.85	68.85	68.85	68.85	68.85
920	960	93.91	71.91	71.91	71.91	71.91	71.91	71.91	71.91	71.91	71.91	71.91
960	1,000	100.97	74.97	74.97	74.97	74.97	74.97	74.97	74.97	74.97	74.97	74.97
1,000	1,040	108.03	78.03	78.03	78.03	78.03	78.03	78.03	78.03	78.03	78.03	78.03
1,040	1,080	115.09	82.09	81.09	81.09	81.09	81.09	81.09	81.09	81.09	81.09	81.09
1,080	1,120	122.15	89.15	84.15	84.15	84.15	84.15	84.15	84.15	84.15	84.15	84.15
1,120	1,160	129.21	96.21	87.21	87.21	87.21	87.21	87.21	87.21	87.21	87.21	87.21
1,160	1,200	136.27	103.27	90.27	90.27	90.27	90.27	90.27	90.27	90.27	90.27	90.27
1,200	1,240	143.33	110.33	93.33	93.33	93.33	93.33	93.33	93.33	93.33	93.33	93.33
1,240	1,280	150.39	117.39	96.39	96.39	96.39	96.39	96.39	96.39	96.39	96.39	96.39
1,280	1,320	157.45	124.45	99.45	99.45	99.45	99.45	99.45	99.45	99.45	99.45	99.45
1,320	1,360	164.51	131.51	102.51	102.51	102.51	102.51	102.51	102.51	102.51	102.51	102.51
1,360	1,400	171.57	138.57	105.57	105.57	105.57	105.57	105.57	105.57	105.57	105.57	105.57
1,400	1,440	178.63	145.63	112.63	108.63	108.63	108.63	108.63	108.63	108.63	108.63	108.63
1,440	1,480	185.69	152.69	119.69	111.69	111.69	111.69	111.69	111.69	111.69	111.69	111.69
1,480	1,520	192.75	159.75	126.75	114.75	114.75	114.75	114.75	114.75	114.75	114.75	114.75
1,520	1,560	199.81	166.81	133.81	117.81	117.81	117.81	117.81	117.81	117.81	117.81	117.81
1,560	1,600	206.87	173.87	140.87	120.87	120.87	120.87	120.87	120.87	120.87	120.87	120.87
1,600	1,640	213.93	180.93	147.93	123.93	123.93	123.93	123.93	123.93	123.93	123.93	123.93
1,640	1,680	220.99	187.99	154.99	126.99	126.99	126.99	126.99	126.99	126.99	126.99	126.99
1,680	1,720	228.05	195.05	162.05	130.05	130.05	130.05	130.05	130.05	130.05	130.05	130.05
1,720	1,760	235.11	202.11	169.11	135.11	133.11	133.11	133.11	133.11	133.11	133.11	133.11
1,760	1,800	242.17	209.17	176.17	142.17	136.17	136.17	136.17	136.17	136.17	136.17	136.17
1,800	1,840	249.23	216.23	183.23	149.23	139.23	139.23	139.23	139.23	139.23	139.23	139.23
1,840	1,880	256.29	223.29	190.29	156.29	142.29	142.29	142.29	142.29	142.29	142.29	142.29
1,880	1,920	263.35	230.35	197.35	163.35	145.35	145.35	145.35	145.35	145.35	145.35	145.35
1,920	1,960	270.41	237.41	204.41	170.41	148.41	148.41	148.41	148.41	148.41	148.41	148.41
1,960	2,000	277.47	244.47	211.47	177.47	151.47	151.47	151.47	151.47	151.47	151.47	151.47
2,000	2,040	284.53	251.53	218.53	184.53	154.53	154.53	154.53	154.53	154.53	154.53	154.53
2,040	2,080	291.59	258.59	225.59	191.59	158.59	157.59	157.59	157.59	157.59	157.59	157.59
2,080	2,120	298.65	265.65	232.65	198.65	165.65	160.65	160.65	160.65	160.65	160.65	160.65
2,120	2,160	305.71	272.71	239.71	205.71	172.71	163.71	163.71	163.71	163.71	163.71	163.71
2,160	2,200	312.77	279.77	246.77	212.77	179.77	166.77	166.77	166.77	166.77	166.77	166.77
2,200	2,240	319.83	286.83	253.83	219.83	186.83	169.83	169.83	169.83	169.83	169.83	169.83
2,240	2,280	327.89	293.89	260.89	226.89	193.89	172.89	172.89	172.89	172.89	172.89	172.89
2,280	2,320	336.95	300.95	267.95	233.95	200.95	175.95	175.95	175.95	175.95	175.95	175.95
2,320	2,360	346.01	308.01	275.01	241.01	208.01	179.01	179.01	179.01	179.01	179.01	179.01
2,360	2,400	355.07	315.07	282.07	248.07	215.07	182.07	182.07	182.07	182.07	182.07	182.07
2,400	2,440	364.13	322.13	289.13	255.13	222.13	189.13	185.13	185.13	185.13	185.13	185.13
2,440	2,480	373.19	329.19	296.19	262.19	229.19	196.19	188.19	188.19	188.19	188.19	188.19
2,480	2,520	382.25	336.25	303.25	269.25	236.25	203.25	191.25	191.25	191.25	191.25	191.25
2,520	2,560	391.31	343.31	310.31	276.31	243.31	210.31	194.31	194.31	194.31	194.31	194.31
2,560	2,600	400.37	350.37	317.37	283.37	250.37	217.37	197.37	197.37	197.37	197.37	197.37
2,600	2,640	409.43	359.43	324.43	290.43	257.43	224.43	200.43	200.43	200.43	200.43	200.43
2,640	2,680	418.49	368.49	331.49	297.49	264.49	231.49	203.49	203.49	203.49	203.49	203.49
2,680	2,720	427.55	377.55	338.55	304.55	271.55	238.55	206.55	206.55	206.55	206.55	206.55
2,720	2,760	436.61	386.61	345.61	311.61	278.61	245.61	211.61	209.61	209.61	209.61	209.61
2,760	2,800	445.67	395.67	352.67	318.67	285.67	252.67	218.67	212.67	212.67	212.67	212.67
2,800	2,840	454.73	404.73	359.73	325.73	292.73	259.73	225.73	215.73	215.73	215.73	215.73
2,840	2,880	463.79	413.79	366.79	332.79	299.79	266.79	232.79	218.79	218.79	218.79	218.79
2,880	2,920	472.85	422.85	373.85	339.85	306.85	273.85	239.85	221.85	221.85	221.85	221.85
2,920	2,960	481.91	431.91	381.91	346.91	313.91	280.91	246.91	224.91	224.91	224.91	224.91
2,960	3,000	490.97	440.97	390.97	353.97	320.97	287.97	253.97	227.97	227.97	227.97	227.97
3,000	3,040	500.03	450.03	400.03	361.03	328.03	295.03	261.03	231.03	231.03	231.03	231.03
3,040	3,080	509.09	459.09	409.09	368.09	335.09	302.09	268.09	235.09	234.09	234.09	234.09
3,080	3,120	518.15	468.15	418.15	375.15	342.15	309.15	275.15	242.15	237.15	237.15	237.15
3,120	3,160	527.21	477.21	427.21	382.21	349.21	316.21	282.21	249.21	240.21	240.21	240.21
3,160	3,200	536.27	486.27	436.27	389.27	356.27	323.27	289.27	256.27	243.27	243.27	243.27
3,200	3,240	545.33	495.33	445.33	396.33	363.33	330.33	296.33	263.33	246.33	246.33	246.33
3,240	3,280	554.39	504.39	454.39	404.39	370.39	337.39	303.39	270.39	249.39	249.39	249.39
3,280	3,320	563.45	513.45	463.45	413.45	377.45	344.45	310.45	277.45	252.45	252.45	252.45
3,320	3,360	572.51	522.51	472.51	422.51	384.51	351.51	317.51	284.51	255.51	255.51	255.51
3,360	3,400	581.57	531.57	481.57	431.57	391.57	358.57	324.57	291.57	258.57	258.57	258.57

Combined Federal Income Tax, Employee Social Security Tax, and Employee Medicare Tax Withholding Tables

MARRIED Persons—MONTHLY Payroll Period

(For Wages Paid through December 2015)

And the wages are—		And the number of withholding allowances claimed is—										
At least	But less than	0	1	2	3	4	5	6	7	8	9	10
		The amount of income, social security, and Medicare taxes to be withheld is—										
$3,400	$3,440	$590.63	$540.63	$490.63	$440.63	$398.63	$365.63	$331.63	$298.63	$265.63	$261.63	$261.63
3,440	3,480	599.69	549.69	499.69	449.69	405.69	372.69	338.69	305.69	272.69	264.69	264.69
3,480	3,520	608.75	558.75	508.75	458.75	412.75	379.75	345.75	312.75	279.75	267.75	267.75
3,520	3,560	617.81	567.81	517.81	467.81	419.81	386.81	352.81	319.81	286.81	270.81	270.81
3,560	3,600	626.87	576.87	526.87	476.87	426.87	393.87	359.87	326.87	293.87	273.87	273.87
3,600	3,640	635.93	585.93	535.93	485.93	435.93	400.93	366.93	333.93	300.93	276.93	276.93
3,640	3,680	644.99	594.99	544.99	494.99	444.99	407.99	373.99	340.99	307.99	279.99	279.99
3,680	3,720	654.05	604.05	554.05	504.05	454.05	415.05	381.05	348.05	315.05	283.05	283.05
3,720	3,760	663.11	613.11	563.11	513.11	463.11	422.11	388.11	355.11	322.11	288.11	286.11
3,760	3,800	672.17	622.17	572.17	522.17	472.17	429.17	395.17	362.17	329.17	295.17	289.17
3,800	3,840	681.23	631.23	581.23	531.23	481.23	436.23	402.23	369.23	336.23	302.23	292.23
3,840	3,880	690.29	640.29	590.29	540.29	490.29	443.29	409.29	376.29	343.29	309.29	295.29
3,880	3,920	699.35	649.35	599.35	549.35	499.35	450.35	416.35	383.35	350.35	316.35	298.35
3,920	3,960	708.41	658.41	608.41	558.41	508.41	458.41	423.41	390.41	357.41	323.41	301.41
3,960	4,000	717.47	667.47	617.47	567.47	517.47	467.47	430.47	397.47	364.47	330.47	304.47
4,000	4,040	726.53	676.53	626.53	576.53	526.53	476.53	437.53	404.53	371.53	337.53	307.53
4,040	4,080	735.59	685.59	635.59	585.59	535.59	485.59	444.59	411.59	378.59	344.59	311.59
4,080	4,120	744.65	694.65	644.65	594.65	544.65	494.65	451.65	418.65	385.65	351.65	318.65
4,120	4,160	753.71	703.71	653.71	603.71	553.71	503.71	458.71	425.71	392.71	358.71	325.71
4,160	4,200	762.77	712.77	662.77	612.77	562.77	512.77	465.77	432.77	399.77	365.77	332.77
4,200	4,240	771.83	721.83	671.83	621.83	571.83	521.83	472.83	439.83	406.83	372.83	339.83
4,240	4,280	780.89	730.89	680.89	630.89	580.89	530.89	480.89	446.89	413.89	379.89	346.89
4,280	4,320	789.95	739.95	689.95	639.95	589.95	539.95	489.95	453.95	420.95	386.95	353.95
4,320	4,360	799.01	749.01	699.01	649.01	599.01	549.01	499.01	461.01	428.01	394.01	361.01
4,360	4,400	808.07	758.07	708.07	658.07	608.07	558.07	508.07	468.07	435.07	401.07	368.07
4,400	4,440	817.13	767.13	717.13	667.13	617.13	567.13	517.13	475.13	442.13	408.13	375.13
4,440	4,480	826.19	776.19	726.19	676.19	626.19	576.19	526.19	482.19	449.19	415.19	382.19
4,480	4,520	835.25	785.25	735.25	685.25	635.25	585.25	535.25	489.25	456.25	422.25	389.25
4,520	4,560	844.31	794.31	744.31	694.31	644.31	594.31	544.31	496.31	463.31	429.31	396.31
4,560	4,600	853.37	803.37	753.37	703.37	653.37	603.37	553.37	503.37	470.37	436.37	403.37
4,600	4,640	862.43	812.43	762.43	712.43	662.43	612.43	562.43	512.43	477.43	443.43	410.43
4,640	4,680	871.49	821.49	771.49	721.49	671.49	621.49	571.49	521.49	484.49	450.49	417.49
4,680	4,720	880.55	830.55	780.55	730.55	680.55	630.55	580.55	530.55	491.55	457.55	424.55
4,720	4,760	889.61	839.61	789.61	739.61	689.61	639.61	589.61	539.61	498.61	464.61	431.61
4,760	4,800	898.67	848.67	798.67	748.67	698.67	648.67	598.67	548.67	505.67	471.67	438.67
4,800	4,840	907.73	857.73	807.73	757.73	707.73	657.73	607.73	557.73	512.73	478.73	445.73
4,840	4,880	916.79	866.79	816.79	766.79	716.79	666.79	616.79	566.79	519.79	485.79	452.79
4,880	4,920	925.85	875.85	825.85	775.85	725.85	675.85	625.85	575.85	526.85	492.85	459.85
4,920	4,960	934.91	884.91	834.91	784.91	734.91	684.91	634.91	584.91	534.91	499.91	466.91
4,960	5,000	943.97	893.97	843.97	793.97	743.97	693.97	643.97	593.97	543.97	506.97	473.97
5,000	5,040	953.03	903.03	853.03	803.03	753.03	703.03	653.03	603.03	553.03	514.03	481.03
5,040	5,080	962.09	912.09	862.09	812.09	762.09	712.09	662.09	612.09	562.09	521.09	488.09
5,080	5,120	971.15	921.15	871.15	821.15	771.15	721.15	671.15	621.15	571.15	528.15	495.15
5,120	5,160	980.21	930.21	880.21	830.21	780.21	730.21	680.21	630.21	580.21	535.21	502.21
5,160	5,200	989.27	939.27	889.27	839.27	789.27	739.27	689.27	639.27	589.27	542.27	509.27
5,200	5,240	998.33	948.33	898.33	848.33	798.33	748.33	698.33	648.33	598.33	549.33	516.33
5,240	5,280	1,007.39	957.39	907.39	857.39	807.39	757.39	707.39	657.39	607.39	557.39	523.39
5,280	5,320	1,016.45	966.45	916.45	866.45	816.45	766.45	716.45	666.45	616.45	566.45	530.45
5,320	5,360	1,025.51	975.51	925.51	875.51	825.51	775.51	725.51	675.51	625.51	575.51	537.51
5,360	5,400	1,034.57	984.57	934.57	884.57	834.57	784.57	734.57	684.57	634.57	584.57	544.57
5,400	5,440	1,043.63	993.63	943.63	893.63	843.63	793.63	743.63	693.63	643.63	593.63	551.63
5,440	5,480	1,052.69	1,002.69	952.69	902.69	852.69	802.69	752.69	702.69	652.69	602.69	558.69
5,480	5,520	1,061.75	1,011.75	961.75	911.75	861.75	811.75	761.75	711.75	661.75	611.75	565.75
5,520	5,560	1,070.81	1,020.81	970.81	920.81	870.81	820.81	770.81	720.81	670.81	620.81	572.81
5,560	5,600	1,079.87	1,029.87	979.87	929.87	879.87	829.87	779.87	729.87	679.87	629.87	579.87
5,600	5,640	1,088.93	1,038.93	988.93	938.93	888.93	838.93	788.93	738.93	688.93	638.93	588.93
5,640	5,680	1,097.99	1,047.99	997.99	947.99	897.99	847.99	797.99	747.99	697.99	647.99	597.99
5,680	5,720	1,107.05	1,057.05	1,007.05	957.05	907.05	857.05	807.05	757.05	707.05	657.05	607.05
5,720	5,760	1,116.11	1,066.11	1,016.11	966.11	916.11	866.11	816.11	766.11	716.11	666.11	616.11
5,760	5,800	1,125.17	1,075.17	1,025.17	975.17	925.17	875.17	825.17	775.17	725.17	675.17	625.17
5,800	5,840	1,134.23	1,084.23	1,034.23	984.23	934.23	884.23	834.23	784.23	734.23	684.23	634.23
5,840	5,880	1,143.29	1,093.29	1,043.29	993.29	943.29	893.29	843.29	793.29	743.29	693.29	643.29
5,880	5,920	1,152.35	1,102.35	1,052.35	1,002.35	952.35	902.35	852.35	802.35	752.35	702.35	652.35
5,920	5,960	1,161.41	1,111.41	1,061.41	1,011.41	961.41	911.41	861.41	811.41	761.41	711.41	661.41
5,960	6,000	1,170.47	1,120.47	1,070.47	1,020.47	970.47	920.47	870.47	820.47	770.47	720.47	670.47
6,000	6,040	1,179.53	1,129.53	1,079.53	1,029.53	979.53	929.53	879.53	829.53	779.53	729.53	679.53
6,040	6,080	1,188.59	1,138.59	1,088.59	1,038.59	988.59	938.59	888.59	838.59	788.59	738.59	688.59

$6,080 and over — Do not use this table. See page 48 for instructions.

APPENDIX A

TAX RESEARCH WORKING PAPER FILE

INDEX TO TAX RESEARCH FILE*

*Most accounting firms maintain a **client file** for each of their clients. Typically, this file contains copies of client letters, memoranda-to-the-file, relevant primary and secondary authorities, and billing information. In our case, the client file for Mercy Hospital would include copies of the following: (1) the December 12 letter to Elizabeth Feghali, (2) the December 9 memorandum-to-the-file, (3) Sec. 119, (4) Reg. Sec. 1.119-1, (5) the *Kowalski* opinion, (6) the *Standard Federal Tax Reporter* annotation, and (7) pertinent billing information.

Tax Research File

As mentioned in Chapter C:1 the tax research process entails six steps.

1. Determine the facts
2. Identify the issues
3. Locate applicable authorities
4. Evaluate these authorities
5. Analyze the facts in terms of applicable authorities
6. Communicate conclusions and recommendations to others.

Let us walk through each of these steps.

Determine the Facts Assume that we have determined the facts to be as follows:

> *Mercy Hospital maintains a cafeteria on its premises. In addition, it rents space to MacDougal's, a privately owned sandwich shop. The cafeteria closes at 8:00 p.m. MacDougal's is open 24 hours. Mercy provides meal vouchers to each of its 240 medical employees to enable them to remain on call in case of emergency. The vouchers are redeemable either at the cafeteria or at MacDougal's. Although the employees are not required to remain on or near the premises during meal hours, they generally do. Elizabeth Fegali, Mercy's Chief Administrator, has approached you with the following question: Is the value of a meal voucher includible in the employees' gross income?*

At this juncture, be sure you understand the facts before proceeding further. Remember, researching the wrong facts could produce the wrong results.

Identify the Issues Identifying the issues presupposes a minimum level of proficiency in tax accounting. This proficiency will come with time, effort, and perseverance. The central issue raised by the facts is the taxability of the meal vouchers. A resolution of this issue will hinge on the resolution of other issues raised in the course of the research.

Locate Applicable Authorities For some students, this step is the most difficult in the research process. It raises the perplexing question, "Where do I begin to look?" The answer depends on the tax resources at one's disposal, as well as one's research preferences. Four rules of thumb apply:

1. *Adopt an approach with which you are comfortable, and that you are confident will produce reliable results.*
2. *Always consult the IRC and other primary authorities.*
3. *Be as thorough as possible, taking into consideration time and billing constraints.*
4. *Make sure that the authorities you consult are current.*

One approach is to conduct a topical search. Begin by consulting the index to the Internal Revenue Code (IRC). Then read the relevant IRC section(s). If the language of the IRC is vague or ambiguous, turn to the Treasury Regulations. Read the relevant regulation section that elaborates or expounds on the IRC provision. If the language of the regulation is confusing or unclear, go to a commercial tax service. Read the relevant tax service paragraphs that explain or analyze the statutory and regulatory provisions. For references to other authorities, browse through the footnotes and annotations of the service. Then, consult these authorities directly. Finally, check the currency of the authorities consulted, with the aid of a citator or status (finding) list.

    If a pertinent court decision or IRS ruling has been called to your attention, consult this authority directly. Alternatively, browse through the status (finding) list of a tax service for references to tax service paragraphs that discuss this authority. Better still, consult a citator or status list for references to court opinions or rulings that cite the authority. If you subscribe to a computerized tax service, conduct a keyword, citation, contents, or topical search. (For a discussion of these types of searches, see the computerized research supplement available for download at *www.prenhall.com/phtax*.) Then, hyperlink to the authorities cited within the text of the documents retrieved. So numerous are the approaches to tax research that one is virtually free to pick and choose. All that is required of the researcher is a basic level of skill and some imagination.

Let us adopt a topical approach to the issue of the meal vouchers. If we consult an index to the IRC, we are likely to find the heading "Meals and Lodging." Below this heading are likely to be several subheadings, some pertaining to deductions, others to exclusions. Because the voucher issue pertains to an exclusion, let us browse through these subheadings. In so doing, we will notice that most of these subheadings refer to Sec. 119. If we look up this IRC section, we will see the following passage:

Sec. 119. Meals or lodging furnished for the convenience of the employer.

(a) **Meals and lodging furnished to employee, his spouse, and his dependents, pursuant to employment.**
There shall be excluded from gross income of an employee the value of any meals or lodging furnished to him . . . by, or on behalf of his employer for the convenience of the employer, but only if—

> (1) in the case of meals, the meals are furnished on the business premises of the employer . . .

(b) **Special rules. For purposes of subsection (a)—**
(4) **Meals furnished to employees on business premises where meals of most employees are otherwise excludable.** All meals furnished on the business premises of an employer to such employer's employees shall be treated as furnished for the convenience of the employer if . . . more than half of the employees to whom such meals are furnished on such premises are furnished such meals for the convenience of the employer.

Section 119 appears to be applicable. It deals with meals furnished to an employee on the business premises of the employer. Our case deals with meal vouchers furnished to employees for redemption at employer-maintained and employer-rented-out facilities. But here, additional issues arise. For purposes of Sec. 119, are meal vouchers the same as "meals"? (Do not assume they are.) Are employer-maintained and employer-rented-out facilities the same as "the business premises of the employer"? (Again, do not assume they are.) And what does the IRC mean by "for the convenience of the employer"? Because the IRC offers no guidance in this respect, let us turn to the Treasury Regulations.

The applicable regulation is Reg. Sec. 1.119-1. How do we know this? Because Treasury Regulation section numbers track the IRC section numbers. Regulation Sec. 1.119-1 is the only regulation under Sec. 119. If we browse through this regulation, we will find the following provision:

(a) Meals . . .
> (2) **Meals furnished without a charge**
> (i) Meals furnished by an employer without charge to the employee will be regarded as furnished for the convenience of the employer if such meals are furnished for a substantial noncompensatory business reason of the employer . . .
> (ii) (a) Meals will be regarded as furnished for a substantial noncompensatory business reason of the employer when the meals are furnished to the employee during his working hours to have the employee available for emergency call during his meal period . . .

(c) **Business premises of the employer.**
> (1) **In general.** For purposes of this section, the term "business premises of the employer" generally means the place of employment of the employee . . .

Based on a reading of this provision, we might conclude that the hospital meals are furnished "for the convenience of the employer." Why? Because they are furnished for a "substantial noncompensatory business reason of the employer," namely, to have the employees available for emergency call during their meal periods. They also are furnished during the employees' working hours. Moreover, under Sec. 119(b)(4), if more than half the employees satisfy the "for the convenience of the employer" test, all employees will be regarded as satisfying the test. But are the meals furnished on "the business premises of the employer"? Under the regulation, the answer would depend. If the meals are furnished in the hospital cafeteria, they probably are furnished on "the business premises of the employer." The hospital is the place of employment of the medical employees. The cafeteria is part of the hospital. On the other hand, if the meals are furnished at MacDougal's, they probably are not furnished on "the business premises of the employer." MacDougal's is not the place of employment of the medical employees. Nor is it a part of the hospital. Thus, Reg. Sec. 1.119-1 is enlightening with respect to two statutory terms: "for the convenience of the employer" and "the business premises of the employer." However, it is obscure with respect to the third term, "meals." Because of this obscurity, let us turn to a tax service.

Although the index to CCH's *Standard Federal Tax Reporter* does not list "meal vouchers," it does list "cash allowances in lieu of meals" as a subtopic under Meals and Lodging. Are meal vouchers the same as cash meal allowances?—perhaps so; let us see. Next to the heading "cash allowances in lieu of meals" is a reference to CCH ¶7222.59. If we look up this reference, we will find the following annotation:

¶7222.59 **Meal allowances.**—Cash meal allowances received by an employee (state trooper) from his employer were not excludible from income. *R.J. Kowalski,* SCt, 77-2 USTC ¶9748, 434 US 77.[1]

Here we discover that, in the *Kowalski* case, the U.S. Supreme Court decided that cash meal allowances received by an employee were not excludible from the employee's income. Is the *Kowalski* case similar to our case? It might be. Let us find out. If we turn to paragraph 9748 of the second 1977 volume of *United States Tax Cases,* we will find the text of the *Kowalski* opinion. A synopsis of this opinion is present below.

In the mid-1970s, the State of New Jersey provided cash meal allowances to its state troopers. The state did not require the troopers to use the allowances exclusively for meals. Nor did it require them to consume their meals on its business premises. One trooper, Robert J. Kowalski, failed to report a portion of his allowance on his tax return. The IRS assessed a deficiency, and Kowalski took the IRS to court. In court, Kowalski argued that the meal allowances were excludible, because they were furnished "for the convenience of the employer." The IRS contended that the allowances were taxable because they amounted to compensation. The Supreme Court took up the case and sided with the IRS. The Court held that the Sec. 119 income exclusion does not apply to cash payments; it applies only to meals in kind.[2]

For the sake of illustration, let us assume that Sec. 119, Reg. Sec. 1.119-1, and the *Kowalski* case are the *only* authorities "on point." How should we evaluate them?

Evaluate Authorities Section 119 is the key authority applicable to our case. It supplies the operative rule for resolving the issue of the meal vouchers. It is vague, however, with respect to three terms: "meals," "business premises of the employer," and "for the convenience of the employer." The principal judicial authority is the *Kowalski* case. It provides an official interpretation of the term "meals." Because the U.S. Supreme Court decided *Kowalski,* the case should be assigned considerable weight. The relevant administrative authority is Reg. Sec. 1.119-1. It expounds on the terms "business premises of the employer" and "for the convenience of the employer." Because neither the IRC nor *Kowalski* explain these terms, Reg. Sec. 1.119-1 should be accorded great weight. But what if *Kowalski* had conflicted with Reg. Sec. 1.119-1? Which should be considered more authoritative? As a general rule, high court decisions "trump" the Treasury Regulations (and all IRS pronouncements for that matter). The more recent the decision, the greater its precedential weight. Had there been no Supreme Court decision and a division of appellate authority, equal weight should have been assigned to each of the appellate court decisions.

Analyze the Facts in Terms of Applicable Authorities Analyzing the facts in terms of applicable authorities involves applying the abstraction of the law to the concreteness of the facts. It entails expressing the generalities of the law in terms of the specifics of the facts. In this process, every legal condition must be satisfied for the result implied by the

[1] The researcher also might read the main *Standard Federal Tax Reporter* paragraph that discusses meals and lodging furnished by the employer (CCH ¶7222.01). Within this paragraph are likely to be references to other primary authorities.

[2] At this juncture, the researcher should consult a citator to determine whether *Kowalski* is still "good law," and to locate other authorities that cite *Kowalski.*

general rule to ensue. Thus, in our case, the conditions of furnishing "meals," "on the business premises of the employer," and "for the convenience of the employer" must be satisfied for the value of the "meals" to be excluded from the employee's income.

When analyzing the facts in terms of case law, the researcher should always draw an *analogy* between case facts and client facts. Likewise, he or she should always draw a *distinction* between case facts and client facts. Remember, under the rule of precedent, a court deciding the client's case will be bound by the precedent of cases involving *similar* facts and issues. By the same token, it will *not* be bound by the precedent of cases involving *dissimilar* facts and issues.

The most useful vehicle for analyzing client facts is the memorandum-to-the-file (see page A-6). The purpose of this document is threefold: first, it assists the researcher in recollecting transactions long transpired; second, it apprises colleagues and supervisors of the nature of one's research; third, it provides "substantial authority" for the tax treatment of a particular item. Let us analyze the facts of our case by way of a memorandum-to-the-file. Notice the format of this document; it generally tracks the steps in the research process itself.

Communicate Conclusions and Recommendations to Others For three practical reasons, research results always should be communicated to the client *in writing*. First, a written communication can be made after extensive revisions. An oral communication cannot. Second, in a written communication, the researcher can delve into the intricacies of tax law. Often, in an oral communication, he or she cannot. Third, a written communication reinforces an oral understanding. Alternatively, it brings to light an oral misunderstanding.

The written communication usually takes the form of a client letter (see page A-7). The purpose of this letter is two-fold: first, it apprises the client of the results of one's research and, second, it recommends to the client a course of action based on these results. A sample client letter is presented below. Notice the organization of this document; it is similar to that of the memorandum-to-the-file.

Memorandum-to-the-File

Date: December 9, 20X1
From: Rosina Havacek
Re: The taxability of meal vouchers furnished by Mercy Hospital to its medical staff.

Facts

[*State only the facts that are relevant to the Issue(s) and necessary for the Analysis.*] Our client, Mercy Hospital ("Mercy"), provides meal vouchers to its medical employees to enable them to remain on emergency call. The vouchers are redeemable at Mercy's onsite cafeteria and at MacDougal's, a privately owned sandwich shop. MacDougal's rents business space from the hospital. Although Mercy does not require its employees to remain on or near its premises during their meal hours, the employees generally do. Elizabeth Fegali, Mercy's Chief Administrator, has asked us to research whether the value of the meal vouchers is taxable to the employees.

Issues

[*Identify the issue(s) raised by the facts. Be specific.*] The taxability of the meal vouchers depends on three issues: first, whether the meals are furnished "for the convenience of the employer"; second, whether they are furnished "on the business premises of the employer"; and third, whether the vouchers are equivalent to cash.

Applicable Law

[*Discuss those legal principles that both strengthen and weaken the client's case. Because the primary authority for tax law is the IRC, begin with the IRC.*] Section 119 provides that the value of meals is excludible from an employee's income if the meals are furnished for the convenience of, and on the business premises of the employer. [*Discuss how administrative and/or judicial authorities expound on statutory terms.*] Under Reg. Sec. 1.119-1, a meal is furnished "for the convenience of the employer" if it is furnished for a "substantial noncompensatory business reason." A "substantial noncompensatory business reason" includes the need to have the employee available for emergency calls during his or her meal period. Under Sec. 119(b)(4), if more than half the employees satisfy the "for the convenience of the employer" test, all employees will be regarded as satisfying the test. Regulation Sec. 1.119-1 defines "business premises of the employer" as the place of employment of the employee.

[*When discussing court cases, present case facts in such a way as to enable the reader to draw an analogy with client facts.*] A Supreme Court case, *Kowalski v. CIR,* 434 U.S. 77, 77-2 USTC ¶9748, discusses what constitutes "meals" for purposes of Sec. 119. In *Kowalski,* the State of New Jersey furnished cash meal allowances to its state troopers to enable them to eat while on duty. It did not require the troopers to use the allowances exclusively for meals. Nor did it require them to consume their meals on its business premises. One trooper, R.J. Kowalski, excluded the value of his allowances from his income. The IRS disputed this treatment, and Kowalski took the IRS to Court. In Court, Kowalski argued that the allowances were excludible because they were furnished "for the convenience of the employer." The IRS contended that the allowances were taxable because they amounted to compensation. The U.S. Supreme Court took up the case and decided for the IRS. The Court held that the Sec. 119 income exlusion does not apply to payments in cash.

Analysis

[*The analysis should (a) apply applicable law to the facts and (b) address the issue(s). In this section, every proposition should be supported by either authority, logic, or plausible assumptions.*]

Issue 1: The meals provided by Mercy seem to be furnished "for the convenience of the employer." They are furnished to have employees available for emergency call during their meal breaks. This is a "substantial noncompensatory reason" within the meaning of Reg. Sec. 1.119-1.

Issue 2: Although the hospital cafeteria appears to be the "business premises of the employer," MacDougal's does not appear to be. The hospital is the place of employment of the medical employees. MacDougal's is not.

Issue 3: [*In applying case law to the facts, indicate how case facts are similar to/dissimilar from client facts. If the analysis does not support a "yes-no" answer, do not give one.*] Based on the foregoing authorities, it is unclear whether the vouchers are equivalent to cash. On the one hand, they are redeemable only in meals. Thus, they resemble meals-in-kind. On the other hand, they are redeemable at more than one institution. Thus, they resemble cash. Nor is it clear whether a court deciding this case would reach the same conclusion as the Supreme Court did in *Kowalski.* In the latter case, the State of New Jersey provided its meal allowances in the form of cash. It did not require its employees to use the allowances exclusively for meals. Nor did it require them to consume their meals on its business premises. In our case, Mercy provides its meal allowances in the form of vouchers. Thus, it indirectly requires its employees to use the allowances exclusively for meals. On the other hand, it does not require them to consume their meals on its business premises.

Conclusion

[*The conclusion should (a) logically flow from the analysis, and (b) address the issue(s).*] Although it appears that the meals acquired by voucher in the hospital cafeteria are furnished "for the convenience of the employer" and "on the business premises of the employer," it is unclear whether the vouchers are equivalent to cash. If they *are* equivalent to cash, *or* if they are redeemed at MacDougal's, their value is likely to be taxable to the employees. On the other hand, if they are not equivalent to cash, *and* they are redeemed only in the hospital cafeteria, their value is likely to be excludible.

Professional Accounting Associates
2701 First City Plaza
Suite 905
Dallas, Texas 75019

December 12, 20X1

Elizabeth Feghali, Chief Administrator
Mercy Hospital
22650 West Haven Drive
Arlington, Texas 75527

Dear Ms. Feghali:

[*Introduction. Set a cordial tone.*] It was great to see you at last Thursday's football game. If not for that last minute fumble, the Longhorns might have taken the Big 12 Conference championship!

[*Issue/Purpose.*] In our meeting of December 6, you asked us to research whether the value of the meal vouchers that Mercy provides to its medical employees is taxable to the employees. [*Short Answer.*] I regret to inform you that if the vouchers are redeemed at MacDougal's, their value is likely to be taxable to the employees. On the other hand, if the vouchers are redeemed in the hospital cafeteria, their value is likely to be excludible from the employee's income. [*The remainder of the letter should elaborate, support, and qualify this answer.*]

[*Steps taken in deriving conclusion.*] In reaching this conclusion, we consulted relevant provisions of the Internal Revenue Code ("IRC"), applicable Treasury Regulations under the IRC, and a pertinent Supreme Court case. In addition, we reviewed the documents on employee benefits that you submitted to us at our earlier meeting.

[*Facts. State only the facts that are relevant to the issue and necessary for the analysis.*] The facts as we understand them are as follows: Mercy provides meal vouchers to its medical employees to enable them to eat while on emergency call. The vouchers are redeemable either in the hospital cafeteria or at MacDougal's. MacDougal's is a privately owned institution that rents business space from the hospital. Although Mercy's employees are not required to remain on or near the premises during their meal hours, they generally do.

[*Applicable law. State, do not interpret.*] Under the IRC, the value of meals is excludible from an employee's income if two conditions are met: first, the meals are furnished "for the convenience of the employer" and second, they are provided "on the business premises of the employer." Although the IRC does not explain what is meant by "for the convenience of the employer," "business premises of the employer," and "meals," other authorities do. Specifically, the Treasury Regulations define "business premises of the employer" to be the place of employment of the employees. The regulations state that providing meals during work hours to have an employee available for emergency calls is "for the convenience of the employer." Moreover, under the IRC, if more than half the employees satisfy the "for the convenience of the employer" test, all the employees will be regarded as satisfying the test. The Supreme Court has interpreted "meals" to mean food-in-kind. The Court has held that cash allowances do not qualify as "meals."

[*Analysis. Express the generalities of applicable law in terms of the specifics of the facts.*] Clearly, the meals furnished by Mercy are "for the convenience of the employer." They are furnished during the employees' work hours to have the employees available for emergency call. Although the meals provided in the hospital cafeteria appear to be furnished "on the business premises of the employer," the meals provided at MacDougal's do not appear to be. The hospital is the place of employment of the medical employees. MacDougal's is not. What is unclear is whether the meal vouchers are equivalent to food-in-kind. On the one hand, they are redeemable at more than one institution and thus resemble cash allowances. On the other hand, they are redeemable only in meals and thus resemble food-in-kind.

[*Conclusion/Recommendation.*] Because of this lack of clarity, we suggest that you modify your employee benefits plan to allow for the provision of meals-in-kind exclusively in the hospital cafeteria. In this way, you will dispel any doubt that Mercy is furnishing "meals," "for the convenience of the employer," "on the premises of the employer."

[*Closing/Follow Up.*] Please call me at 475-2020 if you have any questions concerning this conclusion. May I suggest that we meet next week to discuss the possibility of revising your employee benefits plan.

Very truly yours,
Professional Accounting Associates

By: Rosina Havacek, Junior Associate

B TAX FORMS

Note: Because of the availability of tax forms from many sources, only a limited number of forms are reprinted in this textbook. All federal forms are available from the Internal Revenue Service, either in paper form or from the IRS Web site, http://www.irs.gov.

Facts for Sole Proprietorship (Schedule C)

Andrew Lawrence is the sole proprietor of a business that operates under the name Andrew Lawrence Furniture (Business Code 337000). The proprietorship is located at 1234 First Avenue, City, ST 55555. Andrew started the business with a $200,000 capital investment on June 1, 2008. The proprietorship uses the calendar year as its tax year (the same as its proprietor) and the accrual method of accounting. The following information pertains to its 2014 activities:

A trial balance is included as part of the accompanying worksheet. Notes accompanying the account balances are presented below.

1. Cost of goods sold is determined as follows:

Inventory at beginning of year	$ 64,000
Plus: Purchases	340,800
Cost of labor	143,204
Additional Sec. 263A adjustment	7,000
Other costs	90,000
Goods available for sale	$645,004
Minus: Inventory at end of year	(104,800)
Cost of goods sold	$540,204

The proprietorship values its inventory using the first-in, first-out method and historical costs. The Sec. 263A rules apply to the proprietorship. No change in valuing inventories occurred between the beginning and end of the tax year.

2. The proprietorship uses MACRS depreciation for tax purposes. The current year tax depreciation is $27,476. Of this amount, $15,000 is included in cost of goods sold and inventory. The AMT depreciation adjustment on post-1986 personal property is $1,514. This amount is reported on Andrew Lawrence's Form 6251 (Alternative Minimum Tax—Individuals), which is not reproduced here.

3. Using its excess funds, the proprietorship has purchased various temporary investments, including a 2% investment in Plaza Corporation stock, 50 shares of Service Corporation stock, and some tax-exempt municipal bonds. The proprietorship has held the Plaza stock for two years and sold it in July for $4,500 more than its $7,000 adjusted basis. Prior to the sale, Plaza paid a $1,000 dividend. The 50 shares of Service stock, which had been purchased during the year, was declared worthless during the year. The proprietorship recovered none of its $2,100 adjusted basis.

4. Employees other than Andrew Lawrence receive limited fringe benefits. One employee also receives a $2,000 contribution to an Individual Retirement Account paid by the proprietorship.

5. Miscellaneous expenses include $150 of expenses related to the production of the dividend income.

6. The proprietorship paid no estimated taxes.

7. Balance sheet information is not provided for the sole proprietorship because it is not reported on the Schedule C. Balance sheet information, however, can be found on page 4 of the C corporation tax return.

8. For additional information, see Schedule C and the worksheet on page B-6.

SCHEDULE C
(Form 1040)

Department of the Treasury
Internal Revenue Service (99)

Profit or Loss From Business
(Sole Proprietorship)

► For information on Schedule C and its instructions, go to *www.irs.gov/schedulec.*
► Attach to Form 1040, 1040NR, or 1041; partnerships generally must file Form 1065.

OMB No. 1545-0074

2014

Attachment
Sequence No. **09**

Name of proprietor	Social security number (SSN)
Andrew Lawrence	XXX-XX-XXXX

A Principal business or profession, including product or service (see instructions)
Manufacturing Furniture

B Enter code from instructions ► 3 3 7 0 0 0

C Business name. If no separate business name, leave blank.

D Employer ID number (EIN), (see instr.)
X X X X X X X X X

E Business address (including suite or room no.) ► 1234 Avenue
City, town or post office, state, and ZIP code City, ST 55555

F Accounting method: **(1)** ☐ Cash **(2)** ☒ Accrual **(3)** ☐ Other (specify) ► _____

G Did you "materially participate" in the operation of this business during 2013? If "No," see instructions for limit on losses . ☒ Yes ☐ No

H If you started or acquired this business during 2013, check here . . . . ► ☐

I Did you make any payments in 2013 that would require you to file Form(s) 1099? (see instructions) . . . . . . ☐ Yes ☒ No

J If "Yes," did you or will you file required Forms 1099? . . . . ☐ Yes ☐ No

Part I — Income

1	Gross receipts or sales. See instructions for line 1 and check the box if this income was reported to you on Form W-2 and the "Statutory employee" box on that form was checked . . . . ► ☐	1	869,658
2	Returns and allowances	2	29,242
3	Subtract line 2 from line 1	3	840,416
4	Cost of goods sold (from line 42)	4	540,204
5	**Gross profit.** Subtract line 4 from line 3	5	300,212
6	Other income, including federal and state gasoline or fuel tax credit or refund (see instructions) . . .	6	
7	**Gross income.** Add lines 5 and 6 . . . . ►	7	300,212

Part II — Expenses
Enter expenses for business use of your home only on line 30.

8	Advertising	8	13,000	18 Office expense (see instructions)	18	16,000
9	Car and truck expenses (see instructions)	9	4,000	19 Pension and profit-sharing plans	19	2,000
10	Commissions and fees	10	10,400	20 Rent or lease (see instructions):		
11	Contract labor (see instructions)	11		a Vehicles, machinery, and equipment	20a	36,000
12	Depletion	12		b Other business property	20b	
13	Depreciation and section 179 expense deduction (not included in Part III) (see instructions)	13	12,476	21 Repairs and maintenance	21	
				22 Supplies (not included in Part III)	22	
				23 Taxes and licenses	23	9,840
				24 Travel, meals, and entertainment:		
14	Employee benefit programs (other than on line 19)	14	4,000	a Travel	24a	4,000
15	Insurance (other than health)	15		b Deductible meals and entertainment (see instructions)	24b	4,000
16	Interest:			25 Utilities	25	
a	Mortgage (paid to banks, etc.)	16a		26 Wages (less employment credits)	26	52,000
b	Other	16b	8,000	27a Other expenses (from line 48)	27a	8,650
17	Legal and professional services	17		b **Reserved for future use**	27b	

28	**Total expenses** before expenses for business use of home. Add lines 8 through 27a . . . . . ►	28	184,366
29	Tentative profit or (loss). Subtract line 28 from line 7	29	
30	Expenses for business use of your home. Do not report these expenses elsewhere. Attach Form 8829 unless using the simplified method (see instructions). **Simplified method filers only:** enter the total square footage of: (a) your home: _____ and (b) the part of your home used for business: _____ . Use the Simplified Method Worksheet in the instructions to figure the amount to enter on line 30	30	115,846
31	**Net profit or (loss).** Subtract line 30 from line 29. • If a profit, enter on both **Form 1040, line 12** (or **Form 1040NR, line 13**) and on **Schedule SE, line 2.** (If you checked the box on line 1, see instructions). Estates and trusts, enter on **Form 1041, line 3.** • If a loss, you **must** go to line 32.	31	115,846
32	If you have a loss, check the box that describes your investment in this activity (see instructions). • If you checked 32a, enter the loss on both **Form 1040, line 12,** (or **Form 1040NR, line 13**) and on **Schedule SE, line 2.** (If you checked the box on line 1, see the line 31 instructions). Estates and trusts, enter on **Form 1041, line 3.** • If you checked 32b, you **must** attach **Form 6198.** Your loss may be limited.	32a ☐ All investment is at risk. 32b ☐ Some investment is not at risk.	

For Paperwork Reduction Act Notice, see the separate instructions.　　Cat. No. 11334P　　Schedule C (Form 1040) 2014

Schedule C (Form 1040) 2014

Page **2**

Part III — Cost of Goods Sold (see instructions)

33 Method(s) used to value closing inventory: **a** [X] Cost **b** [ ] Lower of cost or market **c** [ ] Other (attach explanation)

34 Was there any change in determining quantities, costs, or valuations between opening and closing inventory? If "Yes," attach explanation . . . . [ ] Yes [X] No

35 Inventory at beginning of year. If different from last year's closing inventory, attach explanation	35	64,000
36 Purchases less cost of items withdrawn for personal use	36	340,800
37 Cost of labor. Do not include any amounts paid to yourself	37	143,204
38 Materials and supplies	38	
39 Other costs	39	97,000
40 Add lines 35 through 39	40	645,004
41 Inventory at end of year	41	104,800
42 **Cost of goods sold.** Subtract line 41 from line 40. Enter the result here and on line 4	42	540,204

Part IV — Information on Your Vehicle. Complete this part **only** if you are claiming car or truck expenses on line 9 and are not required to file Form 4562 for this business. See the instructions for line 13 to find out if you must file Form 4562.

43 When did you place your vehicle in service for business purposes? (month, day, year) ▶ 3 / 12 / 13

44 Of the total number of miles you drove your vehicle during 2013, enter the number of miles you used your vehicle for:

a Business 17,000 **b** Commuting (see instructions) 4,500 **c** Other 12,000

45 Was your vehicle available for personal use during off-duty hours? . . . . . . [X] Yes [ ] No

46 Do you (or your spouse) have another vehicle available for personal use? . . . [X] Yes [ ] No

47a Do you have evidence to support your deduction? . . . . [X] Yes [ ] No

b If "Yes," is the evidence written? . . . . [X] Yes [ ] No

Part V — Other Expenses. List below business expenses not included on lines 8–26 or line 30.

Repairs	4,800
General and administrative	3,000
Miscellaneous	850
48 **Total other expenses.** Enter here and on line 27a	8,650

Schedule C (Form 1040) 2014

Andrew Lawrence, Sole Proprietorship Reconciliation of Book and Taxable Income for Year Ending December 31, 2014

Account Name	Book Income Debit	Book Income Credit	Adjustments Debit	Adjustments Credit	Taxable Income Debit	Taxable Income Credit	Schedule C	Other Tax Forms	
Sales		$869,658				$869,658	$869,658		
Sales returns & allowances	$ 29,242				$ 29,242		(29,242)		
Cost of sales	540,204				540,204		(540,204)		
Dividends		1,000			1,000	1,000		$ 1,000	(Sch. B)
Tax-exempt interest	$18,000	18,000				0			
Gain on July stock sale		4,500				4,500		4,500	(Sch. D)
Worthless stock loss	2,100				2,100			(2,100)	(Sch. D)
Proprietor's salary(a)	36,000			$36,000	0		0	0	
Other salaries	52,000				52,000		(52,000)		
Rentals	36,000				36,000		(36,000)		
Bad debts	4,000				4,000		(4,000)		
Interest:									
Working capital loans	8,000				8,000		(8,000)		
Purchase tax-exempt bonds	2,000			2,000	0				
Employment taxes	8,320				8,320		(8,320)		
Taxes	1,520				1,520		(1,520)		
Repairs	4,800				4,800		(4,800)		
Depreciation(b)	12,000		476		12,476		(12,476)		
Charitable contributions	12,000				12,000			(12,000)	(Sch. A)
Travel	4,000				4,000		(4,000)		
Meals and entertainment(c)	8,000			4,000	4,000		(4,000)		
Office expenses	16,000				16,000		(16,000)		
Advertising	13,000				13,000		(13,000)		
Transportation expense	10,400				10,400		(10,400)		
General and administrative	3,000				3,000		(3,000)		
Pension plans(d)	2,000				2,000		(2,000)		
Employee benefit programs(e)	4,000				4,000		(4,000)		
Miscellaneous	1,000				1,000		(850)	(150)	(Form 4952)
Net profit/Taxable income	83,572		23,524		107,096		115,846		
Total	$893,158	$893,158	$42,000	$42,000	$875,158	$875,158	$115,846		

(a) The $3,000 monthly salary for Andrew Lawrence is treated as a withdrawal from the proprietorship and is not deducted on Schedule C. The salary does not reduce Schedule C income and therefore is taxed as self-employment income.

(b) MACRS depreciation is $27,476 − $15,000 = $12,476

(c) 50% of the meals and entertainment expense is not deductible for tax purposes.

(d) The pension plan expense is the same for book and tax purposes for this business. No pension expenses relate to pensions for the proprietor.

(e) The employee benefit expense is the same for book and tax purposes for this business. None relates to proprietor benefits.

SCHEDULE SE
(Form 1040)

Department of the Treasury
Internal Revenue Service (99)

Self-Employment Tax

▶ Information about Schedule SE and its separate instructions is at *www.irs.gov/schedulese*.

▶ **Attach to Form 1040 or Form 1040NR.**

OMB No. 1545-0074

2014

Attachment
Sequence No. **17**

Name of person with **self-employment** income (as shown on Form 1040 or Form 1040NR)

Social security number of person
with **self-employment** income ▶

Before you begin: To determine if you must file Schedule SE, see the instructions.

May I Use Short Schedule SE or Must I Use Long Schedule SE?

Note. Use this flowchart **only if** you must file Schedule SE. If unsure, see *Who Must File Schedule SE* in the instructions.

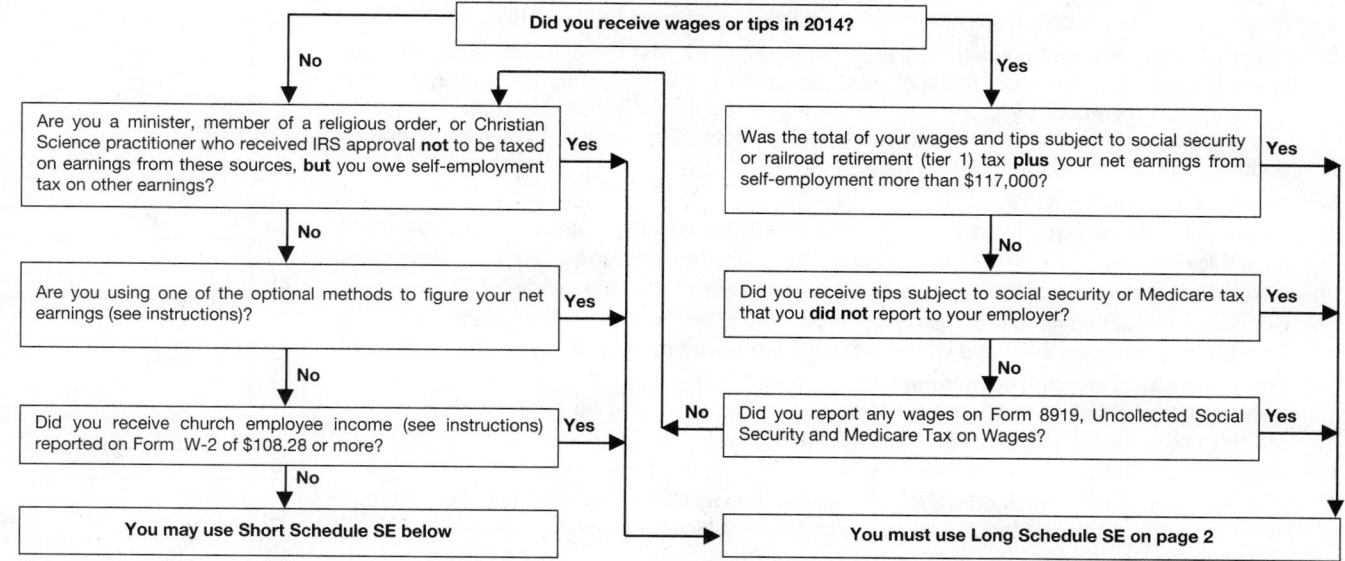

Section A—Short Schedule SE. **Caution.** Read above to see if you can use Short Schedule SE.

1a	Net farm profit or (loss) from Schedule F, line 34, and farm partnerships, Schedule K-1 (Form 1065), box 14, code A	**1a**		
b	If you received social security retirement or disability benefits, enter the amount of Conservation Reserve Program payments included on Schedule F, line 4b, or listed on Schedule K-1 (Form 1065), box 20, code Z	**1b** (		)
2	Net profit or (loss) from Schedule C, line 31; Schedule C-EZ, line 3; Schedule K-1 (Form 1065), box 14, code A (other than farming); and Schedule K-1 (Form 1065-B), box 9, code J1. Ministers and members of religious orders, see instructions for types of income to report on this line. See instructions for other income to report	**2**		
3	Combine lines 1a, 1b, and 2	**3**		
4	Multiply line 3 by 92.35% (.9235). If less than $400, you do not owe self-employment tax; **do not** file this schedule unless you have an amount on line 1b . . . . ▶	**4**		
	Note. If line 4 is less than $400 due to Conservation Reserve Program payments on line 1b, see instructions.			
5	**Self-employment tax.** If the amount on line 4 is: • $117,000 or less, multiply line 4 by 15.3% (.153). Enter the result here and on **Form 1040, line 57,** or **Form 1040NR, line 55** • More than $117,000, multiply line 4 by 2.9% (.029). Then, add $14,508 to the result. Enter the total here and on **Form 1040, line 57,** or **Form 1040NR, line 55**	**5**		
6	**Deduction for one-half of self-employment tax.** Multiply line 5 by 50% (.50). Enter the result here and on **Form 1040, line 27,** or **Form 1040NR, line 27**	**6**		

For Paperwork Reduction Act Notice, see your tax return instructions.   Cat. No. 11358Z   Schedule SE (Form 1040) 2014

Name of person with **self-employment** income (as shown on Form 1040)	Social security number of person with **self-employment** income ▶	

Section B—Long Schedule SE

Part I   **Self-Employment Tax**

Note. If your only income subject to self-employment tax is **church employee income,** see instructions. Also see instructions for the definition of church employee income.

A   If you are a minister, member of a religious order, or Christian Science practitioner **and** you filed Form 4361, but you had $400 or more of **other** net earnings from self-employment, check here and continue with Part I . . . . ▶ ☐

1a	Net farm profit or (loss) from Schedule F, line 34, and farm partnerships, Schedule K-1 (Form 1065), box 14, code A. **Note.** Skip lines 1a and 1b if you use the farm optional method (see instructions)	**1a**		
b	If you received social security retirement or disability benefits, enter the amount of Conservation Reserve Program payments included on Schedule F, line 4b, or listed on Schedule K-1 (Form 1065), box 20, code Z	**1b** (		)
2	Net profit or (loss) from Schedule C, line 31; Schedule C-EZ, line 3; Schedule K-1 (Form 1065), box 14, code A (other than farming); and Schedule K-1 (Form 1065-B), box 9, code J1. Ministers and members of religious orders, see instructions for types of income to report on this line. See instructions for other income to report. **Note.** Skip this line if you use the nonfarm optional method (see instructions)	**2**		
3	Combine lines 1a, 1b, and 2	**3**		
4a	If line 3 is more than zero, multiply line 3 by 92.35% (.9235). Otherwise, enter amount from line 3	**4a**		
	Note. If line 4a is less than $400 due to Conservation Reserve Program payments on line 1b, see instructions.			
b	If you elect one or both of the optional methods, enter the total of lines 15 and 17 here . .	**4b**		
c	Combine lines 4a and 4b. If less than $400, **stop;** you do not owe self-employment tax. **Exception.** If less than $400 and you had **church employee income,** enter -0- and continue ▶	**4c**		
5a	Enter your **church employee income** from Form W-2. See instructions for definition of church employee income . . . **5a**			
b	Multiply line 5a by 92.35% (.9235). If less than $100, enter -0-	**5b**		
6	Add lines 4c and 5b	**6**		
7	Maximum amount of combined wages and self-employment earnings subject to social security tax or the 6.2% portion of the 7.65% railroad retirement (tier 1) tax for 2013	**7**	117,000	00
8a	Total social security wages and tips (total of boxes 3 and 7 on Form(s) W-2) and railroad retirement (tier 1) compensation. If $113,700 or more, skip lines 8b through 10, and go to line 11 **8a**			
b	Unreported tips subject to social security tax (from Form 4137, line 10) **8b**			
c	Wages subject to social security tax (from Form 8919, line 10) **8c**			
d	Add lines 8a, 8b, and 8c	**8d**		
9	Subtract line 8d from line 7. If zero or less, enter -0- here and on line 10 and go to line 11 ▶	**9**		
10	Multiply the **smaller** of line 6 or line 9 by 12.4% (.124)	**10**		
11	Multiply line 6 by 2.9% (.029)	**11**		
12	**Self-employment tax.** Add lines 10 and 11. Enter here and on **Form 1040, line 56,** or **Form 1040NR, line 54**	**12**		
13	**Deduction for one-half of self-employment tax.** Multiply line 12 by 50% (.50). Enter the result here and on **Form 1040, line 27,** or **Form 1040NR, line 27** **13**			

Part II   **Optional Methods To Figure Net Earnings** (see instructions)

Farm Optional Method. You may use this method **only** if **(a)** your gross farm income[1] was not more than $6,960, **or (b)** your net farm profits[2] were less than $5,024.				
14	Maximum income for optional methods	**14**	4,800	00
15	Enter the **smaller** of: two-thirds ($^2/_3$) of gross farm income[1] (not less than zero) or $4,640. Also include this amount on line 4b above	**15**		
Nonfarm Optional Method. You may use this method **only** if **(a)** your net nonfarm profits[3] were less than $5,024 and also less than 72.189% of your gross nonfarm income,[4] **and (b)** you had net earnings from self-employment of at least $400 in 2 of the prior 3 years. **Caution.** You may use this method no more than five times.				
16	Subtract line 15 from line 14	**16**		
17	Enter the **smaller** of: two-thirds ($^2/_3$) of gross nonfarm income[4] (not less than zero) **or** the amount on line 16. Also include this amount on line 4b above	**17**		

[1] From Sch. F, line 9, and Sch. K-1 (Form 1065), box 14, code B.

[2] From Sch. F, line 34, and Sch. K-1 (Form 1065), box 14, code A—minus the amount you would have entered on line 1b had you not used the optional method.

[3] From Sch. C, line 31; Sch. C-EZ, line 3; Sch. K-1 (Form 1065), box 14, code A; and Sch. K-1 (Form 1065-B), box 9, code J1.

[4] From Sch. C, line 7; Sch. C-EZ, line 1; Sch. K-1 (Form 1065), box 14, code C; and Sch. K-1 (Form 1065-B), box 9, code J2.

Form **2210**

Department of the Treasury
Internal Revenue Service

**Underpayment of Estimated Tax by
Individuals, Estates, and Trusts**

▶ Information about Form 2210 and its separate instructions is at *www.irs.gov/form2210.*
▶ Attach to Form 1040, 1040A, 1040NR, 1040NR-EZ, or 1041.

OMB No. 1545-0074

20**14**

Attachment
Sequence No. **06**

Name(s) shown on tax return

Identifying number

Do You Have To File Form 2210?

| Complete lines 1 through 7 below. Is line 7 less than $1,000? | **Yes** ▶ | **Do not file Form 2210.** You do not owe a penalty. |

↓ **No**

| Complete lines 8 and 9 below. Is line 6 equal to or more than line 9? | **Yes** ▶ | You do not owe a penalty. **Do not file Form 2210** (but if box **E** in Part II applies, you must file page 1 of Form 2210). |

↓ **No**

| You may owe a penalty. Does any box in Part II below apply? | **Yes** ▶ | You **must** file Form 2210. Does box **B, C,** or **D** in Part II apply? |

↓ **No**   **No** ↓   **Yes** ▶ You must figure your penalty.

Do not file Form 2210. You are not required to figure your penalty because the IRS will figure it and send you a bill for any unpaid amount. If you want to figure it, you may use Part III or Part IV as a worksheet and enter your penalty amount on your tax return, but **do not file Form 2210.**

You are **not** required to figure your penalty because the IRS will figure it and send you a bill for any unpaid amount. If you want to figure it, you may use Part III or Part IV as a worksheet and enter your penalty amount on your tax return, but **file only page 1 of Form 2210.**

Part I   Required Annual Payment

1	Enter your 2014 tax after credits from Form 1040, line 56 (see instructions if not filing Form 1040)	**1**
2	Other taxes, including self-employment tax and, if applicable, Additional Medicare Tax and/or Net Investment Income Tax (see instructions)	**2**
3	Refundable credits, including the premium tax credit (see instructions)	**3** ( )
4	Current year tax. Combine lines 1, 2, and 3. If less than $1,000, **stop;** you do not owe a penalty. **Do not** file Form 2210	**4**
5	Multiply line 4 by 90% (.90) **5**	
6	Withholding taxes. **Do not** include estimated tax payments (see instructions)	**6**
7	Subtract line 6 from line 4. If less than $1,000, **stop;** you do not owe a penalty. **Do not** file Form 2210	**7**
8	Maximum required annual payment based on prior year's tax (see instructions)	**8**
9	**Required annual payment.** Enter the **smaller** of line 5 or line 8	**9**

Next: Is line 9 more than line 6?

☐ **No.** You **do not** owe a penalty. **Do not** file Form 2210 unless box **E** below applies.

☐ **Yes.** You may owe a penalty, but **do not** file Form 2210 unless one or more boxes in Part II below applies.

• If box **B, C,** or **D** applies, you must figure your penalty and file Form 2210.

• If box **A** or **E** applies (but not **B, C,** or **D**) file only page 1 of Form 2210. You are **not** required to figure your penalty; the IRS will figure it and send you a bill for any unpaid amount. If you want to figure your penalty, you may use Part III or IV as a worksheet and enter your penalty on your tax return, but **file only page 1 of Form 2210.**

Part II   Reasons for Filing. Check applicable boxes. If none apply, **do not** file Form 2210.

A ☐ You request a **waiver** (see instructions) of your entire penalty. You must check this box and file page 1 of Form 2210, but you are not required to figure your penalty.

B ☐ You request a **waiver** (see instructions) of part of your penalty. You must figure your penalty and waiver amount and file Form 2210.

C ☐ Your income varied during the year and your penalty is reduced or eliminated when figured using the **annualized income installment method.** You must figure the penalty using Schedule AI and file Form 2210.

D ☐ Your penalty is lower when figured by treating the federal income tax withheld from your income as paid on the dates it was actually withheld, instead of in equal amounts on the payment due dates. You must figure your penalty and file Form 2210.

E ☐ You filed or are filing a joint return for either 2013 or 2014, but not for both years, and line 8 above is smaller than line 5 above. You must file page 1 of Form 2210, but you are **not** required to figure your penalty (unless box **B, C,** or **D** applies).

For Paperwork Reduction Act Notice, see separate instructions.   Cat. No. 11744P   Form **2210** (2014)

Part III	Short Method

Can You Use the Short Method?	You may use the short method if: • You made no estimated tax payments (or your only payments were withheld federal income tax), **or** • You paid the same amount of estimated tax on each of the four payment due dates.
Must You Use the Regular Method?	You must use the regular method (Part IV) instead of the short method if: • You made any estimated tax payments late, • You checked box **C** or **D** in Part II, **or** • You are filing Form 1040NR or 1040NR-EZ and you did not receive wages as an employee subject to U.S. income tax withholding.

Note: *If any payment was made earlier than the due date, you may use the short method, but using it may cause you to pay a larger penalty than the regular method. If the payment was only a few days early, the difference is likely to be small.*

10	Enter the amount from Form 2210, line 9	**10**		
11	Enter the amount, if any, from Form 2210, line 6	**11**		
12	Enter the total amount, if any, of estimated tax payments you made .	**12**		
13	Add lines 11 and 12	**13**		
14	**Total underpayment for year.** Subtract line 13 from line 10. If zero or less, **stop**; you do not owe a penalty. **Do not file Form 2210 unless you checked box E in Part II**	**14**		
15	Multiply line 14 by .01995	**15**		
16	• If the amount on line 14 was paid **on or after** 4/15/15, enter -0-. • If the amount on line 14 was paid **before** 4/15/15, make the following computation to find the amount to enter on line 16. Amount on Number of days paid line 14 × before 4/15/15 × .00008	**16**		
17	**Penalty.** Subtract line 16 from line 15. Enter the result here and on Form 1040, line 79; Form 1040A, line 51; Form 1040NR, line 76; Form 1040NR-EZ, line 26; or Form 1041, line 26. **Do not file Form 2210 unless you checked a box in Part II** . . . . ▶	**17**		

Form **2210** (2014)

Form 2210 (2014)

Page **3**

Part IV — Regular Method (See the instructions if you are filing Form 1040NR or 1040NR-EZ.)

Section A—Figure Your Underpayment

		Payment Due Dates			
		(a) 4/15/14	**(b)** 6/15/14	**(c)** 9/15/14	**(d)** 1/15/15
18	**Required installments.** If box C in Part II applies, enter the amounts from Schedule AI, line 25. Otherwise, enter 25% (.25) of line 9, Form 2210, in each column **18**				
19	Estimated tax paid and tax withheld (see the instructions). For column (a) only, also enter the amount from line 19 on line 23. If line 19 is equal to or more than line 18 for all payment periods, stop here; you do not owe a penalty. **Do not file Form 2210 unless you checked a box in Part II** **19**				
	Complete lines 20 through 26 of one column before going to line 20 of the next column.				
20	Enter the amount, if any, from line 26 in the previous column **20**				
21	Add lines 19 and 20 . . . . **21**				
22	Add the amounts on lines 24 and 25 in the previous column **22**				
23	Subtract line 22 from line 21. If zero or less, enter -0-. For column (a) only, enter the amount from line 19 . . . . **23**				
24	If line 23 is zero, subtract line 21 from line 22. Otherwise, enter -0- **24**				
25	**Underpayment.** If line 18 is equal to or more than line 23, subtract line 23 from line 18. Then go to line 20 of the next column. Otherwise, go to line 26 . ▶ **25**				
26	**Overpayment.** If line 23 is more than line 18, subtract line 18 from line 23. Then go to line 20 of the next column **26**				

Section B—Figure the Penalty (Use the Worksheet for Form 2210, Part IV, Section B—Figure the Penalty in the instructions.)

27	**Penalty.** Enter the total penalty from line 14 of the Worksheet for Form 2210, Part IV, Section B—Figure the Penalty. Also include this amount on Form 1040, line 79; Form 1040A, line 51; Form 1040NR, line 76; Form 1040NR-EZ, line 26; or Form 1041, line 26. **Do not file Form 2210 unless you checked a box in Part II** . . . . ▶ **27**

Form **2210** (2014)

Form 2210 (2014)

Page **4**

Schedule AI—Annualized Income Installment Method (See the instructions.)

Estates and trusts, **do not** use the period ending dates shown to the right. Instead, use the following: 2/28/14, 4/30/14, 7/31/14, and 11/30/14.

		(a) 1/1/14–3/31/14	**(b)** 1/1/14–5/31/14	**(c)** 1/1/14–8/31/14	**(d)** 1/1/14–12/31/14

Part I Annualized Income Installments

			(a)	(b)	(c)	(d)
1	Enter your adjusted gross income for each period (see instructions). (Estates and trusts, enter your taxable income without your exemption for each period.)	1				
2	Annualization amounts. (Estates and trusts, see instructions)	2	4	2.4	1.5	1
3	Annualized income. Multiply line 1 by line 2	3				
4	If you itemize, enter itemized deductions for the period shown in each column. All others enter -0-, and skip to line 7. **Exception:** Estates and trusts, skip to line 9 and enter amount from line 3	4				
5	Annualization amounts	5	4	2.4	1.5	1
6	Multiply line 4 by line 5 (see instructions if line 3 is more than $152,525)	6				
7	In each column, enter the full amount of your standard deduction from Form 1040, line 40, or Form 1040A, line 24. (Form 1040NR or 1040NR-EZ filers, enter -0-. **Exception:** Indian students and business apprentices, see instructions.)	7				
8	Enter the **larger** of line 6 or line 7	8				
9	Subtract line 8 from line 3	9				
10	In each column, multiply $3,950 by the total number of exemptions claimed. (see instructions if line 3 is more than $152,525) (Estates, trusts, and Form 1040NR or 1040NR-EZ filers, see instructions.)	10				
11	Subtract line 10 from line 9. If zero or less, enter -0-	11				
12	Figure your tax on the amount on line 11 (see instructions)	12				
13	Self-employment tax from line 34 (complete Part II below)	13				
14	Enter other taxes for each payment period including, if applicable, Additional Medicare Tax and/or Net Investment Income Tax (see instructions)	14				
15	Total tax. Add lines 12, 13, and 14	15				
16	For each period, enter the same type of credits as allowed on Form 2210, Part I, lines 1 and 3 (see instructions)	16				
17	Subtract line 16 from line 15. If zero or less, enter -0-	17				
18	Applicable percentage	18	22.5%	45%	67.5%	90%
19	Multiply line 17 by line 18	19				
	Complete lines 20–25 of one column before going to line 20 of the next column.					
20	Enter the total of the amounts in all previous columns of line 25	20				
21	Subtract line 20 from line 19. If zero or less, enter -0-	21				
22	Enter 25% (.25) of line 9 on page 1 of Form 2210 in each column	22				
23	Subtract line 25 of the previous column from line 24 of that column	23				
24	Add lines 22 and 23	24				
25	Enter the **smaller** of line 21 or line 24 here and on Form 2210, Part IV, line 18 ▶	25				

Part II Annualized Self-Employment Tax (Form 1040 and Form 1040NR filers only)

			(a)	(b)	(c)	(d)
26	Net earnings from self-employment for the period (see instructions)	26				
27	Prorated social security tax limit	27	$29,250	$48,750	$78,000	$117,000
28	Enter actual wages for the period subject to social security tax or the 6.2% portion of the 7.65% railroad retirement (tier 1) tax. **Exception:** If you filed Form 4137 or Form 8919, see instructions	28				
29	Subtract line 28 from line 27. If zero or less, enter -0-	29				
30	Annualization amounts	30	0.496	0.2976	0.186	0.124
31	Multiply line 30 by the **smaller** of line 26 or line 29	31				
32	Annualization amounts	32	0.116	0.0696	0.0435	0.029
33	Multiply line 26 by line 32	33				
34	Add lines 31 and 33. Enter here and on line 13 above ▶	34				

Form **2210** (2014)

Form **2441**

Department of the Treasury
Internal Revenue Service (99)

Child and Dependent Care Expenses

▶ Attach to Form 1040, Form 1040A, or Form 1040NR.

▶ Information about Form 2441 and its separate instructions is at
www.irs.gov/form2441.

| 1040 |
| 1040A |
| 1040NR |
| 2441 |

OMB No. 1545-0074

2014

Attachment
Sequence No. **21**

Name(s) shown on return

Your social security number

Part I   **Persons or Organizations Who Provided the Care**—You **must** complete this part.
(If you have more than two care providers, see the instructions.)

1	(a) Care provider's name	(b) Address (number, street, apt. no., city, state, and ZIP code)	(c) Identifying number (SSN or EIN)	(d) Amount paid (see instructions)

Did you receive **dependent care benefits?**

No ────▶ Complete only Part II below.

Yes ────▶ Complete Part III on the back next.

Caution. If the care was provided in your home, you may owe employment taxes. If you do, you cannot file Form 1040A. For details, see the instructions for Form 1040, line 60a, or Form 1040NR, line 59a.

Part II   **Credit for Child and Dependent Care Expenses**

2   Information about your **qualifying person(s).** If you have more than two qualifying persons, see the instructions.

(a) Qualifying person's name		(b) Qualifying person's social security number	(c) Qualified expenses you incurred and paid in 2014 for the person listed in column (a)
First	Last		

3   Add the amounts in column (c) of line 2. **Do not** enter more than $3,000 for one qualifying person or $6,000 for two or more persons. If you completed Part III, enter the amount from line 31 . . . .   **3**

4   Enter your **earned income.** See instructions **4**

5   If married filing jointly, enter your spouse's earned income (if you or your spouse was a student or was disabled, see the instructions); **all others**, enter the amount from line 4   **5**

6   Enter the **smallest** of line 3, 4, or 5 . . . .   **6**

7   Enter the amount from Form 1040, line 38; Form 1040A, line 22; or Form 1040NR, line 37. . . . .   **7**

8   Enter on line 8 the decimal amount shown below that applies to the amount on line 7

If line 7 is:				If line 7 is:		
Over	But not over	Decimal amount is		Over	But not over	Decimal amount is
$0—15,000		.35		$29,000—31,000		.27
15,000—17,000		.34		31,000—33,000		.26
17,000—19,000		.33		33,000—35,000		.25
19,000—21,000		.32		35,000—37,000		.24
21,000—23,000		.31		37,000—39,000		.23
23,000—25,000		.30		39,000—41,000		.22
25,000—27,000		.29		41,000—43,000		.21
27,000—29,000		.28		43,000—No limit		.20

8   X.

9   Multiply line 6 by the decimal amount on line 8. If you paid 2013 expenses in 2014, see the instructions **9**

10   Tax liability limit. Enter the amount from the Credit Limit Worksheet in the instructions. **10**

11   **Credit for child and dependent care expenses.** Enter the **smaller** of line 9 or line 10 here and on Form 1040, line 49; Form 1040A, line 31; or Form 1040NR, line 47 . . . .   **11**

For Paperwork Reduction Act Notice, see your tax return instructions.   Cat. No. 11862M   Form **2441** (2014)

Form 2441 (2014)   Page **2**

Part III Dependent Care Benefits

12 Enter the total amount of **dependent care benefits** you received in 2014. Amounts you received as an employee should be shown in box 10 of your Form(s) W-2. **Do not** include amounts reported as wages in box 1 of Form(s) W-2. If you were self-employed or a partner, include amounts you received under a dependent care assistance program from your sole proprietorship or partnership **12**

13 Enter the amount, if any, you carried over from 2013 and used in 2014 during the grace period. See instructions **13**

14 Enter the amount, if any, you forfeited or carried forward to 2015. See instructions . . . **14** ( )

15 Combine lines 12 through 14. See instructions **15**

16 Enter the total amount of **qualified expenses** incurred in 2014 for the care of the **qualifying person(s)** . . . **16**

17 Enter the **smaller** of line 15 or 16 . . . . **17**

18 Enter your **earned income.** See instructions **18**

19 Enter the amount shown below that applies to you.

- If married filing jointly, enter your spouse's earned income (if you or your spouse was a student or was disabled, see the instructions for line 5).
- If married filing separately, see instructions.
- All others, enter the amount from line 18.
  19

20 Enter the **smallest** of line 17, 18, or 19 . . . . . . **20**

21 Enter $5,000 ($2,500 if married filing separately **and** you were required to enter your spouse's earned income on line 19). **21**

22 Is any amount on line 12 from your sole proprietorship or partnership? (Form 1040A filers go to line 25.)

☐ **No.** Enter -0-.

☐ **Yes.** Enter the amount here **22**

23 Subtract line 22 from line 15 . . . . **23**

24 **Deductible benefits.** Enter the **smallest** of line 20, 21, or 22. Also, include this amount on the appropriate line(s) of your return. See instructions **24**

25 **Excluded benefits. Form 1040 and 1040NR filers:** If you checked "No" on line 22, enter the smaller of line 20 or 21. Otherwise, subtract line 24 from the smaller of line 20 or line 21. If zero or less, enter -0-. **Form 1040A filers:** Enter the **smaller** of line 20 or line 21 . . **25**

26 **Taxable benefits. Form 1040 and 1040NR filers:** Subtract line 25 from line 23. If zero or less, enter -0-. Also, include this amount on Form 1040, line 7, or Form 1040NR, line 8. On the dotted line next to Form 1040, line 7, or Form 1040NR, line 8, enter "DCB." **Form 1040A filers:** Subtract line 25 from line 15. Also, include this amount on Form 1040A, line 7. In the space to the left of line 7, enter "DCB". **26**

To claim the child and dependent care
credit, complete lines 27 through 31 below.

27 Enter $3,000 ($6,000 if two or more qualifying persons) **27**

28 **Form 1040 and 1040NR filers:** Add lines 24 and 25. **Form 1040A filers:** Enter the amount from line 25 . . . . **28**

29 Subtract line 28 from line 27. If zero or less, **stop.** You cannot take the credit. **Exception.** If you paid 2013 expenses in 2014, see the instructions for line 9 . . . . . **29**

30 Complete line 2 on the front of this form. **Do not** include in column (c) any benefits shown on line 28 above. Then, add the amounts in column (c) and enter the total here. **30**

31 Enter the **smaller** of line 29 or 30. Also, enter this amount on line 3 on the front of this form and complete lines 4 through 11 . . . . **31**

Form **2441** (2014)

Form **4684**	**Casualties and Thefts**	OMB No. 1545-0177

Form **4684**

Department of the Treasury
Internal Revenue Service

Casualties and Thefts

► Information about Form 4684 and its separate instructions is at *www.irs.gov/form4684.*
► Attach to your tax return.
► Use a separate Form 4684 for each casualty or theft.

OMB No. 1545-0177

2014

Attachment
Sequence No. **26**

Name(s) shown on tax return	Identifying number

SECTION A—Personal Use Property (Use this section to report casualties and thefts of property **not** used in a trade or business or for income-producing purposes.)

1 Description of properties (show type, location, and date acquired for each property). Use a separate line for each property lost or damaged from the same casualty or theft.

Property **A** _____

Property **B** _____

Property **C** _____

Property **D** _____

			Properties			
			A	**B**	**C**	**D**
2	Cost or other basis of each property	**2**				
3	Insurance or other reimbursement (whether or not you filed a claim) (see instructions)	**3**				
	Note: *If line 2 is more than line 3, skip line 4.*					
4	Gain from casualty or theft. If line 3 is **more** than line 2, enter the difference here and skip lines 5 through 9 for that column. See instructions if line 3 includes insurance or other reimbursement you did not claim, or you received payment for your loss in a later tax year	**4**				
5	Fair market value **before** casualty or theft	**5**				
6	Fair market value **after** casualty or theft	**6**				
7	Subtract line 6 from line 5	**7**				
8	Enter the **smaller** of line 2 or line 7	**8**				
9	Subtract line 3 from line 8. If zero or less, enter -0-	**9**				

10	Casualty or theft loss. Add the amounts on line 9 in columns A through D	**10**	
11	Enter the **smaller** of line 10 or $100	**11**	
12	Subtract line 11 from line 10	**12**	
	Caution: *Use only one Form 4684 for lines 13 through 18.*		
13	Add the amounts on line 12 of all Forms 4684	**13**	
14	Add the amounts on line 4 of all Forms 4684	**14**	
15	• If line 14 is **more** than line 13, enter the difference here and on Schedule D. **Do not** complete the rest of this section (see instructions).	**15**	
	• If line 14 is **less** than line 13, enter -0- here and go to line 16.		
	• If line 14 is **equal** to line 13, enter -0- here. **Do not** complete the rest of this section.		
16	If line 14 is **less** than line 13, enter the difference	**16**	
17	Enter 10% of your adjusted gross income from Form 1040, line 38, or Form 1040NR, line 37. Estates and trusts, see instructions	**17**	
18	Subtract line 17 from line 16. If zero or less, enter -0-. Also enter the result on Schedule A (Form 1040), line 20, or Form 1040NR, Schedule A, line 6. Estates and trusts, enter the result on the "Other deductions" line of your tax return	**18**	

For Paperwork Reduction Act Notice, see instructions.   Cat. No. 12997O   Form **4684** (2014)

Form 4684 (2014)   Attachment Sequence No. **26**   Page **2**

Name(s) shown on tax return. Do not enter name and identifying number if shown on other side. | **Identifying number**

SECTION B—Business and Income-Producing Property

Part I   Casualty or Theft Gain or Loss   (Use a separate Part I for each casualty or theft.)

19 Description of properties (show type, location, and date acquired for each property). Use a separate line for each property lost or damaged from the same casualty or theft. **See instructions if claiming a loss due to a Ponzi-type investment scheme and Section C is not completed.**

Property **A** _____

Property **B** _____

Property **C** _____

Property **D** _____

		Properties		
		A	**B**	**C**	**D**
20 Cost or adjusted basis of each property	**20**				
21 Insurance or other reimbursement (whether or not you filed a claim). See the instructions for line 3	**21**				
Note: *If line 20 is **more** than line 21, skip line 22.*					
22 Gain from casualty or theft. If line 21 is **more** than line 20, enter the difference here and on line 29 or line 34, column (c), except as provided in the instructions for line 33. Also, skip lines 23 through 27 for that column. See the instructions for line 4 if line 21 includes insurance or other reimbursement you did not claim, or you received payment for your loss in a later tax year	**22**				
23 Fair market value **before** casualty or theft	**23**				
24 Fair market value **after** casualty or theft	**24**				
25 Subtract line 24 from line 23	**25**				
26 Enter the **smaller** of line 20 or line 25	**26**				
Note: *If the property was totally destroyed by casualty or lost from theft, enter on line 26 the amount from line 20.*					
27 Subtract line 21 from line 26. If zero or less, enter -0-	**27**				

28 Casualty or theft loss. Add the amounts on line 27. Enter the total here and on line 29 **or** line 34 (see instructions)   **28**

Part II   Summary of Gains and Losses   (from separate Parts I)

(a) Identify casualty or theft	**(b)** Losses from casualties or thefts		**(c)** Gains from casualties or thefts includible in income
	(i) Trade, business, rental or royalty property	*(ii)* Income-producing and employee property	

Casualty or Theft of Property Held One Year or Less

29 _____	( )	( )	
	( )	( )	
30 Totals. Add the amounts on line 29 **30**	( )	( )	

31 Combine line 30, columns (b)(i) and (c). Enter the net gain or (loss) here and on Form 4797, line 14. If Form 4797 is not otherwise required, see instructions   **31**

32 Enter the amount from line 30, column (b)(ii) here. Individuals, enter the amount from income-producing property on Schedule A (Form 1040), line 28, or Form 1040NR, Schedule A, line 14, and enter the amount from property used as an employee on Schedule A (Form 1040), line 23, or Form 1040NR, Schedule A, line 9. Estates and trusts, partnerships, and S corporations, see instructions   **32**

Casualty or Theft of Property Held More Than One Year

33 Casualty or theft gains from Form 4797, line 32   **33**

| **34** | ( ) | ( ) | |
| | ( ) | ( ) | |

35 Total losses. Add amounts on line 34, columns (b)(i) and (b)(ii)   **35** ( ) ( )

36 Total gains. Add lines 33 and 34, column (c)   **36**

37 Add amounts on line 35, columns (b)(i) and (b)(ii)   **37**

38 If the loss on line 37 is **more** than the gain on line 36:

   a Combine line 35, column (b)(i) and line 36, and enter the net gain or (loss) here. Partnerships (except electing large partnerships) and S corporations, see the note below. All others, enter this amount on Form 4797, line 14. If Form 4797 is not otherwise required, see instructions   **38a**

   b Enter the amount from line 35, column (b)(ii) here. Individuals, enter the amount from income-producing property on Schedule A (Form 1040), line 28, or Form 1040NR, Schedule A, line 14, and enter the amount from property used as an employee on Schedule A (Form 1040), line 23, or Form 1040NR, Schedule A, line 9. Estates and trusts, enter on the "Other deductions" line of your tax return. Partnerships (except electing large partnerships) and S corporations, see the note below. Electing large partnerships, enter on Form 1065-B, Part II, line 11   **38b**

39 If the loss on line 37 is **less** than or **equal** to the gain on line 36, combine lines 36 and 37 and enter here. Partnerships (except electing large partnerships), see the note below. All others, enter this amount on Form 4797, line 3   **39**

Note: *Partnerships, enter the amount from line 38a, 38b, or line 39 on Form 1065, Schedule K, line 11. S corporations, enter the amount from line 38a or 38b on Form 1120S, Schedule K, line 10.*

Form **4684** (2014)

Form 6251

Department of the Treasury
Internal Revenue Service (99)

Alternative Minimum Tax—Individuals

► Information about Form 6251 and its separate instructions is at *www.irs.gov/form6251*.
► Attach to Form 1040 or Form 1040NR.

OMB No. 1545-0074

2014

Attachment
Sequence No. **32**

Name(s) shown on Form 1040 or Form 1040NR

Your social security number

Part I Alternative Minimum Taxable Income (See instructions for how to complete each line.)

1	If filing Schedule A (Form 1040), enter the amount from Form 1040, line 41, and go to line 2. Otherwise, enter the amount from Form 1040, line 38, and go to line 7. (If less than zero, enter as a negative amount.)	**1**
2	Medical and dental. If you or your spouse was 65 or older, enter the **smaller** of Schedule A (Form 1040), line 4, **or** 2.5% (.025) of Form 1040, line 38. If zero or less, enter -0-	**2**
3	Taxes from Schedule A (Form 1040), line 9	**3**
4	Enter the home mortgage interest adjustment, if any, from line 6 of the worksheet in the instructions for this line	**4**
5	Miscellaneous deductions from Schedule A (Form 1040), line 27	**5**
6	If Form 1040, line 38, is $152,525 or less, enter -0-. Otherwise, see instructions	**6** ( )
7	Tax refund from Form 1040, line 10 or line 21	**7** ( )
8	Investment interest expense (difference between regular tax and AMT)	**8**
9	Depletion (difference between regular tax and AMT)	**9**
10	Net operating loss deduction from Form 1040, line 21. Enter as a positive amount	**10**
11	Alternative tax net operating loss deduction	**11** ( )
12	Interest from specified private activity bonds exempt from the regular tax	**12**
13	Qualified small business stock (7% of gain excluded under section 1202)	**13**
14	Exercise of incentive stock options (excess of AMT income over regular tax income)	**14**
15	Estates and trusts (amount from Schedule K-1 (Form 1041), box 12, code A)	**15**
16	Electing large partnerships (amount from Schedule K-1 (Form 1065-B), box 6)	**16**
17	Disposition of property (difference between AMT and regular tax gain or loss)	**17**
18	Depreciation on assets placed in service after 1986 (difference between regular tax and AMT)	**18**
19	Passive activities (difference between AMT and regular tax income or loss)	**19**
20	Loss limitations (difference between AMT and regular tax income or loss)	**20**
21	Circulation costs (difference between regular tax and AMT)	**21**
22	Long-term contracts (difference between AMT and regular tax income)	**22**
23	Mining costs (difference between regular tax and AMT)	**23**
24	Research and experimental costs (difference between regular tax and AMT)	**24**
25	Income from certain installment sales before January 1, 1987	**25** ( )
26	Intangible drilling costs preference	**26**
27	Other adjustments, including income-based related adjustments	**27**
28	**Alternative minimum taxable income.** Combine lines 1 through 27. (If married filing separately and line 28 is more than $242,450, see instructions.)	**28**

Part II Alternative Minimum Tax (AMT)

29 Exemption. (If you were under age 24 at the end of 2014, see instructions.)

IF your filing status is . . .	AND line 28 is not over . . .	THEN enter on line 29 . . .	
Single or head of household	$117,300	$52,800	
Married filing jointly or qualifying widow(er)	156,500	82,100	
Married filing separately	78,250	41,050	**29**

If line 28 is **over** the amount shown above for your filing status, see instructions.

30 Subtract line 29 from line 28. If more than zero, go to line 31. If zero or less, enter -0- here and on lines 31, 33, and 35, and go to line 34 — **30**

31 • If you are filing Form 2555 or 2555-EZ, see instructions for the amount to enter.

• If you reported capital gain distributions directly on Form 1040, line 13; you reported qualified dividends on Form 1040, line 9b; **or** you had a gain on both lines 15 and 16 of Schedule D (Form 1040) (as refigured for the AMT, if necessary), complete Part III on the back and enter the amount from line 64 here.

• **All others:** If line 30 is $182,500 or less ($91,250 or less if married filing separately), multiply line 30 by 26% (.26). Otherwise, multiply line 30 by 28% (.28) and subtract $3,650 ($1,825 if married filing separately) from the result. — **31**

32 Alternative minimum tax foreign tax credit (see instructions) — **32**

33 Tentative minimum tax. Subtract line 32 from line 31 — **33**

34 Add Form 1040, line 44 (minus any tax from Form 4972), and Form 1040, line 46. Subtract from the result any foreign tax credit from Form 1040, line 48. If you used Schedule J to figure your tax on Form 1040, line 44, refigure that tax without using Schedule J before completing this line (see instructions) — **34**

35 **AMT.** Subtract line 34 from line 33. If zero or less, enter -0-. Enter here and on Form 1040, line 45 — **35**

For Paperwork Reduction Act Notice, see your tax return instructions.

Cat. No. 13600G

Form **6251** (2014)

Form 6251 (2014)   Page **2**

Part III Tax Computation Using Maximum Capital Gains Rates

Complete Part III only if you are required to do so by line 31 or by the Foreign Earned Income Tax Worksheet in the instructions.

36	Enter the amount from Form 6251, line 30. If you are filing Form 2555 or 2555-EZ, enter the amount from line 3 of the worksheet in the instructions for line 31	**36**
37	Enter the amount from line 6 of the Qualified Dividends and Capital Gain Tax Worksheet in the instructions for Form 1040, line 44, or the amount from line 13 of the Schedule D Tax Worksheet in the instructions for Schedule D (Form 1040), whichever applies (as refigured for the AMT, if necessary) (see instructions). If you are filing Form 2555 or 2555-EZ, see instructions for the amount to enter	**37**
38	Enter the amount from Schedule D (Form 1040), line 19 (as refigured for the AMT, if necessary) (see instructions). If you are filing Form 2555 or 2555-EZ, see instructions for the amount to enter	**38**
39	If you did not complete a Schedule D Tax Worksheet for the regular tax or the AMT, enter the amount from line 37. Otherwise, add lines 37 and 38, and enter the **smaller** of that result or the amount from line 10 of the Schedule D Tax Worksheet (as refigured for the AMT, if necessary). If you are filing Form 2555 or 2555-EZ, see instructions for the amount to enter	**39**
40	Enter the **smaller** of line 36 or line 39	**40**
41	Subtract line 40 from line 36	**41**
42	If line 41 is $182,500 or less ($91,250 or less if married filing separately), multiply line 41 by 26% (.26). Otherwise, multiply line 41 by 28% (.28) and subtract $3,650 ($1,825 if married filing separately) from the result . . . ▶	**42**
43	Enter: • $73,800 if married filing jointly or qualifying widow(er), • $36,900 if single or married filing separately, or • $49,400 if head of household. }	**43**
44	Enter the amount from line 7 of the Qualified Dividends and Capital Gain Tax Worksheet in the instructions for Form 1040, line 44, or the amount from line 14 of the Schedule D Tax Worksheet in the instructions for Schedule D (Form 1040), whichever applies (as figured for the regular tax). If you did not complete either worksheet for the regular tax, enter the amount from Form 1040, line 43; if zero or less, enter -0-. If you are filing Form 2555 or 2555-EZ, see instructions for the amount to enter	**44**
45	Subtract line 44 from line 43. If zero or less, enter -0-	**45**
46	Enter the **smaller** of line 36 or line 37	**46**
47	Enter the **smaller** of line 45 or line 46. This amount is taxed at 0%	**47**
48	Subtract line 47 from line 46	**48**
49	Enter: • $406,750 if single • $228,800 if married filing separately • $457,600 if married filing jointly or qualifying widow(er) • $432,200 if head of household }	**49**
50	Enter the amount from line 45	**50**
51	Enter the amount from line 7 of the Qualified Dividends and Capital Gain Tax Worksheet in the instructions for Form 1040, line 44, or the amount from line 19 of the Schedule D Tax Worksheet, whichever applies (as figured for the regular tax). If you did not complete either worksheet for the regular tax, enter the amount from Form 1040, line 43; if zero or less, enter -0-. If you are filing Form 2555 or Form 2555-EZ, see instructions for the amount to enter	**51**
52	Add line 50 and line 51	**52**
53	Subtract line 52 from line 49. If zero or less, enter -0-	**53**
54	Enter the smaller of line 48 or line 53	**54**
55	Multiply line 54 by 15% (.15) . . . . ▶	**55**
56	Add lines 47 and 54	**56**
	If lines 56 and 36 are the same, skip lines 57 through 61 and go to line 62. Otherwise, go to line 57.	
57	Subtract line 56 from line 46	**57**
58	Multiply line 57 by 20% (.20) . . . . ▶	**58**
	If line 38 is zero or blank, skip lines 59 through 61 and go to line 62. Otherwise, go to line 59.	
59	Add lines 41, 56, and 57	**59**
60	Subtract line 59 from line 36	**60**
61	Multiply line 60 by 25% (.25) . . . . ▶	**61**
62	Add lines 42, 55, 58, and 61	**62**
63	If line 36 is $182,500 or less ($91,250 or less if married filing separately), multiply line 36 by 26% (.26). Otherwise, multiply line 36 by 28% (.28) and subtract $3,650 ($1,825 if married filing separately) from the result	**63**
64	Enter the **smaller** of line 62 or line 63 here and on line 31. If you are filing Form 2555 or 2555-EZ, do not enter this amount on line 31. Instead, enter it on line 4 of the worksheet in the instructions for line 31 . .	**64**

Form **6251** (2014)

Form **8283**

(Rev. December 2014)
Department of the Treasury
Internal Revenue Service

Noncash Charitable Contributions

► **Attach to your tax return if you claimed a total deduction
of over $500 for all contributed property.**
► **Information about Form 8283 and its separate instructions is at** *www.irs.gov/form8283.*

OMB No. 1545-0908

Attachment
Sequence No. **155**

Name(s) shown on your income tax return

Identifying number

Note. Figure the amount of your contribution deduction before completing this form. See your tax return instructions.

Section A. Donated Property of $5,000 or Less and Publicly Traded Securities—List in this section **only** items (or groups of similar items) for which you claimed a deduction of $5,000 or less. Also list publicly traded securities even if the deduction is more than $5,000 (see instructions).

Part I   **Information on Donated Property**—If you need more space, attach a statement.

1	(a) Name and address of the donee organization	(b) If donated property is a vehicle (see instructions), check the box. Also enter the vehicle identification number (unless Form 1098-C is attached).	(c) Description of donated property (For a vehicle, enter the year, make, model, and mileage. For securities, enter the company name and the number of shares.)
A		☐	
B		☐	
C		☐	
D		☐	
E		☐	

Note. If the amount you claimed as a deduction for an item is $500 or less, you do not have to complete columns (e), (f), and (g).

	(d) Date of the contribution	(e) Date acquired by donor (mo., yr.)	(f) How acquired by donor	(g) Donor's cost or adjusted basis	(h) Fair market value (see instructions)	(i) Method used to determine the fair market value
A						
B						
C						
D						
E						

Part II   **Partial Interests and Restricted Use Property**—Complete lines 2a through 2e if you gave less than an entire interest in a property listed in Part I. Complete lines 3a through 3c if conditions were placed on a contribution listed in Part I; also attach the required statement (see instructions).

2a Enter the letter from Part I that identifies the property for which you gave less than an entire interest ► _____
If Part II applies to more than one property, attach a separate statement.

b Total amount claimed as a deduction for the property listed in Part I: **(1)** For this tax year ► _____
(2) For any prior tax years ► _____

c Name and address of each organization to which any such contribution was made in a prior year (complete only if different from the donee organization above):
Name of charitable organization (donee)

Address (number, street, and room or suite no.)

City or town, state, and ZIP code

d For tangible property, enter the place where the property is located or kept ► _____
e Name of any person, other than the donee organization, having actual possession of the property ► _____

		Yes	No
3a	Is there a restriction, either temporary or permanent, on the donee's right to use or dispose of the donated property?		
b	Did you give to anyone (other than the donee organization or another organization participating with the donee organization in cooperative fundraising) the right to the income from the donated property or to the possession of the property, including the right to vote donated securities, to acquire the property by purchase or otherwise, or to designate the person having such income, possession, or right to acquire?		
c	Is there a restriction limiting the donated property for a particular use?		

For Paperwork Reduction Act Notice, see separate instructions.   Cat. No. 62299J   Form **8283** (Rev. 12-2014)

Form 8283 (Rev. 12-2014)   Page **2**

Name(s) shown on your income tax return	Identifying number

Section B. Donated Property Over $5,000 (Except Publicly Traded Securities)—Complete this section for one item (or one group of similar items) for which you claimed a deduction of more than $5,000 per item or group (except contributions of publicly traded securities reported in Section A). Provide a separate form for each property donated unless it is part of a group of similar items. An appraisal is generally required for property listed in Section B. See instructions.

Part I	**Information on Donated Property**—To be completed by the taxpayer and/or the appraiser.

4   Check the box that describes the type of property donated:

a ☐ Art* (contribution of $20,000 or more)   d ☐ Art* (contribution of less than $20,000)   g ☐ Collectibles**   j ☐ Other

b ☐ Qualified Conservation Contribution   e ☐ Other Real Estate   h ☐ Intellectual Property

c ☐ Equipment   f ☐ Securities   i ☐ Vehicles

*Art includes paintings, sculptures, watercolors, prints, drawings, ceramics, antiques, decorative arts, textiles, carpets, silver, rare manuscripts, historical memorabilia, and other similar objects.

**Collectibles include coins, stamps, books, gems, jewelry, sports memorabilia, dolls, etc., but not art as defined above.

Note. In certain cases, you must attach a qualified appraisal of the property. See instructions.

5	**(a)** Description of donated property (if you need more space, attach a separate statement)	**(b)** If tangible property was donated, give a brief summary of the overall physical condition of the property at the time of the gift	**(c)** Appraised fair market value
A			
B			
C			
D			

	(d) Date acquired by donor (mo., yr.)	**(e)** How acquired by donor	**(f)** Donor's cost or adjusted basis	**(g)** For bargain sales, enter amount received	**See instructions** **(h)** Amount claimed as a deduction	**(i)** Date of contribution
A						
B						
C						
D						

Part II	**Taxpayer (Donor) Statement**—List each item included in Part I above that the appraisal identifies as having a value of $500 or less. See instructions.

I declare that the following item(s) included in Part I above has to the best of my knowledge and belief an appraised value of not more than $500 (per item). Enter identifying letter from Part I and describe the specific item. See instructions. ▶ _____

Signature of taxpayer (donor) ▶ _____   Date ▶ _____

Part III	**Declaration of Appraiser**

I declare that I am not the donor, the donee, a party to the transaction in which the donor acquired the property, employed by, or related to any of the foregoing persons, or married to any person who is related to any of the foregoing persons. And, if regularly used by the donor, donee, or party to the transaction, I performed the majority of my appraisals during my tax year for other persons.

Also, I declare that I perform appraisals on a regular basis; and that because of my qualifications as described in the appraisal, I am qualified to make appraisals of the type of property being valued. I certify that the appraisal fees were not based on a percentage of the appraised property value. Furthermore, I understand that a false or fraudulent overstatement of the property value as described in the qualified appraisal or this Form 8283 may subject me to the penalty under section 6701(a) (aiding and abetting the understatement of tax liability). In addition, I understand that I may be subject to a penalty under section 6695A if I know, or reasonably should know, that my appraisal is to be used in connection with a return or claim for refund and a substantial or gross valuation misstatement results from my appraisal. I affirm that I have not been barred from presenting evidence or testimony by the Office of Professional Responsibility.

Sign Here   Signature ▶ _____   Title ▶ _____   Date ▶ _____

Business address (including room or suite no.)	Identifying number
City or town, state, and ZIP code	

Part IV	**Donee Acknowledgment**—To be completed by the charitable organization.

This charitable organization acknowledges that it is a qualified organization under section 170(c) and that it received the donated property as described in Section B, Part I, above on the following date ▶ _____

Furthermore, this organization affirms that in the event it sells, exchanges, or otherwise disposes of the property described in Section B, Part I (or any portion thereof) within 3 years after the date of receipt, it will file **Form 8282,** Donee Information Return, with the IRS and give the donor a copy of that form. This acknowledgment does not represent agreement with the claimed fair market value.

Does the organization intend to use the property for an unrelated use? . . . . ▶ ☐ Yes   ☐ No

Name of charitable organization (donee)	Employer identification number
Address (number, street, and room or suite no.)	City or town, state, and ZIP code
Authorized signature	Title	Date

Form **8283** (Rev. 12-2014)

Form **8582**

Department of the Treasury
Internal Revenue Service (99)

Passive Activity Loss Limitations

▶ See separate instructions.

▶ Attach to Form 1040 or Form 1041.

▶ Information about Form 8582 and its instructions is available at *www.irs.gov/form8582*.

OMB No. 1545-1008

2014

Attachment
Sequence No. **88**

Name(s) shown on return

Identifying number

Part I	**2014 Passive Activity Loss**

Caution: *Complete Worksheets 1, 2, and 3 before completing Part I.*

Rental Real Estate Activities With Active Participation (For the definition of active participation, see **Special Allowance for Rental Real Estate Activities** in the instructions.)

1a	Activities with net income (enter the amount from Worksheet 1, column (a))	**1a**	
b	Activities with net loss (enter the amount from Worksheet 1, column (b))	**1b** ( )	
c	Prior years unallowed losses (enter the amount from Worksheet 1, column (c))	**1c** ( )	
d	Combine lines 1a, 1b, and 1c		**1d**

Commercial Revitalization Deductions From Rental Real Estate Activities

2a	Commercial revitalization deductions from Worksheet 2, column (a) .	**2a** ( )	
b	Prior year unallowed commercial revitalization deductions from Worksheet 2, column (b)	**2b** ( )	
c	Add lines 2a and 2b		**2c** ( )

All Other Passive Activities

3a	Activities with net income (enter the amount from Worksheet 3, column (a))	**3a**	
b	Activities with net loss (enter the amount from Worksheet 3, column (b))	**3b** ( )	
c	Prior years unallowed losses (enter the amount from Worksheet 3, column (c))	**3c** ( )	
d	Combine lines 3a, 3b, and 3c		**3d**
4	Combine lines 1d, 2c, and 3d. If this line is zero or more, stop here and include this form with your return; all losses are allowed, including any prior year unallowed losses entered on line 1c, 2b, or 3c. Report the losses on the forms and schedules normally used		**4**

If line 4 is a loss and: • Line 1d is a loss, go to Part II.

• Line 2c is a loss (and line 1d is zero or more), skip Part II and go to Part III.

• Line 3d is a loss (and lines 1d and 2c are zero or more), skip Parts II and III and go to line 15.

Caution: *If your filing status is married filing separately and you lived with your spouse at any time during the year, **do not** complete Part II or Part III. Instead, go to line 15.*

Part II	**Special Allowance for Rental Real Estate Activities With Active Participation**

Note: *Enter all numbers in Part II as positive amounts. See instructions for an example.*

5	Enter the **smaller** of the loss on line 1d or the loss on line 4		**5**
6	Enter $150,000. If married filing separately, see instructions . .	**6**	
7	Enter modified adjusted gross income, but not less than zero (see instructions)	**7**	
	Note: *If line 7 is greater than or equal to line 6, skip lines 8 and 9, enter -0- on line 10. Otherwise, go to line 8.*		
8	Subtract line 7 from line 6	**8**	
9	Multiply line 8 by 50% (.5). **Do not** enter more than $25,000. If married filing separately, see instructions	**9**	
10	Enter the **smaller** of line 5 or line 9		**10**

If line 2c is a loss, go to Part III. Otherwise, go to line 15.

Part III	**Special Allowance for Commercial Revitalization Deductions From Rental Real Estate Activities**

Note: *Enter all numbers in Part III as positive amounts. See the example for Part II in the instructions.*

11	Enter $25,000 reduced by the amount, if any, on line 10. If married filing separately, see instructions	**11**	
12	Enter the loss from line 4	**12**	
13	Reduce line 12 by the amount on line 10	**13**	
14	Enter the **smallest** of line 2c (treated as a positive amount), line 11, or line 13	**14**	

Part IV	**Total Losses Allowed**

15	Add the income, if any, on lines 1a and 3a and enter the total	**15**	
16	**Total losses allowed from all passive activities for 2014.** Add lines 10, 14, and 15. See instructions to find out how to report the losses on your tax return	**16**	

For Paperwork Reduction Act Notice, see instructions.

Cat. No. 63704F

Form **8582** (2014)

Caution: *The worksheets must be filed with your tax return. Keep a copy for your records.*

Worksheet 1—For Form 8582, Lines 1a, 1b, and 1c (See instructions.)

Name of activity	Current year		Prior years	Overall gain or loss	
	(a) Net income (line 1a)	(b) Net loss (line 1b)	(c) Unallowed loss (line 1c)	(d) Gain	(e) Loss
Total. Enter on Form 8582, lines 1a, 1b, and 1c . . . . ▶					

Worksheet 2—For Form 8582, Lines 2a and 2b (See instructions.)

Name of activity	(a) Current year deductions (line 2a)	(b) Prior year unallowed deductions (line 2b)	(c) Overall loss
Total. Enter on Form 8582, lines 2a and 2b . . . . ▶			

Worksheet 3—For Form 8582, Lines 3a, 3b, and 3c (See instructions.)

Name of activity	Current year		Prior years	Overall gain or loss	
	(a) Net income (line 3a)	(b) Net loss (line 3b)	(c) Unallowed loss (line 3c)	(d) Gain	(e) Loss
Total. Enter on Form 8582, lines 3a, 3b, and 3c . . . . ▶					

Worksheet 4—Use this worksheet if an amount is shown on Form 8582, line 10 or 14 (See instructions.)

Name of activity	Form or schedule and line number to be reported on (see instructions)	(a) Loss	(b) Ratio	(c) Special allowance	(d) Subtract column (c) from column (a)
Total . . . . ▶			1.00		

Worksheet 5—Allocation of Unallowed Losses (See instructions.)

Name of activity	Form or schedule and line number to be reported on (see instructions)	(a) Loss	(b) Ratio	(c) Unallowed loss
Total . . . . ▶			1.00	

Form 8582 (2014)   Page **3**

Worksheet 6—Allowed Losses (See instructions.)

Name of activity	Form or schedule and line number to be reported on (see instructions)	(a) Loss	(b) Unallowed loss	(c) Allowed loss
Total . . . . ▶				

Worksheet 7—Activities With Losses Reported on Two or More Forms or Schedules (See instructions.)

Name of activity:	(a)	(b)	(c) Ratio	(d) Unallowed loss	(e) Allowed loss
Form or schedule and line number to be reported on (see instructions): _____					
1a Net loss plus prior year unallowed loss from form or schedule . ▶					
b Net income from form or schedule . . . . . . ▶					
c Subtract line 1b from line 1a. If zero or less, enter -0- ▶					
Form or schedule and line number to be reported on (see instructions): _____					
1a Net loss plus prior year unallowed loss from form or schedule . ▶					
b Net income from form or schedule . . . . . . ▶					
c Subtract line 1b from line 1a. If zero or less, enter -0- ▶					
Form or schedule and line number to be reported on (see instructions): _____					
1a Net loss plus prior year unallowed loss from form or schedule . ▶					
b Net income from form or schedule . . . . . . ▶					
c Subtract line 1b from line 1a. If zero or less, enter -0- ▶					
Total . . . . ▶			1.00		

Form **8582** (2014)

Form **8615**	Tax for Certain Children Who Have Unearned Income	OMB No. 1545-0074
Department of the Treasury Internal Revenue Service (99)	▶ **Attach only to the child's Form 1040, Form 1040A, or Form 1040NR.** ▶ **Information about Form 8615 and its separate instructions is at** *www.irs.gov/form8615.*	**2014** Attachment Sequence No. **33**

Child's name shown on return	Child's social security number

Before you begin: If the child, the parent, or any of the parent's other children for whom Form 8615 must be filed must use the Schedule D Tax Worksheet or has income from farming or fishing, see **Pub. 929**, Tax Rules for Children and Dependents. It explains how to figure the child's tax using the **Schedule D Tax Worksheet** or **Schedule J** (Form 1040).

A Parent's name (first, initial, and last). **Caution:** *See instructions before completing.*	**B** Parent's social security number

C Parent's filing status (check one):

☐ Single ☐ Married filing jointly ☐ Married filing separately ☐ Head of household ☐ Qualifying widow(er)

Part I   Child's Net Unearned Income

1	Enter the child's unearned income (see instructions)	**1**	
2	If the child **did not** itemize deductions on **Schedule A** (Form 1040 or Form 1040NR), enter $2,000. Otherwise, see instructions	**2**	
3	Subtract line 2 from line 1. If zero or less, **stop;** do not complete the rest of this form but **do** attach it to the child's return	**3**	
4	Enter the child's **taxable income** from Form 1040, line 43; Form 1040A, line 27; or Form 1040NR, line 41. If the child files Form 2555 or 2555-EZ, see the instructions	**4**	
5	Enter the **smaller** of line 3 or line 4. If zero, **stop;** do not complete the rest of this form but **do** attach it to the child's return	**5**	

Part II   Tentative Tax Based on the Tax Rate of the Parent

6	Enter the parent's **taxable income** from Form 1040, line 43; Form 1040A, line 27; Form 1040EZ, line 6; Form 1040NR, line 41; or Form 1040NR-EZ, line 14. If zero or less, enter -0-. If the parent files Form 2555 or 2555-EZ, see the instructions	**6**	
7	Enter the total, if any, from Forms 8615, line 5, of **all other** children of the parent named above. **Do not** include the amount from line 5 above	**7**	
8	Add lines 5, 6, and 7 (see instructions)	**8**	
9	Enter the tax on the amount on line 8 based on the **parent's** filing status above (see instructions). If the Qualified Dividends and Capital Gain Tax Worksheet, Schedule D Tax Worksheet, or Schedule J (Form 1040) is used to figure the tax, check here ▶ ☐	**9**	
10	Enter the parent's tax from Form 1040, line 44; Form 1040A, line 28, minus any alternative minimum tax; Form 1040EZ, line 10; Form 1040NR, line 42; or Form 1040NR-EZ, line 15. **Do not** include any tax from **Form 4972 or 8814** or any tax from recapture of an education credit. If the parent files Form 2555 or 2555-EZ, see the instructions. If the Qualified Dividends and Capital Gain Tax Worksheet, Schedule D Tax Worksheet, or Schedule J (Form 1040) was used to figure the tax, check here ▶ ☐	**10**	
11	Subtract line 10 from line 9 and enter the result. If line 7 is blank, also enter this amount on line 13 and go to **Part III**	**11**	
12a	Add lines 5 and 7	**12a**	
b	Divide line 5 by line 12a. Enter the result as a decimal (rounded to at least three places)	**12b**	× .
13	Multiply line 11 by line 12b	**13**	

Part III   Child's Tax—If lines 4 and 5 above are the same, enter -0- on line 15 and go to line 16.

14	Subtract line 5 from line 4	**14**	
15	Enter the tax on the amount on line 14 based on the **child's** filing status (see instructions). If the Qualified Dividends and Capital Gain Tax Worksheet, Schedule D Tax Worksheet, or Schedule J (Form 1040) is used to figure the tax, check here ▶ ☐	**15**	
16	Add lines 13 and 15	**16**	
17	Enter the tax on the amount on line 4 based on the **child's** filing status (see instructions). If the Qualified Dividends and Capital Gain Tax Worksheet, Schedule D Tax Worksheet, or Schedule J (Form 1040) is used to figure the tax, check here ▶ ☐	**17**	
18	Enter the **larger** of line 16 or line 17 here and on the **child's** Form 1040, line 44; Form 1040A, line 28; or Form 1040NR, line 42. If the child files Form 2555 or 2555-EZ, see the instructions . .	**18**	

For Paperwork Reduction Act Notice, see your tax return instructions.   Cat. No. 64113U   Form **8615** (2014)

C MACRS TABLES

MACRS, ADS and ACRS Depreciation Methods Summary

System	Characteristics	Depreciation Method MACRS	Depreciation Method ADS	Table No.ª MACRS	Table No.ª ADS
MACRS & ADS	Personal Property: 1. Accounting convention	Half-year or mid-quarter	Half-year or mid-quarterᵇ		
	2. Life and method a. 3-year, 5-year, 7-year, 10-year	200% DB or elect straight-line	150% DB or elect straight-line	1, 2, 3, 4, 5	10, 11ᶜ
	b. 15-year, 20-year	150% DB or elect straight-line	150% DB or elect straight-lineᵈ	1, 2, 3, 4, 5 6	
	3. Luxury Automobile Limitations Real property: 1. Accounting convention	Mid-month	Mid-month		
	2. Life and method a. Residential rental property	27.5 years, straight-line	40 years straight-line	7	12
	b. Nonresidential real property	39 years, straight-lineᵉ	40 years straight-line	9	12

	Characteristics	ACRS
ACRSᶠ	Personal Property 1. Accounting convention	Half-year
	2. Life and method a. 3-year, 5-year, 10-year, 15-year	150% DB or elect straight-line
	Real Property 1. Accounting convention	First of month or mid-month
	2. Life a. 15-year property	Placed in service after 12/31/80 and before 3/16/84
	b. 18-year property	Placed in service after 3/15/84 and before 5/9/85
	c. 19-year property	Placed in service after 5/8/85 and before 1/1/87
	3. Method a. All but low-income housing	175% DB or elect straight-line
	b. Low-income housing property	200% DB or elect straight-line

ªAll depreciation tables in this appendix are based upon tables contained in Rev. Proc. 87-57, as amended.
ᵇGeneral and ADS tables are available for property lives from 2.5–50.0 years using the straight-line method. These tables are contained in Rev. Proc. 87-57 and are only partially reproduced here.
ᶜThe mid-quarter tables are available in Rev. Proc. 87-57, but are not reproduced here.
ᵈSpecial recovery periods are assigned certain MACRS properties under the alternative depreciation system.
ᵉA 31.5-year recovery period applied to nonresidential real property placed in service under the MACRS rules prior to May 13, 1993 (see Table 8).
ᶠACRS was effective for years 1981–1986. ACRS tables are no longer reproduced here.

▼ TABLE 1

General Depreciation System—MACRS
Personal Property Placed in Service after 12/31/86
Applicable Convention: Half-year
Applicable Depreciation Method: 200 or 150 Percent Declining Balance Switching to Straight Line

If the Recovery Year Is:	And the Recovery Period Is:					
	3-Year	5-Year	7-Year	10-Year	15-Year	20-Year
	The Depreciation Rate Is:					
1	33.33	20.00	14.29	10.00	5.00	3.750
2	44.45	32.00	24.49	18.00	9.50	7.219
3	14.81	19.20	17.49	14.40	8.55	6.677
4	7.41	11.52	12.49	11.52	7.70	6.177
5		11.52	8.93	9.22	6.93	5.713
6		5.76	8.92	7.37	6.23	5.285
7			8.93	6.55	5.90	4.888
8			4.46	6.55	5.90	4.522
9				6.56	5.91	4.462
10				6.55	5.90	4.461
11				3.28	5.91	4.462
12					5.90	4.461
13					5.91	4.462
14					5.90	4.461
15					5.91	4.462
16					2.95	4.461
17						4.462
18						4.461
19						4.462
20						4.461
21						2.231

▼ TABLE 2

General Depreciation System—MACRS
Personal Property Placed in Service after 12/31/86
Applicable Convention: Mid-quarter (Property Placed in Service in First Quarter)
Applicable Depreciation Method: 200 or 150 Percent Declining Balance Switching to Straight Line

If the Recovery Year Is:	And the Recovery Period Is:					
	3-Year	5-Year	7-Year	10-Year	15-Year	20-Year
	The Depreciation Rate Is:					
1	58.33	35.00	25.00	17.50	8.75	6.563
2	27.78	26.00	21.43	16.50	9.13	7.000
3	12.35	15.60	15.31	13.20	8.21	6.482
4	1.54	11.01	10.93	10.56	7.39	5.996
5		11.01	8.75	8.45	6.65	5.546
6		1.38	8.74	6.76	5.99	5.130
7			8.75	6.55	5.90	4.746
8			1.09	6.55	5.91	4.459
9				6.56	5.90	4.459
10				6.55	5.91	4.459
11				0.82	5.90	4.459
12					5.91	4.460
13					5.90	4.459
14					5.91	4.460
15					5.90	4.459
16					0.74	4.460
17						4.459
18						4.460
19						4.459
20						4.460
21						0.557

▼ TABLE 3

General Depreciation System—MACRS
Personal Property Placed in Service after 12/31/86
Applicable Convention: Mid-quarter (Property Placed in Service in Second Quarter)
Applicable Depreciation Method: 200 or 150 Percent Declining Balance Switching to Straight Line

If the Recovery Year Is:	And the Recovery Period Is:					
	3-Year	5-Year	7-Year	10-Year	15-Year	20-Year
	The Depreciation Rate Is:					
1	41.67	25.00	17.85	12.50	6.25	4.688
2	38.89	30.00	23.47	17.50	9.38	7.148
3	14.14	18.00	16.76	14.00	8.44	6.612
4	5.30	11.37	11.97	11.20	7.59	6.116
5		11.37	8.87	8.96	6.83	5.658
6		4.26	8.87	7.17	6.15	5.233
7			8.87	6.55	5.91	4.841
8			3.33	6.55	5.90	4.478
9				6.56	5.91	4.463
10				6.55	5.90	4.463
11				2.46	5.91	4.463
12					5.90	4.463
13					5.91	4.463
14					5.90	4.463
15					5.91	4.462
16					2.21	4.463
17						4.462
18						4.463
19						4.462
20						4.463
21						1.673

▼ TABLE 4

General Depreciation System—MACRS
Personal Property Placed in Service after 12/31/86
Applicable Convention: Mid-quarter (Property Placed in Service in Third Quarter)
Applicable Depreciation Method: 200 or 150 Percent Declining Balance Switching to Straight Line

If the Recovery Year Is:	And the Recovery Period Is:					
	3-Year	5-Year	7-Year	10-Year	15-Year	20-Year
	The Depreciation Rate Is:					
1	25.00	15.00	10.71	7.50	3.75	2.813
2	50.00	34.00	25.51	18.50	9.63	7.289
3	16.67	20.40	18.22	14.80	8.66	6.742
4	8.33	12.24	13.02	11.84	7.80	6.237
5		11.30	9.30	9.47	7.02	5.769
6		7.06	8.85	7.58	6.31	5.336
7			8.86	6.55	5.90	4.936
8			5.53	6.55	5.90	4.566
9				6.56	5.91	4.460
10				6.55	5.90	4.460
11				4.10	5.91	4.460
12					5.90	4.460
13					5.91	4.461
14					5.90	4.460
15					5.91	4.461
16					3.69	4.460
17						4.461
18						4.460
19						4.461
20						4.460
21						2.788

▼ TABLE 5

General Depreciation System—MACRS
Personal Property Placed in Service after 12/31/86
Applicable Convention: Mid-quarter (Property Placed in Service in Fourth Quarter)
Applicable Depreciation Method: 200 or 150 Percent Declining Balance Switching to Straight Line

If the Recovery Year Is:	And the Recovery Period Is:					
	3-Year	5-Year	7-Year	10-Year	15-Year	20-Year
	The Depreciation Rate Is:					
1	8.33	5.00	3.57	2.50	1.25	0.938
2	61.11	38.00	27.55	19.50	9.88	7.430
3	20.37	22.80	19.68	15.60	8.89	6.872
4	10.19	13.68	14.06	12.48	8.00	6.357
5		10.94	10.04	9.98	7.20	5.880
6		9.58	8.73	7.99	6.48	5.439
7			8.73	6.55	5.90	5.031
8			7.64	6.55	5.90	4.654
9				6.56	5.90	4.458
10				6.55	5.91	4.458
11				5.74	5.90	4.458
12					5.91	4.458
13					5.90	4.458
14					5.91	4.458
15					5.90	4.458
16					5.17	4.458
17						4.458
18						4.459
19						4.458
20						4.459
21						3.901

▼ TABLE 6

Luxury Automobile Depreciation Limits

	Year Automobile is Placed in Service[a]				
	2015	2012–2014	2010–2011	2009	2008
Maximum Allowable Depreciation (100% Business Use):					
Year 1	$3,160	$3,160[b]	$3,060[c]	$2,960[d]	$2,960[e]
Year 2	5,100	5,100	4,900	4,800	4,800
Year 3	3,050	3,050	2,950	2,850	2,850
Year 4 and Each Succeeding Year	1,875	1,875	1,775	1,775	1,775

[a]For years prior to 2008, see the Revenue Procedure for the appropriate year.
[b]$11,160 in Year 1 (2014, 2013, or 2012) if taxpayer claims bonus depreciation.
[c]$11,060 in Year 1 (2011 or 2010) if taxpayer claims bonus depreciation.
[d]$10,960 in Year 1 (2009) if taxpayer claims bonus depreciation.
[e]$10,960 in Year 1 (2008) if taxpayer claimed bonus depreciation.

▼ TABLE 6 (continued)
Truck and Van Depreciation Limits

	Year Truck or Van is Placed in Service[a]							
	2015	2014	2013	2012	2011	2010	2009	2008
Maximum Allowable Depreciation (100% Business Use):								
Year 1	$3,460	$3,460[b]	$3,360[c]	$3,360[c]	$3,260[d]	$3,160[f]	$3,060[e]	$3,160[f]
Year 2	5,600	5,550	5,400	5,300	5,200	5,100	4,900	5,100
Year 3	3,350	3,350	3,250	3,150	3,150	3,050	2,950	3,050
Year 4 and Each								
Succeeding Year	1,975	1,975	1,975	1,875	1,875	1,875	1,775	1,875

[a]For years prior to 2008, see the Revenue Procedure for the appropriate year.
[b]$11,460 in Year 1 (2014) if taxpayer claims bonus depreciation.
[c]$11,360 in Year 1 (2012 and 2013) if taxpayer claims bonus depreciation.
[d]$11,260 in Year 1 (2011) if taxpayer claims bonus depreciation.
[e]$11,060 in Year 1 (2009) if taxpayer claims bonus depreciation.
[f]$11,160 in Year 1 (2010 and 2008) if taxpayer claimed bonus depreciation.

▼ TABLE 7
General Depreciation System—MACRS
Residential Rental Real Property Placed in Service after 12/31/86
Applicable Recovery Period: 27.5 Years
Applicable Convention: Mid-month
Applicable Depreciation Method: Straight Line

If the Recovery Year Is:	And the Month in the First Recovery Year the Property Is Placed in Service Is:											
	1	2	3	4	5	6	7	8	9	10	11	12
	The Depreciation Rate Is:											
1	3.485	3.182	2.879	2.576	2.273	1.970	1.667	1.364	1.061	0.758	0.455	0.152
2	3.636	3.636	3.636	3.636	3.636	3.636	3.636	3.636	3.636	3.636	3.636	3.636
3	3.636	3.636	3.636	3.636	3.636	3.636	3.636	3.636	3.636	3.636	3.636	3.636
4	3.636	3.636	3.636	3.636	3.636	3.636	3.636	3.636	3.636	3.636	3.636	3.636
5	3.636	3.636	3.636	3.636	3.636	3.636	3.636	3.636	3.636	3.636	3.636	3.636
6	3.636	3.636	3.636	3.636	3.636	3.636	3.636	3.636	3.636	3.636	3.636	3.636
7	3.636	3.636	3.636	3.636	3.636	3.636	3.636	3.636	3.636	3.636	3.636	3.636
8	3.636	3.636	3.636	3.636	3.636	3.636	3.636	3.636	3.636	3.636	3.636	3.636
9	3.636	3.636	3.636	3.636	3.636	3.636	3.636	3.636	3.636	3.636	3.636	3.636
10	3.637	3.637	3.637	3.637	3.637	3.637	3.636	3.636	3.636	3.636	3.636	3.636
11	3.636	3.636	3.636	3.636	3.636	3.636	3.637	3.637	3.637	3.637	3.637	3.637
12	3.637	3.637	3.637	3.637	3.637	3.637	3.636	3.636	3.636	3.636	3.636	3.636
13	3.636	3.636	3.636	3.636	3.636	3.636	3.637	3.637	3.637	3.637	3.637	3.637
14	3.637	3.637	3.637	3.637	3.637	3.637	3.636	3.636	3.636	3.636	3.636	3.636
15	3.636	3.636	3.636	3.636	3.636	3.636	3.637	3.637	3.637	3.637	3.637	3.637
16	3.637	3.637	3.637	3.637	3.637	3.637	3.636	3.636	3.636	3.636	3.636	3.636
17	3.636	3.636	3.636	3.636	3.636	3.636	3.637	3.637	3.637	3.637	3.637	3.637
18	3.637	3.637	3.637	3.637	3.637	3.637	3.636	3.636	3.636	3.636	3.636	3.636
19	3.636	3.636	3.636	3.636	3.636	3.636	3.637	3.637	3.637	3.637	3.637	3.637
20	3.637	3.637	3.637	3.637	3.637	3.637	3.636	3.636	3.636	3.636	3.636	3.636
21	3.636	3.636	3.636	3.636	3.636	3.636	3.637	3.637	3.637	3.637	3.637	3.637
22	3.637	3.637	3.637	3.637	3.637	3.637	3.636	3.636	3.636	3.636	3.636	3.636
23	3.636	3.636	3.636	3.636	3.636	3.636	3.637	3.637	3.637	3.637	3.637	3.637
24	3.637	3.637	3.637	3.637	3.637	3.637	3.636	3.636	3.636	3.636	3.636	3.636
25	3.636	3.636	3.636	3.636	3.636	3.636	3.637	3.637	3.637	3.637	3.637	3.637
26	3.637	3.637	3.637	3.637	3.637	3.637	3.636	3.636	3.636	3.636	3.636	3.636
27	3.636	3.636	3.636	3.636	3.636	3.636	3.637	3.637	3.637	3.637	3.637	3.637
28	1.970	2.273	2.576	2.879	3.182	3.485	3.636	3.636	3.636	3.636	3.636	3.636
29	0.000	0.000	0.000	0.000	0.000	0.000	0.152	0.455	0.758	1.061	1.364	1.667

▼ **TABLE 8**

General Depreciation System—MACRS
Nonresidential Real Property Placed in Service after 12/31/86 and before 5/13/93
Applicable Recovery Period: 31.5 Years
Applicable Convention: Mid-month
Applicable Depreciation Method: Straight Line

If the Recovery Year Is:	And the Month in the First Recovery Year the Property Is Placed in Service Is:											
	1	2	3	4	5	6	7	8	9	10	11	12
	The Depreciation Rate Is:											
1	3.042	2.778	2.513	2.249	1.984	1.720	1.455	1.190	0.926	0.661	0.397	0.132
2	3.175	3.175	3.175	3.175	3.175	3.175	3.175	3.175	3.175	3.175	3.175	3.175
3	3.175	3.175	3.175	3.175	3.175	3.175	3.175	3.175	3.175	3.175	3.175	3.175
4	3.175	3.175	3.175	3.175	3.175	3.175	3.175	3.175	3.175	3.175	3.175	3.175
5	3.175	3.175	3.175	3.175	3.175	3.175	3.175	3.175	3.175	3.175	3.175	3.175
6	3.175	3.175	3.175	3.175	3.175	3.175	3.175	3.175	3.175	3.175	3.175	3.175
7	3.175	3.175	3.175	3.175	3.175	3.175	3.175	3.175	3.175	3.175	3.175	3.175
8	3.175	3.174	3.175	3.174	3.175	3.174	3.175	3.175	3.175	3.175	3.175	3.175
9	3.174	3.175	3.174	3.175	3.174	3.175	3.174	3.175	3.174	3.175	3.174	3.175
10	3.175	3.174	3.175	3.174	3.175	3.174	3.175	3.174	3.175	3.174	3.175	3.174
11	3.174	3.175	3.174	3.175	3.174	3.175	3.174	3.175	3.174	3.175	3.174	3.175
12	3.175	3.174	3.175	3.174	3.175	3.174	3.175	3.174	3.175	3.174	3.175	3.174
13	3.174	3.175	3.174	3.175	3.174	3.175	3.174	3.175	3.174	3.175	3.174	3.175
14	3.175	3.174	3.175	3.174	3.175	3.174	3.175	3.174	3.175	3.174	3.175	3.174
15	3.174	3.175	3.174	3.175	3.174	3.175	3.174	3.175	3.174	3.175	3.174	3.175
16	3.175	3.174	3.175	3.174	3.175	3.174	3.175	3.174	3.175	3.174	3.175	3.174
17	3.174	3.175	3.174	3.175	3.174	3.175	3.174	3.175	3.174	3.175	3.174	3.175
18	3.175	3.174	3.175	3.174	3.175	3.174	3.175	3.174	3.175	3.174	3.175	3.174
19	3.174	3.175	3.174	3.175	3.174	3.175	3.174	3.175	3.174	3.175	3.174	3.175
20	3.175	3.174	3.175	3.174	3.175	3.174	3.175	3.174	3.175	3.174	3.175	3.174
21	3.174	3.175	3.174	3.175	3.174	3.175	3.174	3.175	3.174	3.175	3.174	3.175
22	3.175	3.174	3.175	3.174	3.175	3.174	3.175	3.174	3.175	3.174	3.175	3.174
23	3.174	3.175	3.174	3.175	3.174	3.175	3.174	3.175	3.174	3.175	3.174	3.175
24	3.175	3.174	3.175	3.174	3.175	3.174	3.175	3.174	3.175	3.174	3.175	3.174
25	3.174	3.175	3.174	3.175	3.174	3.175	3.174	3.175	3.174	3.175	3.174	3.175
26	3.175	3.174	3.175	3.174	3.175	3.174	3.175	3.174	3.175	3.174	3.175	3.174
27	3.174	3.175	3.174	3.175	3.174	3.175	3.174	3.175	3.174	3.175	3.174	3.175
28	3.175	3.174	3.175	3.174	3.175	3.174	3.175	3.174	3.175	3.174	3.175	3.174
29	3.174	3.175	3.174	3.175	3.174	3.175	3.174	3.175	3.174	3.175	3.174	3.175
30	3.175	3.174	3.175	3.174	3.175	3.174	3.175	3.174	3.175	3.174	3.175	3.174
31	3.174	3.175	3.174	3.175	3.174	3.175	3.174	3.175	3.174	3.175	3.174	3.175
32	1.720	1.984	2.249	2.513	2.778	3.042	3.175	3.174	3.175	3.174	3.175	3.174
33	0.000	0.000	0.000	0.000	0.000	0.000	0.132	0.397	0.661	0.926	1.190	1.455

▼ TABLE 9

General Depreciation System—MACRS
Nonresidential Real Property Placed in Service after 5/12/93
Applicable Recovery Period: 39 years
Applicable Depreciation Method: Straight Line

If the Recovery Year Is:	And the Month in the First Recovery Year the Property Is Placed in Service Is:											
	1	2	3	4	5	6	7	8	9	10	11	12
	The Depreciation Rate Is:											
1	2.461	2.247	2.033	1.819	1.605	1.391	1.177	0.963	0.749	0.535	0.321	0.107
2-39	2.564	2.564	2.564	2.564	2.564	2.564	2.564	2.564	2.564	2.564	2.564	2.564
40	0.107	0.321	0.535	0.749	0.963	1.177	1.391	1.605	1.819	2.033	2.247	2.461

▼ TABLE 10

Alternative Depreciation System—MACRS (Partial Table)
Property Placed in Service after 12/31/86
Applicable Convention: Half-year
Applicable Depreciation Method: 150 Percent Declining Balance Switching to Straight Line

If the Recovery Year Is:	And the Recovery Period Is:					
	3	4	5	7	10	12
	The Depreciation Rate Is:					
1	25.00	18.75	15.00	10.71	7.50	6.25
2	37.50	30.47	25.50	19.13	13.88	11.72
3	25.00	20.31	17.85	15.03	11.79	10.25
4	12.50	20.31	16.66	12.25	10.02	8.97
5		10.16	16.66	12.25	8.74	7.85
6			8.33	12.25	8.74	7.33
7				12.25	8.74	7.33
8				6.13	8.74	7.33
9					8.74	7.33
10					8.74	7.33
11					4.37	7.32
12						7.33
13						3.66

▼ TABLE 11

Alternative Depreciation System—MACRS (Partial Table)
Property Placed in Service after 12/31/86
Applicable Convention: Half-year
Applicable Depreciation Method: Straight Line

If the Recovery Year Is:	And the Recovery Period Is:					
	3	4	5	7	10	12
	The Depreciation Rate Is:					
1	16.67	12.50	10.00	7.14	5.00	4.17
2	33.33	25.00	20.00	14.29	10.00	8.33
3	33.33	25.00	20.00	14.29	10.00	8.33
4	16.67	25.00	20.00	14.28	10.00	8.33
5		12.50	20.00	14.29	10.00	8.33
6			10.00	14.28	10.00	8.33
7				14.29	10.00	8.34
8				7.14	10.00	8.33
9					10.00	8.34
10					10.00	8.33
11					5.00	8.34
12						8.33
13						4.17

▼ TABLE 12

Alternative Depreciation System—MACRS
Real Property Placed into Service after 12/31/86
Applicable Recovery Period: 40 years
Applicable Convention: Mid-month
Applicable Depreciation Method: Straight Line

If the Recovery Year Is:	And the Month in the First Recovery Year the Property Is Placed in Service Is:											
	1	2	3	4	5	6	7	8	9	10	11	12
	The Depreciation Rate Is:											
1	2.396	2.188	1.979	1.771	1.563	1.354	1.146	0.938	0.729	0.521	0.313	0.104
2 to 40	2.500	2.500	2.500	2.500	2.500	2.500	2.500	2.500	2.500	2.500	2.500	2.500
41	0.104	0.312	0.521	0.729	0.937	1.146	1.354	1.562	1.771	1.979	2.187	2.396

▼ TABLE 13

Lease Inclusion Dollar Amounts for Automobiles
(Other Than for Trucks, Vans, or Electronic Automobiles)
With a Lease Term Beginning in Calendar Year 2015

REV. PROC. 2015-19 TABLE 3 *DOLLAR AMOUNTS FOR PASSENGER AUTOMOBILES (THAT ARE NOT TRUCKS OR VANS) WITH A LEASE TERM BEGINNING IN CALENDAR YEAR 2015*

Fair Market Value of Passenger Automobile		Tax Year During Lease				
Over	Not Over	1st	2nd	3rd	4th	5 and Later
$17,500	$18,000	3	6	9	10	11
18,000	18,500	4	7	11	13	15
18,500	19,000	4	9	14	15	18
19,000	19,500	5	11	15	19	21
19,500	20,000	6	12	18	22	24
20,000	20,500	6	14	20	25	27
20,500	21,000	7	15	23	27	31
21,000	21,500	8	17	25	30	34
21,500	22,000	9	18	28	32	38
22,000	23,000	10	21	31	37	42
23,000	24,000	11	24	36	42	49
24,000	25,000	12	27	41	48	55
25,000	26,000	14	30	45	54	62
26,000	27,000	15	34	49	60	68
27,000	28,000	17	37	54	65	75
28,000	29,000	18	40	59	71	81
29,000	30,000	20	43	64	76	87
30,000	31,000	21	46	69	81	95
31,000	32,000	23	49	73	88	100
32,000	33,000	24	52	78	93	107
33,000	34,000	25	56	82	99	114
34,000	35,000	27	59	87	104	120
35,000	36,000	28	62	92	110	126
36,000	37,000	30	65	96	116	133
37,000	38,000	31	68	102	121	139
38,000	39,000	33	71	106	127	146
39,000	40,000	34	75	110	132	153
40,000	41,000	35	78	115	138	159
41,000	42,000	37	81	120	143	166
42,000	43,000	38	84	125	149	172
43,000	44,000	40	87	129	155	179
44,000	45,000	41	90	134	161	185
45,000	46,000	43	93	139	166	191
46,000	47,000	44	97	143	172	198
47,000	48,000	45	100	148	177	205
48,000	49,000	47	103	153	183	210
49,000	50,000	48	106	158	188	218
50,000	51,000	50	109	162	194	224
51,000	52,000	51	112	167	200	230
52,000	53,000	53	115	172	205	237
53,000	54,000	54	119	176	211	243
54,000	55,000	56	122	180	217	250
55,000	56,000	57	125	186	222	256

▼ TABLE 13 (continued)

REV. PROC. 2015-19 TABLE 3 DOLLAR AMOUNTS FOR PASSENGER AUTOMOBILES (THAT ARE NOT TRUCKS OR VANS) WITH A LEASE TERM BEGINNING IN CALENDAR YEAR 2015

Fair Market Value of Passenger Automobile		Tax Year During Lease				
Over	Not Over	1st	2nd	3rd	4th	5 and Later
$ 56,000	$ 57,000	58	128	191	227	263
57,000	58,000	60	131	195	234	269
58,000	59,000	61	135	199	239	276
59,000	60,000	63	137	205	244	283
60,000	62,000	65	142	212	253	292
62,000	64,000	68	149	220	265	304
64,000	66,000	71	155	230	275	318
66,000	68,000	73	162	239	287	331
68,000	70,000	76	168	249	298	343
70,000	72,000	79	174	258	309	357
72,000	74,000	82	180	268	320	370
74,000	76,000	85	186	277	332	383
76,000	78,000	88	193	286	343	396
78,000	80,000	91	199	296	354	408
80,000	85,000	96	210	312	374	431
85,000	90,000	103	226	335	402	464
90,000	95,000	110	242	359	430	496
95,000	100,000	117	258	382	458	529
100,000	110,000	128	281	418	500	577
110,000	120,000	142	313	464	556	643
120,000	130,000	157	344	511	613	707
130,000	140,000	171	376	558	668	772
140,000	150,000	185	408	604	725	837
150,000	160,000	200	439	651	781	902
160,000	170,000	214	470	699	837	966
170,000	180,000	228	502	745	894	1,031
180,000	190,000	243	533	792	950	1,096
190,000	200,000	257	565	839	1,006	1,161
200,000	210,000	271	597	886	1,061	1,226
210,000	220,000	286	628	933	1,118	1,290
220,000	230,000	300	660	979	1,174	1,356
230,000	240,000	315	691	1,026	1,231	1,420
240,000	and over	329	723	1,073	1,286	1,485

▼ TABLE 14

Lease Inclusion Dollar Amounts for Trucks and Vans
With a Lease Term Beginning in Calendar Year 2015

REV. PROC. 2015-19 TABLE 4 *DOLLAR AMOUNTS FOR TRUCKS AND VANS WITH A LEASE TERM BEGINNING IN CALENDAR YEAR 2015*

Fair Market Value of Truck or Van		Tax Year During Lease				
Over	Not Over	1st	2nd	3rd	4th	5 and Later
$18,500	$19,000	2	4	6	8	9
19,000	19,500	3	6	8	11	12
19,500	20,000	4	7	11	13	16
20,000	20,500	4	9	13	16	19
20,500	21,000	5	11	15	19	22
21,000	21,500	6	12	18	22	25
21,500	22,000	6	14	20	25	28
22,000	23,000	7	16	24	29	33
23,000	24,000	9	19	29	34	40
24,000	25,000	10	23	33	40	46
25,000	26,000	12	25	38	46	53
26,000	27,000	13	29	42	51	60
27,000	28,000	15	32	47	57	65
28,000	29,000	16	35	52	62	73
29,000	30,000	18	38	56	68	79
30,000	31,000	19	41	61	74	85
31,000	32,000	20	45	66	79	91
32,000	33,000	22	48	70	85	98
33,000	34,000	23	51	75	91	104
34,000	35,000	25	54	80	96	111
35,000	36,000	26	57	85	101	118
36,000	37,000	28	60	89	108	124
37,000	38,000	29	63	94	113	131
38,000	39,000	30	67	98	119	137
39,000	40,000	32	70	103	124	144
40,000	41,000	33	73	108	130	150
41,000	42,000	35	76	113	135	157
42,000	43,000	36	79	118	141	163
43,000	44,000	38	82	122	147	169
44,000	45,000	39	85	127	153	176
45,000	46,000	40	89	131	158	183
46,000	47,000	42	92	136	163	189
47,000	48,000	43	95	141	169	195
48,000	49,000	45	98	145	175	202
49,000	50,000	46	101	151	180	208
50,000	51,000	48	104	155	186	215
51,000	52,000	49	108	159	192	221
52,000	53,000	51	110	165	197	228
53,000	54,000	52	114	169	203	234
54,000	55,000	53	117	174	208	241
55,000	56,000	55	120	178	214	248
56,000	57,000	56	123	183	220	254
57,000	58,000	58	126	188	225	261
58,000	59,000	59	130	192	231	267
59,000	60,000	61	133	197	236	273
60,000	62,000	63	137	204	245	283
62,000	64,000	66	144	213	256	296
64,000	66,000	68	150	223	268	308

▼ TABLE 14 (continued)

REV. PROC. 2015-19 TABLE 4 *DOLLAR AMOUNTS FOR TRUCKS AND VANS WITH A LEASE TERM BEGINNING IN CALENDAR YEAR 2015*

Fair Market Value of Truck or Van		Tax Year During Lease				
Over	Not Over	1st	2nd	3rd	4th	5 and Later
$ 66,000	$ 68,000	71	157	232	278	322
68,000	70,000	74	163	241	290	335
70,000	72,000	77	169	251	301	348
72,000	74,000	80	175	261	312	361
74,000	76,000	83	182	269	324	374
76,000	78,000	86	188	279	335	386
78,000	80,000	89	194	288	346	400
80,000	85,000	94	205	305	366	422
85,000	90,000	101	221	328	394	455
90,000	95,000	108	237	351	422	488
95,000	100,000	115	253	375	450	519
100,000	110,000	126	276	410	492	569
110,000	120,000	140	308	457	548	633
120,000	130,000	155	339	504	604	698
130,000	140,000	169	371	551	660	763
140,000	150,000	183	403	597	717	827
150,000	160,000	198	434	644	773	893
160,000	170,000	212	466	691	829	957
170,000	180,000	226	497	738	885	1,023
180,000	190,000	241	528	785	942	1,087
190,000	200,000	255	560	832	997	1,152
200,000	210,000	269	592	878	1,054	1,217
210,000	220,000	284	623	925	1,110	1,282
220,000	230,000	298	655	972	1,166	1,346
230,000	240,000	312	687	1,019	1,222	1,411
240,000	and over	327	718	1,066	1,278	1,476

D GLOSSARY

Ability to pay A concept in taxation that holds that taxpayers be taxed according to their ability to pay such taxes, that is, taxpayers that have sufficient financial resources should pay the tax. This concept is an integral part of vertical equity.

Accelerated Cost Recovery System (ACRS) Established by ERTA in 1981, the ACRS provides an accelerated depreciation and shorter cost-recovery period for real and personal property. The Tax Reform Act of 1986 changed the previously allowed depreciation tables and assigned recovery periods that approach the asset's true economic life. The current depreciation system is referred to as MACRS.

Accounting method The method of determining the taxable year in which income and expenses are reported for tax purposes. Generally, the same method must be used for tax purposes as is used for keeping books and records. The accounting treatment used for any item of income or expense and of specific items (e.g., installment sales and contracts) is included in this term. See also each specific accounting method.

Accounting period The period of time, usually 12 months, used by taxpayers to compute their taxable income. Taxpayers who do not keep records must use a calendar year. Taxpayers who do keep books and records may choose between a calendar year or a fiscal year. The accounting period election is made on the taxpayer's first filed return and cannot be changed without IRS consent. The accounting period may be less than 12 months if it is the taxpayer's first or final return or if the taxpayer is changing accounting periods. Certain restrictions upon the use of a fiscal year apply to partnerships, S corporations, and personal service corporations.

Accountable plan A type of employee reimbursement plan that meets two tests, (1) substantiation, and (2) return of excess reimbursement. Under an accountable plan, reimbursements are excluded from the employee's gross income and the expenses are not deductible by the employee.

Accrual method of accounting Accounting method under which income is reported and expenses are deducted when (1) all events have occurred that fix the taxpayer's right to receive the income and (2) the amount of the item can be determined with reasonable accuracy. Taxpayers with inventories to report must use this method to report sales and purchases.

Accumulated earnings tax This penalty tax is intended to discourage companies from retaining excessive amounts of earnings if the funds are invested in earnings that are unrelated to the business's needs. The current tax rate is 20%.

Acquiescence policy IRS policy of announcing whether it agrees or disagrees with a regular Tax Court decision. Such statements are not issued for every case.

ACRS See Accelerated Cost Recovery System.

Active income Income that is produced by the taxpayer's involvement or participation—wages, salaries, and other business income—is considered active income. It is the opposite of passive income.

Additional depreciation The excess of the actual amount of accelerated depreciation (or cost-recovery deductions under ACRS) over the amount of depreciation that would be deductible under the straight-line method. Such depreciation applies to Section 1250 depreciable real property acquired prior to 1987.

Adjusted current earnings An AMT adjustment item for corporations used to compute the Alternative Minimum Tax. The term is a concept based on the traditional earnings and profits definition found in Sec. 312.

Adjusted gross income (AGI) A measure of taxable income that falls between gross income and taxable income. It is the income amount that is used as the basis for calculating the floor or the ceiling for numerous other tax computations.

Adjusted sales price The amount realized from the sale of a residence less any fixing-up expenses.

Ad valorem tax A tax based on the value of real property or personal property. Typically, these taxes are levied at the time of a transaction, as is the case with a sales tax or a value-added tax (VAT). However, the taxes can also be levied annually, as with a real estate tax that a local government levies annually on the value of property.

AGI See Adjusted gross income.

Alimony Payments made pursuant to divorce or separation or written agreement between spouses subject to conditions specified in the tax law. Alimony payments (as contrasted to property settlements) are deductible for AGI by the payor and are included in the gross income of the recipient.

All events test Rule holding that an accrual basis taxpayer must report an item of income (1) when all events have occurred that fix the taxpayer's right to receive the item of income and (2) when the amount of the item can be determined with reasonable accuracy. This test is not satisfied until economic performance has taken place.

Alternative minimum tax (AMT) Applies to individuals, corporations, and estates and trusts only if the tentative minimum tax (TMT) exceeds the taxpayer's regular tax liability. Most taxpayers are not subject to this tax.

Amount realized The amount realized equals the sum of money plus the fair market value of all other property received from the sale or other disposition of the property less any selling expenses (e.g., commissions, advertising, deed preparation costs, and legal expenses) incurred in connection with the sale.

AMT See Alternative Minimum Tax.

Annual accounting period See Accounting period.

Annuity A series of regular payments that will continue for either a fixed period of time or until the death of the recipient. Pensions are usually paid in this way.

Applicable federal rate The rate determined monthly by the federal government which is based on the rate paid by the government on borrowed funds. The rate varies with the term of the loan. Thus, short-term loans are for a period of under three years, mid-term loans are for over three years and under nine years, and long-term loans are for over nine years.

Asset depreciation range (ADR) system of depreciation Depreciation method allowed for property placed in service before January 1, 1981. This method prescribed useful lives for various classes of assets.

Average tax rate The taxpayer's total tax liability divided by the amount of his taxable income.

Backup withholding A modified withholding system intended to prevent abusive noncompliance situations.

Bad debt Bona fide debt that is uncollectible because it is worthless. Such debts are further characterized as "business bad debts," which give rise to an ordinary deduction, and "nonbusiness bad debts," which are treated as a short-term capital loss. A determination of whether a debt is worthless is made by reference to all the pertinent evidence (e.g., the debtor's general financial condition and whether the debt is secured by collateral). Such debts are deductible subject to certain requirements.

Bona fide debt A debt that (1) arises from a valid and enforceable obligation to pay a fixed or determinable sum of money and (2) results in a debtor-creditor relationship.

Bonus depreciation Special first year depreciation on qualified property (non-real estate) placed in service at various times over the past ten years. Most recently, 50% bonus depreciation was allowable in 2008, 2009, and through September 8, 2010. After September 8, 2010 to December 31, 2011, the rate was increased to 100%. For 2012 through 2014, the rate returned to 50%. Congress has not yet extended bonus depreciation to 2015.

Boot Cash and nonlike-kind property given to complete an exchange of like-kind property where the property exchanged is not of equal value. Gain on the exchange is limited to the amount of boot received.

Brother-sister controlled group A group of two or more corporations controlled by five or fewer individuals. There are two definitions, a 80%-50% definition and a 50%-only definition. The definition to be used depends on the specific application.

Business bad debt See Bad debt.

Cafeteria plan Employer-financed plan that offers employees the option of choosing cash or statutory nontaxable fringe benefits (other than scholarships, fellowships, and Sec. 132 benefits such as discounts on merchandise). Such plans may not discriminate in favor of highly compensated individuals or their dependents or spouses.

Capital addition See Capital expenditure.

Capital asset This category of assets includes all assets except inventory, notes and accounts receivable, and depreciable property or land used in a trade or business (e.g., property, plant, and machinery).

Capital expenditure An expenditure that adds to the value of, substantially prolongs the useful life of, or adapts the property to a new or different use qualifies as a capital expenditure.

Capital gain Gain realized on the sale or exchange of a capital asset.

Capital gain dividend A distribution by a regulated investment company (i.e., a mutual fund) of capital gains realized from the sale of investments in the fund. Such dividends also include undistributed capital gains allocated to the shareholders.

Capital gain property Property that is contributed to a public charity upon which a long-term capital gain would be recognized if that property was sold at its fair market value.

Capital loss Loss realized on the sale or exchange of a capital asset.

Capital recovery A capital recovery amount is a deduction for depreciation or cost recovery. It is a factor in the determination of a property's adjusted basis.

Cash method of accounting Accounting method that requires the taxpayer to report income for the taxable year in which payments are actually or constructively received. Expenses are reported in the year they are paid. Most individuals and service businesses (i.e., businesses without inventories) use this method. Small businesses with inventories that have gross receipts of less than $1 million may also use the cash method.

Cash receipts and disbursements method of accounting See Cash method of accounting.

Casualty loss Loss that arises from an identifiable event that was sudden, unexpected, or unusual (e.g., fire, storm, shipwreck, other casualty, or theft). Within certain limitations, individuals may deduct such losses from AGI. Business casualty losses are deductible for AGI.

C Corporation Form of business entity that is taxed as a separate tax-paying entity. Its income is subject to an initial tax at the corporate level. Its shareholders are subject to a second tax when dividends are paid from the corporation's earnings and profits. Under certain conditions, S corporation status may be elected for tax purposes. C corporations are sometimes referred to as "regular corporations."

CD See Certificate of deposit.

Charitable contribution deduction Contributions of money or property made to qualified organizations (i.e., public charities and private nonoperating foundations) may be deducted from AGI. The amount of the deduction depends upon (1) the type of charity receiving the contribution, (2) the type of property contributed, and (3) other limitations mandated by the tax law. See also Unrelated use property.

Child tax credit A credit for individual taxpayers of $1,000 per qualifying child. A qualifying child must be a U.S. citizen, under age 17, qualify as the taxpayer's dependent, and be the taxpayer's descendent, stepchild, or foster child.

Closed-fact situation Situation or transaction that has already occurred.

Closely held C corporation For purposes of the at risk rules, a closely held C corporation is defined as a corporation where more than 50% of the stock is owned by five or fewer individuals at any time during the last half of the corporation's taxable year. These individuals may or may not be members of the same family.

Community income In any of the eight community property states, such income consists of the income from the personal efforts, investments, etc. of either spouse. Community income belongs equally to both spouses.

Compensation Payment for personal services. Salaries, wages, fees, commissions, tips, bonuses, and specialized forms of compensation such as director's fees and jury's fees fall into this category. However, certain fringe benefits and some foreign-earned income are not taxed.

Completed contract method of accounting Accounting method for long-term contracts undertaken by smaller companies. Income from the contract is reported in the taxable year in which the contract is completed. The completed contract method is limited to construction contracts undertaken by smaller companies.

Constant interest rate method Used to amortize the original issue discount ratably over the life of the bond, this method determines the amount of interest income by multiplying the interest yield to maturity by the adjusted issue price.

Constructive dividend Distribution that is intended to result in a deduction to the corporation. For example, excessive salary payments to shareholder-employees may be recharacterized as nondeductible dividends to the corporation to the extent that such amounts are not reasonable. The excess amount may be treated as dividend income to the shareholder-employees rather than as compensation provided that certain conditions are met.

Constructive receipt doctrine Rule holding that cash method taxpayers cannot turn their backs on the receipt of income if the funds are unqualifiedly made available.

Constructive stock ownership Shares that are indirectly or deemed to be owned by another shareholder due to related party situations.

Contributory pension plan A qualified pension plan to which employees make voluntary contributions.

Controlled group A controlled group is two or more separately incorporated businesses owned by the same individuals or entities. Such groups may consist of parent-subsidiary corporations, brother-sister corporations, or a combination of both (combined group).

Cost The amount paid for property in cash or the fair market value of the property given in exchange. The costs of acquiring the property and preparing it for use are included in the cost of the property.

Cost depletion method Calculation of the depletion of an asset (e.g., oil and gas properties) under which the asset's adjusted basis is divided by the estimated recoverable units to arrive at a per-unit depletion. This amount is then multiplied by the number of units sold to determine the cost depletion. This method may be alternated with the percentage depletion method as long as the calculation takes that into account.

Current year's exclusion The amount of the annuity payment that is excluded from gross income. This amount is determined by multiplying the exclusion ratio by the amount received during the year.

Customs duties A federal excise tax on imported goods.

Deductions for AGI Expenses one would see on an income statement prepared for financial accounting purposes, for example, compensation paid to employees, repairs to business property, and depreciation expenses. Certain nonbusiness deductions (e.g., alimony payments, moving expenses, and deductible payments to an individual retirement account (IRA)) are also deductible for AGI.

Deductions from AGI Generally, deductions are allowed for certain personal expenses such as medical deductions and charitable contributions which are referred to as itemized deductions. Alternatively, individuals may deduct the standard deduction. Personal and dependency deductions are also deductions from AGI.

Deferred compensation Methods of compensating employees based upon their current service where the benefits are deferred until future periods (e.g., a pension plan).

Defined benefit pension plan Qualified pension plan which establishes a contribution formula based upon actuarial techniques that are intended to fund a fixed retirement benefit amount. Thus, the amount that will be available at the time of retirement is determined when the contributions are made.

Defined contribution pension plan Qualified pension plan under which a separate account is maintained for each participant and fixed amounts are contributed based upon a specific percentage-of-compensation formula. The retirement benefits are based on the value of the participant's account at the time of retirement. Defined contribution plans for self-employed individuals are referred to as *H.R. 10 plans.*

Dependent care assistance program Employer-financed programs that provide care for an employee's children or other dependents. An employee may exclude up to $5,000 from gross income although the ceiling amount (i.e., $3,000 or $6,000) on the child care credit is reduced by the amount of assistance that is excluded from gross income.

DIF See Discriminate Function System.

Discriminate Function System (DIF) System used by the IRS to select individual returns for audit. This system is intended to identify those tax returns which are most likely to contain errors.

Dividends-received deduction The deduction on dividends received by corporate shareholders that attempts to mitigate the triple taxation that would occur if one corporation paid dividends to a corporate shareholder who, in turn, distributed such amounts to its individual shareholders. Certain restrictions and limitations apply to this deduction.

E&P See Earnings and profits.

Earned income credit A refundable credit that encourages lower income individuals to become gainfully employed. The credit is based on the individual's earned income.

Earnings and profits (E&P) A measure of the corporation's ability to pay a dividend from its current and accumulated earnings without an impairment of capital.

Economic performance test Economic performance occurs when the property or services to be provided are actually delivered.

Education expense Subject to certain limitations and restrictions, education expenses are deductible if they are incurred (1) to improve or maintain the individual's existing skills or (2) to meet requirements that are requisite to continued employment or meet the requirements of state law.

Effective tax rate The taxpayer's total tax liability divided by his total economic income.

Electronic Filing The method of filing a tax return with the IRS by electronic means instead of paper forms.

Employee achievement award Award given under circumstances that does not create a likelihood that it is really disguised compensation. It must be in the form of tangible personal property (other than cash) and be valued at no more than $400.

Employee stock ownership plan (ESOP) A qualified stock bonus plan or combined stock bonus plan and money purchase pension plan. ESOP's are funded by contributions of the employer's stock which are held for the employees' benefit.

Employment taxes Social security (FICA) and federal and state unemployment compensation taxes.

Entertainment expense Entertainment expenses (e.g., business meals) that are either directly related to or associated with the active conduct of a trade or business are deductible within certain limitations and restrictions. Directly related expenses are those that (1) derive a business benefit other than goodwill and (2) are incurred in a clear business setting. Expenses that are associated with the business are those that show a clear business purpose (e.g., obtaining new business) and occur on the same day the business is discussed.

ESOP See Employee stock ownership plan.

Estate tax Part of the federal unified transfer tax system, this tax is based upon the total property transfers an individual makes during his lifetime and at death.

Excess depreciation See Additional depreciation.

Exchange A transaction in which one receives a reciprocal transfer of property rather than cash and/or a cash equivalent.

Excise taxes Federal tax on alcohol, gasoline, telephone usage, oil and gas production, etc. State and local governments may impose similar taxes on goods and services.

Exclusion Any item of income that the tax law says is not taxable.

Exclusion ratio The portion of the annuity payment that is excluded from taxation. This amount equals the investment in the contract (its cost) divided by the expected return from the annuity.

Expected return The amount which a taxpayer can expect to receive from an annuity. It is determined by multiplying the amount of the annuity's annual payment by the expected return multiple.

Expected return multiple The number of years that the annuity is expected to continue. This amount may be a stated term or for the remainder of the taxpayer's life.

Fair market value (FMV) This amount is the price at which property would change hands between a willing buyer and a willing seller where neither party is under any compulsion to buy or sell.

Federal estate tax See estate tax.

Federal Insurance Contributions Act See FICA.

Federal Unemployment Tax Act See FUTA.

FICA Tax withheld through the payment of payroll taxes, FICA is intended to finance social security benefits for individuals who are not self-employed. Employees and employers contribute matching amounts until a federally-set annual earnings ceiling is reached. At that time, no further contributions need be made for that year. No ceiling exists for the hospital insurance (HI) portion of the tax. Self-employed individuals are subject to self-employment tax and currently receive a *for* AGI income tax deduction equal to 50% of their self-employment tax payments.

Field audit procedure Audit procedure generally used by the IRS for corporations or individuals engaged in a trade or business and conducted at either the taxpayer's place of business or his tax advisor's office. Generally, several items on the tax return are examined.

FIFO method of inventory valuation This flow of cost method assumes that the first goods purchased will be the first goods sold. Thus, the ending inventory consists of the last goods purchased.

Fiscal year An annual accounting period that ends on the last day of any month other than December. A fiscal year may be elected by taxpayers that keep books and records, such as businesses.

Flat tax See Proportional tax.

Foreign-earned income An individual's earnings from personal services rendered in a foreign country.

Foreign tax credit Tax credit given to mitigate the possibility of double taxation faced by U.S. taxpayers earning foreign income.

Former passive activity An activity that was formerly considered passive, but which is not considered to be passive with respect to the taxpayer for the current year.

Franchise tax State tax levy sometimes based upon a weighted average formula consisting of net worth, income, and sales.

Functional-use test A test used to determine whether property is considered similar or related in service or use for purposes of involuntary conversions of property under Sec. 1033. The functional-use test requires that the replacement property be functionally the same as the converted property.

FUTA Federal and state unemployment compensation tax.

GAAP See Generally accepted accounting principles.

Gain realized See Realized gain.

General business credit Special credit category consisting of tax credits commonly available to businesses. The more significant credit items are (1) the investment tax credit, (2) the work opportunity credit, (3) the research credit, (4) the low-income housing credit, (5) the empowerment zone employment credit, (6) the disabled access credit.

Generally accepted accounting principles (GAAP) The accounting principles that govern the preparation of financial reports to shareholders. GAAP does not apply to the tax treatment unless the method clearly reflects income. It is used only when the regulations do not specify the treatment of an item or when the regulations provide more than one alternative accounting method.

Gift tax A tax that is imposed upon the donor for transfers that are not supported by full and adequate consideration. A $14,000 annual exclusion is allowed per donee in 2013–2015 and $13,000 for 2009–2012.

Goodwill The excess of the purchase price of a business over the fair market value of all identifiable assets acquired.

Gross income All income received in cash, property, or services, from whatever source derived and from which the taxpayer derives a direct economic benefit.

Gross tax For income tax purposes, the amount determined by multiplying taxable income by the appropriate tax rate(s). The gross tax may also be found in the appropriate tax table for the taxpayer's filing status.

Half year convention An assumption with respect to depreciation that assumes that all asset acquisitions and dispositions are made at the midpoint of the tax year.

Health Savings Account Accounts that may be contributed to a fund by eligible individuals to enable such individuals to accumulate funds on a tax-free basis to pay qualified medical expenses. These accounts may only be set up by individuals who are covered under a high-deductible health plan and, within limits, are tax-deductible.

Holding period The length of time an asset is held before it is disposed of. This period is used to determine whether the gain or loss is long- or short-term.

Horizontal equity A concept in taxation that refers to the notion that similarly-situated taxpayers should be treated equally under the tax law.

H.R. 10 Plan Special retirement plan rules applicable to self-employed individuals. Such plans are often referred to as "Keogh plans."

Hybrid method of accounting Accounting method that combines the cash and accrual methods. Under this method, taxpayers can report sales and purchases under the accrual method and other income and expense items under the cash method. See also the cash method of accounting and the accrual method of accounting.

IDCs See Intangible drilling and development costs.

Imputed interest rule This rule reallocates the payments received in an installment sale between interest (fully taxable) and principal (only gain is taxable). To avoid this, the stated interest rate must equal at least 100% of the applicable federal rate as determined monthly according to the rate paid by the government on borrowed funds.

Incentive stock option plan (ISO) Stock option plan that allows executives to receive a proprietary interest in the corporation. The option to participate in this type of plan must be exercised according to certain requirements and must follow certain procedures.

Income The economic concept of income measures the amount an individual can consume during a period and remain as well off at the end of the period as at the beginning. The accounting concept of income is a measure of the income that is realized in a transaction. The tax concept of income is close to the accounting concept. It includes both taxable and nontaxable income from any source. However, it does not include a return of capital.

Incrementalism A concept in taxation that described how the tax law has been changed or modified over the years. Under incrementalism, the tax law is changed on an incremental basis rather than a complete revision basis.

Indeterminate market value If the market value of the property in question cannot be determined by the usual methods, the "open transaction" doctrine may be applied and the tax consequences may be deferred until the transaction is closed. Alternatively, the property may be valued by using the fair market value of the property that is given in the exchange (e.g., the value of the services rendered).

Individual retirement account (IRA) Contribution for AGI that is deductible if (1) neither the taxpayer nor his spouse are active participants in an employer-sponsored retirement plan or (2) certain income limitations are met. Taxpayers who do not meet these requirements may make nondeductible IRA contributions. See also Roth IRA.

Information Release An administrative pronouncement concerning an issue the IRS thinks the general public will be interested in. Such releases are issued in lay terms.

Innocent spouse rule Rule that exempts a spouse from penalty of from liability for the tax if such spouse had no knowledge of nor reason to know about an item of community income.

Installment sale Any disposition of property which involves receiving at least one payment after the close of the taxable year in which the sale occurs.

Installment sale method of accounting Taxpayers may use this method of accounting to reduce the tax burden from gains on the sale of property paid for in installments. Under this method, payment of the tax is deferred until the sale proceeds are collected. This method is not applicable to sales of publicly traded property or to losses.

Intangible drilling and development costs (IDCs) Expenditures made by an operator for wages, fuel, repairs, hauling supplies, and so forth, incident to and necessary for the preparation and drilling of oil and gas wells.

Intangible property Property that does not have physical substance, such as goodwill, patents, stocks and bonds, etc.

Interest The cost charged by a lender for the use of money. For example, finance charges, loan discounts, premiums, loan origination fees, and points paid by a buyer to obtain a mortgage loan are all interest expenses. The deductibility of the expense depends upon the purpose for which the indebtedness was incurred.

Internal Revenue Code The primary legislative source and authority for tax research, planning, and compliance activities.

Internal Revenue Service (IRS) The branch of the Treasury Department that is responsible for administering the federal tax law.

Interpretative Regulations Treasury Regulations that serve to broadly interpret the provisions of the Internal Revenue Code.

Inter vivos gifts Gifts made during the donor's life-time.

Investment expenses All deductions other than interest that are directly connected with the production of investment income.

Investment income Gross income from property held for investment and any net gain attributable to the disposition of such property. See also Net investment income.

Investment interest Interest expense on indebtedness incurred to purchase or carry property held for investment (e.g., income from interest, dividends, annuities, and royalties). Interest expenses incurred from passive activities are not subject to the investment interest limitations and interest incurred to purchase or carry tax-exempt securities is not deductible. Interest incurred from passive activities is subject to the passive activity loss limitation rules.

Involuntary conversion Such a conversion occurs when property is compulsorily converted into money or other property due to theft, seizure, requisition, condemnation, or partial or complete destruction. For example, an involuntary conversion occurs when the government exercises its right of eminent domain.

IRA See Individual retirement account.

IRC See Internal Revenue Code.

IRR See Internal rate of return.

IRS See Internal Revenue Service.

ISO See Incentive stock option.

Itemized deductions Also known as "deductions from AGI," these personal expenditures are allowable for such items as medical expenses, state and local taxes, charitable contributions, unreimbursed employee business expenses, interest on a personal residence, and casualty and theft losses. There are specific requirements for and limitations on the deductibility of each of these items. In addition, only those taxpayers whose total itemized deductions exceed the standard deduction amount can itemize their deductions. Total itemized deductions are subject to reductions based on AGI. No reduction was required in 2010–2012.

Joint income Income from jointly-held property.

Judicial decisions Decisions of a court of law.

Keogh plan Retirement plan for self-employed individuals. This type of plan is also known as an "H.R. 10 plan."

LCM See Lower of cost or market method of inventory valuation.

Legislative Regulations Treasury Regulations issued at the mandate of the Internal Revenue Code. Legislative regulations have a higher degree of authority than interpretative regulations.

Letter Ruling Letter rulings originate from the IRS at the taxpayer's request. They describe how the IRS will treat a proposed transaction. It is only binding on the person requesting the ruling providing the taxpayer completes the transaction as proposed in the ruling. Those of general interest are published as Revenue Rulings.

LIFO method of inventory valuation This method assumes a last-in, first out flow of cost. It results in the lowest taxable income during periods of inflation because it shows the lowest inventory value. Price indexes are used for the valuation. The information in these indexes is grouped into groups (pools) of similar items. See also Simplified LIFO method.

Like class Classes of assets defined by the Regulations that are considered to be property of a like kind for purposes of Sec. 1031. Like class property is tangible personal property that is in the same General Asset Class or the Same Product Class as other property.

Like-kind exchange A direct exchange of like-kind property. The transferred property and the received property must be held for productive use either (1) in a trade or business or (2) as an investment. Nonrecognition of gain or loss is mandatory. Certain like-kind exchanges between related parties are restricted if either party disposes of the property within two years of the exchange.

Like-kind property Property with a similar nature and character. This term does not refer to either the grade or quality of the property.

Limited liability company (LLC) A corporation that is generally taxed under the partnership rules. Although similar to an S corporation, there is no limit to (1) the number of shareholders, (2) the number of classes of stock, or (3) the types of investments in related entities.

Limited liability partnerships (LLP) LLPs are taxed as partnerships but enjoy limited liability under state partnership laws (i.e., individual partners are liable for their own acts and acts of persons under their direction and control but not for negligence or misconduct by other partners).

Liquidating distribution A distribution that liquidates a partner's entire partnership interest due to retirement, death, or other business reason. Such distributions result in a capital gain or loss to the partner whose interest is liquidated. In a corporate liquidation, the liquidating corporation generally recognizes gains and losses on the distribution of the properties and its shareholders recognize capital gain or loss on the surrender of their stock.

Long-term capital gain (LTCG) Gain realized on the sale or exchange of a capital asset held longer than one year.

Long-term capital loss (LTCL) Loss realized on the sale or exchange of a capital asset held longer than one year.

Long-term contracts Building, manufacturing, installation, and construction contracts that are not completed in the same taxable year in which they are entered into. Service contracts do not qualify as long-term contracts. See also Completed contract method of accounting.

Look-back interest Interest that is assessed on any additional tax that would have been paid if the actual total cost of the contract was used to calculate the tax rather than the estimated cost. Thus, it is applicable to any contract of portion of a contract that is accounted for under either the hybrid or percentage of completion method of accounting.

Lower of cost or market method (LCM) of inventory valuation The valuation method is available to all taxpayers other than those using LIFO valuation. It is applied to each separate item in the inventory.

Marginal tax rate The tax that is applied to an incremental amount of taxable income that is added to the tax base. This rate can be used to measure the tax effect of a proposed transaction. Currently, the highest marginal tax rate for individuals is 39.6%.

Market value This term refers to replacement cost under the lower of cost or market inventory method. That is, it is the price at which the taxpayer can replace the goods in question. See also Fair market value.

Material participation The level of participation by a taxpayer in an activity that determines whether the activity is either passive or active. If a taxpayer does not meet the material participation requirements, the activity is treated as a passive activity.

Medical expense deduction Unreimbursed medical expenses incurred for medical procedures or treatments that are (1) legal in the locality in which they are performed and (2) incurred for the purpose of alleviating a physical or mental defect or illness that affects the body's structure or function are deductible from AGI. Out-of-pocket travel costs incurred while en route to a medical facility, certain capital expenditures affecting the sick person, premiums for medical insurance, and in-patient hospital care are also deductible. Certain

restrictions and limitations apply to this deduction.

Memorandum decision Decision issued by the Tax Court. They deal with factual variations on matters which were decided in earlier cases.

Method of accounting See Accounting method.

Miscellaneous itemized deductions Certain unreimbursed employee expenses (e.g., required uniforms, travel, entertainment, and so on) fall into this category. Miscellaneous itemized deductions also include certain investment expenses, appraisal fees for charitable contributions and fees for tax return preparation. The nature of the deduction depends on whether the taxpayer is an employee or a self-employed individual.

Modified percentage of completion method A variation of the regular percentage of completion method where an election may be made to defer reporting profit from a long-term contract until at least 10% of the estimated total cost has been incurred.

Moving expense Expenses incurred in relation to employment-related job transfers.

Necessary expense Expense that is deductible under Sec. 162 because it is appropriate and helpful in the taxpayer's business. Such expenses must also qualify as ordinary.

Net investment income The excess of the taxpayer's investment income over his investment expenses. See also Investment income.

Net operating loss (NOL) A net operating loss occurs when business expenses exceed business income for any taxable year. Such losses may be carried back two years or carried forward 20 years to a year in which the taxpayer has taxable income. Loss must be carried back first and must be deducted from years in chronological order.

Net Present Value (NPV) Method used by investment analysts to determine the anticipated return on an investment. This method uses a fixed discount rate to compute the net present value of future cash flows.

NOL See Net operating loss.

Net unearned income The amount of unearned income of a child under age 18 (or under 24 if a full-time student and earned income less than 1/2 of his support) that is taxed at the child's parent's top marginal tax rate.

Nonaccountable plan A type of employee reimbursement plan that does not meet either of the two tests for an accountable plan (see accountable plan). Under a nonaccountable plan, reimbursements are included in the employee's gross income and the expenses are deductible by the employee, subject to the 2% of AGI floor.

Nonbusiness bad debt See Bad debt.

Noncontributory pension plan Only the employer makes contributions to this type of pension plan.

Nonliquidating distribution Distribution that reduces but does not eliminate, a partner's partnership interest. Such distributions are generally treated as tax-free returns of capital.

Nonqualified deferred compensation plan Type of plan used by employer to provide incentives or supplementary retirement benefits for executives. Such plans are not subject to the nondiscrimination and vesting rules.

Nonqualified stock option Stock option that does not meet the requirements for an incentive stock option.

Nonrefundable credit Allowances, such as the dependent child care credit, that have been created for various social, economic, and political reasons. The tax credits in this category do not result from payments made to the government in advance. Thus, they can be deducted from the tax, but they are not payable to the taxpayer in situations where the credit exceeds the tax.

NPV See Net Present Value.

Office audit procedure IRS audit of a specific item on an individual's tax return. An office audit takes place at the IRS branch office.

Open-fact situation A situation that has not yet occurred. That is, one for which the facts and events are still controllable and can be planned for.

Ordinary expense An expense that is deductible because it is reasonable in amount and bears a reasonable and proximate relationship to the income-producing activity or property.

Ordinary income property For purposes of the charitable contribution deduction, any property that would result in the recognition of ordinary income if the property were sold. Such property includes inventory, works of art or manuscripts created by the taxpayer, capital assets that have been held for one year or less, and Section 1231 property that results in ordinary income due to depreciation recapture.

Organizational expenditures The amortizable legal, accounting, filing, and other fees incidental to organizing a partnership or a corporation.

Parent-subsidiary controlled group To qualify, a common parent must own at least 80% of the stock of at least one subsidiary corporation and at least 80% of each other component member of the controlled group must be owned by other members of the controlled group.

Partnership Syndicate, group pool, joint venture, or other unincorporateed organization which carries on a business or financial operation or venture.

Partnership interest The capital and/or profits interest in a partnership received in exchange for a contribution of properties or services (e.g., money or business equipment). The nature of a partnership interest is similar to that of corporate stock.

Passive activity To define what constitutes a passive activity for the purpose of applying the passive loss rules, it is necessary to (1) identify what constitutes an activity and (2) determine whether the taxpayer has materially participated in the activity. Temp. Reg. Sec. 1.469-4T contains detailed rules for making these determinations.

Passive income Income from an activity that does not require the taxpayer's material involvement or participation. Thus, income from tax shelters and rental activities fall into the category.

Passive loss Loss generated from a passive activity. Such losses are computed separately. They may be used to offset income from other passive activities, but may not be used to offset either active or portfolio income.

Percentage depletion method Depletion method for assets such as oil and gas that is equal to a specified percentage times the gross income from the property but which may not exceed 100% of the taxable income before depletion is deducted. Lease bonuses, advance royalties, and other amounts payable without regard to production may not be included in the calculation. This method is only available to small oil and gas producers and royalty owners and for certain mineral properties.

Percentage of completion method of accounting Accounting method generally used for long-term contracts under which income is reported in proportion to the amount of work that has been completed in a given year.

Personal exemption A deduction in an amount mandated by Congress. The amount for 2015 is $4,000 ($3,950 for 2014) and is adjusted for increases in the cost of living. An additional exemption is allowed for each individual who is a dependent. Personal and dependency exemptions are phased out for high income taxpayers.

Personal holding company (PHC) A closely held corporation (1) that is owned by a five or fewer shareholders who own more than 50% of the corporation's outstanding stock at any time during the last half of its taxable year and (2) whose PHC income equals at least 60% of the corporation's adjusted gross income for the tax year. Certain corporations (e.g., S corporations) are exempt from this definition.

Personal holding company tax This tax is equal to 20% of the undistributed personal holding company income. It is intended to prevent closely held companies from converting an operating company into a nonoperating investment company.

Personal interest All interest other than active business interest, investment interest, interest incurred in a passive activity, qualified residence interest, and interest incurred when paying the estate tax on an installment basis. Personal interest is currently treated as a nondeductible personal expenditure. See also Interest.

Personal property Property that is other than real property, such as equipment.

Personal service corporation (PSC) A regular C corporation whose principal activity is the performance of personal services that are substantially performed by owner-employees who own more than 10% of the value of the corporation's stock.

PHC See Personal holding company.

Portfolio income Dividends, interest, annuities, and royalties not derived in the ordinary course of business. Gains and losses on property that produces portfolio income are included in such income.

Premium Tax Credit A personal tax credit for a portion of the cost of a taxpayer's health insurance premiums. To be eligible for the credit, the taxpayer must have household income between 100% and 400% of the federal poverty line. The credit is based on the excess of the qualifying premiums over what is deemed to be affordable based on the taxpayer's household income.

Primary cite The highest level official reporter which reports a particular case is called the primary cite.

Principal partner A partner owning 5% or more of the partnership profits and capital interests.

Principal residence The residence that the taxpayer occupies most of the time.

Private activity bond Obligation issued by a state of local government to finance nongovernmental activities (e.g., a sports arena).

Private Letter Ruling See Letter Ruling.

Production activities deduction A special deduction for all taxpayers involved in U.S. manufacturing or production activities. The deduction is 9% of the lesser of qualified production activities income or taxable income (before the deduction).

Production of income An activity of the taxpayer that is generally related to investment activities or matters connected with the determination of any tax. Deductions related to production of income activities are usually *from AGI*, although is some instances they may be *for AGI*, such as expenses connected with rental property.

Profit-sharing plan A qualified defined benefit plan which may be established in lieu of or in addition to a qualified pension plan. Contributions to a profit-sharing plan are usually based upon profits. Incidental benefits may or may not be included. In addition, the plan must meet certain requirements concerning determination of the amount and timing of the employer's contribution, how the employee wants to receive the employer's contribution, vesting, and forfeitures.

Progressive rate Tax that increases as the taxpayer's taxable income increases. The U.S. income tax is an example of a progressive tax.

Property settlement The division of property between spouses upon their separation or divorce.

Property tax Federal, state, or local tax levied on real and/or personal property (e.g., securities, a personal automobile).

Proportional tax A method of taxation under which the tax rate is the same for all taxpayers regardless of their income. State and local sales taxes are examples of this form of tax.

Proposed Regulations Issued following changes in the tax law. May or may not be amended after hearings are conducted and comments received. Proposed regulations are not binding on taxpayers.

PSC See Personal service corporation.

Qualified pension plan Pension plan that includes (1) systematic and definite payments made to a pension trust based upon actuarial methods and (2) usually provides for incidental benefits such as disability, or medical insurance benefits.

Qualified plan award Employee achievement awards given under a written plan or program that does not discriminate in favor of highly compensated employees. Such awards must be in the form of tangible personal property other than cash and be worth no more than $1,600.

Qualified residence interest Interest on an indebtedness which is secured by the taxpayer's qualified residence when it is paid or accrued. A taxpayer may have two qualified residences: a principal residence and a residence that he has personally used more than the greater of 14 days or 10% of the rental days during the year.

Qualifying children A child of the taxpayer who meets the four tests of relationship, age abode, and support. A child who meets these tests may be claimed as a dependency exemption by the taxpayer.

Qualifying relative An individual who may be claimed as a dependent if he or she meets the relationship, gross income, and support tests.

Readily ascertainable fair market value The fair market value of nonqualified stock options can be readily ascertained where the option is traded on an established options exchange.

Real property Property that is land or any structure permanently attached to the land, such as buildings.

Realized gain or loss The gain or loss computed by taking the amount realized from a sale of property and subtracting the property's adjusted basis.

Recapture provision A provision requiring recapture of earlier alimony payments as ordinary income by the payor if the payments decline sharply in either the second or third year.

Recovery of basis doctrine Rule that allows taxpayers to recover the basis of an asset without being taxed. Such amounts are considered a return of capital.

Refundable credit See Tax credit.

Regressive tax A form of taxation under which the tax rate decreases as the tax base (e.g., income) increases.

Regular corporation See C corporation.

Regular decision Tax Court decision that is issued on a particular issue for the first time.

Regulation See Treasury Regulation.

Replacement property Property that is acquired to replace converted property in order to retain nonrecognition of gain status. Such property must generally be functionally the same as the converted property. For example, a business machine must be replaced with a similar business machine. There are exceptions to this rule: The taxpayer-use test applies to the involuntary conversion of rental property owned by an investor; condemnations of real property held for business or investment use may be replaced by like-kind property.

Residential rental property Property from which at least 80% of the gross rental income is rental from dwelling units. Residential units include manufactured homes that are used for rental purposes, but not hotels, motels, or other establishments for transient use.

Restricted property plan Such plans are used to attract and retain key executives by giving them an ownership interest in the corporation. The income recognition rules contained in Sec. 83 govern this type of plan.

Revenue Amounts received by the taxpayer from any source. It includes both taxable and nontaxable amounts and items that are a return of capital. Although closely related to income or gross income, differences between these items do exist.

Revenue Procedure Issued by the national office of the IRS, Revenue Procedures reflect the IRS' position on compliance relating to tax preparation issues. Revenue Procedures, which are published in the Cumulative Bulletin, have less weight than Treasury Regulations.

Revenue Ruling Issued by the national office of the IRS, Revenue Rulings reflect the IRS's interpretation of a narrow tax issue. Revenue Rulings, which are published in the Cumulative Bulletin, have less weight than the Treasury Regulations.

Roth IRA An IRA in which the contributions are nondeductible, but distributions generally are not subject to tax. Therefore, all earnings in a Roth IRA are not subject to taxation.

Royalties Ordinary income arising from amounts paid for the right to use property that belongs to another and is transferred for valuable consideration (e.g., a patent right where substantially all rights are transferred).

Sale A transaction where one receives cash and/or the equivalent of cash, including the assumption of debt, in exchange for an asset.

Sales tax State or local tax on purchases. Generally, food items and medicines are exempt from such tax.

S corporation Small business corporations may elect S corporation status if they meet the 100-shareholder limitation, the type of shareholder restrictions, and the one class of stock restriction. Taxation of such corporations parallels the tax rules that apply to partnerships.

Secondary cite Citation to secondary source (i.e., unofficial reporter).

Section 401(k) plan Type of plan that is often used to supplement a company's regular

qualified pension and profit-sharing plan. Such plans, which generally contain a salary reduction feature, permit the employer to receive either cash or an equivalent contribution to the company's profit-sharing plan. The amount of the contribution is limited.

Section 1231 property Real or depreciable property that is (1) held for more than one year and (2) used in a trade or business. Certain property, such as inventory, U.S. government publications, copyrights, literary, musical, or artistic compositions, and letters, are excluded from this definition.

Section 1245 property Certain property subject to depreciation and, in some cases, amortization. Depreciable personal property such as equipment is Section 1245 property. However, most real property is not.

Section 1250 property Any real property that (1) is not Section 1245 property and (2) is subject to a depreciation allowance.

Security A long-term debt obligation. Long-term is generally defined as 10 years or more.

Self employment tax A tax imposed on self-employed individuals. The SE is comprised of two parts, (1) 12.4% for Social Security taxes (limited to a maximum amount of SE income) and (2) 2.9% for Medicare taxes (no limit on SE income). For 2015, the maximum SE income subject to the tax is $118,500 ($117,000 in 2014). The Medicare tax increases to 3.8% once the self-employment income exceeds a threshold ($200,000 for single taxpayers; $250,000 for married taxpayers).

Separate property All property that is owned before marriage and any gifts or inheritances acquired after marriage are separate property. This distinction depends on the state of residence. However, it is possible even in community property states.

Severance damages Compensation for a decline in the value of the property remaining after part of the taxpayer's property is condemned. The IRS considers such damages analogous to the proceeds from property insurance.

Shared Responsibility Payment An excise tax assessed on taxpayers without the required minimum essential health insurance coverage. The penalty tax is collected with the federal income tax return.

Shifting income The process of transferring income from one family member to another. Methods for shifting income include gifts of stock or bonds to family members who are in lower tax brackets.

Short sale An investment activity where an investor sells a security at its current price and purchases the same security at a future date. A short sale is generally used when the price of a security is expected to decline.

Short-term capital gain (STCG) Gain realized on the sale or exchange of a capital asset held for one year or less.

Short-term capital loss (STCL) Loss realized on the sale or exchange of a capital asset held for one year or less.

Simplified LIFO method This method of inventory valuation allows taxpayers to use a single LIFO pool rather than multiple pools. See also LIFO method.

Small cases procedure When taxes of $50,000 or less are in question for a particular year, the taxpayer may opt to have the case heard by a special commissioner rather than the regular Tax Court. The decision of the commissioner cannot be appealed.

Social security benefits These benefits include (1) the basic monthly retirement and disability benefits paid under social security and (2) tier-one railroad retirement benefits.

Sole proprietorship Form of business entity owned by an individual who reports all items of income, expense, on his individual return on Schedule C.

Specific write-off method of accounting Method of accounting used for bad debts. Under this method, the taxpayer deducts each bad debt individually as it becomes worthless. This is the only allowable accounting method for bad debts arising after 1986.

Splitting income The process of creating additional taxable entities, especially corporations, in order to reduce an individual's effective tax rate.

Standard deduction A floor amount set by Congress to simplify the tax computation. It is used by taxpayers who do not have enough deductions to itemize. The amount of the deduction varies according to the taxpayer's filing status, age, and vision. Taxpayers who use this standard deduction are not required to keep records. See Chapter I:2.

State corporate income tax See Franchise tax.

Statements on Standards for Tax Services (SSTS) Ethical guidelines of the AICPA-Federal Tax Division for CPAs to promote high standards of tax practice.

Statute of Limitations A period of time as provided by law in which a taxpayer's return may not be changed either by the IRS or the taxpayer. The Statute of Limitations is generally three years from the later of the date the tax return is filed or its due date. There is no Statute of Limitations for a fraudulent return.

Stock bonus plan A special type of defined benefit plan under which the employer's stock is contributed to a trust. The stock is then allocated and distributed to the participants. See also Employee stock ownership plan.

Stock dividend A dividend paid in the form of stock in the corporation issuing the dividend.

Stock option plan This category includes incentive stock options and nonqualified Stock option arrangements. Such plans are used to attract and retain key employees.

Substance-over-form doctrine Judicial weighing of a transaction's economic substance more heavily than its legal form.

Surviving spouse A special filing status available to widows and widowers who file a joint return for the year his or her spouse dies and for the following two years. The surviving spouse may not have remarried, must be a U.S. citizen or resident, have qualified to file a joint return for the year, and must have at least one dependent child living at home during the year.

Syndication fees The nonamortizable fees (e.g., brokerage and registration fees) incurred to promote and market partnership interests. Such fees are generally associated with tax-sheltered limited partnership interests.

Tangible property Property that has physical substance, such as land, buildings, natural resources, equipment, etc.

Tax A mandatory assessment levied under the authority of a political entity for the purpose of raising revenue to be used for public or governmental purposes. Such taxes may be levied by the federal, state, or local government.

Taxable income For individuals, taxable income is adjusted gross income reduced by deductions from adjusted gross income.

Tax base The amount to which the tax rate is applied to determine the tax due. For income tax purposes, the tax base is taxable income.

Tax benefit rule Recovery of an amount in a subsequent year that produced a tax benefit in a prior year and is thus taxable to the recipient.

Tax credit Amount that can be deducted from the gross tax to arrive at the net tax due or refund due. Prepaid amounts, that is, amounts paid to the government during the year, are tax credits. Such prepaid amounts are often referred to as "refundable credits."

Tax Deferred Bonds Bonds on which the interest is not subject to current taxation but is deferred to a future period of time, such as Series EE U.S. Savings Bonds.

Tax Exempt Bonds Bonds on which the interest is completely exempt from federal income taxation, such as state and municipal bonds.

Tax law The tax law is comprised of the Internal Revenue Code, administrative and judicial interpretations, and the committee reports issued by the Congressional committees involved in the legislative process.

Taxpayer Compliance Measurement Program (TCMP) A stratified random sample used to select tax returns for audit. The program is intended to test the extent to which taxpayers are in compliance with the law.

Taxpayer-use test A test used to determine whether property is considered similar or related in service or use for purposes of involuntary conversions of property. This test is used by owner-investors (as opposed to owner-users) of property.

Tax research Search for the best possible solution to a problem involving either a proposed or completed transaction.

Tax shelter Passive activity which may lack economic substance other than creating tax deductions and credits that enable taxpayers to reduce or eliminate the income tax liability from their regular business activities. Section 469 restricts the current use of deductions and credits arising from passive activities.

Tax year See Accounting period.

TCMP See Taxpayer Compliance Measurement Program.

Technical Advice Memorandum Such memoranda are administrative interpretations issued in the form of letter ruling. Taxpayers may request them if they need guidance about the tax treatment of complicated technical matters which are being audited.

Temporary Regulations Temporary Regulations are Treasury Regulations that are issued to provide guidance for taxpayers pending the issuance of the final regulations. They are binding upon taxpayers. Temporary Regulations are also required to be issued as proposed regulations and must expire within three years.

Testamentary gift Transfer of property made at the death of the donor (i.e., bequests, devises, and inheritances).

Theft loss Loss of business, investment, or personal-use property due to crimes such as, but not limited to, larceny, embezzlement, robbery, extortion, blackmail, or kidnapping for ransom. Such losses are deductible from AGI, subject to certain limitations.

Total economic income The amount of the taxpayer's income, including exclusions and deductions from the tax base (e.g., tax-exempt bonds), is categorized as total economic income.

Trade or business A business activity of the taxpayer in which deductions are allowed as *for* AGI deductions.

Transportation expense The deductibility of this type of expense depends upon whether it is trade- or business-related, whether it is related to the production of income, whether the expense is employment related and therefore subject to the 2% nondeductible floor for miscellaneous itemized deductions. Commuting expenses are nondeductible. See also Travel expense.

Travel expense Such expenses include transportation, meals, and lodging incurred in the pursuit of a trade, business, or employment-related activity. There are limitations and restrictions on the deductibility of these expenses. See also Transportation expense.

Treasury bill Short-term (i.e., 90-day) obligation that is issued by the government at a discount from the maturity amount. The difference between the issue price and the maturity amount represents the interest income.

Treasury Regulation The principal administrative source of the federal tax law, these regulations reflect the Treasury's and the IRS's interpretation of the Internal Revenue Code. They may be either legislative or interpretative and they may be issued in either proposed, temporary, or final form.

Unfunded deferred compensation plan This type of plan is used for highly-compensated employees who wish to defer the recognition of income until future periods. Funding is generally accomplished through an escrow account for the employee's benefit.

Uniform Capitalization rules (UNICAP) The requirements under the tax law for determining inventory cost. Under UNICAP certain indirect overhead costs are required to be included in inventory for tax purposes which are generally not included for financial accounting.

Unrelated use property Capital gain property which is also tangible personal property and which is contributed to a public charity for a use that is unrelated to the charity's function. The contribution deduction (from AGI) for such property is equal to the property's fair market value minus the capital gain that would be recognized if the property was sold at that value.

Unreported decision District Court decisions that are not officially reported in the Federal Supplement. Such decisions may be reported in secondary reporters that report only tax-related cases.

U.S. Production Activities Deduction See Production Activities Deduction.

U.S. Treasury Bill See Treasury bill.

Vertical equity A concept in taxation that provides that the incidence of taxation should be borne by taxpayers who have the ability to pay the tax. Taxpayers who are not similarly-situated should be treated differently under the tax law.

Wash sale A wash sale results when the taxpayer (1) sells stock or securities and (2) purchases substantially identical stock or securities within the 61-day period extending from 30 days before the date of sale to 30 days after the date of sale.

Wealth transfer tax A tax imposed upon the value of property transferred during one's lifetime (i.e., a gift tax) or upon the death of the transferor (i.e., an estate tax). The tax is imposed upon the transferor of property or upon the estate.

Writ of certiorari A petition to the U.S. Supreme Court to request that the Court agree to hear a case. A writ of certiorari is requested by the party (IRS or taxpayer) that lost at the Court of Appeals level.

Zero coupon bond Bond that is issued at a cost that is substantially less than the current market rate because no interest payments are made. The original issue discount (OID) must be amortized over the term of the bond by investors using the constant rate method. Such bonds offer cash-flow advantages to corporate issuers since no cash outlay for interest is required until the bonds mature.

AICPA STATEMENTS ON STANDARDS FOR TAX SERVICES NOS. 1–7

Note: The AICPA released revised Statements on Standards for Tax Services (SSTS) effective on January 1, 2010. These statements are enforceable standards of tax practice for AICPA members. Changes to Statements No. 1 and 7 (formerly No. 8) were substantive in nature. As a result, Interpretations No. 1-1 and 1-2 relating to former Statement No. 1 are currently being updated. The new statements as well as the old statements can be found on the AICPA website at www.aicpa.org.

PREFACE

1. Standards are the foundation of a profession. The AICPA aids its members in fulfilling their ethical responsibilities by instituting and maintaining standards against which their professional performance can be measured. Compliance with professional standards of tax practice also reaffirms the public's awareness of the professionalism that is associated with CPAs as well as the AICPA.

2. This publication sets forth enforceable tax practice standards for members of the AICPA, Statements on Standards for Tax Services (SSTSs or statements). These statements apply to all members providing tax services regardless of the jurisdictions in which they practice. Interpretations of these statements may be issued as guidance to assist in understanding and applying the statements. The SSTSs and their interpretations are intended to complement other standards of tax practice, such as Treasury Department Circular No. 230, *Regulations Governing the Practice of Attorneys, Certified Public Accountants, Enrolled Agents, Enrolled Actuaries, Enrolled Retirement Plan Agents, and Appraisers before the Internal Revenue Service*; penalty provisions of the Internal Revenue Code; and state boards of accountancy rules.

3. The SSTSs are written in as simple and objective a manner as possible. However, by their nature, practice standards provide for an appropriate range of behavior and need to be interpreted to address a broad range of personal and professional situations. The SSTSs recognize this need by, in some sections, providing relatively subjective rules and by leaving certain terms undefined. These terms are generally rooted in tax concepts and, therefore, should be readily understood by tax practitioners. Accordingly, enforcement of these rules, as part of the AICPA's Code of Professional Conduct Rule 201, *General Standards*, and Rule 202, *Compliance With Standards* (AICPA, *Professional Standards*, vol. 2, ET sec. 201 par. .01 and ET sec. 202 par. .01), will be

undertaken on a case-by-case basis. Members are expected to comply with them.

History

4. The SSTSs have their origin in the Statements on Responsibilities in Tax Practice (SRTPs), which provided a body of advisory opinions on good tax practice. The guidelines as originally set forth in the SRTPs became more important than many members had anticipated when the guidelines were issued. The courts, the IRS, state accountancy boards, and other professional organizations recognized and relied on the SRTPs as the appropriate articulation of professional conduct in a CPA's tax practice. The SRTPs became *de facto* enforceable standards of professional practice, because state disciplinary organizations and courts regularly held CPAs accountable for failure to follow the guidelines set forth in the SRTPs.

5. The AICPA's Tax Executive Committee concluded it was appropriate to issue tax practice standards that would become a part of the AICPA's *Professional Standards*. At its July 1999 meeting, the AICPA Board of Directors approved support of the executive committee's initiative and placed the matter on the agenda of the October 1999 meeting of the AICPA's governing Council. On October 19, 1999, Council approved designating the Tax Executive Committee as a standardsetting body, thus authorizing that committee to promulgate standards of tax practice. As a result, the original SSTSs, largely mirroring the SRTPs, were issued in August 2000.

6. The SRTPs were originally issued between 1964 and 1977. The first nine SRTPs and the introduction were promulgated in 1976; the tenth SRTP was issued in 1977. The original SRTPs concerning the CPA's responsibility to sign the tax return (SRTP No. 1, *Signature of Preparers*, and No. 2, *Signature of Reviewer: Assumption of Preparer's Responsibility*) were withdrawn in 1982 after Treasury Department regulations were issued adopting

substantially the same standards for all tax return preparers. The sixth and seventh SRTPs, concerning the responsibility of a CPA who becomes aware of an error, were revised in 1991. The first interpretation of the SRTPs, Interpretation No. 1-1, "Realistic Possibility Standard," was approved in December 1990. The SSTSs and Interpretation No. 1-1, "Realistic Possibility Standard," of SSTS No. 1, *Tax Return Positions*, superseded and replaced the SRTPs and their Interpretation No. 1-1, effective October 31, 2000. Although the number and names of the SSTSs, and the substance of the rules contained in each of them, remained the same as in the SRTPs, the language was revised to both clarify and reflect the enforceable nature of the SSTSs. In addition, because the applicability of these standards is not limited to federal income tax practice (as was the case with the SRTPs), the language was changed to indicate the broader scope. In 2003, in connection with the tax shelter debate, SSTS Interpretation No. 1-2, "Tax Planning," of SSTS No. 1 was issued to clarify a member's responsibilities in connection with tax planning; that interpretation became effective December 31, 2003.

7. When the original SSTSs were issued, an effort was made to keep to a minimum any changes in the language of the SSTSs from that of the predecessor SRTPs. This was done to alleviate concerns regarding the enforceability of standards that differed from the SRTPs under which members had been practicing. Since the issuance of the original SSTSs, members have asked for clarification on certain matters, such as the duplication of the language in SSTS No. 6, *Knowledge of Error: Return Preparation*, and No. 7, *Knowledge of Error: Administrative Proceedings*. Also, certain changes in federal and state tax laws have raised concerns regarding the need to revise SSTS No. 1. As a result, in 2008, the original SSTS Nos. 1–8 were updated, effective January 1, 2010. The original SSTS Nos. 6–7 were combined into the revised SSTS No. 6, *Knowledge of Error: Return Preparation and Administrative Proceedings*. The original SSTS No. 8, *Form and Content of Advice to Taxpayers*, was renumbered SSTS No. 7. In addition, various revisions were made to the language of the original SSTSs.

Ongoing Process

8. The following SSTSs and any interpretations issued thereunder reflect the AICPA's standards of tax practice and delineate members' responsibilities to taxpayers, the public, the government, and the profession. The statements are intended to be part of an ongoing process of articulating standards of tax practice for members. These standards are subject to change as necessary or appropriate to address changes in the tax law or other developments in the tax practice environment.

9. Members are encouraged to assess the adequacy of their practices and procedures for providing tax services in conformity with these standards. This process will vary according to the size of the practice and the nature of tax services performed.

10. The Tax Executive Committee promulgates the SSTSs and their interpretations. Acknowledgment is also due to the many

members who have devoted their time and efforts over the years to developing and revising the AICPA's standards.

STATEMENT ON STANDARDS FOR TAX SERVICES NO. 1, *TAX RETURN POSITIONS*

Introduction

1. This statement sets forth the applicable standards for members when recommending tax return positions, or preparing or signing tax returns (including amended returns, claims for refund, and information returns) filed with any taxing authority. For purposes of these standards

   a. a *tax return position* is (i) a position reflected on a tax return on which a member has specifically advised a taxpayer or (ii) a position about which a member has knowledge of all material facts and, on the basis of those facts, has concluded whether the position is appropriate.
   b. a *taxpayer* is a client, a member's employer, or any other third-party recipient of tax services.

2. This statement also addresses a member's obligation to advise a taxpayer of relevant tax return disclosure responsibilities and potential penalties.

3. In addition to the AICPA, various taxing authorities, at the federal, state, and local levels, may impose specific reporting and disclosure standards with regard to recommending tax return positions or preparing or signing tax returns.[1] These standards can vary between taxing authorities and by type of tax.

Statement

4. A member should determine and comply with the standards, if any, that are imposed by the applicable taxing authority with respect to recommending a tax return position, or preparing or signing a tax return.

5. If the applicable taxing authority has no written standards with respect to recommending a tax return position or preparing or signing a tax return, or if its standards are lower than the standards set forth in this paragraph, the following standards will apply:

   a. A member should not recommend a tax return position or prepare or sign a tax return taking a position unless the member has a good-faith belief that the position has at least a realistic possibility of being sustained administratively or judicially on its merits if challenged.
   b. Notwithstanding paragraph 5(a), a member may *recommend a tax return position* if the member (i) concludes that there is a reasonable basis for the position and (ii) advises the taxpayer to appropriately disclose that position. Notwithstanding paragraph 5(a), a member may *prepare or sign a tax return* that reflects a position if (i) the member concludes there is a reasonable basis for the position and (ii) the position is appropriately disclosed.

---

[1]A member should refer to the current version of Internal Revenue Code Section 6694, Understatement of taxpayer's liability by tax return preparer, and other relevant federal, state, and jurisdictional authorities to determine the reporting and disclosure standards that are applicable to preparers of tax returns.

6. When recommending a tax return position or when preparing or signing a tax return on which a position is taken, a member should, when relevant, advise the taxpayer regarding potential penalty consequences of such tax return position and the opportunity, if any, to avoid such penalties through disclosure.

7. A member should not recommend a tax return position or prepare or sign a tax return reflecting a position that the member knows

a. exploits the audit selection process of a taxing authority, or
b. serves as a mere arguing position advanced solely to obtain leverage in a negotiation with a taxing authority.

8. When recommending a tax return position, a member has both the right and the responsibility to be an advocate for the taxpayer with respect to any position satisfying the aforementioned standards.

Explanation

9. The AICPA and various taxing authorities impose specific reporting and disclosure standards with respect to tax return positions and preparing or signing tax returns. In a given situation, the standards, if any, imposed by the applicable taxing authority may be higher or lower than the standards set forth in paragraph 5. A member is to comply with the standards, if any, of the applicable taxing authority; if the applicable taxing authority has no standards or if its standards are lower than the standards set forth in paragraph 5, the standards set forth in paragraph 5 will apply.

10. Our self-assessment tax system can function effectively only if taxpayers file tax returns that are true, correct, and complete. A tax return is prepared based on a taxpayer's representation of facts, and the taxpayer has the final responsibility for positions taken on the return. The standards that apply to a taxpayer may differ from those that apply to a member.

11. In addition to a duty to the taxpayer, a member has a duty to the tax system. However, it is well established that the taxpayer has no obligation to pay more taxes than are legally owed, and a member has a duty to the taxpayer to assist in achieving that result. The standards contained in paragraphs 4–8 recognize a member's responsibilities to both the taxpayer and the tax system.

12. In reaching a conclusion concerning whether a given standard in paragraph 4 or 5 has been satisfied, a member may consider a well-reasoned construction of the applicable statute, well-reasoned articles or treatises, or pronouncements issued by the applicable taxing authority, regardless of whether such sources would be treated as *authority* under Internal Revenue Code Section 6662, *Imposition of accuracy-related penalty on underpayments*, and the regulations thereunder. A position would not fail to meet these standards merely because it is later abandoned for practical or procedural considerations during an administrative hearing or in the litigation process.

13. If a member has a good-faith belief that more than one tax return position meets the standards set forth in paragraphs 4–5, a member's advice concerning alternative acceptable positions may include a discussion of the likelihood that each such position might or might not cause the taxpayer's tax return to be examined and whether the position would be challenged in an examination. In such circumstances, such advice is not a violation of paragraph 7.

14. A member's determination of whether information is appropriately disclosed by the taxpayer should be based on the facts and circumstances of the particular case and the disclosure requirements of the applicable taxing authority. If a member recommending a position, but not engaged to prepare or sign the related tax return, advises the taxpayer concerning appropriate disclosure of the position, then the member shall be deemed to meet the disclosure requirements of these standards.

15. If particular facts and circumstances lead a member to believe that a taxpayer penalty might be asserted, the member should so advise the taxpayer and should discuss with the taxpayer the opportunity, if any, to avoid such penalty by disclosing the position on the tax return. Although a member should advise the taxpayer with respect to disclosure, it is the taxpayer's responsibility to decide whether and how to disclose.

16. For purposes of this statement, preparation of a tax return includes giving advice on events that have occurred at the time the advice is given if the advice is directly relevant to determining the existence, character, or amount of a schedule, entry, or other portion of a tax return.

STATEMENT ON STANDARDS FOR TAX SERVICES NO. 2, *ANSWERS TO QUESTIONS ON RETURNS*

Introduction

1. This statement sets forth the applicable standards for members when signing the preparer's declaration on a tax return if one or more questions on the return have not been answered. The term *questions* includes requests for information on the return, in the instructions, or in the regulations, whether or not stated in the form of a question.

Statement

2. A member should make a reasonable effort to obtain from the taxpayer the information necessary to provide appropriate answers to all questions on a tax return before signing as preparer.

Explanation

3. It is recognized that the questions on tax returns are not of uniform importance, and often they are not applicable to the particular taxpayer. Nevertheless, there are at least three reasons why a member should be satisfied that a reasonable effort has been made to obtain information to provide appropriate answers to the questions on the return that are applicable to a taxpayer:

a. A question may be of importance in determining taxable income or loss, or the tax liability shown on the return, in which circumstance an omission may detract from the quality of the return.
b. A request for information may require a disclosure necessary for a complete return or to avoid penalties.
c. A member often must sign a preparer's declaration stating that the return is true, correct, and complete.

4. Reasonable grounds may exist for omitting an answer to a question applicable to a taxpayer. For example, reasonable grounds may include the following:

a. The information is not readily available and the answer is not significant in terms of taxable income or loss, or the tax liability shown on the return.

b. Genuine uncertainty exists regarding the meaning of the question in relation to the particular return.

c. The answer to the question is voluminous; in such cases, a statement should be made on the return that the data will be supplied upon examination.

5. A member should not omit an answer merely because it might prove disadvantageous to a taxpayer.

6. A member should consider whether the omission of an answer to a question may cause the return to be deemed incomplete or result in penalties.

7. If reasonable grounds exist for omission of an answer to an applicable question, a taxpayer is not required to provide on the return an explanation of the reason for the omission.

STATEMENT ON STANDARDS FOR TAX SERVICES NO. 3, *CERTAIN PROCEDURAL ASPECTS OF PREPARING RETURNS*

Introduction

1. This statement sets forth the applicable standards for members concerning the obligation to examine or verify certain supporting data or to consider information related to another taxpayer when preparing a taxpayer's tax return.

Statement

2. In preparing or signing a return, a member may in good faith rely, without verification, on information furnished by the taxpayer or by third parties. However, a member should not ignore the implications of information furnished and should make reasonable inquiries if the information furnished appears to be incorrect, incomplete, or inconsistent either on its face or on the basis of other facts known to the member. Further, a member should refer to the taxpayer's returns for one or more prior years whenever feasible.

3. If the tax law or regulations impose a condition with respect to deductibility or other tax treatment of an item, such as taxpayer maintenance of books and records or substantiating documentation to support the reported deduction or tax treatment, a member should make appropriate inquiries to determine to the member's satisfaction whether such condition has been met.

4. When preparing a tax return, a member should consider information actually known to that member from the tax return of another taxpayer if the information is relevant to that tax return and its consideration is necessary to properly prepare that tax return. In using such information, a member should consider any limitations imposed by any law or rule relating to confidentiality.

Explanation

5. The preparer's declaration on a tax return often states that the information contained therein is true, correct, and complete to the best of the preparer's knowledge and belief based on all information known by the preparer. This type of reference should be understood to include information furnished by the taxpayer or by third parties to a member in connection with the preparation of the return.

6. The preparer's declaration does not require a member to examine or verify supporting data; a member may rely on information furnished by the taxpayer unless it appears to be incorrect, incomplete, or inconsistent. However, there is a need to determine by inquiry that a specifically required condition, such as maintaining books and records or substantiating documentation, has been satisfied and to obtain information when the material furnished appears to be incorrect, incomplete, or inconsistent. Although a member has certain responsibilities in exercising due diligence in preparing a return, the taxpayer has the ultimate responsibility for the contents of the return. Thus, if the taxpayer presents unsupported data in the form of lists of tax information, such as dividends and interest received, charitable contributions, and medical expenses, such information may be used in the preparation of a tax return without verification unless it appears to be incorrect, incomplete, or inconsistent either on its face or on the basis of other facts known to a member.

7. Even though there is no requirement to examine underlying documentation, a member should encourage the taxpayer to provide supporting data where appropriate. For example, a member should encourage the taxpayer to submit underlying documents for use in tax return preparation to permit full consideration of income and deductions arising from security transactions and from pass-through entities, such as estates, trusts, partnerships, and S corporations.

8. The source of information provided to a member by a taxpayer for use in preparing the return is often a pass-through entity, such as a limited partnership, in which the taxpayer has an interest but is not involved in management. A member may accept the information provided by the pass-through entity without further inquiry, unless there is reason to believe it is incorrect, incomplete, or inconsistent, either on its face or on the basis of other facts known to the member. In some instances, it may be appropriate for a member to advise the taxpayer to ascertain the nature and amount of possible exposure to tax deficiencies, interest, and penalties by taxpayer contact with management of the pass-through entity.

9. A member should make use of a taxpayer's returns for one or more prior years in preparing the current return whenever feasible. Reference to prior returns and discussion of prior-year tax determinations with the taxpayer should provide information to determine the taxpayer's general tax status, avoid the omission or duplication of items, and afford a basis for the treatment of similar or related transactions. As with the examination of information supplied for the current year's return, the extent of comparison of the details of income and deduction between years depends on the particular circumstances.

STATEMENT ON STANDARDS FOR TAX SERVICES NO. 4, *USE OF ESTIMATES*

Introduction

1. This statement sets forth the applicable standards for members when using the taxpayer's estimates in the preparation of a tax return. A member may advise on estimates used in the preparation of a tax return, but the taxpayer has the responsibility to provide the estimated data. Appraisals or valuations are not considered estimates for purposes of this statement.

Statement

2. Unless prohibited by statute or by rule, a member may use the taxpayer's estimates in the preparation of a tax return if it is not practical to obtain exact data and if the member determines that the estimates are reasonable based on the facts and circumstances known to the member. The taxpayer's estimates should be presented in a manner that does not imply greater accuracy than exists.

Explanation

3. Accounting requires the exercise of professional judgment and, in many instances, the use of approximations based on judgment. The application of such accounting judgments, as long as not in conflict with methods set forth by a taxing authority, is acceptable. These judgments are not estimates within the purview of this statement. For example, a federal income tax regulation provides that if all other conditions for accrual are met, the exact amount of income or expense need not be known or ascertained at year end if the amount can be determined with reasonable accuracy.

4. When the taxpayer's records do not accurately reflect information related to small expenditures, accuracy in recording some data may be difficult to achieve. Therefore, the use of estimates by a taxpayer in determining the amount to be deducted for such items may be appropriate.

5. When records are missing or precise information about a transaction is not available at the time the return must be filed, a member may prepare a tax return using a taxpayer's estimates of the missing data.

6. Estimated amounts should not be presented in a manner that provides a misleading impression about the degree of factual accuracy.

7. Specific disclosure that an estimate is used for an item in the return is not generally required; however, such disclosure should be made in unusual circumstances where nondisclosure might mislead the taxing authority regarding the degree of accuracy of the return as a whole. Some examples of unusual circumstances include the following:

a. A taxpayer has died or is ill at the time the return must be filed.
b. A taxpayer has not received a Schedule K-1 for a pass-through entity at the time the tax return is to be filed.
c. There is litigation pending (for example, a bankruptcy proceeding) that bears on the return.
d. Fire, computer failure, or natural disaster has destroyed the relevant records.

STATEMENT ON STANDARDS FOR TAX SERVICES NO. 5, *DEPARTURE FROM A POSITION PREVIOUSLY CONCLUDED IN AN ADMINISTRATIVE PROCEEDING OR COURT DECISION*

Introduction

1. This statement sets forth the applicable standards for members in recommending a tax return position that departs from the position determined in an administrative proceeding or in a court decision with respect to the taxpayer's prior return.

2. For purposes of this statement, *administrative proceeding* includes an examination by a taxing authority or an appeals conference relating to a return or a claim for refund.

3. For purposes of this statement, *court decision* means a decision by any court having jurisdiction over tax matters.

Statement

4. The tax return position with respect to an item as determined in an administrative proceeding or court decision does not restrict a member from recommending a different tax position in a later year's return, unless the taxpayer is bound to a specified treatment in the later year, such as by a formal closing agreement. Therefore, the member may recommend a tax return position or prepare or sign a tax return that departs from the treatment of an item as concluded in an administrative proceeding or court decision with respect to a prior return of the taxpayer provided the requirements of Statement on Standards for Tax Services (SSTS) No. 1, *Tax Return Positions*, are satisfied.

Explanation

5. If an administrative proceeding or court decision has resulted in a determination concerning a specific tax treatment of an item in a prior year's return, a member will usually recommend this same tax treatment in subsequent years. However, departures from consistent treatment may be justified under such circumstances as the following:

a. Taxing authorities tend to act consistently in the disposition of an item that was the subject of a prior administrative proceeding but generally are not bound to do so. Similarly, a taxpayer is not bound to follow the tax treatment of an item as consented to in an earlier administrative proceeding.
b. The determination in the administrative proceeding or the court's decision may have been caused by a lack of documentation. Supporting data for the later year may be appropriate.

c. A taxpayer may have yielded in the administrative proceeding for settlement purposes or not appealed the court decision, even though the position met the standards in SSTS No. 1.

d. Court decisions, rulings, or other authorities that are more favorable to a taxpayer's current position may have developed since the prior administrative proceeding was concluded or the prior court decision was rendered.

6. The consent in an earlier administrative proceeding and the existence of an unfavorable court decision are factors that the member should consider in evaluating whether the standards in SSTS No. 1 are met.

STATEMENT ON STANDARDS FOR TAX SERVICES NO. 6, *KNOWLEDGE OF ERROR: RETURN PREPARATION AND ADMINISTRATIVE PROCEEDINGS*

Introduction

1. This statement sets forth the applicable standards for a member who becomes aware of (a) an error in a taxpayer's previously filed tax return; (b) an error in a return that is the subject of an administrative proceeding, such as an examination by a taxing authority or an appeals conference; or (c) a taxpayer's failure to file a required tax return. As used herein, the term *error* includes any position, omission, or method of accounting that, at the time the return is filed, fails to meet the standards set out in Statement on Standards for Tax Services (SSTS) No. 1, *Tax Return Positions*. The term *error* also includes a position taken on a prior year's return that no longer meets these standards due to legislation, judicial decisions, or administrative pronouncements having retroactive effect. However, an error does not include an item that has an insignificant effect on the taxpayer's tax liability. The term *administrative proceeding* does not include a criminal proceeding.

2. This statement applies whether or not the member prepared or signed the return that contains the error.

3. Special considerations may apply when a member has been engaged by legal counsel to provide assistance in a matter relating to the counsel's client.

Statement

4. A member should inform the taxpayer promptly upon becoming aware of an error in a previously filed return, an error in a return that is the subject of an administrative proceeding, or a taxpayer's failure to file a required return. A member also should advise the taxpayer of the potential consequences of the error and recommend the corrective measures to be taken. Such advice and recommendation may be given orally. The member is not allowed to inform the taxing authority without the taxpayer's permission, except when required by law.

5. If a member is requested to prepare the current year's return and the taxpayer has not taken appropriate action to correct an error in a prior year's return, the member should consider whether to withdraw from preparing the return and whether to continue a professional or employment relationship with the taxpayer. If the member does prepare such current year's return, the member should take reasonable steps to ensure that the error is not repeated.

6. If a member is representing a taxpayer in an administrative proceeding with respect to a return that contains an error of which the member is aware, the member should request the taxpayer's agreement to disclose the error to the taxing authority. Lacking such agreement, the member should consider whether to withdraw from representing the taxpayer in the administrative proceeding and whether to continue a professional or employment relationship with the taxpayer.

Explanation

7. While performing services for a taxpayer, a member may become aware of an error in a previously filed return or may become aware that the taxpayer failed to file a required return. The member should advise the taxpayer of the error and the potential consequences, and recommend the measures to be taken. Similarly, when representing the taxpayer before a taxing authority in an administrative proceeding with respect to a return containing an error of which the member is aware, the member should advise the taxpayer to disclose the error to the taxing authority and of the potential consequences of not disclosing the error. Such advice and recommendation may be given orally.

8. It is the taxpayer's responsibility to decide whether to correct the error. If the taxpayer does not correct an error, a member should consider whether to withdraw from the engagement and whether to continue a professional or employment relationship with the taxpayer. Although recognizing that the taxpayer may not be required by statute to correct an error by filing an amended return, a member should consider whether a taxpayer's decision not to file an amended return or otherwise correct an error may predict future behavior that might require termination of the relationship.

9. Once the member has obtained the taxpayer's consent to disclose an error in an administrative proceeding, the disclosure should not be delayed to such a degree that the taxpayer or member might be considered to have failed to act in good faith or to have, in effect, provided misleading information. In any event, disclosure should be made before the conclusion of the administrative proceeding.

10. A conflict between the member's interests and those of the taxpayer may be created by, for example, the potential for violating Code of Professional Conduct Rule 301, *Confidential Client Information* (AICPA, *Professional Standards*, vol. 2, ET sec. 301 par. .01) (relating to the member's confidential client relationship); the tax law and regulations; or laws on privileged communications, as well as by the potential adverse impact on a taxpayer of a member's withdrawal. Therefore, a member should consider consulting with his or her own legal counsel before deciding upon recommendations to the taxpayer and whether to continue a professional or employment relationship with the taxpayer.

11. If a member believes that a taxpayer may face possible exposure to allegations of fraud or other criminal misconduct, the member should advise the taxpayer to consult with an attorney before the taxpayer takes any action.

12. If a member decides to continue a professional or employment relationship with the taxpayer and is requested to prepare a tax return for a year subsequent to that in which the error occurred, the member should take reasonable steps to ensure that the error is not repeated. If the subsequent year's tax return cannot be prepared without perpetuating the error, the member should consider withdrawal from the return preparation. If a member learns that the taxpayer is using an erroneous method of accounting and it is past the due date to request permission to change to a method meeting the standards of SSTS No. 1, the member may sign a tax return for the current year, providing the tax return includes appropriate disclosure of the use of the erroneous method.

13. Whether an error has no more than an insignificant effect on the taxpayer's tax liability is left to the professional judgment of the member based on all the facts and circumstances known to the member. In judging whether an erroneous method of accounting has more than an insignificant effect, a member should consider the method's cumulative effect, as well as its effect on the current year's tax return or the tax return that is the subject of the administrative proceeding.

14. If a member becomes aware of the error while performing services for a taxpayer that do not involve tax return preparation or representation in an administrative proceeding, the member's responsibility is to advise the taxpayer of the existence of the error and to recommend that the error be discussed with the taxpayer's tax return preparer. Such recommendation may be given orally.

STATEMENT ON STANDARDS FOR TAX SERVICES NO. 7, *FORM AND CONTENT OF ADVICE TO TAXPAYERS*

Introduction

1. This statement sets forth the applicable standards for members concerning certain aspects of providing advice to a taxpayer and considers the circumstances in which a member has a responsibility to communicate with a taxpayer when subsequent developments affect advice previously provided. The statement does not, however, cover a member's responsibilities when the expectation is that the advice rendered is likely to be relied on by parties other than the taxpayer.

Statement

2. A member should use professional judgment to ensure that tax advice provided to a taxpayer reflects competence and appropriately serves the taxpayer's needs. When communicating tax advice to a taxpayer in writing, a member should comply with relevant taxing authorities' standards, if any, applicable to written tax advice. A member should use professional judgment about

any need to document oral advice. A member is not required to follow a standard format when communicating or documenting oral advice.

3. A member should assume that tax advice provided to a taxpayer will affect the manner in which the matters or transactions considered would be reported or disclosed on the taxpayer's tax returns. Therefore, for tax advice given to a taxpayer, a member should consider, when relevant (*a*) return reporting and disclosure standards applicable to the related tax return position and (*b*) the potential penalty consequences of the return position. In ascertaining applicable return reporting and disclosure standards, a member should follow the standards in Statement on Standards for Tax Services No. 1, *Tax Return Positions*.

4. A member has no obligation to communicate with a taxpayer when subsequent developments affect advice previously provided with respect to significant matters, except while assisting a taxpayer in implementing procedures or plans associated with the advice provided or when a member undertakes this obligation by specific agreement.

Explanation

5. Tax advice is recognized as a valuable service provided by members. The form of advice may be oral or written and the subject matter may range from routine to complex. Because the range of advice is so extensive and because advice should meet the specific needs of a taxpayer, neither a standard format nor guidelines for communicating or documenting advice to the taxpayer can be established to cover all situations.

6. Although oral advice may serve a taxpayer's needs appropriately in routine matters or in welldefined areas, written communications are recommended in important, unusual, substantial dollar value, or complicated transactions. The member may use professional judgment about whether, subsequently, to document oral advice.

7. In deciding on the form of advice provided to a taxpayer, a member should exercise professional judgment and should consider such factors as the following:

a. The importance of the transaction and amounts involved
b. The specific or general nature of the taxpayer's inquiry
c. The time available for development and submission of the advice
d. The technical complexity involved
e. The existence of authorities and precedents
f. The tax sophistication of the taxpayer
g. The need to seek other professional advice
h. The type of transaction and whether it is subject to heightened reporting or disclosure requirements
i. The potential penalty consequences of the tax return position for which the advice is rendered
j. Whether any potential applicable penalties can be avoided through disclosure
k. Whether the member intends for the taxpayer to rely upon the advice to avoid potential penalties

8. A member may assist a taxpayer in implementing procedures or plans associated with the advice offered. When providing such assistance, the member should review and revise such advice as warranted by new developments and factors affecting the transaction.

9. Sometimes a member is requested to provide tax advice but does not assist in implementing the plans adopted. Although such developments as legislative or administrative changes or future judicial interpretations may affect the advice previously provided, a member cannot be expected to communicate subsequent developments that affect such advice unless the member undertakes this obligation by specific agreement with the taxpayer.

10. Taxpayers should be informed that (*a*) the advice reflects professional judgment based upon the member's understanding of the facts, and the law existing as of the date the advice is rendered and (*b*) subsequent developments could affect previously rendered professional advice. Members may use precautionary language to the effect that their advice is based on facts as stated and authorities that are subject to change.

11. In providing tax advice, a member should be cognizant of applicable confidentiality privileges.

These Statements on Standards for Tax Services were unanimously adopted by the assenting votes of the 17 members of the 18-member Tax Executive Committee who participated in the August 6, 2009, Tax Executive Committee meeting.

Tax Executive Committee (2008–2009)

Alan R. Einhorn, *Chair*	Jeffrey A Porter
Jeffrey R. Hoops, *Immediate Past Chair*	Roby Sawyers
Diane Cornwell	Christopher J. Sokolowski
Eve Elgin	Norman S. Solomon
Andrew D. Gibson	Patricia Thompson
Cherie J. Hennig	Christine Turgeon
Lawrence W. McKoy	Mark Van Deveer
T. Chris Muirhead	Richard P. Weber
Gregory A. Porcaro	Brian T. Whitlock

Tax Practice Responsibilities Committee (2008–2009)

Arthur J. Kip Dellinger, Jr., *Chair*	Douglas Milford
Gregory M. Fowler, *Vice Chair*	Trenton S. Olmstead
Harvey Coustan	Gerald W. Padwe
Todd C. Craft	James W. Sansone
Diane D. Fuller	James H. Schlesser
Jan D. Hayden	Lisa G. Workman
Andrew M. Mattson	

SSTS Revisions Task Force

Conrad M. Davis, *Cochair*	Gregory M. Fowler
Jay M. Levine, *Cochair*	John C. Gardner
Timothy J. Burke, Jr.	Keith R. Lee
Arthur J. Kip Dellinger, Jr.	Mark N. Schneider
Eve Elgin	Gerard H. Schreiber, Jr.
Jeffrey Frishman	J. Edward Swails

AICPA Staff

Thomas P. Ochsenschlager *Vice President—Taxation Tax Division*	Edward S. Karl *Director Tax Division*
	Jean E. Trompeter *Technical Manager Tax Division*

Note: *Statements on Standards for Tax Services are issued by the Tax Executive Committee, the senior technical body of the AICPA designated to promulgate standards of tax practice. Rule 201, General Standards, and Rule 202, Compliance With Standards, of the Code of Professional Conduct (AICPA, Professional Standards, vol. 2, ET sec. 201 par. .01 and ET sec. 202 par. .01), require compliance with these standards.*

F INDEX OF CODE SECTIONS

G INDEX OF TREASURY REGULATIONS

H INDEX OF GOVERNMENT PROMULGATIONS

I INDEX OF COURT CASES

APPENDIX

J SUBJECT INDEX

2015
TAX RATE SCHEDULES

ESTATES AND TRUSTS [§1 (e)]:

If taxable income is:	The tax is:
Not over $2,500	15% of taxable income.
Over $2,500 but not over $5,900	$375 plus 25% of the excess over $2,500.
Over $5,900 but not over $9,050	$1,225 plus 28% of the excess over $5,900.
Over $9,050 but not over $12,300	$2,107 plus 33% of the excess over $9,050.
Over $12,300	$3,179.50 plus 39.6% of the excess over $12,300.

CORPORATIONS

If Taxable Income Is:		The Tax Is:	Of the Amount Over—
Over—	But Not Over—		
$ 0	$ 50,000	15%	$ 0
50,000	75,000	$ 7,500 + 25%	50,000
75,000	100,000	13,750 + 34%	75,000
100,000	335,000	22,250 + 39%	100,000
335,000	10,000,000	113,900 + 34%	335,000
10,000,000	15,000,000	3,400,000 + 35%	10,000,000
15,000,000	18,333,333	5,150,000 + 38%	15,000,000
18,333,333		6,416,667 + 35%	18,333,333

UNIFIED CREDIT AMOUNT FOR ESTATE AND GIFT TAX

Year of Gift/Year of Death	Amount of Credit	Exemption Equivalent[a] (or Applicable Exclusion Amount)
January through June, 1977	$ 30,000 (6,000)[b]	$ 120,666 (30,000)[b]
July through December, 1977	30,000	120,666
1978	34,000	134,000
1979	38,000	147,333
1980	42,500	161,563
1981	47,000	175,625
1982	62,800	225,000
1983	79,300	275,000
1984	96,300	325,000
1985	121,800	400,000
1986	155,800	500,000
1987 through 1997	192,800	600,000
1998	202,050	625,000
1999	211,300	650,000
2000 and 2001	220,550	675,000
2002 and 2003	345,800	1,000,000
2004 and 2005	555,800 (345,800)[b]	1,500,000 (1,000,000)[b]
2006, 2007, and 2008	780,800 (345,800)[b]	2,000,000 (1,000,000)[b]
2009	1,455,800 (345,800)[b]	3,500,000 (1,000,000)[b]
2010	1,730,800[c] (330,800)[b]	5,000,000[c] (1,000,000)[b]
2011	1,730,800	5,000,000
2012	1,772,800	5,120,000
2013	2,045,800	5,250,000
2014	2,081,800	5,340,000
2015	2,117,800	5,430,000

[a] For estate tax purposes in 2011 and 2012, this amount was called the basic exclusion amount.
[b] The numbers in parentheses represent the credit and exemption equivalent amounts for the gift tax.
[c] This amount applied if the executor opted to have the estate subject to the estate tax and FMV basis rule in 2010.